WEBSTER'S NEW WORLD™

Spanish Dictionary

Houghton Mifflin Harcourt
Boston • New York

Webster's New World Spanish Dictionary

Harrap's Pocket Spanish-English Dictionary © CHP 2008; © Larousse 2010. All rights reserved

Published by Houghton Mifflin Harcourt Publishing Company

For information about permission to reproduce selections from this book,
please write Permissions, Houghton Mifflin Harcourt Publishing Company
215 Park Avenue South, New York, New York 10003

www.hmhco.com

ISBN 978-0-470-17825-6

Printed in the United States of America

OPM 10 9

4500468807

Contents/Índice

Preface

This is a revised and expanded edition of our pocket-sized dictionary for students at beginner and intermediate level. We believe it remains the most comprehensive and up-to-date dictionary of its size available.

We have kept track of changes in both languages which reflect the rapid changes in our world. There is excellent coverage of computing terms, and we include terminology relating to cellphones, e-mail and the Internet. The treatment of Latin American Spanish has also been revised.

A major new addition is the Conversation Guide in the supplement. This covers essential phrases for practical and social purposes, from greeting and asking for directions, to expressing opinions, making suggestions and requests, and apologizing. We also include verb tables for Spanish and English in the supplement.

We have retained the "false friend" boxes which help the user avoid common translation pitfalls, and grammar notes to indicate correct usage. We also include detailed pronunciation guides, where special attention is given to the problems English speakers encounter in pronouncing Spanish. The clear page layout, with each new part of speech on a new line, has also been retained.

Prefacio

Les presentamos una nueva edición, revisada y ampliada, de nuestro diccionario de bolsillo, dirigido a estudiantes de nivel elemental e intermedio, obra que creemos continúa siendo la más completa y actualizada de los diccionarios de este tamaño.

Hemos seguido pendientes de la evolución experimentada por ambas lenguas, proceso que refleja los cambios que tiene lugar en el mundo y, como consecuencia, se sigue recogiendo ampliamente la terminología informática, así como el vocabulario de la telefonía celular, el correo electrónico e Internet. Y además, se han revisado los usos tanto del español de América como del inglés norteamericano.

La principal novedad de esta edición es la Guía de conversación del suplemento. En ella se incluyen las frases esenciales para poder comunicarse, que ilustran desde cómo saludar a alguien o preguntar por una dirección hasta cómo expresar una opinión, hacer sugerencias o pedir disculpas. El suplemento incluye también las tablas de conjugación de los verbos ingleses y españoles.

Se mantienen las novedades de la última edición que potencian la utilidad del diccionario como herramienta de aprendizaje: las notas sobre "falsos amigos" para evitar fallos en la traducción y las notas gramaticales que indican el uso correcto de las entradas. Se incluyen también las guías de pronunciación, que prestan especial atención a los problemas que tienen los hispanohablantes al pronunciar el inglés. También se ha mantenido la claridad en la presentación del texto, a la que contribuye la separación en distintos párrafos de cada una de las categorías gramaticales de una misma entrada.

Structure of Entries

> **Amtrak** ['æmtræk] *n* ▨ compañía ferroviaria estadounidense

● The equals sign = introduces an explanation when there is no direct translation.

> **cupcake** ['kʌpkeɪk] *n (cake)* ▨ magdalena *f*

● The sign ≃ introduces a translation that has a roughly equivalent status but is not identical.

> **alert** [ə'lɜːt] **1** *adj (watchful)* alerta; *(lively)* despabilado(a)
> **2** *n* alerta *m*; **to be on the a.** estar alerta
> **3** *vt* **to a. sb to sth** avisar a algn de algo

● The different grammatical categories are cleary indicated, introduced by a bold Arabic numeral.

> **depress** [dɪ'pres] *vt* (**a**) *(person)* deprimir (**b**) *Econ (profits)* reducir; *(trade)* dificultar (**c**) *Fml (switch, lever etc)* presionar; *(clutch, piano pedal)* pisar

● Usage and field labels are clearly shown.

> **reconocer** [34] *vt* (**a**) *(identificar)* to recognize (**b**) *(admitir)* to admit (**c**) *Med (paciente)* to examine

● A number before an irregular Spanish verb refers the user to the verb tables in the middle of the book for information on how to conjugate it.

> **bland** [blænd] *adj (food)* soso(a)
>
> ⌀ Note that the Spanish word **blando** is a false friend and is never a translation for the English word **bland**. In Spanish **blando** means "soft".

● Usage notes warn the user when a word is a false friend.

> **aback** [ə'bæk] *adv* **to be taken a.** quedarse de una pieza *(by por)*

● The most common prepositions used are given after the translation.

> **debris** ['debriː, 'deɪbriː] *n sing* escombros *mpl*

● The number of a noun is indicated where this is ambiguous.

Estructura de las entradas

> **ceviche** *nm* ▦ raw fish marinated in lemon and garlic

- Cuando no es posible dar una traducción se ofrece una explicación precedida por el signo igual (=).

> **inocentada** *nf Fam* ▦ April Fool's joke; **hacer una i. a algn** to play an April Fool's joke on sb

- El signo ≃ precede a una traducción que tiene un significado aproximado pero no idéntico.

> **aflojar 1** *vt* to loosen
> **2** *vi (viento etc)* to abate, to die down
> **3 aflojarse** *upr* to come o work loose; *(rueda)* to go down

- Las diferentes categorías gramaticales vienen precedidas por un número en negrita.

> **abrir²** *(pp* **abierto)** **1** *vi* to open
> **2** *vt* (**a**) *(en general)* to open; *(cremallera)* to undo (**b**) *(gas, grifo)* to turn on (**c**) *Der* **a. (un) expediente** to start proceedings
> **3 abrirse** *upr* (**a**) *(en general)* to open; *Fig* **abrirse paso** to make one's way (**b**) *Fam* **¡me abro!** I'm off!

- Las marcas de uso y de campo semántico están claramente indicadas.

> **reconocer** ⟨34⟩ *vt* (**a**) *(identificar)* to recognize (**b**) *(admitir)* to admit (**c**) *Med (paciente)* to examine

- Los números que aparecen detrás de los verbos irregulares españoles remiten a las conjugaciones que se encuentran en la parte central del diccionario.

> **blando, -a** *adj* soft
>
> ✎ Observa que la palabra inglesa **bland** es un falso amigo y no es la traducción de la palabra española **blando**. En inglés **bland** significa "soso".

- Las notas de uso informan sobre los falsos amigos.

> **acodarse** *upr* to lean **(en on)**

- Las preposiciones de uso más frecuente aparecen después de las traducciones.

> **acústica** *nf* acoustics *sing*

- El número de las traducciones sustantivas aparece en los casos en los que éste es ambiguo.

vii

Abbreviations used in this dictionary
Abreviaturas usadas en este diccionario

abbreviation	*abbr, abr*	abreviatura
adjective	*adj*	adjetivo
adverb	*adv*	adverbio
agriculture	*Agr*	agricultura
somebody, someone	*algn*	alguien
Latin American	*Am*	hispanoamericano
anatomy	*Anat*	anatomía
Andean Spanish (Bolivia, Chile, Colombia, Ecuador, Peru)	*Andes*	español andino (Bolivia, Chile, Colombia, Ecuador, Perú)
approximately	*aprox*	aproximadamente
architecture	*Archit*	arquitectura
Argentinian Spanish	*Arg*	español de Argentina
architecture	*Arquit*	arquitectura
article	*art*	artículo
art	*Art, Arte*	bellas artes
astronomy	*Astron*	astronomía
Australian	*Austr*	australiano
motoring	*Aut*	automóviles
auxiliary	*aux*	auxiliar
aviation	*Av*	aviación
biology	*Biol*	biología
Bolivian	*Bol*	español de Bolivia
botany	*Bot*	botánica
British	*Br*	británico
Central American Spanish	*CAm*	español centroamericano
Canary Islands	*Can*	español de Canarias
Caribbean Spanish (Cuba, Puerto Rico, Dominican republic, Venezuela)	*Carib*	español caribeño (Cuba, Puerto Rico, República Dominicana, Venezuela)
chemistry	*Chem*	químico
Chilean Spanish	*Chile*	español de Chile
cinema	*Cin*	cine
Colombian Spanish	*Col*	español de Colombia
commerce	*Com*	comercio
comparative	*comp*	comparativo
computers	*Comput*	informática
conditional	*cond*	condicional
conjunction	*conj*	conjunción
building industry	*Constr*	construcción
sewing	*Cost*	costura
Costa Rican Spanish	*CRica*	español de Costa Rica
Spanish from the Southern Cone region (Argentina, Uruguay, Paraguay, Chile)	*CSur*	español del Cono Sur (Argentina, Uruguay, Paraguay, Chile)
Cuban Spanish	*Cuba*	español de Cuba
cookery	*Culin*	cocina
definite	*def*	definido
demonstrative	*dem*	demostrativo
sport	*Dep*	deporte
law	*Der*	derecho
ecology	*Ecol*	ecología
economics	*Econ*	economía
Ecuadorian Spanish	*Ecuad*	español de Ecuador
education	*Educ*	educación
electricity	*Elec*	electricidad
especially	*esp*	especialmente
Peninsular Spanish	*Esp*	español de España

specialist term	*Espec*	término especializado
etcetera	*etc*	etcétera
euphemism	*Euph, Euf*	eufemismo
feminine	*f*	femenino
familiar	*Fam*	familiar
railways	*Ferroc*	ferrocarriles
figurative use	*Fig*	uso figurado
finance	*Fin*	finanzas
physics	*Fís*	física
formal use	*Fml*	uso formal
photography	*Fot*	fotografía
feminine plural	*fpl*	plural femenino
football	*Ftb*	fútbol
future	*fut*	futuro
geography	*Geog*	geografía
geology	*Geol*	geología
geometry	*Geom*	geometría
present participle	*ger*	gerundio
Guatemalan Spanish	*Guat*	español de Guatemala
history	*Hist*	historia
humorous	*Hum*	humorístico
imperative	*imperat*	imperativo
imperfect	*imperf*	imperfecto
impersonal	*impers*	impersonal
printing	*Impr*	imprenta
industry	*Ind*	industria
indefinite	*indef*	indefinido
indeterminate	*indet*	indeterminado
indicative	*indic*	indicativo
infinitive	*infin*	infinitivo
computers	*Inform*	informática
insurance	*Ins*	seguros
inseparable	*insep*	inseparable
interjection	*interj*	interjección
interrogative	*interr*	interrogativo
invariable	*inv*	invariable
irregular	*irreg*	irregular
law	*Jur*	derecho
linguistics	*Ling*	lingüística
literature	*Lit*	literatura
phrase	*loc*	locución
masculine	*m*	masculino
mathematics	*Math, Mat*	matemáticas
medicine	*Med*	medicina
meteorology	*Met*	meteorología
Mexican Spanish	*Méx*	español de México
military	*Mil*	militar
mining	*Min*	minas
masculine plural	*mpl*	plural masculino
music	*Mus, Mús*	música
noun	*n*	nombre
nautical	*Naut, Náut*	náutica
neuter	*neut*	neutro
feminine noun	*nf*	nombre femenino
plural feminine noun	*nfpl*	nombre femenino plural
masculine noun	*nm*	nombre masculino
masculine and feminine noun	*nmf/nm,f*	nombre masculino y femenino
plural masculine noun	*nmpl*	nombre masculino plural
plural noun	*npl*	nombre plural
optics	*Opt*	óptica
ornithology	*Orn*	ornitología

ix

Panamanian Spanish	*Pan*	español de Panamá
Paraguayan Spanish	*Par*	español de Paraguay
pejorative	*Pej*	peyorativo
personal	*pers*	personal
Peruvian Spanish	*Perú*	español de Perú
pejorative	*Pey*	peyorativo
photography	*Phot*	fotografía
physics	*Phys*	física
plural	*pl*	plural
politics	*Pol*	política
possessive	*pos, poss*	posesivo
past participle	*pp*	participio pasado
prefix	*pref*	prefijo
preposition	*prep*	preposición
present	*pres*	presente
present participle	*pres p*	gerundio
Puerto Rican Spanish	*PRico*	español de Puerto Rico
pronoun	*pron*	pronombre
psychology	*Psi, Psy*	psicología
past tense	*pt*	pretérito
chemistry	*Quím*	químico
radio	*Rad*	radio
railways	*Rail*	ferrocarriles
Dominican Spanish	*RDom*	español de la República Dominicana
relative	*rel*	relativo
religion	*Rel*	religión
Spanish from the River Plate region (Argentina, Uruguay, Paraguay)	*RP*	español de los países ribereños del Río de la Plata
somebody, someone	*sb*	alguien
school	*Sch*	escuela
Scottish	*Scot*	escocés
separable	*sep*	separable
singular	*sing*	singular
something	*sth*	algo
subjunctive	*subj*	subjuntivo
superlative	*superl*	superlativo
bullfighting	*Taurom*	tauromaquia
technical	*Tech, Téc*	técnica
telephones	*Tel*	teléfonos
textiles	*Tex*	textiles
theatre	*Th*	teatro
television	*TV*	televisión
typography	*Typ*	tipografía
university	*Univ*	universidad
Uruguayan Spanish	*Urug*	español de Uruguay
United States	*US*	Estados Unidos
usually	*usu*	usualmente
verb	*v*	verbo
Venezuelan Spanish	*Ven*	español de Venezuela
intransitive verb	*vi*	verbo intransitivo
reflexive verb	*vpr*	verbo pronominal
transitive verb	*vt*	verbo transitivo
vulgar	*Vulg*	vulgar
zoology	*Zool*	zoología
cultural equivalent	≃	equivalente cultural
registered trademark	®	marca registrada

Spanish Pronunciation Guide

The pronunciation of most Spanish words is predictable as there is a close match between spelling and pronunciation. The table below gives an explanation of that pronunciation. In the dictionary text therefore pronunciation is only given when the word does not follow these rules, often because it is a word of foreign origin. In these cases, the IPA (International Phonetic Alphabet) is used (see column 2 of the table below).

Letter in Spanish	IPA Symbol	Example in Spanish	Pronunciation (example in English)
Vowels			
Note that all vowel sounds in Spanish are shorter than in English			
a	a	**a**la	Similar to the sound in "f**a**ther" but more central
e	e	**e**m**e**	Similar to the sound in "m**e**t"
I	i	**i**r**i**s	Like the vowel sound in "m**ea**t" but much shorter
o	o	**o**s**o**	**o**ff, **o**n
u	u	**u**va	Like the vowel sound in "s**oo**n" but much shorter
Semiconsonants			
"i" in: ia, ie, io, iu	j	h**i**ato, h**i**elo, av**i**ón, v**i**uda	**y**es
"u" in: ua, ue, ui, uo	w	s**u**ave, f**u**ego, h**u**ida	**w**in
Consonants			
b	b	**b**omba (at beginning of word or after m)	**b**oom
	β	a**b**ajo (all other contexts)	A "**b**" pronounced without quite closing the lips completely

Letter in Spanish	IPA Symbol	Example in Spanish	Pronunciation (example in English)
c	θ (in Spain)	ceño (before e) cinco (before i)	thanks (in Spain)
	s (in Southern Spain and Latin America)		sun (in Southern Spain and Latin America)
	k	casa (every context except the preceding ones)	cat
ch	tʃ	caucho	arch
d	d	donde (at beginning of word or after "n") aldea (after "l")	day
	ð	adorno (all other contexts)	Similar to the sound in "mother" but less strong
f	f	furia	fire
g	χ	gema (before "e") girasol (before "i")	Like an "h" but pronounced at the back of the throat (similar to Scottish "loch")
	g	gato (at beginning of word) lengua (after "n")	goose
	ɣ	agua (all other contexts)	Like a "w" pronounced while trying to say "g"
j	χ	jabalí	Like an "h" but pronounced at the back of the throat (similar to Scottish "loch")
l	l	lado	lake
ll	j	lluvia	yellow
	ʒ		In some regions (eg the Rio de la Plata area of South America) it is pronounced as in "pleasure"
m	m	mano	man

Letter in Spanish	IPA Symbol	Example in Spanish	Pronunciation (example in English)
n	n	nulo	no
	ŋ	manco, fango, (before c and g)	parking
ñ	ɲ	año	onion
p	p	papa	pool
q	k	queso	cat
r	r	dorado (in between vowels) hablar (at end of syllable or word)	A rolled "r" sound (similar to Scottish "r")
	rr	rosa (beginning of word) alrededor (after "l") enredo (after "n")	A longer rolled "r" sound (similar to Scottish "r")
rr	rr	arroyo	A much longer rolled "r" sound (similar to Scottish "r")
s	s	saco	sound
sh	ʃ	show	show
t	t	tela	tea
v	b	invierno (after "n")	boom
	β	ave (all other contexts)	A "b" pronounced without quite closing the lips completely
x	ks	examen	extra
y	j	ayer	yes
	ʒ		In some regions (eg the Rio de la Plata area of South America) it is pronounced like the "s" in "pleasure"
z	θ (in Spain)	zapato	thanks (in Spain)
	s (in Southern Spain and Latin America)		sun (in Southern Spain and Latin America)

Pronunciación del inglés

Para ilustrar la pronunciación inglesa, en este diccionario utilizamos los símbolos del AFI (Alfabeto Fonético Internacional). En el siguiente cuadro, para cada sonido del inglés hay ejemplos de palabras en inglés y palabras en español donde aparece un sonido similar. En los casos en los que no hay sonido similar en español, ofrecemos una explicación de cómo pronunciarlos.

Carácter AFI	Ejemplo en inglés	Ejemplo en español
Consonantes		
[b]	babble	bebé
[d]	dig	dedo
[dʒ]	giant, jig	se pronuncia como [ʒ] en "pleasure" pero con una "d" adelante, o como "gi" en italiano: Giovanna
[f]	fit, physics	faro
[g]	grey, big	gris
[h]	happy	"h" aspirada
[j]	yellow	se pronuncia como "y" o "ll" en España: yo, lluvia
[k]	clay, kick	clic
[l]	lip	labio
	pill	papel
[m]	mummy	mamá
[n]	nip, pin	nada
[ŋ]	sing	se pronuncia como "n" antes de "c": banco
[p]	pip	papá
[r]	rig, write	sonido entre "r" y "rr"
[s]	sick, science	sapo
[ʃ]	ship, nation	show
[t]	tip, butt	tela
[tʃ]	chip, batch	caucho
[θ]	thick	zapato (como se pronuncia en España)

Carácter AFI	Ejemplo en inglés	Ejemplo en español
[ð]	this	se pronuncia como la "d" de "hada" pero más fuerte
[v]	vague, give	se pronuncia como "v" de vida, con los dientes apoyados sobre el labio inferior
[w]	wit, why	whisky
[z]	zip, physics	"s" con sonido zumbante
[ʒ]	pleasure	se pronuncia como "y" o "ll" en el Río de la Plata: yo, lluvia
[χ]	loch	jota
Vocales		
[æ]	rag	se pronuncia "a" con posición bucal para "e"
[ɑ:]	large, half	"a" muy alargada
[ʌ]	cup	"a" breve y cerrada
[e]	set	se pronuncia como "e" de elefante pero más corta
[ɜ:]	curtain, were	se pronuncia como una "e" larga con posición bucal entre "o" y "e"
[ə]	utter	se pronuncia como "e" con posición bucal para "o"
[ɪ]	big, women	"i" breve, a medio camino entre "e" e "i"
[i:]	leak, wee	"i" muy alargada
[ɒ]	lock	"o" abierta
[ɔ:]	wall, cork	"o" cerrada y alargada
[ʊ]	put, look	"u" breve
[u:]	moon	"u" muy alargada

Carácter AFI	Ejemplo en inglés	Ejemplo en español
Diptongos		
[aɪ]	why, high, lie	aire
[aʊ]	how	aura
[eə]	bear	"ea" pronunciado muy brevemente y con sonido de "e" más marcado que el de "a"
[eɪ]	day, make, main	reina
[əʊ]	show, go	"ou" como en COU
[ɪə]	here, gear	hielo pronunciado con el sonido de "i" más marcado y alargado que el de "e"
[ɔɪ]	boy, soil	voy
[ʊə]	poor	cuerno pronunciado con el sonido de "u" más marcado y alargado que el de "e"

A, a [a] *nf (letra)* A, a

a¹ *(abr* **área)** area

a² *prep*

> a combines with the article **el** to form the contraction **al** (e.g. **al centro** to the centre).

(a) *(dirección)* to; **ir a Colombia** to go to Colombia; **llegar a Valencia** to arrive in Valencia; **subir al tren** to get on the train; **ir al cine** to go to the cinema; **vete a casa** go home
(b) *(lugar)* at, on; **a la derecha** on the right; **a la entrada** at the entrance; **a lo lejos** in the distance; **a mi lado** at *o* by my side, next to me; **al sol** in the sun; **a la mesa** at (the) table
(c) *(tiempo)* at; **a las doce** at twelve o'clock; **a los sesenta años** at the age of sixty; **a los tres meses/la media hora** three months/half an hour later; **al final** in the end; **al principio** at first
(d) *(distancia)* away; **a 100 km de aquí** 100 km from here
(e) *(manera)* **a la inglesa** in the English fashion *o* style; **escrito a máquina** typed, typewritten; **a mano** by hand
(f) *(proporción)* **a 90 km por hora** at 90 km an hour; **a dos euros el kilo** two euros a kilo; **tres veces a la semana** three times a week
(g) *Dep* **ganar cuatro a dos** to win four (to) two
(h) *(complemento indirecto)* to; *(procedencia)* from; **díselo a Javier** tell Javier; **te lo di a ti** I gave it to you; **comprarle algo a algn** to buy sth from sb; *(para algn)* to buy sth for sb; *(complemento directo de persona)* **saludé a tu tía** I said hello to your aunt
(i) *Fam* **ir a por algn/algo** to go and fetch sb/sth
(j) *(verbo + a + infin)* to; **aprender a nadar** to learn (how) to swim; **fueron a ayudarle** they went to help him
(k) *(nombre + a + infin)* **distancia a recorrer** distance to be covered
(l) **a decir verdad** to tell (you) the truth; **a no ser por ...** if it were not for ...; **a no ser que** unless; **a ver** let's see; **¡a comer!** lunch/dinner/*etc* is ready!; **¡a dormir!** bedtime!; **¿a que no lo haces?** *(desafío)* I bet you don't do it!

abad *nm* abbot

abadía *nf* abbey

abajeño, -a *nm,f Am* lowlander

abajo 1 *adv* **(a)** *(en una casa)* downstairs; **el piso de a.** the downstairs flat **(b)** *(dirección)* down, downwards; **ahí/aquí a.** down there/here; **la parte de a.** the bottom (part); **más a.** further down; **hacia a.** down, downwards; **calle a.** down the street; **echar algo a.** to knock sth down; **venirse a.** *(edificio)* to fall down; *Fig (proyecto)* to fall through
2 *interj* **¡a. la censura!** down with censorship!

abalanzarse [40] *vpr* **a. hacia** to rush towards; **a. sobre** to pounce on

abalear *vt Andes, CAm, Ven* to shoot at

abalorio *nm* **(a)** *(cuenta)* glass bead **(b)** *(baratija)* trinket

abanderado, -a *nm,f* standard bearer

abandonado, -a *adj* **(a)** *(persona, cosa)* abandoned; **tiene a su familia muy abandonada** he takes absolutely no interest in his family **(b)** *(desaseado)* untidy, unkempt

abandonar 1 *vt* **(a)** *(lugar)* to leave, to quit; *(persona, cosa)* to abandon; *(proyecto, plan)* to give up **(b)** *Dep (carrera)* to drop out of
2 abandonarse *vpr* to let oneself go

abandono *nm* **(a)** *(acción)* abandoning, desertion **(b)** *(de proyecto, idea)* giving up **(c)** *(descuido)* neglect

abanicarse *vpr* to fan oneself

abanico *nm* **(a)** *(objeto)* fan **(b)** *(gama)* range; **un amplio a. de posibilidades** a wide range of possibilities

abaratar 1 *vt (precio)* to bring down, to reduce; *(artículo)* to reduce the price of
2 abaratarse *vpr* to become cheaper, to come down in price

abarcar [44] *vt (incluir)* to cover

abarrotado, -a *adj (teatro, autobús)* packed (**de** with); *(desván, baúl)* crammed (**de** with)

abarrotar *vt (teatro, autobús)* to pack (**de** *o* **con** with); *(desván, baúl)* to cram full (**de** *o* **con** of)

abarrotería *nf CAm, Méx* grocer's (shop), grocery store

abarrotero, -a *nm,f CAm, Méx* grocer

abarrotes *nmpl CAm, Méx* groceries; **tienda de a.** grocer's (shop), grocery store

abastecedor, -a *nm,f* supplier

abastecer [33] **1** *vt* to supply
2 abastecerse *vpr* **abastecerse de** to stock up on

abastecimiento *nm* supplying; **a. de agua** water supply

abasto *nm* (a) *Fam* **no doy a.** I can't cope, I can't keep up (b) **mercado de abastos** wholesale food market

abatible *adj* folding, collapsible; **asiento a.** reclining seat

abatido, -a *adj* downcast

abatir 1 *vt* (a) *(derribar)* to knock down, to pull down (b) *(matar)* to kill; **a. a tiros** to shoot down (c) *(desanimar)* to depress, to dishearten
2 abatirse *vpr (desanimarse)* to lose heart, to become depressed

abdicación *nf* abdication

abdicar [44] *vt & vi* to abdicate

abdomen *nm* abdomen

abdominales *nmpl* sit-ups

abecedario *nm* alphabet

abedul *nm* birch

abeja *nf* bee; **a. reina** queen bee

abejorro *nm* bumblebee

aberración *nf* aberration

aberrante *adj* (a) *(absurdo)* ridiculous, idiotic (b) *(perverso)* perverse

abertura *nf (hueco)* opening, gap; *(grieta)* crack, slit

abertzale [aβer't∫ale] *adj & nmf Esp* Basque nationalist

abeto *nm Bot* fir (tree); **a. rojo** spruce

abierto, -a 1 *adj* (a) open; *(grifo)* (turned) on; **a. de par en par** wide open (b) *(persona)* open-minded
2 *pp de* **abrir**

abigarrado, -a *adj (mezclado)* jumbled, mixed up

abismal *adj* abysmal; **una diferencia a.** a world of difference

abismo *nm* abyss; *Fig* **al borde del a.** on the brink of ruin; *Fig* **entre ellos media un a.** they are worlds apart

ablandar 1 *vt* to soften
2 ablandarse *vpr* (a) *(objeto, material)* to soften, to go soft (b) *Fig (persona)* to mellow

abnegación *nf* abnegation, self-denial

abnegado, -a *adj* selfless, self-sacrificing

abocado, -a *adj* destined (**a** to); **está a. al fracaso** it is doomed to failure

abochornar *vt* to embarrass

abofetear *vt* to slap

abogacía *nf* legal profession

abogado, -a *nm,f Br* lawyer, *US* attorney; *(en tribunal supremo)* lawyer, *Br* barrister; **a. de oficio** legal aid lawyer; **a. defensor** counsel for the defence; **a. del diablo** devil's advocate; **a. laboralista** union lawyer

abogar [42] *vi* to plead; **a. a favor de** to plead for, to defend; **a. por algo** to advocate *o* champion sth

abolengo *nm* lineage

abolición *nf* abolition

abolir *vt* to abolish

abolladura *nf* dent

abollar *vt* to dent

abominable *adj* abominable

abominar 1 *vt (detestar)* to abhor, to abominate
2 *vi* **a. de** *(condenar)* to condemn, to criticize

abonado, -a 1 *nm,f (a revista)* subscriber; *(a teléfono, de gas)* customer
2 *adj Fin (pagado)* paid; **a. en cuenta** credited

abonar 1 *vt* (a) *Agr* to fertilize (b) *(pagar)* to pay (for) (c) *(subscribir)* to subscribe
2 abonarse *vpr* to subscribe (**a** to)

abonero, -a *nm,f Méx* hawker, street trader

abono *nm* (a) *Agr (producto)* fertilizer; *(estiércol)* manure·(b) *(pago)* payment (c) *(a revista etc)* subscription; *(billete)* season ticket (d) *Méx (plazo)* instalment; **pagar en abonos** to pay by instalments

abordar *vt (persona)* to approach; *(barco)* to board; **a. un asunto** to tackle a subject

aborigen *(pl* **aborígenes**) **1** *adj* native, indigenous; *esp Austral* aboriginal
2 *nmf* native; *esp Austral* aborigine

aborrecer [33] *vt* to detest, to loathe

abortar 1 *vi (involuntariamente)* to miscarry, to have a miscarriage; *(intencionadamente)* to abort, to have an abortion
2 *vt* to abort

abortista *adj & nmf* abortionist

aborto *nm* miscarriage; *(provocado)* abortion

abotargado, -a *adj* swollen

abotonar *vt (ropa)* to button (up)

abovedado, -a *adj* vaulted

abracadabra *nm* abracadabra

abrasador, -a *adj* scorching

abrasar 1 *vt* to burn oneself
2 abrasarse *upr* to burn

abrazadera *nf* clamp

abrazar [40] **1** *vt* to embrace, to hug; *Fig* (*doctrina*) to embrace
2 abrazarse *upr* **abrazarse a algn** to embrace sb; **se abrazaron** they embraced each other

abrazo *nm* embrace, hug; **un a., abrazos** (*en carta*) best wishes

abrebotellas *nm inv* bottle opener

abrecartas *nm inv* letter-opener, paper-knife

abrefácil *nm* **caja con a.** easy-open carton

abrelatas *nm inv* can opener, *Br* tin-opener

abreviar [43] **1** *vt* to shorten; (*texto*) to abridge; (*palabra*) to abbreviate
2 *vi* to be quick *o* brief; **para a.** to cut a long story short

abreviatura *nf* abbreviation

abridor *nm* (*de latas, botellas*) (can-)opener, *Br* (tin-)opener

abrigado, -a *adj* wrapped-up; **ir muy a.** to be well wrapped-up

abrigar [42] *vt* (**a**) (*dar calor*) to keep warm (**b**) (*proteger*) to protect, to shelter (**c**) (*esperanza*) to cherish; (*duda*) to have, to harbour
2 *vi* to be warm; **esta chaqueta abriga mucho** this cardigan is very warm

abrigo *nm* (**a**) (*prenda*) coat, overcoat; **ropa de a.** warm clothes (**b**) **al a. de** protected *o* sheltered from

abril *nm* April

abrillantador *nm* polish

abrillantar *vt* to polish

abrir¹ *nm* **en un a. y cerrar de ojos** in the twinkling of an eye

abrir² (*pp* **abierto**) **1** *vi* to open
2 *vt* (**a**) (*en general*) to open; (*cremallera*) to undo (**b**) (*gas, grifo*) to turn on (**c**) *Der* **a. (un) expediente** to start proceedings
3 abrirse *upr* (**a**) (*en general*) to open; *Fig* **abrirse paso** to make one's way (**b**) *Fam* **¡me abro!** I'm off!

abrochar 1 *vt* (**a**) (*botones, camisa*) to do up; (*cinturón*) to fasten (**b**) *RP* (*papeles*) to staple
2 abrocharse *upr* (*botones, camisa*) to do up; (*cinturón*) to fasten; **abrocharse la camisa** to do up one's shirt

abrumado, -a *adj* overwhelmed

abrumador, -a *adj* overwhelming

abrumar *vt* to overwhelm, to crush; **tantos problemas me abruman** all these problems are getting on top of me

abrupto, -a *adj* (**a**) (*terreno*) steep, abrupt (**b**) *Fig* abrupt, sudden

absceso *nm* abscess

absentismo *nm Esp* **a. laboral** (*justificado*) absence from work; (*injustificado*) absenteeism

ábside *nm Arquit* apse

absolución *nf* (**a**) *Rel* absolution (**b**) *Der* acquittal

absolutamente *adv* absolutely, completely; **a. nada** nothing at all

absoluto, -a *adj* absolute; **en a.** not at all, by no means

absolutorio, -a *adj Der* **sentencia absolutoria** verdict of not guilty

absolver [4] (*pp* **absuelto**) *vt* (**a**) *Rel* to absolve (**b**) *Der* to acquit

absorbente *adj* (**a**) (*papel*) absorbent (**b**) *Fig* absorbing, engrossing

absorber *vt* (**a**) (*líquido, gas*) to absorb (**b**) (*consumir*) to take up, to soak up (**c**) (*empresa*) to absorb by merger

absorción *nf* (**a**) (*de líquido, gas*) absorption (**b**) (*de empresa*) absorption (by merger)

absorto, -a *adj* absorbed, engrossed (**en** in)

abstemio, -a 1 *adj* teetotal, abstemious
2 *nm,f* teetotaller

abstención *nf* abstention

abstenerse [24] *upr* to abstain (**de** from); (*privarse*) to refrain (**de** from)

abstinencia *nf* abstinence; **síndrome de a.** withdrawal symptoms

abstracción *nf* abstraction

abstracto, -a *adj* abstract

abstraer [25] **1** *vt* to abstract
2 abstraerse *upr* to become lost in thought

abstraído, -a *adj* (*ensimismado*) absorbed, engrossed (**en** in); (*distraído*) absent-minded

absuelto, -a *pp de* **absolver**

absurdo, -a 1 *adj* absurd
2 *nm* absurdity, absurd thing

abuchear *vt* to boo, to jeer at

abucheo *nm* booing, jeering

abuela *nf* grandmother; *Fam* grandma, granny; *Fig* old woman

abuelo *nm* (**a**) (*hombre*) grandfather; *Fam* grandad, grandpa; *Fig* old man (**b**) **abuelos** grandparents

abulense 1 *adj* of/from Avila
2 *nmf* person from Avila

abulia *nf* apathy, lack of willpower

abultado, -a *adj* bulky, big

abultar 1 *vi* to be bulky; **abulta mucho** it takes up a lot of space
2 *vt* to exaggerate

abundancia *nf* abundance, plenty; *Fig* **nadar en la a.** to be rolling in money

abundante *adj* abundant, plentiful

abundar *vi* (**a**) *(ser abundante)* to abound, to be plentiful (**b**) **a. en** *(tener)* to be rich in

aburrido, -a *adj* (**a**) **ser a.** to be boring (**b**) **estar a.** to be bored; **estar a. de** *(harto)* to be tired of

aburrimiento *nm* boredom; **¡qué a.!** how boring!, what a bore!

aburrir 1 *vt* to bore
2 aburrirse *vpr* to get bored; **aburrirse como una ostra** to be bored stiff

abusado, -a *adj Méx Fam* smart, sharp

abusar *vi* (**a**) *(propasarse)* to go too far (**b**) **a. de** *(situación, persona)* to take (unfair) advantage of; *(poder, amabilidad)* to abuse; **a. de la bebida/del tabaco** to drink/smoke too much *o* to excess; *Der* **a. de un niño/una mujer** to abuse a child/woman

abusivo, -a *adj (precio)* exorbitant

abuso *nm* abuse

abyecto, -a *adj* abject

a. C. *(abr antes de Cristo)* BC

a/c *Com (abr a cuenta)* on account

acá *adv* (**a**) *(lugar)* here, over here; **más a.** nearer; **¡ven a.!** come here! (**b**) **de entonces a.** since then

acabado, -a 1 *adj* (**a**) *(terminado)* finished (**b**) *Fig (persona)* worn-out, spent
2 *nm* finish

acabar 1 *vt* to finish (off); *(completar)* to complete
2 *vi* (**a**) *(en general)* to finish, to end; **a. bien** to have a happy ending; **a. con algo** *(terminarlo)* to finish sth; *(romperlo)* to break sth (**b**) **a. de …** to have just …; **acaba de entrar** he has just come in; **no acaba de convencerme** I'm not quite convinced (**c**) **acabaron casándose** *o* **por casarse** they ended up getting married; **acabó en la cárcel** he ended up in jail
3 acabarse *vpr* to finish, to come to an end; **se nos acabó la gasolina** we ran out of *Br* petrol *o US* gas; *Fam* **¡se acabó!** that's that!

acabóse *nm Fam* **esto es el a.** this is the end

acacia *nf* acacia

academia *nf* academy; **a. de idiomas** language school

académico, -a *adj & nm,f* academic

acaecer [33] *v impers* to happen, to occur

acallar *vt* to silence

acalorado, -a *adj* (**a**) *(por calor)* hot (**b**) *Fig (excitado)* worked up, excited; *(debate etc)* heated, angry

acalorarse *vpr* (**a**) *(por calor)* to get hot (**b**) *Fig* to get excited *o* worked up

acampada *nf* camping; **ir de a.** to go camping; **zona de a.** camp site, *US* campground

acampanado, -a *adj* bell-shaped; *(prendas)* flared

acampar *vi* to camp

acantilado *nm* cliff

acantonar *vt (tropas)* to billet, to quarter (**en** in)

acaparar *vt* (**a**) *(productos)* to hoard; *(el mercado)* to corner (**b**) *Fig* to monopolize

acápite *nm* (**a**) *Am (párrafo)* paragraph (**b**) *CAm (título)* title

acaramelado, -a *adj* (**a**) *(color)* caramel-coloured (**b**) *(pareja)* lovey-dovey, starry-eyed

acariciar [43] *vt* to caress; *(pelo, animal)* to stroke; *(esperanza)* to cherish

acarrear *vt* (**a**) *(transportar)* to carry, to transport (**b**) *(conllevar)* to entail

acaso *adv* perhaps, maybe; **¿a. no te lo dije?** did I not tell you, by any chance?; **por si a.** just in case; **si a. viene …** if he should come …

acatamiento *nm* respect; *(de la ley)* observance

acatar *vt* to observe, to comply with

acatarrado, -a *adj* **estar a.** to have a cold

acatarrarse *vpr* to catch a cold

acaudalado, -a *adj* rich, wealthy

acaudillar *vt* to lead

acceder *vi* **a. a** *(consentir)* to accede to, to consent to; *(tener acceso)* to gain admittance to; *Inform* to access

accesible *adj* accessible; *(persona)* approachable

acceso *nm* (**a**) *(entrada)* access, entry; *Inform* **a. aleatorio** random access; *Univ* **prueba de a.** entrance examination; **a. a Internet** Internet access (**b**) *(carretera)* approach, access (**c**) *Med & Fig* fit

accesorio, -a *adj & nm* accessory

accidentado, -a 1 *adj (terreno)* uneven, hilly; *(viaje, vida)* eventful
2 *nm,f* casualty, accident victim

accidental *adj* accidental; **un encuentro a.** a chance meeting

accidente *nm* (**a**) *(suceso)* accident; **por a.** by chance; **a. laboral** industrial accident (**b**) *Geog* **accidentes geográficos** geographical features

acción *nf* (**a**) *(efecto de hacer)* action; **poner en a.** to put into action; **ponerse en**

a. to go into action; **campo de a.** field of action; **película de a.** adventure movie o Br film **(b)** *(hecho)* deed, act; **una buena a.** a good deed **(c)** *Fin* share

accionar 1 *vt* **(a)** *(mecanismo, palanca)* to activate **(b)** *Am Der* to bring a suit against
2 *vi (gesticular)* to gesture, to gesticulate

accionariado *nm Fin Br* shareholders, *US* stockholders

accionista *nmf Br* shareholder, *US* stockholder

acebo *nm (hoja)* holly; *(árbol)* holly tree

acechar *vt* to lie in wait for; **un grave peligro nos acecha** great danger awaits us

acecho *nm* **estar al a. de** *(esperar)* to lie in wait for

aceite *nm* oil; **a. de girasol/maíz/oliva** sunflower/corn/olive oil

aceitera *nf* **(a)** *Culin* **aceiteras** oil and vinegar set **(b)** *Aut* oil can

aceitero, -a 1 *adj* oil
2 *nm,f* oil merchant

aceitoso, -a *adj* oily

aceituna *nf* olive; **a. rellena** stuffed olive

aceitunado, -a *adj* olive, olive-coloured

aceitunero, -a *nm,f* **(a)** *(recolector)* olive picker o harvester **(b)** *(vendedor)* olive seller

acelerado, -a *adj* accelerated, fast; *Fam Fig* **estar a.** to be hyper

acelerador *nm Aut* accelerator

acelerar *vt & vi* to accelerate

acelga *nf* chard

acento *nm* **(a)** *(en una palabra) (escrito)* accent; *(pronunciado)* stress **(b)** *(entonación)* accent

acentuar [30] **1** *vt* **(a)** *(palabra)* to stress **(b)** *Fig* to emphasize, to stress
2 acentuarse *vpr Fig* to become more pronounced o noticeable

acepción *nf* meaning, sense

aceptable *adj* acceptable

aceptación *nf* acceptance; **tener poca a.** to have little success, not to be popular

aceptar *vt* to accept

acequia *nf* irrigation ditch o channel

acera *nf Br* pavement, *US* sidewalk; *Fam Pey* **ser de la a. de enfrente** to be gay o queer

acerbo, -a *adj* **(a)** *(áspero)* bitter **(b)** *(mordaz)* caustic, cutting

acerca *adv* **a. de** about

acercamiento *nm* bringing together, coming together; *Pol* rapprochement

acercar [44] **1** *vt* to bring near o nearer, to bring closer; *Fig* to bring together; **¿te acerco a casa?** can I give you a *Br* lift o *US* ride home?

2 acercarse *vpr* **(a)** to approach **(b)** *(ir)* to go; *(venir)* to come

acerico *nm* pincushion

acero *nm* steel; **a. inoxidable** stainless steel

acérrimo, -a *adj (partidario)* staunch; *(enemigo)* bitter

acertado, -a *adj* **(a)** *(solución)* right, correct; *(decisión)* wise **(b) no estuviste muy a.** al decir eso it wasn't very wise of you to say that

acertante 1 *nmf* winner
2 *adj* winning

acertar [1] **1** *vt (pregunta)* to get right; *(adivinar)* to guess correctly; **a. las quinielas** to win the pools
2 *vi* to be right; **acertó con la calle que buscaba** she found the street she was looking for

acertijo *nm* riddle

acervo *nm* **a. cultural** cultural tradition o heritage

achacar [44] *vt* to attribute **(a** to)

achacoso, -a *adj* ailing, unwell

achaque *nm* ailment, complaint

achicar [44] **1** *vt* **(a)** *(amilanar)* to intimidate **(b)** *(encoger)* to reduce, to make smaller **(c)** *(barco)* to bale out
2 achicarse *vpr* **(a)** *(amilanarse)* to lose heart **(b)** *(encogerse)* to get smaller

achicharrar 1 *vt* to burn to a crisp
2 achicharrarse *vpr Fam (de calor)* to be boiling (hot)

achicoria *nf* chicory

achinado, -a *adj* **(a)** *(ojos)* slanting **(b)** *RP (aindiado)* Indian-looking

acholado, -a *adj Bol, Chile, Perú Pey (mestizo) (físicamente)* Indian-looking; *(culturalmente)* = who has adopted Indian ways

achuchar *vt Fam (empujar)* to shove; *(abrazar)* to hug

achuchón *nm Fam (empujón)* push, shove; *(abrazo)* big hug

aciago, -a *adj* ill-fated, fateful

acicalado, -a *adj* well-dressed, smart

acicalarse *vpr* to dress up, to smarten up

acicate *nm* spur, incentive

acidez *nf (de sabor)* sharpness, sourness; *Quím* acidity; *Med* **a. de estómago** heartburn

ácido, -a 1 *adj (sabor)* sharp, tart; *Quím* acidic; *Fig (tono)* harsh
2 *nm Quím* acid

acierto *nm (buena decisión)* good choice o idea; **con gran a.** very wisely

aclamación *nf* acclamation, acclaim

aclamar *vt* to acclaim

aclaración *nf* explanation, clarification

aclarado *nm Esp* rinsing, rinse

aclarar 1 *vt* (**a**) *(explicar)* to clarify, to explain; *(color)* to lighten, to make lighter (**b**) *Esp (enjuagar)* to rinse
2 *v impers Met* to clear (up)
3 aclararse *vpr* (**a**) *(decidirse)* to make up one's mind; *(entender)* to understand (**b**) *Met* to clear (up)

aclaratorio, -a *adj* explanatory

aclimatación *nf Br* acclimatization, *US* acclimation

aclimatar 1 *vt Br* to acclimatize, *US* to acclimate (**a** to)
2 aclimatarse *vpr Fig* **aclimatarse a algo** to get used to sth

acné *nf* acne

acobardar 1 *vt* to frighten
2 acobardarse *vpr* to get frightened, to lose one's nerve

acodarse *vpr* to lean (**en** on)

acogedor, -a *adj* cosy, warm

acoger [53] **1** *vt* (**a**) *(recibir)* to receive; *(a invitado)* to welcome (**b**) *(persona desvalida)* to take in; *(en familia)* to foster
2 acogerse *vpr Fig* **acogerse a** to take refuge in; *(amnistía)* to avail oneself of; **acogerse a la ley** to have recourse to the law

acogida *nf* (**a**) *(de persona)* reception, welcome (**b**) **a.** *(familiar)* fostering; **familia/hogar de a.** foster parents/home

acojonado, -a *adj Esp muy Fam* shit-scared

acojonante *adj Esp muy Fam* damn *o Br* bloody great *o* terrific

acojonarse *vpr Esp muy Fam* to shit oneself, to be shit-scared

acolchar *vt (rellenar)* to pad; *(prenda)* to quilt

acometer 1 *vt* (**a**) *(emprender)* to undertake (**b**) *(atacar)* to attack
2 *vi (embestir)* **a. contra** to hurtle into

acometida *nf* attack

acomodado, -a *adj* well-off, well-to-do

acomodador, -a *nm,f (hombre)* usher; *(mujer)* usherette

acomodar 1 *vt* (**a**) *(alojar)* to lodge, to accommodate (**b**) *(en cine etc)* to find a place for
2 acomodarse *vpr* (**a**) *(ponerse cómodo)* to make oneself comfortable (**b**) *(adaptarse)* to adapt

acomodaticio, -a *adj* accommodating, easy-going

acompañamiento *nm Culin & Mús* accompaniment

acompañante 1 *nmf* companion
2 *adj* accompanying

acompañar *vt* (**a**) *(persona)* to accompany; **le acompañó hasta la puerta** he saw him to the door; **me acompañó al médico** he came with me to see the doctor; **¿te acompaño a casa?** can I walk you home?; *Fml* **le acompaño en el sentimiento** my condolences (**b**) *(adjuntar)* to enclose

acompasado, -a *adj (crecimiento, desarrollo)* steady; *(pasos)* measured

acomplejado, -a *adj* **estar a.** to have a complex (**por** about)

acomplejar 1 *vt* **a. a algn** to give sb a complex
2 acomplejarse *vpr* **a. por** to develop a complex about

acondicionado, -a *adj* **aire a.** air conditioning

acondicionador *nm* conditioner

acondicionar *vt* to prepare, to set up; *(mejorar)* to improve; *(cabello)* to condition

acongojar *vt* to distress

aconsejable *adj* advisable

aconsejar *vt* to advise

acontecer [33] *v impers* to happen, to take place

acontecimiento *nm* event

acopio *nm* store, stock; **hacer a. de** *(existencias)* to stock up on; *(valor, paciencia)* to summon up

acoplar 1 *vt* (**a**) *(encajar)* to fit (together), to join (**b**) *Téc* to couple, to connect
2 acoplarse *vpr (nave espacial)* to dock

acorazado, -a 1 *adj* armoured, armour-plated
2 *nm* battleship

acordado, -a *adj* agreed; **según lo a.** as agreed

acordar [2] **1** *vt* to agree; *(decidir)* to decide
2 acordarse *vpr* to remember; **no me acuerdo (de Silvia)** I can't remember (Silvia)

acorde 1 *adj* in agreement
2 *nm Mús* chord

acordeón *nm* (**a**) *(instrument)* accordion (**b**) *Col, Méx Fam (en examen)* crib

acordonado, -a *adj* cordoned off

acordonar *vt (zona)* to cordon off

acorralar *vt* to corner

acortar *vt* to shorten; **a. distancias** to cut down the distance

acosar *vt* to harass; *Fig* **a. a algn a preguntas** to bombard sb with questions

acoso *nm* harassment; **a. laboral** (workplace) bullying; **a. sexual** sexual harassment

acostado, -a *adj* (*tumbado*) lying down; (*en la cama*) in bed

acostar [2] **1** *vt* to put to bed
2 acostarse *vpr* to go to bed; *Fam* **acostarse con algn** to sleep with sb, to go to bed with sb

acostumbrado, -a *adj* (**a**) (*habitual*) usual, customary; **es lo a.** it is the custom (**b**) (*habituado*) **a. al frío/calor** used to the cold/heat

acostumbrar 1 *vi* **a. a** (*soler*) to be in the habit of
2 *vt* **a. a algn a algo** (*habituar*) to get sb used to sth
3 acostumbrarse *vpr* (*habituarse*) acostumbrarse a algo to get used to sth

acotación *nf* (**a**) (*en escrito*) (marginal) note; *Teatro* stage direction (**b**) (*en mapa*) elevation mark

acotamiento *nm Méx* (*arcén*) *Br* hard shoulder, *US* shoulder

acotar *vt* (**a**) (*área*) to enclose; *Fig* (*tema*) to delimit (**b**) (*texto*) to annotate (**c**) (*mapa*) to mark with elevations

ácrata *adj & nmf* anarchist

acre 1 *adj* (**a**) (*sabor*) sour, bitter; (*olor*) acrid (**b**) (*palabras*) bitter, harsh; (*crítica*) biting
2 *nm* (*medida*) acre

acrecentar [1] *vt* to increase

acreditación *nf* (*de periodista*) press card; (*de diplomático*) credentials

acreditado *adj* (**a**) (*médico, abogado*) distinguished; (*marca*) reputable (**b**) (*embajador, representante*) accredited

acreditar *vt* (**a**) (*certificar*) to certify; (*autorizar*) to authorize, to entitle (**b**) (*demostrar*) to prove, to confirm (**c**) (*periodista, embajador*) to accredit (**d**) (*dar fama a*) to be a credit to (**e**) *Fin* to credit

acreedor, -a *nm,f Com* creditor

acribillar *vt* to riddle, to pepper; **a. a algn a balazos** to riddle sb with bullets; *Fig* **a. a algn a preguntas** to fire questions at sb

acrílico, -a *adj* acrylic

acriollarse *vpr Am* to adopt local ways

acritud *nf* acrimony

acrobacia *nf* acrobatics *sing*

acróbata *nmf* acrobat

acta *nf* (**a**) (*de reunión*) minutes, record (**b**) (*certificado*) certificate, official document; **a. notarial** affidavit; **A. Única (Europea)** Single European Act

Takes the masculine articles **el** and **un**.

actitud *nf* attitude

activar *vt* to activate

actividad *nf* activity

activista *nmf* activist

activo, -a 1 *adj* active; **en a.** on active service
2 *nm Fin* assets

acto *nm* (**a**) (*hecho*) act, action; **a. sexual** sexual intercourse; **en el a.** at once; **a. seguido** immediately afterwards; *Mil* **en a. de servicio** in action; **hacer a. de presencia** to put in an appearance (**b**) (*ceremonia*) ceremony (**c**) *Teatro* act

actor *nm* actor

actriz *nf* actress

actuación *nf* (**a**) (*de artista*) performance (**b**) (*conducta, proceder*) conduct, behaviour

actual *adj* current, present; (*al día*) up-to-date; **un tema muy a.** a very topical subject

actualidad *nf* current situation; **la a. deportiva** the sports news; **en la a.** at present; **estar de a.** to be topical; **temas de a.** topical subjects

actualizar [40] *vt* to update, to bring up to date; *Inform* (*software, hardware*) to upgrade

actualmente *adv* (*hoy en día*) nowadays, these days; (*ahora*) at the moment, at present

⎧ Observa que las palabras inglesas **actual** y **actually** son falsos amigos y no son la traducción de las palabras españolas **actual** y **actualmente**. En inglés, **actual** significa "real, verdadero", y **actually** significa "en realidad".

actuar [30] *vi* (**a**) (*obrar*) to act; **a. como** *o* **de** to act as (**b**) *Cin & Teatro* to perform, to act

acuarela *nf* watercolour

Acuario *nm* Aquarius

acuario *nm* aquarium

acuartelar *vt* to confine to barracks

acuático, -a *adj* aquatic; **esquí a.** water-skiing

acuchillar *vt* to knife, to stab

acuciante *adj* urgent, pressing

acuciar [43] *vt* (**a**) (*instar*) to goad; **el deseo me acuciaba** I was driven by desire (**b**) (*ser urgente*) **le acucia encontrar un trabajo** he urgently needs to find a job

acudir *vi* (*ir*) to go; (*venir*) to come, to arrive; **nadie acudió en su ayuda** nobody came to help him; **no sé dónde a.** I don't know where to turn

acueducto *nm* aqueduct

acuerdo *nm* agreement; **¡de a.!** all right!, O.K.!; **de a. con** in accordance with; **de común a.** by common consent; **estar de a. en algo** to agree on sth; **ponerse de a.** to agree; **a. marco** framework agreement

acumulación *nf* accumulation

acumular 1 *vt* to accumulate
2 **acumularse** *vpr* to accumulate, to build up

acunar *vt (en cuna)* to rock; *(en brazos)* to cradle

acuñar *vt (moneda)* to mint; *(frase)* to coin

acuoso, -a *adj* watery; *(jugoso)* juicy

acupuntura *nf* acupuncture

acurrucarse [44] *vpr* to curl up, to snuggle up

acusación *nf* accusation; *Der* charge

acusado, -a 1 *nm,f* accused, defendant
2 *adj (marcado)* marked, noticeable

acusar 1 *vt* (a) *(inculpar)* to accuse *(de* of); *Der* to charge *(de* with) (b) *(golpe etc)* to feel; *Fig* **su cara acusaba el cansancio** his exhaustion showed in his face (c) *Com* **a. recibo** to acknowledge receipt
2 **acusarse** *vpr* (a) *(acentuarse)* to become more pronounced (b) *(notarse)* to show

acuse *nm* **a. de recibo** acknowledgement of receipt

acusica *adj & nmf Fam* telltale

acústica *nf* acoustics *sing*

acústico, -a *adj* acoustic

adán *nm Fam* untidy o slovenly person

adaptable *adj* adaptable

adaptación *nf* adaptation

adaptador *nm* adapter

adaptar 1 *vt* to adapt
2 **adaptarse** *vpr* to adjust *(a* to)

adecentar *vt* to tidy (up), to clean (up)

adecuado, -a *adj* appropriate, suitable

adecuar [47] *vt* to adapt

adefesio *nm (persona)* fright, sight; *(cosa)* monstrosity

a. de J.C. *(abr antes de Jesucristo)* BC

adelantado, -a *adj* (a) *(avanzado, precoz)* advanced (b) *(reloj)* fast (c) **pagar por a.** to pay in advance

adelantamiento *nm* overtaking; **hacer un a.** to overtake

adelantar 1 *vt* (a) *Aut* to overtake (b) *(avanzar)* to move o bring forward; *(reloj)* to put forward (c) *(fecha)* to bring forward (d) *(dinero)* to pay in advance (e) *(información)* **no podemos a. nada más por el momento** we can't tell you o say any more for the time being (f) *(conseguir)* **¿qué adelantas con eso?** what do you hope to gain o achieve by that?

2 *vi* (a) *(progresar)* to make progress (b) *(reloj)* to be fast (c) *(en carretera)* to overtake
3 **adelantarse** *vpr* (a) *(ir delante)* to go ahead (b) *(reloj)* to gain, to be fast (c) **el verano se ha adelantado** we are having an early summer (d) **adelantarse a los acontecimientos** to jump the gun

adelante 1 *adv* forward; **más a.** *(lugar)* further on; *(tiempo)* later; **seguir a.** to keep going, to carry on; **llevar a. un plan** to carry out a plan
2 *interj* **¡a!** come in!

adelanto *nm* (a) *(técnico, de dinero)* advance (b) **el reloj lleva diez minutos de a.** the watch is ten minutes fast

adelfa *nf* oleander, rosebay

adelgazamiento *nm* slimming

adelgazar [40] *vi* to slim, to lose weight

ademán *nm (con las manos)* gesture; *(con la cara)* face, expression

además *adv* moreover, furthermore; **a., no lo he visto nunca** what's more, I've never seen him; **a. de él** besides him

adentrarse *vpr* **a. en** *(bosque)* to go deep into; *(asunto)* to study thoroughly

adentro 1 *adv (dentro)* inside; **mar a.** out to sea; **tierra a.** inland
2 **adentros** *nmpl* **decir algo para sus adentros** to say sth to oneself

adepto, -a *nm,f* follower, supporter

> *Observa que la palabra inglesa* **adept** *es un falso amigo y no es la traducción de la palabra española* **adepto.** *En inglés,* **adept** *significa* "experto".

---

aderezar [40] *vt (comida)* to season; *(ensalada)* to dress

aderezo *nm (de comida)* seasoning; *(de ensalada)* dressing

adeudar 1 *vt* to owe; *Fin* to debit
2 **adeudarse** *vpr* to get into debt

adherencia *nf* adherence; *Aut* road-holding

adherente *adj* adhesive, sticky

adherir [5] 1 *vt* to stick on
2 **adherirse** *vpr* **adherirse a** to adhere to; *(partido)* to join

adhesión *nf* adhesion; *(a partido)* joining; *(a teoría)* adherence

adhesivo, -a *adj & nm* adhesive

adicción *nf* addiction; **crear a.** to be addictive

adición *nf* addition

adicional *adj* additional

adicto, -a 1 *nm,f* addict
2 *adj* addicted *(a* to)

adiestrar *vt* to train

adinerado, -a *adj* wealthy, rich

adiós (*pl* **adioses**) **1** *interj* goodbye; *Fam* bye-bye; *(al cruzarse)* hello
2 *nm* goodbye

aditivo, -a *adj & nm* additive

adivinanza *nf* riddle, puzzle

adivinar *vt* to guess; **a. el pensamiento de algn** to read sb's mind

adivino, -a *nm,f* fortune-teller

adjetivo, -a 1 *nm* adjective
2 *adj* adjectival

adjudicación *nf* award; *(en subasta)* sale

adjudicar [44] **1** *vt* (a) *(premio, contrato)* to award (b) *(en subasta)* to sell
2 adjudicarse *upr* to appropriate, to take over

adjuntar *vt* to enclose

adjunto, -a 1 *adj* (a) *(en sobre)* enclosed, attached (b) *Educ* assistant
2 *nm,f Educ* assistant teacher

adm., admón. *(abr* **administración)** admin.

administración *nf* (a) *(gobierno)* **la A.** *Br* the Government, *US* the Administration; *Pol* **a. central** central government; **a. pública** civil service (b) *(de empresa)* administration, management (c) *(oficina)* (branch) office

administrador, -a 1 *nm,f* administrator
2 *nm Inform* **a. de archivos** file manager

administrar 1 *vt* (a) *(dirigir)* to run, to manage (b) *(medicamento, sacramentos)* to administer
2 administrarse *upr* to manage one's own money

administrativo, -a 1 *adj* administrative
2 *nm,f* office worker

admirable *adj* admirable

admiración *nf* (a) *(sentimiento)* admiration; **causar a.** to impress (b) *Ling Br* exclamation mark, *US* exclamation point

admirador, -a *nm,f* admirer

admirar 1 *vt* (a) *(persona, obra)* to admire (b) *(sorprender)* to amaze, to astonish
2 admirarse *upr* to be amazed, to be astonished

admisible *adj* admissible, acceptable

admisión *nf* admission; **reservado el derecho de a.** *(en letrero)* the management reserves the right to refuse admission

admitir *vt* (a) *(dejar entrar)* to admit, to let in (b) *(aceptar)* to accept; **no se admiten cheques** *(en letrero)* no cheques accepted (c) *(tolerar)* to allow (d) *(reconocer)* to admit, to acknowledge; **admito que mentí** I admit that I lied

admón. *(abr* **administración)** admin.

admonición *nf* warning

ADN *nm* *(abr* **ácido desoxirribonucleico)** DNA

adobar *vt Culin* to marinate

adobe *nm* adobe

adobo *nm* marinade

adoctrinar *vt* to indoctrinate

adolecer [33] *vi* **a. de** *(enfermedad)* to suffer from; *(defecto)* to be guilty of

adolescencia *nf* adolescence

adolescente *adj & nmf* adolescent

adonde *adv* where

adónde *adv interr* where (to)?

adondequiera *adv* wherever

adopción *nf* adoption

adoptar *vt* to adopt

adoptivo, -a *adj* *(hijo)* adopted; *(padres)* adoptive; *Fig* **país a.** country of adoption

adoquín *nm* cobble, paving stone

adorable *adj* adorable

adoración *nf* adoration; **sentir a. por algn** to worship sb

adorar *vt* (a) *Rel* to worship (b) *Fig* to adore

adormecer [33] **1** *vt* to lull to sleep
2 adormecerse *upr* to doze off

adormecido, -a *adj* sleepy, drowsy

adormilarse *upr* to doze

adornar *vt* to adorn, to decorate

adorno *nm* decoration, adornment; **de a.** decorative

adosado, -a *adj* adjacent; *(casa)* semi-detached

adquirir [31] *vt* to acquire; *(comprar)* to purchase

adquisición *nf* acquisition; *(compra)* buy, purchase

adquisitivo, -a *adj* **poder a.** purchasing power

adrede *adv* deliberately, on purpose

adrenalina *nf* adrenalin

Adriático *adj & nm* **el (Mar) A.** the Adriatic (Sea)

adscribir *(pp* **adscrito)** **1** *vt* (a) *(asignar)* to assign (b) *(a un trabajo)* to appoint
2 adscribirse *upr* **adscribirse a** *(grupo, partido)* to become a member of; *(ideología)* to subscribe to

aduana *nf* customs

aduanero, -a 1 *adj* customs
2 *nm,f* customs officer

aducir [10] *vt* *(motivo, pretexto)* to give

adueñarse *upr* **a. de** to take over; *(sujeto: pánico)* to take hold of

aduje *pt indef de* **aducir**

adulación *nf* adulation

adular *vt* to flatter

adulterar *vt* to adulterate

adulterio *nm* adultery

adúltero, -a 1 *adj* adulterous
2 *nm,f* *(hombre)* adulterer; *(mujer)* adulteress

adulto, -a *adj & nm,f* adult

adusto, -a *adj* harsh, severe

aduzco *indic pres de* aducir

advenedizo, -a *adj & nm,f* upstart

advenimiento *nm* advent, coming

adverbio *nm* adverb

adversario, -a 1 *nm,f* adversary, opponent
2 *adj* opposing

adversidad *nf* adversity

adverso, -a *adj* *(condiciones)* adverse; *(suerte)* bad; *(viento)* unfavourable

advertencia *nf* warning

advertido, -a *adj* warned; *(informado)* informed; **estás** o **quedas a.** you've been warned

advertir [5] *vt* **(a)** *(de problema)* to warn; *(informar)* to inform, to advise; *Fam* **te advierto que yo tampoco lo vi** mind you, I didn't see it either **(b)** *(notar)* to realize, to notice

adviento *nm* Advent

adyacente *adj* adjacent

aéreo, -a *adj* *(del aire)* aerial; *(de la aviación)* **tráfico a.** air traffic; *Com* **por vía aerea** by air

aeróbic *nm* aerobics *sing*

aerodinámico, -a *adj* aerodynamic; **de línea aerodinámica** streamlined

aeródromo *nm* aerodrome

aeromodelismo *nm* aeroplane modelling

aeromozo, -a *nm,f Am* air steward; *(mujer)* air hostess

aeronáutica *nf* aeronautics *sing*

aeronáutico, -a *adj* **la industria aeronáutica** the aeronautics industry

aeronave *nf* airship

aeroplano *nm* light aeroplane

aeropuerto *nm* airport

aerosol *nm* aerosol

aerostático, -a *adj* **globo a.** hot-air balloon

afable *adj* affable

afamado, -a *adj* famous, well-known

afán *nm* **(a)** *(esfuerzo)* effort **(b)** *(celo)* zeal

afanador, -a *nm,f* **(a)** *Méx (empleado)* (office) cleaner **(b)** *Méx, RP Fam (ladrón)* crook, thief

afanar 1 *vt Fam (robar)* to pinch
2 afanarse *vpr* **a. por conseguir algo** to do one's best to achieve sth

afanoso, -a *adj* keen, eager

afección *nf* disease

afectación *nf* affectation

afectado, -a *adj* affected

afectar *vt* **a. a** to affect; **le afectó mucho** she was deeply affected; **nos afecta a todos** it concerns all of us

afectivo *adj (emocional)* emotional; **tener problemas afectivos** to have emotional problems

afecto *nm* affection; **tomarle a. a algn** to become fond of sb

afectuoso, -a *adj* affectionate

afeitado *nm* shave

afeitar 1 *vt* to shave
2 afeitarse *vpr (uno mismo)* to shave; **se afeitó la barba** he shaved his beard off

afeminado, -a *adj* effeminate

aferrado, -a *adj* **a. a** clinging to

aferrarse *vpr* to clutch, to cling; *Fig* **a. a una creencia** to cling to a belief

Afganistán *n* Afghanistan

afgano, -a *adj & nm,f* Afghan

afianzamiento *nm* strengthening, reinforcement

afianzar [40] **1** *vt* to strengthen, to reinforce
2 afianzarse *vpr (persona)* to establish oneself

afiche *nm Am* poster

afición *nf* **(a)** *(interés)* liking; **tiene a. por la música** he is fond of music **(b)** *(aficionados)* **la a.** the fans

aficionado, -a 1 *nm,f* **(a)** *(interesado)* enthusiast; **un a. a la música** a music lover **(b)** *(no profesional)* amateur
2 *adj* **(a)** *(interesado)* keen, fond; **ser a. a algo** to be fond of sth **(b)** *(no profesional)* amateur

aficionarse *vpr* to become fond **(a** of), to take a liking **(a** to)

afilado, -a *adj* sharp

afilar *vt* to sharpen

afiliación *nf* *(a organización)* membership

afiliado, -a *nm,f* member

afiliarse [43] *vpr* to become a member

afín *adj (semejante)* kindred, similar; *(relacionado)* related

afinar *vt* **(a)** *(puntería)* to sharpen **(b)** *(instrumento)* to tune

afincarse [44] *vpr* to settle **(en** in)

afinidad *nf* affinity

afirmación nf affirmation; **afirmaciones** *(declaración)* statement

afirmar vt (**a**) *(aseverar)* to state, to declare (**b**) *(afianzar)* to strengthen, to reinforce

afirmativo, -a adj affirmative; **en caso a. ...** if the answer is yes ...

aflicción nf suffering, sorrow

afligir [57] **1** vt to afflict
  2 afligirse vpr to grieve, to be distressed

aflojar 1 vt to loosen
  2 vi *(viento etc)* to abate, to die down
  3 aflojarse vpr to come o work loose; *(rueda)* to go down

aflorar vi *(río)* to come to the surface; *(sentimiento)* to surface, to show

afluencia nf inflow, influx; **gran a. de público** great numbers of people

afluente nm tributary

afluir [37] vi to flow (**a** into)

afónico, -a adj **estar a.** to have lost one's voice

aforismo nm aphorism

aforo nm *(capacidad)* seating capacity

afortunadamente adv fortunately, luckily

afortunado, -a adj fortunate; **las Islas Afortunadas** the Canaries

afrenta nf Fml affront

África n Africa

africano, -a adj & nm,f African

afrodisíaco, -a adj & nm aphrodisiac

afrontar vt to confront, to face; **a. las consecuencias** to face the consequences

afrutado, -a adj fruity

afuera 1 adv outside; **la parte de a.** the outside; **más a.** further out; **salir a.** to come o go out
  2 afueras nfpl outskirts

agachar 1 vt to lower
  2 agacharse vpr to crouch down

agalla nf (**a**) *(de pez)* gill (**b**) *(valor)* guts, pluck; **tiene agallas** she's got guts

agarradera nf Am handle

agarrado, -a adj (**a**) Fam *(persona)* stingy, tight (**b**) **baile a.** cheek-to-cheek dancing

agarrar 1 vt (**a**) *(asir)* to grasp, to seize; **agárralo fuerte** hold it tight (**b**) Am *(tomar)* to take; **a. un taxi** to take a taxi (**c**) Fam *(pillar)* to catch; **a. una borrachera** to get drunk o Br pissed
  2 agarrarse vpr to hold on; **agárrate bien** hold tight

agarrotarse vpr (**a**) *(músculo)* to stiffen (**b**) *(máquina)* to seize up

agasajar vt to smother with attentions

ágata nf agate

| Takes the masculine articles **el** and **un**. |

agazaparse vpr to crouch (down)

agencia nf agency; *(sucursal)* branch; **a. de viajes** travel agency; **a. de seguros** insurance agency; **a. inmobiliaria** Br estate agent's, US real estate office

agenciarse [43] vpr to get hold of, to fix oneself up with

agenda nf diary

agente nmf agent; **a. de bolsa** stockbroker; **a. de policía** *(hombre)* policeman; *(mujer)* policewoman; **a. de seguros** insurance broker

agigantado, -a adj **a pasos agigantados** by leaps and bounds

ágil adj agile

agilidad nf agility

agilización nf speeding up

agilizar [40] vt *(trámites)* to speed up

agitación nf *(intranquilidad)* restlessness; *(social, político)* unrest

agitado, -a adj agitated; *(persona)* anxious; *(mar)* rough; **una vida muy agitada** a very hectic life

agitar 1 vt *(botella)* to shake; *(multitud)* to agitate
  2 agitarse vpr *(persona)* to become agitated; *(mar)* to become rough

aglomeración nf agglomeration; *(de gente)* crowd

aglomerar 1 vt to bring together
  2 aglomerarse vpr to mass o gather together

agnóstico, -a adj & nm,f agnostic

agobiado, -a adj Fig **a. de problemas** snowed under with problems; Fig **a. de trabajo** up to one's eyes in work

agobiante adj *(trabajo)* overwhelming; *(lugar)* claustrophobic; *(calor)* oppressive; *(persona)* tiresome, tiring

agobiar [43] **1** vt to overwhelm
  2 agobiarse vpr *(con problemas)* to get over-anxious; *(por el calor)* to suffocate

agobio nm (**a**) *(angustia)* anxiety (**b**) *(sofoco)* suffocation

agolparse vpr to crowd, to throng

agonía nf dying breath, last gasp

agonizante adj dying

agonizar [40] vi to be dying

agosto nm August; Fam **hacer su a.** to make a packet

agotado, -a adj (**a**) *(cansado)* exhausted, worn out (**b**) Com *(entradas)* sold out; *(libro, disco)* out of stock

agotador, -a adj exhausting

agotamiento nm exhaustion

agotar 1 *vt* (**a**) *(cansar)* to exhaust, to wear out (**b**) *(acabar)* to exhaust, to use up (completely)
2 agotarse *vpr* (**a**) *(acabarse)* to run out, to be used up; *(libro, disco, entradas)* to sell out (**b**) *(persona)* to become exhausted *o* tired out

agraciado, -a *adj* (**a**) *(atractivo)* attractive, fetching (**b**) *(ganador)* winning; **ser a. con** to win

agradable *adj* pleasant

agradar *vi* to please; **no me agrada** I don't like it

agradecer [33] *vt* (**a**) *(dar las gracias)* to thank for; **les agradezco su atención** (I) thank you for your attention; **te lo agradezco mucho** thank you very much (**b**) *(estar agradecido)* to be grateful to; **agradecería que vinieras** I'd be grateful if you'd come (**c**) *(uso impers)* **siempre se agradece un descanso** a rest is always welcome

agradecido, -a *adj* grateful; **le estoy muy a.** I am very grateful to you

agradecimiento *nm* gratitude

agrado *nm* pleasure; **no es de su a.** it isn't to his liking

agrandar 1 *vt* to enlarge, to make larger
2 agrandarse *vpr* to enlarge, to become larger

agrario, -a *adj* *(reforma)* agrarian; *(producto, política)* agricultural

agravamiento *nm* aggravation

agravante *Der* **1** *adj* aggravating
2 *nm* aggravating circumstance

agravar 1 *vt* to aggravate
2 agravarse *vpr* to worsen, to get worse

agraviar [43] *vt* to offend, to insult

agravio *nm* offence, insult

agredir *vt* to assault

agregación *nf* addition

agregado, -a 1 *adj* *Educ* **profesor a.** *(escuela)* secondary school teacher; *Univ* assistant teacher
2 *nm,f Pol* attaché

agregar [42] **1** *vt* (**a**) *(añadir)* to add (**b**) *(destinar)* to appoint
2 agregarse *vpr* **agregarse a** to join

agresión *nf* aggression

agresividad *nf* aggressiveness

agresivo, -a *adj* aggressive

agresor, -a 1 *nm,f* aggressor, attacker
2 *adj* attacking

agreste *adj* *(abrupto, rocoso)* rough, rugged; *Fig (basto, rudo)* coarse, uncouth

agriarse *vpr* to turn sour

agrícola *adj* agricultural

agricultor, -a *nm,f* farmer

agricultura *nf* agriculture; **a. biológica** *o* **ecológica** organic farming

agridulce *adj* bittersweet

agrietar 1 *vt* to crack; *(piel, labios)* to chap
2 agrietarse *vpr* to crack; *(piel)* to get chapped

agringarse [42] *vpr Am Pey* = to become like a North American or European

agrio, -a 1 *adj* sour
2 agrios *nmpl* citrus fruits

agrónomo, -a *nm,f* agronomist

agropecuario, -a *adj* farming, agricultural

agroturismo *nm* rural tourism

agrupación *nf* association

agrupar 1 *vt* to group
2 agruparse *vpr* (**a**) *(congregarse)* to group together, to form a group (**b**) *(asociarse)* to associate

agua *nf* water; **a. potable** drinking water; **a. corriente/del grifo** running/tap water; **a. dulce/salada** fresh/salt water; **a. mineral sin/con gas** still/fizzy *o* sparkling mineral water; **a. de colonia** (eau de) cologne; *Fig* **estar con el a. al cuello** to be up to one's neck in it; **aguas jurisdiccionales** territorial waters; **aguas residuales** sewage

> Takes the masculine articles **el** and **un**.

aguacate *nm* *(árbol)* avocado; *(fruto)* avocado (pear)

aguacero *nm* shower, downpour

aguado, -a *adj* watered down

aguafiestas *nmf inv* spoilsport, wet blanket

aguafuerte *nm* (**a**) *Arte* etching (**b**) *Quím* nitric acid

aguamala *nf Carib, Col, Ecuad, Méx* jellyfish

aguamarina *nf* aquamarine

aguamiel *nm o nf* (**a**) *Am (bebida)* = water mixed with honey or cane syrup (**b**) *Carib, Méx (jugo)* maguey juice

aguanieve *nf* sleet

aguantar 1 *vt* (**a**) *(soportar)* to tolerate; **no lo aguanto más** I can't stand it any longer (**b**) *(sostener)* to support, to hold; **aguanta esto** hold this (**c**) **aguanta la respiración** hold your breath
2 aguantarse *vpr* (**a**) *(contenerse)* to restrain oneself; *(lágrimas)* to hold back; **no pude aguantarme la risa** I couldn't help laughing (**b**) *(resignarse)* to resign oneself

aguante *nm* endurance; **tener mucho a.** *(ser paciente)* to be very patient; *(tener resistencia)* to be strong, to have a lot of stamina

aguar [45] *vt* to water down; *Fig* **a. la fiesta a algn** to spoil sb's fun

aguardar 1 *vt* to await
   2 *vi* to wait

aguardiente *nm* liquor, brandy

aguarrás *nm* turpentine

aguatero, -a *nm,f Am* water seller

aguaviva *nf RP* jellyfish

agudeza *nf* (**a**) *(de vista, olfato)* keenness; *(mental)* sharpness, shrewdness (**b**) *(dicho ingenioso)* witticism

agudización *nf (empeoramiento)* worsening

agudizar [40] **1** *vt* to intensify, to make more acute
   2 agudizarse *upr* to intensify, to become more acute

agudo, -a *adj* (**a**) *(vista, olfato)* keen; *(sonido)* high, high-pitched; *(dolor)* sharp; *(crisis, problema, enfermedad)* serious, acute (**b**) *(perspicaz)* keen, sharp; *(ingenioso)* witty

agüero *nm* **de mal a.** that bodes ill

aguijón *nm* sting; *Fig (estímulo)* spur

águila *nf* (**a**) eagle; **á. real** golden eagle (**b**) *Méx (de moneda)* heads; **¿á. o sol?** heads or tails?

> Takes the masculine articles **el** and **un**.

aguileño, -a *adj* aquiline; **nariz aguileña** aquiline nose

aguinaldo *nm* = tip given at Christmas, *Br* Christmas box; **pedir el a.** to go carol singing

agüita *nf Chile* (herbal) tea

aguja *nf* (**a**) *(de coser, jeringuilla)* needle; *(de reloj)* hand; *(de tocadiscos)* stylus (**b**) *Arquit* spire (**c**) *Ferroc* point, *US* switch

agujerear *vt* to make holes in

agujero *nm* (**a**) *(hueco, abertura)* hole; **a. negro** black hole (**b**) *Econ* deficit, shortfall

agujetas *nfpl* (**a**) *Esp (en los músculos)* stiffness; **tener a.** to be stiff (**b**) *Méx* shoelaces

agur *interj Fam* bye!, see you!

aguzar [40] *vt* (**a**) *(afilar)* to sharpen (**b**) *Fig* **a. el oído** to prick up one's ears; **a. la vista** to look attentively; **aguzar el ingenio** to sharpen one's wits

ahí *adv* there; **a. está** there he/she/it is; **ve por a.** go that way; **está por a.** it's over there; **setenta o por a.** seventy or thereabouts; **de a.** hence

ahijado, -a *nm,f* godchild; *(niño)* godson; *(niña)* goddaughter; **ahijados** godchildren

ahínco *nm* eagerness; **con a.** eagerly

ahíto, -a *adj* **estar a. de algo** *(saciado)* to be full of sth; *(harto)* to have had enough of sth

ahogado, -a 1 *adj* (**a**) *(en líquido)* drowned; **morir a.** to drown (**b**) *(asfixiado)* suffocated
   2 *nm,f* drowned person

ahogar [42] **1** *vt* (**a**) *(en líquido)* to drown (**b**) *(asfixiar)* to suffocate
   2 ahogarse *upr* (**a**) *(en líquido)* to drown, to be drowned; *Fig* **ahogarse en un vaso de agua** to make a mountain out of a molehill (**b**) *(asfixiarse)* to suffocate (**c**) *(motor)* to be flooded

ahondar 1 *vt* to deepen
   2 *vi* to go deep; *Fig* **a. en un problema** to go into a problem in depth

ahora 1 *adv* (**a**) *(en este momento)* now; **a. mismo** right now; **de a. en adelante** from now on; **por a.** for the time being (**b**) **a. voy** I'm coming; **a. vuelvo** I'll be back in a minute (**c**) **hasta a.** *(hasta el momento)* until now, so far; *(hasta luego)* see you later
   2 *conj* **a. bien** *(sin embargo)* however; *(y bueno)* well then

ahorcado, -a 1 *nm,f* hanged person
   2 *adj* hanged

ahorcar [44] **1** *vt* to hang
   2 ahorcarse *upr* to hang oneself

ahorita, ahoritita *adv Am salvo RP Fam* (**a**) *(en el presente)* (right) now; **a. voy** I'm just coming (**b**) *(pronto)* in a second (**c**) *(hace poco)* just now, a few minutes ago

ahorrador, -a *adj* thrifty

ahorrar 1 *vt* to save
   2 ahorrarse *upr* **ahórrate los comentarios** keep your comments to yourself

ahorrativo, -a *adj* thrifty

ahorro *nm* (**a**) *(acción)* saving; **a. energético** energy saving (**b**) **ahorros** savings; *Fin* **caja de ahorros** savings bank

ahuecar [44] *vt* (**a**) *(tronco)* to hollow out; *Fam* **a. el ala** to clear off, to beat it (**b**) *(voz)* to deepen

ahuevado, -a *adj CAm, Ecuad, Perú Fam (tonto)* **estar a. con algo** to be bowled over by sth

ahumado, -a *adj (cristal, jamón)* smoked; *(bacon)* smoky; **salmón a.** smoked salmon

ahumar 1 *vt* to smoke
   2 ahumarse *upr* to get all smoky

ahuyentar *vt* to scare away

aindiado, -a *adj* Indian *(used of American Indians)*

airado, -a *adj* angry

airar 1 *vt* to anger
   2 airarse *upr* to get angry

airbag ['erβaɣ, air'βaɣ] (*pl* **airbags**) *nm* airbag

aire *nm* (a) air; **a. acondicionado** air conditioning; **al a.** *(hacia arriba)* into the air; *(al descubierto)* uncovered; **al a. libre** in the open air; **en el a.** *(pendiente)* in the air; *Rad* on the air; **tomar el a.** to get some fresh air; **necesito un cambio de aires** I need a change of scene (b) *(viento)* wind; **hace a.** it's windy (c) *(aspecto)* air, appearance (d) *(expresiones)* **va a su a.** he goes his own sweet way; **darse aires** to put on airs

airear *vt (ropa, lugar)* to air; *Fig (asunto)* to publicize

airoso, -a *adj* graceful, elegant; *Fig* **salir a. de una situación** to come out of a situation with flying colours

aislacionismo *nm* isolationism

aislado, -a *adj* (a) *(lugar, suceso)* isolated (b) *Téc* insulated

aislamiento *nm* (a) *(de lugar, persona)* isolation (b) *Téc* insulation

aislante 1 *adj* **cinta a.** insulating tape
2 *nm* insulator

aislar *vt* (a) *(persona, virus)* to isolate (b) *Téc* to insulate

ajar *vt* to wear out

ajedrez *nm* (a) *(juego)* chess (b) *(piezas y tablero)* chess set

ajeno, -a *adj* belonging to other people; **los bienes ajenos** other people's property; **por causas ajenas a nuestra voluntad** for reasons beyond our control

ajetreado, -a *adj* (very) busy, hectic

ajetreo *nm* activity, hard work, bustle

ají (*pl* **ajís** *o* **ajíes**) *nm* (a) *Andes, RP (pimiento)* chilli (pepper) (b) *Andes, RP (salsa)* = sauce made from oil, vinegar, garlic and chilli

ajiaco *nm* (a) *Andes, Carib (estofado)* = chilli-based stew (b) *Méx (estofado con ajo)* = tripe stew flavoured with garlic

ajillo *nm Culin* **al a.** fried with garlic

ajo *nm* garlic; **cabeza/diente de a.** head/clove of garlic; *Fam* **estar en el a.** to be in on it

ajonjolí (*pl* **ajonjolíes**) *nm* sesame

ajuar *nm (de novia)* trousseau

ajustado, -a *adj* tight

ajustador, -a 1 *nm,f* fitter
2 ajustadores *nmpl Col, Cuba* bra

ajustar 1 *vt* (a) *(encajar) (piezas de motor)* to fit (b) *(arreglar)* to adjust (c) *(apretar)* to tighten
2 *vi (venir justo)* to fit properly, to be a good fit; **la ventana no ajusta bien** the window won't close properly
3 ajustarse *vpr* (a) *(encajarse)* to fit; *Fig*

tu relato no se ajusta a la verdad your account is at variance with the truth, your account doesn't match the facts (b) *(adaptarse)* to fit in (a with); **tenemos que ajustarnos al presupuesto del que disponemos** we have to keep within the limits of our budget

ajuste *nm (de pieza)* fitting; *(de mecanismo)* adjustment; *(de salario)* agreement; **a. de cuentas** settling of scores

ajusticiar [43] *vt* to execute

al *(contracción de a + el)* (a) *ver* **a²** (b) *(al + infin)* **al salir** on leaving; **está al caer** it's about to happen; **al parecer** apparently

ala 1 *nf* (a) *(de ave, avión, edificio)* wing; *Fig* **cortarle las alas a algn** to clip sb's wings (b) *(de sombrero)* brim
2 *nmf Dep* winger

Takes the masculine articles **el** and **un**.

alabanza *nf* praise

alabar *vt* to praise

alabastro *nm* alabaster

alacena *nf (food)* cupboard

alacrán *nm* scorpion

alambicado, -a *adj* intricate

alambique *nm* still

alambrada *nf, Am* **alambrado** *nm* wire fence

alambrar *vt* to fence with wire

alambre *nm* wire; **a. de púas** barbed wire

alameda *nf* (a) *(de álamos)* poplar grove (b) *(paseo)* avenue, boulevard

álamo *nm* poplar

alano, -a *nm,f* **(perro)** a. mastiff

alarde *nm* bragging, boasting; **hacer a. de** to show off

alardear *vi* to brag, to boast; **a. de rico** *o* **de riqueza** to flaunt one's wealth

alargadera *nf Elec* extension

alargado, -a *adj* long

alargar [42] **1** *vt* (a) *(ropa)* to lengthen; *(estirar)* to stretch; **alargó la mano para cogerlo** she stretched out her hand to get it (b) *(prolongar)* to prolong, to extend (c) *(dar)* to pass, to hand over; **alárgame ese jersey** can you pass me that sweater?
2 alargarse *vpr* (a) *(hacerse más largo)* to get longer (b) *(prolongarse)* to go on

alarido *nm* screech, shriek; **dar un a.** to howl

alarma *nf* alarm; **la a. saltó** the alarm went off; **falsa a.** false alarm; **señal de a.** alarm (signal)

alarmado, -a *adj* alarmed

alarmante *adj* alarming

alarmar 1 *vt* to alarm
2 alarmarse *vpr* to be alarmed

alazán, -ana *adj & nm,f* (caballo) a. chestnut

alba *nf* dawn, daybreak

> Takes the masculine articles **el** and **un**.

albacea *nmf (hombre)* executor; *(mujer)* executrix

albahaca *nf* basil

albanés, -esa 1 *adj & nm,f* Albanian
  2 *nm (idioma)* Albanian

Albania *n* Albania

albañil *nm* bricklayer

albañilería *nf* bricklaying; **pared de a.** *(obra)* brick wall

albarán *nm Esp Com* delivery note, despatch note

albaricoque *nm Esp* apricot

albaricoquero *nm Esp* apricot tree

albatros *nm inv* albatross

albedrío *nm* will; **libre a.** free will

alberca *nf* (a) *(depósito)* water tank (b) *Col, Méx (piscina)* swimming pool

albergar [42] **1** *vt (alojar)* to house, to accommodate; *Fig (esperanza)* to cherish; *(odio)* to harbour
  2 albergarse *vpr* to stay

albergue *nm* hostel; **a. juvenil** youth hostel

albino, -a *adj & nm,f* albino

albóndiga *nf* meatball

albores *nmpl* beginning; **en los a. de ...** at the beginning of …

albornoz *nm* bathrobe

alborotado, -a *adj* (a) *(personas)* worked up, agitated (b) *(pelo)* untidy, messy (c) *(mar)* rough; *(tiempo)* stormy

alborotar 1 *vt* (a) *(agitar)* to agitate, to work up (b) *(desordenar)* to mess up
  2 *vi* to kick up a racket
  3 alborotarse *vpr* (a) *(personas)* to get excited *o* worked up (b) *(mar)* to get rough; *(tiempo)* to get stormy

alboroto *nm* (a) *(jaleo)* din, racket (b) *(desorden)* disturbance, uproar

alborozo *nm* merriment, gaiety

albufera *nf* lagoon

álbum *nm* album

alcachofa *nf* (a) *Bot* artichoke (b) *Esp (de regadera)* rose, sprinkler; *(de ducha)* shower head

alcalde *nm* mayor

alcaldesa *nf* mayoress

alcaldía *nf* (a) *(cargo)* mayorship (b) *(oficina)* mayor's office

alcalino, -a *adj* alkaline

alcance *nm* (a) *(de persona)* reach; *(de arma, emisora)* range; **al a. de cualquiera** within everybody's reach; **dar a.** **a** to catch up with; **fuera del a. de los niños** out of the reach of children (b) *(de reformas, medidas)* scope; *(de noticia)* importance

alcancía *nf esp Am* money box

alcanfor *nm* camphor

alcantarilla *nf* sewer; *(boca)* drain

alcantarillado *nm* sewer system

alcanzar [40] **1** *vt* (a) *(llegar a)* to reach; *(persona)* to catch up with; **la producción alcanza dos mil unidades** production is up to two thousand units (b) *(pasar)* **alcánzame la sal** pass me the salt (c) *(conseguir)* to attain, to achieve
  2 *vi* (a) *(ser suficiente)* to be sufficient; **con un kilo no alcanza para todos** one kilo won't be enough for all of us (b) *(poder)* **a. a hacer algo** to be able to do sth; **alcancé a verlo unos segundos** I managed to see him for a few seconds (c) *(llegar)* **no alcanzo** I can't reach it; **hasta donde alcanza la vista** as far as the eye can see

alcaparra *nf (fruto)* caper; *(planta)* caper bush

alcatraz *nm (ave)* gannet

alcaucil *nm RP* artichoke

alcayata *nf* hook

alcazaba *nf* fortress, citadel

alcázar *nm* (a) *(fortaleza)* fortress, citadel (b) *(castillo)* castle, palace

alcista *adj Fin* **mercado a.** bull market; **tendencia a.** upward tendency

alcoba *nf* bedroom

> *Observa que la palabra inglesa **al-cove** es un falso amigo y no es la traducción de la palabra española **alcoba**. En inglés **alcove** significa "hueco".*

alcohol *nm* alcohol

alcoholemia *nf* blood alcohol level; **prueba de a.** Breathalyser® test

alcohólico, -a *adj & nm,f* alcoholic

alcoholímetro *nm Br* Breathalyser®, *US* drunkometer

alcoholismo *nm* alcoholism

alcoholizado, -a *adj & nm,f* alcoholic

alcoholizarse *vpr* to become an alcoholic

alcornoque *nm* cork oak

alcurnia *nf* lineage, ancestry; **de alta a.** of noble lineage

alcuzcuz *nm* couscous

aldaba *nf* door knocker

aldabonazo *nm* (a) *(golpe)* loud knock (b) *(advertencia)* warning

aldea *nf* village

aldeano, -a 1 *adj* village
  2 *nm,f* villager

aleación *nf* alloy

aleatorio, -a *adj* random

alebrestarse *vpr* (**a**) *Méx (alborotarse, entusiasmarse)* to get excited (**b**) *Méx, Ven (rebelarse, indisciplinarse)* to rebel (**c**) *Col (ponerse nervioso)* to get nervous

aleccionador, -a *adj (instructivo)* instructive; *(ejemplar)* exemplary

aleccionar *vt (instruir)* to teach, to instruct; *(adiestrar)* to train

aledaños *nmpl* **en los a. de** in the vicinity of

alegar [42] *vt (motivos, pruebas)* to put forward; **a. que** to claim (that)

alegato *nm Der* plea; *Fig* **hacer un a. a favor de/en contra de** to make a case for/against

alegoría *nf* allegory

alegrar 1 *vt* (**a**) *(complacer)* to make happy o glad; **me alegra que se lo hayas dicho** I am glad you told her (**b**) *Fig (avivar)* to enliven, to brighten up

2 alegrarse *vpr* to be glad, to be happy; **me alegro de verte** I am pleased to see you; **me alegro por ti** I am happy for you

alegre *adj* (**a**) *(contento)* happy, glad (**b**) *(color)* bright; *(música)* lively; *(lugar)* pleasant, cheerful (**c**) *Fig (borracho)* tipsy, merry

alegremente *adv (con alegría)* happily, joyfully; *(irreflexivamente)* blithely

alegría *nf* joy, happiness

alejado, -a *adj* far away, remote

alejar 1 *vt* to move further away

2 alejarse *vpr* to go away, to move away; **no te alejes de mí** keep close to me

aleluya *nm* o *nf* hallelujah, alleluia

alemán, -ana 1 *adj & nm,f* German

2 *nm (idioma)* German

Alemania *n* Germany; **A. del Este/Oeste** East/West Germany; **A. Occidental/Oriental** West/East Germany

alentador, -a *adj* encouraging; **un panorama poco a.** a rather bleak outlook

alentar [1] *vt* to encourage

alergia *nf* allergy

alérgico, -a *adj* allergic

alero *nm* eaves

alerón *nm Av* aileron

alerta *adj & nf* alert; **estar en estado de a.** to be (on the) alert

alertar *vt* to alert (**de** to); **nos alertó del peligro** he alerted us to the danger

aleta *nf (de pez)* fin; *(de foca, de nadador)* flipper

aletargado, -a *adj* lethargic

aletargar [42] **1** *vt* to make lethargic

2 aletargarse *vpr* to become lethargic

aletear *vi* to flutter o flap its wings

alevín *nm (pescado)* young fish; *Fig (principiante)* beginner

alevosía *nf (traición)* treachery; *(premeditación)* premeditation

alevoso, -a *adj (persona)* treacherous; *(acto)* premeditated

alfabético, -a *adj* alphabetical

alfabetización *nf* teaching to read and write; **campaña de a.** literacy campaign

alfabetizar *vt (personas)* to teach to read and write

alfabeto *nm* alphabet

alfajor *nm CSur* = large biscuit filled with toffee and coated with coconut

alfalfa *nf* lucerne, alfalfa

alfarería *nf* (**a**) *(arte)* pottery (**b**) *(taller)* potter's workshop; *(tienda)* pottery shop

alfarero, -a *nm,f* potter

alféizar *nm* windowsill

alférez *nm* second lieutenant

alfil *nm* bishop

alfiler *nm (para coser)* pin; *(broche)* pin, brooch; *(de corbata)* tiepin; *Andes, RP, Ven* **a. de gancho** *(imperdible)* safety pin

alfiletero *nm* pin box, pin case

alfombra *nf (grande)* carpet; *(pequeña)* rug; *Am salvo RP* fitted carpet

alfombrar *vt* to carpet

alfombrilla *nf* rug, mat; *Inform (para ratón)* mouse mat

alforja *nf (para caballos)* saddlebag; *(para persona)* knapsack

alga *nf* alga; *(marina)* seaweed

Takes the masculine articles **el** and **un**.

algarabía *nf* hubbub, hullabaloo

algarrobo *nm* carob tree

algazara *nf* din, row

álgebra *nf* algebra

Takes the masculine articles **el** and **un**.

álgido, -a *adj* culminating, critical; **el punto a.** the climax

algo 1 *pron indef* (**a**) *(afirmativo)* something; *(interrogativo)* anything; **a. así** something like that; **¿a. más?** anything else?; **por a. será** there must be a reason for it; *Fam* **a. es a.** it's better than nothing (**b**) *(cantidad indeterminada)* some; **¿queda a. de pastel?** is there any cake left?

2 *adv (un poco)* quite, somewhat; **se siente a. mejor** she's feeling a bit better

algodón *nm* cotton; **a. (hidrófilo)** *Br* cotton wool, *US* absorbent cotton; **a. de azúcar** *Br* candy floss, *US* cotton candy

algodonero, -a *adj* cotton

alguacil *nm* (a) *(del ayuntamiento)* mayor's assistant (b) *(del juzgado)* bailiff

alguien *pron indef (afirmativo)* somebody, someone; *(interrogativo)* anybody, anyone

alguno, -a 1 *adj* (a) *(delante de nombre)* *(afirmativo)* some; *(interrogativo)* any; **algunos días** some days; **algunas veces** some times; **alguna que otra vez** now and then; **¿has tomado alguna medicina?** have you taken any medicine?; **¿le has visto alguna vez?** have you ever seen him? (b) *(después de nombre)* not at all; **no vino persona alguna** nobody came

> **algún** is used instead of **alguno** before masculine singular nouns (e.g. **algún día** some day).

2 *pron indef* (a) *(singular)* someone, somebody; **a. dirá que ...** someone might say that ...; **a. que otro** some (b) **algunos, -as** some (people)

alhaja *nf* jewel

alhelí *(pl* alhelíes*)* *nm* wallflower, stock

aliado, -a 1 *adj* allied
2 *nm,f* **los Aliados** the Allies

alianza *nf* (a) *(pacto)* alliance (b) *(anillo)* wedding ring

aliarse [29] *vpr* to become allies, to form an alliance

alias *adv & nm inv* alias

alicaído, -a *adj* (a) *(débil)* weak, feeble (b) *(deprimido)* down, depressed

alicatar *vt Esp* to tile

alicates *nmpl* pliers

aliciente *nm* (a) *(atractivo)* lure, charm (b) *(incentivo)* incentive

alienación *nf* alienation

alienado, -a *adj* insane, deranged

alienar *vt* to alienate

alienígena *nmf* alien

aliento *nm* (a) *(respiración)* breath; **sin a.** breathless (b) *(ánimo)* encouragement

aligerar 1 *vt (acelerar)* to speed up; **a. el paso** to quicken one's pace
. 2 *vi Fam* **¡aligera!** hurry up!

alijo *nm* haul; **un a. de drogas** a consignment of drugs

alimaña *nf* vermin

alimentación *nf (comida)* food; *(acción)* feeding; *Téc* supply

alimentar 1 *vt* (a) *(dar alimento)* to feed (b) *Fig (sentimientos)* to nourish (c) *Inform* to feed; *Téc* to supply
2 *vi (ser nutritivo)* to be nutritious
3 alimentarse *vpr* **alimentarse con** *o* **de** to live on

alimentario, -a *adj* food

alimenticio, -a *adj* nutritious; **productos alimenticios** food products, foodstuffs; **valor a.** nutritional value

alimento *nm* (a) *(comida)* food (b) *Fig* **tiene poco a.** it is not very nourishing

alimón *adv* **al a.** together

alineación *nf* (a) *(colocación en línea)* alignment (b) *Dep (equipo)* line-up

alineado, -a *adj* aligned, lined-up; **países no alineados** non-aligned countries

alineamiento *nm* alignment

alinear 1 *vt* to align, to line up
2 alinearse *vpr* to line up

aliñar *vt* to season, to flavour; *(ensalada)* to dress

aliño *nm* seasoning, dressing

alioli *nm* garlic mayonnaise

alisar *vt* to smooth

aliscafo, alíscafo *nm RP* hydrofoil

alistarse *vpr* (a) *Mil* to enlist (b) *Am (prepararse)* to get ready

aliviar [43] **1** *vt (dolor)* to soothe, to relieve; *(carga)* to lighten, to make lighter
2 aliviarse *vpr (dolor)* to ease (off *o* up), to get better

alivio *nm* relief

aljibe *nm* cistern, tank

allá *adv* (a) *(lugar alejado)* there, over there; **a. abajo/arriba** down/up there; **¡a. voy!** here I go!; **más a.** further on; **más a. de** beyond; **el más a.** the beyond (b) *(tiempo)* **a. por los años veinte** back in the twenties (c) **a. tú** that's your problem

allanamiento *nm Der* **a. de morada** breaking and entering

allanar *vt* (a) *(terreno)* to level, to flatten; *Fig (camino)* to smooth (b) *Am (hacer una redada en)* to raid

allegado, -a 1 *adj* close
2 *nm,f* close friend

allende *adv Fml* beyond; **a. los mares** overseas

allí *adv* there, over there; **a. abajo/arriba** down/up there; **de a. para acá** back and forth; **por a.** *(movimiento)* that way; *(posición)* over there

alma *nf* soul; **no había ni un a.** there was not a soul

> Takes the masculine articles **el** and **un**.

almacén *nm* (a) *(local)* warehouse; *(habitación)* storeroom (b) **(grandes) almacenes** department store *sing* (c) *Andes, RP (de alimentos)* grocer's (shop), grocery store (d) *CAm (de ropa)* clothes shop

almacenaje *nm* storage, warehousing

almacenamiento *nm* storage, warehousing; *Inform* storage

almacenar *vt* to store

almanaque *nm* calendar

almeja *nf* clam; *muy Fam* pussy

almena *nf* merlon

almendra *nf* almond; **a. garapiñada** sugared almond

almendrado, -a 1 *adj* almond-shaped; **ojos almendrados** almond eyes
2 *nm Culin* almond paste

almendro *nm* almond tree

almíbar *nm* syrup

almidón *nm* starch

almidonado, -a 1 *adj* starched
2 *nm* starching

almidonar *vt* to starch

alminar *nm* minaret

almirante *nm* admiral

almizcle *nm* musk

almohada *nf* pillow; *Fam* **consultarlo con la a.** to sleep on it

almohadilla *nf* (a) *(cojín)* small cushion (b) *(de animal)* pad

almohadón *nm* pillowcase

almorranas *nfpl* piles

almorzar [2] **1** *vi* to have lunch
2 *vt* to have for lunch

almuerzo *nm* lunch

aló *interj Andes, Carib (al teléfono)* hello!

alocado, -a *adj* thoughtless, rash

alocución *nf* speech, address

alojamiento *nm* accommodation; **dar a.** to accommodate

alojar 1 *vt* to accommodate
2 alojarse *vpr* to stay

alondra *nf* lark; **a. común** skylark

alpaca *nf* alpaca

alpargata *nf* canvas sandal, espadrille

Alpes *npl* **los A.** the Alps

alpinismo *nm* mountaineering, climbing

alpinista *nmf* mountaineer, climber

alpino, -a *adj* Alpine; **esquí a.** downhill skiing

alpiste *nm* (a) *(planta)* canary grass (b) *(semilla)* birdseed

alquilar *vt* to hire; *(pisos, casas)* to rent; **se alquila** *(en letrero)* to let

alquiler *nm* (a) *(de pisos, casas)* renting; **a. de coches** *Br* car hire, *US* car rental; **de a.** *(pisos, casas)* to let, rented; *(coche)* for hire; *(televisión)* for rent (b) *(precio)* hire, rental; *(de pisos, casas)* rent

alquimia *nf* alchemy

alquitrán *nm* tar

alrededor 1 *adv (lugar)* round, around; **mira a.** look around; **a. de la mesa** round the table; **a. de las dos** around two o'clock; **a. de quince** about fifteen
2 alrededores *nmpl* surrounding area; **en los alrededores de Murcia** in the area round Murcia

alta *nf* **dar de** *o* **el a. a algn** *(a un enfermo)* to discharge sb from hospital

Takes the masculine articles **el** and **un**.

altamente *adv* highly, extremely

altanería *nf* haughtiness

altanero, -a *adj* haughty

altar *nm* altar

altavoz *nm* loudspeaker

alteración *nf* (a) *(cambio)* alteration (b) *(alboroto)* quarrel, row; **a. del orden público** disturbance of the peace (c) *(excitación)* agitation

alterar 1 *vt* to alter, to change; **a. el orden público** to disturb the peace
2 alterarse *vpr* (a) *(cambiar)* to change (b) *(inquietarse)* to be upset (c) *(alimentos)* to go off

altercado *nm* quarrel, argument

alternar 1 *vt* to alternate
2 *vi (relacionarse)* to meet people, to socialize
3 alternarse *vpr* to alternate

alternativa *nf* alternative

alternativo, -a *adj* alternative

alterno, -a *adj* alternate; **días alternos** alternate days

alteza *nf* Highness; **Su A. Real** His/Her Royal Highness

altibajos *nmpl* ups and downs

altillo *nm* (a) *(desván)* attic, loft (b) *Esp (armario)* = small storage cupboard above head height, usually above another cupboard

altiplano *nm* high plateau

Altísimo *nm Rel* **el A.** the Almighty

altisonante *adj* grandiloquent

altitud *nf* altitude

altivez *nf* haughtiness

altivo, -a *adj* haughty

alto¹, -a 1 *adj (persona, árbol, edificio)* tall; *(montaña, techo, presión)* high; *(sonido)* loud; *Fig (precio, tecnología)* high; *(tono)* high-pitched; **los pisos altos** the top floors; **en lo a.** at the top; **alta sociedad** high society; **clase alta** upper class; **en voz alta** aloud, in a loud voice; **a altas horas de la noche** late at night
2 *adv* (a) *(en posición)* high, high up (b) *(en volumen)* loud, loudly; **pon la radio**

más alta turn the radio up; **¡habla más a.!** speak up!

3 *nm* (**a**) *(altura)* height; **¿cuánto tiene de a.?** how tall/high is it?; *Fig* **por todo lo a.** in a grand way (**b**) *(elevación)* hill

alto² *nm* (**a**) *(interrupción)* stop, break (**b**) *Mil* halt; **dar el a. a algn** to order sb to halt; **un a. el fuego** a cease-fire

altoparlante *nm Am* loudspeaker

altozano *nm* hillock

altramuz *nm* lupin

altruismo *nm* altruism

altruista 1 *adj* altruistic
  2 *nmf* altruist

altura *nf* (**a**) *(de persona, cosa)* height; **de 10 m de a.** 10 m high (**b**) *(nivel)* level; **a la misma a.** on the same level; *Geog* on the same latitude; **a la a. del cine** by the cinema; *Fig* **estar a la a. de las circunstancias** to meet the challenge; *Fig* **no está a su a.** he does not measure up to him; *Fig* **a estas alturas** at this stage (**c**) *Rel* **alturas** heaven

alubia *nf* bean

alucinación *nf* hallucination

alucinado, -a *adj Fam* staggered, *Br* gobsmacked

alucinante *adj Fam* brilliant, mind-blowing

alucinar *vi* (**a**) *Med* to hallucinate (**b**) *Fam (gustar)* **le alucinan las motos** he's crazy about motorbikes

alucinógeno, -a 1 *adj* hallucinogenic
  2 *nm* hallucinogen

alud *nm* avalanche

aludido, -a *adj Fig* **darse por a.** to take it personally

aludir *vi* to allude to, to mention

alumbrado, -a 1 *adj* lit
  2 *nm Elec* lighting; **a. público** street lighting

alumbrar 1 *vt (iluminar)* to light, to illuminate
  2 *vi (parir)* to give birth

aluminio *nm Br* aluminium, *US* aluminum

alumnado *nm (de colegio)* pupils; *Univ* student body

alumno, -a *nm,f* (**a**) *(de colegio)* pupil; **a. externo** day pupil; **a. interno** boarder (**b**) *Univ* student

alusión *nf* allusion, mention

aluvión *nm (de agua)* flood; **un a. de críticas** a barrage of criticism; **un a. de insultos** a torrent of abuse

alverja *nf Am* pea

alza *nf* rise; **en a.** rising; **jugar al a.** *(bolsa)* to bull the market

---

> Takes the masculine articles **el** and **un**.

alzado, -a 1 *adj* raised, lifted; **votación a mano alzada** vote by a show of hands
  2 *nm Arquit* elevation

alzamiento *nm (rebelión)* uprising

alzar [40] **1** *vt* to raise, to lift; **a. el vuelo** to take off; **a. los ojos/la vista** to look up; **álzate el cuello** turn your collar up
  2 alzarse *vpr* (**a**) *(levantarse)* to get up, to rise (**b**) *(rebelarse)* to rise, to rebel (**c**) **alzarse con la victoria** to win, to be victorious

AM *(abr* **amplitude modulation)** AM

ama *nf (señora)* lady of the house; *(dueña)* owner; **a. de casa** housewife; **a. de llaves** housekeeper

---

> Takes the masculine articles **el** and **un**.

amabilidad *nf* kindness; *Fml* **tenga la a. de esperar** would you be so kind as to wait?

amable *adj* kind, nice; *Fml* **¿sería usted tan a. de ayudarme?** would you be so kind as to help me?

amado, -a 1 *adj* loved, beloved
  2 *nm,f* loved one

amaestrado *adj (animal)* trained; *(en circo)* performing

amaestrar *vt* to train; *(domar)* to tame

amagar [42] *vi* to threaten; **amaga tormenta** a storm is threatening

amago *nm* **hacer a. de** to make as if to; **hizo a. de salir corriendo** he made as if to run off

amainar *vi (viento etc)* to drop, to die down

amalgama *nf* amalgam

amalgamar *vt* to amalgamate

amamantar *vt* to breast-feed; *Zool* to suckle

amancay *nm Andes* golden hurricane lily

amanecer [33] **1** *v impers* to dawn; **¿a qué hora amanece?** when does it get light?; **amaneció lluvioso** it was rainy in the morning
  2 *vi* **amanecimos en Finlandia** we were in Finland at daybreak; **amaneció muy enfermo** he woke up feeling very ill
  3 *nm* dawn, daybreak; **al a.** at dawn

amanerado, -a *adj* mannered, affected

amansar *vt* (**a**) *(fiera)* to tame (**b**) *Fig (apaciguar)* to tame, to calm

amante *nmf* lover; **a. del arte** art lover

amañar *vt* to fix, to fiddle; *(elecciones)* to rig

amapola *nf* poppy

amar 1 *vt* to love
  2 amarse *vpr* to love each other

amaraje *nm Av* landing at sea

amargado, -a 1 *adj (resentido)* bitter; **estar a. de la vida** to be bitter and twisted **2** *nm,f* bitter person

amargar [42] **1** *vt* to make bitter; *Fig* to embitter, to sour **2 amargarse** *vpr Fig* to become embittered *o* bitter; **no te amargues por eso** don't let that make you bitter

amargo, -a *adj* bitter

amargor *nm* bitterness

amargura *nf (pena)* sorrow

amarillear 1 *vt* to turn yellow **2** *vi* to (turn) yellow

amarillento, -a *adj* yellowish

amarillo, -a *adj & nm* yellow; **prensa amarilla** gutter press

amarilloso, -a *adj Col, Méx, Ven* yellowish

amarradero *nm* mooring

amarrar *vt Náut* to moor, to tie up; *(atar)* to tie (up), to bind

amarras *nfpl* **soltar a.** to cast off, to let go

amarre *nm Náut* mooring

amarrete, -a *adj Andes, RP Fam* mean, tight

amasar *vt* **(a)** *Culin* to knead **(b)** *(fortuna)* to amass

amasiato *nm CAm, Chile, Méx* **vivir en a.** to live together

amasijo *nm Fam* hotchpotch, jumble

amasio, -a *nm,f CAm, Méx* live-in lover, common-law partner

amateur [amaˈter] *(pl* **amateurs***) adj & nmf* amateur

amatista *nf* amethyst

amazona *nf* **(a)** *(jinete)* horsewoman **(b)** *(en mitología)* Amazon

Amazonas *n* **el A.** the Amazon

amazónico, -a *adj* Amazonian

ambages *nmpl* **hablar sin a.** to go straight to the point

ámbar *nm* amber

Amberes *n* Antwerp

ambición *nf* ambition

ambicionar *vt* to have as an ambition; **ambiciona ser presidente** his ambition is to become president

ambicioso, -a 1 *adj* ambitious **2** *nm,f* ambitious person

ambidextro, -a 1 *adj* ambidextrous **2** *nm,f* ambidextrous person

ambientación *nf Cin & Teatro* setting

ambientador *nm* air freshener

ambiental *adj* environmental

ambientar 1 *vt* **(a)** *Cin & Teatro* to set **(b)** *(iluminar)* to light; *(decorar)* to decorate

2 ambientarse *vpr (adaptarse)* to adapt, to settle in

ambiente 1 *nm* **(a)** *(gen)* environment; *Fig (medio)* environment, milieu **(b)** *Andes, RP (habitación)* room **2** *adj* environmental; **temperatura a.** room temperature

ambigüedad *nf* ambiguity

ambiguo, -a *adj* ambiguous

ámbito *nm* field, sphere; **empresa de a. nacional** nationwide company

ambos, -as *adj pl Fml* both; **por a. lados** on both sides

ambulancia *nf* ambulance

ambulante *adj* travelling, mobile; **biblioteca a.** mobile library

ambulatorio *nm* surgery, clinic

amedrentar *vt* to frighten, to scare

amén¹ *nm* amen

amén² *adv* **a. de** in addition to

amenaza *nf* threat

amenazador, -a, amenazante *adj* threatening, menacing

amenazar [40] *vt* to threaten; **a. de muerte a algn** to threaten to kill sb

amenizar [40] *vt* to liven up

ameno, -a *adj* entertaining

América *n* America; **A. Central/del Norte/ del Sur** Central/North/South America

americana *nf (prenda)* jacket

americano, -a *adj & nm,f* American

amerindio, -a *adj & nm,f* Amerindian, American Indian

ameritar *vt Am* to deserve

amerizar [40] *vi (hidroavión)* to land at sea; *(vehículo espacial)* to splash down

ametralladora *nf* machine gun

ametrallar *vt* to machine-gun

amianto *nm* asbestos

amigable *adj* friendly

amígdala *nf* tonsil

amigdalitis *nf inv* tonsillitis

amigo, -a 1 *nm,f* friend; **hacerse a. de** to make friends with; **hacerse amigos** to become friends; **son muy amigos** they are very good friends **2** *adj (aficionado)* fond **(de** of)

amilanar 1 *vt* to frighten, to scare **2 amilanarse** *vpr* to be frightened *o* daunted

aminorar *vt* to reduce; **a. el paso** to slow down

amistad *nf* **(a)** *(relación)* friendship **(b)** **amistades** friends

amistoso, -a *adj* friendly

amnesia *nf* amnesia

amnistía *nf* amnesty

amo *nm* (**a**) *(dueño)* owner (**b**) *(señor)* master

amodorrarse *vpr* to get drowsy

amoldar 1 *vt* to adapt, to adjust
2 amoldarse *vpr* to adapt

amonestación *nf* (**a**) *(reprimenda)* rebuke, reprimand; *Dep* warning (**b**) *Rel* **amonestaciones** banns

amonestar *vt* (**a**) *(reprender)* to rebuke, to reprimand; *Dep* to warn (**b**) *Rel* to publish the banns of

amoniaco, amoníaco *nm* ammonia

amontonar 1 *vt* to pile up, to heap up
2 amontonarse *vpr* to pile up, to heap up; *(gente)* to crowd together

amor *nm* love; **hacer el a.** to make love; **a. propio** self-esteem; **¡por el a. de Dios!** for God's sake!

amoral *adj* amoral

amoratado, -a *adj (de frío)* blue with cold; *(de un golpe)* black and blue

amordazar [40] *vt (perro)* to muzzle; *(persona)* to gag

amorfo, -a *adj* amorphous

amorío *nm* love affair, flirtation

amoroso, -a *adj* loving, affectionate

amortajar *vt* to shroud, to wrap in a shroud

amortiguador *nm Aut* shock absorber

amortiguar [45] *vt (golpe)* to cushion; *(ruido)* to muffle; *(luz)* to subdue

amortización *nf* repayment

amortizar [40] *vt* to pay off

amotinado, -a *nm,f* rioter; *Mil* mutineer

amotinamiento *nm* riot, rioting; *Mil* mutiny

amotinar 1 *vt* to incite to riot; *Mil* to incite to mutiny
2 amotinarse *vpr* to rise up; *Mil* to mutiny

amparar 1 *vt* to protect
2 ampararse *vpr* to seek refuge

amparo *nm* protection, shelter; **al a. de la ley** under the protection of the law

amperio *nm Elec* ampère, amp

ampliación *nf* enlargement; *(de plazo, casa)* extension

ampliar [29] *vt* to enlarge; *(casa, plazo)* to extend

amplificador *nm* amplifier

amplificar [44] *vt* to amplify

amplio, -a *adj* large, roomy; *(ancho)* wide, broad; **en el sentido más a. de la palabra** in the broadest sense of the word

amplitud *nf* (**a**) *(cualidad)* roominess, spaciousness; **a. de miras** broad-mindedness (**b**) *Fís (de onda)* amplitude

ampolla *nf* (**a**) *Med* blister; *Fig* **levantar ampollas** to raise people's hackles (**b**) *(de medicina)* ampoule

ampuloso, -a *adj* pompous, bombastic

amputación *nf* amputation

amputar *vt* to amputate

amueblado, -a *adj (piso)* furnished

amueblar *vt* to furnish

amuermar *vt Esp Fam (aburrir)* to bore

amuleto *nm* amulet; **a. de la suerte** lucky charm

amurallar *vt* to wall, to fortify

anacronismo *nm* anachronism

ánade *nm* duck

anales *nmpl* annals

analfabetismo *nm* illiteracy

analfabeto, -a *nm,f* illiterate

analgésico, -a *adj & nm* analgesic

análisis *nm inv* analysis; **a. de sangre** blood test

analista *nmf* analyst; **a. financiero** financial analyst; **a. de sistemas** systems analyst

analítico, -a *adj* analytical

analizar [40] *vt* to analyse

analogía *nf* analogy

analógico, -a *adj* analogue

análogo, -a *adj* analogous, similar

ananá *nm*, **ananás** *nm inv RP* pineapple

anaquel *nm* shelf

anaranjado, -a *adj & nm* orange

anarquía *nf* anarchy

anárquico, -a *adj* anarchic

anarquismo *nm* anarchism

anarquista *adj & nmf* anarchist

anatomía *nf* anatomy

anatómico, -a *adj* anatomical

anca *nf* haunch; **ancas de rana** frogs' legs

> Takes the masculine articles **el** and **un**.

ancestral *adj* ancestral

ancho, -a 1 *adj* wide, broad; **a lo a.** breadthwise; **te está muy a.** it's too big for you
2 *nm* (**a**) *(anchura)* width, breadth; **2 m de a.** 2 m wide; **¿qué a. tiene?** how wide is it? (**b**) *Cost* width
3 anchas *nfpl Esp Fam* **a mis/tus/sus anchas** at ease, comfortable

anchoa *nf* anchovy

anchura *nf* width, breadth

anciano, -a 1 *adj* very old
2 *nm,f* old person; **los ancianos** old people

ancla *nf* anchor

> Takes the masculine articles **el** and **un**.

anclar *vt & vi* to anchor

andadas *nfpl* **volver a las a.** to go back to one's old ways

andaderas *nfpl* baby-walker

andadura *nf* **la a. de un país** the evolution of a country; **el Festival comenzó su a. en 1950** the Festival's history began in 1950

ándale *interj CAm, Méx Fam* come on!

Andalucía *n* Andalusia

andaluz, -a *adj & nm,f* Andalusian

andamio *nm* scaffold

andanzas *nfpl* adventures

andar¹ *nm* **a. o andares** walk, gait

andar² [8] **1** *vi* (**a**) *esp Esp (caminar)* to walk (**b**) *(coche etc)* to move; **este coche anda despacio** this car goes very slowly (**c**) *(funcionar)* to work; **esto no anda** this doesn't work (**d**) *Fam* **anda por los cuarenta** he's about forty; **anda siempre diciendo que …** he's always saying that …; **¿cómo andamos de tiempo?** how are we off for time?; **tu bolso debe a. por ahí** your bag must be over there somewhere **2** *vt (recorrer)* to walk

andarín, -ina *adj* **ser muy a.** to be a very keen walker

ándele *interj CAm, Méx Fam* come on!

andén *nm* (**a**) *(en estación)* platform (**b**) *Andes, CAm (acera) Br* pavement, *US* sidewalk (**c**) *Andes (bancal de tierra)* terrace

Andes *nmpl* Andes

andinismo *nm Am* mountaineering, mountain climbing

andinista *nmf Am* mountaineer, mountain climber

andino, -a *adj* Andean

andrajo *nm* rag

andrajoso, -a *adj* ragged, tattered

androide *nm* android

andurriales *nmpl Fam* out-of-the-way place

anécdota *nf* anecdote

anecdótico, -a *adj* anecdotal

anegar [42] **1** *vt* to flood **2 anegarse** *vpr* to flood; **sus ojos se anegaron de lágrimas** tears welled up in his eyes

anejo, -a *adj (edificio)* connected (**a** to)

anemia *nf* anaemia

anémico, -a 1 *adj* anaemic **2** *nm,f* anaemia sufferer

anestesia *nf (técnica)* anaesthesia; *(sustancia)* anaesthetic

anestésico, -a *adj* anaesthetic

anestesista *nmf* anaesthetist

anexar *vt* to annex

anexión *nf* annexation

anexionar *vt* to annex

anexo, -a 1 *adj (edificio)* connected (**a** to) **2** *nm* annexe

anfetamina *nf* amphetamine

anfibio, -a 1 *adj* amphibious **2** *nm* amphibian

anfiteatro *nm* (**a**) *(romano)* amphitheatre (**b**) *Cin & Teatro* gallery

anfitrión, -ona *nm,f* host, *f* hostess

ángel *nm* (**a**) *(ser)* angel; **á. de la guarda** guardian angel (**b**) *Am (micrófono)* hand-held microphone

angelical *adj* angelic

angina *nf* angina; **tener anginas** to have tonsillitis; *Med* **a. de pecho** angina pectoris

anglófono, -a 1 *adj* English-speaking **2** *nm,f* English speaker

anglosajón, -ona *adj & nm,f* Anglo-Saxon

Angola *n* Angola

angosto, -a *adj Fml* narrow

anguila *nf* eel; **a. de mar** conger eel

angula *nf* elver

angular *adj* angular; *Fot* **(objetivo) gran a.** wide-angle lens; **piedra a.** cornerstone

ángulo *nm* angle; *(rincón)* corner

angustia *nf* anguish

angustiado, -a *adj* anguished, distressed

angustiar [43] *vt* to distress

angustioso, -a *adj* distressing

anhelar *vt* to long for, to yearn for

anhelo *nm* longing, yearning

anhídrido *nm* **a. carbónico** carbon dioxide

anidar *vi* to nest

anilla *nf* ring; **carpeta de anillas** ring-binder

anillo *nm* ring; **a. de boda** wedding ring

ánima *nf* soul

> Takes the masculine articles **el** and **un**.

animación *nf (diversión)* entertainment

animado, -a *adj (fiesta etc)* lively

animador, -a *nm,f* (**a**) *(en espectáculo)* compere; *(en fiesta de niños)* children's entertainer; **a. cultural** cultural organizer (**b**) *Dep* cheerleader

animadversión *nf* ill feeling, animosity

animal 1 *nm* animal; *Fig (basto)* brute; *(necio)* dunce **2** *adj* animal

animar 1 *vt* (**a**) *(alentar)* to encourage (**b**) *(alegrar) (persona)* to cheer up; *(fiesta, bar)* to liven up, to brighten up **2 animarse** *vpr* (**a**) *(persona)* to cheer up;

(fiesta, reunión) to brighten up (**b**) **¿te animas a venir?** do you fancy coming along?

anímico, -a *adj* **estado a.** frame o state of mind

ánimo *nm* (**a**) *(espíritu)* spirit; **estado de á.** frame o state of mind (**b**) **con á. de** *(intención)* with the intention of (**c**) *(valor, coraje)* courage; **dar ánimos a** to encourage; **¡á.!** cheer up!

animosidad *nf* animosity

animoso, -a *adj (valiente)* courageous; *(decidido)* undaunted

aniñado, -a *adj* childlike; *Pey* childish

aniquilación *nf* annihilation

aniquilar *vt* to annihilate

anís *(pl* **anises)** *nm* (**a**) *(bebida)* anisette (**b**) *(grano)* aniseed

anisete *nm* anisette

aniversario *nm* anniversary

ano *nm* anus

anoche *adv* last night; *(por la tarde)* yesterday evening; **antes de a.** the night before last

anochecer [33] **1** *v impers* to get dark; **cuando anochece** at nightfall, at dusk
 2 *vi* to be somewhere at dusk; **anochecimos en Cuenca** we were in Cuenca at dusk
 3 *nm* nightfall, dusk

anodino, -a *adj (insustancial)* insubstantial; *(soso)* insipid, dull

anomalía *nf* anomaly

anómalo, -a *adj* anomalous

anonadado, -a *adj* **me quedé/dejó a.** I was astonished

anonimato *nm* anonymity; **permanecer en el a.** to remain anonymous o nameless

anónimo, -a 1 *adj (desconocido)* anonymous
 2 *nm (carta)* anonymous letter

anorak *(pl* **anoraks)** *nm* anorak

anorexia *nf* anorexia

anormal 1 *adj* (**a**) *(anómalo)* abnormal; **una situación a.** an irregular situation (**b**) *(como insulto)* moronic
 2 *nmf (como insulto)* moron

anotación *nf (nota escrita)* note; *(en registro)* entry; *Com* **a. contable** book entry

anotar 1 *vt* to take down, to make a note of
 2 anotarse *vpr RP (en curso)* to enrol (**en** for); *(para actividad)* to sign up (**en** for)

anquilosado, -a *adj* fossilized; **a. en el pasado** locked in the past

anquilosarse *vpr* to stagnate

ansia *nf* (**a**) *(deseo)* longing, yearning (**b**) *(ansiedad)* anxiety (**c**) *Med* sick feeling

> Takes the masculine articles **el** and **un**.

ansiar [29] *vt* to long for, to yearn for

ansiedad *nf* anxiety; **con a.** anxiously

ansioso, -a *adj* (**a**) *(deseoso)* eager (**por** for) (**b**) *(avaricioso)* greedy

antagónico, -a *adj* antagonistic

antagonismo *nm* antagonism

antagonista 1 *adj* antagonistic
 2 *nmf* antagonist

antaño *adv* in the past, formerly

antártico, -a 1 *adj* Antarctic
 2 *nm* **el A.** the Antarctic

Antártida *nf* Antarctica

ante¹ *nm* (**a**) *Zool* elk, moose (**b**) *(piel)* suede

ante² *prep* (**a**) *(delante de, en presencia de)* before, in the presence of; *Der* **a. notario** in the presence of a notary; **a. todo** most of all (**b**) *(en vista de)* faced with, in view of; **a. la crisis energética** faced with the energy crisis

anteanoche *adv* the night before last

anteayer *adv* the day before yesterday

antebrazo *nm* forearm

antecedente 1 *adj* previous
 2 *nm* antecedent
 3 antecedentes *nmpl (historial)* record; *Der* **antecedentes penales** criminal record; **poner en antecedentes** to put in the picture

anteceder *vt* to precede, to go before

antecesor, -a *nm,f* (**a**) *(en un cargo)* predecessor (**b**) *(antepasado)* ancestor

antedicho, -a *adj* above-mentioned

antelación *nf* notice; **con poca a.** at short notice; **con un mes de a.** a month beforehand, with a month's notice

antemano *adv* **de a.** beforehand, in advance

antena *nf* (**a**) *Rad & TV* aerial; **a. parabólica** satellite dish; **en a.** on the air (**b**) *Zool* antenna, feeler

anteojos *nmpl (prismáticos)* binoculars; *Am (gafas)* spectacles, glasses

antepasado, -a *nm,f* ancestor

antepecho *nm (de ventana)* sill; *(de puente)* parapet

antepenúltimo, -a *adj* antepenultimate; **el capítulo a.** the last chapter but two

anteponer [19] *(pp* **antepuesto)** *vt* to give preference to

anteproyecto *nm Pol* **a. de ley** draft bill

antepuesto, -a *pp de* **anteponer**

antepuse *pt indef de* **anteponer**

anterior adj (a) (previo) previous; **el día a.** the day before (b) (delantero) front; **parte a.** front part

anterioridad nf **con a.** before; **con a. a** prior to, before

anteriormente adv previously, before

antes adv (a) (tiempo) before; **a. de las tres** before three o'clock; **mucho a.** long before; **la noche a.** the night before; **cuanto a.** as soon as possible (b) (antaño) in the past; **a. llovía más** it used to rain more in the past (c) (lugar) before; **a. del semáforo** before the traffic lights (d) **a. prefiero hacerlo yo** I'd rather do it myself; **a. (bien)** on the contrary

antesala nf antechamber, anteroom; Fig **en la a. de** on the eve of

anti- pref anti-

antiabortista 1 adj anti-abortion, pro-life **2** nmf anti-abortion o pro-life campaigner

antiadherente adj nonstick

antiaéreo, -a adj anti-aircraft

antiarrugas adj inv anti-wrinkle

antibiótico, -a adj & nm antibiotic

anticaspa adj anti-dandruff

anticiclón nm anticyclone, high pressure area

anticipación nf **con a.** in advance

anticipadamente adv in advance

anticipado, -a adj brought forward; **elecciones anticipadas** early elections; **gracias anticipadas** thanks in advance; Com **por a.** in advance

anticipar 1 vt (acontecimiento) to bring forward; (dinero) to pay in advance; **no anticipemos acontecimientos** we'll cross that bridge when we come to it
2 anticiparse vpr (a) (adelantarse) **anticiparse a algn** to beat sb to it; **iba a decírtelo, pero él se me anticipó** I was going to tell you, but he beat me to it (b) (llegar pronto) to arrive early; Fig **anticiparse a su tiempo** to be ahead of one's time

anticipo nm (adelanto) advance; **pedir un a.** to ask for an advance (on one's wages)

anticonceptivo, -a adj & nm contraceptive

anticongelante adj & nm antifreeze

anticonstitucional adj unconstitutional

anticuado, -a adj antiquated

anticuario, -a nm,f antique dealer

anticucho nm Andes (brocheta) kebab

anticuerpo nm antibody

antidepresivo, -a 1 adj antidepressant **2** nm antidepressant (drug)

antídoto nm antidote

antier adv Am Fam the day before yesterday

antiestético, -a adj ugly, unsightly

antifaz nm mask

antigás adj careta/mascarilla a. gas mask

antigualla nf Pey museum piece

antiguamente adv (hace mucho) long ago; (previamente) formerly

antigüedad nf (a) (período histórico) antiquity; **en la a.** in olden days, in former times (b) (en cargo) seniority (c) **tienda de antigüedades** antique shop

antiguo, -a adj (a) (viejo) old, ancient (b) (anterior) former (c) (pasado de moda) old-fashioned (d) (en cargo) senior

antihigiénico, -a adj unhygienic, unhealthy

antihistamínico, -a adj & nm antihistamine

antiinflamatorio, -a 1 adj anti-inflammatory **2** nm anti-inflammatory (drug)

Antillas nfpl **las A.** the West Indies, the Antilles

antílope nm antelope

antinatural adj unnatural, contrary to nature

antiniebla adj inv **faros a.** fog lamps

antipatía nf antipathy, dislike; **tener a. a** to dislike

antipático, -a adj unpleasant; **Pedro me es a.** I don't like Pedro

antípodas nfpl **las A.** the Antipodes

antiquísimo, -a (superl de antiguo) adj very old, ancient

antirrobo 1 adj inv antitheft; **alarma a.** burglar alarm; (para coche) car alarm **2** nm (para coche) car alarm; (para casa) burglar alarm

antisemita 1 adj anti-Semitic **2** nmf anti-Semite

antiséptico, -a adj & nm antiseptic

antítesis nf inv antithesis

antivirus nm inv Inform antivirus system

antojadizo, -a adj capricious, unpredictable

antojarse vpr (a) (capricho) **cuando se me antoja** when I feel like it; **se le antojó un helado** he fancied an ice-cream (b) (posibilidad) **se me antoja que ...** I have a feeling that ... (c) Méx (apetecer) to feel like, to want

antojitos nmpl Ecuad, Méx snacks, appetizers

antojo nm (a) (capricho) whim, caprice; (de embarazada) craving; **a su a.** in one's own way, as one pleases (b) (en la piel) birthmark

antología *nf* anthology

antónimo *nm* antonym

antonomasia *nf* **por a.** par excellence

antorcha *nf* torch

antro *nm* dump, hole; *Fig* **a. de perdición** den of iniquity

antropología *nf* anthropology

antropólogo, -a *nm,f* anthropologist

anual *adj* annual; **ingresos anuales** yearly income

anualidad *nf* annual payment, annuity

anuario *nm* yearbook

anudar *vt* to knot, to tie

anulación *nf* cancellation; *(de matrimonio)* annulment; *(de ley)* repeal

anular[1] *nm* ring finger

anular[2] *vt* (**a**) *Com (pedido)* to cancel; *Dep (gol)* to disallow; *(matrimonio)* to annul; *Der (ley)* to repeal (**b**) *Inform* to delete

anunciador, -a *adj* **empresa anunciadora** advertising company

anunciante *nm* advertiser

anunciar [43] **1** *vt* (**a**) *(producto etc)* to advertise (**b**) *(avisar)* to announce
2 anunciarse *vpr* to advertise oneself; **anunciarse en un periódico** to put an advert in a newspaper

anuncio *nm* (**a**) *(comercial)* advertisement, *Br* advert, ad (**b**) *(aviso)* announcement (**c**) *(cartel)* notice, poster

anzuelo *nm* (fish) hook

añadidura *nf* addition; **por a.** besides, on top of everything else

añadir *vt* to add (**a** to)

añejo, -a *adj* (**a**) *(vino, queso)* mature (**b**) *(costumbre)* long-established

añicos *nmpl* smithereens; **hacer a.** to smash to smithereens

añil *adj & nm* indigo

año *nm* (**a**) *(periodo)* year; **el a. pasado** last year; **el a. que viene** next year; **hace años** a long time ago, years ago; **los años noventa** the nineties; **todo el a.** all year (round); **a. luz** light year (**b**) *(edad)* **¿cuántos años tienes?** how old are you?; **tiene seis años** he's six (years old); **entrado en años** getting on

añoranza *nf* longing, yearning

añorar *vt (pasado)* to long for, to yearn for; *(país)* to feel homesick for, to miss

aorta *nf Anat* aorta

APA *nf* (*abr* **Asociación de Padres de Alumnos**) = Spanish association for parents of schoolchildren, ≃ PTA

> Takes the masculine articles **el** and **un**.

apabullar *vt* to overwhelm

apacentar [1] *vt* to put out to pasture, to graze

apache *adj & nmf* Apache

apachurrar *vt Fam* to squash, to crush

apacible *adj* mild, calm

apaciguar [45] **1** *vt (calmar)* to pacify, to appease
2 apaciguarse *vpr (persona)* to calm down; *(tormenta)* to abate

apadrinar *vt* (**a**) *(en bautizo)* to act as godfather to; *(en boda)* to be best man for (**b**) *(artista)* to sponsor

apagado, -a *adj* (**a**) *(luz)* out, off; *(cigarro)* out (**b**) *(color)* dull; *(voz)* sad; *(mirada)* expressionless, lifeless; *(carácter, persona)* spiritless

apagar [42] *vt (fuego)* to put out; *(luz, tele etc)* to turn off, to switch off; *(color)* to soften; *(sed)* to quench

apagón *nm* power cut, blackout

apaisado, -a *adj (papel)* landscape

apalabrar *vt (concertar)* to make a verbal agreement on

apalancado, -a *adj Esp Fam* **se pasó la tarde a. delante del televisor** he spent the afternoon lounging in front of the television

apalancar [44] **1** *vt* to lever up
2 apalancarse *vpr Esp Fam* to install oneself

apalear *vt* to beat, to thrash

apañado, -a *adj Fam* (**a**) *(hábil, mañoso)* clever, resourceful (**b**) **estar a.** to have had it; **¡estamos apañados!** we've had it!

apañar 1 *vt* to mend, to fix
2 apañarse *vpr Esp (arreglarse)* to cope, to manage; **apañárselas (para hacer algo)** to manage (to do sth)

apaño *nm Fam* (**a**) *(reparación)* patch (**b**) *(chanchullo)* fix, shady deal (**c**) *(acuerdo)* compromise

apapachar *vt Méx Fam (mimar)* to cuddle; *(consentir)* to spoil

apapacho *nm Méx Fam (mimo)* cuddle

aparador *nm (mueble)* sideboard; *(de tienda)* shop window

aparato *nm* (**a**) *(dispositivo)* device; *(instrumento)* instrument; **a. de radio/ televisión** radio/television set; **a. digestivo** digestive system; **a. eléctrico** thunder and lightning (**b**) *Tel* **¿quién está al a.?** who's speaking? (**c**) *(ostentación)* display

aparatoso, -a *adj* (**a**) *(pomposo)* ostentatious, showy (**b**) *(espectacular)* spectacular

aparcamiento *nm Esp (parking) Br* car park, *US* parking lot; *(hueco)* parking place

aparcar [44] *Esp* **1** *vt (estacionar)* to park; *Fig (posponer)* to shelve
2 *vi* to park

apareamiento *nm* mating

aparear 1 *vt* to mate
2 aparearse *vpr* to mate

aparecer [33] **1** *vi* (a) *(ante la vista)* to appear; **no aparece en mi lista** he is not on my list (b) *(algo perdido)* to turn up, to show up; **¿apareció el dinero?** did the money turn up?; **no apareció nadie** nobody turned up
2 aparecerse *vpr* to appear

aparejado, -a *adj* **llevar** *o* **traer a.** to entail

aparejador, -a *nm,f* quantity surveyor

aparejar *vt* (a) *(caballo)* to harness (b) *(emparejar)* to pair off

aparejo *nm* (a) *(equipo)* equipment (b) *(de caballo)* harness

aparentar 1 *vt* (a) *(fingir)* to affect (b) *(tener aspecto)* to look; **no aparenta esa edad** she doesn't look that age
2 *vi* to show off

aparente *adj* apparent; **sin motivo a.** for no apparent reason

aparición *nf* (a) *(de persona, cosa)* appearance (b) *(de ser sobrenatural)* apparition

apariencia *nf* appearance; **en a.** apparently; **guardar las apariencias** to keep up appearances

apartado, -a 1 *adj (lugar)* remote, isolated; **mantente a. de él** keep away from him
2 *nm* (a) *(párrafo)* section, paragraph (b) **a. de correos** Post Office Box

apartamento *nm esp Am (en edificio) Br* flat, *US* apartment; *Esp (más pequeño)* apartment

apartar 1 *vt* (a) *(alejar)* to move away, to remove; **a. la mirada** to look away (b) *(guardar)* to put aside
2 *vi* **¡aparta!** move out of the way!
3 apartarse *vpr (alejarse)* to move over, to move away; **apártate de en medio** move out of the way

aparte 1 *adv* (a) *(en otro lugar, a un lado)* aside; **ponlo a.** put it aside; **modestia/bromas a.** modesty/joking apart (b) *(por separado)* separately; **eso hay que pagarlo a.** you have to pay for that separately (c) **a. de eso** apart from that
2 *nm Teatro* aside

apasionado, -a 1 *adj* passionate; **a. de la música** very fond of music
2 *nm,f* enthusiast

apasionante *adj* exciting

apasionar *vt* to excite, to thrill; **le apasiona el jazz** he is mad about jazz

apatía *nf* apathy

apático, -a 1 *adj* apathetic
2 *nm,f* apathetic person

apátrida 1 *adj* stateless
2 *nmf* stateless person

apdo. *(abr* **apartado)** P.O. Box

apeadero *nm* halt

apearse *vpr* **a. (de)** *(tren)* to alight (from), to get off; *(coche, autobús)* to get out (of); *(caballo)* to dismount (from); **se apeó en Jerez** he got off in Jerez

apechugar [42] *vi Fam* **a. con** to shoulder

apedrear *vt (persona)* to stone; *(cosa)* to throw stones at

apegado, -a *adj* attached (**a** to)

apegarse [42] *vpr* to become attached (**a** to)

apego *nm* attachment; **tener a. a** to be attached to

apelación *nf* appeal

apelar *vi* (a) *Der* to (lodge an) appeal; **a. ante/contra** to appeal to/against (b) *(recurrir)* **a. a** *(sentido común, bondad)* to appeal to

apellidarse *vpr* to have as a surname, to be called

apellido *nm* surname; **a. de soltera** maiden name

apelmazado, -a *adj (arroz, bizcocho)* stodgy; **el jersey está a.** the jumper has lost its fluffiness

apelotonar 1 *vt* to bundle up
2 apelotonarse *vpr (gente)* to crowd together

apenado, -a *adj* (a) *(entristecido)* sad (b) *Am salvo RP (avergonzado)* embarrassed; **está muy a. por lo que hizo** he's very embarrassed about what he did

apenar 1 *vt* to sadden
2 apenarse *vpr* (a) *(entristecerse)* to be saddened (b) *Am salvo RP (avergonzarse)* to be embarrassed

apenas *adv* (a) *(casi no)* hardly, scarcely; **a. come** he hardly eats anything; **a. (si) hay nieve** there is hardly any snow (b) *(tan pronto como)* scarcely; **a. llegó, sonó el teléfono** no sooner had he arrived than the phone rang

apéndice *nm* appendix

apendicitis *nf inv* appendicitis

apercibir 1 *vt* to warn
2 apercibirse *vpr* **apercibirse (de)** to notice

aperitivo *nm (bebida)* apéritif; *(comida)* appetizer

aperos *nmpl* **a. de labranza** farming implements

apertura *nf* (a) *(comienzo)* opening (b) *Pol* liberalization

apestar 1 *vi* to stink (**a** of)
2 *vt* to infect with the plague

apetecer [33] *vi Esp* ¿**qué te apetece para cenar?** what would you like for supper?; ¿**te apetece ir al cine?** do you fancy going to the cinema?

apetecible *adj* tempting, inviting

apetito *nm* appetite; **tengo mucho a.** I'm really hungry

apetitoso, -a *adj* appetizing, tempting; *(comida)* delicious, tasty

apiadarse *upr* to take pity (**de** on)

ápice *nm* **ni un á.** not a bit

apicultura *nf* beekeeping, apiculture

apilar 1 *vt* to pile up
2 apilarse *upr* to pile up

apiñado, -a *adj* packed, crammed

apiñarse *upr* to crowd together

apio *nm* celery

apisonadora *nf* roadroller, steamroller

apisonar *vt* to roll

aplacar [44] **1** *vt* to placate, to calm
2 aplacarse *upr* to calm down

aplanar *vt* to level

aplastante *adj* (victoria, derrota) crushing, overwhelming; *(mayoría, superioridad)* overwhelming

aplastar *vt* (a) *(por el peso)* to flatten, to squash (b) *Fig (vencer)* to crush

aplatanado, -a *adj Esp, Méx Fam* listless

aplaudir 1 *vt* to applaud
2 *vi* to applaud, to clap

aplauso *nm (ovación)* round of applause; *Fig (alabanza)* applause; **aplausos** applause

aplazamiento *nm* postponement

aplazar [40] *vt* to postpone

aplicación *nf* application

aplicado, -a *adj* hard-working

aplicar [44] **1** *vt* to apply
2 aplicarse *upr* (a) *(esforzarse)* to apply oneself, to work hard (b) *(norma, ley)* to apply, to be applicable

aplique *nm* wall light, wall lamp

aplomo *nm* aplomb

apocado, -a *adj* shy, timid

apocamiento *nm* timidity

apodar 1 *vt* to nickname
2 apodarse *upr* to be nicknamed

apoderado, -a *nm,f (de torero, deportista)* agent, manager

apoderarse *upr* to take possession (**de** of), to seize; *Fig* **el miedo se apoderó de ella** she was seized by fear

apodo *nm* nickname

apogeo *nm* height; **estar en pleno a.** *(fama etc)* to be at its height

apolillarse *upr* to get moth-eaten

apolítico, -a *adj* apolitical

apología *nf* apology, defence

apoltronarse *upr Fam* to vegetate

apoplejía *nf* apoplexy

apoquinar *vt & vi Esp Fam* to cough up, to fork out

aporrear *vt (puerta)* to bang; **a. el piano** to bang (away) on the piano

aportación *nf* contribution

aportar *vt* to contribute

aposentarse *upr* to take up lodgings

aposento *nm* room

aposta *adv Esp* on purpose, intentionally

apostar¹ [2] **1** *vt* to bet; **te apuesto una cena a que no viene** I bet you a dinner that he won't come
2 *vi* to bet (**por** on); **a. a los caballos** to bet on horses; **apuesto a que sí viene** I bet will come
3 apostarse *upr* to bet; **me apuesto lo que quieras** I bet you anything

apostar² *vt (situar)* to post, to station

apostilla *nf (nota)* note; *(comentario)* comment

apóstol *nm* apostle

apóstrofo *nm* apostrophe

apoteósico, -a *adj* tremendous; **un final a.** a grand finale

apoyacabezas *nm inv Aut* headrest

apoyar *vt* (a) *(inclinar)* to lean, to rest (b) *(causa)* to support
2 apoyarse *upr* (a) *(sostenerse)* **apoyarse en** to lean on; **apóyate en mi brazo** take my arm (b) *(buscar respaldo)* **apoyarse en** to rely on (c) *(basarse)* **apoyarse en** to base one's arguments on

apoyo *nm* support

apreciable *adj* appreciable, noticeable

apreciación *nf* appreciation

apreciado, -a *adj (querido)* esteemed, highly regarded

apreciar [43] **1** *vt* (a) *(sentir afecto por)* to be fond of (b) *(percibir)* to notice, to see (c) *(valorar)* to appreciate
2 apreciarse *upr* to be noticeable

aprecio *nm* regard, esteem; **tener a. a algn** to be fond of sb

aprehender *vt (persona)* to apprehend; *(alijo, mercancía)* to seize

aprehensión *nf (de persona)* arrest, capture; *(de alijo, mercancía)* seizure

apremiante *adj* urgent, pressing

apremiar [43] *vi* to be urgent; **el tiempo apremia** time is short

aprender *vt* to learn; **así aprenderás** that'll teach you

aprendiz, -a *nm,f* apprentice, trainee

aprendizaje *nm* (a) *(adquisición de conocimientos)* learning (b) *(tiempo, situación)* apprenticeship, traineeship

aprensión *nf* apprehension

aprensivo, -a *adj* apprehensive

apresar *vt* to seize, to capture

aprestarse *vpr* **a. a hacer algo** to get ready to do sth

apresurado, -a *adj (persona)* in a hurry; *(cosa)* hurried

apresuramiento *nm* haste, hurry

apresurar 1 *vt (paso etc)* to speed up
2 **apresurarse** *vpr* to hurry up

apretado, -a *adj* (a) *(ropa, cordón)* tight; **íbamos todos apretados en el coche** we were all squashed together in the car (b) *(día, agenda)* busy

apretar [1] 1 *vt (botón)* to press; *(nudo, tornillo)* to tighten; **a. el gatillo** to pull the trigger; **me aprietan las botas** these boots are too tight for me
2 *vi* **apretaba el calor** it was really hot
3 **apretarse** *vpr* to squeeze together, to cram together; *Fig* **apretarse el cinturón** to tighten one's belt

apretón *nm* squeeze; **a. de manos** handshake

apretujar 1 *vt* to squeeze, to crush
2 **apretujarse** *vpr* to squeeze together, to cram together

aprieto *nm* tight spot, fix, jam; **poner a algn en un a.** to put sb in an awkward position

aprisa *adv* quickly

aprisionar *vt (atrapar)* to trap

aprobación *nf* approval

aprobado *nm Educ* pass

aprobar [2] *vt* (a) *(autorizar)* to approve (b) *(estar de acuerdo con)* to approve of (c) *Educ* to pass (d) *Pol (ley)* to pass

aprontar 1 *vt (preparar)* to quickly prepare o get ready
2 **aprontarse** *vpr RP (prepararse)* to get ready; **aprontate para cuando llegue tu papá!** just you wait till your father gets home!

apropiado, -a *adj* suitable, appropriate

apropiarse [43] *vpr* to appropriate

aprovechado, -a *adj* (a) **mal a.** *(recurso, tiempo)* wasted; **bien a.** put to good use (b) *(espacio)* well-planned (c) *(egoísta)* self-seeking

aprovechamiento *nm* use

aprovechar 1 *vt (tiempo, dinero)* to make the most of; *(oferta, ocasión)* to take

advantage of; *(conocimientos, experiencia)* to use, to make use of; **me gustaría a. esta oportunidad para ...** I'd like to take this opportunity to ...
2 *vi* **¡que aproveche!** enjoy your meal!, bon appétit!
3 **aprovecharse** *vpr* to take advantage; **aprovecharse de algn** to take advantage of sb; **aprovecharse de algo** to make the most of sth

aprovisionar 1 *vt* to supply
2 **aprovisionarse** *vpr* **aprovisionarse de algo** to stock up on sth

aproximación *nf* approximation

aproximadamente *adv* approximately, roughly

aproximado, -a *adj* approximate; **un cálculo a.** a rough estimate

aproximar 1 *vt* to bring o put nearer
2 **aproximarse** *vpr* **aproximarse (a)** to approach

aproximativo, -a *adj* approximate, rough

aptitud *nf* aptitude; **prueba de a.** aptitude test

apto, -a *adj* (a) *(apropiado)* suitable, appropriate; *Cin* **a. para todos los públicos** *Br* U, *US* G (b) *(capacitado)* capable, able (c) *Educ* passed

apuesta *nf* bet, wager

apuesto, -a *adj* good-looking; *(hombre)* handsome

apunado, -a *adj Andes* **estar a.** to have altitude sickness

apunarse *vpr Andes* to get altitude sickness

apuntador, -a *nm,f Teatro* prompter

apuntalar *vt* to shore up

apuntar 1 *vt* (a) *(arma)* to aim; **a. a algn** to aim at sb (b) *(señalar)* to point out (c) *(anotar)* to note down, to make a note of
2 *vi* (a) *(indicar)* to indicate, to suggest; **todo parece a. a ...** everything seems to point to ... (b) **cuando apunta el día** when day breaks
3 **apuntarse** *vpr* (a) *(en una lista)* to put one's name down (b) *Fam* **¿te apuntas?** are you game?; **me apunto** count me in

apunte *nm (usu pl)* note; **tomar apuntes** to take notes

apuñalar *vt* to stab

apurado, -a 1 *adj* (a) *(necesitado)* in need; **a. de dinero** hard up for money; **a. de tiempo** in a hurry (b) *(preocupado)* worried; *(avergonzado)* embarrassed (c) *(situación)* awkward, difficult (d) *Esp (afeitado)* close (e) *Am (con prisa)* **estar a.** to be in a hurry
2 *nm Esp (afeitado)* close shave

apurar 1 *vt* (**a**) *(terminar)* to finish off, to end (**b**) *(preocupar)* to worry
 2 apurarse *vpr* (**a**) *Esp, Méx (preocuparse)* to worry, to get worried; **no te apures** don't worry (**b**) *Am (darse prisa)* to rush, to hurry, to pester; **apúrate** get a move on

apuro *nm* (**a**) *(situación difícil)* tight spot, fix, jam; **estar en un a.** to be in a tight spot (**b**) *(escasez de dinero)* hardship; **pasar apuros** to be hard up (**c**) *(vergüenza)* embarrassment; **¡qué a.!** how embarrassing! (**d**) *Am (prisa)* **tener a.** to be in a hurry

aquejado, -a *adj* **a. de** suffering from

aquel, -ella *(pl* **aquellos, -ellas)** *adj dem* (**a**) *(singular)* that; **a. niño** that boy (**b**) **aquellos, -as** those; **aquellas niñas** those girls

aquél, -élla *(pl* **aquéllos, -éllas)** *pron dem m,f* (**a**) *(singular)* that one; *(el anterior)* the former; **aquél/aquélla ... éste/ésta** the former ... the latter (**b**) **todo a. que** anyone who, whoever (**c**) **aquéllos, -as** those; *(los anteriores)* the former

> Note that **aquél** and its various forms can be written without an accent when there is no risk of confusion with the adjective.

aquelarre *nm* coven

aquella *adj dem f ver* **aquel**

aquélla *pron dem f ver* **aquél**

aquello *pron neut f* that, it

aquellos, -as *adj dem pl ver* **aquel**

aquéllos, -as *pron dem m,fpl ver* **aquél**

aquí *adv* (**a**) *(lugar)* here; **a. arriba/fuera** up/out here; **a. está** here it is; **a. mismo** right here; **de a. para allá** up and down, to and fro; **hasta a.** this far; **por a., por favor** this way please; **está por a.** it's around here somewhere (**b**) *(tiempo)* **de a. en adelante** from now on; **de aquí a junio** between now and June; **hasta a.** up till now

aquietar *vt* to pacify, to calm down

árabe 1 *adj (de Arabia)* Arab
 2 *nmf (persona)* Arab
 3 *nm (idioma)* Arabic

Arabia *n* Arabia; **A. Saudí** Saudi Arabia

arado *nm* plough

Aragón *n* Aragon

aragonés, -esa *adj & nm,f* Aragonese

arancel *nm* tariff; **a. aduanero** customs duty

arancelario, -a *adj* tariff; **barreras arancelarias** tariff barriers

arandela *nf Téc* washer; *(anilla)* ring

araña *nf* (**a**) *(insecto)* spider (**b**) *(lámpara)* chandelier

arañar *vt* to scratch

arañazo *nm* scratch

arar *vt* to plough

aras *nfpl Fml* **en a. de** for the sake of

araucaria *nf* araucaria, monkey puzzle tree

arbitraje *nm* (**a**) *Der* arbitration (**b**) *Dep* refereeing; *Ten* umpiring

arbitrar *vt & vi* (**a**) *Der* to arbitrate (**b**) *Dep* to referee; *Ten* to umpire

arbitrariedad *nf* (**a**) *(cualidad)* arbitrariness (**b**) *(acto)* arbitrary action

arbitrario, -a *adj* arbitrary

arbitrio *nm* **dejar algo al a. de algn** to leave sth to sb's discretion

árbitro, -a *nm,f* (**a**) *Dep* referee; *(de tenis)* umpire (**b**) *(mediador)* arbitrator

árbol *nm* (**a**) *Bot* tree (**b**) *Téc* shaft (**c**) *Náut* mast (**d**) *(gráfico)* tree (diagram); **á. genealógico** family o genealogical tree

arbolado, -a 1 *adj* wooded
 2 *nm* woodland

arboleda *nf* grove

arbusto *nm* bush, shrub

arca *nf* (**a**) *(mueble)* chest (**b**) **arcas públicas** Treasury

> Takes the masculine articles **el** and **un**.

arcada *nf* (**a**) *(de estómago)* **me dieron arcadas** I retched (**b**) *Arquit (arcos)* arcade

arcaico, -a *adj* archaic

arcángel *nm* archangel

arcén *nm Esp (en carretera) Br* hard shoulder, *US* shoulder

archi- *pref* super-

archiconocido, -a *adj* extremely well-known

archipiélago *nm* archipelago

archivador *nm* filing cabinet

archivar *vt* (**a**) *(documento etc)* to file (away) (**b**) *(caso, asunto)* to shelve (**c**) *Inform* to save

archivo *nm* (**a**) *(documento)* file (**b**) *(lugar)* archive (**c**) *Inform* file; **a. adjunto** attachment

arcilla *nf* clay

arco *nm* (**a**) *Arquit* arch (**b**) *Mat & Elec* arc (**c**) *(de violín)* bow (**d**) *(para flechas)* bow; **tiro con a.** archery (**e**) **a. iris** rainbow (**f**) *esp Am Dep (portería)* goal, goalmouth

arder *vi* to burn; *Fam* **la conversación está que arde** the conversation is really heating up; **Juan está que arde** Juan is really fuming

ardid *nm* ruse, trick

ardiente *adj* (**a**) *(encendido)* burning; **capilla a.** chapel of rest (**b**) *Fig (fervoroso)* eager

ardilla *nf* squirrel

ardor *nm* (**a**) *(quemazón)* burning (sensation); *Med* **a. de estómago** heartburn (**b**) *(entusiasmo)* fervour

ardoroso, -a *adj* ardent, passionate

arduo, -a *adj* arduous

área *nf* (**a**) *(extensión)* area; *Dep* penalty area (**b**) *(medida)* are *(100 square metres)*

> Takes the masculine articles **el** and **un**.

arena *nf* (**a**) *(material)* sand; **playa de a.** sandy beach (**b**) *Taurom* bullring

arengar [42] *vt* to harangue

arenisca *nf* sandstone

arenoso, -a *adj* sandy

arenque *nm* herring; *Culin* **a. ahumado** kipper

arepa *nf Carib, Col* = pancake made of maize flour

arete *nm Andes, Méx (pendiente)* earring; *Esp (en forma de aro)* hoop earring

argamasa *nf* mortar

Argel *n* Algiers

Argelia *n* Algeria

argelino, -a *adj & nm,f* Algerian

Argentina *n* Argentina

argentino, -a *adj & nm,f* Argentinian, Argentine

argolla *nf* (**a**) *(aro)* (large) ring (**b**) *Andes, Méx (alianza)* wedding ring (**c**) *Carib (pendiente)* hoop earring

argot *(pl* argots) *nm (popular)* slang; *(técnico)* jargon

argucia *nf* ruse

argüende *nm Méx Fam* (**a**) *(chisme)* gossip (**b**) *(fiesta)* party, *Br* rave-up

argüir [62] *vt* (**a**) *(deducir)* to deduce (**b**) *(argumentar)* to argue

argumentación *nf* argument

argumentar 1 *vt (alegar)* to argue
2 *vi (discutir)* to argue

argumento *nm* (**a**) *Lit & Teatro (trama)* plot (**b**) *(razonamiento)* argument

arguyo *indic pres de* **argüir**

aria *nf (de ópera)* aria

aridez *nf* (*de terreno, clima*) aridity, dryness

árido, -a *adj (terreno, clima)* arid, dry; *(libro, tema)* dry

Aries *nm* Aries

ariete *nm Mil* battering ram

ario, -a *adj & nm,f* Aryan

arisco, -a *adj* surly

arista *nf* edge

aristocracia *nf* aristocracy

aristócrata *nmf* aristocrat

aristocrático, -a *adj* aristocratic

aritmética *nf* arithmetic

arlequín *nm* harlequin

arma *nf* weapon; **a. blanca** knife; **a. de fuego** firearm; **a. homicida** murder weapon; **a. nuclear** nuclear weapon; *Fig* **a. de doble filo** double-edged sword

> Takes the masculine articles **el** and **un**.

armada *nf* navy

armadillo *nm* armadillo

armado, -a *adj* armed; **ir a.** to be armed; **lucha armada** armed struggle

armador, -a *nm,f* shipowner

armadura *nf* (**a**) *(armazón)* frame (**b**) *Hist* suit of armour

armamentista *adj* arms; **la carrera a.** the arms race

armamento *nm* armaments; **a. nuclear** nuclear weapons

armar 1 *vt* (**a**) *(tropa, soldado)* to arm (**b**) *(piezas)* to fit *o* put together, to assemble (**c**) *Fam* **armaron un escándalo** they kicked up a fuss
2 armarse *vpr* to arm oneself; *Fig* **armarse de paciencia** to summon up one's patience; *Fig* **armarse de valor** to pluck up courage; *Fam* **se armó la gorda** all hell broke loose

armario *nm (para ropa)* wardrobe; *(de cocina)* cupboard; **a. empotrado** built-in wardrobe *o* cupboard

armatoste *nm (mueble, objeto)* unwieldy object; *(máquina)* contraption

armazón *nm (estructura)* framework, frame; *(de avión, coche)* chassis; *(de edificio)* skeleton

Armenia *n* Armenia

armería *nf* gunsmith's (shop)

armiño *nm* ermine

armisticio *nm* armistice

armonía *nf* harmony

armónica *nf* harmonica, mouth organ

armonioso, -a *adj* harmonious

armonizar [40] *vt & vi* to harmonize

aro *nm* (**a**) *(gen)* hoop; *Fam* **pasar por el a.** to knuckle under (**b**) *Am (pendiente)* earring; *Esp (circular)* hoop earring (**c**) *Ven (alianza)* wedding ring (**d**) *Col (montura)* rim (**e**) *Bol (anillo)* ring

aroma *nm* aroma; *(de vino)* bouquet

aromático, -a *adj* aromatic

arpa *nf* harp

> Takes the masculine articles **el** and **un**.

arpía *nf (en mitología)* harpy; *Fig* harpy, old witch

arpón *nm* harpoon

arquear 1 *vt (madera)* to warp; *(vara, fusta)* to flex; *(cejas, espalda)* to arch
  2 arquearse *upr* to warp

arqueología *nf* archaeology

arqueólogo, -a *nm,f* archaeologist

arquero, -a *nm,f* (a) *(tirador)* archer (b) *Am Ftb* goalkeeper

arquetipo *nm* archetype

arquitecto, -a *nm,f* architect

arquitectónico, -a *adj* architectural

arquitectura *nf* architecture

arrabalero, -a *adj Esp Pey* coarse

arrabales *nmpl* slums

arraigado, -a *adj* deeply rooted

arraigar [42] *vi* to take root

arraigo *nm* roots; **una tradición con mucho a.** a deeply-rooted tradition

arrancar [44] **1** *vt* (a) *(planta)* to uproot, to pull up; **a. de raíz** to uproot (b) *(extraer)* to pull *o* tear off *o* out; *(diente, pelo)* to pull out; *Fig (confesión etc)* to extract; **arranca una hoja del cuaderno** tear a page out of the notebook (c) *(coche, motor)* to start; *Inform* to boot
  2 *vi* (a) *Aut & Téc* to start; *Inform* to boot (up) (b) *(empezar)* to begin; **a. a llorar** to burst out crying

arranque *nm* (a) *Aut & Téc* starting (b) *(comienzo)* start (c) *Fam (arrebato)* outburst, fit

arrasar 1 *vt (edificio, cosecha)* to destroy; *(zona)* to devastate
  2 *vi* (a) **a. con** *(destruir)* to destroy (b) *Fam (triunfar)* to win overwhelmingly

arrastrado, -a 1 *adj* (a) *(vida)* miserable, wretched (b) *Méx, RP (servil)* grovelling
  2 *nm,f Méx, RP* groveller

arrastrar 1 *vt* to pull (along), to drag (along); **vas arrastrando el vestido** your dress is trailing on the ground; **lo arrastró la corriente** he was swept away by the current
  2 arrastrarse *upr* to drag oneself; *Fig (humillarse)* to crawl

arrastre *nm* (a) *(acción)* pulling, dragging; *Esp Fam* **estar para el a.** to have had it (b) **(pesca de) a.** trawling (c) *RP Fam* **tener a.** to have a lot of influence

arrayán *nm* myrtle

arre *interj* gee up!, giddy up!

arrear *vt* (a) *(azuzar)* to gee up (b) *Fam (bofetada)* to give

arrebatador, -a *adj* captivating, fascinating

arrebatar 1 *vt (coger)* to snatch, to seize; *Fig (cautivar)* to captivate, to fascinate
  2 arrebatarse *upr (enfurecerse)* to become furious; *(exaltarse)* to get carried away

arrebato *nm* outburst, fit

arrecho, -a *adj CAm, Méx, Ven Fam (furioso)* mad, furious (b) *CAm, Col, Méx, Ven Vulg (sexualmente)* horny

arreciar [43] *vi (viento, tormenta)* to get worse

arrecife *nm* reef

arreglado, -a *adj* (a) *(reparado)* repaired, fixed (b) *(solucionado)* settled (c) *(habitación)* tidy, neat (d) *(persona)* well-dressed, smart

arreglar 1 *vt* (a) *(reparar)* to repair, to fix (b) *(solucionar)* to sort out (c) *(ordenar)* to tidy (up)
  2 arreglarse *upr* (a) *(vestirse)* to get ready (b) *Fam* **arreglárselas** to manage

arreglo *nm* (a) *(reparación)* repair; **no tiene a.** it is beyond repair; *Fam* **¡no tienes a.!** you're hopeless! (b) *(acuerdo)* agreement; *Fml* **con a. a** in accordance with (c) *Mús* **arreglos musicales** musical arrangements

arrellanarse *upr* to sit back

arremangarse [42] *upr* to roll up one's sleeves

arremeter *vi* **a. contra** to attack

arremolinarse *upr (agua, hojas)* to whirl about; *(personas)* **a. alrededor de** *o* **en torno a** to mill round about, to crowd round

arrendamiento *nm* (a) *(alquiler)* renting, leasing (b) *(precio)* rent

arrendar [1] *vt (dar en arriendo)* to let on lease; *(tomar en arriendo)* to take on lease; *Am* **se arrienda** *(en letrero)* to let

arrendatario, -a *nm,f* leaseholder, tenant

arreos *nmpl* (a) *(de caballería)* harness, trappings (b) *(adornos)* adornments

arrepentido, -a *adj* repentant

arrepentimiento *nm* repentance

arrepentirse [5] *upr* **a. de** to regret; *Rel* to repent

arrestar *vt* to arrest

arresto *nm* (a) *(detención)* arrest; *Der* **a. domiciliario** house arrest (b) **arrestos** courage

arriar [29] *vt (bandera)* to strike; *(velas)* to lower

arriba 1 *adv* up; *(encima)* on the top; **ahí a.** up there; **de a. abajo** from top to bottom; *Fam* **mirar a algn de a. abajo** to look sb up and down; **desde a.** from above; **hacia a.** upwards; **de un millón para a.** from one million upwards; **más a.** higher up, further up; **a. del todo** right on o at the top; **la parte de a.** the top (part); **vive a.** he lives upstairs; **véase más a.** see above

2 *interj* get up!, up you get!; **¡a. la República!** long live the Republic!; **¡a. las manos!** hands up!

3 *prep Am* **a. (de)** on top of

arribar *vi* **a. a** to reach

arribeño, -a *Am* **1** *adj* highland
2 *nm,f* highlander

arribista *nmf* (*profesionalmente*) careerist; (*socialmente*) social climber

arriendo *nm* lease; (*de un piso*) renting; **dar en a.** to let out on lease; **tomar en a.** to take on lease

arriesgado, -a *adj* (a) (*peligroso*) risky (b) (*temerario*) fearless, daring

arriesgar [42] **1** *vt* to risk
2 arriesgarse *vpr* to risk; **se arriesga demasiado** he's taking too many risks

arrimar 1 *vt* to move closer, to bring near o nearer; *Fam* **a. el hombro** to lend a hand
2 arrimarse *vpr* to move o get close, to come near o nearer

arrinconar *vt* (a) (*apartar*) to put in a corner; **a. a algn** to leave sb out in the cold (b) (*abandonar*) to discard (c) (*acorralar*) to corner

arroba *nm Inform* at, @ sign

arrobo *nm* rapture, enthralment

arrocero, -a *adj* (*región*) rice-growing; **la industria arrocera** the rice industry

arrodillarse *vpr* to kneel down

arrogancia *nf* arrogance

arrogante *adj* arrogant

arrojadizo, -a *adj* **arma arrojadiza** missile

arrojado, -a *adj* bold, daring

arrojar 1 *vt* (a) (*tirar*) to throw, to fling (b) *Com* (*saldo*) to show
2 arrojarse *vpr* to throw oneself, to fling oneself

arrojo *nm* daring, courage

arrollador, -a *adj* (*victoria, superioridad*) overwhelming; (*belleza, personalidad*) dazzling

arrollar *vt* **1** to run over, to knock down
2 *vi Dep & Pol* to win easily

arropar 1 *vt* (a) (*con ropa*) to wrap up; (*en la cama*) to tuck in (b) (*proteger*) to support
2 arroparse *vpr* to wrap up (warm)

arrostrar *vt* to face up to

arroyo *nm* brook, stream

arroz *nm* rice; **a. con leche** rice pudding

arruga *nf* (*en la piel*) wrinkle; (*en la ropa*) crease

arrugar [42] **1** *vt* (*piel*) to wrinkle; (*ropa*) to crease; (*papel*) to crumple (up)

2 arrugarse *vpr* (*piel*) to wrinkle; (*ropa*) to crease

arruinado, -a *adj* ruined

arruinar 1 *vt* to ruin
2 arruinarse *vpr* to be ruined

arrullar 1 *vt* (*bebé*) to lull to sleep
2 *vi* (*paloma*) to coo

arrullo *nm* (a) (*de paloma*) cooing (b) (*nana*) lullaby

arrumacos *nmpl Fam* **hacerse a.** (*amantes*) to kiss and cuddle; **hacer a. a** (*bebé*) to coo at

arsenal *nm* (a) *Esp* (*de barcos*) shipyard (b) (*de armas*) arsenal

arsénico *nm* arsenic

arte *nm* o *nf* art; **bellas artes** fine arts; *Fam* **por amor al a.** for the love of it

> Takes the masculine articles **el** and **un**.

artefacto *nm* device; **a. explosivo** explosive device

arteria *nf* artery; (*carretera*) highway

artesanal *adj* handmade

artesanía *nf* (a) (*cualidad*) craftsmanship (b) (*objetos*) crafts, handicrafts

artesano, -a 1 *nm,f* (*hombre*) craftsman; (*mujer*) craftswoman
2 *adj* handmade

ártico, -a 1 *adj* arctic; **el océano Á.** the Arctic Ocean
2 *nm* **el Á.** the Arctic

articulación *nf* (a) *Anat* joint, articulation (b) *Téc* joint

articulado, -a *adj* (*tren etc*) articulated

articular *vt* to articulate

articulista *nmf* feature writer

artículo *nm* article; **a. de fondo** leader (article)

artífice *nmf* architect; **el a. del acuerdo** the architect of the agreement

artificial *adj* artificial; *Tex* man-made, synthetic

artificio *nm* (a) (*falsedad*) artifice; **fuego de a.** firework (b) (*artimaña*) ruse

artillería *nf* artillery; **a. antiaérea** anti-aircraft guns

artillero *nm* artilleryman

artilugio *nm* gadget, device

artimaña *nf* trick, ruse

artista *nmf* artist; **a. de cine** movie o *Br* film actor

artístico, -a *adj* artistic

artritis *nf inv* arthritis

arveja *nf RP* pea

arzobispo *nm* archbishop

as *nm* ace

asa *nf* handle

Takes the masculine articles **el** and **un**.

asado, -a 1 *adj Culin* roast; **pollo a.** roast chicken; *Fig* **a. de calor** roasting, boiling hot
  2 *nm Culin* roast; *Col, CSur (barbacoa)* barbecue

asador *nm* (**a**) *(aparato)* roaster (**b**) *(restaurante)* grill, grillroom

asaduras *nfpl (de cordero, ternera)* offal; *(de ave)* giblets

asalariado, -a 1 *adj* salaried
  2 *nm,f* wage earner, salaried worker

asaltante *nmf* attacker; *(en un robo)* robber

asaltar *vt* to assault, to attack; *(banco)* to rob; **le asaltaron las dudas** he was seized by doubts

asalto *nm* (**a**) *(ataque)* assault, attack; **a. a un banco** bank robbery (**b**) *(en boxeo)* round

asamblea *nf* meeting; **a. general** general meeting

asar 1 *vt* to roast
  2 asarse *upr Fig* to be roasting, to be boiling hot

ascendencia *nf* ancestry, ancestors; **de a. escocesa** of Scottish descent

ascendente 1 *adj* rising
  2 *nm (en astrología)* ascendant

ascender [3] **1** *vt (en un cargo)* to promote
  2 *vi* (**a**) *(subir)* to move upward; *(temperatura)* to rise; *(al trono)* to ascend (**b**) *(de categoría)* to be promoted (**c**) **a. a** *(totalizar)* to come o amount to; **la factura asciende a ...** the bill adds up o comes to ...

ascendiente *nmf* ancestor

ascensión *nf* ascent; *Rel* A. Ascension

ascenso *nm* promotion; *(subida)* rise

ascensor *nm Br* lift, *US* elevator

asco *nm* disgust, repugnance; **me da a.** it makes me (feel) sick; **¡qué a.!** how disgusting o revolting!

ascua *nf* ember; *Fig* **en ascuas** on tenterhooks

Takes the masculine articles **el** and **un**.

aseado, -a *adj* tidy, neat

asear 1 *vt* to clean, to tidy up
  2 asearse *upr* to wash, to get washed

asediar [43] *vt Mil* to lay siege to; *Fig* to pester, to badger

asedio *nm* siege

asegurado, -a 1 *adj* insured
  2 *nm,f* policy holder

asegurador, -a 1 *adj* insurance
  2 *nm,f* insurer

asegurar 1 *vt* (**a**) *(contra riesgos)* to insure (**b**) *(garantizar)* **me aseguró que ...** he assured me that ...; **a. el éxito de un proyecto** to ensure the success of a project (**c**) *(cuerda)* to fasten
  2 asegurarse *upr* (**a**) *(cerciorarse)* to make sure; **asegurarse de que ...** to make sure that ... (**b**) *(contra riesgos)* to insure oneself

asemejarse *upr* **a. a** to look like

asentado, -a *adj (establecido)* established, settled

asentamiento *nm* settlement

asentar [1] **1** *vt* **a. la cabeza** to settle down
  2 asentarse *upr* (**a**) *(establecerse)* to settle down, to establish oneself (**b**) *(té, polvo)* to settle

asentimiento *nm* assent, consent

asentir [5] *vi* to assent, to agree; **a. con la cabeza** to nod

aseo *nm* (**a**) *(limpieza)* cleanliness, tidiness (**b**) *Esp (habitación)* bathroom; **aseos** *Br* toilets, *US* restroom

aséptico, -a *adj Med* aseptic; *Fig (indiferente)* detached

asequible *adj* affordable; *(comprensible)* easy to understand; *(alcanzable)* attainable

asesinar *vt* to murder; *(rey, ministro)* to assassinate

asesinato *nm* murder; *(de rey, ministro)* assassination

asesino, -a 1 *adj* murderous
  2 *nm,f* killer; *(hombre)* murderer; *(mujer)* murderess; *Pol* assassin

asesor, -a 1 *nm,f* adviser; **a. fiscal** tax adviser
  2 *adj* advisory

asesoramiento *nm* advice; *(de empresa)* consultancy

asesorar 1 *vt* to advise; *(empresa)* to provide with consultancy services
  2 asesorarse *upr* to seek advice; **asesorarse de** o **con** to consult

asesoría *nf* (**a**) *(trabajo)* consultancy (**b**) *(oficina)* consultant's office

asestar *vt* to deal; **a. un golpe a algn** to deal sb a blow

aseverar *vt* to assert

asfaltado, -a 1 *adj* asphalt
  2 *nm (acción)* asphalting, surfacing; *(asfalto)* asphalt, (road) surface

asfaltar *vt* to asphalt, to surface

asfalto *nm* asphalt

asfixia *nf* asphyxiation, suffocation

asfixiante *adj* asphyxiating, suffocating; *Fam* **hace un calor a.** it's stifling

asfixiar [43] **1** *vt* to asphyxiate, to suffocate

2 asfixiarse *vpr* to asphyxiate, to suffocate

así *adv* (**a**) *(de esta manera)* like this o that, this way, thus; **ponlo a.** put it this way; **a. de grande/alto** this big/tall; **algo a.** something like this o that; **¿no es a.?** isn't that so o right?; **a. es la vida** such is life; **a. a.** so-so; **a. sin más**, *Am* **a. no más** o **nomás** just like that (**b**) **a las seis o a.** around six o'clock; **diez años o a.** ten years more or less (**c**) **a. como** as well as (**d**) **a. tenga que ... *(aunque)*** even if I have to ... (**e**) **aun a.** and despite that (**f**) **a. pues** so; **a. que ...** so ... (**g**) **a. que llegues** as soon as you arrive

Asia *n* Asia; **A. Menor** Asia Minor

asiático, -a *adj & nm,f* Asian

asidero *nm (asa)* handle; *Fig* pretext, excuse

asiduidad *nf* frequency; **con a.** frequently, regularly

asiduo, -a *adj & nm,f* regular

asiento *nm* (**a**) *(silla, butaca)* seat; **a. trasero/delantero** front/back seat; **tome a.** take a seat (**b**) *(base)* bottom (**c**) *Fin* entry

asignación *nf* (**a**) *(acción)* allocation, assignment (**b**) *(cantidad)* allocation

asignar *vt* to allocate, to assign

asignatura *nf* subject; **a. pendiente** failed subject

asilado, -a *nm,f* refugee

asilar *vt* to grant o give political asylum to

asilo *nm* (**a**) *(amparo)* asylum; *Pol* **a. político** political asylum (**b**) *(hospicio)* home; **a. de ancianos** old people's home

asimilación *nf* assimilation

asimilar *vt* to assimilate

asimismo *adv (también)* also, as well; *(a principio de frase)* likewise

asir [46] **1** *vt* to grasp, to take hold of

2 asirse *vpr también Fig* to cling (**a** to)

asistencia *nf* (**a**) *(presencia)* attendance; **falta de a.** absence (**b**) **a. médica/técnica** medical/technical assistance (**c**) *(público)* audience, public

asistenta *nf Esp* cleaning lady

asistente *nmf* (**a**) *(ayudante)* assistant, helper; **a. social** social worker (**b**) *(presente)* person present; **los asistentes** *(el público)* the audience (**c**) **a. personal** *(computadora)* personal digital assistant

asistido, -a *adj* assisted; **a. por ordenador** computer-assisted; *Esp Aut* **dirección asistida** power steering

asistir 1 *vt* to assist, to help

2 *vi* **a.** (**a**) to attend, to be present (at)

asma *nf* asthma

> Takes the masculine articles **el** and **un**.

asmático, -a *adj & nm,f* asthmatic

asno *nm* donkey, ass

asociación *nf* association

asociado, -a 1 *adj* associated

2 *nm,f* associate, partner

asociar [43] **1** *vt* to associate

2 asociarse *vpr* to form a partnership

asolar [2] *vt* to devastate, to destroy

asomar 1 *vt* asomó **la cabeza por la ventana** he put his head out of the window

2 *vi (sobresalir)* to peep up; *(del interior de algo)* to peep out

3 asomarse *vpr* (**a**) **asomarse a la ventana** to lean out of the window (**b**) *(entrar)* to pop in; *(salir)* to pop out

asombrar 1 *vt* to amaze, to astonish

2 asombrarse *vpr* to be astonished; **asombrarse de algo** to be amazed at sth

asombro *nm* amazement, astonishment

asombroso, -a *adj* amazing, astonishing

asomo *nm* trace, hint; *(de esperanza)* glimmer; **ni por a.** not under any circumstances

asorocharse *vpr Andes* (**a**) *(por la altitud)* to get altitude sickness (**b**) *(sonrojarse)* to blush

aspa *nf* (**a**) *(de molino)* arm; *(de ventilador)* blade (**b**) *(cruz)* cross

> Takes the masculine articles **el** and **un**.

aspaviento *nm* **hacer aspavientos** to wave one's arms about

aspecto *nm* (**a**) *(apariencia)* look, appearance (**b**) *(faceta)* aspect

aspereza *nf* roughness; *Fig* **limar asperezas** to smooth things over

áspero, -a *adj* rough; *Fig (carácter)* surly

aspersión *nf (de jardín)* sprinkling; *(de cultivos)* spraying

aspersor *nm (para jardín)* sprinkler; *(para cultivos)* sprayer

aspiración *nf* (**a**) *(de aire)* inhalation, breathing in (**b**) *(pretensión)* aspiration

aspiradora *nf* vacuum cleaner, *Br* Hoover

aspirante *nmf* candidate, applicant

aspirar 1 *vt* (**a**) *(respirar)* to inhale, to breathe in (**b**) *Téc (absorber)* to suck in, to draw in

2 *vi Fig* **a. a algo** to aspire to sth

aspirina *nf* aspirin

asquear *vt* to disgust, to make sick

asquerosidad *nf* filthy o revolting thing; **¡que a.!** how revolting!

asqueroso, -a 1 *adj (sucio)* filthy; *(desagradable)* revolting, disgusting
  2 *nm,f* filthy o revolting person

asta *nf* (a) *(de bandera)* staff, pole; **a media a.** at half-mast (b) *Zool (cuerno)* horn

> Takes the masculine articles **el** and **un**.

asterisco *nm* asterisk

astilla *nf* splinter

astillero *nm* shipyard

astral *adj* astral; **carta a.** birth chart

astringente *adj* astringent

astro *nm* star

astrología *nf* astrology

astrólogo, -a *nm,f* astrologer

astronauta *nmf* astronaut

astronave *nf* spaceship

astronomía *nf* astronomy

astronómico, -a *adj* astronomical

astrónomo, -a *nm,f* astronomer

astucia *nf (trampas)* cunning; *(sagacidad)* astuteness

asturiano, -a *adj & nm,f* Asturian

Asturias *n* Asturias

astuto, -a *adj (tramposo)* cunning; *(listo)* astute

asumir *vt* to assume

asunción *nf* assumption

asunto *nm* (a) *(cuestión)* matter; *(problema)* issue; **no es a. tuyo** it's none of your business (b) **Asuntos Exteriores** Foreign Affairs

asustar 1 *vt* to frighten, to scare
  2 asustarse *vpr* to be frightened, to be scared

atacante *nmf* attacker, assailant

atacar [44] *vt* to attack, to assault; *Fig* **me ataca los nervios** he gets on my nerves

atado, -a *adj* tied; *(ocupado)* tied up

atadura *nf* tie

atajar 1 *vi* to take a shortcut (**por** across o through)
  2 *vt (contener)* to put a stop to; *(hemorragia, inundación)* to stem

atajo *nm* (a) *(camino corto, medio rápido)* short cut (b) *Esp Pey (panda)* bunch

atalaya *nf* watchtower

atañer *vi* to concern, to have to do with; **eso no te atañe** that has nothing to do with you

ataque *nm* (a) *(acometida)* attack, assault; **a. aéreo** air raid (b) *Med* fit; **a. cardíaco** o **al corazón** heart attack; **a. de nervios/tos** fit of hysterics/coughing

atar 1 *vt* (a) *(nudo, cuerda)* to tie; *(persona caballo, barco)* to tie up; *Fig* **a. cabos** to put

two and two together (b) *Fig (constreñir)* to tie down
  2 atarse *vpr* (a) *(uno mismo)* to tie oneself down (b) **se ató el pelo** she tied her hair up; **atarse los zapatos** to tie one's shoes o shoelaces

atardecer [33] **1** *v impers* to get o grow dark
  2 *nm* evening, dusk

atareado, -a *adj* busy

atascado, -a *adj* stuck

atascar [44] **1** *vt* to block, to obstruct
  2 atascarse *vpr* (a) *(bloquearse)* to become blocked, to become obstructed (b) *Fig (detenerse)* to get stuck

atasco *nm* traffic jam

ataúd *nm* coffin

ataviar [29] **1** *vt* to dress up
  2 ataviarse *vpr* to dress up

atavío *nm* dress, attire

ate *nm Méx* quince jelly

ateísmo *nm* atheism

atemorizar [40] *vt* to frighten, to scare

atemperar *vt* to moderate, to temper

atemporal *adj* timeless

Atenas *n* Athens

atención 1 *nf* attention; **llamar la a.** to attract attention; **prestar/poner a.** to pay attention (**a** to); **a. al cliente** customer care, customer services
  2 *interj* attention!

atender [3] **1** *vt* to attend to; *(petición)* to agree to
  2 *vi (alumno)* to pay attention (**a** to)

atenerse [24] *vpr* **a. a** *(promesa, orden)* to stick to; *(ley, normas)* to observe, to abide by; *(consecuencias)* to bear in mind; **no saber a qué a.** not to know what to expect

atentado *nm* attack; **a. suicida con bomba** suicide bombing; **a. terrorista** terrorist attack

atentamente *adv* **le saluda a.** *(en carta)* yours sincerely/faithfully

atentar *vi* **a. a** o **contra algo** to commit a crime against sth; **a. contra (la vida de) algn** to make an attempt on sb's life

atento, -a *adj* (a) *(pendiente)* attentive; **estar a. a** *(explicación, programa, lección)* to pay attention to; *(ruido, sonido)* to listen out for (b) *(amable)* thoughtful, considerate

atenuante 1 *adj* attenuating
  2 *nm Der* extenuating circumstance

atenuar [30] *vt (disminuir, suavizar)* to diminish; *(dolor)* to ease, to alleviate; *(sonido, luz)* to attenuate

ateo, -a 1 *adj* atheistic
  2 *nm,f* atheist

aterciopelado, -a *adj* velvety

aterido, -a *adj* **a. de frío** stiff with cold, numb

aterrador, -a *adj* terrifying

aterrar 1 *vt* to terrify
   2 aterrarse *upr* to be terrified

aterrizaje *nm Av* landing; **a. forzoso** forced landing

aterrizar [40] *vi* to land

aterrorizar [40] **1** *vt* to terrify; *Mil & Pol* to terrorize
   2 aterrorizarse *upr* to be terrified

atesorar *vt* (*riquezas*) to amass

atestado¹, -a *adj* packed, crammed; **estaba a. de gente** it was full of people

atestado² *nm Der* affidavit, statement; **atestados** testimonials

atestar¹ *vt Der* to testify

atestar² *vt* (*abarrotar*) to pack, to cram (**de** with)

atestiguar [45] *vt* (**a**) *Der* to testify to (**b**) *Fig* to vouch for

atiborrar 1 *vt* to pack, to stuff (**de** with)
   2 atiborrarse *upr Fam* to stuff oneself (**de** with)

ático *nm* (*piso*) = attic *Br* flat *o US* apartment, usually with a roof terrace; (*desván*) attic

atinado, -a *adj* (*juicioso*) sensible; (*pertinente*) pertinent

atinar *vi* to get it right; **a. a hacer algo** to succeed in doing sth; **a. al blanco** to hit the target; **atinó con la solución** he hit on *o* found the solution

atingencia *nf* (**a**) *Am, CAm, Chile, Méx* (*relación*) connection (**b**) *Chile, Méx* (*adecuación*) appropriateness; **la Cámara está estudiando la a. de esa ley** the House is investigating whether the law is appropriate *o* acceptable (**c**) *Méx* (*tino*) good sense

atípico, -a *adj* atypical

atisbar *vt* to make out

atisbo *nm* slight sign, inkling

atizar [40] *vt* (**a**) (*fuego*) to poke, to stir (**b**) (*sospechas, discordias*) to stir up (**c**) *Esp* (*persona*) **me atizó bien fuerte** (*un golpe*) he hit me really hard; (*una paliza*) he gave me a good hiding

atlántico, -a 1 *adj* Atlantic
   2 nm el (océano) A. the Atlantic (Ocean)

atlas *nm inv* atlas

atleta *nmf* athlete

atlético, -a *adj* athletic

atletismo *nm* athletics *sing*

atmósfera *nf* atmosphere

atmosférico, -a *adj* atmospheric

atole, atol *nm CAm, Méx* = thick hot drink made of corn meal

atolladero *nm* fix, jam; **estar en un a.** to be in a jam

atolondrado, -a *adj* foolish, thoughtless

atómico, -a *adj* atomic

átomo *nm* atom

atónito, -a *adj* amazed, astonished

atontado, -a *adj* (**a**) (*tonto*) silly, foolish (**b**) (*aturdido*) bewildered, amazed

atontar *vt* to confuse, to bewilder
   2 atontarse *upr* to be *o* get confused, to be bewildered

atorarse *upr* (**a**) (*atragantarse*) to choke (**con** on) (**b**) *Am* (*atascarse*) to get stuck (**c**) *Am* (*meterse en un lío*) to get into a mess

atormentar 1 *vt* to torment
   2 atormentarse *upr* to torment oneself, to suffer agonies

atornillar *vt* to screw on

atorón *nm Méx* traffic jam

atorrante *adj RP Fam* lazy

atosigar [42] *vt* (*con prisas*) to harass; (*con exigencias*) to pester, to badger

atracador, -a *nm,f* (*de banco*) (bank) robber; (*en la calle*) attacker, mugger

atracar [44] **1** *vt* to hold up; (*persona*) to rob
   2 *vi Náut* to come alongside, to tie up
   3 atracarse *upr* (*de comida*) to stuff oneself (**de** with), to gorge oneself (**de** on)

atracción *nf* attraction; **parque de atracciones** funfair

atraco *nm* hold-up, robbery; **a. a mano armada** armed robbery

atracón *nm Fam* binge, blowout; **darse un a. de comer** to make a pig of oneself

atractivo, -a 1 *adj* attractive, appealing
   2 nm attraction, appeal

atraer [25] *vt* to attract

atragantarse *upr* to choke (**con** on), to swallow the wrong way; *Fig* **esa chica se me ha atragantado** I can't stand that girl

atraigo *indic pres de* **atraer**

atraje *pt indef de* **atraer**

atrancar [44] **1** *vt* (*puerta*) to bolt
   2 atrancarse *upr* to get stuck; (*al hablar, escribir*) to dry up

atrapar *vt* to catch

atrás *adv* (**a**) (*lugar*) at the back, behind; **hacia/para a.** backwards; **puerta de a.** back *o* rear door; *Fig* **echarse a.** to back out (**b**) (*tiempo*) previously, in the past, ago; **un año a.** a year ago; **venir de muy a.** to go *o* date back a long time

atrasado, -a *adj* late, slow; (*pago*) overdue; (*reloj*) slow; (*país*) backward; *Prensa* **número a.** back number

atrasar 1 *vt* to put back
  2 *vi (reloj)* to be slow
  3 atrasarse *upr* (a) *(quedarse atrás)* to remain o stay behind, to lag behind (b) *(en el tiempo)* to be late (c) *(reloj)* to lose time

atraso *nm* (a) *(demora)* delay (b) *(de país)* backwardness (c) *Fin* **atrasos** arrears

atravesado, -a *adj (cruzado)* lying crosswise; **lo tengo a.** I can't stand him

atravesar [1] **1** *vt* (a) *(calle)* to cross (b) *(muro)* to pierce, to go through (c) *(poner a través)* to lay across, to put across, to put crosswise
  2 atravesarse *upr* to get in the way; *Fig* **se me ha atravesado Luis** I can't stand Luis

atrayente *adj* attractive

atreverse *upr* to dare; **a. a hacer algo** to dare to do sth

atrevido, -a *adj* (a) *(osado)* daring, bold (b) *(insolente)* insolent, impudent (c) *(ropa etc)* daring, risqué

atrevimiento *nm* (a) *(osadía)* daring, audacity (b) *(insolencia)* insolence, impudence

atribución *nf* (a) *(imputación)* attribution (b) *(competencia)* responsibility, duty

atribuir [37] **1** *vt* to attribute, to ascribe
  2 atribuirse *upr* to assume

atribular *vt* to distress

atributo *nm* attribute

atril *nm (para partituras)* music stand; *(para libros)* lectern

atrio *nm* (a) *(pórtico)* portico (b) *(patio interior)* atrium

atrocidad *nf* atrocity

atrofiar [43] **1** *vt* to atrophy
  2 atrofiarse *upr* to atrophy

atropellado, -a *adj* hasty, impetuous

atropellar *vt* to knock down, to run over

atropello *nm* (a) *Aut* knocking down, running over (b) *(abuso)* abuse

atroz *adj* (a) *(bárbaro)* atrocious (b) *Fam (hambre, frío)* enormous, tremendous

ATS *nmf Esp (abr* **ayudante técnico sanitario)** qualified nurse

atuendo *nm* dress, attire

atún *nm* (a) tuna, tunny

aturdido, -a *adj* stunned, dazed

aturdimiento *nm* confusion, bewilderment

aturdir *vt* (a) *(con un golpe)* to stun, to daze (b) *(confundir)* to bewilder, to confuse

aturrullar *vt Fam* to fluster

atuve *pt indef de* **atenerse**

audacia *nf* audacity

audaz *adj* audacious, bold

audible *adj* audible

audición *nf* (a) *(acción de oír)* hearing (b) *Mús & Teatro* audition

audiencia *nf* (a) *(público)* audience; *TV & Rad* **horas de máxima a.** prime time; **índice de a.** viewing figures, ratings (b) *(entrevista)* audience (c) *Der* court hearing

audiolibro *nm* audiobook, talking book

audiovisual *adj* audio-visual

auditivo, -a 1 *adj* auditory; **comprensión auditiva** listening comprehension
  2 *nm* receiver

auditor *nm Fin* auditor

auditoría *nf Fin* (a) *(profesión)* auditing (b) *(despacho)* auditor's, auditing company (c) *(balance)* audit; **a. externa/interna** external/internal audit

auditorio *nm* (a) *(público)* audience (b) *(sala)* auditorium, hall

auge *nm* peak; *Econ* boom; *Fig* **estar en a.** to be thriving o booming

augurar *vt (sujeto: persona)* to predict; *(sujeto: suceso)* to augur

augurio *nm* omen

aula *nf (en colegio)* classroom; *Univ* lecture room; **a. magna** amphitheatre

> Takes the masculine articles **el** and **un**.

aullar *vi* to howl, to yell

aullido *nm* howl, yell

aumentar 1 *vt* to increase; *(precios)* to put up; *(producción)* to step up; *Fot* to enlarge; *Opt* to magnify
  2 *vi (precios)* to go up, to rise; *(valor)* to appreciate
  3 aumentarse *upr* to increase, to be on the increase

aumento *nm* increase; *Opt* magnification; **a. de precios** rise in prices; **ir en a.** to be on the increase

aun *adv* even; **a. así** even so, even then; **a. más** even more

aún *adv* still; *(en negativas)* yet; **a. está aquí** he's still here; **ella no ha venido a.** she hasn't come yet

aunar *vt* to unite, to join

aunque *conj* although, though; *(enfático)* even if, even though; **a. no vengas** even if you don't come

aúpa *interj Esp (¡levántate!)* up!, get up!; *(al coger a un niño en brazos)* ups-a-daisy!

aura *nf* aura

> Takes the masculine articles **el** and **un**.

aureola *nf* halo

auricular *nm* (a) *Tel* receiver (b) **auriculares** earphones, headphones

aurora *nf* daybreak, dawn

auscultar *vt* to sound (with a stethoscope)

ausencia *nf* absence

ausentarse *vpr* to leave

ausente 1 *adj* absent
 2 *nmf* absentee

ausentismo *nm Am* **a. laboral** *(justificado)* absence from work; *(injustificado)* absenteeism

austeridad *nf* austerity

austero, -a *adj* austere

austral 1 *adj* southern
 2 *nm Fin* = former standard monetary unit of Argentina

Australia *n* Australia

australiano, -a *adj & nm,f* Australian

Austria *n* Austria

austríaco, -a *adj & nm,f* Austrian

autenticidad *nf* authenticity

auténtico, -a *adj* authentic

autentificar [44] *vt* to authenticate

autismo *nm* autism

autista 1 *adj* autistic
 2 *nmf* autistic person

auto¹ *nm esp CSur (vehículo)* car

auto² *nm Der* decree, writ; **autos** *(pleito)* papers, documents

autoadhesivo, -a *adj* self-adhesive

autoayuda *nf* self-help

autobiografía *nf* autobiography

autobiográfico, -a *adj* autobiographical

autobombo *nm Fam* self-praise, blowing one's own trumpet

autobús *(pl* **autobuses)** *nm* bus

autocar *nm Esp* bus, *Br* coach

autocontrol *nm* self-control

autocrítica *nf* self-criticism

autóctono, -a *adj* indigenous

autodefensa *nf* self-defence

autodisciplina *nf* self-discipline

autoedición *nf Inform* desktop publishing, DTP

autoescuela *nf* driving school, school of motoring

autogobierno *nm* self-government

autógrafo *nm* autograph

autómata *nm* automaton

automático, -a *adj* automatic

automatización *nf* automation

automatizar [40] *vt* to automate

automotor, -triz *adj* self-propelled

automóvil *nm* car, *US* automobile

automovilismo *nm* motoring

automovilista *nmf* motorist

automovilístico, -a *adj* car; **accidente a.** car accident

autonomía *nf* (**a**) *(cualidad)* autonomy (**b**) *(región)* autonomous region

autonómico, -a *adj* autonomous, self-governing; **elecciones autonómicas** elections for the autonomous parliament; **televisión autónomica** regional television

autónomo, -a *adj* autonomous

autopista *nf Br* motorway, *US* freeway; *Inform* **autopista de la información** information superhighway

autopsia *nf* autopsy, postmortem

autor, -a *nm,f (hombre)* author; *(mujer)* authoress; *(de crimen)* perpetrator

autoría *nf (de obra)* authorship; *(de crimen)* perpetration

autoridad *nf* authority

autoritario, -a *adj* authoritarian

autorización *nf* authorization; **dar a. a algn (para hacer algo)** to authorize sb (to do sth)

autorizado, -a *adj* authoritative, official

autorizar [40] *vt* to authorize

autorretrato *nm* self-portrait

autoservicio *nm* self-service; *(supermercado)* supermarket

autostop *nm* hitch-hiking; **hacer a.** to hitch-hike

autostopista *nmf* hitch-hiker

autosuficiencia *nf* self-sufficiency

autosuficiente *adj* self-sufficient

autovía *nf Br* dual carriageway, *US* divided highway

auxiliar [43] **1** *adj* auxiliary
 2 *nmf* assistant; **a. de vuelo** flight attendant
 3 *vt* to help, to assist

auxilio *nm* help, assistance; **primeros auxilios** first aid

auyama *nf Carib, Col* pumpkin

Av. *nf (abr* **Avenida)** Ave

aval *nm Com & Fin* endorsement

avalancha *nf* avalanche

avalar *vt* to guarantee, to endorse

avance *nm* (**a**) *(movimiento, progreso)* advance (**b**) *TV (de futura programación)* preview; **a. informativo** news summary, *US* news in brief (**c**) *Fin (anticipo)* advance payment

avanzado, -a *adj* advanced; **de avanzada edad** advanced in years

avanzar [40] *vt* to advance

avaricia *nf* greed, avarice

avaricioso, -a *adj* greedy, avaricious

avaro, -a 1 *adj* mean, miserly
 2 *nm,f* miser

avasallar *vt* (**a**) *(dominar)* **dejarse a.** to let oneself be pushed *o* ordered around (**b**) *(rival, oponente)* to overwhelm (**c**) *(pueblo)* to subjugate

avatares *nmpl* **los a. de la vida** the ups and downs of life

Avda. = **Av.**

AVE *nf (abr* **Alta Velocidad Española)** High Speed Train

ave *nf* bird; **aves de corral** poultry; **a. de rapiña** bird of prey

> Takes the masculine articles **el** and **un.**

avecinarse *vpr* to approach, to come near

avellana *nf* hazelnut

avellano *nm* hazelnut tree

avena *nf* oats

avendré *indic fut de* **avenir**

avenencia *nf* compromise

avengo *indic pres de* **avenir**

avenida *nf* avenue

avenido, -a *adj* **bien/mal avenidos** on good/bad terms

avenirse [27] *vpr (llevarse bien)* to be on good terms; *(consentir)* to agree (**en** to)

aventajado, -a *adj (destacado)* outstanding, exceptional

aventajar *vt* (**a**) *(estar por delante de)* to be ahead *o* in front (**a** of) (**b**) *(superar)* to surpass, to outdo

aventar [1] **1** *vt* (**a**) *Agr* to winnow (**b**) *(el fuego)* to fan (**c**) *Andes, CAm, Méx Fam (tirar)* to throw; **le aventé una bofetada** I slapped him (**d**) *Andes, CAm, Méx (empujar)* to push, to shove
 2 aventarse *vpr Méx* (**a**) *(tirarse)* to throw oneself (**b**) *(atreverse)* **aventarse a hacer algo** to dare to do sth

aventón *nm CAm, Méx, Perú* **dar a. a algn** to give sb a *Br* lift *o US* ride; **pedir a.** to hitch a *Br* lift *o US* ride

aventura *nf* (**a**) *(suceso, empresa)* adventure (**b**) *(amorosa)* (love) affair

aventurado, -a *adj* risky

aventurarse *vpr* to venture

aventurero, -a *adj* adventurous

avergonzado, -a *adj* ashamed

avergonzar [63] **1** *vt* to shame
 2 avergonzarse *vpr* to be ashamed (**de** of)

avería *nf* breakdown

averiado, -a *adj* out of order; *(coche)* broken down

averiar [29] **1** *vt* to break
 2 averiarse *vpr (estropearse)* to malfunction, to go wrong; *(coche)* to break down

averiguación *nf* enquiry

averiguar [45] *vt* to ascertain

aversión *nf* aversion

avestruz *nm* ostrich

aviación *nf* (**a**) *(navegación)* aviation; **accidente de a.** plane crash; **a. civil** civil aviation (**b**) *(ejército)* airforce

aviador, -a *nm,f* aviator, flier; *Mil (piloto)* air force pilot

aviar[29] *vt (preparar)* to prepare, to get ready

aviar[2] *adj (gripe)* bird

avícola *adj* poultry

avicultura *nf* poultry farming

avidez *nf* avidity, eagerness

ávido, -a *adj* avid; **a. de** eager for

avinagrado, -a *adj* sour

avinagrarse *vpr (vino, alimento)* to turn sour; *(persona, carácter)* to become sour *o* bitter

avión[1] *nm* aircraft, *Br* aeroplane, *US* airplane; **viajar en a.** to fly, to go by plane; **por a.** *(en carta)* airmail

avión[2] *nm (ave)* martin

avioneta *nf* light aircraft *o* plane

avíos *nmpl (equipo)* things

avisar *vt* (**a**) *(informar)* to inform; **avísame cuando hayas acabado** let me know when you've finished (**b**) *(advertir)* to warn; **ya te avisé** I warned you (**c**) *(llamar)* to call for; **a. a la policía** to notify the police; **a. al médico** to send for the doctor

aviso *nm* (**a**) *(advertencia)* warning; **estar sobre a.** to be forewarned (**b**) *(notificación)* notice; *(en teatros, aeropuertos)* call; **hasta nuevo a.** until further notice; **sin previo a.** without notice (**c**) *Am (anuncio)* advertisement; **a. clasificado** classified advertisement

avispa *nf* wasp

avispado, -a *adj Fam* quick-witted

avispero *nm (nido)* wasps' nest

avistar *vt* to see, to sight

avituallamiento *nm* provisioning

avituallar *vt* to provide with food

avivar *vt (fuego)* to stoke (up); *(pasión)* to intensify; *(paso)* to quicken

avizor *adj* **estar ojo a.** to be on the alert *o* on the lookout

axila *nf* armpit, axilla

axioma *nm* axiom

ay *(pl* **ayes)** *interj (dolor)* ouch!

aya *nf (niñera)* nanny

> Takes the masculine articles **el** and **un.**

ayer 1 *adv* yesterday; **a. por la mañana/ por la tarde** yesterday morning/afternoon; **a. por la noche** last night; **antes de**

a. the day before yesterday
  2 *nm* **el a.** yesteryear

ayuda *nf* help, assistance; **ir en a. de algn** to come/go to sb's assistance; **a. al desarrollo** development aid

ayudante *nmf* assistant; *Med* **a. técnico-sanitario** qualified nurse

ayudar 1 *vt* to help; **¿en qué puedo ayudarle?** (how) can I help you?
  2 ayudarse *vpr* (**a**) *(unos a otros)* to help (**b**) **ayudarse de** to use, to make use of

ayunar *vi* to fast

ayunas *nfpl* **en a.** without having eaten breakfast

ayuno *nm* fasting; **guardar/hacer a.** to fast

ayuntamiento *nm* *(institución)* *Br* town council, *US* city council; *(edificio)* *Br* town hall, *US* city hall

azabache *nm* jet; **negro a.** jet black

azada *nf* hoe

azafata *nf* (**a**) *Av* air stewardess, *Br* air hostess (**b**) *(de congresos)* stewardess; *(de concurso)* hostess

azafate *nm* *CAm, Carib, Méx, Perú* tray

azafrán *nm* saffron

azahar *nm* *(del naranjo)* orange blossom; *(del limonero)* lemon blossom

azar *nm* chance; **por a.** by chance; **al a.** at random; **juegos de a.** games of chance;

los azares de la vida the ups and downs of life

azaroso, -a *adj* hazardous, dangerous

azogue *nm* mercury, quicksilver

azorado, -a *adj* embarrassed

azorar 1 *vt* to embarrass
  2 azorarse *vpr* to be embarrassed

Azores *nfpl* **las (Islas) A.** the Azores

azotar *vt* *(pegar, golpear)* to beat; *(con látigo)* to whip, to flog; *Fig* to scourge

azote *nm* (**a**) *(golpe)* smacking; *(latigazo)* lash, stroke (of the whip) (**b**) *Fig* scourge

azotea *nf* flat roof

azteca *adj & nmf* Aztec

azúcar *nm o nf* sugar

azucarado, -a *adj* sweetened

azucarera *nf* *(fábrica)* sugar refinery; *(recipiente)* sugar bowl

azucarero, -a 1 *nm* sugar bowl
  2 *adj* sugar

azucena *nf* white lily

azufre *nm* sulphur

azul *adj & nm* blue; **a. celeste** sky blue; **a. marino** navy blue; **a. turquesa** turquoise; **sangre a.** blue blood

azulado, -a *adj* bluish

azulejo *nm* *(glazed)* tile

azuzar [40] *vt* **a. los perros a algn** to set the dogs on sb

B, b [be] *nf (letra)* B, b

baba *nf* dribble; *Fig* **se le caía la b.** he was delighted

babear *vi (niño)* to dribble; *(adulto, animal)* to slobber

babel *nm o nf* bedlam

babero *nm* bib

Babia *n Fig* **estar en B.** to be daydreaming

babor *nm Náut* port, port side

babosa *nf* slug

babosada *nf CAm, Méx Fam (disparate)* daft thing; **¡no digas babosadas!** don't talk *Br* rubbish *o US* bull!

baboso, -a 1 *adj* (a) *Fam (despreciable)* slimy (b) *Am Fam (tonto)* daft, stupid
   2 *nm,f Fam* (a) *(persona despreciable)* creep (b) *Am (tonto)* twit, idiot

babucha *nf* slipper

baca *nf Aut* roof rack

bacalao *nm (pez)* cod

bacán 1 *Cuba, Perú adj* cool, wicked
   2 *Cuba nm* toff; **como un b.** like a real gentleman

bache *nm* (a) *(en carretera)* pothole (b) *Av* air pocket (c) *Fig* bad patch; **pasar un b.** to go through a bad patch

bachillerato *nm* = academically orientated Spanish secondary school course for pupils aged 14–17

bacilo *nm* bacillus

bacon *nm Esp* bacon

bacteria *nf* bacterium; **bacterias** bacteria

bacteriológico, -a *adj* bacteriological; **guerra bacteriológica** germ warfare

báculo *nm (de obispo)* crosier; **ella será el b. de mi vejez** she'll comfort me in my old age

badén *nm (de carretera)* ditch

bádminton *nm* badminton

bafle, baffle ['bafle] *nm* loudspeaker

bagaje *nm* background; **b. cultural** cultural baggage

bagatela *nf* trifle

Bagdad *n* Baghdad

Bahamas *npl* **las (Islas) B.** the Bahamas

bahía *nf* bay

bailaor, -a *nm,f* flamenco dancer

bailar *vt & vi* to dance; *Fig* **b. al son que le tocan** to toe the line; *Fam* **¡que me quiten lo baila(d)o!** but at least I had a good time!

bailarín, -a *nm,f* dancer; *(clásico)* ballet dancer

baile *nm* (a) *(danza)* dance (b) *(fiesta popular)* dance; *(formal)* ball; **b. de disfraces** fancy dress ball

baja *nf* (a) *(descenso)* drop, fall; *Fin* **jugar a la b.** to bear the market (b) *(cese)* **dar de b. a algn** *(en una empresa)* to lay sb off; *(en un club, sindicato)* to expel sb; **darse de b. (de)** *(dimitir)* to resign (from); *(salirse)* to drop out (of) (c) *Esp (por enfermedad) (permiso)* sick leave; *(documento)* sick note, doctor's certificate; **estar/darse de b.** to be on/take sick leave; **b. por maternidad** maternity leave (d) *Mil* loss, casualty; **bajas civiles** civilian casualties

bajada *nf* (a) *(descenso)* descent (b) *(cuesta)* slope (c) **b. de bandera** *(de taxi)* minimum fare

bajamar *nf* low tide

bajar 1 *vt* (a) *(mover hacia abajo) (libro, cuadro)* to take/bring down; *(telón, ventanilla, mano)* to lower; *(persiana)* to let down; *(cabeza)* to bow *o* lower (b) *(montaña, escaleras)* to go/come down (c) *(reducir) (volumen)* to turn down; *(voz)* to lower; *(precios)* to reduce, to cut (d) *Fam Inform* to download
   2 *vi* (a) *(descender)* to go/come down (b) **b. (de)** *(coche)* to get out (of); *(moto, bicicleta, tren, avión)* to get off; *(caballo)* to get off, to dismount; *(árbol, escalera, silla, mesa)* to come/get down (from) (c) *(disminuir)* to fall, to drop
   3 bajarse *upr* (a) **bajarse (de)** *(coche)* to get out (of); *(moto, bicicleta, tren, avión)* to get off; *(caballo)* to get off, to dismount (from); *(árbol, escalera, silla)* to come/get down (from) (b) *Fam Inform* to download

bajativo *nm Andes, RP (licor)* digestive liqueur; *(tisana)* herbal tea

bajeza *nf* despicable action

bajial *nm Méx, Perú* lowland

bajinis *nm Fam* **decir algo por lo b.** to whisper sth, to say sth under one's breath

bajío *nm* sandbank

bajista 1 *adj Fin* bearish; **tendencia b.** downward trend
2 *nmf Mús* bass guitarist

bajo, -a 1 *adj* low; *(persona)* short; *(sonido)* faint, soft; **en voz baja** in a low voice; **planta baja** *Br* ground floor, *US* first floor; **de baja calidad** of poor quality; **la clase baja** the lower class
2 *nm* (a) *Mús* bass (b) *(planta baja) (piso) Br* ground floor flat, *US* first floor apartment
3 *adv* low; *(hablar)* quietly
4 *prep* under, underneath; **b. cero** below zero; **b. tierra** underground; **b. la lluvia** in the rain

bajón *nm* (a) *(bajada)* slump (b) *(de salud)* relapse, deterioration

bajorrelieve *nm* bas-relief

bajura *nf* **pesca de b.** coastal fishing

bala *nf* bullet; *Fig* **como una b.** like a shot

balacear *vt Am* to shoot

balacera *nf Am* shoot-out

balada *nf* ballad

baladí *(pl baladíes) adj* trivial

balance *nm* (a) *Fin* balance sheet; *Fig* **hacer b. de una situación** to take stock of a situation (b) *(resultado)* outcome

balancear 1 *vt* to rock
2 balancearse *vpr (en mecedora)* to rock; *(en columpio, hamaca)* to swing; *(barco)* to roll

balanceo *nm* (a) *(de columpio, hamaca)* swinging; *(de cuna, mecedora)* rocking; *(de barco)* roll (b) *Am Aut* wheel balance

balancín *nm* (a) *(mecedora)* rocking chair; *(en el jardín)* swing hammock (b) *(columpio)* seesaw

balanza *nf* scales; *Fig* **estar en la b.** to be in the balance o in danger; **b. comercial** balance of trade; **b. de pagos** balance of payments

balar *vi* to bleat

balaustrada *nf* balustrade, railing

balazo *nm* (a) *(disparo)* shot; **matar a algn de un b.** to shoot sb dead (b) *(herida)* bullet wound

balboa *nm Fin* balboa, = standard monetary unit of Panama

balbucear *vt & vi (adulto)* to stutter, stammer; *(niño)* to babble

balbuceo *nm (de adulto)* stuttering, stammering; *(de niño)* babbling

balbucir *vt & vi* = balbucear

Balcanes *nmpl* **los B.** the Balkans

balcón *nm* balcony

balda *nf Esp* shelf

baldado, -a *adj Esp Fam* shattered

balde 1 *nm* pail, bucket
2 de balde *loc adv (gratis)* free
3 en balde *loc adv (en vano)* in vain

baldío, -a 1 *adj (terreno)* uncultivated, waste; *(esfuerzo)* vain, useless
2 *nm Méx, RP (terreno)* vacant lot

baldosa *nf* (ceramic) floor tile; *(para pavimentar)* flagstone, paving stone

balear 1 *vt Am (disparar)* to shoot
2 *adj* Balearic

Baleares *npl* **las (Islas) B.** the Balearic Islands

baleo *nm Am* shoot-out

balido *nm* bleating, bleat

balística *nf* ballistics *sing*

balístico, -a *adj* ballistic

baliza *nf Náut* marker buoy; *Av* beacon; *Aut* warning light *(for roadworks)*

ballena *nf* whale

ballet [ba'le] *(pl ballets) nm* ballet

balneario *nm* spa, health resort

balompié *nm* soccer, *Br* football

balón *nm* ball; *Fig* **b. de oxígeno** boost

baloncesto *nm* basketball

balonmano *nm* handball

balonvolea *nm* volleyball

balsa *nf* (a) *Náut* raft (b) *Fig* **como una b. de aceite** very quiet

bálsamo *nm* balsam, balm

balsero, -a *nm, f (de Cuba)* = refugee fleeing Cuba on a raft

Báltico *nm* **el (Mar) B.** the Baltic (Sea)

baluarte *nm Fig* stronghold

bambas® *nfpl Esp Br* plimsolls, *US* sneakers

bambolear 1 *vt* to shake
2 bambolearse *vpr (árbol, persona)* to sway; *(mesa, silla)* to wobble; *(tren, autobús)* to judder

bambú *(pl bambúes o bambús) nm* bamboo

banal *adj* banal

banalidad *nf* banality

banana *nf* banana

banano *nm* banana tree

banca *nf* (a) *(asiento)* bench (b) *Com & Fin (sector)* (the) banks; *(actividad)* banking; **b. electrónica** electronic banking; **b. por Internet** e-banking (c) *(en juegos)* bank

bancario, -a *adj* bank; **crédito b.** bank loan; **sector b.** banking sector

bancarrota *nf Fin* bankruptcy; **estar en b.** to be bankrupt

banco *nm* (a) *(para sentarse)* bench; *(de iglesia)* pew (b) *Com & Fin* bank (c) *(depósito)* bank; *Inform* **b. de datos** data bank; **b. de sangre** blood bank (**d**) **b. de arena** sandbank (**e**) *(de peces)* shoal, school

banda *nf* (**a**) *Mús* band (**b**) *Inform* **b. ancha** broadband; *Cin* **b. sonora** sound track (**c**) *(cinta)* sash (**d**) *(lado)* side; *Ftb* **línea de b.** touchline; **saque de b.** throw-in

bandada *nf (de aves)* flock; *(de peces)* shoal

bandazo *nm* **dar bandazos** to lurch

bandeja *nf* tray; *Fig* **servir algo a algn en b.** to hand sth to sb on a plate

bandera *nf* flag; **b. azul** *(en playa)* blue flag

banderilla *nf* (**a**) *Taurom* banderilla, = barbed dart thrust into bull's back (**b**) *Esp (aperitivo)* = hors d'œuvre of pickles and olives on a cocktail stick

banderín *nm* pennant, small flag

bandido *nm* bandit, outlaw

bando¹ *nm* (**a**) *Der (edicto)* edict, proclamation (**b**) **bandos** banns

bando² *nm* faction, side; **pasarse al otro b.** to go over to the other side, to change sides

bandolero *nm* bandit, outlaw

banjo ['banjo] *nm* banjo

banquero, -a *nm,f* banker

banqueta *nf* (**a**) *(asiento)* stool (**b**) *(para los pies)* foot-stool (**c**) *CAm, Méx (acera) Br* pavement, *US* sidewalk

banquete *nm* banquet, feast; **b. de bodas** wedding reception

banquillo *nm* (**a**) *Der* dock (**b**) *Dep* bench

banquina *nf RP (arcén) Br* hard shoulder, *US* shoulder

bañadera *nf* (**a**) *Arg (bañera)* bath (**b**) *RP (vehículo)* = old-fashioned school bus

bañado *nm Bol, RP (terreno)* marshy area

bañador *nm Esp (de mujer)* swimsuit; *(de hombre)* swimming trunks

bañar 1 *vt* (**a**) *(con agua)* to bath (**b**) *(cubrir)* to coat, cover; **b. en oro** to goldplate
2 bañarse *vpr (en baño)* to have *o* take a bath; *(en mar, piscina)* to go for a swim; *Am (ducharse)* to have *o* take a shower

bañera *nf* bath, bathtub

bañista *nmf* bather, swimmer

baño *nm* (**a**) *(acción)* bath; *(en playa, piscina)* swim; **darse un b.** *(en bañera)* to have *o* take a bath; *(en playa, piscina)* to go for a swim; **b. María** bain Marie; **b. de sangre** bloodbath (**b**) *(cuarto de aseo)* bathroom; *(servicios) Br* toilet, *US* bathroom (**c**) *(de oro etc)* coat; *(de chocolate etc)* coating, covering (**d**) *(bañera)* bathtub, bath (**e**) *Am (ducha)* shower

bar *nm* bar, pub

barahúnda *nf* din, uproar

baraja *nf Br* pack *o US* deck (of cards)

barajar *vt (cartas)* to shuffle; *Fig (nombres, cifras)* to juggle with

baranda, *Esp* **barandilla** *nf (de escalera)* handrail, banister; *(de balcón)* handrail

baratija *nf* trinket, knick-knack

baratillo *nm* (**a**) *(género)* junk (**b**) *(tienda)* junkshop; *(mercadillo)* flea market

barato, -a 1 *adj* cheap
2 *adv* cheaply

barba *nf* (**a**) *Anat* chin (**b**) *(pelo)* beard; *Esp* **2 euros por b.** 2 euros a head

barbacoa *nf* barbecue

barbaridad *nf* (**a**) *(crueldad)* atrocity (**b**) *(disparate)* piece of nonsense; **no digas barbaridades** don't talk nonsense (**c**) *(montón)* **una b.** a lot; **costar una b.** to cost a fortune

barbarie *nf* savagery, cruelty

bárbaro, -a 1 *adj* (**a**) *Hist* barbarian (**b**) *(cruel)* barbaric, barbarous (**c**) *Fam (enorme)* massive (**d**) *RP Fam (estupendo)* tremendous, terrific
2 *nm,f Hist* barbarian

barbecho *nm (sistema)* land set-aside; *(terreno)* fallow field; **dejar en b.** to leave fallow

barbería *nf* barber's (shop)

barbero *nm* barber

barbilla *nf* chin

barbitúrico *nm* barbiturate

barbudo, -a *adj* with a heavy beard

barca *nf* small boat

barcaza *nf* lighter

Barcelona *n* Barcelona

barcelonés, -esa 1 *adj* of/from Barcelona
2 *nm,f* person from Barcelona

barco *nm* boat, ship; **b. de pasajeros** liner; **b. de vapor** steamer

baremo *nm (escala)* scale; *(norma)* yardstick

barítono *nm* baritone

barlovento *nm* windward (side)

barman *(pl barmans) nm* barman

barniz *nm* (**a**) *(en madera)* varnish; *(en cerámica)* glaze (**b**) *Fig* veneer

barnizado, -a *adj (madera)* varnished; *(cerámica)* glazed

barnizar [40] *vt (madera)* to varnish; *(cerámica)* to glaze

barómetro *nm* barometer

barón *nm* baron

baronesa *nf* baroness

barquero, -a *nm,f (hombre)* boatman; *(mujer)* boatwoman

barquillo nm wafer

barra nf (a) (pieza alargada) bar; **b. de pan** French loaf, baguette; **b. de labios** lipstick (b) (mostrador) bar; **b. americana** = bar where hostesses chat with clients (c) Dep **b. fija** horizontal bar; **barras paralelas** parallel bars (d) (signo gráfico) slash, oblique (e) Andes, RP Fam (de amigos) gang; **b. brava** = group of violent soccer supporters

barraca nf (a) (caseta) shack, hut (b) (en Valencia y Murcia) thatched farmhouse

barracón nm prefabricated hut

barranco nm (despeñadero) cliff, precipice; (torrentera) gully, ravine

barranquismo nm Dep canyoning

barrena nf twist drill

barrenar vt Téc to drill

barrendero, -a nm,f sweeper, street sweeper

barreno nm (a) (taladro) large drill (b) (agujero) (para explosiones) blast hole

barreño nm Esp washing-up bowl

barrer 1 vt to sweep
2 vi (en elecciones) to win by a landslide

barrera nf barrier

barriada nf (a) (barrio popular) neighbourhood, area (b) Am (barrio de chabolas) shanty town

barricada nf barricade

barrida nf sweep

barriga nf belly; Fam tummy

barrigón, -ona, barrigudo, -a adj Fam potbellied

barril nm barrel; **cerveza de b.** draught beer

barrillo nm blackhead

barrio nm area, district, US neighborhood; **del b.** local; **el B. Gótico** the Gothic Quarter; **b. chino** (de chinos) Chinatown; Esp (de prostitución) red-light district; **barrios bajos** slums

barrizal nm mire, quagmire

barro nm (a) (lodo) mud (b) (arcilla) clay; **objetos de b.** earthenware

barroco, -a adj baroque

barruntar vt (sospechar) to suspect; (presentir) to have a feeling

barrunto nm (presentimiento) feeling, presentiment; (sospecha) suspicion

bartola: a la bartola loc adv Fam **tumbarse a la b.** to laze around, to idle away one's time

bártulos nmpl Fam things, bits and pieces

barullo nm (alboroto) row, din; (confusión) confusion

basar 1 vt to base (**en** on)
2 basarse vpr (teoría, película) **basarse en** to be based on; **¿en qué te basas para decir eso?** what grounds do you have for saying that?

basca nf Esp Fam people, crowd

báscula nf scales; (para camiones) weighbridge

bascular vi to tilt

base nf (a) (fundamento, origen) basis; **en b. a** on the basis of; **a b. de estudiar** by studying; **a b. de productos naturales** using natural products (b) (militar, científica) base (c) Quím, Mat & Geom base; Inform **b. de datos** database (d) (de partido) **las bases** the grass roots, the rank and file; **miembro de b.** rank and file member (e) (nociones) grounding

básico, -a adj basic

basílica nf basilica

basket, Am básquet nm basketball

basta interj ¡b.! that's enough!; ¡b. de chistes/tonterías! that's enough jokes/of this nonsense!

bastante 1 adj (a) (suficiente) enough; **b. tiempo/comida** enough time/food; **bastantes platos** enough plates (b) (abundante) quite a lot of; **hace b. calor/frío** it's quite hot/cold; **bastantes amigos** quite a lot of friends
2 adv (a) (suficiente) enough; **con esto hay b.** that is enough; **no soy lo b. rico (como) para ...** I am not rich enough to ... (b) (considerablemente) fairly, quite; **me gusta b.** I quite like it; **vamos b. al cine** we go to the cinema quite o fairly often

bastar 1 vi to be sufficient o enough, to suffice; **basta con tres** three will be enough; ¡basta de tonterías! enough of this nonsense!; **basta con tocarlo para que se abra** you only have to touch it and it opens; ¡basta (ya)! that's enough!, that will do!
2 bastarse vpr **bastarse a sí mismo** to be self-sufficient, to rely only on oneself

bastardilla nf Impr italics

bastardo, -a adj & nm,f bastard

bastidor nm (a) (armazón) frame (b) Teatro **bastidores** wings; Fig **entre bastidores** behind the scenes

bastión nm bastion

basto, -a 1 adj (cosa) rough, coarse; (persona) coarse, uncouth
2 bastos nmpl Naipes = suit in Spanish deck of cards, with the symbol of a wooden club

bastón nm stick, walking stick

bastoncillo nm (de algodón) cotton bud

basura nf Br rubbish, US garbage, US trash

basurero nm (a) (persona) Br dustman, US garbage man (b) (lugar) Br rubbish tip o dump, US garbage dump

bata nf (para casa) dressing gown; (de médico etc) white coat; (de científico) lab coat

batacazo nm (a) (golpe) bump, bang; **los resultados representan un nuevo b. para el partido** the results are another blow for the party (b) CSur Fam (triunfo inesperado) surprise victory

batalla nf battle; **librar b.** to do o join battle; **b. campal** pitched battle

batallar vi (a) (con armas) to fight (b) (con esfuerzo) to battle

batallón nm battalion

batata nf Esp, Arg, Col, Ven sweet potato

bate nm Dep bat; **b. de béisbol** baseball bat

batear Dep **1** vi to bat
2 vt to hit

batería 1 nf (a) Elec battery (b) Mús drums (c) **b. de cocina** pots and pans, set of pans
2 nmf drummer

batiburrillo nm jumble, mess

batida nf (a) (de la policía) raid (b) (en caza) beat

batido, -a 1 adj (a) Culin whipped (b) Dep **tierra batida** clay
2 nm milk shake

batidora nf (eléctrica) mixer

batiente adj **reírse a mandíbula b.** to laugh one's head off

batín nm short dressing gown

batir 1 vt (a) (huevo) to beat; (nata) to whip, to whisk (b) (récord) to break (c) (golpear) to beat against (d) (en caza) to beat
2 batirse vpr to fight

batuta nf Mús baton; Fig **llevar la b.** to be in charge

baúl nm (a) (cofre) trunk (b) Arg, Col (maletero) Br boot, US trunk

bautismo nm baptism, christening

bautizar [40] vt to baptize, to christen; (vino) to water down

bautizo nm baptism, christening

Baviera n Bavaria

baya nf berry

bayeta nf floorcloth

bayoneta nf bayonet

baza nf (a) (en naipes) trick; Fig **meter b.** to butt in (b) (ventaja) advantage

bazar nm bazaar

bazo nm spleen

bazofia nf (a) (comida) pigswill (b) (libro, película) **ser (una) b.** to be Br rubbish o US garbage

be nf (a) Esp (letra) = name of the letter "b" (b) Am **be alta** o **grande** o **larga** b (to distinguish from "v")

beato, -a adj (piadoso) devout; Pey prudish, sanctimonious

bebe, -a nm,f Andes, RP baby

bebé nm baby; **b. probeta** test-tube baby

bebedero nm (a) (abrevadero) drinking trough, water trough (b) Méx, RP (fuente) drinking fountain

bebedor, -a nm,f (hard o heavy) drinker

beber vt & vi to drink

bebible adj drinkable

bebida nf drink; **darse a la b.** to take to drink

bebido, -a adj drunk

beca nf (del gobierno) grant; (de organización privada) scholarship

becar [44] vt (sujeto: gobierno) to award a grant to; (sujeto: organización privada) to award a scholarship to

becario, -a nm,f (a) (estudiante) (del gobierno) grant holder; (de organización privada) scholarship holder (b) (en prácticas) person on a work placement, US intern

becerro nm calf

bechamel nf bechamel; **salsa b.** bechamel sauce, white sauce

bedel nm beadle

begonia nf begonia

beige adj & nm inv beige

béisbol nm baseball

Belén n Bethlehem

belén nm nativity scene, crib

belga adj & nmf Belgian

Bélgica n Belgium

Belgrado n Belgrade

Belice n Belize

bélico, -a adj warlike, bellicose; (preparativos etc) war; **material b.** armaments

belicoso, -a adj warlike, bellicose; (agresivo) aggressive

beligerancia nf belligerence

beligerante adj belligerent; **los países beligerantes** the countries at war

bellaco, -a nm,f villain, scoundrel

belleza nf beauty

bello, -a adj beautiful

bellota nf Bot acorn; Fig **animal de b.** blockhead

bemol 1 adj Mús flat
2 nm Fam **esto tiene bemoles** this is a tough one

bencina nf Chile (gasolina) Br petrol, US gas

bencinera nf Chile Br petrol station, US gas station

bendecir [12] vt to bless; **b. la mesa** to say grace; **¡Dios te bendiga!** God bless you!

bendición nf blessing

bendito, -a 1 adj blessed; (maldito) damned
  2 nm,f (bonachón) good sort, kind soul; (tontorrón) simple soul

beneficencia nf beneficence, charity

beneficiado, -a adj favoured; **salir b. de algo** to do well out of sth

beneficiar [43] **1** vt to benefit
  2 beneficiarse vpr **beneficiarse de** o **con algo** to profit from o by sth

beneficiario, -a nm,f beneficiary

beneficio nm (a) Com & Fin profit (b) (bien) benefit; **en b. propio** in one's own interest; **un concierto a b. de ...** a concert in aid of ...

beneficioso, -a adj beneficial

benéfico, -a adj charitable

beneplácito nm Fml approval, consent

benevolencia nf benevolence

benevolente, benévolo, -a adj benevolent

bengala nf flare

benigno, -a adj (persona) gentle, benign; (clima) mild; (tumor) benign

benjamín, -ina nm,f youngest child

beodo, -a adj & nm,f drunk

berberecho nm (common) cockle

berbiquí (pl berbiquíes o berbiquís) nm Téc brace and bit

berenjena nf Br aubergine, US eggplant

Berlín n Berlin

berlina nf four-door saloon

berlinés, -esa 1 adj of/from Berlin
  2 nm,f Berliner

berma nf Andes (arcén) Br hard shoulder, US shoulder

bermejo, -a adj reddish

bermellón nm vermilion

Bermudas nfpl **las (Islas) B.** Bermuda

bermudas nmpl o nfpl Bermuda shorts

Berna n Bern

berrear vi to bellow, to low

berrido nm bellowing, lowing

berrinche nm Fam tantrum

berro nm cress, watercress

berza nf cabbage

besar 1 vt to kiss
  2 besarse vpr to kiss

beso nm kiss

bestia 1 nf beast, animal; **b. de carga** beast of burden
  2 nmf Fam (persona) brute, beast
  3 adj brutish, boorish; **a lo b.** rudely

bestial adj (brutal) animal, brutal; Fam (enorme) huge, tremendous; (extraordinario) fantastic, terrific

bestialidad nf (a) Fam (estupidez) stupidity (b) (brutalidad) brutality (c) Fam (montón) **una b. de** tons of, stacks of

best-seller [bes'seler] (pl best-sellers) nm best-seller

besugo nm (a) (pez) sea bream (b) Esp (persona) idiot, half-wit

besuquear Fam **1** vt to kiss, to cover with kisses
  2 besuquearse vpr to smooch

betabel nf Méx Br beetroot, US beet

betarraga nf Andes Br beetroot, US beet

betún nm (para el calzado) shoe polish; Quím bitumen

biberón nm baby's bottle, feeding bottle

Biblia nf Bible

bíblico, -a adj biblical

bibliografía nf bibliography

bibliorato nm RP lever arch file

biblioteca nf (a) (institución) library; **b. ambulante** mobile library (b) Chile, Perú, RP (mueble) bookcase

bibliotecario, -a nm,f librarian

bicameral adj Pol bicameral, two-chamber

bicarbonato nm bicarbonate; **b. sódico** bicarbonate of soda

bicentenario nm Br bicentenary, US bicentennial

bíceps nm inv biceps

bicho nm (a) (animal) beast, animal; (insecto) bug; **¿qué b. le ha picado?** Br what's up with him?, US what's eating him? (b) Fam (persona) **todo b. viviente** every living soul; **un b. raro** a weirdo, an oddball

bici nf Fam bike

bicicleta nf bicycle; **montar en b.** to ride a bicycle

bicolor adj two-coloured; Pol **gobierno b.** two-party government

bidé nm bidet

bidón nm drum

biela nf Aut connecting rod

Bielorrusia nf Belarus

bien¹ 1 adv (a) (correctamente) well; **habla b. (el) inglés** she speaks English well; **responder b.** to answer correctly; **hiciste b. en decírmelo** you were right to tell me; **las cosas le van b.** things are going well for him; **¡b.!** good!, great!; **¡muy b.!** excellent,

first class!; **¡qué b.!** great!, fantastic!
(**b**) *(de salud)* well; **sentirse/encontrarse/
estar b.** to feel well
(**c**) **vivir b.** to be comfortably off; **¡está b.!**
(¡de acuerdo!) fine!, all right!; **¡ya está b.!**
that's (quite) enough!; **aquí se está muy b.**
it's really nice here; **esta falda te sienta b.**
this skirt suits you; *Fam* **ese libro está muy
b.** that book is very good; *Fam* **su novia
está muy b.** his girlfriend is very nice
(**d**) *(intensificador)* very, quite; **b.
temprano** very early, nice and early; **b.
caliente** pretty hot; **b. es verdad que … it's**
quite clear that …
(**e**) **más b.** rather, a little
(**f**) **b. podía haberme avisado** she might
have let me know
(**g**) *(de buena gana)* willingly, gladly; **b.
me tomaría una cerveza** I'd really love a
beer
2 *conj* **ahora b.** now, now then; **o b.** or, or
else; **b. … o b. …** either … or …; **no b.** as
soon as; **no b. llegó …** no sooner had she
arrived than …; **si b.** although, even if
3 *adj* **la gente b.** the wealthy, the upper
classes

bien² *nm* (**a**) *(bondad)* good; **el b. y el mal**
good and evil; **un hombre/familia de b.** a
good man/family (**b**) *(bienestar)* **por el b.
de** for the good of; **lo hace por tu b.** he
does it for your own good (**c**) **bienes**
goods; **bienes de equipo** capital goods;
bienes inmuebles real estate, *US* real
property; **bienes de consumo** consumer
goods

bienal *nf* biennial exhibition

bienestar *nm (personal)* well-being,
contentment; *(comodidad)* ease, comfort; **la sociedad del b.** the affluent society

bienhechor, -a *nm,f (hombre)* benefactor; *(mujer)* benefactress

bienintencionado, -a *adj* well-meaning,
well-intentioned

bienio *nm* biennium, two-year period

bienvenida *nf* welcome; **dar la b. a algn** to
welcome sb

bienvenido, -a *adj* welcome

bife *nm* (**a**) *Andes, RP (bistec)* steak (**b**)
Andes, RP (bofetada) slap

bifocal *adj* bifocal; **gafas bifocales**
bifocals

bifurcación *nf (de la carretera)* fork; *Tel*
bifurcation

bifurcarse [44] *vpr* to fork

bigamia *nf* bigamy

bígamo, -a 1 *adj* bigamous
2 *nm,f* bigamist

bigote *nm (de persona)* moustache; *(de
animal) (usu pl)* whiskers

🖉 Observa que la palabra inglesa **bigot**
es un falso amigo y no es la traducción
de la palabra española **bigote**. En inglés, **bigot** significa "intolerante".

bigotudo, -a *adj* with a big moustache

bigudí *(pl* **bigudís** *o* **bigudíes)** *nm* curler

bilateral *adj* bilateral

bilbaíno, -a 1 *adj* of/from Bilbao
2 *nm,f* person from Bilbao

bilingüe *adj* bilingual

bilis *nf inv* bile

billar *nm* (**a**) *(juego)* billiards *sing*; **b.
americano** pool; **b. ruso** snooker (**b**)
(mesa) billiard table

billete *nm* (**a**) *Esp (transporte)* ticket; **b. de
ida** *(en avión)* one-way (ticket); **b. de ida y
vuelta** *Br* return (ticket), *US* round-trip
(ticket) (**b**) *(de banco) Br* note, *US* bill; **un
b. de cinco euros** a five euro note

billetera *nf,* **billetero** *nm* wallet, *US*
billfold

billón *nm* trillion

bimensual *adj* twice-monthly, bi-
monthly

bimestral *adj* two-monthly

bimotor 1 *adj* twin-engined
2 *nm* twin-engined plane

binario, -a *adj* binary

bingo *nm* (**a**) *(juego)* bingo (**b**) *(sala)*
bingo hall

binomio *nm* (**a**) *Mat* binomial (**b**) *(de
personas)* pairing

biodegradable *adj* biodegradable

biodiversidad *nf* biodiversity

biofísica *nf* biophysics *sing*

biografía *nf* biography

biográfico, -a *adj* biographical

biógrafo, -a *nm,f* biographer

biología *nf* biology

biológico, -a *adj* biological; *(agricultura,
productos)* organic

biólogo, -a *nm,f* biologist

biomasa *nf* bio-mass

biombo *nm* (folding) screen

biopsia *nf* biopsy

bioquímica *nf* biochemistry

bioquímico, -a 1 *adj* biochemical
2 *nm,f* biochemist

biotecnología *nf* biotechnology

bióxido *nm* dioxide; **b. de carbono** carbon
dioxide

bipartidismo *nm* two-party system

biquini *nm* bikini

birlar *vt Fam* to pinch, *Br* to nick

Birmania *n Antes* Burma

birmano, -a *adj & nm,f Antes* Burmese

birome *nf RP* Biro®, ballpoint (pen)

birra *nf Fam* beer, *US* brew

birrete *nm* cap, beret; *Rel* biretta; *Univ* mortar-board

birria *nf Fam Br* rubbish, *US* garbage

bis 1 *nm* encore
2 *adv* twice

bisabuelo, -a *nm* (hombre) great-grandfather; (mujer) great-grandmother; **bisabuelos** great-grandparents

bisagra *nf* hinge; **partido b.** party holding the balance of power

bisbisar, bisbisear *vt* to whisper

bisexual *adj & nmf* bisexual

bisiesto *adj* año b. leap year

bisnieto, -a *nm,f* (niño) great-grandson; (niña) great-granddaughter; **mis bisnietos** my great-grandchildren

bisonte *nm* bison, American buffalo

bisoño, -a *adj* inexperienced

bistec (pl bistecs) *nm* steak

bisturí (pl bisturíes) *nm* scalpel

bisutería *nf* imitation jewellery

bit (pl bits) *nm Inform* bit

bitácora *nf Inform* blog

bíter *nm* bitters

bizantino, -a *adj Hist* Byzantine; *Fig* discusiones bizantinas hair-splitting arguments

bizco, -a 1 *adj* cross-eyed
2 *nm,f* cross-eyed person

bizcocho *nm* sponge cake

biznieto, -a *nm,f* = bisnieto

blanca *nf Esp* estar sin b. to be flat broke

blanco¹, -a 1 *adj* white; (tez) fair
2 *nm,f* (hombre) white man; (mujer) white woman; **los blancos** whites

blanco² *nm* (a) (color) white (b) (hueco) blank; **dejó la hoja en b.** he left the page blank; **votos en b.** blank votes; *Fig* pasar la noche en b. to have a sleepless night; **me quedé en b.** my mind went blank (c) (diana) target; **dar en el b.** to hit the target; *Fig* ser el b. de todas las miradas to be the centre of attention

blancura *nf* whiteness

blandengue *adj Pey* weak, soft

blandir *vt* to brandish

blando, -a *adj* soft

> ⚠ Observa que la palabra inglesa **bland** es un falso amigo y no es la traducción de la palabra española **blando**. En inglés **bland** significa "soso".

blanquear *vt* (a) (ropa) to whiten (b) (casa) to whitewash (c) (dinero) to launder

blanquecino, -a *adj* whitish

blanqueo *nm* (a) (de ropa) whitening (b) (de casa) whitewashing (c) (de dinero) laundering

blanquillo *nm* (a) *CAm, Méx* (huevo) egg (b) *Andes* (melocotón) white peach

blasfemar *vi* to blaspheme (**contra** against)

blasfemia *nf* blasphemy

blasón *nm* coat of arms

bledo *nm Fam* me importa un b. I couldn't give a damn

blindado, -a *adj Mil* armoured, armour-plated; (antibalas) bullet-proof; **coche b.** bullet-proof car; **puerta blindada** reinforced door, security door

blindaje *nm* (de puerta) armour-plating; (de vehículo) armour

blindar *vt* to armour-plate

bloc (pl blocs) *nm* pad; **b. de notas** notepad

blog [bloɣ] (pl blogs) *nm Inform* blog

blogger [bloɣer] *nmf Inform* blogger

bloguear *vi Inform* to blog

bloguero, -a *nm,f Inform* blogger

bloomer ['blumer] *nm CAm, Carib* panties, *Br* knickers

bloque *nm* (a) (pieza, edificio) block; **en b.** en bloc; **b. de pisos** *Br* (block of) flats, *US* apartment block (b) *Pol* bloc; **el b. comunista** the Communist Bloc

bloquear 1 *vt* (a) (comunicaciones, carreteras, acuerdo) to block (b) *Mil* to blockade (c) *Fin* (cuentas) to freeze (d) *Inform* (archivo) to lock
2 bloquearse *vpr* (a) (atascarse) to be stuck (b) (persona) to freeze (c) *Aut* (dirección) to lock; (frenos) to jam (d) *Inform* (pantalla) to freeze

bloqueo *nm* (a) (militar, económico) blockade (b) *Fin* (de cuentas) freeze, freezing (c) (de mecanismo) jamming (d) **b. mental** mental block

blues [blus] *nm inv Mús* blues

blúmer (pl blúmers o blúmeres) *nm CAm, Carib* panties, *Br* knickers

blusa *nf* blouse

blusón *nm* loose blouse, smock

bluyín *nm*, **bluyines** *nmpl Andes, Ven* jeans

boato *nm* show, ostentation

bobada *nf* nonsense; **decir bobadas** to talk nonsense

bobalicón, -ona *Fam* **1** *adj* simple, stupid
2 *nm,f* simpleton, idiot

bobería *nf* = bobada

bobina *nf* (a) (de hilo) reel (b) *Elec* coil

bobo, -a 1 adj (tonto) stupid, silly; (ingenuo) naïve
  2 nm,f fool

boca 1 nf (a) (de persona, animal) mouth; **b. abajo** face downward; **b. arriba** face upward; Fig **a pedir de b.** perfectly; Fig **andar de b. en b.** to be the talk of the town; Fam **¡cierra la b!** shut up!; Fam **con la b. abierta** open-mouthed; Fam **se le hizo la b. agua** his mouth watered (b) **b. del metro** Br tube o underground entrance, US subway entrance; **b. de riego** hydrant
  2 nm **el b. a b.** the kiss of life, mouth-to-mouth resuscitation

bocacalle nf entrance to a street

bocadillo nm (a) Esp (con pan) filled roll (made with a baguette); **un b. de jamón/tortilla** a ham/an omelette sandwich (b) (de cómic) balloon

bocado nm (a) (mordedura) bite (b) (de caballo) bit

bocajarro: a bocajarro loc adv (disparar) at point-blank range; **decir algo a b.** to say sth straight out

bocanada nf (de humo) puff; (de viento) gust; Fig **una b. de aire fresco** a breath of fresh air

bocata nm Esp Fam filled roll (made with a baguette)

bocazas nmf inv Fam bigmouth, blabbermouth

boceto nm Arte sketch, outline; (esquema) outline, plan

bochinche nm Am Fam (ruido) racket; (alboroto) fuss

bochorno nm (a) (tiempo) sultry o close weather; (calor sofocante) stifling heat (b) Fig (vergüenza) shame, embarrassment

bochornoso, -a adj (a) (tiempo) sultry, close, muggy; (calor) stifling (b) Fig (vergonzoso) shameful, embarrassing

bocina nf horn; **tocar la b.** to blow o sound one's horn

bocinazo nm hoot, toot

bocón, -ona adj Am Fam **ser b.** to be a bigmouth o blabbermouth

boda nf wedding, marriage; **bodas de plata** silver wedding

bodega nf (a) (cava) wine cellar; (tienda) wine shop (b) Náut hold (c) Méx (almacén) warehouse (d) CAm, Carib (colmado) small grocery store

bodegón nm still-life

bodrio nm Fam **un b.** Br rubbish, US trash

body (pl bodies) nm body (garment)

BOE nm (abr Boletín Oficial del Estado) = official Spanish gazette

bofetada nf, **bofetón** nm slap on the face; **dar una b./un b. a algn** to slap sb's face

boga nf **estar en b.** to be in vogue

bogar [42] vi (a) (remar) to row (b) (navegar) to sail

bogavante nm lobster

bogotano, -a 1 adj of/from Bogotá
  2 nm,f person from Bogotá

bohemio, -a 1 adj (a) (aspecto, vida, barrio) bohemian (b) (de Bohemia) Bohemian
  2 nm,f (a) (artista, vividor) bohemian (b) (de Bohemia) Bohemian

bohío nm Carib hut, cabin

boicot (pl boicots) nm boycott

boicotear vt to boycott

boicoteo nm boycott

bóiler nm Méx boiler

boina nf beret

bol nm bowl

bola nf (a) (objeto) ball; (canica) marble; **b. de nieve** snowball; Fig **no dar pie con b.** to be unable to do anything right (b) Fam (mentira) fib, lie; **meter bolas** to tell fibs (c) (rumor) rumour; **corre la b. por ahí de que te has echado novio** they say you've got yourself a boyfriend

bolchevique adj & nmf Bolshevik

bolear vt Méx (sacar brillo) to shine, to polish

bolera nf bowling alley

bolería nf Méx shoeshine store

bolero nm bolero

boleta nf (a) Cuba, Méx, RP (para votar) ballot, voting slip (b) CSur (comprobante) (de venta, de depósito bancario) receipt (c) CAm, CSur (multa) parking ticket (d) Méx (de calificaciones) Br (school) report, US report card

boletería nf Am (de cine, teatro) box office; (de estación) ticket office

boletero, -a nm,f Am box office attendant

boletín nm bulletin; **B. Oficial del Estado** Official Gazette

boleto nm (a) (de lotería, rifa) ticket (b) Am (para transporte) ticket (c) Col, Méx (para espectáculo) ticket

boli nm Esp Fam pen, Biro®

boliche nm (a) (juego) bowling (b) (bola) jack (c) (lugar) bowling alley (d) CSur Fam (bar) cheap bar; (tienda) small-town store

bólido nm Aut racing car

bolígrafo nm ballpoint (pen), Biro®

bolillo nm (a) (en costura) bobbin (b) Méx (panecillo) bread roll

bolita nf CSur (bola) marble; **jugar a las bolitas** to play marbles

bolívar *nm Fin* bolivar, = standard monetary unit of Venezuela

Bolivia *n* Bolivia

boliviano, -a *adj & nm,f* Bolivian

bollería *nf* (a) *(tienda)* cake shop (b) *(productos)* cakes

bollo *nm* (a) *Culin* bun, bread roll (b) *(abolladura)* dent

bolo¹ *nm (pieza)* skittle, pin; **bolos** *(juego)* (ten-pin) bowling

bolo², -a *nm,f CAm Fam (borracho)* boozer

bolsa¹ *nf* bag; *Méx (de mano) Br* handbag, *US* purse; *Av* **b. de aire** air pocket; **b. de deportes** sports bag; **b. de la compra** shopping bag; **b. de viaje** travel bag

bolsa² *nf Fin* Stock Exchange; **jugar a la b.** to play the market

bolsillo *nm (en prenda)* pocket; **de b.** pocket, pocket-size; **libro de b.** paperback; **lo pagó de su b.** he paid for it out of his own pocket

bolso *nm* (a) *Esp (de mujer) Br* handbag, *US* purse (b) *(de viaje)* bag

boludear *vi RP Fam* (a) *(hacer tonterías)* to mess about (b) *(decir tonterías)* to talk *Br* rubbish *o US* garbage (c) *(perder el tiempo)* to waste one's time

boludo, -a *nm,f RP Fam (estúpido) Br* prat, *US* jerk

bomba¹ *nf* pump; *Chile, Ecuad, Ven (gasolinera) Br* petrol station, *US* gas station; **b. de aire** air pump; **b. de incendios** fire engine; *Chile, Ecuad, Ven* **b. (de gasolina)** *(surtidor) Br* petrol pump, *US* gas pump

bomba² *nf* bomb; **b. atómica/de hidrógeno/de neutrones** atomic/hydrogen/ neutron bomb; **b. de relojería** time bomb; **b. fétida** stink bomb; *Fam* **noticia b.** shattering piece of news; *Esp Fam* **pasarlo b.** to have a whale of a time

bombacha *nf RP (braga) Br* knickers, *US* panties; **bombachas** *(pantalones)* = loose trousers worn by cowboys

bombardear *vt* to bomb, to shell; **b. a algn a preguntas** to bombard sb with questions

bombardeo *nm* bombing, bombardment

bombardero *nm Av* bomber

bombear *vt* to pump

bombeo *nm* pumping; **estación de b.** pumping station

bombero, -a *nm,f* (a) *(de incendios)* firefighter; *(hombre)* fireman; *(mujer)* firewoman; **cuerpo de bomberos** *Br* fire brigade, *US* fire department; **parque de bomberos** fire station (b) *Ven (de gasolinera) Br* petrol-pump *o US* gas-pump attendant

bombilla *Esp nf* (light) bulb

bombillo *nm CAm, Carib, Col, Méx* (light) bulb

bombín *nm* bowler hat

bombita *nf RP* light bulb

bombo *nm* (a) *Mús* bass drum; *Fig* **a b. y platillo(s)** with a great song and dance; *Fam* **darse b.** to blow one's own trumpet (b) *(de sorteo)* lottery drum

bombón *nm* chocolate

bombona *nf* cylinder; **b. de butano** butane gas cylinder

bombonera *nf* chocolate box

bonachón, -ona *adj* good-natured, easy-going

bonaerense 1 *adj* of/from Buenos Aires **2** *nmf* person from Buenos Aires

bonanza *nf* (a) *Náut (tiempo)* fair weather; *(mar)* calm at sea (b) *Fig (prosperidad)* prosperity

bondad *nf* goodness; *Fml* **tenga la b. de esperar** please be so kind as to wait

bondadoso, -a *adj* kind, good-natured

bonete *nm Rel* cap, biretta; *Univ* mortarboard

boniato *nm Esp, Cuba, Urug* sweet potato

bonificación *nf* bonus

bonificar [44] *vt Com* to give a bonus to

bonito¹, -a *adj* pretty, nice

bonito² *nm* tuna

bono *nm* (a) *(vale)* voucher (b) *Fin* bond, debenture; **bonos del tesoro** *o* **del Estado** Treasury bonds

bonobús *(pl bonobuses) nm Esp* = multiple-journey bus ticket

bonoloto *nm* = Spanish state-run lottery

bonsái *nm* bonsai

boñiga *nf* cowpat

boom [bum] *(pl booms) nm* boom

boquerón *nm* anchovy

boquete *nm* hole

boquiabierto, -a *adj* open-mouthed; *Fig* **se quedó b.** he was flabbergasted

boquilla *nf* (a) *(de cigarro)* tip; *(de pipa)* mouthpiece; **decir algo de b.** to pay lip service to sth (b) *Mús* mouthpiece (c) *(orificio)* opening

borbotar, borbotear *vi* to bubble

borbotón *nm* **salir a borbotones** to gush forth

borda *nf Náut* gunwale; **arrojar** *o* **echar por la b.** to throw overboard; **fuera b.** *(motor)* outboard motor

bordado, -a 1 *adj* embroidered; *Esp* **el examen me salió b.** I made a good job of that exam
2 *nm* embroidery

bordar vt (a) (tejido) to embroider (b) Fig to do excellently

borde¹ nm (de mesa, camino) edge; Cost hem, edge; (de vasija) rim, brim; **al b. de** on the brink of, on the verge of; **al b. del mar** at the seaside

borde² Fam **1** adj Esp Fam (antipático) **ser b.** to be Br a ratbag o US an s.o.b.
  2 nmf Esp Fam (antipático) Br ratbag, US s.o.b.

bordear vt to go round the edge of, to skirt

bordillo nm Br kerb, US curb

bordo nm **a b.** on board; **subir a b.** to go on board

bordó adj inv RP burgundy

borla nf tassel

borne nm Elec terminal

borra nf (a) (pelusa) fluff (b) (poso) sediment, dregs

borrachera nf (embriaguez) drunkenness; **agarrarse** o **cogerse una b.** to get drunk

borracho, -a 1 adj (a) (bebido) drunk; **estar b.** to be drunk (b) (bizcocho) with rum
  2 nm,f drunkard, drunk

borrador nm (a) (escrito) rough copy, first draft (b) (croquis) rough o preliminary sketch (c) (para pizarra) board duster

borraja nf **quedar en agua de borrajas** to come to nothing, to fizzle o peter out

borrar 1 vt (a) (con goma) Br to rub out, US to erase; (pizarra) to clean (b) Inform to delete
  2 borrarse vpr (de un club etc) to drop out, to withdraw

borrasca nf area of low pressure

borrascoso, -a adj stormy

borrego, -a nm,f (a) (animal) lamb (b) Fam (persona) **como borregos** like sheep

borrico nm ass, donkey; Fam Fig ass, dimwit

borrón nm blot, smudge

borroso, -a adj blurred; **veo b.** I can't see clearly, everything's blurred

Bosnia n Bosnia

bosnio, -a adj & nm,f Bosnian

bosque nm wood

bosquejar vt (dibujo) to sketch, outline; (plan) to draft, to outline

bosquejo nm (de dibujo) sketch, study; (de plan) draft, outline

bostezar [40] vi to yawn

bostezo nm yawn

bota nf (a) (calzado) boot; Fig **ponerse las botas** to make a killing (b) (de vino) wineskin

botana nf Méx snack, appetizer

botánica nf botany

botánico, -a 1 adj botanic; **jardín b.** botanic gardens
  2 nm,f botanist

botar 1 vi (a) Esp (saltar) to jump (b) (pelota) to bounce
  2 vt (a) (barco) to launch (b) (pelota) to bounce (c) Am salvo RP (tirar) to throw away; **bótalo a la basura** throw it away

botarate nmf madcap, fool

bote nm (a) (envase) (tarro) jar; Esp (lata) tin, can; (de champú, pastillas) bottle; Am **b. de la basura** Br rubbish bin, US garbage can; **b. de humo** smoke canister (b) (barca) boat; **b. salvavidas** lifeboat; **b. de remos** rowing boat (c) (propinas) tips; **para el b.** as a tip (d) (salto) jump; **dar botes** (saltar) to jump up and down; (tren, coche) to bump up and down; **pegar un b.** (de susto) to jump, to give a start (e) (de pelota) bounce; **dar botes** to bounce; Dep **a b. pronto** on the rebound (f) (expresiones) Esp **chupar del b.** to feather one's nest; Esp **tener en el b. a algn** to have sb eating out of one's hand; **a b. pronto** (sin pensar) off the top of one's head

botella nf (a) (recipiente) bottle (b) Cuba (autostop) **dar b. a algn** to give sb a Br lift o US ride; **hacer b.** to hitchhike

botellín nm small bottle

botepronto nm Fam **a b.** all of a sudden

botica nf Anticuado pharmacy, Br chemist's (shop), US drugstore; Fam **hay de todo como en b.** there's everything under the sun

boticario, -a nm,f Anticuado pharmacist, Br chemist, US druggist

botijo nm earthenware pitcher (with spout and handle)

botín¹ nm (de un robo) loot, booty

botín² nm (calzado) ankle boot

botiquín nm (a) (armario) medicine chest o cabinet; (portátil) first-aid kit (b) (enfermería) first-aid post

botón nm button; **pulsar el b.** to press the button; **b. de muestra** sample

botones nm inv (en hotel) bellboy, US bellhop; (recadero) messenger, errand boy

bouquet [bu'ke] (pl bouquets) nm bouquet

boutique [bu'tik] nf boutique

bóveda nf vault

bovino, -a adj bovine; **ganado b.** cattle

box (pl boxes) nm (a) (de caballo) stall (b) (de coches) pit (c) Am (boxeo) boxing

boxeador, -a nm boxer

boxear *vi* to box

boxeo *nm* boxing

boya *nf* (**a**) *Náut* buoy (**b**) *(corcho)* float

boyante *adj (empresa, negocio)* prosperous; *(economía, comercio)* buoyant

boy-scout [bojes'kaut] *(pl* boy scouts) *nm* boy scout

bozal *nm* (**a**) *(para perro)* muzzle (**b**) *Am (cabestro)* halter

bracero *nm* (day) labourer

braga *nf*, **bragas** *nfpl Esp* panties *Br* knickers

bragueta *nf (de pantalón etc) Br* flies, *US* zipper

braguetazo *nm Esp Fam* **dar el b.** to marry for money

braille ['braile] *nm* braille

bramar *vi* to low, to bellow

bramido *nm* lowing, bellowing

brandy *(pl* brandis) *nm* brandy

branquia *nf* gill

brasa *nf* ember, red-hot coal; **a la b.** barbecued

brasero *nm* brazier

brasier *nm Carib, Col, Méx* bra

Brasil *n* Brazil

brasileño, -a, *RP* **brasilero, -a** *adj & nm,f* Brazilian

bravata *nf* piece o act of bravado

bravo, -a 1 *adj* (**a**) *(valiente)* brave, courageous (**b**) *(feroz)* fierce, ferocious; **un toro b.** a fighting bull (**c**) *(mar)* rough, stormy
2 *interj* **¡b.!** well done!, bravo!

bravucón, -ona *nm,f* boaster, braggart

bravura *nf* (**a**) *(de animal)* ferocity, fierceness (**b**) *(de persona)* courage, bravery (**c**) *(de toro)* fighting spirit

braza *nf* (**a**) *(medida)* fathom (**b**) *Esp (en natación)* breaststroke; **nadar a b.** to do the breaststroke

brazada *nf (en natación)* stroke

brazalete *nm* (**a**) *(insignia)* armband (**b**) *(pulsera)* bracelet

brazo *nm* arm; *(de animal)* foreleg; *(de sillón, tocadiscos)* arm; **en brazos** in one's arms; **ir del b.** to walk arm in arm; *Fig* **con los brazos abiertos** with open arms; *Fig* **no dar su b. a torcer** not to give in, to stand firm; **b. de gitano** *Br* Swiss roll, *US* jelly roll

brea *nf* tar, pitch

brebaje *nm* concoction, brew

brecha *nf (en muro)* opening, gap; *Mil & Fig* breach; *Fig* **estar siempre en la b.** to be always in the thick of things

brécol *nm* broccoli

bregar [42] *vi* to fight

Bretaña *nf* (**a**) *(francesa)* Brittany (**b**) **Gran B.** Great Britain

brete *nm* **poner a algn en un b.** to put sb in a tight spot

bretel *nm CSur* strap; **un vestido sin breteles** a strapless dress

breva *nf* (**a**) *(fruta)* early fig (**b**) *Esp Fam* **¡no caerá esa b.!** some chance (of that happening)!

breve *adj* brief; **en b., en breves momentos** shortly, soon; **en breves palabras** in short

brevedad *nf* briefness; *(concisión)* brevity; **con la mayor b. posible** as soon as possible

brevet *nm Chile (de avión)* pilot's licence; *Bol, Ecuad, Perú (de automóvil) Br* driving licence, *US* driver's license; *RP (de velero)* sailor's licence

brezo *nm* heather

bribón, -ona 1 *adj* roguish, dishonest
2 *nm,f* rogue, rascal

bricolaje *nm Br* DIY, do-it-yourself, *US* home improvement

brida *nf* (**a**) *(rienda)* rein, bridle (**b**) *Téc* flange

bridge [britʃ] *nm Naipes* bridge

brigada 1 *nf* (**a**) *Mil* brigade (**b**) *(de policías)* squad; **b. antiterrorista** antiterrorist squad
2 *nm Mil* sergeant major

brillante 1 *adj* (**a**) *(reluciente) (luz, astro)* shining; *(metal, zapatos, pelo)* shiny; *(ojos, joyas)* sparkling (**b**) *(magnífico)* brilliant
2 *nm* diamond

brillantez *nf* brilliance

brillantina *nf* brilliantine

brillar *vi (resplandecer)* to shine; *(ojos, joyas)* to sparkle; *(lentejuelas etc)* to glitter; **b. por su ausencia** to be conspicuous by one's absence

brillo *nm (resplandor)* shine; *(del sol, de la luna)* brightness; *(de lentejuelas etc)* glittering; *(del cabello, tela)* sheen; *(de color)* brilliance; *(de pantalla)* brightness; *(de zapatos)* shine; **sacar b. a** to shine, to polish

brilloso, -a *adj Am* shining

brincar [44] *vi* to skip

brinco *nm* skip

brindar 1 *vi* to drink a toast; **b. por algn/ algo** to drink to sb/sth
2 *vt* (**a**) *(oportunidad)* to offer, to provide (**b**) *Taurom* to dedicate (**a** to)
3 brindarse *vpr* to offer (**a** to), to volunteer (**a** to)

brindis *nm inv* (**a**) *(con bebida)* toast (**b**) *Taurom* dedication (of the bull)

brío *nm* energy

brioso, -a *adj* energetic, vigorous

brisa *nf* breeze; **b. marina** sea breeze

británico, -a 1 *adj* British; **las Islas Británicas** the British Isles
2 *nm,f* Briton; **los británicos** the British

brizna *nf* *(de hierba)* blade; *(de carne)* string

broca *nf* *Téc* bit

brocha *nf* *(para pintar)* paintbrush; **b. de afeitar** shaving brush

broche *nm* **(a)** *(joya)* brooch; *Fig* **poner el b. de oro** to finish with a flourish **(b)** *(de vestido)* fastener

brocheta *nf* *Culin* shish kebab; *(aguja)* skewer

brócoli *nm* broccoli

broma *nf* *(chiste)* joke; **bromas aparte** joking apart; **en b.** as a joke; **¡ni en b.!** not on your life!; **b. pesada** practical joke; **gastar una b.** to play a joke

bromear *vi* to joke

bromista 1 *adj* fond of joking *o* playing jokes
2 *nmf* joker, prankster

bronca *nf* **(a)** *(jaleo)* row; **armar (una) b.** to kick up a row **(b)** *Esp (crítica)* scolding, telling-off; **echar una b. a algn** to bawl sb out **(c)** *RP Fam (rabia)* **me da b.** it hacks me off; **el jefe le tiene b.** the boss can't stand him

bronce *nm* bronze

bronceado, -a 1 *adj* suntanned, tanned
2 *nm* suntan, tan

bronceador, -a 1 *adj* **leche bronceadora** suntan cream
2 *nm* suntan cream *o* lotion

broncearse *vpr* to get a tan *o* a suntan

bronco, -a *adj* rough, coarse

bronquio *nm* bronchial tube

bronquitis *nf inv* bronchitis

brotar *vi* *(planta)* to sprout; *(agua)* to spring, to gush; *(lágrimas)* to well up; *(epidemia)* to break out

brote *nm* **(a)** *Bot (renuevo)* bud, shoot; *(de agua)* gushing **(b)** *(de epidemia, violencia)* outbreak

bruces: de bruces *loc adv* face down; **se cayó de b.** he fell flat on his face

bruja *nf* witch, sorceress

brujería *nf* witchcraft, sorcery

brujo 1 *nm* wizard, sorcerer
2 *adj* *Méx Fam* broke; **estar b.** to be broke

brújula *nf* compass

bruma *nf* mist

brumoso, -a *adj* misty

bruñir *vt* to polish

brusco, -a *adj* **(a)** *(persona)* brusque, abrupt **(b)** *(repentino)* sudden, sharp

Bruselas *n* Brussels

brusquedad *nf* brusqueness, abruptness

brutal *adj* brutal

brutalidad *nf* brutality

bruto, -a 1 *adj* **(a)** *(necio)* stupid, thick; *(grosero)* coarse, uncouth **(b)** *Fin* gross; **peso b.** gross weight **(c)** **un diamante en b.** an uncut diamond
2 *nm,f* blockhead, brute

bucear *vi* to swim under water

buche *nm* maw; *(de ave)* craw; *Fam (estómago)* belly, stomach

bucle *nm* curl, ringlet

bucólico, -a *adj* **(a)** *(campestre)* **un paisaje b.** a charmingly rural landscape **(b)** *Lit* bucolic

budín *nm* pudding

budismo *nm* Buddhism

budista *adj & nmf* Buddhist

buen *adj* good; *ver* **bueno**

buenamente *adv* **haz lo que b. puedas** just do what you can; **si b. puedes** if you possibly can

buenaventura *nf* good fortune, good luck; **echar la b. a algn** to tell sb's fortune

bueno, -a

> grammar note: **buen** is used instead of **bueno** before masculine singular nouns (e.g. **buen hombre** good man). The comparative form of **bueno** is **mejor** (better), and the superlative form is **el mejor** (masculine) or **la mejor** (feminine) (the best).

1 *adj* **(a)** *(en calidad)* good; **un alumno muy b.** a very good pupil; **una buena película** a good movie *o Br* film; **lo b.** the good thing
(b) *(amable) (con ser)* good, kind; **es muy buena persona** he's a very kind soul
(c) *(sano) (con estar)* well, in good health
(d) *(tiempo)* good; **hoy hace buen tiempo** it's fine today; **mañana hará b.** it will be fine *o* a nice day tomorrow
(e) *(conveniente)* good; **no es b. comer tanto** it's not good for you to eat so much; **sería b. que vinieras** it would be a good idea if you came
(f) *(considerable)* considerable; **un buen número de** a good number of; **una buena cantidad** a considerable amount
(g) *(grande)* good, big; **un buen trozo de pastel** a nice *o* good big piece of cake
(h) *Fam (atractivo)* gorgeous, sexy; **Rosa está muy buena** Rosa's a bit of all right!; **una tía buena** a good-looking girl
(i) *Irón* fine, real, proper; **¡en buen lío te**

has metido! that's a fine mess you've got yourself into!

(**j**) **¡buenas!** (*saludos*) hello!; **buenas tardes** (*desde mediodía hasta las cinco*) good afternoon; (*desde las cinco*) good evening; **buenas noches** (*al llegar*) good evening; (*al irse*) good night; **buenos días** good morning

(**k**) (*locuciones*) **de buenas a primeras** suddenly, all at once; **estar de buenas** to be in a good mood; **los buenos tiempos** the good old days; **por las buenas** willingly; **por las buenas o por las malas** willy-nilly; *Irón* **¡buena la has hecho!** that's done it!; **un susto de los buenos** a real fright; *Irón* **¡estaría b.!** I should jolly well hope not!; *Irón* **librarse de una buena** to get off scot-free

2 *nm,f* **el b. de Carlos** good old Carlos

3 *interj* (**a**) (*vale*) all right, OK (**b**) (*expresa sorpresa*) hey! (**c**) *Col, Méx* (*al teléfono*) hello

buey (*pl* **bueyes**) *nm* ox, bullock

búfalo, -a *nm,f* buffalo

bufanda *nf* scarf

bufar *vi* (**a**) (*toro*) to snort; (*gato*) to hiss (**b**) (*persona*) to be fuming

bufé *nm* buffet; **b. libre** self-service buffet meal

bufete *nm* (*de abogado*) lawyer's office

buffet (*pl* **buffets**) *nm* = **bufé**

bufido *nm* (*de toro*) snort; (*de gato*) hiss

bufón *nm* clown, buffoon

buhardilla *nf* attic, garret

búho *nm* owl; **b. real** eagle owl

buhonero, -a *nm,f* pedlar, hawker

buitre *nm* vulture

bujía *nf* (**a**) *Aut* spark plug (**b**) *Fís* candlepower

bula *nf* (*documento*) (papal) bull

bulbo *nm* bulb

buldog (*pl* **buldogs**) *nm* bulldog

bulerías *nfpl* = popular Andalusian song and dance

bulevar *nm* boulevard

Bulgaria *n* Bulgaria

búlgaro, -a *adj & nm,f* Bulgarian

bulín *nm RP Fam* (*picadero*) bachelor pad

bulla *nf Fam* (**a**) (*ruido*) racket, uproar; **armar b.** to kick up a racket (**b**) *Esp* (*prisa*) **meter b. a algn** to hurry sb up

bullicio *nm* (*de ciudad, mercado*) hustle and bustle; (*de multitud*) hubbub

bullicioso, -a 1 *adj* (**a**) (*agitado*) (*reunión, multitud*) noisy; (*calle, mercado*) busy, bustling (**b**) (*inquieto*) rowdy, boisterous

2 *nm,f* boisterous person

bullir *vi* (**a**) (*hervir*) to boil, to bubble (up) (**b**) **b. de gente** to be teeming with people

bulto *nm* (**a**) (*cosa indistinta*) shape, form (**b**) (*maleta, caja*) piece of luggage (**c**) *Med* lump (**d**) **hacer mucho b.** to be very bulky; *Fam* **escurrir el b.** to pass the buck

bumerán *nm* boomerang

bungalow [bunga'lo] (*pl* **bungalows**) *nm* bungalow

búnker (*pl* **bunkeres**) *nm* (**a**) (*refugio*) bunker (**b**) *Esp Pol* reactionary forces

buñuelo *nm* doughnut

BUP *nm Antes* (*abr* **Bachillerato Unificado Polivalente**) = academically orientated Spanish secondary school course for pupils aged 14–17

buque *nm* ship; **b. de guerra** warship; **b. de pasajeros** liner, passenger ship; **b. insignia** flagship

burbuja *nf* bubble; **hacer burbujas** to bubble, make bubbles

burbujear *vi* to bubble

burdel *nm* brothel

Burdeos *n* Bordeaux

burdo, -a *adj* coarse, rough

burgalés, -esa 1 *adj* of/from Burgos

2 *nm,f* person from Burgos

burgués, -esa *adj & nm,f* bourgeois

burguesía *nf* bourgeoisie

burla *nf* gibe, jeer; **hacer b. de algo/algn** to make fun of sth/sb; **hacer b. a algn** to stick one's tongue out at sb

burladero *nm Taurom* = refuge in bullring

burlar 1 *vt* (**a**) (*engañar*) to deceive (**b**) (*eludir*) to dodge, to evade

2 burlarse *vpr* to make fun (**de** of), to laugh (**de** at)

burlón, -ona *adj* mocking

buró *nm* (**a**) *Pol* executive committee (**b**) (*escritorio*) bureau, desk (**c**) *Méx* (*mesa de noche*) bedside table

burocracia *nf* bureaucracy

burócrata *nmf* bureaucrat

burocrático, -a *adj* bureaucratic

burrada *nf* (*comentario*) stupid *o* foolish remark; (*hecho*) stupid *o* foolish act

burro, -a 1 *nm,f* (**a**) (*animal*) donkey, ass; *Fam Fig* **bajarse del b.** to climb *o* back down (**b**) *Fam* (*estúpido*) dimwit, block-head (**c**) **b. de carga** dogsbody, drudge

2 *adj Fam* (**a**) (*necio*) stupid, dumb (**b**) (*obstinado*) stubborn

bursátil *adj* stock-market

bus *nm* bus

busca 1 *nf* search; **ir en b. de** to go in search of

2 *nm Esp* (*buscapersonas*) pager

buscador, -a 1 *nm,f (en general)* hunter; **b. de oro** gold prospector
  2 *nm Inform (en Internet)* search engine

buscapersonas *nm inv* pager

buscapleitos *nmf inv* troubleseeker

buscar [44] **1** *vt* to look *o* search for; **b. una palabra en el diccionario** to look up a word in the dictionary; **ir a b. algo** to go and get sth, to fetch sth; **fue a buscarme a la estación** she picked me up at the station
  2 buscarse *upr Fam* **buscarse la vida** to try and earn one's living; *Fam* **te la estás buscando** you're asking for it; **se busca** *(en anuncios)* wanted

buseta *nf Col, CRica, Ecuad, Ven* minibus

búsqueda *nf* search, quest; *Inform* search

busto *nm* bust

butaca *nf* (**a**) *(sillón)* armchair, easy chair (**b**) *Cin & Teatro* seat; **b. de platea** *o* **patio** seat in the stalls

butano *nm* butane; **(gas) b.** butane gas

butifarra *nf* sausage

buzo *nm* (**a**) *(persona)* diver (**b**) *Arg (sudadera)* sweatshirt (**c**) *Col, Urug (jersey)* sweater, *Br* jumper

buzón *nm* post box, *Br* letter box, *US* mailbox; *Inform (de correo electrónico)* (electronic) mailbox; **echar una carta al b.** to *Br* post *o US* mail a letter; **b. de entrada** in-box; **b. de voz** voice mail

bypass [bai'pas] *nm inv Med* heart bypass operation

byte [bait] *nm Inform* byte

C

C, c [θe] *nf* (*letra*) C, c

C (a) (*abr* **Celsius**) C (b) (*abr* **centígrado**) C

C., Cª (*abr* **compañía**) Co

c (a) (*abr* **calle**) St (b) (*abr* **cargo**) cargo, freight (c) (*abr* **cuenta**) a/c

cabal 1 *adj* (a) (*exacto*) exact, precise (b) (*honesto*) honest, upright
  2 cabales *nmpl Fam* **no está en sus cabales** he's not in his right mind

cábala *nf Fig* **hacer cábalas sobre algo** to speculate about sth

cabalgadura *nf* mount

cabalgar [42] *vt & vi* to ride

cabalgata *nf* cavalcade; **la c. de los Reyes Magos** the procession of the Three Wise Men

caballa *nf* mackerel

caballar *adj* **ganado c.** horses

caballería *nf* (a) (*cabalgadura*) mount, steed (b) *Mil* cavalry

caballeriza *nf* stable

caballero *nm* (a) (*hombre*) gentleman; **¿qué desea, c.?** can I help you, sir?; **ropa de c.** menswear (b) *Hist* knight (c) **caballeros** (*en letrero*) gents

caballeroso, -a *adj* gentlemanly, chivalrous

caballete *nm* (a) (*de pintor*) easel (b) *Téc* trestle (c) (*de nariz*) bridge

caballito *nm* (a) **c. de mar** seahorse (b) **caballitos** merry-go-round, *US* carousel

caballo *nm* (a) (*animal*) horse; **a c.** on horseback; **montar a c.** to ride; *Fig* **a c. entre ...** halfway between ... (b) *Téc* **c. de vapor** horse power (c) (*pieza de ajedrez*) knight (d) *Naipes* queen (e) *Fam* (*heroína*) horse, smack

cabaña *nf* cabin

cabaret (*pl* **cabarets**) *nm* cabaret

cabecear 1 *vi* to nod
  2 *vt Dep* to head

cabecera *nf* (a) (*de fila, mesa*) head; (*de cama*) headboard (b) *Esp* (*de texto*) heading; (*de periódico*) masthead

cabecilla *nmf* leader

cabellera *nf* head of hair

cabello *nm* hair; *Culin* **c. de ángel** = sweet made of gourd and syrup

cabelludo, -a *adj* **cuero c.** scalp

caber [9] *vi* (a) (*haber espacio para*) to fit; **cabe en el maletero** it fits in the *Br* boot o *US* trunk; **¿cabemos todos?** is there room for all of us?; **en este coche/jarro caben ...** this car/jug holds ...; **no cabe por la puerta** it won't go through the door (b) (*expresiones*) **no c. en sí de gozo** to be beside oneself with joy; **no me cabe en la cabeza** I can't understand it; **no cabe duda** there is no doubt; **cabe la posibilidad de que ...** there is a possibility o chance that ...; **no está mal, dentro de lo que cabe** it isn't bad, under the circumstances; **cabe señalar que ...** we should point out that ... (c) *Mat* **doce entre cuatro caben a tres** four into twelve goes three (times)

cabestrillo *nm* sling

cabeza 1 *nf* head; **en c.** in the lead; **por c.** a head, per person; *Fig* **a la c. de** at the front o top of; *Fig* **estar mal de la c.** to be a mental case; **c. de turco** scapegoat; **el o la c. de familia** the head of the family
  2 *nm* **c. rapada** skinhead

cabezada *nf* (a) (*golpe*) butt, blow on the head (b) *Fam* **echar una c.** to have a snooze; **dar cabezadas** to nod

cabezal *nm* (a) (*de aparato*) head (b) (*almohada*) bolster

cabezazo *nm* (*con la cabeza*) headbutt; (*en la cabeza*) blow o bump on the head; *Dep* header

cabezón, -ona *Fam* **1** *adj* (a) (*persona*) **ser c.** (*de cabeza grande*) to have a big head; (*terco*) to be pigheaded (b) *Fam* (*vino*) rough
  2 *nm,f* pigheaded person

cabezota *Fam* **1** *adj* pigheaded
  2 *nmf* pigheaded person

cabezudo *nm* = carnival figure with a huge head

cabida *nf* capacity; **dar c. a** to leave room for

cabildo *nm* (a) (*municipio*) ≃ district council (b) *Rel* chapter

cabina *nf* cabin; **c. telefónica** (*con puerta*) *Br* phone box, *US* phone booth

cabinero, -a *nm,f Col* flight attendant

cabizbajo, -a *adj* crestfallen

cable *nm* cable; *Fam* **echarle un c. a algn** to give sb a hand

cableoperador *nm* cable company, cable operator

cabo *nm* (a) *(extremo)* end; **al c. de** after; **de c. a rabo** from start to finish (b) *Mil* corporal; *(policía)* sergeant (c) *Náut* rope, cable; *Fig* **atar cabos** to put two and two together; *Fig* **no dejar ningún c. suelto** to leave no loose ends (d) *Geog* cape; **Ciudad del C.** Cape Town; **C. Verde** Cape Verde

cabra *nf* goat; *Fam* **estar como una c.** to be off one's head

cabré *indic fut de* **caber**

cabreado, -a *adj muy Fam Br* pissed off, *US* pissed

cabrear *muy Fam* **1** *vt* to make angry, *Br* to piss off
  2 cabrearse *vpr* to get *Br* pissed off *o US* pissed

cabreo *nm muy Fam* rage, fit; **agarrar** *o Esp* **coger un c.** to get really *Br* narked *o US* pissed

cabrío, -a *adj* **macho c.** billy goat; **ganado c.** goats

cabriola *nf* skip

cabrito *nm Zool* kid

cabro, -a *nm,f Chile Fam* kid

cabrón, -ona *nm,f Vulg* bastard, *f* bitch, *US* asshole

cabronada *nf muy Fam* dirty trick

cabuya *nf* (a) *(planta)* agave (b) *(fibra)* fibre hemp (c) *CAm, Col, Ven (cuerda)* rope

caca *nf Fam Br* poo, *US* poop

cacahuete, *CAm, Méx* **cacahuate** *nm* peanut, *US* groundnut

cacao *nm* (a) *Bot* cacao (b) *(polvo, bebida)* cocoa (c) *Fam (lío)* mess

cacarear 1 *vi (gallina)* to cluck
  2 *vt Fig* to boast about

cacareo *nm (de gallina)* clucking

cacatúa *nf* (a) *(ave)* cockatoo (b) *Fam (mujer vieja)* old bat

cacereño, -a 1 *adj* of/from Cáceres
  2 *nm,f* person from Cáceres

cacería *nf* (a) *(actividad)* hunting, shooting (b) *(partida)* hunt, shoot

cacerola *nf* saucepan

cacha *nf Fam (muslo)* thigh; *Esp* **estar cachas** to be well-built

cachalote *nm* sperm whale

cacharro *nm* (a) *(recipiente)* pot; **cacharros** *(de cocina)* pots and pans (b) *Fam (trasto)* thing, piece of junk

caché *nm Inform* **(memoria) c.** cache memory

cachear *vt* to frisk, to search

cachemir *nm,* **cachemira** *nf* cashmere

cacheo *nm* frisk, frisking

cachetada *nf* slap

cachete *nm* (a) *(bofetada)* slap (b) *Am (mejilla)* cheek

cachila *nf RP (automóvil)* vintage car

cachimba *nf* (a) *(pipa)* pipe (b) *RP (pozo)* well

cachiporra *nf* club, truncheon

cachivache *nm Fam* thing, knick-knack

cacho¹ *nm Fam (pedazo)* bit, piece; *Esp* **¡c. tonto!** you idiot!

cacho² *nm* (a) *Andes, Ven (asta)* horn (b) *Andes, Guat, Ven (cuento)* story; **no me vengan a contar cachos, que sé lo que pasó** don't start telling me stories, I know what happened (c) *Andes, Guat, Ven (burla)* joke

cachondearse *vpr Esp Fam* **c. de algn** to make a fool out of sb, *Br* to take the mickey out of sb

cachondeo *nm Esp Fam* **ser un c.** to be a laugh; **tomarse algo a c.** to take sth as a joke

cachondo, -a *adj* (a) *Esp, Méx muy Fam (sexualmente)* **estar c.** to be randy; **ponerse c.** to get randy *o* turned on (b) *Esp Fam (divertido)* **ser c.** to be funny

cachorro, -a *nm,f (de perro)* pup, puppy; *(de gato)* kitten; *(de otros animales)* cub, baby

cacique *nm (jefe)* local boss

caco *nm Fam* thief

cacofonía *nf* cacophony

cacto *nm,* **cactus** *nm inv Bot* cactus

cada *adj (de dos)* each; *(de varios)* each, every; **c. día** every day; **c. dos días** every second day; **c. vez más** more and more; **¿c. cuánto?** how often?; **c. dos por tres** every other minute; **cuatro de c. diez** four out of (every) ten; **¡tienes c. cosa!** you come up with some fine ideas!

cadalso *nm* scaffold

cadáver *nm (de persona)* corpse, (dead) body; *(de animal)* body, carcass; **ingresar c.** to be dead on arrival

cadena *nf* (a) *(de eslabones, tiendas)* chain; *(correa de perro)* lead, leash; *Aut* **cadenas** tyre chains (b) *TV* channel (c) *(de proceso industrial)* line; **c. de montaje** assembly line; **trabajo en c.** assembly line work (d) *Geog* **c. montañosa** mountain range (e) *Der* **c. perpetua** life imprisonment

cadencia *nf* rhythm; *Mús* cadenza

cadera *nf* hip

cadete 1 *nm* (*en ejército*) cadet
2 *nm,f RP* (*chico de los recados*) office junior

caducar [44] *vi* to expire

caducidad *nf* expiry; **fecha de c.** (*en alimento, medicamento*) use-by date

caduco, -a *adj* (a) *Bot* deciduous (b) (*anticuado*) out-of-date

caer [39] **1** *vi* (a) (*hacia abajo*) to fall; **dejar c.** to drop; *Fig* **está al c.** (*llegar*) he'll arrive any minute now; (*ocurrir*) it's on the way (b) (*fecha*) to be; **su cumpleaños cae en sábado** his birthday falls on a Saturday (c) (*entender*) to see, to understand; **ya caigo** I get it; **no caí** I didn't twig (d) *Esp* (*estar, quedar*) **cae cerca de aquí** it's not far from here (e) **me cae bien/mal** I like/don't like her (f) **al c. el día** in the evening; **al c. la noche** at nightfall
2 caerse *vpr* to fall (down); **me caí de la moto** I fell off the motorbike; **se le cayó el pañuelo** he dropped his handkerchief

café *nm* (a) (*bebida*) coffee; **c. con leche** white coffee; *Esp* **c. solo**, *Andes,Ven* **c. tinto** black coffee (b) (*cafetería*) café

cafeína *nf* caffeine

cafetal *nm* coffee plantation

cafetera *nf* coffee-maker

cafetería *nf* snack bar, coffee bar; *Ferroc* buffet car

cafetero, -a *adj* (a) (*de café*) coffee (b) *Fam* **es muy c.** (*persona*) he loves coffee

cafiche *nm Andes Fam* pimp

cafre *nmf* savage, beast

cagado, -a *adj muy Fam* (*cobarde*) chicken, coward; **estar c. de miedo** to be shit-scared

cagar [42] *Fam* **1** *vi* to shit, to crap
2 cagarse *upr* to crap oneself; **cagarse de miedo** to be shit-scared

caída *nf* (a) (*de persona, objeto*) fall; (*de pelo, diente*) loss (b) (*de precios*) drop (c) (*de tela, vestido*) drape (d) *Pol* downfall, collapse

caído, -a 1 *adj* fallen
2 *nmpl* **los caídos** the fallen

caigo *indic pres de* **caer**

caimán *nm* alligator

Cairo *n* **El C.** Cairo

caja *nf* (a) (*recipiente*) box; (*de leche etc*) carton; **c. fuerte** safe; *Fam TV* **la c. tonta** the box, *Br* the telly, *US* the boob tube (b) (*de embalaje*) crate, case; **una c. de cerveza** a crate of beer (c) *Fin* (*en tienda*) cash desk; (*en banco*) cashier's desk (d) *Aut* **c. de cambios** gearbox (e) *Esp* (*entidad financiera*) **c. de ahorros** savings bank (f) (*féretro*) coffin

cajero, -a *nm,f* cashier; **c. automático** cash point, cash dispenser

cajetilla *nf* packet, pack

cajón *nm* (a) (*en un mueble*) drawer; *Fig* **c. de sastre** jumble; *Fam* **de c.** obvious, self-evident (b) (*caja grande*) crate, chest

cajuela *nf CAm, Méx* (*maletero*) *Br* boot, *US* trunk

cal¹ *nf* lime; *Fig* **a c. y canto** hermetically; *Fam* **una de c. y otra de arena** six of one and half a dozen of the other

cal² (*abr* **caloría**) cal

cala *nf* (a) *Geog* creek, cove (b) *Náut* hold

calabacín *nm Bot* (a) (*pequeño*) *Br* courgette, *US* zucchini (b) (*grande*) *Br* marrow, *US* squash

calabaza *nf* pumpkin, gourd

calabobos *nm inv Fam* drizzle

calabozo *nm* (a) (*prisión*) jail, prison (b) (*celda*) cell

calada *nf Esp Fam* (*de cigarrillo*) drag, puff

calado, -a 1 *adj* soaked
2 *nm Náut* draught

calamar *nm* squid *inv*; *Culin* **calamares a la romana** squid rings fried in batter

calambre *nm* (a) *Elec* (*descarga*) electric shock; **ese cable da c.** that wire is live (b) (*en músculo*) cramp

calamidad *nf* calamity

calaña *nf Pey* **de esa c.** of that ilk

calar 1 *vt* (a) (*mojar*) to soak, to drench (b) (*agujerear*) to pierce, to penetrate
2 *vi* (a) (*prenda*) to let in water (b) *Náut* to draw
3 calarse *upr* (a) (*prenda, techo*) to let in water; (*mojarse*) to get soaked (b) (*el sombrero*) to pull down (c) *Esp* (*motor*) to stall

calavera 1 *nf* (a) (*cráneo*) skull (b) *Méx Aut* **calaveras** tail lights
2 *nm* tearaway

calcar [44] *vt* (a) (*un dibujo*) to trace (b) *Fig* (*imitar*) to copy, to imitate

calceta *nf* **hacer c.** to knit

calcetín *nm* sock

calcinar *vt* to burn

calcio *nm* calcium

calco *nm* (a) (*reproducción*) tracing; **papel de c.** carbon paper (b) (*imitación*) carbon copy; **es un c. de** it's a carbon copy of (c) *Ling* calque, loan translation

calcomanía *nf* transfer

calculador, -a *adj también Fig* calculating

calculadora *nf* calculator

calcular *vt* (a) *Mat* to calculate (b) (*evaluar*) to (make an) estimate (c) (*suponer*) to figure, to guess

cálculo *nm* (**a**) *(operación)* calculation; **según mis cálculos** by my reckoning; **hacer cálculos mentales** to do mental arithmetic (**b**) *Med* gallstone (**c**) *Mat (ciencia)* calculus

caldear *vt* to heat up

caldera *nf* (**a**) *(industrial)* boiler; *(olla)* cauldron (**b**) *Urug (hervidor)* kettle

caldereta *nf* stew

calderilla *nf* small change

caldo *nm* stock, broth; **c. de cultivo** culture medium; *Fig* breeding ground

calé *adj & nm* gypsy

calefacción *nf* heating; **c. central** central heating

calefaccionar *vt CSur (calentar)* to heat (up), to warm (up)

calefactor *nm* heater

calefón *nm CSur (calentador)* water heater

caleidoscopio *nm* kaleidoscope

calendario *nm* calendar

calentador *nm* heater

calentamiento *nm Dep* warm-up; **c. global** global warming

calentar [1] **1** *vt* (**a**) *(agua, horno)* to heat; *(comida, habitación)* to warm up; *Fig* **no me calientes la cabeza** don't bug me (**b**) *Fam (pegar)* to smack (**c**) *Fam (excitar)* to arouse (sexually), to turn on
  2 calentarse *vpr* (**a**) *(por calor) (persona)* to warm oneself, to get warm; *(cosa)* to heat up (**b**) *Fam (agitarse)* to get angry *o* annoyed (**c**) *Fig* **se calentaron los ánimos** people became very excited

calentura *nf* (**a**) *(fiebre)* fever, temperature (**b**) *(herida)* cold sore

calesita *nf RP* merry-go-round, *US* carousel

calibrar *vt* to gauge, to bore

calibre *nm* (**a**) *(de arma)* calibre (**b**) *Fig (importancia)* importance

calidad *nf* (**a**) quality; **de primera c.** first-class; **un vino de c.** a good-quality wine (**b**) **en c. de** as

cálido, -a *adj* warm; **una cálida acogida** a warm welcome

calidoscopio *nm* = caleidoscopio

caliente *adj* (**a**) *(a alta temperatura)* hot; *(templado)* warm (**b**) *Fig (debate)* heated; **en c.** in the heat of the moment (**c**) *Fam (cachondo)* hot, randy

calificación *nf Educ Br* mark, *US* grade

calificar [44] *vt* (**a**) *(llamar)* to describe (**de** as); **le calificó de inmoral** he called him immoral (**b**) *(examen) Br* to mark, *US* to grade

calificativo *nm* epithet

caligrafía *nf* calligraphy; *(modo de escribir)* handwriting

calima *nf* haze, mist

calimocho *nm Esp Fam* = drink made with wine and Coca-Cola®

calina *nf* = calima

cáliz *nm* chalice

caliza *nf* limestone

calizo, -a *adj* lime

callado, -a *adj* quiet; **te lo tenías muy c.** you were keeping that quiet

callar 1 *vi* (**a**) *(dejar de hablar)* to stop talking; **¡calla!** be quiet!, *Fam* shut up! (**b**) *(no hablar)* to keep quiet, to say nothing
  2 *vt (noticia)* not to mention, to keep to oneself
  3 callarse *vpr* to stop talking, to be quiet; **¡cállate!** shut up!

calle *nf* (**a**) *(en población)* street, road; **c. de dirección única** one-way street; **c. mayor** *Br* high street, *US* main street; **el hombre de la c.** the man in the street (**b**) *Esp Dep* lane

calleja *nf* narrow street

callejero, -a 1 *nm (mapa)* street directory
  2 *adj (perro)* **gato c.** alley cat

callejón *nm* back alley *o* street; **c. sin salida** cul-de-sac, dead end

callejuela *nf* narrow street, lane

callista *nmf* chiropodist

callo *nm* (**a**) *Med* callus, corn; *Fam* **dar el c.** to slog (**b**) *Esp Culin* **callos** tripe

calma *nf* calm; **¡con c.!** calm down!; **en c.** calm; **tómatelo con c.** take it easy

calmante *nm* painkiller

calmar 1 *vt (persona)* to calm (down); *(dolor)* to soothe, to relieve
  2 calmarse *vpr* (**a**) *(persona)* to calm down (**b**) *(dolor, viento)* to ease off

caló *nm Esp* gypsy dialect

calor *nm* (**a**) *(temperatura)* heat; **hace c.** it's hot; **tengo c.** I'm hot; **entrar en c.** to warm up (**b**) *Fig (afecto)* warmth

caloría *nf* calorie

calote *nm RP Fam* swindle

calumnia *nf (oral)* slander; *(escrita)* libel

calumniar [43] *vt (de palabra)* to slander; *(por escrito)* to libel

calumnioso, -a *adj (de palabra)* slanderous; *(por escrito)* libellous

caluroso, -a *adj* hot; *(acogida etc)* warm

calva *nf* bald patch

calvario *nm (vía crucis)* Calvary, stations of the Cross; *Fig (sufrimiento)* ordeal

calvicie *nf* baldness

calvinismo *nm* Calvinism

calvo, -a 1 *adj* bald; **ni tanto ni tan c.** there's no need to go to extremes
2 *nm* bald man

calza *nf* (a) *(cuña)* wedge (b) *Col (en diente)* filling

calzada *nf* road (surface), *US* pavement

calzado *nm* shoes, footwear

calzador *nm* shoehorn

calzar [40] **1** *vt* (a) *(poner calzado)* to put shoes on; **¿qué número calzas?** what size shoe do you take? (b) *(mueble)* to wedge
2 calzarse *upr* **calzarse los zapatos** to put on one's shoes

calzón *nm* (a) *Esp Dep* shorts (b) *Andes, Méx, RP (bragas)* panties, *Br* knickers; **un c., unos calzones** a pair of panties *o Br* knickers (c) *Bol, Méx* **calzones** *(calzoncillos) Br* underpants, *US* shorts

calzonazos *nm inv Fam* henpecked husband

calzoncillos *nmpl* *(slip)* briefs, *Br* (under)pants, *US* shorts; *(bóxer)* boxer shorts

calzoneta *nm CAm* swimming trunks

cama *nf* bed; **estar en** *o* **guardar c.** to be confined to bed; **hacer la c.** to make the bed; **irse a la c.** to go to bed; **c. doble/ individual** double/single bed; **c. turca** couch

camada *nf* litter

camafeo *nm* cameo

camaleón *nm* chameleon

cámara 1 *nf* (a) *(aparato)* camera; **a c. lenta** in slow motion; **c. de vídeo** video camera; **c. web** webcam, webcam (b) *Pol* Chamber, House; **C. Alta/Baja** Upper/ Lower House (c) *Aut* inner tube (d) *(habitación)* room, chamber; **c. de gas** gas chamber; **c. frigorífica** cold-storage room; **música de c.** chamber music
2 *nmf (hombre)* cameraman; *(mujer)* camerawoman

camarada *nmf* comrade

camaradería *nf* camaraderie

camarera *nf (de hotel)* chambermaid

camarero, -a *nm,f* *(de restaurante) (hombre)* waiter; *(mujer)* waitress; *(tras la barra) (hombre)* barman; *(mujer)* barmaid

camarilla *nf* clique

camarón *nm Br* shrimp, *US* prawn

camarote *nm* cabin

camastro *nm* ramshackle bed

camba *Bol Fam* **1** *adj* of/from the forested lowland region of Bolivia
2 *nmf* person from the forested lowland region of Bolivia

cambalache *nm RP (tienda)* junk shop

cambiante *adj* changing; *(carácter)* changeable

cambiar [43] **1** *vt* (a) *(modificar, reemplazar)* to change; *(trasladar)* to move; **c. algo de sitio** to move sth (b) *(intercambiar)* to swap, to exchange (c) *(dinero)* to change
2 *vi* to change; **c. de casa** to move (house); **c. de idea** to change one's mind; **c. de trabajo** to get another job; **c. de velocidad** to change gear
3 cambiarse *upr* (a) *(de ropa)* to change (clothes) (b) *(de casa)* to move (house)

cambiazo *nm Fam* switch

cambio 1 *nm* (a) *(modificación)* change; **c. de planes** change of plans; **un c. en la opinión pública** a shift in public opinion (b) *(dinero)* change; **¿tienes c. de cinco euros?** have you got change for five euros? (c) *Fin (de divisas)* exchange rate; *(de acciones)* price (d) *Aut* gear change; **c. automático** automatic transmission (e) *(reemplazo, trueque)* exchange; **a c. de** in exchange for
2 en cambio *loc adv* on the other hand

cambista *nmf* moneychanger

Camboya *n* Cambodia

camboyano, -a *adj & nm,f* Cambodian

cambur *nm Ven* banana

camelar *vt Fam* (a) *(convencer)* to cajole (b) *(galantear)* to win over

camelia *nf* camellia

camello, -a 1 *nm,f* camel
2 *nm Fam (traficante de drogas)* (drug) pusher

camellón *nm Col, Méx (en avenida) Br* central reservation, *US* median (strip)

camelo *nm Fam* (a) *(engaño)* hoax (b) *(trola)* cock-and-bull story

camembert ['kamember] *(pl camemberts) nm* camembert

camerino *nm* dressing room

Camerún *n* Cameroon

camilla *nf (con ruedas)* trolley; *(sin ruedas)* stretcher

camillero, -a *nm,f* stretcher-bearer

caminante *nmf* walker

caminar 1 *vi* to walk
2 *vt* to cover, to travel; **caminaron 10 km** they walked for 10 km

caminata *nf* long walk

camino *nm* (a) *(ruta)* route, way; **ir c. de** to be going to; **ponerse en c.** to set off; *Fig* **ir por buen/mal c.** to be on the right/wrong track; **abrirse c.** to break through; **a medio c.** half-way; **en el c.** on the way to; **estar en c.** to be on the way; **nos coge** *o* **pilla de c.** it's on the way (b) *(vía)* path, track (c) *(modo)* way

camión *nm* (a) *(de mercancías)* truck, *Br* lorry; **c. de la basura** *Br* dustcart, *US* garbage truck; **c. cisterna** tanker; **c. frigorífico** refrigerated truck (b) *CAm, Méx (autobús)* bus

camionero, -a *nm,f Br* lorry driver, *US* trucker

camioneta *nf* van

camisa *nf* shirt; **en mangas de c.** in one's shirtsleeves; *Fig* **cambiar de c.** to change sides; **c. de fuerza** straitjacket

camisería *nf (tienda)* shirt shop, outfitter's

camiseta *nf* (a) *(ropa interior) Br* vest, *US* undershirt (b) *(de manga corta)* T-shirt (c) *Dep (de tirantes)* vest; *(con mangas)* shirt; **sudar la c.** to run oneself into the ground

camisola *nf* (a) *(prenda interior)* camisole (b) *Dep* sports shirt

camisón *nm* nightdress; *Fam* nightie

camomila *nf* camomile

camorra *nf Fam* trouble

camorrista 1 *adj* quarrelsome, rowdy
2 *nmf* troublemaker

camote *nm* (a) *Andes, CAm, Méx (batata)* sweet potato; *(bulbo)* tuber, bulb (b) *Méx Fam (complicación)* mess

campal *adj* **batalla c.** pitched battle

campamento *nm* camp

campana *nf* bell; **pantalones de campana** bell-bottom trousers

campanada *nf* (a) *(de campana)* peal (b) *(de reloj)* stroke (c) *Fig (suceso)* sensation; **dar la c.** to make a big splash, to cause a sensation

campanario *nm* belfry, bell tower

campanilla *nf* (a) *(de puerta)* (small) bell (b) *Anat* uvula (c) *Bot* bell flower

campante *adj Fam* **se quedó tan c.** he didn't bat an eyelid

campaña *nf* (a) *(acción organizada)* campaign; **c. electoral** election campaign; **c. publicitaria** advertising campaign (b) *Mil* campaign; **hospital/ambulancia de c.** field hospital/ambulance (c) *RP (campo)* countryside

campar *vi Fam* **c. por sus respetos** to do as one pleases

campechano, -a *adj* unpretentious

campeón, -ona *nm,f* champion; **c. mundial** world champion

campeonato *nm* championship; **un tonto de c.** a prize idiot

campera *nf* (a) *Esp* **camperas** *(botas)* cowboy boots (b) *RP (chaqueta)* jacket

campero, -a 1 *adj Esp* **botas camperas** cowboy boots
2 *nm Andes* Jeep®

campesino, -a *nm,f (hombre)* countryman; *(mujer)* countrywoman

campestre *adj* rural

cámping ['kampin] *(pl* **cámpings)** *nm (terreno)* campsite, *US* campground; **hacer** *o* **ir de c.** to go camping

campiña *nf* countryside

campista *nmf* camper

campo *nm* (a) *(no ciudad)* country, countryside; **a c. traviesa** *o* **través** cross-country; **trabaja (en) el c.** he works (on) the land; **trabajo de c.** fieldwork (b) *Fís, Fot & Inform* field; **c. magnético** magnetic field (c) *(ámbito)* field; **c. de acción** field of action; *Mil* **c. de batalla** battlefield (d) *(campamento)* camp; **c. de concentración** concentration camp; **c. de trabajo** work camp (e) *Esp Dep (de fútbol)* field, *Br* pitch; *(de tenis)* court; *(de golf)* course (f) *Andes (sitio)* room, space; **hazme c. para que me siente** make some room so I can sit down

camposanto *nm* cemetery

campus *nm inv* campus

camuflaje *nm* camouflage

camuflar *vt* to camouflage

cana *nf (gris)* grey hair; *(blanco)* white hair; **tener canas** to have grey hair; *Fam* **echar una c. al aire** to let one's hair down

Canadá *n* Canada

canadiense *adj & nmf* Canadian

canal *nf* (a) *(artificial)* canal; *(natural)* channel; **C. de la Mancha** English Channel (b) *TV, Elec & Inform* channel

canalizar [40] *vt* to channel

canalla 1 *nm* swine, rotter
2 *nf* riffraff, mob

canallesco, -a *adj* rotten, despicable

canalón *nm (de tejado)* gutter; *(en la pared)* drainpipe

canapé *nm* (a) *Culin* canapé (b) *(sofá)* couch, sofa

Canarias *nfpl* **las C.** the Canary Islands, the Canaries

canario, -a 1 *adj & nm,f* Canarian; **Islas Canarias** Canary Islands, Canaries
2 *nm (ave)* canary

canasta *nf* basket

canastilla *nf* small basket; *(de un bebé)* layette

canasto *nm* big basket, hamper

cancán *nm* frilly petticoat; *RP* **cancanes** *(leotardos) Br* tights, *US* pantyhose *(plural)*

cancela *nf* wrought-iron gate

cancelación *nf* cancellation

cancelar *vt* (a) *(acto etc)* to cancel (b) *(deuda)* to pay off (c) *Chile, Ven (compra)* to pay for

Cáncer *nm* Cancer

cáncer *nm* cancer; **c. de pulmón/mama** lung/breast cancer

cancerbero, -a *nm,f Ftb* goalkeeper

cancerígeno, -a *adj* carcinogenic

canceroso, -a *adj (úlcera, tejido)* cancerous; *(enfermo)* suffering from cancer

cancha *nf* **(a)** *(de tenis, baloncesto, squash)* court; *Am (de fútbol)* field, *Br* pitch; *Am (de golf)* course; *Chile* **c. de aterrizaje** runway; *Am* **c. de carreras** racetrack **(b)** *Am (descampado)* open space, open ground; *(corral)* fenced yard **(c)** *Andes, PRico Fam (maíz)* toasted *Br* maize o *US* corn **(d)** *(expresiones)* **dar c. a algn** to give sb a chance; *RP* **tener c.** to be streetwise o savvy

canchero, -a *adj RP Fam* streetwise, savvy

canciller *nm* chancellor

cancillería *nf (de asuntos exteriores)* foreign ministry

canción *nf* song

cancionero *nm* songbook

candado *nm* padlock

candela *nf* fire

candelabro *nm* candelabrum

candelero *nm* candlestick; *Fig* **estar en c.** to be in the limelight

candente *adj* red-hot; *Fig* **tema c.** topical issue

candidato, -a *nm,f* candidate; *(a un puesto)* applicant

candidatura *nf* **(a)** *(lista)* list of candidates **(b)** **presentar su c.** to submit one's application

candidez *nf* candour

cándido, -a *adj* ingenuous, naive

> ⚠️ Observa que la palabra inglesa **candid** es un falso amigo y no es la traducción de la palabra española **cándido**. En inglés, **candid** significa "franco, sincero".

candil *nm* oil lamp; *Méx (candelabro)* chandelier

candilejas *nfpl Teatro* footlights

candor *nm* innocence, naivety

> ⚠️ Observa que la palabra inglesa **candour** es un falso amigo y no es la traducción de la palabra española **candor**. En inglés, **candour** significa "sinceridad, franqueza".

candoroso, -a *adj* innocent, pure

canela *nf* cinnamon

canelones *nmpl Culin* cannelloni

cangrejo *nm (de mar)* crab; *(de río)* freshwater crayfish

canguro 1 *nm* kangaroo
2 *nmf Esp Fam* baby-sitter

caníbal *adj & nmf* cannibal

canica *nf* marble

caniche *nm* poodle

canícula *nf* dog days, midsummer heat

canijo, -a *adj Fam* puny, weak

canilla *nf* **(a)** *Fam (espinilla)* shinbone **(b)** *RP (grifo) Br* tap, *US* faucet **(c)** *Méx (fuerza)* strength

canillera *nf Am (temblor de piernas)* **tenía c.** his legs were trembling o shaking

canillita *nm RP* newspaper vendor

canino, -a 1 *adj* canine; *Fam* **tener un hambre canina** to be starving
2 *nm (colmillo)* canine

canje *nm* exchange

canjeable *adj* exchangeable

canjear *vt* to exchange

cano, -a *adj (blanco)* white; *(gris)* grey

canoa *nf* canoe

canódromo *nm* dog o greyhound track

canon *nm* **(a)** *(norma)* canon, norm **(b)** *Mús & Rel* canon **(c)** *Com* royalty

canónico, -a *adj* canonical; *Der* **derecho c.** canon law

canónigo *nm* canon

canonizar [40] *vt* to canonize

canoso, -a *adj (de pelo blanco)* white-haired; *(de pelo gris)* grey-haired; *(pelo)* white, grey

cansado, -a *adj* **(a)** *(agotado)* tired, weary; **estar c.** to be tired **(b)** **ser c.** *(pesado)* to be boring o tiresome

cansador, -a *adj Andes, RP (que cansa)* tiring; *(que aburre)* boring

cansancio *nm* tiredness, weariness; *Fam* **estoy muerto de c.** I'm on my last legs

cansar 1 *vt* to tire
2 *vi* to be tiring
3 cansarse *vpr* to get tired; **se cansó de esperar** he got fed up (with) waiting

Cantabria *n* Cantabria

cantábrico, -a *adj* Cantabrian; **Mar C.** Bay of Biscay

cántabro, -a *adj & nm,f* Cantabrian

cantaleta *nf Am* **la misma c.** the same old story

cantante 1 *nmf* singer
2 *adj* singing; **llevar la voz c.** to rule the roost

cantaor, -a *nm,f* flamenco singer

cantar¹ *vt & vi* **(a)** *Mús* to sing; *Fig* **en menos que canta un gallo** in a flash **(b)** *Fam (confesar)* to sing, to spill the beans **(c)** *Esp muy Fam (apestar)* to stink

cantar² *nm Literary* song; *Fam* ¡eso es otro c.! that's a totally different thing!

cantarín, -ina *adj (voz)* singsong

cántaro *nm* pitcher; *Fig* **llover a cántaros** to rain cats and dogs

cantautor, -a *nm,f* singer-songwriter

cante *nm* (a) *(canto)* singing; **c. hondo, c. jondo** flamenco (b) *Esp Fam* **dar el c.** to attract attention

cantegril *nm Urug* shanty town

cantera *nf* (a) *(de piedra)* quarry (b) *Fig Ftb* young players

cantero *nm* (a) *(masón)* stonemason (b) *Cuba, RP (parterre)* flowerbed

cantidad **1** *nf* quantity; *(de dinero)* amount, sum; **en c.** a lot; *Fam* **c. de gente** thousands of people
  2 *adv Esp Fam* a lot; **me gusta c.** I really like it a lot

cantimplora *nf* water bottle

cantina *nf (de soldados)* mess; *(en fábrica)* canteen; *(en estación de tren)* buffet

canto¹ *nm* (a) *(arte)* singing (b) *(canción)* song

canto² *nm (borde)* edge; **de c.** on its side

canto³ *nm (guijarro)* pebble, stone; **c. rodado** *(grande)* boulder; *(pequeño)* pebble

cantor, -a 1 *adj* singing; **pájaro c.** songbird
  2 *nm,f* singer

canturrear *vi* to hum, to croon

canutas *nfpl Esp Fam* **pasarlas c.** to have a hard time

canuto *nm* (a) *(tubo)* tube (b) *Fam (porro)* joint

caña *nf* (a) *Esp (de cerveza)* = small glass of beer (b) *Bot* reed; *(tallo)* cane, stem; **c. de azúcar** sugar cane (c) *(de pescar)* rod (d) *Fam* **darle c. al coche** to go at full speed (e) *Andes, Cuba, RP (aguardiente)* caña, = type of rum made using sugar cane spirit

cañada *nf* gully, ravine

cáñamo *nm* hemp

cañaveral *nm* reedbed

cañería *nf* (piece of) piping; **cañerías** plumbing

cañero, -a *nm,f Am (trabajador)* sugar plantation worker; *(propietario)* sugar plantation owner

cañí *adj & nmf Fam* gypsy

caño *nm (tubo)* tube; *(tubería)* pipe

cañón *nm* (a) *(arma)* gun; *Hist* cannon; *Fig* **estar siempre al pie del c.** to be always hard at work (b) *(de fusil)* barrel; *(de chimenea)* flue (c) *Geog* canyon

cañonazo *nm* gunshot

caoba *nf* mahogany

caos *nm inv* chaos

caótico, -a *adj* chaotic

cap. *(abr* **capítulo**) ch

capa *nf* (a) *(prenda)* cloak, cape; **de c. caída** low-spirited (b) *(de pintura)* layer, coat; *Culin* coating (c) *Geol* stratum, layer; **c. de ozono** ozone layer

capacidad *nf* (a) *(cabida)* capacity (b) *(aptitud)* capacity, ability

capacitación *nf* training

capacitar *vt (habilitar)* to entitle; *(formar)* to train

capar *vt* to castrate

caparazón *nm* shell

capataz, -a *nm,f (hombre)* foreman; *(mujer)* forewoman

capaz **1** *adj* capable, able; **ser c. de hacer algo** *(tener la habilidad de)* to be able to do sth; *(atreverse a)* to dare to do sth; **si es entera es c. de despedirle** if he finds out he could quite easily sack him
  2 *adv Andes, RP (tal vez)* maybe

capazo *nm* large wicker basket

capcioso, -a *adj* **pregunta capciosa** trick question

capea *nf* amateur bullfight

capear *vt (dificultad etc)* to dodge, to shirk; *Fig* **c. el temporal** to weather the storm

capellán *nm* chaplain

caperuza *nf (gorro)* hood; *(capuchón)* top, cap

capicúa *adj* **número c.** reversible number; **palabra c.** palindrome

capilar *adj* hair; **loción c.** hair lotion

capilla *nf* chapel; **c. ardiente** chapel of rest

capirote *nm Fam* **tonto de c.** silly idiot

capital **1** *nf* capital
  2 *nm Fin* capital; **c. activo** *o* **social** working *o* share capital
  3 *adj* capital, main; **de importancia c.** of capital importance; **pena c.** capital punishment

capitalismo *nm* capitalism

capitalista *adj & nmf* capitalist

capitalizar [40] *vt* to capitalize

capitán, -ana *nm,f* captain; **c. general** *Br* field marshal, *US* general of the army

capitanear *vt* (a) *Mil & Náut* to captain, to command (b) *(dirigir)* to lead; *Dep* to captain

capitanía *nf Mil* (a) *(empleo)* captaincy (b) *(oficina)* military headquarters; **c. general** Captaincy General

capitel *nm Arquit* capital

capitulación *nf Mil* capitulation; **capitulaciones matrimoniales** marriage settlement

capitular *vi* to capitulate, to surrender

capítulo nm (a) (de libro) chapter (b) Fig **dentro del c. de ...** (tema) under the heading of ...

capó nm Aut Br bonnet, US hood

capón nm rap on the head with the knuckles

capota nf Aut Br convertible roof, US convertible top

capote nm (a) Taurom cape (b) Mil greatcoat

capricho nm (a) (antojo) whim, caprice (b) Mús caprice, capriccio

caprichoso, -a adj whimsical

Capricornio nm Capricorn

cápsula nf capsule

captar vt (a) (ondas) to receive, to pick up (b) (comprender) to understand, to grasp (c) (interés etc) to attract

captura nf capture

capturar vt (criminal) to capture; (cazar, pescar) to catch; Mil to seize

capucha nf hood

capuchino nm (café) cappuccino

capullo 1 nm (a) (de insecto) cocoon (b) (de flor) bud (c) Esp Vulg (glande) head
2 nm,f Esp muy Fam (persona despreciable) jerk, Br dickhead

caqui 1 adj (color) khaki
2 nm (fruto) kaki

cara 1 nf (a) (rostro) face; **c. a c.** face to face; **c. a la pared** facing the wall; **poner mala c.** to pull a long face; **tener buena/mala c.** to look good/bad; Fig **c. de circunstancias** serious look; Fig **dar la c.** to face the consequences (of one's acts); Fig **dar la c. por algn** to stand up for sb; Fig **(de) c. a** with a view to; Fig **echarle a algn algo en c.** to reproach sb for sth; Fig **plantar c. a algn** to face up to sb (b) (lado) (de moneda) right side; **¿c. o cruz?** heads or tails?; **echar algo a c. o cruz** to toss (a coin) for sth, US to flip (a coin) for sth (c) Fam (desfachatez) cheek, nerve; **¡qué c. (más dura) tienes!** you've got a cheek!
2 nmf Fam (desvergonzado) cheeky person

carabela nf caravel

carabina nf (a) (arma) carbine, rifle (b) (persona) chaperone

carabinero nm (a) (marisco) scarlet shrimp, = type of large red prawn (b) Chile (policía) military policeman

caracense 1 adj of/from Guadalajara
2 nmf person from Guadalajara

caracol 1 nm (a) (de tierra) snail; Am shell (b) (rizo) kiss-curl
2 interj **¡caracoles!** good heavens!

caracola nf conch

caracolada nf Culin = stew made with snails

carácter (pl caracteres) nm (a) (temperamento) character; **de mucho c.** with a strong character; **tener buen/mal c.** to be good-natured/bad-tempered (b) Fig (índole) nature; **con c. de invitado** as a guest (c) Impr character

característica nf characteristic

característico, -a adj characteristic

caracterizar [40] vt to characterize

caradura nmf Fam cheeky devil; **¡qué c. eres!** you're so cheeky!

carajillo nm Fam = coffee with a dash of brandy

carajo interj Vulg shit!; **¡vete al c.!** go to hell!

caramba interj Fam (sorpresa) good heavens!, Br blimey!, US jeez!; (enfado) for heaven's sake!

carámbano nm icicle

carambola nf Br cannon, US carom

caramelo nm (a) (dulce) Br (boiled) sweet, US candy (b) (azúcar quemado) caramel; Culin **a punto de c.** syrupy

carantoña nf caress

caraota nf Ven bean

caraqueño, -a 1 adj of/from Caracas
2 nm,f person from Caracas

carátula nf (a) (cubierta) cover (b) (máscara) mask

caravana nf (a) (vehículo) Br caravan, US trailer (b) (de tráfico) Br tailback, US backup (c) Urug (aro, pendiente) earring

caray interj (sorpresa) good heavens!, Br blimey!, US jeez!; (enfado) for heaven's sake!

carbón nm coal; **c. vegetal** charcoal; **c. mineral** coal

carboncillo nm charcoal

carbonero nm coal merchant

carbónico, -a adj carbonic; **agua carbónica** mineral water

carbonilla nf coal dust

carbonizar [40] 1 vt to carbonize, to char; **morir carbonizado** to be burnt to death
2 carbonizarse vpr to carbonize, to char

carbono nm carbon

carburador nm carburettor

carburante nm fuel

carburar vi Fam to work properly

carca Fam 1 adj old fashioned; Pol reactionary
2 nmf old fogey; Pol reactionary

carcaj nm quiver

carcajada nf guffaw

carcamal, *Méx, RP* **carcamán** *nm Fam* old fogey

cárcel *nf* prison, jail

carcelario, -a *adj* prison, jail

carcelero, -a *nm,f* jailer, warder

carcoma *nf* woodworm

carcomer 1 *vt* to eat away

  2 carcomerse *vpr* to be consumed (**de** with)

cardar *vt (lana)* to card; *(pelo)* to backcomb

cardenal *nm* (**a**) *Rel* cardinal (**b**) *Med* bruise

cárdeno, -a *adj* purple

cardiaco, -a, cardíaco, -a 1 *adj* cardiac, heart; **ataque c.** heart attack

  2 *nm,f* person with a heart condition

cardinal *adj* cardinal; **punto/número c.** cardinal point/number

cardiólogo, -a *nm,f* cardiologist

cardo *nm (con espinas)* thistle

carear *vt Der* to bring face to face

carecer [33] *vi* **c. de** to lack

carencia *nf* lack (**de** of)

carente *adj* lacking; **c. de interés** lacking interest

careo *nm Der* confrontation

carestía *nf* **la c. de la vida** the high cost of living

careta *nf* mask; **c. antigás** gas mask

carey *(pl* **careys***) nm* tortoiseshell

carezco *indic pres de* **carecer**

carga *nf* (**a**) *(acción)* loading (**b**) *(cosa cargada)* load; *(de avión, barco)* cargo, freight; *Fig* **c. afectiva** emotional content (**c**) *Fin (gasto)* debit; **c. fiscal** tax charge (**d**) *Fig (obligación)* burden (**e**) *Mil & Elec* charge

cargado, -a *adj* (**a**) *(con peso)* loaded (**b**) *(bebida)* strong; **un café c.** a strong coffee (**c**) *(ambiente)* heavy; **atmósfera cargada** stuffy atmosphere (**d**) *Fig* burdened; **c. de deudas** up to one's eyes in debt (**e**) *Elec* charged

cargador *nm* (**a**) *(de arma)* chamber (**b**) *(persona)* loader; **c. de muelle** docker, stevedore (**c**) *(de baterías)* charger (**d**) *(de celular)* charger

cargamento *nm* (**a**) *(carga)* load (**b**) *(mercancías)* cargo, freight

cargante *adj Fam* annoying

cargar [42] **1** *vt* (**a**) *(con peso)* to load; *(mechero, pluma)* to fill; *(batería)* to charge; *Fig* **c. las culpas a algn** to put the blame on sb (**b**) *Com* to charge; **cárguelo a mi cuenta** charge it to my account; *Fam Educ* **me han cargado las matemáticas** I failed maths

  2 *vi* (**a**) **c. con** *(llevar)* to carry; *Fig* **c. con la responsabilidad** to take the responsibility; *Fig* **c. con las consecuencias** to suffer the consequences (**b**) *Mil* **c. contra** to charge

  3 cargarse *vpr* (**a**) *Esp Fam* **te la vas a cargar** you're asking for trouble and you're going to get it (**b**) *Fam (estropear)* to smash, to ruin (**c**) *Fam (matar)* to kill, to bump off

cargo *nm* (**a**) *(puesto)* post, position; **alto c.** *(puesto)* top job, high ranking position; *(persona)* top person (**b**) **estar al c. de** to be in charge of; **correr a c. de** *(gastos)* to be met by; **hacerse c. de** to take charge of; **hazte c. de mi situación** please try to understand my situation; **c. de conciencia** weight on one's conscience (**c**) *Fin* charge, debit; **con c. a mi cuenta** charged to my account (**d**) *Der* charge, accusation

cargosear *vt CSur* to annoy, to pester

cargoso, -a *adj CSur* annoying

carguero *nm (avión)* transport plane; *(barco)* freighter

cariado, -a *adj* decayed

cariarse *vpr* to decay

Caribe 1 *adj* **el mar C.** the Caribbean (Sea)

  2 **el C.** *(mar)* the Caribbean (Sea); *(región)* the Caribbean

caribeño, -a 1 *adj* Caribbean

  2 *nm,f* person from the Caribbean

caricatura *nf* caricature

caricaturizar [40] *vt* to caricature

caricia *nf* caress, stroke

caridad *nf* charity

caries *nf inv* decay, caries

cariño *nm* (**a**) *(amor)* affection; **coger/ tener c. a algo/algn** to grow/to be fond of sth/sb; **con c.** *(en carta)* dear, love (**b**) *(apelativo)* dear, love, *US* honey (**c**) *(abrazo)* cuddle

cariñoso, -a *adj* loving, affectionate

carisma *nm* charisma

carismático, -a *adj* charismatic

caritativo, -a *adj* charitable

cariz *nm* look

carmesí *(pl* **carmesíes***) adj & nm* crimson

carmín *nm* **(de color) c.** carmine; **c. (de labios)** lipstick

carnal *adj* (**a**) *(de carne)* carnal (**b**) *(pariente)* first; **primo c.** first cousin

carnaval *nm* carnival

carne *nf* (**a**) *(de persona)* flesh; *Fam* **ser de c. y hueso** to be only human; *Fig* **c. de cañón** cannon fodder; **c. de gallina** goosepimples; **c. viva** raw flesh (**b**) *(alimento)* meat; **c. de cerdo/cordero**

ternera/vaca pork/lamb/veal/beef (**c**) *(de fruta)* pulp

carné *nm* = carnet

carnear *vt* (**a**) *Andes, RP (sacrificar)* to slaughter, to butcher (**b**) *Chile (engañar)* to deceive, to take in

carnero *nm* ram; *Culin* mutton

carnet *(pl carnets) nm* card; **c. de conducir** *Br* driving licence, *US* driver's license; **c. de identidad** identity card

carnicería *nf* (**a**) *(tienda)* butcher's (shop) (**b**) *Fig (masacre)* slaughter

carnicero, -a *nm,f* butcher

cárnico, -a *adj* **productos cárnicos** meat products

carnitas *nfpl Méx* = small pieces of braised pork

carnívoro, -a 1 *adj* carnivorous
2 *nm,f* carnivore

carnoso, -a *adj* fleshy

caro, -a 1 *adj* expensive, dear
2 *adv* **salir c.** to cost a lot; **te costará c.** *(amenaza)* you'll pay dearly for this

carozo *nm RP (de fruta, aceituna)* stone, *US* pit

carpa *nf* (**a**) *(pez)* carp (**b**) *(de circo)* big top; *(en parque, la calle)* marquee (**c**) *Am (de tienda de campaña)* tent

Cárpatos *nmpl* Carpathians

carpeta *nf* file, folder

> ✎ Observa que la palabra inglesa **carpet** es un falso amigo y no es la traducción de la palabra española **carpeta**. En inglés **carpet** significa "alfombra".

carpetazo *nm* **dar c. a un asunto** to shelve a matter

carpintería *nf* (**a**) *(oficio)* carpentry; **c. metálica** metalwork (**b**) *(taller)* carpenter's (shop)

carpintero, -a *nm,f* carpenter

carraca *nf* rattle

carraspear *vi* to clear one's throat

carraspeo *nm* clearing of the throat

carraspera *nf* **tener c.** to have a frog in one's throat

carrera *nf* (**a**) *(acción de correr)* run; **a la c.** in a hurry (**b**) *(competición)* race; **c. contra reloj** race against the clock; **c. de coches** rally, meeting; **echar una c. a algn** to race sb; **c. de armamentos** arms race (**c**) *(estudios)* university course; **hacer la c. de derecho/físicas** to study law/physics (at university) (**d**) *(profesión)* career, profession (**e**) *(en medias) Br* ladder, *US* run

carrerilla *nf* **tomar** *o Esp* **coger c.** to take a run; **decir algo de c.** to reel sth off

carreta *nf* cart

carrete *nm (de hilo)* reel; *(de película)* spool; *(de cable)* coil

carretera *nf* road; **c. de acceso** access road; *(en autopista)* slip road; **c. de circunvalación** *Br* ring road, *US* beltway; **c. comarcal** minor road; *Méx* **c. de cuota** toll road; **c. nacional** *Br* ≃ A road, *US* ≃ state highway

carretero, -a *adj Am* road; **un accidente c.** a road accident

carretilla *nf* wheelbarrow

carril *nm* (**a**) *Ferroc* rail (**b**) *Aut* lane

carrillo *nm* cheek; *Fam* **comer a dos carrillos** to devour, to gobble up

carriola *nf Méx (de bebé) Br* pram, *US* baby carriage

carrito *nm* trolley, *US* cart

carro *nm* (**a**) *(carreta)* cart; *Fam* **¡para el c.!** hang on a minute! (**b**) *Mil* **c. de combate** tank (**c**) *(de máquina de escribir)* carriage (**d**) *Am salvo RP (automóvil)* car (**e**) *Méx (vagón)* car; **c. comedor** dining car

carrocería *nf Aut* bodywork

carromato *nm (carro)* wagon

carroña *nf* carrion

carroza 1 *nf* (**a**) *(coche de caballos)* coach, carriage (**b**) *(de carnaval)* float
2 *nmf Fam* old fogey

carruaje *nm* carriage, coach

carrusel *nm (tiovivo)* merry-go-round, *US* carousel

carta *nf* (**a**) *(escrito)* letter; **c. certificada** *Br* recorded *o US* certified letter; **c. urgente** express letter (**b**) *(menú)* menu; **a la c.** à la carte; **c. de vinos** wine list (**c**) *Naipes* card; **echar las cartas a algn** to tell sb's fortune; *Fig* **poner las cartas sobre la mesa** to put *o* lay one's cards on the table, to come clean (**d**) *Geog (mapa)* chart (**e**) *(expresiones)* **adquirir c. de naturaleza** to become widely accepted; **tomar cartas en un asunto** to intervene in an affair

cartabón *nm* set square

cartearse *vpr* to correspond (**con** with), to exchange letters (**con** with)

cartel *nm* poster; **pegar/fijar carteles** to put *o* stick up bills

cártel *nm Com* cartel

cartelera *nf* billboard, *Br* hoarding; *Prensa* **c. de espectáculos** entertainments section *o* page

cartera *nf* (**a**) *(de bolsillo)* wallet, *US* billfold (**b**) *(para documentos)* briefcase; *(de colegial)* satchel, schoolbag (**c**) *Pol (ministerio)* portfolio (**d**) *Com* portfolio; **c. de pedidos** order book (**e**) *Andes, RP (bolso) Br* handbag, *US* purse

carterista nm pickpocket

cartero, -a nm,f (hombre) Br postman, US mailman; (mujer) Br postwoman, US mailwoman

cartilla nf (a) (libreta) book; **c. de ahorros** savings book (b) (libro) first reader; Fam **leerle la c. a algn** to tell sb off

cartografía nf cartography

cartón nm (a) (material) card, cardboard; **c. piedra** papier mâché (b) (de cigarrillos) carton

cartucho nm (a) (de balas) cartridge (b) (de papel) cone

cartulina nf card

casa nf (a) (edificio) house; **c. de huéspedes** Br guesthouse, US rooming house; **c. de socorro** first-aid post (b) (hogar) home; **vete a c.** go home; **en c. de Daniel** at Daniel's; **de andar por c.** everyday (c) (empresa) company, firm; **c. matriz/principal** head/central office

casación nf Der annulment

casadero, -a adj of marrying age

casado, -a 1 adj married
2 nm,f married person; **los recién casados** the newlyweds

casamiento nm marriage; (boda) wedding

casar¹ 1 vt to marry
2 vi to match, to go o fit together
3 casarse vpr to marry, to get married; **casarse por la iglesia/por lo civil** to get married in church/in a registry office

casar² vt Der to annul, to quash

cascabel nm bell

cascada nf waterfall, cascade

cascado, -a 1 adj (a) Esp Fam (estropeado) bust, Br clapped-out; (persona, ropa) worn-out (b) (ronco) rasping

cascanueces nm inv nutcracker

cascar [44] **1** vt (a) (romper) to crack (b) Fam **cascarla** to kick the bucket, to snuff it
2 vi Esp Fam (hablar) to witter on
3 cascarse vpr to crack

cáscara nf shell; (de fruta) skin, peel; (de grano) husk

cascarón nm eggshell

cascarrabias nmf inv Fam grouch, misery guts

casco nm (a) (para la cabeza) helmet (b) (de caballo) hoof (c) Esp, Méx (envase) empty bottle (d) **c. urbano** city centre (e) (de barco) hull (f) **cascos** (auriculares) headphones

cascote nm piece of rubble o debris

caserío nm country house

casero, -a 1 adj (a) (hecho en casa) homemade (b) (persona) home-loving

2 nm,f (dueño) (hombre) landlord; (mujer) landlady

caseta nf hut, booth; (de feria, exposición) stand, stall; Méx **c. de cobro** tollbooth; Méx **c. telefónica** Br phone box, US phone booth

casete 1 nm (magnetófono) cassette player o recorder
2 nf (cinta) cassette (tape)

casi adv almost, nearly; **c. mil personas** almost one thousand people; **c. ni me acuerdo** I can hardly remember it; **c. nunca** hardly ever; **c. nadie** hardly anyone; **c. me caigo** I almost fell

casilla nf (a) (de caja, armario) compartment; (para cartas) pigeonhole; Andes, RP **c. de correos** PO Box; CAm, Carib, Méx **c. postal** PO Box (b) (recuadro) box (c) Fig **sacar a algn de sus casillas** to drive sb mad

casillero nm (set of) pigeonholes

casino nm casino

caso nm case; **el c. es que ...** the fact o thing is that ...; **el c. Mattei** the Mattei affair; **(en) c. contrario** otherwise; **en c. de necesidad** if need be; **en cualquier c.** in any case; **en el mejor/peor de los casos** at best/worst; **en ese c.** in that case; **en todo c.** in any case; **en un c. extremo, en último c.** as a last resort; **hacer c. a o de algn** to pay attention to sb; **hacer c. omiso de** to take no notice of; **no venir al c.** to be beside the point; **pongamos por c.** let's say

caspa nf dandruff

casposo, -a adj Esp Fam (música, película) cheesy; **los famosos casposos** C-list celebs

casquete nm (a) (de bala) case, shell (b) Geog **c. polar** polar icecap

> 📖 Observa que la palabra inglesa **casket** es un falso amigo y no es la traducción de la palabra española **casquete**. En inglés, **casket** significa "cofre, ataúd".

casquillo nm (de bala) case

cassette nm & nf = casete

casta nf (a) (linaje) lineage, descent (b) (animales) breed; **de c.** thoroughbred, purebred (c) (división social) caste

castaña nf chestnut; Fig **sacarle a algn las castañas del fuego** to save sb's bacon

castañetear vi (dientes) to chatter

castaño, -a 1 adj chestnut-brown; (pelo, ojos) brown, dark
2 nm Bot chestnut

castañuela nf castanet

castellano, -a 1 *adj* Castilian
  2 *nm,f (persona)* Castilian
  3 *nm (idioma)* Spanish, Castilian
castidad *nf* chastity
castigar [42] *vt* (**a**) *(imponer castigo)* to punish; *Dep* to penalize (**b**) *(dañar) (piel, salud)* to damage; *(por sol, viento, epidemia)* to devastate
castigo *nm* punishment; *Dep* **área de c.** penalty area
Castilla *n* Castile
castillo *nm* castle
castizo, -a *adj* pure, authentic
casto, -a *adj* chaste
castor *nm* beaver
castrar *vt* to castrate
castrense *adj* military
casual 1 *adj* accidental, chance
  2 *nm Fam* chance
casualidad *nf* chance, coincidence; **de** o **por c.** by chance; **dio la c. que …** it so happened that …; **¿tienes un lápiz, por c.?** do you happen to have a pencil?; **¡que c.!** what a coincidence!

◌ᵍ Observa que la palabra inglesa **ca-sualty** es un falso amigo y no es la traducción de la palabra española **casualidad**. En inglés, **casualty** significa "víctima".

---

casualmente *adv* by chance
cata *nf* tasting
cataclismo *nm* cataclysm
catacumbas *nfpl* catacombs
catador, -a *nm,f* taster
catalán, -ana 1 *adj & nm,f* Catalan
  2 *nm (idioma)* Catalan
catalejo *nm* telescope
catalizador *nm Quím & Fig* catalyst; *Aut* catalytic converter
catalizar [40] *vt* to act as a catalyst for
catalogar [42] *vt* to catalogue; **c. a algn (de)** to class sb (as)
catálogo *nm* catalogue
Cataluña *n* Catalonia
catamarán *nm* catamaran
cataplasma *nf* (**a**) *Med* poultice (**b**) *Fam (pelmazo)* bore
catapulta *nf* catapult
catapultar *vt* to catapult
catar *vt* to taste
catarata *nf* (**a**) *(de agua)* waterfall (**b**) *Med* cataract
catarro *nm* (common) cold
catastral *adj* **valor c.** = value of a property recorded in the land register, *Br* ≃ rateable value, *US* ≃ assessed value

catastro *nm* land registry
catástrofe *nf* catastrophe
catastrófico, -a *adj* catastrophic
catear *vt* (**a**) *Esp Fam (suspender)* to fail, *US* to flunk (**b**) *Am (casa)* to search
catecismo *nm* catechism
cátedra *nf* (professorial) chair; **le han dado la c.** they have appointed him professor
catedral *nf* cathedral
catedrático, -a *nm,f Educ* (**a**) *Univ* professor (**b**) *(de instituto)* head of department
categoría *nf* category; *Fig* class; **de c.** *(persona)* important; *(vino etc)* quality
categórico, -a *adj* categorical
catequesis *nf inv* catechism lesson, ≃ Sunday school
cateto, -a *nm,f Pey* yokel, bumpkin
catire, -a *adj Carib (rubio)* blond, *f* blonde
catolicismo *nm* Catholicism
católico, -a *adj & nm,f* Catholic
catorce *adj & nm inv* fourteen
catre *nm Fam* camp bed, *US* cot
Cáucaso *nm* **el C.** the Caucasus
cauce *nm* (**a**) *(de un río)* bed (**b**) *Fig (canal)* channel; **cauces oficiales** official channels
caucho *nm* (**a**) *(sustancia)* rubber (**b**) *Ven (impermeable) Br* mac, *US* slicker (**c**) *Ven (neumático)* tyre
caudal *nm* (**a**) *(de un río)* flow (**b**) *(riqueza)* wealth, riches
caudaloso, -a *adj (río)* with a large flow
caudillo *nm* leader, head
causa *nf* (**a**) *(motivo)* cause; **a** o **por c. de** because of (**b**) *(ideal)* cause (**c**) *Der (caso)* case; *(juicio)* trial
causante 1 *adj* causal, causing
  2 *nmf* **el c. del incendio** the person who caused the fire
causar *vt* to cause, to bring about; **me causa un gran placer** it gives me great pleasure; **c. buena/mala impresión** to make a good/bad impression
cáustico, -a *adj* caustic
cautela *nf* caution
cautivador, -a 1 *adj* captivating, enchanting
  2 *nm,f* charmer
cautivar *vt* to captivate
cautiverio *nm*, **cautividad** *nf* captivity
cautivo, -a *adj & nm,f* captive
cauto, -a *adj* cautious, wary
cava 1 *nf (bodega)* wine cellar
  2 *nm (vino espumoso)* cava, champagne
cavar *vt* to dig

caverna *nf* cave; **hombre de las cavernas** caveman

cavernícola *nmf* cave dweller

caviar *nm* caviar

cavidad *nf* cavity

cavilar *vt* to ponder

cayado *nm* (de pastor) crook; (de obispo) crosier, crozier

caza 1 *nf* (a) (acción) hunting; **ir de c.** to go hunting; **c. furtiva** poaching (b) (animales) game; **c. mayor/menor** big/small game (c) *Fig* (persecución) hunt; **c. de brujas** witch hunt
2 *nm Av* fighter, fighter plane

cazabe *nm Am* cassava bread

cazabombardero *nm Av* fighter bomber

cazador, -a *nm,f* hunter; **c. furtivo** poacher

cazadora *nf* (waist-length) jacket

cazar [40] *vt* to hunt; *Fam* **cazarlas al vuelo** to be quick on the uptake

cazatalentos *nmf inv* (de artistas, deportistas) talent scout; (de ejecutivos) headhunter

cazo *nm* (a) (cacerola) saucepan (b) (cucharón) ladle

cazuela *nf* saucepan; (guiso) casserole, stew; **a la c.** stewed

cazurro, -a 1 *adj* (bruto) stupid
2 *nm,f* (bruto) idiot, fool

c/c (abr **cuenta corriente**) c/a

CC. OO. *n* (abr **Comisiones Obreras**) = Spanish left-wing trade union

CD (pl **CDs**) *nm* (abr **compact disc**) CD

CD-ROM ['θeðe'rrom] (pl **CD-ROMs**) *nm* CD-ROM

cebada *nf* barley

cebar 1 *vt* (a) (animal) to fatten; (persona) to feed up (b) (anzuelo) to bait (c) (fuego, caldera) to stoke, to fuel; (máquina, arma) to prime (d) *RP* (mate) to prepare, to brew
2 cebarse *vpr* **cebarse con** (ensañarse) to delight in tormenting

cebo *nm* bait

cebolla *nf* onion

cebolleta *nf Br* spring onion, *US* scallion

cebra *nf* zebra; **paso de c.** *Br* zebra crossing, *US* crosswalk

cecear *vi* to lisp

ceceo *nm* lisp

cedazo *nm* sieve

ceder 1 *vt* to give, to hand over; *Aut* **c. el paso** to give way
2 *vi* (a) (cuerda, cable) to give way (b) (lluvia, calor) to ease off *o* up (c) (consentir) to give in

cederrón *nm* CD-ROM

cedro *nm* cedar

cédula *nf* document, certificate; *Am* **c. de identidad** identity card

cegador, -a *adj* blinding

cegar [1] *vt* (a) (persona) to blind (b) (puerta, ventana) to wall up

cegato, -a *Fam* **1** *adj* short-sighted
2 *nm,f* short-sighted person

ceguera *nf* blindness

CEI (abr **Comunidad de Estados Independientes**) CIS

Ceilán *n* Ceylon

ceja *nf* eyebrow

cejar *vi* **c. en el empeño** to give up

celada *nf* trap, ambush

celador, -a *nm,f* (de colegio) *Br* caretaker, *US & Scot* janitor; (de hospital) porter, orderly; (de prisión) *Br* warder, *US* guard; (de museo) attendant

celda *nf* cell; **c. de castigo** punishment cell

celebración *nf* (a) (festejo) celebration (b) (de juicio etc) holding

celebrar 1 *vt* (a) (fiesta, cumpleaños, victoria) to celebrate (b) (reunión, juicio, elecciones) to hold (c) (triunfo) to laud (d) (alegrarse de) **celebro que todo saliera bien** I'm glad everything went well
2 celebrarse *vpr* (llevarse a cabo) to take place, to be held

célebre *adj* famous, well-known

celebridad *nf* (a) (fama) celebrity, fame (b) (persona) celebrity

celeste 1 *adj* (a) (de cielo) celestial (b) (color) sky-blue
2 *nm* sky blue

celestial *adj* celestial, heavenly

celibato *nm* celibacy

célibe *adj & nmf* celibate

celo *nm* (a) (esmero) zeal (b) **en c.** (macho) in rut; (hembra) *Br* on heat, *US* in heat (c) **celos** jealousy; **tener celos (de algn)** to be jealous (of sb)

celo® *nm Fam Br* Sellotape®, *US* Scotch tape®

celofán *nm* cellophane®

celosía *nf* lattice

celoso, -a *adj* (a) (envidioso) jealous (b) (cumplidor) conscientious

celta 1 *adj* Celtic
2 *nmf* Celt
3 *nm* (idioma) Celtic

célula *nf* cell

celular 1 *adj* (a) *Biol* cellular (b) **coche c.** police van (c) *Am* **teléfono c.** mobile phone, cellphone
2 *nm Am* mobile (phone), cellphone

celulitis *nf inv* cellulitis

celuloide nm celluloid

celulosa nf cellulose

cementerio nm cemetery, graveyard; **c. de coches** scrapyard

cemento nm cement; **c. armado** reinforced concrete

cena nf dinner, evening meal; *(antes de acostarse)* supper; **la Última C.** the Last Supper

cenagal nm marsh, swamp

cenar 1 vi to have supper/dinner
2 vt to have for supper/dinner

cencerro nm cowbell

cenefa nf *(de ropa)* edging, trimming; *(de suelo, techo)* ornamental border, frieze

cenetista 1 adj = of or related to the CNT
2 nmf member of the CNT

cenicero nm ashtray

cenit nm zenith

ceniza nf ash

cenizo nm Fam **ser un c.** to be jinxed

censar vt to take a census of

censo nm census; *Esp* **c. electoral** electoral roll

censor nm censor

censura nf (a) *(de libro, película)* censorship (b) *Pol* **moción de c.** vote of no confidence

censurar vt (a) *(libro, película)* to censor (b) *(criticar)* to censure, to criticize

centavo nm *Am Fin* cent, centavo

centella nf spark

centellear vi to flash, to sparkle

centelleo nm flashing, sparkling

centena nf, **centenar** nm hundred; **a centenares** in hundreds

centenar nm hundred; **un c. de** a hundred; **a centenares** by the hundred

centenario nm centenary, hundredth anniversary

centeno nm rye

centésimo, -a adj & nm,f hundredth

centígrado, -a adj centigrade

centilitro nm centilitre

centímetro nm centimetre

céntimo nm cent

centinela nm sentry

centollo nm spider crab

centrado, -a adj (a) *(situado en el centro)* centred (b) *(equilibrado)* stable, balanced

central 1 adj central
2 nf (a) *Elec* **c. nuclear/térmica** nuclear/coal-fired power station (b) *(oficina principal)* head office

centralismo nm centralism

centralita nf Tel switchboard

centralizar [40] vt to centralize

centrar 1 vt (a) *(colocar en el centro)* to centre (b) *(esfuerzos, atención)* to concentrate, to centre (**en** on)
2 centrarse vpr **centrarse en** *(concentrarse)* to concentrate on

céntrico, -a adj centrally situated; **una zona céntrica** an area in the centre of town, US a downtown area

centrifugar [42] vt to centrifuge; *(ropa)* to spin-dry

centrista Pol **1** adj centre; **partido c.** centre party
2 nmf centrist

centro nm (a) *(punto, área)* centre (b) *(establecimiento)* centre; **c. comercial** shopping centre o US mall; **c. docente** educational institution (c) *(de ciudad)* city/town centre; **me voy al c.** I'm going to town

Centroamérica n Central America

centroamericano, -a adj & nm,f Central American

centrocampista nmf Ftb midfielder

centuria nf century

ceñido, -a adj tight-fitting, clinging

ceñirse [6] vpr (a) *(atenerse, limitarse)* to limit oneself, to stick (**a** to); **c. al tema** to keep to the subject; **ciñéndonos a este caso en concreto** coming down to this particular case (b) **c. a** *(prenda)* to cling to

ceño nm scowl, frown; **con el c. fruncido** frowning

CEOE nf *(abr* **Confederación Española de Organizaciones Empresariales)** = Spanish employers' organization, *Br* ≃ CBI

cepa nf (a) *(de vid)* vine (b) *Fig* **vasco de pura c.** *(origen)* Basque through and through

cepillar 1 vt (a) *(con cepillo)* to brush (b) *(en carpintería)* to plane (down) (c) *Fam (robar)* to pinch
2 cepillarse vpr (a) *(con cepillo)* to brush (b) *Fam (matar)* to do in (c) *muy Fam* to lay

cepillo nm brush; *(en carpintería)* plane; **c. de dientes** toothbrush; **c. del pelo** hairbrush

cepo nm (a) *(para cazar)* trap (b) *Aut* clamp

CEPYME nf *(abr* **Confederación Española de la Pequeña y Mediana Empresa)** = Spanish confederation of small and medium-sized businesses

cera nf wax; *(de abeja)* beeswax

cerámica nf ceramics *sing*

ceramista nmf potter

cerca¹ *adv* (a) near, close; **ven más c.** come closer; **ya estamos c.** we are almost there (b) **c. de** *(al lado de)* near, close to; **el colegio está c. de mi casa** the school is near my house (c) **c. de** *(casi)* nearly, around; **c. de cien personas** about one hundred people (d) **de c.** closely; **lo vi muy de c.** I saw it close up

cerca² *nf* fence, wall

cercado *nm* (a) *(lugar cerrado)* enclosure (b) *(valla)* fence, wall

cercanía *nf* (a) *(cualidad)* proximity, nearness (b) **cercanías** *(lugar)* surrounding area; **tren de cercanías** local train

cercano, -a *adj* nearby; **el C. Oriente** the Near East

cercar [44] *vt* (a) *(tapiar)* to fence, to enclose (b) *(rodear)* to surround

cercenar *vt* to cut off, to amputate

cerciorarse *vpr* to make sure (de of)

cerco *nm* (a) *(marca)* circle, ring (b) *Mil (sitio)* siege; **poner c. a (una ciudad)** to besiege (a town)

cerda *nf* (a) *Zool* sow (b) *(pelo)* bristle; **cepillo de c.** bristle brush

Cerdeña *n* Sardinia

cerdo *nm* (a) *(animal)* pig (b) *(carne)* pork (c) *Fam* pig, *Br* arsehole, *US* asshole

cereal *nm* cereal

cerebral *adj Anat & Fig* cerebral

cerebro *nm* brain; *Fig (inteligencia)* brains

ceremonia *nf* ceremony

ceremonioso, -a *adj* ceremonious, formal; *Pey* pompous, stiff

cereza *nf* cherry

cerezo *nm* cherry tree

cerilla *nf Esp* match

cerillo *nm CAm, Ecuad, Méx* match

cernerse [3] *vpr Fig* to loom (**sobre** over)

cernícalo *nm* kestrel

cernirse [54] *vpr* = cernerse

cero *nm* zero; *Dep Br* nil, *US* zero; *Fig* **partir de c.** to start from scratch; *Fig* **ser un c. a la izquierda** to be useless o a good-for-nothing

cerquillo *nm Am Br* fringe, *US* bangs

cerrado, -a *adj* (a) closed, shut; **a puerta cerrada** behind closed doors (b) *(reservado)* reserved; *(intransigente)* uncompromising, unyielding; *Fam (torpe)* thick; *(acento)* broad; *(curva)* tight, sharp (c) *(barba)* bushy

cerradura *nf* lock

cerrajería *nf* (a) *(oficio)* locksmithery (b) *(local)* locksmith's (shop)

cerrajero, -a *nm,f* locksmith

cerrar [1] **1** *vt* to shut, to close; *(grifo, gas)* to turn off; *(luz)* to turn off, to switch off; *(cremallera)* to do up; *(negocio)* to close down; *(cuenta)* to close; *(carta)* to seal; *(puños)* to clench; **c. con llave** to lock; **c. el paso a algn** to block sb's way; *Fam* **c. el pico** to shut one's trap
2 *vi* to close, to shut
3 cerrarse *vpr* to close, to shut; *Fam* **cerrarse en banda** to stick to one's guns

cerro *nm* hill; *Esp Fig* **irse por los cerros de Ubeda** to go off at a tangent, to stray from the point

cerrojo *nm* bolt; **echar el c. de (una puerta)** to bolt (a door)

certamen *nm* competition, contest

certero, -a *adj* accurate

certeza *nf* certainty; **saber (algo) con c.** to be certain (of sth); **tener la c. de que …** to be sure o certain that …

certidumbre *nf* certainty

certificado, -a 1 *adj (documento)* certified; *(carta, paquete)* Br recorded, *US* certified
2 *nm* certificate

certificar [44] *vt (constatar)* to certify

cervatillo *nm* fawn

cervecería *nf* (a) *(bar)* pub, bar (b) *(fábrica)* brewery

cerveza *nf* beer; **c. de barril** draught beer; **c. dorada** o **ligera** lager; **c. negra** stout

cervical 1 *adj* cervical
2 cervicales *nfpl* neck vertebrae

cesante *adj (destituido)* dismissed, *Br* sacked; *CSur, Méx (parado)* unemployed

cesantear *vt Am* to make redundant

cesar 1 *vi* **c. (de)** to stop, to cease; **sin c.** incessantly
2 *vt (empleado)* to dismiss, *Br* to sack

cesárea *nf* Caesarean (section)

cese *nm* (a) *(detención, paro)* stopping, ceasing cessation, suspension (b) *(despido)* dismissal

cesión *nf* cession, transfer; *Der* **c. de bienes** surrender of property

césped *nm* lawn, grass

cesta *nf* basket; **c. de Navidad** Christmas hamper

cesto *nm* basket

cetáceo *nm* cetacean, whale

cetrino, -a *adj* sallow

cetro *nm* sceptre

Ceuta *n* Ceuta

ceutí 1 *adj* of/from Ceuta
2 *nmf* person from Ceuta

ceviche *nm* = raw fish marinated in lemon and garlic

chabacano, -a 1 *adj* cheap
  2 *nm Méx (fruto)* apricot; *(árbol)* apricot tree

chabola *nf Esp* shack; **barrio de chabolas** shanty town

chacal *nm* jackal

chacarero, -a *nm,f Andes, RP* farmer

chacha *nf* maid

cháchara *nf Fam* small talk, chinwag; **estar de c.** to have a yap

chachi *adj Esp Fam* cool, neat

chacinería *nf* pork butcher's (shop)

chacolí *nm* = light wine from the Basque Country

chacra *nf Andes, RP* farm

chafar *vt* **(a)** *Fam (plan etc)* to ruin, to spoil **(b)** *(aplastar)* to squash, to flatten

chal *nm* shawl

chalado, -a *adj Fam* crazy, nuts (**por** about)

chalé *nm* villa

chaleco *nm Br* waistcoat, *US* vest; *(de punto)* sleeveless pullover; **c. antibalas** bullet-proof vest; **c. salvavidas** life jacket

chalet *(pl* **chalets)** *nm* villa

chalupa *nf* **(a)** *(embarcación)* boat, launch **(b)** *Méx (torta)* = small tortilla with a raised rim to contain a filling

chamaco, -a *nm,f Méx Fam* **(a)** *(muchacho)* kid **(b)** *(novio)* boyfriend; *(novia)* girlfriend

chamarra *nf* sheepskin jacket

chamba *nf CAm, Méx, Perú, Ven Fam (trabajo)* job;

chambelán *nm* chamberlain

chambergo *nm* heavy coat

chambón, -ona *nm,f Am Fam* sloppy *o* shoddy worker

chamizo *nm* thatched hut

champa *nf CAm (tienda de campaña)* tent

champán *nm,* **champaña** *nm o nf* champagne

champiñón *nm* mushroom

champú *(pl* **champús** *o* **champúes)** *nm* shampoo

chamuscado, -a *adj (pelo, plumas)* singed; *(tela, papel)* scorched; *(tostada)* burnt

chamuscar [44] *vt* to singe, to scorch

chamusquina *nf* singeing, scorching; *Fam* **esto me huele a c.** there's something fishy going on here

chance 1 *nm o nf Am* opportunity, chance
  2 *adv Méx* maybe

chanchada *nf Am* **(a)** *(porquería)* **¡no hagas chanchadas!** stop that, don't be disgusting! **(b)** *Fam (jugarreta)* dirty trick

chancho, -a *nm,f Am* pig, *f* sow

chanchullo *nm Fam* fiddle, wangle

chancla, chancleta *nf Br* flip-flop, *US & Austr* thong

chanclo *nm (zueco)* clog; *(de goma)* overshoe, galosh

chándal *(pl* **chandals)** *nm Esp* tracksuit

changa *nf Bol, RP (trabajo temporal)* odd job

changador *nm RP (cargador)* porter

changarro *nm Méx (tienda)* small shop; *(puesto)* stand

chantaje *nm* blackmail; **hacer c. a algn** to blackmail sb

chantajear *vt* to blackmail

chantajista *nmf* blackmailer

chanza *nf* joke

chapa *nf* **(a)** *(de metal)* sheet; *(de madera)* panel-board **(b)** *(tapón)* bottle top, cap **(c)** *(de adorno)* badge **(d)** *RP (de matrícula) Br* numberplate, *US* license plate **(e)** *Col, Cuba, Méx (cerradura)* lock

chapado, -a *adj (metal)* plated; **c. en oro** gold-plated; *Fig* **c. a la antigua** old-fashioned

chapapote *nm* oil sludge

chapar 1 *vt (recubrir) (con metal)* to plate; *(con madera)* to veneer
  2 *vi Esp muy Fam (cerrar)* to shut, to close

chaparro, -a 1 *adj* short and squat
  2 *nm Bot* holm oak

chaparrón *nm* downpour, heavy shower

chapopote *nm Carib, Méx* bitumen, pitch

chapotear *vi* to splash about, to paddle

chapucería *nf* botch (job)

chapucero, -a *adj (trabajo)* slapdash, shoddy; *(persona)* bungling

chapulín *nm CAm, Méx (saltamontes)* grasshopper

chapurrear *vt* to speak badly *o* with difficulty; **sólo chapurreaba el francés** he spoke only a few words of French

chapuza 1 *nf* **(a)** *(trabajo mal hecho)* shoddy piece of work **(b)** *(trabajo ocasional)* odd job
  2 chapuzas *nmf inv Fam (persona)* bungler

chapuzón *nm* dip; **darse un c.** to have a dip

chaqué *nm* morning coat

chaqueta *nf* jacket; *Pol* **cambiar de c.** to change sides

chaquetero, -a *nm,f Esp Fam* turncoat

chaquetilla *nf* short jacket

chaquetón *nm* heavy jacket, short coat

charanga *nf Mús* brass band

charca *nf* pond, pool

charco *nm* puddle

charcutería *nf* delicatessen

charla *nf* (*conversación*) talk, chat; (*conferencia*) informal lecture *o* address; *Inform* chat

charlar *vi* to talk, to chat; *Inform* to chat

charlatán, -ana 1 *adj* (*parlanchín*) talkative; (*chismoso*) gossipy
  2 *nm,f* (a) (*parlanchín*) chatterbox; (*chismoso*) gossip; (*bocazas*) bigmouth (b) (*embaucador*) trickster, charmer

charol *nm* (a) (*piel*) patent leather; **zapatos de c.** patent leather shoes (b) *Andes* (*bandeja*) tray

charola *nf Bol, CAm, Méx* tray

charque, charqui *nm Andes, RP* jerked *o* salted beef

charro, -a 1 *adj* (a) *Esp* (*salmantino*) Salamancan (b) (*recargado*) gaudy, showy (c) *Méx* (*líder sindical*) = in league with the bosses
  2 *nm,f* (a) *Esp* (*salmantino*) Salamancan (b) *Méx* (*jinete*) horseman

chárter *adj inv* (*vuelo*) **c.** charter (flight)

chasca *nf Andes* (*greña*) mop of hair

chascar [44] *vt* = **chasquear**

chascarrillo *nm* funny story

chasco *nm Fam* disappointment; **llevarse un c.** to be disappointed

chasis *nm inv* chassis

chasquear *vt* (*lengua*) to click; (*dedos*) to snap; (*látigo*) to crack

chasqui *nm* = Inca messenger or courier

chasquido *nm* (*de la lengua*) click; (*de los dedos*) snap; (*de látigo, madera*) crack

chat (*pl* **chats**) *nm Inform* (*charla*) chat; (*sala*) chat room

chatarra *nf* scrap (metal), scrap iron; *Fam* junk

chatarrero, -a *nm,f* scrap (metal) dealer

chatear *vi Inform* to chat

chato, -a 1 *adj* (a) (*nariz*) snub; (*persona*) snub-nosed (b) (*objeto*) flat, flattened (c) *PRico, RP Fam* (*sin ambiciones*) commonplace; **una vida chata** a humdrum existence
  2 *nm Esp Fam* = small glass of wine

chau *interj Bol, CSur, Perú Fam* bye!, see you!

chaucha 1 *adj RP Fam* dull, boring
  2 *nf* (a) *Bol, RP* green bean (b) *Andes* (*patata*) early potato

chauvinista *adj & nmf* chauvinist

chaval, -a *nm,f Fam* (*chico*) boy, lad; (*chica*) girl

chaveta *nf* (a) (*clavija*) cotter pin (b) *Fam* (*cabeza*) nut, head; **perder la c.** (*volverse loco*) to go off one's rocker (c) *Andes* (*navaja*) penknife

chavo, -a *Fam* 1 *nm,f Méx* (a) (*chico*) guy; (*chica*) girl (b) (*novio*) boyfriend; (*novia*) girlfriend
  2 *nm* (*dinero*) **no tener un c.** to be broke

che *interj RP Fam* **¿qué hacés, c.?, ¿cómo andás, c.?** hey, how's it going, then?; **c., ¡vení para acá!** hey, over here, you!

checo, -a *adj* Czech

checoslovaco, -a 1 *adj* Czechoslovakian, Czech
  2 *nm,f* (*persona*) Czechoslovakian, Czechoslovak, Czech

Checoslovaquia *n* Czechoslovakia

chef [tʃef] (*pl* **chefs**) *nm* chef

chele, -a *CAm* 1 *adj* (*rubio*) blond, *f* blonde; (*de piel blanca*) fair-skinned
  2 *nmf* (*rubio*) blond, *f* blonde; (*de piel blanca*) fair-skinned person

chelín *nm Antes* shilling

chepa *nf Fam* hump

cheque *nm Br* cheque, *US* check; **c. al portador** cheque payable to bearer; **c. de viaje** *o* **(de) viajero** traveller's cheque

chequeo *nm Med* checkup; *Aut* service

chequera *nf Br* chequebook, *US* checkbook

chévere *adj Am salvo RP Fam* great, fantastic

chic *adj inv* chic, elegant

chicano, -a *adj & nm,f* chicano

chicha¹ *nf* (a) *Esp Fam* (*para comer*) meat (b) *Esp Fam* (*de persona*) flesh; **tiene pocas chichas** (*está flaco*) he's as thin as a rake (c) (*bebida alcohólica*) = alcoholic drink made from fermented maize (d) (*bebida refrescante*) = thick, sweet drink made from rice, condensed milk and vanilla

chicha² *adj inv Náut* **calma c.** dead calm

chícharo *nm CAm, Méx* pea

chicharra *nf* (a) (*insecto*) cicada (b) *Méx* (*timbre*) electric buzzer

chiche *nm* (a) *Andes, RP Fam* (*juguete*) toy (b) *Andes, RP* (*adorno*) delicate ornament (c) *CAm, Méx muy Fam* (*pecho*) tit

chichón *nm* bump, lump

chichonera *nf* (*para ciclistas*) hairnet

chicle *nm* chewing gum

chico, -a 1 *nm,f* (*muchacho*) boy, lad; (*muchacha*) girl
  2 *adj* small, little

chicote *nm Am* whip

chiflado, -a *adj Fam* mad, crazy (**por** about)

chiflar *vt* (a) (*silbar*) to hiss (at), to boo (at) (b) *Fam* **le chiflan las motos** he's really into motorbikes

chiflido nm whistling

chigüín, -ina nm,f CAm Fam kid

chiita adj & nmf Shiite

chilango, -a Méx Fam **1** adj of/from Mexico City
2 nm,f person from Mexico City

Chile n Chile

chile nm CAm, Méx chilli

chileno, -a adj & nm,f Chilean

chillar vi (persona) to scream, to shriek; (ratón) to squeak; (frenos) to screech, to squeal; (puerta) to creak, to squeak

chillido nm (de persona) scream, shriek; (de ratón) squeak; (de frenos) screech, squeal; (de puerta) creaking, squeaking

chillón, -ona adj (a) (voz) shrill, high-pitched; (sonido) harsh, strident (b) (color) loud, gaudy

chilpotle nm Méx = smoked or pickled jalapeño chilli

chimbo, -a adj Col, Ven Fam (a) (de mala calidad) lousy (b) (complicado) screwed-up

chimenea nf (a) (hogar abierto) fireplace, hearth (b) (conducto) chimney; (de barco) funnel, stack

chimichurri nm RP = barbecue sauce made from garlic, parsley, oregano and vinegar

chimpancé nm chimpanzee

China n China

china nf (a) (piedra) pebble, small stone; Fam **tocarle a uno la c.** to get the short straw (b) Fam (droga) deal

> ℓ Observa que la palabra inglesa **china** es un falso amigo y no es la traducción de la palabra española **china**. En inglés, **china** significa"loza, porcelana".

chinampa nf Méx = man-made island for growing flowers, fruit and vegetables, in Xochimilco near Mexico City

chinche 1 nf bedbug; Fam **caer como chinches** to drop like flies
2 nmf Fam nuisance, pest

chincheta nf Br drawing pin, US thumbtack

chinchín interj cheers!

chinchulín nm, **chinchulines** nmpl Andes, RP (plato) = piece of sheep or cow intestine, plaited and then roasted

chinesco, -a adj **sombras chinescas** shadow theatre

chingado, -a adj Esp, Méx muy Fam (estropeado) bust, Br knackered

chingana nf Andes Fam = cheap bar or café

chingar [42] **1** vt (a) Esp, Méx muy Fam (estropear) to bust, Br to knacker (b) Esp, Méx muy Fam (molestar) **c. a algn** to piss sb off, to get up sb's nose (c) Esp, Méx Vulg (copular) to fuck; Méx **¡chinga tu madre!** fuck you!
2 vi Esp, Méx Vulg (copular) to screw, to fuck
3 chingarse vpr Méx muy Fam (estropearse) to pack in, to conk out

chino¹ nm (piedrecita) pebble, stone

chino², -a adj (a) (de la China) Chinese; Fam **eso me suena a c.** it's all Greek to me (b) Am (mestizo) of mixed ancestry (c) (rizado) curly

chip (pl chips) nm Inform chip

chipirón nm baby squid

Chipre n Cyprus

chipriota adj & nmf Cypriot

chiqueo nm Méx Fam show of affection; **hacerle chiqueos a algn** to kiss and cuddle sb

chiquilín, -ina nm,f RP (niño) small boy; (niña) small girl

chiquillo, -a nm,f kid

chiquito, -a adj tiny

chirimiri nm Esp drizzle, fine misty rain

chirimoya nf custard apple

chiringuito nm (en playa etc) refreshment stall; (en carretera) roadside snack bar

chiripa nf fluke; Fam Fig **de** o **por c.** by a fluke, by chance; **cogió el tren por c.** it was sheer luck that he caught the train

chiripá (pl chiripaes) nm CSur = garment worn by gauchos over trousers

chirla nf small clam

chirona nf Esp Fam clink, Br nick

chirriar [29] vi (puerta, madera) to creak; (frenos) to screech, to squeal

chirrido nm (de puerta, madera) creak, creaking; (de frenos) screech, squeal

chisme nm (a) (habladuría) piece of gossip (b) Fam (trasto) knick-knack; (cosa) thing

chismorrear vi Fam to gossip

chismorreo nm Fam gossip, gossiping

chismoso, -a 1 adj gossipy
2 nm,f gossip

chispa nf (a) (de fuego, electricidad) spark; Fam Fig **echar chispas** to fume (b) Fam (un poco) bit, tiny amount (c) Fam (agudeza) wit, sparkle; (viveza) liveliness

chispear v impers (lloviznar) to spit

chiste nm joke; **contar un c.** to tell a joke; **c. verde** blue joke, dirty joke

chistera nf top hat

chistorra nf = type of cured pork sausage typical of Aragon and Navarre

chistoso, -a *adj (persona)* funny, witty; *(anécdota)* funny, amusing

chivarse *vpr Esp Fam (niños)* to tell, *Br* to split (**de** on); *(delincuentes)* to squeal, *Br* to grass (**de** on)

chivatazo *nm Esp Fam* tip-off; **dar el c.** to squeal, *Br* to grass

chivato, -a 1 *nm,f Esp Fam (delator) Br* grass, *US* rat; *(acusica)* telltale
  2 *nm* (**a**) *(luz)* warning light (**b**) *(alarma)* alarm bell (**c**) *Ven Fam (pez gordo)* big cheese

chivito *nm* (**a**) *Arg (carne)* roast kid (**b**) *Urug* steak sandwich *(containing cheese and salad)*

chivo, -a *nm,f Zool* kid, young goat; *Fig* **c. expiatorio** scapegoat

chocante *adj (sorprendente)* surprising, startling; *(raro)* strange

chocar [44] **1** *vi* (**a**) *(topar)* to crash, to collide; **c. con** *o* **contra** to run into, to collide with (**b**) *(en discusión)* to clash (**c**) *(extrañar)* **me choca que …** I'm surprised *o* puzzled that …
  2 *vt* (**a**) *(manos)* to shake; *(copas, vasos)* to clink; **¡chócala!, ¡choca esos cinco!** shake (on it)!, put it there!

chochear *vi* (**a**) *(viejo)* to be senile *o* in one's dotage (**b**) *Fam* **c. con algn** to dote on sb

chocho, -a 1 *adj (senil)* senile; **viejo c.** old dodderer
  2 *nm* (**a**) *(altramuz)* lupin (**b**) *Esp, Méx Vulg (vulva) Br* fanny, *US* beaver

choclo *nm Andes, RP* maize, *US* corn

chocolate *nm* (**a**) *(para comer)* chocolate; **c. con leche** milk chocolate (**b**) *Esp Fam (droga)* dope

chocolatería *nf* (**a**) *(fábrica)* chocolate factory (**b**) *(establecimiento)* = café where drinking chocolate is served

chocolatina *nf* bar of chocolate, chocolate bar

chofer *(pl* **choferes)** *nm Am* chauffeur

chófer *(pl* **chóferes)** *nm Esp* chauffeur

chollo *nm Esp Fam (ganga)* bargain

chomba *nf* (**a**) *Arg* polo shirt (**b**) *Chile, Perú (suéter)* sweater, pullover, *Br* jumper

chompa *nf Andes* sweater, pullover, *Br* jumper

chompipe *nm CAm, Méx* turkey

chongo *nm Méx* (**a**) *(moño)* bun (**b**) **chongos zamoranos** *(dulce)* = Mexican dessert made from milk curds, served in syrup

chonta *nf CAm, Perú* = type of palm tree

chop *(pl* **chops)** *nm CSur* (**a**) *(jarra)* beer mug (**b**) *(cerveza)* (mug of) beer

chopo *nm* poplar

chopp *CSur (pl* **chopps)** *nm* = **chop**

choque *nm* (**a**) *(impacto)* impact; *(de coches etc)* crash, collision; **c. frontal** head-on collision; **c. múltiple** pile-up (**b**) *Fig (contienda)* clash

choricear, chorizar *vt Esp Fam* to pinch

chorizo[1] *nm (embutido)* chorizo, = highly-seasoned pork sausage

chorizo[2] **, -a** *nm,f Esp Fam (ladrón)* thief

chorlito *nm (ave)* plover; *Fam Fig* **cabeza de c.** scatterbrain

choro *nm Andes* mussel

chorra *Esp Fam* **1** *nmf (tonto)* idiot, fool; **hacer el c.** to muck about
  2 *nf (suerte)* luck

chorrada *nf Esp Fam* **decir una c.** to say something stupid; **chorradas** *Br* rubbish, *US* garbage

chorrear *vi* to drip, to trickle; *Fam* **c. de sudor** to pour with sweat; *Fam* **tengo el abrigo chorreando** my coat is dripping wet

chorro *nm* (**a**) *(de agua etc)* spurt; *(muy fino)* trickle; **salir a chorros** to gush forth (**b**) *Téc* jet (**c**) *Fig* stream, flood

choto *nm,f* (**a**) *(cabrito)* kid, young goat; *Fam* **estar como una chota** to be crazy, to be off one's rocker (**b**) *(ternero)* calf

chovinismo *nm* chauvinism

chovinista 1 *adj* chauvinistic
  2 *nmf* chauvinist

choza *nf* hut, shack

christmas *nm inv* Christmas card

chubasco *nm* heavy shower, downpour

chubasquero *nm* raincoat, *Br* mac

chúcaro, -a *adj Andes, CAm, RP* (**a**) *(animal)* wild (**b**) *Fam (persona)* **ser c.** to be shy *o* withdrawn

chuchería *nf Fam Br* sweet, *US* candy

chucho *nm Fam* (**a**) *(perro)* mutt, dog (**b**) *RP (susto)* fright; **un c. de frío** a shiver

chueco, -a 1 *adj Am (torcido)* twisted; *(patizambo)* bowlegged; *Méx, Ven Fam (cojo)* lame
  2 *nm,f Am (patizambo)* bowlegged person; *Méx, Ven Fam (cojo)* lame person

chufa *nf* groundnut

chulear *vi Fam* to strut around; **c. de** to go on about

chuleta *nf* (**a**) *(de carne)* chop; **c. de cerdo** pork chop (**b**) *Esp, Ven Fam (en exámenes)* crib note

chullo *nm Andes* woollen cap

chulo, -a *Fam* **1** *nm,f Esp* show-off
  2 *nm (proxeneta)* pimp
  3 *adj Esp, Méx Fam (bonito)* cool, *Br* top, *US* neat

chumbera *nf* prickly pear cactus

chungo, -a *adj Fam* dodgy

chuño *nm Andes, RP* potato starch

chupa *nf Esp Fam* coat

chupachups® *nm inv Esp* lollipop

chupacirios *nmf inv Fam Pey* holy Joe

chupado, -a *adj* (a) *(flaco)* skinny, thin (b) *Fam* **está c.** it's dead easy

chupamedias *nmf Andes, RP, Ven Fam* toady

chupar 1 *vt* (a) *(succionar)* to suck (b) *(lamer)* to lick (c) *(absorber)* to soak up, to absorb
2 *vi* to suck
3 chuparse *vpr* (a) **está para chuparse los dedos** it's really mouthwatering (b) *Esp Fam* to put up with; **nos chupamos toda la película** we sat through the whole film

chupatintas *nm inv Pey* penpusher

chupe *nm* (a) *Andes, Arg (comida)* stew (b) *Méx, RP Fam (bebida)* booze

chupete *nm Br* dummy, *US* pacifier

chupi *adj Esp Fam* great

chupito *nm* shot

chupón, -ona 1 *nm,f Fam (gorrón)* sponger, cadger
2 *nm Méx (chupete) Br* dummy, *US* pacifier

churrasco *nm* barbecued meat

churrería *nf* fritter shop

churrete *nm* dirty mark, grease spot

churro *nm* (a) *(para comer)* = dough formed into sticks or rings, fried in oil and covered in sugar (b) *Fam (chapuza)* mess

chusma *nf* rabble, mob

chutar 1 *vi* (a) *Dep (a gol)* to shoot (b) *Esp Fam (funcionar)* to work; **¡y vas que chutas!** and then you're well away!
2 chutarse *vpr Esp Fam (drogas)* to shoot up

chute *nm* (a) *Dep* shot (b) *Esp Fam (drogas)* fix

CI *nm (abr* **coeficiente intelectual***)* IQ

Cía., cía *(abr* **compañía***)* Co

cianuro *nm* cyanide

cibercafé, Fam ciber *nm Inform* Internet cafe, cybercafe

ciberespacio *nm Inform* cyberspace

cibernética *nf* cybernetics *sing*

cicatero, -a 1 *adj* stingy, mean
2 *nm,f* miser

cicatriz *nf* scar

cicatrizar [40] *vt & vi Med* to heal

cíclico, -a *adj* cyclical

ciclismo *nm* cycling

ciclista 1 *adj* cycling
2 *nmf* cyclist

ciclo *nm* cycle; *(de conferencias etc)* course, series

ciclocross *nm* cyclo-cross

ciclomotor *nm* moped

ciclón *nm* cyclone

ciego, -a 1 *adj* (a) *(invidente)* blind; **a ciegas** blindly (b) *Esp Fam (borracho)* blind drunk; *Br* pissed; *(de droga)* stoned
2 *nm,f* blind person; **los ciegos** the blind

cielo *nm* (a) *(atmósfera)* sky (b) *Rel* heaven; *Fig* **caído del c.** *(oportuno)* heaven-sent; *(inesperado)* out of the blue; **¡c. santo!** good heavens! (c) **c. del paladar** roof of the mouth (d) *(nombre cariñoso)* my love, my dear

ciempiés *nm inv* centipede

cien *adj & nm inv* hundred; **c. libras** a o one hundred pounds; **c. por c.** one hundred per cent

ciénaga *nf* marsh, bog

ciencia *nf* science; *Fig* **saber algo a c. cierta** to know sth for certain; **c. ficción** science fiction; **c. infusa** intuition; **ciencias ocultas** the occult

cieno *nm* mud, mire

científico, -a 1 *adj* scientific
2 *nm,f* scientist

cientista *nmf CSur* **c. social** social scientist

ciento *adj* hundred; **c. tres** one hundred and three; **por c.** percent

ciernes *nmpl* **una campeona en c.** a budding champion; **tenemos un viaje en c.** we're planning a journey

cierre *nm* (a) *(acción)* closing, shutting; *(de fábrica)* closure; *TV* close-down; **c. patronal** lockout (b) *(de bolso)* clasp; *(de puerta)* catch; *(prenda)* fastener; **c. de seguridad** safety lock; **c. centralizado** central locking (c) *Andes, Méx, RP (cremallera) Br* zip *(fastener)*, *US* zipper; **c.** *Andes, Méx* **relámpago** o *Chile* **eclair** o *Urug* **metálico** *Br* zip *(fastener)*, *US* zipper

cierto, -a 1 *adj* (a) *(verdadero)* true; *(seguro)* certain; **estar en lo c.** to be right; **lo c. es que ...** the fact is that ...; **por c.** by the way (b) *(algún)* certain; **ciertas personas** certain o some people
2 *adv* certainly

ciervo, -a *nm,f* deer; *(macho)* stag; *(hembra)* doe, hind

cifra *nf* (a) *(número)* figure, number; *Com* **c. de ventas** sales figures (b) *(código)* cipher, code

cifrar *vt* (a) *(codificar) (mensaje, texto)* to code (b) *(valorar) (pérdidas)* to estimate (c) *(reducir) (aspiraciones, esperanzas)* to pin, to place

cigala *nf* Dublin Bay prawn, scampi

cigarra *nf* cicada

cigarrillo *nm* cigarette

cigarro *nm* (a) *(puro)* cigar (b) *(cigarrillo)* cigarette

cigüeña *nf* (a) *(ave)* stork (b) *Téc* crank

cigüeñal *nm* crankshaft

cilindrada *nf Aut* cylinder capacity

cilíndrico, -a *adj* cylindrical

cilindro *nm* cylinder

cima *nf* summit

cimbrearse *vpr* to sway

cimentar *vt* to lay the foundations of; *Fig (amistad)* to strengthen

cimientos *nmpl* foundations; **echar** *o* **poner los c.** to lay the foundations

cinc *nm* zinc

cincel *nm* chisel

cincelar *vt* to chisel

cinco *adj & nm inv* five

cincuenta *adj & nm inv* fifty

cine *nm* (a) *(local)* cinema, *US* movie theater (b) *(arte)* cinema; **c. mudo** silent movies *o Br* films; **c. sonoro** talking pictures, talkies

cineasta *nmf* movie maker *o* director, *Br* film maker *o* director

cinéfilo, -a *nm,f (que va al cine)* (keen) moviegoer *o Br* filmgoer; *(que entiende de cine)* movie *o Br* film buff

cinematografía *nf* cinematography, *Br* film-making

cinematográfico, -a *adj* movie, *Br* film; **la industria cinematográfica** the movie *o Br* film industry

cíngaro, -a *adj & nm,f* gypsy

cínico, -a 1 *adj* shameless
2 *nm,f* shameless person; **es un c.** he's shameless, he has no shame

> *Observa que la palabra inglesa **cynic** es un falso amigo y no es la traducción de la palabra española **cínico**. En inglés **cynic** significa tanto "descreído, suspicaz" como "desaprensivo".*

cinismo *nm* shamelessness

> *Observa que la palabra inglesa **cynicism** es un falso amigo y no es la traducción de la palabra española **cinismo**. En inglés **cynicism** significa "descreimiento, suspicacia".*

cinta *nf* (a) *(tira)* band, strip; *(para adornar)* ribbon; *Cost* braid, edging (b) *Téc & Mús* tape; **c. adhesiva/aislante** adhesive/insulating tape; **c. de vídeo** video tape; **c. transportadora** conveyor belt (c) *Cin* movie, *Br* film

cinto *nm* belt

cintura *nf* waist

cinturón *nm* belt; *Fig* **apretarse el c.** to tighten one's belt; **c. de seguridad** safety belt; *Am* **c. de miseria** = slum or shanty town area round a large city

cipote [1] *nm* (a) *Fam (bobo)* dimwit, moron (b) *Vulg (pene)* prick, cock

cipote [2], **-a** *nm,f CAm* kid

ciprés *(pl* **cipreses)** *nm* cypress

circense *adj* circus

circo *nm* circus

circuito *nm* circuit

circulación *nf* (a) *(de personas, sangre, dinero)* circulation (b) *(tráfico)* traffic

circular 1 *adj & nf* circular
2 *vi (moverse)* to circulate; *(líquido)* to flow; *(tren, autobús)* to run; *Fig (rumor)* to go round; **circule por la izquierda** *(en letrero)* keep to the left

circulatorio, -a *adj* circulatory; *Aut* **un caos c.** traffic chaos

círculo *nm* circle; *Fig* **c. vicioso** vicious circle

circuncisión *nf* circumcision

circundante *adj* surrounding

circundar *vt* to surround, to encircle

circunferencia *nf* circumference

circunloquio *nm* circumlocution

circunscribir *(pp* **circunscrito) 1** *vt* (a) *(limitar)* to restrict, to confine (b) *Geom* to circumscribe
2 circunscribirse *vpr* to confine *o* limit oneself (**a** to)

circunscripción *nf* district; **c. electoral** electoral district, *Br* constituency

circunscrito, -a 1 *adj* circumscribed
2 *pp de* **circunscribir**

circunspecto, -a *adj* circumspect

circunstancia *nf* circumstance; **en estas circunstancias ...** under the circumstances ...

circunstancial *adj* circumstantial

cirio *nm* wax candle

cirrosis *nf inv* cirrhosis

ciruela *nf* plum; **c. claudia** greengage; **c. pasa** prune

ciruelo *nm* plum tree

cirugía *nf* surgery; **c. estética** *o* **plástica** plastic surgery

cirujano, -a *nm,f* surgeon

cisma *nm* (a) *Rel* schism (b) *Pol* split

cisne *nm* swan

cisterna *nf* cistern, tank

cistitis *nf inv* cystitis

cita *nf* (a) *(profesional)* appointment; **darse c.** to arrange to meet (b) *(amorosa)* date (c) *(mención)* quotation

citación *nf Der* citation, summons *sing*

citado, -a *adj* aforementioned

citar 1 *vt* (a) *(dar cita)* to arrange to meet, to make an appointment with (b) *(mencionar)* to quote (c) *Der* to summons
  2 **citarse** *vpr* **citarse (con algn)** to arrange to meet (sb)

citología *nf Med (análisis)* cervical smear, smear test

cítrico, -a 1 *adj* citric, citrus
  2 **cítricos** *nmpl* citrus fruits

ciudad *nf* town; *(capital)* city; *Méx* **c. perdida** shanty town

ciudadanía *nf* citizenship

ciudadano, -a 1 *nm,f* citizen; **el c. de a pie** the man in the street
  2 *adj* civic

cívico, -a *adj* civic

civil 1 *adj* civil; **matrimonio c.** civil marriage
  2 *nmf* (a) *(no militar)* civilian (b) *Fam (Guardia Civil)* member of the Guardia Civil

civilización *nf* civilization

civilizado, -a *adj* civilized

civilizar [40] *vt* to civilize

civismo *nm* (a) *(urbanidad)* public-spiritedness (b) *(cortesía)* civility

cizaña *nf Bot* bearded darnel; *Fig* **sembrar c.** to sow discord

cl *(abr* **centilitro(s)**) cl

clamar *vt* to cry out for, to clamour for

clamor *nm* clamour

clamoroso, -a *adj* resounding

clan *nm* clan

clandestinidad *nf* **en la c.** underground

clandestino, -a *adj* clandestine, underground; **aborto c.** backstreet abortion

clara *nf* (a) *(de huevo)* white (b) *Esp Fam (bebida)* shandy

claraboya *nf* skylight

clarear *vi* (a) *(amanecer)* to dawn (b) *(despejar)* to clear up (c) *(transparentar)* to wear thin, to become transparent

clarete 1 *adj* **vino c.** light red wine
  2 *nm* light red wine

claridad *nf* (a) *(luz)* light, brightness (b) *(inteligibilidad)* clarity; **con c.** clearly

clarificador, -a *adj* clarifying

clarificar [44] *vt* to clarify

clarín *nm* bugle

clarinete *nm* clarinet

clarividencia *nf* farsightedness, perception

clarividente 1 *adj* farsighted, perceptive
  2 *nmf* clairvoyant

claro, -a 1 *adj* (a) *(luminoso)* bright; *(color)* light; *(día)* clear (b) *(sonido)* clear (c) *(diluido)* *(té, café)* weak; *(salsa)* thin (d) *(poco tupido)* thin, sparse (e) *(explicación, ideas, libro)* clear (f) *(obvio, evidente)* clear; **está c. que …** of course …; **¿está c.?** is that clear?
  2 *interj* of course!; **¡c. que no!** of course not!; **¡c. que sí!** certainly!
  3 *nm* (a) *(espacio)* gap, space; *(en un bosque)* clearing (b) *Met* bright spell
  4 *adv* clearly

clase *nf* (a) *(grupo)* class; **c. alta/media** upper/middle class; **clases pasivas** pensioners; **primera/segunda c.** first/second class (b) *(tipo)* kind, sort; **toda c. de …** all kinds of … (c) *Educ (curso)* class; *(aula)* classroom; **c. particular** private class *o* lesson (d) *(estilo)* class; **tener c.** to have class

clásico, -a 1 *adj* classical; *(típico)* classic; *(en el vestir)* classic
  2 *nm* classic

clasificación *nf* classification; *Dep* league table

clasificador, -a 1 *adj* classifying
  2 *nm (mueble)* filing cabinet

clasificar [44] 1 *vt* to classify, to class
  2 **clasificarse** *vpr Dep* to qualify

claudicar [44] *vi* to give in

claustro *nm* (a) *Arquit* cloister (b) *(reunión)* ≃ staff meeting, *US* faculty meeting

claustrofobia *nf* claustrophobia

cláusula *nf* clause

clausura *nf* (a) *(cierre)* closure; **ceremonia de c.** closing ceremony (b) *Rel* enclosure

clausurar *vt* to close

clavadista *nmf CAm, Méx* diver

clavado, -a *adj* (a) *(con clavos)* nailed (b) *(a la medida)* just right (c) *(parecido)* almost identical; **ser c. a algn** to be the spitting image of sb

clavar 1 *vt* (a) *(con clavos)* to nail; *(clavo)* to bang *o* hammer in; *(estaca)* to drive in (b) *Fam (timar)* to sting, to fleece
  2 **clavarse** *vpr* **clavarse una astilla** to get a splinter

clave 1 *nf* key; **la palabra c.** the key word
  2 *nm* harpsichord

clavel *nm* carnation

clavícula *nf* collarbone

clavija *nf Téc* jack

clavo *nm* (a) *(pieza)* nail; *Fig* **dar en el c.** to hit the nail on the head (b) *(especia)* clove

claxon *nm* horn; **tocar el c.** to sound the horn

clemencia *nf* mercy, clemency

clementina *nf* clementine

cleptomanía *nf* kleptomania

cleptómano, -a *adj & nm,f* kleptomaniac

clerical *adj* clerical

clericó *nm RP* = drink made of white wine and fruit

clérigo *nm* priest

clero *nm* clergy

clic (*pl* **clics**), **click** (*pl* **clicks**) *nm Inform* click; **hacer c. (en)** to click (on); **hacer doble c.** to double-click

cliché *nm* (a) *Fig* (*tópico*) cliché (b) *Fot* negative (c) *Impr* plate

cliente *nmf* customer, client

clientela *nf* clientele

clima *nm* climate

climático, -a *adj* climatic

climatizado, -a *adj* air-conditioned

climatizar [40] *vt* to air-condition

climatología *nf* (a) (*tiempo*) climate (b) (*ciencia*) climatology

clímax *nm inv* climax

clínica *nf* clinic

clínico, -a *adj* clinical

clip (*pl* **clips**) *nm* clip

clítoris *nm inv* clitoris

cloaca *nf* sewer, drain

clorhídrico, -a *adj* hydrochloric

cloro *nm* chlorine

clorofila *nf* chlorophyll

cloroformo *nm* chloroform

cloruro *nm* chloride; **c. sódico** sodium chloride

clóset (*pl* **clósets**) *nm Am* fitted cupboard, *US* closet

club (*pl* **clubs** o **clubes**) *nm* club; **c. náutico** yacht club

cm (*abr* **centímetro(s)**) cm

CNT *nf* (*abr* **Confederación Nacional del Trabajo**) = Spanish anarchist trade union federation

coacción *nf* coercion

coaccionar *vt* to coerce

coactivo, -a *adj* coercive

coagular 1 *vt* (*sangre*) to clot, to coagulate; (*líquido*) to coagulate
  2 coagularse *vpr* (*sangre*) to clot; (*líquido*) to coagulate

coágulo *nm Med* clot

coalición *nf* coalition

coartada *nf* alibi

coartar *vt* to restrict

coba *nf Esp, Méx Fam* (*halago*) flattery; **dar c. a algn** (*adular*) to suck up o crawl to sb; (*aplacar*) to soft-soap sb

cobalto *nm* cobalt

cobarde 1 *adj* cowardly
  2 *nmf* coward

cobardía *nf* cowardice

cobaya *nf* guinea pig

cobertizo *nm* shed, shack

cobertor *nm* bedspread

cobertura *nf* cover; (*de noticia*) coverage

cobija *nf Am* (*manta*) blanket

cobijar 1 *vt* to shelter
  2 cobijarse *vpr* to take shelter

cobijo *nm* shelter; *Fig* (*protección*) protection

cobra *nf* cobra

cobrador, -a *nm,f* (a) (*de autobús*) (*hombre*) conductor; (*mujer*) conductress (b) (*de luz, agua etc*) collector

cobrar 1 *vt* (a) (*dinero*) to charge; (*cheque*) to cash; (*salario*) to earn; **¿me cobra?** how much is that? (b) *Fig* (*fuerza*) to gain, to get; **c. ánimos** to take courage o heart; **c. importancia** to become important
  2 *vi Fam* to catch it
  3 cobrarse *vpr* **¿se cobra?** (*al pagar*) how much is that?

cobre *nm* copper

cobrizo, -a *adj* copper, copper-coloured

cobro *nm* (*pago*) collecting; (*de cheque*) cashing; *Tel* **llamada a c. revertido** *Br* reverse-charge call, *US* collect call

coca *nf* (a) *Bot* coca (b) *Fam* (*droga*) cocaine, coke

cocaína *nf* cocaine

cocainómano, -a *nm,f* cocaine addict

cocalero, -a *Bol, Perú* **1** *adj* **región cocalera** coca-producing area; **productor c.** coca farmer o producer
  2 *nm,f* coca farmer o producer

cocción *nf* cooking; (*en agua*) boiling; (*en horno*) baking

cocear *vi* to kick

cocer [41] **1** *vt* to cook; (*hervir*) to boil; (*hornear*) to bake
  2 *vi* (*hervir*) to boil
  3 cocerse *vpr* (a) (*comida*) to cook; (*hervir*) to boil; (*hornear*) to bake (b) (*tramarse*) to be going on

cochambroso, -a *adj* squalid

cochayuyo *nm Chile, Perú* seaweed

coche *nm* (a) (*automóvil*) car, *US* automobile; **en c.** by car; **c. de carreras** racing car; **c. de bomberos** fire engine, *US* fire truck; **c. fúnebre** hearse (b) *Ferroc* coach, *Br* carriage, *US* car; **c. cama** sleeping car, sleeper (c) (*de caballos*) carriage

cochecito *nm* (*de niño*) *Br* pram, *US* baby carriage

cochera *nf* (a) (*para coches*) garage (b) (*de autobuses*) depot

cochinillo *nm* suckling pig

cochino, -a 1 *nm,f* (**a**) *(macho)* pig; *(hembra)* sow (**b**) *Fam (persona)* filthy person, pig
2 *adj (sucio)* filthy, disgusting

cocido *nm* stew

cociente *nm* quotient

cocina *nf* (**a**) *(habitación)* kitchen (**b**) *(aparato)* cooker, stove; **c. eléctrica/de gas** electric/gas cooker (**c**) *(arte)* cooking; **c. casera** home cooking; **c. española** Spanish cooking *o* cuisine

cocinar *vt & vi* to cook

cocinero, -a *nm,f* cook

cocktail *nm* = **cóctel**

coco¹ *nm* coconut; *Fam (cabeza)* nut; **comerle el c. a algn** to brainwash sb; **comerse el c.** to get obsessed

coco² *nm Fam (fantasma)* bogeyman

cocodrilo *nm* crocodile

cocoliche *nm RP Fam* = pidgin Spanish spoken by Italian immigrants

cocotero *nm* coconut palm

cóctel *nm* cocktail; **c. Molotov** Molotov cocktail

coctelera *nf* cocktail shaker

codazo *nm* (**a**) *(señal)* nudge with one's elbow (**b**) *(golpe)* blow with one's elbow

codearse *vpr* to rub shoulders (**con** with), to hobnob (**con** with)

codeína *nf* codeine

codicia *nf* greed

codiciar [43] *vt* to covet

codicioso, -a *adj* covetous, greedy

codificado, -a *adj (emisión de TV)* scrambled

codificar [44] *vt (ley)* to codify; *(mensajes)* to encode

código *nm* code; **c. de barras** bar code; **c. de circulación** highway code; **c. postal** *Br* postcode, postal code, *US* zip code

codo *nm* elbow; *Fig* **c. con c.** side by side; *Fam* **hablar por los codos** to talk nonstop

codorniz *nf* quail

coeficiente *nm (índice)* rate; *Mat & Fís* coefficient; **c. intelectual** intelligence quotient

coercitivo, -a *adj* coercive

coetáneo, -a *adj & nm,f* contemporary

coexistencia *nf* coexistence

coexistir *vi* to coexist

cofia *nf* bonnet

cofradía *nf (hermandad)* brotherhood; *(asociación)* association

cofre *nm (arca)* trunk, chest; *(para joyas)* box, casket

coger [53] *esp Esp* **1** *vt* (**a**) to take; *(del suelo)* to pick (up); *(fruta, flores)* to pick; *(asir)* to seize, to take hold of; *(bus, tren)* to take, to catch; *(pelota, ladrón, resfriado)* to catch; *(entender)* to grasp; *(costumbre)* to pick up; *(velocidad, fuerza)* to gather; *(atropellar)* to run over, to knock down (**b**) *Am Vulg* to screw, to fuck
2 *vi Fam* **cogió y se fue** he upped and left
3 cogerse *vpr (agarrarse)* to hold on

cogida *nf* goring

cognitivo, -a *adj* cognitive

cogollo *nm (de lechuga)* heart

cogote *nm Esp* nape *o* back of the neck

cohabitación *nf* cohabitation

cohabitar *vi* to live together, to cohabit

cohecho *nm Der* bribery

coherencia *nf* coherence

coherente *adj* coherent

cohesión *nf* cohesion

cohete *nm* rocket; **c. espacial** space rocket

cohibido, -a *adj* inhibited

cohibir 1 *vt* to inhibit
2 cohibirse *vpr* to feel inhibited

COI *nm Dep (abr* **Comité Olímpico Internacional)** IOC

coima *nf Andes, RP Fam* bribe, *Br* backhander

coincidencia *nf* coincidence

coincidir *vi* (**a**) *(versiones, gustos)* to coincide (**b**) *(concordar)* to agree; **todos coincidieron en señalar que ...** everyone agreed that ... (**c**) *(en un sitio)* to meet by chance (**d**) *(en el tiempo)* to coincide

coito *nm* intercourse, coitus

cojear *vi (persona)* to limp, to hobble; *(mueble)* to wobble

cojera *nf* limp

cojín *nm* cushion

cojinete *nm Téc* bearing; **c. de agujas/bolas** needle/ball bearing

cojo, -a 1 *adj (persona)* lame; *(mueble)* rickety
2 *nm,f* lame person

cojón *nm Esp Vulg* ball; **de cojones** *(estupendo) Br* bloody *o US* goddamn brilliant; *(pésimo) Br* bloody *o US* goddamn awful

cojonudo, -a *adj Esp muy Fam Br* bloody *o US* goddamn brilliant

cojudez *nf Andes muy Fam* **¡qué c.!** *(acto)* what a *Br* bloody *o US* goddamn stupid thing to do!; *(dicho)* what a *Br* bloody *o US* goddamn stupid thing to say!

cojudo, -a *adj Andes muy Fam Br* bloody *o US* goddamn stupid

col *nf* cabbage; **c. de Bruselas** Brussels sprout

cola nf (a) *(de animal)* tail; *(de vestido)* train; *(de pelo)* ponytail; **a la c.** at the back o rear; *Fam* **traer c.** to have consequences (**b**) *(fila)* Br queue, US line; **hacer c.** Br to queue (up), US to stand in line (**c**) *(pegamento)* glue

colaboración nf (a) *(cooperación)* collaboration (**b**) *(en prensa)* contribution

colaboracionismo nm Pol collaboration

colaborador, -a nm,f *(compañero)* associate, colleague; *(de prensa)* contributor, writer; **c. externo** freelancer

colaborar vi to collaborate, to co-operate

colación nf sacar o traer (algo) a c. to bring (sth) up

colada nf Esp wash, laundry; **hacer la c.** to do the washing o laundry

colado, -a adj (a) *(líquido)* strained (**b**) *Fam (enamorado)* **estar c. por algn** to have a crush on sb

colador nm colander, sieve; *(de té, café)* strainer

colapsar 1 vt to bring to a standstill
2 colapsarse vpr to come to a standstill

colapso nm (a) *Med* collapse (**b**) *Aut* **c. circulatorio** traffic jam, hold-up

colar [2] **1** vt (a) *(líquido)* to strain, to filter (**b**) *(por agujero)* to slip
2 vi *Fam* **esa mentira no cuela** that lie won't wash
3 colarse vpr (a) *(líquido)* **colarse por** to seep through (**b**) *(persona) (en un sitio)* to slip, to sneak; *(en una cola)* Br to jump the queue, US to cut in line (**c**) *Fam (equivocarse)* to slip up

colateral adj collateral

colcha nf bedspread

colchón nm mattress

colchoneta nf air bed

colear vi (a) *(animal)* to wag its tail; *Fam* **vivito y coleando** alive and kicking (**b**) *Fam* **el asunto aún colea** we haven't heard the last of it yet

colección nf collection

coleccionable adj & nm collectable

coleccionar vt to collect

coleccionista nmf collector

colecta nf collection

colectividad nf community

colectivo, -a 1 adj collective
2 nm (a) *(asociación)* association (**b**) *Andes (taxi)* collective taxi *(with a fixed rate and that travels a fixed route)* (**c**) *Arg, Bol (autobús)* bus

colega nmf (a) *(compañero profesional)* colleague, US co-worker (**b**) *Esp Fam (amigo)* pal, Br mate, US buddy

colegiado, -a nm,f Dep referee

colegial, -a 1 adj *(escolar)* school
2 nm,f *(alumno)* schoolboy; *(alumna)* schoolgirl; **los colegiales** the schoolchildren

colegio nm (a) *(escuela)* school; **c. privado** private school, Br public o independent school (**b**) *(profesional)* association, college; **c. de abogados** the Bar; Pol **c. electoral** electoral college (**c**) Esp **c. mayor** hall of residence

colegir [58] vt to infer, to deduce

cólera[1] nf anger, rage

cólera[2] nm Med cholera

colérico, -a adj furious

colesterol nm cholesterol

coleta nf pigtail, ponytail; *Fig* **cortarse la c.** to retire

coletazo nm dar los últimos coletazos to be on one's last legs

coletilla nf *(de discurso, escrito)* closing comment

colgado, -a adj (a) *Fam* **dejar (a algn) c.** to leave (sb) in the lurch (**b**) *Fam (atontado, loco)* crazy, daft; *(drogado)* high

colgador nm *(percha)* hanger, coathanger; *(gancho)* hook

colgante 1 nm *(joya)* pendant
2 adj hanging

colgar [2] **1** vt *(suspender, ahorcar)* to hang; *(colada)* to hang (out)
2 vi (a) *(pender)* to hang (**de** from); *Fig* **c. de un hilo** to hang by a thread (**b**) *Tel* to hang up
3 colgarse vpr *(ahorcarse)* to hang oneself

colibrí *(pl* colibrís o colibríes*)* nm hummingbird

cólico nm colic

coliflor nf cauliflower

colijo *indic pres de* colegir

colilla nf *(cigarette)* end o butt

colimba nf Arg Fam military service

colina nf hill

colindante adj adjoining, adjacent

colindar vi to be adjacent (**con** to)

colirio nm eye-drops

colisión nf collision, crash

colisionar vi to collide, to crash

colitis nf inv colitis

colla Bol **1** adj of/from the altiplano
2 nmf = indigenous person from the altiplano

collage nm collage

collar nm (a) *(adorno)* necklace (**b**) *(de perro)* collar

collarín nm surgical collar

colmado, -a *adj* full, filled; *(cucharada)* heaped

colmar *vt* (a) *(vaso, copa)* to fill to the brim; **c. a algn de regalos/elogios** to shower gifts/praise on sb (b) *(ambiciones)* to fulfil, to satisfy

colmena *nf* beehive

colmillo *nm* eye o canine tooth; *Zool (de carnívoro)* fang; *(de jabalí, elefante)* tusk

colmo *nm* height; **el c. de** the height of; **¡eso es el c.!** that's the last straw!; **para c.** to top it all

colocación *nf* (a) *(acto)* positioning (b) *(disposición)* lay-out (c) *(empleo)* job, employment

colocado, -a *adj* (a) *(empleado)* employed (b) *Fam (drogado)* high

colocar [44] **1** *vt* (a) *(en una posición, un lugar)* to place, to put (b) *Fin (invertir)* to invest (c) *(emplear)* to find a job for (d) *Fam (drogar)* to give a high to
2 colocarse *vpr* (a) *(situarse)* to put oneself (b) *(emplearse)* to take a job (**de as**) (c) *Fam (drogarse)* to get high

colofón *nm* (a) *(remate, fin)* climax, culmination (b) *(apéndice)* colophon

Colombia *n* Colombia

colombiano, -a *adj & nm,f* Colombian

Colón *n* Columbus

colón *nm Fin* colon, = standard monetary unit of Costa Rica and El Salvador

colonia¹ *nf* colony; *(campamento)* summer camp; *Méx (barrio)* district

colonia² *nf (perfume)* cologne

colonial *adj* colonial

colonialismo *nm* colonialism

colonización *nf* colonization

colonizar [40] *vt* to colonize

colono *nm* settler, colonist

coloquial *adj* colloquial

coloquio *nm* discussion, colloquium

color *nm* colour; *Cin & Fot* **en c.** in colour; **de colores** multicoloured; **de c.** *(persona)* coloured

colorado, -a 1 *adj* red; **ponerse c.** to blush
2 *nm* red

> ℓ Observa que la palabra inglesa **coloured** es un falso amigo y no es la traducción de la palabra española **colorado**. En inglés, **coloured** significa "coloreado".

colorante *nm* colouring

colorear *vt* to colour

colorete *nm* rouge

colorido *nm* colour

colorín *nm* bright colour; **c. colorado, este cuento se ha acabado** and they all lived happily ever after

colosal *adj* colossal

columna *nf* column; *Anat* **c. vertebral** vertebral column, spinal column

columpiar [43] **1** *vt* to swing
2 columpiarse *vpr* to swing

columpio *nm* swing

coma¹ *nf* (a) *Ling & Mús* comma (b) *Mat* point; **tres c. cinco** three point five

coma² *nm Med* coma

comadre *nf* (a) *(madrina)* = godmother of one's child, or mother of one's godchild (b) *Fam (amiga) Br* mate, *US* buddy

comadreja *nf* weasel

comadreo *nm* gossip, gossiping

comadrona *nf* midwife

comal *nm CAm, Méx* = flat clay or metal dish used for baking "tortillas"

comandancia *nf* (a) *(rango)* command (b) *(edificio)* command headquarters (c) *Méx (de policía)* police station

comandante *nm* (a) *Mil* commander, commanding officer (b) *Av* captain

comandar *vt* to command

comando *nm* (a) *Mil* commando (b) *Inform* command

comarca *nf* region

comarcal *adj* regional

comba *nf Esp* (a) *(juego)* skipping; **jugar a la c.** *Br* to skip, *US* to jump rope (b) *(cuerda) Br* skipping rope, *US* jump rope

combar *vt* to bend

combate *nm* combat; *(en boxeo)* fight; *Mil* battle; **fuera de c.** out for the count; *(eliminado)* out of action

combatiente 1 *adj* fighting
2 *nmf* combatant

combatir 1 *vt* to combat
2 *vi* **c. contra** to fight against

combativo, -a *adj* spirited, aggressive

combinación *nf* (a) *(acción)* combination (b) *(prenda)* slip

combinado, -a 1 *adj* combined
2 *nm* (a) *(cóctel)* cocktail (b) *Dep* line-up

combinar 1 *vt* (a) *(mezclar)* to combine; *(bebidas)* to mix; *(colores)* to match
2 *vi* *(colores, ropa)* **c. con** to go with

combustible 1 *nm* fuel
2 *adj* combustible

combustión *nf* combustion

comecocos *nm inv* (a) *Fam (para convencer)* **este panfleto es un c.** this pamphlet is designed to brainwash you (b) *Fam (cosa difícil de comprender)* mindbending problem o puzzle (c) *(juego)* pac-man®

comedia nf comedy

comediante, -a nm,f actor, f actress

comedido, -a adj self-restrained, reserved

comedor nm dining room

comensal nmf companion at table

comentar vt **c. algo con algn** to talk sth over with sb; **me han comentado que …** I've been told that …

comentario nm (a) (observación) comment, remark; **sin c.** no comment (b) (crítica) commentary (c) **comentarios** (cotilleos) gossip

comentarista nmf commentator

comenzar [51] vt & vi to begin, to start; **comenzó a llover** it started raining o to rain; **comenzó diciendo que …** he started by saying that …

comer 1 vt (a) (alimentos) to eat (b) (en juegos) to take, to capture

2 vi (ingerir alimentos) to eat; Esp, Méx (al mediodía) to have lunch; **dar de c. a algn** to feed sb

3 **comerse** vpr (a) (alimentos) to eat (b) (en los juegos de tablero) to take, to capture

comercial adj commercial

comercialización nf marketing

comercializar [40] vt to market

comerciante nmf merchant

comerciar [43] vi to trade; **comercia con oro** he trades in gold

comercio nm (a) (actividad) commerce, trade; **c. exterior** foreign trade; Inform **c. electrónico** e-commerce; **c. justo** fair trade (b) (tienda) shop

comestible 1 adj edible

2 **comestibles** nmpl food, foodstuff(s); **tienda de comestibles** grocer's shop, US grocery store

cometa 1 nm Astron comet

2 nf (juguete) kite

cometer vt (error, falta) to make; (delito, crimen) to commit

cometido nm (a) (tarea) task, assignment (b) (deber) duty; **cumplir su c.** to do one's duty

comezón nm itch

cómic (pl cómics) nm comic

comicios nmpl elections

cómico, -a 1 adj (a) (gracioso) comic, comical (b) (de la comedia) comedy, comic; **actor c.** comedy actor

2 nm,f (humorista) comedian, comic, f comedienne

comida nf (a) (alimento) food; **c. basura** junk food (b) (almuerzo, cena) meal; Esp, Méx (al mediodía) lunch

comidilla nf Fam **la c. del pueblo** the talk of the town

comienzo nm beginning, start; **a comienzos de** at the beginning of; **dar c. (a algo)** to begin o start (sth)

comillas nfpl inverted commas; **entre c.** in inverted commas

comilón, -ona 1 adj greedy, gluttonous

2 nm,f big eater, glutton

comilona nf Fam blow-out, Br slap-up meal

comino nm cumin, cummin; Fam **me importa un c.** I don't give a damn (about it)

comisaría nf police station, US station house

comisario nm (a) (de policía) Br superintendent, US captain (b) (delegado) commissioner; **c. europeo** European Commissioner

comisión nf (a) Com (retribución) commission; **a o con c.** on a commission basis (b) (comité) committee; **la C. Europea** the European Commission

comisura nf corner (of mouth, eyes)

comité nm committee

comitiva nf suite, retinue

como 1 adv (a) (manera) how; **me gusta c. cantas** I like the way you sing; **dilo c. quieras** say it however you like

(b) (comparación) as; **blanco c. la nieve** as white as snow; **habla c. su padre** he talks like his father

(c) (según) as; **c. decíamos ayer** as we were saying yesterday

(d) (en calidad de) as; **c. presidente** as president; **lo compré c. recuerdo** I bought it as a souvenir

(e) (aproximadamente) about; **c. a la mitad de camino** halfway; **c. unos diez** about ten

2 conj (a) Esp (+ subj) (si) if; **c. no estudies vas a suspender** if you don't study, you'll fail (b) (porque) as, since; **c. no venías me marché** as you didn't come, I left (c) **c. si** as if; **c. si nada** o **tal cosa** as if nothing had happened; Fam **c. si lo viera** I can imagine perfectly well

cómo 1 adv (a) ¿**c.?** (¿perdón?) what? (b) (interrogativo) how; ¿**c. estás?** how are you?; ¿**c. lo sabes?** how do you know?; ¿**c. es de grande/ancho?** how big/wide is it?; Esp ¿**a c. están los tomates?** how much are the tomatoes?; ¿**c. es que no viniste a la fiesta?** (por qué) how come you didn't come to the party?; Fam ¿**c. es eso?** how come? (c) (exclamativo) how; ¡**c. has crecido!** you've really grown a lot!; ¡**c. no!** but of course!

2 nm **el c. y el porqué** the whys and wherefores

cómoda nf chest of drawers
comodidad nf (a) (estado, cualidad) comfort (b) (convenciencia) convenience

> ⏺ Observa que la palabra inglesa **commodity** es un falso amigo y no es la traducción de la palabra española **comodidad**. En inglés, **commodity** significa "producto básico".

comodín nm Naipes joker
cómodo, -a adj (a) (confortable) comfortable; **ponerse c.** to make oneself comfortable (b) (útil) handy, convenient
comodón, -ona 1 adj (amante de la comodidad) comfort-loving; (vago) laid-back; **no seas c.** don't be so lazy
  2 nm,f (amante de la comodidad) comfort-lover; (vago) laid-back person
comoquiera adv **c. que** whichever way, however
compa nmf Fam pal, Br mate, US buddy
compact ['kompak] nm inv compact disc
compacto, -a adj compact; **disco c.** compact disc
compadecer [33] **1** vt to feel sorry for, to pity
  2 compadecerse vpr to have o take pity (**de** on)
compadre nm (a) (padrino) = godfather of one's child, or father of one's godchild (b) Fam (amigo) Br mate, US buddy
compadrear vi RP to brag, to boast
compadreo nm (amistad) friendship
compaginar vt to combine
compañerismo nm companionship, comradeship
compañero, -a nm,f companion; **c. de colegio** school friend; Esp **c. de piso** Br flatmate, US roommate
compañía nf company; **hacer c. (a algn)** to keep (sb) company; **c. de seguros/de teatro** insurance/theatre company
comparable adj comparable
comparación nf comparison; **en c.** comparatively; **en c. con** compared to; **sin c.** beyond compare
comparar vt to compare (**con** with)
comparativo, -a adj & nm comparative
comparecencia nf appearance
comparecer [33] vi Der to appear (**ante** before)
comparsa nf band of revellers
compartimento, compartimiento nm compartment; **c. de primera/segunda clase** first-/second-class compartment
compartir vt to share
compás (pl compases) nm (a) Téc (pair of) compasses (b) Náut compass (c) Mús

(división) time; (intervalo) beat; (ritmo) rhythm; **c. de espera** Mús bar rest; Fig (pausa) delay; **al c. de** in time to
compasión nf compassion, pity; **tener c. (de algn)** to feel sorry (for sb)
compasivo, -a adj compassionate
compatible adj compatible
compatriota nmf compatriot; (hombre) fellow countryman; (mujer) fellow countrywoman
compendiar [43] vt to abridge, to summarize
compendio nm compendium
compenetrarse vpr to understand each other o one another
compensación nf compensation
compensar 1 vt (pérdida, error) to make up for; (indemnizar) to compensate (for)
  2 vi to be worthwhile; **este trabajo no compensa** this job's not worth my while
competencia nf (a) (rivalidad, empresas rivales) competition (b) (capacidad) competence (c) (incumbencia) field, province; **no es de mi c.** it's not up to me
competente adj competent
competición nf competition, contest
competido, -a adj hard-fought
competidor, -a 1 nm,f competitor
  2 adj competing
competir [6] vi to compete (**con** with o against; **en** in; **por** for)
competitividad nf competitivity
competitivo, -a adj competitive
compilar vt to compile
compinche nmf (a) (compañero) chum, pal (b) (cómplice) accomplice
complacencia nf (a) (satisfacción) satisfaction (b) (indulgencia) indulgence

> ⏺ Observa que la palabra inglesa **complacency** es un falso amigo y no es la traducción de la palabra española **complacencia**. En inglés, **complacency** significa "autocomplacencia".

complacer [60] **1** vt to please; Fml **me complace presentarles a ...** it gives me great pleasure to introduce to you ...
  2 complacerse vpr to delight (**en** in), to take pleasure (**en** in)
complaciente adj obliging
complejidad nf complexity
complejo, -a adj & nm complex
complementar 1 vt to complement
  2 complementarse vpr to complement (each other), to be complementary to (each other)
complementario, -a adj complementary

complemento *nm* complement; *Ling* object

completamente *adv* completely

completar *vt* to complete

completo, -a *adj* (a) *(terminado)* complete; **por c.** completely (b) *(lleno)* full; **al c.** full up

complexión *nf* build; **de c. fuerte** well-built

> *Observa que la palabra inglesa **complexion** es un falso amigo y no esla traducción de la palabra española **complexión**. En inglés **complexion** significa "tez".*

complicación *nf* complication

complicado, -a *adj* (a) *(complejo)* complicated (b) *(implicado)* involved

complicar [44] **1** *vt* (a) *(dificultar)* to complicate (b) *(involucrar)* **c. a algn en** to involve sb in
2 complicarse *upr* to get complicated; **complicarse la vida** to make life difficult for oneself

cómplice *nmf* accomplice

complot *(pl* **complots)** *nm* conspiracy, plot

componente 1 *adj* component
2 *nm* (a) *(pieza)* component; *(ingrediente)* ingredient (b) *(persona)* member

componer [19] *(pp* **compuesto) 1** *vt* (a) *(formar)* to compose, to make up (b) *Mús & Lit* to compose (c) *(reparar)* to mend, to repair
2 componerse *upr* (a) **componerse de** *(consistir)* to be made up of, to consist of (b) *(arreglarse)* to dress up (c) *Fam* **componérselas** to manage

comportamiento *nm* behaviour

comportar 1 *vt* to entail, to involve
2 comportarse *upr* to behave; **comportarse mal** to misbehave

composición *nf* composition

compositor, -a *nm,f* composer

compostelano, -a *adj* of/from Santiago de Compostela

compostura *nf* composure

compota *nf* compote

compra *nf* *(acción)* buying; *(cosa comprada)* purchase, buy; **hace** *Esp* **la c.** o *Am* **las compras** to do the shopping; **ir de compras** to go shopping

comprador, -a *nm,f* purchaser, buyer

comprar *vt* (a) *(adquirir)* to buy (b) *(sobornar)* to bribe, to buy off

compraventa *nf* trading; **contrato de c.** contract of sale

comprender *vt* (a) *(entender)* to understand; **se comprende** it's understandable (b) *(contener)* to comprise, to include

comprensible *adj* understandable

comprensión *nf* understanding

comprensivo, -a *adj* understanding

> *Observa que la palabra inglesa **comprehensive** es un falso amigo y no es la traducción de la palabra española **comprensivo**. En inglés **comprehensive** significa "amplio, detallado".*

compresa *nf* (a) *(para mujer)* sanitary *Br* towel o *US* napkin (b) *Med* compress

compresor, -a 1 *adj* compressing
2 *nm* compressor

comprimido, -a 1 *nm* pill, tablet
2 *adj* compressed; **escopeta de aire c.** air rifle

comprimir *vt* to compress

comprobación *nf* checking

comprobante *nm* *(de compra etc)* voucher, receipt

comprobar [2] *vt* to check

comprometer 1 *vt* (a) *(arriesgar)* to compromise, to jeopardize (b) *(obligar)* to compel, to force
2 comprometerse *upr* (a) **comprometerse a hacer algo** to undertake to do sth (b) *(novios)* to become engaged

comprometido, -a *adj* (a) *(situación)* difficult (b) *(para casarse)* engaged

compromiso *nm* (a) *(obligación)* obligation, commitment; **sin c.** without obligation; **por c.** out of a sense of duty (b) **poner (a algn) en un c.** to put (sb) in a difficult o embarrassing position (c) *(acuerdo)* agreement; *Fml* **c. matrimonial** engagement; **soltero y sin c.** single and unattached

> *Observa que la palabra inglesa **compromise** es un falso amigo y no es la traducción de la palabra española **compromiso**. En inglés **compromise** significa "solución negociada".*

compuerta *nf* floodgate, sluicegate

compuesto, -a 1 *adj* (a) *(múltiple)* compound (b) **c. de** composed of
2 *nm* compound
3 *pp de* **componer**

compulsar *vt* to make a certified true copy of

compungido, -a *adj* *(arrepentido)* remorseful; *(triste)* sorrowful, sad

compuse *pt indef de* **componer**

computacional *adj* computational, computer

computadora *nf*, **computador** *nm esp Am* computer

cómputo *nm* calculation

comulgar [42] *vi* to receive Holy Communion; *Fig* **no comulgo con sus ideas** I don't share his ideas

común 1 *adj* (**a**) *(compartido) (amigo, interés, acuerdo)* mutual; *(bienes, pastos)* communal; **hacer algo en c.** to do sth together; **tener algo en c.** to have sth in common (**b**) *(habitual)* common; **poco c.** unusual; **por lo c.** generally

2 *Br Pol* **los Comunes** the Commons

comuna *nf* (**a**) *(colectividad)* commune (**b**) *Am (municipalidad)* municipality

comunal *adj* communal

comunero, -a *nm,f Perú, Méx (indígena)* = member of an indigenous village community

comunicación *nf* (**a**) *(contacto)* communication; **ponerse en c. (con algn)** to get in touch (with sb); **se nos cortó la c.** we were cut off (**b**) *(comunicado)* communication; **c. oficial** communiqué

comunicado, -a 1 *adj* **una zona bien comunicada** a well-served zone; **dos ciudades bien comunicadas** two towns with good connections (between them)

2 *nm* communiqué; **c. de prensa** press release

comunicador, -a *nm,f* communicator

comunicar [44] **1** *vt* (**a**) *(transmitir) (sentimientos, ideas)* to convey; *(movimiento, virus)* to transmit (**b**) *(información)* **c. algo a algn** to inform sb of sth, to tell sb sth (**c**) *(conectar)* to connect

2 *vi* (**a**) *(estar conectado)* **c. con** to lead to (**b**) *Esp (por teléfono) Br* to be engaged, *US* to be busy; **está comunicando** it's *Br* engaged *o US* busy

3 *comunicarse vpr (hablarse)* to communicate (with each other)

comunicativo, -a *adj* communicative

comunidad *nf* community; **C. Europea** European Community; **C. de Estados Independientes** Commonwealth of Independent States

comunión *nf* communion

comunismo *nm* communism

comunista *adj & nmf* communist

comunitario, -a *adj* (**a**) *(de la comunidad)* community (**b**) *(de UE)* Community, of the European Union

con *prep* (**a**) *(modo, manera, instrumento)* with; **córtalo c. las tijeras** cut it with the scissors; **voy cómodo c. este jersey** I'm comfortable in this sweater (**b**) *(compañía)* with; **vine c. mi hermana** I came with my sister (**c**) **c. ese frío/niebla** in that cold/fog; **estar c. (la) gripe** to have the flu (**d**) *(contenido)* with; **una bolsa c. dinero** a bag (full) of money (**e**) *(a)* to; **habló c. todos** he spoke to everybody; **sé amable c. ella** be nice to her (**f**) *(con infinitivo)* **c. llamar será suficiente** it will be enough just to phone (**g**) (+ *que* + *subj*) **bastará c. que lo esboces** a general idea will do (**h**) **c. tal (de) que ...** provided that ...; **c. todo (y eso)** even so

conato *nm* attempt; **c. de asesinato** attempted murder

cóncavo, -a *adj* concave

concebible *adj* conceivable, imaginable

concebir [6] **1** *vt* (**a**) *(plan, hijo)* to conceive (**b**) *(entender)* to understand

2 *vi (mujer)* to become pregnant, to conceive

conceder *vt* to grant; *(premio)* to award

concejal, -a *nm,f* town councillor

concejo *nm* council

concentración *nf* concentration; *(de manifestantes)* gathering; *(de coches, motos)* rally; *(de equipo)* base

concentrado *nm* concentrate

concentrar 1 *vt* to concentrate

2 *concentrarse vpr* (**a**) *(mentalmente)* to concentrate (**en** on) (**b**) *(reunirse)* to gather

concepción *nf* conception

concepto *nm* (**a**) *(idea)* concept; **tener buen/mal c. de** to have a good/a bad opinion of; **bajo** *o* **por ningún c.** under no circumstances (**b**) **en c. de** under the heading of (**c**) *(en factura)* item

concerniente *adj* **c.** (**a**) concerning, regarding; *Fml* **en lo c. a** with regard to

concernir [54] *v impers* (**a**) *(afectar)* to concern; **en lo que a mí concierne** as far as I am concerned; **en lo que concierne a** with regard *o* respect to (**b**) *(corresponder)* to be up to

concertación *nf* compromise, agreement

concertar [1] **1** *vt* (**a**) *(cita)* to arrange; *(precio)* to agree on; *(acuerdo)* to reach (**b**) *(una acción etc)* to plan, to co-ordinate

2 *vi* to agree, to tally

concesión *nf* (**a**) *(de préstamo, licencia)* granting; *(de premio)* awarding (**b**) *(cesión) (gen) & Com* concession; **sin hacer concesiones** (**a**) without making concessions (to)

concesionario, -a *nm,f* dealer

concha *nf* (**a**) *Zool (caparazón)* shell; *(carey)* tortoiseshell (**b**) *Andes, RP Vulg (vulva)* cunt (**c**) *Ven (de árbol)* bark; *(de fruta)* peel, rind; *(del pan)* crust; *(de huevo)* shell

conchabarse *vpr Fam* to gang up

concheto, -a *RP Fam* **1** *adj* posh
  2 *nm,f* rich kid

conchudo, -a *nm,f* (**a**) *Andes, Méx,Ven Fam* (*desfachatado*) **ser un c.** to be shameless, *Br* to have a brass neck (**b**) *Andes, Méx,Ven Fam* (*cómodo*) lazybones, layabout (**c**) *Perú, RP muy Fam* jerk, *Br* dickhead

conciencia *nf* (**a**) (*moral*) conscience; **tener la c. tranquila** to have a clear conscience (**b**) (*conocimiento*) consciousness, awareness; **a c.** conscientiously; **tener/tomar c. (de algo)** to be/to become aware (of sth)

concienciar [43], *Am* **concientizar** [40] **1** *vt* to make aware (**de** of)
  2 concienciarse, *Am* **concientizarse** *vpr* to become aware (**de** of)

concienzudo, -a *adj* conscientious

concierto *nm* (**a**) *Mús* concert; (*composición*) concerto (**b**) (*acuerdo*) agreement

conciliación *nf* (*en un litigio*) reconciliation; (*en un conflicto laboral*) conciliation

conciliar [43] *vt* to reconcile; **c. el sueño** to get to sleep

concilio *nm* council

concisión *nf* conciseness

conciso, -a *adj* concise

conciudadano, -a *nm,f* fellow citizen

concluir [37] *vt* to conclude

conclusión *nf* conclusion; **sacar una c.** to draw a conclusion

concluyente *adj* conclusive

concomerse *vpr* to be consumed; **c. de envidia** to be green with envy

concordancia *nf también Ling* agreement

concordar [2] **1** *vi* to agree; **esto no concuerda con lo que dijo ayer** this doesn't fit in with what he said yesterday
  2 *vt* to bring into agreement

concordia *nf* concord

concretamente *adv* specifically

concretar *vt* (*precisar*) to specify, to state explicitly; (*fecha, hora*) to fix

concreto, -a 1 *adj* (**a**) (*preciso, real*) concrete (**b**) (*particular*) specific; **en c.** specifically; **en el caso c. de …** in the specific case of …
  2 *nm Am* concrete

concubina *nf* concubine

concurrencia *nf* (**a**) (*de dos cosas*) concurrence (**b**) (*público*) audience

concurrente 1 *adj* concurrent
  2 *nmf* person present

concurrido, -a *adj* crowded, busy

concurrir *vi* (**a**) (*gente*) to converge (**en** on), to meet (**en** in) (**b**) (*coincidir*) to

concur, to coincide (**c**) (*participar*) to compete; (*en elecciones*) to be a candidate

concursante *nmf* (**a**) (*en competición*) contestant, competitor (**b**) (*para un empleo*) candidate

concursar *vi* to compete, to take part

concurso *nm* (**a**) (*competición*) competition; (*de belleza etc*) contest; *TV* quiz show; **presentar (una obra) a c.** to invite tenders (for a piece of work) (**b**) *Fml* (*ayuda*) help

> 🖉 Observa que la palabra inglesa **concourse** es un falso amigo y no es la traducción de la palabra española **concurso.** En inglés, **concourse** significa "vestíbulo".

condado *nm* (*territorio*) county

condal *adj* of o relating to a count; **la Ciudad C.** Barcelona

conde *nm* count

condecoración *nf* decoration

condecorar *vt* to decorate

condena *nf* (**a**) *Der* sentence (**b**) (*desaprobación*) condemnation, disapproval

condenado, -a 1 *adj* (**a**) *Der* convicted; **c. a muerte** condemned to death (**b**) *Rel & Fam* damned; **c. al fracaso** doomed to failure
  2 *nm,f* (**a**) *Der* convicted person; (*a muerte*) condemned person (**b**) *Rel* damned person

condenar 1 *vt* (**a**) *Der* to convict, to find guilty; **c. a algn a muerte** to condemn sb to death (**b**) (*desaprobar*) to condemn
  2 condenarse *vpr Rel* to be damned

condensación *nf* condensation

condensado, -a *adj* condensed; **leche condensada** condensed milk

condensador *nm* condenser

condensar *vt* to condense

condesa *nf* countess

condescender [3] *vi* **c. a** (*con amabilidad*) to consent to, to accede to; (*con desprecio*) to deign to, to condescend to

condescendiente *adj* obliging

condición *nf* (**a**) (*estado*) condition; **en buenas/malas condiciones** in good/bad condition; **condiciones de trabajo** working conditions (**b**) (*estipulación*) condition; **con la c. de que …** on the condition that … (**c**) (*manera de ser*) nature, character (**d**) (*calidad*) **en su c. de director** in his capacity as director

condicional *adj* conditional

condicionar *vt* **c. algo a algo** to make sth dependent on sth; **una cosa condiciona la otra** one thing determines the other

condimentar *vt* to season, to flavour

condimento *nm* seasoning, flavouring

condolerse [4] *vpr* **c. de** to sympathize with

condominio *nm Am (edificio) Br* block of flats, *US* condominium

condón *nm* condom

condonar *vt (ofensa)* to condone; *(deuda)* to cancel

cóndor *nm* condor

conducción *nf* (a) *Esp (de vehículo)* driving (b) *(por tubería)* piping; *(por cable)* wiring

conducir [10] 1 *vt (coche)* to drive; *(electricidad)* to conduct
2 *vi* (a) *Aut* to drive; **permiso de c.** *Br* driving licence, *US* driver's license (b) *(camino, actitud)* to lead; **eso no conduce a nada** this leads nowhere

conducta *nf* behaviour, conduct; **mala c.** misbehaviour, misconduct

conducto *nm* (a) *(tubería)* pipe; *Fig* **por conductos oficiales** through official channels (b) *Anat* duct, canal

conductor, -a 1 *nm,f Aut* driver
2 *nm Elec* conductor

conectar *vt* to connect; *Elec* to plug in, to switch on

coneja *nf* doe rabbit

conejera *nf (madriguera)* (rabbit) warren; *(para crianza)* rabbit hutch

conejillo *nm* **c. de Indias** guinea pig

conejo *nm* rabbit

conexión *nf* connection

confabularse *vpr* to conspire, to plot

confección *nf* (a) *Cost* dressmaking, tailoring; **el ramo de la c.** the clothing *o US* garment industry (b) *(de un plan etc)* making, making up

confeccionar *vt* to make (up)

confederación *nf* confederation

conferencia *nf* (a) *(charla)* lecture; **dar una c. (sobre algo)** to give a lecture (on sth) (b) *(de prensa)* press conference (c) *Tel* long-distance call

conferenciante *nmf* lecturer

conferir [5] *vt Fml (honor, privilegio)* to confer

confesar [1] 1 *vt* to confess, to admit; *(crimen)* to own up to; *Rel (pecados)* to confess
2 *vi Der* to own up
3 **confesarse** *vpr* to confess; **c. culpable** to admit one's guilt; *Rel* to go to confession

confesión *nf* confession, admission; *Rel* confession

confesionario *nm Rel* confessional

confesor *nm* confessor

confeti *nm* confetti

confiado, -a *adj* (a) *(seguro)* self-confident (b) *(crédulo)* gullible, unsuspecting

confianza *nf* (a) *(seguridad)* confidence; **tener c. en uno mismo** to be self-confident (b) **de c.** reliable (c) **tener c. con algn** to be on intimate terms with sb; **con toda c.** in all confidence; **tomarse (demasiadas) confianzas** to take liberties

confiar [29] 1 *vt (entregar)* to entrust; *(información, secreto)* to confide
2 *vi* **c. en** to trust; **confío en ella** I trust her; **no confíes en su ayuda** don't count on his help
3 **confiarse** *vpr* to confide (**en** *o* **a** in); **confiarse demasiado** to be over-confident

confidencia *nf* confidence

confidencial *adj* confidential

confidente, -a *nm,f* (a) *(hombre)* confidant; *(mujer)* confidante (b) *(de la policía)* informer

configuración *nf también Inform* configuration

configurar *vt* to shape, to form

confín *nm* limit, boundary

confinar *vt Der* to confine

confirmación *nf* confirmation

confirmar *vt* to confirm; *Prov* **la excepción confirma la regla** the exception proves the rule

confiscar [44] *vt* to confiscate

confitado, -a *adj* candied; **frutas confitadas** crystallized fruit

confite *nm Br* sweet, *US* candy

confitería *nf* (a) *(tienda)* confectioner's (b) *RP (café)* café

confitura *nf* preserve, jam

conflagración *nf* **c. mundial** world war

conflictividad *nf* **c. laboral** industrial unrest

conflictivo, -a *adj (asunto)* controversial; *(época)* unsettled; **niño c.** problem child

conflicto *nm* conflict; **c. laboral** industrial dispute

confluencia *nf* confluence

confluir [37] *vi* to converge; *(caminos, ríos)* to meet, to come together

conformar 1 *vt* to shape
2 **conformarse** *vpr* to resign oneself, to be content

conforme 1 *adj* (a) *(satisfecho)* satisfied; **c.** agreed, all right; **no estoy c.** I don't agree (b) **c. a** in accordance *o* keeping with
2 *conj* (a) *(según, como)* as; **c. lo vi/lo oí** as I saw/heard it (b) *(a medida que)* as; **la policía los detenía c. iban saliendo** the

police were arresting them as they came out

conformidad *nf* (**a**) *(aprobación)* approval, consent (**b**) **en c. con** in conformity with

conformismo *nm* conformity

conformista *adj & nmf* conformist

confort *(pl* **conforts)** *nm* comfort; **todo c.** *(en anuncio)* all mod cons

confortable *adj* comfortable

confortar *vt* to comfort

confraternizar [40] *vi* to fraternize

confrontación *nf* (**a**) *(enfrentamiento)* confrontation (**b**) *(comparación)* comparison

confrontar *vt* (**a**) *(enfrentar)* to confront (**b**) *(comparar)* to compare

confundir 1 *vt* (**a**) *(trastocar)* to confuse (**con** with); **c. a una persona con otra** to mistake somebody for somebody else (**b**) *(liar)* to confuse (**c**) *(abrumar)* to confound

2 confundirse *upr* (**a**) *(equivocarse)* to be mistaken; *Tel* **se ha confundido** you've got the wrong number (**b**) *(mezclarse)* to mingle; **se confundió entre el gentío** he disappeared into the crowd

confusión *nf* confusion

confuso, -a *adj* (**a**) *(explicación)* confused; *(formas, recuerdo)* blurred, vague (**b**) *(turbado)* confused, bewildered

congelación *nf* (**a**) *(de alimentos)* freezing (**b**) *Fin* freeze; **c. salarial** wage freeze (**c**) *Med* frostbite

congelado, -a 1 *adj* frozen; *Med* frostbitten

2 congelados *nmpl* frozen food

congelador *nm* freezer

congelar 1 *vt* to freeze

2 congelarse *upr* to freeze; *Med* to get *o* become frostbitten; *Fam* **me estoy congelando** I'm freezing

congeniar [43] *vi* to get on (**con** with)

congénito, -a *adj* congenital

congestión *nf* congestion; *Med* **c. cerebral** stroke

congestionar 1 *vt* to block

2 congestionarse *upr* (**a**) *(calle)* to become congested (**b**) *(cara)* to flush, to turn purple

conglomerado *nm* conglomerate

conglomerar *vt Téc* to conglomerate; *(intereses, tendencias)* to unite

congoja *nf* sorrow, grief

congraciarse [43] *upr* to ingratiate oneself (**con** with)

congratular *vt Fml* to congratulate (**por** on)

congregación *nf* congregation

congregar [42] **1** *vt* to assemble, to bring together

2 congregarse *upr* to assemble, to gather

congresista *nmf* (**a**) *(en un congreso)* delegate (**b**) *(político) (hombre)* congressman; *(mujer)* congresswoman

congreso *nm* congress, conference; *Pol* **C. de los Diputados** = lower house of Spanish Parliament, *Br* ≃ House of Commons, *US* ≃ House of Representatives

congrio *nm* conger (eel)

congruente *adj* consistent, coherent

conjetura *nf* conjecture; **por c.** by guesswork

conjeturar *vt* to conjecture

conjugación *nf* conjugation

conjugar [42] *vt* to conjugate; *Fig (planes, opiniones)* to combine

conjunción *nf* conjunction

conjuntar *vt* to co-ordinate

conjuntivitis *nf inv* conjunctivitis

conjunto, -a 1 *nm* (**a**) *(grupo)* collection, group (**b**) *(todo)* whole; **de c.** overall; **en c.** on the whole (**c**) *Mús (pop)* group, band (**d**) *(prenda)* outfit, ensemble (**e**) *Mat* set (**f**) *Dep* team

2 *adj* joint

conjurar 1 *vt* to exorcise; *(peligro)* to ward off

2 conjurarse *upr* to conspire, to plot

conjuro *nm* (**a**) *(exorcismo)* exorcism (**b**) *(encantamiento)* spell, incantation

conllevar *vt* to entail

conmemoración *nf* commemoration

conmemorar *vt* to commemorate

conmigo *pron pers* with me; **vino c.** he came with me; **él habló c.** he talked to me

conminar *vt* to threaten, to menace

conmoción *nf* commotion, shock; **c. cerebral** concussion

conmocionar *vt* to shock; *Med* to concuss

conmovedor, -a *adj* touching; **una película conmovedora** a moving film

conmover [4] *vt* to touch, to move

conmutador *nm* (**a**) *Elec* switch (**b**) *Am Tel* switchboard

conmutar *vt* to exchange; *Der* to commute; *Elec* to commutate

connivencia *nf* connivance, collusion

connotación *nf* connotation

cono *nm* cone; **C. Sur** = Chile, Argentina, Paraguay and Uruguay

conocedor, -a *adj & nm,f* expert; *(de vino, arte etc)* connoisseur

conocer [34] **1** vt (**a**) (saber acerca de) to know; **dar (algo/algn) a c.** to make (sth/sb) known; **no conozco Rusia** I've never been to Russia (**b**) (a una persona) (por primera vez) to meet; (desde hace tiempo) to know (**c**) (reconocer) to recognize; **te conocí por la voz** I recognized you by your voice
2 conocerse vpr (dos personas) (desde hace tiempo) to know each other; (por primera vez) to meet

conocido, -a 1 adj known; (famoso) well-known
2 nm,f acquaintance

conocimiento nm (**a**) (saber) knowledge; **con c. de causa** with full knowledge of the facts (**b**) (conciencia) consciousness; **perder/recobrar el c.** to lose/regain consciousness (**c**) **conocimientos** knowledge

conque conj so

conquense 1 adj of/from Cuenca
2 nmf person from Cuenca

conquista nf conquest

conquistador, -a nm,f conqueror

conquistar vt (país, ciudad) to conquer; Fig (puesto, título) to win; (a una persona) to win over

consabido, -a adj (**a**) (bien conocido) well-known (**b**) (usual) familiar, usual

consagración nf (**a**) Rel consecration (**b**) (de un artista) recognition

consagrado, -a adj (**a**) Rel consecrated (**b**) (dedicado) dedicated (**c**) (reconocido) recognized, established

consagrar 1 vt (**a**) Rel to consecrate (**b**) (artista) to confirm (**c**) (tiempo, vida) to devote
2 consagrarse vpr (**a**) **consagrarse a** (dedicarse) to devote oneself to, to dedicate oneself to (**b**) (lograr fama) to establish oneself

consciente adj (**a**) Med conscious; **estar c.** to be conscious (**b**) **ser c. de algo** to be aware of sth

conscripto nm Andes, Arg conscript

consecución nf (**a**) (de un objetivo) achievement (**b**) (obtención) obtaining

consecuencia nf (resultado) consequence; **a** o **como c. de** as a consequence o result of; **en c.** therefore; **tener** o **traer (malas) consecuencias** to have (ill) effects; **sacar como** o **en c.** to come to a conclusion (**b**) (coherencia) **actuar en c.** to act accordingly

consecuente adj consistent

consecutivo, -a adj consecutive; **tres días consecutivos** three days in a row

conseguir [6] vt (**a**) (obtener) to get, to obtain; (objetivo) to achieve (**b**) **conseguí terminar** I managed to finish

consejero, -a nm,f (**a**) (asesor) adviser (**b**) Pol councillor (**c**) Com **c. delegado** managing director

consejo nm (**a**) (recomendación) advice; **un c.** a piece of advice (**b**) (junta) council; **c. de ministros** cabinet; (reunión) cabinet meeting; **c. de administración** board of directors; **c. de guerra** court martial

consenso nm consensus

consensuar [30] vt to approve by consensus

consentido, -a adj spoiled

consentimiento nm consent

consentir [5] **1** vt (**a**) (tolerar) to allow, to permit; **no consientas que haga eso** don't allow him to do that (**b**) (mimar) to spoil
2 vi to consent; **c. en** to agree to

conserje nm (de colegio, ministerio) doorman, Br porter; (de bloque de viviendas) Br caretaker, US superintendent, US supervisor

conserjería nf (de colegio, ministerio) porter's lodge; (de bloque de viviendas) Br caretaker's office, US superintendent's o supervisor's office

conserva nf canned food, Br tinned food

conservación nf (**a**) (de alimentos) preservation (**b**) (mantenimiento) maintenance, upkeep

conservador, -a 1 adj & nm,f conservative; Pol Conservative
2 nm (de museo) curator

conservadurismo nm conservatism

conservante nm preservative

conservar 1 vt (**a**) (mantener) (alimento) to preserve; (amistad) to sustain, to keep up; (salud) to look after; (calor) to retain (**b**) (guardar) (libros, cartas, secreto) to keep
2 conservarse vpr (**a**) (tradición etc) to survive (**b**) **conservarse bien** (persona) to age well

conservatorio nm conservatory

considerable adj considerable

consideración nf (**a**) (reflexión) consideration; **tomar algo en c.** to take sth into consideration o account (**b**) (respeto) regard (**c**) **de c.** important, considerable; **herido de c.** seriously injured

considerado, -a adj (**a**) (atento) considerate, thoughtful (**b**) **estar bien/mal c.** to be well/badly thought of

considerar vt to consider; **lo considero imposible** I think it's impossible

consigna nf (**a**) (para maletas) Br left-luggage office, US checkroom (**b**) Mil orders, instructions

consignar *vt* (**a**) *(puesto)* to allocate; *(cantidad)* to assign (**b**) *(mercancía)* to ship, to dispatch

consigo¹ *pron pers* (**a**) *(tercera persona) (hombre)* with him; *(mujer)* with her; *(cosa, animal)* with it; *(plural)* with them; *(usted)* with you (**b**) **hablar c. mismo** to speak to oneself

consigo² *indic pres de* **conseguir**

consiguiente *adj* resulting, consequent; **por c.** therefore, consequently

consistencia *nf* (**a**) *(de masa)* consistency (**b**) *(de argumento)* soundness

consistente *adj* (**a**) *(firme)* firm, solid (**b**) *(teoría)* sound (**c**) **c. en** consisting of

> *ℓ* Observa que la palabra inglesa **consistent** es un falso amigo y no es la traducción de la palabra española **consistente**. En inglés, **consistent** significa "consecuente".

consistir *vi* to consist (**en** of); **el secreto consiste en tener paciencia** the secret lies in being patient

consistorial *adj* **casa c.** town hall

consistorio *nm* town *o* US city council

consola *nf* console table; *Inform* console

consolación *nf* consolation; **premio de c.** consolation prize

consolador, -a 1 *adj* consoling, comforting
  2 *nm* dildo

consolar [2] **1** *vt* to console, to comfort
  2 consolarse *vpr* to console oneself, to take comfort (**con** from)

consolidación *nf* consolidation

consolidar *vt* to consolidate

consomé *nm* clear soup, consommé

consonancia *nf* **en c. con** in keeping with

consonante *adj & nf* consonant

consorcio *nm* consortium

consorte 1 *adj* **príncipe c.** prince consort
  2 *nmf (cónyuge)* partner, spouse

conspicuo, -a *adj* conspicuous

conspiración *nf* conspiracy, plot

conspirar *vi* to conspire, to plot

constancia *nf* (**a**) *(perseverancia)* perseverance (**b**) *(testimonio)* record; **dejar c. de algo** to put sth on record

constante 1 *adj* (**a**) *(persona) (en una empresa)* persistent; *(en ideas, opiniones)* steadfast (**b**) *(acción)* constant
  2 *nf* constant feature; *Mat* constant

constantemente *adv* constantly

constar *vi* (**a**) *(figurar)* to figure, to be included (**en** in); **c. en acta** to be on record (**b**) **me consta que …** I am

absolutely certain that … (**c**) **c. de** to be made up of, to consist of

constatar *vt (observar)* to confirm; *(comprobar)* to check

constelación *nf* constellation

consternación *nf* consternation, dismay

consternar *vt* to dismay

constipado, -a 1 *adj* **estar c.** to have a cold *o* a chill
  2 *nm* cold, chill

> *ℓ* Observa que la palabra inglesa **constipated** es un falso amigo y no es la traducción de la palabra española **constipado**. En inglés **constipated** significa "estreñido".

constiparse *vpr* to catch a cold *o* a chill

constitución *nf* constitution

constitucional *adj* constitutional

constituir [37] **1** *vt* (**a**) *(formar)* to constitute; **estar constituido por** to consist of (**b**) *(suponer)* to represent (**c**) *(fundar)* to constitute, to set up
  2 constituirse *vpr* **constituirse en** to set oneself up as

constituyente *adj & nmf* constituent

constreñir [6] *vt* (**a**) *(forzar)* to compel, to force (**b**) *(oprimir)* to restrict (**c**) *Med* to constrict

construcción *nf* (**a**) *(acción)* construction; *(sector)* the building industry; **en c.** under construction (**b**) *(edificio)* building

constructivo, -a *adj* constructive

constructor, -a 1 *nm,f* builder
  2 *adj* **empresa constructora** builders, construction company

construir [37] *vt* to build, to manufacture

> *ℓ* Observa que el verbo inglés **to construe** es un falso amigo y no es la traducción del verbo español **construir**. En inglés **to construe** significa "interpretar".

consuelo *nm* consolation

cónsul *nmf* consul

consulado *nm* consulate

consulta *nf* (**a**) *(sobre un problema) (acción)* consultation; *(pregunta)* query, enquiry; **obra de c.** reference book (**b**) *(despacho de médico)* Br surgery, US office; **horas de c.** surgery hours

consultar *vt* to consult, to seek advice (**con** from); *(libro)* to look up

consultivo, -a *adj* consultative, advisory

consultorio *nm* (**a**) *(de un médico)* Br surgery, US office (**b**) *Prensa* problem page, advice column

consumado, -a adj (a) hecho c. fait accompli, accomplished fact (b) (artista) consummate

consumar vt (realizar completamente) to complete; (crimen) to commit; (el matrimonio) to consummate

consumición nf (a) (acción) consumption (b) (bebida) drink

consumidor, -a 1 nm,f consumer
2 adj consuming

consumir 1 vt to consume
2 consumirse upr (al hervir) to boil away; Fig (persona) to waste away

consumismo nm consumerism

consumo nm consumption; **bienes de c.** consumer goods; **sociedad de c.** consumer society

contabilidad nf Com (a) (profesión) accountancy (b) (de empresa, sociedad) accounting, book-keeping

contabilizar [40] vt Com to enter in the books; Dep to score

contable nmf Esp accountant

contactar vi **c. con** to contact, to get in touch with

contacto nm contact; Aut ignition; **perder el c.** to lose touch; **ponerse en c.** to get in touch

contado, -a 1 adj few and far between; **contadas veces** very seldom; **tiene los días contados** his days are numbered
2 nm **pagar al c.** to pay cash

contador, -a 1 nm,f Am (persona) accountant; **c. público** Br chartered accountant; US certified public accountant
2 nm (aparato) meter; **c. de agua** water meter

contagiar [43] **1** vt Med to pass on
2 contagiarse upr (a) (persona) to get infected (b) (enfermedad) to be contagious

contagio nm contagion

contagioso, -a adj contagious; Fam (risa) infectious

container (pl **containers**) nm (para mercancías) container

contaminación nf contamination; (del aire) pollution

contaminado, -a adj (alimento) contaminated; (medio ambiente) polluted

contaminar vt to contaminate; (aire, agua) to pollute

contante adj dinero c. (y sonante) hard o ready cash

contar [2] **1** vt (a) (sumar) to count (b) (narrar) to tell
2 vi (a) (hacer cálculos, importar) to count (b) **c. con** (confiar en) to count on; (tener) to have

3 contarse upr Fam **¿qué te cuentas?** how's it going?

contemplación nf (a) (meditación) contemplation (b) (consideración) **contemplaciones** consideration; **tratar a algn sin contemplaciones** not to take into account sb's feelings; **nos echaron sin contemplaciones** they threw us out unceremoniously

contemplar vt to contemplate; (considerar) to consider; (estipular) to stipulate

contemporáneo, -a adj & nm,f contemporary

contención nf muro de c. retaining wall; **c. salarial** wage restraint

contencioso, -a 1 adj (tema, cuestión) contentious; Der litigious
2 nm Der legal dispute

contendiente nmf (en una competición) contender; (en una guerra) warring faction

contenedor nm container; **c. de vidrio** bottle bank

contener [24] **1** vt (a) (incluir) to contain (b) (pasiones etc) to restrain, to hold back
2 contenerse upr to control oneself, to hold (oneself) back

contenido nm content, contents

contentar 1 vt (a) (satisfacer) to please (b) (alegrar) to cheer up
2 contentarse upr (a) (conformarse) to make do (**con** with), to be satisfied (**con** with) (b) (alegrarse) to cheer up

contento, -a adj happy, pleased (**con** with)

contestación nf answer; **dar c.** to answer

contestador nm **c. automático** answering machine

contestar vt (a una pregunta) to answer; Fam (replicar) to answer back

contestatario, -a adj anti-establishment

contexto nm context

contienda nf (competición, combate) contest; (guerra) conflict, war

contigo pron pers with you

contiguo, -a adj contiguous (**a** to), adjoining

continental adj continental

continente nm (a) Geog continent (b) (compostura) countenance

contingencia nf contingency

contingente 1 adj Fml possible
2 nm contingent

continuación nf continuation; **a c.** next

continuamente adv continuously

continuar [30] *vt & vi* to continue, to carry on (with); **continúa en Francia** he's still in France; **continuará** to be continued

continuidad *nf* continuity

continuo, -a 1 *adj* (**a**) *(ininterrumpido)* continuous; *Aut* **línea continua** solid white line (**b**) *(reiterado)* continual, constant
2 *nm* continuum

contonearse *upr* to swing one's hips

contorno *nm Mat* contour; *(línea)* outline; **c. de cintura** waist (measurement)

contorsión *nf* contortion

contorsionarse *upr* to contort o twist oneself

contra 1 *prep* against; **en c. de** against
2 *nm* **los pros y los contras** the pros and cons

contraataque *nm* counterattack

contrabajo, -a *nm* double bass

contrabandista *nmf* smuggler; **c. de armas** gunrunner

contrabando *nm* smuggling; **c. de armas** gunrunning; **pasar algo de c.** to smuggle sth in

contracción *nf* contraction

contracepción *nf* contraception

contrachapado *nm* plywood

contracorriente 1 *nf* crosscurrent
2 *adv* **ir (a) c.** to go against the tide

contradecir [12] *(pp* **contradicho)** *vt* to contradict

contradicción *nf* contradiction

contradicho, -a *pp de* contradecir

contradictorio, -a *adj* contradictory

contraer [25] **1** *vt* to contract; **c. matrimonio con algn** to marry sb
2 contraerse *upr* to contract

contraigo *indic pres de* contraer

contraindicación *nf* contraindication

contraindicado, -a *adj* **está c. beber alcohol durante el embarazo** alcohol should be avoided during pregnancy

contraje *pt indef de* contraer

contralor *nm Am (en institución, empresa)* comptroller

contraloría *nf Am (oficina)* comptroller's office

contraluz *nm* view against the light; **a c.** against the light

contramaestre *nm* (**a**) *(en buque)* boatswain (**b**) *(capataz)* foreman

contramano: a contramano *loc adv* the wrong way

contrapartida *nf* **en c.** in return

contrapelo: a contrapelo *loc adv (acariciar)* the wrong way; **su intervención**

iba a c. del resto his remarks went against the general opinion; **vivir a c.** to have an unconventional lifestyle

contrapeso *nm* counterweight

contraportada *nf* back page

contraposición *nf* contrast

contraproducente *adj* counterproductive

contraprogramación *nf TV* competitive scheduling

contrapunto *nm* counterpoint

contrariamente *adv* **c. a ...** contrary to ...

contrariar [29] *vt* (**a**) *(oponerse a)* to oppose, to go against (**b**) *(disgustar)* to upset

contrariedad *nf* (**a**) *(dificultad)* obstacle, setback (**b**) *(disgusto)* annoyance

contrario, -a 1 *adj* (**a**) *(opuesto) (dirección, sentido, idea)* opposite; *(parte)* opposing; *(equipo)* opposing; **todo lo c.** quite the contrary (**b**) *(desfavorable)* **es c. a nuestros intereses** it goes against our interests (**c**) **ser c. a algo** to be opposed to sth
2 *nm,f* opponent, rival
3 *nf* **llevar la contraria** to be contrary

contrarrestar *vt* to offset, to counteract

contrasentido *nm* **es un c.** it doesn't make sense

contraseña *nf* password

contrastar *vt* to contrast (**con** with)

contraste *nm* contrast

contrata *nf* (fixed price) contract

contratar *vt* (**a**) *(personal)* to hire (**b**) *(servicio, obra, mercancía)* **c. algo a algn** to contract for sth with sb

contratiempo *nm* setback, hitch

contratista *nmf* contractor

contrato *nm* contract; **c. de trabajo** work contract; **c. de alquiler** lease, leasing agreement; **c. basura** short-term contract with poor conditions

contravenir [27] *vt* to contravene, to infringe

contraventana *nf* shutter

contribución *nf* (**a**) *(aporte)* contribution (**b**) *(impuesto)* tax

contribuir [37] **1** *vt* to contribute (**a** to)
2 *vi* to contribute

contribuyente *nmf* taxpayer

contrincante *nmf* rival, opponent

control *nm* (**a**) *(dominio, mando)* control; **c. a distancia** remote control (**b**) *(inspección)* check; *(de policía)* checkpoint

controlador, -a *nm,f* **c. (aéreo)** air traffic controller

controlar 1 *vt* (**a**) *(dominar)* to control (**b**) *(comprobar)* to check (**c**) *(vigilar)* to watch, to keep an eye on
2 controlarse *vpr* to control oneself

controversia *nf* controversy

controvertido, -a *adj* controversial

contumaz *adj* obstinate

contundente *adj* (**a**) *(arma)* blunt (**b**) *(argumento)* forceful, convincing

contusión *nf* contusion, bruise

conuco *nm Carib (parcela)* small plot of land

convalecencia *nf* convalescence

convaleciente *adj & nmf* convalescent

convalidar *vt* to validate; *(documento)* to ratify

convencer [49] *vt* to convince; **c. a algn de algo** to convince sb about sth

convencimiento *nm* conviction; **tener el c. de que …** to be convinced that …

convención *nf* convention

convencional *adj* conventional

convenido, -a *adj* agreed; **según lo c.** as agreed

conveniencia *nf* (**a**) *(provecho)* convenience (**b**) **conveniencias sociales** social proprieties

conveniente *adj* (**a**) *(oportuno)* convenient; *(aconsejable)* advisable (**b**) *(precio)* good, fair

convenio *nm* agreement; **c. laboral** agreement on salary and conditions

convenir [27] *vt & vi* (**a**) *(acordar)* to agree; **c. una fecha** to agree on a date; **sueldo a c.** salary negotiable; **c. en** to agree on (**b**) *(ser oportuno)* to suit, to be good for; **conviene recordar que …** it's as well to remember that …

convento *nm (de monjas)* convent; *(de monjes)* monastery

convergente *adj* convergent

converger [53] *vi* to converge

conversación *nf* conversation

conversada *nf Am Fam* chat

conversar *vi* to converse, to talk

conversión *nf* conversion

converso, -a *nm,f* convert

convertible *adj* convertible

convertir [54] **1** *vt* to change, to convert
2 convertirse *vpr* (**a**) **convertirse en** to turn into, to become (**b**) *Rel* to be converted (**a** to)

convexo, -a *adj* convex

convicción *nf* conviction; **tengo la c. de que …** I am convinced that …

convicto, -a *adj* convicted

convidado, -a *adj & nm,f* guest

convidar *vt* to invite

convincente *adj* convincing

convite *nm* reception

convivencia *nf* life together; *Fig* coexistence

convivir *vi* to live together; *Fig* to coexist (**con** with)

convocar [44] *vt* to summon; *(reunión, elecciones)* to call

convocatoria *nf* (**a**) *(a huelga etc)* call (**b**) *Educ* diet

convulsión *nf Med* convulsion; *(agitación social)* upheaval

convulsivo, -a *adj* convulsive

conyugal *adj* conjugal; **vida c.** married life

cónyuge *nmf* spouse; **cónyuges** married couple, husband and wife

coña *nf Esp muy Fam* **está de c.** he's just pissing around

coñac *(pl coñacs)* *nm* brandy, cognac

coñazo *nm Esp muy Fam* pain, drag; **dar el c.** to be a real pain

coño *esp Esp Vulg* **1** *nm* cunt, twat
2 *interj (enfado)* for fuck's sake!

cooperación *nf* co-operation

cooperador, -a *nm,f* collaborator, co-operator

cooperante *nmf* (overseas) volunteer worker

cooperar *vi* to co-operate (**con** with)

cooperativa *nf* co-operative

coordenada *nf* co-ordinate

coordinación *nf* co-ordination

coordinador, -a *nm,f* co-ordinator

coordinadora *nf* co-ordinating committee; **c. general** joint committee

coordinar *vt* to co-ordinate

copa *nf* (**a**) *(para beber)* glass; **tomar una c.** to have a drink (**b**) *(de árbol)* top (**c**) *Dep* cup (**d**) *Naipes* **copas** = suit in Spanish deck of cards, with the symbol of a goblet

copar *vt* to monopolize

copartícipe *nmf (en empresa)* partner; *(en actividad)* participant

Copenhague *n* Copenhagen

copeo *nm Fam* drinking; **ir de c.** to go out drinking

copetín *nm RP (bebida)* aperitif; *(comida)* appetizer

copia *nf* copy; *Inform* **c. de seguridad** backup; *Inform* **hacer una c. de seguridad de algo** to back sth up

copiar [43] *vt* to copy

copiloto *nm Av* copilot; *Aut* co-driver

copioso, -a *adj* abundant, copious

copistería *nf* copy shop

copla *nf* verse, couplet

copo *nm* flake; *(de nieve)* snowflake; **copos de maíz** cornflakes

coproducción *nf* co-production, joint production

cópula *nf* (a) *(coito)* copulation, intercourse (b) *Ling* conjunction

copular *vt* to copulate (**con** with)

coqueta *nf* dressing table

coquetear *vi* to flirt (**con** with)

coqueto, -a 1 *adj* coquettish
2 *nm,f* flirt

coraje *nm* (a) *(valor)* courage (b) *(ira)* anger, annoyance; *Fig* **dar c. a algn** to infuriate sb; **¡qué c.!** how maddening!

coral¹ *nm Zool* coral

coral² *nf Mús* choral, chorale

Corán *nm Rel* **el C.** the Koran

coránico, -a *adj Rel* Koranic

coraza *nf* (a) *(de soldado)* cuirasse (b) *(de tortuga)* shell (c) *(protección)* shield

corazón *nm* (a) *(de persona, animal)* heart; *Fig* **de (todo) c.** in all sincerity; *Fig* **tener buen c.** to be kind-hearted (b) *(parte central)* heart; *(de fruta)* core (c) *Naipes* **corazones** hearts

corazonada *nf* hunch, feeling

corbata *nf* tie, *US* necktie; **con c.** wearing a tie

Córcega *n* Corsica

corchea *nf Mús Br* quaver, *US* eighth note

corchete *nm* (a) *Impr* square bracket (b) *Cost* hook and eye

corcho *nm* cork; *(de pesca)* float

cordel *nm* rope, cord

cordero, -a *nm,f* lamb

cordial *adj* cordial, warm

cordialidad *nf* cordiality, warmth

cordillera *nf* mountain chain o range

córdoba *nm Fin* cordoba, = monetary unit of Nicaragua

cordón *nm* (a) *(de zapatos)* lace; *(cable eléctrico)* flex; *Anat* **c. umbilical** umbilical cord; **c. policial** police cordon (b) *CSur, Cuba (de la vereda) Br* kerb, *US* curb

cordura *nf* common sense

Corea *n* Korea; **C. del Norte/Sur** North/South Korea

coreano, -a *adj & nm,f* Korean

corear *vt* *(exclamando)* to chorus; *(cantando)* to sing

coreografía *nf* choreography

corista 1 *nmf (en coro)* chorus singer
2 *nf (en cabaret)* chorus girl

cornada *nf Taurom* goring

cornamenta *nf* (a) *(de toro)* horns; *(de ciervo)* antlers (b) *Fam Fig (de marido engañado)* cuckold's horns

córnea *nf* cornea

corneja *nf* crow

córner *(pl* **córners)** *nm Dep* corner (kick); **sacar un c.** to take a corner

corneta *nf* bugle; **c. de llaves** cornet

cornete *nm* (a) *Anat* turbinate bone (b) *(helado)* cornet, cone

cornisa *nf* cornice

cornudo *nm Fam (marido)* cuckold

coro *nm Mús* choir; *Teatro* chorus; *Fig* **a c.** all together

corona *nf* (a) *(de rey)* crown (b) *(de flores etc)* wreath, garland; **c. funeraria** funeral wreath

coronación *nf* (a) *(de monarca)* coronation (b) *(remate, colmo)* culmination

coronar *vt* to crown

coronel *nm* colonel

coronilla *nf* crown of the head; *Fam* **estar hasta la c. (de)** to be fed up (with)

corpiño *nm (vestido)* bodice; *Arg (sostén)* bra

corporación *nf* corporation

corporal *adj* corporal; **castigo c.** corporal punishment; **olor c.** body odour, BO

corporativo, -a *adj* corporative

corpulento, -a *adj* corpulent, stout

corral *nm* farmyard, *US* corral; *(de casa)* courtyard

correa *nf* (a) *(tira)* strap; *(de reloj)* watchstrap; *(de pantalón)* belt; *(de perro)* lead, leash (b) *Téc* belt

corrección *nf* (a) *(rectificación)* correction (b) *(urbanidad)* courtesy, politeness

correcto, -a *adj* (a) *(sin errores)* correct (b) *(educado)* polite, courteous (**con** to); *(conducta)* proper

corredera *nf* **puerta/ventana de c.** sliding door/window

corredizo, -a *adj* sliding; **nudo c.** slipknot; **techo c.** sunroof

corredor, -a *nm,f* (a) *Dep* runner (b) *Fin* **c. de bolsa** stockbroker

corregir [58] **1** *vt* to correct
2 corregirse *vpr* to mend one's ways

correo *nm* (a) *Br* post, *US* mail; **echar algo al c.** to *Br* post o *US* mail sth; **por c.** by *Br* post o *US* mail; *Inform* **c. electrónico** electronic mail, e-mail; *Inform* **me envió un c. (electrónico)** *(un mensaje)* she e-mailed me, she sent me an e-mail; **(tren) c.** mail train (b) *Esp* **Correos** *(institución)* the post office

correr 1 *vi* (a) to run; *(coche)* to go fast; *(conductor)* to drive fast; *(viento)* to blow;

Fig **no corras, habla más despacio** don't rush, speak slower; **c. prisa** to be urgent (**b**) **c. con los gastos** to foot the bill; **corre a mi cargo** I'll take care of it

2 *vt* (**a**) (*cortina*) to draw; (*cerrojo*) to close; (*aventura etc*) to have; **c. el riesgo o peligro** to run the risk (**b**) (*mover*) to pull up, to draw up

3 correrse *vpr* (**a**) (*moverse*) to move over (**b**) *Fam* **correrse una juerga** to go on a spree (**c**) *Andes, Esp muy Fam* (*tener un orgasmo*) to come

correspondencia *nf* (**a**) (*relación, correo*) correspondence (**b**) (*de metro, tren*) connection

corresponder 1 *vi* (**a**) (*compensar*) **c. (con algo) a algn/algo** to repay sb/sth (with sth) (**b**) (*competer*) **c. a algn hacer algo** to be sb's responsibility to do sth (**c**) (*coincidir*) to correspond (**a/con** to/with) (**d**) (*pertenecer*) **me dieron lo que me correspondía** they gave me my share

2 corresponderse *vpr* (**a**) (*ajustarse*) to correspond (**b**) (*dos cosas*) to tally; **no se corresponde con la descripción** it does not match the description (**c**) (*dos personas*) to love each other

correspondiente *adj* corresponding (**a** to)

corresponsal *nmf* correspondent

corrida *nf* **c. (de toros)** bullfight

corrido, -a *adj* (**a**) (*avergonzado*) abashed (**b**) **de c.** without stopping; **se lo sabe de c.** she knows it by heart

corriente 1 *adj* (**a**) (*común*) common (**b**) (*agua*) running (**c**) (*mes, año*) current, present; **el diez del c.** the tenth of this month (**d**) *Fin* (*cuenta*) current (**e**) **estar al c.** to be up to date

2 *nf* (**a**) (*de agua*) current, stream; *Fig* **ir o navegar contra c.** to go against the tide; *Fam* **seguirle o llevarle la c. a algn** to humour sb; *Elec* **c. eléctrica** (electric) current (**b**) (*de aire*) *Br* draught, *US* draft (**c**) (*tendencia*) trend, current

corrijo *indic pres de* **corregir**

corrillo *nm* small group of people talking; *Fig* clique

corro *nm* (**a**) (*círculo*) circle, ring (**b**) (*juego*) ring-a-ring-a-roses

corroborar *vt* to corroborate

corroer [38] *vt* to corrode; *Fig* **la envidia le corroe** envy eats away at him

corromper 1 *vt* (**a**) (*pudrir*) to turn bad, to rot (**b**) (*pervertir*) to corrupt, to pervert

2 corromperse *vpr* (**a**) (*pudrirse*) to go bad, to rot (**b**) (*pervertirse*) to become corrupted

corrosivo, -a *adj* corrosive; *Fig* (*mordaz*) caustic

corrupción *nf* (**a**) (*delito, decadencia*) corruption; *Der* **c. de menores** corruption of minors (**b**) (*de sustancia*) decay

corrupto, -a *adj* corrupt

corsé *nm* corset

corsetería *nf* ladies' underwear shop

cortacésped *nm o nf* lawnmower

cortado, -a 1 *adj* (**a**) (*leche*) sour (**b**) (*labios*) chapped (**c**) *Fam* (*tímido*) shy

2 *nm* = small coffee with a dash of milk

cortafuego *nm* firebreak

cortante *adj* (**a**) (*afilado*) sharp (**b**) *Fig* (*tajante*) (*frase, estilo*) cutting; (*viento*) biting; (*frío*) bitter.

cortapisa *nf* restriction, limitation

cortar 1 *vt* (**a**) to cut; (*carne*) to carve; (*árbol*) to cut down; *Fam* **c. por lo sano** to take drastic measures; *Fam* **cortó con su novio** she split up with her boyfriend (**b**) (*piel*) to chap, to crack (**c**) (*luz, teléfono*) to cut off (**d**) (*paso, carretera*) to block

2 cortarse *vpr* (**a**) (*herirse*) to cut oneself (**b**) **cortarse el pelo** to have one's hair cut (**c**) (*leche etc*) to curdle (**d**) *Tel* **se cortó la comunicación** we were cut off (**e**) *Fam* (*aturdirse*) to become all shy

cortaúñas *nm inv* nail clippers

corte¹ *nm* (**a**) cut; **c. de pelo** haircut; **c. de mangas** ≃ V-sign; *TV* **c. publicitario** commercial break (**b**) (*sección*) section; **c. transversal** cross section (**c**) *Fam* rebuff; **dar un c. a algn** to cut sb dead

corte² *nf* (**a**) (*real*) court (**b**) *Esp* **las Cortes** (Spanish) Parliament

cortejar *vt* to court

cortejo *nm* (**a**) (*galanteo*) courting (**b**) (*comitiva*) entourage, retinue; **c. fúnebre** funeral cortège

cortés (*pl* **corteses**) *adj* courteous, polite

cortesía *nf* courtesy, politeness

corteza *nf* (*de árbol*) bark; (*de queso*) rind; (*de pan*) crust

cortijo *nm* Andalusian farm *o* farmhouse

cortina *nf* curtain; **c. de humo** smoke screen

corto, -a 1 *adj* (**a**) (*distancia, tiempo*) short; *Fam* **c. de luces** dim-witted; **c. de vista** short-sighted; *Aut* **luz corta** dipped headlights (**b**) *Fam* **quedarse c.** (*calcular mal*) to underestimate (**c**) (*apocado*) timid, shy

2 *nm Cin* short (movie *o Br* film)

cortocircuito *nm* short circuit

cortometraje *nm* short (movie *o Br* film)

corvo, -a *adj* curved, bent

cosa *nf* (**a**) thing; **no he visto c. igual** I've never seen anything like it; **no ser gran c.** not to be up to much (**b**) (*asunto*) matter, business; **eso es c. tuya** that's your business o affair; **eso es otra c.** that's different (**c**) **hace c. de una hora** about an hour ago

coscorrón *nm* knock o blow on the head

cosecha *nf* (a) *Agr* harvest, crop (b) *(año del vino)* vintage

cosechadora *nf* combine harvester

cosechar *vt* to harvest, to gather (in)

coser *vt* (a) *(tejido)* to sew; *Fam* **es c. y cantar** it's a piece of cake (b) *Med* to stitch up

cosmético, -a *adj & nm* cosmetic

cósmico, -a *adj* cosmic

cosmonauta *nmf* cosmonaut

cosmopolita *adj & nmf* cosmopolitan

cosmos *nm inv* cosmos

coso *nm* (a) *Taurom* bullring (b) *CSur Fam (objeto)* whatnot, thing; **¿para qué sirve ese c.?** *(en aparato)* what's this thing o thingumajig for?

cosquillas *nfpl* tickling; **hacer c. a algn** to tickle sb; **tener c.** to be ticklish

cosquilleo *nm* tickling

costa[1] *nf* coast; *(litoral)* coastline; *(playa)* beach, seaside

costa[2] *nf* **a c. de** at the expense of; **a toda c.** at all costs, at any price; **vive a c. mía** he lives off me

costado *nm* side; **de c.** sideways; **es catalana por los cuatro costados** she's Catalan through and through

costal *nm* sack

costanera *nf CSur* promenade

costar [2] *vi* (a) *(precio)* to cost; **¿cuánto cuesta?** how much is it?; **c. barato/caro** to be cheap/expensive (b) *Fig* **te va a c. caro** you'll pay dearly for this; **c. trabajo** o **mucho** to be hard; **me cuesta hablar francés** I find it difficult to speak French; **cueste lo que cueste** at any cost

Costa Rica *n* Costa Rica

costarricense *adj & nmf,* **costarriqueño, -a** *adj & nm,f* Costa Rican

coste *nm Esp* cost; **a precio de c.** (at) cost price; **c. de la vida** cost of living

costear 1 *vt* to afford, to pay for; **c. los gastos** to foot the bill
   2 costearse *vpr* to pay for

costero, -a 1 *adj* coastal; **ciudad costera** seaside town
   2 *nf Méx* promenade

costilla *nf* (a) *Anat* rib (b) *Culin* cutlet

costo[1] *nm* cost

costo[2] *nm Esp Fam (hachís)* dope, shit, stuff

costoso, -a *adj* costly, expensive

costra *nf* crust; *Med* scab

costumbre *nf* (a) *(hábito)* habit; **como de c.** as usual; **tengo la c. de levantarme temprano** I usually get up early; **tenía la c. de …** he used to … (b) *(tradición)* custom

costura *nf* (a) *(acción)* sewing (b) *(confección)* dressmaking; **alta c.** haute couture (c) *(línea de puntadas)* seam

costurera *nf* seamstress

costurero *nm* sewing basket

cota *nf Geog* height above sea level; *Fig* rating

cotejar *vt* to compare

cotidiano, -a *adj* daily; **vida cotidiana** everyday life

cotilla *nmf Esp Fam* busybody, gossip

cotillear *vi Esp Fam* to gossip (**de** about)

cotilleo *nm Esp Fam* gossip

cotillón *nm* = party on New Year's Eve or 5th of January

cotización *nf* (a) *Fin* (market) price, quotation (b) *(cuota)* membership fees, subscription

cotizar [40] **1** *vt Fin* to quote
   2 *vi* to pay national insurance
   3 cotizarse *vpr* **cotizarse a** to sell at

coto *nm* (a) *(lugar)* enclosure, reserve; **c. de caza** game reserve (b) **poner c. a** to put a stop to

cotorra *nf* parrot; *Fig (persona)* chatterbox

country *(pl* **countries)** *nm Arg* = luxury suburban housing development

coyote *nm* coyote, prairie wolf

coyuntura *nf* (a) *Anat* articulation, joint (b) *Fig (circunstancia)* juncture; **la c. económica** the economic situation

coz *nf* kick; **dar una c.** to kick

C.P. *(abr* **código postal)** *Br* postcode, *US* zip code

crac(k) *nm* (a) *Fin* crash (b) *(droga)* crack

cráneo *nm* cranium, skull

cráter *nm* crater

creación *nf* creation

creador, -a *nm,f* creator

crear *vt* to create

creatividad *nf* creativity

creativo, -a *adj* creative

crecer [33] *vi* to grow; **c. en importancia** to become more important

creces *nfpl* **con c.** fully, in full; **devolver con c.** to return with interest

crecido, -a *adj (persona)* grown-up

creciente *adj* growing, increasing; **cuarto c.** crescent

crecimiento *nm* growth

credencial *adj* credential; **(cartas) credenciales** credentials

credibilidad *nf* credibility

crédito *nm* (a) *Com & Fin* credit (b) *(confianza)* belief; **dar c. a** to believe

credo *nm* creed

crédulo, -a *adj* credulous, gullible

creencia *nf* belief

creer [36] **1** *vt* (a) *(estar convencido de)* to believe (b) *(pensar)* to think; **creo que no** I don't think so; **creo que sí** I think so; **ya lo creo** I should think so
2 *vi* to believe; **c. en** to believe in
3 creerse *upr* (a) *(considerarse)* to consider oneself to be; **¿qué te has creído?** what o who do you think you are? (b) **no me lo creo** I can't believe it

creíble *adj* credible, believable

creído, -a 1 *adj* arrogant, vain
2 *nm,f* big head

crema *nf* cream

cremallera *nf Br* zip (fastener), *US* zipper

crematorio *nm* **(horno) c.** crematorium

cremoso, -a *adj* creamy

crepe *nm* crêpe, pancake

crepería *nf* creperie

crepitar *vi* to crackle

crepúsculo *nm* twilight

crespo, -a *adj* frizzy

crespón *nm* crepe

cresta *nf* (a) *(de gallo)* comb; *(de punk)* Mohican (b) *(de ola, montaña)* crest

Creta *n* Crete

cretino, -a 1 *adj* stupid, cretinous
2 *nm,f* cretin

creyente *nmf* believer

crezco *indic pres de* crecer

cría *nf* (a) *(cachorro)* young (b) *(crianza)* breeding, raising

criada *nf* maid

criadero *nm* nursery

criadilla *nf Culin* bull's testicle

criado, -a 1 *adj* **mal c.** spoilt
2 *nm,f* servant

crianza *nf (de animales)* breeding; *Fig* **vinos de c.** vintage wines

criar [29] *vt* (a) *(animales)* to breed, to raise; *(niños)* to bring up, to rear (b) *(producir)* to have, to grow

criatura *nf* (a) *(ser)* (living) creature (b) *(crío)* baby, child

criba *nf* sieve

cribar *vt* to sieve, to sift

crimen *nm* murder; **c. de guerra** war crime

criminal *nmf & adj* criminal

crin *nf,* **crines** *nfpl* mane

crío, -a 1 *nm Fam* kid
2 *adj* babyish

criollo, -a *adj & nm,f* Creole

críquet *nm* cricket

crisantemo *nm* chrysanthemum

crisis *nf inv* crisis; **c. nerviosa** nervous breakdown

crispación *nf* tension

crispar *vt* to make tense; *Fig* **eso me crispa los nervios** that sets my nerves on edge

cristal *nm* (a) *(material)* crystal; **c. de roca** rock crystal (b) *Esp (vidrio)* glass; *(de gafas)* lens; *(de ventana)* (window) pane

cristalera *nf (puerta)* French window; *(ventana)* large window

cristalería *nf* (a) *(conjunto)* glassware (b) *(tienda)* glazier's (shop)

cristalino, -a *adj* crystal clear

cristalizar [40] *vi* to crystallize

cristiandad *nf* Christendom

cristianismo *nm* Christianity

cristiano, -a *adj & nm,f* Christian

Cristo *nm* Christ

criterio *nm* (a) *(pauta)* criterion (b) *(opinión)* opinion (c) *(discernimiento)* discretion; **lo dejo a tu c.** I'll leave it up to you

crítica *nf* (a) *(ataque)* criticism (b) *Prensa* review; **tener buena c.** to get good reviews (c) *(conjunto de críticos)* critics

criticar [44] **1** *vt* to criticize
2 *vi (murmurar)* to gossip

crítico, -a 1 *adj* critical
2 *nm,f* critic

criticón, -ona *nm,f Fam* fault-finder

Croacia *n* Croatia

croar *vi* to croak

croata 1 *adj* Croatian
2 *nmf* Croat, Croatian

croché *nm* crochet

croissant [krwa'san] *(pl* croissants*) nm* croissant

croissantería [krwasante'ria] *nf* = shop selling filled croissants

crol *nm* crawl

cromo *nm* (a) *(metal)* chromium, chrome (b) *Esp (estampa)* picture card

cromosoma *nm* chromosome

crónica *nf* (a) *(de la historia)* chronicle (b) *Prensa* feature, article

crónico, -a *adj* chronic

cronista *nmf Prensa* feature writer

cronología *nf* chronology

cronológico, -a *adj* chronological

cronometrar *vt* to time

cronómetro *nm* stopwatch

croqueta *nf* croquette

croquis *nm inv* sketch

cross *nm inv Dep (carrera)* cross-country race; *(deporte)* cross-country (running)

cruce *nm* (a) *(de líneas, paso)* crossing; *(de carreteras)* crossroads; *(de razas)* crossbreeding (b) *Tel* crossed line

crucero *nm Náut* cruise; *(barco)* cruiser

crucial *adj* crucial

crucificar [44] *vt* to crucify

crucifijo *nm* crucifix

crucigrama *nm* crossword (puzzle)

crudeza *nf* (a) *(de clima)* harshness (b) *(de descripción, imágenes)* brutality, harsh realism

crudo, -a 1 *adj* (a) *(natural)* raw; *(comida)* undercooked (b) *(clima)* harsh; *Fam Fig* **lo veo muy c.** it doesn't look too good (c) *(color)* cream
  2 *nm (petróleo)* crude

cruel *adj* cruel

crueldad *nf* cruelty

cruento, -a *adj* bloody

crujido *nm (de madera)* creak, creaking

crujiente *adj (comida)* crunchy

crujir *vi (madera)* to creak; *(comida)* to crunch; *(dientes)* to grind

crustáceo *nm* crustacean

cruz *nf* (a) *(figura)* cross; **C. Roja** Red Cross; **c. gamada** swastika (b) **¿cara o c.?** ≃ heads or tails?

cruza *nf Am* cross, crossbreed

cruzada *nf* crusade

cruzado, -a 1 *adj* (a) *(cheque, piernas, brazos)* crossed (b) *(abrigo, chaqueta)* double-breasted (c) *(atravesado)* lying across (d) *(animal)* crossbred
  2 *nm Hist* crusader

cruzar [40] **1** *vt* (a) *(lugar, piernas)* to cross (b) *(palabras, miradas)* to exchange (c) *(animal, planta)* to cross, to crossbreed
  2 *vi (atravesar)* to cross
  3 cruzarse *vpr* to cross; **cruzarse con algn** to pass sb

cta. *Com (abr cuenta)* a/c

cta. cte. *Com (abr cuenta corriente)* c/a

cte. *(abr corriente)* inst.

cuaderno *nm* notebook

cuadra *nf* (a) *(establo)* stable (b) *Am (en calle)* block (c) *Perú (recibidor)* reception room

cuadrado, -a 1 *adj* (a) *Geom* square (b) *(complexión física)* broad, stocky (c) *Fig (mente)* rigid
  2 *nm* (a) *Geom* square (b) *Mat* square; **elevar (un número) al c.** to square (a number)

cuadrar 1 *vt* (a) *Mat* to square (b) *Andes (aparcar)* to park
  2 *vi (coincidir)* to square, agree (**con** with); *(sumas, cifras)* to tally
  3 cuadrarse *vpr (soldado)* to stand to attention

cuadriculado, -a *adj* **papel c.** square paper

cuadrilátero, -a 1 *adj* quadrilateral
  2 *nm (en boxeo)* ring

cuadrilla *nf (equipo)* gang, team; *Mil* squad; *Taurom* bullfighter's team

cuadro *nm* (a) *Geom* square; **tela a cuadros** checked cloth (b) *Arte* painting, picture (c) *Teatro* scene (d) *Elec & Téc* panel; **c. de mandos** control panel (e) *(gráfico)* chart, graph

cuádruple *adj* quadruple, fourfold

cuajada *nf* curd

cuajar 1 *vt (leche)* to curdle; *(sangre)* to clot
  2 *vi* (a) *(nieve)* to lie (b) *(moda)* to catch on; *(plan)* to get off the ground

cual 1 *pron rel (precedido de artículo)* (a) *(persona) (sujeto)* who; *(objeto)* whom (b) *(cosa)* which
  2 *pron* (a) **tal c.** exactly as (b) *Literario (comparativo)* such as, like

cuál *pron* (a) *(interrogativo)* which (one)?, what?; **¿c. quieres?** which one do you want? (b) *(en oraciones distributivas)* **a c. más tonto** each more stupid than the other

cualidad *nf* quality

cualificado, -a *adj* qualified

cualquier *adj indef* any; **c. cosa** anything; **en c. momento** at any moment o time

cualquiera *(pl* **cualesquiera***)* **1** *adj* (a) *(indefinido)* any; **un profesor c.** any teacher (b) *(corriente)* ordinary

> Note that **cualquier** is used before singular nouns (e.g. **cualquier hombre** any man).

  2 *pron indef* (a) *(persona)* anybody; **c. te lo puede decir** anybody can tell you (b) *(cosa, animal)* any one (c) **c. que sea** whatever it is
  3 *nmf Fig* **ser un c.** to be a nobody; **es una c.** she's a tart

cuando 1 *adv (de tiempo)* when; **c. más** at the most; **c. menos** at least; **de c. en c., de vez en c.** from time to time
  2 *conj* (a) *(temporal)* when; **c. quieras** whenever you want; **c. vengas** when you come (b) *(condicional) (si)* if (c) *(concesiva) (aunque)* **(aun) c.** even if
  3 *prep* during, at the time of; **c. la guerra** during the war; **c. niño** as a child

cuándo *adv interr* when?; **¿desde c.?** since when?; **¿para c. lo quieres?** when do you want it for?

cuantía *nf* quantity, amount

cuantioso, -a *adj* substantial, considerable

cuanto, -a 1 *adj* all; **gasta c. dinero gana** he spends all the money *o* as much as he earns; **unas cuantas niñas** a few girls

2 *pron rel* as much as; **coma c. quiera** eat as much as you want; **regala todo c. tiene** he gives away everything he's got

3 *pron indef pl* **unos cuantos** a few

4 *adv* (a) *(tiempo)* **c. antes** as soon as possible; **en c.** as soon as (b) *(cantidad)* **c. más … más** the more … the more; **c. más lo miro, más me gusta** the more I look at it, the more I like it; **cuantas más personas (haya) mejor** the more the merrier (c) **en c. a** with respect to, regarding; **en c. a Juan** as for Juan, as far as Juan is concerned

cuánto, -a 1 *adj & pron interr (singular)* how much?; *(plural)* how many?; **¿cuántas veces?** how many times?; **¿c. es?** how much is it?

2 *adv* how, how much; **¡cuánta gente hay!** what a lot of people there are!

cuarenta *adj & nm inv* forty; *Fam* **cantarle a algn las c.** to give sb a piece of one's mind

cuarentena *nf Med* quarantine

cuarentón, -ona *nm,f* forty-year-old

cuaresma *nf* Lent

cuartear 1 *vt* to cut *o* chop up

2 cuartearse *upr* to crack

cuartel *nm Mil* barracks; **c. general** headquarters; *Fig* **no dar c.** to give no quarter

cuartelazo *nm* military uprising, revolt

cuartelillo *nm Mil* post, station

cuarteto *nm* quartet

cuartilla *nf* sheet of paper

cuarto, -a 1 *nm* (a) *(habitación)* room; **c. de baño** bathroom; **c. de estar** living room (b) *(cuarta parte)* quarter; **c. de hora** quarter of an hour; *Dep* **cuartos de final** quarter finals (c) *Fam* **cuartos** *(dinero)* dough, money

2 *adj & nm,f* fourth

cuarzo *nm* quartz

cuate *nmf CAm, Ecuad, Méx* (a) *Fam (amigo)* pal, *US* buddy (b) *Fam (persona) (hombre)* guy, *Br* bloke; *(mujer)* woman

cuatro 1 *adj & nm inv* four

2 *nm Fam* a few; **cayeron c. gotas** it rained a little bit

cuatrocientos, -as *adj & nm* four hundred

Cuba *n* Cuba

cuba *nf* cask, barrel; *Fam* **como una c.** (as) drunk as a lord

cubalibre *nm* rum/gin and coke

cubano, -a *adj & nm,f* Cuban

cubata *nm Fam* = **cubalibre**

cubertería *nf* cutlery

cubeta *nf (cuba pequeña)* bucket, pail; *(de barómetro)* bulb; *Fot* tray

cúbico, -a *adj* cubic; *Mat* **raíz cúbica** cube root

cubierta *nf* (a) *(de libro, cama)* cover (b) *(de rueda)* tyre (c) *(de barco)* deck

cubierto, -a 1 *adj* (a) *(tapado)* covered; *(piscina)* indoors; *(cielo)* overcast (b) *(trabajo, plaza)* filled

2 *nm* (a) *(en la mesa)* place setting (b) **cubiertos** cutlery

3 *pp de* **cubrir**

cubil *nm* lair

cubismo *nm* cubism

cubito *nm* little cube; **c. de hielo** ice cube

cúbito *nm Anat* ulna

cubo *nm* (a) *(recipiente)* bucket; **c. de la basura** *Br* rubbish bin, *US* garbage can (b) *Mat* cube (c) *(de rueda)* hub

cubrecama *nm* bedspread

cubrir *(pp cubierto)* **1** *vt* to cover

2 cubrirse *upr (cielo)* to become overcast

cucaracha *nf* cockroach

cuchara *nf* spoon

cucharada *nf* spoonful; **c. rasa/colmada** level/heaped spoonful

cucharilla *nf* teaspoon; **c. de café** coffee spoon

cucharón *nm* ladle

cuchichear *vi* to whisper

cuchicheo *nm* whispering

cuchilla *nf* blade; **c. de afeitar** razor blade

cuchillada *nf*, **cuchillazo** *nm* stab

cuchillo *nm* knife

cuchitril *nm Fam* hovel, hole

cuclillas *nfpl* **en c.** squatting; **ponerse en c.** to squat (down)

cuco, -a 1 *nm* cuckoo

2 *adj Fam (astuto)* shrewd, crafty

cucurucho *nm* (a) *(para helado)* cornet (b) *(de papel)* paper cone

cuello *nm* (a) *(de persona, animal, botella)* neck (b) *(de prendas)* collar

cuenca *nf* (a) *Geog* basin (b) *(del ojo)* socket

cuenco *nm* earthenware bowl

cuenta *nf* (a) *(factura)* bill; *(en restaurante)* *Br* bill, *US* check; *Fin (de banco)* account; **c. corriente** *Br* current account, *US* checking account (c) *(cálculo)* count;

hacer cuentas to do sums; **c. atrás** countdown (d) *(de collar)* bead (e) *Inform* account; **c. de correo (electrónico)** e-mail account (f) *(locuciones)* **caer en la c., darse c.** to realize; **dar c.** to report; **tener en c.** to take into account; **traer c.** to be worthwhile; **más sillas de la c.** too many chairs; **en resumidas cuentas** in short; **pedir cuentas** to ask for an explanation; **trabajar por c. propia** to be self-employed

cuentagotas *nm inv* dropper

cuentakilómetros *nm inv (distancia)* Br ≃ mileometer, US ≃ odometer; *(velocidad)* speedometer

cuentapasos *nm inv* pedometer

cuento *nm* story; *Lit* short story; **contar un c.** to tell a story; *Fig* **eso no viene a c.** that's beside the point; **c. chino** tall story; **c. de hadas** fairy story

cuerda *nf* (a) *(cordel)* rope; *Fig* **bajo c.** dishonestly; **c. floja** tightrope; **cuerdas vocales** vocal cords (b) *(de instrumento)* string (c) *(del reloj)* spring; **dar c. al reloj** to wind up a watch

cuerdo, -a *adj* sane

cueriza *nf Andes Fam* beating, leathering

cuerno *nm* horn; *(de ciervo)* antler; *Fam* **¡vete al c.!** get lost!; *Fam* **ponerle cuernos a algn** to be unfaithful to sb

cuero *nm* (a) *(piel)* leather; **chaqueta de c.** leather jacket (b) **c. cabelludo** scalp; *Fam* **en cueros (vivos)** (stark) naked

cuerpo *nm* (a) body; **de c. entero** full-length; *Fig* **tomar c.** to take shape (b) *(cadáver)* corpse; **de c. presente** lying in state (c) *(parte)* section, part (d) *(grupo)* corps, force; **c. de bomberos** Br fire brigade, US fire department; **c. diplomático** diplomatic corps

cuervo *nm* raven

cuesta 1 *nf* slope; **c. abajo** downhill; **c. arriba** uphill
2 a cuestas *loc adv* on one's back o shoulders

cuestión *nf* (a) *(asunto)* matter, question; **es c. de vida o muerte** it's a matter of life or death; **en c. de unas horas** in just a few hours (b) *(pregunta)* question

cuestionario *nm* questionnaire

cueva *nf* cave

cuezo *indic pres de* cocer

cuico, -a *nm,f Méx Fam* cop

cuidado 1 *nm* care; **con c.** carefully; **tener c.** to be careful; **estar al c. de** *(cosa)* to be in charge of; *(persona)* to look after; **me trae sin c.** I couldn't care less; *Med* **cuidados intensivos** intensive care
2 *interj* **¡c.!** look out!, watch out!; **¡c. con**

lo que dices! watch what you say!; **¡c. con el escalón!** mind the step!

cuidadoso, -a *adj* careful

cuidar 1 *vt* to care for, to look after; **c. de que todo salga bien** to make sure that everything goes all right; **c. los detalles** to pay attention to details
2 cuidarse *vpr* **cuídate** look after yourself

cuitlacoche *nm CAm, Méx* corn smut, = edible fungus which grows on maize

culata *nf* (a) *(de arma)* butt (b) *Aut* cylinder head

culebra *nf* snake

culebrón *nm Esp Fam* soap opera

culinario, -a *adj* culinary

culminación *nf* culmination

culminante *adj (punto)* highest; *(momento)* culminating

culminar *vi* to culminate

culo *nm* (a) *Am Fam (nalgas)* Br bum, US butt; *Esp Vulg* **¡vete a tomar por c.!** fuck off! (b) *(de recipiente)* bottom

culpa *nf* (a) *(responsabilidad)* blame; **echar la c. a algn** to put the blame on sb; **fue c. mía** it was my fault; **por tu c.** because of you (b) *(sentimiento)* guilt

culpabilidad *nf* guilt, culpability

culpable 1 *nmf* offender, culprit
2 *adj* guilty; *Der* **declararse c.** to plead guilty

culpar *vt* to blame; **c. a algn de un delito** to accuse sb of an offence

cultivado, -a *adj* cultivated

cultivar *vt* (a) *(tierra)* to farm, to cultivate; *(plantas)* to grow (b) *(amistad, inteligencia)* to cultivate (c) *(arte)* to practise (d) *(germen)* to culture

cultivo *nm* (a) *(de tierra)* farming; *(de plantas)* growing (b) *(plantación)* crop (c) *(de gérmenes)* culture

culto, -a 1 *adj* educated; *(palabra)* learned
2 *nm* cult; *Rel* worship

cultura *nf* culture

cultural *adj* cultural

culturismo *nm* body building

culturista *nmf* body builder

cumbre *nf* (a) *(de montaña)* summit, top; **(conferencia) c.** summit conference (b) *Fig (culminación)* pinnacle

cumple *nm Fam* birthday

cumpleaños *nm inv* birthday; **¡feliz c.!** happy birthday!

cumplido, -a 1 *adj* (a) *(plazo)* expired; **misión cumplida** mission accomplished (b) *(cortés)* polite
2 *nm* compliment

cumplidor, -a *adj* reliable, dependable

cumplimiento *nm (de deber)* perform-ance; *(de contrato, obligaciones)* ful-filment; *(de la ley)* observance; *(de órdenes)* carrying out; *(de promesa)* fulfilment

cumplir 1 *vt* (a) *(deber)* to do, to carry out, to perform; *(contrato, obligaciones)* to fulfil; *(ley)* to observe; *(orden)* to carry out; *(promesa)* to keep; *(sentencia)* to serve (b) *(años)* **ayer cumplí veinte años** I was twenty (years old) yesterday

2 *vi* (a) *(plazo)* to expire, to end (b) **c. con** *(normas)* to comply; **c. con su deber/trabajo** to do one's duty/job; **c. con algn** to do one's duty by sb

3 cumplirse *upr* (a) *(deseo, sueño)* to be fulfilled, to come true (b) *(plazo)* to expire

cúmulo *nm* pile, load

cuna *nf* (a) *(de bebé)* cot, cradle (b) *(de movimiento, civilización)* cradle; *(de persona)* birthplace

cundir *vi* (a) *(propagarse)* to spread (b) *Esp (dar de sí) (comida, reservas)* to go a long way; *(trabajo, estudio)* to go well; **me cundió mucho el tiempo** I got a lot done

cuneta *nf (de la carretera)* gutter; **quedarse en la c.** to be left behind

cuña *nf* (a) *(pieza)* wedge; **c. publicitaria** commercial break (b) *Andes, RP Fam (enchufe)* **tener c.** to have friends in high places

cuñado, -a *nm,f (hombre)* brother-in-law; *(mujer)* sister-in-law

cuño *nm* **de nuevo c.** newly-coined

cuota *nf* (a) *(de club etc)* membership fees *pl*, dues *pl* (b) *Am (plazo)* instalment; **comprar en cuotas** to buy on *Br* hire purchase *o US* an installment plan (c) *(porción)* quota, share (d) *Méx (importe)* toll; **autopista de c.** toll motorway, *US* turnpike

cupe *pt indef de* **caber**

cupiera *subj imperf de* **caber**

cuplé *nm* popular song

cupo *nm* ceiling; *Mil* **excedente de c.** exempt from military service

cupón *nm* coupon, voucher

cúpula *nf* dome, cupola; *(líderes)* leader-ship

cura 1 *nm Rel* priest
2 *nf Med* cure; *Fig* **no tiene c.** there's no remedy

curación *nf* cure, treatment

curandero, -a *nm,f* quack

curar 1 *vt* (a) *(sanar)* to cure; *(herida)* to dress; *(enfermedad)* to treat (b) *(carne, pescado)* to cure

2 *vi (sanar)* to recover, to get well; *(herida)* to heal up
3 curarse *upr* to recover, to get well; *(herida)* to heal up; **c. en salud** to make sure

curcuncho, -a *adj Andes Fam* hunch-backed

curiosear *vi* to pry

curiosidad *nf* curiosity; **tener c. de** to be curious about

curioso, -a 1 *adj* (a) *(indiscreto)* curious, inquisitive (b) *(extraño)* strange, odd; **lo c. es que …** the strange thing is that … (c) *(limpio)* neat, tidy
2 *nm,f* (a) *(mirón)* onlooker (b) *(chismoso)* nosey-parker, busybody

curita *nf Am Br* (sticking-)plaster, *US* Band-aid®

currante *Esp Fam* **1** *adj* hard-working
2 *nmf* worker

currar *vi Esp Fam* to work

currículum (vitae) [kuˈrrikulum (ˈbite)] *(pl* **currícula** *o* **currículums (vitae))** *nm* curriculum vitae, *Br* CV, *US* résumé

curro *nm Esp Fam* work

curry *(pl* **currys)** *nm* curry; **pollo al c.** chicken curry

cursar *vt* (a) *(estudiar)* to study (b) *(enviar)* to send

cursi *adj (vestido, canción)* tacky, *Br* naff; *(modales, persona)* affected

cursillo *nm* short course; **c. de reciclaje** refresher course

cursivo, -a *adj* **letra cursiva** italics

curso *nm* (a) *(año académico)* year; *(lecciones)* course (b) *(de acontecimientos, río)* course; **en el c. de** during; **año/mes en c.** current year/month (c) *(circulación)* **moneda de c. legal** legal tender

cursor *nm* cursor

curtido, -a *adj* (a) *(piel)* weatherbeaten; *(cuero)* tanned (b) *Fig (persona)* hard-ened

curtiembre *nf Andes, RP* tannery

curtir *vt* (a) *(cuero)* to tan (b) *Fig (avezar)* to harden, to toughen

curva *nf* (a) *(línea, forma)* curve (b) *(en carretera)* bend; **c. cerrada** sharp bend

curvado, -a *adj (forma)* curved; *(espalda)* bent

curvilíneo, -a *adj* curvaceous

curvo, -a *adj* curved

cuscús *nm inv* couscous

cúspide *nf* summit, peak; *Fig* peak

custodia *nf* custody

custodiar [43] *vt* to watch over

cutáneo, -a *adj* cutaneous, skin; *Med*
  erupción cutánea rash
cutícula *nf* cuticle
cutis *nm inv* complexion

cutre *adj Esp Fam (sórdido)* shabby, dingy
cuyo, -a *pron rel & pos (de persona)* whose;
  (de cosa) of which; **en c. caso** in which case
cv *(abr* **caballos de vapor***)* hp

D

D, d [de] *nf (letra)* D, d

D. *(abr* **don)** Mr

Da *(abr* **doña)** Mrs/Ms

dactilar *adj* **huella d.** fingerprint

dádiva *nf (regalo)* gift, present; *(donativo)* donation

dadivoso, -a *adj* generous

dado¹, -a *adj* (**a**) given; **en un momento d.** at a certain point; **ser d. a** to be given to (**b**) **d. que** since, given that

dado² *nm* die, dice

daga *nf* dagger

dalia *nf* dahlia

dálmata *nm* Dalmatian (dog)

daltónico, -a *adj* colour-blind

dama *nf* (**a**) *(señora)* lady (**b**) *(en damas)* king (**c**) **damas** *(juego)* Br draughts, US checkers

damasco *nm* (**a**) *(tela)* damask (**b**) *Andes, RP (albaricoque)* apricot

damnificado, -a *nm,f* victim

danés, -esa 1 *adj* Danish
 2 *nm,f (persona)* Dane
 3 *nm* (**a**) *(idioma)* Danish (**b**) **gran d.** *(perro)* Great Dane

Danubio *nm* **el D.** the Danube

danza *nf* dancing; *(baile)* dance

danzar [40] *vt & vi* to dance

dañar *vt (cosa)* to damage; *(persona)* to hurt, to harm

dañino, -a *adj* harmful, damaging (**para** to)

daño *nm* (**a** *cosa)* damage; *(a persona) (físico)* hurt; *(perjuicio)* harm; **se hizo d. en la pierna** he hurt his leg; *Der* **daños y perjuicios** (legal) damages

dar [11] **1** *vt* (**a**) *(dar)* to give; *(recado, recuerdos)* to pass on, to give; *(noticia)* to tell (**b**) *(mano de pintura, cera)* to apply, to put on (**c**) *(película)* to show, to screen; *(fiesta)* to throw, to give (**d**) *(cosecha)* to produce, to yield; *(fruto, flores)* to bear; *(beneficio, interés)* to give, to yield (**e**) *(bofetada etc)* to deal; **d. a algn en la cabeza** to hit sb on the head (**f**) **dale a la luz** switch the light on; **d. la mano a algn** to shake hands with sb; **d. los buenos días/las buenas noches a algn** to say good morning/good evening to sb; **me da lo mismo, me da igual** it's all the same to me; **¿qué más da?** what difference does it make? (**g**) *(hora)* to strike; **ya han dado las nueve** it's gone nine (o'clock) (**h**) **d. de comer a** to feed (**i**) **d. a conocer** *(noticia)* to release; **d. a entender a algn que ...** to give sb to understand that ... (**j**) **d. por** *(considerar)* to assume, to consider; **lo dieron por muerto** he was assumed dead, he was given up for dead; **d. por descontado** *o* **sabido** to take for granted, to assume
 2 *vi* (**a**) **me dio un ataque de tos/risa** I had a coughing fit/an attack of the giggles (**b**) **d. a** *(ventana, habitación)* to look out onto, to overlook; *(puerta)* to open onto, to lead to (**c**) **d. con** *(persona)* to come across; **d. con la solución** to hit upon the solution (**d**) **d. de sí** *(ropa)* to stretch, to give (**e**) **d. en** to hit; **el sol me daba en los ojos** the sun was (shining) in my eyes (**f**) **d. para** to be enough *o* sufficient for; **el presupuesto no da para más** the budget will not stretch any further (**g**) **le dio por nadar** he took it into his head to go swimming (**h**) **d. que hablar** to set people talking; **el suceso dio que pensar** the incident gave people food for thought
 3 **darse** *vpr* (**a**) **se dio un caso extraño** something strange happened (**b**) *(hallarse)* to be found, to exist (**c**) **darse a** to take to; **se dio a la bebida** he took to drink (**d**) **darse con** *o* **contra** to bump *o* crash into (**e**) **dárselas de** to consider oneself (**f**) **darse por satisfecho** to feel satisfied; **darse por vencido** to give in (**g**) **se le da bien/mal el francés** she's good/bad at French

dardo *nm* dart

dársena *nf* (**a**) *(en puerto)* dock (**b**) *(en estación de autobuses)* bay

datar 1 *vi* **d. de** to date back to *o* from
 2 *vt* to date

dátil *nm* date

dato *nm* (a) *(hecho, cifra)* piece of information; **datos personales** personal details (b) *Inform* **datos** data

d.C. *(abr* **después de Cristo)** AD

dcha. *(abr* **derecha)** rt.

de *prep*

> **de** combines with the article **el** to form the contraction **del** (e.g. **del hombre** of the man).

(a) *(pertenencia)* of; **el título de la novela** the title of the novel; **el coche/hermano de Sofía** Sofía's car/brother; **las bicicletas de los niños** the boys' bicycles (b) *(procedencia)* from; **de Madrid a Valencia** from Madrid to Valencia; **soy de Palencia** I'm from *o* I come from Palencia (c) *(descripción)* **el niño de ojos azules** the boy with blue eyes; **el señor de la chaqueta** the man in the jacket; **el bobo del niño** the silly boy; **un reloj de oro** a gold watch; **un joven de veinte años** a young man of twenty (d) *(contenido)* of; **un saco de patatas** a sack of potatoes (e) **gafas de sol** sunglasses; **goma de borrar** eraser, *Br* rubber (f) *(oficio)* by, as; **es arquitecto de profesión** he's an architect by profession; **trabaja de secretaria** she's working as a secretary (g) *(acerca de)* about; **curso de informática** computer course (h) *(tiempo)* **a las tres de la tarde** at three in the afternoon; **de día** by day; **de noche** at night; **de lunes a jueves** from Monday to Thursday; **de pequeño** as a child; **de año en año** year in year out (i) *(precio)* at; **patatas de 30 céntimos el kilo** potatoes at 30 cents a kilo (j) **una avenida de 15 km** an avenue 15 km long; **una botella de litro** a litre bottle (k) *(con superlativo)* in; **el más largo de España** the longest in Spain (l) *(causa)* with, because of; **llorar de alegría** to cry with joy; **morir de hambre** to die of hunger (m) *(condicional)* **de haber llegado antes** if he had arrived before; **de no ser así** if that wasn't *o* weren't the case; **de ser cierto** if it was *o* were true (n) **lo mismo de siempre** the usual thing (o) **de cuatro en cuatro** in fours, four at a time

deambular *vi* to saunter, to stroll

debajo *adv* underneath, below; **el mío es el de d.** mine is the one below; **está d. de la mesa** it's under the table; **por d. de lo normal** below normal; **salió por d. del coche** he came out from under the car

debate *nm* debate

debatir 1 *vt* to debate
2 debatirse *vpr* to struggle; **debatirse entre la vida y la muerte** to fight for one's life

debe *nm Com* debit, debit side

deber¹ *nm* (a) *(deber)* duty; **cumplir con su d.** to do one's duty (b) *Educ* **deberes** homework

deber² **1** *vt (dinero, explicación)* to owe
2 *vi* (a) *(obligación)* must, to have to; **debe (de) comer** he must eat; **debe (de) irse ahora** she has to leave now; **la factura debe pagarse mañana** the bill must be paid tomorrow; **el tren debe llegar a las dos** the train is expected to arrive at two (b) *(consejo)* **deberías visitar a tus padres** you ought to visit your parents; **debería haber ido ayer** I should have gone yesterday; **no debiste hacerlo** you shouldn't have done it (c) *(suposición)* **deben de estar fuera** they must be out
3 deberse *vpr* **deberse a** to be due to; **esto se debe a la falta de agua** this is due to lack of water

debidamente *adv* duly, properly

debido, -a *adj* (a) *(justo, conveniente)* due; **a su d. tiempo** in due course; **con el d. respeto** with due respect (b) *(adecuado)* proper; **más de lo d.** too much; **tomaron las debidas precauciones** they took the proper precautions; **como es d.** properly (c) **d. a** because of, due to; **d. a que** because of the fact that

débil *adj* weak; *(luz)* dim; **punto d.** weak spot

debilidad *nf* weakness; *Fig* **tener d. por** *(persona)* to have a soft spot for; *(cosa)* to have a weakness for

debilitamiento *nm* weakening

debilitar 1 *vt* to weaken, to debilitate
2 debilitarse *vpr* to weaken, to grow weak

débito *nm (debe)* debit; *(deuda)* debt; *Am* **d. bancario** direct debit

debut *(pl* **debuts)** *nm* début, debut

debutar *vi* to make one's début *o* debut

década *nf* decade; **en la d. de los noventa** during the nineties

decadencia *nf* decadence

decadente *adj & nmf* decadent

decaer [39] *vi* to deteriorate

decaído, -a *adj* down

decaimiento *nm* (a) *(debilidad)* weakness (b) *(desaliento)* low spirits

decano, -a *nm,f Univ* dean

decantarse *vpr* **d. por** to opt for

decapitar *vt* to behead, to decapitate

decena *nf* (about) ten; **una d. de veces** (about) ten times; **por decenas** in tens

decencia *nf* (a) *(decoro)* decency; *(en el vestir)* (b) *(dignidad)* dignity

decenio *nm* decade

decente *adj* (a) *(digno)* decent; **un sueldo d.** a decent salary *o* wage (b) *(en el comportamiento)* proper; *(en el vestir)* modest (c) *(limpio)* clean

decepción *nf* disappointment

📖 Observa que la palabra inglesa **deception** es un falso amigo y no es la traducción de la palabra española **decepción**. En inglés **deception** significa "engaño".

---

decepcionante *adj* disappointing

decepcionar *vt* to disappoint

decididamente *adv* (a) *(con decisión)* resolutely (b) *(sin duda)* definitely

decidido, -a *adj* determined, resolute

decidir 1 *vt & vi* to decide
2 decidirse *vpr* to make up one's mind; **decidirse a hacer algo** to make up one's mind to do sth; **decidirse por algo** to decide on sth

décima *nf* tenth

decimal *adj & nm* decimal; **el sistema métrico d.** the decimal system

décimo, -a 1 *adj & nm,f* tenth
2 *nm* (a) *(parte)* tenth (b) *(billete de lotería)* tenth part of a lottery ticket

decir¹ *nm* saying

decir² [12] *(pp* **dicho)** **1** *vt* (a) *(con palabras)* to say; **dice que no quiere venir** he says he doesn't want to come (b) **d. una mentira/la verdad** to tell a lie/the truth (c) *Esp* **¿diga?, ¿dígame?** *(al teléfono)* hello? (d) **¿qué me dices del nuevo jefe?** what do you think of the new boss? (e) *(mostrar)* to tell, to show; **su cara dice que está mintiendo** you can tell from his face that he's lying (f) *(sugerir)* to mean; **esta película no me dice nada** this film doesn't appeal to me; **¿qué te dice el cuadro?** what does the picture mean to you? (g) **querer d.** to mean (h) *(locuciones)* **es d.** that is (to say); **por así decirlo** as it were, so to speak; **digamos** let's say; **digo yo** in my opinion; **el qué dirán** what people will say; **ni que d. tiene** needless to say; **¡no me digas!** really!; *Esp* **¡y que lo digas!** you can say that again!
2 decirse *vpr* **¿cómo se dice "mesa" en inglés?** how do you say "mesa" in

English?; **se dice que ...** they say that ...; **sé lo que me digo** I know what I am saying

decisión *nf* (a) *(acción)* decision; **tomar una d.** to take *o* make a decision (b) *(cualidad) (firmeza)* determination; *(resolución)* decisiveness; **con d.** decisively

decisivo, -a *adj* decisive

decisorio, -a *adj* decision-making

declamar *vt & vi* to declaim, to recite

declaración *nf* (a) *(afirmación)* declaration; **hacer declaraciones** to comment; **d. de (la) renta** tax return (b) *(ante la policía)* statement; *Der* **prestar d.** to give evidence

declarado, -a *adj (manifiesto)* open, professed; **es un homosexual d.** he is openly gay; **hay un odio d. entre ellos** there is open hostility between them

declarante *nmf Der* witness

declarar 1 *vt* (a) *(ante la autoridad)* to declare; **d. la guerra a** to declare war on (b) *(afirmar)* to state (c) *Der* **d. culpable/inocente a algn** to find sb guilty/not guilty
2 *vi Der* to testify
3 declararse *vpr* (a) **declararse a favor/en contra de** to declare oneself in favour of/against; **declararse en huelga** to go on strike; **declararse a algn** to declare one's love for sb (b) *(guerra, incendio)* to start, to break out (c) *Der* **declararse culpable** to plead guilty

declinar *vt & vi* to decline

declive *nm* (a) *(del terreno)* incline, slope (b) *(de imperio etc)* decline

decolaje *nm Am* take-off

decolar *vi Am* to take off

decolorante *nm* bleaching agent

decolorar 1 *vt* to bleach
2 decolorarse *vpr* to fade

decomisar *vt* to confiscate, to seize

decoración *nf* decoration

decorado *nm* scenery, set

decorador, -a *nm,f* interior designer; *Cin & Teatro* set designer

decorar *vt* to decorate

decorativo, -a *adj* decorative

decoro *nm* (a) *(pudor)* decency, decorum (b) *(dignidad)* dignity

decoroso, -a *adj (decente)* decent; *(correcto)* seemly, proper

decrecer [33] *vi* to decrease, to diminish

decrépito, -a *adj* decrepit

decretar *vt* to decree

decreto *nm* decree; **d.-ley** decree, *Br* order in council

dedal *nm* thimble

dedicación *nf* dedication

dedicar [44] **1** *vt* to dedicate; *(tiempo, esfuerzos)* to devote (**a** to)
  2 dedicarse *vpr* **¿a qué se dedica Vd.?** what do you do for a living?; **los fines de semana ella se dedica a pescar** at weekends she spends her time fishing

dedicatoria *nf* dedication

dedillo *nm* **saber algo al d.** to know sth inside out

dedo *nm (de la mano)* finger; *(del pie)* toe; **d. anular/corazón/índice/meñique** ring/middle/index/little finger; **d. pulgar, d. gordo** thumb; **hacer d.** to hitchhike; *Fig* **elegir a algn a d.** to hand-pick sb

deducción *nf* deduction

deducir [10] *vt* (**a**) *(inferir)* to deduce; **de aquí se deduce que …** from this it follows that … (**b**) *(descontar)* to deduct

deductivo, -a *adj* deductive

defecar [44] *vi* to defecate

defecto *nm* defect, fault; **d. físico** physical defect

defectuoso, -a *adj* defective, faulty

defender [3] **1** *vt* to defend (**de** from); **d. del frío/viento** to shelter from the cold/wind
  2 defenderse *vpr* (**a**) *(contra enemigo, peligro)* to defend oneself (**b**) *Fam* **se defiende en francés** he can get by in French

defendido, -a *nm,f Der* client *(of defence counsel)*

defensa 1 *nf* defence; **en d. propia, en legítima d.** in self-defence; **salir en d. de algn** to come out in defence of sb
  2 *nmf Dep* defender

defensiva *nf* defensive; **estar/ponerse a la d.** to be/go on the defensive

defensivo, -a *adj* defensive

defensor, -a *nm,f* defender; **abogado d.** counsel for the defence; *Esp* **defensor del pueblo** ombudsman

deferencia *nf* deference; **en** *o* **por d. a** out of deference to

deficiencia *nf* deficiency, shortcoming; **d. mental** mental deficiency; **d. renal** kidney failure

deficiente 1 *adj* deficient
  2 *nmf* **d. (mental)** mentally handicapped person
  3 *nm Educ* fail

déficit *(pl* **déficits)** *nm Econ* deficit; *(carencia)* shortage

deficitario, -a *adj (empresa, operación)* loss-making; *(balance)* negative, showing a deficit

definición *nf* definition; **por d.** by definition

definido, -a *adj* (**a**) *(límite, idea)* (clearly) defined (**b**) *Ling* **artículo d.** definite article

definir *vt* to define

definitivamente *adv* (**a**) *(para siempre)* for good, once and for all (**b**) *(con toda seguridad)* definitely

definitivo, -a *adj* definitive; **en definitiva** in short

deflación *nf Econ* deflation

deflacionista *adj Econ* deflationary

deformación *nf* deformation

deformar 1 *vt* to deform, to put out of shape; *(cara)* to disfigure; *Fig (la verdad, una imagen)* to distort
  2 deformarse *vpr* to go out of shape, to become distorted

deforme *adj (cuerpo)* deformed, disfigured; *(imagen)* distorted; *(objeto)* misshapen

defraudación *nf (fiscal)* tax evasion

defraudar *vt* (**a**) *(decepcionar)* to disappoint (**b**) *(estafar)* to defraud; **d. a Hacienda** to evade taxes

defunción *nf Fml* decease, demise

degeneración *nf* degeneration

degenerado, -a *adj & nm,f* degenerate

degenerar *vi* to degenerate

degollar [2] *vt* to behead

degradación *nf* degradation

degradante *adj* degrading

degradar *vt* to degrade

degustación *nf* tasting

degustar *vt* to taste, to sample

dehesa *nf* meadow

dejadez *nf* slovenliness

dejado, -a *adj* careless; *(aspecto)* slovenly

dejar 1 *vt* (**a**) to leave; **déjame en paz** leave me alone; **d. dicho** to leave word *o* a message (**b**) *Esp (prestar)* **d. algo a algn** to lend sb sth, to lend sth to sb (**c**) *(abandonar)* to give up; **d. algo por imposible** to give sth up; **dejé el tabaco y la bebida** I gave up smoking and drinking (**d**) *(permitir)* to let, to allow; **d. caer** to drop; **d. entrar/salir** to let in/out (**e**) *(omitir)* to leave out, to omit (**f**) *(+ adj)* to make; **d. triste** to make sad; **d. preocupado/sorprendido** to worry/surprise (**g**) *(aplazar)* **dejaron el viaje para el verano** they put the trip off until the summer
  2 *v aux* **d. de** + *infin* to stop, to give up; **dejó de fumar el año pasado** he gave up smoking last year; **no deja de llamarme** she's always phoning me up
  3 dejarse *vpr* (**a**) **me he dejado las llaves dentro** I've left the keys inside (**b**) *(locuciones)* **dejarse barba** to grow a

beard; **dejarse caer** to flop down; **dejarse llevar por** to be influenced by

del *(contracción de* de + el*) ver* de

delantal *nm* apron

delante *adv* (**a**) *(en primer lugar, en la parte delantera)* in front; **la entrada de d.** the front entrance (**b**) **d. de** in front of; *(en serie)* ahead of (**c**) **por d.** in front; **se lo lleva todo por d.** he destroys everything in his path; **tiene toda la vida por d.** he has his whole life ahead of him

delantera *nf* lead; **tomar la d.** take the lead

delantero, -a 1 *adj* front
2 *nm Ftb* forward; **d. centro** centre forward

delatar *vt* to inform against; *Fig* to give away

delator, -a *nm,f* informer

delegación *nf* (**a**) *(acto, delegados)* delegation (**b**) *(sucursal)* local office; *Esp* **D. del Gobierno** = office representing central government in each province; *Esp* **D. de Hacienda** = head tax office *(in each province)* (**c**) *Chile, Ecuad, Méx (distrito municipal)* municipal district

delegado, -a *nm,f (representante)* delegate; *(de curso)* reporesentative

delegar [42] *vt* to delegate (**en** to)

deleitar 1 *vt* to delight
2 deleitarse *vpr* to delight in, to take delight in

deleite *nm* delight

deletrear *vt* to spell (out)

deleznable *adj (libro, actuación)* appalling; *(excusa, razón)* contemptible

delfín *nm* dolphin

delgadez *nf* slimness

delgado, -a *adj* slim; *(capa)* fine

deliberación *nf* deliberation

deliberado, -a *adj* deliberate

deliberar *vi* to deliberate (on), to consider

delicadeza *nf* (**a**) *(finura)* delicacy, daintiness (**b**) *(tacto)* tactfulness; **falta de d.** tactlessness

delicado, -a *adj* delicate

delicia *nf* delight; **hacer las delicias de algn** to delight sb

delicioso, -a *adj (comida)* delicious; *(agradable)* delightful

delictivo, -a *adj* criminal, punishable

delimitar *vt (terreno)* to set out the boundaries of; *(funciones)* to define

delincuencia *nf* delinquency

delincuente *adj & nmf* delinquent; **d. juvenil** juvenile delinquent

delineante *nmf (hombre)* draughtsman; *(mujer)* draughtswoman

delinear *vt* to delineate, to outline

delinquir [48] *vi* to commit a crime

delirante *adj* delirious

delirar *vi* to be delirious

delirio *nm* delirium; **delirios de grandeza** delusions of grandeur

delito *nm* crime, offence

delta *nm* delta; **ala d.** hang-glider

demacrado, -a *adj* emaciated

demagogia *nf* demagogy

demagogo, -a *nm,f* demagogue

demanda *nf* (**a**) *Der* lawsuit (**b**) *Com* demand

demandado, -a 1 *nm,f* defendant
2 *adj* in demand

demandante *nmf* claimant

demandar *vt* to sue

demarcar [44] *vt* to demarcate

demás 1 *adj* **los/las d.** the rest of; **la d. gente** the rest of the people
2 *pron* **lo/los/las d.** the rest; **por lo d.** otherwise, apart from that; **y d.** etcetera

demasía *nf* **en d.** excessively

demasiado, -a 1 *adj (singular)* too much; *(plural)* too many; **hay demasiada comida** there is too much food; **quieres demasiadas cosas** you want too many things
2 *adv* too (much); **es d. grande/caro** it is too big/dear; **fumas/trabajas d.** you smoke/work too much

demencia *nf* dementia, insanity

demente 1 *adj* insane, mad
2 *nmf* mental patient

democracia *nf* democracy

demócrata 1 *adj* democratic
2 *nmf* democrat

democrático, -a *adj* democratic

democratizar [40] *vt* to democratize

demografía *nf* demography

demográfico, -a *adj* demographic; **crecimiento d.** population growth

demoledor, -a *adj Fig* devastating

demoler [4] *vt* to demolish

demonio *nm* devil, demon; *Fam* **¿cómo/ dónde demonios …?** how/where the hell …?; *Fam* **¡demonio(s)!** hell!, damn!; *Fam* **¡d. de niño!** you little devil!

demora *nf* delay

demorar 1 *vt* (**a**) *(retrasar)* to delay, hold up (**b**) *(tardar)* **demoraron tres días en pintar la casa** it took them three days to paint the house
2 *vi Am (tardar)* **¡no demores!** don't be late!; **siempre demora en bañarse** he always takes ages in the bathroom; **este quitamanchas demora en actuar** this stain remover takes a while to work

3 demorarse *vpr* (**a**) *(retrasarse)* to be delayed, be held up (**b**) *(detenerse)* to dally (**c**) *esp Am (tardar)* to be late; **no se demoren** don't be late

demostración *nf* demonstration; **una d. de fuerza/afecto** a show of strength

demostrar [2] *vt* (**a**) *(mostrar)* to show, to demonstrate (**b**) *(evidenciar)* to prove

demudado, -a *adj* pale

denegar [1] *vt* to turn down, to reject; *Der* **d. una demanda** to dismiss a claim

denigrante *adj* degrading

denigrar *vt* to denigrate, to vilify

denominación *nf* naming; **d. de origen** = guarantee of region of origin of a wine or other product

denominado, -a *adj* so-called

denominador *nm* denominator; *Mat & Fig* **d. común** common denominator

denominar *vt* to call

denotar *vt* to indicate, to show

densidad *nf* density; **d. de población** population density

denso, -a *adj* dense

dentadura *nf* teeth, set of teeth; **d. postiza** false teeth, dentures

dental *adj* dental

dentera *nf* **me da d.** it sets my teeth on edge

dentífrico, -a 1 *adj* **pasta/crema dentífrica** toothpaste
2 *nm* toothpaste

dentista *nmf* dentist

dentro *adv* (**a**) *(en el interior)* inside; **aquí d.** in here; **por d.** (on the) inside; **por d. está triste** deep down (inside) he feels sad (**b**) **d. de** *(lugar)* inside (**c**) **d. de poco** shortly, soon; **d. de un mes** in a month's time; **d. de lo que cabe** all things considered

denuncia *nf* (**a**) *(a la policía)* complaint (**b**) *(condena)* denunciation

denunciante *nmf* = person who reports a crime

denunciar [43] *vt* (**a**) *(delito)* to report (**a** to) (**b**) *(criticar)* to denounce

deparar *vt* **no sabemos qué nos depara el destino** we don't know what fate has in store for us

departamento *nm* (**a**) *(en organización)* department (**b**) *(territorial)* province, district (**c**) *Arg (piso) Br* flat, *US* apartment

dependencia *nf* (**a**) *(de persona, drogas)* dependence (**b**) **dependencias** *(instalaciones)* outbuildings; **en dependencias policiales** on police premises

depender *vi* to depend (**de** on); *(económicamente)* to be dependent (**de** on)

dependienta *nf Br* shop *or* sales assistant, *US* salesclerk

dependiente 1 *adj* dependent (**de** on)
2 *nm Br* shop *or* sales assistant, *US* salesclerk

depilación *nf* hair removal; **d. a la cera** waxing

depilar *vt* *(piernas, axilas)* to remove the hair from; *(cejas)* to pluck; *(con cera)* to wax

depilatorio, -a 1 *adj* hair-removing
2 *nm* hair-remover

deplorable *adj* deplorable

deplorar *vt* to deplore

deponer [19] *(pp* **depuesto)** *vt* (**a**) *(destituir)* to remove from office; *(líder)* to depose (**b**) *(actitud)* to abandon; *(armas)* to lay down

deportado, -a *nm,f* deportee, deported person

deportar *vt* to deport

deporte *nm* sport; **hacer d.** to practise sports; **d. de aventura** adventure sport

deportista 1 *nmf (hombre)* sportsman; *(mujer)* sportswoman
2 *adj* sporty

deportividad *nf* sportsmanship

deportivo, -a 1 *adj* sports; **club/chaqueta d.** sports club/jacket
2 *nm Aut* sports car

deposición *nf* (**a**) *(de ministro, secretario)* removal from office; *(de líder, rey)* overthrow (**b**) *Med* **deposiciones** stools

depositar 1 *vt* (**a**) *Fin* to deposit (**b**) *(colocar)* to place, to put
2 depositarse *vpr* to settle

depósito *nm* (**a**) *Fin* deposit; **en d.** on deposit (**b**) *(de agua, gasolina)* tank (**c**) **d. de basuras** rubbish tip *o* dump; **d. de cadáveres** mortuary, morgue

depravación *nf* depravity

depravado, -a 1 *adj* depraved
2 *nm,f* **ser un d.** to be depraved *o* degenerate

depre *Fam* **1** *adj* **estar d.** to be feeling down
2 *nf* **tener la d.** to be feeling down

depreciación *nf* depreciation

depreciar [43] **1** *vt* to (cause to) depreciate
2 depreciarse *vpr* to depreciate

depredador, -a 1 *adj* predatory
2 *nm,f* predator

depresión *nf* depression; **d. nerviosa** nervous breakdown

depresivo, -a adj depressive
deprimente adj depressing
deprimido, -a adj depressed
deprimir 1 vt to depress
2 deprimirse vpr to get depressed
deprisa adv quickly
depuesto, -a pp de **deponer**
depuración nf (a) (del agua) purification (b) (purga) purge
depurador, -a adj **planta depuradora** purification plant
depuradora nf purifier
depurar vt (a) (agua) to purify (b) (partido) to purge (c) (estilo) to refine
derecha nf (a) (mano) right hand (b) (lugar) right, right-hand side; **a la d.** to o on the right, on the right-hand side (c) Pol **la d.** the right; Esp **ser de derechas** to be right-wing
derechista nmf right-winger
derecho, -a 1 adj (a) (de la derecha) right (b) (recto) upright, straight
2 nm (a) (privilegio) right; **derechos civiles/humanos** civil/human rights; **tener d. a** to be entitled to, to have the right to; **estar en su d.** to be within one's rights; **no hay d.** it's not fair; **d. de admisión** right to refuse admission (b) Der law; **d. penal/político** criminal/constitutional law (c) Com **derechos** duties; **derechos de autor** royalties; **derechos de matrícula** enrolment fees
3 adv **siga todo d.** go straight ahead
deriva nf drift; **ir a la d.** to drift
derivada nf Mat derivative
derivado nm (producto) by-product
derivar 1 vt to divert; (conversación) to steer
2 vi **d. de** to derive from
3 derivarse vpr (a) **derivarse de** (proceder) to result o stem from (b) **derivarse de** Ling to be derived from
dermatitis nf inv dermatitis
dermatólogo, -a nm,f dermatologist
dermoprotector adj skin-protecting
derogar [42] vt to repeal
derramamiento nm spilling; **d. de sangre** bloodshed
derramar 1 vt to spill; (lágrimas) to shed
2 derramarse vpr to spill
derrame nm Med discharge; **d. cerebral** brain haemorrhage
derrapar vi to skid
derredor nm **en d. de** round, around
derretir [6] **1** vt to melt; (hielo, nieve) to thaw
2 derretirse vpr to melt; (hielo, nieve) to thaw

derribar vt (a) (edificio) to pull down, to knock down (b) (avión) to shoot down (c) (gobierno) to bring down
derrocar [44] vt (gobierno) to topple, to overthrow; (rey) to oust
derrochador, -a 1 adj wasteful
2 nm,f spendthrift
derrochar vt (a) (malgastar) to squander, to waste (b) (rebosar de) to ooze, to be full of
derroche nm (a) (de dinero, energía) waste, squandering (b) (abundancia) profusion, abundance
derrota nf defeat
derrotar vt to defeat, to beat
derrotero nm path, course o plan of action
derrotista adj & nmf defeatist
derruido, -a adj in ruins
derruir [37] vt to demolish
derrumbar 1 vt (edificio) to knock down, to pull down
2 derrumbarse vpr to collapse, to fall down; (techo) to fall in, to cave in
desaborido, -a adj dull
desabrido, -a adj (a) (tiempo) unpleasant (b) Esp (tono) harsh; (persona) moody, irritable
desabrigarse [42] vpr (a) (en la calle) **¡no te desabrigues!** make sure you wrap up warmly! (b) (en la cama) to throw off the covers
desabrochar 1 vt to undo
2 desabrocharse vpr (a) **desabróchate la camisa** undo your shirt (b) (prenda) to come undone
desacato nm lack of respect, disrespect (a for); Der **d. al tribunal** contempt of court
desacertado, -a adj unwise
desacierto nm mistake, error
desaconsejar vt to advise against
desacorde adj (opiniones) differing, conflicting
desacreditar vt (a) (desprestigiar) to discredit, to bring into discredit (b) (criticar) to disparage
desactivar vt (bomba) to defuse
desacuerdo nm disagreement
desafiante adj defiant
desafiar [29] vt to challenge
desafinado, -a adj out of tune
desafinar 1 vi to sing out of tune; (instrumento) to play out of tune
2 desafinarse vpr to go out of tune
desafío nm challenge
desaforado, -a adj (excesivo) uncontrolled; (furioso) furious, wild

desafortunado, -a *adj* unlucky, unfortunate

desagradable *adj* unpleasant, disagreeable

desagradar *vi* to displease

desagradecido, -a 1 *adj* ungrateful
  2 *nm,f* ungrateful person

desagrado *nm* displeasure

desagravio *nm* **en señal de d.** (in order) to make amends

desaguar [45] *vt* to drain

desagüe *nm (vaciado)* drain; *(cañería)* waste pipe, drainpipe

desaguisado *nm (destrozo)* mess; *(desorden)* shambles *sing*

desahogado, -a *adj (acomodado)* well-off, well-to-do; *(espacioso)* spacious, roomy

desahogarse [42] *upr* to let off steam; **d. con algn** to pour out one's woes *o* to tell one's troubles to sb

desahogo *nm (económico)* ease; **vivir con d.** to be comfortably off

desahuciar [43] *vt* (a) *(inquilino)* to evict (b) *(enfermo)* to deprive of all hope

desahucio *nm* eviction

desairado, -a *adj* (a) *(humillado)* spurned (b) *(sin gracia)* awkward

desairar *vt* to slight, to snub

desaire *nm* slight, rebuff

desajustar 1 *vt* to upset
  2 desajustarse *upr (piezas)* to come apart

desajuste *nm* upset; **d. económico** economic imbalance; **un d. de horarios** clashing timetables

desalentador, -a *adj* discouraging, disheartening

desalentar [1] **1** *vt* to discourage, to dishearten
  2 desalentarse *upr* to get discouraged, to lose heart

desaliento *nm* discouragement

desaliñado, -a *adj* scruffy, untidy

desaliño *nm* scruffiness, untidiness

desalmado, -a *adj* cruel, heartless

desalojar *vt* (a) *(por emergencia) (edificio, personas)* to evacuate (b) *(por la fuerza) (ocupantes)* to eject, to remove; *(inquilinos)* to evict

desalojo *nm* (a) *(por emergencia) (de edificio, personas)* evacuation (b) *(por la fuerza) (de ocupantes)* ejection, removal; *(de inquilinos)* eviction

desamor *nm* lack of affection

desamortizar [40] *vt* to alienate, to disentail

desamparado, -a 1 *adj* helpless, unprotected
  2 *nm,f* helpless *o* abandoned person

desamparo *nm* helplessness

desandar [8] *vt* **d. lo andado** to retrace one's steps

desangrarse *upr* to lose (a lot of) blood

desanimado, -a *adj* downhearted, dejected

desanimar 1 *vt* to discourage, to dishearten
  2 desanimarse *upr* to lose heart, to get discouraged

desánimo *nm* discouragement, dejection

desapacible *adj* unpleasant

desaparecer [33] *vi* to disappear

desaparecido, -a 1 *adj* missing
  2 *nm,f* missing person

desaparición *nf* disappearance

desapego *nm* indifference, lack of affection

desapercibido, -a *adj* (a) *(inadvertido)* unnoticed; **pasar d.** to go unnoticed (b) *(desprevenido)* unprepared

desaprensivo, -a 1 *adj* unscrupulous
  2 *nm,f* unscrupulous person

desaprobar [2] *vt (no aprobar)* to disapprove of; *(propuesta, plan)* to reject

desaprovechar *vt (dinero, tiempo)* to waste; **d. una ocasión** to fail to make the most of an opportunity

desarmable *adj (mueble)* that can be dismantled

desarmador *nm Méx* screwdriver

desarmar *vt* (a) *(desmontar)* to dismantle, to take to pieces (b) *Mil* to disarm

desarme *nm* disarmament; **d. nuclear** nuclear disarmament

desarraigado, -a *adj* rootless, without roots

desarraigar [42] *vt* to uproot

desarraigo *nm* rootlessness

desarreglado, -a *adj* (a) *(lugar)* untidy (b) *(persona)* untidy, slovenly

desarreglar *vt* (a) *(desordenar)* to make untidy, to mess up (b) *(planes, horario)* to upset

desarreglo *nm (de vida)* disorder

desarrollado, -a *adj* developed; **país d.** developed country

desarrollar 1 *vt* to develop
  2 desarrollarse *upr* (a) *(persona, enfermedad)* to develop (b) *(tener lugar)* to take place

desarrollo *nm* development; **países en vías de d.** developing countries

desarticular *vt (organización, banda)* to break up; *(plan)* to foil

desaseado, -a *adj* unkempt

desasirse [46] *vpr* to get loose; **d. de** to free *o* rid oneself of

desasosegar [1] *vt* to make restless *o* uneasy

desasosiego *nm* restlessness, uneasiness

desastrado, -a *adj* untidy, scruffy

desastre *nm* disaster; **eres un d.** you're just hopeless

desastroso, -a *adj* disastrous

desatar 1 *vt* to untie, to undo; *(provocar)* to unleash
2 desatarse *vpr* (a) *(zapato, cordón)* to come undone (b) *(tormenta)* to break; *(pasión)* to run wild

desatascar [44] *vt* to unblock, to clear

desatender [3] *vt* to neglect, not to pay attention to

desatento, -a *adj (distraído)* inattentive; *(descortés)* impolite, discourteous

desatinado, -a *adj* unwise

desatino *nm* blunder

desatornillar *vt* to unscrew

desatrancar [44] *vt* to unblock; *(puerta)* to unbolt

desautorizar [40] *vt* (a) *(huelga, manifestación)* to ban, to forbid (b) *(noticia)* to deny (c) *(persona)* to discredit

desavenencia *nf* disagreement

desaventajado, -a *adj* at a disadvantage

desayunar 1 *vi* to have breakfast; *Fml* to breakfast
2 *vt* to have for breakfast

desayuno *nm* breakfast

desazón *nf* unease

desazonar *vt* to cause unease to, to worry

desbancar [44] *vt* to oust

desbandada *nf* scattering; **hubo una d. general** everyone scattered

desbarajuste *nm* confusion, disorder

desbaratar *vt* to ruin, to wreck

desbloquear *vt* (a) *(negociaciones)* to end the deadlock in (b) *(cuenta)* to unfreeze

desbocado, -a *adj (caballo)* runaway

desbocarse [44] *vpr (caballo)* to bolt, to run away

desbolado, -a *RP Fam* **1** *adj* messy, untidy
2 *nm,f* untidy person

desbolarse *vpr RP Fam* to undress, to strip

desbole *nm RP Fam* mess, chaos

desbordante *adj* overflowing, bursting

desbordar 1 *vt* to overflow; *Fig* to overwhelm

2 *vi* to overflow (**de** with)
3 desbordarse *vpr* to overflow, to flood

descabalgar [42] *vi* to dismount

descabellado, -a *adj* crazy, wild

descafeinado, -a *adj* (a) *(café)* decaffeinated (b) *Fig* watered-down, diluted

descalabrar *vt* (a) *(herir)* to wound in the head (b) *(perjudicar)* to do serious damage to

descalabro *nm* major setback, disaster

descalificar [44] *vt* to disqualify

descalzarse [40] *vpr* to take one's shoes off

descalzo, -a *adj* barefoot

descambiar [43] *vt* to exchange

descaminado, -a *adj* **ir d.** to be on the wrong track

descampado *nm* waste ground

descansado, -a *adj* (a) *(persona)* rested (b) *(vida, trabajo)* restful

descansar *vi* to rest, to have a rest; *(por corto tiempo)* to take a break; *Euf* **que en paz descanse** may he/she rest in peace

descansillo *nm* landing

descanso *nm* (a) *(del trabajo)* rest, break; **un día de d.** a day off (b) *(en cine)* intermission; *(en teatro) Br* interval, *US* intermission; *Dep* half-time, interval (c) *(alivio)* relief (d) *(rellano)* landing

descapotable *adj & nm* convertible

descarado, -a 1 *adj* (a) *(insolente)* cheeky, insolent; *(desvergonzado)* shameless (b) *Esp Fam* **d. que sí/no** *(por supuesto)* of course/course not
2 *nm,f* cheeky person

descarga *nf* (a) *(de mercancías, peso)* unloading (b) *Elec & Mil* discharge

descargar [42] **1** *vt* (a) *(mercancías, peso)* to unload (b) *Elec* to discharge (c) *(disparar)* to fire; *(golpe)* to deal
2 *vi (tormenta)* to burst
3 descargarse *vpr (batería)* to go flat

descargo *nm Der* discharge; **testigo de d.** witness for the defence

descarnado, -a *adj* crude

descaro *nm* cheek, nerve; **¡qué d.!** what a cheek!

descarriarse [29] *vpr (ganado)* to stray; *(persona)* to lose one's way, to go astray

descarrilar *vi* to go off the rails, to be derailed

descartar 1 *vt* to rule out
2 descartarse *vpr Naipes* to discard cards; **me descarté de un cinco** I got rid of a five

descascarillarse *vpr* to chip, to peel

descendencia *nf* descendants; **morir sin d.** to die without issue

descendente *adj* *(número, temperatura)* falling; *(movimiento, dirección)* downward, descending

descender [3] **1** *vi* (**a**) *(temperatura, nivel)* to fall, to drop (**b**) **d. de** to descend from **2** *vt* to lower

descendiente *nmf* descendant

descenso *nm* (**a**) *(en el espacio)* descent; *(de temperatura)* fall, drop (**b**) *(en fútbol)* relegation

descentrado, -a *adj* off-centre

descentralizar [40] *vt* to decentralize

descifrar *vt* *(clave, mensaje)* to decipher; *(misterio)* to solve; *(motivos, causas)* to figure out

descojonarse *vpr muy Fam* to piss oneself laughing (**de** at)

descolgar [2] **1** *vt* *(el teléfono)* to pick up; *(cuadro, cortinas)* to take down **2 descolgarse** *vpr* to let oneself down, to slide down

descolorido, -a *adj* faded

descombros *nmpl* rubble, debris

descompasado, -a *adj* excessive, uncontrollable

descomponer [19] *(pp* **descompuesto**) **1** *vt* (**a**) *(dividir)* to break down (**b**) *(corromper)* to rot, decompose **2 descomponerse** *vpr* (**a**) *(corromperse)* to rot, decompose (**b**) *(ponerse nervioso)* to lose one's cool (**c**) *Am* *(el tiempo)* to turn nasty

descomposición *nf* (**a**) *(de carne)* decomposition, rotting; *(de país)* disintegration (**b**) *Quím* breakdown (**c**) *Esp* *(diarrea)* diarrhoea

descompostura *nf* (**a**) *Am* *(malestar)* unpleasant *o* nasty turn (**b**) *Méx, RP* *(avería)* breakdown

descompuesto, -a *adj* **1** (**a**) *(podrido)* rotten, decomposed (**b**) *(furioso)* furious **2** *pp de* **descomponer**

descompuse *pt indef de* **descomponer**

descomunal *adj* huge, massive

desconcertante *adj* disconcerting

desconcertar [1] **1** *vt* to disconcert **2 desconcertarse** *vpr* to be bewildered, to be puzzled

desconchón *nm* bare patch

desconcierto *nm* chaos, confusion

desconectar *vt* to disconnect

desconexión *nf* disconnection

desconfiado, -a *adj* distrustful, wary

desconfianza *nf* distrust, mistrust

desconfiar [29] *vi* **d. (de)** to distrust, to mistrust

descongelar *vt* *(nevera)* to defrost; *(créditos)* to unfreeze

descongestionar *vt* to clear

desconocer [34] *vt* not to know, to be unaware of

desconocido, -a **1** *adj* unknown; *(irreconocible)* unrecognizable **2** *nm* **lo d.** the unknown **3** *nm,f* stranger

desconocimiento *nm* ignorance, lack of knowledge

desconsiderado, -a **1** *adj* inconsiderate, thoughtless **2** *nm,f* inconsiderate *o* thoughtless person

desconsolado, -a *adj* disconsolate, griefstricken

desconsuelo *nm* grief, sorrow

descontado, -a *adj* **por d.** needless to say, of course; **dar por d.** to take for granted

descontar [2] *vt* (**a**) *(cantidad)* to deduct (**b**) *Dep* *(tiempo)* to add on

descontento, -a **1** *adj* unhappy **2** *nm* dissatisfaction

descontrol *nm* *Fam* lack of control; **había un d. total** it was absolute chaos

descontrolarse *vpr* to lose control

desconvocar [44] *vt* to call off

descorchar *vt* to uncork

descornarse [2] *vpr* *Fam* *(trabajar)* to slave (away)

descorrer *vt* to draw back

descortés *adj* impolite, discourteous

descortesía *nf* discourtesy, impoliteness

descoser *vt* to unstitch, to unpick

descosido, -a **1** *nm* *(en ropa)* open seam; *Fam* **como un d.** *(hablar)* endlessly, non-stop; *(beber, comer)* to excess; *(gritar)* wildly

descoyuntar *vt* to dislocate

descrédito *nm* disrepute, discredit

descremado, -a *adj* skimmed

describir *(pp* **descrito**) *vt* to describe

descripción *nf* description

descriptivo, -a *adj* descriptive

descrito, -a *pp de* **describir**

descuajaringar [42] *vt* *Fam* to pull *o* take to pieces

descuartizar [40] *vt* to cut up, to cut into pieces

descubierto, -a **1** *adj* open, uncovered; **a cielo d.** in the open **2** *nm* (**a**) *Fin* overdraft (**b**) **al d.** in the open; **poner al d.** to uncover, to bring out into the open **3** *pp de* **descubrir**

descubridor, -a *nm,f* discoverer

descubrimiento *nm* discovery

descubrir (*pp* **descubierto**) *vt* to discover; (*conspiración*) to uncover; (*placa*) to unveil

descuento *nm* discount

descuidado, -a *adj* (a) (*desaseado*) untidy, neglected (b) (*negligente*) careless, negligent (c) (*desprevenido*) off one's guard

descuidar 1 *vt* to neglect, to overlook
  2 *vi* **descuida, voy yo** don't worry, I'll go
  3 descuidarse *vpr* (*despistarse*) to be careless; **como te descuides, llegarás tarde** if you don't watch out, you'll be late

descuido *nm* (*olvido*) oversight; (*error*) slip; **por d.** inadvertently, by mistake

desde *adv* (a) (*tiempo*) since; **d. ahora** from now on; **d. el lunes/entonces** since Monday/then; **espero d. hace media hora** I've been waiting for half an hour; **no lo he visto d. hace un año** I haven't seen him for a year; **¿d. cuándo?** since when?; **d. siempre** always (b) (*lugar*) from; **d. aquí** from here; **d. arriba/abajo** from above/below (c) **d. luego** of course (d) **d. que** ever since; **d. que lo conozco** ever since I've known him

desdecir [12] (*pp* **desdicho**) **1** *vi* **d. de** not to live up to
  2 desdecirse *vpr* to go back on one's word

desdén *nm* disdain

desdentado, -a *adj* toothless

desdeñar *vt* to disdain

desdeñoso, -a *adj* disdainful

desdibujarse *vpr* to become blurred *o* faint

desdicha *nf* misfortune; **por d.** unfortunately

desdichado, -a 1 *adj* unfortunate
  2 *nm,f* poor devil, wretch

desdicho, -a *pp de* **desdecir**

desdigo *indic pres de* **desdecir**

desdiré *indic fut de* **desdecir**

desdoblar *vt* to unfold

deseable *adj* desirable

desear *vt* (*querer*) to want; (*felicidad*) to wish; (*sexualmente*) to desire; **deja mucho que d.** it leaves a lot to be desired; **¿qué desea?** can I help you?; **estoy deseando que vengas** I'm looking forward to your coming; **te deseo buena suerte/feliz Navidad** I wish you good luck/a merry Christmas

desecar [44] *vt* to dry up

desechable *adj* disposable, throw-away

desechar *vt* (a) (*tirar*) to discard, to throw out *o* away (b) (*oferta*) to turn down, to refuse; (*idea, proyecto*) to drop, to discard

desecho *nm* (a) (*objeto usado*) unwanted object; **material de d.** (*residuos*) waste products (b) (*escoria*) dregs; **desechos** (*basura*) *Br* rubbish, *US* garbage, *US* trash; (*residuos*) waste products

desembalar *vt* to unpack

desembarcar [44] **1** *vt* (*mercancías*) to unload; (*personas*) to disembark
  2 *vi* to disembark

desembarco, desembarque *nm* (*de mercancías*) unloading; (*de personas*) disembarkation

desembocadura *nf* mouth

desembocar [44] *vi* **d. en** (*río*) to flow into; (*calle, situación*) to lead to

desembolsar *vt* to pay out

desembolso *nm* expenditure

desembragar [42] *vt Aut* to declutch

desembrollar *vt Fam* (a) (*aclarar*) to clarify, to clear up (b) (*desenredar*) to disentangle

desembuchar *vi Fam* to spit it out

desempañar *vt* (*con trapo*) to wipe the condensation from; (*electrónicamente*) to demist

desempaquetar *vt* (*paquete*) to unwrap; (*caja*) to unpack

desempatar *vi Dep* to break the deadlock

desempate *nm* play-off; **partido de d.** play-off, deciding match

desempeñar *vt* (a) (*cargo*) to hold, to occupy; (*función*) to fulfil; (*papel*) to play (b) (*recuperar*) to redeem

desempleado, -a 1 *adj* unemployed, out of work
  2 *nm,f* unemployed person; **los desempleados** the unemployed

desempleo *nm* unemployment; **cobrar el d.** to be on the dole

desempolvar *vt* (*pasado*) to revive; **voy a d. los libros de física** I'm going to dig out my physics books

desencadenar 1 *vt* (a) (*prisionero*) to unchain (b) (*suceso, polémica*) to give rise to, to spark off; (*pasión, furia*) to unleash
  2 desencadenarse *vpr* (a) (*pasión, conflicto*) to erupt (b) (*tormenta*) to burst

desencajar 1 *vt* (*pieza*) to knock out; (*hueso*) to dislocate
  2 desencajarse *vpr* (a) (*pieza*) to come out; (*hueso*) to become dislocated (b) (*cara*) to become distorted

desencaminado, -a *adj* = **descaminado**

desencanto *nm* disenchantment

desenchufar *vt* to unplug

desenfadado, -a *adj* carefree, free and easy

desenfado *nm* ease

desenfocado, -a *adj* out of focus

desenfrenado, -a *adj (ritmo)* frantic, frenzied; *(vicio, pasión)* unbridled

desenfreno *nm (descontrol)* lack of restraint; *(vicio)* debauchery

desenganchar *vt (vagón)* to uncouple; *(caballo)* to unhitch; *(pelo, jersey)* to free

desengañar 1 *vt* **d. a algn** to open sb's eyes
  2 desengañarse *upr* to become disillusioned; **desengáñate** stop kidding yourself

desengaño *nm* disappointment; **llevarse** *o* **sufrir un d. con algo** to be disappointed in sth

desengrasar *vt* to degrease, to remove the grease from

desenlace *nm* ending, dénouement

desenmarañar *vt (pelo)* to untangle; *(problema)* to unravel; *(asunto)* to sort out

desenmascarar *vt* to unmask

desenredar *vt* to untangle, to disentangle

desenrollar *vt (hilo, cinta)* to unwind; *(persiana)* to roll down; *(pergamino, papel)* to unroll

desenroscar [44] *vt* to unscrew

desentenderse [3] *upr* **se desentendió de mi problema** he didn't want to have anything to do with my problem

desenterrar [1] *vt* (a) *(cadáver)* to exhume, to disinter; *(tesoro)* to dig up (b) *(recuerdo)* to revive

desentonar *vi* (a) *Mús (cantante)* to sing out of tune; *(instrumento)* to be out of tune (b) *(colores etc)* not to match (c) *(persona, comentario)* to be out of place

desentrañar *vt (misterio)* to unravel, to get to the bottom of

desentrenado, -a *adj* out of training *o* shape

desentumecer [33] *vt* to put the feeling back into

desenvoltura *nf* ease

desenvolver [4] *(pp desenvuelto)* **1** *vt* to unwrap
  2 desenvolverse *upr* (a) *(persona)* to manage, to cope (b) *(hecho)* to develop

desenvuelto, -a 1 *adj* relaxed
  2 *pp de* **desenvolver**

deseo *nm* wish; *(sexual)* desire; **formular un d.** to make a wish

deseoso, -a *adj* eager; **estar d. de** to be eager to

desequilibrado, -a 1 *adj* unbalanced
  2 *nm,f* unbalanced person

desequilibrar 1 *vt* to unbalance, to throw off balance
  2 desequilibrarse *upr* to become mentally disturbed

desequilibrio *nm* imbalance

deserción *nf* desertion

desertar *vi* to desert

desértico, -a *adj* desert

desertización *nf* desertification

desertor, -a *nm,f* deserter

desesperación *nf (desesperanza)* despair; *(exasperación)* desperation

desesperado, -a *adj* (a) *(sin esperanza)* desperate, hopeless (b) *(exasperado)* exasperated, infuriated

desesperante *adj* exasperating

desesperar 1 *vt* (a) *(quitar la esperanza a)* to drive to despair (b) *(exasperar)* to exasperate
  2 desesperarse *upr* to despair

desestabilizar [40] *vt* to destabilize

desestatización *nf Am* privatization, sell-off

desestatizar [40] *vt Am* to privatize, to sell off

desestimar *vt* to reject

desfachatez *nf* cheek, nerve

desfalco *nm* embezzlement

desfallecer [33] *vi* (a) *(debilitarse)* to feel faint; *(desmayarse)* to faint (b) *(desanimarse)* to lose heart

desfasado, -a *adj (persona)* out of touch; *(libro, moda)* out of date

desfase *nm* gap; **d. horario** time lag

desfavorable *adj* unfavourable

desfigurar *vt (cara)* to disfigure; *(verdad)* to distort

desfiladero *nm* narrow pass

desfilar *vi* to parade

desfile *nm Mil* parade, march past; *(de carrozas)* procession; **d. de modas** fashion show

desfogar [42] **1** *vt* to give vent to
  2 desfogarse *upr* to let off steam

desgajar 1 *vt (naranja)* to split into segments; *(rama)* to tear off
  2 desgajarse *upr (rama)* to break off; *(hoja)* to fall

desgana *nf* (a) *(inapetencia)* lack of appetite (b) *(apatía)* apathy, indifference; **con d.** reluctantly, unwillingly

desganado, -a *adj* (a) **estar d.** *(inapetente)* to have no appetite (b) *(apático)* apathetic

desgano *nm Am* = **desgana**

desgañitarse *upr Fam* to shout oneself hoarse

desgarbado, -a *adj* ungraceful, ungainly

desgarrador, -a *adj* harrowing

desgarrar *vt* to tear

desgarrón *nm* big tear, rip

desgastar 1 *vt* to wear out
 2 desgastarse *vpr* to become worn

desgaste *nm* wear; **d. del poder** wear and tear of power

desgracia *nf* (a) *(mala suerte)* misfortune; **por d.** unfortunately (b) *(deshonor)* disgrace (c) **desgracias personales** loss of life

desgraciadamente *adv* unfortunately

desgraciado, -a 1 *adj* (a) *(suceso)* unfortunate (b) *(persona)* unhappy
 2 *nm,f* (a) *(infeliz)* wretch; **un pobre d.** a poor wretch (b) *(canalla)* swine

desgravable *adj* tax-deductible

desgravación *nf* deduction; **d. fiscal** tax deduction

desgravar *vi* to be tax-deductible

desgreñado, -a *adj* dishevelled

desguazar [40] *vt* (barco) to break up; *(vehículo)* to scrap

deshabitado, -a *adj* uninhabited, unoccupied

deshabitar *vt* to abandon, to vacate

deshacer [15] *(pp* **deshecho**) **1** *vt* (a) *(paquete)* to undo; *(maleta)* to unpack (b) *(disolver)* to dissolve; *(derretir)* to melt (c) *(plan)* to destroy, to ruin
 2 deshacerse *vpr* (a) *(nudo, trenza)* to come undone o untied (b) *(disolverse)* to dissolve; *(derretirse)* to melt (c) **deshacerse de algn/algo** to get rid of sb/sth (d) *(afligirse)* to go to pieces; **deshacerse en lágrimas** to cry one's eyes out

deshecho, -a 1 *adj* (a) *(cama)* unmade; *(maleta)* unpacked; *(paquete)* unwrapped (b) *(roto)* broken, smashed (c) *(disuelto)* dissolved; *(derretido)* melted (d) *(abatido)* devastated, shattered (e) *(cansado)* exhausted, tired out
 2 *pp de* **deshacer**

desheredar *vt* to disinherit

deshidratar *vt* to dehydrate

deshielo *nm* thaw

deshilachar *vt* to fray

deshilvanado, -a *adj* (discurso) disjointed

deshonesto, -a *adj* (a) *(sin honradez)* dishonest (b) *(sin pudor)* indecent, improper

deshonor *nm*, **deshonra** *nf* dishonour

deshonrar *vt* to dishonour; *(familia)* to bring disgrace on

deshora: a deshora *loc adv* (en momento inoportuno) at a bad time; *(en horas poco habituales)* at an unearthly hour; **comer a d.** to eat at odd times

deshuesar *vt* (carne) to bone; *(fruto)* Br to stone, US to pit

deshumanizar [40] *vt* to dehumanize

desidia *nf* apathy

desierto, -a 1 *nm* desert
 2 *adj* (a) *(deshabitado)* uninhabited (b) *(vacío)* empty, deserted (c) *(premio)* void

designación *nf* (a) *(nombre)* designation (b) *(nombramiento)* appointment

designar *vt* (a) *(nombrar)* to appoint (b) *(fecha, lugar)* to fix

designio *nm* intention, plan

desigual *adj* (a) *(terreno)* uneven (b) *(actuación)* inconsistent; *(lucha)* unequal (c) *(carácter)* changeable

desigualdad *nf* (a) *(económica, social, racial)* inequality (b) *(del terreno)* unevenness

desilusión *nf* (chasco) disappointment; *(estado de ánimo)* disillusionment

desilusionar 1 *vt* (decepcionar) to disappoint; *(dejar sin ilusiones)* to disillusion
 2 desilusionarse *vpr* (decepcionarse) to be disappointed; *(quedarse sin ilusiones)* to be disillusioned

desinfectante *adj & nm* disinfectant

desinfectar *vt* to disinfect

desinflar 1 *vt* to let down, to deflate
 2 desinflarse *vpr* (balón) to go down; *(neumático)* to go flat

desintegración *nf* disintegration

desintegrar 1 *vt* to disintegrate
 2 desintegrarse *vpr* to disintegrate

desinterés *nm* (pl **desintereses**) (a) *(indiferencia)* lack of interest, apathy (b) *(generosidad)* unselfishness

desinteresado, -a *adj* selfless, unselfish

desintoxicar [44] **1** *vt* to detoxify
 2 desintoxicarse *vpr* (dejar de drogarse) to come off drugs; *(dejar de beber)* to dry out

desistir *vi* to desist

deslavazado, -a *adj* disjointed

deslave *nm* landslide, Br landslip *(caused by flooding or rain)*

desleal *adj* disloyal; *(competencia)* unfair

deslealtad *nf* disloyalty

deslenguado, -a *adj* foul-mouthed

desliar [29] *vt* to unwrap

desligar [42] **1** *vt* (a) *(separar)* to separate (b) *(desatar)* to untie, to unfasten
 2 desligarse *vpr* **d. de** to disassociate oneself from

desliz *nm* mistake, slip; **cometer** *o* **tener un d.** to slip up

deslizar [40] **1** *vi* to slide
2 deslizarse *vpr* (**a**) *(patinar)* to slide (**b**) *(fluir)* to flow

deslucido, -a *adj* (**a**) *(sin brillo)* faded; *(plata)* tarnished (**b**) *(sin gracia) (acto, ceremonia)* dull; *(actuación)* lacklustre, uninspired

deslucir [35] *vt (espectáculo)* to spoil

deslumbrante *adj (luz, belleza)* dazzling; **estaba d.** she looked stunning

deslumbrar *vt* to dazzle

desmadrarse *vpr Esp Fam* to go wild

desmadre *nm Fam (caos)* chaos, utter confusion; *(desenfreno)* rave-up

desmán *nm* (**a**) *(exceso)* excess (**b**) *(abuso de poder)* abuse (of power)

desmandarse *vpr* to get out of hand

desmano: a desmano *loc adv* out of the way; **me coge a d.** it is out of my way

desmantelar *vt (casa, fábrica)* to clear out, to strip; *(arsenal, instalaciones)* to dismantle; *(quiosco, andamios)* to take down; *(organización criminal)* to break up

desmaquillante, desmaquillador *nm* make-up remover

desmaquillarse *vpr* to remove one's make-up

desmarcarse [44] *vpr* (**a**) *Dep* to lose one's marker (**b**) *(apartarse)* **d. de** to distance oneself from

desmayado, -a *adj* unconscious; **caer d.** to faint

desmayarse *vpr* to faint

desmayo *nm* faint, fainting fit; **tener un d.** to faint

desmedido, -a *adj* disproportionate, out of all proportion; *(ambición)* unbounded

desmejorar *vi* to deteriorate, to go downhill

desmelenarse *vpr Fam* to let one's hair down

desmembración *nf,* **desmembramiento** *nm* dismemberment

desmemoriado, -a *adj* forgetful

desmentir [5] *vt* to deny

desmenuzar [40] *vt* (**a**) *(pan, pastel, roca)* to crumble; *(carne)* to chop up (**b**) *(asunto)* to examine in detail

desmerecer [33] *vi* **no desmerece en nada de …** it easily bears comparison with …

desmesura *nf* excess

desmesurado, -a *adj* excessive

desmilitarizar [40] *vt* to demilitarize

desmontable *adj* that can be taken to pieces

desmontar 1 *vt* (**a**) *(desarmar)* to take to pieces, to dismantle (**b**) *(allanar)* to level
2 *vi* **d. (de)** to dismount, to get off

desmoralizar [40] *vt* to demoralize

desmoronarse *vpr* to crumble, to fall to pieces

desnatado, -a *adj (leche)* skimmed

desnivel *nm (en el terreno)* drop, difference in height

desnivelar *vt (terreno)* to make uneven; *(situación)* to upset the balance of; *(encuentro)* to make unequal; *(balanza)* to tip

desnucarse [44] *vpr* to break one's neck

desnuclearizar *vt* to make nuclear-free

desnudar 1 *vt* to undress
2 desnudarse *vpr* to get undressed

desnudez *nf* nakedness, nudity

desnudo, -a 1 *adj* naked, nude
2 *nm Arte* nude

desnutrición *nf* malnutrition

desnutrido, -a *adj* undernourished

desobedecer [33] *vt* to disobey

desobediencia *nf* disobedience

desobediente 1 *adj* disobedient
2 *nmf* disobedient person

desocupado, -a *adj* (**a**) *(vacío)* empty, vacant (**b**) *(ocioso)* free, not busy (**c**) *(sin empleo)* unemployed

desocupar *vt* to empty, to vacate

desodorante *adj & nm* deodorant

desoír [17] *vt* not to listen to, to take no notice of; **d. los consejos de algn** to ignore sb's advice

desolación *nf (destrucción)* desolation; *(desconsuelo)* distress, grief

desolador, a *adj (imagen, espectáculo)* heart-rending; *(noticia)* devastating

desolar *vt* to devastate

desollar [2] *vt* to skin

desorbitado, -a *adj (precio)* exorbitant

desorden *nm* untidiness, mess; **¡qué d.!** what a mess!; **d. público** civil disorder

desordenado, -a *adj* messy, untidy

desordenar *vt* to make untidy, to mess up

desorganización *nf* disorganization

desorganizar [40] *vt* to disorganize, to disrupt

desorientación *nf* disorientation

desorientar 1 *vt* to disorientate
2 desorientarse *vpr* to lose one's sense of direction, to lose one's bearings; *Fig* to become disorientated

despabilado, -a *adj* (**a**) *(sin sueño)* wide awake (**b**) *(listo)* quick, smart

despachar *vt* (**a**) *(asunto)* to get through (**b**) *(correo)* to send, to dispatch (**c**) *(en* *tienda)* to serve (**d**) *Fam (despedir)* to send packing, to sack (**e**) *Am (facturar)* to check in

despacho *nm* (**a**) *(oficina)* office; *(en casa)* study (**b**) *(venta)* sale (**c**) *(comunicación)* dispatch

despachurrar *vt Fam* to squash, to flatten

despacio *adv* (**a**) *(lentamente)* slowly (**b**) *esp Am (en voz baja)* quietly

despampanante *adj Fam* stunning

desparpajo *nm* self-assurance; **con d.** in a carefree manner

desparramar 1 *vt (líquido)* to spill; *(objetos)* to spread, to scatter
 2 desparramarse *vpr (líquido)* to spill; *(objetos, personas)* to scatter, to spread out

despavorido, -a *adj* terrified

despecho *nm* spite; **por d.** out of spite

despectivo, -a *adj* derogatory, disparaging

despedazar [40] *vt* to cut o tear to pieces

despedida *nf* farewell, goodbye; **d. de soltera** hen party o night; **d. de soltero** stag party o night, *US* bachelor party

despedido, -a *adj* (**a**) *(por cierre, reducción de plantilla)* redundant; *(por razones disciplinarias)* sacked (**b**) **salir d.** to be off like a shot

despedir [6] **1** *vt* (**a**) *(decir adiós)* to see off, to say goodbye to (**b**) *(empleado) (por cierre, reducción de plantilla)* to make redundant, to lay off; *(por razones disciplinarias)* to fire, to sack (**c**) *(olor, humo)* to give off
 2 despedirse *vpr (decir adiós)* to say goodbye (**de** to); **ya puedes despedirte del coche** you can say goodbye to the car

despegado, -a *adj* (**a**) *(objeto)* unstuck (**b**) *(persona)* cold, detached

despegar [42] **1** *vt* to take off, to detach
 2 *vi Av* to take off
 3 despegarse *vpr* to come unstuck

despego *nm* detachment

despegue *nm* take-off

despeinado, -a *adj* dishevelled, with untidy hair

despeinar 1 *vt (pelo)* to ruffle; **d. a algn** to mess up sb's hair
 2 despeinarse *vpr* to get one's hair messed up

despejado, -a *adj* clear; *(cielo)* cloudless

despejar 1 *vt* to clear; *(misterio, dudas)* to clear up
 2 despejarse *vpr* (**a**) *(cielo)* to clear (**b**) *(persona)* to clear one's head

despeje *nm Dep* clearance

despellejar *vt* to skin

despelotarse *vpr Esp Fam* (**a**) *(desnudarse)* to strip (**b**) **d. de risa** to laugh one's head off

despensa *nf* pantry, larder

despeñadero *nm* cliff, precipice

despeñarse *vpr* to go over a cliff

desperdiciar [43] *vt* to waste; *(oportunidad)* to throw away

desperdicio *nm* (**a**) *(acto)* waste (**b**) **desperdicios** *(basura)* rubbish; *(desechos)* scraps, leftovers

desperdigar [42] **1** *vt* to scatter, to disperse
 2 desperdigarse *vpr* to scatter

desperezarse [40] *vpr* to stretch (oneself)

desperfecto *nm* (**a**) *(defecto)* flaw, imperfection (**b**) *(daño)* damage

despertador *nm* alarm clock

despertar [1] **1** *vt* to wake (up), to awaken; *Fig (sentimiento etc)* to arouse
 2 despertarse *vpr* to wake (up)

despiadado, -a *adj* merciless

despido *nm (expulsión)* dismissal; *(por cierre, reducción de plantilla)* redundancy

despierto, -a *adj* (**a**) *(desvelado)* awake (**b**) *(vivo)* quick, sharp

despilfarrar *vt* to waste, to squander

despilfarro *nm* wasting, squandering

despiole *nm RP Fam* rumpus, shindy

despistado, -a *adj* (**a**) *(olvidadizo)* absent-minded (**b**) *(momentáneamente)* distracted (**c**) *(confuso)* confused

despistar 1 *vt* (**a**) *(perseguidor)* to shake off; *(perro)* to throw off the scent (**b**) *(confundir)* to mislead (**c**) *(distraer)* to distract
 2 despistarse *vpr* (**a**) *(confundirse)* to get mixed up o confused (**b**) *(distraerse)* to get o be distracted

despiste *nm* (**a**) *(cualidad)* absent-mindedness (**b**) *(error)* slip-up

desplazamiento *nm (viaje)* trip, journey

desplazar [40] **1** *vt* (**a**) *(trasladar)* to move (**a** to) (**b**) *(tomar el lugar de)* to take the place of (**c**) *Náut* to displace
 2 desplazarse *vpr* (**a**) *(viajar)* to travel (**b**) *(moverse)* to move

desplegar [1] **1** *vt* (**a**) *(tela, mapa)* to unfold; *(alas)* to spread, to open (**b**) *(cualidad)* to display (**c**) *Mil* to deploy
 2 desplegarse *vpr* (**a**) *(abrirse)* to open (out), to spread (out) (**b**) *Mil* to deploy

despliegue *nm* (**a**) *Mil* deployment (**b**) *(de medios etc)* display

desplomarse *vpr* to collapse; *(precios)* to slump, to fall sharply

desplumar *vt* (**a**) *(ave)* to pluck (**b**) *Fam (estafar)* to fleece

despoblado, -a 1 *adj* unpopulated, deserted
2 *nm* deserted spot

despoblar [2] *vt* to depopulate

despojar *vt* to strip (**de** of)

despojos *nmpl* (*de animales*) offal; (*cadáver*) remains

desposado, -a *nm,f Fml* (*hombre*) groom; (*mujer*) bride; **los desposados** the newly-weds

desposar *vt Fml* to marry

desposeer [36] *vt* to dispossess (**de** of)

desposeído *nm* **los desposeídos** the have-nots

déspota *nmf* despot

despótico, -a *adj* despotic

despotismo *nm* despotism

despotricar [44] *vi* to rant and rave (**contra** about)

despreciable *adj* despicable, contemptible; (*cantidad*) negligible

despreciar [43] *vt* (**a**) (*desdeñar*) to scorn, to despise (**b**) (*rechazar*) to reject, to spurn

desprecio *nm* (**a**) (*desdén*) scorn, disdain (**b**) (*desaire*) slight, snub

desprender 1 *vt* (**a**) (*separar*) to remove, to detach (**b**) (*olor, humo etc*) to give off
2 desprenderse *vpr* (**a**) (*soltarse*) to come off *o* away (**b**) **desprenderse de** to rid oneself of, to free oneself from (**c**) **de aquí se desprende que ...** it can be deduced from this that ...

desprendido, -a *adj* generous

desprendimiento *nm* (**a**) (*separación*) detachment; **d. de tierras** landslide (**b**) (*generosidad*) generosity

despreocupado, -a *adj* (**a**) (*tranquilo*) unconcerned (**b**) (*descuidado*) careless; (*estilo*) casual

despreocuparse *vpr* (**a**) (*tranquilizarse*) to stop worrying (**b**) (*desentenderse*) to be unconcerned (**de** about), to be indifferent (**de** to)

desprestigiar [43] *vt* to discredit, to run down

desprestigio *nm* discredit, loss of reputation; **campaña de d.** smear campaign

desprevenido, -a *adj* unprepared; **coger** *o* **pillar a algn d.** to catch sb unawares

desprolijo, -a *RP adj* (*casa*) messy, untidy; (*cuaderno*) untidy; (*persona*) unkempt, dishevelled

desproporción *nf* disproportion, lack of proportion

desproporcionado, -a *adj* disproportionate

desprovisto, -a *adj* **d. (de)** lacking, without, devoid (of)

después *adv* (**a**) (*más tarde*) later, afterwards; (*entonces*) then; (*seguidamente*) next; **una semana d.** a week later; **poco d.** soon after (**b**) (*lugar*) next (**c**) **d. de** after; **d. de la guerra** after the war; **mi calle está d. de la tuya** my street is the one after yours; **d. de cenar** after eating; **d. de todo** after all (**d**) **d. de que** after; **d. de que viniera** after he came

despuntar *vi* (**a**) (*día*) to dawn (**b**) (*destacar*) to excel, to stand out

desquiciar [43] **1** *vt* (*persona*) to unhinge
2 desquiciarse *vpr* (*persona*) to go crazy

desquitarse *vpr* to take revenge (**de** for)

desquite *nm* revenge

destacado, -a *adj* outstanding

destacamento *nm* detachment

destacar [44] **1** *vt* to emphasize, to stress
2 *vi* to stand out
3 destacarse *vpr* to stand out

destajo *nm* piecework; **trabajar a d.** to do piecework

destapador *nm Am* bottle opener

destapar 1 *vt* to take the lid off; (*botella*) to open; *Fig* (*asunto*) to uncover; *RP* (*caño*) to unblock
2 destaparse *vpr* to get uncovered

destartalado, -a *adj* rambling; (*desvencijado*) ramshackle

destello *nm* flash, sparkle

destemplado, -a *adj* (**a**) (*voz, gesto*) sharp, snappy; **con cajas destempladas** rudely, brusquely (**b**) (*tiempo*) unpleasant (**c**) (*enfermo*) indisposed, out of sorts (**d**) *Mús* out of tune, discordant

desteñir [6] **1** *vt & vi* to discolour
2 desteñirse *vpr* to lose colour, to fade

desternillarse *vpr* **d. (de risa)** to split one's sides laughing

desterrar [1] *vt* to exile

destiempo: a destiempo *loc adv* at the wrong time *o* moment

destierro *nm* exile

destilación *nf* distillation

destilado, -a *adj* distilled; **agua destilada** distilled water

destilar *vt* to distil

destilería *nf* distillery

destinado, -a *adj* destined, bound; *Fig* **d. al fracaso** doomed to failure

destinar *vt* (**a**) (*dinero etc*) to set aside, to assign (**b**) (*empleado*) to appoint

destinatario, -a *nm,f* (**a**) (*de carta*) addressee (**b**) (*de mercancías*) consignee

destino *nm* (**a**) (*rumbo*) destination; **el avión con d. a Bilbao** the plane to Bilbao (**b**) *(sino)* fate, fortune (**c**) *(de empleo)* post

destitución *nf* dismissal from office

destituir [37] *vt* to dismiss o remove from office

destornillador *nm* screwdriver

destornillar *vt* to unscrew

destreza *nf* skill

destrozado, -a *adj* (**a**) *(roto)* torn-up, smashed (**b**) *(cansado)* worn-out, exhausted (**c**) *(abatido)* shattered

destrozar [40] *vt* (**a**) *(destruir)* to destroy; *(rasgar)* to tear to shreds o pieces (**b**) *(persona)* to shatter; *(vida, reputación)* to ruin

destrozo *nm* damage

destrucción *nf* destruction

destructivo, -a *adj* destructive

destructor, -a 1 *adj* destructive
2 *nm Náut* destroyer

destruir [37] *vt* to destroy

desubicado, -a *nm,f Andes, RP* **es un d.** he has no idea of how to behave

desusado, -a *adj* old-fashioned, outdated

desuso *nm* disuse; **caer en d.** to fall into disuse; **en d.** obsolete, outdated

desvalido, -a *adj* defenceless

desvalijar *vt (robar)* to clean out, to rob; *(casa, tienda)* to burgle

desvalorizar [40] *vt* to devalue

desván *nm* attic, loft

desvanecerse [33] *upr* (**a**) *(disiparse)* to vanish, to fade away (**b**) *(desmayarse)* to faint

desvanecimiento *nm (desmayo)* fainting fit

desvariar [29] *vi* to talk nonsense

desvarío *nm* (**a**) *(delirio)* raving, delirium (**b**) *(disparate)* nonsense

desvelado, -a *adj* awake, wide awake

desvelar 1 *vt* to keep awake
2 desvelarse *upr* (**a**) *(despabilarse)* to stay awake (**b**) *(desvivirse)* to devote oneself (**por** to) (**c**) *CAm, Méx (quedarse despierto)* to stay up o awake

desvencijar 1 *vt* to take apart
2 desvencijarse *upr* to fall apart

desventaja *nf* disadvantage; **estar en d.** to be at a disadvantage

desventura *nf* misfortune, bad luck

desvergonzado, -a 1 *adj* (**a**) *(indecente)* shameless (**b**) *(descarado)* insolent
2 *nm,f* (**a**) *(sinvergüenza)* shameless person (**b**) *(fresco)* insolent o cheeky person

desvergüenza *nf* (**a**) *(indecencia)* shamelessness (**b**) *(atrevimiento)* insolence;

tuvo la d. de negarlo he had the cheek to deny it (**c**) *(impertinencia)* insolent o rude remark

desvestir [6] **1** *vt* to undress
2 desvestirse *upr* to undress (oneself)

desviación *nf (de dirección, cauce, norma)* deviation; *(de carretera) Br* diversion, *US* detour; *Med* **d. de columna** slipped disc

desviar [29] **1** *vt (río, carretera)* to divert; *(golpe, conversación)* to deflect; **d. la mirada** to look away
2 desviarse *upr* to go off course; *(vehículo)* to turn off; *Fig* **desviarse del tema** to digress

desvincular 1 *vt* to dissociate (**de** from)
2 desvincularse *upr* to dissociate oneself (**de** from)

desvío *nm Br* diversion, *US* detour

desvirgar [42] *vt* to deflower

desvirtuar [30] *vt* to distort

desvivirse *upr* **d. por algn** to do everything one can for sb; **d. por hacer algo** to bend over backwards to do sth

detalladamente *adv* in (great) detail

detallado, -a *adj* detailed, thorough

detallar *vt* to give the details of

detalle *nm* (**a**) *(pormenor)* detail; **entrar en detalles** to go into details (**b**) *(delicadeza)* nice thought, nicety; **¡qué d.!** how nice!, how sweet! (**c**) *(toque decorativo)* touch, ornament

detallista 1 *adj* perfectionist
2 *nmf Com* retailer

detectar *vt* to detect

detective *nmf* detective; **d. privado** private detective o eye

detector *nm* detector; **d. de incendios** smoke detector

detención *nf* (**a**) *Der* arrest (**b**) **con d.** carefully, thoroughly

detener [24] **1** *vt (a) (parar)* to stop, to halt (**b**) *Der (arrestar)* to arrest
2 detenerse *upr* to stop

detenidamente *adv* carefully, thoroughly

detenido, -a 1 *adj* (**a**) *(parado)* standing still, stopped (**b**) *(arrestado)* detained (**c**) *(minucioso)* detailed, thorough
2 *nm,f* detainee, person under arrest

detenimiento *nm* **con d.** carefully, thoroughly

detentar *vt* to hold

detergente *nm* detergent; **d. (para la ropa)** washing powder

deteriorar 1 *vt* to spoil, to damage
2 deteriorarse *upr (estropearse)* to deteriorate; *(empeorar)* to deteriorate, to get worse

deterioro nm (empeoramiento) deterioration, worsening; (daño) damage

determinación nf (a) (resolución) determination; **con d.** determinedly (b) (decisión) decision

determinado, -a adj (a) (preciso) definite, precise (b) (resuelto) decisive, resolute (c) Ling definite

determinante adj decisive

determinar 1 vt (a) (fecha etc) to fix, to set (b) (decidir) to decide on (c) (condicionar) to determine (d) (ocasionar) to bring about
  2 determinarse vpr to make up one's mind to

detestable adj detestable, repulsive

detestar vt to detest, to hate

detonante nm detonator; Fig trigger

detonar vt to detonate

detractor, -a nm,f detractor

detrás adv behind; **d. de** behind, on o at the back of

detrimento nm **en d. de** to the detriment of

detuve pt indef de **detener**

deuda nf debt; **estoy en d. contigo** (monetaria) I am in debt to you; (moral) I am indebted to you; **d. pública** (concepto) public debt; (títulos) government stock

deudor, -a 1 adj indebted
  2 nm,f debtor

devaluación nf devaluation

devaluar [30] vt to devalue

devanar 1 vt (hilo) to wind; (alambre) to coil
  2 devanarse vpr Fam **d. los sesos** to rack one's brains

devaneos nmpl (amorosos) flirtation; **tuvo sus d. con la ultraderecha** he flirted with the far right

devastador, -a adj devastating

devastar vt to devastate, to ravage

devengar [42] vt Com to earn, to accrue

devenir [27] vi to become

devoción nf (a) Rel devoutness (b) (al trabajo etc) devotion; Fam **Juan no es santo de mi d.** Juan isn't really my cup of tea

devolución nf (de objeto) return; (de dinero) refund

devolver [4] (pp **devuelto**) **1** vt to give back, return; (dinero) to refund
  2 vi (vomitar) to vomit, throw o bring up
  3 devolverse vpr Am salvo RP to come back

devorar vt to devour

devoto, -a 1 adj pious, devout
  2 nm,f (a) Rel pious person (b) (seguidor) devotee

devuelto, -a pp de **devolver**

DF nm (abr **Distrito Federal**) (en México) Mexico City

DGI nf RP (abr **Dirección General Impositiva**) Br ≃ Inland Revenue, US ≃ IRS

DGT nf (abr **Dirección General de Tráfico**) = government department responsible for road transport

di (a) pt indef de **dar** (b) imperat de **decir**

día nm day; **¿qué d. es hoy?** what's the date today?; **d. a d.** day by day; **de d.** by day; **durante el d.** during the daytime; **de un d. para otro** overnight; **un d. sí y otro no** every other day; **pan del d.** fresh bread; **hoy (en) d.** nowadays; **el d. de mañana** in the future; Fig **estar al d.** to be up to date; Fig **poner al d.** to bring up to date; **d. festivo** holiday; **d. laborable** working day; **d. libre** free day, day off; **es de d.** it is daylight; **hace buen/mal d.** it's a nice/bad day, the weather is nice/bad today

diabetes nf inv diabetes

diabético, -a adj & nm,f diabetic

diablo nm devil; Fam **¡al d. con …!** to hell with …!; Fam **vete al d.** get lost; Fam **¿qué/cómo diablos …?** what/how the hell …?

diablura nf mischief

diabólico, -a adj (a) (del diablo) diabolic (b) (muy malo, difícil) diabolical

diácono nm deacon

diadema nf tiara

diáfano, -a adj (a) (claro) (luz, cielo, ojos) clear; (agua, explicación) crystal-clear (b) Esp (espacio) open-plan

diafragma nm diaphragm

diagnosis nf inv diagnosis

diagnosticar [44] vt to diagnose

diagnóstico nm diagnosis

diagonal adj & nf diagonal; **en d.** diagonally

diagrama nm diagram; Inform **d. de flujo** flowchart

dial nm dial

dialecto nm dialect

dialogar [42] vi to have a conversation; (para negociar) to talk

diálogo nm dialogue

diamante nm diamond

diámetro nm diameter

diana nf (a) Mil reveille (b) (blanco) bull's eye

diapositiva nf slide

diariamente adv daily, every day

diariero, -a *nm,f Andes, RP* newspaper seller

diario, -a 1 *nm* (**a**) *Prensa* (daily) newspaper (**b**) *(memorias)* diary; *Náut* **d. de a bordo, d. de navegación** logbook
2 *adj* daily; **a d.** daily, every day

diarrea *nf* diarrhoea

diatriba *nf* diatribe

dibujante *nmf* (**a**) *(artista)* drawer; *(de cómic)* cartoonist (**b**) *Téc (hombre)* draughtsman; *(mujer)* draughtswoman

dibujar *vt* to draw

dibujo *nm* (**a**) *(técnica, obra)* drawing; **d. artístico** artistic drawing; **d. lineal** draughtsmanship; **dibujos animados** cartoons (**b**) *(en tela)* pattern

diccionario *nm* dictionary; **buscar** *o* **mirar una palabra en el d.** to look up a word in the dictionary

dicha *nf* happiness

dicharachero, -a *adj* talkative

dicho, -a 1 *adj* (**a**) said; **mejor d.** or rather; **d. de otro modo** to put it another way; **d. sea de paso** let it be said in passing; **d. y hecho** no sooner said than done (**b**) *(mencionado)* **dicha persona** the above-mentioned person
2 *pp de* **decir**

dichoso, -a *adj* (**a**) *(feliz)* happy (**b**) *Fam* damned; **¡este d. trabajo!** this damned job!

diciembre *nm* December

dictado *nm* dictation; *Fig* **dictados** dictates

dictador, -a *nm,f* dictator

dictadura *nf* dictatorship

dictáfono® *nm* Dictaphone®

dictamen *nm* *(juicio)* ruling; *(informe)* report

dictaminar *vi* to rule (**sobre** on)

dictar *vt* (**a**) *(texto)* to dictate; *Am (clase)* to teach, to give (**b**) *(sentencia)* to pronounce, to pass; *(ley)* to enact; *(decreto)* to issue

dictatorial *adj* dictatorial

didáctico, -a *adj* didactic

diecinueve *adj & nm inv* nineteen

dieciocho *adj & nm inv* eighteen

dieciséis *adj & nm inv* sixteen

diecisiete *adj & nm inv* seventeen

diente *nm* tooth; *Téc* cog; *(de ajo)* clove; **d. de leche** milk tooth; **dientes postizos** false teeth; *Fig* **hablar entre dientes** to mumble; *Fig* **poner los dientes largos a algn** to make sb green with envy

diera *subj imperf de* **dar**

diéresis *nf inv* diaeresis

diesel *adj & nm* diesel

diestra *nf* right hand

diestro, -a 1 *adj* (**a**) *(hábil)* skilful, clever (**b**) *Esp* **a d. y siniestro** right, left and centre
2 *nm Taurom* bullfighter, matador

dieta *nf* (**a**) diet; **estar a d.** to be on a diet (**b**) **dietas** expense *o* subsistence allowance

dietética *nf* dietetics *sing*

dietista *nmf* dietician

diez *adj & nm inv* ten

difamación *nf* defamation, slander; *(escrita)* libel

difamar *vt* to defame, to slander; *(por escrito)* to libel

diferencia *nf* difference; **a d. de** unlike

diferencial 1 *nm Téc* differential
2 *nf Mat* differential

diferenciar [43] **1** *vt* to differentiate, to distinguish (**entre** between)
2 diferenciarse *vpr* to differ (**de** from), to be different (**de** from *o US* than)

diferente 1 *adj* different (**de** from *o US* than)
2 *adv* differently

diferido, -a *adj* TV **en d.** recorded

diferir [5] **1** *vt (posponer)* to postpone, to put off
2 *vi (diferenciarse)* to differ, to be different; **d. de algn en algo** to differ from sb in sth

difícil *adj* difficult, hard; **d. de creer/hacer** difficult to believe/do; **es d. que venga** it is unlikely that she'll come

dificultad *nf* difficulty; *(aprieto)* trouble, problem

dificultar *vt* **d. algo** to make sth difficult

dificultoso, -a *adj* difficult, hard

difuminar *vt* to blur

difundir 1 *vt (noticia, doctrina, epidemia)* to spread; *(luz, calor)* to diffuse; *(emisión radiofónica)* to broadcast
2 difundirse *vpr (noticia, doctrina, epidemia)* to spread; *(luz, calor)* to be diffused

difunto, -a 1 *adj* late, deceased
2 *nm,f* deceased

difusión *nf* (**a**) *(de noticia)* spreading; **tener gran d.** to be widely broadcast (**b**) *Rad & TV* broadcasting

difuso, -a *adj* diffuse

digerir [5] *vt* to digest; *Fig* to assimilate

digestión *nf* digestion; **corte de d.** sudden indigestion

digestivo, -a *adj* digestive

digitador, -a *nm,f Am* keyboarder

digital *adj* digital; **huellas digitales** fingerprints; **tocadiscos d.** CD player

digitalizar *vt* to digitize

digitar *vt Am* to key, to type

dígito *nm* digit

dignarse *vpr* **d. (a)** to deign to, to condescend to

dignidad *nf* dignity

digno, -a *adj* (**a**) *(merecedor)* worthy; **d. de admiración** worthy of admiration; **d. de mención/verse** worth mentioning/seeing (**b**) *(decoroso)* decent, good

digo *indic pres de* **decir**

dije *pt indef de* **decir**

dilación *nf* delay, hold-up; **sin d.** without delay

dilatado, -a *adj* (**a**) *(agrandado)* dilated (**b**) *(vasto)* vast, extensive

dilatar **1** *vt* (**a**) *(agrandar)* to expand (**b**) *(pupila)* to dilate
　2 dilatarse *vpr* (**a**) *(agrandarse)* to expand (**b**) *(pupila)* to dilate

dilema *nm* dilemma

diligencia *nf* (**a**) *(prontitud)* **con d.** expeditiously (**b**) **diligencias** formalities; *Der* proceedings (**c**) *(vehículo)* stagecoach

diligente *adj (persona)* efficient, swift; *(respuesta)* prompt

dilucidar *vt* to elucidate

diluir [37] **1** *vt* to dilute
　2 diluirse *vpr* to dilute

diluviar [43] *v impers* to pour with rain

diluvio *nm* flood; **el D. (Universal)** the Flood

diluyo *indic pres de* **diluir**

dimensión *nf* (**a**) *(en el espacio, tamaño)* dimension; **de grandes dimensiones** very large (**b**) *(magnitud)* scale

diminutivo, -a *adj & nm* diminutive

diminuto, -a *adj* minute, tiny

dimisión *nf* resignation; **presentar la d.** to hand in one's resignation

dimitir *vi* to resign (**de** from); **d. de un cargo** to give in *o* tender one's resignation

Dinamarca *nf* Denmark

dinámica *nf* dynamics *sing*

dinámico, -a *adj* dynamic

dinamita *nf* dynamite

dinamitar *vt* to dynamite

dinamo, dínamo *nf Esp, nm Am* dynamo

dinar *nm Fin* dinar

dinastía *nf* dynasty

dineral *nm Fam* fortune

dinero *nm* money; **d. contante (y sonante)** cash; **d. efectivo** *o* **en metálico** cash; **gente de d.** wealthy people

dinosaurio *nm* dinosaur

diócesis *nf inv* diocese

dios *nm* god; **¡D. mío!** my God!; **¡por D.!** for goodness sake!; **a la buena de D.** any old how; **hacer algo como D. manda** to do sth properly; *Fam* **ni d.** nobody; *Fam* **todo d.** everybody

diosa *nf* goddess

diploma *nm* diploma

diplomacia *nf* diplomacy

diplomado, -a 1 *adj* qualified
　2 *nm,f* holder of a diploma

diplomarse *vpr* to graduate

diplomático, -a 1 *adj* diplomatic; **cuerpo d.** diplomatic corps
　2 *nm,f* diplomat

diplomatura *nf Educ* ≃ diploma, = qualification obtained after three years of university study

diptongo *nm* diphthong

diputación *nf Esp* **d. provincial** = governing body of each province, ≃ county council

diputado, -a *nm,f Br* ≃ Member of Parliament, MP; *US* ≃ Representative; **Congreso de Diputados** *Br* ≃ House of Commons, *US* ≃ Congress; **d. provincial** ≃ county councillor

dique *nm* dyke

diré *fut de* **decir**

dirección *nf* (**a**) *(sentido, rumbo)* direction; *Aut (en letrero)* **d. prohibida** no entry; **calle de d. única** one-way street (**b**) *(señas)* address; *Inform* **d. de correo electrónico** e-mail address (**c**) *Cin & Teatro* direction (**d**) *(destino)* destination (**e**) *Aut & Téc* steering (**f**) *(mando) (de empresa, hospital)* management; *(de partido)* leadership; *(de colegio)* headship

direccional *nm o nf Col, Ecuad, Méx Br* indicator, *US* turn signal

directa *nf Aut* top gear

directamente *adv* directly, straight away

directiva *nf* (**a**) *(junta)* board (of directors) (**b**) *(ley de la UE)* directive

directivo, -a *adj* directive; **junta directiva** board of directors

directo, -a *adj* direct; *TV & Rad* **en d.** live

director, -a *nm,f (de empresa)* director; *(de hotel, banco)* manager; *(de colegio) Br* headmaster, *f* headmistress, *US* principal; *(de periódico)* editor; **d. de cine** movie *o Br* film director; **d. de orquesta** conductor; **d. gerente** managing director

directorio *nm Inform* directory; *Am salvo RP* **d. telefónico** telephone directory

directriz *nf* (**a**) *(norma)* guideline (**b**) *Mat* directrix

dirigente 1 *adj* leading; **clase d.** ruling class
2 *nmf* leader

dirigir [57] **1** *vt* to direct; *(empresa)* to manage; *(negocio, colegio)* to run; *(orquesta)* to conduct; *(partido)* to lead; *(periódico)* to edit; *(coche, barco)* to steer; **d. la palabra a algn** to speak to sb
2 dirigirse *vpr* **(a) dirigirse a** *o* **hacia** to go to, to make one's way towards **(b)** *(escribir)* to write; **diríjase al apartado de correos 42** write to PO Box 42 **(c)** *(hablar)* to speak

discapacidad *nf* disability

discapacitado, -a 1 *adj* disabled
2 *nm,f* disabled person

discar [44] *vt Andes, RP* to dial

discernir [54] *vt* to discern, to distinguish; **d. algo de algo** to distinguish sth from sth

disciplina *nf* discipline

disciplinado, -a *adj* disciplined

discípulo, -a *nm,f* disciple

disco *nm* **(a)** *Anat, Astron & Geom* disc; **d. de freno** brake disc **(b)** *Mús* record, album; **d. compacto** compact disc **(c)** *Inform* disk; **d. duro** hard disk **(d)** *Dep* discus **(e)** *Tel* dial

discográfico, -a *adj* **casa** *o* **compañía discográfica** record company

disconforme *adj* **estar d. con** to disagree with

discontinuo, -a *adj Aut* **línea discontinua** broken line

discordante *adj* discordant; **ser la nota d.** to be the odd man out

discordia *nf* discord; **la manzana de la d.** the bone of contention; **sembrar d.** to sow discord

discoteca *nf* **(a)** *(lugar)* nightclub **(b)** *(colección)* record collection

discreción *nf* **(a)** *(reserva)* discretion **(b)** **a d.** at will

discrecional *adj* *(cantidad)* according to taste; *(poderes)* discretionary; **parada d.** *(en autobús)* request stop

discrepancia *nf* *(desacuerdo)* disagreement; *(diferencia)* discrepancy

discrepar *vi* *(disentir)* to disagree **(de** with; **en** on); *(diferenciarse)* to be different **(de** from *o US* than)

discreto, -a *adj* **(a)** *(prudente, reservado)* discreet **(b)** *(mediocre)* average

discriminación *nf* discrimination

discriminar *vt* **(a)** *(marginar)* to discriminate against **(b)** *Fml (diferenciar)* to discriminate between, to distinguish

disculpa *nf* excuse; **dar disculpas** to make excuses; **pedir disculpas a algn** to apologize to sb

disculpar 1 *vt* to excuse
2 disculparse *vpr* to apologize (**por** for)

discurrir *vi* **(a)** *(reflexionar)* to think **(b)** *Fig (transcurrir)* to pass, to go by **(c)** *Fml (río)* to wander

discurso *nm* speech; **dar** *o* **pronunciar un d.** to make a speech

discusión *nf* argument

discutible *adj* debatable

discutir 1 *vi* to argue (**de** about)
2 *vt* to discuss, to talk about

disecar [44] *vt* **(a)** *(animal)* to stuff **(b)** *(planta)* to dry

diseminar *vt* to disseminate, to spread

disentir [54] *vi* to dissent, to disagree (**de** with)

diseñador, -a *nm,f* designer; **d. gráfico** graphic designer

diseñar *vt* to design

diseño *nm* design; **ropa de d.** designer clothes; **d. gráfico** graphic design; **d. industrial** industrial design

disertar *vi* to expound (**sobre** *o* upon)

disfraz *nm* disguise; *(para fiesta)* fancy dress; **fiesta de disfraces** fancy dress party

disfrazar [40] **1** *vt* to disguise
2 disfrazarse *vpr* to disguise oneself; **disfrazarse de pirata** to dress up as a pirate

disfrutar 1 *vi* **(a)** *(gozar)* to enjoy oneself **(b)** *(poseer)* **d. (de)** to enjoy
2 *vt* to enjoy

disgregar [42] *vt* **(a)** *(multitud, manifestación)* to disperse, to break up **(b)** *(roca, imperio, Estado)* to break up; *(átomo)* to split

disgustado, -a *adj* upset

disgustar 1 *vt* **(a)** *(apenar)* to upset **(b)** *(desagradar)* **no me disgusta** it's not bad
2 disgustarse *vpr* **(a)** *(enojarse)* to get upset **(b)** *(enemistarse)* to fall out

> ⚘ Observa que el verbo inglés **to disgust** es un falso amigo y no es la traducción del verbo español **disgustar**. En inglés **to disgust** significa "repugnar, indignar".

disgusto *nm* **(a)** *(pena)* **llevarse un d.** to get upset; **dar un d. a algn** to upset sb **(b)** *(desgracia)* trouble **(c)** *(pelea)* fall-out, disagreement **(d)** **estar a d.** to feel uncomfortable *o* uneasy; **hacer algo a d.** to do sth unwillingly *o* reluctantly *ℓ* Observa que la palabra inglesa **disgust** es un falso amigo y no es la traducción de la palabra española **disgusto**. En inglés **disgust** significa "repugnancia, asco".

disidente *adj & nmf* dissident

disimuladamente *adv* quietly, discreetly

disimulado, -a *adj (oculto)* concealed

disimular 1 *vt* to conceal, to hide
2 *vi* to pretend

disimulo *nm* pretence

disipar 1 *vt* (a) *(dudas, sospechas)* to dispel (b) *(fortuna, herencia)* to squander, to throw away (c) *(niebla, humo, vapor)* to drive o blow away
2 disiparse *upr* (a) *(dudas, sospechas)* to be dispelled (b) *(niebla, humo, vapor)* to vanish

dislexia *nf* dyslexia

dislocar [44] *vt* to dislocate

disminución *nf* decrease

disminuir [37] **1** *vt* to reduce
2 *vi* to diminish

disolución *nf (de empresa, partido, matrimonio)* dissolution; *(de manifestación)* breaking up

disolvente *adj & nm* solvent

disolver [4] *(pp disuelto)* **1** *vt* (a) *(en líquido)* to dissolve (b) *(reunión, manifestación)* to break up; *(empresa, partido, matrimonio)* to dissolve
2 disolverse *upr* (a) *(en líquido)* to dissolve (b) *(reunión, manifestación)* to break up

disparar 1 *vt (pistola etc)* to fire; *(flecha, balón)* to shoot; **d. a algn** to shoot at sb
2 dispararse *upr* (a) *(arma)* to go off, to fire (b) *(precios)* to rocket

disparatado, -a *adj* absurd

disparate *nm* (a) *(dicho)* nonsense; **decir disparates** to talk nonsense (b) *(acto)* foolish act

disparidad *nf* disparity

disparo *nm* shot; *Dep* **d. a puerta** shot (at goal)

dispensar *vt* (a) *(disculpar)* to pardon, to forgive (b) *(eximir)* to exempt

dispersar 1 *vt* to disperse; *(esparcir)* to scatter
2 dispersarse *upr* to disperse

disperso, -a *adj (separado)* dispersed; *(esparcido)* scattered

displicencia *nf* condescension, disdain

displicente *adj* condescending, disdainful

disponer [19] *(pp dispuesto)* **1** *vt* (a) *(arreglar)* to arrange, to set out (b) *(ordenar)* to order

2 *vi* **d. de** to have at one's disposal
3 disponerse *upr* to prepare, to get ready

disponible *adj* available

disposición *nf* (a) *(uso)* disposal; **a su d.** at your disposal o service (b) *(colocación)* arrangement, layout (c) **no estar en d. de** not to be prepared to (d) *(orden)* order, law

dispositivo *nm* device

dispuesto, -a 1 *adj* (a) *(ordenado)* arranged (b) *(a punto)* ready (c) *(decidido)* determined; **no estar d. a** not to be prepared to (d) **según lo d. por la ley** in accordance with what the law stipulates
2 *pp de* **disponer**

disputa *nf (discusión)* argument; *(contienda)* contest

disputar 1 *vt* (a) *(premio)* to compete for (b) *Dep (partido)* to play
2 disputarse *upr (premio)* to compete for

disquete *nm* *Inform* diskette, floppy disk

disquetera *nf* *Inform* disk drive

distancia *nf* distance; **a d.** from a distance

distanciamiento *nm* distancing

distanciar [43] **1** *vt* to separate
2 distanciarse *upr* to become separated; *(de otra persona)* to distance oneself

distante *adj* distant, far-off

distar *vi* to be distant o away; *Fig* **d. de** to be far from; **dista mucho de ser perfecto** it's far from (being) perfect

distender [3] *vt* to ease, to relax

distendido, -a *adj* relaxed, informal

distinción *nf* distinction; **a d. de** unlike; **sin d. de** irrespective of

distinguido, -a *adj* distinguished

distinguir [59] **1** *vt* (a) *(diferenciar)* to distinguish (b) *(reconocer)* to recognize (c) *(honrar)* to honour
2 *vi (diferenciar)* to discriminate
3 distinguirse *upr* to distinguish oneself

distintivo, -a 1 *adj* distinctive, distinguishing
2 *nm* distinctive sign o mark

distinto, -a *adj* different

distorsión *nf* distortion

distracción *nf* (a) *(entretenimiento)* entertainment; *(pasatiempo)* pastime, hobby (b) *(descuido)* distraction, absentmindedness

distraer [25] **1** *vt* (a) *(atención)* to distract (b) *(divertir)* to entertain, to amuse
2 distraerse *upr* (a) *(divertirse)* to amuse oneself (b) *(abstraerse)* to let one's mind wander

distraído, -a adj (a) (divertido) entertaining (b) (abstraído) absent-minded

distribución nf (a) (reparto, división) distribution (b) (de casa, habitaciones) layout

distribuidor, -a 1 adj distributing
2 nm,f distributor

distribuir [37] vt to distribute; (trabajo) to share out

distrito nm district; **d. postal** postal district

disturbio nm riot, disturbance

disuadir vt to dissuade

disuasión nf deterrence

disuelto, -a pp de **disolver**

DIU nm (abr **dispositivo intrauterino**) IUD, coil

diurético, -a adj & nm diuretic

diurno, -a adj daytime

diva nf Mús diva, prima donna

divagar [42] vi to digress, to wander

diván nm divan, couch

divergencia nf (de líneas) divergence; (de opiniones) difference of opinion

divergente adj (líneas) divergent, diverging; (opiniones) different, differing

diversidad nf diversity

diversificar [44] **1** vt to diversify
2 diversificarse vpr to be diversified o varied; (empresa) to diversify

diversión nf fun

diverso, -a adj different; **diversos** several, various

divertido, -a adj amusing, funny

divertir [5] **1** vt to amuse, to entertain
2 divertirse vpr to enjoy oneself, to have a good time; **¡que te diviertas!** enjoy yourself!, have fun!

dividendo nm dividend

dividir 1 vt to divide (**en** into); Mat **15 dividido entre 3** 15 divided by 3
2 dividirse vpr to divide, to split up

divinidad nf divinity

divino, -a adj divine

divisa nf (a) (emblema) symbol, emblem (b) Com **divisas** foreign currency

divisar vt to make out, to discern

división nf division

divisorio, -a adj dividing

divorciado, -a 1 adj divorced
2 nm,f (hombre) divorcé; (mujer) divorcée

divorciar [43] **1** vt to divorce
2 divorciarse vpr to get divorced; **se divorció de él** she divorced him, she got a divorce from him

divorcio nm divorce

divulgación nf (de noticia, secreto) revelation; (de cultura, ciencia) popularization; **una obra de d. científica** a work of popular science

divulgar [42] vt (noticia, secreto) to reveal; (cultura, ciencia) to popularize

dizque adv Andes, Carib, Méx Fam apparently

DNI nm (abr **Documento Nacional de Identidad**) Identity Card, ID card

do nm Mús (de solfa) doh, do; (de escala diatónica) C; **do de pecho** high C

dóberman nm Doberman (pinscher)

dobladillo nm (de traje, vestido) hem; (de pantalón) Br turn-up, US cuff

doblaje nm Cin dubbing

doblar 1 vt (a) (duplicar) to double; **me dobla la edad** he is twice as old as I am (b) (plegar) to fold o turn up (c) (torcer) to bend (d) (la esquina) to go round (e) (película) to dub
2 vi (a) (girar) to turn; **d. a la derecha/izquierda** to turn right/left (b) (campanas) to toll
3 doblarse vpr (a) (plegarse) to fold (b) (torcerse) to bend

doble 1 adj double; **arma de d. filo** double-edged weapon
2 nm (a) **el d.** twice as much; **gana el d. que tú** she earns twice as much as you do (b) (persona parecida) double; Cin stand-in

doblegar [42] **1** vt to bend
2 doblegarse vpr to give in

doblez 1 nm (pliegue) fold
2 nm o nf Fig two-facedness, hypocrisy

doce adj & nm inv twelve

docena nf dozen

docencia nf teaching

docente adj teaching; **centro d.** educational centre

dócil adj docile

doctor, -a nm,f doctor

doctorado nm Univ doctorate, PhD

doctorarse vpr to get one's doctorate (**en** in)

doctrina nf doctrine

documentación nf documentation; (DNI, de conducir etc) papers

documental adj & nm documentary

documentar 1 vt to document
2 documentarse vpr **d. (sobre)** to research (about o on)

documento nm document; **d. nacional de identidad** identity card

dogma nm dogma

dogmático, -a adj dogmatic

dogo nm bulldog

dólar *nm* dollar

dolarización *nf Econ* dollarization

dolencia *nf* ailment

doler [4] **1** *vi* to hurt, to ache; **me duele la cabeza** I've got a headache; **me duele la mano** my hand is sore
  2 dolerse *upr* to be sorry *o* sad

dolido, -a *adj* **estar d.** to be hurt

dolor *nm* (a) *Med* pain; **d. de cabeza** headache; **d. de muelas** toothache (b) *(pena)* grief, sorrow

dolorido, -a *adj* (a) *(dañado)* sore, aching (b) *(apenado)* hurt

doloroso, -a *adj* painful

domador, -a *nm,f (de animales salvajes)* tamer; *(de caballos)* breaker; **d. de leones** lion tamer

domar *vt* to tame; *(caballo)* to break in

domesticar [44] *vt* to domesticate; *(animal)* to tame

doméstico, -a *adj* domestic; **animal d.** pet

domiciliación *nf Esp* **pagar mediante d. (bancaria)** to pay by direct debit

domiciliar [43] **1** *vt Esp (pago)* to pay by direct debit
  2 domiciliarse *upr (persona)* to establish residence

domiciliario, -a *adj* **arresto d.** house arrest

domicilio *nm* home, residence; *(señas)* address; **sin d. fijo** of no fixed abode; **d. fiscal** registered office

dominación *nf* rule, dominion

dominante *adj* (a) *(prevaleciente)* dominant (b) *(déspota)* domineering

dominar 1 *vt* (a) *(país, territorio)* to dominate, to rule (b) *(situación)* to control; *(idioma)* to speak very well; *(técnica, tema)* to master; *(paisaje etc)* to overlook
  2 dominarse *upr* to control oneself

domingo *nm inv* Sunday; **D. de Resurrección** *o* **Pascua** Easter Sunday

dominguero, -a *nm,f Fam (excursionista)* weekend tripper; *(conductor)* weekend driver

dominical 1 *adj* Sunday
  2 *nm (suplemento)* Sunday supplement

dominicano, -a *adj & nm,f* Dominican

dominio *nm* (a) *(poder)* control; *(de un idioma)* command; **d. de sí mismo** self-control (b) *(ámbito)* scope, sphere; **ser del d. público** to be public knowledge (c) *(territorio)* dominion (d) *Inform* domain

dominó *nm* dominoes

don¹ *nm* (a) *(habilidad)* gift, talent; **tener el d. de** to have a knack for; **tener d. de gentes** to get on well with people (b) *(regalo)* present, gift

don² *nm* **(Señor)** D. **José García** Mr José García; **D. José** Mr García; **un d. nadie** a nobody

donaire *nm* grace, elegance

donante *nmf* donor; *Med* **d. de sangre** blood donor

donar *vt Fml* to donate; *(sangre)* to give

donativo *nm* donation

doncella *nf Literario* maid, maiden

donde *adv rel* where; **a** *o* **en d.** where; **de** *o* **desde d.** from where; **está d. lo dejaste** it is where you left it; *Fam* **está d. su tía** he's at his aunt's

---

donde combines with the preposition **a** to form **adonde** when following a noun, a pronoun or an adverb expressing location (e.g. **el sitio adonde vamos** the place where we're going; **es allí adonde iban** that's where they were going).

---

dónde *adv interr* where?; **¿de d. eres?** where are you from?; **¿por d. se va a la playa?** which way is it to the beach?

---

dónde can combine with the preposition **a** to form **adónde** (e.g. **¿adónde vamos?** where are we going?).

---

dondequiera *adv* **d. que** wherever; **d. que vaya** wherever I go

donostiarra *Esp* **1** *adj* of/from San Sebastián
  2 *nmf* person from San Sebastián

dónut® *(pl dónuts) nm* doughnut

doña *nf* **(Señora)** D. **Leonor Benítez** Mrs Leonor Benítez; **D. Leonor** Mrs Benítez

dopaje *nm Dep* drug-taking

dopar 1 *vt (caballo etc)* to dope
  2 doparse *upr* to take drugs

doping *(pl dopings) nm Dep* drug-taking

doquier *adv* **por d.** everywhere

dorada *nf (pez)* gilthead bream

dorado, -a 1 *adj* golden
  2 *nm Téc* gilding

dorar *vt* (a) *(con oro)* to gild (b) *Culin* to brown

dormido, -a *adj* (a) *(persona)* asleep; **quedarse d.** to fall asleep; *(no despertarse)* to oversleep, to sleep in (b) *(pierna, brazo)* numb

dormilón, -ona 1 *adj Fam* **ser d.** to be a sleepyhead
  2 *nm,f Fam* sleepyhead
  3 *nf Ven* nightdress

dormir [7] **1** *vi* to sleep; **tener ganas de d.** to feel sleepy
2 *vt* **la siesta** to have an afternoon nap
3 dormirse *upr* to fall asleep; **se me ha dormido el brazo** my arm has gone to sleep

dormitar *vi* to doze, to snooze

dormitorio *nm* (a) *(de una casa)* bedroom (b) *(de colegio, residencia)* dormitory; **ciudad d.** dormitory town

dorsal 1 *adj* **espina d.** spine
2 *nm Dep* number

dorso *nm* back; **instrucciones al d.** instructions over; **véase al d.** see overleaf

dos *adj & nm inv* two; **los d.** both; **nosotros/vosotros d.** both of us/you; *Fam* **cada d. por tres** every other minute; *Fam* **en un d. por tres** in a flash

doscientos, -as *adj & nm* two hundred

dosel *nm* canopy

dosificación *nf* dosage

dosificar [44] *vt* (a) *(fármaco)* to dose (b) *(esfuerzos, energías)* to use sparingly

dosis *nf inv* dose

dossier *nm* dossier

dotación *nf* *(dinero)* amount granted; *(personal)* personnel, staff; *(de barco)* crew

dotado, -a *adj* (a) *(persona)* gifted (b) **d. de** *(persona)* blessed with; *(edificio, instalación, aparato)* equipped with

dotar *vt* **d. de** to provide with

dote *nf* (a) *(de novia)* dowry (b) **dotes** *(talento)* talent

doy *indic pres de* **dar**

dpto. *(abr* **departamento)** Dept

Dr. *(abr* **doctor)** Dr

Dra. *(abr* **doctora)** Dr

dragar [42] *vt* to dredge

dragón *nm* dragon

drama *nm* drama

dramático, -a *adj* dramatic

dramatismo *nm* drama, dramatic quality

dramaturgo, -a *nm,f* playwright, dramatist

drástico, -a *adj* drastic

drenar *vt* to drain

driblar *vi Dep* to dribble

droga *nf* drug; **d. blanda/dura** soft/hard drug

drogadicción *nf* drug addiction

drogadicto, -a *nm,f* drug addict

drogar [42] **1** *vt* to drug
2 drogarse *upr* to take drugs

droguería *nf Esp* = shop selling paint, cleaning materials etc

dto. *(abr* **descuento)** discount

dual *adj* dual

dualidad *nf* duality

dubitativo, -a *adj* doubtful

Dublín *n* Dublin

dublinés, -esa 1 *adj* of/from Dublin
2 *nm,f* Dubliner

ducha *nf* shower; **darse/tomar una d.** to have o take a shower

ducharse *upr* to shower, to have o take a shower

ducho, -a *adj* expert; **ser d. en** to be well versed in

duda *nf* doubt; **sin d.** without a doubt; **no cabe d.** (there is) no doubt; **poner algo en d.** to question sth; **sacar a algn de dudas** to dispel sb's doubts

dudar 1 *vi* *(vacilar)* to hesitate **(en** to); **dudaba entre ir o quedarme** I hesitated whether to go or to stay (b) *(desconfiar)* **d. de algn** to suspect sb
2 *vt* to doubt

dudoso, -a *adj* (a) **ser d.** *(incierto)* to be uncertain o doubtful (b) **estar d.** *(indeciso)* to be undecided (c) *(poco honrado)* dubious

duelo¹ *nm* *(combate)* duel

duelo² *nm* *(luto)* mourning

duende *nm* (a) *(espíritu)* goblin, elf (b) *(encanto)* magic, charm

dueña *nf* owner; *(de pensión)* landlady

dueño *nm* owner; *(de casa etc)* landlord; *Fig* **ser d. de sí mismo** to be self-possessed

Duero *n* **el D.** the Douro

dulce 1 *adj* (a) *(sabor)* sweet (b) *(carácter, voz)* gentle (c) *(metal)* soft (d) **agua d.** fresh water
2 *nm* (a) *Culin (pastel)* cake (b) *(caramelo)* **Br** sweet, **US** candy

dulzura *nf* sweetness

duna *nf* dune

dúo *nm* duet

duodécimo, -a *adj & nm,f* twelfth

dúplex *nm* (a) *(vivienda)* duplex (b) *Elec* linkup

duplicado, -a 1 *adj* **por d.** in duplicate
2 *nm* duplicate, copy

duplicar [44] **1** *vt* to duplicate; *(cifras)* to double
2 duplicarse *upr* to double

duplo *nm* double

duque *nm* duke

duquesa *nf* duchess

duración *nf* duration, length; **disco de larga d.** long-playing record

duradero, -a *adj* durable, lasting

durante *prep* during; **d. el día** during the day; **d. todo el día** all day long; **viví en La Coruña d. un año** I lived in La Coruña for a year

durar *vi* to last; **¿cuánto dura la película?** how long is the film?

durazno *nm (fruto)* peach; *(árbol)* peach tree

Durex® *nm Méx (adhesivo) Br* Sellotape®, *US* Scotch® tape

dureza *nf* (**a**) *(de objeto, material)* hardness (**b**) *(de clima, persona)* harshness (**c**) *(callosidad)* callus, patch of hard skin

✎ Observa que la palabra inglesa **dur-ess** es un falso amigo y no es la traducción de la palabra española **dureza**. En inglés, **duress** significa "coacción".

duro, -a **1** *adj* (**a**) *(material, superficie)* hard; *(carne)* tough; *(pan)* stale (**b**) *(clima)* harsh; *(resistente)* tough; *(severo)* hard (**c**) *(clima)* harsh
2 *nm Esp Antes (moneda)* five-peseta coin
3 *adv* hard; **trabajar d.** to work hard

DVD *nm Inform (abr* **Disco Versátil Digital**) DVD

E, e [e] *nf (letra)* E, e
E *(abr Este)* E
e *conj* and

> *ℓ* **e** is used instead of **y** in front of words beginning with "i" or "hi" (e.g. **apoyo e interés** support and interest; **corazón e hígado** heart and liver)

ebanista *nmf* cabinet-maker
ébano *nm* ebony
ebrio, -a *adj* inebriated; **e. de dicha** drunk with joy
ebullición *nf* boiling; **punto de e.** boiling point
eccema *nm* eczema
echar 1 *vt* (**a**) *(lanzar)* to throw; *Fig* **e. una mano** to give a hand; *Fig* **e. una mirada/una ojeada** to have a look/a quick look *o* glance (**b**) *(carta)* to post, *US* to mail; *(vino, agua)* to pour; **e. sal al estofado** to put salt in the stew; **e. gasolina al coche** to put *Br* petrol *o US* gas in the car (**c**) *(expulsar)* to throw out; *(despedir)* to fire, *Br* to sack (**d**) *(humo, olor etc)* to give off (**e**) *Fam (película)* to show (**f**) **le echó 37 años** he reckoned she was about 37 (**g**) **e. de menos** *o* **en falta** to miss (**h**) **e. abajo** *(edificio)* to demolish
2 *vi* (**+ a + infin**) *(empezar)* to begin to; **echó a correr** he ran off
3 echarse *vpr* (**a**) *(tumbarse)* to lie down; *(lanzarse)* to throw oneself; *Fig* **la noche se nos echó encima** it was night before we knew it (**b**) **échate a un lado** stand aside; *Fig* **echarse atrás** to get cold feet (**c**) *Fam* **echarse novio/novia** to get a boyfriend/girlfriend (**d**) (**+ a + infin**) *(empezar)* to begin to; **echarse a llorar** to burst into tears; **echarse a reír** to burst out laughing; **echarse a perder** *(comida)* to go bad
ecléctico, -a *adj & nm,f* eclectic
eclesiástico, -a 1 *adj* ecclesiastical
2 *nm* clergyman
eclipsar *vt* to eclipse
eclipse *nm* eclipse
eco *nm* echo; *Fig* **hacerse e. de una noticia** to publish an item of news; **tener e.** to arouse interest

ecografía *nf (técnica)* ultrasound scanning; *(imagen)* ultrasound scan
ecología *nf* ecology
ecológico, -a *adj (medioambiental)* ecological; *(alimentos)* organic; *(detergente)* environmentally-friendly
ecologista 1 *adj* environmental, ecological
2 *nmf* environmentalist, ecologist
economía *nf* (**a**) *(actividad productiva)* economy; **e. de mercado** market economy (**b**) *(ciencia)* economics *sing* (**c**) *(ahorro)* **hacer economías** to save
económico, -a *adj* (**a**) *(de la economía) (asunto, doctrina, política)* economic (**b**) *(del dinero) (problemas, situación)* financial (**c**) *(barato)* cheap, low-cost (**d**) *(que gasta poco) (aparato)* economical
economista *nmf* economist
economizar [40] *vt & vi* to economize
ecopunto *nm* recycling bank
ecosistema *nm* ecosystem
ecotasa *nf* ecotax
ecoturismo *nm* ecotourism
ecuación *nf* equation
Ecuador *n* Ecuador
ecuador *nm Geog* equator
ecualizador *nm* **e. (gráfico)** graphic equalizer
ecuánime *adj* (**a**) *(temperamento)* equable, even-tempered (**b**) *(juicio)* impartial
ecuatorial *adj* equatorial
ecuatoriano, -a *adj & nm,f* Ecuadorian
ecuestre *adj* equestrian
ecuménico, -a *adj* ecumenical
eczema *nm* eczema
edad *nf* age; **¿qué e. tienes?** how old are you?; **la tercera e.** senior citizens; **E. Media** Middle Ages
edición *nf* (**a**) *(publicación)* publication; *(de sellos)* issue (**b**) *(conjunto de ejemplares)* edition
edicto *nm* edict, proclamation
edificante *adj* edifying
edificar [44] *vt* to build
edificio *nm* building

edil *nmf* town councillor
Edimburgo *n* Edinburgh
Edipo *n* Oedipus
editar *vt* (**a**) *(libro, periódico)* to publish; *(disco)* to release (**b**) *Inform* to edit
editor, -a 1 *adj* publishing
   2 *nm,f* publisher
editorial 1 *adj* publishing
   2 *nf* publisher, publishing house
   3 *nm Prensa* editorial, leader article
edredón *nm* eiderdown, *Br* duvet
educación *nf* (**a**) *(enseñanza)* education; **e. física** physical education (**b**) *(modales)* **buena/mala e.** good/bad manners; **falta de e.** bad manners
educado, -a *adj* polite
educador, -a *nm,f* educator
educar [44] *vt* (hijos) to raise; *(alumnos)* to educate; *(la voz)* to train
educativo, -a *adj* educational; **sistema e.** education system
edulcorante *nm* sweetener
EE.UU. *(abr* **Estados Unidos**) USA
efectista *adj* designed for effect, dramatic
efectivamente *adv* quite!, yes indeed!
efectividad *nf* effectiveness
efectivo, -a 1 *adj* effective; **hacer algo e.** to carry sth out; *Fin* **hacer e. un cheque** to cash a cheque
   2 *nm* (**a**) *Fin* **en e.** in cash (**b**) *Mil* **efectivos** forces
efecto *nm* (**a**) *(resultado)* effect; **efectos especiales/sonoros** special/sound effects; **efectos personales** personal belongings *o* effects; **a efectos de ...** for the purposes of ...; **en e.** indeed (**b**) *(impresión)* impression; **causar** *o* **hacer e.** to make an impression (**c**) *Dep* spin
efectuar [30] *vt* to carry out; *(viaje)* to make; *Com (pedido)* to place
efeméride *nf* event
efervescente *adj* effervescent; **aspirina e.** soluble aspirin
eficacia *nf (de persona)* efficiency; *(de remedio etc)* effectiveness
eficaz *adj (persona)* efficient; *(remedio, medida etc)* effective
eficiencia *nf* efficiency
eficiente *adj* efficient
efigie *nf* effigy
efímero, -a *adj* ephemeral
efusivo, -a *adj* effusive
Egeo *n* **el (Mar) E.** the Aegean Sea
egipcio, -a *adj & nm,f* Egyptian
Egipto *n* Egypt
egocéntrico, -a *adj* egocentric, self-centred
egoísmo *nm* selfishness, egotsm

egoísta 1 *adj* selfish, egotistic
   2 *nmf* selfish person, egotist
egregio, -a *adj* eminent, illustrious
egresar *vi Am (de escuela)* to leave school after completing one's studies, *US* to graduate; *(de universidad)* to graduate
egreso *nm Am (de universidad)* graduation
Eire *n* Eire, Republic of Ireland
ej. *(abr* **ejemplo**) example
eje *nm* (**a**) *Téc (de rueda)* axle; *(de máquina)* shaft (**b**) *Mat* axis (**c**) *Hist* **El E.** the Axis
ejecución *nf* (**a**) *(de orden)* carrying out (**b**) *(ajusticiamiento)* execution (**c**) *Mús* performance
ejecutar *vt* (**a**) *(orden)* to carry out (**b**) *(ajusticiar)* to execute (**c**) *Mús* to perform, to play (**d**) *Inform* to run
ejecutiva *nf Pol* executive
ejecutivo, -a 1 *adj* executive; *Pol* **el poder e.** the government
   2 *nm* executive
ejecutor, -a *nm,f* (**a**) *Der* executor (**b**) *(verdugo)* executioner
ejemplar 1 *nm* (**a**) *(de libro)* copy; *(de revista, periódico)* number, issue (**b**) *(espécimen)* specimen
   2 *adj* exemplary, model
ejemplificar [44] *vt* to exemplify
ejemplo *nm* example; **por e.** for example; **dar e.** to set an example
ejercer [49] **1** *vt* (**a**) *(profesión etc)* to practise (**b**) *(influencia)* to exert (**c**) **e. el derecho de** *o* **a ...** to exercise one's right to ...
   2 *vi* to practise (**de** as)
ejercicio *nm* (**a**) *(físico)* exercise; **hacer e.** to take *o* do exercise (**b**) *(de profesión)* practice (**c**) *Fin* tax year; **e. económico** financial *o* fiscal year
ejercitar *vt* to practise
ejército *nm* army
ejote *nm CAm, Méx* green bean
el *(f* **la**, *mpl* **los**, *fpl* **las**) **1** *art def* (**a**) the (**b**) *(no se traduce)* **el Sr. García** Mr. García; **el hambre/destino** hunger/fate (**c**) *(con partes del cuerpo, prendas de vestir)* **me he cortado el dedo** I've cut my finger; **métetelo en el bolsillo** put it in your pocket (**d**) *(con días de la semana)* **el lunes** on Monday

---

el is used instead of la before feminine nouns which are stressed on the first syllable and begin with "a" or "ha" (e.g. **el agua, el hacha**). Note that **el** combines with the prepositions **a** and **de** to produce the contracted forms **al** and **del**.

2 pron (**a**) the one; **el de las once** the eleven o'clock one; **el que tienes en la mano** the one you've got in your hand; **el que quieras** whichever one you want (**b**) (no se traduce) **el de tu amigo** your friend's

él pron pers (**a**) (sujeto) (persona) he; (animal, cosa) it (**b**) (complemento) (persona) him; (animal, cosa) it

> Usually omitted in Spanish as a subject except for emphasis or contrast.

elaboración nf (**a**) (de producto) manufacture, production (**b**) (de idea) working out, development

elaborar vt (**a**) (producto) to manufacture, to produce (**b**) (teoría) to develop

elasticidad nf elasticity; Fig flexibility

elástico, -a adj & nm elastic

E/LE (abr **Español como Lengua Extranjera**) Spanish as a foreign language

elección nf choice; Pol **elecciones** election

elector, -a nm,f elector

electorado nm electorate

electoral adj electoral; **campaña e.** election campaign; **colegio e.** polling station

electoralismo nm electioneering

electricidad nf electricity

electricista nmf electrician

eléctrico, -a adj electric

electrificar [44] vt to electrify

electrizar [40] vt to electrify

electrochoque nm electric shock therapy

electrocutar vt to electrocute

electrodo nm electrode

electrodoméstico nm (domestic) electrical appliance

electroimán nm electromagnet

electromagnético, -a adj electromagnetic

electrón nm electron

electrónica nf electronics sing

electrónico, -a adj electronic

elefante nm elephant

elegancia nf elegance

elegante adj elegant

elegía nf elegy

elegir [58] vt (**a**) (escoger) to choose (**b**) (por votación) to elect

elemental adj (**a**) (fundamental) basic, fundamental (**b**) (simple) elementary

elemento nm (**a**) (sustancia, medio, componente) element (**b**) (factor) factor (**c**) Esp Fam (persona) Br chap, US guy; **un e. de cuidado** a bad lot (**d**) **elementos** (atmosféricos) elements; (fundamentos) rudiments

elepé nm LP (record)

elevación nf elevation; **e. de precios** rise in prices; **e. del terreno** rise in the ground

elevado, -a adj (**a**) (alto) high; (edificio) tall (**b**) (pensamiento etc) lofty, noble

elevador nm (**a**) (montacargas) hoist (**b**) Méx (ascensor) Br lift, US elevator

elevalunas nm inv Aut **e. eléctrico** electric windows

elevar 1 vt to raise

2 elevarse upr (**a**) (subir) to rise; (edificio) to stand (**b**) **elevarse a** (cantidad) to amount o come to

elijo indic pres de **elegir**

eliminación nf elimination

eliminar vt to eliminate

eliminatoria nf Dep heat, qualifying round

eliminatorio, -a adj qualifying, eliminatory

élite nf elite, élite

elitista adj elitist

elixir nm (enjuague bucal) mouthwash; Literario elixir

ella pron pers f (**a**) (sujeto) she; (animal, cosa) it, she (**b**) (complemento) her; (animal, cosa) it, her

> Usually omitted in Spanish as a subject except for emphasis or contrast.

ellas pron pers fpl ver **ellos**

ello pron pers neut it; **por e.** for that reason

ellos pron pers mpl (**a**) (sujeto) they (**b**) (complemento) them

> Usually omitted in Spanish as a subject except for emphasis or contrast.

elocuencia nf eloquence

elocuente adj eloquent; **los hechos son elocuentes** the facts speak for themselves

elogiar [43] vt to praise

elogio nm praise

elote nm CAm, Méx (mazorca) corncob, ear of maize o US corn; (granos) sweetcorn, US corn

El Salvador n El Salvador

elucidar vt to elucidate

eludir vt to avoid

e-mail ['imeil] (pl **e-mails**) nm e-mail

emanar vi to emanate (**de** from)

emancipar 1 vt to emancipate

2 emanciparse upr to become emancipated

embadurnar vt to daub, to smear (**de** with)

embajada *nf* embassy

embajador, -a *nm,f* ambassador

embalaje *nm* packing, packaging

embalar 1 *vt* to pack
 2 embalarse *upr* to speed up; *Fig* **no te embales** hold your horses

embalsamar *vt* to embalm

embalsar 1 *vt* to dam
 2 embalsarse *upr* to form a pool

embalse *nm* reservoir

embarazada 1 *adj* pregnant; **dejar e.** to get pregnant
 2 *nf* pregnant woman, expectant mother

> 🖉 Observa que la palabra inglesa **embarrassed** es un falso amigo y no es la traducción de la palabra española **embarazada**. En inglés **embarrassed** significa "avergonzado".

embarazar [40] *vt* to hinder

embarazo *nm* (**a**) *(preñez)* pregnancy (**b**) *(obstáculo)* obstacle (**c**) *(turbación)* embarrassment

embarazoso, -a *adj* awkward, embarrassing

embarcación *nf* (**a**) *(nave)* boat, craft (**b**) *(embarco)* embarkation

embarcadero *nm* quay

embarcar [44] **1** *vt* to ship
 2 *vi* to embark, to go on board
 3 embarcarse *upr* **embarcarse (en)** *Náut* to go on board; *Av* to board (**b**) **embarcarse en un proyecto** to embark on a project

embarco *nm* embarkation

embargar [42] *vt* (**a**) *Der* to seize, to impound (**b**) *Fig* **le embarga la emoción** he's overwhelmed with joy

embargo 1 *nm* (**a**) *Der* seizure of property (**b**) *Com & Pol* embargo
 2 sin embargo *loc adv* however, nevertheless

embarque *nm* *(de persona)* boarding; *(de mercancías)* loading; **tarjeta de e.** boarding card

embarrancar [44] **1** *vi* to run aground
 2 embarrancarse *upr* to run aground

embaucador, -a 1 *adj* deceitful
 2 *nm,f* swindler, cheat

embaucar [44] *vt* to swindle, to cheat

embeber 1 *vt* to soak up
 2 embeberse *upr* to become absorbed *o* engrossed

embelesar *vt* to fascinate

embellecer [33] *vt* to embellish

embestida *nf* *(ataque)* attack; *(de toro)* charge

embestir [6] *vt* *(lanzarse contra)* to attack; *(sujeto: toro)* to charge

emblema *nm* emblem

embobado, -a *adj* fascinated

embobarse *upr* to be fascinated *o* captivated (**con** by)

embolia *nf* embolism

émbolo *nm* piston

embolsarse *upr* to pocket

emborrachar 1 *vt* *(sujeto: persona)* to get drunk; *(sujeto: bebida)* to make *o* get drunk
 2 emborracharse *upr* to get drunk

emboscada *nf* ambush; **tender una e.** to lay an ambush

embotar *vt* *(sentidos)* to dull; *(mente)* to befuddle

embotellamiento *nm* *Aut* traffic jam

embotellar *vt* (**a**) *(líquido)* to bottle (**b**) *(tráfico)* to block

embragar [42] *vi Aut* to engage the clutch

embrague *nm* clutch

embravecerse [33] *upr* *(mar)* to become rough

embriagador, -a *adj* intoxicating

embriagar [42] **1** *vt* to intoxicate
 2 embriagarse *upr* to become intoxicated

embriaguez *nf* intoxication

embridar *vt* to bridle

embrión *nm* embryo

embrollar 1 *vt* to confuse, to muddle
 2 embrollarse *upr* to get muddled *o* confused

embrollo *nm* (**a**) *(lío)* muddle, confusion (**b**) *(aprieto)* fix, jam

embrujado, -a *adj* *(persona)* bewitched; *(sitio)* haunted

embrujar *vt también Fig* to bewitch

embrujo *nm* spell, charm; *Fig* attraction, fascination

embrutecer [33] *vt* to stultify

embuchar *vt* to stuff

embudo *nm* funnel

embuste *nm* lie, trick

embustero, -a *nm,f* cheater, liar

embutido *nm* sausage

embutir *vt* (**a**) *(rellenar)* to stuff (**de** with) (**b**) *(meter)* to stuff (**en** into)

emergencia *nf* emergency; **salida de e.** emergency exit; **en caso de e.** in an emergency

emergente *adj* emerging

emerger [53] *vi* to emerge

emigración *nf* emigration; *(de pájaros)* migration

emigrado, -a *nm,f* emigrant; *Pol* émigré

emigrante *adj & nmf* emigrant

emigrar *vi* to emigrate; *(pájaros)* to migrate

emilio *nm Fam* e-mail (message)

eminencia *nf (persona)* eminent figure, leading light; **e. gris** éminence grise; **Su E.** His Eminence

emirato *nm* emirate

emisario, -a *nm,f* emissary

emisión *nf* (**a**) *(de energía, rayos)* emission (**b**) *(de bonos, sellos)* issue (**c**) *Rad & TV (transmisión)* broadcasting; *(programa)* programme, broadcast

emisora *nf (de radio)* radio station

emitir *vt* (**a**) *(rayos, calor, sonidos)* to emit (**b**) *(opinión, juicio)* to express (**c**) *Rad & TV* to transmit (**d**) *(bonos, sellos)* to issue

emoción *nf* (**a**) *(sentimiento)* emotion (**b**) *(expectación)* excitement; **¡qué e.!** how exciting!

emocionado, -a *adj* deeply moved *o* touched

emocionante *adj* (**a**) *(conmovedor)* moving, touching (**b**) *(excitante)* exciting, thrilling

emocionar 1 *vt* (**a**) *(conmover)* to move, to touch (**b**) *(excitar)* to thrill
  2 emocionarse *vpr* (**a**) *(conmoverse)* to be moved (**b**) *(excitarse)* to get excited

emoticón, emoticono *nm Inform* smiley, emoticon

emotivo, -a *adj* emotional

empacar [44] *vt* (**a**) *(mercancías)* to pack (**b**) *Am* to annoy

empachar *vt* to give indigestion to

empacho *nm (de comida)* indigestion, upset stomach; *Fig* surfeit

empadronarse *vpr* to register on the electoral roll

empalagar [42] *vi* **los bombones me empalagan** I find chocolates sickly; **me empalaga con tanta cortesía** I find his excessive politeness rather cloying

empalagoso, -a *adj* (**a**) *(dulce)* sickly sweet (**b**) *(persona)* smarmy

empalizada *nf* fence; *Mil* stockade

empalmar 1 *vt (tubos, cables)* to connect, to join
  2 empalmarse *vpr Esp Vulg* to get a hard-on

empalme *nm* (**a**) *(de cables, tubos)* connection (**b**) *(de líneas férreas, carreteras)* junction

empanada *nf* pie

empanadilla *nf* pasty

empanado, -a *adj (filete)* breaded, in breadcrumbs

empantanarse *vpr* (**a**) *(inundarse)* to become flooded (**b**) *Fig* to be bogged down

empañar 1 *vt (cristales)* to steam up
  2 empañarse *vpr* to mist up, to steam up

empapado, -a *adj* soaked

empapar 1 *vt* (**a**) *(mojar)* to soak (**b**) *(absorber)* to soak up
  2 empaparse *vpr* (**a**) *(persona)* to get soaked (**b**) *Fam Fig* **empaparse (de)** to take in

empapelar *vt* to paper, to wallpaper

empaque *nm* bearing, presence

empaquetar *vt* to pack

emparedado *nm* sandwich

emparejar *vt (cosas)* to match; *(personas)* to pair off

empastar *vt (diente)* to fill

empaste *nm (de diente)* filling

empatado, -a *adj (partido)* drawn; *(equipos)* level; **estar** *o* **ir empatados** to be drawn

empatar 1 *vi (en competición)* to tie; *(en partido)* to draw
  2 *vt* (**a**) *Dep* **e. el partido** to equalize (**b**) *Andes, Ven (enlazar, empalmar)* to join, to link

empate *nm Dep* draw, tie

empatía *nf* empathy

empecinarse *vpr* to dig one's heels in

empedernido, -a *adj (fumador, bebedor)* hardened

empedrado, -a 1 *adj* cobbled
  2 *nm* (**a**) *(adoquines)* cobblestones (**b**) *(acción)* paving

empeine *nm* instep

empellón *nm* push, shove

empeñar 1 *vt* to pawn
  2 empeñarse *vpr* (**a**) *(insistir)* to insist (**en** on), to be determined (**en** to) (**b**) *(endeudarse)* to get into debt

empeño *nm* (**a**) *(insistencia)* insistence; **poner e. en algo** to put a lot of effort into sth (**b**) *(deuda)* pledge; **casa de empeños** pawnshop

empeoramiento *nm* deterioration, worsening

empeorar 1 *vi* to deteriorate, to worsen
  2 *vt* to make worse
  3 empeorarse *vpr* to deteriorate, to worsen

empequeñecer [33] *vt Fig* to belittle

emperador *nm* emperor

emperatriz *nf* empress

emperifollarse *vpr Fam* to get dolled up

emperrarse *vpr* to insist (**en hacer algo** on doing sth)

empezar [51] *vt* & *vi* (*a hacer algo*) to begin; (*algo*) to start, to commence

empinado, -a *adj* (*cuesta*) steep

empinar 1 *vt* to raise; *Fam* **e. el codo** to drink
2 **empinarse** *upr* (*persona*) to stand on tiptoe

empírico, -a *adj* empirical

emplasto *nm* poultice

emplazamiento *nm* (a) (*lugar*) location (b) *Der* summons *sing*

emplazar¹ [40] *vt* to locate

emplazar² [40] *vt* (*citar*) to summon; *Der* to summons

empleado, -a *nm,f* employee; (*de oficina, banco*) clerk; **empleada del hogar** maid

emplear *vt* (a) (*usar*) to use; (*contratar*) to employ (b) (*dinero, tiempo*) to spend

empleo *nm* (a) (*oficio*) job; *Pol* employment (b) (*uso*) use; **modo de e.** instructions for use

emplomar *vt RP* (*diente*) to fill

empobrecer [33] 1 *vt* to impoverish
2 **empobrecerse** *upr* to become impoverished *o* poor

empobrecimiento *nm* impoverishment

empollar *vt* (a) (*huevos*) to sit on (b) *Esp Fam* (*estudiar*) to bone up on, *Br* to swot up

empollón, -ona *nm,f Esp Fam Br* swot, *US* grind

empolvarse *upr* (*la cara*) to powder

emponzoñar *vt* to poison

emporio *nm* (a) *Com* emporium, trading *o* commercial centre (b) *Am* department store

empotrado, -a *adj* fitted

emprendedor, -a *adj* enterprising

emprender *vt* to undertake; *Fam* **emprenderla con algn** to pick on sb

empresa *nf* (a) *Com & Ind* firm, company; **e. punto com** dot com (company); **e. de trabajo temporal** temping agency (b) *Pol* **la libre e.** free enterprise (c) (*tarea*) undertaking

empresariado *nm* employers

empresarial 1 *adj* (*estructura, crisis*) business; **organización e.** employers' organization
2 **empresariales** *nfpl Esp* business studies

empresario, -a *nm,f* (a) (*hombre*) businessman; (*mujer*) businesswoman (b) (*patrón*) employer

empréstito *nm Fin* debenture loan

empujar *vt* to push, to shove

empuje *nm* (*presión*) pressure; (*brío*) verve, get-up-and-go

empujón *nm* push, shove; **dar empujones** to push and shove

empuñadura *nf* (*de espada*) hilt

empuñar *vt* to grasp, to seize

emular *vt* to emulate

emulsión *nf* emulsion

en *prep* (a) (*posición*) in, on, at; **en Madrid/ Bolivia** in Madrid/Bolivia; **en la mesa** on the table; **en el bolso** in the bag; **en casa/el trabajo** at home/work
(b) (*movimiento*) into; **entró en el cuarto** he went into the room
(c) (*tiempo*) in, on, at; **en 1940** in 1940; **en verano** in summer; *Am* **en la mañana/ tarde** in the morning/afternoon; *Am* **en la noche** at night; **cae en martes** it falls on a Tuesday; **en ese momento** at that moment
(d) (*transporte*) by, in; **en coche/tren** by car/train; **en avión** by air
(e) (*modo*) **en español** in Spanish; **en broma** jokingly; **en serio** seriously
(f) (*reducción, aumento*) by; **los precios aumentaron en un diez por ciento** the prices went up by ten percent
(g) (*tema, materia*) at, in; **bueno en deportes** good at sports; **experto en política** expert in politics
(h) (*división, separación*) in; **lo dividió en tres partes** he divided it in three
(i) (*con infinitivo*) **fue rápido en responder** he was quick to answer; **la conocí en el andar** I recognized her by her walk; **ser sobrio en el vestir** to dress simply

enaguas *nfpl* underskirt, petticoat

enajenación *nf*, **enajenamiento** *nm* (a) **e. mental** mental derangement, insanity (b) *Der* alienation

enajenar *vt* (a) *Der* to alienate (b) (*turbar*) to drive insane

enaltecer [33] *vt* to praise, to extol

enamorado, -a 1 *adj* in love
2 *nm,f* person in love

enamorar 1 *vt* to win the heart of
2 **enamorarse** *upr* to fall in love (**de** with)

enano, -a *adj* & *nm,f* dwarf

enardecer [33] 1 *vt* (*sentimientos*) to rouse, to stir up; (*persona*) to fill with enthusiasm
2 **enardecerse** *upr* to become excited

encabezamiento *nm* (*de carta*) heading; (*de periódico*) headline; (*preámbulo*) foreword, preamble

encabezar [40] *vt* (a) (*carta, lista*) to head; (*periódico*) to lead (b) (*rebelión, carrera, movimiento*) to lead

encabritarse *upr* (a) (*caballo*) to rear (up) (b) (*persona*) to get cross

encadenar *vt* to chain

encajar 1 vt (a) (ajustar) to insert; **e. la puerta** to push the door to (b) Fam (asimilar) to take (c) (comentario) to get in; **e. un golpe a algn** to land sb a blow
2 vi (a) (ajustarse) to fit (b) Fig **e. con** to fit (in) with, to square with

encaje nm lace

encalar vt to whitewash

encallar vi (a) Náut to run aground (b) (proceso, proyecto) to flounder, to fail

encaminado, -a adj estar **bien/mal e.** to be on the right/wrong track

encaminar 1 vt to direct
2 encaminarse vpr to head (**a** for; **hacia** towards)

encamotarse vpr Andes, CAm Fam to fall in love

encandilar vt to dazzle

encantado, -a adj (a) (contento) delighted; **e. de conocerle** pleased to meet you (b) (embrujado) enchanted

encantador, -a 1 adj charming, delightful
2 nm,f magician

encantamiento nm spell

encantar vt (hechizar) to bewitch, to cast a spell on; Fig **me encanta nadar** I love swimming

encanto nm (a) (atractivo) charm; **ser un e.** to be charming (b) (hechizo) spell

encapotado, -a adj overcast

encapricharse vpr (a) (obstinarse) **e. con algo/hacer algo** to set one's mind on sth/doing sth (b) Esp (sentirse atraído) **e. de algn** to become infatuated with sb; **e. de algo** to take a real liking to sth

encapuchado, -a adj hooded

encaramarse vpr to climb up

encarar 1 vt to face, to confront
2 encararse vpr **encararse con** to face up to

encarcelar vt to imprison, to jail

encarecer [33] **1** vt to put up the price of
2 encarecerse vpr to go up (in price)

encarecidamente adv earnestly, insistently; **le rogamos e. que …** we would earnestly request you to …

encarecimiento nm (a) (de producto, coste) increase in price (b) (empeño) **con e.** insistently

encargado, -a 1 nm,f Com (hombre) manager; (mujer) manager, manageress; (responsable) person in charge
2 adj in charge

encargar [42] **1** vt (a) (poner al cargo) **e. a algn de algo** to put sb in charge of sth; **e. a algn que haga algo** to tell sb to do sth (b) (pedido) to order; (obra) to commission

2 encargarse vpr **encargarse de** to see to, to deal with

encargo nm (a) (pedido) order; Esp **hecho de e.** tailor-made (b) (recado) errand (c) (tarea) job, assignment

encariñarse vpr **e. con** to become fond of, to get attached to

encarnación nf incarnation, embodiment

encarnado, -a adj (rojo) red

encarnar vt to personify, to embody

encarnizado, -a adj fierce

encarrilar vt (coche, tren) to put on the road o rails; Fig to put on the right track

encasillar vt to pigeonhole

encausar vt to prosecute

encauzar [40] vt to channel

encendedor nm lighter

encender [3] **1** vt (a) (luz, radio, tele) to switch on, to put on; (cigarro, vela, fuego) to light; (cerilla) to strike, to light (b) Fig to inflame, to stir up
2 encenderse vpr (a) (fuego) to catch; (luz) to go o come on (b) (cara) to blush, to go red

encendido nm ignition

encerado nm (pizarra) Br blackboard, US chalkboard

encerar vt to wax, polish

encerrar [1] **1** vt (a) (recluir) to shut in; (con llave) to lock in (b) Fig (contener) to contain, to include
2 encerrarse vpr to shut oneself up o in; (con llave) to lock oneself in

encestar vi Dep to score (a basket)

encharcar [44] **1** vt to flood, to swamp
2 encharcarse vpr to get flooded

enchilada nf Culin enchilada, = stuffed corn tortilla seasoned with chilli

enchilarse vpr Méx Fam to get angry

enchinar vt Méx to curl

enchufado, -a Fam **1** adj estar **e.** to have good connections o contacts
2 nm,f (favorito) pet

enchufar vt (a) Elec to plug in (b) (unir) to join, to connect (c) Fam (para un trabajo) to pull strings for

enchufe nm (a) Elec (hembra) socket; (macho) plug (b) Fam contact

encía nf gum

enciclopedia nf encyclopedia

encierro nm Pol (protesta) sit-in

encima adv (a) (arriba) on top; **déjalo e.** put it on top; **¿llevas cambio e.?** do you have any change on you?; Fig **quitarse algo de e.** to get rid of sth; **ahí e.** up there (b) (además) besides (c) **e. de** (sobre) on; (en el aire) above; Fig (además) besides; **e.**

de la mesa on the table (**d**) **por e.** above; *Fig* **por e. de sus posibilidades** beyond his abilities; **leer un libro por e.** to skip through a book

encimera *nf Esp (de cocina)* worktop

encina *nf* holm oak

encinta *adj* pregnant

enclaustrarse *vpr* to shut oneself up

enclave *nm* enclave

enclenque *adj (débil)* puny; *(enfermizo)* sickly

encoger [53] **1** *vi (contraerse)* to contract; *(prenda)* to shrink
  2 *vt* to contract; *(prenda)* to shrink
  3 encogerse *vpr (contraerse)* to contract; *(prenda)* to shrink; **encogerse de hombros** to shrug (one's shoulders)

encolar *vt (papel)* to paste; *(madera)* to glue

encolerizar [40] **1** *vt* to infuriate, to anger
  2 encolerizarse *vpr* to become furious

encomendar [1] **1** *vt* to entrust with, to put in charge of
  2 encomendarse *vpr* **e. a** to entrust oneself to

encomienda *nf Am (paquete)* parcel

encomio *nm* praise

enconado, -a *adj (a) (discusión)* bitter, fierce (**b**) *Med* inflamed, sore

encono *nm* spitefulness, ill feeling

encontrado, -a *adj (intereses, opiniones)* conflicting

encontrar [2] **1** *vt (a) (hallar)* to find; **no lo encuentro** I can't find it; **lo encuentro muy agradable** I find it very pleasant (**b**) *(dar con)* to meet; *(problema)* to run into, to come up against
  2 encontrarse *vpr (a) (persona)* to meet (**b**) *(sentirse)* to feel, to be; **encontrarse a gusto** to feel comfortable (**c**) *(estar)* to be

encontronazo *nm (choque)* collision, crash

encorvar 1 *vt* to bend
  2 encorvarse *vpr* to stoop *o* bend (over)

encrespar 1 *vt* (**a**) *(pelo)* to curl (**b**) *(mar)* to make choppy *o* rough (**c**) *(persona)* to infuriate
  2 encresparse *vpr* (**a**) *(mar)* to get rough (**b**) *(persona)* to get cross *o* irritated

encrucijada *nf* crossroads

encuadernación *nf* (**a**) *(oficio)* bookbinding (**b**) *(cubierta)* binding

encuadernador, -a *nm,f* bookbinder

encuadernar *vt* to bind

encuadrar *vt (imagen)* to frame

encuadre *nm Cin & TV* framing

encubierto, -a *adj (secreto)* hidden; *(operación)* covert

encubridor, -a *nm,f Der* accessory (after the fact), abettor

encubrir *vt* to conceal

encuentro *nm* (**a**) *(acción)* encounter, meeting (**b**) *Dep* meeting, match; **e. amistoso** friendly (match)

encuesta *nf* (**a**) *(sondeo)* (opinion) poll, survey (**b**) *(investigación)* investigation, inquiry

encuestador, -a *nm,f* pollster

encuestar *vt* to poll·

encumbrar 1 *vt* to exalt
  2 encumbrarse *vpr* to rise to a high (social) position

ende: por ende *loc adv* therefore

endeble *adj* weak, feeble

endémico, -a *adj Med & Fig* endemic

endemoniado, -a *adj* (**a**) *(poseso)* possessed (**b**) *Fam (molesto) (niño)* wicked; *(trabajo)* very tricky

enderezar [40] **1** *vt (poner derecho)* to straighten out; *(poner vertical)* to set upright
  2 enderezarse *vpr* to straighten up

endeudarse *vpr* to get into debt

endiablado, -a *adj* (**a**) *(poseso)* possessed (**b**) *(travieso)* mischievous, devilish

endibia *nf* endive

endiñar *vt Esp Fam* **e. algo a algn** *(golpe)* to land *o* deal sb sth; *(tarea)* to lumber sb with sth

endiosarse *vpr* to become conceited

endivia *nf* endive

endocrino, -a *Med* **1** *adj* endocrine
  2 *nm,f* endocrinologist

endogamia *nf* endogamy

endomingado, -a *adj Fam* dressed-up, dolled-up

endorfina *nf* endorphin

endosar *vt Fam* **e. algo a algn** *(tarea)* to lumber sb with sth

endoscopia *nf Med* endoscopy

endrina *nf Bot* sloe

endrogarse [42] *vpr Chile, Méx, Perú* to get into debt

endulzar [40] *vt* to sweeten

endurecer [33] **1** *vt* to harden
  2 endurecerse *vpr* to harden, to become hard

enebro *nm* juniper

enema *nm* enema

enemigo, -a 1 *adj* enemy; **soy e. de la bebida** I'm against drink
  2 *nm,f* enemy

enemistad *nf* hostility, enmity

enemistar 1 *vt* to set at odds, to cause a rift between

2 enemistarse *vpr* to become enemies; **e. con algn** to fall out with sb

energético, -a *adj* energy

energía *nf* energy; **e. hidráulica/nuclear** hydro-electric/nuclear power; **e. vital** vitality

enérgico, -a *adj* energetic; *(decisión)* firm; *(tono)* emphatic

energúmeno, -a *nm,f Fam (hombre)* madman; *(mujer)* madwoman; **ponerse como un e.** to go up the wall

enero *nm* January

enervante *adj* exasperating

enervar *vt* to exasperate

enésimo, -a *adj* **(a)** *Mat* nth **(b)** *Fam* umpteenth; **por enésima vez** for the umpteenth time

enfadado, -a *adj esp Esp* **(a)** *(irritado)* angry; *(molesto)* annoyed **(b)** *(peleado)* **estamos enfadados** we've fallen out with each other

enfadar *esp Esp* **1** *vt (irritar)* to anger; *(molestar)* to annoy

2 enfadarse *vpr* **(a)** *(irritarse)* to get angry (**con** with); *(molestarse)* to get annoyed (**con** with) **(b)** *(pelearse)* to fall out

enfado *nm esp Esp* **(a)** *(por irritarse)* anger; *(desavenencia)* fall-out **(b)**

enfangarse [42] *vpr* **e. en un asunto sucio** to get mixed up in a shady business

énfasis *nm inv* emphasis, stress; **poner e. en algo** to lay stress on sth

enfático, -a *adj* emphatic

enfatizar [40] *vt* to emphasize, to stress

enfermar *vi* to become *o* fall ill, to be taken ill

enfermedad *nf* illness; *(contagiosa)* disease

enfermería *nf* infirmary

enfermero, -a *nm,f (mujer)* nurse; *(hombre)* male nurse

enfermizo, -a *adj* unhealthy, sickly

enfermo, -a 1 *adj* ill; **caer e.** to be taken ill; *Fam* **esa gente me pone e.** those people make me sick

2 *nm,f* ill person; *(paciente)* patient

enfervorizar [40] *vt* to enthuse

enfilar *vi* **e. hacia** to make for

enflaquecer [33] *vt* to make thin

enfocado, -a *adj Fot* **bien/mal enfocado** in/out of focus

enfocar [44] *vt* **(a)** *(imagen)* to focus; *(persona)* to focus on **(b)** *(tema)* to approach **(c)** *(con linterna)* to shine a light on

enfoque *nm* **(a)** *(de imagen)* focus **(b)** *(de tema)* approach

enfrentamiento *nm* clash

enfrentar 1 *vt* **(a)** *(situación, peligro)* to confront **(b)** *(enemistar)* to set at odds

2 enfrentarse *vpr* **(a)** **enfrentarse con** *o* **a** to face up to, to confront **(b)** *Dep* **enfrentarse (a)** *(rival)* to meet

enfrente *adv* **(a)** opposite; **la casa de e.** the house opposite *o* across the road **(b)** **e. de.** opposite (to), facing; **e. del colegio** opposite the school

enfriamiento *nm* **(a)** *(proceso)* cooling **(b)** *Med (catarro)* cold, chill

enfriar [29] **1** *vt* to cool (down), to chill **2** *vi* to cool down

3 enfriarse *vpr* **(a)** *(quedarse frío)* to get *o* go cold **(b)** *(resfriarse)* to get *o* catch a cold **(c)** *Fig (pasión)* to cool down

enfurecer [33] **1** *vt* to enrage, to infuriate **2 enfurecerse** *vpr* to get furious, to lose one's temper

enfurruñarse *vpr Fam* to sulk

engalanar 1 *vt* to deck out, to adorn **2 engalanarse** *vpr* to dress up, to get dressed up

enganchado, -a *adj Fam* **estar e. (a la droga)** to be hooked (on drugs)

enganchar 1 *vt* **(a)** *(remolque, caballos)* to hitch up; *(vagones)* to couple **(b)** *Fam (atraer)* **e. a algn para que haga algo** *o* to rope sb into doing sth

2 *vi Fam (hacer adicto)* to be addictive

3 engancharse *vpr* to get caught *o* hooked; *Fam (a la droga)* to get hooked

enganche *nm (gancho)* hook; *(de vagones)* coupling

engañabobos *nm inv (persona)* con man, confidence trickster; *(truco)* con trick

engañar 1 *vt (mentir)* to deceive; *(estafar)* to cheat, to trick; *(al esposo)* to be unfaithful to

2 engañarse *vpr* to deceive oneself

engañifa *nf Fam* swindle

engaño *nm (mentira, broma)* deceit; *(estafa)* swindle; *(ardid)* ploy, trick; **que nadie se llame a e.** let no one have any illusions about it

engañoso, -a *adj (palabras)* deceitful; *(apariencias)* deceptive; *(consejo)* misleading

engarzar [40] *vt* **(a)** *(abalorios)* to thread; *(perlas)* to string **(b)** *(diamante)* to set

engastar *vt* to set, to mount

engatusar *vt Fam* to coax; **e. a algn para que haga algo** to coax sb into doing sth

engendrar *vt* **(a)** *Biol* to engender **(b)** *Fig* to give rise to, to cause

engendro *nm* freak

englobar *vt* to include

engordar 1 *vt* to fatten (up), to make fat **2** *vi* (**a**) *(poner peso)* to put on weight, to get fat; **he engordado 3 kilos** I've put on 3 kilos (**b**) *(comida, bebida)* to be fattening

engorro *nm* bother, nuisance

engorroso, -a *adj* bothersome, tiresome

engranaje *nm* (**a**) *Téc* gearing (**b**) *Fig* machinery

engranar *vt Téc* to engage

engrandecer [33] *vt* to exalt

engrapadora *nf Am* stapler

engrapar *vt Am* to staple

engrasar *vt* (**a**) *(lubricar)* to lubricate, to oil (**b**) *(manchar)* to make greasy, to stain with grease

engrase *nm* lubrication

engreído, -a *adj* vain, conceited

engreírse [56] *vpr* to become vain *o* conceited

engrosar [2] *vt* (*incrementar*) to enlarge; *(cantidad)* to increase, to swell

engrudo *nm* paste

engullir *vt* to gobble up

enharinar *vt* to cover with flour

enhebrar *vt* to thread

enhorabuena *nf* congratulations; **dar la e. a algn** to congratulate sb

enigma *nm* enigma

enigmático, -a *adj* enigmatic

enjabonar *vt* to soap

enjalbegar [42] *vt* to whitewash

enjambre *nm* swarm

enjaular *vt* to cage

enjuagar [42] *vt* to rinse

enjuague *nm* rinse; **e. bucal** mouthwash

enjugar [42] *vt (lágrimas)* to wipe away

enjuiciamiento *nm Der (civil)* lawsuit; *(criminal)* trial, prosecution

enjuiciar [43] *vt Der* to indict, to prosecute

enjundia *nf (sustancia)* substance; *(importancia)* importance

enjuto, -a *adj* lean, skinny

enlace *nm* (**a**) *(unión)* link, connection; **e. químico** chemical bond (**b**) *Ferroc* connection (**c**) *(casamiento)* marriage (**d**) *(persona)* liaison officer; *Esp* **e. sindical** shop steward

enlatado, -a *adj* canned, tinned

enlatar *vt* to can, to tin

enlazar [40] *vt & vi* to link, to connect (**con** with)

enlodar *vt* (**a**) *(enfangar)* to muddy, to cover with mud (**b**) *(reputación)* to stain, to besmirch

enloquecedor, -a *adj* maddening

enloquecer [33] **1** *vi* to go mad **2** *vt* (**a**) *(volver loco)* to drive mad (**b**) *Fam* **me enloquecen las motos** I'm mad about motorbikes **3 enloquecerse** *vpr* to go mad, to go out of one's mind

enlosar *vt* to tile

enlucir [35] *vt (pared)* to plaster; *(plata, oro)* to polish

enlutado, -a *adj* in mourning

enmarañar 1 *vt* (**a**) *(pelo)* to tangle (**b**) *(complicar)* to complicate, to confuse **2 enmarañarse** *vpr* (**a**) *(pelo)* to get tangled (**b**) *(situación)* to get confused, to get into a mess *o* a muddle

enmarcar [44] *vt* to frame

enmascarado, -a *nm,f (hombre)* masked man; *(mujer)* masked woman

enmascarar *vt* (**a**) *(rostro)* to mask (**b**) *(problema, la verdad)* to mask, to disguise

enmendar [1] **1** *vt (corregir)* to correct, to put right; *Der* to amend **2 enmendarse** *vpr (persona)* to reform, to mend one's ways

enmienda *nf* correction; *Der & Pol* amendment

enmohecerse [33] *vpr (metal)* to rust, to get rusty; *Bot* to go mouldy

enmoquetar *vt Esp, RP* to carpet

enmudecer [33] *vi (callar)* to fall silent; *Fig* to be dumbstruck

ennegrecer [33] **1** *vt* to blacken **2 ennegrecerse** *vpr* to become blackened

ennoblecer [33] *vt* to ennoble

enojadizo, -a *adj* irritable, touchy

enojado, -a *adj (irritado)* angry; *(molesto)* annoyed

enojar *esp Am* **1** *vt (irritar)* to anger; *(molestar)* to annoy **2 enojarse** *vpr (irritarse)* to get angry (**con** with); *(molestarse)* to get annoyed (**con** with)

enojo *nm esp Am (irritación)* anger; *(molestia)* annoyance

enorgullecer [33] **1** *vt* to fill with pride **2 enorgullecerse** *vpr* to be *o* feel proud (**de** of)

enorme *adj* enormous

enormidad *nf* enormity; **me gustó una e.** I liked it enormously

enraizado, -a *adj* rooted

enraizarse [40] *vpr (persona)* to put down roots; *(planta, costumbre)* to take root

enrarecerse [33] *vpr (aire)* to become rarefied

enredadera *nf* climbing plant, creeper

enredar 1 *vt* (a) *(pelo)* to entangle, to tangle up (b) *Fig (asunto)* to confuse, to complicate (c) *Fig (implicar)* to involve (en in) (d) *(confundir)* to mix up
2 enredarse *vpr* (a) *(pelo)* to get entangled, to get tangled (up) *o* in a tangle (b) *Fig (asunto)* to get complicated *o* confused (c) *Fig* **enredarse con** *(involucrarse)* to get involved with (d) *(confundirse)* to get mixed up

enredo *nm* (a) *(maraña)* tangle (b) *Fig (lío)* muddle, mess

enrejado *nm (de ventana)* lattice

enrevesado, -a *adj* complicated, difficult

enriquecer [33] **1** *vt* to make rich; *Fig* to enrich
2 enriquecerse *vpr* to get *o* become rich, to prosper; *Fig* to become enriched

enrocar [44] *vi (en ajedrez)* to castle

enrojecer [33] **1** *vt* to redden, to turn red
2 *vi (ruborizarse)* to blush
3 enrojecerse *vpr* to blush

enrolarse *vpr* to enlist

enrollado, -a *adj* (a) *Esp (persona)* great (b) *Fam* **estar e. con algn** *(estar saliendo con)* to go out with sb

enrollar 1 *vt* to roll up; *(cable)* to coil; *(hilo)* to wind up
2 enrollarse *vpr* (a) *Fam (hablar)* to chatter, to go on and on (b) *Fam* **enrollarse con algn** *(tener relaciones)* to have an affair with sb

> 🖉 Observa que el verbo inglés **to enrol** es un falso amigo y no es la traducción del verbo español **enrollar**. En inglés, **to enrol** significa "matricular, inscribir".

enroscar [44] *vt* (a) *(tuerca)* to screw in; *(tapa)* to screw on (b) *(enrollar)* to roll up; *(cuerpo, cola)* to curl up

ensaimada *nf* = kind of spiral pastry from Majorca

ensalada *nf* salad

ensaladera *nf* salad bowl

ensaladilla *nf Esp* **e. rusa** Russian salad

ensalzar [40] *vt* to praise

ensamblador *nm Inform* assembler

ensamblar *vt* to assemble

ensanchar 1 *vt* (a) *(orificio, calle)* to widen; *(ropa)* to let out; *(ciudad)* to expand
2 ensancharse *vpr (orificio, calle)* to widen, to open out

ensanche *nm (de calle)* widening; *(en la ciudad)* new suburb

ensangrentado, -a *adj* bloodstained, covered in blood

ensangrentar [1] *vt* to stain with blood, to cover in blood

ensañarse *vpr* **e. con** to torment, to treat cruelly

ensartar *vt (perlas)* to string together

ensayar *vt* to test, to try out; *Teatro* to rehearse; *Mús* to practise

ensayista *nmf* essayist

ensayo *nm* (a) *(prueba)* test, trial (b) *Teatro* rehearsal; **e. general** dress rehearsal (c) *(escrito)* essay

enseguida *adv (inmediatamente)* immediately, straight away; *(pronto)* very soon; **e. voy** I'll be right there

ensenada *nf* inlet, cove

enseña *nf* ensign, standard

enseñanza *nf* (a) *(educación)* education (b) *(de idioma etc)* teaching (c) **enseñanzas** teachings

enseñar *vt* (a) *(instruir)* to teach; **e. a algn a hacer algo** to teach sb how to do sth (b) *(mostrar)* to show; *(señalar)* to point out

enseres *nmpl (bártulos)* belongings, goods; *(de trabajo)* tools

ensillar *vt* to saddle (up)

ensimismado, -a *adj (en la lectura)* engrossed; *(abstraído)* lost in thought

ensimismarse *vpr (en la lectura)* to become engrossed; *(abstraerse)* to be lost in thought

ensombrecer [33] **1** *vt* to cast a shadow over
2 ensombrecerse *vpr* to darken

ensopar *vt Andes, RP, Ven Fam* to soak

ensordecedor, -a *adj* deafening

ensordecer [33] **1** *vt* to deafen
2 *vi* to go deaf

ensortijado, -a *adj* curly

ensuciar [43] **1** *vt* (a) *(lugar, persona)* to get dirty (b) *Fig (reputación)* to harm, to damage
2 ensuciarse *vpr* to get dirty

ensueño *nm* dream; **una casa de e.** a dream house

entablar *vt* (a) *(conversación)* to open, to begin; *(amistad)* to strike up; *(negocios)* to start (b) *(pleito)* to initiate

entablillar *vt Med* to splint

entallado, -a *adj (vestido)* close-fitting; *(camisa)* fitted

entallar *vt* to take in at the waist

entarimado *nm* parquet floor

ente *nm* (a) *(institución)* organization, body; **e. público** public service organization (b) *(ser)* being

entendederas *nfpl Fam* brains; **ser duro de e.** to be slow on the uptake

entender [3] **1** *vt (comprender)* to understand; **a mi e.** to my way of thinking; **dar a algn a e. que ...** to give sb to understand that ...

2 *vi* (**a**) *(comprender)* to understand (**b**) **e. de** *(saber)* to know about

3 entenderse *vpr* (**a**) *(comprenderse)* to be understood, to be meant (**b**) *Fam* **entenderse (bien) con** to get on (well) with

entendido, -a 1 *nm,f* expert

2 *adj* **tengo e. que …** I understand that …

entendimiento *nm* understanding

enterado, -a 1 *adj* knowledgeable, well-informed; **estar e.** to be in the know; **estar e. de …** to be aware of …

2 *nm,f (listillo)* know-all

enteramente *adv* entirely, completely

enterar 1 *vt* to inform (**de** about *o* of)

2 enterarse *vpr* to find out; **me he enterado de que …** I understand …; **ni me enteré** I didn't even realize it

entereza *nf* strength of character

enternecedor, -a *adj* moving, touching

enternecer [33] **1** *vt* to move, to touch

2 enternecerse *vpr* to be moved *o* touched

entero, -a 1 *adj* (**a**) *(completo)* entire, whole; **por e.** completely (**b**) *Fig (íntegro)* honest, upright (**c**) *Fig (firme)* strong

2 *nm* (**a**) *Mat* whole number (**b**) *Fin* point

enterrador, -a *nm* gravedigger

enterramiento *nm* burial

enterrar [1] *vt* to bury

entidad *nf* organization; **e. comercial** company, firm

entierro *nm (acción)* burial; *(ceremonia)* funeral

entlo. *(abr* **entresuelo)** mezzanine

entomología *nf* entomology

entonación *nf* intonation

entonar 1 *vt* (**a**) *(canto)* to sing (**b**) *Med* to tone up

2 *vi* to be in harmony, to be in tune (**con** with)

entonces *adv* then; **por aquel e.** at that time; **el e. ministro** the then minister

entornar *vt (ojos)* to half-close; *(puerta)* to leave ajar

entorno *nm* environment

entorpecer [33] *vt (obstaculizar)* to hinder, to impede

entrada *nf* (**a**) *(acción)* entry; *(lugar)* entrance (**b**) *(billete)* ticket; *(recaudación)* takings (**c**) *Culin* entrée (**d**) *Com* **anotar una e.** to enter up an item; **entradas** *(ingresos)* receipts, takings (**e**) *Esp (pago inicial)* down payment, deposit (**f**) *(en la frente)* receding hairline (**g**) *Inform* input (**h**) **de e.** for a start

entrado, -a *adj* **e. en años** advanced in years; **hasta bien entrada la noche** well into the night

entramado *nm* framework

entramparse *vpr Fam* to get into debt

entrante 1 *adj* coming; **el mes e.** next month; **el ministro e.** the incoming minister

2 *nm Esp* starter

entrañable *adj* (**a**) *(lugar)* intimate, close (**b**) *(persona)* affectionate, warm-hearted

entrañar *vt* to entail

entrañas *nfpl* bowels

entrar *vi* (**a**) *(introducirse) (viniendo)* to enter, to come in; *(yendo)* to enter, to go in; **el año que entra** next year, the coming year (**b**) *(encajar)* to fit; **no entra en la cerradura** it won't fit in the lock (**c**) *(incorporarse)* **e. en** *(colegio, empresa)* to start at; *(club, partido)* to join (**d**) *(estar incluido)* **e. en, e. dentro de** to be included in (**e**) **entrarle a algn: me entró dolor de cabeza** I got a headache; **me entraron ganas de reír** I felt like laughing; **no me entran las matemáticas** I can't get the hang of maths

entre *prep* (**a**) *(dos)* between (**b**) *(más de dos)* among(st)

entreabierto, -a *adj (ojos etc)* half-open; *(puerta)* ajar

entreacto *nm* interval, intermission

entrecejo *nm* space between the eyebrows; **fruncir el e.** to frown, to knit one's brow

entrecortado, -a *adj (voz)* faltering, hesitant

entrecot *(pl* **entrecots** *o* **entrecotes)** *nm* fillet steak

entrecruzarse [40] *vpr* to entwine

entredicho *nm* **estar en e.** to be suspect; **poner algo en e.** to bring sth into question

entrega *nf* (**a**) *(de productos)* delivery; *(de premios)* presentation (**b**) *(fascículo)* part, instalment (**c**) *(devoción)* selflessness

entregar [42] **1** *vt* to hand over; *(deberes etc)* to hand in; *Com* to deliver

2 entregarse *vpr* (**a**) *(rendirse)* to give in, to surrender (**b**) **entregarse a** to devote oneself to; *Pey* to indulge in

entrelazar [40] *vt* to entwine

entremedias *adv* in between

entremeses *nmpl Culin* hors d'oeuvres

entremeterse *vpr* = **entrometerse**

entremezclarse *vpr* to mix, to mingle

entrenador, -a *nm,f* trainer, coach

entrenamiento *nm* training

entrenar 1 *vt & vi* to train
  2 entrenarse *vpr* to train
entrepierna *nf* crotch, crutch
entresacar [44] *vt* to pick out, to select
entresijos *nmpl* nooks and crannies
entresuelo *nm* mezzanine
entretanto 1 *adv* meanwhile
  2 *nm* **en el e.** in the meantime
entretejer *vt* to interweave
entretención *nf Chile* entertainment
entretener [24] **1** *vt* (**a**) *(divertir)* to entertain, to amuse (**b**) *(retrasar)* to delay; *(detener)* to hold up, to detain
  2 entretenerse *vpr* (**a**) *(distraerse)* to amuse oneself, to while away the time (**b**) *(retrasarse)* to be delayed, to be held up
entretenido, -a *adj* enjoyable, entertaining
entretenimiento *nm* entertainment, amusement
entretiempo 1 *nm CSur* half-time
  2 de entretiempo *loc adj* **ropa de e.** spring/autumn clothes
entrever [28] *vt* to glimpse, to catch sight of; *Fig* **dejó e. que …** she hinted that …
entreverar *CSur* **1** *vt* to mix
  2 entreverarse *vpr* to get tangled
entrevero *nm CSur* tangle, mess
entrevista *nf* interview
entrevistador, -a *nm,f* interviewer
entrevistar 1 *vt* to interview
  2 entrevistarse *vpr* **entrevistarse con algn** to have an interview with sb
entristecer [33] **1** *vt* to sadden, to make sad
  2 entristecerse *vpr* to be sad (**por** about)
entrometerse *vpr* to meddle, to interfere (**en** in)
entrometido, -a 1 *nm,f* meddler, busybody
  2 *adj* interfering
entroncar [44] *vi* to connect
entumecer [33] **1** *vt* to numb
  2 entumecerse *vpr* to go numb
entumecido, -a *adj* numb
enturbiar [43] **1** *vt* (**a**) *(agua)* to make cloudy (**b**) *(asunto)* to cloud, to obscure
  2 enturbiarse *vpr* to become cloudy
entusiasmar 1 *vt* to fill with enthusiasm
  2 entusiasmarse *vpr* to get excited *o* enthusiastic (**con** about)
entusiasmo *nm* enthusiasm; **con e.** enthusiastically
entusiasta 1 *adj* enthusiastic, keen (**de** on)
  2 *nmf* enthusiast
enumerar *vt* to enumerate

enunciado *nm (de teoría, problema)* wording
envainar *vt* to sheathe
envanecer [33] **1** *vt* to make proud *o* vain
  2 envanecerse *vpr* to become conceited *o* proud, to give oneself airs
envasado, -a 1 *nm (en botella)* bottling; *(en paquete)* packing; *(en lata)* canning
  2 *adj* **e. al vacío** vacuum-packed
envasar *vt (embotellar)* to bottle; *(empaquetar)* to pack; *(enlatar)* to can, to tin
envase *nm* (**a**) *(acto)* packing; *(de botella)* bottling; *(de lata)* canning (**b**) *(recipiente)* container (**c**) *(botella vacía)* empty
envejecer [33] **1** *vi* to grow old
  2 *vt* to age
envejecimiento *nm* ageing
envenenamiento *nm* poisoning
envenenar *vt* to poison
envergadura *nf* (**a**) *(importancia)* importance, scope; **de gran e.** large-scale (**b**) *(de pájaro, avión)* span, wingspan; *Náut* breadth (of sail)
envés *(pl* **enveses**) *nm* other side
envestidura *nf* investiture
enviado, -a *nm,f* envoy; *Prensa* **e. especial** special correspondent
enviar [29] *vt* to send
enviciarse [43] *vpr* to become addicted (**con** to)
envidia *nf* envy; **tener e. de algn** to envy sb
envidiable *adj* enviable
envidiar [43] *vt* to envy; **no tener nada que e.** to be in no way inferior (**a** to)
envidioso, -a *adj* envious

> ℓ Observa que la palabra inglesa **invidious** es un falso amigo y no es la traducción de la palabra española **envidioso**. En inglés, **invidious** significa "ingrato" o "injusto".

envilecer [33] *vt* to degrade, to debase
envío *nm* sending; *(remesa)* consignment; *(paquete)* parcel; **gastos de e.** postage and packing; **e. contra reembolso** cash on delivery
enviudar *vi (hombre)* to become a widower, to lose one's wife; *(mujer)* to become a widow, to lose one's husband
envoltorio *nm* wrapper, wrapping
envolver [4] *(pp* **envuelto**) **1** *vt* (**a**) *(con papel)* to wrap (**b**) *(cubrir)* to envelop (**c**) *(en complot etc)* to involve (**en** in)
  2 envolverse *vpr* (**a**) *(cubrirse)* to wrap oneself up (**en** in) (**b**) *(implicarse)* to become involved (**en** in)
enyesar *vt* to plaster; *Med* to put in plaster

enzima *nf* enzyme

épica *nf* epic poetry

epicentro *nm* epicentre

épico, -a *adj* epic

epidemia *nf* epidemic

epidermis *nf inv Anat* epidermis

epilepsia *nf* epilepsy

epílogo *nm* epilogue

episcopal *adj* episcopal

episodio *nm* episode

epístola *nf* epistle

epitafio *nm* epitaph

epíteto *nm* epithet

época *nf* time; *Hist* period, epoch; *Agr* season; **en esta é. del año** at this time of the year; **hacer é.** to be a landmark; **mueble de é.** period furniture

equidad *nf* equity

equilátero *nm* equilateral

equilibrado, -a *adj* (**a**) *(igualado)* balanced (**b**) *(sensato)* sensible

equilibrar *vt* to balance

equilibrio *nm* balance

equilibrismo *nm* balancing act

equilibrista *nmf* tightrope walker

equipaje *nm Br* luggage; *US* baggage; **hacer el e.** to pack, to do the packing

equipar *vt* to equip, to furnish (**con** *o* **de** with)

equiparable *adj* comparable (**a** to; **con** with)

equiparar *vt* to compare (**con** with), to liken (**con** to)

equipo *nm* (**a**) *(de expertos, jugadores)* team (**b**) *(aparatos)* equipment; **e. de alta fidelidad** hi-fi stereo system (**c**) *(ropas)* outfit

equis *nf inv* = name of the letter X

equitación *nf* horse *o US* horseback riding

equitativo, -a *adj* equitable, fair

equivalente *adj* equivalent

equivaler [26] *vi* to be equivalent (**a** to)

equivocación *nf* error, mistake

equivocado, -a *adj* mistaken, wrong

equivocar [44] **1** *vt* to mix up
  2 equivocarse *vpr* to make a mistake; *Tel* **se equivocó de número** he dialled the wrong number; **se equivocó de fecha** he got the wrong date

equívoco, -a 1 *adj* equivocal, misleading
  2 *nm* misunderstanding

era¹ *nf (época)* era, age

era² *nf Agr* threshing floor

era³ *pt indef de* **ser**

erario *nm* exchequer, treasury

eras *pt indef de* **ser**

erección *nf* erection

erecto, -a *adj* upright; *(pene)* erect

eres *indic pres de* **ser**

erguido, -a *adj* upright

erguir [55] **1** *vt* to raise
  2 erguirse *vpr* to rise up

erial *nm* uncultivated land

erigir [57] **1** *vt* to erect
  2 erigirse *vpr* **e. en algo** to set oneself up in sth

erizado, -a *adj* bristly, prickly

erizarse [40] *vpr* to bristle, to stand on end

erizo *nm* hedgehog; **e. de mar** *o* **marino** sea urchin

ermita *nf* hermitage

> 🖉 Observa que la palabra inglesa **hermit** es un falso amigo y no es la traducción de la palabra española **ermita**. En inglés, **hermit** significa "ermitaño".

ermitaño, -a *nm,f* hermit

erosión *nf* erosion

erosionar *vt* to erode

erótico, -a *adj* erotic

erotismo *nm* eroticism

erradicar [44] *vt* to eradicate

errante *adj* wandering

errar [50] **1** *vt* to miss, to get wrong
  2 *vi* (**a**) *(vagar)* to wander, to roam (**b**) *(fallar)* to err

errata *nf* erratum, misprint

erre *nf* **e. que e.** stubbornly, pigheadedly

erróneo, -a *adj* erroneous, wrong

error *nm* error, mistake; *Inform* bug; **por e.** by mistake, in error; *Impr* **e. de imprenta** misprint; **caer en un e.** to make a mistake

Ertzaintza [er'tʃaintʃa] *nf Esp* = Basque police force

eructar *vi* to belch, to burp

eructo *nm* belch, burp

erudición *nf* erudition

erudito, -a 1 *adj* erudite, learned
  2 *nm,f* scholar

erupción *nf* (**a**) *(de volcán)* eruption (**b**) *(en la piel)* rash

es *indic pres de* **ser**

esa *adj dem ver* **ese**

ésa *pron dem ver* **ése**

esbelto, -a *adj* slender

esbirro *nm* henchman

esbozar [40] *vt* to sketch, to outline

esbozo *nm* sketch, outline, rough draft

escabeche *nm* brine

escabechina *nf Fam (destrozo)* destruction

escabroso, -a *adj (tema)* unpleasant; *(detalles)* lurid; *(imágenes)* crude

escabullirse *vpr* to slip away, to scuttle *o* scurry off

escacharrar *vt Esp Fam* to bust

escafandra *nf* diving suit; **e. espacial** spacesuit

escala *nf* (a) *(para medir)* scale; *(de colores)* range; **e. musical** scale; **en gran e.** on a large scale (b) *(parada) Náut* port of call; *Av* stopover; **hacer e. en** to call in at, to stop over in (c) *Mús* scale

escalada *nf* (a) *(de montaña)* climb (b) *(de violencia, precios)* escalation, rise (**de** in)

escalador, -a *nm,f* climber, mountaineer

> *Observa que la palabra inglesa **escalator** es un falso amigo y no es la traducción de la palabra española **escalador**. En inglés, **escalator** significa "escalera mecánica".*

escalafón *nm (graduación)* rank; *(de salarios)* salary *o* wage scale

escalar *vt* to climb, to scale

escaldar *vt* to scald

escalera *nf* (a) *(en edificio)* stairs, staircase; *(de mano)* ladder; **e. de incendios** fire escape; **e. mecánica** escalator; **e. de caracol** spiral staircase (b) *Naipes* run

escalerilla *nf (de piscina)* steps; *Náut* gangway; *Av* (boarding) ramp

escalfar *vt* to poach

escalinata *nf* stoop

escalofriante *adj* hair-raising, bloodcurdling

escalofrío *nm* shiver; **me dio un e.** it gave me the shivers

escalón *nm* step; **e. lateral** *(en letrero)* ramp

escalonar *vt* to place at intervals, to space out

escalope *nm* escalope

escalpelo *nm* scalpel

escama *nf Zool* scale; *(de jabón)* flake

escamarse *vpr* to smell a rat, to become suspicious

escamotear *vt Fam* to diddle out of, to do out of

escampar *vi* to stop raining, to clear up

escanciar [43] *vt (vino)* to pour out, to serve

escandalizar [40] **1** *vt* to scandalize, to shock

2 escandalizarse *vpr* to be shocked (**de** at *o* by)

escándalo *nm* (a) *(alboroto)* racket, din; **armar un e.** to kick up a fuss (b) *(desvergüenza)* scandal

escandaloso, -a *adj* (a) *(ruidoso)* noisy, rowdy (b) *(ofensivo)* scandalous

Escandinavia *n* Scandinavia

escandinavo, -a *adj & nm,f* Scandinavian

escanear *vt Inform & Med* to scan

escáner *nm Inform & Med (aparato)* scanner; *Med (imagen)* scan

escaño *nm (parlamentario)* seat

escapada *nf* (a) *(de prisión)* escape; *(en ciclismo)* breakaway (b) *(viaje rápido)* flying visit, quick trip

> *Observa que la palabra inglesa **escapade** es un falso amigo y no es la traducción de la palabra española **escapada**. En inglés, **escapade** significa "aventura".*

escapar 1 *vi* to escape, to run away

2 escaparse *vpr* (a) *(huir)* to escape, to run away (b) *(gas, agua)* to leak (c) *(dejar ir)* **se me escapó la risa** I let out a laugh; **se me escapó de las manos** it slipped out of my hands (d) *(pasar inadvertido)* **no se le escapa nada** he doesn't miss a thing

escaparate *nm* shop window

escaparatismo *nm* window dressing

escapatoria *nf* **no tener e.** to have no way out

escape *nm* (a) *(de gas)* leak (b) *(de coche)* exhaust; **tubo de e.** exhaust (pipe)

escaquearse *vpr Esp Fam* to duck out; **e. de hacer algo** to worm one's way out of doing sth

escarabajo *nm* beetle

escaramuza *nf Mil & Fig* skirmish

escarbar *vt (suelo)* to scratch; *(fuego)* to poke

escarceos *nmpl* forays; **e. amorosos** flirtations

escarcha *nf* hoarfrost, frost

escarchado, -a *adj (fruta)* crystallized, candied

escarlata *adj & nm* scarlet

escarlatina *nf Med* scarlet fever

escarmentar [1] *vi* to learn one's lesson

escarmiento *nm* punishment, lesson

escarnio *nm* derision, mockery

escarola *nf* curly endive

escarpado, -a *adj (paisaje)* craggy; *(pendiente)* steep

escasear *vi* to be scarce

escasez *nf* scarcity

escaso, -a *adj* scarce; *(dinero)* tight; *(conocimientos)* scant; **e. de dinero** short of money

escatimar *vt* to skimp on; **no escatimó esfuerzos para …** he spared no efforts to …

escayola *nf Constr* plaster of Paris; *Med* plaster; **una e.** a plaster cast

escayolar *vt Med* to put in plaster

escena *nf* (a) *(suceso, acto)* scene (b) *(escenario)* stage; **poner en e.** to stage

escenario *nm* (a) *Teatro* stage (b) *(entorno)* scenario; *(de crimen)* scene; *(de película)* setting

escénico, -a *adj* scenic

escenografía *nf Cin* set design; *Teatro* stage design

escepticismo *nm* scepticism

escéptico, -a *adj & nm,f* sceptic

escindirse *upr* to split (off) **(en** into)

escisión *nf* split

esclarecer [33] *vt* to shed light on

esclava *nf* bangle

esclavitud *nf* slavery

esclavizar [40] *vt* to enslave

esclavo, -a *adj & nm,f* slave

esclusa *nf* lock, sluicegate

escoba *nf* brush, broom

escobilla *nf* brush

escocer [41] **1** *vi* to sting, to smart
  2 escocerse *upr (piel)* to chafe

escocés, -esa 1 *adj* Scottish, Scots; **falda escocesa** kilt
  2 *nm,f (hombre)* Scotsman; *(mujer)* Scotswoman

Escocia *n* Scotland

escoger [53] *vt* to choose

escogido, -a *adj* chosen, selected; *(producto)* choice, select; *Lit* **obras escogidas** selected works

escolar 1 *adj (curso, año)* school
  2 *nmf (niño)* schoolboy; *(niña)* schoolgirl

escolaridad *nf* schooling

escollo *nm* reef; *Fig* pitfall

escolta *nf* escort

escoltar *vt* to escort

escombros *nmpl* rubbish, debris

esconder 1 *vt* to hide **(de** from), to conceal **(de** from)
  2 esconderse *upr* to hide **(de** from)

escondidas *adv* **a e.** secretly

escondite *nm* (a) *(lugar)* hiding place, hide-out (b) *(juego)* hide-and-seek

escondrijo *nm* hiding place, hide-out

escopeta *nf* shotgun; **e. de aire comprimido** air gun; **e. de cañones recortados** *Br* sawn-off shotgun, *US* sawed-off shotgun

escorbuto *nm Med* scurvy

escoria *nf* scum, dregs

Escorpio *nm* Scorpio

escorpión *nm* scorpion

escotado, -a *adj* low-cut

escote *nm* low neckline

escotilla *nf* hatch, hatchway

escozor *nm* stinging, smarting

escribiente *nmf* clerk

escribir *(pp escrito)* **1** *vt* to write; **e. a mano** to write in longhand; **e. a máquina** to type
  2 escribirse *upr* (a) *(dos personas)* to write to each other, to correspond (b) **se escribe con h** it is spelt with an h

escrito, -a 1 *adj* written; **e. a mano** handwritten, in longhand; **por e.** in writing
  2 *nm* writing
  3 *pp de* escribir

escritor, -a *nm,f* writer

escritorio *nm* (a) *(mueble)* writing desk, bureau; *(oficina)* office (b) *Inform* desktop

escritura *nf* (a) *Der* deed, document; **e. de propiedad** title deed (b) *Rel* **Sagradas Escrituras** Holy Scriptures

escrúpulo *nm* (a) *(duda, recelo)* scruple; **una persona sin escrúpulos** an unscrupulous person (b) *(esmero)* scrupulousness, great care (c) *(aprensión)* qualm; **le da e.** he has qualms about it

escrupuloso, -a *adj* (a) *(minucioso)* scrupulous (b) *(aprensivo)* particular, fussy

escrutar *vt* (a) *(con la mirada)* to scrutinize (b) *(votos)* to count

escrutinio *nm (de votos)* count

escuadra *nf* (a) *(instrumento)* square (b) *Mil* squad; *Náut* squadron; *Dep* team; *(de coches)* fleet

escuadrilla *nf Náut* squadron

escuadrón *nm Av* squadron

escuálido, -a *adj* emaciated

escucha *nf* listening; **escuchas telefónicas** phone tapping; **estar a la e. de** to be listening out for

escuchar 1 *vt* to listen to; *(oír)* to hear
  2 *vi* to listen; *(oír)* to hear

escudarse *upr* **e. en algo** to hide behind sth

escudería *nf* motor racing team

escudilla *nf* bowl

escudo *nm* (a) *(arma defensiva)* shield (b) *(blasón)* coat of arms

escudriñar *vt* to scrutinize

escuela *nf* school; **e. de bellas artes** art school; **e. de conducir/de idiomas** driving/language school

escueto, -a *adj* plain, unadorned

escuezo *indic pres de* escocer

esculcar [44] *vt Méx* to search

esculpir *vt* to sculpt; *(madera)* to carve; *(metal)* to engrave

escultor, -a *nm,f (hombre)* sculptor; *(mujer)* sculptress; *(de madera)* woodcarver; *(de metales)* engraver

escultura *nf* sculpture

escultural *adj* sculptural; *(persona)* statuesque

escupidera *nf (orinal)* chamberpot

escupir 1 *vi* to spit
2 *vt* to spit out

escupitajo *nm Fam* spit

escurreplatos *nm inv* dish rack

escurridizo, -a *adj* (a) *(resbaladizo)* slippery (b) *Fig (huidizo)* elusive, slippery

escurridor *nm* colander

escurrir 1 *vt (plato, vaso)* to drain; *(ropa)* to wring out; **e. el bulto** to wriggle out
2 escurrirse *vpr* (a) *(platos etc)* to drip (b) *(escaparse)* to run o slip away (c) *(resbalarse)* to slip

ese, -a *(pl* esos, -as*) adj dem* (a) *(singular)* that (b) **esos, -as** those

ése, -a *(pl* ésos, -as*) pron dem m,f* (a) *(singular)* that one (b) **ésos, -as** those (ones); *Fam* **¡ni por ésas!** no way!; *Fam* **¡no me vengas con ésas!** come off it!

> Note that **ése** and its various forms can be written without an accent when there is no risk of confusion with the adjective.

esencia *nf* essence

esencial *adj* essential; **lo e.** the main thing

esfera *nf* (a) *(figura)* sphere (b) *(de reloj)* face (c) *(social)* circle; **las altas esferas de la política** high political circles

esférico, -a 1 *adj* spherical
2 *nm (balón)* ball

esfinge *nf* sphinx

esforzarse [2] *vpr* to make an effort (**por** to)

esfuerzo *nm* effort

esfumarse *vpr Fam* to beat it

esgrima *nf Dep* fencing

esgrimir *vt* to wield

esguince *nm* sprain

eslabón *nm* link

eslalon *(pl* eslalons*) nm Dep* slalom; **e. gigante** giant slalom

eslavo, -a 1 *adj* Slav, Slavonic
2 *nm,f (persona)* Slav
3 *nm (idioma)* Slavonic

eslip *(pl* eslips*) nm* men's briefs, underpants

eslogan *nm* slogan; **e. publicitario** advertising slogan

eslovaco, -a 1 *adj & nm,f* Slovak, Slovakian
2 *nm (idioma)* Slovak

Eslovaquia *n* Slovakia

Eslovenia *n* Slovenia

esloveno, -a 1 *adj & nm,f* Slovene
2 *nm (idioma)* Slovene

esmaltar *vt* to enamel

esmalte *nm* enamel; *(de uñas)* nail polish o varnish

esmerado, -a *adj* painstaking, careful

esmeralda *nf* emerald

esmerarse *vpr* to be careful; *(esforzarse)* to go to great lengths

esmero *nm* great care

esmoquin *nm Br* dinner jacket, *US* tuxedo

esnifar *vt Fam (drogas)* to sniff

esnob *(pl* esnobs*)* **1** *adj (persona)* snobbish; *(restaurante etc)* posh
2 *nmf* snob

esnobismo *nm* snobbery, snobbishness

ESO *nf (abr* **Enseñanza Secundaria Obligatoria)** = mainstream secondary education in Spain for pupils aged 12–16

eso *pron neut* that; **¡e. es!** that's it!; **por e.** that's why; *Fam* **a e. de las diez** around ten; *Fam* **e. de las Navidades sale muy caro** this whole Christmas thing costs a fortune

esófago *nm* oesophagus

esos, -as *adj dem pl ver* **ese**

ésos, -as *pron dem m,fpl ver* **ése**

esotérico, -a *adj* esoteric

espabilado, -a *adj* (a) *(despierto)* wide awake (b) *(niño)* bright

espabilar 1 *vt* to wake up
2 espabilarse *vpr* to wake up, to waken up

espachurrar *vt* to squash

espacial *adj* spatial; **nave e.** space ship

espaciar [43] *vt* to space out

espacio *nm* (a) *(lugar)* space; *(tiempo)* length; **a doble e.** double-spaced; **el e. (exterior)** (outer) space (b) *Rad & TV* programme

espacioso, -a *adj* spacious, roomy

espada 1 *nf* (a) *(arma)* sword; **estar entre la e. y la pared** to be between the devil and the deep blue sea; **pez e.** swordfish (b) *Naipes* **espadas** = suit in Spanish deck of cards, with the symbol of a sword
2 *nm Taurom* matador

> Observa que la palabra inglesa **spade** es un falso amigo y no es la traducción de la palabra española **espada**. En inglés, **spade** significa "pala".

espadaña nf bullrush

espaguetis nmpl spaghetti

espalda nf (a) Anat back; **espaldas** back; **a espaldas de algn** behind sb's back; **por la e.** from behind; **volver la e. a algn** to turn one's back on sb; Fam **e. mojada** wetback (b) (en natación) backstroke

espaldilla nf shoulder blade

espantapájaros nm inv scarecrow

espantar 1 vt (a) (asustar) to frighten, to scare (b) (ahuyentar) to frighten away
2 espantarse vpr to get o feel frightened (de of), to get o feel scared (de of)

espanto nm fright; Fam **de e.** dreadful, shocking

espantoso, -a adj dreadful

España n Spain

español, -a 1 adj Spanish
2 nm,f Spaniard; **los españoles** the Spanish
3 nm (idioma) Spanish

esparadrapo nm Br (sticking-)plaster, US Band-aid®

esparcimiento nm relaxation

esparcir [52] **1** vt (papeles, semillas) to scatter; Fig (rumor) to spread
2 esparcirse vpr (a) (papeles, semillas) to be scattered (b) (relajarse) to relax

espárrago nm asparagus

espartano, -a adj spartan

espasmo nm spasm

espátula nf Culin spatula; Arte palette knife; Téc stripping knife; (de albañil) trowel

especia nf spice

especial adj special; **en e.** especially; **e. para ...** suitable for ...

especialidad nf speciality, US specialty; Educ main subject

especialista nmf specialist

especializarse [40] vpr to specialize (en in)

especialmente adv (exclusivamente) specially; (muy) especially

especie nf (a) Biol species inv (b) (clase) kind; **una e. de salsa** a kind of sauce (c) Com **en e.** in kind

especificar [44] vt to specify

específico, -a adj specific; **peso e.** specific gravity

espécimen (pl **especímenes**) nm specimen

espectacular adj spectacular

espectáculo nm (a) (escena) spectacle, sight; Fam **dar un e.** to make a spectacle of oneself (b) Teatro, Cin & TV show; **montar un e.** to put on a show

espectador, -a nm,f Dep spectator; (de accidente) onlooker; Teatro & Cin member of the audience; **los espectadores** the audience; TV the viewers

espectro nm (a) Fís spectrum (b) (fantasma) spectre (c) (gama) range

especulación nf speculation; **e. del suelo** land speculation

especulador, -a nm,f Fin speculator

especular vi to speculate

especulativo, -a adj speculative

espejismo nm mirage

espejo nm mirror; Aut **e. retrovisor** rearview mirror

espeleología nf potholing, speleology

espeluznante adj hair-raising, horrifying

espera nf wait; **en e. de ...** waiting for ...; **a la e. de** expecting; **sala de e.** waiting room

esperanza nf hope; **tener la e. puesta en algo** to have one's hopes pinned on sth; **e. de vida** life expectancy; **en estado de buena e.** expecting, pregnant

esperanzador, -a adj encouraging

esperanzar [40] vt to give hope to

esperar 1 vi (a) (aguardar) to wait (b) (tener esperanza de) to hope
2 vt (a) (aguardar) to wait for; **espero a mi hermano** I'm waiting for my brother (b) (tener esperanza de) to hope for; **espero que sí** I hope so; **espero que vengas** I hope you'll come (c) (estar a la espera de) to expect; **te esperábamos ayer** we were expecting you yesterday (d) Fig (bebé) to be expecting

esperma nm sperm

espermatozoide nm spermatozoid

espermicida nm spermicide

esperpéntico, -a adj grotesque

espesar 1 vt to thicken
2 espesarse vpr to thicken, to get thicker

espeso, -a adj (bosque, niebla) dense; (líquido) thick; (masa) stiff

espesor nm thickness; **3 m de e.** 3 m thick

espesura nf denseness

espetar vt (palabras) to blurt out, to tell straight out

espía nmf spy

espiar [29] **1** vi to spy
2 vt to spy on

espichar vi Fam **espichar(la)** (morir) to kick the bucket

espiga nf (a) (de trigo) ear (b) Téc pin

espigado, -a adj slender

espina nf (a) Bot thorn (b) (de pescado) bone (c) Anat **e. dorsal** spinal column, spine (d) Fig **ése me da mala e.** there's something fishy about that one

espinaca *nf* spinach

espinal *adj* spinal; **médula e.** spinal marrow

espinazo *nm* spine, backbone

espinilla *nf* (**a**) *Anat* shin (**b**) *(en la piel)* spot

espinillera *nf Dep* shin pad

espino *nm* hawthorn; **alambre de e.** barbed wire

espionaje *nm* spying, espionage; **novela de e.** spy story

espiral *adj & nf* spiral

espirar *vi* to breathe out, to exhale

espiritismo *nm* spiritualism

espíritu *nm* (**a**) *(mente, actitud)* spirit; **e. deportivo** sportsmanship (**b**) *Rel (alma)* soul; **el E. Santo** the Holy Ghost

espiritual *adj* spiritual

espléndido, -a *adj* (**a**) *(magnífico)* splendid (**b**) *(generoso)* lavish, generous

esplendor *nm* splendour

esplendoroso, -a *adj* magnificent

espliego *nm* lavender

espolear *vt* to spur on

espolvorear *vt* to sprinkle (**de** with)

esponja *nf* sponge

esponjoso, -a *adj* spongy; *(bizcocho)* light

esponsales *nmpl* betrothal, engagement

espontaneidad *nf* spontaneity; **con e.** naturally

espontáneo, -a 1 *adj* spontaneous **2** *nm Taurom* = spectator who spontaneously joins in the bullfight

esporádico, -a *adj* sporadic

esposado, -a *adj* (**a**) *(recién casado)* newly married (**b**) *(con esposas)* handcuffed

esposar *vt* to handcuff

esposas *nfpl* handcuffs

esposo, -a *nm,f* spouse; *(hombre)* husband; *(mujer)* wife

espray (*pl* **esprays**) *nm* spray

esprint (*pl* **esprints**) *nm* sprint

esprintar *vi* to sprint

esprínter *nmf* sprinter

espuela *nf* spur

espuerta *nf* hod

espuma *nf* foam; *(de olas)* surf; *(de cerveza)* froth, head; *(de jabón)* lather; **e. de afeitar** shaving foam

espumoso, -a *adj* frothy; *(vino)* sparkling

esputo *nm* spit

esquela *nf Esp* funeral notice *(in newspaper)*

esquelético, -a *adj* (**a**) *Anat* skeletal (**b**) *(flaco)* skinny

esqueleto *nm* (**a**) *(huesos)* skeleton (**b**) *Constr* framework

esquema *nm* diagram

esquemático, -a *adj (escueto)* schematic; *(con diagramas)* diagrammatic

esquematizar [40] *vt* (**a**) *(en forma de gráfico)* to draw a diagram of (**b**) *(resumir)* to outline

esquí (*pl* **esquíes** o **esquís**) *nm* (**a**) *(objeto)* ski (**b**) *(deporte)* skiing; **e. acuático** waterskiing

esquiador, -a *nm,f* skier

esquiar [29] *vi* to ski

esquilar *vt* to shear

esquimal *adj & nmf* Eskimo

esquina *nf* corner; *Dep* **saque de e.** corner (kick)

esquinazo *nm* **dar e. a algn** to give sb the slip

esquirla *nf* splinter

esquirol *nm Ind* blackleg, scab

esquivar *vt* *(a una persona)* to avoid; *(un golpe)* to dodge

esquivo, -a *adj* cold, aloof

esquizofrenia *nf* schizophrenia

esquizofrénico, -a *adj & nm,f* schizophrenic

esta *adj dem ver* **este²**

está *indic pres de* **estar**

ésta *pron dem f ver* **éste**

estabilidad *nf* stability

estabilizar [40] *vt* to stabilize

estable *adj* stable

establecer [33] **1** *vt* to establish; *(fundar)* to set up, to found; *(récord)* to set **2 establecerse** *vpr* to settle

establecimiento *nm* establishment

establo *nm* cow shed

estaca *nf* stake, post; *(de tienda de campaña)* peg

estacada *nf* fence; *Fig* **dejar a algn en la e.** to leave sb in the lurch

estación *nf* (**a**) *(edificio)* station; **e. de servicio** service station; **e. de esquí** ski resort (**b**) *(del año)* season

estacional *adj* seasonal

estacionamiento *nm Aut (acción)* parking; *(lugar) Br* car park, *US* parking lot

estacionar 1 *vt* to park **2 estacionarse** *vpr Am* to park

estacionario, -a *adj* stationary

estadía *nf Am* stay

estadio *nm* (**a**) *Dep* stadium (**b**) *(fase)* stage

estadista *nmf Pol (hombre)* statesman; *(mujer)* stateswoman

estadística *nf* statistics *sing*; **una e.** a statistic

estado *nm* (a) *Pol* state (b) *(situación)* state, condition; **en buen e.** in good condition; **estar en e.** to be pregnant; **e. de ánimo** state of mind; **e. civil** marital status; *Com* **e. de cuentas** statement of accounts; **e. de excepción** state of emergency; **e. de salud** condition, state of health (c) *Mil* **e. mayor** general staff (d) *(país, división territorial)* state; **Estados Unidos de América** United States of America

estadounidense 1 *adj* United States, American

2 *nmf* American

estafa *nf* swindle

estafador, -a *nm,f* swindler

estafar *vt* to swindle

estafeta *nf* **e. de Correos** sub-post office

estalactita *nf* stalactite

estalagmita *nf* stalagmite

estallar *vi* (a) *(bomba)* to explode, to go off; *(neumático)* to burst; *(guerra)* to break out; *Fig (de cólera etc)* to explode; **e. en sollozos** to burst into tears

estallido *nm (de bomba)* explosion; *(de guerra)* outbreak

estambre *nm Bot* stamen

Estambul *n* Istanbul

estamento *nm Hist* estate; *Fig (grupo)* group

estampa *nf* print, image

🖉 Observa que la palabra inglesa **stamp** es un falso amigo y no es la traducción de la palabra española **estampa**. En inglés, **stamp** significa "sello, tampón".

estampado, -a 1 *adj (tela)* printed

2 *nm* (a) *(tela)* print (b) *(proceso)* printing

estampar *vt* (a) *(tela)* to print (b) *(dejar impreso)* to imprint (c) *(bofetada, beso)* to plant, to place

estampida *nf* (a) *(estampido)* bang (b) *(carrera rápida)* stampede; **de e.** suddenly

estampido *nm* bang

estampilla *nf Am* (postage) stamp

estancado, -a *adj (agua)* stagnant; *Fig* static, at a standstill; **quedarse e.** to get bogged down *o* stuck

estancar [44] **1** *vt* (a) *(agua)* to hold back (b) *Fig (asunto)* to block; *(negociaciones)* to bring to a standstill

2 estancarse *upr* to stagnate; *Fig* to get bogged down

estancia *nf* (a) *Esp, Méx (tiempo)* stay (b) *(habitación)* room (c) *CSur (hacienda)* ranch, farm

estanciero, -a *nm,f CSur* ranch owner, rancher

estanco, -a 1 *nm Esp* tobacconist's

2 *adj* watertight

estándar *adj & nm* standard

estandarizar [40] *vt* to standardize

estandarte *nm* standard, banner

estanque *nm* pool, pond

estanquero, -a *nm,f* tobacconist

estante *nm* shelf; *(para libros)* bookcase

estantería *nf* shelves, shelving

estaño *nm* tin

estar [13] **1** *vi* (a) to be; **está en la playa** he is at the beach; **e. en casa** to be in, to be at home; **estamos en Caracas** we are in Caracas; **¿está tu madre?** is your mother in?; **¿cómo estás?** how are you?; **los precios están bajos** prices are low; **el problema está en el dinero** the problem is money; **e. en lo cierto** to be right; **e. en todo** not to miss a trick

(b) *(+ adj)* to be; **está cansado/enfermo** he's tired/ill; **está vacío** it's empty

(c) *(+ adv)* to be; **está bien/mal** it's all right/wrong; **e. mal de dinero** he's short of money; **estará enseguida** it'll be ready in a minute

(d) *(+ ger)* to be; **está escribiendo** she is writing; **estaba comiendo** he was eating

(e) *(+ a + fecha)* to be; **¿a cuántos estamos?** what's the date (today)?; **estamos a 2 de Noviembre** it is the 2nd of November

(f) *(+ precio)* to be at; **están a dos euros el kilo** they're two euros a kilo

(g) *(locuciones)* **e. al caer** to be just round the corner; **¿estamos?** OK?

(h) *(+ de)* **e. de más** not to be needed; **e. de paseo** to be out for a walk; **e. de vacaciones/viaje** to be (away) on holiday/ a trip; **estoy de jefe hoy** I'm the boss today

(i) *(+ para)* **estará para las seis** it will be finished by six; **hoy no estoy para bromas** I'm in no mood for jokes today; **el tren está para salir** the train is just about to leave

(j) *(+ por)* **está por hacer** it has still to be done; **eso está por ver** it remains to be seen; **estoy por esperar** *(a favor de)* I'm for waiting

(k) *(+ con)* to have; **e. con la gripe** to have the flu, to be down with flu; **estoy con Jaime** *(de acuerdo con)* I agree with Jaime

(l) *(+ sin)* to have no; **e. sin luz/agua** to have no light/water

(m) *(+ que)* **está que se duerme** he is nearly asleep; *Fam* **está que rabia** he's hopping mad

2 estarse *upr* ¡estáte quieto! keep still!, stop fidgeting!

estárter (*pl* **estárters**) *nm* choke

estatal *adj* state; **enseñanza e.** state education

estático, -a *adj* static

estatua *nf* statue

estatura *nf* (a) (*altura*) height; **¿cuál es tu e.?** how tall are you? (b) (*renombre*) stature

estatus *nm inv* status; **e. quo** status quo

estatutario, -a *adj* statutory

estatuto *nm Der* statute; (*de ciudad*) bylaw; (*de empresa etc*) rules

este¹ **1** *adj* eastern; (*dirección*) easterly
2 *nm* east; **al e. de** to the east of

este², -a (*pl* **estos, -as**) *adj dem* (a) (*singular*) this (b) **estos, -as** these

esté *subj pres de* **estar**

éste, -a (*pl* **éstos, -as**) *pron dem m,f* (a) (*singular*) this one; **aquél … é.** the former … the latter (b) **éstos, -as** these (ones); **aquéllos … é.** the former … the latter

> Note that **éste** and its various forms can be written without an accent when there is no risk of confusion with the adjective.

estela *nf* (*de barco*) wake; (*de avión*) vapour trail; (*de cometa*) tail

estelar *adj* (a) *Astron* stellar (b) *Fig Cin & Teatro* star

estentóreo, -a *adj* stentorian, thundering

estepa *nf* steppe

estera *nf* rush mat

estercolero *nm* dunghill

estéreo *nm & adj* stereo

estereofónico, -a *adj* stereophonic, stereo

estereotipar *vt* to stereotype

estereotipo *nm* stereotype

estéril *adj* (a) (*persona*) sterile (b) *Fig* (*esfuerzo*) futile

esterilidad *nf* sterility

esterilizar [40] *vt* to sterilize

esterilla *nf* small mat

esterlina *adj* sterling; **libra e.** pound (sterling)

esternón *nm* sternum, breastbone

estero *nm* (a) (*pantano*) *Am* marsh, swamp (b) *Ven* (*charca*) puddle, pool (c) *Chile* (*arroyo*) stream

estertor *nm* death rattle

estética *nf* aesthetics *sing*

esteticienne *nf* beautician

estético, -a *adj* aesthetic; **cirugía estética** plastic surgery

estibador *nm* docker, stevedore

estiércol *nm* manure, dung

estigma *nm* stigma; *Rel* stigmata

estilarse *upr* to be in vogue, to be fashionable

estilete *nm* (*punzón*) stylus; (*puñal*) stiletto

estilístico, -a *adj* stylistic

estilizar [40] *vt* to stylize

estilo *nm* (a) style; **algo por el e.** something like that; **e. de vida** way of life (b) (*en natación*) stroke (c) *Ling* **e. directo/indirecto** direct/indirect speech

estilográfica *nf* (**pluma**) **e.** fountain pen

estima *nf* esteem, respect

estimación *nf* (a) (*estima*) esteem, respect (b) (*valoración*) evaluation; (*cálculo aproximado*) estimate

estimado, -a *adj* esteemed, respected; **E. Señor** (*en carta*) Dear Sir

estimar *vt* (a) (*apreciar*) to esteem (b) (*considerar*) to consider, to think; **lo estimo conveniente** I think it appropriate (c) (*valorar*) to value

estimativo, -a *adj* approximate, estimated

estimulante **1** *adj* stimulating
2 *nm* stimulant

estimular *vt* to stimulate; *Fig* to encourage

estímulo *nm Biol & Fís* stimulus; *Fig* encouragement

estío *nm* summer

estipendio *nm* stipend, fee

estipular *vt* to stipulate

estirado, -a *adj Fig* stiff

estirar **1** *vt* to stretch; *Fig* (*dinero*) to spin out; *Fig* **e. la pata** to kick the bucket
2 estirarse *upr* to stretch

estirón *nm* **dar** *o* **pegar un e.** to shoot up *o* grow quickly

estirpe *nf* stock, pedigree

estival *adj* summer; **época e.** summertime

esto *pron neut* this, this thing, this matter; *Fam* **e. de la fiesta** this business about the party

estocada *nf Taurom* stab

Estocolmo *n* Stockholm

estofado *nm* stew

estoicismo *nm* stoicism

estoico, -a **1** *adj* stoical
2 *nm,f* stoic

estómago *nm* stomach; **dolor de e.** stomach ache

Estonia *n* Estonia

estonio, -a **1** *adj & nm,f* Estonian
2 *nm* (*idioma*) Estonian

estoque *nm Taurom* sword

estorbar 1 *vt* (**a**) *(dificultar)* to hinder, to get in the way of (**b**) *(molestar)* to disturb

  2 *vi* to be in the way

estorbo *nm* (**a**) *(obstáculo)* obstruction, obstacle (**b**) *(molestia)* nuisance

estornino *nm* starling

estornudar *vi* to sneeze

estornudo *nm* sneeze

estos, -as *adj dem pl ver* **este**

éstos, -as *pron dem m,fpl ver* **éste**

estoy *indic pres de* **estar**

estrabismo *nm* squint

estrado *nm* platform; *Mús* bandstand; *Der* stand

estrafalario, -a *adj Fam* outlandish

estragos *nmpl* **hacer e. en** to wreak havoc with o on

estrambótico, -a *adj Fam* outlandish, eccentric

estrangulador, -a *nm,f* strangler

estrangular *vt* to strangle; *Med* to strangulate

estraperlo *nm* black market

Estrasburgo *n* Strasbourg

estratagema *nf Mil* stratagem; *Fam* trick, ruse

estratega *nmf* strategist

estrategia *nf* strategy

estratégico, -a *adj* strategic

estratificar [44] *vt* to stratify

estrato *nm* stratum

estraza *nf* **papel de e.** brown paper

estrechamente *adv* *(íntimamente)* closely, intimately; **e. relacionados** closely related

estrechamiento *nm* (**a**) *(de calle, tubo)* narrowing (**b**) *(de relaciones entre países)* rapprochement

estrechar 1 *vt* (**a**) *(hacer estrecho)* to narrow; *(ropa)* to take in (**b**) *(mano)* to shake; *(lazos de amistad)* to tighten; **me estrechó entre sus brazos** he hugged me

  2 estrecharse *vpr* to narrow, to become narrower

  ⊘ Observa que el verbo inglés **to stretch** es un falso amigo y no es la traducción del verbo español **estrechar**. En inglés, **to stretch** significa "estirar, desplegar".

estrechez *nf* (**a**) *(falta de anchura)* narrowness; **e. de miras** narrow-mindedness (**b**) *(dificultad económica)* **pasar estrecheces** to be hard up

estrecho, -a 1 *adj* (**a**) narrow; *(ropa, zapato)* tight; *(amistad, relación)* close, intimate (**b**) *Fig* **e. de miras** narrow-minded

  2 *nm Geog* strait, straits

estrella *nf* star; **e. de cine** movie o *Br* film star; *Zool* **e. de mar** starfish; **e. fugaz** shooting star

estrellado, -a *adj* (**a**) *(en forma de estrella)* star-shaped (**b**) *(cielo)* starry (**c**) *(huevos)* scrambled

estrellar 1 *vt Fam* to smash

  2 estrellarse *vpr* *(morir)* to die in a car crash; *Aut & Av* **estrellarse contra** *(chocar)* to crash into

estrellato *nm* stardom

estremecedor, -a *adj* bloodcurdling

estremecer [33] **1** *vt* to shake

  2 estremecerse *vpr* *(de horror, miedo)* to tremble, to shudder (**de** with); *(de frío)* to shiver (**de** with)

estrenar *vt* (**a**) *(objeto)* to use for the first time; *(ropa)* to wear for the first time (**b**) *Teatro & Cin* to premiere

estreno *nm Teatro* first performance; *Cin* premiere

estreñido, -a *adj* constipated

estreñimiento *nm* constipation

estrépito *nm* din, racket

estrepitoso, -a *adj* deafening; *Fig (fracaso)* spectacular

estrés *nm inv* stress

estresado, -a *adj (persona)* stressed

estresante *adj* stressful

estría *nf* (**a**) *(en la piel)* stretch mark (**b**) *Arquit* flute, fluting

estribar *vi* **e. en** to lie in, to be based on

estribillo *nm (en canción)* chorus; *(en poema)* refrain

estribo *nm* (**a**) *(de montura)* stirrup; *Fig* **perder los estribos** to lose one's temper, to lose one's head (**b**) *Arquit* buttress; *(de puente)* pier, support

estribor *nm* starboard

estricto, -a *adj* strict

estridente *adj* strident

estrofa *nf* verse

estropajo *nm* scourer

estropeado, -a *adj* (**a**) *(averiado)* broken (**b**) *(dañado)* damaged (**c**) *(echado a perder)* ruined, spoiled

estropear 1 *vt (averiar)* to break; *(dañar)* to damage; *(echar a perder)* to ruin, to spoil

  2 estropearse *vpr (máquina)* to break down; *(comida)* to go off, to spoil

estropicio *nm* **hacer** o **causar un e.** to wreak havoc

estructura nf structure; (armazón) frame, framework

estructurar vt to structure

estruendo nm roar

estrujar 1 vt (limón etc) to squeeze; (ropa) to wring; (apretar) to crush
2 estrujarse vpr Fam **e. los sesos** o **el cerebro** to rack one's brains

estuario nm estuary

estuche nm case; (para lápices) pencil case

estuco nm stucco

estudiante nmf student

estudiantil adj student

estudiar [43] vt & vi to study

estudio nm (**a**) (actividad) study; (encuesta) survey; Com **e. de mercado** market research (**b**) **estudios** (educación) studies (**c**) (de fotógrafo, pintor) studio; **e. cinematográfico/de grabación** film/recording studio (**d**) (oficina) study; (apartamento) studio Br flat o US apartment

estudioso, -a 1 adj studious
2 nm,f specialist

estufa nf (calentador) heater, Br fire; Méx (cocina) stove

estupefaciente nm drug, narcotic

estupefacto, -a adj astounded, flabbergasted

estupendamente adv wonderfully

estupendo, -a adj wonderful, marvellous; ¡e.! great!

estupidez nf stupidity

estúpido, -a 1 adj stupid
2 nm,f idiot

estupor nm amazement, astonishment

estuve pt indef de estar

esvástica nf swastika

etapa nf stage; **por etapas** in stages

etarra nmf = member of ETA, terrorist Basque separatist organization

etc. (abr etcétera) etc

etcétera adv etcetera

éter nm ether

etéreo, -a adj ethereal

eternidad nf eternity; Fam **una e.** ages

eterno, -a adj eternal

ética nf ethic; (ciencia) ethics sing

ético, -a adj ethical

etílico, -a adj ethylic; **alcohol e.** ethyl alcohol; **en estado e.** intoxicated; **intoxicación etílica** alcohol poisoning

etimología nf etymology

etimológico, -a adj etymological

etíope, etíope adj & nmf Ethiopian

Etiopía nf Ethiopia

etiqueta nf (**a**) (de producto) label (**b**) (ceremonia) etiquette; **de e.** formal

etiquetar vt to label

etnia nf ethnic group

étnico, -a adj ethnic

ETT nf (abr **Empresa de Trabajo Temporal**) temping agency

eucalipto nm eucalyptus

eucaristía nf eucharist

eufemismo nm euphemism

euforia nf euphoria

eufórico, -a adj euphoric

eureka interj eureka!

euro nm (moneda) euro

Eurocámara nf European Parliament

eurodiputado, -a nm,f Euro MP

Europa n Europe

europeísmo nm Europeanism

europeizar [40] vt to europeanize

europeo, -a adj & nm,f European

Euskadi n the Basque Country

euskera adj & nm Basque

eutanasia nf euthanasia

evacuación nf evacuation

evacuar [47] vt to evacuate

evadir 1 vt (respuesta, peligro, impuestos) to avoid; (responsabilidad) to shirk
2 evadirse vpr to escape

evaluación nf evaluation; Educ assessment; **e. continua** continuous assessment

evaluar [30] vt to evaluate, to assess

evangélico, -a adj evangelical

evangelio nm gospel

evangelista nm evangelist

evangelización nf evangelization, evangelizing

evaporación nf evaporation

evaporar 1 vt to evaporate
2 evaporarse vpr to evaporate; Fig to vanish

evasión nf (fuga) escape; Fig evasion; **e. fiscal** o **de impuestos** tax evasion

evasiva nf evasive answer

evasivo, -a adj evasive

evento nm (**a**) (acontecimiento) event (**b**) (incidente) contingency, unforeseen event

eventual adj (**a**) (posible) possible; (gastos) incidental (**b**) (trabajo, obrero) casual, temporary

eventualidad nf contingency

eventualmente adv by chance; **los problemas que e. surjan** such problems as may arise

✒ Observa que las palabras inglesas **eventual** y **eventually** son falsos amigos y no son la traducción de las palabras españolas **eventual** y **eventualmente**. En inglés, **eventual** significa "final" o "consiguiente" y **eventually** "finalmente".

evidencia *nf* obviousness; **poner a algn en e.** to show sb up

evidenciar [43] *vt* to show, to demonstrate

evidente *adj* obvious

evidentemente *adv* obviously

evitar *vt* to avoid; *(prevenir)* to prevent; *(desastre)* to avert

evocador, -a *adj* evocative

evocar [44] *vt (traer a la memoria)* to evoke; *(acordarse de)* to recall

evolución *nf* evolution; *(desarrollo)* development

evolucionar *vi* to develop; *Biol* to evolve; **el enfermo evoluciona favorablemente** the patient is improving

ex 1 *pref* former, ex-; **ex alumno** former pupil, ex-student; **ex combatiente** *Br* ex-serviceman, *f* ex-servicewoman, *US* (war) veteran; **ex marido** ex-husband
2 *nmf Fam* **mi ex** my ex

exabrupto *nm* sharp comment

exacerbar 1 *vt* (a) *(agravar)* to exacerbate, to aggravate (b) *(irritar)* to exasperate, to irritate
2 exacerbarse *vpr* (a) *(agravarse)* to get worse (b) *(irritarse)* to feel exasperated

exactamente *adv* exactly, precisely

exactitud *nf* accuracy; **con e.** precisely

exacto, -a *adj* exact; **¡e.!** precisely!; **para ser e.** to be precise

exageración *nf* exaggeration

exagerado, -a *adj* exaggerated; *(excesivo)* excessive

exagerar 1 *vt* to exaggerate
2 *vi* to overdo it

exaltado, -a 1 *adj* excitable, hot-headed
2 *nm,f* fanatic

exaltar 1 *vt (ensalzar)* to praise, to extol
2 exaltarse *vpr (acalorarse)* to get overexcited, to get carried away

examen *nm* examination, exam; *Esp* **e. de conducir** driving test; *Am* **e. de manejar** driving test; *Med* **e. médico** checkup

examinador, -a *nm,f* examiner

examinar 1 *vt* to examine
2 examinarse *vpr Esp* to take *o* sit an examination

exasperante *adj* exasperating

exasperar 1 *vt* to exasperate
2 exasperarse *vpr* to become exasperated

Exc., Exca., Exc.ª *(abr* **Excelencia)** Excellency

excavación *nf* excavation; *(en arqueología)* dig

excavadora *nf* digger

excavar *vt* to excavate, to dig

excedencia *nf Esp* leave (of absence)

excedente *adj & nm* excess, surplus

exceder 1 *vt* to exceed, to surpass
2 excederse *vpr* to go too far

excelencia *nf* (a) *(cualidad)* excellence; **por e.** par excellence (b) *(título)* **Su E.** His/Her Excellency

excelente *adj* excellent

excelso, -a *adj* sublime, lofty

excentricidad *nf* eccentricity

excéntrico, -a *adj* eccentric

excepción *nf* exception; **a e. de** with the exception of, except for; **de e.** exceptional; *Pol* **estado de e.** state of emergency

excepcional *adj* exceptional

excepto *adv* except (for), apart from

exceptuar [30] *vt* to except, to exclude

excesivo, -a *adj* excessive

exceso *nm* excess; **en e.** in excess, excessively; **e. de equipaje** excess baggage; **e. de velocidad** speeding

excitable *adj* excitable

excitación *nf (sentimiento)* excitement

excitante 1 *adj* exciting; *Med* stimulating
2 *nm* stimulant

excitar 1 *vt* to excite
2 excitarse *vpr* to get excited

exclamación *nf* exclamation

exclamar *vt & vi* to exclaim, to cry out

excluir [37] *vt (dejar fuera)* to exclude (**de** from); *(opción)* to rule out; *(hacer imposible)* to preclude

exclusión *nf* exclusion

exclusiva *nf Prensa* exclusive; *Com* sole right

exclusive *adv (en fechas)* exclusive

exclusivo, -a *adj* exclusive

Excma. *(abr* **Excelentísima)** Most Excellent

Excmo. *(abr* **Excelentísimo)** Most Excellent

excomulgar [42] *vt* to excommunicate

excomunión *nf* excommunication

excremento *nm* excrement

exculpar *vt* to exonerate

excursión *nf* excursion

excursionista *nmf* tripper; *(a pie)* hiker

excusa nf (pretexto) excuse; (disculpa) apology

excusado nm (retrete) toilet

excusar 1 vt (a) (justificar) to excuse (b) (eximir) to exempt (**de** from)
2 excusarse upr (disculparse) to apologize

execrar vt to execrate, to abhor

exención nf exemption; **e. de impuestos** tax exemption

exento, -a adj exempt, free (**de** from)

exequias nfpl funeral rites

exhalar vt to exhale, to breathe out; (gas) to give off, to emit; (suspiro) to heave

exhaustivo, -a adj exhaustive

exhausto, -a adj exhausted

exhibición nf exhibition

exhibicionista nmf exhibitionist

exhibir 1 vt (a) (mostrar) to exhibit, to display (b) (lucir) to show off
2 exhibirse upr to show off, to make an exhibition of oneself

exhortar vt to exhort

exhumar vt to exhume

exigencia nf (a) (petición) demand (b) (requisito) requirement

exigente adj demanding, exacting

exigir [57] vt to demand

exiguo, -a adj minute

exilado, -a 1 adj exiled, in exile
2 nm,f exile

exilar 1 vt to exile
2 exilarse upr to go into exile

exiliado, -a adj & nm,f = **exilado**

exiliar [43] vt = **exilar**

exilio nm exile

eximio, -a adj distinguished, eminent

eximir vt to exempt (**de** from)

existencia nf (a) (vida) existence (b) Com **existencias** stock, stocks

existente adj existing; Com in stock

existir vi to exist, to be (in existence)

éxito nm success; **con é.** successfully; **tener é.** to be successful

---

ℓ Observa que la palabra inglesa **exit** es un falso amigo y no es la traducción de la palabra española **éxito**. En inglés, **exit** significa "salida".

---

exitoso, -a adj successful

éxodo nm exodus

exonerar vt to exonerate

exorbitante adj exorbitant, excessive

exorcista nmf exorcist

exorcizar [40] vt to exorcize

exótico, -a adj exotic

expandir 1 vt to expand
2 expandirse upr to expand

expansión nf (a) (de gas, empresa) expansion (b) (relajación) relaxation; (diversión) recreation

expansionarse upr (divertirse) to relax, to unwind; (divertirse) to have some fun o recreation

expatriado, -a adj & nm,f expatriate

expatriar [29] **1** vt to exile, to banish
2 expatriarse upr to leave one's country

expectación nf expectancy, anticipation

expectativa nf **estar a la e. de** to be on the lookout for

expectorante nm expectorant

expedición nf expedition

expedientar vt to place under enquiry

expediente nm (a) (informe) dossier, record; (ficha) file; Educ **e. académico** academic record, US transcript; **abrirle e. a algn** to place sb under enquiry (b) Der proceedings, action

expedir [6] vt (a) (carta) to send, to dispatch (b) (pasaporte etc) to issue

expedito, -a adj free, clear

expendedor, -a 1 nm,f seller
2 nm **e. automático** vending machine

expendeduría nf Br tobacconist's, US cigar store

expensas nfpl **a e. de** at the expense of

experiencia nf (a) (vivencia) experience; **por e.** from experience (b) (experimento) experiment

experimentado, -a adj experienced

experimental adj experimental

experimentar 1 vi to experiment
2 vt to undergo; (aumento) to show; (pérdida) to suffer; (sensación) to experience, to feel; Med **e. una mejoría** to improve, to make progress

experimento nm experiment

experto, -a nm,f expert

expiar [29] vt to expiate, to atone for

expirar vi to expire

explanada nf esplanade

explayarse upr to talk at length (about)

explicación nf explanation

explicar [44] **1** vt to explain
2 explicarse upr (persona) to explain (oneself); **no me lo explico** I can't understand it

explicativo, -a adj explanatory

explícito, -a adj explicit

exploración nf exploration; Med (interna) exploration; (externa) examination; Téc scanning; Mil reconnaissance

explorador, -a nm,f explorer

explorar *vt* to explore; *Med (internamente)* to explore; *(externamente)* to examine; *Téc* to scan; *Mil* to reconnoitre

explosión *nf* explosion, blast; **hacer e.** to explode; **motor de e.** internal combustion engine; **e. demográfica** population explosion

explosionar *vt & vi* to explode, to blow up

explosivo, -a *adj & nm* explosive

explotación *nf* (a) *(abuso)* exploitation (b) *(uso)* exploitation, working; *Agr* cultivation (of land); *(granja)* farm

explotador, -a *nm,f* exploiter

explotar 1 *vi (bomba)* to explode, to go off
2 *vt* (a) *(aprovechar)* to exploit; *(recursos)* to tap; *(tierra)* to cultivate (b) *(abusar de)* to exploit

expoliar [43] *vt* to plunder, to pillage

exponente *nmf* exponent

exponer [19] *(pp* **expuesto)** **1** *vt* (a) *(mostrar)* to exhibit, to display (b) *(explicar)* to expound, to put forward (c) *(arriesgar)* to expose
2 exponerse *upr* to expose oneself (a to); **te expones a perder el trabajo** you run the risk of losing your job

exportación *nf* export

exportador, -a 1 *adj* exporting
2 *nm,f* exporter

exportar *vt* to export

exposición *nf* (a) *Arte* exhibition; **e. universal** international exposition *o* exhibition, *US* world's fair; **sala de exposiciones** gallery (b) *(de hechos, ideas)* exposé (c) *Fot* exposure

expositor, -a 1 *adj* exponent
2 *nm,f (en feria)* exhibitor; *(de teoría)* exponent

exprés *adj* express; **(olla) e.** pressure cooker; **(café) e.** espresso (coffee)

expresamente *adv* specifically, expressly

expresar 1 *vt* to express; *(manifestar)* to state
2 expresarse *upr* to express oneself

expresión *nf* expression; **la mínima e.** the bare minimum

expresivo, -a *adj* expressive

expreso, -a 1 *adj* express; **con el fin e. de** with the express purpose of
2 *nm Ferroc* express (train)
3 *adv* on purpose, deliberately

exprimidor *nm* squeezer, juicer

exprimir *vt (limón)* to squeeze; *(zumo)* to squeeze out; *Fig (persona)* to exploit, to bleed dry

expropiar [43] *vt* to expropriate

expuesto, -a 1 *adj* (a) *(sin protección)* exposed; **estar e. a** to be exposed to (b) *(peligroso)* risky, dangerous (c) *(exhibido)* on display, on show
2 *pp de* **exponer**

expulsar *vt* (a) *(de local, organización)* to throw out; *(de clase)* to send out; *(de colegio, organización)* to expel; *Dep (jugador)* to send off (b) *(humo)* to emit, to give off; *(objeto, sustancia)* to expel

expulsión *nf* expulsion; *Dep* sending off

expurgar [42] *vt* to expurgate; *Fig* to purge

expuse *pt indef de* **exponer**

exquisitez *nf* (a) *(cualidad)* exquisiteness (b) *(cosa)* exquisite thing; *(comida)* delicacy

exquisito, -a *adj* exquisite; *(comida)* delicious; *(gusto)* refined

extasiado, -a *adj* ecstatic; **quedarse e.** to go into ecstasies *o* raptures

extasiarse [29] *upr* to go into ecstasies *o* raptures

éxtasis *nm inv* ecstasy

extender [3] **1** *vt* (a) *(ampliar)* to extend (b) *(mantel, mapa)* to spread (out), to open (out); *(mano, brazo)* to stretch (out) (c) *(crema, mantequilla)* to spread (d) *(cheque)* to make out; *(documento)* to draw up; *(certificado)* to issue
2 extenderse *upr* (a) *(en el tiempo)* to extend, to last (b) *(en el espacio)* to spread out, to stretch (c) *(rumor, noticia)* to spread, to extend (d) *(hablar demasiado)* to go on

extendido, -a *adj* (a) *(mapa, plano)* spread out, open; *(mano, brazo)* outstretched (b) *(costumbre, rumor)* widespread

extensible *adj* extensible, extendible

extensión *nf (de libro etc)* length; *(de cuerpo)* size; *(de terreno)* area, expanse; *(edificio anexo)* extension; **en toda la e. de la palabra** in every sense of the word; **por e.** by extension

extensivo, -a *adj* **hacer e.** to extend; **ser e. a** to cover

extenso, -a *adj (terreno)* extensive; *(libro, película)* long

extenuar [30] **1** *vt* to exhaust
2 extenuarse *upr* to exhaust oneself

exterior 1 *adj* (a) *(de fuera)* outer; *(puerta)* outside (b) *(política, deuda)* foreign; *Pol* **Ministerio de Asuntos Exteriores** Ministry of Foreign Affairs, *Br* ≃ Foreign Office, *US* ≃ State Department
2 *nm* (a) *(parte de fuera)* exterior, outside (b) *(extranjero)* abroad (c) **exteriores** *Cin* location

exteriorizar [40] *vt* to show

exteriormente *adv* outwardly

exterminar *vt* to exterminate

exterminio *nm* extermination

externalización *nf Com* outsourcing

externalizar [40] *vt Com* to outsource

externo, -a 1 *adj* external; **de uso e.** *(medicamento)* for external use only
  2 *nm,f Educ* day pupil

extinción *nf* extinction

extinguir [59] **1** *vt (fuego)* to extinguish, to put out; *(raza)* to wipe out
  2 extinguirse *vpr (fuego)* to go out; *(especie)* to become extinct, to die out

extinto, -a *adj* extinct

extintor *nm Esp* fire extinguisher

extirpar *vt* (a) *Med* to remove (b) *Fig* to eradicate, to stamp out

extorsión *nf* extortion

extorsionar *vt* to extort

extra 1 *adj* (a) *(suplementario)* extra; **horas e.** overtime; **paga e.** bonus (b) *(superior)* top-quality
  2 *nm* extra
  3 *nmf Cin & Teatro* extra

extra- *pref* extra-; **extramatrimonial** extramarital

extracción *nf* extraction

extracto *nm* (a) *(resumen)* summary; *Fin* **e. de cuenta** statement of account (b) *(concentrado)* extract

extractor *nm* extractor

extradición *nf* extradition

extraer [25] *vt* to extract, to take out

extraescolar *adj* extracurricular

extrafino, -a *adj* superfine

extralimitarse *vpr* to overstep the mark

extranjería *nf* **ley de e.** law on aliens

extranjero, -a 1 *adj* foreign
  2 *nm,f* foreigner
  3 *nm* abroad; **en el e.** abroad

extrañar 1 *vt* (a) *(sorprender)* to surprise; **no es de e.** it's hardly surprising (b) *(echar de menos)* to miss
  2 extrañarse *vpr* **extrañarse de** to be surprised at

extrañeza *nf* (a) *(sorpresa)* surprise, astonishment (b) *(singularidad)* strangeness

extraño, -a 1 *adj* strange; *Med* **cuerpo e.** foreign body
  2 *nm,f* stranger

extraoficial *adj* unofficial

extraordinaria *nf (paga)* bonus

extraordinario, -a *adj* extraordinary; *Prensa* **edición extraordinaria** special edition

extrarradio *nm* outskirts, suburbs

extraterrestre *nmf* alien

extravagancia *nf* eccentricity

extravagante *adj* eccentric, outlandish

extravertido, -a *adj & nm,f* = **extrovertido**

extraviado, -a *adj* lost, missing

extraviar [29] **1** *vt* to mislay, to lose
  2 extraviarse *vpr* to be missing, to get mislaid

extremadamente *adv* extremely

extremado, -a *adj* extreme

Extremadura *n* Extremadura

extremar 1 *vt* **e. la prudencia** to be extremely careful
  2 extremarse *vpr* to take great pains, to do one's utmost

extremaunción *nf* extreme unction

extremeño, -a 1 *adj* of/from Extremadura
  2 *nm,f* person from Extremadura

extremidad *nf* (a) *(extremo)* end, tip (b) *Anat (miembro)* limb, extremity

extremista *adj & nmf* extremist

extremo, -a 1 *nm (de calle, cable)* end; *(máximo)* extreme; **en e.** very much; **en último e.** as a last resort
  2 *nm,f (en fútbol)* winger; **e. derecha/izquierda** outside right/left
  3 *adj* extreme; **E. Oriente** Far East

extrovertido, -a *adj & nm,f* extrovert

exuberante *adj* exuberant; *(vegetación)* lush, abundant

eyaculación *nf* ejaculation; **e. precoz** premature ejaculation

eyacular *vi* to ejaculate

eyectable *adj* **asiento e.** ejector seat

F, f ['efe] *nf (letra)* F, f

fa *nm Mús* F

fabada *nf* stew of beans, pork sausage and bacon

fábrica *nf* factory; **marca de f.** trademark; **precio de f.** factory *o* ex-works price

> Observa que la palabra inglesa **fabric** es un falso amigo y no es la traducción de la palabra española **fábrica**. En inglés **fabric** significa "tejido".

fabricación *nf* manufacture; **de f. casera** home-made; **de f. propia** our own make; **f. en cadena** mass production

fabricante *nmf* manufacturer

fabricar [44] *vt* (**a**) *Ind* to manufacture (**b**) *Fig (mentiras etc)* to fabricate

fabril *adj* manufacturing

fábula *nf* fable

fabuloso, -a *adj* fabulous

facción *nf* (**a**) *Pol* faction (**b**) **facciones** *(rasgos)* features

faceta *nf* facet

facha 1 *nf* (**a**) *(aspecto)* look (**b**) *(mamarracho)* mess; **vas hecho una f.** you look a mess

2 *nmf Esp Fam Pey (fascista)* fascist

fachada *nf* façade

facial *adj* facial

fácil *adj* (**a**) *(sencillo)* easy; **f. de comprender** easy to understand (**b**) *(probable)* likely, probable; **es f. que …** it's (quite) likely that …

facilidad *nf* (**a**) *(sencillez)* easiness (**b**) *(soltura)* ease (**c**) *(servicio)* facility; **dar facilidades** to make things easy; *Com* **facilidades de pago** easy terms (**d**) **f. para los idiomas** gift for languages

facilitar *vt (proporcionar)* to provide, to supply (**a** with)

fácilmente *adv* easily

facsímil, facsímile *nm* facsimile

factible *adj* feasible

fáctico, -a *adj* **los poderes fácticos** the powers that be, the forces of the establishment

factor *nm* factor

factoría *nf* factory

factura *nf* (**a**) *Com* invoice (**b**) *Arg (repostería)* cakes and pastries

facturación *nf* (**a**) *Com* invoicing (**b**) *(de equipajes) (en aeropuerto)* check-in; *(en estación)* registration

facturar *vt* (**a**) *Com* to invoice (**b**) *(en aeropuerto)* to check in; *(en estación)* to register

facultad *nf* faculty; **facultades mentales** faculties

facultativo, -a 1 *adj* optional

2 *nm,f* doctor

faena *nf* (**a**) *(tarea)* task (**b**) *Fam (mala pasada)* dirty trick (**c**) *Taurom* performance

faenar *vi* to fish

fagot *nm Mús* bassoon

fainá *nf Urug (plato)* = baked dough made from chickpea flour, served with pizza

faisán *nm* pheasant

faja *nf* (**a**) *(corsé)* girdle, corset (**b**) *(banda)* sash (**c**) *(de terreno)* strip

fajo *nm (de ropa etc)* bundle; *(de billetes)* wad

falacia *nf* fallacy

falange *nf* (**a**) *Anat & Mil* phalanx (**b**) *Pol* **la F. (Española)** the Falange

falaz *adj* (**a**) *(erróneo)* fallacious (**b**) *(engañoso)* deceitful

falda *nf* (**a**) *(prenda)* skirt; **f. pantalón** culottes (**b**) *(de montaña)* slope, hillside (**c**) *(de mesa)* cover (**d**) *(regazo)* lap

faldero, -a *adj* **perro f.** lapdog

falencia *nf* (**a**) *Am Com (bancarrota)* bankruptcy (**b**) *CSur (error)* fault

falla *nf* (**a**) *(defecto)* defect, fault; **este cajón tiene una f.** there's something wrong with this drawer (**b**) *Am (error)* mistake; **un trabajo lleno de fallas** a piece of work full of mistakes (**c**) *Geol* fault

fallar¹ 1 *vi Der* to rule

2 *vt (premio)* to award

fallar² 1 *vi* to fail; **le falló la puntería** he missed his aim; *Fig* **no me falles** don't let me down

2 *vt* to miss

fallecer [33] *vi Fml* to pass away, to die

fallecido, -a *adj* deceased

fallecimiento *nm* demise

fallido, -a *adj* unsuccessful, vain

fallo¹ *nm Esp* (a) *(error)* mistake; **f. humano** human error (b) *(del corazón, de los frenos)* failure

fallo² *nm* (a) *Der* judgement, sentence (b) *(en concurso)* awarding

falluto, -a *RP Fam* **1** *adj* phoney, hypocritical
2 *nm,f* hypocrite

falo *nm* phallus

falsear *vt (hechos, la verdad)* to distort; *(informe etc)* to falsify

falsedad *nf* (a) *(falta de verdad, autenticidad)* falseness (b) *(mentira)* falsehood

falsete *nm* falsetto; **voz de f.** falsetto voice

falsificar [44] *vt* to falsify; *(cuadro, firma, moneda)* to forge

falso, -a *adj* false; **dar un paso en f.** *(tropezar)* to trip, to stumble; *Fig* to make a blunder; **jurar en f.** to commit perjury (b) *(persona)* insincere

falta *nf* (a) *(carencia)* lack; **por f. de** for want o lack of; **sin f.** without fail; **f. de educación** bad manners (b) *(escasez)* shortage (c) *(ausencia)* absence; **echar algo/a algn en f.** to miss sth/sb (d) *(error)* mistake; *(defecto)* fault, defect; **f. de ortografía** spelling mistake; **sacar faltas a algo/a algn** to find fault with sth/sb (e) *Der* misdemeanour (f) *(en fútbol)* foul; *(en tenis)* fault (g) **hacer f.** to be necessary; **(nos) hace f. una escalera** we need a ladder; **harán f. dos personas para mover el piano** it'll take two people to move the piano; **no hace f. que ...** there is no need for ...

faltante *nm Am* deficit

faltar *vi* (a) *(no estar)* to be missing; **¿quién falta?** who is missing? (b) *(escasear)* to be lacking o needed; **le falta confianza en sí mismo** he lacks confidence in himself; **¡lo que me faltaba!** that's all I needed!; **¡no faltaría o faltaba más!** *(por supuesto)* (but) of course!
(c) *(quedar)* to be left; **¿cuántos kilómetros faltan para Managua?** how many kilometres is it to Managua?; **ya falta poco para las vacaciones** it won't be long now till the holidays; **faltó poco para que me cayera** I very nearly fell
(d) **f. a la verdad** not to tell the truth; **f. al deber** to fail in one's duty; **f. a su palabra/promesa** to break one's word/promise; **f. al respeto a algn** to treat sb with disrespect

falto, -a *adj* **f. de** lacking in

fama *nf* (a) *(renombre)* fame; **tener f.** to be famous o well-known (b) *(reputación)* reputation; **buena/mala f.** good/bad reputation

famélico, -a *adj* starving, famished

familia *nf* family; **estar en f.** to be among friends; **f. numerosa** large family

familiar 1 *adj* (a) *(de la familia)* family; **empresa f.** family business (b) *(conocido)* familiar
2 *nmf* relation, relative

familiaridad *nf* familiarity

familiarizarse [40] *vpr* **f. con** to familiarize oneself with

famoso, -a 1 *adj* famous
2 *nm, f* famous person, celebrity

fan *nmf* fan

fanático, -a 1 *adj* fanatical
2 *nm,f* fanatic

fanatismo *nm* fanaticism

fandango *nm (baile)* fandango

fanfarrón, -ona *Fam* **1** *adj* boastful
2 *nm,f* show-off

fanfarronear *vi Fam* to brag, to boast (**de** about)

fango *nm* (a) *(barro)* mud (b) *Fig* degradation

fantasear *vi* to fantasize

fantasía *nf* fantasy; **joya de f.** imitation jewellery

fantasioso, -a *adj* imaginative

fantasma *nm* (a) *(espectro)* ghost (b) *Esp Fam (fanfarrón)* braggart, show-off

fantasmal *adj* ghostly

fantástico, -a *adj* fantastic

fantoche *nm Pey* nincompoop, ninny

faraón *nm* Pharaoh

fardar *vi Esp Fam* **f. de algo** to show (sth) off

fardo *nm* bundle

farfullar *vt* to jabber

faringe *nf* pharynx

faringitis *nf inv* pharyngitis

fariseo, -a *nm,f Hist* Pharisee; *(falso)* hypocrite

farmacéutico, -a 1 *adj* pharmaceutical
2 *nm,f* pharmacist, *Br* chemist, *US* druggist

farmacia *nf* (a) *(tienda)* pharmacy, *Br* chemist's (shop), *US* drugstore (b) *(ciencia)* pharmacology

fármaco *nm* medicine, medication

faro *nm* (a) *(torre)* lighthouse (b) *(de coche)* headlight, headlamp

farol *nm* (a) *(en la calle)* streetlight, streetlamp; *(lámpara)* lantern (b) *Fam* *(fanfarronada)* bragging; **tirarse un f.** to brag (**c**) *(en naipes)* bluff

farola *nf* streetlight, streetlamp

farolillo *nm Fig* **ser el f. rojo** to bring up the rear

farragoso, -a *adj* confused, rambling

farruco, -a *adj* cocky

farsa *nf* farce

farsante *nmf* fake, impostor

fascículo *nm* instalment

fascinante *adj* fascinating

fascinar *vt* to fascinate

fascismo *nm* fascism

fascista *adj & nmf* fascist

fase *nf* (**a**) *(etapa)* phase, stage (**b**) *Elec & Fís* phase

fastidiado, -a *adj Esp Fam* (**a**) *(roto)* broken (**b**) *(enfermo)* sick; **tiene el estómago f.** he's got a bad stomach

fastidiar [43] **1** *vt* (**a**) *(molestar)* to annoy, to bother; *(dañar)* to hurt; *Fam* **¡no fastidies!** you're kidding! (**b**) *Esp Fam (estropear)* to damage, to ruin; *(planes)* to spoil
2 fastidiarse *vpr Esp (aguantarse)* to put up with it, to resign oneself; **que se fastidie** that's his tough luck (**b**) *Fam (estropearse)* to get damaged, to break down (**c**) **me he fastidiado el tobillo** I've hurt my ankle

fastidio *nm* nuisance

fastuoso, -a *adj (acto)* splendid, lavish

fatal 1 *adj* (**a**) *Esp Fam (muy malo)* terrible, awful (**b**) *(mortal)* deadly, fatal (**c**) *(inexorable)* fateful, inevitable
2 *adv Esp Fam* awfully, terribly; **lo pasó f.** he had a rotten time

fatalidad *nf* (**a**) *(destino)* fate (**b**) *(desgracia)* misfortune

> ⏀ Observa que la palabra inglesa **fatality** es un falso amigo y no es la traducción de la palabra española **fatalidad**. En inglés, **fatality** significa "víctima mortal".

fatalista 1 *adj* fatalistic
2 *nmf* fatalist

fatiga *nf* (**a**) *(cansancio)* fatigue (**b**) **fatigas** *(dificultades)* troubles, difficulties

fatigar [42] **1** *vt* to tire, to weary
2 fatigarse *vpr* to tire, to become tired

fatigoso, -a *adj* tiring, exhausting

fatuo, -a *adj* (**a**) *(envanecido)* conceited (**b**) *(necio)* fatuous, foolish

fauces *nfpl* jaws

fauna *nf* fauna

favor *nm* favour; **por f.** please; **¿puedes hacerme un f.?** can you do me a favour?;

estar a f. de to be in favour of; **haga el f. de sentarse** please sit down

favorable *adj* favourable; **f. a** in favour of

favorecedor, -a *adj* flattering

favorecer [33] *vt* (**a**) *(beneficiar)* to favour (**b**) *(sentar bien)* to flatter

favoritismo *nm* favouritism

favorito, -a *adj & nm,f* favourite

fax *nm* (**a**) *(aparato)* fax (machine); **mandar algo por f.** to fax sth (**b**) *(documento)* fax

fayuca *nf Méx Fam* contraband

faz *nf Fml* face

fe *nf* (**a**) *(creencia)* faith; **de buena/mala fe** with good/dishonest intentions (**b**) *(certificado)* certificate; **fe de bautismo/ matrimonio** baptism/marriage certificate (**c**) *Impr* **fe de erratas** errata

fealdad *nf* ugliness

febrero *nm* February

febril *adj* (**a**) *Med* feverish (**b**) *(actividad)* hectic

fecha *nf* date; **f. límite** *o* **tope** deadline; **f. de caducidad** sell-by date; **hasta la f.** so far; **en f. próxima** at an early date; **el año pasado por estas fechas** this time last year

fechar *vt* to date

fechoría *nf* bad deed, misdemeanour

fécula *nf* starch

fecundación *nf* fertilization; **f. in vitro** in vitro fertilization

fecundar *vt* to fertilize

fecundo, -a *adj* fertile

federación *nf* federation

federal *adj & nmf* federal

fehaciente *adj* irrefutable

felicidad *nf* happiness; **(muchas) felicidades** *(en cumpleaños)* many happy returns

felicitación *nf* **tarjeta de f.** greetings card

felicitar *vt* to congratulate (**por** on); **¡te felicito!** congratulations!

feligrés, -esa *nm,f* parishioner

felino, -a *adj & nm* feline

feliz *adj* (**a**) *(contento)* happy; **¡felices Navidades!** Happy *o* Merry Christmas! (**b**) *(decisión etc)* fortunate

felpa *nf Tex* plush

felpudo *nm* mat, doormat

femenino, -a *adj* (**a**) *(de mujer)* women's; *(sexo, órganos sexuales)* female; **un toque f.** a woman's touch (**b**) *(de la feminidad)* feminine

feminismo *nm* feminism

feminista *adj & nmf* feminist

fémur *nm* femur

fenecer [33] *vi Fml* to pass away, to die

fenomenal 1 *adj* (a) *(magnífico)* great, fantastic (b) *(enorme)* phenomenal
2 *adv Fam* wonderfully, marvellously; **lo pasamos f.** we had a fantastic time

fenómeno, -a 1 *nm* (a) *(suceso)* phenomenon (b) *(prodigio)* genius (c) *(monstruo)* freak
2 *adj Fam* fantastic, terrific
3 *interj* fantastic!, terrific!

feo, -a 1 *adj* ugly; *(asunto etc)* nasty
2 *nm Fam* **hacerle un f. a algn** to offend sb

féretro *nm* coffin

feria *nf* fair; **f. de muestras/del libro** trade/book fair

feriado, -a *Am* **1** *adj* **día f.** (public) holiday
2 *nm* (public) holiday

ferial *adj* **recinto f.** *(de exposiciones)* exhibition centre; *(de fiestas)* fairground

fermentación *nf* fermentation

fermentar *vi* to ferment

fermento *nm* ferment

ferocidad *nf* ferocity, fierceness

feroz *adj* fierce, ferocious; **el lobo f.** the big bad wolf

férreo, -a *adj* iron

ferretería *nf Br* ironmonger's (shop), *US* hardware store

ferrocarril *nm Br* railway, *US* railroad

ferroviario, -a *adj* rail(way), *US* railroad

ferry *(pl* **ferrys** *o* **ferries)** *nm* ferry

fértil *adj* fertile

fertilidad *nf* fertility

fertilizante 1 *adj* fertilizing
2 *nm* fertilizer

fertilizar [40] *vt* to fertilize

ferviente *adj* fervent

fervor *nm* fervour

fervoroso, -a *adj* fervent

festejar *vt* to celebrate

festejos *nmpl* festivities

festín *nm* feast, banquet

festival *nm* festival

festividad *nf* festivity

festivo, -a 1 *adj* (a) *(ambiente etc)* festive (b) **día f.** holiday
2 *nm* holiday

feta *nf RP* slice

fetal *adj* foetal

fetiche *nm* fetish

fétido, -a *adj* stinking, fetid

feto *nm* foetus

feudalismo *nm* feudalism

feudo *nm* fief; *Pol* stronghold

fiabilidad *nf* reliability, trustworthiness

fiable *adj* reliable, trustworthy

fiaca *nf CSur, Méx Fam (pereza)* laziness; **¡qué f. tener que ponerme a planchar!** what a pain *o Br* fag having to do the ironing!

fiador, -a *nm,f* guarantor; **salir** *o* **ser f. de algn** *(pagar fianza)* to stand bail for sb; *(avalar)* to vouch for sb

fiambre *nm* (a) *Culin Br* cold meat, *US* cold cut (b) *Fam (cadáver)* stiff, corpse

fiambrera *nf* lunch box

fianza *nf (depósito)* deposit; *Der* bail; **en libertad bajo f.** on bail

fiar [29] **1** *vt* (a) *(avalar)* to guarantee (b) *(vender sin cobrar)* to sell on credit
2 fiarse *vpr* **fiarse (de)** to trust

fiasco *nm* fiasco

fibra *nf* fibre; *(de madera)* grain; **f. óptica** optical fibre; **f. de vidrio** fibreglass

ficción *nf* fiction

ficha *nf* (a) *(tarjeta)* filing card; **f. técnica** specifications, technical data; *Cin* credits (b) *(en juegos)* counter; *(de ajedrez)* piece, man; *(de dominó)* domino

fichado, -a *adj* **está f. por la policía** he has a police record

fichaje *nm Dep* signing

fichar 1 *vt* (a) *(archivar)* to put on file (b) *Dep* to sign up
2 *vi* (a) *(en el trabajo) (al entrar)* to clock in *o* on, *US* to punch in; *(al salir)* to clock out *o* off, *US* to punch out (b) *Dep* to sign

fichero *nm* card index

ficticio, -a *adj* fictitious

fidedigno, -a *adj* reliable, trustworthy; **fuentes fidedignas** reliable sources

fidelidad *nf* faithfulness; **alta f.** high fidelity, hi-fi

fideo *nm* noodle

fiebre *nf* fever; **tener f.** to have a temperature

fiel 1 *adj* (a) *(leal)* faithful, loyal (b) *(exacto)* accurate, exact
2 *nm* (a) *(de balanza)* needle, pointer (b) *Rel* **los fieles** the congregation

fieltro *nm* felt

fiera *nf* wild animal; *Fam* **estaba hecho una f.** he was hopping mad

fiero, -a *adj* *(salvaje)* wild; *(feroz)* fierce, ferocious

fierro *nm Am (hierro)* iron

fiesta *nf* (a) *(entre amigos)* party (b) **día de f.** holiday (c) *Rel* feast; **f. de guardar** holiday of obligation (d) *(festividad)* celebration, festivity

figura *nf* figure

figurado, -a *adj* figurative; **en sentido f.** figuratively

figurar 1 *vi (en lista)* to figure
  2 figurarse *vpr* to imagine, to suppose; **ya me lo figuraba** I thought as much; **¡figúrate!, ¡figúrese!** just imagine!

figurativo, -a *adj Arte* figurative

figurín *nm* fashion sketch; *Fig* **ir** *o* **estar hecho un f.** to be dressed up to the nines

figurinista *nmf Cin & Teatro* costume designer

fijador *nm* (a) *(gomina)* gel (b) *Fot* fixative

fijamente *adv* **mirar f.** to stare

fijar 1 *vt* to fix; **prohibido f. carteles** *(en letrero)* post no bills
  2 fijarse *vpr* (a) *(darse cuenta)* to notice (b) *(poner atención)* to pay attention, to watch

fijo, -a *adj* (a) *(no variable, inmóvil)* fixed; **sin domicilio f.** of no fixed abode (b) *(empleado, trabajo)* permanent

fila *nf* (a) *(hilera)* file; **en f. india** in single file; **poner en f.** to line up (b) *(de cine, teatro)* row (c) *Mil* **filas** ranks; **llamar a algn a filas** to call sb up; **¡rompan filas!** fall out!, dismiss!

filamento *nm* filament

filantropía *nf* philanthropy

filántropo, -a *nm,f* philanthropist

filarmónico, -a *adj* philharmonic

filatelia *nf* philately, stamp collecting

filete *nm (de carne, pescado)* fillet

filiación *nf Pol* affiliation

filial 1 *adj* (a) *(de hijos)* filial (b) *Com* subsidiary
  2 *nf Com* subsidiary

filigrana *nf* (a) *(en orfebrería)* filigree (b) *Fig* **filigranas** intricacy, intricate work

Filipinas *npl* **(las) F.** (the) Philippines

filipino, -a *adj & nm,f* Philippine, Filipino

film *(pl* **films**) *nm* film

filmar *vt* to film, to shoot

filme *nm* film

fílmico, -a *adj* film

filmoteca *nf (archivo)* film library; *(sala de cine)* film institute

filo *nm* (cutting) edge; **al f. de la medianoche** on the stroke of midnight; *Fig* **de doble f.** double-edged

filón *nm* (a) *Min* seam, vein (b) *Fig (buen negocio)* gold mine

filoso, -a *adj Am* sharp

filosofal *adj* **piedra f.** philosopher's stone

filosofar *vi* to philosophize

filosofía *nf* philosophy; *Fig* **con f.** philosophically

filosófico, -a *adj* philosophical

filósofo, -a *nm,f* philosopher

filtración *nf (de líquido)* filtration; *(de información)* leak

filtrar 1 *vt* (a) *(líquido)* to filter (b) *(información)* to leak
  2 filtrarse *vpr* (a) *(líquido)* to seep (b) *(información)* to leak out

filtro *nm* filter

filudo, -a *adj Andes* sharp

fin *nm* (a) *(final)* end; **dar** *o* **poner f. a** to put an end to; **llegar** *o* **tocar a su f.** to come to an end; **en f.** anyway; **¡por** *o* **al f.!** at last!; **f. de semana** weekend; **al f. y al cabo** when all's said and done; **noche de F. de Año** New Year's Eve (b) *(objetivo)* purpose, aim; **a f. de** in order to, so as to; **a f. de que** in order that, so that; **con el f. de** with the intention of

final 1 *adj* final
  2 *nm* end; **al f.** in the end; **f. de línea** terminal; **f. feliz** happy ending; **a finales de octubre** at the end of October
  3 *nf Dep* final

finalidad *nf* purpose, aim

finalista 1 *nmf* finalist
  2 *adj* in the final

finalizar [40] *vt & vi* to end, to finish

finalmente *adv* finally

financiación *nf* financing

financiar [43] *vt* to finance

financiero, -a 1 *adj* financial
  2 *nm,f* financier

financista *nmf Am* financier

finanzas *nfpl* finances

finca *nf (inmueble)* property; *(de campo)* country house

fingido, -a *adj* feigned, false; **nombre f.** assumed name

fingir [57] **1** *vt* to feign
  2 fingirse *vpr* to pretend to be

finlandés, -esa 1 *adj* Finnish
  2 *nm,f (persona)* Finn
  3 *nm (idioma)* Finnish

Finlandia *n* Finland

fino, -a 1 *adj* (a) *(hilo, capa)* fine (b) *(flaco)* thin (c) *(educado)* refined, polite (d) *(oído)* sharp, acute; *(olfato)* keen (e) *(humor, ironía)* subtle
  2 *nm (vino)* = type of dry sherry

finura *nf* (a) *(refinamiento)* refinement, politeness (b) *(sutileza)* subtlety

fiordo *nm Geog* fiord

firma *nf* (a) *(rúbrica)* signature (b) *(empresa)* firm, company

firmamento *nm* firmament

firmante *adj & nmf* signatory; **el** *o* **la abajo f.** the undersigned

firmar *vt* to sign

firme 1 *adj* (**a**) *(fuerte, sólido)* firm; *Fig* **mantenerse f.** to hold one's ground; **tierra f.** terra firma (**b**) *Mil* **¡firmes!** attention!
2 *nm (de carretera)* road surface
3 *adv* hard

firmemente *adv* firmly

firmeza *nf* firmness

fiscal 1 *adj* fiscal
2 *nmf Der Br* ≃ public prosecutor, *US* ≃ district attorney

fiscalía *nf Der (cargo) Br* ≃ post of public prosecutor, *US* ≃ post of district attorney; *(oficina) Br* ≃ public prosecutor's office, *US* ≃ district attorney's office

fisco *nm* treasury, exchequer

fisgar [42] *vi Fam* to snoop, to pry

fisgón, -ona *nm,f Fam* snooper

fisgonear *vi Fam* to snoop, to pry

física *nf* physics *sing*

físico, -a 1 *adj* physical
2 *nm,f (profesión)* physicist
3 *nm* physique

fisión *nf* fission

fisioterapeuta *nmf* physiotherapist

fisioterapia *nf* physiotherapy

fisonomía *nf* physiognomy

fisonomista *nmf Fam* **ser buen/mal f.** to be good/no good at remembering faces

fisura *nf* fissure

flácido, -a *adj* flaccid, flabby

flaco, -a 1 *adj* (**a**) *(delgado)* skinny (**b**) *Fig* **punto f.** weak spot
2 *nm,f Am Fam (como apelativo)* **¿cómo estás, flaca?** hey, how are you doing?

flagelar *vt* to flagellate

flagelo *nm (látigo)* whip; *Fig* scourge

flagrante *adj* flagrant; **en f. delito** red-handed

flamante *adj* (**a**) *(nuevo)* brand-new (**b**) *(vistoso)* splendid

flamenco, -a 1 *adj* (**a**) *Mús* flamenco (**b**) *(de Flandes)* Flemish
2 *nm* (**a**) *Mús* flamenco (**b**) *(ave)* flamingo (**c**) *(idioma)* Flemish

flan *nm* crème caramel

> ⚠ Observa que la palabra inglesa **flan** es un falso amigo y no es la traducción de la palabra española **flan**. En inglés **flan** significa "tarta".

flanco *nm* flank, side

flanquear *vt* to flank

flaquear *vi (fuerzas, piernas)* to weaken, to give way

flaqueza *nf* weakness

flash [flaʃ, flas] *nm Fot* flash

flato *nm Esp* **tener f.** to have a stitch

flatulencia *nf* flatulence

flauta *nf* flute; **f. dulce** recorder

flautín *nm (instrumento)* piccolo

flautista *nmf* flute player, flautist, *US* flutist

flecha *nf* arrow

flechazo *nm* love at first sight

fleco *nm* fringe

flema *nf* phlegm

flemático, -a *adj* phlegmatic

flemón *nm* gumboil, abscess

flequillo *nm Br* fringe, *US* bangs

fletar *vt* to charter

flete *nm* (**a**) *(alquiler)* charter (**b**) *(carga)* freight

flexibilidad *nf* flexibility

flexible *adj* flexible

flexión *nf* (**a**) *Ling* inflection (**b**) **flexiones de brazo** push-ups, *Br* press-ups

flexionar *vt* to bend

flexo *nm Esp* adjustable table lamp *o* light, Anglepoise® lamp

flipante *adj Esp Fam* great, cool

flipar *Esp Fam* **1** *vi (asombrarse)* to be flabbergasted *o Br* gobsmacked
2 *vt* **le flipan las motos** he's crazy about motorbikes

flirtear *vi* to flirt

flojear *vi (ventas etc)* to fall off, go down; *(piernas)* to weaken, grow weak; *(memoria)* to fail; *Andes Fam (holgazanear)* to laze about *o* around

flojedad *nf* weakness

flojera *nf Fam* weakness, faintness

flojo, -a *adj* (**a**) *(tornillo, cuerda etc)* loose, slack (**b**) *(perezoso)* lazy, idle; *(exámen, trabajo, resultado)* poor

flor *nf* (**a**) *(de planta)* flower; **en f.** in blossom; *Fig* **en la f. de la vida** in the prime of life; *Fig* **la f. y nata** the cream (of society) (**b**) **a f. de piel** skin-deep

flora *nf* flora

floreado, -a *adj* flowery

florecer [33] *vi* (**a**) *(plantas)* to flower (**b**) *(negocio)* to flourish, to thrive

floreciente *adj* flourishing, prosperous

florero *nm* vase

florido, -a *adj* (**a**) *(con flores)* flowery (**b**) *(estilo)* florid

floripondio *nm Pey (adorno)* heavy ornamentation

florista *nmf* florist

floristería *nf* florist's (shop)

flota *nf* fleet

flotador *nm* (**a**) *(de pesca)* float (**b**) *(para nadar)* rubber ring

flotar *vi* to float

flote *nm* floating; **a f.** afloat; **sacar a f. un negocio** to put a business on a sound footing

flotilla *nf* flotilla

fluctuación *nf* fluctuation

fluctuar [30] *vi* to fluctuate

fluidez *nf* fluency

fluido, -a 1 *adj* fluid; *(estilo etc)* fluent **2** *nm* fluid; **f. eléctrico** current

fluir [37] *vi* to flow

flujo *nm* flow; *Fís* flux; *Med* discharge; **f. y reflujo** ebb and flow

flúor *nm* fluorine

fluorescente *adj* fluorescent

fluvial *adj* river

FM *nf (abr* **Frecuencia Modulada)** FM

FMI *nm (abr* **Fondo Monetario Internacional)** IMF

fobia *nf* phobia (**a** about)

foca *nf* seal

foco *nm* (**a**) *Elec* spotlight, floodlight (**b**) *(de ideas, revolución etc)* centre, focal point (**c**) *Am (de vehículo)* (car) headlight; *(farola)* streetlight (**d**) *Andes, Méx (bombilla)* light bulb

fofo, -a *adj* soft; *(persona)* flabby

fogata *nf* bonfire

fogón *nm (de cocina)* ring

fogonazo *nm* flash

fogosidad *nf* ardour, fire

fogoso, -a *adj* fiery, spirited

foguео *nm* **cartucho de f.** blank cartridge

foie-gras [fwa'ɣras] *nm inv* (pâté de) foie-gras

folclore *nm* folklore

folclórico, -a 1 *adj* traditional, popular **2** *nm,f Esp* = singer of traditional Spanish songs

fólder *nm Andes, CAm, Méx (carpeta)* folder

folio *nm* sheet of paper

folklore *nm* folklore

folklórico, -a *adj* = folclórico

follaje *nm* foliage

follar *vi & vt Esp muy Fam* to lay, *Br* to shag

folletín *nm* melodrama

folleto *nm (turístico, publicitario)* brochure; *(explicativo, de instrucciones)* leaflet

follón *nm Esp Fam* (**a**) *(discusión)* row (**b**) *(lío)* mess; **me hice un f. con las listas** I got into a real muddle o mess with the lists

follonero, -a *nm,f Esp Fam* troublemaker

fomentar *vt* to encourage, to promote

fomento *nm* encouragement, promotion; **Ministerio de F.** Ministry of Public Works

fonda *nf* inn

fondear *vi* to anchor

fondo¹ *nm* (**a**) *(parte más baja)* bottom; **a f.** thoroughly; **al f. de la calle** at the bottom of the street; **tocar f.** *Náut* to touch bottom; *Fig* to reach rock bottom; *Fig* **en el f. es bueno** deep down he's kind; **bajos fondos** dregs of society; **doble f.** false bottom (**b**) *(de habitación)* back; *(de pasillo)* end (**c**) *(segundo término)* background; **música de f.** background music (**d**) *Prensa* **artículo de f.** leading article (**e**) *Dep* **corredor de f.** long-distance runner; **esquí de f.** cross-country skiing (**f**) *RP (patio)* back patio (**g**) *Carib, Méx (prenda)* petticoat

fondo² *nm Fin* fund; **cheque sin fondos** bad cheque; *Fam* **f. común** kitty

fonendoscopio *nm* stethoscope

fonética *nf* phonetics *sing*

fonético, -a *adj* phonetic

fono *nm Am Fam* phone

fontanería *nf* plumbing

fontanero, -a *nm,f* plumber

footing *nm* jogging; **hacer f.** to go jogging

forajido, -a *nm,f* outlaw

foráneo, -a *adj* foreign

forastero, -a *nm,f* outsider, stranger

forcejear *vi* to wrestle, to struggle

forcejeo *nm* struggle

fórceps *nm inv* forceps

forense 1 *adj* forensic **2** *nmf* **(médico) f.** forensic surgeon

forestal *adj* forest; **repoblación f.** reafforestation

forfait [for'fait, for'fe] *(pl* forfaits) *nm* (**a**) *(para esquiar)* ski pass (**b**) *Dep* default

forjado, -a *adj (hierro)* wrought

forjar *vt (metal)* to forge; *Fig* to create, to make

forma *nf* (**a**) *(figura)* form, shape; **en f. de L** L-shaped; **¿qué f. tiene?** what shape is it? (**b**) *(manera)* way; **de esta f.** in this way; **de f. que** so that; **de todas formas** anyway, in any case; **no hubo f. de convencerla** there was no way we could convince her; **f. de pago** method of payment (**c**) *Dep* form; **estar en f.** to be on form; **estar en baja f.** to be off form (**d**) *Rel* **Sagrada F.** Host (**e**) **formas** *(modales)* manners

formación *nf* (**a**) *(creación)* formation (**b**) *(educación)* upbringing; *(enseñanza)* training; **f. profesional** vocational training

formal *adj* (a) *(de la forma, legal)* formal (b) *(que se porta bien)* well-behaved, good (c) *(serio)* serious, serious-minded (d) *(fiable)* reliable, dependable

formalidad *nf* (a) *(requisito)* formality (b) *(seriedad)* seriousness (c) *(fiabilidad)* reliability (d) **formalidades** *(trámites)* formalities

formalizar [40] **1** *vt* to formalize
2 formalizarse *vpr* to settle down

formar 1 *vt* (a) *(hacer)* to form; **f. parte de algo** to be a part of sth (b) *(educar)* to bring up; *(enseñar)* to educate, to train
2 formarse *vpr* (a) *(hacerse, crearse)* to be formed, to form; **se formó un charco** a puddle formed; **formarse una impresión de algo** to get an impression of sth (b) *(educarse)* to be educated *o* trained

formatear *vt Inform* to format

formato *nm* format

formica® *nf* Formica®

formidable *adj* (a) *(estupendo)* wonderful, terrific (b) *(espantoso)* formidable

fórmula *nf* formula; *Aut* **f. uno** formula one

formular *vt* *(queja, petición)* to make; *(deseo)* to express; *(pregunta)* to ask; *(teoría)* to formulate

formulario *nm* form

fornicar [44] *vi* to fornicate

fornido, -a *adj* strapping, hefty

foro *nm* (a) *(lugar de discusión)* forum; *Inform* **f. (de discusión)** discussion group (b) *Teatro* back (of the stage)

forofo, -a *nm,f Esp Fam* fan, supporter

forrado, -a *adj* lined; *Fam* **estar f.** to be well-heeled, to be well-off

forraje *nm* fodder

forrar 1 *vt* *(por dentro)* to line; *(por fuera)* to cover
2 forrarse *vpr Fam (de dinero)* to make a packet

forro *nm* (a) *(por dentro)* lining; *(por fuera)* cover, case (b) *RP Fam (preservativo)* rubber, *Br* johnny

fortalecer [33] *vt* to fortify, to strengthen

fortaleza *nf* (a) *(fuerza) (física)* strength; *(de espíritu)* fortitude (b) *Mil* fortress, stronghold

fortificar [44] *vt* to fortify

fortísimo, -a *adj* very strong

fortuito, -a *adj* fortuitous

fortuna *nf* (a) *(destino)* fortune, fate (b) *(suerte)* luck; **por f.** fortunately (c) *(capital)* fortune

forzado, -a *adj* forced; **a marchas forzadas** at a brisk pace; **trabajos forzados** hard labour

forzar [2] *vt* (a) *(obligar)* to force; **f. a algn a hacer algo** to force sb to do sth (b) *(puerta, candado)* to force, to break open

forzosamente *adv* necessarily

forzoso, -a *adj* obligatory, compulsory; *Av* **aterrizaje f.** forced landing

fosa *nf* (a) *(sepultura)* grave (b) *(hoyo)* pit; **f. séptica** septic tank (c) *Anat* **fosas nasales** nostrils

fosforescente *adj* phosphorescent

fósforo *nm (cerilla)* match

fósil *adj & nm* fossil

fosilizarse [40] *vpr* to fossilize, to become fossilized

foso *nm* (a) *(hoyo)* pit (b) *(de fortificación)* moat (c) *(en garage)* inspection pit

foto *nf Fam* photo; **sacar/echar una f.** to take a photo

fotocopia *nf* photocopy

fotocopiadora *nf* photocopier

fotocopiar [43] *vt* to photocopy

fotogénico, -a *adj* photogenic

fotografía *nf* (a) *(imagen)* photograph; **echar** *o* **hacer** *o* **sacar fotografías** to take photographs (b) *(arte)* photography

fotografiar [29] *vt* to photograph, to take a photograph of

fotográfico, -a *adj* photographic

fotógrafo, -a *nm,f* photographer

fotograma *nm Cin* still

fotomatón *nm* passport photo machine

fotómetro *nm* light meter, exposure meter

FP *nf Educ (abr* **Formación Profesional**) vocational training

frac *(pl* **fracs** *o* **fraques)** *nm* dress coat, tails

fracasado, -a 1 *adj* unsuccessful
2 *nm,f (persona)* failure

fracasar *vi* to fail

fracaso *nm* failure; **el f. escolar** educational failure, poor performance at school

> 🖉 Observa que la palabra inglesa **fracas** es un falso amigo y no es la traducción de la palabra española **fracaso**. En inglés, **fracas** significa "gresca, refriega".

fracción *nf* fraction

fraccionamiento *nm Méx* housing estate

fraccionar *vt* to divide, to break up; *(pago)* to split up into instalments

fraccionario, -a *adj* fractional; **moneda fraccionaria** small change

fractura *nf* fracture

fracturar 1 *vt* to fracture
   2 fracturarse *vpr* to fracture
fragancia *nf* fragrance
fragata *nf* frigate
frágil *adj* (a) *(quebradizo)* fragile (b) *(débil)* frail
fragmentar 1 *vt* to fragment
   2 fragmentarse *vpr* to break up
fragmento *nm* fragment; *(de novela etc)* passage
fragor *nm* din
fragua *nf* forge
fraguar [45] *vt* (a) *(metal)* to forge (b) *(plan)* to think up, to fabricate; *(conspiración)* to hatch
fraile *nm* friar, monk
frailecillo *nm* puffin
frambuesa *nf* raspberry
francamente *adv* frankly
francés, -esa 1 *adj* French; *Culin* **tortilla francesa** plain omelette
   2 *nm,f (hombre)* Frenchman; *(mujer)* Frenchwoman
   3 *nm (idioma)* French
Fráncfort *n* Frankfurt; **salchicha de F.** frankfurter
Francia *n* France
francmasón, -ona *nm,f* freemason
franco¹, -a *adj* (a) *(persona)* frank (b) *Com* **f. a bordo** free on board; **f. fábrica** ex-works; **puerto f.** free port (c) *CSur, Méx (día)* **me dieron el día f.** they gave me the day off
franco² *nm Fin (moneda)* franc
francotirador, -a *nm,f* sniper
franela *nf* (a) *(tejido)* flannel (b) *Bol, Col, Ven (camiseta) (interior) Br* vest, *US* undershirt; *(exterior)* T-shirt (c) *Bol, Col, Ven (sudadera)* sweatshirt
franja *nf (de terreno)* strip; *(de bandera)* stripe; *Cost* fringe, border
franquear *vt* (a) *(atravesar)* to cross; *Fig (dificultad, obstáculo)* to overcome (b) *(carta)* to frank (c) *(camino, paso)* to free, to clear
franqueo *nm* postage
franqueza *nf* frankness
franquicia *nf Com* franchise
franquismo *nm Hist* (a) *(ideología)* Francoism (b) **el f.** *(régimen)* the Franco regime
franquista *adj & nmf* Francoist
frasco *nm* small bottle
frase *nf (oración)* sentence; *(expresión)* phrase; **f. hecha** set phrase *o* expression
fraternal *adj* brotherly, fraternal
fraternidad *nf* brotherhood, fraternity

fraternizar [40] *vi* to fraternize
fraterno, -a *adj* fraternal, brotherly
fraude *nm* fraud; **f. fiscal** tax evasion
fraudulento, -a *adj* fraudulent
fray *nm Rel* brother
frazada *nf Am* blanket
frecuencia *nf* frequency; **con f.** frequently, often
frecuentar *vt* to frequent
frecuente *adj* frequent
frecuentemente *adv* frequently, often
fregadero *nm Esp, Méx (kitchen)* sink
fregado¹ *nm* (a) *(lavado)* washing (b) *Fam (follón)* racket
fregado², -a *adj Andes, Méx, Ven Fam* (a) *(persona) (ser)* annoying; **mi vecino es muy f.** my neighbour's a real pain (b) *(persona) (estar)* **perdí las llaves, ¡estoy fregada!** I've lost my keys, I've had it! (c) *(objeto) (roto)* bust
fregar [1] *vt* (a) *(lavar)* to wash; *(suelo)* to mop (b) *Andes, Méx, Ven Fam (molestar)* to annoy, irritate (c) *Andes, Méx, Ven Fam (estropear)* to bust, to break
fregón, -ona *adj Col, Ecuad, Méx (molesto)* annoying
fregona *nf Esp* mop
freidora *nf (deep fat)* fryer
freír [56] *(pp* **frito)** **1** *vt* to fry
   2 freírse *vpr* to fry; *Fig* **freírse de calor** to be roasting
frenar *vt* to brake; *Fig (inflación etc)* to slow down; *(impulsos)* to restrain
frenazo *nm* sudden braking; **dar un f.** to jam on the brakes
frenesí *(pl* **frenesíes)** *nm* frenzy
frenético, -a *adj* frantic
freno *nm* (a) *(de vehículo)* brake; **pisar/ soltar el f.** to press/release the brake; **f. de disco/tambor** disc/drum brake; **f. de mano** *Br* handbrake, *US* emergency brake (b) *(de caballería)* bit (c) *Fig* curb, check; **poner f. a algo** to curb sth
frente 1 *nm* front; **al f. de** at the head of; **chocar de f.** to crash head on; **hacer f. a algo** to face sth, to stand up to sth
   2 *nf Anat* forehead; **f. a f.** face to face
   3 *adv* **f. a** in front of, opposite
fresa *nf* (a) *Esp, CAm, Carib, Méx (planta, fruto)* strawberry (b) *Téc* milling cutter
fresca *nf Fam* cheeky remark
fresco, -a 1 *adj* (a) *(frío)* cool (b) *(comida, fruta)* fresh (c) *(reciente)* fresh, new (d) *(caradura)* cheeky, forward, *US* fresh; **se quedó tan f.** he didn't bat an eyelid; **¡qué f.!** what a nerve!
   2 *nm* (a) *(frescor)* fresh air, cool air; **al f.** in the cool; **hace f.** it's chilly (b) *Arte* fresco

frescor nm freshness

frescura nf (a) (frescor) freshness (b) (desvergüenza) cheek, nerve

fresno nm ash tree

fresón nm (large) strawberry

frialdad nf coldness

fríamente adv coolly

fricción nf (a) (rozamiento, tensión) friction (b) (masaje) massage

friega nf rub

friegaplatos 1 nmf inv (persona) dishwasher
2 nm inf (aparato) dishwaser

frigider nm Andes refrigerator, Br fridge, US icebox

frígido, -a adj frigid

frigorífico, -a 1 nm Esp Br refrigerator, Br fridge, US icebox
2 adj cámara frigorífica cold store

frijol, fríjol nm Am salvo RP bean

frío, -a 1 adj (a) (a baja temperatura) cold (b) (indiferente) cold, cool; **su comentario me dejó f.** her remark left me cold
2 nm cold; **hace f.** it's cold

friolento, -a adj Am sensitive to the cold

friolera nf Fam **la f. de mil euros/dos horas** a mere thousand euros/two hours

friolero, -a adj sensitive to the cold

fritada nf fry-up, dish of fried food

fritanga nf (a) Esp (comida frita) fry-up (b) Am Pey (comida grasienta) greasy food

frito, -a 1 adj (a) Culin fried (b) Fam exasperated, fed up; **me tienes f.** I'm sick to death of you
2 nm **fritos** fried food
3 pp de **freír**

fritura nf fry-up, dish of fried food

frívolo, -a adj frivolous

frondoso, -a adj leafy, luxuriant

frontera nf frontier

fronterizo, -a adj frontier, border; **países fronterizos** neighbouring countries

frontón nm Dep pelota

frotar 1 vt to rub
2 frotarse vpr to rub; **frotarse las manos** to rub one's hands together

fructífero, -a adj fruitful

frugal adj frugal

fruncir [52] vt (a) Cost to gather (b) (labios) to purse, to pucker; **f. el ceño** to frown, to knit one's brow

frustración nf frustration

frustrado, -a adj (persona) frustrated; (plan) failed

frustrante adj frustrating

frustrar 1 vt to frustrate
2 frustrarse vpr (a) (esperanza) to fail, to go awry (b) (persona) to be frustrated

fruta nf fruit; **f. del tiempo** fresh fruit

frutal 1 adj fruit; **árbol f.** fruit tree
2 nm fruit tree

frutería nf fruit shop

frutero, -a 1 nm,f fruit seller, Br fruiterer
2 nm fruit dish o bowl

frutilla nf Bol, CSur, Ecuad strawberry

fruto nm fruit; **frutos secos** nuts; **dar f.** to bear fruit; Fig (dar buen resultado) to be fruitful; **sacar f. de algo** to profit from sth

fu interj **ni fu ni fa** so-so

fucsia nf fuchsia

fuego nm (a) (llamas) fire; **fuegos artificiales** fireworks (b) (lumbre) light; **¿me da f., por favor?** have you got a light, please? (c) Culin **a f. lento** on a low flame; (al horno) in a slow oven

fuel nm fuel oil

fuelle nm (para soplar) bellows

fuente nf (a) (de agua) fountain; Chile, Col, Méx, Ven **f. de soda** (cafetería) = café or counter selling ice cream, soft drinks etc, US soda fountain (serving soft drinks and alcohol) (b) (recipiente) dish, serving dish (c) (de información) source

fuera¹ adv (a) (en el exterior) outside, out; **quédate f.** stay outside; **sal f.** go out; **desde f.** from (the) outside; **por f.** on the outside; **la puerta de f.** the outer door (b) **f. de** out of; **f. de serie** extraordinary; Fig **estar f. de sí** to be beside oneself (c) Dep **el equipo de f.** the away team; **jugar f.** to play away; **f. de juego** offside

fuera² 1 subj imperf de **ir**
2 subj imperf de **ser**

fuero nm (a) Hist code of laws (b) Fig **en tu f. interno** deep down, in your heart of hearts

fuerte 1 adj strong; (dolor) severe; (sonido) loud; (comida) heavy; **el plato f.** the main course; Fig the most important event
2 nm (a) (fortaleza) fort (b) (punto fuerte) forte, strong point
3 adv **¡abrázame f.!** hold me tight!; **comer f.** to eat a lot; **¡habla más f.!** speak up!; **¡pégale f.!** hit him hard!

fuerza nf (a) (fortaleza) strength; Fig **a f. de** by dint of (b) (violencia) force; **a la f.** (por obligación) of necessity; (con violencia) by force; **por f.** of necessity; **f. mayor** force majeure (c) Fís force (d) (cuerpo) force; **las fuerzas del orden** the forces of law and order; **f. aérea** air force; **fuerzas armadas** armed forces

fuese 1 *subj imperf de* **ir**
  2 *subj imperf de* **ser**

fuete *nm Am salvo RP* whip

fuga *nf* (**a**) *(huida)* escape; **darse a la f.** to take flight (**b**) *(de gas etc)* leak

fugarse [42] *upr* to escape; **f. de casa** to run away from home

fugaz *adj* fleeting, brief

fugitivo, -a *nm,f* fugitive

fui 1 *pt indef de* **ir**
  2 *pt indef de* **ser**

fulana *nf* whore, tart

fulano, -a *nm,f* so-and-so, what's-his/her-name; **Doña Fulana de tal** Mrs So-and-so

fular *nm* scarf

fulgor *nm Literario* brilliance, glow

fullero, -a *Fam* **1** *adj* cheating
  2 *nm,f* cheat

fulminante *adj* *(cese)* summary; *(muerte, enfermedad)* sudden; *(mirada)* withering

fulminar *vt* to strike dead; **f. a algn con la mirada** to look daggers at sb

fumador, -a *nm,f* smoker; **los no fumadores** nonsmokers; **f. pasivo** passive smoker

fumar 1 *vt & vi* to smoke; **no f.** *(en letrero)* no smoking
  2 fumarse *upr* to smoke; **fumarse un cigarro** to smoke a cigarette

   Observa que el verbo inglés **to fume** *es un falso amigo y no es la traducción del verbo español* **fumar**. *En inglés,* **to fume** *significa* "despedir humo".

fumigar [42] *vt* to fumigate

funambulista *nmf,* **funámbulo, -a** *nm,f* tightrope walker

función *nf* (**a**) *(papel)* function; **en f. de** depending on (**b**) *(cargo)* **entrar en funciones** to take up one's duties; **presidente en funciones** acting president (**c**) *Teatro* performance (**d**) *Ling & Mat* function

funcionamiento *nm* operation; **poner/entrar en f.** to put/come into operation

funcionar *vi* to work; **no funciona** *(en letrero)* out of order

funcionario, -a *nm,f* *(de la Administración central)* civil servant; *(profesor, bombero, enfermero)* public sector worker; **f. de prisiones** prison officer

funda *nf* cover; *(de gafas etc)* case; *(de espada)* sheath; **f. de almohada** pillowcase

fundación *nf* foundation

fundador, -a *nm,f* founder

fundamental *adj* fundamental

fundamentar *vt* to base (**en** on)

fundamento *nm* basis, grounds; **sin f.** unfounded

fundar 1 *vt* (**a**) *(empresa)* to found (**b**) *(teoría)* to base, to found
  2 fundarse *upr* (**a**) *(empresa)* to be founded (**b**) *(teoría)* to be based (**en** on)

   Observa el verbo inglés **to fund** *es un falso amigo y no es la traducción del verbo español* **fundar**. *En inglés,* **to fund** *significa* "financiar".

fundición *nf* (**a**) *(de metales)* smelting (**b**) *(fábrica)* foundry

fundir 1 *vt* (**a**) *(mantequilla, hielo)* to melt; *(hierro)* to smelt (**b**) *(bombilla, plomos)* to blow
  2 fundirse *upr* (**a**) *(derretirse)* to melt (**b**) *(bombilla, plomos)* to blow (**c**) *Com* to merge (**d**) *Am Fam (arruinarse)* to go bust

fúnebre *adj* (**a**) *(mortuorio)* funeral; **coche f.** hearse (**b**) *(lúgubre)* mournful, lugubrious

funeral *nm* funeral

funeraria *nf* undertaker's, *US* funeral home

funesto, -a *adj* ill-fated, fatal; *(consecuencias)* disastrous

fungir *vi Méx, Perú* to act, to serve (**de** *o* **como** as)

funicular *nm* funicular (railway)

furcia *nf Pey* whore, tart

furgón *nm Aut* van

furgoneta *nf* van

furia *nf* fury; **ponerse hecho una f.** to become furious, to fly into a rage

furibundo, -a *adj* furious, enraged

furioso, -a *adj* furious; **ponerse f.** to become furious

furor *nm* fury, rage; *Fig* **hacer f.** to be all the rage

furtivo, -a *adj* furtive, stealthy; **caza/pesca furtiva** poaching; **cazador/pescador f.** poacher

furúnculo *nm Med* boil

fuselaje *nm* fuselage

fusible *nm* fuse

fusil *nm* gun, rifle

fusilamiento *nm* shooting, execution

fusilar *vt* (**a**) *(ejecutar)* to shoot, to execute (**b**) *Fam (plagiar)* to plagiarize

fusión *nf* (**a**) *(de metales)* fusion; *(del hielo)* thawing, melting; **punto de f.** melting point (**b**) *Com* merger

fusionar 1 *vt* to merge
  2 fusionarse *upr* to merge

fustán *nm Am* petticoat

fútbol *nm* soccer, *Br* football; **f. sala** indoor five-a-side

futbolín *nm Esp Br* table football, *US* foosball

futbolista *nmf* soccer *o Br* football player, *Br* footballer

fútil *adj* futile, trivial

futilidad *nf* futility, triviality

futurista *adj (diseño, ropa)* futuristic; *Arte* futurist

futuro, -a 1 *adj* future

2 *nm* future; **en un f. próximo** in the near future; *CSur, Méx* **a f.** in the future

G, g [xe] *nf (letra)* G, g

g *(abr gramo)* g

gabán *nm* overcoat

gabardina *nf (prenda)* raincoat

gabinete *nm* (**a**) *(despacho)* study; **g. de abogados** lawyers' office (**b**) *Pol* cabinet

gaceta *nf* gazette

gachas *nfpl (corn)* porridge

gacho, -a *adj* **con la cabeza gacha** hanging one's head

gaditano, -a 1 *adj* of/from Cadiz
   2 *nm,f* person from Cadiz

gafar *vt Fam* to put a jinx on, to bring bad luck to

gafas *nfpl* glasses, spectacles; **g. de sol** sunglasses

gafe *Esp Fam* **1** *adj* jinxed; **ser g.** to be jinxed
   2 *nmf* jinxed person

> *Observa que la palabra inglesa* **gaffe** *es un falso amigo y no es la traducción de la palabra española* **gafe**. *En inglés,* **gaffe** *significa "metedura de pata, desliz".*

gafete *nm Méx* badge

gaita *nf* bagpipes

gajes *nmpl Fam Irón* **g. del oficio** occupational hazards

gajo *nm (de fruta)* segment

gala *nf* (**a**) *(vestido)* full dress; **de g.** dressed up; *(ciudad)* decked out (**b**) *Esp (espectáculo)* gala; **hacer g. de** to glory in (**c**) **galas** finery

galán *nm* handsome young man; *Teatro* leading man

galante *adj* gallant

galantear *vt* to court

galanteo *nm* courtship

galantería *nf* gallantry

galápago *nm* turtle

galardón *nm* prize

galardonado, -a *adj* award-winning, prize-winning

galardonar *vt* to award a prize to

galaxia *nf* galaxy

galeón *nm* galleon

galera *nf Náut* galley

galería *nf* (**a**) *Arquit* covered balcony (**b**) *(museo)* art gallery (**c**) *Teatro* gallery

Gales *n* **(el país de) G.** Wales

galés, -esa 1 *adj* Welsh
   2 *nm,f (hombre)* Welshman; *(mujer)* Welshwoman; **los galeses** the Welsh
   3 *nm (idioma)* Welsh

galgo *nm* greyhound

Galicia *n* Galicia

galimatías *nm inv Fam* gibberish

gallardo, -a *adj* (**a**) *(valiente)* brave, dashing (**b**) *(bien parecido)* fine-looking, striking

gallego, -a 1 *adj & nm,f* Galician; *CSur, Cuba Fam* Spanish
   2 *nm (idioma)* Galician

galleta *nf* (**a**) *Culin Br* biscuit, *US* cookie (**b**) *Esp Fam (cachete)* slap

gallina 1 *nf* hen
   2 *nmf Fam* coward, chicken

gallinero *nm* (**a**) *(de gallinas)* hen run (**b**) *Teatro* **el g.** the gods

gallito *adj Fam* cocky

gallo *nm* (**a**) *(ave)* cock, rooster; *Fam Fig* **en menos que canta un g.** before you could say Jack Robinson (**b**) *Fam Mús* off-key note

galón¹ *nm Mil* stripe

galón² *nm (medida)* gallon, *Br* = 4.55 l, *US* = 3.79 l

galopante *adj (inflación)* galloping

galopar *vi* to gallop

galope *nm* gallop; **a g. tendido** flat out

galpón *nm Andes, Carib, RP* shed

gama *nf* range; *Mús* scale

gamba *nf* prawn, *US* shrimp

gamberrismo *nm Esp* hooliganism

gamberro, -a *Esp* **1** *nm,f* hooligan, lout, *Br* yob
   2 *adj* loutish

gamo *nm* fallow deer

gamonal *nm Andes, CAm, Ven* (**a**) *(cacique)* village chief (**b**) *(caudillo)* cacique, local political boss

gamuza *nf* (**a**) *Zool* chamois (**b**) *(trapo)* chamois *o* shammy leather

gana *nf* (**a**) *(deseo)* wish (**de** for); **de buena g.** willingly; **de mala g.** reluctantly; *Fam* **no me da la g.** I don't feel like it (**b**) **tener ganas de (hacer) algo** to feel like (doing) sth; **quedarse con las ganas** not to manage (**c**) *(apetito)* appetite; **comer con ganas** to eat heartily

ganadería *nf* (**a**) *(crianza)* livestock farming (**b**) *(conjunto de ganado)* livestock

ganadero, -a *nm,f* livestock farmer

ganado *nm* livestock; **g. vacuno** cattle

ganador, -a 1 *adj* winning
2 *nm,f* winner

ganancia *nf* profit

ganar 1 *vt* (**a**) *(sueldo)* to earn (**b**) *(premio, competición)* to win (**c**) *(derrotar)* to beat (**d**) *(peso, tiempo)* to gain (**e**) *(alcanzar)* to reach
2 *vi* (**a**) *(vencer)* to win (**b**) *(mejorar)* **g. en algo** to gain in sth
3 ganarse *vpr* (**a**) *(obtener)* to earn; **ganarse el pan** to earn one's daily bread (**b**) *(merecer)* to deserve; **se lo ha ganado** he deserves it (**c**) *(conquistar) (simpatía, respeto)* to earn; *(persona)* to win over

ganchillo *nm* crochet work

gancho *nm* (**a**) *(garfio)* hook (**b**) *Fam Fig (gracia, atractivo)* charm (**c**) *Andes, CAm, Méx (horquilla)* hairpin (**d**) *Andes, CAm, Méx, Ven (percha)* hanger (**e**) *Col, Ven (pinza) Br* (clothes) peg, *US* clothespin

gandul, -a *nm,f* loafer

ganga *nf* bargain

gangoso, -a *adj* nasal

gangrena *nf* gangrene

gansada *nf Fam* silly thing to say/do

ganso, -a 1 *nm,f* (**a**) *(ave)* goose; *(macho)* gander (**b**) *Fam* dolt
2 *adj Fam* ginormous; **pasta gansa** bread, dough

gánster *(pl* **gánsters** *o* **gánsteres)** *nm* gangster

ganzúa *nf* picklock

gañán *nm (obrero)* farmhand; *(hombre rudo)* lout, boor

garabatear *vt* & *vi* to scribble

garabato *nm* scrawl

garaje *nm* garage

garante *nmf Fin* guarantor

garantía *nf* (**a**) *(seguro, promesa)* guarantee; *(de producto)* guarantee, warranty (**b**) *Der (fianza)* security

garantizar [40] *vt* to guarantee

garbanzo *nm* chickpea

garbeo *nm Esp Fam (paseo)* stroll; **darse un g.** to go for a stroll!

garbo *nm* grace

garfio *nm* hook, grappling iron

gargajo *nm* spit

garganta *nf* (**a**) *Anat* throat (**b**) *(desfiladero)* gorge

gargantilla *nf* short necklace

gárgaras *nfpl* gargling *sing*; *Fam* **¡vete a hacer g.!** get lost!

garita *nf* *(de centinela)* sentry box; *(de conserje)* porter's lodge

garito *nm Fam* joint

garra *nf* (**a**) *Zool* claw; *(de ave)* talon (**b**) *Fig (fuerza)* force; **tener g.** to be compelling

garrafa *nf* carafe

garrafal *adj* monumental

garrapata *nf* tick

garrote *nm* (**a**) *(porra)* club (**b**) *Der* garrotte

garrulo, -a *adj Fam* coarse, uncouth

garúa *nf Andes, RP, Ven* drizzle

garza *nf* heron

gas *nm* (**a**) *(fluido)* gas; *Esp* **g. ciudad** town gas; **gases (nocivos)** fumes; **g. de escape** exhaust fumes (**b**) *(en bebida)* fizz; **agua con g.** fizzy water (**c**) *Med* **gases** flatulence

gasa *nf* gauze

gaseosa *nf* (**a**) *Esp, Arg (bebida transparente)* pop, *Br* lemonade (**b**) *CAm, RP (refresco con gas)* fizzy drink, *US* soda

gaseoso, -a *adj (estado)* gaseous; *(bebida)* fizzy

gasfitería *nf Chile, Perú* plumber's (shop)

gasfitero, -a *nm,f Ecuad* plumber

gasoducto *nm* gas pipeline

gasóleo, gasoil *nm* diesel oil

gasolina *nf Br* petrol, *US* gas, *US* gasoline

gasolinera *nf Méx* **gasolinería** *nf Br* petrol *o US* gas station

gastado, -a *adj (objeto)* worn out; *Fig (frase)* hackneyed

gastar 1 *vt* (**a**) *(consumir) (dinero, tiempo)* to spend; *(gasolina, electricidad)* to consume (**b**) *(malgastar)* to waste (**c**) *Esp (ropa)* to wear; **¿qué número gastas?** what size do you take? (**d**) **g. una broma a algn** to play a practical joke on sb
2 gastarse *vpr* (**a**) *(deteriorarse)* to wear out (**b**) *(consumirse)* to run out

gasto *nm* expenditure; **gastos** expenses; **gastos de viaje** travelling expenses

gastritis *nf inv Med* gastritis

gastronomía *nf* gastronomy

gastronómico, -a *adj* gastronomic

gatas: a gatas *loc adv* on all fours

gatear *vi* to crawl

gatillo *nm* trigger; **apretar el g.** to pull the trigger

gato, -a 1 *nm,f (animal)* cat
  2 *nm Aut & Téc* jack
gauchada *nf CSur* favour
gaucho, -a 1 *adj RP Fam (servicial)* helpful, obliging
  2 *nm,f* gaucho
gaveta *nf* drawer
gavilán *nm* sparrowhawk
gaviota *nf* seagull
gay [gai, gei] *(pl gays) adj inv & nm* gay
gazapo *nm (error)* misprint
gaznate *nm* gullet
gazpacho *nm* gazpacho
gel *nm* gel; **g. (de ducha)** shower gel
gelatina *nf (de carne)* gelatine; *(de fruta)* Br jelly, US Jell-O®
gema *nf* gem
gemelo, -a 1 *adj & nm,f (identical)* twin
  2 gemelos *nmpl* (**a**) *(de camisa)* cufflinks (**b**) *(anteojos)* binoculars
gemido *nm* groan
Géminis *nm* Gemini
gemir [6] *vi* to groan
generación *nf* generation
generador *nm Elec* generator
general 1 *adj* general; **por lo** *o* **en g.** in general, generally
  2 *nm Mil & Rel* general
Generalitat *nf* Catalan/Valencian/Balearic parliament
generalización *nf* (**a**) *(comentario)* generalization (**b**) *(extensión)* spread
generalizar [40] **1** *vt* to spread, to make widespread
  2 *vi* to generalize
  3 generalizarse *upr* to become widespread *o* common
generalmente *adv* generally
generar *vt* to generate
género *nm* (**a**) *(clase)* kind, sort (**b**) *Arte & Lit* genre (**c**) *(mercancía)* article (**d**) *Ling* gender (**e**) *Biol* genus; **el g. humano** mankind
generosidad *nf* generosity
generoso, -a *adj* generous (**con** to)
Génesis *nm Rel* Genesis
genética *nf* genetics *sing*
genético, -a *adj* genetic
genial *adj* great, Br brilliant

Observa que la palabra inglesa **genial** es un falso amigo y no es la traducción de la palabra española **genial**. En inglés **genial** significa "cordial, amable".

genio *nm* (**a**) *(carácter)* temperament; *(mal carácter)* temper; **estar de mal g.** to be in a bad mood (**b**) *(facultad)* genius

genital 1 *adj* genital
  2 genitales *nmpl* genitals
genocidio *nm* genocide
genoma *nm* genome
Génova *n* Genoa
gente *nf* (**a**) *(personas)* people (**b**) *(familia)* folks
gentil *adj* (**a**) *(amable)* kind (**b**) *(pagano)* pagan

Observa que la palabra inglesa **genteel** es un falso amigo y no es la traducción de la palabra española **gentil**. En inglés **genteel** significa "fino, distinguido".

gentileza *nf* kindness; *Fml* **por g. de** by courtesy of
gentío *nm* crowd
gentuza *nf Pey* riffraff
genuino, -a *adj (puro)* genuine; *(verdadero)* authentic
geografía *nf* geography
geología *nf* geology
geometría *nf* geometry
geométrico, -a *adj* geometric
geranio *nm* geranium
gerencia *nf* management
gerente *nmf* manager
germano, -a 1 *adj* German, Germanic
  2 *nm,f* German
germen *nm* (**a**) *Biol* germ; **g. de trigo** wheat germ (**b**) *Fig (inicio)* germ; *(fuente)* origin
germinar *vi* to germinate
gerundio *nm* gerund
gesta *nf* heroic exploit
gestación *nf* gestation
gestar *vt* to gestate
gesticular *vi (con manos, brazos)* to gesticulate; *(con la cara)* to pull faces
gestión *nf* (**a**) *(administración)* management (**b**) **gestiones** *(negociaciones)* negotiations; *(trámites)* formalities
gestionar *vt* to take steps to acquire *o* obtain; *(negociar)* to negotiate
gesto *nm* (**a**) *(mueca)* face (**b**) *(con las manos)* gesture
gestor, -a *nm,f* = person who carries out dealings with public bodies on behalf of private customers or companies, combining the roles of solicitor and accountant
gestoría *nf* = office of a "gestor"
giba *nf* hump
Gibraltar *n* Gibraltar
gibraltareño, -a 1 *adj* of/from Gibraltar
  2 *nm,f* Gibraltarian

gigante, -a 1 *nm,f* giant
 2 *adj* giant, enormous

gigantesco, -a *adj* gigantic

gigoló *nm* gigolo

gil, -ila *nm,f CSur Fam* jerk, *Br* twit

gilipollas *nmf inv muy Fam Br* prat, *US* dork

gimnasia *nf* gymnastics *sing*

gimnasio *nm* gymnasium

gimnasta *nmf* gymnast

gimotear *vi* to whine

Ginebra *n* Geneva

ginebra *nf (bebida)* gin

ginecología *nf* gynaecology

ginecólogo, -a *nm,f* gynaecologist

gin-tonic [jin'tonik] *(pl* **gin-tonics)** *nm* gin and tonic

gira *nf Mús & Teatro* tour

girar 1 *vi* (a) *(dar vueltas)* to spin (b) **g. a la derecha/izquierda** to turn right/left
 2 *vt Fin* (a) *(expedir)* to draw (b) *(dinero)* to transfer

girasol *nm* sunflower

giratorio, -a *adj* revolving

giro *nm* (a) *(vuelta)* turn (b) *(de acontecimientos)* direction (c) *(frase)* turn of phrase (d) *Fin* draft; **g. telegráfico** money order; **g. postal** postal *o* money order

gis *nm Méx* chalk

gitano, -a *adj & nm,f* gypsy, gipsy

glacial *adj* icy

glaciar *nm* glacier

glándula *nf* gland

glasear *vt Culin* to glaze

global *adj* comprehensive; **precio g.** all-inclusive price

globalización *nf* globalization

globalmente *adv* as a whole

globo *nm* (a) *(de aire)* balloon (b) *(esfera)* globe (c) *(lámpara)* globe, glass lampshade

glóbulo *nm Med* blood cell, corpuscle

gloria *nf* (a) *(fama)* glory (b) *Rel* heaven; *Fam Fig* **estar en la g.** to be in seventh heaven (c) *Fam (delicia)* delight

glorieta *nf* (a) *(plazoleta)* small square (b) *Esp (rotonda) Br* roundabout, *US* traffic circle (c) *(en un jardín)* arbour

glorificar [44] *vt* to glorify

glorioso, -a *adj* glorious

glosa *nf* marginal note

glosar *vt* (a) *(explicar)* to gloss; *(texto)* to interpret (b) *(comentar)* to comment on

glosario *nm* glossary

glotón, -ona 1 *adj* greedy
 2 *nm,f* glutton

glotonería *nf* gluttony, greed

glucosa *nf* glucose

gobernación *nf* (a) *Col (de provincia)* provincial government (b) *Méx* **G.** *(ministerio) Br* ≃ the Home Office, *US* ≃ the Department of the Interior

gobernador, -a *nm,f* governor

gobernante *adj* ruling

gobernar [1] **1** *vt* to govern; *(país)* to rule
 2 *vi Náut* to steer

gobiernista *Andes, Méx* **1** *adj* government
 2 *nmf* government supporter

gobierno *nm* (a) *Pol* government (b) *(mando)* running (c) *Náut* steering (d) *Náut (timón)* rudder

goce *nm* enjoyment

godo, -a 1 *adj* Gothic
 2 *nm,f Hist* Goth

gofio *nm Andes, Carib, RP (harina)* roasted maize *o US* corn meal

gol *nm* goal

goleada *nf* **ganar por g.** to score a heavy victory

goleador, -a *nm,f* goal scorer

golear *vt* to hammer

golf *nm* golf; **palo de g.** golf club

golfista *nmf* golfer

golfo¹, -a 1 *nm (gamberro)* lout, *Br* yob; *(pillo)* rogue, wide boy
 2 *nf Fam Pey* tart

golfo² *nm Geog* gulf; **el g. Pérsico** the Persian Gulf

golondrina *nf* swallow

golosina *nf Br* sweet, *US* candy

goloso, -a *adj* sweet-toothed

golpe *nm* (a) *(impacto)* blow; *(en puerta)* knock; *(puñetazo)* punch; **de g.** all of a sudden; **g. de estado** coup d'état; **g. de suerte** stroke of luck; **no dar ni g.** not to lift a finger (b) *Aut* bump (c) *(desgracia)* blow; **un duro g.** a great blow (d) *(de humor)* witticism

golpear *vt* to hit; *(con el puño)* to punch; *(puerta, cabeza)* to bang

golpiza *nf Am* beating

goma *nf* (a) *(material)* rubber; **g. de pegar** glue; **g. de borrar** eraser, *Br* rubber (b) *(elástica)* rubber *o Br* elastic band (c) *Cuba, CSur (neumático)* tyre (d) *Fam (preservativo)* rubber

gomaespuma *nf* foam rubber

gomal *nm Am Agr* rubber plantation

gomería *nf CSur* tyre centre

gomero *nm CSur (planta)* rubber plant

gomina *nf* hair cream

góndola *nf* (a) *(embarcación)* gondola (b) *Perú (autobús interurbano)* (intercity) bus (**c**) *Bol (autobús urbano)* city bus (**d**) *(en supermercado)* gondola

gordo, -a 1 *adj* (**a**) *(carnoso)* fat (**b**) *(grueso)* thick (**c**) *(importante)* big; **me cae g.** I can't stand him; **de g.** in a big way

2 *nm,f* (**a**) *(persona)* fat person; *Fam* fatty (**b**) *Am Fam (como apelativo)* **¿cómo estás, g.?** how's it going, big man?

3 *nm* **el g.** *(de lotería)* the jackpot

gordura *nf* fatness

gorgorito *nm* trill

gorila *nm* (**a**) *(animal)* gorilla (**b**) *Esp Fig (en discoteca etc)* bouncer

gorjear *vi (ave)* to chirp

gorjeo *nm* chirping

gorra *nf* cap; *(con visera)* peaked cap; *Esp, Méx Fam* **de g.** for free

gorrión *nm* sparrow

gorro *nm (de lana)* hat; **g. de baño** swimming cap; *Fam* **estar hasta el g. (de)** to be up to here (with)

gorrón, -ona *nm,f Esp, Méx* sponger

gota *nf* (**a**) *(de líquido)* drop; *(de sudor)* bead; **g. a g.** drop by drop; **ni g.** not a bit (**b**) *Med* gout

gotear *v impers* to drip; **el techo gotea** there's a leak in the ceiling

gotera *nf* leak

gotero *nm* (intravenous) drip

gótico, -a *adj* Gothic

gozar [40] *vi* to enjoy oneself; **g. de algo** to enjoy sth

gozne *nm* hinge

gozo *nm* pleasure

grabación *nf* recording

grabado *nm* (**a**) *(arte)* engraving (**b**) *(dibujo)* drawing

grabadora *nf* tape recorder

grabar *vt* (**a**) *(sonidos, imágenes)* to record (**b**) *Inform* to save (**c**) *Arte* to engrave

gracia *nf* (**a**) *(atractivo)* grace (**b**) *(chiste)* joke; **hacer** *o* **tener g.** to be funny (**c**) *(indulto)* pardon

gracias *nfpl (agradecimiento)* thanks; **g. a** thanks to; **g. a Dios** thank God, thank goodness; **muchas** *o* **muchísimas g.** thank you very much

gracioso, -a 1 *adj* (**a**) *(divertido)* funny (**b**) *(garboso)* graceful

2 *nm,f Teatro* comic character

grada *nf* (**a**) *(peldaño)* step (**b**) **gradas** *(en estadio)* terraces

gradación *nf* scale

graderío *nm Esp Teatro* rows; *Dep* terraces

gradiente 1 *nm* gradient

2 *nf CSur, Ecuad* gradient, slope

grado *nm* (**a**) *(unidad)* degree (**b**) *Mil* rank (**c**) **de buen g.** willingly, gladly

graduable *adj* adjustable

graduación *nf* (**a**) *(de la vista)* eye-test; *(de gafas)* strength (**b**) *Educ* graduation (**c**) *(de bebidas)* strength, proof (**d**) *Mil* rank

graduado, -a *nm,f* graduate

gradual *adj* gradual

gradualmente *adv* gradually

graduar [30] **1** *vt* (**a**) *Educ* to confer a degree on (**b**) *Mil* to confer a rank on (**c**) *(regular)* to regulate

2 graduarse *vpr* (**a**) *Educ & Mil* to graduate (**b**) **graduarse la vista** to have one's eyes tested

graffiti *nm* piece of graffiti

grafía *nf* written symbol

gráfico, -a 1 *adj* graphic; **diseño g.** graphic design

2 *nm* graph

grafista *nmf* graphic designer

gragea *nf Med* pill

grajo, -a 1 *nm,f (ave)* rook

2 *nm Andes, Carib Fam (olor)* BO, body odour

gramática *nf* grammar

gramatical *adj* grammatical

gramo *nm* gram, gramme

gran *adj* = **grande**

grana *adj* scarlet

granada *nf* (**a**) *(fruto)* pomegranate (**b**) *Mil* grenade

granate 1 *adj inv (color)* maroon

2 *nm (color)* maroon

grande *adj* (**a**) *(tamaño)* big, large; *Fig (persona)* great; **Gran Bretaña** Great Britain (**b**) *(cantidad)* large; **vivir a lo g.** to live in style; *Fig* **pasarlo en g.** to have a great time

> **gran** is used instead of **grande** before masculine singular nouns (e.g. **gran hombre** great man).

grandeza *nf* (**a**) *(importancia)* greatness (**b**) *(grandiosidad)* grandeur; **delirios de g.** delusions of grandeur

grandioso, -a *adj* grandiose

granel *nm* **a g.** *(sin envase)* loose; *(en gran cantidad)* in bulk; *(en abundancia)* in abundance; **vender/comprar vino a g.** to sell/buy wine from the barrel

granero *nm Agr* granary

granito *nm* granite

granizada *nf* hailstorm

granizado *nm* = drink of flavoured crushed ice

granizar [40] *v impers* to hail

granizo *nm* hail

granja *nf* farm

granjear 1 *vt* to earn
2 granjearse *vpr* to gain, to earn

granjero, -a *nm,f* farmer

grano *nm* (a) *(de cereal, arena)* grain; *(de café)* bean; **ir al g.** to get to the point (b) *(espinilla)* spot

granuja *nm* (a) *(pilluelo)* ragamuffin (b) *(estafador)* con-man

grapa *nf (para papeles)* staple; *(para heridas)* stitch

grapadora *nf* stapler

grapar *vt* to staple

grasa *nf* grease; **grasas saturadas** saturated fats

grasiento, -a *adj* greasy

graso, -a *adj (pelo)* greasy; *(materia)* fatty

gratificar [44] *vt* (a) *(satisfacer)* to gratify (b) *(recompensar)* to reward

gratinado *adj* Culin au gratin

gratinar *vt* Culin to cook au gratin

gratis *adj inv & adv* free

gratitud *nf* gratitude

grato, -a *adj* pleasant

gratuito, -a *adj* (a) *(de balde)* free (of charge) (b) *(arbitrario)* gratuitous

grava *nf* gravel

gravamen *nm* tax

gravar *vt* (a) *(cargar)* to burden (b) *(impuestos)* to tax

grave *adj* (a) *(importante)* serious (b) *(muy enfermo)* seriously ill (c) *(voz, nota)* low

gravedad *nf* (a) *(seriedad, importancia)* seriousness (b) *Fís* gravity

gravilla *nf* chippings

gravitar *vi* (a) *Fís* to gravitate (b) **g. sobre** to rest on

gravoso, -a *adj* (a) *(costoso)* costly (b) *(molesto)* burdensome

graznar *vi (cuervo)* to caw; *(pato)* to quack; *(persona)* to squawk

graznido *nm (de cuervo)* caw; *(de pato)* quack; *(de persona)* squawk

Grecia *n* Greece

gregario, -a *adj* gregarious; **instinto g.** herd instinct

gremio *nm* (a) *Hist* guild (b) *(profesión)* profession, trade

greña *nf* lock of entangled hair; *Fam* **andar a la g.** to squabble

gres *nm* **artículos de g.** stoneware

gresca *nf* row

griego, -a *adj & nm,f* Greek

grieta *nf* crack; *(en la piel)* chap

grifero, -a *nm,f Perú (persona)* Br petrol pump attendant, *US* gas pump attendant

grifo *nm* (a) *Esp (llave)* Br tap, *US* faucet (b) *Perú (gasolinera)* Br petrol station, *US* gas station

grill [gril] *(pl* grills) *nm* grill

grillete *nm* shackle

grillo *nm* cricket

gringo, -a *Fam* **1** *adj* (a) *(estadounidense)* gringo, American (b) *Am (extranjero)* gringo, foreign
2 *nm,f* (a) *(estadounidense)* gringo, American (b) *Am (extranjero)* gringo, foreigner *(from a non-Spanish speaking country)*

gripa *nf* Col, Méx flu

gripe *nf* flu

gris *adj & nm* grey

grisáceo, -a *adj* greyish

gritar *vt & vi* to shout

grito *nm* shout; **a voz en g.** at the top of one's voice

Groenlandia *n* Greenland

grosella *nf (fruto)* redcurrant; **g. negra** blackcurrant; **g. silvestre** gooseberry

grosería *nf* (a) *(ordinariez)* rude word *o* expression (b) *(rusticidad)* rudeness

grosero, -a *adj (tosco)* coarse; *(maleducado)* rude

grosor *nm* thickness

grotesco, -a *adj* grotesque

grúa *nf* (a) *Constr* crane (b) *Aut Br* breakdown van *o* truck, *US* tow truck

grueso, -a 1 *adj* thick; *(persona)* stout
2 *nm (parte principal)* bulk

grulla *nf (ave)* crane

grumo *nm* lump; *(de leche)* curd

gruñido *nm* grunt

gruñir *vi* to grunt

gruñón, -ona *adj* grumpy

grupa *nf* hindquarters

grupo *nm* (a) *(conjunto)* group; *Inform* **g. de noticias** newsgroup (b) *Téc* unit, set

gruta *nf* cave

guaca *nf* (a) *Am (sepultura)* = pre-Columbian Indian tomb (b) *Am (tesoro)* hidden treasure (c) *CRica, Cuba (hucha)* moneybox

guacal *nm* (a) *CAm, Méx (calabaza)* gourd (b) *Carib, Col, Méx (jaula)* cage

guacamayo, -a *nm,f* macaw

guacamol, guacamole *nm* guacamole, avocado dip

guachafita *nf Col, Ven Fam* racket, uproar

guachimán *nm Am* night watchman

guacho, -a *adj & nm,f Andes, RP* (**a**) *muy Fam (persona huérfana)* orphan (**b**) *Fam (sinvergüenza)* bastard, swine

guaco *nm Am (cerámica)* = pottery object found in pre-Columbian Indian tomb

guadaña *nf* scythe

guagua *nf* (**a**) *Andes (niño)* baby (**b**) *Cuba, PRico, RDom* bus

guajiro, -a *nm,f* (**a**) *Cuba Fam (campesino)* peasant (**b**) *(de Guajira)* person from Guajira *(Colombia, Venezuela)*

guajolote *nm CAm, Méx* (**a**) *(pavo)* turkey (**b**) *(tonto)* fool, idiot

guampa *nf Bol, CSur* horn

guanajo *nm Carib* turkey

guantazo *nm* slap

guante *nm* glove

guantera *nf Aut* glove compartment

guapo, -a *adj* (**a**) *esp Esp (atractivo)* good-looking; *(hombre)* handsome; *(mujer)* pretty (**b**) *Am (valiente)* gutsy; **ser g.** to have guts

guaraca *nf Am* sling

guarache *nm Méx (sandalia)* = crude sandal with a sole made from a tyre

guarangada *nf Bol, CSur* rude remark

guarango, -a *adj* rude

guarda *nmf* guard; **g. jurado** security guard

guardabarros *nm inv Esp, Bol, RP (de automóvil, bicicleta) Br* mudguard, *US* fender

guardabosque *nmf* gamekeeper

guardacoches *nmf inv* parking attendant

guardacostas 1 *nmf inv (persona)* coastguard
2 *nm inv (barco)* coastguard boat

guardaespaldas *nmf inv* bodyguard

guardafango *nm inv Andes, CAm, Carib (de vehículo) Br* mudguard, *US* fender

guardameta *nmf Dep* goalkeeper

guardapolvo *nm* overalls

guardar 1 *vt* (**a**) *(conservar)* to keep (**b**) *(un secreto)* to keep; **g. silencio** to remain silent; **g. cama** to stay in bed (**c**) *(poner en un sitio)* to put away (**d**) *(reservar)* to keep (**e**) *Inform* to save
2 guardarse *vpr* **guardarse de hacer algo** *(abstenerse)* to be careful not to do sth; **guardársela a algn** to have it in for sb

guardarropa *nm* (**a**) *(cuarto)* cloakroom (**b**) *(armario)* wardrobe

guardería *nf* **g. infantil** nursery (school)

guardia 1 *nf* (**a**) *(vigilancia)* watch (**b**) **la G. Civil** the Civil Guard (**c**) *(turno de servicio)* duty; **Mil** guard duty; **de g.** on duty; **farmacia de g.** duty chemist
2 *nmf* policeman; *(mujer)* policewoman

guardián, -ana *nm,f* watchman

guarecer [33] **1** *vt* to shelter
2 guarecerse *vpr* to take shelter *o* refuge (**de** from)

guarida *nf (de animal)* lair; *(refugio)* hide-out

guarismo *nm* digit

guarnecer [33] *vt* (**a**) *Culin* to garnish (**b**) *(adornar)* to decorate (**c**) *Mil* to garrison

guarnición *nf* (**a**) *Culin* garnish (**b**) *Mil* garrison

guarro, -a *Esp* **1** *adj* filthy
2 *nm,f* pig

guarura *nm Méx Fam* bodyguard

guasa *nf* mockery

guasca *nf Chile, Perú* whip

guasearse *vpr Fam* to tease

guaso, -a *adj* (**a**) *Chile (campesino)* peasant (**b**) *Andes, RP* **ser un g.** *(grosero)* to be crude *o* coarse; *(maleducado)* to be rude

guasón, -ona 1 *adj* humorous
2 *nm,f* joker

guata *nf* (**a**) *(relleno)* padding (**b**) *Andes Fam (barriga)* belly

Guatemala *n* (**a**) *(país)* Guatemala (**b**) *(ciudad)* Guatemala City

guatemalteco, -a *adj & nm,f* Guatemalan

guay *adj inv Esp Fam* cool, *US* neat

guayaba *nf (fruta)* guava

guayabera *nf CAm, Carib, Col* short jacket

guayabo *nm* (**a**) *(árbol)* guava tree (**b**) *Andes Fam (resaca)* hangover

guepardo *nm* cheetah

güero, -a *adj Méx Fam* blond, *f* blonde, fair-haired

guerra *nf* war; **en g.** at war; **g. bacteriológica** germ warfare; **g. civil/fría/ mundial/nuclear** civil/cold/world/nuclear war; **Fam dar g.** to be a real nuisance

guerrero, -a 1 *nm,f* warrior
2 *adj* warlike

guerrilla *nf* (**a**) *(partida armada)* guerrilla force *o* band (**b**) *(lucha)* guerrilla warfare

guerrillero, -a 1 *adj* guerrilla; **ataque g.** guerrilla attack
2 *nm,f* guerrilla

güevón, -ona *nm,f Andes, Arg, Ven muy Fam (estúpido) Br* prat, *US* jerk

guía 1 *nmf (persona)* guide
2 *nf* (**a**) *(norma)* guideline (**b**) *(libro)* guide; *(lista)* directory; *Esp, RP* **g. telefónica** *o* **de teléfonos** telephone directory

guiar [29] **1** *vt* (**a**) *(indicar el camino)* to guide (**b**) *Aut* to drive; *Náut* to steer; *(caballo, bici)* to ride
2 guiarse *vpr* **guiarse por** to be guided by, to go by

guija *nf* pebble

guijarro *nm* pebble
guillotina *nf* guillotine
guinda *nf (fruto)* morello (cherry)
guindilla *nf* chilli
Guinea Ecuatorial *n* Equatorial Guinea
guineo *nm Andes, CAm* banana
guiñapo *nm* (**a**) *(andrajo)* rag (**b**) *Fig (persona)* wreck; **poner a algn como un g.** to tear sb to pieces
guiñar *vt* to wink
guiño *nm* wink
guiñol *nm* puppet theatre
guión *nm* (**a**) *Cin & TV* script (**b**) *Ling* hyphen, dash (**c**) *(esquema)* sketch
guionista *nmf* scriptwriter
guiri *nmf Esp Fam* foreigner
guirigay *(pl* **guirigays** *o* **guirigáis**) *nm* hubbub
guirnalda *nf* garland
guisa *nf* way, manner; **a g. de** as, by way of
guisado *nm Culin* stew
guisante *nm esp Esp* pea
guisar *vt* to cook
guiso *nm* dish; *(guisado)* stew
guita *nf Esp, RP Fam* dough

guitarra 1 *nf* guitar
    2 *nmf* guitarist
guitarreada *nf CSur* singalong *(to guitars)*
guitarrista *nmf* guitarist
gula *nf* gluttony
gurí, -isa *nm,f RP Fam (niño)* kid, child; *(chico)* lad, boy; *(chica)* lass, girl
gusano *nm* worm; *(oruga)* caterpillar; *Fam Pey (exiliado cubano)* = anti-Castro Cuban living in exile; **g. de seda** silkworm
gustar 1 *vt* (**a**) **me gusta el vino** I like wine; **me gustaban los caramelos** I used to like sweets; **me gusta nadar** I like swimming; **me gustaría ir** I would like to go (**b**) *Fml* **¿gustas?** would you like some?; **cuando gustes** whenever you like
    2 *vi* **g. de** to enjoy
gusto *nm* (**a**) *(sentido)* taste (**b**) *(en fórmulas de cortesía)* pleasure; **con (mucho) g.** with (great) pleasure; **tanto g.** pleased to meet you (**c**) **estar a g.** to feel comfortable *o* at ease; **por g.** for the sake of it; **ser de buen/mal g.** to be in good/bad taste; **tener buen/mal g.** to have good/bad taste; **tenemos el gusto de comunicarle que ...** we are pleased to inform you that ...
gutural *adj* guttural

H

H, h [atʃe] *nf (letra)* H, h; **bomba H** H-bomb

ha *indic pres de* **haber**

haba *nf* broad bean

> Takes the masculine articles **el** and **un**.

Habana *nf* **La H.** Havana

habano *nm* Havana cigar

haber [14] **1** *v aux* (**a**) *(en tiempos compuestos)* to have; **lo he visto** I have seen it; **ya lo había hecho** he had already done it (**b**) **h. de** + *infin (obligación)* to have to; **has de ser bueno** you must be good

2 *v impers (special form of present tense:* **hay**) (**a**) *(existir, estar) (singular used also with plural nouns)* **hay** there is/are; **había** there was/were; **había un gato en el tejado** there was a cat on the roof; **había muchos libros** there were a lot of books; **hay 500 km entre Madrid y Granada** it's 500 km from Madrid to Granada
(**b**) **h. que** + *infin* it is necessary to; **hay que trabajar** you've got to *o* you must work; **habrá que comprobarlo** I/you/we/ *etc* will have to check it
(**c**) *(tener lugar)* **habrá una fiesta** there will be a party; **hoy hay partido** there's a match today; **los accidentes habidos en esta carretera** the accidents which have happened on this road
(**d**) **había una vez ...** once upon a time ...; **no hay de qué** you're welcome, don't mention it; **¿qué hay?** how are things?

3 *nm* (**a**) *Fin* credit; **haberes** assets (**b**) **en su h.** in his possession

habichuela *nf Esp, Carib, Col* bean

hábil *adj* (**a**) *(diestro)* skilful (**b**) *(astuto)* smart (**c**) **días hábiles** working days

habilidad *nf* (**a**) *(destreza)* skill (**b**) *(astucia)* cleverness

habilitar *vt* (**a**) *(espacio)* to fit out (**b**) *Der (autorizar)* to authorize (**c**) *(financiar)* to finance

habiloso, -a *adj Chile* shrewd, astute

habitación *nf (cuarto)* room; *(dormitorio)* bedroom; **h. individual/doble** single/ double room

habitante *nmf* inhabitant

habitar 1 *vt* to live in, to inhabit
2 *vi* to live

hábitat *(pl* **hábitats**) *nm* habitat

hábito *nm* (**a**) *(costumbre)* habit (**b**) *Rel* habit

habitual *adj* usual, habitual; *(cliente, lector)* regular

habituar [30] **1** *vt* to accustom (**a** to)
2 habituarse *vpr* **habituarse a** to get used to, to become accustomed to

habla *nf* (**a**) *(idioma)* language; **países de h. española** Spanish-speaking countries (**b**) *(facultad de hablar)* speech; **quedarse sin h.** to be left speechless (**c**) *Tel* **¡al h.!** speaking!

> Takes the masculine articles **el** and **un**.

hablado, -a *adj* spoken; **el inglés h.** spoken English; **mal h.** coarse, foul-mouthed

hablador, -a *adj (parlanchín)* talkative; *(chismoso)* gossipy

habladuría *nf (rumor)* rumour; *(chisme)* piece of gossip

hablante *nmf* speaker

hablar 1 *vi* to speak, to talk; **h. con algn** to speak to sb; **¡ni h.!** certainly not!; *Fam* **¡quién fue a h.!** look who's talking!
2 *vt* (**a**) *(idioma)* to speak; **habla alemán** he speaks German (**b**) *(tratar un asunto)* to talk over, to discuss
3 hablarse *vpr* (**a**) *(dos personas)* to speak *o* talk to one another (**b**) **se habla español** *(en letrero)* Spanish spoken

habré *indic fut de* **haber**

hacendado, -a *nm,f* (**a**) *(terrateniente)* landowner (**b**) *CSur (ganadero)* rancher

hacendoso, -a *adj* houseproud

hacer [15] **1** *vt* (**a**) *(crear, producir, fabricar)* to make; **h. una casa** to build a house
(**b**) *(obrar, ejecutar)* to do; **eso no se hace** it isn't done; **hazme un favor** do me a favour; **¿qué haces?** *(en este momento)* what are you doing?; *(para vivir)* what do you do *(for a living)?* **tengo mucho que h.** I have a lot to do; **h. deporte** to do sports; **h. una carrera/medicina** to do a degree/medicine
(**c**) *(conseguir) (amigos, dinero)* to make
(**d**) *(obligar)* to make; **hazle callar/ trabajar** make him shut up/work

(**e**) *(arreglar)* to make; **h. la cama** to make the bed
(**f**) *Mat (sumar)* to make; **y con éste hacen cien** and that makes a hundred
(**g**) *(dar aspecto)* to make look; **el negro le hace más delgado** black makes him look slimmer
(**h**) *(sustituyendo a otro verbo)* to do; **ya no puedo leer como solía hacerlo** I can't read as well as I used to
(**i**) *(representar)* to play; **h. el bueno** to play the (part of the) goody
(**j**) **¡bien hecho!** well done!
2 *vi* (**a**) *(actuar)* to play; **hizo de Desdémona** she played Desdemona (**b**) **h. por** *o* **para** + *infin* to try to; **hice por venir** I tried to come (**c**) *(fingir)* to pretend; **h. como si** to act as if (**d**) *(convenir)* to be suitable; **a las ocho si te hace** will eight o'clock be all right for you?
3 *v impers* (**a**) **hace calor/frío** it's hot/cold (**b**) *(tiempo transcurrido)* ago; **hace mucho (tiempo)** a long time ago; **hace dos días que no le veo** I haven't seen him for two days; **hace dos años que vivo en Glasgow** I've been living in Glasgow for two years
4 hacerse *vpr* (**a**) *(volverse)* to become, to grow; **hacerse viejo** to grow old (**b**) *(simular)* to pretend; **hacerse el dormido** to pretend to be sleeping (**c**) **hacerse con** *(apropiarse)* to get hold of (**d**) **hacerse a** *(habituarse)* to get used to; **enseguida me hago a todo** I soon get used to anything
hacha *nf* (**a**) *(herramienta)* axe (**b**) *Fam* **ser un h. en algo** to be an ace *o* a wizard at sth

Takes the masculine articles **el** and **un**.

hachís *nm* hashish

hacia *prep* (**a**) *(dirección)* towards, to; **h. abajo** down, downwards; **h. adelante** forwards; **h. arriba** up, upwards; **h. atrás** back, backwards (**b**) *(tiempo)* at about, at around; **h. las tres** at about three o'clock

hacienda *nf* (**a**) *(finca)* country estate *o* property (**b**) *Fin* **(el Ministerio de) H.** *Br* ≃ the Treasury, *US* ≃ the Department of the Treasury

hacinamiento *nm* *(de gente)* overcrowding

hacinarse *vpr* *(gente)* to be crowded together

hada *nf* fairy; **cuento de hadas** fairy tale; **h. madrina** fairy godmother

Takes the masculine articles **el** and **un**.

hado *nm* destiny

hago *indic pres de* **hacer**

Haití *n* Haiti

hala *interj Esp* **¡h.!** *(para dar ánimo, prisa)* come on!; *(para expresar incredulidad)* no!, you're joking!; *(para expresar admiración, sorpresa)* wow!

halagar [42] *vt* to flatter

halago *nm* flattery

halagüeño, -a *adj (noticia, impresión)* promising

halcón *nm* falcon; **h. peregrino** peregrine (falcon)

hall [ol] *(pl* **halls)** *nm* entrance hall, foyer

hallar 1 *vt (encontrar)* to find; *(averiguar)* to find out; *(descubrir)* to discover
2 hallarse *vpr (estar)* to be, to find oneself; *(estar situado)* to be situated

hallazgo *nm* (**a**) *(descubrimiento)* discovery (**b**) *(cosa encontrada)* find

halógeno, -a *adj Quím* halogenous

halterofilia *nf* weightlifting

hamaca *nf* hammock; *(mecedora)* rocking chair

hambre *nf (apetito)* hunger; *(inanición)* starvation; *(catástrofe)* famine; **tener h.** to be hungry

Takes the masculine articles **el** and **un**.

hambriento, -a *adj* starving

hamburguesa *nf* hamburger, *Br* beefburger

hampa *nf* underworld

Takes the masculine articles **el** and **un**.

hámster ['amster] *(pl* **hámsters)** *nm* hamster

han *indic pres de* **haber**

hangar *nm* hangar

harapo *nm* rag; **hecho un h.** in tatters

hardware ['arwer] *nm Inform* hardware

haré *indic fut de* **hacer**

harén *nm* harem

harina *nf* flour

hartar 1 *vt* (**a**) *(cansar, fastidiar)* to annoy (**b**) *(atiborrar)* to satiate; **el dulce harta enseguida** sweet things soon fill you up
2 hartarse *vpr* (**a**) *(saciar el apetito)* to eat one's fill (**b**) *(cansarse)* to get fed up (**de** with), to grow tired (**de** of)

harto, -a 1 *adj* (**a**) *(de comida)* full (**b**) *(cansado)* fed up; **¡me tienes h.!** I'm fed up with you!; **estoy h. de trabajar** I'm fed up (with) working (**c**) *Am salvo RP (mucho)* lots of; **tiene h. dinero** he's got lots of money
2 *adv* (**a**) *Esp Fml (muy)* very (**b**) *Am salvo RP (muy, mucho)* really

hartura *nf* **¡qué h.!** what a drag!

has *indic pres de* **haber**

hasta 1 *prep* (**a**) *(lugar)* up to, as far as, down to (**b**) *(tiempo)* until, till, up to; **h. el domingo** until Sunday; **h. el final** right to

the end; **h. la fecha** up to now; **h. luego** see you later (**c**) (*con cantidad*) up to, as many as (**d**) (*incluso*) even (**e**) *CAm, Col, Ecuad, Méx* (*no antes de*) **pintaremos la casa h. fin de mes** we won't paint the house till the end of the month
2 *conj* **h. que** until

hastiado, -a *adj* sick, tired (**de** of)

hastiar [29] *vt* to sicken

hastío *nm* weariness

hato *nm* bundle

hay *indic pres de* **haber**

haya[1] *nf* (**a**) *Bot* (*árbol*) beech (**b**) (*madera*) beech (wood)

> Takes the masculine articles **el** and **un**.

haya[2] *subj pres de* **haber**

haz[1] *nm* (**a**) *Agr* sheaf (**b**) (*de luz*) shaft

haz[2] *nf* (*de hoja*) top side

haz[3] *imperat de* **hacer**

hazaña *nf* deed, exploit

hazmerreír *nm* laughing stock

he[1] *adv* **he ahí/aquí ...** there/here you have ...

he[2] *indic pres de* **haber**

hebilla *nf* buckle

hebra *nf* thread; (*de carne*) sinew; (*de madera*) grain; *Esp* **pegar la h.** to chat

hebreo, -a 1 *adj* Hebrew
2 *nm,f* Hebrew

hecatombe *nf* disaster

hechicería *nf* witchcraft

hechicero, -a 1 *adj* bewitching
2 *nm,f* (*hombre*) wizard, sorcerer; (*mujer*) witch, sorceress

hechizar [40] *vt* (**a**) (*embrujar*) to cast a spell on (**b**) *Fig* (*fascinar*) to bewitch, to charm

hechizo *nm* (**a**) (*embrujo*) spell (**b**) *Fig* (*fascinación*) fascination, charm

hecho, -a 1 *adj* (**a**) (*carne*) done (**b**) (*persona*) mature (**c**) (*ropa*) ready-made
2 *nm* (**a**) (*realidad*) fact; **el h. es que ...** the fact is that ...; **de h. in** fact (**b**) (*suceso*) event, incident (**c**) (*acto*) act, deed

hechura *nf* (*forma*) shape; *Cost* cut

hectárea *nf* hectare

hectolitro *nm* hectolitre

heder [3] *vi* to stink, to smell foul

hediondo, -a *adj* foul-smelling

hedor *nm* stink, stench

hegemonía *nf* hegemony

helada *nf* frost

heladera *nf CSur* (*nevera*) refrigerator, *Br* fridge, *US* icebox

heladería *nf* ice-cream parlour

helado, -a 1 *nm* ice cream
2 *adj* (**a**) (*muy frío*) frozen, freezing cold; **estoy h. (de frío)** I'm frozen (**b**) *Fig* **quedarse h.** (*atónito*) to be flabbergasted

helar [1] 1 *vt* (*congelar*) to freeze
2 *v impers* to freeze; **anoche heló** there was a frost last night
3 **helarse** *vpr* (*congelarse*) to freeze

helecho *nm Bot* fern

hélice *nf* (**a**) *Av & Náut* propeller (**b**) *Anat, Arquit & Mat* helix

helicóptero *nm Av* helicopter

helipuerto *nm Av* heliport

hematoma *nm Med* haematoma

hembra *nf* (**a**) *Bot & Zool* female (**b**) (*mujer*) woman (**c**) *Téc* female; (*de tornillo*) nut; (*de enchufe*) socket

hemiciclo *nm* (*en parlamento*) chamber

hemisferio *nm* hemisphere

hemorragia *nf* haemorrhage

hemos *indic pres de* **haber**

henchir [6] *vt* to fill (up)

hender [3] *vt* to crack, to split

hendidura *nf* crack

hendir [5] *vt* = **hender**

heno *nm* hay

hepatitis *nf inv* hepatitis

heráldica *nf* heraldry

herbicida *nm* weedkiller, herbicide

herbívoro, -a 1 *adj* herbivorous, grass-eating
2 *nm,f* herbivore

herbolario *nm* herbalist's (shop)

herboristería *nf* herbalist's (shop)

hercio *nm* Hertz

heredad *nf* (**a**) (*finca*) country estate (**b**) (*conjunto de bienes*) private estate

heredar *vt* (**a**) *Der* to inherit (**b**) **ha heredado la sonrisa de su madre** she's got her mother's smile

heredero, -a *nm,f* (*hombre*) heir; (*mujer*) heiress; **príncipe h.** crown prince

hereditario, -a *adj* hereditary

hereje *nmf Rel* heretic

herejía *nf Rel* heresy

herencia *nf* (**a**) *Der* inheritance, legacy (**b**) *Biol* heredity

herida *nf* (*lesión*) injury; (*corte*) wound

herido, -a *nm,f* injured person; **no hubo heridos** there were no casualties

herir [5] 1 *vt* (**a**) (*físicamente*) (*lesionar*) to injure; (*cortar*) to wound (**b**) (*emocionalmente*) to hurt, to wound (**c**) (*vista*) to offend
2 **herirse** *vpr* to injure *o* hurt oneself

hermana nf (a) (familiar) sister; **h. política** sister-in-law; **prima h.** first cousin (b) Rel (monja) sister

hermanado, -a adj twinned; **ciudad hermanada** twin town

hermanar 1 vt (a) (personas) to unite spiritually (b) (ciudades) to twin (c) (unir) to unite, to combine
2 hermanarse vpr (a) (ciudades) to twin (b) (combinar) to combine

hermanastro, -a nm,f (hombre) stepbrother; (mujer) stepsister

hermandad nf (a) (grupo) fraternity, brotherhood, sisterhood (b) (relación) brotherhood, sisterhood

hermano nm (a) (familiar) brother; **h. político** brother-in-law; **primo h.** first cousin (b) Rel (fraile) brother (c) **hermanos** brothers and sisters

herméticamente adv **h. cerrado** hermetically sealed

hermético, -a adj (a) (cierre) hermetic, airtight (b) (persona) uncommunicative

hermetismo nm uncommunicativeness

hermoso, -a adj (a) (bello) beautiful, lovely (b) (grande) fine

hermosura nf beauty

héroe nm hero

heroico, -a adj heroic

heroína nf (a) (mujer) heroine (b) (droga) heroin

heroinómano, -a nm,f heroin addict

heroísmo nm heroism

herradura nf horseshoe

herramienta nf Téc tool; **caja de herramientas** toolbox

herrar [1] vt (a) (caballo) to shoe (b) (ganado) to brand

herrería nf forge, smithy

herrero nm blacksmith, smith

herrumbre nf rust

hervidero nm (lugar) hotbed

hervir [5] **1** vt to boil
2 vi (a) Culin to boil; **romper a h.** to come to the boil (b) (abundar) to swarm, to seethe (**de** with)

heterodoxo, -a adj unorthodox

heterogéneo, -a adj heterogeneous

heterosexual adj & nmf heterosexual

hez nf (a) (usu pl) (poso) sediment, dregs (b) **heces** faeces

hiato nm Ling hiatus

híbrido, -a adj & nm hybrid

hice pt indef de **hacer**

hiciste pt indef de **hacer**

hidalgo nm Hist nobleman, gentleman

hidalguía nf nobility; Fig chivalry, gentlemanliness

hidratación nf (de la piel) moisturizing

hidratante adj moisturizing; **crema/leche h.** moisturizing cream/lotion

hidratar vt (piel) to moisturize; Quím to hydrate

hidráulico, -a adj hydraulic; **energía hidráulica** hydroelectric energy

hidroavión nm seaplane, US hydroplane

hidrófilo, -a adj **algodón h.** Br cotton wool, Am absorbent cotton

hidrógeno nm Quím hydrogen

hiedra nf ivy

hiel nf (a) (bilis) bile (b) (mala intención) spleen, bitterness

hielo nm ice; Fig **romper el h.** to break the ice

hiena nf hyena

hierba nf (a) (césped) grass; Culin herb; **mala h.** Bot weed; Fig (persona) bad lot; Fam Hum **y otras hierbas** among others; **h. luisa** lemon verbena (b) Fam (marihuana) grass

hierbabuena nf mint

hierro nm (a) (metal) iron; **h. forjado** wrought iron (b) (punta de arma) head, point (c) (marca en el ganado) brand

hígado nm (a) Anat liver (b) Euf guts

higiene nf hygiene

higiénico, -a adj hygienic; **papel h.** toilet paper

higo nm fig; Fam Fig **hecho un h.** wizened, crumpled

higuera nf Bot fig tree

hijastro, -a nm,f (hombre) stepson; (mujer) stepdaughter

hijo, -a nm,f (a) (hombre) son; (mujer) daughter; Pey **h. de papá** rich kid; Vulg **h. de puta** o Méx **de la chingada** bastard, US asshole (b) **hijos** children

hijoputa nm Vulg bastard, US asshole

hilandería nf mill; (de algodón) cotton mill

hilandero, -a nm,f spinner

hilar vt & vi to spin; Fig **h. muy fino** to split hairs

hilaridad nf hilarity, mirth

hilera nf line, row

hilo nm (a) Cost thread; (grueso) yarn; **h. dental** dental floss (b) Fig (de historia, discurso) thread; (de pensamiento) train; **perder el h.** to lose the thread; **h. musical** background music (c) Tex linen

hilvanar vt (a) Cost Br to tack, US to baste (b) Fig (ideas etc) to outline

himno *nm* hymn; **h. nacional** national anthem

hincapié *nm* **hacer h. en** *(insistir)* to insist on; *(subrayar)* to emphasize, to stress

hincar [44] **1** *vt (clavar)* to drive (in); **h. el diente a** to sink one's teeth into
2 hincarse *upr* **hincarse de rodillas** to kneel (down)

hincha *Fam* **1** *nmf Ftb* fan, supporter
2 *nf (antipatía)* grudge, dislike; *Esp* **me tiene h.** he's got it in for me

hinchada *nf Fam Ftb* fans, supporters

hinchado, -a *adj* (a) *(inflado)* inflated, blown up (b) *Med (cara etc)* swollen, puffed up; *(estómago)* bloated (c) *Fig (estilo)* bombastic, pompous

hinchar 1 *vt* (a) *(inflar)* to inflate, to blow up (b) *Fig (exagerar)* to inflate, to exaggerate
2 hincharse *upr* (a) *Med* to swell (up) (b) *Fam* **me hinché de comida** I stuffed myself; **me hinché de llorar** I cried for all I was worth

hinchazón *nf Med* swelling

hindú *adj & nmf* Hindu

hipermercado *nm* hypermarket

hipermetropía *nf* long-sightedness, *Espec* hypermetropia, *US* hypertropia

hipertensión *nf* high blood pressure

hipertexto *nm Inform* hypertext

hípica *nf (carreras de caballos)* horse-racing; *(equitación)* showjumping

hípico, -a *adj* **concurso h.** *(de las carreras)* horseraces; *(de la equitación)* show-jumping

hipnotizar [40] *vt* to hypnotize

hipo *nm* hiccups, hiccoughs; **me ha dado h.** it's given me the hiccups

hipocondríaco, -a *adj & nm,f* hypochondriac

hipocresía *nf* hypocrisy

hipócrita 1 *adj* hypocritical
2 *nmf* hypocrite

hipódromo *nm* racetrack, racecourse

hipopótamo *nm* hippopotamus

hipoteca *nf Fin* mortgage

hipotecar [44] *vt* (a) *Fin* to mortgage (b) *Fig* to jeopardize

hipótesis *nf inv* hypothesis

hipotético, -a *adj* hypothetical

hippy, hippie ['ipi] *(pl hippies) adj & nmf* hippy

hiriente *adj* offensive, wounding; *(palabras)* cutting

hirsuto, -a *adj* hirsute, hairy; *(cerdoso)* bristly

hispánico, -a *adj* Hispanic, Spanish

hispanidad *nf* **el Día de la H.** Columbus Day *(12 October)*

hispano, -a 1 *adj (español)* Spanish; *(español y sudamericano)* Hispanic; *(sudamericano)* Spanish American
2 *nm,f (hispanoamericano)* Spanish American; *(estadounidense)* Hispanic

Hispanoamérica *nf* Latin America

hispanoamericano, -a *adj & nm,f* Latin American

hispanohablante 1 *adj* Spanish-speaking
2 *nmf* Spanish speaker

histeria *nf* hysteria; **un ataque de h.** hysterics

histérico, -a *adj* hysterical; *Fam Fig* **me pones h.** you're driving me mad

historia *nf* (a) *(ciencia)* history; **esto pasará a la h.** this will go down in history (b) *(narración)* story, tale; *Fam* **¡déjate de historias!** don't give me that!

historiador, -a *nm,f* historian

historial *nm* (a) *Med* medical record, case history (b) *(antecedentes)* background

historiar [29] *vt* to recount

histórico, -a *adj* (a) *(novela, legado)* historical; *(centro)* historic (b) *(auténtico)* factual, true; **hechos históricos** true facts (c) *(de gran importancia)* historic; **máximo/mínimo h.** all-time high/low

historieta *nf* (a) *(cuento)* short story, tale (b) *(tira cómica)* comic strip

hito *nm* milestone

hizo *pt indef de* hacer

hnos. *(abr* Hermanos) Bros

hobby ['oβi] *(pl hobbys) nm* hobby

hocico *nm* (a) *(de animal)* snout (b) *(de persona)* mug, snout; *Fam* **meter los hocicos en algo** to stick o poke one's nose into sth

hockey ['okei] *nm* hockey; **h. sobre hielo** *Br* ice hockey, *US* hockey; **h. sobre hierba** *Br* hockey, *US* field hockey

hogar *nm* (a) *(casa)* home (b) *(de la chimenea)* hearth, fireplace (c) *Fig* **formar o crear un h.** *(familia)* to start a family

hogareño, -a *adj (vida)* home, family; *(persona)* home-loving, stay-at-home

hoguera *nf* bonfire

hoja *nf* (a) *Bot* leaf (b) *(pétalo)* petal (c) *(de papel)* sheet, leaf; **h. de cálculo** spreadsheet (d) *(de libro)* leaf, page (e) *(de metal)* sheet (f) *(de cuchillo, espada)* blade (g) *(impreso)* hand-out, printed sheet (h) *(de puerta, ventana)* leaf

hojalata *nf* tin, tin plate

hojaldre *nm Culin* puff pastry

hojarasca *nf* fallen o dead leaves

hojear *vt* to leaf through, to flick through

hola *interj* hello!, hullo!, hi!

Holanda *n* Holland

holandés, -esa 1 *adj* Dutch
2 *nm,f (hombre)* Dutchman; *(mujer)* Dutchwoman
3 *nm (idioma)* Dutch

holding *nm Fin* holding company

holgado, -a *adj* (a) *(ropa)* loose, baggy (b) *(económicamente)* comfortable (c) *(espacio)* roomy; **andar h. de tiempo** to have plenty of time

holgar [2] *vi* (a) *(no trabajar)* to be idle (b) *(sobrar)* **huelga decir que ...** it goes without saying that ...

holgazán, -ana 1 *adj* lazy, idle
2 *nm,f* lazybones, layabout

holgura *nf* (a) *(de ropa)* looseness (b) *(espacio)* space, roominess (c) *(económica)* affluence, comfort; **vivir con h.** to be comfortably off, to be well-off

hollar [2] *vt* to walk on; **terrenos jamás hollados** uncharted territory

hollín *nm* soot

hombre 1 *nm* (a) *(individuo)* man; **de h. a h.** man-to-man; **¡pobre h.!** poor *Br* chap *o US* guy!; **ser muy h.** to be every inch a man; **h. de estado** statesman; **h. de negocios** businessman (b) *(especie)* mankind, man
2 *interj Esp* **¡h.!** *(hey,)* how nice to see you!; **¡sí, h.!** sure!

hombrera *nf* shoulder pad

hombría *nf* manliness, virility

hombrillo *nm Ven (arcén)* (de carretera) verge; (de autopista) *Br* hard shoulder, *US* shoulder

hombro *nm* shoulder; **a hombros** on one's shoulders; **encogerse de hombros** to shrug one's shoulders; **mirar a algn por encima del h.** to look down one's nose at sb

hombruno, -a *adj* mannish, butch

homenaje *nm* homage, tribute; **rendir h. a algn** to pay homage *o* tribute to sb

homenajear *vt* to pay tribute to

homeopatía *nf* homeopathy

homeopático, -a *adj* homeopathic

homicida 1 *nmf (hombre)* murderer; *(mujer)* murderess
2 *adj* homicidal; **el arma h.** the murder weapon

homicidio *nm* homicide

homogéneo, -a *adj* homogeneous, uniform

homologable *adj* comparable (con to)

homologar [42] *vt* to give official approval *o* recognition to

homólogo, -a 1 *adj (semejante)* equivalent
2 *nm,f (persona)* counterpart

homosexual *adj & nmf* homosexual

homosexualidad *nf* homosexuality

honda *nf* sling

hondo, -a *adj* (a) *(profundo)* deep; **plato h.** soup dish (b) *Fig (pesar)* profound, deep

hondonada *nf Geog* hollow, depression

hondura *nf* depth; *Fig* **meterse en honduras** *(profundizar)* to go into too much detail

Honduras *n* Honduras

hondureño, -a *adj & nm,f* Honduran

honestidad *nf* (a) *(honradez)* honesty, uprightness (b) *(decencia)* modesty

honesto, -a *adj* (a) *(honrado)* honest, upright (b) *(decente)* modest

hongo *nm* (a) *Bot* fungus; **h. venenoso** toadstool (b) *(sombrero) Br* bowler (hat), *US* derby

honor *nm* (a) *(virtud)* honour; **palabra de h.** word of honour (b) **en h. a la verdad ...** to be fair ...; **es un h. para mí** it's an honour for me (c) **hacer h. a** to live up to

honorable *adj* honourable

honorario, -a 1 *adj* honorary
2 **honorarios** *nmpl* fees, fee

honorífico, -a *adj* honorific

honra *nf* (a) *(dignidad)* dignity, self-esteem (b) *(fama)* reputation, good name (c) *(honor)* honour; **me cabe la h. de ...** I have the honour of ...; **¡a mucha h.!** and proud of it!

honradez *nf* honesty, integrity

honrado, -a *adj* (a) *(de fiar)* honest (b) *(decente)* upright, respectable

honrar *vt* (a) *(respetar)* to honour (b) *(enaltecer)* to be a credit to

honrilla *nf* self-respect, pride

honroso, -a *adj* honourable

hora *nf* (a) *(60 minutos)* hour; **media h.** half an hour; **a altas horas de la madrugada** in the small hours; **dar la h.** to strike the hour; **(trabajo) por horas** (work) paid by the hour; *Esp* **h. punta**, *Am* **h. pico** *(de mucho tráfico)* rush hour; *(de agua, electricidad)* peak times; **horas extra** overtime (hours) (b) *(en un reloj, momento)* time; **¿qué h. es?** what time is it?; **a su h.** at the proper time; **a última h.** at the last moment; *Esp, Andes, Carib, RP* **la h. de la verdad** the moment of truth (c) *(cita)* appointment; **pedir h.** *(al médico etc)* to ask for an appointment

horadar *vt* to drill *o* bore a hole in

horario, -a 1 *nm Br* timetable, *US* schedule
2 *adj* time; *Rad* **señal horaria** pips

horca *nf* gallows *sing*

horcajadas: a horcajadas *loc adv*
astride

horchata *nf Culin* = cold drink made from
ground tiger nuts, water and sugar

horda *nf* horde, mob

horizontal *adj* horizontal

horizonte *nm* horizon

horma *nf (de zapato)* last

hormiga *nf* ant

hormigón *nm Constr* concrete; **h. armado**
reinforced concrete

hormigonera *nf* concrete mixer

hormiguear *vi* to itch, to tingle; **me
hormigueaba la pierna** I had pins and
needles in my leg

hormigueo *nm* pins and needles, tingling
o itching sensation

hormiguero *nm* (a) *Zool* anthill (b) *Fig*
ser un h. *(lugar)* to be swarming (with
people)

hormona *nf* hormone

hornada *nf* batch

hornear *vt* to bake

hornillo *nm (de cocinar)* stove; *(placa)*
hotplate

horno *nm (cocina)* oven; *Téc* furnace;
(para cerámica, ladrillos) kiln; *Culin*
pescado al h. baked fish; *Fam Fig* **esta
habitación es un h.** this room is boiling
hot

horóscopo *nm* horoscope

horquilla *nf* (a) *(del pelo)* hairpin, *Br*
hairgrip (b) *(estadística)* chart (c) **h. de
precios** price range

horrendo, -a *adj* horrifying, horrible

hórreo *nm Agr* granary

horrible *adj* horrible, dreadful, awful

horripilante *adj* hair-raising, scary

horror *nm* (a) *(miedo)* horror, terror; **¡qué
h.!** how awful!; *Fam* **tengo h. a las motos** I
hate motorbikes (b) *Fam Fig* **me gusta
horrores** *(muchísimo)* I like it an awful lot

horrorizar [40] *vt* to horrify, to terrify

horroroso, -a *adj* (a) *(que da miedo)*
horrifying, terrifying (b) *Fam (muy feo)*
hideous, ghastly (c) *Fam (malísimo)*
awful, dreadful

hortaliza *nf* vegetable

hortelano, -a *nm,f Br* market gardener, *US*
truck farmer

hortensia *nf Bot* hydrangea

hortera *adj Esp Fam (decoración, ropa,
canción)* tacky, *Br* naff; **es muy h.** he has
really tacky o *Br* naff taste

horterada *nf Esp Fam* tacky thing o act

hosco, -a *adj* surly, sullen

hospedaje *nm* lodgings, *Br* accommodation, *US* accommodations

hospedar 1 *vt* to put up, to lodge
2 hospedarse *vpr* to stay **(en at)**

hospicio *nm* orphanage

hospital *nm* hospital

hospitalario, -a *adj* (a) *(acogedor)*
hospitable (b) *Med* hospital; **instalaciones hospitalarias** hospital facilities

hospitalidad *nf* hospitality

hospitalizar [40] *vt* to take o send into
hospital, to hospitalize

hostal *nm* guesthouse

hostelería *nf (negocio)* catering business;
(estudios) hotel management

hostelero, -a *nm,f (hombre)* landlord;
(mujer) landlady

hostería *nf CSur (hotel)* country hotel

hostia 1 *nf* (a) *Rel* host (b) *Esp Vulg
(golpe)* bash (c) *Esp Vulg* **estar de mala h.**
to be in a foul mood; **ser la h.** *(fantástico)*
to be *Br* bloody o *US* goddamn amazing;
(penoso) to be *Br* bloody o *US* goddamn
awful
2 *interj Vulg* damn! *Br* bloody hell!

hostiar [29] *vt Vulg* to bash, to sock

hostigar [42] *vt* to harass

hostil *adj* hostile

hostilidad *nf* hostility

hotel *nm* hotel

hotelero, -a 1 *adj* hotel; **el sector h.** the
hotel sector
2 *nm,f* hotel-keeper, hotelier

hoy *adv* (a) *(día)* today (b) *Fig (presente)*
now; **h. (en) día** nowadays; **h. por h.** at the
present time

hoya *nf Geog* dale, valley

hoyo *nm* (a) *(agujero)* hole, pit (b)
(sepultura) grave (c) *(de golf)* hole

hoyuelo *nm* dimple

hoz *nf Agr* sickle; **la h. y el martillo** the
hammer and sickle

HR *(abr* **Hostal Residencia)** boarding
house

huachafo, -a *adj Perú Fam* tacky

huacho, -a *adj & nm,f Andes, RP =* **guacho**

huasipungo *nm Andes =* small plot of land
given by landowner to Indians in exchange for their labour

huaso, -a *nm,f Chile Fam* farmer, peasant

hube *pt indef de* **haber**

hubiera *subj imperf de* **haber**

hucha *nf Esp* piggy bank

hueco, -a 1 *adj* (a) *(vacío)* empty, hollow
(b) *(sonido)* resonant

2 *nm* (**a**) *(cavidad)* hollow, hole (**b**) *(sitio no ocupado)* empty space (**c**) *(rato libre)* free time

huele *indic pres de* **oler**

huelga *nf* strike; **estar en** *o* **de h.** to be on strike; **h. de brazos caídos** go-slow; **h. de celo** *Br* work-to-rule, *US* job action

huelguista *nmf* striker

huella *nf* (**a**) *(del pie)* footprint; *(de coche)* track; **h. dactilar** fingerprint (**b**) *Fig (vestigio)* trace, sign; **dejar h.** to leave one's mark

huérfano, -a *nm,f* orphan

huero, -a *adj* empty

huerta *nf Agr* (**a**) *(parcela) Br* market garden, *US* truck farm (**b**) *(región)* = irrigated area used for cultivation

huerto *nm (de verduras)* vegetable garden, kitchen garden; *(de frutales)* orchard

hueso *nm* (**a**) *Anat* bone; **estar en los huesos** to be all skin and bone (**b**) *(de fruto) Br* stone, *US* pit (**c**) *Fig (difícil)* hard work; *(profesor)* hard nut (**d**) *Méx (enchufe)* contact; *(trabajo fácil)* cushy job

huésped, -a *nm,f (invitado)* guest; *(en hotel etc)* lodger, boarder; **casa de huéspedes** guesthouse

hueste *nf Mil* army, host

huesudo, -a *adj* bony

huevada *nf Andes, RP muy Fam (dicho)* crap; **lo que dijiste es una h.** what you said is a load of crap

huevo *nm* (**a**) *(de animal)* egg; **h. duro** hard-boiled egg; **h. escalfado** poached egg; **h. frito** fried egg; **h. pasado por agua,** *Andes* **h. a la copa,** *Méx* **h. tibio** soft-boiled egg; **huevos revueltos** scrambled eggs (**b**) *Vulg* **huevos** *(testículos)* balls; **hacer algo por huevos** to do sth even if it kills you; **tener huevos** to have guts

huevón, -ona *nm,f muy Fam* (**a**) *Cuba, Méx (vago)* **es un h.** *Br* he's a lazy sod *o* git, *US* he's so goddamn lazy (**b**) *Andes, Arg, Ven (tonto, torpe) Br* prat, *US* jerk

huida *nf* flight, escape

huidizo, -a *adj* elusive

huipil *nm CAm, Méx* = colourful embroidered dress or blouse traditionally worn by Indian women

huir [37] *vi* to run away (**de** from), to flee; **h. de la cárcel** to escape from prison; **h. de algn** to avoid sb

hule *nm* (**a**) *(tela impermeable)* oilcloth, oilskin (**b**) *(de mesa)* tablecloth (**c**) *CAm, Méx (caucho)* rubber

hulla *nf* soft coal

humanidad *nf* (**a**) *(género humano)* humanity, mankind (**b**) *(cualidad)* humanity, humaneness (**c**) *(bondad)* compassion, kindness

humanitario, -a *adj* humanitarian

humano, -a **1** *adj* (**a**) *(relativo al hombre)* human (**b**) *(compasivo)* humane
2 *nm* human (being); **ser h.** human being

humareda *nf* cloud of smoke; **¡qué h.!** what a lot of smoke!, it's so smoky!

humear *vi (echar humo)* to smoke; *(arrojar vapor)* to steam, to be steaming hot

humedad *nf (atmosférica)* humidity; *(de lugar)* dampness; **a prueba de h.** damp-proof

humedecer [33] **1** *vt* to moisten, to dampen
2 humedecerse *vpr* to become damp *o* wet *o* moist

húmedo, -a *adj (casa, ropa)* damp; *(clima)* humid, damp, moist

humildad *nf* humility

humilde *adj* humble

humillación *nf* humiliation

humillante *adj* humiliating, humbling

humillar **1** *vt (rebajar)* to humiliate, to humble
2 humillarse *vpr* **humillarse ante algn** to humble oneself before sb

humita *nf* (**a**) *Chile (pajarita)* bow tie (**b**) *Andes, Arg (pasta de maíz)* = paste made of mashed *Br* maize *o US* corn kernels mixed with cheese, chilli, onion and other ingredients, wrapped in a *Br* maize *o US* corn husk and steamed

humo *nm (de combustión)* smoke; *(vapor)* steam; *(de vehículo)* fumes; *Fig* **¡qué humos tiene!** she thinks a lot of herself!

humor *nm* (**a**) *(genio)* mood; **estar de buen/mal h.** to be in a good/bad mood (**b**) *(carácter)* temper; **es persona de mal h.** he's bad-tempered (**c**) *(gracia)* humour; **sentido del h.** sense of humour

humorismo *nm* humour

humorista *nmf* humorist; **h. gráfico** cartoonist

humorístico, -a *adj* humorous, funny

hundido, -a *adj* (**a**) *(barco)* sunken; *(ojos)* deep-set (**b**) *Fig (abatido)* down, demoralized

hundimiento *nm* (**a**) *(de barco)* sinking (**b**) *(de edificio)* collapse (**c**) *(de tierra)* subsidence (**d**) *Fin* crash, slump; *(ruina)* downfall

hundir 1 *vt* (**a**) *(barco)* to sink (**b**) *(edificio)* to bring *o* knock down (**c**) *Fig (desmoralizar)* to demoralize
2 hundirse *vpr* (**a**) *(barco)* to sink (**b**)

(edificio) to collapse (**c**) *Fig (empresa)* to collapse, to crash

húngaro, -a 1 *adj* Hungarian
2 *nm,f (persona)* Hungarian
3 *nm (idioma)* Hungarian

Hungría *n* Hungary

huracán *nm* hurricane

huraño, -a *adj Pey* unsociable

hurgar [42] **1** *vi (rebuscar)* to rummage around (**en** in); *(con dedo, palo)* to poke around (**en** in)

2 hurgarse *vpr* **hurgarse la nariz** to pick one's nose

hurón, -ona *nm Zool* ferret

hurtadillas: a hurtadillas *loc adv* stealthily, on the sly

hurtar *vt* to steal, to pilfer

hurto *nm* petty theft, pilfering

husmear 1 *vt (olfatear)* to sniff out, to scent
2 *vi Fig (curiosear)* to snoop, to pry

huyo *indic pres de* **huir**

I, i [i] *nf (letra)* I, i; **i griega** Y, y

ib. *(abr* **ibídem)** ibid.

ibérico, -a *adj* Iberian

Iberoamérica *n* Latin America

iberoamericano, -a *adj & nm,f* Latin American

iceberg *(pl* **icebergs)** *nm* iceberg

icono *nm* icon

iconoclasta 1 *adj* iconoclastic
2 *nmf* iconoclast

iconografía *nf* iconography

ictericia *nf Med* jaundice

I+D *(abr* **Investigación y Desarrollo)** R&D

íd. *(abr* **ídem)** id., idem.

ida *nf* **(billete de) i. y vuelta** *Br* return (ticket), *US* round-trip (ticket); **idas y venidas** comings and goings

idea *nf* **(a)** *(concepto, ocurrencia)* idea; **hacerse a la i. de** to get used to the idea of; *Fam* **ni i.** no idea, not a clue; **i. fija** fixed idea **(b)** *(opinión)* opinion; **cambiar de i.** to change one's mind **(c)** *(intención)* intention; **a mala i.** on purpose

ideal *adj & nm* ideal

idealismo *nm* idealism

idealista 1 *adj* idealistic
2 *nmf* idealist

idealizar [40] *vt* to idealize, to glorify

idear *vt* **(a)** *(inventar)* to devise, to invent **(b)** *(concebir)* to think up, to conceive

ídem *adv* idem, ditto; *Fam* **í. de í.** exactly the same

idéntico, -a *adj* identical

identidad *nf* identity; **carnet de i.** identity card

identificación *nf* identification

identificar [44] **1** *vt* to identify
2 identificarse *upr* to identify oneself; *Fig* **identificarse con** to identify with

ideología *nf* ideology

ideológico, -a *adj* ideological

idílico, -a *adj* idyllic

idilio *nm* **(a)** *Lit* idyll **(b)** *Fig (romance)* romance, love affair

idioma *nm* language

idiomático, -a *adj* idiomatic

idiosincrasia *nf* idiosyncrasy

idiota 1 *adj* idiotic, stupid
2 *nmf* idiot, fool

idiotez *nf* idiocy, stupidity

ido, -a *adj* **(a)** *(distraído)* absent-minded **(b)** *Fam (chiflado)* crazy, nuts

idólatra 1 *adj* idolatrous
2 *nmf (hombre)* idolater; *(mujer)* idolatress

idolatrar *vt* to worship; *Fig* to idolize

idolatría *nf* idolatry

ídolo *nm* idol

idóneo, -a *adj* suitable, fit

iglesia *nf* **(a)** *(edificio)* church **(b)** **la i.** *(institución)* the Church

ignominia *nf* ignominy

ignorancia *nf* ignorance

ignorante 1 *adj* **(a)** *(sin instrucción)* ignorant **(b)** *(no informado)* ignorant, unaware **(de** of)
2 *nmf* ignoramus

ignorar 1 *vt* **(a)** *(algo)* not to know **(b)** *(a algn)* to ignore
2 ignorarse *upr* to be unknown

ignoto, -a *adj* unknown

igual 1 *adj* **(a)** *(idéntico)* the same, alike; **son todos iguales** they're all the same; **es i.** it doesn't matter; **i. que** the same as **(b)** *(equivalente)* equal; **a partes iguales** fifty-fifty **(c)** *Dep (empatados)* even; **treinta iguales** thirty all **(d)** *Mat* equal; **tres más tres i. a seis** three plus three equals six **(e)** **al i. que** just like **(f)** **por i.** equally
2 *nmf* equal; **de i. a i.** on an equal footing; **sin i.** unique, unrivalled
3 *adv* **(a)** **lo haces i. que yo** you do it the same way I do **(b)** *Esp (posiblemente)* perhaps; **i. vengo** I'll probably come **(c)** *Andes, RP (aún así)* all the same; **estaba nublado pero i. fuimos a la playa** it was cloudy but we went to the beach all the same

igualar 1 *vt* **(a)** *(hacer igual)* to make equal **(b)** *(persona)* to be equal to; **nadie la iguala en generosidad** nobody is as generous as she is **(c)** *(nivelar)* to level **(d)** *Dep* **i. el partido** to equalize, to square the match
2 igualarse *upr* **(a)** *(cosas diferentes)* to

become equal (**b**) **igualarse con algn** to place oneself on an equal footing with sb

igualdad *nf* (**a**) *(equivalencia)* equality; **i. ante la ley** equality before the law (**b**) *(identidad)* sameness; **en i. de condiciones** on equal terms

igualitario, -a *adj* egalitarian

igualmente *adv* equally; *(también)* also, likewise; *Fam* **encantado de conocerlo – ¡i.!** pleased to meet you – likewise!

ijada *nf Anat* flank

ikastola *nf* = primary school in the Basque Country where classes are given entirely in Basque

ikurriña *nf* = Basque national flag

ilegal *adj* illegal

ilegalidad *nf* illegality

ilegalmente *adv* illegally

ilegible *adj* illegible, unreadable

ilegítimo, -a *adj* illegitimate

ileso, -a *adj* unhurt, unharmed

ilícito, -a *adj* illicit, unlawful

ilimitado, -a *adj* unlimited, limitless

Ilmo., -a *(abr* **Ilustrísimo)** His Excellence *o* Excellency

ilógico, -a *adj* illogical

iluminación *nf (alumbrado)* illumination, lighting

iluminar *vt* (**a**) *(dar luz a)* to illuminate, to light up; *(adornar con luces)* to light up (**b**) *Fig (a persona)* to enlighten; *(tema)* to throw light upon

ilusión *nf* (**a**) *(esperanza)* hope; *(esperanza vana)* illusion, delusion; **hacerse ilusiones** to build up one's hopes (**b**) *(sueño)* dream (**c**) *Esp (emoción)* excitement, thrill; **me hace i. verla** I'm looking forward to seeing her; **¡qué i.!** how exciting!

ilusionar 1 *vt* (**a**) *(esperanzar)* to build up sb's hopes (**b**) *(entusiasmar)* to excite, to thrill

2 ilusionarse *vpr* (**a**) *(esperanzarse)* to build up one's hopes (**b**) *(entusiasmarse)* to be excited *o* thrilled (**con** about)

iluso, -a *adj* easily deceived, gullible

ilusorio, -a *adj* illusory, unreal

ilustración *nf* (**a**) *(grabado)* illustration, picture; *(ejemplo)* illustration (**b**) *(erudición)* learning, erudition; *Hist* **la I.** the Enlightenment

ilustrado, -a *adj* (**a**) *(con dibujos, ejemplos)* illustrated (**b**) *(erudito)* learned, erudite

ilustrar 1 *vt* (**a**) *(con dibujos, ejemplos)* to illustrate (**b**) *(aclarar)* to explain, to make clear

2 ilustrarse *vpr* to acquire knowledge (**sobre** of), to learn (**sobre** about)

ilustrativo, -a *adj* illustrative

ilustre *adj* illustrious, distinguished

imagen *nf* (**a**) *(figura, apariencia)* image; **ser la viva i. de algn** to be the spitting image of sb; **tener buena i.** to have a good image (**b**) *Rel* image, statue (**c**) *TV* picture; **imágenes de archivo** library pictures

imaginación *nf* imagination; **son imaginaciones tuyas** you're imagining things

imaginar 1 *vt* to imagine

2 imaginarse *vpr* to imagine; **me imagino que sí** I suppose so

imaginario, -a *adj* imaginary

imaginativo, -a *adj* imaginative

imán *nm* magnet

imbatible *adj* unbeatable

imbatido, -a *adj* unbeaten, undefeated

imbécil 1 *adj* stupid, silly

2 *nmf* idiot, imbecile

imbecilidad *nf* stupidity, imbecility

imborrable *adj* indelible

imbuir [37] *vt Fml* to imbue

imitación *nf* imitation

imitar *vt* to imitate; *(gestos)* to mimic; **este collar imita al oro** this necklace is imitation gold

impaciencia *nf* impatience

impacientar 1 *vt* **i. a algn** to make sb lose patience, to exasperate sb

2 impacientarse *vpr* to get *o* grow impatient (**por** at)

impaciente *adj (deseoso)* impatient; *(intranquilo)* anxious

impactante *adj* **una noticia i.** a sensational piece of news

impactar *vt* to shock, to stun

impacto *nm* impact; *Mil* hit

impar *adj Mat* odd; **número i.** odd number

imparable *adj Dep* unstoppable

imparcial *adj* impartial, unbiased

imparcialidad *nf* impartiality

impartir *vt (clases)* to give

impasible *adj* impassive

impávido, -a *adj* fearless

impecable *adj* impeccable

impedido, -a 1 *adj* disabled, handicapped

2 *nm,f* disabled *o* handicapped person

impedimento *nm* impediment; *(obstáculo)* hindrance, obstacle

impedir [6] *vt (obstaculizar)* to impede, to hinder; *(imposibilitar)* to prevent, to stop; **i. el paso** to block the way

impeler *vt Téc* to drive, to propel; *Fig* to drive, to impel

impenetrable *adj* impenetrable

impenitente *adj Rel* impenitent, unrepentant

impensable *adj* unthinkable

impepinable *adj Esp Fam* dead sure, certain

imperante *adj* prevailing

imperar *vi* to prevail

imperativo, -a 1 *adj* imperative
   2 *nm Ling* imperative

imperceptible *adj* imperceptible

imperdible *nm* safety pin

imperdonable *adj* unforgivable, inexcusable

imperecedero, -a *adj* imperishable; *Fig* enduring

imperfección *nf* (a) *(defecto)* defect, fault (b) *(cualidad)* imperfection

imperfecto, -a 1 *adj* (a) *(no perfecto)* imperfect; *(defectuoso)* faulty, defective (b) *Ling* imperfect
   2 *nm Ling* imperfect

imperial *adj* imperial

imperialismo *nm* imperialism

impericia *nf* incompetence

imperio *nm* empire; **el i. de la ley** the rule of law

imperioso, -a *adj* (necesidad) pressing

impermeable 1 *adj* waterproof
   2 *nm* raincoat, *Br* mac

impersonal *adj* impersonal

impertérrito, -a *adj* unperturbed, unmoved

impertinencia *nf* impertinence

impertinente 1 *adj* (insolente) impertinent; *(inoportuno)* irrelevant
   2 impertinentes *nmpl* lorgnette

imperturbable *adj* imperturbable, unruffled

ímpetu *nm* (a) *(impulso)* impetus, momentum (b) *(violencia)* violence (c) *(energía)* energy

impetuoso, -a *adj* (a) *(olas, viento, ataque)* violent (b) *(persona)* impetuous, impulsive

implacable *adj* relentless, implacable

implantar *vt* (costumbres) to implant, to instil; *(reformas)* to introduce; *Med* to implant

implicación *nf* (participación) involvement; *(significado)* implication

implicancia *nf CSur* implication

implicar [44] *vt* (a) *(involucrar)* to involve, to implicate (**en** in) (b) *(conllevar)* to imply

implícito, -a *adj* implicit, implied

implorar *vt* to implore, to beg

impoluto, -a *adj* pure, spotless

imponente *adj* (a) *(impresionante)* imposing, impressive (b) *(sobrecogedor)* stunning (c) *Fam* (atractivo) terrific, tremendous, smashing

imponer [19] *(pp* impuesto*)* **1** *vt* **i. algo (a algn)** *(forzar a aceptar)* to impose sth (on sb); **i. respeto** to command respect
   2 *vi* (impresionar) to be imposing
   3 imponerse *vpr* (a) *(infundir respeto)* to command respect (b) *(prevalecer)* to prevail (c) *(ser necesario)* to be necessary

imponible *adj Fin* taxable

impopular *adj* unpopular, disliked

importación *nf* (mercancía) import; *(acción)* importing; **artículos de i.** imported goods

importancia *nf* importance, significance; **dar i. a** to attach importance to; **sin i.** unimportant

importante *adj* important, significant; **una suma i.** a considerable sum

importar¹ 1 *vi* (a) *(atañer)* **eso no te importa a ti** that doesn't concern you, that's none of your business (b) *(tener importancia)* to be important; **no importa** it doesn't matter; *Fam* **me importa un bledo** *o* **un pito** I couldn't care less (c) *(molestar)* **¿te importaría repetirlo?** would you mind repeating it?; **¿te importa si fumo?** do you mind if I smoke?
   2 *vt* (valer) to amount to; **los libros importan 15 euros** the books come to 15 euros

importar² *vt* to import

importe *nm Com & Fin* amount, total

importunar *vt* to bother, to pester

imposibilidad *nf* impossibility

imposibilitar *vt* (a) *(impedir)* to make impossible, to prevent (b) *(incapacitar)* to disable, to cripple

imposible *adj* impossible; **me es i. hacerlo** I can't (possibly) do it

imposición *nf* (a) *(disciplina, condiciones)* imposing (b) *Fin* deposit; *(impuesto)* taxation

impostor, -a *nm,f* (farsante) impostor

impotencia *nf* powerlessness, helplessness; *Med* impotence

impotente *adj* powerless, helpless; *Med* impotent

impracticable *adj* (a) *(inviable)* impracticable, unviable (b) *(camino)* impassable

imprecar [44] *vt* to imprecate, to curse

imprecisión *nf* imprecision, vagueness

impreciso, -a adj imprecise, vague

impregnar 1 vt to impregnate (**de** with)
  2 impregnarse vpr to become impregnated

imprenta nf (**a**) (taller) printer's, print works (**b**) (aparato) printing press (**c**) **libertad de i.** freedom of the press

imprescindible adj essential, indispensable

impresentable 1 adj unpresentable
  2 nmf **es un i.** he's a disgrace

impresión nf (**a**) Fig (efecto) impression; **causar i.** to make an impression (**b**) Fig (opinión) impression; **cambiar impresiones** to exchange impressions (**c**) Impr (acto) printing; (edición) edition (**d**) (huella) impression, imprint

impresionable adj impressionable

impresionante adj impressive, striking; Fam **un error i.** (tremendo) a terrible mistake

impresionar vt (**a**) (causar admiración) to impress; (sorprender) to stun, to shock (**b**) Fot to expose

impresionismo nm Arte impressionism

impresionista adj & nmf Arte impressionist

impreso, -a 1 adj printed
  2 nm (**a**) (papel, folleto) printed matter (**b**) (formulario) form; **i. de solicitud** application form (**c**) **impresos** (de correos) printed matter
  3 pp de **imprimir**

impresora nf Inform printer; **i. láser** laser printer; **i. de chorro de tinta** inkjet printer

imprevisible adj unforeseeable, unpredictable

imprevisión nf lack of foresight

imprevisto, -a 1 adj unforeseen, unexpected
  2 nm (incidente) unforeseen event

imprimir (pp **impreso**) vt (**a**) Impr & Inform to print (**b**) (marcar) to stamp

improbable adj improbable, unlikely

ímprobo, -a adj Fml (trabajo, esfuerzo) Herculean, strenuous

improcedente adj (**a**) (inoportuno) inappropriate, unsuitable (**b**) Der inadmissible

improductivo, -a adj unproductive

improperio nm insult, offensive remark

impropio, -a adj inappropriate, unsuitable; **i. de** uncharacteristic of

improvisación nf improvisation; Mús extemporization

improvisado, -a adj (espontáneo) improvised, impromptu, ad lib; (provisional) makeshift; **discurso i.** impromptu speech

improvisar vt to improvise; Mús to extemporize

improviso adj **de i.** unexpectedly, suddenly; Fam **pillar a algn de i.** to catch sb unawares

imprudencia nf (**a**) (cualidad) (en los actos) carelessness, recklessness; (en los comentarios) indiscretion (**b**) (acción) careless o reckless act, indiscretion

imprudente adj (en los actos) careless, rash; (en los comentarios) indiscreet

impúdico, -a adj immodest, indecent

impuesto, -a 1 nm Fin tax; **i. sobre la renta** income tax; **libre de impuestos** tax-free; Esp **i. sobre el valor añadido,** Am **i. al valor agregado** value-added tax
  2 adj imposed
  3 pp de **imponer**

impugnar vt (teoría) to refute, to disprove; (decisión) to challenge, to contest

impulsar vt to impel, to drive

impulsivo, -a adj impulsive

impulso nm impulse, thrust; Dep **tomar i.** to take a run-up

impune adj unpunished

impunemente adv with impunity

impunidad nf impunity

impureza nf impurity

impuro, -a adj impure

impuse pt indef de **imponer**

imputar vt **i. algo a algn** (delito) to accuse sb of sth; (fracaso, error) to attribute sth to sb

inabarcable adj unfathomable

inabordable adj unapproachable, inaccessible

inacabable adj interminable, endless

inaccesible adj inaccessible

inaceptable adj unacceptable

inactividad nf inactivity; Fin lull, stagnation

inactivo, -a adj inactive

inadaptación nf maladjustment

inadaptado, -a 1 adj maladjusted
  2 nm,f misfit

inadecuado, -a adj unsuitable, inappropriate

inadmisible adj inadmissible

inadvertido, -a adj unnoticed; **pasar i.** to go unnoticed

inagotable adj (**a**) (recursos) inexhaustible (**b**) (persona) tireless, indefatigable

inaguantable adj unbearable, intolerable

inalámbrico, -a 1 *adj* cordless; *Inform* wireless
2 *nm* cordless phone
inalcanzable *adj* unattainable, unachievable
inalterable *adj* (a) **permanecer i.** to remain unchanged (b) *(persona)* impassive, imperturbable
inamovible *adj* immovable, fixed
inanición *nf* starvation
inanimado, -a *adj* inanimate
inapreciable *adj* (a) *(valioso)* invaluable, inestimable (b) *(pequeño)* imperceptible
inasequible *adj* (a) *(producto)* unaffordable (b) *(meta)* unattainable, unachievable (c) *(persona)* unapproachable, inaccessible
inaudito, -a *adj* (a) *(sin precedente)* unprecedented (b) *(escandaloso)* outrageous
inauguración *nf* inauguration, opening
inaugural *adj* inaugural, opening
inaugurar *vt* to inaugurate, to open
inca *adj & nmf* Inca
incalculable *adj* incalculable, indeterminate
incandescente *adj* white-hot, incandescent
incansable *adj* tireless, indefatigable
incapacidad *nf* (a) *(imposibilidad)* incapacity, inability; **i. física** physical disability; **i. laboral** industrial disability *o Br* disablement (b) *(falta de aptitud)* incompetence
incapacitado, -a *adj (para trabajar)* unfit; *(para ejercer cargos, votar)* disqualified (**para** from); *(para testar, testificar)* incapacitated
incapacitar *vt (para ejercer cargos, votar)* to disqualify (**para** from); *(para trabajar)* (sujeto: circunstancias) to render unfit; *(sujeto: juez)* to declare unfit
incapaz *adj* (a) *(no capaz)* incapable (**de** of); **soy i. de continuar** I can't go on (b) *Der* unfit
incautación *nf Der* seizure, confiscation
incautarse *vpr Der* **i. de** to seize, to confiscate
incauto, -a *adj* (a) *(imprudente)* incautious, unwary (b) *(crédulo)* gullible
incendiar [43] **1** *vt* to set fire to, to set alight
2 incendiarse *vpr* to catch fire
incendiario, -a 1 *adj* incendiary; *Fig (discurso etc)* inflammatory
2 *nm,f (persona)* arsonist, fire-raiser
incendio *nm* fire; **i. forestal** forest fire
incentivar *vt* to give an incentive to

incentivo *nm* incentive
incertidumbre *nf* uncertainty, doubt
incesante *adj* incessant, never-ending
incesto *nm* incest
incestuoso, -a *adj* incestuous
incidencia *nf* (a) *(repercusión)* impact, effect; **la huelga tuvo escasa i.** the strike had little effect (b) *(hecho)* incident (c) *Fís* incidence
incidente *nm* incident
incidir *vi* (a) *(incurrir)* to fall (**en** into) (b) **i. en** *(afectar)* to affect, to influence
incienso *nm* incense
incierto, -a *adj* uncertain
incineración *nf (de basuras)* incineration; *(de cadáveres)* cremation
incineradora *nf (de basura)* incinerator
incinerar *vt (basura)* to incinerate; *(cadáveres)* to cremate
incipiente *adj* incipient, budding
incisión *nf* incision, cut
incisivo, -a 1 *adj (mordaz)* incisive, cutting; *(cortante)* sharp
2 *nm Anat* incisor
inciso *nm (paréntesis)* digression; **a modo de i.** in passing, incidentally
incitación *nf* incitement
incitar *vt* to incite, to urge
inclemencia *nf* inclemency, harshness
inclemente *adj* inclement, harsh
inclinación *nf* (a) *(de terreno)* slope, incline; *(del cuerpo)* stoop (b) *(reverencia)* bow (c) *Fig (tendencia)* tendency, inclination, penchant
inclinado, -a *adj* inclined, slanting; *Fig* **me siento i. a creerle** I feel inclined to believe him
inclinar 1 *vt (doblar)* to incline, to bend; *(cabeza)* to nod; *(ladear)* to tilt
2 inclinarse *vpr* (a) *(doblarse)* to lean (b) *(al saludar)* to bow; **inclinarse ante** to bow down to (c) *(tender)* to be *o* feel inclined (**a** to); **me inclino a pensar que no** I'm rather inclined to think not (d) *(preferir)* **inclinarse por** to favour, to lean towards
incluido, -a *adj* (a) *(después del sustantivo)* included; *(antes del sustantivo)* including; **servicio no i.** service not included; **i. IVA** including VAT; **todos pagan, incluidos los niños** everyone has to pay, including children (b) *(adjunto)* enclosed
incluir [37] *vt* (a) *(comprender)* to include (b) *(adjuntar)* to enclose
inclusión *nf* inclusion
inclusive *adv* (a) *(incluido)* inclusive; **de martes a viernes i.** from Tuesday to Friday inclusive; **hasta la lección ocho i.** up to

and including lesson eight (**b**) *(incluso)*
even

incluso *adv* even; **i. mi madre** even my
mother

incoar *vt Der* to initiate

incógnita *nf* (**a**) *Mat* unknown quantity,
unknown (**b**) *(misterio)* mystery

incógnito *nm* **de i.** incognito

incoherencia *nf (cualidad)* incoherence;
(comentario) nonsensical remark

incoherente *adj (inconexo)* incoherent;
(inconsecuente) inconsistent

incoloro, -a *adj* colourless

incólume *adj Fml* unharmed; **salir i.** to
escape unharmed

incombustible *adj* incombustible, fire-
proof

incomodar 1 *vt* (**a**) *(causar molestia)* to
inconvenience, to put out (**b**) *(fastidiar)*
to bother, to annoy
   2 incomodarse *vpr* (**a**) *(tomarse
molestias)* to put oneself out, to go out of
one's way (**b**) *(disgustarse)* to get annoyed
o angry

incomodidad *nf (falta de comodidad)*
discomfort; *(molestia)* inconvenience

incómodo, -a *adj* uncomfortable;
sentirse i. to feel uncomfortable *o*
awkward

incomparable *adj* incomparable

incompatibilidad *nf* incompatibility; *Der*
i. de caracteres mutual incompatibility

incompatible *adj* incompatible

incompetencia *nf* incompetence

incompetente *adj & nmf* incompetent

incompleto, -a *adj* incomplete; *(inaca-
bado)* unfinished

incomprensible *adj* incomprehensible

incomprensión *nf* lack of understanding, failure to understand; *(indiferencia)*
lack of sympathy

incomunicado, -a *adj* (**a**) *(aislado)*
isolated; **el pueblo se quedó i.** the town
was cut off (**b**) *(en la cárcel)* in solitary
confinement

incomunicar [44] *vt* (**a**) *(ciudad)* to
isolate, to cut off (**b**) *(recluso)* to place in
solitary confinement

inconcebible *adj* inconceivable, unthinkable

inconcluso, -a *adj* unfinished

incondicional 1 *adj* unconditional;
(apoyo) wholehearted; *(amigo)* faithful;
(partidario) staunch
   2 *nm* die-hard

inconexo, -a *adj* incoherent, confused

inconformismo *nm* nonconformity

inconformista *adj & nmf* nonconformist

inconfundible *adj* unmistakable, obvious

incongruencia *nf (cualidad)* inconsistency; **hacer/decir una i.** to do/say sth
incongruous

incongruente *adj (fuera de lugar)*
incongruous; *(desarticulado)* inconsistent; *(absurdo)* crazy, illogical

inconmensurable *adj* immeasurable,
vast

inconsciencia *nf Med* unconsciousness;
Fig (irreflexión) thoughtlessness; *(irres-
ponsabilidad)* irresponsibility

inconsciente *adj* (**a**) *(con estar)*
(desmayado) unconscious (**b**) *(con ser)*
(despreocupado) unaware (**de** of); *Fig
(irreflexivo)* thoughtless, irresponsible

inconsecuente *adj* inconsistent

inconsistente *adj* flimsy; *(argumento)*
weak

inconstancia *nf* inconstancy, fickleness

inconstante *adj* inconstant, fickle

incontable *adj* countless, innumerable

incontenible *adj* uncontrollable, irrepressible

incontestable *adj* indisputable, unquestionable

incontinencia *nf* incontinence

incontrolable *adj* uncontrollable

incontrolado, -a 1 *adj* uncontrolled
   2 *nm,f* troublemaker

inconveniencia *nf* inappropriateness

inconveniente 1 *adj* inappropriate
   2 *nm* (**a**) *(objeción)* objection; **poner
inconvenientes** to raise objections (**b**)
(desventaja) disadvantage, drawback;
(problema) difficulty; **¿tienes i. en
acompañarme?** would you mind coming
with me?

incordiar [43] *vt Esp Fam* to bother, to
pester

incordio *nm Esp Fam* nuisance, pain

incorporación *nf (unión, adición)*
addition; **su i. tendrá lugar el día 31** *(a
trabajo)* he starts work on the 31st

incorporar 1 *vt* (**a**) *(añadir)* to incorporate
(**en** into) (**b**) *(levantar)* to help to sit up
   2 incorporarse *vpr* (**a**) *(incorporarse a
(sociedad)* to join; *(trabajo)* to start; *Mil*
incorporarse a filas to join up (**b**) *(en la
cama)* to sit up

incorrección *nf* (**a**) *(falta)* incorrectness,
inaccuracy; *(gramatical)* mistake (**b**)
(descortesía) discourtesy, impropriety

incorrecto, -a *adj* (**a**) *(equivocado)* incorrect, inaccurate (**b**) *(grosero)* impolite, discourteous

incorregible *adj* incorrigible

incrédulo, -a 1 *adj* sceptical, incredulous; *Rel* unbelieving
2 *nm,f Rel* unbeliever

increíble *adj* incredible, unbelievable

incrementar 1 *vt* to increase
2 incrementarse *vpr* to increase

incremento *nm* (*aumento*) increase; (*crecimiento*) growth; **i. de la temperatura** rise in temperature

increpar *vt Fml* to rebuke, to reprimand

incruento, -a *adj* bloodless

incrustar *vt* (**a**) (*insertar*) to encrust *o* incrust (**b**) (*embutir*) to inlay; **incrustado de perlas** inlaid with pearls

incubadora *nf* incubator

incubar *vt* to incubate

incuestionable *adj* unquestionable, indisputable

inculcar [44] *vt* (*principios, ideas*) to instil (**en** into)

inculpado, -a *nm,f* **el i.** the accused

inculpar *vt* to accuse (**de** of); *Der* to charge (**de** with)

inculto, -a 1 *adj* (*ignorante*) uneducated, uncouth
2 *nm,f* ignoramus

incultura *nf* lack of education

incumbencia *nf* **es/no es de nuestra i.** it is/isn't a matter for us, it falls/doesn't fall within our area of responsibility

incumbir *vi* **i. a algn** to be a matter for sb, to be within sb's area of responsibility

incumplimiento *nm* (*de deber*) non-fulfilment; (*de orden*) failure to execute; **i. de contrato** breach of contract

incumplir *vt* (*deber*) to fail to fulfil; (*promesa, contrato*) to break; (*orden*) to fail to carry out

incurable *adj también Fig* incurable

incurrir *vi* (*cometer*) to fall (**en** into); **i. en delito** to commit a crime; **i. en (un) error** to fall into error

incursión *nf* raid, incursion

incursionar *vi* (**a**) (*territorio*) to make an incursion (**en** into); (*en ciudad*) to make a raid (**en** into) (**b**) (*en tema, asunto*) to dabble

indagar [42] *vt* to investigate, to inquire into

indebido, -a *adj* (*ilegal*) unlawful; (*incorrecto*) improper

indecencia *nf* indecency, obscenity

indecente *adj* (**a**) (*impúdico*) indecent (**b**) (*indigno*) miserable, wretched

indecible *adj* unspeakable; (*inefable*) indescribable; **sufrir lo i.** to suffer agonies

indecisión *nf* indecision, hesitation

indeciso, -a *adj* (**a**) (*vacilante*) hesitant, irresolute (**b**) (*resultados etc*) inconclusive

indefenso, -a *adj* defenceless, helpless

indefinidamente *adv* indefinitely

indefinido, -a *adj* (**a**) (*indeterminado*) indefinite; (*impreciso*) undefined, vague (**b**) *Ling* indefinite

indeleble *adj* indelible

indemne *adj* (*persona*) unharmed, unhurt; (*cosa*) undamaged

indemnización *nf* (**a**) (*acto*) indemnification (**b**) *Fin* (*compensación*) indemnity, compensation; **i. por despido** redundancy payment

indemnizar [40] *vt* to indemnify, to compensate (**por** for)

independencia *nf* independence

independiente *adj* (*libre*) independent; (*individualista*) self-reliant

independientemente *adv* independently (**de** of); (*aparte de*) regardless, irrespective (**de** of)

independizar [40] **1** *vt* to make independent, to grant independence to
2 independizarse *vpr* to become independent

indescifrable *adj* indecipherable

indescriptible *adj* indescribable

indeseable *adj & nmf* undesirable

indeterminado, -a *adj* (**a**) (*sin determinar*) indefinite; (*impreciso*) vague (**b**) *Ling* indefinite

India *n* **la I.** India

indicación *nf* (**a**) (*señal*) indication, sign (**b**) (*instrucción*) instruction, direction; **por i. de algn** at sb's suggestion

indicado, -a *adj* right, suitable; **a la hora indicada** at the specified time; **en el momento menos i.** at the worst possible moment

indicador *nm* (**a**) (*signo*) indicator (**b**) *Téc* gauge, meter; *Aut* **i. del nivel de aceite** (oil) dipstick; *Aut* **i. de velocidad** speedometer

indicar [44] *vt* (*señalar*) to indicate; (*sujeto: flecha*) to point to; **¿me podría i. el camino?** could you show me the way?

indicativo, -a 1 *adj* indicative
2 *nm Ling* indicative

índice *nm* (**a**) (*de libro*) index, table of contents (**b**) (*relación*) index; **i. de natalidad/mortalidad** birth/death rate; *Fin* **i. de precios** price index (**c**) *Anat* (*dedo*) **i.** index finger, forefinger

indicio *nm* (**a**) (*señal*) indication, sign, token (**de** of) (**b**) *Der* **indicios** (*prueba*) evidence

índico, -a *adj* Indian; **Océano Í.** Indian Ocean

indiferencia *nf* indifference, apathy

indiferente *adj* (a) *(no importante)* unimportant; **me es i.** it makes no difference to me (b) *(apático)* indifferent

indígena 1 *adj* indigenous, native (**de** to)
  2 *nmf* native (**de** of)

indigencia *nf Fml* poverty, indigence

indigente *adj Fml* needy, poverty-stricken

indigestarse *vpr* (a) **se le indigestó la comida** the meal gave her indigestion (b) *(sufrir indigestión)* to get indigestion

indigestión *nf* indigestion

indigesto, -a *adj (comida)* indigestible, difficult to digest; **me siento i.** I've got indigestion

indignación *nf* indignation

indignado, -a *adj* indignant (**por** at o about)

indignante *adj* outrageous, infuriating

indignar 1 *vt* to infuriate, to make angry
  2 indignarse *vpr* to be o feel indignant (**por** at o about)

indigno, -a *adj* (a) *(no merecedor)* unworthy (**de** of) (b) *(degradante)* shameful, appalling

indio, -a *adj & nm,f* Indian; **en fila india** in single file; *Esp Fam* **hacer el i.** to play the fool

indirecta *nf Fam (insinuación)* hint, insinuation; **tirar** o **lanzar una i.** to drop a hint; **coger la i.** to get the message

indirecto, -a *adj* indirect; *Ling* **estilo i.** indirect o reported speech

indisciplinado, -a *adj* undisciplined, unruly

indiscreción *nf (cualidad, hecho)* indiscretion; *(comentario)* tactless remark

indiscreto, -a *adj* indiscreet, tactless

indiscriminado, -a *adj* indiscriminate

indiscutible *adj* indisputable, unquestionable

indispensable *adj* indispensable, essential

indisponer [19] *(pp* **indispuesto)** **1** *vt* to upset, to make unwell
  2 indisponerse *vpr* (a) *(enfermar)* to fall ill, to become unwell (b) **indisponerse con algn** to fall out with sb

indispuesto, -a *adj* indisposed, unwell

indispuse *pt indef de* **indisponer**

indistintamente *adv* **utilizan i. el español y el inglés** they use Spanish and English interchangeably

indistinto, -a *adj (indiferente)* immaterial, inconsequential

individual 1 *adj* individual; **habitación i.** single room
  2 individuales *nmpl Dep* singles

individualismo *nm* individualism

individualista 1 *adj* individualistic
  2 *nmf* individualist

individuo *nm* individual

índole *nf* (a) *(carácter)* character, nature (b) *(clase, tipo)* kind, sort

indolencia *nf* indolence, laziness

indolente 1 *adj* indolent, lazy
  2 *nmf* idler

indomable, indómito, -a *adj* (a) *(animal)* untamable (b) *(pueblo)* ungovernable, unruly; *(pasión)* indomitable

Indonesia *n* Indonesia

inducir [10] *vt* (a) *(incitar, mover)* to lead, to induce; **i. a error** to lead into error, to mislead (b) *Elec (corriente)* to induce

inductivo, -a *adj* inductive

indudable *adj* indubitable, unquestionable; **es i. que** there is no doubt that

induje *pt indef de* **inducir**

indulgencia *nf* indulgence, leniency

indulgente *adj* indulgent (**con** towards), lenient (**con** with)

indultar *vt Der* to pardon

indulto *nm Der* pardon, amnesty

indumentaria *nf* clothing, clothes

industria *nf* industry

industrial 1 *adj* industrial
  2 *nmf* industrialist

industrialización *nf* industrialization

industrializado, -a *adj* industrialized

industrializar [40] *vt* to industrialize

induzco *indic pres de* **inducir**

inédito, -a *adj* (a) *(libro, texto)* unpublished (b) *(nuevo)* completely new; *(desconocido)* unknown

inefable *adj* ineffable, indescribable

ineficacia *nf (ineptitud)* inefficiency; *(inutilidad)* ineffectiveness

ineficaz *adj (inepto)* inefficient; *(inefectivo)* ineffective

ineludible *adj* inescapable, unavoidable

ineptitud *nf* ineptitude, incompetence

inepto, -a 1 *adj* inept, incompetent
  2 *nm,f* incompetent person

inequívoco, -a *adj* unmistakable, unequivocal

inercia *nf* (a) *Fís* inertia (b) *(pasividad)* inertia, passivity; **hacer algo por i.** to do sth out of habit

inerte *adj (inanimado)* inert; *(inmóvil)* motionless

inesperado, -a *adj (fortuito)* unexpected, unforeseen; *(imprevisto)* sudden

inestabilidad *nf* instability

inestable *adj* unstable, unsteady

inestimable *adj* inestimable, invaluable

inevitable *adj* inevitable, unavoidable

inexistente *adj* non-existent

inexorable *adj* inexorable

inexperiencia *nf* lack of experience

inexperto, -a *adj (sin habilidad)* inexpert; *(sin experiencia)* inexperienced

inexplicable *adj* inexplicable

inexpugnable *adj Mil* impregnable

infalible *adj* infallible

infame *adj (vil)* infamous, vile; *(despreciable)* dreadful, awful

infamia *nf* disgrace, infamy

infancia *nf* childhood, infancy

infante, -a 1 *nm,f (hijo del rey) (niño)* infante, prince; *(niña)* infanta, princess
  2 *nm (soldado)* infantryman

infantería *nf Mil* infantry; **la i. de marina** the marines

infantil *adj* **(a)** literatura i. *(para niños)* children's literature **(b)** *(aniñado)* childlike; *Pey* childish, infantile

infarto *nm Med* infarction, infarct; **i. (de miocardio)** heart attack, coronary thrombosis; *Fam* **de i.** thrilling, stunning

infatigable *adj* indefatigable, tireless

infección *nf* infection

infeccioso, -a *adj* infectious

infectar 1 *vt* to infect
  2 infectarse *vpr* to become infected (**de** with)

infeliz 1 *adj* unhappy; *(desdichado)* unfortunate
  2 *nmf Fam* simpleton; **es un pobre i.** he is a poor devil

inferior 1 *adj* **(a)** *(más bajo)* lower **(b)** *(calidad)* inferior; **de calidad i.** of inferior quality **(c)** *(cantidad)* lower, less; **i. a la media** below average
  2 *nmf (persona)* subordinate, inferior

inferioridad *nf* inferiority; **estar en i. de condiciones** to be at a disadvantage; **complejo de i.** inferiority complex

inferir [5] *vt Fml* to infer (**de** from)

infernal *adj* infernal, hellish; **había un ruido i.** there was a hell of a noise

infestar *vt* **(a)** **infestado de** *(parásitos)* infested with; *(plantas)* overgrown with **(b)** *Fig (llenar)* to overrun, to invade; **infestado de turistas** swarming with tourists **(c)** *(infectar)* to infect

infición *nf Méx* pollution

infidelidad *nf* infidelity, unfaithfulness

infiel 1 *adj (desleal)* unfaithful
  2 *nmf Rel* infidel

infierno *nm* **(a)** *Rel* hell **(b)** *Fig (tormento)* hell; **su vida es un i.** his life is sheer hell **(c)** *(horno)* inferno; **en verano esto es un i.** in summer it's like an inferno here; *Fam* **¡vete al i.!** go to hell!, get lost!

infiltración *nf* infiltration

infiltrado, -a *nm,f* infiltrator

infiltrar 1 *vt* to infiltrate
  2 infiltrarse *vpr* to infiltrate (**en** into)

ínfimo, -a *adj (mínimo)* extremely low; **detalle í.** smallest detail; **ínfima calidad** very poor quality

infinidad *nf* **una i. de** an infinite number of; *(mucho)* masses of; **en i. de ocasiones** on countless occasions

infinitivo, -a *adj & nm Ling* infinitive

infinito, -a 1 *adj* infinite, endless
  2 *nm* infinity
  3 *adv Fam (muchísimo)* infinitely, immensely

inflación *nf Econ* inflation

inflacionario, -a, inflacionista *adj Econ* inflationary

inflamable *adj* flammable

inflamación *nf Med* inflammation

inflamar 1 *vt* **(a)** *Med* to inflame **(b)** *(encender)* to set on fire, to ignite
  2 inflamarse *vpr* **(a)** *Med* to become inflamed **(b)** *(incendiarse)* to catch fire

inflar 1 *vt* **(a)** *(hinchar)* to inflate, to blow up; *Náut (vela)* to swell **(b)** *Fig (exagerar)* to exaggerate
  2 inflarse *vpr* **(a)** *(hincharse)* to inflate; *Náut (vela)* to swell **(b)** *Fam* **inflarse de** to overdo; **se inflaron de macarrones** they stuffed themselves with macaroni

inflexible *adj* inflexible

infligir [57] *vt* to inflict

influencia *nf* influence; **ejercer** o **tener i. sobre algn** to have an influence on o upon sb; **tener influencias** to be influential; **tráfico de influencias** influence peddling, *US* graft

influenciar [43] *vt* to influence

influir [37] **1** *vt* to influence
  2 *vi* to have influence; **i. en** to influence, to have an influence on

influjo *nm* influence

influyente *adj* influential

información *nf* **(a)** *(conocimiento)* information; **para tu i.** for your information **(b)** *Prensa (noticias)* news *sing*; **i. deportiva** sports news **(c)** *Tel Br* directory enquiries, *US* information **(d)** *(oficina)* information office; *(mostrador)* information desk

informado, -a *adj* informed; **de fuentes bien informadas** from well-informed sources

informal *adj* (a) *(reunión, cena)* informal (b) *(comportamiento)* casual (c) *(persona)* unreliable, untrustworthy

informalidad *nf (incumplimiento)* unreliability; *(desenfado)* informality

informar 1 *vt* to inform (**de** of); *(dar informes)* to report
2 informarse *vpr (procurarse noticias)* to find out (**de** about); *(enterarse)* to inquire (**de** about)

informática *nf* computing, information technology, IT

informático, -a 1 *adj* computer, computing
2 *nm,f* (computer) technician

informativo, -a 1 *adj* (a) *Rad & TV* news; **boletín i.** news (broadcast) (b) *(explicativo)* informative, explanatory
2 *nm Rad & TV* news bulletin

informe *nm* (a) *(documento)* report (b) **informes** references; **pedir informes sobre algn** to make inquiries about sb

infracción *nf (de ley)* infringement, breach (**de** of)

infractor, -a *nm,f* offender

infraestructura *nf* infrastructure

in fraganti *loc adv* in the act; **pillar a algn i.** to catch sb redhanded

infrahumano, -a *adj* subhuman

infranqueable *adj* impassable; *Fig* insurmountable

infrarrojo, -a *adj* infrared

infrautilizar *vt* to underuse

infringir [57] *vt* to infringe, to contravene; **i. una ley** to break a law

infructuoso, -a *adj* fruitless, unsuccessful

infundado, -a *adj* unfounded, groundless

infundir *vt* to infuse; *Fig* to instil; **i. dudas** to give rise to doubt; **i. respeto** to command respect

infusión *nf* infusion

infuso, -a *adj Fam Irón* **ciencia infusa** sheer genius

ingeniar [43] **1** *vt* to invent, to devise
2 ingeniarse *vpr* **ingeniárselas para hacer algo** to manage to do sth

ingeniería *nf* engineering

ingeniero, -a *nm,f* engineer; **i. agrónomo** agricultural engineer; *Esp* **i. de caminos, canales y puertos** civil engineer; **i. de minas/montes** mining/forestry engineer; **i. de telecomunicaciones** telecommunications engineer; **i. técnico** technician

ingenio *nm* (a) *(talento)* talent; *(inventiva)* inventiveness, creativeness; *(agudeza)* wit (b) *(aparato)* device

ingenioso, -a *adj* ingenious, clever; *(vivaz)* witty

ingente *adj* huge, enormous

ingenuidad *nf* ingenuousness, naïveté

ingenuo, -a 1 *adj* ingenuous, naïve
2 *nm,f* naïve person

ingerir [5] *vt (comida)* to ingest, to consume; *(líquidos, alcohol)* to drink, to consume

Inglaterra *n* England

ingle *nf Anat* groin

inglés, -esa 1 *adj* English
2 *nm,f (hombre)* Englishman; *(mujer)* Englishwoman; **los ingleses** the English
3 *nm (idioma)* English

ingratitud *nf* ingratitude, ungratefulness

ingrato, -a 1 *adj* (a) *(persona)* ungrateful (b) *(noticia)* unpleasant (c) *(trabajo)* thankless, unrewarding (d) *(tierra)* unproductive
2 *nm,f* ungrateful person

ingrediente *nm* ingredient

ingresar 1 *vt* (a) *Esp (dinero)* to deposit, to pay in (b) *Med* to admit; **la ingresaron en el hospital** she was admitted to hospital
2 *vi* to enter; **i. en el ejército** to enlist in the army, to join the army; **i. en un club** to join a club; *Esp* **i. cadáver** to be dead on arrival

ingreso *nm* (a) *(de dinero)* deposit; **hacer un i. en una cuenta** to pay money into an account (b) *(entrada)* entry (**en** into); *(admisión)* admission (**en** to) (c) **ingresos** *(sueldo, renta)* income; *(beneficios)* revenue

inhábil *adj* (a) *(incapaz)* unfit; **i. para el trabajo** unfit for work (b) **día i.** non-working day

inhabilitación *nf* (a) *Fml (incapacidad)* disablement (b) *Der* disqualification

inhabilitar *vt* (a) *Fml (incapacitar)* to disable; **inhabilitado para el trabajo** unfit for work (b) *Der* to disqualify

inhabitable *adj* uninhabitable

> 🔎 Observa que la palabra inglesa **inhabitable** es un falso amigo y no es la traducción de la palabra española **inhabitable**. En inglés **inhabitable** significa "habitable".

inhalación *nf* inhalation

inhalador *nm Med* inhaler

inhalar *vt* to inhale

inherente *adj* inherent (**a** in)

inhibición *nf* inhibition

inhibir 1 *vt* to inhibit
2 inhibirse *vpr* (a) *(cohibirse)* to be *o* feel

inhibited (**b**) *(abstenerse)* to refrain (**de** from)

inhóspito, -a *adj* inhospitable

inhumación *nf* burial

inhumano, -a *adj* inhumane; *(cruel)* inhuman

inhumar *vt* to bury

iniciación *nf* (**a**) *(ceremonia)* initiation (**b**) *(principio)* start, beginning

inicial *adj & nf* initial; **punto i.** starting point

iniciar [43] **1** *vt* (**a**) *(empezar)* to begin, to start; *(discusión)* to initiate; *(una cosa nueva)* to pioneer (**b**) *(introducir)* to initiate

2 iniciarse *vpr* (**a**) **iniciarse en algo** *(aprender)* to start to study sth (**b**) *(empezar)* to begin, to start

iniciativa *nf* initiative; **i. privada** private enterprise; **por i. propia** on one's own initiative

inicio *nm* beginning, start; **a inicios de** at the beginning of

inimaginable *adj* unimaginable

inimitable *adj* inimitable

ininterrumpido, -a *adj* uninterrupted, continuous

injerencia *nf* interference, meddling (**en** in)

injerirse *vpr* to interfere, to meddle (**en** in)

injertar *vt Agr & Med* to graft

injerto *nm* graft

injuria *nf (insulto)* insult, affront; *(agravio)* outrage

injuriar [43] *vt (insultar)* to insult; *(ultrajar)* to outrage

injusticia *nf* injustice, unfairness

injustificado, -a *adj* unjustified

injusto, -a *adj* unjust, unfair

inmaculado, -a *adj* immaculate

inmadurez *nf* immaturity

inmaduro, -a *adj* immature

inmediaciones *nfpl* neighbourhood

inmediatamente *adv* immediately, at once

inmediato, -a *adj* (**a**) *(en el tiempo)* immediate; **de i.** at once (**b**) *(en el espacio)* next (**a** to), adjoining

inmejorable *adj (trabajo)* excellent; *(precio)* unbeatable

inmemorial *adj* immemorial; **desde tiempos inmemoriales** since time immemorial

inmensidad *nf* immensity, enormity

inmenso, -a *adj* immense, vast

inmerecido, -a *adj* undeserved, unmerited

inmersión *nf* immersion; *(de submarino)* dive

inmerso, -a *adj* immersed (**en** in)

inmigración *nf* immigration

inmigrante *adj & nmf* immigrant

inmigrar *vi* to immigrate

inminente *adj* imminent, impending

inmiscuirse [37] *vpr* to interfere, to meddle (**en** in)

inmobiliaria *nf Br* estate agency *o* agent's, *US* real estate company

inmobiliario, -a *adj* property, *US* real estate; **agente i.** *Br* estate agent, *US* realtor

inmolar *vt Fml* to immolate, to sacrifice

inmoral *adj* immoral

inmoralidad *nf* immorality

inmortal *adj & nmf* immortal

inmortalidad *nf* immortality

inmortalizar [40] *vt* to immortalize

inmóvil *adj* motionless, immobile

inmovilista *adj* ultra-conservative

inmovilizar [40] *vt* (**a**) *(persona, cosa)* to immobilize (**b**) *Fin (capital)* to immobilize, to tie up

inmueble 1 *adj* **bienes inmuebles** real estate

2 *nm* building

inmundicia *nf* (**a**) *(suciedad)* dirt, filth; *Fig* dirtiness (**b**) *(basura)* rubbish, refuse

inmundo, -a *adj* dirty, filthy; *Fig* nasty

inmune *adj* immune (**a** to), exempt (**de** from)

inmunidad *nf* immunity (**contra** against); **i. diplomática/parlamentaria** diplomatic/ parliamentary immunity

inmunizar [40] *vt* to immunize (**contra** against)

inmutarse *vpr* to change countenance; **ni se inmutó** he didn't turn a hair

innato, -a *adj* innate, inborn

innecesario, -a *adj* unnecessary

innegable *adj* undeniable

innovación *nf* innovation

innovar *vt & vi* to innovate

innumerable *adj* innumerable, countless

inocencia *nf* innocence

inocentada *nf Fam* ≃ April Fool's joke; **hacer una i. a algn** to play an April Fool's joke on sb

inocente 1 *adj* innocent

2 *nmf* innocent; **Día de los Inocentes** Holy Innocents' Day, 28 December, ≃ April Fools' Day

inocuo, -a *adj* innocuous

inodoro, -a 1 *adj* odourless

2 *nm* toilet, lavatory

inofensivo, -a *adj* harmless

inolvidable adj unforgettable

inoperante adj ineffective

inopia nf estar en la i. to be in the clouds, to be miles away

inopinado, -a adj unexpected

inoportuno, -a adj inappropriate; **llegó en un momento muy i.** he turned up at a very awkward moment

inorgánico, -a adj inorganic

inoxidable adj acero i. stainless steel

inquebrantable adj (fe, amistad) unshakeable; (lealtad) unswerving

inquietante adj worrying

inquietar 1 vt to worry
 2 **inquietarse** vpr to worry (**por** about)

inquieto, -a adj (a) (preocupado) worried (**por** about) (b) (intranquilo) restless (c) (emprendedor) eager

inquietud nf (a) (preocupación) worry (b) (agitación) restlessness (c) (anhelo) eagerness

inquilino, -a nm,f tenant

inquirir [31] vt to investigate

inquisición nf (a) (indagación) inquiry, investigation (b) **la I.** (tribunal) the (Spanish) Inquisition

inquisitivo, -a adj inquisitive

inri nm Fam **para más** o **mayor i.** to make matters worse

insaciable adj insatiable

insalubre adj unhealthy

INSALUD nm (abr **Instituto Nacional de la Salud**) = Spanish national health service, Br ≃ NHS, US ≃ Medicaid

insano, -a adj (a) (loco) insane, mad (b) (insalubre) unhealthy

insatisfacción nf (a) (disgusto, descontento) dissatisfaction (b) (falta, carencia) lack of fulfilment

insatisfecho, -a adj dissatisfied

inscribir (pp inscrito) 1 vt (a) (registrar) to register; **i. a un niño en el registro civil** to register a child's birth (b) (matricular) to enrol (c) (grabar) to inscribe
 2 **inscribirse** vpr (a) (registrarse) to register; (hacerse miembro) to join (b) (matricularse) to enrol

inscripción nf (a) (matriculación) enrolment, registration (b) (escrito etc) inscription

inscrito pp de **inscribir**

insecticida nm insecticide

insecto nm insect

inseguridad nf (a) (falta de confianza) insecurity (b) (duda) uncertainty (c) (peligro) lack of safety; **la i. ciudadana** the breakdown of law and order

inseguro, -a adj (a) (poco confiado) insecure (b) (dubitativo) uncertain (c) (peligroso) unsafe

inseminación nf insemination; **i. artificial** artificial insemination

inseminar vt to inseminate

insensatez nf foolishness

insensato, -a 1 adj foolish
 2 nm,f fool

insensibilidad nf insensitivity

insensible adj (a) (indiferente) insensitive (**a** to) (b) (imperceptible) imperceptible (c) Med numb

inseparable adj inseparable

insertar vt to insert

inservible adj useless

insidia nf (a) (trampa) malicious ploy (b) (malicia) maliciousness

insidioso, -a adj insidious

insigne adj distinguished

insignia nf (a) (emblema) badge (b) (bandera) flag

insignificancia nf (a) (intrascendencia) insignificance (b) (nadería) trifle

insignificante adj insignificant

insinuación nf hint, insinuation; **insinuaciones** (amorosas) innuendo

insinuante adj (mirada, ropa) suggestive; (comentarios) full of innuendo

insinuar [30] 1 vt to insinuate
 2 **insinuarse** vpr **insinuarse a algn** to make advances to sb

insípido, -a adj insipid; Fig dull, flat

insistencia nf insistence; **con i.** insistently

insistente adj insistent

insistir vi to insist (**en** on); **insistió en ese punto** he stressed that point

insociable adj unsociable

insolación nf Med sunstroke; **coger una i.** to get sunstroke

insolencia nf insolence

insolente adj insolent

insolidaridad nf unsupportive stance

insólito, -a adj (poco usual) unusual; (extraño) strange, odd

insoluble adj insoluble

insolvencia nf Fin insolvency

insolvente adj Fin insolvent

insomnio nm insomnia; **noche de i.** sleepless night

insondable adj unfathomable

insonorizado, -a adj soundproof

insonorizar [40] vt to soundproof

insoportable adj unbearable

insospechado, -a adj unsuspected

insostenible adj untenable

inspección *nf* inspection

inspeccionar *vt* to inspect

inspector, -a *nm,f* inspector; **i. de Hacienda** tax inspector

inspiración *nf* (**a**) *(mental)* inspiration (**b**) *(inhalación)* inhalation

inspirado, -a *adj* inspired

inspirar 1 *vt* (**a**) *(mentalmente)* to inspire (**b**) *(inhalar)* to inhale, to breathe in
 2 inspirarse *upr* **inspirarse en** to be inspired by

instalación *nf* installation; **instalaciones deportivas** sports facilities

instalar 1 *vt (antena, aparato)* to install, to fit; *(local, puesto)* to set up
 2 instalarse *upr (persona)* to settle (down)

instancia *nf* (**a**) *(solicitud)* request; **a instancia(s) de** at the request of (**b**) *(escrito)* application form (**c**) *Der* **tribunal de primera i.** court of first instance (**d**) **en primera i.** first of all; **en última i.** as a last resort

> 🔎 Observa que la palabra inglesa **instance** es un falso amigo y no es la traducción de la palabra española **instancia**. En inglés, **instance** significa "caso, ejemplo".

instantánea *nf* snapshot

instantáneamente *adv* instantly

instantáneo, -a *adj* instantaneous; **café i.** instant coffee

instante *nm* instant, moment; **a cada i.** constantly; **al i.** immediately, right away; **por instantes** with every second; **¡un i.!** just a moment!

instar *vt* to urge

instauración *nf* founding

instaurar *vt* to found

instigador, -a *nm,f* instigator

instigar [42] *vt* to instigate; **i. a la rebelión** to incite a rebellion

instintivo, -a *adj* instinctive

instinto *nm* instinct; **por i.** instinctively; **i. de conservación** survival instinct

institución *nf* institution

institucional *adj* institutional

instituir [37] *vt* to institute

instituto *nm* (**a**) *(corporación)* institute (**b**) *Esp (centro docente)* high school

institutriz *nf* governess

instituyo *indic pres de* **instituir**

instrucción *nf* (**a**) *(educación)* education (**b**) *(indicación)* instruction; **instrucciones para el o de uso** directions for use (**c**) *Der* preliminary investigation; **la i. del**

sumario proceedings; **juez de i.** examining magistrate (**d**) *Mil* drill

instructivo, -a *adj* instructive

instruido, -a *adj* educated, well-educated

instruir [37] *vt* (**a**) *(enseñar)* to instruct (**b**) *Der* to investigate (**c**) *Mil* to drill

instrumental *adj* instrumental

instrumento *nm* instrument

insubordinación *nf* insubordination

insubordinado, -a *adj* insubordinate

insubordinarse *upr* to rebel (**contra** against)

insuficiencia *nf Med* failure, insufficiency; **i. cardiaca/renal** heart/kidney failure

insuficiente 1 *adj* insufficient
 2 *nm Educ (nota)* fail

insufrible *adj* insufferable

insular 1 *adj* insular, island
 2 *nmf* islander

insulso, -a *adj* insipid

insultante *adj* insulting

insultar *vt* to insult

insulto *nm* insult

insumisión *nf* = refusal to do military service

insumiso, -a 1 *adj* unsubmissive
 2 *nm* = person who refuses to do military service

insuperable *adj* (**a**) *(inmejorable)* unsurpassable (**b**) *(problema)* insurmountable

insurgente *adj & nmf* insurgent

insurrección *nf* insurrection

intachable *adj* irreproachable; **conducta i.** impeccable behaviour

intacto, -a *adj* intact

integración *nf también Mat* integration; **i. racial** racial integration

integral 1 *adj* (**a**) *(total)* total, complete (**b**) *(sin refinar) (pan, harina) Br* wholemeal, *US* wholewheat; *(arroz)* brown (**c**) *(constituyente)* integral; **ser parte i. de algo** to be an integral part of sth
 2 *nf Mat* integral

integrante 1 *adj* integral; **ser parte i. de** to be an integral part of
 2 *nmf* member

integrar 1 *vt (formar)* to compose, to make up; **el equipo lo integran once jugadores** there are eleven players in the team
 2 integrarse *upr* to integrate (**en** with)

integridad *nf* integrity

íntegro, -a *adj* (**a**) *(entero)* whole, entire; *Cin & Lit* **versión íntegra** *(de libro)* unabridged edition; *(de película)* uncut version (**b**) *(honrado)* upright

intelecto *nm* intellect

intelectual *adj & nmf* intellectual

inteligencia *nf (intelecto)* intelligence; **coeficiente de i.** intelligence quotient, IQ

inteligente *adj* intelligent

inteligible *adj* intelligible

intemperie *nf* bad weather; **a la i.** in the open (air)

intempestivo, -a *adj* untimely

intención *nf* intention; **con i.** deliberately, on purpose; **con segunda** *o* **doble i.** with an ulterior motive; **tener la i. de hacer algo** to intend to do sth

intencionado, -a *adj* deliberate

intencional *adj* intentional

intendencia *nf* (**a**) *(militar) Br* ≃ Royal Army Service Corps, *US* ≃ Quartermaster Corps (**b**) *RP (corporación municipal) Br* town council, *US* city council (**c**) *Chile (gobernación)* regional government

intendente *nm* (**a**) *RP (alcalde)* mayor (**b**) *Chile (gobernador)* provincial governor

intensidad *nf* intensity; *(del viento)* force

intensificar [44] **1** *vt* to intensify
2 intensificarse *vpr* to intensify

intensivo, -a *adj* intensive; *Agr* **cultivo i.** intensive farming; *Educ* **curso i.** crash course

intenso, -a *adj* intense

intentar *vt* to try, to attempt; *Fam* **¡inténtalo!** give it a go!

intento *nm* attempt; **i. de suicidio** attempted suicide

intentona *nf Pol* **i. (golpista)** attempted coup

intercalar *vt* to insert

intercambiar [43] *vt* to exchange

intercambio *nm* exchange; **i. comercial** trade

interceder *vi* to intercede

interceptar *vt* (**a**) *(detener)* to intercept (**b**) *(carretera)* to block; *(tráfico)* to hold up

intercesión *nf* intercession

intercontinental *adj* intercontinental

interdicto *nm* prohibition

interés *(pl* **intereses)** *nm* (**a**) *(provecho, curiosidad)* interest; **poner i. en** to take an interest in; **tener i. en** *o* **por** to be interested in (**b**) *(egoísmo)* self-interest; **hacer algo (sólo) por i.** to do sth (purely) out of self-interest; **intereses creados** vested interests (**c**) *Fin* interest; **con un i. del 11 por ciento** at an interest of 11 percent; **tipos de i.** interest rates

interesado, -a 1 *adj* (**a**) *(preocupado, curioso)* interested (**en** in); **las partes interesadas** the interested parties (**b**) *(egoísta)* selfish
2 *nm,f* interested person; **los interesados** those interested *o* concerned

interesante *adj* interesting

interesar 1 *vt* (**a**) *(tener interés)* to interest; **la poesía no me interesa nada** poetry doesn't interest me at all (**b**) *(concernir)* to concern
2 *vi* *(ser importante)* to be of interest, to be important; **interesaría llegar pronto** it is important to get there early
3 interesarse *vpr* **interesarse por** *o* **en** to be interested in; **se interesó por ti** he asked about *o* after you

interferencia *nf* interference; *Rad & TV* jamming

interferir [5] **1** *vt* (**a**) *(interponerse)* to interfere with (**b**) *Rad & TV* to jam
2 *vi* to interfere (**en** in)

interfono *nm Tel* intercom

interinidad *nf* temporariness

interino, -a 1 *adj (persona)* acting
2 *nm,f (suplente)* stand-in, deputy; *(médico, juez)* locum; *(profesor) Br* supply teacher, *US* substitute teacher

interior 1 *adj* (**a**) *(de dentro)* inside, inner; *(patio, jardín)* interior, inside; *(habitación, vida)* inner; **ropa i.** underwear (**b**) *Pol* domestic, internal (**c**) *Geog* inland
2 *nm* (**a**) *(parte de dentro)* interior; **en mi i.** deep down (**b**) *Geog* interior; *Pol* **Ministerio del I.** *Br* ≃ Home Office, *US* ≃ Department of the Interior

interiorizar [40] *vt* to internalize

interjección *nf Ling* interjection

interlocutor, -a *nm,f* speaker; *(negociador)* negotiator

intermediario *nm Com* middleman

intermedio, -a 1 *adj* intermediate
2 *nm TV (intervalo)* break

interminable *adj* endless

intermitente 1 *adj* intermittent
2 *nm Esp, Col (en vehículo) Br* indicator, *US* turn signal

internacional *adj* international

internado, -a 1 *nm,f* inmate
2 *nm (colegio)* boarding school

internar 1 *vt (en hospital)* to confine
2 internarse *vpr* (**a**) *(penetrar)* to advance (**en** into) (**b**) *Dep* to break through

internauta *nmf* Net user

Internet *nf Inform* Internet; **está en I.** it's on the Internet

interno, -a 1 *adj* (**a**) *(de dentro)* internal; **por vía interna** internally (**b**) *Pol* domestic
2 *nm,f (alumno)* boarder; *Med (enfermo)* patient; *(preso)* inmate

3 nm RP (extensión) (telephone) extension; **i. 28, por favor** extension 28, please

interponer [19] (pp **interpuesto**) **1** vt to insert; Der **i. un recurso** to give notice of appeal

2 interponerse upr to intervene

interpretación nf (**a**) (de ideas, significado) interpretation (**b**) Mús & Teatro performance (**c**) (traducción) interpreting

interpretar vt (**a**) (entender, explicar, traducir) to interpret (**b**) Teatro (papel) to play; (obra) to perform; Mús (concierto) to play, to perform; (canción) to sing

intérprete nmf (**a**) (traductor) interpreter (**b**) Teatro performer; Mús (cantante) singer; (músico) performer

interpuesto pp de **interponer**

interpuse pt indef de **interponer**

interrogación nf interrogation; Ling (**signo de**) **i.** question o interrogation mark

interrogante nf Fig question mark

interrogar [42] vt to question; (testigo etc) to interrogate

interrogatorio nm interrogation

interrumpir vt to interrupt; (tráfico) to block

interrupción nf interruption; **i. del embarazo** termination of pregnancy

interruptor nm Elec switch

intersección nf intersection

interurbano, -a adj intercity; Tel **conferencia interurbana** long-distance call

intervalo nm interval; **habrá intervalos de lluvia** there will be periods of rain

intervención nf (**a**) (participación) intervention, participation (**en** in); (aportación) contribution (**en** to) (**b**) Med intervention

intervenir [27] **1** vi (mediar) to intervene (**en** in); (participar) to take part (**en** in); (contribuir) to contribute (**en** to)

2 vt (**a**) (confiscar) to confiscate, to seize (**b**) Tel (teléfono) to tap (**c**) Med to operate on

interventor, -a nm,f (supervisor) inspector; Fin **i. (de cuentas)** auditor

interviú nf interview

intestino, -a 1 adj (luchas) internal

2 nm Anat intestine

intimar vi to become close (**con** to)

intimidad nf (amistad) intimacy; (vida privada) private life; (privacidad) privacy; **en la i.** privately, in private

intimidar vt to intimidate

íntimo, -a 1 adj (vida, fiesta) private; (ambiente, restaurante) intimate; (relación, amistad) close; (sentimiento) innermost

2 nm,f close friend, intimate

intocable adj (persona, institución) above criticism

intolerable adj intolerable

intolerancia nf intolerance

intolerante 1 adj intolerant

2 nmf intolerant person

intoxicación nf poisoning; **i. alimentaria** food poisoning

> ⎰ Observa que la palabra inglesa **intoxication** es un falso amigo y no es la traducción de la palabra española **intoxicación**. En inglés **intoxication** significa "embriaguez".

intoxicar [44] vt to poison

> ⎰ Observa que el verbo inglés **to intoxicate** es un falso amigo y no es la traducción del verbo español **intoxicar**. En inglés **to intoxicate** significa "embriagar, emborrachar".

intranet nf Inform intranet

intranquilidad nf worry

intranquilizarse upr to get worried

intranquilo, -a adj (preocupado) worried; (agitado) restless

intransigente adj intransigent

intransitable adj impassable

intransitivo, -a adj Ling intransitive

intratable adj (**a**) (problema) intractable (**b**) (persona) unsociable

intrépido, -a adj intrepid

intriga nf intrigue; Cin & Teatro plot

intrigante 1 adj (**a**) (interesante) intriguing, interesting (**b**) (maquinador) scheming

2 nmf (persona) schemer

intrigar [42] **1** vt (interesar) to intrigue, to interest

2 vi (maquinar) to plot

intrincado, -a adj (**a**) (cuestión, problema) intricate (**b**) (bosque) dense

intrínseco, -a adj intrinsic

introducción nf introduction

introducir [10] vt (**a**) (meter) (llave, carta) to put in, to insert; Inform (datos) to input, to enter (**b**) (mercancías) to bring in, to introduce (**c**) (dar a conocer) **i. algo en** to introduce o bring sth to

intromisión nf (injerencia) meddling; **perdón por la i.** forgive the intrusion

introspectivo, -a adj introspective

introvertido, -a 1 adj introverted

2 nm,f introvert

intruso, -a 1 *adj* intrusive
2 *nm,f* intruder; *Der* trespasser

intuición *nf* intuition

intuir [37] *vt* to know by intuition, to sense

intuitivo, -a *adj* intuitive

inundación *nf* flood

inundar *vt* to flood; *Fig (de trabajo etc)* to swamp

inusitado, -a *adj* unusual

inusual *adj* unusual

inútil 1 *adj* (a) *(objeto)* useless; *(esfuerzo, intento)* vain, pointless (b) *Mil* unfit (for service)
2 *nmf Fam* good-for-nothing

inutilidad *nf* uselessness

inutilizar [40] *vt* to make o render useless; *(máquina etc)* to put out of action

invadir *vt* to invade; *Fig* **los estudiantes invadieron la calle** students poured out onto the street

invalidar *vt* to invalidate

invalidez *nf* (a) *Der (nulidad)* invalidity (b) *Med (minusvalía)* disability

inválido, -a 1 *adj* (a) *Der (nulo)* invalid (b) *Med (minusválido)* disabled, handicapped
2 *nm,f Med* disabled o handicapped person

invariable *adj* invariable

invasión *nf* invasion

invasor, -a 1 *adj* invading
2 *nm,f* invader

invencible *adj* (a) *(enemigo)* invincible (b) *(obstáculo)* insurmountable

invención *nf (invento)* invention; *(mentira)* fabrication

inventar *vt* to invent; *(excusa, mentira)* to make up, to concoct

inventario *nm* inventory

inventiva *nf* inventiveness; *(imaginación)* imagination

invento *nm* invention

inventor, -a *nm,f* inventor

invernadero *nm* greenhouse; **efecto i.** greenhouse effect

invernal *adj* winter, wintry

invernar [1] *vi* to hibernate

inverosímil *adj* unlikely, improbable

inversión *nf* (a) *(del orden)* inversion (b) *(de dinero, tiempo)* investment

inversionista *nmf* investor

inverso, -a *adj* opposite; **en sentido i.** in the opposite direction; **en orden i.** in reverse order

inversor, -a *nm,f Fin* investor

invertebrado, -a *adj & nm Zool* invertebrate

invertido, -a *adj* inverted, reversed

invertir [5] *vt* (a) *(orden)* to invert, to reverse (b) *(dinero)* to invest (**en** in); *(tiempo)* to spend (**en** on)

investidura *nf* investiture; *Pol* vote of confidence

investigación *nf* (a) *(policial etc)* investigation (b) *(científica)* research

investigador, -a *nm,f* (a) *(detective)* investigator (b) *(científico)* researcher, research worker

investigar [42] *vt* to research; *(indagar)* to investigate

investir [6] *vt* to invest

invidente 1 *adj* unsighted
2 *nmf* unsighted person

invierno *nm* winter

invisible *adj* invisible

invitación *nf* invitation

invitado, -a 1 *adj* invited; **artista i.** guest artist
2 *nm,f* guest

invitar *vt* to invite; **hoy invito yo** it's on me today; **me invitó a una copa** he treated me to a drink

invocar [44] *vt* to invoke

involucrar 1 *vt* to involve (**en** in)
2 involucrarse *vpr* to get involved (**en** in)

involuntario, -a *adj* involuntary; *(impremeditado)* unintentional

invulnerable *adj* invulnerable

inyección *nf* injection; **poner una i.** to give an injection

inyectar *vt* to inject (**en** into); **i. algo a algn** to inject sb with sth

IPC *nm (abr Esp* **Índice de Precios al Consumo** *o Am* **Índice de Precios al Consumidor)** RPI

ir [16] **1** *vi* (a) *(ir)* to go; **¡vamos!** let's go!; **voy a Lima** I'm going to Lima; **¡ya voy!** (I'm) coming!
(b) *(río, camino)* to lead; **esta carretera va a la frontera** this road leads to the border
(c) *(funcionar)* to work (properly); **el ascensor no va** the lift is out of order
(d) *(desenvolverse)* **¿cómo le va el nuevo trabajo?** how is he getting on in his new job?; **¿cómo te va?** how are things?, how are you doing?
(e) *(sentar bien)* to suit; **el verde te va mucho** green really suits you
(f) *(combinar)* to match; **el rojo no va con el verde** red doesn't go with green
(g) *(vestir)* to wear; **ir con falda** to wear a skirt; **ir de blanco/de uniforme** to be dressed in white/in uniform
(h) *Fam (importar, concernir)* to concern;

eso va por ti también and the same goes for you; **ni me va ni me viene** I don't care one way or the other

(**i**) *Fam (comportarse)* to act; **ir de guapo por la vida** to be a flash Harry

(**j**) **va para abogado** he's studying to be a lawyer

(**k**) (+ por) **ir por la derecha** to keep (to the) right; *Esp (ir a buscar)* **ve (a) por agua** go and fetch some water; *(haber llegado)* **voy por la página 90** I've got as far as page 90

(**l**) *(locuciones)* **a eso iba** I was coming to that; **¡ahí va!** catch!; **en lo que va de año** so far this year; **ir a parar** to end up; **¡qué va!** of course not!, nothing of the sort!; **va a lo suyo** he looks after his own interests; **¡vamos a ver!** let's see!; **¡vaya!** fancy that!; **¡vaya moto!** what a bike!

2 *v aux* (**a**) (+ gerundio) **ir andando** to go on foot; **va mejorando** she's improving (**b**) (+ pp) **ya van rotos tres** three (of them) have already been broken (**c**) (ir a + infin) **iba a decir que** I was going to say that; **va a llover** it's going to rain; **vas a caerte** you'll fall

3 **irse** *vpr* (**a**) *(marcharse)* to go away, to leave; **me voy** I'm off; **¡vámonos!** let's go!; **¡vete!** go away!; **vete a casa** go home (**b**) *(líquido, gas) (escaparse)* to leak (**c**) *(direcciones)* **¿por dónde se va a …?** which is the way to …?; **¿por aquí se va al río** is this is the way to the river

ira *nf* wrath, rage, anger

iracundo, -a *adj* (**a**) *(irascible)* irascible (**b**) *(enfadado)* irate, angry

Irak *n* Iraq

Irán *n* Iran

iraní *(pl* iraníes*) adj & nmf* Iranian

Iraq *n* = Irak

iraquí *(pl* iraquíes*) adj & nmf* Iraqi

irascible *adj* irascible, irritable

iris *nm inv Anat* iris; **arco i.** rainbow

Irlanda *n* Ireland; **I. del Norte** Northern Ireland

irlandés, -esa 1 *adj* Irish

2 *nm,f (hombre)* Irishman; *(mujer)* Irishwoman; **los irlandeses** the Irish

3 *nm (idioma)* Irish

ironía *nf* irony

irónico, -a *adj* ironic

IRPF *nm Econ (abr* **impuesto sobre la renta de las personas físicas)** income tax

irracional *adj* irrational

irradiar [43] *vt* (**a**) *(luz, calor)* to radiate (**b**) *(alimentos, enfermo)* to irradiate (**c**) *RP (emitir)* to broadcast

irreal *adj* unreal

irrealizable *adj* unattainable, unfeasible; *Fig* unreachable

irreconocible *adj* unrecognizable

irrecuperable *adj* irretrievable

irreemplazable *adj* = irremplazable

irregular *adj* irregular

irregularidad *nf* irregularity

irremediable *adj* irremediable, incurable

irremplazable *adj* irreplaceable

irreparable *adj* irreparable

irreprochable *adj* irreproachable, blameless

irresistible *adj* (**a**) *(impulso, persona)* irresistible (**b**) *(insoportable)* unbearable

irresoluto, -a *adj* irresolute

irresponsable *adj* irresponsible

irrestricto, -a *adj Am* unconditional, complete

irreverente *adj* irreverent

irreversible *adj* irreversible

irrigación *nf* irrigation

irrigar [42] *vt* to irrigate, to water

irrisorio, -a *adj* derisory, ridiculous

irritable *adj* irritable

irritación *nf* irritation

irritante *adj* irritating

irritar 1 *vt* (**a**) *(enfadar)* to irritate, to exasperate (**b**) *Med* to irritate

2 irritarse *vpr* (**a**) *(enfadarse)* to lose one's temper, to get angry (**b**) *Med* to become irritated

irrompible *adj* unbreakable

irrumpir *vi* to burst (**en** into)

isla *nf* island, isle

islam *nm Rel* Islam

islámico, -a *adj* Islamic

islandés, -esa 1 *adj* Icelandic

2 *nm,f (persona)* Icelander

3 *nm (idioma)* Icelandic

Islandia *n* Iceland

isleño, -a 1 *adj* island

2 *nm,f* islander

islote *nm* small island

ismo *nm Fam* ism

isotónico, -a *adj* isotonic

Israel *n* Israel

israelí *(pl* israelíes*) adj & nmf* Israeli

istmo *nm Geog* isthmus

itacate *nm Méx* packed lunch

Italia *n* Italy

italiano, -a 1 *adj* Italian

2 *nm,f (persona)* Italian

3 *nm (idioma)* Italian

itinerante *adj* itinerant, itinerating

itinerario *nm* itinerary, route

IVA *nm Econ* (*abr Esp* **impuesto sobre el valor añadido,** *Am* **impuesto al valor agregado**) *Br* VAT, *US* ≃ sales tax

izar [40] *vt* to hoist, to raise

izqda., izqdª (*abr* **izquierda**) left

izqdo., izqdº (*abr* **izquierdo**) left

izquierda *nf* (a) (*lado*) left; **a la i.** on the left; **girar a la i.** to turn left (b) (*mano*) left hand (c) *Pol* **la i.** the left; *Esp* **de izquierdas** left-wing; *Am* **de i.** left-wing

izquierdista *Pol* **1** *adj* leftist, left-wing **2** *nmf* leftist, left-winger

izquierdo, -a *adj* left; **brazo i.** left arm; **a mano izquierda** on the left-hand side

izquierdoso, -a *adj Fam* leftish

J, j ['xota] *nf (letra)* J, j

jabalí *(pl jabalíes) nm* wild boar

jabalina *nf Dep* javelin

jabato *nm* young wild boar

jabón *nm* soap; **j. de afeitar/tocador** shaving/toilet soap

jabonera *nf* soap dish

jaca *nf (caballo pequeño)* pony; *(yegua)* mare

jacal *nm Méx* hut

jacinto *nm Bot* hyacinth

jactancia *nf* boastfulness

jactancioso, -a 1 *adj* boastful
2 *nm,f* braggart

jactarse *upr* to boast, to brag (**de** about)

jacuzzi® [ja'kusi] *nm* Jacuzzi®

jade *nm* jade

jadeante *adj* panting, breathless

jadear *vi* to pant, to gasp

jadeo *nm* panting, gasping

jaguar *nm* jaguar

jaiba *nf Am salvo RP* crayfish

jalar *v* (**a**) *Esp Fam (comer)* to eat, *Br* to scoff (**b**) *Am salvo RP (tirar de)* to pull

jalbegar [42] *vt* to whitewash

jalea *nf* jelly; **j. real** royal jelly

jalear *vt* to cheer (on)

jaleo *nm (alboroto)* din, racket; *(riña)* row; *(confusión)* muddle; **armar j.** to make a racket

jalón *nm Am salvo RP* pull

Jamaica *n* Jamaica

jamaicano, -a *adj & nm,f* Jamaican

jamás *adv* never; **j. he estado allí** I have never been there; **nunca j.** never again; **el mejor libro que j. se ha escrito** the best book ever written

jamba *nf Arquit* jamb

jamón *nm* ham; **j. de York/serrano** boiled/cured ham

jamona *adj Fam* buxom

Japón *n* (**el**) **J.** Japan

japonés, -esa 1 *adj* Japanese
2 *nm,f (persona)* Japanese; **los japoneses** the Japanese
3 *nm (idioma)* Japanese

japuta *nf (pez)* Ray's bream

jaque *nm (en ajedrez)* check; **dar j. a** to check; **j. mate** checkmate; **j. al rey** check

jaqueca *nf* migraine

jara *nf Bot* rock rose

jarabe *nm* syrup; **j. para la tos** cough mixture

jarana *nf Fam* **ir de j.** to go on a spree o a binge

jardín *nm Br* garden, *US* yard; **j. botánico** botanical garden; **j. de infancia** nursery school, kindergarten

jardinera *nf* planter

jardinería *nf* gardening

jardinero *nm* gardener

jarra *nf* pitcher; **j. de cerveza** beer mug; *Fig* **de** o **en jarras** (with) arms akimbo, hands on hips

jarro *nm (recipiente)* jug; *(contenido)* jugful; *Fig* **echar un j. de agua fría a** to pour cold water on

jarrón *nm* vase; *(en arqueología)* urn

jaspe *nm* jasper

Jauja *nf* promised land; **¡esto es J.!** this is the life!

jaula *nf* cage

jauría *nf (de perros, periodistas)* pack

jazmín *nm Bot* jasmine

jazz [jas] *nm inv* jazz

J.C. *(abr Jesucristo)* J.C.

jebo, -a *nm,f Ven Fam* = jevo

jeep [jip] *nm Aut* jeep

jefatura *nf* (**a**) *(cargo, dirección)* leadership *(sede)* central office; **j. de policía** police headquarters

jefe, -a *nm (persona al mando)* boss; *(de empresa)* manager; *(de tribu, ejército)* chief; *(de departamento)* head; **J. de Estado** Head of State; **j. de estación** stationmaster; **j. de redacción** editor-in-chief; **j. de ventas** sales manager

Jehová *nm* Jehovah

jején *nm Am* gnat

jengibre *nm Bot* ginger

jeque *nm* sheik, sheikh

jerarquía *nf* hierarchy

jerárquico, -a *adj* hierarchical

jerez *nm* sherry

jerga nf (argot) (técnica) jargon; (vulgar) slang; **la j. legal** legal jargon

jerigonza nf gibberish

jeringa nf syringe

jeringar [42] vt Fam (**a**) (molestar) to pester, to annoy (**b**) (romper) to break

jeringuilla nf (hypodermic) syringe

jeroglífico, -a 1 adj hieroglyphic

2 nm (**a**) Ling hieroglyph, hieroglyphic (**b**) (juego) rebus

jersey (pl jerseys o jerséis) nm Esp sweater, Br jumper

Jerusalén n Jerusalem

Jesucristo nm Jesus Christ

jesuita adj & nmf Jesuit

Jesús 1 n Jesus

2 interj (**a**) (expresa sorpresa) good heavens! (**b**) Esp (al estornudar) bless you!

jet nf Esp **la j.** the jet set

jeta nf Fam (**a**) Esp (descaro) cheek; **tener j.** to be cheeky, to have a nerve (**b**) (cara) mug, face (**c**) (hocico) snout

jet-set Esp nf, Am nm jet set

jeva nf Carib Fam (mujer) chick, Br bird

jevo, -a nm,f Ven Fam (novio) man, boy-friend; (novia) woman, girlfriend

jíbaro, -a nm,f (**a**) (indio) Jivaro (**b**) Ven Fam (traficante) pusher

jícama nf yam bean, jicama

jícara nf CAm, Méx, Ven (**a**) (calabaza) calabash, gourd (**b**) (taza) mug

jilguero nm goldfinch

jinete nm rider, horseman

jinetera nf Cuba Fam prostitute

jiñar vi muy Fam to shit

jirafa nf (**a**) (animal) giraffe (**b**) (de micrófono) boom

jirón nm (**a**) (trozo desgarrado) shred, strip; (pedazo suelto) bit, scrap; **hecho jirones** in shreds o tatters (**b**) Perú (calle) street

jitomate nm Méx tomato

JJOO nmpl (abr **Juegos Olímpicos**) Olympic Games

jocoso, -a adj funny, humorous

joda nf RP, Ven muy Fam (**a**) (fastidio) pain in the Br arse o US ass (**b**) (broma) piss-take; **¡no te enojes!, lo dije/hice en j.** don't be angry, I was just pissing around (**c**) (fiesta) **los espero el sábado en casa, va a haber j.** I'll see you at my place on Saturday, we're having a bash

joder Vulg **1** interj shit!, Br bloody hell!

2 vt (**a**) (fastidiar) to piss off; **¡no me jodas!** come on, don't give me that! (**b**) Esp (copular) to fuck (**c**) (echar a perder) to screw up; **¡la jodiste!** you screwed it up! (**d**) (romper) to bust, Br bugger

3 joderse vpr (**a**) (aguantarse) to put up with it; **¡hay que joderse!** you'll just have to grin and bear it! (**b**) (echarse a perder) to get screwed up; **¡se jodió el invento!** that's really screwed things up!; **¡que se joda!** to hell with him! (**c**) (romperse) to go bust

jodido, -a adj Vulg (**a**) (maldito) damned, Br bloody (**b**) (molesto) annoying (**c**) (enfermo) in a bad way; (cansado) knackered, exhausted (**d**) (estropeado, roto) bust, Br knackered (**e**) (difícil) shitty

jodienda nf Esp Vulg (**a**) (coito) fuck (**b**) (molestia) pain in the Br arse o US ass

jofaina nf washbasin

jogging nm (**a**) (deporte) jogging; **hacer j.** to go jogging (**b**) RP (ropa) track o jogging suit

jolgorio nm Fam (juerga) binge; (algazara) fun

jolín, jolines interj Fam (enfado) blast!, damn!; (sorpresa) gosh!, good grief!

Jordania n Jordan

jornada nf (**a**) **j. (laboral)** (día de trabajo) working day; **j. intensiva** continuous working day; **j. partida** working day with a lunch break; **trabajo de media j./j. completa** part-time/full-time work (**b**) **jornadas** conference

jornal nm (paga) day's wage; **trabajar a j.** to be paid by the day

> ⚠️ Observa que la palabra inglesa **journal** es un falso amigo y no es la traducción de la palabra española **jornal**. En inglés, **journal** significa "revista, diario".

jornalero, -a nm,f day labourer

joroba nf hump

jorobado, -a 1 adj hunchbacked

2 nm,f hunchback

jorobar Fam **1** vt (**a**) (fastidiar) to bug; **me joroba** it really gets up my nose; **¡no jorobes!** (incredulidad) pull the other one! (**b**) (estropear) to bust

2 jorobarse vpr (**a**) (fastidiarse) to grin and bear it (**b**) (estropearse) to bust

jorongo nm Méx (**a**) (manta) blanket (**b**) (poncho) poncho

jota¹ nf (**a**) (letra) = name of the letter J in Spanish (**b**) (cantidad mínima) **j.** not an iota; **no entiendo ni j.** I don't understand a thing

jota² nf Mús = Spanish dance and music

joven 1 adj young; **de aspecto j.** young-looking

2 nmf (hombre) youth, young man; (mujer) girl, young woman; **de j.** as a young man/woman; **los jóvenes** young people, youth

jovial adj jovial, good-humoured

joya *nf* jewel, piece of jewellery; **joyas de imitación** imitation jewellery; *Fig* **ser una j.** *(persona)* to be a real treasure *o* gem

joyería *nf* jewellery shop, jeweller's (shop)

joyero, -a 1 *nm,f* jeweller
2 *nm* jewel case *o* box

joystick ['jɔistik] *(pl* **joysticks)** *nm* joystick

juanete *nm (en el pie)* bunion

jubilación *nf* **(a)** *(acción)* retirement; **j. anticipada** early retirement **(b)** *(pensión)* pension

jubilado, -a 1 *adj* retired
2 *nm,f Br* pensioner, *US* retiree; **los jubilados** retired people

jubilar 1 *vt (retirar)* to retire, to pension off; *Fam Fig* to get rid of, to ditch
2 jubilarse *vpr (retirarse)* to retire, to go into retirement

júbilo *nm* jubilation, joy

judaísmo *nm* Judaism

judería *nf Hist* Jewish quarter

judía *nf* bean; *Esp* **j. verde** green bean

judicial *adj* judicial; **la vía j.** legal channels

judío, -a 1 *adj* Jewish
2 *nm,f* Jew

judo *nm Dep* judo

juego *nm* **(a)** *(acción)* play, playing; *Fig* **j. limpio/sucio** fair/foul play; **j. de palabras** play on words, pun **(b)** *(deporte, diversión)* game; **j. de azar** game of chance; **j. de cartas** card game; **j. de mesa** board game; **Juegos Olímpicos** Olympic Games; **j. de rol** fantasy role-playing game **(c)** *(apuestas)* gambling; *Fig* **poner algo en j.** to put sth at stake **(d)** *(conjunto de piezas)* set; **j. de café/té** coffee/tea service; **ir a j. con** to match

juerga *nf Fam* binge, rave-up; **ir de j.** to go on a binge

juerguista 1 *adj* fun-loving
2 *nmf* fun-loving person, raver

jueves *nm inv* Thursday; **J. Santo** Maundy Thursday

juez *nmf* judge; **j. de instrucción** examining magistrate; **j. de paz** justice of the peace; *Dep* **j. de salida** starter; **j. de línea** *(hombre)* linesman; *(mujer)* lineswoman

jugada *nf* **(a)** *(en deportes, juegos)* move; *(en billar)* shot **(b)** *Fam* dirty trick

jugador, -a *nm,f* player; *(apostador)* gambler

jugar [32] **1** *vi* **(a)** to play; **j. a(l) fútbol/tenis** to play football/tennis; *Fig* **j. sucio** to play dirty **(b)** **j. con** *(no tomar en serio)* to toy with
2 *vt* **(a)** to play **(b)** *(apostar)* to bet, to stake
3 jugarse *vpr* **(a)** *(arriesgar)* to risk; *Fam*

jugarse el pellejo to risk one's neck **(b)** *(apostar)* to bet, to stake

jugarreta *nf Fam* dirty trick

jugo *nm* juice; *Fig* **sacar el j. a** *(aprovechar)* to make the most of; *(explotar)* to squeeze dry

jugoso, -a *adj* **(a)** *(alimento)* juicy; **un filete j.** a juicy steak **(b)** *Fig (sustancioso)* substantial, meaty; **un tema j.** a meaty topic

juguete *nm* toy; **pistola de j.** toy gun; *Fig* **ser el j. de algn** to be sb's plaything

juguetear *vi* to play

juguetería *nf* toy shop

juguetón, -ona *adj* playful

juicio *nm* **(a)** *(facultad mental)* judgement, discernment; *(opinión)* opinion, judgement; **a j. de** in the opinion of; **a mi j.** in my opinion **(b)** *(sensatez)* reason, common sense; **en su sano j.** in one's right mind; **perder el j.** to go mad **(c)** *Der* trial, lawsuit; **llevar a algn a j.** to take legal action against sb, to sue sb

juicioso, -a *adj* judicious, wise

julepe *nm* **(a)** *(juego de naipes)* = type of card game **(b)** *PRico, RP Fam (susto)* scare, fright; **dar un j. a algn** to give sb a scare

julio *nm* July

junco *nm Bot* rush

jungla *nf* jungle

junio *nm* June

júnior *adj Dep* junior; **campeonato j. de golf** junior golf championship

junta *nf* **(a)** *(reunión)* meeting, assembly; *Pol* **j. de gobierno** cabinet meeting **(b)** *(dirección)* board, committee; **j. directiva** board of directors **(c)** *Mil* junta; **j. militar** military junta **(d)** *(parlamento regional)* regional parliament **(e)** *Téc* joint

juntar 1 *vt* **(a)** *(unir)* to join, to put together; *(piezas)* to assemble **(b)** *(reunir) (sellos)* to collect; *(dinero)* to raise
2 juntarse *vpr* **(a)** *(unirse)* to join; *(ríos, caminos)* to meet; *(personas)* to gather **(b)** *(amancebarse)* to live together

junto, -a 1 *adj* together; **dos mesas juntas** two tables side by side; **todos juntos** all together
2 *adv* **j. con** together with; **j. a** next to

juntura *nf Téc* joint, seam

jura *nf (acción)* oath; *(ceremonia)* swearing in; **j. de bandera** oath of allegiance to the flag

jurado *nm* **(a)** *(tribunal)* jury; *(en un concurso)* panel of judges, jury **(b)** *(miembro del tribunal)* juror, member of the jury

juramento *nm* **(a)** *Der* oath; **bajo j.** under oath **(b)** *(blasfemia)* swearword, curse

jurar 1 *vi Der & Rel* to swear, to take an oath
  2 *vt* to swear; **j. el cargo** to take the oath of office; **j. por Dios** to swear to God
  3 jurarse *vpr Fam* **tenérsela jurada a algn** to have it in for sb

jurel *nm (pez)* scad, horse mackerel

jurídico, -a *adj* legal

jurisdicción *nf* jurisdiction

jurisdiccional *adj* jurisdictional; **aguas jurisdiccionales** territorial waters

jurista *nmf* jurist, lawyer

justamente *adv* **¡j.!** precisely!; **j. detrás de** right behind

justicia *nf* justice; **tomarse la j. por su mano** to take the law into one's own hands

justicialismo *nm Pol* = Argentinian nationalistic political movement founded by Juan Domingo Perón

justicialista *adj Pol* = belonging or related to "justicialismo"

justiciero, -a *adj* severe

justificable *adj* justifiable

justificación *nf* justification

justificado, -a *adj* justified, well-grounded

justificante *nm* written proof; **j. de pago** proof of payment

justificar [44] **1** *vt* to justify
  2 justificarse *vpr* to clear oneself, to justify oneself

justo, -a 1 *adj* (a) *(equitativo)* fair; **un trato j.** a fair deal (b) *(apretado) (ropa)* tight; **estamos justos de tiempo** we're pressed for time (c) *(exacto)* right, accurate; **la palabra justa** the right word (d) *(preciso)* **llegamos en el momento j. en que salían** we arrived just as they were leaving (e) **lo j.** just enough
  2 *nm,f* just *o* righteous person; **los justos** the just, the righteous
  3 *adv (exactamente)* exactly, precisely; **j. al lado** right beside

juvenil 1 *adj (aspecto)* youthful, young; **ropa j.** young people's clothes; **delincuencia j.** juvenile delinquency
  2 *nmf Dep* **juveniles** ≃ youth team *(age 16–17)*

juventud *nf* (a) *(edad)* youth (b) *(jóvenes)* young people

juzgado *nm* court, tribunal; **j. de guardia** = court open during the night or at other times when ordinary courts are shut

juzgar [42] *vt* to judge; **a j. por …** judging by …

K

K, k [ka] *nf (letra)* K, k
karaoke *nm* karaoke
kárate *nm Dep* karate
karateka *nmf Dep* person who does karate
karting *nm* go-kart racing, karting
Kenia *n* Kenya
Kg, kg *(abr* **kilogramo(s))** kg
kilo *nm* (a) *(medida)* kilo; *Fam* **pesa un k.** it weighs a ton (b) *Esp Antes Fam (millón)* a million (pesetas)
kilogramo *nm* kilogram, kilogramme
kilolitro *nm* kilolitre
kilometraje *nm* ≃ mileage

kilométrico, -a *adj* kilometric, kilometrical; **billete k.** multiple-journey ticket
kilómetro *nm* kilometre
kilovatio *nm* kilowatt; **k. hora** kilowatt-hour
kimono *nm* kimono
kínder *nm Andes, Méx* kindergarten, nursery school
kiosco *nm* = quiosco
kiwi *nm* (a) *(ave)* kiwi (b) *(fruto)* kiwi (fruit), Chinese gooseberry
kleenex® ['klines, 'klineks] *nm inv* paper hanky, (paper) tissue
km *(abr* **kilómetro(s))** km
Kw, kw *(abr* **kilovatio(s))** kW

L, l ['ele] *nf (letra)* L, l

l *(abr* **litro(s))** l

la¹ 1 *art def* f the; **la mesa** the table
2 *pron dem* the one; **la del vestido azul** the one in the blue dress; **la que vino ayer** the one who came yesterday; *ver* **el**

la² *pron pers* f (*persona*) her; *(usted)* you; *(cosa)* it; **la invitaré** I'll invite her along; **no la dejes abierta** don't leave it open; **ya la avisaremos, señora** we'll let you know, madam; *ver* **le**

la³ *nm Mús* la, A

laberinto *nm* labyrinth

labia *nf Fam* loquacity; *Pey* glibness; **tener mucha l.** to have the gift of the gab

labio *nm* lip

labor *nf* **(a)** *(trabajo)* work; *(tarea)* task; **l. de equipo** teamwork; **profesión: sus labores** occupation: housewife **(b)** *Agr* farmwork **(c)** *(de costura)* needlework

laborable *adj* **(a)** **día l.** *(no festivo)* working day **(b)** *Agr* arable

laboral *adj* industrial; **accidente l.** industrial accident; **conflictividad l.** industrial unrest; **jornada l.** working day; **Universidad L.** technical training college

laboratorio *nm* laboratory

laborioso, -a *adj* **(a)** *(persona)* hard-working **(b)** *(tarea)* laborious

laborista *Pol* **1** *adj* Labour
2 *nmf* Labour (Party) member/supporter

labrador, -a *nm,f (granjero)* farmer; *(trabajador)* farm worker

labranza *nf* farming

labrar 1 *vt* **(a)** *Agr* to till **(b)** *(madera)* to carve; *(piedra)* to cut; *(metal)* to work
2 labrarse *upr Fig* **labrarse un porvenir** to build a future for oneself

laburar *vi RP Fam* to work; **labura de vendedora** she works in a shop

laburo *nm RP Fam* job

laca *nf* **(a)** *(para el pelo)* hair lacquer, hairspray; **l. de uñas** nail polish *o* varnish **(b)** *Arte* lacquer

lacio, -a *adj* **(a)** *(pelo)* lank, limp **(b)** **qué l.!** *(soso)* what a weed!

lacónico, -a *adj* laconic; *(conciso)* terse

lacra *nf* evil, curse; **una l. social** a scourge of society

lacrar *vt* to seal with wax

lacre *nm* sealing wax

lacrimógeno, -a *adj* **(a)** **gas l.** tear gas **(b)** *Fig* **una película lacrimógena** a tear-jerker

lactancia *nf* lactation; **l. artificial** bottle feeding; **l. materna** breastfeeding

lactante *nmf* baby *(not yet eating solid food)*

lactar *vi* to breast-feed

lácteo, -a *adj* **productos lácteos** milk *o* dairy products

ladear 1 *vt* to tilt
2 ladearse *upr* **(a)** *(inclinarse)* to lean, to tilt **(b)** *(desviarse)* to go off to one side

ladera *nf* slope

ladino, -a 1 *adj (astuto)* crafty
2 *nm,f CAm, Méx, Ven (no blanco)* = non-white Spanish-speaking person

lado *nm* **(a)** *(costado, parte)* side; **a un l.** aside; **al l.** close by, nearby; **al l. de** next to, beside; **ponte de l.** stand sideways **(b)** *(lugar)* place; **en otro l.** somewhere else; **por todos lados** everywhere, all around **(c)** *(expresiones)* **dar de l. a algn** to cold-shoulder sb; **por otro l.** *(además)* moreover; **por un l. ..., por otro l. ...** on the one hand ..., on the other hand ...

ladrar *vi* to bark

ladrido *nm también Fig* bark

ladrillo *nm* **(a)** *Constr* brick **(b)** *Fam (pesado)* bore, drag

ladrón, -ona 1 *nm,f* thief, robber; **¡al l.!** stop, thief!
2 *nm Elec* multiple socket

lagartija *nf* small lizard

lagarto *nm* lizard

lago *nm* lake

lágrima *nf* **(a)** *(en los ojos)* tear; **llorar a l. viva** to cry one's eyes out **(b)** *(en lámpara)* teardrop

lagrimoso, -a *adj* tearful

laguna *nf* **(a)** *(lago)* lagoon **(b)** *(en colección, memoria)* gap; *(en leyes, reglamento)* loophole

La Haya *n* The Hague

laico, -a 1 *adj* lay
2 *nm,f* lay person; *(hombre)* layman; *(mujer)* laywoman

lameculos *nmf inv muy Fam* bootlicker, *Br* arselicker, *US* ass-kisser

lamentable *adj* regrettable; *(malo)* lamentable

lamentar 1 *vt* to regret; **lo lamento** I'm sorry
2 lamentarse *vpr* to complain

lamento *nm* moan, wail

lamer *vt* to lick

lámina *nf* (a) *(plancha)* sheet; *(placa)* plate (b) *(rodaja)* slice (c) *(grabado)* engraving (d) *(dibujo)* plate

laminar *vt* (a) *(hacer láminas de)* to roll (b) *(cubrir con láminas)* to laminate

lámpara *nf* (a) *(aparato)* lamp; **l. de pie** *Br* standard lamp, *US* floor lamp (b) *(bombilla)* bulb (c) *Rad* valve (d) *Fam (mancha)* stain

lamparón *nm Fam* oil *o* grease stain

lana *nf* (a) *(de oveja)* wool; **pura l. virgen** pure new wool (b) *Andes, Méx Fam (dinero)* dough, cash

lanar *adj* **ganado l.** sheep

lance *nm Literario (episodio)* event, incident

> *Observa que la palabra inglesa* **lance** *es un falso amigo y no es la traducción de la palabra española* **lance**. *En inglés,* **lance** *significa "lanza".*

lanceta *nf Andes, Méx (aguijón)* sting

lancha *nf* motorboat, launch; **l. motora** speedboat; **l. neumática** rubber dinghy; **l. salvavidas** lifeboat

langosta *nf* (a) *(crustáceo)* lobster (b) *(insecto)* locust

langostino *nm* king prawn

languidecer [33] *vi* to languish

lánguido, -a *adj* languid; *(sin vigor)* listless

lanudo, -a *adj* woolly, fleecy; *(peludo)* furry

lanza *nf* spear, lance; **punta de l.** spearhead; *Fig* **romper una l. en favor de algn/algo** to defend sb/sth

lanzadera *nf* shuttle; **l. espacial** space shuttle

lanzado, -a *adj Fam* reckless; **ir l.** to tear along

lanzamiento *nm* (a) *(de objeto)* throwing, hurling (b) *Dep (de disco, jabalina)* throw; *(de peso)* put (c) *Mil (de cohete etc)* launching (d) *Com* launch; **precio de l.** launch price (e) *Náut* launch

lanzar [40] **1** *vt* (a) *(arrojar)* to throw, to fling (b) *(grito)* to let out (c) *Com, Mil & Náut* to launch
2 lanzarse *vpr* (a) *(arrojarse)* to throw *o* hurl oneself; **lanzarse al suelo** to throw oneself to the ground (b) *(emprender)* **lanzarse a** to embark on; **lanzarse a los negocios** to go into business

lapa *nf* (a) *Zool* limpet (b) **es una verdadera l.** he/she sticks to you like glue

lapicera *nf CSur* ballpoint (pen), Biro®; **l. fuente** fountain pen

lapicero *nm* (a) *Esp (lápiz)* pencil (b) *CAm, Perú (bolígrafo)* ballpoint (pen), Biro®

lápida *nf* headstone

lapidario, -a *adj (frase)* meaningful, oracular

lápiz *nm* pencil; **l. labial** *o* **de labios** lipstick; **l. de ojos** eyeliner

lapso *nm* (a) *(periodo de tiempo)* period (b) *(error)* lapse, slip

lapsus *nm inv* slip; **l. linguae** slip of the tongue

largar [42] **1** *vt* (a) *Fam (golpe, discurso, dinero)* to give (b) *Náut* **l. amarras** to cast off
2 largarse *vpr Fam* to clear off, to split; **¡lárgate!** beat it!

largas *nfpl* **dar l. a algo** to put sth off

largavistas *nm inv Bol, CSur* binoculars

largo, -a 1 *adj* (a) *(espacio)* long; *(tiempo)* long, lengthy; **pasamos un mes l. allí** we spent a good month there; **a lo l. de** *(espacio)* along; *(tiempo)* through; **a la larga** in the long run (b) *(excesivo)* too long; **se hizo l. el día** the day dragged on (c) **largos años** many years
2 *nm* (a) *(longitud)* length; **¿cuánto tiene de l.?** how long is it? (b) *Más* largo
3 *adv* **l. y tendido** at length; *Fam* **¡l. (de aquí)!** clear off!; **esto va para l.** this is going to last a long time

> *Observa que la palabra inglesa* **large** *es un falso amigo y no es la traducción de la palabra española* **largo**. *En inglés* **large** *significa "grande".*

largometraje *nm* feature film, full-length film

laringe *nf* larynx

laringitis *nf inv* laryngitis

las¹ *art def fpl* the; **l. sillas** the chairs; **lávate l. manos** wash your hands; *(no se traduce)* **me gustan l. flores** I like flowers
2 *pron* **l. que** *(personas)* the ones who, those who; *(objetos)* the ones that, those that; **toma l. que quieras** take whichever ones you want; *ver* **la** y **los**

las² *pron pers fpl (ellas)* them; *(ustedes)* you; **l. llamaré mañana (a ustedes)** I'll call you tomorrow; **no l. rompas** don't break them; **Pepa es de l. mías** Pepa thinks the way I do; *ver* **los**

lasaña *nf* lasagna, lasagne

lascivo, -a *adj* lewd, lecherous

láser *adj inv* & *nm inv* laser

lástima *nf* pity; **¡qué l.!** what a pity!, what a shame!; **es una l. que …** it's a pity (that) …; **estar hecho una l.** to be a sorry sight; **tener l. a algn** to feel sorry for sb

lastimar *vt* to hurt, to injure

lastre *nm* (a) *(peso)* ballast (b) *Fig* dead weight

lata¹ *nf* (a) *(envase)* can, *esp Br* tin; **en l.** canned, *esp Br* tinned (b) *(hojalata)* tin(plate); **hecho de l.** made of tin

lata² *nf Esp Fam* nuisance, drag; **dar la l.** to be a nuisance *o* a pest

latente *adj* latent

lateral 1 *adj* side, lateral; **salió por la puerta l.** he went out by the side door; **escalón l.** *(en letrero)* ramp
  2 *nm* side passage; *Aut* **(carril) l.** side lane

latido *nm (del corazón)* beat

latifundio *nm* large landed estate

latigazo *nm* lash

látigo *nm* whip

latín *nm* Latin

latino, -a 1 *adj* Latin; **América Latina** Latin America
  2 *nm,f* Latin American

Latinoamérica *nf* Latin America

latinoamericano, -a *adj* & *nm,f* Latin American

latir *vi* to beat

latitud *nf* (a) *Geog* latitude (b) **latitudes** region, area

latón *nm* brass

latoso, -a *adj Fam* annoying

laucha *nf CSur* (a) *(ratón)* baby *o* small mouse (b) *Fam (persona)* **es una l.** he's a tiny little thing

laúd *nm* lute

laurel *nm Bot* laurel, (sweet) bay; *Culin* bay leaf; *Fig* **dormirse en los laureles** to rest on one's laurels

lava *nf* lava

lavable *adj* washable

lavabo *nm* (a) *(pila)* *Br* washbasin, *US* washbowl (b) *(retrete)* *Br* lavatory, *US* washroom

lavadero *nm (de coches)* carwash

lavado *nm* wash, washing; *Fig* **l. de cerebro** brainwashing; **l. en seco** dry-cleaning

lavadora *nf* washing machine

lavanda *nf* lavender

lavandería *nf* (a) *(automática)* launderette, *US* Laundromat® (b) *(atendida por personal)* laundry

lavaplatos *nm inv* dishwasher

lavar *vt* to wash; **l. en seco** to dry-clean

lavativa *nf* enema

lavatorio *nm* (a) *(en misa)* lavabo (b) *Andes, RP (lavabo)* *Br* washbasin, *US* washbowl

lavavajillas *nm inv (aparato)* dishwasher

laxante *adj* & *nm* laxative

laxitud *nf* laxity, laxness

lazada *nf (nudo)* bow

lazarillo *nm* **(perro) l.** guide dog, *US* seeing-eye dog

lazo *nm* (a) *(adorno)* bow (b) *(nudo)* knot; **l. corredizo** slipknot (c) *(para reses)* lasso (d) *Fig (usu pl) (vínculo)* tie, bond

le 1 *pron pers mf (objeto indirecto) (a él)* (to) him; *(a ella)* (to) her; *(a cosa)* (to) it; *(a usted)* (to) you; **lávale la cara** wash his face; **le compraré uno** I'll buy one for her; **¿qué le pasa (a usted)?** what's the matter with you?
  2 *pron pers m Esp (objeto directo) (él)* him; *(usted)* you; **no le oigo** I can't hear him; **no quiero molestarle** I don't wish to disturb you

leal 1 *adj* loyal, faithful
  2 *nmf* loyalist

lealtad *nf* loyalty, faithfulness

lebrel *nm* greyhound

lección *nf* lesson; *Fig* **dar una l. a algn** to teach sb a lesson; *Fig* **te servirá de l.** let that be a lesson to you

lechal 1 *adj* suckling, sucking
  2 *nm* suckling lamb

lechazo *nm* suckling lamb

leche *nf* (a) *(líquido)* milk; **l. descremada** *o* **desnatada** *Br* skimmed milk, *US* skim milk (b) *muy Fam (humor)* **estar de mala l.** to be in a *Br* bloody *o US* goddamn awful mood (c) *Esp muy Fam (golpe)* knock; **dar** *o* **pegar una l. a algn** to clobber sb

lechera *nf* (a) *(vasija)* churn (b) *Fam* police car

lechería *nf* dairy, creamery

lechero, -a 1 *adj* milk, dairy; **central lechera** dairy co-operative; **vaca lechera** milk cow
  2 *nm* milkman

lecho *nm Lit* bed; **l. del río** river-bed; **l. mortuorio** death-bed

lechón *nm* suckling-pig

lechosa *nf Carib* papaya

lechoso, -a *adj* milky

lechuga *nf* lettuce

lechuza *nf* owl

lectivo, -a *adj* school; **horas lectivas** teaching hours

lector, -a 1 *nm,f* (**a**) *(persona)* reader (**b**) *Esp Univ* lector, (language) assistant
2 *nm* reader; **l. de CD-ROM** CD-ROM drive; **l. de DVD** DVD player

lectura *nf* reading

leer [36] *vt* to read; **léenos el menú** read out the menu for us; *Fig* **l. entre líneas** to read between the lines

legado *nm* legacy

legajo *nm* bundle (of papers)

legal *adj* (**a**) *Der* legal, lawful; **requisitos legales** legal formalities (**b**) *Esp Fam (persona)* honest, decent

legalidad *nf* legality, lawfulness

legalizar [40] *vt* to legalize; *(documento)* to authenticate

legaña *nf* sleep

legar [42] *vt (propiedad)* to bequeath; *Fig (tradiciones)* to hand down, to pass on

legendario, -a *adj* legendary

legible *adj* legible

legión *nf* legion

legionella *nf* Legionnaire's Disease

legislación *nf* legislation

legislar *vi* to legislate

legislativo, -a *adj* legislative; **el poder l.** parliament

legislatura *nf* legislature

legitimar *vt (justificar)* to legitimize; *(autentificar)* to authenticate

legitimidad *nf* legitimacy

legítimo, -a *adj* (**a**) *Der* legitimate; **en legítima defensa** in self-defence (**b**) *(auténtico)* authentic, real; **oro l.** pure gold

lego, -a 1 *adj Rel* lay
2 *nm* (**a**) *(profano)* layman; **ser l. en la materia** to know nothing about the subject (**b**) *Rel* lay brother

legua *nf (medida)* league; *Fig* **se nota a la l.** it stands out a mile

legumbre *nf* pulse, pod vegetable; **legumbres secas** dried pulses; **legumbres verdes** green vegetables

lehendakari *nmf* = head of the Basque government

lejanía *nf* distance

lejano, -a *adj* distant, far-off; **parientes lejanos** distant relatives; **el L. Oriente** the Far East

lejía *nf* bleach

lejos *adv* far (away); **a lo l.** in the distance; **de l.** from a distance; *Fig* **ir demasiado l.** to go too far; *Fig* **llegar l.** to go a long way; *Fig* **sin ir más l.** to take an obvious example

lelo, -a *Fam* **1** *adj* stupid, silly
2 *nm,f* ninny

lema *nm* (**a**) *(divisa)* motto, slogan (**b**) *(contraseña)* code name

lencería *nf* (**a**) *(prendas)* lingerie (**b**) *(ropa blanca)* linen (goods)

lengua *nf* (**a**) *Anat* tongue; *Fig* **malas lenguas** gossips; *Fam Fig* **irse de la l.** to spill the beans; *Fam Fig* **tirarle a algn de la l.** to draw sb out (**b**) *Ling* language; **l. materna** native o mother tongue

lenguado *nm (pez)* sole

lenguaje *nm* language; *Inform* language; **l. corporal** body language

lengüeta *nf* (**a**) *(de zapato)* tongue (**b**) *Mús* reed

lente 1 *nf* lens; **lentes de contacto** contact lenses
2 lentes *nmpl Am* glasses; **lentes de contacto** contact lenses

lenteja *nf* lentil

lentejuela *nf* sequin, spangle

lentilla *nf Esp* contact lens; **lentillas blandas/duras** soft/hard lenses

lentitud *nf* slowness; **con l.** slowly

lento, -a *adj* slow; **a fuego l.** on a low heat

leña *nf* (**a**) *(madera)* firewood; *Fig* **echar l. al fuego** to add fuel to the fire (**b**) *Fam (golpes)* knocks

leñador, -a *nm,f* woodcutter

leñazo *nm Fam (golpe)* blow, smash

leñe *interj Esp Fam* damn it!

leño *nm* log

Leo *nm* Leo

león *nm* lion

leona *nf* lioness

leonera *nf* lion's den; *Fig (habitación)* den

leopardo *nm* leopard

leotardos *nmpl Esp* thick tights

lépero, -a *Fam adj* (**a**) *CAm, Méx (vulgar)* coarse, vulgar (**b**) *Cuba (ladino)* smart, crafty

lepra *nf* leprosy

leproso, -a 1 *adj* leprous
2 *nm,f* leper

les 1 *pron pers mfpl (objeto indirecto)* (*a ellos, -as)* them; *(a ustedes)* you; **dales el dinero** give them the money; **l. he comprado un regalo** I've bought you a present
2 *pron pers mpl Esp (objeto directo) (ellos)* them; *(ustedes)* you; **l. esperaré** I shall wait for you; **no quiero molestarles** I don't wish to disturb you

lesbiana *nf* lesbian

leseras *nfpl Chile Fam (tonterías)* nonsense, *Br* rubbish

lesión *nf* (a) *(corporal)* injury (b) *Der (perjuicio)* damage

lesionar *vt* to injure

leso, -a *adj Der* **crimen de lesa humanidad** crime against humanity

letal *adj* lethal, deadly

letanía *nf* litany

letargo *nm* lethargy

letón, -ona 1 *adj* Latvian
  2 *nm,f* Latvian
  3 *nm (idioma)* Latvian, Lettish

Letonia *n* Latvia

letra *nf* (a) *(signo)* letter; **l. de imprenta** block capitals; **l. mayúscula** capital letter; **l. minúscula** small letter; **l. pequeña** small print (b) *(escritura)* (hand)writing (c) *Mús (texto)* lyrics, words (d) *Fin* **l. (de cambio)** bill of exchange, draft (e) *Univ* **letras** arts

letrado, -a *nm,f* lawyer

letrero *nm (aviso)* notice, sign; *(cartel)* poster; **l. luminoso** neon sign

leucemia *nf* leukaemia

levadizo, -a *adj* **puente l.** drawbridge

levadura *nf* yeast; **l. en polvo** baking powder

levantamiento *nm* (a) *Dep* **l. de pesos** weightlifting (b) *(insurrección)* uprising

levantar 1 *vt* (a) *(alzar, elevar)* to raise, to lift; *(mano, voz)* to raise; *(edificio)* to erect; *Fig (ánimos)* to raise; **l. los ojos** to look up (b) *(castigo)* to suspend
  2 levantarse *upr* (a) *(ponerse de pie)* to stand up, to rise (b) *(salir de la cama)* to get up (c) *(concluir)* to finish; **se levanta la sesión** the meeting is closed (d) *Pol* to rise, to revolt; **levantarse en armas** to rise up in arms (e) *(viento)* to come up; *(tormenta)* to gather

levante *nm* (a) **(el) L.** Levante, = the regions of Valencia and Murcia (b) *(viento)* east wind, Levanter

levar *vt* **l. ancla** to weigh anchor

leve *adj (ligero)* light; *Fig (de poca importancia)* slight

levedad *nf (ligereza)* lightness; *Fig* slightness; **heridas de l.** minor injuries

levemente *adv* slightly

levitar *vi* to levitate

léxico, -a *Ling* **1** *nm (diccionario)* lexicon; *(vocabulario)* vocabulary, word list
  2 *adj* lexical

ley *(pl* **leyes)** *nf* (a) *(norma)* law; *(parlamentaria)* act; **leyes** *(derecho)* law (b) **oro de l.** pure gold; **plata de l.** sterling silver

leyenda *nf* (a) *(relato)* legend (b) *(en un mapa)* legend; *(en una moneda)* inscription; *(bajo ilustración)* caption

liar [29] **1** *vt* (a) *(envolver)* to wrap up; *(un cigarrillo)* to roll (b) *(enredar)* to muddle up; *(confundir)* to confuse
  2 liarse *upr* (a) *(embarullarse)* to get muddled up (b) *Esp Fam (salir)* to get involved **(con** with); *(besarse)* to neck (c) *Esp* **liarse a bofetadas** to come to blows

libanés, -esa *adj & nm,f* Lebanese

Líbano *n* **el L.** (the) Lebanon

libelo *nm* lampoon, satire

libélula *nf* dragonfly

liberación *nf (de país)* liberation; *(de prisionero)* release, freeing

liberal *adj & nm,f* liberal

liberalizar [40] *vt* to liberalize

liberar *vt (país)* to liberate; *(prisionero)* to free, to release

libertad *nf* freedom, liberty; **en l.** free; *Der* **(en) l. bajo palabra/fianza** (on) parole/bail; *Der* **(en) l. condicional** (on) parole; **l. de comercio** free trade; **l. de expresión** freedom of speech

libertador, -a *nm,f* liberator

libertar *vt* to set free, to release

libertinaje *nm* licentiousness

libertino, -a *adj & nm,f* libertine

Libia *n* Libya

libio, -a *adj & nm,f* Libyan

Libra *nm* Libra

libra *nf (unidad de peso, moneda)* pound; **l. esterlina** pound sterling

librar 1 *vt* (a) **l. a algn de algo** to free sb from sth (b) *Com (letra)* to draw (c) **l. batalla** to do o join battle
  2 *vi Esp (no trabajar)* to be off work; **libro los martes** I have Tuesdays off
  3 librarse *upr* to escape; **librarse de algn** to get rid of sb

libre *adj* free; **entrada l.** *(gratis)* admission free; *(sin restricción)* open to the public; **l. cambio** free trade; **l. de impuestos** tax-free

librería *nf* (a) *(tienda)* bookshop, *US* bookstore (b) *Esp (mueble)* bookcase

> Observa que la palabra inglesa **library** es un falso amigo y no es la traducción de la palabra española **librería**. En inglés **library** significa "biblioteca".

librero, -a 1 *nm,f* bookseller
  2 *nm CAm, Col, Méx (mueble)* bookcase

> Observa que la palabra inglesa **librarian** es un falso amigo y no es la traducción de la palabra española **librero**. En inglés **librarian** significa "bibliotecario".

libreta *nf* notebook; **l. (de ahorro)** savings book

libretista *nmf Am (guionista)* screenwriter, scriptwriter

libreto *nm Am (guión)* script

libro *nm* book; **l. de texto** textbook; *Com* **l. de caja** cashbook; *Fin* **l. mayor** ledger

liceal *nmf Urug Br* secondary school *o US* high school pupil

liceano, -a *nm,f Chile Br* secondary school *o US* high school pupil

liceísta *nmf Ven Br* secondary school *o US* high school pupil

licencia *nf* (a) *(permiso)* permission; *(documento)* permit, licence; **l. de armas/ caza** gun/hunting licence; *Carib, Chile, Ecuad* **l. de conducir,** *Méx* **l. para conducir** *Br* driving licence, *US* driver's license (b) *(libertad abusiva)* licence, licentiousness

licenciado, -a *nm,f* (a) *Univ* graduate; **l. en Ciencias** Bachelor of Science (b) *Am salvo RP (forma de tratamiento)* = form of address used to indicate respect; **el l. Pérez** Mr Pérez

licenciar [43] **1** *vt* (a) *Mil* to discharge (b) *Univ* to confer a degree on
2 licenciarse *vpr Univ* to graduate

licenciatura *nf Univ (título)* (bachelor's) degree (course); *(carrera)* degree (course)

liceo *nm* (a) *(sociedad literaria)* literary society (b) *(escuela) Br* secondary school, *US* high school

licitar *vt Com (pujar)* to bid for

lícito, -a *adj (permisible)* allowed; *Der* lawful

licor *nm* liquor, *US* spirits

licorería *nf* (a) *(fábrica)* distillery (b) *(tienda) Br* off-licence, *US* liquor store

licuadora *nf* (a) *Esp (para extraer zumo)* juice extractor, juicer (b) *Am (para batir)* blender, *Br* liquidizer

licuar [30] *vt* to liquidize

lid *nf* contest

líder *nmf* leader

liderar *vt* to lead, to head

liderato, liderazgo *nm* leadership; *Dep* top *o* first position

lidia *nf* bullfight, bullfighting

lidiador *nm* bullfighter

lidiar [43] **1** *vt Taurom* to fight
2 *vi* to fight; **l. con** to contend with, to fight against

liebre *nf* hare

liendre *nf* nit

lienzo *nm* (a) *Tex* linen (b) *Arte* canvas

lifting ['liftin] *(pl* **liftings)** *nm* face-lift

liga *nf* (a) *Dep & Pol* league; **hacer buena l.** to get on well together (b) *(para medias) (elástico)* garter; *(colgante) Br* suspender, *US* garter

ligamento *nm* ligament

ligar [42] **1** *vt (unir, aglutinar)* to bind; *(atar)* to tie (up); *(salsa)* to thicken
2 *vi Fam (encontrar pareja)* to score, *Br* to pull; **l. con algn** *(entablar relaciones) Br* to get off with sb, *US* to make out with sb
3 ligarse *vpr Esp Fam* **ligarse a algn** *Br* to get off with sb, *US* to make out with sb

ligazón *nf* bond, tie

ligeramente *adv* (a) *(levemente)* lightly (b) *(un poco)* slightly

ligereza *nf* (a) *(levedad)* lightness (b) *(irreflexión)* rashness (c) *(rapidez)* speed

ligero, -a 1 *adj* (a) *(de poco peso)* light, lightweight; **l. de ropa** lightly clad (b) *(leve)* (brisa, comida, roce) light; *(dolor, diferencia)* slight (c) *(veloz)* swift, quick; *(ágil)* agile, nimble (d) **hacer algo a la ligera** to do sth without much thought; **tomarse algo a la ligera** not to take sth seriously
2 *adv (rápido)* fast, swiftly

light [lait] *adj inv (tabaco)* `mild; *Fig (persona)* lightweight

ligón, -ona *adj Esp Fam* **es muy l.** he's always *Br* getting off *o US* making out with somebody or other

ligue *nm Esp Fam (novio) Br* bloke, *US* squeeze; *(novia) Br* bird, *US* squeeze

liguero, -a 1 *adj Dep* league; **partido l.** league game *o Br* match
2 *nm Br* suspender belt, *US* garter belt

lija *nf* sandpaper; **papel de l.** sandpaper

lijar *vt* to sand *o* sandpaper (down)

lila¹ 1 *nm (color)* lilac
2 *nf (flor)* lilac
3 *adj inv* lilac

lila² 1 *Fam (tonto)* dumb, stupid
2 *nmf (tonto)* twit

lima¹ *nf (fruto)* lime

lima² *nf (herramienta)* file; **l. de uñas** nail-file

limar *vt* to file; *Fig* **l. asperezas** to smooth things over

limbo *nm* limbo

limitación *nf* limitation; **l. de velocidad** speed limit

limitar 1 *vt* to limit, to restrict
2 *vi* to border; **l. con** to border on

límite *nm* limit; *Geog & Pol* boundary, border; **caso l.** borderline case; **fecha l.** deadline; **velocidad l.** maximum speed

limítrofe *adj* neighbouring

limón *nm* lemon

limonada *nf* lemonade, = iced, sweetened lemon juice drink

limonero *nm* lemon tree

limosna *nf* alms; **pedir l.** to beg

limpiabotas *nm inv* shoeshine, *Br* bootblack

limpiacristales *nm inv* window cleaner

limpiador, -a 1 *adj* cleansing
2 *nm,f (persona)* cleaner
3 *nm (producto)* cleaner

limpiaparabrisas *nm inv Br* windscreen *o US* windshield wiper

limpiar [43] *vt* to clean; *(con trapo)* to wipe; *(zapatos)* to polish

limpieza *nf (calidad)* cleanliness; *(acción)* cleaning; **con l.** cleanly

limpio, -a 1 *adj* (a) *(aseado)* clean (b) *Dep* **juego l.** fair play (c) *Fin (neto)* net; **beneficios en l.** net profit (d) **pasar algo** *Esp* a *o Am* **en l.** to produce a fair copy of sth
2 *adv* fairly; **jugar l.** to play fair

linaje *nm* lineage

linaza *nf* **aceite de l.** linseed oil

lince *nm* lynx; **tiene ojos de l.** he's eagle-eyed

linchar *vt* to lynch

lindante *adj* bordering

lindar *vi* **con** to border on

linde *nm o nf* boundary, limit

lindero, -a 1 *adj* bordering, adjoining
2 *nm* boundary, limit

lindo, -a 1 *adj esp Am (bonito)* pretty, lovely; **de lo l.** a great deal
2 *adv Am (bien)* very well, beautifully; **dibuja muy l.** he draws very well *o* beautifully

línea *nf* (a) line; **l. aérea** airline; **en líneas generales** roughly speaking; *Inform* **en l.** on-line (b) **guardar la l.** to watch one's figure

lineal 1 *adj* linear; **dibujo l.** line drawing
2 *nm (en supermercado)* shelf

lingote *nm* ingot; *(de oro, plata)* bar

lingüista *nmf* linguist

lingüística *nf* linguistics *sing*

lingüístico, -a *adj* linguistic

lino *nm* (a) *Bot* flax (b) *Tex* linen

linterna *nf Br* torch, *US* flashlight

linyera *nmf RP (vagabundo)* tramp, *US* bum

lío *nm* (a) *(paquete)* bundle (b) *Fam (embrollo)* mess, muddle; **hacerse un l.** to get mixed up; **meterse en líos** to get into trouble; **armar un l.** to kick up a fuss (c) *Fam (relación amorosa)* affair

lioso, -a *adj Fam (asunto)* confusing

lipotimia *nf* fainting fit

liquidación *nf* (a) *Com (saldo)* clearance sale (b) *Fin* liquidation

liquidar 1 *vt* (a) *(deuda, cuenta)* to settle; *(mercancías)* to sell off (b) *Fam (matar)* to liquidate
2 liquidarse *vpr Fam (gastar)* to spend

liquidez *nf Fin* liquidity

líquido, -a 1 *adj* (a) liquid (b) *Fin* net
2 *nm* (a) *(sustancia)* liquid; *Med* fluid (b) *Fin* liquid assets

lira *nf* (a) *Antes (moneda)* lira (b) *Mús* lyre

lírico, -a *adj* lyrical

lirio *nm* iris

lirismo *nm* lyricism

lirón *nm* dormouse; *Fig* **dormir como un l.** to sleep like a log

Lisboa *n* Lisbon

lisiado, -a 1 *adj* crippled
2 *nm,f* cripple

lisiar [43] *vt* to maim, to cripple

liso, -a 1 *adj* (a) *(superficie)* smooth, even; *Esp* **los cien metros lisos** the one hundred metres sprint (b) *(pelo, falda)* straight (c) *(tela)* self-coloured
2 *nm,f Andes, CAm,Ven* cheeky; **es un l.** he's so cheeky

lisonjero, -a 1 *adj* flattering
2 *nm,f* flatterer

lista *nf* (a) *(relación)* list; **l. de espera** waiting list; *(en avión)* standby; **pasar l.** to call the register *o* the roll; *Inform* **l. de correo** mailing list (b) *(franja)* stripe; **a listas** striped

listado, -a 1 *adj* striped
2 *nm* list; *Inform* listing

listar *vt* (a) *Inform* to list (b) *Am (hacer una lista de)* to list

listín *nm Esp* **l. telefónico** telephone directory

listo, -a *adj* (a) **ser l.** *(inteligente)* to be clever *o* smart (b) **estar l.** *(a punto)* to be ready

listón *nm Dep* bar; *Fig* **subir el l.** to raise the requirements level

lisura *nf* (a) *Andes, CAm, Ven (atrevimiento)* cheek (b) *Andes, CAm, Ven (dicho grosero)* rude remark (c) *Perú (donaire)* grace

litera *nf (cama)* bunk bed; *(en tren)* couchette

literal *adj* literal

literario, -a *adj* literary

literato, -a *nm,f* writer, author

> 🖉 Observa que la palabra inglesa **literate** es un falso amigo y no es la traducción de la palabra española **literato**. En inglés, **literate** significa "alfabetizado".

literatura *nf* literature

litigar [42] *vi Der* to litigate

litigio *nm Der* lawsuit; *Fig* dispute; **en l. in** dispute

litografía *nf* (a) *(técnica)* lithography (b) *(imagen)* lithograph

litoral 1 *nm* coast, seaboard
2 *adj* coastal

litro *nm* litre

Lituania *n* Lithuania

lituano, -a 1 *adj & nm,f* Lithuanian
2 *nm (idioma)* Lithuanian

liturgia *nf* liturgy

liviano, -a *adj* lightweight

lívido, -a *adj* livid

liza *nf* contest

llaga *nf* sore; *(herida)* wound

llama *nf* flame; **en llamas** in flames, ablaze

llamada *nf* call; *Tel* **l. interurbana** long-distance call; **señal de l.** ringing tone

llamado, -a 1 *adj* so-called
2 *nm Am* (a) *(en general)* call; *(a la puerta)* knock; *(con timbre)* ring (b) *(telefónico)* call; **hacer un l.** to make a phone call (c) *(apelación)* appeal, call; **hacer un l. a algn para que haga algo** to call upon sb to do sth; **hacer un l. a la huelga** to call a strike

llamamiento *nm* appeal

llamar 1 *vt* (a) to call; **l. (por teléfono)** to call, to phone (b) *(atraer)* to draw, to attract; **l. la atención** to attract attention
2 *vi (a la puerta)* to knock
3 llamarse *vpr* to be called; **¿cómo te llamas?** what's your name?

llamarada *nf* blaze

llamativo, -a *adj* (a) *(color, ropa)* loud, flashy (b) *(persona)* striking

llaneza *nf* simplicity

llano, -a 1 *adj* (a) *(superficie)* flat, level (b) *(claro)* clear (c) *(sencillo)* simple; **el pueblo l.** the common people
2 *nm* plain

llanta *nf* (a) *(aro metálico)* rim (b) *Am (neumático)* tyre

llanto *nm* crying, weeping

llanura *nf* plain

llave *nf* (a) *(de cerradura)* key; **bajo l.** under lock and key; **echar la l., cerrar con l.** to lock up; **l. en mano** *(vivienda)* ready for immediate occupation; **l. maestra** master key (b) *(grifo) Br* tap, *US* faucet; **l. de paso** stopcock; **cerrar la l. de paso** to turn the water/gas off at the *Br* mains o *US* main value (c) *(interruptor)* **l. de la luz** light switch (d) *(herramienta)* spanner; **l. allen** Allen key; **l. inglesa** monkey wrench, *Br* adjustable spanner (e) *(de judo)* hold, lock (f) *(signo ortográfico)*

curly bracket (**g**) *Inform* **l. USB** memory stick

llavero *nm* key-ring

llegada *nf* arrival; *Dep* finish

llegar [42] **1** *vi* (a) *(a un lugar)* to arrive; **l. a Madrid** to arrive in Madrid (b) *(ser bastante)* to be enough (c) *(alcanzar)* **l. a** to reach; **¿llegas al techo?** can you reach the ceiling?; *Fig* **l. a las manos** to come to blows; **l. a presidente** to become president (d) **l. a +** *infin* to go so far as to (e) **l. a ser** to become
2 llegarse *vpr* to stop by

llenar 1 *vt* (a) *(recipiente)* to fill; *(superficie)* to cover; **l. a algn de** to fill sb with (b) *(satisfacer)* to satisfy
2 *vi (comida)* to be filling
3 llenarse *vpr* to fill (up), to become full

lleno, -a 1 *adj* full (up); *Fig* **de l.** fully
2 *nm Teatro* full house

llevadero, -a *adj* bearable, tolerable

llevar 1 *vt* (a) *(de un lugar a otro)* to take; *(hacia el oyente)* to bring; **l. algo/a algn a** to take sth/sb to; **me llevó en coche** he drove me there (b) *(transportar)* to carry; **dejarse l.** to get carried away (c) *(prenda)* to wear; **lle-vaba una falda** she was wearing a skirt (d) *(soportar)* to bear; **¿cómo lleva lo de su enfermedad?** how's he bearing up? (e) *(tiempo)* **llevo dos años aquí** I've been here for two years; **esto lleva mucho tiempo** this takes a long time (f) *(ocuparse de) (problema, asunto)* to handle, to deal with; *(casa, negocio)* to look after, to run
2 *vi* (a) **l. +** *gerundio* to have been + *present participle*; **llevo dos años estudiando español** I've been studying Spanish for two years (b) **l. +** *participio* to have + *past participle*; **llevaba escritas seis cartas** I had written six letters
3 llevarse *vpr* (a) *(consigo)* to take; *(premio)* to win; *(recibir)* to get (b) *(arrastrar)* to carry away (c) *(estar de moda)* to be fashionable (d) **llevarse bien con algn** to get on well with sb

llorar *vi* to cry; *Lit* to weep

llorica *nmf Fam* crybaby

lloriquear *vi* to whimper, to snivel

llorón, -ona *adj* **un bebé l.** a baby which cries a lot

lloroso, -a *adj* tearful

llover [4] *v impers* to rain

llovizna *nf* drizzle

lloviznar *v impers* to drizzle

lluvia *nf* rain; **una l. de** lots of; **l. radiactiva** (nuclear) fallout; **l. ácida** acid rain

lluvioso, -a *adj* rainy

lo¹ *art neut* the; **lo mejor** the best (part); **lo mismo** the same thing; **lo mío** mine; **lo tuyo** yours

lo² *pron pers m & neut* (*mpl* **los**, *fpl* **las**) (**a**) *(cosa)* it; **debes hacerlo** you must do it; **no lo creo** I don't think so; *(no se traduce)* **no se lo dije** I didn't tell her; *ver* **le** (**b**) **lo que ...** what ...; **no sé lo que pasa** I don't know what's going on (**c**) **lo cual ...** which ... (**d**) **lo de ...** the business of ...; **cuéntame lo del juicio** tell me about the trial

loable *adj* praiseworthy, laudable

loar *vt* to praise

lobo *nm* wolf; **como boca de l.** pitch-dark; *Fam* **¡menos lobos!** pull the other one!

lóbrego, -a *adj* gloomy

lóbulo *nm* lobe

local 1 *adj* local
2 *nm (recinto)* premises, site

localidad *nf* (**a**) *(pueblo)* locality; *(en impreso)* place of residence (**b**) *Cin & Teatro (asiento)* seat; *(entrada)* ticket

localización *nf* localization

localizar [40] *vt* (**a**) *(encontrar)* to find (**b**) *(restringir)* to localize

loción *nf* lotion

loco, -a 1 *adj* mad, crazy; **a lo l.** crazily; **l. por** crazy about; **volverse l.** to go mad; *Fam* **¡ni l.!** I'd sooner die!
2 *nm,f* madman, madwoman; **hacerse el l.** to act the fool
3 *nm Chile (molusco)* false abalone

locomotor, -triz *adj* locomotive

locomotora *nf* locomotive

locuaz *adj* loquacious, talkative

locución *nf* phrase

locura *nf (enfermedad)* madness, insanity; **con l.** madly; *Fam* **esto es una l.** this is crazy

locutor, -a *nm,f TV & Rad (de noticias) Br* newsreader, *US* news announcer; *(de programa de radio) Br* presenter, *US* host, *f* hostess

locutorio *nm* telephone booth

lodo *nm* mud

logaritmo *nm* logarithm

lógica *nf* logic; **no tiene l.** there's no logic to it

lógico, -a *adj* logical; **era l. que ocurriera** it was bound to happen

logística *nf* logistics *sing o pl*

logotipo *nm* logo

logrado, -a *adj (bien hecho)* accomplished

lograr *vt* (**a**) *(objetivo)* to achieve; *(puesto, beca, divorcio)* to get, to obtain; *(resultado)* to obtain, to achieve; *(premio)* to win (**b**) **l. hacer algo** to manage to do sth

logro *nm* achievement

loma *nf* hillock, rise

lombriz *nf* worm, earthworm

lomo *nm* (**a**) *(de animal)* back; **a lomo(s)** on the back (**b**) *Culin* loin (**c**) *(de libro)* spine

lona *nf* canvas

loncha *nf* slice; **l. de bacon** rasher of bacon

lonche *nm* (**a**) *Perú, Ven (merienda) (en escuela)* = snack eaten during break time; *(en casa)* (afternoon) tea (**b**) *Am (comida fría)* (packed) lunch (**c**) *Méx (torta)* filled roll

lonchería *nf Méx, Ven* = small fast food restaurant selling snacks, sandwiches etc

londinense 1 *adj* of/from London
2 *nmf* Londoner

Londres *n* London

longaniza *nf* spicy (pork) sausage

longevo, -a *adj* long-lived

longitud *nf* (**a**) *(dimensión)* length; **2 m de l.** 2 m long; **l. de onda** wavelength (**b**) *Geog* longitude

lonja¹ *nf (loncha)* slice

lonja² *nf Esp* **l. de pescado** fish market

loquería *nf Am* mental asylum, mental hospital

lord (*pl* **lores**) *nm* lord

loro *nm* parrot

los¹ 1 *art def mpl* the; **l. libros** the books; **cierra l. ojos** close your eyes; **l. García** the Garcías; *ver* **el, las** y **los**
2 *pron* **l. que** *(personas)* the ones who, those who; *(cosas)* the ones (that); **toma l. que quieras** take whichever ones you want; **esos son l. míos/tuyos** these are mine/yours; *ver* **les**

los² *pron pers mpl* them; **¿l. has visto?** have you seen them?

losa *nf* (stone) slab, flagstone

lote *nm* (**a**) *(para vender, subastar)* share (**b**) *(conjunto)* batch, lot (**c**) *Inform* batch (**d**) *Esp Fam* **darse el l. (con)** to neck (with), *Br* to snog (**e**) *Am (solar)* plot (of land)

loteamiento *nm Bol, Urug* parcelling out, division into plots

loteo *nm Andes, Méx, RP* parcelling out, division into plots

lotería *nf* lottery; **me tocó la l.** I won a prize in the lottery

lotización *nf Ecuad, Perú* parcelling out, division into plots

loto 1 *nm Bot* lotus
2 *nf Esp Fam* = weekly state-run lottery, *Br* ≃ National Lottery

loza *nf* (**a**) *(material)* earthenware (**b**) *(de cocina)* crockery

lozano, -a *adj* (**a**) *(persona)* healthy-looking (**b**) *(plantas)* lush, luxuriant

Ltda. *(abr* **Limitada)** Ltd

lubina *nf* sea bass

lubricante *nm* lubricant

lubricar [44] *vt* to lubricate

lucero *nm* (bright) star

lucha *nf* (**a**) *(combate, enfrentamiento)* fight, struggle; *(esfuerzo)* struggle; **l. de clases** class struggle (**b**) *Dep* wrestling; **l. libre** freestyle wrestling

luchador, -a *nm,f* (**a**) *(persona tenaz)* fighter (**b**) *Dep* wrestler

luchar *vi* (**a**) *(combatir)* to fight; *(esforzarse)* to struggle; **l. contra** to fight (against); **l. por** to fight for (**b**) *Dep* to wrestle

lucidez *nf* lucidity

lúcido, -a *adj* lucid, clear

luciérnaga *nf* glow-worm

lucir [35] **1** *vi* (**a**) *(brillar)* to shine (**b**) *Am (parecer)* to look; **luces cansada** you seem o look tired (**c**) *Fam (compensar)* **no le luce lo que estudia** his studies don't get him anywhere
2 *vt (ropas)* to sport; *(talento)* to display
3 lucirse *vpr* (**a**) *(hacer buen papel)* to do very well (**b**) *(pavonearse)* to show off

lucrativo, -a *adj* lucrative, profitable

lucro *nm* profit, gain; **afán de l.** greed for money

lúcuma *nf Andes* lucuma, = sweet, pear-shaped fruit

lúdico, -a *adj* relating to games, recreational

luego 1 *adv* (**a**) *(después)* then, next, afterwards (**b**) *(más tarde)* later (on); **¡hasta l.!** so long!; **l. de** after (**c**) **desde l.** of course (**d**) *Chile, Ven (pronto)* soon; **acaba l., te estoy esperando** hurry up and finish, I'm waiting for you; *Méx Fam* **l., l. lueguito** immediately, straight away
2 *conj* therefore

lugar *nm* (**a**) *(sitio)* place; **en primer l.** in the first place; **en l. de** instead of; **sin l. a dudas** without a doubt; **tener l.** to take place (**b**) **dar l. a** to cause, to give rise to

lugareño, -a *nm,f* local

lugarteniente *nmf* lieutenant

lúgubre *adj* gloomy, lugubrious

lujo *nm* luxury; **productos de l.** luxury products; **no puedo permitirme ese l.** I can't afford that

lujoso, -a *adj* luxurious

lujuria *nf* lust

> *ℓ* Observa que la palabra inglesa **lux-ury** es un falso amigo y no es la traducción de la palabra española **lujuria**. En inglés, **luxury** significa "lujo".

lujurioso, -a *adj* lecherous, lustful

lumbago *nm* lumbago

lumbre *nf* fire

lumbrera *nf* luminary

luminoso, -a *adj* luminous; *Fig* bright

luna *nf* (**a**) *(astro)* moon; *Fig* **estar en la l.** to have one's head in the clouds; **l. creciente/llena** crescent/full moon; **l. de miel** honeymoon (**b**) *(de escaparate)* pane; *(espejo)* mirror

lunar 1 *adj* lunar
2 *nm (redondel)* dot; *(en la piel)* mole, beauty spot; **vestido de lunares** spotted dress

lunático, -a *nm,f* lunatic

lunes *nm inv* Monday; **vendré el l.** I'll come on Monday

lupa *nf* magnifying glass

luso, -a *adj & nm,f* Portuguese

lustrabotas *nm,f inv,* **lustrador, -a** *nm,f Andes, RP* shoeshine, *Br* bootblack

lustradora *nf Andes, RP* floor polisher

lustrar *vt* to polish; *(zapatos)* to shine

lustre *nm (brillo)* shine, lustre; *Fig (esplendor)* splendour, glory; **dar** *o* **sacar l. a algo** to polish sth

lustro *nm* five-year period

lustroso, -a *adj* shiny, glossy

luto *nm* mourning

Luxemburgo *n* Luxembourg

luz *nf* (**a**) light; **apagar la l.** to put out the light; **a la l. de** in the light of; **a todas luces** obviously; *Fig* **dar a l. (a un niño)** to give birth (to a child) (**b**) *Aut* light; **luces de cruce** *Br* dipped headlights, *US* low beams; **luces de posición** sidelights (**c**) **luces** *(inteligencia)* intelligence; **corto de luces** dim-witted (**d**) **traje de luces** bullfighter's costume

luzco *indic pres de* **lucir**

lycra® *nf* Lycra®

M

M, m ['eme] *nf (letra)* M, m

m (**a**) *(abr* metro(s)) m (**b**) *(abr* minuto(s)) min

macabro, -a *adj* macabre

macana *nf* (**a**) *Andes, Carib, Méx (garrote)* wooden *Br* truncheon *o US* billy club (**b**) *CSur, Perú, Ven Fam (fastidio)* pain, drag (**c**) *CAm, Cuba (azada)* hoe

macanear *vt CSur, Ven (hacer mal)* to botch, to do badly

macanudo, -a *adj Fam* great, terrific

macarra *nm Fam* lout, *Br* yob

macarrón *nm* (**a**) *(dulce)* macaroon (**b**) *Elec* sheath

macarrones *nmpl* macaroni

macedonia *nf* fruit salad

macerar *vt* to soak, to macerate

maceta *nf (tiesto)* plant-pot, flowerpot

machacar [44] **1** *vt* (**a**) *(aplastar)* to crush; *Dep* to smash (**b**) *Esp Fam (estudiar) Br* to swot up on, *US* to bone up on (**c**) *Fam (insistir en)* to harp on about, to go on about

  2 *vi* (**a**) *Fam (insistir mucho)* to harp on, to go on (**b**) *Fam (estudiar con ahínco) Br* to swot, *US* to grind (**c**) *(en baloncesto)* to dunk

machacón, -ona *Fam* **1** *adj (repetitivo)* repetitious; *(pesado)* boring, tiresome

  2 *nm,f (muy estudioso) Br* swot, *US* grind

machamartillo: a machamartillo *loc adv (con firmeza)* firmly; *(con obstinación)* obstinately

machete *nm* (**a**) *(arma)* machete (**b**) *Ven (amigo)* pal, *Br* mate, *US* buddy (**c**) *Arg Fam (chuleta)* crib note

machismo *nm* machismo, male chauvinism

machista *adj & nm* male chauvinist

macho 1 *adj* (**a**) *(animal, planta)* male (**b**) *Fam (viril)* manly, virile, macho

  2 *nm* (**a**) *(animal, planta)* male (**b**) *Téc (pieza)* male piece *o* part; *(de enchufe)* (male) plug (**c**) *Fam (hombre viril)* macho man, he-man (**d**) *Esp Fam (como apelativo)* ¡oye, m.! *Br* hey, mate!, *US* hey, buddy!

machote *nm CAm, Méx (borrador)* rough draft

macilento, -a *adj* wan

macizo, -a 1 *adj* (**a**) *(sólido)* solid; **de oro m.** of solid gold (**b**) *(robusto)* solid, robust; *Fam (atractivo)* well-built

  2 *nm (masa sólida)* mass

macramé *nm* macramé

macro *nf Inform* macro

macro- *pref* macro-

macroeconomía *nf* macroeconomics sing

macrofestival *nm* = large open-air music festival

macuto *nm (morral)* knapsack, haversack

madeja *nf (de lana etc)* hank, skein

madera *nf* (**a**) *(material)* wood; *(de construcción)* timber, *US* lumber; **de m.** wood, wooden (**b**) *Fig* **tiene m. de líder** he has all the makings of a leader (**c**) *Esp Fam (policía)* **la m.** the pigs

madero *nm* (**a**) *(de construcción)* timber, *US* lumber; *(leño)* log (**b**) *Fam (policía)* pig

madrastra *nf* stepmother

madre 1 *nf* (**a**) *(persona)* mother; **es m. de tres hijos** she is a mother of three (children); **m. adoptiva** adoptive mother; **m. aquilada** surrogate mother; **m. de familia** mother, housewife; **m. política** mother-in-law; **m. soltera** unmarried mother; *Fig* **la m. patria** one's motherland; *Méx muy Fam* **me vale m.** I couldn't give a damn *o Br* a toss (**b**) *(de río)* bed

  2 *interj* ¡m. de Dios!, ¡m. mía! good heavens!

madreperla *nf (nácar)* mother-of-pearl

madreselva *nf* honeysuckle

Madrid *n* Madrid

madriguera *nf* burrow, hole

madrileño, -a 1 *adj* of/from Madrid

  2 *nm,f* person from Madrid

madrina *nf* (**a**) *(de bautizo)* godmother (**b**) *(de boda)* ≃ bridesmaid (**c**) *Fig (protectora)* protectress

madrugada *nf* (**a**) *(amanecer)* dawn; **de m.** at dawn (**b**) *(noche)* early morning; **las tres de la m.** three in the morning

madrugador, -a 1 *adj* early-rising

  2 *nm,f* early riser

madrugar [42] *vi* to get up early

maduración *nf (de fruta)* ripening

madurar 1 *vt (plan)* to think out
2 *vi* (a) *(persona)* to mature (b) *(fruta)* to ripen

madurez *nf* (a) *(de la fruta)* ripeness (b) *(sensatez, juicio)* maturity (c) *(edad adulta)* adulthood

maduro, -a *adj* (a) *(persona)* mature; **de edad madura** middle-aged (b) *(fruta)* ripe

maestría *nf* (a) *(habilidad)* mastery, skill (b) *Am (título)* master's degree

maestro, -a 1 *nm,f* (a) *Educ* teacher; **m. de escuela** schoolteacher (b) *Méx (en universidad)* Br lecturer, US professor (c) *(especialista)* master; **m. de obras** foreman (d) *Mús* maestro
2 *adj* **obra maestra** masterpiece; **llave maestra** master key

mafia *nf* mafia

mafioso, -a 1 *adj* of/relating to the mafia
2 *nm,f* member of the mafia, mafioso

magdalena *nf* = small sponge cake

magia *nf* magic; **por arte de m.** as if by magic

mágico, -a *adj* (a) *(palabra, alfombra, varita)* magic (b) *(momento, situación)* magical

magisterio *nm* teaching

magistrado, -a *nm,f* judge

magistral *adj (excelente)* masterly; **una jugada m.** a master stroke

magistratura *nf (jueces)* magistrature; *(tribunal)* tribunal

magnánimo, -a *adj* magnanimous

magnate *nm* magnate, tycoon

magnesio *nm* magnesium

magnético, -a *adj* magnetic

magnetizar [40] *vt* (a) *(imantar)* to magnetize (b) *Fig (hipnotizar)* to hypnotize

magnetofónico, -a *adj* magnetic

magnetófono *nm* tape recorder

magnífico, -a *adj* magnificent, splendid

magnitud *nf* magnitude, dimension; **de primera m.** of the first order

magno, -a *adj Literario* great; **aula magna** main amphitheatre

magnolia *nf* magnolia

mago, -a *nm,f* wizard, magician; **los tres Reyes Magos** the Three Wise Men, the Three Kings

magrear *vt muy Fam* to fondle, to grope

magro, -a 1 *nm (de cerdo)* lean meat
2 *adj (sin grasa)* lean

magullar 1 *vt* to bruise, to damage
2 magullarse *vpr* to get bruised, to get damaged

mahometano, -a *adj & nm,f Rel* Mohammedan, Muslim

mahonesa *nf* mayonnaise

maillot [ma'jot] *(pl maillots) nm (malla)* leotard; *Dep* shirt

maíz *nm (planta) Br* maize, US (Indian) corn; *(utilizado en cocina) Br* sweetcorn, US corn

maizal *nm Br* maize field, US cornfield

majadería *nf* silly thing, absurdity

majadero, -a *nm,f* fool, idiot

majareta, *Esp* **majara** *adj Fam* loony, nutty

majestad *nf* majesty

majestuosidad *nf* majesty

majestuoso, -a *adj* majestic, stately

majo, -a *adj Esp (bonito)* pretty, nice; *Fam (simpático)* nice; **tiene un hijo muy m.** she's got a lovely little boy; *Fam* **ven aquí, m.** come here, dear

mal 1 *nm* (a) *(maldad)* evil; **el m.** evil (b) *(daño)* harm; **no le deseo ningún m.** I don't wish him any harm (c) *(enfermedad)* illness, disease; *Fam* **el m. de las vacas locas** mad cow disease
2 *adj* bad; **un m. año** a bad year; *ver* **malo**
3 *adv* badly, wrong; **lo hizo muy m.** he did it very badly; **menos m. que …** it's a good job (that) …; **no está (nada) m.** it is not bad (at all); **te oigo/veo (muy) m.** I can hardly hear/see you; **tomar a m.** *(enfadarse)* to take badly

malabar *adj* **juegos malabares** juggling

malabarista *nmf* juggler

malaria *nf* malaria

malcriado, -a *adj* ill-mannered, ill-bred

malcriar [29] *vt* to spoil

maldad *nf* (a) *(cualidad)* badness, evil (b) *(acción)* evil *o* wicked thing

maldecir [12] **1** *vt* to curse
2 *vi* (a) *(blasfemar)* to curse (b) *(criticar)* to speak ill (**de** of)

maldición 1 *nf* curse
2 *interj* damnation!

maldito, -a *adj* (a) *Fam (molesto)* damned, *Br* bloody (b) *(endemoniado)* damned, cursed; **¡maldita sea!** damn it!

maleable *adj también Fig* malleable

maleante *nmf* crook

malear *vt* to corrupt

malecón *nm* jetty

maleducado, -a 1 *adj* bad-mannered
2 *nm,f* bad-mannered person

maleficio *nm* curse, spell

maléfico, -a *adj* evil, harmful

malentendido *nm* misunderstanding

malestar nm (a) (molestia) discomfort (b) (inquietud) uneasiness; **tengo m.** I feel uneasy

maleta nf suitcase, case; **hacer la m.** to pack one's things o case

maletero nm Esp, Cuba, **maletera** nf Am (de automóvil) Br boot, US trunk

maletín nm briefcase

malévolo, -a adj malevolent

maleza nf (a) (arbustos) thicket, undergrowth (b) (malas hierbas) weeds

malformación nf malformation

malgastar vt to waste, to squander

malhablado, -a 1 adj foul-mouthed
2 nm,f foul-mouthed person

malhechor, -a nm,f wrongdoer, criminal

malhumor nm bad temper

malhumorado, -a adj (de mal carácter) bad-tempered; (enfadado) in a bad mood

malicia nf (a) (mala intención) malice, maliciousness (b) (astucia) cunning, slyness (c) (maldad) badness, evil

malicioso, -a 1 adj malicious, spiteful
2 nm,f malicious o spiteful person

maligno, -a adj malignant

malintencionado, -a adj ill-intentioned

malla nf (a) Esp **mallas** (de gimnasia) leotard; (de ballet) tights (b) (red) mesh (c) Ecuad, Perú, RP (traje de baño) swimsuit

Mallorca n Majorca

mallorquín, -ina adj & nm,f Majorcan

malo, -a 1 adj (a) bad; **un año m.** a bad year; **estar a malas** to be on bad terms; **por las malas** by force (b) (persona) (malvado) wicked, bad; (travieso) naughty (c) (de poca calidad) bad, poor; **una mala canción/comida** a poor song/meal (d) (perjudicial) harmful; **el tabaco es m.** tobacco is harmful (e) **lo m. es que ...** the problem is that ... (f) (enfermo) ill, sick

> **Mal** is used instead of **malo** before masculine singular nouns (e.g. **un mal ejemplo** a bad example). The comparative form of **malo** (= worse) is **peor**, the superlative forms (= the worst) are **el peor** (masculine) and **la peor** (feminine).

2 nm,f Fam **el m.** the baddy o villain

malograr 1 vt Andes (estropear) to make a mess of, to ruin
2 malograrse vpr (a) (fracasar) to fail, fall through (b) Andes (estropearse) (máquina) to break down; (alimento) to go off, to spoil; **se malogró el día** the day turned nasty

maloliente adj foul-smelling

malparado, -a adj **salir m.** to end up in a sorry state

malpensado, -a 1 adj nasty-minded
2 nm,f nasty-minded person

malsonante adj (grosero) rude, offensive; **palabras malsonantes** foul language

malta nf (cebada) malt

maltratado, -a adj battered

maltratar vt to ill-treat, to mistreat

maltrato nm ill-treatment; **m. psicológico** psychological abuse

maltrecho, -a adj in a sorry state, wrecked

malva 1 adj inv mauve
2 nm (color) mauve
3 nf Bot mallow

malvado, -a 1 adj evil, wicked
2 nm,f villain, evil person

malvender vt to sell at a loss

malversar vt to misappropriate, to embezzle

Malvinas npl **las (Islas) M.** the Falkland Islands

malviviente nmf CSur criminal

malvivir vi to live very badly

mama nf (a) (de mujer) breast; (de animal) teat (b) Fam (mamá) Br mummy, US mommy

mamá nf Fam Br mum, US mom; Col, Méx Fam **m. grande** grandma

mamada nf (a) (bebé) (breast) feed (b) Vulg (felatio) blowjob

mamadera nf RP (baby's) bottle

mamar vt (leche) to suck; **lo mamó desde pequeño** (lo aprendió) he was immersed in it as a child

mamarracho, -a nm,f Fam (persona) ridiculous-looking person, mess, sight; (cosa) mess

mameluco nm (a) Fam (torpe, necio) idiot (b) Méx (con mangas) Br overalls, US coveralls; CSur (de peto) Br dungarees, US overalls

mamey nm (a) (árbol) mamey, mammee (b) (fruto) mamey, mammee (apple)

mamífero, -a nm,f mammal

mamón nm muy Fam (insulto) Br prat, US jerk

mampara nf screen

mamporro nm Fam wallop

mampostería nf masonry

mamut (pl **mamuts**) nm mammoth

manada nf (a) Zool (de vacas, elefantes) herd; (de ovejas) flock; (de lobos, perros) pack; (de leones) pride (b) Fam (multitud) crowd, mob; **en manada(s)** in crowds

manager ['manajer] (*pl* **managers**) *nmf Dep & Mús* manager

manantial *nm* spring

manar 1 *vi* to flow, to run (**de** from)
  2 *vt* **la herida manaba sangre** blood flowed from his wound

manazas *nmf inv Fam* ham-fisted person

mancebo *nm Literario* young man

Mancha *n* **el Canal de la M.** the English Channel

mancha *nf* stain, spot; **m. solar** sunspot; **m. de tinta/vino** ink/wine stain

manchado, -a *adj* dirty, stained; **leche manchada** milky coffee

manchar 1 *vt* to stain, to dirty; *Fig* to stain, to blemish
  2 mancharse *vpr* to get dirty

manchego, -a 1 *adj* of/from La Mancha
  2 *nm,f* person from La Mancha

manco, -a 1 *adj* (**a**) *(de un brazo)* one-armed; *(sin brazos)* armless (**b**) *(de una mano)* one-handed; *(sin manos)* handless
  2 *nm,f* (**a**) *(de brazos)* one-armed/armless person (**b**) *(de manos)* one-handed/handless person

mancomunidad *nf* community, association

mancuerna *nf* (**a**) *(pesa)* dumbbell (**b**) *CAm, Chile, Col, Méx, Ven (gemelo)* cufflink

mandado, -a *nm* order, errand

mandamás (*pl* **mandamases**) *nmf Fam Br* big boss, *US* head honcho

mandamiento *nm* (**a**) *(orden)* order, command (**b**) **los Diez Mandamientos** the Ten Commandments

mandar *vt* (**a**) *(ordenar)* to order; *Fam* **¿mande?** pardon? (**b**) *(grupo)* to lead, to be in charge o command of; *Mil* to command (**c**) *(enviar)* to send; **m. (a) por** to send for; **m. algo por correo** to post sth, to send sth by post; **m. recuerdos** to send regards

mandarina *nf* mandarin (orange), tangerine

mandatario, -a *nm,f Pol* president

mandato *nm* (**a**) *(orden)* order, command (**b**) *Der* writ, warrant (**c**) *Pol (legislatura)* mandate, term of office

mandíbula *nf* jaw; *Fam* **reír a m. batiente** to laugh one's head off

mandil *nm* apron

Mandinga *nm Am* the devil

mando *nm* (**a**) *(autoridad)* command, control (**b**) **los altos mandos del ejército** high-ranking army officers (**c**) *Téc (control)* controls; *Aut* **cuadro** o **tablero de mandos** dashboard; **m. a distancia** remote control; **palanca de m.** *Téc*

control lever; *(de avión, videojuego)* joystick

mandón, -ona 1 *adj Fam* bossy, domineering
  2 *nm,f Fam* bossy o domineering person
  3 *nm Chile (de mina)* foreman

manecilla *nf (de reloj)* hand

manejable *adj* manageable; *(herramienta)* easy-to-use; *(coche)* manoeuvrable

manejar 1 *vt* (**a**) *(máquina)* to handle, to operate; *Fig (situación)* to handle (**b**) *(negocio)* to run, to manage (**c**) *(a otra persona)* to domineer, to boss about (**d**) *Am (conducir)* to drive
  2 *vi Am (conducir)* to drive
  3 manejarse *vpr* to manage

manejo *nm* (**a**) *(uso)* handling, use; **de fácil m.** easy-to-use (**b**) *(de un negocio)* management; *(de un coche)* driving

manera *nf* (**a**) *(forma)* way, manner; **a mi/tu m.** (in) my/your way; **de cualquier m.** *(mal)* carelessly, any old how; *(en cualquier caso)* in any case; **de esta m.** (in) this way; **de ninguna m.** in no way, certainly not; **de todas maneras** anyway, at any rate, in any case; **es mi m. de ser** that's the way I am; **en modo m.** it's impossible (**b**) **de m. que** so; **de tal m. que** in such a way that (**c**) **maneras** *(modales)* manners; **de buenas maneras** politely

manga *nf* (**a**) *(de ropa)* sleeve; **de m. corta/larga** short-/long-sleeved; **sin mangas** sleeveless; *Fig* **hacer un corte de mangas a algn** ≃ to give sb the finger; *Fig* **m. por hombro** messy and untidy; *Fig* **sacarse algo de la m.** to pull sth out of one's hat (**b**) *(de riego)* hose (**c**) *(del mar)* arm (**d**) *Dep* leg, round; *Ten* set

mangante *nmf Fam* thief

mangar [42] *vt Fam* to pinch, *Br* to nick

mango *nm* (**a**) *(asa)* handle (**b**) *(fruta)* mango (**c**) *RP Fam (dinero)* **no tengo un m.** I haven't got a bean, I'm broke

mangonear *vi Fam* (**a**) *(entrometerse)* to meddle (**b**) *(dar órdenes)* to throw one's weight around

manguera *nf* hose

manguito *nm* (**a**) *(para las mangas)* oversleeve; *(para flotar)* armband (**b**) *Téc* sleeve

maní (*pl* **maníes**) *nm Andes, Carib, RP* peanut

manía *nf* (**a**) *(costumbre)* habit; **tiene la m. de morderse las uñas** he's always biting his fingernails (**b**) *(afición exagerada)* craze; **la m. de las motos** the motorbike craze (**c**) *Fam (ojeriza)* dislike; **me tiene m.** he has it in for me (**d**) *Med* mania

maniaco, -a, maníaco, -a 1 adj manic
2 nm, f maniac

maniatar vt to tie the hands of

maniático, -a 1 adj fussy
2 nm,f fusspot

manicomio nm Br mental o psychiatric hospital, US insane asylum

manicura nf manicure

manido, -a adj trite, hackneyed

manifestación nf (a) (política) demonstration (b) (expresión) manifestation, expression

manifestante nmf demonstrator

manifestar [1] **1** vt (a) (declarar) to state, to declare (b) (mostrar) to show, to display
2 manifestarse vpr (a) (por la calle) to demonstrate (b) (declararse) to declare oneself; se manifestó contrario a … he spoke out against …

manifiesto, -a 1 adj clear, obvious; poner de m. (revelar) to reveal, to show; (hacer patente) to make clear
2 nm manifesto

manigua nf, **manigual** nm Carib, Col (selva) marshy tropical forest

manilla nf (a) (de reloj) hand (b) esp Am (manivela) crank

manillar nm handlebar

maniobra nf manoeuvre

maniobrar vi to manoeuvre

manipulación nf manipulation

manipular vt to manipulate; (máquina) to handle

maniquí (pl maniquíes) nm (muñeco) dummy

manitas nmf inv Esp Fam (a) ser un m. to be handy, to be very good with one's hands (b) hacer m. to hold hands

manito nm Méx Fam pal, Br mate, US buddy

manivela nf Téc crank

manjar nm delicacy (food)

mano 1 nf (a) (de persona) hand; a m. (sin máquina) by hand; (asequible) at hand; escrito a m. hand-written; hecho a m. hand-made; a m. armada armed; estrechar la m. a algn to shake hands with sb; de segunda m. second-hand; echar una m. a algn to give sb a hand; ¡manos a la obra! shoulders to the wheel!; meter m. (a problema) to tackle; Vulg (a persona) to touch up; traerse algo entre manos to be up to sth; equipaje de m. hand luggage (b) (lado) side; a m. derecha/izquierda on the right/left(-hand side) (c) m. de pintura coat of paint (d) m. de obra labour (force) (e) RP (dirección) direction (of traffic); calle de una/doble m. one-/two-way street
2 nm Am salvo RP Fam pal, Br mate, US buddy
3 manos libres nm inv (teléfono) hands-free set

manojo nm bunch; ser un m. de nervios to be a bundle of nerves

manopla nf mitten

manoseado, -a adj (objeto) worn(-out); (tema) hackneyed

manosear vt to touch repeatedly, to finger; Fam to paw

manotazo nm cuff, slap

mansalva: a mansalva loc adv (en gran cantidad) galore

mansedumbre nf (a) (de persona) meekness, gentleness (b) (de animal) tameness, docility

mansión nf mansion

manso, -a adj (a) (persona) gentle, meek (b) (animal) tame, docile (c) Chile Fam (extraordinario) tremendous; tiene la mansa casa he has a gigantic o massive house

manta 1 nf (a) (de cama) blanket; m. eléctrica electric blanket (b) (zurra) beating, hiding (c) Méx (algodón) = coarse cotton cloth (d) Ven (vestido) = traditional Indian woman's dress
2 nmf Esp Fam layabout

manteca nf (a) Esp (de animal) fat; m. de cacao/cacahuete cocoa/peanut butter; m. de cerdo lard (b) RP, Ven (mantequilla) butter

mantecado nm Esp = very crumbly shortbread biscuit

mantel nm tablecloth

> *Observa que la palabra inglesa* **mantle** *es un falso amigo y no es la traducción de la palabra española* **mantel**. *En inglés,* **mantle** *significa "manto, capa".*

mantelería nf set of table linen

mantener [24] **1** vt (a) (conservar) to keep; mantén el fuego encendido keep the fire burning; m. la línea to keep in trim (b) (entrevista, reunión) to have; m. correspondencia con algn to correspond with sb (c) (ideas, opiniones) to defend, to maintain (d) (familia) to support, to feed (e) (peso) to support, to hold up
2 mantenerse vpr (a) (sostenerse) to stand (b) mantenerse firme (perseverar) to hold one's ground (c) (sustentarse) to live (de on)

mantenimiento nm (a) Téc maintenance, upkeep; servicio de m. maintenance service (b) (alimento) sustenance, support (c) **gimnasia de m.** keep fit

mantequilla *nf* butter

mantilla *nf (de mujer)* mantilla; *(de bebé)* shawl

manto *nm* cloak

mantón *nm* shawl

mantuve *pt indef de* **mantener**

manual 1 *adj* manual; **trabajo m.** manual labour; *Educ* **trabajos manuales** handicrafts

2 *nm* manual, handbook

manubrio *nm Am* handlebars

manufactura *nf* (a) *(fabricación)* manufacture (b) *(fábrica)* factory

manufacturar *vt* to manufacture

manuscrito *nm* manuscript

manutención *nf* maintenance

manzana *nf* (a) *(fruta)* apple (b) *(de edificios)* block

manzanilla *nf* (a) *Bot* camomile (b) *(infusión)* camomile tea (c) *(vino)* manzanilla

manzano *nm* apple tree

maña *nf* (a) *(astucia)* cunning (b) *(habilidad)* skill

mañana 1 *nf* morning; **a las dos de la m.** at two in the morning; **de m.** early in the morning; *Esp* **por la m.,** *Am* **en la m.** in the morning

2 *nm* **el m.** tomorrow, the future

3 *adv* tomorrow; **¡hasta m.!** see you to-morrow!; **m. por la m.** tomorrow morning; **pasado m.** the day after tomorrow

mañanitas *nfpl Méx* birthday song

mañoco *nm Ven* tapioca

mañoso, -a *adj Esp* skilful

mapa *nm* map; **m. mudo** blank map; *Fam* **borrar del m.** to wipe out

maqueta *nf* (a) *(miniatura)* scale model, maquette (b) *Mús* demo (tape)

maquiavélico, -a *adj* Machiavellian

maquila *nf CAm, Méx (de artículos electrónicos)* assembly; *(de ropa)* making-up

maquiladora *nf CAm, Méx* = bonded assembly plant set up by a foreign firm near the US border, *US* maquiladora

maquillaje *nm* make-up

maquillar 1 *vt* to make up

2 maquillarse *vpr* (a) *(ponerse maquillaje)* to put one's make-up on, to make (oneself) up (b) *(usar maquillaje)* to wear make-up

máquina *nf* (a) machine; **escrito a m.** typewritten; **hecho a m.** machine-made; *Fam* **a toda m.** at full speed; **m. de afeitar**

(eléctrica) (electric) razor *o* shaver; **m. de coser** sewing machine; **m. de escribir** typewriter; **m. fotográfica** *o* **de fotos** camera; **m.** *Esp* **tragaperras** *o* *Am* **tragamonedas** slot machine, *Br* fruit machine (b) *Cuba (automóvil)* car

maquinar *vt* to plot, to scheme

maquinaria *nf* (a) *(aparatos)* machinery (b) *(mecanismo)* *(de reloj, aparato)* mechanism (c) *(de Estado, partido)* machinery

maquinilla *nf* **m. de afeitar** safety razor

maquinista *nmf Br* engine driver, *US* engineer

mar 1 *nm o nf* (a) sea; **en alta m.** on the high seas; **m. adentro** out to sea; **por m.** by sea; **m. gruesa** heavy sea; **m. picada** rough sea; *Fam* **está la m. de guapa** she's looking really beautiful; **llover a mares** to rain cats and dogs

> Note that the feminine is used in literary language, by people such as fishermen with a close connection with the sea, and in some idiomatic expressions.

2 *nm* sea; **M. del Norte** North Sea; **M. Muerto/Negro** Dead/Black Sea

maraca *nf* maraca

maracuyá *nf* passion fruit

maraña *nf* tangle

maratón *nm* marathon

maratoniano, -a *adj* marathon

maravilla *nf* marvel, wonder; **de m.** wonderfully; **¡qué m. de película!** what a wonderful film!; *Fam* **a las mil maravillas** marvellously

maravillar 1 *vt* to amaze, to astonish

2 maravillarse *vpr* to marvel (**con** at), to wonder (**con** at)

maravilloso, -a *adj* wonderful, marvellous

marca *nf* (a) *(señal)* mark; *(de rueda, animal)* track (b) *Com (de tabaco, café)* brand; *(de vehículo, máquina)* make; **ropa de m.** designer clothes; **m. de fábrica** trademark; **m. registrada** registered trademark (c) *Dep (récord)* record; *(tiempo)* time

marcador *nm* (a) *Dep (tablero)* scoreboard; *(goleador)* scorer (b) *(para libros)* bookmark (c) *Am (rotulador)* felt-tip pen; *Méx (fluorescente)* highlighter pen

marcaje *nm Dep* marking

marcapasos *nm inv Med* pacemaker

marcar [44] **1** *vt* (a) *(poner o dejar marca en)* to mark (b) *Tel* to dial (c) *(indicar)* to indicate, to show; *(en termómetro, contador)* to read (d) *Dep (gol, puntos)* to score; *(jugador)* to mark (**e**) *(cabello)* to set

2 marcarse *upr Esp Fam* **marcarse un detalle** to do something nice o kind

marcha *nf* (**a**) *Mil, Pol & Mús* march; **hacer algo sobre la m.** to do sth as one goes along; *Esp* **a marchas forzadas** against the clock (**b**) **estar en m.** *(vehículo)* to be in motion; *(máquina)* to be working; *(proyecto)* to be under way; **poner en m.** to start (**c**) *Aut* gear; **m. atrás** reverse (gear) (**d**) *Esp Fam (animación)* liveliness, life; **hay mucha m.** there's a great atmosphere (**e**) *(partida)* departure

marchante, -a *nm,f* (**a**) *(de arte)* dealer (**b**) *CAm, Méx, Ven Fam (cliente)* customer, patron

marchar 1 *vi* (**a**) *(ir)* to go, to walk; *Fam* **¡marchando!** on your way!; **¡una cerveza! – ¡marchando!** a beer, please! – coming right up! (**b**) *(aparato)* to be on; **m. bien** *(negocio)* to be going well (**c**) *Mil* to march

2 marcharse *upr (irse)* to leave, to go away

marchitarse *upr* to shrivel, to wither

marchito, -a *adj* shrivelled, withered

marchoso, -a *Esp Fam* **1** *adj (persona)* fun-loving, wild

2 *nm,f* raver, fun-lover

marcial *adj* martial; **artes marciales** martial arts

marciano, -a *adj & nm,f* Martian

marco *nm* (**a**) *(de cuadro, foto)* frame (**b**) *(ámbito)* framework; **acuerdo m.** framework agreement (**c**) *(moneda)* mark

marea *nf* (**a**) *(del mar)* tide; **m. alta/baja** high/low tide; **m. negra** oil slick (**b**) *(multitud)* crowd, mob

mareado, -a *adj* (**a**) *(con náuseas)* sick; *(en coche)* car-sick, travel-sick; *(en el mar)* seasick; *(en avión)* airsick (**b**) *(aturdido)* dizzy (**c**) *Euf (bebido)* tipsy

marear 1 *vt* (**a**) *(con náuseas)* to make sick; *(en coche)* to make car-sick o travel-sick; *(en el mar)* to make seasick; *(en avión)* to make airsick (**b**) *(aturdir)* to make dizzy (**c**) *Fam (fastidiar)* to annoy, to pester

2 marearse *upr* (**a**) *(con náuseas)* to get sick/car-sick o travel-sick/seasick/airsick (**b**) *(quedar aturdido)* to get dizzy (**c**) *Euf (emborracharse)* to get tipsy

marejada *nf* heavy sea

maremoto *nm* tidal wave

mareo *nm* (**a**) *(náusea)* sickness; *(en el mar)* seasickness; *(en un avión)* airsickness; *(en un coche)* car-sickness, travel-sickness (**b**) *(aturdimiento)* dizziness, light-headedness

marfil *nm* ivory

margarina *nf* margarine

margarita *nf* daisy

margen 1 *nm* (**a**) *(de página)* margin (**b**) *(de camino)* side (**c**) *(límite)* margin; *Com* **m. de beneficio** profit margin (**d**) **dejar algn/algo al m.** to leave sb/sth out; **mantenerse al m.** not to get involved; **al m. de** leaving aside

2 *nf (de río)* bank

marginación *nf* exclusion

marginado, -a 1 *adj* excluded

2 *nm,f* socially excluded person

marginal (**a**) *(de fuera de la sociedad)* socially excluded (**b**) *Econ* marginal

marginar *vt* to exclude

maría *nf Fam* (**a**) *Esp, Ven (droga)* marijuana, pot (**b**) *Esp (asignatura fácil)* easy subject (**c**) *(mujer sencilla)* (typical) housewife

mariachi *nm* (**a**) *(música)* mariachi (music) (**b**) *(orquesta)* mariachi band; *(músico)* mariachi (musician)

marica *nm Fam Br* poof, *US* fag

maricón *nm muy Fam Br* poof, *US* fag

marido *nm* husband

marihuana *nf* marijuana

marimacho *nm Fam* mannish woman, butch woman

marimandón, -ona *Esp nm,f Fam* domineering person

marimorena *nf Fam* row, fuss; *Fam* **armar(se) la m.** to kick up a racket

marina *nf* (**a**) *Náut* seamanship (**b**) *Mil* navy; **m. de guerra** navy; **m. mercante** merchant navy

marinero, -a 1 *nm* sailor, seaman

2 *adj* seafaring

marino, -a 1 *adj* marine; **brisa marina** sea breeze

2 *nm* sailor

marioneta *nf* marionette, puppet

mariposa *nf* (**a**) *(insecto)* butterfly (**b**) *(lamparilla)* oil lamp (**c**) *(en natación)* butterfly

mariposear *vi* (**a**) *(flirtear)* to flirt (**b**) *(ser inconstante)* to be fickle

mariposón *nm Fam* fairy, pansy

mariquita 1 *nf (insecto) Br* ladybird, *US* ladybug

2 *nm Fam (marica)* fairy

mariscada *nf* seafood meal

mariscal *nm Mil* marshal; **m. de campo** *Br* field marshal, *US* general of the army

marisco(s) *nm(pl)* shellfish, seafood

marisma *nf* marsh

marisquería *nf* seafood restaurant, shellfish bar

marítimo, -a *adj* maritime, sea; **ciudad marítima** coastal town; **paseo m.** promenade

marketing ['marketin] (*pl* **marketings**) *nm* marketing

mármol *nm* marble

marmóreo, -a *adj* marble

maroma *nf* (a) *Náut* cable (b) *(cuerda)* thick rope

marqués (*pl* **marqueses**) *nm* marquis

marquesa *nf* marchioness

marquesina *nf* canopy; **m. (del autobús)** bus shelter

marquetería *nf* marquetry, inlaid work

marrano, -a 1 *adj* (sucio) filthy, dirty
2 *nm,f* (a) *Fam* (persona) dirty pig, slob (b) *(animal)* pig

marras: de marras *loc adv* **el individuo de m.** the man in question

marrón *adj & nm* brown

marroquí (*pl* **marroquíes**) *adj & nmf* Moroccan

marroquinería *nf* leather goods

Marruecos *n* Morocco

marrullero, -a 1 *adj* cajoling, wheedling
2 *nm,f* cajoler, wheedler

Marte *n* Mars

martes *nm inv* Tuesday; **m. y trece** ≃ Friday the thirteenth

martillero *nm CSur* auctioneer

martillo *nm* hammer

mártir *nmf* martyr

martirio *nm* (a) *Rel* martyrdom (b) *Fig (sufrimiento)* torment

martirizar [40] *vt* (a) *(torturar)* to martyr (b) *Fig (hacer sufrir)* to torture, to torment

marxista *adj & nmf* Marxist

marzo *nm* March

mas *conj Literario* but

más 1 *adv* (a) *(adicional)* more; **no tengo m.** I haven't got any more
(b) *(comparativo)* more; **es m. alta/inteligente que yo** she's taller/more intelligent than me; **tengo m. dinero que tú** I've more money than you; **m. gente de la que esperas** more people than you're expecting; **m. de** *(con numerales, cantidad)* more than, over
(c) *(superlativo)* most; **es el m. bonito/caro** it's the prettiest/most expensive
(d) *(como interjección)* so …, what a …; **¡qué casa m. bonita!** what a lovely house!; **¡está m. guapa!** she looks so beautiful!
(e) *(después de pron interr e indef)* else; **¿algo m.?** anything else?; **no, nada m.** no, nothing else; **¿quién m.?** who else?; **nadie/alguien m.** nobody/somebody else
(f) **cada día** *o* **vez m.** more and more;

estar de m. to be unnecessary; **traje uno de m.** I brought a spare one; **es m.** what's more, furthermore; **lo m. posible** as much as possible; **m. bien** rather; **m. o menos** more or less; **m. aún** even more; **¿qué m. da?** what's the difference?; **todo lo m.** at the most
(g) **por m.** (+ *adj/adv*) **+ que** (+ *subjunctive*) however (much), no matter how (much); **por m. fuerte que sea** however strong he may be; **por m. que grites no te oirá nadie** no matter how much you shout nobody will hear you
2 *nm inv* **los m.** the majority, most people; **sus m. y sus menos** its pros and cons
3 *prep Mat* plus; **dos m. dos** two plus *o* and two

masa *nf* (a) *(de materia)* mass; **m. salarial** total wage bill (b) *(multitud)* throng; **en m.** en masse; **las masas** the masses (c) *Culin* dough (d) *Elec (tierra)* Br earth, US ground (e) *RP (pastelito)* cake

masacrar *vt* to massacre

masacre *nf* massacre

masaje *nm* massage; **dar un masaje a algn** to give sb a massage

masajista *nmf (hombre)* masseur; *(mujer)* masseuse

mascar [44] *vt & vi* to chew, to masticate

máscara *nf* mask; **m. de gas** gas mask

> 🖉 Observa que la palabra inglesa **mascara** es un falso amigo y no es la traducción de la palabra española **máscara**. En inglés **mascara** significa "rímel".

mascarilla *nf* (a) *(de protección)* mask; **m. de oxígeno** oxygen mask (b) *Med* face mask (c) *(cosmética)* face pack

mascota *nf* mascot

masculino, -a *adj* (a) *Zool & Bot* male (b) *(de hombre)* male, manly; **una voz masculina** a manly voice (c) *(para hombre)* men's; **ropa masculina** men's clothes, menswear (d) *Ling* masculine

mascullar *vt* to mumble

masía *nf* ≃ traditional Catalan or Aragonese farmhouse

masificación *nf* overcrowding

masificado, -a *adj* overcrowded

masilla *nf* putty

masivo, -a *adj* massive

masón *nm* freemason, mason

masonería *nf* freemasonry, masonry

masoquista 1 *adj* masochistic
2 *nmf* masochist

master (*pl* **masters**) *nm* Master's (degree)

masticar [44] *vt* to chew

mástil *nm* (**a**) *(asta)* mast, pole (**b**) *Náut* mast (**c**) *(de guitarra)* neck

mastín *nm* mastiff

masturbación *nf* masturbation

masturbar 1 *vt* to masturbate
2 masturbarse *vpr* to masturbate

mata *nf* (**a**) *(matorral)* bush, shrub; **m. de pelo** head of hair (**b**) *(ramita)* sprig

matadero *nm* slaughterhouse, abattoir

matador *nm* matador, bullfighter

matambre *nm Andes, RP* (**a**) *(carne)* flank *o Br* skirt steak (**b**) *(plato)* = flank steak rolled with boiled egg, olives and red pepper, which is cooked, then sliced and served cold

matanza *nf* slaughter

matar 1 *vt* to kill; *Fam* **m. el tiempo** to kill time; **comer algo para m. el hambre** to eat sth to keep one going
2 matarse *vpr (morir)* to die; *(suicidarse)* to kill oneself; **se mató en un accidente de coche** he was killed in a car accident

matarratas *nm inv* rat poison

matasellos *nm inv* postmark

matasuegras *nm inv* party blower

mate¹ *adj (sin brillo)* matt

mate² *nm (en ajedrez)* mate; **jaque m.** checkmate

mate³ *nm CSur (infusión)* maté

matemáticas *nfpl* mathematics *sing*

matemático, -a 1 *adj* mathematical
2 *nm,f* mathematician

materia *nf* (**a**) *(sustancia, asunto)* matter; **m. gris** grey matter (**b**) *(material)* material; **m. prima** raw material (**c**) *Educ (asignatura)* subject

material 1 *adj* material, physical; **daños materiales** damage to property
2 *nm* (**a**) *(sustancia)* material (**b**) *(equipo)* equipment; **m. escolar/de construcción** school/building materials; **m. de oficina** office stationery

materialista *adj & nmf* materialist

materialmente *adv* physically

maternal *adj* maternal, motherly

maternidad *nf (estado)* motherhood; **permiso de/sala de m.** maternity leave/ward

materno, -a *adj* maternal; **abuelo m.** maternal grandfather; **lengua materna** native *o* mother tongue

matinal *adj* morning; **televisión m.** breakfast television

matiz *nm* (**a**) *(de color)* shade (**b**) *(de palabra)* shade of meaning, nuance; **un m. irónico** a touch of irony

matización *nf* clarification, explanation to add a rider

matizar [40] *vt* (**a**) *(puntualizar)* to clarify, to explain (**b**) *(teñir)* to tinge (**de** with) (**c**) *Arte* to blend

matón *nm Fam* thug, bully

matorral *nm* brushwood, thicket

matraca *nf (ruido)* rattle; *Fam* **dar la m. a algn** to pester *o* bother sb

matrero, -a *nm,f Andes, RP (fugitivo)* outlaw

matriarcado *nm* matriarchy

matriarcal *adj* matriarchal

matrícula *nf* (**a**) *(acción)* registration; **derechos de m.** registration fee; **m. de honor** distinction; **plazo de m.** registration period (**b**) *Aut Br* number plate, *US* license plate

matriculación *nf* registration

matricular 1 *vt* to register
2 matricularse *vpr* to register

matrimonial *adj* matrimonial; **agencia m.** marriage bureau; **enlace m.** wedding; **vida m.** married life

matrimonio *nm* (**a**) *(institución)* marriage; **contraer m.** to marry; **m. civil/religioso** registry office/church wedding; **cama de m.** double bed (**b**) *(pareja casada)* married couple; **el m. y los niños** the couple and their children; **el m. Romero** Mr and Mrs Romero, the Romeros

matriz *nf* (**a**) *Anat* womb, uterus (**b**) *Mat* matrix (**c**) *(de documento) (original)* original, master copy (**d**) *Téc* mould
2 *adj (empresa)* parent; **casa m.** head office

matrona *nf* midwife

matutino, -a *adj* morning; **prensa matutina** morning papers

maullar *vi* to miaow

maullido *nm* miaowing, miaow

maxilar *nm* jaw, jawbone

máxima *nf* (**a**) *Met* maximum temperature (**b**) *(aforismo)* maxim

máxime *adv* especially, all the more so

máximo, -a 1 *adj* maximum, highest; **la máxima puntuación** the highest score
2 *nm* maximum; **al m.** to the utmost; **como m.** *(como mucho)* at the most; *(lo más tarde)* at the latest

maya 1 *adj* Mayan
2 *nmf* Maya, Mayan
3 *nm (idioma)* Maya

mayo *nm* May

mayonesa *nf* mayonnaise

mayor 1 *adj* (**a**) *(comparativo) (tamaño)* larger, bigger (**que** than); *(edad)* older, elder; **m. que yo** older than me (**b**) *(superlativo) (tamaño)* largest, biggest; *(edad)* oldest, eldest; **la m. parte** the majority; **la m. parte de las veces** most often (**c**) *(adulto)* grown-up; **ser m. de edad** to be of age (**d**) *(maduro)* elderly, mature (**e**) *(principal)* major, main; *Educ* **colegio m.** *Br* hall of residence, *US* residence hall, *US* dormitory (**f**) *Mús* major (**g**) *Com* **al por m.** wholesale; *Fig (en abundancia)* by the score, galore

2 *nm* (**a**) *Mil* major (**b**) **mayores** *(adultos)* grown-ups, adults

mayordomo *nm* butler

mayoreo *nm Am* wholesale

mayoría *nf* majority; **en su m.** in the main; **la m. de los niños** most children; **m. absoluta** absolute majority; **m. relativa** *Br* relative majority, *US* plurality; **m. de edad** majority

mayorista 1 *adj* wholesale
2 *nmf* wholesaler; **precios de m.** whole-sale prices

mayoritario, -a *adj* majority; **un gobierno m.** a majority government

mayúscula *nf* capital letter

mayúsculo, -a *adj* (**a**) *Ling (letra)* capital (**b**) *(error)* very big, enormous

mazacote *nm* (**a**) *Culin* solid mass, stodge (**b**) *(mezcla confusa)* hotchpotch

mazapán *nm* marzipan

mazmorra *nf* dungeon

mazo *nm* mallet

mazorca *nf Agr* cob

me *pron pers* (**a**) *(objeto directo)* me; **no me mires** don't look at me (**b**) *(objeto indirecto)* me, to me, for me; **¿me das un caramelo?** will you give me a sweet?; **me lo dio** he gave it to me; **me es difícil hacerlo** it is difficult for me to do it (**c**) *(pron reflexivo)* myself; **me he cortado** I've cut myself; **me voy/muero** *(no se traduce)* I'm off/dying

meada *nf Fam* piss; **echar una m.** to have a piss

meadero *nm Fam Br* bog, *US* john

meandro *nm* meander

mear *Fam* **1** *vi* to (have a) piss
2 mearse *vpr* to wet oneself; *Fig* **mearse de risa** to piss oneself (laughing)

mecachis *interj Fam Br* sugar!, *US* shoot!

mecánica *nf* (**a**) *(ciencia)* mechanics *sing* (**b**) *(mecanismo)* mechanism, works

mecánico, -a 1 *adj* mechanical
2 *nm,f* mechanic

mecanismo *nm* mechanism

mecanizar [40] *vt* to mechanize

mecanografía *nf* typewriting, typing

mecanografiar [29] *vt* to type

mecanógrafo, -a *nm,f* typist

mecapal *nm CAm, Méx* = porter's leather harness

mecedora *nf* rocking-chair

mecenas *nmf inv* patron

mecer [49] **1** *vt* to rock
2 mecerse *vpr* to swing, to rock

mecha *nf* (**a**) *(de vela)* wick (**b**) *Mil & Min* fuse; *Fam* **aguantar m.** to grin and bear it (**c**) *(de pelo)* streak; **hacerse mechas** to have one's hair streaked

mechar *vt (carne)* to lard

mechero *nm Esp* (cigarette) lighter

mechón *nm* (**a**) *(de pelo)* lock (**b**) *(de lana)* tuft

medalla *nf* medal

medallón *nm* medallion

media *nf* (**a**) *(prenda interior)* **medias** *(hasta la cintura)* *Br* tights, *US* pantyhose; *(hasta medio muslo)* stockings (**b**) *(calcetín) (hasta la rodilla)* (knee-length) sock; *Am (de cualquier longitud)* sock (**c**) *(promedio)* average; *Mat* mean; **m. aritmética/geométrica** arithmetic/geo-metric mean (**d**) *(incompleto)* unfinished; *(entre dos)* half and half; **ir a medias** to go halves

> 🖉 Observa que la palabra inglesa **media** es un falso amigo y no es la traducción de la palabra española **media**. En inglés, **media** significa "medios de comunicación".

mediación *nf* mediation, intervention; **por m. de un amigo** through a friend

mediado, -a 1 *adj* half-full, half-empty
2 a mediados de *loc prep* about the middle of

mediador, -a *nm,f* mediator

medialuna *nf* (**a**) *(símbolo musulmán)* crescent (**b**) *Am (bollo)* croissant

mediana *nf* (**a**) *(de autopista)* *Br* central reservation, *US* median (strip) (**b**) *Mat* median

mediano, -a *adj* (**a**) *(de tamaño)* medium; *(de calidad)* average (**b**) *(mediocre)* average, ordinary

medianoche *nf* midnight

mediante *prep* by means of, with the help of, using; **Dios m.** God willing

mediar [43] *vi* (**a**) *(intervenir)* to mediate, to intervene; **m. en favor de algn** to intercede on behalf of sb (**b**) *(tiempo)* to pass; **mediaron tres semanas** three weeks passed

mediático, -a *adj* media

medicación nf medication

medicamento nm medicine

medicina nf medicine; **estudiante de m.** medical student

medicinal adj medicinal

médico, -a 1 nm,f doctor; **m. de cabecera** family doctor, general practitioner; **m. interno (residente)** Br house officer, US intern
  2 adj medical

medida 1 nf (a) (dimensión) measurement; **tomar las medidas a algn** to take sb's measurements; **a (la) m.** (ropa) made-to-measure; **m. de capacidad** measure (liquid or dry) (b) (grado) extent, degree; **en gran m.** to a great extent (c) (disposición) measure; **adoptar** o **tomar medidas** to take measures o steps
  2 a medida que loc conj as; **a m. que avanzaba** as he advanced

medidor nm Am meter

medieval adj medieval

medievo nm Middle Ages

medio, -a 1 adj (a) (mitad) half; **m. kilo** half a kilo; **una hora y media** one and a half hours, an hour and a half; **a m. camino** halfway; **a media mañana/tarde** in the middle of the morning/afternoon (b) (intermedio) (estatura, tamaño) medium; (posición, punto) middle; **de clase media** middle-class (c) (normal) average; **salario m.** average wage
  2 adv half; **está m. muerta** she is half dead
  3 nm (a) (mitad) half (b) (centro) middle; **en m. (de)** (en el centro) in the middle (of); (entre dos) in between (c) **medios de transporte** means of transport; **por m. de ...** by means of ...; **medios económicos** means; **medios de comunicación (de masas)** (mass) media (d) **m. ambiente** environment (e) Dep (jugador) half back

medioambiental adj environmental

mediocre adj mediocre

mediocridad nf mediocrity

mediodía nm (a) (hora exacta) midday, noon (b) (período aproximado) early afternoon, lunch-time

medir [6] **1** vt (a) (distancia, superficie, temperatura) to measure (b) (moderar) to weigh; **mide tus palabras** weigh your words
  2 vi to measure, to be; **¿cuánto mides?** how tall are you?; **mide 2 m** he is 2 m tall; **mide 2 m de alto/ancho/largo** it is 2 m high/wide/long

meditar vt & vi to meditate, to ponder; **m. sobre algo** to ponder over sth

mediterráneo, -a 1 adj Mediterranean
  2 nm **el M.** the Mediterranean

médium nmf inv medium

medrar vi to climb the social ladder

médula nf (a) Anat (bone) marrow; **m. espinal** spinal cord (b) (lo más profundo) marrow, pith; **hasta la m.** to the marrow

medusa nf jellyfish

megabit (pl **megabits**) nm Inform megabit

megafonía nf public-address system, PA system

megáfono nm megaphone

megalito nm megalith

megalómano, -a adj megalomaniac

mejicano, -a adj & nm,f Mexican

Méjico n Mexico; **ciudad de M.** Mexico City; **Nuevo M.** New Mexico

mejilla nf cheek

mejillón nm mussel

mejor 1 adj (a) (comparativo) better (que than); **es m. no decírselo** it's better not to tell her; **es m. que vayas** you'd better go (b) (superlativo) best; **tu m. amiga** your best friend; **lo m.** the best thing
  2 adv (a) (comparativo) better (que than); **cada vez m.** better and better; **ella conduce m.** she drives better; **m. dicho** or rather; **¡mucho** o **tanto m.!** so much the better! (b) (superlativo) best; **es el que m. canta** he is the one who sings the best; **a lo m.** (quizás) perhaps; (ojalá) hopefully
  3 nmf **el/la m.** the best; **el m. de los dos** the better of the two; **el m. de los tres** best of the three

mejora nf improvement

mejorar 1 vt to improve; **m. la red vial** to improve the road system; **m. una marca** o **un récord** to break a record
  2 vi to improve, to get better
  3 mejorarse upr to get better; **¡que te mejores!** get well soon!

mejoría nf improvement

melancolía nf melancholy

melancólico, -a adj melancholic, melancholy

melé nf Esp Dep scrum

melena nf (head of) hair; (de león) mane

melindroso, -a 1 adj affected, fussy, finicky
  2 nm,f affected o finicky person

mella nf (a) (hendedura) nick, notch; (en plato, taza etc) chip (b) (en dentadura) gap (c) Fig impression; **hacer m. en algn** to make an impression on sb

mellado, -a adj (sin dientes) gap-toothed

mellizo, -a adj & nm,f twin

melocotón nm esp Esp peach

melocotonero *nm esp Esp* peach tree

melodía *nf* melody, tune; *(de teléfono)* ringtone

melodrama *nm* melodrama

melodramático, -a *adj* melodramatic

melón *nm* (a) *(fruto)* melon (b) *Fam (tonto)* ninny (c) *muy Fam* **melones** *(tetas)* boobs

melopea *nf Esp Fam* **coger** *o* **agarrar/ llevar una m.** to get/be drunk *o Br* pissed

meloso, -a *adj* sweet, honeyed

membrana *nf* membrane

membresía *nf Am* membership

membrete *nm* letterhead

membrillo *nm* (a) *Bot (fruto)* quince; *(árbol)* quince tree; *(dulce)* quince preserve *o* jelly (b) *Fam (tonto)* dimwit

memela *nf Méx* = thick corn tortilla, oval in shape

memo, -a *Fam* **1** *adj* silly, stupid
  2 *nm,f* nincompoop, ninny

memorable *adj* memorable

memorándum *(pl* **memorándums)** *nm* memorandum

memoria *nf* (a) *(capacidad de recordar)* memory; **aprender/saber algo de m.** to learn/know sth by heart; **irse de la m.** to slip one's mind (b) *(recuerdo)* memory, recollection (c) *(informe)* report, statement; **m. anual** annual report (d) **memorias** *(biografía)* memoirs

memorístico, -a *adj* acquired by memory

memorizar [40] *vt* to memorize

menaje *nm* furniture and furnishing; **m. de cocina** kitchen equipment *o* utensils

mención *nf* mention; **m. honorífica** honourable mention

mencionar *vt* to mention

mendicidad *nf* begging

mendigar [42] *vt & vi* to beg

mendigo, -a *nm,f* beggar

mendrugo *nm* (a) *(de pan)* crust (of bread) (b) *Esp Fam (idiota)* fathead, idiot

mene *nm Ven* = deposit of oil at surface level

menear **1** *vt (mover)* to move; *(cabeza)* to shake; *(cola)* to wag
  2 menearse *vpr (moverse)* to move (about); *(agitarse)* to shake

meneo *nm* shake; *(de cola)* wag, waggle

menester *nm* (a) **es m.** it is necessary (b) **menesteres** *(deberes)* jobs

menestra *nf* vegetable stew

mengano, -a *nm,f Fam* so-and-so, what's-his/her-name

menguante *adj* waning, on the wane; **cuarto m.** last quarter

menguar [45] **1** *vt* (a) *(disminuir)* to diminish, to reduce (b) *(en labor de punto)* to decrease
  2 *vi* (a) *(disminuir)* to diminish, to decrease (b) *(luna)* to wane

menopausia *nf* menopause

menor **1** *adj* (a) *(comparativo)* *(de tamaño)* smaller (**que** than); *(de edad)* younger (**que** than); **el mal m.** the lesser of two evils; **ser m. de edad** to be a minor *o* under age (b) *(superlativo)* *(de tamaño)* smallest; *(de intensidad)* least, slightest; *(de edad)* youngest; **al m. ruido** at the slightest noise (c) *Mús* minor (d) *Com* **al por m.** retail
  2 *nmf* (b) *Der* minor; **tribunal de menores** juvenile court (b) *(superlativo)* **el/la m.** *(hijo, hermano)* the youngest; **el m. de los dos** the smaller of the two; **el m. de los tres** the youngest of the three; **es la m.** she's the youngest child

Menorca *n* Minorca

menos **1** *adj* (a) *(comparativo)* *(con singular)* less; *(con plural)* fewer; **m. dinero/leche/tiempo que** less money/milk/time than; **m. libros/pisos que** fewer books/flats than; *(con cláusula)* **tiene m. años de lo que parece** he's younger than he looks (b) *(superlativo)* **fui el que perdí m. dinero** I lost the least money
  2 *adv* (a) **m. de** *(con singular)* less than; *(con plural)* fewer than, less than; **m. de media hora** less than half an hour (b) *(superlativo)* *(con singular)* least; *(con plural)* the fewest; *(con cantidad)* the least; **el m. inteligente de la clase** the least intelligent boy in the class; **ayer fue cuando vinieron m. personas** yesterday was when the fewest people came (c) *Esp, RP (con las horas)* to; **son las dos m. diez** it's ten to two, it's ten to
  3 *(locuciones)* **a m. que** (+ *subjunctive*) unless; **al** *o* **por lo m.** at least; **echar a algn de m.** to miss sb; **eso es lo de m.** that's the least of it; **¡m. mal!** just as well!; **nada m. que** no less/no fewer than; **ni mucho m.** far from it
  4 *prep* (a) *(excepto)* but, except; **todo m. eso** anything but that (b) *Mat* minus; **tres m. uno** three minus one

menoscabar *vt* (a) *(perjudicar)* to damage (b) *(desacreditar)* to discredit

menoscabo *nm* (de fama, honra)* damage; *(de derechos, intereses, salud)* harm; *(de belleza, perfección)* diminishing; **ir en m. de algo** to be to the detriment of sth

menospreciar [43] *vt* to scorn, to disdain

menosprecio *nm* contempt, scorn, disdain

mensáfono *nm* pager
mensaje *nm* message; **m. de texto** text (message)
mensajería *nf* (a) *(de paquetes, cartas)* courier service (b) *(por teléfono)* messaging (c) *Inform* **m. instantánea** instant messaging
mensajero, -a *nm,f* messenger, courier
menso, -a *adj Méx Fam* foolish, stupid
menstruación *nf* menstruation
menstruar [30] *vi* to menstruate
mensual *adj* monthly; **dos visitas mensuales** two visits a month
mensualidad *nf (pago)* monthly payment; *(sueldo)* monthly salary o wage
menta *nf* (a) *Bot* mint (b) *(licor)* crème de menthe
mental *adj* mental
mentalidad *nf* mentality; **de m. abierta/cerrada** open-/narrow-minded
mentalizar [40] **1** *vt* to make aware
  2 mentalizarse *vpr* to get into a frame of mind; **mentalizarse de que ...** to get used to the idea that ...
mentar [1] *vt* to mention, to name
mente *nf* mind; **se me quedó la m. en blanco** my mind went blank; **m. abierta/tolerante/cerrada** open/broad/closed mind
mentecato, -a *nm,f* fool, idiot
mentir [5] *vi* to lie, to tell lies
mentira *nf* lie; **aunque parezca m.** strange as it may seem; **parece m.** it is unbelievable
mentiroso, -a 1 *adj* lying
  2 *nm,f* liar
mentís *nm inv* denial
mentón *nm Anat* chin
menú *nm* menu; **m. del día** set meal
menudeo *nm Andes, Méx* retailing
menudillos *nmpl* giblets
menudo, -a 1 *adj* minute, tiny; *(irónico)* tremendous; **la gente menuda** the little ones; **¡m. lío/susto!** what a mess/fright!
  2 *adv* **a m.** often
meñique *adj & nm (dedo)* **m.** little finger, *US & Scot* pinkie
meollo *nm* core, heart; **el m. de la cuestión** the nub of the question, the heart of the matter
mercadillo *nm* flea market
mercado *nm* market; *Antes* **M. Común** Common Market; **m. financiero** financial market; **m. negro** black market; **m. único** single market; **m. de valores** securities market; **sacar algo al m.** to put sth on the market

mercadotecnia *nf* marketing
mercancía *nf* merchandise, goods
mercante *adj* merchant; **barco/marina m.** merchant ship/navy
mercantil *adj* mercantile, commercial
merced *nf Fml* favour, grace; **a m. de** at the mercy of
mercenario, -a *adj & nm,f* mercenary
mercería *nf Br* haberdasher's (shop), *US* notions store
Mercosur *nm (abr* **Mercado Común del Sur)** MERCOSUR, = South American economic community consisting of Argentina, Brazil, Paraguay and Uruguay
mercurio *nm Quím* mercury, quicksilver
merecer [33] **1** *vt* (a) to deserve (b) **no merece la pena hacerlo** it's not worth (while) doing it
  2 merecerse *vpr* to deserve
merecido, -a 1 *adj* deserved; **ella lo tiene m.** *(recompensa)* she deserves it; *(castigo)* it serves her right
  2 *nm* just deserts
merendar [1] **1** *vt* to have as an afternoon snack, to have for tea
  2 *vi* to have an afternoon snack, to have tea
merendero *nm (establecimiento)* tea room, snack-bar; *(en el campo)* picnic spot
merengue *nm* (a) *Culin* meringue (b) *(baile)* merengue
merezco *indic pres de* **merecer**
meridiano *nm* meridian
meridional 1 *adj* southern
  2 *nmf* southerner
merienda *nf* afternoon snack, tea
mérito *nm* merit, worth; **hacer méritos para algo** to strive to deserve sth
merluza *nf* hake
merma *nf* decrease, reduction
mermar 1 *vt* to cause to decrease o diminish
  2 *vi* to decrease, to diminish
mermelada *nf* jam; *(de agrios)* marmalade; **m. de fresa** strawberry jam; **m. de naranja** orange marmalade
mero, -a *adj* (a) *(simple)* mere; **por el m. hecho de** through the mere fact of (b) *CAm, Méx Fam* **en el m. centro** right in the centre; *Méx* **el m. m.** the big shot
merodear *vi* to prowl
mes *nm* (a) *(tiempo)* month; **el m. pasado/que viene** last/next month (b) *(cobro)* monthly salary o wages; *(pago)* monthly payment (c) *Fam (menstruación)* period
mesa *nf* (a) *(mueble)* table; *(de despacho, oficina)* desk; **poner/recoger la m.** to set/

clear the table; **m. camilla** = small round table under which a heater is placed (**b**) *(comité)* board, committee; *(en un debate)* panel; **el presidente de la m.** the chairman; **m. electoral** electoral college; **m. redonda** *(coloquio)* round table

mesada *nf* (**a**) *Am (pago mensual)* monthly payment, monthly instalment (**b**) *RP (para adolescentes)* pocket money, *US* allowance (**c**) *RP (encimera)* worktop

mesero, -a *nm,f Col, Guat, Méx, Salv (hombre)* waiter; *(mujer)* waitress

meseta *nf* plateau, tableland, meseta; **la M.** the plateau of Castile

mesilla *nf* **m. de noche** bedside table

mesón *nm* = old-style tavern

mesonero, -a *nm,f* (**a**) *Esp (en mesón)* innkeeper (**b**) *Chile, Ven (camarero) (hombre)* waiter; *(mujer)* waitress

mestizo, -a 1 *adj (persona)* of mixed race, half-caste; *(animal, planta)* cross-bred
2 *nm,f* person of mixed race, half-caste

mesura *nf Fml* moderation, restraint

⏀ Observa que la palabra inglesa **mea-sure** es un falso amigo y no es la traduc-ción de la palabra española **mesura**. En inglés, **mesura** significa "medida".

---

meta *nf* (**a**) *(objetivo)* goal, aim, objective (**b**) *(de carrera)* finish, finishing line (**c**) *Ftb (portería)* goal

metabolismo *nm* metabolism

metadona *nf* methadone

metafísica *nf* metaphysics *sing*

metáfora *nf* metaphor

metal *nm* (**a**) *(material)* metal; **metales preciosos** precious metals (**b**) *Mús* brass

metálico, -a 1 *adj* metallic
2 *nm* cash; **pagar en m.** to pay (in) cash

metalizado, -a *adj (pintura)* metallic

metalúrgico, -a 1 *adj* metallurgical
2 *nm,f* metallurgist

metamorfosis *nf inv también Fig* metamorphosis

metate *nm Guat, Méx* grinding stone

metedura *nf Fam* **m. de pata** blunder, *Br* clanger

meteorito *nm* meteorite

meteoro *nm* meteor

meteorología *nf* meteorology

meteorológico, -a *adj* meteorological; **parte m.** weather report *o* forecast

meter 1 *vt* (**a**) *(poner)* to put (**en** in); *Fig* **m. las narices en algo** to poke one's nose into sth (**b**) *(comprometer)* to involve (**en** in), to get mixed up (**en** in) (**c**) *Fam Fig (dar)* to give; **m. un rollo** to go on and on; **m. prisa**

a algn to hurry sb up (**d**) *(hacer)* to make; **m. ruido** to make a noise
2 meterse *vpr* (**a**) *(entrar)* to go/come in, to get in (**b**) *(estar)* to be; **¿dónde te habías metido?** where have you been (all this time)? (**c**) *(entrometerse)* to meddle (**d**) **meterse con algn** *(en broma)* to get at sb

metiche *Méx, Ven Fam nmf* busybody, *Br* nosey-parker

meticuloso, -a *adj* meticulous

metido, -a *adj Fam* **estar muy m. en algo** to be deeply involved in sth; **m. en años** getting on (in years)

metódico, -a *adj* methodical

método *nm* method

metodología *nf* methodology

metomentodo *nmf inv Fam* busybody, *Br* nosey-parker

metralla *nf* shrapnel

metralleta *nf* submachine-gun

métrico, -a *adj* metric; **sistema m.** metric system

metro *nm* (**a**) *(medida)* metre (**b**) *(tren) Br* underground, *US* subway (**c**) *(cinta métrica)* tape measure

metrópoli *nf* metropolis

metropolitano, -a 1 *adj* metropolitan
2 *nm Fml Br* underground, *US* subway

mexicano, -a *adj & nm,f* Mexican

México *n* Mexico

mezcla *nf* (**a**) *(acción)* mixing, blending; *Rad & Cin* mixing (**b**) *(producto)* mixture, blend

mezclar 1 *vt* (**a**) *(dos o más cosas)* to mix, to blend (**b**) *(desordenar)* to mix up (**c**) *(involucrar)* to involve, to mix up
2 mezclarse *vpr* (**a**) *(cosas)* to get mixed up; *(gente)* to mingle (**b**) *(relacionarse)* to get involved (**con** with)

mezcolanza *nf Fml* strange mixture, hotch-potch

mezquino, -a *adj* (**a**) *(persona)* mean, stingy (**b**) *(sueldo)* miserable

mezquita *nf* mosque

mg *(abr* **miligramo(s))** mg

mi¹ *adj* my; **mi casa/trabajo** my house/job; **mis cosas/libros** my things/books

mi² *(pl* **mis)** *nm Mús* E; **mi menor** E minor

mí *pron pers* me; **a mí me dio tres** he gave me three; **compra otro para mí** buy one for me too; **por mí mismo** just by myself

mía *adj & pron pos f ver* **mío**

miaja *nf* crumb; *Fig* bit

miche *nm Ven* = cane spirit flavoured with herbs and spices

michelín *nm Fam* spare tyre

mico *nm* (**a**) *Zool* (long-tailed) monkey (**b**) *Fam (pequeño)* **es un m.** he's a midget *o Br* titch

micra *nf* micron

micro 1 *nm Fam* mike, microphone
2 *nm o nf Arg, Bol, Chile (autobús)* minibus

microbio *nm* microbe

microbús (*pl* **microbuses**) *nm* (**a**) *(autobús)* minibus (**b**) *Méx (taxi)* (collective) taxi

microchip (*pl* **microchips**) *nm Inform* microchip

microclima *nm* microclimate

microcrédito *nm Econ* microcredit

microficha *nf* microfiche

micrófono *nm* microphone

microondas *nm inv* **un (horno) m.** a microwave (oven)

microscopio *nm* microscope

miedica *nmf Esp Fam* scaredy-cat

miedo *nm (pavor)* fear; *(temor)* apprehension; **una película de m.** a horror movie *o Br* film; **tener m. de algn/algo** to be afraid of sb/sth; *Esp Fam* **de m.: lo pasamos de m.** we had a fantastic time; **un calor de m.** sizzling heat

miedoso, -a *adj* fearful

miel *nf* honey; **luna de m.** honeymoon

miembro *nm* (**a**) *(socio)* member; **estado m.** member state (**b**) *Anat* limb; **m. viril** penis

mientras 1 *conj* (**a**) *(al mismo tiempo que)* while (**b**) *(durante el tiempo que)* when, while; **m. viví en Barcelona** when I lived in Barcelona (**c**) **m. que** *(por el contrario)* whereas (**d**) *Fam (cuanto más)* **m. más/menos …** the more/less …
2 *adv* **m. (tanto)** meanwhile, in the meantime

miércoles *nm inv* Wednesday; **M. de Ceniza** Ash Wednesday

mierda *nf Vulg* (**a**) *(excremento)* shit; *(suciedad)* crap; **ese libro es una m.** that book is crap; **¡vete a la m.!** piss off! (**b**) *Esp (borrachera)* bender

miga *nf (de pan etc)* crumb; *Fig* **hacer buenas migas con algn** to get on well with sb

migaja *nf* (**a**) *(trozo)* bit; *(de pan)* crumb (**b**) *(pizca)* scrap; **migajas** *(restos)* leftovers

migra *nf Méx Fam Pey* **la m.** = US police border patrol

migraña *nf* migraine

migrar *vi* to migrate

mijo *nm* millet

mil *adj & nm* thousand; **m. euros** a *o* one thousand euros

milagro *nm* miracle

milagroso, -a *adj* miraculous

milano *nm* kite

milenario, -a *adj* ancient

milenio *nm* millennium

milésima *nf* thousandth; **m. de segundo** millisecond

milésimo, -a *adj & nm* thousandth; **la milésima parte** a thousandth

mili *nf Esp Antes Fam* military *o* national service

milicia *nf (grupo armado)* militia

milico *nm Andes, RP Fam Pey* soldier; **los milicos** the military

miligramo *nm* milligram

mililitro *nm* millilitre

milímetro *nm* millimetre

militante *adj & nmf* militant

militar 1 *adj* military
2 *nm* military man, soldier; **los militares** the military
3 *vi Pol (en partido)* to be a member

milla *nf* mile

millar *nm* thousand

millardo *nm* billion, thousand million

millón *nm* million; **dos millones** two million

millonario, -a *adj & nm,f* millionaire

millonésimo, -a *adj & nm* millionth

milpa *nf CAm, Méx* cornfield

mimado, -a *adj* spoilt

mimar *vt* to spoil, to pamper

> 🖉 Observa que el verbo inglés **to mime** es un falso amigo y no es la traducción del verbo español **mimar**. En inglés, **to mime** significa "representar con gestos".

mimbre *nm* wicker

mímica *nf* mimicry

mimo *nm* (**a**) *(delicadeza)* care (**b**) *Fig (zalamería)* pampering (**c**) *Teatro (actor)* mime

mimosa *nf Bot* mimosa

mimoso, -a *adj* **está m.** he wants a cuddle

mina *nf* (**a**) *Geol & Mil* mine (**b**) *(de lápiz)* lead; (**c**) *Fig (cosa rentable)* goldmine (**d**) *CSur Fam (chica) Br* bird, *US* chick

minar *vt* (**a**) *Mil* to mine (**b**) *Fig (desgastar)* to undermine

mineral 1 *adj* mineral
2 *nm* (**a**) *Geol* mineral (**b**) *Min* ore; **m. de hierro** iron ore

minería *nf (técnica)* mining; *(sector)* mining industry

minero, -a 1 *nm,f* miner
2 *adj* mining

miniatura *nf* miniature

mini disk, mini disc *nm inv* mini disc

minifalda *nf* miniskirt

minifundio *nm* smallholding

minigolf (*pl* **minigolfs**) *nm* crazy golf

mínima *nf* minimum temperature

minimizar *vt* to minimize

mínimo, -a 1 *adj* (a) (*lo más bajo posible*) minimum (b) (*muy pequeño*) (*efecto, importancia*) minimal, very small; (*ruido, idea*) slightest; **como m.** at the very least
  2 *nm* (*límite*) minimum; **m. común múltiplo** lowest common multiple

minipimer® (*pl* **minipímers**) *nm o nf* hand-held mixer

ministerio *nm* (a) *Pol Br* ministry, *US* department (b) *Rel* ministry

ministro, -a *nm,f* (a) *Pol Br* minister, *US* secretary; **primer m.** prime minister (b) *Rel* minister

minoría *nf* minority; *Der* **m. de edad** minority

minorista *nmf* retailer

minoritario, -a *adj* minority

minucioso, -a *adj* (a) (*persona*) meticulous (b) (*informe, trabajo*) minute, detailed

minúscula *nf* small letter, lower-case letter

minúsculo, -a *adj* minuscule, minute; **letra minúscula** lower-case *o* small letter

minusvalía *nf* (a) *Fin* capital loss (b) (*física*) disability, handicap

minusválido, -a 1 *adj* disabled, handicapped
  2 *nm,f* disabled person, handicapped person

minuta *nf* (*factura*) fee

minutero *nm* minute hand

minuto *nm* minute

mío, -a 1 *adj pos* of mine; **un amigo m.** a friend of mine; **no es asunto m.** it is none of my business
  2 *pron pos* mine; **ese libro es m.** that book is mine; **lo m. es el tenis** tennis is my strong point; *Fam* **los míos** my people *o* folks

miope *nmf* short-sighted *o US* nearsighted person, *Espec* myopic person

miopía *nf* short-sightedness, *US* nearsightedness, *Espec* myopia

mira *nf* (a) *Téc* sight (b) (*objetivo*) aim, target; **con miras a** with a view to; **amplitud de miras** broad-mindedness

mirada *nf* look; **lanzar** *o* **echar una m.** a to glance at; **levantar la m.** to look up; **m. fija** stare

mirador *nm* (a) (*lugar con vista*) viewpoint (b) (*balcón*) bay window, windowed balcony

mirar 1 *vt* to look at; (*observar*) to watch; (*fijamente*) to stare at; **mirándolo bien ...** if you think about it ...
  2 *vi* (a) (*dirigir la vista*) to look; (*observar*) to watch; (*fijamente*) to stare; **¡mira!** look (at that!) (b) (*dar a*) to look, to face; **la casa mira al sur** the house faces south (c) **m. por algn/algo** (*cuidar*) to look after sb/sth

mirilla *nf* spyhole

mirlo *nm* blackbird

mirón, -ona *Fam* **1** *adj* (*curioso*) nosey; (*con lascivia*) peeping
  2 *nm,f* (*espectador*) onlooker; (*curioso*) busybody, *Br* nosy parker; (*voyeur*) peeping Tom

mirra *nf* myrrh

misántropo, -a 1 *adj* misanthropic
  2 *nm,f* misanthrope, misanthropist

miscelánea *nf* (a) (*mezcla*) miscellany (b) *Méx* (*tienda*) = small general store

miserable 1 *adj* (a) (*mezquino*) (*persona*) despicable; (*sueldo etc*) miserable (b) (*pobre*) wretched, poor; **una vida m.** a wretched life
  2 *nmf* (a) (*mezquino*) miser (b) (*canalla*) wretch

miseria *nf* (a) (*pobreza extrema*) extreme poverty (b) (*insignificancia*) pittance; **ganar una m.** to earn next to nothing (c) (*tacañería*) miserliness, meanness

misericordia *nf* mercy, compassion

mísero, -a *adj* miserable, wretched

misil *nm* missile

misión *nf* mission; **m. cumplida** mission accomplished

misionero, -a *nm,f* missionary

mismísimo, -a *adj superl Fam* (*en persona*) in person

mismo, -a 1 *adj* (a) (*igual, no otro*) same (b) (*uso enfático*) **yo m.** I myself; **aquí m.** right here
  2 *pron* same; **es el m. de ayer** it's the same one as yesterday; **estamos en las mismas** we're back to square one; **lo m.** the same (thing); **dar** *o* **ser lo m.** to make no difference; **por eso m.** that is why; **por uno** *o* **sí m.** by oneself
  3 *adv* (a) (*por ejemplo*) for instance; **que venga alguien, Juan m.** ask one of them to come, Juan, for instance (b) **así m.** likewise

misógino, -a 1 *adj* misogynous
  2 *nm,f* misogynist

miss *nf* beauty queen

misterio *nm* mystery

misterioso, -a *adj* mysterious

místico, -a 1 *adj* mystical
2 *nm,f* mystic

mitad *nf* (**a**) **la m.** half; **a m. de precio** half-price; **a m. de película** halfway through the movie *o Br* film (**b**) *(centro)* middle; **en m. de** in the middle of; **en m. del primer acto** halfway through the first act

mítico, -a *adj* mythical

mitigar [42] *vt* to mitigate; *(daño)* to reduce

mitin *nm Pol* meeting, rally

mito *nm* myth

mitología *nf* mythology

mitote *nm Méx Fam (alboroto)* racket

mixto, -a *adj* mixed

mm *(abr* milímetro(s)*)* mm

mobiliario *nm* furniture

moca *nm* mocha

mocasín *nm* moccasin

mochila *nf* rucksack, backpack

mochuelo *nm Zool* little owl

moción *nf* motion; **m. de censura** vote of censure

moco *nm* snot; **sonarse los mocos** to blow one's nose; **tener mocos** to have a runny nose

mocoso, -a *nm,f Fam* brat

moda *nf* fashion; *(furor pasajero)* craze; **a la m., de m.** in fashion; **pasado de m.** old-fashioned

modales *nmpl* manners

modalidad *nf* form, type; *Com* **m. de pago** method of payment; *Dep* **m. deportiva** discipline

modelar *vt* to model, to shape; *Am (ropa)* to model

modélico, -a *adj* model

modelo 1 *adj inv & nm* model
2 *nmf* (fashion) model; **desfile de modelos** fashion show

módem *(pl* modems*)* *nm Inform* modem

moderación *nf* moderation

moderado, -a *adj* moderate; **un m. aumento de temperatura** a mild increase in temperature

moderador, -a *nm,f* chairperson; *(hombre)* chairman; *(mujer)* chairwoman

moderar 1 *vt* (**a**) *(atenuar)* to moderate; *(velocidad)* to reduce (**b**) *(debate)* to chair
2 moderarse *vpr* to be moderate

modernizar [40] **1** *vt* to modernize
2 modernizarse *vpr* to modernize

moderno, -a *adj* modern

modestia *nf* modesty; **m. aparte** without wishing to be immodest

modesto, -a *adj* modest

módico, -a *adj* moderate; **una módica suma** a modest *o* small sum

modificación *nf* alteration

modificar [44] *vt* to modify

modismo *nm* idiom

modisto, -a *nm,f* (**a**) *(diseñador)* fashion designer (**b**) *(sastre) (hombre)* couturier; *(mujer)* couturière

modo *nm* (**a**) *(manera)* way, manner; **de todos modos** in any case, anyway; **de m. que** *(así que)* so; **m. de empleo** instructions for use (**b**) **modos** manners (**c**) *Ling* mood

modorra *nf* drowsiness

modoso, -a *adj* *(recatado)* modest; *(educado)* well-behaved

modular *vt* to modulate

módulo *nm* module

mofa *nf* mockery; **en tono de m.** in a gibing tone

mofarse *vpr* to laugh (**de** at), to make fun (**de** of)

moflete *nm* chubby cheek

mogollón *Esp Fam* **1** *nm* (**a**) **m. de** loads of (**b**) *(confusión)* commotion
2 *adv* loads, *Br* heaps; **me gusta m.** I like it loads

moho *nm* mould

mohoso, -a *adj* mouldy

moisés *nm inv* Moses basket

mojado, -a *adj (empapado)* wet; *(húmedo)* damp

mojar 1 *vt* to wet; *(humedecer)* to dampen; **m. pan en la leche** to dip *o* dunk bread in one's milk
2 mojarse *vpr* to get wet

mojigato, -a *adj (beato)* prudish; *(falsamente humilde)* sanctimonious

mojón *nm* **m. kilométrico** ≃ milestone

moka *nm* mocha

molar 1 *vi Esp Fam* **me mola cantidad** I really love it, it's brilliant
2 *adj & nm Anat* molar

molcajete *nm Méx* mortar

molde *nm* mould; **letras de m.** print; **pan de m.** ≃ sliced bread

moldeador *nm Esp (del pelo)* soft perm

moldear *vt* to mould

mole 1 *nf* mass, bulk
2 *nm Méx* = thick, cooked chilli sauce

molécula *nf* molecule

moler [4] *vt* (**a**) *(triturar)* to grind (**b**) **m. a algn a golpes** to beat sb up

molestar 1 *vt* (**a**) *(incomodar)* to disturb, to bother; **¿le molestaría esperar fuera?** would you mind waiting outside? (**b**) *(ofender)* to upset (**c**) *(doler)* **me molesta**

la pierna my leg is giving me a bit of trouble
  2 molestarse *vpr* (a) *(tomarse la molestia)* to bother (b) *(ofenderse)* to take offence, to get upset

molestia *nf* (a) *(incomodidad)* bother, trouble; **no es ninguna m.** it's no trouble at all; **perdone las molestias** forgive the inconvenience (b) *(dolor)* trouble, slight pain

molesto, -a *adj* (a) **ser m.** *(costumbre, ruido)* to be annoying; *(humo, sensación)* to be unpleasant (b) **estar m.** *(ofendido)* to be upset; *(con malestar)* to be in discomfort; *(incómodo)* to be uncomfortable

molestoso, -a *Am salvo RP Fam* **1** *adj* annoying
  2 *nm,f* nuisance

molido, -a *adj Fam (cansado)* worn out

molinillo *nm* grinder

molino *nm* mill; **m. de viento** windmill

mollera *nf Fam* nut, *Br* bonce; **duro de m.** *(tonto)* dense, thick; *(testarudo)* pigheaded

molón, -ona *adj Esp Fam* (a) *(que gusta) Br* brilliant, *US* neat (b) *(elegante)* smart

molusco *nm* mollusc

momentáneo, -a *adj* momentary

momento *nm* (a) *(instante)* moment; **al m.** at once; **por momentos** by the minute (b) *(periodo)* time; **de m.** for the time being; **en cualquier m.** at any time

momia *nf* mummy

mona *nf Fam* **dormir la m.** to sleep it off

Mónaco *n* Monaco

monada *nf Fam* **¡qué m.!** how cute!

monaguillo *nm Rel* altar boy

monarca *nmf* monarch

monarquía *nf* monarchy

monasterio *nm Rel* monastery

monda *nf* (a) *(piel)* peel, skin (b) *Esp Fam* **ser la m.** *(divertido)* to be a scream

mondadientes *nm inv* toothpick

mondar 1 *vt* to peel
  2 mondarse *vpr Esp Fam* **mondarse (de risa)** to laugh one's head off

moneda *nf* (a) *(pieza)* coin; **m. suelta** small change; **acuñar m.** to mint money (b) *Fin* currency; **m. única** single currency

monedero *nm Br* purse, *US* change purse

monería *nf Fam* = monada

monetario, -a *adj* monetary

mongol 1 *adj & nmf* Mongolian
  2 *nm (idioma)* Mongolian

mongólico, -a *Med* **1** *adj* Down's syndrome
  2 *nm,f* **ser m.** to have Down's syndrome

monigote *nm* (a) *Pey (persona)* wimp (b) *(dibujo)* rough drawing o sketch (of a person)

monitor, -a 1 *nm,f (persona)* instructor; **m. de esquí** skiing instructor
  2 *nm Inform & Mec* monitor

monja *nf* nun

monje *nm* monk

mono, -a 1 *nm* (a) *(animal)* monkey (b) *(prenda) (con mangas) Br* overalls, *US* coveralls; *(con peto) Br* dungarees, *US* overalls; *Ven (de deporte)* tracksuit (c) *Esp Fam (síndrome de abstinencia)* cold turkey
  2 *adj Fam (bonito)* pretty, cute

monobloque *nm Arg* tower block

monografía *nf* monograph

monográfico, -a 1 *adj* monographic
  2 *nm* monograph

monolingüe *adj* monolingual

monólogo *nm* monologue

monoparental *adj* **familia m.** one-parent o single-parent family

monopatín *nm Esp* skateboard

monopolio *nm* monopoly

monopolizar [40] *vt* to monopolize

monótono, -a *adj* monotonous

monovolumen *nm* people carrier

monserga *nf Esp Fam* drivel

monstruo *nm* (a) *(ser fantástico)* monster (b) *(genio)* genius

monstruoso, -a *adj* (a) *(repugnante)* monstrous (b) *(enorme)* massive, huge

monta *nf Fig* **de poca m.** of little importance

montacargas *nm inv Br* goods lift, *US* freight elevator

montado, -a 1 *adj (nata)* whipped
  2 *nm Esp (bocadillo)* = small piece of bread with a savoury topping

montador, -a *nm,f* (a) *(operario)* fitter (b) *Cin & TV* film editor

montaje *nm* (a) *Téc (instalación)* fitting; *(ensamblaje)* assembling; **cadena de m.** assembly line (b) *Cin* editing and mounting (c) *Teatro* staging (d) *Fot* montage (e) *Fam (farsa)* farce

montante *nm Fin* amount

montaña *nf* mountain; **m. rusa** big dipper

montañero, -a *nm,f* mountaineer

montañismo *nm* mountaineering

montañoso, -a *adj* mountainous

montar 1 *vi* (a) *(subirse)* to get on; *(en coche)* to get in; *(en bici, a caballo)* to ride (**b**) *Fin (ascender)* **m. a** to amount to, to come to

2 *vt* (**a**) *(colocar)* to put on (**b**) *(máquina etc)* to assemble; *(negocio)* to set up, to start (**c**) *Esp Culin (nata)* to whip (**d**) *Cin & Fot (película)* to edit, to mount; *(fotografía)* to mount (**e**) *Teatro (obra)* to stage, to mount (**f**) *Zool (cubrir)* to mount **3 montarse** *upr* (**a**) *(subirse)* to get on; *(en coche)* to get in (**en** to) (**b**) *Fam (organizarse)* **se montó un gran escándalo** there was a huge fuss (**c**) *Esp Fam* **montárselo bien** to have things (nicely) worked out *o* set up

monte *nm* (**a**) *(montaña)* mountain; *(con nombre propio)* mount; **de m.** wild (**b**) **el m.** *(zona)* the hills

montera *nf* bullfighter's hat

montés *adj (animal)* wild

montevideano, -a 1 *adj* of/from Montevideo

2 *nm,f* person from Montevideo

monto *nm* total

montón *nm* heap, pile; **un m. de** a load of; *Fam* **me gusta un m.** I really love it; *Fam* **del m.** run-of-the-mill, nothing special

montura *nf* (**a**) *(cabalgadura)* mount (**b**) *(de gafas)* frame

monumental *adj* (**a**) *(ciudad, lugar)* famous for its monuments (**b**) *(fracaso, éxito)* monumental

monumento *nm* monument

monzón *nm* monsoon

moño *nm* (**a**) *(de pelo)* bun (**b**) *Am (lazo)* bow (**c**) *Méx (pajarita)* bow tie

moquear *vi* to have a runny nose

moqueta *nf Esp* fitted carpet

mora *nf* blackberry

morado, -a 1 *adj* (**a**) purple; *Esp Fam* **pasarlas moradas** to have a tough time; *Esp Fam* **ponerse m.** to stuff oneself

2 *nm* purple

moral 1 *adj* moral

2 *nf* (**a**) *(ética)* morals (**b**) *(ánimo)* morale, spirits; **levantar la m. a algn** to raise sb's spirits

moraleja *nf* moral

moralista 1 *adj* moralistic

2 *nmf* moralist

moratón *nm* bruise

moratoria *nf* moratorium

morbo *nm Fam* morbid curiosity

morboso, -a *adj* morbid, ghoulish

morcilla *nf Br* black pudding, *US* blood sausage; *Esp Fam* **que te/os den m.** you can stuff it, then!

mordaz *adj* biting

mordaza *nf* gag

mordedura *nf* bite

morder [4] *vt* to bite; **me ha mordido** it bit me; *Fig* **m. el anzuelo** to take the bait

mordida *nf CAm, Méx Fam* bribe, *Br* backhander

mordisco *nm* bite

mordisquear *vt* to nibble (at)

moreno, -a 1 *adj* (**a**) *(pelo, piel)* dark (**b**) *(bronceado)* tanned; **ponerse m.** to get a suntan; **pan/azúcar m.** brown bread/ sugar

2 *nm,f (persona) (de pelo)* dark-haired person; *(de piel)* dark-skinned person

morera *nf Bot* white mulberry

moretón *nm* bruise

morfina *nf* morphine

morfinómano, -a 1 *nm,f* morphine addict

2 *adj* addicted to morphine

morgue *nf* morgue

moribundo, -a *adj* dying

morir [7] **1** *vi* to die; **m. de frío/hambre/ cáncer** to die of cold/hunger/cancer; **m. de amor** *o* **pena** to die from a broken heart **2 morirse** *upr* to die; **morirse de hambre** to starve to death; *Fig* to be starving; **morirse de aburrimiento** to be bored to death; **morirse de ganas (de hacer algo)** to be dying (to do sth); **morirse de risa** to die laughing

mormón, -ona *adj & nm,f* Mormon

moro, -a *nm,f* (**a**) *Hist* Moor; *Fam* **no hay moros en la costa** the coast is clear (**b**) *Esp Fam Pey (árabe)* Arab, = pejorative term referring to a North African or Arab person

morocho, -a *adj Andes, RP (moreno)* dark-haired

moronga *nf CAm, Méx Br* black pudding, *US* blood sausage

moroso, -a *nm,f* bad debtor

> ⎘ Observa que la palabra inglesa **morose** es un falso amigo y no es la traducción de la palabra española **moroso**. En inglés **morose** significa "hosco, huraño".

morral *nm (de cazador)* game bag

morralla *nf Pey (personas)* scum; *(cosas)* junk

morrear *vi Esp Fam* to smooch

morriña *nf Esp (por el país)* homesickness; *(por el pasado)* nostalgia

morro *nm* (**a**) *(de animal) (hocico)* snout (**b**) *Esp (de avión)* nose; *(de coche)* front (**c**) *Esp Fam* **morros** *(labios)* lips; *(boca)* mouth; **caerse de m.** to fall flat on one's face (**d**) *Esp Fam (caradura)* **¡qué m. tiene!** he's got a real nerve!

morrón *adj* pimiento m. (fleshy) red pepper

morsa *nf* walrus

morse *nm* Morse

mortadela *nf* mortadella

mortaja *nf* shroud

mortal 1 *adj (no inmortal)* mortal; *(caída, enfermedad)* fatal; *(aburrimiento, odio, enemigo)* deadly
  2 *nmf* mortal

mortalidad *nf* mortality; **índice de m.** death rate

mortandad *nf* death toll

mortecino, -a *adj* colourless

mortero *nm* Culin & Mil mortar

mortífero, -a *adj* deadly, lethal

mortificar [44] *vt* to mortify

mortuorio, -a *adj* death; **lecho m.** deathbed

moruno, -a *adj* Moorish; *Esp Culin* pincho m. = kebab of marinated pork

mosaico *nm* mosaic

mosca *nf* fly; peso m. flyweight; *Esp Fam* estar m. to be suspicious; *Fam* por si las moscas just in case; *Fam* ¿qué m. te ha picado? what's up with you?

moscada *adj* nuez m. nutmeg

moscardón *nm* (a) *(insecto)* blowfly (b) *Fam (pesado)* pest

moscatel *nm* Muscatel, = dessert wine made from muscat grapes; uvas de m. muscat grapes

moscovita *adj & nmf* Muscovite

Moscú *n* Moscow

mosquear 1 *vt* (a) *(enfadar)* m. a algn *Br* to get up sb's nose, *US* to tick sb off (b) *(hacer sospechar)* to make suspicious; me mosquea que no haya llamado todavía I'm a bit surprised he hasn't phoned yet
  2 mosquearse *vpr (enfadarse)* to get in a huff

mosqueo *nm Fam* tener un m. *(enfado)* to be hacked off; *(sospechas)* to be suspicious

mosquetero *nm Hist* musketeer

mosquitero *nm* mosquito net

mosquito *nm* mosquito

mostaza *nf Bot & Culin* mustard

mosto *nm (bebida)* grape juice; *(residuo)* must

mostrador *nm (en tienda)* counter; *(en bar)* bar; *(en aeropuerto, de información)* desk

mostrar 1 *vt* to show; **muéstramelo** show it to me
  2 mostrarse *vpr* to be; se mostró muy comprensiva she was very understanding

mota *nf* speck

mote¹ *nm* nickname

mote² *nm Andes* stewed *Br* maize *o US* corn

moteado, -a *adj* dotted

motel *nm* motel

motero, -a *nm,f Fam* biker

motín *nm (de tropas, en barco)* mutiny; *(en cárcel)* riot

motivación *nf* motivation

motivar *vt (impulsar)* to motivate; *(causar)* to cause

motivo *nm* (a) *(causa)* reason; *(usu pl)* grounds; con este o tal m. for this reason; con m. de on the occasion of; sin m. for no reason at all; bajo ningún m. under no circumstances (b) *Arte & Mús* motif, leitmotiv

moto *nf* motorbike, motorcycle; m. náutica *o* acuática jet ski

motocicleta *nf* motorbike, motorcycle

motociclismo *nm* motorcycling

motociclista *nmf* motorcyclist

motocross *nm* motocross

motoesquí *(pl* motoesquís *o* motoesquíes) *nm* snowbike

motoneta *nf Am (motor)* scooter

motonetista *nmf Am* scooter rider

motor, -a 1 *nm (grande)* engine; *(pequeño)* motor; m. de reacción jet engine; m. de explosión internal combustion engine; m. eléctrico electric motor; *Inform* m. de búsqueda search engine
  2 *adj Téc* motive

motora *nf* motorboat

motorista *nmf Esp* motorcyclist

motorizar [40] **1** *vt* to motorize
  2 motorizarse *vpr Fam* to get oneself a car/motorbike

motosierra *nf* power saw

motricidad *nf* motor function

motriz *adj* fuerza m. motive power

mouse [maus] *nm inv Am Inform* mouse

mousse [mus] *nf, Esp nm* mousse

movedizo, -a *adj* arenas movedizas quicksand

mover [4] **1** *vt* (a) *(desplazar)* to move; m. algo de su sitio to move sth out of its place (b) *(hacer funcionar)* to drive; el motor mueve el coche the engine drives the car (c) *(impulsar)* m. a algn a hacer algo to prompt sb to do sth
  2 moverse *vpr* (a) *(desplazarse)* to move (b) *(darse prisa)* to hurry up; ¡muévete! get a move on!

movida *nf Esp, RP Fam* hay mucha m. there's a lot going on

movido, -a adj (**a**) Fot blurred (**b**) (jornada, viaje) hectic

móvil 1 adj mobile; **teléfono m.** mobile phone; **TV & Rad unidad m.** outside broadcast unit
2 nm (**a**) (de delito) motive (**b**) (teléfono) mobile (**c**) (juguete) mobile

movilizar [40] vt to mobilize

movimiento nm (**a**) (desplazamiento, corriente) movement; Fís & Téc motion; (poner algo) **en m.** (to set sth) in motion; **m. sísmico** earth tremor (**b**) (actividad) activity (**c**) Com & Fin (entradas y salidas) operations

moviola nf editing projector

mozárabe 1 adj Mozarabic, = Christian in the time of Moorish Spain
2 nmf (habitante) Mozarab, = Christian of Moorish Spain
3 nm (idioma) Mozarabic

mozo, -a 1 nmf (**a**) (niño) young boy, young lad; (niña) young girl (**b**) Andes, RP (camarero) waiter; (camarera) waitress (**c**) Col (novio) boyfriend; (novia) girlfriend
2 nm (**a**) (de estación) porter; (de hotel) bellboy, US bellhop (**b**) Esp (recluta) conscript

mucamo, -a Andes, RP nm,f chamberperson; (mujer) chambermaid

muchacho, -a nm,f (hombre) boy; (mujer) girl

muchedumbre nf crowd

mucho, -a 1 adj (**a**) (singular) (usu en frases afirmativas) a lot of, lots of; (usu en frases negativas) much; **m. tiempo** a long time; **tengo m. sueño/mucha sed** I am very sleepy/thirsty; **hay m. tonto suelto** there are lots of idiots around; **¿bebes m. café?** – **no, no m.** do you drink a lot of coffee? – no, not much (**b**) (demasiado) **es m. coche para mí** this car is a bit too much for me (**c**) **muchos, -as** (usu en frases afirmativas) a lot of, lots of; (usu en frases neg) many; **tiene muchos años** he is very old
2 pron (**a**) (singular) a lot, a great deal; **¿cuánta leche queda?** – **mucha** how much milk is there left? – a lot (**b**) (plural) **muchos, -as** a lot, lots, many; **¿cuántos libros tienes?** – **muchos** how many books have you got? – lots or a lot; **muchos creemos que ...** many of us believe that ...
3 adv (**a**) (singular) a lot, very much; **lo siento m.** I'm very sorry; **como m.** at the most; **con m.** by far; **m. antes/después** long before/after; **¡ni mucho menos!** not by a long way!; **por m. (que)** (+ subjunctive) however much (**b**) (tiempo) **hace m. que no viene por aquí** he has not been to see us for a long time (**c**) (a menudo) often; **vamos m. al cine** we go to the cinema quite often

muda nf (ropa) change of underwear

mudanza nf move; **estar de m.** to be moving; **camión de m.** Br removal van, US moving van

mudar 1 vt (**a**) (ropa) to change (**b**) (plumas, pelo) to moult; (piel) to shed, to slough
2 mudarse vpr **mudarse de casa/ropa** to move house/to change one's clothes

mudéjar adj & nmf Mudejar

mudo, -a 1 adj (**a**) (que no habla) dumb; **cine m.** silent movies o Br films (**b**) (callado) speechless
2 nm,f mute

mueble 1 nm piece of furniture; **muebles** furniture; **con/sin muebles** furnished/ unfurnished; **m. bar** cocktail cabinet
2 adj Der **bienes muebles** personal property

mueca nf (gesto) face, expression; (de dolor) grimace; **hacer muecas** to pull faces

muela nf Anat molar; **dolor de muelas** toothache; **m. del juicio** wisdom tooth (**b**) Téc (de molino) millstone

muelle nm (**a**) (resorte) spring (**b**) (en puerto) dock, quay

muerdo nm Esp Fam bite

muermo nm Esp Fam **ser un m.** (situación) to be boring; (persona) to be a bore; **tener un m.** to be bored

muerte nf death; **m. natural** natural death; **dar m. a algn** to kill sb; **odiar a algn a m.** to loathe sb; Esp **de mala m.** badly; Fam **un susto de m.** the fright of one's life

muerto, -a 1 adj dead; **caer m.** to drop dead; **m. de hambre** starving; **m. de frío** frozen to death; **m. de miedo** scared stiff; **m. de risa** laughing one's head off; **horas muertas** spare time; Aut **(en) punto m.** (in) neutral
2 nm,f (**a**) (difunto) dead person; **hacerse el m.** to pretend to be dead; Fam **cargar con el m.** to do the dirty work (**b**) (víctima) fatality; **hubo dos muertos** two (people) died

muesca nf notch

muestra nf (**a**) (espécimen) sample, specimen (**b**) (prueba, señal) sign; **dar muestras de** to show signs of; **m. de cariño/respeto** token of affection/respect; **una m. más de ...** yet another example of ... (**c**) (modelo a copiar) model

muestreo nm sampling

mugido nm (de vaca) moo; (de toro) bellow

mugir [57] *vi (vaca)* to moo, to low; *(toro)* to bellow

mugre *nf* filth

mugriento, -a *adj* filthy

mujer *nf* (a) woman; **dos mujeres** two women; **m. de la limpieza** cleaner; **m. de su casa** houseproud woman (b) *(esposa)* wife; **su futura m.** his bride-to-be

mujeriego 1 *adj* woman-chasing
2 *nm* womanizer, woman chaser

mulato, -a *adj & nm,f* mulatto

muleta *nf* (a) *(prótesis)* crutch (b) *Taurom* muleta

muletilla *nf (frase)* pet phrase; *(palabra)* pet word

mullido, -a *adj* soft

mulo *nm* mule

multa *nf* fine; **poner una m. a algn** to fine sb

multar *vt* to fine

multicolor *adj* multicoloured

multilateral *adj* multilateral

multimedia *adj inv Inform* multimedia

multinacional *adj & nf* multinacional

múltiple *adj (variado)* multiple; **múltiples** *(numerosos)* many, numerous

multiplicación *nf* multiplication

multiplicar [44] **1** *vt & vi* to multiply (**por** by)
2 multiplicarse *vpr (reproducirse, aumentar)* to multiply

múltiplo, -a *adj & nm* multiple

multipropiedad *nf* time-sharing

multirriesgo *adj inv* **póliza m.** multiple risk policy

multitud *nf (de personas)* crowd; **m. de cosas** a huge number of things

multiusuario *adj inv* multi-user

mundano, -a *adj* worldly

> 🖉 Observa que la palabra inglesa **mundane** es un falso amigo y no es la traducción de la palabra española **mundano**. En inglés, **mundane** significa "prosaico".

mundial 1 *adj (política, economía, guerra)* world; *(tratado, organización, fama)* worldwide; **campeón m.** world champion; **de fama m.** world-famous
2 *nm* World Championship(s); *(en fútbol)* World Cup

mundialmente *adv* **m. famoso** world-famous, famous worldwide

mundo *nm* world; **todo el m.** everyone; **correr** *o* **ver m.** to travel widely; **nada del otro m.** nothing special; **el otro m.** the hereafter

munición *nf* ammunition

municipal 1 *adj* municipal
2 *nmf Esp* (local) policeman, *f* (local) policewoman

municipio *nm* (a) *(corporación)* local council (b) *(territorio)* town, municipality

muñeca *nf* (a) *(del cuerpo)* wrist (b) *(juguete, muchacha)* doll (c) *Andes, RP Fam* **tener m.** *(enchufe)* to have friends in high places; *(habilidad)* to have the knack (d) *Méx (mazorca)* baby sweetcorn

muñeco *nm (juguete)* doll; **m. de trapo** rag doll; **m. de nieve** snowman

muñeira *nf* = popular Galician dance and music

muñequera *nf* wristband

muñón *nm Anat* stump

mural 1 *adj (pintura)* mural; *(mapa)* wall
2 *nm* mural

muralla *nf* wall

Murcia *n* Murcia

murciélago *nm Zool* bat

murmullo *nm* murmur

murmuración *nf* gossip

murmurar *vi* (a) *(criticar)* to gossip (b) *(susurrar)* to whisper; *(refunfuñar)* to grumble (c) *Fig (río)* to murmur

muro *nm* wall

musa *nf* muse

musaraña *nf Fam* **estar pensando en las musarañas** to be daydreaming *o* in the clouds

musculación *nf* body-building

musculatura *nf* muscles

músculo *nm* muscle

musculoso, -a *adj* muscular

museo *nm (de ciencias, historia)* museum; *(de arte)* art gallery

musgo *nm* moss

música *nf* music; **m. clásica** classical music; **m. de fondo** background music

musical 1 *adj* musical
2 *nm* musical

músico, -a 1 *adj* musical
2 *nm,f* musician

muslo *nm (de persona)* thigh; *(de pollo, pavo) (entero)* leg; *(parte inferior)* drumstick

mustio, -a *adj* (a) *(plantas)* wilted, withered (b) *(persona)* sad, gloomy

musulmán, -ana *adj & nm,f* Muslim, Moslem

mutación *nf Biol* mutation

mutilación *nf* mutilation

mutilado, -a *nm,f* disabled person; **m. de guerra** disabled serviceman

mutilar *vt* to mutilate

mutis *nm inv Teatro* exit

mutismo *nm* silence

mutua *nf Br* friendly society, *US* mutual benefit society

mutual *nf CSur, Perú Br* friendly society, *US* mutual benefit society

mutualidad *nf Br* friendly society, *US* mutual benefit society

mutuo, -a *adj* mutual

muy *adv* very; **m. bueno/malo** very good/bad; **¡m. bien!** very good!; **M. señor mío** Dear Sir; **m. de los andaluces** typically Andalusian; **m. de mañana/noche** very early/late

N, n ['ene] *nf (letra)* N, n

N (*abr* **Norte**) N

nabo *nm* (**a**) *Bot* turnip (**b**) *muy Fam (pene)* tool, *Br* knob

nácar *nm* mother-of-pearl

nacer [60] *vi* (**a**) *(persona)* to be born; **nací en Salamanca** I was born in Salamanca; **al n.** at birth (**b**) *(pájaro)* to hatch (out) (**c**) *(pelo)* to begin to grow (**d**) *(río)* to rise

nacido, -a *adj* born

naciente *adj (sol)* rising

nacimiento *nm* (**a**) *(de persona, animal)* birth; **sordo de n.** deaf from birth; **lugar de n.** birthplace, place of birth (**b**) *Fig (principio)* origin, beginning; *(de río)* source (**c**) *(belén)* Nativity scene, crib

nación *nf* nation; **las Naciones Unidas** the United Nations

nacional 1 *adj (equipo, moneda, monumento)* national; *(mercado, vuelo)* domestic

2 *nmf* national; *Hist* **los nacionales** the Francoist forces

nacionalidad *nf* nationality

nacionalismo *nm* nationalism

nacionalista *adj & nmf* nationalist

nacionalizar [40] **1** *vt* (**a**) *Econ (banca, industria)* to nationalize (**b**) *(naturalizar)* to naturalize

2 **nacionalizarse** *vpr* to become naturalized; **n. español** to take up Spanish citizenship

nada 1 *pron* (**a**) *(como respuesta)* nothing; **¿qué quieres? – n.** what do you want? – nothing

(**b**) *(con verbo)* not … anything; *(enfático)* nothing; **no sé n.** I don't know anything; **yo no digo n.** I'm saying nothing

(**c**) *(con otro negativo)* anything; **no hace nunca n.** he never does anything; **nadie sabía n.** nobody knew anything

(**d**) *(en ciertas construcciones)* anything; **más que n.** more than anything; **sin decir n.** without saying anything; **casi n.** hardly anything

(**e**) **gracias – de n.** thanks – don't mention it; *Fam* **para n.** not at all; **casi n.** almost nothing; **como si n.** just like that; **un rasguño de n.** an insignificant little scratch; **n. de eso** nothing of the kind; **n. de n.** nothing at all; **n. más verla** as soon as he saw her

2 *adv* not at all; **no me gusta n.** I don't like it at all; **no lo encuentro n. interesante** I don't find it remotely interesting

3 *nf* nothingness; **salir de la n.** to come out of nowhere

nadador, -a *nm,f* swimmer

nadar *vi* (**a**) *Dep* to swim; **n. a braza** to do the breaststroke (**b**) *(flotar)* to float

nadie 1 *pron* (**a**) *(como respuesta)* no one, nobody; **¿quién vino? – n.** who came? – no one (**b**) *(con verbo)* not … anyone, not … anybody; *(enfático)* no one, nobody; **no conozco a n.** I don't know anyone *o* anybody; **no vi a n.** I didn't see anyone *o* anybody, I saw no one (**c**) *(con otro negativo)* anyone, anybody; **nunca habla con n.** he never speaks to anybody (**d**) *(en ciertas construcciones)* anybody, anyone; **más que n.** more than anyone; **sin decírselo a n.** without telling anyone; **casi n.** hardly anyone

2 *nm* nobody; **ser un don n.** to be a nobody

nado: a nado *loc adv* swimming; **cruzar** *o* **pasar a n.** to swim across

NAFTA *nm* (*abr* **North American Free Trade Agreement**) NAFTA

nafta *nf RP (gasolina) Br* petrol, *US* gas, *US* gasoline

nahua, náhuatl 1 *adj* Nahuatl

2 *nmf (individuo)* Nahuatl (Indian)

nailon *nm* nylon

naipe *nm* playing card

nalga *nf* buttock; **nalgas** bottom, buttocks

nana *nf* (**a**) *(canción)* lullaby (**b**) *Col, Méx (niñera)* nanny (**c**) *Col, Méx (nodriza)* wet nurse

napalm *nm* napalm

napias *nfpl Fam* snout

Nápoles *n* Naples

napolitano, -a *adj & nm,f* Neapolitan

naranja 1 *nf* orange; *Fig* **mi media n.** my better half

2 *adj & nm (color)* orange

naranjada *nf* orangeade

naranjo *nm* orange tree

narciso *nm* (a) *(blanco)* narcissus; *(amarillo)* daffodil (b) *Fig (hombre)* narcissist

narcótico *nm (somnífero)* narcotic; *(droga)* drug

narcotizar [40] *vt (drogar)* to drug

narcotraficante *nmf* drug trafficker

narcotráfico *nm* drug trafficking

nariz *nf* (a) *Anat* nose; *Fam* **me da en la n. que ...** I've got this feeling that ... (b) *Fam* **narices** nose; **en mis (propias) narices** right under my very nose; **estar hasta las narices de** to be fed up to the back teeth with; **meter las narices en algo** to poke one's nose into sth; *Esp* **tenemos que ir por narices** we have to go whether we like it or not; *Esp* **me estás hinchando las narices** you're beginning to get on my nerves

narración *nf* narration

narrador, -a *nm,f* narrator

narrar *vt* to narrate, to tell

narrativa *nf* narrative

narrativo, -a *adj & nf* narrative

nata *nf* (a) *Esp (crema de leche)* cream; **n. batida** o **montada** whipped cream (b) *(de leche hervida)* skin (c) *Fig* cream, best

natación *nf Dep* swimming

natal *adj* **mi país n.** my native country; **su pueblo n.** his home town

natalidad *nf* birth rate; **control de n.** birth control

natillas *nfpl Esp* custard

natividad *nf* Nativity

nativo, -a *adj & nm,f* native

nato, -a *adj* born

natura *nf Literario* nature; **contra n.** against nature

natural 1 *adj* natural; *(fruta, flor)* fresh; **de tamaño n.** life-size; **en estado n.** in its natural state; *Der* **hijo n.** illegitimate child
2 *nmf* native

naturaleza *nf* (a) nature; **en plena n.** in the wild, in unspoilt countryside; *Arte* **n. muerta** still life (b) *(complexión)* constitution

naturalidad *nf (sencillez)* naturalness; **con n.** naturally, straightforwardly

naturalismo *nm* naturalism

naturalista 1 *adj* naturalistic
2 *nmf* naturalist

naturalización *nf* naturalization

naturalizar [40] **1** *vt* to naturalize
2 naturalizarse *upr* to become naturalized

naturalmente *adv* naturally; **¡n.!** of course!

naturismo *nm* naturism

naturista *nmf* naturist

naufragar [42] *vi (barco)* to sink, to be wrecked; *(persona)* to be shipwrecked

naufragio *nm Náut* shipwreck

náufrago, -a *nm,f* shipwrecked person, castaway

náusea *nf (usu pl)* nausea, sickness; **me da n.** it makes me sick; **sentir náuseas** to feel sick

nauseabundo, -a *adj* nauseating, sickening

náutico, -a *adj* nautical

navaja *nf* (a) *(cuchillo)* penknife, pocketknife; **n. de afeitar** razor (b) *(molusco)* razor-shell

navajazo *nm* stab, gash

navajero *nm Fam* thug

naval *adj* naval

Navarra *n* Navarre

navarro, -a 1 *adj* Navarrese, of/from Navarre
2 *nm,f* person from Navarre

nave *nf* (a) *(barco)* ship; **n. (espacial)** spaceship, spacecraft (b) *Ind* plant, building (c) *(de iglesia)* nave; **n. lateral** aisle

navegable *adj* navigable

navegación *nf* navigation; **n. costera** coastal shipping

navegador *nm Inform* browser

navegar [42] *vi* (a) *(en barco)* to navigate, to sail (b) *Av* to navigate, to fly (c) **n. por Internet** to surf the Net

Navidad *nf* Christmas; **árbol de N.** Christmas tree; **Feliz N., Felices Navidades** Merry Christmas

navideño, -a *adj* Christmas

navío *nm* ship

nazareno, -a 1 *adj & nm,f* Nazarene
2 *nm* = penitent in Holy Week processions; **el N.** Jesus of Nazareth

nazi *adj & nmf* Nazi

nazismo *nm* Nazism

n/c., n/cta. *(abr* **nuestra cuenta)** our account, our acct

neblina *nf* mist, thin fog

nebulosa *nf Astron* nebula

nebuloso, -a *adj* (a) *Met* cloudy, hazy (b) *Fig* nebulous, vague

necedad *nf* (a) *(estupidez)* stupidity, foolishness (b) *(tontería)* stupid thing to say/to do

necesario, -a *adj* necessary; **es n. hacerlo** it has to be done; **es n. que vayas** you must go; **no es n. que vayas** there is no need for you to go; **si fuera n.** if need be

neceser *nm (de aseo)* toilet bag; *(de maquillaje)* make-up bag

necesidad *nf* (**a**) need; **tener n. de** to need; **artículos de primera n.** essentials; **por n.** of necessity (**b**) *(pobreza)* poverty, hardship (**c**) **hacer sus necesidades** to relieve oneself

necesitado, -a 1 *adj (pobre)* needy, poor; **n. de** in need of
2 *nm, f* needy *o* poor person; **los necesitados** the poor

necesitar *vt* to need; **se necesita chico** *(en anuncios)* boy wanted

necio, -a 1 *adj* (**a**) *(tonto)* silly, stupid (**b**) *Am (terco)* stubborn, pigheaded (**c**) *Méx (susceptible)* touchy
2 *nm,f* (**a**) *(tonto)* fool, idiot (**b**) *Am (terco)* stubborn *o* pigheaded person (**c**) *Méx (susceptible)* touchy person; **es un n.** he's really touchy

nécora *nf* = small edible crab

necrológica *nm,f* obituary

necrológico, -a *adj* **nota necrológica** obituary

néctar *nm* nectar

nectarina *nf* nectarine

neerlandés, -esa 1 *adj* Dutch, of/from the Netherlands
2 *nm, f (persona) (hombre)* Dutchman; *(mujer)* Dutchwoman; **los neerlandeses** the Dutch
3 *nm (idioma)* Dutch

nefasto, -a *adj* (**a**) *(perjudicial)* harmful (**b**) *(funesto)* unlucky, ill-fated (**c**) *(inútil)* hopeless

negación *nf* (**a**) *(lo contrario)* negation (**b**) *(negativa)* denial; *(rechazo)* refusal (**c**) *Ling* negative

negado, -a 1 *adj* **ser n. para algo** to be hopeless *o* useless at sth
2 *nm,f* no-hoper

negar [1] **1** *vt* (**a**) *(desmentir)* to deny; **negó haberlo robado** he denied stealing it (**b**) *(rechazar)* to refuse, to deny; **le negaron la beca** they refused him the grant
2 negarse *vpr* to refuse (**a** to)

negativa *nf* denial

negativo, -a *adj & nm* negative

negligencia *nf* negligence

negociable *adj* negotiable

negociación *nf* negotiation

negociado *nm Andes, RP (chanchullo)* shady deal

negociador, -a *adj* negotiating; **comité n.** negotiating committee

negociante *nmf* dealer; *(hombre)* businessman; *(mujer)* businesswoman

negociar [43] **1** *vt Fin & Pol* to negotiate
2 *vi (comerciar)* to do business, to deal

negocio *nm Com & Fin* business; *(transacción)* deal, transaction; *(asunto)* affair; **hombre de negocios** businessman; **mujer de negocios** businesswoman

negra *nf* (**a**) *Mús Br* crotchet, *US* quarter note (**b**) *(mala suerte)* **tener la n.** to be very unlucky

negrita *adj & nf Impr* bold (face)

negro, -a 1 *adj* (**a**) *(color)* black; **estar n.** *(bronceado)* to be suntanned (**b**) *Fig (suerte)* awful; *(porvenir)* black, gloomy; **verlo todo n.** to be very pessimistic; **vérselas negras para hacer algo** to have a tough time doing sth (**c**) *Fam (furioso)* furious, fuming; **me pone n.** it makes me mad
2 *nm,f (hombre)* black; *(mujer)* black (woman)
3 *nm (color)* black

nene, -a *nm,f (niño)* baby boy; *(niña)* baby girl

nenúfar *nm Bot* waterlily

neocelandés, -esa 1 *adj* of/from New Zealand
2 *nm,f* New Zealander

neoclásico, -a *adj Arte & Lit* neoclassic, neoclassical

neologismo *nm* neologism

neón *nm* neon

neoyorquino, -a 1 *adj* of/from New York
2 *nm,f* New Yorker

neozelandés, -esa *adj & nm,f* = **neocelandés**

nepotismo *nm* nepotism

Neptuno *n* Neptune

nervio *nm* (**a**) *Anat & Bot* nerve; *(de la carne)* sinew (**b**) *Fig (fuerza, vigor)* nerve, courage (**c**) **nervios** nerves; **ataque de nervios** fit of hysterics; **ser un manojo de nervios** to be a bundle of nerves; **tener los nervios de acero** to have nerves of steel

nerviosismo *nm* nerves

nervioso, -a *adj* nervous; **poner n. a algn** to get on sb's nerves

neto, -a *adj* (**a**) *(peso, cantidad)* net (**b**) *(nítido)* neat, clear

neumático, -a 1 *adj* pneumatic
2 *nm* tyre; **n. de recambio** spare tyre

neumonía *nf* pneumonia

neurálgico, -a *adj Med* neuralgic; *Fig* **centro n.** nerve centre

neurólogo, -a *nm,f* neurologist

neurosis *nf inv* neurosis

neurótico, -a *adj & nm,f* neurotic

neutral *adj* neutral

neutralidad *nf* neutrality

neutralizar [40] *vt* to neutralize

neutro, -a *adj* (a) *(imparcial)* neutral (b) *Ling* neuter

neutrón *nm Fís* neutron

nevada *nf* snowfall

nevar [1] *v impers* to snow

nevera *nf* (a) *(frigorífico)* refrigerator, *Br* fridge, *US* icebox (b) *(portátil)* cool box

nexo *nm* connection, link

ni *conj* (a) no … ni, ni … ni neither … nor, not … or; **no tengo tiempo ni dinero** I have got neither time nor money; **ni ha venido ni ha llamado** he hasn't come or phoned; **no vengas ni hoy ni mañana** don't come today or tomorrow (b) *(ni siquiera)* not even; **ni por dinero** not even for money; **ni se te ocurra** don't even think about it; **¡ni hablar!** no way!

Nicaragua *n* Nicaragua

nicaragüense *adj & nmf* Nicaraguan

nicho *nm* niche

nicotina *nf* nicotine

nido *nm* nest

niebla *nf* fog; **hay mucha n.** it is very foggy

nieto, -a *nm,f (niño)* grandson; *(niña)* granddaughter; **mis nietos** my grand-children

nieve *nf* (a) *Met* snow; *Culin* **batir a punto de n.** to beat until stiff (b) *Fam (cocaína)* snow (c) *Carib, Méx (dulce)* sorbet

nigeriano, -a *adj & nm,f* Nigerian

Nilo *n* **el N.** the Nile

nilón *nm Tex* nylon

nimio, -a *adj* insignificant, petty

ninfómana *nf* nymphomaniac

ninguno, -a 1 *adj* (a) *(con verbo)* not … any; **no leí ninguna revista** I didn't read any magazines; **no tiene ninguna gracia** it is not funny at all (b) **en ninguna parte** nowhere; **de ningún modo** no way

> **Ningún** is used instead of **ninguno** before masculine singular nouns (e.g. **ningún hombre** no man).

2 *pron* (a) *(persona)* nobody, no one; **n. lo vio** no one saw it; **n. de los dos** neither of the two; **n. de ellos** none of them (b) *(cosa)* not … any of them; *(enfático)* none of them; **no me gusta n.** I don't like any of them; **no vi n.** I saw none of them

niña *nf Anat* pupil; *Fig* **es la n. de sus ojos** she's the apple of his eye

niñera *nf* nursemaid, nanny

niñez *nf* infancy; *(a partir de los cuatro años)* childhood

niño, -a *nm,f* (a) *(crío) (varón)* child, boy; *(hembra)* child, girl; *(bebé)* baby; **de n.** as a child; **n. prodigio** child prodigy; *Pey* **n. bien** o **de papá** rich boy, rich kid; *Pey* **n.**

bonito o **mimado** mummy's/daddy's boy (b) **niños** children; *Fig* **juego de niños** child's play

nipón, -ona *adj & nm,f* Japanese; **los nipones** the Japanese

níquel *nm* nickel

niqui *nm Esp* polo shirt

níspero *nm (fruto)* medlar; *(árbol)* medlar tree

nítido, -a *adj (claro)* clear; *(imagen)* sharp

nitrógeno *nm* nitrogen

nitroglicerina *nf* nitroglycerine

nivel *nm* (a) *(altura)* level; **a n. del mar** at sea level (b) *(categoría)* standard; **n. de vida** standard of living (c) *(instrumento)* level; **n. de aire** spirit level (d) *Ferroc* **paso a n.** *Br* level crossing, *US* grade crossing

nivelar *vt* (a) *(allanar)* to level out o off (b) *(equilibrar)* to even out

no *(abr número)* no

no *(pl* noes*)* 1 *adv* (a) *(como respuesta)* no; **¿te gusta? – no** do you like it? – no (b) *(en otros contextos)* not; **no vi a nadie** I didn't see anyone; **aún no** not yet; **ya no** no longer, not any more; **no sin antes …** not without first …; **¿por qué no?** why not? (c) **no fumar/aparcar** *(en letrero)* no smoking/parking (d) **no sea que** (+ *subjunctive)* in case (e) **es rubia, ¿no?** she's blonde, isn't she?; **llegaron ayer, ¿no?** they arrived yesterday, didn't they? (f) *(como prefijo negativo)* non-; **la no violencia** non-violence

2 *nm* no; **un no rotundo** a definite no

noble 1 *adj* noble

2 *nmf (hombre)* nobleman; *(mujer)* noblewoman; **los nobles** the nobility

nobleza *nf* nobility

noche *nf* evening; *(después de las diez)* night, night-time; **de n.,** *Esp* **por la n.,** *Am* **en la n.** at night; **esta n.** tonight; **mañana por la n.** tomorrow night/evening; **buenas noches** *(saludo)* good evening; *(despedida)* good night; **son las nueve de la n.** it's nine p.m.

nochebuena *nf* Christmas Eve

nochero *nm* (a) *CSur (vigilante)* night watchman (b) *Col (mesilla de noche)* bedside table

nochevieja *nf* New Year's Eve

noción *nf* (a) *(concepto)* notion, idea (b) **nociones** smattering, basic knowledge; **nociones de español** a smattering of Spanish

nocivo, -a *adj* noxious, harmful

noctámbulo, -a *nm,f* sleepwalker; *Fam* nightbird

nocturno, -a *adj* (**a**) night; **vida nocturna** night life; **clases nocturnas** evening classes (**b**) *Bot & Zool* nocturnal

nodriza 1 *nf* wet nurse
2 *adj* **buque/avión n.** refuelling ship/plane

nogal *nm Bot* walnut (tree)

nómada 1 *adj* nomadic
2 *nmf* nomad

nombrado, -a *adj* (*célebre*) famous, well-known

nombramiento *nm* appointment

nombrar *vt* (**a**) (*designar*) to name, to appoint; **n. a algn director** to appoint sb director (**b**) (*mencionar*) to name, to mention

nombre *nm* (**a**) (*apelativo*) name; **n. de pila** Christian name; **n. y apellidos** full name; **a n. de** (*carta*) addressed to; (*cheque*) made out to; **en n. de** on behalf of (**b**) *Ling* noun; **n. propio** proper noun

nomeolvides *nm inv* (**a**) (*flor*) forget-me-not (**b**) (*pulsera*) identity bracelet

nómina *nf* (**a**) (*de sueldo*) pay slip (**b**) (*plantilla*) payroll

nominar *vt* to nominate

nominativo, -a *adj* **cheque n.** a cheque made out to

non *nm* (**a**) *Mat* odd number; **pares y nones** odds and evens (**b**) *Fam* **nones** (*negación*) no; **decir (que) nones** to refuse

nono, -a *adj* = **noveno**

norcoreano, -a *adj & nm,f* North Korean

nordeste *nm* = **noreste**

nórdico, -a 1 *adj* (**a**) (*del norte*) northern (**b**) (*escandinavo*) Nordic
2 *nm,f* Nordic person

noreste *nm* northeast

noria *nf* (**a**) *Esp* (*de feria*) *Br* big wheel, *US* Ferris wheel (**b**) (*para agua*) water wheel

norirlandés, -esa 1 *adj* Northern Irish
2 *nm,f* (*persona*) (*hombre*) Northern Irishman; (*mujer*) Northern Irishwoman; **los norirlandeses** the Northern Irish

norma *nf* (*patrón, modelo*) standard; (*regla*) rule

normal *adj* normal, usual; **lo n.** the normal thing, what usually happens

normalidad *nf* normality; **volver a la n.** to return to normal

normalizar [40] **1** *vt* to normalize, to restore to normal
2 normalizarse *vpr* to return to normal

normativa *nf* rules

noroeste *nm* northwest

norte *nm* (**a**) (*geográfico*) north; **al n. de** to the north of (**b**) (*meta*) aim, goal

norteafricano, -a *adj & nm,f* North African

Norteamérica *n* North America

norteamericano, -a *adj & nm,f* (North) American

norteño, -a 1 *adj* northern
2 *nm,f* Northerner

Noruega *n* Norway

noruego, -a 1 *adj* Norwegian
2 *nm,f* Norwegian
3 *nm* (*idioma*) Norwegian

nos 1 *pron pers* (*directo*) us; (*indirecto*) (to) us; **n. ha visto** he has seen us; **n. trajo un regalo** he brought us a present; **n. lo dio** he gave it to us
2 *pron* (*reflexivo*) ourselves; (*recíproco*) each other; **n. hemos divertido mucho** we enjoyed ourselves a lot; **n. queremos mucho** we love each other very much

nosotros, -as *pron pers pl* (**a**) (*sujeto*) we; **n. lo vimos** we saw it; **somos n.** it is us (**b**) (*complemento*) us; **con n.** with us

> Usually omitted in Spanish except for emphasis or contrast.

nostalgia *nf* nostalgia; (*morriña*) homesickness

nostálgico, -a *adj* nostalgic; (*con morriña*) homesick

nota *nf* (**a**) (*anotación*) note (**b**) (*calificación*) *Br* mark, *US* grade; **sacar** *o* **tener buenas notas** to get good *Br* marks *o US* grades (**c**) *Fig* (*detalle*) element, quality; **la n. dominante** the prevailing quality (**d**) *Mús* note; *Fam* **dar la n.** to make oneself noticed

notable 1 *adj* (*apreciable*) noticeable; (*destacado*) outstanding, remarkable
2 *nm* (*nota*) very good

notar 1 *vt* (*percibir*) to notice, to note
2 notarse *vpr* to be noticeable *o* evident, to show; **no se nota** it doesn't show; **se nota que …** one can see that …

notaría *nf* (*despacho*) notary's office

notarial *adj* notarial; **acta n.** affidavit

notario, -a *nm,f* notary (public), solicitor

noticia *nf* news *sing*; **una n.** a piece of news; **una buena n.** good news; **no tengo n. de esto** I don't know anything about it

> 🖉 Observa que la palabra inglesa **notice** es un falso amigo y no es la traducción de la palabra española **noticia**. En inglés **notice** significa "aviso, anuncio".

noticiario, *Am* **noticiero** *nm* (**a**) *Cin* newsreel (**b**) *Rad & TV* television news

notificación *nf* notification; **sin n. previa** without (previous) notice; *Der* **n. judicial** summons *sing*

notificar [44] *vt* to notify

notorio, -a *adj* (a) *(evidente)* obvious, evident (b) *(famoso)* famous, well-known

> 🔎 Observa que la palabra inglesa **notorious** es un falso amigo y no es la traducción de la palabra española **notorio**. En inglés, **notorious** significa "tristemente célebre".

novatada *nf* (a) *(broma)* rough joke, rag (b) **pagar la n.** to learn the hard way

novato, -a 1 *adj (persona)* inexperienced; *Fam* green
  2 *nm,f* (a) *(principiante)* novice, beginner (b) *Univ* fresher

novecientos, -as *adj & nm* nine hundred

novedad *nf* (a) *(cosa nueva)* novelty; **últimas novedades** latest arrivals (b) *(cambio)* change, development (c) *(cualidad)* newness

novedoso, -a *adj* (a) *(nuevo)* new, full of novelties (b) *(innovador)* innovative

novel 1 *adj* new, inexperienced
  2 *nmf* beginner, novice

novela *nf Lit* novel; **n. corta** short story; **n. policíaca** detective story

novelero, -a *adj* fond of new things

novelesco, -a *adj* (a) *(de novela)* novelistic, fictional (b) *(extraordinario)* bizarre, fantastic

novelista *nmf* novelist

noveno, -a *adj & nm* ninth; **novena parte** ninth

noventa *adj & nm inv* ninety

novia *nf* (a) *(amiga)* girlfriend (b) *(prometida)* fiancée (c) *(en boda)* bride

noviar *vi CSur, Méx Fam* **n. con algn** to go out with sb, *US* to date sb; **novian hace tiempo** they've been going out together *o US* dating for a while

noviazgo *nm* engagement

noviembre *nm* November

novillada *nf Taurom* = bullfight with young bulls

novillero, -a *nm,f Taurom* apprentice matador

novillo, -a *nm,f* (a) *(toro)* young bull; *(vaca)* young cow (b) *Esp Fam* **hacer novillos** to play *Br* truant *o US* hookey

novio *nm* (a) *(amigo)* boyfriend (b) *(prometido)* fiancé (c) *(en boda)* bridegroom; **los novios** the bride and groom

nubarrón *nm Fam* storm cloud

nube *nf* cloud; *Fig* **vivir en las nubes** to have one's head in the clouds; *Fig* **poner a algn por las nubes** to praise sb to the skies

nublado, -a *adj* cloudy, overcast

nublarse *vpr* to become cloudy, to cloud over; *Fig* **se le nubló la vista** his eyes clouded over

nubosidad *nf* cloudiness, clouds

nuboso, -a *adj* cloudy

nuca *nf* nape, back of the neck

nuclear *adj* nuclear; **central n.** nuclear power station

núcleo *nm* nucleus; *(parte central)* core; **n. urbano** city centre

nudillo *nm (usu pl)* knuckle

nudismo *nm* nudism

nudista *adj & nmf* nudist

nudo *nm* (a) *(lazo)* knot; **hacer un n.** to tie a knot; *Fig* **se me hizo un n. en la garganta** I got a lump in my throat (b) *(de comunicaciones)* junction

nuera *nf* daughter-in-law

nuestro, -a 1 *adj pos* (a) *(antes del sustantivo)* our; **nuestra familia** our family (b) *(después del sustantivo)* of ours; **un amigo n.** a friend of ours
  2 *pron pos* ours; **este libro es n.** this book is ours

nuevamente *adv* again

Nueva Zelanda *n* New Zealand

nueve *adj & nm inv* nine

nuevo, -a 1 *adj* (a) new; *Fam* **¿qué hay de n.?** what's new?; **de n.** again; **Nueva York** New York; **Nueva Zelanda** New Zealand (b) *(adicional)* further
  2 *nm,f* newcomer; *(principiante)* beginner

nuez *nf* (a) *(fruto)* walnut; **n. moscada** nutmeg (b) *Anat* **n. (de Adán)** Adam's apple

nulidad *nf* (a) *(ineptitud)* incompetence (b) *Der* nullity

nulo, -a *adj* (a) *(inepto)* useless, totally incapable (b) *(sin valor)* null and void, invalid; **voto n.** invalid vote (c) **crecimiento n.** zero growth

núm. *(abr número)* no

numeral *adj & nm* numeral

numerar *vt* to number

numerario, -a 1 *adj* **profesor no n.** teacher on a temporary contract
  2 *nm (miembro)* full member

numérico, -a *adj* numerical

número *nm* (a) *(signo)* number; **n. de matrícula** *Br* registration number, *US* license number; **n. de serie** serial number; *Fig* **sin n.** countless (b) *(de zapatos)* size (c) *Prensa* number, issue; **n. atrasado** back number (d) *(en espectáculo)* sketch, act; *Fam* **montar un n.** to make a scene

numeroso, -a *adj* numerous

numismática *nf* *(estudio)* numismatics *sing*

nunca *adv* (**a**) *(como respuesta)* never; **¿cuándo volverás? – n.** when will you come back? – never (**b**) *(con verbo)* never; *(enfático)* not … ever; **no he estado n. en España** I've never been to Spain; **yo no haría n. eso** I wouldn't ever do that (**c**) *(en ciertas construcciones)* ever; **casi n.** hardly ever; **más que n.** more than ever (**d**) **n. jamás** never ever; *(futuro)* never again

nupcial *adj* wedding, nuptial; **marcha n.** wedding march

nupcias *nfpl* *Fml* wedding, nuptials; **casarse en segundas n.** to marry again

nutria *nf* otter

nutrición *nf* nutrition

nutricionista *nmf* nutritionist

nutrir 1 *vt* to nourish, to feed
2 nutrirse *upr* to feed (**de** *o* **con** on)

nutritivo, -a *adj* nutritious, nourishing; **valor n.** nutritional value

ñandutí *nm Par* fine lace
ñapa *Ven Fam nf* bonus, extra; **ni de ñ.** no way
ñato, -a *adj Andes, RP* snub-nosed

ñoñería, ñoñez *nf* inanity
ñoño, -a *adj* (**a**) *(remilgado)* squeamish; *(quejica)* whining (**b**) *(soso)* dull, insipid
ñoqui *nm Culin* gnocchi

O, o [o] *nf (letra)* O, o

O. *(abr* **Oeste)** W

o *conj* or; **jueves o viernes** Thursday or Friday; **o ... o** either ... or; **o sea** that is (to say), in other words

---

u is used instead of **o** in front of words beginning with "o" or "ho" (e.g. **mujer u hombre** woman or man). Note that **ó** (with acute accent) is used between figures.

---

oasis *nm inv* oasis

obcecado, -a *adj* stubborn

obcecar [44] **1** *vt* to blind; **la ira lo obceca** he is blinded by anger

   2 obcecarse *vpr* to become stubborn; **obcecarse en hacer algo** to stubbornly insist on doing sth

obedecer [33] **1** *vt* to obey

   2 *vi* **o. a** *(provenir)* to be due to; **¿a qué obedece esa actitud?** what's the reason behind this attitude?

obediencia *nf* obedience

obediente *adj* obedient

obertura *nf* overture

obesidad *nf* obesity

obeso, -a *adj* obese

óbice *nm* obstacle; **eso no es ó. para que yo no lo haga** it won't prevent me from doing it

obispo *nm* bishop

objeción *nf* objection; **poner una o.** to raise an objection, to object

objetar *vt* to object to

objetividad *nf* objectivity

objetivo, -a 1 *nm* (a) *(fin, meta)* objective, aim (b) *Mil* target (c) *Cin & Fot* lens; **o. zoom** zoom lens
   2 *adj* objective

objeto *nm* (a) *(cosa)* object; **objetos perdidos** lost property, *US* lost and found; **mujer o. sex** object (b) *(fin)* aim, purpose; **con o. de ...** in order to ...; **tiene por o. ...** it is designed to ... (c) *Ling* object

objetor, -a *nm,f* objector; **o. de conciencia** conscientious objector

obligación *nf* (a) *(deber)* obligation; **por o.** out of a sense of duty; **tengo o. de ...** I have to ... (b) *Fin* bond, security

obligado, -a *adj* obliged; **verse** *o* **estar o. a** to be obliged to

obligar [42] *vt* to compel, to force

obligatorio, -a *adj* compulsory, obligatory

obra *nf* (a) *(trabajo)* (piece of) work; **por o. de** thanks to (b) *Arte* work; **o. maestra** masterpiece (c) *(acto)* deed (d) *Constr* building site (e) **obras** *(arreglos)* repairs; **carretera en obras** *(en letrero)* roadworks; **cerrado por obras** *(en letrero)* closed for repairs

obrar 1 *vi* (a) *(proceder)* to act, to behave; **o. bien/mal** to do the right/wrong thing (b) *Fml* **obra en nuestro poder ...** we are in receipt of ...
   2 *vt (milagro)* to work

obrero, -a 1 *nm,f* worker, labourer
   2 *adj* working; **clase obrera** working class; **movimiento o.** labour movement

obscenidad *nf* obscenity

obsceno, -a *adj* obscene

obscurecer [33] *v impers, vt & vpr* = oscurecer

obscuridad *nf* = oscuridad

obscuro, -a *adj* = oscuro

obsequiar [43] *vt Esp* **o. a algn con algo,** *Am* **o. algo a algn** to present sb with sth

obsequio *nm* gift, present

observación *nf* observation

observador, -a 1 *nm,f* observer
   2 *adj* observant

observancia *nf* observance

observar *vt* (a) *(mirar)* to observe, to watch (b) *(notar)* to notice (c) *(cumplir)* to observe

observatorio *nm* observatory

obsesión *nf* obsession

obsesionar 1 *vt* to obsess; **estoy obsesionado con eso** I can't get it out of my mind
   2 obsesionarse *vpr* to get obsessed

obsesivo, -a *adj* obsessive

obseso, -a *nm,f* obsessed person; **un o. sexual** a sex maniac

obsoleto, -a *adj* obsolete

obstaculizar [40] *vt* to obstruct, to get in the way of

obstáculo *nm* obstacle

obstante *adv* **no o.** nevertheless, however

obstetricia *nf* obstetrics *sing*

obstinación *nf* obstinacy

obstinado, -a *adj* obstinate

obstinarse *upr* to persist (**en** in)

obstrucción *nf* obstruction; *Med* blockage

obstruir [37] **1** *vt* (**a**) *(salida, paso)* to block, to obstruct (**b**) *(progreso)* to impede, to block
  2 obstruirse *upr* to get blocked up

obtención *nf* obtaining

obtener [24] **1** *vt* *(alcanzar)* to obtain, to get
  2 obtenerse *upr* **obtenerse de** *(provenir)* to come from

obturador *nm Fot* shutter

obtuso, -a *adj* obtuse

obús *nm* shell

obviar [43] *vt* *(problema)* to get round

obvio, -a *adj* obvious

oca *nf* goose

ocasión *nf* (**a**) *(momento)* occasion; **con o. de ...** on the occasion of ...; **en cierta o.** once (**b**) *(oportunidad)* opportunity, chance; **aprovechar una o.** to make the most of an opportunity (**c**) *Com* bargain; **de o.** cheap; **precios de o.** bargain prices

ocasional *adj* (**a**) *(eventual)* occasional; **trabajo o.** casual work; **de forma o.** occasionally (**b**) *(fortuito)* accidental, chance

ocasionar *vt* to cause, to bring about

ocaso *nm* *(anochecer)* sunset; *Fig (declive)* fall, decline

occidental *adj* western, occidental

occidente *nm* west; **el O.** the West

OCDE *nf* (*abr* **Organización para la Cooperación y el Desarrollo Económico**) OECD

Oceanía *n* Oceania

oceánico, -a *adj* oceanic

océano *nm* ocean

ochenta *adj & nm inv* eighty

ocho *adj & nm inv* eight

ochocientos, -as *adj & nm* eight hundred

ocio *nm* leisure; **en mis ratos de o.** in my spare *o* leisure time

ocioso, -a *adj* (**a**) *(inactivo)* idle (**b**) *(inútil)* pointless

ocre *nm* ochre

octavilla *nf (panfleto)* handout, leaflet

octavo, -a *adj & nm,f* eighth

octogenario, -a *adj & nm,f* octogenarian

octogésimo, -a *adj & nm,f* eightieth

octubre *nm* October

ocular *adj* **testigo o.** eye witness

oculista *nmf* ophthalmologist

ocultar **1** *vt* to conceal, to hide; **o. algo a algn** to hide sth from sb
  2 ocultarse *upr* to hide

oculto, -a *adj* concealed, hidden

ocupación *nf* occupation

ocupado, -a *adj (persona)* busy; *(asiento)* taken; *(teléfono) Br* engaged, *US* busy; *(lavabo)* engaged; *(puesto de trabajo)* filled

ocupante *nmf (de casa)* occupant, occupier; *(ilegal)* squatter; *(de vehículo)* occupant

ocupar **1** *vt* (**a**) *(invadir) (territorio, edificio)* to occupy (**b**) *(espacio, tiempo)* to take up; *(cargo)* to hold, fill (**c**) *CAm, Méx (usar, emplear)* to use
  2 ocuparse *upr* **ocuparse de** *(cuidar)* to look after; *(encargarse)* to see to

ocurrencia *nf (agudeza)* witty remark, wisecrack; *(idea)* bright idea

> *Observa que la palabra inglesa* **occurrence** *es un falso amigo y no es la traducción de la palabra española* **ocurrencia**. *En inglés,* **occurrence** *significa "suceso, incidencia".*

ocurrente *adj* witty

ocurrir **1** *v impers* to happen, to occur; **¿qué ocurre?** what's going on?; **¿qué te ocurre?** what's the matter with you?
  2 ocurrirse *upr* **no se me ocurre nada** I can't think of anything; **se me ocurre que ...** it occurs to me that ...

odiar [43] *vt* to detest, to hate; **odio tener que ...** I hate having to ...

odio *nm* hatred, loathing; **mirada de o.** hateful look

odioso, -a *adj* hateful

odontología *nf* dentistry, odontology

odontólogo, -a *nm,f* dental surgeon, odontologist

odre *nm* wineskin

OEA *nf* (*abr* **Organización de Estados Americanos**) OAS

oeste *nm* west

ofender **1** *vt* to offend
  2 ofenderse *upr* to be offended (**por** by), to take offence (**por** at)

ofensa *nf* offence

ofensiva *nf* offensive

ofensivo, -a *adj* offensive

oferta *nf* offer; *Fin & Ind* bid, tender, proposal; *Com* **de** o **en o.** on (special) offer; **o. y demanda** supply and demand

ofertar *vt* to offer

off *adj* **voz en o.** *Cin & TV* voice-over; *Teatro* voice offstage

offset *nm Impr* offset

oficial 1 *adj* official
2 *nmf* (**a**) *Mil & Náut* officer (**b**) *(empleado)* clerk (**c**) *(obrero)* skilled worker

oficialismo *nm Am* (**a**) **el o.** *(gobierno)* the Government (**b**) **el o.** *(partidarios del gobierno)* government supporters

oficialista *Am* **1** *adj* pro-government
2 *nm,f* government supporter

oficina *nf* office; **o. de empleo** *Br* job centre, *US* job office; **o. de turismo** tourist office; **o. de correos** post office; **horas/ horario de o.** office hours

oficinista *nmf* office worker, clerk

oficio *nm* (**a**) *(ocupación)* job, occupation; *(profesión)* trade; **ser del o.** to be in the trade (**b**) *(comunicación oficial)* official letter o note; **de o.** ex-officio; **abogado de o.** state-appointed lawyer (**c**) *Rel* service

oficioso, -a *adj (noticia, fuente)* unofficial

> 🖉 Observa que la palabra inglesa **officious** es un falso amigo y no es la traducción de la palabra española **oficioso**. En inglés, **officious** significa "excesivamente celoso o diligente".

ofimática *nf* office automation

ofrecer [33] **1** *vt* (**a**) *(dar)* to offer (**b**) *(tener) (aspecto, dificultades)* to present
2 ofrecerse *vpr* (**a**) *(prestarse)* to offer, to volunteer (**b**) *(situación)* to present itself (**c**) *Fml* **¿qué se le ofrece?** what can I do for you?

ofrecimiento *nm* offering

ofrendar *vt Rel* to offer up

ofrezco *indic pres de* **ofrecer**

oftalmología *nf* ophthalmology

oftalmólogo, -a *nm,f* ophthalmologist

ofuscación *nf*, **ofuscamiento** *nm* blindness

ofuscar [44] *vt* (**a**) *(confundir)* to blind (**b**) *(deslumbrar)* to dazzle

ogro *nm también Fig* ogre

oídas: de oídas *loc adv* by hearsay

oído *nm* (**a**) *(sentido)* hearing (**b**) *(órgano)* ear; **aprender de o.** to learn by ear; *Fig* **hacer oídos sordos** to turn a deaf ear

oír [17] *vt* to hear; **¡oye!** hey!; **¡oiga!** excuse me!; *Fam* **como lo oyes** believe it or not

ojal *nm* buttonhole

ojalá 1 *interj* let's hope so!, I hope so!
2 *conj* (+ *subjunctive*) **¡o. sea cierto!** I hope it's true!

ojeada *nf* **echar una o.** to have a quick look

ojeras *nfpl* rings o bags under the eyes

ojeriza *nf* dislike

ojo 1 *nm* (**a**) *(para ver)* eye; **o. morado** black eye; **ojos saltones** bulging eyes; *Fig* **a ojos vista** clearly, openly; *Fig* **calcular a o.** to guess; *Fam* **no pegué o.** I didn't sleep a wink (**b**) *(de aguja)* eye; *(de cerradura)* keyhole (**c**) *(de un puente)* span
2 *interj* careful!, look out!

ojota *nf* (**a**) *Andes (zapatilla)* sandal (**b**) *RP (chancleta)* *Br* flip-flop, *US, Austr* thong

okupa *nmf Esp Fam* squatter

ola *nf* wave; **o. de calor** heat wave

ole, olé *interj* bravo!

oleada *nf* wave; *Fig* **o. de turistas** influx of tourists

oleaje *nm* swell

óleo *nm Arte* oil; **pintura** o **cuadro al ó.** oil painting

oleoducto *nm* (oil) pipeline

oler [65] **1** *vt* (**a**) *(percibir olor)* to smell (**b**) *Fig (adivinar)* to smell, to feel
2 *vi* (**a**) *(exhalar)* to smell; **o. a** to smell of; **o. bien/mal** to smell good/bad (**b**) *Fig (parecer)* to smack (**a** of)
3 olerse *vpr Fig (adivinar)* to feel, to sense; **me lo olía** I thought as much

olfatear *vt* (**a**) *(oler)* to sniff (**b**) *Fig (indagar)* to pry into

olfato *nm* sense of smell; *Fig* good nose, instinct

oligarquía *nf* oligarchy

olimpiada *nf Dep* Olympiad, Olympic Games; **las olimpiadas** the Olympic Games

olímpicamente *adv Fam* **paso o. de estudiar** I couldn't give a damn about studying

olímpico, -a *adj* Olympic; **Juegos Olímpicos** Olympic Games

oliva *nf* olive; **aceite de o.** olive oil

olivar *nm* olive grove

olivo *nm* olive (tree)

olla *nf* saucepan, pot; **o. exprés** o **a presión** pressure cooker

olmo *nm* smooth-leaved elm

olor *nm* smell; **o. corporal** body odour

oloroso, -a *adj* fragrant, sweet-smelling

OLP *nf (abr* **Organización para la Liberación de Palestina**) PLO

olvidadizo, -a *adj* forgetful

olvidar 1 *vt* (**a**) *(hecho, dato, persona)* to forget; *Fam* **¡olvídame!** leave me alone!

(**b**) *(dejarse)* to leave; **olvidé el paraguas allí** I left my umbrella there

2 olvidarse *upr* to forget; **se me ha olvidado hacerlo** I forgot to do it

olvido *nm* (**a**) *(desmemoria)* oblivion (**b**) *(lapsus)* oversight

ombligo *nm* navel

ominoso, -a *adj* abominable

omisión *nf* omission

omiso, -a *adj* **hacer caso o. de** to take no notice of

omitir *vt* to omit, to leave out

ómnibus (*pl* **ómnibus** *o* **ómnibuses**) *nm* Cuba, Urug *(urbano)* bus; Andes, Cuba, Urug *(interurbano, internacional)* Br coach, US bus

omnipotente *adj* omnipotent, almighty

omnipresente *adj* omnipresent

omnisciente *adj* omniscient, all-knowing

omnívoro, -a 1 *adj* omnivorous
2 *nm,f* omnivore

omoplato *nm* shoulder blade

OMS *nf (abr* **Organización Mundial de la Salud)** WHO

ONCE *nf (abr* **Organización Nacional de Ciegos Españolas)** ≃ RNIB

once *adj & nm inv* eleven

onda *nf* (**a**) *Fís* wave; *Fam Fig* **estar en la o.** to be with it; **o. expansiva** shock wave; *Rad* **o. larga/media/corta** long/medium/ short wave (**b**) *(en el agua)* ripple (**c**) *(de pelo)* wave (**d**) *Méx, RP* **¿qué o.?** *(¿qué tal?)* how's it going?, how are things?; *Méx, RP* **captar** *o* **agarrar la onda** *(entender)* to catch the drift

ondear *vi (bandera)* to flutter

ondulación *nf (onda)* ripple; *(del pelo)* wave

ondulado, -a *adj (pelo)* wavy; *(paisaje)* rolling

ondulante *adj* undulating

ondular 1 *vt (pelo)* to wave
2 *vi (moverse)* to undulate

oneroso, -a *adj (impuesto)* heavy

ONG *nf inv (abr* **Organización no Gubernamental)** NGO

onomástica *nf* saint's day

onomatopeya *nf* onomatopoeia

ONU *nf (abr* **Organización de las Naciones Unidas)** UN

onubense 1 *adj* of/from Huelva
2 *nmf* person from Huelva

onza *nf (medida)* ounce

OPA *nf (abr* **Oferta Pública de Adquisición)** takeover bid

opaco, -a *adj* opaque

ópalo *nm* opal

opción *nf* (**a**) *(elección)* option, choice; *(alternativa)* alternative (**b**) *(posibilidad)* opportunity, chance

opcional *adj* optional

open *nm Dep* open

OPEP *nf (abr* **Organización de los Países Exportadores de Petróleo)** OPEC

ópera *nf Mús* opera

operación *nf* (**a**) *Med* operation; **o. quirúrgica** surgical operation (**b**) *Fin* transaction, deal; **operaciones bursátiles** stock exchange transactions (**c**) *Mat* operation

operador, -a *nm,f* (**a**) *(técnico)* operator (**b**) *Cin (de cámara) (hombre)* cameraman; *(mujer)* camerawoman; *(del proyector)* projectionist (**c**) *Tel* operator

operante *adj* operative

operar 1 *vt* (**a**) *Med* **o. a algn (de algo)** to operate on sb (for sth) (**b**) *(cambio etc)* to bring about
2 *vi Fin* to deal, to do business (**con** with)
3 operarse *upr* (**a**) *Med* to have an operation (**de** for) (**b**) *(producirse)* to occur, to come about

operario, -a *nm,f* operator; *(obrero)* worker

operativo, -a 1 *adj* operative
2 *nm* operation

opereta *nf* operetta

opinar 1 *vt (pensar)* to think
2 *vi (declarar)* to give one's opinion

opinión *nf (juicio)* opinion; **cambiar de o.** to change one's mind

opio *nm* opium

oponente *nmf* opponent

oponer [19] *(pp* **opuesto) 1** *vt (resistencia)* to offer
2 oponerse *upr (estar en contra)* to be opposed; **se opone a aceptarlo** he refuses to accept it

oporto *nm (vino)* port

oportunidad *nf* opportunity, chance

oportunista *adj & nmf* opportunist

oportuno, -a *adj* (**a**) *(adecuado)* timely; **¡qué o.!** what good timing! (**b**) *(conveniente)* appropriate; **si te parece o.** if you think it appropriate

oposición *nf* (**a**) *(resistencia)* opposition (**b**) *(examen)* = competitive examination for public sector jobs (**c**) *Pol* **la o.** the opposition

opositar *vi* = to sit a competitive public examination

opositor, -a *nm,f* (**a**) *(candidato)* = candidate in a competitive public examination (**b**) *Am Pol* opponent

opresión nf oppression; **o. en el pecho** tightness of the chest

opresivo, -a adj oppressive

opresor, -a 1 nm,f oppressor
2 adj oppressive, oppressing

oprimir vt (a) *(pulsar)* to press (b) *(subyugar)* to oppress

oprobio nm ignominy, opprobrium

optar vi (a) *(elegir)* to choose (**entre** between); **opté por ir yo mismo** I decided to go myself (b) *(aspirar)* to apply (**a** for); **puede o. a medalla** he's in with a chance of winning a medal

optativo, -a adj optional, *US* elective

óptica nf (a) *(tienda)* optician's (shop) (b) *(punto de vista)* angle

óptico, -a 1 adj optical
2 nm,f optician

optimismo nm optimism

optimista 1 adj optimistic
2 nmf optimist

óptimo, -a adj optimum, excellent

opuesto, -a 1 adj (a) *(contrario)* contrary; **en direcciones opuestas** in opposite directions; **gustos opuestos** conflicting tastes (b) *(de enfrente)* opposite; **el extremo o.** the other end
2 pp de **oponer**

opulencia nf opulence

opulento, -a adj opulent

opuse pt indef de **oponer**

oración nf (a) *Rel* prayer (b) *Ling* clause, sentence

oráculo nm oracle

orador, -a nm,f speaker, orator

oral adj oral; *Med* **por vía o.** to be taken orally

órale interj *Méx Fam* (a) *(venga)* come on! (b) *(de acuerdo)* right!, OK!

orangután nm orang-outang, orang-utan

orar vi *Rel* to pray

oratoria nf oratory

órbita nf (a) *(de planeta)* orbit (b) *Anat* eye socket

orca nf killer whale

orden 1 nm order; **o. público** law and order; **por o. alfabético** in alphabetical order; **de primer o.** first-rate; **o. del día** agenda; **del o. de** approximately
2 nf (a) *(mandato)* order; *Mil* **¡a la o.!** sir! (b) *Der* warrant, order; **o. de registro** search warrant; **o. judicial** court order

ordenado, -a adj tidy

ordenador nm *Esp* computer; **o. personal** personal computer

ordenamiento nm ordering

ordenanza 1 nm *(empleado)* office boy
2 nf regulations; **o. municipal** bylaw

ordenar 1 vt (a) *(organizar)* to put in order; *(habitación)* to tidy up (b) *(mandar)* to order (c) *Am (pedir)* to order
2 ordenarse upr *Rel* to be ordained (**de** as), take holy orders

ordeñar vt to milk

ordinario, -a adj (a) *(corriente)* ordinary, common (b) *(grosero)* vulgar, common

orégano nm oregano, marjoram

oreja nf ear; *(de sillón)* wing

orfanato nm orphanage

orfebre nmf *(del oro)* goldsmith; *(de la plata)* silversmith

orfebrería nf gold/silver work

orfelinato nm orphanage

orgánico, -a adj organic

organigrama nm organization chart; *Inform* flow chart

organillo nm barrel organ

organismo nm (a) *(ser vivo)* organism (b) *(institución)* organization, body

organización nf organization

organizado, -a adj organized; **viaje o.** package tour

organizador, -a 1 adj organizing
2 nm,f organizer

organizar [40] **1** vt to organize
2 organizarse upr *(persona)* to organize oneself

órgano nm organ

orgasmo nm orgasm

orgía nf orgy

orgullo nm (a) *(propia estima)* pride (b) *(arrogancia)* arrogance

orgulloso, -a adj (a) **estar o.** *(satisfecho)* to be proud (b) **ser o.** *(arrogante)* to be arrogant o haughty

orientación nf (a) *(dirección)* orientation, direction (b) *(guía)* guidance; **curso de o.** induction course

oriental 1 adj (a) *(del este)* eastern, oriental; *(del Lejano Oriente)* oriental (b) *Am (uruguayo)* Uruguayan
2 nmf (a) *(del Lejano Oriente)* oriental (b) *Am (uruguayo)* Uruguayan

orientar 1 vt (a) *(enfocar)* to aim (**a** at), to intend (**a** for); **orientado al consumo** intended for consumption (b) *(indicar camino)* to give directions to; *Fig (aconsejar)* to advise (c) **una casa orientada al sur** a house facing south (d) *(esfuerzo)* to direct
2 orientarse upr *(encontrar el camino)* to get one's bearings, to find one's way about

oriente *nm* East, Orient; **el Extremo** *o* **Lejano/Medio/Próximo O.** the Far/Middle/Near East

orificio *nm* hole, opening; *Anat & Téc* orifice; **o. de entrada** inlet; **o. de salida** outlet

origen *nm* origin; **país de o.** country of origin; **dar o. a** to give rise to

original *adj & nm* original

originalidad *nf* originality

originar 1 *vt* to cause, to give rise to
2 originarse *vpr* to originate

originariamente *adv* originally

originario, -a *adj* native

orilla *nf* *(borde)* edge; *(del río)* bank; *(del mar)* shore

orillero, -a *adj* *RP, Ven* common, low-class

orín[1] *nm* *(herrumbre)* rust

orín[2] *nm* orines *(orina)* urine

orina *nf* urine

orinal *nm* chamberpot; *Fam* potty

orinar 1 *vi* to urinate
2 orinarse *vpr* to wet oneself

oriundo, -a *adj* ser o. de to come from

orla *nf* *Univ* graduation photograph

ornamento *nm* ornament

ornar *vt* to adorn, to embellish

ornato *nm* *(atavío)* finery; *(adorno)* decoration

ornitología *nf* ornithology

ornitólogo, -a *nm,f* ornithologist

oro *nm* **(a)** *(metal)* gold; **de o.** gold, golden; **o. de ley** pure *o* real gold, standard gold **(b)** *Naipes* oros = suit in Spanish deck of cards, with the symbol of a gold coin

orquesta *nf* orchestra; *(de verbena)* dance band

orquestar *vt* to orchestrate

orquídea *nf* orchid

ortiga *nf* (stinging) nettle

ortodoxia *nf* orthodoxy

ortodoxo, -a *adj* orthodox

ortografía *nf* spelling, orthography; **faltas de o.** spelling mistakes

ortográfico, -a *adj* spelling; **signos ortográficos** punctuation

ortopédico, -a *adj* orthopaedic; **pierna ortopédica** artificial leg

oruga *nf* caterpillar

orzuelo *nm* *Med* sty, stye

os *pron pers pl* **(a)** *(complemento directo)* you; **os veo mañana** I'll see you tomorrow **(b)** *(complemento indirecto)* you, to you; **os daré el dinero** I'll give you the money; **os escribiré** I'll write to you **(c)** *(con verbo reflexivo)* yourselves **(d)** *(con verbo*

recíproco) each other; **os queréis mucho** you love each other very much

osa *nf* **O. Mayor** *Br* Great Bear, *US* Big Dipper; **O. Menor** *Br* Little Bear, *US* Little Dipper

osadía *nf* **(a)** *(audacia)* daring **(b)** *(desvergüenza)* impudence

osado, -a *adj* **(a)** *(audaz)* daring **(b)** *(desvergonzado)* shameless

osar *vi* to dare

osario *nm* ossuary

Óscar *nm Cin* Oscar

oscilación *nf* **(a)** *Fís* oscillation **(b)** *(de precios)* fluctuation

oscilar *vi* **(a)** *Fís* to oscillate **(b)** *(variar)* to vary, to fluctuate

oscuras: a oscuras *loc adv* in the dark; **nos quedamos a o.** we were left in darkness

oscurecer [33] **1** *v impers* to get dark
2 *vt* to darken
3 oscurecerse *vpr* to darken

oscuridad *nf* darkness; *Fig* obscurity

oscuro, -a *adj* **(a)** *(sin luz)* dark **(b)** *(origen, idea)* obscure; *(asunto)* shady; *(nublado)* overcast

óseo, -a *adj* osseous, bony; **tejido ó.** bone tissue

osito *nm Fam* **o. (de peluche)** teddy bear

ósmosis, osmosis *nf inv* osmosis

oso *nm* bear; **o. polar** polar bear; **o. hormiguero** anteater; **o. marino** fur seal; *Fam Fig* **hacer el o.** to play the fool

osobuco *nm Culin* osso bucco

ostensible *adj* ostensible

ostentación *nf* ostentation; **hacer o. de algo** to show sth off

ostentar *vt* **(a)** *(lucir)* to flaunt **(b)** *(cargo)* to hold

ostentoso, -a *adj* ostentatious

osteópata *nmf* osteopath

osteopatía *nf* osteopathy

ostión *nm* **(a)** *Méx (ostra)* Portuguese oyster, Pacific oyser **(b)** *Chile (vieira)* scallop

ostra *nf* oyster; *Fig* **aburrirse como una o.** to be bored stiff; *Esp Fam* **¡ostras!** *Br* crikey!, *US* gee!

ostracismo *nm* ostracism

OTAN *nf* *(abr* **Organización del Tratado del Atlántico Norte)** NATO

otear *vt (horizonte)* to scan, to search

OTI *nf (abr* **Organización de Televisiones Iberoamericanas)** = association of all Spanish-speaking television networks

otitis *nf inv* infection and inflammation of the ear, *Espec* otitis

otoñal *adj* autumn, autumnal, *US* fall

otoño *nm* autumn, *US* fall

otorgamiento *nm (concesión)* granting; *(de un premio)* awarding

otorgar [42] *vt* (**a**) *(premio)* to award (**a** to); **o. un indulto** to grant pardon (**b**) *(permiso)* to grant (**a** to)

otorrino, -a *nm,f Fam* ear, nose and throat specialist

otorrinolaringólogo, -a *nm,f* ear, nose and throat specialist

otro, -a 1 *adj indef* (**a**) *(sin artículo) (singular)* another; *(plural)* other; **o. coche** another car; **otras personas** other people (**b**) *(con artículo definido)* other; **el o. coche** the other car (**c**) *otra cosa* something else; **otra vez** again

2 *pron indef* (**a**) *(sin artículo) (sing)* another (one); *(pl) (personas)* others; *(cosas)* other ones; **dame o.** give me another (one); **no es mío, es de o.** it's not mine, it's somebody else's (**b**) *(con artículo definido) (sing)* **el o./la otra** the other (one); *(pl) (personas)* **los otros/las otras** the others; *(cosas)* the other ones (**c**) **hacer o. tanto** to do likewise

ovación *nf* ovation

ovacionar *vt* to give an ovation to, to applaud

oval, ovalado, -a *adj* oval

óvalo *nm* oval

ovario *nm* ovary

oveja *nf* sheep; *(hembra)* ewe; *Fig* **la o. negra** the black sheep

overol *nm Am (de peto) Br* dungarees, *US* overalls; *(completo)* overalls, *Br* boilersuit

ovillo *nm* ball (of wool); *Fig* **hacerse un o.** to curl up into a ball

ovino, -a *adj* ovine; **ganado o.** sheep *pl*

OVNI *nm (abr* **objeto volador no identificado)** UFO

ovular 1 *adj* ovular
   2 *vi* to ovulate

óvulo *nm* ovule

oxidación *nf Quím* oxidation; *(de metal)* rusting

oxidado, -a *adj* rusty

oxidar 1 *vt Quím* to oxidize; *(metal)* to rust
   2 oxidarse *vpr Quím* to oxidize; *(metal)* to go rusty

óxido *nm* (**a**) *Quím* oxide; **ó. de carbono** carbon monoxide (**b**) *(herrumbre)* rust

oxigenado, -a *adj* oxygenated; **agua oxigenada** (hydrogen) peroxide

oxígeno *nm* oxygen; **bomba de o.** oxygen cylinder *o* tank

oye *indic pres & imperat de* **oír**

oyente *nmf* (**a**) *Rad* listener (**b**) *Univ Br* occasional student, *US* auditing student

ozono *nm* ozone; **capa de o.** ozone layer

P

P, p [pe] *nf (letra)* P, p

pabellón *nm* (a) p. de deportes sports centre (b) *(en feria)* stand (c) *(bloque)* wing (d) *(bandera)* flag

pábulo *nm Fml* dar p. a to encourage

pacer [60] *vt & vi* to graze, to pasture

pachá *nm Fam* vivir como un p. to live like a king

pachanguero, -a *adj Fam Pey (música)* catchy

pacharán *nm* = liqueur made from brandy and sloes

pachorra *nf Fam* tener p. to be phlegmatic

paciencia *nf* patience; **armarse de p.** to grin and bear it

paciente *adj & nmf* patient

pacificación *nf* pacification

pacificador, -a 1 *adj* pacifying
2 *nm,f* peacemaker

pacificar [44] **1** *vt* to pacify; *Fig (apaciguar)* to appease, to calm
2 pacificarse *vpr* to calm down

Pacífico *nm* el (océano) P. the Pacific (Ocean)

pacífico, -a *adj* peaceful

pacifismo *nm* pacifism

pacifista *adj & nmf* pacifist

pack [pak] *(pl* packs*)* *nm* pack; **un p. de seis** a six-pack

paco, -a *nm,f Andes, Pan Fam (policía)* cop

pacotilla *nf Fam* de p. second-rate

pactar *vt* to agree to

pacto *nm* pact; **el P. de Varsovia** the Warsaw Pact; **p. de caballeros** gentlemen's agreement

padecer [33] *vt & vi* to suffer; **padece del corazón** he suffers from heart trouble

padecimiento *nm* suffering

padrastro *nm* (a) *(hombre)* stepfather (b) *(pellejo)* hangnail

padrazo *nm* easy-going *o* indulgent father

padre 1 *nm* (a) *(hombre)* father; **p. de familia** family man (b) **padres** parents
2 *adj Fam* (a) *Esp (tremendo)* huge; **fue el cachondeo p.** it was a great laugh (b) *Méx (genial)* great, fantastic

padrenuestro *nm* Lord's Prayer

padrino *nm* (a) *(de bautizo)* godfather; *(de boda)* best man; **padrinos** godparents (b) *(espónsor)* sponsor

padrísimo, -a *adj Méx Fam* fantastic, great

padrón *nm* census

padrote *nm* (a) *Méx Fam (proxeneta)* pimp (b) *CAm, Ven (caballo)* stallion

paella *nf* paella, = rice dish made with vegetables, meat and/or seafood

paellera *nf* paella pan

pág. *(abr* página*)* p

paga *nf (salario)* wage; *(de niños)* pocket money, *US* allowance; **p. extra** bonus

pagadero, -a *adj* payable; *Fin* **cheque p. al portador** cheque payable to bearer

pagado, -a *adj* paid

pagano, -a *adj & nm,f* pagan, heathen

pagar [42] *vt (persona, factura)* to pay; *(gastos, delito)* to pay for; *(deuda)* to pay off, to settle; *(ayuda, favor)* to repay; **p. en metálico** *o* **al contado** to pay cash; **p. por** *(producto, mala acción)* to pay for; *Fig* **lo ha pagado caro** he's paid dearly for it

pagaré *nm Fin* promissory note, IOU; **p. del tesoro** treasury note

página *nf* page; **en la p. 3** on page 3; *Fig* **una p. importante de la historia** an important chapter in history; *Inform* **p. personal** home page; *Inform* **p. de inicio** home page; *Inform* **p. web** web page

pago *nm* payment; **p. adelantado** *o* **anticipado** advance payment; **p. contra reembolso** cash on delivery; **p. inicial** down payment; **p. por visión** pay-per-view

paila *nf Andes, CAm, Carib (sartén)* frying pan

paipái *(pl* paipáis*)*, **paipay** *(pl* paipays*)* *nm* = large palm fan

país *nm* country, land; **vino del p.** local wine; **los Países Bajos** the Netherlands; **P. Vasco** Basque Country; **P. Valenciano** Valencia

paisaje *nm* landscape, scenery

paisano, -a 1 *adj* of the same country
2 *nm,f (compatriota)* fellow countryman/ countrywoman, compatriot; **en traje de p.** in plain clothes

paja nf (**a**) (*hierba, caña*) straw (**b**) Fig (*relleno*) padding, waffle (**c**) Vulg **hacerse una o** Am **la p.** to jerk off, Br to have a wank

pajar nm hayloft

pajarita nf (**a**) Esp (*corbata*) bow tie (**b**) (*de papel*) paper bird

pájaro nm bird; **Madrid a vista de p.** a bird's-eye view of Madrid; **p. carpintero** woodpecker

paje nm page

pajita nf (drinking) straw

Pakistán n Pakistan

pakistaní adj & nmf Pakistani

pala nf (**a**) (*herramienta*) spade; (*para recoger*) shovel; (*de cocina*) slice (**b**) Dep (*de ping-pong, frontón*) bat, US paddle; (*de remo*) blade

palabra nf (**a**) (*vocablo*) word; **de p.** by word of mouth; **dirigir la p. a algn** to address sb; **juego de palabras** pun (**b**) (*promesa*) word; **p. de honor** word of honour (**c**) (*turno para hablar*) right to speak; **tener la p.** to have the floor

palabrería nf Fam hot air, talk

palabrota nf swearword

palacio nm (*grande*) palace; (*pequeño*) mansion; **P. de Justicia** Law Courts

paladar nm (**a**) (*en la boca*) palate (**b**) (*sabor*) taste

paladear vt to savour, to relish

palanca nf (**a**) (*barra, mando*) lever; Aut **p. de cambio** Br gear lever, gearstick, US gearshift, stick shift; **p. de mando** joystick (**b**) (*trampolín*) diving board

palangana nf Br washbasin, US washbowl

palco nm box

paleolítico, -a adj palaeolithic, paleolithic

paleontología nf palaeontology, paleontology

Palestina n Palestine

palestino, -a adj & nm,f Palestinian

palestra nf arena; Fig **salir o saltar a la p.** to enter the fray, to take the field

paleta nf (**a**) (*espátula*) slice (**b**) (*de pintor*) palette; (*de albañil*) trowel (**c**) Dep (*de pingpong*) bat, US paddle (**d**) Andes, CAm, Méx (*piruli*) lollipop; Bol, Col, Perú (*polo*) Br ice lolly, US Popsicle®

paletilla nf Culin shoulder

paleto, -a Esp Fam Pey **1** adj unsophisticated, boorish

2 nm,f country bumpkin, yokel

paliar [43] vt to alleviate, to palliate

paliativo, -a adj & nm palliative

palidecer [33] vi (**a**) (*persona*) to turn pale (**b**) Fig (*perder importancia*) to pale, to fade

palidez nf paleness, pallor

pálido, -a adj pale

palillero nm toothpick case

palillo nm (**a**) (*mondadientes*) toothpick; **palillos chinos** chopsticks (**b**) Mús drumstick

palio nm canopy

palique nm Fam chat, small talk

paliza nf (**a**) (*zurra*) thrashing, beating; **darle a algn una p.** to beat sb up (**b**) (*derrota*) beating (**c**) Fam (*pesadez*) bore, pain (in the neck)

palma nf (**a**) Anat palm (**b**) Bot palm tree (**c**) **hacer palmas** to applaud

palmada nf (**a**) (*golpe*) slap (**b**) **palmadas** applause, clapping

palmar vi Fam to kick the bucket, to snuff it

palmarés (pl **palmareses**) nm (**a**) (*historial*) record (**b**) (*vencedores*) list of winners

palmatoria nf candlestick

palmera nf palm tree

palmo nm (*medida*) span; Fig **p. a p.** inch by inch

palo nm (**a**) (*de madera*) stick; (*vara*) rod; (*de escoba*) broomstick; Fig **a p. seco** on its own (**b**) (*golpe*) blow; Fig **dar un p. a algn** to let sb down (**c**) **de p.** wooden (**d**) Dep (*de portería*) woodwork (**e**) (*de golf*) club (**f**) Naipes suit

paloma nf pigeon; Lit dove; **p. mensajera** homing o carrier pigeon

palomar nm pigeon house, dovecot

palomilla nf wing o butterfly nut

palomitas nfpl **p. (de maíz)** popcorn

palpable adj palpable

palpar vt to touch, to feel; Med to palpate

palpitación nf beating; (*con fuerza*) throbbing; Med **palpitaciones** palpitations

palpitante adj (**a**) (*corazón*) beating; (*con fuerza*) throbbing (**b**) (*cuestión*) burning

palpitar vi to beat; (*con fuerza*) to throb

palta nf Andes, RP (*fruto*) avocado

palúdico, -a adj malarial

paludismo nm malaria

palurdo, -a adj uncouth, boorish

pamela nf broad-brimmed hat

pampa nf pampa, pampas

pamplinas nfpl Fam nonsense

pan nm bread; **p. de molde** packaged sliced bread; **p. integral** Br wholemeal o US wholewheat bread; **p. rallado** breadcrumbs pl; **p. dulce** Méx (*bollo*) bun; RP (*panetone*) panettone; Arg **p. lactal** sliced bread; Fam Fig **más bueno que el p.** as good as gold; *Fam Fig* **es p. comido** it's a piece of cake

pana *nf* corduroy

panacea *nf* panacea

panadería *nf* baker's (shop), bakery

panadero, -a *nm,f* baker

panal *nm* honeycomb

Panamá *n* Panama

panamá *nm (sombrero)* Panama hat

panameño, -a *adj & nm,f* Panamanian

pancarta *nf* placard; *(en manifestación)* banner

pancho *nm RP* hot dog

páncreas *nm inv* pancreas

panda 1 *adj* **oso p.** panda
   2 *nm* panda
   3 *nf Esp (de amigos)* crowd, gang; *(de gamberros, delincuentes)* gang

pandereta *nf* tambourine

pandilla *nf Fam* gang

panecillo *nm* bread roll

panel *nm* panel

panera *nf (para guardar) Br* bread bin, *US* bread box; *(para servir)* bread basket

pánfilo, -a *adj Fam (bobo)* silly, stupid; *(crédulo)* gullible

panfleto *nm* lampoon, political pamphlet

pánico *nm* panic; **sembrar el p.** to cause panic

panocha *nf (de maíz)* ear, cob

panorama *nm (vista)* panorama, view; *(situación)* overall state; *(perspectiva)* outlook

panorámica *nf* panorama

panorámico, -a *adj* panoramic

panqueque *nm Am* pancake

pantaleta *nf,* **pantaletas** *nfpl CAm, Carib, Méx (bragas)* panties, *Br* knickers

pantalla *nf (a) Cin,TV & Inform* screen *(b) (de lámpara)* shade *(c) Fig* **servir de p.** to act as a decoy

pantalón *nm (usu pl)* trousers, *US* pants; **p. vaquero** jeans

pantano *nm Geog (a) (natural)* marsh, bog *(b) (artificial)* reservoir

panteón *nm* pantheon, mausoleum; **p. familiar** family vault

pantera *nf* panther

pantimedias *nfpl Méx Br* tights, *US* pantyhose

pantomima *nf Teatro* pantomime, mime; *Pey (farsa)* farce

pantorrilla *nf Anat* calf

pants *nmpl Méx (traje)* tracksuit, jogging suit; *(pantalón)* tracksuit bottoms *o US* pants

pantufla *nf* slipper

panty *(pl* **pantis***) nm Br* tights, *US* pantyhose

> 🔎 Observa que la palabra inglesa **panties** es un falso amigo y no es la traducción de la palabra española **panty**. En inglés **panties** significa "bragas".

panza *nf Fam* belly, paunch

panzada *nf Fam* bellyful

pañal *nm Br* nappy, *US* diaper; *Fam Fig* **estar en pañales** to be in its infancy

paño *nm (tela)* cloth, material; *(de lana)* woollen cloth; *(para polvo)* duster, rag; *(de cocina) Br* tea towel, *US* dish towel; *Fig* **paños calientes** half-measures; **en paños menores** in one's underclothes

pañoleta *nf* shawl

pañuelo *nm (de nariz)* handkerchief; *(para el cuello)* scarf; *(para la cabeza)* headscarf; **p. de papel** tissue, paper handkerchief

Papa *nm* **el P.** the Pope

papa *nf esp Am* potato; *Fam* **no saber ni p. (de algo)** not to have the faintest idea (about sth)

papá *nm Fam* dad, daddy, *US* pop

papachar *vt Méx* to cuddle, to pamper

papada *nf* double chin

papagayo *nm (a) (animal)* parrot *(b) Carib, Méx (cometa)* kite

papalote *nm CAm, Méx* kite

papamoscas *nm inv* flycatcher

papanatas *nmf inv* sucker, twit

paparrucha *nf (piece of)* nonsense

papaya *nf* papaya *o* pawpaw fruit

papear *vt & vi Esp, Ven Fam* to eat, to scoff

papel *nm (a) (material)* paper; *(hoja)* piece *o* sheet of paper; **p. higiénico** toilet paper; **p. carbón** *o RP* **carbónico** carbon paper; **p. de carta** writing paper, stationery; *Chile* **p. confort** toilet paper; **p. de alumimio/de estraza** aluminium foil/brown paper; **p. de fumar** cigarette paper; **p. de lija** sandpaper; **p. moneda** paper money, banknotes *pl*; **p. pintado** wallpaper; *Cuba* **p. sanitario** toilet paper; **p. secante** blotting paper; *Guat,Ven* **p. toilette** *o* **tualé** toilet paper *(b) Cin & Teatro* role, part *(c)* **papeles** *(documentos)* documents, identification papers; **los sin papeles** undocumented immigrants

papeleo *nm Fam* paperwork

papelera *nf (a) (en despacho)* wastepaper basket *o Br* bin; *(en calle) Br* litter bin, *US* garbage can *(b) Inform (en Windows)* recycle bin; *(en Macintosh) Br* wastebasket, *US* trash can

papelería *nf (tienda)* stationer's (shop)

papeleta *nf* (a) *(de rifa)* ticket; *(de votación)* ballot paper; *(de resultados)* report (b) *Fam (dificultad)* tricky problem, difficult job

papeo *nm Fam* grub

paperas *nfpl Med* mumps *sing*

papilla *nf (de niños)* baby food, *US* formula

papista *adj & nmf* papist

Papúa Nueva Guinea *n* Papua New Guinea

paquete *nm* (a) *(de cigarrillos etc)* pack, packet; *(postal)* parcel, package (b) *(conjunto)* set, package; *Fin* **p. de acciones** share package (c) *Inform* software package (d) *Fam (castigo)* punishment (e) *Esp muy Fam (genitales)* packet, bulge

Paquistán *n* Pakistan

paquistaní *(pl paquistaníes) adj & nmf* Pakistani

par 1 *adj Mat* even
2 *nm* (a) *(pareja)* pair; *(dos)* couple (b) *Mat* even number; **pares y nones** odds and evens (c) *(noble)* peer (d) *(locuciones)* **a la p.** *(a la vez)* at the same time; **de p. en p.** wide open; *Fig* **sin p.** matchless

para *prep* (a) *(finalidad)* for; **bueno p. la salud** good for your health; **¿p. qué?** what for?; **p. que lo disfrutes** for you to enjoy (b) *(con infinitivo)* to, in order to; **p. terminar antes** to o in order to finish earlier (c) *(tiempo)* by; **p. entonces** by then (d) *(comparación)* **p. ser inglés habla muy bien español** for an Englishman he speaks very good Spanish (e) *(expresiones)* **decir p. sí** to say to oneself; **ir p. viejo** to be getting old; **no es p. tanto** it's not as bad as all that; **p. mí** in my opinion

parábola *nf* (a) *Geom* parabola (b) *Rel* parable

parabólica *nf* satellite dish

parabólico, -a *adj* parabolic; *TV* **antena parabólica** satellite dish

parabrisas *nm inv Br* windscreen, *US* windshield

paracaídas *nm inv* parachute

paracaidista *nmf Dep* parachutist; *Mil* paratrooper

parachoques *nm inv* bumper, *US* fender

parada *nf* (a) *(detención)* stop; **p. de autobús** bus stop; **p. de taxis** taxi stand o rank (b) *Ftb* save, stop

paradero *nm* (a) *(lugar)* whereabouts *sing* (b) *Chile, Col, Méx, Perú (de autobús)* stop

parado, -a 1 *adj* (a) *(inmóvil) (vehículo)* stationary, standing; *(persona)* still,

motionless; *(fábrica)* at a standstill (b) *Esp (desempleado)* unemployed, out of work (c) *Esp (pasivo)* **ser muy p.** to lack initiative (d) *Am (en pie)* standing (e) *Chile, PRico (orgulloso)* vain, conceited (f) **salir bien/mal p.** to come off well/badly
2 *nm,f Esp* unemployed person

paradoja *nf* paradox

paradójico, -a *adj* paradoxical

parador *nm* roadside inn; **p. (nacional)** = state-owned luxury hotel, usually a building of historic or artistic importance

parafernalia *nf* paraphernalia *pl*

parafrasear *vt* to paraphrase

paráfrasis *nf inv* paraphrase

paragolpes *nmpl inv RP* bumper, *US* fender

paraguas *nm inv* umbrella

Paraguay *n* Paraguay

paraguayo, -a 1 *adj & nm,f* Paraguayan
2 *nm (fruta)* = fruit similar to peach

paragüero *nm* umbrella stand

paraíso *nm* (a) *(lugar perfecto)* paradise; **p. terrenal** heaven on earth; *Fin* **p. fiscal** tax haven (b) *Teatro* gods, gallery

paraje *nm* spot, place

paralelo, -a *adj & nm* parallel

parálisis *nf inv* paralysis; **p. infantil** poliomyelitis

paralítico, -a *adj & nm,f* paralytic

paralización *nf* (a) *Med* paralysis (b) *(detención)* halting, stopping

paralizar [40] **1** *vt* to paralyse
2 **paralizarse** *vpr (producción, proyecto)* to come to a standstill

parámetro *nm* parameter

paramilitar *adj* paramilitary

páramo *nm* bleak plain o plateau, moor

parangón *nm Fml* comparison; **sin p.** incomparable

paranoia *nf* paranoia

paranoico, -a *adj & nm,f* paranoiac, paranoid

parapente *nm (desde montaña)* paragliding, parapenting

parapeto *nm* parapet

parapléjico, -a *adj & nm,f* paraplegic

parar 1 *vt* (a) *(detener)* to stop (b) *Dep* to save (c) *Am (levantar)* to raise
2 *vi* (a) to stop; **p. de hacer algo** to stop doing sth; **sin p.** nonstop, without stopping; *Fam* **no p.** to be always on the go (b) *(acabar)* **fue a p. a la cárcel** he ended up in jail
3 **pararse** *vpr* (a) to stop; **p. a pensar** to stop to think (b) *Am (ponerse en pie)* to stand up

pararrayos nm inv lightning rod o conductor

parásito, -a 1 adj parasitic
2 nm parasite

parasol nm sunshade, parasol

parcela nf plot

parche nm (a) (de tela, goma) patch (b) (para salir del paso) makeshift solution

parchís (pl parchises) nm Br ≃ ludo, US ≃ Parcheesi®

parcial 1 adj (a) (partidario) biased (b) (no completo) partial; **a tiempo p.** part-time
2 nm **(examen) p.** class examination

parcialmente adv partially, partly

parco, -a adj (a) (moderado) sparing (en in) (b) (escaso) meagre; (cena) frugal; (explicación) brief, concise

pardillo, -a 1 nm,f Esp Fam (a) (ingenuo) naive person (b) (palurdo) Br bumpkin, US hick
2 nm (ave) linnet

pardo, -a adj (marrón) brown; (gris) dark grey

parecer¹ nm (a) (opinión) opinion (b) (aspecto) appearance

parecer² [33] **1** vi to seem, to look (like); **parece difícil** it seems o looks difficult; **parecía (de) cera** it looked like wax; (uso impers) **parece que no arranca** it looks as if it won't start; **como te parezca** whatever you like; **¿te parece?** is that okay with you?; **parece que sí/no** I think/don't think so; **¿qué te parece?** what do you think of it?
2 parecerse vpr (a) to be alike; **no se parecen** they're not alike (b) **parecerse a** to look like, to resemble; **se parecen a su madre** they look like their mother

parecido, -a 1 adj (a) (similar) alike, similar (b) **bien p.** good-looking
2 nm likeness, resemblance; **tener p. con algn** to bear a resemblance to sb

pared nf wall

paredón nm **le llevaron al p.** he was executed by firing squad

pareja nf (a) (de cosas, personas) pair; **por parejas** in pairs (b) (hombre y mujer) couple; (hijo e hija) boy and girl; **hacen buena p.** they make a nice couple, they're well matched; **p. de hecho** = common-law heterosexual or homosexual relationship (c) (en naipes) pair; **doble p.** two pairs (d) (de baile, juego) partner

parejo, -a adj (a) (parecido) similar, alike (b) **ir parejos** to be neck and neck

parentela nf Fam relations, relatives

parentesco nm relationship, kinship

paréntesis nm inv (a) (signo) bracket, parenthesis; **entre p.** in brackets o parentheses (b) (descanso) break; (digresión) digression

pareo nm wraparound skirt

parezco indic pres de parecer

paria nmf pariah

parida nf Esp Fam **decir paridas** to talk Br rubbish o US garbage

pariente nmf relative, relation

> ⚠ Observa que la palabra inglesa **parent** es un falso amigo y no es la traducción de la palabra española **pariente**. En inglés **parent** significa tanto "padre" como "madre".

parir 1 vi to give birth; Esp Fam **poner algo/a algn a p.** Br to slag sth/sb off, US to badmouth sth/sb
2 vt to give birth to

París n Paris

parking (pl parkings) nm Br car park, US parking lot

parlamentario, -a 1 adj parliamentary
2 nm,f member of parliament

parlamento nm parliament

parlanchín, -ina adj Fam talkative, chatty

paro nm (a) (huelga) strike, stoppage (b) Esp (desempleo) unemployment; **estar en p.** to be unemployed; **cobrar el p.** to receive unemployment benefit, Br to be on the dole

parodia nf parody

parodiar [43] vt to parody

parpadear vi (ojos) to blink; Fig (luz) to flicker

parpadeo nm (de ojos) blinking; Fig (de luz) flickering

párpado nm eyelid

parque nm (a) (zona) park; **p. de atracciones** funfair; **p. eólico** wind farm; **p. infantil** playground; **p. nacional/natural** national park/nature reserve; **p. temático** theme park (b) (de niños) playpen (c) (vehículos) fleet; **p. móvil** fleet

parqué nm parquet

parqueadero nm Col, Ecuad, Pan, Ven Br car park, US parking lot

parquear vt Bol, Carib, Col to park

parquet [par'ke] (pl parquets) nm (suelo) parquet (floor)

parquímetro nm Aut parking meter

parra nf grapevine

párrafo nm paragraph

parranda nf Fam spree

parricidio nm parricide

parrilla *nf* (a) *Culin* grill; **pescado a la p.** grilled fish (b) *Téc* grate (c) *Aut & Dep* starting grid

parrillada *nf* mixed grill

párroco *nm* parish priest

parronal *nm Chile* vineyard

parroquia *nf* parish; *(iglesia)* parish church

parroquiano, -a *nm,f* (regular) customer

parsimonia *nf* phlegm, calmness

parte 1 *nf* (a) *(sección)* part (b) *(en una repartición)* share (c) *(lugar)* place, spot; **en** *o* **por todas partes** everywhere; **se fue por otra p.** he went another way (d) *Der* party (e) *(bando)* side; **estoy de tu p.** I'm on your side (f) *Euf* **partes** *(genitales)* private parts (g) *(locuciones)* **por mí p.** as far as I am concerned; **de p. de ... on** behalf of ...; *Tel* **¿de p. de quién?** who's calling?; **en gran p.** to a large extent; **en p.** partly; **la mayor p.** the majority; **por otra p.** on the other hand; **tomar p. en** to take part in

2 *nm (informe)* report

partición *nf* *(reparto)* division; *(de herencia, territorio)* partitioning

participación *nf* (a) *(colaboración, intervención)* participation (b) *Fin (acción)* share; **p. en los beneficios** profit-sharing (c) *(en lotería)* part of a lottery ticket (d) *(notificación)* notice, notification

participante 1 *adj* participating

2 *nmf* participant

participar 1 *vi* (a) *(colaborar, intervenir)* to take part, to participate (**en** in) (b) *Fin* to have a share (**en** in) (c) *(compartir)* **p. de** to share

2 *vt (notificar)* to notify

partícipe *nmf* **hacer p. de algo a algn** *(notificar)* to notify sb of sth; *(compartir)* to share sth with sb

participio *nm Ling* participle

partícula *nf* particle

particular 1 *adj* (a) *(concreto)* particular (b) *(privado)* private, personal (c) *(raro)* peculiar

2 *nmf (individuo)* private individual

3 *nm (asunto)* subject, matter

particularidad *nf* special feature

partida *nf* (a) *(salida)* departure (b) *Com (remesa)* batch, consignment (c) *(juego)* game (d) *Fin (entrada)* item (e) *Der (certificado)* certificate; **p. de nacimiento** birth certificate

partidario, -a 1 *adj* **ser/no ser p. de algo** to be for/against sth

2 *nm,f* supporter, follower; **es p. del aborto** he is in favour of abortion

partidista *adj* biased, partisan

partido *nm* (a) *Pol* party (b) *Dep* game, *Br* match; **p. amistoso** friendly; **p. de vuelta** return game *o Br* match (c) *(provecho)* advantage; **sacar p. de** to profit from (d) *Der (distrito)* district (e) **tomar p. por** *o* side with (f) **ser un buen p.** to be a good catch

partir 1 *vt* to break; *(dividir)* to split, to divide; *(cortar)* to cut; **p. a algn por la mitad** to mess things up for sb

2 *vi* (a) *(marcharse)* to leave, to set out *o* off (b) **a p. de** from

3 **partirse** *vpr* to split (up), to break (up); *Fam* **partirse de risa** to split one's sides laughing

partisano, -a *nm,f* partisan

partitura *nf Mús* score

parto *nm* childbirth, labour; **estar de p.** to be in labour

parvulario *nm* nursery school, kindergarten

párvulo, -a *nm,f Br* infant, *US* preschooler

pasa *nf* raisin; **p. de Corinto** currant

pasable *adj* passable, tolerable

pasaboca *nm Col* snack, appetizer

pasacalle *nm* (a) *(procesión)* street procession *(during town festival)* (b) *(banderola) Col, Urug* banner *(hung across street)*

pasada *nf* (a) **de p.** in passing (b) *(jugarreta)* dirty trick (c) *Esp Fam* **es una p.** *(una barbaridad)* it's way over the top

pasadizo *nm* passage

pasado, -a 1 *adj* (a) *(último)* last; **el año/lunes p.** last year/Monday (b) *(anticuado)* dated, old-fashioned; **p. (de moda)** out of date *o* fashion (c) *(alimento)* bad (d) *Culin* cooked; **lo quiero muy p.** I want it well done (e) **p. mañana** the day after tomorrow

2 *nm* past

pasador *nm* (a) *(para el pelo) Br* (hair) slide, *US* barrette (b) *(pestillo)* bolt

pasaje *nm* (a) *(calle)* passage (b) *(pasajeros)* passengers (c) *(billete)* ticket

pasajero, -a 1 *adj* passing, temporary; **aventura pasajera** fling

2 *nm,f* passenger

pasamanos *nm inv (barra)* handrail; *(de escalera)* banister, bannister

pasamontañas *nm inv* balaclava

pasapalo *nm Ven* snack, appetizer

pasaporte *nm* passport

pasapurés *nm inv Culin* potato masher

pasar 1 *vt* (a) *(dar, transmitir)* to pass; *(noticia, aviso)* to pass on; *(página)* to turn; **p. algo** *Esp* **a** *o Am* **en limpio** to make a fair copy of sth (b) *(tiempo)* to spend, to pass; **p. el rato** to kill time (c) *(experimentar)* to go through, to experience; **p. hambre** to go hungry; **pasarlo bien** to enjoy oneself, to have a good time; **pasarlo mal** to have a hard time of it (**d**) *(cruzar) (río, calle)* to cross; *(barrera)* to pass through o over; *(límite)* to go beyond (**e**) *(trasladar)* **p. algo a** to move sth to (**f**) *(consentir)* **p. algo a algn** to let sb get away with sth (**g**) *(examen)* to pass (**h**) *Cin* to run, to show

2 *vi* (**a**) *(ir, moverse)* to pass; **¿ha pasado el autobús?** has the bus gone by?; **ha pasado un hombre corriendo** a man has run past; **p. de largo** to go by (without stopping); **el tren pasa por Burgos** the train goes via Burgos; **pasa por casa mañana** come round to my house tomorrow

(**b**) **p. a** *(continuar)* to go on to; **p. a ser** to become

(**c**) *(entrar)* to come in

(**d**) *(tiempo)* to pass, to go by

(**e**) *(suceder)* to happen; **¿qué pasa aquí?** what's going on here?; **¿qué te pasa?** what's the matter?; **pase lo que pase** whatever happens, come what may; *Fam* **¿qué pasa?** *(saludo)* how are you?

(**f**) **p. sin** to do without; *Fam* **paso de tí** I couldn't care less about you; *Fam* **yo paso** count me out

3 pasarse *vpr* (**a**) **se me pasó la ocasión** I missed my chance; **se le pasó llamarme** he forgot to phone me (**b**) *(gastar) (tiempo)* to spend, to pass; **pasárselo bien/mal** to have a good/bad time (**c**) *(comida)* to go off (**d**) *Fam (excederse)* to go too far; **no te pases** don't overdo it (**e**) **pásate por mi casa** call round at my place

pasarela *nf (puente)* footbridge; *(de barco)* gangway; *(de moda) Br* catwalk, *US* runway

pasatiempo *nm* pastime, hobby

pascua *nf* (**a**) *(de los cristianos)* Easter; *(de los judíos)* Passover (**b**) **Pascuas** *(Navidad)* Christmas; **¡felices Pascuas!** Merry Christmas!

pascualina *nf RP, Ven* = tart with spinach and hard-boiled egg

pase *nm* (**a**) *(permiso)* pass, permit (**b**) *Esp (proyección)* showing

pasear 1 *vi* to go for a walk, to take a walk
2 *vt* (**a**) *(persona)* to take for a walk; *(perro)* to walk (**b**) *Fig (exhibir)* to show off
3 pasearse *vpr* to go for a walk

paseíllo *nm Taurom* opening parade

paseo *nm* (**a**) *(a pie)* walk; *(en bicicleta, caballo)* ride; *(en coche)* drive; **dar un p.** to go for a walk/a ride (**b**) *(avenida)* avenue

pasillo *nm* corridor; *Av* **p. aéreo** air corridor

pasión *nf* passion

pasional *adj* passionate; **crimen p.** crime of passion

pasividad *nf* passivity, passiveness

pasivo, -a 1 *adj* passive; *(inactivo)* inactive
2 *nm Com* liabilities

pasmado, -a *adj (asombrado)* astounded, amazed; *(atontado)* flabbergasted; **dejar p.** to astonish; **quedarse p.** to be amazed

pasmo *nm* astonishment, amazement

paso¹, -a *adj* **ciruela pasa** prune; **uva pasa** raisin

paso² *nm* (**a**) *(con el pie)* step; *(modo de andar)* gait, walk; *(ruido al andar)* footstep; *Mil* **llevar el p.** to keep in step; *Fig* **a dos pasos** a short distance away; *Fig* **seguir los pasos de algn** to follow in sb's footsteps (**b**) *(camino)* passage, way; **abrirse p.** to force one's way through; *Aut* **ceda el p.** *(en letrero) Br* give way, *US* yield; **prohibido el p.** *(en letrero)* no entry; **p. de cebra** *Br* zebra crossing, = pedestrian crossing marked with black and white lines; **p. elevado** *Br* flyover, *US* overpass; **p. a nivel** *Br* level crossing, *US* grade crossing; **p. peatonal** o **de peatones** *Br* pedestrian crossing, *US* crosswalk; **p. subterráneo** *(para peatones) Br* subway, *US* underpass; *(para coches)* underpass (**c**) *(acción)* passing; **a su p. por la ciudad** when he was in town; **el p. del tiempo** the passage of time; **estar de p.** to be just passing through

pasodoble *nm* paso doble

pasota *adj Esp Fam* apathetic

pasta *nf* (**a**) *(masa)* paste; **p. de dientes** o **dentífrica** toothpaste (**b**) *(de pasteles)* dough; *(italiana)* pasta (**c**) *(pastelito)* shortcake *Br* biscuit o *US* cookie (**d**) *Esp Fam (dinero)* dough

pastar *vi* to graze, to pasture

pastel *nm* (**a**) *(dulce)* cake; *(de carne, fruta)* pie (**b**) *Arte* pastel (**c**) *Fam* **descubrir el p.** to spill the beans

pastelería *nf* (**a**) *(tienda)* cake shop, patisserie (**b**) *(repostería)* pastries

pastelero, -a *nm,f* pastry cook, confectioner

pastiche *nm* pastiche

pastilla *nf* (**a**) *Med* tablet, pill; **pastillas para la tos** cough drops (**b**) *(de jabón)* bar (**c**) *Esp Fam* **a toda p.** at top speed, *Br* like the clappers

pastizal *nm* grazing land, pasture

pasto *nm* (**a**) *(hierba)* grass (**b**) *(alimento)* fodder; **ser p. de** to fall prey to (**c**) *Am (césped)* lawn, grass

pastor, -a 1 *nm,f* shepherd; *(mujer)* shepherdess; **perro p.** sheepdog
2 *nm* (a) *Rel* pastor, minister (b) *(perro)* **p. alemán** Alsatian

pastoreo *nm* shepherding

pastoso, -a *adj (blando)* pasty; *(arroz)* sticky; **tener la boca pastosa** to have a furry tongue

pata 1 *nf* leg; *Fig* **patas arriba** upside down; **estirar la p.** to kick the bucket; **mala p.** bad luck; **meter la p.** to put one's foot in it; **p. de gallo** crow's foot
2 *nm Perú Fam (amigo)* pal, *Br* mate, *US* buddy; *(tipo)* guy, *Br* bloke

patada *nf (puntapié)* kick, stamp

patalear *vi (en el aire)* to kick about; *(en el suelo)* to stamp one's feet

pataleo *nm (en el aire)* kicking; *(de rabia)* stamping

patán *nm* bumpkin, yokel

patata *nf Esp* potato; **patatas fritas** *(de sartén)* *Br* chips, *US* (French) fries; *(de bolsa)* *Br* crisps, *US* (potato) chips

patatús *nm inv Fam* dizzy spell, queer turn

paté *nm* pâté

patear 1 *vt (pisotear)* to stamp on
2 *vi (patalear)* to stamp one's feet
3 **patearse** *upr Fam (recorrer)* to tramp; **se pateó toda la ciudad** he tramped *o* traipsed all over town

patena *nf* paten; *Esp* **limpio** *o* **blanco como una p.** as clean as a new pin

patentar *vt* to patent

patente 1 *nf* (a) *(autorización)* licence; *(de invención)* patent (b) *CSur (matrícula)* *Br* number plate, *US* license plate
2 *adj (evidente)* patent, obvious

paternal *adj* paternal, fatherly

paternalista *adj* paternalistic

paternidad *nf (estado)* fatherhood; *Der* paternity

paterno, -a *adj* paternal

patético, -a *adj* (a) *(emotivo)* pathetic, moving (b) *(ridículo)* pathetic

patíbulo *nm* scaffold, gallows *sing*

patidifuso, -a *adj Fam* dumbfounded, flabbergasted

patilla *nf* (a) *(de gafas)* leg (b) **patillas** *(pelo)* sideburns

patín *nm* (a) *(para el pie)* skate; **p. de ruedas/de hielo** roller-/ice-skate; **p. en línea** rollerblade (b) *(patinete)* scooter (c) *Esp (embarcación)* pedal boat

patinaje *nm* skating; **p. artístico** figure skating; **p. sobre hielo/ruedas** ice-/roller-skating

patinar *vi* (a) *(sobre hielo)* to skate; *(sobre ruedas)* to roller-skate; *(con patines en línea)* to roller-blade (b) *(deslizarse)* to slide; *(resbalar)* to slip; *(vehículo)* to skid (c) *Fam (equivocarse)* to put one's foot in it, to slip up

patinazo *nm* (a) *(de vehículo)* skid (b) *Fam (equivocación)* blunder, boob

patinete *nm* scooter

patio *nm* (a) *(de una casa)* yard, patio; *(de recreo)* playground (b) *Esp Teatro & Cin* **p. de butacas** stalls

pato *nm* duck; *Fam* **pagar el p.** *Br* to carry the can, *US* to pick up the tab

patógeno, -a *adj* pathogenic

patología *nf* pathology

patológico, -a *adj* pathological

patoso, -a *adj Esp* clumsy

patota *nf Perú, RP (de gamberros)* street gang

patraña *nf* absurd story

patria *nf* fatherland, native country; **madre p.** motherland; **p. chica** one's home town/region

patriarca *nm* patriarch

patrimonio *nm (de empresa)* assets; *(propios)* estate, assets; *(herencia)* inheritance

patriota *nmf* patriot

patriótico, -a *adj* patriotic

patriotismo *nm* patriotism

patrocinador, -a 1 *adj* sponsoring
2 *nm,f* sponsor

patrocinar *vt* to sponsor

patrocinio *nm* sponsorship, patronage

patrón, -ona 1 *nm,f* (a) *(jefe)* boss (b) *Esp (de pensión) (hombre)* landlord; *(mujer)* landlady (c) *Rel* patron saint
2 *nm* (a) *(modelo)* pattern (b) *(medida)* standard

patronal 1 *adj* employers'; **cierre p.** lockout; **clase p.** managerial class
2 *nf (dirección)* management

patronato *nm* trust

patronazgo *nm* patronage

patrono, -a *nm,f* (a) *(de empresa) (encargado)* boss; *(empresario)* employer (b) *Rel* patron saint

patrulla *nf* patrol; **estar de p.** to be on patrol; **coche p.** patrol car

patrullar 1 *vt* to patrol
2 *vi* to be on patrol

patrullero *nm* (a) *(barco)* patrol boat (b) *CSur (auto)* police (patrol) car, *US* cruiser

paulatino, -a *adj* gradual

paupérrimo, -a *adj* extremely poor, poverty-stricken

pausa *nf* pause, break; *Mús* rest

pausado, -a *adj* unhurried, calm

pauta *nf* guidelines

pava *nf* (**a**) *CAm (flequillo) Br* fringe, *US* bangs (**b**) *Chile, Perú (broma)* coarse o tasteless joke (**c**) *Arg (hervidor)* kettle

pavada *nf RP* (**a**) *Fam (estupidez)* **decir una pavada** to say something stupid; **decir pavadas** to talk nonsense (**b**) *(cosa sin importancia)* silly little thing

pavesa *nf* ash

pavimentar *vt (carretera)* to surface; *(acera)* to pave; *(suelo)* to floor

pavimento *nm (de carretera)* road (surface), *US* pavement; *(de acera)* paving; *(de habitación)* flooring

pavo *nm* (**a**) *(ave)* turkey; *Fam* **no ser moco de p.** to be nothing to scoff at; *Fam* **estar en la edad del p.** to be growing up (**b**) *Fam (tonto)* twit

pavonearse *upr Fam* to show off, to strut

pavoneo *nm Fam* showing off, strutting

pavor *nm* terror, dread

pay *(pl pays) nm Chile, Méx, Ven* pie

payaso *nm* clown; **hacer el p.** to act the clown

payés, -esa *nm,f* = Catalan or Balearic peasant

payo, -a *nm,f* non-gipsy person

paz *nf* peace; *(sosiego)* peacefulness; *Fam* **¡déjame en p.!** leave me alone!; **hacer las paces** to make (it) up

pazguato, -a *adj* (**a**) *(estúpido)* silly, stupid (**b**) *(mojigato)* prudish

pazo *nm* = Galician mansion, belonging to noble family

PC *nm (abr* **personal computer)** PC

PDA *nm (abr* **personal digital assistant)** PDA

pe *nf Fam* **de pe a pa** from A to Z

peaje *nm* toll; **autopista de p.** *Br* toll motorway, *US* turnpike

peatón *nm* pedestrian

peatonal *adj* pedestrian; **calle p.** pedestrian street

peca *nf* freckle

pecado *nm Rel* sin; **p. capital** o **mortal** deadly sin

pecador, -a *nm,f* sinner

pecaminoso, -a *adj* sinful

pecar [44] *vi* to sin; *Fig* **p. por defecto** to fall short of the mark

pecera *nf* fish bowl, fish tank

pecho *nm* (**a**) *Anat* chest; *(de mujer)* breast, bust; *(de animal)* breast; **dar el p. (a un bebé)** to breast-feed (a baby); *Fig* **tomar(se) algo a p.** to take sth to heart (**b**)

Am (en natación) breaststroke; **nadar p.** to do the breaststroke

pechuga *nf* (**a**) *(de ave)* breast (**b**) *Fam (de mujer)* bust

pecoso, -a *adj* freckly

pectoral *adj* pectoral, chest

peculiar *adj (raro)* peculiar; *(característico)* characteristic

peculiaridad *nf* (**a**) *(cualidad)* uniqueness (**b**) *(detalle)* particular feature o characteristic

pedagogía *nf* pedagogy

pedagógico, -a *adj* pedagogical

pedagogo, -a *nm,f (especialista)* educationalist; *(profesor)* teacher, educator

pedal *nm* pedal

pedalear *vi* to pedal

pedante 1 *adj* pretentious

2 *nmf* pretentious person

pedantería *nf (cualidad)* pretentiousness; *(dicho, hecho)* piece of pretentiousness

pedazo *nm* piece, bit; **a pedazos** in pieces; **caerse a pedazos** to fall apart o to pieces; **hacer pedazos** to break o tear to pieces, to smash (up); *Fam* **¡qué p. de coche!** what a terrific car!

pederasta *nm* pederast

pedernal *nm* flint

pedestal *nm* pedestal

pediatra *nmf* paediatrician

pediatría *nf* paediatrics *sing*

pedicura *nf* pedicure

pedido *nm* (**a**) *Com* order; **hacer un p.** to place an order with (**b**) *(petición)* request

pedigrí *nm* pedigree

pedir [6] **1** *vt* (**a**) *(solicitar)* to ask for; **p. algo a algn** to ask sb for sth; **p. a algn que haga algo** to ask sb to do sth; **p. prestado** to borrow; *Fig* **p. cuentas** to ask for an explanation (**b**) *(en bares, restaurantes)* to order

2 *vi* (**a**) *(mendigar)* to beg (**b**) *(rezar)* **p. por ...** to pray for ...

pedo *nm* (**a**) *(ventosidad)* fart; **tirarse un p.** to fart (**b**) *Fam (borrachera)* bender

pedrada *nf* **a pedradas** by stoning; **rompió la ventana de una p.** he smashed the window with a stone

pedrea *nf Esp (en lotería)* small prizes

pedregoso, -a *adj* stony, rocky

pedrería *nf* precious stones, gems

pedrisco *nm* hailstorm

pega *nf* (**a**) *Fam (obstáculo)* difficulty, hitch; **poner pegas (a)** to find problems (with) (**b**) **de p.** *(falso)* false, fake

pegadizo, -a *adj* catchy

pegado, -a *adj* (**a**) *(adherido)* stuck (**b**) *(quemado)* burnt

pegajoso, -a *adj (pegadizo)* sticky; *Fig (persona)* tiresome, hard to get rid of

pegamento *nm* glue

pegar [42] **1** *vt* (**a**) *(adherir)* to stick; *(con pegamento)* to glue; *(coser)* to sew on; *Fam* **no pegó ojo** he didn't sleep a wink; **p. fuego a** to set fire to (**b**) *(golpear)* to hit (**c**) **p. un grito** to shout; **p. un salto** to jump (**d**) *Fam (contagiar)* to give; **me ha pegado sus manías** I've caught his bad habits (**e**) *(arrimar)* **p. algo a** *o* **contra algo** to put *o* place sth against sth

2 *vi* (**a**) *(adherirse)* to stick (**b**) *(armonizar)* to match, to go; **el azul no pega con el verde** blue and green don't go together *o* don't match; *Fig* **ella no pegaría aquí** she wouldn't fit in here (**c**) *(sol)* to beat down

3 pegarse *upr* (**a**) *(adherirse)* to stick; *(pelearse)* to fight (**b**) *(darse)* to have, to get; **pegarse un tiro** to shoot oneself (**c**) *-(comida)* to get burnt; **se me ha pegado el sol** I've got a touch of the sun (**d**) *Esp Fam* **pegársela a algn** to trick *o* deceive sb (**e**) *(arrimarse)* to get close (**f**) *Fam Fig* to stick (**g**) *Med (enfermedad)* to be catching *o* contagious; *Fig (melodía)* to be catchy

pegatina *nf Esp* sticker

peinado *nm* hairstyle; *Fam* hairdo

peinar 1 *vt* (**a**) *(pelo)* to comb (**b**) *(registrar)* to comb

2 peinarse *upr* to comb one's hair

peine *nm* comb

peineta *nf* = ornamental comb worn in hair

p.ej. *(abr por ejemplo)* e.g

peladilla *nf* sugared almond

pelado, -a 1 *adj* (**a**) *(cabeza)* shorn; *(piel, fruta)* peeled; *(terreno)* bare (**b**) *Fam* **saqué un cinco p.** *(en escuela)* I just scraped a pass; **a grito p.** shouting and bawling (**c**) *Fam (arruinado)* broke, *Br* skint (**d**) *(desvergonzado)* impudent, insolent

2 *nm Fam* haircut

3 *nm,f* (**a**) *Andes Fam (niño, adolescente)* kid (**b**) *CAm, Méx Fam (persona humilde)* common person, *Br* pleb, *Br* oik

pelagatos *nmf inv Fam Pey* poor devil, nobody

pelaje *nm (de gato, oso, conejo)* fur; *(de perro, caballo)* coat

pelambrera *nf Fam* long thick hair

pelapatatas *nm inv* potato peeler

pelar 1 *vt* (**a**) *Fam (cortar el pelo a)* to cut the hair of (**b**) *(fruta, patata)* to peel; *Fam* **hace un frío que pela** it's brass monkey weather

2 *vi (despellejar)* to peel

3 pelarse *upr Fam* (**a**) *(cortarse el pelo)* to get one's hair cut (**b**) **corre que se las pela** she runs like the wind

peldaño *nm* step; *(de escalera de mano)* rung

pelea *nf* fight; *(riña)* row, quarrel; **buscar p.** to look for trouble

peleado, -a *adj* **estar p. (con algn)** not to be on speaking terms (with sb)

pelear 1 *vi* to fight; *(reñir)* to quarrel

2 pelearse *upr* (**a**) *(luchar)* to fight; *(reñir)* to quarrel (**b**) *(enemistarse)* to fall out

pelele *nm* (**a**) *Fam Pey (persona)* puppet (**b**) *(muñeco)* guy, straw doll

peleón, -ona *adj* (**a**) *(persona)* quarrelsome, aggressive (**b**) *(vino)* cheap

peletería *nf* furrier's; *(tienda)* fur shop

peletero, -a *nm,f* furrier

peliagudo, -a *adj* difficult, tricky

pelícano *nm* pelican

película *nf* (**a**) *Cin* movie, *Br* film; **p. de miedo** *o* **terror** horror movie *o Br* film; **p. del Oeste** Western; *Fam* **de p.** fabulous (**b**) *Fot* film

peligrar *vi* to be in danger, to be threatened; **hacer p.** to endanger, to jeopardize

peligro *nm* danger; *(riesgo)* risk; **con p. de ...** at the risk of ...; **correr (el) p. de ...** to run the risk of ...; **poner en p.** to endanger

peligroso, -a *adj* dangerous, risky

pelirrojo, -a 1 *adj* red-haired; *(anaranjado)* ginger-haired

2 *nm,f* redhead

pellejo *nm* (**a**) *(piel)* skin (**b**) *(odre)* wineskin (**c**) *Fam* **arriesgar** *o* **jugarse el p.** to risk one's neck

pelliza *nf* fur jacket

pellizcar [44] *vt* to pinch, to nip

pellizco *nm* pinch, nip

pelma *nmf,* **pelmazo, -a** *nm,f Esp (persona)* bore, drag

pelo *nm* (**a**) *(de persona)* hair; **cortarse el p.** *(uno mismo)* to cut one's hair; *(en la peluquería)* to have one's hair cut; *Fig* **no tiene ni un p. de tonto** he's no fool; *Fig* **no tener pelos en la lengua** to be very outspoken; *Fig* **tomar el p. a algn** to pull sb's leg, *Br* to take the mickey out of sb; *Fam* **con pelos y señales** in full detail; *Fam* **por los pelos** by the skin of one's teeth; *Fam* **me puso el p. de punta** it gave me the creeps (**b**) *(de animal)* fur, coat, hair (**c**) *Tex (de una tela)* nap, pile (**d**) *(cerda)* bristle

pelón, -ona *adj (sin pelo)* bald

pelota 1 *nf* (**a**) *(para jugar)* ball; *Fam* **devolver la p.** to give tit for tat; **p. vasca** pelota (**b**) *Fam (cabeza)* nut (**c**) *Esp* **hacer la p. a algn** to toady to sb, to butter sb up (**d**) *muy Fam* **pelotas** *(testículos)* balls; **en pelotas** *Br* starkers, *US* butt-naked
2 *nmf Esp Fam (persona)* crawler

pelotari *nm* pelota player

peloteo *nm Ten* knock-up

pelotilla *nf Esp Fam* **hacer la p. (a algn)** to fawn (on sb)

pelotillero, -a *nm,f Esp Fam* crawler

pelotón *nm* (**a**) *Mil* squad (**b**) *Fam (grupo)* small crowd, bunch; *(en ciclismo)* pack (**c**) *(amasijo)* bundle

pelotudo, -a *adj RP Fam* (**a**) *(estúpido)* damn stupid (**b**) *(grande)* massive

peluca *nf* wig

peluche *nm* **(osito de) p.** teddy bear

peludo, -a *adj* hairy, furry

peluquería *nf* hairdresser's (shop)

peluquero, -a *nm,f* hairdresser

peluquín *nm* toupee

pelusa *nf (de tela)* fluff; *(de polvo)* ball of fluff

pelvis *nf inv* pelvis

pena *nf* (**a**) *(tristeza)* grief, sorrow; *Fig* **me da p. de ella** I feel sorry for her; **¡qué p.!** what a pity! (**b**) *(dificultad)* hardships *pl*, trouble; **no merece** *o* **vale la p. (ir)** it's not worth while (going); **a duras penas** with great difficulty (**c**) *(castigo)* punishment, penalty; **p. de muerte** *o* **capital** death penalty (**d**) *CAm, Carib, Col, Méx (vergüenza)* embarrassment; **me da p.** I'm embarrassed about it

penacho *nm* (**a**) *(de ave)* crest, tuft (**b**) *Mil (de plumas)* plume

penal 1 *adj* penal; *Der* **código p.** penal code
2 *nm* prison, jail

penalidades *nfpl* hardships, troubles

penalización *nf* penalization; *Dep* penalty

penalizar [40] *vt* to penalize

penalti *nm Dep* penalty; *Esp Fam* **casarse de p.** to have a shotgun wedding

penar *vi* to be in torment, to suffer

pendejo, -a *nm,f* (**a**) *Am muy Fam (tonto)* jerk, *Br* tosser (**b**) *RP Fam Pey (adolescente)* spotty teenager

pendenciero, -a *adj* quarrelsome, argumentative

pendiente 1 *adj* (**a**) *(por resolver)* pending; *Educ* **asignatura p.** failed subject; *Com* **p. de pago** unpaid (**b**) **estar p. de** *(esperar)* to be waiting for; *(vigilar)*

to be on the lookout for (**c**) *(colgante)* hanging (**de** from)
2 *nm Esp* earring
3 *nf* slope; *(de tejado)* pitch

pendón *nm* (**a**) *(bandera)* banner (**b**) *Pey (mujer)* floozy; *(hombre)* layabout, good-for-nothing

péndulo *nm* pendulum

pene *nm* penis

penetración *nf* (**a**) *(introducción)* penetration (**b**) *(perspicacia)* insight, perception

penetrante *adj* penetrating; *(frío, voz)* piercing

penetrar 1 *vt* to penetrate; **p. un misterio** to get to the bottom of a mystery
2 *vi (entrar)* to go *o* get (**en** in)

penicilina *nf* penicillin

península *nf* peninsula

peninsular *adj* peninsular

penique *nm* penny; **peniques** pence

penitencia *nf* penance

penitenciaría *nf* prison

penitenciario, -a *adj* penitentiary, prison

penitente *nmf* penitent

penoso, -a *adj* (**a**) *(lamentable)* sorry, distressing (**b**) *(laborioso)* laborious, difficult (**c**) *CAm, Carib, Col, Méx (embarazoso)* embarrassing (**d**) *CAm, Carib, Col, Méx (persona)* shy

pensado, -a *adj* **bien p., ...** on reflection, ...; **en el momento menos p.** when least expected; **mal p.** twisted; **tener algo p.** to have sth planned, to have sth in mind; **tengo p. ir** I intend to go

pensador, -a *nm,f* thinker

pensamiento *nm* (**a**) *(facultad, idea)* thought (**b**) *(máxima)* saying, motto (**c**) *Bot* pansy

pensar [1] **1** *vi* to think (**en** of *o* about; **sobre** about *o* over); *Fig* **sin p.** *(con precipitación)* without thinking; *(involuntariamente)* involuntarily
2 *vt* (**a**) *(opinar, creer)* to think (**de** of); *(considerar)* to think over *o* about; **piénsalo bien** think it over; *Fam* **¡ni pensarlo!** not on your life! (**b**) *(proponerse)* to intend; **pienso quedarme** I plan to stay (**c**) *(idear)* to think up

pensativo, -a *adj* pensive, thoughtful

pensión *nf* (**a**) *(residencia)* boarding house; *(hotel)* guesthouse; **media p.** half board; **p. completa** full board (**b**) *(paga)* pension, allowance; **p. vitalicia** life annuity

pensionista *nmf (jubilado)* pensioner

pentágono *nm* pentagon

pentagrama *nm* staff, stave

penthouse *nm CSur, Ven* penthouse

penúltimo, -a *adj & nm,f* next to the last, penultimate

penumbra *nf* penumbra, half-light

penuria *nf* scarcity, shortage

peña *nf* (a) *(roca)* rock, crag (b) *(de amigos)* club (c) *Esp Fam (gente)* people

peñasco *nm* rock, crag

peñón *nm* rock; **el P. de Gibraltar** the Rock of Gibraltar

peón *nm* (a) *(obrero)* unskilled labourer; **p. agrícola** farmhand (b) *(en ajedrez)* pawn

peonada *nf* day's work

peonza *nf* (spinning) top

peor **1** *adj* (a) *(comparativo)* worse (b) *(superlativo)* worst; **en el p. de los casos** if the worst comes to the worst; **lo p. es que** the worst of it is that

2 *adv* (a) *(comparativo)* worse; **¡p. para mí/ti/etc.!** too bad! (b) *(superlativo)* worst

pepa *nf* (a) *Am salvo RP (pepita)* pip; *(hueso)* stone (b) *Méx, RP, Ven muy Fam (vulva)* pussy (c) *Ven (en la piel)* blackhead

pepenador, -a *CAm, Méx nm,f* scavenger (on rubbish tip)

pepián *nm Andes, CAm, Méx* = pipián

pepinillo *nm* gherkin

pepino *nm* cucumber; *Fam* **me importa un p.** I don't give a toss

pepita *nf* *(de fruta)* pip, seed; *(de metal)* nugget

pepito *nm Esp (de carne)* grilled meat sandwich

pepitoria *nf* fricassee; **pollo en p.** fricassee of chicken

peque *nmf Fam (niño)* kid

pequeño, -a **1** *adj* small, little; *(bajo)* short

2 *nm,f* child; **de p.** as a child

Pequín *n* Peking

pera *nf* (a) *Bot* pear; **p. de agua** juicy pear (b) *CSur Fam (mentón)* chin

peral *nm* pear tree

percance *nm* mishap, setback

percatarse *upr* **p. de** to realize

percebe *nm* (a) *(marisco)* goose barnacle (b) *Fam (persona)* twit

percepción *nf* perception

perceptible *adj* perceptible

percha *nf* *(colgador)* (coat) hanger; *(de gallina)* perch

perchero *nm* coat rack

percibir *vt* (a) *(notar)* to perceive, to notice (b) *(cobrar)* to receive

percusión *nf* percussion

percutor *nm* hammer, firing pin

perdedor, -a **1** *adj* losing

2 *nm,f* loser

perder [3] **1** *vt* (a) *(dinero, objeto, amigo)* to lose (b) *(tren, vuelo)* to miss; *(tiempo)* to waste; *(oportunidad)* to miss (c) *(pervertir)* to be the ruin o downfall of

2 *vi* to lose; **echar (algo) a p.** to spoil (sth); **echarse a p.** to be spoilt; **salir perdiendo** to come off worst

3 perderse *upr* (a) *(extraviarse) (persona)* to get lost; **se me ha perdido la llave** I've lost my key; **no te lo pierdas** don't miss it (b) *(pervertirse)* to go to rack and ruin

perdición *nf* undoing, downfall

pérdida *nf* (a) *(de objeto, persona, peso)* loss; *Esp* **no tiene p.** you can't miss it (b) *(de tiempo, esfuerzos)* waste (c) *Mil* **pérdidas** losses

perdido, -a *adj* (a) *(extraviado)* lost (b) *Fam (sucio)* filthy (c) *Fam* **loco p.** mad as a hatter (d) **estar p. por algn** *(enamorado)* to be crazy about sb (e) *(acabado)* finished; **¡estoy p.!** I'm a goner!

perdigón *nm* pellet

perdiguero, -a *adj* partridge-hunting; **perro p.** setter

perdiz *nf* partridge

perdón *nm* pardon, forgiveness; **¡p.!** sorry!; **pedir p.** to apologize

perdonar *vt* (a) *(remitir)* to forgive (b) **¡perdone!** sorry!; **perdone que le moleste** sorry to bother you (c) *(eximir)* to pardon; **perdonarle la vida a algn** to spare sb's life; **p. una deuda** to write off a debt

perdurable *adj* (a) *(eterno)* everlasting (b) *(duradero)* durable, long-lasting

perdurar *vi* (a) *(durar)* to endure, to last (b) *(persistir)* to persist, to continue to exist

perecedero, -a *adj* perishable; **artículos perecederos** perishables

perecer [33] *vi* to perish, to die

peregrinación *nf*, **peregrinaje** *nm* pilgrimage

peregrino, -a **1** *nm,f* pilgrim

2 *adj* **ideas peregrinas** crazy ideas

perejil *nm* parsley

perenne *adj* perennial, everlasting

perentorio, -a *adj* peremptory, urgent

pereza *nf* laziness, idleness

perezoso, -a *adj (vago)* lazy, idle

perfección *nf* perfection; **a la p.** to perfection

perfeccionamiento *nm* (a) *(acción)* perfecting (b) *(mejora)* improvement

perfeccionar *vt* to perfect; *(mejorar)* to improve, to make better

perfeccionista *adj & nmf* perfectionist

perfectamente *adv* perfectly; **¡p.!** *(de acuerdo)* agreed!, all right!

perfecto, -a *adj* perfect

perfidia *nf* perfidy, treachery

perfil *nm* (a) *(físico, psicológico)* profile; *(contorno)* outline, contour; **de p.** in profile (b) *Geom* cross-section

perfilar 1 *vt (dar forma a)* to shape, to outline
  2 perfilarse *vpr (tomar forma)* to take shape

perforación *nf* perforation; *Min* drilling, boring; *Inform (de tarjetas)* punching

perforadora *nf (para papel)* punch; *(herramienta)* drill

perforar *vt* to perforate; *(con taladro)* to drill, to bore

perfumar 1 *vt* to perfume
  2 perfumarse *vpr* to put on perfume

perfume *nm* perfume, scent

perfumería *nf (tienda, arte)* perfumery

pergamino *nm* parchment

pérgola *nf* pergola

pericia *nf* expertise, skill

periferia *nf* periphery; *(alrededores)* outskirts

periférico, -a 1 *adj* peripheral
  2 *nm* (a) *Inform* peripheral (b) *CAm, Méx (carretera)* Br ring road, *US* beltway

perífrasis *nf inv Ling* **p. verbal** compound verb

perilla *nf (barba)* goatee; *Fam* **venir de p.** *o* **perillas** to be just the right thing

perímetro *nm* perimeter

periódico, -a 1 *nm* newspaper
  2 *adj* periodic(al); *Quím* **tabla periódica** periodic table

periodismo *nm* journalism

periodista *nmf* journalist, reporter

periodo, período *nm* period

peripecia *nf* incident, adventure

periplo *nm* voyage, tour

periquete *nm Fam* **en un p.** in a jiffy

periquito *nm* budgerigar; *Fam* budgie

periscopio *nm* periscope

peritaje *nm (estudios)* technical studies

perito, -a *nm,f* technician, expert; **p. industrial/agrónomo** ≃ industrial/agricultural expert

peritonitis *nf inv Med* peritonitis

perjudicar [44] *vt* to harm, to injure; *(intereses)* to prejudice

perjudicial *adj* prejudicial, harmful

perjuicio *nm* harm, damage; **en p. de** to the detriment of; **sin p. de** without prejudice to

perjurar *vi* to commit perjury

perjurio *nm* perjury

perla *nf* pearl; *Fig (persona)* gem, jewel; *Fam* **me viene de perlas** it's just the ticket

permanecer [33] *vi* to remain, to stay

permanencia *nf* (a) *(inmutabilidad)* permanence (b) *(estancia)* stay

permanente 1 *adj* permanent
  2 *nf (de pelo)* permanent wave, perm; **hacerse la p.** to have one's hair permed

permisivo, -a *adj* permissive

permiso *nm* (a) *(autorización)* permission (b) *(licencia)* licence, permit; **p. de conducción** *o* **de conducir** *Br* driving licence, *US* driver's license; **p. de residencia/trabajo** residence/work permit (c) *Mil* leave; **estar de p.** to be on leave

permitir 1 *vt* to permit, to allow; **¿me permite?** may I?
  2 permitirse *vpr* (a) *(uno mismo)* to allow oneself; **me permito recordarle que** let me remind you that (b) *(económicamente)* **no puedo permitírmelo** I can't afford it

permutar *vt* to exchange

pernicioso, -a *adj* pernicious

pernil *nm (de pantalón)* leg; *(jamón)* leg of pork

pernocta *nf Mil* **(pase de) p.** overnight pass

pernoctar *vi* to stay overnight

pero 1 *conj* but; **p., ¿qué pasa aquí?** now, what's going on here?
  2 *nm* objection

perogrullada *nf* truism, platitude

perol *nm* large saucepan, pot

perorata *nf* boring speech

perpendicular *adj & nf* perpendicular

perpetrar *vt* to perpetrate, to commit

perpetuar [30] *vt* to perpetuate

perpetuo, -a *adj* perpetual, everlasting; *Der* **cadena perpetua** life imprisonment

perplejidad *nf* perplexity, bewilderment

perplejo, -a *adj* perplexed, bewildered

perra *nf* (a) *(animal)* bitch (b) *Esp Fam (dinero)* penny; **estar sin una p.** to be broke

perrera *nf* kennel, kennels

perrería *nf Fam* dirty trick

perro, -a 1 *nm* dog; *Fam* **un día de perros** a lousy day; *Fam* **vida de perros** dog's life; *Culin* **p. caliente** hot dog
  2 *adj Fam (vago)* lazy

persa 1 *adj & nmf* Persian
  2 *nm (idioma)* Persian, Farsi

persecución *nf* (a) *(seguimiento)* pursuit (b) *(acoso)* persecution

perseguir [6] *vt* (a) *(seguir)* to pursue, to chase; *(correr trás)* to run after, to follow (b) *(acosar)* to persecute (c) *(tratar de obtener)* to pursue

perseverante *adj* persevering

perseverar *vi* to persevere, to persist

persiana *nf* blind

pérsico, -a *adj* Persian; **golfo P.** Persian Gulf

persignarse *upr* to cross oneself

persistencia *nf* persistence

persistente *adj* persistent

persistir *vi* to persist

persona *nf* person; **algunas personas** some people; *Fam* **p. mayor** grown-up

personaje *nm* (a) *Cin, Lit & Teatro* character (b) *(celebridad)* celebrity, important person

personal 1 *adj* personal, private
　2 *nm* (a) *(plantilla)* staff, personnel (b) *Esp Fam (gente)* people

personalidad *nf* personality

personarse *upr* to present oneself, to appear in person

personero, -a *nm,f Am* (a) *(representante)* representative (b) *(portavoz)* spokesperson

personificar [44] *vt* to personify

perspectiva *nf* (a) *(en dibujo, punto de vista)* perspective (b) *(futuro, posibilidad)* prospect

perspicacia *nf* insight, perspicacity

perspicaz *adj* sharp, perspicacious

persuadir *vt* to persuade; **estar persuadido de que** to be convinced that

persuasión *nf* persuasion

persuasivo, -a *adj* persuasive, convincing

pertenecer [33] *vi* to belong (a to)

perteneciente *adj* belonging

pertenencia 1 *nf* *(a un partido etc)* affiliation, membership
　2 pertenencias *nfpl* belongings

pértiga *nf* pole; *Dep* **salto con p.** pole vault

pertinaz *adj* (a) *(persistente)* persistent (b) *(obstinado)* obstinate, stubborn

pertinente *adj* *(adecuado)* appropriate; *(relevante)* pertinent, relevant

perturbación *nf* disturbance; **p. del orden público** breach of the peace; *Med* **p. mental** mental disorder

perturbado, -a *adj* (mentally) deranged o unbalanced

perturbador, -a 1 *adj* disturbing
　2 *nm,f* unruly person

perturbar *vt (el orden)* to disturb

Perú *n* Peru

peruano, -a *adj & nm,f* Peruvian

perversión *nf* perversion

perverso, -a *adj* perverse, evil

pervertir [5] *vt* to pervert, to corrupt

pervivir *vi* to survive

pesa *nf* weight; **levantamiento de pesas** weightlifting

pesadez *nf* (a) *(sensación)* heaviness; *(de estómago)* fullness (b) *Fam (fastidio)* drag, pain

pesadilla *nf* nightmare; **de p.** nightmarish

pesado, -a 1 *adj* (a) *(que pesa)* heavy (b) *(sueño)* deep (c) *(aburrido)* tedious, dull (d) *(molesto)* annoying; **ponerse p.** to be a pain
　2 *nm,f* bore

pesadumbre *nf* grief, affliction

pésame *nm* condolences, sympathy; **dar el p.** to offer one's condolences; **mi más sentido p.** my deepest sympathy

pesar 1 *vt* to weigh
　2 *vi* (a) *(tener peso)* to weigh; **¿cuánto pesas?** how much do you weigh? (b) *(ser pesado)* to be heavy; **pesa mucho** it's very heavy (c) *(tener importancia)* **este factor pesa mucho** this is a very important factor (d) *(entristecer)* **me pesa tener que hacerlo** I regret having to do it
　3 *nm* (a) *(pena)* sorrow, grief (b) *(arrepentimiento)* regret; **a su p.** to his regret
　4 a pesar de *loc prep* in spite of

pesaroso, -a *adj* (a) *(triste)* sorrowful, sad (b) *(arrepentido)* regretful, sorry

pesca *nf* fishing; *Fam* **y toda la p.** and all that

pescadería *nf* fish shop, fishmonger's (shop)

pescadero, -a *nm,f* fishmonger

pescadilla *nf* whiting

pescado *nm* fish

pescador, -a 1 *adj* fishing
　2 *nm,f (hombre)* fisherman; *(mujer)* fisherwoman

pescar [44] **1** *vi* to fish
　2 *vt* (a) *(peces)* to fish (b) *Fam (coger)* to catch

pescozón *nm* slap on the neck/head

pescuezo *nm Fam* neck

pese: pese a que *loc adv* in spite of (the fact that)

pesebre *nm* manger, stall

pesero *nm Méx* (a) *(vehículo)* collective taxi *(with a fixed rate and that travels a fixed route)* (b) *(persona)* collective taxi driver

peseta *nf Antes* peseta

pesetero, -a *nm,f Esp Fam Pey* skinflint

pesimismo *nm* pessimism

pesimista 1 *adj* pessimistic
2 *nmf* pessimist

pésimo, -a *adj* very bad, awful, terrible

peso *nm* (a) weight; **al p.** by weight; **p. bruto/neto** gross/net weight; *Fig* **me quité un p. de encima** it took a load off my mind; **p. mosca/pesado** *(en boxeo)* flyweight/heavyweight (b) *(importancia)* importance; **de p.** *(persona)* influential; *(razón)* convincing (c) *(moneda)* peso

pespunte *nm* backstitch

pesquero, -a 1 *adj* fishing
2 *nm* fishing boat

pesquisa *nf* inquiry

pestaña *nf* (a) *(del ojo)* eyelash, lash (b) *(en página Web)* tab

pestañear *vi* to blink; **sin p.** without batting an eyelid

peste *nf* (a) *(hedor)* stench, stink (b) *Med* plague; *Hist* **la p. negra** the Black Death (c) **decir** *o* **echar pestes de algn** *Br* to slag sb off, *US* to badmouth sb

pesticida *nm* pesticide

pestilencia *nf* stench, stink

pestilente *adj* stinking, foul

pestillo *nm* bolt, latch

petaca *nf* (a) *(para cigarrillos)* cigarette case; *(para bebidas)* flask (b) *Méx (maleta)* suitcase (c) *Méx Fam* **petacas** *(nalgas)* buttocks

pétalo *nm* petal

petanca *nf* petanque

petardo *nm* (a) *(cohete)* firecracker, *Br* banger; *Mil* petard (b) *Fam (persona aburrida)* bore (c) *Esp Fam (porro)* joint

petate *nm Mil* luggage

petenera *nf Esp Fam* **salir por peteneras** to go off at a tangent

petición *nf* request; *Der* petition, plea

petiso, -a *adj Andes, RP Fam* short

peto *nm* **pantalón de p.** dungarees

petrificar [44] *vt* to petrify

petróleo *nm* petroleum, oil

> *Observa* que en el inglés británico **petrol** es un falso amigo y no es la traducción de la palabra española **petróleo**. En inglés británico **petrol** significa "gasolina".

petrolero *nm* oil tanker

petrolífero, -a *adj* oil; **pozo p.** oil well

petulancia *nf* arrogance

petulante *adj* arrogant, vain

> *Observa* que la palabra inglesa **petulant** es un falso amigo y no es la traducción de la palabra española **petulante**. En inglés **petulant** significa "caprichoso".

petunia *nf* petunia

peúco *nm* bootee

peyorativo, -a *adj* pejorative, derogatory

pez¹ *nm* fish; **ella está como p. en el agua** she's in her element; **p. gordo** big shot

pez² *nf* pitch, tar

pezón *nm* nipple

pezuña *nf* hoof

piadoso, -a *adj* (a) *(devoto)* pious (b) *(compasivo)* compassionate; **mentira piadosa** white lie

pianista *nmf* pianist, piano player

piano *nm* piano

piar [29] *vi* to chirp, to tweet

piara *nf* herd of pigs

PIB *nm Fin (abr* **producto** *Esp* **interior** *o Am* **bruto)** GDP

pibe, -a *nm,f Fam* (a) *Esp (hombre)* guy; *(mujer)* girl (b) *Arg (niño)* kid, boy; *(niña)* kid, girl

pica *nf* (a) *(lanza)* pike (b) **picas** *(palo de baraja)* spades

picada *nf* (a) *RP (tapas)* appetizers, snacks (b) *RP Br* mince, *US* ground beef (c) *Am (de avión)* nose dive; **hacer una p.** to dive

picadero *nm* riding school

picadillo *nm* (a) *(de carne)* minced meat; *(de verduras)* vegetable salad (b) *Chile (tapas)* appetizers, snacks

picado, -a 1 *adj* (a) *Esp, RP (carne) Br* minced, *US* ground (b) *(fruta)* bad; *(diente)* decayed (c) *(mar)* choppy (d) **estar p. con** *(en competición)* to be at loggerheads with
2 *nm Esp Av* dive; **caer en p.** to plummet

picador *nm Taurom* mounted bullfighter, picador

picadora *nf Esp, RP* mincer

picadura *nf* (a) *(mordedura)* bite; *(de avispa, abeja)* sting (b) *(en fruta)* spot; *Med (de viruela)* pockmark; *(en diente)* decay, caries *sing*; *(en metalurgia)* pitting

picajoso, -a *adj* touchy

picante *adj* (a) *Culin* hot, spicy (b) *(chiste etc)* risqué, spicy

picantería *nf Andes (restaurante)* cheap restaurant

picapica *nm* **(polvos de) p.** itching powder

picaporte *nm* *(aldaba)* door knocker; *(pomo)* door handle

picar [44] **1** *vt* (**a**) *(de insecto, serpiente)* to bite; *(de avispas, abejas)* to sting; *(barba)* to prick (**b**) *(comer) (de aves)* to peck (at); *(de persona)* to nibble, to pick at (**c**) *(de pez)* to bite (**d**) *(perforar)* to prick, to puncture (**e**) *Culin Esp, RP (carne) Br* to mince, *US* to grind (**f**) *(incitar)* to incite, to goad; **p. la curiosidad (de algn)** to arouse (sb's) curiosity

2 *vi* (**a**) *(escocer)* to itch; *(herida)* to smart; *(el sol)* to burn (**b**) *Culin* to be hot (**c**) *(pez)* to bite (**d**) *Fig (dejarse engañar)* to swallow it

3 picarse *vpr* (**a**) *(hacerse rivales)* to be at loggerheads (**b**) *(fruta)* to spot, to rot; *(ropa)* to become moth-eaten; *(dientes)* to decay (**c**) *(enfadarse)* to get cross (**d**) *(drogadicto)* to shoot up

picardía 1 *nf* (**a**) *(astucia)* craftiness (**b**) *(de niño)* mischief

2 picardías *nm inv (prenda femenina)* negligee

pícaro, -a 1 *adj* (**a**) *(travieso)* naughty, mischievous; *(astuto)* sly, crafty (**b**) *(procaz)* risqué

2 *nm,f* rascal, rogue

picatoste *nm* crouton

pichi *nm Br* pinafore dress, *US* jumper

pichincha *nf RP Fam* snip, bargain

pichón *nm* young pigeon; **tiro al** *o* **de p.** pigeon shooting

pickles *nmpl RP* pickles

picnic (*pl* **picnics**) *nm* picnic

pico *nm* (**a**) *(de ave)* beak, bill; *Fam (boca)* mouth, *esp Br* gob; **tener un p. de oro** to have the gift of the gab (**b**) *(punta)* corner (**c**) *Geog* peak (**d**) *(herramienta)* pick, pickaxe (**e**) *(cantidad)* odd amount; **cincuenta y p.** fifty odd; **las dos y p.** just after two (**f**) *(drogas)* fix

picor *nm* itch, tingling

picoso, -a *adj Méx* spicy, hot

picotazo *nm* peck

picotear *vt & vi* (**a**) *(pájaro)* to peck (**b**) *(comer)* to nibble

pictórico, -a *adj* pictorial

pie *nm* (**a**) *(de persona)* foot; **pies** feet; **a p.** on foot; **de p.** standing up; **de pies a cabeza** from head to foot; **en p.** standing; **el acuerdo sigue en p.** the agreement still stands; **hacer p.** to touch the bottom; **perder p.** to get out of one's depth; *Fig* **a pies juntillas** blindly; *Fig* **al p. de la letra** to the letter, word for word; *Fig* **con buen/mal p.** on the right/wrong footing; *Fig* **con pies de plomo** gingerly, cautiously; *Fig* **dar p. a** to give cause for (**b**) *(de instrumento)* stand; *(de copa)* stem (**c**) *(de página)* foot; *(de ilustración)* caption (**d**) *(medida)* foot (**e**) *Teatro* cue (**f**) *Lit* foot

piedad *nf* (**a**) *(religiosidad)* piety (**b**) *(compasión)* pity

piedra *nf* stone; *(de mechero)* flint; **poner la primera p.** to lay the foundation stone; *Fam Fig* **me dejó** *o* **me quedé de p.** I was flabbergasted

piel *nf* (**a**) *(de persona)* skin; **p. de gallina** goose pimples (**b**) *(de fruta, de patata)* skin, peel (**c**) *Esp, Méx (cuero)* leather (**d**) *(pelo)* fur

pienso *nm* fodder, feed; **piensos compuestos** mixed feed

pierna *nf* leg

pieza *nf* (**a**) *(pedazo, parte)* piece; **p. de recambio** spare part, *US* extra; *Fig* **me dejó** *o* **me quedé de una p.** I was speechless *o* dumbfounded *o* flabbergasted (**b**) *(habitación)* room (**c**) *Teatro* play

pigmento *nm* pigment

pigmeo, -a *nm, f* pygmy, pigmy

pijama *nm* pyjamas

pijo, -a *Esp* **1** *adj Fam* posh; **un barrio p.** a posh area

2 *nm,f Fam* rich kid

3 *nm muy Fam (pene)* prick, cock

pila *nf* (**a**) *Elec* battery (**b**) *(montón)* pile, heap; *Fig* **una p. de** *(muchos)* piles *o* heaps *o* loads of (**c**) *(lavadero)* basin (**d**) *Fig* **nombre de p.** Christian name

pilar *nm* (**a**) *Arquit* pillar (**b**) *(fuente)* waterhole

píldora *nf* pill; **p. abortiva** morning-after pill; *Fig* **dorar la p. a algn** to butter sb up

pileta *nf RP* (**a**) *(en baño)* wasbasin; *(en cocina)* sink (**b**) *(piscina)* swimming pool

pilila *nf Fam Br* willy, *US* peter

pillaje *nm* looting, pillage

pillar 1 *vt* (**a**) *(robar)* to plunder, to loot (**b**) *(coger)* to catch; *(alcanzar)* to catch up with; **lo pilló un coche** he was run over by a car (**c**) *Fam* to be; **me pilla un poco lejos** it's a bit far for *o* from me

2 pillarse *vpr* to catch; **pillarse un dedo/una mano** to catch one's finger/hand

pillo, -a 1 *adj* (**a**) *(travieso)* naughty (**b**) *(astuto)* sly, cunning

2 *nm,f* rogue

pilotar *vt Av* to pilot, to fly; *Aut* to drive; *Náut* to pilot, to steer

piloto *nm* (**a**) *Av & Náut* pilot; *Aut* driver; **piso p.** show flat; **programa p.** pilot programme (**b**) *(luz)* pilot lamp *o* light

piltrafa *nf Fam* **estar hecho una p.** to be on one's last legs

pimentón *nm* paprika, red pepper

pimienta *nf* pepper

pimiento *nm (fruto)* pepper; *(planta)* pimiento; **p. morrón** sweet pepper; *Fam*

me importa un p. I don't give a damn, I couldn't care less

pimpollo *nm* (a) *Bot* shoot (b) *Fam (hombre)* hunk; *(mujer)* babe

pin *(pl* **pins)** *nm* pin, (lapel) badge

pinacoteca *nf* art gallery

pináculo *nm* pinnacle

pinar *nm* pine grove, pine wood

pincel *nm* brush, paintbrush

pincelada *nf* brushstroke, stroke of a brush

pinchadiscos *nmf inv Esp* disc jockey, DJ

pinchar 1 *vt* (a) *(punzar)* to prick; *(balón, globo)* to burst; *(rueda)* to puncture (b) *Fam (incitar)* to prod; *(molestar)* to get at, to nag (c) *Med* to give an injection to (d) *Tel* to bug

2 *vi* (a) *Aut* to get a puncture (b) *Fam* **ni pincha ni corta** his opinion doesn't count for anything

⚬ Observa que el verbo inglés **to pinch** es un falso amigo y no es la traducción del verbo español **pinchar**. En inglés, **to pinch** significa "pellizcar".

pinchazo *nm* (a) *(punzadura)* prick; *Aut* puncture, blowout (b) *(de dolor)* sudden o sharp pain

pinche¹ *nmf* (a) *(de cocina) (hombre)* kitchen boy; *(mujer)* maid (b) *RP Fam (en oficina)* office junior

pinche² *adj Méx Fam* damn, *Br* bloody; **¡ese p. perro!** that damn o *Br* bloody dog!

pincho *nm* (a) *(púa)* barb (b) *Esp (tapa)* bar snack, aperitif; **p. moruno** ≃ shish kebab; **p. de tortilla** = small portion of omelette

pinga *nf Andes, Méx, Ven Vulg* prick, cock

ping-pong [pim'pon] *nm* ping-pong, table-tennis

pingüe *adj* abundant, plentiful; **pingües beneficios** fat profits

pingüino *nm* penguin

pino *nm* pine; *Esp Fig* **hacer el p.** to do a handstand; *Esp Fam* **en el quinto p.** in the back of beyond

pinol, pinole *nm CAm, Méx Br* maize flour, *US* corn flour

pinta 1 *nf* (a) *Fam (aspecto)* look; **tiene p. de ser interesante** it looks interesting (b) *(mota)* dot; *(lunar)* spot (c) *(medida)* pint

2 *nmf Fam* shameless person

pintada *nf* graffiti

pintado, -a *adj* **recién p.** *(en letrero)* wet paint; *Fam Fig* **nos viene que ni p.** it is just the ticket; *Fam Fig* **te está que ni p.** it suits you to a T

pintalabios *nm inv* lipstick

pintar 1 *vt* (a) *(dar color)* to paint (b) *(dibujar)* to draw, to sketch

2 *vi (importar)* to count; *Fig* **yo aquí no pinto nada** I am out of place here

3 **pintarse** *upr* (a) *(maquillarse)* to put make-up on (b) *Fam* **pintárselas** to manage

pintarrajear *vt* to daub

pintor, -a *nm,f* painter

pintoresco, -a *adj* (a) *(lugar)* picturesque (b) *(raro)* eccentric, bizarre

pintura *nf* (a) *(técnica, cuadro)* painting; **p. rupestre** cave painting; *Fam Fig* **no la puedo ver ni en p.** I can't stand the sight of her (b) *(materia)* paint (c) *(lápiz)* colour pencil; *(de cera)* crayon

pinza *nf (para tender) Br* clothes peg, *US* clothespin; *(de animal)* pincer, claw; **pinzas** *(para depilar)* tweezers; *(para hielo)* tongs

piña *nf* (a) *(de pino)* pine cone; *(ananás)* pineapple (b) *Fig (grupo)* clan, clique (c) *Fam (golpe)* thump

piñón *nm* (a) *(del pino)* pine seed o nut (b) *Téc* pinion

pío¹ *nm* **¡p., p.!** cheep, cheep!; *Fam* **no dijo ni p.** there wasn't a cheep out of him

pío², -a *adj* pious

piojo *nm* louse

piola *adj RP Fam* (a) *(simpático)* fun (b) *Irón (listo)* smart, clever (c) *(lugar)* cosy

piolín *nm Andes, RP* cord

pionero, -a *nm,f* pioneer

pipa *nf* (a) *(de fumar)* pipe; **fumar en p.** to smoke a pipe (b) *(de fruta)* pip; *(de girasol)* sunflower seed

pipí *nm Fam* pee, *Br* wee-wee; **hacer p.** to have a pee

pipián *nm Andes, CAm, Méx* (a) *(salsa)* = sauce thickened with ground nuts or seeds (b) *(guiso)* = type of stew in which the sauce is thickened with ground nuts or seeds

pique *nm* (a) *(enfado)* grudge (b) *(rivalidad)* needle (c) **a p. de** on the point of (d) **irse a p.** *Náut* to sink; *(un plan)* to fall through; *(un negocio)* to go bust

piqueta *nf* pickaxe

piquete *nm* (a) *(de huelga)* picket (b) *Mil* **p. de ejecución** firing squad

pira *nf* pyre

pirado, -a *Fam* **1** *adj* crazy

2 *nm,f* loony, *Br* nutter

piragua *nf* canoe

piragüismo *nm* canoeing

piragüista *nmf* canoeist

pirámide *nf* pyramid

piraña *nf* piranha

pirarse *upr Esp, RP Fam* to clear off, to hop it

pirata *adj & nmf* pirate

piratear *vt Fig* to pirate

Pirineo(s) *nm(pl)* Pyrenees

pirita *nf* pyrite

pirómano, -a *nm,f Med* pyromaniac; *Der* arsonist

piropo *nm* echar un p. to pay a compliment

pirueta *nf* pirouette; *Fig Pol* hacer una p. to do a U-turn

piruja *nf Col, Méx muy Fam* whore, *US* hooker

pirulí *nm* lollipop

pis *nm Fam* pee; hacer p. to have a pee

pisada *nf* step, footstep; *(huella)* footprint

pisapapeles *nm inv* paperweight

pisar *vt* to tread on, to step on

piscifactoría *nf* fish farm

piscina *nf* swimming pool

Piscis *nm inv* Pisces

pisco *nm* pisco, = Andean grape brandy

piscolabis *nm inv Esp Fam* snack

piso *nm* (a) *Esp (vivienda)* apartment, *Br* flat; *Pol* p. franco safe house (b) *(planta)* floor; *(de carretera)* surface

pisotear *vt (aplastar)* to stamp on; *(pisar)* to trample on

pisotón *nm* me dio un p. he stood on my foot

pista *nf* (a) *(de atletismo, forestal)* track; **p. de baile** dance floor; *Dep* **p. de esquí** ski run *o* slope; *Dep* **p. de patinaje** ice rink; *Dep* **p. de tenis** tennis court; **p. de aterrizaje** landing strip; **p. de despegue** runway (b) *(rastro)* trail, track (c) *(indicio)* clue; **dame una p.** give me a clue

pistacho *nm* pistachio nut

pisto *nm Culin* ≃ ratatouille

pistola *nf* (a) *(arma)* gun, pistol (b) *(para pintar)* spray gun

pistolero *nm* gunman, gangster

pistón *nm* (a) *Téc (émbolo)* piston (b) *Mús* key

pita *nf* agave

pitada *nf* (a) *(silbidos de protesta)* booing, whistling (b) *Am Fam (calada)* drag, puff

pitar 1 *vt* (a) *(silbato)* to blow (b) *Dep* **el árbitro pitó un penalti** the referee awarded a penalty

2 *vi* (a) *(con silbato)* to whistle (b) *Aut* to toot one's horn (c) *Dep* to referee (d) *Esp Fam* **salir pitando** to fly off

pitido *nm* whistle

pitillera *nf* cigarette case

pitillo *nm* (a) *(cigarrillo)* cigarette (b) *Col (paja)* drinking straw

pito *nm* (a) *(silbato)* whistle; *Aut* horn; *Fam* **me importa un p.** I don't give a hoot (b) *Fam (cigarrillo)* fag (c) *Fam (pene) Br* willy, *US* peter

pitón *nm* (a) *(serpiente)* python (b) *(de toro)* horn

pitorreo *nm Esp Fam* scoffing, teasing; **hacer algo de p.** to do sth for a laugh

pivote *nmf* (a) *(eje)* pivot (b) *Dep* pivot

pizarra *nf* (a) *(encerado) Br* blackboard, *US* chalkboard (b) *(roca, material)* slate

pizarrón *nm Am Br* blackboard, *US* chalkboard

pizca *nf* little bit, tiny piece; **ni p.** not a bit; **una p. de sal** a pinch of salt

pizza ['pitsa] *nf* pizza

pizzería [pitse'ria] *nf* pizzeria, pizza parlour

placa *nf* (a) *(lámina)* plate; **p. solar** solar panel (b) *(conmemorativa)* plaque (c) *Med* **p. dental** dental plaque

placaje *nm Dep* tackle

placentero, -a *adj* pleasant, agreeable

placer [33] **1** *vt* to please

2 *nm* pleasure; **ha sido un p. (conocerle)** it's been a pleasure (meeting you); *Fml* **tengo el p. de** it gives me great pleasure to; **un viaje de p.** a holiday trip

placidez *nf* placidity

plácido, -a *adj* placid, easy-going

plaga *nf* (a) *(de insectos)* plague (b) *Agr* pest, blight

plagar [42] *vt* to cover, to fill

plagiar [43] *vt* (a) *(copiar)* to plagiarize (b) *CAm, Col, Perú, Méx (secuestrar)* to kidnap

plagiario, -a *nm,f CAm, Col, Perú, Méx* kidnapper

plagio *nm* (a) *(copia)* plagiarism (b) *CAm, Col, Perú, Ven (secuestro)* kidnapping

plan *nm* (a) *(proyecto)* plan (b) *(programa)* scheme, programme; *Educ* **p. de estudios** syllabus; **estar a p.** to be on a diet (c) *Fam* **en p. de broma** for a laugh; **si te pones en ese p.** if you're going to be like that (about it); **en p. barato** cheaply (d) *Fam (cita)* date

plana *nf* (a) *(página)* page; **a toda p.** full page; **primera p.** front page (b) *Mil* **p. mayor** staff

plancha *nf* (a) *(para la ropa)* iron; *(de metal)* plate (b) *Culin* hotplate; **sardinas a la p.** grilled sardines (c) *Impr* plate

planchado *nm* ironing

planchar *vt* to iron

planchazo *nm Fam* blunder, boob

planeador *nm* glider

planear 1 *vt* to plan
 2 *vi* to glide

planeta *nm* planet

planetario, -a 1 *adj* planetary
 2 *nm* planetarium

planicie *nf* plain

planificación *nf* planning; **p. familiar** family planning

planificar [44] *vt* to plan

planilla *nf* (**a**) *Am (formulario)* form (**b**) *Am (nómina)* payroll

plano, -a 1 *nm* (**a**) *(de ciudad)* map; *Arquit* plan, draft (**b**) *Cin* shot; **un primer p.** a close-up; *Fig* **estar en primer/segundo p.** to be in the limelight/in the background (**c**) *Mat* plane
 2 *adj* flat, even

planta *nf* (**a**) *(vegetal)* plant (**b**) *(del pie)* sole (**c**) *(piso)* floor, storey; **p. baja** *Br* ground floor, *US* first floor (**d**) *(fábrica)* plant

plantación *nf* (**a**) *(terreno)* plantation (**b**) *(acción)* planting

plantado, -a *adj Fam* **dejar a algn p.** to stand sb up

plantar 1 *vt* (**a**) *(árboles, campo)* to plant (**b**) *(poner)* to put, to place; **p. cara a algn** to stand up to sb (**c**) *Fam* **p. a algn en la calle** to throw sb out; **le ha plantado su novia** his girlfriend has ditched him
 2 plantarse *upr* (**a**) *(ponerse)* to plant oneself (**b**) *(en un sitio con rapidez)* **plantarse en** to get to, to make it to

planteamiento *nm (enfoque)* approach

plantear 1 *vt* (**a**) *(problema)* to pose, to raise (**b**) *(planear)* to plan (**c**) *(proponer)* to put forward (**d**) *(exponer)* to present
 2 plantearse *upr* (**a**) *(considerar)* to consider (**b**) *(problema)* to arise

plantel *nm* team

plantilla *nf* (**a**) *(personal)* staff, personnel (**b**) *(de zapato)* insole (**c**) *(patrón)* model, pattern

plantón *nm Fam* **dar un p. a algn** to stand sb up

plañir *vi* to mourn

plasmar 1 *vt* (**a**) *(reproducir)* to capture (**b**) *(expresar)* to express
 2 plasmarse *upr* **p. en** to take the shape of

plasta *nmf Esp Fam* bore

plástico, -a *adj & nm* plastic

plastificar [44] *vt* to coat *o* cover with plastic

plastilina® *nf* Plasticine®

plata *nf* (**a**) *(metal)* silver; *(objetos de plata)* silverware; *Fam* **hablar en p.** to lay (it) on the line; **p. de ley** sterling silver (**b**) *Am Fam (dinero)* money

plataforma *nf* platform

plátano *nm* (**a**) *(fruta)* banana (**b**) *(árbol)* plane tree; **falso p.** sycamore

platea *nf Br* stalls, *US* orchestra

plateado, -a *adj* (**a**) *(con plata)* silver-plated (**b**) *(color)* silvery

platense 1 *adj* of/from the River Plate
 2 *nmf* person from the River Plate

plateresco *nm* plateresque, = 15–16th century Spanish architectural style

plática *nf CAm, Méx (charla)* talk, chat

platicar [44] *vi CAm, Méx* to chat, to talk

platillo *nm* (**a**) *(para taza)* saucer; **p. volador,** *Esp* **p. volante** flying saucer (**b**) *Mús* cymbal

platina *nf* deck; **doble p.** double deck

platino *nm* (**a**) *(metal)* platinum (**b**) *Aut* **platinos** contact breaker, points

plato *nm* (**a**) *(recipiente)* plate, dish (**b**) *(parte de una comida)* course; **de primer p.** for starters; **p. fuerte** main course; **p. combinado** one-meal meal (**c**) *(guiso)* dish (**d**) *(de balanza)* pan, tray (**e**) *(de tocadiscos)* turntable

plató *nm Cin & TV (film)* set

platudo, -a *adj Am Fam* loaded, rolling in it

plausible *adj* (**a**) *(admisible)* plausible, acceptable (**b**) *(loable)* commendable

playa *nf* (**a**) *(junto al mar)* beach (**b**) *Am* **p. de estacionamiento** *Br* car park, *US* parking lot

play-back ['pleɪak] *(pl* **play-backs**) *nm* **hacer p.** to mime (the lyrics)

playera *nf* (**a**) *(zapatilla)* *Br* sandshoe, *US* sneaker (**b**) *Méx (camiseta)* teeshirt

plaza *nf* (**a**) *(en población)* square (**b**) *(sitio)* place; **tenemos plazas limitadas** there are a limited number of places available; **p. de aparcamiento** parking space (**c**) *(mercado)* market, market-place (**d**) *Aut (asiento)* seat (**e**) *(laboral)* post, position (**f**) **p. de toros** bullring

plazo *nm* (**a**) *(periodo)* time, period; *(término)* deadline; **a corto/largo p.** in the short term/in the long run; **el p. termina el viernes** Friday is the deadline (**b**) *Fin* **comprar a plazos** to buy on *Br* hire purchase *o US* an installment plan; **en seis plazos** in six instalments

pleamar *nf* high tide

plebe *nf* masses, plebs

plebeyo, -a 1 *adj* plebeian
 2 *nm,f* plebeian, pleb

plebiscito *nm* plebiscite

plegable *adj* folding, collapsible

plegar [1] **1** *vt* to fold
 2 plegarse *upr* to give way, to bow

plegaria *nf* prayer

pleitear *vi* to conduct a lawsuit, to plead

pleito *nm* (**a**) *Der* lawsuit, litigation; **poner un p. (a algn)** to sue (sb) (**b**) *Am (discusión)* argument

plenilunio *nm* full moon

plenitud *nf* plenitude, fullness; **en la p. de la vida** in the prime of life

pleno, -a 1 *adj* full; **en plena noche** in the middle of the night; **los empleados en p.** the entire staff

 2 *nm* plenary meeting

pletórico, -a *adj* abundant

plexiglás® *nm* Perspex®, *US* Plexiglass®

pliego *nm (hoja)* sheet *o* piece of paper; **p. de condiciones** bidding specifications

pliegue *nm* (**a**) *(doblez)* fold (**b**) *(en plisado)* pleat

plinto *nm Dep* vaulting box

plisar *vt* to pleat

plomería *nf Méx, RP, Ven* (**a**) *(negocio)* plumber's (**b**) *(instalación)* plumbing

plomero *nm Méx, RP, Ven* plumber

plomizo, -a *adj (color, cielo)* leaden

plomo *nm* (**a**) *(en metalurgia)* lead (**b**) *Elec (fusible)* fuse (**c**) *(bala)* slug, pellet

pluma *nf* (**a**) *(de ave)* feather (**b**) *(estilográfica)* fountain pen (**c**) *Carib, Méx (bolígrafo)* (ballpoint) pen (**d**) *Carib, Col, Méx (grifo) Br* tap, *US* faucet

plumaje *nm* plumage

plumazo *nm* **de un p.** at a stroke

plumero *nm* (**a**) *(para el polvo)* feather duster (**b**) *Fam* **se te ve el p.** I can see through you

plumier *(pl* plumiers*)* *nm* pencil box

plumón *nm (de ave)* down

plural *adj & nm* plural

pluralidad *nf* diversity

pluralismo *nm* pluralism

pluriempleo *nm* **hacer p.** to have more than one job

plus *nm* bonus

plusmarca *nf* record

plusmarquista *nmf* record breaker

plusvalía *nf (tras venta)* capital gain; *Econ* surplus value

Plza. *(abr* Plaza*)* Sq

PM *nf (abr* policía militar*)* MP

p.m. *(abr* post meridiem*)* p.m.

población *nf* (**a**) *(ciudad)* town; *(pueblo)* village (**b**) *(habitantes)* population (**c**) *Chile (barrio)* **p. (callampa)** shanty town

poblado, -a *adj (zona)* populated; *Fig* **p. de** full of (**b**) *(barba)* bushy, thick

poblador, -a *nm,f* settler

poblar [2] *vt* (**a**) *(con gente)* to settle, to people; *(con plantas)* to plant (**b**) *(vivir en)* to inhabit

pobre 1 *adj* poor; **¡p.!** poor thing!; **un hombre p.** a poor man; **un p. hombre** a poor devil

 2 *nmf* poor person; **los pobres** the poor

pobreza *nf* poverty; *Fig (de medios, recursos)* lack

pocho, -a *adj* (**a**) *(fruta)* bad, overripe (**b**) *Fig (persona) (débil)* off-colour; *(triste)* depressed, down (**c**) *Méx Fam (americanizado)* Americanized

pochoclo *nm Arg* popcorn

pocilga *nf* pigsty

pocillo *nm* (**a**) *RP (pequeño)* small cup (**b**) *Méx, Ven (grande)* enamel mug

pócima *nf* potion; *Pey* concoction, brew

poción *nf* potion

poco, -a 1 *nm* (**a**) **un p.** *(con adj o adv)* a little; **un p. tarde/frío** a little late/cold (**b**) **un p.** *(con sustantivo)* a little; **un p. de azúcar** a little sugar

 2 *adj* (**a**) *(en singular)* not much, little; **p. sitio/tiempo** not much *o* little space/time; **poca cosa** not much (**b**) **pocos, -as** not many, few; **pocas personas** not many *o* few people

 3 *pron* (**a**) *(escasa cantidad)* not much; **queda p.** there isn't much left (**b**) *(breve tiempo)* **p. antes/después** shortly *o* a little before/afterwards; **a p. de** shortly *o* a little after; **dentro de p.** soon (**c**) **pocos, -as** *(cosas)* few, not many; **tengo muy pocos** I have very few, I don't have very many (**d**) **pocos, -as** *(personas)* few people, not many people; **vinieron pocos** few people came, not many people came; **unos pocos** a few

 4 *adv* (**a**) *(con verbo)* not (very) much, little; **ella come p.** she doesn't eat much, she eats little (**b**) *(con adj)* not very; **es p. probable** it's not very likely (**c**) *(en frases)* **p. a p.** little by little, gradually; **por p.** almost

podadera, *Am* **podadora** *nf* garden shears

podar *vt* to prune

podcast *nm* podcast

poder¹ *nm* power; *Econ* **p. adquisitivo** purchasing power

poder² [18] **1** *vi* (**a**) *(capacidad)* to be able to; **no puede hablar** she can't speak; **no podré llamarte** I won't be able to phone; **no puedo más** I can't take any more; **guapa a más no p.** unbelievably pretty (**b**) *(permiso)* can, may; **¿puedo pasar?** can *o* may I come in?; **¿se puede (entrar)?** may I (come in)?; **aquí no se puede fumar** you can't smoke here

(**c**) *(uso impers) (posibilidad)* may; might; **puede que no lo sepan** they may o might not know; **no puede ser** that's impossible; **puede (ser) (que sí)** maybe, perhaps (**d**) *(deber)* **no podemos portarnos así con él** we can't treat him like that (**e**) **p. con** *(enfermedad, rival)* to be able to overcome; *(tarea, problema)* to be able to cope with
  2 *vt (batir)* to be stronger than; **les puede a todos** he can take on anybody

poderoso, -a *adj* powerful

podio, pódium *nm Dep* podium

podómetro *nm* pedometer

podré *indic fut de* **poder²**

podrido, -a *adj* (**a**) *(putrefacto)* rotten, putrid (**b**) *(corrupto)* rotten; *Fam* **estar p. de dinero** o *Am* **en plata** to be filthy rich (**c**) *RP Fam (harto)* fed up, sick

poema *nm* poem

poesía *nf* (**a**) *(género)* poetry (**b**) *(poema)* poem

poeta *nmf* poet

poético, -a *adj* poetic

póker *nm* poker

polaco, -a 1 *adj* Polish
  2 *nm,f* Pole
  3 *nm (idioma)* Polish

polar *adj* polar

polaridad *nf* polarity

polarizar [40] *vt* (**a**) *Fís* to polarize (**b**) *Fig (ánimo, atención)* to concentrate

polea *nf* pulley

polémica *nf* controversy

polémico, -a *adj* controversial

polemizar [40] *vi* to argue, to debate

polen *nm* pollen

polera *nf* (**a**) *Arg, Chile (polo)* polo shirt (**b**) *Urug (de cuello alto)* turtleneck o *Br* polo neck sweater

poli *Fam* **1** *nmf* cop
  2 *nf* **la p.** the fuzz *pl*

polichinela *nm* (**a**) *(personaje)* Punchinello (**b**) *(títere)* puppet, marionette

policía 1 *nf* police (force)
  2 *nmf (hombre)* policeman; *(mujer)* policewoman

policíaco, -a, policiaco, -a, policial *adj* police; **novela/película policíaca** detective story/movie o *Br* film

polideportivo *nm* sports centre

poliéster *nm* polyester

polietileno *nm Br* polythene, *US* polyethylene

polifacético, -a *adj* versatile, many-sided; **es un hombre muy p.** he's a man of many talents

poligamia *nf* polygamy

políglota *adj & nmf* polyglot

polígono *nm* polygon; **p. industrial** *Br* industrial estate, *US* industrial area

polilla *nf* moth

polio *nf* polio

politécnico, -a *adj & nm* polytechnic

política *nf* (**a**) *(ciencia, actividad)* politics *sing* (**b**) *(medidas)* policy

políticamente *adv* **p. correcto** politically correct

político, -a 1 *adj* (**a**) *(de gobierno)* political (**b**) *(pariente)* in-law; **hermano p.** brother-in-law; **su familia política** her in-laws
  2 *nm,f* politician

póliza *nf* (**a**) *(sello)* stamp (**b**) **p. de seguros** insurance policy

polizón *nm* stowaway

polla *nf Vulg* prick

pollera *nf* (**a**) *CSur (occidental)* skirt (**b**) *Andes (indígena)* = long skirt worn in layers by Indian women

pollo *nm* (**a**) *(ave)* chicken (**b**) *Fam (joven)* lad

polo *nm* (**a**) *Elec & Geog* pole; **P. Norte/ Sur** North/South Pole (**b**) *(helado)* Br ice lolly, *US* Popsicle® (**c**) *(prenda)* polo shirt (**d**) *Dep* polo

pololear *vi Chile Fam* to go out (together)

pololo, -a *nm,f Chile Fam (hombre)* boyfriend; *(mujer)* girlfriend

Polonia *n* Poland

poltrona *nf* easy chair

polución *nf* pollution

polvareda *nf* cloud of dust

polvera *nf* powder compact

polvo *nm* (**a**) *(en el aire)* dust; **limpiar** o **quitar el p.** to dust (**b**) *(de producto)* powder; **en p.** powdered; **polvo(s) de talco** talcum powder (**c**) *Fam* **estar hecho p.** *(cansado)* to be *Br* knackered o *US* bushed; *(deprimido)* to be depressed (**d**) *muy Fam* **echar un p.** to have a screw o *Br* a shag

pólvora *nf* gunpowder

polvoriento, -a *adj* dusty

polvorín *nm* gunpowder arsenal; *Fig* powder keg

polvorón *nm* sweet pastry

pomada *nf* ointment

pomelo *nm (fruto)* grapefruit; *(árbol)* grapefruit tree

pómez *adj inv* **piedra p.** pumice (stone)

pomo *nm (de puerta)* knob

pompa *nf* (**a**) **p. (de jabón)** (soap) bubble (**b**) *(suntuosidad)* pomp (**c**) *Méx Fam* **pompas** behind, bottom

pompis *nm inv Fam* botty

pomposo, -a *adj* pompous

pómulo *nm* cheekbone

ponchar 1 *vt* (**a**) *(asunto)* CAm, Carib, Méx *(rueda)* to puncture (**b**) *Am (en béisbol)* to strike out **2 poncharse** *vpr* (**a**) *CAm, Carib, Méx (rueda)* to blow (**b**) *Am (en béisbol)* to strike out

ponche *nm* punch

poncho *nm* poncho

ponderar *vt* (**a**) *(asunto)* to weigh up *o* consider (**b**) *(alabar)* to praise

pondré *indic fut de* **poner**

ponencia *nf* paper

poner [19] *(pp* **puesto**) **1** *vt* (**a**) *(colocar, meter)* to put; *(mesa, huevo)* to lay; *(gesto)* to make; *(multa)* to impose; *(telegrama)* to send; *(negocio)* to set up
(**b**) *(tele, radio etc)* to turn *o* switch on
(**c**) (+ *adj*) to make; **p. triste a algn** to make sb sad; **p. colorado a algn** to make sb blush
(**d**) **¿qué llevaba puesto?** what was he wearing?
(**e**) *Esp (decir)* **¿qué pone aquí?** what does it say here?
(**f**) *(suponer)* to suppose; **pongamos que Ana no viene** supposing Ana doesn't turn up
(**g**) *TV & Cin* to put on, to show; **¿qué ponen en la tele?** what's on the telly?
(**h**) *Esp Tel* **ponme con Manuel** put me through to Manuel
(**i**) *(nombrar)* **le pondremos (de nombre) Pilar** we are going to call her Pilar
2 *v impers Am Fam (parecer)* **se me pone que …** it seems to me that …
3 ponerse *vpr* (**a**) *(colocarse)* to put oneself; **ponte en mi lugar** put yourself in my place; **ponte más cerca** come closer (**b**) *(vestirse)* to put on; **ella se puso el jersey** she put her sweater on (**c**) (+ *adj*) to become; **ponerse furioso/malo** to become furious/ill (**d**) *(sol)* to set (**e**) *Tel* **ponerse al teléfono** to answer the phone (**f**) **ponerse a** to start to; **ponerse a trabajar** to get down to work

poney (*pl* **poneys**) *nm* pony

pongo *indic pres de* **poner**

poniente *nm* (**a**) *(occidente)* West (**b**) *(viento)* westerly (wind)

ponqué *nm Col, Ven* = fruit or custard-filled cake

pontífice *nm* Pontiff; **el Sumo P.** His Holiness the Pope

ponzoña *nf* venom, poison

ponzoñoso, -a *adj* venomous, poisonous

popa *nf* stern; *Fig* **ir viento en p.** to go full speed ahead

popote *nm Méx* (drinking) straw

populacho *nm Pey* plebs, masses

popular *adj* (**a**) *(creencia, movimiento, revuelta)* popular; *(arte, música)* folk; *(lenguaje)* colloquial (**b**) *(famoso, aceptado)* popular

popularidad *nf* popularity

popularizar [40] *vt* to popularize

populoso, -a *adj* densely populated

popurrí *nm Mús* medley

póquer *nm* poker

por *prep* (**a**) *(agente)* by; **pintado p. Picasso** painted by Picasso
(**b**) **p. qué** why
(**c**) *(causa)* because of; **p. sus ideas** because of her ideas; **p. necesidad/amor** out of need/love; **suspendió p. no estudiar** he failed because he didn't study
(**d**) *(tiempo)* **p. la mañana/noche** in the morning/at night; **p. ahora** for the time being; **p. entonces** at that time
(**e**) *(en favor de)* for; **lo hago p. mi hermano** I'm doing it for my brother('s sake)
(**f**) *(lugar)* **pasamos p. Córdoba** we went through Córdoba; **p. ahí** over there; **¿p. dónde vamos?** which way are we taking *o* going?; **p. la calle** in the street; **mirar p. la ventana** to look out the window; **entrar p. la ventana** to get in through the window
(**g**) *(medio)* by; **p. avión/correo** by plane/post
(**h**) *(a cambio de)* for; **cambiar algo p. otra cosa** to exchange sth for something else
(**i**) *(distributivo)* **p. cabeza** a head, per person; **p. hora/mes** per hour/month
(**j**) *Mat* **dos p. tres, seis** two times three is six; **un 10 p. ciento** 10 percent
(**k**) *(con infinitivo)* in order to, so as to; **hablar p. hablar** to talk for the sake of it
(**l**) *(locuciones)* **p. así decirlo** so to speak; **p. más** *o* **muy … que sea** no matter how … he/she is; **p. mí** as far as I'm concerned

porcelana *nf* porcelain

porcentaje *nm* percentage

porche *nm* porch

porcino, -a *adj* **ganado p.** pigs

porción *nf* portion, part

pordiosero, -a *nm,f* tramp, *US* bum

porfiado, -a *adj (insistente)* persistent; *(tozudo)* stubborn

pormenor *nm* detail; **venta al p.** retail

porno *adj inv Fam* porn

pornografía *nf* pornography

pornográfico, -a *adj* pornographic

poro *nm* pore

poroso, -a *adj* porous

poroto *nm Andes, RP (judía)* kidney bean

porque *conj* (**a**) *(causal)* because; **¡p. no!** just because! (**b**) *(final)* *(+ subj)* so that, in order that

porqué *nm* reason

porquería *nf* (**a**) *(suciedad)* dirt, filth (**b**) *(cosa de mala calidad)* Br rubbish, US garbage (**c**) **porquerías** *(comida)* Br rubbish, US garbage

porra *nf* (**a**) *(de policía)* truncheon, baton (**b**) *Fam (locuciones)* **¡una p.!** *Br* rubbish!, US garbage!; **¡vete a la p.!** get lost!

porrazo *nm* thump

porro *nm* (**a**) *Fam (de droga)* joint (**b**) *Am (puerro)* leek

porrón *nm* = glass wine vessel used for drinking wine from its long spout

portaaviones *nm inv* aircraft carrier

portada *nf* (**a**) *(de libro etc)* cover; *(de periódico)* front page; *(de disco)* sleeve (**b**) *(fachada)* front, facade

portador, -a *nm,f Com* bearer; *Med* carrier

portaequipajes *nm inv* (**a**) *Aut (maletero)* Br boot, US trunk; *(baca)* roof o luggage rack (**b**) *(carrito)* luggage trolley

portafolios *nm inv* briefcase

portal *nm* (**a**) *(zaguán)* porch, entrance hall (**b**) *(puerta de la calle)* main door (**c**) **p. de Belén** Nativity scene (**d**) *Inform* portal

portamaletas *nm inv* = **portaequipajes**

portaminas *nm inv* propelling pencil

portamonedas *nm inv* purse

portarse *vpr* to behave; **p. mal** to misbehave

portátil *adj* portable

portaviones *nm inv* = **portaaviones**

portavoz *nmf* spokesperson; *(hombre)* spokesman; *(mujer)* spokeswoman

portazo *nm* **oímos un p.** we heard a slam o bang; **dar un p.** to slam the door

porte *nm* (**a**) *(aspecto)* bearing (**b**) *(transporte)* carriage

portento *nm* (**a**) *(cosa)* wonder, marvel (**b**) *(persona)* genius

portentoso, -a *adj* extraordinary, prodigious

porteño, -a 1 *adj* of/from Buenos Aires **2** *nm,f* person from Buenos Aires

portería *nf* (**a**) *(de casa, colegio)* Br caretaker's office, US super(intendent)'s office; *(de hotel, ministerio)* porter's office (**b**) *Dep* goal, goalmouth

portero, -a 1 *nm,f* (**a**) *(de casa, colegio)* Br caretaker, US super(intendent); *(de hotel, ministerio) (en recepción)* porter; *(a la puerta)* doorman (**b**) *Dep* goalkeeper **2** *nm* **p. automático** entryphone

pórtico *nm* (**a**) *(portal)* portico, porch (**b**) *(con arcadas)* arcade

portorriqueño, -a *adj & nm,f* Puerto Rican

portuario, -a *adj* harbour, port

Portugal *n* Portugal

portugués, -esa 1 *adj & nm,f* Portuguese **2** *nm (idioma)* Portuguese

porvenir *nm* future; **sin p.** with no prospects

pos *adv* **en p. de** after

posada *nf* inn

posaderas *nfpl Fam* buttocks

posadero, -a *nm,f* innkeeper

posar 1 *vi (para retrato etc)* to pose **2** *vt* to put o lay down **3 posarse** *vpr* to settle, to alight

posavasos *nm inv* coaster

posdata *nf* postscript

pose *nf* (**a**) *(postura)* pose (**b**) *(afectación)* posing

poseedor, -a *nm,f* possessor

poseer [36] *vt* to possess, to own

poseído, -a *adj* possessed

posesión *nf* possession; **estar en p. de** to have; **tomar p. (de un cargo)** to take up (a post)

posesivo, -a *adj* possessive

poseso, -a *adj & nm,f* possessed

posguerra *nf* postwar period

posibilidad *nf* possibility; *(oportunidad)* chance

posibilitar *vt* to make possible

posible *adj* possible; **de ser p.** if possible; **en (la medida de) lo p.** as far as possible; **haré todo lo p.** I'll do everything I can; **lo antes p.** as soon as possible; **es p. que venga** he might come

posición *nf* position

positivo, -a *adj* positive

posmoderno, -a *adj* postmodern

poso *nm* dregs, sediment

posponer [19] *vt* (*pp* **pospuesto**) (**a**) *(aplazar)* to postpone, to put off (**b**) *(relegar)* to put in second place o behind, to relegate

posta *nf* **a p.** on purpose

postal 1 *adj* postal **2** *nf* postcard

poste *nm* pole; *Dep (de portería)* post

póster *nm* (*pl* **pósters** o **posters**) *nm* poster

postergar [42] *vt* (**a**) *(relegar)* to relegate (**b**) *(retrasar)* to delay; *(aplazar)* to postpone

posteridad *nf* posterity; **pasar a la p.** to go down in history

posterior *adj* (**a**) *(lugar)* posterior, rear (**b**) *(tiempo)* later (**a** than), subsequent (**a** to)

posterioridad *nf* posteriority; **con p.** later

posteriormente *adv* subsequently, later

postgrado *nm* postgraduate; **estudios de p.** postgraduate studies

postgraduado, -a *adj & nm,f* postgraduate

postigo *nm* (*de puerta*) wicket; (*de ventana*) shutter

postín *nm Fam* boasting, showing off; **darse p.** to show off, to swank; **de p.** posh, swanky

postizo, -a 1 *adj* false; **dentadura postiza** false teeth, dentures
   2 *nm* hairpiece

postor *nm* bidder

postrarse *upr* to prostrate oneself, to kneel down

postre *nm* dessert, *Br* pudding

postrero, -a *adj* last

> Postrer is used instead of postrero before masculine singular nouns (e.g. **el postrer día** the last day).

postrimerías *nfpl* final stages

postular 1 *vt* (**a**) *(defender)* to call for (**b**) *Am (candidatar)* to nominate
   2 *vi (en colecta)* to collect
   3 postularse *upr Am* (**a**) *Pol (para cargo)* to stand, to run (**b**) *CSur (para trabajo)* to apply (**para** for)

póstumo, -a *adj* posthumous

postura *nf* (**a**) *(física)* position, posture (**b**) *(actitud)* attitude

posventa, postventa *adj inv* **servicio p.** after-sales service

potable *adj* drinkable; **agua p./no p.** drinking water/not drinking water

potaje *nm* hotpot, stew

pote *nm* pot

potencia *nf* power; **en p.** potential

potencial 1 *adj* potential
   2 *nm* potential; **p. eléctrico** voltage; **p. humano** manpower

potenciar [43] *vt* to promote, to strengthen

potente *adj* powerful, strong

potestad *nf* power, authority

potingue *nm Fam (cosmético)* potion

potra *nf Fam* luck

potrero *nm Am* field, pasture

potro *nm Zool* colt; *(de gimnasia)* horse

poyo *nm* stone bench

pozo *nm* well; *Min* shaft, pit

pozole *nm CAm, Carib, Méx (guiso)* = stew made with maize kernels, pork or chicken and vegetables

PP *nm (abr* **Partido Popular**) = Spanish political party to the right of the political spectrum

práctica *nf* (**a**) *(ejercicio, destreza)* practice; **en la p.** in practice (**b**) *(clase no teórica)* practical (**c**) **prácticas** *(laborales)* training

practicante 1 *adj Rel* practising
   2 *nmf Med* medical assistant

practicar [44] **1** *vt* to practise; *(operación)* to carry out
   2 *vi* to practise

práctico, -a *adj* practical; *(útil)* handy, useful

pradera *nf* meadow

prado *nm* meadow, field

Praga *n* Prague

pragmático, -a 1 *adj* pragmatic
   2 *nm,f* pragmatist

preámbulo *nm* (**a**) *(introducción)* preamble (**b**) *(rodeo)* circumlocution

preaviso *nm* previous warning, notice

precalentamiento *nm* warm-up

precalentar [1] *vt* to preheat

precario, -a *adj* precarious

precaución *nf* (**a**) *(cautela)* caution; **con p.** cautiously (**b**) *(medida)* precaution

precaver 1 *vt* to guard against
   2 precaverse *upr* to take precautions (**de** o **contra** against)

precavido, -a *adj* cautious, prudent

precedencia *nf* precedence, priority

precedente 1 *adj* preceding
   2 *nmf* predecessor
   3 *nm* precedent; **sin p.** unprecedented

preceder *vt* to precede

precepto *nm* precept

preciarse [43] *upr* to have self-respect; **p. de** to pride oneself on

precintar *vt* to seal

precinto *nm* seal

> ⚠ Observa que la palabra inglesa **precinct** es un falso amigo y no es la traducción de la palabra española **precinto**. En inglés, **precinct** significa "recinto" o "distrito".

precio *nm* price; **p. de costo** cost price; **a cualquier p.** at any price

preciosidad *nf* (**a**) *(hermosura) (cosa)* lovely thing; *(persona)* darling (**b**) *Fml (cualidad)* preciousness

precioso, -a *adj* (**a**) *(hermoso)* lovely, beautiful (**b**) *(valioso)* precious, valuable

precipicio *nm* precipice

precipitación *nf* (**a**) *(prisa)* haste (**b**) *(lluvia)* rainfall

precipitado, -a *adj* *(apresurado)* hasty, hurried; *(irreflexivo)* rash

precipitar 1 *vt* (**a**) *(acelerar)* to hurry, to rush (**b**) *(arrojar)* to throw, to hurl down

2 precipitarse *upr* (**a**) *(persona)* to hurl oneself; *(acontecimientos)* to gather speed (**b**) *(actuar irreflexivamente)* to hurry, to rush

precisamente *adv* *(con precisión)* precisely; *(exactamente)* exactly; **p. por eso** for that very reason

precisar *vt* (**a**) *(determinar)* to determine, to give full details of; *(especificar)* to specify (**b**) *(necesitar)* to require, to need

precisión *nf* (**a**) *(exactitud)* precision, accuracy; **con p.** precisely, accurately (**b**) *(aclaración)* clarification

preciso, -a *adj* (**a**) *(necesario)* necessary, essential (**b**) *(exacto)* accurate, exact; **en este p. momento** at this very moment (**c**) *(claro)* concise, clear

preconizar [40] *vt* to advocate

precoz *adj* (**a**) *(persona)* precocious (**b**) *(fruta)* early

precursor, -a *nm,f* precursor

predecesor, -a *nm,f* predecessor

predecir [12] *(pp* predicho*)* *vt* to foretell, to predict

predestinado, -a *adj* predestined

predeterminar *vt* to predetermine

predicado *nm* *Ling* predicate

predicador, -a *nm,f* preacher

predicar [44] *vt* to preach

predicción *nf* prediction, forecast

predice *indic pres de* **predecir**

predicho, -a *pp de* **predecir**

predije *pt indef de* **predecir**

predilección *nf* predilection

predilecto, -a *adj* favourite, preferred

predisponer [19] *(pp* predispuesto*)* *vt* to predispose

predisposición *nf* predisposition

predispuesto, -a *pp de* **predisponer**

predominante *adj* predominant

predominar *vi* to predominate

predominio *nm* predominance

preeminente *adj* preeminent

preescolar *adj* preschool; **en p.** in nursery school

prefabricado, -a *adj* prefabricated

prefacio *nm* preface

preferencia *nf* preference

preferente, preferencial *adj* preferential

preferible *adj* preferable; **es p. que no vengas** you'd better not come

preferido, -a *nm,f* favourite

preferir [5] *vt* to prefer

prefijo *nm* (**a**) *Tel Br* dialling code, *US* area code (**b**) *Ling* prefix

pregón *nm* (**a**) *(bando)* proclamation, announcement (**b**) *(discurso)* speech

pregonar *vt* *(anunciar)* to announce publicly; *Fig (divulgar)* to reveal, to disclose

pregonero, -a *nm,f* *(de pueblo)* town crier; *Fig (bocazas)* blabbermouth

pregunta *nf* question; **hacer una p.** to ask a question

preguntar 1 *vt* to ask; **p. algo a algn** to ask sb sth; **p. por algn** to ask after *o* about sb

2 preguntarse *upr* to wonder; **me pregunto si ...** I wonder whether ...

preguntón, -ona *nm,f* *Fam* nosey person, *Br* nosey parker

prehistoria *nf* prehistory

prehistórico, -a *adj* prehistoric

prejubilación *nf* = voluntary redundancy before entitlement to early retirement

prejuicio *nm* prejudice; **tener prejuicios** to be prejudiced, to be biased

preliminar *adj & nm* preliminary

preludio *nm* prelude

prematrimonial *adj* premarital

prematuro, -a *adj* premature

premeditación *nf* premeditation; **con p.** deliberately

premeditado, -a *adj* premeditated, deliberate

premiado, -a *adj* prize-winning

premiar [43] *vt* (**a**) *(en competición, sorteo)* to award a prize to (**b**) *(recompensar)* to reward

premio *nm* (**a**) *(en competición, sorteo)* prize, award (**b**) *(recompensa)* reward

premisa *nf* premise

premonición *nf* premonition

premura *nf* urgency; **p. de tiempo** haste

prenatal *adj* antenatal, prenatal

prenda *nf* (**a**) *(prenda)* garment (**b**) *(garantía)* token, pledge

prendar 1 *vt* to captivate, to delight

2 prendarse *upr* to fall in love (**de** with)

prendedor *nm* brooch, pin

prender 1 *vt* (**a**) *(arrestar)* to arrest, to apprehend (**b**) *(sujetar)* to fasten (**c**) *(encender)* *esp Am (luz, interruptor)* to light; **p. fuego a algo** to set fire to sth, to set sth on fire

2 *vi* (a) *(arder)* to catch (fire) (b) *(planta)* to take root

3 prenderse *upr* to catch fire

prensa *nf* press; *Fig* **tener buena/mala p.** to have a good/bad press

prensar *vt* to press

preñado, -a *adj* (a) *(hembra)* pregnant (b) *Fig (lleno)* pregnant (**de** with), full (**de** of)

preñar *vt* to make pregnant

preocupación *nf* worry, concern

preocupado, -a *adj* worried, concerned

preocupar 1 *vt* to worry; **me preocupa que llegue tan tarde** I'm worried about him arriving so late

2 preocuparse *upr* to worry, to get worried (**por** about); **no te preocupes** don't worry; **preocuparse de algn** to look after sb; **preocuparse de algo** to see to sth

prepago *nm Tel* pay-as-you-go

preparación *nf* preparation; *(formación)* training

preparado, -a 1 *adj* (a) *(dispuesto)* ready, prepared; **comidas preparadas** ready-cooked meals (b) *(capacitado)* trained, qualified

2 *nm (medicamento)* preparation

preparador, -a *nm,f* coach, trainer

preparar 1 *vt* (a) *(disponer, elaborar)* to prepare, to get ready; **p. un examen** to prepare for an exam (b) *Dep (entrenar)* to train, to coach

2 prepararse *upr* (a) *(disponerse)* to prepare oneself, to get ready (b) *Dep (entrenarse)* to train

preparativo *nm* preparation

preparatorio, -a *adj* preparatory

preponderante *adj* preponderant

preposición *nf Ling* preposition

prepotente *adj* domineering; *(arrogante)* overbearing

prerrogativa *nf* prerogative

presa *nf* (a) *(de animal)* prey; *Fig* **ser p. de** to be a victim of; **p. del pánico** panic-stricken (b) *(embalse)* dam

presagiar [43] *vt* to predict, to foretell

presagio *nm* (a) *(señal)* omen; **buen/mal p.** good/bad omen (b) *(premonición)* premonition

presbiteriano, -a *adj & nm,f* Presbyterian

presbítero *nm* priest

prescindir *vi* **p. de** to do without

prescribir *(pp* prescrito*) vt* to prescribe

prescripción *nf* prescription; **p. facultativa** medical prescription

prescrito, -a *pp de* prescribir

presencia *nf* presence; **hacer acto de p.** to put in an appearance; **p. de ánimo** presence of mind

presencial *adj* **testigo p.** eyewitness

presenciar [43] *vt (ver)* to witness

presentable *adj* presentable; **no estoy p.** I'm not dressed for the occasion

presentación *nf* presentation; *(aspecto)* appearance; *(de personas)* introduction

presentador, -a *nm,f Rad & TV* presenter

presentar 1 *vt* (a) *(mostrar, anunciar)* to present (b) *(una persona a otra)* to introduce; **le presento al doctor Ruiz** may I introduce you to Dr Ruiz (c) *(ofrecer) (disculpas, excusas)* to make; *(respetos)* to pay (d) *(tener) (aspecto)* to have, to show

2 presentarse *upr* (a) *(comparecer)* to present oneself; *(inesperadamente)* to turn o come up (b) *(ocasión, oportunidad)* to present itself, to arise (c) *(candidato)* to stand; **presentarse a unas elecciones** to stand for election, *US* to run for office; **presentarse a un examen** to sit an examination (d) *(darse a conocer)* to introduce oneself (**a** to)

presente 1 *adj* present; **la p. (carta)** this letter; **hacer p.** to declare, to state; **tener p.** *(tener en cuenta)* to bear in mind; *(recordar)* to remember

2 *nm* present

presentimiento *nm* presentiment, premonition; **tengo el p. de que ...** I have the feeling that ...

presentir [5] *vt* to have a presentiment o premonition of

preservación *nf* preservation, protection

preservar *vt* to preserve, to protect (**de** from; **contra** against)

preservativo *nm* sheath, condom

presidencia *nf* (a) *Pol* presidency (b) *(de una reunión) (hombre)* chairmanship; *(mujer)* chairwomanship

presidenciable *nmf esp Am* potential presidential candidate

presidencial *adj* presidential

presidente, -a *nm,f* (a) *Pol (de nación)* president; **p. (del gobierno)** prime minister (b) *(de una reunión)* chairperson

presidiario, -a *nm,f* prisoner, convict

presidio *nm* prison, penitentiary

presidir *vt* (a) *Pol* to rule, to head (b) *(reunión)* to chair, to preside over

presión *nf* pressure; **a** o **bajo p.** under pressure; **grupo de p.** pressure group, lobby; **p. arterial** o **sanguínea** blood pressure; **p. atmosférica** atmospheric pressure

presionar *vt* to press; *Fig* to pressurize, to put pressure on

preso, -a 1 *adj* imprisoned
  2 *nm,f* prisoner

prestación *nf* (a) *(de servicio) (acción)* provision; *(resultado)* service (b) *(subsidio)* benefit (c) **prestaciones** *(de vehículo)* performance

prestado, -a *adj* **dejar p.** to lend; **pedir p.** to borrow; **vivir de p.** to scrounge

prestamista *nmf* moneylender

préstamo *nm* loan

prestar 1 *vt* (a) *(dejar) (dinero, cosa)* to lend, to loan; **¿me prestas tu pluma?** can I borrow your pen? (b) *(atención)* to pay; *(ayuda)* to give; *(servicio)* to do
  2 prestarse *vpr* (a) *(ofrecerse)* to offer oneself (a to) (b) **prestarse a** *(dar motivo)* to cause; **se presta a (crear) malentendidos** it makes for misunderstandings

presteza *nf* promptness; **con p.** promptly

prestidigitador, -a *nm,f* conjuror, magician

prestigiar [43] *vt* to give prestige to

prestigio *nm* prestige

prestigioso, -a *adj* prestigious

presto, -a *adj Fml* (a) *(dispuesto)* ready, prepared (b) *(rápido)* swift, prompt

presumible *adj* probable, likely

presumido, -a 1 *adj* vain, conceited
  2 *nm,f* vain person

presumir 1 *vt (suponer)* to presume, to suppose
  2 *vi* (a) *(ser vanidoso)* to show off (b) **presume de guapo** he thinks he's good-looking

presunción *nf* (a) *(suposición)* presumption, supposition (b) *(vanidad)* vanity, conceit

presunto, -a *adj* supposed; *Der* alleged

presuntuoso, -a *adj* (a) *(vanidoso)* vain, conceited (b) *(pretencioso)* pretentious, showy

┌─────────────────────────────────────┐
│ 𝒪 Observa que la palabra inglesa **presumptuous** es un falso amigo y no es la traducción de la palabra española **presuntuoso**. En inglés **presumptuous** significa "impertinente". │
└─────────────────────────────────────┘

presuponer [19] *(pp* **presupuesto)** *vt* to presuppose

presupuestar *vt* to budget

presupuestario, -a *adj* budgetary

presupuesto, -a 1 *nm* (a) *Fin* budget; *(cálculo)* estimate (b) *(supuesto)* supposition, assumption
  2 *pp de* **presuponer**

presuroso, -a *adj (rápido)* quick; *(con prisa)* in a hurry

pretencioso, -a *adj* pretentious

pretender *vt* (a) *(intentar)* to try; **¿qué pretendes insinuar?** what are you getting at? (b) *(afirmar)* to claim (c) *(aspirar a)* to try for (d) *(cortejar)* to court, to woo

pretendiente, -a *nm,f* (a) *(al trono)* pretender (b) *(a un cargo)* applicant, candidate (c) *(amante)* suitor

pretensión *nf* (a) *(aspiración)* aim, aspiration (b) *(presunción)* pretentiousness

pretérito, -a 1 *adj* past, former
  2 *nm Ling* preterite, simple past tense

pretextar *vt* to plead, to allege

pretexto *nm* pretext, excuse

pretil *nm* parapet

prevalecer [33] *vi* to prevail

prevención *nf* (a) *(precaución)* prevention; **en p. de** as a prevention against (b) *(medida)* precaution

prevenir [27] *vt* (a) *(preparar)* to prepare, to get ready (b) *(prever)* to prevent, to forestall; *(evitar)* to avoid; **para p. la gripe** to prevent flu; *Prov* **más vale p. que curar** prevention is better than cure (c) *(advertir)* to warn

preventivo, -a *adj* preventive; *(medidas)* precautionary; *Der* **detención** *o* **prisión preventiva** remand in custody

prever [28] *(pp* **previsto)** *vt* (a) *(prevenir)* to foresee, to forecast (b) *(preparar de antemano)* to cater for

previo, -a *adj* previous, prior; **p. pago de su importe** only on payment; **sin p. aviso** without prior notice

previsible *adj* predictable

previsión *nf* (a) *(predicción)* forecast; **p. del tiempo** weather forecast (b) *(precaución)* precaution; **en p. de** as a precaution against (c) *Andes, RP* **p. social** social security

previsor, -a *adj* careful, far-sighted

previsto, -a 1 *adj* foreseen, forecast; **según lo p.** as expected
  2 *pp de* **prever**

prieto, -a *adj* (a) *(ceñido)* tight; **íbamos muy prietos en el coche** we were really squashed together in the car (b) *Méx (oscuro)* dark

prima *nf* *(gratificación)* bonus; **p. de seguro** insurance premium

primacía *nf* primacy

primar 1 *vi* to have priority, to prevail
  2 *vt* to give a bonus to

primaria *nf* *(enseñanza)* primary education

primario, -a adj primary

primavera nf spring

primer adj (delante de nm) ver **primero**

primera nf (a) (en tren) first class (b) Aut (marcha) first gear (c) **a la p.** at the first attempt; Fam **de p.** great, first-class

primero, -a 1 adj first; **a primera hora de la mañana** first thing in the morning; **primera página** o **plana** front page; **de primera necesidad** basic

> **Primer** is used instead of **primero** before masculine singular nouns (e.g. **el primer hombre** the first man).

2 nm,f first; **a primero(s) de mes** at the beginning of the month
3 adv (a) (en primer lugar) first (b) (más bien) rather, sooner

primicia nf scoop, exclusive

primitivo, -a adj primitive

primo, -a 1 nm,f (a) (familiar) cousin; **p. hermano** first cousin (b) Fam (tonto) fool, drip, dunce
2 adj (a) **materia prima** raw material (b) (número) prime

primogénito, -a adj & nm,f first-born

primor nm (a) (delicadeza) delicacy (b) (belleza) beauty

primordial adj essential, fundamental

primoroso, -a adj delicate, exquisite

princesa nf princess

principado nm principality

principal adj main, principal; **lo p. es que ...** the main thing is that ...; **puerta p.** front door

príncipe nm prince

principiante 1 adj novice
2 nmf beginner, novice

principio nm (a) (comienzo) beginning, start; **a principio(s) de** at the beginning of; **al p., en un p.** at first, in the beginning (b) (fundamento) principle; **en p.** in principle (c) **principios** rudiments, basics

pringar [42] **1** vt (ensuciar) to make greasy/dirty
2 vi Fam (trabajar) to work hard
3 pringarse upr (a) (ensuciarse) to get greasy/dirty (b) Fam (meterse de lleno) to get involved

pringoso, -a adj (grasiento) greasy; (sucio) dirty

pringue nm (grasa) grease

prior, -a nm,f (hombre) prior; (mujer) prioress

priori: a priori loc adv a priori

prioridad nf priority

prioritario, -a adj priority

prisa nf (a) (rapidez) hurry; **date p.** hurry up; **tener p.** to be in a hurry; **de/a p.** in a hurry (b) **correr p.** to be urgent; **me corre mucha p.** I need it right away

prisión nf prison, jail

prisionero, -a nm,f prisoner

prisma nm prism

prismáticos nmpl binoculars, field glasses

priva nf Esp Fam booze

privación nf deprivation

privado, -a adj private

privar 1 vt (despojar) to deprive (**de** of)
2 vi (a) Fam (gustar) to like; (estar de moda) to be fashionable o popular (b) Fam (beber) to booze
3 privarse upr (abstenerse) to deprive oneself (**de** of), to go without

privativo, -a adj exclusive (**de** of)

privilegiado, -a 1 adj privileged
2 nm,f privileged person

privilegio nm privilege

pro 1 nm advantage; **los pros y los contras** the pros and cons; **en p. de** in favour of
2 prep in favour of; **campaña p. desarme** campaign for disarmament, disarmament campaign

proa nf prow, bows

probabilidad nf probability, likelihood; **tiene pocas probabilidades** he stands little chance

probable adj probable, likely; **es p. que llueva** it'll probably rain

probador nm fitting room

probar [2] **1** vt (a) (comida, bebida) to try (b) (comprobar) to test, to check (c) (intentar) to try (d) (demostrar) to prove, to show
2 vi to try; **p. a** to attempt o try to
3 probarse upr (ropa) to try on

probeta nf test tube; **niño p.** test-tube baby

problema nm problem

problemático, -a adj problematic

procedencia nf origin, source

procedente adj (a) (originario) coming (**de** from) (b) (adecuado) appropriate; Der proper

proceder 1 vi (a) **p. de** (provenir) to come from (b) (actuar) to act (c) (ser oportuno) to be advisable o appropriate; Der **la protesta no procede** objection overruled (d) **p. a** (continuar) to go on to
2 nm (comportamiento) behaviour

procedimiento nm (a) (método) procedure (b) Der (trámites) proceedings

procesado, -a 1 nm,f accused
2 nm Inform processing

procesador *nm* processor; **p. de textos** word processor

procesamiento *nm* (a) *Der* prosecution (b) *Inform* **p. de datos/textos** data/word processing

procesar *vt* (a) *Der* to prosecute (b) *(elaborar, transformar)* to process; *Inform* to process

procesión *nf* procession

proceso *nm* (a) *(operación)* process; *Inform* **p. de datos** data processing (b) *Der* trial

proclamación *nf* proclamation

proclamar *vt* to proclaim

proclive *adj* prone, inclined

procreación *nf* procreation

procrear *vt* to procreate

procurador, -a *nm,f Der* attorney

procuraduría *nf Méx* **p. general de justicia** Ministry of Justice

procurar *vt* (a) *(intentar)* to try, to attempt; **procura que no te vean** make sure they don't see you (b) *(proporcionar)* (to manage) to get

prodigar [42] *Fml* **1** *vt* *(dar generosamente)* to lavish

 2 prodigarse *vpr* **prodigarse en** to be lavish in

prodigio *nm* prodigy, miracle; **hacer prodigios** to work wonders; **niño p.** child prodigy

prodigioso, -a *adj* *(sobrenatural)* prodigious; *(maravilloso)* wonderful, marvellous

pródigo, -a *adj* generous, lavish; **es p. en regalos** he's very generous with presents

producción *nf* (a) *(acción)* production; *(producto)* product; **p. en cadena/serie** assembly-line/mass production (b) *Cin & TV* production

producir [10] **1** *vt* (a) *(producto, sonido)* to produce; *(fruto, cosecha)* to yield, to bear; *(ganancias)* to yield (b) *Fig* *(originar)* to cause, to bring about (c) *Cine & TV* to produce

 2 producirse *vpr* to take place, to happen

productividad *nf* productivity

productivo, -a *adj* productive; *(beneficioso)* profitable

producto *nm* product; *Agr* *(producción)* produce

productor, -a 1 *adj* producing

 2 *nm,f* producer

proeza *nf* heroic deed, exploit

profanación *nf* desecration, profanation

profanar *vt* to desecrate, to profane

profano, -a 1 *adj* profane, secular

 2 *nm,f (hombre)* layman; *(mujer)* laywoman

profecía *nf* prophecy

proferir [31] *vt* to utter; **p. insultos** to hurl insults

profesar *vt* to profess

profesión *nf* profession; **de p.** by profession

profesional *adj & nmf* professional

profesionista *adj & nmf Méx* professional

profeso: ex profeso *loc adv* intentionally

profesor, -a *nm,f* teacher; *Univ Br* lecturer, *US* professor

profesorado *nm* *(profesión)* teaching; *(grupo de profesores)* staff

profeta *nm* prophet

profetizar [40] *vt* to prophesy, to foretell

profiláctico, -a 1 *adj* prophylactic

 2 *nm* condom

prófugo, -a 1 *adj & nm,f* fugitive

 2 *nm Mil* deserter

profundidad *nf* depth; *Fig (de ideas etc)* profundity, depth; **un metro de p.** one metre deep *o* in depth

profundizar [40] **1** *vt (hoyo, conocimientos)* to deepen

 2 *vi (en excavación)* to dig deeper; *(en estudio, conocimientos)* to go into depth; **p. en** *(tema)* to study in depth

profundo, -a *adj* deep; *Fig (idea, sentimiento)* profound

profusión *nf* profusion

progenitor, -a *nm,f (antepasado)* ancestor, progenitor; **progenitores** *(padres)* parents

programa *nm* programme; *Inform* program; *Educ* syllabus

programación *nf Rad & TV* programme planning

programador, -a *nm,f Inform* programmer

programar *vt* to programme; *Inform* to program

progre *adj & nmf Fam* lefty

progresar *vi* to progress, to make progress

progresista *adj & nmf* progressive

progresivo, -a *adj* progressive

progreso *nm* progress; **hace grandes progresos** he's making great progress

prohibición *nf* prohibition, ban

prohibido, -a *adj* forbidden, prohibited; **prohibida la entrada** *(en letrero)* no admittance; **p. aparcar/fumar** *(en letrero)* no parking/smoking

prohibir *vt* to forbid, to prohibit; **se prohíbe pasar** (*en letrero*) no admittance o entry

prohibitivo, -a *adj* prohibitive

prójimo, -a *nm,f* one's fellow man, one's neighbour

proletariado *nm* proletariat

proletario, -a *adj & nm,f* proletarian

proliferación *nf* proliferation; **p. nuclear** proliferation (of nuclear arms)

proliferar *vi* to proliferate

prolífico, -a *adj* prolific

prolijo, -a *adj* verbose, long-winded

prólogo *nm* prologue

prolongación *nf* prolonging, extension, prolongation

prolongado, -a *adj* long

prolongar [42] **1** *vt* (*alargar*) to prolong, to extend
　2 prolongarse *vpr* (*continuar*) to carry on

promedio *nm* average; **como p.** on average

promesa *nf* promise; *Fig* **la joven p. de la música** the promising young musician

prometedor, -a *adj* promising

prometer 1 *vt* to promise; **te lo prometo** I promise
　2 *vi* to be promising
　3 prometerse *vpr* (*pareja*) to get engaged

prometido, -a 1 *adj* promised
　2 *nm,f* (*hombre*) fiancé; (*mujer*) fiancée

prominente *adj* (*elevado*) protruding, projecting; (*importante*) prominent

promiscuo, -a *adj* promiscuous

promoción *nf* promotion; *Educ* **p. universitaria** class, year

promocionar *vt* (*cosas*) to promote; (*personas*) to promote

promotor, -a 1 *adj* promoting
　2 *nm,f* promoter

promover [4] *vt* (**a**) (*cosas, personas*) to promote; (*juicio, querella*) to initiate (**b**) (*causar*) to cause, to give rise to

promulgar [42] *vt* to promulgate

pronombre *nm* pronoun

pronosticar [44] *vt* to predict, to forecast; *Med* to make a prognosis of

pronóstico *nm* (*del tiempo*) forecast; *Med* prognosis

pronto, -a 1 *adj* quick, prompt; *Fml* (*dispuesto*) prepared
　2 *nm* (*impulso*) sudden impulse
　3 *adv* (**a**) (*deprisa*) quickly, rapidly; **al p.** at first; **de p.** suddenly; **por de o lo p.** (*para empezar*) to start with (**b**) (*dentro de poco*) soon; **¡hasta p.!** see you soon! (**c**) *Esp* (*temprano*) early; **salimos p.** we left early

pronunciación *nf* pronunciation

pronunciamiento *nm* (**a**) *Mil* uprising, insurrection (**b**) *Der* pronouncement

pronunciar [43] **1** *vt* to pronounce; (*discurso*) to deliver
　2 pronunciarse *vpr* (**a**) (*opinar*) to declare oneself (**b**) (*sublevarse*) to rise up

propagación *nf* propagation, spreading

propagador, -a *nm,f* propagator

propaganda *nf* (*política*) propaganda; (*comercial*) advertising, publicity

propagar [42] **1** *vt* to propagate, to spread
　2 propagarse *vpr* to spread

propano *nm* propane

propasarse *vpr* to go too far

propensión *nf* tendency, inclination

propenso, -a *adj* (**a**) (*inclinado*) prone, inclined (**b**) *Med* susceptible

propiamente *adv* **p. dicho** strictly speaking

propiciar [43] *vt* (*causar*) to cause

propicio, -a *adj* propitious, suitable; **ser p. a** to be inclined to

propiedad *nf* (**a**) (*posesión*) ownership; (*cosa poseída*) property (**b**) (*cualidad*) property, quality; *Fig* **con p.** properly, appropriately

propietario, -a *nm,f* owner

propina *nf* tip; **dar p. (a algn)** to tip (sb)

propinar *vt* to give

propio, -a *adj* (**a**) (*de uno*) own; **en su propia casa** in his own house (**b**) (*correcto*) suitable, appropriate; **juegos propios para su edad** games suitable for their age (**c**) (*característico*) typical, peculiar (**d**) (*mismo*) (*hombre*) himself; (*mujer*) herself; (*animal, cosa*) itself; **el p. autor** the author himself (**e**) **propios, -as** themselves; **los propios inquilinos** the tenants themselves (**f**) *Ling* proper

proponer [19] (*pp* **propuesto**) **1** *vt* to propose, to suggest
　2 proponerse *vpr* to intend

proporción *nf* (**a**) (*relación*) proportion; **en p. con** in proportion to (**b**) **proporciones** (*tamaño*) size

proporcionado, -a *adj* (*mesurado*) proportionate, in proportion

proporcional *adj* proportional

proporcionar *vt* (*dar*) to give, to supply, to provide

proposición *nf* (**a**) (*propuesta*) proposal (**b**) (*oración*) clause

propósito *nm* (**a**) (*intención*) intention (**b**) **a p.** (*por cierto*) by the way; (*adrede*) on purpose, intentionally; **a p. de viajes** ... speaking of travelling ...

propuesta *nf* suggestion, proposal

propuesto, -a *pp de* **proponer**

propugnar *vt* to advocate

propulsar *vt (vehículo)* to drive; *Fig (idea)* to promote

propulsión *nf* propulsion

propulsor, -a *nm,f* promoter

propuse *pt indef de* **proponer**

prórroga *nf* (a) *(prolongación)* extension; *Dep Br* extra time, *US* overtime (b) *(aplazamiento)* postponement; *Mil* deferment

prorrogar [42] *vt* (a) *(prolongar)* to extend (b) *(aplazar)* to postpone; *Mil* to defer

prorrumpir *vi* to burst (**en** into)

prosa *nf* prose

proscrito, -a 1 *adj (persona)* exiled, banished; *(cosa)* banned
   2 *nm,f* exile, outlaw

proseguir [6] *vt & vi* to carry on, to continue

prospección *nf* (a) *Min* prospect (b) *Com* survey

prospecto *nm* leaflet, prospectus

prosperar *vi (negocio, país)* to prosper, to thrive; *(propuesta)* to be accepted

prosperidad *nf* prosperity

próspero, -a *adj* prosperous, thriving; **¡p. año nuevo!** Happy New Year!

prostíbulo *nm* brothel

prostitución *nf* prostitution

prostituir [37] **1** *vt* to prostitute
   2 prostituirse *vpr* to prostitute oneself

prostituta *nf* prostitute

protagonista *nmf* (a) *(de obra, película)* main character, leading role; **¿quién es el p.?** who plays the lead? (b) *Fig* **ser p. de** *(acontecimiento histórico)* to play a leading part in; *(accidente)* to be one of the main people involved in

protagonizar [40] *vt* (a) *(obra, película)* to play the lead in, to star in (b) *(acontecimiento histórico)* to play a leading part in; *(accidente)* to be one of the main people involved in

protección *nf* protection

proteccionismo *nm* protectionism

protector, -a 1 *adj* protecting, protective
   2 *nm,f* protector

proteger [53] *vt* to protect, to defend

protegido, -a *nm,f (hombre)* protégé; *(mujer)* protégée

proteína *nf* protein

prótesis *nf inv* prosthesis

protesta *nf* protest; *Der* objection

protestante *adj & nmf Rel* Protestant

protestar *vi* (a) *(quejarse)* to complain (**por** about); *Der* to object (**b**) *Pol* to protest

protestón, -ona *nm,f Fam* moaner

protocolo *nm* protocol

protón *nm* proton

prototipo *nm* prototype

protuberancia *nf* protuberance

protuberante *adj* protuberant, bulging

prov. *(abr* **provincia)** prov

provecho *nm* profit, benefit; **¡buen p.!** enjoy your meal!; **sacar p. de algo** to benefit from sth

provechoso, -a *adj* beneficial

proveedor, -a *nm,f* supplier, purveyor; *Inform* **p. de acceso (a Internet)** Internet access provider

proveer [36] *(pp* **provisto)** *vt* to supply, to provide

proveniente *adj (procedente)* coming; *(resultante)* arising, resulting

provenir [27] *vi* **p. de** to come from

proverbio *nm* proverb

providencia *nf* providence

provincia *nf* province

provincial *adj* provincial

provinciano, -a *adj & nm,f Pey* provincial

provisión *nf* provision

provisional, *Am* **provisorio, -a** *adj* provisional

provisto, -a 1 *adj* **p. de** equipped with
   2 *pp de* **proveer**

provocación *nf* provocation

provocado, -a *adj* provoked, caused; **incendio p.** arson

provocador, -a 1 *nm,f* instigator, agent provocateur
   2 *adj* provocative

provocar [44] *vt* (a) *(causar)* to cause; **p. un incendio** to start a fire (b) *(instigar)* to provoke (c) *Carib, Col, Méx Fam (apetecer)* **¿te provoca ir al cine?** would you like to go to the movies?, *Br* do you fancy going to the cinema?

provocativo, -a *adj* provocative

proxeneta *nmf* procurer, pimp

próximamente *adv (pronto)* soon; *Cin & Teatro (en letrero)* coming soon

proximidad *nf* proximity, closeness; **en las proximidades de** close to, in the vicinity of

próximo, -a *adj* (a) *(cercano)* near, close (b) *(siguiente)* next

proyección *nf* (a) *(de mapa)* projection (b) *Cin* screening, showing

proyectar *vt* (a) *(luz)* to project (b) *(planear)* to plan (c) *Cin* to project, to screen

proyectil *nm* projectile

proyecto *nm (plan)* project, plan; **tener algo en p.** to be planning sth; **p. de ley** bill

proyector *nm Cin* projector

prudencia *nf* prudence, discretion; *(moderación)* care

prudente *adj* prudent, sensible; *(conductor)* careful; **a una hora p.** at a reasonable time

prueba *nf* (a) *(demostración)* piece of evidence; *(concluyente)* proof; **en p. de** as a sign of (b) *(examen etc)* test; **a p.** on trial; **a p. de agua/balas** waterproof/bullet-proof; **haz la p.** try it (c) *Dep* event

psicoanálisis *nm inv* psychoanalysis

psicodélico, -a *adj* psychedelic

psicología *nf* psychology

psicológico, -a *adj* psychological

psicólogo, -a *nm,f* psychologist

psicópata *nmf* psychopath

psicosis *nf inv* psychosis

psicotécnico, -a *adj* psychometric

psicoterapeuta *nmf* psychotherapist

psicoterapia *nf* psychotherapy

psicótico, -a *adj & nm,f* psychotic

psique *nf* psyche

psiquiatra *nmf* psychiatrist

psiquiatría *nf* psychiatry

psiquiátrico, -a 1 *adj* psychiatric; **hospital p.** psychiatric hospital
2 *nm* psychiatric hospital

psíquico, -a *adj* psychic

PSOE *nm Pol (abr* **Partido Socialista Obrero Español)** = Spanish political party to the centre-left of the political spectrum

pta. *(pl* **ptas.)** *Antes (abr* **peseta)** peseta

púa *nf* (a) *(de planta)* thorn; *(de animal)* quill, spine; *(de peine)* tooth; **alambre de púas** barbed wire (b) *Mús* plectrum

pub [pa, paf] *(pl* **pubs)** *nm* pub

pubertad *nf* puberty

pubis *nm inv* pubes

publicación *nf* publication

publicar [44] *vt* (a) *(libro etc)* to publish (b) *(secreto)* to publicize

publicidad *nf* (a) *Com* advertising (b) *(conocimiento público)* publicity

publicitario, -a *adj* advertising

público, -a 1 *adj* public
2 *nm* public; *Teatro* audience; *Dep* spectators

pucha *interj Andes, RP Fam Euf* (a) *(lamento, enojo) Br* sugar!, *US* shoot! (b) *(sorpresa)* wow!

pucherazo *nm* rigging of an election

puchero *nm* (a) *(olla)* cooking pot; *(cocido)* stew (b) **hacer pucheros** to pout

pucho *nm Fam* (a) *Andes, RP (cigarrillo)* cigarette, *Br* fag (b) *Andes, RP (colilla)* cigarette butt (c) *Chile, Ecuad (hijo menor)* youngest child

pude *pt indef de* **poder**

pudendo, -a *adj* **partes pudendas** private parts

púdico, -a *adj* modest

pudiente *adj* rich, wealthy

pudor *nm* modesty

pudoroso, -a *adj* modest

pudrir 1 *vt* to rot
2 pudrirse *vpr* to rot

pueblerino, -a *adj Pey* countrified, provincial

pueblo *nm* (a) *(población) (pequeña)* village; *(grande)* town (b) *(gente)* people; **el p. español** the Spanish people

puente *nm* (a) *(construcción)* bridge; *Av* **p. aéreo** *(civil)* air shuttle service; *Mil* airlift; **p. colgante** suspension bridge; **p. levadizo** drawbridge (b) *(vacaciones)* ≃ long weekend (c) *(en dientes)* bridge

puerco, -a 1 *adj* filthy
2 *nm,f* pig
3 *nm* **p. espín** porcupine

puericultura *nf* paediatrics *sing*

pueril *adj* childish, puerile

puerro *nm* leek

puerta *nf* door; *(verja, en aeropuerto)* gate; *Dep* goal; **p. corredera/giratoria** sliding/revolving door; *Fig* **a las puertas, en puertas** imminent; *Fig* **a p. cerrada** behind closed doors

puerto *nm* (a) *(de mar)* port, harbour; **p. deportivo** marina (b) *(de montaña)* (mountain) pass

Puerto Rico *n* Puerto Rico

puertorriqueño, -a *adj & nm,f* Puerto Rican

pues *conj* (a) *(puesto que)* as, since (b) *(por lo tanto)* therefore (c) *(entonces)* so (d) *(para reforzar)* **¡p. claro que sí!** but of course!; **p. como iba diciendo** well, as I was saying; **¡p. mejor!** so much the better!; **¡p. no!** certainly not! (e) *(como pregunta)* **¿p.?** why?

puesta *nf* (a) **p. de sol** sunset (b) *Fig* **p. a punto** tuning, adjusting; *Fig* **p. al día** updating; *Teatro* **p. en escena** staging; **p. en marcha** starting-up, start-up

puestero, -a *nm,f Am* stallholder

puesto, -a 1 *conj* **p. que** since, as
2 *nm* (a) *(lugar)* place; *(asiento)* seat (b) *(empleo)* position, post, job; **p. de trabajo**

job, post (**c**) *(tienda)* stall (**d**) *Mil* post
   3 *adj* (**a**) *(colocado)* set, put (**b**) **llevar p.**
(ropa) to have on; *Fam* **ir muy p.** to be all
dressed up (**c**) *Fam (borracho)* drunk (**d**)
Fam **estar p. en una materia** to be well up
in a subject
   4 *pp de* **poner**

púgil *nm* boxer

pugna *nf* battle, fight

pugnar *vi* to fight, to struggle (**por** for)

puja *nf (acción)* bidding; *(cantidad)* bid

pujante *adj* thriving, prosperous

pujanza *nf* strength, vigour

pujar *vi* (**a**) *(pugnar)* to struggle (**b**) *(en
subasta)* to bid higher

pulcro, -a *adj* (extremely) neat

pulga *nf* flea; *Fam* **tener malas pulgas** to
be bad-tempered, *Br* to be stroppy

pulgada *nf* inch

pulgar *nm* thumb

pulidora *nf* polisher

pulimentar *vt* to polish

pulir *vt* (**a**) *(metal, madera)* to polish (**b**)
(mejorar) to polish up

pulla *nf* dig

pulmón *nm* lung

pulmonía *nf* pneumonia

pulpa *nf* pulp

pulpería *nf Am* general store

púlpito *nm* pulpit

pulpo *nm* octopus

pulque *nm CAm, Méx* pulque, = fermented
agave cactus juice

pulquería *nf CAm, Méx* "pulque" bar

pulsación *nf* keystroke

pulsar *vt (timbre, botón)* to press; *(tecla)* to
hit, to strike

pulsera *nf (aro)* bracelet; *(de reloj)*
watchstrap; **reloj de p.** wristwatch

pulso *nm* (**a**) *(latido)* pulse; *Fig* **tomar el p.
a la opinión pública** to sound out opinion
(**b**) *(firmeza)* **tener buen p.** to have a
steady hand; **a p.** freehand (**c**) *(lucha)*
echar un p. (con algn) to arm-wrestle
(with sb) (**d**) *(situación conflictiva)* battle
of wills

pulverizador *nm* spray, atomizer

pulverizar [40] *vt (sólidos)* to pulverize;
(líquidos) to spray; *(récord)* to smash

puma *nm* puma

puna *nf Andes* (**a**) *(llanura)* Andean
plateau (**b**) *(mal de altura)* altitude
sickness

pundonor *nm* self-respect, self-esteem

punk [pank] *(pl* punks*) adj nm & nmf* punk

punki ['panki] *adj & nmf* punk

punta *nf* (**a**) *(extremo)* tip; *(extremo
afilado)* point; *(de cabello)* end; **sacar p. a
un lápiz** to sharpen a pencil; **tecnología p.**
state-of-the-art technology; **me pone los
nervios de p.** he makes me very nervous
(**b**) *(periodo)* peak; **hora p.** rush hour (**c**)
(pequeña cantidad) bit; **una p. de sal** a
pinch of salt (**d**) *(clavo)* nail

puntada *nf* (**a**) *(pespunte)* stitch (**b**) *RP
(dolor)* stabbing pain (**c**) *Méx (broma)*
witticism

puntaje *nf Am (calificación)* mark, *US*
grade; *(en concursos, competiciones)*
score

puntal *nm (madero)* prop; *Fig (soporte)*
pillar, support

puntapié *nm* kick

puntear *vt* (**a**) *(dibujar)* to dot (**b**) *Mús
(guitarra)* to pluck

punteo *nm* plucking

puntera *nf (de zapato)* toecap; *(de
calcetín)* toe

puntería *nf* aim; **tener buena/mala p.** to
be a good/bad shot

puntero, -a **1** *adj* leading
   2 *nm,f CSur Dep* winger

puntiagudo, -a *adj* pointed, sharp

puntilla *nf* (**a**) *(encaje)* lace (**b**) **dar la
p.** *Taurom* to finish (the bull) off; *Fig
(liquidar)* to finish off (**c**) **de puntillas** on
tiptoe

puntilloso, -a *adj* touchy

punto *nm* (**a**) *(unidad, tanto)* point; **p.
muerto** *Aut* neutral; *Fig (impase)*
deadlock; **p. de vista** point of view (**b**)
(marca) dot; **línea de puntos** dotted line
(**c**) *(lugar)* place, point (**d**) *(signo
ortográfico)* **p. y aparte** *Br* full stop *o US*
period, new paragraph; **p. y coma**
semicolon; **p. y seguido** *Br* full stop, *US*
period *(no new paragraph)*; **dos puntos**
colon (**e**) *Cost & Med* stitch; **hacer p.** to
knit (**f**) *(expresiones)* **a p.** ready; *Culin* **en
su p.** just right; **a p. de** on the point of;
hasta cierto p. to a certain *o* some extent;
en p. *(tiempo)* sharp, on the dot

puntocom *nf (empresa)* dotcom

puntuable *adj Dep* **una prueba p. para** a
race counting towards

puntuación *nf* (**a**) *Ling* punctuation (**b**)
Dep score (**c**) *Educ* mark

puntual 1 *adj* (**a**) *(en el tiempo)* punctual
(**b**) *(exacto)* accurate, precise (**c**) *(aislado)* specific
   2 *adv* punctually

puntualidad *nf* punctuality

puntualización *nf* clarification

puntualizar [40] *vt* to specify, to clarify

puntuar [30] **1** *vt* *(al escribir)* to punctuate **2** *vi* (**a**) *(marcar)* to score (**b**) *(ser puntuable)* to count

punzada *nf (de dolor)* sudden sharp pain

punzante *adj (objeto)* sharp; *(dolor)* acute, piercing

punzar [40] *vt Téc* to punch

punzón *nm (herramienta)* punch

puñado *nm* handful; *Fam* **a puñados** by the score, galore

puñal *nm* dagger

puñalada *nf* stab; *Fig* **p. trapera** stab in the back

puñeta *nf Fam* **hacer la p. a algn** to pester sb, to annoy sb; **¡puñetas!** damn!; **¡vete a hacer puñetas!** go to hell!

puñetazo *nm* punch

puñetero, -a *Esp Fam* **1** *adj* (**a**) *(persona)* damn (**b**) *(cosa)* tricky, awkward **2** *nm,f* pain

puño *nm* (**a**) *(mano cerrada)* fist (**b**) *(de camisa etc)* cuff (**c**) *(de herramienta)* handle

pupa *nf* (**a**) *(herida)* cold sore (**b**) *Fam (daño)* pain

pupila *nf (de ojo)* pupil

pupilo, -a *nm,f* pupil

pupitre *nm* desk

purasangre *adj & nm* thoroughbred

puré *nm* purée; **p. de patatas** mashed potatoes; **p. de verduras** thick vegetable soup

pureta *nmf Fam* old fogey

pureza *nf* purity

purga *nf Med* purgative; *Fig* purge

purgante *adj & nm* purgative

purgar [42] *vt Med & Fig* to purge

purgatorio *nm* purgatory

purificación *nf* purification

purificar [44] *vt* to purify

purista *nmf* purist

puritano, -a 1 *adj* puritanical **2** *nm,f* puritan, Puritan

puro, -a 1 *adj* (**a**) *(sin mezclas)* pure; **aire p.** fresh air; **la pura verdad** the plain truth; *Pol* **p. y duro** hardline (**b**) *(mero)* sheer, mere; **por pura curiosidad** out of sheer curiosity (**c**) *(casto)* chaste, pure **2** *nm (cigarro)* cigar

púrpura *adj inv* purple

purpúreo, -a *adj* purple

pus *nm* pus

puse *pt indef de* **poner**

pusilánime *adj* faint-hearted

pústula *nf* sore, pustule

puta *nf Vulg* whore; **de p. madre** great, terrific; **de p. pena** *Br* bloody *o US* goddamn awful; **no tengo ni p. idea** I haven't (got) a *Br* bloody *o US* goddamn clue; **pasarlas putas** to go through hell, to have a rotten time

putada *nf muy Fam* dirty trick; **¡qué p.!** what a bugger!

puteada *nf RP muy Fam (insulto)* swear word

putear *vt muy Fam* (**a**) *(fastidiar)* **p. a algn** to screw *o* bugger sb around (**b**) *Am (insultar)* **p. a algn** to call sb for everything, to call sb every name under the sun

puticlub *nm Fam* brothel

puto, -a 1 *adj Vulg* fucking **2** *nm* male prostitute, stud

putrefacto, -a, pútrido, -a *adj* putrefied, rotten

puzzle *nm* jigsaw puzzle

PVC *nm (abr* **cloruro de polivinilo***)* PVC

PVP *nm (abr* **precio de venta al público***)* RRP

PYME *nf (abr* **Pequeña y Mediana Empresa***)* SME

Pza. *(abr* **Plaza***)* Sq

Q, q [ku] *nf (letra)* Q, q

que¹ *pron rel* **(a)** *(sujeto) (persona)* who; *(cosa)* that, which; **el hombre q. vino** the man who came; **la bomba q. estalló** the bomb that *o* which went off **(b)** *(complemento) (persona)* no se traduce *o* that *o* who *o* Fml whom; *(cosa)* no se traduce *o* that *o* which; **la chica q. conocí** the girl (that *o* who *o* whom) I met; **el coche q. compré** the car (that *o* which) I bought **(c) lo q.** what; **lo q. más me gusta** what I like best **(d)** *(con infinitivo)* no se traduce **hay mucho q. hacer** there's a lot to do

que² *conj* **(a)** no se traduce *o* that; **dijo q. llamaría** he said (that) he would call; **quiero q. vengas** I want you to come **(b)** *(consecutivo)* no se traduce *o* that; *(en comparativas)* than; **habla tan bajo q. no se le oye** he speaks so quietly (that) he can't be heard; **más alto q. yo** taller than me **(c)** *(causal)* no se traduce **date deprisa q. no tenemos mucho tiempo** hurry up, we haven't got much time **(d)** *(enfático)* no se traduce **¡q. no!** no!; **¡q. te calles!** I said be quiet! **(e)** *(deseo, mandato)* (+ subjunctive) no se traduce; **¡q. te diviertas!** enjoy yourself! **(f)** *(final)* so that; **ven q. te dé un beso** come and let me give you a kiss **(g)** *(disyuntivo)* whether; **me da igual q. suba o no** it doesn't matter to me whether he comes up or not **(h)** *(locuciones)* **¿a q. no …?** I bet you can't …!; **q. yo sepa** as far as I know; **yo q. tú** if I were you

qué 1 *pron* **(a)** what; **¿q. quieres?** what do you want?; *Fam* **¿y q.?** so what? **(b)** *(exclamativo)* (+ adj) how; (+ n) what a; **¡q. bonito!** how pretty!; **¡q. lástima!** what a pity!; *Fam* **¡q. de …!** what a lot of …! **2** *adj* which; **¿q. libro quieres?** which book do you want?

quebrada *nf Am (arroyo)* stream

quebradero *nm* **q. de cabeza** headache

quebradizo, -a *adj (débil)* fragile; *(cabello, hielo)* brittle

quebrado *nm Mat* fraction

quebrantamiento *nm (de ley)* violation, infringement

quebrantar *vt* **(a)** *(promesa, ley)* to break **(b)** *(moral, resistencia)* to break

quebrar [1] **1** *vt (romper)* to break **2** *vi Fin* to go bankrupt **3 quebrarse** *upr* to break; *Med* to rupture oneself

queda *nf* **toque de q.** curfew

quedar 1 *vi* **(a)** *(restar)* to be left, to remain; **quedan dos** there are two left **(b)** *(en un lugar)* to arrange to meet; **quedamos en el bar** I'll meet you in the bar **(c) me queda corta** *(ropa)* it is too short for me; **quedaría muy bien allí** *(objeto)* it would look very nice there **(d)** *(acordar)* to agree **(en** to); **¿en qué quedamos?** so what's it to be? **(e)** *(estar situado)* to be; **¿dónde queda la estación?** where's the station? **(f) q. bien/mal** to make a good/bad impression **2 quedarse** *upr* **(a)** *(permanecer)* to stay; **se quedó en casa** she stayed (at) home; **quedarse sin dinero/pan** to run out of money/bread; **quedarse con hambre** to still be hungry **(b) quedarse (con)** *(retener)* to keep; **quédese (con) el cambio** keep the change **(c)** *Esp Fam* **quedarse con algn** to make a fool of sb

quedo *adv* softly, quietly

quehacer *nm* task, chore

queja *nf* complaint; *(de dolor)* groan, moan

quejarse *upr* to complain (**de** about)

quejica *Fam* **1** *adj* grumpy **2** *nmf* moaner

quejido *nm* groan, cry

quemado, -a *adj* **(a)** *(por el fuego)* burnt, burned; *(por el sol)* sunburnt **(b)** *Fig (agotado)* burnt-out

quemador *nm (de cocina)* burner

quemadura *nf* burn

quemar 1 *vt* to burn; *Fig (agotar)* to burn out **2** *vi* to be burning hot; **este café quema** this coffee's boiling hot **3 quemarse** *upr Fig* to burn out

quemarropa: a quemarropa *loc adv* point-blank

quemazón *nf* smarting

quena *nf* Andean flute

quepa *etc ver* **caber**

quepo *indic pres de* **caber**

queque *nm Andes, CAm, Méx* sponge (cake)

querella *nf Der* lawsuit

querer [20] **1** *vt* (**a**) *(amar)* to love (**b**) *(desear)* to want; **¿cuánto quiere por la casa?** how much does he want for the house?; **sin q.** without meaning to; **queriendo** on purpose; **¡por lo que más quieras!** for heaven's sake!; **¿quiere pasarme el pan?** would you pass me the bread? (**c**) **q. decir** to mean (**d**) **no quiso darme permiso** he refused me permission **2 quererse** *vpr* to love each other **3** *nm* love, affection

querido, -a 1 *adj* dear, beloved; **q. amigo** *(en carta)* dear friend **2** *nm,f (amante)* lover; *(mujer)* mistress

queroseno, *Am* **querosén** *nm* kerosene, kerosine

querré *indic fut de* **querer**

quesadilla *nf* (**a**) *CAm, Méx (salada)* = filled fried tortilla (**b**) *Ecuad (dulce)* = sweet, cheese-filled pasty

queso *nm* cheese; **q. rallado** grated cheese; **q. de cerdo** *Br* brawn, *US* headcheese

quetzal *nm* quetzal, = standard monetary unit of Guatemala

quicio *nm (de puerta)* doorpost; *Fig* **sacar de q.** *(persona)* to infuriate; *(cosa)* to take too far

quid *nm* crux; **has dado en el q.** you've hit the nail on the head

quiebra *nf Fin (bancarrota)* bankruptcy; *(crack)* crash

quiebro *nm (con el cuerpo)* dodge; *Ftb* dribbling

quien *pron rel* (**a**) *(con prep)* no se traduce *o Fml* whom; **el hombre con q. vino** the man she came with; *Fml* the man with whom she came (**b**) *(indefinido)* whoever, anyone who; **q. quiera venir que venga** whoever wants to can come; **hay q. dice lo contrario** some people say the opposite; *Fig* **q. más q. menos** everybody

quién *pron interr* (**a**) *(sujeto)* who?; **¿q. es?** who is it? (**b**) *(complemento)* who, *Fml* whom; **¿para q. es?** who is it for?; **¿de q. es esa bici?** whose bike is that?

quienquiera *(pl* **quienesquiera)** *pron* whoever; **q. que venga** whoever comes

quieto, -a *adj* still; *(mar)* calm; **¡estáte q.!** keep still!, don't move!

quietud *nf (inmovilidad)* stillness; *(calma)* calm

quijada *nf* jawbone

quilate *nm* carat

quilla *nf* keel

quillango *nm Arg, Chile* fur blanket

quilo *nm* = **kilo**

quilombo *nm RP muy Fam* (**a**) *(burdel)* whorehouse (**b**) *(lío, desorden)* **se armó un gran q.** all hell broke loose

quimera *nf* fantasy, pipe dream

química *nf* chemistry

químico, -a 1 *adj* chemical **2** *nm,f* chemist

quimioterapia *nf* chemotherapy

quimono *nm* kimono

quincallería *nf* trinkets

quince *adj & nm inv* fifteen

quinceañero, -a *adj & nm,f* fifteen-year-old

quincena *nf* fortnight, two weeks

quincenal *adj* fortnightly

quincho *nm* (**a**) *Andes, RP (techo)* thatched roof (**b**) *Andes, RP (refugio)* thatched shelter

quinielas *nfpl Esp Br* (football) pools, *US* sports lottery

quinientos, -as *adj & nm* five hundred

quinina *nf* quinine

quinqué *nm* oil lamp

quinquenal *adj* quinquennial, five-year

quinta *nf* (**a**) *(casa)* country house (**b**) *Mil* call-up year

quintaesencia *nf* quintessence

quintal *nm (medida)* = 46 kg; **q. métrico** ≃ 100 kg

quinteto *nm* quintet

quinto, -a 1 *adj & nm,f* fifth **2** *nm Mil* conscript, recruit

quiosco *nm* kiosk; **q. de periódicos** newspaper stand

quipos, quipus *nmpl Andes* quipus, = knotted cords used for record keeping by the Incas

quirófano *nm* operating *Br* theatre *o US* room

quiromancia *nf* palmistry

quirúrgico, -a *adj* surgical

quise *indic fut de* **querer**

quisque, quisqui *pron Fam* **todo** *o* **cada q.** everyone, everybody

quisquilloso, -a 1 *adj* fussy, finicky **2** *nm,f* fusspot

quiste *nm* cyst

quitaesmalte *nm inv* nail varnish *o* polish remover

quitamanchas *nm inv* stain remover

quitanieves *nm inv* snow plough

quitar 1 *vt* (**a**) to remove; *(ropa)* to take off; *(la mesa)* to clear; *(mancha)* to remove; *(dolor)* to relieve; *(hipo)* to stop; *(sed)* to quench; *(hambre)* to take away (**b**) *(apartar)* to take away, to take off; **q. importancia a algo** to play sth down; **q. las ganas a algn** to put sb off (**c**) *(robar)* to steal, to take; *(tiempo)* to take up; *(sitio)* to take (**d**) *(descontar)* to take off (**e**) *Fam (apagar)* to turn off (**f**) **eso no quita para que …** that's no reason not to be … (**g**) **¡quita!** go away!

2 quitarse *vpr* (**a**) *(apartarse)* to move away (**b**) *(mancha)* to come out; *(dolor)* to go away; **se me han quitado las ganas** I don't feel like it any more (**c**) *(ropa, gafas)* to take off (**d**) **quitarse de beber/fumar** to give up drinking/smoking (**e**) **quitarse a algn de encima** to get rid of sb

> 🖉 Observa que el verbo inglés **to quit** es un falso amigo y no es la traducción del verbo español **quitar**. En inglés, **to quit** significa "dejar, abandonar".

quizá(s) *adv* perhaps, maybe

R, r ['erre] *nf (letra)* R, r

rábano *nm* radish; *Fam* **me importa un r.** I couldn't care less

rabia *nf* (a) *Fig (ira)* fury, rage; **¡qué r.!** how annoying!; **me da r.** it gets up my nose; **me tiene r.** he's got it in for me (b) *Med* rabies *sing*

rabiar [43] *vi (enfadar)* to rage; **hacer r. a algn** to make sb see red

rabieta *nf Fam* tantrum; **coger una r.** to throw a tantrum

rabillo *nm (del ojo)* corner

rabino *nm* rabbi

rabioso, -a *adj* (a) *Med* rabid; **perro r.** rabid dog (b) *Fig (enfadado)* furious (c) **de rabiosa actualidad** up-to-the-minute

rabo *nm* tail; *(de fruta etc)* stalk

racanear *vi Fam* to be stingy

rácano, -a *adj Fam* stingy, mean

racha *nf (de viento)* gust, squall; *Fam (período)* spell, patch; **a rachas** in fits and starts

racial *adj* **discriminación r.** racial discrimination; **disturbios raciales** race riots

racimo *nm* bunch, cluster

raciocinio *nm* reason

ración *nf* portion

racional *adj* rational

racionalizar [40] *vt* to rationalize

racionamiento *nm* rationing; **cartilla de r.** ration book

racionar *vt (limitar)* to ration; *(repartir)* to ration out

racismo *nm* racism

racista *adj & nmf* racist

radar *nm Téc* radar

radiación *nf* radiation

radiactividad *nf* radioactivity

radiactivo, -a *adj* radioactive

radiador *nm* radiator

radial *adj* (a) *(en forma de estrella)* radial (b) *Am (de la radio)* radio

radiante *adj* radiant (**de** with)

radiar [43] *vt* to broadcast, to transmit

radical *adj* radical

radicalizar [40] **1** *vt* to harden, to make more radical

2 radicalizarse *vpr* to become more radical *o* extreme

radicar [44] *vi (estar)* to be (situated) (**en** in), to be rooted (**en** in)

radio 1 *nf (medio)* radio; *Esp, CSur (aparato)* radio (set)

2 *nm* (a) *Anat & Geom* radius; **r. de acción** field of action, scope (b) *(de rueda)* spoke (c) *Quím* radium (d) *Am salvo CSur (transistor)* radio

radioactividad *nf* radioactivity

radioactivo, -a *adj* radioactive

radioaficionado, -a *nm,f* radio ham

radiocasete *nm* radio cassette

radiodespertador *nm* clock radio

radiodifusión *nf* broadcasting

radioescucha *nmf* listener

radiograbador *nm*, **radiograbadora** *nf CSur* radio cassette

radiografía *nf (imagen)* X-ray

radiólogo, -a *nm,f* radiologist

radionovela *nf* radio soap opera

radiotaxi *nm (aparato de radio)* = taxi-driver's two-way radio; *(taxi)* taxi *(fitted with two-way radio)*

radioyente *nmf* listener

ráfaga *nf (de viento)* gust, squall; *(de disparos)* burst

rafting *nm Dep* rafting

raído, -a *adj* worn

raigambre *nf* roots

raíl *nm* rail

raíz *nf* root; **r. cuadrada** square root; *Fig* **a r. de** as a result of

raja *nf (corte)* cut, slit; *(hendidura)* crack, split

rajar 1 *vt (hender)* to crack, split; *Fam (acuchillar)* to cut up

2 *vi Esp Fam* to natter on, to witter on

3 rajarse *vpr* (a) *(partirse)* to crack (b) *Esp Fam (echarse atrás)* to back *o* pull out

rajatabla: a rajatabla *loc adv* to the letter, strictly

ralea *nf Pey* type, sort

ralentí *nm* neutral; **estar al r.** to be ticking over

ralentizar *vt* to slow down

rallado, -a *adj* **queso r.** grated cheese; **pan r.** breadcrumbs

rallador *nm* grater

ralladura *nf* gratings

rallar *vt* to grate

rally ['rrali] (*pl* **rallys**) *nm* rally

ralo, -a *adj* sparse, thin

rama *nf* branch; *Fam* **andarse** *o* **irse por las ramas** to beat about the bush

ramaje *nm* branches

ramalazo *nm Fam* **cuando le da el r.** when the mood takes him

rambla *nf* (*avenida*) boulevard, avenue

ramera *nf* prostitute, whore

ramificación *nf* ramification

ramificarse [44] *vpr* to ramify, to branch (out)

ramillete *nm* (*de flores*) posy

ramo *nm* (a) (*de flores*) bunch, bouquet (b) (*sector*) branch

rampa *nf* ramp; **r. de lanzamiento** launch pad

ramplón, -ona *adj* coarse, vulgar

rana *nf* frog; *Fam* **salir r.** to be a disappointment

ranchera *nf* (a) *Mús* = popular Mexican song (b) (*automóvil*) *Br* estate (car), *US* station wagon

ranchero, -a *nm,f* rancher, farmer

rancho *nm* (a) (*granja*) ranch (b) *Mil* (*comida*) mess (c) *RP* (*en la playa*) = thatched beach-side building (d) *CSur, Ven* (*en la ciudad*) shack, shanty (e) *Méx* (*pequeña finca*) = small farmhouse and outbuildings

rancio, -a *adj* (a) (*comida*) stale (b) (*antiguo*) ancient

rango *nm* rank; (*jerarquía elevada*) high social standing

ranura *nf* slot

rapar *vt* (*afeitar*) to shave; (*pelo*) to crop

rapaz¹ *adj* predatory; **ave r.** bird of prey

rapaz², -aza *nm,f* youngster; (*muchacho*) lad; (*muchacha*) lass

rape *nm* (a) (*pez*) angler fish (b) *Fam* **cortado al r.** close-cropped

rapero, -a *nm,f Mús* rapper

rápidamente *adv* quickly

rapidez *nf* speed, rapidity

rápido, -a 1 *adj* quick, fast, rapid
　　2 *adv* quickly
　　3 *nm* (a) (*tren*) fast train (b) **rápidos** (*de un río*) rapids

rapiña *nf* robbery, theft; **ave de r.** bird of prey

raptar *vt* to kidnap, to abduct

rapto *nm* (a) (*secuestro*) kidnapping, abduction (b) *Fig* (*arrebato*) outburst, fit

raqueta *nf* (a) (*de tenis*) racquet; (*de ping-pong*) *Br* bat, *US* paddle (b) (*de nieve*) snowshoe

raquítico, -a *adj Fam* (*escaso*) small, meagre; (*delgado*) emaciated

raquitismo *nm* rickets *sing*

rareza *nf* (a) (*de persona, cosa*) rarity (b) (*extravagancia*) eccentricity

raro, -a *adj* (a) (*extraño*) odd, strange (b) (*excepcional*) rare; **rara vez** seldom

ras *nm* level; **a r. de** (on a) level with; **a r. de tierra** at ground level

rasante 1 *nf Aut* **cambio de r.** brow of a hill
　　2 *adj* (*vuelo*) low

rasar *vt* (*nivelar*) to level

rasca *nf Esp Fam* (*frío*) cold

rascacielos *nm inv* skyscraper

rascador *nm* (*herramienta*) scraper

rascar [44] **1** *vt* (a) (*con las uñas*) to scratch; (*guitarra*) to strum
　　2 *vi* to chafe

rasero *nm Fig* **medir con el mismo r.** to treat impartially

rasgado, -a *adj* (*ojos*) slit, almond-shaped

rasgar [42] *vt* to tear, to rip

rasgo *nm* (*característica*) characteristic, feature; (*de la cara*) feature; *Fig* **a grandes rasgos** broadly speaking

rasgón *nm* tear, rip

rasguñar *vt* to scratch, to scrape

rasguño *nm* scratch, scrape

raso, -a 1 *adj* (*llano*) flat, level; (*vuelo*) low; (*cielo*) clear, cloudless; **soldado r.** private
　　2 *nm* satin

raspa *nf* (*de pescado*) bone, backbone

raspadita *nf Arg* ≃ scratchcard

raspador *nm* scraper

raspadura *nf* scraping, scrapings

raspar 1 *vt* to scrape (off)
　　2 *vi* (*ropa etc*) to chafe

rastra *nf* **a la r.**, **a rastras** dragging; *Fig* (*de mal grado*) grudgingly

rastreador *nm* tracker

rastrear *vt* to search, to comb

rastreo *nm* searching, combing

rastrero, -a *adj* despicable

rastrillo *nm* (a) (*herramienta*) rake (b) (*mercado*) flea market (c) *Méx* (*para afeitarse*) razor

rastro *nm* (a) (*pista*) trace; (*en el suelo*) trail (b) (*mercado*) flea market

rastrojo *nm* stubble

rasurar *vt* to shave

rata 1 *nf* rat
  2 *nm Fam (tacaño)* mean o stingy person
ratero, -a *nm,f* pickpocket
ratificar [44] *vt* to ratify
rato *nm* (a) *(momento)* while, time; **a ratos** at times; **al poco r.** shortly after; **hay para r.** it'll take a while; **pasar un buen/mal r.** to have a good/bad time; **ratos libres** free time (b) *Esp Fam* **un r.** *(mucho)* very, a lot
ratón *nm* mouse; *Esp Inform* mouse
ratonera *nf* mousetrap
raudal *nm* torrent, flood; *Fig* **a raudales** in abundance
raya *nf* (a) *(línea)* line; *(del pantalón)* crease; *Esp, Andes, RP (del pelo) Br* parting, *US* part; **camisa a rayas** striped shirt (b) *Fig* **tener a r.** to keep at bay; **pasarse de la r.** to go over the score (c) *(de droga)* fix, dose
rayano, -a *adj* bordering (**en** on)
rayar 1 *vt (arañar)* to scratch
  2 *vi* **r. en** o **con** to border on
rayo *nm* (a) *(de luz)* ray; *Fís* ray, beam; **rayos X** X-rays (b) *(relámpago)* (flash of) lightning; **¡mal r. la parta!** to hell with her!
rayón *nm* rayon
rayuela *nf* hopscotch
raza *nf* (a) *(humana)* race (b) *(de animal)* breed (c) *Méx Pey (populacho)* **la r.** the masses (d) *Perú (descaro)* cheek, nerve
razón *nf* (a) *(facultad)* reason; **uso de r.** power of reasoning (b) *(motivo)* reason; **r. de más para** all the more reason to (c) *(justicia)* rightness, justice; **dar la r. a algn** to say that sb is right; **tienes r.** you're right (d) *(proporción)* ratio, rate; **a r. de** at the rate of (e) **r. aquí** *(en letrero)* enquire within, apply within
razonable *adj* reasonable
razonado, -a *adj* reasoned, well-reasoned
razonamiento *nm* reasoning
razonar 1 *vt (argumentar)* to reason out
  2 *vi (discurrir)* to reason
reacción *nf* reaction; **avión de r.** jet (plane); **r. en cadena** chain reaction
reaccionar *vi* to react
reaccionario, -a *adj & nm,f* reactionary
reacio, -a *adj* reluctant, unwilling
reactor *nm* reactor; *(avión)* jet (plane)
readaptación *nf* readjustment
reafirmar *vt* to reaffirm, to reassert
reagrupar *vt* to regroup
reajuste *nm* readjustment; *Com* **r. de plantillas** downsizing; **r. ministerial** cabinet reshuffle
real¹ *adj (efectivo, verdadero)* real; **en la vida r.** in real life

real² *adj (regio)* royal
realce *nm (relieve)* relief; *Fig (esplendor)* splendour
realeza *nf* royalty
realidad *nf* reality; **en r.** in fact, actually; **la r. es que …** the fact of the matter is that …
realismo *nm* realism
realista 1 *adj* realistic
  2 *nmf* realist
realizable *adj* feasible
realización *nf (ejecución)* carrying out; *Cin & TV* production
realizador, -a *nm,f Cin & TV* producer
realizar [40] **1** *vt* (a) *(hacer)* to carry out; *(ambición)* to achieve, to fulfil (b) *Cin & TV* to produce (c) *Fin* to realize
  2 realizarse *vpr (persona)* to fulfil oneself; *(sueño)* to come true
realmente *adv* really; *(en realidad)* actually, in fact
realzar [40] *vt (belleza, importancia)* to enhance, to heighten
reanimación *nf* (a) *(física, moral)* recovery (b) *Med* resuscitation
reanimar 1 *vt* (a) *(físicamente)* to revive (b) *(moralmente)* to cheer up (c) *Med* to resuscitate
  2 reanimarse *vpr* to revive
reanudación *nf* renewal, resumption; **r. de las clases** return to school
reanudar 1 *vt* to renew, to resume; **r. el paso** o **la marcha** to set off again; **r. las clases** to go back to school
  2 reanudarse *vpr* to start again, to resume
reaparición *nf* reappearance, recurrence; *(de artista etc)* comeback
reapertura *nf* reopening
rearme *nm* rearmament
reaseguro *nm* reinsurance
reavivar *vt* to revive
rebaja *nf (descuento)* reduction, discount; **rebajas** sales; **precio de r.** sale price
rebajado, -a *adj* (a) *(precio)* reduced (b) *(diluido)* diluted (**con** with)
rebajar 1 *vt* (a) *(precio)* to cut, to reduce; *(cantidad)* to take off (b) *(color)* to tone down, to soften; *(intensidad)* to diminish (c) *(trabajador)* to excuse, to exempt (**de** from) (d) *(humillar)* to humiliate
  2 rebajarse *vpr (humillarse)* to humble oneself
rebanada *nf* slice
rebanar *vt* to slice, to cut into slices
rebañar *vt* to scrape clean
rebaño *nm (de ovejas)* flock; *(de otros animales)* herd

rebasar *vt* (**a**) *(exceder)* to exceed, to go beyond (**b**) *Aut* to overtake

rebatir *vt* to refute

> *𝓁* Observa que la palabra inglesa **rebate** es un falso amigo y no es la traducción del verbo español **rebatir**. En inglés, **rebate** significa "devolución".

rebeca *nf* cardigan

rebelarse *vpr* to rebel, to revolt

rebelde 1 *nmf* rebel
    2 *adj* rebellious; *Fig* **una tos r.** a persistent cough

rebeldía *nf* (**a**) *(cualidad)* rebelliousness (**b**) *Der* default

rebelión *nf* rebellion, revolt

rebenque *nm RP (fusta)* (riding) crop, whip

reblandecer [33] *vt* to soften

rebobinar *vt* to rewind

rebosante *adj* overflowing (**de** with), brimming (**de** with)

rebosar 1 *vi* to overflow, to brim over; *Fig* **r. de** to be overflowing *o* brimming with
    2 *vt (irradiar)* to radiate

rebotar *vi* to bounce (**en** off), to rebound (**en** off)

rebote *nm* (**a**) *(bote)* bounce, bouncing; *Fig* **de r.** by chance, indirectly (**b**) *Dep* rebound; **de r.** on the rebound

rebozado, -a *adj Culin* coated in batter/breadcrumbs; *Fig* **r. de** *o* **en** *(barro)* covered in

rebozar [40] *vt* to coat in batter/breadcrumbs

rebozo *nm Am* wrap, shawl; **sin r.** *(con franqueza)* frankly

rebullirse *vpr* to stir

rebuscado, -a *adj* recherché

rebuznar *vi* to bray

recabar *vt (información)* to obtain, to manage to get

recado *nm (mandado)* errand; *(mensaje)* message; **dejar un r.** to leave a message

recaer [39] *vi* (**a**) *Med* to relapse (**b**) *(culpa, responsabilidad)* to fall (**sobre** on)

recaída *nf* relapse

recalcar [44] *vt* to stress, to emphasize

recalcitrante *adj* recalcitrant

recalentar [1] *vt (comida)* to reheat, to warm up; *(calentar demasiado)* to overheat

recámara *nf* (**a**) *(de rueda)* tube (**b**) *(habitación)* dressing room (**c**) *CAm, Col, Méx (dormitorio)* bedroom

recamarera *nf CAm, Col, Méx* chambermaid

recambiar [43] *vt* to change (over)

recambio *nm* (**a**) *(repuesto)* spare (part); **rueda de r.** spare wheel (**b**) *(de pluma etc)* refill

recapacitar *vi* to reflect, to think

recarga *nf (de móvil)* top-up

recargable *adj (pluma)* refillable; *(mechero)* rechargeable

recargado, -a *adj* overloaded; *Fig (estilo)* overelaborate, affected

recargar [42] **1** *vt* (**a**) *Elec* to recharge (**b**) *(sobrecargar)* to overload; *(adornar mucho)* to overelaborate (**c**) *Fin* to increase
    2 recargarse *vpr Méx (apoyarse)* to lean (**contra** against)

recargo *nm* extra charge, surcharge

recatado, -a *adj (modesto)* modest, decent

recato *nm (pudor)* modesty; **sin r.** openly, without reserve

recaudación *nf (cobro)* collection; *(cantidad recaudada)* takings; *Dep* gate

recaudador, -a *nm,f* tax collector

recaudar *vt* to collect

recaudo *nm* **estar a buen r.** to be in safekeeping

recelar *vi* **r. de** to distrust

recelo *nm* suspicion, distrust

receloso, -a *adj* suspicious, distrustful

recepción *nf* reception; *(en hotel)* reception (desk)

recepcionista *nmf* receptionist

receptivo, -a *adj* receptive

receptor, -a *nm,f (persona)* recipient
    2 *nm Rad & TV* receiver

recesión *nf* recession

receta *nf* recipe; *Med* prescription

recetar *vt Med* to prescribe

rechazar [40] *vt* to reject, to turn down; *Mil* to repel, to drive back

rechazo *nm* rejection

rechiflar *vt* (**a**) *(silbar)* to hiss, to boo (**b**) *(mofarse)* to mock, to jeer at

rechinar *vi (dientes)* to grind; *(madera)* to creak; *(metal)* to squeak, to screech

rechistar *vi* **sin r.** without a word of protest

rechoncho, -a *adj Fam* chubby, tubby

rechupete: de rechupete *loc Fam* **estaba de r.** it was mouthwateringly good

recibidor *nm* entrance hall

recibimiento *nm* reception, welcome

recibir 1 *vt* to receive; *(en casa)* to welcome; *(en la estación etc)* to meet
    2 recibirse *vpr Am (graduarse)* to graduate, to qualify (**de** as)

recibo *nm* (**a**) *(factura)* invoice, bill; *(resguardo)* receipt; **r. de la luz** electricity bill (**b**) **acusar r. de** to acknowledge receipt of

reciclado, -a 1 *adj* recycled
  2 *nm (reciclaje)* recycling

reciclaje *nm (de residuos)* recycling; *Fig (renovación)* retraining; **curso de r.** refresher course

reciclar *vt (residuos)* to recycle; *Fig (profesores etc)* to retrain

recién *adv* (**a**) *(recientemente) (antes de pp)* recently, newly; **café r. hecho** freshly-made coffee; **r. casados** newlyweds; **r. nacido** newborn baby (**b**) *Am (apenas)* just now, recently; **regresó r. ayer** she only *o* just got back yesterday (**c**) *Am (ahora mismo)* (only) just; **r. me entero** I've (only) just heard (**d**) *Am (sólo)* only; **r. el martes sabremos el resultado** we'll only know the result on Tuesday, we won't know the result until Tuesday

reciente *adj* recent

recientemente *adv* recently, lately

recinto *nm (cercado)* enclosure; **r. comercial** shopping precinct

recio, -a 1 *adj (robusto)* strong, sturdy; *(grueso)* thick; *(voz)* loud
  2 *adv* hard

recipiente *nm* receptacle, container

> *Observa que la palabra inglesa **recipient** es un falso amigo y no es la traducción de la palabra española **recipiente**. En inglés **recipient** significa "receptor, destinatario".*

recíproco, -a *adj* reciprocal

recital *nm Mús* recital; *Lit* reading

recitar *vt* to recite

reclamación *nf* (**a**) *(demanda)* claim, demand (**b**) *(queja)* complaint

reclamar 1 *vt* to demand, to ask for
  2 *vi* (**a**) *(quejarse)* to complain (**contra** about) (**b**) *Der* to appeal

reclamo *nm* (**a**) *(publicitario)* appeal (**b**) *(en caza)* decoy bird, lure; *Fig* inducement (**c**) *Am (queja)* complaint (**d**) *Am (reivindicación)* claim

reclinar 1 *vt* to lean (**sobre** on)
  2 reclinarse *vpr* to lean back, to recline

recluir [37] *vt* to shut away, to lock away; *(encarcelar)* to imprison, to intern

reclusión *nf* seclusion; *(encarcelamiento)* imprisonment, internment

recluso, -a *nm,f* prisoner

> *Observa que la palabra inglesa **recluse** es un falso amigo y no es la traducción de la palabra española **recluso**. En inglés, **recluse** significa "solitario".*

recluta *nmf* recruit

reclutamiento *nm (voluntario)* recruitment; *(obligatorio)* conscription

recobrar 1 *vt* to recover, to retrieve; *(conocimiento)* to regain; **r. el aliento** to get one's breath back
  2 recobrarse *vpr* to recover, to recuperate

recochineo *nm Fam* mockery

recodo *nm (de río)* twist, turn; *(de camino)* bend

recogedor *nm* dustpan

recoger [53] **1** *vt* (**a**) *(del suelo etc)* to pick up (**b**) *(datos etc)* to gather, to collect (**c**) *(ordenar, limpiar)* to clean; **r. la mesa** to clear the table (**d**) *(ira buscar)* to pick up, to fetch (**e**) *(cosecha)* to gather, to pick
  2 recogerse *vpr* (**a**) *(irse a casa)* to go home (**b**) *(pelo)* to lift up

recogida *nf* collection; *Agr (cosecha)* harvest, harvesting

recolección *nf Agr* harvest, harvesting; *(recogida)* collection, gathering

> *Observa que la palabra inglesa **recollection** es un falso amigo y no es la traducción de la palabra española **recolección**. En inglés, **recollection** significa "recuerdo".*

recomendable *adj* recommendable

recomendación *nf* recommendation, reference

recomendado, -a *adj Am (carta, paquete)* registered

recomendar [1] *vt* to recommend

recompensa *nf* reward

recompensar *vt* to reward

recomponer [19] *(pp recompuesto)* *vt* to repair, to mend

reconciliación *nf* reconciliation

reconciliar [43] **1** *vt* to reconcile
  2 reconciliarse *vpr* to be reconciled

recóndito, -a *adj* hidden, secret

reconfortante *adj* comforting

reconfortar *vt* to comfort

reconocer [34] *vt* (**a**) *(identificar)* to recognize (**b**) *(admitir)* to admit (**c**) *Med (paciente)* to examine

reconocimiento *nm* (**a**) *(identificación, admisión)* recognition (**b**) *Med* examination, checkup (**c**) *(agradecimiento)* gratitude

reconquista *nf* reconquest

reconstruir [37] *vt* to reconstruct

reconversión *nf* restructuring; **r. industrial** rationalization of industry

reconvertir [5] *vt (reestructurar)* to restructure; *(industria)* to rationalize

recopilación *nf* compilation, collection

recopilar *vt* to compile, to collect

récord *(pl* **récords)** *nm* record

recordar [2] **1** *vt* (**a**) *(rememorar)* to remember (**b**) **r. algo a algn** to remind sb of sth
  2 *vi* to remember

recordatorio *nm (aviso)* reminder; *(de defunción)* notice of death

recorrer *vt (distancia)* to cover, to travel; *(país)* to tour, to travel through *o* round; *(ciudad)* to visit, to walk round

recorrido *nm, Am* **recorrida** *nf (distancia)* distance travelled; *(trayecto)* trip, journey; *(itinerario)* itinerary, route

recortable *adj & nm* cutout

recortar *vt* to cut out

recorte *nm (acción, de periódico)* cutting; *(de salarios etc)* cut

recostado, -a *adj* reclining, leaning

recostar [2] **1** *vt* to lean
  2 recostarse *upr (tumbarse)* to lie down

recoveco *nm* nook, corner

recrear 1 *vt* to recreate
  2 recrearse *upr* **r. con** to take pleasure *o* delight in

recreativo, -a *adj* recreational

recreo *nm (en el colegio)* break, recreation

recriminar *vt* to reproach

recrudecerse [33] *upr* to worsen

recrudecimiento *nm* worsening

recta *nf Geom* straight line; *(de carretera)* straight stretch; *Dep* **la r. final** the home straight

rectangular *adj* rectangular

rectángulo *nm* rectangle

rectificación *nf (de error)* rectification; *(en periódico)* correction

rectificar [44] *vt (error)* to rectify; *(conducta, actitud)* to improve

rectilíneo, -a *adj* straight

rectitud *nf* straightness; *Fig* uprightness, rectitude

recto, -a 1 *adj* (**a**) *(derecho)* straight (**b**) *(honesto)* upright, honest (**c**) *Geom* right
  2 *nm Anat* rectum
  3 *adv* straight (on)

rector, -a 1 *adj (principio)* guiding, ruling
  2 *nm Rel* rector

recua *nf* string, series

recuadro *nm* box

recubrir *(pp* **recubierto)** *vt* to cover

recuento *nm* count; **hacer (el) r. de** to count

recuerdo *nm* (**a**) *(memoria)* memory (**b**) *(regalo etc)* souvenir (**c**) **recuerdos** regards

recuperación *nf* recovery; *(examen)* resit

recuperar 1 *vt (salud)* to recover; *(conocimiento)* to regain; *(tiempo, clases)* to make up
  2 recuperarse *upr* to recover

recurrir *vi* (**a**) *Der* to appeal (**b**) **r. a** *(a algn)* to turn to; *(a algo)* to make use of, to resort to

> 🖉 Observa que el verbo inglés **to recur** es un falso amigo y no es la traducción del verbo español **recurrir.** En inglés, **to recur** significa "repetirse".

recurso *nm* (**a**) *(bien, riqueza)* resource; **recursos humanos** human resources; **recursos naturales** natural resources; **como último r.** as a last resort (**b**) *Der* appeal

red *nf* net; *(sistema)* network; *Com (cadena)* chain of supermarkets; *Fig (trampa)* trap; **la R.** *(Internet)* the Net

redacción *nf (escrito)* composition, essay; *(acción)* writing; *Prensa* editing; *(redactores)* editorial staff

redactar *vt* to draft; *Prensa* to edit

redactor, -a *nm,f Prensa* editor

redada *nf* **r. policial** *(en un solo sitio)* raid; *(en varios lugares a la vez)* round-up

redentor, -a *nm,f* redeemer

redil *nm* fold, sheepfold

redimir *vt* to redeem

redoblar 1 *vt* to redouble
  2 *vi (tambor)* to roll

redoble *nm* roll; *(de campanas)* peal

redomado, -a *adj* utter, out-and-out

redonda *nf* **a la r.** around

redondeado, -a *adj* rounded

redondear *vt (objeto)* to round, to make round; *(cantidad)* to round up

redondel *nm Fam (círculo)* circle, ring; *Taurom* ring, arena

redondo, -a *adj* (**a**) *(circular)* round; *Fig* **caer r.** to collapse (**b**) *(rotundo)* categorical; *(perfecto)* perfect

reducción *nf* reduction

reducido, -a *adj (disminuido)* reduced, decreased; *(pequeño)* limited, small

reducir [10] **1** *vt (disminuir)* to reduce
  2 reducirse *upr* (**a**) *(disminuirse)* to be reduced, to diminish (**b**) *(limitarse)* to confine oneself

redundancia *nf* redundancy, superfluousness; **valga la r.** if I might say so again

redundante *adj* redundant

redundar *vi* **r. en** to result in, to lead to

reembolsar *vt* to reimburse; *(deuda)* to repay; *(importe)* to refund

reembolso *nm* reimbursement; *(de deuda)* repayment; *(devolución)* refund; **contra r.** cash on delivery

reemplazar [40] *vt* to replace (**con** with)

reemplazo *nm* replacement; *Mil* call-up

reestrenar *vt Cin* to rerun; *Teatro* to revive

reestreno *nm* (a) *Cin* rerun, re-release; **cine de r.** second-run cinema (b) *Teatro* revival

reestructuración *nf* restructuring

reestructurar *vt* to restructure

refacción *nf* (a) *Andes, CAm, RP, Ven (reforma)* refurbishment; *(reparación)* restoration (b) *Méx (recambio)* spare part

refaccionar *vt Andes, CAm, Ven (reformar)* to refurbish; *(reparar)* to restore

referencia *nf* reference; **con r.** a with reference to

referéndum *(pl* referéndums) *nm* referendum

referente *adj* **r.** a concerning, regarding

referir [5] **1** *vt* to tell, to relate
  2 referirse *vpr (aludir)* to refer (**a** to); **¿a qué te refieres?** what do you mean?

refilón: de refilón *loc adv (de pasada)* briefly; **mirar algo de r.** to look at sth out of the corner of one's eye

refinado, -a *adj* refined

refinamiento *nm* refinement

refinar *vt* to refine

refinería *nf* refinery

reflector, -a 1 *adj* reflecting
  2 *nm Elec* spotlight, searchlight

reflejar 1 *vt* to reflect
  2 reflejarse *vpr* to be reflected (**en** in)

reflejo, -a 1 *nm* (a) *(imagen)* reflection (b) *(destello)* gleam, glint (c) *Anat* reflex (d) **reflejos** *(en el cabello)* streaks, highlights
  2 *adj (movimiento)* reflex

reflexión *nf* reflection

reflexionar *vi* to reflect (**sobre** on), to think (**sobre** about)

reflexivo, -a *adj* (a) *(persona)* thoughtful (b) *Ling* reflexive

reflujo *nm* ebb (tide)

reforma *nf* (a) *(modificación)* reform; **r. fiscal** tax reform (b) *(en local, casa)* alterations

reformar 1 *vt* to reform; *(edificio)* to renovate
  2 reformarse *vpr* to reform

reformatorio *nm* reformatory, reform school

reforzar [2] *vt* to reinforce, to strengthen

refractario, -a *adj Téc* heat-resistant

refrán *nm* proverb, saying

refregar [1] *vt* to rub vigorously; *Fig* **no me lo refriegues** don't rub it in

refrenar 1 *vt* to restrain, to curb
  2 refrenarse *vpr* to restrain oneself

refrendar *vt (firmar)* to endorse, to countersign; *(aprobar)* to approve

refrescante *adj* refreshing

refrescar [44] **1** *vt* to refresh
  2 *vi* (a) *(tiempo)* to turn cool (b) *(bebida)* to be refreshing
  3 refrescarse *vpr* to cool down

refresco *nm* soft drink, refreshments

refriega *nf (lucha)* scuffle, brawl; *(escaramuza)* skirmish

refrigeración *nf* refrigeration

refrigerado, -a *adj* air-conditioned

refrigerador *nm* refrigerator, *Br* fridge, *US* icebox

refrigerar *vt* to refrigerate

refrigerio *nm* refreshments

refuerzo *nm* reinforcement

refugiado, -a *adj & nm,f* refugee

refugiarse [43] *vpr* to shelter, to take refuge

refugio *nm* refuge

refulgir [57] *vi (brillar)* to shine; *(resplandecer)* to glitter, to sparkle

refunfuñar *vi* to grumble, to moan

refutar *vt* to refute

regadera *nf* (a) *(para regar)* watering can; *Esp Fam* **estar como una r.** to be as mad as a hatter (b) *Col, Méx, Ven (ducha)* shower

regadío *nm (tierra)* irrigated land

regalado, -a *adj* (a) *(gratis)* free; *(muy barato)* dirt-cheap (b) **una vida regalada** an easy life

regalar *vt* (a) *(dar)* to give (as a present); *(en ofertas etc)* to give away (b) **r. el oído** a **algn** to flatter sb

regaliz *nm* liquorice

regalo *nm* present, gift; **de r.** as a present

regalón, -ona *adj CSur Fam (niño)* spoilt

regañadientes: a regañadientes *loc adv* reluctantly, unwillingly

regañar *vt* to tell off

regañina *nf* telling-off

regar [1] *vt* to water

regata *nf* boat race

regatear 1 *vi* (a) *(al comprar)* to haggle (b) *Dep* to dribble
  2 *vt* **no r. esfuerzos** to spare no effort

regateo *nm* (a) *(de precios)* haggling (b) *Dep* dribbling

regazo *nm* lap

regeneración *nf* regeneration

regenerar *vt* to regenerate

regentar *vt* to rule, to govern; *(cargo)* to hold

regente 1 *nmf Pol* regent
2 *nmf* **(a)** *(director)* manager **(b)** *Méx (alcalde)* mayor, *f* mayoress

régimen *(pl* **regímenes)** *nm* **(a)** *Pol* regime **(b)** *Med* diet; **estar a r.** to be on a diet

regimiento *nm* regiment

regio, -a *adj* **(a)** *(real)* royal, regal **(b)** *Andes, RP (genial)* great, fabulous

región *nf* region

regional *adj* regional

regir [58] **1** *vt* to govern
2 *vi* to be in force
3 regirse *vpr* to be guided, to go **(por** by)

registrado, -a *adj* **(a)** *(patentado, inscrito)* registered; **marca registrada** registered trademark **(b)** *Am (certificado)* registered

registrador, -a *adj* **caja registradora** cash register

registradora *nf Am* cash register

registrar 1 *vt* **(a)** *(examinar)* to search **(b)** *(inscribir)* to register **(c)** *(grabar)* to record
2 registrarse *vpr* **(a)** *(inscribirse)* to register, to enrol **(b)** *(detectarse)* to be recorded

registro *nm* **(a)** *(inspección)* inspection **(b)** *(inscripción)* registration; *(oficina)* registry office; *(libro)* register **(c)** *Ling & Mús* register

regla *nf* **(a)** *(norma)* rule; **en r.** in order; **por r. general** as a (general) rule; **r. de oro** golden rule **(b)** *(instrumento)* ruler **(c)** *Mat* rule **(d)** *Med (periodo)* period

reglamentación *nf* regulation

reglamentar *vt* to regulate

reglamentario, -a *adj* statutory; *Mil* **arma reglamentaria** regulation gun

reglamento *nm* regulations, rules

reglar *vt* to regulate

regocijar 1 *vt* to delight, to amuse
2 regocijarse *vpr* to be delighted, to rejoice

regocijo *nm (placer)* delight, joy; *(alborozo)* rejoicing, merriment

regodearse *vpr Fam* to delight **(con** in)

regodeo *nm Fam* delight

regordete, -a *adj Fam* plump, chubby

regresar 1 *vi* to return
2 *vt Am salvo RP (devolver)* to give back
3 regresarse *vpr Am salvo RP (yendo)* to go back, to return; *(viniendo)* to come back, to return

regresión *nf* regression

regreso *nm* return

reguero *nm (de líquido)* trickle; *(de humo, arena)* trail

regulable *adj* adjustable

regular 1 *vt* **(a)** *(actividad, economía, tráfico)* to regulate, to control **(b)** *(mecanismo)* to adjust
2 *adj* **(a)** *(uniforme)* regular; **vuelo r.** scheduled flight; **por lo r.** as a rule **(b)** *(mediano)* average, so-so
3 *adv* so-so

regularidad *nf* regularity; **con r.** regularly

regularizar [40] *vt* to regularize

regusto *nm* aftertaste

rehabilitar *vt* to rehabilitate; *(edificio)* to convert

rehacer [15] *(pp* **rehecho)** **1** *vt* to redo
2 rehacerse *vpr* to recover, to recuperate

rehén *nm* hostage

rehogar [42] *vt* to brown

rehuir [37] *vt* to shun, to avoid

rehusar *vt* to refuse

reina *nf* queen

reinado *nm* reign

reinante *adj (que reina)* reigning, ruling; *(prevaleciente)* prevailing

reinar *vi* to reign

reincidente *nmf Der* recidivist

reincidir *vi* to relapse, to fall back **(en** into)

reincorporarse *vpr* **r. al trabajo** to return to work

reino *nm* kingdom; **el R. Unido** the United Kingdom

reinserción *nf (social)* reintegration, rehabilitation

reinsertar *vt (en sociedad)* to reintegrate, to rehabilitate

reintegrar *vt* **(a)** *(trabajador)* to reinstate **(b)** *(dinero)* to reimburse, to refund

reintegro *nm (en lotería)* winning of one's stake

reír [56] **1** *vi* to laugh
2 reírse *vpr* to laugh **(de** at)

reiterar *vt* to reiterate, to repeat

reivindicación *nf* claim, demand

reivindicar [44] *vt* to claim, to demand; **el atentado fue reivindicado por los terroristas** the terrorists claimed responsibility for the attack

reivindicativo, -a *adj* protest

reja *nf* **(a)** *(de ventana)* grill, grating; *Fam* **estar entre rejas** to be behind bars **(b)** *Agr* ploughshare

rejilla *nf (de ventana, ventilador, radiador)* grill; *(de horno)* gridiron; *(para equipaje)* luggage rack

rejoneador, -a *nm,f Taurom* = bullfighter on horseback

rejonear *vt Taurom* to fight on horseback

rejuvenecer [33] *vt* to rejuvenate

relación *nf* (a) *(conexión)* relation, connection; **con** *o* **en r. a** with regard to (b) *(entre personas)* relations, relationship; **relaciones públicas** public relations; **relaciones sexuales** sexual relations (c) *(lista)* list; *(relato)* account (d) *Mat & Téc* ratio

relacionado, -a *adj* related (**con** to), connected (**con** with)

relacionar 1 *vt* to relate (**con** to), to connect (**con** with)
 2 relacionarse *vpr (alternar)* to mix (**con** with)

relajación *nf* relaxation

relajante *adj* relaxing

relajar 1 *vt* to relax
 2 relajarse *vpr* to relax; *(moral)* to deteriorate

relajo *nm* (a) *Am Fam (alboroto)* **se armó un r.** there was an almighty row; **esta mesa es un r.** this table is a complete mess (b) *Méx, RP (complicación)* nuisance, hassle (c) *CAm, Carib, Méx (broma)* joke

relamerse *vpr* to lick one's lips

relamido, -a *adj (afectado)* affected; *(pulcro)* prim and proper

relámpago *nm* flash of lightning; *Fig* **pasó como un r.** he flashed past; *Fig* **visita r.** flying visit

relampaguear *v impers* to flash

relanzar *vt* to relaunch

relatar *vt* to narrate, to relate

relatividad *nf* relativity

relativo, -a *adj* relative (**a** to); **en lo r. a** with regard to, concerning

relato *nm (cuento)* tale, story

relax *nm Fam* relaxation

relegar [42] *vt* to relegate

relevancia *nf* importance

> *Ø* Observa que la palabra inglesa **relevance** es un falso amigo y no es la traducción de la palabra española **relevancia**. En inglés, **relevance** significa "pertinencia".

relevante *adj* important

relevar 1 *vt* to relieve, to take over from; **fue relevado del cargo** he was relieved of his duties
 2 relevarse *vpr (turnarse)* to relieve one another

relevo *nm* relief; *Dep* relay

relieve *nm Arte* relief; *Fig* **poner de r.** to emphasize

religión *nf* religion

religioso, -a 1 *adj* religious
 2 *nm,f (hombre)* monk; *(mujer)* nun

relinchar *vi* to neigh, to whinny

relincho *nm* neigh, whinny

reliquia *nf* relic

rellamada *nf Tel* redial

rellano *nm* landing

rellenar *vt* (a) *(impreso etc)* to fill in (b) *(un ave)* to stuff; *(un pastel)* to fill

relleno, -a 1 *nm (de aves)* stuffing; *(de pasteles)* filling
 2 *adj* stuffed

reloj *nm* clock; *(de pulsera)* watch; **r. de arena** hourglass; **r. de sol** sundial; **r. despertador** alarm clock

relojería *nf (tienda)* watchmaker's, clockmaker's; **bomba de r.** time bomb

relojero, -a *nm,f* watchmaker, clockmaker

reluciente *adj* shining, gleaming

relucir [35] *vi* to shine, to gleam; **sacar a r. un tema** to bring up a subject

relumbrar *vi* to shine, to gleam

reluzco *indic pres de* relucir

remachar *vt* to drive home, to hammer home

remache *nm* rivet

remanente *nm (restos)* remainder; *(extra)* surplus

remangar [42] **1** *vt* to roll up
 2 remangarse *vpr (mangas, camisa)* to roll up one's sleeves; **remangarse los pantalones** to roll up one's trouser legs

remanso *nm* still pool; **r. de paz** oasis of peace

remar *vi* to row

remarcar [44] *vt* to stress, to underline

> *Ø* Observa que el verbo inglés **to remark** es un falso amigo y no es la traducción del verbo español **remarcar**. En inglés, **to remark** significa "comentar, observar".

rematadamente *adv* **r. loco** as mad as a hatter

rematar *vt* (a) *(acabar)* to finish off, to put the finishing touches to (b) *Com* to sell off cheaply

remate *nm* (a) *(final)* end, finish; **para r.** to crown it all (b) *Dep* shot at goal (c) **de r.** utter, utterly

rembolsar *vt* = reembolsar

rembolso *nm* = reembolso

remedar *vt* to imitate, to copy

remediar [43] *vt* (a) *(daño)* to remedy; *(problema)* to solve; *(crisis, situación)* to resolve (**b**) *(evitar)* to avoid, to prevent; **no pude remediarlo** I couldn't help it

remedio *nm (cura)* remedy, cure; *(solución)* solution; **¡qué r.!** what else can I do?; **no hay más r.** there's no choice; **sin r.** without fail; *Fam* **¡no tienes r.!** you're hopeless!

remedo *nm (imitación)* imitation, copy; *(parodia)* parody

rememorar *vt* to remember, to recall

remendar [1] *vt (ropa)* to patch

remera *nf RP (prenda)* T-shirt

remero, -a *nm,f* rower

remesa *nf (de mercancías)* consignment, shipment; *(de dinero)* remittance

remiendo *nm (parche)* patch

remilgado, -a *adj (afectado)* affected; *(melindroso)* fussy, finicky; *(gazmoño)* prudish

remilgo *nm* affectation; *(gazmoñería)* prudishness

reminiscencia *nf* reminiscence

remise *nm RP* taxi *(in private car without meter)*

remisero, -a *nm,f RP* taxi driver *(of private car without meter)*

remiso, -a *adj* reluctant

remite *nm (en carta)* = sender's name and address

remitente *nmf* sender

remitir 1 *vt (**a**) (enviar)* to send (**b**) *(referir)* to refer
2 *vi (fiebre, temporal)* to subside
3 **remitirse** *vpr* **si nos remitimos a los hechos** if we look at the facts; **remítase a la página 10** see page 10

remo *nm* oar; *(deporte)* rowing

remoción *nf Andes, RP (de escombros)* removal; *(de heridos)* transport

remodelación *nf* reshaping; *(reorganización)* reorganization; *Pol* **r. ministerial** o **del gobierno** cabinet reshuffle

remodelar *vt* to reshape; *(reorganizar)* to reorganize

remojar *vt* to soak (**en** in)

remojo *nm* **dejar** o **poner en r.** to soak, to leave to soak

remojón *nm Fam* **darse un r.** to go for a dip

remolacha *nf (planta) Br* beetroot, *US* beet

remolcador *nm* (**a**) *Náut* tug, tugboat (**b**) *Aut Br* breakdown van o truck, *US* tow truck

remolcar [44] *vt* to tow

remolino *nm (de agua)* whirlpool, eddy; *(de aire)* whirlwind

remolón, -ona 1 *adj* lazy
2 *nm,f* **hacerse el r.** to shirk, to slack

remolonear *vi* to shirk, to slack

remolque *nm (acción)* towing; *(vehículo)* trailer; *Fig* **ir a r. de algn** to trundle along behind sb

remontar 1 *vt* (**a**) *(subir)* to go up (**b**) *(superar)* to overcome
2 **remontarse** *vpr* (**a**) *(pájaros, aviones)* to soar (**b**) *(datar)* to go back, to date back (**a** to)

remorder [4] *vt* **me remuerde la conciencia por …** I've got a bad conscience about …

remordimiento *nm* remorse

remoto, -a *adj* remote, faraway; **no tengo la más remota idea** I haven't got the faintest idea

remover [4] *vt* (**a**) *(trasladar)* to move over (**b**) *(tierra)* to turn over; *(líquido)* to shake up; *(comida etc)* to stir; *(asunto)* to stir up

> Observa que el verbo inglés **to remove** es un falso amigo y no es la traducción del verbo español **remover**. En inglés, **to remove** significa "quitar, despedir".

remozar [40] *vt* to modernize

remplazar [40] *vt* = reemplazar

remplazo *nm* = reemplazo

remuneración *nf* remuneration

remunerar *vt* to remunerate

renacentista *adj* Renaissance

renacer [60] *vi* (**a**) *(flores, hojas)* to grow again (**b**) *(sentimiento, interés)* to return, to revive; **sentirse r.** to feel reborn, to feel one has a new lease of life

Renacimiento *nm* Renaissance

renacuajo *nm* tadpole; *Fam (niño pequeño)* shrimp

renal *adj* kidney; **insuficiencia r.** kidney failure

rencilla *nf* quarrel

rencor *nm* rancour; *(resentimiento)* resentment; **guardar r. a algn** to have a grudge against sb

rencoroso, -a *adj (hostil)* rancorous; *(resentido)* resentful

rendición *nf* surrender

rendido, -a *adj* exhausted, worn out

rendija *nf* crack, split

rendimiento *nm (producción)* yield, output; *(de máquina, motor)* efficiency, performance

rendir [6] **1** *vt* (**a**) *(fruto, beneficios)* to yield, to produce (**b**) *(cansar)* to exhaust, to wear out (**c**) **r. culto a** to worship; **r. homenaje a** to pay homage to
2 *vi (dar beneficios)* to pay, to be profitable

3 rendirse *vpr* (**a**) *(entregarse)* to give oneself up, to surrender; *(ceder, abandonar)* to give in; **¡me rindo!** I give in o up! (**b**) *(cansarse)* to wear oneself out

renegado, -a *adj & nm,f* renegade

renegar [1] *vt* **r. de** to renounce, to disown

renegrido, -a *adj* blackened

RENFE *nf* (*abr* **Red Nacional de los Ferrocarriles Españoles**) = Spanish state railway company

renglón *nm* line; **a r. seguido** immediately afterwards

rengo, -a *adj Andes, RP* lame

renguear *vi Andes, RP* to limp, to hobble

reno *nm* reindeer

renombrado, -a *adj* renowned, famous

renombre *nm* renown, fame

renovable *adj* renewable

renovación *nf* *(de contrato, pasaporte)* renewal; *(de una casa)* renovation

renovar [2] *vt* to renew; *(edificio)* to renovate

renta *nf* (**a**) *Fin (ingresos)* income; *(beneficio)* interest, return; **r. per cápita** per capita income; **r. fija** fixed-interest security (**b**) *(alquiler)* rent

rentable *adj* profitable

rentar 1 *vt* (**a**) *(rendir)* to produce, yield (**b**) *Méx (alquilar)* to rent; *(vehículo)* to hire
2 *vi* to be profitable

renuncia *nf* (**a**) *(abandono)* giving up (**b**) *(dimisión)* resignation

renunciar [43] *vi* (**a**) **r. a** to renounce, to give up; *(no aceptar)* to decline (**b**) *(dimitir)* to resign

reñido, -a *adj* *(disputado)* tough, hard-fought

reñir [6] **1** *vt (regañar)* to scold, to tell off
2 *vi (discutir)* to quarrel, to argue; *(pelear)* to fight; **r. con algn** to fall out with sb

reo *nmf (acusado)* defendant, accused; *(culpable)* culprit

reojo: de reojo *loc adv* **mirar algo de r.** to look at sth out of the corner of one's eye

reparación *nf* repair; *(compensación)* reparation, amends

reparar 1 *vt* to repair; *(ofensa, injuria)* to make amends for; *(daño)* to make good
2 *vi* **r. en** *(darse cuenta de)* to notice; *(reflexionar sobre)* to think about

reparo *nm* **no tener reparos en** not to hesitate to; **me da r.** I feel embarrassed

repartidor, -a *nm,f* distributor

repartir *vt* (**a**) *(dividir)* to distribute, to share out (**b**) *(regalo, premio)* to give out, to hand out; *(correo)* to deliver; *Naipes* to deal

reparto *nm* (**a**) *(división)* distribution, sharing out (**b**) *(distribución)* handing out; *(de mercancías)* delivery (**c**) *Cin & Teatro* cast

repasador *nm RP (trapo)* tea towel

repasar *vt* (**a**) *(revisar)* to revise, to go over; *(estudiar)* to revise (**b**) *(ropa)* to mend

repaso *nm* revision

repatear *vt Fam* to annoy

repatriar [29] *vt* to repatriate

repecho *nm* steep slope

repelente *adj* repulsive, repellent; *Fam* **niño r.** little know-all

repeler *vt (rechazar)* to repel, to repulse; *(repugnar)* to disgust

repente 1 *nm (arrebato)* fit
2 de repente *loc adv* suddenly

repentino, -a *adj* sudden

repercusión *nf* repercussion

repercutir *vi* **r. en** to have repercussions on, to affect

repertorio *nm* repertoire, repertory

repesca *nf Fam (examen)* resit

repetición *nf* repetition; **r. de la jugada** action replay

repetido, -a *adj* **repetidas veces** repeatedly

repetidor, -a 1 *adj* repeating
2 *nm,f Fam Educ* = student who is repeating a year

repetir [6] **1** *vt* to repeat; *(plato)* to have a second helping of
2 *vi Educ* to repeat a year
3 repetirse *vpr* (**a**) *(persona)* to repeat oneself (**b**) *(hecho)* to recur (**c**) **el pepino se repite** cucumber repeats (on me/you/him/etc)

repicar [44] *vt & vi* to ring

repipi *adj Fam* **niño r.** precocious brat

repique *nm Fam* ringing

repiquetear *vt & vi (campanas)* to ring; *(tambor)* to beat

repisa *nf* shelf, ledge

replantear 1 *vt* (**a**) *(situación, problema)* to restate (**b**) *(cuestión) (de nuevo)* to raise again
2 replantearse *vpr* to reconsider

replegarse [1] *vpr* to fall back, to retreat

repleto, -a *adj* full (up), jam-packed; **r. de** packed with, crammed with

réplica *nf* (**a**) *(respuesta)* reply (**b**) *(copia)* replica

replicar [44] **1** *vt* (**a**) *(responder)* to answer back (**b**) *(objetar)* to answer back, to retort
2 *vi (objetar)* to answer back

repliegue *nm Mil* withdrawal, retreat

repoblación *nf* repopulation; **r. forestal** reafforestation

repoblar [2] *vt* to repopulate; *(bosque)* to reafforest

repollo *nm* cabbage

reponer [19] *(pp* repuesto) **1** *vt* (a) *(existencias)* to replace (b) *Cine & Teatro* to re-run; *TV (programa)* to repeat
2 reponerse *upr* to recover (**de** from)

reportaje *nm Prensa & Rad* report; *(noticias)* article, news item

reportar 1 *vt* (a) *(beneficios etc)* to bring (b) *Andes, CAm, Méx, Ven (informar)* to report (c) *CAm, Méx (denunciar)* to report (to the police)
2 reportarse *upr CAm, Méx, Ven (presentarse)* to report (**a** to)

reporte *nm Andes, CAm, Méx, Ven (informe)* report; *(noticia)* news item *o* report; **recibí reportes de mi hermano** I was sent news by my brother; **el r. del tiempo** weather report *o* forecast

reportero, -a *nm,f* reporter

reposacabezas *nm inv Aut* headrest

reposar 1 *vt* to rest (**en** on)
2 *vi (descansar)* to rest, to take a rest; *(té)* to infuse; *(comida)* to stand

reposera *nf RP (silla) Br* sun-lounger, *US* beach recliner

reposición *nf TV* repeat; *Cin* rerun, reshowing

reposo *nm* rest; **en r.** at rest

repostar *vt (provisiones)* to stock up with; *(gasolina)* to fill up with

repostería *nf* confectionery; *(tienda)* confectioner's (shop)

repostero, -a *nm,f* confectioner

reprender *vt* to reprimand, to scold

represalia *nf* reprisal

representación *nf* (a) *(gen) & Com* representation; **en r. de** on behalf of (b) *Teatro* performance

representante *nmf* representative

representar *vt* (a) *(simbolizar, sustituir)* to represent (b) *(significar)* to mean, to represent (c) *Teatro (obra)* to perform

representativo, -a *adj* representative

represión *nf* repression

represivo, -a *adj* repressive

reprimenda *nf* reprimand

reprimir *vt* to repress

reprobar [2] *vt* (a) *(cosa)* to condemn; *(persona)* to reproach, reprove (b) *Am (estudiante, examen)* to fail

réprobo, -a *adj & nm,f* reprobate

reprochar *vt* to reproach; **r. algo a algn** to reproach sb for sth

reproche *nm* reproach

reproducción *nf* reproduction

reproducir [10] **1** *vt* to reproduce
2 reproducirse *upr* (a) *(procrear)* to reproduce, to breed (b) *(repetirse)* to recur, to happen again

reproductor, -a *adj* reproductive

reptar *vi* to slither

reptil *nm* reptile

república *nf* republic; **la R. Checa** the Czech Republic; **la R. Dominicana** the Dominican Republic

republicano, -a *adj & nm,f* republican

repudiar [43] *vt* to repudiate

repuesto 1 *nm (recambio)* spare part, spare; *Aut* **rueda de r.** spare wheel
2 *pp de* **reponer**

repugnancia *nf* loathing, disgust

repugnante *adj* disgusting, revolting

repugnar *vt* to disgust, to revolt

repujar *vt* to emboss

repulsa *nf* rebuff

repulsión *nf* repulsion, repugnance

repulsivo, -a *adj* repulsive, revolting

repuntar *vi Am (mejorar)* to improve

repunte *nm (aumento)* rise, increase; **un r. en las ventas** an improvement *o* increase in sales

repuse *pt indef de* **reponer**

reputación *nf* reputation

reputado, -a *adj* highly reputed

requemar *vt* to scorch

requerimiento *nm* (a) *(súplica)* request (b) *Der (aviso)* summons *sing*

> 🔎 Observa que la palabra inglesa **requirement** es un falso amigo y no es la traducción de la palabra española **requerimiento**. En inglés, **requirement** significa "requisito".

requerir [5] *vt* (a) *(necesitar)* to require (b) *(solicitar)* to request (c) *Der (avisar)* to summon

requesón *nm* cottage cheese

requete- *pref Fam* really, very, incredibly; **requetebueno** brilliant

réquiem *(pl* réquiems) *nm* requiem

requisa *nf* (a) *(inspección)* inspection (b) *Mil* requisition

requisar *vt* to requisition

requisito *nm* requirement, requisite

res *nf* animal

resabiado, -a *adj Pey* pedantic

resabio *nm* (a) *(mal sabor)* unpleasant *o* bad aftertaste (b) *(vicio)* bad habit

resaca *nf* (a) *(de alcohol)* hangover (b) *Náut* undertow, undercurrent

resaltar *vi* to stand out

resarcir [52] *vt* to compensate

resbalada *nf Am Fam* slip; **dar** *o* **pegar una r.** to slip

resbaladizo, -a *adj* slippery

resbalar 1 *vi* (a) *(caer)* to slip (**con** *o* **en** on) (b) *(estar resbaladizo)* to be slippery
2 resbalarse *upr* to slip (over)

resbalón *nm* slip

rescatar *vt (persona)* to rescue; *(objeto)* to recover

rescate *nm* (a) *(salvamento)* rescue; *(recuperación)* recovery (b) *(suma)* ransom

rescindir *vt* to rescind, to cancel

rescisión *nf* cancellation

rescoldo *nm* embers

resecarse [44] *upr* to dry up, to become parched

reseco, -a *adj* very dry, parched

resentido, -a *adj* resentful

resentimiento *nm* resentment

resentirse [5] *upr* (a) *(sufrir)* to suffer from, to feel the effects of (b) *(ofenderse)* to feel offended; **r. por algo** to take offence at sth, to feel bitter about sth

reseña *nf* review; *Prensa* write-up

reserva 1 *nf* (a) *(de entradas etc)* reservation, booking (b) *(provisión)* reserve, stock; **un vino de r.** a vintage wine (c) *Mil* reserve, reserves (d) *(duda)* reservation
2 *nmf Dep* reserve, substitute

reservación *nf Méx* reservation

reservado, -a 1 *adj (persona)* reserved, quiet
2 *nm* private room

reservar 1 *vt* (a) *(billetes etc)* to reserve, to book (b) *(dinero, tiempo etc)* to keep, to save
2 reservarse *upr* (a) *(uno mismo)* to save oneself (**para** for) (b) *(sentimientos)* to keep to oneself (c) **reservarse el derecho de** to reserve the right to

resfriado, -a 1 *nm (catarro)* cold; **coger un r.** to catch (a) cold
2 *adj* **estar r.** to have a cold

resfriarse *upr* to catch (a) cold

resfrío *nm Andes, RP* cold

resguardar *vt (proteger)* to protect, to shelter (**de** from)

resguardo *nm* (a) *(recibo)* receipt (b) *(protección)* protection, shelter

residencia *nf* residence; **r. de ancianos** old people's home

residencial *adj* residential

residente *adj & nmf* resident

residir *vi* to reside, to live (**en** in); *Fig* to lie (**en** in)

residuo *nm* (a) *Quím* residue (b) **residuos** waste

resignación *nf* resignation

resignado, -a *adj* resigned

resignarse *upr* to resign oneself (**a** to)

resina *nf* resin

resistencia *nf* (a) *(oposición)* resistance (b) *(aguante)* stamina (c) *Elec* resistance

resistente *adj (fuerte)* tough, strong; **r. al calor** heat-resistant

resistir 1 *vt (peso, dolor, ataque)* to withstand; *(tentación)* to resist; *(situación, persona)* to put up with
2 *vi* (a) *(ejército, ciudad)* to resist (b) *(persona)* to keep going
3 resistirse *upr* **resistirse (a algo)** to resist (sth); **resistirse a hacer algo** to refuse to do sth

resollar [2] *vi* to breathe heavily; *(con silbido)* to wheeze

resolución *nf* (a) *(solución)* solution (b) *(decisión)* resolution

resolver [4] *(pp* **resuelto)** **1** *vt (problema)* to solve; *(asunto)* to settle
2 *vi (decidir)* to resolve, to decide
3 resolverse *upr* (a) *(solucionarse)* to be solved (b) *(decidirse)* to resolve, to make up one's mind (**a** to)

resonancia *nf* (a) *(sonora)* resonance (b) *(repercusión)* repercussions

resonar [2] *vi* to resound; *(tener eco)* to echo

resoplar *vi (respirar)* to breathe heavily; *(de cansancio)* to puff and pant; *(de enfado)* to huff and puff

resoplido *nm (silbido)* wheezing; *(de cansancio)* panting; *(de enfado)* snort

resorte *nm* spring

> Observa que la palabra inglesa **resort** es un falso amigo y no es la traducción de la palabra española **resorte**. En inglés, **resort** significa "recurso" o "lugar de vacaciones; ".

respaldar *vt* to support, to back (up)

respaldo *nm (de asiento)* back; *Fig (apoyo)* support, backing

respetar *vt* to concern, to regard; **por lo que a mí respecta** as far as I'm concerned

respectivo, -a *adj* respective; **en lo r.** a with regard to, regarding

respecto *nm* **al r., a este r.** in this respect; **con r. a, r. a, r. de** with regard to; **r. a mí** as for me, as far as I am concerned

respetable 1 *adj* respectable
2 *nm Fam* **el r.** the audience

respetar *vt* to respect; **hacerse r. de todos** to command everyone's respect

respeto *nm* respect; **por r.** out of consideration

respetuoso, -a *adj* respectful

respingo *nm* start, jump

respingón, -ona *adj (nariz)* snub, upturned

respiración *nf (acción)* breathing, respiration; *(aliento)* breath; **r. artificial** artificial resuscitation

respirar *vi* to breathe; **¡por fin respiro!** well, that's a relief!

respiratorio, -a *adj* respiratory

respiro *nm (descanso)* breather, break; *(alivio)* relief, respite

resplandecer [33] *vi* to shine

resplandeciente *adj (brillante)* shining; *(esplendoroso)* resplendent, radiant

resplandor *nm (brillo)* brightness; *(muy intenso)* brilliance; *(de fuego)* glow, blaze

responder 1 *vt* to answer
  2 *vi* **(a)** *(una carta)* to reply **(b)** *(reaccionar)* to respond **(c)** *(protestar)* to answer back **(d)** **r. de algn** to be responsible for sb; **r. por algn** to vouch for sb

respondón, -ona *adj Fam* argumentative, cheeky

responsabilidad *nf* responsibility

responsabilizar [40] **1** *vt* to make o hold responsible **(de** for)
  2 responsabilizarse *upr* to assume o claim responsibility **(de** for)

responsable 1 *adj* responsible
  2 *nmf* **el/la r.** *(encargado)* the person in charge; *(de robo etc)* the perpetrator

respuesta *nf* answer, reply; *(reacción)* response

resquebrajarse *upr* to crack

resquemor *nm* resentment, ill feeling

resquicio *nm* crack, chink

resta *nf* subtraction

restablecer [33] **1** *vt* to re-establish; *(el orden)* to restore
  2 restablecerse *upr Med* to recover

restablecimiento *nm* re-establishment; *(del orden etc)* restoration; *Med* recovery

restante *adj* remaining; **lo r.** the rest, the remainder

restar 1 *vt* **(a)** *Mat* to subtract, to take away **(b)** **r. importancia a algo** to play sth down
  2 *vi (quedar)* to be left, to remain

restauración *nf* restoration

restaurador, -a 1 *nm,f* restorer
  2 *adj* restoring

restaurante *nm* restaurant

restaurar *vt* to restore

restitución *nf* restitution

restituir [37] *vt (restablecer)* to restore; *(devolver)* to return, to give back

resto *nm* **(a)** **el r.** the rest; *Mat* the remainder **(b)** **restos** remains; *(de comida)* leftovers

restregar [1] *vt* to rub hard, to scrub

restricción *nf* restriction

restrictivo, -a *adj* restrictive

restringir [57] *vt* to restrict, to limit

resucitar *vt & vi* to resuscitate

resuello *nm* breath, gasp

resuelto, -a 1 *adj (decidido)* resolute, determined
  2 *pp de* **resolver**

resultado *nm* result; *(consecuencia)* outcome; **dar buen r.** to work, to give results

resultante *adj* resulting

resultar *vi* **(a)** *(ser)* to turn o work out; **así resulta más barato** this way; **me resultó fácil** it turned out to be easy for me **(b)** *(ocurrir)* **resulta que ...** the thing is ...; **y ahora resulta que no puede venir** and now it turns out that she can't come **(c)** *(tener éxito)* to be successful; **la fiesta no resultó** the party wasn't a success

resultas *nfpl* **a r. de** as a result of

resumen *nm* summary; **en r.** in short, to sum up

resumir 1 *vt* to sum up; *(recapitular)* to summarize
  2 resumirse *upr* **(a)** *(abreviarse)* **se resume en pocas palabras** it can be summed up in a few words **(b)** **resumirse en** *(saldarse con)* to result in

> 🖉 Observa que la palabra inglesa **resume** es un falso amigo y no es la traducción de la palabra española **resumir**. En inglés **resume** significa "reanudar".

resurgir [57] *vi* to reappear

resurrección *nf* resurrection

retablo *nm* altarpiece

retaguardia *nf* rearguard

retahíla *nf* series *sing*, string

retal *nm* remnant

retar *vt* to challenge

retardo *nm* delay

retazo *nm (pedazo)* scrap; *(fragmento)* fragment, piece

retén *nm* **(a)** **r. (de bomberos)** squad (of firefighters) **(b)** *Am (de menores)* reformatory, reform school

retención *nf* retention; *Fin* deduction; **r. de tráfico** (traffic) hold-up, traffic jam

retener [24] *vt* (**a**) *(conservar)* to retain (**b**) *Fin (descontar)* to deduct (**c**) *(detener)* to detain

reticencia *nf* reticence, reserve

reticente *adj* reticent, reserved

retina *nf* retina

retintín *nm* innuendo, sarcastic tone

retirada *nf* retreat, withdrawal

retirado, -a **1** *adj* (**a**) *(alejado)* remote (**b**) *(jubilado)* retired
2 *nm,f* retired person, *US* retiree

retirar **1** *vt* to take away, to remove; *(dinero)* to withdraw; *(ofensa)* to take back
2 retirarse *upr* (**a**) *(apartarse)* to withdraw, to draw back; *(irse)* to retire (**b**) *(jubilarse)* to retire (**c**) *Mil* to retreat, to withdraw

retiro *nm* (**a**) *(jubilación)* retirement; *(pensión)* pension (**b**) *(lugar tranquilo)* retreat (**c**) *Rel* retreat

reto *nm* challenge

retocar [44] *vt* to touch up

retoño *nm* *(rebrote)* shoot, sprout; *(niño)* kid

retoque *nm* retouching, touching up; **los últimos retoques** the finishing touches

retorcer [41] **1** *vt (cuerda, hilo)* to twist; *(ropa)* to wring (out)
2 retorcerse *upr* to twist, to become twisted; **retorcerse de dolor** to writhe in pain

retorcido, -a *adj (malintencionado)* twisted

retórica *nf* rhetoric

retórico, -a *adj* rhetorical

retornable *adj* returnable; **envase no r.** non-deposit bottle

retornar **1** *vt* to return, to give back
2 *vi* to return, to come back, to go back

retorno *nm* return

retortijón *nm* stomach cramp

retozar [40] *vi* to frolic, to romp

retracción *nf* retraction

retractar **1** *vt* to retract
2 retractarse *upr* **r. (de)** to retract, to take back

retraerse *upr (retirarse)* to withdraw; *(por miedo)* to shy away

retraído, -a *adj* shy, reserved

retraimiento *nm* shyness

retransmisión *nf* broadcast, transmission

retransmitir *vt* to broadcast

retrasado, -a **1** *adj* (**a**) *(tren)* late; *(reloj)* slow; **voy r.** I'm behind schedule (**b**) *(país)* backward, underdeveloped (**c**) *(mental)* retarded, backward

2 *nm,f* **r. (mental)** mentally retarded person

retrasar **1** *vt* (**a**) *(retardar)* to slow down (**b**) *(atrasar)* to delay, to postpone (**c**) *(reloj)* to put back
2 retrasarse *upr* to be late, to be delayed; *(reloj)* to be slow

retraso *nm* delay; **con r.** late; **una hora de r.** an hour behind schedule; **r. mental** mental deficiency

retratar **1** *vt (pintar)* to paint a portrait of; *Fot* to take a photograph of; *Fig (describir)* to describe, to depict
2 retratarse *upr* *Fot* to have one's photograph taken

retrato *nm (pintura)* portrait; *Fot* photograph; **r. robot** Identikit® picture, *Br* Photofit® picture; **ser el vivo r. de** to be the spitting image of

retreta *nf* retreat

retrete *nm* toilet, *Br* bathroom

retribución *nf (pago)* payment; *(recompensa)* reward

> *✎* Observa que la palabra inglesa **retribution** es un falso amigo y no es la traducción de la palabra española **retribución**. En inglés, **retribution** significa "represalias".

retribuir *vt (pagar)* to pay; *(recompensar)* to reward

retro *adj inv (estilo, moda)* retro

retroactivo, -a *adj* retroactive; **con efecto r.** retrospectively

retroceder *vi* to move back, to back away

retroceso *nm* (**a**) *(movimiento)* backward movement (**b**) *(en enfermedad)* deterioration, worsening

retrógrado, -a *adj & nm,f (en política)* reactionary

retropropulsión *nf Av* jet propulsion

retrospectivo, -a *adj & nf* retrospective

retrovisor *nm Aut* rear-view mirror

retumbar *vi (resonar)* to resound; *(tronar)* to thunder, to boom

retuve *pt indef de* retener

reúma *nm* rheumatism

reumático, -a *adj & nm,f* rheumatic

reumatismo *nm* rheumatism

reunión *nf* meeting; *(reencuentro)* reunion

reunir **1** *vt* to gather together; *(dinero)* to raise; *(cualidades)* to have, to possess; *(requisitos)* to fulfil
2 reunirse *upr* to meet, to gather; **reunirse con algn** to meet sb

revalidar *vt* to ratify, to confirm; *Dep (título)* to retain

revalorizar [40] **1** vt (aumentar el valor de) to increase the value of; (moneda) to revalue

2 revalorizarse vpr (aumentar de valor) to appreciate; (moneda) to be revalued

revancha nf revenge; Dep return match

revanchista adj vengeful, vindictive

revelación nf revelation

revelado nm Fot developing

revelar vt (a) (descubrir) to reveal, to disclose (b) Fot (película) to develop

revender vt (entradas) to tout

reventa nf (de entradas) touting

reventado, -a adj Fam (cansado) knackered

reventar [1] **1** vt (a) (explotar) to burst (b) (romper) to break, to smash (c) Fam (fastidiar) to annoy, to bother

2 vi (explotar) to burst; **r. de** (estar lleno) to be bursting with; **r. de ganas de hacer algo** to be dying to do sth

3 reventarse vpr (explotar) to burst, to explode

reventón nm (de neumático) blowout, Br puncture, US flat

reverberación nf reverberation

reverberar vi to reverberate

reverencia nf (a) (respeto) reverence (b) (inclinación) (de hombre) bow; (de mujer) curtsy

reverenciar [43] vt to revere, to venerate

reverendo, -a adj & nm,f reverend

reversa nf Méx reverse

reversible adj reversible

reverso nm reverse, back

revertido, -a adj ver **cobro**

revertir [5] vi to result (**en** in)

revés (pl **reveses**) nm (a) (reverso) reverse; **al o del r.** (al contrario) the other way round; (la parte interior en el exterior) inside out; (boca abajo) upside down; (la parte de detrás delante) back to front; **al r. de lo que dicen** contrary to what they say (b) (bofetada) slap; Ten backhand (stroke) (c) Fig (contrariedad) setback, reverse; **los reveses de la vida** life's misfortunes; **reveses de fortuna** setbacks, blows of fate

revestimiento nm Téc covering, coating

revestir [6] vt (recubrir) to cover (**de** with); (con pintura) to coat (**de** with); **la herida no reviste importancia** the wound is not serious

revisar vt to check; (coche) to service

revisión nf checking; (de coche) service, overhaul; **r. médica** checkup

revisor, -a nm,f ticket inspector

revista nf (a) (publicación) magazine; (académica) journal (b) **pasar r. a** to inspect, to review (c) Teatro revue

revistero nm (mueble) magazine rack

revitalizar [40] vt to revitalize

revivir vt & vi to revive

revocar [44] vt to revoke, to repeal

revolcar [2] **1** vt Fam (oponente) to floor, to crush

2 revolcarse vpr to roll about

revolcón nm fall, tumble; Fam (sexual) romp

revolotear vi to fly about, to flutter about

revoltijo, revoltillo nm jumble

revoltoso, -a adj (travieso) mischievous, naughty

revolución nf revolution

revolucionar vt to revolutionize

revolucionario, -a adj & nm,f revolutionary

revolver [4] (pp **revuelto**) **1** vt (mezclar) to stir, to mix; (desordenar) to mess up; **me revuelve el estómago** it turns my stomach

2 revolverse vpr (a) (agitarse) to roll (b) Fig **revolverse contra algn** to turn against sb (c) (el tiempo) to turn stormy; (el mar) to become rough

> 🖉 Observa que el verbo inglés **to revolve** es un falso amigo y no es la traducción del verbo español **revolver**. En inglés, **to revolve** significa "girar".

revólver nm revolver

revuelo nm stir, commotion

revuelta nf (a) (insurrección) revolt (b) (curva) bend, turn

revuelto, -a **1** adj (a) (desordenado) jumbled, in a mess (b) (tiempo) stormy, unsettled; (mar) rough (c) (agitado) excited

2 pp de **revolver**

revulsivo nm (a) (fármaco) counterirritant, Espec revulsive (b) (estímulo) kick-start, stimulus

rey (pl **reyes**) nm king; Rel (**el día de**) **Reyes** (the) Epiphany, 6 January

reyerta nf quarrel, dispute

rezagado, -a nm,f straggler, latecomer

rezagarse [42] vpr to lag o fall behind

rezar [40] **1** vi (a) (orar) to pray (b) (decir) to say, to read

2 vt (oración) to say

rezo nm prayer

rezumar vt to ooze; Fig to exude

ría nf estuary

riachuelo nm brook, stream

riada nf flood

ribera *nf (de río)* bank; *(zona)* riverside, waterfront

ribete *nm* edging, border

ribetear *vt* to edge, to border

ricamente *adv Fam* tan r. quite happily

rico, -a 1 *adj* (a) ser r. *(adinerado)* to be rich o wealthy; *(abundante)* to be rich; *(bonito)* to be lovely o adorable; *(fértil)* to be rich o fertile (b) estar r. *(delicioso)* to be delicious
2 *nm,f* rich person

rictus *nm inv (de dolor)* wince; un r. de amargura a bitter expression

ridiculez *nf* ridiculous thing; *(cualidad)* ridiculousness

ridiculizar [40] *vt* to ridicule

ridículo, -a 1 *adj* ridiculous
2 *nm* ridicule; hacer el r., quedar en r. to make a fool of oneself; poner a algn en r. to make a fool of sb

riego *nm* watering, irrigation; r. sanguíneo blood circulation

riel *nm* rail

rienda *nf* rein; *Fig* dar r. suelta a to give free rein to; *Fig* llevar las riendas to hold the reins, to be in control

riesgo *nm* risk; correr el r. de to run the risk of; seguro a todo r. fully comprehensive insurance

riesgoso, -a *adj Am* risky

rifa *nf* raffle

rifar *vt* to raffle (off)

rifle *nm* rifle

rigidez *nf* rigidity, stiffness; *Fig (severidad)* strictness, inflexibility

rígido, -a *adj* rigid, stiff; *Fig (severo)* strict, inflexible

rigor *nm* rigour; *(severidad)* severity; con r. rigorously; de r. indispensable

rigurosamente *adv (severamente)* strictly; r. cierto absolutely true

riguroso, -a *adj* (a) *(severo)* strict (b) *(exacto)* rigorous, disciplined (c) *(inclemente)* harsh

rijo *indic pres de* regir

rima *nf* rhyme

rimar *vt & vi* to rhyme (con with)

rimbombante *adj (lenguaje)* pompous, pretentious

rímel *nm* mascara

rincón *nm* corner; *Fam (lugar remoto)* nook

ring [rrin] *(pl rings) nm* (boxing) ring

rinoceronte *nm* rhinoceros

riña *nf (pelea)* fight; *(discusión)* row, quarrel

riñón *nm* kidney; *Fam* costar un r. to cost an arm and a leg; *Med* r. artificial kidney machine

riñonera *nf (pequeño bolso) Br* bum bag, *US* fanny pack

río *nm* river; r. abajo downstream; r. arriba upstream

rioja *nm* Rioja (wine)

rioplatense *adj* of/from the River Plate region

RIP *(abr requiescat in pace)* RIP

ripio *nm Lit* = word or phrase included to complete a rhyme; *Fam* no perder r. not to miss a trick

riqueza *nf* (a) *(fortuna)* wealth (b) *(cualidad)* wealthiness

risa *nf* laugh; *(carcajadas)* laughter; es (cosa) de r. it's laughable; me da r. it makes me laugh; tomarse algo a r. to laugh sth off; *Fig* morirse o mondarse de r. to die o fall about laughing; *Fam* mi hermano es una r. my brother is a laugh; *Fam Fig* tener algo muerto de r. to leave sth lying around

risco *nm* crag, cliff

risible *adj* laughable

risilla, risita *nf* giggle, titter; *(risa falsa)* false laugh

risotada *nf* guffaw

ristra *nf* string

ristre *nm* en r. at the ready

risueño, -a *adj* smiling

rítmico, -a *adj* rhythmic

ritmo *nm* (a) *(compás, repetición)* rhythm, beat; *(cardíaco)* beat (b) *(velocidad)* rate; llevar un buen r. de trabajo to work at a good pace

rito *nm* (a) *Rel* rite (b) *(costumbre)* ritual

ritual *adj & nm* ritual

rival *adj & nmf* rival

rivalidad *nf* rivalry

rivalizar [40] *vi* to rival (en in)

rizado, -a *adj* (a) *(pelo)* curly (b) *(mar)* choppy

rizar [40] **1** *vt (pelo)* to curl; *(tela, papel)* to crease; *Fig* r. el rizo to make things even more complicated
2 rizarse *vpr (pelo)* to curl, to go curly

rizo *nm* (a) *(de pelo)* curl (b) *(en el agua)* ripple

RNE *nf (abr Radio Nacional de España)* = Spanish state radio station

robar *vt* (a) *(objeto)* to steal; *(banco, persona)* to rob; *(casa)* to burgle; *Fig* en aquel supermercado te roban they really rip you off in that supermarket (b) *Naipes* to draw

roble *nm* oak (tree)

robo *nm* robbery, theft; *(en casa)* burglary; *Fam (timo)* rip-off; **r. de identidad** identity theft

robot *(pl robots) nm* robot; **r. de cocina** food processor

robustecer [33] *vt* to strengthen

robusto, -a *adj* robust, sturdy

roca *nf* rock

rocambolesco, -a *adj* incredible, far-fetched

roce *nm* **(a)** *(fricción)* rubbing; *(en la piel)* chafing **(b)** *(marca) (en la pared etc)* scuff mark; *(en la piel)* chafing mark, graze **(c)** *(contacto ligero)* brush, light touch **(d)** *Fam (trato entre personas)* contact **(e)** *Fam (discusión)* brush

rociar [29] *vt (salpicar)* to spray, to sprinkle

rocín *nm* nag, hack

rocío *nm* dew

rock *nm inv* rock; **r. duro** hard rock; **r. and roll** rock and roll

Rocosas *nfpl* **las R.** the Rockies

rocoso, -a *adj* rocky, stony

rodaballo *nm (pez)* turbot

rodado, -a *adj* **(a)** *canto* **r.** boulder **(b)** *tráfico* **r.** road traffic, vehicular traffic

rodaja *nf* slice; **en rodajas** sliced

rodaje *nm* **(a)** *(filmación)* filming, shooting **(b)** *Aut* running in

rodante *adj* rolling

rodar [2] **1** *vt (película etc)* to film, to shoot
2 *vi* to roll, to turn

rodear 1 *vt* to surround, to encircle
2 rodearse *upr* to surround oneself **(de** with)

rodeo *nm* **(a)** *(desvío)* detour **(b)** *(al hablar)* evasiveness; **andarse con rodeos** to beat about the bush; **no andarse con rodeos** to get straight to the point **(c)** *(espectáculo)* rodeo

rodilla *nf* knee; **de rodillas** *(arrodillado)* kneeling; **hincarse** *o* **ponerse de rodillas** to kneel down, to go down on one's knees

rodillera *nf (de pantalón)* knee patch; *Dep* knee pad

rodillo *nm* roller; **r. de cocina** rolling pin

rododendro *nm* rhododendron

roedor *nm* rodent

roer [38] *vt (hueso)* to gnaw; *(galleta)* to nibble at; *Fig (conciencia)* to gnaw at, to nag at; *Fig* **un hueso duro de r.** a hard nut to crack

rogar [2] *vt (pedir)* to request, to ask; *(implorar)* to beg; **hacerse de r.** to play hard to get; **se ruega silencio** *(en letrero)* silence please; **rogamos disculpen la molestia** please forgive the inconvenience

roído, -a *adj* gnawed, eaten away

rojizo, -a *adj* reddish

rojo, -a 1 *adj* **(a)** *(color)* red; *Fin* **estar en números rojos** to be in the red **(b)** *Pol (comunista)* red
2 *nm (color)* red; **al r. vivo** *(caliente)* red-hot; *Fig (tenso)* very tense
3 *nm,f Pol (comunista)* red

rol *nm* role

rollizo, -a *adj* chubby, plump

rollo *nm* **(a)** *(de papel etc)* roll **(b)** *Fam (pesadez)* drag, bore; **es el mismo r. de siempre** it's the same old story; **un r. de libro** a boring book **(c)** *Esp Fam (amorío)* affair

Roma *n* Rome

romance *nm* **(a)** *(aventura amorosa)* romance **(b)** *(idioma)* Romance **(c)** *Lit* narrative poem, ballad

románico, -a *adj & nm* Romanesque

romano, -a *adj & nm,f* Roman

romanticismo *nm* romanticism

romántico, -a *adj & nm,f* romantic

rombo *nm* rhombus

romería *nf Rel* pilgrimage

romero *nm Bot* rosemary

romo, -a *adj* **(a)** *(sin filo)* blunt **(b)** *(nariz)* snub

rompecabezas *nm inv (juego)* (jigsaw) puzzle; *Fig (problema)* riddle, puzzle

rompeolas *nm inv* breakwater, jetty

romper *(pp* **roto) 1** *vt* **(a)** *(partir, estropear) (papel, tela)* to tear; *(vajilla, cristal)* to smash, to shatter **(b)** *(relaciones)* to break off
2 *vi* **(a)** *(olas, día)* to break **(b)** *(acabar)* to break **(con** with); **rompió con su novio** she broke it off with her boyfriend **(c) r. a llorar** to burst out crying; **r. en llanto** to burst into tears
3 romperse *upr* to break; *(papel, tela)* to tear; **se rompió por la mitad** it broke o split in half; *Fig* **romperse la cabeza** to rack one's brains

rompevientos *nm inv RP (jersey) Br* polo neck, *US* turtleneck; *(anorak)* windcheater

rompimiento *nm Am* break

ron *nm* rum

roncar [44] *vi* to snore

roncha *nf (en la piel)* swelling, lump

ronco, -a *adj* hoarse; **quedarse r.** to lose one's voice

ronda *nf* **(a)** *(de vigilancia)* patrol **(b)** *(en el juego, de conversaciones, bebidas)* round **(c)** *(carretera) Br* ring road, *US* beltway; *(avenida)* avenue

rondar 1 *vt* (**a**) *(vigilar)* to patrol, to do the rounds of (**b**) *Pey (merodear)* to prowl around, to hang about (**c**) *(estar cerca de)* to be about *o* approximately; **ronda los cuarenta** he is about forty

2 *vi* (**a**) *(vigilar)* to patrol (**b**) *(merodear)* to prowl around, to roam around

rondín *nm Andes* (**a**) *(vigilante)* watchman, guard (**b**) *(armónica)* mouth organ

ronquera *nf* hoarseness

ronquido *nm* snore

ronronear *vi* to purr

ronroneo *nm* purring

roña *nf* (**a**) *(mugre)* filth, dirt (**b**) *(sarna)* mange

roñica *Fam* **1** *adj* mean, stingy
2 *nmf* scrooge, miser

roñoso, -a *adj* (**a**) *(mugriento)* filthy, dirty (**b**) *(sarnoso)* mangy (**c**) *Fam (tacaño)* mean, stingy

ropa *nf* clothes, clothing; *Fig* **a quema r.** point-blank; **r. blanca** (household) linen; **r. interior** underwear

---

ℓ Observa que la palabra inglesa **rope** es un falso amigo y no es la traducción de la palabra española **ropa**. En inglés, **rope** significa "cuerda, soga".

---

ropaje *nm* clothes

ropero *nm* **(armario)** **r.** wardrobe

roque *adj Fam* **quedarse r.** to fall fast asleep

roquefort [rroke'for] *nm* Roquefort (cheese)

rosa 1 *adj inv (color)* pink; **novela r.** romantic novel
2 *nf (Bot)* rose; *(en la piel)* birthmark; **r. de los vientos** compass (rose)
3 *nm (color)* pink

rosáceo, -a *adj* rose-coloured, rosy

rosado, -a 1 *adj (color)* pink, rosy; *(vino)* rosé
2 *nm (vino)* rosé

rosal *nm* rosebush

rosaleda *nf* rose garden

rosario *nm Rel* rosary; *(sarta)* string, series *sing*

rosbif *nm* roast beef

rosca *nf* (**a**) *(de tornillo)* thread; **tapón de r.** screw top; *Fig* **pasarse de r.** to go too far (**b**) *(espiral)* spiral, coil

rosco *nm* = ring-shaped bread roll; *Esp Fam* **nunca se come un r.** he never gets off with anyone

roscón *nm* = ring-shaped bread roll; **r. de Reyes** = ring-shaped pastry eaten on 6th January

rosetón *nm* rose window

rosquilla *nf* ring-shaped pastry; *Fam Fig* **venderse como rosquillas** to sell like hot cakes

rosticería *nf Chile, Méx* = shop selling roast chicken

rostro *nm* face; *Fam* **tener mucho r.** to have a lot of nerve; *Fam* **¡vaya r.!** what a cheek!

ℓ Observa que la palabra inglesa **rostrum** es un falso amigo y no es la traducción de la palabra española **rostro**. En inglés, **rostrum** significa "estrado".

---

rotación *nf* rotation

rotativo, -a 1 *adj* rotary, revolving
2 *nm* newspaper

roto, -a 1 *adj* broken; *(papel)* torn; *(ropa)* in tatters, tattered
2 *nm (agujero)* hole, tear
3 *nm,f Chile Fam* (**a**) *(tipo)* guy; *(mujer)* woman (**b**) *Pey (trabajador)* worker
4 *pp de* **romper**

rotonda *nf* (**a**) *(glorieta)* roundabout (**b**) *(plaza)* circus

rotoso, -a *Andes, RP adj* ragged, in tatters

rótula *nf* (**a**) *Anat* kneecap (**b**) *Téc* ball-and-socket joint

rotulador *nm* felt-tip pen

rotular *vt* to letter, to label

rótulo *nm (letrero)* sign, notice; *(titular)* title, heading

rotundo, -a *adj* categorical; **éxito r.** resounding success; **un no r.** a flat refusal

rotura *nf (ruptura)* breaking; *Med* fracture

roturar *vt* to plough

roulotte [rru'lot] *nf Br* caravan, *US* trailer

rozadura *nf* scratch, abrasion

rozamiento *nm* rubbing, friction

rozar [40] **1** *vt* to touch, to rub against, to brush against
2 *vi* to rub
3 **rozarse** *vpr* to rub, to brush (**con** against)

Rte. *(abr* **remite, remitente)** sender

ruana *nf Andes (cerrada)* poncho; *RP (abierta)* wrap-around poncho

rubeola *nf* German measles *sing*, rubella

rubí *(pl* **rubís** *o* **rubíes)** *nm* ruby

rubicundo, -a *adj* rosy, reddish

rubio, -a 1 *adj (pelo, persona)* fair, blond, *f* blonde; **r. de bote** peroxide blonde; **tabaco r.** Virginia tobacco
2 *nm,f* blond, *f* blonde

rublo *nm* rouble

rubor *nm* blush, flush

ruborizarse [40] *vpr* to blush, to go red

ruboroso, -a *adj* blushing, bashful

rúbrica *nf* (**a**) *(de firma)* = flourish added to a signature (**b**) *(título)* title, heading

rudeza *nf* roughness, coarseness

rudimentario, -a *adj* rudimentary

rudimento *nm* rudiment

rudo, -a *adj* rough, coarse

rueda *nf* (**a**) *(pieza)* wheel; *Aut* **r. de recambio** spare wheel; *Aut* **r. delantera/ trasera** front/rear wheel; **r. de prensa** press conference; *Fam* **ir sobre ruedas** to go very smoothly (**b**) *(rodaja)* round slice

ruedo *nm* (**a**) *Taurom* bullring, arena (**b**) *(de falda)* hem

ruego *nm* request

rufián *nm* villain, scoundrel

rugby *nm* rugby

rugido *nm* *(de animal)* roar; *(del viento)* howl; *(de tripas)* rumbling

rugir [57] *vi* to roar; *(viento)* to howl

rugoso, -a *adj* rough

ruibarbo *nm* rhubarb

ruido *nm* noise; *(sonido)* sound; *(jaleo)* din, row; *Fig* stir, commotion; **hacer r.** to make a noise

ruidoso, -a *adj* noisy, loud

ruin *adj* (**a**) *(vil)* vile, despicable (**b**) *(tacaño)* mean, stingy

ruina *nf* ruin; *(derrumbamiento)* collapse; *(de persona)* downfall

ruindad *nf* *(cualidad)* vileness, meanness; *(acto)* mean act, low trick

ruinoso, -a *adj* dilapidated, tumbledown

ruiseñor *nm* nightingale

ruleta *nf* roulette

ruletear *vi CAm, Méx Fam (en taxi)* to drive a taxi

ruletero *nm CAm, Méx Fam (de taxi)* taxi driver

rulo *nm* (**a**) *(para el pelo)* curler, roller (**b**) *Culin* rolling pin

rulot *(pl* rulots*) nf Br* caravan, *US* trailer

ruma *nf Andes, Ven* heap, pile

Rumanía *n* Romania

rumano, -a 1 *adj & nm,f* Romanian
2 *nm (idioma)* Romanian

rumba *nf* rhumba, rumba

rumbo *nm* direction, course; **(con) r. a** bound for, heading for

rumiante *nm* ruminant

rumiar [43] **1** *vt* (**a**) *(mascar)* to chew (**b**) *Fig (pensar)* to ruminate, to reflect on, to chew over
2 *vi* to ruminate, to chew the cud

rumor *nm* (**a**) *(chisme)* rumour (**b**) *(ruido sordo)* murmur

rumorearse *v impers* to be rumoured

runrún, runruneo *nm* buzz, noise

rupestre *adj* **pintura r.** cave painting

ruptura *nf* breaking; *(de relaciones)* breaking off

rural *adj* rural, country

Rusia *n* Russia

ruso, -a 1 *adj & nm,f* Russian
2 *nm (idioma)* Russian

rústico, -a *adj* rustic, rural

ruta *nf* route, road

rutilante *adj* sparkling

rutina *nf* routine; **por r.** as a matter of course

rutinario, -a *adj* routine

S, s ['ese] *nf (letra)* S, s

S *(abr* **Sur)** S

S. *(abr* **San, Santo)** St

s. *(abr* **siglo)** c

S.A. *(abr* **Sociedad Anónima)** *Br* ≃ PLC, *US* ≃ Inc

sábado *nm* Saturday

sabana *nf* savannah

sábana *nf* sheet; *Fam* **se me pegaron las sábanas** I overslept

sabandija *nf (insecto)* creepy-crawly; *(persona)* creep

sabañón *nm* chilblain

sabático, -a *adj* sabbatical

sabelotodo *nmf inv* know-all

saber¹ *nm* knowledge

saber² [21] **1** *vt* (**a**) *(conocer)* to know; **hacer s.** to inform; **para que lo sepas** for your information; **que yo sepa** as far as I know; **vete tú a s.** goodness knows; **¡y yo qué sé!** how should I know!; *Fig* **a s.** namely (**b**) *(tener habilidad)* to be able to; **¿sabes cocinar?** can you cook?; **¿sabes hablar inglés?** can you speak English? (**c**) *(enterarse)* to learn, to find out; **lo supe ayer** I found this out yesterday

2 *vi* (**a**) *(tener sabor a)* to taste (**a** of); **sabe a fresa** it tastes of strawberries; *Fig* **me sabe mal** I feel guilty o bad about that (**b**) *Am (soler)* **s. hacer algo** to be in the habit of doing sth

sabido, -a *adj* known; **como es s.** as everyone knows

sabiduría *nf* wisdom

sabiendas: a sabiendas *loc adv* **lo hizo a s.** he did it in the full knowledge of what he was doing; **a s. de que ...** knowing full well that ...

sabihondo, -a *nm,f Fam* know-all

sabio, -a 1 *adj (prudente)* wise
2 *nm,f* scholar

sabiondo, -a *nm,f Fam* = sabihondo

sable *nm* sabre

sabor *nm (gusto)* taste, flavour; **con s. a limón** lemon-flavoured; **sin s.** tasteless; **me deja mal s. de boca** it leaves a bad taste in my mouth

saborear *vt (degustar)* to taste; *Fig (apreciar)* to savour

sabotaje *nm* sabotage

saboteador, -a *nm,f* saboteur

sabotear *vt* to sabotage

sabré *indic fut de* saber²

sabroso, -a *adj* (**a**) *(gustoso)* tasty (**b**) *Carib, Col, Méx (grato)* pleasant, nice; *(entretenido)* entertaining (**c**) *Carib, Col, Méx (contagioso) (ritmo)* catchy; *(risa)* contagious

sabueso *nm* bloodhound

sacacorchos *nm inv* corkscrew

sacapuntas *nm inv* pencil sharpener

sacar [44] *vt* (**a**) *(extraer)* to take out; *(con más fuerza)* to pull out; **s. dinero del banco** to withdraw money from the bank; **s. la lengua** to stick one's tongue out; *Fig* **s. faltas a algo** to find fault with sth; *Fig* **s. adelante** to help to get on; **s. provecho de algo** to benefit from sth; **s. algo en claro** o **en limpio** to make sense of sth (**b**) *(obtener)* to get; *(dinero)* to get, to make; *(conclusiones)* to draw, to reach; *(entrada)* to get, to buy (**c**) *(producto, libro, disco)* to bring out; *(nueva moda)* to bring in (**d**) *(fotografía)* to take; *(fotocopia)* to make (**e**) *Ten* to serve; *Ftb* to kick off

sacarina *nf* saccharin

sacerdotal *adj* priestly

sacerdote *nm* priest; **sumo s.** high priest

saciar [43] *vt* to satiate; *(sed)* to quench; *(deseos, hambre)* to satisfy; *(ambiciones)* to fulfil

saciedad *nf* satiety; **repetir algo hasta la s.** to repeat sth ad nauseam

saco *nm* (**a**) *(bolsa)* sack; **s. de dormir** sleeping bag (**b**) *Mil* **entrar a s. en una ciudad** to pillage a town (**c**) *Am (abrigo)* jacket; *(de tela)* jacket; *(de punto)* cardigan

sacralizar [40] *vt* to consecrate

sacramento *nm* sacrament

sacrificar [44] **1** *vt* to sacrifice
2 sacrificarse *upr* to make a sacrifice o sacrifices

sacrificio *nm* sacrifice

sacrilegio *nm* sacrilege

sacrílego, -a *adj* sacrilegious

sacristán *nm* verger, sexton

sacristía *nf* vestry, sacristy

sacro, -a *adj* sacred

sacudida *nf* (a) *(movimiento)* shake; *(espasmo)* jolt, jerk; **s. eléctrica** electric shock (b) *(de terremoto)* tremor

sacudir *vt* (a) *(agitar)* to shake; *(alfombra, sábana)* to shake out; *(arena, polvo)* to shake off (b) *(golpear)* to beat (c) *(conmover)* to shock, to stun

sádico, -a 1 *adj* sadistic
2 *nm,f* sadist

sadismo *nm* sadism

sadomasoquista 1 *adj* sadomasochistic
2 *nmf* sadomasochist

saeta *nf* (a) *(dardo)* dart (b) *(canción)* = flamenco-style song sung on religious occasions

safari *nm* *(cacería)* safari; *(parque)* safari park

sagacidad *nf* *(del listo)* cleverness; *(del astuto)* astuteness, shrewdness

sagaz *adj* *(listo)* clever; *(astuto)* astute, shrewd

Sagitario *nm* Sagittarius

sagrado, -a *adj* sacred

sagrario *nm* tabernacle

Sáhara ['saara], **Sahara** [sa'ara] *n* Sahara

saharaui [saa'rawi] *adj & nmf* Saharan

sahariana [saa'rjana] *nf* safari jacket

sainete *nm Teatro* comic sketch, one-act farce

sajón, -ona *adj & nm,f* Saxon

sal¹ *nf* (a) *Culin & Quím* **s. fina** table salt; **s. gema** salt crystals; *Esp* **s. gorda** cooking salt (b) *Fig (gracia)* wit

sal² *imperat de* salir

sala *nf* room; *(en un hospital)* ward; *Der* courtroom; **s. de estar** lounge, living room; **s. de espera** waiting room; **s. de exposiciones** exhibition hall; **s. de fiestas** nightclub, discotheque; **s. de lectura** reading room

saladito *nm RP* savoury snack *o* appetizer

salado, -a *adj* (a) *(con sal)* salted; *(con exceso de sal)* salty; **agua salada** salt water (b) *Esp (gracioso, simpático)* amusing; *(encantador)* charming (c) *CAm, Carib, Méx (desgraciado)* unlucky

salamandra *nf* salamander

salamanquesa *nf* gecko

salame *nm CSur* salami

salar *vt* to salt, to add salt to

salarial *adj* salary, wage

salario *nm* salary, wages; **s. mínimo** minimum wage

salazones *nfpl* salted meat/fish

salchicha *nf* sausage

salchichón *nm* = salami-type sausage

salchichonería *nf Méx* delicatessen

saldar *vt* (a) *Fin (cuenta)* to settle; *(deuda)* to pay off (b) *Com (vender barato)* to sell off (c) *Fig (diferencias)* to settle, to resolve

saldo *nm* (a) **saldos** sales; **a precio de s.** at bargain prices (b) *Fin* balance (c) *(de una deuda)* liquidation, settlement (d) *(resto de mercancía)* remainder, leftover

saldré *indic fut de* salir

salero *nm* (a) *(recipiente)* saltcellar, *US* saltshaker (b) *Fig (gracia)* charm

salgo *indic pres de* salir

salida *nf* (a) *(partida)* departure; *(puerta etc)* exit, way out; **callejón sin s.** dead end; **s. de emergencia** emergency exit (b) *Dep* start; **línea de s.** starting line; **s. nula** false start (c) **te vi a la s. del cine** I saw you leaving the cinema (d) *(de un astro)* rising; **s. del sol** sunrise (e) *(profesional)* opening; *Com* outlet (f) *(recurso)* solution, way out; **no tengo otra s.** I have no other option (g) *Fam (ocurrencia)* witty remark, witticism (h) *Inform* output

salido, -a *adj muy Fam (persona)* horny

saliente *adj* (a) *(destacable)* salient (b) *(cesante)* outgoing

salina *nf* salt mine

salino, -a *adj* saline

salir [22] **1** *vi* (a) *(de un sitio)* to go out, to leave; *(venir de dentro)* to come out; **salió de la habitación** she left the room; **s. de la carretera** to turn off the road
(b) *(tren etc)* to depart
(c) *(novios)* to go out (**con** with)
(d) *(aparecer)* to appear; *(revista, disco)* to come out; *(ley)* to come in; *(trabajo, vacante)* to come up
(e) *(resultar)* to turn out, to turn out to be; **el pequeño les ha salido muy listo** their son has turned out to be very clever; **¿cómo te salió el examen?** how did your exam go?; **s. ganando** to come out ahead *o* on top; **salió presidente** he was elected president
(f) **s. a** *(precio)* to come to, to work out at; **s. barato/caro** to work out cheap/ expensive
(g) **ha salido al abuelo** she takes after her grandfather
(h) *(problema)* to work out; **esta cuenta no me sale** I can't work this sum out
(i) **¡con qué cosas sales!** the things you come out with!

2 salirse *vpr* (a) *(líquido, gas)* to leak (out); *Fig* **salirse de lo normal** to be out of the ordinary; **se salió de la carretera** he went off the road (**b**) *Fam* **salirse con la suya** to get one's own way

saliva *nf* saliva

salivar *vi* to salivate

salivazo *nm* spit

salmantino, -a 1 *adj* of/from Salamanca
   2 *nm,f* person from Salamanca

salmo *nm* psalm

salmón 1 *nm* (*pescado*) salmon
   2 *adj inv* (*color*) salmon pink, salmon

salmonete *nm* (*pescado*) red mullet

salmorejo *nm* (*salsa*) = sauce made from vinegar, water, pepper and salt

salmuera *nf* brine

salobre *adj* (*agua*) brackish; (*gusto*) salty, briny

salón *nm* (**a**) (*en una casa*) lounge, sitting room (**b**) **s. de actos** assembly hall; **s. de baile** dance hall (**c**) **s. de belleza** beauty salon; **s. de té** tearoom, teashop (**d**) **s. dei automóvil** motor show

salpicadera *nf Méx Br* mudguard, *US* fender

salpicadero *nm Esp* dashboard

salpicadura *nf* splashing

salpicar [44] *vt* (**a**) (*rociar*) to splash; **me salpicó el abrigo de barro** he splashed mud on my coat (**b**) *Fig* (*esparcir*) to sprinkle

salpicón *nm Culin* = cold dish of chopped fish or meat, seasoned with pepper, salt, vinegar and onion

salpimentar [1] *vt* to season

salpullido *nm* rash

salsa *nf* sauce; (*de carne*) gravy; *Fig* **en su (propia) s.** in one's element

salsera *nf* gravy boat

saltamontes *nm inv* grasshopper

saltar 1 *vt* (*obstáculo, valla*) to jump (over)
   2 *vi* (**a**) (*moverse*) to jump; *Fig* **s. a la vista** to be obvious (**b**) (*cristal etc*) to break, to shatter; (*plomos*) to go, to blow (**c**) (*desprenderse*) to come off (**d**) (*encolerizarse*) to explode, to blow up; **por menos de nada salta** the smallest thing makes him explode
   3 saltarse *vpr* (**a**) (*omitir*) to skip, to miss out; **saltarse el semáforo/turno** to jump the lights/the queue (**b**) (*botón*) to come off; **se me saltaron las lágrimas** tears came to my eyes

salteado, -a *adj* (**a**) (*espaciado*) spaced out (**b**) *Culin* sauté, sautéed

saltear *vt Culin* to sauté

saltimbanqui *nmf* acrobat, tumbler

salto *nm* (**a**) (*acción*) jump, leap; *Fig* (*paso adelante*) leap forward; **a saltos** in leaps and bounds; **dar** o **pegar un s.** to jump, to

leap; **de un s.** in a flash; *Fig* **a s. de mata** every now and then; **s. de agua** waterfall; **s. de cama** negligée (**b**) *Dep* jump; **s. de altura** high jump; **s. de longitud** long jump; **s. mortal** somersault

saltón, -ona *adj* **ojos saltones** bulging eyes

salubre *adj* salubrious

salubridad *nf* healthiness; **por razones de s.** for health reasons

salud *nf* health; **beber a la s. de algn** to drink to sb's health; *Fam* **¡s.!** cheers!

saludable *adj* (**a**) (*sano*) healthy, wholesome (**b**) (*beneficioso*) good, beneficial

saludar *vt* (**a**) (*decir hola a*) to say hello to, to greet; **saluda de mi parte a** give my regards to; **le saluda atentamente** (*en una carta*) yours faithfully; *Mil* to salute

saludo *nm* greeting; *Mil* salute; **un s. de** best wishes from

salva *nf Mil* salvo, volley

salvación *nf* salvation

salvado *nm* bran

Salvador *nm* (**a**) *Rel* **el S.** the Saviour (**b**) *Geog* **El S.** El Salvador

salvador, -a *nm,f* saviour

salvadoreño, -a *adj & nm,f* Salvadoran, Salvadorian

salvaguarda *nf* (*defensa*) protection

salvaguardar *vt* to safeguard (**de** from), to protect (**de** from)

salvaguardia *nf* = **salvaguarda**

salvajada *nf* brutal act

salvaje *adj* (**a**) *Bot* wild, uncultivated; *Zool* (*pueblo, tribu*) savage, uncivilized (**b**) *Fam* (*violento*) savage, wild

salvajismo *nm* savagery

salvamanteles *nm inv* (*plano*) table mat; (*con pies*) trivet

salvamento *nm* rescue

salvar 1 *vt* (**a**) (*de peligro*) to save, to rescue (**de** from) (**b**) (*obstáculo*) to clear; (*dificultad*) to get round, to overcome (**c**) (*exceptuar*) to exclude, to except; **salvando ciertos errores** except for a few mistakes
   2 salvarse *vpr* (**a**) (*sobrevivir*) to survive, to come out alive; *Fam* (*escaparse*) to escape (**de** from); **¡sálvese quien pueda!** every man for himself!; *Fam* **salvarse por los pelos** to have a narrow escape (**b**) *Rel* to be saved, to save one's soul

salvavidas *nm inv* life belt

salvedad *nf* exception

salvia *nf Bot* sage

salvo, -a 1 *adj* unharmed, safe; **a s.** safe
   2 *adv* (*exceptuando*) except (for); **s. que** unless

salvoconducto *nm* safe-conduct

San *adj* Saint

sanar 1 *vt (curar)* to cure, to heal
2 *vi* (**a**) *(persona)* to recover, to get better (**b**) *(herida)* to heal

sanatorio *nm* sanatorium

sanción *nf* (**a**) *(castigo)* penalty; *Econ* sanction (**b**) *(aprobación)* approval, sanction

sancionar *vt* (**a**) *(castigar)* to penalize (**b**) *(aprobar)* to sanction

sancocho *nm Andes (comida)* = stew of beef, chicken or fish, vegetables and green bananas

sandalia *nf* sandal

sándalo *nm* sandalwood

sandez *nf* piece of nonsense

sandía *nf* watermelon

sándwich ['sanwitʃ, 'sanwis] *(pl* **sándwiches)** *nm* sandwich

sandwichera *nf* toasted sandwich maker

saneamiento *nm* (*de terreno*) drainage, draining; *(de una empresa)* reorganization

sanear *vt (terrenos)* to drain; *(empresa)* to reorganize

sangrar 1 *vt* (**a**) *(sacar sangre)* to bleed (**b**) *Fam (sacar dinero)* to bleed dry
2 *vi* to bleed

sangre *nf* blood; **donar s.** to give blood; **s. fría** sangfroid; **a s. fría** in cold blood

sangría *nf* (**a**) *Med* bleeding, bloodletting; *Fig* drain (**b**) *(timo)* rip-off (**c**) *(bebida)* sangria

sangriento, -a *adj (guerra etc)* bloody

sanguijuela *nf* leech, bloodsucker

sanguinario, -a *adj* bloodthirsty

sanguíneo, -a *adj* blood; **grupo s.** blood group

sanidad *nf* health; **Ministerio de S.** Department of Health

> ℰ Observa que la palabra inglesa **sanity** es un falso amigo y no es la traducción de la palabra española **sanidad**. En inglés **sanity** significa "cordura, sensatez".

sanitario, -a 1 *adj* health
2 *nm* toilet, *US* bathroom

sano, -a *adj* (**a**) *(bien de salud)* healthy; **s. y salvo** safe and sound (**b**) *(comida)* healthy, wholesome (**c**) **en su s. juicio** in one's right mind

> ℰ Observa que la palabra inglesa **sane** es un falso amigo y no es la traducción de la palabra española **sano**. En inglés, **sane** significa "cuerdo, sensato".

Santa Claus, *Méx,Ven* **Santa Clos** *n* Santa Claus

santería *nf* (**a**) *(religión)* santería, = form of religion common in the Caribbean in which people allegedly have contact with the spirit world (**b**) *Am (tienda)* = shop selling religious mementoes such as statues of saints

santero, -a *nm,f (curandero)* = faith healer who calls on the saints to assist with the healing process

santiamén *nm Fam* **en un s.** in a flash, in no time at all

santidad *nf* saintliness, holiness

santificar [44] *vt* to sanctify

santiguarse [45] *vpr* to cross oneself

santo, -a 1 *adj* (**a**) *(sagrado)* holy (**b**) *(bueno)* saintly; **un s. varón** a saint
2 *nm,f Rel & Fig* saint; *Fam* **¡por todos los santos!** for heaven's sake!; *Fig* **se me fue el s. al cielo** I clean forgot
3 *nm (onomástica)* saint's day; *Fig* **¿a s. de qué?** why on earth?

santuario *nm* sanctuary, shrine

saña *nf* fury; **con s.** furiously

sapo *nm* toad; *Fam* **echar sapos y culebras** to rant and rave

saque *nm* (**a**) *Ftb* **s. inicial** kick-off; **s. de banda** throw-in; **s. de esquina** corner kick (**b**) *Ten* service

saquear *vt (ciudad)* to sack, to plunder; *(casas, tiendas)* to loot

saqueo *nm (de ciudad)* sacking, plundering; *(de casas, tiendas)* looting

S.A.R. *(abr* **Su Alteza Real)** H.R.H.

sarampión *nm* measles *sing*

sarao *nm* knees-up

sarcasmo *nm* sarcasm

sarcástico, -a *adj* sarcastic

sarcófago *nm* sarcophagus

sardana *nf* sardana, = Catalan dance and music

sardina *nf* sardine

sardónico, -a *adj* sardonic

sargento *nm* sergeant

sarmiento *nm* vine shoot

sarna *nf Med* scabies *sing; Zool* mange

sarpullido *nm* rash

sarro *nm (sedimento)* deposit; *(en los dientes)* tartar; *(en la lengua)* fur

sarta *nf* string

sartén *nf* frying pan, *US* fry-pan; *Fam Fig* **tener la s. por el mango** to call the shots

sastre *nm* tailor

sastrería *nf (oficio)* tailoring; *(taller)* tailor's (shop); *Cin & Teatro* wardrobe (department)

Satanás *n* Satan

satánico, -a *adj* satanic

satélite *nm* satellite; *Fig* **país s.** satellite state; **televisión vía s.** satelliteTV

satén *nm* satin

satinar *vt* to gloss, to make glossy

sátira *nf* satire

satírico, -a *adj* satirical

satirizar [40] *vt* to satirize

satisfacción *nf* satisfaction; **s. de un deseo** fulfilment of a desire

satisfacer [15] (*pp* **satisfecho**) *vt* (a) *(deseos, necesidades)* to satisfy (b) *(requisitos)* to meet, to satisfy (c) *(deuda)* to pay

satisfactorio, -a *adj* satisfactory

satisfecho, -a 1 *adj* satisfied; **me doy por s.** that's good enough for me; **s. de sí mismo** self-satisfied, smug
2 *pp de* **satisfacer**

saturar *vt* to saturate

Saturno *n* Saturn

sauce *nm* willow; **s. llorón** weeping willow

saudí, saudita *adj & nmf* Saudi; **Arabia Saudita** Saudi Arabia

sauna *nf* sauna

savia *nf* sap

saxo *nm Fam Mús* sax

saxofón *nm* saxophone

saxofonista *nmf* saxophonist

sayo *nm* cassock, smock

sazonar *vt* to season, to flavour

s/c. (*abr* **su cuenta**) your account

Sdad. (*abr* **sociedad**) Soc.

se¹ *pron* (a) *(reflexivo) (objeto directo) (a él mismo)* himself; *(animal)* itself; *(a ella misma)* herself; *(animal)* itself; *(a usted mismo)* yourself; *(a ellos mismos)* themselves; *(a ustedes mismos)* yourselves
(b) *(objeto indirecto) (a él mismo)* (to/for) himself; *(animal)* (to/for) itself; *(a ella misma)* (to/for) herself; *(animal)* (to/for) itself; *(a usted mismo)* (to/for) yourself; *(a ellos mismos)* (to/for) themselves; *(a ustedes mismos)* (to/for) yourselves; **se compró un nuevo coche** he bought himself a new car; **todos los días se lava el pelo** she washes her hair every day
(c) *(recíproco)* one another, each other
(d) *(voz pasiva)* **el vino se guarda en cubas** wine is kept in casks
(e) *(uso impers)* **nunca se sabe** you never know; **se habla inglés** *(en letrero)* English spoken here; **se dice que ...** it is said that ...

se² *pron pers (a él)* (to/for) him; *(a ella)* (to/for) her; *(a usted o ustedes)* (to/for) you; *(a ellos)* (to/for) them; **se lo diré en cuanto les vea** I'll tell them as soon as I see them; **¿se lo explico?** shall I explain it to you?; **¿se lo has dado ya?** have you given it to him yet?

sé¹ *indic pres de* **saber**

sé² *imperat de* **ser**

sea *subj pres de* **ser**

sebo *nm* fat

secado *nm* drying

secador *nm* dryer; **s. de pelo** hairdryer

secadora *nf* tumble dryer

secano *nm* dry land

secante *adj* **papel s.** blotting paper

secar [44] **1** *vt* to dry
2 secarse *vpr* (a) *(objeto, suelo)* to dry; **sécate** dry yourself; **secarse las manos** to dry one's hands (b) *(planta, pozo)* to dry up

sección *nf* section

seco, -a *adj* (a) *(sin humedad)* dry; *(higos, pasas)* dried; **limpieza en s.** dry-cleaning; *Fig* **a secas** just, only (b) *(tono)* curt, sharp; *(golpe, ruido)* sharp; *Fig* **frenar en s.** to pull up sharply; *Fig* **parar en s.** to stop dead (c) *(delgado)* skinny

secreción *nf* secretion

secretaría *nf* *(oficina)* secretary's office; **S. de Estado** *(en España)* = government department under the control of *Br* a junior minister *o US* an under-secretary; *(en Latinoamérica)* ministry; *(en Estados Unidos)* State Department

secretariado *nm* (a) *(oficina)* secretariat (b) *Educ* secretarial course

secretario, -a *nm,f* secretary; **s. de dirección** secretary to the director; **s. de Estado** *(en España) Br* junior minister, *US* under-secretary; *(en Latinoamérica) Br* minister, *US* secretary; *(en Estados Unidos)* Secretary of State

secreto, -a 1 *adj* secret; **en s.** in secret, secretly
2 *nm* secret; **guardar un s.** to keep a secret; **con mucho s.** in great secrecy

secta *nf* sect

sectario, -a *adj* sectarian

sector *nm* (a) *(división)* section; *Econ* industry, sector (b) *(zona)* area; **un s. de la ciudad** an area of the city

sectorial *adj* sectoral

secuela *nf* consequence

secuencia *nf* sequence

secuestrador, -a *nm,f* (a) *(de persona)* kidnapper; *(de un avión)* hijacker (b) *Der* sequestrator

secuestrar *vt* (a) *(persona)* to kidnap; *(aviones)* to hijack (b) *Der* to confiscate

secuestro *nm* (a) *(de persona)* kidnapping; *(de un avión)* hijacking (b) *Der* confiscation

secular *adj* (a) *Rel* secular, lay (b) *(antiquísimo)* ancient, age-old

secundar *vt* to back

secundario, -a *adj* secondary

secuoya *nf Bot* redwood, sequoia; **s. gigante** giant sequoia

sed *nf* thirst; **tener s.** to be thirsty

seda *nf* silk

sedal *nm* fishing line

sedante *adj & nm* sedative

sede *nf* (a) *(de organización, empresa)* headquarters; *(de gobierno)* seat; *(de acontecimiento)* venue; **s. social** head office (b) **la Santa S.** the Holy See

sedentario, -a *adj* sedentary

sedición *nf* sedition

sedicioso, -a 1 *adj* rebellious
　2 *nm,f* rebel

sediento, -a *adj* thirsty; *Fig* **s. de poder** hungry for power

sedimentario, -a *adj* sedimentary

sedimentarse *upr* to settle

sedimento *nm* sediment, deposit

sedoso, -a *adj* silky, silken

seducción *nf* seduction

seducir [10] *vt* to seduce; *(persuadir)* to tempt

seductor, -a 1 *adj* seductive; *(persuasivo)* tempting
　2 *nm,f* seducer

segador, -a *nm,f (agricultor)* reaper

segadora *nf (máquina)* reaper, harvester

segar [1] *vt* to reap, to cut

seglar 1 *adj* secular, lay
　2 *nmf* lay person; *(hombre)* layman; *(mujer)* laywoman

segmento *nm* segment

segregación *nf* (a) *(separación)* segregation (b) *(secreción)* secretion

segregar [42] *vt* (a) *(separar)* to segregate (b) *(secretar)* to secrete

seguida: en seguida *loc adv* = enseguida

seguido, -a 1 *adj* (a) *(continuo)* continuous (b) *(consecutivo)* consecutive, successive; **tres veces seguidas** on three consecutive occasions; **tres lunes seguidos** three Mondays in a row
　2 *adv* (a) *(en línea recta)* straight on; **todo s.** straight on *o* ahead (b) *Am (a menudo)* often

seguidor, -a *nm,f* follower

seguimiento *nm (de elecciones, enfermedad)* monitoring; *(por radio, radar)* tracking; *(de persona, noticia)* following

seguir [6] **1** *vt* (a) *(ir detrás de)* to follow (b) *(camino)* to continue (c) *(perseguir)* to chase
　2 *vi* (a) *(sucederse)* **s. a algo** to follow sth (b) *(continuar)* to continue, to go on; **siguió hablando** he continued *o* went on *o* kept on speaking; **sigo resfriado** I've still got a cold; **sigue con vida** he's still alive
　3 **seguirse** *upr* to follow, to ensue

según 1 *prep* (a) *(de acuerdo con)* according to; **s. la Biblia** according to the Bible (b) *(en función de)* depending on; **varía s. el tiempo (que haga)** it varies depending on the weather
　2 *adv* (a) *(en función de cómo)* depending on; **s. estén las cosas** depending on how things stand; **¿vendrás mañana? – s.** will you come tomorrow? – it depends (b) *(tal como)* just as; **estaba s. lo dejé** it was just as I had left it (c) *(a medida que)* as; **s. iba leyendo …** as I read on …

segunda *nf* (a) *Aut* second (gear); **meter (la) s.** to go into second (gear) (b) *Av & Ferroc* second class; **viajar en s.** to travel second class

segundero *nm* second hand

segundo¹, -a 1 *adj* second; *Fig* **decir algo con segundas (intenciones)** to say sth with a double meaning
　2 *nm,f (de una serie)* second (one)

segundo² *nm (tiempo)* second; **sesenta segundos** sixty seconds

seguramente *adv* (a) *(seguro)* surely (b) *(probablemente)* most probably; **s. no lloverá** it isn't likely to rain

seguridad *nf* (a) *(física)* safety; **s. en carretera** road safety; **para mayor s.** to be on the safe side (b) *(protección)* security; **cerradura de s.** security lock (c) *(confianza)* confidence; **s. en sí mismo** self-confidence (d) *(certeza)* certainty; **con toda s.** most probably; **tener la s. de que …** to be certain that … (e) **S. Social** ≃ Social Security, *Br* ≃ National Health Service

seguro, -a 1 *adj* (a) *(sin peligro)* safe; *Fig* **ir sobre s.** to play safe (b) *(protegido, estable)* secure (c) *(cierto)* definite, certain; **tener por s. que …** to be sure that … (d) *(confiado)* sure; **estoy s. de que …** I am sure that …
　2 *nm* (a) *(contrato)* insurance; **s. a todo riesgo** fully comprehensive insurance; **s. contra terceros** third party insurance; **s. de vida** life insurance (b) *(dispositivo)*

safety catch o device (**c**) *CAm, Méx* (*imperdible*) safety pin
3 *adv* for sure, definitely

seis *adj & nm inv* six

seiscientos, -as *adj & nm* six hundred

seísmo *nm* (*terremoto*) earthquake; (*temblor de tierra*) earth tremor

selección *nf* (**a**) (*acción*) selection (**b**) *Dep* team

seleccionador, -a *nm,f Dep* manager

seleccionar *vt* to select

selectividad *nf* selectivity; *Esp* (*examen*) (prueba de) s. entrance examination

selectivo, -a *adj* selective

selecto, -a *adj* select; **ambiente s.** exclusive atmosphere

selector, -a 1 *adj* selecting
2 *nm* selector (button)

self-service *nm* self-service cafeteria

sellar *vt* (*documento*) to seal; (*carta*) to stamp

sello *nm* (**a**) (*de correos*) stamp; (*para documentos*) seal (**b**) (*precinto*) seal

selva *nf* jungle

semáforo *nm* traffic lights

semana *nf* week; **entre s.** during the week; **S. Santa** Holy Week

semanada *nf Am* (weekly) pocket money

semanal *adj & nm* weekly

semanario *nm* weekly magazine

semblante *nm Literario* (*cara*) face; *Fig* (*aspecto*) look

sembrado *nm* sown field

sembrar [1] *vt* (**a**) *Agr* to sow (**b**) *Fig* **s. el pánico** to spread panic

semejante 1 *adj* (**a**) · (*parecido*) similar; **nunca he visto nada s.** I've never seen anything like it (**b**) *Pey* (*comparativo*) such; **s. desvergüenza** such insolence
2 *nm* (*prójimo*) fellow being

semejanza *nf* similarity, likeness

semen *nm* semen

semental *nm* stud

semestral *adj* half-yearly

semestre *nm* six-month period, *US* semester

semicírculo *nm* semicircle

semidesnatado, -a *adj* semi-skimmed

semidirecto, -a 1 *adj* express
2 *nm* (*tren*) = through train, a section of which becomes a stopping train

semifinal *nf* semifinal

semifinalista *nmf* semifinalist

semilla *nf* seed

semillero *nm* seedbed

seminario *nm* (**a**) *Educ* seminar (**b**) *Rel* seminary

sémola *nf* semolina

Sena *n* **el S.** the Seine

senado *nm* senate

senador, -a *nm,f* senator

sencillez *nf* simplicity

sencillo, -a 1 *adj* (**a**) (*fácil*) simple, easy (**b**) (*natural*) natural, unaffected (**c**) (*billete*) *Br* single, *US* one-way (**d**) (*sin adornos*) simple, plain
2 *nm Andes, CAm, Méx Fam* (*cambio*) loose change

senda *nf*, **sendero** *nm* path

sendos, -as *adj pl* **con sendas carteras** each carrying a briefcase

senil *adj* senile

seno *nm* (**a**) (*pecho*) breast (**b**) *Fig* bosom, heart; **en el s. de** within (**c**) *Mat* sine

sensación *nf* (**a**) (*percepción*) sensation, feeling; **tengo la s. de que ...** I have a feeling that ... (**b**) (*efecto*) sensation; **causar s.** to cause a sensation

sensacional *adj* sensational

sensacionalismo *nm* sensationalism

sensacionalista *adj* sensationalist; **prensa s.** gutter press

sensato, -a *adj* sensible

sensibilidad *nf* (**a**) (*percepción*) feeling; **no tiene s. en los brazos** she has no feeling in her arms (**b**) (*emotividad*) sensitivity; **tener la s. a flor de piel** to be easily hurt, to be very sensitive

sensibilizar [40] *vt* to make aware; **s.·a la opinión pública** to increase public awareness

sensible *adj* (**a**) (*gen*) sensitive (**b**) (*evidente*) noticeable; (*importante*) significant

sensiblemente *adv* noticeably, considerably

⌐ Observa que la palabra inglesa **sensible** es un falso amigo y no es la traducción de la palabra española **sensible**. En inglés, **sensible** significa tanto "sensato" como "práctico".

sensiblero, -a *adj* over-sentimental, mawkish

sensitivo, -a *adj* (**a**) (*de los sentidos*) sensory (**b**) (*receptible*) sensitive

sensorial *adj* sensory

sensual *adj* sensual

sensualidad *nf* sensuality

sentada *nf* (**a**) (*protesta*) sit-in (**b**) *Fam* **de una s.** at one sitting, in one go

sentado, -a *adj* (*establecido*) established, settled; **dar algo por s.** to take sth for granted; **dejar s. que ...** to make it clear that ...

sentar [1] **1** *vt* (**a**) *(en asiento)* to seat, to sit (**b**) *(establecer)* to establish; **s. las bases** to lay the foundations
2 *vi* (**a**) *(color, ropa etc)* to suit; **el pelo corto te sienta mal** short hair doesn't suit you (**b**) **s. bien/mal a** *(comida)* to agree/disagree with; **la sopa te sentará bien** the soup will do you good (**c**) **le sentó mal la broma** she didn't like the joke
3 sentarse *upr* to sit, to sit down

sentencia *nf* (**a**) *Der* sentence; **visto para s.** ready for judgement (**b**) *(aforismo)* maxim, saying

sentenciar [43] *vt Der* to sentence (**a** to)

sentido, -a 1 *nm* (**a**) *(capacidad)* sense; **los cinco sentidos** the five senses; **s. común** common sense; **s. del humor** sense of humour (**b**) *(significado)* meaning; **doble s.** double meaning; **no tiene s.** it doesn't make sense (**c**) *(dirección)* direction; **(de) s. único** one-way (**d**) *(conciencia)* consciousness; **perder el s.** to faint
2 *adj* deeply felt; *Fml* **mi más s. pésame** my deepest sympathy

sentimental 1 *adj* sentimental; **vida s.** love life
2 *nmf* sentimental person

sentimiento *nm* feeling; *Fml* **le acompaño en el s.** my deepest sympathy

sentir¹ *nm* (**a**) *(sentimiento)* feeling (**b**) *(opinión)* opinion, view

sentir² [5] **1** *vt* (**a**) *(notar)* to feel; **s. hambre/calor** to feel hungry/hot (**b**) *(lamentar)* to regret, to be sorry about; **lo siento (mucho)** I'm (very) sorry; **siento molestarle** I'm sorry to bother you
2 sentirse *upr* to feel; **me siento mal** I feel ill; **sentirse con ánimos de hacer algo** to feel like doing sth

seña *nf* (**a**) *(gesto, indicio)* sign, signal; **hacer señas a algn** to signal to sb (**b**) **señas** *(dirección)* address

señal *nf* (**a**) *(indicio)* sign, indication; **en s. de** as a sign of, as a token of (**b**) *(placa)* sign; **s. de tráfico** road sign (**c**) *(gesto etc)* signal, sign (**d**) *(marca)* mark; *(vestigio)* trace (**e**) *Tel* tone; **s. de llamada** *Br* dialling tone, *US* dial tone (**f**) *Com* deposit

señalado, -a *adj (importante)* important; **un día s.** a red-letter day

señalar *vt* (**a**) *(indicar)* to mark, to indicate; **s. con el dedo** to point at (**b**) *(resaltar)* to point out (**c**) *(precio, fecha)* to fix, to arrange

señalero *nm Urug Br* indicator, *US* turn signal

señor *nm* (**a**) *(hombre)* man; *(caballero)* gentleman (**b**) *Rel* **El S.** the Lord (**c**) *(con apellido)* Mr; *(tratamiento de respeto)* sir; **el Sr. Gutiérrez** Mr Gutiérrez; **muy s. mío** *(en carta)* Dear Sir (**d**) *(con título) (no se traduce)* **el s. ministro** the Minister

señora *nf* (**a**) *(mujer)* woman, *Fml* lady; **¡señoras y señores!** ladies and gentlemen! (**b**) *Rel* **Nuestra S.** Our Lady (**c**) *(con apellido)* Mrs; *(tratamiento de respeto)* madam; **la Sra. Salinas** Mrs Salinas; **muy s. mía** *(en carta)* Dear Madam (**d**) *(con título) (no se traduce)* **la s. ministra** the Minister (**e**) *(esposa)* wife

señoría *nf* (**a**) *Der (hombre)* lordship; *(mujer)* ladyship (**b**) *Pol* **sus señorías** the honourable gentlemen

señorita *nf* (**a**) *(joven)* young woman, *Fml* young lady (**b**) *(tratamiento de respeto)* Miss; **S. Padilla** Miss Padilla (**c**) *Educ* **la s.** the teacher, Miss

señorito, -a 1 *adj Fam Pey (refinado)* lordly
2 *nm* (**a**) *Anticuado (hijo del amo)* master (**b**) *Fam Pey (niñato)* rich kid

señuelo *nm* decoy

sepa *subj pres de* **saber**

separación *nf* (**a**) *(acción)* separation; *Der* **s. conyugal** legal separation (**b**) *(espacio)* space, distance

separado, -a *adj* (**a**) *(apartado)* separate; **por s.** separately, individually (**b**) *(divorciado)* separated

separar 1 *vt* (**a**) *(desunir, alejar)* to separate (**de** from) (**b**) *(apartar)* to move away
2 separarse *upr* (**a**) *(ir por distinto lugar)* to separate, to part company (**b**) *(matrimonio)* to separate (**c**) *(apartarse)* to move away (**de** from)

separata *nf* offprint

separatismo *nm* separatism

separatista *adj & nmf* separatist

separo *nm Méx* cell

sepia 1 *nf (pez)* cuttlefish
2 *adj & nm (color)* sepia

septentrional *adj* northern

septiembre *nm* September; **el 5 de s.** the 5th of September; **en s.** in September

séptimo, -a *adj & nm,f* seventh; **la** *o* **una séptima parte** a seventh

sepulcral *adj (silencio)* deathly

sepulcro *nm* tomb

sepultura *nf* grave

sepulturero, -a *nm,f* gravedigger

sequía *nf* drought

séquito *nm* entourage, retinue

ser¹ nm being; **s. humano** human being; **s. vivo** living being

ser² [23] vi (a) (+ adj) to be; **es alto y rubio** he is tall and fair; **el edificio es gris** the building is grey
(b) (+ profesión) to be a(n); **Rafael es músico** Rafael is a musician
(c) **s. de** (procedencia) to be o come from; **¿de dónde eres?** where are you from?, where do you come from?
(d) **s. de** (+ material) to be made of
(e) **s. de** (+ poseedor) to belong to; **el perro es de Miguel** the dog belongs to Miguel; **¿de quién es este abrigo?** whose coat is this?
(f) **s. para** (finalidad) to be for; **esta agua es para lavar** this water is for washing
(g) (+ día, hora) to be; **hoy es 2 de noviembre** today is the 2nd of November; **son las cinco de la tarde** it's five o'clock (in the afternoon), its five p.m.
(h) (+ cantidad) **¿cuántos estaremos en la fiesta?** how many of us will there be at the party?
(i) (costar) to be, to cost; **¿cuánto es?** how much is it?
(j) (tener lugar) to be; **el estreno será mañana** tomorrow is the opening night
(k) **¿qué es de Gonzalo?** what has become of Gonzalo?
(l) (auxiliar en pasiva) to be; **fue asesinado** he was murdered
(m) (locuciones) **¿cómo es eso?, ¿cómo puede s.?** how can that be?; **es más** furthermore; **es que ...** it's just that ...; **como sea** anyhow; **lo que sea** whatever; **o sea** that is (to say); **por si fuera poco** to top it all; **sea como sea** in any case, be that as it may; **a no s. que** unless; **de no s. por ...** had it not been for ...; **eso era de esperar** it was to be expected

The auxiliary verb **ser** is used with the past participle of a verb to form the passive (e.g. **la película fue criticada** the film was criticized).

serenar 1 vt (calmar) to calm
2 serenarse vpr (calmarse) to calm down
serenidad nf serenity
sereno¹ nm (vigilante) nightwatchman
sereno², **-a** adj (a) (en calma) calm (b) Fam (sobrio) sober
serial nm Rad & TV serial
serie nf (a) (sucesión, conjunto) series sing; **fabricación en s.** mass production; **lleva ABS de s.** it has ABS fitted as standard; **fuera de s.** out of the ordinary (b) Rad & TV series sing

seriedad nf (a) (gravedad) seriousness (b) (formalidad) reliability, dependability; **falta de s.** irresponsibility

serio, **-a 1** adj (a) (grave) serious (b) (formal) reliable, responsible
2 en serio loc adv seriously
sermón nm sermon
sermonear vt & vi Fam to lecture
seropositivo, **-a** adj HIV-positive
serpentear vi to wind one's way, to meander
serpentina nf (de papel) streamer
serpiente nf snake; **s. de cascabel** rattlesnake; **s. pitón** python
serranía nf mountainous area/country
serrar [1] vt to saw
serrín nm sawdust
serrucho nm handsaw
servicial adj helpful, obliging
servicio nm (a) (asistencia) service; **s. a domicilio** home delivery service; **s. público** public service (b) (funcionamiento) service; **estar fuera de s.** (máquina) to be out of order (c) Mil service; **s. militar** military service; **estar de s.** to be on duty (d) Esp (WC) toilet, US bathroom (e) Econ **servicios** (sector terciario) services (f) Dep serve, service
servidor, **-a 1** nm,f servant; Fam **un s.** yours truly
2 nm Inform server
servidumbre nf (a) (criados) servants (b) (dependencia) servitude
servil adj servile
servilleta nf napkin, Br serviette
servilletero nm serviette ring, napkin ring
servir [6] **1** vt to serve; **¿en qué puedo servirle?** what can I do for you?, may I help you?; **¿te sirvo una copa?** will I pour you a drink?
2 vi (a) (prestar servicio) to serve (b) (valer) to be useful, to be suitable; **no sirve de nada llorar** it's no use crying; **ya no sirve** it's no use; **¿para qué sirve esto?** what is this (used) for?; **s. de** to serve as, to act as
3 servirse vpr (a) (comida) to help oneself (b) Fml **sírvase comunicarnos su decisión** please inform us of your decision
sésamo nm sesame
sesenta adj & num inv sixty
sesgar [42] vt (a) (cortar) to cut diagonally (b) (torcer) to slant
sesgo nm Fig slant, turn; **tomar un s. favorable** to take a turn for the better

sesión *nf* (a) *(reunión)* meeting, session; *Der* session, sitting (b) *Cin* showing

seso *nm* brain

set *nm Ten* set

seta *nf Esp (comestible)* mushroom; **s. venenosa** toadstool

setecientos, -as *adj & nm* seven hundred

setenta *adj & nm inv* seventy

setiembre *nm* = **septiembre**

seto *nm* hedge

seudónimo *nm* pseudonym; *(de escritores)* pen name

severidad *nf* severity

severo, -a *adj* severe

Sevilla *n* Seville

sevillana *nf* = Andalusian dance and song

sexismo *nm* sexism

sexista *adj* sexist

sexo *nm* (a) *(género, actividad)* sex (b) *(órgano)* genitals

sexólogo, -a *nm,f* sexologist

sexto, -a *adj & nm,f* sixth

sexual *adj* sexual; **vida s.** sex life

sexualidad *nf* sexuality

sexy *adj* sexy

shock *nm* shock

shorts [ʃorts] *nmpl, Am* **short** [ʃor, ʃort] (*pl* **shores**) *nm* shorts

show [ʃou, tʃou] (*pl* **shows**) *nm* show

si¹ *conj* (a) *(condicional)* if; **como si** as if; **si no** if not; **si quieres** if you like, if you wish (b) *(pregunta indirecta)* whether, if; **me preguntó si me gustaba** he asked me if I liked it; **no sé si ir o no** *(disyuntivo)* I don't know whether to go or not (c) *(sorpresa)* **¡si está llorando!** but she's crying!

si² *nm Mús* B; *(en solfeo)* ti

sí¹ *pron pers* (a) *(singular)* *(él)* himself; *(ella)* herself; *(cosa)* itself; *(plural)* themselves; **de por sí, en sí** in itself; **hablaban entre sí** they were talking among themselves *o* to each other; **por sí mismo** by himself (b) *(uno mismo)* oneself; **decir para sí** to say to oneself

sí² (*pl* **síes**) **1** *adv* (a) *(afirmación)* yes; **dije que sí** I said yes, I accepted, I agreed; **porque sí** just because; **¡que sí!** yes, I tell you!; **un día sí y otro no** every other day (b) *(uso enfático) (no se traduce)* **sí que me gusta** of course I like it; **¡eso sí que no!** certainly not!

2 *nm* yes; **los síes** *(en parlamento)* the ayes

siamés, -esa *nmf* Siamese twin

sibarita *nmf* sybarite

sicario *nm* hired gunman; *Fam* hitman

Sicilia *n* Sicily

sico- = **psico-**

sicómoro *nm* sycamore

sida *nm* *(abr* **síndrome de inmunodeficiencia adquirida***)* AIDS

sidecar *nm* sidecar

siderurgia *nf* iron and steel industry

siderúrgico, -a *adj* iron and steel; **la industria siderúrgica** the iron and steel industry

sidra *nf Br* cider, *US* hard cider

siega 1 *ver* **segar**

2 *nf* (a) *(acción)* reaping, harvesting (b) *(época)* harvest (time)

siembra 1 *ver* **sembrar**

2 *nf* (a) *(acción)* sowing (b) *(época)* sowing time

siempre *adv* (a) *(todo el tiempo)* always; **s. pasa lo mismo** it's always the same; **como s.** as usual; **a la hora de s.** at the usual time; **eso es así desde s.** it has always been like that; **para s.** for ever; **s. que** *(cada vez que)* whenever; *(a condición de que)* provided, as long as; **s. y cuando** provided, as long as (b) *Am (todavía)* still; **s. viven allí** they still live there (c) *Méx Fam (enfático)* **s. sí quiero ir** I do still want to go; **s. no me marcho** I'm still not leaving

sien *nf* temple

sierra *nf* (a) *(herramienta)* saw; **s. mecánica** power saw (b) *Geog* mountain range, sierra

siervo, -a *nm,f* slave

siesta *nf* siesta, nap; **dormir la s.** to have a siesta *o* an afternoon nap

siete 1 *adj* seven

2 *nm inv* seven

3 *nf RP Fam Euf* **¡la gran s.!** *Br* sugar!, *US* shoot!

sietemesino, -a *nm,f* seven-month-old baby, premature baby

sífilis *nf inv* syphilis

sifón *nm* siphon; **whisky con s.** whisky and soda

sig. *(abr* **siguiente***)* following

sigilo *nm* secrecy; **entrar con mucho s.** to tiptoe in

sigilosamente *adv* *(secretamente)* secretly; **entró s. en la habitación** she crept *o* slipped into the room

sigiloso, -a *adj* secretive

sigla *nf* acronym

siglo *nm* century; **el s. veintiuno** the twenty-first century; *Fam* **hace siglos que no le veo** I haven't seen him for ages

signatario, -a *adj & nm,f* signatory

significación *nf* (a) *(sentido)* meaning (b) *(importancia)* significance

significado *nm* meaning

significar [44] *vt* to mean

significativo, -a *adj* significant; *(expresivo)* meaningful

signo *nm* (a) *(señal)* sign (b) *Ling* mark; **s. de interrogación** question mark (c) *(del zodiaco)* sign

sigo *indic pres de* **seguir**

siguiente *adj* following, next; **¡el s.!** next, please!; **al día s.** the following day

sílaba *nf* syllable

silbar *vi* to whistle; *(abuchear)* to hiss, to boo

silbato *nm* whistle

silbido *nm* whistle, whistling; *(agudo)* hiss

silenciador *nm* (de arma) silencer; *(de coche, moto)* Br silencer, US muffler

silenciar [43] *vt* (a) *(sonido)* to muffle (b) *(noticia)* to hush up

silencio *nm* silence; **imponer s. a algn** to make sb be quiet

silencioso, -a *adj* quiet, silent

silicio *nm* silicon

silicona *nf* silicone

silla *nf* (a) *(mueble)* chair; **s. de ruedas** wheelchair; **s. giratoria** swivel chair (b) *(de montura)* saddle

sillín *nm* saddle

sillón *nm* armchair

silo *nm* silo

silueta *nf* silhouette; *(de cuerpo)* figure

silvestre *adj* wild

simbólico, -a *adj* symbolic; **precio s.** token price

simbolizar [40] *vt* to symbolize

símbolo *nm* symbol

simetría *nf* symmetry

simétrico, -a *adj* symmetrical

simiente *nf* seed

similar *adj* similar

similitud *nf* similarity

simio *nm* monkey

simpatía *nf* liking, affection; **le tengo mucha s.** I am very fond of him

> *Observa que la palabra inglesa **sympathy** es un falso amigo y no es la traducción de la palabra española **simpatía**. En inglés **sympathy** significa tanto "compasión" como "comprensión".*

simpático, -a *adj* nice, likeable; **me cae s.** I like him

> *Observa que la palabra inglesa **sympathetic** es un falso amigo y no es la traducción de la palabra española **simpático**. En inglés **sympathetic** significa tanto "comprensivo" como "compasivo".*

simpatizante *nmf* sympathizer

simpatizar [40] *vi* (a) *(persona)* to hit it off (**con** with) (b) *(idea)* to sympathize (**con** with)

simple 1 *adj* (a) *(sencillo)* simple (b) *(fácil)* simple, easy (c) *(mero)* mere (d) *(persona)* simple, simple-minded
2 *nm (persona)* simpleton

simpleza *nf (de persona)* simple-mindedness

simplicidad *nf* simplicity

simplificar [44] *vt* to simplify

simposio *nm* symposium

simulacro *nm* sham, pretence; **un s. de ataque** a mock attack

simular *vt* to simulate

simultanear *vt* to combine; **simultanea el trabajo y los estudios** he's working and studying at the same time

simultáneo, -a *adj* simultaneous

sin *prep* (a) without; **s. dinero/tí** without money/you; **estamos s. pan** we're out of bread; **s. hacer nada** without doing any-thing; **cerveza s.** alcohol-free beer; **s. más ni más** without further ado (b) (+ *infin*) **está s. secar** it hasn't been dried

sinagoga *nf* synagogue

sincerarse *vpr* to open one's heart (**con** to)

sinceridad *nf* sincerity; **con toda s.** in all sincerity

sincero, -a *adj* sincere

sincronizar [40] *vt* to synchronize

sindical *adj* (Br trade o US labor) union

sindicalista *nmf* union member, Br trade unionist

sindicar [44] *vt Andes, RP, Ven* to accuse; **s. a algn de algo** to accuse sb of sth

sindicato *nm* (Br trade o US labor) union

síndrome *nm* syndrome

sinfín *nm* endless number; **un s. de** lots of

sinfonía *nf* symphony

sinfónico, -a *adj* symphonic

singani *nm Bol* grape brandy

singular 1 *adj* (a) *(excepcional)* exceptional, unique (b) *(raro)* peculiar, odd (c) *Ling* singular
2 *nm Ling* singular; **en s.** in the singular

siniestrado, -a *adj* stricken

siniestro, -a 1 *adj* sinister, ominous
2 *nm* disaster, catastrophe

sinnúmero *nm* **un s. de** countless

sino¹ *nm Fml* fate, destiny

sino² *conj* (a) but; **no fui a Madrid, s. a Barcelona** I didn't go to Madrid but to

Barcelona (**b**) *(excepto)* **nadie s. él** no one but him; **no quiero s. que me oigan** I only want them to listen (to me)

sinónimo, -a 1 *adj* synonymous
  2 *nm* synonym

sinóptico, -a *adj* **cuadro s.** diagram, chart

sinsabor *nm (usu pl)* trouble, worry

síntesis *nf inv* synthesis; **en s.** in short

sintético, -a *adj* synthetic

sintetizador *nm* synthesizer

sintetizar [40] *vt* to synthesize

síntoma *nm* symptom

sintonía *nf* (**a**) *Elec & Rad* tuning (**b**) *Mús & Rad (de programa)* theme tune, *Br* signature tune (**c**) *Fig* harmony

sintonizador *nm Rad* tuning knob

sintonizar [40] *vt* (**a**) *Rad* to tune in to (**b**) *(simpatizar)* **sintonizaron muy bien** they clicked straight away

sinuoso, -a *adj (camino)* winding

sinvergüenza 1 *adj (desvergonzado)* shameless; *(descarado)* cheeky
  2 *nmf (desvergonzado)* rogue; *(caradura)* cheeky devil

sionismo *nm* Zionism

siquiera 1 *adv (por lo menos)* at least; **ni s.** not even
  2 *conj Fml (aunque)* although, even though

sirena *nf* (**a**) *(mujer)* mermaid, siren (**b**) *(señal acústica)* siren

Siria *n* Syria

sirimiri *nm* fine drizzle

sirio, -a *adj & nm,f* Syrian

sirviente, -a *nm,f* servant

sisa *nf* (**a**) *(de manga)* armhole (**b**) *(de dinero)* pilfering

sisar *vt* to pilfer, to filch

sisear *vi* to hiss

sísmico, -a *adj* seismic

sismógrafo *nm* seismograph

sistema *nm* system; **por s.** as a rule; **s. nervioso** nervous system; **s. montañoso** mountain chain

sistemático, -a *adj* systematic

sitiar [43] *vt* to besiege

sitio¹ *nm* (**a**) *(lugar)* place; **en cualquier s.** anywhere; **en todos los sitios** everywhere; *Fig* **quedarse en el s.** to die (**b**) *(espacio)* room; **hacer s.** to make room (**c**) *Méx (parada de taxis)* taxi *Br* rank o *US* stand (**d**) *Inform* site; **s. web** website

sitio² *nm* siege; **estado de s.** state of emergency

sito, -a *adj Fml* situated, located

situación *nf* (**a**) *(circunstancias)* situation; *(legal, social)* status; **su s. económica es** buena his financial position is good; **estar en s. de hacer algo** to be in a position to do sth (**b**) *(ubicación)* location, situation

situado, -a *adj* situated; *Fig* **estar bien s.** to have a good position

situar [30] **1** *vt* to locate
  2 situarse *vpr* to be situated o located

sketch *(pl* **sketches)** *nm Cin & Teatro* sketch

skin [es'kin] *(pl* **skin** o **skins**), **skinhead** [es'kineð] *(pl* **skinheads)** *nmf* skinhead

S.L. *(abr* **Sociedad Limitada)** *Br* ≃ Ltd, *US* ≃ Inc

slip *(pl* **slips)** *nm* briefs

slogan *nm* slogan

S.M. *(abr* **Su Majestad)** *(rey)* His Majesty; *(reina)* Her Majesty

SMS *nm inv Tel (abr* **short message service)** SMS; **un S.** an SMS

s/n. *(abr* **sin número)** = abbreviation used in addresses after the street name, where the building has no number

snob *adj & nmf* = **esnob**

snobismo *nm* = **esnobismo**

so¹ *prep (bajo)* under; **so pena de** under penalty of

so² *nm Fam* **¡so imbécil!** you damned idiot!

sobaco *nm* armpit

sobar *vt (tocar)* to finger, to paw; *Fam (persona)* to touch up, to fondle

soberanía *nf* sovereignty

soberano, -a 1 *adj* (**a**) *(independiente)* sovereign (**b**) *Fam (grande)* massive
  2 *nm,f (monarca)* sovereign

soberbia *nf* pride

soberbio, -a *adj* (**a**) *(arrogante)* proud (**b**) *(magnífico)* splendid, magnificent

sobornar *vt* to bribe

soborno *nm (acción)* bribery; *(dinero etc)* bribe

sobra *nf* (**a**) **de s.** *(no necesario)* superfluous; **tener de s.** to have plenty; **estar de s.** not to be needed; **saber algo de s.** to know sth only too well (**b**) **sobras** *(restos)* leftovers

sobradamente *adv* only too well

sobrado, -a *adj (que sobra)* abundant, more than enough; **sobradas veces** repeatedly; **andar s. de tiempo/dinero** to have plenty of time/money

sobrante 1 *adj* remaining, spare
  2 *nm* surplus, excess

sobrar *vi* (**a**) *(haber de más)* to be more than enough, *(singular)* to be too much, *(plural)* to be too many; **sobran tres sillas** there are three chairs too many; **sobran comentarios** I've nothing further to add;

Fam **tú sobras aquí** you are not wanted here (**b**) *(quedar)* to be left over; **ha sobrado carne** there's still some meat left

sobrasada *nf* sausage spread

sobre[1] *nm* (**a**) *(para carta)* envelope (**b**) *(de sopa etc)* packet

sobre[2] *prep* (**a**) *(encima de)* on, upon, on top of (**b**) *(por encima)* over, above (**c**) *(acerca de)* about, on (**d**) *(aproximadamente)* about; **vendré s. las ocho** I'll come at about eight o'clock (**e**) **s. todo** especially, above all

sobre- *pref* super-, over-

sobrealimentado, -a *adj* overfed

sobrecarga *nf* overload

sobrecargar [42] *vt* to overload

sobrecogedor, -a *adj* dramatic, awesome

sobrecoger [53] *vt (impresionar)* to shock; *(asustar)* to frighten, to startle

sobredosis *nf inv* overdose

sobreentenderse *vpr* **se sobreentiende** that goes without saying

sobrehumano, -a *adj* superhuman

sobreimpresión *nf Fot & Cin* superimposing

sobrellevar *vt* to endure, to bear

sobremesa[1] *nf* afternoon

sobremesa[2] *nf* **ordenador de s.** desktop computer

sobrenatural *adj* supernatural

sobrenombre *nm* nickname

sobrepasar 1 *vt* to exceed, to surpass; *(rival)* to beat
  2 sobrepasarse *vpr* to go too far

sobrepeso *nm (de carga)* overload, excess weight; *(de persona)* excess weight

sobreponer [19] *(pp* **sobrepuesto**) **1** *vt* (**a**) *(poner encima)* to put on top (**b**) *Fig (anteponer)* **s. algo a algo** to put sth before sth
  2 sobreponerse *vpr* **sobreponerse a algo** to overcome sth

sobreproducción *nf* overproduction

sobrepuesto, -a *pp de* **sobreponer**

sobresaliente 1 *nm (nota)* ≃ A
  2 *adj (que destaca)* outstanding, excellent

sobresalir [22] *vi* to stick out, to protrude; *Fig (destacar)* to stand out, to excel

sobresaltar 1 *vt* to startle
  2 sobresaltarse *vpr* to be startled, to start

sobresalto *nm (movimiento)* start; *(susto)* fright

sobreseer [36] *vt Der* to stay; **s. una causa** to stay proceedings

sobretiempo *nm Andes* (**a**) *(en trabajo)* overtime (**b**) *(en deporte) Br* extra time, *US* overtime

sobrevalorar *vt* to overestimate

sobrevenir [27] *vi* to happen unexpectedly

sobreviviente 1 *adj* surviving
  2 *nmf* survivor

sobrevivir *vi* to survive

sobrevolar [2] *vt* to fly over

sobriedad *nf* sobriety; *(en la bebida)* soberness

sobrino, -a *nm (hombre)* nephew; *(mujer)* niece; **mis sobrinos** my nieces and nephews

sobrio, -a *adj* sober

socarrón, -ona *adj* sarcastic

socavar *vt* to undermine

socavón *nm (hoyo)* hollow; *(en la carretera)* pothole

sociable *adj* sociable, friendly

social *adj* social

socialdemócrata 1 *adj* social democratic
  2 *nmf* social democrat

socialismo *nm* socialism

socialista *adj & nmf* socialist

socializar [40] *vt* to socialize

sociedad *nf* (**a**) *(de seres vivos)* society; **s. de consumo** consumer society (**b**) *(asociación)* association, society (**c**) *Com (empresa)* company; **s. anónima** *Br* public (limited) company, *US* incorporated company; **s. limitada** private limited company

socio, -a *nm,f* (**a**) *(miembro)* member; **hacerse s. de un club** to become a member of a club, to join a club (**b**) *Com (asociado)* partner

sociología *nf* sociology

sociológico, -a *adj* sociological

sociólogo, -a *nm,f* sociologist

socorrer *vt* to help, to assist

socorrido, -a *adj* handy, useful

socorrismo *nm* first aid; *(en la playa)* lifesaving

socorrista *nmf* life-saver, lifeguard

socorro *nm* help, assistance; **¡s.!** help!; **puesto de s.** first-aid post

soda *nf* soda water

soez *adj* vulgar, crude

sofá *nm* sofa, settee; **s. cama** sofa bed, studio couch

sofisticado, -a *adj* sophisticated

sofocado, -a *adj* suffocated

sofocante *adj* suffocating, stifling; **hacía un calor s.** it was unbearably hot

sofocar [44] **1** *vt* (**a**) *(ahogar)* to suffocate, to smother (**b**) *(incendio)* to extinguish, to put out
2 sofocarse *upr* (**a**) *(ahogarse)* to suffocate, to stifle (**b**) *Fam (irritarse)* to get upset

sofoco *nm Fig (vergüenza)* embarrassment; **le dio un s.** *(disgusto)* it gave her quite a turn

sofocón *nm Fam* shock; **llevarse un s.** to get upset

sofreír [56] *vt* to fry lightly, to brown

sofrito *nm* = fried tomato and onion sauce

software ['sofwer] *nm* software

soga *nf* rope; *Fig* **estar con la s. al cuello** to be in dire straits

soja *nf* (**a**) *(planta, fruto) Br* soya bean, *US* soy bean (**b**) *(proteína)* soya

sojuzgar [42] *vt* to subjugate

sol[1] *nm* (**a**) *(astro)* sun (**b**) *(luz)* sunlight; *(luz y calor)* sunshine; **hace s.** it's sunny, the sun is shining; **tomar el s.** to sunbathe; **al o bajo el s.** in the sun; **de s. a s.** from sunrise to sunset (**c**) *Fin* = standard monetary unit of Peru

sol[2] *nm Mús* G; *(solfeo)* so

solamente *adv* only; **no s.** not only; **s. con mirarte lo sé** I know just by looking at you; **s. que ...** except that ...

solapa *nf (de chaqueta)* lapel; *(de sobre, bolsillo, libro)* flap

solapadamente *adv* stealthily, in an underhand way

solapado, -a *adj (persona)* sly

solapamiento *nm* overlap

solapar *vt* to cover up

solar[1] *adj* solar; **luz s.** sunlight

solar[2] *nm (terreno)* plot; *(en obras)* building site

solario, solárium *(pl* solariums*) nm* solarium

solaz *nm Fml (descanso)* rest, relaxation; *(esparcimiento)* recreation, entertainment

solazarse [40] *upr (relajar)* to relax; *(divertir)* to entertain oneself, to amuse oneself

soldado *nm* soldier; **s. raso** private

soldador, -a 1 *nm,f* welder
2 *nm* soldering iron

soldar [2] *vt (cable)* to solder; *(chapa)* to weld

soleado, -a *adj* sunny

soledad *nf (estado)* solitude; *(sentimiento)* loneliness

solemne *adj* (**a**) *(majestuoso)* solemn (**b**) *Pey* downright

solemnidad *nf* solemnity

soler [4] *vi* (**a**) *(en presente)* to be in the habit of; **solemos ir en coche** we usually go by car; **sueles equivocarte** you are usually wrong (**b**) *(en pasado)* **solía pasear por aquí** he used to walk round here

solera *nf* **de s.** old-established; **vino de s.** vintage wine

solfa *nf Mús* solfa; *Fam* **poner en s.** to ridicule

solicitar *vt (información etc)* to request, to ask for; *(trabajo)* to apply for

solícito, -a *adj* obliging, attentive

solicitud *nf (petición)* request; *(de trabajo)* application

solidaridad *nf* solidarity

solidario, -a *adj (actitud)* supportive; (**con** of); **ser s. con algn** to show solidarity with sb

solidarizarse *upr* to show one's solidarity (**con** with)

solidez *nf* solidity, strength

sólido, -a *adj* solid, strong

soliloquio *nm* soliloquy

solista *nmf* soloist

solitario, -a 1 *adj (que está solo)* solitary, lone; *(que se siente solo)* lonely
2 *nm* (**a**) *(diamante)* solitaire (**b**) *Naipes Br* patience, *US* solitaire

soliviantar *vt (incitar)* to stir up; *(indignar)* to exasperate

sollozar [40] *vi* to sob

sollozo *nm* sob

solo, -a 1 *adj* (**a**) *(sin nadie)* alone; *(único)* single; **ni un s. día** not a single day; **una sola vez** only once, just once (**b**) *(solitario)* lonely (**c**) **hablar s.** to talk to oneself; **se enciende s.** it switches itself on automatically; **a solas** alone, by oneself
2 *nm Mús* solo

sólo *adv* only; **tan s.** only; **no s. ... sino (también)** not only ... but (also); **con s., (tan) s. con** just by

> Note that the adverb **sólo** can be written without an accent when there is no risk of confusion with the adjective.

solomillo *nm* sirloin

soltar [2] **1** *vt* (**a**) *(desasir)* to let go of; **¡suéltame!** let me go! (**b**) *(prisionero)* to release (**c**) *(humo, olor)* to give off (**d**) *(bofetada)* to deal; *(carcajada)* to let out; **me soltó un rollo** he bored me to tears
2 soltarse *upr* (**a**) *(desatarse)* to come loose (**b**) *(perro etc)* to get loose, to break loose (**c**) *(desprenderse)* to come off

soltero, -a 1 *adj* single, unmarried
2 *nm (hombre)* bachelor, single man
3 *nf* **soltera** *(mujer)* single woman, spinster

solterón, -ona *nm,f* old bachelor, *f* old maid

soltura *nf (agilidad)* agility; *(seguridad)* confidence, assurance; **habla italiano con s.** he speaks Italian fluently

soluble *adj* soluble; **café s.** instant coffee

solución *nf* solution

solucionar *vt* to solve; *(arreglar)* to settle

solvencia *nf* **(a)** *Fin* solvency **(b)** *(fiabilidad)* reliability; **fuentes de toda s.** completely reliable sources

solventar *vt (problema)* to solve, to resolve; *(deuda, asunto)* to settle

solvente *adj* **(a)** *Fin* solvent **(b)** *(fiable)* reliable

sombra *nf* **(a)** *(silueta proyectada)* shadow; **s. de ojos** eyeshadow; *Fam Fig* **tener mala s.** to be nasty *o* a swine **(b)** *(zona)* shade; **a la s.** in the shade

sombrero *nm* hat; **s. de copa** top hat; **s. hongo** *Br* bowler hat, *US* derby

sombrilla *nf* parasol, sunshade

sombrío, -a *adj (oscuro)* dark; *(tenebroso)* sombre, gloomy; *Fig (persona)* gloomy, sullen

somero, -a *adj* superficial, shallow

someter 1 *vt* **(a)** **s. a algn a algo** to subject sb to sth; **s. a prueba** to put to the test; **s. algo a votación** to put sth to the vote **(b)** *(rebeldes)* to subdue, to put down
2 someterse *vpr* **(a)** *(subordinarse)* to submit **(b)** *(rendirse)* to surrender, to yield **(c)** **someterse a un tratamiento** to undergo treatment

somier *nm* spring mattress

somnífero *nm* sleeping pill

somnoliento, -a *adj* sleepy, drowsy

son *nm* sound; **al s. del tambor** to the sound of the drum; **venir en s. de paz** to come in peace

sonado, -a *adj* **(a)** *(renombrado)* much talked of **(b)** *Fam (trastocado)* mad, crazy

sonajero *nm* rattle

sonámbulo, -a *nm,f* somnambulist, sleepwalker

sonar [2] **1** *vi* **(a)** *(producir sonido)* to sound; **sonaba una sirena** you could hear (the sound of) a siren; **s. a** to sound like; **suena bien** it sounds good **(b)** *(timbre, teléfono)* to ring; **sonaron las cinco** the clock struck five **(c)** *(ser familiar)* **tu nombre/cara me suena** your name/face rings a bell
2 sonarse *vpr* **sonarse (la nariz)** to blow one's nose

sonda *nf* **(a)** *Med* sound, probe **(b)** **s. espacial** space probe

sondear *vt* **(a)** *(opinión)* to test, to sound out **(b)** *Med* to sound, to probe **(c)** *Náut* to sound

sondeo *nm* **(a)** *(encuesta)* poll **(b)** *Med* sounding, probing **(c)** *Náut* sounding

soneto *nm Lit* sonnet

sonido *nm* sound

sonoro, -a *adj* **(a)** *Cin* sound; **banda sonora** soundtrack **(b)** *(resonante)* loud, resounding **(c)** *Ling* voiced

sonreír [56] **1** *vi* to smile; **me sonrió** she smiled at me
2 sonreírse *vpr* to smile

sonriente *adj* smiling

sonrisa *nf* smile

sonrojarse *vpr* to blush

sonsacar [44] *vt* **s. algo a algn** to extract sth from sb

sonso, -a *adj Am* foolish, silly

soñador, -a *nm,f* dreamer

soñar [2] *vt & vi* to dream; **s. con** to dream of *o* about; *Fig* **¡ni soñarlo!** not on your life!; **s. despierto** to daydream

soñoliento, -a *adj* sleepy, drowsy

sopa *nf* soup; **s. juliana** spring vegetable soup; *Fig* **quedar hecho una s.** to get soaked to the skin

sope *nm Méx* = fried corn tortilla, with beans and cheese or other toppings

sopera *nf* soup tureen

sopero, -a *adj* **cucharada sopera** soup spoon

sopesar *vt* to weigh up

sopetón *nm Fam* **de s.** all of a sudden

soplagaitas *nmf inv Fam* jerk, *Br* prat

soplar 1 *vi (viento)* to blow
2 *vt* **(a)** *(polvo etc)* to blow away **(b)** *(para enfriar)* to blow on **(c)** *(para apagar)* to blow out **(d)** *(para inflar)* to blow up **(e)** *(en examen etc)* **me sopló las respuestas** he whispered the answers to me

soplete *nm* blowlamp, blowtorch

soplido *nm* blow, puff

soplillo *nm Fam* **orejas de s.** sticky-out ears

soplo *nm* **(a)** *(acción)* blow, puff; *(de viento)* gust **(b)** *Med* murmur

soplón, -ona *nm,f Fam (niño)* telltale, sneak; *(delator) Br* grass, *US* rat

soporífero, -a *adj* **(a)** *(que adormece)* soporific, sleep-inducing **(b)** *(aburrido)* boring, dull

soportable *adj* bearable

soportal *nm* porch; **soportales** arcade

soportar *vt* (**a**) *(peso)* to support, to bear (**b**) *Fig (calor, ruido)* to bear, to endure; *(situación)* to put up with, to bear; **no te soporto** I can't stand you

soporte *nm* support; **s. publicitario** advertising medium

soprano *nmf* soprano

sorber *vt* (**a**) *(beber)* to sip (**b**) *(absorber)* to soak up, to absorb

sorbete *nm* sorbet, sherbet

sorbo *nm* sip; *(trago)* gulp; **de un s.** in one gulp

sordera *nf* deafness

sórdido, -a *adj* squalid, sordid

sordo, -a 1 *adj* (**a**) *(persona)* deaf; **s. como una tapia** stone-deaf (**b**) *(golpe, ruido, dolor)* dull
2 *nm,f* deaf person; **los sordos** the deaf *pl*; *Fam Fig* **hacerse el s.** to turn a deaf ear

sordomudo, -a 1 *adj* deaf and dumb, deaf-mute
2 *nm,f* deaf and dumb person, deaf-mute

soroche *nm* (**a**) *Andes, Arg (mal de altura)* altitude sickness (**b**) *Chile (rubor)* blush, flush

sorprendente *adj* surprising

sorprender *vt* (**a**) *(extrañar)* to surprise (**b**) *(coger desprevenido)* to catch unawares, to take by surprise

sorpresa *nf* surprise; **coger de** *o* **por s.** to take by surprise

sorpresivo, -a *adj* unexpected, surprising

sortear *vt* (**a**) *(echar a suertes)* to draw lots for; *(rifar)* to raffle (off) (**b**) *(evitar)* to avoid, to get round

sorteo *nm* draw; *(rifa)* raffle

sortija *nf* ring

sortilegio *nm* spell

SOS *nm* SOS

sosa *nf* soda; **s. cáustica** caustic soda

sosegado, -a *adj* calm, quiet

sosegar [1] **1** *vt* to calm, to quieten
2 sosegarse *vpr* to calm down

sosiego *nm* *(calma)* calmness; *(paz)* peace, tranquillity

soslayo: de soslayo *loc adv* **mirar de s.** to look sideways (at)

soso, -a *adj* lacking in salt; *Fig (persona)* insipid, dull

sospecha *nf* suspicion

sospechar 1 *vi* to suspect; **s. de algn** to suspect sb
2 *vt* to suspect

sospechoso, -a 1 *adj* suspicious; **s. de** suspected of
2 *nm,f* suspect

sostén *nm* (**a**) *(apoyo)* support (**b**) *(sustento)* sustenance (**c**) *(prenda)* bra, brassière

sostener [24] **1** *vt* (**a**) *(sujetar)* to support, to hold up (**b**) *(con la mano)* to hold (**c**) *Fig (teoría etc)* to defend, to uphold; **s. que … to maintain that … (d**) *(conversación)* to hold, to sustain (**e**) *(familia)* to support
2 sostenerse *vpr* (**a**) *(mantenerse)* to support oneself (**b**) *(permanecer)* to stay, to remain

sostenible *adj (desarrollo)* sustainable

sostenido, -a *adj* (**a**) *(continuado)* sustained (**b**) *Mús* sharp

sostuve *pt indef de* **sostener**

sota *nf Naipes* jack, knave

sotana *nf* cassock, soutane

sótano *nm* basement, cellar

soto *nm* grove

soviético, -a *adj & nm,f* Soviet; *Hist* **la Unión Soviética** the Soviet Union

soy *indic pres de* **ser**

sport: de sport *loc adj* casual, sports; **chaqueta de s.** sports jacket

spot *(pl* **spots)** *nm TV* commercial, advert, ad

spray *(pl* **sprays)** *nm* spray

sprint *(pl* **sprints)** *nm* sprint

squash *nm inv Dep* squash

Sr. *(abr* **Señor)** Mr

Sra. *(abr* **Señora)** Mrs

S.R.C., s.r.c. *(abr* **se ruega contestación)** please reply, R.S.V.P.

Sres. *(abr* **señores)** Messrs

Srta. *(abr* **Señorita)** Miss

SS.AA. *(abr* **Sus Altezas)** Their Royal Highnesses

SS.MM. *(abr* **Sus Majestades)** their Royal Highnesses

Sta. *(abr* **Santa)** St

stand *(pl* **stands)** *nm Com* stand

standard *adj & nm* standard

standing *(pl* **standings)** *nm* standing, social status; **un apartamento de alto s.** a luxury flat

status *nm inv* status

Sto. *(abr* **Santo)** St

stock *(pl* **stocks)** *nm Com* stock

stop *(pl* **stops)** *nm (señal)* stop sign

su *(pl* **sus)** *adj pos (de él)* his; *(de ella)* her; *(de usted, ustedes)* your; *(de animales o cosas)* its; *(impersonal)* one's; *(de ellos)* their; **su coche** his/her/your/their car; **su pata** its leg; **sus libros** his/her/your/their books; **sus patas** its legs

suave adj (piel, color, voz) soft; (jabón, sabor, clima) mild; (movimiento) smooth; (cuesta, brisa, carácter) gentle

> 🖉 Observa que la palabra inglesa **suave** es un falso amigo y no es la traducción de la palabra española **suave**. En inglés **suave** significa "fino, cortés".

suavidad nf (de piel, color, voz) softness; (de jabón, sabor, clima) mildness; (de movimiento) smoothness; (de cuesta, brisa, carácter) gentleness

suavizante nm (para el pelo) (hair) conditioner; (para la ropa) fabric softener

suavizar [40] **1** vt (poner blando) to soften; (hacer liso) to smooth; (ropa, cabello) to condition
2 suavizarse vpr (temperatura) to get milder; (persona) to calm down

subacuático, -a adj underwater

subalimentado, -a adj undernourished, underfed

subalterno, -a adj & nm,f subordinate, subaltern

subarrendar [1] vt to sublet, to sublease

subasta nf (a) (venta) auction (b) (contrata) tender

subastar vt to auction (off), to sell at auction

subcampeón, -ona nm,f Dep runner-up

subconsciente adj & nm subconscious

subcontratación nf Com outsourcing

subdesarrollado, -a adj underdeveloped

subdesarrollo nm underdevelopment

subdirector, -a nm,f assistant manager

subdirectorio nm Inform subdirectory

súbdito, -a nm,f subject, citizen; **s. francés** French citizen

subdividir vt to subdivide

subestimar vt to underestimate

subida nf (a) (de temperatura) rise; (de precios, salarios) rise, increase (b) (ascenso) ascent, climb (c) (pendiente) slope, hill (d) Fam (drogas) high

subido, -a adj **s. de tono** daring, risqué

subir 1 vt (a) (calle, escaleras, montaña) to go up (b) (llevar arriba) to take/bring up; (poner arriba) to lift up (c) (precio, salario) to raise, to put up; (volumen) to turn up; (voz) to raise
2 vi (a) (ir arriba) to go/come up (b) **s. a** (coche) to get into; (autobús) to get on; (barco, avión, tren) to board, to get on (c) (precio, temperatura) to rise, to go up
3 subirse vpr (a) **subirse a** (árbol) to climb up; (mesa) to climb onto; Fig **el vino se le subió a la cabeza** the wine

went to his head (b) **subirse a** (coche) to get into; (autobús, avión, tren) to get on, to board; (caballo, bici) to get on (c) (cremallera) to do up; (mangas) to roll up

súbitamente adv suddenly

súbito, -a adj sudden

subjetivo, -a adj subjective

subjuntivo, -a adj & nm subjunctive

sublevación nf rising, rebellion

sublevar 1 vt Fig (indignar) to infuriate, to enrage
2 sublevarse vpr to rebel, to revolt

sublime adj sublime

submarinismo nm skin-diving

submarinista nmf scuba diver

submarino, -a 1 adj submarine, underwater
2 nm submarine

subnormal 1 adj (retrasado) mentally retarded; (insulto) moronic
2 nmf (retrasado) mentally retarded person; (insulto) moron, cretin

suboficial nmf Mil noncommissioned officer

subordinado, -a adj & nm,f subordinate

subordinar vt to subordinate

subproducto nm by-product

subrayar vt to underline

subrepticio, -a adj surreptitious

subrutina nf subroutine

subsanar vt (error) to rectify, to put right; (daño) to make up for

subscribir (pp subscrito) vt = suscribir

subscripción nf subscription

subscrito, -a pp de subscribir

subsecretario, -a nm,f undersecretary

subsidiario, -a adj subsidiary

subsidio nm allowance, benefit; **s. de desempleo** unemployment benefit

subsistencia nf subsistence

subsistir vi to subsist, to remain; (vivir) to live on, to survive

subsuelo nm subsoil

subte nm RP metro, Br underground, US subway

subterráneo, -a 1 adj underground
2 nm (túnel) tunnel, underground passage

subtítulo nm subtitle

suburbano, -a 1 adj suburban
2 nm (tren) suburban train

suburbio nm poor suburb

subvención nf subsidy

subvencionar vt to subsidize

subversión nf subversion

subversivo, -a adj subversive
subyacente adj underlying
subyugar [42] vt to subjugate
succionar vt to suck (in)
sucedáneo, -a adj & nm substitute
suceder 1 vi (**a**) (ocurrir) (uso impers) to happen, to occur; **¿qué sucede?** what's going on?, what's the matter? (**b**) (seguir) to follow, to succeed
　2 sucederse vpr to follow one another, to come one after the other
sucesión nf (**a**) (serie) series sing, succession (**b**) (al trono) succession (**c**) (descendencia) issue, heirs
sucesivamente adv **y así s.** and so on
sucesivo, -a adj following, successive; **en lo s.** from now on
suceso nm (hecho) event, occurrence; (incidente) incident; Prensa **sección de sucesos** accident and crime reports

⚠ Observa que la palabra inglesa **success** es un falso amigo y no es la traducción de la palabra española **suceso**. En inglés, **success** significa "éxito".

sucesor, -a nm,f successor
suciedad nf (**a**) (porquería) dirt (**b**) (calidad) dirtiness
sucinto, -a adj concise, succinct
sucio, -a 1 adj dirty; **en s.** in rough; Fig **juego s.** foul play; Fig **negocio s.** shady business
　2 adv **jugar s.** to play dirty
sucre nm Fin sucre, = standard monetary unit of Ecuador
suculento, -a adj succulent, juicy
sucumbir vi to succumb, to yield
sucursal nf Com & Fin branch, branch office
sudaca nmf Fam Pey South American
sudadera nf sweatshirt
Sudáfrica n South Africa
sudafricano, -a adj & nm,f South African
Sudamérica n South America
sudamericano, -a adj & nm,f South American
sudar vt & vi to sweat; Fam Fig **s. la gota gorda** to sweat blood
sudeste nm southeast
sudoeste nm southwest
sudor nm sweat; Fig **con el s. de mi frente** by the sweat of my brow
sudoroso, -a adj sweaty
Suecia n Sweden
sueco, -a 1 adj Swedish
　2 nm,f (persona) Swede
　3 nm (idioma) Swedish

suegro, -a nm (hombre) father-in-law; (mujer) mother-in-law; **mis suegros** my in-laws
suela nf (de zapato) sole
sueldo nm salary, wages; **sueldo mínimo** minimum wage
suelo nm (**a**) (superficie) ground; (de interior) floor; Fig **estar por los suelos** (precios) to be rock-bottom (**b**) (territorio) soil, land (**c**) (campo, terreno) land; **s. cultivable** arable land (**d**) (de carretera) surface
suelto, -a 1 adj (**a**) (animal, criminal, tornillo) loose (**b**) (no envasado, separado) loose; **hojas sueltas** loose sheets (of paper); **se venden sueltos** they are sold singly o separately o loose; **dinero s.** loose change
　2 nm (dinero) (loose) change
sueño nm (**a**) (estado) sleep; (ganas de dormir) sleepiness; **tener s.** to feel o be sleepy (**b**) (cosa soñada) dream
suero nm Med serum; (de la leche) whey
suerte nf (**a**) (fortuna) luck; **por s.** fortunately; **probar s.** to try one's luck; **tener s.** to be lucky; **¡que tengas s.!** good luck! (**b**) **echar algo** Esp **a suertes** o Am **a la s.** to draw lots for sth (**c**) (destino) fate, destiny (**d**) Fml (género) kind, sort, type
suéter nm sweater
suficiente 1 adj (bastante) sufficient, enough
　2 nm Educ pass
suficientemente adv sufficiently; **no es lo s. rico como para …** he isn't rich enough to …
sufijo nm suffix
sufragar [42] **1** vt (gastos) to pay, defray
　2 vi Am to vote
sufragio nm Pol suffrage; (voto) vote
sufrido, -a adj (persona) long-suffering
sufrimiento nm suffering
sufrir 1 vi to suffer; **s. del corazón** to have a heart condition
　2 vt (**a**) (accidente) to have; (operación) to undergo; (dificultades, cambios) to experience; **s. dolores de cabeza** to suffer from headaches (**b**) (aguantar) to bear, to put up with
sugerencia nf suggestion
sugerente adj suggestive
sugerir [5] vt to suggest
sugestión nf suggestion
sugestionar 1 vt to influence
　2 sugestionarse vpr to become obsessed
sugestivo, -a adj suggestive; (atractivo) alluring
suiche nm Col, Ven switch

suicida 1 *nmf (persona)* suicide
  2 *adj* suicidal

suicidarse *upr* to commit suicide, to kill oneself

suicidio *nm* suicide

suite *nf* suite

Suiza *n* Switzerland

suizo, -a 1 *adj* Swiss
  2 *nm,f (persona)* Swiss
  3 *nm Esp (bollo)* = type of sugared bun

sujetador *nm Esp* bra, brassière

sujetar 1 *vt* (a) *(agarrar)* to hold (b) *(fijar)* to hold down, to hold in place (c) *Fig (someter)* to restrain
  2 sujetarse *upr (agarrarse)* to hold on

sujeto, -a 1 *nm* subject; *(individuo)* fellow, individual
  2 *adj (atado)* fastened, secure; **s. a** *(sometido)* subject to, liable to

sulfato *nm* sulphate

sulfurar 1 *vt Fam (exasperar)* to exasperate, to infuriate
  2 sulfurarse *upr Fam* to lose one's temper, to blow one's top

sultán *nm* sultan

suma *nf* (a) *(cantidad)* sum, amount (b) *Mat* sum, addition; **s. total** sum total (c) **en s.** in short

sumamente *adv* extremely, highly

sumar 1 *vt Mat* to add, to add up
  2 sumarse *upr* **sumarse a** *(huelga)* to join; *(propuesta)* to support

sumario, -a 1 *adj* summary, brief; *Der* **juicio s.** summary proceedings
  2 *nm Der* summary

sumarísimo, -a *adj Der* swift, expeditious

sumergible *adj & nm* submersible

sumergir [57] **1** *vt* to submerge, to submerse; *(hundir)* to sink, to plunge
  2 sumergirse *upr* to submerge, to go underwater; *(hundirse)* to sink

sumidero *nm* drain, sewer

suministrar *vt* to supply, to provide; **s. algo a algn** to supply sb with sth

suministro *nm* supply

sumir *vt* **s. a algn en** to plunge sb into

sumiso, -a *adj* submissive, obedient

sumo, -a *adj (supremo)* supreme; **con s. cuidado** with extreme care; **a lo s.** at (the) most

suntuoso, -a *adj* sumptuous, magnificent

supe *pt indef de* saber²

supeditar *vt* to subject (a to)

súper *Fam* **1** *adj* super, great
  2 *nm* (a) *(supermercado)* supermarket (b) *(gasolina) Br* four-star (petrol), *US* regular

superación *nf* overcoming; **afán de s.** drive to improve

superado, -a *adj* outdated, obsolete

superar 1 *vt* (a) *(obstáculo etc)* to overcome, to surmount; *(prueba)* to pass (b) *(aventajar)* to surpass, to excel
  2 superarse *upr* to improve o better oneself

superávit *nm* surplus

superdotado, -a 1 *adj* exceptionally gifted
  2 *nm,f* genius

superficial *adj* superficial

superficialidad *nf* superficiality

superficie *nf* surface; *(área)* area; *Com* **grandes superficies** hypermarkets

superfluo, -a *adj* superfluous

superhombre *nm* superman

superior 1 *adj* (a) *(posición)* top, upper (b) *(cantidad)* greater, higher, larger (a than) (c) *(calidad)* superior; **calidad s.** top quality (d) *Educ* higher
  2 *nm (jefe)* superior

superioridad *nf* superiority

supermán *nm* superman

supermercado *nm* supermarket

superpoblación *nf* overpopulation

superponer [19] *(pp* superpuesto*)* *vt* to superimpose

superpotencia *nf* superpower

superproducción *nf* (a) *Ind* overproduction (b) *Cin* mammoth production

superpuesto, -a 1 *adj* superimposed
  2 *pp de* superponer

supersónico, -a *adj* supersonic

superstición *nf* superstition

supersticioso, -a *adj* superstitious

supervisar *vt* to supervise

supervisor, -a *nm,f* supervisor

supervivencia *nf* survival

superviviente 1 *adj* surviving
  2 *nmf* survivor

supino, -a *adj* (a) *(boca arriba)* supine, face up (b) *(absoluto)* total, absolute

suplantar *vt* to supplant, to take the place of

suplementario, -a *adj* supplementary, additional

suplemento *nm* supplement; **sin s.** without extra charge

suplente *adj & nmf (sustituto)* substitute, stand-in; *Dep* substitute

supletorio, -a *adj* supplementary, additional; **cama supletoria** extra bed; **teléfono s.** extension

súplica *nf* entreaty, plea

suplicar [44] *vt* to beseech, to beg

suplicio nm (tortura) torture; Fig (tormento) torment

suplir vt (a) (reemplazar) to replace, to substitute (b) (compensar) to make up for

suponer [19] (pp **supuesto**) vt (a) (significar) to mean (b) (implicar) to entail (c) (representar) to account for (d) (pensar) to suppose; **supongo que sí** I suppose so; **supongamos que … let's** assume that … (e) (adivinar) to guess; **(me) lo suponía** I guessed as much

suposición nf supposition

supositorio nm suppository

supremacía nf supremacy

supremo, -a adj supreme

supresión nf (de ley) abolition; (de restricción) lifting; (de palabra) deletion; (de rebelión) suppression

suprimir vt (a) (ley, impuesto) to abolish; (restricción) to lift; (palabra) to delete, to take/leave out; (rebelión) to suppress (b) (omitir) to omit

supuesto, -a 1 adj (a) (asumido) supposed, assumed; **¡por s.!** of course!; **dar algo por s.** to take sth for granted (b) (presunto) alleged
2 nm assumption; **en el s. de que** on the assumption that
3 pp de **suponer**

supurar vi to suppurate, to fester

supuse pt indef de **suponer**

sur nm south

Suramérica n South America

suramericano, -a adj & nm,f South American

surcar [44] vt Agr to plough; Fig (olas) to cut through

surco nm Agr furrow; (en un disco) groove

sureño, -a 1 adj southern
2 nm,f southerner

sureste nm = **sudeste**

surf, surfing nm surfing

surfista nmf surfer

surgir [57] vi (aparecer) to arise, to emerge, to appear; (problema, dificultad) to crop up

suroeste nm = **sudoeste**

surrealista adj & nmf surrealist

surtido, -a 1 adj (a) (variado) assorted (b) **bien s.** well-stocked
2 nm selection, assortment

surtidor nm spout; **s. de gasolina** Br petrol pump, US gas pump

surtir vt (a) (proveer) to supply (de with) (b) **s. efecto** to have the desired effect

susceptible adj (a) (sensible) oversensitive (b) (posible) **s. de** liable to

suscitar vt (provocar) to cause, to provoke; (rebelión) to stir up, to arouse; (interés etc) to arouse

suscribir (pp **suscrito**) **1** vt (a) (ratificar) to subscribe to, to endorse (b) (firmar) to sign
2 suscribirse vpr to subscribe (a to)

suscripción nf subscription

suscrito, -a pp de **suscribir**

susodicho, -a adj above-mentioned, aforesaid

suspender 1 vt (a) (interrumpir) to suspend; (reunión) to adjourn (b) Esp (estudiante, examen) to fail (c) (colgar) to hang, to suspend
2 vi (alumno) to fail

suspense nm suspense; **novela/película de s.** thriller

suspensión nf (a) (de servicio) suspension; Fin & Der **s. de pagos** suspension of payments (b) Aut suspension

suspensivo, -a adj **puntos suspensivos** suspension points

suspenso nm (a) Esp (nota) **sacar un s.** to fail (b) **en s.** (asunto, trabajo) pending; **estar en s.** to be pending

suspicacia nf suspicion

suspicaz adj suspicious

suspirar vi to sigh

suspiro nm sigh

sustancia nf substance

sustancial adj substantial

sustantivo, -a 1 adj substantive
2 nm Ling noun

sustentar vt (a) (familia) to support (b) (teoría) to support, to defend

sustento nm (a) (alimento) sustenance, food (b) (apoyo) support

sustitución nf replacement

sustituir [37] vt to replace (**por** with); (temporalmente) to substitute for

sustituto, -a nm,f substitute, replacement

susto nm fright, scare; **llevarse o darse un s.** to get a fright

sustracción nf (a) (robo) theft (b) Mat subtraction

sustraer [25] vt (a) Mat to subtract (b) (robar) to steal, to remove

sustrato nm substratum

susurrar vt to whisper

susurro nm whisper

sutil adj (a) (diferencia, pregunta) subtle (b) (aroma) delicate

sutileza nf (dicho) subtlety

suyo, -a *adj & pron pos (de él)* his; *(de ella)* hers; *(de usted, ustedes)* yours; *(de animal o cosa)* its; *(de ellos, ellas)* theirs; **los zapatos no son suyos** the shoes aren't hers; **varios amigos suyos** several friends of his/hers/yours/theirs; *Fam* **es muy s.** he's very aloof; *Fam* **hacer de las suyas** to be up to one's tricks; *Fam* **ir (cada uno) a lo s.** to mind one's own business; *Fam* **salirse con la suya** to get one's (own) way

T, t [te] *nf (letra)* T, t

t *(abr* **tonelada(s))** t

tabaco *nm* (a) *(planta, hoja)* tobacco; **t. rubio** Virginia tobacco (b) *(cigarrillos)* cigarettes

tábano *nm* horsefly

tabaquismo *nm* smoking; **t. pasivo** passive smoking

tabarra *nf Fam* **dar la t.** to go on and on

tabasco® *nm*Tabasco® *(sauce)*

taberna *nf* pub, bar; *(antiguamente)* tavern

tabernero, -a *nm,f* publican; *(hombre)* landlord; *(mujer)* landlady

tabique *nm* (a) *(pared)* partition (wall) (b) *Anat* **t. nasal** nasal wall

tabla *nf* (a) *(de madera)* plank; *Dep (de surf, vela, trampolín)* board; **t. de planchar** ironing board; **t. de quesos** cheeseboard (b) *(lista, gráfico)* table; **t. de multiplicación** multiplication table (c) *(de vestido)* pleat (d) **tablas** *(en ajedrez)* stalemate, draw; **quedar en tablas** *(juego)* to end in a draw (e) *Fig* **tener (muchas) tablas** to be an old hand

tablado *nm (de teatro)* stage; *(de baile)* dancefloor; *(plataforma)* platform

tablao *nm Fam* = flamenco bar or show

tablero *nm* (a) *(tablón)* panel, board; **t. de mandos** *(de coche)* dash(board) (b) *(en juegos)* board; **t. de ajedrez** chessboard

tableta *nf (de chocolate)* bar

tablón *nm* plank; *(en construcción)* beam; **t. de anuncios** *Br* noticeboard, *US* bulletin board

tabú *(pl* **tabúes)** *adj & nm* taboo

tabular *vt* to tabulate

taburete *nm* stool

tacaño, -a 1 *adj* mean, stingy
2 *nm,f* miser

tacatá, tacataca *nm* baby-walker

tacha *nf* **sin t.** flawless, without blemish

tachar *vt* (a) *(lo escrito)* to cross out (b) *(acusar)* **t. de** to accuse of

tachero *nm RP Fam (de taxi)* taxi driver

tacho *nm Andes, RP (metálico, de hojalata)* tin; *(de plástico)* container; *(papelera) Br*
waste-paper bin *o* basket, *US* waste basket

tachón *nm (borrón)* crossing out

tachuela *nf* tack, stud

tácito, -a *adj* tacit

taciturno, -a *adj* (a) *(callado)* taciturn (b) *(triste)* sullen

taco *nm* (a) *(tarugo)* plug; *(de billetes)* wad; *(de bota de fútbol)* stud; *(en billar)* cue (b) *(cubo) (de jamón, queso)* cube, piece (c) *Culin (tortilla de maíz)* taco, = rolled-up tortilla pancake (d) *Esp Fam (palabrota)* swearword (e) *Esp Fam (lío)* mess, muddle; **armarse** *o* **hacerse un t.** to get all mixed up (f) **me gusta un t.** I like it a lot (g) *Esp Fam* **tacos** *(años)* years

tacón *nm* heel; **zapatos de t.** high-heeled shoes

taconeo *nm (pisada)* heel-tapping; *(golpe)* stamping with the heels

táctica *nf* tactics

táctico, -a *adj* tactical

táctil *adj* tactile; **pantalla t.** touch screen

tacto *nm* (a) *(sentido)* touch (b) *Fig (delicadeza)* tact; **tener t.** to be tactful

taekwondo *nm* tae kwon do

tafetán *nm* taffeta

tai-chi *nm* tai chi

tailandés, -esa 1 *adj & nm,f* Thai
2 *nm (idioma)* Thai

Tailandia *n* Thailand

taimado, -a *adj* sly, crafty

Taiwán [tai'wan] *n* Taiwan

tajada *nf* (a) *(de comida)* slice; *Fig* **sacar** *o* **llevarse t.** to take one's share (b) *Esp Fam (borrachera)* drunkenness

tajante *adj* incisive

Tajo *n* **el T.** the Tagus

tajo *nm* (a) *(corte)* deep cut (b) *Esp (trabajo)* workplace, work

tal 1 *adj* (a) *(semejante)* such; *(más sustantivo singular contable)* such a; **en tales condiciones** in such conditions; **nunca dije t. cosa** I never said such a thing (b) *(indeterminado)* such and such; **t. día y a t. hora** such and such a day and at such and such a time (c) *(persona)* person called …; **te llamó una t. Amelia**

someone called Amelia phoned you (**d**) (*locuciones*) **t. vez** perhaps, maybe; **como si t. cosa** as if nothing had happened

2 *adv* (**a**) (*así*) just; **t. cual** just as it is; (**y**) **como** just as (**b**) **¿qué t.?** how are things?; **¿qué t. ese vino?** how do you find this wine?

3 *conj* as; **con t. (de) que** (+ *subjunctive*) so long as, provided

4 *pron* (*cosa*) something; (*persona*) someone, somebody; **t. para cual** two of a kind; **y t. y cual** and so on

tala *nf* felling

taladradora *nf* drill

taladrar *vt* to drill; (*pared*) to bore through; (*papeles*) to punch

taladro *nm* (**a**) (*herramienta*) drill (**b**) (*agujero*) hole

talante *nm* (**a**) (*carácter*) character, disposition (**b**) (*voluntad*) **de buen t.** willingly; **de mal t.** unwillingly, reluctantly

talar *vt* (*árboles*) to fell, to cut down

talco *nm* talc; **polvos de t.** talcum powder

talego *nm Esp Fam* (*cárcel*) clink, hole

talento *nm* talent

Talgo *nm* = fast passenger train

talibán *adj & nmf* Taliban

talismán *nm* talisman, lucky charm

talla *nf* (**a**) (*de prenda*) size; **¿qué t. usas?** what size are you? (**b**) (*estatura*) height; *Fig* stature; *Fig* **dar la t.** to make the grade (**c**) (*escultura*) carving, sculpture (**d**) (*tallado*) cutting, carving

tallado *nm* (*de madera*) carving; (*de piedras preciosas*) cutting; (*de metales*) engraving

tallar *vt* (*madera, piedra*) to carve; (*piedras preciosas*) to cut; (*metales*) to engrave

tallarines *nmpl* tagliatelle

talle *nm* (**a**) (*cintura*) waist (**b**) (*cuerpo*) (*de hombre*) build, physique; (*de mujer*) figure, shape

taller *nm* (**a**) (*obrador*) workshop; *Aut* **t. de reparaciones** garage (**b**) *Ind* factory, mill

tallo *nm* stem, stalk

talón *nm* (**a**) (*del pie*) heel (**b**) (*cheque*) cheque

> ⏿ Observa que la palabra inglesa **talon** es un falso amigo y no es la traducción de la palabra española **talón**. En inglés, **talon** significa "garra".

talonario *nm* (*de cheques*) cheque book; (*de billetes*) book of tickets

tamal *nm* (*comida*) tamale, = steamed maize dumpling with savoury or sweet filling, wrapped in maize husks or a banana leaf

tamaño, -a 1 *adj* such a big, so big a

2 *nm* size; **de gran t.** large; **del t. de** as large as, as big as

tamarindo *nm* tamarind

tambalearse *vpr* (*persona*) to stagger; (*mesa*) to wobble; *Fig* to teeter

tambero *nm* (**a**) *RP* (*granjero*) dairy farmer (**b**) (*dueño*) (*de una tienda*) shopkeeper; (*de un tenderete*) stall holder

también *adv* (*igualmente*) too, also, as well; **tú t. puedes venir** you can come too; **¿lo harás? yo t.** are you going to do it? so am I

tambo *nm* (**a**) *Andes* (*posada*) wayside inn (**b**) *Andes* (*tienda*) shop; (*tenderete*) stall (**c**) *RP* (*granja*) dairy farm (**d**) *Méx* (*recipiente*) drum

tambor *nm* (**a**) (*musical, de lavadora*) drum (**b**) *Anat* eardrum

Támesis *n* **el T.** the Thames

tamiz *nm* sieve

tamizar [40] *vt* to sieve

tampoco *adv* (**a**) (*en afirmativas*) nor, neither; **Juan no vendrá y María t.** Juan won't come and neither will Maria; **no lo sé – yo t.** I don't know – neither do I (**b**) (*en negativas*) either, not … either; **la Bolsa no sube, pero t. baja** the stock market isn't going up, but it's not going down either

tampón *nm* tampon

tan *adv* (**a**) (*con adjetivo*) so; (*con sustantivo singular*) such a; **no me gusta t. dulce** I don't like it so sweet; **t. grande/ deprisa que …** so big/quickly that …; **nunca había visto una casa t. grande** I had never seen such a big house; **¡qué vestido t. bonito!** what a beautiful dress! (**b**) (*comparativo*) **t. … como** as … as; **t. alto como tú** as tall as you (are) (**c**) **t. siquiera** at least; **t. sólo** only

tanda *nf* (*conjunto*) batch, lot; (*serie*) series *sing*; **por tandas** in groups

tándem *nm* tandem

tanga *nm* tanga

tangente *nf* tangent; *Fig* **salirse** *o* **escaparse por la t.** to go off at a tangent

tangible *adj* tangible

tango *nm* tango

tanguero, -a 1 *adj* **ser muy t.** to love the tango

2 *nm,f* (*aficionado*) tango enthusiast

tanque *nm* tank

tantear 1 *vt* (**a**) **t. a algn** to sound sb out; **t. el terreno** to see how the land lies (**b**) (*calcular*) to estimate, to guess

2 *vi Dep* to (keep) score

tanteo nm (**a**) *(cálculo)* estimate, guess (**b**) *Dep* score

tanto, -a 1 nm (**a**) *(punto)* point (**b**) *(cantidad imprecisa)* so much, a certain amount; **t. por ciento** percentage (**c**) **un t.** a bit; **la casa es un t. pequeña** the house is rather o somewhat small (**d**) **estar al t.** *(informado)* to be informed; *(pendiente)* to be on the lookout

2 adj (**a**) (+ *singular*) so much; (+ *plural*) so many; **no le des t. dinero** don't give him so much money; **¡ha pasado t. tiempo!** it's been so long!; **no comas tantas manzanas** don't eat so many apples (**b**) **cincuenta y tantas personas** fifty-odd people; **en el año sesenta y tantos** in nineteen sixty-something (**c**) **t. como** as much as; **tantos como** as many as

3 pron (**a**) (+ *singular*) so much; **otro t.** as much again, the same again; **no es o hay para t.** it's not that bad (**b**) (+ *plural*) so many; **otros tantos** as many again; **uno de tantos** run-of-the-mill; *Fam* **a las tantas** very late, at an unearthly hour

4 adv (**a**) *(cantidad)* so much; **t. mejor/ peor** so much the better/worse; **t. más cuanto que** all the more so because (**b**) *(tiempo)* so long (**c**) *(frecuencia)* so often (**d**) **t. ... como** both ... and; **t. tú como yo** both you and I; **t. si vienes como si no** whether you come or not (**e**) *(locuciones)* **por lo t.** therefore; **¡y t.!** oh yes!, and how!

tañer vt to play

tapa nf (**a**) *(cubierta)* lid; *Andes, RP (de botella)* top; *(de libro)* cover; *(de zapato)* heelplate; *Aut (de cilindro)* head (**b**) *(aperitivo)* appetizer, snack

tapabarros nm inv (**a**) *(de hombre primitivo)* loincloth (**b**) *(tanga)* tanga briefs

tapadera nf *(tapa)* cover, lid; *Fig* cover, front

tapadillo: de tapadillo loc adv on the sly

tapado nm *CSur (abrigo)* overcoat

tapar 1 vt (**a**) *(cerrar) (recipiente)* to put the lid/top on; *(con ropa o manta)* to wrap up (**b**) *(ocultar)* to cover; *(vista)* to block (**c**) *(encubrir)* to cover up

2 taparse upr *(cubrirse)* to cover oneself; *(abrigarse)* to wrap up

taparrabos nm inv loincloth

tapeo nm *Esp* **ir de t.** to go out for some tapas

tapete nm (table) cover; *Fig* **poner algo sobre el t.** to table sth

tapia nf garden wall

tapiar [43] vt (**a**) *(área)* to wall off (**b**) *(puerta, ventana)* to wall, to close up

tapicería nf (**a**) *(de muebles, coche)* upholstery (**b**) *(tienda)* upholsterer's shop/ workshop (**c**) *(arte)* tapestry

tapioca nf tapioca

tapiz nm tapestry

tapizar [40] vt to upholster

tapón nm (**a**) *(de lavabo etc)* stopper, plug; *(de botella)* cap, cork; **t. de rosca** screw-on cap (**b**) *(de oídos)* earplug (**c**) *(en baloncesto)* block (**d**) *Aut* traffic jam (**e**) *Am (plomo)* fuse

taponar 1 vt (**a**) *(tubería, hueco)* to plug (**b**) *Med (herida)* to tampon

2 taponarse upr **se me han taponado los oídos** my ears are all blocked up

taquería nf *Méx (quiosco)* taco stall; *(restaurante)* taco restaurant

taquigrafía nf shorthand

taquígrafo, -a nm,f shorthand writer

taquilla nf (**a**) *(ventanilla)* ticket office, booking office; *Cin & Teatro* box-office; **un éxito de t.** a box-office success (**b**) *(recaudación)* takings (**c**) *(armario)* locker

taquillero, -a 1 adj popular; **película taquillera** box-office hit

2 nm,f booking o ticket clerk

tara nf (**a**) *(peso)* tare (**b**) *(defecto)* defect, fault

tarántula nf tarantula

tararear vt & vi to hum

tardanza nf delay

tardar 1 vt *(llevar tiempo)* to take; **¿cuánto va a t.?** how long will it take?; **tardé dos horas en venir** it took me two hours to get here

2 vi *(demorar)* to take long; **si tarda mucho, me voy** if it takes much longer, I'm going; **no tardes** don't be long; **a más t.** at the latest

3 tardarse upr **¿cuánto se tarda en llegar?** how long does it take to get there?

tarde 1 nf (**a**) *(hasta las cinco)* afternoon (**b**) *(después de las cinco)* evening (**c**) **la t. noche** late evening

2 adv late; **siento llegar t.** sorry I'm late; **de t. en t.** very rarely, not very often; **(más) t. o (más) temprano** sooner or later

tardío, -a adj late, belated

tarea nf job, task; **tareas** *(de ama de casa)* housework; *(de estudiante)* homework

tarifa nf (**a**) *(precio)* tariff, rate; *(en transportes)* fare (**b**) *(lista de precios)* price list

tarima nf platform, dais

tarjeta nf card; **t. de crédito** credit card; **t. postal** postcard; **t. de rasca y gana** scratchcard; **t. telefónica** phonecard; **t. de visita** visiting card, *US* calling card

tarraconense 1 *adj* of/from Tarragona
2 *nmf* person from Tarragona

tarro *nm* (**a**) *(vasija)* jar, pot (**b**) *Esp Fam (cabeza)* nut, *Br* bonce

tarta *nf* tart, pie

tartamudear *vi* to stutter, to stammer

tartamudo, -a 1 *adj* stuttering, stammering
2 *nm,f* stutterer, stammerer

tartana *nf Fam (coche viejo)* banger, heap

tártaro, -a *adj & nm, f* Tartar

tartera *nf* lunch box

tarugo *nm* (**a**) *(de madera)* lump of wood (**b**) *Fam (persona)* blockhead

tarumba *adj Fam* crazy, mad; **estar t.** to be bonkers

tasa *nf* (**a**) *(precio)* fee; **tasas académicas** course fees (**b**) *(impuesto)* tax; **tasas de aeropuerto** airport tax (**c**) *(índice)* rate; **t. de natalidad/mortalidad** birth/death rate (**d**) *(valoración)* valuation, appraisal

tasación *nf* valuation

tasador, -a *nm,f* valuer

tasar *vt* (**a**) *(valorar)* to value; **t. una casa en 10 millones de euros** to value a house at 10 million euros (**b**) *(poner precio)* to set *o* fix the price of

tasca *nf* cheap bar

tata 1 *nf Esp (niñera)* nanny
2 *nm Am Fam (papá)* dad, *US* pop

tatarabuelo, -a *nm,f (hombre)* great-great-grandfather; *(mujer)* great-great-grandmother; **tatarabuelos** great-great-grandparents

tataranieto, -a *nm,f (hombre)* great-great-grandson; *(mujer)* great-great-granddaughter; **tataranietos** great-great-grandchildren

tatuaje *nm* tattoo

tatuar [30] *vt* to tattoo

taurino, -a *adj* bullfighting

Tauro *nm* Taurus

tauromaquia *nf* tauromachy, (art of) bullfighting

taxativo, -a *adj* categorical

taxi *nm* taxi

taxímetro *nm* taximeter, clock

taxista *nmf* taxi driver

taza *nf* (**a**) *(para líquido)* cup; **una t. de café** *(recipiente)* coffee cup; *(contenido)* a cup of coffee (**b**) *(de retrete)* bowl

tazón *nm* bowl

te *pron pers* (**a**) *(complemento directo)* you; *(complemento indirecto)* (to/for) you; **no quiero verte** I don't want to see you; **te compraré uno** I'll buy one for you, I'll buy you one; **te lo dije** I told you so (**b**) *(reflexivo)* yourself; **lávate** wash yourself;

(sin traducción) **bébetelo todo** drink it up; **no te vayas** don't go

té *nm* tea; **té con limón** lemon tea

tea *nf* torch

teatral *adj* (**a**) **grupo t.** theatre company; **obra t.** play (**b**) *Fig (teatrero)* theatrical

teatrero, -a *adj* theatrical

teatro *nm* (**a**) *(espectáculo, edificio)* theatre; **obra de t.** play; **autor de t.** playwright (**b**) *(fingimiento)* play-acting

tebeo *nm Esp* (children's) comic

techar *vt* to roof

techo *nm (de habitación)* ceiling; *(tejado)* roof; *Aut* **t. corredizo** sun roof

tecla *nf* key; *Fig* **dar en la t.** to get it right

teclado *nm* keyboard; *Inform* **t. expandido** expanded keyboard

teclear 1 *vt* to key in
2 *vi* to drum with one's fingers

técnica *nf* (**a**) *(tecnología)* technology (**b**) *(método)* technique (**c**) *(habilidad)* skill

técnico, -a 1 *adj* technical
2 *nm,f* technician, technical expert

tecnócrata *nmf* technocrat

tecnología *nf* technology

tecnológico, -a *adj* technological

tecolote *nm CAm, Méx* owl

tedio *nm* tedium, boredom

tedioso, -a *adj* tedious, boring

teja *nf* tile; *Fam Fig* **a toca t.** on the nail

tejado *nm* roof

tejanos *nmpl* jeans

tejemaneje *nm Fam* intrigue, scheming

tejer *vt (en el telar)* to weave; *(hacer punto)* to knit; *(telaraña)* to spin; *Fig (plan)* to plot, to scheme

tejido *nm* (**a**) *(material)* fabric; **t. de punto** knitted fabric (**b**) *Anat* tissue

tejo *nm Esp Fam* **tirar los tejos a algn** to make a play for sb

tejón *nm* badger

tel. *(abr* **teléfono)** tel.

tela *nf* (**a**) *Tex* material, fabric, cloth; *(de la leche)* skin; **t. de araña** cobweb; **t. metálica** gauze (**b**) *Fam (dinero)* dough (**c**) *Arte* canvas (**d**) *Fig* **poner en t. de juicio** to question; *Fig* **tiene mucha t.** it's not an easy thing

telar *nm* loom

telaraña *nf* cobweb, spider's web

tele *nf Fam* TV, *Br* telly

telearrastre *nm* ski lift

telebanca *nf* telephone banking, home banking

telebasura *nf Fam* junk TV

telecabina *nf* cable car

telecomunicaciones *nfpl* telecommunications

telediario *nm* television news

teledirigido, -a *adj* remote-controlled

telefax *nm* telefax, fax

teleférico *nm* cable car

telefilm, telefilme *nm* TV film

telefonazo *nm* **dar un t. (a algn)** to give (sb) a buzz *o* *Br* ring

telefonear *vt & vi* to phone, *Br* to ring

telefonía *nf* **t. móvil** mobile phones

telefónica *nf* **Compañía T.** ≃ British Telecom

telefónico, -a *adj* telephone; **llamada telefónica** telephone call

telefonista *nmf* (telephone) operator

teléfono *nm* telephone, phone; **t. móvil** *or* *Am* **celular** *Br* mobile phone, *US* cellphone; **t. fijo** land line (phone); **t. inalámbrico** cordless telephone; **está hablando por t.** she's on the phone; **te llamó por t.** she phoned you

telegrafiar [29] *vt* to telegraph, to wire

telegráfico, -a *adj* telegraphic; **giro t.** giro, money order

telégrafo *nm* (a) *(medio, aparato)* telegraph (b) **telégrafos** telegraph office

telegrama *nm* telegram, cable

teleimpresora *nf* teleprinter

telele *nm Fam* **darle a uno un t.** to have a fit

telemando *nm* remote control (unit)

telemarketing *nm* telemarketing

telenovela *nf* television serial

teleobjetivo *nm* telephoto lens *sing*

telepatía *nf* telepathy

telepático, -a *adj* telepathic

telescopio *nm* telescope

teleserie *nf* television series *sing*

telesilla *nm* chair lift

telespectador, -a *nm,f* TV viewer

telesquí *(pl* telesquíes *o* telesquís*) nm* ski lift

teletexto *nm* teletext

teletienda *nf* home shopping programme

teletipo *nm* teleprinter

teletrabajador, -a *nm,f* teleworker

teletrabajo *nm* teleworking

televenta *nf* (por teléfono) telesales

televidente *nmf* TV viewer

televisar *vt* to televise

televisión *nf* (a) *(sistema)* television (b) *Fam (aparato)* television set; **t. en color/ en blanco y negro** colour/black-and-white television; **t. digital** digital television; **t. por cable** cable television; **ver la t.** to watch television

televisivo, -a *adj* television; **espacio t.** television programme

televisor *nm* television set

télex *nm inv* telex

telón *nm Teatro* curtain; *Pol & Hist* **t. de acero** Iron Curtain; **t. de fondo** *Teatro* backdrop; *Fig* background

telonero, -a *nm,f (grupo)* support (band); *(cantante)* supporting artist

tema *nm* (a) *(asunto)* topic, subject; *(de examen)* subject; **temas de actualidad** current affairs (b) *Mús* theme

temario *nm (de examen)* programme

temática *nf* subject matter

temático, -a *adj* thematic

temblar [1] *vi* (de frío) to shiver; *(de miedo, por nervios)* to tremble, to shake (de with); *(voz)* to quiver

tembleque *nm Fam* shaking fit

temblón, -ona *adj Fam* trembling, shaky

temblor *nm* tremor, shudder; **t. de tierra** earth tremor

tembloroso, -a *adj* shaking; *(voz)* quivering; *(de frío)* shivering; *(de miedo)* trembling; **manos temblorosas** shaky hands

temer 1 *vt* to fear, to be afraid of; **temo que esté muerto** I fear he's dead; **temo que no podrá recibirle** I'm afraid (that) he won't be able to see you
   2 *vi* to be afraid
   3 temerse *vpr* to fear, to be afraid; **¡me lo temía!** I was afraid this would happen!

temerario, -a *adj* reckless, rash

temeridad *nf* (a) *(actitud)* temerity, rashness (b) *(acto temerario)* reckless act

temeroso, -a *adj* fearful, timid

temible *adj* fearful, frightful

temor *nm* (a) *(miedo)* fear (b) *(recelo)* worry, apprehension

témpano *nm* ice floe

temperamental *adj* temperamental

temperamento *nm* temperament; **tener t.** to have a strong character

temperatura *nf* temperature

tempestad *nf* storm; *Fig* turmoil, uproar

tempestuoso, -a *adj* stormy, tempestuous

templado, -a *adj* (a) *(agua)* lukewarm; *(clima)* mild, temperate (b) *Mús (afinado)* tuned

templanza *nf* moderation, restraint

templar *vt* (a) *(algo frío)* to warm up; *(algo caliente)* to cool down (b) *(calmar)* (nervios, ánimos) to calm; *(ira, pasiones)* to restrain; *(voz)* to soften (c) *Mús (instrumento)* to tune (d) *Téc (metal)* to temper

temple *nm* (a) *(fortaleza)* boldness, courage (b) *Arte* tempera

templete *nm* bandstand

templo *nm* temple

temporada *nf* (a) *(periodo concreto)* season; **t. alta** high *o* peak season; **t. baja** low *o* off season (b) *(periodo indefinido)* (period of) time; **por temporadas** on and off

temporal 1 *adj* temporary, provisional
2 *nm* storm

temporario, -a *adj Am* temporary

temporero, -a *nm,f* seasonal *o* temporary worker

tempranero, -a *adj* (a) *(persona)* early-rising (b) *(cosecha)* early

temprano, -a *adj & adv* early

tenacidad *nf* tenacity, perseverance

tenacillas *nfpl* *(para pelo)* curling tongs

tenaz *adj* tenacious

tenaza *nf*, **tenazas** *nfpl* *(herramienta)* pliers, pincers; *(para el fuego)* tongs

tendedero *nm* clothes line, drying place

tendencia *nf* tendency

tendencioso, -a *adj* tendentious, biased

tender [3] **1** *vt* (a) *(mantel etc)* to spread out; *(para secar)* to hang out (b) *Am (cama)* to make; *(mesa)* to set, to lay (c) *(red)* to cast; *(puente)* to build; *(vía, cable)* to lay; *(trampa)* to lay, to set (d) *(mano)* to stretch *o* hold out (e) *(tumbar)* to lay
2 *vi* to tend (a to), have a tendency (a to)
3 tenderse *upr* to lie down, stretch out

tenderete *nm* *(puesto)* market stall

tendero, -a *nm,f* shopkeeper

tendido *nm* (a) *(de vía, cable)* laying; *(de puente)* construction; **t. eléctrico** electrical installation (b) *Taurom (asientos)* = front tiers of seats

tendón *nm* tendon, sinew

tenebroso, -a *adj* *(sombrío)* dark, gloomy; *(siniestro)* sinister, shady

tenedor *nm* fork

teneduría *nf* **t. de libros** bookkeeping

tenencia *nf* *Der* **t. ilícita de armas** illegal possession of arms

tener [24] **1** *vt* (a) to have, have got; **tenemos un examen** we've got *o* we have an exam; **va a t. un niño** she's going to have a baby, she's expecting; **¡ahí (lo) tienes!** there you are!
(b) *(poseer)* to own, possess
(c) *(sostener)* to hold; **tenme el bolso un momento** hold my bag a minute; **ten, es para ti** take this *o* here you are, it's for you
(d) **t. calor/frío** to be hot/cold; **t. cariño a algn** to be fond of sb; **t. miedo** to be frightened

(e) *(edad)* to be; **tiene dieciocho (años)** he's eighteen (years old)
(f) *Am (llevar)* **tengo tres años aquí** I've been here for three years
(g) *(medida)* **la casa tiene 100 metros cuadrados** the house is 100 square metres
(h) *(contener)* to hold, to contain
(i) *(mantener)* to keep; **me tuvo despierto toda la noche** he kept me up all night
(j) **t. por** *(considerar)* to consider, to think; **me tienen por estúpido** they think I'm a fool; **ten por seguro que lloverá** you can be sure it'll rain
(k) **t. que** to have (got) to; **tengo que irme** I must leave; **tienes/tendrías que verlo** you must/should see it
2 tenerse *upr* (a) **tenerse en pie** to stand (up) (b) **tenerse por** *(considerarse)* to think *o* consider oneself; **se tiene por muy inteligente** he thinks he's very intelligent

tenga *subj pres de* **tener**

tengo *indic pres de* **tener**

teniente *nm* (a) *Mil* lieutenant (b) **t. (de) alcalde** deputy mayor

tenis *nm* tennis

tenista *nmf* tennis player

tenor¹ *nm* *Mús* tenor

tenor² *nm* **a t. de** according to

tensar *vt* *(cable etc)* to tighten; *(arco)* to draw

tensión *nf* (a) *(estado emocional)* tension; **en t.** tense; **t. nerviosa** nervous tension (b) *(de la sangre)* **t. (arterial)** blood pressure (c) *Elec* voltage (d) *Téc* stress

tenso, -a *adj* (a) *(cuerda, cable)* tense, taut (b) *(persona)* tense; *(relaciones)* strained

tentación *nf* temptation

tentáculo *nm* tentacle

tentador, -a *adj* tempting

tentar [1] *vt* (a) *(palpar)* to feel, to touch (b) *(incitar)* to tempt

tentativa *nf* attempt; *Der* **t. de asesinato** attempted murder

tentempié *nm* *Fam* (a) *(comida)* snack, bite (b) *(juguete)* tumbler

tenue *adj* (a) *(luz, sonido)* subdued, faint (b) *(delgado)* thin, light

teñir [6] **1** *vt* (a) *(pelo etc)* to dye (b) *Fig* to tinge with
2 teñirse *upr* **teñirse el pelo** to dye one's hair

teología *nf* theology

teorema *nm* theorem

teoría *nf* theory; **en t.** theoretically

teórico, -a *adj* theoretical

teorizar [40] *vi* to theorize (**sobre** on)

tepache nm = non-alcoholic Mexican drink made from fermented pineapple peelings and unrefined sugar

tequila nf tequila

terapeuta nmf therapist

terapia nf therapy

tercer adj third; **el t. mundo** the third world

tercera nf Aut third (gear)

tercerización nf Am Com outsourcing

tercermundista adj third-world

tercero, -a 1 adj third

> **Tercer** is used instead of **tercero** before masculine singular nouns (e.g. **el tercer piso** the third floor).

2 nm,f (de una serie) third; Esp **a la tercera va la vencida** third time lucky
3 nm (mediador) mediator; Der third party

terceto nm Mús trio

terciar [43] **1** vi (a) (mediar) to mediate, to arbitrate (b) (participar) to take part, to participate
2 terciarse vpr **si se tercia** should the occasion arise

terciario, -a adj tertiary

tercio nm (a) (parte) (one) third (b) (de cerveza) = medium-sized bottle of beer (c) Taurom stage, part (of a bullfight)

terciopelo nm velvet

terco, -a adj stubborn, obstinate

tereré nm Arg, Par (mate) cold maté

tergal® nm = type of synthetic fibre containing polyester

tergiversar vt (verdad) to distort; (palabras) to twist

termal adj thermal

termas nfpl (baños) spa, hot baths o springs

térmico, -a adj thermal; **central térmica** coal-fired power station

terminación nf completion

terminal 1 adj terminal
2 nf (de aeropuerto) terminal; (de autobús) terminus
3 nm Elec & Inform terminal

terminante adj (a) (categórico) categorical, final (b) (dato, resultado) conclusive

terminantemente adv categorically; **t. prohibido** strictly forbidden

terminar 1 vt (acabar) to finish, to complete; (completamente) to finish off
2 vi (a) (acabarse) to finish, to end; **termina en seis** it ends with a six; **no termina de convencerse** he still isn't quite convinced (b) (ir a parar) to end up (**en**

in); **terminó por comprarlo** he ended up buying it (c) **t. con** (eliminar) to put an end to
3 terminarse vpr (a) (finalizar) to finish, to end, to be over (b) (vino, dinero etc) to run out

término nm (a) (final) end, finish (b) (palabra) term, word; **en otros términos** in other words; **en términos generales** generally speaking (c) **t. municipal** district (d) **por t. medio** on average (e) Fig **en último t.** as a last resort

terminología nf terminology

termita nf termite

termo nm Thermos® (flask), flask

termodinámico, -a adj thermodynamic

termómetro nm thermometer

termonuclear adj thermonuclear

termostato nm thermostat

ternera nf (carne) veal

ternero, -a nm, f (animal) calf

terno nm (a) (trío) trio (b) (traje) three-piece suit

ternura nf tenderness

terquedad nf stubbornness, obstinacy

terracota nf terracotta

terraja adj RP Fam (persona) flashy, tacky; (decoración, ropa, canción) tacky, Br naff

terrajada nf RP Fam **esos zapatos son una t.** those shoes are tacky

terral nm Am (polvareda) dust cloud

Terranova n Newfoundland

terraplén nm embankment

terráqueo, -a adj globo t. (tierra) (the) earth; (esfera) globe

terrateniente nmf landowner

terraza nf (a) (balcón) balcony (b) (de café) terrace, patio (c) (azotea) terrace roof

terremoto nm earthquake

terrenal adj un paraíso t. a heaven on earth

terreno nm (a) (tierra) (piece of) land, ground; (por su relieve) terrain; (campo) field; **ganar/perder t.** to gain/lose ground (b) Dep **t. de juego** Ten court; Ftb field (c) Fig field, sphere

terrestre adj (a) (de la tierra) terrestrial, earthly (b) (por tierra) by land; **por vía t.** by land

terrible adj terrible, awful

terrícola nmf (en ciencia ficción) earthling

terrier nm terrier

territorio nm territory

terrón nm (de azúcar) lump; (de tierra) clod

terror nm terror; Cin horror

terrorífico, -a adj terrifying, frightening

terrorismo nm terrorism

terrorista adj & nmf terrorist

terroso, -a adj (color) earth-coloured

terruño nm (terreno) piece of land; (patria chica) homeland, native land

terso, -a adj smooth

tersura nf smoothness

tertulia nf get-together; **t. literaria** literary gathering

tesina nf (undergraduate) dissertation

tesis nf inv thesis; (opinión) view, theory

tesón nm tenacity, firmness

tesorero, -a nm,f treasurer

tesoro nm también Fig treasure

test (pl tests) nm test

testaferro nm front man

testamentario, -a Der **1** adj testamentary
   2 nm,f executor

testamento nm (a) Der will; **hacer** o **otorgar t.** to make o draw up one's will
   (b) Rel Testament

testar vi to make o draw up one's will

testarudo, -a adj stubborn, obstinate

testear vt CSur to test

testículo nm testicle

testificar [44] vt to testify

testigo **1** nmf witness; Der **t. de cargo/descargo** witness for the prosecution/defence; Der **t. ocular/presencial** eyewitness; Rel **Testigos de Jehová** Jehovah's Witnesses
   2 nm Dep baton

testimoniar [43] vt to testify to, to attest to

testimonio nm Der testimony; (prueba) proof

teta nf Fam (a) (de mujer) tit, boob; **niño de t.** breastfeeding baby (b) (de animal) teat

tétanos nm inv tetanus

tetera nf teapot

tetero nm Col,Ven (biberón) baby's bottle

tetilla nf (a) (de hombre, animal) nipple (b) (de biberón) teat

tetina nf teat

tetrabrik® (pl tetrabriks) nm **un t. de leche** a carton of milk

tétrico, -a adj gloomy, dull

textil adj & nm textile

texto nm text; **libro de t.** textbook

textual adj textual; (exacto) literal; **en palabras textuales** literally

textura nf texture

tez nf complexion

ti pron pers you; **es para ti** it's for you; **hazlo por ti** do it for your own sake; **piensas demasiado en ti mismo** you think too much about yourself

tianguis nm inv CAm, Méx open-air market

tibia nf shinbone, tibia

tibieza nf tepidity

tibio, -a adj tepid, lukewarm; Fam **ponerse t. de cerveza** to down bucketfuls of beer

tiburón nm shark

tic (pl tics) nm tic, twitch; **t. nervioso** nervous tic o twitch

ticket (pl tickets) nm (billete) ticket; (recibo) receipt

tictac nm tick-tock, ticking

tiempo nm (a) time; **a t.** in time; **a su (debido) t.** in due course; **a un t., al mismo t.** at the same time; **al poco t.** soon afterwards; **antes de t.** (too) early o soon; **con el t.** in the course of time, with time; **con t.** in advance; **¿cuánto t.?** how long?; **¿cuánto t. hace?** how long ago?; **demasiado t.** too long; **estar a t. de** to still have time to; **hacer t.** to kill time; **¿nos da t. de llegar?** have we got (enough) time to get there?; **t. libre** free time; Fig **dar t. al t.** to let matters take their course
   (b) (meteorológico) weather; **¿qué t. hace?** what's the weather like?; **hace buen/mal t.** the weather is good/bad
   (c) (edad) age; **¿cuánto** o **qué t. tiene tu niño?** how old is your baby/child?
   (d) Mús movement
   (e) Dep half
   (f) Ling tense

tienda nf (a) (establecimiento) shop, store; **ir de tiendas** to go shopping (b) **t. (de campaña)** tent

tientas: a tientas loc adv **andar a t.** to feel one's way; **buscar (algo) a t.** to grope (for sth)

tiento nm tact; **con t.** tactfully

tierno, -a adj (a) (blando) tender, soft (b) (reciente) fresh

tierra nf (a) (planeta) earth (b) Agr land, soil (c) (continente) land; **tocar t.** to land (d) (país) country; **t. de nadie** no-man's-land (e) (suelo) ground; Fig **echar** o **tirar por t.** to spoil (f) Elec **(toma de) t.** Br earth, US ground

tierral nm Am (polvareda) dust cloud

tieso, -a adj (rígido) stiff, rigid; (erguido) upright, erect

tiesto nm flowerpot

tifoideo, -a adj typhoid

tifón nm typhoon

tifus nm inv typhus (fever)

tigre nm tiger; Am (jaguar) jaguar

tijeras *nfpl* (pair of) scissors

tijereta *nf* (**a**) *(insecto)* earwig (**b**) *Dep* scissors kick

tila *nf (flor)* lime *o* linden blossom; *(infusión)* lime *o* linden blossom tea

tildar *vt* to call, to brand; **me tildó de ladrón** he called me a thief

tilde *nf* written accent

tilín *nm (sonido)* ting-a-ling; *Fam Fig* **Raúl le hace t.** she fancies Raúl

tilma *nf Méx* woollen blanket

tilo *nm* lime tree

timar *vt* to swindle; **me han timado** they did me

timbal *nm* kettledrum

timbrar *vt (carta)* to stamp; *(documento)* to seal

timbre *nm* (**a**) *(de puerta)* bell (**b**) *(sello)* stamp, seal; *Fin* fiscal *o* revenue stamp (**c**) *Mús (sonido)* timbre

timidez *nf* shyness

tímido, -a *adj* shy; *Fig (mejoría)* light; *(intento)* cautious

timo *nm* swindle, fiddle; **es un t.** it's a rip-off

timón *nm* (**a**) *(de barco) (palanca)* tiller, helm; *(rueda)* wheel, helm; *(pieza articulada)* rudder; **estar al t.** to be at the helm (**b**) *Andes, Cuba (steering wheel)* steering wheel

timonel *nm* helmsman

tímpano *nm Anat* eardrum

tina *nf* (**a**) *(tinaja)* pitcher (**b**) *(gran cuba)* vat (**c**) *CAm, Col, Méx (bañera)* bathtub

tinaja *nf* large earthenware jar

tinerfeño, -a **1** *adj* of/from Tenerife
2 *nm,f* person from Tenerife

tinglado *nm Fam* (**a**) **todo el t.** the whole caboodle (**b**) *(desorden)* chaos

tinieblas *nfpl* darkness

tino *nm* (**a**) *(puntería)* (good) aim; **tener buen t.** to be a good shot (**b**) *(tacto)* (common) sense, good judgement

tinta *nf* ink; **t. china** Indian ink; **t. simpática** invisible ink; *Fig* **medias tintas** ambiguities, half measures

tinte *nm* (**a**) *(color)* dye (**b**) *Fig (matiz)* shade, overtone

tintero *nm* inkpot, inkwell; *Fig* **se quedó en el t.** it wasn't said

tintinear *vi (vidrio)* to clink; *(campana)* to jingle, to tinkle

tintineo *nm (de vidrio)* clinking; *(de campana)* jingling

tinto 1 *adj (vino)* red
2 *nm* (**a**) *(vino)* red wine (**b**) *Col, Ven (café)* black coffee

tintorería *nf* dry-cleaner's

tintura *nf Quím* tincture; **t. de yodo** iodine

tío, -a *nm,f* (**a**) *(pariente) (hombre)* uncle; *(mujer)* aunt; **mis tíos** my uncle and aunt (**b**) *Esp Fam (persona) (hombre)* guy, *Br* bloke; *(mujer)* girl, woman

tiovivo *nm* merry-go-round, *US* carousel

tipazo *nm Fam* good figure

tipear *vt & vi Am* to type

típico, -a *adj* (**a**) *(característico)* typical; **eso es t. de Antonio** that's just like Antonio (**b**) *(baile, traje)* traditional

tipificar [44] *vt* to classify

tipismo *nm* local colour

tipo *nm* (**a**) *(clase)* type, kind (**b**) *Fam (persona)* guy, *Br* bloke; **t. raro** weirdo (**c**) *Anat (de hombre)* build, physique; *(de mujer)* figure (**d**) *Fin* rate; **t. de cambio/interés** rate of exchange/interest (**e**) **el político t. de la izquierda** the typical left-wing politician

tipografía *nf* typography

tipográfico, -a *adj* typographic; **error t.** printing error

tipógrafo, -a *nm,f* typographer

tiquismiquis *nmf inv Fam* fusspot

tira 1 *nf* (**a**) *(banda, cinta)* strip (**b**) *(de dibujos)* comic strip (**c**) *Fam* **la t. de gente** a lot *o* loads of people (**d**) *Méx Fam* **la t.** *(la policía)* the law, *US* the heat
2 tira y afloja *nm* tug of war

tirabuzón *nm* ringlet

tirachinas *nm inv Br* catapult, *US* slingshot

tirada *nf* (**a**) *(lanzamiento)* throw (**b**) *(impresión)* print run

tirado, -a *adj Fam* (**a**) *(barato)* dirt-cheap (**b**) *(fácil)* dead easy (**c**) *Fam* **dejar t. (a algn)** to let (sb) down

tirador *nm* (**a**) *(persona)* marksman (**b**) *(pomo)* knob, handle; *(cordón)* bell pull (**c**) *(tirachinas) Br* catapult, *US* slingshot

tiraje *nm Am* print run

tiralíneas *nm inv* tracer, drawing *o* ruling pen

tiranía *nf* tyranny

tiránico, -a *adj* tyrannical

tiranizar [40] *vt* to tyrannize

tirano, -a *nm,f* tyrant

tirante 1 *adj (cable etc)* tight, taut; *(situación, relación)* tense
2 *nm* (**a**) *(de vestido etc)* strap; **tirantes** *Br* braces, *US* suspenders (**b**) *Téc* brace, stay

tirar 1 *vt* (**a**) *(echar)* to throw (**b**) *(dejar caer)* to drop (**c**) *(desechar)* to throw away; *Fig (dinero)* to squander (**d**) *(derribar)* to knock down; **t. la puerta (abajo)** to smash the door in (**e**) *(foto)* to take (**f**) *Impr* to print (**g**) *(beso)* to blow

2 *vi* (**a**) **t. de** *(cuerda, puerta)* to pull (**b**) *(chimenea, estufa)* to draw (**c**) *(funcionar)* to work, to run (**d**) **ir tirando** to get by (**e**) **t. a** to tend towards; **tira a rojo** it's reddish (**f**) **tira a la izquierda** turn left; **¡venga, tira ya!** come on, get going! (**g**) *(disparar)* to shoot, to fire; *Ftb* **t. a puerta** to shoot at goal

3 tirarse *upr* (**a**) *(lanzarse)* to throw o hurl oneself; **tirarse de cabeza al agua** to dive into the water (**b**) *(tumbarse)* to lie down (**c**) *Fam (tiempo)* to spend; **me tiré una hora esperando** I waited (for) a good hour (**d**) *Vulg* **tirarse a algn** to lay sb

tirita *nf Br* (sticking) plaster, *US* Band-aid®

tiritar *vi* to shiver, to shake

tiro *nm* (**a**) *(lanzamiento)* throw (**b**) *(disparo, ruido)* shot; *Ftb* **t. a gol** shot at goal; **t. al blanco** target shooting; **t. al plato** clay pigeon shooting; **t. con arco** archery (**c**) *(de vestido)* shoulder width (**d**) *(de chimenea)* draught; **animal de t.** draught animal

tirón *nm* pull, tug; *(de bolso)* snatch; *Fam* **de un t.** in one go

tirotear *vt* to shoot at, to snipe at

tiroteo *nm* shooting, firing to and fro

tirria *nf Fam* **le tengo t.** I can't stand him

tísico, -a *adj* tubercular, consumptive

tisis *nf inv* tuberculosis, consumption

tisú *nm* tissue, paper hankie

títere *nm (marioneta)* puppet; **no dejar t. con cabeza** to spare no one

titilar *vi (luz)* to flicker; *(estrella)* to twinkle

titiritero, -a *nm,f* puppeteer

titubeante *adj (actitud)* hesitant; *(voz)* hesitant, faltering

titubear *vi (dudar)* to hesitate; *(al hablar)* to falter, to hesitate

titubeo *nm* hesitation, hesitancy

titulación *nf* qualifications

titulado, -a *adj (licenciado)* graduate; *(diplomado)* qualified

titular¹ 1 *nmf (persona)* holder
2 *nm Prensa* headline
3 *adj* appointed, official

titular² 1 *vt (poner título)* to call
2 titularse *upr* (**a**) *(película etc)* to be called; **¿cómo se titula?** what is it called? (**b**) *Educ* to graduate (**en** in)

titularidad *nf Educ* tenure

título *nm* (**a**) *(de obra)* title (**b**) *Educ* degree; *(diploma)* diploma (**c**) *Prensa (titular)* headline (**d**) **a t. de ejemplo** by way of example

tiza *nf* chalk; **una t.** a piece of chalk

tiznar *vt* to blacken (with soot)

tizón *nm* half-burnt stick, brand

tlapalería *nf Méx* ironmonger's (shop)

toalla *nf* towel; **tirar la t.** to throw in the towel

toallero *nm* towel *Br* rail o *US* bar

tobillo *nm* ankle

tobogán *nm* slide, chute

toca *nf (sombrero)* headdress; *(de monja)* wimple

tocadiscos *nm inv* record player; **t. digital** o **compacto** CD player

tocado¹ *nm* (**a**) *(peinado)* coiffure, hairdo (**b**) *(prenda)* headdress

tocado², -a *adj Fam* crazy, touched

tocador *nm* (**a**) *(mueble)* dressing table (**b**) *(habitación)* dressing room; **t. de señoras** powder room

tocante *adj* **en lo t. a …** with reference to …

tocar [44] **1** *vt* (**a**) *(entrar en contacto con)* to touch; *Fam Fig* **toca madera** touch wood (**b**) *(instrumento, canción)* to play; *(timbre, campana)* to ring; *(bocina)* to blow (**c**) *(tema, asunto)* to touch on (**d**) *(afectar)* to concern; **por lo que a mí me toca** as far as I am concerned

2 *vi* (**a**) **¿a quién le toca?** *(en juegos)* whose turn is it? (**b**) **me tocó el gordo** *(en rifa)* I won the jackpot (**c**) **t. con** to be next to; *Fig* **t. a su fin** to be coming to an end (**d**) *(llamar)* **t. a la puerta** to knock on the door

3 tocarse *upr* (**a**) *(una cosa con otra)* to touch each other (**b**) **¿os tocáis algo?** *(ser parientes)* are you related? (**c**) *(cubrirse la cabeza)* to cover one's head

tocata 1 *nf Mús* toccata
2 *nm Fam* record player

tocateja: a tocateja *loc adv* **pagar a t.** to pay on the nail

tocayo, -a *nm,f* namesake

tocho *nm Fam (libro grande)* tome

tocino *nm* pork o bacon fat; **t. de cielo** = sweet made with egg yolk

tocólogo, -a *nm,f* obstetrician

tocuyo *nm Andes, Arg* coarse cotton cloth

todavía *adv* (**a**) *(aún)* still; *(en negativas)* yet; **t. la quiere** he still loves her; **t. no** not yet; **no mires t.** don't look yet (**b**) *(para reforzar)* even, still; **t. más/menos** even more/less

todo, -a 1 *adj* (**a**) *(el total de)* all; **t. el pan** all the bread; **t. el mundo** (absolutely) everybody; **t. el día** all day, the whole o entire day; **todas las manzanas** all the apples; *Fam* **t. quisqui** every Tom, Dick and Harry (**b**) *(cada)* every; **t. ciudadano de más de dieciocho años** every citizen over eighteen years of age (**c**) *(entero)* complete, thorough; **es toda una mujer**

she is every inch a woman (**d**) *(con expresiones de tiempo)* every; **todos los niños** all the children; **todos los martes** every Tuesday

2 *nm (totalidad)* whole

3 *pron* (**a**) *(sin excluir nada)* all, everything; **ante t.** first of all; **con t.** in spite of everything; **del t.** completely; **después de t.** after all; **eso es t.** that's all, that's it; **estar en t.** to be really with it; **hay de t.** there are all sorts; **lo sé t.** I know all about it; **t. lo contrario** quite the contrary *o* opposite; **t. lo más** at the most (**b**) *(cualquiera)* anybody; **t. aquél** *o* **el que quiera** anybody who wants (to) (**c**) *(cada uno)* **todos aprobamos** we all passed; **todos fueron** they all went

4 *adv* completely, totally; **volvió t. sucio** he was all dirty when he got back

todopoderoso, -a *adj* all-powerful, almighty

todoterreno *nm* four-wheel drive (vehicle), SUV

toga *nf* (**a**) *(de académico)* gown; *(de magistrado)* robes (**b**) *Hist* toga

Tokio *n* Tokyo

toldo *nm (cubierta)* awning

tolerancia *nf* tolerance

tolerante *adj* tolerant

tolerar *vt* to tolerate; *(situación)* to stand; *(gente)* to put up with

toma *nf* (**a**) *(acción)* taking; *Elec* **t. de corriente** power point, socket (**b**) *Med* dose (**c**) *Mil* capture (**d**) *Cin* take, shot (**e**) **t. de posesión** swearing in (**f**) *Fam Fig* **t. y daca** give and take

tomado, -a *adj* (**a**) *(voz)* hoarse (**b**) *Am Fam (persona)* tight, tanked up (**c**) **tenerla tomada con algn** to have it in for sb

tomadura *nf Fam* **t. de pelo** leg-pull; *(timo)* rip-off

tomar 1 *vt* (**a**) *(coger)* to take; *(autobús, tren)* to catch; *(decisión)* to make, to take; **toma** here (you are); **t. el sol** to sunbathe; *Av* **t. tierra** to land; *Fam* **tomarla con algn** to have it in for sb (**b**) *(comer, beber)* to have (**c**) **t. algo a mal** to take sth badly; **t. en serio/broma** to take seriously/as a joke (**d**) *(confundir)* to take (**por** for) (**e**) *Mil* to take

2 *vi Am (beber alcohol)* to drink

3 tomarse *upr* (**a**) *(comer)* to eat; *(beber)* to drink (**b**) *Fam* **no te lo tomes así** don't take it like that

tomate *nm* tomato; **salsa de t.** *(de lata)* tomato sauce; *(de botella)* ketchup

tomavistas *nm inv* cine *o* movie camera

tómbola *nf* tombola

tomillo *nm* thyme

tomo *nm* volume; *Fam* **de t. y lomo** utter, out-and-out

ton *nm* **sin t. ni son** without rhyme or reason

tonada *nf* (**a**) *Mús* tune, song (**b**) *Am (acento)* (regional) accent

tonalidad *nf* tonality

tonel *nm* barrel, cask

tonelada *nf* ton; **t. métrica** tonne

tonelaje *nm* tonnage

tonelero, -a *nm,f* cooper

tongo *nm* fix

tónico, -a 1 *nm Med* tonic; *(cosmético)* skin tonic

2 tónica *nf* (**a**) *(tendencia)* tendency, trend; **tónica general** overall trend (**b**) *(bebida)* tonic (water) (**c**) *Mús* tonic

3 (**a**) *Ling* tonic, stressed (**b**) *Med & Mús* tonic

tonificante *adj* invigorating

tonificar [44] *vt* to tone up, to invigorate

tono *nm* tone; **a t. con** in tune *o* harmony with; **subir de t.** *o* **el t.** to speak louder; **un t. alto/bajo** a high/low pitch; **dar el t.** to set the tone; *Fig* **darse t.** to put on airs; *Fig* **fuera de t.** inappropriate, out of place

tontear *vi* to flirt

tontería *nf* (**a**) *(dicho, hecho)* silly *o* stupid thing (**b**) *(insignificancia)* trifle

tonto, -a 1 *adj* silly, dumb

2 *nm,f* fool, idiot; **t. de remate** *o* **de capirote** prize idiot

topacio *nm* topaz

topadora *nf RP* bulldozer

toparse *upr* **t. con** to bump into; *(dificultades)* to run up against, to encounter; **t. con algo** to come across sth

tope 1 *nm* (**a**) *(límite)* limit, end; *Fam* **a t.** *(al máximo)* flat out; *Fig* **estar hasta los topes** to be full up; **fecha t.** deadline (**b**) *Téc* stop, check (**c**) *Ferroc* buffer

2 *adv Fam* incredibly; **t. difícil** really difficult

tópico, -a 1 *nm* cliché

2 *adj Med* for external use

> Observa que la palabra inglesa **topic** es un falso amigo y no es la traducción de la palabra española **tópico**. En inglés **topic** significa "tema".

---

topo *nm* mole

topografía *nf* topography

topónimo *nm* place name

toque *nm* (**a**) *(detalle, retoque)* touch (**b**) *(de campanas)* peal; **t. de queda** curfew (**c**) *Fam* **dar un t. a algn** *(avisar)* to let sb know; *(advertir)* to warn sb

toquetear *vt* to fiddle with, to finger

toquilla *nf* (knitted) shawl

tórax *nm* thorax

torbellino *nm* (a) *(de viento)* whirlwind (b) *Fig (confusión)* whirl, turmoil

torcedura *nf (acción)* twist, twisting; *Med* sprain

torcer [41] **1** *vt* (a) *(metal)* to bend; *(cuerda, hilo)* to twist; *Med* to sprain; *Fig (esquina)* to turn (b) *(inclinar)* to slant
2 *vi* to turn (left o right)
3 torcerse *vpr* (a) *(doblarse)* to twist, to bend (b) *Med* **se me torció el tobillo** I sprained my ankle (c) *(plan)* to fall through (d) *(desviarse)* to go off to the side

torcido, -a *adj* twisted; *(ladeado)* slanted, lopsided; *(corbata)* crooked

tordo, -a 1 *adj* dapple-grey
2 *nm (ave)* thrush

torear 1 *vt* to fight; *Fam* **t. a algn** to tease o confuse sb; *Fam* **t. un asunto** to tackle a matter skilfully
2 *vi* to bullfight

toreo *nm* bullfighting

torera *nf (prenda)* bolero (jacket)

torero, -a *nm,f* bullfighter

tormenta *nf* storm

tormento *nm (tortura)* torture; *(padecimiento)* torment

tormentoso, -a *adj* stormy

tornado *nm* tornado

tornar *Fml* **1** *vt (convertir)* to transform, to turn (**en** into)
2 *vi (regresar)* to return, to go back; **t. en sí** to regain consciousness
3 tornarse *vpr* to become, to turn

tornasolado, -a *adj* iridescent

torneo *nm* (a) *Dep* tournament, *US* tourney (b) *Hist* tourney, joust

tornillo *nm* screw

torniquete *nm* (a) *(en entrada)* turnstile (b) *Med* tourniquet

torno 1 *nm (de carpintero)* lathe; *(de alfarero)* wheel
2 en torno a *loc prep (alrededor de)* around, round; *(aproximadamente)* around, about

toro *nm* bull; **¿te gustan los toros?** do you like bullfighting?

toronja *nf* grapefruit

torpe *adj* (a) *(sin habilidad)* clumsy (b) *(tonto)* dim, thick (c) *(movimiento)* slow, awkward

torpedear *vt* to torpedo

torpedo *nm* torpedo

torpeza *nf* (a) *(física)* clumsiness; *(mental)* dimness, stupidity (b) *(lentitud)* slowness, heaviness (c) *(error)* blunder

torre *nf* (a) *(construcción)* tower (b) *Mil* turret (c) *(en ajedrez)* rook, castle

torrefacto, -a *adj* roasted; **café t.** high roast coffee

torrencial *adj* torrential

torrente *nm* (a) *(de agua)* torrent (b) *Fig* **t. de voz** strong o powerful voice

torrezno *nm* = rasher of fried bacon

tórrido, -a *adj* torrid

torrija *nf* ≃ French toast *(sweetened)*

torsión *nf* (a) *(torcedura)* twist, twisting (b) *Téc* torsion

torso *nm* (a) *Anat* torso (b) *Arte* bust

torta *nf* (a) *Culin Esp (de harina)* = flat, round plain cake; *CSur, Ven (dulce)* cake; *Andes, CAm, Carib, RP (salada)* pie; *Méx (sandwich)* filled roll (b) *Fam (golpe)* slap, punch

tortazo *nm Fam* (a) *(bofetada)* slap, punch (b) *(golpe)* whack, thump

tortícolis *nf inv* crick in the neck

tortilla *nf* (a) *(egg)* omelette; **t. española** Spanish o potato omelette; **t. francesa** French o plain omelette (b) *(de maíz)* tortilla, = thin maize pancake

tortillera *nf muy Fam* dyke, lesbian

tórtola *nf* dove

tortuga *nf (de tierra)* tortoise, *US* turtle; *(de mar)* turtle

tortuoso, -a *adj* tortuous

tortura *nf* torture

torturar *vt* to torture

tos *nf* cough; **t. ferina** whooping cough

tosco, -a *adj (basto)* rustic, rough; *(persona)* uncouth

toser *vi* to cough

tosquedad *nf* roughness

tostada *nf* (slice of) toast

tostado, -a *adj* (a) *(pan)* toasted (b) *(moreno)* tanned, brown

tostador *nm* toaster

tostar [2] *vt (pan)* to toast; *(café)* to roast; *(carne, pescado)* to brown; *Fig (la piel)* to tan

tostón *nm* (a) *(cochinillo)* roast sucking pig (b) *(de pan)* crouton (c) *Fam (tabarra)* bore, drag

total 1 *adj (completo)* total
2 *nm* (a) *(todo)* whole; **en t.** in all (b) *Mat* total
3 *adv* so, in short; **¿t. para qué?** what's the point anyhow?; *Fam* **t. que ...** so ...; **t., tampoco te hará caso** he won't listen to you anyway

totalidad *nf* whole, totality; **la t. de** all of; **en su t.** as a whole

totalitario, -a *adj* totalitarian

totalizar [40] **1** *vt* to total
  2 *vi* to amount to

tóxico, -a *adj* toxic, poisonous
  2 *nm* poison

toxicomanía *nf* drug addiction

toxicómano, -a *Med* **1** *adj* addicted to drugs
  2 *nm,f* drug addict

tozudo, -a *adj* obstinate, stubborn

traba *nf* (**a**) *(de rueda)* chock; *(enlace)* bond, tie (**b**) *Fig (obstáculo)* hindrance, obstacle

trabajador, -a **1** *nm,f* worker, labourer
  2 *adj* hard-working

trabajar **1** *vi* to work; **trabaja mucho** he works hard; **t. de camarera** to work as a waitress
  2 *vt* (**a**) *(hierro, barro, tierra)* to work; *(masa)* to knead (**b**) *(vender) (producto, género, marca)* to sell, to stock (**c**) *(mejorar)* to work on o at

trabajo *nm* (**a**) *(ocupación)* work; **t. a destajo** piecework; **t. eventual** casual labour; **trabajos manuales** arts and crafts (**b**) *(empleo)* employment, job (**c**) *(tarea)* task, job (**d**) *Educ (redacción)* report, paper (**e**) *(esfuerzo)* effort; **cuesta t. creerlo** it's hard to believe

trabajoso, -a *adj* *(laborioso)* hard, laborious; *(difícil)* difficult

trabalenguas *nm inv* tongue twister

trabar **1** *vt* (**a**) *(sujetar)* to lock, to fasten; *(plan)* to obstruct (**b**) *(conversación, amistad)* to start, to strike up (**c**) *(salsa)* to thicken
  2 trabarse *vpr* (**a**) *(cuerdas)* to get tangled up (**b**) *Fig* **se le trabó la lengua** he got tongue-tied

trabazón *nf* *(de ideas)* link

trabilla *nf* *(de pantalón)* belt loop

traca *nf* string of firecrackers

tracción *nf* traction; *Aut* **t. delantera/trasera** front-/rear-wheel drive; *Aut* **t. en las cuatro ruedas** four-wheel drive

tractor *nm* tractor

tradición *nf* tradition

tradicional *adj* traditional

traducción *nf* translation; **t. directa/inversa** translation from/into a foreign language

traducir [10] **1** *vt* to translate (**a** into)
  2 traducirse *vpr Fig* to result (**en** in)

traductor, -a *nm,f* translator

traer [25] **1** *vt* (**a**) *(de un lugar a otro)* to bring; **trae** give it to me (**b**) *(llevar encima, consigo)* to carry (**c**) *(llevar puesto)* to wear (**d**) *(problemas)* to cause; **traerá como consecuencia …** it will result in …
  2 traerse *vpr (llevar consigo)* to bring

along; *Fig* **¿qué se trae entre manos?** what is he up to?

traficante *nmf (de drogas etc)* trafficker, pusher

traficar [44] *vi (ilegalmente)* to traffic (**con** in)

tráfico *nm* (**a**) *Aut* traffic; **t. rodado** road traffic (**b**) *Com* traffic, trade; **t. de drogas** drug traffic

tragaluz *nm* skylight

tragaperras, *Am* **tragamonedas** *nf inv* *Fam (máquina)* **t.** slot machine

tragar [42] **1** *vt* (**a**) *(ingerir)* to swallow (**b**) *Fam (engullir)* to gobble up, to tuck away (**c**) *Fig (soportar) (persona)* to stand, to stomach (**d**) *Fig (creer)* to believe, to swallow
  2 tragarse *vpr* (**a**) *(ingerir)* to swallow (**b**) *Fig (creer)* to believe, to swallow

tragedia *nf* tragedy

trágico, -a *adj* tragic

tragicomedia *nf* tragicomedy

trago *nm* (**a**) *(bebida)* swig; **de un t.** in one go (**b**) *Fig* **pasar un mal t.** to have a bad time of it

tragón, -ona *nm,f* big eater

traición *nf* treason, betrayal; **a t.** treacherously; **alta t.** high treason

traicionar *vt (amigo, ideal, país)* to betray; *(descubrir)* to give away

traicionero, -a *adj* treacherous

traidor, -a **1** *adj* treacherous
  2 *nm,f* traitor

traigo *indic pres de* **traer**

tráiler *(pl* **tráilers***)* *nm* (**a**) *Cin* trailer, *US* preview (**b**) *Aut Br* articulated lorry, *US* semitrailer (**c**) *Méx (casa rodante)* *Br* caravan, *US* trailer

traje¹ *nm* (**a**) *(de hombre)* suit; **t. de baño** swimming costume, bathing suit o *Br* costume; **t. de luces** bullfighter's costume; **t. de paisano** civilian clothes (**b**) *(de mujer)* dress; **t. de chaqueta** two-piece suit; **t. de novia** wedding dress

traje² *pt indef de* **traer**

trajeado, -a *adj Fam* sharp, dapper

trajín *nm Fam* comings and goings, hustle and bustle

trajinar *vi* to run o bustle about

trama *nf* (**a**) *Tex* weft, woof (**b**) *Lit* plot

tramar *vt* to plot, to cook up; **¿qué tramas?** what are you up to?

tramitar *vt* (**a**) *(gestionar)* to take the necessary (legal) steps to obtain (**b**) *Fml (despachar)* to convey, to transmit (**c**) *Com, Der & Fin* to carry out, to process

trámite *nm (paso)* step; *(formalidad)* formality; *Com, Der & Fin* **trámites** procedures, proceedings

tramo *nm (de carretera)* section, stretch; *(de escalera)* flight

tramontana *nf* north wind

tramoya *nf (maquinaria)* stage machinery; *(trama)* plot, scheme

trampa *nf* **(a)** *(de caza)* trap, snare **(b)** *(puerta)* trapdoor **(c)** *(engaño)* fiddle; **hacer trampa(s)** to cheat **(d)** *(truco)* trick

> Observa que la palabra inglesa **tramp** es un falso amigo y no es la traducción de la palabra española **trampa**. En inglés, **tramp** significa "vagabundo".

trampilla *nf* trapdoor, hatch

trampolín *nm* **(a)** *(de piscina)* diving board **(b)** *(de esquí)* ski jump

> Observa que la palabra inglesa **trampoline** es un falso amigo y no es la traducción de la palabra española **trampolín**. En inglés, **trampoline** significa "cama elástica".

tramposo, -a 1 *adj* cheating
2 *nm,f* cheat

tranca *nf (en puerta, ventana)* bar; *Fam* **a trancas y barrancas** with great difficulty

trancar 1 *vt (asegurar) (con cerrojo)* to bolt; *(con tranca)* to bar
2 trancarse *upr Am (atascarse)* to get stuck; **la llave se trancó en la cerradura** the key got stuck in the lock

trance *nm* **(a)** *(coyuntura)* (critical) moment; **estar en t. de ...** to be on the point of ... **(b)** *(éxtasis)* trance

tranquilidad *nf* calmness, tranquillity; **con t.** calmly; **pídemelo con toda t.** don't hesitate to ask me

tranquilizante *nm* tranquillizer

tranquilizar [40] **1** *vt* to calm down; **lo dijo para tranquilizarme** he said it to reassure me
2 tranquilizarse *upr* to calm down

tranquillo *nm* knack; **coger el t. a algo** to get the knack of sth

tranquilo, -a *adj* **(a)** *(persona, lugar)* calm; *(agua)* still; *(conciencia)* clear; *Fam* **tú t.** don't you worry **(b)** *(despreocupado)* placid, easy-going

transacción *nf* transaction, deal

transar *vi Fam* **(a)** *Am (transigir)* to compromise, to give in **(b)** *Am (negociar)* to come to an arrangement, to reach a compromise **(c)** *RP (droga)* to deal

transatlántico, -a 1 *adj* transatlantic
2 *nm Náut* (ocean) liner

transbordador *nm* (car) ferry; **t. espacial** space shuttle

transbordar 1 *vt* to transfer; *Náut (mercancías)* to tranship
2 *vi Ferroc* to change trains, *US* to transfer

transbordo *nm* **(a)** *Ferroc* change, *US* transfer; **hacer t.** to change, *US* to transfer **(b)** *Náut* transhipment

transcurrir *vi* **(a)** *(tiempo)* to pass, to go by **(b)** *(acontecer)* to take place

transcurso *nm* course o passing (of time); **en el t. de** in the course of, during

transeúnte *nmf* passer-by

transferencia *nf* transfer

transferible *adj* transferable

transferir [5] *vt* to transfer

transformación *nf* transformation

transformador *nm Elec* transformer

transformar 1 *vt* to transform, to change
2 transformarse *upr* to change, to turn (**en** into); *(algo plegable)* to convert

tránsfuga *nmf* **(a)** *Mil* deserter **(b)** *Pol* turncoat

transfusión *nf* transfusion

transgénico, -a 1 *adj* transgenic
2 transgénicos *nmpl* GM foods

transgredir *vt* to transgress, to break

transgresor, -a *nm,f* transgressor, law-breaker

transición *nf* transition

transido, -a *adj Fml* **t. de dolor** racked with pain

transigente *adj* tolerant

transigir [57] *vi* to compromise

transistor *nm* transistor

transitable *adj* passable

transitado, -a *adj* busy

transitar *vi* to pass

transitivo, -a *adj Ling* transitive

tránsito *nm* **(a)** *Aut* traffic **(b)** *(movimiento)* movement, passage; **pasajeros en t.** passengers in transit

transitorio, -a *adj* transitory

translúcido, -a *adj* translucent

translucirse [35] *upr* = traslucirse

transmisión *nf* **(a)** *(de sonido, datos, virus)* transmission **(b)** *Rad & TV (programa)* broadcast; *(servicio)* broadcasting **(c)** *Téc* drive; **t. delantera/trasera** front-/rear-wheel drive

transmisor *nm* transmitter

transmitir *vt* **(a)** *(sonido, datos, virus)* to transmit **(b)** *Rad & TV* to broadcast

transparencia *nf* transparency

transparentarse *upr (tela)* to be see-through; *(cristal, líquido)* to be transparent; **esta tela se transparenta** this is see-through material; **se le transparentaban las bragas** you could see her panties

transparente *adj* transparent

transpiración *nf* perspiration

transpirar *vi* to perspire

transplantar *vt* = trasplantar

transplante *nm* = trasplante

transponer [19] (*pp* **transpuesto**) **1** *vt* to transpose, to move about

2 transponerse *vpr (desmayarse)* to faint

transportar *vt* to transport; *(pasajeros)* to carry; *(mercancías)* to ship

transporte *nm* transport, *US* transportation; **t. de mercancías** freight transport; **t. marítimo** shipment

transportista *nmf* carrier

transpuesto *pp de* transponer

transvase *nm* (**a**) *(de líquidos)* decanting (**b**) *(de ríos)* transfer

transversal *adj* transverse, cross

tranvía *nm Br* tram, *US* streetcar

trapecio *nm* trapeze

trapecista *nmf* trapeze artist

trapero, -a 1 *nm Br* rag-and-bone man, *US* junkman

2 *adj* **puñalada trapera** stab in the back

trapichear *vi Fam* to be on the fiddle

trapicheo *nm Fam* (**a**) *(negocio sucio)* fiddle (**b**) *(tejemaneje)* scheme

trapo *nm* (**a**) *(viejo, roto)* rag (**b**) *(bayeta)* cloth; *Fam* **poner a algn como un t.** to tear sb to pieces; **t. de cocina** *Br* tea towel, *US* dish towel; **t. del polvo** dust cloth, *Br* duster

tráquea *nf* trachea, windpipe

traqueteo *nm* rattle, clatter

tras *prep* (**a**) *(después de)* after; **uno t. otro** one after the other (**b**) *(detrás)* behind; **sentados uno t. otro** sitting one behind the other (**c**) **andar/ir t.** to be after; **la policía iba t. ella** the police were after her

trasatlántico, -a *adj & nm* = transatlántico

trasbordador *nm* = transbordador

trasbordar *vt & vi* = transbordar

trasbordo *nm* = transbordo

trascendencia *nf* (**a**) *(importancia)* importance, significance (**b**) *(en filosofía)* transcendence

trascendental, trascendente *adj* (**a**) *(importante)* momentous (**b**) *(en filosofía)* transcendental

trascender [3] *vi* (**a**) *(noticia)* to become known, to leak out (**b**) *(tener consecuencias)* to have far-reaching consequences (**c**) **t. de** to go beyond

trascurrir *vi* = transcurrir

trascurso *nm* = transcurso

trasero, -a 1 *adj* back, rear; **en la parte trasera** at the back

2 *nm Euf* backside

trasferencia *nf* = transferencia

trasferible *adj* = transferible

trasferir [5] *vt* = transferir

trasfondo *nm* background

trasformación *nf* = transformación

trasformador *nm* = transformador

trasformar *vt* = transformar

trásfuga *nmf* = tránsfuga

trasfusión *nf* = transfusión

trasgredir *vt* = transgredir

trasgresor, -a *nm,f* = transgresor

trashumancia *nf* = seasonal movement of livestock

trasiego *nm* comings and goings, hustle and bustle

trasladar 1 *vt (cosa)* to move; *(persona)* to move, to transfer

2 trasladarse *vpr* to go, to move

traslado *nm (de casa)* move, removal; *(de personal)* transfer; *Educ* **t. de expediente** transfer of student record

traslucirse [35] *vpr* to show through

trasluz *nm* **mirar algo al t.** to hold sth against the light

trasmano: a trasmano *loc adv* out of reach; **(me) coge a t.** it's out of my way

trasmisión *nf* = transmisión

trasmisor *nm* = transmisor

trasmitir *vt* = transmitir

trasnochado, -a *adj* old, hackneyed

trasnochador, -a 1 *adj* given to staying up late

2 *nm,f* night owl

trasnochar *vi* to stay up (very) late

traspapelar 1 *vt* to mislay, to misplace

2 traspapelarse *vpr* to get mislaid *o* misplaced

trasparencia *nf* = transparencia

trasparentarse *vpr* = transparentarse

trasparente *adj* = transparente

traspasar *vt* (**a**) *(atravesar)* to go through (**b**) *(negocio, jugador)* to transfer; **se traspasa** *(en letrero)* (business) for sale

> 🖉 Observa que el verbo inglés **to trespass** es un falso amigo y no es la traducción del verbo español **traspasar**. En inglés, **to trespass** significa "entrar sin autorización".

traspaso *nm (de propiedad, jugador)* transfer; *(de negocio)* sale (as a going concern); **t. de competencias** devolution

traspié *nm* stumble, trip; **dar un t.** to trip; *Fig* to slip up

traspiración *nf* = transpiración

traspirar *vi* = transpirar

trasplantar *vt* to transplant

trasplante *nm* transplant; **t. de corazón** heart transplant

trasponer [19] *vt* = transponer

trasportar *vt* = transportar

trasporte *nm* = transporte

traspuesto, -a *adj* **quedarse t.** to doze off

trasquilar *vt* (*oveja*) to shear; (*pelo*) to crop

trastabillar *vi* to stagger, to totter

trastada *nf Fam* **hacer trastadas** to be up to mischief

trastazo *nm Fam* wallop, thump

traste¹ *nm Mús* fret

traste² *nm* (**a**) *Am salvo RP* (*utensilio de cocina*) cooking utensil; **fregar los trastes** to wash the dishes (**b**) *CSur Fam* (*trasero*) bottom, *US* tush (**c**) *Fig* **dar al t. (con un plan)** to spoil (a plan); **irse al t.** to fall through

trastear *vi* to rummage about

trastero *nm* (**cuarto**) **t.** junk room

trastienda *nf* back shop

trasto *nm* (*objeto cualquiera*) thing; (*cosa inservible*) piece of junk

trastocar [44] *vt* = trastornar

trastornado, -a *adj* (*loco*) mad, unhinged

trastornar 1 *vt* (**a**) (*planes*) to disrupt (**b**) *Fig* (*persona*) to unhinge
2 **trastornarse** *vpr* (*enloquecer*) to go out of one's mind, to go mad

trastorno *nm* (*molestia*) trouble, inconvenience; **t. mental** mental disorder *o* disturbance

trasvase *nm* = transvase

trasversal *adj* = transversal

trata *nf* slave trade *o* traffic; **t. de blancas** white slave trade

tratado *nm* (**a**) (*pacto*) treaty (**b**) (*estudio*) treatise

tratamiento *nm* (**a**) (*hacia persona*) treatment; (*título*) title, form of address (**b**) (*de enfermo, sustancia, tema*) treatment (**c**) *Inform* processing; **t. de textos** word processing

tratar 1 *vt* (**a**) (*comportarse con*) to treat; **t. bien/mal** to treat well/badly (**b**) (*enfermo, sustancia, tema*) to treat (**c**) *Inform* to process (**d**) (*tener trato*) **la traté muy poco** I didn't have much to do with her; **me trata de tú** he addresses me as "tú"
2 *vi* (**a**) **t. de** (*intentar*) to try (**b**) **t. de** *o* **sobre** *o* **acerca de** to be about; **¿de qué trata?**

what is it about? (**c**) **t. con** (*tener tratos*) to deal with; (*negociar*) to negotiate with; (*relacionarse*) to move among (**d**) *Com* **t. en** to deal in
3 **tratarse** *upr* (**a**) (*relacionarse*) to be on speaking terms (**b**) **se trata de** (*es cuestión de*) it's a question of; **se trata de un caso excepcional** it's an exceptional case

tratativas *nfpl CSur* negotiation

trato *nm* (**a**) (*de personas*) manner; (*contacto*) contact; **malos tratos** ill-treatment (**b**) (*acuerdo*) agreement; **¡t. hecho!** it's a deal! (**c**) *Com* deal

trauma *nm* trauma

traumático, -a *adj* traumatic

traumatizar *vt Med* to traumatize; *Fam* to shock

través 1 *prep* (**a**) **a t. de** (*superficie*) across, over; (*agujero etc*) through; **a t. del río** across the river; **a t. del agujero** through the hole (**b**) *Fig* **a t. de** through; **a t. del periódico** through the newspaper
2 *adv* **de t.** (*en diagonal*) crosswise; (*de lado*) sideways
3 *nm* (*pl* **traveses**) *Fig* (*desgracia*) misfortune

travesaño *nm Ftb* crossbar

travesía *nf* (*viaje*) crossing

travestí (*pl* **travestíes** *o* **travestís**), **travestí** *nmf* (*que se viste de mujer*) transvestite, cross-dresser; (*artista*) drag artist

> 🖉 Observa que la palabra inglesa **travesty** es un falso amigo y no es la traducción de la palabra española **travestí**. En inglés, **travesty** significa "parodia burda".

travesura *nf* mischief, childish prank

travieso, -a *adj* mischievous

trayecto *nm* (**a**) (*distancia*) distance; (*recorrido*) route; (*trecho*) stretch (**b**) (*viaje*) journey

trayectoria *nf* (**a**) (*de proyectil, geométrica*) trajectory (**b**) *Fig* (*orientación*) line, course

traza *nf* (*apariencia*) looks, appearance; **no lleva trazas de curarse** it doesn't look as if he's going to get better

trazado *nm* (**a**) (*plano*) layout, plan (**b**) (*de carretera, ferrocarril*) route

trazar [40] *vt* (*línea*) to draw; (*plano*) to design; *Fig* (*plan*) to sketch out

trazo *nm* (**a**) (*línea*) line (**b**) (*de letra*) stroke

trébol *nm* (**a**) (*planta*) clover (**b**) *Naipes* club

trece 1 *adj inv* thirteen
  2 *nm inv* thirteen; *Fig* **estar** *o* **mantenerse** *o* **seguir en sus t.** to stick to one's guns

trecho *nm* distance, way; *(tramo)* stretch; **de t. en t.** from time to time

tregua *nf Mil* truce; *Fig* respite

treinta *adj & nm inv* thirty

treintavo, -a *adj & nm* thirtieth

treintena *nf* **una t. de** (about) thirty

tremendista *adj* over the top

tremendo, -a *adj* (a) *(terrible)* terrible, dreadful (b) *(muy grande)* enormous; *Fig* tremendous

trementina *nf* turpentine

trémulo, -a *adj Literario (vacilante)* quivering, tremulous; *(luz)* flickering

tren *nm* (a) *(ferrocarril)* train (b) *Av* **t. de aterrizaje** undercarriage; **t. de lavado** car wash (c) **t. de vida** lifestyle

trenca *nf* duffle coat

trenza *nf (de pelo)* plait, *esp US* braid

trepador, -a *adj* climbing

trepar *vt & vi* to climb

trepidante *adj* vibrating, shaking; *Fig* **lleva un ritmo de vida t.** he leads a hectic *o* frantic life

trepidar *vi* to vibrate, to shake

tres 1 *adj inv (cardinal)* three; *(ordinal)* third; *Fam* **de t. al cuarto** cheap, of little value
  2 *nm* three; **t. en raya** *Br* noughts and crosses, *US* tick-tack-toe

trescientos, -as *adj & nm* three hundred

tresillo *nm* (a) *(mueble)* (three-piece) suite (b) *Mús* triplet

treta *nf* trick, ruse

trial *nm Dep* trial

triangular *adj* triangular

triángulo *nm* triangle; *Fig* **t. amoroso** eternal triangle

tribal *adj* tribal

tribu *nf* tribe

tribuna *nf* (a) *(plataforma)* rostrum, dais; **t. de (la) prensa** press box (b) *Dep* stand

tribunal *nm* (a) *Der* court; **t. de apelación** court of appeal; **el T. Supremo** *Br* ≃ the High Court, *US* ≃ the Supreme Court (b) *(de examen)* board of examiners

tributar *vt* to pay

tributario, -a *adj* **sistema t.** tax system

tributo *nm* (a) *Com* tax (b) *(homenaje)* tribute

triciclo *nm* tricycle

tricornio *nm* three-cornered hat

tricotar *vt & vi* to knit

tridimensional *adj* three-dimensional

trienio *nm* three-year period

trifásico, -a 1 *adj Elec* three-phase
  2 *nm* adapter

trigésimo, -a *adj & nm,f* thirtieth; **t. primero** thirty-first

trigo *nm* wheat

trigueño, -a *adj Am (pelo)* light brown, corn-coloured; *(persona)* light brown-skinned

trilla *nf* threshing

trillado, -a *adj Fig* well-worn

trilladora *nf* threshing machine; **t. segadora** combine harvester

trillar *vt* to thresh

trillizo, -a *nm,f* triplet

trilogía *nf* trilogy

trimestral *adj* quarterly, three-monthly

trimestre *nm* quarter; *Educ* term

trinar *vi* (a) *(pájaro)* to warble (b) *Fam* **está que trina** he's really fuming

trincar¹ [44] *vt Fam (capturar)* to catch

trincar² *vt Fam* to drink

trinchar *vt (carne)* to carve, to slice (up)

trinchera *nf* trench

trineo *nm* sledge, sleigh

Trinidad *nf* **la Santísima T.** the Holy Trinity

trino *nm* warble, trill

trío *nm* trio

tripa *nf* (a) *(intestino)* gut, intestine; *Esp Fam* tummy; **dolor de t.** stomach ache (b) **tripas** innards

triple *adj & nm* triple

triplicado, -a *adj* triplicate; **por t.** in triplicate

triplicar [44] *vt* to triple, to treble

trípode *nm* tripod

tríptico *nm* (a) *(cuadro)* triptych (b) *(folleto)* leaflet *(folded twice to form three parts)*

tripulación *nf* crew

tripulante *nmf* crew member

tripular *vt* to man

triquiñuela *nf Fam* trick, dodge

tris *nm* **estar en un t. de** to be on the verge of

triste *adj* (a) *(persona, situación)* sad (b) *(lugar)* gloomy

tristeza *nf* sadness

triturar *vt (machacar)* to grind (up)

triunfador, -a 1 *adj* winning
  2 *nm,f* winner

triunfal *adj* triumphant

triunfar *vi* to triumph

triunfo *nm* (a) *(victoria)* triumph, victory; *Dep* win (b) *(éxito)* success

trivial *adj* trivial

trivialidad *nf* triviality

trivializar *vt* to trivialize, to minimize

triza *nf* bit, fragment; **hacer trizas** to tear to shreds

trocar [64] *vt* (a) *(transformar)* **t. algo (en algo)** to change sth (into sth) (b) *(intercambiar)* to swap, to exchange

trocear *vt* to cut up (into bits o pieces)

trocha *nf Am* path

trofeo *nm* trophy

trola *nf Fam* fib

tromba *nf* **t. de agua** violent downpour

trombón *nm* trombone

trombosis *nf inv* thrombosis

trompa *nf* (a) *Mús* horn (b) *(de elefante)* trunk (c) *Anat* tube (d) *Fam* **estar t.** to be sloshed o plastered

trompazo *nm Fam* bump; **darse o pegarse un t.** to have a bump

trompeta *nf* trumpet

trompetista *nmf* trumpet player, trumpeter

trompicón *nm* trip, stumble; **hacer algo a trompicones** to do sth in fits and starts

trompo *nm* spinning top

trona *nf* high chair

tronar [2] **1** *vi* to thunder
2 *vt Méx Fam* (a) *(destruir, acabar con)* to get rid of (b) *(suspender)* to fail

tronchar 1 *vt (partir)* to snap
2 troncharse *vpr Fam* **troncharse de risa** to split one's sides laughing

tronco *nm* (a) *Anat* trunk, torso (b) *Bot (de árbol)* trunk; *(leño)* log; *Fam Fig* **dormir como un t.** to sleep like a log

tronera *nf* (a) *(de billar)* pocket (b) *(ventana)* small window; *(de fortificación)* loophole; *Náut* porthole

trono *nm* throne

tropa *nf (no oficiales)* rank and file; *(ejército)* troops

tropel *nm* throng, mob; **en t.** in a mad rush

tropezar [1] *vi* (a) *(con los pies)* to trip, to stumble (**con** on) (b) *(por casualidad)* **t. con algo** to come across sth; **t. con algn/ dificultades** to run into sb/difficulties

tropezón *nm* (a) *(con los pies)* trip, stumble; **dar un t.** to trip (b) *(error)* slip-up, faux pas (c) *(de comida)* chunk of meat

tropical *adj* tropical

trópico *nm* tropic

tropiezo 1 *nm* (a) *(con los pies)* trip, stumble (b) *Fig (error)* blunder, faux pas
2 *indic pres de* **tropezar**

trotamundos *nmf inv* globetrotter

trotar *vi* to trot

trote *nm* (a) *(de caballo)* trot; **al t.** at a trot (b) *Fam* **ya no está para esos trotes** he cannot keep up the pace any more

trovador *nm* troubadour

trozar *vt Am (carne)* to cut up; *(res, tronco)* to butcher, to cut up

trozo *nm* piece

trucar [44] *vt* to doctor, to alter

trucha *nf* trout

truco *nm* (a) *(ardid)* trick; **aquí hay t.** there's something fishy going on here (b) **coger el t. (a algo)** to get the knack o hang (of sth)

truculento, -a *adj* horrifying, terrifying

> 🖉 Observa que la palabra inglesa **truculent** es un falso amigo y no es la traducción de la palabra española **truculento**. En inglés, **truculent** significa "agresivo, airado".

trueno *nm* thunder; **un t.** a thunderclap

trueque *nm* barter

trufa *nf* truffle

truhán, -ana *nm,f* rogue, crook

truncar [44] *vt (vida, carrera)* to cut short; *(esperanzas)* to shatter

trusa *nf* (a) *Carib (traje de baño)* swimsuit (b) *Perú (short)* briefs (c) *RP (faja)* girdle

trust [trus(t)] *(pl trusts)* *nm* trust, cartel

tu *(pl tus) adj pos* your; **tu libro** your book; **tus libros** your books

tú *pron* you; **de tú a tú** on equal terms

> Usually omitted in Spanish except for emphasis or contrast.

tuba *nf* tuba

tubérculo *nm* (a) *Bot* tuber (b) *Med* tubercle

tuberculosis *nf inv* tuberculosis

tubería *nf* (a) *(de agua)* piping, pipes (b) *(de gas)* pipeline

tubo *nm* (a) *(cilindro, recipiente)* tube; **t. de ensayo** test tube (b) *(tubería)* pipe; *Aut* **t. de escape** exhaust (pipe)

tucán *nm* toucan

tuerca *nf* nut

tuerto, -a 1 *adj* one-eyed, blind in one eye
2 *nm,f* one-eyed person

tuerzo *indic pres de* **torcer**

tuétano *nm* marrow; *Fig* **hasta el t.** to one's fingertips

tufo *nm Fam* stench, foul smell

tugurio *nm Fam* hovel

tul *nm* tulle

tulipa *nf (de lámpara)* tulip-shaped lampshade

tulipán *nm* tulip

tullido, -a *adj* crippled, disabled

tullir *vt* to cripple

tumba *nf* grave, tomb

tumbar 1 *vt* to knock down o over
2 tumbarse *vpr (acostarse)* to lie down, to stretch out

tumbo *nm* **dar tumbos** to reel

tumbona *nf Br* sun-lounger, *US* (beach) recliner

tumor *nm* tumour

tumulto *nm* tumult, commotion

tumultuoso, -a *adj* tumultuous, riotous

tuna *nf* (**a**) *(agrupación musical)* = group of student minstrels (**b**) *Am (higo chumbo)* prickly pear

> 🖉 Observa que la palabra inglesa **tuna** es un falso amigo y no es la traducción de la palabra española **tuna**. En inglés, **tuna** significa "atún, bonito".

tunante, -a *nm,f* rogue, crook

túnel *nm* tunnel; **el T. del Canal de la Mancha** the Channel Tunnel

Túnez *n* (**a**) *(país)* Tunisia (**b**) *(ciudad)* Tunis

túnica *nf* tunic

tuno, -a 1 *nm,f (bribón)* rogue, crook
2 *nm* = member of a "tuna"

tuntún: al tuntún *loc adv* haphazardly, any old how

tupé *nm* quiff

tupido, -a *adj* thick, dense

turba¹ *nf (combustible)* peat

turba² *nf (muchedumbre)* mob, crowd

turbado, -a *adj* (**a**) *(alterado)* disturbed (**b**) *(preocupado)* worried, anxious (**c**) *(desconcertado)* confused

turbante *nm* turban

turbar 1 *vt* (**a**) *(alterar)* to unsettle (**b**) *(preocupar)* to upset o worry (**c**) *(desconcertar)* to baffle, to put off
2 turbarse *vpr* (**a**) *(preocuparse)* to be o become upset (**b**) *(desconcertarse)* to be o become confused o baffled

turbina *nf* turbine

turbio, -a *adj (agua)* cloudy; *(negocio etc)* shady, dubious

turbulencia *nf* turbulence

turbulento, -a *adj* turbulent

turco, -a 1 *adj* Turkish
2 *nm,f (persona)* Turk
3 *nm (idioma)* Turkish

turismo *nm* (**a**) *(actividad)* tourism; **hacer t. (por)** to go touring (round); **t. rural** country holidays, rural tourism (**b**) *Aut* private car

turista *nmf* tourist

turístico, -a *adj* tourist; **de interés t.** of interest to tourists

túrmix® *nf inv* blender, liquidizer

turnarse *vpr* to take turns

turno *nm* (**a**) *(en juegos etc)* turn, go (**b**) *(de trabajo)* shift; **estar de t.** to be on duty; **t. de día/noche** day/night shift

turquesa *adj inv & nf* turquoise

Turquía *n* Turkey

turrón *nm* nougat

tute *nm Fam* **darse un t. de algo** to go to town doing sth

tutear 1 *vt* = to address as "tú"
2 tutearse *vpr* = to address each other as "tú"

tutela *nf* (**a**) *Der* guardianship, tutelage (**b**) *Fig (protección)* protection, guidance

tuteo *nm* = use of the "tú" form of address

tutor *nm* (**a**) *Der* guardian (**b**) *Educ* tutor

tuve *pt indef de* tener

tuyo, -a 1 *adj pos (con personas)* of yours; *(con objetos)* one of your; **¿es amigo t.?** is he a friend of yours?; **unas amigas tuyas** some friends of yours; **un libro t.** one of your books
2 *pron pos* yours; **éste es t.** this one is yours; *Fam* **los tuyos** *(familiares)* your family

U, u [u] *nf (letra)* U, u

u *conj (delante de palabras que empiecen por o o ho)* or; **siete u ocho** seven or eight; **ayer u hoy** yesterday or today

ubicación *nf* location, position

ubicar [44] **1** *vt* (a) *(situar) (edificio, fábrica)* to locate (b) *Am (colocar)* to put (c) *Am (encontrar)* to find, to locate; **no veo su ficha por acá, pero en cuanto la ubique le aviso** I can't see your card here, but as soon as I find it I'll let you know
2 ubicarse *upr* (a) *(edificio)* to be situated o located (b) *Am (persona)* to get one's bearings; **¿ya te ubicas en la ciudad?** are you finding your way around the city all right?

ubicuo, -a *adj* ubiquitous

ubre *nf* udder

UCI *nf (abr* **unidad de cuidados intensivos)** ICU

Ucrania *n* Ukraine

ucraniano, -a *adj & nm,f* Ukrainian

Ud., Uds. *(abr* **usted, ustedes)** you

UE *nf (abr* **Unión Europea)** EU

ufanarse *upr* to boast (**de** of)

ufano, -a *adj* conceited

UGT *nf (abr* **Unión General de Traba-jadores)** = major socialist trade union in Spain

ujier *nm* usher

úlcera *nf* ulcer

ulcerarse *upr* to ulcerate

ulterior *adj* subsequent

últimamente *adv* lately, recently

ultimar *vt* (a) *(terminar)* to finalize (b) *Am (asesinar)* to kill

ultimátum *(pl* **ultimátums)** *nm* ultimatum

último, -a 1 *adj* (a) *(en una serie, en el tiempo)* last; **el ú. día** the last day; **por ú.** finally (b) *(más reciente)* latest; **últimas noticias** latest news (c) *(más alto)* top; *(más bajo)* bottom; **el ú. piso** the top floor; **la última fila** the back row (d) *(definitivo)* final
2 *nm,f* **llegar el ú.** to arrive last; **a últimos de mes** at the end of the month; **en las últimas** on one's last legs; *Fam* **a la última**

up to the minute; **el ú. de la lista** the lowest in the list

ultra *nmf Pol* extreme right-winger

ultraderecha *nf Pol* extreme right

ultrajar *vt* to outrage, to offend

ultraje *nm* outrage, offence

ultramarinos *nm inv (tienda)* grocer's (shop)

ultranza: a ultranza 1 *loc adj* die-hard, hardline
2 *loc adv* to the last, at any price

ultratumba *nf* afterlife

ultravioleta *adj inv* ultraviolet

ulular *vi (viento)* to howl; *(búho)* to hoot

umbral *nm* threshold

umbrío, -a, umbroso, -a *adj* shady

un, una 1 *art indef* (a) *(singular)* a; *(antes de vocal)* an; **un coche** a car; **un huevo** an egg; **una flor** a flower (b) *(plural)* some; **unas flores** some flowers
2 *adj (delante de nm sing)* one; **un chico y dos chicas** one boy and two girls; *ver también* **uno**

unánime *adj* unanimous

unanimidad *nf* unanimity; **por u.** unanimously

unción *nf* unction

undécimo, -a *adj* eleventh

UNED *nf (abr* **Universidad Nacional de Educación a Distancia)** = Spanish open university

ungir [57] *vt Rel* to anoint

ungüento *nm* ointment

únicamente *adv* only, solely

único, -a *adj* (a) *(solo)* only; **es el ú. que tengo** it's the only one I've got; **hijo ú.** only child; **lo ú. que quiero** the only thing I want; **el Mercado Ú.** the Single Market; **el Acta Única** the Single European Act (b) *(extraordinario)* unique

unidad *nf* (a) *(elemento, medida, sección)* unit; **u. de cuidados intensivos** intensive care unit (b) *(cohesión)* unity

unido, -a *adj* united; **están muy unidos** they are very attached to one another; **una familia muy unida** a very close family

unifamiliar *adj* **vivienda u.** detached house

unificación *nf* unification

unificar [44] *vt* to unify

uniformar *vt* (**a**) *(igualar)* to make uniform, to standardize (**b**) *(poner un uniforme a)* to put into uniform, to give a uniform to

uniforme 1 *nm (prenda)* uniform
2 *adj* (**a**) *(igual)* uniform (**b**) *(superficie)* even

uniformidad *nf* (**a**) *(igualdad)* uniformity (**b**) *(de superficie)* evenness

unilateral *adj* unilateral

unión *nf* union

Unión Soviética *n Hist* Soviet Union

unir 1 *vt (juntar)* to unite, to join (together); **esta carretera une las dos comarcas** this road links both districts
2 **unirse** *vpr (juntarse)* to unite, to join

unisex *adj inv* unisex

unísono *nm* unison; **al u.** in unison

unitario, -a *adj* unitary; **precio u.** unit price

universal *adj* universal; **historia u.** world history

universidad *nf* university; **u. a distancia** = distance learning university, ≃ Open University; **u. laboral** technical college

universitario, -a 1 *adj* university
2 *nm,f* university student

universo *nm* universe

uno, -a 1 *nm inv* one; **el u.** (number) one; **el u. de mayo** the first of May
2 *nf* **es la una** *(hora)* it's one o'clock
3 *adj* **unos, -as** some; **unas cajas** some boxes; **habrá unos** *o* **unas veinte** there must be around twenty
4 *pron* (**a**) *(indefinido, numeral)* one; **u. (de ellos), una (de ellas)** one of them; **unos cuantos** a few; **se miraron el u. al otro** they looked at each other; **de u. en u.** one by one; **un trás otro** one after the other; **una de dos** one of the two (**b**) *(persona)* someone, somebody; **u. que pasaba por allí** some passer-by; **vive con u.** she's living with some man; **unos ... otros** some people ... others (**c**) *(impersonal)* you, one; **u. tiene que ...** you have to ...

untar *vt* to grease, to smear; *(mantequilla)* to spread

uña *nf* (**a**) *(de mano)* nail, fingernail; *(de pie)* toenail; **morderse** *o* **comerse las uñas** to bite one's fingernails; *Fig* **ser u. y carne** to be hand in glove (**b**) *Zool (garra)* claw; *(pezuña)* hoof

uperizado, -a *adj* **leche uperizada** UHT milk

uralita® *nf* = material made of asbestos and cement, usually corrugated and used mainly for roofing

uranio *nm* uranium

Urano *nm* Uranus

urbanidad *nf* urbanity, politeness

urbanismo *nm* town planning

urbanístico, -a *adj* town-planning

urbanización *nf* (**a**) *(barrio)* housing development *o* estate (**b**) *(proceso)* urbanization

urbanizar *vt* to build up

urbano, -a *adj* urban, city; **guardia u.** (traffic) policeman

urbe *nf* large city

urdimbre *nf* (**a**) *Tex* warp (**b**) *(trama)* intrigue

urdir *vt* (**a**) *Tex* to warp (**b**) *(tramar)* to plot, to scheme

urgencia *nf* (**a**) *(cualidad)* urgency; **con u.** urgently (**b**) *(en hospital) (caso)* emergency (case); **urgencias** *Br* casualty (department), accident and emergency (department), *US* emergency room

urgente *adj* urgent; **correo u.** express mail

urgir [57] *vi* to be urgent *o* pressing; **me urge (tenerlo)** I need it urgently

urinario *nm* urinal, *US* comfort station

urna *nf* (**a**) *Pol* ballot box (**b**) *(vasija)* urn

urólogo, -a *nm,f Med* urologist

urraca *nf* magpie

URSS *nf Hist (abr* **Unión de Repúblicas Socialistas Soviéticas***)* USSR

urticaria *nf Med* hives

Uruguay *n* **(el) U.** Uruguay

uruguayo, -a *adj & nm,f* Uruguayan

usado, -a *adj (ropa)* second-hand, used

usanza *nf Literario* **a la antigua u.** in the old style

usar 1 *vt* (**a**) *(aparato, término)* to use (**b**) *(prenda)* to wear
2 **usarse** *vpr* to be used *o* in fashion

usina *nf Andes, RP* plant; **u. eléctrica** power station, power plant; **u. nuclear** nuclear power station, nuclear power plant

uso *nm* (**a**) use; **hacer u. de** *(utilizar)* to make use of, to use; *(de prerrogativa, derecho)* to exercise; **de u. externo** *(medicamento)* for external use only (**b**) *(de prenda)* wearing; **haga u. del casco** wear a helmet (**c**) *(costumbre)* usage, custom; **al u.** conventional

usted *(pl* **ustedes***) pron pers Fml* you; **¿quién es u.?, ¿quiénes son ustedes?** who are you?

Usually omitted in Spanish except for emphasis or contrast. Although formal in peninsular Spanish, it is not necessarily so in Latin American Spanish.

usual *adj* usual, common

usuario, -a *nm,f* user

usura *nf* usury

usurero, -a *nm,f* usurer

usurpar *vt* to usurp

utensilio *nm* utensil; *(herramienta)* tool

útero *nm* uterus, womb

útil 1 *adj* useful; *(día)* working
2 *nm (herramienta)* tool, instrument

utilidad *nf* usefulness, utility; *(beneficio)* profit

utilitario, -a 1 *adj* utilitarian
2 *nm (coche)* utility vehicle

utilización *nf* use, utilization

utilizar [40] *vt* to use, to utilize

utopía *nf* utopia

utópico, -a *adj & nm,f* utopian

uva *nf* grape; **u. blanca** green grape

UVI *nf (abr* **unidad de vigilancia intensiva)** ICU

V, v ['ue] *nf (letra)* V, v

V *Elec (abr* **voltio(s)**) V

vaca *nf* (a) *(animal)* cow (b) *(carne)* beef

vacaciones *nfpl* holiday, *Br* holidays, *US* vacation; **durante las v.** during the holidays; **estar/irse de v.** to be/go on *Br* holiday *o US* vacation

vacacionista *nmf Am Br* holidaymaker, *US* vacationer

vacante 1 *adj* vacant
2 *nf* vacancy

vaciar [29] **1** *vt* (a) *(recipiente)* to empty; *(contenido)* to empty out (b) *(terreno)* to hollow out (c) *Arte* to cast, to mould
2 vaciarse *vpr* to empty

vacilación *nf* hesitation

vacilante *adj* (a) *(persona)* hesitant, irresolute (b) *(voz)* hesitant, faltering (c) *(luz)* flickering

vacilar *vi* (a) *(dudar)* to hesitate; **sin v.** without hesitation (b) *(voz)* to falter (c) *(luz)* to flicker (d) *Fam (jactarse)* to show off

vacilón, -ona *Fam* **1** *adj* (a) *(fanfarrón)* swanky (b) *Esp, Carib, Méx (bromista)* jokey, teasing
2 *nm,f* (a) *(fanfarrón)* show-off (b) *Esp, Carib, Méx (bromista)* tease
3 *nm CAm, Carib, Méx (fiesta)* party

vacío, -a 1 *adj* (a) *(recipiente, palabras, vida)* empty (b) *(sin ocupar)* vacant, unoccupied
2 *nm* (a) *(abismo, carencia)* void (b) *Fís* vacuum; **envasado al v.** vacuum-packed (c) *(hueco)* gap; *(espacio)* (empty) space

vacuna *nf* vaccine

vacunación *nf* vaccination

vacunar 1 *vt* to vaccinate (**contra** against); *Fig* to inure
2 vacunarse *vpr* to get oneself vaccinated

vacuno, -a *adj* bovine; **ganado v.** cattle

vacuo, -a *adj* vacuous, empty

vadear *vt (río)* to ford; *Fig (dificultad)* to overcome

vado *nm* (a) *(de río)* ford (b) *Aut* **v. permanente** *(en letrero)* keep clear

vagabundear *vi* to wander, to roam

vagabundo, -a 1 *adj (persona)* vagrant; **perro v.** stray dog
2 *nm,f (sin casa)* tramp, vagrant, *US* bum

vagancia *nf* idleness, laziness

vagar [42] *vi* to wander about, to roam about

vagina *nf* vagina

vago, -a 1 *adj* (a) *(perezoso)* lazy (b) *(indefinido)* vague
2 *nm,f* (a) *(holgazán)* layabout (b) *Der* vagrant

vagón *nm (para pasajeros)* carriage, coach, *US* car; *(para mercancías)* truck, wagon, *US* freight car, *US* boxcar

vagoneta *nf* wagon

vaguedad *nf* vagueness

vaho *nm (de aliento)* breath; *(vapor)* vapour

vaina 1 *nf* (a) *(de espada)* sheath, scabbard (b) *Bot* pod (c) *Col, Perú, Ven muy Fam (cosa molesta)* pain (in the neck)
2 *nmf Col, Perú, Ven muy Fam* **ése es un v.** he's a pain

vainilla *nf* vanilla

vaivén *nm* (a) *(oscilación)* swinging, to-and-fro movement (b) *(de gente)* coming and going, bustle; *Fig* **vaivenes** ups and downs

vajilla *nf* crockery, dishes; **una v.** a set of dishes, a dinner service

valdré *indic fut de* **valer**

vale¹ *interj Esp* all right!, O.K.!

vale² *nm* (a) *(comprobante)* voucher (b) *(pagaré)* promissory note, IOU (I owe you) (c) *Méx, Ven Fam (amigo)* pal, *Br* mate, *US* buddy

valedero, -a *adj* valid

valenciano, -a 1 *adj & nm,f* Valencian
2 *nm (idioma)* Valencian

valentía *nf* courage, bravery

valentón, -ona *Pey* **1** *adj* bragging, boastful
2 *nm,f* braggart

valer [26] **1** *vt* (a) *(tener un valor de)* to be worth; **no vale nada** it is worthless; **vale una fortuna** it is worth a fortune; **no vale la pena (ir)** it's not worth while (going) (b) *(costar)* to cost;

¿cuánto vale? how much is it? (c) *(proporcionar)* to earn

2 *vi* (a) *(servir)* to be useful, to be of use (b) *(ser válido)* to be valid, to count; **no vale hacer trampa** cheating isn't on (c) **más vale** it is better; **más vale que te vayas ya** you had better leave now

3 valerse *vpr* **valerse de** to use, to make use of; **valerse por sí mismo** to be able to manage on one's own

valeriana *nf* valerian, allheal

valeroso, -a *adj* brave, courageous

valgo *indic pres de* **valer**

valía *nf* value, worth

validez *nf* validity

válido, -a *adj* valid

valiente *adj* (a) *(valeroso)* brave, courageous (b) *Irón* **¡v. amigo eres tú!** a fine friend you are!

valija *nf* (a) *(maleta)* case, suitcase; **v. diplomática** diplomatic bag (b) *(de correos)* mailbag

valioso, -a *adj* valuable

valla *nf* (a) *(cerca)* fence; *(muro)* wall; **v. publicitaria** billboard, *Br* hoarding (b) *Dep* hurdle; **los 100 metros vallas** the 100 metres hurdle race

vallado *nm* fence

vallar *vt* to fence (in)

valle *nm* valley

vallisoletano, -a 1 *adj* of/from Valladolid

2 *nm,f* person from Valladolid

valor *nm* (a) *(precio, utilidad, mérito)* value; **objetos de v.** valuables; **sin v.** worthless; **v. alimenticio** food value (b) *(valentía)* courage (c) *(desvergüenza)* cheek, nerve (d) **valores** *(principios)* values; *Fin* securities

valoración *nf* *(de propiedad, obra)* valuation; *(de pérdidas, daños)* assessment, estimation

valorar *vt* (a) *(tasar) (propiedad, obra)* to value; *(pérdidas, daños)* to assess, to estimate (b) *(apreciar)* to value

valorizar [40] *vt* to raise the value of

vals *nm* waltz

válvula *nf* valve; **v. de seguridad** safety valve

vampiro *nm* vampire

vanagloriarse [43] *vpr* to boast (**de** of)

vandalismo *nm* vandalism

vándalo, -a *nm,f* vandal

vanguardia *nf* (a) *(cultural)* avant-garde, vanguard; **ir a la v. de** to be at the forefront of (b) *Mil* vanguard

vanguardista 1 *adj* avant-garde

2 *nmf* avant-gardist

vanidad *nf* vanity

vanidoso, -a *adj* vain, conceited

vano, -a *adj* (a) *(vanidoso)* vain, conceited (b) *(esfuerzo, esperanza)* vain, futile; **en v.** in vain

vapor *nm* (a) *(de agua hirviendo)* steam; *Culin* **al v.** steamed (b) *(gas)* vapour; **v. de agua** water vapour

vaporizador *nm* vaporizer, spray

vaporizar [40] **1** *vt* to vaporize

2 vaporizarse *vpr* to vaporize, to evaporate

vaporoso, -a *adj* vaporous

vapulear *vt* *(físicamente)* to shake; *(con palabras)* to slate

vaquero 1 *nm* cowboy

2 *adj* **pantalón v.** jeans, pair of jeans

3 vaqueros *nmpl* *(prenda)* jeans, pair of jeans

vara *nf* pole, rod

varar 1 *vt* to beach, to dock

2 *vi* to run aground

variable *adj & nf* variable

variación *nf* variation

variado, -a *adj* varied; **galletas variadas** assorted *Br* biscuits *o US* cookies

variante *nf* variant

variar [29] **1** *vt* to vary, to change

2 *vi* to vary, to change; *Irón* **para v.** as usual, just for a change

varicela *nf* chickenpox

variedad *nf* (a) *(cualidad)* variety (b) *Teatro* **variedades** variety, *Br* music hall, *US* vaudeville

varilla *nf* *(vara)* rod, stick; *(de abanico, paraguas)* rib

variopinto, -a *adj* diverse, assorted; **un público v.** a varied audience

varios, -as *adj* several

varita *nf* **v. mágica** magic wand

variz *nf* varicose vein

varón *nm* *(hombre)* man; *(chico)* boy; **hijo v.** male child; **sexo v.** male sex

varonil *adj* manly, virile

Varsovia *n* Warsaw

vas *indic pres de* **ir**

vasallo, -a *nm,f* *Hist* vassal

vasco, -a 1 *adj* Basque; **el País V.** the Basque Country

2 *nm,f* Basque

3 *nm (idioma)* Basque

vascuence *nm (idioma)* Basque

vasectomía *nf* vasectomy

vaselina *nf* Vaseline®

vasija *nf* pot

vaso *nm* (a) *(para beber)* glass (b) *Anat* vessel

📖 Observa que la palabra inglesa **vase** es un falso amigo y no es la traducción de la palabra española **vaso**. En inglés, **vase** significa "jarrón".

vástago nm (descendiente) offspring

vasto, -a adj vast

váter nm toilet

Vaticano nm **el V.** the Vatican

vaticinar vt to prophesy, to predict

vaticinio nm prophecy, prediction

vatio nm watt

vaya¹ interj **¡v. lío!** what a mess!

vaya² subj pres de **ir**

Vd., Vds. (abr **usted, ustedes**) you

ve 1 imperat de **ir**
　2 indic pres de **ver**

vecinal adj local

vecindad nf (a) (barrio) neighbourhood (b) (alrededores) vicinity

vecindario nm neighbourhood

vecino, -a 1 nm,f (a) (persona) neighbour; **el v. de al lado** the next-door neighbour (b) (residente) resident
　2 adj neighbouring, nearby

veda nf (de caza) closed season; **levantar la v.** to open the season

vedado, -a adj **coto v. de caza** private hunting ground

vedar vt to forbid, to prohibit

vega nf fertile plain o lowland

vegetación nf (a) Bot vegetation (b) Med **vegetaciones** adenoids

vegetal nm vegetable

vegetar vi to vegetate

vegetariano, -a adj & nm,f vegetarian

vehemencia nf vehemence

vehemente adj vehement

vehículo nm vehicle

veinte adj & nm inv twenty

veintena nf (veinte) twenty; **una v. de** about twenty

vejación nf humiliation

vejar vt to humiliate

vejatorio, -a adj humiliating

vejez nf old age

vejiga nf bladder

vela¹ nf (a) (de cera) candle; Fam **quedarse a dos velas** to be in the dark (b) (vigilia) **pasar la noche en v.** to have a sleepless night

vela² nf Náut sail

velada nf evening (party)

velado, -a adj veiled, hidden

velador nm (a) (mesa) table (b) Andes, Méx (mesilla) bedside table (c) Méx, RP (lámpara) bedside lamp

velar 1 vi **v. por** to watch over
　2 vt (muerto) to keep a vigil over; (enfermo) to sit up with

velatorio nm vigil, wake

velcro® nm Velcro®

veleidad nf fickleness

veleidoso, -a adj fickle

velero nm sailing boat o ship

veleta 1 nf weather vane, weathercock
　2 nmf Fam fickle o changeable person

veliz nf Méx suitcase

vello nm hair

vellón nm fleece

velloso, -a, velludo, -a adj downy

velo nm veil

velocidad nf (a) (rapidez) speed; (de proyectil etc) velocity; Aut **v. máxima** speed limit; Inform **v. de transmisión** bit rate; Inform **v. operativa** operating speed (b) Aut (marcha) gear

velocímetro nm speedometer

velocista nmf sprinter

velódromo nm cycle track, velodrome

velomotor nm moped

velorio nm wake

veloz 1 adj swift, rapid
　2 adv quickly, fast

vena nf vein

venado nm deer, stag; Culin venison

vencedor, -a 1 nm,f winner
　2 adj winning

vencejo nm swift

vencer [49] **1** vt (a) (al enemigo) to defeat; (al contrincante) to beat (b) (dificultad) to overcome, to surmount
　2 vi (a) (pago, deuda) to fall due, to be payable (b) (plazo) to expire
　3 vencerse vpr (torcerse) to warp

vencido, -a adj (a) Mil (derrotado) defeated; Dep beaten; Fig **darse por v.** to give up, to accept defeat (b) (pago, deuda) due, payable (c) (plazo) expired (d) Fam **a la tercera va la vencida** third time lucky

vencimiento nm (a) Com maturity (b) (de un plazo) expiry

venda nf bandage

vendaje nm bandaging, dressing

vendar vt to bandage; Fig **v. los ojos a algn** to blindfold sb

vendaval nm gale

vendedor, -a nm,f seller; (hombre) salesman; (mujer) saleswoman

vender 1 *vt* to sell; **v. a plazos/al contado** to sell on credit/for cash; **v. al por mayor/menor** to (sell) wholesale/retail
2 venderse *vpr* (**a**) *(producto)* to sell; **este disco se vende bien** this record is selling well; **se vende** *(en letrero)* for sale (**b**) *(claudicar)* to sell out

vendimia *nf* grape harvest

vendimiador, -a *nm,f* grape picker

vendimiar [43] **1** *vt* to harvest *(grapes)*
2 *vi* to pick grapes

vendré *indic fut de* **venir**

Venecia *n* Venice

veneno *nm* poison; *(de serpiente)* venom

venenoso, -a *adj* poisonous

venerable *adj* venerable

veneración *nf* veneration

venerar *vt* to venerate, to revere

venéreo, -a *adj* venereal

venezolano, -a *adj & nm,f* Venezuelan

Venezuela *n* Venezuela

venga *subj pres de* **venir**

venganza *nf* vengeance, revenge

vengar [42] **1** *vt* to avenge
2 vengarse *vpr* to avenge oneself; **vengarse de algn** to take revenge on sb

vengativo, -a *adj* vengeful, vindictive

vengo *indic pres de* **venir**

venia *nf* (**a**) *Fml (permiso)* permission (**b**) *(perdón)* pardon

venial *adj* venial

venida *nf* coming, arrival

venidero, -a *adj* future, coming

venir [27] **1** *vi* (**a**) to come; *Fig* **v. a menos** to come down in the world; *Fig* **v. al mundo** to be born; **el año que viene** next year; *Fig* **me viene a la memoria** I remember; *Fam* **¡venga ya!** *(vamos)* come on!; *(expresa incredulidad)* come off it! (**b**) **v. grande/pequeño** *(ropa)* to be too big/small; **v. mal/bien** to be inconvenient/convenient; **el metro me viene muy bien** I find the *Br* underground o *US* subway very handy (**c**) *(en pasivas)* **esto vino provocado por ...** this was brought about by ... (**d**) **esto viene ocurriendo desde hace mucho tiempo** this has been going on for a long time now
2 venirse *vpr* **venirse abajo** to collapse

venta *nf* (**a**) *(acción)* sale; **en v.** for sale; **a la v.** on sale; **v. al contado** cash sale; **v. al por mayor/menor** wholesale/retail; **v. a plazos** sale by instalments, *Br* hire purchase (**b**) *(posada)* country inn

ventaja *nf* advantage; **llevar v. a** to have the advantage over; **le sacó 2 m de v.** he beat him by 2 m

ventajoso, -a *adj* advantageous

ventana *nf* (**a**) *(en edificio)* window (**b**) *(de la nariz)* nostril

ventanal *nm* large window

ventanilla *nf* (**a**) *(de vehículo, sobre)* window (**b**) *(taquilla)* counter

ventanuco *nm* small window

ventilación *nf* ventilation; **sin v.** unventilated

ventilador *nm* ventilator; *(de coche)* fan

ventilar 1 *vt* *(habitación)* to ventilate, to air
2 ventilarse *vpr* *Fam (terminar)* to finish off

ventisca *nf* blizzard; *(de nieve)* snowstorm

ventosa *nf* sucker; *Med* cupping glass

ventosear *vi* to break wind

ventoso, -a *adj* windy

ventrílocuo, -a *nm,f* ventriloquist

ventura *nf* (**a**) *(felicidad)* happiness (**b**) *(suerte)* luck; *(casualidad)* chance

venturoso, -a *adj* lucky, fortunate

Venus *nm* Venus

veo-veo *nm Fam* **el (juego del) v.** I-spy

ver¹ *nm* **de buen v.** good-looking

ver² [28] **1** *vt* to see; *(televisión)* to watch; **a v.** let me see, let's see; **a v. si escribes** I hope you'll write; **(ya) veremos** we'll see; **no tener nada que v. con** to have nothing to do with
2 a ver *loc adv (veamos)* let's see; *(al empezar algo)* right!;**¿a ver?** let me see, let's have a look
3 verse *vpr* (**a**) *(imagen etc)* to be seen (**b**) *(encontrarse con algn)* to meet, see each other; **¡nos vemos!** see you later!

vera *nf* edge, border; **a la v. de** beside, next to

veracidad *nf* veracity, truthfulness

veraneante *nmf* *Br* holidaymaker, *US* (summer) vacationer

veranear *vi* **v. en** to spend one's summer *Br* holidays o *US* vacation in

veraneo *nm* summer *Br* holidays o *US* vacation

veraniego, -a *adj* summer

veranillo *nm* Indian summer

verano *nm* summer

veras *nfpl* **de v.** really, seriously

veraz *adj* veracious, truthful

verbal *adj* verbal

verbena *nf* street party

verbo *nm* verb

verborrea *nf* *Fam* verbosity, verbal diarrhoea

verdad *nf* (**a**) **la v.** the truth; **es v.** it is true; **a decir v.** to tell the truth; **¡de v!** really!, truly!; **un amigo de v.** a real friend (**b**) *(buscando confirmación)* está muy bien, ¿(no es) v.? it is very good, isn't it?; **no te gusta, ¿v.?** you don't like it, do you?

verdaderamente *adv* truly, really

verdadero, -a *adj* true, real

verde 1 *adj* (a) *(color)* green (b) *(poco maduro) (fruta)* unripe, green; *(proyecto, plan)* in its early stages (c) *(ecologista)* Green, green (d) *Fam (obsceno)* blue, dirty; **viejo v.** dirty old man (e) *Fam Fig* **poner v. a algn** to call sb every name under the sun
2 *nm* (a) *(color)* green (b) *Pol* **los Verdes** the Greens

verdear *vi* to turn green

verdor *nm* greenness

verdoso, -a *adj* greenish

verdugo *nm* (a) *(de preso)* executioner; *(que ahorca)* hangman (b) *(pasamontañas)* balaclava

verdulería *nf* greengrocer's (shop)

verdulero, -a *nm,f* greengrocer

verdura(s) *nf(pl)* vegetables, greens

vereda *nf* (a) *(camino)* path, lane (b) *CSur, Perú (acera) Br* pavement, *US* sidewalk (c) *Col (distrito)* area, district

veredicto *nm* verdict

verga *nf* penis

vergonzoso, -a *adj* (a) *(penoso)* shameful, disgraceful (b) *(tímido)* shy, bashful

vergüenza *nf* (a) *(deshonra)* shame; **¿no te da v.?** aren't you ashamed?, have you no shame?; **¡es una v.!** it's a disgrace! (b) *(bochorno)* embarrassment; **me da v.** I'm too embarrassed; **sentir v. ajena** to feel embarrassed for sb (c) *(timidez)* shyness, bashfulness

vericueto *nm* winding path; *Fig* **los vericuetos** the ins and outs

verídico, -a *adj* truthful, true

verificar [44] **1** *vt (comprobar)* to check
2 verificarse *vpr* to take place, to occur

verja *nf (reja)* grating; *(cerca)* railing, railings; *(puerta)* iron gate

vermut *(pl* **vermuts)**, **vermú 1** *nm* (a) *(licor)* vermouth (b) *(aperitivo)* aperitif
2 *nf esp Andes, RP (en cine)* early-evening showing; *(en teatro)* early-evening performance

verosímil *adj* probable, likely; *(creíble)* credible

verruga *nf* wart

versado, -a *adj* well-versed (**en** in)

versar *vi* **v. sobre** to be about, to deal with

versátil *adj* (a) *(polifacético)* versatile (b) *(voluble)* changeable, inconstant

versículo *nm* verse

versión *nf* version; **película en v. original** movie *o Br* film in the original language

verso *nm* (a) *(poesía)* verse (b) *(línea)* line

vértebra *nf* vertebra

vertebrado, -a *adj & nm* vertebrate

vertedero *nm (de basura) Br* rubbish tip *o* dump, *US* garbage dump

verter [3] **1** *vt* (a) *(líquido)* to pour (out) (b) *(basura)* to dump
2 *vi (río)* to flow, to run (**a** into)

vertical *adj* vertical

vértice *nm* vertex

vertidos *nmpl (residuo)* waste; **vertidos radiactivos** radioactive waste

vertiente *nf* (a) *(de una montaña, un tejado)* slope; *Fig* aspect (b) *CSur (manantial)* spring

vertiginoso, -a *adj (aumento, desarrollo)* dramatic, spectacular; *(velocidad)* dizzying; *(ritmo)* frenetic

vértigo *nm* vertigo; **me da v.** it makes me dizzy

vesícula *nf* vesicle; **v. biliar** gall bladder

vespa® *nf (motor)* scooter

vespertino, -a 1 *adj* evening
2 *nm Prensa* evening newspaper

vespino® *nm* moped

vestíbulo *nm (de casa)* hall; *(de edificio público)* foyer

vestido, -a 1 *nm (ropa)* clothes; *(de mujer)* dress
2 *adj* dressed; **policía v. de paisano** plainclothes policeman

vestiduras *nfpl (ropa)* clothes; *(sacerdotales)* vestments

vestigio *nm* vestige, trace

vestimenta *nf* clothes, garments

vestir [6] **1** *vt* (a) *(a algn)* to dress (b) *(llevar puesto)* to wear
2 *vi* (a) *(llevar ropa)* to dress (b) *(ser elegante)* **ropa de (mucho) v.** formal dress; *Fam* **la seda viste mucho** silk always looks very elegant
3 vestirse *vpr (ponerse ropa)* to get dressed, to dress; **vestirse de** to wear, to dress in; *(disfrazarse)* to dress up as

vestuario *nm* (a) *(conjunto de vestidos)* clothes, wardrobe; *Teatro* wardrobe, costumes (b) *(camerino)* dressing room (c) *Dep* changing room, *US* locker room

veta *nf Min* vein, seam; *(de carne)* streak

vetar *vt* to veto

veterano, -a *adj & nm,f* veteran

veterinaria *nf (ciencia)* veterinary medicine *o* science

veterinario, -a *nm,f (persona)* vet, *Br* veterinary surgeon, *US* veterinarian

veto *nm* veto; **derecho a v.** power *o* right of veto

vetusto, -a *adj Fml* ancient

vez *nf* (a) *(ocasión)* time; **una v.** once; **dos veces** twice; **cinco veces** five times; **a** *o* **algunas veces** sometimes; **cada v.** each *o* every time; **cada v. más** more and more; **de v. en cuando** now and again, every now and then; **¿le has visto alguna v.?** have you ever seen him?; **otra v.** again; **a la v.** at the same time; **tal v.** perhaps, maybe; **de una v.** in one go; **de una v. para siempre** once and for all; **en v. de** instead of; **érase** *o* **había una v.** *(en cuentos etc)* once upon a time (b) *(turno)* turn (c) **hacer las veces de** to do duty as

v.g(r). *(abr* **verbigracia)** eg

vía 1 *nf* (a) *Ferroc* track, line (b) *(camino)* road; **v. pública** public thoroughfare; **V. Láctea** Milky Way (c) *Anat* passage, tract; **(por) v. oral** to be taken orally (d) *Fig* **por v. oficial** through official channels; **por v. aérea/marítima** by air/sea (e) **en vías de** in the process of; **países en vías de desarrollo** developing countries
 2 *prep (a través de)* via, through; **v. París** via Paris; **transmisión v. satélite** satellite transmission

viable *adj* viable

viaducto *nm* viaduct

viajante *nmf (hombre)* travelling salesman; *(mujer)* travelling saleswoman

viajar *vi* to travel

viaje *nm (recorrido)* journey, trip; *(largo, en barco)* voyage; **¡buen v.!** bon voyage!, have a good trip!; **estar de v.** to be away (on a trip); **irse** *o* **marcharse de v.** to go on a journey *o* trip; **v. de negocios** business trip; **v. de novios** honeymoon

viajero, -a *nm,f* traveller; *(en transporte público)* passenger

vianda *nf Méx, RP (tentempié)* packed lunch; *(fiambrera)* lunchbox

viandante *nmf* passer-by

viario, -a *adj* road, highway; **red viaria** road network

víbora *nf* viper

vibración *nf* vibration

vibrador *nm* vibrator

vibrar *vt & vi* to vibrate

vicario, -a *nm,f* vicar

vicepresidente, -a *nm,f* (a) *Pol* vice-president (b) *(de compañía, comité)* vice-chairperson, *US* vice-president; *(hombre)* vice-chairman; *(mujer)* vice-chairwoman

vicesecretario, -a *nm,f* assistant secretary

viceversa *adv* vice versa

viciado, -a *adj* (a) *(corrompido)* corrupt (b) *(aire)* stuffy

viciar [43] **1** *vt* (a) *(corromper)* to corrupt (b) *(estropear)* to ruin
 2 viciarse *vpr* (a) *(deformarse)* to go out of shape (b) *(corromperse)* to become corrupted; *(enviciarse)* to get into a bad habit

vicio *nm* (a) *(libertinaje, actividad inmoral)* vice (b) *(mala costumbre)* bad habit (c) *(defecto, error)* defect

vicioso, -a 1 *adj* (a) *(persona)* depraved, perverted (b) *círculo* v. vicious circle
 2 *nm,f* depraved person; **v. del trabajo** workaholic

vicisitud *nf (usu pl)* vicissitude

víctima *nf* victim

victimar *vt Am* to kill, to murder

victimario, -a *nm,f Am* killer, murderer

victoria *nf* victory

victorioso, -a *adj* victorious

vicuña *nf* vicuña

vid *nf* vine, grapevine

vida *nf* life; *(período)* lifetime; **de toda la v.** lifelong; **en mi v.** never in my life; **de por v.** for life; **ganarse la v.** to earn one's living; **¿qué es de tu v.?** how's life?; **estar con/sin v.** to be alive/dead

vidente *nmf* clairvoyant

vídeo, *Am* **video** *nm* video; **grabar en v.** to videotape

videocámara *nf* video camera

videocasete *nm* video, video cassette

videoclub *nm* video club

videoconferencia *nf (concepto)* video-conferencing; *(sesión)* videoconference

videoconsola *nf* game console

videojuego *nm* video game

vidriera *nf* (a) *(ventana)* glass window; *(en catedrales)* stained glass window (b) *Am (escaparate)* shop window

vidrio *nm* glass

vieira *nf* scallop

viejo, -a 1 *adj* old; **hacerse v.** to grow old; **un v. amigo** an old friend
 2 *nm,f* (a) *(hombre, padre)* old man; *(mujer, madre)* old woman; **los viejos** old people; *Fam* **mis viejos** my parents (b) *Am Fam (amigo)* pal, *Br* mate, *US* buddy; *(amiga)* girl, *US* girlfriend (c) *Chile* **el V. de Pascua** *o* **Pascuero** Father Christmas

Viena *n* Vienna

vienés, -esa *adj & nm,f* Viennese

viento *nm* wind; **hace** *o* **sopla mucho v.** it is very windy; *Fam Fig* **¡vete a tomar v.!** get lost!

vientre *nm* stomach, belly; **hacer de v.** to have a bowel movement

viernes *nm inv* Friday; **V. Santo** Good Friday

Vietnam *n* Vietnam

vietnamita *adj & nmf* Vietnamese

viga *nf (de madera)* beam; *(de hierro)* girder

vigencia *nf* validity; **entrar en v.** to come into force o effect

vigente *adj* in force

vigésimo, -a *adj & nm,f* twentieth

vigía 1 *nf* watchtower, lookout post
  2 *nmf* lookout; *(hombre)* watchman; *(mujer)* watchwoman

vigilancia *nf* (a) *(cuidado)* vigilance; *Med* **v. intensiva** intensive care (b) *(control)* surveillance

vigilante *nmf* guard; **v. nocturno** night watchman

vigilar 1 *vt (lugar)* to guard; *(espiar)* to watch; **vigila que no entren** make sure they don't get in
  2 *vi* to keep watch

vigilia *nf* (a) *(vela)* wakefulness (b) *(víspera)* eve (c) *Rel (abstinencia)* abstinence

vigor *nm* (a) *(fuerza)* vigour (b) **en v.** *(ley)* in force; *(contrato, tarifa)* current

vigoroso, -a *adj* vigorous

VIH *nm (abr* **virus de la inmunodeficiencia humana)** HIV

vikingo, -a *adj & nm, f* Viking

vil *adj* vile, base

vileza *nf* (a) *(cualidad)* vileness, baseness (b) *(acto)* vile act, despicable deed

vilipendiar [43] *vt Fml* to vilify, to revile

villa *nf* (a) *(población)* town (b) *(casa)* villa, country house (c) *Arg, Bol* **v. miseria** shanty town

villancico *nm* (Christmas) carol

vilo: en vilo *loc adv* on tenterhooks

vinagre *nm* vinegar

vinagrera *nf* **vinagreras** oil and vinegar cruets, cruet (stand)

vinagreta *nf* vinaigrette sauce

vinajeras *nfpl* cruets

vincha *nf Andes, RP* headband

vinculación *nf* link, connection

vinculante *adj* binding

vincular *vt* to link, to bind; *(relacionar)* to relate, to connect

vínculo *nm* link

vine *pt indef de* **venir**

vinícola *adj* wine-producing

vinicultor, -a *nm,f* wine producer

vinicultura *nf* wine production o growing

vinilo *nm* vinyl

vino *nm* wine; **tomar un v.** to have a glass of wine; **v. blanco/tinto** white/red wine; **v. dulce/seco** sweet/dry wine; **v. rosado** rosé

viña *nf* vineyard

viñedo *nm* vineyard

viñeta *nf* illustration

viola *nf* viola

violación *nf* (a) *(de una persona)* rape (b) *(de ley, derecho)* violation, infringement

violador *nm* rapist

violar *vt* (a) *(persona)* to rape (b) *(ley, derecho)* to violate, to infringe

violencia *nf* (a) *(agresividad)* violence; **v. doméstica** domestic violence (b) *(incomodidad)* awkwardness

violentar *vt* (a) *(forzar)* to force, to break open; *(sitio)* to break into, to enter by force (b) *(enojar)* to infuriate

violento, -a *adj* (a) *(agresivo)* violent (b) *(incómodo) (situación)* embarrassing, awkward; **sentirse v.** to feel embarrassed o awkward

violeta 1 *adj & nm (color)* violet
  2 *nf (flor)* violet

violín *nm* violin; *Fam* fiddle

violinista *nmf* violinist

violón *nm* double bass

violoncelista, violonchelista *nmf* cellist

violoncelo, violonchelo *nm* violoncello, cello

VIP *nmf (abr* **very important person)** VIP

viraje *nm (en coche)* swerve; *(en barco)* tack

virar *vi (girar)* to turn round o around

virgen 1 *adj* (a) *(persona, selva)* virgin (b) *(aceite, lana)* pure; *(cinta)* blank
  2 *nmf* virgin; *Fam* **ser un viva la v.** to be a devil-may-care person

virginidad *nf* virginity

Virgo *nm* Virgo

virgo *nm* hymen

virguería *nf Fam* **hacer virguerías** to work wonders, to be a dab hand

vírico, -a *adj* viral

viril *adj* virile, manly; **miembro v.** penis

virilidad *nf* virility

virtual *adj* virtual

virtud *nf* (a) *(moral)* virtue (b) *(facultad)* power; **tener la v. de** to have the power o ability to (c) **en v. de** by virtue of

virtuoso, -a 1 *adj* virtuous
  2 *nm,f (músico)* virtuoso

viruela *nf* smallpox; **viruelas** pockmarks

virulé: a la virulé *loc adj Fam* (a) *(torcido)* crooked, twisted (b) **un ojo a la v.** a black eye

virulencia *nf* virulence
virulento, -a *adj* virulent
virus *nm inv* virus
viruta *nf* shaving
visado *nm, Am* **visa** *nf* visa
víscera *nf* internal organ; **vísceras** *(órganos)* entrails; *(comida)* offal
visceral *adj* profound, deep-rooted
viscosa *nf (tejido)* viscose
viscoso, -a *adj* viscous
visera *nf (de gorra)* peak; *(de casco)* visor
visibilidad *nf* visibility; **curva con mala v.** blind corner
visible *adj* visible; *(evidente)* evident
visillo *nm* net curtain, lace curtain
visión *nf* (a) *(capacidad)* vision, sight (b) *(interpretación)* view; **con v. de conjunto** overall view; **con v. de futuro** forward-looking (c) *(aparición)* vision
visionario, -a *adj & nm,f* visionary
visita *nf* (a) *(acción)* visit; **hacer una v.** to pay a visit; **estar de v.** to be visiting (b) *(invitado)* visitor, guest
visitante 1 *nmf* visitor
2 *adj (equipo)* away
visitar *vt* to visit
vislumbrar *vt* to glimpse
viso *nm* (a) *(reflejo)* sheen (b) *Fig* **tener visos de** to seem, to appear
visón *nm* mink
visor *nm Fot* viewfinder

> ♪ Observa que la palabra inglesa **visor** es un falso amigo y no es la traducción de la palabra española **visor**. En inglés, **visor** significa "visera".

víspera *nf (día anterior)* day before; *(de festivo)* eve; **en vísperas de** in the period leading up to
vista *nf* (a) *(sentido)* sight; **a la v.** visible; **a primera** *o* **simple v.** at first sight, on the face of it; **corto de v.** short-sighted; **conocer a algn de v.** to know sb by sight; **perder de v. a** to lose sight of; **quítalo de mi v.** take it away; *Fig* **tener mucha v. para** to have a good eye for; *Fig* **volver la v. atrás** to look back; *Fam* **¡hasta la v.!** goodbye!, see you!; *Fam* **hacer la v. gorda** to turn a blind eye (b) *(panorama)* view; **con vista(s) al mar** overlooking the sea (c) *Der* trial, hearing (d) *(locuciones)* **con vistas a** with a view to; **en v. de** in view of, considering
vistazo *nm* glance; **echar un v. a algo** *(ojear)* to have a (quick) look at sth; *(tener cuidado de)* to keep an eye on sth
visto, -a 1 *adj* (a) **está v. que ...** it is obvious that ...; **por lo v.** evidently,

apparently; **v. que** in view of the fact that, seeing *o* given that (b) **estar bien v.** to be well looked upon, to be considered acceptable; **estar mal v.** to be frowned upon (c) **estar muy v.** to be old hat
2 *nm* **v. bueno** approval, O.K.
vistoso, -a *adj* eye-catching
visual *adj* visual; **campo v.** field of vision
visualizar [40] *vt* to visualize; *(película)* to view
vital *adj* (a) *(órgano, energía)* vital; **es v.** it is vital (b) *(persona)* full of vitality
vitalicio, -a *adj* life, for life; **cargo v.** position held for life; **pensión v.** life pension
vitalidad *nf* vitality
vitamina *nf* vitamin
vitamínico, -a *adj* vitamin; **complejo v.** multivitamins
viticultor, -a *nm,f* wine grower
viticultura *nf* wine growing
vitorear *vt* to cheer
vítreo, -a *adj* vitreous
vitrina *nf (aparador)* glass *o* display cabinet; *(de exposición)* glass case, showcase; *Am (escaparate)* shop window
vituallas *nfpl* provisions
vituperar *vt* to condemn
vituperio *nm* condemnation
viudo, -a *nm,f (hombre)* widower; *(mujer)* widow
viva *interj* **¡v.!** hurrah!
vivacidad *nf* vivacity
vivaracho, -a *adj* lively, sprightly
vivaz *adj* alert, lively
vivencias *nfpl* personal experience
víveres *nmpl* provisions, supplies
vivero *nm (de plantas)* nursery; *(de peces)* fish farm *o* hatchery; **v. (de empresas)** business incubator
viveza *nf* (a) *(de colorido, descripción)* vividness (b) *(de persona, discusión, ojos)* liveliness; *(de ingenio, inteligencia)* sharpness
vividor, -a *nm,f Pey* sponger, scrounger
vivienda *nf (casa)* home; *(alojamiento)* housing
vivir 1 *vi* to live; **vive de sus ahorros** she lives off her savings; **viven de la pesca** they make their living by fishing
2 *vt* to live through
3 *nm* life
vivito, -a *adj Fam* **v. y coleando** alive and kicking
vivo, -a 1 *adj* (a) *(ser, lengua)* living; **un animal v.** a live animal; **estar v.** to be alive; **de viva voz** verbally, by word of mouth; **en**

v. *(programa)* live (**b**) *(gestos, ojos, descripción)* lively, vivid; *(dolor, deseo)* intense; *(luz, color)* bright; *(ingenio)* quick, sharp
  2 *nm,f* **los vivos** the living

Vizcaya *n* **el golfo de V.** the Bay of Biscay

V.o B.o *(abr* **visto bueno)** *(en documento)* approved

vocablo *nm* word, term

vocabulario *nm* vocabulary

vocación *nf* vocation, calling; **con v. europea** with leanings towards Europe

vocacional *adj* vocational

vocal 1 *nf Ling* vowel
  2 *nmf* member

vocalista *nmf Mús* vocalist, singer

vocalizar [40] *vt & vi* to vocalize

voceador, -a *nm,f Col, Ecuad, Méx* newspaper seller

vocerío *nm* shouting

vocero, -a *nm,f esp Am (hombre)* spokesperson, spokesman; *(mujer)* spokesperson, spokeswoman

vociferante *adj* vociferous

vociferar *vt & vi* to vociferate

vodka *nm* vodka

vol. *(abr* **volumen)** vol

volado, -a *adj Fam* **estar v.** to have a screw loose

volador, -a *adj* flying

volandas: en volandas *loc adv* in the air, flying through the air

volante 1 *nm* (**a**) *Aut* steering wheel; **ir al v.** to be driving; **un as del v.** a motor-racing champion (**b**) *Cost* frill, ruffle (**c**) *Esp (del médico)* (referral) note
  2 *adj* flying; **platillo v.** flying saucer

volantín *nm Carib, Chile* kite

volar [2] **1** *vi* (**a**) *(en el aire)* to fly; *Fig* **lo hizo volando** he did it in a flash (**b**) *Fam (desaparecer)* to disappear, to vanish
  2 *vt (edificio)* to blow up; *(caja fuerte)* to blow open; *Min* to blast
  3 *volarse vpr (papel etc)* to be blown away

volátil *adj* volatile

volcán *nm* volcano

volcánico, -a *adj* volcanic

volcar [2] **1** *vt* (**a**) *(cubo etc)* to knock over; *(barco, bote)* to capsize (**b**) *(vaciar)* to empty out (**c**) *(tiempo)* to invest
  2 *vi (coche)* to turn over; *(barco)* to capsize
  3 *volcarse vpr (vaso, jarra)* to fall over, to tip over; *(coche)* to turn over; *(barco)* to capsize (**b**) *Fig* **volcarse con** to do one's utmost for

voleibol *nm* volleyball

voleo *nm* **a v.** at random, haphazardly

volquete *nm* dumper truck, *US* dump truck

voltaje *nm* voltage

voltear 1 *vt* (**a**) *Am (derribar) (objeto)* to knock over; *(gobierno)* to overthrow, to bring down (**b**) *Am salvo RP (poner del revés) (boca abajo)* to turn upside down; *(lo de dentro fuera)* to turn inside out; *(lo de detrás delante)* to turn back to front (**c**) *Am salvo RP (cabeza, espalda)* to turn
  2 *vi Méx (doblar la esquina)* to turn
  3 *voltearse vpr* (**a**) *Am (volverse)* to turn round o around (**b**) *Méx (vehículo)* to overturn

voltereta *nf* somersault

voltio *nm* volt

voluble *adj* fickle, changeable

> 🖉 Observa que la palabra inglesa **voluble** es un falso amigo y no es la traducción de la palabra española **voluble**. En inglés, **voluble** significa "locuaz".

---

volumen *nm* volume

voluminoso, -a *adj* voluminous; *(enorme)* massive, bulky

voluntad *nf* will; **fuerza de v.** willpower; **tiene mucha v.** he is very strong-willed; **a v.** at will

voluntario, -a 1 *adj* voluntary
  2 *nm,f* volunteer; **ofrecerse v.** to volunteer

voluntarioso, -a *adj* willing

voluptuoso, -a *adj* voluptuous

volver [4] *(pp* **vuelto) 1** *vi* (**a**) *(ir)* to go back, to return; *(venir)* to come back, to return; **v. en sí** to come round, to recover consciousness (**b**) **v. a hacer algo** to do sth again
  2 *vt* (**a**) *(convertir)* to turn, to make; **me vas a v. loco** you are driving me mad (**b**) *(dar la vuelta a)* to turn over; *(boca abajo)* to turn upside down; *(de fuera adentro)* to turn inside out; *(de atrás adelante)* to turn back to front; **volverle la espalda a algn** to turn one's back on sb; *Fig* **v. la vista atrás** to look back; **al v. la esquina** on turning the corner
  3 *volverse vpr* (**a**) *(girar)* to turn (**b**) *(regresar) (venir)* to come back; *(ir)* to go back (**c**) *(convertirse)* to become; **volverse loco(a)** to go mad

vomitar 1 *vi* to vomit, to be sick; **tengo ganas de v.** I feel sick, I want to be sick
  2 *vt* to vomit, to bring up

vómito *nm (lo vomitado)* vomit; *(acción)* vomiting

vomitona *nf Fam* vomit

voracidad *nf* voracity, voraciousness

vorágine *nf* confusion, whirl

voraz *adj* voracious

vórtice *nm* vortex

vos *pron pers Am (tú)* you

> The **vos** form is used alongside **tú** in many Latin American countries, and in some countries (Argentina, Paraguay and Uruguay) is the preferred form.

V.O.S.E. *nf (abr* **versión original subtitulada en español**) = original language version subtitled in Spanish

vosotros, -as *pron pers pl Esp* (a) *(sujeto)* you (b) *(con prep)* you; **entre v.** among yourselves; **sin vosotras** without you

> Usually omitted in Spanish except for emphasis or contrast. In Latin America, **vosotros** is not used. Instead, **ustedes** is used as the second person plural in all contexts, without necessarily suggesting formality.

votación *nf* (a) *(voto)* vote, ballot (b) *(acción)* voting

votante *nmf* voter

votar *vi* to vote; **v. a algn** to vote for sb

voto *nm* (a) *(en elección)* vote; **tener v.** to have a vote; **v. secreto** secret ballot (b) *Rel* vow

vox *nf* **v. populi** common knowledge

voy *indic pres de* **ir**

voz *nf* (a) *(sonido, tono)* voice; **en v. alta** aloud; **en v. baja** in a low voice; **a media v.** in a low voice, softly; **de viva v.** verbally (b) *(grito)* shout; **a voces** shouting; **dar voces** to shout; *Fig* **estar pidiendo algo a voces** to be crying out for sth; *Fig* **secreto a voces** open secret; **a v. en grito** at the top of one's voice (c) **no tener ni v. ni voto** to have no say in the matter; *Fig* **llevar la v. cantante** to rule the roost (d) *Ling* **v. pasiva** passive voice

vudú *(pl* **vudús** *o* **vudúes)** *nm* voodoo

vuelco *nm* upset, tumble; **dar un v.** *(coche)* to overturn; *Fig* **me dio un v. el corazón** my heart missed a beat

vuelo *nm* (a) flight; **v. chárter/regular** charter/scheduled flight; **v. sin motor** gliding; *Fig* **cazarlas** *o* **cogerlas al v.** to be quick on the uptake (b) *Cost* **una falda de v.** a full skirt

vuelta *nf* (a) *(regreso)* return; *(viaje)* return journey; **a v. de correo** by return of post; **estar de v.** to be back; *Dep* **partido de v.** return match (b) *(giro)* turn; *(en carreras)* lap; *Dep (ciclista)* tour; **dar media v.** to turn round *o* around; *Fig* **la cabeza me da vueltas** my head is spinning; *Fig* **no le des más vueltas** stop worrying about it; **v. de campana** somersault (c) *(dinero)* change (d) **dar una v.** *(a pie)* to go for a walk *o* stroll; *(en coche)* to go for a drive *o* a spin (in the car) (e) *Fig* **no tiene v. de hoja** there's no doubt about it

vuelto, -a 1 *adj* **jersey de cuello v.** rollneck sweater

2 *nm Am* change

3 *pp de* **volver**

vuestro, -a *Esp* **1** *adj pos (antes del sustantivo)* your; *(después del sustantivo)* of yours; **v. libro** your book; **un amigo v.** a friend of yours

2 *pron pos* yours; **éstos son los vuestros** these are yours; **lo v.** what is yours, what belongs to you

vulgar *adj* (a) *(no refinado)* vulgar (b) *(no técnico)* **el término v.** the everyday term

vulgaridad *nf* vulgarity

vulgarizar [40] *vt* to popularize

vulgarmente *adv* **v. llamado** commonly known as

vulgo *nm* **el v.** the common people; *Pey* the masses

vulnerable *adj* vulnerable

vulnerar *vt (ley, acuerdo)* to violate

vulva *nf* vulva

W, w [ue'ðole] *nf (letra)* W, w

W *Elec (abr* vatio(s)) W

walkie-talkie [*Esp* 'walki'talki, *Am* 'woki'toki] *nm* walkie-talkie

walkman® ['walman] *(pl* **walkmans**) *nm* Walkman®

WAP [wæp] *nm (abr* **Wireless Application Protocol**) WAP

wáter [*Esp* 'bater, *Am* 'water] *nm* toilet

waterpolo [water'polo] *nm* water polo

WC [*Esp* ue'θe, *Am* dolee'se] *nm (abr* **water closet**) WC

Web, web [web] *Inform* **1** *nf (World Wide Web)* la W. the Web
2 *nm* o *nf (página web)* web site

whisky ['wiski] *(pl* **whiskys**) *nm (escocés)* whisky; *(irlandés, US)* whiskey

windsurf ['winsurf], **windsurfing** ['win-surfin] *nm* windsurfing

windsurfista [winsur'fista] *nmf* wind-surfer

wireless ['waiales] *adj Inform (tecnología, red)* wireless

xenofobia *nf* xenophobia

xenófobo, -a 1 *adj* xenophobic
2 *nmf* xenophobe

xilofón, xilófono *nm* xylophone

Y, y [iɣri'eɣa] *nf (letra)* Y, y

y *conj* (**a**) *and;* **una chica alta y morena** a tall, dark-haired girl; **son las tres y cuarto** it's a quarter past three (**b**) *¿y qué?* so what?; *¿y si no llega a tiempo?* what if he doesn't arrive in time?; *¿y tú?* what about you?; *¿y eso?* how come?; **y eso que** although, even though; **¡y tanto!** you bet!, and how!; *ver* **e**

ya 1 *adv* (**a**) *(en el pasado)* already; **ya lo sabía** I already knew; **ya en la Edad Media** as far back as the Middle Ages (**b**) *(ahora mismo)* now; **es preciso actuar ya** it is vital that we act now; **¡hazlo ya!** do it at once!; **ya mismo** right away (**c**) *(en el futuro)* **ya hablaremos luego** we'll talk about it later; **ya nos veremos** see you!; **ya verás** you'll see (**d**) **ya no** no longer; **ya no viene por aquí** he doesn't come round here any more (**e**) *(refuerza el verbo)* **ya era hora** about time too; **ya lo creo** of course, I should think so; **¡ya voy!** coming!; **¡ya está!** that's it!
2 *conj* **ya que** since

yacer [61] *vi* (**a**) *(estar tumbado, enterrado)* to lie; **aquí yace ...** here lies ... (**b**) *(tener relaciones sexuales)* to lie together

yacimiento *nm* bed, deposit; **yacimientos petrolíferos** oilfields

yaguar *nm* jaguar

yanqui *Pey* **1** *adj* Yankee
2 *nmf* Yankee, Yank

yarará *nf Am* = large poisonous snake

yaraví *(pl* **yaravíes** o **yaravís**) *nm Am* = type of melancholy Indian song

yarda *nf* yard

yate *nm* yacht

yaya *nf* (**a**) *Perú (insecto)* mite (**b**) *Cuba, PRico (árbol)* lancewood

yayo, -a *nm,f Fam (hombre)* grandad; *(mujer)* grandma

yegua *nf* mare

yema *nf* (**a**) *(de huevo)* yolk (**b**) *Bot* bud (**c**) **y. del dedo** fingertip (**d**) *Culin* = sweet made from sugar and egg yolk

Yemen *n* (el) Y. Yemen

yen *(moneda)* yen

yendo *gerundio de* **ir**

yerba *nf* (**a**) = **hierba** (**b**) *RP* maté; **y. mate** *(yerba)* maté leaves

yerbatero, -a 1 *nm,f Andes, Carib (curandero)* witch doctor who uses herbs; *(vendedor de hierbas)* herbalist
2 *adj RP* maté

yermo, -a *adj* barren, uncultivated

yerno *nm* son-in-law

yerro *indic pres de* **errar**

yeso *nm* (**a**) *Geol* gypsum (**b**) *Constr* plaster

Yibuti *n* Djibouti

yiu-yitsu *nm* ju-jitsu

yo *pron pers* I; **entre tú y yo** between you and me; *¿quién es? – soy yo* who is it? – it's me; **yo no** not me; **yo que tú** if I were you; **yo mismo** I myself

Usually omitted as a personal pronoun in Spanish except for emphasis or contrast.

yodo *nm* iodine

yoga *nm* yoga

yogur (*pl* **yogures**), **yogurt** (*pl* **yogurts**) *nm* yogurt, yoghurt

yogurtera *nf* yoghurt maker

yonqui *nmf Fam* junkie, drug addict

yoyó *nm* yo-yo

yuca *nf* yucca

yudo *nm* judo

yudoka *nmf* judoka

yugo *nm* yoke

Yugoslavia *n* Yugoslavia

yugoslavo, -a *adj & nm,f* Yugoslav, Yugoslavian

yugular *nf* jugular

yunque *nm* anvil

yunta *nf* yoke o team of oxen

yuxtaponer [19] (*pp* **yuxtapuesto**) *vt* to juxtapose

yuxtaposición *nf* juxtaposition

yuxtapuesto, -a *pp de* **yuxtaponer**

yuyo *nm* (**a**) *CSur (mala hierba)* weed; *(hierba medicinal)* medicinal herb (**b**) *Andes (hierba silvestre)* wild herb

Z

Z, z ['θeta] *nf (letra)* Z, z

zacate *nm CAm, Méx* fodder

zafarse *vpr (librarse)* to get away, to escape (**de** from)

zafio, -a *adj* uncouth

zafiro *nm* sapphire

zaga *nf* **a la z.** behind, at the rear

zaguán *nm* hall, hallway

zaherir *vt* to hurt

Zaire *n* Zaire

zalamero, -a 1 *nm,f* flatterer, fawner
2 *adj* flattering, fawning

zamarra *nf* sheepskin jacket

Zambia *n* Zambia

zambo, -a 1 *adj (piernas, persona)* knock-kneed
2 *nm,f Am* = person who has one Black and one Indian parent

zambomba *nf* = kind of primitive drum

zambullida *nf* plunge

zambullirse *vpr* to plunge

zamparse *vpr Fam* to gobble down

zanahoria *nf* carrot

zancada *nf* stride

zancadilla *nf* **ponerle la z. a algn** to trip sb up

zanco *nm* stilt

zancudo, -a 1 *adj* (**a**) *(ave)* wading (**b**) *(persona)* long-legged
2 *nm Am* mosquito

zángano, -a 1 *nm (insecto)* drone
2 *nm,f Fam (persona)* idler, lazybones *inv*

zanja *nf* ditch, trench

zanjar *vt (asunto)* to settle

zapallito *nm CSur Br* courgette, *US* zucchini

zapallo *nm* (**a**) *Andes, RP* **z. (italiano)** *Br* courgette, *US* zucchini (**b**) *Andes, RP (calabaza)* pumpkin (**c**) *RP Fam (bobo)* mug, *Br* wally

zapata *nf* (**a**) *(cuña)* wedge (**b**) *Téc* shoe

zapateado *nm* = type of flamenco dance where the dancers stamp their feet rhythmically

zapatear *vi* to tap one's feet

zapatería *nf* shoe shop

zapatero, -a *nm,f (vendedor)* shoe dealer; *(fabricante)* shoemaker, cobbler

zapatilla *nf* slipper; **zapatillas de deporte** *Br* trainers, *US* sneakers

zapato *nm* shoe; **zapatos de tacón** high-heeled shoes

zapping ['θapin] *nm inv Fam* channel-hopping, *US* channel surfing; **hacer z.** to channel-hop

zar *nm* czar, tsar

Zaragoza *n* Saragossa

zaragozano, -a 1 *adj* of/from Saragossa
2 *nm,f* person from Saragossa

zarandear *vt* to shake

zarandeo *nm* shaking

zarina *nf* czarina, tsarina

zarpa *nf (uña)* claw; *(mano)* paw

zarpar *vi* to weigh anchor, to set sail

zarpazo *nm* clawing; **dar o pegar un z. a** to claw

zarza *nf* bramble, blackberry bush

zarzal *nm* bramble patch

zarzamora *nf (zarza)* blackberry bush; *(fruto)* blackberry

zarzuela *nf* (**a**) *Mús* = Spanish operetta (**b**) **la Z.** = royal residence in Madrid (**c**) *Culin* = fish stew

zenit *nm* zenith

zigzag *(pl* **zigzags** *o* **zigzagues)** *nm* zigzag

zigzaguear *vi* to zigzag

Zimbabwe *n* Zimbabwe

zinc *nm* zinc

zíper *nm CAm, Méx Br* zip, *US* zipper

zipizape *nm Fam* squabble, set-to

zócalo *nm* (**a**) *(de pared)* skirting board (**b**) *(pedestal)* plinth

zodiaco, zodíaco *nm* zodiac

zona *nf* zone; *(región)* region; **z. euro** euro zone; **z. verde** park, green area

zoo *nm* zoo

zoología *nf* zoology

zoológico, -a 1 *adj* zoological; **parque z.** zoo
2 *nm* zoo

zoom *nm Cin & Fot* zoom

zopenco, -a *nm,f Fam* dope, halfwit

zopilote *nm CAm, Méx* black vulture

zoquete 1 *nmf Fam* blockhead
  2 *nm CSur* *(calcetín)* ankle sock

zorra *nf* (**a**) *(animal)* vixen (**b**) *Esp Fam* slut

zorro, -a 1 *nm* fox
  2 *adj* (**a**) *(astuto)* cunning, sly (**b**) *Esp muy Fam* **no tengo ni zorra (idea)** I haven't got a *Br* bloody *o US* goddamn clue

zorzal *nm (ave)* thrush

zozobrar *vi* to be in danger of going under

zueco *nm* clog

zumbado, -a *adj Fam* crazy, mad

zumbar 1 *vi* to buzz, to hum; **me zumban los oídos** my ears are buzzing; *Fam* **salir zumbando** to zoom off
  2 *vt Fam* to thrash

zumbido *nm* buzzing, humming

zumo *nm Esp* juice

zurcir [52] *vt Cost* to darn; *Fam* **¡que te zurzan!** go to hell!

zurda *nf (mano)* left hand

zurdo, -a 1 *nm,f (persona)* left-handed person
  2 *adj* left-handed

zurrar *vt (pegar)* to beat, to flog

zutano, -a *nm,f Fam* so-and-so, what's-his/her-name

Spanish Verbs

◆

Regular Spelling Changes

The rules of spelling in Spanish cause a number of verbs to have regular spelling changes. These are listed below.

Spanish verbs fall into three groups depending on whether their infinitive ends in **-ar, -er** or **-ir**. The stem of the verb is the part which is left when the **-ar, -er** or **-ir** is removed from the infinitive. For example, the stem of **tomar** is **tom**, the stem of **beber** is **beb**, and the stem of **salir** is **sal**.

In the examples given below, the following indicators are used:

> (**1**) = first person singular present indicative
> (**2**) = present subjunctive, all persons
> (**3**) = first person singular preterite

Verbs ending in -ar

Verbs with a stem ending in **c**, for example **buscar**

The **c** changes to **qu** in:

> (**2**) busque, busques, busque, busquemos, busquéis, busquen
> (**3**) busqué

Verbs with a stem ending in **g**, for example **cargar**

The **g** changes to **gu** in:

> (**2**) cargue, cargues, cargue, carguemos, carguéis, carguen
> (**3**) cargué

Verbs with a stem ending in **gu**, for example **averiguar**

The **gu** changes to **gü** in:

> (**2**) averigüe, averigües, averigüe, averigüemos, averigüéis, averigüen
> (**3**) averigüé

Verbs with a stem ending in **z**, for example **realizar**

The **z** changes to **c** in:

> (**2**) realice, realices, realice, realicemos, realicéis, realicen
> (**3**) realicé

Verbs ending in -er *or* -ir

Verbs with a stem ending in **c**, for example **esparcir**

The **c** changes to **z** in:

> (**1**) esparzo
> (**2**) esparza, esparzas, esparza, esparzamos, esparzáis, esparzan

Verbs with a stem ending in **g**, for example **coger**

The **g** changes to **j** in:

> (**1**) cojo
> (**2**) coja, cojas, coja, cojamos, cojáis, cojan

Verbs with a stem ending in **qu**, for example **delinquir**

The **qu** changes to **c** in:

> (**1**) delinco
> (**2**) delinca, delincas, delinca, delincamos, delincáis, delincan

Verbs with a stem ending in **gu**, for example **distinguir**

The **gu** changes to **g** in:

> (**1**) distingo
> (**2**) distinga, distingas, distinga, distingamos, distingáis, distingan

Models for Regular Conjugation

TOMAR to take

INDICATIVE

PRESENT	FUTURE	CONDITIONAL
1. tomo	tomaré	tomaría
2. tomas	tomarás	tomarías
3. toma	tomará	tomaría
1. tomamos	tomaremos	tomaríamos
2. tomáis	tomaréis	tomaríais
3. toman	tomarán	tomarían

IMPERFECT	PRETERITE	PERFECT
1. tomaba	tomé	he tomado
2. tomabas	tomaste	has tomado
3. tomaba	tomó	ha tomado
1. tomábamos	tomamos	hemos tomado
2. tomabais	tomasteis	habéis tomado
3. tomaban	tomaron	han tomado

FUTURE PERFECT	CONDITIONAL PERFECT	PLUPERFECT
1. habré tomado	habría tomado	había tomado
2. habrás tomado	habrías tomado	habías tomado
3. habrá tomado	habría tomado	había tomado
1. habremos tomado	habríamos tomado	habíamos tomado
2. habréis tomado	habríais tomado	habíais tomado
3. habrán tomado	habrían tomado	habían tomado

SUBJUNCTIVE

PRESENT	IMPERFECT	PERFECT/PLUPERFECT
1. tome	tom-ara/ase	haya/hubiera* tomado
2. tomes	tom-aras/ases	hayas/hubieras tomado
3. tome	tom-ara/ase	haya/hubiera tomado
1. tomemos	tom-áramos/ásemos	hayamos/hubiéramos tomado
2. toméis	tom-arais/aseis	hayáis/hubierais tomado
3. tomen	tom-aran/asen	hayan/hubieran tomado

IMPERATIVE / INFINITIVE / PARTICIPLE

IMPERATIVE	INFINITIVE	PARTICIPLE
(tú) toma	**PRESENT**	**PRESENT**
(Vd) tome	tomar	tomando
(nosotros) tomemos		
(vosotros) tomad	**PERFECT**	**PAST**
(Vds) tomen	haber tomado	tomado

* the alternative form 'hubiese' etc is also possible

COMER to eat

INDICATIVE

PRESENT	FUTURE	CONDITIONAL
1. como	comeré	comería
2. comes	comerás	comerías
3. come	comerá	comería
1. comemos	comeremos	comeríamos
2. coméis	comeréis	comeríais
3. comen	comerán	comerían

IMPERFECT	PRETERITE	PERFECT
1. comía	comí	he comido
2. comías	comiste	has comido
3. comía	comió	ha comido
1. comíamos	comimos	hemos comido
2. comíais	comisteis	habéis comido
3. comían	comieron	han comido

FUTURE PERFECT	CONDITIONAL PERFECT	PLUPERFECT
1. habré comido	habría comido	había comido
2. habrás comido	habrías comido	habías comido
3. habrá comido	habría comido	había comido
1. habremos comido	habríamos comido	habíamos comido
2. habréis comido	habríais comido	habíais comido
3. habrán comido	habrían comido	habían comido

SUBJUNCTIVE

PRESENT	IMPERFECT	PERFECT/PLUPERFECT
1. coma	com-iera/iese	haya/hubiera* comido
2. comas	com-ieras/ieses	hayas/hubieras comido
3. coma	com-iera/iese	haya/hubiera comido
1. comamos	com-iéramos/iésemos	hayamos/hubiéramos comido
2. comáis	com-ierais/ieseis	hayáis/hubierais comido
3. coman	com-ieran/iesen	hayan/hubieran comido

IMPERATIVE	INFINITIVE	PARTICIPLE
(tú) come	**PRESENT**	**PRESENT**
(Vd) coma	comer	comiendo
(nosotros) comamos		
(vosotros) comed	**PERFECT**	**PAST**
(Vds) coman	haber comido	comido

* the alternative form 'hubiese' etc is also possible

PARTIR to leave

INDICATIVE

PRESENT	FUTURE	CONDITIONAL
1. parto	partiré	partiría
2. partes	partirás	partirías
3. parte	partirá	partiría
1. partimos	partiremos	partiríamos
2. partís	partiréis	partiríais
3. parten	partirán	partirían

IMPERFECT	PRETERITE	PERFECT
1. partía	partí	he partido
2. partías	partiste	has partido
3. partía	partió	ha partido
1. partíamos	partimos	hemos partido
2. partíais	partisteis	habéis partido
3. partían	partieron	han partido

FUTURE PERFECT	CONDITIONAL PERFECT	PLUPERFECT
1. habré partido	habría partido	había partido
2. habrás partido	habrías partido	habías partido
3. habrá partido	habría partido	había partido
1. habremos partido	habríamos partido	habíamos partido
2. habréis partido	habríais partido	habíais partido
3. habrán partido	habrían partido	habían partido

SUBJUNCTIVE

PRESENT	IMPERFECT	PERFECT/PLUPERFECT
parta	parti-era/ese	haya/hubiera* partido
partas	parti-eras/eses	hayas/hubieras partido
parta	parti-era/ese	haya/hubiera partido
partamos	parti-éramos/ésemos	hayamos/hubiéramos partido
partáis	parti-erais/eseis	hayáis/hubierais partido
partan	parti-eran/esen	hayan/hubieran partido

IMPERATIVE   INFINITIVE   PARTICIPLE

IMPERATIVE	INFINITIVE	PARTICIPLE
(tú) parte	**PRESENT**	**PRESENT**
(Vd) parta	partir	partiendo
(nosotros) partamos		
(vosotros) partid	**PERFECT**	**PAST**
(Vds) partan	haber partido	partido

* the alternative form 'hubiese' etc is also possible

Models for Irregular Conjugation

[1] **pensar PRES** pienso, piensas, piensa, pensamos, penséis, piensan; **PRES SUBJ** piense, pienses, piense, pensemos, penséis, piensen; **IMPERAT** piensa, piense, pensemos, pensad, piensen

[2] **contar PRES** cuento, cuentas, cuenta, contamos, contáis, cuentan; **PRES SUBJ** cuente, cuentes, cuente, contemos, contéis, cuenten; **IMPERAT** cuenta, cuente, contemos, contad, cuenten

[3] **perder PRES** pierdo, pierdes, pierde, perdemos, perdéis, pierden; **PRES SUBJ** pierda, pierdas, pierda, perdamos, perdáis, pierdan; **IMPERAT** pierde, pierda, perdamos, perded, pierdan

[4] **morder PRES** muerdo, muerdes, muerde, mordemos, mordéis, muerden; **PRES SUBJ** muerda, muerdas, muerda, mordamos, mordáis, muerdan; **IMPERAT** muerde, muerda, mordamos, morded, muerdan

[5] **sentir PRES** siento, sientes, siente, sentimos, sentís, sienten; **PRES SUBJ** sienta, sientas, sienta, sintamos, sintáis, sientan; **PRES P** sintiendo; **IMPERAT** siente, sienta, sintamos, sentid, sientan

[6] **vestir PRES** visto, vistes, viste, vestimos, vestís, visten; **PRES SUBJ** vista, vistas, vista, vistamos, vistáis, vistan; **PRES P** vistiendo; **IMPERAT** viste, vista, vistamos, vestid, vistan

[7] **dormir PRES** duermo, duermes, duerme, dormimos, dormís, duermen; **PRES SUBJ** duerma, duermas, duerma, durmamos, durmáis, duerman; **PRES P** durmiendo; **IMPERAT** duerme, duerma, durmamos, dormid, duerman

[8] **andar PRET** anduve, anduviste, anduvo, anduvimos, anduvisteis, anduvieron; **IMPERF SUBJ** anduviera/anduviese

[9] **caber PRES** quepo, cabes, cabe, cabemos, cabéis, caben; **PRES SUBJ** quepa, quepas, quepa, quepamos, quepáis, quepan; **FUT** cabré; **COND** cabría; **PRET** cupe, cupiste, cupo, cupimos, cupisteis, cupieron; **IMPERF SUBJ** cupiera/cupiese; **IMPERAT** cabe, quepa, quepamos, cabed, quepan

[10] **conducir PRES** conduzco, conduces, conduce, conducimos, conducís, conducen; **PRES SUBJ** conduzca, conduzcas, conduzca, conduzcamos, conduzcáis, conduzcan; **PRET** conduje, condujiste, condujo, condujimos, condujisteis, condujeron; **IMPERF SUBJ** condujera/condujese; **IMPERAT** conduce, conduzca, conduzcamos, conducid, conduzcan

[11] **dar PRES** doy, das, da, damos, dais, dan; **PRES SUBJ** dé, des, dé, demos, deis, den; **PRET** di, diste, dio, dimos, disteis, dieron; **IMPERF SUBJ** diera/diese; **IMPERAT** da, dé, demos, dad, den

[12] **decir PRES** digo, dices, dice, decimos, decís, dicen; **PRES SUBJ** diga, digas, diga, digamos, digáis, digan; **FUT** diré; **COND** diría; **PRET** dije, dijiste, dijo, dijimos, dijisteis, dijeron; **IMPERF SUBJ** dijera/dijese; **PRES P** diciendo; **PP** dicho; **IMPERAT** di, diga, digamos, decid, digan

[13] **ESTAR** to be

INDICATIVE

PRESENT	FUTURE	CONDITIONAL
1. estoy	estaré	estaría
2. estás	estarás	estarías
3. está	estará	estaría
1. estamos	estaremos	estaríamos
2. estáis	estaréis	estaríais
3. están	estarán	estarían

IMPERFECT	PRETERITE	PERFECT
1. estaba	estuve	he estado
2. estabas	estuviste	has estado
3. estaba	estuvo	ha estado
1. estábamos	estuvimos	hemos estado
2. estabais	estuvisteis	habéis estado
3. estaban	estuvieron	han estado

FUTURE PERFECT	CONDITIONAL PERFECT	PLUPERFECT
1. habré estado	habría estado	había estado
2. habrás estado	habrías estado	habías estado
3. habrá estado	habría estado	había estado
1. habremos estado	habríamos estado	habíamos estado
2. habréis estado	habríais estado	habíais estado
3. habrán estado	habrían estado	habían estado

SUBJUNCTIVE

PRESENT	IMPERFECT	PERFECT/PLUPERFECT
1. esté	estuv-iera/iese	haya/hubiera* estado
2. estés	estuv-ieras/ieses	hayas/hubieras estado
3. esté	estuv-iera/iese	haya/hubiera estado
1. estemos	esuv-iéramos/iésemos	hayamos/hubiéramos estado
2. estéis	estuv-ierais/ieseis	hayáis/hubierais estado
3. estén	estuv-ieran/iesen	hayan/hubieran estado

IMPERATIVE   INFINITIVE   PARTICIPLE

IMPERATIVE	INFINITIVE	PARTICIPLE
(tú) está	**PRESENT**	**PRESENT**
(Vd) esté	estar	estando
(nosotros) estemos		
(vosotros) estad	**PERFECT**	**PAST**
(Vds) estén	haber estado	estado

* the alternative form 'hubiese' etc is also possible

[14] **HABER** to have (*auxiliary*)

INDICATIVE

PRESENT	FUTURE	CONDITIONAL
1. he	habré	habría
2. has	habrás	habrías
3. ha/hay*	habrá	habría
1. hemos	habremos	habríamos
2. habéis	habréis	habríais
3. han	habrán	habrían

IMPERFECT	PRETERITE	PERFECT
1. había	hube	
2. habías	hubiste	
3. había	hubo	ha habido*
1. habíamos	hubimos	
2. habíais	hubisteis	
3. habían	hubieron	

FUTURE PERFECT	CONDITIONAL PERFECT	PLUPERFECT
1.		
2.		
3. habrá habido*	habría habido*	había habido*
1.		
2.		
3.		

SUBJUNCTIVE

PRESENT	IMPERFECT	PERFECT/PLUPERFECT
1. haya	hub-iera/iese	
2. hayas	hub-ieras/ieses	
3. haya	hub-iera/iese	haya/hubiera** habido*
1. hayamos	hub-iéramos/iésemos	
2. hayáis	hub-ierais/ieseis	
3. hayan	hub-ieran/iesen	

INFINITIVE

PRESENT
haber
PERFECT
haber habido*

PARTICIPLE

PRESENT
habiendo
PAST
habido

* 'haber' is an auxiliary verb used with the participle of another verb to form compound tenses (eg he bebido - I have drunk). 'hay' means 'there is/are' and all third person singular forms in their respective tenses have this meaning. The forms highlighted with an asterisk are used only for this latter construction.

** the alternative form 'hubiese' is also possible.

[15] **hacer PRES** hago, haces, hace, hacemos, hacéis, hacen; **PRES SUBJ** haga, hagas, haga hagamos, hagáis, hagan; **FUT** haré; **COND** haría; **PRET** hice, hiciste, hizo, hicimos, hicisteis, hicieron; **IMPERF SUBJ** hiciera/hiciese; **PP** hecho; **IMPERAT** haz, haga, hagamos, haced, hagan

[16] **ir PRES** voy, vas, va, vamos, vais, van; **PRES SUBJ** vaya, vayas, vaya, vayamos, vayáis, vayan; **IMPERF** iba, ibas, iba, íbamos, ibais, iban; **PRET** fui, fuiste, fue, fuimos, fuisteis, fueron; **IMPERF SUBJ** fuera/fuese; **PRES P** yendo; **IMPERAT** ve, vaya, vamos, id, vayan

[17] **oír PRES** oigo, oyes, oye, oímos, oís, oyen; **PRES SUBJ** oiga, oigas, oiga, oigamos, oigáis, oigan; **PRET** oí, oíste, oyó, oímos, oísteis, oyeron; **IMPERF SUBJ** oyera/oyese; **PRES P** oyendo; **PP** oído; **IMPERAT** oye, oiga, oigamos, oíd, oigan

[18] **poder PRES** puedo, puedes, puede, podemos, podéis, pueden; **PRES SUBJ** pueda, puedas, pueda, podamos, podáis, puedan; **FUT** podré; **COND** podría; **PRET** pude, pudiste, pudo, pudimos, pudisteis, pudieron; **IMPERF SUBJ** pudiera/pudiese; **PRES P** pudiendo; **IMPERAT** puede, pueda, podamos, poded, puedan

[19] **poner PRES** pongo, pones, pone, ponemos, ponéis, ponen; **PRES SUBJ** ponga, pongas, ponga, pongamos, pongáis, pongan; **FUT** pondré; **PRET** puse, pusiste, puso, pusimos, pusisteis, pusieron; **IMPERF SUBJ** pusiera/pusiese; **PP** puesto; **IMPERAT** pon, ponga, pongamos, poned, pongan

[20] **querer PRES** quiero, quieres, quiere, queremos, queréis, quieren; **PRES SUBJ** quiera, quieras, quiera, queramos, queráis, quieran; **FUT** querré; **COND** querría; **PRET** quise, quisiste, quiso, quisimos, quisisteis, quisieron; **IMPERF SUBJ** quisiera/quisiese; **IMPERAT** quiere, quiera, queramos, quered, quieran

[21] **saber PRES** sé, sabes, sabe, sabemos, sabéis, saben; **PRES SUBJ** sepa, sepas, sepa, sepamos, sepáis, sepan; **FUT** sabré; **COND** sabría; **PRET** supe, supiste, supo, supimos, supisteis, supieron; **IMPERF SUBJ** supiera/supiese; **IMPERAT** sabe, sepa, sepamos, sabed, sepan

[22] **salir PRES** salgo, sales, sale, salimos, salís, salen; **PRES SUBJ** salga, salgas, salga, salgamos, salgáis, salgan; **FUT** saldré; **COND** saldría; **IMPERAT** sal, salga salgamos, salid, salgan

[23] **ser PRES** soy, eres, es, somos, sois, son; **PRES SUBJ** sea, seas, sea, seamos, seáis, sean; **IMPERF** era, eras, era, éramos, erais, eran; **PRET** fui, fuiste, fue, fuimos, fuisteis, fueron; **IMPERF SUBJ** fuera/fuese; **IMPERAT** sé, sea, seamos, sed, sean

[24] **tener PRES** tengo, tienes, tiene, tenemos, tenéis, tienen; **PRES SUBJ** tenga, tengas, tenga, tengamos, tengáis, tengan; **FUT** tendré; **COND** tendría; **PRET** tuve, tuviste, tuvo, tuvimos, tuvisteis, tuvieron; **IMPERF SUBJ** tuviera/tuviese; **IMPERAT** ten, tenga, tengamos, tened tengan

[25] **traer PRES** traigo, traes, trae, traemos, traéis, traen; **PRES SUBJ** traiga, traigas, traiga, traigamos, traigáis, traigan; **PRET** traje, trajiste, trajo, trajimos, trajisteis, trajeron; **IMPERF SUBJ** trajera/trajese; **IMPERAT** trae, traiga, traigamos, traed, traigan

[26] **valer PRES** valgo, vales, vale, valemos, valéis, valen; **PRES SUBJ** valga, valgas, valga, valgamos, valgáis, valgan; **FUT** valdré; **COND** valdría; **IMPERAT** vale, valga, valemos, valed, valgan

[27] **venir PRES** vengo, vienes, viene, venimos, venís, vienen; **PRES SUBJ** venga, vengas, venga, vengamos, vengáis, vengan; **FUT** vendré; **COND** vendría; **PRET** vine, viniste, vino, vinimos, vinisteis, vinieron; **IMPERF SUBJ** viniera/viniese; **PRES P** viniendo; **IMPERAT** ven, venga, vengamos, venid, vengan

[28] **ver PRES** veo, ves, ve, vemos, veis, ven; **PRES SUBJ** vea, veas, vea, veamos, veáis, vean; **IMPERF** veía, veías, veía, veíamos, veíais, veían; **PRET** vi, viste, vio, vimos, visteis, vieron; **IMPERF SUBJ** viera/viese; **IMPERAT** ve, vea, veamos, ved, vean

[29] **desviar PRES** desvío, desvías, desvía, desviamos, desviáis, desvían; **PRES SUBJ** desvíe, desvíes, desvíe, desviemos, desviéis, desvíen; **IMPERAT** desvía, desvíe, desviemos, desviéis, desvíen

[30] **continuar PRES** continúo, continúas, continúa, continuamos, continuáis, continúan; **PRES SUBJ** continúe, continúes, continúe, continuemos, continuéis, continúen; **IMPERAT** continúa, continúe, continuemos, continuad, continúen

[31] **adquirir PRES** adquiero, adquieres, adquiere, adquirimos, adquirís, adquieren; **PRES SUBJ** adquiera, adquiras, adquiera, adquiramos, adquiráis, adquieran; **IMPERAT** adquiere, adquiera, adquiramos, adquirid, adquieran

[32] **jugar PRES** juego, juegas, juega, jugamos, jugáis, juegan; **PRES SUBJ** juegue, juegues, juegue, juguemos, juguéis, jueguen; **IMPERAT** juega, juegue, juguemos, jugad, jueguen

[33] **agradecer PRES** agradezco, agradeces, agradece, agradecemos, agradecéis, agradecen; **PRES SUBJ** agradezca, agradezcas, agradezca, agradezcamos, agradezcáis, agradezcan; **IMPERAT** agradece, agradezca, agradezcamos, agradeced, agradezcan

[34] **conocer PRES** conozco, conoces, conoce, conocemos, conocéis, conocen; **PRES SUBJ** conozca, conozcas, conozca, conozcamos, conozcáis, conozcan; **IMPERAT** conoce, conozca, conozcamos, conoced, conozcan

[35] **lucir PRES** luzco, luces, luce, lucimos, lucís, lucen; **PRES SUBJ** luzca, luzcas, luzca, luzcamos, luzcáis, luzcan; **IMPERAT** luce, luzca, luzcamos, lucid, luzcan

[36] **leer PRET** leí, leíste, leyó, leímos, leísteis, leyeron; **IMPERF SUBJ** leyera/leyese; **PRES P** leyendo; **PP** leído; **IMPERAT** lee, lea, leamos, leed, lean

[37] **huir PRES** huyo, huyes, huye, huimos, huís, huyen; **PRES SUBJ** huya, huyas, huya, huyamos, huyáis, huyan; **PRET** huí, huiste, huyó, huimos, huisteis, huyeron; **IMPERF SUBJ** huyera/huyese; **PRES P** huyendo; **PP** huido; **IMPERAT** huye, huya, huyamos, huid, huyan

[38] **roer PRES** roo/roigo/royo, roes, roe, roemos, roéis, roen; **PRES SUBJ** roa/roiga/roya, roas, roa, roamos, roáis, roan; **PRET** roí, roíste, royó, roímos, roísteis, royeron; **IMPERF SUBJ** royera/royese; **PRES P** royendo; **PP** roído; **IMPERAT** roe, roa, roamos, roed, roan

[39] **caer** PRES caigo, caes, cae, caemos, caéis, caen; PRES SUBJ caiga, caigas, caiga, caigamos, caigáis, caigan; PRES P cayendo; PP caído; IMPERAT cae, caiga caigamos, caed, caigan

[40] **cazar** PRET cacé, cazaste, cazó, cazamos, cazasteis, cazaron; PRES SUBJ cace, caces, cacen, cacemos, cacéis, cacen

[41] **cocer** PRES cuezo, cueces, cuece, cocemos, cocéis, cuecen; PRES SUBJ cueza, cuezas, cueza, cozamos, cozáis, cuezan; IMPERAT cuece, cueza, cozamos, coced, cuezan

[42] **llegar** PRET llegué, llegaste, llegó, llegamos, llegasteis, llegaron; PRES SUBJ llegue, llegues, llegue, lleguemos, lleguéis, lleguen

[43] **cambiar** PRES cambio, cambias, cambia, cambiamos, cambiáis, cambian; PRES SUBJ cambie, cambies, cambie, cambiemos, cambiéis, cambien; IMPERAT cambia, cambie, cambiemos, cambiad, cambien

[44] **sacar** PRET saqué, sacaste, sacó, sacamos, sacasteis, sacaron; PRES SUBJ saque, saques, saque, saquemos, saquéis, saquen; IMPERAT saca, saque, saquemos, sacad, saquen

[45] **averiguar** PRET averigüé, averiguaste, averiguó, averiguamos, averiguasteis, averiguaron; PRES SUBJ averigüe, averigües, averigüe, averigüemos, averigüéis, averigüen; IMPERAT averigua, averigüe, averigüemos, averiguad, averigüen

[46] **asir** PRES asgo, ases, ase, asimos, asís, asen; PRES SUBJ asga, asgas, asga, asgamos, asgáis, asgan; IMPERAT ase, asga, asgamos, asid, asgan

[47] **adecuar** PRES adecuo, adecuas, adecua, adecuamos, adecuáis, adecuan; PRES SUBJ adecue, adecues, adecue, adecuemos, adecuéis, adecuen; IMPERAT adecua, adecuen, adecuemos, adecuad, adecuen

[48] **delinquir** PRES delinco, delinques, delinque, delinquimos, delinquís, delinquen; PRES SUBJ delinca, delincas, delinca, delincamos, delincáis, delincan; IMPERAT delinque, delinca, delincamos, delinquid, delincan

[49] **mecer** PRES mezo, meces, mece, mecemos, mecéis, mecen; PRES SUBJ meza, mezas, meza, mezamos, mezáis, mezan; IMPERAT mece, meza, mezamos, meced, mezan

[50] **errar** PRES yerro, yerras, yerra, erramos, erráis, yerran; PRES SUBJ yerre, yerres, yerre, erremos, erréis, yerren; IMPERAT yerra, yerre, erremos, errad, yerren

[51] **comenzar** PRES comienzo, comienzas, comienza, comenzamos, comenzáis, comienzan; PRES SUBJ comience, comiences, comience, comencemos, comencéis, comiencen; IMPERAT comienza, comience, comencemos, comenzad, comiencen

[52] **zurcir** PRES zurzo, zurces, zurce, zurcimos, zurcís, zurcen; PRES SUBJ zurza, zurzas, zurza, zurzamos, zurzáis, zurzan; IMPERAT zurce, zurza, zurzamos, zurcid, zurzan

[53] **proteger** PRES protejo, proteges, protege, protegemos, protegéis, protegen; PRES SUBJ proteja, protejas, proteja, protejamos, protejáis, protejan; IMPERAT protege, proteja, protejamos, proteged, protejan

[54] **discernir PRES** discierno, disciernes, discierne, discernimos, discernís, disciernen; **PRES SUBJ** discierna, disciernas, discierna, discernamos, discernáis, disciernan; **IMPERAT** discierne, discierna, discernamos, discernid, disciernan

[55] **erguir PRES** irgo/yergo, irgues/yergues, irgue/yergue, erguimos, erguís, irguen/yerguen; **PRET** erguí, erguiste, irguió, erguimos, erguisteis, irguieron; **PRES SUBJ** irga/yerga, irgas/yergas, irga/yerga, irgamos/yergamos, irgáis/yergáis, irgan/yergan; **IMPERF SUBJ** irguiera/irguiese; **IMPERAT** irgue/yergue, irga/yerga, irgamos/yergamos, erguid, irgan/yergan

[56] **reír PRES** río, ríes, ríe, reímos, reís, ríen; **PRET** reí, reíste, rió, reímos, reísteis, rieron; **PRES SUBJ** ría, rías, ría, riamos, riáis, rían; **IMPERF SUBJ** riera/riese; **IMPERAT** ríe, ría, riamos, reíd, rían

[57] **dirigir PRES** dirijo, diriges, dirige, dirigimos, dirigís, dirigen; **PRES SUBJ** dirija, dirijas, dirija, dirijamos, dirijáis, dirijan; **IMPERAT** dirige, dirija, dirijamos, dirigid, dirijan

[58] **regir PRES** rijo, riges, rige, regimos, regís, rigen; **PRES SUBJ** rija, rijas, rija, rijamos, rijáis, rijan; **IMPERAT** rige, rija, rijamos, regid, rijan

[59] **distinguir PRES** distingo, distingues, distingue, distinguimos, distinguís, distinguen; **PRES SUBJ** distinga, distingas, distinga, distingamos, distingáis, distingan; **IMPERAT** distingue, distinga, distingamos, distinguid, distingan

[60] **nacer PRES** nazco, naces, nace, nacemos, nacéis, nacen; **PRES SUBJ** nazca, nazcas, nazca, nazcamos, nazcáis, nazcan; **IMPERAT** nace, nazca, nazcamos, naced, nazcan

[61] **yacer PRES** yazco/yazgo/yago, yaces, yace, yacemos, yacéis, yacen; **PRES SUBJ** yazca/yazga/yaga; **IMPERAT** yace/yaz, yazca/yazga/yaga, yazcamos/yazgamos/yagamos, yaced, yazcan/yazgan/yagan

[62] **argüir PRES** arguyo, arguyes, arguye, argüimos, argüís, arguyen; **PRET** argüí, argüiste, arguyó, argüimos, argüisteis, arguyeron; **PRES SUBJ** arguya, arguyas, arguya, arguyamos, arguyáis, arguyan; **IMPERF SUBJ** arguyera/arguyese; **IMPERAT** arguye, arguya, arguyamos, argüid, arguyan

[63] **avergonzar PRES** avergüenzo, avergüenzas, avergüenza, avergonzamos, avergonzáis, avergüenzan; **PRET** avergoncé, avergonzaste, avergonzó, avergonzamos, avergonzasteis, avergonzaron; **PRES SUBJ** avergüence, avergüences, avergüence, avergoncemos, avergoncéis, avergüencen; **IMPERAT** avergüenza, avergüence, avergoncemos, avergonzad, avergüencen

[64] **trocar PRES** trueco, truecas, trueca, trocamos, trocáis, truecan; **PRET** troqué, trocaste, trocó, trocamos, trocasteis, trocaron; **PRES SUBJ** trueque, trueques, trueque, troquemos, troquéis, truequen; **IMPERAT** trueca, trueque, troquemos, trocad, truequen

[65] **oler PRES** huelo, hueles, huele, olemos, oléis, huelen; **PRES SUBJ** huela, huelas, huela, olamos, oláis, huelan; **IMPERAT** huele, huela, olamos, oled, huelan

Verbos irregulares ingleses

INFINITIVO	PRETÉRITO	PARTICIPIO
arise	arose	arisen
awake	awoke	awoken
awaken	awoke, awakened	awakened, awoken
be	were/was	been
bear	bore	borne
beat	beat	beaten
become	became	become
begin	began	begun
bend	bent	bent
beseech	besought, beseeched	besought, beseeched
bet	bet, betted	bet, betted
bid	bade, bid	bidden, bid
bind	bound	bound
bite	bit	bitten
bleed	bled	bled
blow	blew	blown
break	broke	broken
breed	bred	bred
bring	brought	brought
build	built	built
burn	burnt, burned	burnt, burned
burst	burst	burst
buy	bought	bought
cast	cast	cast
catch	caught	caught
choose	chose	chosen
cling	clung	clung
clothe	clad, clothed	clad, clothed
come	came	come
cost	cost	cost
creep	crept	crept
cut	cut	cut
deal	dealt	dealt
dig	dug	dug
do	did	done
draw	drew	drawn
dream	dreamt, dreamed	dreamt, dreamed
drink	drank	drunk
drive	drove	driven
dwell	dwelt	dwelt
eat	ate	eaten
fall	fell	fallen
feed	fed	fed
feel	felt	felt

INFINITIVO	PRETÉRITO	PARTICIPIO
fight	fought	fought
find	found	found
flee	fled	fled
fling	flung	flung
fly	flew	flown
forget	forgot	forgotten
forgive	forgave	forgiven
forsake	forsook	forsaken
freeze	froze	frozen
get	got	got, *US* gotten
give	gave	given
go	went	gone
grind	ground	ground
grow	grew	grown
hang	hung/hanged	hung/hanged
have	had	had
hear	heard	heard
hide	hid	hidden
hit	hit	hit
hold	held	held
hurt	hurt	hurt
keep	kept	kept
kneel	knelt	knelt
knit	knitted, knit	knitted, knit
know	knew	known
lay	laid	laid
lead	led	led
lean	leant, leaned	leant, leaned
leap	leapt, leaped	leapt, leaped
learn	learnt, learned	learnt, learned
leave	left	left
lend	lent	lent
let	let	let
lie	lay	lain
light	lit	lit
lose	lost	lost
make	made	made
mean	meant	meant
meet	met	met
mow	mowed	mown, mowed
pay	paid	paid
put	put	put
quit	quit	quit
read	read	read
rend	rent	rent
rid	rid	rid
ride	rode	ridden
ring	rang	rung
rise	rose	risen
run	ran	run
saw	sawed	sawn, sawed

INFINITIVO	PRETÉRITO	PARTICIPIO
say	said	said
see	saw	seen
seek	sought	sought
sell	sold	sold
send	sent	sent
set	set	set
sew	sewed	sewn
shake	shook	shaken
shear	sheared	shorn, sheared
shed	shed	shed
shine	shone	shone
shoe	shod	shod
shoot	shot	shot
show	showed	shown
shrink	shrank	shrunk
shut	shut	shut
sing	sang	sung
sink	sank	sunk
sit	sat	sat
slay	slew	slain
sleep	slept	slept
slide	slid	slid
sling	slung	slung
slink	slunk	slunk
slit	slit	slit
smell	smelled, smelt	smelled, smelt
sow	sowed	sown, sowed
speak	spoke	spoken
speed	sped, speeded	sped, speeded
spell	spelt, spelled	spelt, spelled
spend	spent	spent
spill	spilt, spilled	spilt, spilled
spin	span	spun
spit	spat	spat
split	split	split
spoil	spoilt, spoiled	spoilt, spoiled
spread	spread	spread
spring	sprang	sprung
stand	stood	stood
steal	stole	stolen
stick	stuck	stuck
sting	stung	stung
stink	stank, stunk	stunk
strew	strewed	strewed, strewn
stride	strode	stridden
strike	struck	struck
string	strung	strung
strive	strove	striven
swear	swore	sworn
sweep	swept	swept
swell	swelled	swollen

INFINITIVO	PRETÉRITO	PARTICIPIO
swing	swung	swung
swim	swam	swum
take	took	taken
teach	taught	taught
tear	tore	torn
tell	told	told
think	thought	thought
thrive	thrived, throve	thrived, thriven
throw	threw	thrown
thrust	thrust	thrust
tread	trod	trodden
wake	woke	woken
wear	wore	worn
weave	wove	woven
weep	wept	wept
wet	wet	wet
win	won	won
wind	wound	wound
wring	wrung	wrung
write	wrote	written

CONVERSATION GUIDE

Spanish has two main ways of saying *you*: **tú** and **usted**. **Tú** is informal and should be used when speaking to a friend or young person. **Usted** is used when addressing older people or people you don't know, and in formal contexts. The plural form **ustedes** is also used when addressing more than one person (formally or informally). Note that **tú** and **usted** take different verb forms.

The direct and indirect pronoun associated with **tú** is **te**, and **ti** is used after prepositions; the possessive adjective is **tuyo(a)**, and the possessive pronoun is (**el/la**) **tuyo(a)**. The **usted** equivalents are **lo/la** (direct), **le** (indirect), **usted** after propositions, and **suyo(a)** and (**el/la**) **suyo(a)**.

It's best to start off addressing people as **usted**; if they want you to use the **tú** form, they may say "**podemos tutearnos**".

Greetings and introductions

Hello, how are you?
Hola, ¿cómo le/te va?

Fine thank you, how are you?
Bien, gracias, ¿y a usted/ti?

Hi, how's it going?
Hola, ¿qué tal?

Good, and you?
Bien, ¿y tú?

How are the kids?
¿Cómo están los niños?

They're fine thanks.
Están bien, gracias.

Good morning/afternoon.
Buen día or *Buenos días.*

Good evening.
Buenas noches.

Good afternoon
Buenas tardes.

What's your name?
¿Cómo se llama?/ ¿Cómo te llamas?

My name's Steve.
Me llamo Steve.

I'm Elaine and this is my husband David.
Yo soy Elaine y este es David, mi marido.

Pleased to meet you.
Encantado(a).

How old are you?
¿Qué edad tiene?/¿Cuántos años tienes?

I'm 18/32 (years old).
Tengo dieciocho/treinta y dos años.

Where are you from?
¿De dónde es?/¿De dónde eres?

I'm from the US.
Soy de Estados Unidos.

Conversation Guide

Where do you live?
¿Dónde vive?/¿Dónde vives?

I live near Boston.
Vivo cerca de Boston.

We live in Florida.
Vivimos en Florida.

We're American.
Somos estadounidenses or
americanos or *norteamericanos.*

What do you do?
¿A qué se dedica?/¿A qué te dedicas?

I'm a lawyer/a student.
Soy abogado(a)/estudiante.

I'm in high school/college.
Voy al colegio/a la universidad.

I'm a stay-at-home mom.
Soy ama de casa.

I work in publishing.
Trabajo en el campo editorial.

I'm retired.
Estoy jubilado(a).

Do you have any brothers and sisters?
¿Tiene/Tienes hermanos?

I've got two older sisters and a little brother.
Tengo dos hermanas mayores y un hermano menor.

I'm an only child.
Soy hijo(a) único(a).

I'm the eldest/the youngest.
Soy el mayor/el menor.
Soy la mayor/la menor.

Do you have kids?
¿Tienen hijos?

We have a nine-year-old daughter named Alice.
Tenemos una hija de nueve años que se llama Alice.

Are you married?
¿Está casado(a)? ¿Estás casado(a)?

I'm divorced/separated/widowed
Estoy divorciado(a)/separado(a)./Soy viudo(a).

What do you do in your free time?
¿Qué hace en su tiempo libre?
¿Qué haces en tu tiempo libre?

I like swimming/going to the movies.
Me gusta nadar/ir al cine.

I run/play tennis/do yoga.
Corro/juego al tenis/hago yoga.

I'm taking Spanish classes.
Estoy tomando clases de español.

See you soon/later!
¡Hasta luego!

See you tomorrow/on Monday.
Hasta mañana/el lunes.

Goodbye!/Bye!
¡Adiós!/¡Chau!

Good night.
Buenas noches.

We should keep in touch, here's my e-mail address.
Tenemos que seguir en contacto, esta es mi dirección electrónica.

Come see us if you're ever in New York!
¡Venga/Ven a vernos si pasa/pasas por Nueva York!

Directions

Can you tell me where the tourist information office is, please?
¿Podría/Podrías decirme dónde queda la oficina de información turística, por favor?

I'm lost.
Estoy perdido(a).

How do I get to the train station?
¿Cómo puedo llegar a la estación?

Is there a bank around here?
¿Hay algún banco cerca de aquí?

Where's the nearest supermarket
¿Dónde está/queda el supermercado más cercano?

Do you have a map of the town?
¿Tiene/Tienes un plano de la ciudad?

Can you show me on the map?
¿Podría/Podrías mostrármelo en el plano?

I'm looking for the Hotel Royal.
Busco el hotel Royal.

Is it far?
¿Está/Queda lejos?

Turn right and then go straight on.
Doble/Tuerza a la derecha y continúe recto.
Dobla/Tuerce a la derecha y continúa recto.

Take the next exit.
Tome/Toma la próxima salida.

It's just around the corner.
Está/Queda aquí a la vuelta.

Take the second left after the traffic lights.
Tome/Toma la segunda a la izquierda, después del semáforo.

Understanding

I don't understand.
No entiendo.

I didn't understand.
No entendí.

Excuse me?
¿Cómo?/¿Perdón?

Could you repeat that?
¿Podría repetírmelo?

Can you speak more slowly, please?
¿Podría hablar más despacio, por favor?

I don't speak much Spanish.
No hablo mucho español.

I can understand a little bit.
Entiendo un poquito.

Conversation Guide

Sorry, I misunderstood.
Perdóneme, entendí mal.

What's going on?
¿Qué pasa/sucede?

I took Spanish in high school but I've forgotten everything.
Estudié español en el colegio, pero ya me olvidé de todo.

Do you speak English?
¿Habla/Hablas inglés?

You speak very good English.
Habla/Hablas muy bien inglés.

What does that mean?
¿Qué quiere decir?

What is it?
¿Qué es?

What's that called in Spanish?
¿Cómo se llama eso en español?

How do you say … in Spanish?
¿Cómo se dice … en español?

How do you spell it?
¿Cómo se escribe?

Could you write it down for me?
¿Podría/Podrías escribírmelo?

I don't know how to pronounce it.
No sé cómo se pronuncia.

I think it's a difficult language.
Me parece una lengua difícil.

Suggestions and invitations

What do you want to do?
¿Qué le/te gustaría hacer?

What would you rather do?
¿Qué prefiere/prefieres hacer?

Shall we go for a drink?
¿Vamos a tomar algo?

Would you like to go for a coffee?
¿Quiere/Quieres ir a tomar un café?

How about going to the movies?
¿Y si vamos al cine?

Let's go for a swim!
¡Vamos a nadar un rato!

Why don't we have a barbecue tonight?
¿Y si hiciéramos una barbacoa/ un asado esta noche?

Do you feel like a drink before dinner?
¿ Le/Te gustaría tomar un aperitivo antes de cenar?

Let's meet at noon/outside the museum.
¿Nos encontramos al mediodía/en la puerta del museo?

I think we should leave around 9.
Creo que deberíamos salir alrededor de las nueve.

Are you free tomorrow night?
¿Está/Estás libre mañana de noche?

What shall we do tomorrow?
¿Qué podemos hacer mañana?

Wishes and desires

I'd like to go to the pool.
Me gustaría ir a la piscina.

I don't want to go to the art gallery.
No quiero ir al museo de arte.

I feel like an ice-cream.
Tengo ganas de tomar un helado.

I don't feel like going downtown.
No tengo ganas de ir al centro.

I'd rather stay here.
Preferiría quedarme aquí.

I wouldn't mind buying a souvenir.
Me gustaría comprar algún recuerdo.

I'd like to learn Spanish.
Me gustaría aprender español.

I wish we could stay longer!
¡Ojalá pudiéramos quedarnos más tiempo!

Accepting and refusing offers

I'd love to!
¡Encantado(a)!/¡Me encantaría!

I don't feel like it.
No tengo ganas.

That's a good idea.
Es una buena idea.

That sounds nice.
Eso suena bien.

I'm sorry, I can't.
Lo siento/lamento, no puedo.

I'm afraid I already have plans.
Lo siento/lamento, ya tengo planes.

That's very kind of you.
Es muy amable de su/tu parte.

Thank you for offering.
Gracias por el ofrecimiento.

I don't mind.
Para mí es lo mismo.

It's up to you.
Depende de lo que quiera/quieras.

Agreeing and disagreeing

I agree (with you).
Estoy de acuerdo (con usted/ contigo).

I disagree (with you).
No estoy de acuerdo (con usted/ contigo).

You're (quite) right).
Tiene/Tienes toda la razón.

I think you're wrong.
Creo que está/estás equivocado(a).

That's true.
Es verdad.

That's not true (at all).
No es verdad (en absoluto).

Conversation Guide

I see your point, but...
Entiendo lo que dice/dices, pero...

Sure!/Of course!
¡Claro!/¡Por supuesto!

Of course not!
¡Claro que no!

Requests

Could I have a glass of water?
¿Me daría un vaso de agua?

I'd like the steak, please.
Yo quiero la carne, por favor.

Could you bring us some more bread, please?
¿Podría traernos un poco más de pan, por favor?

Could we have some clean towels/extra pillows?
¿Podría traernos unas toallas limpias/algunas almohadas más?

Is it ok if I smoke?
¿Le/Te molesta si fumo?

Do you have a cigarette/a light?
¿Tiene/Tienes cigarrillos/fuego?

Can I borrow a pencil?
¿Puede/Puedes prestarme un lápiz?

Could I use your cellphone?
¿Puedo usar su/tu celular or móvil?

Do you mind if I open the window?
¿Le/Te molesta que abra la ventana?

Can I have your e-mail address?
¿Me daría su dirección electrónica?
¿Me darías tu dirección electrónica?

Likes, dislikes and preferences

I like swimming/playing golf.
Me gusta nadar/jugar al golf.

I love ballet/playing cards.
Me encanta el ballet/jugar a las cartas.

I don't like modern art/shopping.
No me gusta el arte moderno/ir de compras.

I hate tomatoes/watching sports.
Detesto los tomates/mirar deportes.

I really enjoyed the movie.
La película me gustó mucho.

I didn't like the museum that much.
El museo no me gustó demasiado.

I'm a big baseball fan.
Soy fanático(a) del béisbol.

I'm not really into classical music.
La música clásica no me entusiasma.

What's your favourite dish?
¿Cuál es su/tu plato preferido?

The restaurant was nothing special.
El restaurante no era nada especial/del otro mundo.

I prefer Diet Coke®.
Prefiero la Coca Light®.

I'd rather have chips than salad.
Preferiría las papas fritas en vez de la ensalada.

Opinions

What do you think?
¿Qué le/te parece?

Do you agree?
¿Está/Estás de acuerdo?

What did you think of the exhibition?
¿Qué le/te pareció la exposición?

It was good, wasn't it?
Estuvo bien, ¿no es verdad?

It was OK.
No estuvo mal.

I think it's a great idea.
Creo que es una excelente idea.

I don't think it's possible.
No creo que sea posible.

We found the hotel quite noisy.
El hotel nos pareció demasiado ruidoso.

I thought the museum was boring.
El museo me pareció aburrido.

In my opinion, the tour of the castle is overpriced.
En mi opinión, la visita al castillo es demasiado cara.

I think she's very nice.
Me parece muy simpática.

I'm not sure.
No estoy seguro(a).

I've changed my mind.
Cambié de idea.

I don't know.
No sé.

Advice and recommendations

Can you recommend a good restaurant?
¿Podría/Podrías recomendar un buen restaurante?

I'd like some information on bus routes.
Precisaría información sobre las líneas de bus.

Can you help me?
¿Podría ayudarme?

I need some advice (on...).
Preciso un consejo (sobre...).

Conversation Guide

I recommend the Hostería San Miguel.
Le/Te recomiendo la Hostería San Miguel.

I'd advise you to go early in the morning.
Le/Te aconsejo que vaya/vayas temprano por la mañana.

I wouldn't recommend that bar.
No le/te recomiendo ese bar.

You really must visit the cathedral.
Tiene/Tienes que visitar la catedral. No se puede/te puedes perder la catedral.

It's best to take a cab.
Lo mejor es tomar un taxi.

You should take a warm coat.
Sería bueno que trajera/trajeras un abrigo.

It's not advisable to swim here.
No es recomendable bañarse aquí.

Be careful!
¡Cuidado!

Gratitude

Thank you (very much).
(Muchas) Gracias.

You're welcome!
¡De nada!/¡Por favor!

Thanks, that's very kind.
Gracias, muy amable.

That would be great, thank you.
Sería sensacional, gracias.

Thank you for having me.
Gracias por haberme invitado.

Thanks a lot for your help.
Muchas gracias por su ayuda.

Apologies

I'm (so) sorry.
Lo siento muchísimo.

Excuse me.
Discúlpeme. Perdóneme.

Sorry I'm late.
Siento muchísimo llegar tarde.

Sorry to bother you, but…
Disculpe/Disculpa que lo/te moleste, pero…

Sorry, it's my fault.
Lo siento, es mi culpa.

Sorry, I didn't mean to!
Lo siento, ¡no lo hice a propósito!

I apologize for waking you up last night.
Disculpe que lo(a) haya despertado anoche.
Disculpa que te haya despertado anoche.

No problem.
No es nada./No hay problema.

That's ok.	Don't worry about it.
Está bien./No hay problema.	*No se preocupe./No te preocupes.*

Feelings and emotions

I'm really happy to be here.
Me alegro mucho de estar aquí.

I'm sad to be leaving tomorrow.
Me da tristeza irme mañana.

I'm delighted to meet you.
*Encantado(a) de conocerlo(a)/
conocerte.*

I'm so excited!
¡Estoy tan entusiasmado(a)!

I miss my family.
Extraño a mi familia.

I'll miss you.
Lo(a)/Te voy a extrañar.

I'm nervous about flying.
Volar me pone nervioso(a).

The rollercoaster was really
scary!
*¡La montaña rusa me dio mucho
miedo!*

I'm worried about him/her.
Estoy preocupado(a) por él/ella.

I'm scared we're going to miss
our flight.
Tengo miedo de perder el avión.

I'm angry about my flight being
cancelled.
*Estoy enojado(a) por la cancelación
del vuelo.*

I'm really mad at them!
¡Estoy muy enojado(a) con ellos!

I'm a little tired.
Estoy un poco cansado(a).

I'm hot/cold/hungry/thirsty.
Tengo calor/frío/hambre/sed.

Surprise

Really?
¿Ah sí?/¿De verdad?

No way!
¡No puede ser!

Are you kidding?
¿Está/Estás bromeando?

That's amazing!
¡Es increíble !

What a surprise!
¡Qué sorpresa!

How strange!
¡Qué raro!

Disappointment

What a pity!
¡Qué lástima/pena!

How disappointing!
¡Es realmente una lástima/pena!

It's a shame you couldn't come.
Es una lástima que no haya/hayas podido venir.

I was a bit disappointed that the store was closed.
Me decepcionó un poco que la tienda estuviera cerrada.

Congratulations and compliments

Congratulations!
¡Felicitaciones!

Well done!
¡Bravo!

That's great news!
¡Excelente noticia!

I'm so pleased for you.
Me alegro mucho por usted/ti.

Thank you, that was delicious.
Gracias, estaba delicioso.

What a lovely house/view!
¡Qué bonita casa/vista!

You look great!
¡Es/Eres sensacional!

I had a great time.
Me divertí muchísimo.

Good wishes

Happy birthday!
¡Feliz cumpleaños!

Merry Christmas!
¡Feliz navidad!

Happy New Year!
¡Feliz año nuevo!

Best wishes.
Los mejores deseos.

Good luck!
¡Buena suerte!

Cheers!
¡Salud!

Take care!
¡Cuídese!/¡Cuídate!

Get well soon!
¡Que se mejore!/¡Que te mejores!

Have a nice day/evening!
¡Buen día!/¡Buenas noches!

Have a good weekend/trip!
¡Buen fin de semana/viaje!

A, a [eɪ] *n* (**a**) *(the letter)* A, a *f* (**b**) *Mus* A la *m* (**c**) *Br* **A road** ≃ carretera *f* nacional

a [eɪ, *unstressed* ə] *indef art (before vowel or silent h* **an**) (**a**) *(in general)* un, una; **a man/a woman** un hombre/una mujer; **he has a big nose** tiene la nariz grande (**b**) *(omitted in Spanish)* **half a litre/an hour** medio litro/media hora; **a hundred/thousand people** cien/mil personas; **let's have a drink** vamos a beber algo; **he's a teacher** es profesor; **what a pity** qué pena (**c**) *(each)* **60 pence a kilo** 60 peniques el kilo; **to eat grapes two at a time** comer las uvas de dos en dos; **three times a week** tres veces a la semana (**d**) *(a certain)* **a Mr Rees phoned** llamó un tal Sr. Rees

AA [eɪ'eɪ] *n* (**a**) *(abbr* **Alcoholics Anonymous**) AA, alcohólicos *mpl* anónimos (**b**) *(abbr* **Automobile Association**) = asociación automovilística británica, *Esp* ≃ RACE *m*, *Arg* ≃ ACA *m*

AAA [eɪeɪ'eɪ] *n* (**a**) *Br (abbr* **Amateur Athletic Association**) = federación británica de atletismo aficionado (**b**) *US (abbr* **American Automobile Association**) = asociación automovilística estadounidense, *Esp* ≃ RACE *m*, *Arg* ≃ ACA *m*

aback [ə'bæk] *adv* **to be taken a.** quedarse de una pieza (**by** por)

abandon [ə'bændən] **1** *n* desenfreno *m*; **with reckless a.** desenfrenadamente **2** *vt (child)* abandonar; *(job)* dejar; *(project)* renunciar a

abase [ə'beɪs] *vt* **to a. oneself** humillarse

abashed [ə'bæʃt] *adj* avergonzado(a), abochornado(a), *Am salvo RP* apenado(a)

abate [ə'beɪt] *vi (anger)* apaciguarse; *(storm)* amainar

abattoir ['æbətwɑː(r)] *n* matadero *m*

abbey ['æbɪ] *n* abadía *f*

abbot ['æbət] *n* abad *m*

abbreviate [ə'briːvɪeɪt] *vt* abreviar

abbreviation [əbriːvɪ'eɪʃən] *n* abreviatura *f*

abdicate ['æbdɪkeɪt] *vt & vi* abdicar

abdication [æbdɪ'keɪʃən] *n* abdicación *f*

abdomen ['æbdəmən] *n* abdomen *m*

abduct [æb'dʌkt] *vt* raptar, secuestrar

abduction [əb'dʌkʃən] *n* rapto *m*, secuestro *m*

aberration [æbə'reɪʃən] *n* aberración *f*

abet [ə'bet] *vt* **to aid and a. sb** ser cómplice de algn

abeyance [ə'beɪəns] *n* **to be in a.** estar en desuso

abhor [əb'hɔː(r)] *vt* aborrecer

abhorrent [əb'hɒrənt] *adj* aborrecible

abide [ə'baɪd] *vt* aguantar; **I can't a. it** no lo aguanto

▸ **abide by** *vt insep (promise)* cumplir con; *(rules)* atenerse a

ability [ə'bɪlɪtɪ] *n (capability)* capacidad *f*, aptitud *f*; *(talent)* talento *m*

abject ['æbdʒekt] *adj (state)* miserable; *(apology)* rastrero(a)

ablaze [ə'bleɪz] *adj & adv* en llamas, ardiendo

able ['eɪbəl] *adj (capable)* capaz; **will you be a. to come on Tuesday?** ¿podrás venir el martes?

able-bodied [eɪbəl'bɒdɪd] *adj* sano(a); **a. seaman** marinero *m* de primera

abnormal [æb'nɔːməl] *adj* anormal

abnormally [æb'nɔːməlɪ] *adv* anormalmente; *(large, quiet)* excepcionalmente

aboard [ə'bɔːd] **1** *adv* a bordo; **to go a.** *(ship)* embarcarse; *(train)* subir **2** *prep* a bordo de

abode [ə'bəʊd] *n Jur* **of no fixed a.** sin domicilio fijo

abolish [ə'bɒlɪʃ] *vt* abolir

abolition [æbə'lɪʃən] *n* abolición *f*

abominable [ə'bɒmɪnəbəl] *adj* deplorable, abominable; **her handwriting is a.** tiene una letra malísima *or* lamentable

aborigine [æbə'rɪdʒɪnɪ] *n* aborigen *mf* australiano(a)

abort [ə'bɔːt] **1** *vt Med* hacer abortar; *Fig (plan etc)* archivar **2** *vi Med* abortar

abortion [ə'bɔːʃən] *n Med* aborto *m*; **a. law** ley *f* del aborto; **to have an a.** abortar

abortive [ə'bɔːtɪv] *adj (plan)* fracasado(a); *(attempt)* frustrado(a)

abound [ə'baʊnd] *vi* **to a. in** *or* **with** abundar en

about [ə'baʊt] *adv & prep* (**a**) *(concerning)* acerca de, sobre; **a programme a. Paris** un programa sobre París; **to be worried a. sth** estar preocupado(a) por algo; **to speak a. sth** hablar de algo; **what's it all a.?** *(what's happening?)* ¿qué pasa?; *(story etc)* ¿de qué se trata?; *Fam* **how a. a game of tennis?** ¿qué te parece un partido de tenis? (**b**) *(around)* por todas partes; **don't leave things lying a.** no dejes las cosas por medio; **there's nobody a.** no hay nadie; **to look a.** mirar alrededor; **to rush a.** correr de un lado para otro; **we went for a walk a. the town** dimos una vuelta por el pueblo (**c**) *(approximately)* más o menos; **it's a. three o'clock** son más o menos las tres; **it's a. time you got up** ya es hora de que te levantes; **it's just a. finished** está casi terminado; **she's a. forty** tiene unos cuarenta años (**d**) **it's a. to start** está a punto de empezar; **not to be a. to do sth** no estar dispuesto(a) a hacer algo

about-face [əbaʊt'feɪs], *Br* **about-turn** [əbaʊt'tɜːn] *n* media vuelta *f*; **to do a.** dar media vuelta; *Fig* cambiar de idea por completo

above [ə'bʌv] *adv & prep* (**a**) *(higher than)* encima de, sobre, arriba; **100 m a. sea level** 100 m sobre el nivel del mar; **it's a. the door** está encima de la puerta; **the flat a.** el piso de arriba (**b**) *(greater than)* superior (a); **amounts a. £10** cantidades superiores a las 10 libras; *Fig* **a policy imposed from a.** una política impuesta desde arriba (**c**) **a. all** sobre todo; **he's not a. stealing** es capaz incluso de robar (**d**) *(in book etc)* más arriba

above-board [ə'bʌv'bɔːd] *adj (scheme)* legítimo(a)

above-mentioned [ə'bʌvmenʃənd] *adj* susodicho(a)

abrasive [ə'breɪsɪv] **1** *adj (substance)* abrasivo(a); *Fig (voice, wit etc)* cáustico(a)
2 *n* abrasivo *m*

abreast [ə'brest] *adv* **to walk three a.** ir de tres en fondo; *Fig* **to keep a. of things** mantenerse al día

abridged [ə'brɪdʒd] *adj (book)* abreviado(a)

abroad [ə'brɔːd] *adv* **to be a.** estar en el extranjero; **to go a.** irse al extranjero

abrupt [ə'brʌpt] *adj (manner)* brusco(a); *(tone)* áspero(a); *(change)* súbito(a)

abruptly [ə'brʌptlɪ] *adv (act)* bruscamente; *(speak)* con aspereza; *(change)* repentinamente

abscess ['æbses] *n* absceso *m*; *(on gum)* flemón *m*

abscond [əb'skɒnd] *vi* huir

absence ['æbsəns] *n (of person)* ausencia *f*; *(of thing)* falta *f*

absent ['æbsənt] *adj* ausente; *Fig* **an a. look** una mirada distraída

absentee [æbsən'tiː] *n* ausente *mf*; **a. landlord** (propietario(a) *m,f*) ausentista *mf or Esp* absentista *mf*

absenteeism [æbsən'tiːɪzəm] *n* ausentismo *m, Esp* absentismo *m*

absently ['æbsəntlɪ] *adv* distraídamente

absent-minded [æbsən'maɪndɪd] *adj* distraído(a)

absolute ['æbsəluːt] *adj (complete, total)* absoluto(a); *(for emphasis)* absoluto(a), auténtico(a); **it's an a. disgrace** es una auténtica vergüenza

absolutely [æbsə'luːtlɪ] **1** *adv (completely)* completamente; **a. wrong** totalmente equivocado(a); **a. not** en absoluto; **you're a. right** tienes toda la razón
2 *interj* **a.!** ¡desde luego!

absolve [əb'zɒlv] *vt* absolver (**from** de)

absorb [əb'zɔːb] *vt (liquid)* absorber; *(sound, blow)* amortiguar; *Fig* **to be absorbed in sth** estar absorto(a) en algo

absorbing [əb'zɔːbɪŋ] *adj (book, work)* absorbente

abstain [əb'steɪn] *vi (not vote)* abstenerse (**from** de); *(not drink alcohol)* no beber alcohol, *Am* no tomar

abstemious [əb'stiːmɪəs] *adj* abstemio(a)

abstention [əb'stenʃən] *n* abstención *f*

abstinence ['æbstɪnəns] *n* abstinencia *f*

abstract ['æbstrækt] **1** *adj* abstracto(a)
2 *n (of thesis etc)* resumen *m*

abstruse [əb'struːs] *adj* abstruso(a)

absurd [əb'sɜːd] *adj* absurdo(a)

abundance [ə'bʌndəns] *n* abundancia *f*

abundant [ə'bʌndənt] *adj* abundante, rico(a) (**in** en)

abuse 1 *n* [ə'bjuːs] (**a**) *(ill-treatment)* malos tratos; *(misuse)* abuso *m* (**b**) *(insults)* injurias *fpl*
2 *vt* [ə'bjuːz] (**a**) *(ill-treat)* maltratar; *(misuse)* abusar de (**b**) *(insult)* injuriar

abusive [əb'juːsɪv] *adj (insulting)* insultante

abysmal [ə'bɪzməl] *adj (conditions)* extremo(a); *Fam (very bad)* fatal, pésimo(a)

abyss [ə'bɪs] *n* abismo *m*; *Fig* extremo *m*

AC [eɪ'siː] *(abbr* **alternating current)** CA

academic [ækə'demɪk] **1** *adj (of school, university)* académico(a); *(intellectual)* académico(a), intelectual; **a. year** año *m* escolar

2 *n* (*university teacher*) profesor(a) *m,f* de universidad

academy [əˈkædəmɪ] *n* (*society*) academia *f*; *Educ* instituto *m* de enseñanza media; **a. of music** conservatorio *m*

accede [ækˈsiːd] *vi* acceder (**to** a)

accelerate [ækˈseləreɪt] **1** *vt* (*engine*) acelerar; (*step*) aligerar

2 *vi* (*car, engine*) acelerar

acceleration [ækseləˈreɪʃən] *n* aceleración *f*

accelerator [ækˈseləreɪtə(r)] *n* acelerador *m*

accent [ˈæksənt] *n* acento *m*

accentuate [ækˈsentʃʊeɪt] *vt* subrayar

accept [əkˈsept] **1** *vt* (*in general*) aceptar; (*reasons*) aceptar, admitir; (*blame*) admitir, reconocer; **do you a. that …?** ¿estás de acuerdo en que …?

2 *vi* aceptar

acceptable [əkˈseptəbəl] *adj* (*satisfactory*) aceptable; (*tolerable*) admisible

acceptance [əkˈseptəns] *n* (*act of accepting*) aceptación *f*; (*good reception*) aprobación *f*

access [ˈækses] *n* acceso *m*; *Comput* **a. provider** proveedor *m* de acceso (a Internet); **a. road** carretera *f* de acceso; **to have a. to sth** tener libre acceso a algo

accessible [əkˈsesəbəl] *adj* accesible

accession [əkˈseʃən] *n* subida *f* (al trono)

accessory [əkˈsesərɪ] *n* (**a**) *Jur* cómplice *mf* (**b**) **accessories** accesorios *mpl*; (*for outfit*) complementos *mpl*

accident [ˈæksɪdənt] *n* accidente *m*; (*coincidence*) casualidad *f*; **it was an a. on my part** lo hice sin querer; **car a.** accidente *m* de carretera; **by a.** por casualidad

accidental [æksɪˈdentəl] *adj* accidental, casual

accidentally [æksɪˈdentəlɪ] *adv* (*by chance*) por casualidad; **he did it a.** lo hizo sin querer

accident-prone [ˈæksɪdəntprəʊn] *adj* propenso(a) a los accidentes

acclaim [əˈkleɪm] **1** *n* aclamación *f*

2 *vt* aclamar

acclimatization [əklaɪmətaɪˈzeɪʃən], *US* **acclimation** [æklɪˈmeɪʃən] *n* aclimatación *f*

acclimatize [əˈklaɪmətaɪz], *US* **acclimate** [ˈæklɪmeɪt] *vt* aclimatar

acclimatized [əˈklaɪmətaɪzd] *adj* aclimatado(a); **to become a.** aclimatarse

accolade [ˈækəleɪd] *n* elogio *m*

accommodate [əˈkɒmədeɪt] *vt* (**a**) (*guests*) alojar (**b**) **to a. sb's wishes** complacer a algn

accommodating [əˈkɒmədeɪtɪŋ] *adj* (*obliging*) complaciente; (*understanding*) comprensivo(a)

accommodation [əkɒməˈdeɪʃən] *n* (*US also* **accommodations**) (*lodgings*) alojamiento *m*

accompany [əˈkʌmpənɪ] *vt* acompañar

accomplice [əˈkʌmplɪs] *n* cómplice *mf*

accomplish [əˈkʌmplɪʃ] *vt* (*aim*) conseguir; (*task, mission*) llevar a cabo

accomplished [əˈkʌmplɪʃt] *adj* dotado(a), experto(a)

accomplishment [əˈkʌmplɪʃmənt] *n* (**a**) (*of task*) realización *f*; (*of duty*) cumplimiento *m* (**b**) **accomplishments** (*talents*) dotes *fpl*

accord [əˈkɔːd] **1** *n* (*agreement*) acuerdo *m*; **of her/his own a.** espontáneamente

2 *vt* (*honour etc*) conceder

accordance [əˈkɔːdəns] *n* **in a. with** de acuerdo con

according [əˈkɔːdɪŋ] *prep* **a. to** según; **everything went a. to plan** todo salió conforme a los planes

accordingly [əˈkɔːdɪŋlɪ] *adv* (**a**) **to act a.** (*appropriately*) obrar según y conforme (**b**) (*therefore*) así pues

accordion [əˈkɔːdɪən] *n* acordeón *m*

account [əˈkaʊnt] *n* (**a**) (*report*) informe *m*; **by all accounts** al decir de todos (**b**) **I was fearful on her a.** sufría por ella; **it's of no a.** no tiene importancia; **on a. of** a causa de; **on no a.** bajo ningún concepto; **to take a. of, to take into a.** tener en cuenta (**c**) *Com* cuenta *f*; **to keep the accounts** llevar las cuentas; **accounts department** servicio *m* de contabilidad; **to open/close an a.** abrir/cancelar una cuenta; **current a.** cuenta corriente; **a. number** número *m* de cuenta

► **account for** *vt insep* (*explain*) explicar

accountable [əˈkaʊntəbəl] *adj* **to be a. to sb for sth** ser responsable ante algn de algo

accountancy [əˈkaʊntənsɪ] *n* contabilidad *f*

accountant [əˈkaʊntənt] *n* *Esp* contable *mf*, *Am* contador(a) *m,f*

accounting [əˈkaʊntɪŋ] *n* contabilidad *f*

accredited [əˈkredɪtɪd] *adj* acreditado(a)

accrue [əˈkruː] *vi* (*interest*) acumularse

accumulate [əˈkjuːmjʊleɪt] **1** *vt* acumular

2 *vi* acumularse

accuracy ['ækjʊrəsɪ] n (of number etc) exactitud f; (of shot, criticism) certeza f

accurate ['ækjʊrət] adj (number) exacto(a); (shot, criticism) certero(a); (answer)· correcto(a); (observation) acertado(a); (instrument) de precisión; (translation) fiel

accusation [ækjʊ'zeɪʃən] n acusación f

accuse [ə'kju:z] vt acusar

accused [ə'kju:zd] n the a. el/la acusado(a)

accustom [ə'kʌstəm] vt acostumbrar; to be accustomed to doing sth estar acostumbrado(a) a hacer algo

ace [eɪs] n (a) Cards & Fig as m (b) (in tennis) ace m

acetate ['æsɪteɪt] n acetato m

acetone ['æsɪtəʊn] n acetona f

ache [eɪk] 1 n dolor m; aches and pains achaques mpl
2 vi doler; my back aches me duele la espalda

achieve [ə'tʃi:v] vt (attain) conseguir, alcanzar; (accomplish) llevar a cabo, realizar

achievement [ə'tʃi:vmənt] n (attainment) logro m; (completion) realización f; (feat) hazaña f

acid ['æsɪd] 1 adj (chemical, taste) ácido(a); (remark) sarcástico(a); a. rain lluvia ácida; Fig a. test prueba f de fuego
2 n ácido m

acknowledge [ək'nɒlɪdʒ] vt (a) (recognize) reconocer; (claim, defeat) admitir; (present) agradecer; (letter) acusar recibo de (b) (greet) saludar

acknowledgement [ək'nɒlɪdʒmənt] n (a) (recognition) reconocimiento m; (of letter) acuse m de recibo (b) acknowledgements (in preface) menciones fpl

acne ['æknɪ] n acné m

acorn ['eɪkɔːn] n bellota f

acoustic [ə'ku:stɪk] 1 adj acústico(a)
2 npl acoustics acústica f

acquaint [ə'kweɪnt] vt to a. sb with the facts informar a algn de los detalles; to be acquainted with the procedure estar al corriente de como se procede; to be acquainted with sb conocer a algn

acquaintance [ə'kweɪntəns] n (a) (familiarity) (with person) relación f; (with facts) conocimiento m; to make sb's a. conocer a algn (b) (person) conocido(a) m,f

acquiesce [ækwɪ'es] vi consentir (in en)

acquiescent [ækwɪ'esənt] adj conforme

acquire [ə'kwaɪə(r)] vt adquirir

acquisition [ækwɪ'zɪʃən] n adquisición f

acquisitive [ə'kwɪzɪtɪv] adj codicioso(a)

acquit [ə'kwɪt] vt (a) Jur to a. sb of sth absolver a algn de algo (b) to a. oneself well defenderse bien

acquittal [ə'kwɪtəl] n absolución f

acre ['eɪkə(r)] n acre m (= 4.047m²)

acrid ['ækrɪd] adj (smell, taste) acre

acrimonious [ækrɪ'məʊnɪəs] adj (remark) cáustico(a); (dispute) encona-do(a)

acrobat ['ækrəbæt] n acróbata mf

acrobatic [ækrə'bætɪk] adj acrobático(a)

acronym ['ækrənɪm] n siglas fpl, acrónimo m

across [ə'krɒs] 1 adv a través; the river is 30 m a. el río mide 30 m de ancho; to go a. atravesar; to run a. atravesar corriendo
2 prep (a) (from one side to the other of) a través de; to go a. the street cruzar la calle (b) (on the other side of) al otro lado de; they live a. the road viven enfrente

acrylic [ə'krɪlɪk] adj acrílico(a)

act [ækt] 1 n (a) (action) acto m, acción f; a. of God caso m de fuerza mayor (b) (law) a. (Br of parliament or US of Congress) ley f (c) Th acto m; (turn in show) número m
2 vt Th (part) interpretar; (character) representar; Fig to a. the fool hacer el tonto
3 vi (a) Th hacer teatro; Cin hacer cine; Fig (pretend) fingir (b) (behave) comportarse (c) (take action) actuar, obrar; to a. on sb's advice seguir el consejo de algn (d) (work) funcionar; (drug etc) actuar; to a. as a deterrent servir de disuasivo (e) to a. as director hacer de director

▸ **act out** vt sep exteriorizar

▸ **act up** vi Fam (machine) funcionar mal; (child) dar guerra

acting ['æktɪŋ] 1 adj interino(a)
2 n (profession) teatro m; he's done some a. ha hecho algo de teatro

action ['ækʃən] n (a) (deed) acción f; Mil acción de combate; to be out of a. (person) estar fuera de servicio; (machine) estar estropeado(a); to take a. tomar medidas (b) Jur demanda f (c) Br TV a. replay repetición f

activate ['æktɪveɪt] vt activar

active ['æktɪv] adj (person, imagination, life) activo(a); (interest, dislike) profundo(a); Gram a. voice voz activa; Comput a. window ventana activa

activist ['æktɪvɪst] n activista mf

activity [æk'tɪvɪtɪ] n (of person) actividad f; (on street etc) bullicio m

actor ['æktə(r)] *n* actor *m*

actress ['æktrɪs] *n* actriz *f*

actual ['æktʃʊəl] *adj* real, verdadero(a)

> *Note that the Spanish word **actual** is a false friend and is never a translation for the English word **actual**. In Spanish **actual** means "current, up-to-date, topical".*

actually ['æktʃʊəlɪ] *adv* (*really*) en efecto, realmente; (*even*) incluso, hasta; (*in fact*) de hecho

> *Note that the Spanish word **actualmente** is a false friend and is never a translation for the English word **actually**. In Spanish **actualmente** means "nowadays, at the moment".*

actuary ['æktʃʊərɪ] *n* actuario(a) *m,f* de seguros

acumen ['ækjʊmən] *n* perspicacia *f*

acupuncture ['ækjʊpʌŋktʃə(r)] *n* acupuntura *f*

acute [ə'kjuːt] *adj* (*pain, mind, eyesight*) agudo(a); (*hearing, sense of smell*) muy fino(a); (*problem, shortage*) aciciante; (*embarrassment*) intenso(a); (*person*) perspicaz

AD [eɪ'diː] (*abbr* **Anno Domini**) d.J.C., d.C.

ad [æd] *n Fam* anuncio *m*

adamant ['ædəmənt] *adj* firme, inflexible

adapt [ə'dæpt] **1** *vt* adaptar (**to** a); **to a. oneself to sth** adaptarse a algo
2 *vi* adaptarse

adaptable [ə'dæptəbəl] *adj* (*instrument*) ajustable; **he's very a.** se amolda fácilmente a las circunstancias

adaptation [ædəp'teɪʃən] *n* adaptación *f*

adapter, adaptor [ə'dæptə(r)] *n Elec* ladrón *m*

add [æd] **1** *vt* (*numbers*) sumar; (*one thing to another*) añadir
2 *vi* (*count*) sumar

▶ **add to** *vt insep* aumentar

▶ **add up 1** *vt sep* sumar
2 *vi* (*numbers*) sumar; *Fig* **it doesn't a. up** no tiene sentido; **it doesn't a. up to much** no es gran cosa

added ['ædɪd] *adj* adicional

adder ['ædə(r)] *n* víbora *f*

addict ['ædɪkt] *n* adicto(a) *m,f*; *Fam* **television a.** teleadicto(a) *m,f*

addicted [ə'dɪktɪd] *adj* adicto(a); **to become a. to sth** enviciarse con algo

addiction [ə'dɪkʃən] *n* (*to gambling etc*) vicio *m*; (*to drugs*) adicción *f*

addictive [ə'dɪktɪv] *adj* que crea adicción

addition [ə'dɪʃən] *n Math* adición *f*; (*increase*) aumento *m*; **an a. to the family** un nuevo miembro de la familia; **in a. to** además de

additional [ə'dɪʃənəl] *adj* adicional

additive ['ædɪtɪv] *n* aditivo *m*

address [ə'dres] **1** *n* (**a**) (*on letter*) dirección *f*, señas *fpl* (**b**) (*speech*) discurso *m*
2 *vt* (**a**) (*letter*) dirigir (**to** a) (**b**) (*speak to*) dirigirse a; **to a. the floor** tomar la palabra (**c**) (*use form of address to*) tratar (**as** de)

adenoids ['ædɪnɔɪdz] *npl* vegetaciones *fpl* (adenoideas)

adept 1 [ə'dept] *adj* experto(a) (**at** en)
2 ['ædept] *n* experto(a) *m,f*

> *Note that the Spanish word **adepto** is a false friend and is never a translation for the English word **adept**. In Spanish **adepto** means "follower, supporter".*

adequate ['ædɪkwɪt] *adj* (*enough*) suficiente; (*satisfactory*) adecuado(a)

adhere [əd'hɪə(r)] *vi* (*stick*) pegarse (**to** a)

▶ **adhere to** *vt insep* (*policy*) adherirse a; (*contract*) cumplir con

adherent [əd'hɪərənt] *n* partidario(a) *m,f*

adhesive [əd'hiːsɪv] **1** *adj* adhesivo(a), adherente; **a. tape** cinta adhesiva
2 *n* adhesivo *m*

ad hoc [æd'hɒk] *adj* (*remark*) improvisado(a); **an a. committee** un comité especial

ad infinitum [ædɪnfɪ'naɪtəm] *adv* hasta el infinito

adjacent [ə'dʒeɪsənt] *adj* (*building*) contiguo(a); (*land*) colindante; **a. to** contiguo(a) a

adjective ['ædʒɪktɪv] *n* adjetivo *m*

adjoining [ə'dʒɔɪnɪŋ] *adj* (*building, room*) contiguo(a)

adjourn [ə'dʒɜːn] **1** *vt* (*postpone*) aplazar; (*court*) levantar
2 *vi* **the meeting adjourned** se levantó la sesión

adjudicate [ə'dʒuːdɪkeɪt] *vt* juzgar

adjudicator [ə'dʒuːdɪkeɪtə(r)] *n* juez(a) *m,f*

adjust [ə'dʒʌst] **1** *vt* (*machine etc*) ajustar; *Fig* (*methods*) variar
2 *vi* (*person*) adaptarse (**to** a)

adjustable [ə'dʒʌstəbəl] *adj* ajustable; **a.** *Br* **spanner** *or US* **wrench** llave *f* inglesa

adjustment [ə'dʒʌstmənt] *n* (**a**) (*to machine etc*) ajuste *m*; (*by person*) adaptación *f* (**b**) (*change*) modificación *f*

ad lib [æd'lɪb] **1** *adv* (*speak*) sin preparación; (*continue*) a voluntad

2 *adj (speech)* improvisado(a)
3 ad-lib *vi* improvisar

administer [əd'mɪnɪstə(r)] *vt (country)* gobernar; *(justice)* administrar

administration [ədmɪnɪ'streɪʃən] *n (management) (of justice)* administración *f*; *(governing body)* dirección *f*; *US (government)* gobierno *m*, administración *f*

administrative [əd'mɪnɪstrətɪv] *adj* administrativo(a)

administrator [əd'mɪnɪstreɪtə(r)] *n* administrador(a) *m,f*

admirable ['ædmərəbəl] *adj* admirable

admiral ['ædmərəl] *n* almirante *m*

admiration [ædmə'reɪʃən] *n* admiración *f*

admire [əd'maɪə(r)] *vt* admirar

admirer [əd'maɪərə(r)] *n* admirador(a) *m,f*

admissible [əd'mɪsəbəl] *adj* admisible

admission [əd'mɪʃən] *n* (**a**) *(to school etc)* ingreso *m*; *(price)* entrada *f* (**b**) *(of fact)* reconocimiento *m*; *(confession)* confesión *f*

admit [əd'mɪt] *vt* (**a**) *(person)* dejar entrar; **to be admitted to hospital** ser ingresado(a) en el hospital (**b**) *(acknowledge)* reconocer; *(crime, guilt)* confesar

admittance [əd'mɪtəns] *n (entry)* entrada *f*

admittedly [əd'mɪtɪdlɪ] *adv* la verdad es que …

admonish [əd'mɒnɪʃ] *vt* amonestar

ad nauseam [æd'nɔːzɪæm] *adv* hasta la saciedad

ado [ə'duː] *n* without further a. sin más

adolescence [ædə'lesəns] *n* adolescencia *f*

adolescent [ædə'lesənt] *n* adolescente *mf*

adopt [ə'dɒpt] *vt (child, approach, measure)* adoptar; *(candidate)* nombrar

adopted [ə'dɒptɪd] *adj* **a. child** hijo(a) adoptivo(a)

adoption [ə'dɒpʃən] *n* adopción *f*; **country of a.** país adoptivo

adorable [ə'dɔːrəbəl] *adj* encantador(a)

adore [ə'dɔː(r)] *vt* adorar

adorn [ə'dɔːn] *vt* adornar

adornment [ə'dɔːnmənt] *n* adorno *m*

adrenalin [ə'drenəlɪn] *n* adrenalina *f*

Adriatic [eɪdrɪ'ætɪk] *adj* **the A. (Sea)** el (mar) Adriático

adrift [ə'drɪft] *adv* **to come a.** *(boat)* irse a la deriva; *(rope)* soltarse; *Fig* **to go a.** *(plans)* ir a la deriva

ADSL [eɪdiːes'el] *n Comput (abbr* **asymmetrical digital subscriber line)** ADSL *m*

adult ['ædʌlt] **1** *adj (person)* adulto(a), mayor; *(film)* para adultos; *(education)* de adultos
2 *n* adulto(a) *m,f*

adulterate [ə'dʌltəreɪt] *vt* adulterar

adulterer [ə'dʌltərə(r)] *n* adúltero *m*

adulteress [ə'dʌltrɪs] *n* adúltera *f*

adultery [ə'dʌltərɪ] *n* adulterio *m*

advance [əd'vɑːns] **1** *n* (**a**) *(movement)* avance *m*; *Fig (progress)* progreso *m*; **to have sth ready in a.** tener algo preparado de antemano; **to make advances (to)** *(person)* insinuarse (a) (**b**) *(loan)* anticipo *m*
2 *adj (before time)* adelantado(a); *Cin & Th* **a. bookings** reservas *fpl* por adelantado
3 *vt* (**a**) *(troops)* avanzar; *(time, date)* adelantar (**b**) *(idea)* proponer; *(opinion)* dar
4 *vi (move forward)* avanzar, adelantarse; *(make progress)* hacer progresos; *(gain promotion)* ascender

advanced [əd'vɑːnst] *adj (developed)* avanzado(a); *(student)* adelantado(a); *(course)* superior; *Br* **A. level** = examen final o diploma en una asignatura de los estudios preuniversitarios

advancement [əd'vɑːnsmənt] *n (progress)* adelanto *m*; *(promotion)* ascenso *m*

advantage [əd'vɑːntɪdʒ] *n* ventaja *f*; *(in tennis)* **a.** Velasco ventaja para Velasco; **to take a. of** *(person)* aprovecharse de; *(opportunity)* aprovechar

advantageous [ædvən'teɪdʒəs] *adj* ventajoso(a)

advent ['ædvent] *n (arrival)* llegada *f*; *(of Christ)* advenimiento *m*; **A.** Adviento *m*

adventure [əd'ventʃə(r)] *n* aventura *f*; **a. sport** deporte *m* de aventura

adventurous [əd'ventʃərəs] *adj* aventurero(a)

adverb ['ædvɜːb] *n* adverbio *m*

adversary ['ædvəsərɪ] *n* adversario(a) *m,f*

adverse ['ædvɜːs] *adj (effect)* desfavorable; *(conditions)* adverso(a); *(winds)* contrario(a)

adversity [əd'vɜːsɪtɪ] *n* adversidad *f*

advert ['ædvɜːt] *n Br Fam* anuncio *m*

advertise ['ædvətaɪz] **1** *vt* anunciar
2 *vi* poner un anuncio (**for sth/sb** pidiendo algo/a alguien)

advertisement [əd'vɜːtɪsmənt] *n* anuncio *m*; **advertisements** publicidad *f*

advertiser ['ædvətaɪzə(r)] *n* anunciante *mf*

advertising ['ædvətaızıŋ] **1** n publicidad f, propaganda f; (in newspaper) anuncios mpl
  2 adj publicitario(a); **a. agency** agencia f de publicidad

advice [əd'vaıs] n consejos mpl; **a piece of a.** un consejo; **to take legal a.** on a matter consultar un caso con un abogado; **to take sb's a.** seguir los consejos de algn

advisable [əd'vaızəbəl] adj aconsejable

advise [əd'vaız] vt (give advice to) aconsejar; (give professional guidance) asesorar (**on** sobre); **I a. you to do it** te aconsejo que lo hagas

adviser [əd'vaızə(r)] n consejero(a) m,f; (professional) asesor(a) m,f

advisory [əd'vaızərı] adj asesor(a)

advocate 1 n ['ædvəkıt] Scot Jur abogado(a) m,f; (supporter) defensor(a) m,f
  2 vt ['ædvəkeıt] (reform) abogar por; (plan) apoyar

aerial ['eərıəl] **1** adj aéreo(a)
  2 n antena f

aerobics [eə'rəʊbıks] n sing aerobic m

aerodrome ['eərədrəʊm] n Br aeródromo m

aerodynamics [eərəʊdaı'næmıks] n sing aerodinámica f

aeroplane ['eərəpleın] n Br avión m

aerosol ['eərəsɒl] n aerosol m

aerospace ['eərəʊspeıs] adj aeroespacial

aesthetic [iːs'θetık] adj estético(a)

afar [ə'fɑː(r)] adv lejos; **from a.** desde lejos

affair [ə'feə(r)] n (matter) asunto m; (event) acontecimiento m; **that's my a.** eso es asunto mío; **business affairs** negocios mpl; **foreign affairs** asuntos exteriores; **love a.** aventura amorosa

affect [ə'fekt] vt (person, health) afectar; (prices, future) influir en; (touch emotionally) conmover

affected [ə'fektıd] adj (**a**) (unnatural) afectado(a) (**b**) (influenced) influido(a) (**c**) (touched emotionally) conmovido(a) (**d**) (pretended) fingido(a)

affection [ə'fekʃən] n afecto m, cariño m

affectionate [ə'fekʃənıt] adj cariñoso(a)

affidavit [æfı'deıvıt] n declaración escrita y jurada

affiliated [ə'fılıeıtıd] adj afiliado(a); **to be/become a.** (**to** or **with**) afiliarse (a)

affinity [ə'fınıtı] n afinidad f; (liking) simpatía f

affirm [ə'fɜːm] vt afirmar, sostener

affirmation [æfə'meıʃən] n afirmación f

affirmative [ə'fɜːmətıv] **1** adj (answer) afirmativo(a); US **a. action** discriminación positiva
  2 n **he answered in the a.** contestó que sí

affix [ə'fıks] vt (stamp) pegar

afflict [ə'flıkt] vt afligir

affluence ['æfluəns] n opulencia f

affluent ['æfluənt] adj (society) opulento(a); (person) rico(a)

afford [ə'fɔːd] vt (**a**) (be able to buy) permitirse el lujo de; **I can't a. a new car** no puedo pagar un coche nuevo (**b**) (be able to do) permitirse; **you can't a. to miss the opportunity** no puedes perderte la ocasión

affordable [ə'fɔːdəbəl] adj (price, purchase) asequible

affront [ə'frʌnt] **1** n afrenta f
  2 vt afrentar

Afghanistan [æf'gænıstɑːn] n Afganistán

afield [ə'fiːld] adv far **a.** muy lejos

afloat [ə'fləʊt] adv **to keep a.** mantenerse a flote

afoot [ə'fʊt] adv **there's a plan a.** hay un proyecto en marcha; **there's something strange a.** se está tramando algo

aforementioned [ə'fɔːmenʃənd], **aforesaid** [ə'fɔːsed] adj susodicho(a)

afraid [ə'freıd] adj (**a**) **to be a.** tener miedo (**of sb/sth** a algn/de algo); **I'm a. of it** me da miedo (**b**) **I'm a.** not temo que no; **I'm a. so** me temo que sí; **I'm a. you're wrong** me temo que estás equivocado(a)

afresh [ə'freʃ] adv de nuevo

Africa ['æfrıkə] n Africa

African ['æfrıkən] adj & n africano(a) (m,f)

Afro ['æfrəʊ] adj & n Fam (hairstyle) afro (m)

aft [ɑːft] adv en popa; **to go a.** ir en popa

after ['ɑːftə(r)] **1** adv después; **soon a.** poco después; **the day a.** el día siguiente
  2 prep (**a**) (later) después de; US **it's ten a. five** son las cinco y diez; **soon a. arriving** al poco rato de llegar; **the day a. tomorrow** pasado mañana (**b**) (behind) detrás de, tras; **a. you!** ¡pase usted!; **they went in one a. the other** entraron uno tras otro; **the police are a. them** la policía anda tras ellos (**c**) (about) por; **they asked a. you** preguntaron por ti; **what's he a.?** ¿qué pretende?
  3 conj después (de) que; **a. it happened** después de que ocurriera

after-effect ['ɑːftərıfekt] n efecto secundario

afterlife ['ɑːftəlaɪf] *n* vida *f* después de la muerte

aftermath ['ɑːftəmæθ] *n* secuelas *fpl*

afternoon [ɑːftə'nuːn] *n* tarde *f*; **good a.!** ¡buenas tardes!; **in the a.** por la tarde

afternoons [ɑːftə'nuːnz] *adv US* por las tardes

afters ['ɑːftəz] *npl Fam* postre *m*

after-sales service [ɑːftəseɪlz'sɜːvɪs] *n Com* servicio *m* posventa

aftershave ['ɑːftəʃeɪv] *n* (*as perfume*) colonia f; **a. (balm** *or* **lotion)** loción *f* para después del afeitado *or Méx* rasurado

afterthought ['ɑːftəθɔːt] *n* ocurrencia *f* tardía

afterward(s) ['ɑːftəwəd(z)] *adv* después, más tarde

again [ə'gen] *adv* (**a**) (*in general*) de nuevo, otra vez; **I tried a. and a.** lo intenté una y otra vez; **to do sth a.** volver a hacer algo; **never a.!** ¡nunca más!; **now and a.** de vez en cuando; **once a.** otra vez (**b**) (*besides*) además; **then a.** por otra parte

against [ə'genst] *prep* (**a**) (*touching*) contra (**b**) (*opposing*) contra, en contra (de); **a. the grain** a contrapelo; **it's a. the law** es ilegal (**c**) **as a.** en contraste con, comparado con

age [eɪdʒ] **1** *n* (**a**) (*of person, object*) edad *f*; **she's eighteen years of a.** tiene dieciocho años; **to be under a.** ser menor de edad; **to come of a.** llegar a la mayoría de edad; **a. limit** límite *m* de edad; **old a.** vejez *f* (**b**) (*period*) época *f*; **the Iron A.** la Edad de Hierro (**c**) *Fam* (*long time*) eternidad *f*; **it's ages since I last saw her** hace siglos que.no la veo
2 *vt & vi* envejecer

aged¹ [eɪdʒd] *adj* de *or* a la edad de

aged² ['eɪdʒɪd] *npl* **the a.** los ancianos

agency ['eɪdʒənsɪ] *n* (**a**) *Com* agencia *f* (**b**) **by the a. of** por medio de

agenda [ə'dʒendə] *n* orden *m* del día

agent ['eɪdʒənt] *n* agente *mf*; (*representative*) representante *mf*

aggravate ['ægrəveɪt] *vt* (*worsen*) agravar; (*annoy*) fastidiar, molestar, *RP* hinchar

aggregate ['ægrɪgɪt] *n* conjunto *m*; **on a.** en conjunto

aggression [ə'greʃən] *n* agresión *f*

aggressive [ə'gresɪv] *adj* (*violent*) agresivo(a), violento(a); (*dynamic*) dinámico(a)

aggrieved [ə'griːvd] *adj* apenado(a)

aghast [ə'gɑːst] *adj* espantado(a)

agile [*Br* 'ædʒaɪl, *US* 'ædʒəl] *adj* ágil

agitate ['ædʒɪteɪt] **1** *vt* (*shake*) agitar; *Fig* (*worry*) perturbar
2 *vi Pol* **to a. against sth** hacer campaña en contra de algo

agitated [ædʒɪteɪtɪd] *adj* ·inquieto(a), agitado(a); **to be a.** estar inquieto(a) *or* agitado(a)

agitator ['ædʒɪteɪtə(r)] *n Pol* agitador(a) *m,f*

AGM [eɪdʒiː'em] *n Br* (*abbr* **annual general meeting**) junta *f* general anual

agnostic [æg'nɒstɪk] *n* agnóstico(a) *m,f*

ago [ə'gəʊ] *adv* **a long time a.** hace mucho tiempo; **as long a. as 1910** ya en 1910; **a week a.** hace una semana; **how long a.?** ¿hace cuánto tiempo?

agog [ə'gɒg] *adj* ansioso(a)

agonizing ['ægənaɪzɪŋ] *adj* (*pain*) atroz; (*decision*) desesperante

agony ['ægənɪ] *n* dolor *m* muy fuerte; (*anguish*) angustia *f*; **he was in a. with his back** tenía un dolor insoportable de espalda

agree [ə'griː] **1** *vi* (**a**) (*be in agreement*) estar de acuerdo; (*reach agreement*) ponerse de acuerdo; (*consent*) consentir; **to a. to do sth** consentir en hacer algo; **to a. with sb** estar de acuerdo con algn (**b**) (*harmonize*) (*things*) concordar; (*people*) congeniar; **onions don't a. with me** la cebolla no me sienta bien
2 *vt* acordar

agreeable [ə'griːəbəl] *adj* (*pleasant*) agradable; (*person*) simpático(a); (*in agreement*) de acuerdo

agreement [ə'griːmənt] *n* (*arrangement*) acuerdo *m*; *Com* contrato *m*; **to reach an a.** llegar a un acuerdo

agricultural [ægrɪ'kʌltʃərəl] *adj* agrícola; **a. college** escuela *f* de agricultura

agriculture ['ægrɪkʌltʃə(r)] *n* agricultura *f*

aground [ə'graʊnd] *adv* **to run a.** encallar, varar

ahead [ə'hed] *adv* (*forwards*) adelante; (*in front*) delante, *Am* adelante; (*early*) antes; **go a.!** ¡adelante!; **to be a.** llevar la ventaja; **to go a.** ir adelante; *Fig* **to go a. with sth** llevar algo adelante; (*start*) comenzar algo; **to get a.** triunfar; **to look a.** pensar en el futuro

aid [eɪd] **1** *n* ayuda *f*; (*rescue*) auxilio *m*; **in a. of** a beneficio de; **to come to the a. of sb** acudir en ayuda de algn; **a. worker** cooperante *mf*
2 *vt* ayudar; **to a. and abet sb** ser cómplice de algn

aide [eɪd] *n* ayudante *mf*

AIDS [eɪdz] *n* (*abbr* **Acquired Immune Deficiency Syndrome**) sida *m*

ailing ['eɪlɪŋ] *adj* achacoso(a)

ailment ['eɪlmənt] *n* enfermedad *f* (leve), achaque *m*

aim [eɪm] **1** *n* (*with weapon*) puntería *f*; (*target*) propósito *m*
2 *vt* (*gun*) apuntar (**at** a *or* hacia); (*attack, action*) dirigir (**at** a *or* hacia)
▸ **aim at** *vt insep* (*target*) tirar para; **to a. at doing sth** tener pensado hacer algo
▸ **aim to** *vt insep* **to a. to do sth** tener la intención de hacer algo

aimless ['eɪmlɪs] *adj* sin objeto, sin propósito

aimlessly ['eɪmlɪslɪ] *adv* (*wander*) sin rumbo fijo

air [eə(r)] **1** *n* (**a**) (*atmosphere, sky*) aire *m*; **to throw sth up in the a.** lanzar algo al aire; *Fig* **it's still in the a.** todavía queda por resolver; *Aut* **a. bag** airbag *m*; **a. bed** colchón *m* hinchable; **a. conditioning** aire acondicionado; **a. freshener** ambientador *m*; **a. gun** pistola *f* de aire comprimido; **a. pocket** bache *m*; **a. pressure** presión atmosférica (**b**) (*relating to air travel*) **to travel by a.** viajar en avión; **a. base** base aérea; **a. fare** (precio *m* del) *Esp* billete *m or Am* boleto *m or Am* pasaje *m*; **A. Force** Fuerzas Aéreas; **a. hostess** azafata *f* de vuelo, *Am* aeromoza *f*; **a. raid** ataque aéreo; **a. terminal** terminal aérea; **a. traffic control** control *m* de tráfico aéreo; **a. traffic controller** controlador(a) aéreo(a) (**c**) *Rad & TV* **to be on the a.** (*programme*) estar emitiendo; (*person*) estar transmitiendo (**d**) (*melody*) melodía *f*, aire *m* (**e**) (*look, manner*) aire *m*
2 *vt* (*bed, clothes*) airear; (*room*) ventilar; *Fig* (*grievance*) airear; (*knowledge*) hacer alarde de

airborne ['eəbɔːn] *adj* (*aircraft*) en vuelo; (*troops*) aerotransportado(a)

air-conditioned ['eəkɒndɪʃənd] *adj* climatizado(a)

aircraft ['eəkrɑːft] *n* (*pl* **aircraft**) avión *m*; **a. carrier** portaviones *m inv*

airfield ['eəfiːld] *n* campo *m* de aviación

airlift ['eəlɪft] *n* puente aéreo

airline ['eəlaɪn] *n* línea aérea

airlock ['eəlɒk] *n* (*in pipe*) bolsa *f* de aire; (*in spacecraft*) esclusa *f* de aire

airmail ['eəmeɪl] *n* correo aéreo; **by a.** por avión

airplane ['eəpleɪn] *n US* avión *m*

airport ['eəpɔːt] *n* aeropuerto *m*; **a. tax** tasas *fpl* de aeropuerto

airsick ['eəsɪk] *adj* **to be a.** marearse en avión

airstrip ['eəstrɪp] *n* pista *f* de aterrizaje

airtight ['eətaɪt] *adj* hermético(a)

airy ['eərɪ] *adj* (**airier, airiest**) (*well-ventilated*) bien ventilado(a); (*vague, carefree*) ligero(a)

aisle [aɪl] *n* (*in church*) nave *f*; (*in theatre*) pasillo *m*

ajar [ə'dʒɑː(r)] *adj & adv* entreabierto(a)

akin [ə'kɪn] *adj* semejante

alacrity [ə'lækrɪtɪ] *n Fml* **with a.** con presteza

à la mode [ælə'məʊd] *adj US* (*dessert*) con helado

alarm [ə'lɑːm] **1** *n* (**a**) (*warning, alert*) alarma *f*; **a. clock** despertador *m* (**b**) (*anxiety*) inquietud *f*; **to cause a.** provocar temor
2 *vt* alarmar

alas [ə'læs] *interj* ¡ay!, ¡ay de mí!

Albania [æl'beɪnɪə] *n* Albania

Albanian [æl'beɪnɪən] **1** *n* (**a**) (*person*) albanés(esa) *m,f* (**b**) (*language*) albanés *m*
2 *adj* albanés(esa)

albatross ['ælbətrɒs] *n* albatros *m*

albeit [ɔːl'biːɪt] *conj* aunque, no obstante

album ['ælbəm] *n* álbum *m*

alcohol ['ælkəhɒl] *n* alcohol *m*

alcoholic [ælkə'hɒlɪk] *adj & n* alcohólico(a) *(m,f)*

alcopop ['ælkəʊpɒp] *n Br* = combinado alcohólico con aspecto de refresco que se comercializa envasado

alcove ['ælkəʊv] *n* hueco *m*

> 🔔 Note that the Spanish word **alcoba** is a false friend and is never a translation for the English word **alcove**. In Spanish **alcoba** means "bedroom".

---

ale [eɪl] *n* cerveza *f*; **brown/pale a.** cerveza negra/rubia

alert [ə'lɜːt] **1** *adj* (*watchful*) alerta; (*lively*) despabilado(a)
2 *n* alerta *m*; **to be on the a.** estar alerta
3 *vt* **to a. sb to sth** avisar a algn de algo

A-level ['eɪlevəl] *n Br Educ* (*abbr* **Advanced level**) = examen final o diploma en una asignatura de los estudios preuniversitarios

algae ['ældʒiː] *npl* algas *fpl*

algebra ['ældʒɪbrə] *n* álgebra *f*

Algeria [æl'dʒɪərɪə] *n* Argelia

Algerian [æl'dʒɪərɪən] *adj & n* argelino(a) *(m,f)*

Algiers [æl'dʒɪəz] *n* Argel

alias ['eɪlɪəs] **1** n alias m
2 adv alias

alibi ['ælɪbaɪ] n coartada f

alien ['eɪlɪən] **1** adj (foreign) extranjero(a); (from space) extraterrestre; **a. to** ajeno(a) a
2 n (foreigner) extranjero(a) m,f; (from space) extraterrestre mf

alienate ['eɪlɪəneɪt] vt (**a**) **to a. sb** ofender a algn; **to a. oneself from sb** alejarse de algn (**b**) Jur enajenar

alight¹ [ə'laɪt] adj (burning) **to be a.** estar ardiendo or en llamas

alight² [ə'laɪt] vi (get off) apearse (**from** de)

align [ə'laɪn] vt alinear

alike [ə'laɪk] **1** adj (similar) parecidos(as); (the same) iguales
2 adv (in the same way) de la misma manera, igualmente; **dressed a.** vestidos(as) iguales

alimony ['ælɪmənɪ] n Jur pensión alimenticia

alive [ə'laɪv] adj vivo(a); **to be a.** estar vivo(a); Fig **to be a. with** (teeming) ser un hervidero de

alkaline ['ælkəlaɪn] adj alcalino(a)

all [ɔːl] **1** adj todo(a), todos(as); **a. year** (durante) todo el año; **a. kinds of things** todo tipo de cosas; **at a. hours** a todas horas; **at a. times** siempre; **she works a. the time** siempre está trabajando; **a. six of us were there** los seis estábamos allí
2 pron todo(a), todos(as); **after a.** al fin y al cabo; **a. of his work** toda su obra; **a. of us** todos(as) nosotros(as); **a. who saw it** todos los que lo vieron; **a. you can do is wait** lo único que puedes hacer es esperar; **I don't like it at a.** no me gusta en absoluto; **is that a.?** ¿eso es todo?; **most of** or **above a.** sobre todo; **once and for a.** de una vez por todas; **thanks − not at a.** gracias − de nada; **a. in a.** en conjunto; **that's a.** ya está; **the score was one a.** empataron a uno
3 adv **a. by myself** completamente solo(a); **a. at once** (suddenly) de repente; (altogether) de una vez; **a. the better** tanto mejor; **he knew a. along** no lo sabía desde el principio; **it's a. but impossible** es casi imposible; **I'm not a. that tired** no estoy tan cansado(a) como eso

Allah ['ælə] n Alá m

all-around ['ɔːləraʊnd] adj US = **all-round**

allay [ə'leɪ] vt (fears, doubts) apaciguar

allegation [ælɪ'geɪʃən] n alegato m

allege [ə'ledʒ] vt sostener, pretender (**that** que); **it is alleged that she ac-** cepted a bribe supuestamente aceptó un soborno

allegedly [ə'ledʒɪdlɪ] adv supuestamente

allegiance [ə'liːdʒəns] n lealtad f

allergic [ə'lɜːdʒɪk] adj alérgico(a) (**to** a)

allergy ['ælədʒɪ] n alergia f

alleviate [ə'liːvɪeɪt] vt (pain) aliviar

alley ['ælɪ] n callejón m

alliance [ə'laɪəns] n alianza f

allied ['ælaɪd] adj aliado(a)

alligator ['ælɪgeɪtə(r)] n caimán m

all-in ['ɔːlɪn] adj (price) todo incluido; Sport **a. wrestling** lucha f libre

alliteration [əlɪtə'reɪʃən] n aliteración f

all-night ['ɔːlnaɪt] adj (café etc) abierto(a) toda la noche; (vigil) que dura toda la noche

allocate ['æləkeɪt] vt destinar (**to** para)

allocation [ælə'keɪʃən] n (**a**) (distribution) asignación f (**b**) (amount allocated) cuota f

allot [ə'lɒt] vt asignar

allotment [ə'lɒtmənt] n (**a**) (of time, money) asignación f (**b**) Br (plot of land) huerto m de ocio, parcela f (arrendada por el ayuntamiento para cultivo)

all-out ['ɔːlaʊt] **1** adj (effort) supremo(a); (attack) concentrado(a)
2 all out adv **to go all out to do sth** emplearse a fondo para hacer algo

allow [ə'laʊ] vt (**a**) (permit) permitir; (a request) acceder a; **to a. sb to do sth** permitir que algn haga algo (**b**) (allot) (time) dejar; (money) destinar

▸ **allow for** vt insep tener en cuenta

allowance [ə'laʊəns] n (money given) asignación f; US (pocket money) paga f; **to make allowances for sb/sth** disculpar a algn/tener algo en cuenta; **tax a.** desgravación f fiscal; **travel a.** dietas fpl de viaje

alloy ['ælɔɪ] n aleación f

all-purpose ['ɔːl'pɜːpəs] adj (cleaner, adhesive) multiuso

all right [ɔːl'raɪt] **1** adj (okay) bien; **thank you very much − that's a.** muchas gracias − de nada
2 adv (**a**) (well) bien (**b**) (definitely) sin duda (**c**) (okay) de acuerdo, vale

all-round ['ɔːlraʊnd] adj (athlete) completo(a)

all-terrain [ɔːltə'reɪn] adj **a. vehicle** todoterreno m

all-time ['ɔːltaɪm] adj **an a. low** una baja sin antecedente; **the a. greats** los grandes de siempre

allude [ə'luːd] vi **to a. to** aludir a

alluring [ə'ljʊərɪŋ] *adj* atractivo(a)

allusion [ə'luːʒən] *n* alusión *f*

ally ['ælaɪ] **1** *n* aliado(a) *m,f*
　2 *vt* **to a. oneself to/with sb** aliarse a/ con algn

almighty [ɔːl'maɪtɪ] **1** *adj (all-powerful)* todopoderoso(a)
　2 *n* **the A.** El Todopoderoso

almond ['ɑːmənd] *n* almendra *f*

almost ['ɔːlməʊst] *adv* casi

alms [ɑːmz] *npl* limosna *f*

aloft [ə'lɒft] *adv* arriba

alone [ə'ləʊn] **1** *adj* solo(a); **can I speak to you a.?** ¿puedo hablar contigo a solas?; **let a.** ni mucho menos; **leave it a.!** ¡no lo toques!; **leave me a.** déjame en paz; **to be a.** estar solo(a)
　2 *adv* solamente, sólo

along [ə'lɒŋ] **1** *adv* **come a.!** ¡anda, ven!; **he'll be a. in ten minutes** llegará dentro de diez minutos; **a. with** junto con
　2 *prep (the length of)* a lo largo de; **to walk a. the street** andar por la calle; **it's just a. the street** está un poco más abajo

alongside [ə'lɒŋsaɪd] **1** *adv Naut* de costado
　2 *prep* al lado de

aloof [ə'luːf] **1** *adj (person)* distante
　2 *adv* **to keep oneself a. (from)** mantenerse a distancia (de)

aloud [ə'laʊd] *adv* en voz alta

alphabet ['ælfəbet] *n* alfabeto *m*

alphabetical [ælfə'betɪkəl] *adj* alfabético(a)

alphabetically [ælfə'betɪkəlɪ] *adv* por orden alfabético

alpine ['ælpaɪn] *adj* alpino(a)

Alps [ælps] *npl* **the A.** los Alpes

already [ɔːl'redɪ] *adv* ya

alright [ɔːl'raɪt] *adj & adv* = **all right**

Alsatian [æl'seɪʃən] *n* pastor *m* alemán

also ['ɔːlsəʊ] *adv* también, además

also-ran ['ɔːlsəʊræn] *n Fam (person)* segundo(ona) *m,f*

altar ['ɔːltə(r)] *n* altar *m*

alter ['ɔːltə(r)] **1** *vt (plan)* cambiar, retocar; *(project)* modificar; *(clothing)* arreglar; *(timetable)* revisar
　2 *vi* cambiar, cambiarse

alteration [ɔːltə'reɪʃən] *n (to plan)* cambio *m*; *(to project)* modificación *f*; *(to clothing)* arreglo *m*; *(to timetable)* revisión *f*; **alterations** *(to building)* reformas *fpl*

alternate 1 *adj* [ɔːl'tɜːnɪt] alterno(a); **on a. days** cada dos días
　2 *vt* ['ɔːltəneɪt] alternar

alternately [ɔːl'tɜːnɪtlɪ] *adv* **a. hot and cold** ahora caliente, ahora frío

alternative [ɔːl'tɜːnətɪv] **1** *adj* alternativo(a)
　2 *n* alternativa *f*; **I have no a. but to accept** no tengo más remedio que aceptar

alternatively [ɔːl'tɜːnətɪvlɪ] *adv* o bien; **a., you could walk** o bien podrías ir andando

alternator ['ɔːltəneɪtə(r)] *n Aut* alternador *m*

although [ɔːl'ðəʊ] *conj* aunque

altitude ['æltɪtjuːd] *n* altitud *f*

alto ['æltəʊ] *adj & n (male singer, instrument)* alto *(m)*; *(female singer)* contralto *(f)*

altogether [ɔːltə'geðə(r)] *adv (in total)* en conjunto, en total; *(completely)* completamente, del todo

altruism ['æltruːɪzəm] *n* altruismo *m*

aluminium [æljʊ'mɪnɪəm], *US* **aluminum** [ə'luːmɪnəm] *n* aluminio *m*

alumnus [ə'lʌmnəs] *n (pl* **alumni** [ə'lʌmnaɪ]) *US* antiguo alumno

always ['ɔːlweɪz] *adv* siempre

AM [eɪ'em] *Rad (abbr* **amplitude modulation)** AM

am [æm] *1st person sing pres of* **be**

a.m. [eɪ'em] *(abbr* **ante meridiem)** a.m., de la mañana

amalgamate [ə'mælgəmeɪt] **1** *vt (metals)* amalgamar
　2 *vi (metals)* amalgamarse; *(companies)* fusionarse

amalgamation [əmælgə'meɪʃən] *n* fusión *f*

amass [ə'mæs] *vt (money)* amontonar; *(information)* acumular

amateur ['æmətə(r)] **1** *n* amateur *mf*, aficionado(a) *m,f*
　2 *adj (painter, musician)* aficionado(a); *Pej (work etc)* chapucero(a), de aficionado

amateurish ['æmətərɪʃ] *adj* chapucero(a)

amaze [ə'meɪz] *vt* asombrar, pasmar; **to be amazed at sth** quedarse pasmado(a) de algo

amazement [ə'meɪzmənt] *n* asombro *m*, sorpresa *f*

amazing [ə'meɪzɪŋ] *adj* asombroso(a), increíble

ambassador [æm'bæsədə(r)] *n* embajador(a) *m,f*

amber ['æmbə(r)] **1** *n* ámbar *m*
　2 *adj* ambarino(a); *Br* **a. light** semáforo *m* en ámbar

ambiguity [æmbɪ'gjuːɪtɪ] *n* ambigüedad *f*

ambiguous [æm'bɪgjʊəs] *adj* ambiguo(a)

ambition [æm'bɪʃən] n ambición f
ambitious [æm'bɪʃəs] adj ambicioso(a)
ambivalent [æm'bɪvələnt] adj ambivalente
amble ['æmbəl] vi deambular
ambulance ['æmbjʊləns] n ambulancia f; **a. man** ambulanciero m
ambush ['æmbʊʃ] **1** n also Fig emboscada f
2 vt also Fig tender una emboscada a
amen [ɑː'men] interj amén
amenable [ə'miːnəbəl] adj **I'd be quite a. to doing** that no me importaría nada hacer eso; **a. to reason** razonable
amend [ə'mend] vt (law) enmendar; (error) subsanar
amendment [ə'mendmənt] n enmienda f
amends [ə'mendz] npl **to make a. to sb for sth** compensar a algn por algo
amenities [ə'miːnɪtɪz] npl comodidades fpl
America [ə'merɪkə] n (continent) América f; (USA) (los) Estados Unidos; **South A.** América del Sur, Sudamérica f
American [ə'merɪkən] adj & n americano(a) (m,f); (of USA) norteamericano(a) (m,f), estadounidense (mf)
amiable ['eɪmɪəbəl] adj amable, afable
amicable ['æmɪkəbəl] adj amistoso(a)
amid(st) [ə'mɪd(st)] prep entre, en medio de
amiss [ə'mɪs] adj & adv mal; **there's sth a.** algo anda mal; **to take sth a.** tomar algo a mal
ammonia [ə'məʊnɪə] n amoníaco m
ammunition [æmjʊ'nɪʃən] n municiones fpl
amnesia [æm'niːʒə] n amnesia f
amnesty ['æmnɪstɪ] n amnistía f
amok [ə'mɒk] adv Fig **to run a.** (child) desmadrarse; (inflation etc) dispararse
among(st) [ə'mʌŋ(st)] prep entre
amoral [eɪ'mɒrəl] adj amoral
amorous ['æmərəs] adj cariñoso(a)
amorphous [ə'mɔːfəs] adj amorfo(a)
amount [ə'maʊnt] n cantidad f; (of money) suma f; (of bill) importe m
▸ **amount to** vt insep (add up to) ascender a; Fig (mean) equivaler a
amp [æmp], **ampère** ['æmpeə(r)] n amperio m
amphetamine [æm'fetəmiːn] n anfetamina f
amphibian [æm'fɪbɪən] adj & n anfibio(a) (m)
amphibious [æm'fɪbɪəs] adj anfibio(a)

amphitheatre, US **amphitheater** ['æmfɪθɪətə(r)] n anfiteatro m
ample ['æmpəl] adj (enough) bastante; (more than enough) abundante; (large) amplio(a)
amplifier ['æmplɪfaɪə(r)] n amplificador m
amplify ['æmplɪfaɪ] vt (essay, remarks) ampliar; (current, volume) amplificar
amputate ['æmpjʊteɪt] vt amputar
Amtrak ['æmtræk] n = compañía ferroviaria estadounidense
amuck [ə'mʌk] adv = amok
amuse [ə'mjuːz] vt divertir, entretener
amusement [ə'mjuːzmənt] n (enjoyment) diversión f; (laughter) risa f; (pastime) pasatiempo m; **a. arcade** salón m de juegos; **a. park** parque m de atracciones
amusing [ə'mjuːzɪŋ] adj divertido(a)
an [æn, unstressed ən] see a
anabolic steroid [ænəbɒlɪk'stɪərɔɪd] n esteroide m anabolizante
anaemia [ə'niːmɪə] n anemia f
anaemic [ə'niːmɪk] adj Med anémico(a); Fig (weak) pobre
anaesthetic [ænɪs'θetɪk] n anestesia f
anaesthetist [ə'niːsθətɪst] n anestesista mf
analog(ue) ['ænəlɒg] n análogo m; **a. computer** ordenador analógico, Am computadora analógica; **a. watch** reloj m de agujas
analogy [ə'nælədʒɪ] n analogía f
analyse ['ænəlaɪz] vt analizar
analysis [ə'nælɪsɪs] n (pl **analyses** [ə'nælɪsiːz]) análisis m inv
analyst ['ænəlɪst] n analista mf; (psychoanalyst) psicoanalista mf
analytic(al) [ænə'lɪtɪk(əl)] adj analítico(a)
analyze ['ænəlaɪz] vt US = analyse
anarchist ['ænəkɪst] n anarquista mf
anarchy ['ænəkɪ] n anarquía f
anathema [ə'næθəmə] n **the very idea was a. to him** le repugnaba sólo de pensarlo
anatomy [ə'nætəmɪ] n anatomía f
ancestor ['ænsestə(r)] n antepasado m
anchor ['æŋkə(r)] **1** n Naut ancla f; Fig áncora f
2 vt Naut anclar; Fig (fix securely) sujetar
3 vi anclar
anchovy [Br 'æntʃəvɪ, Am æn'tʃəʊvɪ] n anchoa f
ancient ['eɪnʃənt] adj antiguo(a)
ancillary [æn'sɪlərɪ] adj & n auxiliar (mf)

and [ænd, *unstressed* ənd, ən] *conj* y; *(before* **i, hi)** e; **a hundred a. one** ciento uno; **a. so on** etcétera; **Bill a. Pat** Bill y Pat; **Chinese a. Indian** chino e indio; **come a. see us** ven a vernos; **four a. a half** cuatro y medio; **she cried a. cried** no paró de llorar; **try a. help me** trata de ayudarme; **wait a. see** espera a ver; **worse a. worse** cada vez peor

Andalusia [ændə'lu:zɪə] *n* Andalucía

Andalusian [ændə'lu:zɪən] *adj* andaluz(a)

Andes ['ændi:z] *npl* **the A.** los Andes

Andorra [æn'dɔːrə] *n* Andorra

anecdote ['ænɪkdəʊt] *n* anécdota *f*

anemia [ə'ni:mɪə] *n US* = **anaemia**

anemic [ə'ni:mɪk] *n US* = **anaemic**

anesthetic [ænɪs'θetɪk] *n US* = **anaesthetic**

anesthetist [ə'ni:sθətɪst] *n US* = **anaesthetist**

angel ['eɪndʒəl] *n* ángel *m*

anger ['æŋɡə(r)] **1** *n* ira *f*, *esp Esp* enfado *m*, *esp Am* enojo *m*
2 *vt esp Esp* enfadar, *esp Am* enojar

angina [æn'dʒaɪnə] *n* angina *f* (de pecho)

angle ['æŋɡəl] *n* ángulo *m*; *Fig* punto *m* de vista

angler ['æŋɡlə(r)] *n* pescador(a) *m,f* de caña

Anglican ['æŋɡlɪkən] *adj & n* anglicano(a) *(m,f)*

Anglo-Saxon [æŋɡləʊ'sæksən] *adj & n* anglosajón(ona) *(m,f)*

Angola [æŋ'ɡəʊlə] *n* Angola

angrily ['æŋɡrɪlɪ] *adv* airadamente, con *esp Esp* enfado *or esp Am* enojo

angry ['æŋɡrɪ] *adj* (**angrier, angriest**) *(person) esp Esp* enfadado(a), *esp Am* enojado(a); *(voice, letter)* airado(a); **to get a.** estar *esp Esp* enfadado(a) *or esp Am* enojado(a)

anguish ['æŋɡwɪʃ] *n* angustia *f*

angular ['æŋɡjʊlə(r)] *adj (shape)* angular; *(face)* anguloso(a)

animal ['ænɪməl] **1** *adj* animal
2 *n* animal *m*; *Fig* bestia *f*

animate 1 *adj* ['ænɪmət] vivo(a)
2 *vt* ['ænɪmeɪt] animar

animated ['ænɪmeɪtɪd] *adj (lively)* animado(a)

animation [ænɪ'meɪʃən] *n* animación *f*

animosity [ænɪ'mɒsɪtɪ] *n* animosidad *f*

aniseed ['ænɪsi:d] *n* anís *m*

ankle ['æŋkəl] *n* tobillo *m*; **a. boots** botines *mpl*; **a. socks** calcetines cortos, *CSur* zoquetes *mpl*, *Col* medias tobilleras

annex [ə'neks] *vt (territory)* anexionar

annexe, *US* **annex** ['æneks] *n (building)* (edificio *m*) anexo *m*

annihilate [ə'naɪəleɪt] *vt* aniquilar

anniversary [ænɪ'vɜːsərɪ] *n* aniversario *m*; **wedding a.** aniversario de bodas

announce [ə'naʊns] *vt* anunciar

announcement [ə'naʊnsmənt] *n* anuncio *m*; *(news)* comunicación *f*; *(statement)* declaración *f*

announcer [ə'naʊnsə(r)] *n Rad & TV* locutor(a) *m,f*

annoy [ə'nɔɪ] *vt* fastidiar, molestar, *esp Am* enojar; **to get annoyed** molestarse, *esp Esp* enfadarse, *esp Am* enojarse

annoyance [ə'nɔɪəns] *n (feeling) esp Esp* enfado *m*, *esp Am* enojo *m*; *(thing)* molestia *f*, fastidio *m*

annoying [ə'nɔɪɪŋ] *adj* molesto(a), fastidioso(a)

annual ['ænjʊəl] **1** *adj* anual
2 *n (book)* anuario *m*; *(plant)* anual *m*

annually ['ænjʊəlɪ] *adv* anualmente

annuity [ə'njuːɪtɪ] *n Fin* anualidad *f*

annul [ə'nʌl] *vt* anular

annulment [ə'nʌlmənt] *n* anulación *f*

anomaly [ə'nɒməlɪ] *n* anomalía *f*

anonymity [ænə'nɪmɪtɪ] *n* anonimato *m*

anonymous [ə'nɒnɪməs] *adj* anónimo(a)

anorak ['ænəræk] *n* anorak *m*

anorexia [ænə'reksɪə] *n* anorexia *f*

another [ə'nʌðə(r)] **1** *adj* otro(a); **a. one** otro(a); **without a. word** sin más
2 *pron* otro(a); **have a.** toma otro(a); **to love one a.** quererse el uno al otro

Ansaphone® ['ɑːnsəfəʊn] *n* mensáfono *m*

answer ['ɑːnsə(r)] **1** *n (to question, letter)* respuesta *f*, contestación *f*; *(to problem)* solución *f*; **in a. to your letter** contestando a su carta; **there's no a.** *(on telephone)* no contestan; *(at door)* no abren
2 *vt (person, question, letter)* responder a, contestar; *(problem)* solucionar; *(door)* abrir; *(phone)* contestar, *Esp* coger
3 *vi* contestar, responder

▸ **answer back** *vi* replicar; **don't a. back!** ¡no seas respondón!

▸ **answer for** *vt insep* responder de; **he's got a lot to a. for** es responsable de muchas cosas

▸ **answer to** *vt insep (name)* responder a; *(description)* corresponder a; **to a. to sb (for sth)** ser responsable ante algn (de algo)

answerable [ˈɑːnsərəbəl] *adj* to be a. to sb for sth ser responsable ante algn de algo

answering machine [ˈɑːnsərɪŋməʃiːn] *n* contestador automático

ant [ænt] *n* hormiga *f*; **a. hill** hormiguero *m*

antagonism [ænˈtægənɪzəm] *n* antagonismo *m* (**between** entre), hostilidad *f* (**towards** hacia)

antagonize [ænˈtægənaɪz] *vt* enemistar, malquistar

Antarctic [ænˈtɑːktɪk] **1** *adj* antártico(a); **A. Ocean** océano Antártico **2** *n* the A. la Antártida

Antarctica [ænˈtɑːktɪkə] *n* Antártida

antecedent [æntɪˈsiːdənt] *n* antecedente *m*

antelope [ˈæntɪləʊp] *n* antílope *m*

antenatal [æntɪˈneɪtəl] *adj* prenatal; **a. clinic** clínica *f* de obstetricia *or* de preparación al parto

antenna [ænˈtenə] *n* (**a**) (*pl* **antennae** [ænˈteniː]) (*of animal, insect*) antena *f* (**b**) (*pl* **antennas**) *Rad & TV* antena *f*

anthem [ˈænθəm] *n* motete *m*; **national a.** himno *m* nacional

anthology [ænˈθɒlədʒɪ] *n* antología *f*

anthracite [ˈænθrəsaɪt] *n* antracita *f*

anthropology [ænθrəˈpɒlədʒɪ] *n* antropología *f*

anti-aircraft [æntɪˈeəkrɑːft] *adj* antiaéreo(a)

antibiotic [æntɪbaɪˈɒtɪk] *n* antibiótico *m*

antibody [ˈæntɪbɒdɪ] *n* anticuerpo *m*

anticipate [ænˈtɪsɪpeɪt] *vt* (**a**) (*expect*) esperar (**b**) (*predict*) prever; (*get ahead of*) anticiparse a, adelantarse a

anticipation [æntɪsɪˈpeɪʃən] *n* (*expectation*) esperanza *f*; (*expectancy*) ilusión *f*

anticlimax [æntɪˈklaɪmæks] *n* (*disappointment*) decepción *f*

anticlockwise [æntɪˈklɒkwaɪz] *adv Br* en sentido opuesto al de las agujas del reloj

antics [ˈæntɪks] *npl* payasadas *fpl*; (*naughtiness*) travesuras *fpl*

anticyclone [æntɪˈsaɪkləʊn] *n* anticiclón *m*

antidote [ˈæntɪdəʊt] *n* antídoto *m*

antifreeze [ˈæntɪfriːz] *n* anticongelante *m*

antihistamine [æntɪˈhɪstəmɪn] *n* antihistamínico *m*

antinuclear [æntɪˈnjuːklɪə(r)] *adj* antinuclear

antipathy [ænˈtɪpəθɪ] *n* antipatía *f* (**to** a)

antiperspirant [æntɪˈpɜːspɪrənt] *n* antitranspirante *m*

antiquated [ˈæntɪkweɪtɪd] *adj* anticuado(a)

antique [ænˈtiːk] **1** *adj* antiguo(a) **2** *n* antigüedad *f*; **a. dealer** anticuario(a) *m,f*; **a. shop** tienda *f* de antigüedades

antiquity [ænˈtɪkwɪtɪ] *n* antigüedad *f*

antisemitic [æntɪsɪˈmɪtɪk] *adj* (*person*) antisemita; (*beliefs, remarks*) antisemítico(a)

anti-Semitism [æntɪˈsemɪtɪzəm] *n* antisemitismo *m*

antiseptic [æntɪˈseptɪk] *adj & n* antiséptico(a) (*m*)

antisocial [æntɪˈsəʊʃəl] *adj* (*delinquent*) antisocial; (*unsociable*) insociable

antithesis [ænˈtɪθɪsɪs] *n* antítesis *f*

antivirus [ˈæntɪˈvaɪrəs] *adj* Comput (*program, software*) antivirus

antler [ˈæntlə(r)] *n* cuerna *f*; **antlers** cornamenta *f*

Antwerp [ˈæntwɜːp] *n* Amberes

anus [ˈeɪnəs] *n* ano *m*

anvil [ˈænvɪl] *n* yunque *m*

anxiety [æŋˈzaɪtɪ] *n* (*concern*) inquietud *f*; (*worry*) preocupación *f*; (*fear*) angustia *f*; (*eagerness*) ansia *f*

anxious [ˈæŋkʃəs] *adj* (*concerned*) inquieto(a); (*worried*) preocupado(a); (*fearful*) angustiado(a); (*eager*) ansioso(a); **to be a. about sth** estar preocupado(a) por algo

any [ˈenɪ] **1** *adj* (**a**) (*in questions, conditionals*) algún(una); **are there a. seats left?** ¿quedan plazas?; **have you a. apples?** ¿tienes manzanas?; **have you a. money?** ¿tienes (algo de) dinero? (**b**) (*in negative clauses*) ningún(una); **I don't have a. time** no tengo tiempo (**c**) (*no matter which*) cualquier(a); **a. doctor will say the same** cualquier médico te dirá lo mismo; **at a. moment** en cualquier momento (**d**) (*every*) todo(a); **in a. case** de todas formas

2 *pron* (**a**) (*in questions*) alguno(a); **do they have a.?** ¿tienen alguno?; **I need some paper, have you a.?** necesito papel, ¿tienes? (**b**) (*in negative clauses*) ninguno(a); **I don't want a.** no quiero ninguno (**c**) (*no matter which*) cualquiera; **you can have a. (one)** coge el/la que quieras

3 *adv* **is there a. more?** ¿hay más?; **I used to like it, but not a. more/longer** antes me gustaba pero ya no; **is he a. better?** ¿está mejor?

anybody [ˈenɪbɒdɪ] *pron* (*in questions, conditionals*) alguien, alguno(a); (*in negative clauses*) nadie, ninguno(a); (*no matter who*) cualquiera; **a. but me**

cualquiera menos yo; **bring a. you like** trae a quien quieras; **do you see a. over there?** ¿ves a alguien allí?; **I can't find a.** no encuentro a nadie

anyhow ['enɪhaʊ] *adv* (**a**) *(in spite of that)* en todo caso, de todas formas; *(changing the subject)* bueno, pues (**b**) *(carelessly)* desordenadamente, de cualquier modo or forma

anyone ['enɪwʌn] *pron* = **anybody**

anyplace ['enɪpleɪs] *adv US* = **anywhere**

anything ['enɪθɪŋ] **1** *pron (in questions, conditionals)* algo, alguna cosa; *(in negative clauses)* nada; *(no matter what)* cualquier cosa; **a. but that** cualquier cosa menos eso; **a. else?** ¿algo más?; **can I do a. for you?** ¿puedo ayudarte en algo?; **hardly a.** casi nada; **if a., I'd buy the big one** de comprar uno compraría el grande; **to run/work like a.** correr/trabajar a más no poder
2 *adv* **is this a. like what you wanted?** ¿viene a ser éste lo que querías?

anyway ['enɪweɪ] *adv* = **anyhow (a)**

anywhere ['enɪweə(r)] *adv* (**a**) *(in questions, conditionals) (situation)* en alguna parte; *(movement)* a alguna parte; **could it be a. else?** ¿podría estar en otro sitio? (**b**) *(in negative clauses) (situation)* en ninguna parte; *(movement)* a ninguna parte; *(no matter where)* dondequiera, en cualquier parte; **go a. you like** ve a donde quieras; **we aren't a. near finished** no hemos terminado ni mucho menos

apart [ə'pɑːt] *adv* (**a**) *(at a distance)* alejado(a), separado(a); **to be poles a.** ser polos opuestos; **you can't tell the twins a.** no se puede distinguir los mellizos el uno del otro (**b**) *(to pieces)* **to fall a.** deshacerse; **to take sth a.** desmontar algo (**c**) **a. from** *(excepting)* aparte de

apartheid [ə'pɑːtheɪt] *n* apartheid *m*

apartment [ə'pɑːtmənt] *n US* apartamento *m Esp* piso *m*, *Arg* departamento *m*; **a. block** edificio *m* or bloque *m* de apartamentos *or Esp* pisos *or Arg* departamentos

apathetic [æpə'θetɪk] *adj* apático(a)

apathy ['æpəθɪ] *n* apatía *f*

ape [eɪp] **1** *n* mono *m*
2 *vt* imitar, copiar

apéritif [ə'perɪtiːf] *n* aperitivo *m*

aperture ['æpətʃə(r)] *n* (*hole, crack*) resquicio *m*, rendija *f*; *Phot* abertura *f*

APEX ['eɪpeks] *adj* **A. ticket** billete *m* or*Am* boleto *m* or*Am* pasaje *m* (con tarifa) APEX

apex ['eɪpeks] *n (of triangle)* vértice *m*; *Fig* cumbre *f*

aphrodisiac [æfrə'dɪzɪæk] *n* afrodisíaco *m*

apiece [ə'piːs] *adv* cada uno(a)

aplomb [ə'plɒm] *n* aplomo *m*

apocalypse [ə'pɒkəlɪps] *n* apocalipsis *m inv*

apolitical [eɪpə'lɪtɪkəl] *adj* apolítico(a)

apologetic [əpɒlə'dʒetɪk] *adj (remorseful)* de disculpa; **he was very a.** pidió mil perdones

apologetically [əpɒlə'dʒetɪklɪ] *adv* disculpándose, pidiendo perdón

apologize [ə'pɒlədʒaɪz] *vi (say sorry)* disculparse; **they apologized to us for the delay** se disculparon con nosotros por el retraso

apology [ə'pɒlədʒɪ] *n* disculpa *f*, excusa *f*; *Fam* **what an a. for a meal!** ¡vaya birria de comida!

apoplectic [æpə'plektɪk] *adj Med* apopléctico(a); *Fam* **to be a. with rage** estar furioso(a)

apostle [ə'pɒsəl] *n* apóstol *m*

apostrophe [ə'pɒstrəfɪ] *n* apóstrofo *m*

appal, *US* **appall** [ə'pɔːl] *vt* horrorizar

appalling [ə'pɔːlɪŋ] *adj (horrifying)* horroroso(a); *Fam (very bad)* pésimo(a), fatal

apparatus [æpə'reɪtəs] *n* aparato *m*; *(equipment)* equipo *m*

apparel [ə'pærəl] *n US* indumentaria *f*, ropa *f*

apparent [ə'pærənt] *adj (obvious)* evidente; *(seeming)* aparente; **to become a.** ponerse de manifiesto

apparently [ə'pærəntlɪ] *adv (seemingly)* por lo visto

apparition [æpə'rɪʃən] *n* aparición *f*

appeal [ə'piːl] **1** *n* (**a**) *(request)* solicitud *f*; *(plea)* súplica *f* (**b**) *(attraction)* atractivo *m*; *(interest)* interés *m* (**c**) *Jur* apelación *f*
2 *vi* (**a**) *(plead)* rogar, suplicar (**to a**); **to a. for help** solicitar ayuda (**b**) *(attract)* atraer; *(interest)* interesar; **it doesn't a. to me** no me dice nada (**c**) *Jur* apelar

appealing [ə'piːlɪŋ] *adj (moving)* conmovedor(a); *(attractive)* atractivo(a); *(tempting)* atrayente

appear [ə'pɪə(r)] *vi* (**a**) *(become visible)* aparecer; *(publicly)* presentarse; *(on stage)* actuar; **to a. before a court** comparecer ante un tribunal; **to a. on television** salir en la televisión (**b**) *(seem)* parecer; **he appears relaxed** parece relajado; **so it appears** según parece

appearance [ə'pɪərəns] *n* (**a**) *(becoming visible)* aparición *f*; *(publicly)* presentación *f*; *(on stage)* actuación *f*; *(before court)* comparecencia *f*; *(of book etc)* publicación f; **to put in an a.** hacer acto de presencia (**b**) *(look)* apariencia f, aspecto m; **to all appearances** al parecer

appease [ə'piːz] *vt (anger)* aplacar, apaciguar; *(person)* calmar, apaciguar; *Pol* contemporizar con

appeasement [ə'piːzmənt] *n Pol* contemporización f

appendices [ə'pendɪsiːz] *pl of* appendix

appendicitis [əpendɪ'saɪtɪs] *n* apendicitis f

appendix [ə'pendɪks] *n (pl* **appendices)** apéndice m

appetite ['æpɪtaɪt] *n* apetito m; *Fig* deseo m

appetizer ['æpɪtaɪzə(r)] *n (drink)* aperitivo m; *(snack)* tapa f, pincho m

appetizing ['æpɪtaɪzɪŋ] *adj* apetitoso(a)

applaud [ə'plɔːd] *vt & vi* aplaudir

applause [ə'plɔːz] *n* aplausos *mpl*

apple ['æpəl] *n* manzana f; **a. tree** manzano m

appliance [ə'plaɪəns] *n* dispositivo m

applicable [ə'plɪkəbəl] *adj* aplicable

applicant ['æplɪkənt] *n (for post)* candidato(a) m,f; *(to court, for tickets)* solicitante mf

application [æplɪ'keɪʃən] *n (a) (of cream)* aplicación f (**b**) *(for post etc)* solicitud f; **a. form** solicitud; **job a.** solicitud de empleo (**c**) *(effort)* aplicación f; **she lacks a.** no se aplica

applied [ə'plaɪd] *adj* aplicado(a)

apply [ə'plaɪ] **1** *vt* aplicar; *(brake)* emplear; *(law)* recurrir a; *(pressure)* ejercer; **to a. oneself to** dedicarse a

2 *vi* (**a**) *(law, rule)* aplicarse; **that applies to you too!** ¡esto es válido *or* vale para tí también! (**b**) **to apply (to sb) for sth** *(job, grant)* solicitar algo (a algn)

▸ **apply for** *vt insep (post, information)* solicitar; *(tickets)* pedir

appoint [ə'pɔɪnt] *vt (person)* nombrar; *(time, place etc)* fijar, señalar

appointment [ə'pɔɪntmənt] *n* (**a**) *(to post)* nombramiento m; *(post)* cargo m (**b**) *(meeting)* cita f; **to make an a. with** citarse con; *(at doctor's)* pedir hora a

apportion [ə'pɔːʃən] *vt Fig (blame)* echar

appraisal [ə'preɪzəl] *n* evaluación f

appreciable [ə'priːʃəbəl] *adj (difference)* apreciable; *(sum)* importante

appreciate [ə'priːʃɪeɪt] **1** *vt* (**a**) *(be thankful for)* agradecer (**b**) *(understand)* entender (**c**) *(value)* apreciar, valorar

2 *vi (increase in value)* apreciarse

appreciation [əpriːʃɪ'eɪʃən] *n* (**a**) *(of help, advice)* agradecimiento m; *(of difficulty)*

comprensión f; *(of wine etc)* aprecio m; *(appraisal)* evaluación f (**b**) *(increase in value)* apreciación f

appreciative [ə'priːʃɪətɪv] *adj (thankful)* agradecido(a); *(responsive)* apreciativo(a)

apprehend [æprɪ'hend] *vt (arrest)* detener

apprehension [æprɪ'henʃən] *n* (**a**) *(arrest)* detención f (**b**) *(fear)* aprensión f

apprehensive [æprɪ'hensɪv] *adj (fearful)* aprensivo(a)

apprentice [ə'prentɪs] *n* aprendiz(a) m,f

apprenticeship [ə'prentɪsʃɪp] *n* aprendizaje m

approach [ə'prəutʃ] **1** *n* (**a**) *(coming near)* acercamiento m; *(to town)* acceso m; **a. road** vía f de acceso (**b**) *(to problem)* enfoque m

2 *vt (come near to)* acercarse a; *(be similar to)* aproximarse a; *Fig (problem)* abordar; *(person)* dirigirse a; **to a. sb about sth** dirigirse a algn a propósito de algo

3 *vi* acercarse

approachable [ə'prəutʃəbəl] *adj (person)* accesible

appropriate¹ [ə'prəupriət] *adj (suitable)* apropiado(a), adecuado(a); *(convenient)* oportuno(a)

appropriate² [ə'prəuprieɪt] *vt (allocate)* asignar; *(steal)* apropiarse de

approval [ə'pruːvəl] *n* aprobación f, visto bueno; *Com* **to get sth on a.** adquirir algo sin compromiso de compra

approve [ə'pruːv] *vt* aprobar; *Br Formerly* **approved school** reformatorio m, correccional m

▸ **approve of** *vt insep* aprobar

approving [ə'pruːvɪŋ] *adj (look etc)* aprobatorio(a)

approx [ə'prɒks] *(abbr* **approximately)** aprox.

approximate 1 *adj* [ə'prɒksɪmɪt] aproximado(a)

2 *vt* [ə'prɒksɪmeɪt] aproximarse a

approximately [ə'prɒksɪmɪtlɪ] *adv* aproximadamente

apricot ['eɪprɪkɒt] *n (fruit) Esp* albaricoque m, *Andes, RP* damasco m, *Méx* chabacano m; **a. tree** *Esp* albaricoquero m, *Andes, RP* damasco m, *Méx* chabacano m

April ['eɪprəl] *n* abril m; **A. Fools' Day** día m uno de abril, ≃ día de los Inocentes (28 de diciembre)

apron ['eɪprən] *n* delantal m; *(for workman)* mandil m

apt [æpt] *adj* (**a**) *(suitable)* apropiado(a); *(remark)* acertado(a), oportuno(a); *(name)* justo(a); *(description)* exacto(a) (**b**) **to be a. to do sth** ser propenso(a) a hacer algo

aptitude ['æptɪtjuːd] *n* capacidad *f*; **a. test** prueba *f* de aptitud

aptly ['æptlɪ] *adv* acertadamente

aqualung ['ækwəlʌŋ] *n* botella *f* de oxígeno

aquamarine [ækwəmə'riːn] **1** *n* *(gem)* aguamarina *f*
2 *adj* de color de aguamarina

aquarium [ə'kweərɪəm] *n* acuario *m*

Aquarius [ə'kweərɪəs] *n* Acuario *m*

aquatic [ə'kwætɪk] *adj* acuático(a)

aqueduct ['ækwɪdʌkt] *n* acueducto *m*

Arab ['ærəb] *adj & n* árabe *(mf)*

Arabian [ə'reɪbɪən] *adj* árabe

Arabic ['ærəbɪk] **1** *adj* árabe, arábigo(a); **A. numerals** numeración arábiga
2 *n* *(language)* árabe *m*

arable ['ærəbəl] *adj* cultivable

Aragon ['ærəgən] *n* Aragón

arbitrary ['ɑːbɪtrərɪ] *adj* arbitrario(a)

arbitrate ['ɑːbɪtreɪt] *vt & vi* arbitrar

arbitration [ɑːbɪ'treɪʃən] *n* arbitraje *m*

arc [ɑːk] *n* arco *m*; **a. lamp** arco voltaico

arcade [ɑː'keɪd] *n* arcada *f*; *(passageway)* pasaje *m*; **shopping a.** galerías *fpl* (comerciales)

arch [ɑːtʃ] **1** *n* (**a**) *Archit* arco *m*; *(vault)* bóveda *f* (**b**) *Anat* empeine *m*
2 *vt (back)* arquear

archaeologist [ɑːkɪ'ɒlədʒɪst] *n* arqueólogo(a) *m,f*

archaeology [ɑːkɪ'ɒlədʒɪ] *n* arqueología *f*

archaic [ɑː'keɪɪk] *adj* arcaico(a)

archbishop [ɑːtʃ'bɪʃəp] *n* arzobispo *m*

arched [ɑːtʃt] *adj* arqueado(a)

archeologist [ɑːkɪ'ɒlədʒɪst] *n US* = archaeologist

archeology [ɑːkɪ'ɒlədʒɪ] *n US* = archaeology

archer ['ɑːtʃə(r)] *n* arquero(a) *m,f*

archery ['ɑːtʃərɪ] *n* tiro *m* con arco

archetypal ['ɑːkɪtaɪpəl] *adj* arquetípico(a)

archipelago [ɑːkɪ'pelɪgəʊ] *n* archipiélago *m*

architect ['ɑːkɪtekt] *n* arquitecto(a) *m,f*

architectural [ɑːkɪ'tektʃərəl] *adj* arquitectónico(a)

architecture ['ɑːkɪtektʃə(r)] *n* arquitectura *f*

archives ['ɑːkaɪvz] *npl* archivos *mpl*

archway ['ɑːtʃweɪ] *n (arch)* arco *m*; *(vault)* bóveda *f*; *(in church)* atrio *m*; *(passage)* pasaje *m*

arctic ['ɑːktɪk] **1** *adj* ártico(a); **A. Circle** círculo polar Ártico
2 *n* **the A.** el Ártico

ardent ['ɑːdənt] *adj (supporter etc)* apasionado(a); *(desire)* ardiente

ardour, *US* **ardor** ['ɑːdə(r)] *n* pasión *f*, ardor *m*

arduous ['ɑːdjʊəs] *adj* arduo(a), penoso(a)

are [ɑː(r)] *2nd person sing pres, 1st, 2nd, 3rd person pl pres of* **be**

area ['eərɪə] *n (surface)* área *f*, superficie *f*; *(space)* extensión *f*; *(region)* región *f*; *(of town)* zona *f*; *Fig (field)* campo *m*; *US Tel* **a. code** prefijo *m* local

arena [ə'riːnə] *n (stadium)* estadio *m*; *(bullring)* plaza *f*; *(circus)* pista *f*; *Fig (stage)* campo *m* de batalla

Argentina [ɑːdʒən'tiːnə] *n* Argentina

Argentinian [ɑːdʒən'tɪnɪən] *adj & n* argentino(a) *(m,f)*

arguable ['ɑːgjʊəbəl] *adj* discutible

arguably ['ɑːgjʊəblɪ] *adv* **it's a. the best** hay quienes dicen que es el mejor

argue ['ɑːgjuː] **1** *vt (reason)* discutir; *(point of view)* mantener
2 *vi (quarrel)* discutir; *(reason)* argumentar, razonar; **to a. for** abogar por; **to a. against sth** ponerse en contra de algo

argument ['ɑːgjʊmənt] *n (reason)* argumento *m* (**for** a favor de; **against** en contra de); *(quarrel)* discusión *f*, disputa *f*; **for the sake of a.** por decir algo

argumentative [ɑːgjʊ'mentətɪv] *adj* **she's very a.** le gusta discutir por todo

aria ['ɑːrɪə] *n* aria *f*

arid ['ærɪd] *adj* árido(a)

Aries ['eəriːz] *n* Aries *m*

arise [ə'raɪz] *vi (pt* **arose***; pp* **arisen** [ə'rɪzən]) *(get up)* levantarse; *(happen)* surgir; **should the occasion a.** si se presenta la ocasión

aristocracy [ærɪ'stɒkrəsɪ] *n* aristocracia *f*

aristocrat [*Br* 'ærɪstəkræt, *US* ə'rɪstəkræt] *n* aristócrata *mf*

arithmetic [ə'rɪθmətɪk] *n* aritmética *f*

ark [ɑːk] *n* arca *f*; **Noah's A.** el arca de Noé

arm [ɑːm] **1** *n* (**a**) *(of person, chair)* brazo *m*; *(of garment)* manga *f*; **to walk a. in a.** ir cogidos(as) del brazo (**b**) *Mil* **arms** armas *fpl*; **arms race** carrera armamentística; **coat of arms** escudo *m*
2 *vt* armar; **to a. oneself against sth** armarse contra algo

armaments ['ɑːməmənts] *npl* armamentos *mpl*

armband ['ɑːmbænd] *n (at funeral, for swimming)* brazalete *m*

armchair ['ɑːmtʃeə(r)] *n* sillón *m*

armed ['ɑːmd] *adj* armado(a); **a. forces** fuerzas armadas; **a. robbery** robo *m* a mano armada

Armenia [ɑːˈmiːnɪə] *n* Armenia

armistice ['ɑːmɪstɪs] *n* armisticio *m*

armour, *US* **armor** ['ɑːmə(r)] *n (on vehicle)* blindaje *m*; **(suit of) a.** armadura *f*

armoured car, *US* **armored car** ['ɑːməd'kɑː(r)] *n* coche blindado

armour-plated, *US* **armor-plated** ['ɑːmə'pleɪtɪd] *adj* acorazado(a)

armoury, *US* **armory** ['ɑːmərɪ] *n* arsenal *m*

armpit ['ɑːmpɪt] *n* axila *f*, sobaco *m*

army ['ɑːmɪ] *n* ejército *m*

aroma [əˈrəʊmə] *n* aroma *m*

aromatic [ærəʊˈmætɪk] *adj* aromático(a)

arose [əˈrəʊz] *pt of* **arise**

around [əˈraʊnd] **1** *adv* alrededor; **all a.** por todos los lados; **are the children a.?** ¿están los niños por aquí?; **he looked a.** miró a su alrededor

2 *prep* **(a)** *(indicating position)* alrededor de; **a. the corner** a la vuelta de la esquina; **a. here** por aquí **(b)** *(approximately)* aproximadamente

arouse [əˈraʊz] *vt (sleeper, emotion)* despertar; *(sexually)* excitar

arrange [əˈreɪndʒ] **1** *vt* **(a)** *(order)* ordenar; *(hair, flowers)* arreglar; *Mus* adaptar **(b)** *(plan)* organizar; *(agree on)* quedar en; **to a. a time** fijar una hora; **arranged marriage** boda arreglada

2 *vi* **I shall a. for him to be there** lo arreglaré para que pueda asistir

arrangement [əˈreɪndʒmənt] *n* **(a)** *(display)* colocación *f*; *Mus* adaptación *f* **(b)** *(agreement)* acuerdo *m* **(c)** **arrangements** *(plans)* planes *mpl*; *(preparations)* preparativos *mpl*

array [əˈreɪ] *n* colección *f*; **a great a. of goods** un gran surtido de productos

arrears [əˈrɪəz] *npl* atrasos *mpl*; **to be in a. with the rent** estar atrasado(a) en el pago del alquiler *or Méx* de la renta; **to be paid in a.** cobrar con retraso

arrest [əˈrest] **1** *n* detención *f*; **to be under a.** estar detenido(a)

2 *vt (criminal)* detener; *Fig (progress)* frenar

arresting [əˈrestɪŋ] *adj* llamativo(a)

arrival [əˈraɪvəl] *n* llegada *f*; **a new a.** un(a) recién llegado(a)

arrive [əˈraɪv] *vi* llegar (**at/in** a)

arrogance ['ærəgəns] *n* arrogancia *f*

arrogant ['ærəgənt] *adj* arrogante

arrow ['ærəʊ] *n* flecha *f*

arse [ɑːs] *n Br Vulg (buttocks)* culo *m*

arsenal ['ɑːsənəl] *n* arsenal *m*

arsenic ['ɑːsənɪk] *n* arsénico *m*

arson ['ɑːsən] *n* incendio provocado

art [ɑːt] *n* **(a)** *(in general)* arte *m*; **the arts** las bellas artes; **arts and crafts** artes *fpl* y oficios *mpl*; **a. gallery** galería *f* de arte **(b)** **arts** *(branch of knowledge)* letras *fpl*

artefact ['ɑːtɪfækt] *n* artefacto *m*; *(in archaeology)* objeto *m* de arte

artery ['ɑːtərɪ] *n* arteria *f*

artful ['ɑːtfʊl] *adj (cunning)* ladino(a)

arthritis [ɑːˈθraɪtɪs] *n* artritis *f*

artichoke ['ɑːtɪtʃəʊk] *n* alcachofa *f*, *Am* alcaucil *m*

article ['ɑːtɪkəl] **1** *n* artículo *m*; **a. of clothing** prenda *f* de vestir

2 *vt* **to be articled to a firm of solicitors** trabajar en prácticas o hacer una pasantía en un bufete de abogados

articulate[1] [ɑːˈtɪkjʊlɪt] *adj (speech)* claro(a); *(person)* elocuente

articulate[2] [ɑːˈtɪkjʊleɪt] *vt (word)* articular; *(idea, feeling)* formular, expresar

articulated lorry [ɑːˈtɪkjʊleɪtɪdˈlɒrɪ] *n Br* camión articulado

artificial [ɑːtɪˈfɪʃəl] *adj* artificial; *(limb)* postizo(a); **a. intelligence** inteligencia *f* artificial

artillery [ɑːˈtɪlərɪ] *n* artillería *f*

artisan ['ɑːtɪzæn] *n* artesano(a) *m,f*

artist ['ɑːtɪst] *n* artista *mf*; *(painter)* pintor(a) *m,f*

artistic [ɑːˈtɪstɪk] *adj* artístico(a)

artistry ['ɑːtɪstrɪ] *n* arte *m*, talento artístico

arty ['ɑːtɪ] *adj* (**artier**, **artiest**) *Fam (person)* = que se interesa por las artes

as [æz, *unstressed* əz] **1** *adv & conj* **(a)** *(comparison)* **as ... as ...** tan ... como ...; **as far as** hasta; *Fig* **as far as I'm concerned** por lo que a mí respecta; **as many as** tantos(as) como; **as much as** tanto(a) como; **as tall as me** tan alto(a) como yo; **as opposed to** a diferencia de; **as little as £5** tan sólo 5 libras; **as soon as they arrive** en cuanto lleguen; **I'll stay as long as I can** quedaré todo el tiempo que pueda; **just as big** igual de grande; **three times as fast** tres veces más rápido; **the same as** igual que

(b) *(manner)* como; **as a rule** por regla general; **as you know** como ya sabéis; **as you like** como quieras; **do as I say** haz lo que yo te digo; **he's working as a doctor** está trabajando de médico; **I thought as much** ya me lo suponía; **it serves as a table** sirve de mesa; **leave it as it is** déjalo tal como está; **he was dressed as a pirate** iba vestido de pirata

(**c**) *(while, when)* mientras (que); **as a child** de niño(a); **as I was eating** mientras comía; **as we were leaving, we saw Pat** al salir vimos a Pat

(**d**) *(though)* aunque; **be that as it may** por mucho que así sea; **young as he is** aunque es joven

(**e**) *(because)* como, ya que

(**f**) *(and so)* igual que; **as do I** igual que yo; **as well** también

(**g**) *(purpose)* para; **so as to do sth** para hacer algo

(**h**) **as for my brother** en cuanto a mi hermano

(**i**) **as from, as of** a partir de

(**j**) **to act as if** actuar como si *(+ subj)*; **it looks as if the concert is off** parece ser que no habrá concierto

(**k**) **it's late enough as it is** ya es muy tarde; **as it were** por así decirlo

(**l**) **as long as** *(only if)* siempre que, con tal de que

(**m**) **as regards** en cuanto a, por lo que se refiere a; **as usual** como siempre; **as yet** aún, todavía

2 *rel pron* **such as** tal(es) como

asap [ˈeɪeseɪˈpiː] *adv* (*abbr* **as soon as possible**) cuanto antes, lo antes posible

asbestos [æzˈbestəs] *n* amianto *m*, asbesto *m*

ascend [əˈsend] *vi* subir, ascender

ascendancy [əˈsendənsɪ] *n* dominio *m*, influencia *f*

ascendant [əˈsendənt] *n* **to be in the a.** estar en auge

ascent [əˈsent] *n* subida *f*

ascertain [æsəˈteɪn] *vt* averiguar, enterarse de

ascribe [əˈskraɪb] *vt* **to a. sth to sth/sb** imputar algo a algo/algn

aseptic [əˈseptɪk] *adj* aséptico(a)

ash[1] [æʃ] *n Bot* fresno *m*

ash[2] [æʃ] *n* ceniza *f*; **a. bin,** *US* **a. can** cubo *m* de la basura; **Rel A. Wednesday** miércoles *m inv* de ceniza

ashamed [əˈʃeɪmd] *adj* avergonzado(a), *Am salvo RP* apenado(a); **you ought to be a. of yourself!** ¡debería darte vergüenza *or Am salvo RP* pena!

ashen [ˈæʃən] *adj (face)* pálido(a)

ashore [əˈʃɔː(r)] *adv (position)* en tierra; **to go a.** desembarcar; **to swim a.** nadar hacia tierra

ashtray [ˈæʃtreɪ] *n* cenicero *m*

Asia [ˈeɪʒə] *n* Asia; **A. Minor** Asia Menor

Asian [ˈeɪʒən] **1** *n* asiático(a) *m,f*; *Br (person from Indian subcontinent)* = persona de la India, Paquistán o Bangladesh

2 *adj* asiático(a); *Br (from Indian subcontinent)* = de la India, Paquistán o Bangladesh

aside [əˈsaɪd] **1** *adv* al lado, aparte; **to cast a.** echar a un lado; **to stand a.** apartarse

2 *prep* **a. from** *(apart from)* aparte de; *(as well as)* además de

3 *n Th* aparte *m*

ask [ɑːsk] **1** *vt* (**a**) *(enquire about)* preguntar; **to a. sb a question** hacer una pregunta a algn (**b**) *(request)* pedir, solicitar; **she asked me to post it** me pidió que lo echara al buzón (**c**) *(invite)* invitar

2 *vi (enquire)* preguntar; *(request)* pedir

▸ **ask after** *vt insep* **to a. after sb** preguntar por algn

▸ **ask for** *vt insep (help)* pedir, solicitar; *(person)* preguntar por

▸ **ask out** *vt sep* **to a. sb out** invitar a algn a salir

askance [əˈskæns] *adv* **to look a. at sb** mirar a algn con recelo

askew [əˈskjuː] **1** *adj* ladeado(a)

2 *adv* de lado

asleep [əˈsliːp] *adj (person)* dormido(a); *(limb)* adormecido(a); **to fall a.** quedarse dormido(a)

asparagus [əˈspærəgəs] *n inv* espárragos *mpl*

aspect [ˈæspekt] *n* (**a**) *(of question)* aspecto *m* (**b**) *(of building)* orientación *f*

aspersions [əˈspɜːʃənz] *npl* **to cast a. on sb** difamar a algn

asphalt [ˈæsfælt] *n* asfalto *m*

asphyxiate [æsˈfɪksɪeɪt] **1** *vt* asfixiar

2 *vi* asfixiarse

asphyxiation [æsfɪksɪˈeɪʃən] *n* asfixia *f*

aspiration [æspəˈreɪʃən] *n* aspiración *f*

aspire [əˈspaɪə(r)] *vi* **to a. to** aspirar a

aspirin [ˈæsprɪn] *n* aspirina *f*

ass[1] [æs] *n* asno(a) *m,f*, burro(a) *m,f*

ass[2] [æs] *n US Vulg* culo *m*

assailant [əˈseɪlənt] *n* agresor(a) *m,f*, atacante *mf*

assassin [əˈsæsɪn] *n* asesino(a) *m,f*

assassinate [əˈsæsɪneɪt] *vt* asesinar

assassination [əsæsɪˈneɪʃən] *n* asesinato *m*

assault [əˈsɔːlt] **1** *n Mil* ataque *m* (**on** a); *Jur* agresión *f*

2 *vt Mil* asaltar, atacar; *Jur* agredir; *(sexually)* violar

assemble [ə'sembəl] **1** *vt (people)* reunir, juntar; *(furniture)* montar
  2 *vi (people)* reunirse, juntarse

assembly [ə'semblɪ] *n* reunión *f*, asamblea *f*; *Tech* montaje *m*; *Br Sch* = reunión de todos los profesores y los alumnos al principio de la jornada escolar; *Ind* **a. line** cadena *f* de montaje

assent [ə'sent] **1** *n (agreement)* asentimiento *m*; *(consent)* consentimiento *m*; *(approval)* aprobación *f*
  2 *vi* asentir, consentir (**to** en)

assert [ə'sɜːt] *vt* afirmar; **to a. oneself** imponerse; **to a. one's rights** hacer valer sus derechos

assertion [ə'sɜːʃən] *n* afirmación *f*

assertive [ə'sɜːtɪv] *adj* enérgico(a)

assess [ə'ses] *vt (estimate value of)* valorar; *(damages, price)* calcular; *(tax)* gravar; *Fig (effect)* evaluar

assessment [ə'sesmənt] *n (of value)* valoración *f*; *(of damages etc)* cálculo *m*; *(of taxes)* gravamen *m*; *Fig* juicio *m*

assessor [ə'sesə(r)] *n* asesor(a) *m,f*

asset ['æset] *n* (**a**) *(benefit)* ventaja *f*; **to be an a.** *(person)* ser de gran valor (**b**) *Fin* **assets** bienes *mpl*; **fixed assets** bienes raíces

asshole ['æshəʊl] *n US Vulg (unpleasant person)* hijo(a) *m,f* de puta, cabrón(ona) *m,f*

assiduous [ə'sɪdjʊəs] *adj* asiduo(a)

assign [ə'saɪn] *vt (task)* asignar; *(property etc)* ceder; **to a. sb to a job** designar a algn para un trabajo

assignment [ə'saɪnmənt] *n (allocation)* asignación *f*; *(task)* tarea *f*; *(mission)* misión *f*; *(appointment)* cita *f*

assimilate [ə'sɪmɪleɪt] *vt* asimilar

assist [ə'sɪst] *vt & vi* ayudar

assistance [ə'sɪstəns] *n* ayuda *f*, auxilio *m*

assistant [ə'sɪstənt] *n* ayudante *mf*; **a. manager** subdirector(a) *m,f*; **shop a.** dependiente(a) *m,f*; *Br* **(language) a.** *(in school)* auxiliar *mf* de conversación; *(in university)* lector(a) *m,f* de lengua extranjera

associate¹ [ə'səʊʃɪeɪt] **1** *vt (ideas)* relacionar; *(companies)* asociar; **to be associated with sth** estar relacionado(a) con algo
  2 *vi* **to a. with** tratar con

associate² [ə'səʊʃɪt] **1** *adj* asociado(a)
  2 *n (colleague)* colega *mf*; *(partner)* socio(a) *m,f*; *(accomplice)* cómplice *mf*

association [əsəʊsɪ'eɪʃən] *n* asociación *f*, *(company)* sociedad *f*

assorted [ə'sɔːtɪd] *adj* surtido(a), variado(a)

assortment [ə'sɔːtmənt] *n* surtido *m*, variedad *f*

assume [ə'sjuːm] **1** *vt (power)* asumir; *(attitude, name)* adoptar; **an assumed name** un nombre falso
  2 *vi (suppose)* suponer

assumption [ə'sʌmpʃən] *n* (**a**) *(of power)* toma *f*; **a. of office** toma de posesión (**b**) *(supposition)* suposición *f*

assurance [ə'ʃʊərəns] *n* (**a**) *(guarantee)* garantía *f* (**b**) *(confidence)* confianza *f* (**c**) *Br (insurance)* seguro *m*

assure [ə'ʃʊə(r)] *vt* asegurar

asterisk ['æstərɪsk] *n* asterisco *m*

astern [ə'stɜːn] *adv* a popa

asthma ['æsmə] *n* asma *f*

astonish [ə'stɒnɪʃ] *vt* asombrar, pasmar; **I was astonished** me quedé pasmado(a)

astonishing [ə'stɒnɪʃɪŋ] *adj* asombroso(a), pasmoso(a)

astonishment [ə'stɒnɪʃmənt] *n* asombro *m*; **to my a.** para gran sorpresa mía

astound [ə'staʊnd] *vt* asombrar, pasmar

astounding [ə'staʊndɪŋ] *adj* pasmoso(a), asombroso(a)

astray [ə'streɪ] *adv* **to go a.** extraviarse; *Fig* equivocarse; **to lead sb a.** llevar a algn por mal camino

astride [ə'straɪd] *prep* a horcajadas sobre

astrology [ə'strɒlədʒɪ] *n* astrología *f*

astronaut ['æstrənɔːt] *n* astronauta *mf*

astronomer [ə'strɒnəmə(r)] *n* astrónomo(a) *m,f*

astronomical [æstrə'nɒmɪkəl] *adj* astronómico(a)

astronomy [ə'strɒnəmɪ] *n* astronomía *f*

Asturias [æ'stʊərɪæs] *n* Asturias

astute [ə'stjuːt] *adj* astuto(a)

asylum [ə'saɪləm] *n* (**a**) *(protection)* asilo *m*; **to seek political a.** pedir asilo político (**b**) **mental a.** manicomio *m*

at [æt, *unstressed* ət] *prep* (**a**) *(position)* a, en; **at school/work** en el colegio/trabajo; **at the window** a la ventana; **at the top** en lo alto
  (**b**) *(direction)* a; **to be angry at sb** estar *esp Esp* enfadado(a) *or esp Am* enojado(a) con algn; **to laugh at sb** reírse de algn; **to look at sth/sb** mirar algo/a algn; **to shout at sb** gritarle a algn
  (**c**) *(time)* a; **at Easter/Christmas** en Semana Santa/Navidad; **at six o'clock** a las seis; **at night** *Esp* por la noche, *Am* en la noche; **at first** al principio; **at last** por fin; **at once** enseguida; **at that time** entonces; **at the moment** ahora
  (**d**) *(manner)* a, en; **at best/worst** en el mejor/peor de los casos; **at hand** a mano;

at least por lo menos; **not at all** en absoluto; *(don't mention it)* de nada (**e**) *(rate)* a; **they retail at 100 euros each** se venden a 100 euros la unidad; **two at a time** de dos en dos

ate [et, eɪt] *pt of* **eat**

atheist ['eɪθɪɪst] *n* ateo(a) *m,f*

Athens ['æθɪnz] *n* Atenas

athlete ['æθliːt] *n* atleta *mf*

athletic [æθ'letɪk] **1** *adj* atlético(a) **2** *npl* **athletics** *Br (track and field)* atletismo *m*; *US* deportes *mpl*

Atlantic [ət'læntɪk] *adj* **the A. (Ocean)** el (océano) Atlántico

atlas ['ætləs] *n* atlas *m*

ATM [eɪtiː'em] *n Fin (abbr* **automated teller machine)** cajero automático

atmosphere ['ætməsfɪə(r)] *n* atmósfera *f*; *Fig (ambience)* ambiente *m*

atmospheric [ætməs'ferɪk] *adj* atmosférico(a)

atom ['ætəm] *n* átomo *m*; **a. bomb** bomba atómica

atomic [ə'tɒmɪk] *adj* atómico(a)

atone [ə'təʊn] *vi* **to a. for** expiar

atrocious [ə'trəʊʃəs] *adj* atroz

atrocity [ə'trɒsɪtɪ] *n* atrocidad *f*

attach [ə'tætʃ] *vt (stick)* pegar; *(fasten)* sujetar; *(document)* adjuntar; **to a. importance to sth** dar importancia a algo; *Fig* **to be attached to** *(be fond of)* tener cariño a

attaché [ə'tæʃeɪ] *n* agregado(a) *m,f*; **a. case** maletín *m*

attachment [ə'tætʃmənt] *n* (**a**) *Tech* accesorio *m*; *(action)* acoplamiento *m* (**b**) *(fondness)* apego *m* (**to** por) (**c**) *Comput (to e-mail)* archivo adjunto, anexo *m*

attack [ə'tæk] **1** *n* (**a**) *(assault)* ataque *m*, asalto *m*; **an a. on sb's life** un atentado contra la vida de algn (**b**) *Med* ataque *m* **2** *vt (assault)* atacar, asaltar; *Fig (problem)* abordar; *(job)* emprender; *Fig (criticize)* atacar

attacker [ə'tækə(r)] *n* asaltante *mf*, agresor(a) *m,f*

attain [ə'teɪn] *vt (aim)* lograr; *(rank, age)* llegar a

attainment [ə'teɪnmənt] *n (achievement)* logro *m*; *(skill)* talento *m*

attempt [ə'tempt] **1** *n* intento *m*, tentativa *f*; **at the second a.** a la segunda; **an a. on sb's life** un atentado contra la vida de algn **2** *vt* intentar; **to a. to do sth** tratar de *or* intentar hacer algo; *Jur* **attempted**

murder/rape intento *m* de asesinato/ violación

attend [ə'tend] **1** *vt (be present at)* asistir a; *(care for, wait on)* atender **2** *vi (be present)* asistir; *(pay attention)* prestar atención

▸**attend to** *vt insep (business)* ocuparse de; *(in shop)* atender a

attendance [ə'tendəns] *n* asistencia *f*

attendant [ə'tendənt] *n (in cinema etc)* acomodador(a) *m,f*; *(in museum)* guía *mf*; *(in car park)* vigilante(a) *m,f*

attention [ə'tenʃən] *n* (**a**) *(in general)* atención *f*; **for the a. of Miss Jones** a la atención de la Srta. Jones; **pay a.!** ¡atiende!; **to pay a. to sth/sb** prestar atención a algo/algn (**b**) *Mil* **a.!** ¡firmes!; **to stand to a.** estar firmes

attentive [ə'tentɪv] *adj (listener)* atento(a); *(helpful)* solícito(a)

attest [ə'test] *vi* **to a.** dar testimonio de

attic ['ætɪk] *n* ático *m*

attire [ə'taɪə(r)] *n Fml* traje *m*

attitude ['ætɪtjuːd] *n* actitud *f*; *(position of body)* postura *f*; **an a. of mind** un estado de ánimo

attorney [ə'tɜːnɪ] *n* (**a**) *US (lawyer)* abogado(a) *m,f*; **A. General** ≃ Ministro(a) *m,f* de Justicia; **district a.** fiscal *mf* (**b**) *Jur* **power of a.** poderes *mpl*

attract [ə'trækt] *vt* atraer; **to a. attention** llamar la atención; **to a. a waiter's attention** llamar a un camarero

attraction [ə'trækʃən] *n* (**a**) *(power)* atracción *f* (**b**) *(attractive thing)* atractivo *m*; *(charm)* encanto *m*; *(incentive)* aliciente *m*; **the main a.** el número fuerte

attractive [ə'træktɪv] *adj* atractivo(a)

attribute¹ ['ætrɪbjuːt] *n (quality)* atributo *m*

attribute² [ə'trɪbjuːt] *vt* atribuir

attrition [ə'trɪʃən] *n* **war of a.** guerra *f* de desgaste

aubergine ['əʊbəʒiːn] *n Br* berenjena *f*

auburn ['ɔːbən] *adj* castaño rojizo *inv*

auction ['ɔːkʃən] **1** *n* subasta *f* **2** *vt* subastar

auctioneer [ɔːkʃə'nɪə(r)] *n* subastador(a) *m,f*

audacious [ɔː'deɪʃəs] *adj (daring)* audaz; *(bold)* atrevido(a); *(impudent)* descarado(a)

audacity [ɔː'dæsɪtɪ] *n* audacia *f*

audible ['ɔːdɪbəl] *adj* audible

audience ['ɔːdɪəns] *n* (**a**) *(spectators)* público *m*; *(at concert, conference)* auditorio *m*; *(television)* telespectadores *mpl* (**b**) *(meeting)* audiencia *f*

audiobook ['ɔːdɪəʊbʊk] *n* audiolibro *m*

audio-visual [ˌɔːdɪəʊ'vɪzjʊəl] *adj* audiovisual; **a. aids** apoyo *m* audiovisual

audit ['ɔːdɪt] **1** *n* revisión *f* de cuentas
2 *vt* revisar, intervenir

audition [ɔː'dɪʃən] **1** *n* prueba *f*
2 *vt* **to a. sb for a part** probar a algn para un papel

auditor ['ɔːdɪtə(r)] *n* revisor(a) *m,f* de cuentas

auditorium [ɔːdɪ'tɔːrɪəm] *n* auditorio *m*

augment [ɔːg'ment] *vt* aumentar

augur ['ɔːgə(r)] *vi* **to a. well** ser de buen agüero

August ['ɔːgəst] *n* agosto *m*

aunt [ɑːnt] *n* (*also Fam* **auntie, aunty** ['ɑːntɪ]) tía *f*

au pair [əʊ'peə(r)] *n* **au pair (girl)** au pair *f*

aura ['ɔːrə] *n* aura *f*; *Rel* aureola *f*

aural ['ɔːrəl] *adj* auditivo(a), del oído

auspices ['ɔːspɪsɪz] *npl* **under the a. of** bajo los auspicios de

auspicious [ɔː'spɪʃəs] *adj* de buen augurio

austere [ɒ'stɪə(r)] *adj* austero(a)

austerity [ɒ'sterɪtɪ] *n* austeridad *f*

Australia [ɒ'streɪlɪə] *n* Australia

Australian [ɒ'streɪlɪən] *adj & n* australiano(a) *(m,f)*

Austria ['ɒstrɪə] *n* Austria

Austrian ['ɒstrɪən] *adj & n* austríaco(a) *(m,f)*

authentic [ɔː'θentɪk] *adj* auténtico(a)

author ['ɔːθə(r)] *n* autor(a) *m,f*

authoritarian [ɔːθɒrɪ'teərɪən] *adj* autoritario(a)

authoritative [ɔː'θɒrɪtətɪv] *adj* (*reliable*) autorizado(a); (*authoritarian*) autoritario(a)

authority [ɔː'θɒrɪtɪ] *n* autoridad *f*; **local a.** ayuntamiento *m*

authorization [ɔːθəraɪ'zeɪʃən] *n* autorización *f*

authorize ['ɔːθəraɪz] *vt* autorizar; **to a. sb to do sth** autorizar a algn a hacer algo

autistic [ɔː'tɪstɪk] *adj* autista

auto ['ɔːtəʊ] *n US* automóvil *m*, *Esp* coche *m*, *Am* carro *m*, *RP* auto *m*

autobiography [ɔːtəʊbaɪ'ɒgrəfɪ] *n* autobiografía *f*

autograph ['ɔːtəgrɑːf] **1** *n* autógrafo *m*
2 *vt* (*sign*) firmar; (*book, photo*) dedicar

automata [ɔː'tɒmətə] *pl of* **automaton**

automatic [ɔːtə'mætɪk] **1** *adj* automático(a)
2 *n* (*car*) *Esp* coche *or Am* carro *or RP* auto (con cambio) automático; (*gun*) pistola automática

automatically [ɔːtə'mætɪklɪ] *adv* automáticamente

automation [ɔːtə'meɪʃən] *n* automatización *f*; **office a.** ofimática *f*

automaton [ɔː'tɒmətən] *n* (*pl* **automata**) autómata *m*

automobile ['ɔːtəməbiːl] *n US* automóvil *m*, *Esp* coche *m*, *Am* carro *m*, *RP* auto *m*

autonomous [ɔː'tɒnəməs] *adj* autónomo(a)

autonomy [ɔː'tɒnəmɪ] *n* autonomía *f*

autopsy ['ɔːtɒpsɪ] *n* autopsia *f*

autumn ['ɔːtəm] *n* otoño *m*

auxiliary [ɔːg'zɪljərɪ] *adj* auxiliar

Av., av. (*abbr* **Avenue**) Av., Avda.

avail [ə'veɪl] **1** *n* **to no a.** en vano
2 *vt* **to a. oneself of sth** aprovecharse de algo

availability [əveɪlə'bɪlɪtɪ] *n* disponibilidad *f*

available [ə'veɪləbəl] *adj* (*thing*) disponible; (*person*) libre

avalanche ['ævəlɑːnʃ] *n* avalancha *f*

avarice ['ævərɪs] *n* avaricia *f*

Ave (*abbr* **Avenue**) Av., Avda.

avenge [ə'vendʒ] *vt* vengar

avenue ['ævɪnjuː] *n* avenida *f*; *Fig* vía *f*

average ['ævərɪdʒ] **1** *n* promedio *m*, media *f*; **on a.** por término medio
2 *adj* (*mean, typical*) medio(a); (*unexceptional*) regular
3 *vt* sacar la media de; **he averages eight hours' work a day** trabaja una media de ocho horas al día
▸ **average out at** *vt insep* salir a una media de

averse [ə'vɜːs] *adj* **to be a. to sth** ser reacio(a) a algo

aversion [ə'vɜːʃən] *n* (*feeling*) aversión *f*; (*thing*) bestia negra

avert [ə'vɜːt] *vt* (*eyes, thoughts*) apartar (**from** de); (*accident*) impedir; (*danger*) evitar

aviation [eɪvɪ'eɪʃən] *n* aviación *f*

avid ['ævɪd] *adj* (*reader*) voraz

avidly ['ævɪdlɪ] *adv* vorazmente

avocado [ævə'kɑːdəʊ] *n* **a. (pear)** aguacate *m*, *Andes, CSur* palta *f*

avoid [ə'vɔɪd] *vt* (*person, thing*) evitar; (*punishment, danger, question*) evitar, eludir

avoidable [ə'vɔɪdəbəl] *adj* evitable

await [ə'weɪt] *vt* esperar, *Esp* aguardar

awake [ə'weɪk] **1** *adj* despierto(a); **to be a.** estar despierto(a)

2 *vt* (*pt* **awoke, awaked**; *pp* **awoken, awaked**) despertar

awaken [ə'weɪkən] *vt & vi* (*pt* **awakened**; *pp* **awoken**) = **awake 2**

awakening [ə'weɪkənɪŋ] *n* despertar *m*

award [ə'wɔːd] **1** *n* (*prize*) premio *m*; (*medal*) condecoración *f*; *Jur* indemnización *f*; (*grant*) beca *f*

  2 *vt* (*prize*) conceder, otorgar; (*medal*) dar; (*damages*) adjudicar

aware [ə'weə(r)] *adj* (*informed*) enterado(a); **not that I'm a. of** que yo sepa no; **to be a. of sth** ser consciente de algo; **to become a. of sth** darse cuenta de algo

awareness [ə'weənɪs] *n* conciencia *f* (**of** de)

awash [ə'wɒʃ] *adj* inundado(a) (**with** de)

away [ə'weɪ] *adv* **far a.** lejos; **go a.!** ¡lárgate!; **it's 3 miles a.** está a 3 millas (de distancia); **keep a. from the fire!** ¡no te acerques al fuego!; **right a.** en seguida; **to be a.** (*absent*) estar ausente; (*out*) estar fuera; **to die a.** desvanecerse; **to give sth a.** regalar algo; (*secret*) revelar algo; **to go a.** irse; *Sport* **to play a.** jugar fuera; **to turn a.** volver la cara; **to work a.** trabajar

awe [ɔː] *n* (*fear*) temor *m*; (*amazement*) asombro *m*; **he was in a. of his father** le intimidaba su padre

awe-inspiring ['ɔːɪnspaɪərɪŋ] *adj* impresionante, imponente

awesome ['ɔːsəm] *adj* impresionante

awful ['ɔːfʊl] *adj Fam* espantoso(a); **an a. lot of people** un montón de gente, *Am salvo RP* harta gente

awfully ['ɔːfʊlɪ] *adv Fam* terriblemente

awkward ['ɔːkwəd] *adj* (*clumsy*) torpe; (*difficult*) pesado(a); (*object*) incómodo(a); (*moment*) inoportuno(a); (*situation*) embarazoso(a); (*problem*) difícil

awning ['ɔːnɪŋ] *n* (*on ship*) toldo *m*; (*on shop*) marquesina *f*

awoke [ə'wəʊk] *pt of* **awake**

awoken [ə'wəʊkən] *pp of* **awake, awaken**

axe, *US* **ax** [æks] **1** *n* hacha *f*

  2 *vt Fig* (*jobs*) eliminar; (*costs*) reducir; (*plan*) cancelar; (*person*) despedir

axis ['æksɪs] *n* (*pl* **axes** ['æksiːz]) eje *m*

axle ['æksəl] *n* eje *m*; *Tech* árbol *m*

ayatollah [aɪə'tɒlə] *n* ayatolá *m*

Aztec ['æztek] *adj & n* azteca (*mf*)

B

B, b [biː] *n* (a) *(the letter)* B, b *f*; *BrAut* **B road** carretera secundaria (b) *Mus* **B** si *m*; **B flat** si bemol

BA [biːˈeɪ] *n* *(abbr* **Bachelor of Arts)** *(person)* licenciado(a) *m,f* en Filosofía y Letras

babble [ˈbæbəl] *vi* (baby) balbucear; *(brook)* murmurar

babe [beɪb] *n* (a) *(baby)* bebé *m*, *Andes* guagua *mf*, *RP* nene(a) *m,f*(b) *Fam* nena *f*, bombón *m*

baboon [bəˈbuːn] *n* zambo *m*

baby [ˈbeɪbɪ] *n* (a) *(infant)* bebé *m*, *Andes* guagua *mf*, *RP* nene(a) *m,f*; *Br* **B. Buggy®** sillita *f* de paseo *or* de niño; *US* **b. buggy** *or* **carriage** cochecito *m* de niño; **b. face** cara *f* de niño (b) *Fam (darling)* querido(a) *m,f*

baby-sit [ˈbeɪbɪsɪt] *vi* cuidar a niños, hacer de *Esp* canguro *or* *Am* babysitter

baby-sitter [ˈbeɪbɪsɪtə(r)] *n* *Esp* canguro *mf*, *Am* babysitter *mf*

baby-walker [ˈbeɪbɪwɔːkə(r)] *n* *Br* taca-taca *m*

bachelor [ˈbætʃələ(r)] *n* soltero *m*; *Univ* **B. of Arts/Science** licenciado(a) *m,f* en Filosofía y Letras/Ciencias

back [bæk] **1** *n* (a) *(of person)* espalda *f*; *(of animal)* lomo *m*; **b. to front** al revés; *Fig* **to get sb's b. up** poner negro a algn; *Fig* **to have one's b. to the wall** estar en un aprieto (b) *(of book)* lomo *m*; *(of chair)* respaldo *m*; *(of coin)* reverso *m*; *(of hand)* dorso *m*; *(of house, car)* parte *f* de atrás (c) *(of stage, cupboard)* fondo *m* (d) *Ftb* defensa *mf* (e) *US* **in b. (of)** *(behind)* en la parte de atrás (de), detrás (de); *(to the rear of)* al fondo de)

2 *adj* (a) *(in space)* trasero(a), de atrás; **b. door** puerta *f* de atrás; **b. seat** asiento *m* de detrás (b) *(in time)* **b. rent** alquiler *m* or *Am* renta *f* pendiente de pago; **b. pay** atrasos *mpl*

3 *adv* (c) *(to the rear)* atrás; *(towards the rear)* hacia atrás; **b. and forth** de acá para allá (d) **some years b.** hace unos años

4 *vt* (a) *(support)* apoyar, respaldar (b) *Fin* financiar (c) *(bet on)* apostar por (d) *(car etc)* dar marcha atrás a

5 *vi* (a) *(move backwards)* retroceder (b) *(car etc)* dar marcha atrás

▸ **back away** *vi* retirarse

▸ **back down** *vi* echarse atrás

▸ **back off** *vi* desistir

▸ **back out** *vi* *(withdraw)* retractarse, volverse atrás

▸ **back up 1** *vt sep* (a) *(support)* apoyar (b) *Comput (file)* hacer una copia de seguridad de
2 *vi Aut* ir marcha atrás

backache [ˈbækeɪk] *n* dolor *m* de espalda

backbencher [bækˈbentʃə(r)] *n* *Br* diputado(a) *m,f* ordinario(a) *(sin cargo en el Gobierno o la oposición)*

backbiting [ˈbækbaɪtɪŋ] *n* *Fam* chismorreo *m*, murmuración *f*, *RP* chusmerío *m*

backbone [ˈbækbəʊn] *n* *Anat* columna *f*

backcloth [ˈbækklɒθ] *n* telón *m* de fondo

backdate [bækˈdeɪt] *vt* antedatar

backdated [bækˈdeɪtɪd] *adj* con efecto retroactivo

backdrop [ˈbækdrɒp] *n* telón *m* de fondo

backer [ˈbækə(r)] *n* (a) *Fin* promotor(a) *m,f* (b) *Pol* partidario(a) *m,f* (c) *(person who bets)* apostante *mf*

backfire [bækˈfaɪə(r)] *vi* (a) *Aut* petardear (b) *Fig* **our plan backfired** nos salió el tiro por la culata

background [ˈbækgraʊnd] *n* (a) *(in scene, painting, view)* fondo *m*; **to stay in the b.** quedarse en segundo plano; **b. music** música *f* de fondo (b) *(of person) (social)* origen *m*; *(past)* pasado *m*; *(education)* formación *f* (c) *(circumstances)* antecedentes *mpl*

backhand [ˈbækhænd] *n* *Sport* revés *m*

backhanded [ˈbækhændɪd] *adj* equívoco(a), ambiguo(a)

backhander [ˈbækhændə(r)] *n* *Br Fam (bribe)* soborno *m*, *Andes, RP* coima *f*, *CAm, Méx* mordida *f*

backing [ˈbækɪŋ] *n* (a) *(support)* apoyo *m*; *Com & Fin* respaldo financiero (b) *Mus* acompañamiento *m*

backlash [ˈbæklæʃ] *n* reacción violenta y repentina

backlog [ˈbæklɒg] *n* **to have a b. of work** tener un montón de trabajo atrasado

backpack ['bækpæk] *n* mochila *f*

backpedal [bæk'pedəl] *vi Fam* dar marcha atrás

backside [bæk'saɪd] *n Fam* trasero *m*, culo *m*

backstage [bæk'steɪdʒ] *adv* entre bastidores

backstroke ['bækstrəʊk] *n* espalda *f*

backtrack ['bæktræk] *vi Fig* volverse atrás

backup ['bækʌp] *n* (a) *(support)* apoyo *m*, respaldo *m*; *Comput* b. (file) fichero *m* de apoyo (b) *US (of traffic)* caravana *f*

backward ['bækwəd] **1** *adj* (a) *(movement)* hacia atrás (b) *(country)* subdesarrollado(a); *(child)* retrasado(a)
2 *adv esp US* hacia atrás

backwards ['bækwədz] *adv* hacia atrás; **to walk b.** andar de espaldas

backyard [bæk'jɑːd] *n* patio trasero; *US* jardín trasero

bacon ['beɪkən] *n* panceta *f*, *Méx* tocino *m*, *Esp* bacon, *Esp* beicon *m*

bacteria [bæk'tɪərɪə] *npl* bacterias *fpl*

bad [bæd] *adj* (a) *(worse, worst)* (a) *(poor)* malo(a); **to go from b. to worse** ir de mal en peor (b) *(decayed)* podrido(a); **to go b.** echarse a perder (c) **that's too b.!** ¡qué pena! (d) *(wicked)* malo(a); **to use b. language** ser mal hablado(a) (e) *(accident)* grave; *(headache)* fuerte (f) *(ill)* enfermo(a) (g) *Fin* **b. debt** deuda *f* incobrable

bade [bæd, beɪd] *pt of* bid

badge [bædʒ] *n* insignia *f*; *(metal disc)* chapa *f*

badger ['bædʒə(r)] **1** *n* tejón *m*
2 *vt* acosar

badly ['bædlɪ] *adv* (a) *(not well)* mal; **he did b. in the exam** le salió mal el examen; **to be b. off** andar mal de dinero (b) *(seriously)* gravemente (c) *(very much)* mucho; **to miss sb b.** echar mucho de menos a algn; **we need it b.** nos hace mucha falta

bad-mannered [bæd'mænəd] *adj* maleducado(a)

badminton ['bædmɪntən] *n* bádminton *m*

bad-tempered [bæd'tempəd] *adj* **to be b.** *(temperament)* tener mal genio; *(temporarily)* estar de mal humor

baffle ['bæfəl] **1** *vt* desconcertar
2 *n Tech* pantalla acústica

baffling ['bæflɪŋ] *adj* incomprensible, enigmático(a)

bag [bæg] *n* (a) *(large)* bolsa *f*; *(handbag)* bolso *m*, *Andes*, *RP* cartera *f*, *Méx* bolsa; *Fam* **bags of** montones de; **travel b.** bolsa de viaje (b) *(hunting)* caza *f*; *Fam* **it's in** **the b.** es cosa hecha (c) *Br very Fam Pej* **old b.** *(woman)* bruja *f* (d) **to have bags under one's eyes** tener ojeras

baggage ['bægɪdʒ] *n* equipaje *m*; **b. handler** mozo(a) *m,f* de equipajes

baggy ['bægɪ] *adj* (**baggier, baggiest**) holgado(a); **b. trousers** pantalones anchos

bagpipes ['bægpaɪps] *npl* gaita *f*

Bahamas [bə'hɑːməz] *npl* **the B.** las Bahamas

bail¹ [beɪl] *n Jur* fianza *f*; **on b.** bajo fianza; **to stand** *or US* **post b. for sb** salir fiador por algn
▸ **bail out** *vt sep Fig (person)* sacar de apuros a

bail² [beɪl] *vi Naut* **to b. (out)** achicar

bailiff ['beɪlɪf] *n* (a) *Jur* alguacil *m* (b) *(steward)* administrador *m*

bait [beɪt] **1** *n* cebo *m*; **to rise to the b.** tragar el anzuelo, picar
2 *vt* (a) *(for fishing)* cebar (b) *(torment)* hostigar

baize [beɪz] *n* bayeta *f*; **green b.** tapete *m* verde

bake [beɪk] **1** *vt* (a) *(bread, cake)* cocer al horno; *(potatoes)* asar (b) *(dry, harden)* resecar
2 *vi Fam* hacer mucho calor

baked [beɪkt] *adj* al horno; **b. potato** patata *f or Am* papa *f* al horno

baker ['beɪkə(r)] *n* panadero(a) *m,f*

bakery ['beɪkərɪ] *n* panadería *f*

baking ['beɪkɪŋ] *n* cocción *f*; **b. dish** fuente *f* para horno; **b. powder** levadura *f* en polvo; **b. tin** molde *m*

balaclava [bælə'klɑːvə] *n* pasamontañas *m inv*

balance ['bæləns] **1** *n* (a) *(scales)* balanza *f*; *Fig* **to hang in the b.** estar en juego (b) *(equilibrium)* equilibrio *m*; *Pol* **b. of power** equilibrio de fuerzas (c) *Fin* saldo *m*; **b. of payments** balanza *f* de pagos; **b. sheet** balance *m*; **credit b.** saldo acreedor (d) *(remainder)* resto *m*
2 *vt* (a) *(object)* poner en equilibrio (**on** en) (b) *(budget)* ajustar; **to b. the books** hacer que cuadren las cuentas (c) *(consider)* sopesar
3 *vi* guardar el equilibrio
▸ **balance out** *vi (figures)* corresponderse

balanced ['bælənst] *adj* equilibrado(a)

balcony ['bælkənɪ] *n* balcón *m*; *Th* anfiteatro *m*

bald [bɔːld] *adj* (a) *(person)* calvo(a) (b) *(tyre)* desgastado(a) (c) *(style)* escueto(a)

baldness ['bɔːldnɪs] *n* (a) *(of person)* calvicie *f* (b) *(of tyre)* desgaste *m* (c) *(of style)* sencillez *f*

bale¹ [beɪl] **1** n (of cloth) fardo m
2 vt embalar

bale² [beɪl] vt = **bail²**

▸ **bale out 1** vi Av saltar en paracaídas de un avión
2 vt sep Fig (person) sacar de apuros a

Balearic [bælɪˈærɪk] adj the B. Islands las Islas Baleares

baleful [ˈbeɪlfʊl] adj funesto(a), siniestro(a)

Balkans [ˈbɔːlkəns] npl the B. los Balcanes

ball¹ [bɔːl] n (a) (in cricket, tennis etc) pelota f; Ftb balón m; (in billiards, golf etc) bola f; Fig the b. is in your court ahora te toca a ti; Fig to play b. with sb cooperar con algn; Fam to be on the b. ser un(a) espabilado(a); Tech b. bearing rodamiento m de bolas; b. game (in general) juego m de pelota; US (baseball match) partido m de béisbol m; Fig it's a whole new b. game es otra historia (b) (of paper) bola f; (of wool) ovillo m

ball² [bɔːl] n (dance) baile m

ballad [ˈbæləd] n balada f

ballast [ˈbæləst] n Naut lastre m

ballerina [bæləˈriːnə] n bailarina f

ballet [ˈbæleɪ] n ballet m; b. dancer bailarín(ina) m,f

ballistic [bəˈlɪstɪk] adj balístico(a)

ballistics [bəˈlɪstɪks] n sing balística f

balloon [bəˈluːn] **1** n (a) (for party, travel) globo m (b) (in cartoon) bocadillo m
2 vi (swell) hincharse como un globo; (grow dramatically) dispararse

ballot [ˈbælət] **1** n votación f; b. box urna f; b. paper papeleta f (de voto), Chile, Méx voto m, Col tarjetón m, RP boleta f
2 vt (membership) consultar por votación

ballpark [ˈbɔːlpɑːk] n US campo m de béisbol; Fig a b. figure una cifra aproximada

ballpoint [ˈbɔːlpɔɪnt] n b. (pen) bolígrafo m, Carib, Méx pluma f, Col, Ecuad estereográfico m, CSur lapicera f

ballroom [ˈbɔːlruːm] n salón m de baile

ballyhoo [bælɪˈhuː] n Fam (fuss) alboroto m, Esp escandalera f, RP batifondo m

balm [bɑːm] n bálsamo m

balmy [ˈbɑːmɪ] adj (balmier, balmiest) (weather) suave

Baltic [ˈbɔːltɪk] adj báltico(a); the B. (Sea) el (mar) Báltico

balustrade [ˈbæləstreɪd] n barandilla f

bamboo [bæmˈbuː] n bambú m

bamboozle [bæmˈbuːzəl] vt Fam (a) (puzzle) dejar perplejo(a) (b) (trick) engañar, embaucar

ban [bæn] **1** n prohibición f
2 vt (a) (prohibit) prohibir (b) (exclude) excluir

banal [bəˈnɑːl] adj banal, trivial

banana [bəˈnɑːnə] n plátano m, CAm, Col banano m, Ven cambur m, RP banana f; Fam to be bananas (mad) estar como una cabra or Méx destrompado(a) or RP de la nuca

band [bænd] **1** n (a) (strip) tira f; (ribbon) cinta f (b) (stripe) raya f (c) (group) grupo m; (of youths) pandilla f; (of thieves) banda f (d) Mus banda f
2 vi to b. together unirse, juntarse

bandage [ˈbændɪdʒ] **1** n venda f
2 vt vendar

Band-Aid® [ˈbændeɪd] n US Esp tirita® f, Am curita f

bandit [ˈbændɪt] n bandido m

bandstand [ˈbændstænd] n quiosco m de música

bandwagon [ˈbændwægən] n Fig to jump on the b. subirse al tren

bandwidth [ˈbændwɪdθ] n Comput ancho m de banda

bandy [ˈbændɪ] **1** vt (words, ideas) intercambiar
2 adj (bandier, bandiest) torcido(a) hacia fuera

▸ **bandy about** vt sep (ideas) propagar, difundir

bandy-legged [ˈbændɪˈleg(ɪ)d] adj patizambo(a)

bang [bæŋ] **1** n (a) (blow) golpe m (b) (noise) ruido m; (explosion) estallido m; (of gun) estampido m
2 npl US bangs flequillo m, Am cerquillo m (corto)
3 vt golpear; to b. sth shut cerrar algo de golpe
4 vi golpear; to b. shut cerrarse de golpe
5 interj (blow) ¡zas!; b., b.! (of gun) ¡pum, pum!
6 adv Fam justo

banger [ˈbæŋə(r)] n (a) (firework) petardo m (b) Fam (sausage) salchicha f (c) Fam old b. (car) tartana f

bangle [ˈbæŋgəl] n brazalete m

banish [ˈbænɪʃ] vt desterrar

banister [ˈbænɪstə(r)] n pasamanos m inv

banjo [ˈbændʒəʊ] n (pl banjos) banjo m

bank¹ [bæŋk] **1** n (a) (financial institution) banco m; b. account cuenta bancaria; b. card tarjeta bancaria; b. clerk empleado(a) m,f de banca; b. draft letra bancaria; Br b. holiday fiesta f nacional; b. statement extracto m de cuenta (b) (in gambling) banca f (c) (store) banco m

2 *vt (money, cheque)* depositar, *Esp* ingresar
3 *vi* **to b. with** tener una cuenta en
▸ **bank on** *vt insep* contar con
bank² [bæŋk] **1** *n* (**a**) *(mound)* loma *f*; *(embankment)* terraplén *m* (**b**) *(of river)* ribera *f*; *(edge)* orilla *f*
2 *vt Av* ladear
3 *vi Av* ladearse
bankbook ['bæŋkbʊk] *n* libreta *f* de ahorros
banker ['bæŋkə(r)] *n* banquero(a) *m,f*
banking ['bæŋkɪŋ] *n* banca *f*
banknote ['bæŋknəʊt] *n* billete *m* de banco
bankrupt ['bæŋkrʌpt] **1** *adj* en quiebra; **to go b.** quebrar
2 *vt* llevar a la bancarrota
bankruptcy ['bæŋkrʌptsɪ] *n* quiebra *f*, bancarrota *f*
banner ['bænə(r)] *n (in demonstration)* pancarta *f*; *(flag)* bandera *f*
banns [bænz] *npl* amonestaciones *fpl*
banquet ['bæŋkwɪt] *n* banquete *m*
banter ['bæntə(r)] **1** *n* bromas *fpl*
2 *vi* bromear
bap [bæp] *n Br* = panecillo blando redondo
baptism ['bæptɪzəm] *n* bautismo *m*
Baptist ['bæptɪst] *n* baptista *mf*, bautista *mf*
baptize [bæp'taɪz, *US* 'bæptaɪz] *vt* bautizar
bar [bɑː(r)] **1** *n* (**a**) *(of gold)* barra *f*; *(of chocolate)* tableta *f*; *(of soap)* pastilla *f*; *Com* **b. code** código *m* de barras (**b**) *(of cage)* barrote *m*; *Fam* **to be behind bars** estar en la cárcel (**c**) *(obstacle)* obstáculo *m* (**d**) *Jur (dock)* banquillo *m*; *(court)* tribunal *m* (**e**) *Jur* **the B.** *Br (barristers)* = conjunto de los abogados que ejercen en tribunales superiores; *US (lawyers in general)* la abogacía (**f**) *(pub)* bar *m*; *(counter)* barra *f* (**g**) *Mus* compás *m*
2 *vt* (**a**) *(door)* atrancar; *(road)* cortar (**b**) *(exclude)* excluir (**from** de) (**c**) *(prohibit)* prohibir
3 *prep* salvo; **b. none** sin excepción
barbarian [bɑː'beərɪən] *adj & n* bárbaro(a) *(m,f)*
barbaric [bɑː'bærɪk] *adj* bárbaro(a)
barbecue ['bɑːbɪkjuː] **1** *n* barbacoa *f*, *Andes, RP* asado *m*
2 *vt* asar en la barbacoa
barbed [bɑːbd] *adj* (**a**) **b. wire** alambre *m* de púas (**b**) *Fig (remark)* mordaz
barber ['bɑːbə(r)] *n* barbero(a) *m,f*; **b.'s (shop)** barbería *f*

barbiturate [bɑː'bɪtjʊrɪt] *n* barbitúrico *m*
bare [beə(r)] **1** *adj* (**a**) *(not covered)* desnudo(a); *(head)* descubierto(a); *(foot)* descalzo(a); *(room)* vacío(a); **to lay b.** poner al descubierto; **with his b. hands** sólo con las manos (**b**) *(basic)* mero(a); **the b. minimum** lo mínimo
2 *vt* descubrir
bareback(ed) ['beə'bæk(t)] *adv* **to ride b.** montar un caballo a pelo
barefaced ['beəfeɪst] *adj* desvergonzado(a)
barefoot ['beə'fʊt] *adj & adv* descalzo(a)
barely ['beəlɪ] *adv* apenas
bargain ['bɑːgɪn] **1** *n* (**a**) *(agreement)* pacto *m*; *(deal)* negocio *m*; **into the b.** por añadidura, además; **to drive a hard b.** imponer condiciones duras; **to strike a b.** cerrar un trato (**b**) *(cheap purchase)* ganga *f*; **b. price** precio *m* de oferta
2 *vi* (**a**) *(negotiate)* negociar (**b**) *(haggle)* regatear
▸ **bargain for** *vt insep* esperar, contar con
barge [bɑːdʒ] **1** *n* gabarra *f*
2 *vi Fam* **to b. into** *(room)* irrumpir en; *(person)* tropezar con
▸ **barge in** *vi Fam* (**a**) *(go in)* entrar sin permiso (**b**) *(interfere)* entrometerse
baritone ['bærɪtəʊn] *adj & n* barítono *(m)*
bark¹ [bɑːk] **1** *n* ladrido *m*
2 *vi (dog)* ladrar
bark² [bɑːk] *n Bot* corteza *f*
barley ['bɑːlɪ] *n* cebada *f*; **b. sugar** azúcar *m* cande
barmaid ['bɑːmeɪd] *n esp Br* camarera *f*, *Am* mesera *f*, *RP* moza *f*
barman ['bɑːmən] *n* camarero *m*, *Am* mesero *m*, *RP* mozo *m*
barn [bɑːn] *n* granero *m*; **b. dance** baile *m* popular
barnacle ['bɑːnəkəl] *n* percebe *m*
barnyard ['bɑːnjɑːd] *n* corral *m*
barometer [bə'rɒmɪtə(r)] *n* barómetro *m*
baron ['bærən] *n* barón *m*
baroness ['bærənɪs] *n* baronesa *f*
baroque [bə'rɒk] *adj* barroco(a)
barrack ['bærək] *vt Br (heckle)* abuchear
barracks ['bærəks] *n Mil* cuartel *m*
barrage ['bærɑːdʒ] *n* (**a**) *(dam)* presa *f* (**b**) *Mil* barrera *f* de fuego (**c**) *Fig (of questions)* lluvia *f*
barrel ['bærəl] *n* (**a**) *(of wine)* tonel *m*; *(of beer, oil)* barril *m* (**b**) *(of firearm)* cañón *m*
barren ['bærən] *adj (land, woman)* yermo(a); *(landscape)* árido(a)
barricade [bærɪ'keɪd] **1** *n* barricada *f*
2 *vt* poner barricadas en; **to b. oneself in** parapetarse

barrier ['bærɪə(r)] n barrera f

barring ['bɑːrɪŋ] prep salvo, excepto; **b. a miracle** a menos que ocurra un milagro

barrister ['bærɪstə(r)] n Br abogado(a) m,f (que ejerce en tribunales superiores)

barrow ['bærəʊ] n carretilla f

bartender ['bɑːtendə(r)] n US camarero m, Am mesero m, RP barman m

barter ['bɑːtə(r)] vt trocar (**for** por)

base [beɪs] **1** n base f; (of company) sede f central; **air/naval b.** base aérea/naval
2 vt (**a**) (found) basar (**on** en) (**b**) (troops) estacionar
3 adj (**a**) Fml (despicable) bajo(a), despreciable (**b**) (metal) común

baseball ['beɪsbɔːl] n béisbol m

baseline ['beɪslaɪn] n (in tennis) línea f de saque

basement ['beɪsmənt] n sótano m

bases ['beɪsiːz] pl of **basis**

bash [bæʃ] **1** n (heavy blow) golpetazo m; (dent) bollo m; Fam (attempt) intento m
2 vt golpear

bashful ['bæʃfʊl] adj tímido(a)

basic ['beɪsɪk] **1** adj básico(a); **b. pay** sueldo m base
2 npl **the basics** lo fundamental

basically ['beɪsɪklɪ] adv fundamentalmente

basil [Br 'bæzəl, US 'beɪzəl] n albahaca f

basin ['beɪsən] n (**a**) (for cooking) recipiente m, bol m; (for washing hands) lavabo m, Am lavamanos m inv; (plastic, for washing up) palangana f, Esp barreño m (**b**) (of river) cuenca f

basis ['beɪsɪs] n (pl **bases**) base f; **on the b. of** en base a

bask [bɑːsk] vi tostarse; **to b. in the sun** tomar el sol

basket ['bɑːskɪt] n cesta f; (in basketball) canasta f

basketball ['bɑːskɪtbɔːl] n baloncesto m

Basque [bæsk, bɑːsk] **1** adj vasco(a); **B. Country** País Vasco, Euskadi; **B. flag** ikurriña f; **B. nationalist** abertzale mf
2 n (**a**) (person) vasco(a) m,f (**b**) (language) vasco m, euskera m

bass¹ [bæs] n inv (seawater) lubina f; (freshwater) perca f

bass² [beɪs] **1** n (**a**) (singer) bajo m (**b**) (notes) graves mpl; **b. drum** bombo m; **b. guitar** bajo m
2 adj bajo(a)

bassoon [bə'suːn] n fagot m

bastard ['bɑːstəd, 'bæstəd] **1** n (**a**) (illegitimate child) hijo(a) ilegítimo(a), (hijo(a) bastardo(a) m,f (**b**) very Fam (unpleasant person) cabrón m, hijo m de puta; **poor b.!** ¡el pobre!
2 adj bastardo(a)

baste [beɪst] vt Culin regar con grasa

bastion ['bæstɪən] n baluarte m, bastión m

bat¹ [bæt] **1** n (in cricket, baseball) bate m; (in table tennis) pala f; Br Fam **to do sth off one's own b.** hacer algo por cuenta propia
2 vi (in cricket, baseball) batear

bat² [bæt] n Zool murciélago m

bat³ [bæt] vt Fam **without batting an eyelid** sin pestañear

batch [bætʃ] n (of bread) hornada f; (of goods) lote m; Comput **b. processing** procesamiento m por lotes

bated ['beɪtɪd] adj **with b. breath** sin respirar

bath [bɑːθ] **1** n (**a**) (action) baño m; **to have a b.** bañarse; **b. towel** toalla f de baño (**b**) (tub) bañera f, Am tina f (**c**) Br (swimming) **baths** piscina f, Méx alberca f, RP pileta f
2 vt bañar

bathe [beɪð] **1** vi bañarse
2 vt (**a**) (wound) lavar (**b**) **he was bathed in sweat** (covered) estaba empapado de sudor

bather ['beɪðə(r)] n bañista mf

bathing ['beɪðɪŋ] n baño m; **b. cap** gorro m de baño; **b. costume** bañador m, traje m de baño, Col vestido m de baño, RP malla f; **b. trunks** bañador m (de hombre)

bathrobe ['bɑːθrəʊb] n albornoz m

bathroom ['bɑːθruːm] n (with bath) cuarto m de baño; (toilet) baño m, servicio m, CSur toilette m

bathtub ['bɑːθtʌb] n bañera f, Am tina f

baton ['bætən, 'bætɒn] n (**a**) Mus batuta f (**b**) Br (of policeman) porra f (**c**) Sport testigo m

battalion [bə'tæljən] n batallón m

batter¹ ['bætə(r)] vt aporrear, apalear

batter² ['bætə(r)] n (in cricket, baseball) bateador(a) m,f

batter³ ['bætə(r)] Culin **1** n pasta f (para rebozar); **fish in b.** pescado rebozado
2 vt rebozar

battered ['bætəd] adj (car) abollado(a); (person) maltratado(a)

battering ['bætərɪŋ] n paliza f; **to take a b.** recibir una paliza; Mil **b. ram** ariete m

battery ['bætərɪ] n (**a**) (for torch, radio) pila f, Aut batería f (**b**) Jur **assault and b.** lesiones fpl

battle ['bætəl] **1** n batalla f; Fig lucha f; **to do b.** librar batalla; Fig **b. cry** lema m
2 vi luchar

battlefield ['bætəlfi:ld] n campo m de batalla

battleship ['bætəlʃɪp] n acorazado m

bauble ['bɔ:bəl] n chuchería f

baulk [bɔ:k] 1 vt (frustrate, defeat) frustrar, hacer fracasar
2 vi **to b. at sth** (of person) mostrarse reticente or echarse atrás ante algo

bawdy ['bɔ:dɪ] adj (**bawdier, bawdiest**) (joke etc) verde

bawl [bɔ:l] vi gritar, chillar

bay¹ [beɪ] n Geog bahía f; (large) golfo m; **B. of Biscay** golfo de Vizcaya; **B. of Bengal** golfo de Bengala

bay² [beɪ] n (a) (recess) hueco m; **b. window** ventana saladiza (b) (in factory) nave f; **cargo b.** bodega f de carga

bay³ [beɪ] n Bot laurel m

bay⁴ [beɪ] 1 vi (dog) aullar
2 n ladrido m; Fig **at b.** acorralado(a); Fig **to keep sb at b.** mantener a algn a raya

bayonet ['beɪənɪt] n bayoneta f

bazaar [bə'zɑ:(r)] n (a) (market) bazar m (b) (**church**) **b.** (charity sale) rastrillo benéfico

B & B [bi:ən'bi:] n Br (abbr **bed and breakfast**) (hotel) = hostal familiar en el que el desayuno está incluido en el precio de la habitación

BBC [bi:bi:'si:] n (abbr **British Broadcasting Corporation**) BBC f

BC [bi:'si:] (abbr **before Christ**) a.d.C.

be [bi:, unstressed bɪ]

En el inglés hablado, y en el escrito en estilo coloquial, el verbo **be** se contrae de forma que **I am** se transforma en **I'm**, **he/she/it is** se transforman en **he's/ she's/it's** y **you/we/they are** se transforman en **you're/we're/they're**. Las formas negativas **is not**, **are not**, **was not** y **were not** se transforman en **isn't**, **aren't**, **wasn't** y **weren't**.

1 vi (pres 1st person sing **am**; 3rd person sing **is**; 2nd person sing & all persons pl **are**; pt 1st & 3rd persons sing **was**; 2nd person sing & all persons pl **were**; pp **been**) (a) (indicating permanent quality, condition) ser; **he is very tall** es muy alto; **Madrid is the capital** Madrid es la capital; **sugar is sweet** el azúcar es dulce (b) (nationality, occupation) ser; **he's Italian** es italiano
(c) (origin, ownership) ser; **the car is Domingo's** el coche es de Domingo
(d) (price) costar; (total) ser; **a return ticket is £24** un billete de ida y vuelta cuesta £24; **how much is it?** ¿cuánto es? (e) (temporary state) estar; **how are you?**

– **I'm very well** ¿cómo estás? – estoy muy bien; **this soup is cold** esta sopa está fría; **to be cold/afraid/hungry** (person) tener frío/miedo/hambre
(f) (location) estar; **Birmingham is 120 miles from London** Birmingham está a 120 millas de Londres
(g) (age) tener; **she is thirty (years old)** tiene treinta años

2 v aux (a) (with pres p) estar; **he is writing a letter** está escribiendo una carta; **she was singing** estaba cantando; **they are leaving next week** se van la semana que viene; **we have been waiting for a long time** hace mucho que estamos esperando; **he is coming** (emphatic) es seguro que viene
(b) (passive) ser; **he was murdered** fue asesinado; **she is allowed to smoke** se le permite fumar
(c) (obligation) **I am to see him this afternoon** debo verle esta tarde; **you are not to smoke here** no se puede fumar aquí

3 v impers (a) (with **there**) haber; **there is, there are** hay; **there was, there were** había; **there will be** habrá; **there would be** habría; **there have been a lot of complaints** ha habido muchas quejas; **there were ten of us** éramos diez
(b) (with **it**) **it's late** es tarde; **it is said that …** se dice que …; **who is it? – it's me** ¿quién es? – soy yo; **what is it?** ¿qué pasa?
(c) (weather) **it's foggy** hay niebla; **it's cold/hot** hace frío/calor
(d) (time) ser; **it's one o'clock** es la una; **it's four o'clock** son las cuatro
(e) (date) **it's the 11th/Tuesday today** hoy es 11/martes
(f) (in tag questions) **it's lovely, isn't it?** es bonito, ¿no?; **you're happy, aren't you?** estás contento, ¿verdad?; **he's not very clever, is he?** no es muy listo, ¿verdad?
(g) (unreal conditions) **if I was/were you …** yo en tu lugar …; **if you were a millionaire …** si fueras millonario …
(h) (as past participle of **go**) **I've been to Paris** he estado en París

beach [bi:tʃ] 1 n playa f
2 vt varar

beacon ['bi:kən] n (a) Av & Naut baliza f (b) (lighthouse) faro m

bead [bi:d] n (a) (of necklace etc) cuenta f; **glass b.** abalorio m (b) (of liquid) gota f

beady ['bi:dɪ] adj (**beadier, beadiest**) (eyes) pequeños y brillantes

beagle ['bi:gəl] n beagle m

beak [bi:k] n (a) (of bird) pico m (b) Fam (nose) nariz ganchuda

beaker ['biːkə(r)] *n (tumbler)* taza alta, jarra *f*

beam [biːm] **1** *n* (a) *(in building)* viga *f* (b) *(of light)* rayo *m*; *Phys* haz *m*
2 *vi* (a) *(sun)* brillar (b) *(smile)* sonreír
3 *vt (broadcast)* difundir, emitir

beaming ['biːmɪŋ] *adj (smiling)* radiante

bean [biːn] *n (vegetable) Esp* alubia *f*, *Esp* judía *f*, *Am salvo RP* frijol *m*, *Andes, RP* poroto *m*; *(of coffee)* grano *m*; **to be full of beans** estar lleno(a) de vitalidad

beansprout ['biːnspraʊt] *n* brote *m* de soja

bear¹ [beə(r)] *(pt* **bore***, pp* **borne***)* **1** *vt* (a) *(carry)* llevar; **to b. in mind** tener presente (b) *(support)* sostener (c) *(endure)* soportar, aguantar; **I can't b. him** no lo soporto (d) *(pt* **born** *passive only, not followed by* **by***) (give birth to)* dar a luz a; **he was born in Wakefield** nació en Wakefield
2 *vi (turn)* girar, torcer; **to b. left** girar a la izquierda

▸**bear down** *vi (approach)* correr (**on** sobre)

▸**bear out** *vt sep (confirm)* confirmar

▸**bear up** *vi (endure)* resistir

▸**bear with** *vt insep* tener paciencia con

bear² [beə(r)] *n (animal)* oso *m*; **b. cub** osezno *m*

bearable ['beərəbəl] *adj* soportable

beard [bɪəd] *n* barba *f*

bearer ['beərə(r)] *n* portador(a) *m,f*; *(of passport, office)* titular *mf*

bearing ['beərɪŋ] *n* (a) *(posture)* porte *m* (b) *(relevance)* relación *f*; **to have a b.** on estar relacionado(a) con (c) *Tech* cojinete *m* (d) *Naut* **bearings** posición *f*, orientación *f*; **to get one's bearings** orientarse

beast [biːst] *n* (a) *(animal)* bestia *f*; **b. of burden** bestia de carga (b) *Fam (unpleasant person)* bestia *f*, bruto *m*

beastly ['biːstlɪ] *adj* (**beastlier**, **beastliest**) *Fam* asqueroso(a)

beat [biːt] **1** *vt (pt* **beat***; pp* **beaten** ['biːtən]*)* (a) *(hit)* pegar, golpear; *(drum)* tocar; *Fam* **b. it!** ¡largo!, ¡esfúmate!; *RP* ¡bórrate! (b) *Culin* batir (c) *(defeat)* batir, vencer; **we b. them 5-2** les ganamos 5 a 2; *Fam* **it beats me** *(puzzle)* no lo entiendo (d) *Mus (time)* marcar
2 *vi* (a) *(heart)* latir (b) *(strike)* dar golpes; *Fam* **to b. about the bush** andarse por las ramas
3 *n* (a) *(of heart)* latido *m* (b) *Mus* ritmo *m*, compás *m* (c) *Br (of policeman)* ronda *f*

▸**beat down** *vi (sun)* apretar

▸**beat off** *vt sep* rechazar

▸**beat up** *vt sep Fam* dar una paliza a

beater ['biːtə(r)] *n* (a) *(in hunting)* ojeador(a) *m,f* (b) *(in cookery)* batidora *f*, batidor *m*

beating ['biːtɪŋ] *n* (a) *(thrashing)* paliza *f* (b) *(defeat)* derrota *f* (c) *(of drum)* toque *m* (d) *(of heart)* latido *m*

beautician [bjuː'tɪʃən] *n* esteticista *mf*

beautiful ['bjuːtɪfʊl] *adj (woman)* bonita, *esp Esp* guapa; *(child, animal)* bonito(a), precioso(a); *(music, dress, landscape)* hermoso(a), precioso(a); *(smell, taste)* delicioso(a)

beauty ['bjuːtɪ] *n* belleza *f*, hermosura *f*; **b. contest** concurso *m* de belleza; **b. parlour** salón *m* de belleza; **b. queen** miss *f*; **b. salon** salón de belleza; **b. spot** *(on face)* lunar *m*; *(place)* lugar pintoresco

beaver ['biːvə(r)] **1** *n* castor *m*
2 *vi* **to b. away at sth** meterse de lleno en algo

became [bɪ'keɪm] *pt of* **become**

because [bɪ'kɒz] **1** *conj* porque
2 *prep* **b. of** a causa de, debido a

beckon ['bekən] *vt & vi* llamar (con la mano); **to b. to sb** llamar a algn con señas

become [bɪ'kʌm] **1** *vi (pt* **became***; pp* **become***) (a teacher, doctor)* hacerse; *(boring, jealous, suspicious)* volverse; *(old, difficult, stronger)* hacerse; *(happy, sad, thin)* ponerse; **to b. angry** *Esp* enfadarse, *esp Am* enojarse; **to b. interested** interesarse; **what will b. of him?** ¿qué va a ser de él?
2 *vt Fml (of clothes, colour)* sentar bien a

becoming [bɪ'kʌmɪŋ] *adj* (a) *(dress)* favorecedor(a) (b) *(behaviour)* conveniente, apropiado(a)

bed [bed] *n* (a) *(for sleeping)* cama *f*; **to get out of b.** levantarse de la cama; **to go to b.** acostarse; **to make the b.** hacer la cama; *Br* **b. and breakfast** *(service)* cama y desayuno *m*; *(sign)* pensión *f*; **b. linen** ropa *f* de cama (b) *(of river)* lecho *m*; *(of sea)* fondo *m* (c) *Geol* estrato *m* (d) *(flower)* **b.** arriate *m*

bedbug ['bedbʌg] *n* chinche *f* o *m*

bedclothes ['bedkləʊðz] *npl*, **bedding** ['bdɪŋ] *n* ropa *f* de cama

bedlam ['bedləm] *n* algarabía *f*, alboroto *m*

bedraggled [bɪ'drægəld] *adj (wet)* mojado(a); *(dirty)* ensuciado(a)

bedridden ['bedrɪdən] *adj* postrado(a) en cama

bedroom ['bedruːm] *n (in house)* dormitorio *m*, habitación *f*, cuarto *m*, *CAm, Col, Méx* recámara *f*; *(in hotel)* habitación *f*, *Am* cuarto *m*, *CAm, Col, Méx* recámara *f*

bedside ['bedsaɪd] *n* **at sb's b.** al lado de la cama de algn; **b. table** mesilla *f* or mesita *f* (de noche), *Andes* velador *m*, *Méx* buró *m*, *RP* mesa *f* de luz

bedsit ['bedsɪt], *Fam* **bedsitter** [bed-'sɪtə(r)] *n Br* estudio *m*

bedspread ['bedspred] *n* colcha *f*

bedtime ['bedtaɪm] *n* hora *f* de acostarse

bee [biː] *n* abeja *f*

beech [biːtʃ] *n* haya *f*

beef [biːf] *n* carne *f* de vaca, *Am* carne de res; **roast b.** rosbif *m*

▸ **beef up** *vt sep Fam* reforzar

beefburger ['biːfbɜːgə(r)] *n* hamburguesa *f*

beefsteak ['biːfsteɪk] *n* filete *m*, bistec *m*, *RP* bife *m*

beehive ['biːhaɪv] *n* colmena *f*

beeline ['biːlaɪn] *n Fam* **to make a b. for sth** ir directo hacia algo

been [biːn, bɪn] *pp of* **be**

beep [biːp] *n* (*of apparatus*) pitido *m*; (*of horn*) pito *m*

beer [bɪə(r)] *n* cerveza *f*; **a glass of b.** una caña

beet [biːt] *n US* remolacha *f*, *Méx* betabel *m*

beetle ['biːtəl] *n* escarabajo *m*

beetroot ['biːtruːt] *n Br* remolacha *f*, *Méx* betabel *m*

befit [bɪ'fɪt] *vt* convenir a, corresponder a

before [bɪ'fɔː(r)] **1** *conj* (a) (*earlier than*) antes de que (+ *subj*), antes de (+ *infin*); **b. she goes** antes de que se vaya; **b. leaving** antes de salir (b) (*rather than*) antes que (+ *infin*)
2 *prep* (a) (*place*) delante de; (*in the presence of*) ante (b) (*order, time*) antes de; **b. Christ** antes de Cristo; **b. long** dentro de poco; **b. 1950** antes de 1950; **I saw it b. you** lo vi antes que tú
3 *adv* (a) (*time*) antes; **I have met him b.** ya lo conozco; **not long b.** poco antes; **the night b.** la noche anterior (b) (*place*) delante, por delante

beforehand [bɪ'fɔːhænd] *adv* (a) (*earlier*) antes (b) (*in advance*) de antemano, con anticipación

befriend [bɪ'frend] *vt* trabar amistad con

beg [beg] **1** *vt* (a) (*money etc*) pedir (b) (*beseech*) rogar, suplicar; **I b. your pardon!** ¡perdone usted!; **I b. your pardon?** ¿cómo ha dicho usted?
2 *vi* (a) (*solicit*) mendigar; (*dog*) pedir; **to b. for money** pedir limosna (b) **to b. for help/mercy** (*beseech*) implorar ayuda/compasión

began [bɪ'gæn] *pt of* **begin**

beggar ['begə(r)] *n* mendigo(a) *m,f*; *Br Fam* **poor b.!** ¡pobre diablo!

begin [bɪ'gɪn] *vt & vi* (*pt* **began**; *pp* **begun**) empezar, comenzar; **to b. again** volver a empezar; **to b. at the beginning** empezar por el principio; **to b. doing** *or* **to do sth** empezar a hacer algo; **to b. with ...** (*initially*) para empezar ...

beginner [bɪ'gɪnə(r)] *n* principiante *mf*

beginning [bɪ'gɪnɪŋ] *n* principio *m*, comienzo *m*; **at the b. of May** a principios de mayo; **from the b.** desde el principio; **in the b.** al principio; **the beginnings of civilization** los orígenes de la civilización

begonia [bɪ'gəʊnɪə] *n* begonia *f*

begrudge [bɪ'grʌdʒ] *vt* (*resent*) dar de mala gana; (*envy*) envidiar

beguile [bɪ'gaɪl] *vt* (*charm*) seducir

begun [bɪ'gʌn] *pp of* **begin**

behalf [bɪ'hɑːf] *n* **on b. of**, *US* **in b. of** en nombre de, de parte de; **don't worry on my b.** no te preocupes por mí

behave [bɪ'heɪv] *vi* (a) (*person*) portarse, comportarse; **b. yourself!** ¡pórtate bien!; **to b. well/badly** portarse bien/mal (b) (*machine*) funcionar

behaviour, *US* **behavior** [bɪ'heɪvjə(r)] *n* (a) (*of person*) comportamiento *m*, conducta *f* (b) (*of machine*) funcionamiento *m*

behead [bɪ'hed] *vt* decapitar

beheld [bɪ'held] *pt & pp of* **behold**

behind [bɪ'haɪnd] **1** *prep* detrás de; **b. sb's back** a espaldas de algn; **b. the scenes** entre bastidores; **b. the times** (*less advanced than*) anticuado(a); **to be b. sb** (*support*) apoyar a algn; **what motive was there b. the crime?** ¿cuál fue el móvil del crimen?
2 *adv* (a) (*in the rear*) detrás, atrás; **I've left my umbrella b.** se me ha olvidado el paraguas (b) **to be b. with one's payments** (*late*) estar atrasado(a) en los pagos
3 *n Fam* trasero *m*

behold [bɪ'həʊld] *vt* (*pt & pp* **beheld**) *Literary* contemplar

beige [beɪʒ] *adj & n* beige (*m inv*), *Esp* beis (*m inv*)

Beijing [beɪ'ʒɪŋ] *n* Pekín

being ['biːɪŋ] *n* (a) (*creature*) ser *m* (b) (*existence*) existencia *f*; **to come into b.** nacer

Belarus [belə'ruːs] *n* Bielorrusia

belated [bɪ'leɪtɪd] *adj* tardío(a)

belch [beltʃ] **1** *vi* (*person*) eructar
2 *vt* (*smoke, flames*) vomitar, arrojar
3 *n* eructo *m*

beleaguered [bɪˈliːgəd] *adj* asediado(a)

belfry [ˈbelfrɪ] *n* campanario *m*

Belgian [ˈbeldʒən] *adj & n* belga *(mf)*

Belgium [ˈbeldʒəm] *n* Bélgica

Belgrade [belˈgreɪd] *n* Belgrado

belie [bɪˈlaɪ] *vt* desmentir

belief [bɪˈliːf] *n* (**a**) *(conviction)* creencia *f*; **it is my b. that ...** estoy convencido(a) de que ...; **beyond b.** increíble (**b**) *(religious faith)* creencias *fpl*, fe *f* (**c**) *(confidence)* confianza *f* (**in** en)

believable [bɪˈliːvəbəl] *adj* verosímil

believe [bɪˈliːv] **1** *vi* (**a**) *(have faith)* creer (**b**) **to b. in** *(be in favour of)* ser partidario(a) de (**c**) *(think)* creer; **I b. so** creo que sí
2 *vt* creer

believer [bɪˈliːvə(r)] *n* (**a**) *Rel* creyente *mf* (**b**) *(supporter)* partidario(a) *m,f* (**in** de)

belittle [bɪˈlɪtəl] *vt* *(person)* menospreciar; *(problem)* minimizar

bell [bel] *n* *(of church)* campana *f*; *(small)* campanilla *f*; *(of school, door, bicycle etc)* timbre *m*; *(on cat)* cascabel *m*; *(on cow)* cencerro *m*; *Fig* **that rings a b.** eso me suena; **b. jar** campana de vidrio *or Esp* cristal; **b. tower** campanario *m*

bell-bottoms [ˈbelbɒtəmz] *npl* pantalones *mpl* de campana

bellboy [ˈbelbɔɪ], **bellhop** [ˈbelhɒp] *n US* botones *m inv*

belligerent [bɪˈlɪdʒərənt] *adj* agresivo(a)

bellow [ˈbeləʊ] *vi* *(bull)* bramar; *(person)* rugir

bellows [ˈbeləʊz] *npl* **(pair of) b.** fuelle *m*

belly [ˈbelɪ] *n* (**a**) *(of person)* vientre *m*, barriga *f*; **b. flop** panzazo *m* (**b**) *(of animal)* panza *f*

bellyache [ˈbelieɪk] *n Fam* dolor *m* de barriga

belong [bɪˈlɒŋ] *vi* (**a**) **to b. to** *(be property of)* pertenecer a (**b**) *(be a member)* ser socio(a) (**to** de); *Pol* **to b. to a party** ser miembro de un partido (**c**) *(have a proper place)* corresponder a; **this chair belongs here** esta silla va aquí

belongings [bɪˈlɒŋɪŋz] *npl* efectos *mpl* personales

beloved [bɪˈlʌvɪd, bɪˈlʌvd] **1** *adj* amado(a), querido(a)
2 *n* amado(a) *m,f*

below [bɪˈləʊ] **1** *prep* debajo de, bajo, *Am* abajo de; **b. average** por debajo de la media; **10 degrees b. zero** 10 grados bajo cero
2 *adv* abajo; **above and b.** arriba y abajo; **see b.** véase más abajo

belt [belt] **1** *n* (**a**) *(for trousers)* cinturón *m*, correa *f*; **blow below the b.** golpe bajo (**b**) *(of machine)* correa *f* (**c**) *(of land)* franja *f*, cinturón *m*
2 *vt Fam* pegar una paliza a

▸ **belt along** *vi Fam* ir a todo gas

▸ **belt out** *vt sep Fam (song)* cantar a voz en grito

▸ **belt up** *vi Br Fam* callarse

beltway [ˈbeltweɪ] *n US* carretera *f* de circunvalación

bemused [bɪˈmjuːzd] *adj* perplejo(a)

bench [bentʃ] *n* (**a**) *(seat)* banco *m* (**b**) *(in parliament)* escaño *m* (**c**) *Br* **the B.** *(judges)* la magistratura (**d**) *Sport* banquillo *m*

bend [bend] **1** *vt* *(pt & pp bent)* doblar; *Fam* **to b. the rules** hacer una excepción
2 *vi* (**a**) *(road, river)* hacer una curva, girar; *(tree)* doblarse (**b**) **to b. (over)** inclinarse; *Fam* **he bends over backwards to please her** hace lo imposible por complacerla
3 *n* *(of river, road)* curva *f*; *(of pipe, arm)* codo *m*; *Br Fam* **to be round the b.** estar *Esp* majara *or Am* zafado(a) *or RP* piantado(a)

▸ **bend down** *vi* inclinarse

beneath [bɪˈniːθ] **1** *prep* *(below)* bajo, debajo de; *Fig* **it's b. him** es indigno de él
2 *adv* debajo

benefactor [ˈbenɪfæktə(r)] *n* bienhechor(a) *m,f*

beneficial [benɪˈfɪʃəl] *adj* (**a**) *(doing good)* benéfico(a) (**b**) *(advantageous)* beneficioso(a)

beneficiary [benɪˈfɪʃərɪ] *n* beneficiario(a) *m,f*

benefit [ˈbenɪfɪt] **1** *vt* beneficiar
2 *vi* sacar provecho (**from** *or* **by** de)
3 *n* (**a**) *(advantage)* beneficio *m*, provecho *m*; **for the b. of** en beneficio de; **I did it for your b.** lo hice por tu bien (**b**) *(allowance)* subsidio *m*; **unemployment b.** subsidio de desempleo (**c**) *(event)* función benéfica

benevolent [bɪˈnevələnt] *adj* benévolo(a)

Bengal [beŋˈɡɔːl] *n* Bengala

benign [bɪˈnaɪn] *adj* benigno(a)

bent [bent] **1** *adj* (**a**) *(curved)* curvado(a) (**b**) **to be b. on doing sth** *(determined)* estar empeñado(a) en hacer algo (**c**) *Br Fam (dishonest)* deshonesto(a)
2 *n* *(inclination)* inclinación *f* (**towards** hacia)
3 *pt & pp of* bend

benzine [ˈbenziːn] *n Chem* bencina *f*

bequeath [bɪˈkwiːð] *vt Jur* legar

bequest [bɪ'kwest] *n Jur* legado *m*

bereaved [bɪ'riːvd] *npl* **the b.** los familiares del/de un difunto

bereavement [bɪ'riːvmənt] *n (mourning)* duelo *m*

bereft [bɪ'reft] *adj* **b. of** privado(a) de

beret ['bereɪ] *n* boina *f*

Berlin [bɜː'lɪn] *n* Berlín

Bermuda [bə'mjuːdə] *n* las (Islas) Bermudas; **B. shorts** bermudas *fpl*

Bern [bɜːn] *n* Berna

berry ['berɪ] *n* baya *f*

berserk [bə'sɜːk, bə'zɜːk] *adj* **to go b.** volverse loco(a)

berth [bɜːθ] *Naut* **1** *n* (a) *(mooring)* amarradero *m*; *Fig* **to give sb a wide b.** evitar a algn (b) *(bed)* litera *f*
2 *vi* atracar

beseech [bɪ'siːtʃ] *vt (pt & pp* **besought** *or* **beseeched)** suplicar, implorar

beset [bɪ'set] *vt (pt & pp* **beset)** acosar; **it is b. with dangers** está plagado de peligros

beside [bɪ'saɪd] *prep* (a) *(next to)* al lado de, junto a (b) *(compared with)* comparado con (c) **he was b. himself with joy** estaba loco de alegría; **that's b. the point** eso no viene al caso; **to be b. oneself** estar fuera de sí

besides [bɪ'saɪdz] **1** *prep* (a) *(in addition to)* además de (b) *(except)* excepto, menos; **no one b. me** nadie más que yo
2 *adv* además

besiege [bɪ'siːdʒ] *vt (city)* sitiar; *Fig* asediar

besought [bɪ'sɔːt] *pt & pp of* **beseech**

best [best] **1** *adj (superl of* **good)** mejor; **b. man** ≃ padrino *m* de boda; **her b. friend** su mejor amiga; **the b. thing would be to phone them** lo mejor sería llamarles; **we had to wait the b. part of a year** tuvimos que esperar casi un año; **with b. wishes from Mary** *(in letter)* con mis mejores deseos, Mary
2 *adv (superl of* **well)** mejor; **as b. I can** lo mejor que pueda; **I like this one b.** éste es el que más me gusta; **the world's b. dressed man** el hombre mejor vestido del mundo
3 *n* **the b.** el/la/lo mejor; **all the b.!** *(at the end of letter)* ¡un saludo!, *RP* cariños; **at b.** a lo más; **to be at one's b.** estar en plena forma; **to do one's b.** hacer todo lo posible; **to make the b. of sth** sacar el mejor partido de algo; **to the b. of my knowledge** que yo sepa

bestiality [bestɪ'ælɪtɪ] *n* bestialidad *f*

bestow [bɪ'stəʊ] *vt (favour etc)* conceder; *(honours, power)* otorgar (**on** a); *(title etc)* conferir (**on** a)

best-seller [best'selə(r)] *n* best-seller *m*

best-selling ['bestselɪŋ] *adj* **a b. author** un autor de superventas

bet [bet] **1** *n* apuesta *f*
2 *vt (pt* **bet** *or* **betted)** apostar
3 *vi* apostar (**on** por); *Fam* **you b.!** ¡y tanto!

Bethlehem ['beθlɪhem] *n* Belén

betray [bɪ'treɪ] *vt (person, country)* traicionar; *(spouse)* engañar; *(secret, fact)* revelar

betrayal [bɪ'treɪəl] *n* traición *f*

better ['betə(r)] **1** *adj* (a) *(comp of* **good)** mejor; **that's b.!** ¡así está mejor!; **the weather is b. than last week** hace mejor tiempo que la semana pasada; **to be b. than …** no ser más que …; **to get b.** mejorar (b) *(healthier)* mejor (de salud) (c) **b. off** *(better)* mejor; *(richer)* más rico(a); **you'd be b. off going home** lo mejor es que te vayas a casa (d) **the b. part of the day** la mayor parte del día
2 *adv (comp of* **well)** mejor; **we had b. leave** más vale que nos vayamos; **to think b. of** *(plan)* cambiar de; **all the b., so much the b.** tanto mejor; **b. and b.** cada vez mejor; *Prov* **b. late than never** más vale tarde que nunca
3 *n* mejor; **a change for the b.** una mejora; **to get the b. of sb** vencer a algn
4 *vt* (a) *(improve)* mejorar (b) *(surpass)* superar

betting ['betɪŋ] *n* apuestas *fpl*; **b. shop** quiosco *m* de apuestas

between [bɪ'twiːn] **1** *prep* entre; **b. you and me** entre nosotros; **closed b. one and two** cerrado de una a dos
2 *adv* **in b.** *(position)* en medio; *(time)* entretanto, mientras (tanto)

beverage ['bevərɪdʒ] *n* bebida *f*

bevy ['bevɪ] *n* bandada *f*

beware [bɪ'weə(r)] *vi* tener cuidado (**of** con); **b.!** ¡cuidado!; **b. of the dog** *(sign)* cuidado con el perro

bewildered [bɪ'wɪldəd] *adj* desconcertado(a)

bewilderment [bɪ'wɪldəmənt] *n* desconcierto *m*

bewitching [bɪ'wɪtʃɪŋ] *adj* fascinador(a)

beyond [bɪ'jɒnd] **1** *prep* más allá de; **b. belief** increíble; **b. doubt** sin lugar a dudas; **it is b. me why …** no comprendo por qué …; **it's b. a joke** eso ya no tiene gracia; **she is b. caring** ya no le importa; **this task is b. me** no puedo con esta tarea
2 *adv* más allá, más lejos

bias ['baɪəs] *n (tendency)* tendencia *f* (**towards** hacia); *(prejudice)* prejuicio *m*

bias(s)ed ['baɪəst] *adj* parcial; **to be b. against sth/sb** tener prejuicio en contra de algo/algn

bib [bɪb] *n* (*for baby*) babero *m*; (*of apron*) peto *m*

Bible ['baɪbəl] *n* Biblia *f*; *Fam Pej* **B. thumper** *or Br* **basher** evangelista *mf*

biblical ['bɪblɪkəl] *adj* bíblico(a)

bibliography [bɪblɪ'ɒgrəfɪ] *n* bibliografía *f*

bicarbonate [baɪ'kɑːbənɪt] *n* bicarbonato *m*; **b. of soda** bicarbonato sódico

bicentenary [baɪsen'tiːnərɪ], *US* **bicentennial** [baɪsen'tenɪəl] *n* bicentenario *m*

biceps ['baɪseps] *n* bíceps *m*

bicker ['bɪkə(r)] *vi* reñir

bicycle ['baɪsɪkəl] *n* bicicleta *f*; **b. pump** bomba *f* (de aire); **to go by b.** ir en bicicleta

bid [bɪd] **1** *vt* (*pt* bid *or* bade; *pp* bid *or* bidden ['bɪdən]) (a) *Literary* (*say*) decir; (*command*) mandar, ordenar; **to b. sb farewell** despedirse de algn (b) (*at auction*) (*pt & pp* bid) pujar
  2 *vi* (*pt & pp* bid) (*at auction*) pujar (**for** por)
  3 *n* (a) (*offer*) oferta *f* (b) (*at auction*) puja *f* (c) (*attempt*) intento *m*, tentativa *f*

bidder ['bɪdə(r)] *n* **the highest b.** el mejor postor

bidding ['bɪdɪŋ] *n* (a) (*at auction*) puja *f* (b) (*order*) orden *f*; **to do sb's b.** cumplir la orden de algn

bide [baɪd] *vt* (*pt* bided *or* bode; *pp* bided) esperar; **to b. one's time** esperar el momento oportuno

bidet ['biːdeɪ] *n* bidé *m*

bifocal [baɪ'fəʊkəl] **1** *adj* bifocal
  2 *npl* **bifocals** gafas *fpl or Am* anteojos *fpl* (con lentes) bifocales

big [bɪg] **1** *adj* grande (gran *before singular noun*); **a b. clock** un reloj grande; **a b. surprise** una gran sorpresa; **my b. brother** mi hermano mayor; *Fam Ironic* **b. deal!** ¡y qué?; **b. business** los grandes negocios; **b. dipper** montaña rusa; *US Astron* **B. Dipper** Osa *f* Mayor; *Fam* **b. gun, b. shot** pez gordo; *Fam* **to make the b. time** tener éxito; **b. toe** dedo gordo del pie; *Fam* **b. top** carpa *f*
  2 *adv* (a) (*on a grand scale*) a lo grande (b) (*well*) de manera excepcional

bigamy ['bɪgəmɪ] *n* bigamia *f*

bighead ['bɪghed] *n* *Fam* creído(a) *m,f*, engreído(a) *m,f*

bigheaded [bɪg'hedɪd] *adj* creído(a), engreído(a)

bigot ['bɪgət] *n* intolerante *mf*

> 🖉 Note that the Spanish word **bigote** is a false friend and is never a translation for the English word **bigot**. In Spanish **bigote** means "moustache".

bigoted ['bɪgətɪd] *adj* intolerante

bigotry ['bɪgətrɪ] *n* intolerancia *f*

bigwig ['bɪgwɪg] *n* *Fam* pez gordo

bike [baɪk] *n* *Fam* (*abbr* **bicycle** *or* **motorbike**) (*bicycle*) bici *f*; (*motorcycle*) moto *f*; *Br* **on your b.!** (*go away*) ¡largo!, ¡piérdete!; (*don't talk nonsense*) ¡no digas *Esp* chorradas *or Am* pendejadas *or RP* pavadas!

bikini [bɪ'kiːnɪ] *n* bikini *m*

bilateral [baɪ'lætərəl] *adj* bilateral

bile [baɪl] *n* bilis *f*

bilingual [baɪ'lɪŋgwəl] *adj* bilingüe

Bill [bɪl] *n* *Br Fam* **the Old B.** *Esp* la pasma, *Andes* los pacos, *Méx* los cuicos, *RP* la cana

bill¹ [bɪl] **1** *n* (a) (*for gas etc*) factura *f*, recibo *m* (b) *esp Br* (*in restaurant*) cuenta *f* (c) *Pol* proyecto *m* de ley; **B. of Rights =** las diez primeras enmiendas a la constitución estadounidense, relacionadas con la garantía de las libertades individuales (d) *US* (*banknote*) billete *m* de banco (e) (*poster*) cartel *m* (f) *Fin* **b. of exchange** letra *f* de cambio
  2 *vt* (a) (*send bill to*) facturar (b) *Th* programar

bill² [bɪl] *n* (*of bird*) pico *m*

billboard ['bɪlbɔːd] *n* (*hoarding*) cartelera *f*

billet ['bɪlɪt] **1** *n* alojamiento *m*
  2 *vt* alojar

billfold ['bɪlfəʊld] *n US* cartera *f*, billetero *m*

billiards ['bɪljədz] *n sing* billar *m*

billion ['bɪljən] *n* mil millones *mpl*, millardo *m*; *Br Old-fashioned* billón *m*

billionaire [bɪljə'neə(r)] *n* multimillonario(a) *m,f*

billow ['bɪləʊ] **1** *n* (*of water*) ola *f*; (*of smoke*) nube *f*
  2 *vi* (*sea*) ondear; (*sail*) hincharse

billy goat ['bɪlɪgəʊt] *n* macho cabrío

bin [bɪn] *n* (*for storage*) cajón *m*; *Br* **bread b.** panera *f*; *Br* (*rubbish*) **b.** cubo *m or Am* bote *m* de la basura

binary ['baɪnərɪ] *adj* **b. number** número binario

bind [baɪnd] *vt* (*pt & pp* bound) (a) (*tie up*) atar (b) *Med* (*bandage*) vendar (c) (*book*) encuadernar (d) (*require*) obligar (e) (*join etc*) unir

▸ **bind over** *vt sep Jur* obligar legalmente

binder ['baɪndə(r)] n (file) carpeta f

binding ['baɪndɪŋ] adj (promise) comprometedor(a); (contract) vinculante

binge [bɪndʒ] n Fam borrachera f; **to go on a b.** irse de juerga

bingo ['bɪŋɡəʊ] n bingo m

binoculars [bɪ'nɒkjʊləz] npl prismáticos mpl, gemelos mpl

biochemistry [baɪəʊ'kemɪstrɪ] n bioquímica f

biodegradable [baɪəʊdɪ'ɡreɪdəbəl] adj biodegradable

biodiversity [baɪəʊdaɪ'vɜːsɪtɪ] n biodiversidad f

biography [baɪ'ɒɡrəfɪ] n biografía f

biological [baɪə'lɒdʒɪkəl] adj biológico(a); **b. warfare** guerra biológica

biologist [baɪ'ɒlədʒɪst] n biólogo(a) m,f

biology [baɪ'ɒlədʒɪ] n biología f

biorhythm ['baɪəʊrɪðəm] n biorritmo m

biosphere ['baɪəsfɪə(r)] n biosfera f

biotechnology [baɪəʊtek'nɒlədʒɪ] n biotecnología f

birch [bɜːtʃ] n (a) (Bot) abedul m (b) Br (rod for whipping) vara f
2 vt azotar

bird [bɜːd] n (a) (in general) pájaro m, (as opposed to mammals, reptiles etc) ave f; Fig **to kill two birds with one stone** matar dos pájaros de un tiro; **they're birds of a feather** son tal para cual; **b. of prey** ave de rapiña (b) Br Fam (woman) nena f, Arg piba f

birdcage ['bɜːdkeɪdʒ] n jaula f

birdie ['bɜːdɪ] n (in golf) birdie m

bird's-eye view [bɜːdzaɪ'vjuː] n vista f de pájaro

bird-watcher ['bɜːdwɒtʃə(r)] n ornitólogo(a) m,f

Biro® ['baɪrəʊ] n (pl Biros) Br bolígrafo m, Carib, Méx pluma f, Col, Ecuad esferográfico m, CSur lapicera f

birth [bɜːθ] n also Fig nacimiento m; (childbirth) parto m; **by b.** de nacimiento; **of noble b.** (parentage) de noble linaje; **to give b. to a child** dar a luz a un niño; **b. certificate** partida f de nacimiento; **b. control** (family planning) control m de la natalidad; (contraception) métodos anticonceptivos; **b. rate** índice m de natalidad

birthday ['bɜːθdeɪ] n cumpleaños m inv

birthmark ['bɜːθmɑːk] n antojo m

birthplace ['bɜːθpleɪs] n lugar m de nacimiento

Biscay ['bɪskeɪ] n Vizcaya; **the Bay of B.** el golfo de Vizcaya

biscuit ['bɪskɪt] n (a) Br (sweet, salted) galleta f; Fam **that really takes the b.!** ¡eso ya es el colmo! (b) US (muffin) tortita f, bollo m

bisect [baɪ'sekt] vt Geom bisecar; (town, area) dividir por la mitad

bisexual [baɪ'seksjʊəl] adj bisexual

bishop ['bɪʃəp] n (a) Rel obispo m (b) (in chess) alfil m

bison ['baɪsən] n inv bisonte m

bit¹ [bɪt] n (a) (small piece) trozo m, pedazo m; **to smash sth to bits** hacer añicos algo (b) (small quantity) poco m; **a b. of advice** un consejo; **bits and pieces** trastos mpl; Fig **b. by b.** poco a poco (c) **a b.** (slightly) un poco; **a b. longer** un ratito más; **a b. worried** un poco preocupado(a) (d) (coin) moneda f

bit² [bɪt] n (of tool) broca f

bit³ [bɪt] n Comput bit m

bit⁴ [bɪt] pt of **bite**

bitch [bɪtʃ] **1** n (a) Zool (female) hembra f; (dog) perra f (b) Fam (spiteful woman) bruja f
2 vi Fam (complain) quejarse, Esp dar la tabarra

bitchy ['bɪtʃɪ] adj (bitchier, bitchiest) Fam malicioso(a), Esp puñetero(a)

bite [baɪt] **1** n (a) (of person, dog) mordisco m; (of insect) picadura f; (of snake) mordedura f, picadura f (b) (mouthful) bocado m (c) Fam (snack) bocado m
2 vt (pt **bit**; pp **bitten**) (of person, dog) morder; (of insect, snake) picar; **to b. one's nails** morderse las uñas; Fam **to b. sb's head off** echarle una bronca a algn
3 vi (person, dog) morder; (insect, snake) picar

biting ['baɪtɪŋ] adj (wind) cortante; Fig (criticism) mordaz

bitten ['bɪtən] pp of **bite**

bitter ['bɪtə(r)] **1** adj (a) (taste) amargo(a) (b) (wind, cold, weather) recio(a) (c) (person) amargado(a), resentido(a) (d) (struggle) encarnizado(a); (hatred) implacable
2 n Br (beer) = cerveza sin burbujas y de tono castaño

bitterly ['bɪtəlɪ] adv **she was b. disappointed** sufrió una terrible decepción

bitterness ['bɪtənɪs] n (a) (taste) amargor m (b) (of wind, cold, weather) crudeza f (c) (of person) amargura f, amargor m

bittersweet [bɪtə'swiːt] adj agridulce

bitumen ['bɪtjʊmɪn] n betún m

bizarre [bɪ'zɑː(r)] adj (odd) extraño(a); (eccentric) estrafalario(a)

blab [blæb] *vi Fam* parlotear; *Esp* largar, *Méx* platicar; *(let out a secret)* chivarse

black [blæk] **1** *adj* (**a**) *(colour)* negro(a); **a b. and white television** un televisor en blanco y negro; *Fig* **b. and blue** amoratado(a); **to put sth down in b. and white** poner algo por escrito; *Av* **b. box** caja negra; **b. coffee** café solo; **the B. Country** = la región industrial de los Midlands; **b. eye** ojo morado; **b. hole** agujero negro; **b. humour** humor negro; **b. magic** magia negra; **b. market** mercado negro; *esp Br* **b. pudding** morcilla *f*; **the B. Sea** el Mar Negro; *Fig* **b. sheep** oveja negra (**b**) *(gloomy)* negro(a); *Fig* **a b. day** un día aciago; *Aut* **b. spot** punto negro
2 *n* (**a**) *(colour)* negro *m* (**b**) *(person)* negro(a) *m,f*
3 *vt* (**a**) *(make black)* ennegrecer (**b**) *(polish)* lustrar (**c**) *Br (boycott)* boicotear
▸ **black out 1** *vt sep* (**a**) *(extinguish lights in)* apagar las luces de (**b**) *(censor)* censurar
2 *vi (faint)* desmayarse

blackberry ['blækbərɪ] *n* zarzamora *f*

blackbird ['blækbɜːd] *n* mirlo *m*

blackboard ['blækbɔːd] *n* pizarra *f*, encerado *m*, *Am* pizarrón *m*

blackcurrant [blæk'kʌrənt] *n* grosella negra

blacken ['blækən] *vt* (**a**) *(make black)* ennegrecer (**b**) *Fig (defame)* manchar

blackhead ['blækhed] *n* espinilla *f*

blackjack ['blækdʒæk] *n* (**a**) *US (truncheon)* porra *f* (**b**) *(card game)* veintiuna *f*

blackleg ['blækleg] *n* esquirol *m*

blacklist ['blæklɪst] *n* lista negra

blackmail ['blækmeɪl] **1** *n* chantaje *m*
2 *vt* chantajear

blackout ['blækaʊt] *n* (**a**) *(of lights)* apagón *m* (**b**) *Rad & TV* censura *f* (**c**) *(fainting)* pérdida *f* de conocimiento

blacksmith ['blæksmɪθ] *n* herrero *m*

bladder ['blædə(r)] *n* vejiga *f*; **gall b.** vesícula *f* biliar

blade [bleɪd] *n* (**a**) *(of grass)* brizna *f* (**b**) *(of knife etc)* hoja *f* (**c**) *(of propeller, oar)* pala *f*

blame [bleɪm] **1** *n* culpa *f*; **to take the b. for sth** asumir la responsabilidad de algo
2 *vt* echar la culpa a; **he is to b.** él tiene la culpa

blameless ['bleɪmlɪs] *adj (person)* inocente; *(conduct)* intachable

blanch [blɑːntʃ] **1** *vt Culin* escaldar
2 *vi (go pale)* palidecer, ponerse pálido(a)

blancmange [blə'mɒnʒ] *n* = tipo de budín dulce

bland [blænd] *adj (food)* soso(a)

> *Note that the Spanish word* **blando** *is a false friend and is never a translation for the English word* **bland***. In Spanish* **blando** *means* "soft".

blank [blæŋk] **1** *adj* (**a**) *(without writing)* en blanco; *Fin* **b. cheque** cheque *m* en blanco (**b**) *(empty)* vacío(a); **a b. look** una mirada inexpresiva (**c**) **a b. refusal** *(absolute)* una negativa rotunda
2 *n* (**a**) *(space)* espacio *m* en blanco; **to draw a b.** no tener éxito (**b**) *Mil* cartucho *m* de fogueo (**c**) *US (form)* impreso *m*

blanket ['blæŋkɪt] **1** *n* manta *f*, *Am* cobija *f*, *Am* frazada *f*; *Fig* capa *f*
2 *adj* general

blare [bleə(r)] *vi* resonar
▸ **blare out** *vt sep* pregonar

blasé [*Br* 'blɑːzeɪ, *US* blɑː'zeɪ] *adj* de vuelta (de todo)

blasphemous ['blæsfəməs] *adj* blasfemo(a)

blasphemy ['blæsfəmɪ] *n* blasfemia *f*

blast [blɑːst] **1** *n* (**a**) *(of wind)* ráfaga *f* (**b**) *(of horn etc)* toque *m*; **at full b.** a toda marcha (**c**) *(explosion)* explosión *f* (**d**) *(shock wave)* onda *f* de choque
2 *vt* (**a**) *(blow up)* volar; *Br Fam* **b. (it)!** ¡maldito sea! (**b**) *Fig (destroy)* arruinar (**c**) *Fig (criticize)* criticar

blasted ['blɑːstɪd] *adj* maldito(a)

blast-off ['blɑːstɒf] *n* despegue *m*

blatant ['bleɪtənt] *adj (very obvious)* evidente; *(shameless)* descarado(a); **a b. lie** una mentira patente

blaze[1] [bleɪz] **1** *n* (**a**) *(burst of flame)* llamarada *f* (**b**) *(fierce fire)* incendio *m* (**c**) *(of sun)* resplandor *m* (**d**) *Fig (of anger)* arranque *m*
2 *vi* (**a**) *(fire)* arder (**b**) *(sun etc)* brillar

blaze[2] [bleɪz] *vt* **to b. a trail** abrir un camino

blazer ['bleɪzə(r)] *n* chaqueta *f* sport

blazing ['bleɪzɪŋ] *adj (building)* en llamas; *Fig* **a b. row** una discusión violenta

bleach [bliːtʃ] **1** *n* *(household)* lejía *f*, *Arg* lavandina *f*, *CAm, Chile, Méx, Ven* cloro *m*, *Col* clorol *m*, *Urug* jane *f*
2 *vt* (**a**) *(whiten)* blanquear; *(fade)* descolorir (**b**) *(hair)* decolorar

bleachers ['bliːtʃəz] *npl US Sport (seats)* gradas *fpl*

bleak [bliːk] *adj* (**a**) *(countryside)* desolado(a) (**b**) *(weather)* desapacible (**c**) *(future)* poco prometedor(a)

bleary ['blɪərɪ] *adj (blearier, bleariest)* *(eyes)* *(due to tears)* lloroso(a); *(due to tiredness)* cansado(a)

bleary-eyed [blɪərɪ'aɪd] *adj* con los ojos llorosos/cansados

bleat [bliːt] **1** *n* balido *m*
2 *vi (animal)* balar

bleed [bliːd] **1** *vi (pt & pp* **bled** [bled]) sangrar
2 *vt Med* sangrar; *Fam* **to b. sb dry** sacarle a algn hasta el último céntimo

bleeding ['bliːdɪŋ] **1** *n* hemorragia *f*
2 *adj* (**a**) *(wound)* sangrante (**b**) *Br Fam (for emphasis)* **you b. liar!** ¡pedazo de *or* **Méx** pinche mentiroso!

bleep [bliːp] **1** *n* bip *m*, pitido *m*
2 *vi* pitar

bleeper ['bliːpə(r)] *n Br* buscapersonas *m inv*, *Esp* busca *m*, **Méx** localizador *m*, *RP* radiomensaje *m*

blemish ['blemɪʃ] *n (flaw)* defecto *m*; *(on fruit)* maca *f*; *Fig* mancha *f*; *Fig* **without b.** sin tacha

blend [blend] **1** *n* mezcla *f*
2 *vt (mix)* mezclar; *(colours)* armonizar
3 *vi (mix)* mezclarse; *(colours)* armonizar

blender ['blendə(r)] *n Esp* batidora *f*, *Am* licuadora *f*

bless [bles] *vt (pt & pp* **blessed** *or* **blest**) *(say blessing for)* bendecir; **b. you!** *(when someone sneezes)* ¡salud! *Esp* ¡¡jesús!; **blessed with good eyesight** dotado(a) de buena vista

blessed ['blesɪd] *adj* (**a**) *(holy)* sagrado(a), santo(a) (**b**) *Fam (for emphasis)* dichoso(a)

blessing ['blesɪŋ] *n* bendición *f*; *(advantage)* ventaja *f*; **a mixed b.** una ventaja relativa

blest [blest] *pt & pp of* **bless**

blew [bluː] *pt of* **blow**

blight [blaɪt] **1** *n* plaga *f*
2 *vt Fig (spoil)* arruinar; *(frustrate)* frustrar

blimey ['blaɪmɪ] *interj Br Fam* ¡miércoles!, ¡caramba!, **Méx** ¡ay güey!

blind [blaɪnd] **1** *adj* ciego(a); **a b. man** un ciego; **a b. woman** una ciega; *Fig* **b. faith** fe ciega; *Fig* **to turn a b. eye** hacer la vista gorda; **b. alley** callejón *m* sin salida; **b. spot** ángulo muerto; *Fam* **b. date** cita *f* a ciegas
2 *adv* a ciegas; *Fam* **to get b. drunk** agarrar una curda
3 *n* (**a**) *Br (on window)* persiana *f* (**b**) *pl* **the b.** los ciegos
4 *vt (deprive of sight, dazzle)* cegar, dejar ciego

blinders ['blaɪndəz] *npl US* anteojeras *fpl*

blindfold ['blaɪndfəʊld] **1** *n* venda *f*
2 *vt* vendar los ojos a

blinding ['blaɪndɪŋ] *adj* cegador(a), deslumbrante

blindly ['blaɪndlɪ] *adv* a ciegas, ciegamente

blindness ['blaɪndnɪs] *n* ceguera *f*

blink [blɪŋk] *vi (eyes)* pestañear; *(lights)* parpadear

blinkered ['blɪŋkəd] *adj Fig* de miras estrechas

blinkers ['blɪŋkəz] *npl (on horse)* anteojeras *fpl*

bliss [blɪs] *n* felicidad *f*; **it was b.!** ¡fue maravilloso!

blissful ['blɪsfʊl] *adj (happy)* feliz; *(marvellous)* maravilloso(a)

blister ['blɪstə(r)] **1** *n (on skin)* ampolla *f*; *(on paint)* burbuja *f*
2 *vi* ampollarse

blithe [blaɪð] *adj* alegre

blithely ['blaɪðlɪ] *adv* alegremente

blitz [blɪts] **1** *n* bombardeo aéreo
2 *vt* bombardear

blizzard ['blɪzəd] *n* ventisca *f*

bloated ['bləʊtɪd] *adj* hinchado(a)

blob [blɒb] *n (drop)* gota *f*; *(spot)* mancha *f*

bloc [blɒk] *n Pol* bloque *m*

block [blɒk] **1** *n* (**a**) *(of ice, wood, stone)* bloque *m*; *(of butcher, for execution)* tajo *m*; **in b. capitals** en mayúsculas (**b**) *Br* **a b. of flats** un bloque de pisos (**c**) *(group of buildings)* manzana *f*, *Am* cuadra *f* (**d**) *(obstruction)* bloqueo *m*
2 *vt (obstruct)* obstruir; **to b. the way** cerrar el paso

▶ **block up** *vt sep* bloquear, obstruir; **to get blocked up** *(pipe)* obstruirse

blockade [blɒ'keɪd] *n* bloqueo *m*

blockage ['blɒkɪdʒ] *n* bloqueo *m*, obstrucción *f*

blockbuster ['blɒkbʌstə(r)] *n Fam* exitazo *m*; *Cin & TV* gran éxito *m* de taquilla; *(book)* éxito de ventas

blog [blɒg] **1** *n Comput (abbr* **weblog***)* blog *m*, bitácora *f*
2 *vi* bloguear, tener un blog

blogger ['blɒgə(r)] *n* blogger *mf*, bloguero(a) *mf*, bitacorero(a) *m,f*

bloke [bləʊk] *n Br Fam* tipo *m*, *Esp* tío *m*

blond [blɒnd] **1** *n (man)* rubio *m*, **Méx** güero *m*, *CAm* chele *m*, *Carib* catire *m*, *Col* mono *m*
2 *adj* rubio(a), **Méx** güero(a), *CAm* chele(a), *Carib* catire(a), *Col* mono(a)

blonde [blɒnd] **1** *n (man, woman)* rubio(a) *m,f*, **Méx** güero(a) *m,f*, *CAm* chele(a) *m,f*, *Carib* catire(a) *m,f*, *Col* mono(a) *m,f*

2 *adj* rubio(a), *Méx* güero(a), *CAm* chele(a), *Carib* catire(a), *Col* mono(a)

blood [blʌd] *n* (**a**) *(body fluid)* sangre *f*; **b. bank** banco *m* de sangre; **b. cell** glóbulo *m*; **b. donor** donante *mf* de sangre; **b. group** grupo sanguíneo; **b. pressure** tensión *f* arterial; *US* **b. sausage** morcilla *f*; **b. test** análisis *m* de sangre; **b. transfusion** transfusión *f* de sangre; **b. vessel** vaso sanguíneo; **blue b.** sangre azul; **high/low b. pressure** hipertensión *f*/hipotensión *f* (**b**) *(breeding, kinship)* **of noble/Italian b.** de sangre noble/italiana

bloodbath [ˈblʌdbɑːθ] *n Fig* baño *m* de sangre

bloodhound [ˈblʌdhaʊnd] *n* sabueso *m*

bloodshed [ˈblʌdʃed] *n* derramamiento *m* de sangre

bloodshot [ˈblʌdʃɒt] *adj* inyectado(a) de sangre

bloodstream [ˈblʌdstriːm] *n* corriente sanguínea

bloodthirsty [ˈblʌdθɜːstɪ] *adj* sanguinario(a)

bloody [ˈblʌdɪ] **1** *adj* (**bloodier, bloodiest**) (**a**) *(bleeding)* sanguinolento(a), sangriento(a); *(bloodstained)* ensangrentado(a); *(battle, revolution)* sangriento(a); *Fig* **to give sb a b. nose** poner a algn en su sitio (**b**) *Br, Austr very Fam (for emphasis)* maldito(a), *Esp* puñetero(a), *Méx* pinche; **a b. liar** un(a) mentiroso(a) de mierda; **b. hell!** ¡me cago en la mar!, ¡mierda!, *Méx* ¡en la madre!
2 *adv Br, Austr very Fam* **it's b. hot!** hace un calor del carajo *or Esp* de la leche *or RP* de mierda; **he can b. well do it himself!** ¡que lo haga él, carajo *or Esp* joder!

bloody-minded [blʌdɪˈmaɪndɪd] *adj Br Fam* terco(a)

bloom [bluːm] **1** *n* (**a**) *(flower)* flor *f*; **in full b.** en flor (**b**) *(on fruit)* vello *m*
2 *vi (blossom)* florecer

blooming [ˈbluːmɪŋ] *adj* (**a**) *(blossoming)* floreciente (**b**) *Br Fam (for emphasis)* condenado(a)

blossom [ˈblɒsəm] **1** *n (flower)* flor *f*
2 *vi* florecer; *Fig* **to b. out** alcanzar la plenitud

blot [blɒt] **1** *n (of ink)* borrón *m*; *Fig* mancha *f*
2 *vt* (**a**) *(with ink)* emborronar (**b**) *(dry)* secar
3 *vi (ink)* correrse

▸ **blot out** *vt sep (memories)* borrar; *(view)* ocultar

blotch [blɒtʃ] *n (on skin)* mancha *f*, enrojecimiento *m*

blotchy [ˈblɒtʃɪ] *adj* (**blotchier, blotchiest**) *(skin etc)* enrojecido(a); *(paint etc)* cubierto(a) de manchas

blotting-paper [ˈblɒtɪŋpeɪpə(r)] *n* papel *m* secante

blouse [blaʊz] *n* blusa *f*

blow¹ [bləʊ] *n* golpe *m*; **to come to blows** llegar a las manos; **it came as a terrible b.** fue un duro golpe

blow² [bləʊ] **1** *vi* (*pt* **blew**; *pp* **blown**) (**a**) *(wind)* soplar (**b**) *(fuse)* fundirse (**c**) *(tyre)* reventar
2 *vt* (**a**) *(kiss)* mandar (**b**) *(trumpet etc)* tocar (**c**) *(one's nose)* sonarse (**d**) *(fuse)* fundir (**e**) *Br Fam (money)* fundir, *RP* fumar

▸ **blow away** *vt sep & vi* = **blow off**

▸ **blow down** *vt sep* derribar

▸ **blow off 1** *vt sep (by wind)* llevarse
2 *vi (hat)* salir volando

▸ **blow out** *vt sep* apagar
2 *vi* apagarse

▸ **blow over** *vi (storm)* calmarse; *(scandal)* olvidarse

▸ **blow up 1** *vt sep* (**a**) *(building)* volar (**b**) *(inflate)* inflar (**c**) *Phot* ampliar
2 *vi (explode)* explotar

blowlamp [ˈbləʊlæmp] *n Br* soplete *m*

blown [bləʊn] *pp of* **blow**

blowout [ˈbləʊaʊt] *n* (**a**) *(of tyre)* reventón *m*, *Am* ponchadura *f* (**b**) *Fam (big meal)* comilona *f*, *Esp* cuchipanda *f*

blowtorch [ˈbləʊtɔːtʃ] *n US* soplete *m*

blow-up [ˈbləʊʌp] *n Phot* ampliación *f*

blubber [ˈblʌbə(r)] **1** *n* grasa *f* de ballena
2 *vi Fam* llorar a moco tendido

bludgeon [ˈblʌdʒən] *vt* aporrear; *Fig* **to b. sb into doing sth** forzar a algn a hacer algo

blue [bluː] **1** *adj* (**a**) *(colour)* azul; *Fig* **once in a b. moon** de uvas a peras, *RP* cada muerte de obispo; *Fam* **to scream b. murder** gritar como un loco; **b. jeans** vaqueros *mpl*, tejanos *mpl* (**b**) *(sad)* triste; **to feel b.** sentirse deprimido(a) (**c**) *(obscene)* verde; **b. joke** chiste *m* verde
2 *n* (**a**) *(colour)* azul *m*; *Fam* **the boys in b.** los maderos (**b**) **out of the b.** *(suddenly)* de repente; *(unexpectedly)* como llovido del cielo

bluebell [ˈbluːbel] *n* campanilla *f*

blueberry [ˈbluːbərɪ] *n* arándano *m*

bluebottle [ˈbluːbɒtəl] *n* moscarda *f*, mosca *f* azul

blue-collar [ˈbluːkɒlə(r)] *adj* **b. worker** obrero(a) *m,f*

blueprint [ˈbluːprɪnt] *n* anteproyecto *m*

blues [bluːz] *n* (**a**) *Mus* **the b.** el blues (**b**) *Fam (sadness)* tristeza *f*, melancolía *f*; **to have the b.** estar muy depre

bluetit ['bluːtɪt] *n* herrerillo *m* común

bluff [blʌf] **1** *n (trick)* farol *m*; **to call sb's b.** hacer que algn ponga sus cartas encima de la mesa
  2 *adj (abrupt)* brusco(a); *(forthright)* francote(a)
  3 *vi* tirarse un farol; **to b. one's way through sth** hacer colar algo

blunder ['blʌndə(r)] **1** *n* metedura *f o Am* metida *f* de pata; *Fam* patinazo *m*
  2 *vi* meter la pata, pegar un patinazo

blunt [blʌnt] **1** *adj* (**a**) *(knife)* desafilado(a); *(pencil)* despuntado(a); **b. instrument** instrumento *m* contundente (**b**) *(frank)* directo(a), francote(a); *(statement)* tajante
  2 *vt (pencil)* despuntar; *(knife)* desafilar

bluntly ['blʌntlɪ] *adv* francamente

blur [blɜː(r)] **1** *n* aspecto borroso
  2 *vt (windows)* empañar; *(shape)* desdibujar; *(memory)* enturbiar

blurb [blɜːb] *n (in book)* resumen *m*

blurred [blɜːd] *adj* borroso(a)

blurt [blɜːt] *vt* **to b. out** dejar escapar

blush [blʌʃ] **1** *n* rubor *m*
  2 *vi* ruborizarse

blusher ['blʌʃə(r)] *n* colorete *m*

blustery ['blʌstərɪ] *adj* borrascoso(a)

BO [biː'əʊ] *n Fam (abbr* **body odour)** sobaquina *f*, olor *m* a sudor

boar [bɔː(r)] *n* verraco *m*; **wild b.** jabalí *m*

board [bɔːd] **1** *n* (**a**) *(plank)* tabla *f* (**b**) *(work surface)* mesa *f*; *(blackboard)* pizarra *f, Am* pizarrón *m*; *(for games)* tablero *m* (**c**) *(meals)* pensión *f*; **full b.** pensión completa; **b. and lodging** *or US* **room** casa *f* y comida (**d**) *(committee)* junta *f*, consejo *m*; **b. of directors** consejo de administración; **b. room** sala *f* del consejo (**e**) *Naut* **on b.** a bordo (**f**) *Fig* **above b.** en regla; **across-the-b.** general; **to let sth go by the b.** abandonar algo
  2 *vt (ship, plane etc)* embarcarse en, subir a
  3 *vi* (**a**) *(lodge)* alojarse (**b**) *(at school)* estar interno(a)
  ▸ **board up** *vt sep* tapar

boarder ['bɔːdə(r)] *n* (**a**) *(in boarding house)* huésped *mf* (**b**) *(at school)* interno(a) *m,f*

boarding ['bɔːdɪŋ] *n* (**a**) *(embarkation)* embarque *m*; **b. card, b. pass** tarjeta *f* de embarque (**b**) *(lodging)* alojamiento *m*, pensión *f*; **b. house** pensión; **b. school** internado *m*

boardwalk ['bɔːdwɔːk] *n US* paseo marítimo entarimado

boast [bəʊst] **1** *n* jactancia *f*, alarde *m*
  2 *vi* jactarse, alardear (**about** de)
  3 *vt* presumir de, alardear de; **the town boasts an Olympic swimming pool** la ciudad disfruta de una piscina olímpica

boastful ['bəʊstfʊl] *adj* jactancioso(a), presuntuoso(a)

boat [bəʊt] *n* barco *m*; *(small)* barca *f*, bote *m*; *(launch)* lancha *f*; *(large)* buque *m*; *Fig* **we're all in the same b.** todos estamos en el mismo barco; **fishing b.** barco de pesca

boater ['bəʊtə(r)] *n* canotié *m*, canotier *m*

boatswain ['bəʊsən] *n* contramaestre *m*

boatyard ['bəʊtjɑːd] *n* astillero *m*

bob [bɒb] **1** *n* (**a**) *(haircut)* pelo *m* a lo chico (**b**) *Fam (pl* **bob)** *Br Formerly (shilling)* chelín *m*
  2 *vi* **to b. up and down** subir y bajar

bobbin ['bɒbɪn] *n (of sewing machine)* canilla *f*; *(for lace-making)* bolillo *m*

bobby ['bɒbɪ] *n Br Fam (policeman)* poli *m*

bobby-pin ['bɒbɪpɪn] *n US (hairgrip)* horquilla *f*

bobsleigh ['bɒbsleɪ] *n* bobsleigh *m*

bode[1] [bəʊd] *pt of* **bide**

bode[2] [bəʊd] **1** *vt* presagiar
  2 *vi* **to b. well/ill** ser de buen/mal agüero

bodice ['bɒdɪs] *n* (**a**) *(sleeveless undergarment)* corpiño *m* (**b**) *(of dress)* cuerpo *m*

bodily ['bɒdɪlɪ] **1** *adj* físico(a); **b. harm** daños *mpl* corporales
  2 *adv* **to carry sb b.** llevar a algn en brazos

body ['bɒdɪ] *n* (**a**) *(of person, animal)* cuerpo *m*; **b. odour** olor *m* corporal (**b**) *(corpse)* cadáver *m* (**c**) *(main part)* parte *f* principal (**d**) *Aut* carrocería *f* (**e**) *(organization)* entidad *f* (**f**) *(group of people)* conjunto *m*, grupo *m*

body-blow ['bɒdɪbləʊ] *n Fig* duro golpe

body-builder ['bɒdɪbɪldə(r)] *n* culturista *mf*

body-building ['bɒdɪbɪldɪŋ] *n* culturismo *m*

bodyguard ['bɒdɪgɑːd] *n* guardaespaldas *mf inv*

bodywork ['bɒdɪwɜːk] *n Aut* carrocería *f*

Boer ['bəʊə(r)] *adj* **the B. War** la guerra del Transvaal

bog [bɒg] *n* (**a**) *(marsh)* ciénaga *f* (**b**) *Br Fam (lavatory)* baño *m, Esp* tiger *m*
  ▸ **bog down** *vt sep* **to get bogged down** atascarse

bogey ['bəʊgɪ] *n* (**a**) *(spectre)* espectro *m*, fantasma *m* (**b**) *(bugbear)* pesadilla *f* (**c**) *(in golf)* bogey *m* (**d**) *Br Fam (mucus)* moco *m*

boggle ['bɒgəl] *vi Fam* **the mind boggles!** ¡es alucinante!

bogus ['bəʊgəs] *adj* falso(a); **b. company** compañía *f* fantasma

boil¹ [bɔɪl] **1** *n* **to come to the b.** empezar a hervir
2 *vt (water)* hervir; *(food)* cocer; *(egg)* cocer, pasar por agua
3 *vi* hervir; *Fig* **to b. with rage** estar furioso(a)
► **boil down** *vi* reducirse (**to** a)
► **boil over** *vi (milk)* salirse

boil² [bɔɪl] *n Med* furúnculo *m*

boiled [bɔɪld] *adj* **b. egg** huevo cocido *or* pasado por agua

boiler ['bɔɪlə(r)] *n* caldera *f*; *Br* **b. suit** mono *m* (de trabajo), *Am* overol *m*, *CSur, Cuba* mameluco *m*

boiling ['bɔɪlɪŋ] *adj* **b. water** agua *f* hirviendo; **it's b. hot** *(food)* quema; *(weather)* hace un calor agobiante; **b. point** punto *m* de ebullición

boisterous ['bɔɪstərəs] *adj* (**a**) *(person, party)* bullicioso(a) (**b**) *(weather)* borrascoso(a)

bold [bəʊld] *adj* (**a**) *(brave)* valiente (**b**) *(daring)* audaz (**c**) *Typ* **b. type** negrita *f*

Bolivia [bə'lɪvɪə] *n* Bolivia

Bolivian [bə'lɪvɪən] *adj & n* boliviano(a) *(m,f)*

bollard ['bɒlɑːd] *n Br (traffic barrier)* hito *m*

bollocks ['bɒləks] *npl Br very Fam* cojones *mpl*; **b.!** *(disagreement)* ¡y un huevo!

Bolshevik ['bɒlʃəvɪk] *adj & n* bolchevique *(mf)*

bolster ['bəʊlstə(r)] **1** *n (pillow)* cabezal *m*, travesaño *m*
2 *vt (strengthen)* reforzar; *(support)* apoyar

bolt [bəʊlt] **1** *n* (**a**) *(on door)* cerrojo *m*; *(small)* pestillo *m* (**b**) *Tech* perno *m*, tornillo *m* (**c**) *(of lightning)* rayo *m*
2 *vt* (**a**) *(lock)* cerrar con cerrojo (**b**) *Tech* sujetar con pernos (**c**) *Fam (food)* engullir
3 *vi (person)* largarse; *(horse)* desbocarse
4 *adv* **b. upright** derecho(a)

bomb [bɒm] **1** *n* bomba *f*; *Br Fam* **to cost a b.** costar un ojo de la cara; **car b.** coche-bomba *m*; **letter b.** carta-bomba *f*; **b. disposal squad** brigada *f* de artificieros; **b. scare** amenaza *f* de bomba
2 *vt (city etc)* bombardear; *(by terrorists)* volar
3 *vi Br Fam* **to b. (along)** *(car)* ir a toda pastilla

bombard [bɒm'bɑːd] *vt* bombardear

bombardment [bɒm'bɑːdmənt] *n* bombardeo *m*

bombastic [bɒm'bæstɪk] *adj* rimbombante

bomber ['bɒmə(r)] *n* (**a**) *Av* bombardero *m*; **b. jacket** cazadora *f or CSur* campera *f or Méx* chamarra *f* de aviador (**b**) *(person)* terrorista *mf (que coloca bombas)*

bombshell ['bɒmʃel] *n* (**a**) *Mil* obús *m* (**b**) *Fig (surprise)* bomba *f* (**c**) *Fam* **a blonde b.** una rubia explosiva

bona fide [bəʊnə'faɪd] *adj* (**a**) *(genuine)* auténtico(a) (**b**) *(in good faith)* bienintencionado(a)

bond [bɒnd] **1** *n* (**a**) *(link)* lazo *m*, vínculo *m* (**b**) *Fin* bono *m* (**c**) *(binding agreement)* acuerdo *m*
2 *vt (stick)* pegar
3 *vi (form attachment)* unirse (**with** a)

bondage ['bɒndɪdʒ] *n* esclavitud *f*

bone [bəʊn] **1** *n* (**a**) *(of person, animal)* hueso *m*; *(in fish)* espina *f*; *Fig* **b. of contention** manzana *f* de la discordia; *Fig* **he made no bones about it** no trató de disimularlo; **b. china** porcelana fina (**b**) **bones** *(remains)* restos *mpl*; **the bare bones** lo esencial
2 *vt (meat)* deshuesar; *(fish)* quitar las espinas a
► **bone up on** *vt insep Fam* empollar

bone-dry ['bəʊn'draɪ] *adj* completamente seco(a)

bone-idle ['bəʊn'aɪdəl] *adj* gandul(a)

bonfire ['bɒnfaɪə(r)] *n* hoguera *f*, fogata *f*; *Br* **B. Night** = fiesta del 5 de noviembre en que de noche se hacen hogueras y hay fuegos artificiales

bonkers ['bɒŋkəz] *adj Br Fam* **to be b.** estar chiflado(a) *or Esp* majareta

bonnet ['bɒnɪt] *n* (**a**) *(child's)* gorra *f* (**b**) *Br (of car)* capó *m*, *CAm, Méx* cofre *m*

bonus ['bəʊnəs] *n* (**a**) *(on wages)* prima *f* (**b**) *Fin (on shares)* dividendo *m* extraordinario (**c**) *Br Ins* beneficio *m*

bony ['bəʊnɪ] *adj* (**bonier, boniest**) *(person)* huesudo(a); *(fish)* lleno(a) de espinas

boo [buː] **1** *interj* ¡bu!
2 *n* abucheo *m*
3 *vt* abuchear

boob [buːb] *n Br Fam* (**a**) *(silly mistake)* metedura *f or Am* metida *f* de pata (**b**) **boobs** *(breasts)* tetas *fpl*

booby ['buːbɪ] *n* **b. prize** premio *m* de consolación; **b. trap** *(trick)* trampa *f*; *(explosive device)* trampa explosiva, bomba trampa *or* camuflada

booby-trap ['buːbɪtræp] *vt (pt & pp* **booby-trapped)** colocar una bomba trampa en

boogie ['buːgɪ] *vi Fam* bailar

book [bʊk] **1** *n* (**a**) *(printed volume)* libro *m; Fig* **by the b.** según las reglas; **b. end** sujetalibros *m inv* (**b**) *(of stamps)* carpeta *f;* (**c**) *(of matches)* cajetilla *f* (**c**) *Com* **books** cuentas *fpl*
  2 *vt* (**a**) *(reserve)* reservar; *(return flight)* cerrar (**b**) *(engage)* contratar (**c**) *(by police)* poner una multa a
▸ **book into** *vt insep (hotel)* reservar una habitación en
▸ **book out** *vi (of hotel)* marcharse
▸ **book up** *vt sep* **booked up** *(sign)* completo

bookcase ['bʊkkeɪs] *n* librería *f*, estantería *f*

booking ['bʊkɪŋ] *n esp Br (reservation)* reserva *f;* **b. office** taquilla *f, Am* boletería *f*

bookkeeping ['bʊkiːpɪŋ] *n Fin* contabilidad *f*

booklet ['bʊklɪt] *n* folleto *m*

bookmaker ['bʊkmeɪkə(r)] *n* corredor(a) *m,f* de apuestas

bookmark ['bʊkmɑːk] *n* marcador *m*

bookseller ['bʊkselə(r)] *n* librero(a) *m,f*

bookshelf ['bʊkʃelf] *n* **bookshelves** estantería *f*

bookshop ['bʊkʃɒp] *n* librería *f*

bookstall ['bʊkstɔːl] *n (in street)* puesto *m* de libros; *Br (in railway station)* quiosco *m* de prensa

bookstore ['bʊkstɔː(r)] *n US* librería *f*

bookworm ['bʊkwɜːm] *n Fam* ratón *m* de biblioteca

boom¹ [buːm] **1** *n* (**a**) *(noise)* estampido *m*, trueno *m* (**b**) *(sudden prosperity)* boom *m*, auge *m*
  2 *vi* (**a**) *(thunder)* retumbar; *(cannon)* tronar (**b**) *(prosper)* estar en auge

boom² [buːm] *n (of microphone)* jirafa *f*

boomerang ['buːməræŋ] *n* bumerang *m*, bumerán *m*

booming ['buːmɪŋ] *adj* (**a**) *(voice, thunder)* que retumba (**b**) *(prosperous)* en auge

boon [buːn] *n (blessing)* bendición *f*

boor [bʊə(r)] *n* grosero(a) *m,f*, cafre *mf*

boost [buːst] **1** *n* estímulo *m*, empujón *m*
  2 *vt* (**a**) *(increase)* aumentar (**b**) **to b. sb's confidence** subirle la moral a algn (**c**) *(tourism, exports)* fomentar (**d**) *(voltage)* elevar

booster ['buːstə(r)] *n* (**a**) *Elec* elevador *m* de voltaje (**b**) *Rad & TV (amplifier)*

amplificador *m* (**c**) *Med* **b. (shot)** revacunación *f*

boot¹ [buːt] **1** *n* (**a**) *(footwear)* bota *f;* *(ankle-length)* botín *m; Fig* **he's too big for his boots** es muy creído; *Br Fam* **to put the b. in** pisotear; *Fam* **she got the b.** la echaron (del trabajo); **b. polish** betún *m* (**b**) *Br (of car)* maletero *m, CAm, Méx* cajuela *f, CSur* baúl *m*
  2 *vt Fam* (**a**) *Ftb (ball)* chutar (**b**) **to b. (out)** echar a patadas (**c**) *Comput* arrancar
  3 *vi Comput* **to b. (up)** arrancar

boot² [buːt] *n* **to b.** además

bootblack ['buːtblæk] *n esp US* limpiabotas *mf inv*

booth [buːð, buːθ] *n* (**a**) *(in language lab etc)* cabina *f;* **telephone b.** cabina telefónica (**b**) *(at fair)* puesto *m*

bootleg ['buːtleg] *adj* de contrabando

bootlegger ['buːtlegə(r)] *n* contrabandista *mf*

booty ['buːtɪ] *n* botín *m*

booze [buːz] *Fam* **1** *n* bebida *f, Esp* priva *f, RP* chupi *m*
  2 *vi* empinar el codo, *Esp* privar, *RP* chupar

bop [bɒp] *Br Fam* **1** *n (dance)* baile *m*
  2 *vi Fam (dance)* bailar

Bordeaux [bɔːˈdəʊ] *n* (**a**) *(city)* Burdeos (**b**) *(wine)* burdeos *m*

border ['bɔːdə(r)] *n* (**a**) *(edge)* borde *m; (on clothes)* ribete *m* (**b**) *(frontier)* frontera *f* (**c**) *(flowerbed)* arriate *m*
▸ **border on** *vt insep* (**a**) *Geog* lindar con (**b**) *Fig* rayar en

borderline ['bɔːdəlaɪn] **1** *n* (**a**) *(border)* frontera *f* (**b**) *(dividing line)* línea divisoria
  2 *adj (case etc)* dudoso(a)

bore¹ [bɔː(r)] **1** *vt Tech* taladrar, perforar
  2 *n* (**a**) *Tech (hole)* taladro *m* (**b**) *(of gun)* calibre *m*

bore² [bɔː(r)] **1** *vt* aburrir
  2 *n (person)* pesado(a) *m,f*, pelma *mf; (thing)* lata *f*, rollo *m;* **what a b.!** ¡qué rollo!

bore³ [bɔː(r)] *pt of* **bear**

bored [bɔːd] *adj* aburrido(a); **to be b. stiff** *or* **to tears** estar aburrido(a) como una ostra *or RP* un perro

boredom ['bɔːdəm] *n* aburrimiento *m*

boring ['bɔːrɪŋ] *adj (uninteresting)* aburrido(a); *(tedious)* pesado(a), latoso(a)

born [bɔːn] **1** *pp of* **bear**; **to be b.** nacer; **I wasn't b. yesterday** no nací ayer
  2 *adj (having natural ability)* nato(a); **b. poet** poeta nato

born-again ['bɔːnəgen] *adj Rel* converso(a)

borne [bɔːn] *pp of* **bear**

borough ['bʌrə] n (a) (town) ciudad f; US (municipality) municipio m (b) Br (constituency) = división administrativa y electoral que comprende un municipio o un distrito urbano

borrow ['bɒrəʊ] 1 vt (a) (take on loan) tomar prestado(a); **can I b. your pen?** ¿me prestas or dejas tu bolígrafo? (b) (ideas etc) apropiarse
2 vi **she's always borrowing from other people** siempre está pidiendo cosas prestadas a los demás

borstal ['bɔːstəl] n Br Formerly correccional m, reformatorio m

Bosnia ['bɒznɪə] n Bosnia

Bosnia-Herzegovina ['bɒznɪəhɜːtsəgə'viːnə] n Bosnia y Herce-góvina

Bosnian ['bɒznɪən] adj & n bosnio(a) (m,f)

bosom ['bʊzəm] n (a) (breast) pecho m; (breasts) pechos mpl; **b. friend** amigo(a) m,f del alma (b) Fig seno m

boss [bɒs] n (a) (head) jefe(a) m,f; (factory owner etc) patrón(ona) m,f (b) esp US Pol jefe m; Pej cacique m
2 vt **to b. sb about** or **around** mandar sobre algn

bossy ['bɒsɪ] adj (**bossier, bossiest**) Fam mandón(ona)

bosun ['bəʊsən] n contramaestre m

botanic(al) [bə'tænɪk(əl)] adj botáni-co(a); **b. garden** jardín botánico

botany ['bɒtənɪ] n botánica f

botch [bɒtʃ] 1 vt chapucear; **a botched job** una chapuza
2 n chapuza f

both [bəʊθ] 1 adj ambos(as), los dos/las dos; **b. men are teachers** ambos son profesores; **hold it with b. hands** sujétalo con las dos manos
2 pron **b. (of them)** ambos(as), los dos/las dos; **b. of you** vosotros dos
3 conj a la vez; **b. England and Spain are in Europe** tanto Inglaterra como España están en Europa

bother ['bɒðə(r)] 1 vt (a) (disturb) molestar; (be a nuisance to) dar la lata a (b) (worry) preocupar; Fam **I can't be bothered** no tengo ganas
2 vi molestarse; **don't b. about me** no te preocupes por mí; **he didn't b. shaving** no se molestó en afeitarse
3 n (a) (disturbance) molestia f; (nuis-ance) lata f (b) (trouble) problemas mpl
4 interj Br ¡maldito sea!

bothersome ['bɒðəsəm] adj molesto(a)

bottle ['bɒtəl] 1 n botella f; (of perfume, ink) frasco m; **baby's b.** biberón m; **b. bank**

contenedor m de vidrio; **b. opener** abre-botellas m inv
2 vt (wine) embotellar; (fruit) enfrascar

▸ **bottle out** vi Br Fam rajarse

▸ **bottle up** vt sep reprimir

bottled ['bɒtəld] adj (beer, wine) en botella, embotellado(a); (fruit) envasa-do(a)

bottle-green ['bɒtəlɡriːn] adj verde botella

bottleneck ['bɒtəlnek] n Aut embote-llamiento m, atasco m

bottom ['bɒtəm] 1 adj (a) (lowest) más bajo(a); (drawer, shelf) de abajo; Aut **b. gear** primera f (b) (last) último(a); Fin **saldo m final**; Fig resultado m final
2 n (a) (lowest part) (of well, sea) fondo m; (of stairs, mountain, page) pie m; (of list) final m; Educ **to be (at) the b. of the class** ser el último/la última de la clase; **to touch b.** tocar fondo; Fam **bottoms up!** ¡salud! (b) (fundamental part, source) **to get to the b. of a matter** llegar al meollo de una cuestión; **who is at the b. of all this?** ¿quién está detrás de todo esto? (c) Fam (buttocks) trasero m

▸ **bottom out** vi Fin tocar fondo

bottomless ['bɒtəmlɪs] adj (abyss) sin fondo; (reserve) inagotable

boudoir ['buːdwɑː(r)] n tocador m

bough [baʊ] n rama f

bought [bɔːt] pt & pp of **buy**

bouillon ['buːjɒn] n caldo m; US **b. cube** pastilla f or cubito m de caldo (concentrado)

boulder ['bəʊldə(r)] n canto rodado

boulevard ['buːlvɑː(r)] n bulevar m

bounce [baʊns] 1 vi (a) (ball) rebotar (b) (jump) saltar (c) Fam (cheque) ser rechazado (por el banco)
2 vt (ball) botar
3 n (a) (of ball) bote m (b) (jump) salto m (c) (energy) vitalidad f

▸ **bounce back** vi (recover health) recuperarse, recobrarse

bouncer ['baʊnsə(r)] n Fam gorila m

bound¹ [baʊnd] adj (a) (tied up) atado(a) (b) (obliged) obligado(a) (c) (linked) vinculado(a) (with a) (d) **it's b. to happen** sucederá con toda seguridad; **it was b. to fail** estaba destinado al fracaso

bound² [baʊnd] 1 vi saltar
2 n salto m

bound³ [baʊnd] pt & pp of **bind**

bound⁴ [baʊnd] adj **b. for** con destino a, rumbo a; **to be b. for** dirigirse a

boundary ['baʊndərɪ] n límite m

boundless ['baʊndlɪs] *adj* ilimitado(a), sin límites

bounds [baʊndz] *npl* **beyond the b. of reality** más allá de la realidad; **her ambition knows no b.** su ambición no conoce límites; **the river is out of b.** está prohibido bajar al río

bounty ['baʊntɪ] *n* prima *f*, gratificación *f*

bouquet [buːˈkeɪ] *n* (**a**) *(of flowers)* ramillete *m* (**b**) *(of wine)* aroma *m*, buqué *m*

bourbon ['bɜːbən] *n US (whiskey)* whisky americano, bourbon *m*

bourgeois ['bʊəʒwɑː] *adj & n* burgués(esa) (*m,f*)

bourgeoisie [bʊəʒwɑːˈziː] *n* burguesía *f*

bout [baʊt] *n* (**a**) *(of work)* turno *m*; *(of illness)* ataque *m* (**b**) *(in boxing)* combate *m*

boutique [buːˈtiːk] *n* boutique *f*, tienda *f*

bow¹ [baʊ] **1** *vi* (**a**) *(as greeting, sign of respect)* inclinar la cabeza (**b**) *(give in)* ceder
2 *n (with head, body)* reverencia *f*
▶ **bow out** *vi* retirarse (**of** de)

bow² [bəʊ] *n* (**a**) *Sport & Mus* arco *m*; *Fig* **to have more than one string to one's b.** ser una persona de recursos (**b**) *(knot)* lazo *m*; **b. tie** *Esp* pajarita *f*, *CAm, Carib, Col* corbatín *m*, *Méx* corbata *f* de moño

bow³ [baʊ] *n (of ship)* proa *f*

bowel ['baʊəl] *n* intestino *m*; **bowels** entrañas *fpl*

bowl¹ [bəʊl] *n* (**a**) *(dish)* cuenco *m*; *(for soup)* tazón *m*; *(for washing hands)* palangana *f*; *(for washing clothes, dishes)* barreño *m*; *(of toilet)* taza *f* (**b**) *Geol* cuenca *f*

bowl² [bəʊl] **1** *n* bola *f*
2 *vt (in cricket)* lanzar
3 *vi* (**a**) *(play bowls)* jugar a los bolos (**b**) *(in cricket)* lanzar la pelota
▶ **bowl along** *vi Fam (car)* ir volando
▶ **bowl out** *vt sep (in cricket)* eliminar
▶ **bowl over** *vt sep* (**a**) *(knock down)* derribar (**b**) *Fig (astonish)* desconcertar

bow-legged ['bəʊleg(ɪ)d] *adj* patizambo(a)

bowler¹ ['bəʊlə(r)] *n (in cricket)* lanzador(a) *m,f*

bowler² ['bəʊlə(r)] *n (hat)* bombín *m*

bowling ['bəʊlɪŋ] *n (game)* bolos *mpl*; **b. alley** bolera *f*; **b. ball** bola *f* (de jugar a los bolos)

bowls [bəʊlz] *npl Sport* bolos *mpl*

box¹ [bɒks] **1** *n* (**a**) *(container)* caja *f*; *(of matches)* cajetilla *f*; *Cin & Th* **b. office**

taquilla *f* (**b**) *Th* palco *m* (**c**) *Br Fam (television)* **the b.** la tele
2 *vt (pack)* embalar

box² [bɒks] *Sport* **1** *vi* boxear
2 *vt (hit)* pegar; **to b. sb's ears** dar un cachete a algn

boxcar ['bɒkskɑː(r)] *n US* vagón *m* de mercancías, furgón *m* (de mercancías)

boxer ['bɒksə(r)] *n* (**a**) *(fighter)* boxeador *m* (**b**) *(dog)* bóxer *m*

boxing ['bɒksɪŋ] *n* boxeo *m*, *CAm, Méx* box *m*; **b. ring** cuadrilátero *m*

Boxing Day ['bɒksɪŋdeɪ] *n Br* = el día de San Esteban *(26 de diciembre)*

boxroom ['bɒksruːm] *n Br* = en una vivienda, cuarto pequeño sin ventana que se suele usar como trastero

boy [bɔɪ] *n* (**a**) *(child)* niño *m*, chico *m*; *(youth)* joven *m*; **b. band** = grupo musical juvenil compuesto por adolescentes varones; *Fam* **oh b.!** ¡vaya! (**b**) *(son)* hijo *m*

boycott ['bɔɪkɒt] **1** *n* boicot *m*
2 *vt* boicotear

boyfriend ['bɔɪfrend] *n* novio *m*; *(live-in)* compañero *m*

boyhood ['bɔɪhʊd] *n* niñez *f*, juventud *f*

boyish ['bɔɪɪʃ] *adj* juvenil, de muchacho

bra [brɑː] *n* sostén *m*, *Esp* sujetador *m*, *Carib, Col, Méx* brasier *m*, *RP* corpiño *m*

brace [breɪs] **1** *n* (**a**) *(clamp)* abrazadera *f*; *(of drill)* berbiquí *m*; *(for teeth)* aparato *m* (**b**) *Br* **braces** *(for trousers)* tirantes *mpl*
2 *vt* (**a**) *(reinforce)* reforzar (**b**) **to b. oneself (for)** prepararse *or Chile, Méx, Ven* alistarse (para)
▶ **brace up** *vi* cobrar ánimo

bracelet ['breɪslɪt] *n* pulsera *f*

bracing ['breɪsɪŋ] *adj (wind)* fresco(a); *(stimulating)* tonificante

bracken ['brækən] *n* helecho *m*

bracket ['brækɪt] **1** *n* (**a**) *Typ (round)* paréntesis *m*; *(square)* corchete *m*; *(curly)* llave *f*; **in brackets** entre paréntesis (**b**) *(support)* soporte *m*; *(for lamp)* brazo *m*; *(shelf)* repisa *f* (**c**) *(for tax)* sector *m*
2 *vt* (**a**) *(phrase etc)* poner entre paréntesis (**b**) *(group together)* agrupar, juntar

brag [bræg] *vi* jactarse (**about** de)

braggart ['brægət] *n* fanfarrón(ona) *m,f*

braid [breɪd] **1** *vt* trenzar
2 *n* (**a**) *Sewing* galón *m* (**b**) *esp US (plait)* trenza *f*

Braille [breɪl] *n* braille *m*

brain [breɪn] *n* (**a**) *(organ)* cerebro *m*; **she's got cars on the b.** está obsesionada por los coches; *Med* **b. death** muerte *f* cerebral; *Fig* **b. drain** fuga *f* de cerebros;

b. wave idea *f* genial (**b**) *Fam* **brains** inteligencia *f*; **to have brains** ser inteligente; *Br* **brains** *or US* **b. trust** grupo *m* de expertos (**c**) *Culin* **brains** sesos *mpl*

brainchild ['breɪntʃaɪld] *n* invento *m*, idea *f* genial

brainpower ['breɪnpaʊə(r)] *n* capacidad *f* intelectual

brainstorm ['breɪnstɔːm] *n* (**a**) *(outburst)* arranque *m* (**b**) *(brainwave)* genialidad *f*, lluvia *f* de ideas

brainwash ['breɪnwɒʃ] *vt* lavar el cerebro a

brainy ['breɪnɪ] *adj* (**brainier, brainiest**) *Fam* listo(a)

braise [breɪz] *vt* estofar, *Andes, Méx* ahogar

brake [breɪk] **1** *n Aut (also pl)* freno *m*; **b. drum** tambor *m* del freno; **b. fluid** líquido *m* de frenos; **b. light** luz *f* de freno
2 *vi* frenar, echar el freno

bramble ['bræmbəl] *n* zarza *f*, zarzamora *f*

bran [bræn] *n* salvado *m*

branch [brɑːntʃ] **1** *n (of tree)* rama *f*; *(of road)* bifurcación *f*; *(of science etc)* ramo *m*; *Com* **b. (office)** sucursal *f*
2 *vi (road)* bifurcarse

▸ **branch off** *vi* desviarse

▸ **branch out** *vi* diversificarse

brand [brænd] **1** *n* (**a**) *Com* marca *f*; **b. name** marca de fábrica (**b**) *(type)* clase *f* (**c**) *(on cattle)* hierro *m*
2 *vt* (**a**) *(animal)* marcar con hierro candente (**b**) *(label)* tildar

brandish ['brændɪʃ] *vt* blandir

brand-new ['brænd'njuː] *adj* flamante

brandy ['brændɪ] *n* brandy *m*, coñac *m*, *RP* cognac *m*

brash [bræʃ] *adj* (**a**) *(impudent)* descarado(a) (**b**) *(reckless)* temerario(a) (**c**) *(loud, showy)* chillón(ona)

brass [brɑːs] *n* (**a**) *(metal)* latón *m* (**b**) *Br Fam (money) Esp* pasta *f*, *Esp, RP* guita *f*, *Am* plata *f*, *Méx* lana *f* (**c**) *Mus* instrumentos *mpl* de metal; **b. band** banda *f* de metal

brassiere ['bræzɪə(r)] *n* sostén *m*, *Esp* sujetador *m*, *Carib, Col, Méx* brasier *m*, *RP* corpiño *m*

brat [bræt] *n Fam* mocoso(a) *m,f*

bravado [brə'vɑːdəʊ] *n* bravuconería *f*

brave [breɪv] **1** *adj* valiente, valeroso(a)
2 *n US* (**Indian**) **b.** guerrero indio
3 *vt* (**a**) *(face)* hacer frente a (**b**) *(defy)* desafiar

bravely ['breɪvlɪ] *adv* valientemente

bravery ['breɪvərɪ] *n* valentía *f*, valor *m*

bravo [brɑː'vəʊ] *interj* ¡bravo!

brawl [brɔːl] **1** *n* reyerta *f*
2 *vi* pelearse

brawn [brɔːn] *n* (**a**) *(strength)* fuerza física (**b**) *Br Culin* queso *m* de cerdo

bray [breɪ] **1** *n (of donkey)* rebuzno *m*
2 *vi* rebuznar

brazen ['breɪzən] *adj* descarado(a)

Brazil [brə'zɪl] *n* (el) Brasil

brazil [brə'zɪl] *n* **b. nut** nuez *f* del Brasil

Brazilian [brə'zɪlɪən] *adj & n* brasileño(a) *(m,f)*

breach [briːtʃ] **1** *n* (**a**) *(in wall)* brecha *f* (**b**) *(violation)* incumplimiento *m*; **b. of confidence** abuso *m* de confianza; **b. of contract** incumplimiento de contrato; **b. of the law** violación *f* de la ley; **b. of the peace** alteración *f* del orden público (**c**) *(in relations)* ruptura *f*
2 *vt* violar

bread [bred] *n* (**a**) *(food)* pan *m*; **b. and butter** pan con mantequilla, *Am* pan con manteca; *Fig* **our daily b.** el pan nuestro de cada día (**b**) *Fam (money) Esp* pasta *f*, *Esp, RP* guita *f*, *Am* plata *f*, *Méx* lana *f*

breadboard ['bredbɔːd] *n* tabla *f* (para cortar el pan)

breadcrumb ['bredkrʌm] *n* miga *f* de pan; **breadcrumbs** pan rallado

breadline ['bredlaɪn] *n Fam* miseria *f*; **to be on the b.** vivir en la miseria

breadth [bredθ] *n* (**a**) *(width)* anchura *f*; **it is 2 m in b.** tiene 2 m de ancho (**b**) *(extent)* amplitud *f*

breadwinner ['bredwɪnə(r)] *n* cabeza *mf* de familia

break [breɪk] **1** *vt (pt broke; pp broken)* (**a**) *(in general)* romper; **to b. a leg** romperse la pierna; **to b. a record** batir un récord; *Fig* **to b. sb's heart** partirle el corazón a algn (**b**) *(fail to keep)* faltar a; **to b. a contract** romper un contrato; **to b. the law** violar la ley (**c**) *(destroy)* destrozar; *Fin* arruinar (**d**) *(interrupt)* interrumpir (**e**) *(soften) (fall)* amortiguar (**f**) **she broke the news to him** le comunicó la noticia
2 *vi* (**a**) *(glass, machine, bone)* romperse; *(waves)* romper (**b**) *(storm)* estallar (**c**) *(voice)* cambiar (**d**) *(health)* resentirse (**e**) **when day breaks** al rayar el alba (**f**) *(story)* divulgarse
3 *n* (**a**) *(fracture)* rotura *f*; *(crack)* grieta *f*; *(opening)* abertura *f* (**b**) *(in relationship)* ruptura *f* (**c**) *(pause)* pausa *f*, descanso *m*; *(at school)* recreo *m*; **to take a b.** descansar un rato; *(holiday)* tomar unos días libres; (**d**) *Fam (chance)* oportunidad *f*

▸ **break away** *vi* (**a**) *(become separate)* desprenderse (**from** de) (**b**) *(escape)* escaparse

▸ **break down** 1 *vt sep* (**a**) *(door)* derribar (**b**) *(resistance)* acabar con (**c**) *(costs)* desglosar

2 *vi* (**a**) *Aut* tener una avería (**b**) *(resistance)* ceder (**c**) *(health)* debilitarse (**d**) *(weep)* ponerse a llorar

▸ **break in** 1 *vt sep* acostumbrar; **to b. in a pair of shoes** cogerle la forma a los zapatos

2 *vi (burglar)* entrar por la fuerza

▸ **break into** *vt insep* (**a**) *(burgle) (house)* allanar; *(safe)* forzar (**b**) **to b. into song** empezar a cantar

▸ **break off** 1 *vt sep* partir

2 *vi* (**a**) *(become detached)* desprenderse (**b**) *(talks)* interrumpirse (**c**) *(stop)* pararse

▸ **break out** *vi* (**a**) *(prisoners)* escaparse (**b**) *(war etc)* estallar; **she broke out in a rash** le salió un sarpullido

▸ **break through** 1 *vt insep* (**a**) *(crowd)* abrirse paso por; *(cordon)* romper (**b**) *(clouds)* atravesar

2 *vi* (**a**) *(crowd)* abrirse paso (**b**) *(sun)* salir

▸ **break up** 1 *vt sep (object)* romper; *(car)* desguazar; *(crowd)* disolver

2 *vi* (**a**) *(object)* romperse (**b**) *(crowd)* disolverse; *(meeting)* levantarse (**c**) *(relationship)* fracasar; *(couple)* separarse (**d**) *Educ* terminar

▸ **break with** *vt insep (past)* romper con

breakable ['breɪkəbəl] *adj* frágil

breakage ['breɪkɪdʒ] *n (breaking)* rotura *f*

breakaway ['breɪkəweɪ] *adj* disidente

breakdown ['breɪkdaʊn] *n* (**a**) *Aut* avería *f*; *Br* **b. truck** grúa *f* (**b**) *(nervous)* **b.** crisis nerviosa (**c**) *(in communications) Esp* fallo *m*, *Am* falla *f* (**d**) *(analysis)* análisis *m*; *Fin* desglose *m*

breaker ['breɪkə(r)] *n* (**a**) *(wave)* ola *f* grande (**b**) *Tech* trituradora *f* (**c**) *(switch)* interruptor automático

breakfast ['brekfəst] 1 *n* desayuno *m*; **to have b.** desayunar

2 *vi* desayunar

break-in ['breɪkɪn] *n* robo *m (con allanamiento de morada)*

breaking ['breɪkɪŋ] *n* (**a**) **b. point** *(of person, patience)* límite *m* (**b**) *Jur* **b. and entering** allanamiento *m* de morada

breakthrough ['breɪkθruː] *n* paso *m* adelante, avance *m*

breakwater ['breɪkwɔːtə(r)] *n* rompeolas *m inv*

breast [brest] *n (chest)* pecho *m*; *(of woman)* pecho, seno *m*; *(of chicken etc)* pechuga *f*; *Fig* **to make a clean b. of it** dar la cara

breast-feed ['brestfiːd] *vt* dar el pecho a, amamantar a

breaststroke ['breststrəʊk] *n* braza *f*

breath [breθ] *n* respiración *f*; **in the same b.** al mismo tiempo; **out of b.** sin aliento; **to catch one's b.** recobrar el aliento; **to draw b.** respirar; **under one's b.** en voz baja; *Fig* **to take sb's b. away** dejar pasmado(a) a algn; **to go out for a b. of fresh air** salir a tomar el aire; *Aut* **b. test** alcoholemia *f*

Breathalyser®, *US* **Breathalyzer®** ['breθəlaɪzə(r)] *n* alcoholímetro *m*

breathe [briːð] 1 *vt* respirar; **to b. a sigh of relief** dar un suspiro de alivio

2 *vi* respirar; **to b. in** aspirar; **to b. out** espirar; **to b. heavily** resoplar

breather ['briːðə(r)] *n* Fam (rest) descanso *m*

breathing ['briːðɪŋ] *n* respiración *f*; **b. space** pausa *f*, respiro *m*

breathless ['breθlɪs] *adj* sin aliento, jadeante

breathtaking ['breθteɪkɪŋ] *adj* impresionante

bred [bred] *pt & pp of* **breed**

breeches ['brɪtʃɪz, 'briːtʃɪz] *npl* bombachos *mpl*; **knee b., riding b.** pantalones *mpl* de montar

breed [briːd] 1 *n (of animal)* raza *f*; *Fig (class)* clase *f*

2 *vt (pt & pp* **bred**) *(animals)* criar; *Fig (ideas)* engendrar

3 *vi (animals)* reproducirse

breeder ['briːdə(r)] *n* (**a**) *(person)* criador(a) *m,f* (**b**) **(fast) b. reactor** reactor *m* generador

breeding ['briːdɪŋ] *n* (**a**) *(of animals)* cría *f*; *Fig* **b. ground** caldo *m* de cultivo (**b**) *(of person)* educación *f*

breeze [briːz] 1 *n* brisa *f*; *Br Constr* **b. block** bloque *m* de cemento

2 *vi* **to b. in/out** entrar/salir despreocupadamente

breezy ['briːzɪ] *adj* (**breezier, breeziest**) (**a**) *(weather)* ventoso(a) (**b**) *(person)* despreocupado(a)

brevity ['brevɪtɪ] *n* brevedad *f*

brew [bruː] 1 *vt (beer)* elaborar; *(hot drink)* preparar

2 *vi (tea)* reposar; *Fig* **a storm is brewing** se prepara una tormenta; *Fam* **something's brewing** algo se está cociendo

3 n (a) (of tea) infusión f; Fam (of beer) birra f (b) (magic potion) brebaje m

brewer ['bruːə(r)] n cervecero(a) m,f

brewery ['bruːərɪ] n cervecería f

brewing ['bruːɪŋ] **1** adj cervecero(a)
2 n (of beer) elaboración f de la cerveza

briar ['braɪə(r)] n brezo m

bribe [braɪb] **1** vt sobornar
2 n soborno m, Andes, CSur coima f, CAm, Méx mordida f

bribery ['braɪbərɪ] n soborno m

bric-a-brac ['brɪkəbræk] n baratijas fpl

brick [brɪk] n ladrillo m; Br Fam Old-fashioned **he's a b.** es un gran tipo

bricklayer ['brɪkleɪə(r)] n albañil m

brickwork ['brɪkwɜːk] n ladrillos mpl

bridal ['braɪdəl] adj nupcial

bride [braɪd] n novia f; **the b. and groom** los novios

bridegroom ['braɪdgruːm] n novio m

bridesmaid ['braɪdzmeɪd] n dama f de honor

bridge¹ [brɪdʒ] **1** n puente m; (of nose) caballete m; (of ship) puente m de mando
2 vt (a) (river) tender un puente sobre (b) (gap) llenar; Br Fin **bridging loan** crédito m a corto plazo

bridge² [brɪdʒ] n Cards bridge m

bridle ['braɪdəl] **1** n brida f; (bit) freno m; **b. path** camino m de herradura
2 vt (horse) embridar

brief [briːf] **1** adj (a) (short) breve (b) (concise) conciso(a)
2 n (a) (report) informe m; **in b.** en resumen (b) Jur expediente m (c) Mil instrucciones fpl (d) **briefs** (for men) calzoncillos mpl, Chile fundillos mpl, Méx calzones mpl; (for women) Esp bragas fpl, Chile, Col, Méx calzones mpl, RP bombacha f
3 vt (a) (inform) informar (b) (instruct) dar instrucciones a

briefcase ['briːfkeɪs] n cartera f, portafolios m inv

briefing ['briːfɪŋ] n (meeting) reunión informativa

briefly ['briːflɪ] adv brevemente; **as b. as possible** con la mayor brevedad (posible)

brigade [brɪ'geɪd] n brigada f

brigadier [brɪgə'dɪə(r)] n Br general m de brigada; US **b. general** general de brigada

bright [braɪt] adj (a) (light, sun, eyes) brillante; (colour) vivo(a); (day) claro(a) (b) (cheerful) alegre (c) (clever) listo(a), espabilado(a) (d) (promising) prometedor(a)

brighten ['braɪtən] vi (prospects) mejorarse; (face) iluminarse

▸ **brighten up 1** vt sep (room etc) alegrar
2 vi (weather) despejarse; (person) animarse

brightly ['braɪtlɪ] adv brillantemente

brightness ['braɪtnɪs] n (a) (of sun) resplandor m; (of day) claridad f; (of colour) viveza f (b) (cleverness) inteligencia f

brilliance ['brɪljəns] n (a) (of light) brillo m; (of colour) viveza f (b) (of person) brillantez f

brilliant ['brɪljənt] **1** adj (a) (bright, intense) radiante, resplandeciente; (colour) brillante (b) (person, idea) genial (c) Br (excellent) genial, Am salvo RP chévere, Andes, CSur macanudo(a), Méx padre, RP bárbaro(a)
2 n brillante m

brim [brɪm] **1** n borde m; (of hat) ala f; **full to the b.** lleno(a) hasta el borde
2 vi rebosar (**with** de)

▸ **brim over** vi rebosar

brine [braɪn] n salmuera f

bring [brɪŋ] vt (pt & pp brought) (a) (carry, take) traer; (lead) llevar (b) (cause) provocar; **he brought it upon himself** se lo buscó (c) (persuade) convencer; **how did they b. themselves to do it?** ¿cómo llegaron a hacerlo?

▸ **bring about** vt sep provocar

▸ **bring along** vt sep traer

▸ **bring back** vt sep (a) (return) devolver (b) (reintroduce) volver a introducir (c) (make one remember) traerle a la memoria

▸ **bring down** vt sep (a) (from upstairs) bajar (b) (government) derribar; Th **to b. the house down** echar el teatro abajo con los aplausos (c) (reduce) rebajar

▸ **bring forward** vt sep (a) (meeting etc) adelantar (b) (present) presentar (c) Fin **brought forward** suma y sigue

▸ **bring in** vt sep (a) (yield) dar (b) (show in) hacer entrar (c) (law etc) introducir; (fashion) lanzar

▸ **bring off** vt sep lograr, conseguir

▸ **bring on** vt sep provocar

▸ **bring out** vt sep (a) (publish) publicar (b) (reveal) recalcar; **he brings out the worst in me** despierta lo peor que hay en mí

▸ **bring round** vt sep (a) (revive) hacer volver en sí (b) (persuade) convencer

▸ **bring to** vt sep reanimar

▸ **bring up** vt sep (a) (educate) criar, educar (b) (subject) plantear (c) (vomit) devolver

brink [brɪŋk] n (edge) borde m; Fig **on the b. of ruin** al borde de la ruina; **on the b. of tears** a punto de llorar

brisk [brɪsk] *adj (person, manner)* enérgico(a); *(pace)* rápido(a); *(trade)* activo(a); *(weather, wind)* fresco(a)

bristle ['brɪsəl] **1** *n* cerda *f*
  2 *vi* (**a**) *(animal's fur)* erizarse (**b**) *(show anger)* enfurecerse (**at** con)
► **bristle with** *vt insep (be full of)* estar lleno(a) de

Brit [brɪt] *n Fam* británico(a) *m,f*

Britain ['brɪtən] *n* (**Great**) **B.** Gran Bretaña

British ['brɪtɪʃ] **1** *adj* británico(a); **the B. Isles** las Islas Británicas
  2 *npl* the **B.** los británicos

Brittany ['brɪtənɪ] *n* Bretaña

brittle ['brɪtəl] *adj* quebradizo(a), frágil

broach [brəʊtʃ] *vt (subject)* abordar

broad [brɔːd] *adj* (**a**) *(wide)* ancho(a); *(large)* extenso(a) (**b**) **a b. hint** *(clear)* una indirecta clara (**c**) *(daylight)* pleno(a) (**d**) *(not detailed)* general (**e**) *(accent)* marcado(a), cerrado(a)

broadband ['brɔːdbænd] **1** *n Tel* banda *f* ancha
  2 *adj Comput* de banda ancha

broadcast ['brɔːdkɑːst] *Rad & TV* **1** *n* emisión *f*
  2 *vt (pt & pp* **broadcast)** emitir, transmitir

broadcaster ['brɔːdkɑːstə(r)] *n* locutor(a) *m,f*

broadcasting ['brɔːdkɑːstɪŋ] *n Rad* radiodifusión *f; TV* transmisión *f; Rad* **b. station** emisora *f*

broaden ['brɔːdən] *vt* ensanchar

broadly ['brɔːdlɪ] *adv* en términos generales

broad-minded [brɔːd'maɪndɪd] *adj* liberal, tolerante

broadsheet ['brɔːdʃiːt] *n* folleto *m*

broccoli ['brɒkəlɪ] *n* brécol *m*

brochure ['brəʊʃə(r), 'brəʊʃʊə(r)] *n* folleto *m*

broil [brɔɪl] *vt US (grill)* asar a la parrilla

broiler ['brɔɪlə(r)] *n* (**a**) *(chicken)* pollo (tomatero) (**b**) *US (grill)* parrilla *f*

broke [brəʊk] **1** *adj Fam* **to be b.** estar sin un centavo *or Méx* sin un peso *or Esp* sin blanca
  2 *pt of* **break**

broken ['brəʊkən] **1** *adj* (**a**) *(object, bone, promise)* roto(a); *(machinery)* estropeado(a); (**b**) *(home)* deshecho(a); *(person)* destrozado(a); *(ground)* accidentado(a); **to speak b. English** chapurrear el inglés
  2 *pp of* **break**

broken-hearted [brəʊkən'hɑːtɪd] *adj Fig* con el corazón destrozado

broker ['brəʊkə(r)] *n* corredor *m*, agente *mf* de Bolsa

brolly ['brɒlɪ] *n Br Fam* paraguas *m inv*

bronchitis [brɒŋ'kaɪtɪs] *n* bronquitis *f*

bronze [brɒnz] **1** *n* bronce *m*
  2 *adj (material)* de bronce; *(colour)* bronceado(a)

bronzed [brɒnzd] *adj (suntanned)* bronceado(a)

brooch [brəʊtʃ] *n* broche *m*

brood [bruːd] **1** *n (birds)* cría *f; Hum (children)* prole *f*
  2 *vi (hen)* empollar; *Fig* **to b. over a problem** darle vueltas a un problema

broody ['bruːdɪ] *adj* (**broodier, broodiest**) (**a**) *(pensive)* pensativo(a) (**b**) *(moody)* melancólico(a) (**c**) *Br Fam (woman)* con ganas de tener hijos

brook¹ [brʊk] *n* arroyo *m*

brook² [brʊk] *vt Fml (tolerate)* soportar, consentir

broom [bruːm] *n* (**a**) *(for cleaning)* escoba *f* (**b**) *Bot* retama *f*

broomstick ['bruːmstɪk] *n* palo *m* de escoba

Bros *Com (abbr* **Brothers)** Hnos

broth [brɒθ] *n* caldo *m*

brothel ['brɒθəl] *n* burdel *m*

brother ['brʌðə(r)] *n* hermano *m*; **brothers and sisters** hermanos

brotherhood ['brʌðəhʊd] *n* hermandad *f*

brother-in-law ['brʌðərɪnlɔː] *n (pl* **brothers-in-law)** cuñado *m*

brotherly ['brʌðəlɪ] *adj* fraternal

brought [brɔːt] *pt & pp of* **bring**

brow [braʊ] *n* (**a**) *(forehead)* frente *f* (**b**) *(eyebrow)* ceja *f* (**c**) *(of hill)* cima *f*

brown [braʊn] **1** *adj* marrón, *Am* café; *(hair, eyes)* castaño(a); *(skin)* moreno(a); **b. bread** pan *m* integral; **b. paper** papel *m* de estraza; **b. sugar** azúcar moreno
  2 *n* marrón *m*, *Am* color *m* café
  3 *vt Culin* dorar; *(tan)* broncear

Brownie ['braʊnɪ] *n* escultista *f*

brownish ['braʊnɪʃ] *adj* pardusco(a)

browse [braʊz] **1** *vi (in shop)* mirar; *(through book)* hojear
  2 *vt Comput* **to b. the Web** navegar por la Web
  3 *n* **to have a b. (in)** dar un vistazo (a)

browser ['braʊzə(r)] *n Comput* navegador *m*

bruise [bruːz] **1** *n* morado *m*, cardenal *m*
  2 *vt (body)* contusionar; *(fruit)* estropear
  3 *vi (body)* magullarse; *(fruit)* estropearse

brunch [brʌntʃ] *n Fam* desayuno-comida *m, RP* brunch *m*

brunette [bruːˈnet] adj & n morena (f)

brunt [brʌnt] n **the b.** lo peor; **to bear the b.** llevar el peso

brush¹ [brʌʃ] 1 n (a) (for hair, teeth) cepillo m; Art pincel m; (for house-painting) brocha f (b) (with the law) roce m
2 vt (a) (clean) cepillar; **to b. one's hair** cepillarse el pelo; **to b. one's teeth** cepillarse los dientes (b) (touch lightly) rozar
3 vi **to b. against** rozar al pasar
▸ **brush aside** vt sep dejar de lado
▸ **brush off** vt sep Fam no hacer caso a, Esp pasar de
▸ **brush up** vt sep repasar

brush² [brʌʃ] n (undergrowth) broza f, maleza f

brush-off [ˈbrʌʃɒf] n Fam **to give sb the b.** no hacer ni caso a algn

brushwood [ˈbrʌʃwʊd] n maleza f

brusque [bruːsk, brʊsk] adj brusco(a)

Brussels [ˈbrʌsəlz] n Bruselas

brutal [ˈbruːtəl] adj brutal, cruel

brute [bruːt] 1 adj bruto(a); **b. force** fuerza bruta
2 n (animal) bruto m; (person) bestia f

BSc [biːesˈsiː] n (abbr **Bachelor of Science**) (person) licenciado(a) m,f en Ciencias

BSE [biːesˈiː] n (abbr **bovine spongiform encephalopathy**) encefalopatía f espongiforme bovina (enfermedad de las vacas locas)

bubble [ˈbʌbəl] 1 n burbuja f; **b. bath** espuma f de baño; **b. gum** chicle m; **soap b.** pompa f de jabón
2 vi (form bubbles) burbujear, borbotear

bubbly [ˈbʌblɪ] 1 adj (**bubblier, bubbliest**) efervescente
2 n Fam champán m, cava m

buck¹ [bʌk] 1 n (male deer) ciervo m; (male goat) macho cabrío; Fam **to pass the b. to sb** echarle el muerto a algn
2 vi (horse) corcovear
▸ **buck up** vt sep Fam **b. your ideas up!** ¡espabílate!
2 vi (cheer up) animarse

buck² [bʌk] n US, Austr Fam dólar m

bucket [ˈbʌkɪt] 1 n balde m, Esp cubo m; Br Fam **it's raining buckets** llueve a cántaros or RP a baldes
2 vi Fam **it's bucketing (down)** llueve a cántaros or RP a baldes

buckle [ˈbʌkəl] 1 n hebilla f
2 vt abrochar (con hebilla)
3 vi (a) (wall, metal) combarse (b) (knees) doblarse

bud [bʌd] 1 n (shoot) brote m; (flower) capullo m

2 vi (plant) brotar, salir; Fig (talent) brotar, nacer

Buddhism [ˈbʊdɪzəm] n budismo m

Buddhist [ˈbʊdɪst] adj & n budista (mf)

budding [ˈbʌdɪŋ] adj en ciernes

buddy [ˈbʌdɪ] n US Fam Esp colega mf, Am compadre m, Am hermano(a) m,f, Méx cuate m

budge [bʌdʒ] vi (a) (move) moverse (b) (yield) ceder

budgerigar [ˈbʌdʒərɪgɑː(r)] n periquito (australiano)

budget [ˈbʌdʒɪt] 1 n presupuesto m; Br Pol **the B.** ≃ los Presupuestos Generales del Estado
2 vi hacer un presupuesto (**for** para)

budgie [ˈbʌdʒɪ] n Br Fam = **budgerigar**

buff¹ [bʌf] 1 adj & n (colour) color (m) de ante
2 vt dar brillo a

buff² [bʌf] n Fam (enthusiast) aficionado(a) m,f

buffalo [ˈbʌfələʊ] n (pl **buffaloes** or **buffalo**) búfalo m

buffer [ˈbʌfə(r)] 1 n (a) (device) amortiguador m; Rail tope m; **b. zone** zona f de seguridad (b) Comput memoria intermedia
2 vt amortiguar

buffet¹ [ˈbʊfeɪ] n (a) (snack bar) bar m; (at railway station) cantina f; Rail **b. car** coche m restaurante (b) (self-service meal) bufet m libre (c) (item of furniture) aparador m

buffet² [ˈbʌfɪt] vt golpear

buffoon [bəˈfuːn] n bufón m, payaso m

bug [bʌg] 1 n (a) (insect) bicho m (b) Fam (microbe) microbio m; **the flu b.** el virus de la gripe (c) (hidden microphone) micrófono oculto (d) Comput error m
2 vt Fam (a) **to b. a room** ocultar micrófonos en una habitación (b) (annoy) fastidiar, molestar

bugger [ˈbʌgə(r)] 1 n Br very Fam (unpleasant person) cabrón(ona) m,f; **you silly b.** ¡qué tonto(a) eres!; **the poor b.!** ¡pobre desgraciado!; **b. all** nada de nada
2 vt (a) (sodomize) sodomizar (b) Br very Fam **b. (it)!** ¡carajo!, Esp ¡joder!, RP ¡la puta (digo)!
▸ **bugger about** very Fam 1 vi hacer chorradas
2 vt sep **they really buggered him about** se las hicieron pasar canutas
▸ **bugger off** vi very Fam Pej pirarse; **b. off!** ¡vete a la mierda!
▸ **bugger up** vt sep very Fam jorobar

buggy ['bʌgɪ] n (**a**) Br (baby's pushchair) sillita f de niño (**b**) US (pram) cochecito m (de niño)

bugle ['bju:gəl] n bugle m

build [bɪld] **1** vt (pt & pp **built**) construir **2** n (physique) tipo m, físico m

▸ **build up** vt sep (accumulate) acumular; **to b. up a reputation** labrarse una buena reputación

builder ['bɪldə(r)] n constructor(a) m,f; (contractor) contratista mf

building ['bɪldɪŋ] n edificio m, construcción f; **b. site** obra f; Br **b. society** sociedad hipotecaria

build-up ['bɪldʌp] n (**a**) (accumulation) aumento m; (of gas) acumulación f (**b**) (publicity) propaganda f

built [bɪlt] pt & pp of build

built-in ['bɪlt'ɪn] adj (**a**) (cupboard) empotrado(a) (**b**) (incorporated) incorporado(a)

built-up [bɪlt'ʌp] adj urbanizado(a)

bulb [bʌlb] n (**a**) Bot bulbo m (**b**) (light bulb) Esp bombilla f, Andes, Méx foco m, CAm, Carib bombillo m, RP lamparita f

Bulgaria [bʌl'geərɪə] n Bulgaria

Bulgarian [bʌl'geərɪən] **1** adj búlgaro(a) **2** n (**a**) (person) búlgaro(a) m,f (**b**) (language) búlgaro m

bulge [bʌldʒ] **1** n protuberancia f; (in pocket) bulto m **2** vi (swell) hincharse; (be full) estar repleto(a)

bulimia [bu:'lɪmɪə] n Med bulimia f

bulk [bʌlk] n (**a**) (mass) masa f, volumen m; Com **in b.** a granel; **to buy sth in b.** comprar algo al por mayor (**b**) (greater part) mayor parte f

bulky ['bʌlkɪ] adj (**bulkier, bulkiest**) (**a**) (large) voluminoso(a) (**b**) **this crate is rather b.** esta caja es un armatoste

bull [bʊl] n (**a**) (animal) toro m; Fig **to take the b. by the horns** agarrar or Esp coger el toro por los cuernos (**b**) Fin **b. market** mercado m al alza

bulldog ['bʊldɒg] n buldog m

bulldoze ['bʊldəʊz] vt (land) nivelar; (building) derribar

bulldozer ['bʊldəʊzə(r)] n bulldozer m

bullet ['bʊlɪt] n bala f; **b. wound** balazo m

bulletin ['bʊlɪtɪn] n boletín m; Rad & TV **news b.** boletín de noticias; US **b. board** tablón m de anuncios

bullet-proof ['bʊlɪtpru:f] adj a prueba de balas; **b. vest** chaleco m antibalas

bullfight ['bʊlfaɪt] n corrida f de toros

bullfighter ['bʊlfaɪtə(r)] n torero(a) m,f

bullfighting ['bʊlfaɪtɪŋ] n los toros mpl; (art) tauromaquia f

bullion ['bʊljən] n **gold/silver b.** oro/plata en lingotes

bullish ['bʊlɪʃ] adj Fin (market) en alza

bullock ['bʊlək] n buey m

bullring ['bʊlrɪŋ] n plaza f de toros

bull's-eye ['bʊlzaɪ] n (of target) blanco m

bully ['bʊlɪ] **1** n matón m; (at school) Esp abusón(ona) m,f, Am abusador(a) m,f **2** vt (terrorize) intimidar; (bulldoze) tiranizar **3** interj Ironic **b. for you!** ¡bravo!

bulwark ['bʊlwək] n baluarte m

bum¹ [bʌm] n Br Fam (bottom) culo m, Am cola f

bum² [bʌm] Fam **1** n (**a**) US (tramp) vagabundo m (**b**) (idler) holgazán(ana) m,f **2** vi gorronear

▸ **bum around** vi Fam vaguear

bumblebee ['bʌmblbi:] n abejorro m

bumbling ['bʌmblɪŋ] adj torpe

bump [bʌmp] **1** n (**a**) (swelling) chichón m; (lump) abolladura f; (on road) bache m (**b**) (blow) choque m, golpe m (**c**) (jolt) sacudida f **2** vt golpear; **to b. one's head** darse un golpe en la cabeza **3** vi chocar (**into** contra)

▸ **bump into** vt insep (meet) tropezar con

▸ **bump off** vt sep Fam liquidar

bumper ['bʌmpə(r)] **1** adj abundante; Br **b. issue** número m especial **2** n Br (of car) parachoques m inv, Méx defensas fpl, RP paragolpes m inv

bumptious ['bʌmpʃəs] adj presuntuoso(a), engreído(a)

bumpy ['bʌmpɪ] adj (**bumpier, bumpiest**) con muchos baches

bun [bʌn] n (**a**) (bread) panecillo m; (sweet) bollo m; Fig Euph **she's got a b. in the oven** está preñada (**b**) (of hair) moño m

bunch [bʌntʃ] **1** n (of keys) manojo m; (of flowers) ramo m; (of grapes) racimo m; (of people) grupo m; (gang) pandilla f **2** vi **to b. together** juntarse, agruparse

bundle ['bʌndəl] **1** n (of clothes) bulto m, fardo m; (of papers) fajo m; (of wood) haz m **2** vt (**a**) (make a bundle of) liar, atar (**b**) (push) empujar

bung [bʌŋ] **1** n tapón m **2** vt Fam (put, throw) echar, Am botar

▸ **bung up** vt sep Fam atascar

bungalow ['bʌŋgələʊ] n chalé m, bungalow m

bungle ['bʌŋgəl] *vt* chapucear

bunion ['bʌnjən] *n* juanete *m*

bunk [bʌŋk] *n (bed)* litera *f*

bunker ['bʌŋkə(r)] *n* (a) *(coal)* carbonera *f* (b) *Mil* búnker *m* (c) *Br (on golf course)* búnker *m*

bunny ['bʌnɪ] *n Fam (baby talk)* b. **(rabbit)** conejito *m*

bunting ['bʌntɪŋ] *n (material)* lanilla *f*; *(flags)* banderines *mpl*; *Naut* empavesada *f*

buoy [bɔɪ] *n* boya *f*

▸ **buoy up** *vt sep* (a) *(keep afloat)* mantener a flote (b) *(person, spirits)* alentar, animar

buoyancy ['bɔɪənsɪ] *n* (a) *(of object)* flotabilidad *f* (b) *Fin* tendencia *f* alcista (c) *(optimism)* optimismo *m*

buoyant ['bɔɪənt] *adj* (a) *(object)* flotante (b) *Fin* con tendencia alcista (c) *(optimistic)* optimista

burble ['bɜːbəl] *vi* (a) *(stream)* murmurar; *(baby)* balbucear (b) *(talk quickly)* farfullar

burden ['bɜːdən] **1** *n* carga *f*; *Fig* **to be a b. to sb** ser una carga para algn
2 *vt* cargar (**with** con)

bureau ['bjʊərəʊ] *n (pl bureaux)* (a) *(office)* agencia *f*, oficina *f* (b) *Br (desk)* escritorio *m* (c) *US (chest of drawers)* cómoda *f*

bureaucracy [bjʊə'rɒkrəsɪ] *n* burocracia *f*

bureaucrat ['bjʊərəkræt] *n* burócrata *mf*

bureaucratic [bjʊərə'krætɪk] *adj* burocrático(a)

burgeon ['bɜːdʒən] *vi* florecer

burger ['bɜːgə(r)] *n Fam (hamburger)* hamburguesa *f*

burglar ['bɜːglə(r)] *n* ladrón(ona) *m,f*; **b. alarm** alarma *f* antirrobo

burglarize ['bɜːgləraɪz] *vt US* robar, desvalijar

burglary ['bɜːglərɪ] *n* robo *m* con allanamiento de morada

burgle ['bɜːgəl] *vt* robar, desvalijar

burial ['berɪəl] *n* entierro *m*

burly ['bɜːlɪ] *adj* (**burlier, burliest**) fornido(a), fuerte

Burma ['bɜːmə] *n* Birmania

Burmese [bɜː'miːz] **1** *adj* birmano(a)
2 *n* (a) *(person)* birmano(a) *m,f* (b) *(language)* birmano *m*

burn [bɜːn] **1** *n* quemadura *f*
2 *vt (pt & pp* **burnt** *or* **burned)** quemar
3 *vi* (a) *(fire)* arder; *(building, food)* quemarse (b) *(lamp)* estar encendido(a) (c) *(sore)* escocer

▸ **burn down 1** *vt sep* incendiar
. **2** *vi* incendiarse

▸ **burn out** *vi (person)* quemarse

▸ **burn up** *vt sep (energy, calories)* quemar

burner ['bɜːnə(r)] *n* quemador *m*

burning ['bɜːnɪŋ] *adj* (a) *(on fire)* incendiado(a); *(hot)* abrasador(a) (b) *(passionate)* ardiente (c) **a b. question** una cuestión candente

burnt [bɜːnt] **1** *adj* quemado(a); **b. almonds** almendras tostadas
2 *pt & pp of* **burn**

burp [bɜːp] **1** *n* eructo *m*
2 *vi* eructar

burrow ['bʌrəʊ] **1** *n (animal)* madriguera *f*
2 *vi* (a) *(dig) (person, animal)* excavar (b) *(search)* rebuscar

bursar ['bɜːsə(r)] *n* tesorero(a) *m,f*

bursary ['bɜːsərɪ] *n Br (scholarship)* beca *f*

burst [bɜːst] **1** *n* (a) *(explosion)* estallido *m*; *(of tyre)* reventón *m* (b) *(of applause)* arranque *m*; *(of rage)* arrebato *m*; **b. of gunfire** ráfaga *f* de tiros; **b. of laughter** carcajadas *fpl*
2 *vt (pt & pp* **burst**) *(balloon)* reventar; *Fig* **the river b. its banks** el río se salió de madre
3 *vi (balloon, tyre, pipe)* reventarse; *(shell)* estallar

▸ **burst into** *vt insep* (a) *(enter)* irrumpir en (b) *(suddenly start)* **b. into laughter/ tears** echarse a reír/llorar

▸ **burst open** *vi* abrirse violentamente

▸ **burst out** *vi* **to b. out laughing** echarse a reír

bursting ['bɜːstɪŋ] *adj* **the bar was b. with people** el bar estaba atestado de gente; *Fam* **to be b. to do sth** reventar por hacer algo

bury ['berɪ] *vt* (a) *(body, treasure)* enterrar; **to be buried in thought** estar absorto(a) en pensamientos (b) *(hide)* ocultar

bus [bʌs] *n (pl* **buses,** *US* **busses)** autobús *m, Andes* buseta *f, Bol, RP* colectivo *m, CAm, Carib* guagua *f, CAm, Méx* camión *m, Urug* ómnibus *m, Ven* microbusete *m*; **b. conductor** cobrador(a) *m,f* de autobús; **b. driver** conductor(a) *m,f* de autobús; **b. stop** parada *f* de autobús

bush [bʊʃ] *n* (a) *(shrub)* arbusto *m* (b) *Austr* **the b.** el monte; *Fam* **b. telegraph** *Esp* radio *f* macuto, *Cuba, CRica, Pan* radio *f* bemba

bushy ['bʊʃɪ] *adj* (**bushier, bushiest**) espeso(a), tupido(a)

business ['bɪznɪs] *n* (a) *(commerce)* negocios *mpl*; **how's b.?** ¿cómo andan los negocios?; **to be away on b.** estar en viaje de negocios; **b. deal** negocio *m*; **b. hours** horas *fpl* de oficina; **b. trip** viaje *m* de negocios (**b**) *(firm)* empresa *f* (**c**) *(matter)* asunto *m*; **I mean b.** estoy hablando en serio; **it's no b. of mine** no es asunto mío; **to make it one's b. to …** encargarse de …; **to get down to b.** ir al grano; **to go about one's b.** ocuparse de sus asuntos

businesslike ['bɪznɪslaɪk] *adj (practical)* eficiente; *(methodical)* metódico(a); *(serious)* serio(a)

businessman ['bɪznɪsmən] *n* hombre *m* de negocios

businesswoman ['bɪznɪswʊmən] *n* mujer *f* de negocios

busker ['bʌskə(r)] *n Br Fam* músico(a) *m,f* callejero(a)

bust¹ [bʌst] *n* (**a**) *(of woman)* pecho *m* (**b**) *Art* busto *m*

bust² [bʌst] *Fam* **1** *vt* (**a**) *(break)* estropear, *Esp* escacharrar (**b**) *(person)* trincar; *(place)* hacer una redada en
2 *adj* (**a**) *(broken)* **to be b.** estar estropeado(a) *or Esp* escacharrado(a) (**b**) **to go b.** *(bankrupt)* quebrar

bustle ['bʌsəl] **1** *n (activity, noise)* bullicio *m*
2 *vi* **to b. about** ir y venir

bustling ['bʌslɪŋ] *adj* bullicioso(a)

bust-up ['bʌstʌp] *n Br Fam* bronca *f*

busy ['bɪzɪ] **1** *adj* (**busier, busiest**) (**a**) *(person)* ocupado(a); *(day, office)* ajetreado(a); *(street)* transitado(a) (**b**) *US Tel* ocupado(a); **b. signal** señal *f* de comunicado
2 *vt* **to b. oneself doing sth** ocuparse haciendo algo

busybody ['bɪzɪbɒdɪ] *n* entrometido(a) *m,f*

but [bʌt] **1** *conj* (**a**) *(in general)* pero; **b. yet** a pesar de todo (**b**) *(after negative)* sino; **not two b. three** no dos sino tres
2 *adv* **b. for her we would have drowned** si no hubiera sido por ella, nos habríamos ahogado
3 *prep* salvo, menos; **everyone b. her** todos menos ella

butane ['bjuːteɪn] *n* butano *m*; **b. gas** gas butano

butcher ['bʊtʃə(r)] **1** *n* carnicero(a) *m,f*; **b.'s (shop)** carnicería *f*
2 *vt (animals)* matar; *(people)* masacrar

butler ['bʌtlə(r)] *n* mayordomo *m*

butt¹ [bʌt] *n* (**a**) *(of rifle)* culata *f*; *(of cigarette)* colilla *f* (**b**) *US Fam (bottom)* culo *m*

butt² [bʌt] **1** *n (with head)* cabezazo *m*
2 *vt (strike with head)* dar un cabezazo a

▸ **butt in** *vi* entrar en la conversación

butter ['bʌtə(r)] **1** *n* mantequilla *f, RP* manteca *f*; **b. dish** mantequera *f*
2 *vt* untar con mantequilla *or RP* manteca

buttercup ['bʌtəkʌp] *n* ranúnculo *m*, botón *m* de oro

butterfingers ['bʌtəfɪŋgəz] *n sing Fam* manazas *mf inv*

butterfly ['bʌtəflaɪ] *n* mariposa *f*

buttock ['bʌtək] *n* nalga *f*; **buttocks** nalgas *fpl*

button ['bʌtən] **1** *n* (**a**) *(on clothes, machine)* botón *m* (**b**) *US (badge)* chapa *f*
2 *vt* **to b. (up)** abrochar(se), abotonar(se)

buttonhole ['bʌtənhəʊl] *n* ojal *m*

buttress ['bʌtrɪs] **1** *n* (**a**) *Archit* contrafuerte *m* (**b**) *(support)* apoyo *m*
2 *vt (support) (argument, system)* respaldar

buxom ['bʌksəm] *adj (woman)* pechugona

buy [baɪ] **1** *n* compra *f*; **a good b.** una ganga
2 *vt (pt & pp* **bought**) (**a**) *(purchase)* comprar; **she bought that car from a neighbour** compró ese coche a un vecino (**b**) *Fam (believe)* tragar

▸ **buy off** *vt sep* sobornar

▸ **buy out** *vt sep* adquirir la parte de

▸ **buy up** *vt sep* comprar en grandes cantidades

buyer ['baɪə(r)] *n* comprador(a) *m,f*

buzz [bʌz] **1** *n* (**a**) *(of bee)* zumbido *m*; *(of conversation)* rumor *m* (**b**) *Fam (telephone call)* telefonazo *m*
2 *vi* zumbar

buzzer ['bʌzə(r)] *n* timbre *m*

by [baɪ] **1** *prep* (**a**) *(indicating agent)* por; **composed by Bach** compuesto(a) por Bach; **a film by Almodóvar** una película de Almodóvar
(**b**) *(via)* por; **he left by the back door** salió por la puerta trasera
(**c**) *(manner)* por; **by car/train** en coche/tren; **by credit card** con tarjeta de crédito; **by day/night** de día/noche; **by chance** por casualidad; **by oneself** solo(a); **made by hand** hecho(a) a mano
(**d**) *(amount)* por; **little by little** poco a poco; **they are sold by the dozen** se venden por docenas; **to be paid by the hour** cobrar por horas; **by far** con mucho
(**e**) *(beside)* al lado de, junto a; **side by side** juntos(as)
(**f**) **to walk by a building** *(pass)* pasar por delante de un edificio
(**g**) *(time)* para; **by now** ya; **by then** para entonces; **we have to be there by nine**

tenemos que estar allí para las nueve
(**h**) *Math* por
(**i**) *(according to)* según; **is that O.K. by
you?** ¿te viene bien?
(**j**) *(phrases)* **bit by bit** poco a poco; **day by
day** día a día; **what do you mean by that?**
¿qué quieres decir con eso?; **by the way** a
propósito
  2 *adv* (**a**) **to go by** *(past)* pasar; **she
just walked by** pasó de largo (**b**) **by and
by** con el tiempo; **by and large** en conjunto

bye [baɪ] **1** *n* **by the b.** por cierto
  2 *interj Fam* ¡adiós!, ¡hasta luego!, *Am*
¡bye!, *Am* ¡chau!

bye-bye ['baɪ'baɪ] *interj Fam* ¡adiós!,
¡hasta luego!, *Am* ¡bye!, *Am* ¡chau!

by-election ['baɪɪlekʃən] *n Br* elección *f*
parcial

bygone ['baɪɡɒn] **1** *adj* pasado(a)
  2 *npl* **let bygones be bygones** lo pasado
pasado está, *Am* lo pasado, pisado

by-law ['baɪlɔ:] *n* ley *f* municipal

bypass ['baɪpɑ:s] **1** *n* (**a**) *(road)* carretera *f*
de circunvalación (**b**) *Med* **b. surgery**
cirugía *f* de bypass
  2 *vt* evitar

by-product ['baɪprɒdʌkt] *n Chem & Ind*
derivado *m*, subproducto *m*; *Fig* consecuencia *f*

byroad ['baɪrəʊd] *n* carretera secundaria

bystander ['baɪstændə(r)] *n* testigo *mf*

byte [baɪt] *n Comput* byte *m*, octeto *m*

byword ['baɪwɜ:d] *n* **it became a b. for
modernity** se convirtió en sinónimo de
modernidad

C

C, c [si:] n (**a**) (*letter*) C, c (**b**) *Mus* do m (**c**) *Sch* (*grade*) aprobado m; **to get a C** (*in exam, essay*) sacar un aprobado

C [si:] (**a**) (*abbr* **celsius** *or* **centigrade**) C, centígrado (**b**) (*abbr* **century**) s., siglo; **C. 16** s. XVI

cab [kæb] n taxi m; **c. driver** taxista mf

cabaret ['kæbəreɪ] n cabaret m

cabbage ['kæbɪdʒ] n col f, berza f; **red c.** (col) lombarda f

cabin ['kæbɪn] n (**a**) (*hut*) choza f; **log c.** cabaña f (**b**) *Naut* camarote m (**c**) (*of lorry, plane*) cabina f

cabinet ['kæbɪnɪt] n (**a**) (*item of furniture*) armario m; (*glass-fronted*) vitrina f; **c. maker** ebanista mf (**b**) *Pol* gabinete m, consejo m de ministros

cable ['keɪbəl] **1** n cable m; **c. car** teleférico m; **c. company** cableoperador(a) m,f; **c. TV** televisión f por cable **2** vt & vi cablegrafiar, telegrafiar

caboose [kə'buːs] n US (*on train*) furgón m de cola

cache [kæʃ] n (**a**) (*place*) alijo m (**b**) *Comput* caché f

cackle ['kækəl] vi cacarear

cactus ['kæktəs] n (*pl* **cacti** ['kæktaɪ]) cactus m

CAD [kæd] n (*abbr* **computer-aided** *or -***assisted design**) CAD m, diseño asistido por *Esp* ordenador *or Am* computadora

cad [kæd] n *Br Fam Old-fashioned* canalla m

caddie ['kædɪ] n (*in golf*) cadi m

cadet [kə'det] n *Mil* cadete m

cadge [kædʒ] vt & vi *Fam* gorrear, *Esp, Méx* gorronear, *RP* garronear (**from** *or* **off** a)

Caesarean [siː'zeərɪən] n *Med* **she had a C.** le hicieron una cesárea; **C. section** operación cesárea

café ['kæfeɪ] , **cafeteria** [kæfɪ'tɪərɪə] n cafetería f

cafetiere [kæfə'tjɜː(r)] n *Br* cafetera f (de émbolo)

caffeine ['kæfiːn] n cafeína f

cage [keɪdʒ] **1** n jaula f **2** vt enjaular

cagey ['keɪdʒɪ] adj (**cagier, cagiest**) **to be c.** (**about sth**) (*cautious*) ir *or Esp* andar con tiento (con algo); (*evasive*) salirse por la tangente (en cuanto a algo)

cagoule [kə'guːl] n *Br* (*garment*) chubasquero m

Cairo ['kaɪrəʊ] n (el) Cairo

cajole [kə'dʒəʊl] vt engatusar

cake [keɪk] n pastel m, tarta f

calamity [kə'læmɪtɪ] n calamidad f

calcium ['kælsɪəm] n calcio m

calculate ['kælkjʊleɪt] vt calcular

calculated ['kælkjʊleɪtɪd] adj intencionado(a)

calculating ['kælkjʊleɪtɪŋ] adj (**a**) **c. machine** calculadora f (**b**) *Pej* (*person*) calculador(a)

calculation [kælkjʊ'leɪʃən] n cálculo m

calculator ['kælkjʊleɪtə(r)] n calculadora f

calendar ['kælɪndə(r)] n calendario m; **c. year** año m natural, *Am* año calendario

calf¹ [kɑːf] n (*pl* **calves**) (*of cattle*) becerro(a) m,f, ternero(a) m,f, (*of other animals*) cría f

calf² [kɑːf] n (*pl* **calves**) *Anat* pantorilla f

calfskin ['kɑːfskɪn] n piel f de becerro

calibre, *US* **caliber** ['kælɪbə(r)] n calibre m

call [kɔːl] **1** vt (**a**) (*on phone*) llamar, telefonear, *Am* hablar; **to c. sb names** poner verde a algn; **what's he called?** ¿cómo se llama? (**b**) (*meeting etc*) convocar; **to c. sth to mind** traer algo a la memoria
2 vi (**a**) (*on phone*) llamar, *Am* hablar; *Tel* **who's calling?** ¿de parte de quién? (**b**) **to c. at sb's** (**house**) pasar por casa de algn; **to c. for sth/sb** pasar a recoger algo/a algn (**c**) (*trains*) parar (**d**) **to c. for** (*require*) exigir; **that wasn't called for** eso no estaba justificado
3 n (**a**) (*shout*) (*of person*) llamada f, grito m, *Am* llamado m (**b**) (*visit*) visita f; **to pay a c. on sb** visitar a algn (**c**) *Tel* (**phone**) **c.** llamada f, *Am* llamado m; **c. box** *Br* cabina telefónica; *US* teléfono m de emergencia; **c. centre** centro m de atención telefónica

▸ **call away** *vt sep* **to be called away on business** tener que ausentarse por motivos de trabajo

▸ **call back** *vi (phone again)* volver a llamar *or Am* hablar; *(visit again)* volver

▸ **call in** *vt sep (doctor)* llamar

2 *vi* (a) **I'll c. in tomorrow** *(visit)* mañana me paso (b) *Naut* hacer escala (**at** en)

▸ **call off** *vt sep* suspender

▸ **call on** *vt insep* (a) *(visit)* visitar (b) **to c. on sb for support** recurrir a algn en busca de apoyo

▸ **call out 1** *vt sep* (a) *(shout)* gritar (b) *(doctor)* hacer venir; *(workers)* convocar a la huelga

2 *vi* gritar

▸ **call up** *vt sep* (a) *Tel* llamar, *Am* hablar (b) *Mil* llamar a filas, reclutar

caller ['kɔːlə(r)] *n* visita *mf; Tel* persona *f* que llama

calling ['kɔːlɪŋ] *n esp Rel* vocación *f; US* **c. card** tarjeta *f* de visita

callous ['kæləs] *adj* insensible, duro(a)

call-up ['kɔːlʌp] *n Mil* llamada *f or Am* llamado *m* a filas, reclutamiento *m*

calm [kɑːm] **1** *adj* (a) *(weather, sea)* en calma (b) *(relaxed)* tranquilo(a); **keep c.!** ¡tranquilo(a)!

2 *n* (a) *(of weather, sea)* calma *f* (b) *(tranquillity)* tranquilidad *f*

3 *vt* calmar, tranquilizar

4 *vi* **to c. (down)** calmarse, tranquilizarse

Calor Gas® ['kælǝgæs] *n Br* butano *m*

calorie, calory ['kælǝrɪ] *n* caloría *f*

calve [kɑːv] *vi (cow)* parir (un becerro)

calves [kɑːvz] *pl of* **calf¹, calf²**

Cambodia [kæm'bǝʊdɪǝ] *n* Camboya

camcorder ['kæmkɔːdǝ(r)] *n* videocámara *f (portátil)*

came [keɪm] *pt of* **come**

camel ['kæmǝl] *n* camello(a) *m,f*

cameo ['kæmɪǝʊ] *n* camafeo *m*

camera ['kæmǝrǝ] *n* (a) *(photographic)* cámara *f (fotográfica); Cin & TV* cámara (b) *Jur* **in c.** a puerta cerrada

cameraman ['kæmǝrǝmǝn] *n* cámara *m*

Cameroon [kæmǝ'ruːn] *n* Camerún

camomile ['kæmǝmaɪl] *n* camomila *f;* **c. tea** *(infusión f de)* manzanilla *f*

camouflage ['kæmǝflɑːʒ] **1** *n* camuflaje *m*

2 *vt* camuflar

camp¹ [kæmp] **1** *n* campamento *m;* **c. bed** cama *f* plegable; **c. site** camping *m*

2 *vi* **to go camping** ir de camping

camp² [kæmp] *adj Fam* afeminado(a); *(affected)* amanerado(a)

campaign [kæm'peɪn] **1** *n* campaña *f*

2 *vi* **to c. for/against** hacer campaña a favor de/en contra de

campaigner [kæm'peɪnǝ(r)] *n* defensor(a) *m,f* (**for** de)

camper ['kæmpǝ(r)] *n* (a) *(person)* campista *mf* (b) *US (vehicle)* caravana *f*

camping ['kæmpɪŋ] *n* **c. ground, c. site** camping *m*

campus ['kæmpǝs] *n* campus *m,* ciudad universitaria

can¹ [kæn, *unstressed* kǝn] *v aux (pt* **could***)*

El verbo **can** carece de infinitivo, de gerundio y de participio. En infinitivo o en participio, se empleará la forma correspondiente de **be able to**, por ejemplo: **he wanted to be able to speak English**; **she has always been able to swim**. En el inglés hablado, y en el escrito en estilo coloquial, la forma negativa **cannot** se transforma en **can't** y la forma negativa **could not** se transforma en **couldn't**.

(a) *(be able to)* poder; **he could have come** podría haber venido; **I'll phone you as soon as I c.** te llamaré en cuanto pueda; **she can't do it** no puede hacerlo; **I can't understand why** no entiendo por qué (b) *(know how to)* saber; **c. you ski?** ¿sabes esquiar?; **I can't speak English** no sé hablar inglés (c) *(be permitted to)* poder; **he can't go out tonight** no le dejan salir esta noche (d) *(be possible)* poder; **she could have forgotten** puede (ser) que lo haya olvidado; **they can't be very poor** no deben ser muy pobres; **what c. it be?** ¿qué será?

can² [kæn] **1** *n* (a) *(of oil)* bidón *m* (b) *(container)* lata *f, Am* tarro *m;* **c. opener** abrelatas *m inv*

2 *vt (fish, fruit)* enlatar

Canada ['kænǝdǝ] *n* Canadá

Canadian [kǝ'neɪdɪǝn] *adj & n* canadiense *(mf)*

canal [kǝ'næl] *n* canal *m*

canary [kǝ'neǝrɪ] *n* canario *m*

Canary Islands [kǝ'neǝraɪlǝndz] *npl* (Islas *fpl*) Canarias *fpl*

cancel ['kænsǝl] *vt (train, contract)* cancelar; *Com* anular; *(permission)* retirar; *(decree)* revocar

cancellation [kænsɪ'leɪʃǝn] *n* cancelación *f, Com* anulación *f*

cancer ['kænsǝ(r)] *n* (a) *Med* cáncer *m;* **breast c.** cáncer de mama; **c. research** cancerología *f* (b) **C.** *(in astrology)* Cáncer *m*

candelabra [kændɪ'lɑːbrǝ] *n* candelabro *m*

candid ['kændɪd] *adj* franco(a), sincero(a)

> *Note that the Spanish word **cándido** is a false friend and is never a translation for the English word **candid**. In Spanish **cándido** means "ingenuous, naive".*

candidate ['kændɪdeɪt, 'kændɪdɪt] *n* candidato(a) *m,f*; *(in exam)* opositor(a) *m,f*

candle ['kændəl] *n* vela *f*; *(in church)* cirio *m*

candlelight ['kændəllaɪt] *n* luz *f* de vela; **by c.** a la luz de las velas

candlestick ['kændəlstɪk] *n* candelero *m*, palmatoria *f*; *(in church)* cirial *m*

candour, *US* **candor** ['kændə(r)] *n* sinceridad *f*, franqueza *f*

> *Note that the Spanish word **candor** is a false friend and is never a translation for the English word **candour**. In Spanish, **candor** means "innocence, naïvety".*

candy ['kændɪ] *n US (sweet)* caramelo *m*; *(sweets)* dulces *mpl*; **c. store** confitería *f*

candyfloss ['kændɪflɒs] *n Br* algodón *m* dulce

cane [keɪn] **1** *n* (a) *Bot* caña *f*; **c. sugar** azúcar *m* de caña (b) *(wicker)* mimbre *m* (c) *(walking stick)* bastón *m*; *(for punishment)* palmeta *f*
2 *vt* castigar con la palmeta

canine ['keɪnaɪn] *adj Zool* canino(a); **c. tooth** colmillo *m*

canister ['kænɪstə(r)] *n* bote *m*

cannabis ['kænəbɪs] *n* hachís *m*, cannabis *m*

canned [kænd] *adj* enlatado(a); **c. foods** conservas *fpl*

cannelloni [kænə'ləʊnɪ] *n* canelones *mpl*

cannibal ['kænɪbəl] *adj & n* caníbal *(mf)*

cannon ['kænən] **1** *n* (a) *(pl* **cannons** *or* **cannon)** cañón *m*; *Fig* **c. fodder** carne *f* de cañón (b) *Br (in billiards, snooker)* carambola *f*
2 *vi* chocar **(into** contra)

cannonball ['kænənbɔːl] *n* bala *f* de cañón

cannot ['kænɒt, kæ'nɒt] = **can not**

canoe [kə'nuː] *n* canoa *f*; *Sport* piragua *f*

canoeing [kə'nuːɪŋ] *n* piragüismo *m*; **to go c.** ir a hacer piragüismo

canon ['kænən] *n Rel* canon *m*

canopy ['kænəpɪ] *n* (a) *(on throne)* dosel *m* (b) *(awning)* toldo *m*

can't [kɑːnt] = **can not**

Cantabria [kæn'tæbrɪə] *n* Cantabria

cantankerous [kæn'tæŋkərəs] *adj* intratable

canteen [kæn'tiːn] *n* (a) *(restaurant)* cantina *f* (b) *Br (set of cutlery)* juego *m* de cubiertos (c) *(flask)* cantimplora *f*

canter ['kæntə(r)] **1** *n* medio galope
2 *vi* ir a medio galope

canvas ['kænvəs] *n* (a) *Tex* lona *f* (b) *(painting)* lienzo *m*

canvass ['kænvəs] *vi* (a) *Pol* hacer propaganda electoral (b) *Com* hacer promoción, buscar clientes

canvasser ['kænvəsə(r)] *n Pol* = persona que hace propaganda electoral de puerta en puerta

canyon ['kænjən] *n* cañón *m*; **the Grand C.** el Gran Cañón

canyoning ['kænjənɪŋ] *n Sport* barranquismo *m*

CAP [siːeɪ'piː] *n (abbr* **Common Agricultural Policy)** PAC *f*

cap [kæp] **1** *n* (a) *(headgear) (without peak)* gorro *m*; *(with peak)* gorra *f* (b) *Br Sport* **to win a c. for England** ser seleccionado(a) para el equipo de Inglaterra (c) *(of pen)* capuchón *m*; *(of bottle)* chapa *f*
2 *vt* (a) *(bottle)* poner la chapa a; *Fig* **to c. it all** para colmo (b) *Br Sport* seleccionar

capability [keɪpə'bɪlɪtɪ] *n* habilidad *f*

capable ['keɪpəbəl] *adj* (a) *(skilful)* hábil (b) *(able)* capaz **(of** de)

capacity [kə'pæsɪtɪ] *n* (a) *(of container, theatre)* capacidad *f* (b) *(aptitude)* **to have a c. for sth** tener capacidad para algo (c) *(role)* **in her c. as manageress** en calidad de gerente

cape¹ [keɪp] *n (garment)* capa *f*

cape² [keɪp] *n Geog* cabo *m*, promontorio *m*; **C. Horn** Cabo de Hornos; **C. Town** Ciudad del Cabo; **C. Verde** Cabo Verde

caper ['keɪpə(r)] *n (prank)* travesura *f*

capital ['kæpɪtəl] **1** *n* (a) *(town)* capital *f* (b) *(letter)* mayúscula *f* (c) *Fin* capital *m*
2 *adj* (a) *(city)* capital (b) **c. punishment** pena *f* capital (c) **c. letter** mayúscula *f*

capitalism ['kæpɪtəlɪzəm] *n* capitalismo *m*

capitalist ['kæpɪtəlɪst] *adj & n* capitalista *(mf)*

capitalize ['kæpɪtəlaɪz] **1** *vt Fin* capitalizar
2 *vi* **to c. on sth** sacar provecho *or* beneficio de algo

capitulate [kə'pɪtjʊleɪt] *vi* capitular

cappuccino [kæpə'tʃiːnəʊ] *n* (café *m*) capuchino *m*

Capricorn ['kæprɪkɔːn] *n* Capricornio *m*

capsicum ['kæpsɪkəm] *n* pimiento *m*

capsize [kæp'saɪz] **1** *vt* hacer zozobrar
2 *vi* zozobrar

capsule ['kæpsjuːl] *n* cápsula *f*

captain ['kæptɪn] **1** *n* capitán *m*
2 *vt* capitanear

caption ['kæpʃən] *n (under picture)* pie *m*
de foto; *Cin* subtítulo *m*

captivating ['kæptɪveɪtɪŋ] *adj* seduc-
tor(a)

captive ['kæptɪv] **1** *n* cautivo(a) *m,f*
2 *adj* cautivo(a)

captivity [kæp'tɪvɪtɪ] *n* cautiverio *m*

capture ['kæptʃə(r)] **1** *vt* (**a**) *(person)*
capturar; *Mil (town)* tomar; *(in chess,*
draughts) comer (**b**) *(market)* acaparar
(**c**) *Fig (mood)* reflejar
2 *n (of fugitive)* captura *f; (of town)* toma *f*

car [kɑː(r)] *n* (**a**) *(automobile)* coche *m, Am*
carro *m, CSur* auto *m; Br* **c. park** parking *m,*
Esp aparcamiento *m;* **c. wash** túnel *m* de
lavado (**b**) *US Rail* coche *m*

carafe [kə'ræf, kə'rɑːf] *n* jarra *f*

caramel ['kærəmel] *n* azúcar quemado;
(sweet) caramelo *m*

carat ['kærət] *n* quilate *m*

caravan ['kærəvæn] *n* (**a**) *Br (vehicle)*
caravana *f* (**b**) *(in desert)* caravana *f*

carbohydrate [kɑːbəʊ'haɪdreɪt] *n* hidra-
to *m* de carbono, carbohidrato *m*

carbon ['kɑːbən] *n* carbono *m;* **c. copy**
copia *f* al papel carbón; *Fig* copia exacta;
c. dioxide dióxido *m* de carbono; **c. paper**
papel *m* carbón

carburettor [kɑːbjʊ'retə(r)], *US* **carbu-
retor** ['kɑːbəreɪtər] *n* carburador *m*

carcass ['kɑːkəs] *n* res muerta

card [kɑːd] *n* (**a**) *(thin cardboard)*
cartulina *f* (**b**) *(with printed information)*
tarjeta *f; (postcard)* (tarjeta) postal *f;*
birthday/Christmas c. tarjeta de cum-
pleaños/de Navidad (**c**) *(in file)* ficha *f;*
(for identification) carné *m, CSur, Méx*
credencial *m;* **c. index** fichero *m* (**d**)
(playing) naipe *m,* carta *f;* **pack of
cards** baraja *f,* cartas *fpl; Fig Br* **on** *or US* **in**
the cards previsto(a)

cardboard ['kɑːdbɔːd] *n* cartón *m;* **c. box**
caja *f* de cartón; **c. cutout** recortable *m*

cardiac ['kɑːdɪæk] *adj* cardíaco(a); **c.
arrest** paro cardíaco

cardigan ['kɑːdɪgən] *n* rebeca *f*

cardinal ['kɑːdɪnəl] **1** *n Rel* cardenal *m*
2 *adj* cardinal; **c. numbers** números *mpl*
cardinales

care [keə(r)] **1** *vi (be concerned)*
preocuparse (**about** por); **I don't c.** no
me importa; *Fam* **for all I c.** me trae sin

cuidado; *Fam* **he couldn't c. less** le
importa un bledo
2 *n* (**a**) *(attention, protection)* cuidado *m,*
atención *f;* **c. of ...** *(on letter)* al cuidado de
...; **medical c.** asistencia médica; **to take
c. of** cuidar; *(business)* ocuparse de (**b**)
(carefulness) cuidado *m;* **take c.** *(be*
careful) ten cuidado; *(as farewell)*
¡cuídate! (**c**) *(worry)* preocupación *f*

▸ **care for** *vt insep* (**a**) *(look after)* cuidar
(**b**) *Fml (like)* **would you c. for a coffee?**
¿te apetece *or Carib, Col, Méx* provoca un
café?

career [kə'rɪə(r)] **1** *n* carrera *f*
2 *vi* correr a toda velocidad

carefree ['keəfriː] *adj* despreocupado(a)

careful ['keəfʊl] *adj (taking care,*
thorough) cuidadoso(a); *(prudent)* cau-
to(a), precavido(a); **be c.!** ¡ojo!; **to be c.**
tener cuidado

carefully ['keəfʊlɪ] *adv (painstakingly)*
cuidadosamente; *(cautiously)* con cuidado

careless ['keəlɪs] *adj (negligent)* descui-
dado(a); **c. driving** conducción temeraria; **a c. mistake** un descuido

carelessly ['keəlɪslɪ] *adv* descuida-
damente, a la ligera

carelessness ['keəlɪsnɪs] *n* descuido *m*

carer ['keərə(r)] *n* = persona que cuida de
un familiar enfermo o anciano, sin que
necesariamente reciba compensación
económica por ello

caress [kə'res] **1** *n* caricia *f*
2 *vt* acariciar

caretaker ['keəteɪkə(r)] *n Br (of building)*
conserje *m,* portero(a) *m,f; (of school)*
conserje *m*

carfare ['kɑːrfeər] *n US* (precio *m* del)
billete *m* or *Am* boleto *m*

cargo ['kɑːgəʊ] *n (pl* **cargoes** *or US* **cargos**)
carga *f,* cargamento *m; Naut* **c. boat**
buque *m* de carga, carguero *m*

Caribbean [kærɪ'bɪən, *US* kə'rɪbɪən] *adj*
caribe, caribeño(a); **the C. (Sea)** el (mar)
Caribe

caricature ['kærɪkətjʊə(r)] *n* caricatura *f*

caring ['keərɪŋ] *adj* solidario(a)

carnage ['kɑːnɪdʒ] *n Fig* carnicería *f*

carnal ['kɑːnəl] *adj* carnal

carnation [kɑː'neɪʃən] *n* clavel *m*

carnival ['kɑːnɪvəl] *n* carnaval *m*

carnivorous [kɑː'nɪvərəs] *adj* carní-
voro(a)

carol ['kærəl] *n* villancico *m*

carom ['kærəm] *n US (in billiards, pool)*
carambola *f*

carousel [kærə'sel] n (a) *US (at fair)* tiovivo m (b) *(at airport)* cinta transportadora de equipajes

carp¹ [kɑːp] n *(fish)* carpa f

carp² [kɑːp] vi refunfuñar

carpenter ['kɑːpɪntə(r)] n carpintero(a) m,f

carpentry ['kɑːpɪntrɪ] n carpintería f

carpet ['kɑːpɪt] **1** n alfombra f
2 vt *(floor)* Esp enmoquetar, Am alfombrar

> *Note that the Spanish word **carpeta** is a false friend and is never a translation for the English word **carpet**. In Spanish **carpeta** means "file, folder".*

carriage ['kærɪdʒ] n (a) *(horse-drawn)* carruaje m (b) *Br (of train)* vagón m, coche m (c) *(of gun)* cureña f (d) *(of typewriter)* carro m (e) *(of goods)* porte m, transporte m

carriageway ['kærɪdʒweɪ] n Br calzada f; **dual c.** autovía

carrier ['kærɪə(r)] n (a) *(company)* transportista mf; Br **c. bag** bolsa f de plástico; **c. pigeon** paloma mensajera (b) Med portador(a) m,f

carrot ['kærət] n zanahoria f

carry ['kærɪ] **1** vt (a) *(transport, convey)* llevar; *(goods, passengers)* transportar (b) *(stock)* tener; *(responsibility, penalty)* conllevar, implicar (c) *(disease)* ser portador(a) de
2 vi *(sound)* oírse

▸ **carry away** vt sep llevarse; **to get carried away** entusiasmarse

▸ **carry forward** vt sep Fin **carried forward** suma y sigue

▸ **carry off** vt sep *(prize)* llevarse; Fam **to c. it off** salir airoso(a)

▸ **carry on 1** vt sep *(business)* dirigir, gestionar; *(conversation)* mantener
2 vi (a) *(continue)* continuar, seguir; **c. on!** ¡sigue!, ¡adelante! (b) Fam *(make a fuss)* hacer una escena; **don't c. on about it!** ¡no te enrolles! (c) Fam **to c. on with sb** tener un lío or Méx una movida or RP un asunto con algn

▸ **carry out** vt sep *(plan)* llevar a cabo, realizar; *(test)* verificar

carryall ['kærɪɔːl] n US bolsa f *(de viaje o de deporte)*

carrycot ['kærɪkɒt] n Br moisés m, capazo m

car-sick ['kɑːsɪk] adj mareado(a) *(en el coche)*

cart [kɑːt] **1** n *(horse-drawn)* carro m; *(handcart)* carretilla f; US *(in supermarket)* carrito m
2 vt carretear

cartel [kɑː'tel] n cártel m

cartilage ['kɑːtɪlɪdʒ] n cartílago m

carton ['kɑːtən] n *(of cream etc)* caja f

cartoon [kɑː'tuːn] n *(strip)* tira cómica, historieta f; Art cartón m; *(animated)* dibujos animados

cartoonist [kɑː'tuːnɪst] n caricaturista mf

cartridge ['kɑːtrɪdʒ] n (a) *(for firearm, of film)* cartucho m (b) *(for pen)* recambio m; **c. paper** papel guarro

carve [kɑːv] vt (a) *(wood)* tallar; *(stone, metal)* cincelar, esculpir (b) *(meat)* trinchar

carving ['kɑːvɪŋ] n (a) Art talla f (b) **c. knife** *(for meat)* cuchillo m de trinchar

cascade [kæ'skeɪd] n cascada f

case¹ [keɪs] n (a) *(instance, situation)* caso m; **a c. in point** un buen ejemplo; **in any c.** en cualquier caso, de todas formas; **in c. of doubt** en caso de duda; **just in c.** por si acaso (b) Med caso m; **c. history** historial clínico (c) Jur causa f

case² [keɪs] n (a) *(suitcase)* maleta f, RP valija f; *(small)* estuche m; *(soft)* funda f (b) **a c. of wine** una caja de botellas de vino (c) Typ **lower c.** minúscula f; **upper c.** mayúscula f

cash [kæʃ] **1** n dinero efectivo; **to pay c.** pagar al contado or en efectivo; Br **c. desk** caja f; **c. on delivery** entrega f contra reembolso; **c. dispenser** cajero automático; **c. register** caja registradora
2 vt *(cheque)* cobrar

▸ **cash in** vi Fam Fig **to c. in on sth** sacar provecho de algo
2 vt sep hacer efectivo(a)

cash-and-carry [kæʃən'kærɪ] adj & adv = de venta al por mayor y pago al contado

cashew ['kæʃuː] n **c.** *(nut)* anacardo m

cashier [kæ'ʃɪə(r)] n cajero(a) m,f

cashmere ['kæʃmɪə(r)] n cachemira f

casino [kə'siːnəʊ] n casino m

cask [kɑːsk] n tonel m, barril m

casket ['kɑːskɪt] n *(box)* cofre m; US *(coffin)* ataúd m

> *Note that the Spanish word **casquete** is a false friend and is never a translation for the English word **casket**. In Spanish **casquete** means "shell case".*

casserole ['kæsərəʊl] n (a) *(container)* cacerola f (b) Culin guisado m

cassette [kə'set] n cinta f, casete f; **c. recorder** casete m

cast [kɑːst] **1** vt *(pt & pp cast)* (a) *(net, fishing line)* echar, arrojar; *(light)* proyectar; *(glance)* lanzar; *(vote)* emitir (b) Fig **to c. doubt on sth** poner algo en duda; **to c. suspicion on sb** levantar

sospechas sobre algn (**c**) *(metal)* moldear; **c. iron** hierro fundido (**d**) *Th (play)* hacer el reparto de
2 *n* (**a**) *(mould)* molde *m*; *(product)* pieza *f* (**b**) *Med* **(plaster) c.** escayola *f*, *esp Am* yeso *m* (**c**) *Th* reparto *m*
▸ **cast off** *vi Naut* soltar (las) amarras
castanets [kæstə'nets] *npl* castañuelas *fpl*
castaway ['kɑːstəweɪ] *n* náufrago(a) *m,f*
caste [kɑːst] *n* casta *f*
caster sugar ['kɑːstə(r)'ʃʊgə(r)] *n Br* azúcar extrafino *f*
Castile [kæ'stiːl] *n* Castilla
Castilian [kæ'stɪlɪən] **1** *adj* castellano(a)
2 *n* **C. (Spanish)** *(language)* castellano *m*
casting ['kɑːstɪŋ] *n* **c. vote** voto *m* de calidad
cast-iron ['kɑːstaɪən] *adj* de hierro fundido
castle ['kɑːsəl] **1** *n* (**a**) *(building)* castillo *m* (**b**) *(in chess)* torre *f*
2 *vi (in chess)* enrocar
castor[1] ['kɑːstə(r)] *n* **c. oil** aceite *m* de ricino
castor[2] ['kɑːstə(r)] *n (on furniture)* ruedecilla *f*
castrate [kæ'streɪt] *vt* castrar
casual ['kæʒʊəl] *adj* (**a**) *(meeting etc)* fortuito(a) (**b**) *(worker)* eventual (**c**) *(clothes)* (de) sport (**d**) *(visit)* de paso (**e**) *(person, attitude)* despreocupado(a), informal
casualty ['kæʒʊəltɪ] *n* (**a**) *Mil* baja *f*, **casualties** pérdidas *fpl* (**b**) *(injured)* herido(a) *m,f*

⌗ Note that the Spanish word **casualidad** is a false friend and is never a translation for the English word **casualty**. In Spanish **casualidad** means "chance, coincidence".

cat [kæt] *n* gato(a) *m,f*, *Fig* **to let the c. out of the bag** revelar el secreto, *Esp* descubrir el pastel
Catalan ['kætəlæn] **1** *adj* catalán(ana)
2 *n* (**a**) *(person)* catalán(ana) *m,f* (**b**) *(language)* catalán *m*
catalogue, *US* **catalog** ['kætəlɒg] **1** *n* catálogo *m*
2 *vt* catalogar
Catalonia [kætə'ləʊnɪə] *n* Cataluña
catalyst ['kætəlɪst] *n* catalizador *m*
catapult ['kætəpʌlt] *n Br* tirachinas *m inv*
cataract ['kætərækt] *n (in river)* & *Med* catarata *f*
catarrh [kə'tɑː(r)] *n* catarro *m*
catastrophe [kə'tæstrəfɪ] *n* catástrofe *f*

catastrophic [kætə'strɒfɪk] *adj* catastrófico(a)
catch [kætʃ] **1** *vt (pt & pp* **caught***)* (**a**) *(thrown object, falling object)* atrapar, *Esp* coger, *Am* agarrar; *(fish)* pescar; *(prey, mouse, thief)* atrapar, capturar; **c. (it)!** *(when throwing something)* ¡agárralo!, *Esp* ¡cógelo!; *(train, bus)* tomar, *Esp* coger, *Am* agarrar; **to c. a cold** *Esp* coger *or Am* agarrar un resfriado; **to c. fire** *(log)* prenderse; *(building)* incendiarse; **to c. hold of** agarrar; **to c. sb's eye** captar la atención de algn; **to c. sight of** entrever (**b**) *(surprise)* pillar, sorprender (**c**) *(hear)* (alcanzar a) oír (**d**) **to c. one's breath** *(hold)* sostener la respiración; *(recover)* recuperar el aliento
2 *vi (sleeve etc)* engancharse (**on** en); *(fire)* encenderse
3 *n* (**a**) *(of ball)* parada *f*; *(of fish)* presa *f* (**b**) *(on door)* pestillo *m* (**c**) *(disadvantage)* trampa *f*
▸ **catch on** *vi Fam* (**a**) *(become popular)* ganar popularidad (**b**) *(understand)* caer en la cuenta
▸ **catch out** *vt sep Fam* **to c. sb out** *(discover, trick)* *Esp* pillar *or Am* agarrar a algn
▸ **catch up** *vi* (**a**) **to c. up with sb** *(reach)* alcanzar a algn (**b**) *(with news)* ponerse al corriente (**on** de); **to c. up on sleep** recuperar el sueño perdido; **to c. up with work** ponerse al día de trabajo
catching ['kætʃɪŋ] *adj (disease)* contagioso(a)
catchment ['kætʃmənt] *n* **c. area** zona *f* de captación
catchword ['kætʃwɜːd] *n* lema *m*
catchy ['kætʃɪ] *adj* (**catchier, catchiest**) *Fam (tune)* pegadizo(a)
categoric(al) [kætɪ'gɒrɪk(əl)] *adj* categórico(a)
categorize ['kætɪgəraɪz] *vt* clasificar
category ['kætɪgərɪ] *n* categoría *f*
cater ['keɪtə(r)] *vi* (**a**) **to c. for** *(wedding etc)* proveer comida para (**b**) **to c. for** *(taste)* atender a
caterer ['keɪtərə(r)] *n* proveedor(a) *m,f*
catering ['keɪtərɪŋ] *n* abastecimiento *m* (de comidas por encargo)
caterpillar ['kætəpɪlə(r)] *n* oruga *f*; **c. (tractor)** tractor *m* de oruga
cathedral [kə'θiːdrəl] *n* catedral *f*
Catholic ['kæθəlɪk] *adj & n* católico(a) *(m,f)*
catholic ['kæθəlɪk] *adj* católico(a)
Catholicism [kə'θɒlɪsɪzəm] *n* catolicismo *m*
cat's-eye® ['kætsaɪ] *n Br* captafaro *m*, = baliza reflectante en la calzada

cattle ['kætəl] *npl* ganado (vacuno)

catty ['kætɪ] *adj* (**cattier, cattiest**) *Fam (remark)* malintencionado(a); *(person)* malicioso(a)

catwalk ['kætwɔːk] *n* pasarela *f*

Caucasian [kɔːˈkeɪzɪən] *adj & n* caucásico(a) *(m,f)*, blanco(a) *(m,f)*

caucus ['kɔːkəs] *n* comité *m* central, ejecutiva *f*

caught [kɔːt] *pt & pp of* **catch**

cauliflower ['kɒlɪflaʊə(r)] *n* coliflor *f*

cause [kɔːz] **1** *n* (**a**) *(origin)* causa *f* (**b**) *(reason)* motivo *m* (**c**) **for a good c.** por una buena causa
  2 *vt* causar; **to c. sb to do sth** hacer que algn haga algo

caustic ['kɔːstɪk] *adj Chem* cáustico(a); *Fig (sarcastic)* cáustico(a), mordaz

caution ['kɔːʃən] **1** *n* (**a**) *(care)* cautela *f*, prudencia *f* (**b**) *(warning)* aviso *m*, advertencia *f* (**c**) *BrJur* reprensión *f*
  2 *vt* advertir, amonestar

cautious ['kɔːʃəs] *adj* cauteloso(a), prudente

cavalcade [kævəlˈkeɪd] *n* cabalgata *f*

cavalier [kævəˈlɪə(r)] **1** *adj* arrogante
  2 *n* caballero *m*

cavalry ['kævəlrɪ] *n* caballería *f*

cave [keɪv] *n* cueva *f*
  ▸ **cave in** *vi (roof etc)* derrumbarse, hundirse

caveman ['keɪvmæn] *n* hombre *m* de las cavernas

cavern ['kævən] *n* caverna *f*

caviar(e) ['kævɪɑː(r)] *n* caviar *m*

cavity ['kævɪtɪ] *n* (**a**) *(hole)* cavidad *f* (**b**) *(in tooth)* caries *f inv*

cavort [kəˈvɔːt] *vi* retozar, brincar

CB [siːˈbiː] *n (abbr* **Citizens' Band**) banda ciudadana

CBI [siːbiːˈaɪ] *n Br (abbr* **Confederation of British Industry**) = organización empresarial británica, ≃ CEOE *f*

cc [siːˈsiː] *(abbr* **cubic centimetre(s)**) cc

CCTV [siːsiːtiːˈviː] *n (abbr* **closed-circuit television**) circuito cerrado de televisión

CD [siːˈdiː] *n (abbr* **compact disc**) CD *m*; **CD player** (lector *m or* reproductor *m* de) CD *m*

CD-ROM [siːdiːˈrɒm] *n Comput (abbr* **compact disc read-only memory**) CD-ROM *m*

cease [siːs] **1** *vt* cesar; **to c. doing** *or* **to do sth** dejar de hacer algo
  2 *vi* terminar

cease-fire [siːsˈfaɪə(r)] *n* alto *m* el fuego

ceaseless ['siːslɪs] *adj* incesante

cedar ['siːdə(r)] *n* cedro *m*

cede [siːd] *vt* ceder

ceiling ['siːlɪŋ] *n* techo *m*

celebrate ['selɪbreɪt] **1** *vt (occasion)* celebrar
  2 *vi* divertirse

celebrated ['selɪbreɪtɪd] *adj* célebre

celebration [selɪˈbreɪʃən] *n* celebración *f*; **celebrations** festividades *fpl*

celebrity [sɪˈlebrɪtɪ] *n* celebridad *f*

celery ['selərɪ] *n* apio *m*

celibate ['selɪbɪt] *adj & n* célibe *(mf)*

cell [sel] *n* (**a**) *(in prison)* celda *f* (**b**) *Biol & Pol* célula *f* (**c**) *Elec* pila *f*

cellar ['selə(r)] *n* sótano *m*; *(for wine)* bodega *f*

cello ['tʃeləʊ] *n* violoncelo *m*

Cellophane® ['seləfeɪn] *n Br* celofán *m*

cellphone ['selfəʊn] *n* teléfono *m* móvil *or Am* celular

cellular ['seljʊlə(r)] *adj* celular; **c. phone** teléfono *m* móvil *or Am* celular

celluloid ['seljʊlɔɪd] *n* celuloide *m*

cellulose ['seljʊləʊs] *n* celulosa *f*

Celsius ['selsɪəs] *adj* Celsio

Celt [kelt, selt] *n* celta *mf*

Celtic ['keltɪk, 'seltɪk] **1** *n (language)* celta *m*
  2 *adj* celta

cement [sɪˈment] **1** *n* cemento *m*; **c. mixer** hormigonera *f*
  2 *vt Constr* unir con cemento; *Fig (friendship)* cimentar

cemetery ['semɪtrɪ] *n* cementerio *m*

censor ['sensə(r)] **1** *n* censor(a) *m,f*
  2 *vt* censurar

censorship ['sensəʃɪp] *n* censura *f*

censure ['senʃə(r)] **1** *n* censura *f*
  2 *vt* censurar

census ['sensəs] *n* censo *m*

cent [sent] *n* centavo *m*, céntimo *m*

centenary [senˈtiːnərɪ] *n* centenario *m*

center ['sentər] *n & vt US* = **centre**

centigrade ['sentɪgreɪd] *adj* centígrado(a)

centilitre, *US* **centiliter** ['sentɪliːtə(r)] *n* centilitro *m*

centimetre, *US* **centimeter** ['sentɪmiːtə(r)] *n* centímetro *m*

centipede ['sentɪpiːd] *n* ciempiés *m inv*

central ['sentrəl] *adj* central; **c. heating** calefacción *f* central; **C. America** Centroamérica; **C. American** centroamericano(a) *m,f*; *Br* **c. reservation** *(on motorway)* mediana *f*, *Col, Méx* camellón *m*

centralize ['sentrəlaɪz] *vt* centralizar

centrally ['sentrəlɪ] *adv* c. heated con calefacción central; c. situated céntrico(a)

centre, *US* **center** ['sentə(r)] **1** *n* centro *m*; **town** c. centro de la ciudad; *Ftb* c. **forward** delantero centro; *Ftb* c. **half** medio centro; *Pol* c. **party** partido *m* centrista; **sports** c. centro deportivo
2 *vt (attention etc)* centrar (**on** en)

century ['sentʃərɪ] *n* siglo *m*; **the nineteenth** c. el siglo diecinueve

ceramic [sɪ'ræmɪk] **1** *n* cerámica *f*
2 *adj* de cerámica

ceramics [sɪ'ræmɪks] *n sing* cerámica *f*

cereal ['sɪərɪəl] *n* cereal *m*

cerebral ['serɪbrəl, sɪ'riːbrəl] *adj* cerebral; c. **palsy** parálisis *f* cerebral

ceremony ['serɪmənɪ] *n* ceremonia *f*

certain ['sɜːtən] *adj* (**a**) *(sure)* seguro(a); **to be** c. estar seguro(a); **to make** c. **of sth** asegurarse de algo; **for** c. a ciencia cierta (**b**) **to a** c. **extent** hasta cierto punto (**c**) *(not known)* cierto(a); **a** c. **Miss Ward** una tal señorita Ward (**d**) *(true)* cierto(a)

certainly ['sɜːtənlɪ] *adv* desde luego; c. **not** de ninguna manera

certainty ['sɜːtəntɪ] *n* certeza *f*; *(assurance)* seguridad *f*

certificate [sə'tɪfɪkɪt] *n* certificado *m*; *Educ* diploma *m*

certified ['sɜːtɪfaɪd] *adj* *(qualified)* diplomado(a); *(document)* certificado(a); *US* c. **public accountant** censor(a) jurado(a) de cuentas, auditor(a) *m,f*, *Am* contador(a) público(a)

certify ['sɜːtɪfaɪ] *vt* certificar

cervical ['sɜːvɪkəl, sə'vaɪkəl] *adj* c. **cancer** cáncer *m* del útero; c. **smear** frotis *m* cervical

cervix ['sɜːvɪks] *n* (**a**) *(uterus)* cuello *m* del útero (**b**) *(neck)* cerviz *f*, cuello *m*

cessation [se'seɪʃən] *n* cese *m*

cesspit ['sespɪt] *n* pozo negro

Ceylon [sɪ'lɒn] *n* Ceilán *m*

cf [siː'ef] *(abbr* **confer, compare)** cf., cfr.

chador ['tʃʌdə(r)] *n* chador *m*

chafe [tʃeɪf] **1** *vt (make sore)* rozar
2 *vi (skin)* irritarse; *(item of clothing)* rozar

chaffinch ['tʃæfɪntʃ] *n* pinzón *m* vulgar

chagrin ['ʃægrɪn] *n* disgusto *m*, desilusión *f*

chain [tʃeɪn] **1** *n* cadena *f*; *Fig (of events)* serie *f*; c. **of mountains** cordillera *f*; c. **reaction** reacción *f* en cadena; c. **saw** sierra mecánica
2 *vt* **to** c. (**up**) encadenar

chain-smoke ['tʃeɪnsməʊk] *vi* fumar un pitillo tras otro

chair [tʃeə(r)] **1** *n* (**a**) *(seat)* silla *f*; *(armchair)* sillón *m*; c. **lift** telesilla *m* (**b**) *(of meeting)* presidente(a) *m,f* (**c**) *Univ (of professor)* cátedra *f*
2 *vt (meeting)* presidir

chairman ['tʃeəmən] *n* presidente *m*

chairperson ['tʃeəpɜːsən] *n* presidente(a) *m,f*

chalet ['ʃæleɪ] *n* chalet *m*, chalé *m*

chalk [tʃɔːk] *n (for writing)* tiza *f*, *Méx* gis *m*
▶**chalk up** *vt sep* *Fam (victory etc)* apuntarse

challenge ['tʃælɪndʒ] **1** *vt* (**a**) *(to a contest, fight)* retar, desafiar; **to** c. **sb to do sth** retar a algn a que haga algo (**b**) *(authority, statement)* cuestionar, poner en duda (**c**) *Mil* dar el alto a
2 *n* (**a**) *(exacting task, to duel)* reto *m*, desafío *m* (**b**) *Mil* quién vive m

challenger ['tʃælɪndʒə(r)] *n* aspirante *mf*

challenging ['tʃælɪndʒɪŋ] *adj* *(idea)* desafiante; *(task)* que presenta un desafío

chamber ['tʃeɪmbə(r)] *n* (**a**) *(hall)* cámara *f*; **C. of Commerce** Cámara de Comercio (**b**) *Mus* c. **music** música *f* de cámara (**c**) *Br Jur* **chambers** gabinete *m*

chambermaid ['tʃeɪmbəmeɪd] *n* camarera *f*

chameleon [kə'miːlɪən] *n* camaleón *m*

champagne [ʃæm'peɪn] *n* *(French)* champán *m*; *(from Catalonia)* cava *m*

champion ['tʃæmpɪən] *n* campeón(ona) *m,f*; *Fig* c. **of human rights** defensor(a) *m,f* de los derechos humanos

championship ['tʃæmpɪənʃɪp] *n* campeonato *m*

chance [tʃɑːns] **1** *n* (**a**) *(fortune)* casualidad *f*, azar *m*; **by** c. por casualidad; **to take a** c. arriesgarse; c. **meeting** encuentro *m* casual (**b**) *(likelihood)* posibilidad *f*; (**the**) **chances are that …** lo más posible es que … (**c**) *(opportunity)* oportunidad *f*, *Am* chance *f*
2 *vt* arriesgar
▶**chance upon** *vt insep* encontrar por casualidad

chancellor ['tʃɑːnsələ(r)] *n* (**a**) *(head of state, in embassy)* canciller *m* (**b**) *Univ Br* rector(a) honorario(a); *US* rector(a) *m,f* (**c**) *Br* **C. of the Exchequer** ≃ ministro(a) *m,f* de Hacienda

chandelier [ʃændɪ'lɪə(r)] *n* araña *f* (de luces)

change [tʃeɪndʒ] **1** *vt* cambiar; **to** c. **gear** cambiar de marcha; **to** c. **one's mind/the subject** cambiar de opinión/de tema; **to** c.

trains hacer transbordo; **to get changed** cambiarse de ropa; *Fig* **to c. hands** cambiar de dueño(a)

2 *vi* cambiar, cambiarse; **to c. for the better/worse** mejorar/empeorar; **to c. into** convertirse en

3 *n* (a) *(alteration)* cambio *m*; **for a c.** para variar; **c. of heart** cambio de parecer; **c. of scene** cambio de aires (b) *(money)* cambio *m*, *Andes, CAm, Méx* sencillo *m*, *RP* vuelto *m*; **small c.** suelto *m*

▸ **change over** *vi* cambiarse

changeable [ˈtʃeɪndʒəbəl] *adj (weather)* variable; *(person)* inconstante

changeover [ˈtʃeɪndʒəʊvə(r)] *n* conversión *f*

changing [ˈtʃeɪndʒɪŋ] **1** *n* (a) **c. room** vestuario *m* (b) *Mil* relevo *m (de la guardia)*

2 *adj* cambiante

channel [ˈtʃænəl] **1** *n* (a) *Geog* canal *m*; *(of river)* cauce *m*; **the C. Islands** las Islas Anglonormandas; **the English C.** el Canal de la Mancha (b) *(administrative)* vía *f* (c) *Rad & TV* canal *m*, cadena *f*

2 *vt Fig (ideas etc)* canalizar, encauzar

chant [tʃɑːnt] **1** *n* (a) *Rel* cántico *m*; *(of demonstrators)* slogan *m*

2 *vt & vi Rel* cantar; *(demonstrators)* corear

chaos [ˈkeɪɒs] *n* caos *m*

chaotic [keɪˈɒtɪk] *adj* caótico(a)

chap [tʃæp] *n Fam (man)* tipo *m*, *Esp* tío *m*; **a good c.** un buen tipo

chapel [ˈtʃæpəl] *n* capilla *f*

chaperon(e) [ˈʃæpərəʊn] *n* señora *f* de compañía, *Esp* carabina *f*, *Am* chaperona *f*

chaplain [ˈtʃæplɪn] *n* capellán *m*

chapter [ˈtʃæptə(r)] *n* (a) *(of book)* capítulo *m* (b) *Rel* cabildo *m*

char [tʃɑː(r)] *vt* chamuscar, carbonizar

character [ˈkærɪktə(r)] *n* (a) *(nature, personality)* carácter *m* (b) *(unusual person)* personaje *m*; *Pej* **some c. in a uniform** un tipo de uniforme (c) *(in novel, play)* personaje *m* (d) *Typ & Comput* carácter *m*

characteristic [kærɪktəˈrɪstɪk] **1** *n* característica *f*

2 *adj* característico(a)

characterize [ˈkærɪktəraɪz] *vt* caracterizar

charcoal [ˈtʃɑːkəʊl] *n* carbón *m* vegetal; *Art* **c. drawing** carboncillo *m*; **c. grey** gris marengo *or* oscuro

charge [tʃɑːdʒ] **1** *vt* (a) *(price)* cobrar; **c. it to my account** cárguelo en mi cuenta (b) **to c. sb with a crime** acusar a algn de un delito (c) *Mil* cargar contra (d) *Elec* cargar

2 *vi Elec & Mil* cargar; **to c. about** andar a lo loco

3 *n* (a) *(cost)* precio *m*; **free of c.** gratis (b) **to be in c.** of estar a cargo de; **to take c. of** hacerse cargo de (c) *Jur* cargo *m*, acusación *f* (d) *(explosive)* carga explosiva (e) *Mil* carga *f* (f) *Elec* carga *f*

charged [tʃɑːdʒd] *adj Fig* emotivo(a)

charger [ˈtʃɑːdʒə(r)] *n (for phone)* cargador *m*

charismatic [kærɪzˈmætɪk] *adj* carismático(a)

charitable [ˈtʃærɪtəbəl] *adj (person, action)* caritativo(a); *(organization)* benéfico(a)

charity [ˈtʃærɪtɪ] *n* caridad *f*; *(organization)* institución benéfica

charlady [ˈtʃɑːleɪdɪ] *n Br* señora *f* de la limpieza

charlatan [ˈʃɑːlətən] *n (doctor)* curandero(a) *m,f*

charm [tʃɑːm] **1** *n* (a) *(quality)* encanto *m* (b) *(spell)* hechizo *m*; **lucky c.** amuleto *m*

2 *vt* encantar

charming [ˈtʃɑːmɪŋ] *adj* encantador(a)

chart [tʃɑːt] **1** *n* (a) *(giving information)* tabla *f*; *(graph)* gráfico *m* (b) *(map)* carta *f* de navegación (c) *Mus* **the charts** la lista de éxitos

2 *vt Av & Naut (on map)* trazar

charter [ˈtʃɑːtə(r)] **1** *n* (a) *(of institution)* estatutos *mpl*; *(of rights)* carta *f* (b) **c. flight** vuelo *m* chárter

2 *vt (plane, boat)* fletar

chartered accountant [tʃɑːtədəˈkaʊntənt] *n Br* censor(a) *m,f* jurado(a) de cuentas, *Am* contador(a) *m,f* público(a)

chase [tʃeɪs] **1** *vt (pursue)* perseguir

2 *n (pursuit)* persecución *f*

chasm [ˈkæzəm] *n Geog* sima *f*; *Fig* abismo *m*

chassis [ˈʃæsɪ] *n* chasis *m inv*

chaste [tʃeɪst] *adj* casto(a)

chastise [tʃæsˈtaɪz] *vt* castigar

chastity [ˈtʃæstɪtɪ] *n* castidad *f*

chat [tʃæt] **1** *n* (a) *(informal conversation)* charla *f* *CAm, Méx* plática *f*; *Br* **c. show** coloquio *m* (b) *Comput* chat *m*; **c. room** sala *f* de conversación

2 *vi* (a) *(talk informally)* charlar, *CAm, Méx* platicar (b) *Comput* chatear (**to** *or* **with** con)

▸ **chat up** *vt sep Br Fam* **to chat sb up** intentar ligar con algn, *RP* intentar levantar a algn

chatter [ˈtʃætə(r)] **1** *vi (person)* parlotear; *(bird)* piar; *(teeth)* castañetear

2 *n* (of person) parloteo *m*; (of birds) gorjeo *m*; (of teeth) castañeteo *m*

chatterbox ['tʃætəbɒks] *n Fam* parlanchín(ina) *m,f*

chatty ['tʃætɪ] *adj* (**chattier, chattiest**) hablador(a)

chauffeur ['ʃəʊfə(r), ʃəʊ'fɜ:(r)] *n Esp* chófer *m*, *Am* chofer *m*

chauvinism ['ʃəʊvɪnɪzəm] *n* chovinismo *m*; **male c.** machismo *m*

chauvinist ['ʃəʊvɪnɪst] *adj & n* chovinista (*mf*); **male c.** machista *m*

cheap [tʃi:p] **1** *adj* (inexpensive) barato(a); (fare, rate) económico(a), reducido(a); (joke) de mal gusto; (contemptible) bajo(a)
2 *n Br Fam* **on the c.** en plan barato
3 *adv* barato

cheapen ['tʃi:pən] *vt Fig* degradar

cheaply ['tʃi:plɪ] *adv* barato, en plan económico

cheat [tʃi:t] **1** *vt* engañar; **to c. sb out of sth** estafar algo a algn
2 *vi* (**a**) (at games) hacer trampa; (in exam etc) copiar(se) (**b**) *Fam* (husband, wife) poner cuernos (**on** a)
3 *n* (trickster) tramposo(a) *m,f*

check [tʃek] **1** *vt* (**a**) (verify, examine) (information) comprobar, *Guat, Méx* checar; (passport, ticket) revisar (**b**) (restrain) (inflation, enemy advance) frenar; (emotion, impulse) contener, reprimir
2 *vi* comprobar, *Guat, Méx* checar
3 *n* (**a**) (inspection) control *m*, inspección *f* (**b**) (in chess) jaque *m* (**c**) (pattern) cuadro *m* (**d**) **to keep in c.** (feelings) contener; (enemy) mantener a raya (**e**) *US* = **cheque**
▸ **check in** *vi* (at airport) facturar; (at hotel) registrarse (**at** en)
▸ **check out 1** *vi* (of hotel) dejar el hotel
2 *vt sep* (facts) verificar
▸ **check up** *vi* **to c. up on sb** hacer averiguaciones sobre algn; **to c. up on sth** comprobar algo

checked [tʃekt] *adj* a cuadros

checker ['tʃekər] *n US* (cashier) cajero(a) *m,f*

checkered ['tʃekərd] *adj US* = **chequered**

checkers ['tʃekərz] *n sing US* (game) damas *fpl*

check-in ['tʃekɪn] *n* **c. desk** (at airport) mostrador *m* de facturación

checking account ['tʃekɪŋ ə'kaʊnt] *n US* cuenta *f* corriente

checkmate ['tʃekmeɪt] **1** *n* (in chess) jaque mate *m*
2 *vt* (in chess) dar jaque mate a; *Fig* (opponent) frustrar

checkout ['tʃekaʊt] *n* (counter) caja *f*

checkpoint ['tʃekpɔɪnt] *n* control *m*

checkroom ['tʃekru:m] *n US* (for coats, hats) guardarropa *m*; (for luggage) consigna *f*

checkup ['tʃekʌp] *n Med* chequeo *m*, examen médico

cheek [tʃi:k] *n* (**a**) (of face) mejilla *f* (**b**) *Fam* (nerve) cara *f*; **he's got a c.!** ¡qué caradura!, *Esp* ¡vaya morro!

cheekbone ['tʃi:kbəʊn] *n* pómulo *m*

cheeky ['tʃi:kɪ] *adj* (**cheekier, cheekiest**) *Fam* fresco(a), descarado(a)

cheep [tʃi:p] **1** *n* (of bird) pío *m*
2 *vi* piar

cheer [tʃɪə(r)] **1** *vt* aplaudir, aclamar
2 *vt* (**a**) (applaud) vitorear, aclamar (**b**) (make hopeful) animar
3 *n* viva *m*; **cheers** aplausos *mpl*; *Br Fam* **cheers!** (thank you) ¡gracias!; (before drinking) ¡salud!
▸ **cheer up 1** *vi* animarse
2 *vt sep* **to c. sb up** alegrar or animar a algn

cheerful ['tʃɪəfʊl] *adj* alegre

cheerio [tʃɪərɪ'əʊ] *interj Br Fam* ¡chao!, *Am* ¡chau!

cheese [tʃi:z] *n* queso *m*

cheesecake ['tʃi:zkeɪk] *n* tarta *f* de queso

cheetah ['tʃi:tə] *n* guepardo *m*

chef [ʃef] *n* chef *m*

chemical ['kemɪkəl] **1** *n* sustancia química, producto químico
2 *adj* químico(a)

chemist ['kemɪst] *n* (**a**) (scientist) químico(a) *m,f* (**b**) *Br* (pharmacist) farmacéutico(a) *m,f*; **c.'s (shop)** farmacia *f*

chemistry ['kemɪstrɪ] *n* química *f*

chemotherapy ['ki:məʊ'θerəpɪ] *n Med* quimioterapia *f*

cheque [tʃek] *n* cheque *m*; **to pay by c.** pagar con (un) cheque; *Br* **c. book** talonario *m* (de cheques); *Br* **c. card** = tarjeta que avala los cheques

chequered ['tʃekəd] *adj* a cuadros; *Fig* **a c. career** una carrera con altibajos

cherish ['tʃerɪʃ] *vt* (**a**) (person) tenerle mucho cariño a (**b**) *Fig* (hopes etc) abrigar

cherry ['tʃerɪ] *n* cereza *f*

chess [tʃes] *n* ajedrez *m*

chessboard ['tʃesbɔ:d] *n* tablero *m* de ajedrez

chesspiece ['tʃespi:s] *n* pieza *f* de ajedrez

chest [tʃest] *n* (**a**) *Anat* pecho *m* (**b**) (for linen) arca *f*; (for valuables) cofre *m*; **c. of drawers** cómoda *f*

chestnut ['tʃesnʌt] *n* (tree, colour) castaño *m*; (nut) castaña *f*

chew [tʃuː] *vt* masticar, mascar

chewing gum [ˈtʃuːɪŋʌm] *n* chicle *m*

chewy [ˈtʃuːɪ] *adj* (**chewier, chewiest**) *(meat, bread)* correoso(a); *(confectionery)* gomoso(a), correoso(a)

chic [ʃiːk] *adj* elegante

chick [tʃɪk] *n* (**a**) *(young chicken)* pollito *m* (**b**) *Fam (woman)* nena *f*, *Arg* piba *f*, *Méx* chava *f*

chicken [ˈtʃɪkɪn] **1** *n* (**a**) *(bird)* gallina *f*; *(meat)* pollo *m* (**b**) *Fam (coward)* gallina *mf*, *Esp* miedica *mf*
 2 *vi Fam* **to c. out** acobardarse, *Méx* ciscarse, *RP* achicarse

chickenpox [ˈtʃɪkɪnpɒks] *n* varicela *f*

chickpea [ˈtʃɪkpiː] *n* garbanzo *m*

chicory [ˈtʃɪkərɪ] *n* achicoria *f*

chief [tʃiːf] **1** *n* jefe *m*
 2 *adj* principal

chiefly [ˈtʃiːflɪ] *adv (above all)* sobre todo; *(mainly)* principalmente

chiffon [ˈʃɪfɒn] *n* gasa *f*

chilblain [ˈtʃɪlbleɪn] *n* sabañón *m*

child [tʃaɪld] *n* (*pl* **children**) niño(a) *m,f*, *(son)* hijo *m*; *(daughter)* hija *f*; **c. minder** = persona que cuida niños en su propia casa

childbirth [ˈtʃaɪldbɜːθ] *n* parto *m*

childhood [ˈtʃaɪldhʊd] *n* infancia *f*, niñez *f*

childish [ˈtʃaɪldɪʃ] *adj* pueril, aniñado(a)

childlike [ˈtʃaɪldlaɪk] *adj* infantil

children [ˈtʃɪldrən] *pl of* **child**

Chile [ˈtʃɪlɪ] *n* Chile

Chilean [ˈtʃɪlɪən] *adj & n* chileno(a) *(m,f)*

chili [ˈtʃɪlɪ] *n* = **chilli**

chill [tʃɪl] **1** *n* (**a**) *Med* resfriado *m* (**b**) *(coldness)* fresco *m*
 2 *adj* frío(a)
 3 *vt (meat)* refrigerar; *(wine)* enfriar
▸ **chill out** *vi Fam* relajarse, estar tranqui

chilli [ˈtʃɪlɪ] *n* **c. (pepper)** chile *m*, *Esp* guindilla *f*, *Andes, RP* ají *m*

chilly [ˈtʃɪlɪ] *adj* (**chillier, chilliest**) frío(a)

chime [tʃaɪm] **1** *n* (*peal*) campanada *f*
 2 *vt* **to c. five o'clock** *(of clock)* dar las cinco
 3 *vi* sonar
▸ **chime in** *vi Fam* meter baza or *Méx*, *RP* la cuchara

chimney [ˈtʃɪmnɪ] *n* chimenea *f*; **c. sweep** deshollinador *m*

chimpanzee [tʃɪmpænˈziː] *n* chimpancé *m*

chin [tʃɪn] *n* barbilla *f*, mentón *m*; **double c.** papada *f*

China [ˈtʃaɪnə] *n* China

china [ˈtʃaɪnə] *n* loza *f*, porcelana *f*

> *ℓ* Note that the Spanish word **china** is a false friend and is never a translation for the English word **china**. In Spanish **china** means "pebble, small stone".

Chinese [tʃaɪˈniːz] **1** *adj* chino(a)
 2 *n* (**a**) *(person)* chino(a) *m,f* (**b**) *(language)* chino *m*

chink¹ [tʃɪŋk] *n (opening)* resquicio *m*; *(crack)* grieta *f*

chink² [tʃɪŋk] **1** *vi* tintinear
 2 *n* tintineo *m*

chip [tʃɪp] **1** *n* (**a**) *(of wood)* astilla *f*; *(of stone)* lasca *f*; *(in cup)* mella *f* (**b**) *Br Culin* **chips** *Esp* patatas or *Am* papas fritas; *US* **(potato) chips** *(crisps) Esp* patatas or *Am* papas fritas *(de bolsa)* (**c**) *Comput* chip *m* (**d**) *(in gambling)* ficha *f*
 2 *vt (wood)* astillar; *(stone)* resquebrajar; *(china, glass)* mellar
 3 *vi (wood)* astillarse; *(china, glass)* mellarse; *(paint)* desconcharse
▸ **chip in** *vi Fam* (**a**) *(in discussion)* meter baza or *Méx*, *RP* la cuchara, terciar (**b**) *(with money)* poner algo (de dinero)

chiropodist [kɪˈrɒpədɪst] *n* podólogo(a) *m,f*, *Am* podiatra *mf*

chirp [tʃɜːp] *vi (birds)* gorjear

chisel [ˈtʃɪzəl] *n* cincel *m*

chit [tʃɪt] *n* nota *f*; *(small invoice)* vale *m*

chitchat [ˈtʃɪttʃæt] *n Fam* charla *f*, cháchara *f*, *CAm*, *Méx* plática *f*

chivalry [ˈʃɪvəlrɪ] *n* caballerosidad *f*

chives [tʃaɪvz] *npl* cebolleta *f*

chlorine [ˈklɔːriːn] *n* cloro *m*

chock-a-block [tʃɒkəˈblɒk], **chock-full** [tʃɒkˈfʊl] *adj Fam* (lleno(a)) hasta los topes

chocolate [ˈtʃɒkəlɪt] **1** *n* chocolate *m*; **chocolates** bombones *mpl*
 2 *adj* de chocolate

choice [tʃɔɪs] **1** *n* elección *f*; **a wide c.** un gran surtido; **by c.** por gusto
 2 *adj* selecto(a)

choir [ˈkwaɪə(r)] *n* coro *m*, coral *f*

choirboy [ˈkwaɪəbɔɪ] *n* niño *m* de coro

choke [tʃəʊk] **1** *vt* (**a**) *(person)* ahogar (**b**) *(obstruct)* obstruir
 2 *vi* ahogarse; **to c. on food** atragantarse con la comida
 3 *n Aut* estárter *m*
▸ **choke back** *vt sep (emotions)* tragarse

cholera [ˈkɒlərə] *n* cólera *m*

cholesterol [kəˈlestərɒl] *n* colesterol *m*

choose [tʃuːz] **1** vt (pt **chose**; pp **chosen**) elegir, escoger; **to c. to do sth** decidir hacer algo
2 vi elegir, escoger

choos(e)y ['tʃuːzɪ] adj (**choosier**, **choosiest**) Fam exigente

chop [tʃɒp] **1** vt (**a**) (wood) cortar; (tree) talar (**b**) Culin cortar a pedacitos
2 n (**a**) (blow) tajo m; (with axe) hachazo m (**b**) Culin chuleta f

chopper ['tʃɒpə(r)] n Fam helicóptero m

choppy ['tʃɒpɪ] adj (**choppier**, **choppiest**) (sea) picado(a)

chopsticks ['tʃɒpstɪks] npl palillos mpl

choral ['kɔːrəl] adj coral

chord [kɔːd] n Mus acorde m; Fig **it strikes a c.** (me) suena

chore [tʃɔː(r)] n quehacer m, tarea f

chortle ['tʃɔːtəl] vi reír con ganas

chorus ['kɔːrəs] n Mus & Th coro m; (in a song) estribillo m; **c. girl** corista f

chose [tʃəʊz] pt of **choose**

chosen ['tʃəʊzən] pp of **choose**

Christ [kraɪst] n Cristo m, Jesucristo m

christen ['krɪsən] vt bautizar

christening ['krɪsənɪŋ] n bautizo m

Christian ['krɪstʃən] **1** adj cristiano(a); **c. name** nombre m de pila
2 n cristiano(a) m,f

Christianity [krɪstɪ'ænɪtɪ] n cristianismo m

Christmas ['krɪsməs] n Navidad f; **merry C.!** ¡feliz Navidad!; **C. carol** villancico m; **C. Day** día m de Navidad; **C. Eve** Nochebuena f

chrome [krəʊm] n cromo m

chromium ['krəʊmɪəm] n cromo m; **c. plating** cromado m

chromosome ['krəʊməsəʊm] n cromosoma m

chronic ['krɒnɪk] adj crónico(a)

chronicle ['krɒnɪkəl] **1** n crónica f
2 vt hacer la crónica de

chronological [krɒnə'lɒdʒɪkəl] adj cronológico(a)

chrysanthemum [krɪ'sænθəməm] n crisantemo m

chubby ['tʃʌbɪ] adj (**chubbier**, **chubbiest**) rellenito(a)

chuck [tʃʌk] vt Fam tirar, Am botar **to c. one's job in** or **up** dejar el trabajo; **to c. sb out** echar a algn; **to c. sth away** or **out** tirar or Am botar algo

chuckle ['tʃʌkəl] **1** vi reír entre dientes
2 n sonrisita f

chug [tʃʌg] vi traquetear

chum [tʃʌm] n compinche mf, compañero(a) m,f

chunk [tʃʌŋk] n Fam cacho m, pedazo m

church [tʃɜːtʃ] n iglesia f; **to go to c.** ir a misa; **C. of England** Iglesia Anglicana

churchyard ['tʃɜːtʃjɑːd] n cementerio m, campo santo

churlish ['tʃɜːlɪʃ] adj grosero(a)

churn [tʃɜːn] **1** n (for butter) mantequera f; Br (for milk) lechera f
2 vt (butter) hacer
3 vi revolverse, agitarse
▸ **churn out** vt sep Fam producir en serie

chute [ʃuːt] n (channel) conducto m; (slide) tobogán m

chutney ['tʃʌtnɪ] n conserva f (de frutas) picante

CIA [siːaɪ'eɪ] n US (abbr **Central Intelligence Agency**) CIA f

CID [siːaɪ'diː] n Br (abbr **Criminal Investigation Department**) = policía judicial británica

cider ['saɪdə(r)] n sidra f

cigar [sɪ'gɑː(r)] n puro m

cigarette [sɪgə'ret] n cigarrillo m; **c. case** pitillera f; **c. end** colilla f, Am pucho m; **c. holder** boquilla f; **c. lighter** encendedor m, Esp mechero m

cinder ['sɪndə(r)] n **cinders** cenizas fpl; **burnt to a c.** completamente carbonizado(a)

Cinderella [sɪndə'relə] n Cenicienta f

cine camera ['sɪnɪkæmərə] n Br cámara f de cine

cinema ['sɪnɪmə] n (**a**) Br (building) cine m (**b**) (art) cine m

cinnamon ['sɪnəmən] n canela f

cipher ['saɪfə(r)] n (numeral) cifra f

circle ['sɜːkəl] **1** n (**a**) (shape, group) círculo m; **in business circles** en el mundo de los negocios (**b**) Th anfiteatro m
2 vt (surround) rodear; (move round) dar la vuelta a
3 vi dar vueltas

circuit ['sɜːkɪt] n (**a**) (journey) recorrido m (**b**) Elec circuito m (**c**) Br (motor-racing track) circuito m

circular ['sɜːkjʊlə(r)] adj & n circular (f)

circulate ['sɜːkjʊleɪt] **1** vt (news) hacer circular
2 vi circular

circulation [sɜːkjʊ'leɪʃən] n (**a**) (of blood) circulación f (**b**) (of newspaper) tirada f

circumcise ['sɜːkəmsaɪz] vt circuncidar

circumference [sə'kʌmfərəns] n circunferencia f

circumspect ['sɜːkəmspekt] *adj* circunspecto(a), *Esp* comedido(a)

circumstance ['sɜːkəmstəns] *n (situation)* circunstancia *f*; **under no circumstances** en ningún caso; **economic circumstances** situación económica

circumvent [sɜːkəm'vent] *vt Fig* burlar

circus ['sɜːkəs] *n* circo *m*

cirrhosis [sɪ'rəʊsɪs] *n* cirrosis *f*

CIS [siːaɪ'es] *n (abbr* **Commonwealth of Independent States)** CEI *f*

cistern ['sɪstən] *n* cisterna *f*

cite [saɪt] *vt (quote)* citar

citizen ['sɪtɪzən] *n* ciudadano(a) *m,f*

citizenship ['sɪtɪzənʃɪp] *n* ciudadanía *f*

citrus ['sɪtrəs] *adj* **c. fruits** agrios *mpl*

city ['sɪtɪ] *n* ciudad *f*; **the C.** la City (de Londres), = el barrio financiero y bursátil de Londres; *US* **c. council** ayuntamiento *m*; *US* **c. hall** ayuntamiento

civic ['sɪvɪk] *adj* cívico(a); *Br* **c. centre** centro cívico; **c. duties** obligaciones cívicas

civics ['sɪvɪks] *n sing (subject)* educación *f* cívica

civil ['sɪvəl] *adj* **(a)** *(of society)* civil; **c. defence** defensa *f* civil; **c. engineer** ingeniero(a) *m,f* de caminos; **c. rights** derechos *mpl* civiles; **c. servant** funcionario(a) *m,f*; *Pol* **c. service** administración pública *f*; **(b)** *(polite)* cortés

civilian [sɪ'vɪljən] *adj & n* civil *(mf)*; **c. clothing** traje *m* de paisano

civilization [sɪvɪlaɪ'zeɪʃən] *n* civilización *f*

civilized ['sɪvɪlaɪzd] *adj* civilizado(a)

clad [klæd] **1** *adj Literary* vestido(a)
2 *pt & pp of* **clothe**

claim [kleɪm] **1** *vt* **(a)** *(benefits, rights)* reclamar; *Jur (compensation)* exigir **(b)** *(assert)* afirmar
2 *n* **(a)** *(demand)* reclamación *f*; *Jur* demanda *f*; **to put in a c.** reclamar una indemnización **(b)** *(right)* derecho *m* **(c)** *(assertion)* pretensión *f*

claimant ['kleɪmənt] *n Jur* demandante *mf*

clairvoyant [kleə'vɔɪənt] *n* clarividente *mf*

clam [klæm] *n* almeja *f*
▸ **clam up** *vi Fam* callarse

clamber ['klæmbə(r)] *vi* trepar (**over** por)

clammy ['klæmɪ] *adj* (**clammier, clammiest**) *(weather)* bochornoso(a); *(hand)* pegajoso(a)

clamour, *US* **clamor** ['klæmə(r)] **1** *n* clamor *m*
2 *vi* clamar; **to c. for** pedir a gritos

clamp [klæmp] **1** *n (for carpentry)* tornillo *m* de banco; *Tech* abrazadera *f*; **wheel c.** cepo *m*
2 *vt* sujetar con abrazaderas
▸ **clamp down on** *vt insep* aumentar los esfuerzos contra

clan [klæn] *n* clan *m*

clandestine [klæn'destɪn] *adj* clandestino(a)

clang [klæŋ] **1** *vi* sonar
2 *n* sonido metálico

clap [klæp] **1** *vi* aplaudir
2 *n* **(a)** *(with hands)* **to give sb a c.** aplaudir a algn **(b)** *(noise)* **a c. of thunder** un trueno

clapping ['klæpɪŋ] *n* aplausos *mpl*

claret ['klærət] *n Br (wine)* clarete *m*; *(colour)* burdeos *m*

clarification [klærɪfɪ'keɪʃən] *n* aclaración *f*

clarify ['klærɪfaɪ] *vt* aclarar

clarinet [klærɪ'net] *n* clarinete *m*

clarity ['klærɪtɪ] *n* claridad *f*

clash [klæʃ] **1** *vi* **(a)** *(cymbals)* sonar; *(swords)* chocar; *Fig (disagree)* estar en desacuerdo **(b)** *(colours)* desentonar **(c)** *(dates)* coincidir
2 *n* **(a)** *(sound)* sonido *m* **(b)** *(fight)* choque *m*; *Fig (conflict)* conflicto *m*

clasp [klɑːsp] **1** *n* **(a)** *(on belt)* cierre *m*; *(on necklace)* broche *m* **(b)** *(grasp)* apretón *m*; **c. knife** navaja *f*
2 *vt (object)* agarrar; **to c. hands** juntar las manos

class [klɑːs] **1** *n* clase *f*; **c. struggle** lucha *f* de clases; *US Educ* **c. of 2004** promoción *f* de 2004
2 *vt* clasificar

classic ['klæsɪk] **1** *adj* clásico(a)
2 *n* **(a)** *(author)* autor clásico; *(work)* obra clásica **(b)** **the classics** *(literature)* las obras clásicas; **classics** *(languages)* clásicas *fpl*

classical ['klæsɪkəl] *adj* clásico(a)

classification [klæsɪfɪ'keɪʃən] *n* clasificación *f*

classified ['klæsɪfaɪd] *adj (information)* secreto(a); **c. advertisements** anuncios *mpl* por palabras

classify ['klæsɪfaɪ] *vt* clasificar

classless ['klɑːslɪs] *adj* sin clases

classmate ['klɑːsmeɪt] *n* compañero(a) *m,f* de clase

classroom ['klɑːsruːm] *n* aula *f*, clase *f*

classy ['klɑːsɪ] *adj* (**classier, classiest**) *Fam* con clase, elegante

clatter ['klætə(r)] 1 *vi* he clattered up the stairs subió las escaleras con estrépito
 2 *n* ruido *m*, estrépito *m*

clause [klɔ:z] *n* (a) *Jur* cláusula *f* (b) *Gram* oración *f*

claustrophobic [klɔ:strə'fəʊbɪk] *adj* claustrofóbico(a)

claw [klɔ:] 1 *n* (of bird, animal) garra *f*; (of crab, lobster) pinza *f*
 2 *vt* (scratch) arañar
▸ **claw at** *vt insep* agarrar, arañar

clay [kleɪ] *n* arcilla *f*; **c. pigeon shooting** tiro *m* al plato

clean [kli:n] 1 *adj* (a) (not dirty) limpio(a) (b) (unmarked, pure) sin defecto; **to have a c. record** no tener antecedentes (penales) (c) (not obscene) decente
 2 *adv* (a) **to play c.** jugar limpio; *Fam* **to come c.** confesarlo todo (b) *Fam* por completo; **it went c. through the middle** pasó justo por el medio
 3 *vt* (room) limpiar; **to c. one's teeth** lavarse los dientes
▸ **clean out** *vt sep* (room) limpiar a fondo
▸ **clean up** *vt sep & vi* limpiar

clean-cut ['kli:n'kʌt] *adj* (person) limpio(a), pulcro(a)

cleaner ['kli:nə(r)] *n* limpiador(a) *m,f*

cleaning ['kli:nɪŋ] *n* limpieza *f*

cleanliness ['klenlɪnɪs] *n* limpieza *f*

cleanse [klenz] *vt* limpiar

clean-shaven ['kli:n'ʃeɪvən] *adj* (man, face) (bien) afeitado(a)

cleansing ['klenzɪŋ] *n* **c. lotion** loción limpiadora

clear [klɪə(r)] 1 *adj* (a) (liquid, explanation) claro(a); (road, day) despejado(a); **c. conscience** conciencia tranquila (b) (obvious) claro(a); **to make sth c.** aclarar algo (c) (majority) absoluto(a); (profit) neto(a) (d) (free) libre
 2 *adv* (a) *Fig* **loud and c.** claramente (b) **stand c.!** ¡apártese!; **to stay c. of** evitar
 3 *vt* (a) (room) vaciar; *Com* liquidar; **to c. one's throat** aclararse la garganta; **to c. the table** quitar la mesa (b) (authorize) autorizar (c) (hurdle) salvar (d) **to c. sb of a charge** exculpar a algn de un delito
 4 *vi* (sky) despejarse
▸ **clear away** *vt sep* quitar
▸ **clear off** *vi Br Fam* largarse; **c. off!** ¡largo!
▸ **clear out** *vt sep* (room) limpiar a fondo; (cupboard) vaciar
▸ **clear up** 1 *vt sep* (a) (tidy) recoger; (arrange) ordenar (b) (mystery) resolver; (misunderstanding) aclarar
 2 *vi* (weather) despejarse; (problem) desaparecer

clearance ['klɪərəns] *n* (a) (of area) despeje *m*; *Com* **c. sale** liquidación *f* (de existencias) (b) (space) espacio *m* libre (c) (authorization) autorización *f*

clear-cut [klɪə'kʌt] *adj* claro(a)

clearing ['klɪərɪŋ] *n* (a) (in wood) claro *m* (b) (of rubbish) limpieza *f* (c) (of cheque) compensación *f*

clearly ['klɪəlɪ] *adv* claramente

clearway ['klɪəweɪ] *n Br* = carretera donde está prohibido parar

cleaver ['kli:və(r)] *n* cuchillo *m* de carnicero

clef [klef] *n* clave *f*; **bass/treble c.** clave de fa/de sol

cleft [kleft] *n* hendidura *f*, grieta *f*

clementine ['kleməntaɪn] *n Br* clementina *f*

clench [klentʃ] *vt* (teeth, fist) apretar

clergy ['klɜ:dʒɪ] *n* clero *m*

clergyman ['klɜ:dʒɪmən] *n* clérigo *m*

cleric ['klerɪk] *n Rel* clérigo *m*

clerical ['klerɪkəl] *adj* (a) *Rel* clerical (b) (staff, work) de oficina

clerk [klɑ:k, *US* klɜ:rk] *n* (a) (office worker) oficinista *mf*; (civil servant) funcionario(a) *m,f* (b) *US Com* dependiente(a) *m,f*, vendedor(a) *m,f*

clever ['klevə(r)] *adj* (a) (person) inteligente, listo(a); **to be c. at sth** tener aptitud para algo; *Br Fam Pej* **c. clogs** or **dick** sabelotodo *mf*, *Esp* listillo(a) *m,f* (b) (argument) ingenioso(a)

cliché ['kli:ʃeɪ] *n* cliché *m*

click [klɪk] 1 *n* (sound) clic *m*
 2 *vt* (tongue) chasquear
 3 *vi* (a) **it didn't c.** (I didn't realize) no me di cuenta (b) *Comput* hacer clic (on en)

client ['klaɪənt] *n* cliente *mf*

clientele [kli:ɒn'tel] *n* clientela *f*

cliff [klɪf] *n* acantilado *m*

climate ['klaɪmɪt] *n* clima *m*

climax ['klaɪmæks] *n* (a) (peak) clímax *m*, punto *m* culminante (b) (sexual) orgasmo *m*

climb [klaɪm] 1 *vt* (ladder) subir a; (mountain) escalar; (tree) trepar a
 2 *vi* (plants) trepar; *Av* subir; *Fig* (socially) ascender
 3 *n* subida *f*, ascensión *f*
▸ **climb down** *vi* (descend) bajar; *Fig* (in argument) echarse atrás

climber ['klaɪmə(r)] *n* alpinista *mf*, *Am* andinista *mf*

climbing ['klaɪmɪŋ] *n Sport* montañismo *m*, alpinismo *m*, *Am* andinismo *m*

clinch [klɪntʃ] **1** *vt* (*deal*) cerrar; (*argument*) zanjar
2 *n* (*of lovers, fighters*) abrazo *m*

cling [klɪŋ] *vi* (*pt & pp* **clung**) (*hang on*) agarrarse; (*clothes*) ajustarse; (*smell*) pegarse; **to c. together** unirse

clingfilm ['klɪŋfɪlm] *n Br* plástico *m* transparente (*para envolver alimentos*)

clinic ['klɪnɪk] *n* (*in state hospital*) ambulatorio *m*; (*specialized*) clínica *f*

clinical ['klɪnɪkəl] *adj* (**a**) *Med* clínico(a) (**b**) (*detached*) frío(a)

clink [klɪŋk] **1** *vi* tintinear
2 *n* tintineo *m*

clip¹ [klɪp] **1** *vt* (*cut*) cortar; (*ticket*) picar
2 *n* (**a**) (*of film*) extracto *m* (**b**) (*with scissors*) tijeretada *f*

clip² [klɪp] **1** *n* (*for hair*) pasador *m*; (*for paper*) clip *m*, sujetapapeles *m inv*; (*brooch*) clip
2 *vt* sujetar

clippers ['klɪpəz] *npl* (*for hair*) maquinilla *f* para rapar; (*for nails*) cortauñas *m inv*; (*for hedge*) tijeras *fpl* de podar

clipping ['klɪpɪŋ] *n* recorte *m*

clique [kli:k] *n Pej* camarilla *f*

cloak [kləʊk] **1** *n* (*garment*) capa *f*
2 *vt* encubrir

cloakroom ['kləʊkru:m] *n* guardarropa *m*; *Br Euph* (*toilets*) servicios *mpl*

clock [klɒk] **1** *n* reloj *m*
2 *vt* (*race*) cronometrar
▸ **clock in, clock on** *vi* fichar (a la entrada), *Am* marcar tarjeta (a la entrada)
▸ **clock off, clock out** *vi* fichar (a la salida), *Am* marcar tarjeta (a la salida)
▸ **clock up** *vt sep* (*mileage*) hacer

clockwise ['klɒkwaɪz] *adj & adv* en el sentido de las agujas del reloj

clockwork ['klɒkwɜːk] *n* mecanismo *m*; **c. toy** juguete *m* de cuerda

clog [klɒg] **1** *vt* obstruir, atascar; **to get clogged up** atascarse
2 *n* (*footwear*) zueco *m*

cloister ['klɔɪstə(r)] *n* claustro *m*

clone [kləʊn] **1** *n* clon *m*
2 *vt Biol* clonar

close¹ [kləʊs] **1** *adj* (**a**) (*in space, time*) cercano(a); (*contact*) directo(a); **c. to** cerca de; **c. together** juntos(as) (**b**) (*relationship*) estrecho(a); (*friend*) íntimo(a) (**c**) (*inspection*) detallado(a); (*watch*) atento(a) (**d**) (*contest*) reñido(a); **a c. resemblance** un gran parecido (**e**) (*air*) cargado(a); (*weather*) bochornoso(a)
2 *adv* cerca; **they live c. by** *or* **c. at hand** viven cerca; **to stand c. together** estar apretados(as)

close² [kləʊz] **1** *vt* (**a**) (*door, eyes, shop*) cerrar; **closing time** hora *f* de cierre (**b**) (*meeting, debate*) terminar; (*conference*) clausurar
2 *vi* (**a**) (*shut*) cerrar, cerrarse (**b**) (*end*) concluirse, terminarse
3 *n* fin *m*, final *m*
▸ **close down** *vi* (*business*) cerrar para siempre; *Br Rad & TV* finalizar la emisión
▸ **close in** *vi* **to c. in on sb** rodear a algn

closed [kləʊzd] *adj* cerrado(a); *Ind* **c. shop** = empresa que emplea solamente a miembros de un sindicato

close-knit [kləʊs'nɪt] *adj Fig* unido(a)

closely ['kləʊslɪ] *adv* (**a**) (*tightly*) estrechamente, muy; **c. contested** muy reñido(a); **they are c. related** (*people*) son parientes próximos (**b**) (*attentively*) con atención; **to follow (events) c.** seguir de cerca los acontecimientos

closet ['klɒzɪt] *n US* armario *m*

close-up ['kləʊsʌp] *n* primer plano *m*

closure ['kləʊʒə(r)] *n* cierre *m*

clot [klɒt] **1** *n* (**a**) (*of blood*) coágulo *m*; *Med* **c. on the brain** embolia *f* cerebral (**b**) *Br Fam* lelo(a) *m,f*, *Esp* memo(a) *m,f*
2 *vi* coagularse

cloth [klɒθ] *n* tela *f*, paño *m*; (*rag*) trapo *m*; (*tablecloth*) mantel *m*

clothe [kləʊð] *vt* (*pt & pp* **clothed** *or* **clad**) vestir (**in** *or* **with** de); *Fig* revestir, cubrir (**in** *or* **with** de)

clothes [kləʊðz] *npl* ropa *f*, vestidos *mpl*; **c. brush** cepillo *m* de la ropa; **c. hanger** percha *f*; **c. horse** tendedero *m* plegable; **c. line** tendedero *m*; **c.** *Br* **peg** *or US* **pin** pinza *f*

clothing ['kləʊðɪŋ] *n* ropa *f*

cloud [klaʊd] **1** *n* nube *f*
2 *vt* nublar; *Fig* **to c. the issue** complicar el asunto
3 *vi* **to c. over** nublarse

cloudy ['klaʊdɪ] *adj* (**cloudier, cloudiest**) (**a**) (*sky*) nublado(a) (**b**) (*liquid*) turbio(a)

clout [klaʊt] *Fam* **1** *n* (**a**) (*blow*) tortazo *m* (**b**) (*influence*) influencia *f*
2 *vt* (*hit*) sacudir, *Esp* atizar, *RP* mandar

clove¹ [kləʊv] *n* (*spice*) clavo *m*

clove² [kləʊv] *n* (*of garlic*) diente *m*

clover ['kləʊvə(r)] *n* trébol *m*

clown [klaʊn] **1** *n* payaso *m*
2 *vi* **to c.** (**about** *or* **around**) hacer el payaso

cloying ['klɔɪɪŋ] *adj* empalagoso(a)

club [klʌb] **1** *n* (**a**) (*society*) club *m*; **sports c.** club deportivo (**b**) (*nightclub*) discoteca *f*, sala *f* (de fiestas) (**c**) (*heavy stick*) garrote *m*, porra *f*; (*in golf*) palo *m* (**d**) *Cards* trébol *m*

2 *vt* aporrear

3 *vi* **to c. together** pagar entre varios

clubhouse ['klʌbhaʊs] *n* sede *f* de un club

cluck [klʌk] **1** *n* cloqueo *m*

2 *vi* cloquear

clue [klu:] *n (sign)* indicio *m*; *(to mystery)* pista *f*; *(in crossword)* clave *f*; *Fam* **I haven't a c.** no tengo ni idea

clump [klʌmp] *n (of trees)* grupo *m*; *(of plants)* mata *f*

clumsy ['klʌmzɪ] *adj* (**clumsier, clumsiest**) *(person, movement)* torpe

clung [klʌŋ] *pt & pp of* **cling**

cluster ['klʌstə(r)] **1** *n* grupo *m*; *(of grapes)* racimo *m*

2 *vi* agruparse

clutch [klʌtʃ] **1** *vt* agarrar

2 *vi Fig* **to c. at straws** aferrarse a cualquier cosa

3 *n* **(a)** *Aut* embrague *m* **(b)** *Fig* **to fall into sb's clutches** caer en las garras de algn

clutter ['klʌtə(r)] *vt* **to c. (up)** llenar, atestar

cm *(abbr* **centimetre(s))** cm

CND [si:n'di:] *n Br (abbr* **Campaign for Nuclear Disarmament)** = organización británica en favor del desarme nuclear

Co **(a)** *Com (abbr* **Company)** Cía. **(b)** *(abbr* **County)** condado

c/o [si:'əʊ] *(abbr* **care of)** en el domicilio de

coach [kəʊtʃ] **1** *n* **(a)** *esp Br (bus)* autobús *m*, *Esp* autocar *m*; *(carriage)* carruaje *m*; **c. tour** excursión *f* en autocar **(b)** *Rail* coche *m*, vagón *m* **(c)** *Sport* entrenador(a) *m,f*

2 *vt Sport* entrenar; *Educ* dar clases particulares a

coagulate [kəʊ'ægjʊleɪt] *vi* coagularse

coal [kəʊl] *n* carbón *m*, hulla *f*; **c. bunker** carbonera *f*; **c. merchant** carbonero *m*; **c. mine** mina *f* de carbón

coalfield ['kəʊlfi:ld] *n* yacimiento *m* de carbón

coalition [kəʊə'lɪʃən] *n* coalición *f*

coarse [kɔ:s] *adj (material)* basto(a); *(skin)* áspero(a); *(language)* grosero(a), ordinario(a)

coast [kəʊst] *n* costa *f*, litoral *m*

coastal ['kəʊstəl] *adj* costero(a)

coaster ['kəʊstə(r)] *n (mat)* salvamanteles *m inv*

coastguard ['kəʊstgɑ:d] *n esp Br (person)* guardacostas *mf inv*

coastline ['kəʊstlaɪn] *n* litoral *m*, costa *f*

coat [kəʊt] **1** *n* **(a)** *(overcoat)* abrigo *m*; *(jacket)* chaqueta *f*, *Méx* chamarra *f*, *RP* campera *f*; **c. hanger** percha *f* **(b)** *(of*

animal) pelo *m* **(c)** *(of paint)* mano *f*, capa *f*

2 *vt* cubrir (**with**·de); *(with liquid)* bañar (**with** en)

coating ['kəʊtɪŋ] *n* capa *f*, baño *m*

coax [kəʊks] *vt* engatusar

cob [kɒb] *n* mazorca *f*

cobble ['kɒbəl] *n* adoquín *m*

cobbled ['kɒbəld] *adj (path, street)* adoquinado(a)

cobbler ['kɒblə(r)] *n* zapatero *m*

cobweb ['kɒbweb] *n* telaraña *f*

cocaine [kə'keɪn] *n* cocaína *f*

cock [kɒk] **1** *n* **(a)** *(male fowl)* gallo *m*; *(male bird)* macho *m* **(b)** *Vulg (penis) Esp* polla *f*, *Am* verga *f*, *Chile* pico *m*, *Méx* pito *m*, *RP* pija *f*

2 *vt (gun)* amartillar; *(ears)* erguir

▸ **cock up** *vt sep Br very Fam* **to c. sth up** cagar *or Esp* joder *or Méx* madrear algo

cocker ['kɒkə(r)] *n* **c. spaniel** cocker *m*

cockerel ['kɒkərəl] *n* gallo *m* joven

cockeyed ['kɒkaɪd] *adj Fam (lopsided)* torcido(a); *(scheme)* disparatado(a)

cockle ['kɒkəl] *n* berberecho *m*

cockney ['kɒknɪ] **1** *adj* = del East End londinense

2 *n* = persona del East End londinense

cockpit ['kɒkpɪt] *n* cabina *f* del piloto

cockroach ['kɒkrəʊtʃ] *n* cucaracha *f*

cocktail ['kɒkteɪl] *n* cóctel *m*; **c. lounge** bar *m*; **c. party** cóctel; **prawn c.** cóctel de gambas; **Molotov c.** cóctel Molotov

cocky ['kɒkɪ] *adj* (**cockier, cockiest**) *Fam* gallito(a), engreído(a), *Esp* chulo(a)

cocoa ['kəʊkəʊ] *n* cacao *m*

coconut ['kəʊkənʌt] *n* coco *m*

cocoon [kə'ku:n] *n* capullo *m*

COD [si:əʊ'di:] *Br (abbr* **cash on delivery)** CAE

cod [kɒd] *n* bacalao *m*; **c. liver oil** aceite *m* de hígado de bacalao

code [kəʊd] **1** *n* código *m*; *(symbol)* clave *f*; *Tel* prefijo *m*

2 *vt (message)* cifrar, poner en clave

co-ed [kəʊ'ed] *Fam* **1** *adj* mixto(a)

2 *n* colegio mixto

coeducational ['kəʊedjʊ'keɪʃənəl] *adj* mixto(a)

coerce [kəʊ'ɜ:s] *vt* coaccionar

coercion [kəʊ'ɜ:ʃən] *n* coacción *f*

coexist [kəʊɪg'zɪst] *vi* coexistir

coffee ['kɒfɪ] *n* café *m*; **c. bar/shop** cafetería *f*; **c. break** descanso *m*; **c. table** mesita *f* de café

coffeepot ['kɒfɪpɒt] *n* cafetera *f*

coffer ['kɒfə(r)] *n* arca *f*

coffin ['kɒfɪn] n ataúd m
cog [kɒg] n diente m
cognac ['kɒnjæk] n coñac m
cognitive ['kɒgnɪtɪv] adj cognitivo(a)
cohabit [kəʊ'hæbɪt] vi cohabitar, convivir
coherent [kəʊ'hɪərənt] adj coherente
coil [kɔɪl] 1 vt to c. (up) enrollar
2 vi enroscarse
3 n (a) (loop) vuelta f; (of rope) rollo m; (of hair) rizo m (b) Br (contraceptive) espiral f (c) Elec carrete m, bobina f
coin [kɔɪn] 1 n moneda f
2 vt (a) (money) acuñar (b) Fig to c. a phrase por así decirlo
coinage ['kɔɪnɪdʒ] n moneda f, sistema monetario
coincide [kəʊɪn'saɪd] vi coincidir (with con)
coincidence [kəʊ'ɪnsɪdəns] n coincidencia f
coincidental [kəʊɪnsɪ'dentəl] adj casual
coincidentally [kəʊɪnsɪ'dentəlɪ] adv por casualidad or coincidencia
Coke® [kəʊk] n Fam Coca-Cola® f
coke [kəʊk] n (coal) coque m
colander ['kɒləndə(r)] n colador m
cold [kəʊld] 1 adj frío(a); I'm c. tengo frío; it's c. (weather) hace frío; (thing) está frío(a); Fig to get c. feet (about doing sth) entrarle miedo a algn (de hacer algo); c. cream crema f hidratante; Fig it leaves me c. ni me va ni me viene, Esp me deja frío(a); c. sore herpes m inv labial, Esp calentura f, Méx fuego m; c. war guerra fría
2 n (a) (low temperature) frío m (b) (illness) catarro m, Esp, Méx resfriado m, Andes, RP resfrío m; to have a c. estar acatarrado(a), tener un Esp, Méx resfriado or Andes, RP resfrío
cold-blooded [kəʊld'blʌdɪd] adj (a) (animal) de sangre fría (b) Fig (person) frío(a); (crime) a sangre fría
coldness ['kəʊldnɪs] n (of weather, manner) frialdad f
coleslaw ['kəʊlslɔː] n ensalada f de col
collaborate [kə'læbəreɪt] vi colaborar (with con)
collaboration [kəlæbə'reɪʃən] n also Pej colaboración f
collaborator [kə'læbəreɪtə(r)] n Pol colaboracionista mf
collapse [kə'læps] 1 vi (break down) derrumbarse; (cave in) hundirse; Fig (prices) caer en picado; Med sufrir un colapso
2 vt (table) plegar

3 n (breaking down) derrumbamiento m; (caving in) hundimiento m; Med colapso m
collapsible [kə'læpsəbəl] adj plegable
collar ['kɒlə(r)] 1 n (of garment) cuello m; (for dog) collar m
2 vt Fam pescar, agarrar
collarbone ['kɒləbəʊn] n clavícula f
collateral [kɒ'lætərəl] 1 n Fin garantía subsidiaria
2 adj colateral
colleague ['kɒliːg] n colega mf
collect [kə'lekt] 1 vt (a) (gather) recoger (b) (stamps etc) coleccionar (c) (taxes) recaudar
2 vi (a) (people) reunirse (b) (for charity) hacer una colecta (for para)
3 adv US to call sb c. llamar or Am hablar a algn a cobro revertido
collection [kə'lekʃən] n (a) (of mail) recogida f; (of money) colecta f (b) (of stamps) colección f
collective [kə'lektɪv] 1 adj colectivo(a); c. bargaining negociación colectiva
2 n colectivo m
collector [kə'lektə(r)] n (of stamps) coleccionista m f
college ['kɒlɪdʒ] n colegio m; Br (of university) colegio universitario; US (university) universidad f
collide [kə'laɪd] vi chocar, colisionar
collie ['kɒlɪ] n perro m pastor escocés
colliery ['kɒljərɪ] n Br mina f de carbón
collision [kə'lɪʒən] n choque m
colloquial [kə'ləʊkwɪəl] adj coloquial
collusion [kə'luːʒən] n conspiración f
cologne [kə'ləʊn] n (agua f de) colonia f
Colombia [kə'lɒmbɪə] n Colombia
Colombian [kə'lɒmbɪən] adj & n colombiano(a) (m,f)
colon¹ ['kəʊlən] n Typ dos puntos mpl
colon² ['kəʊlən] n Anat colon m
colonel ['kɜːnəl] n coronel m
colonial [kə'ləʊnɪəl] adj colonial
colonize ['kɒlənaɪz] vt colonizar
colony ['kɒlənɪ] n colonia f
color ['kʌlər] n, vt & vi US = colour
colossal [kə'lɒsəl] adj colosal
colour ['kʌlə(r)] 1 n (a) (hue) color m; what c. is it? ¿de qué color es?; c. film/television película f/televisión f en color; c. scheme combinación f de colores (b) (skin colour) color m de la piel; c. bar discriminación f racial ; colours Br Sport colores mpl; Mil (flag) bandera f
2 vt colorear
3 vi to c. (up) ruborizarse

colour-blind ['kʌləblaɪnd] *adj* daltónico(a)

coloured ['kʌləd] *adj (clothes)* de color; *(photograph)* en color

> 🖉 Note that the Spanish word **colorado** is a false friend and is never a translation for the English word **coloured**. In Spanish **colorado** means "red".

colourful ['kʌləfʊl] *adj* (a) *(having bright colours)* de colores vivos (b) *(interesting, exciting)* lleno(a) de colorido; *(person)* pintoresco(a)

colouring ['kʌlərɪŋ] *n (colour)* colorido *m*

colourless ['kʌlələs] *adj (clear)* incoloro(a); *Fig (dull)* insulso(a)

colt [kəʊlt] *n* potro *m*

column ['kɒləm] *n* columna *f*

columnist ['kɒləmnɪst] *n* columnista *mf*

coma ['kəʊmə] *n* coma *m*; **to go into a c.** entrar en coma

comb [kəʊm] **1** *n* peine *m*
2 *vt* peinar; **to c. one's hair** peinarse

combat ['kɒmbæt] **1** *n* combate *m*
2 *vt (enemy, disease)* combatir
3 *vi* combatir (**against** contra)

combination [kɒmbɪ'neɪʃən] *n* combinación *f*

combine [kəm'baɪn] **1** *vt* combinar
2 *vi (merge)* unirse, combinarse; *(people)* unirse
3 *n* ['kɒmbaɪn] (a) *Com* asociación *f* (b) **c. harvester** cosechadora *f*

combustion [kəm'bʌstʃən] *n* combustión *f*

come [kʌm] *vi (pt* came) *(pp* come) (a) *(in general)* venir (**from** de); *(arrive)* venir, llegar; **coming!** ¡voy!; **to c. and go** ir y venir; *Fig* **in years to c.** en el futuro (b) *(happen)* suceder; **c. what may** pase lo que pase (c) **I came to believe that ...** llegué a creer que …

▸ **come about** *vi* ocurrir, suceder

▸ **come across 1** *vt insep (thing)* encontrar por casualidad; **to c. across sb** tropezar con algn
2 *vi Fig* **to c. across well** causar buena impresión

▸ **come along** *vi* (a) *(arrive)* venir; **c. along!** ¡vamos!, *Esp* ¡venga! (b) *(make progress)* progresar

▸ **come away** *vi (leave)* salir; *(part)* desprenderse (**from** de)

▸ **come back** *vi (return)* volver, *Col, Méx* regresarse

▸ **come before** *vt insep* (a) *(in time)* preceder (b) *(court)* comparecer ante

▸ **come by** *vt insep* adquirir

▸ **come down** *vi (descend)* bajar; *(rain)* caer; *(building)* ser derribado(a); **to c. down with the flu** *Esp* pillar un resfriado, *Am* agarrarse un resfrío

▸ **come forward** *vi (advance)* avanzar; *(volunteer)* ofrecerse

▸ **come in** *vi* (a) *(enter)* entrar; **c. in!** ¡pase! (b) *(arrive) (train)* llegar; *(tide)* subir; *Fam Fig* **where do I c. in?** y yo ¿qué pinto? (c) **to c. in handy** venir bien (d) **to c. in for** ser objeto de

▸ **come into** *vt insep* (a) *(enter)* entrar en (b) *(inherit)* heredar

▸ **come off 1** *vt insep (fall from)* caerse de; *Fam* **c. off it!** ¡venga ya!
2 *vi* (a) *(fall)* caerse; *(stain)* quitarse; *(button)* caerse (b) *Fam (take place)* pasar; *(succeed)* salir bien; **to c. off badly** salir mal

▸ **come on** *vi* (a) **c. on!** *(hurry)* ¡vamos!, *Esp* ¡venga! (b) *(make progress)* progresar (c) *(rain, illness)* comenzar

▸ **come out** *vi* (a) *(person, sun, book)* salir; *(product)* estrenarse; *(facts)* revelarse (b) *(stain)* quitarse; *(colour)* desteñir (c) **to c. out against/in favour of sth** declararse en contra/a favor de algo; *Br Ind* **to c. out (on strike)** declararse en huelga (d) *(turn out)* salir

▸ **come over 1** *vi* venir
2 *vt insep* (a) *(hill)* aparecer en lo alto de (b) *Fam* **what's c. over you?** ¿qué te pasa?

▸ **come round 1** *vt insep (corner)* dar la vuelta a
2 *vi* (a) *(visit)* venir (b) *(regain consciousness)* volver en sí (c) **to c. round to sb's way of thinking** dejarse convencer por algn

▸ **come through 1** *vt insep* (a) *(cross)* cruzar (b) *(illness)* recuperarse de; *(accident)* sobrevivir
2 *vi (message)* llegar

▸ **come to 1** *vi (regain consciousness)* volver en sí
2 *vt insep* (a) *Fig* **to c. to one's senses** recobrar la razón (b) *(amount to)* costar (c) *(arrive at)* llegar a; **to c. to an end** terminar; *Fam* **c. to that** a propósito

▸ **come under** *vt insep Fig* **to c. under fire from sb** ser criticado(a) por algn

▸ **come up** *vi* (a) *(rise)* subir; *(approach)* acercarse (**to** a) (b) *(difficulty, question)* surgir; **to c. up with a solution** encontrar una solución; **to c. up against problems** encontrarse con problemas (c) *(sun)* salir (d) **to c. up to** igualar; **to c. up to sb's expectations** satisfacer a algn (e) *Br Fam* **three chips, coming up!** ¡van tres de patatas fritas!

▸ **come upon** *vt insep* = **come across 1**

comeback ['kʌmbæk] n Fam (a) (of person) reaparición f; **to make a c.** reaparecer (b) (answer) réplica f

comedian [kə'miːdɪən] n cómico m

comedienne [kəmiːdɪ'en] n cómica f

comedown ['kʌmdaʊn] n Fam desilusión f, revés m

comedy ['kɒmɪdɪ] n comedia f

comet ['kɒmɪt] n cometa m

comeuppance [kʌm'ʌpəns] n Fam **to get one's c.** llevarse su merecido

comfort ['kʌmfət] **1** n (a) (ease) comodidad f; US **c. station** servicios mpl, Esp aseos mpl, Am baños mpl (b) (consolation) consuelo m; **to take c. in** or **from sth** consolarse con algo
2 vt consolar

comfortable ['kʌmfətəbəl] adj (chair, person, margin) cómodo(a); (temperature) agradable

comfortably ['kʌmfətəblɪ] adv (win) con facilidad; **to be c. off** vivir cómodamente

comforter ['kʌmfətə(r)] n (a) Br (scarf) bufanda f (b) (for baby) chupete m (c) US (quilt) edredón m

comforting ['kʌmfətɪŋ] adj consolador(a)

comic ['kɒmɪk] **1** adj cómico(a); **c. strip** tira cómica, historieta f
2 n (a) (person) cómico m,f (b) **c. (book)** (for children) Esp tebeo m, Am revista f de historietas; (for adults) cómic m

coming ['kʌmɪŋ] **1** adj (year) próximo(a); (generation) futuro(a)
2 n venida f, llegada f; **comings and goings** idas fpl y venidas; Fig **c. and going** ajetreo m

comma ['kɒmə] n coma f

command [kə'mɑːnd] **1** vt (a) (order) mandar (b) (respect) infundir; (attention) obtener (c) (have at one's disposal) disponer de
2 n (a) (order) orden f; (authority) mando m; **to be at sb's c.** estar a las órdenes de algn (b) (of language) dominio m (c) (disposal) disposición f (d) Comput comando m, instrucción f

commandeer [kɒmən'dɪə(r)] vt requisar

commander [kə'mɑːndə(r)] n comandante m

commanding [kə'mɑːndɪŋ] adj dominante; Mil **c. officer** comandante m

commandment [kə'mɑːndmənt] n mandamiento m

commando [kə'mɑːndəʊ] n comando m

commemorate [kə'meməreɪt] vt conmemorar

commemoration [kəmemə'reɪʃən] n conmemoración f; **in c. of** en conmemoración de

commence [kə'mens] vt & vi Fml comenzar

commend [kə'mend] vt (a) (praise) alabar, elogiar (b) (entrust) encomendar (c) (recommend) recomendar

commendable [kə'mendəbəl] adj encomiable

commensurate [kə'menʃərɪt] adj proporcional; **c. to** or **with** en proporción con

comment ['kɒment] **1** n comentario m; **no c.** sin comentario
2 vi hacer comentarios

commentary ['kɒməntərɪ] n comentario m

commentator ['kɒmənteɪtə(r)] n comentarista mf

commerce ['kɒmɜːs] n comercio m

commercial [kə'mɜːʃəl] **1** adj comercial; TV **c. break** corte publicitario
2 n TV anuncio m

commercialize [kə'mɜːʃəlaɪz] vt explotar

commiserate [kə'mɪzəreɪt] vi compadecerse (**with** de)

commission [kə'mɪʃən] **1** n (a) Mil despacho m (de oficial); **out of c.** fuera de servicio (b) (of inquiry) comisión f; (job) encargo m (c) (payment) comisión f
2 vt (a) Mil nombrar (b) (order) encargar (c) Naut poner en servicio

commissionaire [kəmɪʃə'neə(r)] n Br (at hotel, cinema) portero m de librea

commissioner [kə'mɪʃənə(r)] n (official) comisario m; **c. of police** comisario de policía

commit [kə'mɪt] vt (a) (crime) cometer; **to c. suicide** suicidarse (b) **to c. oneself (to do sth)** comprometerse (a hacer algo) (c) **to c. sth to sb's care** confiar algo a algn

commitment [kə'mɪtmənt] n compromiso m

committee [kə'mɪtɪ] n comisión f, comité m

commode [kə'məʊd] n (chair) silla f con orinal; (chest of drawers) cómoda f

commodity [kə'mɒdɪtɪ] n producto básico

> 🖉 Note that the Spanish word **comodidad** is a false friend and is never a translation for the English word **commodity**. In Spanish **comodidad** means "comfort, convenience".

common ['kɒmən] **1** adj (a) (frequent) común, frecuente (b) (shared) común;

that's **c. knowledge** eso lo sabe todo el mundo; **c. law** derecho consuetudinario; **C. Market** Mercado *m* Común; **c. room** *(for students)* sala *f* de estudiantes; *(for teachers)* sala *f* de profesores (**c**) *(ordinary)* corriente (**d**) *(vulgar)* ordinario(a), maleducado(a)
2 *n (land)* campo *m or* terreno *m* comunal

commonly ['kɒmənlɪ] *adv* comúnmente

commonplace ['kɒmənpleɪs] *adj* corriente

Commons ['kɒmənz] *npl Br, Can* **the (House of) C.** la Cámara de los Comunes

Commonwealth ['kɒmənwelθ] *n Br* **the C.** la Commonwealth; **C. of Independent States** Comunidad *f* de Estados Independientes

commotion [kə'məʊʃən] *n* alboroto *m*

communal ['kɒmjʊnəl] *adj* comunal

commune¹ [kə'mjuːn] *vi (converse)* conversar íntimamente; *(with nature)* estar en comunión (**with** con)

commune² ['kɒmjuːn] *n* comuna *f*

communicate [kə'mjuːnɪkeɪt] **1** *vi* comunicarse (**with** con)
2 *vt* comunicar

communication [kəmjuːnɪ'keɪʃən] *n* comunicación *f*; *Br Rail* **c. cord** timbre *m* de alarma

communicator [kə'mjuːnɪkeɪtə(r)] *n* comunicador(a) *m,f*

communion [kə'mjuːnɪən] *n* comunión *f*; **to take c.** comulgar

communiqué [kə'mjuːnɪkeɪ] *n* comunicado *m* oficial

communism ['kɒmjʊnɪzəm] *n* comunismo *m*

communist ['kɒmjʊnɪst] *adj & n* comunista *(mf)*

community [kə'mjuːnɪtɪ] *n* comunidad *f*; *(people)* colectividad *f*; **c. centre** centro *m* social

commute [kə'mjuːt] **1** *vi* = viajar diariamente al lugar de trabajo
2 *vt Jur* conmutar

commuter [kə'mjuːtə(r)] *n* = persona que viaja diariamente al lugar de trabajo

compact¹ **1** *adj* [kəm'pækt] compacto(a)
2 *n* ['kɒmpækt] *(for powder)* polvera *f*

compact² ['kɒmpækt] *n Pol* pacto *m*

compact disc ['kɒmpækt'dɪsk] *n* disco compacto

companion [kəm'pænjən] *n* compañero(a) *m,f*

companionship [kəm'pænjənʃɪp] *n* compañerismo *m*

company ['kʌmpənɪ] *n* (**a**) *(companionship)* compañía *f*; **to keep sb c.** hacer compañía a algn (**b**) *Com* empresa *f*, compañía *f*

comparable ['kɒmpərəbəl] *adj* comparable (**to** *or* **with** con)

comparative [kəm'pærətɪv] **1** *adj (comfort, wealth)* relativo(a); *(study, research)* comparado(a)
2 *n Gram* comparativo *m*

comparatively [kəm'pærətɪvlɪ] *adv* relativamente

compare [kəm'peə(r)] **1** *vt* comparar (**to** *or* **with** con); **(as) compared with** en comparación con
2 *vi* compararse

comparison [kəm'pærɪsən] *n* comparación *f*; **by c.** en comparación; **there's no c.** no se puede comparar

compartment [kəm'pɑːtmənt] *n (section)* compartimiento *m*; *Rail* departamento *m*

compass ['kʌmpəs] *n* (**a**) *(for finding direction)* brújula *f* (**b**) **(pair of) compasses** compás *m* (**c**) *Fig (range)* límites *mpl*

compassion [kəm'pæʃən] *n* compasión *f*

compassionate [kəm'pæʃənət] *adj* compasivo(a)

compatible [kəm'pætəbəl] *adj* compatible

compatriot [kəm'pætrɪət] *n* compatriota *mf*

compel [kəm'pel] *vt* (**a**) *(oblige)* obligar; **to c. sb to do sth** obligar a algn a hacer algo (**b**) *(admiration)* despertar

compelling [kəm'pelɪŋ] *adj* irresistible

compensate ['kɒmpənseɪt] **1** *vt* compensar; **to c. sb for sth** indemnizar a algn de algo
2 *vi* compensar

compensation [kɒmpən'seɪʃən] *n* compensación *f*; *(for loss)* indemnización *f*

compere ['kɒmpeə(r)] *n Br* animador(a) *m,f*

compete [kəm'piːt] *vi* competir

competence ['kɒmpɪtəns] *n* (**a**) *(ability)* aptitud *f* (**b**) *(of court etc)* competencia *f*

competent ['kɒmpɪtənt] *adj* competente

competition [kɒmpɪ'tɪʃən] *n* (**a**) *(contest)* concurso *m* (**b**) *Com* competencia *f*

competitive [kəm'petɪtɪv] *adj* competitivo(a)

competitor [kəm'petɪtə(r)] *n* competidor(a) *m,f*

compilation [kɒmpɪ'leɪʃən] *n* recopilación *f*

compile [kəm'paɪl] *vt* compilar, recopilar

complacency [kəm'pleɪsənsɪ] *n* autocomplacencia *f*

> 🖉 Note that the Spanish word **complacencia** is a false friend and is never a translation for the English word **complacency**. In Spanish, **complacencia** means "satisfaction, indulgence".

complacent [kəm'pleɪsənt] *adj* autocomplaciente

complain [kəm'pleɪn] *vi* quejarse (**of/about** de)

complaint [kəm'pleɪnt] *n* (**a**) *(grievance)* queja *f*; *Com (formal protest)* queja *f*, reclamación *f*, *Am* reclamo *m* (**b**) *Med* afección *f*, problema *m*

complement ['kɒmplɪmənt] **1** *n* (**a**) *Ling* complemento *m* (**b**) *Naut* dotación *f*
  2 *vt* complementar

complementary [kɒmplɪ'mentərɪ] *adj* complementario(a)

complete [kəm'pliːt] **1** *adj* (**a**) *(entire)* completo(a) (**b**) *(absolute)* total
  2 *vt* completar; **to c. a form** rellenar un formulario

completely [kəm'pliːtlɪ] *adv* completamente, por completo

completion [kəm'pliːʃən] *n* terminación *f*; **near c.** casi terminado(a); **on c.** en cuanto se termine

complex ['kɒmpleks] **1** *adj* complejo(a)
  2 *n* complejo *m*; **inferiority c.** complejo de inferioridad

complexion [kəm'plekʃən] *n* tez *f*; *Fig* aspecto *m*

> 🖉 Note that the Spanish word **complexión** is a false friend and is never a translation for the English word **complexion**. In Spanish **complexión** means "build".

compliance [kəm'plaɪəns] *n* conformidad *f*; **in c. with** de acuerdo con

complicate ['kɒmplɪkeɪt] *vt* complicar

complicated ['kɒmplɪkeɪtɪd] *adj* complicado(a)

complication [kɒmplɪ'keɪʃən] *n* complicación *f*

complicity [kəm'plɪsɪtɪ] *n* complicidad *f*

compliment 1 *n* ['kɒmplɪmənt] cumplido *m*; **to pay sb a c.** hacerle un cumplido a algn; **with compliments** con mis mejores deseos
  2 *vt* ['kɒmplɪment] felicitar; **to c. sb on sth** felicitar a algn por algo

complimentary [kɒmplɪ'mentərɪ] *adj* (**a**) *(praising)* elogioso(a) (**b**) *(free)* gratis

comply [kəm'plaɪ] *vi* obedecer; **to c. with** *(order)* cumplir con; *(request)* acceder a

component [kəm'pəʊnənt] **1** *n* componente *m*
  2 *adj* componente; **c. part** parte *f*

compose [kəm'pəʊz] **1** *vt* (**a**) *(music, poetry)* componer (**b**) *(constitute)* **to be composed of** estar compuesto(a) de (**c**) *(calm)* **to c. oneself** calmarse
  2 *vi* *(create music)* componer

composed [kəm'pəʊzd] *adj* *(calm)* sereno(a)

composer [kəm'pəʊzə(r)] *n* compositor(a) *m,f*

composite ['kɒmpəzɪt] *adj* compuesto(a)

composition [kɒmpə'zɪʃən] *n* composición *f*; *(essay)* redacción *f*

compost ['kɒmpɒst] *n* abono *m*

composure [kəm'pəʊʒə(r)] *n* calma *f*, serenidad *f*

compound¹ ['kɒmpaʊnd] **1** *n* compuesto *m*
  2 *adj* compuesto(a); **c. fracture** fractura abierta
  3 *vt* [kəm'paʊnd] *(problem)* agravar

compound² ['kɒmpaʊnd] *n* *(enclosure)* recinto *m*

comprehend [kɒmprɪ'hend] *vt* comprender

comprehensible [kɒmprɪ'hensəbəl] *adj* comprensible

comprehension [kɒmprɪ'henʃən] *n* comprensión *f*

comprehensive [kɒmprɪ'hensɪv] *adj* (**a**) *(knowledge)* amplio(a); *(study)* detallado(a) (**b**) *Ins* a todo riesgo (**c**) *Br* **c. school** ≃ instituto *m* de segunda enseñanza

> 🖉 Note that the Spanish word **comprensivo** is a false friend and is never a translation for the English word **comprehensive**. In Spanish **comprensivo** means "understanding".

compress 1 *vt* [kəm'pres] comprimir
  2 *n* ['kɒmpres] compresa *f*

comprise [kəm'praɪz] *vt* *(include)* comprender; **to be comprised of** constar de

compromise ['kɒmprəmaɪz] **1** *n* solución negociada; **to reach a c.** llegar a un acuerdo
  2 *vi* *(two people)* llegar a un acuerdo; *(individual)* transigir
  3 *vt* *(person)* comprometer

*Note that the Spanish word **compromiso** is a false friend and is never a translation for the English word **compromise**. In Spanish **compromiso** means "obligation, commitment, agreement".*

compulsion [kəm'pʌlʃən] *n* obligación *f*

compulsive [kəm'pʌlsɪv] *adj* compulsivo(a)

compulsory [kəm'pʌlsərɪ] *adj* obligatorio(a)

computational [kɒmpju:'teɪʃənəl] *adj* computacional

computer [kəm'pju:tə(r)] *n* *Esp* ordenador *m*, *Am* computadora *f*; **personal c.** ordenador personal, *Am* computadora personal; **c. programmer** programador(a) *m,f*; **c. science** informática *f*

computerize [kəm'pju:təraɪz] *vt* informatizar, *Am* computarizar, *Am* computadorizar

computing [kəm'pju:tɪŋ] *n* informática *f*, *Am* computación *f*

comrade ['kɒmreɪd] *n* (**a**) *(companion)* compañero(a) *m,f* (**b**) *Pol* camarada *mf*

comradeship ['kɒmreɪdʃɪp] *n* camaradería *f*

con [kɒn] *Fam* **1** *vt* timar, *RP* cagar
2 *n* timo *m*, *Andes*, *RP* truchada *f*; **c. man** timador *m*, *Andes*, *RP* cagador *m*

concave ['kɒnkeɪv] *adj* cóncavo(a)

conceal [kən'si:l] *vt* *(object)* ocultar, esconder (**from** de); *(fact)* ocultar (**from** de)

concede [kən'si:d] *vt* conceder

conceit [kən'si:t] *n* presunción *f*, vanidad *f*

conceited [kən'si:tɪd] *adj* presuntuoso(a)

conceivable [kən'si:vəbəl] *adj* concebible

conceive [kən'si:v] *vt & vi* concebir

concentrate ['kɒnsəntreɪt] **1** *vt* concentrar
2 *vi* **to c. on sth** concentrarse en algo

concentration [kɒnsən'treɪʃən] *n* concentración *f*; **c. camp** campo *m* de concentración

concept ['kɒnsept] *n* concepto *m*

conception [kən'sepʃən] *n* *Med* concepción *f*; *(understanding)* concepto *m*, idea *f*

concern [kən'sɜːn] **1** *vt* (**a**) *(affect)* concernir, incumbir; **as far as I'm concerned** por lo que a mí se refiere (**b**) *(worry)* preocupar
2 *n* (**a**) **it's no c. of mine** no es asunto mío (**b**) *(worry)* preocupación *f* (**c**) *Com* negocio *m*

concerned [kən'sɜːnd] *adj* (**a**) *(affected)* afectado(a) (**b**) *(worried)* preocupado(a) (**about** por)

concerning [kən'sɜːnɪŋ] *prep* con respecto a, en cuanto a

concert ['kɒnsət] *n* *Mus* concierto *m*; **c. hall** sala *f* de conciertos

concerted [kən'sɜːtɪd] *adj* concertado(a)

concertina [kɒnsə'ti:nə] *n* concertina *f*

concerto [kən'tʃɜːtəʊ] *n* concierto *m*

concession [kən'seʃən] *n* (**a**) *(compromise)* concesión *f* (**b**) *Br (discount)* descuento *m*

conciliatory [kən'sɪliətərɪ] *adj* conciliador(a)

concise [kən'saɪs] *adj* conciso(a)

conclude [kən'klu:d] *vt & vi* concluir

conclusion [kən'klu:ʒən] *n* conclusión *f*; **to reach a c.** llegar a una conclusión

conclusive [kən'klu:sɪv] *adj* concluyente

concoct [kən'kɒkt] *vt* *(dish)* confeccionar; *Fig (plan)* fraguar; *(excuse)* inventar

concoction [kən'kɒkʃən] *n* *(mixture)* mezcolanza *f*; *Pej (brew)* brebaje *m*

concourse ['kɒŋkɔːs] *n* explanada *f*

*Note that the Spanish word **concurso** is a false friend and is never a translation for the English word **concourse**. In Spanish **concurso** means "competition, contest".*

concrete ['kɒnkri:t] **1** *n* hormigón *m*, *Am* concreto *m*; **c. mixer** hormigonera *f*
2 *adj* (**a**) *(definite)* concreto(a) (**b**) *(made of concrete)* de hormigón

concur [kən'kɜː(r)] *vi* (**a**) **to c. with** *(agree)* estar de acuerdo con (**b**) *(coincide)* coincidir

concurrent [kən'kʌrənt] *adj* simultáneo(a)

concussion [kən'kʌʃən] *n* conmoción *f* cerebral

condemn [kən'dem] *vt* condenar

condemnation [kɒndem'neɪʃən] *n* condena *f*

condensation [kɒnden'seɪʃən] *n* condensación *f*

condense [kən'dens] **1** *vt* condensar
2 *vi* condensarse

condensed [kən'denst] *adj* **c. milk** leche condensada

condescending [kɒndɪ'sendɪŋ] *adj* condescendiente

condition [kən'dɪʃən] **1** *n* condición *f*; **to be in good c.** estar en buen estado; **on c. that ...** a condición de que ...; **on one c.** con una condición; **heart c.** enfermedad

cardíaca; **conditions** *(circumstances)* circunstancias *fpl*
  2 *vt* condicionar

conditional [kən'dɪʃənəl] *adj* condicional

conditioner [kən'dɪʃənə(r)] *n* acondicionador *m*

condo ['kɒndəʊ] *n US Fam* = **condominium**

condolences [kən'dəʊlənsɪz] *npl* pésame *m*; **please accept my c.** le acompaño en el sentimiento

condom ['kɒndəm] *n* preservativo *m*

condominium [kɒndə'mɪnɪəm] *n US (building)* = bloque de apartamentos poseídos por diferentes propietarios; *(apartment)* apartamento *m, Esp* piso *m, Arg* departamento *m (en propiedad)*

condone [kən'dəʊn] *vt* perdonar, consentir

condor ['kɒndɔ:(r)] *n* cóndor *m*

conducive [kən'dju:sɪv] *adj* conducente

conduct 1 *n* ['kɒndʌkt] *(behaviour)* conducta *f*, comportamiento *m*
  2 *vt* [kən'dʌkt] *(lead)* guiar; *(business, orchestra)* dirigir; **conducted tour** visita acompañada; **to c. oneself** comportarse
  3 *vi Mus* dirigir

conductor [kən'dʌktə(r)] *n* **(a)** *Br (on bus)* cobrador(a) *m,f, RP* guarda *mf* **(b)** *US Rail* revisor(a) *m,f* **(c)** *Mus* director(a) *m,f* **(d)** *Phys* conductor *m*

conductress [kən'dʌktrɪs] *n Br (on bus)* cobradora *f, RP* guarda *f*

cone [kəʊn] *n* **(a)** *(shape)* cono *m*; **ice-cream c.** cucurucho *m*; *(for traffic)* cono *m (de tráfico)* **(b)** *Bot* piña *f*

confectioner [kən'fekʃənə(r)] *n* confitero(a) *m,f*; **c.'s (shop)** *(sweet shop)* confitería *f*

confectionery [kən'fekʃənərɪ] *n* dulces *mpl*

confederate [kən'fedərɪt] **1** *adj* confederado(a)
  2 *n* confederado(a) *m,f, Jur* cómplice *mf*

confederation [kənfedə'reɪʃən] *n* confederación *f*

confer [kən'fɜ:(r)] **1** *vt* **to c. a title on sb** conferir un título a algn
  2 *vi* consultar

conference ['kɒnfərəns] *n* conferencia *f*

confess [kən'fes] **1** *vi* confesar; *Rel* confesarse
  2 *vt* confesar, admitir; *Rel* confesar

confession [kən'feʃən] *n* confesión *f*

confessional [kən'feʃənəl] *n* confesionario *m*

confetti [kən'fetɪ] *n* confeti *m*

confide [kən'faɪd] *vi* **to c. in sb** confiar en algn

confidence ['kɒnfɪdəns] *n* **(a)** *(trust)* confianza *f*; *(self-assurance)* confianza *f* (en uno mismo); **vote of c./no c.** voto *m* de confianza/de censura; **c. trick** camelo *m* **(b)** *(secret)* confidencia *f*; **in c.** en confianza

confident ['kɒnfɪdənt] *adj* seguro(a)

confidential [kɒnfɪ'denʃəl] *adj (secret)* confidencial; *(entrusted)* de confianza

confidently ['kɒnfɪdəntlɪ] *adv* con seguridad

confine [kən'faɪn] *vt* confinar, recluir; **to c. oneself to sth** *(limit)* limitarse a algo

confinement [kən'faɪnmənt] *n* **(a)** *(prison)* reclusión *f*, encierro *m*; **to be in solitary c.** estar incomunicado(a) **(b)** *Old-fashioned Med* parto *m*

confirm [kən'fɜ:m] *vt* confirmar

confirmation [kɒnfə'meɪʃən] *n* confirmación *f*

confirmed [kən'fɜ:md] *adj* empedernido(a)

confiscate ['kɒnfɪskeɪt] *vt* confiscar

conflict 1 *n* ['kɒnflɪkt] conflicto *m*
  2 *vi* [kən'flɪkt] chocar (**with** con)

conflicting [kən'flɪktɪŋ] *adj* contradictorio(a)

conform [kən'fɔ:m] *vi* conformarse; **to c. to** *or* **with** *(customs)* amoldarse a; *(rules)* someterse a

confound [kən'faʊnd] *vt* confundir, desconcertar

confront [kən'frʌnt] *vt* hacer frente a

confrontation [kɒnfrʌn'teɪʃən] *n* confrontación *f*

confuse [kən'fju:z] *vt (person)* despistar; *(thing)* confundir (**with** con); **to get confused** confundirse

confused [kən'fju:zd] *adj (person)* confundido(a); *(mind, ideas)* confuso(a)

confusing [kən'fju:zɪŋ] *adj* confuso(a)

confusion [kən'fju:ʒən] *n* confusión *f*

congeal [kən'dʒi:l] *vi* coagularse

congenial [kən'dʒi:nɪəl] *adj* agradable

congenital [kən'dʒenɪtəl] *adj* congénito(a)

congested [kən'dʒestɪd] *adj* **(a)** *(street)* repleto(a) de gente; *(city)* superpoblado(a) **(b)** *Med* congestionado(a)

congestion [kən'dʒestʃən] *n* congestión *f*

conglomeration [kənglɒmə'reɪʃən] *n* conglomeración *f*

congratulate [kən'grætjʊleɪt] *vt* felicitar

congratulations [kəngrætjʊ'leɪʃənz] *npl* felicitaciones *fpl*; **c.!** ¡enhorabuena!

congregate ['kɒŋgrɪgeɪt] *vi* congregarse

congregation [kɒŋgrɪ'geɪʃən] n (group) congregación f; Rel fieles mpl

congress ['kɒŋgres] n (a) (conference) congreso m (b) US Pol **C.** el Congreso (de los Estados Unidos)

Congressman ['kɒŋgresmən] n US Pol congresista m, Am congresal m

Congresswoman ['kɒŋgreswʊmən] n US Pol congresista f, Am congresal f

conifer ['kɒnɪfə(r)] n conífera f

conjecture [kən'dʒektʃə(r)] **1** n conjetura f
2 vt conjeturar
3 vi hacer conjeturas

conjugal ['kɒndʒʊgəl] adj conyugal

conjugate ['kɒndʒʊgeɪt] vt conjugar

conjunction [kən'dʒʌŋkʃən] n conjunción f; Fig **in c. with** conjuntamente con

conjunctivitis [kəndʒʌŋktɪ'vaɪtɪs] n conjuntivitis f

conjure ['kʌndʒə(r)] **1** vt **to c. (up)** (of magician) hacer aparecer; (memories) evocar
2 vi hacer juegos de manos

conjurer ['kʌndʒərə(r)] n prestidigitador(a) m,f

conker ['kɒŋkə(r)] n Fam castaña f

connect [kə'nekt] **1** vt (a) (pipes, wires, gas) conectar, empalmar (**to** con or a) (b) (link) conectar; Fig **to be connected by marriage** estar emparentado(a) por matrimonio (**c**) Tel (person) pasar, Esp poner (**d**) (associate) (person, problem) relacionar (**with** con)
2 vi (wires, roads, pipes) conectarse, empalmarse; (train, flight) enlazar (**with** con)

connected [kə'nektɪd] adj (events) relacionado(a); Fig **to be well c.** (person) (socially) estar bien relacionado(a)

connection [kə'nekʃən] n (a) (joint) juntura f, unión f; Elec conexión f; Tel instalación f (b) Rail correspondencia f (c) Fig (of ideas) relación f; **in c. with** (regarding) con respecto a (d) (person) contacto m

connive [kə'naɪv] vi **to c. at** hacer la vista gorda con

connoisseur [kɒnɪ'sɜː(r)] n conocedor(a) m,f

connotation [kɒnə'teɪʃən] n connotación f

conquer ['kɒŋkə(r)] vt (enemy, bad habit) vencer; (country) conquistar

conqueror ['kɒŋkərə(r)] n conquistador m

conquest ['kɒŋkwest] n conquista f

conscience ['kɒnʃəns] n conciencia f; **to have a clear c.** tener la conciencia tranquila; **to have a guilty c.** sentirse culpable

conscientious [kɒnʃɪ'enʃəs] adj concienzudo(a); **c. objector** objetor(a) m,f de conciencia

conscious ['kɒnʃəs] adj (aware) consciente; (choice etc) deliberado(a)

consciousness ['kɒnʃəsnɪs] n Med conocimiento m; (awareness) conciencia f

conscript ['kɒnskrɪpt] n recluta m

conscription [kən'skrɪpʃən] n servicio militar obligatorio

consecrate ['kɒnsɪkreɪt] vt consagrar

consecutive [kən'sekjʊtɪv] adj consecutivo(a)

consensus [kən'sensəs] n consenso m

consent [kən'sent] **1** n consentimiento m; **by common c.** de común acuerdo
2 vi consentir (**to** en)

consequence ['kɒnsɪkwəns] n consecuencia f

consequent ['kɒnsɪkwənt] adj consiguiente

consequently ['kɒnsɪkwəntlɪ] adv por consiguiente

conservation [kɒnsə'veɪʃən] n conservación f

conservative [kən'sɜːvətɪv] **1** adj cauteloso(a)
2 adj & n Br Pol **C.** conservador(a) (m,f)

conservatory [kən'sɜːvətrɪ] n (a) (greenhouse) invernadero m (b) Mus conservatorio m

conserve 1 vt [kən'sɜːv] conservar
2 n ['kɒnsɜːv] conserva f

consider [kən'sɪdə(r)] vt (a) (ponder on, regard) considerar; **to c. doing sth** pensar hacer algo (b) (keep in mind) tener en cuenta

considerable [kən'sɪdərəbəl] adj considerable

considerably [kən'sɪdərəblɪ] adv bastante

considerate [kən'sɪdərɪt] adj considerado(a)

consideration [kənsɪdə'reɪʃən] n consideración f; **without due c.** sin reflexión

considering [kən'sɪdərɪŋ] prep teniendo en cuenta

consign [kən'saɪn] vt Com consignar; Fig entregar

consignment [kən'saɪnmənt] n envío m

consist [kən'sɪst] vi **to c. of** consistir en

consistency [kən'sɪstənsɪ] n (a) (of actions) consecuencia f (b) (of mixture) consistencia f

consistent [kən'sɪstənt] *adj* consecuente; **c. with** de acuerdo con

> 🖉 Note that the Spanish word **consistente** is a false friend and is never a translation for the English word **consistent**. In Spanish **consistente** means "firm, solid, sound".

consolation [kɒnsə'leɪʃən] *n* consuelo *m*; **c. prize** premio *m* de consolación

console[1] [kən'səʊl] *vt* consolar

console[2] ['kɒnsəʊl] *n* consola *f*; **(game) c.** videoconsola *f*

consolidate [kən'sɒlɪdeɪt] **1** *vt* consolidar
  2 *vi* consolidarse

consonant ['kɒnsənənt] *n* consonante *f*

consortium [kən'sɔːtɪəm] *n* consorcio *m*

conspicuous [kən'spɪkjʊəs] *adj (striking)* llamativo(a); *(easily seen)* visible; *(mistake)* evidente

conspiracy [kən'spɪrəsɪ] *n* conjura *f*

conspire [kən'spaɪə(r)] *vi* conspirar

constable ['kʌnstəbəl] *n Br* policía *mf*; **chief c.** jefe *m* de policía

constabulary [kən'stæbjʊlərɪ] *n Br* (cuerpo *m* de) policía *f*

constant ['kɒnstənt] **1** *adj (price, temperature)* constante; *(continuous)* continuo(a), constante
  2 *n* constante *f*

constellation [kɒnstɪ'leɪʃən] *n* constelación *f*

consternation [kɒnstə'neɪʃən] *n* consternación *f*

constipated ['kɒnstɪpeɪtɪd] *adj* **to be c.** estar estreñido(a)

> 🖉 Note that the Spanish word **constipado** is a false friend and is never a translation for the English word **constipated**. In Spanish **constipado** means both "cold, chill" and "suffering from a cold".

constipation [kɒnstɪ'peɪʃən] *n* estreñimiento *m*

constituency [kən'stɪtjʊənsɪ] *n* circunscripción *f* electoral

constituent [kən'stɪtjʊənt] **1** *adj (component)* constituyente
  2 *n* **(a)** *(part)* componente *m* **(b)** *Pol* votante *mf*

constitute ['kɒnstɪtjuːt] *vt* constituir

constitution [kɒnstɪ'tjuːʃən] *n* constitución *f*

constitutional [kɒnstɪ'tjuːʃənəl] *adj* constitucional

constrained [kən'streɪnd] *adj* **to feel c. to do sth** sentirse obligado(a) a hacer algo

constraint [kən'streɪnt] *n* coacción *f*; **to feel c. in sb's presence** sentirse cohibido(a) ante algn

construct [kən'strʌkt] *vt* construir

construction [kən'strʌkʃən] *n* construcción *f*

constructive [kən'strʌktɪv] *adj* constructivo(a)

construe [kən'struː] *vt* interpretar

> 🖉 Note that the Spanish verb **construir** is a false friend and is never a translation for the English verb **to construe**. In Spanish, **construir** means "to build, to manufacture".

consul ['kɒnsəl] *n* cónsul *mf*

consulate ['kɒnsjʊlɪt] *n* consulado *m*

consult [kən'sʌlt] *vt & vi* consultar **(about** sobre)

consultancy [kən'sʌltənsɪ] *n Com* asesoría *f*, consultoría *f*

consultant [kən'sʌltənt] *n Med* especialista *mf*; *Com & Ind* asesor(a) *m,f*

consultation [kɒnsəl'teɪʃən] *n* consulta *f*

consulting [kən'sʌltɪŋ] *adj* **c. room** consulta *f*

consume [kən'sjuːm] *vt* consumir

consumer [kən'sjuːmə(r)] *n* consumidor(a) *m,f*; **c. goods** bienes *mpl* de consumo

consummate 1 *vt* ['kɒnsəmeɪt] consumar
  2 *adj* ['kɒnsəmɪt] consumado(a)

consumption [kən'sʌmpʃən] *n* **(a)** *(of food)* consumo *m*; **fit for c.** apto(a) para el consumo **(b)** *Med* tisis *f*

cont. *(abbr* **continued)** sigue

contact ['kɒntækt] **1** *n* contacto *m*; **c. lens** lente *f* de contacto, *Esp* lentilla *f*, *Méx* pupilente *f*
  2 *vt* ponerse en contacto con

contagious [kən'teɪdʒəs] *adj* contagioso(a)

contain [kən'teɪn] *vt* contener; **to c. oneself** contenerse

container [kən'teɪnə(r)] *n* **(a)** *(box, package)* recipiente *m*; *(bottle)* envase *m* **(b)** *Naut* contenedor *m*

contaminate [kən'tæmɪneɪt] *vt* contaminar

contamination [kəntæmɪ'neɪʃən] *n* contaminación *f*

contd. *(abbr* **continued)** sigue

contemplate ['kɒntempleɪt] *vt* **(a)** *(consider)* considerar, pensar en **(b)** *(look at)* contemplar

contemporary [kən'temprərɪ] *adj & n* contemporáneo(a) *(m,f)*

contempt [kən'tempt] *n* desprecio *m*; **to hold in c.** despreciar; **c. of court** desacato *m* a los tribunales

contemptible [kən'temptəbəl] *adj* despreciable

contemptuous [kən'temptjʊəs] *adj* despectivo(a)

contend [kən'tend] **1** *vi* competir; *Fig* **there are many problems to c. with** se han planteado muchos problemas
2 *vt* afirmar

contender [kən'tendə(r)] *n* contendiente *mf*

content¹ ['kɒntent] *n* contenido *m*; **table of contents** índice *m* de materias

content² [kən'tent] **1** *adj* contento(a)
2 *vt* contentar
3 *n* contento *m*; **to one's heart's c.** todo lo que uno quiera

contented [kən'tentɪd] *adj* contento(a), satisfecho(a)

contention [kən'tenʃən] *n* (a) *(dispute)* controversia *f* (b) *(point)* punto *m* de vista

contentment [kən'tentmənt] *n* contento *m*

contest 1 *n* ['kɒntest] concurso *m*; *Sport* prueba *f*
2 *vt* [kən'test] (a) *(matter)* rebatir; *(verdict)* impugnar; *Fig (will)* disputar (b) *Pol (seat)* luchar por

contestant [kən'testənt] *n* concursante *mf*

context ['kɒntekst] *n* contexto *m*

continent ['kɒntɪnənt] *n* continente *m*; *Br* **(on) the C.** (en) Europa

continental [kɒntɪ'nentəl] *adj* (a) *(in geography)* continental; **c. shelf** plataforma *f* continental (b) *Br* de la Europa continental; **c. quilt** edredón *m*

contingency [kən'tɪndʒənsɪ] *n* contingencia *f*; **c. plans** planes *mpl* para casos de emergencia

contingent [kən'tɪndʒənt] *adj & n* contingente *(m)*

continual [kən'tɪnjʊəl] *adj* continuo(a), constante

continuation [kəntɪnjʊ'eɪʃən] *n (sequel etc)* continuación *f*; *(extension)* prolongación *f*

continue [kən'tɪnjuː] *vt & vi* continuar, seguir; **to c. to do sth** seguir *or* continuar haciendo algo

continuous [kən'tɪnjʊəs] *adj* continuo(a)

contort [kən'tɔːt] *vt* retorcer

contortion [kən'tɔːʃən] *n* contorsión *f*

contour ['kɒntʊə(r)] *n* contorno *m*; **c. line** línea *f* de nivel

contraband ['kɒntrəbænd] *n* contrabando *m*

contraception [kɒntrə'sepʃən] *n* anticoncepción *f*

contraceptive [kɒntrə'septɪv] *adj & n* anticonceptivo *(m)*

contract [kən'trækt] **1** *vi (shrink)* contraerse
2 *vt* (a) *(illness, debt)* contraer (b) **to c. to do sth** *(make agreement)* firmar un contrato para hacer algo
3 *n* ['kɒntrækt] contrato *m*; **to enter into a c.** hacer un contrato

contraction [kən'trækʃən] *n* contracción *f*

contractor [kən'træktə(r)] *n* contratista *mf*

contradict [kɒntrə'dɪkt] *vt* contradecir

contradiction [kɒntrə'dɪkʃən] *n* contradicción *f*; **it's a c. in terms** no tiene lógica

contradictory [kɒntrə'dɪktərɪ] *adj* contradictorio(a)

contraption [kən'træpʃən] *n* *Fam* cacharro *m*

contrary ['kɒntrərɪ] **1** *adj* (a) *(opposite)* contrario(a) (b) [kən'treərɪ] *(awkward)* terco(a)
2 *n* **on the c.** todo lo contrario; **unless I tell you to the c.** a menos que te diga lo contrario
3 *adv* **c. to** en contra de

contrast 1 *vi* [kən'trɑːst] contrastar
2 *n* ['kɒntrɑːst] contraste *m*

contrasting [kən'trɑːstɪŋ] *adj* opuesto(a)

contravene [kɒntrə'viːn] *vt* contravenir

contribute [kən'trɪbjuːt] **1** *vt* contribuir con, aportar
2 *vi* contribuir; **to c. to a newspaper** escribir para un periódico

contribution [kɒntrɪ'bjuːʃən] *n* (a) *(of money)* contribución *f*; *(of ideas etc)* aportación *f* (b) *Press* colaboración *f*

contributor [kən'trɪbjutə(r)] *n* *(to newspaper)* colaborador(a) *m,f*

contrive [kən'traɪv] *vt* inventar, idear; **to c. to do sth** buscar la forma de hacer algo

contrived [kən'traɪvd] *adj* artificial, forzado(a)

control [kən'trəʊl] **1** *vt (company, country)* controlar, regular; *(child, pupils, animal)* controlar, dominar; *(vehicle)* manejar, controlar; **to c. one's temper** controlarse
2 *n* (a) *(power)* control *m*, dominio *m*; *(authority)* autoridad *f*; **to be out of c.** fuera de control; **to be in c.** estar al mando; **to be under c.** *(situation)* estar bajo control; **to go out of c.** descontrolarse; **to lose/**

regain c. perder/recuperar el control (**b**) *Aut & Av (device)* mando *m*; *Rad & TV* botón *m* de control; **c. panel** tablero *m* de instrumentos; **c. room** sala *f* de control; *Av* **c. tower** torre *f* de control

controversial [kɒntrə'vɜ:ʃəl] *adj* controvertido(a), polémico(a)

controversy ['kɒntrəvɜ:sɪ, kən'trɒvəsɪ] *n* polémica *f*

conurbation [kɒnɜ:'beɪʃən] *n* conurbación *f*

convalesce [kɒnvə'les] *vi* convalecer

convalescence [kɒnvə'lesəns] *n* convalecencia *f*

convalescent [kɒnvə'lesənt] *adj* convaleciente; **c. home** clínica *f* de reposo

convene [kən'vi:n] **1** *vt* convocar
2 *vi* reunirse

convenience [kən'vi:nɪəns] *n* conveniencia *f*, comodidad *f*; **all modern conveniences** todas las comodidades; **at your c.** cuando le convenga; **c. food** comida precocinada; *Br* **public conveniences** servicio *m* público, *Esp* aseos *mpl*, *Am* baños *mpl* públicos

convenient [kən'vi:nɪənt] *adj (time, arrangement)* conveniente, oportuno(a); *(place)* bien situado(a)

convent ['kɒnvənt] *n* convento *m*

convention [kən'venʃən] *n* convención *f*

conventional [kən'venʃənəl] *adj* convencional

converge [kən'vɜ:dʒ] *vi* convergir

conversant [kən'vɜ:sənt] *adj Fml* **to be c. with a subject** ser versado(a) en una materia

conversation [kɒnvə'seɪʃən] *n* conversación *f*, *CAm, Méx* plática *f*

conversational [kɒnvə'seɪʃənəl] *adj* coloquial

converse[1] [kən'vɜ:s] *vi* conversar

converse[2] ['kɒnvɜ:s] *n* **the c.** lo opuesto

conversely ['kɒnvɜ:slɪ] *adv* a la inversa

conversion [kən'vɜ:ʃən] *n Math & Rel* conversión *f* (**to** a; **into** en)

convert 1 *vt* [kən'vɜ:t] convertir
2 *n* ['kɒnvɜ:t] converso(a) *m,f*

convertible [kən'vɜ:təbəl] **1** *adj* convertible
2 *n (car)* descapotable *m*, *Am* convertible *m*

convex ['kɒnveks, kɒn'veks] *adj* convexo(a)

convey [kən'veɪ] *vt* (**a**) *(carry)* transportar (**b**) *(sound)* transmitir; *(idea)* comunicar

conveyor [kən'veɪə(r)] *n* **c. belt** cinta transportadora

convict 1 *vt* [kən'vɪkt] declarar culpable a, condenar
2 *n* ['kɒnvɪkt] presidiario(a) *m,f*

conviction [kən'vɪkʃən] *n* (**a**) *(belief)* creencia *f*, convicción *f* (**b**) *Jur* condena *f*

convince [kən'vɪns] *vt* convencer

convincing [kən'vɪnsɪŋ] *adj* convincente

convoluted ['kɒnvəlu:tɪd] *adj* intrincado(a)

convoy ['kɒnvɔɪ] *n* convoy *m*

convulse [kən'vʌls] *vt* convulsionar; *Fam* **to be convulsed with laughter** troncharse de risa

convulsion [kən'vʌlʃən] *n* convulsión *f*

coo [ku:] *vi (pigeon)* arrullar

cook [kʊk] **1** *vt (boil, bake, fry)* guisar, cocinar; *(dinner)* preparar; *Fam* **to c. the books** falsificar las cuentas
2 *vi (person)* cocinar, guisar; *(food)* cocerse
3 *n* cocinero(a) *m,f*

cookbook ['kʊkbʊk] *n US* libro *m* de cocina

cooker ['kʊkə(r)] *n* cocina *f*, *Col, Méx, Ven* estufa *f*

cookery ['kʊkərɪ] *n* cocina *f*; **c. book** libro *m* de cocina

cookie ['kʊkɪ] *n US* galleta *f*

cooking ['kʊkɪŋ] *n* cocina *f*

cool [ku:l] **1** *adj* (**a**) *(cold)* fresco(a); **it's c.** hace fresco (**b**) *(person) (calm)* tranquilo(a); *(reserved)* frío(a)
2 *n* (**a**) *(coldness)* fresco *m* (**b**) *(calm)* **to lose one's c.** perder la calma
3 *vt (air)* refrescar; *(drink)* enfriar
4 *adv Fam* **to play it c.** aparentar calma
▸ **cool down, cool off** *vi Fig* calmarse; *(feelings)* enfriarse

coolness ['ku:lnɪs] *n* (**a**) *Fig (calmness)* calma *f*, *(composure)* aplomo *m* (**b**) *Fam (nerve, cheek)* frescura *f*

coop [ku:p] **1** *n* gallinero *m*
2 *vt* **to c. (up)** encerrar

co-op ['kəʊɒp] *n* cooperativa *f*

co-operate [kəʊ'ɒpəreɪt] *vi* cooperar

co-operation [kəʊɒpə'reɪʃən] *n* cooperación *f*

co-operative [kəʊ'ɒpərətɪv] **1** *adj (helpful)* cooperador(a)
2 *n* cooperativa *f*

co-ordinate *vt* [kəʊ'ɔ:dɪneɪt] coordinar
2 *n* [kəʊ'ɔ:dɪnɪt] (**a**) *Math* coordenada *f* (**b**) **co-ordinates** *(clothes)* conjunto *m*

co-ordination [kəʊɔ:dɪ'neɪʃən] *n* coordinación *f*

cop [kɒp] *Fam* **1** *n (policeman)* poli *m*
2 *vt Br* **you'll c. it** te vas a ganar una buena

▸ **cop out** vi Fam zafarse, Esp escaquearse, RP zafar

cope [kəʊp] vi arreglárselas; **to c. with** (person, work) poder con; (problem) hacer frente a

Copenhagen [kəʊpən'heɪgən] n Copenhague

copier ['kɒpɪə(r)] n (photocopying machine) fotocopiadora f

copious ['kəʊpɪəs] adj copioso(a), abundante

copper[1] ['kɒpə(r)] 1 n (metal) cobre m
2 adj (colour) cobrizo(a)

copper[2] ['kɒpə(r)] n Fam poli mf

coppice ['kɒpɪs], **copse** [kɒps] n arboleda f, bosquecillo m

copulate ['kɒpjʊleɪt] vi copular

copy ['kɒpɪ] 1 n (a) (in general) copia f (b) (of book) ejemplar m
2 vt & vi copiar

copycat ['kɒpɪkæt] n Fam copión(ona) m,f

copyright ['kɒpɪraɪt] n derechos mpl de autor

coral ['kɒrəl] n coral m; **c. reef** arrecife m de coral

cord [kɔːd] n (a) (string) cuerda f; Elec cordón m (b) Tex (corduroy) pana f; **cords** pantalones mpl de pana

cordial ['kɔːdɪəl] 1 adj cordial
2 n licor m

cordless ['kɔːdlɪs] adj **c. phone** teléfono inalámbrico

cordon ['kɔːdən] 1 n cordón m
2 vt to **c. off a street** acordonar una calle

corduroy ['kɔːdərɔɪ] n pana f

core [kɔː(r)] 1 n (of fruit) corazón m; Elec núcleo m; Fig **the hard c.** los incondicionales
2 vt quitarle el corazón a

coriander [kɒrɪ'ændə(r)] n culantro m

cork [kɔːk] n corcho m; **c. oak** alcornoque m

corkscrew ['kɔːkskruː] n sacacorchos m inv

corn[1] [kɔːn] n (a) Br (wheat) trigo m; (b) (maize) maíz m, Andes, RP cochlo m; **c. bread** pan m de maíz orAndes, RP choclo; **c. on the cob** mazorca f de maíz orAndes, RP choclo, Méx elote m

corn[2] [kɔːn] n Med callo m

corncob ['kɔːnkɒb] n mazorca f

cornea ['kɔːnɪə] n córnea f

corner ['kɔːnə(r)] 1 n (a) (of street) esquina f; (bend in road) curva f; **round the c.** a la vuelta de la esquina; Ftb **c. kick** córner m; **c.** Br **shop** or US **store** tienda pequeña de barrio (b) (of room) rincón m

2 vt (a) (enemy) arrinconar (b) Com acaparar
3 vi Aut tomar una curva

cornerstone ['kɔːnəstəʊn] n piedra f angular

cornet [Br 'kɔːnɪt, US kɔː'net] n (a) Mus corneta f (b) Br (for ice cream) cucurucho m

cornflakes ['kɔːnfleɪks] npl copos mpl de maíz, cornflakes mpl

cornflour ['kɔːnflaʊə(r)], US **cornstarch** ['kɔːnstɑːrtʃ] n harina f de maíz orAndes, RP choclo, maicena® f

Cornwall ['kɔːnwəl] n Cornualles

corny ['kɔːnɪ] adj (**cornier, corniest**) Fam gastado(a)

corollary [kə'rɒlərɪ] n corolario m

coronary ['kɒrənərɪ] adj coronario(a); **c. thrombosis** trombosis coronaria

coronation [kɒrə'neɪʃən] n coronación f

coroner ['kɒrənə(r)] n juez mf de instrucción

corporal[1] ['kɔːpərəl] adj corporal; **c. punishment** castigo m corporal

corporal[2] ['kɔːpərəl] n Mil cabo m

corporate ['kɔːpərɪt] adj corporativo(a)

corporation [kɔːpə'reɪʃən] n (a) (business) sociedad anónima (b) (of city) ayuntamiento m

corps [kɔː(r)] n (pl corps [kɔːz]) cuerpo m

corpse [kɔːps] n cadáver m

corpulent ['kɔːpjʊlənt] adj corpulento(a)

corpuscle ['kɔːpʌsəl] n corpúsculo m

corral [kə'rɑːl] n US corral m

correct [kə'rekt] 1 vt corregir
2 adj (a) (amount, figure) exacto(a); (information, use, spelling) correcto(a) (b) (person, behaviour) correcto(a)

correction [kə'rekʃən] n corrección f

correlation [kɒrə'leɪʃən] n correlación f

correspond [kɒrɪ'spɒnd] vi (a) (be in accordance, be equivalent) corresponder (**with** or **to** con or a), corresponderse (**with** or **to** con) (b) (by letter) mantener correspondencia (**with** con)

correspondence [kɒrɪ'spɒndəns] n correspondencia f; **c. course** curso m por correspondencia

correspondent [kɒrɪ'spɒndənt] n Press corresponsal mf; **special c.** enviado(a) m,f especial

corresponding [kɒrɪ'spɒndɪŋ] adj correspondiente

corridor ['kɒrɪdɔː(r)] n pasillo m

corroborate [kə'rɒbəreɪt] vt corroborar

corrode [kə'rəʊd] 1 vt corroer
2 vi corroerse

corrosion [kəˈrəʊʒən] *n* corrosión *f*

corrugated [ˈkɒrʊɡeɪtɪd] *adj* **c. iron** hierro ondulado

corrupt [kəˈrʌpt] **1** *adj (person)* corrompido(a), corrupto(a); *(actions)* deshonesto(a)
2 *vt & vi* corromper

corruption [kəˈrʌpʃən] *n* corrupción *f*

corset [ˈkɔːsɪt] *n (garment)* faja *f*

Corsica [ˈkɔːsɪkə] *n* Córcega

cortège [kɔːˈteɪʒ] *n* cortejo *m*, comitiva *f*

cosh [kɒʃ] *n Br* porra *f*

cosmetic [kɒzˈmetɪk] **1** *n* cosmético *m*
2 *adj* cosmético(a); **c. surgery** cirugía plástica

cosmic [ˈkɒzmɪk] *adj* cósmico(a)

cosmonaut [ˈkɒzmənɔːt] *n* cosmonauta *mf*

cosmopolitan [kɒzməˈpɒlɪtən] *adj* cosmopolita

cosset [ˈkɒsɪt] *vt* mimar

cost [kɒst] **1** *n (price)* costo *m, Esp* coste *m*; **c. of living** costo *or Esp* coste de la vida; **to count the c.** considerar las desventajas; **at all costs** a toda costa
2 *vt & vi (pt & pp cost)* costar, valer; **how much does it c.?** ¿cuánto cuesta?; **whatever it costs** cueste lo que cueste
3 *vt (pt & pp costed) Com & Ind* calcular el costo *or Esp* coste de

co-star [ˈkəʊstɑː(r)] *n Cin & Th* coprotagonista *mf*

Costa Rica [kɒstəˈriːkə] *n* Costa Rica

Costa Rican [kɒstəˈriːkən] *adj & n* costarricense *(mf)*

cost-effective [kɒstɪˈfektɪv] *adj* rentable

costly [ˈkɒstlɪ] *adj* (**costlier, costliest**) costoso(a)

costume [ˈkɒstjuːm] *n* traje *m*; (swimming) **c.** traje *m* de baño, *Esp* bañador *m*, *RP* malla *f*; **c. jewellery** bisutería *f*

cosy [ˈkəʊzɪ] *adj* (**cosier, cosiest**) *(atmosphere)* acogedor(a); *(bed)* calentito(a); **it's c. in here** aquí se está bien

cot [kɒt] *n* (a) *Br (for child)* cuna *f* (b) *US (folding bed)* catre *m*, cama *f* plegable

cottage [ˈkɒtɪdʒ] *n* casa *f* de campo; **c. cheese** queso fresco; **c. industry** industria casera; *Br* **c. pie** = pastel de carne picada y puré de *Esp* patata *or Am* papa

cotton [ˈkɒtən] *n* algodón *m, Am* cotón *m*; **a c. shirt** una camisa de algodón; **c. bud** bastoncillo *m* (de algodón); *US* **c. candy** algodón dulce; *Br* **c. wool** algodón (hidrófilo)

▸ **cotton on** *vi Fam* enterarse, *Esp* coscarse, *RP* captar

couch [kaʊtʃ] *n* sofá *m*; *(in surgery)* camilla *f*

couchette [kuːˈʃet] *n Rail* litera *f*

cough [kɒf] **1** *vi* toser
2 *n* tos *f*; **c. drop** pastilla *f* para la tos; **c. mixture** jarabe *m* para la tos

▸ **cough up** *vt sep Fam (money)* poner, *Esp* apoquinar, *RP* garpar

could [kʊd] *v aux see* **can¹**

council [ˈkaʊnsəl] *n (body)* consejo *m*; *Br* **c. house** vivienda *f* de protección oficial; **town c.** consejo municipal, ayuntamiento *m*

councillor, *US* **councilor** [ˈkaʊnsələ(r)] *n* concejal *mf*

counsel [ˈkaʊnsəl] **1** *n* (a) *(advice)* consejo *m* (b) *Jur* abogado(a) *m,f*
2 *vt* aconsejar

counselling [ˈkaʊnsəlɪŋ] *n* apoyo *m* psicológico, orientación *f* psicológica

counsellor, *US* **counselor** [ˈkaʊnsələ(r)] *n* (a) *(adviser)* asesor(a) *m,f* (b) *US Jur* abogado(a) *m,f*

count¹ [kaʊnt] **1** *vt* (a) *(enumerate)* contar (b) *Fig* **to c. oneself lucky** considerarse afortunado(a)
2 *vi* contar; **that doesn't c.** eso no vale; **to c. to ten** contar hasta diez
3 *n* (a) *(calculation)* cuenta *f*, *(of votes)* recuento *m* (b) *Jur* cargo *m*

▸ **count on** *vt insep* contar con

count² [kaʊnt] *n (nobleman)* conde *m*

countdown [ˈkaʊntdaʊn] *n* cuenta *f* atrás

countenance [ˈkaʊntɪnəns] **1** *n* semblante *m*, rostro *m*
2 *vt* aprobar

counter¹ [ˈkaʊntə(r)] *n* (a) *(in shop)* mostrador *m*; *(in bank)* ventanilla *f* (b) *(in board games)* ficha *f*

counter² [ˈkaʊntə(r)] *n* contador *m*

counter³ [ˈkaʊntə(r)] **1** *adv* **c. to** en contra de
2 *vt (attack)* contestar a; *(trend)* contrarrestar
3 *vi* contestar

counteract [kaʊntərˈækt] *vt* contrarrestar

counterattack [ˈkaʊntərətæk] *n* contraataque *m*

counter-clockwise [ˈkaʊntəˈklɒkwaɪz] *adv US* en sentido opuesto al de las agujas del reloj

counterfeit [ˈkaʊntəfɪt] **1** *adj* falsificado(a); **c. coin** moneda falsa
2 *n* falsificación *f*
3 *vt* falsificar

counterfoil [ˈkaʊntəfɔɪl] *n Br (of cheque)* matriz *f*

countermand [kaʊntə'mɑːnd] *vt (command)* revocar; *Com (order)* anular

counterpart ['kaʊntəpɑːt] *n* homólogo(a) *m,f*

counterproductive [kaʊntəprə'dʌktɪv] *adj* contraproducente

countersign ['kaʊntəsaɪn] *vt* refrendar

countess ['kaʊntɪs] *n* condesa *f*

countless ['kaʊntlɪs] *adj* innumerable, incontable

country ['kʌntrɪ] *n* **(a)** *(state)* país *m*; **native c.** patria *f* **(b)** *(rural area)* campo *m*; **c. dancing** baile *m* popular

countryman ['kʌntrɪmən] *n* **(a)** *(rural)* hombre *m* del campo **(b)** *(compatriot)* compatriota *m*

countryside ['kʌntrɪsaɪd] *n (area)* campo *m*; *(scenery)* paisaje *m*

county ['kaʊntɪ] *n* condado *m*

coup [kuː] *n (pl* **coups** [kuːz]*)* golpe *m*; **c. d'état** golpe de estado

couple ['kʌpəl] **1** *n* **(a)** *(of people)* pareja *f*; **a married c.** un matrimonio **(b)** *(of things)* par *m*; *Fam* **a c. of times** un par de veces

2 *vt (wagons)* enganchar

coupling ['kʌplɪŋ] *n Rail* enganche *m*

coupon ['kuːpɒn] *n* **(a)** *(for discount, rationing)* cupón *m* **(b)** *Br* **football** *or* **pools c.** boleto *m* (de las quinielas)

courage ['kʌrɪdʒ] *n* coraje *m*, valentía *f*

courageous [kə'reɪdʒəs] *adj* valeroso(a), valiente

courgette [kʊə'ʒet] *n Br* calabacín *m*, *CSur* zapallito *m*, *Méx* calabacita *f*

courier ['kʊrɪə(r)] *n* **(a)** *(messenger)* mensajero(a) *m,f*; **c. service** mensajería *f* **(b)** *(guide)* guía *mf* turístico(a)

course [kɔːs] *n* **(a)** *(of river)* curso *m*; *Naut & Av* rumbo *m* **(b)** *Fig* desarrollo *m*; **in the c. of construction** en vías de construcción; **in the c. of time** con el tiempo **(c)** *(series)* ciclo *m*; **a c. of treatment** un tratamiento **(d)** *Educ* curso *m*; *Univ* asignatura *f* **(e)** *(for golf) Esp* campo *m*, *Am* cancha *f*; *(for horse-racing)* hipódromo *m* **(f)** *Culin* plato *m* **(g)** **of c.** claro, por supuesto; **of c. not!** ¡claro que no!

court [kɔːt] **1** *n* **(a)** *Jur* tribunal *m*; **c. martial** consejo *m* de guerra; **c. order** orden *f* judicial **(b)** *(royal)* corte *f* **(c)** *Sport* pista *f*, cancha *f*

2 *vt (woman)* hacer la corte a; *Fig* **to c. danger** buscar el peligro; *Fig* **to c. disaster** exponerse al desastre

3 *vi (couple)* tener relaciones

courteous ['kɜːtɪəs] *adj* cortés

courtesy ['kɜːtɪsɪ] *n* cortesía *f*; **by c. of** por cortesía de

courthouse ['kɔːthaʊs] *n US* palacio *m* de justicia

courtier ['kɔːtɪə(r)] *n* cortesano(a) *m,f*

court-martial [kɔːt'mɑːʃəl] *vt* hacer un consejo de guerra a

courtroom ['kɔːtruːm] *n* sala *f* de justicia

courtyard ['kɔːtjɑːd] *n* patio *m*

cousin ['kʌzən] *n* primo(a) *m,f*; **first c.** primo(a) hermano(a)

cove [kəʊv] *n* cala *f*, ensenada *f*

covenant ['kʌvənənt] *n* convenio *m*, pacto *m*

cover ['kʌvə(r)] **1** *vt* **(a)** *(person, object)* cubrir **(with** de); *(with lid)* tapar; *(book)* forrar **(b)** *(hide)* disimular **(c)** *(protect)* abrigar **(d)** *(distance)* recorrer **(e)** *Press (story)* cubrir **(f)** *(deal with)* abarcar **(g)** *(include)* incluir

2 *vi* **to c. for sb** sustituir a algn

3 *n* **(a)** *(lid)* tapa *f*; *(on bed)* manta *f*, *Am* frazada *f*, cobija *f*; *(of chair etc)* funda *f* **(b)** *(of book)* tapa *f*; *(of magazine)* portada *f* **(c)** *(in restaurant)* cubierto *m* **(d)** *(protection)* abrigo *m*; **to take c.** abrigarse; **under c.** al abrigo; *(indoors)* bajo techo

▸ **cover up 1** *vt sep* **(a)** *(person, object)* cubrir; *(with a lid)* tapar **(b)** *(conceal)* ocultar

2 *vi* **(a)** *(person)* abrigarse **(b)** **to c. up for sb** encubrir a algn

coverage ['kʌvərɪdʒ] *n* cobertura *f*

coveralls ['kʌvərɔːlz] *npl US* mono *m* (de trabajo), *Am* overol *m*

covering ['kʌvərɪŋ] **1** *n (on furniture)* funda *f*; *(of snow, dust, chocolate)* capa *f*

2 *adj (letter)* explicatorio(a)

covert ['kʌvət] *adj* disimulado(a), secreto(a)

cover-up ['kʌvərʌp] *n* encubrimiento *m*

covet ['kʌvɪt] *vt* codiciar

cow[1] [kaʊ] *n* vaca *f*; *Pej (woman)* arpía *f*, bruja *f*

cow[2] [kaʊ] *vt* intimidar

coward ['kaʊəd] *n* cobarde *mf*

cowardice ['kaʊədɪs] *n* cobardía *f*

cowardly ['kaʊədlɪ] *adj* cobarde

cowboy ['kaʊbɔɪ] *n* vaquero *m*

cower ['kaʊə(r)] *vi (with fear)* encogerse

cox [kɒks] *n* timonel *m*

coy [kɔɪ] *adj* (**coyer, coyest**) *(shy)* tímido(a); *(demure)* coquetón(ona)

cozy ['kəʊzɪ] *adj US* = **cosy**

CPA [siːpiː'eɪ] *n US (abbr* **certified public accountant)** *Esp* censor(a) *m,f* jurado(a) de cuentas, *Am* contador(a) *m,f* público(a)

crab [kræb] n (a) (crustacean) cangrejo m, Am jaiba f (b) **c. apple** manzana f silvestre

crack [kræk] **1** vt (a) (cup) partir; (bone) fracturar; (nut) cascar; (safe) forzar (b) (whip) hacer restallar (c) Fig (problem) dar con la solución de; (joke) contar

2 vi (a) (glass) partirse; (wall) agrietarse (b) (whip) restallar (c) Fam **to get cracking on sth** ponerse a hacer algo

3 n (a) (in cup) raja f; (in wall, ground) grieta f (b) (of whip) restallido m; (of gun) detonación f (c) Fam (drug) crack m

4 adj Fam de primera

▶ **crack down on** vt insep atajar con mano dura

▶ **crack up** vi Fam Fig (go mad) desquiciarse; (with laughter) partirse de risa, Méx atacarse de risa

cracker ['krækə(r)] n (a) (biscuit) galleta salada (b) (firework) petardo m

crackle ['krækəl] vi (twigs) crujir; (fire) crepitar

cradle ['kreɪdəl] n (baby's) cuna f

craft [krɑːft] n (a) (occupation) oficio m; (art) arte m; (skill) destreza f (b) (cunning) maña f (c) Naut embarcación f

craftsman ['krɑːftsmən] n artesano m

craftsmanship ['krɑːftsmənʃɪp] n arte f

crafty ['krɑːftɪ] adj (**craftier, craftiest**) astuto(a)

crag [kræg] n peña f, peñasco m

cram [kræm] **1** vt atiborrar; **crammed with** atestado(a) de

2 vi Fam Educ matarse estudiando, Esp empollar, RP tragar

cramp[1] [kræmp] n Med calambre m; **cramps** retortijones mpl

cramp[2] [kræmp] vt (development etc) poner trabas a

cramped [kræmpt] adj (room) estrecho(a); (writing) apretado(a)

cranberry ['krænbərɪ] n arándano m

crane [kreɪn] **1** n (a) Zool grulla f común (b) (device) grúa f

2 vt estirar

crank [kræŋk] n (a) Tech manivela f (b) Fam (eccentric) rarito(a) m,f

crankshaft ['kræŋkʃɑːft] n árbol m del cigüeñal

cranny ['krænɪ] n Fig **in every nook and c.** en todos los rincones

crap [kræp] n very Fam (a) (excrement) mierda f (b) (worthless things) mierdas fpl, porquerías fpl; (nonsense) Esp gilipolleces fpl, Esp paridas fpl, Col, Méx pendejadas fpl, RP pelotudeces fpl

crash [kræʃ] **1** vi **to c. one's car** tener un accidente con el coche or Am carro or CSur auto

2 vi (a) (car, plane) estrellarse; (collide) chocar; **to c. into** estrellarse contra (b) (business, economy) quebrar (c) Comput bloquearse, colgarse

3 n (a) (noise) estrépito m (b) (collision) choque m; **car/plane c.** accidente m de coche or Am carro or CSur auto/de avión; Fig **c. course** curso m intensivo; **c. helmet** casco m (protector) (c) (financial) quiebra f (financiera), crac m

crash-land [kræʃ'lænd] vi hacer un aterrizaje forzoso

crass [kræs] adj (person) grosero(a); (error) garrafal

crate [kreɪt] n caja f, cajón m (para embalaje)

crater ['kreɪtə(r)] n cráter m

cravat [krə'væt] n pañuelo m (de hombre)

crave [kreɪv] vi **to c. for sth** ansiar algo

craving ['kreɪvɪŋ] n ansia f; (in pregnancy) antojo m

crawfish ['krɔːfɪʃ] n langosta f

crawl [krɔːl] **1** vi (baby) gatear; (vehicle) avanzar lentamente; Fig **to c. to sb** arrastrarse a los pies de algn

2 n (swimming) crol m

crayfish ['kreɪfɪʃ] n cangrejo m de río

crayon ['kreɪɒn] n cera f

craze [kreɪz] n manía f; (fashion) moda f; **it's the latest c.** es el último grito

crazy ['kreɪzɪ] adj (**crazier, craziest**) Fam loco(a), chalado(a)

creak [kriːk] vi (floor) crujir; (hinge) chirriar

cream [kriːm] **1** n (a) (of milk) Esp nata f, Am crema f (de leche); **c.-coloured** color crema; Fig **the c.** la flor y nata; **c. cheese** queso blanco para untar (b) (cosmetic) crema f

2 vt (a) (milk) desnatar (b) Culin batir; **creamed potatoes** puré m de patatas or Am papas

creamy ['kriːmɪ] adj (**creamier, creamiest**) cremoso(a)

crease [kriːs] **1** n (wrinkle) arruga f; (fold) pliegue m; (on trousers) raya f

2 vt (clothes) arrugar

3 vi arrugarse

create [kriː'eɪt] vt crear

creation [kriː'eɪʃən] n creación f

creative [kriː'eɪtɪv] adj (person) creativo(a)

creativity [kriːeɪ'tɪvɪtɪ] n creatividad f

creator [kriː'eɪtə(r)] n creador(a) m,f

creature ['kriːtʃə(r)] n (animal) criatura f

crèche [kreɪʃ, kreʃ] n Br guardería f (infantil)

credence ['kri:dəns] *n* **to give c.** to dar crédito a

credentials [krɪ'denʃəlz] *npl* credenciales *fpl*

credibility [kredɪ'bɪlɪtɪ] *n* credibilidad *f*

credible ['kredɪbəl] *adj* creíble

credit ['kredɪt] **1** *n* (a) *Fin* crédito *m*; **on c.** a crédito; **c. card** tarjeta *f* de crédito (b) **to give c. to sb for sth** reconocer algo a algn (c) *(benefit)* honor *m*; **to be a c. to** hacer honor a (d) *Cin & TV* **credits** créditos *mpl*

   2 *vt* (a) *Fin* abonar (b) *(believe)* creer (c) *Fig* atribuir; **he is credited with having ...** se le atribuye haber ...

creditor ['kredɪtə(r)] *n* acreedor(a) *m,f*

creed [kri:d] *n* credo *m*

creek [kri:k] *n* (a) *Br* cala *f* (b) *US, Austr* riachuelo *m*

creep [kri:p] **1** *vi* (*pt & pp* **crept**) *(animal, person)* andar silenciosamente; *(plant)* trepar; **to c. up on sb** sorprender a algn

   2 *n Fam (unpleasant person)* asqueroso(a) *m,f*; *Am* arrastrado(a) *m,f*, *Méx* lambiscón(ona) *m,f*, *RP* chupamedias *mf inv*

creeper ['kri:pə(r)] *n Bot* trepadora *f*

creepy ['kri:pɪ] *adj* (**creepier, creepiest**) *Fam* espeluznante

cremate [krɪ'meɪt] *vt* incinerar

cremation [krɪ'meɪʃən] *n* incineración *f*, cremación *f*

crematorium [kremə'tɔ:rɪəm] *n* crematorio *m*

crêpe [kreɪp] *n* (a) *Tex* crepé *m* (b) **c. paper** papel *m* crespón

crept [krept] *pt & pp of* **creep**

crescendo [krɪ'ʃendəʊ] *n* crescendo *m*

crescent ['kresənt] **1** *n (shape)* medialuna *f*; *Br (street)* calle *f* en medialuna

   2 *adj* creciente

cress [kres] *n* berro *m*

crest [krest] *n* (a) *(of cock, wave)* cresta *f*; *(on helmet)* penacho *m*; *(of hill)* cima *f* (b) *(heraldic)* blasón *m*

crestfallen ['krestfɔ:lən] *adj* abatido(a)

Crete [kri:t] *n* Creta

cretin ['kretɪn] *n* cretino(a) *m,f*

crevasse [krɪ'væs] *n* grieta *f*, fisura *f*

crevice ['krevɪs] *n* grieta *f*, hendedura *f*

crew [kru:] *n Av & Naut* tripulación *f*; **c. cut** corte *m* al rape; **c.-neck sweater** jersey *m* con cuello redondo

crib [krɪb] **1** *n* (a) *(manger)* pesebre *m* (b) *(for baby)* cuna *f* (c) *Fam (in exam)* *Esp, Ven* chuleta *f*, *Arg* machete *m*, *Col, Méx* acordeón *m*

   2 *vt Fam* (a) *(copy)* copiar (b) *(steal)* quitar

crick [krɪk] *n Fam* **a c. in the neck** una tortícolis

cricket¹ ['krɪkɪt] *n (insect)* grillo *m*

cricket² ['krɪkɪt] *n Sport* cricket *m*

crikey ['kraɪkɪ] *interj Fam Old-fashioned* ¡caramba!

crime [kraɪm] *n* delincuencia *f*; *(offence)* delito *m*

criminal ['krɪmɪnəl] *adj & n* criminal *(mf)*; **c. law** derecho *m* penal; **c. record** antecedentes *mpl* penales

crimson ['krɪmzən] *adj & n* carmesí *(m)*

cringe [krɪndʒ] *vi* abatirse, encogerse

crinkle ['krɪŋkəl] *vt* fruncir, arrugar

cripple ['krɪpəl] **1** *n* lisiado(a) *m,f*, mutilado(a) *m,f*

   2 *vt (person)* dejar inválido(a), lisiar; *Fig (industry, system)* deteriorar, arruinar

crisis ['kraɪsɪs] *n (pl* **crises** ['kraɪsi:z]*)* crisis *f inv*

crisp [krɪsp] **1** *adj* (a) *(pastry, bacon)* crujiente; *(apple, lettuce)* fresco(a) (b) *(clothing, linen)* fresco(a); *(banknote)* nuevo(a) (c) *(air, breeze)* fresco(a) (d) *(style)* conciso(a)

   2 *n Br* **crisps** patatas *or Am* papas fritas (de bolsa)

crisscross ['krɪskrɒs] *n* líneas entrecruzadas

criterion [kraɪ'tɪərɪən] *n (pl* **criteria** [kraɪ'tɪərɪə]*)* criterio *m*

critic ['krɪtɪk] *n Art & Th* crítico(a) *m,f*

critical ['krɪtɪkəl] *adj* crítico(a)

critically ['krɪtɪkəlɪ] *adv* críticamente; **c. ill** gravemente enfermo(a)

criticism ['krɪtɪsɪzəm] *n* crítica *f*

criticize ['krɪtɪsaɪz] *vt* criticar

croak [krəʊk] *vi (frog)* croar; *(raven)* graznar; *(person)* hablar con voz ronca

Croat ['krəʊæt] **1** *adj* croata

   2 *n* (a) *(person)* croata *mf* (b) *(language)* croata *m*

Croatia [krəʊ'eɪʃə] *n* Croacia

Croatian [krəʊ'eɪʃən] *adj & n* = **Croat**

crochet ['krəʊʃeɪ] *n* ganchillo *m*, *Col, CSur* crochet *m*, *Méx* gancho *m*

crockery ['krɒkərɪ] *n* loza *f*

crocodile ['krɒkədaɪl] *n* cocodrilo *m*

crocus ['krəʊkəs] *n* azafrán *m*

crony ['krəʊnɪ] *n* compinche *mf*

crook [krʊk] **1** *n* (a) *(of shepherd)* cayado *m* (b) *Fam* caco *m*

   2 *vt (arm)* doblar

crooked ['krʊkɪd] *adj* (**a**) *(stick, picture)* torcido(a); *(path)* tortuoso(a) (**b**) *Fam (dishonest)* deshonesto(a)

crop [krɒp] **1** *n* (**a**) *(variety)* cultivo *m*; *(harvest)* cosecha *f* (**b**) *(whip)* fusta *f*
2 *vt (hair)* rapar; *(grass)* cortar

▸ **crop up** *vi Fam* surgir, presentarse

croquet ['krəʊkeɪ] *n* croquet *m*

croquette [krɒ'ket] *n Culin* croqueta *f*

cross [krɒs] **1** *n* (**a**) *(religious symbol)* cruz *f* (**b**) *(breeds)* cruce *m*, *Am* cruza *f*
2 *vt* (**a**) *(go across)* cruzar (**b**) *Rel* **to c. oneself** hacer la señal de la cruz; *Fam* **c. my heart!** ¡te lo juro!
3 *vi (pass over)* cruzar; *(roads)* cruzarse; **to c. over** cruzar
4 *adj (annoyed) esp Esp* enfadado(a), *esp Am* enojado(a)

▸ **cross off, cross out** *vt sep* tachar, rayar

crossbar ['krɒsbɑː(r)] *n* travesaño *m*

cross-country 1 *adj* ['krɒskʌntrɪ] **c. race** cros *m*
2 *adv* [krɒs'kʌntrɪ] campo través

cross-examine [krɒsɪg'zæmɪn] *vt* interrogar

cross-eyed ['krɒsaɪd] *adj* bizco(a)

crossfire ['krɒsfaɪə(r)] *n also Fig* fuego cruzado

crossing ['krɒsɪŋ] *n* cruce *m*; **pedestrian c.** paso *m* de peatones; **sea c.** travesía *f*

cross-legged [krɒs'leg(ɪ)d] *adj* con las piernas cruzadas

cross-reference [krɒs'refərəns] *n* remisión *f*

crossroads ['krɒsrəʊdz] *n* cruce *m*; *Fig* encrucijada *f*

cross-section ['krɒs'sekʃən] *n* sección *f* transversal

crosswalk ['krɒswɔːk] *n US* paso *m* de peatones

crosswind ['krɒswɪnd] *n* viento *m* lateral

crossword ['krɒswɜːd] *n* **c. (puzzle)** crucigrama *m*

crotch [krɒtʃ] *n* entrepierna *f*

crotchet ['krɒtʃɪt] *n Br Mus* negra *f*

crotchety ['krɒtʃɪtɪ] *adj Fam* gruñón(ona)

crouch [kraʊtʃ] *vi* **to c. (down)** agacharse

crow¹ [krəʊ] *n* cuervo *m*; *Fig* **as the c. flies** en línea recta; **c.'s-feet** patas *fpl* de gallo

crow² [krəʊ] **1** *vi* (**a**) *(cock)* cantar; *Fig* **to c. over sth** jactarse de algo (**b**) *(baby)* balbucir
2 *n (of cock)* canto *m*

crowbar ['krəʊbɑː(r)] *n* palanca *f*

crowd [kraʊd] **1** *n* muchedumbre *f*, *Fam (gang)* pandilla *f*, *Méx* bola *f*, *RP* barra *f*; **the c.** el populacho
2 *vt (streets)* llenar

3 *vi* apiñarse; **to c. in/out** entrar/salir en tropel

crowded ['kraʊdɪd] *adj* atestado(a), lleno(a)

crown [kraʊn] **1** *n* (**a**) *(of king)* corona *f*; **the c. jewels** las joyas de la corona (**b**) *(of head)* coronilla *f*
2 *vt* coronar

crucial ['kruːʃəl] *adj* decisivo(a)

crucifix ['kruːsɪfɪks] *n* crucifijo *m*

crucifixion [kruːsɪ'fɪkʃən] *n* crucifixión *f*

crucify ['kruːsɪfaɪ] *vt* crucificar

crude [kruːd] *adj* (**a**) *(manners, style)* tosco(a), grosero(a); *(tool)* primitivo(a) (**b**) **c. oil** crudo *m*

cruel [kruːəl] *adj* cruel (**to con**)

cruelty ['kruːəltɪ] *n* crueldad *f* (**to hacia**)

cruet ['kruːɪt] *n* **c. set** vinagreras *fpl*

cruise [kruːz] **1** *vi* (**a**) *Naut* hacer un crucero (**b**) *Aut* viajar a velocidad constante; *Av* viajar a velocidad de crucero
2 *n* (**a**) *Naut* crucero *m* (**b**) **c. missile** misil teledirigido

cruiser ['kruːzə(r)] *n* (barco *m*) crucero *m*

crumb [krʌm] *n* miga *f*, migaja *f*

crumble ['krʌmbəl] **1** *vt* desmigar
2 *vi (wall)* desmoronarse; *Fig (hopes)* desvanecerse

crumbly ['krʌmblɪ] *adj* (**crumblier, crumbliest**) que se desmigaja

crumpet ['krʌmpɪt] *n* = torta pequeña que se come con mantequilla

crumple ['krʌmpəl] *vt* arrugar

crunch [krʌntʃ] **1** *vt (food)* ronchar; *(with feet)* hacer crujir
2 *n Fam* **when it comes to the c.** a la hora de la verdad

crunchy ['krʌntʃɪ] *adj* (**crunchier, crunchiest**) crujiente

crusade [kruː'seɪd] *n* cruzada *f*

crush [krʌʃ] **1** *vt* (**a**) *(squash) (person, thing)* estrujar, aplastar; *(grapes, garlic)* prensar, aplastar (**b**) *(squeeze, press)* apretujar (**c**) *(wrinkle)* arrugar (**d**) *(opponent, revolt)* aplastar, destrozar
2 *n* (**a**) *(of people)* gentío *m* (**b**) **orange c.** naranjada *f*

crushing ['krʌʃɪŋ] *adj Fig (defeat, reply)* aplastante

crust [krʌst] *n* corteza *f*

crutch [krʌtʃ] *n Med* muleta *f*; *Fig* apoyo *m*

crux [krʌks] *n* **the c. of the matter** el quid de la cuestión

cry [kraɪ] **1** *vi* (*pt & pp* **cried**) (**a**) *(shout, call)* gritar (**b**) *(weep)* llorar

2 *vt* gritar; *Fig* **to c. wolf** dar una falsa alarma
3 *n* (**a**) *(call)* grito *m* (**b**) *(weep)* llanto *m*
▸ **cry off** *vi Fam* rajarse
▸ **cry out** *vi* gritar; **to c. out for sth** pedir algo a gritos
crying ['kraɪɪŋ] *adj* **it's a c. shame** es una vergüenza
crypt [krɪpt] *n* cripta *f*
cryptic ['krɪptɪk] *adj* enigmático(a)
crystal ['krɪstəl] *n* cristal *m*
crystal-clear [krɪstəl'klɪə(r)] *adj* claro(a) como el agua
crystallize ['krɪstəlaɪz] **1** *vt* cristalizar **2** *vi* cristalizar
cub [kʌb] *n* (**a**) *(animal)* cachorro *m* (**b**) *(junior scout)* niño *m* explorador
Cuba ['kjuːbə] *n* Cuba
Cuban ['kjuːbən] *adj & n* cubano(a) *(m,f)*
cubbyhole ['kʌbɪhəʊl] *n* cuchitril *m*
cube [kjuːb] **1** *n* cubo *m*; *(of sugar)* terrón *m*; **c. root** raíz cúbica **2** *vt Math* elevar al cubo
cubic ['kjuːbɪk] *adj* cúbico(a)
cubicle ['kjuːbɪkəl] *n* cubículo *m*; *(at swimming pool)* caseta *f*
cuckoo ['kʊkuː] **1** *n* cuco *m*; **c. clock** reloj *m* de cuco, *RP* reloj *m* cucú **2** *adj Fam (mad)* **to be c.** estar pirado(a), *Méx* estar zafado(a)
cucumber ['kjuːkʌmbə(r)] *n* pepino *m*
cuddle ['kʌdəl] **1** *vt* abrazar **2** *vi* abrazarse
cuddly ['kʌdlɪ] *adj* (**cuddlier, cuddliest**) **c. toy** muñeco *m* de peluche
cue¹ [kjuː] *n Th* pie *m*
cue² [kjuː] *n (in billiards)* taco *m*; **c. ball** bola blanca
cuff¹ [kʌf] *n (of sleeve)* puño *m*; *US (of trousers)* dobladillo *m*; *Fig* **to do sth off the c.** improvisar algo
cuff² [kʌf] **1** *vt (hit)* dar un sopapo *or Am* una cachetada a **2** *n (blow)* cachete *m*, cate *m*
cufflinks ['kʌflɪŋks] *npl* gemelos *mpl*
cul-de-sac ['kʌldəsæk] *n* callejón *m* sin salida
culinary ['kʌlɪnərɪ] *adj* culinario(a)
cull [kʌl] *vt* (**a**) *(choose)* escoger (**b**) *(animals)* eliminar
culminate ['kʌlmɪneɪt] *vi* **to c. in** terminar en
culmination [kʌlmɪ'neɪʃən] *n* culminación *f*, punto *m* culminante
culottes [kjuː'lɒts] *npl* falda *f or Am* pollera *f* pantalón
culprit ['kʌlprɪt] *n* culpable *mf*

cult [kʌlt] *n* culto *m*; **c. figure** ídolo *m*
cultivate ['kʌltɪveɪt] *vt* cultivar
cultivated ['kʌltɪveɪtɪd] *adj (person)* culto(a)
cultivation [kʌltɪ'veɪʃən] *n* cultivo *m* (de la tierra)
cultural ['kʌltʃərəl] *adj* cultural
culture ['kʌltʃə(r)] *n* cultura *f*
cultured ['kʌltʃəd] *adj* = **cultivated**
cumbersome ['kʌmbəsəm] *adj (awkward)* incómodo(a); *(bulky)* voluminoso(a)
cum(m)in ['kʌmɪn] *n* comino *m*
cumulative ['kjuːmjʊlətɪv] *adj* acumulativo(a)
cunning ['kʌnɪŋ] **1** *adj* astuto(a) **2** *n* astucia *f*
cup [kʌp] **1** *n* taza *f*; *Sport* copa *f*; **C. Final** final *f* de copa; **c. tie** partido *m* de copa **2** *vt (hands)* ahuecar
cupboard ['kʌbəd] *n* armario *m*; *(on wall)* alacena *f*
cupcake ['kʌpkeɪk] *n (cake)* ≃ magdalena *f*
curable ['kjʊərəbəl] *adj* curable
curate ['kjʊərɪt] *n* cura *m* coadjutor
curator [kjʊə'reɪtə(r)] *n* conservador(a) *m,f*
curb [kɜːb] **1** *n* (**a**) *(limit)* freno *m* (**b**) *US (kerb)* bordillo *m* (de la acera), *Chile* solera *f*, *Col, Perú* sardinel *m*, *CSur* cordón *m* (de la vereda), *Méx* borde *m* (de la banqueta) **2** *vt (horse)* refrenar; *Fig (public spending)* contener
curd [kɜːd] *n* cuajada *f*
curdle ['kɜːdəl] *vi* cuajarse
cure [kjʊə(r)] **1** *vt* curar **2** *n (remedy)* cura *f*, remedio *m*
curfew ['kɜːfjuː] *n* toque *m* de queda
curiosity [kjʊərɪ'ɒsɪtɪ] *n* curiosidad *f*
curious ['kjʊərɪəs] *adj* (**a**) *(inquisitive)* curioso(a) (**b**) *(odd)* extraño(a)
curl [kɜːl] **1** *vt (hair)* rizar; *(lip)* fruncir **2** *vi* rizarse **3** *n (of hair)* rizo *m*, *Andes, RP* rulo *m*; *(of smoke)* espiral *f*
▸ **curl up** *vi* enroscarse
curler ['kɜːlə(r)] *n (for hair)* rulo *m*, *Chile* tubo *m*, *RP* rulero *m*, *Ven* rollo *m*
curly ['kɜːlɪ] *adj* (**curlier, curliest**) rizado(a), *Chile, Col* crespo(a), *Méx* quebrado(a), *RP* enrulado(a)
currant ['kʌrənt] *n* pasa *f* (de Corinto)
currency ['kʌrənsɪ] *n* (**a**) *Fin* moneda *f*; **foreign c.** divisa *f* (**b**) *(acceptance)* **to gain c.** cobrar fuerza

current ['kʌrənt] **1** adj **(a)** (opinion) general; (word) en uso; (year) en curso; Br **c. account** cuenta f corriente; **c. affairs** actualidad (política); Fin **c. assets** activo m disponible **(b) the c. issue** (of magazine, newspaper) el último número
2 n corriente f

currently ['kʌrəntlɪ] adv actualmente

curriculum [kə'rɪkjʊləm] n (pl **curricula** [kə'rɪkjʊlə]) plan m de estudios; esp Br **c. vitae** curriculum m (vitae)

curry¹ ['kʌrɪ] n curry m; **chicken c.** pollo m al curry

curry² ['kʌrɪ] vt **to c. favour with** congraciarse con

curse [kɜːs] **1** n maldición f; (oath) palabrota f; Fig azote m
2 vt maldecir
3 vi blasfemar

cursor ['kɜːsə(r)] n cursor m

cursory ['kɜːsərɪ] adj rápido(a)

curt [kɜːt] adj brusco(a), seco(a)

curtail [kɜː'teɪl] vt (expenses) reducir; (text) acortar

curtain ['kɜːtən] n cortina f; Th telón m; Fig velo m

curts(e)y ['kɜːtsɪ] **1** n reverencia f
2 vi hacer una reverencia (**to** a)

curve [kɜːv] **1** n curva f
2 vt encorvar
3 vi torcerse, describir una curva

cushion ['kʊʃən] **1** n cojín m; (large) almohadón m; (of billiard table) banda f
2 vt Fig amortiguar; (person) proteger

cushy ['kʊʃɪ] adj (**cushier, cushiest**) Fam fácil; **a c. number** una ganga, Esp un chollo, Méx pan m comido

custard ['kʌstəd] n natillas fpl; **c. powder** polvos mpl para hacer natillas

custodian [kʌ'stəʊdɪən] n conserje mf, guarda mf

custody ['kʌstədɪ] n custodia f; **to take into c.** detener

custom ['kʌstəm] n **(a)** (habit) costumbre f **(b)** Com clientela f

customary ['kʌstəmərɪ] adj habitual

customer ['kʌstəmə(r)] n cliente mf; **c. care** or **services** atención f al cliente

customize ['kʌstəmaɪz] vt hacer por encargo

custom-made [kʌstəm'meɪd] adj hecho(a) a la medida

customs ['kʌstəmz] npl aduana f; **c. duty** derechos mpl de aduana; **c. officer** agente mf de aduana

cut [kʌt] **1** n **(a)** (in flesh, wood, cloth) corte m **(b)** (of meat) clase f de carne **(c)** (in wages, prices) recorte m **(d)** (style) (of clothes, hair) corte m
2 vt (pt & pp **cut**) **(a)** (in general) cortar; (stone) tallar; (in slices) rebanar; **to c. one's finger** cortarse el dedo; Fig **to c. a long story short** en resumidas cuentas; Fig **to c. corners** recortar presupuestos **(b)** (wages, prices) recortar **(c)** (divide up) dividir (**into** en)
3 vi (of knife, scissors) cortar
▸ **cut back** vt sep (expenses) reducir; (production) disminuir
▸ **cut down 1** vt sep (tree) talar
2 vt insep **to c. down on** reducir
▸ **cut in** vi (driver) adelantar bruscamente
▸ **cut off** vt sep (water etc) cortar; (place) aislar; (heir) excluir; Tel **I've been c. off** me han cortado (la comunicación)
▸ **cut out 1** vt sep **(a)** (from newspaper) recortar; (person) **to be c. out for sth** estar hecho(a) para algo **(b)** (delete) suprimir
2 vi (engine) calarse
▸ **cut up** vt sep cortar en pedazos

cutback ['kʌtbæk] n reducción f (**in** de)

cute [kjuːt] adj **(a)** (sweet) bonito(a), mono(a) **(b)** US Fam Pej (clever) listo(a)

cuticle ['kjuːtɪkəl] n cutícula f

cutlery ['kʌtlərɪ] n cubiertos mpl

cutlet ['kʌtlɪt] n chuleta f

cut-price [kʌt'praɪs] adj (article) a precio rebajado

cutthroat ['kʌtθrəʊt] **1** n asesino(a) m,f, matón m
2 adj (cruel) cruel; (competition) feroz

cutting ['kʌtɪŋ] **1** n (of plant) esqueje m; (from newspaper) recorte m; Rail desmonte m
2 adj (wind) cortante; (remark) hiriente, cortante

CV, cv [siː'viː] n (abbr **curriculum vitae**) CV m

cwt. (abbr **hundredweight**) (metric) 50 kg; Br (112 lb) = 50,8 kg; US (100 lb) = 45,36 kg

cyanide ['saɪənaɪd] n cianuro m

cybercafe ['saɪbəkæfeɪ] n Comput cibercafé m

cybernetics [saɪbə'netɪks] n Comput cibernética f

cyberspace ['saɪbəspeɪs] n Comput ciberespacio m

cycle ['saɪkəl] **1** n **(a)** (pattern) ciclo m **(b)** (bicycle) bicicleta f; (motorcycle) moto f
2 vi ir en bicicleta

cycling ['saɪklɪŋ] n ciclismo m

cyclist ['saɪklɪst] n ciclista mf

cyclone ['saɪkləʊn] n ciclón m

cygnet ['sɪgnɪt] n pollo m de cisne

cylinder ['sɪlɪndə(r)] *n* (**a**) *(shape, in engine)* cilindro *m* (**b**) *(for gas)* bombona *f*

cymbal ['sɪmbəl] *n* címbalo *m*, platillo *m*

cynic ['sɪnɪk] *n* descreído(a) *m,f*, suspicaz *mf*

> ° Note that the Spanish word **cínico** is a false friend and is never a translation for the English word **cynic**. In Spanish, **cínico** means "shameless person".

cynical ['sɪnɪkəl] *adj* (**a**) *(sceptical)* descreído(a), suspicaz (**b**) *(unscrupulous)* desaprensivo(a), sin escrúpulos

> ° Note that the Spanish word **cínico** is a false friend and is never a translation for the English word **cynical**. In Spanish **cínico** means "shameless".

cynicism ['sɪnɪsɪzəm] *n* descreimiento *m*, suspicacia *f*

> ° Note that the Spanish word **cinismo** is a false friend and is never a translation for the English word **cynicism**. In Spanish, **cinismo** means "shamelessness".

cypress ['saɪprəs] *n* ciprés *m*

Cypriot ['sɪprɪət] *adj & n* chipriota *(mf)*

Cyprus ['saɪprəs] *n* Chipre

cyst [sɪst] *n* quiste *m*

cystitis [sɪ'staɪtɪs] *n* cistitis *f*

czar [zɑː(r)] *n* zar *m*

Czech [tʃek] **1** *adj* checo(a); **the C. Republic** la República Checa
2 *n* (**a**) *(person)* checo(a) *m,f* (**b**) *(language)* checo *m*

Czechoslovakia [tʃekəʊslə'vækɪə] *n* Hist Checoslovaquia

D, d [di:] n (a) *(the letter)* D, d f (b) *Mus* **D** re m

DA [di:'eɪ] n US *(abbr* **district attorney)** fiscal mf *(del distrito)*

dab [dæb] 1 n *(small quantity)* toque m
   2 vt (a) *(apply)* aplicar (b) *(touch lightly)* tocar ligeramente

dabble ['dæbəl] vi to d. in politics meterse en política

dachshund ['dækshʊnd] n perro m salchicha

dad [dæd], **daddy** ['dædɪ] n *Fam* papá m

daddy-longlegs [dædɪ'lɒŋlegz] n inv *Fam* (a) *Br (cranefly)* típula f (b) *US (harvestman)* segador m

daffodil ['dæfədɪl] n narciso m

daft [dɑːft] adj *Br Fam (persona, idea)* tonto(a), *Am* sonso(a), *Am* zonzo(a)

dagger ['dægə(r)] n puñal m, daga f

dahlia ['deɪlɪə] n dalia f

daily ['deɪlɪ] 1 adj diario(a), cotidiano(a)
   2 adv diariamente; **three times d.** tres veces al día
   3 n (a) *(newspaper)* diario m (b) *Br Fam (cleaning lady)* asistenta f

dainty ['deɪntɪ] adj *(daintier, daintiest) (movement)* grácil; *(features, lace)* delicado(a), fino(a)

dairy ['deərɪ] n *(on farm)* vaquería f; *(shop)* lechería f; **d. farming** industria lechera; **d. produce** productos lácteos

dais ['deɪs] n *(in hall)* tarima f; *(in ceremony)* estrado m

daisy ['deɪzɪ] n margarita f

daisywheel ['deɪzɪwiːl] n *(printer)* margarita f

dale [deɪl] n valle m, hondonada f

Dalmatian [dæl'meɪʃən] n *(perro m)* dálmata m

dam [dæm] 1 n *(barrier)* dique m; *(lake)* presa f
   2 vt *(water)* represar
   ▸ **dam up** vt sep *Fig (emotion)* contener

damage ['dæmɪdʒ] 1 n (a) *(to machine, building)* daños mpl; *(to health, reputation)* perjuicio m (b) *Jur* **damages** daños mpl y perjuicios mpl
   2 vt *(machine, building)* dañar; *(health, reputation)* perjudicar

damaging ['dæmɪdʒɪŋ] adj perjudicial

damn [dæm] 1 vt condenar
   2 interj *Fam* **d. (it)!** ¡maldito(a) sea!; **well, I'll be damned!** ¡vaya por Dios!
   3 n *Fam* **I don't give a d.** me importa un bledo
   4 adj *Fam* maldito(a)
   5 adv *Fam* muy, sumamente

damned [dæmd] adj & adv = **damn**

damnedest ['dæmdɪst] n *Fam* **to do one's d. to …** hacer todo lo posible para …

damning ['dæmɪŋ] adj *(evidence)* irrefutable; *(criticism)* mordaz

damp [dæmp] 1 adj húmedo(a)
   2 n humedad f
   3 vt (a) *(for ironing)* humedecer (b) **to d. (down)** *(fire)* sofocar; *Fig (violence)* frenar

dampen ['dæmpən] vt humedecer; *Fig* frenar

damper ['dæmpə(r)] n *Fig* **to put a d. on sth** poner freno a algo

damsel ['dæmzəl] n *Literary* doncella f

damson ['dæmzən] n ciruela damascena

dance [dɑːns] 1 n baile m; *(classical, tribal)* danza f; **d. band** orquesta f de baile; **d. floor** pista f de baile; **d. hall** salón m de baile
   2 vi & vt bailar

dancer ['dɑːnsə(r)] n *(by profession)* bailarín(ina) m,f

dancing ['dɑːnsɪŋ] n baile m

dandelion ['dændɪlaɪən] n diente m de león

dandruff ['dændrəf] n caspa f

Dane [deɪn] n danés(esa) m,f

danger ['deɪndʒə(r)] n (a) *(risk)* riesgo m; *(of war etc)* amenaza f (b) *(peril)* peligro m; **d. (sign)** peligro; **out of d.** fuera de peligro

dangerous ['deɪndʒərəs] adj peligroso(a); **d. driving** conducción temeraria

dangerously ['deɪndʒərəslɪ] adv peligrosamente

dangle ['dæŋgəl] 1 vi *(hang)* colgar; *(swing)* balancearse

2 vt (legs) colgar; (bait) dejar colgado(a); (swing) balancear en el aire

Danish ['deɪnɪʃ] adj danés(esa); **D. pastry** pastel m de hojaldre
2 n (language) danés m

dapper ['dæpə(r)] adj pulcro(a)

dappled ['dæpəld] adj (shade) moteado(a)

dare [deə(r)] **1** vi atreverse, osar; **he doesn't d. be late** no se atreve a llegar tarde; **how d. you!** ¿cómo te atreves?; esp Br **I d. say** quizás; Ironic ya (lo creo)
2 vt (challenge) desafiar
3 n desafío m

daredevil ['deədevəl] adj & n atrevido(a) (m,f), temerario(a) (m,f)

daring ['deərɪŋ] **1** adj (a) (bold) audaz, osado(a) (b) (clothes) atrevido(a)
2 n atrevimiento m, osadía f

dark [dɑːk] **1** adj (a) (room, colour) oscuro(a); (hair, complexion) moreno(a); (eyes, future) negro(a) (b) Fig (gloomy) triste (c) Fig (sinister) siniestro(a)
2 n (a) (darkness) oscuridad f, tinieblas fpl; **after d.** después del anochecer (b) Fig **to be in the d. (about sth)** Esp estar in albis (sobre algo), Am no tener ni idea (sobre algo)

darken ['dɑːkən] **1** vt (sky, colour) oscurecer
2 vi (sky, colour) oscurecerse; Fig (thoughts, mood) ensombrecerse

darkness ['dɑːknɪs] n oscuridad f, tinieblas fpl

darkroom ['dɑːkruːm] n cuarto m oscuro

darling ['dɑːlɪŋ] adj & n querido(a) (m,f)

darn [dɑːn] **1** vt zurcir
2 n zurcido m

dart [dɑːt] **1** n (a) (missile) dardo m (b) **darts** (game) dardos mpl
2 vi (fly about) revolotear; **to d. in/out** entrar/salir corriendo

dartboard ['dɑːtbɔːd] n diana f

dash [dæʃ] **1** n (a) (rush) carrera f (b) esp US (race) sprint m (c) (small amount) poquito m; (of salt) pizca f; (of liquid) gota f (d) Typ guión largo; (hyphen) guión
2 vt (throw) arrojar
3 vi (rush) correr; **to d. around** correr de un lado a otro; **to d. out** salir corriendo
▸ **dash off** vi salir corriendo

dashboard ['dæʃbɔːd] n tablero m de mandos, Esp salpicadero m

dashing ['dæʃɪŋ] adj (appearance) garboso(a)

data ['deɪtə, 'dɑːtə] npl datos mpl; **d. bank** or **base** banco m de datos; **d. processing**

(act) proceso m de datos; (science) informática f; **d. protection act** ley f de informática

date¹ [deɪt] **1** n (a) (day) fecha f; **what's the d. today?** ¿a qué (fecha) estamos hoy?, ¿qué fecha es hoy?, Am ¿a cómo estamos?; **out of d. (ideas)** anticuado(a); (expression) desusado(a); (invalid) caducado(a); **to d.** hasta la fecha; Fig **to be up to d.** estar al día; **d. of birth** fecha de nacimiento (b) (social event) compromiso m; Fam (with girl, boy) cita f (c) US Fam (person dated) ligue m
2 vt (ruins) datar
3 vi (ideas) quedar anticuado(a)
▸ **date back to, date from** vt insep remontar a, datar de

date² [deɪt] n (fruit) dátil m; **d. palm** datilera f

dated ['deɪtɪd] adj (idea) anticuado(a); (fashion) pasado(a) de moda; (expression) desusado(a)

daub [dɔːb] vt embadurnar (**with** de)

daughter ['dɔːtə(r)] n hija f

daughter-in-law ['dɔːtərɪnlɔː] n nuera f, hija política

daunting ['dɔːntɪŋ] adj desalentador(a)

dawdle ['dɔːdəl] vi Fam (walk slowly) andar despacio; (waste time) perder el tiempo

dawn [dɔːn] **1** n alba f, amanecer m
2 vi (a) (day) amanecer (b) Fig (age, hope) comenzar (c) Fig **suddenly it dawned on him that …** de repente cayó en la cuenta de que …

day [deɪ] n (a) (period of 24 hours) día m; **one of these days** un día de éstos; **(on) the next** or **following d.** el or al día siguiente; **the d. after tomorrow** pasado mañana; **the d. before yesterday** anteayer; **the other d.** el otro día (b) (daylight) día m; **by d.** de día (c) (era) **in those days** en aquellos tiempos; **these days** hoy (en) día

daybreak ['deɪbreɪk] n amanecer m

daydream ['deɪdriːm] **1** n fantasía f
2 vi fantasear, soñar despierto(a)

daylight ['deɪlaɪt] n luz f del día; **in broad d.** en pleno día; **to scare the (living) daylights out of sb** pegarle a algn un susto de muerte

daytime ['deɪtaɪm] n día m; **in the d.** de día

day-to-day ['deɪtədeɪ] adj cotidiano(a), diario(a)

daze [deɪz] n aturdimiento m; **in a d.** aturdido(a)

dazed [deɪzd] adj aturdido(a), atontado(a)

dazzle ['dæzəl] *vt* deslumbrar

D-day ['di:dei] *n* día *m* D

deacon ['di:kən] *n* diácono *m*

dead [ded] **1** *adj* (a) *(not alive)* muerto(a); **to be d.** estar muerto(a); **a d. man** un muerto (b) *(battery)* gastado(a), agotado(a); **the phone is d.** no hay línea (c) *(numb)* dormido(a); **my leg went d.** se me durmió la pierna (d) *(silence, secrecy)* total; **d. end** callejón *m* sin salida

2 *adv* *(very)* muy; *Fam* **you're d. right** tienes toda la razón; **to stop d.** pararse en seco

3 *npl* **the d.** los muertos

deaden ['dedən] *vt* *(impact, noise)* amortiguar; *Fig (pain, feeling)* calmar, aliviar

deadline ['dedlain] *n* *(date)* fecha *f* tope; *(time)* hora *f* tope; **we have to meet the d.** tenemos que hacerlo dentro del plazo

deadlock ['dedlɒk] *n* punto muerto

deadly ['dedli] **1** *adj* **(deadlier, deadliest)** *(poison, blow, enemy)* mortal; *(weapon)* mortífero(a); *(aim)* certero(a)

2 *adv* *(extremely)* terriblemente, sumamente

deadpan ['dedpæn] *adj* *Fam (face)* sin expresión; *(humour)* guasón(ona)

deaf [def] **1** *adj* sordo(a); *Fig* **to turn a d. ear** hacerse el sordo; **d. mute** sordomudo(a) *m,f*

2 *npl* **the d.** los sordos; **the d. and dumb** los sordomudos

deafen ['defən] *vt* ensordecer

deafening ['defəniŋ] *adj* ensordecedor(a)

deafness ['defnis] *n* sordera *f*

deal [di:l] **1** *n* (a) *Com & Pol* trato *m*, pacto *m*; **business d.** negocio *m*, transacción *f*; **to do a d. with sb** *(transaction)* cerrar un trato con algn; *(agreement)* pactar algo con algn; *Fam* **it's a d.!** ¡trato hecho! (b) *(amount)* cantidad *f*; **a good d. of criticism** muchas críticas; **a good d. slower** mucho más despacio (c) *Cards* reparto *m*

2 *vt* *(pt & pp* **dealt)** (a) *Cards* dar *(to a)* (b) **to d. sb a blow** asestarle un golpe a algn

▸ **deal in** *vt insep (goods)* comerciar en, tratar en; *(drugs)* traficar con

▸ **deal out** *vt sep* repartir

▸ **deal with** *vt insep (firm, person)* tratar con; *(subject, problem)* abordar, ocuparse de; *(in book etc)* tratar de

dealer ['di:lə(r)] *n* (a) *Com (in goods)* comerciante *mf*; *(in drugs)* traficante *mf* (b) *Cards* repartidor(a) *m,f*

dealings ['di:liŋz] *npl* (a) *(relations)* trato *m* (b) *Com* negocios *mpl*

dealt [delt] *pt & pp of* **deal**

dean [di:n] *n* (a) *Rel* deán *m* (b) *Univ* decano *m*

dear [diə(r)] **1** *adj* (a) *(loved)* querido(a); **D. Andrew** *(in letter)* Querido Andrew; *Fml* **D. Madam** Estimada señora; *Fml* **D. Sir(s)** Muy señor(es) mío(s) (b) *(expensive)* caro(a)

2 *n* querido(a) *m,f*; **my d.** mi vida

3 *interj* **oh d.!, d. me!** *(surprise)* ¡caramba!; *(disappointment)* ¡qué pena!

dearly ['diəli] *adv* muchísimo; *Fig* **he paid d. for his mistake** su error le costó caro

dearth [dɜ:θ] *n Fml* escasez *f*

death [deθ] *n* muerte *f*; *Fml* fallecimiento *m*; *Fam* **to be bored to d.** aburrirse como una ostra; *Fam* **to be scared to d.** estar muerto(a) de miedo; *Fam Fig* **to be sick to d. of** estar hasta la coronilla de; **d. certificate** certificado *m* de defunción; **d. penalty, d. sentence** pena *f* de muerte

deathbed ['deθbed] *n* **to be on one's d.** estar en el lecho de muerte

deathly ['deθli] *adj* **(deathlier, deathliest)** *(silence)* sepulcral; **d. pale** pálido(a) como un muerto

debacle [dei'bɑ:kəl] *n* debacle *f*

debar [di'bɑ:(r)] *vt Fml* excluir, prohibir

debase [di'beis] *vt Fig* envilecer; **to d. oneself** humillarse

debatable [di'beitəbəl] *adj* discutible

debate [di'beit] **1** *n* debate *m*; **a heated d.** una discusión acalorada

2 *vt* (a) *(discuss)* discutir (b) *(wonder about)* dar vueltas a

3 *vi* discutir

debateable [di'beitəbəl] *adj* = **debatable**

debauchery [di'bɔ:tʃəri] *n* libertinaje *m*

debilitating [di'biliteitiŋ] *adj* debilitador(a), debilitante

debit ['debit] **1** *n* débito *m*; **d. balance** saldo negativo

2 *vt* **d. Mr Jones with £20** cargar la suma de 20 libras en la cuenta del Sr. Jones

debris ['debri:, 'deibri:] *n sing* escombros *mpl*

debt [det] *n* deuda *f*; **to be deeply in d.** estar cargado(a) de deudas; *Fig* **to be in sb's d.** estar en deuda con algn

debtor ['detə(r)] *n* deudor(a) *m,f*

debug [di:'bʌg] *vt Comput* eliminar fallos de

debunk [di:'bʌŋk] *vt Fam* desacreditar, desprestigiar

debut ['debju:, 'deibju:] *n* debut *m*; **to make one's d.** debutar

debutante ['debjʊtɑːnt] *n* debutante *f*

decade [de'keɪd, 'dekeɪd] *n* decenio *m*, década *f*

decadence ['dekədəns] *n* decadencia *f*

decadent ['dekədənt] *adj* decadente

decaffeinated [dɪ'kæfɪneɪtɪd] *adj* descafeinado(a)

decanter [dɪ'kæntə(r)] *n* jarra *f*, jarro *m*

decapitate [dɪ'kæpɪteɪt] *vt* decapitar

decay [dɪ'keɪ] **1** *n* (of food, body) putrefacción *f*, descomposición *f*; (of teeth) caries *f inv*; (of building) ruina *f*; (of civilization) decadencia *f*
  2 *vi* (food, body) pudrirse, descomponerse; (teeth) cariarse; (decline) declinarse

deceased [dɪ'siːst] *adj Fml* difunto(a), fallecido(a)

deceit [dɪ'siːt] *n* (**a**) (dishonesty) falta *f* de honradez, falsedad *f* (**b**) (trick) engaño *m*, mentira *f*

deceitful [dɪ'siːtfʊl] *adj* falso(a)

deceive [dɪ'siːv] *vt* (mislead) engañar; (lie to) mentir

December [dɪ'sembə(r)] *n* diciembre *m*

decency ['diːsənsɪ] *n* decencia *f*; (modesty) pudor *m*; (morality) moralidad *f*

decent ['diːsənt] *adj* (**a**) (respectable) decente, decoroso(a); **a d. wage** un sueldo decente (**b**) Fam (kind) **a d. chap** un buen tipo

decentralize [diː'sentrəlaɪz] *vt* descentralizar

deception [dɪ'sepʃən] *n* engaño *m*

> *ℓ* Note that the Spanish word **decepción** is a false friend and is never a translation for the English word "**deception**". In Spanish **decepción** means "disappointment".

deceptive [dɪ'septɪv] *adj* engañoso(a)

deceptively [dɪ'septɪvlɪ] *adv* **it looks d. simple** parece engañosamente sencillo(a)

decibel ['desɪbel] *n* decibelio *m*

decide [dɪ'saɪd] **1** *vt* (**a**) (choose, resolve) decidir; **to d. to do sth** decidir hacer algo (**b**) (matter, question) resolver, determinar
  2 *vi* (reach decision) decidirse; **to d. against sth** decidirse en contra de algo
  ▸ **decide on** *vt insep* (choose) optar por

decided [dɪ'saɪdɪd] *adj* (**a**) (noticeable) marcado(a) (**b**) (resolute) decidido(a); (views) categórico(a)

decidedly [dɪ'saɪdɪdlɪ] *adv Fml* (**a**) (clearly) indudablemente (**b**) (resolutely) decididamente

deciding [dɪ'saɪdɪŋ] *adj* decisivo(a)

deciduous [dɪ'sɪdjʊəs] *adj* de hoja caduca

decimal ['desɪməl] **1** *adj* decimal; **d. point** coma *f* (de fracción decimal)
  2 *n* decimal *m*

decimate ['desɪmeɪt] *vt* diezmar

decipher [dɪ'saɪfə(r)] *vt* descifrar

decision [dɪ'sɪʒən] *n* (**a**) (choice, judgement) decisión *f*; **to come to a d.** llegar a una decisión; **to make** *or* **take a d.** tomar una decisión (**b**) Fml (decisiveness) **to act with d.** actuar con decisión

decisive [dɪ'saɪsɪv] *adj* (**a**) (resolute) decidido(a), resuelto(a) (**b**) (conclusive) decisivo(a)

deck [dek] **1** *n* (**a**) (of ship) cubierta *f*; **d. chair** tumbona *f* (**b**) (of bus) piso *m*; **top d.** piso de arriba (**c**) *esp US* (of cards) baraja *f* (**d**) (of record player) plato *m*
  2 *vt* **to d. out** adornar

declaration [deklə'reɪʃən] *n* declaración *f*

declare [dɪ'kleə(r)] *vt* declarar; **to d. war (on)** declarar la guerra (a); **to d. sb guilty/innocent** declarar a algn culpable/inocente

declared [dɪ'kleəd] *adj* (opponent) declarado(a); (intention) manifiesto(a)

decline [dɪ'klaɪn] **1** *n* (**a**) (decrease) disminución *f* (**b**) (deterioration) deterioro *m*; (of health) empeoramiento *m*; **to fall into d.** empezar a decaer
  2 *vi* (**a**) (decrease) disminuir; (amount) bajar; (business) decaer (**b**) (deteriorate) deteriorarse; (health) empeorar (**c**) (refuse) negarse
  3 *vt* (**a**) (refuse) rechazar (**b**) Gram declinar

declutch [diː'klʌtʃ] *vi* soltar el embrague

decode [diː'kəʊd] *vt* descifrar

decompose [diːkəm'pəʊz] *vi* descomponerse

décor ['deɪkɔː(r)] *n* decoración *f*; *Th* decorado *m*

decorate ['dekəreɪt] *vt* (**a**) (adorn) decorar, adornar (**with** con) (**b**) (paint) pintar; (wallpaper) empapelar (**c**) (honour) condecorar

decoration [dekə'reɪʃən] *n* (**a**) (decor) decoración *f*; **Christmas decorations** adornos navideños (**b**) (medal) condecoración *f*

decorative ['dekərətɪv] *adj* decorativo(a)

decorator ['dekəreɪtə(r)] *n* decorador(a) *m,f*; (painter) pintor(a) *m,f*; (paperhanger) empapelador(a) *m,f*

decorum [dɪ'kɔːrəm] *n* decoro *m*

decoy ['diːkɔɪ] *n Fig* señuelo *m*

decrease **1** *n* ['diːkriːs] reducción *f*, disminución *f* (**in** en)

2 vi [dɪ'kriːs] disminuir, reducirse
3 vt disminuir, reducir
decree [dɪ'kriː] **1** n (a) Pol & Rel decreto m (**b**) esp US Jur sentencia f; **d. absolute** sentencia definitiva de divorcio; **d. nisi** sentencia provisional de divorcio
2 vt Pol & Rel decretar, pronunciar
decrepit [dɪ'krepɪt] adj decrépito(a)
dedicate ['dedɪkeɪt] vt consagrar, dedicar
dedicated ['dedɪkeɪtɪd] adj ardiente; **d. to** entregado(a) a
dedication [dedɪ'keɪʃən] n (act) dedicación f; (commitment) entrega f; (in book) dedicatoria f
deduce [dɪ'djuːs] vt deducir (**from** de)
deduct [dɪ'dʌkt] vt descontar (**from** de)
deduction [dɪ'dʌkʃən] n (a) (conclusion) conclusión f (**b**) (subtraction) descuento m
deed [diːd] n (a) (act) acto m; (feat) hazaña f (**b**) Jur escritura f; **title deeds** título m de propiedad
deem [diːm] vt Fml estimar
deep [diːp] **1** adj (a) (water, sleep, thinker) profundo(a); (breath, sigh) hondo(a); **it's 10 m d.** tiene 10 m de profundidad (**b**) (voice) grave (**c**) (colour) intenso(a)
2 adv **to be d. in thought** estar absorto(a); **to look d. into sb's eyes** penetrar a algn con la mirada
deepen ['diːpən] **1** vt (well) profundizar, ahondar; Fig (knowledge) aumentar
2 vi (river etc) hacerse más hondo or profundo; Fig (knowledge) aumentar; (colour, emotion) intensificarse; (sound, voice) hacerse más grave
deep-freeze [diːp'friːz] **1** n congelador m
2 vt congelar
deep-fry [diːp'fraɪ] vt freír en mucho aceite
deeply ['diːplɪ] adv profundamente; **to care d. about** preocuparse profundamente por
deep-rooted [diːp'ruːtɪd], **deep-seated** [diːp'siːtɪd] adj (fear, prejudice) arraigado(a)
deep-set [diːp'set] adj (eyes) hundido(a)
deer [dɪə(r)] n inv ciervo m
deface [dɪ'feɪs] vt (book, poster) garabatear
de facto [deɪ'fæktəʊ] adj & adv Fml de hecho
defamation [defə'meɪʃən] n difamación f
default [dɪ'fɔːlt] **1** vi (a) (not act) faltar a sus compromisos (**b**) Jur estar en rebeldía (**c**) (not pay) suspender pagos
2 n (a) (failure to act) omisión f (**b**)

(failure to pay) incumplimiento m de pago (**c**) Jur rebeldía f; **in d. of** a falta de; **to win by d.** ganar por incomparecencia del adversario
defaulter [dɪ'fɔːltə(r)] n (on loan) moroso(a) m,f, Jur & Mil rebelde mf
defeat [dɪ'fiːt] **1** vt (opponent) derrotar, vencer; (proposal, bill) rechazar
2 n (of opponent) derrota f; (of proposal, bill) rechazo m
defeatist [dɪ'fiːtɪst] adj & n derrotista (mf)
defect 1 n ['diːfekt] defecto m; (flaw) desperfecto m
2 vi [dɪ'fekt] desertar (**from** de); (from country) huir
defective [dɪ'fektɪv] adj (faulty) defectuoso(a); (flawed) con desperfectos; (lacking) incompleto(a)
defector [dɪ'fektə(r)] n Pol tránsfuga mf, trásfuga mf
defence [dɪ'fens] n (a) (of country) defensa f, Br **the Ministry of D.**, US **the Department of Defense** el Ministerio de Defensa; **to come to sb's d.** salir en defensa de algn (**b**) Jur defensa f (**c**) Sport [Br dɪ'fens, US 'diːfens] **the d.** la defensa
defenceless [dɪ'fenslɪs] adj indefenso(a)
defend [dɪ'fend] vt defender
defendant [dɪ'fendənt] n Jur acusado(a) m,f
defender [dɪ'fendə(r)] n defensor(a) m,f, Sport defensa mf
defending [dɪ'fendɪŋ] adj Sport defensor(a); **d. champion** campeón(ona) m,f titular
defense [dɪ'fens, 'diːfens] n US = **defence**
defensive [dɪ'fensɪv] **1** adj defensivo(a)
2 n **to be on the d.** estar a la defensiva
defer¹ [dɪ'fɜː(r)] vt aplazar, retrasar
defer² [dɪ'fɜː(r)] vi **to d. to** deferir a
deference ['defərəns] n Fml deferencia f, respeto m; **out of** or **in d. to** por respeto or por deferencia a
defiance [dɪ'faɪəns] n (a) (challenge) desafío m; **in d. of** a despecho de (**b**) (resistance) resistencia f
defiant [dɪ'faɪənt] adj (challenging) desafiante; (bold) insolente
deficiency [dɪ'fɪʃənsɪ] n (a) (lack) falta f, carencia f (**b**) (shortcoming) defecto m
deficient [dɪ'fɪʃənt] adj deficiente; **to be d. in sth** carecer de algo
deficit ['defɪsɪt] n déficit m
defile [dɪ'faɪl] vt Fml (a) (mind) corromper; (honour) manchar; (woman) deshonrar (**b**) (desecrate) profanar

define [dɪ'faɪn] vt (term, word) definir; (duties, powers) delimitar

definite ['defɪnɪt] adj (a) (clear) claro(a); (progress) notable (b) (date, place) determinado(a); **is it d.?** ¿es seguro?

definitely ['defɪnɪtlɪ] **1** adv sin duda; **he was d. drunk** no cabe duda de que estaba borracho
2 interj ¡desde luego!

definition [defɪ'nɪʃən] n definición f; **by d.** por definición

definitive [dɪ'fɪnɪtɪv] adj definitivo(a)

deflate [dɪ'fleɪt] vt (a) (tyre etc) desinflar (b) Fig rebajar; **to d. sb** hacer bajar los humos a algn (c) **to d. the economy** tomar medidas deflacionistas

deflationary [dɪ'fleɪʃənərɪ] adj Econ deflacionista

deflect [dɪ'flekt] vt desviar

deflection [dɪ'flekʃən] n desviación f

deforestation [diːfɒrɪ'steɪʃən] n deforestación f

deformed [dɪ'fɔːmd] adj deforme

deformity [dɪ'fɔːmɪtɪ] n deformidad f

defraud [dɪ'frɔːd] vt estafar

defrost [diː'frɒst] vt (a) (freezer, food) descongelar (b) US (windscreen) desempañar

deft [deft] adj hábil, diestro(a)

defunct [dɪ'fʌŋkt] adj (person) difunto(a); (thing) en desuso

defuse [diː'fjuːz] vt (bomb) desactivar; Fig **to d. a situation** reducir la tensión de una situación

defy [dɪ'faɪ] vt (a) (person) desafiar; (law, order) contravenir (b) (challenge) retar, desafiar

degenerate 1 vi [dɪ'dʒenəreɪt] degenerar (into en)
2 adj & n [dɪ'dʒenərɪt] degenerado(a) (m,f)

degrading [dɪ'greɪdɪŋ] adj degradante

degree [dɪ'griː] n (a) (extent, level) & Geom & Phys grado m; **to some d.** hasta cierto punto; **by degrees** poco a poco (b) (qualification) título m; (doctorate) doctorado m; **to have a d. in science** ser licenciado(a) en ciencias

dehydrated [diːhaɪ'dreɪtɪd] adj (person) deshidratado(a); (vegetables) seco(a)

de-ice [diː'aɪs] vt quitar el hielo a, deshelar

de-icer [diː'aɪsə(r)] n anticongelante m

deign [deɪn] vi dignarse

deity ['deɪtɪ] n deidad f

dejected [dɪ'dʒektɪd] adj desalentado(a), abatido(a)

delay [dɪ'leɪ] **1** vt (a) (flight, train) retrasar; (person) entretener; **delayed action** acción retardada (b) (postpone) aplazar
2 vi **don't d.** no lo deje para más tarde
3 n retraso m, Am demora f

delectable [dɪ'lektəbəl] adj delicioso(a)

delegate 1 n ['delɪgɪt] delegado(a) m,f
2 vt ['delɪgeɪt] delegar (**to** en); **to d. sb to do sth** encargar a algn que haga algo

delegation [delɪ'geɪʃən] n delegación f

delete [dɪ'liːt] vt tachar, suprimir

deliberate 1 adj [dɪ'lɪbərɪt] (intentional) deliberado(a), intencionado(a); (studied) premeditado(a); (careful) prudente; (unhurried) pausado(a)
2 vt [dɪ'lɪbəreɪt] deliberar
3 vi deliberar (**on** or **about** sobre)

deliberately [dɪ'lɪbərɪtlɪ] adv (intentionally) a propósito; (unhurriedly) pausadamente

deliberation [dɪlɪbə'reɪʃən] n (a) (consideration) deliberación f (b) (care) cuidado m; (unhurriedness) pausa f

delicacy ['delɪkəsɪ] n (a) (fineness) delicadeza f (b) (food) manjar (exquisito)

delicate ['delɪkɪt] adj (glass, situation) delicado(a); (health) frágil, delicado(a); (flavour, colour) suave

delicatessen [delɪkə'tesən] n (shop) = tienda de ultramarinos or Am enlatados de calidad

delicious [dɪ'lɪʃəs] adj delicioso(a)

delight [dɪ'laɪt] **1** n (a) (pleasure) placer m; **he took d. in it** le encantó (b) (source of pleasure) encanto m, delicia f
2 vt encantar

delighted [dɪ'laɪtɪd] adj encantado(a); **I'm d. to see you** me alegro mucho de verte

delightful [dɪ'laɪtfʊl] adj (person, smile) encantador(a); (meal, evening) delicioso(a)

delinquency [dɪ'lɪŋkwənsɪ] n delincuencia f; **juvenile d.** delincuencia juvenil

delinquent [dɪ'lɪŋkwənt] adj & n delincuente (mf)

delirious [dɪ'lɪrɪəs] adj delirante

deliver [dɪ'lɪvə(r)] vt (a) (goods) repartir, entregar; (message) dar; (order) despachar (b) (blow) asestar; (speech, verdict) pronunciar (c) Med ayudar en el nacimiento de (d) Fml (rescue) liberar

delivery [dɪ'lɪvərɪ] n (a) (of goods) reparto m, entrega f (b) (of speech) declamación f (c) (of baby) parto m

delta ['deltə] n Geog delta m

delude [dɪ'luːd] vt engañar; **don't d. yourself** no te hagas ilusiones

deluge ['delju:dʒ] **1** n *(flood)* inundación f; *(rain)* diluvio m; *Fig (of letters etc)* avalancha f
2 vt Fml inundar

delusion [dɪ'lu:ʒən] n **(a)** *(state, act)* engaño m **(b)** *(false belief)* ilusión (vana); **delusions of grandeur** delirios mpl de grandeza

de luxe [də'lʌks, də'lʊks] adj de lujo inv

delve [delv] vi **to d. into** *(pocket)* hurgar en; *(subject)* profundizar en

demagogue ['deməgɒg] n demagogo(a) m,f

demand [dɪ'mɑːnd] **1** n **(a)** *(request)* exigencia f; **on d.** a petición **(b)** *(for goods)* demanda f (**for** de); **to be in d.** estar muy solicitado(a) **(c)** Econ demanda f
2 vt **(a)** *(request)* exigir; **to d. that ...** insistir en que ... (+ subj) **(b)** *(require)* requerir

demanding [dɪ'mɑːndɪŋ] adj **(a)** *(person)* exigente **(b)** *(job)* agotador(a)

demean [dɪ'miːn] vt Fml **to d. oneself** rebajarse

demeaning [dɪ'miːnɪŋ] adj Fml humillante

demeanour, US **demeanor** [dɪ'miːnə(r)] n Fml **(a)** *(behaviour)* comportamiento m, conducta f **(b)** *(bearing)* porte m

demented [dɪ'mentɪd] adj Med demente; Fam loco(a)

demise [dɪ'maɪz] n Fml *(death)* fallecimiento m; Fig *(of institution)* desaparición f; *(of ambition etc)* fracaso m

demister [diː'mɪstə(r)] n Br Aut luneta f térmica, dispositivo m antivaho

demo ['deməʊ] n Fam manifestación f; **d. tape** maqueta f

demobilize [diː'məʊbɪlaɪz] vt desmovilizar

democracy [dɪ'mɒkrəsɪ] n democracia f

democrat ['deməkræt] n demócrata mf; Pol **Christian D.** democratacristiano(a) m,f; **Social D.** socialdemócrata mf

democratic [demə'krætɪk] adj democrático(a); US Pol **D. party** partido m demócrata

demographic [demə'græfɪk] adj demográfico(a)

demolish [dɪ'mɒlɪʃ] vt *(building)* derribar, demoler; Fig *(theory, proposal)* echar por tierra

demolition [demə'lɪʃən] n demolición f

demon ['diːmən] n demonio m

demonstrate ['demənstreɪt] **1** vt demostrar
2 vi Pol manifestarse

demonstration [demən'streɪʃən] n **(a)** *(proof)* demostración f, prueba f **(b)** *(explanation)* explicación f **(c)** Pol manifestación f

demonstrative [dɪ'mɒnstrətɪv] adj expresivo(a)

demonstrator ['demənstreɪtə(r)] n manifestante mf

demoralize [dɪ'mɒrəlaɪz] vt desmoralizar

demoralizing [dɪ'mɒrəlaɪzɪŋ] adj desmoralizador(a), desmoralizante

demote [dɪ'məʊt] vt rebajar de graduación a

demure [dɪ'mjʊə(r)] adj *(person)* recatado(a)

den [den] n **(a)** *(of animal)* guarida f **(b)** Fam *(study)* estudio m

denial [dɪ'naɪəl] n **(a)** *(of charge)* desmentido m **(b)** *(of rights)* denegación f; *(of request)* negativa f

denim ['denɪm] n tela f vaquera; **denims** *(jeans)* vaqueros mpl, Andes, Ven bluyíns nmpl, Méx pantalones mpl de mezclilla; **d. skirt/shirt** falda f/camisa f vaquera

Denmark ['denmɑːk] n Dinamarca

denomination [dɪnɒmɪ'neɪʃən] n **(a)** Rel confesión f **(b)** Fin *(of coins)* valor m

denominator [dɪ'nɒmɪneɪtə(r)] n denominador m

denote [dɪ'nəʊt] vt *(show)* indicar; *(mean)* significar

denounce [dɪ'naʊns] vt denunciar; *(criticize)* censurar

dense [dens] adj **(a)** *(smoke, fog)* denso(a); *(crowd)* nutrido(a) **(b)** Fam *(stupid)* corto(a)

densely ['denslɪ] adv densamente

density ['densɪtɪ] n densidad f

dent [dent] **1** n abolladura f
2 vt *(car)* abollar

dental ['dentəl] adj dental; **d. floss** hilo m dental; **d. surgeon** odontólogo m,f; **d. surgery** *(place)* clínica f dental; *(treatment)* cirugía f dental

dentist ['dentɪst] n dentista mf

dentistry ['dentɪstrɪ] n odontología f

dentures ['dentʃəz] n **(set of) d.** dentadura postiza

denunciation [dɪnʌnsɪ'eɪʃən] n denuncia f, condena f

deny [dɪ'naɪ] vt **(a)** *(repudiate)* negar; *(rumour, report)* desmentir; *(charge)* rechazar **(b)** *(refuse)* negar

deodorant [diː'əʊdərənt] n desodorante m

depart [dɪ'pɑːt] vi marcharse, irse; Fig *(from subject)* desviarse (**from** de)

department [dɪ'pɑ:tmənt] *n* sección *f*; *(in university)* departamento *m*; *(in government)* ministerio *m*; **d. store** grandes almacenes *mpl*; *US* **D. of the Interior** Ministerio *m* del Interior

departure [dɪ'pɑ:tʃə(r)] *n* partida *f*; *Av & Rail* salida *f*; *Av* **d. lounge** sala *f* de embarque

depend [dɪ'pend] **1** *vi* (rely) fiarse (**on** or **upon** de)
2 *v impers* (be determined by) depender (**on** or **upon** de); **it depends on the weather** según el tiempo que haga; **that depends** según

dependable [dɪ'pendəbəl] *adj* (person) formal; (friend) leal; (car) fiable, *Am* confiable

dependant [dɪ'pendənt] *n* dependiente *mf*

dependence [dɪ'pendəns] *n* dependencia *f*

dependent [dɪ'pendənt] **1** *adj* dependiente; **to be d. on sth** depender de algo
2 *n US* = **dependant**

depict [dɪ'pɪkt] *vt Art* representar; *Fig* describir

deplete [dɪ'pli:t] *vt* reducir

deplorable [dɪ'plɔ:rəbəl] *adj* lamentable

deplore [dɪ'plɔ:(r)] *vt* deplorar

deploy [dɪ'plɔɪ] *vt Mil* desplegar; *Fig* utilizar

depopulate [di:'pɒpjʊleɪt] *vt* despoblar

deport [dɪ'pɔ:t] *vt* expulsar (**from** de; **to** a)

deportation [di:pɔ:'teɪʃən] *n* expulsión *f*

deportment [dɪ'pɔ:tmənt] *n Fml* porte *m*

depose [dɪ'pəʊz] *vt* deponer

deposit [dɪ'pɒzɪt] **1** *n* (a) (in bank) depósito *m*; *Br* **d. account** cuenta *f* de ahorros (b) (returnable) señal *f*, fianza *f*; (first payment) entrega *f* inicial, *Esp* entrada *f* (c) (of minerals) yacimiento *m*; (in wine) poso *m*
2 *vt* depositar; (in bank account) *Esp* ingresar, *Am* depositar

deposition [depə'zɪʃən] *n* (a) (of leader) destitución *f* (b) *Jur* (of witness) declaración *f*

depositor [dɪ'pɒzɪtə(r)] *n* depositante *mf*

depot [*Br* 'depəʊ, *US* 'di:pəʊ] *n* almacén *m*; *Mil* depósito *m*; *Br* (for keeping and repairing buses) cochera *f*; *US* (bus station) estación *f* de autobuses, *CAm*, *Méx* central *f* camionera

depraved [dɪ'preɪvd] *adj* (person) depravado(a)

deprecate ['deprɪkeɪt] *vt* desaprobar, censurar

depreciate [dɪ'pri:ʃɪeɪt] *vi* depreciarse

depreciation [dɪpri:ʃɪ'eɪʃən] *n* depreciación *f*

depress [dɪ'pres] *vt* (a) (person) deprimir (b) *Econ* (profits) reducir; (trade) dificultar (c) *Fml* (switch, lever etc) presionar; (clutch, piano pedal) pisar

depressed [dɪ'prest] *adj* (a) (person) deprimido(a); **to get d.** deprimirse (b) (market) en crisis (c) (surface) hundido(a)

depressing [dɪ'presɪŋ] *adj* deprimente

depression [dɪ'preʃən] *n* depresión *f*

deprivation [deprɪ'veɪʃən] *n* (hardship) privación *f*; (loss) pérdida *f*

deprive [dɪ'praɪv] *vt* privar (**of** de)

deprived [dɪ'praɪvd] *adj* necesitado(a)

dept (abbr **department**) dpt, dpto

depth [depθ] *n* profundidad *f*; **to be in the depths of despair** estar completamente desesperado(a); **in d.** (investigate, discuss) a fondo, en profundidad

deputation [depjʊ'teɪʃən] *n* delegación *f*

deputy ['depjʊtɪ] *n* (a) (substitute) suplente *mf*; **d. chairman** vicepresidente *m*; **d. head** subdirector(a) *m,f* (b) *Pol* diputado(a) *m,f*

derail [dɪ'reɪl] *vt* hacer descarrilar

deranged [dɪ'reɪndʒd] *adj* trastornado(a)

derby [*Br* 'dɑ:bɪ, *US* 'dɜ:rbɪ] *n* (a) *Sport* derby *m* (b) *US* bombín *m*, sombrero hongo

derelict ['derɪlɪkt] *adj* abandonado(a), en ruinas

deride [dɪ'raɪd] *vt* ridiculizar, burlarse de

derisive [dɪ'raɪsɪv] *adj* burlón(ona)

derisory [dɪ'raɪsərɪ] *adj* irrisorio(a)

derivative [dɪ'rɪvətɪv] **1** *adj* (art, writing) sin originalidad
2 *n* (of word, substance) derivado *m*

derive [dɪ'raɪv] **1** *vt* sacar
2 *vi* (word) derivarse (**from** de); (skill) provenir (**from** de)

derogatory [dɪ'rɒgətərɪ] *adj* (remark, article) despectivo(a); (meaning) peyorativo(a)

derrick ['derɪk] *n* torre *f* de perforación

descend [dɪ'send] **1** *vi* descender; **to d. from** (be related to) descender de
2 *vt* (stairs) bajar

descendant [dɪ'sendənt] *n* descendiente *mf*

descent [dɪ'sent] *n* (a) (downward movement) descenso *m* (b) (ancestry) ascendencia *f*

describe [dɪˈskraɪb] vt (**a**) (depict verbally) describir; (characterize) definir (**b**) Fml (draw) (circle) trazar

description [dɪˈskrɪpʃən] n descripción f; **to defy d.** superar la descripción

desecrate [ˈdesɪkreɪt] vt profanar

desert¹ [ˈdezət] n desierto m

desert² [dɪˈzɜːt] **1** vt (place, family) abandonar
  2 vi Mil desertar (**from** de)

deserted [dɪˈzɜːtɪd] adj desierto(a)

deserter [dɪˈzɜːtə(r)] n desertor(a) m,f

desertion [dɪˈzɜːʃən] n abandono m; Pol defección f; Mil deserción f

deserts [dɪˈzɜːts] npl **to get one's just d.** llevarse su merecido

deserve [dɪˈzɜːv] vt merecer, merecerse, Am ameritar

deservedly [dɪˈzɜːvɪdlɪ] adv con (toda) razón

deserving [dɪˈzɜːvɪŋ] adj (person) de valía; (cause) meritorio(a)

design [dɪˈzaɪn] **1** n (**a**) (of car, furniture, clothes) diseño m (**b**) (drawing, blueprint) plano m (**c**) (layout) disposición f (**d**) (pattern) dibujo m (**e**) Fig (scheme) intención f; **by d.** a propósito; Fam **to have designs on** tener puestas las miras en
  2 vt diseñar

designate 1 vt [ˈdezɪgneɪt] (**a**) (appoint) designar, nombrar (**b**) Fml (boundary) señalar
  2 adj [ˈdezɪgnɪt] designado(a)

designer [dɪˈzaɪnə(r)] n Art diseñador(a) m,f; **d. jeans** pantalones mpl de marca

desirable [dɪˈzaɪərəbəl] adj deseable; (asset, offer) atractivo(a)

desire [dɪˈzaɪə(r)] **1** n deseo m; **I feel no d. to go** no me Esp apetece or Carib, Col, Méx provoca nada ir, no tengo nada de ganas de ir
  2 vt desear

desist [dɪˈzɪst] vi Fml desistir (**from** de)

desk [desk] n (in school) pupitre m; (in office) escritorio m; US **d. clerk** recepcionista mf; **d. job** trabajo m de oficina; **news d.** redacción f; **reception d.** recepción f

desktop [ˈdesktɒp] n Comput escritorio m; **d. computer** Esp ordenador m or Am computadora de sobremesa; **d. publishing** autoedición f

desolate [ˈdesəlɪt] adj (**a**) (uninhabited) desierto(a); (barren) yermo(a) (**b**) (person) desconsolado(a)

desolation [desəˈleɪʃən] n (**a**) (of place) desolación f; (by destruction) asolamiento m (**b**) (of person) desconsuelo m

despair [dɪˈspeə(r)] **1** n desesperación f; **to drive sb to d.** desesperar a algn
  2 vi desesperar(se) (**of** de)

despairing [dɪˈspeərɪŋ] adj desesperado(a)

despatch [dɪˈspætʃ] n & vt = **dispatch**

desperate [ˈdespərɪt] adj (person, situation) desesperado(a); (struggle) encarnizado(a)

desperately [ˈdespərɪtlɪ] adv (fight, plead) desesperadamente; (struggle) encarnizadamente; (ill) gravísimamente; (in love) locamente

desperation [despəˈreɪʃən] n desesperación f; **in d.** a la desesperada

despicable [dɪˈspɪkəbəl] adj despreciable; (behaviour) indigno(a)

despise [dɪˈspaɪz] vt despreciar, menospreciar

despite [dɪˈspaɪt] prep Fml a pesar de

despondent [dɪˈspɒndənt] adj abatido(a)

despot [ˈdespɒt] n déspota mf

dessert [dɪˈzɜːt] n postre m; **d. wine** vino m dulce

dessertspoon [dɪˈzɜːtspuːn] n cuchara f or Ven cucharilla f de postre; (as measurement) cucharada f de las de postre

destination [destɪˈneɪʃən] n destino m

destined [ˈdestɪnd] adj (**a**) **d. to fail** condenado(a) al fracaso (**b**) (bound) con destino (**for** a)

destiny [ˈdestɪnɪ] n destino m

destitute [ˈdestɪtjuːt] adj indigente

destroy [dɪˈstrɔɪ] vt destruir; (vehicle, old furniture) destrozar

destroyer [dɪˈstrɔɪə(r)] n Naut destructor m

destruction [dɪˈstrʌkʃən] n destrucción f; Fig ruina f

destructive [dɪˈstrʌktɪv] adj (gale etc) destructor(a); (tendency, criticism) destructivo(a)

detach [dɪˈtætʃ] vt (remove) separar

detachable [dɪˈtætʃəbəl] adj separable (**from** de)

detached [dɪˈtætʃt] adj (**a**) (separated) separado(a); esp Br **d. house** casa f independiente (**b**) (impartial) objetivo(a)

detachment [dɪˈtætʃmənt] n (**a**) (impartiality) objetividad f; (aloofness) desapego m (**b**) Mil destacamento m

detail [Br ˈdiːteɪl, US dɪˈteɪl] **1** n (**a**) (item of information) detalle m; **without going into detail(s)** sin entrar en detalles; **details** (information) detalles mpl; (address and phone number) datos mpl (**b**) Mil destacamento m

2 vt (**a**) (list) detallar, enumerar (**b**) Mil (appoint) destacar

detailed ['di:teɪld] adj detallado(a), minucioso(a)

detain [dɪ'teɪn] vt (**a**) Jur detener (**b**) (delay) retener

detainee [di:teɪ'ni:] n Pol preso(a) m,f

detect [dɪ'tekt] vt (of person) percibir; (of machine) detectar; (source of a problem) identificar, hallar

detection [dɪ'tekʃən] n (of mines, plane) detección f; (by detective) investigación f

detective [dɪ'tektɪv] n detective mf; d. story novela policíaca

detector [dɪ'tektə(r)] n aparato m detector

detention [dɪ'tenʃən] n (of suspect etc) detención f, arresto m; Educ to get d. quedarse castigado(a)

deter [dɪ'tɜ:(r)] vt (dissuade) disuadir (from de); (stop) impedir

detergent [dɪ'tɜ:dʒənt] n detergente m

deteriorate [dɪ'tɪərɪəreɪt] vi deteriorarse

deterioration [dɪtɪərɪə'reɪʃən] n empeoramiento m; (of substance, friendship) deterioro m

determination [dɪtɜ:mɪ'neɪʃən] n (resolution) resolución f

determine [dɪ'tɜ:mɪn] vt determinar

determined [dɪ'tɜ:mɪnd] adj (person) decidido(a); (effort) enérgico(a)

deterrent [dɪ'terənt] **1** adj disuasivo(a); **2** n fuerza disuasoria

detest [dɪ'test] vt detestar, odiar

detonate ['detəneɪt] vt & vi detonar

detonation [detə'neɪʃən] n detonación f

detour ['di:tʊə(r)] n desvío m

detract [dɪ'trækt] vi quitar mérito (from a)

detractor [dɪ'træktə(r)] n detractor(a) m,f

detriment ['detrɪmənt] n perjuicio m (to de)

detrimental [detrɪ'mentəl] adj perjudicial (to para)

deuce [dju:s] n (in tennis) cuarenta iguales mpl

devaluation [di:vælju:'eɪʃən] n devaluación f

devastate ['devəsteɪt] vt (city, area) asolar; Fig (person) desolar

devastating ['devəsteɪtɪŋ] adj (fire) devastador(a); (wind, flood) arrollador(a)

devastation [devə'steɪʃən] n asolación f

develop [dɪ'veləp] **1** vt (**a**) (theory, argument, design) desarrollar; (skills) perfeccionar (**b**) (natural resources) aprovechar; (site, land) urbanizar (**c**) (habit) adquirir; (interest) mostrar (**d**) Phot revelar
2 vi (**a**) (body, industry) desarrollarse; (system) perfeccionarse; (interest) crecer (**b**) (appear) crearse; (evolve) evolucionar

developer [dɪ'veləpə(r)] n (property) d. inmobiliaria f

development [dɪ'veləpmənt] n (**a**) (of theory, argument, design) desarrollo m; (of trade) fomento m; (of skill) perfección f; (of character) formación f (**b**) (progress, change) cambio m, variación f; there are no new developments no hay ninguna novedad (**c**) (exploitation) explotación f (**d**) (housing project) urbanización f

deviate ['di:vɪeɪt] vi desviarse (from de)

deviation [di:vɪ'eɪʃən] n (from norm, route) desviación f (from de); (from truth) alejamiento m

device [dɪ'vaɪs] n (**a**) (for measuring, processing, cutting) aparato m; (for safety, security) dispositivo m (**b**) (method, scheme) estratagema f

devil ['devəl] n diablo m, demonio m; d.'s advocate abogado(a) m,f del diablo; Fam where the d. did you put it? ¿dónde demonios lo pusiste?; you lucky d.! ¡vaya suerte que tienes!

devious ['di:vɪəs] adj (**a**) (winding) tortuoso(a) (**b**) (person, mind) retorcido(a)

devise [dɪ'vaɪz] vt idear, concebir

devoid [dɪ'vɔɪd] adj desprovisto(a) (of de)

devolution [di:və'lu:ʃən] n Pol = transmisión de poderes a las regiones

devote [dɪ'vəʊt] vt dedicar; she devoted her life to helping the poor consagró su vida a la ayuda de los pobres

devoted [dɪ'vəʊtɪd] adj fiel, leal (to a)

devotee [devə'ti:] n (of religion) devoto(a) m,f; (of theatre, sport) aficionado(a) m,f; Pol partidario(a) m,f

devotion [dɪ'vəʊʃən] n devoción f; (to cause) dedicación f

devour [dɪ'vaʊə(r)] vt devorar

devout [dɪ'vaʊt] adj devoto(a)

dew [dju:] n rocío m

dexterity [dek'sterɪtɪ] n destreza f

dext(e)rous ['dekstrəs] adj diestro(a)

diabetes [daɪə'bi:ti:z, daɪə'bi:tɪs] n diabetes f

diabetic [daɪə'betɪk] adj & n diabético(a) (m,f)

diabolical [daɪə'bɒlɪkəl] adj (**a**) (evil) diabólico(a) (**b**) Br Fam (very bad) espantoso(a)

diagnose ['daɪəgnəʊz] *vt* diagnosticar

diagnosis [daɪəg'nəʊsɪs] *n* (*pl* **diagnoses** [daɪəg'nəʊsiːz]) diagnóstico *m*

diagonal [daɪ'ægənəl] *adj & n* diagonal (*f*)

diagonally [daɪ'ægənəlɪ] *adv* en diagonal, diagonalmente

diagram ['daɪəgræm] *n* diagrama *m*; (*of process, system*) esquema *m*; (*of workings*) gráfico *m*

dial ['daɪəl, daɪl] **1** *n* (*of clock*) esfera *f*; (*of radio*) cuadrante *m*; (*of telephone*) disco *m*; (*of machine*) botón *m* selector
2 *vt & vi Tel* marcar, *Andes, CSur* discar; *Br* **dialling** *or US* **d. code** prefijo *m*; *Br* **dialling** *or US* **d. tone** señal *f* de marcar *or Andes, CSur* discar

dialect ['daɪəlekt] *n* dialecto *m*

dialogue, *US* **dialog** ['daɪəlɒg] *n* diálogo *m*

dialysis [daɪ'ælɪsɪs] *n Med* diálisis *f inv*

diameter [daɪ'æmɪtə(r)] *n* diámetro *m*

diametrically [daɪə'metrɪkəlɪ] *adv* diametralmente

diamond ['daɪəmənd] *n* (**a**) (*gem*) diamante *m* (**b**) (*shape*) rombo *m*

diaper ['daɪəpə(r)] *n US* pañal *m*

diaphragm ['daɪəfræm] *n* diafragma *m*

diarrhoea, *US* **diarrhea** [daɪə'rɪə] *n* diarrea *f*

diary ['daɪərɪ] *n* (**a**) (*as record*) diario *m*; **to keep a d.** llevar un diario (**b**) (*for appointments*) agenda *f*

dice [daɪs] **1** *n* (*pl* **dice**) dado *m*
2 *vt Culin* cortar en cuadritos

dichotomy [daɪ'kɒtəmɪ] *n* dicotomía *f*

dictate 1 *vt* [dɪk'teɪt] (*letter, order*) dictar
2 *vi* **to d. to sb** dar órdenes a algn
3 *n* ['dɪkteɪt] *Fig* **the dictates of conscience** los dictados de la conciencia

dictation [dɪk'teɪʃən] *n* dictado *m*

dictator [dɪk'teɪtə(r)] *n* dictador(a) *m,f*

dictatorship [dɪk'teɪtəʃɪp] *n* dictadura *f*

diction ['dɪkʃən] *n* dicción *f*

dictionary ['dɪkʃənərɪ] *n* diccionario *m*

did [dɪd] *pt of* do

die [daɪ] *vi* morir, morirse; *Fam Fig* **to be dying for sth/to do sth** morirse por algo/ de ganas de hacer algo

▶ **die away** *vi* desvanecerse

▶ **die down** *vi* (*fire*) extinguirse; (*wind*) amainar; (*noise, excitement*) disminuir

▶ **die off** *vi* morir uno por uno

▶ **die out** *vi* extinguirse

die-hard ['daɪhɑːd] *n* reaccionario(a) *m,f*

diesel ['diːzəl] *n* (**a**) (*oil*) gasoil *m*; **d. engine** motor *m* diesel (**b**) *Fam* (*vehicle*) vehículo *m* diesel

diet ['daɪət] **1** *n* (*normal food*) dieta *f*; (*selected food*) régimen *m*; **to be on a d.** estar a régimen
2 *vi* estar a régimen

dietician [daɪə'tɪʃən] *n* especialista *mf* en dietética, *Am* dietista *mf*

differ ['dɪfə(r)] *vi* (*be unlike*) ser distinto(a); (*disagree*) discrepar

difference ['dɪfərəns] *n* (**a**) (*dissimilarity*) diferencia *f*; **it makes no d. (to me)** (me) da igual; **what d. does it make?** ¿qué más da? (**b**) (*disagreement*) desacuerdo *m*

different ['dɪfərənt] *adj* diferente, distinto(a); **you look d.** pareces otro(a)

differentiate [dɪfə'renʃɪeɪt] **1** *vt* distinguir, diferenciar (**from** de)
2 *vi* distinguir (**between** entre)

differently ['dɪfərəntlɪ] *adv* de otra manera

difficult ['dɪfɪkəlt] *adj* difícil

difficulty ['dɪfɪkəltɪ] *n* dificultad *f*; (*problem*) problema *m*; **to be in difficulties** estar en un apuro

diffident ['dɪfɪdənt] *adj* tímido(a)

diffuse 1 *adj* [dɪ'fjuːs] (*light*) difuso(a); *Fig* vago(a)
2 *vt* [dɪ'fjuːz] difundir; (*heat*) desprender

dig [dɪg] **1** *n* (**a**) (*poke*) codazo *m* (**b**) *Fam* (*gibe*) pulla *f*
2 *vt* (*pt & pp* **dug**) (**a**) (*earth*) cavar; (*tunnel*) excavar (**b**) *Fam Fig* **to d. one's heels in** mantenerse en sus trece
3 *vi* (*person*) cavar; (*animal*) escarbar

▶ **dig in** *vi Mil* atrincherarse

▶ **dig out** *vt sep Fig* (*old suit*) sacar; (*information*) descubrir

▶ **dig up** *vt sep* (*weeds*) arrancar; (*buried object*) desenterrar; (*road*) levantar; *Fig* sacar a relucir

digest 1 *n* ['daɪdʒest] (*summary*) resumen *m*
2 *vt* [dɪ'dʒest] (*food*) digerir; *Fig* (*facts*) asimilar

digestion [dɪ'dʒestʃən] *n* digestión *f*

digestive [dɪ'dʒestɪv] *adj* digestivo(a); *Br* **d. biscuit** galleta *f* integral

digger ['dɪgə(r)] *n* excavadora *f*

digit ['dɪdʒɪt] *n* (**a**) *Math* dígito *m* (**b**) *Fml Anat* dedo *m*

digital ['dɪdʒɪtəl] *adj* digital; **d. television** televisión *f* digital

dignified ['dɪgnɪfaɪd] *adj* (*manner*) solemne, serio(a); (*appearance*) majestuoso(a)

dignitary ['dɪgnɪtərɪ] *n* dignatario *m*

dignity ['dɪgnɪtɪ] n dignidad f
digress [daɪ'gres] vi apartarse del tema
dike [daɪk] n US = **dyke**
dilapidated [dɪ'læpɪdeɪtɪd] adj en mal estado
dilemma [dɪ'lemə, daɪ'lemə] n dilema m
diligent ['dɪlɪdʒənt] adj (worker) diligente; (inquiries, search) esmerado(a)
dilute [daɪ'lu:t] **1** vt diluir; (wine, milk) aguar; Fig (effect, influence) atenuar
2 vi diluirse
dim [dɪm] **1** adj (**dimmer, dimmest**) (a) (light) débil, tenue; (room) oscuro(a); (outline) borroso(a); (eyesight) defectuoso(a); Fig (memory) vago(a); Fig (future) sombrío(a) (b) Fam (stupid) tonto(a), corto de alcances, Am sonso(a)
2 vt (light) bajar
3 vi (light) bajarse; (sight) nublarse; Fig (joy) extinguirse
dime [daɪm] n US moneda f de diez centavos
dimension [daɪ'menʃən] n dimensión f
diminish [dɪ'mɪnɪʃ] vt & vi disminuir
diminutive [dɪ'mɪnjʊtɪv] **1** adj diminuto(a)
2 n Gram diminutivo m
dimly ['dɪmlɪ] adv vagamente
dimmer ['dɪmə(r)] n **d. (switch)** regulador m de voltaje
dimple ['dɪmpəl] n hoyuelo m
din [dɪn] n (of crowd) alboroto m; (of machinery) estruendo m
dine [daɪn] vi Fml cenar; **to d. out** cenar fuera
diner ['daɪnə(r)] n (a) (person) comensal mf (b) US (restaurant) restaurante barato
dinghy ['dɪŋɪ] n bote m; (**rubber**) **d.** bote neumático
dingy ['dɪndʒɪ] adj (**dingier, dingiest**) (a) (dark) oscuro(a) (b) (dirty) sucio(a) (c) (colour) desteñido(a)
dining car ['daɪnɪŋkɑ:(r)] n vagón m restaurante
dining room ['daɪnɪŋruːm] n comedor m
dinner ['dɪnə(r)] n (at midday) comida f; (in evening) cena f; **d. jacket** smoking m; **d. service** vajilla f; **d. table** mesa f de comedor
dinosaur ['daɪnəsɔ:(r)] n dinosaurio m
dint [dɪnt] n **by d. of** a fuerza de
diocese ['daɪəsɪs] n diócesis f inv
dioxide [daɪ'ɒksaɪd] n bióxido m
dip [dɪp] **1** n (a) Fam (bathe) chapuzón m (b) (of road) pendiente f; (in ground)

depresión f (c) Culin salsa f (para mojar aperitivos)
2 vt (a) (immerse) meter (**in(to)** en); (food) mojar (**in(to)** en) (b) Br Aut **to d. one's headlights** poner las luces de cruce
3 vi (road) bajar
▶ **dip into** vt insep (a) (savings) echar mano de (b) (book) hojear
diphthong ['dɪfθɒŋ] n diptongo m
diploma [dɪ'pləʊmə] n diploma m
diplomacy [dɪ'pləʊməsɪ] n diplomacia f
diplomat ['dɪpləmæt] n diplomático(a) m,f
diplomatic [dɪplə'mætɪk] adj diplomático(a)
dipstick ['dɪpstɪk] n indicador m de nivel del aceite
dire ['daɪə(r)] adj (urgent) extremo(a); (serious) grave
direct [dɪ'rekt, 'daɪrekt] **1** adj directo(a); **the d. opposite** todo lo contrario; Elec **d. current** corriente continua
3 vt (a) (remark, gaze, effort) dirigir (**at** a); **can you d. me to a bank? ¿**me puede indicar dónde hay un banco? (b) (instruct) mandar
direction [dɪ'rekʃən, daɪ'rekʃən] n (a) (way) dirección f; **sense of d.** sentido m de la orientación (b) **directions** (to place) señas fpl; **directions for use** modo m de empleo (c) (of play, film) dirección f
directive [dɪ'rektɪv, daɪ'rektɪv] n directiva f
directly [dɪ'rektlɪ, daɪ'rektlɪ] **1** adv (a) (above etc) exactamente, justo (b) (speak) francamente (c) (descend) directamente (d) (come) en seguida
2 conj Fam en cuanto
director [dɪ'rektə(r), daɪ'rektə(r)] n director(a) m,f
directory [dɪ'rektərɪ, daɪ'rektərɪ] n Tel guía telefónica, Am directorio m de teléfonos; **d. enquiries** (servicio m de) información f
dirt [dɜːt] n suciedad f
dirt-cheap [dɜːt'tʃiːp] adv & adj Fam tirado(a)
dirty ['dɜːtɪ] **1** adj (**dirtier, dirtiest**) (a) (unclean) sucio(a) (b) **to give sb a d. look** fulminar a algn con la mirada (c) (joke) verde; (mind) pervertido(a); **d. word** palabrota f; **d. old man** viejo m verde
2 vt ensuciar
disability [dɪsə'bɪlɪtɪ] n incapacidad f, discapacidad f; **d. pension** pensión f por invalidez

disabled [dɪ'seɪbəld] **1** *adj* minusválido(a)
2 *npl* **the d.** los minusválidos

disadvantage [dɪsəd'vɑːntɪdʒ] *n* desventaja *f*; *(obstacle)* inconveniente *m*

disaffection [dɪsə'fekʃən] *n* descontento *m*

disagree [dɪsə'griː] *vi* (**a**) *(differ)* no estar de acuerdo (**with** con); **to d. on** or **over sth** reñir por algo (**b**) *(not match)* discrepar (**with** de *or* con) (**c**) **garlic disagrees with me** el ajo no me sienta bien

disagreeable [dɪsə'griːəbəl] *adj* desagradable

disagreement [dɪsə'griːmənt] *n* (**a**) *(failure to agree)* desacuerdo *m*; *(argument)* discusión *f* (**b**) *(discrepancy)* discrepancia *f*

disallow [dɪsə'laʊ] *vt* *(goal)* anular; *(objection)* rechazar

disappear [dɪsə'pɪə(r)] *vi* desaparecer

disappearance [dɪsə'pɪərəns] *n* desaparición *f*

disappoint [dɪsə'pɔɪnt] *vt* *(person)* decepcionar, defraudar; *(hope, ambition)* frustrar

disappointed [dɪsə'pɔɪntɪd] *adj* decepcionado(a)

disappointing [dɪsə'pɔɪntɪŋ] *adj* decepcionante

disappointment [dɪsə'pɔɪntmənt] *n* decepción *f*

disapproval [dɪsə'pruːvəl] *n* desaprobación *f*

disapprove [dɪsə'pruːv] *vi* **to d. of** desaprobar

disarm [dɪs'ɑːm] **1** *vt* desarmar
2 *vi* desarmarse

disarmament [dɪs'ɑːməmənt] *n* desarme *m*

disarray [dɪsə'reɪ] *n* *Fml* **in d.** *(room, papers)* en desorden; *(hair)* desarreglado(a); *(thoughts)* confuso(a)

disaster [dɪ'zɑːstə(r)] *n* desastre *m*

disastrous [dɪ'zɑːstrəs] *adj* desastroso(a)

disband [dɪs'bænd] **1** *vt* disolver
2 *vi* disolverse

disbelief [dɪsbɪ'liːf] *n* incredulidad *f*

disc [dɪsk] *n* disco *m*; *Comput* disquete *m*; **d. jockey** disc-jockey *mf*, pinchadiscos *mf inv*

discard [dɪs'kɑːd] *vt* *(old things)* deshacerse de; *(plan)* descartar

discern [dɪ'sɜːn] *vt* *(shape, difference)* percibir; *(truth)* darse cuenta de

discerning [dɪ'sɜːnɪŋ] *adj* *(person)* perspicaz; *(taste)* refinado(a)

discharge *Fml* **1** *vt* [dɪs'tʃɑːdʒ] *(prisoner)* soltar; *(patient)* dar de alta a; *(soldier)* licenciar; *(employee)* despedir; *(gun)* descargar
2 *n* ['dɪstʃɑːdʒ] (**a**) *(of current, load, gas)* descarga *f*; *(of gases)* escape *m* (**b**) *(of prisoner)* liberación *f*; *(of patient)* alta *f*; *(of soldier)* licencia *f*

disciple [dɪ'saɪpəl] *n* discípulo(a) *m,f*

discipline ['dɪsɪplɪn] **1** *n* disciplina *f*
2 *vt* *(child)* castigar; *(worker)* sancionar; *(official)* expedientar

disclaim [dɪs'kleɪm] *vt Fml* negar tener

disclose [dɪs'kləʊz] *vt* revelar

disclosure [dɪs'kləʊʒə(r)] *n* revelación *f*

disco ['dɪskəʊ] *n Fam* (*abbr* **discotheque**) disco *f*

discolour, *US* **discolor** [dɪs'kʌlə(r)] *vt* descolorir

discomfort [dɪs'kʌmfət] *n* (**a**) *(lack of comfort)* incomodidad *f* (**b**) *(pain)* malestar *m* (**c**) *(unease)* inquietud *f*

disconcert [dɪskən'sɜːt] *vt* desconcertar

disconcerting [dɪskən'sɜːtɪŋ] *adj* desconcertante

disconnect [dɪskə'nekt] *vt* desconectar (**from** de); *(gas, electricity)* cortar

disconnected [dɪskə'nektɪd] *adj* inconexo(a)

disconsolate [dɪs'kɒnsəlɪt] *adj* desconsolado(a)

discontent [dɪskən'tent] *n* descontento *m*

discontented [dɪskən'tentɪd] *adj* descontento(a)

discontinue [dɪskən'tɪnjuː] *vt Fml* abandonar; *(work)* interrumpir

discord ['dɪskɔːd] *n* (**a**) *Fml* discordia *f* (**b**) *Mus* disonancia *f*

discordant [dɪs'kɔːdənt] *adj* discordante

discotheque ['dɪskətek] *n* discoteca *f*

discount **1** *n* ['dɪskaʊnt] descuento *m*
2 *vt* [dɪs'kaʊnt] (**a**) *(price)* rebajar (**b**) *(view, suggestion)* descartar

discourage [dɪs'kʌrɪdʒ] *vt* *(dishearten)* desanimar; *(advances)* rechazar

discouraging [dɪs'kʌrɪdʒɪŋ] *adj* desalentador(a)

discover [dɪ'skʌvə(r)] *vt* descubrir; *(missing person, object)* encontrar

discovery [dɪ'skʌvərɪ] *n* descubrimiento *m*

discredit [dɪs'kredɪt] **1** *n* descrédito *m*
2 *vt* *(person, régime)* desacreditar; *(theory)* poner en duda

discreet [dɪ'skriːt] *adj* discreto(a); *(distance, silence)* prudente; *(hat, house)* modesto(a)

discrepancy [dɪ'skrepənsɪ] *n* diferencia *f*

discretion [dɪ'skreʃən] *n* discreción *f*; *(prudence)* prudencia *f*; **at the d. of ...** a juicio de ...

discriminate [dɪ'skrɪmɪneɪt] *vi* discriminar (**between** entre); **to d. against sth/sb** discriminar algo/a algn

discriminating [dɪ'skrɪmɪneɪtɪŋ] *adj* *(person)* entendido(a); *(taste)* refinado(a)

discrimination [dɪskrɪmɪ'neɪʃən] *n* (**a**) *(bias)* discriminación *f* (**b**) *(distinction)* diferenciación *f*

discus ['dɪskəs] *n* disco *m* *(para lanzamientos)*

discuss [dɪ'skʌs] *vt* discutir; *(in writing)* tratar de

discussion [dɪ'skʌʃən] *n* discusión *f*; *Comput* **d. group** foro *m* (de discusión)

disdain [dɪs'deɪn] *Fml* **1** *n* desdén *m*
2 *vt* desdeñar

disdainful [dɪs'deɪnfʊl] *adj Fml* desdeñoso(a)

disease [dɪ'ziːz] *n* enfermedad *f*; *Fig* mal *m*

disembark [dɪsɪm'bɑːk] *vt & vi* desembarcar

disenchanted [dɪsɪn'tʃɑːntɪd] *adj* desencantado(a), desilusionado(a)

disengage [dɪsɪn'geɪdʒ] *vt* soltar; *Aut* **to d. the clutch** soltar el embrague, desembragar

disentangle [dɪsɪn'tæŋɡəl] *vt* desenredar

disfigure [dɪs'fɪɡə(r)] *vt* desfigurar

disgrace [dɪs'ɡreɪs] **1** *n* (**a**) *(disfavour)* desgracia *f*; **to be in d.** estar desacreditado(a); **to fall into d.** caer en desgracia (**b**) *(shame)* vergüenza *f*, escándalo *m*
2 *vt* deshonrar, desacreditar

disgraceful [dɪs'ɡreɪsfʊl] *adj* vergonzoso(a)

disgruntled [dɪs'ɡrʌntəld] *adj* contrariado(a), disgustado(a)

disguise [dɪs'ɡaɪz] **1** *n* disfraz *m*; **in d.** disfrazado(a)
2 *vt* (**a**) *(person)* disfrazar (**as** de) (**b**) *(feelings)* disimular

disgust [dɪs'ɡʌst] **1** *n* (**a**) *(loathing)* repugnancia *f*, asco *m* (**b**) *(strong disapproval)* indignación *f*
2 *vt* (**a**) *(revolt)* repugnar, dar asco a (**b**) *(offend)* indignar

> ✏ Note that the Spanish words **disgusto** and **disgustar** are false friends and are never a translation for the English word **disgust**. In Spanish **disgusto** means "annoyance, trouble" and **disgustar** means "to upset".

disgusting [dɪs'ɡʌstɪŋ] *adj* asqueroso(a), repugnante; *(behaviour, state of affairs)* intolerable

dish [dɪʃ] *n* *(for serving)* fuente *f*; *(course)* plato *m*; **to wash** *or* **do the dishes** fregar los platos

▸ **dish out** *vt sep Fam (food)* servir; *(books, advice)* repartir; **to d. it out (to sb)** *(criticize)* criticar (a algn)

▸ **dish up** *vt sep (meal)* servir

dishcloth ['dɪʃklɒθ] *n* *(for washing)* bayeta *f*; *(for drying)* paño *m* (de cocina), *CAm* secador *m*, *Méx* trapón *m*, *RP* repasador *m*

dishearten [dɪs'hɑːtən] *vt* desanimar

dishevelled, *US* **disheveled** [dɪ'ʃevəld] *adj* *(hair)* despeinado(a); *(appearance)* desaliñado(a)

dishonest [dɪs'ɒnɪst] *adj* *(person)* poco honrado(a); *(means)* fraudulento(a)

dishonesty [dɪs'ɒnɪstɪ] *n* *(of person)* falta *f* de honradez

dishonour, *US* **dishonor** [dɪs'ɒnə(r)] **1** *n* *Fml* deshonra *f*
2 *vt (name)* deshonrar

dishonourable, *US* **dishonorable** [dɪs'ɒnərəbəl] *adj* deshonroso(a)

dishtowel ['dɪʃtaʊəl] *n* paño *m* (de cocina), *CAm* secador *m*, *Méx* trapón *m*, *RP* repasador *m*

dishwasher ['dɪʃwɒʃə(r)] *n* lavaplatos *m inv*; *(person)* lavaplatos *mf inv*

disillusion [dɪsɪ'luːʒən] *vt* desilusionar

disincentive [dɪsɪn'sentɪv] *n* freno *m*

disinfect [dɪsɪn'fekt] *vt* desinfectar

disinfectant [dɪsɪn'fektənt] *n* desinfectante *m*

disinherit [dɪsɪn'herɪt] *vt* desheredar

disintegrate [dɪs'ɪntɪɡreɪt] *vi* desintegrarse

disintegration [dɪsɪntɪ'ɡreɪʃən] *n* desintegración *f*

disinterested [dɪs'ɪntrɪstɪd] *adj* desinteresado(a)

disjointed [dɪs'dʒɔɪntɪd] *adj* inconexo(a)

disk [dɪsk] *n US* disco *m*; *Comput* disquete *m*; **on d.** en disco; **d. drive** disquetera *f*, disketera *f*

diskette [dɪs'ket] *n Comput* disquete *m*

dislike [dɪs'laɪk] **1** *n* antipatía *f*, aversión *f* (**of a** *or* hacia)
2 *vt* tener antipatía *or* aversión a *or* hacia
dislocate ['dɪsləkeɪt] *vt (joint)* dislocar
dislodge [dɪs'lɒdʒ] *vt* sacar
disloyal [dɪs'lɔɪəl] *adj* desleal
dismal ['dɪzməl] *adj* (**a**) *(prospect)* sombrío(a); *(place, weather)* deprimente; *(person)* triste (**b**) *(failure)* horroroso(a)
dismantle [dɪs'mæntəl] *vt* desmontar
dismay [dɪs'meɪ] **1** *n* consternación *f*
2 *vt* consternar
dismiss [dɪs'mɪs] *vt* (**a**) *(idea)* descartar (**b**) *(employee)* despedir; *(official)* destituir (**c**) **to d. sb** *(from room, presence)* dar permiso a algn para retirarse (**d**) *Jur (case)* sobreseer
dismissal [dɪs'mɪsəl] *n* (**a**) *(of employee)* despido *m*; *(of official)* destitución *f* (**b**) *Jur (of case)* sobreseimiento *m*
dismount [dɪs'maʊnt] *vi Fml* apearse (**from** de)
disobedience [dɪsə'biːdɪəns] *n* desobediencia *f*
disobedient [dɪsə'biːdɪənt] *adj* desobediente
disobey [dɪsə'beɪ] *vt & vi* desobedecer; *(law)* violar
disorder [dɪs'ɔːdə(r)] *n* (**a**) *(untidiness)* desorden *m* (**b**) *(riot)* disturbio *m* (**c**) *(of organ, mind)* trastorno *m*; *(of speech)* defecto *m*
disorderly [dɪs'ɔːdəlɪ] *adj* (**a**) *(untidy)* desordenado(a) (**b**) *(meeting)* alborotado(a); *(conduct)* escandaloso(a)
disorganized [dɪs'ɔːɡənaɪzd] *adj* desorganizado(a)
disorient [dɪs'ɔːrɪənt], **disorientate** [dɪs'ɔːrɪenteɪt] *vt* desorientar
disown [dɪs'əʊn] *vt* desconocer
disparaging [dɪ'spærɪdʒɪŋ] *adj* despectivo(a)
disparity [dɪ'spærɪtɪ] *n Fml* disparidad *f*
dispassionate [dɪs'pæʃənɪt] *adj* desapasionado(a)
dispatch [dɪ'spætʃ] **1** *n* (**a**) *(official message)* despacho *m*; *(journalist's report)* reportaje *m*; *(military message)* parte *m* (**b**) *(of mail)* envío *m*; *(of goods)* consignación *f*
2 *vt* (**a**) *(mail)* enviar; *(goods)* expedir (**b**) *Fam (food)* zamparse; *(job)* despachar
dispel [dɪ'spel] *vt* disipar
dispensary [dɪ'spensərɪ] *n* dispensario *m*
dispense [dɪ'spens] *vt (supplies)* repartir; *(justice)* administrar
▸ **dispense with** *vt insep (do without)* prescindir de

dispenser [dɪ'spensə(r)] *n* máquina expendedora; **cash d.** cajero automático; **soap d.** dosificador *m* de jabón
dispensing chemist [dɪspensɪŋ'kemɪst] *n Br* farmacéutico(a) *m,f*
dispersal [dɪ'spɜːsəl] *n* dispersión *f*
disperse [dɪ'spɜːs] **1** *vt* dispersar
2 *vi* dispersarse; *(fog)* disiparse
dispirited [dɪ'spɪrɪtɪd] *adj* abatido(a)
displace [dɪs'pleɪs] *vt* (**a**) *(shift)* desplazar; **displaced person** desplazado(a) *m,f* (**b**) *(supplant)* sustituir
display [dɪ'spleɪ] **1** *n* (**a**) *(exhibition)* exposición *f*; *Comput* visualización *f*; *(of feelings, skills)* demostración *f*; *(of force)* despliegue *m*; **d. window** escaparate *m*, *Am* vidriera *f*, *Chile, Col, Méx* vitrina *f*; **military d.** desfile *m* militar
2 *vt* (**a**) *(on sign, screen)* mostrar; *(goods)* exponer; *Comput* visualizar (**b**) *(feelings)* manifestar
displease [dɪs'pliːz] *vt* disgustar; *(offend)* ofender
displeasure [dɪs'pleʒə(r)] *n* disgusto *m*
disposable [dɪ'spəʊzəbəl] *adj* (**a**) *(throwaway)* desechable (**b**) *(available)* disponible
disposal [dɪ'spəʊzəl] *n* (**a**) *(of rubbish)* eliminación *f* (**b**) **at my d.** *(available)* a mi disposición
dispose [dɪ'spəʊz] **1** *vi* **to d. of** *(remove)* eliminar; *(rubbish)* tirar; *(unwanted object)* deshacerse de; *(matter)* resolver; *(sell)* vender; *(property)* traspasar
2 *vt Fml (arrange)* disponer
disposed [dɪ'spəʊzd] *adj (inclined)* dispuesto(a)
disposition [dɪspə'zɪʃən] *n* (**a**) *(temperament)* genio *m* (**b**) *Fml (arrangement)* disposición *f*
dispossess [dɪspə'zes] *vt* desposeer (**of** de)
disproportionate [dɪsprə'pɔːʃənɪt] *adj* desproporcionado(a) (**to a**)
disprove [dɪs'pruːv] *vt* refutar
dispute **1** *n* ['dɪspjuːt] *(disagreement)* discusión *f*; *(quarrel)* disputa *f*; **industrial d.** conflicto *m* laboral
2 *vt* [dɪ'spjuːt] *(claim)* refutar; *(territory)* disputar; *(matter)* discutir
3 *vi* discutir (**about** *or* **over** de *or* sobre)
disqualify [dɪs'kwɒlɪfaɪ] *vt* (**a**) *Sport* descalificar (**b**) *(make ineligible)* incapacitar
disquiet [dɪs'kwaɪət] *n* preocupación *f*, inquietud *f*
disregard [dɪsrɪ'ɡɑːd] **1** *n* indiferencia *f*; *(for safety)* despreocupación *f*
2 *vt* descuidar; *(ignore)* ignorar

disrepair [dɪsrɪ'peə(r)] n mal estado m; **in (a state of) d.** en mal estado; **to fall into d.** deteriorarse

disreputable [dɪs'repjʊtəbəl] adj (person, area) de mala fama; (behaviour) vergonzoso(a)

disrepute [dɪsrɪ'pju:t] n mala fama, oprobio m

disrespectful [dɪsrɪ'spektfʊl] adj irrespetuoso(a)

disrupt [dɪs'rʌpt] vt (meeting, traffic) interrumpir; (schedule etc) desbaratar

disruption [dɪs'rʌpʃən] n (of meeting, traffic) interrupción f; (of schedule etc) desbaratamiento m

disruptive [dɪs'rʌptɪv] adj **to be d.** ocasionar trastornos

dissatisfaction [dɪssætɪs'fækʃən] n descontento m, insatisfacción f

dissatisfied [dɪs'sætɪsfaɪd] adj descontento(a)

dissect [dɪ'sekt, daɪ'sekt] vt disecar

disseminate [dɪ'semɪneɪt] vt Fml diseminar, difundir

dissent [dɪ'sent] **1** n disentimiento m **2** vi disentir

dissertation [dɪsə'teɪʃən] n Univ Br (for higher degree) tesina f; US (doctoral) tesis f

disservice [dɪs'sɜ:vɪs] n perjuicio m; **to do sth/sb a d.** perjudicar algo/a algn

dissident ['dɪsɪdənt] adj & n disidente (mf)

dissimilar [dɪ'sɪmɪlə(r)] adj distinto(a)

dissipate ['dɪsɪpeɪt] **1** vt (fears, doubts) disipar; (fortune, one's energy) derrochar **2** vi (mist, doubts) disiparse

dissociate [dɪ'səʊʃɪeɪt] vt **to d. oneself (from)** desmarcarse (de)

dissolute ['dɪsəlu:t] adj disoluto(a)

dissolution [dɪsə'lu:ʃən] n disolución f; (of agreement) rescisión f

dissolve [dɪ'zɒlv] **1** vt disolver **2** vi disolverse

dissuade [dɪ'sweɪd] vt disuadir (**from** de)

distance ['dɪstəns] **1** n distancia f; **in the d.** a lo lejos; Fam **to stay the d.** completar la prueba **2** vt **to d. oneself (from)** distanciarse (de)

distant ['dɪstənt] adj (a) (place, time) lejano(a); (look) distraído(a) (b) (aloof) distante, frío(a)

distaste [dɪs'teɪst] n aversión f

distasteful [dɪs'teɪstfʊl] adj desagradable

distend [dɪ'stend] Fml **1** vt dilatar **2** vi dilatarse

distil, US **distill** [dɪ'stɪl] vt destilar

distillery [dɪ'stɪlərɪ] n destilería f

distinct [dɪ'stɪŋkt] adj (a) (different) diferente; **as d. from** a diferencia de (b) (smell, change) marcado(a); (idea, intention) claro(a)

distinction [dɪ'stɪŋkʃən] n (a) (difference) diferencia f (b) (excellence) distinción f (c) Educ sobresaliente m

distinctive [dɪ'stɪŋktɪv] adj distintivo(a)

distinctly [dɪs'tɪŋktlɪ] adv (a) (clearly) (speak, hear) claramente, con claridad (b) (decidedly) (better, easier) claramente; (ill-mannered, stupid) verdaderamente

distinguish [dɪ'stɪŋgwɪʃ] vt distinguir

distinguished [dɪ'stɪŋgwɪʃt] adj distinguido(a)

distinguishing [dɪ'stɪŋgwɪʃɪŋ] adj distintivo(a), característico(a)

distort [dɪ'stɔ:t] vt (misrepresent) deformar; (words) tergiversar

distortion [dɪ'stɔ:ʃən] n deformación f; (of sound, image) distorsión f

distract [dɪ'strækt] vt distraer

distracted [dɪ'stræktɪd] adj distraído(a)

distraction [dɪ'strækʃən] n (interruption) distracción f; (confusion) confusión f; **to drive sb to d.** sacar a algn de quicio

distraught [dɪ'strɔ:t] adj (anguished) afligido(a)

distress [dɪ'stres] **1** n (mental) angustia f; (physical) dolor m; **d. signal** señal f de socorro **2** vt (upset) apenar

distressing [dɪ'stresɪŋ] adj penoso(a)

distribute [dɪ'strɪbju:t] vt distribuir, repartir

distribution [dɪstrɪ'bju:ʃən] n distribución f

distributor [dɪ'strɪbjʊtə(r)] n (a) Com distribuidor(a) m,f (b) Aut distribuidor m, Esp delco® m

district ['dɪstrɪkt] n (of country) región f; (of town) barrio m; US **d. attorney** fiscal m; **d. council** corporación f local; Br **d. nurse** practicante mf

distrust [dɪs'trʌst] **1** n recelo m **2** vt desconfiar de

disturb [dɪ'stɜ:b] vt (a) (inconvenience) molestar (b) (silence) romper; (sleep) interrumpir (c) (worry) perturbar (d) (papers) desordenar

disturbance [dɪ'stɜ:bəns] n (a) (of routine) alteración f (b) (commotion) disturbio m, alboroto m

disturbed [dɪ'stɜ:bd] adj (mentally) inestable

disturbing [dɪ'stɜːbɪŋ] *adj* inquietante

disuse [dɪs'juːs] *n* desuso *m*

disused [dɪs'juːzd] *adj* abandonado(a)

ditch [dɪtʃ] **1** *n* zanja *f*; *(at roadside)* cuneta *f*; *(for irrigation)* acequia *f*
   2 *vt Fam (plan, friend)* abandonar

dither ['dɪðə(r)] *vi Br Fam* vacilar, titubear

ditto ['dɪtəʊ] *adv* ídem, lo mismo

dive [daɪv] **1** *n* (a) *(into water)* salto *m* de cabeza; *(of submarine)* inmersión *f*; *(of plane) Esp* picado *m, Am* picada *f*; *Sport* salto (b) *Fam (bar)* antro *m*
   2 *vi* (a) *(from poolside, diving board)* tirarse de cabeza; *(submarine)* sumergirse; *(plane) Esp* picado *m* *or Am* picada; *Sport* saltar (b) *(move quickly)* **he dived for the phone** se precipitó hacia el teléfono

diver ['daɪvə(r)] *n (person)* buceador(a) *m,f; (professional)* buzo *m; Sport* saltador(a) *m,f*

diverge [daɪ'vɜːdʒ] *vi* divergir

diverse [daɪ'vɜːs] *adj (varied)* diverso(a), variado(a); *(different)* distinto(a), diferente

diversify [daɪ'vɜːsɪfaɪ] **1** *vt* diversificar
   2 *vi (of company)* diversificarse

diversion [daɪ'vɜːʃən] *n* (a) *(distraction)* distracción *f* (b) *Br (detour)* desvío *m*

diversity [daɪ'vɜːsɪtɪ] *n* diversidad *f*

divert [daɪ'vɜːt] *vt* desviar

divide [dɪ'vaɪd] **1** *vt* dividir
   2 *vi (road, stream)* bifurcarse
   3 *n* división *f*, diferencia *f*

dividend ['dɪvɪdend] *n Fin* dividendo *m; Fig* beneficio *m*

divine [dɪ'vaɪn] *adj* divino(a)

diving board ['daɪvɪŋbɔːd] *n* trampolín *m*

divinity [dɪ'vɪnɪtɪ] *n* (a) *(divine nature, god)* divinidad *f* (b) *(subject)* teología *f*

division [dɪ'vɪʒən] *n* (a) *(separation, in maths)* división *f* (b) *(distribution)* reparto *m* (c) *(of organization)* división *f*

divorce [dɪ'vɔːs] **1** *n* divorcio *m*
   2 *vt* **she divorced him, she got divorced from him** se divorció de él
   3 *vi* divorciarse

divorcee [dɪvɔː'siː] *n* divorciado(a) *m,f*

divorcée [dɪvɔː'seɪ] *n* divorciada *f*

divulge [daɪ'vʌldʒ] *vt Fml* divulgar, revelar

DIY [diːaɪ'waɪ] *n Br (abbr* **do-it-yourself**) bricolaje *m*

dizziness ['dɪzɪnɪs] *n* vértigo *m*

dizzy ['dɪzɪ] *adj* (**dizzier, dizziest**) (a) *(person) (unwell)* mareado(a) (b) *(height, pace)* vertiginoso(a)

DJ ['diːdʒeɪ] *n Fam (abbr* **disc jockey**) pinchadiscos *mf inv,* disc-jockey *mf*

DNA [diːen'eɪ] *n (abbr* **deoxyribonucleic acid**) ADN *m*

do [duː, *unstressed* dʊ, də] **1** *v aux*

En el inglés hablado, y en el escrito en estilo coloquial, las formas negativas **do not, does not** y **did not** se transforman en **don't, doesn't** y **didn't**.

(3rd person sing pres **does***; pt* **did***; pp* **done***)* (a) *(in negatives and questions) (not translated in Spanish)* **do you want some coffee?** ¿quieres café?; **do you drive?** ¿tienes carnet de conducir?; **don't you want to come?** ¿no quieres venir?; **he doesn't smoke** no fuma
   (b) *(emphatic) (not translated in Spanish)* **DO come with us!** ¡ánimo, vente con nosotros!; **I DO like your bag** me encanta tu bolso
   (c) *(substituting main verb in sentence) (not translated in Spanish)* **neither/so do I** yo tampoco/también; **I'll go if you do** si vas tú, voy yo; **I think it's dear, but he doesn't** a mí me parece caro pero a él no; **who went? – I did** ¿quién asistió? – yo
   (d) *(in question tags)* **he refused, didn't he?** dijo que no, ¿verdad?; **I don't like it, do you?** a mí no me gusta, ¿y a ti?
   2 *vt* hacer; *(task)* realizar; *(duty)* cumplir con; **to do one's best** hacer todo lo posible; **to do sth again** volver a hacer algo; **to do sth for sb** hacer algo por algn; **to do the cooking/cleaning** cocinar/limpiar; **what can I do for you?** ¿en qué puedo servirle?; **what do you do (for a living)?** ¿a qué te dedicas?; *Fam* **he's done it!** ¡lo ha conseguido!

Do, unido a muchos nombres, expresa actividades, como **to do the gardening, to do the ironing,** *etc.* En este diccionario, estas estructuras se encuentran bajo los nombres respectivos.

---

3 *vi* (a) *(act)* hacer; **do as I tell you** haz lo que te digo; **you did right** hiciste bien (b) **he did badly in the exams** los exámenes le salieron mal; **how are you doing?** ¿qué tal?; **how do you do?** *(greeting)* ¿cómo está usted?; *(answer)* mucho gusto; **to do well** *(person)* tener éxito; *(business)* ir bien (c) **£5 will do** *(suffice)* con 5 libras será suficiente; *Fam* **that will do!** ¡basta ya! (d) **this cushion will do as a pillow** *(be suitable)* este cojín servirá de almohada; **this won't do** esto no puede ser
   4 *n Br Fam (party)* fiesta *f; (event)* ceremonia *f*

▶**do away with** *vt insep* (a) *(abolish)* abolir; *(discard)* deshacerse de (b) *(kill)* asesinar

▶**do down** *vt sep Br (criticize)* desacreditar, menospreciar

▶**do for** *vt insep Fam (destroy, ruin)* arruinar; *Fig* **I'm done for if I don't finish this** estoy perdido(a) si no acabo esto

▶**do in** *vt sep Fam* (a) *(kill)* cargarse (b) *esp Br* **I'm done in** *(exhausted)* estoy hecho(a) polvo

▶**do over** *vt sep Fam* (a) *US (repeat)* repetir (b) *Br (thrash)* dar una paliza a

▶**do up** *vt sep* (a) *(wrap)* envolver (b) *(belt etc)* abrochar; *(laces)* atar (c) *(dress up)* arreglar (d) *Fam (redecorate)* renovar

▶**do with** *vt insep* (a) **I could do with a rest** *(need)* un descanso no me vendría nada mal (b) **to have** *or* **be to do with** *(concern)* tener que ver con

▶**do without** *vt insep* pasar sin, prescindir de

docile ['dəʊsaɪl] *adj* dócil; *(animal)* manso(a)

dock¹ [dɒk] **1** *n Naut* **the docks** el muelle
2 *vi* (a) *(ship)* atracar (b) *(spacecraft)* acoplarse

dock² [dɒk] *vt (reduce)* descontar

dock³ [dɒk] *n Jur* banquillo *m* (de los acusados)

docker ['dɒkə(r)] *n* estibador *m*

dockland ['dɒklænd] *n* zona *f* del puerto

dockyard ['dɒkjɑːd] *n* astillero *m*

doctor ['dɒktə(r)] **1** *n* (a) *Med* médico(a) *m,f* (b) *Univ* doctor(a) *m,f*; **D. of Law** doctor(a) en derecho
2 *vt Pej (figures)* falsificar; *(text)* arreglar; *(drink etc)* adulterar

doctorate ['dɒktərɪt] *n* doctorado *m*

doctrine ['dɒktrɪn] *n* doctrina *f*

document 1 *n* ['dɒkjʊmənt] documento *m*; **documents** *(of vehicle, cargo)* documentación *f*
2 *vt* ['dɒkjʊment] documentar

documentary [dɒkjʊ'mentərɪ] *adj & n* documental *(m)*

dodge [dɒdʒ] **1** *vt* (a) *(blow)* esquivar; *(pursuer)* despistar; *Fig* eludir (b) *Fam* **to d. one's taxes** engañar a Hacienda
2 *vi (move aside)* echarse a un lado
3 *n* (a) *(movement)* regate *m* (b) *Fam (trick)* truco *m*

Dodgems® ['dɒdʒəmz] *npl Br* autos *mpl* or coches *mpl* de choque, *Méx* carritos *mpl* chocones, *CSur* autitos *mpl* chocadores

dodgy ['dɒdʒɪ] *adj* (**dodgier, dodgiest**) *Br Fam (risky)* peligroso(a), *Esp* chungo; *(untrustworthy)* dudoso; **a d. business**

deal un chanchullo; **the engine sounds a bit d.** el motor no suena nada bien

doe [dəʊ] *n (of deer)* gama *f*; *(of rabbit)* coneja *f*

does [dʌz] *3rd person sing pres of* **do**

doesn't ['dʌzənt] = **does not**

dog [dɒg] **1** *n* perro(a) *m,f*
2 *vt* acosar; **to d. sb's footsteps** seguir los pasos de algn

dog-eared ['dɒgɪəd] *adj (book)* con los bordes de las páginas doblados; *(shabby)* sobado(a)

dogged ['dɒgɪd] *adj* obstinado(a), tenaz

doghouse ['dɒghaʊs] *n US Fam* perrera *f*; *Fig* **to be in the d.** estar castigado(a)

dogma ['dɒgmə] *n* dogma *m*

dogmatic [dɒg'mætɪk] *adj* dogmático(a)

dogsbody ['dɒgzbɒdɪ] *n Br Fam (drudge)* burro *m* de carga

doh [dəʊ] *n Mus* do *m*

doing ['duːɪŋ] *n* (a) *(action)* obra *f*; **it was none of my d.** yo no tuve nada que ver; *Fig* **it took some d.** costó trabajo hacerlo (b) **doings** *(activities)* actividades *fpl*

do-it-yourself [duːɪtjə'self] *n* bricolaje *m*

doldrums ['dɒldrəmz] *npl Fam Fig* **to be in the d.** *(person)* estar con la moral baja, *Am* estar con el ánimo por el piso; *(trade)* estar estancado(a)

dole [dəʊl] *Fam* **1** *n Br Fam* subsidio *m* de desempleo, *Esp* paro *m*; **to be on the d.** cobrar el subsidio de desempleo *or Esp* el paro; **to go on the d.** apuntarse para cobrar el desempleo, *Esp* apuntarse al paro
2 *vt* **to d. (out)** repartir

doleful ['dəʊlfʊl] *adj* triste, afligido(a)

doll [dɒl] **1** *n* (a) *(toy)* muñeca *f* (b) *US Fam (girl)* muñeca *f*
2 *vt Fam* **to d. oneself up** ponerse guapa

dollar ['dɒlə(r)] *n* dólar *m*

dolphin ['dɒlfɪn] *n* delfín *m*

domain [də'meɪn] *n* (a) *(sphere)* campo *m*, esfera *f*; **that's not my d.** no es de mi competencia (b) *(territory)* dominio *m* (c) *Comput* dominio *m*; **d. name** nombre *m* de dominio

dome [dəʊm] *n (roof)* cúpula *f*; *(ceiling)* bóveda *f*

domestic [də'mestɪk] *adj* (a) *(appliance, pet)* doméstico(a); *Br* **d. science** economía doméstica; **d. violence** violencia doméstica (b) *(home-loving)* casero(a) (c) *(flight, news)* nacional; *(trade, policy)* interior

domesticate [də'mestɪkeɪt] *vt (make home-loving)* volver hogareño(a) *or* casero(a)

domicile ['dɒmɪsaɪl] n domicilio m

dominant ['dɒmɪnənt] adj dominante

dominate ['dɒmɪneɪt] vt & vi dominar

domineering [dɒmɪ'nɪərɪŋ] adj dominante

Dominican [də'mɪnɪkən] adj & n (of Dominica) dominicano(a) (m,f); **D. Republic** República Dominicana

dominion [də'mɪnjən] n dominio m

domino ['dɒmɪnəʊ] n (pl dominoes) (piece) ficha f de dominó; **dominoes** (game) dominó m

don [dɒn] n Br Univ profesor(a) m,f

donate [dəʊ'neɪt] vt donar

donation [dəʊ'neɪʃən] n donativo m

done [dʌn] **1** adj (a) (finished) terminado(a); **it's over and d. with** se acabó (b) Fam (tired) rendido(a) (c) (meat) hecho(a); (vegetables) cocido(a)
2 pp of **do**

donkey ['dɒŋkɪ] n burro(a) m,f

donor ['dəʊnə(r)] n donante m

don't [dəʊnt] = **do not**

donut ['dəʊnʌt] n US dónut m

doodle ['duːdəl] vi Fam (write) garabatear; (draw) hacer dibujos

doom [duːm] **1** n (fate) destino (funesto); (ruin) perdición f; (death) muerte f
2 **to be doomed** (about to die) ir hacia una muerte segura; (plan, marriage) estar condenado(a) al fracaso

doomsday ['duːmzdeɪ] n día m del juicio final

door [dɔː(r)] n puerta f; **front/back d.** puerta principal/trasera; Fig **behind closed doors** a puerta cerrada; **d. handle** manilla f (de la puerta); **d. knocker** picaporte m; **next d. (to)** (en) la casa de al lado (de)

doorbell ['dɔːbel] n timbre m (de la puerta)

doorknob ['dɔːnɒb] n pomo m

doorman ['dɔːmən] n portero m

doormat ['dɔːmæt] n felpudo m, esterilla f

doorstep ['dɔːstep] n peldaño m; Fig **on one's d.** a la vuelta de la esquina

door-to-door ['dɔːtə'dɔː(r)] adj a domicilio

doorway ['dɔːweɪ] n portal m, entrada f

dope [dəʊp] **1** n (a) Fam (drug) chocolate m (b) Fam (person) tonto(a) mf, Am zonzo(a) m,f
2 vt (food, drink) adulterar con drogas; Sport dopar

dop(e)y ['dəʊpɪ] adj (dopier, dopiest) Fam (stupid) tonto(a), bobo(a), Am sonso(a), Am zonzo(a)

dork [dɔːk] n US Fam petardo(a) m,f

dormant ['dɔːmənt] adj inactivo(a); Fig (rivalry) latente

dormitory ['dɔːmɪtərɪ] n (a) (in school) dormitorio m (b) US (in university) colegio m mayor

dosage ['dəʊsɪdʒ] n Fml (amount) dosis f inv

dose [dəʊs] **1** n dosis f inv
2 vt (patient) medicar

doss [dɒs] vi Br Fam sobar

dosshouse ['dɒshaʊs] n Br Fam pensión f de mala muerte

dossier ['dɒsɪeɪ] n expediente m

dot [dɒt] **1** n punto m; **on the d.** en punto; Comput **d. matrix printer** impresora f matricial or de agujas
2 vt (a) Fam **to d. one's i's and cross one's t's** poner los puntos sobre las íes (b) (scatter) esparcir, salpicar

dotcom ['dɒtkɒm] n (company) punto-com f

dote [dəʊt] vi **to d. on sb** chochear con algn

double ['dʌbəl] **1** adj doble; **it's d. the price** cuesta dos veces más; **d. bass** contrabajo m; **d. bed** cama f de matrimonio; Br **d. cream** Esp nata f para montar, Am crema líquida enriquecida, RP crema f doble
2 adv doble; **folded d.** doblado(a) por la mitad; **to earn d.** ganar el doble
3 n vivo retrato m; Cin & Th doble m
4 vt doblar; Fig (efforts) redoblar
5 vi (a) (increase) doblarse (b) **to d. as** (serve) hacer las veces de

▸ **double back** vi **to d. back on one's tracks** volver sobre sus pasos

▸ **double up 1** vt sep (bend) doblar
2 vi (a) (bend) doblarse (b) (share room) compartir la habitación (**with** con)

double-barrelled ['dʌbəlbærəld] adj (a) (gun) de dos cañones (b) Br (surname) compuesto(a)

double-breasted ['dʌbəlbrestɪd] adj cruzado(a)

double-check [dʌbəl'tʃek] vt & vi repasar dos veces

double-cross [dʌbəl'krɒs] Fam **1** vt engañar, traicionar
2 n engaño m, traición f

double-decker [dʌbəl'dekə(r)] n Br **d. (bus)** autobús m de dos pisos

double-edged ['dʌbəledʒd] adj de doble filo

double-glazing ['dʌbəl'gleɪzɪŋ] n doble acristalamiento m

doubt [daʊt] **1** n duda f; **beyond (all) d.** sin duda alguna; **no d.** sin duda; **there's no d. about it** no cabe la menor duda; **to be in**

d. about sth dudar algo; **to be open to d.** *(fact)* ser dudoso(a); *(outcome)* ser incierto(a)
2 *vt* (**a**) *(distrust)* desconfiar de (**b**) *(not be sure of)* dudar; **I d. if** *or* **whether he'll come** dudo que venga

doubtful ['daʊtfʊl] *adj* (**a**) *(future)* dudoso(a), *(look)* dubitativo(a); **I'm a bit d. about it** no me convence del todo; **it's d. whether …** no se sabe seguro si … (**b**) *(questionable)* sospechoso(a)

doubtless ['daʊtlɪs] *adv* sin duda, seguramente

dough [dəʊ] *n* (**a**) *(for bread)* masa *f* (**b**) *Fam (money)* Esp pasta *f*, Esp, RP guita *f*, Am plata *f*, Méx lana *f*

doughnut ['dəʊnʌt] *n* rosquilla *f*, dónut® *m*

douse [daʊs] *vt* (**a**) *(soak)* mojar (**b**) *(extinguish)* apagar

dove [dʌv] *n* paloma *f*

dovetail ['dʌvteɪl] *vt Fig (plans)* sincronizar

dowdy ['daʊdɪ] *adj* (**dowdier, dowdiest**) poco elegante

down [daʊn] **1** *prep* (**a**) *(to or at a lower level)* **d. the river** río abajo; **to go d. the road** bajar la calle (**b**) *(along)* por
2 *adv* (**a**) *(to lower level)* (hacia) abajo; *(to floor)* al suelo; *(to ground)* a tierra; **sales are d. by 5 percent** las ventas han bajado un 5 por ciento; **to fall d.** caerse (**b**) *(at lower level)* abajo; **d. there** allí abajo; *Fam Fig* **to feel d.** estar deprimido(a); *Br Fam* **d. under** en/a Australia y Nueva Zelanda
3 *adj (payment)* al contado; *(on property)* de entrada
4 *vt Fam (drink)* tomarse de un trago; *(food)* zamparse

down-and-out ['daʊnən'aʊt] **1** *adj* en las últimas
2 *n* vagabundo(a) *m,f*

downbeat ['daʊnbiːt] *adj Fam (gloomy)* deprimido(a)

downcast ['daʊnkɑːst] *adj* abatido(a)

downfall ['daʊnfɔːl] *n (of regime)* caída *f*; *(of person)* perdición *f*

downgrade ['daʊngreɪd] *vt* degradar

downhearted [daʊn'hɑːtɪd] *adj* desalentado(a)

downhill [daʊn'hɪl] **1** *adj (skiing)* de descenso; *Fam* **after the first exam, the rest were all d.** después del primer examen, los demás le fueron sobre ruedas
2 *adv* **to go d.** ir cuesta abajo; *Fig (standards)* deteriorarse

download ['daʊnləʊd] *vt Comput* bajar, descargar

down-market [daʊn'mɑːkɪt] **1** *adj* barato(a)
2 *adv* **to move d.** *(of company)* producir artículos más asequibles

downpour ['daʊnpɔː(r)] *n* chaparrón *m*

downright ['daʊnraɪt] *Fam* **1** *adj (blunt)* tajante; *(categorical)* categórico(a); **it's a d. lie** es una mentira y gorda
2 *adv (totally)* completamente

downsizing ['daʊnsaɪzɪŋ] *n Com* reajuste *m* de plantillas

downstairs 1 *adv* [daʊn'steəz] abajo; *(to ground floor)* a la planta baja; **to go d.** bajar la escalera
2 *adj* ['daʊnsteəz] *(on ground floor)* de la planta baja

downstream [daʊn'striːm] *adv* río abajo

down-to-earth [daʊntʊ'ɜːθ] *adj* realista

downtown [daʊn'taʊn] *adv US* en el centro (de la ciudad)

downturn ['daʊntɜːn] *n* baja *f*

downward ['daʊnwəd] **1** *adj (slope)* descendente; *(look)* hacia abajo; *Fin (tendency)* a la baja
2 *adv* = **downwards**

downwards ['daʊnwədz] *adv* hacia abajo

dowry ['daʊərɪ] *n* dote *f*

doz *(abbr* **dozen**) docena *f*

doze [dəʊz] **1** *vi* dormitar
2 *n* cabezada *f*; **to have a d.** echar una cabezada
▸ **doze off** *vi* quedarse dormido(a)

dozen ['dʌzən] *n* docena *f*; **half a d./a d. eggs** media docena/una docena de huevos; *Fam* **dozens of** un montón de

Dr *(abbr* **Doctor**) Dr., Dra.

drab [dræb] *adj* (**drabber, drabbest**) (**a**) *(ugly)* feo(a); *(dreary)* monótono(a), gris (**b**) *(colour)* pardo(a)

draft [drɑːft] **1** *n* (**a**) *(of letter, text)* borrador *m* (**b**) *US* servicio militar obligatorio (**c**) *US* = **draught**
2 *vt* (**a**) *(of letter, text)* hacer un borrador de (**b**) *US Mil* reclutar

draftsman ['drɑːftsmən] *n US* = **draughtsman**

drag [dræg] **1** *vt (pull)* arrastrar
2 *vi (trail)* arrastrarse
3 *n Fam (nuisance)* lata *f*
▸ **drag off** *vt sep* llevarse arrastrando
▸ **drag on** *vi (war, strike)* hacerse interminable
▸ **drag out** *vt sep (speech etc)* alargar

dragon ['drægən] *n* dragón *m*

dragonfly ['drægənflaɪ] *n* libélula *f*

drain [dreɪn] **1** *n* (**a**) *(for water)* desagüe *m*; *(for sewage)* alcantarilla *f* (**b**) *(grating)* sumidero *m* (**c**) *Fig* **the boys are a d. on her strength** los niños la dejan agotada
2 *vt* (**a**) *(marsh etc)* avenar; *(reservoir)* desecar (**b**) *(crockery)* escurrir (**c**) *(empty) (glass)* apurar; *Fig (capital etc)* agotar
3 *vi* (**a**) *(crockery)* escurrirse (**b**) **to d. (away)** *(liquid)* irse

drainage ['dreɪnɪdʒ] *n (of marsh)* drenaje *m*; *(of reservoir, building)* desagüe *m*; *(of town)* alcantarillado *m*

drainpipe ['dreɪnpaɪp] *n* tubo *m* de desagüe

dram [dræm] *n Fam* trago *m (de whisky)*

drama ['drɑːmə] *n* (**a**) *(play)* obra *f* de teatro; *Fig* drama *m* (**b**) *(subject)* teatro *m*

dramatic [drə'mætɪk] *adj* (**a**) *(change)* impresionante; *(moment)* emocionante (**b**) *Th* dramático(a), teatral

dramatist ['dræmətɪst] *n* dramaturgo(a) *m,f*

dramatization [dræmətaɪ'zeɪʃən] *n* adaptación *f* teatral

dramatize ['dræmətaɪz] *vt* (**a**) *(adapt)* hacer una adaptación teatral de (**b**) *(exaggerate)* dramatizar

drank [dræŋk] *pt of* **drink**

drape [dreɪp] **1** *vt* **to d. sth over sth** colgar algo sobre algo; **draped with** cubierto(a) de
2 *n* (**a**) *(of fabric)* caída *f* (**b**) *US* cortina *f*

draper ['dreɪpə(r)] *n Br* pañero(a) *m,f*

drastic ['dræstɪk] *adj* (**a**) *(measures)* drástico(a), severo(a) (**b**) *(change)* radical

draught [drɑːft] *n* (**a**) *(of cold air)* corriente *f* (de aire) (**b**) *(of liquid)* trago *m*; **d. (beer)** cerveza *f* de barril (**c**) *Br* **draughts** *(game)* damas *fpl*

draughtboard ['drɑːftbɔːd] *n Br* tablero *m* de damas

draughtsman ['drɑːftsmən] *n* delineante *mf*

draw [drɔː] **1** *vt (pt* **drew***; pp* **drawn**) (**a**) *(picture)* dibujar; *(line)* trazar (**b**) *(pull)* tirar de; *(train, carriage)* arrastrar; *(curtains) (open)* descorrer; *(close)* correr; *(blinds)* bajar (**c**) *(extract)* sacar; *(salary)* cobrar; *(cheque)* librar (**d**) *(attract)* atraer; *(attention)* llamar (**e**) *Fig (strength)* sacar (**f**) *(comparison)* hacer; *(conclusion)* sacar
2 *vi* (**a**) *(sketch)* dibujar (**b**) *(move)* **the train drew into/out of the station** el tren entró en/salió de la estación; **to d. apart**

(**from**) separarse (de) (**c**) *Sport* **they drew two all** empataron a dos
3 *n* (**a**) *(raffle)* sorteo *m* (**b**) *Sport* empate *m* (**c**) *(attraction)* atracción *f*

▸ **draw in** *vi (days)* acortarse

▸ **draw on** *vt insep (savings)* recurrir a; *(experience)* aprovecharse de

▸ **draw out** *vt sep* (**a**) *(make long)* alargar (**b**) *(encourage to speak)* desatar la lengua a (**c**) *(from pocket, drawer etc)* sacar

▸ **draw up** *vt sep (contract)* preparar; *(plan)* esbozar

drawback ['drɔːbæk] *n* desventaja *f*, inconveniente *m*

drawbridge ['drɔːbrɪdʒ] *n* puente levadizo

drawer ['drɔːə(r)] *n* cajón *m*

drawing ['drɔːɪŋ] *n* dibujo *m*; *Br* **d. pin** *Esp* chincheta *f*, *Am* chinche *m*; *Fml* **d. room** sala *f* de estar

drawl [drɔːl] **1** *vi* hablar arrastrando las palabras
2 *n* voz cansina; *US* **a Southern d.** un acento sureño

drawn [drɔːn] **1** *adj (tired)* ojeroso(a)
2 *pp of* **draw**

dread [dred] **1** *vt* temer a, tener pavor a
2 *n* temor *m*

dreadful ['dredfʊl] *adj* (**a**) *(shocking)* espantoso(a) (**b**) *Fam (awful)* fatal; **how d.!** ¡qué horror!

dreadfully ['dredfʊlɪ] *adv Fam* terriblemente

dreadlocks ['dredlɒks] *npl* trenzas *fpl* rastafari

dream [driːm] **1** *n* sueño *m*; **it worked like a d.** salió a la perfección
2 *vt (pt & pp* **dreamed** *or* **dreamt**) soñar
3 *vi* soñar (**of** *or* **about** con)

dreamer ['driːmə(r)] *n* soñador(a) *m,f*

dreamt [dremt] *pt & pp of* **dream**

dreamy ['driːmɪ] *adj* (**dreamier, dreamiest**) *(absent-minded)* distraído(a); *(wonderful)* de ensueño

dreary ['drɪərɪ] *adj* (**drearier, dreariest**) (**a**) *(gloomy)* triste (**b**) *Fam (boring)* aburrido(a), pesado(a)

dredge [dredʒ] *vt & vi* dragar, rastrear

▸ **dredge up** *vt sep* (**a**) *(body)* sacar del agua (**b**) *Fam Fig* sacar a relucir

dregs [dregz] *npl* poso *m*

drench [drentʃ] *vt* empapar

dress [dres] **1** *n* (**a**) *(frock)* vestido *m* (**b**) *(clothing)* ropa *f*; **d. rehearsal** ensayo *m* general; **d. shirt** camisa *f* de etiqueta
2 *vt* (**a**) *(person)* vestir; **he was dressed in a grey suit** llevaba (puesto) un traje gris

(**b**) *(salad)* aderezar, *Esp* aliñar (**c**) *(wound)* vendar

3 *vi* vestirse

▸**dress up 1** *vi* (**a**) *(in disguise)* disfrazarse (**as de**) (**b**) *(in best clothes)* vestirse elegante

2 *vt sep Fig* disfrazar

dresser ['dresə(r)] *n* (**a**) *Br (in kitchen)* aparador *m* (**b**) *US (in bedroom)* cómoda *f* (**c**) *Th* ayudante *mf* de camerino

dressing ['dresɪŋ] *n* (**a**) *(bandage)* vendaje *m* (**b**) **(salad)** **d.** aliño *m* (**c**) **d. gown** bata *f*; **d. room** *Th* camerino *m*; *Sport* vestuario *m*; **d. table** tocador *m*

dressmaker ['dresmeɪkə(r)] *n* modista *mf*

dressy ['dresɪ] *adj* (**dressier, dressiest**) vistoso(a)

drew [druː] *pt of* **draw**

dribble ['drɪbəl] **1** *vi* (**a**) *(baby)* babear (**b**) *(liquid)* gotear

2 *vt Sport (ball)* driblar

3 *n (saliva)* saliva *f*; *(of water, blood)* gotas *fpl*

dried [draɪd] *adj (fruit)* seco(a); *(milk)* en polvo

drier ['draɪə(r)] *n* = **dryer**

drift [drɪft] **1** *vi* (**a**) *(boat)* ir a la deriva; *Fig (person)* ir sin rumbo, vagar; **they drifted away** se marcharon poco a poco (**b**) *(snow)* amontonarse

2 *n* (**a**) *(flow)* flujo *m* (**b**) *(of snow)* ventisquero *m*; *(of sand)* montón *m* (**c**) *Fig (meaning)* idea *f*

driftwood ['drɪftwʊd] *n* madera *f* flotante

drill [drɪl] **1** *n* (**a**) *(hand tool)* taladro *m*; *Min* barrena *f*; **dentist's d.** fresa *f*; **pneumatic d.** martillo neumático (**b**) *esp Mil* instrucción *f*

2 *vt* (**a**) *(wood etc)* taladrar (**b**) *(soldiers, children)* instruir

3 *vi (by hand)* taladrar; *(for oil, coal)* perforar, sondar

drink [drɪŋk] **1** *vt (pt* **drank**; *pp* **drunk**) beber

2 *vi* beber; **to have sth to d.** tomarse algo; **to d. to sth/sb** brindar por algo/algn

3 *n* bebida *f*; *(alcoholic)* copa *f*

drinker [drɪŋkə(r)] *n* bebedor(a) *m,f*

drinking ['drɪŋkɪŋ] *n* **d. water** agua *f* potable

drip [drɪp] **1** *n* (**a**) *(drop)* gota *f*; *(sound)* goteo *m* (**b**) *Med* gota a gota *m inv* (**c**) *Fam (weak person)* sosaina *mf*

2 *vi* gotear; **he was dripping with sweat** el sudor le caía a gotas

drip-dry ['drɪp'draɪ] *adj* que no necesita planchado

dripping ['drɪpɪŋ] *n Culin* pringue *f*

drive [draɪv] **1** *vt (pt* **drove**; *pp* **driven**) (**a**) *(vehicle)* conducir, *Am* manejar; *(person)* llevar (**b**) *(power)* impulsar (**c**) *(compel)* forzar, obligar; **to d. sb mad** volver loco(a) a algn; **to d. off** rechazar

2 *vi Aut* conducir, *Am* manejar

3 *n* (**a**) *(trip)* paseo *m* en coche *or Am* carro *or CSur* auto; **to go for a d.** dar una vuelta en coche *or Am* carro *or CSur* carro (**b**) *(to house)* camino *m* de entrada (**c**) *(campaign)* campaña *f* (**d**) *(energy)* energía *f*, vigor *m* (**e**) *Comput* unidad *f* de disco

drive-in ['draɪvɪn] *n US (cinema)* autocine *m*

drivel ['drɪvəl] *n Fam Esp* chorradas *fpl*, *CAm, Méx* babosadas *fpl*, *Chile* leseras *fpl*, *CSur, Perú, Ven* macanas *fpl*;

driven ['drɪvən] *pp of* **drive**

driver ['draɪvə(r)] *n (of car, bus)* conductor(a) *m,f*; *(of train)* maquinista *mf*, *Am* chofer *mf*; *(of lorry)* camionero(a) *m,f*; *(of racing car)* piloto *mf*; *US* **d.'s license** *Esp* carné *m or* permiso *m* de conducir, *Bol, Ecuad, Perú* brevet *m*, *Carib* licencia *f* de conducir, *Méx* licencia *f* de manejar *or* para manejar, *RP* permiso *m* de conductor

driveway ['draɪvweɪ] *n (to house)* camino *m* de entrada

driving ['draɪvɪŋ] **1** *n* conducción *f*, *Am* manejo *m*; *Br* **d. licence** *Esp* carné *m or* permiso *m* de conducir, *Bol, Ecuad, Perú* brevet *m*, *Carib* licencia *f* de conducir, *Méx* licencia *f* de manejar *or* para manejar, *RP* permiso *m* de conductor; **d. school** autoescuela *f*; **d. test** examen *m* de conducir

2 *adj* **d. force** fuerza *f* motriz

drizzle ['drɪzəl] **1** *n* llovizna *f*, *Andes, RP* garúa *f*

2 *vi* lloviznar, chispear, *Andes, RP* garuar

droll [drəʊl] *adj* gracioso(a)

dromedary ['drɒmədərɪ] *n* dromedario *m*

drone [drəʊn] *vi (bee etc)* zumbar

droop [druːp] *vi (flower)* marchitarse; *(eyelids)* caerse

drop [drɒp] **1** *n* (**a**) *(of liquid)* gota *f*; **eye drops** colirio *m* (**b**) *(descent)* desnivel *m* (**c**) *(in price)* bajada *f*; *(in temperature)* descenso *m*

2 *vt* (**a**) *(let fall)* dejar caer; *(lower)* bajar; *(reduce)* disminuir; **to d. a hint** soltar una indirecta (**b**) *(abandon) (subject, charge etc)* abandonar, dejar; *Sport* **he was dropped from the team** le echaron del equipo

3 *vi (object)* caerse; *(person)* tirarse;

(voice, price, temperature) bajar; *(wind)* amainar; *(speed)* disminuir

▸ **drop by, drop in** *vi Fam (visit)* pasarse (**at** por)

▸ **drop off 1** *vi Fam (fall asleep)* quedarse dormido(a)
2 *vt sep (deliver)* dejar

▸ **drop out** *vi (from college)* dejar los estudios; *(from society)* marginarse; *(from competition)* retirarse

▸ **drop round** *vi Fam =* **drop by**

dropout ['drɒpaʊt] *n Fam Pej* automarginado(a) *m,f*

dropper ['drɒpə(r)] *n* cuentagotas *m inv*

droppings ['drɒpɪŋz] *npl* excrementos *mpl*

drought [draʊt] *n* sequía *f*

drove [drəʊv] **1** *n (of cattle)* manada *f*
2 *pt of* **drive**

drown [draʊn] **1** *vt* **(a)** *(kill by drowning)* ahogar **(b)** *(flood)* inundar **(c)** *(make inaudible)* ahogar
2 *vi* ahogarse; **he (was) drowned** murió ahogado

drowsy ['draʊzɪ] *adj* **(drowsier, drowsiest)** soñoliento(a); **to feel d.** tener sueño

drudgery ['drʌdʒərɪ] *n* trabajo duro y pesado

drug [drʌg] **1** *n* **(a)** *(medicine)* medicamento *m* **(b)** *(narcotic)* droga *f*, estupefaciente *m*; **to be on drugs** drogarse; **d. addict** drogadicto(a) *m,f*; **d. addiction** drogadicción *f*; **d. squad** brigada *f* antidroga
2 *vt (person)* drogar; *(food, drink)* adulterar con drogas

druggist ['drʌgɪst] *n US* farmacéutico(a) *m,f*

drugstore ['drʌgstɔːr] *n US =* establecimiento donde se compran medicamentos, periódicos, etc

drum [drʌm] **1** *n* **(a)** *(musical instrument)* tambor *m*; **to play the drums** tocar la batería **(b)** *(container)* barril *m*; *(for oil)* bidón *m*
2 *vi Fig (with fingers)* tabalear
3 *vt Fig* **to d. sth into sb** enseñar algo a algn a machamartillo

▸ **drum up** *vt sep Fam* solicitar

drummer ['drʌmə(r)] *n (in band)* tambor *mf*; *(in pop group)* batería *mf*, *Am* baterista *mf*

drumstick ['drʌmstɪk] *n* **(a)** *Mus* baqueta *f* **(b)** *(chicken leg)* muslo *m*

drunk [drʌŋk] **1** *adj* borracho(a); **to get d.** emborracharse
2 *n* borracho(a) *m,f*
3 *pp of* **drink**

drunkard ['drʌŋkəd] *n* borracho(a) *m,f*

drunken ['drʌŋkən] *adj (person)* borracho(a); **d. brawl** trifulca *f* de borrachos

dry [draɪ] **1** *adj* **(drier, driest** *or* **dryer, dryest)** **(a)** *(weather, clothing, wine)* seco(a); *US* **d. goods store** mercería *f*, tienda *f* de confección **(b)** *(wry)* socarrón(ona)
2 *vt (pt & pp* **dried)** secar
3 *vi* **to d. (off)** secarse

dry-clean [draɪ'kliːn] *vt* limpiar *or* lavar en seco

dryer ['draɪə(r)] *n* secadora *f*

DTP [diːtiː'piː] *n Comput (abbr* **desktop publishing)** autoedición *f*

dual ['djʊəl] *adj* doble; *Br* **d. carriageway** *(road)* (tramo *m* de) autovía *f*

dub¹ [dʌb] *vt (subtitle)* doblar

dub² [dʌb] *vt* **(a)** *(give nickname to)* apodar **(b)** *(knight)* armar

dubious ['djuːbɪəs] *adj* **(a)** *(morals etc)* dudoso(a); *(compliment)* equívoco(a) **(b)** *(doubting)* indeciso(a)

Dublin ['dʌblɪn] *n* Dublín

duchess ['dʌtʃɪs] *n* duquesa *f*

duck¹ [dʌk] *n* pato(a) *m,f*; *Culin* pato *m*

duck² [dʌk] **1** *vt* **(a)** *(submerge)* dar una ahogadilla a **(b)** *(evade)* esquivar
2 *vi* **(a)** *(evade blow)* esquivar **(b)** *Fam* **to d. (out)** rajarse

duckling ['dʌklɪŋ] *n* patito *m*

duct [dʌkt] *n (for fuel etc)* conducto *m*; *Anat* canal *m*

dud [dʌd] *Fam* **1** *adj* **(a)** *(useless)* inútil; *(defective)* estropeado(a) **(b)** *(banknote)* falso(a); *(cheque)* sin fondos
2 *n (useless thing)* engañifa *f*; *(person)* desastre *m*

dude [duːd] *n US Fam (man)* tipo *m*, *Esp* tío *m*

due [djuː] *adj* **(a)** *(expected)* esperado(a); **the train is d. (to arrive) at ten** el tren debe llegar a las diez **(b)** *Fml (proper)* debido(a); **in d. course** a su debido tiempo **(c)** *(owing)* pagadero(a); **how much are you d.?** *(owed)* ¿cuánto te deben? **(d)** **to be d. to** *(caused by)* deberse a; **d. to** *(because of)* debido de

duel ['djuːəl] *n* duelo *m*

duet [djuː'et] *n* dúo *m*

duffel ['dʌfəl] *n* **d. bag** petate *m*; **d. coat** trenca *f*

dug [dʌg] *pt & pp of* **dig**

duke [djuːk] *n* duque *m*

dull [dʌl] **1** *adj* **(a)** *(boring)* pesado(a); *(place)* sin interés **(b)** *(light)* apagado(a); *(weather)* gris **(c)** *(sound, ache)* sordo(a) (**d**) *(not intelligent)* tonto(a), torpe, *Am* sonso(a)

2 *vt (pain)* aliviar

duly ['djuːlɪ] *adv Fml (properly)* debidamente; *(as expected)* como era de esperar; *(in due course)* a su debido tiempo

dumb [dʌm] **1** *adj* (**a**) *Med* mudo(a) (**b**) *Fam (stupid)* tonto(a)

2 *npl* **the d.** los mudos

dumbbell ['dʌmbel] *n Sport* pesa *f*

dumbfounded [dʌm'faʊndɪd] *adj* pasmado(a)

dumbstruck ['dʌmstrʌk] *adj* pasmado(a)

dummy ['dʌmɪ] *n* (**a**) *(sham)* imitación *f* (**b**) *(in shop window)* maniquí *m*; *(of ventriloquist)* muñeco *m* (**c**) *Br (for baby)* chupete *m*

dump [dʌmp] **1** *n* (**a**) *(tip)* vertedero *m*; *(for old cars)* cementerio *m* (de coches) (**b**) *Fam Pej (place)* estercolero *m*; *(town)* poblacho *m*; *(dwelling)* tugurio *m* (**c**) *Mil* depósito *m*

2 *vt* (**a**) *(rubbish)* verter; *(truck contents)* descargar (**b**) *(person)* dejar; *Com* inundar el mercado con (**c**) *Comput (transfer)* copiar de memoria interna

dumping ['dʌmpɪŋ] *n* vertido *m*

dumpling ['dʌmplɪŋ] *n Culin* = bola de masa hervida

Dumpster® ['dʌmpstə(r)] *n* contenedor *m* (de escombros)

dumpy ['dʌmpɪ] *adj* (**dumpier, dumpiest**) *Fam* rechoncho(a)

dunce [dʌns] *n Fam* tonto(a) *m,f*

dune [djuːn] *n* (**sand**) **d.** duna *f*

dung [dʌŋ] *n* estiércol *m*

dungarees [dʌŋgə'riːz] *npl* mono *m*

dungeon ['dʌndʒən] *n* calabozo *m*, mazmorra *f*

duo ['djuːəʊ] *n Mus* dúo *m*; *Fam* pareja *f*

dupe [djuːp] **1** *vt* engañar

2 *n* ingenuo(a) *m,f*

duplex ['djuːpleks] *n US (house)* casa adosada; **d. apartment** dúplex *m inv*

duplicate 1 *vt* ['djuːplɪkeɪt] (**a**) *(copy)* duplicar; *(film, tape)* reproducir (**b**) *(repeat)* repetir

2 *n* ['djuːplɪkɪt] duplicado *m*; **in d.** por duplicado

durable ['djʊərəbəl] *adj* duradero(a)

duration [djʊ'reɪʃən] *n Fml* duración *f*

duress [djʊ'res] *n Fml* coacción *f*

---

during ['djʊərɪŋ] *prep* durante

dusk [dʌsk] *n Fml* crepúsculo *m*; **at d.** al anochecer

dust [dʌst] **1** *n* polvo *m*; **d. cloud** polvareda *f*; **d. jacket** sobrecubierta *f*

2 *vt* (**a**) *(furniture)* quitar el polvo a (**b**) *(cake)* espolvorear

dustbin ['dʌstbɪn] *n Br* cubo *m or Am* bote *m* de la basura

dustcart ['dʌstkɑːt] *n Br* camión *m* de la basura

duster ['dʌstə(r)] *n Br (cloth)* trapo *m or* bayeta *f* (del polvo); **feather d.** plumero *m*

dustman ['dʌstmən] *n Br* basurero *m*

dustpan ['dʌstpæn] *n* recogedor *m*

dusty ['dʌstɪ] *adj* (**dustier, dustiest**) polvoriento(a)

Dutch [dʌtʃ] **1** *adj* holandés(esa); *Fig* **D. cap** diafragma *m*

2 *n* (**a**) *pl* **the D.** los holandeses (**b**) *(language)* holandés *m*; **it's double D. to me** me suena a chino

3 *adv Fam* **to go D.** pagar cada uno lo suyo, *Esp* pagar a escote

Dutchman ['dʌtʃmən] *n* holandés *m*

Dutchwoman ['dʌtʃwʊmən] *n* holandesa *f*

duty ['djuːtɪ] *n* (**a**) *(obligation)* deber *m*; **to do one's d.** cumplir con su deber (**b**) *(task)* duties tareas *fpl* (**c**) **to be on d.** estar de servicio; *Med & Mil* estar de guardia (**d**) *(tax)* impuesto *m*

duty-free [djuːtɪ'friː] *adj* libre de impuestos

duvet ['duːveɪ] *n Br* edredón *m*

DVD [diːviː'diː] *n Comput (abbr* **Digital Versatile Disk, Digital Video Disk)** DVD *m*

dwarf [dwɔːf] **1** *n (pl* **dwarves** [dwɔːvz]) *(person)* enano(a) *m,f*

2 *vt* hacer parecer pequeño(a) a

dwell [dwel] *vi (pt & pp* **dwelt**) *Fml* morar

▸ **dwell on** *vt insep* hablar extensamente de; **let's not d. on it** olvidémoslo

dwelling ['dwelɪŋ] *n Fml & Hum* morada *f*, vivienda *f*

dwelt [dwelt] *pt & pp of* **dwell**

dwindle ['dwɪndəl] *vi* menguar, disminuir

dye [daɪ] **1** *n* tinte *m*

2 *vt (pres p* **dyeing**; *pt & pp* **dyed**) teñir; **to d. one's hair black** teñirse el pelo de negro

dying ['daɪɪŋ] *adj (person)* moribundo(a), agonizante; *Fig (custom)* en vías de desaparición

dyke [daɪk] *n* (**a**) *(bank)* dique *m*; *(causeway)* terraplén *m* (**b**) *very Fam Pej* tortillera *f*

ℓ Note that the Spanish word **dureza** is a false friend and is never a translation for the English word **duress**. In Spanish, **dureza** means "hardness, harshness".

dynamic [daɪˈnæmɪk] *adj* dinámico(a)
dynamics [daɪˈnæmɪks] *n sing* dinámica*f*
dynamism [ˈdaɪnəmɪzəm] *n* dinamismo *m*
dynamite [ˈdaɪnəmaɪt] *n* dinamita *f*

dynamo [ˈdaɪnəməʊ] *n* dínamo *f*
dynasty [ˈdɪnəstɪ] *n* dinastía *f*
dysentery [ˈdɪsəntrɪ] *n* disentería *f*
dyslexia [dɪsˈleksɪə] *n* dislexia *f*

E, e [iː] *n* (**a**) (*the letter*) E, e *f* (**b**) *Mus* E mi *m*

E [iː] *n* (**a**) (*abbr* **East**) E (**b**) *Fam* (*abbr* **ecstasy**) (*drug*) éxtasis *m inv*

each [iːtʃ] **1** *adj* cada; **e. day/month** todos los días/meses; **e. person** cada cual; **e. time I see him** cada vez que lo veo
2 *pron* (**a**) (*both, all*) cada uno(a); **£2 e. 2** libras cada uno; **we bought one e.** nos compramos uno cada uno (**b**) (*reciprocal*) **e. other** el uno al otro; **they hate e. other** se odian

eager ['iːgə(r)] *adj* (*anxious*) impaciente; (*desirous*) deseoso(a); **e. to begin** impaciente por empezar; **to be e. for success** codiciar el éxito

eagerly ['iːgəlɪ] *adv* (*anxiously*) con impaciencia; (*keenly*) con ilusión

eagle ['iːgəl] *n* águila *f*

ear [ɪə(r)] *n* (**a**) (*external part*) oreja *f*; (*internal part, sense of hearing*) oído *m* (**b**) (*of wheat*) espiga *f*

earache ['ɪəreɪk] *n* dolor *m* de oídos

eardrum ['ɪədrʌm] *n* tímpano *m*

earl [ɜːl] *n* conde *m*

earlobe ['ɪələʊb] *n* lóbulo *m*

early ['ɜːlɪ] (**earlier, earliest**) **1** *adj* (**a**) (*before the usual time*) temprano(a); **to have an e. night** acostarse pronto; **you're e.!** ¡qué pronto has venido! (**b**) (*at first stage, period*) **at an e. age** siendo joven; **in e. July** a principios de julio; **e. work** obra de juventud; **in her e. forties** a los cuarenta y pocos
2 *adv* (**a**) (*before the expected time*) temprano, *Esp* pronto; **earlier on** antes; **five minutes e.** con cinco minutos de adelanto; (*near the beginning*) **as e. as 1914** ya en 1914; **as e. as possible** tan pronto como sea posible; **to book e.** reservar con tiempo; **e. on** temprano

earmark ['ɪəmɑːk] *vt* destinar (**for** para or a)

earn [ɜːn] *vt* (**a**) (*money*) ganar; **to e. one's living** ganarse la vida (**b**) (*reputation*) ganarse (**c**) **to e. interest** cobrar interés or intereses

earnest ['ɜːnɪst] **1** *adj* serio(a), formal
2 *n* **in e. de veras**, en serio

earnings ['ɜːnɪŋz] *npl* ingresos *mpl*

earphones ['ɪəfəʊnz] *npl* auriculares *mpl*

earring ['ɪərɪŋ] *n* pendiente *m*, *Am* arete *m*

earshot ['ɪəʃɒt] *n* **out of e.** fuera del alcance del oído; **within e.** al alcance del oído

earth [ɜːθ] **1** *n* (**a**) (*soil*) tierra *f*; **the E.** la Tierra; *Fig* **to be down to e.** ser práctico; *Fam* **where/why on e. …?** ¿pero dónde/por qué demonios …? (**b**) *Br Elec* toma *f* de tierra
2 *vt Br Elec* conectar a tierra

earthenware ['ɜːθənweə(r)] **1** *n* loza *f*
2 *adj* de barro

earthquake ['ɜːθkweɪk] *n* terremoto *m*

earthshattering ['ɜːθʃætərɪŋ] *adj* trascendental; **e. news** noticia bomba

earthworm ['ɜːθwɜːm] *n* lombriz *f* de tierra

earthy ['ɜːθɪ] *adj* (**earthier, earthiest**) (**a**) (*taste*) terroso(a) (**b**) (*bawdy*) tosco(a)

earwig ['ɪəwɪg] *n* tijereta *f*

ease [iːz] **1** *n* (**a**) (*freedom from discomfort*) tranquilidad *f*; **at e.** relajado(a) (**b**) (*lack of difficulty*) facilidad *f*
2 *vt* (*pain*) aliviar

▸**ease off, ease up** *vi* (**a**) (*decrease*) disminuir (**b**) (*slow-down*) ir más despacio

easel ['iːzəl] *n* caballete *m*

easily ['iːzɪlɪ] *adv* fácilmente; **e. the best** con mucho el mejor

east [iːst] **1** *n* este *m*; **the Middle E.** el Oriente Medio
2 *adj* del este, oriental; **E. Germany** Alemania Oriental
3 *adv* al or hacia el este

Easter ['iːstə(r)] *n* Semana Santa, Pascua *f*; **E. egg** huevo *m* de Pascua; **E. Sunday** Domingo *m* de Resurrección

easterly ['iːstəlɪ] *adj* (*from the east*) del este; (*to the east*) hacia al este

eastern ['iːstən] *adj* oriental, del este

eastward(s) ['iːstwəd(z)] *adv* hacia el este

easy ['iːzɪ] (**easier, easiest**) **1** *adj* (**a**) (*simple*) fácil, sencillo(a) (**b**) (*unworried, comfortable*) cómodo(a), tranquilo(a); *Fam* **I'm e.!** ¡me da lo mismo!; **e. chair** butacón *m*

2 *adv* **go e. on the wine** no te pases con el vino; *Fam* **to take things e.** tomarse las cosas con calma; *Fam* **take it e.!** ¡tranquilo!

easy-going [iːzɪˈgəʊɪŋ] *adj (calm)* tranquilo(a); *(lax)* despreocupado(a); *(undemanding)* poco exigente

eat [iːt] *vt (pt* ate; *pp* eaten) comer

▸ **eat away** *vt sep* desgastar; *(metal)* corroer

▸ **eat into** *vt insep* (**a**) *(wood)* roer (**b**) *Fig (savings)* consumir

▸ **eat out** *vi* comer fuera

▸ **eat up** *vt sep* (**a**) *(meal)* terminar (**b**) *Fig (petrol)* consumir; *(miles)* recorrer rápidamente

eatable [ˈiːtəbəl] *adj* comestible

eaten [ˈiːtən] *pp of* eat

eau de Cologne [əʊdəkəˈləʊn] *n* colonia *f*

eaves [iːvz] *npl* alero *m*

eavesdrop [ˈiːvzdrɒp] *vi* escuchar disimuladamente

e-banking [ˈiːˈbæŋkɪŋ] *n* banca *f* por Internet

ebb [eb] **1** *n* reflujo *m*; *Fig* **the e. and flow** *(of events)* los vaivenes; *Fig* **to be at a low e.** estar decaído
2 *vi* (**a**) *(tide)* bajar; **to e. and flow** subir y bajar (**b**) *Fig* **to e. away** decaer

ebony [ˈebənɪ] **1** *n* ébano *m*
2 *adj* de ébano

eccentric [ɪkˈsentrɪk] *adj & n* excéntrico(a) *(m,f)*

ecclesiastic [ɪkliːzɪˈæstɪk] *adj & n* eclesiástico(a) *(m,f)*

echelon [ˈeʃəlɒn] *n* escalafón *m*

echo [ˈekəʊ] **1** *n (pl* echoes) eco *m*
2 *vt (repeat)* repetir
3 *vi* resonar, hacer eco

eclectic [ɪˈklektɪk] *adj* ecléctico(a)

eclipse [ɪˈklɪps] **1** *n* eclipse *m*
2 *vt* eclipsar

ecological [iːkəˈlɒdʒɪkəl] *adj* ecológico(a)

ecology [ɪˈkɒlədʒɪ] *n* ecología *f*

e-commerce [iːˈkɒmɜːs] *n* comercio electrónico

economic [iːkəˈnɒmɪk] *adj* económico(a); *(profitable)* rentable

economical [iːkəˈnɒmɪkəl] *adj* económico(a)

economics [iːkəˈnɒmɪks] *n sing (science)* economía *f*; *Educ* (ciencias *fpl*) económicas *fpl*

economist [ɪˈkɒnəmɪst] *n* economista *mf*

economize [ɪˈkɒnəmaɪz] *vi* economizar

economy [ɪˈkɒnəmɪ] *n* (**a**) *Pol* **the e.** la economía *f* (**b**) *(saving)* ahorro *m*; **e. class** clase *f* turista

ecosystem [ˈiːkəʊsɪstəm] *n* ecosistema *m*

ecotax [ˈiːkəʊtæks] *n* ecotasa *f*

ecotourism [ˈiːkəʊtɔːrɪzəm] *n* ecoturismo *m*

ecstasy [ˈekstəsɪ] *n* éxtasis *m inv*

ecstatic [ekˈstætɪk] *adj* extático(a)

Ecuador [ˈekwədɔː(r)] *n* Ecuador

eczema [ˈeksɪmə] *n* eczema *m*

eddy [ˈedɪ] **1** *n* remolino *m*
2 *vi* arremolinarse

edge [edʒ] **1** *n* borde *m*; *(of knife)* filo *m*; *(of coin)* canto *m*; *(of water)* orilla *f*; **on the e. of town** en las afueras de la ciudad
2 *vt Sewing* ribetear
3 *vi* **to e. forward** avanzar poco a poco

edgeways [ˈedʒweɪz], **edgewise** [ˈedʒwaɪz] *adv* de lado; *Fig* **I couldn't get a word in e.** no pude decir ni pío

edging [ˈedʒɪŋ] *n* borde *m*; *Sewing* ribete *m*

edgy [ˈedʒɪ] *adj* (**edgier, edgiest**) nervioso(a)

edible [ˈedɪbəl] *adj* comestible

edict [ˈiːdɪkt] *n Hist* edicto *m*; *Jur* decreto *m*

Edinburgh [ˈedɪnbrə] *n* Edimburgo

edit [ˈedɪt] *vt* (**a**) *(prepare for printing)* preparar para la imprenta (**b**) *(rewrite)* corregir (**c**) *Press* ser redactor(a) de (**d**) *Cin, Rad & TV* montar; *(cut)* cortar

edition [ɪˈdɪʃən] *n* edición *f*

editor [ˈedɪtə(r)] *n (of book)* editor(a) *m,f*; *Press* redactor(a) *m,f*; *Cin & TV* montador(a) *m,f*

editorial [edɪˈtɔːrɪəl] **1** *adj* editorial; **e. staff** redacción *f*
2 *n* editorial *m*

educate [ˈedjʊkeɪt] *vt* educar

educated [ˈedjʊkeɪtɪd] *adj* culto(a)

education [edjʊˈkeɪʃən] *n* (**a**) *(schooling)* enseñanza *f*; **Ministry of E.** Ministerio *m* de Educación (**b**) *(training)* formación *f* (**c**) *(studies)* estudios *mpl* (**d**) *(culture)* cultura *f*

educational [edjʊˈkeɪʃənəl] *adj* educativo(a), educacional

eel [iːl] *n* anguila *f*

eerie [ˈɪərɪ] *adj* (**eerier, eeriest**) siniestro(a)

efface [ɪˈfeɪs] *vt* borrar

effect [ɪˈfekt] **1** *n* (**a**) *(result)* efecto *m*; **in e.** efectivamente; **to come into e.** entrar en vigor; **to have an e. on** afectar a; **to take e.** *(drug)* surtir efecto; *(law)* entrar en vigor

(**b**) *(impression)* impresión *f*
2 *vt Fml* provocar
effective [ɪ'fektɪv] *adj* (**a**) *(successful)* eficaz (**b**) *(real)* efectivo(a) (**c**) *(impressive)* impresionante
effectively [ɪ'fektɪvlɪ] *adv* (**a**) *(successfully)* eficazmente (**b**) *(in fact)* en efecto
effeminate [ɪ'femɪnɪt] *adj* afeminado(a)
effervescent [efə'vesənt] *adj* efervescente
efficiency [ɪ'fɪʃənsɪ] *n (of person)* eficacia *f*; *(of machine)* rendimiento *m*
efficient [ɪ'fɪʃənt] *adj* eficaz, eficiente; *(machine)* de buen rendimiento
effigy ['efɪdʒɪ] *n* efigie *f*
effluent ['efluənt] *n* vertidos *mpl*
effort ['efət] *n* (**a**) *(exertion)* esfuerzo *m*; **to make an e.** hacer un esfuerzo, esforzarse (**b**) *(attempt)* intento *m*
effortless ['efətlɪs] *adj* sin esfuerzo
effrontery [ɪ'frʌntərɪ] *n* desfachatez *f*
effusive [ɪ'fjuːsɪv] *adj* efusivo(a)
eg [iː'dʒiː] *(abbr exempli gratia)* p. ej.
egalitarian [ɪgælɪ'teərɪən] *adj* igualitario(a)
egg [eg] **1** *n* huevo *m*, *CAm, Méx* blanquillo *m*; **e. cup** huevera *f*; **e. timer** reloj *m* de arena; **e. white** clara *f* de huevo
2 *vt* **to e. sb on (to do sth)** empujar a algn (a hacer algo)
eggplant ['egplɑːnt] *n US* berenjena *f*
eggshell ['egʃel] *n* cáscara *f* de huevo
ego ['iːgəʊ, 'egəʊ] *n* (**a**) *Psy* ego *m*; *Fam* **e. trip** autobombo *m* (**b**) *(self-esteem)* amor *m* propio
egocentric(al) [iːgəʊ'sentrɪk(əl)] *adj* egocéntrico(a)
egotism ['iːgəʊɪzəm] *n* egoísmo *m*
egotist ['iːgəʊɪst] *n* egoísta *mf*
egotistic(al) [iːgəʊ'tɪstɪk(əl)] *adj* egotista
Egypt ['iːdʒɪpt] *n* Egipto
Egyptian [ɪ'dʒɪpʃən] *adj & n* egipcio(a) *(m,f)*
eiderdown ['aɪdədaʊn] *n* edredón *m*
eight [eɪt] *adj & n* ocho *(m inv)*
eighteen [eɪ'tiːn] *adj & n* dieciocho *(m inv)*
eighteenth [eɪ'tiːnθ] **1** *adj & n* decimoctavo *(m,f)*
2 *n (fraction)* decimoctavo *m*
eighth [eɪtθ] **1** *adj & n* octavo(a) *(m,f)*
2 *n (fraction)* octavo *m*
eighty ['eɪtɪ] *adj & n* ochenta *(m inv)*
Eire ['eərə] *n* Eire
either ['aɪðə(r), 'iːðə(r)] **1** *pron* (**a**) *(affirmative)* cualquiera; **e. of them**

cualquiera de los dos; **e. of us** cualquiera de nosotros dos (**b**) *(negative)* ninguno/ ninguna, ni el uno ni el otro/ni la una ni la otra; **I don't want e. of them** no quiero ninguno de los dos
2 *adj (both)* cada, los dos/las dos; **on e. side** en ambos lados; **in e. case** en cualquier de los dos casos
3 *conj* o; **e. ... or ...** o ... o ...; **e. Friday or Saturday** o (bien) el viernes o el sábado
4 *adv (after negative)* tampoco; **I don't want to do it e.** yo tampoco quiero hacerlo
ejaculate [ɪ'dʒækjʊleɪt] *vi (man)* eyacular
eject [ɪ'dʒekt] **1** *vt* expulsar
2 *vi Av* eyectarse
eke [iːk] *vt* **to e. out a living** ganarse la vida a duras penas
elaborate 1 *vt* [ɪ'læbəreɪt] (**a**) *(devise)* elaborar (**b**) *(explain)* explicar detalladamente
2 *vi* explicarse; **to e. on sth** explicar algo con más detalles
3 *adj* [ɪ'læbərɪt] (**a**) *(complicated)* complicado(a) (**b**) *(detailed)* detallado(a); *(style)* esmerado(a)
elapse [ɪ'læps] *vi* transcurrir, pasar
elastic [ɪ'læstɪk] **1** *adj* elástico(a); *Fig* flexible; **e. band** goma elástica
2 *n* elástico *m*
Elastoplast® [ɪ'lɑːstəplɑːst] *n Br Esp* tirita *f*, *Am* curita *f*
elated [ɪ'leɪtɪd] *adj* eufórico(a)
elation [ɪ'leɪʃən] *n* regocijo *m*
elbow ['elbəʊ] **1** *n* codo *m*; *Fig* **e. room** espacio *m*
2 *vt* **to e. sb** dar un codazo a algn
elder[1] ['eldə(r)] **1** *adj* mayor
2 *n* **the elders** los ancianos
elder[2] ['eldə(r)] *n Bot* saúco *m*
elderly ['eldəlɪ] **1** *adj* anciano(a)
2 *npl* **the e.** los ancianos
eldest ['eldɪst] **1** *adj* mayor
2 *n* **the e.** el/la mayor
elect [ɪ'lekt] **1** *vt* (**a**) *Pol* elegir (**b**) **to e. to do sth** *(choose)* decidir hacer algo
2 *adj* **the president e.** el presidente electo
election [ɪ'lekʃən] **1** *n* elección *f*; **general e.** elecciones *fpl* generales
2 *adj* electoral
electioneering [ɪlekʃə'nɪərɪŋ] *n* electoralismo *m*
elective [ɪ'lektɪv] *adj Univ (course)* optativo(a), opcional
elector [ɪ'lektə(r)] *n* elector(a) *m,f*
electoral [ɪ'lektərəl] *adj* electoral
electorate [ɪ'lektərɪt] *n* electorado *m*

electric [ɪ'lektrɪk] *adj* eléctrico(a); *Fig (atmosphere)* electrizado(a); **e. blanket** manta eléctrica, *Am* frazada eléctrica; **e. chair** silla eléctrica; **e. shock** electrochoque *m*

electrical [ɪ'lektrɪkəl] *adj* eléctrico(a)

electrician [ɪlek'trɪʃən] *n* electricista *mf*

electricity [ɪlek'trɪsɪtɪ] *n* electricidad *f*; **e. bill** recibo *m* de la luz

electrify [ɪ'lektrɪfaɪ] *vt* (a) *(railway line)* electrificar (b) *Fig (excite)* electrizar

electrocute [ɪ'lektrəkju:t] *vt* electrocutar

electron [ɪ'lektrɒn] *n* electrón *m*

electronic [ɪlek'trɒnɪk] *adj* electrónico(a); **e. banking** banca electrónica, telebanca *f*

electronics [ɪlek'trɒnɪks] **1** *n sing (science)* electrónica *f*
2 *npl (of machine)* componentes *mpl* electrónicos

elegant ['elɪgənt] *adj* elegante

element ['elɪmənt] *n* (a) *(constituent part)* elemento *m* (b) *(factor)* componente *m*, elemento *m* (c) *(electrical)* resistencia *f* (d) *Fam Fig* **to be in one's e.** estar en su salsa

elementary [elɪ'mentərɪ] *adj (basic)* elemental; *(not developed)* rudimentario(a); *(easy)* fácil; *US* **e. school** escuela primaria

elephant ['elɪfənt] *n* elefante *m*

elevate ['elɪveɪt] *vt* elevar; *(in rank)* ascender

elevation [elɪ'veɪʃən] *n* (a) *(above sea level)* altitud *f* (b) *Archit* alzado *m*

elevator ['elɪveɪtə(r)] *n US* ascensor *m*

eleven [ɪ'levən] *adj & n* once *(m inv)*

elevenses [ɪ'levənzɪz] *npl Br Fam* tentempié *m* (de la mañana), *Am* onces *fpl*

eleventh [ɪ'levənθ] **1** *adj & n* undécimo(a) *(m,f)*
2 *n (fraction)* undécimo *m*

elicit [ɪ'lɪsɪt] *vt* obtener

eligible ['elɪdʒəbəl] *adj* apto(a); **he isn't e. to vote** no tiene derecho al voto

eliminate [ɪ'lɪmɪneɪt] *vt* eliminar

elite [ɪ'li:t] *n* elite *f*

elitist [ɪ'li:tɪst] *adj* elitista

elm [elm] *n* olmo *m*

elocution [elə'kju:ʃən] *n* elocución *f*

elongate ['i:lɒŋgeɪt] *vt* alargar

elope [ɪ'ləʊp] *vi* fugarse para casarse

eloquent ['eləkwənt] *adj* elocuente

else [els] *adv* (a) **anyone e.** alguien más; **anything e.?** ¿algo más?; **everything e.** todo lo demás; **no one e.** nadie más; **someone e.** otro(a); **something e.** otra

cosa, algo más; **somewhere e.** en otra parte; **what e.?** ¿qué más?; **where e.?** ¿en qué otro sitio? (b) **or e.** *(otherwise)* si no

elsewhere [els'weə(r)] *adv* en otra parte

elucidate [ɪ'lu:sɪdeɪt] *vt* aclarar

elude [ɪ'lu:d] *vt* (a) *(escape)* eludir; **his name eludes me** no consigo acordarme de su nombre (b) *(avoid)* esquivar

elusive [ɪ'lu:sɪv] *adj* esquivo(a); *(evasive)* evasivo(a)

emaciated [ɪ'meɪsɪeɪtɪd] *adj* demacrado(a)

e-mail ['i:meɪl] *Comput* **1** *n (system)* correo *m* electrónico; *(message)* mensaje *m* por) correo electrónico; **e. address** dirección *f* de correo electrónico
2 *vt (person)* enviar un correo electrónico a; *(file)* enviar por correo electrónico

emanate ['eməneɪt] *vi* provenir (**from** de)

emancipate [ɪ'mænsɪpeɪt] *vt* emancipar

emancipation [ɪmænsɪ'peɪʃən] *n* emancipación *f*

embankment [ɪm'bæŋkmənt] *n* (a) *(made of earth)* terraplén *m* (b) *(of river)* dique *m*

embargo [em'bɑ:gəʊ] *n (pl embargoes)* embargo *m*

embark [em'bɑ:k] **1** *vt (merchandise)* embarcar
2 *vi* embarcar, embarcarse; *Fig* **to e. upon** emprender; *(sth difficult)* embarcarse en

embarkation [embɑ:'keɪʃən] *n* embarque *m*

embarrass [ɪm'bærəs] *vt* avergonzar, *Am salvo RP* apenar

embarrassed [ɪm'bærəst] *adj (ashamed)* avergonzado(a), *Am salvo RP* apenado(a); *(uncomfortable)* azorado(a), violento(a)

> *⚠ Note that the Spanish word **embarazado** is a false friend and is never a translation for the English word **embarrassed**. In Spanish, **embarazado** means "pregnant".*

embarrassing [ɪm'bærəsɪŋ] *adj* embarazoso(a), *Am salvo RP* penoso(a)

embarrassment [ɪm'bærəsmənt] *n (shame)* vergüenza *f*, *Am salvo RP* pena *f*; *(discomfort)* apuro *m*, embarazo *m*

embassy ['embəsɪ] *n* embajada *f*

embed [ɪm'bed] *vt (jewels)* incrustar; *Fig* grabar

embellish [ɪm'belɪʃ] *vt* embellecer; *(story)* exagerar

ember ['embə(r)] *n* ascua *f*, rescoldo *m*

embezzle [ɪm'bezəl] *vt* desfalcar, malversar

embezzlement [ɪm'bezəlmənt] n malversación f

embitter [ɪm'bɪtə(r)] vt amargar

embittered [ɪm'bɪtəd] adj amargado(a), resentido(a)

emblem ['embləm] n emblema m

embody [ɪm'bɒdɪ] vt (a) (include) abarcar (b) (personify) encarnar

embossed [ɪm'bɒst] adj en relieve

embrace [ɪm'breɪs] 1 vt (person, belief) abrazar; (include) abarcar
2 vi abrazarse
3 n abrazo m

embroider [ɪm'brɔɪdə(r)] vt (a) Sewing bordar (b) Fig (story, truth) adornar, embellecer

embroidery [ɪm'brɔɪdərɪ] n bordado m

embryo ['embrɪəʊ] n embrión m

emerald ['emərəld] n esmeralda f

emerge [ɪ'mɜːdʒ] vi salir; (problem) surgir; **it emerged that ...** resultó que ...

emergence [ɪ'mɜːdʒəns] n aparición f

emergency [ɪ'mɜːdʒənsɪ] n emergencia f; Med urgencia f; **in an e.** en caso de emergencia; **e. exit** salida f de emergencia; **e. landing** aterrizaje forzoso; **e. measures** medidas fpl de urgencia; US **e. room** sala f de urgencias; Aut **e. stop** frenazo m en seco; Pol **state of e.** estado m de excepción

emery ['emərɪ] n **e. board** lima f de uñas

emigrant ['emɪgrənt] n emigrante mf

emigrate ['emɪgreɪt] vi emigrar

emigration [emɪ'greɪʃən] n emigración f

eminent ['emɪnənt] adj eminente

emission [ɪ'mɪʃən] n emisión f

emit [ɪ'mɪt] vt (signals) emitir; (smells) despedir; (sound) producir

emoticon [ɪ'mɒtɪkɒn] n Comput emoticono m

emotion [ɪ'məʊʃən] n emoción f

emotional [ɪ'məʊʃənəl] adj (problem, reaction) emocional; (film, farewell) conmovedor(a)

emotive [ɪ'məʊtɪv] adj emotivo(a)

empathy ['empəθɪ] n empatía f

emperor ['empərə(r)] n emperador m

emphasis ['emfəsɪs] n (pl **emphases** ['emfəsɪːz]) énfasis m; **to place e. on sth** hacer hincapié en algo

emphasize ['emfəsaɪz] vt subrayar, hacer hincapié en; (insist) insistir; (highlight) hacer resaltar

emphatic [em'fætɪk] adj (forceful) enfático(a); (convinced) categórico(a)

emphatically [em'fætɪklɪ] adv categóricamente

empire ['empaɪə(r)] n imperio m

employ [ɪm'plɔɪ] vt emplear; (time) ocupar

employee [em'plɔɪiː, emplɔɪ'iː] n empleado(a) m,f

employer [ɪm'plɔɪə(r)] n patrón(ona) m,f

employment [ɪm'plɔɪmənt] n empleo m; **e. agency** agencia f de colocaciones; **full e.** pleno empleo

empower [ɪm'paʊə(r)] vt autorizar

empress ['emprɪs] n emperatriz f

emptiness ['emptɪnɪs] n vacío m

empty ['emptɪ] 1 adj (emptier, emptiest) vacío(a); **an e. house** una casa deshabitada; **e. promises** promesas fpl vanas
2 vt vaciar
3 vi vaciarse
4 npl **empties** (bottles) cascos mpl

empty-handed [emptɪ'hændɪd] adj con las manos vacías

emulate ['emjʊleɪt] vt emular

emulsion [ɪ'mʌlʃən] n emulsión f; **e. paint** pintura f mate

enable [ɪn'eɪbəl] vt permitir

enact [ɪn'ækt] vt (play) representar; (law) promulgar

enamel [ɪ'næməl] n esmalte m

enamoured, US **enamored** [ɪn'æməd] adj **to be e. of** estar enamorado(a) de; **I'm not greatly e. of the idea** no me entusiasma la idea

encase [ɪn'keɪs] vt **encased in** revestido(a) de

enchant [ɪn'tʃɑːnt] vt encantar

enchanting [ɪn'tʃɑːntɪŋ] adj encantador(a)

encircle [ɪn'sɜːkəl] vt rodear

enclave ['enkleɪv] n enclave m

enclose [ɪn'kləʊz] vt (a) (surround) rodear (b) (fence in) cercar (c) (in envelope) adjuntar; **please find enclosed** le enviamos adjunto

enclosure [ɪn'kləʊʒə(r)] n (a) (fenced area) cercado m (b) (in envelope) documento adjunto (c) (of racecourse) recinto m

encompass [ɪn'kʌmpəs] vt abarcar

encore ['ɒŋkɔː(r)] 1 interj ¡otra!, ¡bis!
2 n repetición f, bis m

encounter [ɪn'kaʊntə(r)] 1 n (meeting) encuentro m
2 vt encontrar, encontrarse con; (problems) tropezar con

encourage [ɪn'kʌrɪdʒ] vt (a) (person) animar (b) (tourism, trade) fomentar

encouragement [ɪn'kʌrɪdʒmənt] n estímulo m

encroach [ɪn'krəʊtʃ] *vi* **to e. on** *(territory)* invadir; *(rights)* usurpar; *(time, freedom)* quitar

encrusted [ɪn'krʌstɪd] *adj* incrustado(a) **(with** de)

encumber [ɪn'kʌmbə(r)] *vt* estorbar; *(with debts)* gravar

encyclop(a)edia [ensaɪkləʊ'piːdɪə] *n* enciclopedia *f*

end [end] **1** *n* (**a**) *(of stick)* punta *f*; *(of street)* final *m*; *(of table)* extremo *m*; Fig **to make ends meet** llegar a final de mes (**b**) *(conclusion)* fin *m*, final *m*; **in the e.** al final; **for hours on e.** hora tras hora; **to bring an e. to sth** poner fin a algo; **to put an e. to** acabar con (**c**) *(aim)* objetivo *m*, fin *m*

2 *vt* acabar, terminar

3 *vi* acabarse, terminarse

▸ **end up** *vi* terminar; **it ended up in the dustbin** fue a parar al cubo de la basura; **to e. up doing sth** terminar por hacer algo

endanger [ɪn'deɪndʒə(r)] *vt* poner en peligro

endangered [ɪn'deɪndʒəd] *adj* en peligro

endearing [ɪn'dɪərɪŋ] *adj* simpático(a)

endeavour, *US* **endeavor** [ɪn'devə(r)] **1** *n* esfuerzo *m*

2 *vt* intentar, procurar

ending ['endɪŋ] *n* final *m*

endive ['endaɪv] *n Bot* (**a**) *(curly)* escarola *f* (**b**) *esp US (chicory)* endibia *f*, achicoria *f*

endless ['endlɪs] *adj* interminable

endorse [ɪn'dɔːs] *vt* (**a**) *(document, cheque)* endosar (**b**) *(approve) (opinion, action)* apoyar, respaldar

endorsement [ɪn'dɔːsmənt] *n* (**a**) *(on document, cheque)* endoso *m* (**b**) *Br (on driving licence)* infracción *f* anotada (**c**) *(approval)* aprobación *f*

endow [ɪn'daʊ] *vt* dotar; **to be endowed with** estar dotado(a) de

endurance [ɪn'djʊərəns] *n* resistencia *f*

endure [ɪn'djʊə(r)] **1** *vt (bear)* aguantar, soportar

2 *vi* perdurar

enemy ['enəmɪ] *adj & n* enemigo(a) *(m,f)*

energetic [enə'dʒetɪk] *adj* enérgico(a)

energy ['enədʒɪ] *n* energía *f*

enforce [ɪn'fɔːs] *vt (law)* hacer cumplir

enforcement [ɪn'fɔːsmənt] *n* aplicación *f*

engage [ɪn'geɪdʒ] *vt* (**a**) *(hire)* contratar (**b**) *(attention)* llamar (**c**) *(in conversation)* entablar

engaged [ɪn'geɪdʒd] *adj* (**a**) *(betrothed)* prometido(a); **to get e.** prometerse (**b**) *(busy)* ocupado(a); *Br Tel* **it's e.** está comunicando

engagement [ɪn'geɪdʒmənt] *n* (**a**) *(betrothal)* petición *f* de mano; *(period)* noviazgo *m*; **e. ring** anillo *m* de compromiso (**b**) *(appointment)* cita *f* (**c**) *Mil* combate *m*

engaging [ɪn'geɪdʒɪŋ] *adj* simpático(a), agradable

engender [ɪn'dʒendə(r)] *vt* engendrar

engine ['endʒɪn] *n* motor *m*; *Rail* locomotora *f*; **e. room** sala *f* de máquinas; **e. driver** maquinista *mf*

engineer [endʒɪ'nɪə(r)] **1** *n* ingeniero(a) *m,f*; *Naut & US Rail* maquinista *mf*

2 *vt (cause, bring about)* urdir

engineering [endʒɪ'nɪərɪŋ] *n* ingeniería *f*; **electrical e.** electrotecnia *f*; **civil e.** ingeniería civil

England ['ɪŋglənd] *n* Inglaterra

English ['ɪŋglɪʃ] **1** *adj* inglés(esa)

2 *n* (**a**) *(language)* inglés *m* (**b**) *pl* **the E.** los ingleses

Englishman ['ɪŋglɪʃmən] *n* inglés *m*

English-speaking ['ɪŋglɪʃspiːkɪŋ] *adj* de habla inglesa

Englishwoman ['ɪŋglɪʃwʊmən] *n* inglesa *f*

engraving [ɪn'greɪvɪŋ] *n* grabado *m*

engrossed [ɪn'grəʊst] *adj* absorto(a) (**in** en)

engulf [ɪn'gʌlf] *vt* tragarse

enhance [ɪn'hɑːns] *vt (beauty)* realzar; *(power, chances)* aumentar

enigma [ɪ'nɪgmə] *n* enigma *m*

enjoy [ɪn'dʒɔɪ] *vt* (**a**) *(take pleasure from)* disfrutar de; **to e. oneself** pasarlo bien (**b**) *(benefit from)* gozar de

enjoyable [ɪn'dʒɔɪəbəl] *adj* agradable; *(amusing)* divertido(a)

enjoyment [ɪn'dʒɔɪmənt] *n* placer *m*, gusto *m*

enlarge [ɪn'lɑːdʒ] **1** *vt* extender, ampliar; *Phot* ampliar

2 *vi* **to e. upon a subject** extenderse sobre un tema

enlargement [ɪn'lɑːdʒmənt] *n Phot* ampliación *f*

enlighten [ɪn'laɪtən] *vt* iluminar

enlightened [ɪn'laɪtənd] *adj* (**a**) *(learned)* culto(a); *(informed)* bien informado(a) (**b**) *Hist* ilustrado(a)

enlightenment [ɪn'laɪtənmənt] *n* **the Age of E.** el Siglo de las Luces

enlist [ɪn'lɪst] **1** *vt Mil* reclutar; **to e. sb's help** conseguir ayuda de algn

2 *vi Mil* alistarse

enmity ['enmɪtɪ] *n* enemistad *f*, hostilidad *f*

enormous [ɪ'nɔːməs] *adj* enorme

enormously [ɪˈnɔːməslɪ] *adv* enormemente; **I enjoyed myself e.** lo pasé genial

enough [ɪˈnʌf] **1** *adj* bastante, suficiente; **e. books** bastantes libros; **e. money** bastante dinero; **have we got e. petrol?** ¿tenemos suficiente gasolina?

2 *adv* bastante; **oddly e. ...** lo curioso es que ...; **sure e.** en efecto

3 *pron* lo bastante, lo suficiente; **e. to live on** lo suficiente para vivir; **it isn't e.** no basta; **more than e.** más que suficiente; *Fam* **I've had e.!** ¡estoy harto!

enquire [ɪnˈkwaɪə(r)] *vi* preguntar

enquiry [ɪnˈkwaɪərɪ] *n* (**a**) *(question)* pregunta *f*; **to make an e.** preguntar; **enquiries** información *f* (**b**) *(investigation)* investigación *f*

enrage [ɪnˈreɪdʒ] *vt* enfurecer

enrich [ɪnˈrɪtʃ] *vt* enriquecer

enrol, *US* **enroll** [ɪnˈrəʊl] **1** *vt* matricular, inscribir

2 *vi* matricularse, inscribirse

⚠ Note that the Spanish verb **enrollar** is a false friend and is never a translation for the English verb **enrol**. In Spanish **enrollar** means "to roll up".

enrolment, *US* **enrollment** [ɪnˈrəʊlmənt] *n* matrícula *f*

en route [ɒnˈruːt] *adv* en or por el camino

ensign [ˈensaɪn] *n* (**a**) *(flag)* bandera *f*, enseña *f* (**b**) *US (naval officer)* alférez *m* de fragata

enslave [ɪnˈsleɪv] *vt* esclavizar

ensue [ɪnˈsjuː] *vi* (**a**) *(follow)* seguir (**b**) *(result)* resultar (**from** de)

ensure [ɪnˈʃʊə(r)] *vt* asegurar

entail [ɪnˈteɪl] *vt (involve)* suponer

entangle [ɪnˈtæŋɡəl] *vt* enredar

enter [ˈentə(r)] **1** *vt* (**a**) *(go into)* entrar en; *Fig (join)* ingresar en (**b**) *(write down)* apuntar, anotar (**c**) *Comput* dar entrada a

2 *vi* entrar

▸ **enter into** *vt insep* (**a**) *(agreement)* firmar; *(negotiations)* iniciar; *(bargain)* cerrar (**b**) *(relations)* establecer; *(conversation)* entablar

enterprise [ˈentəpraɪz] *n* empresa *f*; **free e.** libre empresa; **private e.** iniciativa privada; *(as a whole)* el sector privado; **public e.** el sector público

enterprising [ˈentəpraɪzɪŋ] *adj* emprendedor(a)

entertain [entəˈteɪn] **1** *vt* (**a**) *(amuse)* divertir (**b**) *(consider)* considerar; **to e. an idea** abrigar una idea

2 *vi* tener invitados

entertainer [entəˈteɪnə(r)] *n* artista *mf*

entertaining [entəˈteɪnɪŋ] *adj* divertido(a)

entertainment [entəˈteɪnmənt] *n* (**a**) *(amusement)* entretenimiento *m*, diversión *f* (**b**) *Th* espectáculo *m*

enthralling [ɪnˈθrɔːlɪŋ] *adj* fascinante

enthuse [ɪnˈθjuːz] *vi* entusiasmarse (**over** por)

enthusiasm [ɪnˈθjuːzɪæzəm] *n* entusiasmo *m*

enthusiast [ɪnˈθjuːzɪæst] *n* entusiasta *mf*

enthusiastic [ɪnθjuːzɪˈæstɪk] *adj* entusiasta; *(praise)* caluroso(a); **to be e. about sth** entusiasmarse por algo

entice [ɪnˈtaɪs] *vt* seducir, atraer

enticing [ɪnˈtaɪsɪŋ] *adj* atractivo(a), tentador(a)

entire [ɪnˈtaɪə(r)] *adj* entero(a), todo(a)

entirely [ɪnˈtaɪəlɪ] *adv* (**a**) *(completely)* totalmente (**b**) *(solely)* exclusivamente

entirety [ɪnˈtaɪərɪtɪ] *n* **in its e.** en su totalidad

entitle [ɪnˈtaɪtəl] *vt* (**a**) *(allow)* dar derecho a; **to be entitled to** tener derecho a (**b**) *(book etc)* titular

entity [ˈentɪtɪ] *n* entidad *f*

entourage [ɒntuːˈrɑːʒ] *n* séquito *m*

entrails [ˈentreɪlz] *npl* tripas *fpl*; *Fig* entrañas *fpl*

entrance¹ [ˈentrəns] *n* (**a**) *(way in, act of entering)* entrada *f*; **e. fee** *(to museum etc)* entrada; *(to organization)* cuota *f* (**b**) *(admission)* entrada *f*, ingreso *m*; **e. examination** examen *m* de ingreso

entrance² [ɪnˈtrɑːns] *vt* encantar

entrant [ˈentrənt] *n* *(in competition)* participante *mf*; *(applicant)* aspirante *mf*

entreat [ɪnˈtriːt] *vt Fml* suplicar, rogar

entrée [ˈɒntreɪ] *n Br (first course)* entrada *f*, primer plato *m*; *US (main course)* plato *m* principal

entrenched [ɪnˈtrentʃt] *adj* firmemente enraizado(a)

entrepreneur [ɒntrəprəˈnɜː(r)] *n* empresario(a) *m,f*

entrust [ɪnˈtrʌst] *vt* encargar (**with** de); **to e. sth to sb** dejar algo al cuidado de algn

entry [ˈentrɪ] *n* (**a**) *(entrance)* entrada *f*; **no e.** *(sign)* dirección prohibida (**b**) *(in competition)* participante *mf*

enumerate [ɪˈnjuːməreɪt] *vt* enumerar

enunciate [ɪˈnʌnsɪeɪt] *vt (words)* articular; *(ideas)* formular

envelop [ɪnˈveləp] *vt* envolver

envelope [ˈenvələup] *n* sobre *m*

envious [ˈenvɪəs] *adj* envidioso(a); **to feel e.** tener envidia

environment [ɪn'vaɪərənmənt] *n* medio *m* ambiente

environmental [ɪnvaɪərən'mentəl] *adj* medioambiental

environmentally [ɪnvaɪərən'mentəlɪ] *adv* ecológicamente; **e. friendly** ecológico(a), que no daña el medio ambiente

envisage [ɪn'vɪzɪdʒ] *vt (imagine)* imaginarse; *(foresee)* prever

envoy ['envɔɪ] *n* enviado(a) *m,f*

envy ['envɪ] **1** *n* envidia *f*
2 *vt* envidiar, tener envidia de

enzyme ['enzaɪm] *n* enzima *m*

ephemeral [ɪ'femərəl] *adj* efímero(a)

epic ['epɪk] **1** *n* epopeya *f*
2 *adj* épico(a)

epidemic [epɪ'demɪk] *n* epidemia *f; Fig (of crime etc)* ola *f*

epilepsy ['epɪlepsɪ] *n* epilepsia *f*

epilogue, *US* **epilog** ['epɪlɒg] *n* epílogo *m*

episode ['epɪsəʊd] *n* episodio *m*

epistle [ɪ'pɪsəl] *n* epístola *f*

epitaph ['epɪtɑːf] *n* epitafio *m*

epitome [ɪ'pɪtəmɪ] *n Fml* personificación *f*

epitomize [ɪ'pɪtəmaɪz] *vt Fml* personificar

epoch ['iːpɒk] *n* época *f*

equable ['ekwəbəl] *adj* (a) *(person)* ecuánime (b) *(climate)* uniforme

equal ['iːkwəl] **1** *adj* igual; **to be e. to the occasion** estar a la altura de las circunstancias; **e. pay** igualdad *f* de salarios
2 *n* igual *mf*; **to treat sb as an e.** tratar a algn de igual a igual
3 *vt (pt & pp* **equalled,** *US* **equaled**) (a) *Math* equivaler (b) *(match)* igualar

equality [iː'kwɒlɪtɪ] *n* igualdad *f*

equalize ['iːkwəlaɪz] **1** *vi Ftb* empatar
2 *vt* igualar

equalizer ['iːkwəlaɪzə(r)] *n Ftb* gol *m* del empate; *(of sound)* ecualizador *m*

equally ['iːkwəlɪ] *adv* igualmente; **e. pretty** igual de bonito(a); **to share sth e.** dividir algo en partes iguales

equanimity [ekwə'nɪmɪtɪ] *n* ecuanimidad *f*

equate [ɪ'kweɪt] *vt* equiparar, comparar **(to** con)

equation [ɪ'kweɪʒən, ɪ'kweɪʃən] *n Math* ecuación *f*

equator [ɪ'kweɪtə(r)] *n* ecuador *m*

equatorial [ekwə'tɔːrɪəl] *adj* ecuatorial

equestrian [ɪ'kwestrɪən] *adj* ecuestre

equilibrium [iːkwɪ'lɪbrɪəm] *n* equilibrio *m*

equinox ['iːkwɪnɒks] *n* equinoccio *m*

equip [ɪ'kwɪp] *vt (with tools, machines)* equipar; *(with food)* proveer

equipment [ɪ'kwɪpmənt] *n (materials)* equipo *m*; **office e.** material *m* de oficina

equipped [ɪ'kwɪpt] *adj (with tools, machines)* equipado(a); *(with skills)* dotado(a)

equitable ['ekwɪtəbəl] *adj* equitativo(a)

equities ['ekwɪtɪz] *npl* acciones ordinarias

equivalent [ɪ'kwɪvələnt] *adj & n* equivalente *(m);* **to be e.** equivaler a, ser equivalente a

equivocal [ɪ'kwɪvəkəl] *adj* equívoco(a)

era ['ɪərə] *n* era *f*

eradicate [ɪ'rædɪkeɪt] *vt* erradicar

erase [ɪ'reɪz] *vt* borrar

eraser [*Br* ɪ'reɪzə(r), *US* ɪ'reɪsər] *n* goma *f* de borrar

erect [ɪ'rekt] **1** *adj* (a) *(upright)* erguido(a) (b) *(penis)* erecto(a)
2 *vt (monument)* levantar, erigir

erection [ɪ'rekʃən] *n* (a) *(of building)* construcción *f* (b) *(penis)* erección *f*

ermine ['ɜːmɪn] *n* armiño *m*

erode [ɪ'rəʊd] *vt* (a) *(rock, soil)* erosionar (b) *(metal)* corroer, desgastar; *Fig (power, confidence)* hacer perder

erosion [ɪ'rəʊʒən] *n Geol* erosión *f*

erotic [ɪ'rɒtɪk] *adj* erótico(a)

err [ɜː(r)] *vi* errar; **to e. on the side of caution** pecar de prudente

errand ['erənd] *n* recado *m*; **e. boy** recadero *m*

erratic [ɪ'rætɪk] *adj (performance, behaviour)* irregular; *(weather)* muy variable; *(person)* caprichoso(a)

erroneous [ɪ'rəʊnɪəs] *adj* erróneo(a)

error ['erə(r)] *n* error *m*, equivocación *f*

erupt [ɪ'rʌpt] *vi* (a) *(volcano)* entrar en erupción; *(violence)* estallar (b) **his skin erupted in a rash** le salió una erupción

eruption [ɪ'rʌpʃən] *n* erupción *f*

escalate ['eskəleɪt] *vi (war)* intensificarse; *(prices)* aumentar; *(change)* convertirse **(into** en)

escalation [eskə'leɪʃən] *n (of war)* intensificación *f*, escalada *f; (of prices)* subida *f*

escalator ['eskəleɪtə(r)] *n* escalera mecánica

> 🖉 Note that the Spanish word **escalador** is a false friend and is never a translation for the English word **escalator**. In Spanish **escalador** means "climber, mountaineer".

escalope ['eskələp] *n* escalope *m*

escapade ['eskəpeɪd] n aventura f

> 🖉 Note that the Spanish word **escapada** is a false friend and is never a translation for the English word **escapade**. In Spanish **escapada** means both "escape" and "quick trip".

escape [ɪ'skeɪp] **1** n huída f, fuga f; (of gas) escape m; **e. route** vía f de escape
2 vi escaparse
3 vt (a) (avoid) evitar, huir de; **to e. punishment** librarse del castigo (b) Fig **his name escapes me** no recuerdo su nombre

escapism [ɪ'skeɪpɪzəm] n evasión f

escort 1 n ['eskɔ:t] (a) (companion) acompañante mf (b) Mil escolta f
2 vt [ɪ'skɔ:t] (a) (accompany) acompañar (b) (protect) escoltar

Eskimo ['eskɪməʊ] adj & n esquimal (mf)

esoteric [esəʊ'terɪk] adj esotérico(a)

especial [ɪ'speʃəl] adj especial

especially [ɪ'speʃəlɪ] adv especialmente, sobre todo

espionage ['espɪənɑ:ʒ] n espionaje m

esplanade [esplə'neɪd] n paseo marítimo

espouse [ɪ'spaʊz] vt Fml (cause) abrazar, adoptar

espresso [e'spresəʊ] n **e. (coffee)** café m exprés or Esp solo or Am negro

esquire [ɪ'skwaɪə(r)] n Br señor m; **Timothy Whiteman E.** Sr. Don Timothy Whiteman

essay ['eseɪ] n Educ redacción f

essence ['esəns] n esencia f; **in e.** esencialmente

essential [ɪ'senʃəl] **1** adj esencial, imprescindible
2 n necesidad básica; **the essentials** lo fundamental

essentially [ɪ'senʃəlɪ] adv esencialmente

establish [ɪ'stæblɪʃ] vt (a) (found) establecer; (business) montar (b) Jur **to e. a fact** probar un hecho; **to e. the truth** demostrar la ver-dad

established [ɪ'stæblɪʃt] adj (person) establecido(a); (fact) conocido(a)

establishment [ɪ'stæblɪʃmənt] n establecimiento m; **the E.** el sistema

estate [ɪ'steɪt] n (a) (land) finca f; Br **e. agent** agente mf inmobiliario(a); Br **e. (car)** ranchera f, Esp coche m modelo familiar (b) Br **(housing) e.** urbanización f (c) Jur (of deceased person) herencia f

esteem [ɪ'sti:m] **1** n **to hold sb in great e.** apreciar mucho a algn
2 vt estimar

esthetic [es'θetɪk] adj US = aesthetic

estimate 1 n ['estɪmɪt] (calculation) cálculo m; (likely cost of work) presupuesto m; **rough e.** cálculo aproximado
2 vt ['estɪmeɪt] calcular; Fig pensar, creer

estimation [estɪ'meɪʃən] n (a) (opinion) juicio m, opinión f (b) (esteem) estima f

Estonia [e'stəʊnɪə] n Estonia

Estonian [e'stəʊnɪən] **1** adj estonio(a)
2 n (a) (person) estonio(a) m,f (b) (language) estonio m

estrange [ɪ'streɪndʒ] vt **to become estranged (from)** alejarse (de)

estuary ['estjʊərɪ] n estuario m

etc [et'setrə] adv (abbr et cetera) etc., etcétera

etching ['etʃɪŋ] n aguafuerte m

eternal [ɪ'tɜ:nəl] adj eterno(a), incesante; **e. triangle** triángulo amoroso

eternity [ɪ'tɜ:nɪtɪ] n eternidad f

ether ['i:θə(r)] n éter m

ethereal [ɪ'θɪərɪəl] adj etéreo(a)

ethical ['eθɪkəl] adj ético(a)

ethics ['eθɪks] n ética f

Ethiopia [i:θɪ'əʊpɪə] n Etiopía

ethnic ['eθnɪk] adj étnico(a)

ethos ['i:θɒs] n carácter distintivo

e-ticket ['i:'tɪkɪt] n Esp billete m or Am boleto m or Am pasaje m electrónico

etiquette ['etɪket] n protocolo m, etiqueta f

etymology [etɪ'mɒlədʒɪ] n etimología f

EU [i:'ju:] n (abbr **European Union**) UE f

eucalyptus [ju:kə'lɪptəs] n eucalipto m

euphemism ['ju:fɪmɪzəm] n eufemismo m

euphoria [ju:'fɔ:rɪə] n euforia f

euro ['jʊərəʊ] n (pl **euros**) (European currency) euro m

Eurocrat ['jʊərəʊkræt] n eurócrata mf

Euro-MP ['jʊərəʊempi:] n eurodiputado(a) m,f

Europe ['jʊərəp] n Europa

European [jʊərə'pi:ən] adj & n europeo(a) (m,f); **E. Union** Unión Europea

Eurosceptic ['jʊərəʊskeptɪk] n Br euroescéptico(a) m,f

euthanasia [ju:θə'neɪzɪə] n eutanasia f

evacuate [ɪ'vækjʊeɪt] vt evacuar

evacuation [ɪvækjʊ'eɪʃən] n evacuación f

evade [ɪ'veɪd] vt evadir

evaluate [ɪ'væljʊeɪt] vt evaluar

evaluation [ɪvæljʊ'eɪʃən] n evaluación f

evangelical [i:væn'dʒelɪkəl] adj evangélico(a)

evangelist [ɪ'vændʒɪlɪst] n evangelista mf

evaporate [ɪ'væpəreɪt] **1** vt evaporar; **evaporated milk** leche condensada sin endulzar

2 vi evaporarse; Fig desvanecerse

evasion [ɪ'veɪʒən] n (**a**) (of pursuer, question) evasión f (**b**) (evasive answer) evasiva f

evasive [ɪ'veɪsɪv] adj evasivo(a)

eve [iːv] n víspera f; **on the e. of** en vísperas de

even ['iːvən] **1** adj (**a**) (smooth) liso(a); (level) llano(a) (**b**) (regular) uniforme (**c**) (equally balanced) igual; **to get e. with sb** desquitarse con algn (**d**) (number) par (**e**) (at the same level) a nivel (**f**) (quantity) exacto(a)

2 adv (**a**) (for emphasis) incluso, aun; **e. now** incluso ahora; **e. so** aun así; **e. the children knew** hasta los niños lo sabían (**b**) (negative) **not e.** ni siquiera; **she can't e.** write her name ni siquiera sabe escribir su nombre (**c**) (before comparative) aun, todavía; **e. worse** aun peor (**d**) **e. if** incluso si; **e. though** aunque

3 vt igualar

evening ['iːvnɪŋ] n (**a**) (early) tarde f; (late) noche f; **in the e.** por la tarde; **tomorrow e.** mañana por la tarde; **e. class** clase nocturna; **e. dress** (for man) traje m de etiqueta; (for woman) traje m de noche; **e. paper** periódico vespertino (**b**) (greeting) **good e.!** (early) ¡buenas tardes!; (late) ¡buenas noches!

evenly ['iːvənlɪ] adv (uniformly) uniformemente; (fairly) equitativamente

event [ɪ'vent] n (**a**) (happening) suceso m, acontecimiento m (**b**) (case) caso m; **in the e. of fire** en caso de incendio (**c**) Sport prueba f

eventful [ɪ'ventfʊl] adj **an e. day** (busy) un día agitado; (memorable) un día memorable

eventual [ɪ'ventʃʊəl] adj (ultimate) final; (resulting) consiguiente

> 🖉 Note that the Spanish word **eventual** is a false friend and is never a translation for the English word **eventual**. In Spanish **eventual** means both "possible" and "temporary".

eventuality [ɪventʃʊ'ælɪtɪ] n eventualidad f

eventually [ɪ'ventʃʊəlɪ] adv finalmente

> 🖉 Note that the Spanish word **eventual-mente** is a false friend and is never a translation for the English word **eventually**. In Spanish **eventualmente** means both "by chance" and "possibly".

ever ['evə(r)] adv (**a**) (always, at any time) siempre; **for e.** para siempre; **stronger than e.** más fuerte que nunca (**b**) (with negative sense) **not e.** nunca (**c**) (in questions) alguna vez; **have you e. been there?** ¿has estado allí alguna vez? (**d**) (emphasis) **how e. did you manage it?** ¿cómo diablos lo conseguiste?; **thank you e. so much** muchísimas gracias

evergreen ['evəɡriːn] **1** adj de hoja perenne

2 n árbol m de hoja perenne

everlasting [evə'lɑːstɪŋ] adj eterno(a)

evermore [evə'mɔː(r)] adv **for e.** para siempre jamás

every ['evrɪ] adj (**a**) (each) cada; **e. now and then** de vez en cuando; **e. day** todos los días; **e. other day** cada dos días; **e. one of you** todos(as) vosotros(as); **e. citizen** todo ciudadano (**b**) **you had e. right to be angry** tenías toda la razón para estar esp Esp enfadado or esp Am enojado

everybody ['evrɪbɒdɪ] pron todo el mundo, todos(as)

everyday ['evrɪdeɪ] adj diario(a), de todos los días; **an e. occurrence** un suceso cotidiano

everyone ['evrɪwʌn] pron todo el mundo, todos(as)

everyplace ['evrɪpleɪs] adv US = **every-where**

everything ['evrɪθɪŋ] pron todo; **he eats e.** come de todo; **she means e. to me** ella lo es todo para mí

everywhere ['evrɪweə(r)] adv en todas partes, por todas partes

evict [ɪ'vɪkt] vt desahuciar

evidence ['evɪdəns] n (**a**) (proof) evidencia f (**b**) Jur testimonio m; **to give e.** prestar declaración (**c**) (sign) indicio m, señal f; **to be in e.** dejarse notar

evident ['evɪdənt] adj evidente, manifiesto(a)

evidently ['evɪdəntlɪ] adv evidentemente, al parecer

evil ['iːvəl] **1** adj (wicked) malo(a), malvado(a); (harmful) nocivo(a); (unfortunate) aciago(a)

2 n mal m

evocative [ɪ'vɒkətɪv] adj evocador(a)

evoke [ɪ'vəʊk] vt evocar

evolution [iːvə'luːʃən] n evolución f; Biol desarrollo m

evolve [ɪ'vɒlv] **1** vi (species) evolucionar; (ideas) desarrollarse

2 vt desarrollar

ewe [juː] n oveja f

ex [eks] n **her ex** su ex marido; **his ex** su ex mujer

ex- [eks] *pref* ex, antiguo(a); **ex-minister** ex ministro

exacerbate [ɪgˈzæsəbeɪt] *vt* exacerbar

exact [ɪgˈzækt] **1** *adj (accurate)* exacto(a); *(definition)* preciso(a); **this e. spot** ese mismo lugar
2 *vt* exigir

exacting [ɪgˈzæktɪŋ] *adj* exigente

exactly [ɪgˈzæktlɪ] *adv* exactamente; precisamente; **e.!** ¡exacto!

exaggerate [ɪgˈzædʒəreɪt] *vi & vt* exagerar

exaggeration [ɪgzædʒəˈreɪʃən] *n* exageración *f*

exalt [ɪgˈzɔːlt] *vt Fml* exaltar

exam [ɪgˈzæm] *n Fam* examen *m*

examination [ɪgzæmɪˈneɪʃən] *n* (a) *Educ* examen *m*; **to sit an e.** hacer un examen (b) *Med* reconocimiento *m* (c) *Jur* interrogatorio *m*

examine [ɪgˈzæmɪn] *vt Educ* examinar; *(customs)* registrar; *Med* hacer un reconocimiento médico a; *Jur* interrogar

examiner [ɪgˈzæmɪnə(r)] *n* examinador(a) *m,f*

example [ɪgˈzɑːmpəl] *n* ejemplo *m*; *(specimen)* ejemplar *m*; **for e.** por ejemplo

exasperate [ɪgˈzɑːspəreɪt] *vt* exasperar

exasperation [ɪgzɑːspəˈreɪʃən] *n* exasperación *f*

excavate [ˈekskəveɪt] *vt* excavar

excavation [ekskəˈveɪʃən] *n* excavación *f*

exceed [ekˈsiːd] *vt* exceder, sobrepasar

exceedingly [ekˈsiːdɪŋlɪ] *adv* extremadamente, sumamente

excel [ɪkˈsel] **1** *vi* sobresalir
2 *vt* superar

excellency [ˈeksələnsɪ] *n* **His E.** Su Excelencia

excellent [ˈeksələnt] *adj* excelente

except [ɪkˈsept] **1** *prep* excepto, salvo; **e. for the little ones** excepto los pequeños; **e. that …** salvo que …
2 *vt* exceptuar

exception [ɪkˈsepʃən] *n* excepción *f*; **with the e. of** a excepción de; **without e.** sin excepción; **to take e. to sth** *(be offended)* ofenderse por algo

exceptional [ɪkˈsepʃənəl] *adj* excepcional

excerpt [ˈeksɜːpt] *n* extracto *m*

excess **1** *n* [ɪkˈses] exceso *m*
2 *adj* [ˈekses] excedente; **e. baggage** exceso *m* de equipaje; **e. fare** suplemento *m*

excessive [ɪkˈsesɪv] *adj* excesivo(a)

excessively [ɪkˈsesɪvlɪ] *adv* excesivamente, en exceso

exchange [ɪksˈtʃeɪndʒ] **1** *n* (a) *(of prisoners, ideas)* intercambio *m*; **e. of ideas** intercambio *m* de ideas; **in e. for** a cambio de (b) *Fin* **e. rate** tipo *m* de cambio (c) **(telephone) e.** central telefónica
2 *vt* (a) *(insults, gifts, information)* intercambiar; **to e. blows** golpearse (b) *Fin (currency)* cambiar

exchequer [ɪksˈtʃekə(r)] *n Br* **the E.** Hacienda *f*; **Chancellor of the E.** Ministro *m* de Hacienda

excise [ˈeksaɪz] *n* impuesto *m* sobre el consumo; **e. duty** derechos *mpl* de aduana

excitable [ɪkˈsaɪtəbəl] *adj* excitable

excite [ɪkˈsaɪt] *vt (person)* entusiasmar, emocionar; *(stimulate)* excitar

excited [ɪkˈsaɪtɪd] *adj* entusiasmado(a), emocionado(a)

excitement [ɪkˈsaɪtmənt] *n (stimulation)* excitación *f*; *(emotion)* emoción *f*; *(commotion)* agitación *f*

exciting [ɪkˈsaɪtɪŋ] *adj* apasionante, emocionante

exclaim [ɪkˈskleɪm] **1** *vi* exclamar
2 *vt* gritar

exclamation [eksкləˈmeɪʃən] *n* exclamación *f*; **e.** *Br* **mark** *or US* **point** signo *m* de admiración

exclude [ɪkˈskluːd] *vt* excluir; *(from club)* no admitir

excluding [ɪkˈskluːdɪŋ] *prep* excepto

exclusion [ɪkˈskluːʒən] *n* exclusión *f*

exclusive [ɪkˈskluːsɪv] **1** *adj* exclusivo(a); *(neighbourhood)* selecto(a); *(club)* cerrado(a)
2 *n Press* exclusiva *f*

exclusively [ɪkˈskluːsɪvlɪ] *adv* exclusivamente

excommunicate [ekskəˈmjuːnɪkeɪt] *vt* excomulgar

excrement [ˈekskrɪmənt] *n* excremento *m*

excruciating [ɪkˈskruːʃɪeɪtɪŋ] *adj* insoportable

excruciatingly [ɪkˈskruːʃɪeɪtɪŋlɪ] *adv* horriblemente

excursion [ɪkˈskɜːʃən] *n* excursión *f*

excusable [ɪkˈskjuːzəbəl] *adj* perdonable

excuse **1** *vt* [ɪkˈskjuːz] (a) *(forgive)* disculpar, excusar; **e. me!** *(to attract attention)* ¡perdón!, ¡oiga (por favor)!; *(when trying to get past)* con permiso; **may I be excused for a moment?** ¿puedo salir un momento? (b) *(exempt)* dispensar (c) *(justify)* justificar
2 *n* [ɪkˈskjuːs] excusa *f*; **to make an e.** dar excusas

ex-directory [eksdɪ'rektərɪ] *adj Br* **e. (telephone) number** = número de teléfono que no figura en la guía *or Am* en el directorio

execute ['eksɪkjuːt] *vt* (**a**) *(order)* cumplir; *(task)* realizar (**b**) *Jur* cumplir (**c**) *(person)* ejecutar

execution [eksɪ'kjuːʃən] *n* (**a**) *(of order)* cumplimiento *m*; *(of task)* realización *f* (**b**) *Jur* cumplimiento *m* (**c**) *(of person)* ejecución *f*

executioner [eksɪ'kjuːʃənə(r)] *n* verdugo *m*

executive [ɪg'zekjʊtɪv] **1** *adj* ejecutivo(a) **2** *n* ejecutivo(a) *m,f*

executor [ɪg'zekjʊtə(r)] *n* albacea *m*

exemplary [ɪg'zemplərɪ] *adj* ejemplar

exemplify [ɪg'zemplɪfaɪ] *vt* ejemplificar

exempt [ɪg'zempt] **1** *vt* eximir (**from** de) **2** *adj* exento(a); **e. from tax** libre de impuesto

exemption [ɪg'zempʃən] *n* exención *f*

exercise ['eksəsaɪz] **1** *n* ejercicio *m*; **e. book** cuaderno *m* **2** *vt* (**a**) *(rights, duties)* ejercer (**b**) *(dog)* sacar de paseo **3** *vi* hacer ejercicio

exert [ɪg'zɜːt] *vt* *(influence)* ejercer; **to e. oneself** esforzarse

exertion [ɪg'zɜːʃən] *n* esfuerzo *m*

exhale [eks'heɪl] **1** *vt* *(breathe)* exhalar **2** *vi* espirar

exhaust [ɪg'zɔːst] **1** *vt* agotar **2** *n* *(gas)* gases *mpl* de combustión; **e. pipe** tubo *m* de escape

exhausted [ɪg'zɔːstɪd] *adj* agotado(a)

exhausting [ɪg'zɔːstɪŋ] *adj* agotador(a)

exhaustion [ɪg'zɔːstʃən] *n* agotamiento *m*

exhaustive [ɪg'zɔːstɪv] *adj* exhaustivo(a)

exhibit [ɪg'zɪbɪt] **1** *n* *Art* objeto expuesto; *Jur* prueba *f* instrumental **2** *vt Art* exponer; *(surprise etc)* mostrar

exhibition [eksɪ'bɪʃən] *n* exposición *f*

exhibitionist [eksɪ'bɪʃənɪst] *adj & n* exhibicionista *(mf)*

exhilarating [ɪg'zɪləreɪtɪŋ] *adj* estimulante

exhilaration [ɪgzɪlə'reɪʃən] *n* regocijo *m*

exhume [eks'hjuːm] *vt* exhumar

exile ['eksaɪl] **1** *n* (**a**) *(banishment)* exilio *m* (**b**) *(person)* exiliado(a) *m,f* **2** *vt* exiliar

exist [ɪg'zɪst] *vi* existir; *(have little money)* malvivir

existence [ɪg'zɪstəns] *n* existencia *f*

existing [ɪg'zɪstɪŋ] *adj* existente, actual

exit ['eksɪt] **1** *n* salida *f*; **to make an e.** salir **2** *vi* *(leave)* & *Comput* salir

📌 Note that the Spanish word **éxito** is a false friend and is never a translation for the English word **exit**. In Spanish **éxito** means "success".

exodus ['eksədəs] *n* éxodo *m*

exonerate [ɪg'zɒnəreɪt] *vt Fml* exonerar (**from** de)

exorbitant [ɪg'zɔːbɪtənt] *adj* exorbitante, desorbitado(a)

exotic [ɪg'zɒtɪk] *adj* exótico(a)

expand [ɪk'spænd] **1** *vt* *(enlarge)* ampliar; *(gas, metal)* dilatar **2** *vi* *(grow)* ampliarse; *(metal)* dilatarse; *(become more friendly)* abrirse

▶ **expand on** *vt insep* ampliar

expanse [ɪk'spæns] *n* extensión *f*

expansion [ɪk'spænʃən] *n* *(in size)* expansión *f*; *(of gas, metal)* dilatación *f*

expatriate 1 *adj & n* [eks'pætrɪt] expatriado(a) *(m,f)* **2** *vt* [eks'pætrɪeɪt] expatriar

expect [ɪk'spekt] **1** *vt* (**a**) *(anticipate)* esperar; **I half expected that to happen** suponía que iba a ocurrir (**b**) *(demand)* contar con (**c**) *(suppose)* suponer **2** *vi Fam* **to be expecting** estar embarazada

expectancy [ɪk'spektənsɪ] *n* expectación *f*

expectant [ɪk'spektənt] *adj* ilusionado(a); **e. mother** mujer embarazada

expectation [ekspek'teɪʃən] *n* esperanza *f*; **contrary to e.** contrariamente a lo que se esperaba

expedient [ɪk'spiːdɪənt] **1** *adj* conveniente, oportuno(a) **2** *n* expediente *m*, recurso *m*

expedition [ekspɪ'dɪʃən] *n* expedición *f*

expel [ɪk'spel] *vt* expulsar

expend [ɪk'spend] *vt* gastar

expendable [ɪk'spendəbəl] *adj* prescindible

expenditure [ɪk'spendɪtʃə(r)] *n* desembolso *m*

expense [ɪk'spens] *n* gasto *m*; **all expenses paid** con todos los gastos pagados; **to spare no e.** no escatimar gastos; *Fig* **at the e. of** a costa de; **e. account** cuenta *f* de gastos de representación

expensive [ɪk'spensɪv] *adj* caro(a), costoso(a)

experience [ɪk'spɪərɪəns] **1** *n* experiencia *f* **2** *vt* *(sensation)* experimentar; *(difficulty, loss)* sufrir

experienced [ɪk'spɪərɪənst] *adj* experimentado(a)

experiment [ɪk'sperɪmənt] **1** *n* experimento *m*
2 *vi* experimentar, hacer experimentos (on *or* with con)

experimental [ɪksperɪ'mentəl] *adj* experimental

expert ['eksp3ːt] **1** *adj* experto(a)
2 *n* experto(a) *m,f*, especialista *mf*

expertise [eksp3ː'tiːz] *n* pericia *f*

expire [ɪk'spaɪə(r)] *vi* (a) *(die)* expirar; *(mandate)* terminar (b) *Com & Ins* vencer; *(ticket)* caducar

expiry [ɪk'spaɪərɪ] *n* vencimiento *m*; **e. date** fecha *f* de caducidad

explain [ɪk'spleɪn] **1** *vt* explicar; *(clarify)* aclarar; **to e. oneself** justificarse
2 *vi* explicarse

explanation [eksplə'neɪʃən] *n* explicación *f*; *(clarification)* aclaración *f*

explanatory [ɪk'splænətərɪ] *adj* explicativo(a), aclaratorio(a)

expletive [ɪk'spliːtɪv] *n* palabrota *f*, *Esp* taco *m*

explicit [ɪk'splɪsɪt] *adj* explícito(a)

explode [ɪk'spləʊd] **1** *vt* (a) *(bomb)* hacer explotar (b) *Fig (theory)* echar por tierra
2 *vi (bomb)* estallar, explotar; *Fig* **to e. with** *or* **in anger** montar en cólera

exploit 1 *n* ['eksplɔɪt] proeza *f*, hazaña *f*
2 *vt* [ɪk'splɔɪt] explotar

exploitation [eksplɔɪ'teɪʃən] *n* explotación *f*

exploratory [ek'splɒrətərɪ] *adj* exploratorio(a)

explore [ɪk'splɔː(r)] *vt* explorar

explorer [ɪk'splɔːrə(r)] *n* explorador(a) *m,f*

explosion [ɪk'spləʊʒən] *n* explosión *f*

explosive [ɪk'spləʊsɪv] **1** *adj* explosivo(a); **e. issue** asunto delicado
2 *n* explosivo *m*

exponent [ɪk'spəʊnənt] *n* exponente *m*; *(supporter)* defensor(a) *m,f*

export 1 *vt* [ɪk'spɔːt] exportar
2 *n* ['ekspɔːt] (a) *(trade)* exportación *f* (b) *(commodity)* artículo *m* de exportación

exporter [ɪk'spɔːtə(r)] *n* exportador(a) *m,f*

expose [ɪk'spəʊz] *vt (uncover)* exponer; *(secret)* revelar; *(plot)* descubrir; **to e. oneself** exhibirse desnudo

exposed [ɪk'spəʊzd] *adj* expuesto(a)

exposure [ɪk'spəʊʒə(r)] *n* (a) *(to light, cold, heat)* exposición *f*; **to die of e.** morir de frío (b) *Phot* fotografía *f*; **e. meter**

fotómetro *m* (c) *(of criminal)* descubrimiento *m*

expound [ɪk'spaʊnd] *vt* exponer

express [ɪk'spres] **1** *adj* (a) *(explicit)* expreso(a) (b) *Br (letter)* urgente; **e. train** expreso *m*
2 *n Rail* expreso *m*
3 *vt* expresar
4 *adv* **send it e.** mándalo urgente

expression [ɪk'spreʃən] *n* expresión *f*

expressive [ɪk'spresɪv] *adj* expresivo(a)

expressly [ɪk'spreslɪ] *adv Fml* expresamente

expressway [ɪk'spresweɪ] *n US* autopista *f*

expulsion [ɪk'spʌlʃən] *n* expulsión *f*

exquisite [ɪk'skwɪzɪt] *adj* exquisito(a)

extend [ɪk'stend] **1** *vt* (a) *(enlarge)* ampliar; *(lengthen)* alargar; *(increase)* aumentar; *Fig* **the prohibition was extended to cover cigarettes** extendieron la prohibición a los cigarrillos (b) *(give)* rendir, dar; **to e. a welcome to sb** recibir a algn (c) *(prolong)* prolongar
2 *vi* (a) *(stretch)* extenderse (b) *(last)* prolongarse

extension [ɪk'stenʃən] *n* (a) *(on building)* ampliación *f*, *(of time)* prórroga *f* (b) *(for telephone)* extensión *f*, *RP* interno *m*

extensive [ɪk'stensɪv] *adj* extenso(a)

extent [ɪk'stent] *n* (a) *(area)* extensión *f* (b) **to some e.** hasta cierto punto; **to a large e.** en gran parte; **to a lesser e.** en menor grado; **to such an e.** hasta tal punto

extenuating [ɪk'stenjʊeɪtɪŋ] *adj* atenuante

exterior [ɪk'stɪərɪə(r)] **1** *adj* exterior, externo(a)
2 *n* exterior *m*

exterminate [ɪk'st3ːmɪneɪt] *vt* exterminar

extermination [ɪkst3ːmɪ'neɪʃən] *n* exterminación *f*, exterminio *m*

external [ɪk'st3ːnəl] *adj* externo(a), exterior

extinct [ɪk'stɪŋkt] *adj* extinguido(a)

extinction [ɪk'stɪŋkʃən] *n* extinción *f*

extinguish [ɪk'stɪŋwɪʃ] *vt* extinguir, apagar

extinguisher [ɪk'stɪŋwɪʃə(r)] *n* extintor *m*

extol, *US* **extoll** [ɪk'stəʊl] *vt* ensalzar

extort [ɪk'stɔːt] *vt* arrancar; *(money)* sacar

extortion [ɪk'stɔːʃən] *n* extorsión *f*

extortionate [ɪk'stɔːʃənɪt] *adj* desorbitado(a)

extra ['ekstrə] **1** *adj* extra; *(spare)* de sobra; **e. time** *(in soccer match)* prórroga *f*
2 *adv* extra; **e. fine** extra fino

3 *n (additional charge)* suplemento *m*; *Cin* extra *mf*; *(newspaper)* edición *f* especial

extract 1 *n* ['ekstrækt] extracto *m*
  2 *vt* [ɪk'strækt] *(tooth, information)* extraer; *(confession)* arrancar

extraction [ɪk'strækʃən] *n* extracción *f*

extracurricular [ekstrəkə'rɪkjʊlə(r)] *adj* extracurricular

extradite ['ekstrədaɪt] *vt* extraditar

extramarital [ekstrə'mærɪtəl] *adj* extramatrimonial

extramural [ekstrə'mjʊərəl] *adj* **e. course** = curso para estudiantes libres

extraordinary [ɪk'strɔːdənərɪ] *adj (meeting)* extraordinario(a); *(behaviour etc)* extraño(a)

extravagance [ɪk'strævəgəns] *n (with money)* derroche *m*; *(of behaviour)* extravagancia *f*

extravagant [ɪk'strævəgənt] *adj (wasteful)* derrochador(a); *(excessive)* exagerado(a); *(luxurious)* lujoso(a)

Extremadura [ekstrəmə'djuːrə] *n* Extremadura

extreme [ɪk'striːm] **1** *adj* extremo(a); **an e. case** un caso excepcional; **to hold e. views** tener opiniones radicales
  2 *n* extremo *m*; **in the e.** en sumo grado

extremely [ɪk'striːmlɪ] *adv* extremadamente; **I'm e. sorry** lo siento de veras

extremist [ɪk'striːmɪst] *n* extremista *mf*

extremity [ɪk'stremɪtɪ] *n* extremidad *f*

extricate ['ekstrɪkeɪt] *vt* sacar; **to e. oneself (from)** lograr salir (de)

extrovert ['ekstrəvɜːt] *adj & n* extrovertido(a) *(m,f)*

exuberant [ɪg'zjuːbərənt] *adj* exuberante

exude [ɪg'zjuːd] *vt & vi (moisture, sap)* exudar; *Fig* rebosar

exultant [ɪg'zʌltənt] *adj* jubiloso(a)

eye [aɪ] **1** *n* ojo *m*; *Fig* **I couldn't believe my eyes** no podía creerlo; *Fig* **in the eyes of** según; *Fig* **not to take one's eyes off sb/ sth** no quitar la vista de encima a algo/ algn; *Fig* **to catch sb's e.** llamar la atención a algn; *Fig* **to have an e. for** tener buen ojo para; *Fig* **to make eyes at sb** echar miraditas a algn; *Fig* **to see e. to e. with sb** estar de acuerdo con algn; *Fig* **to turn a blind e. (to)** hacer la vista gorda (a); *Fig* **with an e. to** con miras a; **to keep an e. on sb/sth** vigilar a algo/algn; **to keep an e. out for** estar pendiente de; **black e.** ojo morado; *US* **e. doctor** óptico(a) *m,f*
  2 *vt* observar

eyeball ['aɪbɔːl] *n* globo *m* ocular

eyebrow ['aɪbraʊ] *n* ceja *f*

eyecatching ['aɪkætʃɪŋ] *adj* llamativo(a)

eye-drops ['aɪdrɒps] *npl (medicine)* colirio *m*

eyeglasses ['aɪglɑːsɪz] *npl US (spectacles)* gafas *fpl*, *Am* lentes *mpl*, anteojos *mpl*

eyelash ['aɪlæʃ] *n* pestaña *f*

eyelid ['aɪlɪd] *n* párpado *m*

eyeliner ['aɪlaɪnə(r)] *n* lápiz *m* de ojos

eye-opener ['aɪəʊpənə(r)] *n* revelación *f*, gran sorpresa *f*

eyeshadow ['aɪʃædəʊ] *n* sombra *f* de ojos

eyesight ['aɪsaɪt] *n* vista *f*

eyesore ['aɪsɔː(r)] *n* monstruosidad *f*

eyestrain ['aɪstreɪn] *n* vista cansada

eyewash ['aɪwɒʃ] *n* colirio *m*; *Fig* **it's all e.** eso son disparates

eyewitness ['aɪwɪtnɪs] *n* testigo *mf* ocular

F

F, f [ef] *n* (**a**) *(the letter)* F, f *f* (**b**) *Mus* F fa *m*
F *(abbr* **Fahrenheit**) F

fable ['feɪbəl] *n* fábula *f*

fabric ['fæbrɪk] *n* (**a**) *Tex* tejido *m* (**b**) *Constr* estructura *f*

*Note that the Spanish word **fábrica** is a false friend and is never a translation for the English word **fabric**. In Spanish **fábrica** means "factory".*

fabricate ['fæbrɪkeɪt] *vt* fabricar

fabrication [fæbrɪ'keɪʃən] *n Fig* fabricación *f*

fabulous ['fæbjʊləs] *adj* fabuloso(a)

façade [fə'sɑːd, fæ'sɑːd] *n* fachada *f*

face [feɪs] **1** *n* (**a**) *(of person)* cara *f*, rostro *m*; **f. to f.** cara a cara; **f. cloth** paño *m* (**b**) *(expression)* cara *f*, expresión *f*; **to pull faces** hacer muecas (**c**) *(surface)* superficie *f*; *(of card, coin)* cara *f*, *(of watch)* esfera *f*; **f. down/up** boca abajo/arriba (**d**) *(appearance)* aspecto *m*; **to take sth at f. value** entender algo sólo en su sentido literal; **to lose f.** desprestigiarse; **to save f.** salvar las apariencias
2 *vt* (**a**) *(look on to)* dar a; *(be opposite)* estar enfrente de (**b**) **to f. the wall/window** *(of person)* estar de cara a la pared/ventana (**c**) *(problem)* hacer frente a; **to f. up to** hacer cara a
3 *vi* **to f. on to** dar a; **to f. towards** mirar hacia; **f. this way** vuélvase de este lado

faceless ['feɪsləs] *adj* anónimo(a)

facelift ['feɪslɪft] *n Med* lifting *m*; *Fig* renovación *f*

facet ['fæsɪt] *n* faceta *f*

facetious [fə'siːʃəs] *adj* bromista

facial ['feɪʃəl] *adj* facial

facile ['fæsaɪl] *adj* superficial

facilitate [fə'sɪlɪteɪt] *vt* facilitar

facility [fə'sɪlɪtɪ] *n* (**a**) *(ease)* facilidad *f* (**b**) **facilities** *(means)* facilidades *fpl*; **credit facilities** facilidades de crédito (**c**) **facilities** *(rooms, equipment)* instalaciones *fpl*; **cooking facilities** derecho *m* a cocina

facing ['feɪsɪŋ] *adj* de enfrente

facsimile [fæk'sɪmɪlɪ] *n* (**a**) *(copy)* facsímil *m* (**b**) *(message)* telefax *m* (**c**) *(machine)* facsímil *m*

fact [fækt] *n* hecho *m*; **as a matter of f.** de hecho; **the f. that he confessed** el hecho de que confesara; **in f.** en realidad

fact-finding ['fæktfaɪndɪŋ] *adj* investigador(a)

faction ['fækʃən] *n (group)* facción *f*

factor ['fæktə(r)] *n* factor *m*

factory ['fæktərɪ] *n* fábrica *f*

factual ['fæktʃʊəl] *adj* **a f. error** un error de hecho

faculty ['fækəltɪ] *n* (**a**) *(of mind, section of university)* facultad *f* (**b**) *US Univ* cuerpo *m* docente

fad [fæd] *n Fam (craze)* moda pasajera; *(whim)* capricho *m*

fade [feɪd] *vi (colour)* desteñirse; *(flower)* marchitarse; *(light)* apagarse
▸ **fade away** *vi* desvanecerse
▸ **fade in, fade out** *vt sep Cin & TV* fundir

faded ['feɪdɪd] *adj (colour)* desteñido(a); *(flower)* marchito(a)

fag [fæg] *n* (**a**) *Br Fam (cigarette)* pitillo *m* (**b**) *US very Fam (homosexual)* maricón *m*, *Méx* tortillón *m*, *RP* trolo *m*

faggot ['fægət] *n* (**a**) *Br (meatball)* albóndiga *f* (**b**) *US very Fam (homosexual)* maricón *m*, *Méx* tortillón *m*, *RP* trolo *m*

fail [feɪl] **1** *n* (**a**) *(in exam) Esp* suspenso *m*, *Am* reprobado *m* (**b**) **without f.** sin falta
2 *vt* (**a**) **don't f. me** no me falles (**b**) *(exam)* suspender (**c**) *(be unable)* no lograr (**d**) *(neglect)* dejar de
3 *vi (show, film)* fracasar; *(in exam) Esp* suspender, *Am* reprobar; *(brakes)* fallar (**b**) *(business)* quebrar (**c**) *(of health)* deteriorarse

failing ['feɪlɪŋ] **1** *n* (**a**) *(shortcoming)* defecto *m* (**b**) *(weakness)* punto *m* débil
2 *prep* a falta de

failure ['feɪljə(r)] *n* (**a**) *(lack of success)* fracaso *m* (**b**) *(of company)* quiebra *f* (**c**) *(in exam, course) Esp* suspenso *m*, *Am* reprobado *m* (**d**) *(person)* fracasado(a) *m,f*

faint [feɪnt] **1** *adj* (**a**) *(sound)* débil; *(colour)* pálido(a); *(outline)* borroso(a); *(recollection)* vago(a) (**b**) *(giddy)* mareado(a)
2 *n* desmayo *m*
3 *vi* desmayarse

faint-hearted [feɪntˈhɑːtɪd] *adj* temeroso(a)

fair¹ [feə(r)] **1** *adj* (a) *(impartial)* imparcial; *(just)* justo(a); **it's not f.** no hay derecho; *Fam* **f. enough!** de acuerdo *or Esp* vale (b) *(hair)* rubio(a), *Méx* güero(a); *(skin)* claro(a) (c) *(weather)* bueno(a) (d) *(beautiful)* bello(a) (e) **a f. number** un buen número; **he has a f. chance** tiene bastantes probabilidades
2 *adv* **to play f.** jugar limpio

fair² [feə(r)] *n* (a) *Br (funfair)* feria *f* (b) **trade f.** feria de muestras

fairground [ˈfeəgraʊnd] *n* real *m* de la feria

fairly [ˈfeəlɪ] *adv* (a) *(justly)* justamente (b) *(moderately)* bastante

fairness [ˈfeənɪs] *n* justicia *f*, equidad *f*; **in all f.** para ser justo(a)

fairy [ˈfeərɪ] *n* (a) *(in folklore)* hada *f*; **f. godmother** hada madrina; **f. tale** cuento *m* de hadas (b) *Fam Pej (homosexual)* mariquita *m*

fait accompli [feɪtəˈkɒmpliː] *n Fml* hecho consumado

faith [feɪθ] *n* (a) *Rel* fe *f* (b) *(trust)* confianza *f*; **in good f.** de buena fe

faithful [ˈfeɪθfʊl] **1** *adj* fiel
2 *npl* **the f.** los fieles

faithfully [ˈfeɪθfʊlɪ] *adv* fielmente; **yours f.** *(in letter)* le saluda atentamente

fake [feɪk] **1** *adj* falso(a)
2 *n* (a) *(object)* falsificación *f* (b) *(person)* impostor(a) *m,f*
3 *vt* (a) *(forge)* falsificar (b) *(feign)* fingir
4 *vi (pretend)* fingir

falcon [ˈfɔːlkən] *n* halcón *m*

Falklands [ˈfɔːlkləndz] *npl* **the F.** las (Islas) Malvinas

fall [fɔːl] **1** *n* (a) *(of person, prices, besieged city)* caída *f* (b) *(decrease)* baja *f* (c) *US (autumn)* otoño *m* (d) **falls** *(waterfall)* cascada *f*; **Niagara Falls** las cataratas del Niágara
2 *vi* *(pt* **fell**; *pp* **fallen**) (a) *(drop)* caer; *(trip, tumble)* caerse; **they f. into two categories** se dividen en dos categorías; *Fig* **night was falling** anochecía; *Fig* **to f. short (of)** no alcanzar (b) *(in battle)* caer (c) *(temperature, prices)* bajar (d) *(become)* **to f. asleep** dormirse; **to f. ill** caer enfermo(a), enfermar, *RP, Ven* enfermarse; **to f. in love** enamorarse
▸ **fall back** *vi* replegarse
▸ **fall back on** *vt insep* echar mano a, recurrir a
▸ **fall behind** *vi (in race)* quedarse atrás; **to f. behind with one's work** retrasarse en el trabajo

▸ **fall down** *vi* (a) *(picture etc)* caerse (b) *(building)* derrumbarse
▸ **fall for** *vt insep* (a) *(person)* enamorarse de (b) *(trick)* dejarse engañar por
▸ **fall in** *vi* (a) *(roof)* desplomarse (b) *Mil* formar filas
▸ **fall off 1** *vi* (a) *(drop off)* caerse (b) *(part)* desprenderse (c) *(diminish)* disminuir
2 *vt insep* **to f. off sth** caerse de algo
▸ **fall out** *vi* (a) *(hair)* caerse (b) *Mil* romper filas (c) *(quarrel)* pelearse
▸ **fall over** *vi* caerse
▸ **fall through** *vi (plan)* fracasar

fallacy [ˈfæləsɪ] *n* falacia *f*

fallen [ˈfɔːlən] *pp of* **fall**

fallible [ˈfælɪbəl] *adj* falible

fall-out [ˈfɔːlaʊt] *n* **(radioactive) f.** lluvia radioactiva; **f. shelter** refugio antiatómico

fallow [ˈfæləʊ] *adj Agr* en barbecho

false [fɔːls] *adj* falso(a); **f. teeth** dentadura postiza; **f. alarm** falsa alarma

falsehood [ˈfɔːlshʊd] *n* falsedad *f*

falsify [ˈfɔːlsɪfaɪ] *vt (records, accounts)* falsificar; *(story)* falsear

falter [ˈfɔːltə(r)] *vi* vacilar; *(voice)* fallar

faltering [ˈfɔːltərɪŋ] *adj* vacilante

fame [feɪm] *n* fama *f*

familiar [fəˈmɪljə(r)] *adj* (a) *(common)* familiar, conocido(a); **his face is f.** su cara me suena (b) *(aware, knowledgeable)* enterado(a), al corriente (**with** de) (c) **to be on f. terms with sb** *(know well)* tener confianza con algn

familiarity [fəmɪlɪˈærɪtɪ] *n* (a) *(awareness, knowledge)* familiaridad *f* (**with** con) (b) *(intimacy)* confianza *f*

familiarize [fəˈmɪljəraɪz] *vt* (a) *(become acquainted)* familiarizar (**with** con); **to f. oneself with sth** familiarizarse con algo (b) *(make widely known)* popularizar

family [ˈfæmɪlɪ] *n* familia *f*; **f. allowance** subsidio *m* familiar; **f. doctor** médico *m* de cabecera; **f. man** hombre hogareño; **f. planning** planificación *f* familiar; **f. tree** árbol genealógico

famine [ˈfæmɪn] *n* hambre *f*, escasez *f* de alimentos

famished [ˈfæmɪʃt] *adj Fam* muerto(a) de hambre

famous [ˈfeɪməs] *adj* célebre, famoso(a) (**for** por)

famously [ˈfeɪməslɪ] *adv Fam* estupendamente

fan [fæn] **1** *n* (a) *(cooling device) (handheld)* abanico *m*; *(mechanical)* ventilador *m* (b) *(person)* aficionado(a) *m,f*; *(of pop*

star etc) fan *mf*; **f. club** club *m* de fans; **football f.** hincha *mf*
  2 *vt* (**a**) *(with fan)* abanicar (**b**) *(fire, passions)* avivar
▸**fan out** *vi (troops)* desplegarse en abanico

fanatic [fə'nætɪk] *adj & n* fanático(a) *(m,f)*

fanatical [fə'nætɪkəl] *adj* fanático(a)

fanciful ['fænsɪfʊl] *adj* (**a**) *(person)* caprichoso(a) (**b**) *(idea)* fantástico(a)

fancy ['fænsɪ] **1** *adj* (**fancier, fanciest**) de fantasía; **f. dress** disfraz *m*
  2 *n* (**a**) *(imagination)* fantasía *f* (**b**) *(whim)* capricho *m*, antojo *m*; **to take a f. to sb** cogerle cariño a algn; **to take a f. to sth** encapricharse con algo
  3 *vt* (**a**) *(imagine)* imaginarse; *Fam* **f. seeing you here!** ¡qué casualidad verte por aquí! (**b**) *(like, want)* apetecer; **do you f. a drink?** ¿te apetece una copa?; *Br Fam* **I f. her** ella me gusta

fanfare ['fænfeə(r)] *n* fanfarria *f*

fang [fæŋ] *n* colmillo *m*

fanny ['fænɪ] *n* (**a**) *US Fam (buttocks)* culo *m* (**b**) *Br Vulg (vagina) Esp* coño *m*, *Andes, RP* concha *f*; *Méx* paloma *f*

fantasize ['fæntəsaɪz] *vi* fantasear

fantastic [fæn'tæstɪk] *adj* fantástico(a)

fantasy ['fæntəsɪ] *n* fantasía *f*

FAQ [fæk] *(abbr* **frequently asked questions**) *n Comput* preguntas *fpl* más frecuentes

far [fɑː(r)] (**farther** *or* **further, farthest** *or* **furthest**) **1** *adj* (**a**) *(distant)* lejano(a); **the F. East** el Lejano Oriente (**b**) *(at the f.* end en el otro extremo (**c**) *Pol* **the f. left/right** la extrema izquierda/derecha
  2 *adv* (**a**) *(distant)* lejos; **f. off** a lo lejos; **farther back/north** más atrás/al norte; **how f. is it to Cardiff?** ¿cuánto hay de aquí a Cardiff?; **as f. as I know** que yo sepa; **as f. as possible** en lo posible; *Fig* **f. from complaining, he seemed pleased** lejos de quejarse, parecía contento; *Fig* **I'm f. from satisfied** no estoy satisfecho(a) ni mucho menos; *Fam* **to go too f.** pasarse de la raya (**b**) *(in time)* **as f. back as the fifties** ya en los años cincuenta; **so f.** hasta ahora (**c**) *(much)* mucho; **by f.** con diferencia *or* mucho, *RP* por lejos; **f. cleverer** mucho más listo(a); **f. too much** demasiado

faraway ['fɑːrəweɪ] *adj* lejano(a), remoto(a)

farce [fɑːs] *n* farsa *f*

farcical ['fɑːsɪkəl] *adj* absurdo(a)

fare [feə(r)] **1** *n* (**a**) *(ticket price)* tarifa *f*, precio *m* del billete; *(for boat)* pasaje *m*; **half f.** media tarifa (**b**) *(passenger)*

pasajero(a) *m,f* (**c**) *(food)* comida *f*
  2 *vi* **how did you f.?** ¿qué tal te fue?

farewell [feə'wel] **1** *interj Literary* ¡adiós!
  2 *n* despedida *f*

far-fetched [fɑː'fetʃt] *adj* rebuscado(a)

farm [fɑːm] **1** *n (small)* granja *f*; *(large)* hacienda *f*, *CSur* estancia *f*
  2 *vt* cultivar, labrar
▸**farm out** *vt sep* encargar fuera

farmer ['fɑːmə(r)] *n* granjero(a) *m,f*, *Am* hacendado *m,f*

farmhand ['fɑːmhænd] *n* peón *m*, labriego(a) *m,f*

farmhouse ['fɑːmhaʊs] *n* granja *f*, *Am* hacienda *f*

farming ['fɑːmɪŋ] **1** *n* (**a**) *(agriculture)* agricultura *f* (**b**) *(of land)* cultivo *m*, labranza *f*
  2 *adj* agrícola

farmyard ['fɑːmjɑːd] *n* corral *m*

far-reaching [fɑː'riːtʃɪŋ] *adj* de gran alcance

far-sighted [fɑː'saɪtɪd] *adj* (**a**) *(person)* con visión de futuro (**b**) *(plan)* con miras al futuro

fart [fɑːt] *Fam* **1** *n* pedo *m*
  2 *vi* echarse un pedo

farther ['fɑːðə(r)] *adj & adv comp of* **far**

farthest ['fɑːðɪst] *adj & adv superl of* **far**

fascinate ['fæsɪneɪt] *vt* fascinar

fascinating ['fæsɪneɪtɪŋ] *adj* fascinante

fascination [fæsɪ'neɪʃən] *n* fascinación *f*

fascism ['fæʃɪzəm] *n* fascismo *m*

fascist ['fæʃɪst] *adj & n* fascista *(mf)*

fashion ['fæʃən] **1** *n* (**a**) *(manner)* manera *f*, modo *m*; **after a f.** más o menos (**b**) *(latest style)* moda *f*; **to go/be out of f.** pasar/no estar de moda; **f. designer** diseñador(a) *m,f* de modas; **f. parade** desfile *m* de modelos
  2 *vt (metal)* labrar; *(clay)* formar

fashionable ['fæʃənəbəl] *adj* de moda

fast¹ [fɑːst] **1** *adj* (**a**) *(quick)* rápido(a) (**b**) **hard and f. rules** reglas estrictas (**c**) *(clock)* adelantado(a)
  2 *adv* (**a**) *(rapidly)* rápido, deprisa; **how f.?** ¿a qué velocidad? (**b**) *(securely)* firmemente; **f. asleep** profundamente dormido(a)

fast² [fɑːst] **1** *n* ayuno *m*
  2 *vi* ayunar

fasten ['fɑːsən] **1** *vt* (**a**) *(attach)* sujetar; *(fix)* fijar (**b**) *(belt)* abrochar; *(bag)* asegurar; *(shoelaces)* atar
  2 *vi (dress)* abrocharse

fastener ['fɑːsənə(r)] *n* cierre *m*

fastidious [fæ'stɪdɪəs] *adj* quisquilloso(a)

fat [fæt] **1** *adj* (**fatter, fattest**) (**a**) (*person*) gordo(a) (**b**) (*book, file*) grueso(a) (**c**) (*meat*) que tiene mucha grasa
2 *n* grasa *f*; **cooking f.** manteca *f* de cerdo

fatal ['feɪtəl] *adj* (**a**) (*accident, illness*) mortal (**b**) (*ill-fated*) fatal, funesto(a) (**c**) (*fateful*) fatídico(a)

fatalistic [feɪtə'lɪstɪk] *adj* fatalista

fatality [fə'tælɪtɪ] *n* víctima *f* mortal

> *Note that the Spanish word **fatalidad** is a false friend and is never a translation for the English word **fatality**. In Spanish **fatalidad** means both "fate" and "misfortune".*

fatally ['feɪtəlɪ] *adv* **f. wounded** mortalmente herido(a)

fate [feɪt] *n* destino *m*, suerte *f*

fateful ['feɪtfʊl] *adj* fatídico(a), aciago(a)

father ['fɑːðə(r)] *n* (**a**) (*parent*) padre *m*; **my f. and mother** mis padres; **F. Christmas** Papá *m* Noel (**b**) *Rel* padre *m*

fatherhood ['fɑːðəhʊd] *n* paternidad *f*

father-in-law ['fɑːðərɪnlɔː] *n* suegro *m*

fatherland ['fɑːðəlænd] *n* patria *f*

fatherly ['fɑːðəlɪ] *adj* paternal

fathom ['fæðəm] **1** *n* *Naut* braza *f*
2 *vt* comprender
▸ **fathom out** *vt sep* comprobar; **I can't f. it out** no me lo explico

fatigue [fə'tiːg] *n* (**a**) (*tiredness*) fatiga *f* (**b**) *Mil* faena *f*; **f. dress** traje *m* de faena

fatten ['fætən] *vt* engordar

fattening ['fætənɪŋ] *adj* que engorda

fatty ['fætɪ] **1** *adj* (**fattier, fattiest**) (*food*) graso(a); *Anat* (*tissue*) adiposo(a)
2 *n* *Fam* (*person*) gordinflón(ona) *m,f*

fatuous ['fætjʊəs] *adj* necio(a)

faucet ['fɔːsɪt] *n* *US* *Esp* grifo *m*, *Chile, Col, Méx* llave *f*, *RP* canilla *f*

fault [fɔːlt] **1** *n* (**a**) (*defect*) defecto *m*; (*in merchandise*) desperfecto *m* (**b**) (*blame*) culpa *f*; **to be at f.** tener la culpa (**c**) (*mistake*) error *m* (**d**) *Geol* falla *f*
2 *vt* criticar

faultless ['fɔːltlɪs] *adj* intachable

faulty ['fɔːltɪ] *adj* (**faultier, faultiest**) defectuoso(a)

fauna ['fɔːnə] *n* fauna *f*

faux pas [fəʊ'pɑː] *n* (*pl* **faux pas**) *Fml* (*mistake*) paso *m* en falso; (*blunder*) metedura *f* de pata

favour, *US* **favor** ['feɪvə(r)] **1** *n* favor *m*; **in f. of** a favor de; **to be in f. with sb** gozar del favor de algn; **to ask sb a f.** pedirle un favor a algn; **1-0 in our f.** (*advantage*) 1-0 a favor nuestro

2 *vt* (**a**) (*person*) favorecer a (**b**) (*approve*) estar a favor de

favourable, *US* **favorable** ['feɪvərəbəl] *adj* favorable

favourite, *US* **favorite** ['feɪvərɪt] *adj & n* favorito(a) (*m,f*)

favouritism, *US* **favoritism** ['feɪvərɪtɪzəm] *n* favoritismo *m*

fawn[1] [fɔːn] **1** *adj* beige, *Esp* beis
2 *n* (**a**) *Zool* cervatillo *m* (**b**) (*colour*) beige *m*, *Esp* beis *m*

fawn[2] [fɔːn] *vi* adular (**on** a)

fax [fæks] **1** *n* (*machine, message*) fax *m*; **f. modem** modem *m* fax
2 *vt* mandar por fax

fear [fɪə(r)] **1** *n* miedo *m*, temor *m*; **for f. of** por temor a; *Fam* **no f.!** ¡ni pensarlo!
2 *vt* temer; **I f. it's too late** me temo que ya es tarde
3 *vi* temer (**for** por)

fearful ['fɪəfʊl] *adj* (**a**) (*person*) temeroso(a) (**b**) (*frightening*) espantoso(a)

fearless ['fɪəlɪs] *adj* intrépido(a)

feasibility [fiːzə'bɪlɪtɪ] *n* viabilidad *f*

feasible ['fiːzəbəl] *adj* (*practicable*) factible; (*possible*) viable

feast [fiːst] *n* banquete *m*; *Rel* **f. day** fiesta *f* de guardar

feat [fiːt] *n* hazaña *f*

feather ['feðə(r)] **1** *n* pluma *f*; **f. duster** plumero *m*
2 *vt* *Fam* **to f. one's nest** hacer su agosto

feature ['fiːtʃə(r)] **1** *n* (**a**) (*of face*) rasgo *m*, facción *f* (**b**) (*characteristic*) característica *f* (**c**) **f. film** largometraje *m* (**d**) *Press* crónica *f* especial
2 *vt* (**a**) (*of car, appliance, house*) contar *or* estar equipado(a) con (**b**) *Cin* tener como protagonista a
3 *vi* figurar

February ['februərɪ] *n* febrero *m*

fed [fed] **1** *adj* *Fam* **f. up (with)** harto(a) (de)
2 *pt & pp of* **feed**

federal ['fedərəl] *adj* federal

federation [fedə'reɪʃən] *n* federación *f*

fee [fiː] *n* (*of lawyer, doctor*) honorarios *mpl*; *Ftb* **transfer f.** prima *f* de traslado; *Univ* **tuition fees** derechos *mpl* de matrícula

feeble ['fiːbəl] *adj* débil

feed [fiːd] **1** *vt* (*pt & pp* **fed**) (**a**) (*give food to*) dar de comer a; *Fig* (*fire*) alimentar; **to f. a baby** (*breast-feed*) amamantar a un bebé; (*with bottle*) dar el biberón a un bebé (**b**) *Elec* alimentar (**c**) (*insert*) introducir
2 *vi* (*cows, sheep*) pacer; **to f. on sth** (*person*) comer algo

3 *n* (**a**) *(food)* comida *f*; **cattle f.** pienso *m* (**b**) *Fig* reacción *f*
▸ **feed up** *vt sep* cebar
feedback ['fiːdbæk] *n* (**a**) *Tech* feedback *m* (**b**) *Fig* reacción *f*
feeder ['fiːdə(r)] *n Tech* alimentador *m*
feeding ['fiːdɪŋ] *n* **f. bottle** biberón *m*
feel [fiːl] **1** *vi* (*pt & pp* **felt**) (**a**) *(emotion, sensation)* sentir; **how do you f.?** ¿qué tal te encuentras?; **I f. bad about it** me da pena; **to f. happy/uncomfortable** sentirse feliz/incómodo; **to f. cold/sleepy** tener frío/sueño (**b**) *(seem)* **your hand feels cold** tienes la mano fría; **it feels like summer** parece verano (**c**) *(opinion)* opinar; **I f. sure that ...** estoy seguro(a) de que ... (**d**) **I f. like an ice cream** me tomaría *or Esp* me apetece un helado, *Carib, Col, Méx* me provoca un sorbete; **to f. like doing sth** tener ganas de hacer algo
2 *vt* (**a**) *(touch)* tocar (**b**) **she feels a failure** se siente inútil (**c**) *(notice, be aware of)* notar
3 *n* (**a**) *(touch, sensation)* tacto *m*; *Fig* **to get the f. for sth** *Esp* cogerle el truco a algo, *Am* agarrar la onda a algo (**b**) *(atmosphere)* ambiente *m*
▸ **feel for** *vt insep* (**a**) *(search for)* buscar (**b**) *(have sympathy for)* compadecer
feeler ['fiːlə(r)] *n (of insect)* antena *f*; *Fig* **to put one's feelers out** tantear el terreno
feeling ['fiːlɪŋ] **1** *n* (**a**) *(emotion)* sentimiento *m*; **ill f.** rencor *m* (**b**) *(compassion)* compasión *f* (**c**) **I had the f. that ...** *(impression)* tuve la impresión de que ... (**d**) *(sensitivity)* sensibilidad *f* (**e**) *(opinion)* opinión *f*; **to express one's feelings** expresar sus opiniones
2 *adj* sensible, compasivo(a)
feet [fiːt] *pl of* **foot**
feign [feɪn] *vt* fingir
feint [feɪnt] *Sport* **1** *n* finta *f*
2 *vi* fintar
feline ['fiːlaɪn] **1** *n* felino *m*, félido *m*
2 *adj* felino(a)
fell[1] [fel] *pt of* **fall**
fell[2] [fel] *vt (trees)* talar; *Fig (enemy)* derribar
fellow ['feləʊ] *n* (**a**) *(companion)* compañero(a) *m,f*; **f. citizen** conciudadano(a) *m,f*; **f. countryman/countrywoman** compatriota *mf*; **f. men** prójimos *mpl*; **f. passenger/student** compañero(a) *m,f* de viaje/estudios (**b**) *Fam (chap)* tipo *m*, tío *m* (**c**) *(of society)* socio(a) *m,f*
fellowship ['feləʊʃɪp] *n* (**a**) *(comradeship)* camaradería *f* (**b**) *Univ* beca *f* de investigación

felony ['felənɪ] *n US Jur* crimen *m*, delito *m* grave
felt[1] [felt] *pt & pp of* **feel**
felt[2] [felt] *n Tex* fieltro *m*
felt-tip(ped) ['felttɪp(t)] *adj* **f. pen** rotulador *m*
female ['fiːmeɪl] **1** *adj* (**a**) *Zool* hembra (**b**) *(person)* femenino(a)
2 *n* (**a**) *Zool* hembra *f* (**b**) *(woman)* mujer *f*; *(girl)* chica *f*
feminine ['femɪnɪn] *adj* femenino(a)
feminism ['femɪnɪzəm] *n* feminismo *m*
feminist ['femɪnɪst] *adj & n* feminista *(mf)*
fence [fens] **1** *n* cerca *f*, valla *f*; *Fig* **to sit on the f.** ver los toros desde la barrera
2 *vi Sport* practicar la esgrima
▸ **fence in** *vt sep* meter en un cercado
fencing ['fensɪŋ] *n Sport* esgrima *f*
fend [fend] *vi* **to f. for oneself** valerse por sí mismo
▸ **fend off** *vt sep (blow)* parar; *(question)* rehuir; *(attack)* rechazar
fender ['fendə(r)] *n* (**a**) *(fireplace)* pantalla *f* (**b**) *US Aut Esp, Bol, RP* guardabarros *mpl*, *Andes, CAm, Carib* guardafango *m*, *Méx* salpicadera *f* (**c**) *Naut* defensa *f*
ferment *vt & vi* [fə'ment] fermentar
fern [fɜːn] *n* helecho *m*
ferocious [fə'rəʊʃəs] *adj* feroz
ferocity [fə'rɒsɪtɪ] *n* ferocidad *f*
ferret ['ferɪt] **1** *n* hurón *m*
2 *vi* huronear, husmear
▸ **ferret out** *vt sep* descubrir
ferry ['ferɪ] **1** *n* (**a**) *(small)* barca *f* de pasaje (**b**) *(large, for cars)* transbordador *m*, ferry *m*
2 *vt* transportar
fertile ['fɜːtaɪl] *adj* fértil
fertility [fə'tɪlɪtɪ] *n (of soil)* fertilidad *f*
fertilize ['fɜːtɪlaɪz] *vt* (**a**) *(soil)* abonar (**b**) *(egg)* fecundar
fertilizer ['fɜːtɪlaɪzə(r)] *n* abono *m*
fervent ['fɜːvənt] *adj* ferviente
fervour, *US* **fervor** ['fɜːvə(r)] *n* fervor *m*
fester ['festə(r)] *vi* supurar
festival ['festɪvəl] *n (event)* festival *m*; *(celebration)* fiesta *f*
festive ['festɪv] *adj* festivo(a); **the f. season** las fiestas de Navidad
festivity [fe'stɪvɪtɪ] *n* **the festivities** las fiestas
festoon [fe'stuːn] *vt* adornar
fetch [fetʃ] *vt* (**a**) *(go for)* ir a buscar (**b**) *(bring)* traer (**c**) **how much did it f.?** *(sell for)* ¿por cuánto se vendió?
fetching ['fetʃɪŋ] *adj* atractivo(a)

fete [feɪt] **1** n fiesta f
 2 vt festejar
fetish ['fetɪʃ, 'fiːtɪʃ] n fetiche m
fetus ['fiːtəs] n US = **foetus**
feud [fjuːd] **1** n enemistad duradera
 2 vi pelear
feudal ['fjuːdəl] adj feudal
fever ['fiːvə(r)] n fiebre f
feverish ['fiːvərɪʃ] adj febril
few [fjuː] **1** adj (**a**) (not many) pocos(as);
 as f. as solamente (**b**) (some) algunos(as),
 unos(as) cuantos(as); **a f. books** unos or
 algunos libros; **she has fewer books than
 I thought** tiene menos libros de lo que
 pensaba; **for the past f. years** durante
 estos últimos años; **in the next f. days**
 dentro de unos días; **quite a f.** bastantes
 2 pron (**a**) (not many) pocos(as); **there
 are too f.** no hay suficientes (**b**) (some)
 algunos(as), unos(as) cuantos(as); **who
 has the fewest?** ¿quién tiene menos?
fiancé [fɪ'ɒnseɪ] n prometido m
fiancée [fɪ'ɒnseɪ] n prometida f
fiasco [fɪ'æskəʊ] n (pl Br **fiascos**, US
 fiascoes) fiasco m
fib [fɪb] Fam **1** n trola f
 2 vi contar trolas
fibre, US **fiber** ['faɪbə(r)] n fibra f
fibreglass, US **fiberglass** ['faɪbəglɑːs] n
 fibra f de vidrio
fickle ['fɪkəl] adj inconstante, voluble
fiction ['fɪkʃən] n ficción f
fictional ['fɪkʃənəl] adj (**a**) Lit nove-
 lesco(a) (**b**) (imaginative) ficticio(a)
fictitious ['fɪk'tɪʃəs] adj ficticio(a)
fiddle ['fɪdəl] **1** n (**a**) (violin) violín m (en
 música folk) (**b**) esp Br Fam (swindle) timo
 m
 2 vt Br Fam amañar
 3 vi juguetear (**with** con)
▸ **fiddle about** vi perder tiempo
fiddly ['fɪdlɪ] adj (**fiddlier, fiddliest**) Fam
 laborioso(a)
fidelity [fɪ'delətɪ] n fidelidad f
fidget ['fɪdʒɪt] vi enredar, trastear; **stop
 fidgeting!** ¡estáte quieto!
field [fiːld] **1** n (**a**) (of crops) & Comput
 campo m; **f. glasses** gemelos mpl; **f.
 marshal** mariscal m de campo (**b**) Geol &
 Min yacimiento m (**c**) **f. trip** viaje m de
 estudios; **f. work** trabajo m de campo
 2 vt Sport (**a**) (ball) parar y devolver (**b**)
 (team) presentar
fiend [fiːnd] n demonio m; Fam (fanatic)
 fanático(a) m,f
fiendish ['fiːndɪʃ] adj Fam diabólico(a)

fierce [fɪəs] adj (animal) feroz; (argument)
 acalorado(a); (heat, competition) inten-
 so(a); (wind) violento(a)
fiery ['faɪərɪ] adj (**fierier, fieriest**) (temper)
 fogoso(a); (speech) acalorado(a); (colour)
 encendido(a)
fifteen [fɪf'tiːn] adj & n quince (m inv)
fifteenth [fɪf'tiːnθ] **1** adj & n decimo-
 quinto(a) (m,f)
 2 n (fraction) quinzavo m
fifth [fɪfθ] **1** adj & n quinto(a) (m,f)
 2 n (fraction) quinto m
fifty ['fɪftɪ] adj & n cincuenta (m inv)
fifty-fifty ['fɪftɪ'fɪftɪ] Fam **1** adj **a f. chance**
 una probabilidad del cincuenta por
 ciento
 2 adv **to go f.** ir a medias
fig¹ [fɪg] n (fruit) higo m
fig² [fɪg] (abbr **figure**) fig
fight [faɪt] **1** vt (pt & pp **fought**) (**a**) (enemy,
 rivals) luchar contra; (of boxer) pelear
 contra; Fig (corruption) combatir (**b**)
 (war, battle) librar (**c**) (decision) recurrir
 contra
 2 vi (**a**) (physically) luchar (**about/with**
 por/contra) (**b**) (quarrel) reñir; **to f. over
 sth** disputarse la posesión de algo (**c**) Fig
 (struggle) luchar (**for/against** por/contra)
 3 n (**a**) (physical, verbal) pelea f; (in
 boxing) combate m (**b**) (quarrel) riña f
 (**c**) Fig (struggle) lucha f
▸ **fight back 1** vt sep (tears) contener
 2 vi contraatacar
▸ **fight off** vt sep (**a**) (attack) rechazar (**b**)
 (illness) cortar
▸ **fight out** vt sep discutir
fighter ['faɪtə(r)] n (**a**) (person) combatiente mf; (in boxing) púgil m (**b**) Fig
 luchador(a) m,f; **f. (plane)** (avión m de)
 caza m; **f. bomber** cazabombardero m
fighting ['faɪtɪŋ] **1** adj **he's got a f. chance**
 tiene verdaderas posibilidades
 2 n lucha f
figment ['fɪgmənt] n **it's a f. of your
 imagination** es un producto de tu imaginación
figurative ['fɪgərətɪv] adj figurado(a)
figure ['fɪgə(r), US 'fɪgjər] **1** n (**a**) (form,
 outline) forma f, silueta f (**b**) (shape,
 statue, character) figura f; **she has a good
 f.** tiene buen tipo (**c**) (in book) dibujo m
 (**d**) **f. of speech** figura retórica (**e**) Math
 cifra f
 2 vt US Fam pensar, figurarse
 3 vi (**a**) (appear) (in list, book) figurar (**b**)
 Fam (make sense) **that figures!** (es) normal or lógico
▸ **figure out** vt sep Fam comprender; **I can't
 f. it out** no me lo explico

figurehead ['fɪgəhed] *n Fig* figura deco-
rativa

filament ['fɪləmənt] *n* filamento *m*

filch [fɪltʃ] *vt Fam* afanar, *Esp* mangar

file [faɪl] **1** *n* (**a**) *(tool)* lima *f* (**b**) *(folder)*
carpeta *f* (**c**) *(archive, of computer)*
archivo *m*; **on f.** archivado(a); **f. manager**
administrador *m* de archivos (**d**) *(line)* fila
f; **in single f.** en fila india
  2 *vt* (**a**) *(smooth)* limar (**b**) *(put away)*
archivar
  3 *vi* **to f. past** desfilar

filing ['faɪlɪŋ] *n* clasificación *f*; **f. cabinet**
archivador *m*; *(for cards)* fichero *m*

Filipino [fɪlɪ'piːnəʊ] *n* filipino(a) *m,f*

fill [fɪl] **1** *vt* (**a**) *(space, time)* llenar (**with**
de) (**b**) *(post, requirements)* cubrir (**c**)
Culin rellenar
  2 *vi* llenarse (**with** de)
  3 *n* **to eat one's f.** comer hasta hartarse
▸ **fill in** *vt sep* (**a**) *(space, form)* rellenar
(**b**) *Fam (inform)* poner al corriente (**on**
de) (**c**) *(time)* pasar
  2 *vi* **to f. in for sb** sustituir a algn
▸ **fill out** *vt sep US (form)* llenar
  2 *vi Fam* engordar
▸ **fill up** *vt sep* llenar hasta arriba; *Fam Aut*
f. her up! ¡llénelo!
  2 *vi* llenarse

fillet ['fɪlɪt] *n* filete *m*; **f. steak** filete

filling ['fɪlɪŋ] **1** *adj* que llena mucho
  2 *n* (**a**) *(stuffing)* relleno *m* (**b**) *(in*
tooth) empaste *m* (**c**) *Br* **f. station**
gasolinera *f*, estación *f* de servicio, *Andes,*
Ven bomba *f*, *Méx* gasolinería *f*, *Perú* grifo
m

fillip ['fɪlɪp] *n Fam* estímulo *m*

film [fɪlm] **1** *n* (**a**) *esp Br (at cinema)*
película *f*; **f. star** estrella *f* de cine (**b**)
(layer) capa *f* (**c**) *(photographic)* **a (roll**
of) f. un rollo *or* carrete
  2 *vt Cin* filmar
  3 *vi Cin* rodar

film-strip ['fɪlmstrɪp] *n* cortometraje
m

filter ['fɪltə(r)] **1** *n* filtro *m*; *Aut* **f. lane** carril
m de acceso
  2 *vt* filtrar
▸ **filter through** *vi Fig* filtrarse (**to** a)

filter-tip ['fɪltətɪp] *n (cigarette)* cigarrillo
m con filtro

filth [fɪlθ] *n (dirt)* porquería *f*; *Fig* porquerías *fpl*

filthy ['fɪlθɪ] *adj* (**filthier, filthiest**) (**a**)
(dirty) asqueroso(a) (**b**) *(obscene)* obsce-
no(a)

fin [fɪn] *n Zool & Av* aleta *f*

final ['faɪnəl] **1** *adj* (**a**) *(last)* último(a),
final (**b**) *(definitive)* definitivo(a)

2 *n* (**a**) *Sport* final *f* (**b**) *Univ* **finals** *Br*
exámenes *mpl* de fin de carrera; *US*
exámenes *mpl* finales

finale [fɪ'nɑːlɪ] *n* final *m*

finalist ['faɪnəlɪst] *n* finalista *mf*

finalize ['faɪnəlaɪz] *vt* ultimar; *(date)* fijar

finally ['faɪnəlɪ] *adv (lastly)* por último; *(at*
last) por fin

finance ['faɪnæns, fɪ'næns] **1** *n* (**a**) *(busi-*
ness, funding) finanzas *fpl* (**b**) **finances**
(funds) finanzas *fpl*
  2 *vt* financiar

financial [faɪ'nænʃəl, fɪ'nænʃəl] *adj* fi-
nanciero(a); **f. crisis** crisis económica; *Br*
f. year *(for budget)* ejercicio (económico);
(for tax) año *m* fiscal

financier [faɪ'nænsɪə(r), fɪ'nænsɪə(r)] *n*
financiero(a) *m,f*

finch [fɪntʃ] *n* pinzón *m*

find [faɪnd] **1** *vt (pt & pp* **found**) (**a**) *(locate)*
encontrar (**b**) *(think)* encontrar (**c**)
(discover) descubrir (**d**) *Jur* **to f. sb**
guilty/not guilty declarar culpable/
inocente a algn (**e**) **I can't f. the courage**
to tell him no tengo valor para decírselo; **I**
found it impossible to get away me
resultó imposible irme
  2 *n* hallazgo *m*
▸ **find out 1** *vt sep* (**a**) *(inquire)* averiguar
(**b**) *(discover)* descubrir
  2 *vi* (**a**) **to f. out about sth** informarse
sobre algo (**b**) *(discover)* enterarse

findings ['faɪndɪŋz] *npl* conclusiones *fpl*

fine¹ [faɪn] **1** *n* multa *f*
  2 *vt* multar

fine² [faɪn] **1** *adj* (**a**) *(delicate etc)* fino(a)
(**b**) *(subtle)* sutil (**c**) *(excellent)* excelente
(**d**) *(weather)* bueno(a) (**e**) *(all right)* bien
  2 *adv Fam* muy bien
  3 *interj* ¡vale!

finely ['faɪnlɪ] *adv* (**a**) *(skilfully)* acertadamente, hábilmente (**b**) *(chopped,*
sliced) muy fino (**c**) **f. tuned** a punto

finery ['faɪnərɪ] *n* galas *fpl*

finesse [fɪ'nes] *n (delicacy)* finura *f*;
(cunning) astucia *f*; *(tact)* diplomacia *f*

finger ['fɪŋgə(r)] **1** *n* dedo *m* (de la mano)
  2 *vt* tocar; *Pej* manosear

fingernail ['fɪŋgəneɪl] *n* uña *f*

fingerprint ['fɪŋgəprɪnt] *n* huella *f*
dactilar

fingertip ['fɪŋgətɪp] *n* punta *f or* yema *f*
del dedo

finicky ['fɪnɪkɪ] *adj (person)* quisqui-
lloso(a)

finish ['fɪnɪʃ] **1** *n* (**a**) *(of day, meeting)* final
m; *(of race)* llegada *f* (**b**) *(surface)* acabado
m
  2 *vt* (**a**) *(complete)* acabar, terminar; **to f.**

doing sth terminar de hacer algo (**b**) *(use up)* agotar

3 *vi* acabar, terminar; **to f. second** quedar el segundo

▸ **finish off** *vt sep* (**a**) *(complete)* terminar completamente (**b**) *Fam (kill)* rematar

▸ **finish up 1** *vt sep* acabar, agotar

2 *vi* to **f. up in jail** ir a parar a la cárcel

finished ['fɪnɪʃt] *adj* (**a**) *(product)* acabado(a) (**b**) *Fam (exhausted)* rendido(a)

finishing ['fɪnɪʃɪŋ] *adj* **to put the f. touch(es) to sth** darle los últimos toques a algo; **f. line** (línea *f* de) meta *f*; **f. school** = escuela privada de modales para señoritas

finite ['faɪnaɪt] *adj* finito(a); *(verb)* conjugable

Finland ['fɪnlənd] *n* Finlandia

Finn [fɪn] *n* finlandés(esa) *m,f*

Finnish ['fɪnɪʃ] **1** *adj* finlandés(esa)

2 *n (language)* finlandés *m*

fir [fɜː(r)] *n* abeto *m*

fire ['faɪə(r)] **1** *n* (**a**) *(element, in hearth)* fuego *m* (**b**) *(accident etc)* incendio *m*; **to be on f.** estar en llamas; **to catch f.** incendiarse; **f. alarm** alarma *f* de incendios; *Br* **f. brigade**, *US* **f. department** (cuerpo *m* de) bomberos *mpl*; **f. engine** coche *m* de bomberos; **f. escape** escalera *f* de incendios; **f. exit** salida *f* de emergencia; **f. extinguisher** extintor *m*; **f. fighter** bombero(a) *m,f*; **f. station** parque *m* de bomberos (**c**) *(heater)* estufa *f* (**d**) *Mil* fuego *m*; **to open f.** abrir fuego

2 *vt* (**a**) *(gun)* disparar (**at** a); *(rocket)* lanzar; *Fig* **to f. questions at sb** bombardear a algn a preguntas (**b**) *Fam (dismiss)* despedir

3 *vi (shoot)* disparar (**at** sobre)

firearm ['faɪərɑːm] *n* arma *f* de fuego

fireman ['faɪəmən] *n* bombero *m*

fireplace ['faɪəpleɪs] *n* chimenea *f*, *(hearth)* hogar *m*

fireside ['faɪəsaɪd] *n* hogar *m*; **by the f.** al calor de la lumbre

firewood ['faɪəwʊd] *n* leña *f*

fireworks ['faɪəwɜːks] *npl* fuegos *mpl* artificiales

firing ['faɪərɪŋ] *n Mil* tiroteo *m*; **f. line** línea *f* de fuego; **f. squad** pelotón *m* de fusilamiento

firm [fɜːm] **1** *adj* firme; **to be f. with sb** *(strict)* tratar a algn con firmeza

2 *n Com* empresa *f*, firma *f*

firmly ['fɜːmlɪ] *adv* firmemente

firmness ['fɜːmnɪs] *n* firmeza *f*

first [fɜːst] **1** *adj* primero(a); *(before masculine singular noun)* primer; **Charles the F.** Carlos Primero; **for the f. time** por

primera vez; **in the f. place** en primer lugar; **f. aid** primeros auxilios; **f. floor** *Br* primer piso, *US* planta baja; **f. name** nombre *m* de pila

2 *adv (before anything else)* primero; **f. of all** en primer lugar

3 *n* (**a**) **the f.** el primero/la primera; **the f. of April** el primero *or Esp* el uno de abril (**b**) **at f.** al principio; **from the (very) f.** desde el principio (**c**) *Aut* primera *f*

first-class ['fɜːst'klɑːs] **1** *adj* de primera clase

2 *adv* **to travel f.** viajar en primera

first-hand ['fɜːst'hænd] *adv & adj* de primera mano

firstly ['fɜːstlɪ] *adv* en primer lugar

first-rate ['fɜːst'reɪt] *adj* de primera

fiscal ['fɪskəl] *adj* fiscal

fish [fɪʃ] **1** *n (pl* fish) *(animal)* pez *m*; *(food)* pescado *m*; **f. shop** pescadería *f*; *Br* **f. and chips** = pescado frito con patatas *or Am* papas fritas; **f.** *Br* **finger** *or US* **stick** palito *m* de pescado

2 *vi* pescar; *Fig* **to f. in one's pocket for sth** buscar algo en el bolsillo

fishbone ['fɪʃbəʊn] *n* espina *f*, raspa *f*

fisherman ['fɪʃəmən] *n* pescador *m*

fishing ['fɪʃɪŋ] *n* pesca *f*; **to go f.** ir de pesca; **f. net** red *f* de pesca; **f. rod** caña *f* de pescar; **f. tackle** aparejo *m* de pescar

fishmonger ['fɪʃmʌŋgə(r)] *n Br* pescadero(a) *m,f*; **f.'s (shop)** pescadería *f*

fishy ['fɪʃɪ] *adj* (**fishier, fishiest**) de pescado; *Fam (suspicious)* sospechoso(a)

fist [fɪst] *n* puño *m*

fit[1] [fɪt] **1** *vt* (**a**) *(match)* ajustarse a, adecuarse a; **that suit doesn't f. you** ese traje no te entalla; **the key doesn't f. the lock** la llave no es de esta cerradura; *Fig* **she doesn't f. the description** no responde a la descripción (**b**) *(install)* colocar; **a car fitted with a radio** un coche provisto de radio

2 *vi* (**a**) *(be of right size)* caber (**b**) *(facts etc)* cuadrar

3 *adj* (**a**) *(suitable)* apto(a), adecuado(a) (**for** para); **are you f. to drive?** ¿estás en condiciones de conducir? (**b**) *(healthy)* en (plena) forma; **to keep f.** mantenerse en forma

4 *n* ajuste *m*; **to be a good f.** encajar bien

▸ **fit in 1** *vi* **he didn't f. in with his colleagues** no encajó con sus compañeros de trabajo (**b**) *(tally)* cuadrar (**with** con)

2 *vt sep (find time for)* encontrar un hueco para

▸ **fit out** *vt sep* equipar

fit² [fɪt] *n* (**a**) *Med* ataque *m* (**b**) *Fig* arrebato *m*; **f. of anger** arranque *m* de cólera; *Fig* **by fits and starts** a trompicones

fitful ['fɪtfʊl] *adj* discontinuo(a)

fitness ['fɪtnɪs] *n* (**a**) *(aptitude)* aptitud *f*, capacidad *f* (**b**) *(health)* (buen) estado físico

fitted ['fɪtɪd] *adj* empotrado(a); **f. carpet** moqueta *f*; **f. cupboard** armario empotrado

fitter ['fɪtə(r)] *n* ajustador(a) *m,f*

fitting ['fɪtɪŋ] **1** *adj* apropiado(a)
2 *n* (**a**) *(of dress)* prueba *f*; **f. room** probador *m* (**b**) *(of office)* equipamiento *m*; **fittings** *(of bathroom)* accesorios *mpl*

five [faɪv] *adj & n* cinco (*m inv*)

fiver ['faɪvə(r)] *n Fam Br* cinco libras *fpl*; *US* cinco dólares *mpl*

fix [fɪks] **1** *n* (**a**) *Fam* **to be in a f.** estar en un apuro (**b**) *Fam (drugs)* chute *m*
2 *vt* (**a**) *(fasten)* fijar, asegurar (**b**) *(date, price)* fijar; *(limit)* señalar (**c**) *(repair)* arreglar (**d**) *US (food, drink)* preparar
▸ **fix up** *vt sep (arrange)* arreglar; **to f. sb up with sth** proveer a algn de algo

fixation [fɪk'seɪʃən] *n* idea fija

fixed [fɪkst] *adj* (**a**) *(unchanging)* fijo(a) (**b**) *Fam (match etc)* amañado(a)

fixture ['fɪkstʃə(r)] *n* (**a**) *Br (in football)* encuentro *m* (**b**) **fixtures** *(in building)* accesorios *mpl*

fizz [fɪz] **1** *n* burbujeo *m*
2 *vi* burbujear
▸ **fizzle out** ['fɪzəl] *vi Fam (plan)* quedarse en nada *or Esp* en agua de borrajas

fizzy ['fɪzɪ] *adj* (**fizzier, fizziest**) *(water)* con gas

flabbergasted ['flæbəgɑːstɪd] *adj* pasmado(a)

flabby ['flæbɪ] *adj* (**flabbier, flabbiest**) fofo(a)

flag [flæg] **1** *n* bandera *f*; *Naut* pabellón *m*
2 *vt Fig* **to f. down a car** hacer señales a un coche para que pare
3 *vi (interest)* decaer; *(conversation)* languidecer

flagpole ['flægpəʊl] *n* asta *f* de bandera

flagrant ['fleɪgrənt] *adj* flagrante

flagship ['flægʃɪp] *n* buque *m* insignia

flagstone ['flægstəʊn] *n* losa *f*

flair [fleə(r)] *n* facilidad *f*

flak [flæk] *n* (**a**) *Mil* fuego antiaéreo (**b**) *Fam* críticas *fpl*

flake [fleɪk] **1** *n* *(of snow)* copo *m*; *(of skin, soap)* escama *f*; *(of paint)* desconchón *m*
2 *vi (skin)* descamarse; *(paint)* desconcharse

flamboyant [flæm'bɔɪənt] *adj* extravagante

flame [fleɪm] *n* (**a**) *(of fire)* llama *f*; **to go up in flames** incendiarse (**b**) *Comput* llamarada *f*, = mensaje ofensivo

flameproof ['fleɪmpruːf] *adj* ininflamable

flamingo [flə'mɪŋgəʊ] *n* flamenco *m*

flammable ['flæməbəl] *adj* inflamable

flan [flæn] *n* tarta *f*; **fruit f.** tarta de fruta

📎 Note that the Spanish word **flan** is a false friend and is never a translation for the English word **flan**. In Spanish **flan** means "crème caramel".

---

flank [flæŋk] **1** *n* (**a**) *(of animal)* ijada *f* (**b**) *Mil* flanco *m*
2 *vt* flanquear

flannel ['flænəl] *n* (**a**) *Tex* franela *f* (**b**) *Br (face-cloth)* toallita *f*

flap [flæp] **1** *vt (wings, arms)* batir
2 *vi (wings)* aletear; *(flag)* ondear
3 *n* (**a**) *(of envelope, pocket)* solapa *f*; *(of tent)* faldón *m* (**b**) *(of wing)* aletazo *m* (**c**) *Fam* **to get into a f.** ponerse nervioso(a)

flare [fleə(r)] **1** *n* (**a**) *(flame)* llamarada *f* (**b**) *Mil & Naut* bengala *f*
2 *vi* **to f. (up)** *(fire)* llamear; *Fig (person)* encolerizarse; *(trouble)* estallar

flared [fleəd] *adj (trousers etc)* acampanado(a)

flash [flæʃ] **1** *n* (**a**) *(of light)* destello *m*; *(of lightning)* relámpago *m*; *Fig* **in a f.** en un santiamén (**b**) **news f.** noticia *f* de última hora (**c**) *Phot* flash *m*
2 *adj Br Fam (showy)* llamativo(a), ostentoso(a)
3 *vt* (**a**) *(torch)* dirigir (**b**) *Rad & TV* transmitir
4 *vi* (**a**) *(light)* destellar (**b**) **a car flashed past** un coche pasó como un rayo

flashback ['flæʃbæk] *n* flashback *m*

flashcube ['flæʃkjuːb] *n* cubo *m* flash

flashlight ['flæʃlaɪt] *n US* linterna *f*

flashy ['flæʃɪ] *adj* (**flashier, flashiest**) *Fam* chillón(ona)

flask [flɑːsk] *n* frasco *m*; **(Thermos®) f.** termo *m*

flat [flæt] **1** *adj* (**flatter, flattest**) (**a**) *(surface)* llano(a) (**b**) *(beer)* sin gas (**c**) *(battery)* descargado(a); *(tyre)* desinflado(a) (**d**) *(rate)* fijo(a) (**e**) *(dull)* soso(a) (**f**) *Mus* **B f.** si *m* bemol
2 *adv* (**a**) **to fall f. on one's face** caerse de bruces (**b**) **in ten seconds f.** en diez segundos justos (**c**) *Fam* **to go f. out** ir a todo gas
3 *n* (**a**) *Br (apartment)* apartamento *m*,

Esp piso *m*, *Arg* departamento *m* (**b**) *US Aut* pinchazo *m*

flatly ['flætlɪ] *adv* rotundamente

flatmate ['flætmeɪt] *n Br* compañero(a) *m*,*f* de apartamento *or Esp* piso *or Arg* departamento

flatten ['flætən] *vt* (**a**) *(make level)* allanar (**b**) *(crush)* aplastar

flatter ['flætə(r)] *vt* (**a**) *(of person)* adular, halagar (**b**) *(of clothes, portrait)* favorecer (**c**) **to f. oneself** hacerse ilusiones

flattering ['flætərɪŋ] *adj* (**a**) *(words)* halagador(a) (**b**) *(dress, portrait)* favorecedor(a)

flattery ['flætərɪ] *n* adulación *f*, halago *m*

flaunt [flɔːnt] *vt* hacer alarde de

flavour, *US* **flavor** ['fleɪvə(r)] **1** *n* sabor *m*
2 *vt Culin* sazonar (**with** con)

flavoured, *US* **flavored** ['fleɪvəd] *adj* **strawberry f.** con sabor a fresa *or Bol, CSur, Ecuad* frutilla

flavouring, *US* **flavoring** ['fleɪvərɪŋ] *n* condimento *m*; **artificial f.** aroma *m* artificial

flaw [flɔː] *n* *(failing)* defecto *m*; *(fault)* desperfecto *m*

flawed [flɔːd] *adj* defectuoso(a)

flawless ['flɔːlɪs] *adj* perfecto(a)

flax [flæks] *n* lino *m*

flaxen ['flæksən] *adj* *(hair)* rubio(a) pajizo(a)

flea [fliː] *n* pulga *f*; **f. market** rastro *m*

fleck [flek] *n (speck)* mota *f*, punto *m*

fled [fled] *pt & pp of* **flee**

fledg(e)ling ['fledʒlɪŋ] *adj Fig* novato(a)

flee [fliː] **1** *vt (pt & pp* **fled)** huir de
2 *vi* huir (**from** de)

fleece [fliːs] **1** *n* (**a**) *(sheep's coat)* lana *f* (**b**) *(sheared)* vellón *m*
2 *vt Fam (cheat)* sangrar

fleet [fliːt] *n* flota *f*

fleeting ['fliːtɪŋ] *adj* fugaz

Flemish ['flemɪʃ] **1** *adj* flamenco(a)
2 *n (language)* flamenco *m*

flesh [fleʃ] *n* (**a**) *(of person, animal)* carne *f*; *Fig* **in the f.** en persona; *Fig* **to be of f. and blood** ser de carne y hueso; **f. wound** herida *f* superficial (**b**) *(of fruit)* pulpa *f*

flew [fluː] *pt of* **fly**[1]

flex [fleks] **1** *n Br Elec* cable *m*
2 *vt (muscles)* flexionar

flexibility [fleksɪ'bɪlɪtɪ] *n* flexibilidad *f*

flexible ['fleksɪbəl] *adj* flexible

flexitime ['fleksɪtaɪm] *n* horario *m* flexible

flick [flɪk] **1** *n* movimiento rápido; *(of finger)* capirotazo *m*
2 *vt (with finger)* dar un capirotazo a
▸ **flick through** *vt insep (book)* hojear

flicker ['flɪkə(r)] **1** *n* parpadeo *m*; *Fig* **a f. of hope** un destello de esperanza
2 *vi (flame)* parpadear

flier ['flaɪə(r)] *n* aviador(a) *m*,*f*

flight [flaɪt] *n* (**a**) *(act of flying)* vuelo *m*; **f. attendant** auxiliar *mf* de vuelo; **f. path** trayectoria *f* de vuelo (**b**) *(of ball)* trayectoria *f* (**c**) *(escape)* huida *f*, fuga *f*; **to take f.** darse a la fuga (**d**) *(of stairs)* tramo *m*

flight-deck ['flaɪtdek] *n (cockpit)* cabina *f* del piloto

flimsy ['flɪmzɪ] *adj* **(flimsier, flimsiest)** *(cloth)* ligero(a); *(paper)* fino(a); *(structure)* poco sólido(a); *(excuse)* poco convincente

flinch [flɪntʃ] *vi (wince)* estremecerse

fling [flɪŋ] **1** *vt (pt & pp* **flung)** arrojar
2 *n Fam* **to have a f.** echar una cana al aire

flint [flɪnt] *n* (**a**) *(stone)* pedernal *m* (**b**) *(in lighter)* piedra *f* de mechero

flip [flɪp] **1** *n (flick)* capirotazo *m*; **f. chart** flip chart *m*, pizarra *f* de conferencia *(con bloc)*
2 *vt (toss)* tirar (al aire); **to f. a coin** echar a cara o cruz

flip-flop ['flɪpflɒp] *n* (**a**) *Comput* báscula *f* biestable (**b**) *Br (footwear)* chancla *f*

flippant ['flɪpənt] *adj* frívolo(a)

flipper ['flɪpə(r)] *n* aleta *f*

flirt [flɜːt] **1** *n* coqueto(a) *m*,*f*
2 *vi* flirtear, coquetear; **to f. with death** jugar con la muerte

flirtation [flɜː'teɪʃən] *n* flirteo *m*, coqueteo *m*

flit [flɪt] *vi* **to f. about** *(bird)* revolotear; *Fig* **to f. from one thing to another** saltar de una cosa a otra

float [fləʊt] **1** *n* (**a**) *(on fishing line, as swimming aid)* flotador *m* (**b**) *(in procession)* carroza *f*
2 *vt* (**a**) *(ship)* flotar (**b**) *(shares)* emitir; *(currency, business)* hacer flotar
3 *vi* flotar

floating ['fləʊtɪŋ] *adj* flotante; *(voter)* indeciso(a)

flock [flɒk] **1** *n Zool* rebaño *m*; *(of birds)* bandada *f*; *Rel* grey *f*; *(crowd)* multitud *f*
2 *vi* acudir en masa

flog [flɒg] *vt* (**a**) *(beat)* azotar; *Fam* **to f. a subject to death** agotar completamente un tema (**b**) *Br Fam (sell)* enchufar, vender

flood [flʌd] **1** *n* inundación *f*; *(of river)* riada *f*; *Fig* torrente *m*

2 *vt* inundar

3 *vi* (*river*) desbordarse; *Fig* **to f. in** entrar a raudales

flooding ['flʌdɪŋ] *n* inundaciones *fpl*

floodlight ['flʌdlaɪt] *n* foco *m*

floor [flɔː(r)] **1** *n* (**a**) (*of room*) suelo *m*; **dance f.** pista *f* de baile (**b**) (*of ocean, forest*) fondo *m* (**c**) (*storey*) piso *m*; **first f.** *Br* primer piso, *US* planta baja; *Br* **ground f.** planta baja

2 *vt Fig* dejar perplejo(a)

floorboard ['flɔːbɔːd] *n* tabla *f* (del suelo)

flop [flɒp] **1** *n Fam* fracaso *m*

2 *vi* (**a**) **to f. down on the bed** tumbarse en la cama (**b**) *Fig* fracasar

floppy ['flɒpɪ] *adj* (**floppier, floppiest**) flojo(a); *Comput* **f. disk** disco *m* flexible

flora ['flɔːrə] *n* flora *f*

florid ['flɒrɪd] *adj* (*style*) florido(a)

florist ['flɒrɪst] *n* florista *mf*; **f.'s shop** floristería *f*

flounce¹ [flaʊns] *vi* **to f. in/out** entrar/salir airadamente

flounce² [flaʊns] *n Sewing* volante *m*, *Chile* vuelo *m*, *RP*, *Ven* volado *m*

flounder¹ ['flaʊndə(r)] *n* (*fish*) platija *f*

flounder² ['flaʊndə(r)] *vi* (**a**) (*struggle*) forcejear; *Fig* enredarse (**b**) (*be at a loss*) no saber que decir/hacer

flour ['flaʊə(r)] *n* harina *f*

flourish ['flʌrɪʃ] **1** *n* (**a**) (*gesture*) ademán *m* (teatral) (**b**) (*under signature*) rúbrica *f*

2 *vt* (*brandish*) agitar

3 *vi* (*thrive*) florecer; (*plant*) crecer

flourishing ['flʌrɪʃɪŋ] *adj* floreciente

flout [flaʊt] *vt Jur* desacatar

flow [fləʊ] **1** *n* flujo *m*; (*of river*) corriente *f*; (*of traffic*) circulación *f*; (*of capital*) movimiento *m*; (*of people, goods*) afluencia *f*; **f. chart** diagrama *m* de flujo; *Comput* organigrama *m*

2 *vi* (*blood, river*) fluir; (*sea*) subir; (*traffic*) circular

flower ['flaʊə(r)] **1** *n* flor *f*; **f. bed** arriate *m*

2 *vi* florecer

flowerpot ['flaʊəpɒt] *n* maceta *f*

flowery ['flaʊərɪ] *adj Fig* florido(a)

flowing ['fləʊɪŋ] *adj* (*hair*) suelto(a); (*dress*) de mucho vuelo; (*style*) fluido(a); (*shape, movement*) natural

flown [fləʊn] *pp* of **fly¹**

flu [fluː] *n* (*abbr* **influenza**) gripe *f*, *Am* gripa *f*

fluctuate ['flʌktjʊeɪt] *vi* fluctuar

fluctuation [flʌktjʊ'eɪʃən] *n* fluctuación *f*

flue [fluː] *n* conducto *m* de humos; (*chimney*) cañón *m*

fluent ['fluːənt] *adj* (**a**) **he speaks f. German** habla el alemán con soltura (**b**) (*eloquent*) fluido(a)

fluff [flʌf] **1** *n* (*down*) pelusa *f*

2 *vt Fam* **to f. sth** hacer algo mal

fluffy ['flʌfɪ] *adj* (**fluffier, fluffiest**) (*pillow*) mullido(a); (*toy*) de peluche; (*cake*) esponjoso(a)

fluid ['fluːɪd] **1** *adj* (*movement*) natural; (*style, prose*) fluido(a); (*situation*) incierto(a)

2 *n* fluido *m*, líquido *m*

fluke [fluːk] *n Fam* chiripa *f*; **by a f.** por chiripa

flummox ['flʌməks] *vt Fam* desconcertar

flung [flʌŋ] *pt & pp* of **fling**

flunk [flʌŋk] *vt & vi US Fam Esp* catear, *Am* reprobar, *Méx* tronar

fluorescent [flʊə'resənt] *adj* fluorescente

fluoride ['flʊəraɪd] *n* fluoruro *m*

flurry ['flʌrɪ] *n* (**a**) (*of wind*) ráfaga *f*; (*of snow*) nevasca *f* (**b**) *Fig* (*bustle*) agitación *f*

flush [flʌʃ] **1** *adj* **f. with** (*level*) a ras de

2 *n* (*blush*) rubor *m*

3 *vt* **to f. the lavatory** tirar de la cadena

4 *vi* (*blush*) ruborizarse

flushed [flʌʃt] *adj* (*cheeks*) rojo(a), encendido(a); *Fig* **f. with success** emocionado(a) ante el éxito

fluster ['flʌstə(r)] *vt* **to get flustered** ponerse nervioso(a)

flute [fluːt] *n* flauta *f*

flutist ['fluːtɪst] *n US Mus* flautista *mf*

flutter ['flʌtə(r)] **1** *vi* (*leaves, birds*) revolotear; (*flag*) ondear

2 *n Br Fam* (*bet*) apuesta *f*

flux [flʌks] *n* (*flow*) flujo *m*; (*instability*) inestabilidad *f*, *Fig* **to be in a state of f.** estar cambiando constantemente

fly¹ [flaɪ] **1** *vt* (*pt* **flew**; *pp* **flown**) (**a**) *Av* pilotar (**b**) (*merchandise, troops*) transportar (**c**) (*distance*) recorrer (**d**) (*kite*) hacer volar

2 *vi* (**a**) (*bird, plane*) volar (**b**) (*go by plane*) ir en avión (**c**) (*flag*) ondear (**d**) **to f. into a rage** montar en cólera (**e**) *Fam* **to go flying** (*fall*) caerse

3 *n* **f., flies** bragueta *f*

fly² [flaɪ] *n* (*insect*) mosca *f*; **f. spray** spray *m* matamoscas

flying ['flaɪɪŋ] **1** *adj* volador(a); (*rapid*) rápido(a); **a f. visit** una visita relámpago; *Fig* **to come out of an affair with f. colours** salir airoso(a) en un asunto; *Fig* **to get off to a f. start** empezar con buen pie; **f. saucer** platillo *m* volante

2 *n* (**a**) *(action)* vuelo *m* (**b**) *(aviation)* aviación *f*

flyleaf ['flaɪliːf] *n (of book)* guarda *f*

flyover ['flaɪəʊvə(r)] *n Br* paso elevado

flypast ['flaɪpɑːst] *n BrAv* desfile aéreo

flyweight ['flaɪweɪt] *n (in boxing)* peso *m* mosca

FM [ef'em] *n Rad (abbr* **frequency modulation)** FM *f,* frecuencia *f* modulada

foal [fəʊl] *n* potro/a *m,f*

foam [fəʊm] **1** *n* espuma *f;* **f. bath** espuma de baño; **f. rubber** goma espuma
  2 *vi* hacer espuma

fob [fɒb] *n (chain)* cadena *f (de reloj)*
▸**fob off** *vt sep Fam* **he fobbed off his old radio on a stranger** le colocó su radio vieja a un desconocido; **to f. sb off with excuses** darle largas a algn

focus ['fəʊkəs] **1** *vt* centrarse (**on** en)
  2 *vi* enfocar; **f. on sth** *Phot* enfocar algo; *Fig* centrarse en algo
  3 *n (pl* **focuses)** foco *m* inv; **to be in f./out of f.** estar enfocado(a)/desenfocado(a)

fodder ['fɒdə(r)] *n* pienso *m*

foe [fəʊ] *n Fml* enemigo(a) *m,f*

foetus ['fiːtəs] *n* feto *m*

fog [fɒg] *n* niebla *f; (at sea)* bruma *f*

fogey ['fəʊgɪ] *n Fam* **old f.** cascarrabias *mf inv*

foggy ['fɒgɪ] *adj (***foggier, foggiest)** **it is f.** hay niebla; *Fam* **I haven't the foggiest (idea)** no tengo la más mínima idea

foghorn ['fɒghɔːn] *n* sirena *f (de niebla)*

foglamp ['fɒglæmp], *US* **foglight** ['fɒglaɪt] *n* faro *m* antiniebla

foil [fɔɪl] **1** *n* (**a**) **aluminium f.** papel *m* de aluminio (**b**) *(in fencing)* florete *m*
  2 *vt (plot)* desbaratar

fold [fəʊld] **1** *n (crease)* pliegue *m*
  2 *vt* plegar, doblar; **to f. one's arms** cruzar los brazos
  3 *vi* **to f. (up)** *(chair etc)* plegarse; *Com* quebrar

folder ['fəʊldə(r)] *n* carpeta *f*

folding ['fəʊldɪŋ] *adj (chair etc)* plegable

foliage ['fəʊlɪɪdʒ] *n* follaje *m*

folk [fəʊk] **1** *npl Fam* (**a**) *(people)* gente *f* (**b**) **my/your folks** mi/tu familia; *US (parents)* mis/tus padres
  2 *adj* popular; **f. music** música *f* folk; **f. song** canción *f* popular

folklore ['fəʊklɔː(r)] *n* folklore *m*

follow ['fɒləʊ] **1** *vt* seguir; *(pursue)* perseguir; *(understand)* comprender; *(way of life)* llevar
  2 *vi* (**a**) *(come after)* seguir; **as follows** como sigue (**b**) *(result)* resultar; **that**

doesn't f. eso no es lógico (**c**) *(understand)* entender
▸**follow through, follow up** *vt sep (idea)* llevar a cabo; *(clue)* investigar

follower ['fɒləʊə(r)] *n* seguidor(a) *m,f*

following ['fɒləʊɪŋ] **1** *adj* siguiente
  2 *n* seguidores *mpl*

folly ['fɒlɪ] *n* locura *f,* desatino *m*

fond [fɒnd] *adj (loving)* cariñoso(a); **to be f. of sb** tenerle mucho cariño a algn; **to be f. of doing sth** ser aficionado(a) a hacer algo

fondle ['fɒndəl] *vt* acariciar

fondly ['fɒndlɪ] *adv* (**a**) *(lovingly)* cariñosamente (**b**) *(naively)* **to f. imagine that …** creer ingenuamente que …

fondness ['fɒndnɪs] *n (love)* cariño *m* (**for** a); *(liking)* afición *f* (**for** a)

font [fɒnt] *n Rel* pila *f*

food [fuːd] *n* comida *f;* **f. chain** cadena trófica; **f. poisoning** intoxicación alimenticia

foodstuffs ['fuːdstʌfs] *npl* productos alimenticios

fool [fuːl] **1** *n* (**a**) *(stupid person)* idiota *mf;* **to make a f. of sb** poner a algn en ridículo (**b**) *Culin* ≃ mousse *f* de fruta
  2 *vt (deceive)* engañar
  3 *vi (joke)* bromear; **to f. about** *or* **around** hacer el tonto

foolhardy ['fuːlhɑːdɪ] *adj (***foolhardier, foolhardiest)** temerario(a); *(person)* intrépido(a)

foolish ['fuːlɪʃ] *adj* estúpido(a)

foolproof ['fuːlpruːf] *adj* infalible

foot [fʊt] **1** *n (pl* **feet)** pie *m; Zool* pata *f;* **on f. a pie,** *Esp* andando
  2 *vt (bill)* pagar

footage ['fʊtɪdʒ] *n Cin* metraje *m*

football ['fʊtbɔːl] *n* (**a**) *(soccer)* fútbol *m;* **bar f.** futbolín *m;* **f. ground** campo *m* de fútbol; **f. match** partido *m* de fútbol; *Br* **f. pools** quinielas *fpl* (**b**) *(ball)* balón *m*

footballer ['fʊtbɔːlə(r)] *n* futbolista *mf*

footbridge ['fʊtbrɪdʒ] *n* puente *m* para peatones

foothills ['fʊthɪlz] *npl* estribaciones *fpl*

foothold ['fʊthəʊld] *n Fig* **to gain a f.** afianzarse en una posición

footing ['fʊtɪŋ] *n* **to lose one's f.** perder el equilibrio; **on a friendly f.** en plan amistoso; **on an equal f.** en pie de igualdad

footlights ['fʊtlaɪts] *npl* candilejas *fpl*

footman ['fʊtmən] *n* lacayo *m*

footnote ['fʊtnəʊt] *n* nota *f* a pie de página

footpath ['fʊtpɑːθ] *n (track)* sendero *m*

footprint ['fʊtprɪnt] n pisada f

footsore ['fʊtsɔː(r)] adj con los pies doloridos

footstep ['fʊtstep] n paso m

footwear ['fʊtweə(r)] n calzado m

for [fɔː(r), unstressed fə(r)] **1** prep (a) (intended) para; **curtains f. the bedroom** cortinas para el dormitorio
(b) (representing) por; **a cheque f. £10** un cheque de 10 libras; **what's the Spanish f. "rivet"?** ¿cómo se dice "rivet" en español? (c) (purpose) para; **what's this f.?** ¿para qué sirve esto?
(d) (because of) por; **famous f. its cuisine** famoso(a) por su cocina
(e) (on behalf of) por; **will you do it f. me?** ¿lo harás por mí?
(f) (during) por, durante; **I shall stay f. two weeks** me quedaré dos semanas; **I've been here f. three months** hace tres meses que estoy aquí
(g) (distance) **I walked f. 10 km** caminé 10 km
(h) (at a point in time) para; **I can do it f. next Monday** puedo hacerlo para el lunes que viene; **f. the last time** por última vez
(i) (destination) para
(j) (in exchange) por; **I got the car f. £500** conseguí el coche por 500 libras; **how much did you sell it f.?** ¿por cuánto lo vendiste?
(k) (in favour of) a favor de; **are you f. or against?** ¿estás a favor o en contra?; **to vote f. sb** votar a algn
(l) (to obtain) para; **to run f. the bus** correr para alcanzar el autobús; **to send sb f. water** mandar a algn a por agua
(m) (with respect to) en cuanto a; **as f. him** en cuanto a él; **f. all I know** que yo sepa
(n) (despite) a pesar de; **he's tall f. his age** está muy alto para su edad
(o) (towards) hacia, por; **his love f. you** su amor por ti
(p) (as) por; **what do you use f. fuel?** ¿qué utilizan como combustible?
(q) (+ object + infin) **it's time f. you to go** es hora de que os marchéis; **it's easy f. him to say that** le es fácil decir eso
2 conj (since, as) ya que, puesto que

forage ['fɒrɪdʒ] **1** n forraje m
2 vi hurgar

foray ['fɒreɪ] n incursión f

forbade [fə'beɪd] pt of **forbid**

forbearance [fɔː'beərəns] n paciencia f

forbid [fə'bɪd] vt (pt **forbade**; pp **forbidden** [fə'bɪdən]) prohibir; **to f. sb to do sth** prohibirle a algn hacer algo

forbidding [fə'bɪdɪŋ] adj (stern) severo(a); (bleak) inhóspito(a)

force [fɔːs] **1** n (a) (strength, violence, influence) fuerza f; **by f.** por la fuerza; **to come into f.** entrar en vigor (b) Mil fuerza f; **the (armed) forces** las fuerzas armadas; **the police f.** la policía
2 vt forzar; **to f. sb to do sth** forzar a algn a hacer algo

forced [fɔːst] adj forzado(a); **f. landing** aterrizaje forzoso

force-feed ['fɔːsfiːd] vt alimentar a la fuerza

forceful ['fɔːsfʊl] adj (a) (person) enérgico(a) (b) (argument) convincente

forceps ['fɔːseps] npl fórceps m

forcible ['fɔːsəbəl] adj Jur **f. entry** allanamiento m de morada, Am invasión f de domicilio

forcibly ['fɔːsəblɪ] adv a or por la fuerza

ford [fɔːd] **1** n vado m
2 vt vadear

fore [fɔː(r)] n Fig **to come to the f.** empezar a destacar

forearm ['fɔːrɑːm] n antebrazo m

foreboding [fɔː'bəʊdɪŋ] n presentimiento m

forecast ['fɔːkɑːst] **1** n pronóstico m
2 vt (pt & pp **forecast** or **forecasted**) pronosticar

forecourt ['fɔːkɔːt] n (of garage) área f de servicio

forefathers ['fɔːfɑːðəz] npl antepasados mpl

forefinger ['fɔːfɪŋgə(r)] n (dedo m) índice m

forefront ['fɔːfrʌnt] n **in the f.** a la vanguardia

forego [fɔː'gəʊ] vt (pt **forewent**; pp **foregone** [fɔː'gɒn]) Fml renunciar a

foregone ['fɔːgɒn] adj **a f. conclusion** un resultado inevitable

foreground ['fɔːgraʊnd] n primer plano m

forehead ['fɒrɪd, 'fɔːhed] n frente f

foreign ['fɒrɪn] adj extranjero(a); (trade, policy) exterior; **f. exchange** divisas fpl; Br **the F. Office** el Ministerio de Asuntos Exteriores; **f. body** cuerpo extraño

foreigner ['fɒrɪnə(r)] n extranjero(a) m,f

foreman ['fɔːmən] n (a) Ind capataz m (b) Jur presidente m del jurado

foremost ['fɔːməʊst] adj principal; **first and f.** ante todo

forename ['fɔːneɪm] n nombre m de pila

forensic [fə'rensɪk] adj forense

forerunner ['fɔːrʌnə(r)] n precursor(a) m,f

foresee [fɔː'siː] vt (pt **foresaw** [fɔː'sɔː]; pp **foreseen**) prever

foreseeable [fɔːˈsiːəbəl] *adj* previsible; **in the f. future** en un futuro próximo

foreseen [fɔːˈsiːn] *pp* of **foresee**

foreshadow [fɔːˈʃædəʊ] *vt* presagiar

foresight [ˈfɔːsaɪt] *n* previsión *f*

forest [ˈfɒrɪst] *n* bosque *m*

forestall [fɔːˈstɔːl] *vt* (*plan*) anticiparse a; (*danger*) prevenir

forestry [ˈfɒrɪstrɪ] *n* silvicultura *f*

foretaste [ˈfɔːteɪst] *n* anticipo *m* (**of** de)

foretell [fɔːˈtel] *vt* (*pt & pp* **foretold** [fɔːˈtəʊld]) presagiar

forever [fəˈrevə(r)] *adv* (a) (*eternally*) siempre (b) (*for good*) para siempre (c) *Fam* (*ages*) siglos *mpl*

forewent [fɔːˈwent] *pt* of **forego**

foreword [ˈfɔːwɜːd] *n* prefacio *m*

forfeit [ˈfɔːfɪt] **1** *n* (*penalty*) pena *f*; (*in games*) prenda *f*
2 *vt* perder

forgave [fəˈɡeɪv] *pt* of **forgive**

forge [fɔːdʒ] **1** *n* (a) (*furnace*) fragua *f* (b) (*blacksmith's*) herrería *f*
2 *vt* (a) (*counterfeit*) falsificar (b) (*metal*) forjar
3 *vi* **to f. ahead** hacer grandes progresos

forged [fɔːdʒd] *adj* (*banknote, letter*) falso(a), falsificado(a)

forger [ˈfɔːdʒə(r)] *n* falsificador(a) *m,f*

forgery [ˈfɔːdʒərɪ] *n* falsificación *f*

forget [fəˈɡet] **1** *vt* (*pt* **forgot**; *pp* **forgotten**) olvidar, olvidarse de; **I've forgotten my key** he olvidado la llave
2 *vi* olvidarse

forgetful [fəˈɡetfʊl] *adj* olvidadizo(a)

forget-me-not [fəˈɡetmɪnɒt] *n* nomeolvides *f inv*

forgive [fəˈɡɪv] *vt* (*pt* **forgave**; *pp* **forgiven** [fəˈɡɪvən]) perdonar; **to f. sb for sth** perdonarle algo a algn

forgiveness [fəˈɡɪvnɪs] *n* perdón *m*

forgo [fɔːˈɡəʊ] *vt Fml* = **forego**

forgot [fəˈɡɒt] *pt* of **forget**

forgotten [fəˈɡɒtən] *pp* of **forget**

fork [fɔːk] **1** *n* (a) *Agr* horca *f* (b) (*cutlery*) tenedor *m* (c) (*in road*) bifurcación *f*
2 *vi* (*roads*) bifurcarse

▸ **fork out** *vt sep Fam* (*money*) aflojar, *Esp* apoquinar, *RP* garpar

fork-lift truck [fɔːklɪftˈtrʌk] *n* carretilla *f* elevadora de horquilla

forlorn [fəˈlɔːn] *adj* (*forsaken*) abandonado(a); (*desolate*) triste; (*without hope*) desesperado(a)

form [fɔːm] **1** *n* (a) (*shape*) forma *f* (b) (*type*) clase *f* (c) (*document*) formulario *m* (d) **on/on top/off f.** en/en plena/en baja

forma (e) *Br Educ* clase *f*; **the first f.** el primer curso
2 *vt* formar; **to f. an impression** formarse una impresión
3 *vi* formarse

formal [ˈfɔːməl] *adj* (a) (*official*) oficial; **a f. application** una solicitud en forma (b) (*party, dress*) de etiqueta (c) (*ordered*) formal (d) (*person*) formalista

formality [fɔːˈmælɪtɪ] *n* formalidad *f*

formally [ˈfɔːməlɪ] *adv* oficialmente

format [ˈfɔːmæt] **1** *n* formato *m*
2 *vt Comput* formatear

formation [fɔːˈmeɪʃən] *n* formación *f*

formative [ˈfɔːmətɪv] *adj* formativo(a)

former [ˈfɔːmə(r)] *adj* (a) (*time*) anterior (b) (*one-time*) antiguo(a); (*person*) ex; **the f. champion** el excampeón (c) (*first*) aquél/aquélla; **Peter and Lisa came, the f. wearing a hat** vinieron Peter y Lisa, aquél llevaba sombrero

formerly [ˈfɔːməlɪ] *adv* antiguamente

formidable [ˈfɔːmɪdəbəl] *adj* (*prodigious*) formidable; (*daunting*) terrible

formula [ˈfɔːmjʊlə] *n* fórmula *f*

formulate [ˈfɔːmjʊleɪt] *vt* formular

forsake [fəˈseɪk] *vt* (*pt* **forsook** [fəˈsʊk]; *pp* **forsaken** [fəˈseɪkən]) *Literary* (a) (*abandon, desert*) abandonar (b) (*give up*) renunciar a

fort [fɔːt] *n* fortaleza *f*

forte [ˈfɔːteɪ] *n* fuerte *m*

forth [fɔːθ] *adv Fml* **and so f.** y así sucesivamente; **to go back and f.** ir de acá para allá

forthcoming [fɔːθˈkʌmɪŋ] *adj* (a) (*event*) próximo(a) (b) **no money was f.** no hubo oferta de dinero (c) (*communicative*) comunicativo(a)

forthright [ˈfɔːθraɪt] *adj* franco(a)

fortieth [ˈfɔːtɪəθ] *adj & n* cuadragésimo(a) (*m,f*)

fortification [fɔːtɪfɪˈkeɪʃən] *n* fortificación *f*

fortify [ˈfɔːtɪfaɪ] *vt* fortificar

fortitude [ˈfɔːtɪtjuːd] *n* fortaleza *f*, fuerza *f*

fortnight [ˈfɔːtnaɪt] *n Br* quincena *f*

fortnightly [ˈfɔːtnaɪtlɪ] *Br* **1** *adj* quincenal
2 *adv* cada quince días

fortress [ˈfɔːtrɪs] *n* fortaleza *f*

fortunate [ˈfɔːtʃənɪt] *adj* afortunado(a); **it was f. that he came** fue una suerte que viniera

fortunately [ˈfɔːtʃənɪtlɪ] *adv* afortunadamente

fortune ['fɔːtʃən] n (a) (luck, fate) suerte f; **to tell sb's f.** echar la buenaventura a algn (b) (money) fortuna f

fortune-teller ['fɔːtʃəntelə(r)] n adivino(a) m,f

forty ['fɔːtɪ] adj & n cuarenta (m inv)

forum ['fɔːrəm] n foro m

forward ['fɔːwəd] 1 adv (a) (also **forwards**) (direction and movement) hacia adelante (b) Fig **to come f.** ofrecerse (c) **from this day f.** de ahora en adelante
2 adj (a) (movement) hacia adelante; (position) delantero(a) (b) (person) fresco(a)
3 n Sport delantero(a) m,f
4 vt (a) (send on) remitir (b) Fml (send goods) expedir (c) Fml (further) fomentar

fossil ['fɒsəl] n fósil m; **f. fuel** combustible m fósil

foster ['fɒstə(r)] 1 vt (a) (child) adoptar (temporalmente), acoger (b) Fml (hopes) abrigar; (relations) fomentar
2 adj **f. child** niño(a) m,f en régimen de acogida; **f. parents** familia f de acogida

fostering ['fɒstərɪŋ] n acogida f familiar (de un niño)

fought [fɔːt] pt & pp of **fight**

foul [faʊl] 1 adj (a) (smell) fétido(a); (taste) asqueroso(a) (b) (deed) atroz; (weather) de perros (c) (language) grosero(a) (d) Sport **f. play** juego sucio
2 n Sport falta f
3 vt (a) (dirty) ensuciar; (air) contaminar (b) Sport cometer una falta contra

found¹ [faʊnd] pt & pp of **find**

found² [faʊnd] vt (establish) fundar

foundation [faʊn'deɪʃən] n (a) (establishment) fundación f (b) (basis) fundamento m (c) Constr **foundations** cimientos mpl

founder¹ ['faʊndə(r)] n fundador(a) m,f

founder² ['faʊndə(r)] vi (a) Fml (sink) hundirse (b) Fig (plan, hopes) fracasar

foundry ['faʊndrɪ] n fundición f

fountain ['faʊntɪn] n (structure) fuente f; (jet) surtidor m; **f. pen** pluma estilográfica, CSur lapicera f fuente, Perú lapicero m

four [fɔː(r)] adj & n cuatro (m inv); **on all fours** a gatas

four-door ['fɔːdɔː(r)] adj Aut de cuatro puertas

four-poster [fɔː'pəʊstə(r)] adj & n **f. (bed)** cama f con dosel

foursome ['fɔːsəm] n grupo m de cuatro personas

fourteen [fɔː'tiːn] adj & n catorce (m inv)

fourteenth [fɔː'tiːnθ] 1 adj & n decimocuarto(a) (m,f)
2 n (fraction) catorceavo m

fourth [fɔːθ] 1 adj & n cuarto(a) (m,f)
2 n (a) (fraction) cuarto m (b) Aut cuarta f (velocidad)

fowl [faʊl] n (pl **fowl**) ave f de corral

fox [fɒks] 1 n zorro(a) m,f
2 vt (a) (perplex) dejar perplejo(a) (b) (deceive) engañar

foyer ['fɔɪeɪ, 'fɔɪə(r)] n vestíbulo m

fracas ['frækɑː] n gresca f, refriega f

> 🔎 Note that the Spanish word **fracaso** is a false friend and is never a translation for the English word **fracas**. In Spanish, **fracaso** means "failure".

fraction ['frækʃən] n fracción f

fracture ['fræktʃə(r)] 1 n fractura f
2 vt fracturar

fragile ['frædʒaɪl] adj frágil

fragment ['frægmənt] n fragmento m

fragrance ['freɪgrəns] n fragancia f, perfume m

fragrant ['freɪgrənt] adj fragante, aromático(a)

frail [freɪl] adj frágil, delicado(a)

frame [freɪm] 1 n (a) (of window, door, picture) marco m; (of machine) armazón m; (of bicycle) cuadro m; (of spectacles) montura f; Fig **f. of mind** estado m de ánimo (b) Cin & TV fotograma m
2 vt (a) (picture) enmarcar (b) (question) formular (c) Fam (innocent person) incriminar

framework ['freɪmwɜːk] n Fig **within the f. of ...** dentro del marco de ...

franc [fræŋk] n franco m

France [frɑːns] n Francia f

franchise ['fræntʃaɪz] n (a) Pol derecho m al voto (b) Com concesión f, licencia f

frank [fræŋk] 1 adj franco(a)
2 vt (mail) franquear

frankly ['fræŋklɪ] adv francamente

frankness ['fræŋknɪs] n franqueza f

frantic ['fræntɪk] adj (anxious) desesperado(a); (hectic) frenético(a)

fraternal [frə'tɜːnəl] adj fraterno(a)

fraternity [frə'tɜːnɪtɪ] n (society) asociación f, Rel hermandad f, cofradía f; US Univ = asociación de estudiantes que suele funcionar como club social

fraternize ['frætənaɪz] vi confraternizar (with con)

fraud [frɔːd] n (a) (deception) fraude m (b) (person) impostor(a) m,f

fraught [frɔːt] adj (a) (full) cargado(a) (with de) (b) (tense) nervioso(a)

fray¹ [freɪ] *vi* (**a**) *(cloth)* deshilacharse (**b**) *(nerves)* crisparse; **his temper frequently frayed** se irritaba a menudo

fray² [freɪ] *n* combate *m*

freak [friːk] **1** *n* (**a**) *(monster)* monstruo *m* (**b**) *Fam (eccentric)* estrafalario(a) *m,f* (**c**) *Fam (fan)* fanático(a) *m,f*
2 *adj* (**a**) *(unexpected)* inesperado(a) (**b**) *(unusual)* insólito(a)

freckle ['frekəl] *n* peca *f*

free [friː] **1** *adj* (**a**) *(unrestricted, unoccupied)* libre; **to set sb f.** poner en libertad a algn; **f. kick** tiro *m* libre; **f. speech** libertad *f* de expresión; **f. will** libre albedrío *m* (**b**) **f. (of charge)** *(gratis)* gratuito(a); **f. gift** obsequio *m*
2 *adv* (**a**) **(for) f.** gratis (**b**) *(loose)* suelto(a)
3 *vt* (**a**) *(liberate)* poner en libertad (**b**) *(let loose, work loose)* soltar (**c**) *(untie)* desatar (**d**) *(exempt)* eximir (**from** de)

freebie ['friːbɪ] *n Fam* regalito *m*

freedom ['friːdəm] *n* (**a**) *(liberty)* libertad *f*; **f. of the press** libertad de prensa (**b**) *(exemption)* exención *f*

free-for-all ['friːfərɔːl] *n Fam (fight, discussion)* bronca *f*, gresca *f*, *Méx* agarrón *m*

freehold ['friːhəʊld] *adj* en propiedad absoluta

freelance ['friːlɑːns] *adj* independiente

freely ['friːlɪ] *adv* libremente; **to be f. available** encontrarse fácilmente

freemason ['friːmeɪsən] *n* francmasón *m*

free-range ['friːreɪndʒ] *adj Br* de granja

free-style ['friːstaɪl] *n* estilo *m* libre

freeway ['friːweɪ] *n US* autopista *f*

freewheel [friːˈwiːl] *vi* ir en punto muerto

freeze [friːz] **1** *vt* (*pt* **froze**; *pp* **frozen**) congelar
2 *n Met* helada *f*; **price f.** congelación *f* de precios; *TV & Cin* **f. frame** imagen congelada
3 *vi (liquid)* helarse; *(food)* congelarse

freeze-dried ['friːzdraɪd] *adj* liofilizado(a)

freezer ['friːzə(r)] *n* congelador *m*

freezing ['friːzɪŋ] *adj* (**a**) *(rain, wind)* helado(a); *(weather, temperature)* muy frío(a) (**b**) **f. point** punto *m* de congelación; **above/below f. point** sobre/bajo cero

freight [freɪt] *n* (**a**) *(transport)* transporte *m* (**b**) *(goods, price)* flete *m*; *US* **f. car** vagón *m*; *US* **f. elevator** montacargas *m inv*; **f. train** tren *m* de mercancías

French [frentʃ] **1** *adj* francés(esa); **F. bean** judía *f* verde, *Bol, RP* chaucha *f*, *CAm* ejote *m*, *Col, Cuba* habichuela *f*, *Chile* poroto *m* verde, *Ven* vainita *f*; **F. dressing** vinagreta *f*; *US* **F. fries** patatas *fpl* or *Am* papas *fpl* fritas; **F. window** puerta *f* vidriera
2 *n* (**a**) *(language)* francés *m* (**b**) *pl* **the F.** los franceses

Frenchman ['frentʃmən] *n* francés *m*

Frenchwoman ['frentʃwʊmən] *n* francesa *f*

frenetic [frɪˈnetɪk] *adj* frenético(a)

frenzy ['frenzɪ] *n* frenesí *m*

frequency ['friːkwənsɪ] *n* frecuencia *f*

frequent 1 *adj* ['friːkwənt] frecuente
2 *vt* [frɪˈkwent] frecuentar

frequently ['friːkwəntlɪ] *adv* frecuentemente, a menudo

fresh [freʃ] *adj* (**a**) *(food, air)* fresco(a); **f. water** agua *f* dulce; **f. bread** pan *m* del día (**b**) *(page, attempt)* nuevo(a) (**c**) *(original)* novedoso(a), original (**d**) *US Fam (cheeky)* fresco(a)

freshen ['freʃən] *vi (wind)* refrescar
▸ **freshen up** *vi* asearse

fresher ['freʃə(r)] *n Br Univ* novato(a) *m,f*

freshly ['freʃlɪ] *adv* recién, recientemente

freshman ['freʃmən] *n US* = **fresher**

freshness ['freʃnɪs] *n* frescura *f*

freshwater ['freʃwɔːtə(r)] *adj* de agua dulce

fret [fret] *vi* preocuparse (**about** por)

FRG [efaːˈdʒiː] *n (abbr* **Federal Republic of Germany)** RFA *f*

friar ['fraɪə(r)] *n* fraile *m*

friction ['frɪkʃən] *n* fricción *f*

Friday ['fraɪdɪ] *n* viernes *m*

fridge [frɪdʒ] *n esp Br* nevera *f*, frigorífico *m*, *Andes* frigider *m*, *RP* heladera *f*

fried [fraɪd] *adj* frito(a)

friend [frend] *n* amigo(a) *m,f*; **a f. of mine** un(a) amigo(a) mío(a); **to make friends with sb** hacerse amigo(a) de algn; **to make friends again** hacer las paces

friendliness ['frendlɪnɪs] *n* amabilidad *f*, simpatía *f*

friendly ['frendlɪ] *adj* (**friendlier, friendliest**) *(person)* simpático(a); *(atmosphere)* acogedor(a); **f. advice** consejo *m* de amigo; **f. nation** nación amiga

friendship ['frendʃɪp] *n* amistad *f*

frieze [friːz] *n* friso *m*

frigate ['frɪgɪt] *n* fragata *f*

fright [fraɪt] *n* (**a**) *(fear)* miedo *m*; **to take f.** asustarse (**b**) *(shock)* susto *m*; **to get a f.** pegarse un susto

frighten ['fraɪtən] *vt* asustar
▸ **frighten away, frighten off** *vt sep* ahuyentar

frightened ['fraɪtənd] adj asustado(a); **to be f. of sb** tenerle miedo a algn

frightening ['fraɪtənɪŋ] adj espantoso(a)

frightful ['fraɪtfʊl] adj espantoso(a), horroroso(a)

frightfully ['fraɪtfʊlɪ] adv tremendamente, terriblemente

frigid ['frɪdʒɪd] adj frígido(a)

frill [frɪl] n (on dress) volante m; Fig **frills** (decorations) adornos mpl

fringe [frɪndʒ] n (a) Br (of hair) flequillo m, Am cerquillo m (b) (edge) borde m; Fig **on the f. of society** al margen de la sociedad; **f. theatre** teatro m experimental; **f. benefits** extras mpl

Frisbee® ['frɪzbɪ] n platillo m

frisk [frɪsk] vt Fam (search) registrar

frisky ['frɪskɪ] adj (**friskier, friskiest**) (a) (children, animals) juguetón(ona) (b) (adult) vivo(a)

fritter ['frɪtə(r)] n buñuelo m

▸ **fritter away** vt sep malgastar

frivolous ['frɪvələs] adj frívolo(a)

frizzy ['frɪzɪ] adj (**frizzier, frizziest**) crespo(a)

frock [frɒk] n vestido m; **f. coat** levita f

frog [frɒg] n rana f

frogman ['frɒgmən] n hombre m rana

frolic ['frɒlɪk] vi retozar, juguetear

from [frɒm, unstressed frəm] prep (a) (time) desde, a partir de; **f. now on** a partir de ahora; **Monday to Friday** de lunes a viernes; **f. the 8th to the 17th** desde el 8 hasta el 17 (b) (price, number) desde, de; **a number f. one to ten** un número del uno a diez (c) (origin) de; **a letter f. her father** una carta de su padre; **f. English into Spanish** del inglés al español; **he's f. Malaga** es de Málaga; **the train f. Bilbao** el tren procedente de Bilbao (d) (distance) de; **the town is 4 miles f. the coast** el pueblo está a 4 millas de la costa (e) (out of) de; **bread is made f. flour** el pan se hace con harina (f) (remove, subtract) a; **he took the book f. the child** le quitó el libro al niño; **take three f. five** restar tres a cinco (g) (according to) según, por; **f. what the author said** según lo que dijo el autor (h) (position) desde, de; **f. here** desde aquí (i) **can you tell margarine f. butter?** ¿puedes distinguir entre la margarina y la mantequilla?

front [frʌnt] 1 n (a) (not back) parte delantera; **in f. (of)** delante (de) (b) (of building) fachada f (c) Mil, Pol & Met

frente m (d) (seaside) paseo marítimo (e) Fig **she put on a brave f.** hizo de tripas corazón

2 adj delantero(a), de delante; **f. door** puerta f principal; **f. seat** asiento m de delante

frontier ['frʌntɪə(r)] n frontera f

front-page ['frʌntpeɪdʒ] adj de primera página

frost [frɒst] 1 n (a) (covering) escarcha f (b) (freezing) helada f

2 vt US Culin recubrir con azúcar glas

▸ **frost over** vi escarchar

frostbite ['frɒstbaɪt] n congelación f

frosted ['frɒstɪd] adj (a) (glass) esmerilado(a) (b) US Culin recubierto(a) de azúcar glas

frosty ['frɒstɪ] adj (**frostier, frostiest**) (a) **it will be a f. night tonight** esta noche habrá helada (b) Fig glacial

froth [frɒθ] 1 n espuma f; (from mouth) espumarajos mpl

2 vi espumar

frothy ['frɒθɪ] adj (**frothier, frothiest**) espumoso(a)

frown [fraʊn] vi fruncir el ceño

▸ **frown upon** vt insep desaprobar

froze [frəʊz] pt of **freeze**

frozen ['frəʊzən] 1 adj (liquid, feet etc) helado(a); (food) congelado(a)

2 pp of **freeze**

frugal ['fruːgəl] adj frugal

fruit [fruːt] n (a) Bot fruto m (b) (apple, orange etc) fruta f; **f. cake** pastel m con fruto seco; **f. machine** (máquina f) tragaperras f inv; **f. salad** macedonia de frutas (c) **fruits** (rewards) frutos mpl

fruitful ['fruːtfʊl] adj Fig provechoso(a)

fruition [fruː'ɪʃən] n Fml **to come to f.** realizarse

fruitless ['fruːtlɪs] adj infructuoso(a)

frustrate [frʌ'streɪt] vt frustrar

frustrated [frʌ'streɪtɪd] adj frustrado(a)

frustrating [frʌ'streɪtɪŋ] adj frustrante

frustration [frʌ'streɪʃən] n frustración f

fry¹ [fraɪ] 1 vt (pt & pp **fried**) freír

2 vi Fig asarse

fry² [fraɪ] npl **small f.** gente f de poca monta

frying pan ['fraɪŋpæn], US **fry-pan** ['fraɪpæn] n sartén f

ft (abbr **foot**) pie m; (abbr **feet**) pies mpl

fuck [fʌk] Vulg 1 vt (a) (have sex with) Esp follar, Am coger, Méx chingar (b) (expressing surprise, irritation) **f. (it)!** ¡carajo!, Esp ¡joder!

2 vi Esp follar, Am coger, Méx chingar

▸**fuck off** *vi Vulg* **f. off!** *Esp* ¡vete a tomar por (el) culo!, *Méx* ¡vete a la chingada!, *RP* ¡ándate a la puta que te parió!

▸**fuck up** *vt sep Vulg* joder

fucking [ˈfʌkɪŋ] *Vulg* **1** *adj* **f. idiot!** *Esp* ¡gilipollas!, *Am* ¡pendejo!, *RP* ¡boludo! **where's the f. key?** ¿dónde está la puta llave?

2 *adv* **a f. good film** una película de puta madre

fuddy-duddy [ˈfʌdɪdʌdɪ] *n Fam* **an old f.** un carcamal *or Am* carcamán

fudge [fʌdʒ] **1** *n Culin* = dulce hecho con azúcar, leche y mantequilla

2 *vt (figures)* amañar

fuel [ˈfjʊəl] **1** *n* combustible *m*; *(for engines)* carburante *m*; **f. tank** depósito *m* de combustible

2 *vt Fig (ambition)* estimular; *(difficult situation)* empeorar

fugitive [ˈfjuːdʒɪtɪv] *n Fml* fugitivo(a) *m,f*

fulfil, *US* **fulfill** [fʊlˈfɪl] *vt* **(a)** *(task, ambition)* realizar; *(promise)* cumplir; *(role)* desempeñar **(b)** *(wishes)* satisfacer

fulfilment, *US* **fulfillment** [fʊlˈfɪlmənt] *n* **(a)** *(of ambition)* realización *f* **(b)** *(of duty, promise)* cumplimiento *m*

full [fʊl] **1** *adj* **(a)** *(container, room)* lleno(a); **f. of** lleno(a) de; **I'm f. (up)** no puedo más **(b)** *(complete) (amount, support)* total; *(explanation, recovery)* completo(a); **at f. speed** a toda velocidad; **f. employment** pleno empleo; **f. moon** luna llena; **f. stop** punto *m*

2 *n* **in f.** en su totalidad; **name in f.** nombre y apellidos completos

3 *adv* **f. well** perfectamente

full-blown [ˈfʊlbləʊn] *adj* auténtico(a)

full-fledged [ˈfʊlfledʒd] *adj US =* **fully-fledged**

fullness [ˈfʊlnɪs] *n* **in the f. of time** con el tiempo

full-scale [ˈfʊlskeɪl] *adj* **(a)** *(model)* de tamaño natural **(b)** **f. search** registro *m* a fondo; **f. war** guerra generalizada *or* total

full-time [ˈfʊlˈtaɪm] **1** *adj* de jornada completa

2 *adv* **to work f.** trabajar a tiempo completo

fully [ˈfʊlɪ] *adv* completamente

fully-fledged [ˈfʊlfledʒd] *adj Br Fig* hecho(a) y derecho(a)

fulsome [ˈfʊlsəm] *adj* excesivo(a), exagerado(a)

fumble [ˈfʌmbəl] *vi* hurgar; **to f. for sth** buscar algo a tientas; **to f. with sth** manejar algo con torpeza

fume [fjuːm] **1** *n* **fumes** humos *mpl*

2 *vi* despedir humo

> *Note that the Spanish verb **fumar** is a false friend and is never a translation for the English verb **to fume**. In Spanish **fumar** means "to smoke".*

fun [fʌn] **1** *n (amusement)* diversión *f*; **in** *or* **for f.** en broma; **to have f.** divertirse, pasarlo bien; **to make f. of sb** reírse de algn

2 *adj* divertido(a)

function [ˈfʌŋkʃən] **1** *n* **(a)** *(of machine, person, institution)* función *f* **(b)** *(ceremony)* acto *m*; *(party)* recepción *f*

2 *vi* funcionar

functional [ˈfʌŋkʃənəl] *adj* funcional

fund [fʌnd] **1** *n* **(a)** *Fin* fondo *m* **(b)** **funds** *(available money)* fondos *mpl*

2 *vt (finance)* financiar

> *Note that the Spanish verb **fundar** is a false friend and is never a translation for the English verb **to fund**. In Spanish **fundar** means "to found".*

fundamental [fʌndəˈmentəl] **1** *adj* fundamental

2 *npl* **fundamentals** principios básicos

funeral [ˈfjuːnərəl] *n* funeral *m*; *US* **f. home** funeraria *f*; **f. march** marcha *f* fúnebre; *Br* **f. parlour** funeraria *f*; **f. service** misa *f* de cuerpo presente

funfair [ˈfʌnfeə(r)] *n Br* parque *m* de atracciones

fungus [ˈfʌŋɡəs] *n (pl* **fungi** [ˈfʌŋɡaɪ]*)* **(a)** *Bot* hongo *m* **(b)** *Med* hongo *m*

funnel [ˈfʌnəl] **1** *n* **(a)** *(for liquids)* embudo *m* **(b)** *Naut* chimenea *f*

2 *vt (pt & pp* **funnelled**, *US* **funneled)** *Fig (funds, energy)* encauzar

funnily [ˈfʌnɪlɪ] *adv Fam* **f. enough** aunque parezca extraño

funny [ˈfʌnɪ] *adj (funnier, funniest)* **(a)** *(peculiar)* raro(a), extraño(a); **that's f.!** ¡qué raro! **(b)** *(amusing)* divertido(a), gracioso(a); **I found it very f.** me hizo mucha gracia **(c)** *Fam (ill)* mal

fur [fɜː(r)] **1** *n* **(a)** *(of living animal)* pelo *m* **(b)** *(of dead animal)* piel *f* **(c)** *(in kettle, on tongue)* sarro *m*

2 *adj* de piel; **f. coat** abrigo *m* de pieles

furious [ˈfjʊərɪəs] *adj* **(a)** *(angry)* furioso(a) **(b)** *(vigorous)* violento(a)

furlong [ˈfɜːlɒŋ] *n (measurement) =* aprox 201 m

furnace [ˈfɜːnɪs] *n* horno *m*

furnish [ˈfɜːnɪʃ] *vt* **(a)** *(house)* amueblar **(b)** *Fml (food)* suministrar; *(details)* facilitar

furnishings [ˈfɜːnɪʃɪŋz] *npl (furniture, fittings)* mobiliario *m*, muebles *mpl*

furniture ['fɜːnɪtʃə(r)] *n* muebles *mpl*; **a piece of f.** un mueble

furrow ['fʌrəʊ] *n Agr* surco *m*; (*on forehead*) arruga *f*

furry ['fɜːrɪ] *adj* (**furrier, furriest**) (**a**) (*hairy*) peludo(a) (**b**) (*tongue, kettle*) sarroso(a)

further ['fɜːðə(r)] (*comp of* **far**) **1** *adj* (**a**) (*new*) nuevo(a); **until f. notice** hasta nuevo aviso (**b**) (*additional*) otro(a), adicional (**c**) (*later*) posterior; *Br* **f. education** estudios *mpl* superiores
  2 *adv* (**a**) (*more*) más; **f. back** más atrás; **f. along** más adelante (**b**) *Fml* (*besides*) además
  3 *vt* fomentar

furthermore [fɜːðə'mɔː(r)] *adv Fml* además

furthest ['fɜːðɪst] *adj* (*superl of* **far**) más lejano(a)

furtive ['fɜːtɪv] *adj* furtivo(a)

fury ['fjʊərɪ] *n* furia *f*, furor *m*

fuse [fjuːz] **1** *n* (**a**) *Elec* fusible *m*; **f. box** caja *f* de fusibles (**b**) (*of bomb*) mecha *f*
  2 *vi* (**a**) *Br Elec* **the lights fused** se fundieron los plomos (**b**) *Fig* (*merge*) fusionarse (**c**) (*melt*) fundirse
  3 *vt* (**a**) *Br Elec* **a surge of power fused the lights** se fundieron los plomos y se fue la luz por una subida de corriente (**b**) *Fig* (*merge*) fusionar (**c**) (*melt*) fundir

fuselage ['fjuːzɪlɑːʒ] *n* fuselaje *m*

fusion ['fjuːʒən] *n* fusión *f*

fuss [fʌs] **1** *n* (*commotion*) jaleo *m*; **to kick up a f.** armar un escándalo; **stop making a f.** (*complaining*) deja ya de quejarte; **to make a f. of** (*pay attention to*) mimar a
  2 *vi* preocuparse (**about** por)

fussy ['fʌsɪ] *adj* (**fussier, fussiest**) exigente; (*nitpicking*) quisquilloso(a)

futile ['fjuːtaɪl] *adj* inútil, vano(a)

futility [fjuː'tɪlɪtɪ] *n* inutilidad *f*

futon ['fuːtɒn] *n* futón *m*

future ['fjuːtʃə(r)] **1** *n* futuro *m*, porvenir *m*; **in the near f.** en un futuro próximo; **in f.** de aquí en adelante
  2 *adj* futuro(a)

futuristic [fjuːtʃə'rɪstɪk] *adj* futurista

fuze [fjuːz] *n*, *vi & vt US* = **fuse**

fuzzy ['fʌzɪ] *adj* (**fuzzier, fuzziest**) (**a**) (*hair*) muy rizado(a) (**b**) (*blurred*) borroso(a)

FYI (*abbr* **for your information**) para tu información

G

G, g [dʒiː] n (**a**) *(the letter)* G, g f (**b**) *Mus* G sol m

G [dʒiː] adj US Cin ≃ (apta) para todos los públicos

g *(abbr* **gramme)** g

gabble ['gæbəl] **1** n chapurreo m
2 vi hablar atropelladamente

gable ['geɪbəl] n aguilón m

gadget ['gædʒɪt] n artilugio m, aparato m

Gaelic ['geɪlɪk] **1** adj gaélico(a)
2 n *(language)* gaélico m

gaffe [gæf] n metedura f de pata, desliz m; **to make a g.** meter la pata, patinar

> ✍ Note that the Spanish word **gafe** is a false friend and is never a translation for the English word **gaffe**. In Spanish **gafe** means "jinxed person".

gag [gæg] **1** n (**a**) *(on mouth)* mordaza f (**b**) *Fam (joke)* chiste m
2 vt amordazar

gage [geɪdʒ] n & vt US = **gauge**

gaiety ['geɪətɪ] n regocijo m

gaily ['geɪlɪ] adv alegremente

gain [geɪn] **1** n ganancia f, beneficio m; *(increase)* aumento m
2 vt ganar; *Fig* **to g. ground** ganar terreno; **to g. speed** ganar velocidad, acelerar; **to g. weight** aumentar de peso

gait [geɪt] n paso m, manera f de caminar or Esp andar m

gal *(abbr* **gallon)** galón m

gala ['gɑːlə, 'geɪlə] n gala f, fiesta f

galaxy ['gæləksɪ] n galaxia f

gale [geɪl] n vendaval m

Galicia [gə'lɪʃə] n Galicia

Galician [gə'lɪʃɪən, gə'lɪʃən] **1** adj gallego(a)
2 n (**a**) *(person)* gallego(a) m,f (**b**) *(language)* gallego m

gall [gɔːl] **1** n *Fam* descaro m
2 vt molestar, irritar

gallant ['gælənt] adj *(brave)* valiente; *(also* [gə'lænt]) *(chivalrous)* galante

gallantry ['gæləntrɪ] n *(bravery)* gallardía f; *(politeness)* galantería f

galleon ['gælɪən] n galeón m

gallery ['gælərɪ] n (**a**) **(art) g.** *(for sale)* galería f de arte; *(for exhibition)* museo m (de arte) (**b**) *Th* galería f

galley ['gælɪ] n (**a**) *(ship)* galera f; **g. slave** galeote m (**b**) *(kitchen)* cocina f

Gallicism ['gælɪsɪzəm] n galicismo m

gallivant ['gælɪvænt] vi *Fam* callejear

gallon ['gælən] n galón m *(Br = 4,55 l; US = 3,79 l)*

gallop ['gæləp] **1** n galope m
2 vi galopar

gallows ['gæləʊz] n sing horca f, patíbulo m

gallstone ['gɔːlstəʊn] n cálculo m biliar

galore [gə'lɔː(r)] adv *Fam* en cantidad, en abundancia

galvanize ['gælvənaɪz] vt *(metal)* galvanizar; *Fig* **to g. sb into action** galvanizar a algn

galvanized ['gælvənaɪzd] adj galvanizado(a)

gambit ['gæmbɪt] n *(in chess)* gambito m; *Fig* táctica f

gamble ['gæmbəl] **1** n *(risk)* riesgo m; *(risky undertaking)* empresa arriesgada; *(bet)* apuesta f
2 vi *(bet)* jugar; *(take a risk)* arriesgarse

gambler ['gæmblə(r)] n jugador(a) m,f

gambling ['gæmblɪŋ] n juego m

gambol ['gæmbəl] vi brincar

game [geɪm] **1** n (**a**) *(activity, sport)* juego m; **g. of chance** juego de azar (**b**) *(match)* partido m; *(of bridge)* partida f (**c**) **games** *(sporting event)* juegos mpl; *Br (school subject)* deportes mpl (**d**) *(hunting)* caza f; *Fig* presa f
2 adj **g. for anything** dispuesto(a) a todo

gamekeeper ['geɪmkiːpə(r)] n guardabosque mf

gamely ['geɪmlɪ] adv resueltamente

gammon ['gæmən] n *Br* jamón curado

gamut ['gæmət] n gama f; **to run the g. of ...** experimentar todas las posibilidades de ...

gang [gæŋ] n *(of criminals)* banda f; *(of youths)* pandilla f; *(of workers)* cuadrilla f
▸ **gang up** vi *Fam* confabularse **(on** contra)

gangplank ['gæŋplæŋk] n plancha f

gangrene ['gæŋgriːn] n gangrena f

gangster ['gæŋstə(r)] n gángster m

gangway ['gæŋweɪ] n Naut pasarela f; Th pasillo m

gantry ['gæntrɪ] n puente m transversal

gaol [dʒeɪl] n & vt Br = **jail**

gap [gæp] n (a) (physical opening) hueco m; (blank space) espacio m en blanco (b) (in time) intervalo m; (in age, ability) diferencia f; (in knowledge) laguna f

gape [geɪp] vi (person) quedarse boquiabierto(a), mirar boquiabierto(a); (thing) estar abierto(a)

gaping ['geɪpɪŋ] adj Fig profundo(a)

garage ['gæraːʒ, 'gærɪdʒ, US gəˈraːʒ] n garaje m; (for repairs) taller mecánico; (filling station) gasolinera f, estación f de servicio, Andes, Ven bomba f, Méx gasolinería f, Perú grifo m

garbage ['gaːbɪdʒ] n US basura f, Méx cochera f, Fig tonterías fpl

garbanzo [gaːˈbaːnzəʊ] n (pl garbanzos) US g. (bean) garbanzo m;

garbled ['gaːbəld] adj embrollado(a); **g. account** relato confuso

garden ['gaːdən] n jardín m; **g. centre** centro m de jardinería; **g. party** recepción f al aire libre

gardener ['gaːdənə(r)] n jardinero(a) m,f

gardenia [gaːˈdiːnɪə] n gardenia f

gardening ['gaːdənɪŋ] n jardinería f; **his mother does the g.** su madre es la que cuida el jardín

gargle ['gaːgəl] vi hacer gárgaras

gargoyle ['gaːgɔɪl] n gárgola f

garish ['geərɪʃ] adj chillón(ona)

garland ['gaːlənd] n guirnalda f

garlic ['gaːlɪk] n ajo m

garment ['gaːmənt] n prenda f

garnish ['gaːnɪʃ] vt guarnecer

garrison ['gærɪsən] n guarnición f

garrulous ['gærʊləs] adj locuaz

garter ['gaːtə(r)] n liga f

gas [gæs] **1** n (a) (for cooking, heating) gas m; **g. cooker** cocina f de gas; **g. fire** estufa f de gas; **g. mask** careta f antigás; **g. ring** hornillo m de gas (b) US gasolina f, RP nafta f; **g. pump** surtidor m de gasolina; **g. station** gasolinera f, estación f de servicio, Andes, Ven bomba f, Méx gasolinería f, Perú grifo m; **g. tank** depósito m de la gasolina
2 vt (asphyxiate) asfixiar con gas
3 vi Fam (talk) charlotear

gash [gæʃ] **1** n herida profunda
2 vt hacer un corte en; **he gashed his forehead** se hizo una herida en la frente

gasket ['gæskɪt] n junta f

gasoline ['gæsəliːn] n US gasolina f, RP nafta f

gasp [gaːsp] **1** n (cry) grito sordo; (breath) bocanada f, Fig **to be at one's last g.** estar en las últimas
2 vi (in surprise) quedar boquiabierto(a); (breathe) jadear

gassy ['gæsɪ] adj (**gassier, gassiest**) gaseoso(a)

gastric ['gæstrɪk] adj gástrico(a)

gastronomic [gæstrəˈnɒmɪk] adj gastronómico(a)

gate [geɪt] n (a) (entrance) puerta f (b) Sport (spectators) entrada f; **g. (money)** taquilla f

gateau ['gætəʊ] n (pl gateaux ['gætəʊz]) pastel m con nata

gatecrash ['geɪtkræʃ] **1** vt colarse en
2 vi colarse

gateway ['geɪtweɪ] n puerta f, Fig pasaporte m

gather ['gæðə(r)] **1** vt (a) (collect) reunir; (fruit, flowers) recoger (b) (bring together) reunir (c) (harvest) cosechar (d) **to g. speed** ir ganando velocidad; **to g. strength** cobrar fuerzas (e) (understand) suponer; **I g. that ...** tengo entendido que ...
2 vi (a) (come together) reunirse (b) (form) formarse

▸ **gather round** vi agruparse

gathering ['gæðərɪŋ] **1** adj creciente
2 n reunión f

gauche [gəʊʃ] adj (clumsy) torpe; (tactless) sin tacto

gaudy ['gɔːdɪ] adj (**gaudier, gaudiest**) chillón(ona)

gauge [geɪdʒ] **1** n (a) (of gun, screw, wire) calibre m; (of railway track) ancho m de vía (b) (instrument) calibrador m (c) Fig (indicator) indicador m
2 vt (a) (measure) medir, calibrar (b) Fig (judge) juzgar

gaunt [gɔːnt] adj (lean) demacrado(a); (desolate) lúgubre

gauntlet ['gɔːntlɪt] n guantelete m; Fig **to run the g. of ...** estar sometido(a) a ...; Fig **to throw down the g.** arrojar el guante, Am desafiar a algn

gauze [gɔːz] n gasa f

gave [geɪv] pt of **give**

gawky ['gɔːkɪ] adj (**gawkier, gawkiest**) desgarbado(a)

gay [geɪ] adj (a) (homosexual) gay (b) (happy) alegre

gaze [geɪz] **1** n mirada fija
2 vi mirar fijamente

gazelle [gəˈzel] n gacela f

gazette [gə'zet] *n* gaceta *f*; *US* periódico *m*

gazump [gə'zʌmp] *vi Br Fam* = romper un compromiso de venta para vender a un precio más alto

GB [dʒi:'bi:] (*abbr* **Great Britain**) GB

GCSE [dʒi:si:es'i:] *n Br* (*abbr* **General Certificate of Secondary Education**) = certificado de enseñanza secundaria

GDP [dʒi:di:'pi:] *n* (*abbr* **gross domestic product**) PIB *m*

GDR [dʒi:di:'ɑ:(r)] *n Hist* (*abbr* **German Democratic Republic**) RDA *f*

gear [gɪə(r)] **1** *n* (a) (*equipment*) equipo *m* (b) *Fam* (*belongings*) bártulos *mpl* (c) *Fam* (*clothing*) ropa *f* (d) *Tech* engranaje *m* (e) *Aut* velocidad *f*, marcha *f*; **first g.** primera *f* (velocidad *f*); **g. lever** *or US* **shift** palanca *f* de cambio
   2 *vt* ajustar, adaptar

gearbox ['gɪəbɒks] *n* caja *f* de cambios

gearstick ['gɪəstɪk], *US* **gearshift** ['gɪəʃɪft] *n* palanca *f* de cambio

gee [dʒi:] *interj US* **g. (whizz)!** ¡anda!, ¡caramba!

geek [gi:k] *n Fam* lelo(a) *m,f*, tontaina *mf*

geese [gi:s] *pl of* **goose**

gel [dʒel] **1** *n* gel *m*; (*for hair*) gomina *f*
   2 *vi Fig* (*ideas etc*) cuajar
   3 *vt* (*hair*) engominar

gelatin ['dʒelətɪn] *n* gelatina *f*

gelignite ['dʒelɪgnaɪt] *n* gelignita *f*

gem [dʒem] *n* piedra preciosa; *Fig* (*person*) joya *f*

Gemini ['dʒemɪnaɪ] *n* Géminis *m inv*

gen [dʒen] *n Br Fam* (*information*) información *f*, datos *mpl*

gender ['dʒendə(r)] *n* género *m*

gene [dʒi:n] *n* gene *m*, gen *m*

general ['dʒenərəl] **1** *adj* general; **g. knowledge** conocimientos *mpl* generales; **in g.** en general; **the g. public** el público; **g. practitioner** médico *m* de cabecera
   2 *n Mil* general *m*; *US* **g. of the army** mariscal *m* de campo

generalization [dʒenərəlaɪ'zeɪʃən] *n* generalización *f*

generalize ['dʒenərəlaɪz] *vt & vi* generalizar

generally ['dʒenərəlɪ] *adv* generalmente, en general

generate ['dʒenəreɪt] *vt* generar

generation [dʒenə'reɪʃən] *n* generación *f*; **g. gap** abismo *m* or conflicto *m* generacional

generator ['dʒenəreɪtə(r)] *n* generador *m*

generosity [dʒenə'rɒsɪtɪ] *n* generosidad *f*

generous ['dʒenərəs] *adj* generoso(a); (*plentiful*) copioso(a)

genetic [dʒɪ'netɪk] *adj* genético(a); **g. engineering** ingeniería genética

genetically [dʒɪ'netɪklɪ] *adv* **g. modified** (*plant, food*) modificado(a) genéticamente

genetics [dʒɪ'netɪks] *n sing* genética *f*

Geneva [dʒɪ'ni:və] *n* Ginebra

genial ['dʒi:nɪəl, 'dʒi:njəl] *adj* cordial, amable

> *📝 Note that the Spanish word **genial** is a false friend and is never a translation for the English word **genial**. In Spanish, **genial** means both "brilliant" and "terrific".*

genie ['dʒi:nɪ] *n* duende *m*, genio *m*

genitals ['dʒenɪtəlz] *npl* órganos *mpl* genitales

genius ['dʒi:njəs, 'dʒi:nɪəs] *n* (a) (*person*) genio *m* (b) (*gift*) don *m*

genome ['dʒi:nəʊm] *n Biol* genoma *m*

genre ['ʒɑ:nrə] *n* género *m*

gent [dʒent] *n Br Fam* (*abbr* **gentleman**) señor *m*, caballero *m*; **the gents** (*toilets*) el baño *or Esp* el servicio *or CSur* la toilette de caballeros

genteel [dʒen'ti:l] *adj* fino(a), distinguido(a)

> *📝 Note that the Spanish word **gentil** is a false friend and is never a translation for the English word **genteel**. In Spanish, **gentil** means both "kind" and "pagan".*

gentle ['dʒentəl] *adj* dulce, tierno(a); (*breeze*) suave

gentleman ['dʒentəlmən] *n* caballero *m*; **g.'s agreement** pacto *m* de caballeros

gently ['dʒentlɪ] *adv* con cuidado

gentry ['dʒentrɪ] *n* pequeña nobleza, alta burguesía

genuine ['dʒenjʊɪn] *adj* auténtico(a), genuino(a); (*sincere*) sincero(a)

genuinely ['dʒenjʊɪnlɪ] *adv* auténticamente

geographic(al) [dʒɪə'græfɪk(əl)] *adj* geográfico(a)

geography [dʒɪ'ɒgrəfɪ] *n* geografía *f*

geologic(al) [dʒɪə'lɒdʒɪk(əl)] *adj* geológico(a)

geology [dʒɪ'ɒlədʒɪ] *n* geología *f*

geometric(al) [dʒɪə'metrɪk(əl)] *adj* geométrico(a)

geometry [dʒɪ'ɒmɪtrɪ] *n* geometría *f*

geopolitical [dʒi:əʊpə'lɪtɪkəl] *adj* geopolítico(a)

geranium [dʒɪ'reɪnɪəm] *n* geranio *m*

geriatric [dʒerɪ'ætrɪk] *adj* geriátrico(a)

▸**germ** [dʒɜːm] *n* (**a**) *Biol & Fig* germen *m* (**b**) *Med* microbio *m*

German ['dʒɜːmən] **1** *adj* alemán(ana); **G. measles** rubeola *f*
　2 *n* (**a**) *(person)* alemán(ana) *m,f* (**b**) *(language)* alemán *m*

Germany ['dʒɜːmənɪ] *n* Alemania

germinate ['dʒɜːmɪneɪt] *vi* germinar

gestation [dʒe'steɪʃən] *n* gestación *f*

gesticulate [dʒe'stɪkjʊleɪt] *vi* gesticular

gesture ['dʒestʃə(r)] **1** *n* gesto *m*, ademán *m*; **it's an empty g.** es pura formalidad
　2 *vi* gesticular, hacer gestos

get [get] **1** *vt* (*pt & pp* **got**, *US pp* **gotten**) (**a**) *(obtain)* obtener, conseguir; *(receive)* recibir; *(earn)* ganar (**b**) *(fetch) (something)* traer; *(somebody)* ir a por; **can I g. you something to eat?** ¿quieres comer algo?; **g. the police!** ¡llama a la policía! (**c**) *(bus, train)* tomar, *Esp* coger, *Am* agarrar (**d**) *(have done)* **g. him to call me** dile que me llame; **to g. sb to agree to sth** conseguir que algn acepte algo; **to g. one's hair cut** cortarse el pelo (**e**) **have got, have got to** *see* **have** (**f**) *Fam (understand)* entender
　2 *vi* (**a**) *(become)* ponerse; **to g. dressed** vestirse; **to g. drunk** emborracharse; **to g. married** casarse; **to g. paid** cobrar (**b**) **to g. to** *(arrive, come to)* llegar a; **to g. to know sb** llegar a conocer a algn

▸**get about** *vi (person)* salir; *(news)* difundirse

▸**get across** *vt sep (idea etc)* hacer comprender

▸**get ahead** *vi* progresar

▸**get along** *vi* (**a**) *(leave)* marcharse (**b**) *(manage)* arreglárselas (**c**) *(two people)* llevarse bien

▸**get around** *vi (person)* salir; *(travel)* viajar; *(news)* difundirse

▸**get at** *vt insep* (**a**) *(reach)* alcanzar (**b**) *(insinuate)* insinuar; **what are you getting at?** ¿a dónde quieres llegar?

▸**get away** *vi* escaparse

▸**get away with** *vt insep* salir impune de

▸**get back 1** *vi* (**a**) *(return)* regresar, volver (**b**) **g. back!** *(move backwards)* ¡atrás!
　2 *vt sep (recover)* recuperar; *Fam* **to g. one's own back on sb** vengarse de algn

▸**get by** *vi (manage)* arreglárselas; **she can g. by in French** sabe defenderse en francés

▸**get down 1** *vt sep (depress)* deprimir
　2 *vi (descend)* bajar

▸**get down to** *vt insep* ponerse a; **to g. down to the facts** ir al grano

▸**get in 1** *vi* (**a**) *(arrive)* llegar (**b**) *Pol* ser elegido(a)
　2 *vt sep* (**a**) *(buy)* comprar (**b**) *(collect)* recoger

▸**get into** *vt insep Fig* **to g. into bad habits** adquirir malas costumbres; **to g. into trouble** meterse en un lío

▸**get off 1** *vt insep (bus etc)* bajarse de
　2 *vt sep (remove)* quitar, *Andes, RP* sacar
　3 *vi* (**a**) *(descend from vehicle)* bajarse; *Fam* **g. off!** ¡fuera! (**b**) **to g. off to a good start** *(begin)* empezar bien (**c**) *(go unpunished)* librarse

▸**get off with** *vt insep Fam* ligar

▸**get on 1** *vt insep (board)* subir a
　2 *vi* (**a**) *(board)* subirse (**b**) *(make progress)* hacer progresos; **how are you getting on?** ¿cómo te van las cosas? (**c**) **to g. on well (with sb)** llevarse bien (con algn) (**d**) *(continue)* seguir; **to g. on with one's work** seguir trabajando

▸**get on to** *vt insep* (**a**) *(find a person)* localizar; *(find out)* descubrir (**b**) *(continue)* pasar a

▸**get out 1** *vt sep (object)* sacar
　2 *vi* (**a**) *(room etc)* salir (**of** de); *(train)* bajar (**of** de) (**b**) *(escape)* escaparse (**of** de); **to g. out of an obligation** librarse de un compromiso (**c**) *(news)* difundirse; *(secret)* hacerse público

▸**get over 1** *vt insep* (**a**) *(illness)* recuperarse de (**b**) *(difficulty)* vencer
　2 *vt sep (convey)* hacer comprender

▸**get round** *vt insep* (**a**) *(problem)* salvar; *(difficulty)* vencer (**b**) *(rule)* soslayar

▸**get round to** *vt insep* **if I g. round to it** si tengo tiempo

▸**get through 1** *vi* (**a**) *(message)* llegar (**b**) *Educ* aprobar (**c**) *Tel* **to g. through to sb** conseguir comunicar con algn
　2 *vt insep* (**a**) **to g. through a lot of work** trabajar mucho (**b**) *(consume)* consumir

▸**get together 1** *vi (people)* juntarse, reunirse
　2 *vt sep (people)* juntar, reunir

▸**get up 1** *vi (rise)* levantarse, *Am* pararse
　2 *vt sep (wake)* despertar

▸**get up to** *vt insep* hacer; **to g. up to mischief** hacer de las suyas

getaway ['getəweɪ] *n* fuga *f*; **to make one's g.** fugarse

get-together ['gettəgeðə(r)] *n* reunión *f*

geyser ['giːzə(r), *US* 'gaɪzər] *n* (**a**) *Geog* géiser *m* (**b**) *(water heater)* calentador *m* de agua

ghastly ['gɑːstlɪ] *adj* (**ghastlier, ghastliest**) horrible, espantoso(a)

gherkin ['gɜːkɪn] *n* pepinillo *m*

ghetto ['getəʊ] *n* gueto *m*

ghost [gəʊst] n fantasma m; **g. story** cuento m de fantasmas; **g. town** pueblo m fantasma

ghost-writer ['gəʊstraɪtə(r)] n negro(a) m,f

ghoulish ['guːlɪʃ] adj macabro(a)

giant ['dʒaɪənt] adj & n gigante (m)

gibberish ['dʒɪbərɪʃ] n galimatías m inv

gibe [dʒaɪb] 1 n mofa f
2 vi mofarse (**at** de)

giblets ['dʒɪblɪts] npl menudillos mpl

Gibraltar [dʒɪ'brɔːltə(r)] n Gibraltar

Gibraltarian [dʒɪbrɔːl'teərɪən] adj & n gibraltareño(a) (m,f)

giddiness ['gɪdɪnɪs] n mareo m; (vertigo) vértigo m

giddy ['gɪdɪ] adj (**giddier, giddiest**) mareado(a); **it makes me g.** me da vértigo; **to feel g.** sentirse mareado(a)

gift [gɪft] n (**a**) (present) regalo m, obsequio m; **g. token** vale m (**b**) (talent) don m; **to have a g. for music** estar muy dotado(a) para la música

gifted ['gɪftɪd] adj dotado(a)

gig [gɪg] n Fam Mus actuación f

gigabyte ['dʒɪgəbaɪt] n Comput gigabyte m

gigantic [dʒaɪ'gæntɪk] adj gigantesco(a)

giggle ['gɪgəl] 1 n risita f; esp Br Fam **to do sth for a g.** hacer algo de broma
2 vi soltar risitas

gild [gɪld] vt dorar

gill¹ [dʒɪl] n (liquid measure) = 0,142 l

gill² [gɪl] n (of fish) branquia f, agalla f

gilt [gɪlt] 1 adj dorado(a)
2 n (colour) dorado m

gilt-edged ['gɪltedʒd] adj **g. securities** or **stock** Br títulos mpl de deuda pública, valores mpl del Estado; US títulos mpl or valores mpl de máxima garantía

gimmick ['gɪmɪk] n truco m; (in advertising) reclamo m

gin [dʒɪn] n ginebra f; **g. and tonic** gin tonic m

ginger ['dʒɪndʒə(r)] 1 n jengibre m; **g. ale** ginger ale m
2 adj (hair) pelirrojo(a)

gingerbread ['dʒɪndʒəbred] n pan m de jengibre

gingerly ['dʒɪndʒəlɪ] adv cautelosamente

gipsy ['dʒɪpsɪ] adj & n gitano(a) (m,f)

giraffe [dʒɪ'rɑːf] n jirafa f

girder ['gɜːdə(r)] n viga f

girdle ['gɜːdəl] n faja f

girl [gɜːl] n (**a**) (young woman) chica f; (child, baby) niña f; Br **g. guide**, US **g. scout**

exploradora f (**b**) (daughter) hija f (**c**) (sweetheart) novia f

girlfriend ['gɜːlfrend] n (**a**) (lover) novia f (**b**) (female friend) amiga f

girlhood ['gɜːlhʊd] n niñez f

girlish ['gɜːlɪʃ] adj (**a**) (of girl, young woman) de niña (**b**) (effeminate) afeminado(a)

giro ['dʒaɪrəʊ] n Br Fam (unemployment cheque) cheque m del desempleo or Esp paro

gist [dʒɪst] n esencia f; **did you get the g. of what he was saying?** ¿cogiste la idea de lo que decía?

give [gɪv] 1 n (elasticity) elasticidad f
2 vt (pt **gave**; pp **given**) (**a**) (in general) dar; (as present) regalar; **to g. sth to sb** dar algo a algn; **to g. sb sth** dar de comer a algn (**b**) (pay) pagar (**c**) (speech) pronunciar (**d**) (grant) otorgar; **to g. sb one's attention** prestar atención a algn (**e**) (yield) ceder; **to g. way** Aut ceder el paso; Fig ceder; (of legs) flaquear
3 vi (yield) ceder; (fabric) dar de sí

▸ **give away** vt sep (**a**) (prize) repartir; (present) regalar (**b**) (reveal) revelar; **to g. the game away** descubrir el pastel (**c**) (betray) traicionar

▸ **give back** vt sep devolver

▸ **give in** 1 vi (**a**) (admit defeat) darse por vencido(a); (surrender) rendirse (**b**) **to g. in to** ceder ante
2 vt sep (hand in) entregar

▸ **give off** vt sep (smell etc) despedir

▸ **give out** vt sep distribuir, repartir

▸ **give over** vt sep (hand over) entregar; (devote) dedicar

▸ **give up** 1 vt sep (**a**) (idea) abandonar; **to g. up smoking** dejar de fumar (**b**) (hand over) entregar; **to g. oneself up** entregarse
2 vi (admit defeat) darse por vencido(a), rendirse

▸ **give up on** vt insep darse por vencido con

given ['gɪvən] 1 adj (**a**) (particular) dado(a); **at a g. time** en un momento dado (**b**) **g. to** dado(a) a
2 conj (considering) dado(a)
3 pp of **give**

glacial ['gleɪsɪəl] adj (**a**) Geol glaciar (**b**) (icy) glacial; Fig **g. look** mirada f glacial

glacier ['glæsɪə(r)] n glaciar m

glad [glæd] adj (**gladder, gladdest**) contento(a); (happy) alegre; **he'll be only too g. to help you** tendrá mucho gusto en ayudarle; **to be g.** alegrarse

gladiator ['glædɪeɪtə(r)] n Hist gladiador m

gladly ['glædlɪ] *adv* con mucho gusto

glamor ['glæmər] *n US* = **glamour**

glamorous ['glæmərəs] *adj* atractivo(a), encantador(a)

glamour ['glæmə(r)] *n* atractivo *m*; *(charm)* encanto *m*; *Fam* **g. girl** bombón *m*, *Am* muñequita *f*

glance [glɑːns] **1** *n* mirada *f*, vistazo *m*; **at a g.** de un vistazo; **at first g.** a primera vista
2 *vi* echar un vistazo (**at** a)
▸ **glance off** *vt insep (of ball etc)* rebotar de

glancing ['glɑːnsɪŋ] *adj (blow)* oblicuo(a)

gland [glænd] *n* glándula *f*

glandular ['glændjʊlə(r)] *adj* glandular; **g. fever** mononucleosis infecciosa

glare [gleə(r)] **1** *n (light)* luz *f* deslumbrante; *(dazzle)* deslumbramiento *m*; *(look)* mirada *f* feroz
2 *vi (dazzle)* deslumbrar; *(look)* lanzar una mirada furiosa (**at** a)

glaring ['gleərɪŋ] *adj (light)* deslumbrante; *(colour)* chillón(ona); *(obvious)* evidente

glass [glɑːs] *n* (**a**) *(material)* vidrio *m*; **pane of g.** cristal *m* (**b**) *(drinking vessel)* vaso *m*; **wine g.** copa *f* (para vino) (**c**) **glasses** *(spectacles)* gafas *fpl*, *Am* lentes *mpl*, anteojos *mpl*; **to wear glasses** llevar gafas *or Am* lentes *or* anteojos

glasshouse ['glɑːshaʊs] *n Br* invernadero *m*

glassware ['glɑːsweə(r)] *n* cristalería *f*

glassy ['glɑːsɪ] *adj* (**glassier, glassiest**) *(water)* cristalino(a); *(eyes)* vidrioso(a)

glaze [gleɪz] **1** *n (varnish)* barniz *m*; *(for pottery)* vidriado *m*
2 *vt* (**a**) *(windows)* acristalar; (**b**) *(varnish)* barnizar; *(ceramics)* vidriar (**c**) *Culin* glasear

glazed [gleɪzd] *adj (eyes)* de mirada ausente

glazier ['gleɪzɪə(r)] *n* vidriero(a) *m,f*

gleam [gliːm] **1** *n (of light)* destello *m*
2 *vi* resplandecer, relucir

gleaming ['gliːmɪŋ] *adj* brillante, reluciente

glean [gliːn] *vt Fig* recoger, cosechar

glee [gliː] *n* gozo *m*

gleeful ['gliːfʊl] *adj* gozoso(a)

glen [glen] *n* cañada *f*

glib [glɪb] *adj* (**glibber, glibbest**) *Pej (person)* con mucha labia, *CAm, Ecuad, Méx* labioso(a); *(excuse, answer)* fácil

glide [glaɪd] *vi* (**a**) *(slip, slide)* deslizarse (**b**) *Av* planear

glider ['glaɪdə(r)] *n* planeador *m*

gliding ['glaɪdɪŋ] *n* vuelo *m* sin motor

glimmer ['glɪmə(r)] *n* (**a**) *(light)* luz *f* tenue (**b**) *Fig (trace)* destello *m*

glimpse [glɪmps] **1** *n* atisbo *m*
2 *vt* atisbar

glint [glɪnt] **1** *n* destello *m*, centelleo *m*; **he had a g. in his eye** le brillaban los ojos
2 *vi* destellar, centellear

glisten ['glɪsən] *vi* relucir, brillar

glitter ['glɪtə(r)] **1** *n* brillo *m*
2 *vi* relucir

gloat [gləʊt] *vi* jactarse; **to g. over another's misfortune** recrearse con la desgracia de otro

global ['gləʊbəl] *adj* (**a**) *(of the world)* mundial; **g. warming** calentamiento *m* global (**b**) *(overall)* global

globalization [gləʊbəlaɪˈzeɪʃən] *n* mundialización *f*, globalización *f*

globe [gləʊb] *n* globo *m*, esfera *f*

gloom [gluːm] *n (obscurity)* penumbra *f*; *(melancholy)* melancolía *f*; *(despair)* desolación *f*

gloomy ['gluːmɪ] *adj* (**gloomier, gloomiest**) *(dark)* oscuro(a); *(weather)* gris; *(dismal)* deprimente; *(despairing)* pesimista; *(sad)* triste

glorify ['glɔːrɪfaɪ] *vt* glorificar

glorious ['glɔːrɪəs] *adj (momentous)* glorioso(a); *(splendid)* magnífico(a), espléndido(a)

glory ['glɔːrɪ] *n (honour, praise)* gloria *f*; *(splendour)* esplendor *m*; *(triumph)* triunfo *m*

gloss [glɒs] **1** *n* (**a**) *(explanation)* glosa *f* (**b**) *(sheen)* brillo *m*; **g. (paint)** pintura *f* brillante
2 *vi* glosar
▸ **gloss over** *vt insep Fig* encubrir

glossary ['glɒsərɪ] *n* glosario *m*

glossy ['glɒsɪ] *adj* (**glossier, glossiest**) lustroso(a); **g. magazine** revista *f* de lujo

glove [glʌv] *n* guante *m*; *Aut* **g. compartment** guantera *f*

glow [gləʊ] **1** *n* brillo *m*; *(of fire)* incandescencia *f*; *(of sun)* arrebol *m*; *(heat)* calor *m*; *(light)* luz *f*; *(in cheeks)* rubor *m*
2 *vi* brillar; *(fire)* arder; *Fig* rebosar de

glower ['glaʊə(r)] *vi* poner cara de enfadado(a)

glowing ['gləʊɪŋ] *adj* (**a**) *(fire)* incandescente; *(colour)* vivo(a); *(light)* brillante (**b**) *(cheeks)* encendido(a) (**c**) *Fig (report)* entusiasta

glucose ['gluːkəʊz] *n* glucosa *f*

glue [gluː] **1** *n* pegamento *m*, cola *f*
2 *vt* pegar (**to** a)

glum [glʌm] *adj* (**glummer, glummest**) alicaído(a)

glut [glʌt] *n* superabundancia *f*, exceso *m*

glutton ['glʌtən] *n* glotón(ona) *m,f*

GM [dʒiːˈem] *adj* (*abbr* **genetically modified**) transgénico(a), modificado(a) genéticamente; **GM food** (alimentos) transgénicos

GMO [dʒiːemˈəʊ] *n* (*abbr* **genetically modified organism**) OMG *m*

GMT [dʒiːemˈtiː] *n* (*abbr* **Greenwich Mean Time**) hora *f* del meridiano de Greenwich

gnarled [nɑːld] *adj* nudoso(a)

gnash [næʃ] *vt* rechinar

gnat [næt] *n* mosquito *m*

gnaw [nɔː] *vt & vi* (*chew*) roer

gnome [nəʊm] *n* gnomo *m*

GNP [dʒiːenˈpiː] *n* (*abbr* **gross national product**) PNB *m*

go [gəʊ] **1** *vi* (*3rd person sing pres* **goes**; *pt* **went**; *pp* **gone**) (**a**) (*in general*) ir; **to go for a walk** (ir a) dar un paseo (**b**) (*depart*) irse, marcharse (**c**) (*function*) funcionar (**d**) (*be sold*) venderse (**e**) (*become*) quedarse, volverse; **to go blind** quedarse ciego(a); **to go mad** volverse loco(a) (**f**) (*progress*) ir, marchar; **everything went well** todo salió bien; **how's it going?** ¿qué tal (te van las cosas)? (**g**) **to be going to** (*in the future*) ir a; (*on the point of*) estar a punto de (**h**) (*fit*) caber (**i**) (*be available*) quedar; **I'll take whatever's going** me conformo con lo que hay (**j**) (*be acceptable*) valer; **anything goes** todo vale (**k**) (*time*) pasar; **there are only two weeks to go** sólo quedan dos semanas (**l**) (*say*) decir; **as the saying goes** según lo dicho (**m**) **to let sth go** soltar algo **2** *vt* (**a**) (*travel*) hacer, recorrer (**b**) **to go it alone** apañárselas solo **3** *n* (**a**) (*energy*) energía *f*, dinamismo *m* (**b**) (*try*) intento *m*; **to have a go at sth** probar suerte con algo; **to have a go at sb** criticar a algn (**c**) (*turn*) turno *m*; **it's your go** te toca a ti (**d**) **to make a go of sth** tener éxito en algo

▸ **go about 1** *vt insep* (**a**) (*task*) emprender; **how do you go about it?** ¿cómo hay que hacerlo? (**b**) **to go about one's business** ocuparse de sus asuntos **2** *vi* (*rumour*) correr

▸ **go after** *vt insep* (*pursue*) ir tras

▸ **go against** *vt insep* (*oppose*) ir en contra de; (*verdict*) ser desfavorable a

▸ **go ahead** *vi* (**a**) (*proceed*) proceder (**b**) **we'll go on ahead** iremos delante

▸ **go along 1** *vt insep* (*street*) pasar por **2** *vi* (*progress*) progresar

▸ **go along with** *vt insep* (**a**) (*agree with*) estar de acuerdo con (**b**) (*accompany*) acompañar

▸ **go around** *vi* (**a**) (*rumour*) correr (**b**) **there's enough to go around** hay para todos

▸ **go away** *vi* marcharse

▸ **go back** *vi* (**a**) (*return*) volver, regresar (**b**) *Fig* **to go back to** (*date from*) datar de

▸ **go back on** *vt insep* **to go back on one's word** faltar a su palabra

▸ **go back to** *vt insep* volver a

▸ **go by** *vi* pasar; **as time goes by** con el tiempo

▸ **go down** *vi* (**a**) (*descend*) bajar; (*sun*) ponerse; (*ship*) hundirse (**b**) (*diminish*) disminuir; (*temperature*) bajar (**c**) (*be received*) ser acogido(a)

▸ **go down with** *vt insep* (*contract*) agarrar, *Esp* coger

▸ **go for** *vt insep* (**a**) (*attack*) lanzarse sobre (**b**) (*fetch*) ir por

▸ **go in** *vi* entrar

▸ **go in for** *vt insep* (*exam*) presentarse a; (*hobby*) dedicarse a

▸ **go into** *vt insep* (**a**) (*enter*) entrar en; **to go into journalism** dedicarse al periodismo (**b**) (*study*) examinar; (*matter*) investigar

▸ **go off 1** *vi* (**a**) (*leave*) irse, marcharse (**b**) (*bomb*) explotar; (*gun*) dispararse; (*alarm*) sonar (**c**) (*food*) pasarse **2** *vt insep Fam* **to go off sth** perder el gusto *or* el interés por algo

▸ **go on** *vi* (**a**) (*continue*) seguir, continuar; **to go on talking** seguir hablando; *Fam* **to go on and on about sth** no parar de hablar sobre algo; (*complain*) quejarse constantemente de algo (**b**) (*time*) transcurrir, pasar (**c**) (*light*) encenderse, *Am* prenderse

▸ **go out** *vi* (**a**) (*leave*) salir; **to go out for a meal** comer *or* cenar fuera (**b**) (*boy and girl*) salir juntos (**c**) (*fire, light*) apagarse (**d**) (*tide*) bajar

▸ **go over** *vt insep* (*revise*) repasar

▸ **go over to** *vt insep* (**a**) (*approach*) acercarse a (**b**) (*switch to*) **to go over to a different system** cambiar de sistema; **to go over to the enemy** pasarse al enemigo

▸ **go round** *vi* (**a**) (*revolve*) dar vueltas (**b**) **to go round to sb's house** pasar por casa de algn

▸ **go through 1** *vi (bill)* ser aprobado(a) **2** *vt insep* (**a**) *(examine)* examinar; *(search)* registrar (**b**) *(rehearse)* ensayar (**c**) *(spend)* gastar (**d**) *(list etc)* explicar (**e**) *(endure)* sufrir

▸ **go through with** *vt insep* llevar a cabo

▸ **go under** *vi* (**a**) *(ship)* hundirse (**b**) *(business)* fracasar

▸ **go up** *vi* (**a**) *(price etc)* subir (**b**) **to go up to sb** acercarse a algn (**c**) *(in a lift)* subir

▸ **go with** *vt insep* (**a**) *(accompany)* ir con (**b**) *(colours)* hacer juego con

▸ **go without** *vt insep* pasarse sin, prescindir de

goad [gəʊd] *vt* aguijonear

go-ahead ['gəʊəhed] *n Fam* **to give sb the g.** dar luz verde a algn

goal [gəʊl] *n* (**a**) *Sport* gol *m*; **g. post** poste *m* (**b**) *(aim, objective)* meta *f*, objetivo *m*

goalkeeper ['gəʊlki:pə(r)] *n* portero(a) *m,f*

goat [gəʊt] *n (female)* cabra *f*; *(male)* macho cabrío

gob [gɒb] *n esp Br very Fam* pico *m*

gobble ['gɒbəl] *vt* engullir

go-between ['gəʊbɪtwi:n] *n* intermediario(a) *m,f*

goblet ['gɒblɪt] *n* copa *f*

god [gɒd] *n* dios *m*; **G.** Dios; **(my) G.!** ¡Dios mío!

godchild ['gɒdtʃaɪld] *n* ahijado(a) *m,f*

goddam(n) ['gɒdæm] *US Fam* **1** *adj* maldito(a), dichoso(a), *Méx* pinche **2** *adv* **that was g. stupid!** ¡eso fue una auténtica estupidez!

goddaughter ['gɒddɔːtə(r)] *n* ahijada *f*

goddess ['gɒdɪs] *n* diosa *f*

godfather ['gɒdfɑːðə(r)] *n* padrino *m*

godforsaken ['gɒdfəseɪkən] *adj (place)* remoto(a)

godmother ['gɒdmʌðə(r)] *n* madrina *f*

godparents ['gɒdpeərənts] *npl* padrinos *mpl*

godsend ['gɒdsend] *n* regalo inesperado

godson ['gɒdsʌn] *n* ahijado *m*

goggles ['gɒgəlz] *npl* gafas *fpl* protectoras, *CSur* antiparras *fpl*

going ['gəʊɪŋ] **1** *adj* (**a**) *(price)* corriente; **the g. rate** el precio medio (**b**) **a g. concern** un negocio que marcha bien (**c**) **to get** *or* **be g.** marcharse (**d**) **to keep g.** resistir **2** *n* **to get out while the g. is good** retirarse antes que sea demasiado tarde

goings-on [gəʊɪŋz'ɒn] *npl Fam* tejemanejes *mpl*

go-kart ['gəʊkɑːt] *n Sport* kart *m*

gold [gəʊld] **1** *n* oro *m*; **g. leaf** pan *m* de oro; **g. medal** medalla *f* de oro; **g. mine** mina *f* de oro **2** *adj* de oro; *(colour)* oro, dorado(a)

golden ['gəʊldən] *adj* de oro; *(colour)* dorado(a); *Fig* **a g. opportunity** una excelente oportunidad; **g. eagle** águila *f* real; *Fig* **g. handshake** indemnización *f* por despido; **g. wedding** bodas *fpl* de oro

goldfish ['gəʊldfɪʃ] *n* pez *m* de colores

gold-plated [gəʊld'pleɪtɪd] *adj* chapado(a) en oro

goldsmith ['gəʊldsmɪθ] *n* orfebre *m*

golf [gɒlf] *n* golf *m*; **g. ball** pelota *f* de golf; **g. club** *(stick)* palo *m* de golf; *(place)* club *m* de golf; **g. course** campo *m* de golf

golfer ['gɒlfə(r)] *n* golfista *mf*

golly ['gɒlɪ] *interj* ¡vaya!

gone [gɒn] **1** *adj* desaparecido(a) **2** *pp of* **go**

gong [gɒŋ] *n* gong *m*

good [gʊd] **1** *adj* (**better, best**) (**a**) *(before noun)* buen(a); *(after noun)* bueno(a); **a g. book** un buen libro; **g. afternoon/evening** buenas tardes; **g. morning** buenos días; **g. night** buenas noches; **it looks g.** tiene buena pinta; **to feel g.** sentirse bien; **to smell g.** oler bien; **to have a g. time** pasarlo bien (**b**) *(kind)* amable (**c**) *(morally correct)* correcto(a); **be g.!** ¡pórtate bien! (**d**) **he's g. at languages** tiene facilidad para los idiomas (**e**) *(attractive)* bonito(a); **g. looks** atractivo *m*, belleza *f* (**f**) *(propitious)* propicio(a) (**g**) *(character)* agradable; **he's in a g. mood** está de buen humor **2** *n* (**a**) *(in general)* bien *m*; **g. and evil** el bien y el mal; **to do g.** hacer el bien (**b**) *(advantage)* bien *m*, provecho *m*; **for your own g.** para tu propio bien; **it's no g. waiting** no sirve de nada esperar; **it will do you g.** te hará bien (**c**) *Com* **goods** artículos *mpl*, géneros *mpl*; **goods train** tren *m* de mercancías **3 for good** *adv* **she's gone for g.** se ha ido para siempre **4** *interj* ¡muy bien!

goodbye [gʊd'baɪ] **1** *interj* ¡adiós! **2** *n* adiós *m*, despedida *f*; **to say g. to sb** despedirse de algn

good-for-nothing ['gʊdfənʌθɪŋ] *adj & n* inútil *(mf)*

good-hearted [gʊd'hɑːtɪd] *adj* de buen corazón

good-looking [gʊd'lʊkɪŋ] *adj* guapo(a)

good-natured [gʊd'neɪtʃəd] *adj* amable, bondadoso(a)

goodness ['gʊdnɪs] n bondad f; **my g.!** ¡Dios mío!; **thank g.!** ¡gracias a Dios!; **for g. sake!** ¡por Dios!

good-tempered [gʊd'tempəd] adj apacible

goodwill [gʊd'wɪl] n (a) (benevolence) buena voluntad (b) Com fondo m de comercio

goof [guːf] US Fam 1 n metedura f or Am metida f de pata
2 vi meter la pata

goose [guːs] n (pl geese) ganso m, oca f

gooseberry ['gʊzbərɪ, 'guːsbərɪ] n uva espina, grosella espinosa; Br Fam **to play g.** Esp hacer de carabina or de sujetavelas, Méx hacer mal tercio, RP estar de paleta

gooseflesh ['guːsfleʃ] n, **goosepimples** ['guːspɪmpəlz] npl carne f de gallina

goose-step ['guːsstep] vi ir a paso de la oca

gore¹ [gɔː(r)] n sangre derramada

gore² [gɔː(r)] vt (of bull) cornear, dar cornadas a

gorge [gɔːdʒ] 1 n desfiladero m
2 vt & vi **to g. (oneself) (on)** atiborrarse (de)

gorgeous ['gɔːdʒəs] adj magnífico(a), estupendo(a); (person) atractivo(a), guapo(a)

gorilla [gə'rɪlə] n gorila m

gorse [gɔːs] n aulaga f

gory ['gɔːrɪ] adj (**gorier, goriest**) sangriento(a)

gosh [gɒʃ] interj Fam ¡cielos!, ¡caray!

go-slow [gəʊ'sləʊ] n Br huelga f de celo

gospel ['gɒspəl] n **the G.** el Evangelio; Fam **it's the g. truth** es la pura verdad

gossip ['gɒsɪp] 1 n (a) (rumour) cotilleo m; **g. column** ecos mpl de sociedad (b) (person) chismoso(a) m,f, cotilla mf
2 vi (natter) cotillear, chismorrear

got [gɒt] pt & pp of **get**

Gothic ['gɒθɪk] adj gótico(a)

gotten ['gɒtən] US pp of **get**

gourmet ['gʊəmeɪ] n gourmet mf

gout [gaʊt] n gota f

govern ['gʌvən] vt (a) (state, country) gobernar; (emotions) dominar (b) (of scientific law) regir, determinar

governess ['gʌvənɪs] n institutriz f

governing ['gʌvənɪŋ] adj gobernante; **g. body** consejo m de administración

government ['gʌvənmənt] n gobierno m

governmental [gʌvən'mentəl] adj gubernamental

governor ['gʌvənə(r)] n (ruler) gobernador(a) m,f, (of prison) director(a) m,f, (of school) administrador(a) m,f

gown [gaʊn] n (dress) vestido largo; Jur & Univ toga f

GP [dʒiː'piː] n Br (abbr **general practitioner**) médico(a) m,f de familia or de cabecera

GPO [dʒiːpiː'əʊ] n Br Formerly (abbr **General Post Office**) ≃ (Administración f Central de) Correos mpl

grab [græb] 1 n agarrón m; Fam **to be up for grabs** estar disponible
2 vt (a) (snatch) agarrar; **to g. hold of sb** agarrarse a algn (b) Fam (take hurriedly) **to g. a bite to eat** comer algo en cualquier parte (c) Fam (attract, interest) **how does that g. you?** ¿qué te parece?

grace [greɪs] 1 n (a) (of movement, language) gracia f, elegancia f (b) Rel gracia f (c) **to say g.** bendecir la mesa (d) **five days' g.** (reprieve) un plazo de cinco días
2 vt (a) (adorn) adornar (b) (honour) honrar

graceful ['greɪsfʊl] adj elegante; (movement) garboso(a)

gracefully ['greɪsfʊlɪ] adv (a) (beautifully) con gracia, con elegancia (b) (accept) con cortesía

gracious ['greɪʃəs] 1 adj (a) (elegant) elegante (b) (courteous) cortés (c) (kind) amable
2 interj **good g. (me)!, goodness g.!** ¡santo cielo!

grade [greɪd] 1 n (a) (quality) grado m; (rank) categoría f; Mil rango m (b) US Educ (mark) nota f (c) US Educ (class) clase f; **g. school** escuela primaria (d) (level) nivel m (e) US **g. crossing** paso m a nivel
2 vt clasificar

gradient ['greɪdɪənt] n (graph) declive m; (hill) cuesta f, pendiente f

gradual ['grædjʊəl] adj gradual, progresivo(a)

gradually ['grædjʊəlɪ] adv poco a poco

graduate 1 n ['grædjʊɪt] Univ licenciado(a) m,f, US (from high school) ≃ bachiller mf
2 vi ['grædjʊeɪt] (a) Univ licenciarse (in en) (b) US (from high school) ≃ sacar el bachillerato

graduation [grædjʊ'eɪʃən] n graduación f; Univ **g. ceremony** ceremonia f de entrega de los títulos

graffiti [grə'fiːtɪ] npl grafiti mpl

graft [grɑːft] 1 n (a) Med injerto m (b) Br Fam (work) trabajo m (c) US (bribery) corruptelas fpl
2 vt Med injertar (on to en)
3 vi Br Fam trabajar mucho, Esp currar a tope, Méx chambear duro, RP laburar como loco

grain [greɪn] n (a) (cereals) cereales mpl (b) (particle) grano m; Fig **there's not a g. of truth in it** no tiene ni pizca de verdad (c) (in wood) fibra f; (in stone) veta f; (in leather) flor f; Fig **to go against the g.** ir a contrapelo

gram [græm] n gramo m

grammar ['græmə(r)] n gramática f; **g. (book)** libro m de gramática; Br **g. school** instituto m de enseñanza secundaria (al que sólo se accede después de superar un examen de ingreso)

grammatical [grə'mætɪkəl] adj gramatical

gramme [græm] n gramo m

gramophone ['græməfəʊn] n gramófono m

granary ['grænərɪ] n granero m

grand [grænd] **1** adj (a) (imposing) grandioso(a), imponente; (plan, scheme) ambicioso(a); **g. piano** piano m de cola (b) (overall) global; **g. total** total m (c) Fam (excellent) genial, Am salvo RP chévere, Méx padre, RP bárbaro(a)
2 n Fam mil libras fpl; US mil dólares mpl

grandchild ['græntʃaɪld] n nieto(a) m,f

granddad ['grændæd] n Fam abuelo m

granddaughter ['grændɔːtə(r)] n nieta f

grandeur ['grændʒə(r)] n grandeza f, grandiosidad f

grandfather ['grænfɑːðə(r)] n abuelo m; **g. clock** reloj m de caja

grandiose ['grændɪəʊs] adj grandioso(a)

grandma ['grænmɑː] n Fam abuelita f

grandmother ['grænmʌðə(r)] n abuela f

grandpa ['grænpɑː] n Fam abuelito m

grandparents ['grænpeərənts] npl abuelos mpl

grandson ['grænsʌn] n nieto m

grandstand ['grænstænd] n tribuna f

granite ['grænɪt] n granito m

granny ['grænɪ] n Fam abuelita f

grant [grɑːnt] **1** vt (a) (allow) conceder, otorgar (b) (admit) admitir; **to take sb for granted** no apreciar a algn en lo que vale; **to take sth for granted** dar algo por sentado
2 n Educ beca f; (subsidy) subvención f

granulated ['grænjʊleɪtɪd] adj granulado(a)

granule ['grænjuːl] n gránulo m

grape [greɪp] n uva f; **g. juice** mosto m

grapefruit ['greɪpfruːt] n pomelo m, Am toronja f

grapevine ['greɪpvaɪn] n Bot vid f; (against wall) parra f; Fam **I heard it on** or **through the g.** me enteré por ahí

graph [grɑːf, græf] n gráfica f

graphic ['græfɪk] adj gráfico(a); **g. arts** artes gráficas; **g. designer** grafista mf

graphics ['græfɪks] **1** n (study) grafismo m
2 npl Comput gráficas fpl

grapple ['græpəl] **1** vi (struggle) luchar cuerpo a cuerpo (with con); Fig **to g. with a problem** intentar resolver un problema
2 n (hook) garfio m

grasp [grɑːsp] **1** vt (a) (hold firmly) agarrar, asir (b) (understand) comprender
2 n (a) (grip) agarrón m (b) (understanding) comprensión f; **within sb's g.** al alcance de algn

grasping ['grɑːspɪŋ] adj avaro(a)

grass [grɑːs] n hierba f; (lawn) césped m; Fig **g. roots** base f

▶ **grass over** vi cubrirse de hierba

grasshopper ['grɑːshɒpə(r)] n saltamontes m inv

grassland ['grɑːslænd] n pradera f

grass-roots ['grɑːsruːts] adj de base; **at g. level** a nivel popular

grassy ['grɑːsɪ] adj (grassier, grassiest) cubierto(a) de hierba

grate¹ [greɪt] **1** vt Culin rallar
2 vi chirriar

grate² [greɪt] n (a) (in fireplace) rejilla f (b) (fireplace) chimenea f (c) Constr rejilla f, reja f

grateful ['greɪtfʊl] adj agradecido(a); **to be g. for** agradecer

grater ['greɪtə(r)] n Culin rallador m

gratification [grætɪfɪ'keɪʃən] n (pleasure) placer m, satisfacción f

gratify ['grætɪfaɪ] vt (a) (please) complacer (b) (yield to) sucumbir a

gratifying ['grætɪfaɪɪŋ] adj grato(a)

grating¹ ['greɪtɪŋ] n rejilla f, reja f

grating² ['greɪtɪŋ] adj chirriante; (tone) áspero(a)

gratis ['greɪtɪs, 'grætɪs] adv gratis

gratitude ['grætɪtjuːd] n agradecimiento m

gratuitous [grə'tjuːɪtəs] adj gratuito(a)

gratuity [grə'tjuːɪtɪ] n gratificación f

grave¹ [greɪv] n sepultura f, tumba f

grave² [greɪv] adj (look etc) serio(a); (situation) grave

gravel ['grævəl] n grava f, gravilla f

gravestone ['greɪvstəʊn] n lápida f sepulcral

graveyard ['greɪvjɑːd] n cementerio m

gravity ['grævɪtɪ] n gravedad f

gravy ['greɪvɪ] n salsa f, jugo m (de la carne)

gray [greɪ] adj & n US = **grey**

graze¹ [greɪz] vi pacer, pastar

graze² [greɪz] **1** vt (scratch) rasguñar; (brush against) rozar
  2 n rasguño m

grease [griːs, griːz] **1** n grasa f
  2 vt engrasar

greaseproof ['griːspruːf] adj Br **g. paper** papel graso

greasy ['griːsɪ, 'griːzɪ] adj (**greasier, greasiest**) (**a**) (oily) grasiento(a); (hair, food) graso(a) (**b**) (slippery) resbaladizo(a) (**c**) Fam (manner) adulador(a), Méx, RP arrastrado(a)

great [greɪt] **1** adj (**a**) (large, important) grande; (before singular noun) gran; (pain, heat) fuerte; **a g. many** muchos(as); **G. Britain** Gran Bretaña; Br **G. Bear** Osa f Mayor (**b**) Fam (excellent) genial, Am salvo RP chévere, Méx padre, RP bárbaro(a); **to have a g. time** pasarlo muy bien
  2 adv Fam muy bien, estupendamente

great-aunt [greɪt'ɑːnt] n tía abuela

great-grandchild [greɪt'grænt∫aɪld] n bisnieto(a) m,f

great-grandfather [greɪt'grænfɑːðə(r)] n bisabuelo m

great-grandmother [greɪt'grænmʌðə(r)] n bisabuela f

greatly ['greɪtlɪ] adv muy, mucho

greatness ['greɪtnɪs] n grandeza f

great-uncle [greɪt'ʌŋkəl] n tío abuelo

Greece [griːs] n Grecia

greed, greediness ['griːd, 'griːdɪnɪs] n (for food) gula f; (for money) codicia f, avaricia f

greedy ['griːdɪ] adj (**greedier, greediest**) (for food) glotón(ona); (for money) codicioso(a) (**for** de)

Greek [griːk] **1** adj griego(a)
  2 n (**a**) (person) griego(a) m,f (**b**) (language) griego m

green [griːn] **1** n (**a**) (colour) verde m (**b**) (in golf) green m (**c**) **village g. plaza** f (del pueblo) (**d**) **greens** (vegetables) verdura(s) f(pl)
  2 adj (**a**) (colour) verde; **g. bean** judía f verde, Bol, RP chaucha f, CAm ejote m, Col, Cuba habichuela f, Chile poroto m verde, Ven vainita f; **g. belt** zona f verde; US **G. card** (work permit) permiso m de trabajo; **g. pepper** pimiento m verde; **she was g. with envy** se la comía la envidia (**b**) (inexperienced) verde, novato(a); (gullible) crédulo(a) (**c**) Pol **G. Party** Partido m Verde

greenery ['griːnərɪ] n follaje m

greenfly ['griːnflaɪ] n pulgón m

greengage ['griːngeɪdʒ] n ciruela claudia

greengrocer ['griːngrəʊsə(r)] n Br verdulero(a) m,f

greenhouse ['griːnhaʊs] n invernadero m; **g. effect** efecto invernadero

greenish ['griːnɪ∫] adj verdoso(a)

Greenland ['griːnlənd] n Groenlandia

greet [griːt] vt (wave at) saludar; (receive) recibir; (welcome) dar la bienvenida a

greeting ['griːtɪŋ] n saludo m; **New Year/birthday greetings** felicitaciones fpl de Año Nuevo/cumpleaños; Br **greetings** or US **g. card** tarjeta f de felicitación

gregarious [grɪ'geərɪəs] adj gregario(a), sociable

Grenada [gre'neɪdə] n Granada

grenade [grɪ'neɪd] n granada f

grew [gruː] pt of **grow**

grey [greɪ] **1** adj (colour) gris; (hair) cano(a); (sky) nublado(a); **g. matter** materia f gris
  2 n (**a**) (colour) gris m (**b**) (horse) caballo tordo

grey-haired ['greɪheəd] adj canoso(a)

greyhound ['greɪhaʊnd] n galgo m

greyish ['greɪɪ∫] adj grisáceo(a)

grid [grɪd] n (**a**) (on map) cuadrícula f (**b**) (of electricity etc) red f nacional (**c**) (for cooking) parrilla f

griddle ['grɪdəl] n (for cooking) plancha f

gridiron ['grɪdaɪən] n Culin parrilla f

grief [griːf] n dolor m, pena f; Fam **to come to g.** (car, driver) sufrir un accidente; (plans) irse al traste

grievance ['griːvəns] n (wrong) agravio m; (resentment) queja f

grieve [griːv] **1** vt apenar, dar pena a
  2 vi apenarse, afligirse; **to g. for sb** llorar la muerte de algn

grievous ['griːvəs] adj (offence) grave; Br Jur **g. bodily harm** lesiones fpl corporales graves

grill [grɪl] **1** vt (**a**) Culin asar (a la parrilla) (**b**) Fam (interrogate) interrogar duramente
  2 n Br (on cooker) grill m; (for open fire) parrilla f; (dish) parrillada f

grill(e) [grɪl] n (grating) reja f

grim [grɪm] adj (**grimmer, grimmest**) (**a**) (sinister) macabro(a); (landscape) lúgubre (**b**) (person) ceñudo(a) (**c**) Fam (unpleasant) desagradable

grimace [grɪ'meɪs] **1** n mueca f
  2 vi hacer una mueca

grime [graɪm] n mugre f, porquería f

grimy ['graɪmɪ] adj (**grimier, grimiest**) mugriento(a)

grin [grɪn] **1** *vi* sonreír abiertamente
2 *n* sonrisa abierta

grind [graɪnd] **1** *vt* (*pt & pp* **ground**) (*mill*) moler; (*crush*) triturar; (*sharpen*) afilar; *US* (*meat*) picar
2 *vi* (**a**) (*wheels, gears*) chirriar; **to g. to a halt** (*vehicle*) pararse lentamente; (*production etc*) pararse poco a poco (**b**) *US Fam* empollar
3 *n* (**a**) *Fam* **the daily g.** la rutina cotidiana (**b**) *US Fam* (*studious pupil*) empollón(ona) *m,f*
▸ **grind down** *vt sep Fig* **to g. down the opposition** acabar con la oposición

grinder ['graɪndə(r)] *n* (*for coffee, pepper*) molinillo *m*; (*crusher*) trituradora *f*; (*for sharpening*) afilador *m*

grip [grɪp] **1** *n* (**a**) (*hold*) agarrón *m*; (*handshake*) apretón *m*; **to get to grips with a problem** superar un problema (**b**) (*handle*) (*of oar, handlebars, racket*) empuñadura *f* (**c**) *US* (*bag*) bolsa *f* de viaje
2 *vt* (**a**) (*seize*) agarrar, asir; (*hand*) apretar (**b**) *Fig* (*of film, story*) captar la atención de; **to be gripped by fear** ser presa del miedo

gripe [graɪp] **1** *vi Fam* (*complain*) quejarse
2 *n* (**a**) *Med* (*pain*) retortijón *m* (**b**) *Fam* (*complaint*) queja *f*

gripping ['grɪpɪŋ] *adj* (*film, story*) apasionante

grisly ['grɪzlɪ] *adj* (**grislier, grisliest**) espeluznante

gristle ['grɪsəl] *n* cartílago *m*, ternilla *f*

grit [grɪt] **1** *n* (**a**) (*gravel*) grava *f* (**b**) *Fam* (*courage*) valor *m*
2 *vt Fig* **to g. one's teeth** apretar los dientes

gritty ['grɪtɪ] *adj* (**grittier, grittiest**) valiente

grizzly ['grɪzlɪ] *adj* **g. bear** oso pardo

groan [grəʊn] **1** *n* (**a**) (*of pain*) gemido *m* (**b**) *Fam* (*of disapproval*) gruñido *m*
2 *vi* (**a**) (*in pain*) gemir (**b**) *Fam* (*complain*) quejarse (**about** de)

grocer ['grəʊsə(r)] *n* tendero(a) *m,f*; *Br* **g.'s (shop)** tienda *f* de comestibles *or* de ultramarinos, *Andes, CSur* bodega *f*, *CAm, Méx* (tienda *f* de) abarrotes *mpl*

groceries ['grəʊsərɪz] *npl* comestibles *mpl*

grocery ['grəʊsərɪ] *n esp US* **g. (store)** tienda *f* de comestibles *or* de ultramarinos, *Andes, CSur* bodega *f*, *CAm, Méx* (tienda *f* de) abarrotes *mpl*

groggy ['grɒgɪ] *adj* (**groggier, groggiest**) *Fam* (*boxer*) grogui; *Fig* (*unsteady*) atontado(a); (*weak*) débil

groin [grɔɪn] *n* ingle *f*

groom [gruːm] **1** *n* (**a**) (*of horse*) mozo *m* de cuadra (**b**) (*bridegroom*) novio *m*
2 *vt* (*horse*) almohazar; (*clothes, appearance*) cuidar

groove [gruːv] *n* (*furrow etc*) ranura *f*; (*of record*) surco *m*

grope [grəʊp] *vi* (**a**) (*search about*) andar a tientas; **to g. for sth** buscar algo a tientas (**b**) *Fam* (*fondle*) meter mano

gross [grəʊs] **1** *adj* (**a**) (*fat*) muy gordo(a) (**b**) (*vulgar*) (*joke, person*) basto(a), grosero(a) (**c**) (*blatant*) (*indecency, incompetence*) tremendo(a); (*error, ignorance*) craso(a) (**d**) (*profit, income*) bruto(a); *Econ* **g. national product** producto nacional bruto
2 *vt* (*earn*) ganar en bruto

grossly ['grəʊslɪ] *adv* enormemente

grotesque [grəʊ'tesk] *adj* grotesco(a)

grotto ['grɒtəʊ] *n* gruta *f*

ground¹ [graʊnd] **1** *n* (**a**) (*earth*) suelo *m*, tierra *f*; **at g. level** al nivel del suelo; *Br* **g. floor** planta baja (**b**) (*land*) terreno *m* (**c**) *US Elec* toma *f* de tierra (**d**) **grounds** (*gardens*) jardines *mpl* (**e**) **grounds** (*reason*) motivo *m* (**f**) **grounds** (*sediment*) poso *m*
2 *vt* (**a**) *Av* obligar a quedarse en tierra; *Naut* varar (**b**) *US Elec* conectar con tierra

ground² [graʊnd] **1** *adj* (*coffee*) molido(a); *US* (*meat*) *Esp, RP* picado(a); *Am* molido(a)
2 *pt & pp of* **grind**

grounding ['graʊndɪŋ] *n* base *f*; **to have a good g. in** tener buenos conocimientos de

groundless ['graʊndlɪs] *adj* infundado(a)

groundsheet ['graʊndʃiːt] *n Br* (*of tent*) suelo *m*

groundsman ['graʊndzmən] *n Br* encargado(a) *m,f* del mantenimiento del campo de juego

groundwork ['graʊndwɜːk] *n* trabajo preparatorio

group [gruːp] **1** *n* grupo *m*, conjunto *m*
2 *vt* agrupar, juntar (**into** en)
3 *vi* **to g. (together)** agruparse, juntarse

grouse¹ [graʊs] *n* (*bird*) urogallo *m*

grouse² [graʊs] *Fam* **1** *vi* quejarse (**about** de)
2 *n* queja *f*

grove [grəʊv] *n* arboleda *f*

grovel ['grɒvəl] *vi* (*pt & pp* **grovelled**, *US* **groveled**) humillarse (**to** ante); (*crawl*) arrastrarse (**to** ante)

grow [grəʊ] **1** *vt* (*pt* **grew**; *pp* **grown**) (*cultivate*) cultivar; **to g. a beard** dejarse (crecer) la barba

  2 *vi* (**a**) (*increase in size*) crecer (**b**) (*become*) hacerse, volverse; **to g. accustomed to** acostumbrarse a; **to g. dark** oscurecer; **to g. old** envejecer

▸ **grow out of** *vt insep* (**a**) **he's grown out of his shirt** se le ha quedado pequeña la camisa (**b**) *Fig* (*phase etc*) superar

▸ **grow up** *vi* crecer, hacerse mayor

grower ['grəʊə(r)] *n* cultivador(a) *m,f*

growing ['grəʊɪŋ] *adj* (*child*) que crece; (*problem etc*) creciente; **he's a g. boy** está dando el estirón

growl [graʊl] **1** *vi* gruñir
  2 *n* gruñido *m*

grown [grəʊn] **1** *adj* crecido(a), adulto(a)
  2 *pp of* **grow**

grown-up ['grəʊnʌp] *adj & n* adulto(a) (*m,f*); **the grown-ups** los mayores

growth [grəʊθ] *n* (**a**) (*increase in size*) crecimiento *m*; (*development*) desarrollo *m* (**b**) (*lump*) bulto *m*

grub [grʌb] *n* (**a**) (*larva*) gusano *m* (**b**) *Fam* (*food*) papeo *m*

grubby ['grʌbɪ] *adj* (**grubbier**, **grubbiest**) sucio(a)

grudge [grʌdʒ] **1** *n* rencor *m*; **to bear sb a g.** guardar rencor a algn
  2 *vt* (*give unwillingly*) dar a regañadientes; **he grudges me my success** me envidia el éxito

grudgingly ['grʌdʒɪŋlɪ] *adv* a regañadientes

gruelling, *US* **grueling** ['gruːəlɪŋ] *adj* penoso(a)

gruesome ['gruːsəm] *adj* espantoso(a), horrible

gruff [grʌf] *adj* (*manner*) brusco(a); (*voice*) áspero(a)

grumble ['grʌmbəl] **1** *vi* refunfuñar
  2 *n* queja *f*

grumpy ['grʌmpɪ] *adj* (**grumpier**, **grumpiest**) gruñón(ona)

grunt [grʌnt] **1** *vi* gruñir
  2 *n* gruñido *m*

guarantee [gærən'tiː] **1** *n* garantía *f*; (*certificate*) certificado *m* de garantía
  2 *vt* garantizar; (*assure*) asegurar

guard [gɑːd] **1** *vt* (**a**) (*protect*) defender, proteger; (*keep watch over*) vigilar (**b**) (*control*) guardar
  2 *vi* protegerse (**against** de *or* contra)
  3 *n* (**a**) **to be on one's g.** estar en guardia; **to catch sb off his g.** pillar *or Esp* coger *or Am* agarrar desprevenido a algn (**b**) (*sentry*) guardia *mf*; **g. dog** perro *m* guardián (**c**) *Br Rail* jefe *m* de tren; **g.'s**

van furgón *m* de cola (**d**) (*on machine*) dispositivo *m* de seguridad; **fire g.** pantalla *f*

guarded ['gɑːdɪd] *adj* cauteloso(a), precavido(a)

guardhouse ['gɑːdhaʊs] *n Mil* (**a**) (*headquarters*) cuerpo *m* de guardia (**b**) (*prison*) prisión *f* militar

guardian ['gɑːdɪən] *n* (**a**) (*of standards*) guardián(ana) *m,f*; **g. angel** ángel *m* de la guarda (**b**) *Jur* (*of minor*) tutor(a) *m,f*

Guatemala [gwaːtə'maːlə] *n* Guatemala

Guatemalan [gwaːtə'maːlən] *adj & n* guatemalteco(a) (*m,f*)

guava ['gwaːvə] *n Bot* guayaba *f*; **g. tree** guayabo *m*

guer(r)illa [gə'rɪlə] *n* guerrillero(a) *m,f*; **g. warfare** guerra *f* de guerrillas

guess [ges] **1** *vt & vi* (**a**) (*estimate*) adivinar; **I guessed as much** me lo imaginaba; **to g. right/wrong** acertar/no acertar (**b**) (*suppose*) suponer; **I g. so** supongo que sí
  2 *n* conjetura *f*; (*estimate*) cálculo *m*; **at a rough g.** a ojo de buen cubero; **to have** *or* **make a g.** intentar adivinar

guesswork ['geswɜːk] *n* conjetura *f*

guest [gest] *n* (*at home*) invitado(a) *m,f*; (*in hotel*) cliente(a) *m,f*, huésped(a) *m,f*; **g. artist** artista *mf* invitado(a); **g. room** cuarto *m* de los invitados

guesthouse ['gesthaʊs] *n* casa *f* de huéspedes

guffaw [gʌ'fɔː] *vi* reírse a carcajadas

guidance ['gaɪdəns] *n* orientación *f*, consejos *mpl*; **for your g.** a título de información

guide [gaɪd] **1** *vt* guiar, dirigir
  2 *n* (**a**) (*person*) guía *mf*; *Br* **girl g.** exploradora *f*; **g. dog** perro lazarillo (**b**) (*guidebook*) guía *f*

guidebook ['gaɪdbʊk] *n* guía *f*

guided ['gaɪdɪd] *adj* dirigido(a); **g. tour** visita con guía; **g. missile** misil teledirigido

guideline ['gaɪdlaɪn] *n* pauta *f*

guild [gɪld] *n* gremio *m*

guile [gaɪl] *n* astucia *f*

guillotine ['gɪlətiːn] *n* guillotina *f*

guilt [gɪlt] *n* (**a**) (*blame*) culpa *f* (**b**) (*emotion*) culpabilidad *f*

guilty ['gɪltɪ] *adj* (**guiltier**, **guiltiest**) culpable (**of** de); **to have a g. conscience** remorderle a uno la conciencia

guinea¹ ['gɪnɪ] *n* **g. pig** conejillo *m* de Indias, cobayo *m*; *Fig* **to act as a g. pig** servir de conejillo de Indias

guinea² ['gɪnɪ] n Br (coin) guinea f (= 21 chelines)

guise [gaɪz] n under the g. of so pretexto de

guitar [gɪ'tɑː(r)] n guitarra f

guitarist [gɪ'tɑːrɪst] n guitarrista mf

gulf [gʌlf] n (a) (bay) golfo m; G. of Mexico Golfo de Méjico; G. Stream corriente f del Golfo de Méjico; the G. War la guerra del Golfo (b) Fig abismo m

gull [gʌl] n gaviota f

gulley ['gʌlɪ] n = gully

gullible ['gʌləbəl] adj crédulo(a)

gully ['gʌlɪ] n barranco m, hondonada f

gulp [gʌlp] 1 n trago m
2 vt tragar; to g. sth down (drink) tomarse algo de un trago; (food) engullir algo
3 vi (a) (swallow air) tragar aire (b) Fig (with fear) tragar saliva

gum¹ [gʌm] 1 n (a) (adhesive) goma f (b) Br (sweet) chicle m
2 vt pegar con goma

gum² [gʌm] n Anat encía f

gumboot ['gʌmbuːt] n bota f de agua or goma or Méx, Ven caucho

gun [gʌn] n arma f de fuego; (handgun) pistola f, revólver m; (rifle) fusil m, escopeta f; (cannon) cañón m; Fam the big guns los peces gordos
► gun down vt sep matar a tiros

gunboat ['gʌnbəʊt] n cañonero m

gunfire ['gʌnfaɪə(r)] n tiros mpl

gunman ['gʌnmən] n pistolero m, gángster m

gunpoint ['gʌnpoɪnt] n at g. a punta de pistola

gunpowder ['gʌnpaʊdə(r)] n pólvora f

gunrunner ['gʌnrʌnə(r)] n traficante mf de armas

gunshot ['gʌnʃɒt] n disparo m, tiro m

gunsmith ['gʌnsmɪθ] n armero m

gurgle ['gɜːgəl] vi (baby) gorjear; (liquid) gorgotear; (stream) murmurar

guru ['gʊruː, 'guːruː] n gurú m

gush [gʌʃ] 1 vi (a) (spurt, pour) manar, correr (b) Fig to g. about sth hablar con excesiva entusiasmo de algo
2 n (of water) chorro m; (of words) torrente m

gushing ['gʌʃɪŋ] adj Fig (person) efusivo(a)

gusset ['gʌsɪt] n escudete m

gust [gʌst] n (of wind) ráfaga f, racha f

gusto ['gʌstəʊ] n entusiasmo m

gut [gʌt] 1 n (a) Anat intestino m (b) guts (entrails) tripas fpl; Fam to have guts tener agallas
2 vt (a) (fish) destripar (b) (destroy) destruir por dentro
3 adj Fam g. reaction reacción f visceral

gutter ['gʌtə(r)] n (in street) arroyo m; (on roof) canalón m; Fig g. press prensa amarilla

guttural ['gʌtərəl] adj gutural

guy¹ [gaɪ] n Fam (man) tipo m, Esp tío m

guy² [gaɪ] n (rope) viento m, cuerda f

guzzle ['gʌzəl] vt & vi Fam (food etc) zamparse; (car) tragar mucho

gym [dʒɪm] n Fam (a) (gymnasium) gimnasio m (b) (gymnastics) gimnasia f; g. shoes zapatillas fpl de deporte

gymnasium [dʒɪm'neɪzɪəm] n gimnasio m

gymnast ['dʒɪmnæst] n gimnasta mf

gymnastics [dʒɪm'næstɪks] n sing gimnasia f

gynaecologist, US **gynecologist** [gaɪnɪ'kɒlədʒɪst] n ginecólogo(a) m,f

gypsy ['dʒɪpsɪ] adj & n gitano(a) (m,f)

gyrate [dʒaɪ'reɪt] vi girar

H, h [eɪtʃ] *n (the letter)* H, h *f*

haberdashery [hæbə'dæʃərɪ] *n* (**a**) *Br (sewing items, shop)* mercería *f* (**b**) *US (men's clothes)* ropa *f* de caballero; *(shop)* tienda *f* de confección de caballero

habit ['hæbɪt] *n* (**a**) *(custom)* hábito *m*, costumbre *f* (**b**) *(garment)* hábito *m*

habitable ['hæbɪtəbəl] *adj* habitable

habitat ['hæbɪtæt] *n* hábitat *m*

habitual [hə'bɪtjʊəl] *adj* habitual; *(drinker, liar)* empedernido(a)

habitually [hə'bɪtjʊəlɪ] *adv* por costumbre

hack¹ [hæk] **1** *n (cut)* corte *m*; *(with axe)* hachazo *m*
  2 *vt (with knife, axe)* cortar; *(kick)* dar un puntapié a

hack² [hæk] *n Fam (writer)* escritorzuelo(a) *m,f*; *(journalist)* gacetillero(a) *m,f*

hacker ['hækə(r)] *n Comput* pirata *mf* informático(a), hacker *mf*

hackneyed ['hæknɪd] *adj* trillado(a)

hacksaw ['hæksɔː] *n* sierra *f* para metales

had [hæd] *pt & pp of* **have**

haddock ['hædək] *n* abadejo *m*

haemophilia [hiːməʊ'fɪlɪə] *n* hemofilia *f*

haemophiliac [hiːməʊ'fɪlɪæk] *adj & n* hemofílico(a) *(m,f)*

haemorrhage ['hemərɪdʒ] *n* hemorragia *f*

haemorrhoids ['hemərɔɪdz] *npl* hemorroides *fpl*

hag [hæg] *n Pej* bruja *f*, arpía *f*

haggard ['hægəd] *adj* ojeroso(a)

haggle ['hægəl] *vi* regatear

Hague [heɪg] *n* The H. La Haya

hail¹ [heɪl] **1** *n* granizo *m*; *Fig* a h. of bullets/insults una lluvia de balas/insultos
  2 *vi* granizar

hail² [heɪl] **1** *vt* (**a**) *(taxi etc)* parar (**b**) *(acclaim)* aclamar
  2 *vi* to h. from *(originate)* ser nativo(a) de

hailstone ['heɪlstəʊn] *n* granizo *m*

hailstorm ['heɪlstɔːm] *n* granizada *f*

hair [heə(r)] *n (strand)* pelo *m*, cabello *m*; *(mass)* pelo, cabellos *mpl*; *(on arm, leg)* vello *m*; to have long h. tener el pelo largo

hairbrush ['heəbrʌʃ] *n* cepillo *m* (para el pelo)

haircut ['heəkʌt] *n* corte *m* de pelo; to have a h. cortarse el pelo

hairdo ['heəduː] *n Fam* peinado *m*

hairdresser ['heədresə(r)] *n* peluquero(a) *m,f*; h.'s (shop) peluquería *f*

hairdryer, hairdrier ['heədraɪə(r)] *n* secador *m* (de pelo)

hairgrip ['heəgrɪp] *n Br* horquilla *f*

hairline ['heəlaɪn] **1** *adj* muy fino(a)
  2 *n* nacimiento *m* del pelo; receding h. entradas *fpl*

hairnet ['heənet] *n* redecilla *f*

hairpiece ['heəpiːs] *n* postizo *m*

hairpin ['heəpɪn] *n* horquilla *f*; h. bend curva muy cerrada

hair-raising ['heəreɪzɪŋ] *adj* espeluznante

hair-remover ['heərɪmuːvə(r)] *n* depilatorio *m*

hairspray ['heəspreɪ] *n* laca *f* (para el pelo)

hairstyle ['heəstaɪl] *n* peinado *m*, corte *m* de pelo

hairy ['heərɪ] *adj* (**hairier, hairiest**) (**a**) *(with hair)* peludo(a) (**b**) *Fig (frightening)* enervante, espantoso(a)

hake [heɪk] *n* merluza *f*; *(young)* pescadilla *f*

half [hɑːf] **1** *n (pl* **halves**) mitad *f*; *Sport (period)* tiempo *m*; he's four and a h. tiene cuatro años y medio; to cut in h. cortar por la mitad
  2 *adj* medio(a); h. a dozen/an hour media docena/hora; h. board media pensión; h. fare media tarifa; h. term medio trimestre
  3 *adv* medio, a medias; h. asleep medio dormido(a)

half-caste ['hɑːfkɑːst] *adj & n* mestizo(a) *(m,f)*

half-day [hɑːf'deɪ] *n* media jornada

half-hearted [hɑːf'hɑːtɪd] *adj* poco entusiasta

half-hour [hɑːf'aʊə(r)] *n* media hora

half-life ['hɑːflaɪf] *n* media vida

half-mast [hɑːfˈmɑːst] n Br **at h.** a media asta

half-price [hɑːfˈprais] adv a mitad de precio

half-time [hɑːfˈtaim] n descanso m

half-way [ˈhɑːfwei] **1** adj intermedio(a)
2 halfway [hɑːfˈwei] adv a medio camino, a mitad de camino

half-yearly [ˈhɑːfjiəli] adj semestral

halibut [ˈhælibət] n mero m

hall [hɔːl] n (a) (lobby) vestíbulo m (b) (building) sala f; Br Univ **h. of residence** residencia f de estudiantes, Esp colegio m mayor

hallmark [ˈhɔːlmɑːk] n (a) (on gold, silver) contraste m (b) Fig sello m

hallo [həˈləʊ] interj ¡hola!

hallowed [ˈhæləʊd] adj santificado(a)

Hallowe(')en [hæləʊˈiːn] n víspera f de Todos los Santos

hallucinate [həˈluːsineit] vi alucinar

hallucination [həluːsiˈneiʃən] n alucinación f

hallucinogenic [həluːsinəʊˈdʒenik] adj alucinógeno(a)

hallway [ˈhɔːlwei] n vestíbulo m

halo [ˈheiləʊ] n (a) Rel aureola f (b) Astron halo m

halt [hɔːlt] **1** n (stop) alto m, parada f; **to call a h. to sth** poner fin a algo
2 vt parar
3 vi pararse

halting [ˈhɔːltiŋ] adj vacilante

halve [hɑːv] vt (a) (divide in two) dividir (en dos); (cake, fruit) partir por la mitad (b) (reduce by half) reducir a la mitad

halves [hɑːvz] pl of **half**

ham [hæm] n jamón m; **boiled h.** jamón de York; **Parma** or **cured h.** jamón serrano

hamburger [ˈhæmbɜːgə(r)] n hamburguesa f

hamlet [ˈhæmlit] n aldea f

hammer [ˈhæmə(r)] **1** n (a) (tool) & Sport martillo m; (b) (of gun) percutor m
2 vt (a) (hit with hammer) martillear; Fig **to h. home** insistir sobre (b) Fam (defeat) dar una paliza a
3 vi martillar, dar golpes

hammering [ˈhæməriŋ] n Fam paliza f

hammock [ˈhæmək] n hamaca f; Naut coy m

hamper[1] [ˈhæmpə(r)] n cesta f

hamper[2] [ˈhæmpə(r)] vt estorbar, dificultar

hamster [ˈhæmstə(r)] n hámster m

hamstring [ˈhæmstriŋ] n tendón m de la corva

hand [hænd] **1** n (a) (part of body) mano f; **by h.** a mano; **(close) at h.** a mano; **hands up!** ¡manos arriba!; **on the one/other h.** por una/otra parte; Fig **to get out of h.** descontrolarse; Fig **to wash one's hands of sth** lavarse las manos de algo; Fig **to give sb a h.** echarle una mano a algn; **h. grenade** granada f de mano (b) (worker) trabajador(a) m,f; Naut tripulante m (c) (of clock) manecilla f (d) (handwriting) letra f
2 vt (give) dar, entregar

▶ **hand back** vt sep devolver

▶ **hand down** vt sep dejar en herencia

▶ **hand in** vt sep (homework) entregar; (resignation) presentar

▶ **hand out** vt sep repartir

▶ **hand over** vt sep entregar

▶ **hand round** vt sep repartir

handbag [ˈhændbæg] n Br (woman's) Esp bolso m, Col, CSur cartera f, Méx bolsa f

handball [ˈhændbɔːl] n Sport balonmano m

handbook [ˈhændbʊk] n manual m

handbrake [ˈhændbreik] n freno m de mano

handcuff [ˈhændkʌf] **1** vt esposar
2 npl **handcuffs** esposas fpl

handful [ˈhændfʊl] n puñado m

handicap [ˈhændikæp] **1** n (a) Med minusvalía f (b) Sport hándicap m, desventaja f
2 vt impedir

handicapped [ˈhændikæpt] adj (a) (physically) minusválido(a); (mentally) retrasado(a) (b) Sport en desventaja (c) Fig desfavorecido(a)

handicraft [ˈhændikrɑːft] n artesanía f

handiwork [ˈhændiwɜːk] n (work) obra f; (craft) artesanía f

handkerchief [ˈhæŋkətʃiːf] n pañuelo m

handle [ˈhændəl] **1** n (of knife) mango m; (of cup) asa f; (of door) pomo m; (of drawer) tirador m
2 vt (a) (touch, hold) manejar; **h. with care** (sign) frágil (b) (problem) encargarse de; (people) tratar; Fam (put up with) soportar

handlebars [ˈhændəlbɑːz] n (of bicycle, motorbike) manillar m, Am manubrio m

handmade [hændˈmeid] adj hecho(a) a mano

hand-out [ˈhændaʊt] n (a) (leaflet) folleto m; Press nota f de prensa (b) (charity) limosna f

hand-picked [hændˈpikt] adj selecto(a)

handrail [ˈhændreil] n pasamanos m inv, baranda f, Esp barandilla f

hands-free ['hænzfriː] *adj (telephone)* de manos libres

handshake ['hændʃeɪk] *n* apretón *m* de manos

handsome ['hænsəm] *adj* (**a**) *(person)* guapo(a) (**b**) *(substantial)* considerable

handwriting ['hændraɪtɪŋ] *n* letra *f*

handwritten ['hændrɪtən] *adj* manuscrito(a), escrito(a) a mano

handy ['hændɪ] *adj* (**handier, handiest**) (**a**) *(useful)* útil, práctico(a); *(nearby)* a mano (**b**) *(dextrous)* diestro(a)

handyman ['hændɪmæn] *n (person good at odd jobs)* persona *f* habilidosa, *Esp* manitas *mf inv*

hang [hæŋ] **1** *vt (pt & pp* **hung**) (**a**) *(suspend)* colgar (**b**) *(head)* bajar (**c**) *(pt* **hanged**) ahorcar
2 *vi* (**a**) *(be suspended)* colgar (**from** de); *(in air)* flotar (**b**) *(criminal)* ser ahorcado(a); **to h. oneself** ahorcarse
▸ **hang about, hang around** *vi Fam (wait)* esperar
▸ **hang on** *vi* (**a**) *(hold)* agarrarse (**b**) *(wait)* esperar
▸ **hang out 1** *vt sep (washing)* tender
2 *vi Fam (frequent)* frecuentar
▸ **hang round** *vi Fam* = **hang about**
▸ **hang together** *vi (ideas)* ser coherente
▸ **hang up** *vt sep (picture, telephone)* colgar

hangar ['hæŋə(r)] *n* hangar *m*

hanger ['hæŋə(r)] *n* percha *f*

hang-glider ['hæŋɡlaɪdə(r)] *n* ala delta

hang-gliding ['hæŋɡlaɪdɪŋ] *n* vuelo *m* libre

hangman ['hæŋmən] *n* verdugo *m*

hangover ['hæŋəʊvə(r)] *n* resaca *f*

hang-up ['hæŋʌp] *n Fam (complex)* complejo *m*

hanker ['hæŋkə(r)] *vi* **to h. after sth** anhelar algo

hankie, hanky ['hæŋkɪ] *n Fam* pañuelo *m*

haphazard [hæp'hæzəd] *adj* caótico(a), desordenado(a)

happen ['hæpən] *vi* suceder, ocurrir; **it so happens that** lo que pasa es que; **if you h. to see my friend** si por casualidad ves a mi amigo

happening ['hæpənɪŋ] *n* acontecimiento *m*

happily ['hæpɪlɪ] *adv (with pleasure)* felizmente; *(fortunately)* afortunadamente

happiness ['hæpɪnɪs] *n* felicidad *f*

happy ['hæpɪ] *adj* (**happier, happiest**) *(cheerful)* feliz, contento(a); *(fortunate)* afortunado(a); **h. birthday!** ¡feliz cumpleaños!

happy-go-lucky [hæpɪɡəʊ'lʌkɪ] *adj* despreocupado(a); **a h. fellow** un viva la virgen

harangue [hə'ræŋ] **1** *vt* arengar
2 *n* arenga *f*

harass ['hærəs] *vt* acosar

harassment ['hærəsmənt, hə'ræsmənt] *n* hostigamiento *m*, acoso *m*

harbour, *US* **harbor** ['hɑːbə(r)] **1** *n* puerto *m*
2 *vt* (**a**) *(criminal)* encubrir (**b**) *(doubts)* abrigar

hard [hɑːd] **1** *adj* (**a**) *(substance)* duro(a); *Comput* **h. disk** disco duro; *Br Aut* **h. shoulder** *Esp* arcén *m*, *Andes* berma *f*, *Méx* acotamiento *m*, *RP* banquina *f* (**b**) *(difficult)* difícil; **h. of hearing** duro(a) de oído; *Fam Fig* **to be h. up** estar sin blanca (**c**) *(harsh)* severo(a); *(strict)* estricto(a); **h. drugs** drogas duras; *Pol* **h. left** extrema izquierda; **h. sell** promoción *f* de venta agresiva (**d**) **a h. worker** un trabajador concienzudo (**e**) **h. luck!** ¡mala suerte! (**f**) **h. evidence** pruebas definitivas; **h. currency** divisa *f* fuerte
2 *adv* (**a**) *(hit)* fuerte (**b**) *(work)* mucho, concienzudamente

hardback ['hɑːdbæk] *n* edición *f* de tapas duras

hardball ['hɑːdbɔːl] *n US (baseball)* béisbol *m*

hard-boiled ['hɑːdbɔɪld] *adj* duro(a)

hard-core ['hɑːdkɔː(r)] *adj* irreductible

harden ['hɑːdən] **1** *vt* endurecer
2 *vi* endurecerse

hardened ['hɑːdənd] *adj Fig* habitual

hard-headed [hɑːd'hedɪd] *adj* realista

hard-hearted [hɑːd'hɑːtɪd] *adj* insensible

hardliner [hɑːd'laɪnə(r)] *n* duro(a) *m,f*

hardly ['hɑːdlɪ] *adv* apenas; **h. anyone/ ever** casi nadie/nunca; **he had h. begun when …** apenas había comenzado cuando …; **I can h. believe it** apenas lo puedo creer

hardship ['hɑːdʃɪp] *n* privación *f*, apuro *m*

hardware ['hɑːdweə(r)] *n* (**a**) *(goods)* ferretería *f*; *US* **h. store** *(ironmonger's)* ferretería (**b**) *Comput* hardware *m*

hardwearing [hɑːd'weərɪŋ] *adj* duradero(a)

hardworking ['hɑːdwɜːkɪŋ] *adj* muy trabajador(a)

hardy ['hɑːdɪ] *adj* (**hardier, hardiest**) *(person)* robusto(a), fuerte; *(plant)* resistente

hare [heə(r)] **1** *n* liebre *f*
2 *vi* correr muy de prisa

haricot [ˈhærɪkəʊ] n **h. (bean)** alubia f blanca, Esp judía f blanca, Am salvo RP frijol m blanco, Andes, RP poroto m blanco

harm [haːm] **1** n daño m, perjuicio m; **to be out of h.'s way** estar a salvo
2 vt hacer daño a, perjudicar

harmful [ˈhaːmfʊl] adj perjudicial (**to** para)

harmless [ˈhaːmlɪs] adj inofensivo(a)

harmonica [haːˈmɒnɪkə] n armónica f

harmonious [haːˈməʊnɪəs] adj armonioso(a)

harmonize [ˈhaːmənaɪz] vt & vi armonizar

harmony [ˈhaːmənɪ] n armonía f

harness [ˈhaːnɪs] **1** n (for horse) arreos mpl
2 vt (**a**) (horse) enjaezar (**b**) Fig (resources etc) aprovechar

harp [haːp] n arpa f
▸ **harp on** vi Fam hablar sin parar

harpoon [haːˈpuːn] **1** n arpón m
2 vt arponear

harrowing [ˈhærəʊɪŋ] adj angustioso(a)

harsh [haːʃ] adj severo(a); (voice) áspero(a); (sound) discordante

harvest [ˈhaːvɪst] **1** n cosecha f; (of grapes) vendimia f
2 vt cosechar, recoger

harvester [ˈhaːvɪstə(r)] n (**a**) (person) segador(a) m,f (**b**) (machine) cosechadora f

has [hæz] 3rd person sing pres of **have**

has-been [ˈhæzbiːn] n Fam Pej vieja gloria f

hash[1] [hæʃ] n Culin guiso m de carne con Esp patatas or Am papas, Andes, Méx ahogado m de carne con papas; Fam Fig **to make a h. of sth** hacer algo muy mal; **h. browns** = fritura de Esp patata or Am papa y cebolla

hash[2] [hæʃ] n Fam chocolate m, Esp costo m

hashish [ˈhæʃiːʃ] n hachís m

hassle [ˈhæsəl] Fam **1** n (**a**) (trouble, inconvenience) lío m, Esp follón m; **to give sb h.** dar la lata a algn (**b**) (wrangle) trifulca f
2 vt fastidiar

haste [heɪst] n Fml prisa f; **to make h.** darse prisa

hasten [ˈheɪsən] vi apresurarse

hastily [ˈheɪstɪlɪ] adv (quickly) de prisa

hasty [ˈheɪstɪ] adj (hastier, hastiest) apresurado(a); (rash) precipitado(a)

hat [hæt] n sombrero m

hatch[1] [hætʃ] n escotilla f; **serving h.** ventanilla f

hatch[2] [hætʃ] **1** vt (**a**) (eggs) empollar (**b**) Fig (plan) tramar
2 vi **to h. (out)** salirse del huevo

hatchback [ˈhætʃbæk] n coche m de 3/5 puertas

hatchet [ˈhætʃɪt] n hacha f; Fam **h. man** matón m

hate [heɪt] **1** n odio m
2 vt odiar

hateful [ˈheɪtfʊl] adj odioso(a)

hatred [ˈheɪtrɪd] n odio m

haughty [ˈhɔːtɪ] adj (haughtier, haughtiest) altanero(a), arrogante

haul [hɔːl] **1** n (**a**) (journey) trayecto m (**b**) (of fish) redada f (**c**) (loot) botín m
2 vt (**a**) (pull) arrastrar (**b**) (transport) acarrear
▸ **haul up** vt sep Fam (to court) llevar

haulage [ˈhɔːlɪdʒ] n transporte m

haulier [ˈhɔːljə(r)], US **hauler** [ˈhɔːlə(r)] n (company) empresa f de transportes, transportista mf

haunch [hɔːntʃ] n (of person) cadera f; **to sit or squat on one's haunches** ponerse en cuclillas

haunt [hɔːnt] **1** n guarida f
2 vt (**a**) (of ghost) aparecerse en (**b**) Fig atormentar (**c**) (frequent) frecuentar

haunted [ˈhɔːntɪd] adj encantado(a), embrujado(a)

Havana [həˈvænə] n La Habana; **H. cigar** habano m

have [hæv] (3rd person sing pres **has**; pt & pp **had**)

En el inglés hablado, y en el escrito en estilo coloquial, el verbo auxiliar **have** se contrae de forma que **I have** se transforma en **I've**, **he/she/it has** se transforman en **he's/she's/it's** y **you/we/they have** se transforman en **you've/we've/they've**. Las formas de pasado **I/you/he** etc **had** se transforman en **I'd, you'd, he'd** etc. Las formas negativas **has not** y **had not** se transforman en **hasn't, haven't** y **hadn't**.

1 vt (**a**) (possess) tener; **h. you got** or **do you h. a car?** ¿tienes coche?
(**b**) (get, experience, suffer) tener; **to h. a holiday** tomarse unas vacaciones
(**c**) (partake of) (drink) tomar; **to h. breakfast/dinner/lunch/tea** desayunar/cenar/comer/merendar; **to h. a bath/shave** bañarse/afeitarse
(**d**) **to h. (got) to** (obligation) tener que, deber
(**e**) (make happen) hacer que; **I'll h. someone come round** haré que venga alguien

(**f**) *(receive)* recibir; **to h. people round** invitar a gente

(**g**) *(party, meeting)* hacer, celebrar

(**h**) **to h. a baby** tener un niño

(**i**) **we won't h. it** *(allow)* no lo consentiremos

(**j**) *(hold)* tener; *Fig* **to h. sth against sb** tener algo en contra de algn

(**k**) *Fam (deceive)* engañar

(**l**) **you'd better stay** más vale que te quedes

2 *v aux* (**a**) *(compound)* haber; **I had been waiting for half an hour** hacía media hora que esperaba; **he hasn't eaten yet** no ha comido aún; **she had broken the window** había roto el cristal; **we h. lived here for ten years** hace diez años que vivimos aquí; **so I h.!** *(emphatic)* ¡ay, sí!, es verdad; **yes I h.!** ¡que sí! (**b**) *(tag questions)* **you haven't seen my book, h. you?** no has visto mi libro, ¿verdad?; **he's been to France, hasn't he?** ha estado en Francia, ¿verdad? *or* ¿no? (**c**) *(have + just)* **to h. just done sth** acabar de hacer algo

▸ **have on** *vt sep* (**a**) *(wear)* vestir (**b**) *Fam* **to h. sb on** tomarle el pelo *or Esp, Carib, Méx* vacilar a algn

▸ **have out** *vt sep Fam* **to h. it out with sb** ajustar cuentas con algn

▸ **have over** *vt sep (invite)* recibir

haven ['heɪvən] *n* puerto *m*; *Fig* refugio *m*

haversack ['hævəsæk] *n* mochila *f*

havoc ['hævək] *n* **to play h. with** hacer estragos en

hawk [hɔːk] *n (bird) & Pol* halcón *m*

hawker ['hɔːkə(r)] *n* vendedor(a) *m,f* ambulante

hawthorn ['hɔːθɔːn] *n* espino *m* albar

hay [heɪ] *n* heno *m*; **h. fever** fiebre *f* del heno

haystack ['heɪstæk] *n* almiar *m*

haywire ['heɪwaɪə(r)] *adj Fam* en desorden; **to go h.** *(machine etc)* estropearse; *(person)* volverse loco(a)

hazard ['hæzəd] **1** *n* peligro *m*, riesgo *m*; *(in golf)* obstáculo *m*
2 *vt Fml* arriesgar; **to h. a guess** intentar adivinar

hazardous ['hæzədəs] *adj* arriesgado(a), peligroso(a)

haze [heɪz] *n (mist)* neblina *f*; *Fig (blur)* confusión *f*

hazel ['heɪzəl] *adj (de color)* avellana

hazelnut ['heɪzəlnʌt] *n* avellana *f*

hazy ['heɪzɪ] *adj* (**hazier, haziest**) nebuloso(a)

he [hiː] *pers pron* él *(usually omitted in Spanish, except for contrast)*; HE **did it** ha sido él; **he who** el que

head [hed] **1** *n* (**a**) *(of person)* cabeza *f*; *(mind)* mente *f*; **£3 a h.** *(each)* 3 libras por cabeza; *Fig* **to lose one's h.** perder la cabeza; **success went to his h.** se le subió el éxito a cabeza (**b**) *(of nail)* cabeza *f*; *(of beer)* espuma *f* (**c**) *(boss)* cabeza *m*; *(of company)* director(a) *m,f*, *Br* **h. (teacher)** director(a) *m,f* (**d**) *(of coin)* cara *f*; **heads or tails** cara o cruz
2 *adj* principal; **h. office** oficina *f* central
3 *vt* (**a**) *(list etc)* encabezar (**b**) *Ftb* cabecear

▸ **head for** *vt insep* dirigirse hacia

▸ **head off 1** *vi* irse
2 *vt sep (avert)* evitar

headache ['hedeɪk] *n* dolor *m* de cabeza; *Fig* quebradero *m* de cabeza

headband ['hedbænd] *n* cinta *f* para la cabeza

headcheese ['hedtʃiːz] *n US* queso *m* de cerdo

header ['hedə(r)] *n Ftb* cabezazo *m*

head-first [hed'fɜːst] *adv* de cabeza

head-hunter ['hedhʌntə(r)] *n Fig* cazatalentos *mf inv*

heading ['hedɪŋ] *n* título *m*; *(of letter)* membrete *m*

headlamp ['hedlæmp] *n* faro *m*

headland ['hedlənd] *n* punta *f*, cabo *m*

headlight ['hedlaɪt] *n* faro *m*

headline ['hedlaɪn] *n* titular *m*; **the headlines** *(on radio, TV)* los titulares

headlong ['hedlɒŋ] *adj & adv* de cabeza; **to rush h. into sth** lanzarse a hacer algo sin pensar

headmaster [hed'mɑːstə(r)] *n* director *m*

headmistress [hed'mɪstrɪs] *n* directora *f*

head-on ['hedɒn] *adj* **a h. collision** un choque frontal

headphones ['hedfəʊnz] *npl* auriculares *mpl*

headquarters ['hedkwɔːtəz] *npl* (**a**) *(of organization)* central *f*, sede *f* (**b**) *Mil* cuartel *m* general

headrest ['hedrest] *n Aut* apoyacabezas *m inv*

headroom ['hedruːm] *n* altura *f* libre

headscarf ['hedskɑːf] *n* pañuelo *m*

headstrong ['hedstrɒŋ] *adj* testarudo(a)

headway ['hedweɪ] *n* **to make h.** avanzar, progresar

headwind ['hedwɪnd] *n* viento *m* de proa

heady ['hedɪ] *adj* (**headier, headiest**) embriagador(a)

heal [hiːl] **1** vt (wound) curar
2 vi cicatrizar

health [helθ] n salud f; Fig prosperidad f;
to be in good/bad h. estar bien/mal de
salud; **your good h.!** ¡salud!; **h. foods**
alimentos mpl naturales; **h. food shop**
tienda f de alimentos naturales; Br **the H.
Service** el sistema de sanidad pública
británico

healthy [ˈhelθɪ] adj (**healthier, healthi-
est**) sano(a); (good for health) saludable;
(thriving) próspero(a).

heap [hiːp] **1** n montón m
2 vt amontonar; Fig **to h. praise on sb**
colmar a algn de alabanzas; **a heaped
spoonful** una cucharada colmada

hear [hɪə(r)] **1** vt (pt & pp **heard** [hɜːd]) (**a**)
(perceive) oír (**b**) (listen to) escuchar (**c**)
(find out) enterarse (**d**) Jur ver; (evidence)
oír
2 vi **to h. from sb** tener noticias de algn

hearing [ˈhɪərɪŋ] n (**a**) (sense) oído m; **h.
aid** audífono m (**b**) Jur audiencia f

hearsay [ˈhɪəseɪ] n rumores mpl

hearse [hɜːs] n coche m fúnebre

heart [hɑːt] n (**a**) (organ, seat of emotions)
corazón m; **h. attack** infarto m de
miocardio; Med **h. failure** insuficiencia
cardíaca; **h. transplant** trasplante m de
corazón; **a broken h.** un corazón roto; **at
h.** en el fondo; **to take sth to h.** tomarse
algo a pecho; **to have a good h.** (be kind)
tener buen corazón (**b**) (courage,
enthusiasm) valor m; **his h. wasn't in it** no
ponía interés en ello; **to lose h.**
desanimarse (**c**) (core) meollo m; (of
lettuce) cogollo m

heartache [ˈhɑːteɪk] n dolor m, tristeza f

heartbeat [ˈhɑːtbiːt] n latido m del corazón

heart-breaking [ˈhɑːtbreɪkɪŋ] adj des-
garrador(a)

heart-broken [ˈhɑːtbrəʊkən] adj hun-
dido(a); **he's h.** tiene el corazón destrozado

heartburn [ˈhɑːtbɜːn] n acedía f

heartening [ˈhɑːtənɪŋ] adj alentador(a)

heartfelt [ˈhɑːtfelt] adj sincero(a)

hearth [hɑːθ] n (**a**) (fireplace) chimenea f
(**b**) Fml (home) hogar m

heartless [ˈhɑːtlɪs] adj cruel, insensible

heart-throb [ˈhɑːtθrɒb] n ídolo m

hearty [ˈhɑːtɪ] adj (**heartier, heartiest**)
(person) francote; (meal) abundante;
(welcome) cordial; **to have a h. appetite**
ser de buen comer

heat [hiːt] **1** n (**a**) (high temperature) calor
m (**b**) Sport eliminatoria f (**c**) Zool **in** or Br
on h. en celo
2 vt calentar

▸ **heat up** vi (**a**) (warm up) calentarse (**b**)
(increase excitement) acalorarse

heated [ˈhiːtɪd] adj Fig (argument)
acalorado(a)

heater [ˈhiːtə(r)] n calentador m

heath [hiːθ] n (land) brezal m

heathen [ˈhiːðən] adj & n pagano(a) (m,f)

heather [ˈheðə(r)] n brezo m

heating [ˈhiːtɪŋ] n calefacción f

heatwave [ˈhiːtweɪv] n ola f de calor

heave [hiːv] **1** n (pull) tirón m; (push)
empujón m
2 vt (**a**) (lift) levantar; (haul) tirar; (push)
empujar (**b**) (throw) arrojar
3 vi subir y bajar

heaven [ˈhevən] **1** n cielo m; **the heavens**
(sky) cielo m; **for h.'s sake!** ¡por Dios!; **h. on
earth** un paraíso en la tierra
2 interj (**good**) **heavens!** ¡por Dios!

heavenly [ˈhevənlɪ] adj celestial

heavily [ˈhevɪlɪ] adv **it rained h.** llovió
mucho; **to sleep h.** dormir profundamente

heavy [ˈhevɪ] **1** adj (**heavier, heaviest**)
pesado(a); (rain, meal) fuerte; (traffic)
denso(a); (loss) grande; **h. going** duro(a);
is it h.? ¿pesa mucho?; **a h. drinker/
smoker** un(a) bebedor(a)/fumador(a)
empedernido(a); Mus **h. metal** heavy
metal m
2 n Fam gorila m

heavyweight [ˈhevɪweɪt] n peso pesado

Hebrew [ˈhiːbruː] **1** adj hebreo(a)
2 n (person) hebreo(a) m,f; (language)
hebreo m

Hebrides [ˈhebrɪdiːz] npl **the H.** las (Islas)
Hébridas

heckle [ˈhekəl] vt interrumpir

heckler [ˈheklə(r)] n altercador(a) m,f

hectare [ˈhektɑː(r)] n hectárea f

hectic [ˈhektɪk] adj agitado(a)

hedge [hedʒ] **1** n seto m
2 vt cercar con un seto; Fig **to h. one's
bets** cubrirse

hedgehog [ˈhedʒhɒg] n erizo m

hedgerow [ˈhedʒrəʊ] n seto vivo

heed [hiːd] n **to take h. of** hacer caso de

heedless [ˈhiːdlɪs] adj desatento(a)

heel [hiːl] n (of foot) talón m; (of shoe)
tacón m; (of palm) pulpejo m; Fig **to be on
sb's heels** pisarle los talones a algn; **high
heels** zapatos mpl de tacón alto

hefty [ˈheftɪ] adj (**heftier, heftiest**) (**a**)
(person) fornido(a); (package) pesado(a)
(**b**) (large) grande

height [haɪt] n (of building, mountain,
tree) altura f; (of person) estatura f; Av **to
gain/lose h.** subir/bajar; **what h. are you?**

¿cuánto mides?; *Fig* **the h. of ignorance** el colmo de la ignorancia

heighten ['haɪtən] *vt (intensify)* realzar; *(increase)* aumentar

heir [eə(r)] *n* heredero *m*

heiress ['eərɪs] *n* heredera *f*

heirloom ['eəluːm] *n* reliquia *f*/joya *f* de familia

held [held] *pt & pp of* **hold**

helicopter ['helɪkɒptə(r)] *n* helicóptero *m*

helium ['hiːlɪəm] *n* helio *m*

hell [hel] *n* infierno *m; Fam* **what the h. are you doing?** ¿qué diablos estás haciendo?; *Fam Pej* **go to h.!** ¡vete a hacer puñetas!; *Fam* **a h. of a party** una fiesta estupenda; *Fam* **she's had a h. of a day** ha tenido un día fatal

hellish ['helɪʃ] *adj Fam* infernal

hello [hə'ləʊ, he'ləʊ] *interj* ¡hola!; *(on phone) (when answering)* ¿sí?, ¿diga?, *Am* ¿aló?, *Méx* ¿bueno?; *(showing surprise)* ¡hala!

helm [helm] *n* timón *m;* **to be at the h.** llevar el timón

helmet ['helmɪt] *n* casco *m*

help [help] **1** *n* (a) *(aid)* ayuda *f;* **h.!** ¡socorro! (b) *(person)* **(daily) h.** asistenta *f*
2 *vt* (a) *(aid)* ayudar; **can I h. you?** *(in shop)* ¿qué desea? (b) *(alleviate)* aliviar (c) **h. yourself!** *(to food etc)* ¡sírvete! (d) *(avoid)* evitar; **I can't h. it** no lo puedo remediar

▸ **help out** *vt sep* **to h. sb out** echarle una mano a algn

helper ['helpə(r)] *n* ayudante(a) *m,f*

helpful ['helpfʊl] *adj (person)* amable; *(thing)* útil

helping ['helpɪŋ] *n* ración *f;* **who wants a second h.?** ¿quién quiere repetir?

helpless ['helplɪs] *adj (defenceless)* desamparado(a); *(powerless)* incapaz

helplessly ['helplɪslɪ] *adv* inútilmente, en vano

helpline ['helplaɪn] *n* teléfono *m* de asistencia *or* ayuda

helter-skelter [heltə'skeltə(r)] **1** *n Br (at fairground)* tobogán *m*
2 *adj* atropellado(a)
3 *adv* atropelladamente

hem [hem] **1** *n Sewing* dobladillo *m*
2 *vt Sewing* hacer un dobladillo a

▸ **hem in** *vt sep* cercar, rodear

hemisphere ['hemɪsfɪə(r)] *n* hemisferio *m*

hemophilia [hiːməʊ'fɪlɪə] *n US* = **haemophilia**

hemophiliac [hiːməʊ'fɪlɪæk] *adj & n US* = **haemophiliac**

hemorrhage ['hemərɪdʒ] *n US* = **haemorrhage**

hemorrhoids ['hemərɔɪdz] *npl US* = **haemorrhoids**

hen [hen] *n* gallina *f; Fam* **h. party** reunión *f* de mujeres

hence [hens] *adv Fml* (a) **six months h.** *(from now)* de aquí a seis meses (b) *(consequently)* por lo tanto

henceforth [hens'fɔːθ] *adv Fml* de ahora en adelante

henchman ['hentʃmən] *n Pej* secuaz *m*

henna ['henə] *n Bot* alheña *f; (dye)* henna *f*

henpecked ['henpekt] *adj Fam* **a h. husband** un calzonazos

hepatitis [hepə'taɪtɪs] *n* hepatitis *f*

her [hɜː(r), *unstressed* hə(r)] **1** *poss adj (one thing)* su; *(more than one)* sus; *(to distinguish)* de ella; **are they h. books or his?** ¿los libros son de ella o de él?; **she has cut h. finger** se ha cortado el dedo
2 *pron* (a) *(direct object)* la; **I saw h. recently** la vi hace poco (b) *(indirect object)* le; *(with other third person pronouns)* se; **he gave h. money** le dio dinero; **they handed it to h.** se lo entregaron (c) *(after prep)* ella; **for h.** para ella (d) *(as subject) Fam* ella; **look, it's h.!** ¡mira, es ella!

herald ['herəld] **1** *n* heraldo *m*
2 *vt* anunciar

heraldry ['herəldrɪ] *n* heráldica *f*

herb [hɜːb, *US* ɜːrb] *n* hierba *f;* **h. tea** infusión *f*

herbal ['hɜːbəl] *adj* herbario(a); **h. remedies** curas *fpl* de hierbas

herd [hɜːd] *n (of cattle)* manada *f; (of goats)* rebaño *m; Fig (large group)* multitud *f*

here [hɪə(r)] *adv* aquí; **come h.** ven aquí; **h.!** ¡presente!; **h. goes!** ¡vamos a ver!; **h.'s to success!** ¡brindemos por el éxito!; **h. you are!** ¡toma!; **look h., you can't do that!** ¡oiga, que no se permite hacer eso!

hereafter [hɪər'ɑːftə(r)] *Fml* **1** *adv* de ahora en adelante
2 *n* **the h.** la otra vida, el más allá

hereby [hɪə'baɪ] *adv Fml* por la presente

hereditary [hɪ'redɪtərɪ] *adj* hereditario(a)

heresy ['herəsɪ] *n* herejía *f*

heretic ['herətɪk] *n* hereje *mf*

heritage ['herɪtɪdʒ] *n* patrimonio *m; Jur* herencia *f*

hermetically [hɜː'metɪklɪ] *adv* **h. sealed** herméticamente cerrado(a)

hermit ['hɜːmɪt] *n* ermitaño(a) *m,f*

𝒜 Note that the Spanish word **ermita** is a false friend and is never a translation for the English word **hermit**. In Spanish, **ermita** means "hermitage".

hermitage ['hɜːmɪtɪdʒ] *n* ermita *f*

hernia ['hɜːnɪə] *n* hernia *f*

hero ['hɪərəʊ] *n (pl* **heroes**) héroe *m; (in novel)* protagonista *m;* **h. worship** idolatría *f*

heroic [hɪ'rəʊɪk] *adj* heroico(a)

heroin ['herəʊɪn] *n* heroína *f*

heroine ['herəʊɪn] *n* heroína *f; (in novel)* protagonista *f*

heron ['herən] *n* garza *f*

herring ['herɪŋ] *n* arenque *m*

hers [hɜːz] *poss pron* (**a**) *(attribute) (one thing)* suyo(a); *(more than one)* suyos(as); *(to distinguish)* de ella; **they are h.,** not his son de ella, no de él (**b**) *(noun reference) (one thing)* el suyo/la suya; *(more than one)* los suyos/las suyas; **my car is blue and h. is red** mi coche es azul y el suyo es rojo

herself [hɜː'self] *pers pron* (**a**) *(reflexive)* se; **she dressed h.** se vistió (**b**) *(alone)* ella misma; **she was by h.** estaba sola (**c**) *(emphatic)* **she told me so h.** eso me dijo ella

hesitant ['hezɪtənt] *adj* vacilante

hesitate ['hezɪteɪt] *vi* vacilar

hesitation [hezɪ'teɪʃən] *n* indecisión *f*

heterogeneous [hetərəʊ'dʒiːnɪəs] *adj* heterogéneo(a)

heterosexual [hetərəʊ'seksjʊəl] *adj & n* heterosexual *(mf)*

hexagon ['heksəgən] *n* hexágono *m*

hey [heɪ] *interj* ¡oye!, ¡eh!

heyday ['heɪdeɪ] *n* auge *m*, apogeo *m*

HGV [eɪtʃdʒiː'viː] *n Br (abbr* **heavy goods vehicle)** vehículo *m* de carga pesada

hi [haɪ] *interj Fam* ¡hola!

hiatus [haɪ'eɪtəs] *n Fml* laguna *f*

hibernate ['haɪbəneɪt] *vi* hibernar

hibernation [haɪbə'neɪʃən] *n* hibernación *f*

hibiscus [haɪ'bɪskəs] *n* hibisco *m*

hiccup, hiccough ['hɪkʌp] *n* hipo *m; Fam (minor problem)* problemilla *m;* **to have hiccups** tener hipo

hide¹ [haɪd] **1** *vt (pt* **hid** [hɪd]; *pp* **hidden** ['hɪdən]) *(conceal)* esconder; *(obscure)* ocultar
2 *vi* esconderse, ocultarse
3 *n* puesto *m*

hide² [haɪd] *n (of animal)* piel *f*

hide-and-seek [haɪdən'siːk] *n* escondite *m*

hideous ['hɪdɪəs] *adj (horrific)* horroroso(a); *(extremely ugly)* espantoso(a)

hide-out ['haɪdaʊt] *n* escondrijo *m*, guarida *f*

hiding¹ ['haɪdɪŋ] *n* **to go into h.** esconderse

hiding² ['haɪdɪŋ] *n Fam* paliza *f*

hierarchy ['haɪərɑːkɪ] *n* jerarquía *f*

hi-fi ['haɪfaɪ] *n* hifi *m;* **h. equipment** equipo *m* de alta fidelidad

high [haɪ] **1** *adj* (**a**) *(mountain, building)* alto(a); **how h. is that wall?** ¿qué altura tiene esa pared?; **it's 3 feet h.** tiene 3 pies de alto; **h. chair** silla alta para niños; **h. jump** salto *m* de altura (**b**) *(price, speed, standards)* alto(a), elevado(a); **to have a h. opinion of sb** tener muy buena opinión de algn; **h. blood pressure** tensión alta (**c**) *(rank, position)* elevado(a), alto(a); **h. wind** viento *m* fuerte; **h. school** instituto *m* de enseñanza media; *Br* **the H. Street** la Calle Mayor (**d**) *Fam (drugged)* colocado(a)
2 *adv* alto; **to fly h.** volar a gran altura
3 *n (high point)* punto máximo

highbrow ['haɪbraʊ] *adj & n* intelectual *(mf)*

high-class ['haɪklɑːs] *adj* de alta categoría

higher ['haɪə(r)] **1** *adj* superior; **h. education** enseñanza *f* superior
2 *n Scot Educ* **H.** = examen final de los estudios preuniversitarios

high-five ['haɪfaɪv] *n US Fam* palmada *f* en el aire *(saludo entre dos)*

high-flier, high-flyer [haɪ'flaɪə(r)] *n Fig* = persona dotada y ambiciosa

high-handed [haɪ'hændɪd] *adj* despótico(a)

high-heeled ['haɪhiːld] *adj* de tacón, *Am* de taco alto

highlands ['haɪləndz] *npl* tierras altas

highlight ['haɪlaɪt] **1** *n* (**a**) *(in hair)* reflejo *m* (**b**) *(of event)* atracción *f* principal
2 *vt* (**a**) *(problem, difference)* destacar (**b**) *(text)* resaltar *(con rotulador fluorescente)*

highly ['haɪlɪ] *adv (very)* sumamente; **to speak h. of sb** hablar muy bien de algn

highly-strung [haɪlɪ'strʌŋ] *adj* muy nervioso(a)

Highness ['haɪnɪs] *n* **Your H.** Su Alteza

high-pitched ['haɪpɪtʃt] *adj* estridente

high-powered ['haɪpaʊəd] *adj (person)* dinámico(a)

high-ranking ['haɪræŋkɪŋ] *adj* **h. official** alto funcionario

high-rise ['haɪraɪz] *adj* **h. building** rascacielos *m inv*

high-speed ['haɪspiːd] *adj* h. **lens** objetivo ultrarrápido; h. **train** tren *m* de alta velocidad

high-tech ['haɪtek] *adj* de alta tecnología

highway ['haɪweɪ] *n US* carretera *f*, autopista *f*; *Br* **H. Code** código *m* de la circulación

highwayman ['haɪweɪmən] *n* salteador *m* de caminos

hijack ['haɪdʒæk] **1** *vt* secuestrar
2 *n* secuestro *m*

hijacker ['haɪdʒækə(r)] *n* secuestrador(a) *m,f*, *(of planes)* pirata *mf* del aire

hike [haɪk] **1** *n* (**a**) *(walk)* excursión *f* (**b**) **price h.** aumento *m* de precio
2 *vi* ir de excursión

hiker ['haɪkə(r)] *n* excursionista *mf*

hilarious [hɪ'leərɪəs] *adj* graciosísimo(a)

hill [hɪl] *n* colina *f*; *(slope)* cuesta *f*

hillside ['hɪlsaɪd] *n* ladera *f*

hilltop ['hɪltɒp] *n* cima *f* de una colina

hilly ['hɪlɪ] *adj* (**hillier, hilliest**) accidentado(a)

hilt [hɪlt] *n* puño *m*, empuñadura *f*; **I'll support you up to the h.** te daré mi apoyo total

him [hɪm] *pron* (**a**) *(direct object)* lo, le; **hit h.!** ¡pégale!; **she loves h.** lo quiere (**b**) *(indirect object)* le; *(with other third person pronouns)* se; **give h. the money** dale el dinero; **give it to h.** dáselo (**c**) *(after prep)* él; **it's not like h. to say that** no es propio de él decir eso (**d**) *Fam (as subject)* él; **it's h.** es él

himself [hɪm'self] *pers pron* (**a**) *(reflexive)* se; **he hurt h.** se hizo daño (**b**) *(alone)* solo, por sí mismo; **by h.** solo (**c**) *(emphatic)* él mismo

hind[1] [haɪnd] *adj* trasero(a); **h. legs** patas traseras

hind[2] [haɪnd] *n Zool* cierva *f*

hinder ['hɪndə(r)] *vt* dificultar, estorbar; **to h. sb from doing sth** impedir a algn hacer algo

hindrance ['hɪndrəns] *n* estorbo *m*

hindsight ['haɪndsaɪt] *n* retrospectiva *f*

Hindu [hɪn'duː, 'hɪnduː] *adj & n* hindú *(mf)*

Hinduism ['hɪnduɪzəm] *n* hinduismo *m*

hinge [hɪndʒ] **1** *n* bisagra *f*, *Fig* eje *m*
2 *vt* engoznar
▸ **hinge on** *vt insep* depender de

hint [hɪnt] **1** *n* (**a**) *(allusion)* indirecta *f*; **to take the h.** pillar *or Esp* coger la indirecta (**b**) *(clue)* pista *f* (**c**) *(trace)* pizca *f* (**d**) *(advice)* consejo *m*
2 *vt* **to h. that …** insinuar que …

hip[1] [hɪp] *n* cadera *f*; **h. flask** petaca *f*

hip[2] [hɪp] *adj Fam (trendy)* moderno(a), a la última, *Am* de onda

hip-hop ['hɪphɒp] *n* hip-hop *m*

hippie ['hɪpɪ] *adj & n Fam* hippy *(mf)*

hippopotamus [hɪpə'pɒtəməs] *n* (*pl* **hippopotami** [hɪpə'pɒtəmaɪ]) hipopótamo *m*

hire ['haɪə(r)] **1** *n Br (of car, room, suit)* alquiler *m*, *Méx* renta *f*; **bicycles for h.** se alquilan bicicletas; **for h.** *(taxi)* libre; **h. purchase** compra *f* a plazos
2 *vt* (**a**) *Br (rent)* alquilar, *Méx* rentar (**b**) *(employ)* contratar
▸ **hire out** *vt sep Br (car)* alquilar, *Méx* rentar; *(one's services)* ofrecer

his [hɪz] **1** *poss adj (one thing)* su; *(more than one)* sus; *(to distinguish)* de él; **he washed h. face** se lavó la cara; **is it h. dog or hers?** ¿el perro es de él o de ella?
2 *poss pron* (**a**) *(attribute) (one thing)* suyo(a); *(more than one)* suyos(as); *(to distinguish)* de él (**b**) *(noun reference) (one thing)* el suyo/la suya; *(more than one)* los suyos/las suyas; **my car is blue and h. is red** mi coche es azul y el suyo es rojo

Hispanic [hɪ'spænɪk] **1** *adj* hispánico(a)
2 *n US* hispano(a) *m,f*, latino(a) *m,f*

hiss [hɪs] **1** *n* siseo *m*; *Th* silbido *m*
2 *vt & vi* silbar

historian [hɪ'stɔːrɪən] *n* historiador(a) *m,f*

historic [hɪ'stɒrɪk] *adj* histórico(a)

historical [hɪ'stɒrɪkəl] *adj* histórico(a); **h. novel** novela histórica

history ['hɪstərɪ] *n* historia *f*

hit [hɪt] **1** *n* (**a**) *(blow)* golpe *m*; **direct h.** impacto directo; *Fam* **h. list** lista negra; *Fam* **h. man** asesino *m* a sueldo (**b**) *(success)* éxito *m*; **h. parade** lista *f* de éxitos (**c**) *Comput (visit to website)* acceso *m*, visita *f*
2 *vt* (*pt & pp* **hit**) (**a**) *(strike)* golpear, pegar; **he was h. in the leg** le dieron en la pierna; **the car h. the kerb** el coche chocó contra el bordillo (**b**) *(affect)* afectar (**c**) **to h. the headlines** salir en primera plana
▸ **hit back** *vi (reply to criticism)* replicar
▸ **hit on** *vt insep* dar con; **we h. on the idea of …** se nos ocurrió la idea de …
▸ **hit out** *vi* **to h. out at sb** atacar a algn
▸ **hit upon** *vt insep* = **hit on**

hit-and-run [hɪtən'rʌn] *adj* **h. driver** = conductor que atropella a algn y no para

hitch [hɪtʃ] **1** *n* dificultad *f*
2 *vt (fasten)* atar
3 *vi Fam (hitch-hike)* hacer autostop
▸ **hitch up** *vt sep* remangarse

hitch-hike ['hɪtʃhaɪk] *vi* hacer autostop *or* dedo

hitch-hiker ['hɪtʃhaɪkə(r)] *n* autostopista *mf*

hitherto [hɪðə'tuː] *adv Fml* hasta la fecha

HIV [eɪtʃaɪ'viː] *n (abbr* **human immuno-deficiency virus)** VIH *m;* **to be diagnosed HIV positive/negative** dar seropositivo(a)/ seronegativo(a) en la prueba del SIDA

hive [haɪv] *n* colmena *f; Fig* lugar muy activo

HM (*abbr* **His/Her Majesty**) SM

hoard [hɔːd] **1** *n (provisions)* reservas *fpl; (money etc)* tesoro *m*
2 *vt (objects)* acumular; *(money)* atesorar

hoarding ['hɔːdɪŋ] *n (temporary fence)* valla *f; Br (billboard)* valla publicitaria

hoarfrost ['hɔːfrɒst] *n* escarcha *f*

hoarse [hɔːs] *adj* ronco(a); **to be h.** tener la voz ronca

hoax [həʊks] *n (joke)* broma pesada; *(trick)* engaño *m*

hob [hɒb] *n (of cooker)* fuego *m, Esp, Andes, Méx* hornilla *f, RP* hornalla *f*

hobble ['hɒbəl] *vi* cojear, *Andes, RP* renguear

hobby ['hɒbɪ] *n* pasatiempo *m,* afición *f*

hobbyhorse ['hɒbɪhɔːs] *n (toy)* caballito *m* de juguete; *Fig (fixed idea)* idea fija, manía *f*

hobo ['həʊbəʊ] *n US* vagabundo(a) *m,f*

hockey ['hɒkɪ] *n Br (on grass)* hockey *m* (sobre hierba *or Am* césped); *US (on ice)* hockey (sobre hielo)

hog [hɒg] **1** *n* cerdo *m,* puerco *m; Fam* **to go the whole h.** liarse la manta a la cabeza
2 *vt Fam* acaparar

hoist [hɔɪst] **1** *n (crane)* grúa *f; (lift)* montacargas *m inv*
2 *vt* levantar, subir

hold [həʊld] **1** *vt (pt & pp* **held)** (**a**) *(keep in hand)* aguantar, tener (en la mano); *(grip)* agarrar; *(support) (weight)* soportar; *(opinion)* sostener; **to h. sb** abrazar a algn; **to h. sb's hand** cogerle la mano a algn (**b**) *(contain)* dar cabida a; **the jug holds a litre** en la jarra cabe un litro (**c**) *(meeting)* celebrar; *(conversation)* mantener (**d**) *(keep)* Tel **h. the line** no colgar (**e**) **h. office** ocupar un puesto (**e**) **he was held for two hours at the police station** estuvo detenido durante dos horas en la comisaría; **to h. one's breath** contener la respiración; **to h. sb hostage** retener a algn como rehén (**f**) *Tel* **to h. the line** no colgar
2 *vi (rope)* aguantar
3 *n* (**a**) **to get h. of** *(grip)* agarrar, *Esp*

coger; *Fig* localizar (**b**) *Naut* bodega *f* (**c**) *(in wrestling)* llave *f*

▸**hold back 1** *vt sep (crowd)* contener; *(feelings)* reprimir; *(truth)* ocultar; **I don't want to h. you back** *(delay)* no quiero entretenerte
2 *vi (hesitate)* vacilar

▸**hold down** *vt sep* (**a**) *(control)* dominar (**b**) *Fam (job)* desempeñar

▸**hold off** *vt sep* mantener a distancia

▸**hold on** *vi* (**a**) *(keep a firm grasp)* agarrarse bien (**b**) *(wait)* esperar; *Tel* **h. on!** ¡no cuelgue!

▸**hold out 1** *vt sep (hand)* tender
2 *vi (last) (things)* durar; *(person)* resistir

▸**hold up** *vt sep* (**a**) *(rob) (train)* asaltar; *(bank)* atracar (**b**) *(delay)* retrasar (**c**) *(raise)* levantar (**d**) *(support)* apuntalar

holdall ['həʊldɔːl] *n esp Br* bolsa *f (de viaje o de deporte)*

holder ['həʊldə(r)] *n* (**a**) *(receptacle)* recipiente *m* (**b**) *(owner)* poseedor(a) *m,f; (of passport)* titular *mf;* **record h.** plusmarquista *mf*

holding ['həʊldɪŋ] *n* (**a**) *(property)* propiedad *f* (**b**) *Fin* valor *m* en cartera; **h. company** holding *m*

hold-up ['həʊldʌp] *n* (**a**) *(robbery)* atraco *m* (**b**) *(delay)* retraso *m; (in traffic)* atasco *m*

hole [həʊl] *n* (**a**) *(in roof, clothing)* agujero *m; (in ground)* hoyo *m; (in the road)* bache *m* (**b**) *(in golf)* hoyo *m* (**c**) *Fam (of place)* antro *m*

holiday ['hɒlɪdeɪ] **1** *n (one day) Esp* (día *m* de) fiesta, *Am* feriado *m; Br (several days)* vacaciones *fpl;* **to be/go on h.** estar/irse de vacaciones; **h. resort** lugar turístico
2 *vi Br* pasar las vacaciones; *(in summer)* veranear

holidaymaker ['hɒlɪdeɪmeɪkə(r)] *n esp Br* turista *mf; (in summer)* veraneante *mf*

holiness ['həʊlɪnɪs] *n* santidad *f*

Holland ['hɒlənd] *n* Holanda

hollow ['hɒləʊ] **1** *adj* (**a**) *(container, log)* hueco(a) (**b**) *(cheeks, eyes)* hundido(a) (**c**) *Fig (insincere)* falso(a); *(empty)* vacío(a)
2 *n* hueco *m; Geog* hondonada *f*
3 *vt* **to h. (out)** hacer un hueco en

holly ['hɒlɪ] *n* acebo *m*

holocaust ['hɒləkɔːst] *n* holocausto *m*

hologram ['hɒləgræm] *n* holograma *m*

holster ['həʊlstə(r)] *n* pistolera *f*

holy ['həʊlɪ] *adj* (**holier, holiest**) sagrado(a), santo(a); *(blessed)* bendito(a); **H. Ghost** Espíritu Santo; **H. Land** Tierra Santa; **H. See** Santa Sede

homage ['hɒmɪdʒ] *n* homenaje *m;* **to pay h. to sb** rendir homenaje a algn

home [həʊm] **1** n (**a**) *(house)* casa f; *(family)* hogar m; **at h.** en casa; *Fig* **make yourself at h.!** ¡estás en tu casa!; *Fig* **to feel at h.** estar a gusto; **h. banking** telebanco m; *Comput* **h. page** *(initial page)* portada f, página f inicial or de inicio; *(personal page)* página personal; **h. shopping** telecompra f (**b**) *(institution)* residencia f; **old people's h.** asilo de ancianos m; *Sport* **to play at h.** jugar en casa; **h. run** carrera completa

2 adj (**a**) *(domestic)* del hogar; *Br* **h. help** asistenta f (**b**) *Pol* interior; *Br* **H. Office** Ministerio m del Interior; *Br* **H. Secretary** Ministro(a) m,f del Interior (**c**) *(native)* natal

3 adv en casa; **to go h.** irse a casa; **to leave h.** irse de casa

homeland ['həʊmlænd] n patria f; *(birthplace)* tierra f natal

homeless ['həʊmlɪs] **1** adj sin techo
2 npl **the h.** los sin techo

homely ['həʊmlɪ] adj (**homelier**, **homeliest**) (**a**) *Br (person)* casero(a); *(atmosphere)* familiar (**b**) *US (ugly)* feúcho(a)

home-made ['həʊmmeɪd] adj casero(a)

homeopathy [həʊmɪ'ɒpəθɪ] n *US* = **homeopathy**

homesick ['həʊmsɪk] adj **to be h.** tener morriña

homeward(s) ['həʊmwəd(z)] adv hacia casa

homework ['həʊmwɜːk] n deberes mpl

homey ['həʊmɪ] adj *US Fam* hogareño(a)

homicide ['hɒmɪsaɪd] n homicidio m

homing ['həʊmɪŋ] adj (**a**) **h. device** cabeza buscadora (**b**) **h. pigeon** paloma mensajera

homoeopathy [həʊmɪ'ɒpəθɪ] n homeopatía f

homogeneous [hɒmə'dʒiːnɪəs] adj homogéneo(a)

homosexual [həʊməʊ'seksjʊəl] adj & n homosexual (mf)

Honduran [hɒn'djʊərən] adj & n hondureño(a) (m,f)

Honduras [hɒn'djʊərəs] n Honduras

honest ['ɒnɪst] adj honrado(a); *(sincere)* sincero(a), franco(a); *(fair)* justo(a); **the h. truth** la pura verdad

honestly ['ɒnɪstlɪ] adv honradamente; *(question)* ¿de verdad?; *(exclamation)* ¡hay que ver!; **h., it doesn't matter** de verdad, no tiene importancia

honesty ['ɒnɪstɪ] n honradez f

honey ['hʌnɪ] n miel f; *esp US Fam (endearment)* cariño m

honeycomb ['hʌnɪkəʊm] n panal m

honeymoon ['hʌnɪmuːn] n luna f de miel

honeysuckle ['hʌnɪsʌkəl] n madreselva f

honk [hɒŋk] vi *Aut* tocar la bocina

honor ['ɒnə(r)] n & vt *US* = **honour**

honorable ['ɒnərəbəl] adj *US* = **honourable**

honorary ['ɒnərərɪ] adj *(member)* honorario(a); *(duties)* honorífico(a)

honour ['ɒnə(r)] **1** n (**a**) *(respect)* honor m (**b**) *US Jur* **Her H.**/**His H.**/**Your H.** Su Señoría f (**c**) *Mil* **honours** honores mpl (**d**) **Honours degree** licenciatura f superior

2 vt (**a**) *(respect)* honrar (**b**) *(obligation)* cumplir con

honourable ['ɒnərəbəl] adj *(person)* honrado(a); *(action)* honroso(a)

hood [hʊd] n (**a**) *(of garment)* capucha f (**b**) *Br (of car, pram)* capota f; *US (car bonnet)* capó m (**c**) *US Fam (gangster)* matón(ona) m,f

hoodlum ['huːdləm] n matón(ona) m,f

hoodwink ['hʊdwɪŋk] vt *Fam* engañar, *Esp* timar

hoof [huːf] n (pl **hoofs** or **hooves**) *(of horse)* casco m; *(of cow, sheep)* pezuña f

hook [hʊk] **1** n (**a**) *(in general)* gancho m; *(in fishing)* anzuelo m; *Sewing* **hooks and eyes** corchetes mpl; **to take the phone off the h.** descolgar el teléfono (**b**) *(in boxing)* gancho m

2 vt enganchar

▸ **hook up** vt sep & vi *Rad, TV & Comput* conectar (**with** con)

hooked [hʊkt] adj (**a**) *(nose)* aguileño(a) (**b**) *Fam (addicted)* enganchado(a) (**on** a); **to get h.** engancharse

hooker ['hʊkə(r)] n *US Fam (prostitute)* fulana f, puta f

hookey ['hʊkɪ] n *US Fam* **to play h.** faltar a clase, *Esp* hacer novillos, *Col* capar clase, *Méx* irse de pinta, *RP* hacerse la rabona

hook-up ['hʊkʌp] n (**a**) *Comput* conexión f (**b**) *Rad & TV* emisión f múltiple

hooky ['hʊkɪ] n *US Fam* = **hookey**

hooligan ['huːlɪgən] n *Fam* gamberro(a) m,f

hoop [huːp] n aro m; *(of barrel)* fleje m

hooray [huː'reɪ] interj ¡hurra!

hoot [huːt] **1** n (**a**) *(of owl)* ululato m; *Fam* **hoots of laughter** carcajadas fpl; *Fam* **I don't care a h.** me importa un pepino (**b**) *(of car horn)* bocinazo m

2 vi (**a**) *(owl)* ulular (**b**) *(car)* dar un bocinazo; *(train)* silbar; *(siren)* pitar

hooter ['huːtə(r)] n *Br (of car)* bocina f; *(of ship, factory)* sirena f

Hoover® ['huːvə(r)] *Br* **1** n aspiradora f
2 vt **to h.** pasar la aspiradora por

hooves [huːvz] *pl of* hoof

hop¹ [hɒp] **1** *vi* saltar; **to h. on one leg** andar a la pata coja
2 *n (small jump)* brinco *m*

hop² [hɒp] *n Bot* lúpulo *m*

hope [həʊp] **1** *n* esperanza *f; (false)* ilusión *f;* **to have little h. of doing sth** tener pocas posibilidades de hacer algo
2 *vt & vi* esperar; **I h. so/not** espero que sí/no; **we h. you're well** esperamos que estés bien

hopeful ['həʊpfʊl] *adj (confident)* optimista; *(promising)* prometedor(a)

hopefully ['həʊpfʊlɪ] *adv* (**a**) *(confidently)* con optimismo (**b**) **h. the weather will be fine** *(it is hoped)* esperemos que haga buen tiempo

hopeless ['həʊplɪs] *adj* desesperado(a); *Fam* **to be h. at sports** ser negado(a) para los deportes

hopelessly ['həʊplɪslɪ] *adv* desesperadamente; **h. lost** completamente perdido(a)

horde [hɔːd] *n* multitud *f*

horizon [hə'raɪzən] *n* horizonte *m*

horizontal [hɒrɪ'zɒntəl] *adj* horizontal

hormone ['hɔːməʊn] *n* hormona *f*

horn [hɔːn] *n* (**a**) *(of animal)* cuerno *m* (**b**) *Fam Mus* trompeta *f;* **French h.** trompa *f;* **hunting h.** cuerno *m* de caza (**c**) *Aut* bocina *f*

hornet ['hɔːnɪt] *n* avispón *m*

horny ['hɔːnɪ] *adj* (**hornier, horniest**) (**a**) *(hands)* calloso(a) (**b**) *very Fam (sexually aroused) Esp, Méx* cachondo(a), *CAm, Col, Méx, Ven* arrecho(a), *RP* caliente

horoscope ['hɒrəskəʊp] *n* horóscopo *m*

horrendous [hɒ'rendəs] *adj* horrendo(a)

horrible ['hɒrəbəl] *adj* horrible

horrid ['hɒrɪd] *adj* horrible

horrific [hə'rɪfɪk] *adj* horrendo(a)

horrify ['hɒrɪfaɪ] *vt* horrorizar

horror ['hɒrə(r)] *n* horror *m; Fam* **a little h.** un diablillo; **h. film** película *f* de miedo *or* de terror

hors d'oeuvre [ɔː'dɜːvr] *n (pl* **hors d'oeuvres**) entremés *m*

horse [hɔːs] *n* (**a**) *(animal)* caballo *m;* **h. race** carrera *f* de caballos (**b**) **h. chestnut** *(tree)* castaño *m* de Indias

horseback ['hɔːsbæk] *n* **on h.** a caballo; *US* **h. riding** equitación *f*

horseman ['hɔːsmən] *n* jinete *m*

horseplay ['hɔːspleɪ] *n* payasadas *fpl*

horsepower ['hɔːspaʊə(r)] *n* caballo *m* (de vapor)

horseradish ['hɔːsrædɪʃ] *n* rábano rusticano

horseshoe ['hɔːsʃuː] *n* herradura *f*

horsewoman ['hɔːswʊmən] *n* amazona *f*

horticulture ['hɔːtɪkʌltʃə(r)] *n* horticultura *f*

hose [həʊz] *n (pipe)* manguera *f*

hosepipe ['həʊzpaɪp] *n* manguera *f*

hosiery ['həʊzɪərɪ] *n* medias *fpl* y calcetines *mpl*

hospice ['hɒspɪs] *n* residencia *f* para enfermos terminales

hospitable ['hɒspɪtəbəl, hɒ'spɪtəbəl] *adj* hospitalario(a); **h. atmosphere** ambiente acogedor

hospital ['hɒspɪtəl] *n* hospital *m*

hospitality [hɒspɪ'tælɪtɪ] *n* hospitalidad *f*

host¹ [həʊst] **1** *n* (**a**) *(at home, party)* anfitrión *m* (**b**) *Th & TV* presentador *m* (**c**) *Biol* huésped *m*
2 *vt Th & TV* presentar

host² [həʊst] *n (large number)* montón *m*

host³ [həʊst] *n Rel* hostia *f*

hostage ['hɒstɪdʒ] *n* rehén *m*

hostel ['hɒstəl] *n* hostal *m*

hostess ['həʊstɪs] *n* (**a**) *(at home, party)* anfitriona *f* (**b**) *Th & TV* presentadora *f* (**c**) *(air)* **h.** azafata *f*

hostile ['hɒstaɪl, *US* 'hɒstəl] *adj* hostil

hostility [hɒ'stɪlɪtɪ] *n* hostilidad *f*

hot [hɒt] *adj* (**hotter, hottest**) (**a**) *(high in temperature)* caliente; *Fig* **h. line** teléfono rojo (**b**) *(day, weather)* caluroso(a); **it's very h.** hace mucho calor; **to feel h.** tener calor (**c**) *(spicy)* picante; **h. dog** perrito *m* caliente, *Col, Méx* perro *m* caliente, *RP* pancho *m* (**d**) *(temper)* fuerte (**e**) *Fam (good)* bueno(a); **it's not so h.** no es nada del otro mundo (**f**) *(popular)* popular

▸ **hot up** *vi Fam (situation, contest) Esp* calentarse, *Am* ponerse bravo(a)

hotbed ['hɒtbed] *n Fig* hervidero *m*

hotcake ['hɒtkeɪk] *n US* crepe *f,* panqueque *m, Esp* tortita *f*

hotel [həʊ'tel] *n* hotel *m*

hotelier [həʊ'teljeɪ] *n* hotelero(a) *m,f*

hot-headed [hɒt'hedɪd] *adj* impetuoso(a)

hothouse ['hɒthaʊs] *n* invernadero *m*

hotplate ['hɒtpleɪt] *n (cooker)* placa *f* de cocina; *(to keep food warm)* calientaplatos *m inv*

hotshot ['hɒtʃɒt] *n Fam* as *m, Esp* hacha *f*

hot-water [hɒt'wɔːtə(r)] *adj* **h. bottle** bolsa *f* de agua caliente

hound [haʊnd] **1** *n* perro *m* de caza
2 *vt* acosar

hour [ˈaʊə(r)] *n* hora *f*; **60 miles an h.** 60 millas por hora; **by the h.** por horas; **h. hand** manecilla *f*

hourly [ˈaʊəlɪ] **1** *adj* cada hora
　2 *adv* por horas

house 1 *n* [haʊs] (**a**) *(dwelling)* casa *f*; **at my h.** en mi casa; *Fig* **on the h.** cortesía de la casa; **h. plant** planta *f* de interior (**b**) *Pol* **H. of Commons** Cámara *f* de los Comunes; **H. of Lords** Cámara de los Lores; *US* **H. of Representatives** Cámara de Representantes; **Houses of Parliament** Parlamento *m* (**c**) *(company)* empresa *f*; **publishing h.** editorial *f* (**d**) *Th* sala *f*
　2 *vt* [haʊz] alojar; *(store)* guardar

houseboat [ˈhaʊsbəʊt] *n* casa *f* flotante

housebound [ˈhaʊsbaʊnd] *adj* **to be h.** estar confinado(a) en casa

housebreaking [ˈhaʊsbreɪkɪŋ] *n* robos *mpl* de casas, *RP* escruche *m*

housebroken [ˈhaʊsbrəʊkən] *adj US (pet)* = que ya ha aprendido a no hacer sus necesidades en casa

housecoat [ˈhaʊskəʊt] *n* bata *f*

household [ˈhaʊshəʊld] *n* hogar *m*, *Esp* unidad *f* familiar; **h. products** productos domésticos

housekeeper [ˈhaʊskiːpə(r)] *n* ama *f* de llaves

housekeeping [ˈhaʊskiːpɪŋ] *n* administración doméstica; **h. money** dinero *m* para los gastos domésticos

house-train [ˈhaʊstreɪn] *vt (pet)* educar

house-warming [ˈhaʊswɔːmɪŋ] *n* **h. (party)** = fiesta que se da al estrenar casa

housewife [ˈhaʊswaɪf] *n* ama *f* de casa

housework [ˈhaʊswɜːk] *n* trabajo doméstico

housing [ˈhaʊzɪŋ] *n* vivienda *f*; *Br* **h. estate** *(public housing)* ≃ viviendas *fpl* de protección oficial; *(private housing)* urbanización *f*, *Am* condominio *m*

hovel [ˈhʌvəl, ˈhɒvəl] *n* casucha *f*

hover [ˈhɒvə(r)] *vi (bird)* cernerse; *(aircraft)* permanecer inmóvil (en el aire)

hovercraft [ˈhɒvəkrɑːft] *n* aerodeslizador *m*

how [haʊ] *adv* (**a**) *(direct question)* ¿cómo?; **h. are you?** ¿cómo estás?; *Fam* **h. come?** ¿por qué? (**b**) *(indirect question)* cómo (**c**) *(very)* qué; **h. funny!** ¡qué divertido! (**d**) *(suggestion)* **h. about going to the cinema?** ¿te apetece ir al cine? (**e**) *(quantity)* cuánto; **h. old is she?** ¿cuántos años tiene?; **h. tall are you?** ¿cuánto mides? (**f**) *(many)* ¿cuántos(as)?; **h. much?** ¿cuánto(a)?

however [haʊˈevə(r)] *adv* (**a**) *(nevertheless)* no obstante, sin embargo (**b**)

(with adjective) **h. difficult it may be** por difícil que sea; **h. much** por mucho que *(+ subj)*

howl [haʊl] **1** *n* aullido *m*
　2 *vi* aullar

howler [ˈhaʊlə(r)] *n Fam* error *m* grave *or Esp* de bulto

HP, hp [eɪtʃˈpiː] *n* (**a**) *Br (abbr* **hire purchase)** compra *f* a plazos (**b**) *(abbr* **horsepower)** cv *mpl*

HQ [eɪtʃˈkjuː] *n (abbr* **headquarters)** sede *f*, central *f*

hub [hʌb] *n Aut* cubo *m*; *Fig* eje *m*

hubbub [ˈhʌbʌb] *n* alboroto *m*

hubcap [ˈhʌbkæp] *n Aut* tapacubos *m inv*

huddle [ˈhʌdəl] **1** *n* grupo *m*
　2 *vi* **to h. (up** *or* **together)** acurrucarse

hue[1] [hjuː] *n (colour)* tinte *m*; *(shade)* matiz *m*

hue[2] [hjuː] *n* **h. and cry** fuerte protesta *f*

huff [hʌf] *n* **to be in a h.** estar mosqueado(a) *or Esp* enfurruñado(a)

hug [hʌg] **1** *vt* abrazar
　2 *n* abrazo *m*

huge [hjuːdʒ] *adj* enorme

hugely [ˈhjuːdʒlɪ] *adv* enormemente

hulk [hʌlk] *n* (**a**) *Naut* casco *m* (**b**) *(thing, person)* armatoste *m*

hull [hʌl] *n Naut* casco *m*

hullabal(l)oo [hʌləbəˈluː] *n Fam* follón *m*

hullo [hʌˈləʊ] *interj Br* ¡hola!

hum [hʌm] **1** *vt (tune)* tararear
　2 *vi (bees, engine)* zumbar; *(sing)* tararear
　3 *n (of bees)* zumbido *m*

human [ˈhjuːmən] **1** *adj* humano(a); **h. race** raza humana; **h. being** ser humano
　2 *n* ser humano

humane [hjuːˈmeɪn] *adj* humano(a)

humanitarian [hjuːmænɪˈteərɪən] *adj* humanitario(a)

humanity [hjuːˈmænɪtɪ] *n* humanidad *f*; *Univ* **the humanities** las humanidades

humble [ˈhʌmbəl] **1** *adj* humilde
　2 *vt* humillar

humbug [ˈhʌmbʌg] *n* (**a**) *Fam* tonterías *fpl* (**b**) *Br (mint)* **h.** caramelo *m* de menta

humdrum [ˈhʌmdrʌm] *adj* monótono(a), aburrido(a)

humid [ˈhjuːmɪd] *adj* húmedo(a)

humidity [hjuːˈmɪdɪtɪ] *n* humedad *f*

humiliate [hjuːˈmɪlɪeɪt] *vt* humillar

humiliation [hjuːmɪlɪˈeɪʃən] *n* humillación *f*

humility [hjuːˈmɪlɪtɪ] *n* humildad *f*

humor [ˈhjuːmə(r)] *n & vt US* = **humour**

humorous ['hju:mərəs] *adj (writer)* humorístico(a); *(person, story)* gracioso(a), divertido(a)

humour ['hju:mə(r)] **1** *n* humor *m*
2 *vt* seguir la corriente a

hump [hʌmp] **1** *n* (**a**) *(on back)* joroba *f* (**b**) *(small hill)* montículo *m*
2 *vt esp Br Fam (carry)* acarrear

humus ['hju:məs] *n* mantillo *m*, humus *m*

hunch [hʌntʃ] *n Fam* corazonada *f*

hunchback ['hʌntʃbæk] *n* jorobado(a) *m,f*

hundred ['hʌndrəd] **1** *n* cien *m*, ciento *m*; *(rough number)* centenar *m*; **a h. and twenty-five** ciento veinticinco; **five h.** quinientos
2 *adj* cien; **a h. people** cien personas; **a h. percent** cien por cien; **two h. chairs** doscientas sillas

hundredth ['hʌndrədθ] *adj & n* centésimo(a) *(m,f)*

hundredweight ['hʌndrədweɪt] *n Br* = 50,8 kg; *US* = 45,36 kg

hung [hʌŋ] **1** *adj Fam* (**a**) **h. over** con resaca (**b**) **h. up** acomplejado(a)
2 *pt & pp of* **hang**

Hungarian [hʌŋ'geərɪən] *adj & n* húngaro(a) *(m,f)*

Hungary ['hʌŋgərɪ] *n* Hungría

hunger ['hʌŋgə(r)] **1** *n* hambre *f*; **h. strike** huelga *f* de hambre
2 *vi Fig* tener hambre (**for** de)

hungry ['hʌŋgrɪ] *adj* (**hungrier, hungriest**) hambriento(a); **to be h.** tener hambre; **to go h.** pasar hambre

hunk [hʌŋk] *n* (**a**) *(piece)* buen pedazo *m* (**b**) *Fam (man)* machote *m*

hunt [hʌnt] **1** *vt* cazar
2 *vi (for game)* cazar; *(search)* buscar
3 *n* caza *f*; *(search)* búsqueda *f*
► **hunt down** *vt sep* perseguir

hunter ['hʌntə(r)] *n* cazador(a) *m,f*

hunting ['hʌntɪŋ] *n* caza *f*; *(expedition)* cacería *f*

hurdle ['hɜ:dəl] *n Sport* valla *f*; *Fig* obstáculo *m*

hurl [hɜ:l] *vt* arrojar, lanzar

hurrah [hʊ'rɑ:], **hurray** [hʊ'reɪ] *interj* ¡hurra!; **h. for John!** ¡viva John!

hurricane ['hʌrɪkən, US 'hʌrɪkeɪn] *n* huracán *m*

hurried ['hʌrɪd] *adj* apresurado(a); *(action etc)* hecho(a) de prisa

hurriedly ['hʌrɪdlɪ] *adv* deprisa, apresuradamente

hurry ['hʌrɪ] **1** *vt* meter prisa a
2 *vi* darse prisa, apresurarse, *Am* apurarse
3 *n* **to be in a h.** tener prisa *or Am* apuro

hurt [hɜ:t] **1** *vt (pt & pp* **hurt**) hacer daño a; *(wound)* herir; *(feelings)* ofender
2 *vi* doler; **my arm hurts** me duele el brazo
3 *adj (physically)* herido(a); *(mentally)* dolido(a)

hurtful ['hɜ:tfʊl] *adj* hiriente

hurtle ['hɜ:təl] *vi* lanzarse; **to h. down** desplomarse

husband ['hʌzbənd] *n* marido *m*, esposo *m*

hush [hʌʃ] **1** *vt* callar; **to h. sth up** echar tierra a un asunto
2 *n* silencio *m*
3 *interj* ¡silencio!

hush-hush [hʌʃ'hʌʃ] *adj Fam* confidencial

husky¹ ['hʌskɪ] *adj* (**huskier, huskiest**) ronco(a)

husky² ['hʌskɪ] *n (dog)* perro *m* esquimal

hustings ['hʌstɪŋz] *npl Pol* (**a**) *(platform)* tribuna *f* electoral (**b**) *(election)* elecciones *fpl*

hustle ['hʌsəl] **1** *vt* (**a**) *(jostle)* empujar (**b**) *Fam* meter prisa a
2 *n* bullicio *m*; **h. and bustle** ajetreo *m*

hut [hʌt] *n* cabaña *f*; *(shed)* cobertizo *m*; *Mil* barraca *f*

hutch [hʌtʃ] *n* jaula *f*; **rabbit h.** conejera *f*

hyacinth ['haɪəsɪnθ] *n* jacinto *m*

hybrid ['haɪbrɪd] *adj & n* híbrido(a) *(m,f)*

hydrant ['haɪdrənt] *n* **fire h.** boca *f* de incendio

hydraulic [haɪ'drɒlɪk] *adj* hidráulico(a)

hydrocarbon [haɪdrəʊ'kɑ:bən] *n* hidrocarburo *m*

hydrochloric [haɪdrəʊ'klɒrɪk] *adj* **h. acid** ácido clorhídrico

hydroelectric [haɪdrəʊ'lektrɪk] *adj* hidroeléctrico(a)

hydrofoil ['haɪdrəfɔɪl] *n* hidroala *f*, *RP* alíscafo *m*

hydrogen ['haɪdrədʒən] *n* hidrógeno *m*

hydroplane ['haɪdrəpleɪn] *n US (seaplane)* hidroavión *m*

hyena [haɪ'i:nə] *n* hiena *f*

hygiene ['haɪdʒi:n] *n* higiene *f*

hygienic [haɪ'dʒi:nɪk] *adj* higiénico(a)

hymn [hɪm] *n* himno *m*; **h. book** cantoral *m*

hype [haɪp] *n Fam* campaña publicitaria, movida *f*

hyper- ['haɪpə(r)] *pref* hiper-; **hyperactive** hiperactivo(a)

hypermarket ['haɪpəmɑ:kɪt] *n Br* hipermercado *m*

hypersensitive [haɪpə'sensɪtɪv] *adj* hipersensible

hypertext [ˈhaɪpətekst] *n Comput* hipertexto *m*

hyphen [ˈhaɪfən] *n* guión *m*

hypnosis [hɪpˈnəʊsɪs] *n* hipnosis *f*

hypnotist [ˈhɪpnətɪst] *n* hipnotizador(a) *m,f*

hypnotize [ˈhɪpnətaɪz] *vt* hipnotizar

hypoallergenic [haɪpəʊæləˈdʒenɪk] *adj* hipoalergénico(a)

hypochondriac [haɪpəˈkɒndrɪæk] *adj & n* hipocondríaco(a) *(m,f)*

hypocrisy [hɪˈpɒkrəsɪ] *n* hipocresía *f*

hypocrite [ˈhɪpəkrɪt] *n* hipócrita *mf*

hypocritical [hɪpəˈkrɪtɪkəl] *adj* hipócrita

hypodermic [haɪpəˈdɜːmɪk] *adj Med* hipodérmico(a); **h. needle** aguja hipodérmica

hypothesis [haɪˈpɒθɪsɪs] *n (pl* **hypotheses** [haɪˈpɒθɪsiːz]) hipótesis *f*

hypothetic(al) [haɪpəˈθetɪk(əl)] *adj* hipotético(a)

hysteria [hɪˈstɪərɪə] *n* histeria *f*

hysterical [hɪˈsterɪkəl] *adj* histérico(a)

hysterics [hɪˈsterɪks] *npl* (**a**) *(panic)* ataque *m* de histeria (**b**) *Fam (of laughter)* ataque *m* de risa

l, i [aɪ] *n (the letter)* l, i *f*

I [aɪ] *pers pron* yo *(usually omitted in Spanish, except for contrast)*; **I know her** (yo) la conozco

IAEA [aɪeiː'eɪ] *n (abbr* **International Atomic Energy Agency)** AIEA *f*

ICBM [aɪsiːbiː'em] *n (abbr* **intercontinental ballistic missile)** misil *m* balístico intercontinental

ice [aɪs] **1** *n* hielo *m*; **i. axe** pico *m* (de alpinista); **i. cream** helado *m, Am* sorbete; **i. cube** cubito *m* de hielo; **i. hockey** hockey *m* sobre hielo; *Br* **i. lolly** polo *m*; **i. rink** pista *f* de patinaje; **i. skate** patín *m* de cuchilla
2 *vt (cake)* alcorzar

▸ **ice over, ice up** *vi (pond etc)* helarse; *(windscreen, plane wings)* cubrirse de hielo

iceberg ['aɪsbɜːg] *n* iceberg *m*

icebox ['aɪsbɒks] *n* (**a**) *Br (compartment of fridge)* congelador *m* (**b**) *US (fridge)* nevera *f, Méx* refrigerador *m, RP* heladera *f*

icecap ['aɪskæp] *n* casquete *m* glaciar

Iceland ['aɪslənd] *n* Islandia

ice-skating ['aɪsskeɪtɪŋ] *n* patinaje *m* sobre hielo

icicle ['aɪsɪkəl] *n* carámbano *m*

icing ['aɪsɪŋ] *n* alcorza *f; Br* **i. sugar** azúcar *m Esp, Méx* glas *or Esp* de lustre *or Chile* flor *or RP* impalpable

icon ['aɪkɒn] *n* icono *m*

icy ['aɪsɪ] *adj* (**icier, iciest**) *(road etc)* helado(a); *Fig (smile)* glacial

ID [aɪ'diː] *n US* documentación *f*; **ID card** DNI *m*

I'd [aɪd] = I would; I had

idea [aɪ'dɪə] *n* idea *f*; **(I've) no idea** (no tengo) ni idea; *Fam* **what's the big i.?** ¿a qué viene esto?

ideal [aɪ'dɪəl] *adj & n* ideal (*m*)

idealist [aɪ'dɪəlɪst] *n* idealista *mf*

idealistic [aɪdɪə'lɪstɪk] *adj* idealista

idealize [aɪ'dɪəlaɪz] *vt* idealizar

ideally [aɪ'dɪəlɪ] *adv* (**a**) *(perfectly)* perfectamente (**b**) *(in the best conditions)* de ser posible

identical [aɪ'dentɪkəl] *adj* idéntico(a)

identification [aɪdentɪfɪ'keɪʃən] *n* (**a**) *(of body, criminal)* identificación *f* (**b**) *(papers)* documentación *f*

identify [aɪ'dentɪfaɪ] **1** *vt (body)* identificar; *(cause)* descubrir
2 *vi* identificarse (**with** con)

Identikit® [aɪ'dentɪkɪt] *n* **i. picture** retrato *m* robot

identity [aɪ'dentɪtɪ] *n* identidad *f*; **i. card** carné *m* de identidad; **proof of i.** prueba *f* de identidad; **i. theft** robo *m* de identidad

ideological [aɪdɪə'lɒdʒɪkəl] *adj* ideológico(a)

ideology [aɪdɪ'ɒlədʒɪ] *n* ideología *f*

idiom ['ɪdɪəm] *n* modismo *m; Fig (style)* lenguaje *m*

idiomatic [ɪdɪə'mætɪk] *adj* idiomático(a)

idiosyncrasy [ɪdɪəʊ'sɪŋkrəsɪ] *n* idiosincrasia *f*

idiot ['ɪdɪət] *n* idiota *mf*, tonto(a) *m,f*

idiotic [ɪdɪ'ɒtɪk] *adj (behaviour)* idiota, tonto(a); *(joke, plan)* estúpido(a)

idle ['aɪdəl] **1** *adj* holgazán(ana); *(not working) (person)* desempleado(a); *(machinery)* parado(a); *(gossip)* frívolo(a); *(threat)* vano(a)
2 *vi (engine)* funcionar en vacío

▸ **idle away** *vt sep (time)* desperdiciar

idleness ['aɪdəlnɪs] *n (laziness)* holgazanería *f*, *(unemployment)* desempleo *m*; *(stoppage)* paro *m*

idol ['aɪdəl] *n* ídolo *m*

idolize ['aɪdəlaɪz] *vt* idolatrar

idyllic [ɪ'dɪlɪk] *adj* idílico(a)

i.e. ['aɪ'iː] *(abbr* **id est)** i.e., es decir

if [ɪf] **1** *conj* (**a**) *(conditional)* si; **if not** si no; **if so** de ser así; **if I were you** en tu lugar; **if only she were here!** ¡ojalá estuviera aquí! (**b**) *(whenever)* si; **if you need help, ask** siempre que necesites ayuda, pídela
2 *n* **ifs and buts** pegas *fpl*

igloo ['ɪgluː] *n* iglú *m*

ignite [ɪg'naɪt] **1** *vt* encender
2 *vi* encenderse

ignition [ɪg'nɪʃən] *n* ignición *f; Aut* encendido *m*; **i. key** llave *f* de contacto

ignorance ['ɪgnərəns] *n* ignorancia *f*

ignorant ['ɪgnərənt] *adj* ignorante (**of** de); **to be i. of the facts** ignorar *or* desconocer los hechos

ignore [ɪg'nɔː(r)] *vt (warning, remark)* no hacer caso de; *(behaviour, fact)* pasar por alto

ill [ɪl] **1** *adj* (**a**) *(unwell)* enfermo(a); **to feel i.** encontrarse mal (**b**) *(bad)* malo(a); **i. feeling** resentimiento *m*; **i. will** mala voluntad
  2 *n* mal *m*
  3 *adv* difícilmente

I'll [aɪl] = **I shall; I will**

ill-advised [ɪləd'vaɪzd] *adj (person)* imprudente; *(act)* desatinado(a); **you'd be i. to go** harías mal en ir

ill-disposed [ɪldɪ'spəʊzd] *adj* poco dispuesto(a)

illegal [ɪ'liːgəl] *adj* ilegal

illegible [ɪ'ledʒɪbəl] *adj* ilegible

illegitimate [ɪlɪ'dʒɪtɪmɪt] *adj* ilegítimo(a)

ill-fated [ɪl'feɪtɪd] *adj* abocado(a) al fracaso

ill-founded [ɪl'faʊndɪd] *adj* infundado(a)

illicit [ɪ'lɪsɪt] *adj* ilícito(a)

illiteracy [ɪ'lɪtərəsɪ] *n* analfabetismo *m*

illiterate [ɪ'lɪtərɪt] *adj (person)* analfabeto(a); *Fam (uneducated)* inculto(a)

illness ['ɪlnɪs] *n* enfermedad *f*

illogical [ɪ'lɒdʒɪkəl] *adj* ilógico(a)

ill-treat [ɪl'triːt] *vt* maltratar

illuminate [ɪ'luːmɪneɪt] *vt* (**a**) *(light up)* iluminar, alumbrar; *Fig (clarify)* aclarar (**b**) *(manuscript)* iluminar

illuminating [ɪ'luːmɪneɪtɪŋ] *adj (experience, book)* instructivo(a); *(remark)* revelador(a)

illumination [ɪluːmɪ'neɪʃən] *n* (**a**) *(lighting)* iluminación *f*; *Fig (clarification)* aclaración *f* (**b**) **illuminations** *(decorative lights)* iluminación *f*

illusion [i'luːʒən] *n* ilusión *f*; **to be under the i. that ...** engañarse pensando que ...

illusory [ɪ'luːsərɪ] *adj* ilusorio(a)

illustrate ['ɪləstreɪt] *vt* ilustrar

illustration [ɪlə'streɪʃən] *n* ilustración *f*; *(example)* ejemplo *m*

illustrious [ɪ'lʌstrɪəs] *adj* ilustre

I'm [aɪm] = **I am**

image ['ɪmɪdʒ] *n* imagen *f*

imagery ['ɪmɪdʒərɪ] *n Lit* imágenes *fpl*

imaginary [ɪ'mædʒɪnərɪ] *adj* imaginario(a)

imagination [ɪmædʒɪ'neɪʃən] *n* imaginación *f*; *(inventiveness)* inventiva *f*

imaginative [ɪ'mædʒɪnətɪv] *adj* imaginativo(a)

imagine [ɪ'mædʒɪn] *vt (visualize)* imaginar; *(think)* suponer, imaginarse; **just i.!** ¡imagínate!

imbalance [ɪm'bæləns] *n* desequilibrio *m*

imbecile ['ɪmbɪsiːl] *n* imbécil *mf*

IMF [aɪɛ'mef] *n (abbr* **International Monetary Fund)** FMI *m*

imitate ['ɪmɪteɪt] *vt* imitar

imitation [ɪmɪ'teɪʃən] **1** *n* imitación *f*, copia *f*; *Pej* remedo *m*
  2 *adj* de imitación

immaculate [ɪ'mækjʊlɪt] *adj (clean)* inmaculado(a); *(tidy)* perfectamente ordenado(a); *(clothes)* impecable; *(work)* perfecto(a); **the I. Conception** la Inmaculada Concepción

immaterial [ɪmə'tɪərɪəl] *adj* irrelevante; **it's i. to me whether ...** me trae sin cuidado si ...

immature [ɪmə'tjʊə(r)] *adj* inmaduro(a)

immediate [ɪ'miːdɪət] *adj* inmediato(a); **in the i. future** en un futuro inmediato; **the i. family** la familia más cercana

immediately [ɪ'miːdɪətlɪ] **1** *adv* inmediatamente
  2 *conj* en cuanto

immense [ɪ'mens] *adj* inmenso(a), enorme

immensely [ɪ'menslɪ] *adv (rich)* enormemente; *(interesting, difficult)* sumamente

immerse [ɪ'mɜːs] *vt* sumergir (**in** en); *Fig* **to be immersed in sth** estar absorto(a) en algo

immersion [ɪ'mɜːʃən] *n* inmersión *f*; *Br* **i. heater** calentador *m* de inmersión; **i. course** cursillo intensivo

immigrant ['ɪmɪgrənt] *adj* & *n* inmigrante *(mf)*

immigrate ['ɪmɪgreɪt] *vi* inmigrar

immigration [ɪmɪ'greɪʃən] *n* inmigración *f*

imminent ['ɪmɪnənt] *adj* inminente

immobile [ɪ'məʊbaɪl] *adj* inmóvil

immobilize [ɪ'məʊbɪlaɪz] *vt* inmovilizar

immodest [ɪ'mɒdɪst] *adj* indecente

immoral [ɪ'mɒrəl] *adj* inmoral

immortal [ɪ'mɔːtəl] *adj* inmortal

immortality [ɪmɔː'tælɪtɪ] *n* inmortalidad *f*

immortalize [ɪ'mɔːtəlaɪz] *vt* inmortalizar

immune [ɪ'mjuːn] *adj* inmune; *(exempt)* exento(a)

immunity [ɪ'mjuːnɪtɪ] *n* inmunidad *f*

immunize ['ɪmjʊnaɪz] *vt* inmunizar (**against** contra)

impact ['ɪmpækt] n impacto m; (crash) choque m

impair [ɪm'peə(r)] vt perjudicar; (sight etc) dañar

impart [ɪm'pɑːt] vt Fml (news) comunicar; (knowledge) transmitir

impartial [ɪm'pɑːʃəl] adj imparcial

impassable [ɪm'pɑːsəbəl] adj (road, ground) intransitable; (barrier) infranqueable

impasse [æm'pɑːs] n punto muerto

impassive [ɪm'pæsɪv] adj impasible

impatience [ɪm'peɪʃəns] n impaciencia f

impatient [ɪm'peɪʃənt] adj impaciente; (fretful) irritable; **to get i.** perder la paciencia

impeccable [ɪm'pekəbəl] adj impecable

impede [ɪm'piːd] vt (prevent) impedir; (hinder) estorbar; (obstruct) poner trabas a

impediment [ɪm'pedɪmənt] n impedimento m; (obstacle) estorbo m; **speech i.** defecto m del habla

impending [ɪm'pendɪŋ] adj Fml inminente

impenetrable [ɪm'penɪtrəbəl] adj impenetrable; Fig (mystery, thoughts) insondable

imperative [ɪm'perətɪv] **1** adj Fml imperativo(a); (tone) imperioso(a); (urgent) urgente
2 n Gram imperativo m

imperceptible [ɪmpə'septəbəl] adj imperceptible

imperfect [ɪm'pɜːfɪkt] **1** adj imperfecto(a); (goods) defectuoso(a)
2 n Gram imperfecto m

imperfection [ɪmpə'fekʃən] n defecto m

imperial [ɪm'pɪərɪəl] adj (a) (of empire) imperial (b) (measure) **i. gallon** galón británico (aprox 4,546 l)

imperialism [ɪm'pɪərɪəlɪzəm] n imperialismo m

imperialist [ɪm'pɪərɪəlɪst] adj & n imperialista (mf)

imperious [ɪm'pɪərɪəs] adj imperioso(a)

impersonal [ɪm'pɜːsənəl] adj impersonal

impersonate [ɪm'pɜːsəneɪt] vt hacerse pasar por; (famous people) imitar

impersonation [ɪmpɜːsə'neɪʃən] n imitación f

impertinent [ɪm'pɜːtɪnənt] adj impertinente

impervious [ɪm'pɜːvɪəs] adj (rock) impermeable; Fig **to be i. to reason** no atender a razones

impetuous [ɪm'petjʊəs] adj impetuoso(a)

impetus ['ɪmpɪtəs] n ímpetu m; Fig impulso m

impinge [ɪm'pɪndʒ] vi Fml afectar (on a)

implant Med **1** vt [ɪm'plɑːnt] implantar
2 n ['ɪmplɑːnt] implantación f

implement 1 n ['ɪmplɪmənt] (tool) herramienta f; (instrument) instrumento m; **farm implements** aperos mpl de labranza
2 vt ['ɪmplɪment] (decision, plan) llevar a cabo; (law, policy) aplicar

implicate ['ɪmplɪkeɪt] vt implicar (in en)

implication [ɪmplɪ'keɪʃən] n implicación f; (consequence) consecuencia f

implicit [ɪm'plɪsɪt] adj (implied) implícito(a); (trust) absoluto(a); (faith) incondicional

implore [ɪm'plɔː(r)] vt implorar, suplicar

imply [ɪm'plaɪ] vt (a) (involve) implicar (b) (hint) dar a entender; (mean) significar

impolite [ɪmpə'laɪt] adj maleducado(a)

import 1 n ['ɪmpɔːt] (a) Com importación f; **i. duty** derechos mpl de importación (b) Fml (meaning) sentido m
2 vt [ɪm'pɔːt] Com importar

importance [ɪm'pɔːtəns] n importancia f; (standing) envergadura f; **of little i.** de poca monta

important [ɪm'pɔːtənt] adj importante; **it's not i.** no importa

importer [ɪm'pɔːtə(r)] n Com importador(a) m,f

impose [ɪm'pəʊz] **1** vt imponer (on or upon a)
2 vi **to i. on** or **upon** (take advantage of) abusar de

imposing [ɪm'pəʊzɪŋ] adj imponente, impresionante

imposition [ɪmpə'zɪʃən] n (of tax etc) imposición f; (unfair demand) abuso m; **would it be an i. if …?** ¿le molestaría si …?

impossibility [ɪmpɒsə'bɪlɪtɪ] n imposibilidad f

impossible [ɪm'pɒsəbəl] **1** adj imposible; (person) insoportable
2 n **to do the i.** hacer lo imposible

impossibly [ɪm'pɒsəblɪ] adv de manera insoportable; **i. difficult** de una dificultad insuperable

impostor [ɪm'pɒstə(r)] n impostor(a) m,f

impotent ['ɪmpətənt] adj impotente

impound [ɪm'paʊnd] vt incautarse de

impoverished [ɪmˈpɒvərɪʃt] *adj (person, country)* empobrecido(a); *(soil)* agotado(a)

impracticable [ɪmˈpræktɪkəbəl] *adj* impracticable, irrealizable

impractical [ɪmˈpræktɪkəl] *adj (person)* poco práctico(a); *(project, solution etc)* poco viable

imprecise [ɪmprɪˈsaɪs] *adj* impreciso(a)

impregnable [ɪmˈpregnəbəl] *adj* inexpugnable

impregnate [ˈɪmpregneɪt] *vt* (a) *(soak)* impregnar (**with** de) (b) *Fml (fertilize)* fecundar

impress [ɪmˈpres] *vt* (a) *(make an impression on)* impresionar; **to i. sb favourably/unfavourably** dar a algn buena/mala impresión (b) *(mark)* imprimir (**on** en); *(pattern)* estampar (**on** en); *Fig* **to i. sth on sb** convencer a algn de la importancia de algo

impression [ɪmˈpreʃən] *n* (a) *(effect)* impresión *f*; **to be under the i. that ...** tener la impresión de que ...; **to give the i. of ...** dar la impresión de ... (b) *(imprint)* marca *f*; *(in snow)* huella *f* (c) *(imitation)* imitación *f*

impressionist [ɪmˈpreʃənɪst] *adj & n* impresionista *(mf)*

impressive [ɪmˈpresɪv] *adj* impresionante

imprint 1 *vt* [ɪmˈprɪnt] *(mark)* dejar huella (**on** en)
2 *n* [ˈɪmprɪnt] (a) *(mark)* marca *f*; *(left by foot etc)* huella *f* (b) *(publisher's name)* pie *m* de imprenta

imprison [ɪmˈprɪzən] *vt* encarcelar

imprisonment [ɪmˈprɪzənmənt] *n* encarcelamiento *m*

improbable [ɪmˈprɒbəbəl] *adj (event)* improbable; *(story)* inverosímil

impromptu [ɪmˈprɒmptjuː] **1** *adj (speech)* improvisado(a); *(visit)* imprevisto(a)
2 *adv* de improviso

improper [ɪmˈprɒpə(r)] *adj* (a) *(use, purpose)* impropio(a), incorrecto(a); *(suggestion, behaviour)* indecoroso(a) (b) *(dishonest)* impropio(a), irregular

improve [ɪmˈpruːv] **1** *vt* mejorar; *(knowledge)* perfeccionar; *(mind)* cultivar; *(increase)* aumentar
2 *vi* mejorarse; *(increase)* aumentar
▸ **improve on** *vt insep* superar; *(offer, bid)* sobrepujar

improvement [ɪmˈpruːvmənt] *n* mejora *f*; *(in skill)* perfeccionamiento *m*; *(increase)* aumento *m*

improvise [ˈɪmprəvaɪz] *vt & vi* improvisar

imprudent [ɪmˈpruːdənt] *adj* imprudente

impudence [ˈɪmpjʊdəns] *n* insolencia *f*

impudent [ˈɪmpjʊdənt] *adj* insolente

impulse [ˈɪmpʌls] *n* impulso *m*; **to act on (an) i.** dejarse llevar por un impulso

impulsive [ɪmˈpʌlsɪv] *adj* irreflexivo(a)

impunity [ɪmˈpjuːnɪtɪ] *n* impunidad *f*

impure [ɪmˈpjʊə(r)] *adj* (a) *(act)* impuro(a); *(thought)* impúdico(a) (b) *(air)* contaminado(a)

impurity [ɪmˈpjʊərɪtɪ] *n* (a) *(of act)* deshonestidad *f* (b) *(in air, substance)* impureza *f*

in [ɪn] **1** *prep* (a) *(place)* en; *(within)* dentro de; **in bed** en la cama; **in Brazil** en Brasil; **in prison** en la cárcel
(b) *(motion)* en; **she arrived in Paris** llegó a París
(c) *(time) (during)* en, durante; **I haven't seen her in years** hace años que no la veo; **in May/1945** en mayo/1945; **in spring** en primavera; **in the daytime** durante el día; **in the morning** por la mañana; **at ten in the morning** a las diez de la mañana
(d) *(time) (within)* dentro de; **I arrived in time** llegué a tiempo
(e) *(time) (after)* al cabo de
(f) *(manner)* en; **in a loud/quiet voice** en voz alta/baja; **in fashion** de moda; **in French** en francés; **in writing** por escrito; **write in pencil** escribe con lápiz
(g) *(wearing)* **dressed in blue** vestido(a) de azul; **in uniform** de uniforme
(h) *(weather etc)* a, en; **in the rain** bajo la lluvia; **in the sun** al sol; en la oscuridad; **in daylight** a la luz del día
(i) *(state, emotion)* en; **in danger/public/ silence** en peligro/público/silencio; **in love** enamorado(a); **in tears** llorando
(j) *(ratio, numbers)* de; **in threes** de tres en tres; **one in six** uno de cada seis; **2 m in length** 2 m de largo
(k) *(after superlative)* de; **the smallest car in the world** el coche más pequeño del mundo
(l) *(phrases)* **in all** en total; **in itself/ himself/herself** en sí; **in that ...** dado que ...
2 *adv* **in here/there** aquí/allí dentro; **let's go in** vamos adentro; **to be in** *(at home)* estar (en casa); *(at work)* estar; *(tide)* estar alta; *Fam (in fashion)* estar de moda; **the bus is in** el autobús ha llegado; *Fam* **to be in on sth** estar enterado(a) de algo
3 *adj Fam* (a) *(fashionable) (place)* de moda; *(clothes)* del último grito (b) **an in joke** una broma privada
4 *n Fam* **ins and outs** detalles *mpl*

inability [ɪnəˈbɪlɪtɪ] *n* incapacidad *f*

inaccessible [ɪnæk'sesəbəl] *adj* inaccesible

inaccurate [ɪn'ækjʊrɪt] *adj* inexacto(a); *(statement)* erróneo(a); *(figures, total)* incorrecto(a)

inactivity [ɪnæk'tɪvɪtɪ] *n* inactividad *f*

inadequate [ɪn'ædɪkwɪt] *adj* (a) *(lacking)* insuficiente (b) *(not capable)* incapaz; *(unsuitable)* inadecuado(a) (c) *(defective)* defectuoso(a)

inadvertent [ɪnəd'vɜːtənt] *adj* involuntario(a)

inadvertently [ɪnəd'vɜːtəntlɪ] *adv* involuntariamente

inadvisable [ɪnəd'vaɪzəbəl] *adj* imprudente

inane [ɪ'neɪn] *adj* necio(a), fatuo(a)

inanimate [ɪn'ænɪmɪt] *adj* inanimado(a)

inappropriate [ɪnə'prəʊprɪɪt] *adj* inoportuno(a); *(behaviour)* poco apropiado(a)

inarticulate [ɪnɑː'tɪkjʊlɪt] *adj* *(cry, sound)* inarticulado(a); **to be i.** *(person)* expresarse mal

inasmuch as [ɪnəz'mʌtʃəz] *conj Fml* (a) *(since)* puesto que, ya que (b) *(insofar as)* en la medida en que

inattentive [ɪnə'tentɪv] *adj* desatento(a)

inaudible [ɪn'ɔːdəbəl] *adj* inaudible

inaugural [ɪn'ɔːgjʊrəl] *adj* inaugural

inaugurate [ɪn'ɔːgjʊreɪt] *vt* *(building)* inaugurar; *(president)* investir

inauguration [ɪnɔːgjʊ'reɪʃən] *n* *(of building)* inauguración *f*; *(of president)* investidura *f*

inauspicious [ɪnɔː'spɪʃəs] *adj* *(start)* poco prometedor(a); *(circumstances)* desfavorable

inborn ['ɪnbɔːn] *adj* innato(a)

in-box ['ɪnbɒks] *n* *(for e-mail)* buzón *m* de entrada

inbred ['ɪnbred] *adj* (a) *(quality)* innato(a) (b) *(family)* endogámico(a)

Inc, inc *US Com (abbr* **Incorporated)** ≃ S.A.

incalculable [ɪn'kælkjʊləbəl] *adj* incalculable

incapable [ɪn'keɪpəbəl] *adj* incapaz

incapacitate [ɪnkə'pæsɪteɪt] *vt Fml* incapacitar

incapacity [ɪnkə'pæsɪtɪ] *n* incapacidad *f*

incarcerate [ɪn'kɑːsəreɪt] *vt Fml* encarcelar

incarnation [ɪnkɑː'neɪʃən] *n* encarnación *f*

incendiary [ɪn'sendɪərɪ] **1** *adj* incendiario(a)
2 *n* bomba incendiaria

incense¹ ['ɪnsens] *n* incienso *m*

incense² [ɪn'sens] *vt* enfurecer, sacar de quicio

incentive [ɪn'sentɪv] *n* incentivo *m*

incessant [ɪn'sesənt] *adj* incesante; *(demands)* constante

incessantly [ɪn'sesəntlɪ] *adv* sin cesar

incest ['ɪnsest] *n* incesto *m*

inch [ɪntʃ] *n* pulgada *f* *(aprox 2,54 cm)*; *Fig* **i. by i.** poco a poco; *Fig* **she wouldn't give an i.** no quería ceder ni un ápice
▸ **inch forward** *vt sep & vi* avanzar poco a poco

incidence ['ɪnsɪdəns] *n* frecuencia *f*

incident ['ɪnsɪdənt] *n* incidente *m*

incidental [ɪnsɪ'dentəl] *adj* *(accessory)* incidental, accesorio(a); *(risk)* inherente (**to** a); **i. music** música *f* de fondo

incidentally [ɪnsɪ'dentəlɪ] *adv* a propósito

incinerator [ɪn'sɪnəreɪtə(r)] *n* incinerador *m*

incipient [ɪn'sɪpɪənt] *adj Fml* incipiente

incision [ɪn'sɪʒən] *n* incisión *f*

incisive [ɪn'saɪsɪv] *adj* *(comment)* incisivo(a); *(reply)* tajante; *(mind)* penetrante

incite [ɪn'saɪt] *vt* incitar; **to i. sb to do sth** incitar a algn a hacer algo

inclination [ɪnklɪ'neɪʃən] *n* inclinación *f*; **my i. is to stay** yo prefiero quedarme

incline [ɪn'klaɪn] **1** *vt* (a) **I'm inclined to believe him** me inclino a creerlo; **she's inclined to be aggressive** tiende a ser agresiva (b) *(head etc)* inclinar
2 *vi* *(slope)* inclinarse
3 *n* ['ɪnklaɪn] *(slope)* pendiente *f*

include [ɪn'kluːd] *vt* incluir (**in** en); *(in price)* comprender (**in** en); *(in list)* figurar (**in** en)

including [ɪn'kluːdɪŋ] *prep* incluso, inclusive

inclusion [ɪn'kluːʒən] *n* inclusión *f*

inclusive [ɪn'kluːsɪv] *adj* inclusivo(a); **pages 6 to 10 i.** de la página 6 a la 10, ambas inclusive; **the rent is i. of bills** el alquiler incluye las facturas

incognito [ɪnkɒg'niːtəʊ] *adv* de incógnito

incoherent [ɪnkəʊ'hɪərənt] *adj* incoherente

income ['ɪnkʌm] *n* ingresos *mpl*; *(from investment)* réditos *mpl*; **i. tax** impuesto *m* sobre la renta; **i. tax return** declaración *f* de la renta

incoming ['ɪnkʌmɪŋ] *adj* *(flight)* de llegada; *(president)* entrante; *(tide)* ascendente; *(mail)* recibido(a); *(phone call)* de fuera

incomparable [ɪn'kɒmpərəbəl] *adj* incomparable, sin par

incompatible [ɪnkəm'pætəbəl] *adj* incompatible (**with** con)

incompetence [ɪn'kɒmpɪtəns] *n* incompetencia *f*

incompetent [ɪn'kɒmpɪtənt] *adj* incompetente

incomplete [ɪnkəm'pli:t] *adj* incompleto(a)

incomprehensible [ɪnkɒmprɪ'hensəbəl] *adj* incomprensible

inconceivable [ɪnkən'si:vəbəl] *adj* inconcebible

inconclusive [ɪnkən'klu:sɪv] *adj* (*vote*) no decisivo(a); (*proof*) no concluyente

incongruous [ɪn'kɒŋgrʊəs] *adj* incongruente

inconsiderate [ɪnkən'sɪdərɪt] *adj* desconsiderado(a); **how i. of you!** ¡qué falta de consideración por tu parte!

inconsistency [ɪnkən'sɪstənsɪ] *n* inconsecuencia *f*; (*contradiction*) contradicción *f*

inconsistent [ɪnkən'sɪstənt] *adj* inconsecuente; (*contradictory*) contradictorio(a); **your evidence is i. with the facts** su testimonio no concuerda con los hechos

inconspicuous [ɪnkən'spɪkjʊəs] *adj* que pasa desapercibido(a); (*discreet*) discreto(a)

incontrovertible [ɪnkɒntrə'vɜ:təbəl] *adj Fml* incontrovertible

inconvenience [ɪnkən'vi:nɪəns] **1** *n* inconveniente *f*; (*annoyance*) molestia *f* **2** *vt* (*annoy*) molestar; (*cause difficulty to*) incomodar

inconvenient [ɪnkən'vi:nɪənt] *adj* molesto(a); (*time*) inoportuno(a); (*design*) poco práctico(a)

incorporate [ɪn'kɔ:pəreɪt] *vt* incorporar (**in** *or* **into** a); (*include*) incluir; (*contain*) contener

incorporated [ɪn'kɔ:pəreɪtɪd] *adj US Com* **i. company** sociedad anónima

incorrect [ɪnkə'rekt] *adj* incorrecto(a)

incorrigible [ɪn'kɒrɪdʒəbəl] *adj* incorregible

increase 1 *n* ['ɪnkri:s] aumento *m*; (*in number*) incremento *m*; (*in price etc*) subida *f* **2** *vt* [ɪn'kri:s] aumentar; (*price etc*) subir **3** *vi* aumentar

increasing [ɪn'kri:sɪŋ] *adj* creciente

increasingly [ɪn'kri:sɪŋlɪ] *adv* cada vez más

incredible [ɪn'kredəbəl] *adj* increíble

incredulous [ɪn'kredjʊləs] *adj* incrédulo(a)

increment ['ɪnkrɪmənt] *n* incremento *m*

incriminate [ɪn'krɪmɪneɪt] *vt* incriminar

incriminating [ɪn'krɪmɪneɪtɪŋ] *adj* incriminatorio(a)

incubation [ɪnkjʊ'beɪʃən] *n* incubación *f*

incubator ['ɪnkjʊbeɪtə(r)] *n* incubadora *f*

incumbent [ɪn'kʌmbənt] **1** *n* titular *mf* **2** *adj Fml* **to be i. on sb to do sth** ser la obligación de algn hacer algo

incur [ɪn'kɜ:(r)] *vt* (*blame*) incurrir en; (*risk*) correr; (*debt*) contraer; (*loss*) sufrir

incurable [ɪn'kjʊərəbəl] *adj* incurable

indebted [ɪn'detɪd] *adj* endeudado(a); *Fig* (*grateful*) agradecido(a); *Fig* **to be i. to sb** estar en deuda con algn

indecent [ɪn'di:sənt] *adj* indecente; **i. assault** atentado *m* contra el pudor; **i. exposure** exhibicionismo *m*

indecision [ɪndɪ'sɪʒən] *n* indecisión *f*

indecisive [ɪndɪ'saɪsɪv] *adj* (*person*) indeciso(a); (*evidence*) poco concluyente; (*victory*) no decisivo(a)

indeed [ɪn'di:d] *adv* (**a**) *Fml* (*in fact*) efectivamente, en realidad (**b**) **I'm very sorry i.** lo siento de veras; **it's very hard i.** es verdaderamente difícil; **thank you very much i.** muchísimas gracias

indefinite [ɪn'defɪnɪt] *adj* indefinido(a)

indefinitely [ɪn'defɪnɪtlɪ] *adv* indefinidamente

indelible [ɪn'deləbəl] *adj* indeleble

indemnify [ɪn'demnɪfaɪ] *vt* indemnizar (**for** por)

indemnity [ɪn'demnɪtɪ] *n* (**a**) (*insurance*) indemnidad *f* (**b**) (*compensation*) indemnización *f*

indentation [ɪnden'teɪʃən] *n* (**a**) *Typ* sangría *f* (**b**) (*of edge*) muesca *f*; (*of surface*) depresión *f*

independence [ɪndɪ'pendəns] *n* independencia *f*; *US* **I. Day** Día *m* de la Independencia (*4 julio*)

independent [ɪndɪ'pendənt] *adj* independiente; *Br* **i. school** colegio *m* privado; **to become i.** independizarse

in-depth ['ɪndepθ] *adj* minucioso(a), exhaustivo(a)

indescribable [ɪndɪs'kraɪbəbəl] *adj* (*pain, beauty*) indescriptible

indestructible [ɪndɪ'strʌktəbəl] *adj* indestructible

indeterminate [ɪndɪ'tɜ:mɪnɪt] *adj* indeterminado(a)

index ['ɪndeks] **1** *n* (*pl* **indexes** *or* **indices**) (**a**) (*in book*) índice *m*; (*in library*) catálogo *m*; **i. card** ficha *f* (**b**) *Math* exponente

m; *Econ* índice *m* (**c**) **i. finger** dedo *m* índice
  2 *vt* catalogar

index-linked ['ɪndeks'lɪŋkt] *adj* sujeto(a) al aumento de la inflación

India ['ɪndɪə] *n* (la) India

Indian ['ɪndɪən] *adj & n* (*of America*) indio(a) (*m,f*), *Am* indígena (*mf*); (*of India*) indio(a), hindú (*mf*); **I. Ocean** Océano Índico; **I. summer** veranillo *m* de San Martín

indicate ['ɪndɪkeɪt] **1** *vt* indicar
  2 *vi BrAut* poner el intermitente

indication [ɪndɪ'keɪʃən] *n* indicio *m*

indicative [ɪn'dɪkətɪv] **1** *adj* indicativo(a)
  2 *n Gram* indicativo *m*

indicator ['ɪndɪkeɪtə(r)] *n* indicador *m*; *Br Aut* intermitente *m*

indices ['ɪndɪsi:z] *pl of* **index**

indict [ɪn'daɪt] *vt* acusar (**for** de)

indictment [ɪn'daɪtmənt] *n Jur* acusación *f*; *Fig* **a damning i. of his books** una crítica feroz de sus libros

indifference [ɪn'dɪfərəns] *n* indiferencia *f*

indifferent [ɪn'dɪfərənt] *adj* (**a**) (*uninterested*) indiferente (**b**) (*mediocre*) regular

indigenous [ɪn'dɪdʒɪnəs] *adj* indígena

indigestion [ɪndɪ'dʒestʃən] *n* indigestión *f*; **to suffer from i.** tener un empacho

indignant [ɪn'dɪgnənt] *adj* indignado(a); (*look*) de indignación; **to get i. about sth** indignarse por algo

indignity [ɪn'dɪgnɪtɪ] *n* indignidad *f*

indigo ['ɪndɪgəʊ] **1** *n* añil *m*
  2 *adj* (de color) añil

indirect [ɪndɪ'rekt, ɪndaɪ'rekt] *adj* indirecto(a)

indiscreet [ɪndɪ'skri:t] *adj* indiscreto(a)

indiscretion [ɪndɪ'skreʃən] *n* indiscreción *f*

indiscriminate [ɪndɪs'krɪmɪnɪt] *adj* indiscriminado(a)

indispensable [ɪndɪ'spensəbəl] *adj* indispensable, imprescindible

indisposed [ɪndɪ'spəʊzd] *adj Fml* indispuesto(a)

indisputable [ɪndɪ'spju:təbəl] *adj* indiscutible, incontestable

indistinct [ɪndɪ'stɪŋkt] *adj* indistinto(a); (*memory*) confuso(a), vago(a); (*shape etc*) borroso(a)

indistinguishable [ɪndɪ'stɪŋgwɪʃəbəl] *adj* indistinguible

individual [ɪndɪ'vɪdjʊəl] **1** *adj* (**a**) (*separate*) individual; (*for one*) particular; (*personal*) personal (**b**) (*characteristic*) particular; (*original*) original

  2 *n* (*person*) individuo *m*; **private i.** particular *m*

individualist [ɪndɪ'vɪdjʊəlɪst] *n* individualista *mf*

indoctrinate [ɪn'dɒktrɪneɪt] *vt* adoctrinar

indoctrination [ɪndɒktrɪ'neɪʃən] *n* adoctrinamiento *m*

indolent ['ɪndələnt] *adj Fml* indolente

Indonesia [ɪndəʊ'ni:zɪə] *n* Indonesia

Indonesian [ɪndəʊ'ni:zɪən] **1** *adj* indonesio(a)
  2 *n* (**a**) (*person*) indonesio(a) *m,f* (**b**) (*language*) indonesio *m*

indoor ['ɪndɔ:(r)] *adj* (*plant*) de interior; **i. football** fútbol *m* sala; **i. pool** piscina cubierta

indoors [ɪn'dɔ:z] *adv* (*inside*) dentro (de casa); (*at home*) en casa; **let's go i.** vamos adentro

induce [ɪn'dju:s] *vt* (**a**) (*persuade*) inducir, persuadir (**b**) (*cause*) producir; *Med* (*labour*) provocar

inducement [ɪn'dju:smənt] *n* incentivo *m*, aliciente *m*

induction [ɪn'dʌkʃən] *n* (**a**) *Med* (*of labour*) inducción *f* (**b**) (*into new job, group*) iniciación *f* (**c**) *Elec* inducción *f*

indulge [ɪn'dʌldʒ] **1** *vt* (**a**) (*child*) consentir; (*person*) complacer; **to i. oneself** darse gusto (**b**) (*whim*) ceder a, satisfacer
  2 *vi* darse el gusto (**in** de)

indulgence [ɪn'dʌldʒəns] *n* (**a**) (*of child*) mimo *m*; (*of attitude*) indulgencia *f* (**b**) (*of whim*) satisfacción *f*

indulgent [ɪn'dʌldʒənt] *adj* indulgente

industrial [ɪn'dʌstrɪəl] *adj* industrial; **to take i. action** declararse en huelga; *Br* **i. estate**, *US* **i. park** polígono *m* industrial

industrialist [ɪn'dʌstrɪəlɪst] *n* industrial *mf*

industrialize [ɪn'dʌstrɪəlaɪz] *vt* industrializar; **to become industrialized** industrializarse

industrious [ɪn'dʌstrɪəs] *adj* trabajador(a)

industry ['ɪndəstrɪ] *n* (**a**) (*economic*) industria *f* (**b**) (*hard work*) aplicación *f*

inebriated [ɪn'i:brɪeɪtɪd] *adj* embriagado(a)

inedible [ɪn'edəbəl] *adj* incomible

ineffective [ɪnɪ'fektɪv] *adj* ineficaz

ineffectual [ɪnɪ'fektʃʊəl] *adj* (*aim, protest*) ineficaz; (*person*) incompetente

inefficiency [ɪnɪ'fɪʃənsɪ] *n* ineficacia *f*; (*of person*) incompetencia *f*

inefficient [ɪnɪ'fɪʃənt] *adj* ineficaz; *(person)* inepto(a)

ineligible [ɪn'elɪdʒəbəl] *adj* no apto(a) (**for** para)

inept [ɪn'ept] *adj (person)* inepto(a); *(remark)* estúpido(a)

inequality [ɪnɪ'kwɒlɪtɪ] *n* desigualdad *f*

inert [ɪn'ɜːt] *adj* inerte

inertia [ɪn'ɜːʃə] *n* inercia *f*

inescapable [ɪnɪ'skeɪpəbəl] *adj* ineludible

inevitability [ɪnevɪtə'bɪlɪtɪ] *n* inevitabilidad *f*

inevitable [ɪn'evɪtəbəl] *adj* inevitable

inexcusable [ɪnɪk'skjuːzəbəl] *adj* inexcusable, imperdonable

inexhaustible [ɪnɪg'zɔːstəbəl] *adj* inagotable

inexorable [ɪn'eksərəbəl] *adj Fml* inexorable

inexpensive [ɪnɪk'spensɪv] *adj* económico(a)

inexperience [ɪnɪk'spɪərɪəns] *n* inexperiencia *f*

inexperienced [ɪnɪk'spɪərɪənst] *adj* inexperto(a)

inexplicable [ɪnɪk'splɪkəbəl] *adj* inexplicable

infallible [ɪn'fæləbəl] *adj* infalible

infamous ['ɪnfəməs] *adj* infame

infancy ['ɪnfənsɪ] *n* infancia *f*

infant ['ɪnfənt] *n* niño(a) *m,f*; *Br* **i. school** parvulario *m*

infantile ['ɪnfəntaɪl] *adj* infantil

infantry ['ɪnfəntrɪ] *n* infantería *f*

infatuated [ɪn'fætjʊeɪtɪd] *adj* encaprichado(a)

infatuation [ɪnfætjʊ'eɪʃən] *n* encaprichamiento *m*

infect [ɪn'fekt] *vt (cut)* infectar; *(water)* contaminar; *(person)* contagiar

infection [ɪn'fekʃən] *n (of cut)* infección *f*; *(of water)* contaminación *f*; *(with illness)* contagio *m*

infectious [ɪn'fekʃəs] *adj (disease)* infeccioso(a); *Fig* contagioso(a)

infer [ɪn'fɜː(r)] *vt* inferir (**from** de)

inference ['ɪnfərəns] *n* inferencia *f*

inferior [ɪn'fɪərɪə(r)] **1** *adj* inferior (**to** a) **2** *n Pej* inferior *mf*

inferiority [ɪnfɪərɪ'ɒrɪtɪ] *n* inferioridad *f*

inferno [ɪn'fɜːnəʊ] *n Literary* infierno *m*; *Fig* **the house was a raging i.** la casa ardía en llamas

infertile [ɪn'fɜːtaɪl] *adj* estéril

infertility [ɪnfə'tɪlɪtɪ] *n* esterilidad *f*

infest [ɪn'fest] *vt* infestar, plagar (**with** de)

infidelity [ɪnfɪ'delɪtɪ] *n* infidelidad *f*

infighting ['ɪnfaɪtɪŋ] *n Fig* luchas internas

infiltrate ['ɪnfɪltreɪt] *vt* infiltrarse (**into** en)

infinite ['ɪnfɪnɪt] *adj* infinito(a)

infinitive [ɪn'fɪnɪtɪv] *n* infinitivo *m*

infinity [ɪn'fɪnɪtɪ] *n* infinidad *f*; *Math* infinito *m*

infirm [ɪn'fɜːm] **1** *adj (ailing)* enfermizo(a); *(weak)* débil **2** *npl* **the i.** los inválidos

infirmary [ɪn'fɜːmərɪ] *n* hospital *m*

infirmity [ɪn'fɜːmɪtɪ] *n Fml (ailment)* enfermedad *f*; *(weakness)* debilidad *f*

inflame [ɪn'fleɪm] *vt (passion)* encender; *(curiosity)* avivar; *(crowd)* enardecer

inflamed [ɪn'fleɪmd] *adj* inflamado(a); **to become i.** inflamarse

inflammable [ɪn'flæməbəl] *adj (material)* inflamable; *Fig (situation)* explosivo(a)

inflammation [ɪnflə'meɪʃən] *n* inflamación *f*

inflatable [ɪn'fleɪtəbəl] *adj* inflable

inflate [ɪn'fleɪt] **1** *vt* inflar **2** *vi* inflarse

inflated [ɪn'fleɪtɪd] *adj* (**a**) *Fig (prices)* inflacionista (**b**) *Pej (view, idea)* exagerado(a)

inflation [ɪn'fleɪʃən] *n* inflación *f*

inflexible [ɪn'fleksəbəl] *adj* inflexible

inflict [ɪn'flɪkt] *vt (blow)* asestar (**on** a); *(damage)* causar (**on** a); *(defeat)* infligir (**on** a)

in-flight ['ɪnflaɪt] *adj* durante el vuelo

influence ['ɪnflʊəns] **1** *n* influencia *f*; *Fam* **to be under the i.** llevar una copa de más **2** *vt* influir en

influential [ɪnflʊ'enʃəl] *adj* influyente

influenza [ɪnflʊ'enzə] *n* gripe *f*

influx ['ɪnflʌks] *n* afluencia *f*

info ['ɪnfəʊ] *n Fam* información *f*

inform [ɪn'fɔːm] **1** *vt* informar *or CAm, Méx* reportar (**of/about** de/sobre); *(police)* avisar (**of/about** de) **2** *vi* **to i. against** *or* **on** denunciar

informal [ɪn'fɔːməl] *adj* (**a**) *(occasion, behaviour)* informal; *(language, treatment)* familiar (**b**) *(unofficial)* no oficial

informality [ɪnfɔː'mælɪtɪ] *n (of occasion, behaviour)* sencillez *f*; *(of treatment)* familiaridad *f*

informant [ɪn'fɔːmənt] *n* informante *mf*

information [ɪnfə'meɪʃən] *n* (**a**) *(news, facts)* información *f*; *(details)* detalles *mpl*; *(knowledge)* conocimientos *mpl*; **a piece of i.** un dato; **i. bureau** centro *m* de información; **i. (super)highway** autopista f de la información; **i. technology** informática f (**b**) US Tel información f, Am informaciones fpl

informative [ɪnˈfɔːmətɪv] adj informativo(a)

informed [ɪnˈfɔːmd] adj enterado(a); **keep me i.** téngame al corriente

informer [ɪnˈfɔːmə(r)] n delator(a) m,f; (to the police) soplón(ona) m,f

infrared [ɪnfrəˈred] adj infrarrojo(a)

infrastructure [ˈɪnfrəstrʌktʃə(r)] n infraestructura f

infrequent [ɪnˈfriːkwənt] adj infrecuente

infringe [ɪnˈfrɪndʒ] **1** vt (law, rule) infringir; (copyright) no respetar
2 vi **to i. on** or **upon** (rights) violar; (privacy) invadir

infringement [ɪnˈfrɪndʒmənt] n (of law, rule) infracción f; (of rights) violación f

infuriate [ɪnˈfjʊərɪeɪt] vt poner furioso(a)

infuriating [ɪnˈfjʊərɪeɪtɪŋ] adj exasperante

infusion [ɪnˈfjuːʒən] n infusión f

ingenious [ɪnˈdʒiːnɪəs] adj ingenioso(a)

ingenuity [ɪndʒɪˈnjuːɪt] n ingenio m

ingenuous [ɪnˈdʒenjʊəs] adj ingenuo(a)

ingot [ˈɪŋgət] n lingote m

ingrained [ɪnˈgreɪnd] adj Fig arraigado(a)

ingratiate [ɪnˈgreɪʃɪeɪt] vt **to i. oneself with sb** congraciarse con algn

ingratiating [ɪnˈgreɪʃɪeɪtɪŋ] adj zalamero(a)

ingratitude [ɪnˈgrætɪtjuːd] n ingratitud f

ingredient [ɪnˈgriːdɪənt] n ingrediente m

inhabit [ɪnˈhæbɪt] vt vivir en, ocupar

inhabitable [ɪnˈhæbɪtəbəl] adj habitable

> *Note that the Spanish word **inhabitable** is a false friend and is never a translation for the English word **inhabitable**. In Spanish, **inhabitable** means "uninhabitable".*

inhabitant [ɪnˈhæbɪtənt] n habitante mf

inhale [ɪnˈheɪl] **1** vt (gas) inhalar; (air) aspirar
2 vi aspirar; (smoker) tragar el humo

inherent [ɪnˈhɪərənt] adj inherente

inherit [ɪnˈherɪt] vt heredar (**from** de)

inheritance [ɪnˈherɪtəns] n herencia f

inhibit [ɪnˈhɪbɪt] vt limitar; (person) cohibir; **to i. sb from doing sth** impedir a algn hacer algo

inhibited [ɪnˈhɪbɪtɪd] adj cohibido(a)

inhibition [ɪnhɪˈbɪʃən] n cohibición f

inhospitable [ɪnhɒˈspɪtəbəl] adj inhospitalario(a); (climate, place) inhóspito(a)

inhuman [ɪnˈhjuːmən] adj inhumano(a)

inhumane [ɪnhjuːˈmeɪn] adj inhumano(a)

iniquity [ɪˈnɪkwɪt] n Fml iniquidad f

initial [ɪˈnɪʃəl] **1** adj inicial, primero(a)
2 n inicial f; **initials** iniciales fpl
3 vt (pt & pp **initialled,** US **initialed**) firmar con las iniciales

initially [ɪˈnɪʃəlɪ] adv al principio

initiate [ɪˈnɪʃɪeɪt] vt (**a**) Fml (begin) iniciar; (legal proceedings) emprender (**b**) (into secret society) admitir (**into** en)

initiation [ɪnɪʃɪˈeɪʃən] n (**a**) (start) principio m (**b**) (admission) iniciación f

initiative [ɪˈnɪʃətɪv] n iniciativa f

inject [ɪnˈdʒekt] vt (**a**) (drug etc) inyectar (**b**) Fig (capital) invertir; (life, hope) infundir

injection [ɪnˈdʒekʃən] n inyección f; **to give sb an i.** poner una inyección a algn

injunction [ɪnˈdʒʌŋkʃən] n interdicto m

injure [ˈɪndʒə(r)] vt herir; **to i. oneself** hacerse daño; Fig (health, reputation) perjudicar

injured [ˈɪndʒəd] **1** adj herido(a); Fig (look, tone) ofendido(a)
2 npl **the i.** los heridos

injury [ˈɪndʒərɪ] n (hurt) herida f; Fig (harm) daño m; Sport **i. time** (tiempo m de) descuento m

injustice [ɪnˈdʒʌstɪs] n injusticia f

ink [ɪŋk] n tinta f; **invisible i.** tinta simpática

inkjet printer [ˈɪŋkdʒetˈprɪntə(r)] n Comput impresora f de chorro de tinta

inkling [ˈɪŋklɪŋ] n (idea) idea f; (suspicion) sospecha f; (sign) señal f

inkwell [ˈɪŋkwel] n tintero m

inlaid [ɪnˈleɪd] adj (wood) taraceado(a); (ivory, gems) incrustado(a)

inland 1 adj [ˈɪnlənd] (del) interior; Br **I. Revenue** ≃ Hacienda f
2 adv [ɪnˈlænd] (travel) tierra adentro

in-laws [ˈɪnlɔːz] npl Fam familia f política

inlet [ˈɪnlet] n (**a**) (in coastline) ensenada f, cala f (**b**) (in pipe, machine) entrada f, admisión f

inline [ˈɪnlaɪn] adj **i. skates** patines mpl en línea

inmate [ˈɪnmeɪt] n (of prison) preso(a) m,f; (of hospital) enfermo(a) m,f; (of asylum, camp) internado(a) m,f

inn [ɪn] n (with lodging) posada f, mesón m

innate [ɪ'neɪt] *adj* innato(a)

inner ['ɪnə(r)] *adj* (**a**) *(region)* interior; *(structure)* interno(a); **i. city** zona urbana desfavorecida; **i. tube** cámara *f* de aire (**b**) *Fig (thoughts)* íntimo(a); *(peace etc)* interior

innermost ['ɪnəməʊst] *adj (room)* más interior; *Fig (thoughts)* más íntimo(a)

innings ['ɪnɪŋz] *npl (in cricket)* turno *m* para batear, *Am* inning *m*

innocence ['ɪnəsəns] *n* inocencia *f*

innocent ['ɪnəsənt] *adj & n* inocente *(mf)*

innocuous [ɪ'nɒkjʊəs] *adj* inocuo(a)

innovation [ɪnə'veɪʃən] *n* novedad *f*

innuendo [ɪnjʊ'endəʊ] *n* indirecta *f*

innumerable [ɪ'njuːmərəbəl] *adj* innumerable

inoculate [ɪ'nɒkjʊleɪt] *vt* inocular

inoculation [ɪnɒkjʊ'leɪʃən] *n* inoculación *f*

inoffensive [ɪnə'fensɪv] *adj* inofensivo(a)

inopportune [ɪn'ɒpətjuːn, ɪnɒpə'tjuːn] *adj* inoportuno(a)

inordinate [ɪ'nɔːdɪnɪt] *adj* desmesurado(a)

inpatient ['ɪnpeɪʃənt] *n* interno(a) *m,f*

input ['ɪnpʊt] *n (of resources)* inversión *f*; *(of power)* entrada *f*; *Comput (of data)* input *m*, entrada

inquest ['ɪnkwest] *n* investigación *f* judicial

inquire [ɪn'kwaɪə(r)] **1** *vt* preguntar; *(find out)* averiguar

    2 *vi* preguntar (**about** por); *(find out)* informarse (**about** de)

▸ **inquire after** *vt insep* preguntar por

▸ **inquire into** *vt insep* investigar, indagar

inquiry [ɪn'kwaɪərɪ] *n* (**a**) *(request for information)* consulta *f*; **inquiries** *(sign)* información (**b**) *(investigation)* investigación *f* (oficial)

inquisitive [ɪn'kwɪzɪtɪv] *adj (curious)* curioso(a); *(questioning)* preguntón(ona)

inroads ['ɪnrəʊdz] *npl* the firm is making **i. into the market** la empresa está ganando terreno en el mercado; **to make i. into one's capital** reducir su capital

insane [ɪn'seɪn] *adj* loco(a); *(act)* insensato(a); *Fig* **to drive sb i.** volver loco(a) a algn

insanity [ɪn'sænɪtɪ] *n* demencia *f*, locura *f*

insatiable [ɪn'seɪʃəbəl] *adj* insaciable

inscribe [ɪn'skraɪb] *vt Fml* inscribir; *(book)* dedicar

inscription [ɪn'skrɪpʃən] *n* (*on stone, coin*) inscripción *f*; *(in book, on photo)* dedicatoria *f*

inscrutable [ɪn'skruːtəbəl] *adj* inescrutable, insondable

insect ['ɪnsekt] *n* insecto *m*; **i. bite** picadura *f*

insecticide [ɪn'sektɪsaɪd] *n* insecticida *m*

insecure [ɪnsɪ'kjʊə(r)] *adj* inseguro(a)

insecurity [ɪnsɪ'kjʊərɪtɪ] *n* inseguridad *f*

insemination [ɪnsemɪ'neɪʃən] *n* inseminación *f*

insensible [ɪn'sensəbəl] *adj Fml* inconsciente

insensitive [ɪn'sensɪtɪv] *adj* insensible

inseparable [ɪn'sepərəbəl] *adj* inseparable

insert 1 ['ɪnsɜːt] encarte *m*

    2 *vt* [ɪn'sɜːt] introducir

insertion [ɪn'sɜːʃən] *n* introducción *f*; *(of clause, text)* inserción *f*

inshore 1 *adj* ['ɪnʃɔː(r)] *(fishing)* de bajura

    2 *adv* [ɪn'ʃɔː(r)] cerca de la costa

inside [ɪn'saɪd] **1** *n* (**a**) *(of house)* interior *m*; **on the i.** por dentro; **to turn sth i. out** volver algo al revés (**b**) *Fam* **insides** tripas *fpl*

    2 *adj* ['ɪnsaɪd] interior; *Aut* **i. lane** carril *m* interior

    3 *adv (be)* dentro, adentro; *(run etc)* (hacia) adentro; **to come i.** entrar

    4 *prep* (**a**) *(place)* dentro de (**b**) *Fam* **i. (of)** *(time)* en menos de

insider [ɪn'saɪdə(r)] *n* **i. dealing** = uso indebido de información privilegiada y confidencial para operaciones comerciales

insidious [ɪn'sɪdɪəs] *adj* insidioso(a)

insight ['ɪnsaɪt] *n* perspicacia *f*

insignia [ɪn'sɪgnɪə] *n inv* insignia *f*

insignificant [ɪnsɪg'nɪfɪkənt] *adj* insignificante

insincere [ɪnsɪn'sɪə(r)] *adj* poco sincero(a)

insinuate [ɪn'sɪnjʊeɪt] *vt* insinuar

insipid [ɪn'sɪpɪd] *adj* soso(a), insulso(a)

insist [ɪn'sɪst] **1** *vi* insistir (**on** en); *(argue)* obstinarse (**on** en)

    2 *vt* **to i. that …** insistir en que …

insistence [ɪn'sɪstəns] *n* insistencia *f*

insistent [ɪn'sɪstənt] *adj* insistente

insofar as [ɪnsəʊ'fɑːræz] *adv* en tanto que

insole ['ɪnsəʊl] *n (of shoe)* plantilla *f*

insolent ['ɪnsələnt] *adj* insolente

insoluble [ɪn'sɒljʊbəl] *adj* insoluble

insolvent [ɪn'sɒlvənt] *adj Fin* insolvente

insomnia [ɪn'sɒmnɪə] *n* insomnio *m*

insomniac [ɪn'sɒmnɪæk] *n* insomne *mf*

inspect [ɪn'spekt] *vt* inspeccionar, examinar; *(troops)* pasar revista a

inspection [ɪn'spekʃən] n inspección f; (of troops) revista f

inspector [ɪn'spektə(r)] n inspector(a) m,f; Br (on bus, train) revisor(a) m,f

inspiration [ɪnspɪ'reɪʃən] n inspiración f; **to get i. from sth/sb** inspirarse en algo/algn

inspire [ɪn'spaɪə(r)] vt inspirar; **to i. respect in sb** infundir respeto a algn; **to i. sb to do sth** animar a algn a hacer algo

inspired [ɪn'spaɪəd] adj inspirado(a)

instability [ɪnstə'bɪlɪtɪ] n inestabilidad f

install, US **instal** [ɪn'stɔːl] vt instalar

installation [ɪnstə'leɪʃən] n instalación f

instalment, US **installment** [ɪn'stɔːl- mənt] n (a) (of payment) plazo m; **to pay by instalments** pagar a plazos; US **i. plan** venta f/compra f a plazos (b) (of novel, programme) entrega f; (of journal) fascículo m

instance ['ɪnstəns] n caso m, ejemplo m; **for i.** por ejemplo; **in the first i.** en primer lugar

> *𝒥* Note that the Spanish word **instancia** is a false friend and is never a translation for the English word **instance**. In Spanish **instancia** means "request".

instant ['ɪnstənt] **1** n (moment) instante m, momento m; **in an i.** en un instante **2** adj inmediato(a); (coffee, meal) instantáneo(a); **i. messaging** mensajería f instantánea

instantaneous [ɪnstən'teɪnɪəs] adj in-stantáneo(a)

instantly ['ɪnstəntlɪ] adv inmediatamen-te

instead [ɪn'sted] **1** adv en cambio **2** prep **i. of** en vez de, en lugar de

instep ['ɪnstep] n empeine m

instigate ['ɪnstɪgeɪt] vt (strike, violence) instigar; (inquiry, changes) iniciar

instigation [ɪnstɪ'geɪʃən] n instigación f

instil, US **instill** [ɪn'stɪl] vt (idea, habit) inculcar (**in** a or en); (courage, respect) infundir (**in** a)

instinct ['ɪnstɪŋkt] n instinto m

instinctive [ɪn'stɪŋktɪv] adj instintivo(a)

institute ['ɪnstɪtjuːt] **1** n instituto m; (centre) centro m; (professional body) colegio m **2** vt Fml (a) (system) establecer (b) (start) iniciar; (proceedings) entablar

institution [ɪnstɪ'tjuːʃən] n (a) (organization) institución f (b) (home) asilo m; (asylum) manicomio m

instruct [ɪn'strʌkt] vt instruir; (order) mandar; **I am instructed to say that ...** me han encargado decir que ...

instruction [ɪn'strʌkʃən] n (a) (training) instrucción f (b) **instructions** instruc-ciones fpl; **instructions for use** modo de empleo

instructive [ɪn'strʌktɪv] adj instruc-tivo(a)

instructor [ɪn'strʌktə(r)] n instructor(a) m,f; (of driving) profesor(a) m,f

instrument ['ɪnstrəmənt] n instrumento m; **i. panel** tablero m de mandos

instrumental [ɪnstrə'mentəl] adj (a) Mus instrumental (b) **to be i. in sth** contribuir decisivamente a algo

insubordinate [ɪnsə'bɔːdɪnɪt] adj insubordinado(a)

insubstantial [ɪnsəb'stænʃəl] adj insubstancial; (structure) poco sólido(a)

insufferable [ɪn'sʌfərəbəl] adj insopor-table

insufficient [ɪnsə'fɪʃənt] adj insuficiente

insular ['ɪnsjʊlə(r)] adj (a) Geog insular (b) Fig Pej estrecho(a) de miras

insulate ['ɪnsjʊleɪt] vt aislar (**against** or **from** de)

insulating tape ['ɪnsjʊleɪtɪŋteɪp] n Br cinta f aislante

insulation [ɪnsjʊ'leɪʃən] n aislamiento m

insulin ['ɪnsjʊlɪn] n insulina f

insult 1 n. ['ɪnsʌlt] (words) insulto m; (action) afrenta f, ofensa f **2** vt [ɪn'sʌlt] insultar, ofender

insulting [ɪn'sʌltɪŋ] adj insultante, ofensivo(a)

insuperable [ɪn'suːpərəbəl] adj insu-perable

insurance [ɪn'ʃʊərəns] n seguro m; **fire i.** seguro contra incendios; **i. broker** agente mf de seguros; **i. company** compañía f de seguros; **i. policy** póliza f (de seguros); **private health i.** seguro médico privado

insure [ɪn'ʃʊə(r)] vt asegurar (**against** contra)

insurgent [ɪn'sɜːdʒənt] adj & n insur-recto(a) (m,f)

insurmountable [ɪnsə'maʊntəbəl] adj (problem etc) insuperable; (barrier) infranqueable

intact [ɪn'tækt] adj intacto(a)

intake ['ɪnteɪk] n (a) (of air, water) entrada f; (of electricity etc) toma f (b) (of food, calories) consumo m (c) (of students, recruits) número m de admitidos

integral ['ɪntɪgrəl] **1** adj (**a**) (intrinsic) integrante (**b**) (whole) íntegro(a) (**c**) Math integral
  2 n Math integral f

integrate ['ɪntɪgreɪt] **1** vt integrar
  2 vi integrarse

integration [ɪntɪ'greɪʃən] n integración f

integrity [ɪn'tegrɪtɪ] n integridad f, honradez f

intellect ['ɪntɪlekt] n intelecto m

intellectual [ɪntɪ'lektʃʊəl] adj & n intelectual (mf)

intelligence [ɪn'telɪdʒəns] n (**a**) (faculty) inteligencia f (**b**) (information) información f

intelligent [ɪn'telɪdʒənt] adj inteligente

intelligentsia [ɪntelɪ'dʒentsɪə] n intelectualidad f

intelligible [ɪn'telɪdʒəbəl] adj inteligible

intend [ɪn'tend] vt (**a**) (mean) tener la intención de (**b**) **to i. sth for sb** destinar algo a algn

intended [ɪn'tendɪd] adj (planned) previsto(a)

intense [ɪn'tens] adj intenso(a); (person) muy serio(a)

intensely [ɪn'tenslɪ] adv (extremely) enormemente, sumamente

intensify [ɪn'tensɪfaɪ] vt (search) intensificar; (effort) redoblar; (production, pollution) aumentar

intensity [ɪn'tensɪtɪ] n intensidad f

intensive [ɪn'tensɪv] adj intensivo(a); Med **i. care unit** unidad f de vigilancia intensiva

intent [ɪn'tent] **1** adj (absorbed) absorto(a); (gaze etc) atento(a); **to be i. on doing sth** estar resuelto(a) a hacer algo
  2 n Fml intención f, propósito m; **to all intents and purposes** a todos los efectos

intention [ɪn'tenʃən] n intención f

intentional [ɪn'tenʃənəl] adj deliberado(a)

intentionally [ɪn'tenʃənəlɪ] adv a propósito

interact [ɪntər'ækt] vi (people) interrelacionarse

interaction [ɪntər'ækʃən] n interacción f

interactive [ɪntər'æktɪv] adj interactivo(a)

intercede [ɪntə'siːd] vi interceder (**with** ante)

intercept [ɪntə'sept] vt interceptar

interchange 1 n ['ɪntətʃeɪndʒ] (**a**) (exchange) intercambio m (**b**) (on motorway) cruce m
  2 vt [ɪntə'tʃeɪndʒ] intercambiar (**with** con)

interchangeable [ɪntə'tʃeɪndʒəbəl] adj intercambiable

intercity [ɪntə'sɪtɪ] n Rail Esp intercity m, Am interurbano m

intercom ['ɪntəkɒm] n portero automático

intercontinental [ɪntəkɒntɪ'nentəl] adj **i. ballistic missile** misil balístico intercontinental

intercourse ['ɪntəkɔːs] n (**a**) (dealings) trato m (**b**) (sexual) relaciones fpl sexuales

interest ['ɪntrɪst] **1** n (**a**) (curiosity) interés m; (hobby) afición f (**b**) (benefit) **in the i. of** en pro de (**c**) (financial stake) participación f (**d**) Fin interés m; **i. rate** tipo m de interés
  2 vt interesar; **he's interested in politics** le interesa la política

interesting ['ɪntrɪstɪŋ] adj interesante

interface ['ɪntəfeɪs] n Comput interface f

interfere [ɪntə'fɪə(r)] vi (**a**) (meddle) entrometerse (**in** en); **to i. with** (hinder) dificultar; (spoil) estropear; (prevent) impedir (**b**) Rad & TV interferir (**with** con)

interference [ɪntə'fɪərəns] n (meddling) intromisión f; (hindrance) estorbo m; Rad & TV interferencia f

interim ['ɪntərɪm] **1** n Fml **in the i.** en el ínterin
  2 adj interino(a), provisional

interior [ɪn'tɪərɪə(r)] **1** adj interior
  2 n interior m; **i. design** diseño m de interiores

interlock [ɪntə'lɒk] vi encajarse; (fingers) entrelazarse; (cogs) engranarse

interloper ['ɪntələʊpə(r)] n intruso(a) m,f

interlude ['ɪntəluːd] n (break) intervalo m; Cin & Th intermedio m; Mus interludio m

intermediary [ɪntə'miːdɪərɪ] n intermediario(a) m,f

intermediate [ɪntə'miːdɪt] adj intermedio(a)

interminable [ɪn'tɜːmɪnəbəl] adj interminable

intermission [ɪntə'mɪʃən] n Cin & Th intermedio m

intermittent [ɪntə'mɪtənt] adj intermitente

intern 1 vt [ɪn'tɜːn] recluir
  2 n ['ɪntɜːn] (**a**) US Med médico(a) m,f interno(a) residente (**b**) Com (on work placement) becario(a) m,f

internal [ɪn'tɜːnəl] adj interior; (dispute, injury) interno(a); US **I. Revenue Service** ≃ Hacienda f

internally [ɪn'tɜːnəlɪ] *adv* interiormente; **not to be taken i.** *(on medicine)* uso externo

international [ɪntə'næʃənəl] **1** *adj* internacional
2 *n Sport (player)* internacional *mf*; *(match)* partido *m* internacional

Internet ['ɪntənet] *n Comput* **the I.** Internet *f*; **it's on the I.** está en Internet; **I. access provider** proveedor *m* de acceso a Internet; **I. service provider** proveedor *m* de (acceso a) Internet

interplay ['ɪntəpleɪ] *n* interacción *f*

interpret [ɪn'tɜːprɪt] **1** *vt* interpretar
2 *vi* actuar de intérprete

interpretation [ɪntɜːprɪ'teɪʃən] *n* interpretación *f*

interpreter [ɪn'tɜːprɪtə(r)] *n* intérprete *mf*

interrelated [ɪntərɪ'leɪtɪd] *adj* estrechamente relacionado(a)

interrogate [ɪn'terəgeɪt] *vt* interrogar

interrogation [ɪnterə'geɪʃən] *n* interrogatorio *m*

interrogative [ɪntə'rɒgətɪv] *Gram* **1** *adj* interrogativo(a)
2 *n (word)* palabra interrogativa

interrupt [ɪntə'rʌpt] *vt & vi* interrumpir

interruption [ɪntə'rʌpʃən] *n* interrupción *f*

intersect [ɪntə'sekt] **1** *vt* cruzar
2 *vi* cruzarse

intersection [ɪntə'sekʃən] *n* **(a)** *(crossroads)* cruce *m* **(b)** *(of two lines)* intersección *f*

intersperse [ɪntə'spɜːs] *vt* esparcir

interstate ['ɪntəsteɪt] *n US* autopista *f* interestatal

intertwine [ɪntə'twaɪn] **1** *vt* entrelazar (**with** con)
2 *vi* entrelazarse (**with** con)

interval ['ɪntəvəl] *n* **(a)** *(of time, space)* intervalo *m*; **at intervals** *(time, space)* a intervalos; *(time)* de vez en cuando **(b)** *Br Cin & Th* intermedio *m*

intervene [ɪntə'viːn] *vi* **(a)** *(person)* intervenir (**in** en) **(b)** *(event)* sobrevenir **(c)** *(time)* transcurrir

intervention [ɪntə'venʃən] *n* intervención *f*

interview ['ɪntəvjuː] **1** *n* entrevista *f*; **to give an i.** conceder una entrevista
2 *vt* entrevistar

interviewer ['ɪntəvjuːə(r)] *n* entrevistador(a) *m,f*

intestine [ɪn'testɪn] *n* intestino *m*; **large/ small i.** intestino grueso/delgado

intimacy ['ɪntɪməsɪ] *n (closeness)* intimidad *f*, *Euph (sex)* relación íntima; **intimacies** intimidades *fpl*

intimate¹ ['ɪntɪmɪt] *adj* íntimo(a); *(knowledge)* profundo(a)

intimate² ['ɪntɪmeɪt] *vt Fml* dar a entender

intimidate [ɪn'tɪmɪdeɪt] *vt* intimidar

intimidating [ɪn'tɪmɪdeɪtɪŋ] *adj* atemorizante

into ['ɪntuː, *unstressed* 'ɪntə] *prep* **(a)** *(motion)* en, a, con; **he fell i. the water** se cayó al agua; **to get i. a car** subir a un coche; **to go i. a house** entrar en una casa **(b)** *(state)* en, a; **to change pounds i. euros** cambiar libras en *or* por euros; **to translate sth i. French** traducir algo al francés **(c)** **to divide sth i. three** dividir algo en tres **(d)** *Fam* **to be i. sth** ser aficionado(a) a algo

intolerable [ɪn'tɒlərəbəl] *adj* intolerable

intolerance [ɪn'tɒlərəns] *n* intolerancia *f*

intolerant [ɪn'tɒlərənt] *adj* intolerante

intonation [ɪntə'neɪʃən] *n* entonación *f*

intoxicated [ɪn'tɒksɪkeɪtɪd] *adj* borracho(a)

> 🖉 Note that the Spanish word **intoxicado** is a false friend and is never a translation for the English word **intoxicated**. In Spanish **intoxicado** means "poisoned".

intoxicating [ɪn'tɒksɪkeɪtɪŋ] *adj* embriagador(a); **i. liquor** bebida alcohólica

intoxication [ɪntɒksɪ'keɪʃən] *n* embriaguez *f*

> 🖉 Note that the Spanish word **intoxicación** is a false friend and is never a translation for the English word **intoxication**. In Spanish, **intoxicación** means "poisoning".

intractable [ɪn'træktəbəl] *adj Fml (person)* intratable; *(problem)* insoluble

intranet ['ɪntrənet] *n Comput* intranet *f*

intransigent [ɪn'trænsɪdʒənt] *adj Fml* intransigente, intolerante

intransitive [ɪn'trænsɪtɪv] *adj* intransitivo(a)

intravenous [ɪntrə'viːnəs] *adj* intravenoso(a)

in-tray ['ɪntreɪ] *n* bandeja *f* de asuntos pendientes

intrepid [ɪn'trepɪd] *adj* intrépido(a), audaz

intricate ['ɪntrɪkɪt] *adj* intrincado(a)

intrigue 1 *n* [ɪn'triːg, 'ɪntriːg] intriga *f*
2 *vt* [ɪn'triːg] intrigar
3 *vi* intrigar, conspirar

intriguing [ɪnˈtriːgɪŋ] *adj* intrigante
intrinsic [ɪnˈtrɪnsɪk] *adj Fml* intrínseco(a)
introduce [ɪntrəˈdjuːs] *vt* (**a**) *(person, programme)* presentar (**to** a) (**b**) *(bring in)* introducir (**into** *or* **to** en); *Com (product)* lanzar (**into** *or* **to** a); *(topic)* proponer
introduction [ɪntrəˈdʌkʃən] *n* (**a**) *(of person, programme)* presentación *f*, *(in book)* introducción *f* (**b**) *(bringing in)* introducción *f*, *Com (of product)* lanzamiento *m*
introductory [ɪntrəˈdʌktəri] *adj* introductorio(a); *(remarks)* preliminar; *Com* de lanzamiento
introspective [ɪntrəˈspektɪv] *adj* introspectivo(a)
introvert [ˈɪntrəvɜːt] *n* introvertido(a) *m,f*
intrude [ɪnˈtruːd] *vi* entrometerse (**into** *or* **on** en); *(disturb)* molestar
intruder [ɪnˈtruːdə(r)] *n* intruso(a) *m,f*
intrusion [ɪnˈtruːʒən] *n* incursión *f*
intuition [ɪntjʊˈɪʃən] *n* intuición *f*
inundate [ˈɪnʌndeɪt] *vt* inundar (**with** de)
invade [ɪnˈveɪd] *vt* invadir
invader [ɪnˈveɪdə(r)] *n* invasor(a) *m,f*
invalid¹ [ˈɪnvəlɪd] *n (disabled person)* minusválido(a) *m,f*; *(sick person)* enfermo(a) *m,f*
invalid² [ɪnˈvælɪd] *adj* inválido(a), nulo(a)
invalidate [ɪnˈvælɪdeɪt] *vt* invalidar
invaluable [ɪnˈvæljʊəbəl] *adj* inestimable
invariable [ɪnˈveərɪəbəl] *adj* invariable
invariably [ɪnˈveərɪəblɪ] *adv* invariablemente
invasion [ɪnˈveɪʒən] *n* invasión *f*
invent [ɪnˈvent] *vt* inventar
invention [ɪnˈvenʃən] *n* invento *m*; *(creativity)* inventiva *f*; *(lie)* mentira *f*
inventive [ɪnˈventɪv] *adj* inventivo(a)
inventor [ɪnˈventə(r)] *n* inventor(a) *m,f*
inventory [ˈɪnvəntəri] *n* inventario *m*
invert [ɪnˈvɜːt] *vt* invertir
invertebrate [ɪnˈvɜːtɪbrɪt] **1** *adj* invertebrado(a)
  2 *n* invertebrado *m*
inverted [ɪnˈvɜːtɪd] *adj* (**in**) **i. commas** *(entre)* comillas *fpl*
invest [ɪnˈvest] **1** *vt* invertir (**in** en); **to i. sb with sth** conferir algo a algn
  2 *vi* invertir (**in** en)
investigate [ɪnˈvestɪgeɪt] *vt (crime, subject)* investigar; *(cause, possibility)* estudiar
investigation [ɪnvestɪˈgeɪʃən] *n (of crime)* investigación *f*; *(of cause)* examen *m*

investigator [ɪnˈvestɪgeɪtə(r)] *n* investigador(a) *m,f*; **private i.** detective privado
investment [ɪnˈvestmənt] *n* inversión *f*
investor [ɪnˈvestə(r)] *n* inversor(a) *m,f*
inveterate [ɪnˈvetərɪt] *adj* empedernido(a)
invidious [ɪnˈvɪdɪəs] *adj (task)* ingrato(a); *(comparison)* injusto(a)

> 🖉 Note that the Spanish word **envidioso** is a false friend and is never a translation for the English word **invidious**. In Spanish, **envidioso** means "envious".

invigilator [ɪnˈvɪdʒɪleɪtə(r)] *n Br (in exam)* vigilante *mf*
invigorating [ɪnˈvɪgəreɪtɪŋ] *adj* vigorizante
invincible [ɪnˈvɪnsəbəl] *adj* invencible
invisible [ɪnˈvɪzəbəl] *adj* invisible
invitation [ɪnvɪˈteɪʃən] *n* invitación *f*
invite [ɪnˈvaɪt] *vt* (**a**) *(guest)* invitar (**to** a) (**b**) *(comments etc)* solicitar; *(criticism)* provocar; **to i. trouble** buscarse problemas
inviting [ɪnˈvaɪtɪŋ] *adj (attractive)* atractivo(a); *(food)* apetitoso(a)
invoice [ˈɪnvɔɪs] **1** *n* factura *f*
  2 *vt* facturar
invoke [ɪnˈvəʊk] *vt Fml* invocar
involuntary [ɪnˈvɒləntəri] *adj* involuntario(a)
involve [ɪnˈvɒlv] *vt* (**a**) *(concern)* implicar (**in** en); **the issues involved** las cuestiones en juego; **to be involved in an accident** sufrir un accidente (**b**) *(entail)* suponer, implicar; *(trouble, risk)* acarrear
involved [ɪnˈvɒlvd] *adj (complicated)* complicado(a); *Fam (romantically attached)* enredado(a), liado(a)
involvement [ɪnˈvɒlvmənt] *n (participation)* participación *f*; *(in crime)* implicación *f*
invulnerable [ɪnˈvʌlnərəbəl] *adj* invulnerable
inward [ˈɪnwəd] **1** *adj* interior
  2 *adv* = **inwards**
inwardly [ˈɪnwədlɪ] *adv* interiormente, por dentro
inwards [ˈɪnwədz] *adv* hacia dentro
in-your-face [ˈɪnjəˈfeɪs] *adj Fam (style)* descarado(a); *(movie, advert)* impactante, fuerte
iodine [ˈaɪədiːn] *n* yodo *m*
iota [aɪˈəʊtə] *n* pizca *f*, ápice *m*
IOU [aɪəʊˈjuː] *n (abbr* **I owe you)** pagaré *m*
IQ [aɪˈkjuː] *n (abbr* **intelligence quotient)** CI *m*

IRA [aɪɑːˈreɪ] n (a) (abbr Irish Republican Army) IRA m (b) US (abbr individual retirement account) cuenta f de retiro or jubilación individual

Iran [ɪˈrɑːn] n Irán

Iranian [ɪˈreɪnɪən] adj & n iraní (mf)

Iraq [ɪˈrɑːk] n Irak

Iraqi [ɪˈrɑːkɪ] adj & n iraquí (mf)

irascible [ɪˈræsɪbəl] adj Fml irascible

irate [aɪˈreɪt] adj airado(a), furioso(a)

Ireland [ˈaɪələnd] n Irlanda; **Republic of I.** República de Irlanda

iris [ˈaɪərɪs] n (a) Anat iris m inv (b) Bot lirio m

Irish [ˈaɪrɪʃ] **1** adj irlandés(esa); **I. coffee** café m irlandés; **I. Sea** Mar m de Irlanda
2 n (a) (language) irlandés m (b) pl **the I.** los irlandeses

Irishman [ˈaɪrɪʃmən] n irlandés m

Irishwoman [ˈaɪrɪʃwomən] n irlandesa f

irksome [ˈɜːksəm] adj fastidioso(a)

iron [ˈaɪən] **1** n (a) (metal) hierro m; **the i. and steel industry** la industria siderúrgica (b) (for clothes) plancha f
2 vt (clothes) planchar
▸ **iron out** vt sep (a) (crease) planchar (b) Fam Fig (problem) resolver

ironic(al) [aɪˈrɒnɪk(əl)] adj irónico(a)

ironing [ˈaɪənɪŋ] n (a) **to do the i.** planchar; **i. board** mesa f de la plancha (b) (clothes to be ironed) ropa f para planchar; (clothes ironed) ropa planchada

ironmonger [ˈaɪənmʌŋgə(r)] n Br ferretero(a) m,f; **i.'s (shop)** ferretería f

irony [ˈaɪrənɪ] n ironía f

irradiate [ɪˈreɪdɪeɪt] vt irradiar

irrational [ɪˈræʃənəl] adj irracional

irreconcilable [ɪrekənˈsaɪləbəl] adj irreconciliable

irrefutable [ɪrɪˈfjuːtəbəl] adj Fml irrefutable

irregular [ɪˈregjʊlə(r)] adj irregular

irrelevant [ɪˈreləvənt] adj no pertinente

irreparable [ɪˈrepərəbəl] adj irreparable

irreplaceable [ɪrɪˈpleɪsəbəl] adj irremplazable

irrepressible [ɪrɪˈpresəbəl] adj incontenible

irresistible [ɪrɪˈzɪstəbəl] adj irresistible

irresolute [ɪˈrezəluːt] adj Fml indeciso(a)

irrespective [ɪrɪˈspektɪv] adj **i. of** sin tener en cuenta

irresponsible [ɪrɪˈspɒnsəbəl] adj irresponsable

irreverent [ɪˈrevərənt] adj irreverente

irrevocable [ɪˈrevəkəbəl] adj irrevocable

irrigate [ˈɪrɪgeɪt] vt regar

irrigation [ɪrɪˈgeɪʃən] n riego m; **i. channel** acequia f; **i. system** sistema m de regadío

irritable [ˈɪrɪtəbəl] adj irritable

irritate [ˈɪrɪteɪt] vt (annoy) fastidiar; Med irritar

irritating [ˈɪrɪteɪtɪŋ] adj irritante

irritation [ɪrɪˈteɪʃən] n (a) (annoyance) fastidio m; (ill humour) mal humor m (b) Med irritación f

IRS [aɪɑːˈres] n US (abbr Internal Revenue Service) **the I.** Hacienda, Esp ≃ la Agencia Tributaria, Méx ≃ el Servicio de Administración Tributaria

is [ɪz] 3rd person sing pres of be

Islam [ˈɪzlɑːm] n islam m

Islamic [ɪzˈlæmɪk] adj islámico(a)

island [ˈaɪlənd] n isla f; (traffic) i. isleta f

islander [ˈaɪləndə(r)] n isleño(a) m,f

isle [aɪl] n isla f

isn't [ˈɪzənt] = **is not**

isolate [ˈaɪsəleɪt] vt aislar (from de)

isolated [ˈaɪsəleɪtɪd] adj aislado(a)

isolation [aɪsəˈleɪʃən] n aislamiento m

ISP [aɪesˈpiː] n Comput (abbr Internet Service Provider) PSI m

Israel [ˈɪzreɪəl] n Israel

Israeli [ɪzˈreɪlɪ] adj & n israelí (mf)

issue [ˈɪʃuː] **1** n (a) (matter) cuestión f; **to take i. with sb (over sth)** manifestar su desacuerdo con algn (en algo) (b) (of magazine) ejemplar m (c) Fml (outcome) resultado m (d) Jur (offspring) descendencia f
2 vt (a) (book) publicar; (banknotes etc) emitir; (passport) expedir (b) (supplies) repartir (c) (order, instructions) dar; (warrant) dictar

isthmus [ˈɪsməs] n istmo m

IT [aɪˈtiː] n Comput (abbr information technology) informática f

it [ɪt] pers pron (a) (subject) él/ella/ello (usually omitted in Spanish, except for contrast); **it's here** está aquí (b) (direct object) lo/la; **I don't believe it** no me lo creo; **I liked the house and bought it** me gustó la casa y la compré (c) (indirect object) le; **give it a kick** dale una patada (d) (after prep) él/ella/ello; **I saw the beach and ran towards it** vi la playa y fui corriendo hacia ella; **we'll talk about it later** ya hablaremos de ello (e) (abstract) ello; **let's get down to it!** ¡vamos a ello! (f) (impersonal) **it's late** es tarde; **it's me** soy yo; **it's raining** está lloviendo; **it's 2 miles to town** hay 2 millas de aquí al pueblo; **who is it?** ¿quién es?

Italian [ɪˈtæljən] **1** *adj* italiano(a)
 2 *n* (**a**) *(person)* italiano(a) *m,f* (**b**)
 (language) italiano *m*
italic [ɪˈtælɪk] *n* **i., italics** cursiva *f*
Italy [ˈɪtəlɪ] *n* Italia
itch [ɪtʃ] **1** *n* picor *m*; *Fig* **an i. to travel** unas
 ganas locas de viajar
 2 *vi* (**a**) *(skin)* picar (**b**) *Fig* anhelar; *Fam*
 to be itching to do sth tener muchas
 ganas de hacer algo
itchy [ˈɪtʃɪ] *adj* (**itchier, itchiest**) que pica
item [ˈaɪtəm] *n* (**a**) *(in list)* artículo *m*; *(in
 collection)* pieza *f*; **i. of clothing** prenda *f*
 de vestir (**b**) *(on agenda)* asunto *m*; *(in
 show)* número *m*; **news i.** noticia *f*
itemize [ˈaɪtəmaɪz] *vt* detallar
itinerant [ɪˈtɪnərənt] *adj Fml* itinerante
itinerary [aɪˈtɪnərərɪ] *n* itinerario *m*

it'll [ˈɪtəl] = **it will**
its [ɪts] *poss adj (one thing)* su; *(more than
 one)* sus
itself [ɪtˈself] *pers pron* (**a**) *(reflexive)* se;
 the cat scratched i. el gato se arañó (**b**)
 (emphatic) él mismo/ella misma/ello
 mismo; *(after prep)* sí (mismo(a)); **in i.** en
 sí
ITV [aɪtiːˈviː] *n Br (abbr* **Independent
 Television***)* = canal privado de televisión
 británico
IUD [aɪjuːˈdiː] *n (abbr* **intrauterine (contraceptive) device***)* DIU *m*
IVF [aɪviːˈef] *n Med (abbr* **in vitro fertilization***)* fertilización *f* in vitro
ivory [ˈaɪvərɪ] *n* marfil *m*
ivy [ˈaɪvɪ] *n* hiedra *f*

— J —

J, j [dʒeɪ] *n (the letter)* J, j *f*

jab [dʒæb] **1** *n* pinchazo *m; (poke)* golpe seco
2 *vt* pinchar; *(with fist)* dar un puñetazo a

jabber ['dʒæbə(r)] *vi Fam (chatter)* charlotear; *(speak quickly)* hablar atropelladamente

jack [dʒæk] *n* (a) *Aut* gato *m* (b) *Cards* sota *f* (c) *(bowls)* boliche *m*
▸ **jack in** *vt sep Br Fam (job)* dejar
▸ **jack up** *vt sep Fam (price, salaries)* subir

jackal ['dʒækɔːl] *n* chacal *m*

jackdaw ['dʒækdɔː] *n* grajilla *f*

jacket ['dʒækɪt] *n* (a) *(coat) (formal)* chaqueta *f*, americana *f*, *Am* saco *m; (casual)* cazadora *f*, *(bomber jacket)* cazadora *f* (b) *(of book)* sobrecubierta *f*, *US (of record)* funda *f* (c) **j. potatoes** patatas *fpl or Am* papas *fpl* al horno

jack-knife ['dʒæknaɪf] **1** *n* navaja *f*
2 *vi* colear

jack-of-all-trades [dʒækəv'ɔːltreɪdz] *n* persona *f* mañosa *or* de muchos oficios

jackpot ['dʒækpɒt] *n* (premio *m*) gordo *m*

Jacuzzi® [dʒə'kuːzɪ] *n* jacuzzi® *m*

jade [dʒeɪd] *n* jade *m*

jaded ['dʒeɪdɪd] *adj (tired)* agotado(a); *(palate)* hastiado(a)

jagged ['dʒægɪd] *adj* dentado(a)

jaguar [*Br* 'dʒægjʊə(r), *US* 'dʒægwɑː(r)] *n* jaguar *m*

jail [dʒeɪl] **1** *n* cárcel *f*, prisión *f*
2 *vt* encarcelar

jailbreak ['dʒeɪlbreɪk] *n* fuga *f*, evasión *f*

jailer ['dʒeɪlə(r)] *n* carcelero(a) *m,f*

jam¹ [dʒæm] *n Culin* mermelada *f*

jam² [dʒæm] **1** *n (blockage)* atasco *m; Fam (fix)* apuro *m*
2 *vt* (a) *(cram)* meter a la fuerza (b) *(block)* atascar; *Rad* interferir
3 *vi (door)* atrancarse; *(brakes)* agarrotarse

Jamaica [dʒə'meɪkə] *n* Jamaica *f*

jam-packed [dʒæm'pækt] *adj Fam (with people)* atestado(a); *(with things)* atiborrado(a)

jangle ['dʒæŋgəl] *vi* tintinear

janitor ['dʒænɪtə(r)] *n US, Scot (caretaker)* conserje *m*, bedel *m*

January ['dʒænjʊərɪ] *n* enero *m*

Japan [dʒə'pæn] *n* (el) Japón

Japanese [dʒæpə'niːz] **1** *adj* japonés(esa)
2 *n (person)* japonés(esa) *m,f, (language)* japonés *m*

jar¹ [dʒɑː(r)] *n (container)* tarro *m; Br Fam* **to have a j.** tomar una copa

jar² [dʒɑː(r)] *vi (sounds)* chirriar; *(appearance)* chocar; *(colours)* desentonar; *Fig* **to j. on one's nerves** ponerle a uno los nervios de punta

jargon ['dʒɑːgən] *n* jerga *f*, argot *m*

jasmin(e) ['dʒæzmɪn] *n* jazmín *m*

jaundice ['dʒɔːndɪs] *n* ictericia *f*

jaundiced ['dʒɔːndɪst] *adj Med* ictérico(a); *Fig (bitter)* amargado(a)

jaunt [dʒɔːnt] *n (walk)* paseo *m; (trip)* excursión *f*

jaunty ['dʒɔːntɪ] *adj* (**jauntier, jauntiest**) *(sprightly)* garboso(a); *(lively)* vivaz

javelin ['dʒævəlɪn] *n* jabalina *f*

jaw [dʒɔː] **1** *n* mandíbula *f*
2 *vi Fam* estar de palique

jay [dʒeɪ] *n* arrendajo *m* (común)

jaywalker ['dʒeɪwɔːkə(r)] *n* peatón *m* imprudente

jaywalking ['dʒeɪwɔːkɪŋ] *n* imprudencia *f* peatonal

jazz [dʒæz] *n* jazz *m*
▸ **jazz up** *vt sep* alegrar; *(premises)* arreglar

jazzy ['dʒæzɪ] *adj* (**jazzier, jazziest**) *Fam (showy)* llamativo(a); *(brightly coloured)* de colores chillones

jealous ['dʒeləs] *adj* celoso(a); *(envious)* envidioso(a); **to be j. of …** tener celos de …

jealousy ['dʒeləsɪ] *n* celos *mpl; (envy)* envidia *f*

jeans [dʒiːnz] *npl* vaqueros *mpl*, tejanos *mpl*

Jeep® [dʒiːp] *n* jeep *m*, todo terreno *m inv*

jeer [dʒɪə(r)] **1** *n (boo)* abucheo *m; (mocking)* mofa *f*
2 *vi (boo)* abuchear; *(mock)* burlarse

jeering ['dʒɪərɪŋ] *adj* burlón(ona)

Jehovah [dʒɪˈhəʊvə] n **J.'s Witness** testigo mf de Jehová

Jell-O®, jello [ˈdʒeləʊ] n US gelatina f

jelly [ˈdʒelɪ] n Br (dessert) gelatina f; esp US (jam) mermelada f, confitura f

jellyfish [ˈdʒelɪfɪʃ] n medusa f

jeopardize [ˈdʒepədaɪz] vt poner en peligro; (agreement etc) comprometer

jeopardy [ˈdʒepədɪ] n riesgo m, peligro m

jerk [dʒɜːk] 1 n (a) (jolt) sacudida f; (pull) tirón m (b) Pej (idiot) imbécil mf
2 vt (shake) sacudir; (pull) dar un tirón a
3 vi (move suddenly) dar una sacudida

jerkin [ˈdʒɜːkɪn] n chaleco m

jersey [ˈdʒɜːzɪ] n suéter m, Esp jersey m, RP pulóver m

jest [dʒest] 1 n broma f
2 vi bromear

Jesuit [ˈdʒezjʊɪt] adj & n jesuita (m)

Jesus [ˈdʒiːzəs] n Jesús m; **J. Christ** Jesucristo m

jet¹ [dʒet] 1 n (a) (stream of water) chorro m (b) (spout) surtidor m (c) Av reactor m; **j. engine** reactor m; **j. lag** = cansancio debido al desfase horario; **j. ski** moto náutica or acuática; **the j. set** Esp la jet(-set), Am el jet-set
2 vi Fam volar

jet² [dʒet] n **j. black** negro(a) como el azabache

jettison [ˈdʒetɪsən] vt also Fig tirar or echar por la borda, Am salvo RP botar por la borda

jetty [ˈdʒetɪ] n muelle m, malecón m

Jew [dʒuː] n judío(a) m,f

jewel [ˈdʒuːəl] n joya f; (stone) piedra preciosa; (in watch) rubí m; Fig (person) joya

jeweller, US jeweler [ˈdʒuːələ(r)] n joyero(a) m,f; **j.'s (shop)** joyería f

jewellery, US jewelry [ˈdʒuːəlrɪ] n joyas fpl, alhajas fpl

Jewess [ˈdʒuːɪs] n judía f

Jewish [ˈdʒuːɪʃ] adj judío(a)

jibe [dʒaɪb] n & vi = gibe

jiffy [ˈdʒɪfɪ] n Fam momento m; **in a j.** en un santiamén; **just a j.!** ¡un momento!

jig [dʒɪg] n Mus giga f

jigsaw [ˈdʒɪgsɔː] n (puzzle) rompecabezas m inv

jilt [dʒɪlt] vt Fam dejar plantado(a)

jingle [ˈdʒɪŋgəl] 1 n Rad & TV = canción que acompaña un anuncio
2 vi tintinear

jingoistic [dʒɪŋgəʊˈɪstɪk] adj patriotero(a)

jinx [dʒɪŋks] 1 n (person) gafe mf
2 vt gafar

jitters [ˈdʒɪtəz] npl Fam **to get the j.** tener canguelo

jive [dʒaɪv] 1 n swing m
2 vi bailar el swing

job [dʒɒb] n (a) (task) tarea f (b) (post) (puesto m de) trabajo m, empleo con; US **j. office** oficina f de empleo; **j. sharing** trabajo compartido a tiempo parcial (c) Fam **we had a j. to …** nos costó (trabajo) … (d) Br Fam **it's a good j. that …** menos mal que …

Jobcentre [ˈdʒɒbsentə(r)] n Br oficina f de empleo

jobless [ˈdʒɒblɪs] adj parado(a)

jockey [ˈdʒɒkɪ] 1 n jinete m, jockey m
2 vi **to j. for position** luchar para conseguir una posición aventajada

jocular [ˈdʒɒkjʊlə(r)] adj jocoso(a)

jog [dʒɒg] 1 n trote m
2 vt empujar; Fig (memory) refrescar
3 vi Sport hacer footing

jogging [ˈdʒɒgɪŋ] n footing m

john [dʒɒn] n US Fam **the j.** (lavatory) el váter

join [dʒɔɪn] 1 vt (a) (unite, connect) unir; **to j. forces with sb** unir fuerzas con algn (b) (road) empalmar con; (river) desembocar en (c) (meet) reunirse con (d) (institution) entrar; (army) alistarse a; (discussion, game) unirse a (e) (party, union) afiliarse a; (club) ingresar en
2 vi (a) (pipes, roads, rivers) juntarse, unirse (b) (in party, union) afiliarse; (in club) ingresar
3 n juntura f

▸ **join in** 1 vi participar, tomar parte; (debate) intervenir
2 vt insep participar en, tomar parte en

▸ **join up** 1 vt sep juntar
2 vi (of roads) unirse; Mil alistarse

joiner [ˈdʒɔɪnə(r)] n carpintero(a) m,f

joinery [ˈdʒɔɪnərɪ] n carpintería f

joint [dʒɔɪnt] 1 n (a) Anat & Tech articulación f (b) (in woodwork) junta f, juntura f (c) (of meat) (raw) pieza f; (roasted) asado m (d) Fam (nightclub etc) garito m (e) Fam (drug) porro m
2 adj colectivo(a); **j. (bank) account** cuenta conjunta; **j. venture** empresa conjunta

jointly [ˈdʒɔɪntlɪ] adv conjuntamente, en común

joist [dʒɔɪst] n vigueta f

joke [dʒəʊk] 1 n (a) (funny story) chiste m; (prank) broma f; **to play a j. on sb** gastarle una broma a algn; **to tell a j.** contar un chiste (b) Fam (person) hazmerreír m, payaso(a) m,f; **to be a j.** (of thing) ser de chiste

2 *vi* estar de broma; **you must be joking!** ¡no hablarás en serio!

joker ['dʒəʊkə(r)] *n* (**a**) *(clown)* bromista *mf* (**b**) *Cards* comodín *m*

jolly ['dʒɒlɪ] **1** *adj* (jollier, jolliest) alegre
2 *adv Br Fam (very)* bien; **she played j. well** jugó muy bien

jolt [dʒəʊlt] **1** *n (shake)* sacudida *f*; *(shock, surprise)* susto *m*
2 *vt (shake)* sacudir
3 *vi (shake)* dar sacudidas

Jordan ['dʒɔːdən] *n* (**a**) *(river)* Jordán *m* (**b**) *(country)* Jordania

joss-stick ['dʒɒsstɪk] *n* varita *f* de incienso

jostle ['dʒɒsəl] **1** *vt* dar empujones a
2 *vi* dar empujones

jot [dʒɒt] *n* jota *f*, pizca *f*; **not a j.** ni jota
▸ **jot down** *vt sep* apuntar

jotter ['dʒɒtə(r)] *n Br* bloc *m*

journal ['dʒɜːnəl] *n* (**a**) *(publication)* revista *f* (especializada) (**b**) *(diary)* diario *m*

⚠ Note that the Spanish word **jornal** is a false friend and is never a translation for the English word **journal**. In Spanish **jornal** means "day's wage".

journalism ['dʒɜːnəlɪzəm] *n* periodismo *m*

journalist ['dʒɜːnəlɪst] *n* periodista *mf*

journey ['dʒɜːnɪ] **1** *n* viaje *m*; *(distance)* trayecto *m*
2 *vi Fml* viajar

jovial ['dʒəʊvɪəl] *adj* jovial

jowl [dʒaʊl] *n* quijada *f*

joy [dʒɔɪ] *n* alegría *f*; *(pleasure)* placer *m*

joyful ['dʒɔɪfʊl] *adj* alegre, contento(a)

joyous ['dʒɔɪəs] *adj Literary* alegre

joyride ['dʒɔɪraɪd] *n Fam* paseo *m* en un coche robado

joystick ['dʒɔɪstɪk] *n Av* palanca *f* de mando; *(of video game)* joystick *m*

JP [dʒeɪ'piː] *n Br Jur (abbr Justice of the Peace)* juez *mf* de paz

Jr *(abbr Junior)* Neil Smith, Jr Neil Smith, hijo

jubilant ['dʒuːbɪlənt] *adj* jubiloso(a)

jubilation [dʒuːbɪ'leɪʃən] *n* júbilo *m*

jubilee ['dʒuːbɪliː] *n* festejos *mpl*; **golden j.** quincuagésimo aniversario

judge [dʒʌdʒ] **1** *n* juez *mf*, jueza *f*; *(in competition)* jurado *m*
2 *vt* (**a**) *Jur* juzgar (**b**) *(estimate)* considerar (**c**) *(competition)* actuar de juez de (**a**) *(assess)* juzgar
3 *vi* juzgar; **judging from what you say** a juzgar por lo que dices

judg(e)ment ['dʒʌdʒmənt] *n* (**a**) *Jur* sentencia *f*, fallo *m* (**b**) *(opinion)* juicio *m* (**c**) *(ability)* buen juicio *m*

judicial [dʒuː'dɪʃəl] *adj* judicial

judiciary [dʒuː'dɪʃərɪ] *n* magistratura *f*

judicious [dʒuː'dɪʃəs] *adj Fml* juicioso(a)

judo ['dʒuːdəʊ] *n* judo *m*

jug [dʒʌg] *n Br* jarra *f*; **milk j.** jarra de leche

juggernaut ['dʒʌgənɔːt] *n Br* camión *m* grande, tráiler *m*

juggle ['dʒʌgəl] *vi (perform)* hacer juegos malabares (**with** con); *Fig (responsibilities)* ajustar

juggler ['dʒʌglə(r)] *n* malabarista *mf*

juice [dʒuːs] *n (of fruit)* zumo *m*, *Am* jugo *m*; *(of meat)* jugo *m*

juicy ['dʒuːsɪ] *adj* (juicier, juiciest) *also Fig* jugoso(a)

jukebox ['dʒuːkbɒks] *n* rocola *f*

July [dʒuː'laɪ, dʒə'laɪ] *n* julio *m*

jumble ['dʒʌmbəl] **1** *n* revoltijo *m*; *Br* **j. sale** rastrillo benéfico
2 *vt* revolver

jumbo ['dʒʌmbəʊ] *n* **j. (jet)** jumbo *m*

jump [dʒʌmp] **1** *n (leap)* salto *m*; *(sudden increase)* subida repentina; **j. suit** mono *m*
2 *vi* (**a**) *(leap) (person, animal)* saltar, brincar; *Fig* **to j. to conclusions** sacar conclusiones precipitadas (**b**) *Fig (start)* sobresaltarse (**c**) *(increase)* aumentar de golpe
3 *vt* saltar; *Br* **to j. the queue** colarse; *US* **to j. rope** saltar a la comba
▸ **jump at** *vt insep* aceptar sin pensarlo

jumper ['dʒʌmpə(r)] *n* (**a**) *Br (sweater)* suéter *m*, *Esp* jersey *m*, *RP* pulóver *m* (**b**) *US (dress)* *Esp* pichi *m*, *CSur, Méx* jumper *m* (**c**) *US Aut* **j. cables** cables *mpl* de emergencia

jumpy ['dʒʌmpɪ] *adj* (jumpier, jumpiest) *Fam* nervioso(a)

junction ['dʒʌŋkʃən] *n (of roads)* cruce *m*; *Elec & Rail* empalme *m*

juncture ['dʒʌŋktʃə(r)] *n Fml* **at this j.** en esta coyuntura

June [dʒuːn] *n* junio *m*

jungle ['dʒʌŋgəl] *n* jungla *f*, selva *f*; *Fig* laberinto *m*; **the concrete j.** la jungla de asfalto

junior ['dʒuːnjə(r)] **1** *adj* (**a**) *(son of)* hijo; **David Hughes J.** David Hughes hijo (**b**) *US* **j. high (school)** *(between 11 and 15)* escuela secundaria; *Br* **j. school** *(between 7 and 11)* escuela primaria; **j. team** equipo *m* juvenil (**c**) *(lower in rank)* subalterno(a)
2 *n* (**a**) *(person of lower rank)* subalterno(a) *m,f* (**b**) *(younger person)* menor *mf*

junk [dʒʌŋk] n (**a**) *Fam* trastos *mpl*; **j. food** comida basura; **j. mail** propaganda f (por correo); **j. shop** tienda f de segunda mano (**b**) *(boat)* junco m

junkie [ˈdʒʌŋkɪ] n *Fam* yonqui *mf*

junkman [ˈdʒʌŋkmæn] n *US* trapero m

junta [ˈdʒʌntə, *US* ˈhʊntə] n junta f militar

jurisdiction [dʒʊərɪsˈdɪkʃən] n *Fml* jurisdicción f

juror [ˈdʒʊərə(r)] n jurado(a) m,f

jury [ˈdʒʊərɪ] n jurado m

just [dʒʌst] **1** adj *(fair)* justo(a); *Fml (well-founded)* justificado(a)
   2 adv (**a**) he had **j. arrived** acababa de llegar (**b**) *(at this very moment)* ahora mismo, en este momento; **he was j. leaving when ...** estaba a punto de salir cuando ...; **I'm j. coming!** ¡ya voy!; (**c**) *(only)* solamente; **j. in case** por si acaso; **j. a minute!** ¡un momento! (**d**) *(barely)* por poco; **j. about** casi; **j. enough** justo lo suficiente (**e**) *(emphatic)* **it's j. fantastic!**

¡es sencillamente fantástico! (**f**) *(exactly)* exactamente, justo; **j. as I thought** me lo figuraba; **j. as fast as** tan rápido como

justice [ˈdʒʌstɪs] n (**a**) *(power of law, fairness)* justicia f; **you didn't do yourself j.** no diste lo mejor de ti (**b**) *Jur (judge)* juez *mf*; **J. of the Peace** juez de paz

justifiable [ˈdʒʌstɪfaɪəbəl] adj justificable

justification [dʒʌstɪfɪˈkeɪʃən] n justificación f

justified [ˈdʒʌstɪfaɪd] adj **to be j. in doing sth** tener razón en hacer algo

justify [ˈdʒʌstɪfaɪ] vt justificar

jut [dʒʌt] vi sobresalir; **to j. out over** proyectarse sobre

juvenile [ˈdʒuːvənaɪl] **1** adj (**a**) *(for young people)* juvenil; **j. court** tribunal m de menores; **j. delinquent** delincuente *mf* juvenil (**b**) *(immature)* infantil
   2 n menor *mf*, joven *mf*

juxtapose [dʒʌkstəˈpəʊz] vt yuxtaponer

K, k [keɪ] n (the letter) K, k f

kaleidoscope [kə'laɪdəskəʊp] n caleidoscopio m

Kampuchea [kæmpʊ'tʃɪə] n Kampuchea

kangaroo [kæŋgə'ruː] n canguro m

karaoke [kærɪ'əʊkɪ] n karaoke m

karat ['kærət] n US quilate m

karate [kə'rɑːtɪ] n kárate m

kebab [kə'bæb] n Culin pincho moruno, brocheta f

keel [kiːl] n quilla f; Fig **to be on an even k.** estar en calma

▸ **keel over** vi Fam desmayarse

keen [kiːn] adj (a) (eager) entusiasta (b) (intense) profundo(a) (c) (mind, senses) agudo(a); (look) penetrante; (blade) afilado(a); (competition) fuerte

keep [kiːp] 1 n (a) **to earn one's k.** ganarse el pan (b) Fam **for keeps** para siempre
2 vt (pt & pp kept) (a) (retain) quedarse con, guardar; (store) guardar (b) (maintain) (diary, accounts) llevar; (a promise) cumplir; (a secret) guardar (c) (maintain in a certain state) mantener; **to k. one's room tidy** mantener su cuarto limpio; **to k. sb waiting** hacer esperar a algn (d) (look after) (animals) tener; (shop, hotel) llevar (e) (detain) entretener (f) (prevent) **to k. sb from doing sth** impedir a algn hacer algo
3 vi (a) (remain) seguir; **k. still!** ¡estáte quieto(a)!; **to k. fit** mantenerse en forma; **to k. going** seguir adelante (b) (do frequently) no dejar de: **she keeps forgetting her keys** siempre se olvida las llaves (c) (food) conservarse

▸ **keep at** vt insep perseverar en

▸ **keep away 1** vt sep mantener a distancia
2 vi mantenerse a distancia

▸ **keep back** vt sep (information) ocultar, callar; (money etc) retener

▸ **keep down** vt sep **to k. prices down** mantener los precios bajos

▸ **keep off** vt insep **k. off the grass** (sign) prohibido pisar la hierba

▸ **keep on 1** vt sep (a) (clothes etc) no quitarse; **to k. an eye on sth/sb** vigilar algo/a algn (b) (continue to employ) no despedir a
2 vi (continue to do) seguir

▸ **keep out 1** vt sep no dejar pasar
2 vi no entrar; **k. out!** (sign) ¡prohibida la entrada!

▸ **keep to** vt insep (subject) limitarse a; **to k. to one's room** quedarse en el cuarto; **k. to the point!** ¡cíñete a la cuestión!; **to k. to the left** circular por la izquierda

▸ **keep up** vt sep (a) (custom) mantener; **to k. up appearances** guardar las apariencias (b) **k. it up!** ¡sigue así! (c) (prevent from sleeping) mantener despierto(a)

▸ **keep up with** vt insep **to k. up with the times** estar al día

keeper ['kiːpə(r)] n (in zoo) guarda mf; (in record office) archivero(a) m,f; (in museum) conservador(a) m,f

keeping ['kiːpɪŋ] n (a) (care) cuidado m (b) **in k. with** en armonía con; **out of k. with** en desacuerdo con

keepsake ['kiːpseɪk] n recuerdo m

keg [keg] n barril m

kennel ['kenəl] n caseta f para perros; **kennels** hotel m de perros

Kenya ['kenjə, 'kiːnjə] n Kenia

Kenyan ['kenjən, 'kiːnjən] adj & n keniano(a) (m,f)

kept [kept] pt & pp of **keep**

kerb [kɜːb] n Br bordillo m (de la acera), Chile solera f, Col, Perú sardinel m, CSur cordón m (de la vereda), Méx borde m (de la banqueta)

kernel ['kɜːnəl] n (of fruit, nut) pepita f; (of wheat) grano m; Fig meollo m

kerosene, kerosine ['kerəsiːn] n US queroseno m

ketchup ['ketʃəp] n ketchup m, salsa f de tomate

kettle ['ketəl] n hervidor m; **that's a different k. of fish** eso es harina de otro costal

key [kiː] 1 n (a) (for lock) llave f; **k. ring** llavero m (b) (of piano, typewriter) tecla f (c) Mus tono m
2 adj clave
3 vt Comput teclear

▸ **key in** vt sep Comput introducir

keyboard ['kiːbɔːd] n teclado m

keyed up [kiːd'ʌp] adj nervioso(a)

keyhole ['kiːhəʊl] *n* ojo *m* de la cerradura

keynote ['kiːnəʊt] *n Mus* tónica *f*; *Fig* nota *f* dominante

kg (*abbr* **kilogram(s)**) kg

khaki ['kɑːkɪ] *adj & n* caqui (*m*)

kick [kɪk] **1** *n* (*from person*) patada *f*, puntapié *m*; (*from horse etc*) coz *f*
  2 *vt* dar un puntapié a
  3 *vi* (*animal*) cocear; (*person*) dar patadas
▸ **kick off** *vi Fam* empezar; *Ftb* sacar
▸ **kick out** *vt sep* echar a patadas
▸ **kick up** *vt insep Fam* **to k. up a fuss** armar *or Esp* montar un alboroto

kick-off ['kɪkɒf] *n Ftb* saque *m* inicial

kid¹ [kɪd] *n* (**a**) *Zool* cabrito *m*; *Fig* **to handle sb with k. gloves** tratar a algn con guante blanco (**b**) *Fam* niño(a) *m,f*, *CAm* chavalo(a) *m,f*, *Méx* chavo(a) *mf*; **the kids** los críos

kid² [kɪd] **1** *vt* tomar el pelo a; **to k. oneself** (*fool*) hacerse ilusiones
  2 *vi Fam* tomar el pelo; **no kidding!** ¡va en serio!

kidnap ['kɪdnæp] *vt* secuestrar

kidnapper ['kɪdnæpə(r)] *n* secuestrador(a) *m,f*

kidnapping ['kɪdnæpɪŋ] *n* secuestro *m*

kidney ['kɪdnɪ] *n* riñón *m*

kill [kɪl] *vt* matar; *Fig* **to k. time** pasar el rato; *Fam* **my feet are killing me!** ¡cómo me duelen los pies!
▸ **kill off** *vt sep* exterminar

killer ['kɪlə(r)] *n* asesino(a) *m,f*; **k. whale** orca *f*

killing ['kɪlɪŋ] *n* asesinato *m*; *Fig* **to make a k.** forrarse de dinero

killjoy ['kɪldʒɔɪ] *n* aguafiestas *mf inv*

kiln [kɪln] *n* horno *m*

kilo ['kiːləʊ] *n* kilo *m*

kilobyte ['kɪləbaɪt] *n Comput* kilobyte *m*

kilogram(me) ['kɪləʊgræm] *n* kilogramo *m*

kilometre, *US* **kilometer** [kɪ'lɒmɪtə(r)] *n* kilómetro *m*

kilowatt ['kɪləʊwɒt] *n* kilovatio *m*

kilt [kɪlt] *n* falda escocesa, kilt *m*

kin [kɪn] *n* familiares *mpl*, parientes *mpl*

kind¹ [kaɪnd] **1** *n* tipo *m*, clase *f*; **they are two of a k.** son tal para cual; **in k.** (*payment*) en especie; (*treatment*) con la misma moneda
  2 *adv* **Fam k. of** en cierta manera

kind² ['kaɪnd] *adj* amable, simpático(a); *Fml* **would you be so k. as to …?** ¿me haría usted el favor de …?

kindergarten ['kɪndəgɑːtən] *n* jardín *m* de infancia

kind-hearted [kaɪnd'hɑːtɪd] *adj* bondadoso(a)

kindle ['kɪndəl] *vt* encender, *Am* prender

kindly ['kaɪndlɪ] **1** *adj* (**kindlier, kindliest**) amable, bondadoso(a)
  2 *adv Fml* (*please*) por favor; **k. remit a cheque** sírvase enviar cheque; **to look k. on** aprobar

kindness ['kaɪndnɪs] *n* bondad *f*, amabilidad *f*

kindred ['kɪndrɪd] *adj* **k. spirits** almas gemelas

kinetic [kɪ'netɪk] *adj* cinético(a)

king [kɪŋ] *n* rey *m*; (*draughts*) dama *f*

kingdom ['kɪŋdəm] *n* reino *m*

kingfisher ['kɪŋfɪʃə(r)] *n* martín *m* pescador

king-size ['kɪŋsaɪz] *adj* extralargo(a)

kink [kɪŋk] *n* (*in rope*) coca *f*, (*in hair*) rizo *m*

kinky ['kɪŋkɪ] *adj* (**kinkier, kinkiest**) *Fam* (*person*) aberrante, pervertido(a); (*erotic, pornographic*) erótico(a)

kiosk ['kiːɒsk] *n* quiosco *m*

kip [kɪp] *Br Fam*
  1 *n* **to have a k.** echar un sueño
  2 *vi* (*pt & pp* **kipped**) dormir

kipper ['kɪpə(r)] *n* arenque *m* ahumado

kiss [kɪs] **1** *n* beso *m*
  2 *vt* besar
  3 *vi* besarse

kit [kɪt] *n* (**a**) (*gear*) equipo *m*; *Mil* avíos *mpl* (**b**) (*clothing*) ropa *f* (**c**) (*toy model*) maqueta *f*
▸ **kit out** *vt sep* equipar

kitchen ['kɪtʃɪn] *n* cocina *f*; **k. sink** fregadero *m*

kite [kaɪt] *n* (**a**) (*toy*) cometa *f* (**b**) (*bird*) milano *m*

kitten ['kɪtən] *n* gatito(a) *m,f*

kitty ['kɪtɪ] *n* (*money*) fondo *m* común; *Cards* bote *m*

kiwi ['kiːwiː] *n* (**a**) (*bird*) kiwi *m* (**b**) **k. (fruit)** kiwi *m*

klutz [klʌts] *n US Fam* (*stupid person*) bobo(a) *m,f*, *Esp* chorra *mf*; (*clumsy person*) torpe, *Esp* patoso(a) *m,f*

km (*pl* **km** *or* **kms**) (*abbr* **kilometre(s)**) km

knack [næk] *n* **to get the k. of doing sth** cogerle el truquillo a algo

knackered ['nækəd] *adj Br Fam* **to be k.** (*tired*) estar hecho(a) polvo *or* reventado(a); (*broken, damaged*) estar hecho(a) polvo

knapsack ['næpsæk] *n* mochila *f*

knead [niːd] *vt* dar masaje a; *(bread etc)* amasar

knee [niː] **1** *n* rodilla *f*
2 *vt* dar un rodillazo a

kneecap ['niːkæp] **1** *n* rótula *f*
2 *vt* romper la rótula a

kneel [niːl] *vi (pt & pp* **knelt) to k. (down)** arrodillarse

knell [nel] *n Literary* toque *m* de difuntos

knelt [nelt] *pt & pp of* **kneel**

knew [njuː] *pt of* **know**

knickers ['nɪkəz] *npl Br* bragas *fpl, Chile, Col, Méx* calzones *mpl, RP* bombacha *f*

knick-knack ['nɪknæk] *n Fam* chuchería *f*, baratija *f*

knife [naɪf] **1** *n (pl* **knives)** cuchillo *m*
2 *vt* apuñalar, dar una puñalada a

knight [naɪt] **1** *n Hist* caballero *m*; *(in chess)* caballo *m*
2 *vt* armar caballero

knighthood ['naɪthʊd] *n (rank)* título *m* de caballero

knit [nɪt] **1** *vt (pt & pp* **knitted** *or* **knit) (a)** *(sweater)* tejer **(b) to k. (together)** *(join)* juntar; *Fig* **to k. one's brow** fruncir el ceño
2 *vi* **(a)** *(with wool)* tejer, hacer punto **(b)** *(bone)* soldarse

knitting ['nɪtɪŋ] *n* punto *m*; **k. machine** máquina *f* de tejer; **k. needle** aguja *f* de tejer

knitwear ['nɪtweə(r)] *n* prendas *fpl* de punto *or Am* tejidas

knives [naɪvz] *pl of* **knife**

knob [nɒb] *n* **(a)** *(of stick)* puño *m*; *(of drawer)* tirador *m*; *(button)* botón *m* **(b)** *(small portion)* trozo *m*

knock [nɒk] **1** *n* golpe *m*; *Fig* revés *m*
2 *vt* **(a)** *(hit)* golpear **(b)** *Fam (criticize)* criticar
3 *vi* chocar **(against** *or* **into** contra); *(at door)* llamar **(at** a)

▸ **knock down** *vt sep* **(a)** *(demolish)* derribar **(b)** *Aut* atropellar **(c)** *(price)* rebajar

▸ **knock off** *vt sep* **(a)** *(cause to fall off)* tirar **(b)** *Fam (steal) Esp* mangar, *Am* volar **(c)** *Fam (kill)* asesinar a, *Esp* cepillarse a
2 *vi Fam* **they k. off at five** se piran a las cinco

▸ **knock out** *vt sep* **(a)** *(make unconscious)* dejar sin conocimiento, *(in boxing)* poner fuera de combate, derrotar por K.O. **(b)** *(surprise)* dejar pasmado(a)

▸ **knock over** *vt sep (cup)* volcar; *(with car)* atropellar

knocker ['nɒkə(r)] *n (on door)* aldaba *f*

knock-kneed [nɒk'niːd] *adj* patizambo(a), *Am* chueco(a)

knockout ['nɒkaʊt] *n* **(a)** *(in boxing)* K.O. *m,* knock-out *m, Fam* maravilla *f*

knot [nɒt] **1** *n* nudo *m*; *(group of people)* corro *m*
2 *vt* anudar

knotty ['nɒtɪ] *adj* **(knottier, knottiest)** nudoso(a); *Fig* **a k. problem** un problema espinoso

know [nəʊ] **1** *vt (pt* **knew;** *pp* **known) (a)** *(have knowledge of)* saber; **she knows how to ski** sabe esquiar; **to get to k. sth** enterarse de algo **(b)** *(be acquainted with)* conocer; **we got to k. each other at the party** nos conocimos en la fiesta
2 *vi* saber; **as far as I k.** que yo sepa; **to let sb k.** avisar a algn

know-all ['nəʊɔːl] *n Fam* sabelotodo *mf*

know-how ['nəʊhaʊ] *n Fam* conocimiento práctico

knowing ['nəʊɪŋ] *adj (deliberate)* deliberado(a); **a k. smile** una sonrisa de complicidad

knowingly ['nəʊɪŋlɪ] *adv (shrewdly)* a sabiendas; *(deliberately)* deliberadamente

know-it-all ['nəʊɪtɔːl] *n Fam* sabihondo(a) *m,f,* sabelotodo *mf*

knowledge ['nɒlɪdʒ] *n* **(a)** *(awareness)* conocimiento *m*; **without my k.** sin saberlo yo **(b)** *(learning)* conocimientos *mpl*

knowledgeable ['nɒlɪdʒəbəl] *adj* erudito(a); **k. about** muy entendido(a) en

known [nəʊn] **1** *adj* conocido(a)
2 *pp of* **know**

knuckle ['nʌkəl] *n Anat* nudillo *m*; *Culin* hueso *m*

▸ **knuckle down** *vi Fam* ponerse a trabajar en serio

KO [keɪ'əʊ] *n Fam (abbr* **knockout)** K.O. *m*

Koran [kɔː'rɑːn] *n* Corán *m*

Koranic [kə'rænɪk] *adj* coránico(a)

Korea [kə'riːə] *n* Corea

Korean [kə'riːən] *adj & n* coreano(a) *(m,f)*

Kurd [kɜːd] *n* curdo(a) *m,f*

Kuwait [kʊ'weɪt] *n* Kuwait

L, l [el] *n (the letter)* L, l *f*

lab [læb] *n Fam (abbr* **laboratory)** laboratorio *m*

label ['leɪbəl] **1** *n* etiqueta *f*; **record l.** ≃ casa discográfica
2 *vt (pt & pp* **labelled,** *US* **labeled)** poner etiqueta a

labor ['leɪbə(r)] *n, adj, vt & vi US =* **labour**

laboratory [lə'bɒrətəri, *US* 'læbrətɔːrɪ] *n* laboratorio *m*

labored ['leɪbəd] *adj US =* **laboured**

laborer ['leɪbərə(r)] *n US =* **labourer**

laborious [lə'bɔːrɪəs] *adj* penoso(a)

labour ['leɪbə(r)] **1** *n* **(a)** *(work)* trabajo *m* **(b)** *(workforce)* mano *f* de obra **(c) labours** esfuerzos *mpl* **(d) the L. Party** el Partido Laborista **(e)** *(childbirth)* **to be in l.** estar de parto
2 *adj* laboral
3 *vt (stress, linger on)* machacar; *(a point)* insistir en
4 *vi (work)* trabajar (duro)

laboured ['leɪbəd] *adj (breathing)* fatigoso(a); *(style)* forzado(a)

labourer ['leɪbərə(r)] *n* peón *m*; **farm l.** peón *m* agrícola

labour-saving ['leɪbəseɪvɪŋ] *adj* **l. devices** electrodomésticos *mpl*

labyrinth ['læbərɪnθ] *n* laberinto *m*

lace [leɪs] **1** *n* **(a)** *(fabric)* encaje *m* **(b) laces** cordones *mpl*
2 *vt* **(a)** *(shoes)* atar (los cordones de) **(b)** *(add spirits to)* echar licor a
▸ **lace up** *vt sep* atar con cordones

lacerate ['læsəreɪt] *vt* lacerar

lack [læk] **1** *n* falta *f*, escasez *f*; **for l. of** por falta de
2 *vt* carecer de
3 *vi* carecer (**in** de)

lackadaisical [lækə'deɪzɪkəl] *adj (lazy)* perezoso(a); *(indifferent)* indiferente

lacklustre, *US* **lackluster** ['læklʌstə(r)] *adj (eyes)* apagado(a); *(performance)* anodino(a)

laconic [lə'kɒnɪk] *adj* lacónico(a)

lacquer ['lækə(r)] **1** *n* laca *f*
2 *vt (hair)* poner laca en

lad [læd] *n Fam* chaval *m*, muchacho *m*; **(stable) l.** mozo *m* de cuadra

ladder ['lædə(r)] **1** *n* **(a)** *(for climbing)* escalera *f*; *Fig* escala *f* **(b)** *(in stocking)* carrera *f*
2 *vt* **I've laddered my stocking** me he hecho una carrera en las medias

laden ['leɪdən] *adj* cargado(a) (**with** de)

ladle ['leɪdəl] *n* cucharón *m*

lady ['leɪdɪ] *n* señora *f*; *Pol* **First L.** primera dama; **Ladies** *(sign on WC)* Señoras; **ladies and gentlemen!** ¡señoras y señores!; **L. Brown** Lady Brown

ladybird ['leɪdɪbɜːd], *US* **ladybug** ['leɪdɪbʌg] *n* mariquita *f*

lady-in-waiting [leɪdɪn'weɪtɪŋ] *n* dama *f* de honor

ladylike ['leɪdɪlaɪk] *adj* elegante

ladyship ['leɪdɪʃɪp] *n* **Her/Your L.** su señoría

lag [læg] **1** *n* **time l.** demora *f*
2 *vt Tech* revestir
3 *vi* **to l. (behind)** quedarse atrás, retrasarse

lager ['lɑːgə(r)] *n* cerveza rubia

lagoon [lə'guːn] *n* laguna *f*

laid [leɪd] *pt & pp of* **lay**

laid-back [leɪd'bæk] *adj Fam* tranquilo(a), *Esp* cachazudo(a)

lain [leɪn] *pp of* **lie²**

lair [leə(r)] *n* guarida *f*

lake [leɪk] *n* lago *m*

lamb [læm] *n* cordero *m*; *(meat)* carne *f* de cordero; **l. chop** chuleta *f* de cordero; **l.'s wool** lana *f* de cordero

lame [leɪm] *adj* **(a)** *(person, animal)* cojo(a) **(b)** *(excuse, argument)* endeble, pobre

lament [lə'ment] **1** *n Mus* elegía *f*
2 *vt (death)* llorar, lamentar
3 *vi* llorar (**for** a), lamentarse (**over** de)

lamentable ['læməntəbəl] *adj* lamentable

laminated ['læmɪneɪtɪd] *adj (metal)* laminado(a); *(glass)* inastillable; *(paper)* plastificado(a)

lamp [læmp] *n* lámpara *f*; *Aut* faro *m*

lampoon [læm'puːn] **1** n sátira f
  2 vt satirizar

lamp-post ['læmppəʊst] n farola f

lampshade ['læmpʃeɪd] n pantalla f

lance [lɑːns] **1** n lanza f; Br Mil **l. corporal** cabo interino
  2 vt Med abrir con lanceta

> *Note that the Spanish word **lance** is a false friend and is never a translation for the English word **lance**. In Spanish **lance** means "event, incident".*

land [lænd] **1** n (a) (not sea) tierra f; **by l.** por tierra (b) Literary (country) país m (c) (property) tierras fpl; **piece of l.** terreno m
  2 vt (a) (plane) hacer aterrizar (b) (disembark) desembarcar (c) Fam (obtain) conseguir; (contract) ganar (d) Fam **she got landed with the responsibility** tuvo que cargar con la responsabilidad (e) Fam (blow) asestar
  3 vi (a) (plane) aterrizar (b) (disembark) desembarcar
▸ **land up** vi Fam ir a parar

landing ['lændɪŋ] n (a) (of staircase) rellano m (b) (of plane) aterrizaje m; **l. strip** pista f de aterrizaje (c) (of passengers) desembarco m; **l. stage** desembarcadero m

landlady ['lændleɪdɪ] n (of flat) dueña f, propietaria f; (of boarding house) patrona f; (of pub) dueña f

landlord ['lændlɔːd] n (of flat) dueño m, propietario m; (of pub) patrón m, dueño m

landmark ['lændmɑːk] n (a) (distinctive feature) punto m de referencia (b) Fig (in history) hito m

landowner ['lændəʊnə(r)] n terrateniente mf

landscape ['lændskeɪp] **1** n paisaje m
  2 vt ajardinar

landslide ['lændslaɪd] n desprendimiento m de tierras; **l. victory** victoria arrolladora

lane [leɪn] n (in country) camino m; (in town) callejón m; (of motorway) carril m; Sport calle f; Naut ruta f

language ['læŋgwɪdʒ] n (a) (of a people) idioma m, lengua f; **l. laboratory** laboratorio m de idiomas; **l. school** academia f de idiomas (b) (style of speech or writing) lenguaje m; **bad l.** palabrotas fpl

languid ['læŋgwɪd] adj lánguido(a)

languish ['læŋgwɪʃ] vi languidecer; (project, plan etc) quedar abandonado(a); (in prison) pudrirse

lank [læŋk] adj (hair) lacio(a)

lanky ['læŋkɪ] adj (lankier, lankiest) larguirucho(a)

lantern ['læntən] n farol m

lap¹ [læp] n Anat regazo m

lap² [læp] **1** n (circuit) vuelta f; Fig etapa f
  2 vt (overtake) doblar

lap³ [læp] **1** vt (pt & pp lapped) (of cat) beber a lengüetadas
  2 vi (waves) lamer, besar
▸ **lap up** vt sep (a) (of cat) beber a lengüetadas (b) Fig (wallow in) disfrutar con; (flattery) recibir con entusiasmo (c) Fig (believe) tragar

lapel [lə'pel] n solapa f

Lapland ['læplænd] n Laponia

lapse [læps] **1** n (a) (of time) lapso m (b) (error) error m, desliz m; (of memory) fallo m
  2 vi (a) (time) pasar, transcurrir (b) (expire) caducar (c) (err) cometer un error; (fall back) caer (into en)

laptop ['læptɒp] n Comput **l. (computer)** Esp ordenador m or Am computadora f portátil

larceny ['lɑːsənɪ] n Jur (delito m de) robo m or latrocinio m

larch [lɑːtʃ] n alerce m

lard [lɑːd] n manteca f de cerdo

larder ['lɑːdə(r)] n despensa f

large [lɑːdʒ] adj grande; (amount) importante; (extensive) amplio(a); **by and l.** por lo general
  2 n **to be at l.** andar suelto(a); **the public at l.** el público en general

> *Note that the Spanish word **largo** is a false friend and is never a translation for the English word **large**. In Spanish **largo** means "long".*

largely ['lɑːdʒlɪ] adv (mainly) en gran parte; (chiefly) principalmente

large-scale ['lɑːdʒskeɪl] adj (project, problem etc) de gran envergadura; (map) a gran escala

lark¹ [lɑːk] n (bird) alondra f

lark² [lɑːk] n Fam (joke) broma f; **what a l.!** ¡qué risa!
▸ **lark about, lark around** vi Fam hacer el tonto

larva ['lɑːvə] n larva f

laryngitis [lærɪn'dʒaɪtɪs] n laringitis f

larynx ['lærɪŋks] n Anat laringe f

laser ['leɪzə(r)] n láser m; **l. printer** impresora f láser

lash [læʃ] **1** n (a) (eyelash) pestaña f (b) (blow with whip) latigazo m
  2 vt (a) (beat) azotar (b) (rain) azotar (c) (tie) atar

▸ **lash out** *vi* (a) *(with fists)* repartir golpes a diestro y siniestro; *(verbally)* criticar (**at** a) (b) *Fam (spend money)* tirar *or Am salvo RP* botar la casa por la ventana

lass [læs] *n Fam* chavala *f*, muchacha *f*

lasso [læ'su:] 1 *n* lazo *m (para ganado)* 2 *vt* capturar con lazo, *CSur* lacear

last [lɑːst] 1 *adj* (a) *(final)* último(a), final; *Fam* **the l. straw** el colmo (b) *(most recent)* último(a) (c) *(past)* pasado(a); *(previous)* anterior; **l. but one** penúltimo(a); **l. month** el mes pasado; **l. night** anoche
  2 *adv* (a) **when I l. saw her** la última vez que la vi (b) *(at the end)* en último lugar; *(in race etc)* último; **at (long) l.** por fin; **l. but not least** el último en orden pero no en importancia
  3 *n* **the l.** el último/la última
  4 *vi* (a) *(time)* durar; *(hold out)* aguantar (b) *(be enough for)* llegar, alcanzar

last-ditch [lɑːst'dɪtʃ] *adj (effort, attempt)* último(a) y desesperado(a)

lasting [lɑːstɪŋ] *adj* duradero(a)

lastly [lɑːstlɪ] *adv* por último, finalmente

last-minute [lɑːst'mɪnɪt] *adj* de última hora

latch [lætʃ] *n* picaporte *m*, pestillo *m*

late [leɪt] 1 *adj* (a) *(not on time)* tardío(a); *(hour)* avanzado(a); **to be five minutes l.** llegar con cinco minutos de retraso (b) *(far on in time)* tarde; **in l. autumn** a finales del otoño; **in the l. afternoon** a última hora de la tarde; **she's in her l. twenties** ronda los treinta (c) *(dead)* difunto(a)
  2 *adv* (a) *(not on time)* tarde; **to arrive l.** llegar tarde (b) *(far on in time)* tarde; **l. at night** a altas horas de la noche; **l. in life** a una edad avanzada (c) **as l. as 1950** todavía en 1950; **of l.** últimamente

latecomer [leɪtkʌmə(r)] *n* tardón(ona) *m,f*

lately [leɪtlɪ] *adv* últimamente, recientemente

latent [leɪtənt] *adj* latente

later [leɪtə(r)] 1 *adj* (a) *(subsequent)* posterior; **in her l. novels** en sus novelas posteriores (b) *(more recent)* más reciente
  2 *adv* más tarde, después; **l. on** más adelante, más tarde

lateral [lætərəl] *adj* lateral

latest [leɪtɪst] *adj (superl of* late*) (most recent)* último(a), más reciente
  2 *n* **the l.** lo último; **have you heard the l.?** ¿te enteraste de lo último?; **Friday at the l.** el viernes a más tardar

lathe [leɪð] *n Tech* torno *m*

lather [lɑːðə(r)] 1 *n (of soap)* espuma *f*; *(horse's sweat)* sudor *m*
  2 *vt (with soap)* enjabonar

Latin [lætɪn] 1 *adj & n* latino(a) *(m,f)*; **L. America** América Latina, Latinoamérica *f*; **L. American** latinoamericano(a) *(m,f)*
  2 *n (language)* latín *m*

latitude [lætɪtjuːd] *n* latitud *f*

latrine [lə'triːn] *n* letrina *f*

latter [lætə(r)] 1 *adj* (a) *(last)* último(a) (b) *(second of two)* segundo(a)
  2 *pron* éste(a); **the former … the l.** aquél … éste/aquélla … ésta

lattice [lætɪs] *n* enrejado *m*, rejilla *f*

laudable [lɔːdəbəl] *adj* loable

laugh [lɑːf] 1 *n* risa *f*; *(guffaw)* carcajada *f*; **for a l.** para divertirse
  2 *vi* reír, reírse

▸ **laugh about** *vt insep* **to l. about sth/sb** reírse de algo/algn

▸ **laugh at** *vt insep* **to l. at sth/sb** reírse de algo/algn

▸ **laugh off** *vt sep* tomar a risa

laughable [lɑːfəbəl] *adj (situation, suggestion)* ridículo(a); *(amount, offer)* irrisorio(a)

laughing-stock [lɑːfɪŋstɒk] *n* hazmerreír *m inv*

laughter [lɑːftə(r)] *n* risa *f*

launch [lɔːntʃ] 1 *n* (a) *(vessel)* lancha *f* (b) *(of product)* lanzamiento *f*
  2 *vt* (a) *(attack, rocket, new product)* lanzar; *(ship)* botar (b) *(company)* fundar; *(scheme)* iniciar

launching [lɔːntʃɪŋ] *n* (a) *(of rocket, new product)* lanzamiento *m* (b) *(of ship)* botadura *f* (c) *(of film, play)* estreno *m* (d) *(of new company)* fundación *f*

launchpad [lɔːntʃpæd] *n* plataforma *f* de lanzamiento

launder [lɔːndə(r)] *vt* lavar y planchar; *Fig (money)* blanquear

laund(e)rette [lɔːndə'ret], *US* **Laundromat®** [lɔːndrəmæt] *n* lavandería *f*

laundry [lɔːndrɪ] *n* (a) *(place)* lavandería *f* (b) *(dirty clothes)* ropa sucia; **to do the l.** lavar la ropa

laurel [lɒrəl] *n* laurel *m*; *Fam Fig* **to rest on one's laurels** dormirse en los laureles

lava [lɑːvə] *n* lava *f*

lavatory [lævətərɪ] *n* (a) *(receptacle)* váter *m*, retrete *m* (b) *(room)* (cuarto *m* de) baño *m*; **public l.** servicios *mpl*, *Esp* aseos *mpl*

lavender [lævəndə(r)] *n* lavanda *f*

lavish [lævɪʃ] 1 *adj* (a) *(generous)* pródigo(a) (b) *(abundant)* abundante (c) *(luxurious)* lujoso(a)

2 *vt* **to l. praise on sb** colmar de alabanzas a algn; **to l. attention on sb** prodigarse en atenciones con algn

law [lɔː] *n* (**a**) *(rule, set of rules)* ley *f*; **by l.** según la ley; **l. and order** el orden público; **to lay down the l.** dictar la ley (**b**) *(as subject)* derecho *m*; **l. court** tribunal *m* de justicia (**c**) *Fam* **the l.** *(police)* la poli

law-abiding ['lɔːəbaɪdɪŋ] *adj* respetuoso(a) de la ley

lawful ['lɔːfʊl] *adj* legal; *(permitted by law)* lícito(a); *(legitimate)* legítimo(a)

lawn [lɔːn] *n* césped *m*; **l. tennis** tenis *m* sobre hierba

lawnmower ['lɔːnməʊə(r)] *n* cortacésped *m*

lawsuit ['lɔːsjuːt] *n* pleito *m*

lawyer ['lɔːjə(r)] *n* abogado(a) *m,f*; **l.'s office** bufete *m* de abogados

lax [læks] *adj (morals, discipline)* relajado(a), laxo(a); *(person)* negligente, poco riguroso(a); *(security, standards)* descuidado(a), poco riguroso(a)

laxative ['læksətɪv] *adj & n* laxante *(m)*

laxity ['læksɪtɪ] *n (of morals, discipline)* laxitud *f*, *Esp* relajo *m*; *(of person)* negligencia *f* (**in doing sth** al hacer algo); *(of security, standards)* falta *f* de rigor

lay¹ [leɪ] *adj* (**a**) *Rel* laico(a) (**b**) *(non-specialist)* lego(a)

lay² [leɪ] *vt (pt & pp* **laid**)
1 (**a**) *(place)* poner, colocar; *(cable, trap)* tender; *(foundations)* echar (**b**) *(fire)* preparar; *(table)* poner (**c**) *(eggs)* poner
2 *pt of* **lie²**

▸ **lay aside** *vt sep* dejar a un lado

▸ **lay by** *vt sep (save)* guardar; *(money)* ahorrar

▸ **lay down** *vt sep* (**a**) *(put down)* poner; *(let go)* dejar; **to l. down one's arms** rendir las armas (**b**) *(establish)* fijar, imponer; *(principles)* sentar

▸ **lay into** *vt insep Fam (physically)* dar una paliza a; *(verbally)* arremeter contra

▸ **lay off 1** *vt sep (dismiss)* despedir
2 *vt insep Fam* dejar en paz

▸ **lay on** *vt sep (provide)* proveer de; *(food)* preparar

▸ **lay out** *vt sep* (**a**) *(open out)* extender (**b**) *(arrange)* disponer (**c**) *(ideas)* exponer (**d**) *(plan)* trazar (**e**) *Fam (spend)* gastar

▸ **lay up** *vt sep* (**a**) *(store)* guardar (**b**) *(accumulate)* almacenar (**c**) *Fam* **to be laid up** tener que guardar cama

layabout ['leɪəbaʊt] *n Fam* vago(a) *m,f*

lay-by ['leɪbaɪ] *n Br* área *f* de descanso

layer ['leɪə(r)] *n* capa *f*

layman ['leɪmən] *n* lego(a) *m,f*

layout ['leɪaʊt] *n (arrangement)* disposición *f*; *(presentation)* presentación *f*; *Typ* composición *f*; *(plan)* diseño *m*, trazado *m*

laze [leɪz] *vi* **to l.** **(about/around)** holgazanear, gandulear

laziness ['leɪzɪnɪs] *n* pereza *f*, holgazanería *f*

lazy ['leɪzɪ] *adj (lazier, laziest)* perezoso(a), holgazán(ana); **at a l. pace** a paso lento

lb *(abbr* **pound**) libra *f*

lead¹ [led] *n* (**a**) *(metal)* plomo *m* (**b**) *(in pencil)* mina *f*

lead² [liːd] **1** *n* (**a**) *(front position)* delantera *f*; *(advantage)* ventaja *f*; **to take the l.** *(in race)* tomar la delantera (**b**) *(clue)* pista *f* (**c**) *Th* primer papel *m* (**d**) *(leash)* correa *f* (**e**) *Elec* cable *m*
2 *vt (pt & pp* **led**) (**a**) *(conduct)* llevar, conducir (**b**) *(be the leader of)* dirigir, encabezar (**c**) *(influence)* llevar a; **this leads me to believe that** esto me lleva a creer que (**d**) *(life)* llevar
3 *vi (road)* llevar, conducir **(to** a) (**b**) *(go first)* ir delante; *(in race)* llevar la delantera (**c**) **to l. to** llevar a

▸ **lead away** *vt sep* llevar

▸ **lead on 1** *vt sep (deceive)* engañar, timar
2 *vi (go ahead)* ir adelante

▸ **lead up to** *vt insep* llevar a

leaden ['ledən] *adj (sky)* plomizo(a); *(food)* pesado(a)

leader ['liːdə(r)] *n* (**a**) *(of group, in race)* líder (**b**) *Press* editorial *m*

leadership ['liːdəʃɪp] *n* (**a**) *(command)* dirección *f*, mando *m*; *Pol* liderazgo *m* (**b**) *(leaders)* dirigentes *mpl*, cúpula *f*

lead-free ['ledfriː] *adj* sin plomo

leading ['liːdɪŋ] *adj* (**a**) *(main)* principal (**b**) *(outstanding)* destacado(a)

leaf [liːf] *n (pl* **leaves**) hoja *f*; **to turn over a new l.** hacer borrón y cuenta nueva

▸ **leaf through** *vt insep* hojear

leaflet ['liːflɪt] *n* folleto *m*

league [liːg] *n* (**a**) *(alliance)* alianza *f*; *(association)* sociedad *f*; *Fam* **to be in l. with sb** estar conchabado(a) con algn (**b**) *Sport* liga *f*

leak [liːk] **1** *n* (**a**) *(hole)* agujero *m*; *(in roof)* gotera *f* (**b**) *(of gas, liquid)* fuga *f*, escape *m*; *(of information)* filtración *f*
2 *vt (information)* filtrar (**to** a)
3 *vi* (**a**) *(container)* tener un agujero; *(pipe)* tener un escape; *(roof)* gotear; *(boat)* hacer agua (**b**) *(gas, liquid)* escaparse; *(information)* filtrarse; *(news)* trascender

leaky ['li:kɪ] adj (**leakier, leakiest**) (container) agujereado(a); (roof) que tiene goteras; (ship) que hace agua

lean¹ [li:n] adj (meat) magro(a); (person) flaco(a); (harvest) escaso(a)

lean² [li:n] 1 vt apoyar (**on** en)
  2 vi (pt & pp **leaned** or **leant**) (a) (building, tree) inclinarse (b) (for support) **to l. on/against** apoyarse en/ contra; Fig **to l. on sb** (pressurize) presionar a algn; (depend) depender de algn
  ▸ **lean back** vi reclinarse
  ▸ **lean forward** vi inclinarse hacia delante
  ▸ **lean out** vi asomarse
  ▸ **lean over** vi inclinarse

leaning ['li:nɪŋ] 1 adj inclinado(a)
  2 n Fig (tendency) inclinación f, tendencia f

leant [lent] Br pt & pp of **lean**

lean-to ['li:ntu:] n (hut) cobertizo m

leap [li:p] 1 n (jump) salto m; Fig paso m; **l. year** año bisiesto
  2 vi (pt & pp **leaped** or **leapt**) saltar; Fig **her heart leapt** su corazón dio un vuelco
  ▸ **leap at** vt insep Fig (chance) no dejar escapar

leapfrog ['li:pfrɒg] n pídola f

leapt [lept] pt & pp of **leap**

learn [lɜ:n] 1 vt (pt & pp **learned** or **learnt**) (a) (language, skill) aprender; **to l. (how) to ski** aprender a esquiar (b) (find out about) **to l. that** enterarse de que
  2 vi (a) (acquire knowledge) aprender (b) (find out) **to l. about** or **of** enterarse de

learned ['lɜ:nɪd] adj erudito(a)

learner ['lɜ:nə(r)] n (beginner) principiante mf; **l. driver** aprendiz(a) m,f de conductor

learning ['lɜ:nɪŋ] n (knowledge) conocimientos mpl; (erudition) saber m

learnt [lɜ:nt] Br pt & pp of **learn**

lease [li:s] 1 n contrato m de arrendamiento; Fig **to give sb a new l.** Br of or US **on life** dar nueva vida a algn
  2 vt arrendar

leasehold ['li:shəʊld] 1 n derechos mpl de arrendamiento
  2 adj (property) arrendado(a)

leash [li:ʃ] n correa f

least [li:st] (superl of **little**) 1 adj menor, mínimo(a); **he has the l. time** él es quien menos tiempo tiene
  2 adv menos; **l. of all him** él menos que nadie
  3 n **the l.** lo menos; **at l.** por lo menos, al menos; **to say the l.** por no decir más

leather ['leðə(r)] 1 n piel f, cuero m
  2 adj de piel

leave¹ [li:v] 1 vt (pt & pp **left**) (a) (depart from) (place) irse de, marcharse de; (room) salir de; (person) dejar (b) (allow to remain) dejar; **l. him alone!** ¡déjale en paz!; Fam **l. it to me** yo me encargo (c) (put, deposit) **to l. sth somewhere** (deliberately) dejar algo en algún sitio; (by mistake) dejarse algo en algún sitio (d) (bequeath) legar (e) (remain) **to be left** quedar
  2 vi (go away) irse, marcharse; (go out) salir; **the train leaves in five minutes** el tren sale dentro de cinco minutos
  ▸ **leave behind** vt sep **to l. sth behind** dejarse algo
  ▸ **leave on** vt sep (a) (clothes) dejar puesto(a) (b) (lights, radio) dejar encendido(a) or Am prendido(a)
  ▸ **leave out** vt sep (omit) omitir; Fig **to feel left out** sentirse excluido(a)
  ▸ **leave over** vt sep **to be left over** (food, money) sobrar

leave² [li:v] n (a) (permission) permiso m (b) (time off) vacaciones fpl; Mil **on l.** de permiso; **l. of absence** excedencia f (c) **to take one's l. of sb** despedirse de algn

leaves [li:vz] pl of **leaf**

Lebanon ['lebənən] n (**the**) **L.** (el) Líbano

lecherous ['letʃərəs] adj lascivo(a)

lecture ['lektʃə(r)] 1 n (a) (public speech) conferencia f; Univ clase f; **to give a l. (on)** dar una conferencia (sobre); **l. theatre** sala f de conferencias; Univ aula f (b) (rebuke) sermón m
  2 vt (reproach) sermonear
  3 vi dar una conferencia; Univ dar clases

lecturer ['lektʃərə(r)] n conferenciante mf; Br Univ profesor(a) m,f de universidad

led [led] pt & pp of **lead**

ledge [ledʒ] n (a) (shelf) repisa f; (of window) alféizar m (b) (on mountain) saliente m

ledger ['ledʒə(r)] n libro m mayor

lee [li:] n (a) Naut sotavento m (b) Fig abrigo m

leech [li:tʃ] n sanguijuela f

leek [li:k] n puerro m

leer [lɪə(r)] vi mirar con lascivia

leeway ['li:weɪ] n libertad f; **this gives me a certain amount of l.** esto me da cierto margen de libertad

left¹ [left] 1 adj izquierdo(a); Pol **l. wing** izquierda f
  2 adv a la izquierda
  3 n izquierda f; **on the l.** a mano izquierda; Pol **to be on the l.** ser de izquierdas

left² [left] *pt & pp of* **leave**
left-hand ['lefthænd] *adj* **l. drive** con el volante a la izquierda; **on the l. side** a mano izquierda
left-handed [left'hændɪd] *adj* zurdo(a)
left-luggage [left'lʌgɪdʒ] *n Br* **l. office** consigna *f*
leftovers ['leftəʊvəz] *npl* sobras *fpl*
left-wing ['leftwɪŋ] *adj* de izquierdas, izquierdista
leg [leg] *n* (**a**) *(of person)* pierna *f*; *(of animal, table)* pata *f*; *Culin (of lamb)* pierna; *(of trousers)* pernera *f* (**b**) *(stage)* etapa *f*
legacy ['legəsɪ] *n* herencia *f*, legado *m*
legal ['li:gəl] *adj* (**a**) *(lawful, legitimate)* legal; **l. tender** moneda *f* de curso legal (**b**) *(relating to the law)* legal, jurídico(a); **l. aid** asesoramiento jurídico gratuito; **l. dispute** contencioso *m*; *US* **l. holiday** fiesta *f* nacional
legalize ['li:gəlaɪz] *vt* legalizar
legally ['li:gəlɪ] *adv* legalmente
legend ['ledʒənd] *n* leyenda *f*
legendary ['ledʒəndərɪ] *adj* legendario(a)
leggings ['legɪŋz] *npl* polainas *fpl*
legible ['ledʒəbəl] *adj* legible
legion ['li:dʒən] *n* legión *f*
legislation [ledʒɪs'leɪʃən] *n* legislación *f*
legislative ['ledʒɪslətɪv] *adj* legislativo(a)
legislator ['ledʒɪsleɪtə(r)] *n* legislador(a) *m,f*
legislature ['ledʒɪsleɪtʃə(r)] *n* asamblea legislativa
legitimate [lɪ'dʒɪtɪmɪt] *adj* legítimo(a)
legroom ['legru:m] *n* espacio *m* para las piernas
leisure ['leʒə(r), *US* 'li:ʒər] *n* ocio *m*, tiempo *m* libre; **at l.** con calma; **do it at your l.** hazlo cuando tengas tiempo; **l. activities** pasatiempos *mpl*; **l. centre** centro recreativo
leisurely ['leʒəlɪ, *US* 'li:ʒərlɪ] *adj* *(unhurried)* tranquilo(a); *(slow)* lento(a)
lemon ['lemən] *n* limón *m*; **l. curd** crema *f* de limón; **l. juice** zumo *m* de limón; **l. tea** té *m* con limón
lemonade [lemə'neɪd] *n* *(still)* limonada *f*; *Br (fizzy) Esp, Arg* gaseosa *f*, *Am* gaseosa *f* de lima *or* limón
lend [lend] *vt* *(pt & pp lent)* prestar; **to l. oneself/itself to sth** prestarse a *or* para algo
lender ['lendə(r)] *n Fin* prestamista *mf*
lending ['lendɪŋ] *n* **l. library** biblioteca *f* de préstamo

length [leŋkθ, leŋθ] *n* (**a**) *(in space)* longitud *f*; **it is 5 m in l.** tiene 5 m de largo; *Fig* **to go to any lengths to achieve sth** hacer lo que sea para conseguir algo (**b**) *(duration)* duración *f* (**c**) *(of string)* trozo *m*; *(of cloth)* retal *m* (**d**) **at l.** *(finally)* finalmente; *(in depth)* a fondo
lengthen ['leŋkθən, 'leŋθən] **1** *vt* alargar; *(lifetime)* prolongar
2 *vi* alargarse; *(lifetime)* prolongarse
lengthways ['leŋθweɪz] *adv* a lo largo
lengthy ['leŋkθɪ, 'leŋθɪ] *adj* (**lengthier, lengthiest**) largo(a); *(film, illness)* de larga duración; *(meeting, discussion)* prolongado(a)
lenient ['li:nɪənt] *adj* indulgente
lens [lenz] *n* *(of eye)* cristalino *m*; *(of spectacles)* lente *f*; *Phot* objetivo *m*
Lent [lent] *n* Cuaresma *f*
lent [lent] *pt & pp of* **lend**
lentil ['lentɪl] *n* lenteja *f*
Leo ['li:əʊ] *n* Leo *m*
leopard ['lepəd] *n* leopardo *m*
leotard ['li:əta:d] *n* leotardo *m*
leper ['lepə(r)] *n* leproso(a) *m,f*
leprosy ['leprəsɪ] *n* lepra *f*
lesbian ['lezbɪən] *adj & n* lesbiana (*f*)
less [les] **1** *adj* (*comp of* **little**) menos
2 *pron* menos; **the l. said about it, the better** cuanto menos se hable de eso mejor
3 *adv* menos; **l. and l.** cada vez menos
4 *prep* menos
lessen ['lesən] *vt & vi* disminuir
lesser ['lesə(r)] *adj* menor; **to a l. extent** en menor grado
lesson ['lesən] *n* (**a**) *(session)* clase *f*; *(in book)* lección *f*; **Spanish lessons** clases de español (**b**) *Rel* lectura *f*
lest [lest] *conj Fml (in case)* para que no; **l. we forget** para que no olvidemos
let [let] **1** *vt* *(pt & pp let)* (**a**) *(allow)* dejar, permitir; **to l. go of sth** soltar algo; **to l. sb know** avisar a algn; *Fig* **to l. oneself go** dejarse ir (**b**) *(rent out)* alquilar, *Méx* rentar; **to l.** *(sign)* se alquila (**c**) **l. alone** ni mucho menos
2 *v aux* **l. him wait** que espere; **l. me go!** ¡suéltame!; **l.'s go!** ¡vamos!, ¡vámonos!; **l.'s see** a ver
▸ **let down** *vt sep* (**a**) *(lower)* bajar; *(lengthen)* alargar (**b**) *(deflate)* desinflar (**c**) *(fail)* fallar, defraudar
▸ **let in** *vt sep* (**a**) *(admit)* dejar entrar (**b**) **to l. oneself in for** meterse en
▸ **let off** *vt sep* (**a**) *(bomb)* hacer explotar; *(fireworks)* hacer estallar (**b**) *(liquid, air)*

soltar (**c**) *Fam* **to l. sb off** *(pardon)* perdonar

▸ **let on** *vi Fam* **don't l. on** *(reveal information)* no se lo digas

▸ **let out** *vt sep* (**a**) *(release)* soltar; *(news)* divulgar, *(secret)* revelar (**b**) *(air, water)* dejar salir (**c**) *(cry)* soltar (**d**) *Sewing* ensanchar

▸ **let up** *vi* cesar, parar

letdown ['letdaʊn] *n* decepción *f*

lethal ['li:θəl] *adj* letal

lethargic [lɪ'θɑ:dʒɪk] *adj* aletargado(a)

letter ['letə(r)] *n* (**a**) *(of alphabet)* letra *f*; *Fig* **to the l.** al pie de la letra (**b**) *(written message)* carta *f*; *Br* **l. box** buzón *m*; *Com* **l. of credit** carta de crédito

letterhead ['letəhed] *n* membrete *m*

lettering ['letərɪŋ] *n* rótulo *m*

lettuce ['letɪs] *n* lechuga *f*

let-up ['letʌp] *n Fam* descanso *m*, respiro *m*

leukaemia, *US* **leukemia** [lu:'ki:mɪə] *n* leucemia *f*

level ['levəl] **1** *adj* (**a**) *(flat)* llano(a); *(even)* nivelado(a); *(equal)* igual, parejo(a); **a l. spoonful of** una cucharada rasa de; **to be l. with** estar a nivel de; *Br* **l. crossing** paso *m* a nivel (**b**) *(steady)* estable; *(tone)* uniforme

2 *vt* (*pt & pp* **levelled**, *US* **leveled**) (**a**) *(make level)* nivelar (**b**) *(building)* arrasar (**c**) *(stare, criticism)* dirigir

3 *n* nivel *m*; **to be on a l. with** estar al mismo nivel que

▸ **level off**, **level out** *vi* estabilizarse

▸ **level with** *vt insep Fam* ser franco(a) con

level-headed [levəl'hedɪd] *adj* sensato(a)

lever ['li:və(r), *US* 'levə(r)] **1** *n* palanca *f*
2 *vt* apalancar; **to l. sth out** sacar algo con palanca

leverage ['li:vərɪdʒ] *n Fig* influencia *f*

levy ['levɪ] **1** *vt (tax)* recaudar; *(fine)* imponer
2 *n (of tax)* recaudación *f*; *(of fine)* imposición *f*

lewd [lu:d] *adj (person)* lascivo(a); *(story)* obsceno(a)

liability [laɪə'bɪlɪtɪ] *n* (**a**) *Jur* responsabilidad *f* (**b**) *(handicap)* estorbo *m* (**c**) *Fin* **liabilities** pasivo *m*

liable ['laɪəbəl] *adj* (**a**) *Jur* responsable; *(susceptible)* sujeto(a); **to be l. for** ser responsable de (**b**) **to be l. to do sth** ser propenso(a) a hacer algo; **it's l. to happen** es muy probable que (así) suceda

liaise [lɪ'eɪz] *vi* comunicarse (**with** con)

liaison [lɪ'eɪzɒn] *n* (**a**) *(cooperation)* coordinación *f*; **l. officer** oficial *mf* de enlace (**b**) *(love affair)* amorío *m*

liar ['laɪə(r)] *n* mentiroso(a) *m,f*, embustero(a) *m,f*

libel ['laɪbəl] **1** *n* libelo *m*
2 *vt* (*pt & pp* **libelled**, *US* **libeled**) difamar, calumniar

liberal ['lɪbərəl] **1** *adj* (**a**) *(tolerant)* liberal; **L. Party** Partido *m* Liberal (**b**) *(abundant)* abundante
2 *n Pol* **L.** liberal *mf*

liberate ['lɪbəreɪt] *vt* liberar; *(prisoner etc)* poner en libertad; **liberated woman** mujer liberada

liberation [lɪbə'reɪʃən] *n* liberación *f*

liberty ['lɪbətɪ] *n* libertad *f*; **to be at l. to say sth** ser libre de decir algo; **to take liberties** tomarse libertades

Libra ['li:brə] *n* Libra *m*

librarian [laɪ'breərɪən] *n* bibliotecario(a) *m,f*

> 🖉 Note that the Spanish word **librero** is a false friend and is never a translation for the English word **librarian**. In Spanish **librero** means "bookseller".

library ['laɪbrərɪ] *n* biblioteca *f*

> 🖉 Note that the Spanish word **librería** is a false friend and is never a translation for the English word **library**. In Spanish **librería** means "bookshop".

Libya ['lɪbɪə] *n* Libia

Libyan ['lɪbɪən] *adj & n* libio(a) *(m,f)*

lice [laɪs] *pl of* **louse**

licence, *US* **license** ['laɪsəns] *n* (**a**) *(permit)* licencia *f*, permiso *m*; *Aut* **l. number** matrícula *f*; *US* **l. plate** (placa *f* de la) matrícula (**b**) *(freedom)* libertad *f*; *(excessive freedom)* libertinaje *m*

license ['laɪsəns] **1** *vt* dar licencia a, autorizar
2 *n US =* **licence**

licensed ['laɪsənst] *adj Br* **l. premises =** local autorizado para la venta de bebidas alcohólicas; **l. restaurant =** restaurante con licencia para vender bebidas alcohólicas

licentious [laɪ'senʃəs] *adj* licencioso(a)

lichen ['laɪkən, 'lɪtʃən] *n* liquen *m*

lick [lɪk] **1** *vt* lamer; **to l. one's lips** relamerse
2 *n* lamedura *f*; *Fam* **a l. of paint** una mano de pintura

licorice ['lɪkərɪs] *n US =* **liquorice**

lid [lɪd] *n* (**a**) *(cover)* tapa *f* (**b**) *(of eye)* párpado *m*

'lie¹ [laɪ] **1** *vi* mentir
2 *n* mentira *f*

lie² [laɪ] **1** *vi* (*pt* **lay**; *pp* **lain**) (**a**) (*act*) echarse, acostarse; (*state*) estar echado(a), estar acostado(a); (*be buried*) yacer (**b**) (*be situated*) encontrarse, hallarse; **the valley lay before us** el valle se extendía ante nosotros (**c**) (*remain*) quedarse
2 *n* (*position*) situación *f*; (*direction*) orientación *f*
▶ **lie about, lie around** *vi* (*person*) estar tumbado(a); (*things*) estar tirado(a)
▶ **lie down** *vi* acostarse, echarse

lie-in ['laɪɪn] *n Fam* **to have a l.** levantarse tarde

lieu [ljuː, luː] *n* **in l. of** en lugar de

lieutenant [*Br* lef'tenənt, *US* luː'tenənt] *n* (**a**) *Mil* teniente *m* (**b**) (*deputy, assistant*) lugarteniente *m*

life [laɪf] *n* (*pl* **lives**) (**a**) (*in general*) vida *f*; **to come to l.** cobrar vida; **to take one's own l.** suicidarse; *Fam* **how's l.?** ¿qué tal?; **l. belt** cinturón *m* salvavidas; **l. imprisonment** cadena perpetua; **l. insurance** seguro *m* de vida; **l. jacket** chaleco *m* salvavidas; **l. style** estilo *m* de vida; **l. story** biografía *f* (**b**) (*liveliness*) vitalidad *f*

lifeboat ['laɪfbəʊt] *n* (*on ship*) bote *m* salvavidas; (*on shore*) lancha *f* de socorro

lifeguard ['laɪfgɑːd] *n* socorrista *mf*

lifeless ['laɪflɪs] *adj* sin vida

lifelike ['laɪflaɪk] *adj* natural; (*portrait*) fiel

lifeline ['laɪflaɪn] *n Fig* cordón *m* umbilical

lifelong ['laɪflɒŋ] *adj* de toda la vida

life-size(d) ['laɪfsaɪz(d)] *adj* (de) tamaño natural

lifetime ['laɪftaɪm] *n* vida *f*; **in his l.** durante su vida; **it's the chance of a l.** es una ocasión única

lift [lɪft] **1** *vt* (**a**) (*raise, move*) levantar (**b**) (*troops*) transportar (**c**) *Fam* (*steal*) birlar
2 *vi* (*clouds, mist*) disiparse
3 *n* (**a**) *Br* (*elevator*) ascensor *m* (**b**) **to give sb a l.** llevar a algn en coche (**c**) *Fig* (*boost*) estímulo *m*
▶ **lift up** *vt sep* levantar, alzar

lift-off ['lɪftɒf] *n* despegue *m*

ligament ['lɪgəmənt] *n* ligamento *m*

light¹ [laɪt] **1** *n* (**a**) (*illumination*) luz *f*; **by the l. of** en vista de; *Fig* **to bring sth to l.** sacar algo a la luz; *Fig* **to come to l.** salir a la luz; **l. switch** interruptor *m* de la luz; **l. year** año *m* luz (**b**) (*lamp*) luz *f*, lámpara *f*; (*traffic light*) semáforo *m*; (*headlight*) faro *m* (**c**) (*flame*)

lumbre *f*; **to set l. to sth** prender fuego a algo; *Fam* **have you got a l.?** ¿tiene fuego?
2 *vt* (*pt & pp* **lighted** *or* **lit**) (**a**) (*illuminate*) iluminar, alumbrar (**b**) (*ignite*) encender
3 *adj* claro(a); (*hair*) rubio(a)
▶ **light up 1** *vt sep* iluminar, alumbrar
2 *vi* (**a**) (*sky*) iluminarse (**b**) *Fam* encender un cigarrillo

light² [laɪt] **1** *adj* ligero(a); (*rain*) fino(a); (*breeze*) suave; *Fig* (*sentence etc*) leve; *Fig* **to make l. of sth** dar poca importancia a algo
2 *adv* **to travel l.** ir ligero(a) de equipaje

lighten¹ ['laɪtən] **1** *vt* (**a**) (*colour*) aclarar (**b**) (*illuminate*) iluminar
2 *vi* aclararse

lighten² ['laɪtən] *vt* (**a**) (*weight*) aligerar (**b**) *Fig* (*mitigate*) aliviar; (*heart*) alegrar

lighter ['laɪtə(r)] *n* (**cigarette**) **l.** encendedor *m*, mechero *m*

light-headed [laɪt'hedɪd] *adj* (**a**) (*dizzy*) mareado(a) (**b**) (*frivolous*) frívolo(a)

light-hearted [laɪt'hɑːtɪd] *adj* alegre

lighthouse ['laɪthaʊs] *n* faro *m*

lighting ['laɪtɪŋ] *n* (**a**) (*act*) iluminación *f* (**b**) (*system*) alumbrado *m*

lightly ['laɪtlɪ] *adv* ligeramente; **to get off l.** salir casi indemne

lightness¹ ['laɪtnɪs] *n* luminosidad *f*, claridad *f*

lightness² ['laɪtnɪs] *n* (*of weight*) ligereza *f*

lightning ['laɪtnɪŋ] *n* (*flash*) relámpago *m*; (*stroke*) rayo *m*; **l. conductor** *or* **rod** pararrayos *m inv*; **l. strike** huelga *f* relámpago

lightweight ['laɪtweɪt] *adj* (*suit etc*) ligero(a); (*boxer*) de peso ligero; *Fig* (*person*) light

like¹ [laɪk] **1** *adj* (*similar*) parecido(a), similar
2 *adv* (**as**) **l. as not** a lo mejor
3 *prep* (**a**) (*similar to*) como, parecido(a) a; (*the same as*) igual que; **it's not l. her to do that** no es propio de ella hacer eso; **I've never seen anything l. it** nunca he visto cosa igual; **l. that** así; **people l. that** son tipo de gente; **what's he l.?** ¿cómo es? (**b**) **to feel l.** (*want*) tener ganas de; **I feel l. a change** me apetece un cambio
4 *n* **brushes, combs and the l.** cepillos, peines y cosas por el estilo

like² [laɪk] **1** *vt* (**a**) **do you l. chocolate?** ¿te gusta el chocolate?; **he likes dancing** le gusta bailar; **she likes children** le gustan los niños (**b**) (*want*) querer; **whether you l. it or not** quieras o no (quieras); **would you l. a drink?** ¿te apetece tomar algo?

2 *vi* querer, gustar; **as you l.** como quieras

3 *n* gusto *m*

likeable ['laɪkəbəl] *adj* simpático(a)

likelihood ['laɪklɪhʊd] *n* probabilidad *f*

likely ['laɪklɪ] **1** *adj* (**likelier, likeliest**) probable; **he's l. to cause trouble** es probable que cause problemas; **where are you l. to be this afternoon?** ¿dónde piensas estar esta tarde?

2 *adv* probablemente; **not l.!** ¡ni hablar!

liken ['laɪkən] *vt* comparar (**to** a *or* con)

likeness ['laɪknɪs] *n* (**a**) *(similarity)* parecido *m* (**b**) *(portrait)* retrato *m*

likewise ['laɪkwaɪz] *adv* (**a**) *(also)* también, asimismo (**b**) *(the same)* lo mismo, igual

liking ['laɪkɪŋ] *n* (*for thing*) afición *f*; (*for person*) simpatía *f*; (*for friend*) cariño *m*; **to take a l. to sth** cogerle el gusto a algo; **to take a l. to sb** tomar *or Esp* coger cariño a algn

lilac ['laɪlək] **1** *n* (**a**) *Bot* lila *f* (**b**) *(colour)* lila *m*

2 *adj* lila, de color lila

lilt [lɪlt] *n* melodía *f*

lily ['lɪlɪ] *n* lirio *m*, azucena *f*; **l. of the valley** lirio de los valles

limb [lɪm] *n* miembro *m*; *Fig* **to be out on a l.** *(in danger)* estar en peligro; *Br (isolated)* estar aislado(a)

▸ **limber up** ['lɪmbə(r)] *vi Sport* entrar en calor; *Fig* prepararse (**for** para)

limbo ['lɪmbəʊ] *n* limbo *m*; *Fig* olvido *m*; **to be in l.** caer en el olvido

lime¹ [laɪm] *n Chem* cal *f*

lime² [laɪm] *n* (*fruit*) lima *f*; (*tree*) limero *m*

limelight ['laɪmlaɪt] *n Fig* **to be in the l.** estar en el candelero

limerick ['lɪmərɪk] *n* quintilla humorística

limestone ['laɪmstəʊn] *n* piedra caliza

limit ['lɪmɪt] **1** *n* límite *m*; *(maximum)* máximo *m*; *(minimum)* mínimo *m*

2 *vt* (*restrict*) limitar

limitation [lɪmɪ'teɪʃən] *n* limitación *f*

limited ['lɪmɪtɪd] *adj* limitado(a); *US (train)* semidirecto(a); **l. company** sociedad (de responsabilidad) limitada; **l. edition** edición limitada; **l. liability** responsabilidad limitada

limitless ['lɪmɪtlɪs] *adj* ilimitado(a)

limousine ['lɪməziːn, lɪmə'ziːn] *n* limusina *f*

limp¹ [lɪmp] **1** *vi* cojear

2 *n* cojera *f*

limp² [lɪmp] *adj* (**a**) *(floppy)* flojo(a) (**b**) *(weak)* débil

limpet ['lɪmpɪt] *n* lapa *f*

linchpin ['lɪntʃpɪn] *n Tech* pezonera *f*; *Fig* eje *m*

line¹ [laɪn] *n* (**a**) *(in general)* línea *f*; *(straight)* raya *f* (**b**) *(of writing)* renglón *m*; *(of poetry)* verso *m*; *Th* **to learn one's lines** aprenderse el papel (**c**) *(row)* fila *f*; *(of trees)* hilera *f*; *US (queue)* cola *f*; *Fig* **to be in l. (with)** coincidir (con); *US* **to stand in l.** *(queue)* hacer cola; *Fig* **sth along these lines** algo por el estilo; **l. dancing** baile *m* en línea, = baile al ritmo de música country en el que los participantes se colocan en hileras y dan los mismos pasos (**d**) *(rope)* cuerda *f*; *(wire)* cable *m* (**e**) *Tel* línea *f*; **hold the l.!** ¡no cuelgue! (**f**) *Br Rail* vía *f* (**g**) *(range of goods)* surtido *m*; **a new l.** una nueva línea

▸ **line up 1** *vt sep (arrange in rows)* poner en fila

2 *vi (people)* ponerse en fila; *(troops)* formar; *(in queue)* hacer cola

line² [laɪn] *vt (pipe etc)* revestir; *Sewing* forrar; *Fam* **to l. one's pockets** forrarse

linear ['lɪnɪə(r)] *adj* lineal

lined [laɪnd] *adj* (**a**) *(paper)* rayado(a); *(face)* arrugado(a) (**b**) *(garment)* forrado(a)

linen ['lɪnɪn] *n* (**a**) *(cloth)* lino *m* (**b**) *(clothes)* ropa *f*; *(sheets etc)* ropa blanca

liner ['laɪnə(r)] *n* transatlántico *m*

linesman ['laɪnzmən] *n Sport* juez *m* de línea

line-up ['laɪnʌp] *n Sport* alineación *f*

linger ['lɪŋgə(r)] *vi* tardar; *(dawdle)* rezagarse; *(smell, doubt)* persistir; *Fig (memory)* perdurar

lingerie ['lænʒəriː] *n Fml* ropa *f* interior (de mujer)

lingering ['lɪŋgərɪŋ] *adj (doubt)* persistente; *(look)* fijo(a)

lingo ['lɪŋgəʊ] *n (pl* **lingoes)** *Fam* (**a**) *(language)* lengua *f*, idioma *m* (**b**) *(jargon)* jerga *f*

linguist ['lɪŋgwɪst] *n* lingüista *mf*; **he's a good l.** se le dan bien los idiomas

linguistic [lɪŋ'gwɪstɪk] *adj* lingüístico(a)

linguistics [lɪŋ'gwɪstɪks] *n sing* lingüística *f*

lining ['laɪnɪŋ] *n* forro *m*

link [lɪŋk] **1** *n* (**a**) *(of chain)* eslabón *m* (**b**) *(connection)* conexión *f*; *Fig* vínculo *m*; **rail l.** enlace ferroviario (**c**) **links** campo *m* de golf

2 *vt* unir

▸ **link up** *vi* unirse; *(meet)* encontrarse; *(spaceships)* acoplarse

link-up ['lɪŋkʌp] n Tel & TV conexión f; (meeting) encuentro m; (of spaceships) acoplamiento m

lino ['laɪnəʊ] n Fam linóleo m

linoleum [lɪ'nəʊlɪəm] n linóleo m, linóleum m

lint [lɪnt] n (for wounds) hilas fpl

lion ['laɪən] n león m

lioness ['laɪənɪs] n leona f

lip [lɪp] n (a) (of mouth) labio m (b) (of jug) pico m

lip-read ['lɪpriːd] vt & vi leer en los labios

lip-service ['lɪpsɜːvɪs] n palabrería f

lipstick ['lɪpstɪk] n lápiz m de labios

liqueur [lɪ'kjʊə(r)] n licor m

liquid ['lɪkwɪd] adj & n líquido(a) (m)

liquidate ['lɪkwɪdeɪt] vt liquidar

liquidation [lɪkwɪ'deɪʃən] n liquidación f; to go into l. entrar en liquidación

liquidize ['lɪkwɪdaɪz] vt licuar

liquidizer ['lɪkwɪdaɪzə(r)] n Br Esp batidora f, Am licuadora f

liquor ['lɪkər] n US alcohol m, bebidas alcohólicas; l. store tienda f de bebidas alcohólicas

liquorice ['lɪkərɪs] n regaliz m

Lisbon ['lɪzbən] n Lisboa

lisp [lɪsp] 1 n ceceo m
2 vi cecear

list¹ [lɪst] 1 n lista f; (catalogue) catálogo m
2 vt (make a list of) hacer una lista de; (put on a list) poner en una lista; it is not listed no figura en la lista

list² [lɪst] Naut 1 n escora f
2 vi escorar

listen ['lɪsən] vi escuchar; (pay attention) prestar atención
▸ listen out for vt insep estar atento(a) a

listener ['lɪsənə(r)] n oyente mf

listless ['lɪstlɪs] adj apático(a)

lit [lɪt] pt & pp of light

liter ['liːtə(r)] n US = litre

literacy ['lɪtərəsɪ] n alfabetización f

literal ['lɪtərəl] adj literal

literally ['lɪtərəlɪ] adv literalmente

literary ['lɪtərərɪ] adj literario(a)

literate ['lɪtərɪt] adj alfabetizado(a)

> Note that the Spanish word literato is a false friend and is never a translation for the English word literate. In Spanish literato means "writer, author".

literature ['lɪtərətʃə(r)] n (a) (fiction, poetry) literatura f (b) Fam (documentation) folleto informativo

lithe [laɪð] adj Fml ágil

Lithuania [lɪθjʊ'eɪnɪə] n Lituania

Lithuanian [lɪθjʊ'eɪnɪən] 1 adj lituano(a)
2 n (person) lituano(a) m,f; (language) lituano m

litigation [lɪtɪ'geɪʃən] n litigio m

litmus ['lɪtməs] n Fig l. test prueba f contundente

litre ['liːtə(r)] n litro m

litter ['lɪtə(r)] 1 n (a) (rubbish) basura f; (papers) papeles mpl; l. bin papelera f (b) (offspring) camada f
2 vt ensuciar

littered ['lɪtəd] adj cubierto(a) (with de)

little ['lɪtəl] 1 adj (a) (small) pequeño(a); a l. dog un perrito; a l. house una casita; l. finger (dedo m) meñique m (b) (not much) poco(a); a l. cheese un poco de queso
2 pron poco m; save me a l. guárdame un poco
3 adv poco; l. by l. poco a poco; as l. as possible lo menos posible

live¹ [lɪv] 1 vt vivir; to l. an interesting life vivir una vida interesante
2 vi vivir; long l. the King! ¡viva el Rey!
▸ live down vt sep conseguir que se olvide
▸ live for vt insep vivir para
▸ live off vt insep vivir de
▸ live on 1 vt insep (food, money) vivir de
2 vi (memory) persistir
▸ live through vt insep vivir durante
▸ live together vi vivir juntos
▸ live up vt sep Fam to l. it up pegarse la gran vida
▸ live up to vt insep (promises) cumplir con; it didn't l. up to expectations no fue lo que se esperaba
▸ live with vt insep (a) (cohabit with) vivir con (b) Fig (accept) aceptar

live² [laɪv] adj (a) (living) vivo(a) (b) Rad & TV en directo, en vivo (c) (ammunition) real; (bomb) sin explotar; Elec con corriente; Fam he's a real l. wire! ¡éste no para nunca!

livelihood ['laɪvlɪhʊd] n sustento m

lively ['laɪvlɪ] adj (livelier, liveliest) (person) vivo(a); (place) animado(a); Fig (interest) entusiástico(a)

liven ['laɪvən] vt to l. (up) animar

liver ['lɪvə(r)] n hígado m

livery ['lɪvərɪ] n librea f

lives [laɪvz] pl of life

livestock ['laɪvstɒk] n ganado m

livid ['lɪvɪd] adj lívido(a); Fam (angry) furioso(a)

living ['lɪvɪŋ] 1 adj vivo(a)
2 n vida f; l. conditions condiciones fpl de vida; l. expenses dietas fpl; to earn or

make one's l. ganarse la vida; **l. room** sala f de estar; **l. standards** nivel m de vida; **l. wage** sueldo mínimo

lizard ['lɪzəd] n (large) lagarto m; (small) lagartija f

llama ['lɑːmə] n llama f

load [ləʊd] **1** n (cargo) carga f; (weight) peso m; Elec & Tech carga; Fam **loads (of)** montones de; Fam **that's a l. of rubbish!** ¡no son más que tonterías! **2** vt cargar

► **load up** vt sep & vi cargar

loaded ['ləʊdɪd] adj (a) (lorry, gun) cargado(a) (**with** de); Fig **a l. question** una pregunta intencionada (**b**) Fam **to be l.** (rich) estar forrado(a)

loading ['ləʊdɪŋ] n carga f; **l. bay** cargadero m

loaf[1] [ləʊf] n (pl loaves) pan m; (French stick) barra f de pan; (sliced) pan de molde

loaf[2] [ləʊf] vi **to l. (about** or **around)** holgazanear

loan [ləʊn] **1** n préstamo m; Fin empréstito m; **on l.** prestado(a); (footballer) cedido(a) **2** vt prestar

loath [ləʊθ] adj **to be l. to do sth** ser reacio(a) a hacer algo

loathe [ləʊð] vt aborrecer, odiar

loathing ['ləʊðɪŋ] n aborrecimiento m, odio m

loathsome ['ləʊðsəm] adj odioso(a), repugnante

loaves [ləʊvz] pl of loaf

lobby ['lɒbɪ] **1** n (**a**) (hall) vestíbulo m (**b**) (pressure group) grupo m de presión, lobby m **2** vt presionar **3** vi ejercer presiones

lobe [ləʊb] n lóbulo m

lobster ['lɒbstə(r)] n langosta f

local ['ləʊkəl] **1** adj local; (person) del pueblo; Med **l. anaesthetic** anestesia f local; Tel **l. call** llamada urbana; **l. government** gobierno m municipal **2** n Fam (**a**) **the locals** los vecinos (**b**) Br (pub) bar m del barrio

locality [ləʊ'kælɪtɪ] n localidad f

localize ['ləʊkəlaɪz] vt (restrict) localizar

locally ['ləʊkəlɪ] adv en or de la localidad

locate [ləʊ'keɪt] vt (situate) situar, ubicar; (find) localizar

location [ləʊ'keɪʃən] n (**a**) (place) emplazamiento m, ubicación f (**b**) Cin **l. shots** exteriores mpl; **they're on l. in Australia** están rodando en Australia

loch [lɒχ, lɒk] n Scot (lake) lago m; (inlet) ría f

lock[1] [lɒk] **1** n (**a**) (on door etc) cerradura f; (bolt) cerrojo m; (padlock) candado m (**b**) (on canal) esclusa f **2** vt cerrar con llave/cerrojo/candado **3** vi (door etc) cerrarse; (wheels) trabarse

► **lock up** vt sep (house) cerrar; (jail) meter en la cárcel

lock[2] [lɒk] n Literary (of hair) mechón m

locker ['lɒkə(r)] n (cupboard) armario ropero; US **l. room** vestuarios mpl

locket ['lɒkɪt] n medallón m

lockout ['lɒkaʊt] n cierre m patronal

locksmith ['lɒksmɪθ] n cerrajero m

lockup ['lɒkʌp] n (**a**) (for storage) garaje m, Am cochera f (**b**) Fam (police cells) calabozo m

loco ['ləʊkəʊ] adj US Fam pirado(a)

locomotive [ləʊkə'məʊtɪv] n locomotora f

locust ['ləʊkəst] n langosta f

lodge [lɒdʒ] **1** n (gamekeeper's) casa f del guarda; (porter's) portería f; (hunter's) refugio m **2** vt (**a**) (accommodate) alojar (**b**) (complaint) presentar **3** vi (**a**) (live) alojarse (**b**) (get stuck) meterse (**in** en)

lodger ['lɒdʒə(r)] n huésped a m,f

lodging ['lɒdʒɪŋ] n alojamiento m; **l. house** casa f de huéspedes

loft [lɒft] n desván m

lofty ['lɒftɪ] adj (loftier, loftiest) Literary (high) alto(a); Pej (haughty) altivo(a)

log [lɒg] **1** n (**a**) (tree-trunk) tronco m; (for fuel) leño m; **l. cabin** cabaña f de troncos (**b**) Naut diario m de a bordo **2** vt (record) registrar

► **log in, log on** vi Comput entrar (en sistema)

► **log out, log off** vi Comput salir (del sistema)

logarithm ['lɒgərɪðəm] n logaritmo m

log-book ['lɒgbʊk] n Naut diario m de a bordo; Av diario de vuelo; Aut documentación f (del coche)

loggerheads ['lɒgəhedz] npl Fam **to be at l. with sb** estar peleado(a) or Esp andar a la greña con algn

logic ['lɒdʒɪk] n lógica f

logical ['lɒdʒɪkəl] adj lógico(a)

logistics [lə'dʒɪstɪks] npl logística f

logo ['ləʊgəʊ] n logotipo m

loin [lɔɪn] n (of animal) ijada f; Culin (of pork) lomo m; (of beef) solomillo m

loiter ['lɔɪtə(r)] vi (hang about) holgazanear; (lag behind) rezagarse; (prowl) merodear

loll [lɒl] *vi (tongue, head)* colgar
▸ **loll about, loll around** *vi* repantigarse

lollipop ['lɒlɪpɒp] *n* pirulí *m*, chupa-chup® *m*; *Br Fam* **l. lady/man** = persona encargada de ayudar a cruzar la calle a los colegiales

lolly ['lɒlɪ] *n Fam* (a) *(sweet)* pirulí *m*, chupachup® *m*; **ice(d) l.** polo *m* (b) *Br Fam (money) Esp* pasta *f*, *Am* plata *f*

London ['lʌndən] *n* Londres

Londoner ['lʌndənə(r)] *n* londinense *mf*

lone [ləʊn] *adj (solitary)* solitario(a); *(single)* solo(a)

loneliness ['ləʊnlɪnɪs] *n* soledad *f*

lonely ['ləʊnlɪ] *adj* (**lonelier, loneliest**) solo(a), solitario(a)

long¹ [lɒŋ] **1** *adj* (a) *(size)* largo(a); **how l. is the table?** ¿cuánto tiene de largo la mesa?; **it's 3 m l.** tiene 3 m de largo; **l. jump** salto *m* de longitud (b) *(time)* mucho(a); **at l. last** por fin; **how l. is the film?** ¿cuánto tiempo dura la película?
2 *adv* mucho, mucho tiempo; **all day l.** todo el día; **as l. as the exhibition lasts** mientras dura la exposición; **as l. as** *or* **so l. as you don't mind** con tal de que no te importe; **before l.** dentro de poco; **how l. have you been here?** ¿cuánto tiempo llevas aquí?

long² [lɒŋ] *vi* añorar; **to l. for** anhelar

long-distance ['lɒŋdɪstəns] *adj* de larga distancia; **l. call** conferencia interurbana; **l. runner** corredor(a) *m,f* de fondo

longhand ['lɒŋhænd] *n* escritura *f* a mano

longing ['lɒŋɪŋ] *n (desire)* anhelo *m*; *(nostalgia)* nostalgia *f*

longitude ['lɒndʒɪtjuːd] *n* longitud *f*

long-playing ['lɒŋpleɪɪŋ] *adj* de larga duración; **l. record** elepé *m*

long-range ['lɒŋreɪndʒ] *adj (missile etc)* de largo alcance; *(weather forecast)* de largo plazo

long-sighted [lɒŋ'saɪtɪd] *adj* (a) *Med* présbita (b) *Fig* previsor(a)

long-standing ['lɒŋstændɪŋ] *adj* antiguo(a), de mucho tiempo

long-suffering ['lɒŋsʌfərɪŋ] *adj* sufrido(a)

long-term ['lɒŋtɜːm] *adj* a largo plazo

long-winded [lɒŋ'wɪndɪd] *adj* prolijo(a)

loo [luː] *n Br Fam* baño *m*, wáter *m*

look [lʊk] **1** *n* (a) *(glance)* mirada *f*; **to take a l. at** *(peep)* echar un vistazo a; *(examine)* examinar (b) *(appearance)* aspecto *m*, apariencia *f*; **I don't like the l. of it** me da mala espina (c) *(fashion)* moda *f* (d) *(good)* **looks** belleza *f*
2 *vi* (a) *(in general)* mirar, *Am* ver (b)

(seem) parecer; **it looks delicious** tiene un aspecto buenísimo; **she looks like her father** *(resembles)* se parece a su padre
3 *vt* mirar
▸ **look after** *vt insep* cuidar a, ocuparse de
▸ **look at** *vt insep* mirar; *Fig* **whichever way you l. at it** desde cualquier punto de vista
▸ **look away** *vi* apartar la mirada
▸ **look back** *vi* (a) *(in space)* mirar atrás; *Fig* **since then he has never looked back** desde entonces ha ido prosperando (b) *(remember)* recordar
▸ **look down** *vi Fig* **to l. down on sth/sb** despreciar algo/a algn
▸ **look for** *vt insep* buscar
▸ **look forward to** *vt insep* esperar con ansia; **I l. forward to hearing from you** *(in letter)* espero noticias suyas
▸ **look into** *vt insep* examinar, investigar
▸ **look on 1** *vt insep (consider)* considerar
2 *vi* quedarse mirando
▸ **look onto** *vt insep* dar a
▸ **look out** *vi* (a) **the bedroom looks out onto the garden** el dormitorio da al jardín (b) **l. out!** *(take care)* ¡cuidado!, ¡ojo!
▸ **look over** *vt sep (examine)* revisar; *(place)* inspeccionar
▸ **look round 1** *vt insep (house, shop)* ver
2 *vi* mirar alrededor; *(turn head)* volver la cabeza
▸ **look through** *vt insep* (a) *(window)* mirar por (b) *(leaf through)* hojear; *(examine)* revisar; *(check)* registrar
▸ **look to** *vt insep* (a) *(take care of)* velar por (b) *(turn to)* recurrir a
▸ **look up 1** *vt sep* (a) *(look for)* buscar (b) *(visit)* ir a visitar
2 *vi* (a) *(glance upwards)* alzar la vista (b) *Fam (improve)* mejorar
▸ **look upon** *vt insep* considerar
▸ **look up to** *vt insep (person)* respetar

lookout ['lʊkaʊt] *n (person)* centinela *mf*; *(place)* mirador *m*; **to be on the l. for** estar al acecho de; *Fam* **that's his l.!** ¡eso es asunto suyo!

loom¹ [luːm] *n* telar *m*

loom² [luːm] *vi* alzarse; *Fig (threaten)* amenazar

loony ['luːnɪ] *adj* (**loonier, looniest**) *Fam* loco(a)

loop [luːp] **1** *n* (a) *(of rope, ribbon)* lazo *m* (b) *Comput* bucle *m*
2 *vt* (a) *(string)* enrollar (b) *Av* **to l. the l.** rizar el rizo

loophole ['luːphəʊl] *n Fig* escapatoria *f*

loose [luːs] *adj* (**a**) *(not secure)* flojo(a); *(papers, hair, clothes)* suelto(a); *(tongue)* desatado(a); *(baggy)* holgado(a); **to set sb l.** soltar a algn (**b**) *(not packaged)* a granel; **l. change** suelto *m* (**c**) *(not exact)* vago(a); *(translation)* libre (**d**) *(lax)* relajado(a); **a l. woman** una mujer fácil

loosely [ˈluːslɪ] *adv* (**a**) *(approximately)* aproximadamente (**b**) *(vaguely)* vagamente

loosen [ˈluːsən] **1** *vt* aflojar; *(belt)* desabrochar; *Fig (restrictions)* flexibilizar
2 *vi (slacken)* aflojarse

loot [luːt] **1** *n* botín *m*
2 *vt* saquear

looting [ˈluːtɪŋ] *n* saqueo *m*, pillaje *m*

lop [lɒp] *vt* podar
▸ **lop off** *vt sep* cortar

lope [ləʊp] *vi* andar a zancadas

lopsided [lɒpˈsaɪdɪd] *adj* ladeado(a)

lord [lɔːd] *n* (**a**) *(aristocrat)* señor *m*, lord *m*; *Br* **the (House of) Lords** la cámara de los lores; **the L. Mayor** el señor alcalde (**b**) *Rel* **the L.** El Señor; **good L.!** ¡Dios mío!; **the L.'s Prayer** el Padrenuestro (**c**) *(judge)* señoría *mf*

lordship [ˈlɔːdʃɪp] *n Br* **His/Your L.** su señoría

lorry [ˈlɒrɪ] *n Br* camión *m*; **l. driver** camionero(a) *m,f*; **l. load** carga *f*

lose [luːz] **1** *vt (pt & pp* lost*)* perder; **to l. time** *(of clock)* atrasarse
2 *vi* perder; **to l. to sb** perder contra algn; **to l. out** salir perdiendo

loser [ˈluːzə(r)] *n* perdedor(a) *m,f*

loss [lɒs] *n* pérdida *f*; **to make a l.** perder; *Fig* **to be at a l. for words** quedarse de una pieza; **to be at a l. what to do** no saber qué hacer

lost [lɒst] **1** *adj* (**a**) *(missing)* perdido(a); **to get l.** perderse; *Fam* **get l.!** ¡vete a la porra!; **l. property office,** *US* **l. and found department** oficina *f* de objetos perdidos (**b**) *(disoriented)* desorientado(a); *(distracted)* distraído(a); **l. in thought** ensimismado(a)
2 *pt & pp of* **lose**

lot [lɒt] *n* (**a**) *(fate)* suerte *f* (**b**) *US (plot of land)* parcela *f* (**c**) *(in an auction)* lote *m* (**d**) *(everything)* todo *m*; **he ate the l.** se lo comió todo (**e**) **a l. of** *(much)* mucho(a); *(many)* muchos(as); **he feels a l. better** se encuentra mucho mejor; *Fam* **lots of** montones de, cantidad de

lotion [ˈləʊʃən] *n* loción *f*

lottery [ˈlɒtərɪ] *n* lotería *f*; **l. ticket** ≃ décimo *m* de lotería

loud [laʊd] **1** *adj* (**a**) *(voice)* alto(a); *(noise)* fuerte; *(laugh)* estrepitoso(a); *(applause)* clamoroso(a); *(protests, party)* ruidoso(a) (**b**) *(flashy)* chillón(ona) (**c**) *(vulgar)* hortera
2 *adv* **to read/think out l.** leer/pensar en voz alta

loudhailer [laʊdˈheɪlə(r)] *n Br* megáfono *m*

loudspeaker [laʊdˈspiːkə(r)] *n* altavoz *m*

lounge [laʊndʒ] **1** *n Br* salón *m*, sala *f* de estar
2 *vi* hacer el vago

louse [laʊs] *n (pl* lice*)* piojo *m*

lousy [ˈlaʊzɪ] *adj* (**lousier, lousiest**) *Fam* fatal; **a l. trick** una cochinada

lout [laʊt] *n* gamberro *m*

lovable [ˈlʌvəbəl] *adj* adorable

love [lʌv] **1** *n* (**a**) *(between lovers or members of a family)* amor *m* (**for** por); *(affection)* cariño *m*; **to be in l. with sb** estar enamorado(a) de algn; **to fall in l.** enamorarse; **to make l.** hacer el amor; **(with) l. (from) Mary** *(in letter)* un abrazo, Mary; **l. affair** amorío *m*; **l. letter/story** carta *f*/historia *f* de amor; **l. life** vida *f* sentimental (**b**) *(person)* amor *m*, cariño *m*; *Fam* chato(a) *m,f*; **my l.** mi amor (**c**) *(in tennis)* **forty l.** cuarenta a cero
2 *vt (person)* querer a, amar a; **he loves cooking/football** le encanta cocinar/el fútbol

lovely [ˈlʌvlɪ] *adj* (**lovelier, loveliest**) *(charming)* encantador(a); *(beautiful)* precioso(a), *Am* lindo(a); *(delicious)* riquísimo(a)

lover [ˈlʌvə(r)] *n* (**a**) *(sexual partner)* amante *mf* (**b**) *(enthusiast)* aficionado(a) *m,f*, amigo(a) *m,f*

loving [ˈlʌvɪŋ] *adj* cariñoso(a)

low¹ [ləʊ] **1** *adj* (**a**) *(not high, not loud)* bajo(a); *(neckline)* escotado(a) (**b**) *(small in quantity)* bajo(a) (**c**) *(poor)* pobre (**d**) *(battery)* gastado(a); **l. frequency** baja frecuencia (**e**) **to feel l.** sentirse deprimido(a) (**f**) *(reprehensible)* malo(a)
2 *adv* bajo
3 *n* (**a**) *Met* área *f* de baja presión (**b**) *(low point)* punto más bajo; **to reach an all-time l.** tocar fondo

low² [ləʊ] *vi (cow)* mugir

lowdown [ˈləʊdaʊn] *n Fam* pormenores *mpl*

lower [ˈləʊə(r)] **1** *adj (comp of* low*)* inferior; *Typ* **l. case** minúscula *f*; **l. class** clase baja
2 *adv comp of* **low**
3 *vt* bajar; *(flag)* arriar; *(reduce)* reducir; *(price)* rebajar

lower-class ['ləʊəklɑːs] *adj* de clase baja

lowest ['ləʊɪst] **1** *adj* (*superl* of **low**) más bajo(a); *(price, speed)* mínimo(a)
2 *n* **at the l.** como mínimo

low-key [ləʊ'kiː] *adj* sin ceremonia

lowlands ['ləʊləndz] *npl* tierras bajas

lowly ['ləʊlɪ] *adj* (**lowlier, lowliest**) humilde

low-necked ['ləʊnekt] *adj* escotado(a)

loyal ['lɔɪəl] *adj* leal, fiel

loyalty ['lɔɪəltɪ] *n* lealtad *f*, fidelidad *f*

lozenge ['lɒzɪndʒ] *n* pastilla *f*

LP [el'piː] *n* (*abbr* **long-playing record**) LP *m*

L-plate ['elpleɪt] *n Br* placa *f* de la "L"

LSD [eles'diː] *n* (*abbr* **lysergic acid diethylamide**) LSD *m*

Ltd *Br Com* (*abbr* **limited**) S.L.

lubricant ['luːbrɪkənt] *n* lubricante *m*

lubricate ['luːbrɪkeɪt] *vt* lubricar; *(engine)* engrasar

lubrication [luːbrɪ'keɪʃən] *n* engrase *m*

lucid ['luːsɪd] *adj* lúcido(a)

luck [lʌk] *n* suerte *f*; **bad l.!** ¡mala suerte!; **good l.!** ¡(buena) suerte!; **to be l.** estar de suerte; **to be out of l.** no tener suerte; *Fig* **to push one's l.** tentar la suerte; *Fig* **to try one's l.** probar fortuna

luckily ['lʌkɪlɪ] *adv* por suerte, afortunadamente

lucky ['lʌkɪ] *adj* (**luckier, luckiest**) *(person)* afortunado(a); *(day)* de suerte; *(move)* oportuno(a); *(charm)* de la suerte; **to be lucky** tener suerte; **a l. break** una oportunidad

lucrative ['luːkrətɪv] *adj* lucrativo(a)

ludicrous ['luːdɪkrəs] *adj* absurdo(a), ridículo(a)

lug [lʌg] *vt Fam* arrastrar

luggage ['lʌgɪdʒ] *n* equipaje *m*; **l. rack** *Aut* baca *f*; *Rail* portaequipajes *m inv*

lukewarm ['luːkwɔːm] *adj* *(water etc)* tibio(a); *Fig (reception etc)* poco entusiasta

lull [lʌl] **1** *n* *(in storm)* calma chicha; *(in fighting)* tregua *f*
2 *vt (cause to sleep)* adormecer; **to l. sb into a false sense of security** infundir una falsa seguridad a algn

lullaby ['lʌləbaɪ] *n* canción *f* de cuna, nana *f*

lumbago [lʌm'beɪgəʊ] *n* lumbago *m*

lumber ['lʌmbə(r)] **1** *n* (**a**) *Br (junk)* trastos viejos (**b**) *US (wood)* maderos *mpl*
2 *vt Fam* cargar (**with** de)

lumberjack ['lʌmbədʒæk] *n* leñador *m*

lumberyard ['lʌmbəjɑːd] *n US* almacén *m* maderero, maderería *f*, *RP* barraca *f* maderera

luminous ['luːmɪnəs] *adj* luminoso(a)

lump [lʌmp] **1** *n* *(of coal etc)* trozo *m*; *(of sugar, earth)* terrón *m*; *(in sauce)* grumo *m*; *(swelling)* bulto *m*; *Fam Fig (in throat)* nudo *m*; **l. sum** cantidad *f* global
2 *vt Fam (endure)* aguantar
▸ **lump together** *vt sep* apelotonar

lumpy ['lʌmpɪ] *adj* (**lumpier, lumpiest**) *(bed)* lleno(a) de bultos; *(sauce)* grumoso(a)

lunacy ['luːnəsɪ] *n* locura *f*

lunar ['luːnə(r)] *adj* lunar

lunatic ['luːnətɪk] *adj & n* loco(a) *(m,f)*; **l. asylum** manicomio *m*

lunch [lʌntʃ] **1** *n* comida *f*, almuerzo *m*; **l. box** tartera *f*, fiambrera *f*; **l. hour** hora *f* de comer
2 *vi* comer, almorzar

luncheon ['lʌntʃən] *n Old-fashioned Fml* almuerzo *m*; **l. voucher** vale *m* de comida; **(pork) l. meat** carne *f* de cerdo troceada, chopped *m*

lunchtime ['lʌntʃtaɪm] *n* hora *f* de comer

lung [lʌŋ] *n* pulmón *m*

lunge [lʌndʒ] **1** *n* arremetida *f*
2 *vi* **to l. (forward)** arremeter; **to l. (out) at sb** arremeter contra algn

lurch [lɜːtʃ] **1** *n* (**a**) *(of vehicle)* sacudida *f*; *(of person)* tambaleo *m* (**b**) *Fam* **to leave sb in the l.** dejar a algn en la cuneta
2 *vi (vehicle)* dar sacudidas; *(person)* tambalearse

lure [lʊə(r)] **1** *n* *(decoy)* señuelo *m*; *(bait)* cebo *m*; *Fig (charm)* aliciente *m*
2 *vt* atraer con engaños

lurid ['lʊərɪd] *adj* (**a**) *(gruesome)* espeluznante; *(sensational)* sensacionalista (**b**) *(gaudy)* chillón(ona)

lurk [lɜːk] *vi (lie in wait)* estar al acecho; *(hide)* esconderse

luscious ['lʌʃəs] *adj (food)* delicioso(a)

lush [lʌʃ] *adj (vegetation)* exuberante

lust [lʌst] **1** *n* *(sexual desire)* lujuria *f*; *(craving)* ansia *f*; *(greed)* codicia *f*
2 *vi* **to l. after sth/sb** codiciar algo/ desear a algn

lustre, *US* **luster** ['lʌstə(r)] *n* lustre *m*

lusty ['lʌstɪ] *adj* (**lustier, lustiest**) robusto(a)

lute [luːt] *n* laúd *m*

Luxembourg ['lʌksəmbɜːg] *n* Luxemburgo

luxuriant [lʌg'zjʊərɪənt] *adj (plants)* exuberante; *(hair etc)* abundante

luxurious [lʌgˈzjʊərɪəs] *adj* lujoso(a)
luxury [ˈlʌkʃərɪ] *n* lujo *m*; **l. flat** piso *m* de
lujo

> 🖉 Note that the Spanish word **lujuria** is a
> false friend and is never a translation for
> the English word **luxury**. In Spanish **lu-**
> **juria** means "lust".

lychee [ˈlaɪtʃiː] *n* lichi *m*

lying [ˈlaɪɪŋ] **1** *adj* mentiroso(a)
   2 *n* mentiras *fpl*
lynch [lɪntʃ] *vt* linchar
lyre [laɪə(r)] *n Mus* lira *f*
lyric [ˈlɪrɪk] **1** *adj* lírico(a)
   2 *n* (**a**) *(poem)* poema lírico (**b**) **lyrics**
   (words of song) letra *f*
lyrical [ˈlɪrɪkəl] *adj* lírico(a)

M, m [em] *n (the letter)* M, m *f*

m (**a**) *(abbr* **metre(s))** m (**b**) *(abbr* **million(s))** m

MA [em'eɪ] *n Univ (abbr* **Master of Arts)** máster *m or Am* maestría *f* (en Humanidades)

mac [mæk] *n Br Fam (raincoat)* impermeable *m*, gabardina *f*

macabre [mə'kɑːbrə] *adj* macabro(a)

mac(c)aroni [mækə'rəʊnɪ] *n* macarrones *mpl*

mace¹ [meɪs] *n (club, ceremonial staff)* maza *f*

mace² [meɪs] *n (spice)* macis *f inv*

Macedonia [mæsə'dəʊnɪə] *n* Macedonia

Macedonian [mæsə'dəʊnɪən] *adj & n* macedonio(a) *(m,f)*

machine [mə'ʃiːn] **1** *n* máquina *f*; **m. gun** ametralladora *f*
  2 *vt* trabajar a máquina

machine-gun [mə'ʃiːngʌn] *vt* ametrallar

machine-readable [mə'ʃiːn'riːdəbəl] *adj Comput* legible para *Esp* el ordenador *or Am* la computadora

machinery [mə'ʃiːnərɪ] *n (machines)* maquinaria *f*; *(workings of machine)* mecanismo *m*

macho ['mætʃəʊ] *adj (remark, attitude)* muy de macho

macintosh 'mækɪntɒʃ *n* = **mackintosh**

mackerel ['mækrəl] *n (pl* **mackerel)** caballa *f*

mackintosh ['mækɪntɒʃ] *n* impermeable *m*

macro ['mækrəʊ] *n (pl* **macros)** *Comput* macro *m or f*

macrobiotic [mækrəʊbaɪ'ɒtɪk] *adj* macrobiótico(a)

macroeconomics [mækrəʊiːkə'nɒmɪks] *n sing* macroeconomía *f*

mad [mæd] *adj* (**madder, maddest**) (**a**) *(insane) (person)* loco(a); *(dog)* rabioso(a); **to be/go m.** estar/volverse loco(a); *Fam* **to run/work like m.** correr/trabajar como (un(a)) loco(a); *Fam* **m. cow disease** el mal de las vacas locas (**b**) *(idea, plan)* disparatado(a) (**c**) *Fam* **to be m. about sth/sb** estar loco(a) por algo/

algn (**d**) *esp US Fam (angry) esp Esp* enfadado(a), *esp Am* enojado(a); **to be m. with** *or* **at sb** estar muy *esp Esp* enfadado(a) *or esp Am* enojado(a) con algn

madam ['mædəm] *n* señora *f*; **Dear M.** *(in letter)* Muy señora mía, Estimada señora

madden ['mædən] *vt* volver loco(a)

maddening ['mædənɪŋ] *adj* exasperante

made [meɪd] *pt & pp of* **make**

Madeira [mə'dɪərə] *n* (**a**) *(island)* Madeira (**b**) *(wine)* madeira *m*; **M. cake** bizcocho *m*

made-to-measure ['meɪdtə'meʒə(r)] *adj* hecho(a) a (la) medida

made-up ['meɪdʌp] *adj* (**a**) *(face, person)* maquillado(a); *(eyes, lips)* pintado(a) (**b**) *(story, excuse)* inventado(a)

madly ['mædlɪ] *adv* (**a**) *(desperately) (rush, struggle)* como loco(a) (**b**) *Fam (extremely)* terriblemente; **to be m. in love with sb** estar locamente enamorado(a) de algn

madman ['mædmən] *n* loco *m*

madness ['mædnɪs] *n* locura *f*

Madrid [mə'drɪd] *n* Madrid

Mafia ['mæfɪə] *n* mafia *f*

magazine [mægə'ziːn] *n* (**a**) *(periodical)* revista *f* (**b**) *(in rifle)* recámara *f* (**c**) *Mil (storehouse)* almacén *m*; *(for explosives)* polvorín *m*

maggot ['mægət] *n* larva *f*, gusano *m*

magic ['mædʒɪk] **1** *n* magia *f*
  2 *adj* (**a**) *(spell, trick)* mágico(a); **m. wand** varita mágica (**b**) *Fam (excellent)* genial, *Esp* guay, *Am salvo RP* chévere, *Méx* padrísimo(a), *RP* bárbaro(a)

magical ['mædʒɪkəl] *adj* mágico(a)

magician [mə'dʒɪʃən] *n* (**a**) *(wizard)* mago *m,f* (**b**) *(conjurer)* prestidigitador(a) *m,f*

magistrate ['mædʒɪstreɪt] *n Br* juez *mf* de primera instancia; **magistrates' court** juzgado *m* de primera instancia

magnanimous [mæg'nænɪməs] *adj* magnánimo(a)

magnesium [mæg'niːzɪəm] *n Chem* magnesio *m*

magnet ['mægnɪt] *n* imán *m*

magnetic [mæg'netɪk] *adj* magnético(a); *Fig (personality)* carismático(a); **m. tape** cinta magnetofónica

magnetism ['mægnɪtɪzəm] *n* magnetismo *m*

magnificence [mæg'nɪfɪsəns] *n* magnificencia *f*

magnificent [mæg'nɪfɪsənt] *adj* magnífico(a)

magnify ['mægnɪfaɪ] *vt* (a) *(enlarge)* aumentar (b) *Fig (exaggerate)* exagerar

magnifying glass ['mægnɪfaɪŋɡlɑːs] *n* lupa *f*

magnitude ['mægnɪtjuːd] *n* magnitud *f*

magpie ['mægpaɪ] *n* urraca *f*

mahogany [mə'hɒɡənɪ] **1** *n* caoba *f*
2 *adj* de caoba

maid [meɪd] *n* (a) *(servant)* criada *f*, *Andes, RP* mucama *f* (b) *Pej old m.* solterona *f*

maiden ['meɪdən] *adj* (a) *(unmarried)* soltera; **m. name** apellido *m* de soltera (b) *(voyage, flight)* inaugural

mail [meɪl] **1** *n* correo *m*; **by m.** por correo; **m. order** venta *f* por correo
2 *vt esp US* enviar or mandar (por correo)

mailbox ['meɪlbɒks] *n US* buzón *m*

mailing list ['meɪlɪŋlɪst] *n* lista *f* de direcciones *(para envío de publicidad)*

mailman ['meɪlmæn] *n US* cartero *m*

maim [meɪm] *vt* lisiar

main [meɪn] **1** *adj (problem, door etc)* principal; *(square, mast, sail)* mayor; *(office)* central; *Culin* **m. course** plato *m* principal; **m. road** carretera *f* principal; *US* **M. Street** la Calle Mayor
2 *n* (a) *(pipe, wire)* conducto *m* principal; **the mains** *(water or gas system)* la cañería maestra; *Elec* la red eléctrica (b) **in the m.** por regla general

mainframe ['meɪnfreɪm] *n* **m. (computer)** *Esp* ordenador *m* or *Am* computadora *f* central

mainland ['meɪnlənd] *n* continente *m*

mainly ['meɪnlɪ] *adv* principalmente, sobre todo; *(for the most part)* en su mayoría

mainstay ['meɪnsteɪ] *n Fig* sustento *m*, sostén *m*

mainstream ['meɪnstriːm] *n* corriente *f* principal

maintain [meɪn'teɪn] *vt* mantener; *(conversation)* sostener; *(silence, appearances)* guardar; *(road, machine)* conservar en buen estado

maintenance ['meɪntənəns] *n* (a) *(of car, equipment, roads)* mantenimiento *m* (b) *(divorce allowance)* pensión *f*

maisonette [meɪzə'net] *n* dúplex *m*

maître d' ['meɪtrə'diː] *n US* maître *mf* (d'hôtel)

maize [meɪz] *n* maíz *m*, *Andes, RP* choclo *m*

majestic [mə'dʒestɪk] *adj* majestuoso(a)

majesty ['mædʒɪstɪ] *n* majestad *f*

major ['meɪdʒə(r)] **1** *adj* (a) *(important)* importante, de primer orden (b) *Mus* mayor
2 *n* (a) *Mil* comandante *m* (b) *US Univ* especialidad *f*
3 *vi US Univ* **to m. in** especializarse en

Majorca [mə'jɔːkə] *n* Mallorca

Majorcan [mə'jɔːkən] *adj & n* mallorquín(ina) *(m,f)*

majority [mə'dʒɒrɪtɪ] *n* mayoría *f*; **to be in the m.** ser (la) mayoría

make [meɪk] *(pt & pp* **made**) **1** *vt* (a) *(produce, prepare, perform)* hacer; *(manufacture)* hacer, fabricar; *(clothes, curtains)* confeccionar; *(meal)* preparar; *(payment)* efectuar; *(speech)* pronunciar; *(decision)* tomar; *(mistake)* cometer; **to be made of** ser de; **to m. a noise** hacer ruido (b) *(cause to be)* hacer; **to m. sb happy** hacer feliz a algn; **to m. sb sad** entristecer a algn; **he made it clear that ...** dejó claro que ...
(c) *(convert)* convertir (**into** en); *(appoint)* nombrar
(d) *(force, compel)* obligar; **to m. sb do sth** hacer que algn haga algo
(e) *(earn)* ganar; **to m. a living** ganarse la vida
(f) **7 and 5 m. 12** 7 y 5 son 12
(g) **to m. do with sth** arreglárselas con algo
(h) *(calculate, reckon)* calcular; **I don't know what to m. of it** no sé qué pensar de eso; **what time do you m. it?** ¿qué hora tienes?
(i) *(reach) Fam* **to m. it** *(arrive in time)* llegar (a tiempo); *(finish in time)* terminar a tiempo; **to m. the charts** *(record)* llegar a las listas de éxitos
(j) *(become, be)* ser; **he'll m. a good doctor/singer** será un buen médico/cantante
2 *vi* (a) **to m. sure** or **certain (of sth)** asegurarse (de algo) (b) **she made as if** or **as though to leave** hizo como si quisiera marcharse
3 *n (brand)* marca *f*

▸ **make for** *vt insep (move towards)* dirigirse hacia

▸ **make out 1** *vt sep* (a) *(list, receipt)* hacer; *(cheque)* extender (b) *(perceive)* distinguir; *(writing)* descifrar (c) *(understand)* entender (d) *Fam (claim)* **to m. out (that) ...** decir or pretender que ...
2 *vi* (a) *(get on)* **how did you m. out?** ¿qué

tal te fue? (**b**) *US Fam (sexually) (neck)*
meterse mano, *Esp* darse el lote; *(have
sex)* enrollarse
▸**make up 1** *vt sep* (**a**) *(parcel, list)* hacer;
(prescription) preparar; *(assemble)* montar (**b**) *(story)* inventar (**c**) *(apply
cosmetics to)* maquillar; *(one's face)*
maquillarse (**d**) *(loss)* compensar; *(lost
time)* recuperar (**e**) *(constitute)* componer (**f**) **to m. it up (with sb)** hacer las
paces (con algn)
 2 *vi* maquillarse
▸**make up for** *vt insep (losses)* compensar;
(lost time) recuperar
▸**make up to** *vt sep* **to m. it up to sb for sth**
compensar a algn por algo
make-believe ['meɪkbɪliːv] *n (fantasy)*
fantasía *f*; *(pretence)* fingimiento *m*; **to
live in a world of m.** vivir en un mundo
de ensueño
makeover ['meɪkəʊvə(r)] *n* renovación *f*
or cambio *m* de imagen
maker ['meɪkə(r)] *n* fabricante *mf*
makeshift ['meɪkʃɪft] *adj (improvised)*
improvisado(a); *(temporary)* provisional
make-up ['meɪkʌp] *n* (**a**) *(cosmetics)*
maquillaje *m*; **m. remover** desmaquillador *m* (**b**) *(composition)* composición
f; *(character)* carácter *m*
making ['meɪkɪŋ] *n* (**a**) *(manufacture)*
fabricación *f*; *(preparation)* preparación *f*
(**b**) **he has the makings of a politician**
tiene madera de político
maladjusted [mælə'dʒʌstɪd] *adj* ina-
daptado(a)
malaise [mæ'leɪz] *n* malestar *m*
malaria [mə'leərɪə] *n* malaria *f*
Malay [mə'leɪ] **1** *adj* malayo(a)
 2 *n* (**a**) *(person)* malayo(a) *m,f* (**b**)
(language) malayo *m*
Malaysia [mə'leɪzɪə] *n* Malasia
male [meɪl] **1** *adj (animal, plant)* macho;
(person) varón; *(sex)* masculino; *Pej* **m.
chauvinism** machismo *m*
 2 *n (person)* varón *m*; *(animal, plant)*
macho *m*
malevolent [mə'levələnt] *adj* malé-
volo(a)
malfunction [mæl'fʌŋkʃən] **1** *n Esp* fallo
m, *Am* falla *f*
 2 *vi* funcionar mal
malice ['mælɪs] *n* malicia *f*; *Jur* **with m.
aforethought** con premeditación
malicious [mə'lɪʃəs] *adj* malévolo(a)
malign [mə'laɪn] **1** *adj* perjudicial,
pernicioso(a)
 2 *vt* difamar
malignant [mə'lɪgnənt] *adj* (**a**) *(person)*
malvado(a) (**b**) *Med* maligno(a)

malingerer [mə'lɪŋgərə(r)] *n* = persona
que se finge enferma (para no ir a
trabajar)
mall [mɔːl] *n US* centro *m* comercial
malleable ['mælɪəbəl] *adj* maleable
mallet ['mælɪt] *n* mazo *m*
malnutrition [mælnjuː'trɪʃən] *n* desnutrición *f*
malpractice [mæl'præktɪs] *n* negligencia
f (profesional); *esp US Jur* **m. suit**
demanda *f* por negligencia (profesional)
malt [mɔːlt] *n* malta *f*
Malta ['mɔːltə] *n* Malta
mammal ['mæməl] *n* mamífero *m*
mammary ['mæmərɪ] *adj* **m. gland** mama
f
mammoth ['mæməθ] **1** *n Zool* mamut *m*
 2 *adj* gigantesco(a)
man [mæn] **1** *n (pl* **men**) (**a**) *(adult male)*
hombre *m*; **old m.** viejo *m*; **young m.** joven
m; *Fig* **the m. in the street** el hombre de la
calle (**b**) *(humanity)* el hombre (**c**)
(husband) marido *m*; *(partner)* pareja *f*
(**d**) *(in chess)* pieza *f*; *(in draughts)* ficha *f*
 2 *vt (boat, plane)* tripular; *(post)* servir;
manned flight vuelo tripulado
manacles ['mænəkəlz] *npl (for hands)*
esposas *fpl*; *(for feet)* grilletes *mpl*
manage ['mænɪdʒ] **1** *vt* (**a**) *(company,
household)* llevar; *(money, affairs, person)* manejar (**b**) *(succeed)* conseguir; **to
m. to do sth** lograr hacer algo
 2 *vi (cope physically)* poder; *(esp
financially)* arreglárselas; **we're managing** vamos tirando
manageable ['mænɪdʒəbəl] *adj* manejable
management ['mænɪdʒmənt] *n* dirección *f*
manager ['mænɪdʒə(r)] *n* (**a**) *(of
company, bank)* director(a) *m,f*; *(head of
department)* jefe(a) *m,f* (**b**) *(of pop group
etc)* mánager *m* (**c**) *Sport* entrenador(a)
m,f
manageress [mænɪdʒə'res] *n (of shop,
restaurant)* encargada *f*; *(of company)*
directora *f*
managerial [mænɪ'dʒɪərɪəl] *adj* direc-
tivo(a)
managing ['mænɪdʒɪŋ] *adj esp Br* **m.
director** director(a) *m,f* gerente
mandarin ['mændərɪn] *n* **m. (orange)**
mandarina *f*
mandate ['mændeɪt] *n* mandato *m*
mandatory ['mændətərɪ] *adj Fml* obliga-
torio(a)
mane [meɪn] *n (of horse)* crin *f*; *(of lion)*
melena *f*

maneuver [mə'nu:vər] *n, vt & vi US* = **manoeuvre**

manfully ['mænfʊlɪ] *adv* con hombría, valientemente

manger ['meɪndʒə(r)] *n* pesebre *m*

mangle¹ ['mæŋɡəl] *n (for wringing)* rodillo *m*

mangle² ['mæŋɡəl] *vt (crush)* aplastar; *(destroy by cutting)* despedazar

mango ['mæŋɡəʊ] *n (pl* mangoes) mango *m*

mangy ['meɪndʒɪ] *adj* (mangier, mangiest) *(animal)* sarnoso(a); *Fam (carpet)* raído(a)

manhandle ['mænhændəl] *vt* they manhandled him into the car lo metieron en el coche *or Am* carro *or CSur* auto a empujones

manhole ['mænhəʊl] *n* (boca *f* de) alcantarilla *f*

manhood ['mænhʊd] *n* (**a**) *(age)* madurez *f*; **to reach m.** alcanzar la madurez (**b**) *(masculinity)* hombría *f*

mania ['meɪnɪə] *n* manía *f*

maniac ['meɪnɪæk] *n* maníaco(a) *m,f*; **to drive like a m.** *Esp* conducir *or Am* manejar como un loco

manic ['mænɪk] *adj* maníaco(a)

manic-depressive ['mænɪkɪ'presɪv] *adj & n* maníaco(a) depresivo(a)

manicure ['mænɪkjʊə(r)] **1** *n* manicura *f* **2** *vt* **to m. one's nails** hacerse la manicura

manifest ['mænɪfest] *Fml* **1** *adj* manifiesto(a) **2** *vt* manifestar

manifesto [mænɪ'festəʊ] *n* programa *m* electoral

manifold ['mænɪfəʊld] *adj Fml (numerous)* múltiple; *(varied)* diverso(a)

manipulate [mə'nɪpjʊleɪt] *vt (controls, people, statistics)* manipular

mankind [mæn'kaɪnd] *n* la humanidad, el género humano

manly ['mænlɪ] *adj* (manlier, manliest) varonil, viril

man-made ['mænmeɪd] *adj (lake)* artificial; *(fibres, fabric)* sintético(a)

manner ['mænə(r)] *n* (**a**) *(way, method)* manera *f*, modo *m*; **in this m.** de esta manera (**b**) *(attitude, behaviour)* actitud *f* (**c**) *(type)* **all m. of …** toda clase de … (**d**) *(etiquette)* **(good) manners** buenos modales; **bad manners** falta *f* de educación

mannerism ['mænərɪzəm] *n (gesture)* gesto *m*; *(affectation)* amaneramiento *m*

manoeuvre [mə'nu:və(r)] **1** *n* maniobra *f* **2** *vt* maniobrar; *(person)* manejar **3** *vi* maniobrar

manor ['mænə(r)] *n* **m. (house)** casa solariega

manpower ['mænpaʊə(r)] *n* mano *f* de obra

mansion ['mænʃən] *n* casa *f* grande; *(in country)* casa solariega

manslaughter ['mænslɔːtə(r)] *n* homicidio involuntario

mantelpiece ['mæntəlpiːs] *n (shelf)* repisa *f* de chimenea; *(fireplace)* chimenea *f*

mantle ['mæntəl] *n Fig (of lava, snow)* manto *m*, capa *f*

> 🖉 Note that the Spanish word **mantel** is a false friend and is never a translation for the English word **mantle**. In Spanish, **mantel** means "tablecloth".

manual ['mænjʊəl] *adj & n* manual *(m)*

manufacture [mænjʊ'fæktʃə(r)] **1** *vt* fabricar **2** *n* fabricación *f*

manufacturer [mænjʊ'fæktʃərə(r)] *n* fabricante *mf*

manure [mə'njʊə(r)] *n* abono *m*, estiércol *m*

manuscript ['mænjʊskrɪpt] *n* manuscrito *m*

many ['menɪ] **1** *adj* (more, most) mucho(a)/muchos(as); **a great m.** muchísimos(as); **as m. … as …** tantos(as) … como …; **how m. days?** ¿cuántos días?; **too m.** demasiados(as) **2** *pron* muchos(as)

map [mæp] **1** *n (of country)* mapa *m*; *(of town, bus route)* plano *m* **2** *vt* trazar un mapa de

▸ **map out** *vt sep (route)* trazar en un mapa; *Fig (future etc)* planear

maple ['meɪpəl] *n* arce *m*

mar [mɑ:(r)] *vt* estropear; **to m. sb's enjoyment** aguarle la fiesta a algn

marathon ['mærəθən] *n* maratón *m*

marble ['mɑ:bəl] **1** *n* (**a**) *(stone)* mármol *m* (**b**) *(glass ball)* canica *f* **2** *adj* de mármol

March [mɑ:tʃ] *n* marzo *m*

march [mɑ:tʃ] **1** *n* (**a**) *(of soldiers)* marcha *f* (**b**) *(demonstration)* manifestación *f* **2** *vi* (**a**) *(soldiers)* marchar; *(at ceremony, on parade)* desfilar (**b**) *(demonstrate)* manifestarse **3** *vt Mil* hacer marchar

mare [meə(r)] *n* yegua *f*

margarine [mɑ:dʒə'ri:n] *n* margarina *f*

margin ['mɑ:dʒɪn] *n* margen *m*; *Fig* **to win by a narrow m.** ganar por escaso margen

marginal ['mɑːdʒɪnəl] adj (**a**) (*improvement, increase*) marginal (**b**) Br Pol (*seat, constituency*) muy reñido(a)

marginally ['mɑːdʒɪnəlɪ] adv ligeramente

marigold ['mærɪɡəʊld] n caléndula f

marijuana, marihuana [mærɪ'hwɑːnə] n marihuana f, marijuana f

marina [mə'riːnə] n puerto deportivo

marinade [mærɪ'neɪd] Culin **1** n adobo m
 2 vt = marinate

marinate ['mærɪneɪt] vt Culin adobar

marine [mə'riːn] **1** adj marino(a)
 2 n marine mf, infante mf de marina, Am fusilero m naval

marital ['mærɪtəl] adj matrimonial; **m. status** estado m civil

maritime ['mærɪtaɪm] adj marítimo(a)

marjoram ['mɑːdʒərəm] n mejorana f

mark¹ [mɑːk] **1** n (**a**) (*left by blow etc*) señal f; (*stain*) mancha f (**b**) (*sign, token*) señal f (**c**) (*in exam etc*) nota f
 2 vt (**a**) (*stain*) manchar (**b**) (*with tick, cross*) señalar (**c**) (*exam*) corregir; (*student*) dar notas a (**d**) **m. my words** fíjate en lo que te digo
 ▸ **mark out** vt sep (**a**) (*area*) delimitar (**b**) **to m. sb out for** destinar a algn a

mark² [mɑːk] n (*unit of currency*) marco m

marked [mɑːkt] adj (*noticeable*) marcado(a), acusado(a)

marker ['mɑːkə(r)] n (**a**) (*of essay, exam*) examinador(a) m,f, corrector(a) m,f de exámenes (**b**) Sport marcador(a) m,f (**c**) (*indicator*) señal f (**d**) (*pen*) **m. (pen)** rotulador m, Col marcador m, Méx plumón m

market ['mɑːkɪt] **1** n mercado m, CSur feria f, CAm, Méx tianguis m; **on the m.** en venta; **m. forces** tendencias fpl del mercado; **m. price** precio m de mercado; **m. research** estudio m de mercado
 2 vt (*sell*) poner en venta; (*promote*) promocionar

marketable ['mɑːkɪtəbəl] adj comerciable

marketing ['mɑːkɪtɪŋ] n marketing m, mercadotecnia f

marketplace ['mɑːkɪtpleɪs] n mercado m

marking ['mɑːkɪŋ] n (**a**) **markings** (*on animal*) marcas fpl, manchas fpl; (*on plane*) distintivo m (**b**) (*of essay, exam*) corrección f

marksman ['mɑːksmən] n tirador m

marmalade ['mɑːməleɪd] n mermelada f (*de cítricos*)

maroon [mə'ruːn] adj (*de color*) granate

marooned [mə'ruːnd] adj bloqueado(a)

marquee [mɑː'kiː] n (**a**) Br (*tent*) carpa f (**b**) US (*of building*) marquesina f

marquess, marquis ['mɑːkwɪs] n marqués m

marriage ['mærɪdʒ] n (*wedding*) boda f, Andes matrimonio m, RP casamiento m; (*institution, period, relationship*) matrimonio m; **m. bureau** agencia f matrimonial; **m. certificate** certificado m de matrimonio

married ['mærɪd] adj casado(a); **to be m.** estar or Am ser casado(a)

marrow ['mærəʊ] n (**a**) (*bone*) **m.** médula f (**b**) Br (*vegetable*) **m.** calabacín m

marry ['mærɪ] vt (*take in marriage*) casarse con; (*give in marriage*) casar (**to** con); (*unite in marriage*) casar; **to get married** casarse

Mars [mɑːz] n Marte m

marsh [mɑːʃ] n pantano m; **salt m.** marisma f

marshal ['mɑːʃəl] **1** n (*army officer*) mariscal m; US (*police chief*) jefe(a) m,f de policía; (*fire chief*) jefe(a) m,f de bomberos; (*police officer*) policía mf
 2 vt (pt & pp **marshalled**, US **marshaled**) (**a**) (*people, troops*) dirigir (**b**) (*arguments, thoughts*) poner en orden

marshy ['mɑːʃɪ] adj (**marshier, marshiest**) pantanoso(a)

martial ['mɑːʃəl] adj marcial; **m. arts** artes fpl marciales

Martian ['mɑːʃən] adj & n marciano(a) (m,f)

martyr ['mɑːtə(r)] **1** n mártir mf
 2 vt martirizar

martyrdom ['mɑːtədəm] n martirio m

marvel ['mɑːvəl] **1** n maravilla f
 2 vi **to m. at** maravillarse de

marvellous, US marvelous ['mɑːvələs] adj maravilloso(a)

Marxism ['mɑːksɪzəm] n marxismo m

Marxist ['mɑːksɪst] adj & n marxista (mf)

marzipan ['mɑːzɪpæn] n mazapán m

mascara [mæ'skɑːrə] n rímel m

✎ Note that the Spanish word **máscara** is a false friend and is never a translation for the English word **mascara**. In Spanish **máscara** means "mask".

---

mascot ['mæskət] n mascota f

masculine ['mæskjʊlɪn] adj masculino(a); (*woman*) hombruna

mash [mæʃ] **1** n (*for animals*) afrecho m
 2 vt **to m. (up)** machacar; **mashed potatoes** puré m de Esp patatas or Am papas

mask [mɑːsk] **1** n máscara f; (of doctor, dentist etc) mascarilla f
2 vt enmascarar; Fig (conceal) ocultar (**from** de)

masochism ['mæsəkızəm] n masoquismo m

masochist ['mæsəkıst] adj & n masoquista (mf)

mason ['meısən] n (**a**) (builder) albañil m (**b**) (freemason) masón m, francmasón m

masonic [mə'sɒnık] adj masónico(a)

masonry ['meısənrı] n (stonework) albañilería f

masquerade [mæskə'reıd] **1** n (pretence) farsa f
2 vi to m. **as** hacerse pasar por

mass¹ [mæs] n Rel misa f; **to say m.** decir misa

mass² [mæs] **1** n (**a**) (shapeless substance) & Phys masa f (**b**) (large number) sinnúmero m; (of people) multitud f (**c**) Pol **the masses** las masas
2 adj masivo(a); **m. media** medios mpl de comunicación (de masas); **m. production** fabricación f en serie
3 vi (troops, people) congregarse, concentrarse

massacre ['mæsəkə(r)] **1** n masacre f
2 vt masacrar

massage ['mæsɑːʒ, mə'sɑːdʒ] **1** n masaje m
2 vt (**a**) (body, scalp) dar un masaje a (**b**) Fig (figures) maquillar

masseur [mæ'sɜː(r)] n masajista m

masseuse [mæ'sɜːz] n masajista f

massive ['mæsıv] adj enorme; (heart attack) grave

mast [mɑːst] n (**a**) Naut mástil m (**b**) Rad & TV torre f

master ['mɑːstə(r)] **1** n (**a**) (of servants) señor m; (of ship) patrón m; (of slave, dog) amo m (**b**) Br (teacher) profesor m (**c**) Univ **m.'s degree** ≃ máster m (**d**) (expert) maestro m
2 adj (**a**) **m. copy** original m; **m. key** llave maestra (**b**) (expert) maestro(a)
3 vt (**a**) (person, situation) dominar (**b**) (subject, skill) llegar a dominar

masterful ['mɑːstəfʊl] adj autoritario(a); (imperious) imperioso(a); (personality) dominante

masterly ['mɑːstəlı] adj magistral

mastermind ['mɑːstəmaınd] **1** n (person) cerebro m
2 vt ser el cerebro de

masterpiece ['mɑːstəpiːs] n obra maestra

mastery ['mɑːstərı] n (**a**) (control) dominio m (**of** de) (**b**) (skill, expertise) maestría f

masturbate ['mæstəbeıt] vi masturbarse

mat¹ [mæt] n (rug) alfombrilla f; (doormat) felpudo m; (rush mat) estera f; Sport colchoneta f

mat² [mæt] adj mate

match¹ [mætʃ] n fósforo m, Esp cerilla f, Am cerillo m

match² [mætʃ] **1** n (**a**) Sport partido m; (in boxing) combate m (**b**) Fig **to meet one's m.** (equal) encontrar uno la horma de su zapato
2 vt (**a**) (equal, be the equal of) igualar (**b**) (be in harmony with) armonizar; **they are well matched** (teams) van iguales; (couple) hacen buena pareja (**c**) (colours, clothes) hacer juego con; (pair of socks, gloves) ser el compañero de
3 vi (harmonize) hacer juego

matchbox ['mætʃbɒks] n caja f de fósforos or Esp cerillas or Am cerillos

matching ['mætʃıŋ] adj que hace juego

matchstick ['mætʃstık] n fósforo m, Esp cerilla f, Am cerillo m

mate [meıt] **1** n (**a**) Br, Austr Fam (friend) amigo(a) m,f, Esp colega mf, Méx cuate mf (**b**) Zool (male) macho m; (female) hembra f (**c**) (assistant) ayudante mf (**d**) (on ship) oficial m; (first) **m.** primer oficial
2 vi Zool aparearse

material [mə'tıərıəl] **1** n (**a**) (substance) materia f (**b**) (cloth) tejido m, tela f (**c**) **materials** (ingredients, equipment) materiales mpl
2 adj (**a**) (important) substancial (**b**) (physical) material

materialistic [mətıərıə'lıstık] adj materialista

materialize [mə'tıərıəlaız] vi (**a**) (hopes) realizarse; (plan, idea) concretarse (**b**) (show up) presentarse

maternal [mə'tɜːnəl] adj maternal; (uncle etc) materno(a)

maternity [mə'tɜːnıtı] n maternidad f; **m. dress** vestido m premamá; **m. hospital** maternidad

math [mæθ] n US = **maths**

mathematical [mæθə'mætıkəl] adj matemático(a)

mathematician [mæθəmə'tıʃən] n matemático(a) m,f

mathematics [mæθə'mætıks] n sing matemáticas fpl

maths [mæθs] n sing Br Fam matemáticas fpl

matinée ['mætıneı] n Cin sesión f de tarde; Th función f de tarde

mating ['meɪtɪŋ] n apareamiento m; **m. call** reclamo m; **m. season** época f de celo

matrices ['meɪtrɪsiːz] pl of **matrix**

matriculate [mə'trɪkjʊleɪt] vi Univ matricularse

matriculation [mətrɪkjʊ'leɪʃən] n Univ matriculación f

matrimonial [mætrɪ'məʊnɪəl] adj matrimonial

matrimony ['mætrɪmənɪ] n matrimonio m; (married life) vida f conyugal

matrix ['meɪtrɪks] n (pl **matrices**) matriz f

matron ['meɪtrən] n (in hospital) enfermera f jefe

matronly ['meɪtrənlɪ] adj madura y recia

matt [mæt] adj mate

matted ['mætɪd] adj enmarañado(a)

matter ['mætə(r)] **1** n (a) (affair, question) asunto m; **a m. of opinion/taste** una cuestión de opinión/gustos; **as a m. of fact** en realidad (b) (problem) **what's the m.?** ¿qué pasa? (c) **no m. what he does** haga lo que haga; **no m. where you go** dondequiera que vayas; **no m. how** como sea (d) (substance) materia f, sustancia f (e) (content) contenido m; (subject) tema m
2 vi importar; **it doesn't m.** no importa, da igual

matter-of-fact ['mætərəv'fækt] adj (person) práctico(a); (account) realista; (style) prosaico(a)

mattress ['mætrɪs] n colchón f

mature [mə't∫ʊə(r)] **1** adj maduro(a); Fin vencido(a)
2 vi madurar; Fin vencer
3 vt madurar

maturity [mə't∫ʊərɪtɪ] n madurez f

maul [mɔːl] vt (a) (wound) agredir (b) (handle roughly) maltratar (c) (touch in unpleasant way) sobar

mausoleum [mɔːsə'liːəm] n (pl **mausoleums** or **mausolea** [mɔːsə'liːə]) mausoleo m

mauve [məʊv] adj & n malva (m)

maverick ['mævərɪk] adj & n inconformista (mf), disidente (mf)

mawkish ['mɔːkɪ∫] adj Pej empalagoso(a)

max [mæks] n (abbr **maximum**) máx

maxim ['mæksɪm] n máxima f

maxima ['mæksɪmə] pl of **maximum**

maximize ['mæksɪmaɪz] vt maximizar

maximum ['mæksɪməm] **1** n (pl **maxima**) máximo m
2 adj máximo(a)

May [meɪ] n mayo m; **M. Day** el Primero or el Uno de Mayo

may [meɪ] v aux (pt **might**)

En el inglés hablado, y en el escrito en estilo coloquial, la forma negativa **might not** se transforma en **mightn't**. La forma **might have** se transforma en **might've**.

(a) (expressing possibility) poder, ser posible; **come what m.** pase lo que pase; **he m.** or **might come** puede que venga; **you m.** or **might as well stay** más vale que te quedes (b) (permission) poder; **m. I?** ¿me permite?; **you m. smoke** pueden fumar (c) (wish) ojalá (+ subj); **m. you always be happy!** ¡ojalá seas siempre feliz!

maybe ['meɪbiː] adv quizá(s), tal vez

mayhem ['meɪhem] n (disturbance) alboroto m; (havoc) estragos mpl

mayonnaise [meɪə'neɪz] n mayonesa f, mahonesa f

mayor [meə(r)] n (man) alcalde m; (woman) alcaldesa f

mayoress ['meəres] n alcaldesa f

maze [meɪz] n laberinto m

MB Comput (abbr **megabyte**) MB

MBA [embiː'eɪ] n Univ (abbr **Master of Business Administration**) MBA m, máster m en administración de empresas

MD [em'diː] n (a) (abbr **Doctor of Medicine**) Doctor(a) m,f en Medicina (b) Fam (abbr **Managing Director**) director(a) m,f gerente

me [miː, unstressed mɪ] pron (a) (as object) me; **he gave it to me** me lo dio; **listen to me** escúchame; **she knows me** me conoce (b) (after prep) mí; **it's for me** es para mí; **with me** conmigo (c) (emphatic) yo; **it's me** soy yo; **what about ME?** ¿y yo, qué?

meadow ['medəʊ] n prado m, pradera f

meagre, US **meager** ['miːgə(r)] adj exiguo(a)

meal¹ [miːl] n (flour) harina f

meal² [miːl] n (food) comida f

mealtime ['miːltaɪm] n hora f de comer

mealy-mouthed [miːlɪ'maʊðd] adj Pej evasivo(a); **to be m.** andarse con rodeos

mean¹ [miːn] vt (pt & pp **meant**) (a) (signify) (of word, event) significar; (of person) querer decir; **what do you m. by that?** ¿qué quieres decir con eso?; **it means a lot to me** significa mucho para mí (b) (intend) pensar, tener la intención de; **I m. it** (te) lo digo en serio; **she didn't m. to do it** lo hizo sin querer (c) (entail) suponer; **it would m. having to give up smoking** significaría tener que dejar de fumar (d) (refer to) referirse a (e) (destine) destinar (**for** a or para)

mean² [mi:n] *adj* (**a**) *(miserly)* tacaño(a) (**b**) *(unkind)* malo(a); *(petty)* mezquino(a); *US (bad-tempered)* malhumorado(a); **to be m. to sb** tratar mal a algn (**c**) **it was no m. feat** fue toda una hazaña (**d**) *US Fam (good)* genial, *Esp* guay, *Am salvo RP* chévere, *Méx* padre, *RP* macanudo(a)

mean³ [mi:n] **1** *adj (average)* medio(a)
2 *n (average)* promedio *m*; *Math* media *f*

meander [mɪ'ændə(r)] *vi (river)* serpentear; *(person)* vagar; *Fig (digress)* divagar

meaning ['mi:nɪŋ] *n* sentido *m*, significado *m*

meaningful ['mi:nɪŋfʊl] *adj* significativo(a)

meaningless ['mi:nɪŋlɪs] *adj* sin sentido

meanness ['mi:nnɪs] *n* (**a**) *(miserliness)* tacañería *f* (**b**) *(nastiness)* maldad *f*

means [mi:nz] *n* (**a**) *sing or pl (method)* medio *m*, manera *f*; **by m. of** por medio de, mediante (**b**) *pl (resources, wealth)* medios *mpl* (de vida), recursos (económicos) *mpl* (**c**) **by all m.!** ¡por supuesto!

meant [ment] *pt & pp of* **mean**

meantime ['mi:ntaɪm] **1** *adv* mientras tanto
2 *n* **in the m.** mientras tanto

meanwhile ['mi:nwaɪl] *adv* mientras tanto

measles ['mi:zəlz] *n sing* sarampión *m*

measly ['mi:zlɪ] *adj* (**measlier, measliest**) *Fam* ridículo(a), irrisorio(a)

measure ['meʒə(r)] **1** *n* (**a**) *(action, step)* medida *f* (**b**) *(measurement, quantity)* medida *f*; *(means of estimating)* indicador *m*, índice *m*; *(ruler)* regla *f* (**c**) **in some m.** hasta cierto punto (**d**) *Mus* compás *m*
2 *vt (object, area)* medir; *(person)* tomar las medidas de

⌨ Note that the Spanish word **mesura** is a false friend and is never a translation for the English word **measure**. In Spanish **mesura** means "moderation, restraint".

▸ **measure up** *vi* **to m. up (to sth)** estar a la altura (de algo)

measurement ['meʒəmənt] *n* medida *f*

meat [mi:t] *n* carne *f*; *Culin* **m. pie** empanada *f* de carne

meatball ['mi:tbɔ:l] *n* albóndiga *f*

meaty ['mi:tɪ] *adj* (**meatier, meatiest**) (**a**) *(fleshy)* carnoso(a) (**b**) *Fig (story)* jugoso(a)

Mecca ['mekə] *n* la Meca

mechanic [mɪ'kænɪk] *n (person)* mecánico(a) *m,f*

mechanical [mɪ'kænɪkəl] *adj* mecánico(a)

mechanics [mɪ'kænɪks] **1** *n sing (science)* mecánica *f*
2 *npl (technical aspects)* mecanismo *m*

mechanism ['mekənɪzəm] *n* mecanismo *m*

medal ['medəl] *n* medalla *f*

medalist ['medəlɪst] *US* = **medallist**

medallion [mɪ'dæljən] *n* medallón *m*

medallist ['medəlɪst] *n* medallista *mf*

meddle ['medəl] *vi* entrometerse (**in** en); **to m. with sth** manosear algo

media ['mi:dɪə] *npl* medios *mpl* de comunicación; **m. coverage** cobertura periodística

⌨ Note that the Spanish word **media** is a false friend and is never a translation for the English word **media**. In Spanish **media** means both "stocking, sock" and "average".

median ['mi:dɪən] **1** *adj* mediano(a); *US Aut* **m. (strip)** mediana *f*, *Col, Méx* camellón *m*
2 *n Geom* mediana *f*; *Math* valor mediano

mediate ['mi:dɪeɪt] *vi* mediar

mediator ['mi:dɪeɪtə(r)] *n* mediador(a) *m,f*

Medicaid ['medɪkeɪd] *n (in US)* = seguro médico estatal para personas con renta baja

medical ['medɪkəl] **1** *adj (treatment)* médico(a); *(book)* de medicina
2 *n Fam* reconocimiento médico

Medicare ['medɪkeə(r)] *n (in US)* = seguro médico para ancianos y algunos discapacitados

medicated ['medɪkeɪtɪd] *adj* medicinal

medication [medɪ'keɪʃən] *n* medicamento *m*, medicina *f*

medicine ['medsɪn] *n (science)* medicina *f*; *(drugs etc)* medicamento *m*

medieval [medɪ'i:vəl] *adj* medieval

mediocre [mi:dɪ'əʊkə(r)] *adj* mediocre

meditate ['medɪteɪt] *vi* meditar (**on** sobre)

meditation [medɪ'teɪʃən] *n* meditación *f*

Mediterranean [medɪtə'reɪnɪən] **1** *adj* mediterráneo(a)
2 *n* **the M.** el Mediterráneo

medium ['mi:dɪəm] **1** *adj (average)* mediano(a); *Br Rad* **m. wave** onda media
2 *n* (**a**) *(pl* **media**) *(means)* medio *m* (**b**) *(pl* **mediums**) *(spiritualist)* médium *mf*

medley ['medlɪ] *n (mixture)* mezcla *f*; *Mus* popurrí *m*

meek [miːk] *adj* manso(a), sumiso(a); *(humble)* humilde

meet [miːt] **1** *vt* (*pt & pp* **met**) (a) *(encounter) (by chance)* encontrar, encontrarse con; *(by arrangement)* reunirse con; *(in formal meeting)* entrevistarse con (b) *(become acquainted with)* conocer; **I'd like you to m. my mother** quiero presentarte a mi madre; **the first time I met him** cuando lo conocí (c) *(join with)* unirse con, juntarse con; **where East meets West** donde se encuentran el Oriente y el Occidente (d) *(encounter) (danger)* encontrar; *(opponent)* enfrentarse con (e) *(satisfy) (demand, need, condition)* satisfacer; *(objection, criticism)* responder a
2 *vi* (a) *(by chance)* encontrarse; *(by arrangement)* reunirse; *(for formal meeting)* entrevistarse (b) *(become acquainted)* conocerse (c) *Sport* enfrentarse (d) *(rivers, roads)* encontrarse, unirse
3 *n (sports event)* encuentro *m*; *(in athletics)* reunión *f* atlética

▸**meet up** *vi* encontrarse, quedar (**with** con)

▸**meet with** *vt insep (difficulty)* tropezar con; *(loss)* sufrir; *(success)* tener; *esp US (person)* reunirse con

meeting ['miːtɪŋ] *n (chance encounter)* encuentro *m*; *(prearranged)* cita *f*; *(formal)* entrevista *f*; *(of committee etc)* reunión *f*; *(of assembly)* sesión *f*; *(of shareholders)* junta *f*; *(rally)* mitin *m*; *Sport* encuentro *m*; *(of rivers)* confluencia *f*

mega ['megə] *adj Fam (excellent)* genial, guay, *Andes, CAm, Carib, Méx* chévere, *RP* bárbaro(a)

megabyte ['megəbaɪt] *n Comput* megabyte *m*

megalomania [megələʊ'meɪnɪə] *n* megalomanía *f*

megaphone ['megəfəʊn] *n* megáfono *m*

melancholy ['melənkəlɪ] **1** *n* melancolía *f*
2 *adj* melancólico(a)

Melilla [me'liːjə] *n* Melilla

mellow ['meləʊ] **1** *adj* maduro(a); *(wine)* añejo(a); *(colour, voice)* suave; *(person)* apacible
2 *vi (fruit)* madurar; *(colour, voice)* suavizarse

melodrama ['melədrɑːmə] *n* melodrama *m*

melodramatic [melədrə'mætɪk] *adj* melodramático(a)

melody ['melədɪ] *n* melodía *f*

melon ['melən] *n* melón *m*

melt [melt] **1** *vt (metal)* fundir; *Fig (sb's heart)* ablandar
2 *vi (snow)* derretirse; *(metal)* fundirse; *Fig* ablandarse

▸**melt away** *vi (snow)* derretirse; *Fig (money)* desaparecer; *Fig (confidence)* desvanecerse

▸**melt down** *vt sep (metal)* fundir

melting ['meltɪŋ] *n* fundición *f*; **m. point** punto *m* de fusión; **m. pot** crisol *m*

member ['membə(r)] *n* miembro *mf*; *(of a society)* socio(a) *m,f*; *(of party, union)* afiliado(a) *m,f*; *US* **M. of Congress** congresista *mf*; *Br* **M. of Parliament** diputado(a) *m,f*

membership ['membəʃɪp] *n (state)* calidad *f* de socio; *(entry)* ingreso *m*; *Pol* afiliación *f*; *(number of members)* número *m* de socios; **m. card** carnet *m* de socio

memento [mə'mentəʊ] *n* recuerdo *m*

memo ['meməʊ] *n (official note)* memorándum *m*; *(personal note)* nota *f*, apunte *m*

memoirs ['memwɑːz] *npl* memorias *fpl*

memorabilia [memərə'bɪlɪə] *npl* wartime **m.** objetos *mpl* de la época de la guerra

memorable ['memərəbəl] *adj* memorable

memorandum [memə'rændəm] *n (pl* **memoranda**) *(official note)* memorándum *m*; *(personal note)* nota *f*, apunte *m*

memorial [mɪ'mɔːrɪəl] **1** *adj (plaque etc)* conmemorativo(a)
2 *n* monumento conmemorativo

memorize ['meməraɪz] *vt* memorizar, aprender de memoria

memory ['memərɪ] *n* memoria *f*; *(recollection)* recuerdo *m*; *Comput* **m. stick** llave *f* USB

men [men] *pl of* **man**

menace ['menɪs] **1** *n (threat)* amenaza *f*; *(danger)* peligro *m*; *Fam (person)* pesado(a) *m,f*
2 *vt* amenazar

menacing ['menɪsɪŋ] *adj* amenazador(a)

menagerie [mɪ'nædʒərɪ] *n* casa *f* de fieras

mend [mend] **1** *vt* reparar, arreglar; *(clothes)* remendar; *(socks etc)* zurcir
2 *vi (ill person)* reponerse
3 *n (patch)* remiendo *m*; *(darn)* zurcido *m*

mending ['mendɪŋ] *n (repair)* reparación *f*; *(darning)* zurcido *m*; *(clothes for mending)* ropa *f* para remendar

menial ['miːnɪəl] *adj (task)* servil, bajo(a)

meningitis [menɪn'dʒaɪtɪs] *n* meningitis *f inv*

menopause ['menəpɔːz] *n* menopausia *f*

menstrual ['menstrʊəl] *adj* menstrual

menstruation [menstru'eɪʃən] *n* menstruación *f*

menswear ['menzweə(r)] *n* ropa *f* de caballero *or* hombre

mental ['mentəl] *adj* (**a**) *(state, age)* mental; **m. hospital** hospital psiquiátrico; **m. illness** enfermedad *f* mental (**b**) *Br Fam (mad)* pirado(a), *CSur* rayado(a)

mentality [men'tælɪtɪ] *n* mentalidad *f*

mentally ['mentəlɪ] *adv* **m. ill** enfermo(a) mental; **to be m. handicapped** ser un/una disminuido(a) psíquico(a)

mention ['menʃən] **1** *n* mención *f*
2 *vt* mencionar; **don't m. it!** ¡de nada!

mentor ['mentɔ:(r)] *n* mentor *m*

menu ['menju:] *n* (**a**) *(card)* carta *f*; *(fixed meal)* menú *m*; **today's m.** el menú del día (**b**) *Comput* menú *m*

MEP [emi:'pi:] *n Br (abbr* **Member of the European Parliament**) eurodiputado(a) *m,f*

mercenary ['mɜ:sɪnərɪ] *adj & n* mercenario(a) *(m,f)*

merchandise ['mɜ:tʃəndaɪz] *n* mercancías *fpl*, géneros *mpl*

merchant ['mɜːtʃənt] *n Com & Fin* comerciante *mf*; *(retailer)* detallista *mf*; **m. bank** banco *m* comercial

merciful ['mɜːsɪfʊl] *adj* clemente, compasivo(a) (**towards** con)

merciless ['mɜːsɪlɪs] *adj* despiadado(a)

Mercury ['mɜːkjʊrɪ] *n* Mercurio *m*

mercury ['mɜːkjʊrɪ] *n* mercurio *m*

mercy ['mɜːsɪ] *n* misericordia *f*, compasión *f*; **at the m. of** a la merced de; **to have m. on** tener compasión de

mere [mɪə(r)] *adj* mero(a), simple

merely ['mɪəlɪ] *adv* simplemente

merge [mɜːdʒ] **1** *vt (blend)* unir (**with** con); *Com* fusionar
2 *vi* unirse; *(roads)* empalmar; *Com* fusionarse

merger ['mɜːdʒə(r)] *n Com* fusión *f*

meridian [mə'rɪdɪən] *n Geog & Astron* meridiano *m*

meringue [mə'ræŋ] *n* merengue *m*

merit ['merɪt] **1** *n (of person)* mérito *m*; *(of plan etc)* ventaja *f*
2 *vt* merecer, *Am* ameritar

mermaid ['mɜːmeɪd] *n* sirena *f*

merry ['merɪ] *adj (merrier, merriest) (happy)* alegre; *Fam (slightly drunk)* alegre, *Esp* piripi; **m. Christmas!** ¡felices Navidades!

merry-go-round ['merɪɡəʊraʊnd] *n* tiovivo *m*, carrusel *m*, *RP* calesita *f*

mesh [meʃ] **1** *n Tex* malla *f*; *Tech* engranaje *m*; *Fig* red *f*
2 *vt Tech* engranar

mesmerize ['mezməraɪz] *vt* hipnotizar

mess [mes] *n* (**a**) *(confusion)* confusión *f*; *(disorder)* desorden *m*; **to be in a m.** *(of room etc)* estar desordenado(a) (**b**) *(in life, affairs)* lío *m*; **to get into a m.** meterse en un lío (**c**) *(dirt)* suciedad *f* (**d**) *Mil (room)* comedor *m*
▸ **mess about, mess around** *Fam* **1** *vt sep* fastidiar
2 *vi (act the fool)* hacer el primo; *(idle)* gandulear; *(kill time)* pasar el rato
▸ **mess about with** *vt insep Fam (fiddle with)* manosear; **to m. about with sb** tener un lío con algn
▸ **mess up** *vt sep Fam (make untidy)* desordenar; *(dirty)* ensuciar; *(spoil)* estropear

message ['mesɪdʒ] *n (communication)* recado *m*; *(of story etc)* mensaje *m*; *Fam* **to get the m.** comprender

messaging ['mesɪdʒɪŋ] *n* mensajería *f*

messenger ['mesɪndʒə(r)] *n* mensajero(a) *m,f*

Messiah [mɪ'saɪə] *n Rel* Mesías *m inv*

Messrs ['mesəz] *npl (abbr* **Messieurs**) Sres.

messy ['mesɪ] *adj (messier, messiest)* (**a**) *(untidy) (room)* desordenado(a); *(person)* desaliñado(a) (**b**) *(dirty)* sucio(a) (**c**) *(confused)* enredado(a)

met [met] *pt & pp of* **meet**

metabolism [me'tæbəlɪzəm] *n* metabolismo *m*

metal ['metəl] **1** *n* metal *m*
2 *adj* metálico(a)

metallic [mɪ'tælɪk] *adj* metálico(a); **m. blue** azul metalizado

metallurgy [me'tælədʒɪ] *n* metalurgia *f*

metalwork ['metəlwɜːk] *n (craft)* metalistería *f*; *(objects)* objetos *mpl* de metal

metamorphosis [metə'mɔːfəsɪs] *n (pl* **metamorphoses** [metə'mɔːfəsiːz]) metamorfosis *f inv*

metaphor ['metəfə(r)] *n* metáfora *f*

mete [miːt] *vt* **to m. out** imponer

meteor ['miːtɪə(r)] *n* bólido *m*

meteoric [miːtɪ'ɒrɪk] *adj* meteórico(a)

meteorite ['miːtɪəraɪt] *n* meteorito *m*

meteorology [miːtɪə'rɒlədʒɪ] *n* meteorología *f*

meter[1] ['miːtə(r)] *n* contador *m*

meter[2] ['miːtər] *n US =* **metre**

method ['meθəd] *n* método *m*

methodical [mɪ'θɒdɪkəl] *adj* metódico(a)

Methodist ['meθədɪst] *adj & n* metodista *(mf)*

methylated spirits ['meθɪleɪtɪd'spɪrɪts], *Br Fam* **meths** [meθs] *n* alcohol desnaturalizado *(con metanol)*, alcohol *m* de quemar

meticulous [mə'tɪkjʊləs] *adj* meticuloso(a)

metre ['miːtə(r)] *n* metro *m*

metric ['metrɪk] *adj* métrico(a)

metropolis [mɪ'trɒpəlɪs] *n* metrópoli *f*

metropolitan [metrə'pɒlɪtən] *adj* metropolitano(a)

mettle ['metəl] *n* valor *m*

mew [mjuː] *vi (cat)* maullar

mews [mjuːz] *n sing Br (street)* callejuela *f*; **m. flat** = apartamento de lujo en unas caballerizas reconvertidas

Mexican ['meksɪkən] *adj & n* mejicano(a) *(m,f)*, mexicano(a) *(m,f)*

Mexico ['meksɪkəʊ] *n* México, Méjico

mezzanine ['metsəniːn] *n* **m. (floor)** entreplanta *f*

miaow [miː'aʊ] **1** *vi* maullar

   2 *n* maullido *m*

mice [maɪs] *pl of* **mouse**

mickey ['mɪkɪ] *n Fam* **to take the m. (out of sb)** tomar el pelo (a algn)

microbe ['maɪkrəʊb] *n* microbio *m*

microchip ['maɪkrəʊtʃɪp] *n* microplaqueta *f*, microchip *m*

microcomputer ['maɪkrəʊkəm'pjuːtə(r)] *n Esp.* microordenador *m*, *Am* microcomputadora *f*

microcosm ['maɪkrəʊkɒzəm] *n* microcosmo *m*

microfiche ['maɪkrəʊfiːʃ] *n* microficha *f*

microfilm ['maɪkrəʊfɪlm] *n* microfilm *m*

microphone ['maɪkrəfəʊn] *n* micrófono *m*

microprocessor [maɪkrəʊ'prəʊsesə(r)] *n* microprocesador *m*

microscope ['maɪkrəskəʊp] *n* microscopio *m*

microwave ['maɪkrəʊweɪv] *n* microonda *f*; **m. (oven)** (horno *m*) microondas *m inv*

mid [mɪd] *adj* **(in) m. afternoon** a media tarde; **(in) m. April** a mediados de abril; **to be in one's m. thirties** tener unos treinta y cinco años

midair **1** *adj* ['mɪdeə(r)] *(collision, explosion)* en el aire

   2 *n* [mɪd'eə(r)] *Fig* **to leave sth in m.** dejar algo en el aire

midday **1** *n* [mɪd'deɪ] mediodía *m*

   2 *adj* ['mɪddeɪ] de mediodía

middle ['mɪdəl] **1** *adj* de en medio; **m. age** mediana edad; **the M. Ages** la Edad Media; **the m. class** la clase media

   2 *n* **(a)** *(in general)* medio *m*; **in the m. of** en medio de; **in the m. of winter** en pleno invierno; *Fam* **in the m. of nowhere** en el quinto pino **(b)** *(waist)* cintura *f*

middle-aged [mɪdəl'eɪʒd] *adj* de mediana edad

middle-class [mɪdəl'klɑːs] *adj* de clase media

middleman ['mɪdəlmæn] *n* intermediario *m*

middleweight ['mɪdəlweɪt] *n* peso medio

middling ['mɪdlɪŋ] *adj* mediano(a)

midfielder [mɪd'fiːldə(r)] *n Sport* centrocampista *mf*

midge [mɪdʒ] *n* mosca enana

midget ['mɪdʒɪt] *n* enano(a) *m,f*

Midlands ['mɪdləndz] *npl* **the M.** = la región central de Inglaterra

midnight ['mɪdnaɪt] *n* medianoche *f*

midriff ['mɪdrɪf] *n* diafragma *m*

midst [mɪdst] *n* **in the m. of** en medio de

midsummer [mɪd'sʌmə(r)] *n* pleno verano; **M.'s Day** Día *m* de San Juan *(24 de junio)*

midterm ['mɪd'tɜːm] *adj* **(a)** *Pol Br* **m. by-election** = elecciones parciales a mitad de legislatura; *US* **m. elections** = elecciones a mitad del mandato presidencial **(b)** *Sch Univ* de mitad de trimestre

midway ['mɪdweɪ] *adv* a medio camino

midweek **1** *adv* [mɪd'wiːk] entre semana

   2 *adj* ['mɪdwiːk] de entre semana

Mid-West ['mɪd'west] *n* Medio Oeste *m* (de Estados Unidos)

midwife ['mɪdwaɪf] *n* comadrona *f*, partera *f*

midwifery ['mɪdwɪfərɪ] *n* obstetricia *f*

midwinter [mɪd'wɪntə(r)] *n* pleno invierno *m*

might[1] [maɪt] *v aux see* **may**

might[2] [maɪt] *n Fml* fuerza *f*, poder *m*

mighty ['maɪtɪ] **1** *adj* (**mightier, mightiest**) *(strong)* fuerte; *(powerful)* poderoso(a); *(great)* enorme

   2 *adv US Fam* un montón, *Esp* cantidad

migraine ['miːgreɪn, 'maɪgreɪn] *n* jaqueca *f*

migrant ['maɪgrənt] **1** *adj* migratorio(a)

   2 *n (person)* emigrante *mf*; *(bird)* ave migratoria

migrate [maɪ'greɪt] *vi* emigrar

migration [maɪ'greɪʃən] *n* migración *f*

mike [maɪk] *n Fam* micro *m*

mild [maɪld] *adj (person, character)* apacible; *(climate)* templado(a); *(punishment)* leve; *(tobacco, taste)* suave

mildew ['mɪldjuː] n moho m; (on plants) añublo m

mildly ['maɪldlɪ] adv (softly, gently) suavemente; (slightly) ligeramente; **and that's putting it m.** y esto es decir poco

mildness ['maɪldnɪs] n (of character) apacibilidad f; (of climate, taste) suavidad f; (of punishment) levedad f

mile [maɪl] n milla f; Fam **miles better** muchísimo mejor

mileage ['maɪlɪdʒ] n kilometraje m

milestone ['maɪlstəʊn] n hito m

milieu ['miːljɜː] n medio m ambiente

militant ['mɪlɪtənt] adj & n militante (mf)

military ['mɪlɪtərɪ] adj militar; **to do one's m. service** hacer el servicio militar

militia [mɪ'lɪʃə] n milicia f

milk [mɪlk] **1** n leche f; **m. chocolate** chocolate m con leche; **m. shake** batido m, Am licuado m
2 vt (a) (cow, goat) ordeñar (b) Fam **they milked him of all his money** le sangraron hasta el último centavo

milkman ['mɪlkmən] n lechero m

milky ['mɪlkɪ] adj (**milkier, milkiest**) lechoso(a); (colour) pálido(a); **M. Way** Vía Láctea

mill [mɪl] **1** n (grinder) molino m; (for coffee) molinillo m; (factory) fábrica f; **cotton m.** hilandería f
2 vt moler

▸ **mill about, mill around** vi arremolinarse

millennium [mɪ'lenɪəm] n (pl **millenniums** or **millennia** [mɪ'lenɪə]) milenio m

miller ['mɪlə(r)] n molinero(a) m,f

millet ['mɪlɪt] n mijo m

milligram(me) ['mɪlɪgræm] n miligramo m

millilitre, US **milliliter** ['mɪlɪliːtə(r)] n mililitro m

millimetre, US **millimeter** ['mɪlɪmiːtə(r)] n milímetro m

milliner ['mɪlɪnə(r)] n sombrerero(a) m,f

millinery ['mɪlɪnərɪ] n sombreros mpl de señora

million ['mɪljən] n millón m

millionaire [mɪljə'neə(r)] n millonario(a) m,f

millstone ['mɪlstəʊn] n muela f; Fig carga f

mime [maɪm] **1** n (art) mímica f; (play) pantomima f
2 vt representar con gestos

<hr>

> 🖉 Note that the Spanish verb **mimar** is a false friend and is never a translation for the English verb **to mime**. In Spanish **mimar** means "to spoil, to pamper".

<hr>

mimic ['mɪmɪk] **1** adj & n mímico(a) (m,f)
2 vt imitar

mimicry ['mɪmɪkrɪ] n imitación f

minaret ['mɪnəret] n alminar m, minarete m

mince [mɪns] **1** n Br (meat) carne Esp, RP picada or Am molida; **m. pie** (containing meat) = empanada de carne picada; (containing fruit) = pastel navideño relleno de "mincemeat"
2 vt picar

mincemeat ['mɪnsmiːt] n (meat) carne Esp, RP picada or Am molida; (fruit) = relleno a base de fruta escarchada, frutos secos y especias

mincer ['mɪnsə(r)] n picadora f de carne

mind [maɪnd] **1** n (a) (thoughts, intellect) mente f; **to bear** or **keep sth in m.** tener algo en cuenta; **what kind of car do you have in m.?** ¿en qué clase de coche estás pensando?; **to lose one's m.** perder el juicio; **I'm sure if you put your m. to it you could do it** estoy seguro de que podrías hacerlo si pusieses tus cinco sentidos (en ello); **it slipped my m.** lo olvidé por completo (b) (opinion) **to be in two minds (about sth)** estar indeciso(a) (acerca de algo); **to have a m. of one's own** ser capaz de pensar or decidir por sí mismo(a); **to my m.** a mi parecer; Fam **I gave him a piece of my m.** le canté las cuarenta
2 vt (a) (child) cuidar; (house) vigilar; (be careful of) tener cuidado con; **m. the step!** ¡ojo con el escalón!; **m. your own business!** ¡no te metas donde no te llaman!; **m. you, he is fifty** ten en cuenta que tiene cincuenta años (b) (object to) **I don't m. the cold** el frío no me importa or no me molesta; **I wouldn't m. a cup of coffee** me vendría bien un café; **would you m. not doing that?** ¿te importaría no hacer eso?
3 vi (a) (object) importar; **do you m. if I open the window?** ¿le importa que abra la ventana?; **never m.!** ¡es igual!

mind-boggling ['maɪndbɒglɪŋ], **mind-blowing** ['maɪndbləʊɪŋ] adj Fam alucinante

minder ['maɪndə(r)] n (a) Br Fam (bodyguard) gorila m, Méx guarura m (b) (child or baby) **m.** Esp canguro mf, Am baby-sitter f, Méx niñera f

mindful ['maɪndfʊl] adj consciente

mindless ['maɪndlɪs] adj (task) de autómata; (violence) injustificable

mine[1] [maɪn] poss pron (el) mío/(la) mía, (los) míos/(las) mías, lo mío; **a friend of m.** un amigo mío; **these gloves are m.** estos guantes son míos; **which is m.?** ¿cuál es el mío?

mine² [maɪn] **1** n mina f; Fig **a m. of information** un pozo de información
2 vt (coal etc) extraer; Mil minar

minefield ['maɪnfiːld] n campo m de minas

miner ['maɪnə(r)] n minero(a) m,f

mineral ['mɪnərəl] **1** adj mineral; **m. water** agua f mineral
2 n mineral m

minesweeper ['maɪnswiːpə(r)] n dragaminas m inv

mingle ['mɪŋgəl] vi mezclarse

miniature ['mɪnɪtʃə(r)] **1** n miniatura f
2 adj (railway) en miniatura; (camera, garden) diminuto(a)

minibus ['mɪnɪbʌs] n microbús m

minicab ['mɪnɪkæb] n Br taxi m (que sólo se puede pedir por teléfono)

minim ['mɪnɪm] n Br Mus blanca f

minimal ['mɪnɪməl] adj mínimo(a)

minimize ['mɪnɪmaɪz] vt minimizar, reducir al mínimo

minimum ['mɪnɪməm] **1** adj mínimo(a); **m. wage** salario mínimo
2 n mínimo m

mining ['maɪnɪŋ] **1** n minería f, explotación f de minas; Mil & Naut minado m
2 adj minero(a)

miniskirt ['mɪnɪskɜːt] n minifalda f

minister ['mɪnɪstə(r)] **1** n Pol ministro(a) m,f; Rel pastor(a) m,f
2 vi **to m. to sb** atender a algn

ministerial [mɪnɪ'stɪərɪəl] adj Pol ministerial

ministry ['mɪnɪstrɪ] n Pol ministerio m; Rel sacerdocio m

mink [mɪŋk] n visón m; **m. coat** abrigo m de visón

minnow ['mɪnəʊ] n alevín m

minor ['maɪnə(r)] **1** adj (lesser) menor; (unimportant) sin importancia; (role) secundario(a); Mus menor
2 n Jur menor mf de edad

Minorca [mɪ'nɔːkə] n Menorca f

minority [maɪ'nɒrɪtɪ] n minoría f; **to be in the m.** ser (la) minoría; Pol **m. party** partido minoritario

mint¹ [mɪnt] **1** n Fin **the (Royal) M.** ≃ la Casa de la Moneda, Esp ≃ la Fábrica Nacional de Moneda y Timbre
2 vt (coin, words) acuñar

mint² [mɪnt] n Bot menta f; (sweet) pastilla f de menta

minus ['maɪnəs] **1** prep **5 m. 3** 5 menos 3; **m. 10 degrees** 10 grados bajo cero
2 adj negativo(a)
3 n **m. (sign)** signo m (de) menos

minute¹ ['mɪnɪt] n (a) (of time) minuto m; **at the last m.** a última hora; **just a m.** (espera) un momento; **this very m.** ahora mismo (b) **the minutes** (notes) el acta

minute² [maɪ'njuːt] adj (tiny) diminuto(a); (examination) minucioso(a)

miracle ['mɪrəkəl] n milagro m

miraculous [mɪ'rækjʊləs] adj milagroso(a)

mirage [mɪ'rɑːʒ] n espejismo m

mire [maɪə(r)] n fango m, lodo m; (muddy place) lodazal m

mirror ['mɪrə(r)] **1** n espejo m; Fig reflejo m; **rear-view m.** retrovisor m
2 vt reflejar

mirth [mɜːθ] n alegría f; (laughter) risas fpl

misadventure [mɪsəd'ventʃə(r)] n desgracia f; **death by m.** muerte f accidental

misanthropist [mɪ'zænθrəpɪst] n misántropo(a) m,f

misapprehension [mɪsæprɪ'henʃən] n malentendido m

misbehave [mɪsbɪ'heɪv] vi portarse mal

miscalculate [mɪs'kælkjʊleɪt] vt & vi calcular mal

miscarriage ['mɪskærɪdʒ] n Med aborto (espontáneo); **m. of justice** error m judicial

miscellaneous [mɪsɪ'leɪnɪəs] adj variado(a); **m. expenses** gastos diversos

mischief ['mɪstʃɪf] n (naughtiness) travesura f, Fml (evil) malicia f; **to get up to m.** hacer travesuras; Br Fam Hum (injury) **to do oneself a m.** hacerse daño

mischievous ['mɪstʃɪvəs] adj (naughty) travieso(a); (playful) juguetón(ona); Fml (wicked) malicioso(a)

misconception [mɪskən'sepʃən] n concepto erróneo

misconduct [mɪs'kɒndʌkt] n mala conducta

misconstrue [mɪskən'struː] vt interpretar mal

miscount [mɪs'kaʊnt] vt (votes etc) contar mal

misdeed [mɪs'diːd] n fechoría f

misdemeanour, US **misdemeanor** [mɪsdɪ'miːnə(r)] n (misdeed) fechoría f; Jur falta m

miser ['maɪzə(r)] n avaro(a) m,f

miserable ['mɪzərəbəl] adj (a) (sad) triste (b) (unpleasant) lamentable; (weather) horroroso(a) (c) (wretched) miserable

miserly ['maɪzəlɪ] adj avaro(a), tacaño(a)

misery ['mɪzərɪ] n (sadness) tristeza f; (wretchedness) desgracia f; (suffering)

sufrimiento *m*; *(poverty)* miseria *f*; *Fam*
(person) aguafiestas *mf*

misfire [mɪsˈfaɪə(r)] *vi (engine, plan etc)*
fallar

misfit [ˈmɪsfɪt] *n (person)* inadaptado(a)
m,f

misfortune [mɪsˈfɔːtʃən] *n* desgracia *f*

misgiving [mɪsˈgɪvɪŋ] *n (doubt)* recelo *m*;
(fear) temor *m*

misguided [mɪsˈgaɪdɪd] *adj* equivoca-
do(a)

mishandle [mɪsˈhændəl] *vt* llevar *or*
manejar mal

mishap [ˈmɪshæp] *n* contratiempo *m*

misinform [mɪsɪnˈfɔːm] *vt* informar mal

misinterpret [mɪsɪnˈtɜːprɪt] *vt* interpretar mal

misjudge [mɪsˈdʒʌdʒ] *vt* juzgar mal

mislay [mɪsˈleɪ] *vt* extraviar

mislead [mɪsˈliːd] *vt* despistar; *(deliberately)* engañar

misleading [mɪsˈliːdɪŋ] *adj (erroneous)*
erróneo(a); *(deliberately)* engañoso(a)

mismanagement [mɪsˈmænɪdʒmənt] *n*
mala administración

misnomer [mɪsˈnəʊmə(r)] *n* nombre
equivocado

misogynist [mɪˈsɒdʒɪnɪst] *n* misógino(a)
m,f

misplace [mɪsˈpleɪs] *vt (trust)* encauzar
mal; *(book, spectacles etc)* extraviar

misprint [ˈmɪsprɪnt] *n* errata *f*, error *m* de
imprenta

misquote [mɪsˈkwəʊt] *vt* (**a**) *(accidentally)* citar equivocadamente (**b**) *(deliberately) (person)* tergiversar las palabras de;
(words) tergiversar

misrepresent [mɪsreprɪˈzent] *vt (facts)*
desvirtuar; *(words)* tergiversar

miss¹ [mɪs] *n* señorita *f*

▸ **miss out 1** *vt sep (omit)* saltarse; *(on
purpose)* pasar por alto

2 *vt insep* **to m. out on** perderse

miss² [mɪs] **1** *n (throw etc)* Esp fallo *m*, Am
falla *f*, Fam **to give sth a m.** pasar de algo
2 *vt* (**a**) *(target)* no acertar en; *(shot,
penalty) Esp* fallar, Am errar; **the car just
missed me** el coche *or Am* carro *or CSur*
auto no me atropelló por poco (**b**) *(train
etc)* perder; *(opportunity)* dejar pasar; **you
have missed the point** no has captado la
idea (**c**) *(feel lack of)* echar de menos, *esp
Am* extrañar; **I m. you** te echo de menos,
esp Am te extraño
3 *vi* (**a**) *(miss target) (when throwing)*
fallar; *(when shooting)* errar (**b**) *(be
absent)* **to be missing** faltar

misshapen [mɪsˈʃeɪpən] *adj* deforme

missile [ˈmɪsaɪl, *US* ˈmɪsəl] *n Mil* misil *m*;
(object thrown) proyectil *m*

missing [ˈmɪsɪŋ] *adj (object)* perdido(a);
(person) desaparecido(a); *(from meeting
etc)* ausente; **m. person** desaparecido(a)
m,f, **three cups are m.** faltan tres tazas

mission [ˈmɪʃən] *n* misión *f*; **m. (station)**
misión *f*; Com **m. statement** declaración *f*
de (la) misión, misión *f*

missionary [ˈmɪʃənərɪ] *n* misionero(a)
m,f

misspell [ˈmɪsˈspel] *(pt & pp* **misspelt**
[ˈmɪsˈspelt]) *vt* escribir incorrectamente

misspent [ˈmɪsspent] *adj (youth)*
malgastado(a)

mist [mɪst] **1** *n* neblina *f*; *(thick)* niebla *f*; *(at
sea)* bruma *f*
2 *vi* **to m. over** *or* **up** *(countryside)*
cubrirse de neblina; *(window etc)*
empañarse

mistake [mɪsˈteɪk] **1** *n* error *m*; **by m.** por
equivocación; **I hurt him by m.** le golpeé
sin querer; **to make a m.** equivocarse,
cometer un error
2 *vt (pt* **mistook***; pp* **mistaken***) (meaning)*
malentender; **to m. Jack for Bill** confundir
a Jack con Bill

mistaken [mɪsˈteɪkən] *adj* equivocado(a),
erróneo(a); **you are m.** estás equi-
vocado(a)

mister [ˈmɪstə(r)] *n* señor *m*

mistletoe [ˈmɪsəltəʊ] *n* muérdago *m*

mistook [mɪsˈtʊk] *pt of* **mistake**

mistreat [mɪsˈtriːt] *vt* tratar mal

mistress [ˈmɪstrɪs] *n* (**a**) *(of servant,
house)* señora *f*, ama *f* (**b**) *(lover)* amante
f (**c**) *Educ (primary school)* maestra *f*;
(secondary school) profesora *f*

mistrust [mɪsˈtrʌst] **1** *n* recelo *m*
2 *vt* desconfiar de

misty [ˈmɪstɪ] *adj* (**mistier, mistiest**) *(day)*
de niebla; *(window etc)* empañado(a)

misunderstand [mɪsʌndəˈstænd] *vt & vi*
malentender

misunderstanding [mɪsʌndəˈstændɪŋ] *n*
malentendido *m*; *(disagreement)* desavenencia *f*

misuse 1 *n* [mɪsˈjuːs] mal uso *m*; *(of funds)*
malversación *f*; *(of power)* abuso *m*
2 *vt* [mɪsˈjuːz] emplear mal; *(funds)*
malversar; *(power)* abusar de

miter [ˈmaɪtər] *n US =* **mitre**

mitigate [ˈmɪtɪgeɪt] *vt* atenuar

mitigating [ˈmɪtɪgeɪtɪŋ] *adj* **m. circumstances** circunstancias *fpl* atenuantes

mitre [ˈmaɪtə(r)] *n* mitra *f*

mitten [ˈmɪtən] *n* manopla *f*; *(fingerless)*
mitón *m*

mix [mɪks] **1** *n* mezcla *f*
2 *vt* mezclar
3 *vi (blend)* mezclarse *(with* con); *(go well together)* ir bien juntos(as)
▸ **mix up** *vt sep (confuse)* confundir *(with* con); *(papers)* revolver; **to be mixed up in sth** estar involucrado(a) en algo

mixed [mɪkst] *adj (assorted)* surtido(a); *(varied)* variado(a); *(school)* mixto(a); *(feelings)* contradictorio(a)

mixed-up [mɪkst'ʌp] *adj (objects, papers etc)* revuelto(a); *(person)* confuso(a)

mixer ['mɪksə(r)] *n* (**a**) *(for cooking)* batidora *f* (**b**) **to be a good m.** *(person)* tener don de gentes

mixture ['mɪkstʃə(r)] *n* mezcla *f*

mix-up ['mɪksʌp] *n Fam* confusión *f*, lío *m*

mm *(abbr* **millimetre(s))** mm

moan [məʊn] **1** *n (groan)* gemido *m*, quejido *m*
2 *vi (groan)* gemir; *(complain)* quejarse *(about* de)

moat [məʊt] *n* foso *m*

mob [mɒb] **1** *n* multitud *f*; *(riff-raff)* gentuza *f*; **the m.** el populacho
2 *vt* acosar

mobile ['məʊbaɪl, *US* 'məʊbəl] **1** *adj* móvil; **m. home** caravana *f*; **m. phone** teléfono *m* móvil, *Am* teléfono *m* celular
2 *n* (**a**) *(hanging ornament)* móvil *m* (**b**) *Fam (mobile phone)* móvil *m*, *Am* celular *m*

mobility [məʊ'bɪlɪtɪ] *n* movilidad *f*

mobilize ['məʊbɪlaɪz] *vt* movilizar

moccasin ['mɒkəsɪn] *n* mocasín *m*

mock [mɒk] **1** *adj (sympathy etc)* fingido(a); *(objects)* de imitación
2 *vt (make fun of)* burlarse de
3 *vi* burlarse *(at* de)

mockery ['mɒkərɪ] *n* burla *f*

mod cons ['mɒd'kɒnz] *npl Br Fam* **with all m.** con todas las comodidades

mode [məʊd] *n (manner)* modo *m*, estilo *m*; *(fashion)* moda *f*

model ['mɒdəl] **1** *n (person, example)* modelo *m*; **(scale) m.** maqueta *f*
2 *adj (railway)* en miniatura; *(pupil)* ejemplar; *(school)* modelo
3 *vt (clay etc)* modelar; *(clothes)* presentar; *Comput* simular por *Esp* ordenador *or Am* computadora
4 *vi (make models)* modelar; *(work as model)* trabajar de modelo

modem ['məʊdem] *n Comput* modem *m*

moderate¹ ['mɒdərɪt] **1** *adj* moderado(a); *(reasonable)* razonable; *(average)* regular; *(ability)* mediocre
2 *n Pol* moderado(a) *m,f*

moderate² ['mɒdəreɪt] **1** *vt* moderar
2 *vi* moderarse; *(wind)* calmarse; *(in debate)* arbitrar

moderately ['mɒdərɪtlɪ] *adv* medianamente

moderation [mɒdə'reɪʃən] *n* moderación *f*; **in m.** con moderación

modern ['mɒdən] *adj* moderno(a); *(history)* contemporáneo(a); **m. languages** lenguas modernas

modernize ['mɒdənaɪz] *vt* modernizar

modest ['mɒdɪst] *adj* modesto(a); *(chaste)* púdico(a); *(price)* módico(a); *(success)* discreto(a)

modesty ['mɒdɪstɪ] *n (humility)* modestia *f*; *(chastity)* pudor *m*

modification [mɒdɪfɪ'keɪʃən] *n* modificación *f*

modify ['mɒdɪfaɪ] *vt* modificar

module ['mɒdjuːl] *n* módulo *m*

mogul ['məʊgʌl] *n* magnate *m*

mohair ['məʊheə(r)] **1** *n* mohair *m*
2 *adj* de mohair

moist [mɔɪst] *adj* húmedo(a)

moisten ['mɔɪsən] *vt* humedecer

moisture ['mɔɪstʃə(r)] *n* humedad *f*

moisturizer ['mɔɪstʃəraɪzə(r)] *n* crema *f* or leche *f* hidratante

molar ['məʊlə(r)] *n* muela *f*

molasses [mə'læsɪz] *n sing* melaza *f*

mold¹ [məʊld] *n US* = **mould¹**

mold² [məʊld] *n & vt US* = **mould²**

molder ['məʊldər] *vi US* = **moulder**

molding ['məʊldɪŋ] *n US* = **moulding**

moldy ['məʊldɪ] *adj US* = **mouldy**

mole¹ [məʊl] *n (beauty spot)* lunar *m*

mole² [məʊl] *n (animal)* topo *m*

molecule ['mɒlɪkjuːl] *n* molécula *f*

molest [mə'lest] *vt* importunar; *(sexually assault)* acosar (sexualmente)

mollycoddle ['mɒlɪkɒdəl] *vt Fam* mimar, consentir

molt [məʊlt] *vi US* = **moult**

molten ['məʊltən] *adj* fundido(a); *(lava)* líquido(a)

mom [mɒm] *n US Fam* mamá *f*

moment ['məʊmənt] *n* momento *m*; **at the m.** en este momento; **for the m.** de momento; **in a m.** dentro de un momento; **at any m.** de un momento a otro

momentarily ['məʊməntərɪlɪ] *adv* momentáneamente; *US (soon)* dentro de poco

momentary ['məʊməntərɪ] *adj* momentáneo(a)

momentous [məʊ'mentəs] *adj* trascendental

momentum [məʊ'mentəm] *n Phys* momento *m*; *(speed)* velocidad *f*; *Fig* **to gather m.** cobrar velocidad

mommy ['mɒmɪ] *n US Fam* mamá *f*

Monaco ['mɒnəkəʊ] *n* Mónaco

monarch ['mɒnək] *n* monarca *m*

monarchy ['mɒnəkɪ] *n* monarquía *f*

monastery ['mɒnəstərɪ] *n* monasterio *m*

Monday ['mʌndɪ] *n* lunes *m*

monetarism ['mʌnɪtərɪzəm] *n* monetarismo *m*

monetary ['mʌnɪtərɪ] *adj* monetario(a)

money ['mʌnɪ] *n* dinero *m*; *(currency)* moneda *f*; **to make m.** ganar dinero

moneylender ['mʌnɪlendə(r)] *n* prestamista *mf*

money-spinner ['mʌnɪspɪnə(r)] *n Fam* negocio *m* rentable

Mongolia [mɒŋ'gəʊlɪə] *n* Mongolia

mongolism ['mɒŋgəlɪzəm] *n* mongolismo *m*

mongrel ['mʌŋgrəl] *n* perro mestizo

monitor ['mɒnɪtə(r)] **1** *n (screen)* monitor *m*; *Educ* delegado(a) *m,f*
2 *vt (check)* controlar; *(progress, events)* seguir de cerca

monk [mʌŋk] *n* monje *m*

monkey ['mʌŋkɪ] *n* mono *m*; *Br* **m. nut** *Esp* cacahuete *m*, *Am* maní *m*, *CAm*, *Méx* cacahuate *m*

monochrome ['mɒnəkrəʊm] *adj* monocromo(a); *(television, photo)* en blanco y negro

monocle ['mɒnəkəl] *n* monóculo *m*

monogamous [mɒ'nɒgəməs] *adj* monógamo(a)

monolingual [mɒnəʊ'lɪŋgwəl] *adj* monolingüe

monologue, *US* **monolog** ['mɒnəlɒg] *n* monólogo *m*

monopolize [mə'nɒpəlaɪz] *vt Fin* monopolizar; *(attention etc)* acaparar

monopoly [mə'nɒpəlɪ] *n* monopolio *m*

monosyllable [mɒnəʊ'sɪləbəl] *n* monosílabo *m*

monotone ['mɒnətəʊn] *n* **in a m.** con una voz monótona

monotonous [mə'nɒtənəs] *adj* monótono(a)

monotony [mə'nɒtənɪ] *n* monotonía *f*

monsoon [mɒn'suːn] *n* monzón *m*

monster ['mɒnstə(r)] *n* monstruo *m*

monstrosity [mɒn'strɒsɪtɪ] *n* monstruosidad *f*

monstrous ['mɒnstrəs] *adj (huge)* enorme; *(hideous)* monstruoso(a); *(outrageous)* escandaloso(a)

montage ['mɒntɑːʒ] *n* montaje *m*

month [mʌnθ] *n* mes *m*

monthly ['mʌnθlɪ] **1** *adj* mensual; **m. instalment** mensualidad *f*
2 *n (periodical)* revista *f* mensual
3 *adv* mensualmente, cada mes

monument ['mɒnjʊmənt] *n* monumento *m*

monumental [mɒnjʊ'mentəl] *adj* monumental; *Fam (huge)* enorme

moo [muː] **1** *n* mugido *m*
2 *vi* mugir

mooch [muːtʃ] *Fam* **1** *vi* **to m. around** vagar, dar vueltas
2 *vt* **to m. sth off sb** *(cadge)* gorronearle algo a algn

mood [muːd] *n* humor *m*; **to be in a good/bad m.** estar de buen/mal humor; **to be in the m. for (doing) sth** estar de humor para (hacer) algo

moody ['muːdɪ] *adj (moodier, moodiest) (changeable)* de humor variable; *(bad-tempered)* malhumorado(a)

moon [muːn] *n* luna *f*; *Fam* **over the m.** en el séptimo cielo

moonlight ['muːnlaɪt] *n* luz *f* de la luna

moonlighting ['muːnlaɪtɪŋ] *n Fam* pluriempleo *m*

moonlit ['muːnlɪt] *adj* iluminado(a) por la luna

Moor [mʊə(r)] *n* moro(a) *m,f*

moor[1] [mʊə(r)] *n (heath)* páramo *m*

moor[2] [mʊə(r)] *vt Naut* amarrar

Moorish ['mʊərɪʃ] *adj* moro(a)

moorland ['mʊələnd] *n* páramo *m*

moose ['muːs] *n (pl moose)* alce *m*

moot [muːt] *adj* **it's a m. point** es discutible

mop [mɒp] **1** *n (for floor)* fregona *f*
2 *vt* fregar

▸ **mop up** *vt sep (liquids)* enjugar; *(enemy forces)* acabar con

▸ **mope about, mope around** *vi* andar abatido(a)

mope [məʊp] *vi* estar alicaído(a)

moped ['məʊped] *n* ciclomotor *m*, vespa *f*

moral ['mɒrəl] **1** *adj* moral
2 *n* moraleja *f*; **morals** moral *f*, moralidad *f*

morale [mə'rɑːl] *n* moral *f*, estado *m* de ánimo

morality [mə'rælɪtɪ] *n* moralidad *f*

morass [mə'ræs] *n* pantano *m*; *Fig* lío *m*

moratorium [mɒrə'tɔːrɪəm] *n (pl moratoriums or moratoria* [mɒrə'tɔːrɪə]*)* moratoria *f* (**on** en)

morbid ['mɔːbɪd] *adj Med* mórbido(a); *(mind)* morboso(a)

more [mɔː(r)] **1** *adj* más; **is there any m. tea?** ¿queda más té?; **I've no m. money** no me queda más dinero; **m. tourists** más turistas

2 *pron* más; **how many m.?** ¿cuántos más?; **many/much m.** muchos(as)/ mucho más; **m. than a hundred** más de cien; **the m. he has, the m. he wants** cuanto más tiene más quiere; **and what is m.** y lo que es más

3 *adv* más; **I won't do it any m.** no lo volveré a hacer; **she doesn't live here any m.** ya no vive aquí; **m. and m. difficult** cada vez más difícil; **m. or less** más o menos

moreish ['mɔːrɪʃ] *adj Fam (food)* irresistible, adictivo(a)

moreover [mɔː'rəʊvə(r)] *adv* además

morgue [mɔːg] *n* depósito *m* de cadáveres

morning ['mɔːnɪŋ] **1** *n* mañana *f*; *(before dawn)* madrugada *f*; **in the m.** por la mañana; **on Monday mornings** los lunes por la mañana; **tomorrow m.** mañana por la mañana

2 *adj* matutino(a)

Moroccan [mə'rɒkən] *adj & n* marroquí *(mf)*

Morocco [mə'rɒkəʊ] *n* Marruecos

moron ['mɔːrɒn] *n Fam* subnormal *mf*, *Am* zonzo(a) *m,f*

morose [mə'rəʊs] *adj* hosco(a), huraño(a)

𝒪 Note that the Spanish word **moroso** is a false friend and is never a translation for the English word **morose**. In Spanish, **moroso** means "bad debtor".

---

morphine ['mɔːfiːn] *n* morfina *f*

Morse [mɔːs] *n* **M. (code)** (alfabeto *m*) Morse *m*

morsel ['mɔːsəl] *n (of food)* bocado *m*; *Fig* trozo *m*

mortal ['mɔːtəl] **1** *adj* mortal
2 *n* mortal *mf*

mortality [mɔː'tælɪtɪ] *n* mortalidad *f*

mortally ['mɔːtəlɪ] *adv* mortalmente; **m. wounded** herido(a) de muerte

mortar ['mɔːtə(r)] *n* mortero *m*

mortgage ['mɔːgɪdʒ] **1** *n* hipoteca *f*
2 *vt* hipotecar

mortician [mɔː'tɪʃən] *n US (undertaker)* encargado(a) *m,f* de funeraria

mortify ['mɔːtɪfaɪ] *vt* mortificar; *Fam* **I was mortified** me sentí avergonzado(a)

mortuary ['mɔːtʃʊərɪ] *n* depósito *m* de cadáveres

mosaic [mə'zeɪɪk] *n* mosaico *m*

Moscow ['mɒskəʊ, *US* 'mɒskaʊ] *n* Moscú

Moslem ['mɒzləm] *adj & n* musulmán(ana) *(m,f)*

mosque [mɒsk] *n* mezquita *f*

mosquito [mɒs'kiːtəʊ] *n (pl* **mosquitoes)** mosquito *m*, *Am* zancudo *m*; **m. net** mosquitero *m*

moss [mɒs] *n* musgo *m*

most [məʊst] **1** *adj (superl of* **much, many)** (**a**) *(greatest in quantity etc)* más; **this house suffered (the) m. damage** esta casa fue la más afectada; **who made (the) m. mistakes?** ¿quién cometió más errores? (**b**) *(the majority of)* la mayoría de, la mayor parte de; **m. people** la mayoría de la gente

2 *pron (greatest part)* la mayor parte; *(greatest number)* lo máximo, lo más; *(the majority of people)* la mayoría; **at the (very) m.** como máximo; **to make the m. of sth** aprovechar algo al máximo

3 *adv (superl of* **much)** (**a**) *(to form superlative)* más; **the m.** el/la más; **the m. intelligent student** el estudiante más inteligente (**b**) *(with verbs)* más; **what I like m.** lo que más me gusta (**c**) *(very)* muy; **m. of all** sobre todo

mostly ['məʊstlɪ] *adv (chiefly)* en su mayor parte; *(generally)* generalmente; *(usually)* normalmente

MOT [eməʊ'tiː] *n Br (abbr* **Ministry of Transport) M. test** inspección técnica de vehículos, *Esp* ≃ ITV; *Esp* ≃ VTV *f*

motel [məʊ'tel] *n* motel *m*

moth [mɒθ] *n* mariposa nocturna; **clothes m.** polilla *f*

mother ['mʌðə(r)] **1** *n* madre *f*; **M.'s Day** Día *m* de la Madre; **m. tongue** lengua materna

2 *vt* cuidar maternalmente

motherhood ['mʌðəhʊd] *n* maternidad *f*

mother-in-law ['mʌðərɪnlɔː] *n (pl* **mothers-in-law)** suegra *f*

motherly ['mʌðəlɪ] *adj* maternal

mother-of-pearl [mʌðərəv'pɜːl] *n* madreperla *f*, nácar *m*

mother-to-be [mʌðətə'biː] *n (pl* **mothers-to-be)** futura madre

motif [məʊ'tiːf] *n Art & Mus* motivo *m*; *(embroidered etc)* adorno *m*; *Fig (main subject)* tema *m*

motion ['məʊʃən] **1** *n (movement)* movimiento *m*; *(gesture)* ademán *m*; *(proposal)* moción *f*

2 *vt & vi* **to m. (to) sb to do sth** hacer señas a algn para que haga algo

motionless ['məʊʃənlɪs] *adj* inmóvil

motivate ['məʊtɪveɪt] *vt* motivar

motivation [ˌməʊtɪ'veɪʃən] n motivación f

motive ['məʊtɪv] **1** adj (force) motriz
2 n (reason) motivo m; Jur móvil m

motley ['mɒtlɪ] adj (**motlier, motliest**) (multicoloured) abigarrado(a); (varied) variado(a)

motor ['məʊtə(r)] n (engine) motor m; Br Fam (car) coche m, Am carro m, CSur auto m; **m. racing** carreras fpl de coches or Am carros or CSur autos

motorbike ['məʊtəbaɪk] n Fam motocicleta f, moto f

motorboat ['məʊtəbəʊt] n (lancha) motora f

motorcar ['məʊtəkɑː(r)] n Br coche m, automóvil m

motorcycle ['məʊtəsaɪkəl] n motocicleta f

motorcyclist ['məʊtəsaɪklɪst] n motociclista mf

motoring ['məʊtərɪŋ] n automovilismo m

motorist ['məʊtərɪst] n automovilista m

motorway ['məʊtəweɪ] n Br autopista f

mottled ['mɒtəld] adj (skin, animal) con manchas; (surface) moteado(a)

motto ['mɒtəʊ] n lema m

mould¹ [məʊld] n (fungus) moho m

mould² [məʊld] **1** n molde m
2 vt moldear; (clay) modelar

moulder ['məʊldə(r)] vi to **m. (away)** desmoronarse

moulding ['məʊldɪŋ] n moldura f

mouldy ['məʊldɪ] adj (**mouldier, mouldiest**) mohoso(a); **to go m.** enmohecerse

moult [məʊlt] vi mudar

mound [maʊnd] n montón m; (small hill) montículo m

mount¹ [maʊnt] n monte m; **M. Everest** (Monte) Everest m

▸ **mount up** vi (accumulate) acumularse

mount² [maʊnt] **1** n (horse) montura f, (support) soporte m, base f, (for photograph) marco m; (for jewel) engaste m
2 vt (horse) subirse or montar a; (campaign) organizar; (photograph) enmarcar; (jewel) engastar
3 vi (go up) subir; (get on horse, bike) montar; (increase) subir

mountain ['maʊntɪn] **1** n montaña f, Fig (pile) montón m
2 adj de montaña, montañés(esa); **m. range** sierra f, cordillera f

mountaineer [ˌmaʊntɪ'nɪə(r)] n montañero(a) m,f, alpinista mf, Am andinista mf

mountaineering [ˌmaʊntɪ'nɪərɪŋ] n montañismo m, alpinismo m, Am andinismo m

mountainous ['maʊntɪnəs] adj montañoso(a)

mourn [mɔːn] **1** vt llorar la muerte de
2 vi to **m. for sb** llorar la muerte de algn

mourner ['mɔːnə(r)] n doliente mf

mournful ['mɔːnfʊl] adj triste; (voice) lúgubre

mourning ['mɔːnɪŋ] n luto m; **in m.** de luto

mouse [maʊs] n (pl **mice**) (a) (animal) ratón m (b) Comput Esp ratón m, Am mouse m

mousetrap ['maʊstræp] n ratonera f

mousse [muːs] n Culin mousse f, (for hair) (styling) **m.** espuma (moldeadora)

moustache [mə'stɑːʃ] n bigote m

mousy ['maʊsɪ] adj (**mousier, mousiest**) (colour) pardusco(a); (hair) castaño claro; (shy) tímido(a)

mouth [maʊθ] **1** n (pl **mouths** [maʊðz]) (a) (of person, animal, tunnel) boca f (b) (of river) desembocadura f
2 vt [maʊð] (without sincerity) decir mecánicamente; (silently) decir moviendo sólo los labios

mouthful ['maʊθfʊl] n (of food) bocado m; (of drink) trago m

mouth organ ['maʊθɔːgən] n armónica f

mouthpiece ['maʊθpiːs] n Mus boquilla f, (of telephone) micrófono m; Fig (spokesman) portavoz m

mouthwash ['maʊθwɒʃ] n elixir m, enjuague m bucal

mouthwatering ['maʊθwɔːtərɪŋ] adj muy apetitoso(a), que le hace a uno la boca agua

movable ['muːvəbəl] adj movible, móvil

move [muːv] **1** n (a) (movement) movimiento m; **to be on the m.** estar en marcha; **we must make a m.** debemos irnos ya; Fam **get a m. on!** ¡date prisa!, Am ¡apúrate!; (step) paso m; **to make the first m.** dar el primer paso (c) (in game) jugada f, (turn) turno m (d) (to new home) mudanza f, (to new job) traslado m
2 vt (a) (shift) mover; (furniture etc) cambiar de sitio; (transfer) trasladar; **to m. house** mudarse (de casa) (b) (in game) mover (c) (motivate) inducir; (persuade) persuadir; **I won't be moved** no me harán cambiar de parecer (d) (affect emotionally) conmover
3 vi (a) (change position) moverse, desplazarse; (change house) mudarse de casa; (change post) trasladarse (b) (train etc) estar en marcha; **to start moving** ponerse en marcha (c) (leave) irse,

marcharse (**d**) *(in game)* hacer una jugada

► **move about 1** *vt sep* cambiar de sitio

 2 *vi (be restless)* ir y venir; *(travel)* viajar de un lugar a otro

► **move along 1** *vt sep (move forward)* hacer avanzar; *(keep moving)* hacer circular

 2 *vi (move forward)* avanzar; *(keep moving)* circular; **m. along!** *(to person on bench)* ¡haz sitio!

► **move around** *vt sep & vi* = **move about**

► **move away 1** *vt sep* alejar, apartar (**from** de)

 2 *vi (move aside)* alejarse, apartarse; *(leave)* irse; *(change house)* mudarse (de casa)

► **move back 1** *vt sep (to original place)* volver

 2 *vi (withdraw)* retirarse; *(to original place)* volver

► **move forward 1** *vt sep* avanzar

 2 *vi* avanzar, adelantarse

► **move in** *vi (into new home)* instalarse

► **move off** *vi (go away)* irse, marcharse; *(train)* salir

► **move on** *vi (keep moving)* circular; *(go forward)* avanzar; *(time)* transcurrir

► **move out** *vi (leave)* irse, marcharse; *(leave house)* mudarse

► **move over** *vi* correrse

► **move up** *vi (go up)* subir; *Fig (be promoted)* ser ascendido(a), ascender; *(move along)* correrse, hacer sitio

movement ['mu:vmənt] *n* (**a**) *(change of position, location)* movimiento *m*; *(gesture)* gesto *m*, ademán *m* (**b**) *(of goods)* transporte *m*; *(of employees)* traslado *m* (**c**) *(of goods, capital)* circulación *f*

movie ['mu:vɪ] *n* película *f*; **to go to the movies** ir al cine; **m. star** estrella *f* de cine; *US* **m. theater** cine *m*

moving ['mu:vɪŋ] *adj (that moves)* móvil; *(car etc)* en marcha; *Fig (touching)* conmovedor(a)

mow [məʊ] *vt (pt* mowed; *pp* mown *or* mowed) *(lawn)* cortar; *(corn, wheat)* segar; *Fig* **to m. down** segar

mower ['məʊə(r)] *n* cortacésped *m*

mown [məʊn] *pp of* **mow**

MP [em'pi:] *n Br Pol (abbr* **Member of Parliament)** diputado(a) *m,f*

mph [empi:'eɪtʃ] *(abbr* **miles per hour)** millas *fpl* por hora

MPhil [em'fɪl] *n (abbr* **Master of Philosophy)** = curso de posgrado de dos años de duración, superior a un máster e inferior a un doctorado

Mr ['mɪstə(r)] *(abbr* **Mister)** Sr

Mrs ['mɪsɪz] *(abbr* **Missus)** Sra

Ms [məz] *n* Sra/Srta

> **Ms** es el equivalente femenino de **Mr**, y se utiliza para dirigirse a una mujer sin precisar su estado civil.

MSc [emes'si:] *n (abbr* **Master of Science)** máster *m or Am* maestría *f* en Ciencias

much [mʌtʃ] **1** *adj* mucho(a); **as m. ... as** tanto(a) ... como; **how m. chocolate?** ¿cuánto chocolate?; **so m.** tanto(a)

 2 *adv* mucho; **as m. as** tanto como; **as m. as possible** todo lo posible; **how m.?** ¿cuánto?; **how m. is it?** ¿cuánto es?, ¿cuánto vale?; **m. better** mucho mejor; **m. more** mucho más; **thank you very m.** muchísimas gracias; **too m.** demasiado

 3 *pron* mucho; **I thought as m.** lo suponía; **m. of the town was destroyed** gran parte de la ciudad quedó destruida; **m. remains to be done** queda mucho por hacer

muck [mʌk] *n (dirt)* suciedad *f*; *(mud)* lodo *m*; *Fig* porquería *f*

► **muck about, muck around** *Br Fam* **1** *vi (idle)* perder el tiempo; *(play the fool)* hacer el tonto

 2 *vt sep* **to m. sb about** fastidiar a algn

► **muck up** *vt sep (dirty)* ensuciar; *Fig (spoil)* echar a perder

mucky ['mʌkɪ] *adj* (**muckier, muckiest**) sucio(a)

mucus ['mju:kəs] *n* moco *m*, mucosidad *f*

mud [mʌd] *n* lodo *m*, barro *m*; *(thick)* fango *m*; *Fig* **to sling m. at sb** poner a algn por los suelos; **m. flat** marisma *f*

muddle ['mʌdəl] **1** *n* desorden *m*; *Fig (mix-up)* embrollo *m*, lío *m*; **to get into a m.** hacerse un lío

 2 *vt* confundir

► **muddle through** *vi* arreglárselas, ingeniárselas

► **muddle up** *vt sep* confundir

muddy ['mʌdɪ] *adj* (**muddier, muddiest**) *(lane)* fangoso(a); *(hands)* cubierto(a) de lodo; *(liquid)* turbio(a)

mudguard ['mʌdgɑ:d] *n Br Esp, RP* guardabarros *m inv, Andes, CAm, Carib* guardafango *m, Méx* salpicadera *f*

muff¹ [mʌf] *n* manguito *m*; **ear muffs** orejeras *fpl*

muff² [mʌf] *vt Fam* pifiar; **to m. it (up)** estropearlo

muffin ['mʌfɪn] *n Br (teacake)* tortita *f; US* ≃ magdalena *f*

muffle ['mʌfəl] *vt (sound)* amortiguar; **to m. (up)** *(person)* abrigar

muffler ['mʌflə(r)] *n US Aut* silenciador *m*

mug¹ [mʌg] n *(large cup)* tazón m; *(beer tankard)* jarra f

mug² [mʌg] **1** n *Br Fam (gullible person)* bobo(a) m,f, primo(a) m,f, *Am* zonzo(a) m,f; *(face)* jeta f
  2 vt atracar, asaltar

mugger ['mʌgə(r)] n atracador(a) m,f

mugging ['mʌgɪŋ] n asalto m

muggy ['mʌgɪ] adj *(muggier, muggiest)* bochornoso(a)

mule [mjuːl] n mulo(a) m,f

mull [mʌl] vt mulled wine = vino caliente con especias
  ▸mull over vtsep to m. sth over darle vueltas a algo

multicoloured, *US* **multicolored** ['mʌltɪkʌləd] adj multicolor

multicultural [mʌltɪ'kʌltʃərəl] adj multicultural

multilingual [mʌltɪ'lɪŋgwəl] adj *(person)* políglota(a); *(dictionary, document)* multilingüe

multimedia [mʌltɪ'miːdɪə] **1** n multimedia f
  2 adj multimedia inv

multimillionaire [mʌltɪmɪljə'neə(r)] n multimillonario(a) m,f

multinational [mʌltɪ'næʃənəl] adj & n multinacional (f)

multiple ['mʌltɪpəl] **1** adj múltiple; m. sclerosis esclerosis f múltiple
  2 n múltiplo m

multiplex ['mʌltɪpleks] n multicine m

multiplication [mʌltɪplɪ'keɪʃən] n multiplicación f; m. sign signo m de multiplicar

multiply ['mʌltɪplaɪ] **1** vt multiplicar (by por)
  2 vi multiplicarse

multipurpose [mʌltɪ'pɜːpəs] adj multiuso inv

multiracial [mʌltɪ'reɪʃəl] adj multirracial

multistorey, *US* **multistory** [mʌltɪ'stɔːrɪ] adj *(building)* de varios pisos; m. car park estacionamiento m or *Esp* aparcamiento m or *Col* parqueadero m de varias plantas

multitude ['mʌltɪtjuːd] n multitud f, muchedumbre f

mum¹ [mʌm] n *Br Fam* mamá f

mum² [mʌm] adj to keep m. no decir ni pío

mumble ['mʌmbəl] **1** vi hablar entre dientes
  2 vt decir entre dientes

mumbo-jumbo ['mʌmbəʊ'dʒʌmbəʊ] n *(nonsense)* palabrería f, monsergas fpl

mummy¹ ['mʌmɪ] n *Br Fam (mother)* mamá f

mummy² ['mʌmɪ] n *(body)* momia f

mumps [mʌmps] n sing paperas fpl

munch [mʌntʃ] vt & vi mascar

mundane [mʌn'deɪn] adj *Pej (ordinary)* prosaico(a); *(job, life)* rutinario(a)

> 🖉 Note that the Spanish word **mundano** is a false friend and is never a translation for the English word **mundane**. In Spanish, **mundano** means "worldly".

municipal [mjuː'nɪsɪpəl] adj municipal

municipality [mjuːnɪsɪ'pælɪtɪ] n municipio m

munitions [mjuː'nɪʃənz] npl municiones fpl, armamento m

mural ['mjʊərəl] adj & n mural (m)

murder ['mɜːdə(r)] **1** n asesinato m, homicidio m
  2 vt asesinar

murderer ['mɜːdərə(r)] n asesino(a) m,f

murderess ['mɜːdərɪs] n asesina f

murderous ['mɜːdərəs] adj homicida

murky ['mɜːkɪ] adj *(murkier, murkiest)* oscuro(a); *(water)* turbio(a)

murmur ['mɜːmə(r)] **1** n murmullo m; *(of traffic)* ruido m; *(complaint)* queja f
  2 vt & vi murmurar

muscle ['mʌsəl] **1** n músculo m
  2 vi *Fam* to m. in on sth entrometerse en algo

muscular ['mʌskjʊlə(r)] adj *(pain, tissue)* muscular; *(person)* musculoso(a)

Muse [mjuːz] n *(in mythology)* musa f

muse [mjuːz] vi to m. on or about sth meditar algo

museum [mjuː'zɪəm] n museo m

mushroom ['mʌʃruːm] **1** n hongo m, *Esp* seta f; *(button mushroom)* champiñón m
  2 vi *Fig* crecer de la noche a la mañana

music ['mjuːzɪk] n música f; m. hall teatro m de variedades; m. library fonoteca f

musical ['mjuːzɪkəl] **1** adj musical; to be m. estar dotado(a) para la música
  2 n musical m

musician [mjuː'zɪʃən] n músico(a) m,f

musk [mʌsk] n almizcle m

Muslim ['mʊzlɪm] adj & n musulmán(ana) (m,f)

muslin ['mʌzlɪn] n muselina f

mussel ['mʌsəl] n mejillón m

must [mʌst] **1** v aux (a) *(obligation)* deber, tener que; you m. arrive on time tienes que or debes llegar a la hora (b) *(probability)* deber de; he m. be ill debe de estar enfermo
  2 n *Fam* to be a m. ser imprescindible

mustache ['mʌstæʃ] n *US* bigote m

mustard ['mʌstəd] *n* mostaza *f*
muster ['mʌstə(r)] **1** *vt Fig* **to m. (up) courage** cobrar fuerzas
2 *vi* reunirse, juntarse
mustn't ['mʌsənt] = **must not**
musty ['mʌstɪ] *adj* (**mustier, mustiest**) que huele a cerrado *or* a humedad
mutant ['mjuːtənt] *adj & n* mutante *(mf)*
mute ['mjuːt] **1** *adj* mudo(a)
2 *n* (*person*) mudo(a) *m,f*; *Mus* sordina *f*
muted ['mjuːtɪd] *adj* (*sound*) sordo(a); (*colour*) suave
mutilate ['mjuːtɪleɪt] *vt* mutilar
mutiny ['mjuːtɪnɪ] **1** *n* motín *m*
2 *vi* amotinarse
mutter ['mʌtə(r)] **1** *n* (*mumble*) murmullo *m*
2 *vt* murmurar, decir entre dientes
3 *vi* (*angrily*) refunfuñar
mutton ['mʌtən] *n* (carne *f* de) cordero *m*
mutual ['mjuːtʃʊəl] *adj* mutuo(a); (*shared*) común
mutually ['mjuːtʃʊəlɪ] *adv* mutuamente
Muzak® ['mjuːzæk] *n* música *f* de supermercado

muzzle ['mʌzəl] **1** *n* (*snout*) hocico *m*; (*for dog*) bozal *m*; (*of gun*) boca *f*
2 *vt* (*dog*) abozalar; *Fig* amordazar
my [maɪ] *poss adj* mi; **my cousins** mis primos; **my father** mi padre; **one of my friends** un amigo mío; **I washed my hair** me lavé el pelo; **I twisted my ankle** me torcí el tobillo
myriad ['mɪrɪəd] *n Literary* miríada *f*
myself [maɪ'self] *pers pron* (**a**) (*emphatic*) yo mismo(a); **my husband and m.** mi marido y yo (**b**) (*reflexive*) me; **I hurt m.** me hice daño (**c**) (*after prep*) mí (mismo(a))
mysterious [mɪ'stɪərɪəs] *adj* misterioso(a)
mystery ['mɪstərɪ] *n* misterio *m*
mystical ['mɪstɪkəl] *adj* místico(a)
mystify ['mɪstɪfaɪ] *vt* dejar perplejo(a)
mystique [mɪ'stiːk] *n* aureola *f* de misterio
myth [mɪθ] *n* mito *m*; **it's a complete m.** es pura fantasía
mythology [mɪ'θɒlədʒɪ] *n* mitología *f*

N, n [en] n *(the letter)* N, n f

N *(abbr* **North)** N

nab [næb] vt *Fam (catch)* pescar, *Esp* trincar

naff [næf] adj *Br Fam (tasteless)* ordinario(a), *Esp* hortera, *Esp* cutre, *Chile* cuico(a), *RP* terraja; *(comment, behaviour)* de mal gusto; **a n. remark** una bordería

NAFTA ['næftə] n *(abbr* **North American Free Trade Agreement)** NAFTA f, TLC m

nag [næg] **1** vt fastidiar, dar la lata a; **to n. sb to do sth** fastidiar *or* dar la lata a algn para que haga algo
2 vi quejarse

nagging ['nægɪŋ] adj *(persistent)* continuo(a)

nail [neɪl] **1** n **(a)** *(of finger, toe)* uña f; **n. clippers** cortaúñas m inv; **n. polish** *or* **varnish** esmalte m *or* laca f de uñas **(b)** *(metal)* clavo m
2 vt **(a)** *(in carpentry)* clavar **(b)** *Fam (catch, trap)* pillar, pescar

nailbrush ['neɪlbrʌʃ] n cepillo m de uñas

nailfile ['neɪlfaɪl] n lima f de uñas

nail-scissors ['neɪlsɪzəz] npl tijeras fpl de uñas

naïve [naɪ'iːv] adj ingenuo(a)

naked ['neɪkɪd] adj desnudo(a); *(flame)* sin protección; **the n. truth** la pura verdad

name [neɪm] **1** n **(a)** *(of person)* nombre m; *(surname)* apellido m; **what's your n.?** ¿cómo te llamas?; **to call sb names** poner verde a algn **(b)** *(reputation)* reputación f; **to make a n. for oneself** hacerse famoso(a)
2 vt **(a)** *(give name to)* poner nombre a, bautizar; **to n. sb after** *or US* **for sb** poner a algn el nombre de algn **(b)** *(appoint)* nombrar **(c)** *(refer to)* mencionar

nameless ['neɪmlɪs] adj anónimo(a); **to remain n.** permanecer en el anonimato

namely ['neɪmlɪ] adv a saber

namesake ['neɪmseɪk] n tocayo(a) m,f

nanny ['nænɪ] n niñera f

nap [næp] **1** n *(sleep)* siesta f; **to have a n.** echar la *or* una siesta
2 vi *Fig* **to catch sb napping** pillar *or Esp*

coger *or Am* agarrar a algn desprevenido(a)

napalm ['neɪpɑːm] n napalm m

nape [neɪp] n nuca f, cogote m

napkin ['næpkɪn] n **(table)** n. servilleta f

Naples ['neɪpəlz] n Nápoles

nappy ['næpɪ] n *Br* pañal m

narcissus [nɑː'sɪsəs] n *Bot* narciso m

narcotic [nɑː'kɒtɪk] **1** adj narcótico(a)
2 n narcótico m

narrate [nə'reɪt] vt narrar, relatar

narration [nə'reɪʃən] n narración f, relato m

narrative ['nærətɪv] **1** n *Lit* narrativa f; *(story)* narración f
2 adj narrativo(a)

narrator [nə'reɪtə(r)] n narrador(a) m,f

narrow ['nærəʊ] **1** adj **(a)** *(passage, road etc)* estrecho(a), angosto(a) **(b)** *(restricted)* reducido(a); *(sense)* estricto(a); **to have a n. escape** librarse por los pelos
2 vi estrecharse
▸ **narrow down 1** vt sep reducir, limitar
2 vi **to n. down to** reducirse a

narrowly ['nærəʊlɪ] adv **(a)** *(closely)* de cerca **(b)** *(by a small margin)* por poco

narrow-minded ['nærəʊ'maɪndɪd] adj de miras estrechas

nasal ['neɪzəl] adj nasal; *(voice)* gangoso(a)

nastiness ['nɑːstɪnɪs] n **(a)** *(unpleasantness)* carácter m desagradable **(b)** *(maliciousness)* mala intención

nasty ['nɑːstɪ] adj **(nastier, nastiest)** **(a)** *(person)* desagradable; **to turn n.** *(of weather, situation)* ponerse feo(a) **(b)** *(unfriendly)* antipático(a); *(malicious)* mal intencionado(a); *Br Fam* **he's a n. piece of work** es un asco de tío **(c)** *(illness, accident)* grave

nation ['neɪʃən] n nación f

national ['næʃnəl] **1** adj nacional; **n. anthem** himno m nacional; **n. insurance** seguridad f social; *Mil* **n. service** servicio m militar
2 n súbdito(a) m,f

nationalism ['næʃnəlɪzəm] n nacionalismo m

nationalist ['næʃnəlɪst] *adj & n* nacionalista *(mf)*

nationality [næʃə'nælɪtɪ] *n* nacionalidad *f*

nationalization [næʃnəlaɪ'zeɪʃən] *n* nacionalización *f*

nationalize ['næʃnəlaɪz] *vt* nacionalizar

nationwide ['neɪʃənwaɪd] *adj* de ámbito nacional

native ['neɪtɪv] **1** *adj* (**a**) *(place)* natal; **n. land** patria *f*; **n. language** lengua materna (**b**) *(plant, animal)* originario(a) (**to** de)
2 *n* nativo(a) *m,f*, natural *mf*; *(original inhabitant)* indígena *mf*

NATO, Nato ['neɪtəʊ] *n (abbr* **North Atlantic Treaty Organization)** OTAN *f*

natter ['nætə(r)] *Fam* **1** *vi* charlar, darle a la lengua, *CAm, Méx* platicar
2 *n* charla *f*, *CAm, Méx* plática *f*

natural ['nætʃərəl] **1** *adj* (**a**) *(colour, taste)* natural (**b**) *(normal)* normal; **it's only n. that …** es lógico que … (**c**) *(born)* nato(a)
2 *n* (**a**) **she's a n. for the job** es la persona ideal para el trabajo (**b**) *Mus* becuadro *m*

naturalize ['nætʃərəlaɪz] *vt* **to become naturalized** naturalizarse

naturally ['nætʃərəlɪ] *adv* (**a**) *(of course)* naturalmente (**b**) *(by nature)* por naturaleza (**c**) *(in a relaxed manner)* con naturalidad

nature ['neɪtʃə(r)] *n* (**a**) *(the natural world)* naturaleza *f* (**b**) *(character)* naturaleza *f*, carácter *m*; **by n.** por naturaleza; **human n.** la naturaleza humana (**c**) *(sort, kind)* índole *f*, clase *f*

naught [nɔːt] *US =* **nought**

naughtily ['nɔːtɪlɪ] *adv* **to behave n.** portarse mal

naughty ['nɔːtɪ] *adj* (**naughtier, naughtiest**) (**a**) *(child)* travieso(a) (**b**) *(joke, story)* atrevido(a), picante

nausea ['nɔːzɪə] *n Med (sickness)* náusea *f*

nauseate ['nɔːzɪeɪt] *vt (disgust)* dar asco a

nauseating ['nɔːzɪeɪtɪŋ] *adj* nauseabundo(a)

nautical ['nɔːtɪkəl] *adj* náutico(a); **n. mile** milla marítima

naval ['neɪvəl] *adj* naval; **n. officer** oficial *mf* de marina; **n. power** potencia marítima *or* naval

Navarre [nə'vɑː(r)] *n* Navarra

nave [neɪv] *n Archit* nave *f*

navel ['neɪvəl] *n Anat* ombligo *m*

navigate ['nævɪgeɪt] **1** *vt (river)* navegar por; *Naut (ship)* gobernar
2 *vi* navegar; *(in driving)* indicar la dirección

navigation [nævɪ'geɪʃən] *n Naut* navegación *f*

navigator ['nævɪgeɪtə(r)] *n* (**a**) *Naut* navegante *mf*, oficial *mf* de derrota (**b**) *Aut & Av* copiloto *mf*

navvy ['nævɪ] *n Br Fam* peón *m*

navy ['neɪvɪ] *n* marina *f*; **n. blue** azul marino

Nazi ['nɑːtsɪ] *adj & n* nazi *(mf)*

Nazism ['nɑːtsɪzəm] *n* nazismo *m*

NB, nb [en'biː] *(abbr* **nota bene)** N.B.

neap [niːp] *n* **n. (tide)** marea muerta

near [nɪə(r)] **1** *adj (in space)* cercano(a); *(in time)* próximo(a); **in the n. future** en un futuro próximo
2 *adv (in space)* cerca; **that's n. enough** (ya) vale, está bien
3 *prep* cerca de; **n. the end of the film** hacia el final de la película
4 *vt* acercarse a

nearby **1** *adj* ['nɪəbaɪ] cercano(a)
2 *adv* ['nɪə'baɪ] cerca

nearly ['nɪəlɪ] *adv* casi; **we haven't n. enough** no alcanza ni con mucho

nearside ['nɪəsaɪd] *n Br Aut* lado *m* del copiloto

near-sighted [nɪə'saɪtɪd] *adj* miope

neat [niːt] *adj* (**a**) *(room, habits etc)* ordenado(a); *(handwriting)* claro(a); *(appearance)* pulcro(a) (**b**) *(idea)* ingenioso(a) (**c**) *(whisky etc)* solo(a) (**d**) *US Fam (fine)* genial, fenomenal

neatly ['niːtlɪ] *adv* (**a**) *(carefully)* cuidadosamente (**b**) *(cleverly)* hábilmente

necessarily [nesɪ'serəlɪ] *adv* necesariamente, por fuerza

necessary ['nesɪsərɪ] **1** *adj* (**a**) *(essential)* necesario(a); **if n.** si es preciso (**b**) *(unavoidable)* inevitable
2 *n* **the n.** lo necesario

necessitate [nɪ'sesɪteɪt] *vt* necesitar, exigir

necessity [nɪ'sesɪtɪ] *n* (**a**) *(need)* necesidad *f*; **out of n.** por necesidad (**b**) **necessities** *(articles)* necesidades *fpl*

neck [nek] *n* (**a**) cuello *m*; *(of animal)* pescuezo *m*; **to stick one's n. out** arriesgarse

necklace ['neklɪs] *n* collar *m*

neckline ['neklaɪn] *n (of dress)* escote *m*

necktie ['nektaɪ] *n US* corbata *f*

nectar ['nektə(r)] *n* néctar *m*

nectarine ['nektəriːn] *n* nectarina *f*

née [neɪ] *adj* **n. Brown** de soltera Brown

need [niːd] *n* (**a**) *(necessity, requirement)* necesidad *f*; **there's no n. for you to do that** no hace falta que hagas eso (**b**) *(poverty)* indigencia *f*; **to be in** n. estar necesitado(a)

2 *vt (of person)* necesitar; **I n. to see him** tengo que verle; **you'll n. to take more money** te hará falta más dinero; **this work needs a lot of patience** este trabajo requiere mucha paciencia; *Ironic* **that's all I n.** sólo me faltaba eso

3 *v aux* tener que, deber; **n. he go?** ¿tiene que ir?; **you needn't wait** no hace falta que esperes

> Cuando se emplea como verbo modal sólo existe una forma, y los auxiliares **do/does** no se usan: **he need only worry about himself**; **need she go?**; **it needn't matter**.

needle ['niːdəl] *n* (**a**) *(for sewing, knitting)* aguja *f* (**b**) *Bot* hoja *f*

needless ['niːdlɪs] *adj* innecesario(a); **n. to say** huelga decir

needlessly ['niːdlɪslɪ] *adv* innecesariamente

needlework ['niːdəlwɜːk] *n (sewing)* costura *f*; *(embroidery)* bordado *m*

needy ['niːdɪ] *adj* (**needier, neediest**) necesitado(a)

negate [nɪ'geɪt] *vt* (**a**) *(deny)* negar (**b**) *(nullify)* anular

negative ['negətɪv] **1** *adj* negativo(a)
2 *n* (**a**) *Ling* negación *f* (**b**) *Phot* negativo *m*

neglect [nɪ'glekt] **1** *vt* (**a**) *(child, duty etc)* descuidar, desatender (**b**) **to n. to do sth** *(omit to do)* no hacer algo
2 *n* dejadez *f*

neglectful [nɪ'glektfʊl] *adj* descuidado(a), negligente

negligée ['neglɪʒeɪ] *n* salto *m* de cama

negligence ['neglɪdʒəns] *n* negligencia *f*, descuido *m*

negligent ['neglɪdʒənt] *adj* negligente, descuidado(a)

negligible ['neglɪdʒɪbəl] *adj* insignificante

negotiate [nɪ'gəʊʃɪeɪt] **1** *vt* (**a**) *(contract)* negociar (**b**) *Fig (obstacle)* salvar, franquear
2 *vi* negociar

negotiation [nɪgəʊʃɪ'eɪʃən] *n* negociación *f*

negro ['niːgrəʊ] *n (pl* **negroes**) negro(a) *m,f*

neigh [neɪ] **1** *n* relincho *m*
2 *vi* relinchar

neighbour, *US* **neighbor** ['neɪbə(r)] *n* vecino(a) *m,f*; *Rel* prójimo *m*

neighbourhood, *US* **neighborhood** ['neɪbəhʊd] *n (district)* vecindad *f*, barrio *m*; *(people)* vecindario *m*

neighbouring, *US* **neighboring** ['neɪbərɪŋ] *adj* vecino(a)

neither ['naɪðə(r), 'niːðə(r)] **1** *adj & pron* ninguno de los dos/ninguna de las dos
2 *adv* **n. … nor** ni … ni
3 *conj* tampoco; **she was not there and n. was her sister** ella no estaba, ni su hermana tampoco

neon ['niːɒn] *n* neón *m*; **n. light** luz *f* de neón

nephew ['nefjuː] *n* sobrino *m*

nerd [nɜːd] *n Fam* (**a**) *(boring person)* petardo(a) *m,f*, *RP* nerd *mf* (**b**) *(as insult)* bobo(a) *m,f*

nerve [nɜːv] *n* (**a**) *Anat* nervio *m*; **to get on sb's nerves** poner los nervios de punta a algn (**b**) *(courage)* valor *m* (**c**) *Fam (cheek)* cara *f*, descaro *m*; **what a n.!** ¡qué cara!

nerve-racking ['nɜːvrækɪŋ] *adj* crispante, exasperante

nervous ['nɜːvəs] *adj* (**a**) *(of the nerve system)* nervioso(a); **n. breakdown** depresión nerviosa (**b**) *(apprehensive)* nervioso(a), inquieto(a)

nest [nest] **1** *n (of bird)* nido *m*; *(hen's)* nidal *m*; *(animal's)* madriguera *f*; *Fig* **n. egg** ahorros *mpl*
2 *vi (birds)* anidar

nestle ['nesəl] **1** *vt* recostar
2 *vi (settle comfortably)* acomodarse

Net [net] *n Fam Comput* **the N.** *(Internet)* la Red; **N. user** internauta *mf*

net¹ [net] *n* red *f*; *Br* **n. curtains** visillos *mpl*

net² [net] **1** *adj* neto(a); **n. weight** peso neto
2 *vt (earn)* ganar neto

netball ['netbɔːl] *n Sport* baloncesto femenino

Netherlands ['neðələndz] *npl* **the N.** los Países Bajos

netiquette ['netɪket] *n Comput* netiqueta *f*

netting ['netɪŋ] *n* redes *fpl*, malla *f*

nettle ['netəl] **1** *n Bot* ortiga *f*
2 *vt Fam* irritar

network ['netwɜːk] **1** *n* red *f*
2 *vi (establish contacts)* establecer contactos

neurosis [njʊ'rəʊsɪs] *n* neurosis *f*

neurotic [njʊ'rɒtɪk] *adj & n* neurótico(a) *(m,f)*

neuter ['njuːtə(r)] **1** *adj* neutro(a)
2 *n Ling* neutro *m*
3 *vt (geld)* castrar

neutral ['nju:trəl] **1** adj neutro(a); Pol **to remain n.** permanecer neutral
2 n Aut punto muerto

neutrality [nju:'trælɪtɪ] n neutralidad f

neutralize ['nju:trəlaɪz] vt neutralizar

neutron ['nju:trɒn] n Phys neutrón m; **n. bomb** bomba f de neutrones

never ['nevə(r)] adv nunca, jamás; **n. again** nunca (ja)más; Fam **n. mind** da igual, no importa

never-ending ['nevər'endɪŋ] adj sin fin, interminable

nevertheless [nevəðə'les] adv sin embargo, no obstante

new [nju:] adj nuevo(a); **as good as n.** como nuevo; **n. moon** luna nueva; **N. Year** Año nuevo; **N. Year's Eve** Nochevieja f

newborn ['nju:bɔ:n] adj recién nacido(a)

newcomer ['nju:kʌmə(r)] n recién llegado(a) m,f; (to job etc) nuevo(a) m,f

newfangled ['nju:fæŋgəld] adj novedoso(a)

newly ['nju:lɪ] adv recién, recientemente

newlywed ['nju:lɪwed] n recién casado(a) m,f

news [nju:z] n sing noticias fpl; (TV programme) telediario m, Am noticiero m, Andes, RP noticioso m; **a piece of n.** una noticia; **n. agency** agencia f de información; US **n. in brief** avance informativo; **n. bulletin** boletín informativo; **n. summary** avance informativo

newsagent ['nju:zeɪdʒənt] n Br vendedor(a) m,f de periódicos

newsflash ['nju:zflæʃ] n noticia f de última hora

newsgroup ['nju:zgru:p] n Comput grupo m de noticias

newsletter ['nju:zletə(r)] n hoja f informativa

newspaper ['nju:zpeɪpə(r)] n periódico m, diario m

newsprint ['nju:zprɪnt] n papel m de periódico

newsreader ['nju:zri:də(r)] n Rad & TV presentador(a) m,f de los informativos

newsreel ['nju:zri:l] n noticiario m

news-stand ['nju:zstænd] n quiosco m de periódicos

newt [nju:t] n Zool tritón m

next [nekst] **1** adj (a) (in place) de al lado (b) (in time) próximo(a); **the n. day** el día siguiente; **n. Friday** el viernes que viene; **n. time** la próxima vez; **the week after n.** dentro de dos semanas (c) (in order) siguiente, próximo(a); **n. of kin** pariente m más cercano

2 adv después, luego; **what shall we do n.?** ¿qué hacemos ahora?
3 prep **n. to** al lado de, junto a; **n. to nothing** casi nada

next-door 1 adj ['neksdɔ:(r)] de al lado; **our n. neighbour** el vecino/la vecina de al lado
2 adv [neks'dɔ:(r)] al lado

NGO [endʒi:'əʊ] n (pl NGOs) (abbr non-governmental organization) ONG f

NHS [eneɪtʃ'es] n Br (abbr National Health Service) = la sanidad pública británica

nib [nɪb] n plumilla f

nibble ['nɪbəl] vt & vi mordisquear

nice [naɪs] adj (a) (person) simpático(a), Esp majo(a), RP dulce; (thing) agradable; **n. and cool** fresquito(a); **to smell/taste n.** oler/saber bien (b) (nice-looking) bonito(a), Am lindo(a) (c) Ironic menudo(a)

nicely ['naɪslɪ] adv muy bien

niche [ni:ʃ] n (a) Archit hornacina f, nicho m (b) Fig hueco m

nick [nɪk] **1** n (a) (notch) muesca f; (cut) herida pequeña; Fam **in the n. of time** en el momento preciso (b) Br Fam (prison) cárcel f, Esp trullo m, Andes, RP cana f, Méx bote m
2 vt Br Fam (a) (steal) afanar, Esp mangar (b) (arrest) detener, Esp trincar

nickel ['nɪkəl] n (a) (metal) níquel m (b) US moneda f de 5 centavos

nickname ['nɪkneɪm] **1** n apodo m
2 vt apodar

nicotine ['nɪkəti:n] n nicotina f

niece [ni:s] n sobrina f

nifty ['nɪftɪ] adj (niftier, niftiest) (a) (quick) rápido(a); (agile) ágil (b) (ingenious) ingenioso(a)

Nigeria [naɪ'dʒɪərɪə] n Nigeria

nigger ['nɪgə(r)] n Fam Pej = término generalmente ofensivo para referirse a un negro, RP grone m

niggling ['nɪgəlɪŋ] adj (trifling) insignificante; (irritating) molesto(a)

night [naɪt] n noche f; **at n.** de noche; **at twelve o'clock at n.** a las doce de la noche; **last n.** anoche; **n. life** vida nocturna; **n. school** escuela nocturna; **n. shift** turno m de noche; US **n. stand** or **table** mesita f or mesilla f de noche

nightclub ['naɪtklʌb] n sala f de fiestas; (disco) discoteca f

nightdress ['naɪtdres] n camisón m

nightfall ['naɪtfɔ:l] n anochecer m

nightgown ['naɪtgaʊn] n camisón m

nightie ['naɪtɪ] n Fam camisón m

nightingale ['naɪtɪŋgeɪl] n ruiseñor m

nightly ['naɪtlɪ] **1** adj de cada noche
2 adv todas las noches

nightmare ['naɪtmeə(r)] n pesadilla f

nightshade ['naɪtʃeɪd] n Bot **deadly n.**
belladona f

night-time ['naɪttaɪm] n noche f; **at n.** por
la noche

nil [nɪl] n nada f; Sport cero m; Br **two n.**
dos a cero

Nile [naɪl] n the N. el Nilo

nimble ['nɪmbəl] adj ágil, rápido(a)

nine [naɪn] adj & n nueve (m inv)

nineteen [naɪn'tiːn] adj & n diecinueve
(m inv)

nineteenth [naɪn'tiːnθ] adj decimono-
veno(a)

ninety ['naɪntɪ] adj & n noventa (m inv)

ninth [naɪnθ] **1** adj & n noveno(a) (m,f)
2 n (fraction) noveno m

nip [nɪp] **1** vt (a) (pinch) pellizcar (b) (bite)
morder; **to n. sth in the bud** cortar algo de
raíz
2 n (a) (pinch) pellizco m (b) (bite)
mordisco m

nipple ['nɪpəl] n (a) Anat (female) pezón
m; (male) tetilla f (b) US (on baby's bottle)
tetilla f, tetina f

nippy ['nɪpɪ] adj (nippier, nippiest) Fam
(a) Br (quick) rápido(a) (b) (cold)
fresquito(a)

nit [nɪt] n (insect) piojo m; (insect's egg)
liendre f

nitrogen ['naɪtrədʒən] n Chem nitrógeno
m

nitroglycerin(e) [naɪtrəʊ'glɪsəriːn] n
Chem nitroglicerina f

nitty-gritty [nɪtɪ'grɪtɪ] n Fam **to get down
to the n.** ir al grano

nitwit ['nɪtwɪt] n Fam imbécil mf

no [nəʊ] **1** adv no; **come here! – no!** ¡ven
aquí! – ¡no!; **no longer** ya no; **no less than**
no menos de
2 adj ninguno(a); **she has no children** no
tiene hijos; **I have no idea** no tengo (ni)
idea; **it's no good** or **use** no vale la pena;
Aut **no parking** (sign) prohibido aparcar;
Fam **no way!** ¡ni hablar!
3 n no m; **to say no** decir que no

no. (pl **nos.**) (abbr **number**) no, núm.

nobility [nəʊ'bɪlɪtɪ] n nobleza f

noble ['nəʊbəl] adj noble

nobleman ['nəʊbəlmən] n noble m

noblewoman ['nəʊbəlwʊmən] n noble f

nobody ['nəʊbədɪ] **1** pron nadie; **there
was n. there** no había nadie; **n. else**
nadie más
2 n nadie m; **he's a n.** es un don nadie

no-brainer ['nəʊ'breɪnə(r)] n Fam **it's a n.**
está tirado

nocturnal [nɒk'tɜːnəl] adj nocturno(a)

nod [nɒd] **1** n (of greeting) saludo m (con la
cabeza); (of agreement) señal f de
asentimiento
2 vi (greet) saludar con la cabeza; (agree)
asentir con la cabeza
3 vt **to n. one's head** inclinar la cabeza
▸ **nod off** vi dormirse

no-go ['nəʊ'gəʊ] adj **n. area** zona
prohibida

noise [nɔɪz] n ruido m; **to make a n.** hacer
ruido

noiseless ['nɔɪzlɪs] adj silencioso(a), sin
ruido

noisy ['nɔɪzɪ] adj (noisier, noisiest)
ruidoso(a)

nomad ['nəʊmæd] n nómada mf

no-man's-land ['nəʊmænzlænd] n tierra
f de nadie

nominal ['nɒmɪnəl] adj nominal; (payment, rent) simbólico(a)

nominate ['nɒmɪneɪt] vt (a) (propose)
designar, proponer (b) (appoint) nombrar

nomination [nɒmɪ'neɪʃən] n (a) (proposal) propuesta f (b) (appointment)
nombramiento m

nominative ['nɒmɪnətɪv] n nominativo m

nominee [nɒmɪ'niː] n persona propuesta

non- [nɒn] pref no

non-aggression [nɒnə'greʃən] n Pol no
agresión f; **n. pact** pacto m de no agresión

non-alcoholic [nɒnælkə'hɒlɪk] adj sin
alcohol

non-aligned [nɒnə'laɪnd] adj Pol no
alineado(a)

nonchalant ['nɒnʃələnt] adj (indifferent)
indiferente; (calm) imperturbable, impasible

noncommittal [nɒnkə'mɪtəl] adj (person) evasivo(a); (answer) que no
compromete (a nada)

nonconformist [nɒnkən'fɔːmɪst] n
inconformista mf

nondescript [Br 'nɒndɪskrɪpt, US
nɒndɪ'skrɪpt] adj indescriptible; (uninteresting) soso(a)

none [nʌn] **1** pron ninguno(a); **I know n.
of them** no conozco a ninguno de ellos; **n.
at all** nada en absoluto; **n. other than ...**
nada menos que ...
2 adv de ningún modo; **she's n. the worse
for it** no se ha visto afectada or perjudi-
cada por ello; **n. too soon** a buena hora

nonentity [nɒ'nentɪtɪ] n (person) cero m a
la izquierda

nonetheless [nʌnðəˈles] *adv* no obstante, sin embargo

nonevent [nɒnɪˈvent] *n* fracaso *m*

nonexistent [nɒnɪgˈzɪstənt] *adj* inexistente

nonfiction [nɒnˈfɪkʃən] *n* no ficción *f*

no-nonsense [ˈnəʊˈnɒnsəns] *adj (person)* recto(a), serio(a)

nonplussed [nɒnˈplʌst] *adj* perplejo(a)

non-profit(-making) [nɒnˈprɒfɪt(meɪkɪŋ)] *adj* sin fines lucrativos

nonreturnable [nɒnrɪˈtɜːnəbəl] *adj* no retornable

nonsense [ˈnɒnsəns] *n* tonterías *fpl*, disparates *mpl*; **that's n.** eso es absurdo

nonsmoker [nɒnˈsməʊkə(r)] *n* no fumador(a) *m,f*, persona *f* que no fuma

nonstarter [nɒnˈstɑːtə(r)] *n Fig* **to be a n.** *(plan)* ser irrealizable

nonstick [nɒnˈstɪk] *adj* antiadherente

nonstop [nɒnˈstɒp] **1** *adj* sin parar; *(train)* directo(a)
2 *adv* sin parar

noodles [ˈnuːdəlz] *npl Culin* tallarines *mpl (chinos)*

nook [nʊk] *n* recoveco *m*, rincón *m*

noon [nuːn] *n* mediodía *m*; **at n.** a mediodía

no one [ˈnəʊwʌn] *pron* nadie; **n. came** no vino nadie

noose [nuːs] *n* lazo *m*; *(hangman's)* soga *f*

nor [nɔː(r)] *conj* ni, ni tampoco; **neither ... n.** ni ... ni; **neither you n. I** ni tú ni yo; **n. do I** (ni) yo tampoco

norm [nɔːm] *n* norma *f*

normal [ˈnɔːməl] *adj* normal

normality [nɔːˈmælɪtɪ], *US* **normalcy** [ˈnɔːməlsɪ] *n* normalidad *f*

normally [ˈnɔːməlɪ] *adv* normalmente

Normandy [ˈnɔːməndɪ] *n* Normandía

north [nɔːθ] **1** *n* norte *m*; **the N.** el norte; **N. America** América del Norte, Norteamérica; **N. Korea** Corea del Norte; **N. Pole** Polo *m* Norte
2 *adv* hacia el norte, al norte
3 *adj* del norte; **n. wind** viento *m* del norte

northeast [nɔːθˈiːst] *n* nor(d)este *m*

northerly [ˈnɔːðəlɪ] *adj* norte, del norte

northern [ˈnɔːðən] *adj* del norte, septentrional; **n. hemisphere** hemisferio *m* norte; **N. Ireland** Irlanda del Norte

northerner [ˈnɔːðənə(r)] *n* norteño(a) *m,f*

northward [ˈnɔːθwəd] *adj & adv* hacia el norte

northwest [nɔːθˈwest] *n* noroeste *m*

Norway [ˈnɔːweɪ] *n* Noruega

Norwegian [nɔːˈwiːdʒən] **1** *adj* noruego(a)
2 *n* **(a)** *(person)* noruego(a) *m,f* **(b)** *(language)* noruego *m*

nose [nəʊz] *n* **(a)** *(of person)* nariz *f*; *(of animal)* hocico *m* **(b)** *(sense of smell)* olfato *m* **(c)** *(of car, plane)* morro *m*
▸ **nose about, nose around** *vi* curiosear

nosebleed [ˈnəʊzbliːd] *n* hemorragia *f* nasal

nosedive [ˈnəʊzdaɪv] *Av* **1** *n Esp* picado *m*, *Am* picada *f*
2 *vi* hacer *Esp* un picado *or Am* una picada

no-smoking [nəʊˈsməʊkɪŋ] *adj (carriage, area)* de or para no fumadores

nostalgia [nɒˈstældʒɪə] *n* nostalgia *f*

nostalgic [nɒˈstældʒɪk] *adj* nostálgico(a)

nostril [ˈnɒstrɪl] *n Anat* orificio *m* nasal

nosy [ˈnəʊzɪ] *adj* **(nosier, nosiest)** *Fam* entrometido(a)

not [nɒt] *adv* no; **he's n. in today** hoy no está; **n. at all** en absoluto; **thank you — n. at all** gracias – no hay de qué; **n. too well** bastante mal; *Fam* **n. likely!** ¡ni hablar!

En el inglés hablado, y en el escrito en estilo coloquial, **not** se contrae después de verbos modales y auxiliares.

---

notable [ˈnəʊtəbəl] *adj* notable

notably [ˈnəʊtəblɪ] *adv* notablemente

notary [ˈnəʊtərɪ] *n Jur* **n. (public)** notario(a) *m,f*, escribano(a) *m,f*

notch [nɒtʃ] *n* muesca *f*; *(cut)* corte *m*
▸ **notch up** *vt sep Fig* **to n. up a victory** apuntarse una victoria

note [nəʊt] **1** *n* **(a)** *Mus* nota *f* **(b)** *(on paper)* nota *f* **(c) to take n. of** *(notice)* prestar atención a **(d)** *esp Br (banknote)* billete *m* (de banco) **(e) notes** apuntes *mpl*; **to take n.** tomar apuntes
2 *vt* **(a)** *(write down)* apuntar, anotar **(b)** *(notice)* notar, fijarse en

notebook [ˈnəʊtbʊk] *n* **(a)** cuaderno *m*, libreta *f* **(b)** *Comput Esp* ordenador *m* or *Am* computadora *f* portátil

noted [ˈnəʊtɪd] *adj* notable, célebre

notepad [ˈnəʊtpæd] *n* bloc *m* de notas

notepaper [ˈnəʊtpeɪpə(r)] *n* papel *m* de carta

noteworthy [ˈnəʊtwɜːðɪ] *adj* digno(a) de mención

nothing [ˈnʌθɪŋ] **1** *n* nada; **I saw n.** no vi nada; **for n.** *(free of charge)* gratis; **it's n.** no es nada; **it's n. to do with you** no tiene nada que ver contigo; **n. else** nada más; *Fam* **n. much** poca cosa
2 *adv* **she looks n. like her sister** no se parece en nada a su hermana

notice ['nəʊtɪs] **1** n (**a**) *(warning)* aviso m; **he gave a month's n.** presentó la dimisión con un mes de antelación; **at short n.** con poca antelación; **until further n.** hasta nuevo aviso; **without n.** sin previo aviso (**b**) *(attention)* atención f; **to take no n. of sth** no hacer caso de algo; **to take n. of sth** prestar atención a algo; **to come to one's n.** llegar al conocimiento de uno (**c**) *(in newspaper etc)* anuncio m (**d**) *(sign)* letrero m, aviso m
2 vt darse cuenta de, notar

> ♦ Note that the Spanish word **noticia** is a false friend and is never a translation for the English word **notice**. In Spanish **noticia** means "(piece of) news".

noticeable ['nəʊtɪsəbəl] *adj* que se nota, evidente
noticeboard ['nəʊtɪsbɔːd] n Br tablón m de anuncios
notification [nəʊtɪfɪ'keɪʃən] n aviso m
notify ['nəʊtɪfaɪ] vt avisar
notion ['nəʊʃən] n (**a**) *(idea, concept)* idea f, noción f (**b**) *(whim)* capricho m
notorious [nəʊ'tɔːrɪəs] *adj Pej* tristemente célebre

> ♦ Note that the Spanish word **notorio** is a false friend and is never a translation for the English word **notorious**. In Spanish **notorio** means both "obvious" and "famous, well-known".

notwithstanding [nɒtwɪθ'stændɪŋ] **1** *prep* a pesar de
2 *adv* sin embargo, no obstante
nougat ['nuːgɑː] n turrón blando
nought [nɔːt] n cero m
noun [naʊn] n nombre m, sustantivo m
nourish ['nʌrɪʃ] vt nutrir; Fig (hopes) abrigar
nourishing ['nʌrɪʃɪŋ] *adj* nutritivo(a)
nourishment ['nʌrɪʃmənt] n alimentación f, nutrición f
novel[1] ['nɒvəl] n novela f
novel[2] ['nɒvəl] *adj* original, novedoso(a)
novelist ['nɒvəlɪst] n novelista mf
novelty ['nɒvəltɪ] n novedad f
November [nəʊ'vembə(r)] n noviembre m
novice ['nɒvɪs] n (**a**) *(beginner)* novato(a) m,f, principiante mf (**b**) Rel novicio(a) m,f
now [naʊ] **1** adv (**a**) *(at this moment)* ahora; **just n., right n.** ahora mismo; **from n. on** de ahora en adelante; **n. and then, n. and again** de vez en cuando (**b**) *(for events in past)* entonces (**c**) *(at present, these days)* actualmente, hoy (en) día (**d**)

(not related to time) **n. (then)** ahora bien; **n., n.!** ¡vamos!, ¡ya está bien!
2 conj n. (**that**) ahora que, ya que
3 n **until n.** hasta ahora; **he'll be home by n.** ya habrá llegado a casa
nowadays ['naʊədeɪz] adv hoy (en) día, actualmente
nowhere ['nəʊweə(r)] adv en ninguna parte; **that will get you n.** eso no te servirá de nada; **it's n. near ready** no está preparado, ni mucho menos
noxious ['nɒkʃəs] *adj* nocivo(a)
nozzle ['nɒzəl] n boca f, boquilla f
nuance ['njuːɑːns] n matiz m
nub [nʌb] n **the n. of the matter** el quid de la cuestión
nuclear ['njuːklɪə(r)] *adj* nuclear; **n. arms** armas fpl nucleares; **n. power** energía f nuclear; **n. power station** central f nuclear
nucleus ['njuːklɪəs] n núcleo m
nude [njuːd] **1** *adj* desnudo(a)
2 n Art & Phot desnudo m; **in the n.** al desnudo
nudge [nʌdʒ] **1** vt dar un codazo a
2 n codazo m
nudist ['njuːdɪst] *adj & n* nudista (mf)
nudity ['njuːdɪtɪ] n desnudez f
nugget ['nʌgɪt] n Min pepita f; **gold n.** pepita de oro
nuisance ['njuːsəns] n (**a**) *(annoying thing)* molestia f, pesadez f; **what a n.!** ¡qué lata! (**b**) *(person)* pesado(a) m,f
nuke [njuːk] Fam **1** n *(bomb)* bomba f nuclear or atómica
2 vt atacar con armas nucleares
null [nʌl] *adj* nulo(a); **n. and void** nulo(a) y sin valor
nullify ['nʌlɪfaɪ] vt anular
numb [nʌm] **1** *adj (without feeling)* entumecido(a); Fig paralizado(a); **n. with fear** paralizado(a) de miedo
2 vt *(with cold)* entumecer (de frío); *(with anaesthetic)* adormecer
number ['nʌmbə(r)] **1** n (**a**) *(figure)* número m; Tel **have you got my n.?** ¿tienes mi (número de) teléfono? (**b**) *(quantity)* **a n. of people** varias personas (**c**) Br *(of car)* matrícula f; **n. plate** (placa f de la) matrícula f
2 vt (**a**) *(put a number on)* numerar (**b**) *(count)* contar
numeral ['njuːmərəl] n número m, cifra f
numerate ['njuːmərət] *adj* **to be n.** tener un conocimiento básico de matemáticas
numerical [njuː'merɪkəl] *adj* numérico(a)

numerically [njuːˈmerɪkəlɪ] *adv* numéricamente

numerous [ˈnjuːmərəs] *adj* numeroso(a)

numismatics [njuːmɪzˈmætɪks] *n sing* numismática *f*

nun [nʌn] *n* monja *f*

nuptial [ˈnʌpʃəl] *adj* nupcial

nurse [nɜːs] **1** *n* enfermera *f*; *(male)* enfermero *m*
2 *vt* (**a**) *(look after)* cuidar, atender (**b**) *(baby)* acunar (**c**) *(suckle)* amamantar (**d**) *Fig (grudge etc)* guardar

nursery [ˈnɜːsərɪ] *n* (**a**) *(institution)* guardería *f*; **n. school** jardín *m* de infancia (**b**) *(in house)* cuarto *m* de los niños; **n. rhyme** poema *m* infantil (**c**) *(garden centre)* vivero *m*

nursing [ˈnɜːsɪŋ] *n* **n. home** *Br (where children are born)* maternidad *f*; *(for old people, war veterans)* residencia *f*

nurture [ˈnɜːtʃə(r)] *vt (animal)* alimentar; *(feelings)* abrigar

nut [nʌt] *n* (**a**) *(fruit)* fruto seco (**b**) *Fam (head)* coco *m* (**c**) *Fam (mad person)* chiflado(a) *m,f*, chalado(a) *m,f* (**d**) *Tech* tuerca *f*

nutcase [ˈnʌtkeɪs] *n Fam* chalado(a) *m,f*

nutcracker [ˈnʌtkrækə(r)] *n* cascanueces *m inv*

nutmeg [ˈnʌtmeg] *n* nuez moscada

nutrition [njuːˈtrɪʃən] *n* nutrición *f*

nutritious [njuːˈtrɪʃəs] *adj* nutritivo(a), alimenticio(a)

nuts [nʌts] *adj Fam* chiflado(a), *Esp* majara; **to be n.** estar chiflado(a) *or Esp* majara

nutshell [ˈnʌtʃel] *n* cáscara *f*; *Fig* **in a n.** en pocas palabras

nylon [ˈnaɪlɒn] **1** *n* (**a**) *(textile)* nilón *m*, nailon *m* (**b**) **nylons** medias *fpl* de nilón
2 *adj* de nilón

nymph [nɪmf] *n* ninfa *f*

nymphomaniac [nɪmfəˈmeɪnɪæk] *n* ninfómana *f*

O

O, o [əʊ] n (**a**) *(the letter)* O, o f (**b**) *Math & Tel* cero m

oaf [əʊf] n tarugo m, zote m

oak [əʊk] n roble m

OAP [əʊer'pi:] n *Br* *(abbr* **old-age pensioner)** pensionista mf, jubilado(a) m,f

oar [ɔ:(r)] n remo m

oarsman [ˈɔːzmən] n remero m

oasis [əʊˈeɪsɪs] n *(pl* **oases** [əʊˈeɪsiːz]) oasis m inv

oat [əʊt] n avena f; **rolled oats** copos mpl de avena

oath [əʊθ] n *(pl* **oaths** [əʊðz]) (**a**) *Jur* juramento m; **to take an o.** prestar juramento (**b**) *(swearword)* palabrota f

oatmeal [ˈəʊtmiːl] n harina f de avena

obedience [əˈbiːdɪəns] n obediencia f

obedient [əˈbiːdɪənt] adj obediente

obese [əʊˈbiːs] adj obeso(a)

obey [əˈbeɪ] vt obedecer; *(law)* cumplir con

obituary [əˈbɪtjʊərɪ] n necrología f

object¹ [ˈɒbdʒɪkt] n (**a**) *(thing)* objeto m (**b**) *(aim, purpose)* fin m, objetivo m (**c**) *(obstacle)* inconveniente m (**d**) *Ling* complemento m

object² [əbˈdʒekt] vi oponerse (**to** a); **do you o. to my smoking?** ¿le molesta que fume?

objection [əbˈdʒekʃən] n (**a**) *(protest)* objeción f (**b**) *(drawback)* inconveniente m; **provided there's no o.** si no hay inconveniente

objectionable [əbˈdʒekʃənəbəl] adj *(unacceptable)* inaceptable; *(unpleasant)* ofensivo(a)

objective [əbˈdʒektɪv] **1** adj objetivo(a) **2** n objetivo m

objector [əbˈdʒektə(r)] n objetor(a) m,f

obligation [ɒblɪˈgeɪʃən] n obligación f; **to be under an o. to sb** estarle muy agradecido(a) a algn

obligatory [ɒˈblɪgətərɪ] adj obligatorio(a)

oblige [əˈblaɪdʒ] vt (**a**) *(compel)* obligar; **I'm obliged to do it** me veo obligado(a) a hacerlo (**b**) *(do a favour for)* hacer un favor a (**c**) **to be obliged** *(grateful)* estar agradecido(a)

obliging [əˈblaɪdʒɪŋ] adj solícito(a)

oblique [əˈbliːk] adj oblicuo(a), inclinado(a); *Fig* **an o. reference** una alusión indirecta

obliterate [əˈblɪtəreɪt] vt (**a**) *(memory)* borrar (**b**) *(species, race)* eliminar; *(village)* arrasar

oblivion [əˈblɪvɪən] n olvido m; **to sink into o.** caer en el olvido

oblivious [əˈblɪvɪəs] adj inconsciente

oblong [ˈɒblɒŋ] **1** adj oblongo(a) **2** n rectángulo m

obnoxious [əbˈnɒkʃəs] adj repugnante

oboe [ˈəʊbəʊ] n oboe m

obscene [əbˈsiːn] adj obsceno(a)

obscenity [əbˈsenɪtɪ] n obscenidad f

obscure [əbˈskjʊə(r)] **1** adj (**a**) *(not clear)* oscuro(a); *(vague)* vago(a) (**b**) *(little-known)* *(author, poet etc)* desconocido(a) **2** vt *(truth)* ocultar

obsequious [əbˈsiːkwɪəs] adj servil

observance [əbˈzɜːvəns] n (**a**) *(of law, custom)* observancia f (**b**) *Rel* **observances** prácticas religiosas

observant [əbˈzɜːvənt] adj observador(a)

observation [ɒbzəˈveɪʃən] n observación f; *(surveillance)* vigilancia f

observatory [əbˈzɜːvətərɪ] n observatorio m

observe [əbˈzɜːv] vt (**a**) *(watch)* observar; *(in surveillance)* vigilar (**b**) *(remark)* advertir (**c**) *(law, customs)* observar, acatar

observer [əbˈzɜːvə(r)] n observador(a) m,f

obsess [əbˈses] vt obsesionar; **to be obsessed (with** or **by)** estar obsesionado(a) (con)

obsession [əbˈseʃən] n obsesión f

obsessive [əbˈsesɪv] adj obsesivo(a)

obsolete [ˈɒbsəliːt, ɒbsəˈliːt] adj obsoleto(a)

obstacle [ˈɒbstəkəl] n obstáculo m; *Fig* impedimento m; **o. race** carrera f de obstáculos

obstinate [ˈɒbstɪnɪt] adj (**a**) *(person)* obstinado(a), terco(a) (**b**) *(pain)* persistente

obstruct [əb'strʌkt] *vt* (a) *(block)* (road, pipe) obstruir, bloquear; *(view)* impedir (b) *(hinder)* estorbar; *(progress)* dificultar

obstruction [əb'strʌkʃən] *n* (a) *(action)* obstrucción *f* (b) *(hindrance)* obstáculo *m*

obtain [əb'teɪn] *vt* obtener, conseguir

obtainable [əb'teɪnəbəl] *adj* obtenible

obtrusive [əb'truːsɪv] *adj* (a) *(interfering)* entrometido(a) (b) *(noticeable)* llamativo(a)

obtuse [əb'tjuːs] *adj* obtuso(a)

obviate ['ɒbvɪeɪt] *vt Fml* obviar

obvious ['ɒbvɪəs] *adj* obvio(a), evidente

obviously ['ɒbvɪəslɪ] *adv* evidentemente; **o.!** ¡claro!, ¡por supuesto!

occasion [ə'keɪʒən] **1** *n* (a) *(time)* ocasión *f*; **on o.** de vez en cuando (b) *(event)* acontecimiento *m*; **on the o. of** con ocasión de (c) *Fml (cause)* motivo *m*
2 *vt Fml* ocasionar

occasional [ə'keɪʒənəl] *adj* esporádico(a), eventual

occasionally [ə'keɪʒənəlɪ] *adv* de vez en cuando

occupant ['ɒkjʊpənt] *n* ocupante *mf*; *(tenant)* inquilino(a) *m,f*

occupation [ɒkjʊ'peɪʃən] *n* (a) *(job, profession)* profesión *f*, ocupación *f* (b) *(pastime)* pasatiempo *m* (c) *(of building, house, country)* ocupación *f*

occupational [ɒkjʊ'peɪʃənəl] *adj* profesional, laboral; **o. hazard** gaje *m* del oficio

occupied ['ɒkjʊpaɪd] *adj* ocupado(a)

occupier ['ɒkjʊpaɪə(r)] *n Br* ocupante *mf*; *(tenant)* inquilino(a) *m,f*

occupy ['ɒkjʊpaɪ] *vt* (a) *(live in)* ocupar, habitar (b) *(time)* pasar; **to o. one's time in doing sth** dedicar su tiempo a hacer algo (c) *(building, factory etc in protest)* tomar posesión de

occur [ə'kɜː(r)] *vi* (a) *(event)* suceder, acaecer; *(change)* producirse (b) *(be found)* encontrarse (c) **it occurred to me that …** se me ocurrió que …

occurrence [ə'kʌrəns] *n* suceso *m*, incidencia *f*

> *Note that the Spanish word **ocurrencia** is a false friend and is never a translation for the English word **occurrence**. In Spanish **ocurrencia** means "witty remark" and "bright idea".*

ocean ['əʊʃən] *n* océano *m*

ocean-going ['əʊʃəngəʊɪŋ] *adj* de alta mar

ochre, *US* **ocher** ['əʊkə(r)] **1** *n* ocre *m*; **red o.** almagre *m*; **yellow o.** ocre amarillo
2 *adj* (de color) ocre

o'clock [ə'klɒk] *adv* **(it's) one o.** (es) la una; **(it's) two o.** (son) las dos

octave ['ɒktɪv] *n* octava *f*

October [ɒk'təʊbə(r)] *n* octubre *m*

octogenarian [ɒktəʊdʒɪ'neərɪən] *adj & n* octogenario(a) *(m,f)*

octopus ['ɒktəpəs] *n* pulpo *m*

OD [əʊ'diː] *(pt & pp* **OD'd** *or* **OD'ed)** *vi Fam* meterse una sobredosis

odd [ɒd] **1** *adj* (a) *(strange)* raro(a), extraño(a) (b) *(occasional)* esporádico(a); **o. job** trabajillo *m* (c) **an o. number** *(not even)* un impar (d) *(unpaired)* desparejado(a); **an o. sock** un calcetín suelto
2 *adv* y pico; **twenty o. people** veinte y pico *or* y tantas personas

oddity ['ɒdɪtɪ] *n* (a) *(thing)* curiosidad *f*; *(person)* estrafalario(a) *m,f* (b) *(quality)* rareza *f*

oddly ['ɒdlɪ] *adv* extrañamente; **o. enough** por extraño que parezca

odds [ɒdz] *npl* (a) *(chances)* probabilidades *fpl*; **the o. are that …** lo más probable es que … (+ *subj*) (b) *(in betting)* puntos *mpl* de ventaja; **the o. are five to one** las apuestas están cinco a uno (c) *Br* **it makes no o.** da lo mismo (d) **at o. with sb** *(in disagreement)* reñido(a) con algn (e) **o. and ends** *(small things)* cositas *fpl*; *(trinkets)* chucherías *fpl*

odds-on ['ɒdzɒn] *adj* seguro(a); **o. favourite** *(horse)* caballo favorito

ode [əʊd] *n* oda *f*

odious ['əʊdɪəs] *adj* repugnante

odour, *US* **odor** ['əʊdə(r)] *n* olor *m*; *(fragrance)* perfume *m*

OECD [əʊiːsiː'diː] *n (abbr* **Organization for Economic Co-operation and Development)** OCDE *f*

of [ɒv, *unstressed* əv] *prep* de; **a friend of mine** un amigo mío; **a bottle of wine** una botella de vino; **a dress (made) of silk** un vestido de seda; **that's very kind of you** es usted muy amable; **there are four of us** somos cuatro; **two of them** dos de ellos; **south of** al sur de; **the 7th of November** 7 de noviembre

off [ɒf] **1** *prep* de; **she fell o. her horse** se cayó del caballo; **a few kilometres o. the coast** a unos kilómetros de la costa; **I'm o. wine** he perdido el gusto al vino
2 *adv* (a) **he turned o. the radio** apagó la radio (b) *(absent)* fuera; **I have a day o.** tengo un día libre; **to be o. sick** estar de baja por enfermedad (c) *(distant)* **6 miles**

o. a 6 millas (**d**) **I'm o. to London** me voy a Londres (**e**) **10 percent o.** un descuento del 10 por ciento (**f**) **o. and on** de vez en cuando
　3 *adj* (**a**) *(gas etc)* apagado(a); *(water)* cortado(a) (**b**) *(cancelled)* cancelado(a) (**c**) *(low)* bajo(a); *(unsatisfactory)* malo(a); **on the o. chance** por si acaso; **the o. season** la temporada baja (**d**) *(gone bad) (meat, fish)* malo(a), pasado(a); *(milk)* agrio(a)

offal ['ɒfəl] *n (of chicken etc)* menudillos *mpl*; *(of cattle, pigs)* asaduras *fpl*

off-colour, *US* **off-color** ['ɒf'kʌlə(r)] *adj* (**a**) *Br (ill)* indispuesto(a) (**b**) *(joke, story)* indecente

offence [ə'fens] *n* (**a**) *Jur* delito *m* (**b**) *(insult)* ofensa *f*; **to give o.** ofender; **to take o. at sth** ofenderse por algo (**c**) *Mil (attack)* ofensiva *f*

offend [ə'fend] *vt* ofender

offender [ə'fendə(r)] *n (criminal)* delincuente *mf*

offense [ə'fens] *n US* = **offence**

offensive [ə'fensɪv] **1** *adj* (**a**) *(insulting)* ofensivo(a) (**b**) *(repulsive)* repugnante
　2 *n Mil* ofensiva *f*; **to be on the o.** estar a la ofensiva

offer ['ɒfə(r)] **1** *vt* ofrecer; **to o. to do a job** ofrecerse para hacer un trabajo
　2 *n* oferta *f*; **on o.** *(reduced)* de oferta; *(available)* disponible; **o. of marriage** proposición *f* de matrimonio

offering ['ɒfərɪŋ] *n* (**a**) *(thing presented)* entrega *f* (**b**) *Rel* ofrenda *f*

offhand **1** *adj* [ɒf'hænd] *(abrupt)* brusco(a); *(inconsiderate)* descortés
　2 *adv* [ɒf'hænd] **I don't know o.** así sin pensarlo, no lo sé

office ['ɒfɪs] *n* (**a**) *(room)* despacho *m*; *(building)* oficina *f*; *(of lawyer)* despacho, bufete *m*; *US (of doctor, dentist)* consulta *f*; **o. hours** horas *fpl* de oficina (**b**) *Br Pol* ministerio *m* (**c**) *US (federal agency)* agencia *f* gubernamental (**d**) *(position)* cargo *m* (**e**) *Pol* **to be in o.** estar en el poder

officer ['ɒfɪsə(r)] *n* (**a**) *Mil* oficial *mf* (**b**) **(police) o.** agente *mf* de policía (**c**) *(government official)* funcionario(a) *m,f* (**d**) *(of company, society)* director(a) *m,f*

official [ə'fɪʃəl] **1** *adj* oficial
　2 *n* funcionario(a) *m,f*

officially [ə'fɪʃəlɪ] *adv* oficialmente

officiate [ə'fɪʃɪeɪt] *vi* (**a**) *(act in official capacity)* oficiar; **to o. as** ejercer funciones de (**b**) *Rel* oficiar

officious [ə'fɪʃəs] *adj Pej* excesivamente celoso(a) *or* diligente

---

> ✎ Note that the Spanish word **oficioso** is a false friend and is never a translation for the English word **officious**. In Spanish, **oficioso** means "unofficial".

off-licence ['ɒflaɪsəns] *n Br* tienda *f* de bebidas alcohólicas

off-line ['ɒflaɪn] *adj Comput* desconectado(a)

off-peak [ɒf'piːk] *adj (flight)* de temporada baja; *(rate)* de fuera de las horas punta

off-putting ['ɒfpʊtɪŋ] *adj Br Fam* desconcertante

offset [ɒf'set] *vt (pt & pp offset) (balance out)* compensar

offshoot ['ɒfʃuːt] *n* (**a**) *Bot* renuevo *m* (**b**) *Fig (of organization)* ramificación *f*

offshore ['ɒf'ʃɔː(r)] *adj* (**a**) *(breeze etc)* terral (**b**) *(oil rig)* costa afuera (**c**) *(overseas)* en el extranjero; **o. investment** inversión *f* en el extranjero

offside 1 *adv* [ɒf'saɪd] *Ftb* fuera de juego
　2 *n* ['ɒfsaɪd] *Aut (with left-hand drive)* lado derecho; *(with right-hand drive)* lado izquierdo

offspring ['ɒfsprɪŋ] *n (pl* **offspring**) *(child)* vástago *m*; *(children)* progenitura *f*

offstage 1 *adv* [ɒf'steɪdʒ] fuera del escenario
　2 *adj* ['ɒfsteɪdʒ] de fuera del escenario

often ['ɒfən, 'ɒftən] *adv* a menudo, con frecuencia; **every so o.** de vez en cuando

ogle ['əʊgəl] *vt & vi* **to o. (at) sb** comerse a algn con los ojos

oh [əʊ] *interj* ¡oh!, ¡ay!; **oh, my God!** ¡Dios mío!

oil [ɔɪl] **1** *n* (**a**) *(for cooking, lubricating)* aceite *m*; **o. lamp** lámpara *f* de aceite, quinqué *m*; **o. slick** mancha *f* de aceite (**b**) *(petroleum)* petróleo *m*; **o. rig** plataforma petrolera; **o. tanker** petrolero *m* (**c**) *(paint)* **o. paint** pintura *f* al óleo
　2 *vt* engrasar

oilcan ['ɔɪlkæn] *n* aceitera *f*

oilfield ['ɔɪlfiːld] *n* yacimiento petrolífero

oilskin ['ɔɪlskɪn] *n* (**a**) *(fabric)* hule *m* (**b**) **oilskins** chubasquero *m*, impermeable *m* de hule

oily ['ɔɪlɪ] *adj (oilier, oiliest)* aceitoso(a), grasiento(a); *(hair, skin)* graso(a)

ointment ['ɔɪntmənt] *n* ungüento *m*, pomada *f*

O.K., okay [əʊ'keɪ] *Fam* **1** *interj* de acuerdo, *Esp* vale, *Am* ok, *Méx* ándale
　2 *adj* bien; **is it O.K. if …?** ¿está bien si …?
　3 *vt* dar el visto bueno a

old [əʊld] **1** *adj* (**a**) *(not young, not new)* viejo(a); **an o. man** un anciano; **o. age** vejez *f*; *Br* **o. age pensioner** pensionista *mf*; *Br* **o. boy** *(addressing sb)* muchacho; **o. hand** veterano(a) *m,f*; **good o. John!** ¡el bueno de John! (**b**) **how o. are you?** ¿cuántos años tienes?; **she's five years o.** tiene cinco años (**c**) *(previous)* antiguo(a); **o. boy** antiguo alumno **2** *n* **of o.** de antaño

old-fashioned [əʊld'fæʃənd] *adj (outdated)* a la antigua; *(unfashionable)* anticuado(a), pasado(a) de moda

olive ['ɒlɪv] *n* (**a**) *(tree)* olivo *m* (**b**) *(fruit)* aceituna *f*, oliva *f*; **o. oil** aceite *m* de oliva

Olympic [ə'lɪmpɪk] **1** *adj* olímpico(a); **O. Games** Juegos Olímpicos **2** *npl* **the Olympics** las Olimpiadas

omelette, *US* **omelet** ['ɒmlɪt] *n* tortilla *f*; **Spanish o.** tortilla española *or* de patatas *or Am* de papas

omen ['əʊmen] *n* presagio *m*

ominous ['ɒmɪnəs] *adj* de mal agüero

omission [əʊ'mɪʃən] *n* omisión *f*, *Fig* olvido *m*

omit [əʊ'mɪt] *vt* omitir; *(accidentally)* pasar por alto; *(forget)* olvidarse (**to** de)

omnipotent [ɒm'nɪpətənt] **1** *adj* omnipotente **2** *n* **the O.** el Todopoderoso

on [ɒn] **1** *prep* (**a**) *(location)* sobre, encima de, en; **I hit him on the head** le di un golpe en la cabeza; **it's on the desk** está encima de *or* sobre el escritorio; **hanging on the wall** colgado de la pared; **on page 4** en la página 4 (**b**) *(alongside)* en; **a town on the coast** un pueblo en la costa (**c**) *(direction)* en, a; **on the right** a la derecha; **on the way** en el camino (**d**) *(time)* en; **on 3 April** el 3 de abril; **on a sunny day** un día de sol; **on Monday** el lunes; **on Mondays** los lunes; **on time** a tiempo (**e**) *(indicating medium)* **on TV/the radio** en la tele/radio; **on the phone** al teléfono (**f**) *(at the time of)* a; **on his arrival** a su llegada; **on learning of this** al conocer esto (**g**) *(transport)* en, a; **on foot** a pie (**h**) *(state, process)* en, de; **on holiday/business** de vacaciones/negocios (**i**) *(regarding)* sobre; **a lecture on numismatics** una conferencia sobre numismática (**j**) *(against)* contra; **an attack on** un ataque contra **2** *adv* (**a**) *(covering)* encima, puesto; **she had a coat on** llevaba puesto un abrigo (**b**) *Fam* **have you anything on tonight?**

¿tienes algún plan para esta noche? (**c**) **and so on** y así sucesivamente; **he talks on and on** habla sin parar; **to work on** seguir trabajando (**d**) **from that day on** a partir de aquel día; **later on** más tarde **3** *adj Fam* (**a**) **to be on** *(TV, radio, light)* estar encendido(a) *or Am* prendido(a); *(film, play)* estar en cartelera (**b**) *(definitely planned)* previsto(a); **you're on!** ¡trato hecho! (**c**) *Br Fam (acceptable)* **that isn't on** eso no está bien

once [wʌns] **1** *adv* (**a**) *(one time)* una vez; **o. a week** una vez por semana; **o. more** una vez más; **o. or twice** un par de veces; *Fig* **o. and for all** de una vez por todas (**b**) *(formerly)* en otro tiempo; **o. (upon a time) there was ...** érase una vez ... (**c**) **at o.** en seguida, inmediatamente **2** *conj* una vez que (+ *subj*), en cuanto (+ *subj*)

oncoming ['ɒnkʌmɪŋ] *adj (car, traffic)* que viene en dirección contraria

one [wʌn] **1** *adj* (**a**) *(number)* un(a); **for o. thing** primero; **you're the o. person who knows** tú eres el único que lo sabe (**b**) *(indefinite)* un(a); **he'll come back o. day** un día volverá **2** *pron* (**a**) *(identifying)* **that o.** ése/ésa; **this o.** éste/ésta; *(distant)* aquél/aquélla; **any o.** cualquiera; **the blue ones** los azules/las azules; **the o. on the table** el/la que está encima de la mesa; **the ones that, the ones who** los/las que (**b**) *(indefinite)* uno(a) *m,f*; **o. at a time** de uno en uno; **o. by o.** uno tras otro (**c**) *(impersonal)* uno(a) *m,f*; **o. has to fight** hay que luchar; **o. hopes that will never happen** esperemos que no ocurra (**d**) *(reciprocal)* **o. another** el uno al otro; **they love o. another** se aman **3** *n* *(digit)* uno *m*; **o. hundred/thousand** cien/mil

one-armed ['wʌnɑːmd] *adj (person)* manco(a); *Br Fam* **o. bandit** *(machine f)* tragaperras *f inv*, *RP* tragamonedas *f inv*

one-man ['wʌnmæn] *adj* **a o. show** un espectáculo con un solo artista

one-man band [wʌnmæn'bænd] *n* hombre *m* orquesta

one-off ['wʌnɒf] *adj Br Fam* único(a), fuera de serie

oneself [wʌn'self] *pron* (**a**) *(reflexive)* uno(a) mismo(a) *m,f*, sí mismo(a) *m,f*; **to talk to o.** hablar para sí (**b**) *(alone)* uno(a) mismo(a) *m,f*; **by o.** solo(a)

one-sided [wʌn'saɪdɪd] *adj (bargain)* desigual; *(judgement)* parcial; *(decision)* unilateral

one-to-one ['wʌntə'wʌn] *adj* **o. tuition** clases *fpl* individuales

one-way ['wʌnweɪ] adj (a) US (ticket) de ida (b) (street) de dirección única

ongoing ['ɒngəʊɪŋ] adj (a) (in progress) en curso, actual (b) (developing) en desarrollo

onion ['ʌnjən] n cebolla f

on-line ['ɒnlaɪn] adj Comput conectado(a)

onlooker ['ɒnlʊkə(r)] n espectador(a) m,f

only ['əʊnlɪ] 1 adj único(a); o. son hijo único
2 adv solamente, sólo; staff o. (sign) reservado al personal; he has o. just left acaba de marcharse hace un momento; o. yesterday ayer mismo
3 conj pero

onset ['ɒnset] n (start) comienzo m

onslaught ['ɒnslɔːt] n embestida f

onto ['ɒntʊ, unstressed 'ɒntə] prep sobre, encima de

onus ['əʊnəs] n responsabilidad f

onward ['ɒnwəd] adj hacia adelante

onward(s) ['ɒnwəd(z)] adv a partir de, en adelante; from this time o. de ahora en adelante

ooze [uːz] 1 vi rezumar
2 vt rebosar

opaque [əʊ'peɪk] adj opaco(a)

OPEC ['əʊpek] n (abbr Organization of Petroleum-Exporting Countries) OPEP f

open ['əʊpən] 1 adj (a) (in general) abierto(a); in the o. air al aire libre; to be o. with sb ser sincero(a) con algn; to keep an o. mind no tener prejuicios; I am o. to suggestions acepto cualquier sugerencia; o. to criticism susceptible a la crítica; an o. question una cuestión sin resolver; o. season (in hunting) temporada f de caza; Av & Rail o. ticket billete or Am boleto abierto; o. verdict veredicto inconcluso (b) (opposition) manifiesto(a)
2 vt (in general) abrir; (exhibition etc) inaugurar; (negotiations, conversation) entablar; to o. fire abrir fuego
3 vi (a) (door, window, flower) abrirse; (shop, bank) abrir; to o. onto (of door, window) dar a (b) (start) empezar; Th & Cin estrenarse
4 n in the o. al aire libre
▸ **open out 1** vt sep abrir, desplegar
2 vi (flowers) abrirse; (view) extenderse
▸ **open up 1** vt sep (market etc) abrir; (possibilities) crear
2 vi (shopkeeper, new shop) abrir; (flower, new market) abrirse; Fam o. up! ¡abre la puerta!

opener ['əʊpənə(r)] n tin or US can o. abrelatas m inv

opening ['əʊpənɪŋ] n (a) (act) apertura f; o. night noche f de estreno (b) (beginning) comienzo m (c) (aperture) abertura f; (gap) brecha f (d) Com oportunidad f (e) (vacancy) vacante f

openly ['əʊpənlɪ] adv abiertamente

open-minded [əʊpən'maɪndɪd] adj sin prejuicios

openness ['əʊpənnɪs] n franqueza f

open-plan ['əʊpənplæn] adj (office) abierto(a)

opera ['ɒpərə] n ópera f; o. house ópera, teatro m de la ópera

operate ['ɒpəreɪt] 1 vi (a) (function) funcionar (b) Med operar; to o. on sb for appendicitis operar a algn de apendicitis
2 vt (a) (control) manejar (b) (business) dirigir

operatic [ɒpə'rætɪk] adj de ópera

operating ['ɒpəreɪtɪŋ] n (a) o. costs gastos mpl or Esp costes mpl de explotación; Comput o. system sistema operativo (b) Med o. table mesa f de operaciones; o. theatre or US room quirófano m

operation [ɒpə'reɪʃən] n (a) (of machine) funcionamiento m; (by person) manejo m (b) Mil maniobra f (c) Med operación f, intervención quirúrgica; to undergo an o. for ser operado(a) de

operational [ɒpə'reɪʃənəl] adj (a) (ready for use) operativo(a) (b) Mil operacional

operative ['ɒpərətɪv] adj (a) Jur (in force) vigente; to become o. entrar en vigor (b) (significant) clave, significativo(a); the o. word la palabra clave

operator ['ɒpəreɪtə(r)] n (a) Ind operario(a) m,f (b) Tel operador(a) m,f (c) (dealer) negociante mf, agente mf; tour o. agente de viajes

opinion [ə'pɪnjən] n opinión f; in my o. en mi opinión, a mi juicio; it's a matter of o. es cuestión de opiniones; to have a high o. of sb tener buen concepto de algn; o. poll encuesta f, sondeo m

opinionated [ə'pɪnjəneɪtɪd] adj dogmático(a)

opium ['əʊpɪəm] n opio m

opponent [ə'pəʊnənt] n adversario(a) m,f

opportune ['ɒpətjuːn] adj oportuno(a)

opportunist [ɒpə'tjuːnɪst] adj & n oportunista (mf)

opportunity [ɒpə'tjuːnɪtɪ] n oportunidad f, ocasión f; a job with opportunities un trabajo con buenas perspectivas

oppose [ə'pəʊz] vt oponerse a

opposed [ə'pəʊzd] *adj* opuesto(a); **to be o. to sth** estar en contra de algo; **as o. to** comparado(a) con

opposing [ə'pəʊzɪŋ] *adj* adversario(a)

opposite ['ɒpəzɪt] **1** *adj* (**a**) *(facing)* de enfrente; *(page)* contiguo(a) (**b**) *(contrary)* opuesto(a), contrario(a); **in the o. direction** en dirección contraria
2 *n* **the o.** lo contrario; **quite the o.!** ¡al contrario!
3 *prep* enfrente de, frente a
4 *adv* enfrente

opposition [ɒpə'zɪʃən] *n* (**a**) *(resistance)* oposición *f*; **in o. to** en contra de (**b**) *Br Pol* **the O.** la oposición

oppress [ə'pres] *vt* oprimir

oppression [ə'preʃən] *n* opresión *f*

oppressive [ə'presɪv] *adj* opresivo(a); *(atmosphere)* agobiante; *(heat)* sofocante

opt [ɒpt] *vi* optar; **to o. for** optar por; **to o. to do sth** optar por hacer algo
▸ **opt out** *vi* retirarse; **to o. out of doing sth** decidir no hacer algo

optical ['ɒptɪkəl] *adj* óptico(a)

optician [ɒp'tɪʃən] *n* óptico(a) *m,f*

optics ['ɒptɪks] *n sing* óptica *f*

optimism ['ɒptɪmɪzəm] *n* optimismo *m*

optimist ['ɒptɪmɪst] *n* optimista *mf*

optimistic [ɒptɪ'mɪstɪk] *adj* optimista

optimistically [ɒptɪ'mɪstɪkəlɪ] *adv* con optimismo

optimum ['ɒptɪməm] **1** *n* grado óptimo
2 *adj* óptimo(a)

option ['ɒpʃən] *n* opción *f*; **I have no o.** no tengo más remedio; **to keep one's options open** no comprometerse; **with the o. of** con opción a

optional ['ɒpʃənəl] *adj* optativo(a), facultativo(a); *Educ* **o. subject** (asignatura) optativa

opulence ['ɒpjʊləns] *n* opulencia *f*

or [ɔː(r), *unstressed* ə(r)] *conj* (**a**) *(in general)* o; *(before a word beginning with* **o** *or* **ho**) u; **or else** si no, o bien; **whether you like it or not** tanto si te gusta como si no; **either a bun or a piece of cake** (o) una magdalena o un trozo de pastel (**b**) *(with negative)* ni; **he can't read or write** no sabe leer ni escribir; *see* **nor**

oral ['ɔːrəl, 'ɒrəl] **1** *adj* oral
2 *n* examen *m* oral

orally ['ɔːrəlɪ, 'ɒrəlɪ] *adv* **to be taken o.** *(on medicine)* por vía oral

orange ['ɒrɪndʒ] **1** *n* naranja *f*; **o. juice** *Esp* zumo *m or Am* jugo *m* de naranja
2 *adj* de color naranja

orator ['ɒrətə(r)] *n* orador(a) *m,f*

oratory ['ɒrətərɪ] *n* oratoria *f*

orbit ['ɔːbɪt] **1** *n Astron* órbita *f*
2 *vt* girar alrededor de
3 *vi* girar

orchard ['ɔːtʃəd] *n* huerto *m*

orchestra ['ɔːkɪstrə] *n* orquesta *f*; *US (in theatre)* platea *f*, patio *m* de butacas

orchestral [ɔː'kestrəl] *adj* orquestal

orchid ['ɔːkɪd] *n* orquídea *f*

ordain [ɔː'deɪn] *vt* (**a**) *Rel* ordenar; **to be ordained** ordenarse (**b**) *(decree)* decretar

ordeal [ɔː'diːl] *n* mala experiencia

order ['ɔːdə(r)] **1** *n* (**a**) *(sequence)* orden *m*; **to put in o.** ordenar (**b**) *(condition)* estado *m*; **out of o.** *(sign)* averiado(a) (**c**) *(peace)* orden *m*; **to restore o.** reestablecer el orden público (**d**) *(command)* orden *f* (**e**) *Com* pedido *m*, encargo *m*; **o. form** hoja *f* de pedido (**f**) *Rel* orden *f* (**g**) **in o. that** para que *(+ subj)*, a fin de que *(+ subj)*; **in o. to** *(+ infin)* para *(+ infin)*, a fin de *(+ infin)*
2 *vt* (**a**) *(command)* ordenar, mandar; **to o. sb to do sth** mandar a algn hacer algo (**b**) *Com* pedir, encargar

orderly ['ɔːdəlɪ] *adj (tidy etc)* ordenado(a)

ordinal ['ɔːdɪnəl] *adj & n* ordinal *(m)*

ordinance ['ɔːdɪnəns] *n Fml (decree)* ordenanza *f*, decreto *m*

ordinary ['ɔːdənrɪ] **1** *adj* usual, normal; *(average)* corriente, común; **the o. citizen** el ciudadano de a pie
2 *n* **the o.** lo corriente, lo normal; **out of the o.** fuera de lo común

ordnance ['ɔːdnəns] *n Br* **O. Survey** = instituto británico de cartografía

ore [ɔː(r)] *n* mineral *m*

organ ['ɔːgən] *n Mus & Anat* órgano *m*

organic [ɔː'gænɪk] *adj* orgánico(a); *(farming, food)* biológico(a), ecológico(a)

organism ['ɔːgənɪzəm] *n* organismo *m*

organization [ɔːgənaɪ'zeɪʃən] *n* organización *f*

organize ['ɔːgənaɪz] *vt* organizar

organizer ['ɔːgənaɪzə(r)] *n* organizador(a) *m,f*

orgasm ['ɔːgæzəm] *n* orgasmo *m*

orgy ['ɔːdʒɪ] *n* orgía *f*

Orient ['ɔːrɪənt] *n* **the O.** el Oriente

Oriental [ɔːrɪ'entəl] *adj & n* oriental *(mf)*

orientate ['ɔːrɪənteɪt] *vt* orientar

origin ['ɒrɪdʒɪn] *n* origen *m*; **country of o.** país *m* natal *or* de origen

original [ə'rɪdʒɪnəl] **1** *adj (first, innovative)* original; *Rel* **o. sin** pecado *m* original
2 *n* original *m*

originality [ərɪdʒɪ'nælɪtɪ] *n* originalidad *f*

originally [ə'rɪdʒɪnəlɪ] adv (**a**) (at first) en un principio (**b**) (with imagination) con originalidad

originate [ə'rɪdʒɪneɪt] **1** vt originar

2 vi **to o. from** or **in** tener su origen en

Orkneys ['ɔːknɪz] npl **the O.** las (Islas) Orcadas

ornament ['ɔːnəmənt] n ornamento m, adorno m

ornamental [ɔːnə'mentəl] adj decorativo(a)

ornate [ɔː'neɪt] adj vistoso(a)

ornithology [ɔːnɪ'θɒlədʒɪ] n ornitología f

orphan ['ɔːfən] **1** n huérfano(a) m,f

2 vt **she was orphaned** quedó huérfana

orphanage ['ɔːfənɪdʒ] n orfanato m

orthodox ['ɔːθədɒks] adj ortodoxo(a)

orthodoxy ['ɔːθədɒksɪ] n ortodoxia f

orthopaedic, US **orthopedic** [ɔːθəʊ-'piːdɪk] adj ortopédico(a)

Oscar ['ɒskə(r)] n Óscar m

oscillate ['ɒsɪleɪt] vi oscilar

ostensible [ɒ'stensɪbəl] adj (**a**) (apparent) ostensible (**b**) (pretended) aparente

ostentatious [ɒsten'teɪʃəs] adj ostentoso(a)

osteopath ['ɒstɪəpæθ] n osteópata mf

ostracize ['ɒstrəsaɪz] vt (from society) condenar al ostracismo; (from group) aislar, excluir

ostrich ['ɒstrɪtʃ] n avestruz f

other ['ʌðə(r)] **1** adj otro(a); **every o. day** cada dos días; **on the o. hand** por otra parte; **o. people have seen it** otros lo han visto; **the o. four** los otros cuatro; **the o. one** el otro/la otra; **the o. thing** lo otro

2 pron otro(a) m,f; **many others** otros muchos; **the others** los otros, los demás; **we see each o. quite often** nos vemos con bastante frecuencia; **he must be somewhere or o.** debe de estar en alguna parte

otherwise ['ʌðəwaɪz] **1** adv (**a**) (if not) si no (**b**) (differently) de otra manera (**c**) (in other respects) por lo demás

2 adj distinto(a)

OTT [əʊtiː'tiː] adj Br Fam (abbr **over the top**) exagerado(a)

otter ['ɒtə(r)] n nutria f

ouch [aʊtʃ] interj (expressing pain) ¡ay!

ought [ɔːt] v aux

En el inglés hablado, y en el escrito en estilo coloquial, la forma negativa **ought not** se transforma en **oughtn't**.

(**a**) (obligation) deber; **I thought I o. to tell you** creí que debía decírtelo; **she o. to do it** debería hacerlo (**b**) (vague desirability) tener que, deber; **you o. to see the exhibition** deberías ver la exposición (**c**) (expectation) **he o. to pass the exam** seguramente aprobará el examen; **that o. to do** con eso bastará

ounce [aʊns] n onza f

our [aʊə(r)] poss adj nuestro(a)

ours [aʊəz] poss pron (**a**) (singular) el nuestro m, la nuestra f; (plural) los nuestros mpl, las nuestras fpl (**b**) **of o.** nuestro(a); **a friend of o.** un amigo nuestro

ourselves [aʊə'selvz] pers pron pl (**a**) (reflexive) nos (**b**) (emphatic) nosotros mismos/nosotras mismas (**c**) **by o.** a solas

oust [aʊst] vt (**a**) (from a post) desbancar (**b**) (from property etc) desalojar

out [aʊt] **1** adv (outside, away) fuera; **to go o.** salir

2 adj (**a**) **the sun is o.** ha salido el sol (**b**) (unfashionable) pasado(a) de moda (**c**) (fire) apagado(a) (**d**) **she's o.** (not in) ha salido, no está (**e**) (inaccurate) equivocado(a); **to be o. in one's calculations** equivocarse en los cálculos (**f**) **before the week is o.** antes de que acabe la semana

3 prep Fam (out of) por; **he jumped o. the window** saltó por la ventana

4 out of adv (**a**) (place, control, danger) fuera de; **to go o. of the room** salir de la habitación (**b**) (cause, motive) por; **o. of love** por amor (**c**) (made from) de; **made o. wood** hechode madera (**d**) (short of, without) sin; **I'm o. of cash** me he quedado sin dinero (**e**) (in proportions) de; **three days o. of four** tres días de cada cuatro

out-and-out ['aʊtənaʊt] adj redomado(a)

outboard ['aʊtbɔːd] adj **o. motor** fueraborda m

outbreak ['aʊtbreɪk] n (of war) comienzo m; (of disease) brote m; (of violence) ola f; **at the o. of war** cuando estalló la guerra

outbuilding ['aʊtbɪldɪŋ] n dependencia f

outburst ['aʊtbɜːst] n (of anger) arrebato m; (of generosity) arranque m

outcast ['aʊtkɑːst] n marginado(a) m,f

outcome ['aʊtkʌm] n resultado m

outcrop ['aʊtkrɒp] n Geol afloramiento m

outcry ['aʊtkraɪ] n **there was an o.** hubo fuertes protestas

outdated [aʊt'deɪtɪd] adj anticuado(a), obsoleto(a)

outdo [aʊt'duː] vt (pt **outdid** [aʊt'dɪd]; pp **outdone** [aʊt'dʌn]) **to o. sb** superar a algn

outdoor ['aʊtdɔː(r)] *adj* (**a**) *(games, sports, work)* al aire libre (**b**) *(clothes)* de calle

outdoors [aʊt'dɔːz] *adv* fuera, al aire libre

outer ['aʊtə(r)] *adj* exterior, externo(a)

outfit ['aʊtfɪt] *n* (**a**) *(kit, equipment)* equipo *m* (**b**) *(set of clothes)* conjunto *m* (**c**) *Fam (group)* grupo *m*

outgoing ['aʊtgəʊɪŋ] **1** *adj* (**a**) *(departing)* saliente (**b**) *(sociable)* extrovertido(a)
2 *npl Br* **outgoings** gastos *mpl*

outgrow [aʊt'grəʊ] *vt* (*pt* **outgrew** [aʊt'gruː]; *pp* **outgrown** [aʊt'grən]) **he's outgrowing all his clothes** toda la ropa se le está quedando pequeña; **she'll o. it** se le pasará con la edad

outhouse ['aʊthaʊs] *n* = **outbuilding**

outing ['aʊtɪŋ] *n* excursión *f*

outlandish [aʊt'lændɪʃ] *adj* estrafalario(a), extravagante

outlast [aʊt'lɑːst] *vt (person)* sobrevivir a; *(thing)* durar más que

outlaw ['aʊtlɔː] **1** *n* proscrito(a) *m,f*
2 *vt* prohibir

outlay ['aʊtleɪ] *n (expense)* desembolso *m*

outlet ['aʊtlet] *n* (**a**) *(opening)* salida *f* (**b**) *(for emotions)* válvula *f* de escape (**c**) *Com* mercado *m*

outline ['aʊtlaɪn] **1** *n* (**a**) *(draft)* bosquejo *m* (**b**) *(outer line)* contorno *m*; *(silhouette)* perfil *m*
2 *vt* (**a**) *(draw lines of)* perfilar (**b**) *(summarize)* resumir (**c**) *(describe roughly)* trazar las líneas generales de

outlive [aʊt'lɪv] *vt* sobrevivir a

outlook ['aʊtlʊk] *n* (**a**) *(point of view)* punto *m* de vista (**b**) *(prospect)* perspectiva *f*; *Met* previsión *f*

outlying ['aʊtlaɪɪŋ] *adj (remote)* periférico(a)

outmoded [aʊt'məʊdɪd] *adj* anticuado(a)

outnumber [aʊt'nʌmbə(r)] *vt* exceder en número

out-of-the-way ['aʊtəvðə'weɪ] *adj* (**a**) *(distant)* apartado(a), remoto(a) (**b**) *(uncommon)* fuera de lo común

outpatient ['aʊtpeɪʃənt] *n* paciente externo(a); **outpatients' department** clínica ambulatoria

outpost ['aʊtpəʊst] *n* enclave *m*

output ['aʊtpʊt] *n* (**a**) *(of goods, of author)* producción *f*, *(of machine)* rendimiento *m* (**b**) *Elec* potencia *f* (**c**) *Comput* salida *f*

outrage ['aʊtreɪdʒ] **1** *n* ultraje *m*; **it's an o.!** ¡es un escándalo!
2 *vt* **to be outraged by sth** indignarse por algo

outrageous [aʊt'reɪdʒəs] *adj (behaviour)* escandaloso(a); *(clothes)* extravagante; *(price)* exorbitante

outright 1 *adj* ['aʊtraɪt] *(absolute)* absoluto(a)
2 *adv* [aʊt'raɪt] (**a**) *(completely)* por completo (**b**) *(directly)* directamente, sin reserva (**c**) *(immediately)* en el acto

outset ['aʊtset] *n* comienzo *m*, principio *m*

outside 1 *prep* [aʊt'saɪd, 'aʊtsaɪd] (**a**) *(physically)* fuera de (**b**) *(beyond)* más allá de (**c**) *(other than)* aparte de
2 *adj* ['aʊtsaɪd] (**a**) *(exterior)* exterior, externo(a) (**b**) *(remote)* remoto(a)
3 *adv* [aʊt'saɪd] fuera, afuera
4 *n* [aʊt'saɪd, 'aʊtsaɪd] exterior *m*; **on the o.** por fuera; *Fam* **at the o.** como mucho

outsider [aʊt'saɪdə(r)] *n* (**a**) *(stranger)* extraño(a) *m,f*, extraño(a) *m,f* (**b**) *Pol* = candidato(a) con pocas posibilidades de ganar

outsize(d) ['aʊtsaɪz(d)] *adj (clothes)* de talla especial; *(appetite, ego)* desmedido(a)

outskirts ['aʊtskɜːts] *npl* afueras *fpl*

outsourcing ['aʊtsɔːsɪŋ] *n Com* externalización *f*, subcontratación *f*, *Am* tercerización *f*; *Am* terciarización *f*

outspoken [aʊt'spəʊkən] *adj* directo(a), abierto(a)

outstanding [aʊt'stændɪŋ] *adj* (**a**) *(exceptional)* destacado(a) (**b**) *(unpaid, unresolved)* pendiente

outstretched [aʊt'stretʃt] *adj* extendido(a)

outward ['aʊtwəd] **1** *adj* (**a**) *(external)* exterior, externo(a) (**b**) **the o. journey** el viaje de ida
2 *adv* = **outwards**

outwardly ['aʊtwədlɪ] *adv* aparentemente, en apariencia

outwards ['aʊtwədz] *adv* hacia (a)fuera

outweigh [aʊt'weɪ] *vt* (**a**) *(be more important than)* tener más peso que (**b**) *(weigh more than)* pesar más que

oval ['əʊvəl] **1** *adj* oval, ovalado(a)
2 *n* óvalo *m*

ovary ['əʊvərɪ] *n* ovario *m*

ovation [əʊ'veɪʃən] *n* ovación *f*

oven ['ʌvən] *n* horno *m*

ovenproof ['ʌvənpruːf] *adj* refractario(a)

over ['əʊvə(r)] **1** *prep* (**a**) *(above, on top of)* sobre, encima de, *Am* arriba de (**b**) *(across)* al otro lado de; **the bridge o. the**

river el puente que cruza el río (**c**) *(during)* durante (**d**) *(throughout)* por (**e**) *(by the agency of)* por; **o. the phone** por teléfono (**f**) *(more than)* más de; **men o. twenty-five** hombres mayores de veinticinco años; **o. and above** además de (**g**) *(recovered from)* recuperado(a) de
2 *adv* (**a**) **o. here/there** aquí/allí, *Am* acá/allá (**b**) *(throughout)* por; **all o.** por todas partes (**c**) *(more)* más (**d**) *(again)* otra vez; **o. and o. (again)** una y otra vez (**e**) *(in excess)* de más
3 *adj (finished)* acabado(a); **it's (all) o.** se acabó

overall ['ǝʊvǝrɔːl] **1** *adj* total, global
2 *n Br* **overalls** *(boiler suit)* mono *m* (de trabajo), *Am* overol *m*
3 *adv* [ǝʊvǝr'ɔːl] *(on the whole)* por lo general, en conjunto

overawe [ǝʊvǝr'ɔː] *vt* **to be overawed by sth/sb** quedarse anonadado(a) por algo/algn

overbearing [ǝʊvǝ'beǝrɪŋ] *adj (domineering)* dominante; *(important)* significativo(a)

overboard ['ǝʊvǝbɔːd] *adv* por la borda; **man o.!** ¡hombre al agua!; *Fam* **to go o.** pasarse

overbook ['ǝʊvǝ'bʊk] *vt (flight, holiday)* **they've overbooked this flight** este vuelo tiene overbooking

overcast ['ǝʊvǝkɑːst] *adj* nublado(a)

overcharge [ǝʊvǝ'tʃɑːdʒ] *vt* (**a**) *(charge too much)* cobrar demasiado a (**b**) *(overload)* sobrecargar

overcoat ['ǝʊvǝkǝʊt] *n* abrigo *m*

overcome [ǝʊvǝ'kʌm] *vt* (**a**) *(conquer)* vencer; **o. by grief** deshecho(a) por el dolor (**b**) *(obstacle)* superar

overconfident [ǝʊvǝ'kɒnfɪdǝnt] *adj* demasiado confiado(a)

overcrowded [ǝʊvǝ'kraʊdɪd] *adj (room)* atestado(a) (de gente); *(country)* superpoblado(a)

overcrowding [ǝʊvǝ'kraʊdɪŋ] *n (of slums, prisons)* hacinamiento *m*; *(of classrooms)* masificación *f*, *(of country)* superpoblación *f*

overdo [ǝʊvǝ'duː] *vt (pt overdid* [ǝʊvǝ-'dɪd]; *pp overdone* [ǝʊvǝ'dʌn]) (**a**) *(carry too far)* exagerar; **don't o. it** no te pases (**b**) *Culin* cocer *or* asar demasiado

overdose [ǝʊvǝdǝʊs] *n* sobredosis *f*

overdraft ['ǝʊvǝdrɑːft] *n* giro *m* en descubierto; *(amount)* saldo *m* deudor

overdrawn [ǝʊvǝ'drɔːn] *vt* **to be o.** tener la cuenta en descubierto

overdue [ǝʊvǝ'djuː] *adj* **to be o.** *(person, train)* retrasarse, venir con retraso *or Am* demora; *(bill)* estar sin pagar

overestimate [ǝʊvǝr'estɪmeɪt] *vt* sobreestimar

overflow 1 *vi* [ǝʊvǝ'flǝʊ] *(river)* desbordarse; *(cup etc)* derramarse
2 *n* ['ǝʊvǝflǝʊ] *(of river etc)* desbordamiento *m*; **o. pipe** cañería *f* de desagüe

overgrown [ǝʊvǝ'grǝʊn] *adj* (**a**) *(with grass)* cubierto(a) (de hierba) (**b**) *(in size)* demasiado grande

overhaul 1 *vt* [ǝʊvǝ'hɔːl] revisar
2 *n* ['ǝʊvǝhɔːl] revisión *f* y reparación *f*

overhead 1 *adj* ['ǝʊvǝhed] *(por)* encima de la cabeza; **o. cable** cable aéreo
2 *adv* [ǝʊvǝ'hed] arriba, por encima de la cabeza
3 *n* [ǝʊvǝhed] *US* = **overheads**

overheads ['ǝʊvǝhedz] *npl Br* gastos *mpl* generales

overhear [ǝʊvǝ'hɪǝ(r)] *vt (pt & pp overheard* [ǝʊvǝ'hɜːd]) oír por casualidad

overheat [ǝʊvǝ'hiːt] *vi* recalentarse

overjoyed [ǝʊvǝ'dʒɔɪd] *adj* rebosante de alegría

overlap [ǝʊvǝ'læp] *vi* superponerse; *Fig* **our plans o.** nuestros planes coinciden parcialmente

overleaf [ǝʊvǝ'liːf] *adv* al dorso

overload 1 *vt* [ǝʊvǝ'lǝʊd] sobrecargar
2 *n* ['ǝʊvǝlǝʊd] sobrecarga *f*

overlook [ǝʊvǝ'lʊk] *vt* (**a**) *(fail to notice)* saltarse (**b**) *(ignore)* no hacer caso de; **we'll o. it this time** esta vez lo pasaremos por alto (**c**) *(have a view of)* dar a, tener vista a

overmanning [ǝʊvǝ'mænɪŋ] *n Ind* exceso *m* de empleados

overnight 1 *adv* [ǝʊvǝ'naɪt] (**a**) *(during the night)* por la noche; **we stayed there o.** pasamos la noche allí (**b**) *(suddenly)* de la noche a la mañana
2 *adj* ['ǝʊvǝnaɪt] *(sudden)* repentino(a); **o. stay** *Esp, Méx* estancia *f or Am* estadia *f* de una noche

overpass ['ǝʊvǝpɑːs] *n US* paso elevado

overpay [ǝʊvǝ'peɪ] *vt (pt & pp overpaid* [ǝʊvǝ'peɪd]) pagar demasiado a

overpower [ǝʊvǝ'paʊǝ(r)] *vt* (**a**) *(subdue)* dominar (**b**) *(affect strongly)* abrumar

overpowering [ǝʊvǝ'paʊǝrɪŋ] *adj (emotion, heat)* tremendo(a), desmesurado(a); *(smell, taste)* fortísimo(a), intensísimo(a)

overpriced [ǝʊvǝ'praɪst] *adj* excesivamente caro(a)

overrate [əʊvəˈreɪt] *vt* sobreestimar, supervalorar

overreact [əʊvərɪˈækt] *vi* reaccionar exageradamente

override [əʊvəˈraɪd] *vt (pt* **overrode**; *pp* **overridden** [əʊvəˈrɪdən] (**a**) *(disregard)* hacer caso omiso de (**b**) *(annul, cancel out)* anular (**c**) *(be more important than)* contar más que

overriding [əʊvəˈraɪdɪŋ] *adj* principal; *(importance)* primordial; *(need)* imperioso(a)

overrode [əʊvəˈrəʊd] *pt of* override

overrule [əʊvəˈruːl] *vt* invalidar; *Jur* denegar

overrun [əʊvəˈrʌn] *vt* (**a**) *(country)* invadir (**b**) *(allotted time)* rebasar, excederse de

oversaw [əʊvəˈsɔː] *pt of* oversee

overseas 1 *adv* [əʊvəˈsiːz] en ultramar; **to live o.** vivir en el extranjero
2 *adj* [ˈəʊvəsiːz] de ultramar; *(visitor)* extranjero(a); *(trade)* exterior

oversee [əʊvəˈsiː] *vt (pt* **oversaw**; *pp* **overseen** [əʊvəˈsiːn]) supervisar

overseer [ˈəʊvəsiːə(r)] *n* supervisor(a) *m,f*; *(foreman)* capataz *m*

overshadow [əʊvəˈʃædəʊ] *vt Fig* eclipsar

overshoot [əʊvəˈʃuːt] *vt (pt & pp* **overshot** [əʊvəˈʃɒt]) **to o. a turning** pasarse un cruce; *Fig* **to o. the mark** pasarse de la raya

oversight [ˈəʊvəsaɪt] *n* descuido *m*

oversleep [əʊvəˈsliːp] *vi (pt & pp* **overslept** [əʊvəˈslept]) quedarse dormido(a)

overspill [ˈəʊvəspɪl] *n esp Br* exceso *m* de población

overstate [əʊvəˈsteɪt] *vt* exagerar

overstep [əʊvəˈstep] *vt Fig* **to o. the mark** pasarse de la raya

overt [əʊˈvɜːt] *adj* patente

overtake [əʊvəˈteɪk] *vt (pt* **overtook**; *pp* **overtaken** [əʊvəˈteɪkən]) (**a**) *Br Aut* adelantar (**b**) *(surpass)* superar a (**c**) *(of night)* sorprender

overthrow [əʊvəˈθrəʊ] *vt (pt* **overthrew** [əʊvəˈθruː]; *pp* **overthrown** [əʊvəˈθrəʊn]) *(government)* derribar

overtime [ˈəʊvətaɪm] *n* (**a**) *(work)* horas *fpl* extra (**b**) *US* prórroga *f*

overtone [ˈəʊvətəʊn] *n* matiz *m*

overtook [əʊvəˈtʊk] *pt of* overtake

overture [ˈəʊvətjʊə(r)] *n* (**a**) *Mus* obertura *f*; *Fig (introduction)* introducción *f* (**b**) *(proposal)* propuesta *f*

overturn [əʊvəˈtɜːn] *vt & vi* volcar

overweight [əʊvəˈweɪt] *adj* demasiado pesado(a)

overwhelm [əʊvəˈwelm] *vt* (**a**) *(defeat)* aplastar; *(overpower)* abrumar; **I'm overwhelmed** estoy abrumado (**b**) *(with letters, work etc)* inundar

overwhelming [əʊvəˈwelmɪŋ] *adj (defeat)* aplastante; *(desire etc)* irresistible

overwork [əʊvəˈwɜːk] **1** *vi* trabajar demasiado
2 *vt (person)* forzar; *(excuse etc)* abusar de

overwrought [əʊvəˈrɔːt] *adj* (**a**) *(tense)* muy nervioso(a) (**b**) *Literary (too elaborate)* forzado(a)

owe [əʊ] *vt* deber

owing [ˈəʊɪŋ] *adj* **o. to** debido a, a causa de

owl [aʊl] *n* **(short-eared) o.** búho *m*, *CAm, Méx* tecolote *m*; **(barn) o.** lechuza *f*

own [əʊn] **1** *adj* propio(a); **it's his o. fault** es culpa suya
2 *pron* (**a**) **my o./your o./his o./etc** lo mío/lo tuyo/lo suyo/*etc*; *Fam* **to get one's o. back** tomarse la revancha (**b**) **on one's o.** *(without help)* uno(a) mismo(a); *(alone)* solo(a)
3 *vt* poseer, ser dueño(a) de
▸ **own up** *vi* **to o. up (to sth)** confesar (algo)

own-brand [ˈəʊnˈbrænd] *adj Br Com* de marca blanca

owner [ˈəʊnə(r)] *n* propietario(a) *m,f*, dueño(a) *m,f*

ownership [ˈəʊnəʃɪp] *n* propiedad *f*, posesión *f*

ox [ɒks] *n (pl* **oxen** [ˈɒksən]) buey *m*

oxide [ˈɒksaɪd] *n Chem* óxido *m*

oxtail [ˈɒksteɪl] *n* rabo *m* de buey

oxygen [ˈɒksɪdʒən] *n* oxígeno *m*; **o. mask** máscara *f* de oxígeno

oyster [ˈɔɪstə(r)] *n* ostra *f*

Oz [ɒz] *n Fam* Australia

oz *(abbr* **ounce(s))** onza(s) *f(pl)*

ozone [ˈəʊzəʊn] *n* ozono *m*; **o. layer** capa *f* de ozono

P, p [pi:] *n (the letter)* P, p *f*

p (**a**) (*pl* **pp**) (*abbr* **page**) pág., p (**b**) [pi:] *Br Fam* (*abbr* **penny, pence**) penique(s) *m(pl)*

PA [pi:'eɪ] *n Fam* (**a**) (*abbr* **personal assistant**) ayudante *mf* personal (**b**) (*abbr* **public-address (system)**) megafonía *f*

pa [pɑː] *n US Fam (dad)* papá *m*

p.a. (*abbr* **per annum**) al año

pace [peɪs] **1** *n (step)* paso *m; (speed)* ritmo *m;* **to keep p. with** seguir a; *Fig* avanzar al mismo ritmo que; **to set the p.** marcar el paso; *Fig* marcar la pauta
2 *vi* **to p. up and down** ir de un lado a otro

pacemaker ['peɪsmeɪkə(r)] *n Sport* liebre *f; Med* marcapasos *m inv*

Pacific [pə'sɪfɪk] *adj* **the P. (Ocean)** el (océano) Pacífico

pacifier ['pæsɪfaɪə(r)] *n US (for baby)* chupete *m*

pacifist ['pæsɪfɪst] *adj & n* pacifista (*mf*)

pacify ['pæsɪfaɪ] *vt (person)* calmar; *(country)* pacificar

pack¹ [pæk] **1** *n (parcel)* paquete *m; (bundle)* bulto *m; US (of cigarettes)* paquete *m; Br (of playing cards)* baraja *f; (of hounds)* jauría *f*
2 *vt* (**a**) *(goods)* embalar, envasar; *(in suitcase)* poner; **to p. one's suitcase** hacer la maleta *or Am* valija; *Fig* **to p. one's bags** marcharse (**b**) *(fill)* atestar (**c**) *(press down)* (snow) apretar
3 *vi* (**a**) *(prepare luggage)* hacer las maletas; *Fam* **to send sb packing** mandar a paseo a algn (**b**) *(of people)* apiñarse (**into** en)

▸ **pack in** *vt sep Fam (give up)* dejar

▸ **pack off** *vt sep Fam* mandar

▸ **pack up** *Fam* **1** *vt sep (give up)* dejar
2 *vi (stop working)* dejarlo, parar de trabajar; *(machine etc)* estropearse

pack² [pæk] *vt (meeting)* llenar de partidarios

package ['pækɪdʒ] **1** *n* (**a**) *(parcel)* paquete *m; (bundle)* bulto *m* (**b**) *(of proposals etc)* paquete *m; (agreement)* acuerdo *m;* **p. deal** convenio *m* general; **p. tour** viaje *m* todo incluido
2 *vt (goods)* envasar, embalar

packaging ['pækɪdʒɪŋ] *n (for transport, freight)* embalaje *m; (of product)* envasado *m*

packed [pækt] *adj* (**a**) *(crowded)* abarrotado(a) (**b**) **p. lunch** comida preparada de casa *(para excursión, trabajo, colegio)*

packet ['pækɪt] *n* (**a**) *(of tea, cigarettes)* paquete *m; (bag)* bolsa *f* (**b**) *Fam (lot of money)* **to make** *or* **earn a p.** ganar una millonada *or Méx* un chorro de lana *or RP* una ponchada de guita

packing ['pækɪŋ] *n* embalaje *m;* **p. case** caja *f* de embalar; **to do one's p.** hacer las maletas

pact [pækt] *n* pacto *m*

pad¹ [pæd] **1** *n* (**a**) *(for protection)* almohadilla *f; (of paper)* bloc *m*, taco *m* (**b**) **launch p.** plataforma *f* de lanzamiento (**c**) *Fam (flat)* casa *f, Esp* choza *f*
2 *vt (chair)* acolchar

▸ **pad out** *vt sep Fig* meter paja en

pad² [pæd] *vi* **to p. about** *or* **around** andar silenciosamente

padded ['pædɪd] *adj (envelope, jacket)* acolchado(a); **p. cell** celda acolchada

padding ['pædɪŋ] *n (material)* relleno *m; Fig (in speech etc)* paja *f*

paddle¹ ['pædəl] **1** *n* (**a**) *(oar)* pala *f;* **p. boat** *or* **steamer** vapor *m* de ruedas (**b**) *US (for table tennis)* pala *f*
2 *vt (boat)* remar con pala en
3 *vi (in boat)* remar con pala

paddle² ['pædəl] *vi* chapotear

paddling pool ['pædlɪŋpuːl] *n (inflatable)* piscina *f or Méx* alberca *f or RP* pileta *f* hinchable; *(in park)* piscina *f or Méx* alberca *f or RP* pileta *f* para niños

paddock ['pædək] *n* potrero *m; (in race course)* paddock *m*

paddy ['pædɪ] *n* arrozal *m*

padlock ['pædlɒk] **1** *n* candado *m*
2 *vt* cerrar con candado

paediatrician [piːdɪə'trɪʃən] *n* pediatra *mf*

paedophile ['piːdəʊfaɪl] *n* pedófilo(a) *m,f*

pagan ['peɪɡən] *adj & n* pagano(a) (*m,f*)

page¹ [peɪdʒ] *n* página *f*

page² [peɪdʒ] **1** n (servant) paje m; (of knight) escudero m; (at club) botones m inv
2 vt (call) avisar por megafonía

pageant ['pædʒənt] n (show) espectáculo m; (procession) desfile m; (on horses) cabalgata f

pageantry ['pædʒəntrɪ] n pompa f, boato m

pager ['peɪdʒə(r)] n buscapersonas m inv, Esp busca m, Méx localizador m, RP radiomensaje m

paid [peɪd] **1** adj pagado(a); Fig **to put p. to sth** acabar con algo
2 pt & pp of **pay**

pail [peɪl] n cubo m; (child's) cubito m

pain [peɪn] **1** n (a) (physical) dolor m; (grief) sufrimiento m; Fam **he's a p. (in the neck)** es un plomazo or pelmazo or Méx sangrón; **on p. of death** so pena de muerte (b) **to take pains over sth** esmerarse en algo
2 vt (grieve) dar pena a

pained [peɪnd] adj de reproche

painful ['peɪnfʊl] adj doloroso(a); Fam (very bad) malísimo(a)

painfully ['peɪnfʊlɪ] adv (a) **p. shy** lastimosamente tímido(a) (b) Fam terriblemente

painkiller ['peɪnkɪlə(r)] n analgésico m

painless ['peɪnlɪs] adj sin dolor; Fig sin dificultades

painstaking ['peɪnzteɪkɪŋ] adj (person) concienzudo(a); (care, research) esmerado(a)

paint [peɪnt] **1** n pintura f
2 vt pintar; **to p. sth white** pintar algo de blanco
3 vi pintar

paintbrush ['peɪntbrʌʃ] n Art pincel m; (for walls) brocha f

painter ['peɪntə(r)] n pintor(a) m,f

painting ['peɪntɪŋ] n cuadro m; (activity) pintura f

paintwork ['peɪntwɜːk] n pintura f

pair [peə(r)] n (of gloves, shoes) par m; (of people, cards) pareja f; **a p. of scissors** unas tijeras; **a p. of trousers** un pantalón, unos pantalones

pajamas [pə'dʒæməz] npl US = **pyjamas**

Pakistan [pɑːkɪ'stɑːn] n Paquistán

Pakistani [pɑːkɪ'stɑːnɪ] adj & n paquistaní (mf)

pal [pæl] n Fam amiguete(a) m,f, Esp colega mf

palace ['pælɪs] n palacio m

palatable ['pælətəbəl] adj (tasty) sabroso(a); Fig aceptable

palate ['pælɪt] n paladar m

palatial [pə'leɪʃəl] adj suntuoso(a), señorial

palaver [pə'lɑːvə(r)] n Br Fam lío m, Esp follón m

pale¹ [peɪl] **1** adj (skin) pálido(a); (colour) claro(a); (light) tenue; **to turn p.** palidecer
2 vi palidecer

pale² [peɪl] n Fig **to be beyond the p.** ser inaceptable

Palestine ['pælɪstaɪn] n Palestina

Palestinian [pælɪ'stɪnɪən] adj & n palestino(a) (m,f)

palette ['pælɪt] n paleta f; **p. knife** espátula f

paling ['peɪlɪŋ] n valla f

palisade [pælɪ'seɪd] n palizada f, estacada f

pall¹ [pɔːl] n Fig manto m; (of smoke) cortina f

pall² [pɔːl] vi aburrir; **it never palls** nunca cansa

pallet ['pælɪt] n plataforma f de carga

pallid ['pælɪd] adj pálido(a)

pallor ['pælə(r)] n palidez f

palm¹ [pɑːm] n (tree) palmera f; (leaf) palma f; **date p.** palma datilera; **P. Sunday** domingo m de Ramos

► **palm off** vt sep **to p. sth off on sb** colocar or endosar algo a algn

palm² [pɑːm] n Anat palma f

palmistry ['pɑːmɪstrɪ] n quiromancia f

palpable ['pælpəbəl] adj palpable

palpitate ['pælpɪteɪt] vi palpitar

palpitation [pælpɪ'teɪʃən] n palpitación f

paltry ['pɔːltrɪ] adj (paltrier, paltriest) insignificante

pamper ['pæmpə(r)] vt mimar, consentir

pamphlet ['pæmflɪt] n folleto m

pan¹ [pæn] **1** n (a) (saucepan) cazuela f, cacerola f (b) (of scales) platillo m (c) Br (of lavatory) taza f
2 vt Fam (criticize) vapulear, Esp poner por los suelos

pan² [pæn] vi Cin tomar vistas panorámicas

panacea [pænə'sɪə] n panacea f

panache [pə'næʃ] n garbo m, salero m

Panama ['pænəmɑː] n Panamá; **P. Canal** Canal m de Panamá

pancake ['pænkeɪk] n crepe f

panda ['pændə] n panda m; Br **p. car** coche m or Am carro m or CSur auto m patrulla

pandemonium [pændɪ'məʊnɪəm] n alboroto m

pander ['pændə(r)] vi **to p. to** (person) complacer a; (wishes) acceder a

pane [peɪn] *n* **p. (of glass)** hoja *m* de vidrio *or Esp* cristal

panel ['pænəl] *n* (**a**) *(of wall)* panel *m*; *(flat surface)* tabla *f*; *(of instruments)* tablero *m*; *(of ceiling)* artesón *m* (**b**) *(jury)* jurado *m*; *Rad & TV* concursantes *mpl*

panelling, *US* **paneling** ['pænəlɪŋ] *n* paneles *mpl*

pang [pæŋ] *n (of pain, hunger)* punzada *f*; *Fig (of conscience)* remordimiento *m*; **birth pangs** dolores *mpl* del parto

panic ['pænɪk] **1** *n* pánico *m*; **to get into a p.** ponerse histérico(a)
2 *vi* aterrarse

panicky ['pænɪkɪ] *adj* asustadizo(a)

panic-stricken ['pænɪkstrɪkən] *adj* aterrado(a)

panorama [pænə'rɑːmə] *n* panorama *m*

pansy ['pænzɪ] *n Bot* pensamiento *m*; *Fam Pej* mariquita *m*

pant [pænt] **1** *n* jadeo *m*
2 *vi* jadear

panther ['pænθə(r)] *n* pantera *f*

panties ['pæntɪz] *npl esp US Esp* bragas *fpl*, *Chile, Col, Méx* calzones *mpl*, *Ecuad* follones *mpl*, *RP* bombacha *f*

> *Note that the Spanish word* **panty** *is a false friend and is never a translation for the English word* **panties***. In Spanish,* **panty** *means "(pair of) tights".*

pantomime ['pæntəmaɪm] *n BrTh* = obra de teatro musical para niños basada en un cuento de hadas y representada en Navidad

pantry ['pæntrɪ] *n* despensa *f*

pants [pænts] *npl* (**a**) *Br (men's underwear)* calzoncillos *mpl*, *Chile* fundillos *mpl*, *Col* pantaloncillos *mpl*, *Méx* calzones *mpl*, *Méx* chones *mpl*; *(women's underwear) Esp* bragas *fpl*, *Chile, Col, Méx* calzones *mpl*, *RP* bombacha *f* (**b**) *US (trousers)* pantalones *mpl*

pantyhose ['pæntɪhəʊz] *n US* medias *fpl*, pantis *mpl*

papal ['peɪpəl] *adj* papal

paparazzo [pæpə'rætsəʊ] *n (pl* paparazzi [pæpə'rætsiː]) paparazzi *mf*

paper ['peɪpə(r)] **1** *n* (**a**) *(material)* papel *m*; *Fig* **on p.** en teoría; **writing p.** papel de escribir (**b**) *(exam)* examen *m*; *(essay)* trabajo (escrito) (**c**) *Pol* libro *m* (**d**) *(newspaper)* periódico *m*; **the papers** la prensa (**e**) **papers** *(documents)* documentos *mpl*
2 *vt* empapelar

paperback ['peɪpəbæk] *n* libro *m* en rústica

paperclip ['peɪpəklɪp] *n* clip *m*, sujetapapeles *m inv*

paperweight ['peɪpəweɪt] *n* pisapapeles *m inv*

paperwork ['peɪpəwɜːk] *n* papeleo *m*

papier-mâché [pæpjeɪ'mæʃeɪ] *n* cartón *m* piedra

paprika ['pæprɪkə] *n* pimentón molido

par [pɑː(r)] *n (parity)* igualdad *f*; *(in golf)* par *m*; *Fig* **it's p. for the course** es lo normal en estos casos; *Fig* **to feel below p.** estar en baja forma

parable ['pærəbəl] *n* parábola *f*

paracetamol [pærə'siːtəmɒl] *n* paracetamol *m*

parachute ['pærəʃuːt] **1** *n* paracaídas *m inv*
2 *vi* **to p. (down)** saltar *or* lanzarse en paracaídas

parade [pə'reɪd] **1** *n* desfile *m*; *Mil* **to be on p.** pasar revista
2 *vt Mil* hacer desfilar; *Fig (flaunt)* hacer alarde de
3 *vi (troops)* pasar revista; *(procession)* desfilar

paradise ['pærədaɪs] *n* paraíso *m*

paradox ['pærədɒks] *n* paradoja *f*

paradoxical [pærə'dɒksɪkəl] *adj* paradójico(a)

paraffin ['pærəfɪn] *n* parafina *f*; **liquid p.** aceite *m* de parafina; **p. lamp** lámpara *f* de petróleo

paragliding ['pærəglaɪdɪŋ] *n* parapente *m*

paragon ['pærəgən] *n* modelo *m*

paragraph ['pærəgrɑːf] *n* párrafo *m*

Paraguay ['pærəgwaɪ] *n* Paraguay *m*

Paraguayan [pærə'gwaɪən] *adj & n* paraguayo(a) *(m,f)*

paralegal [pærə'liːgəl] *n US* ayudante *mf* de un abogado, *RP* procurador(a) *m,f*

parallel ['pærəlel] **1** *adj* paralelo(a) (**to** *or* **with** a); *Fig* comparable (**to** *or* **with** a)
2 *n Geog* paralelo *m*; *Geom* paralela *f*; *Fig* paralelo
3 *vt Fig* ser paralelo(a) a

paralyse ['pærəlaɪz] *vt* paralizar

paralysis [pə'rælɪsɪs] *n* parálisis *f*

paralyze ['pærəlaɪz] *vt US* = **paralyse**

paramedic [pærə'medɪk] *n* auxiliar *mf* sanitario(a)

parameter [pə'ræmɪtə(r)] *n* parámetro *m*

paramilitary [pærə'mɪlɪtərɪ] *adj* paramilitar

paramount ['pærəmaʊnt] *adj* **of p. importance** de suma importancia

paranoid ['pærənɔɪd] *adj & n* paranoico(a) *(m,f)*

paraphernalia [pærəfə'neɪlɪə] *n* parafernalia *f*

paraphrase ['pærəfreɪz] *vt* parafrasear

parasite ['pærəsaɪt] *n* parásito *m*

parasol ['pærəsɒl] *n* sombrilla *f*

paratrooper ['pærətru:p(r)] *n* paracaidista *mf*

parcel ['pɑ:səl] **1** *n* paquete *m*; **p. bomb** paquete bomba
   2 *vt* **to p. up** envolver, empaquetar

parched [pɑ:tʃt] *adj (land)* reseco(a); *(lips, mouth)* seco(a); *Fig* **to be p.** estar muerto(a) de sed

parchment ['pɑ:tʃmənt] *n* pergamino *m*

pardon ['pɑ:dən] **1** *n* perdón *m*; *Jur* indulto *m*; **I beg your p.** (Usted) perdone; **(I beg your) p.?** ¿cómo (dice)?
   2 *vt* perdonar; *Jur* indultar; **p. me!** ¡(Usted) perdone!

parent ['peərənt] *n* **parents** padres *mpl*

> *♪* Note that the Spanish word **pariente** is a false friend and is never a translation for the English word **parent**. In Spanish **pariente** means "relative, relation".

parental [pə'rentəl] *adj* paternal; **p. guidance** consejos *mpl* paternales

parenthesis [pə'renθɪsɪs] *n (pl* **parentheses** [pə'renθɪsi:z]) paréntesis *m inv*; **in p.** entre paréntesis

pariah [pə'raɪə] *n* paria *mf*

Paris ['pærɪs] *n* París

parish ['pærɪʃ] *n* parroquia *f*

Parisian [pə'rɪzɪən] *adj & n* parisino(a) *(m,f)*

parity ['pærɪtɪ] *n* igualdad *f*; *(of shares)* paridad *f*

park [pɑ:k] **1** *n* parque *m*
   2 *vt* estacionar, *Esp* aparcar

parking ['pɑ:kɪŋ] *n* estacionamiento *m*, *Esp* aparcamiento *m*; **no p.** *(sign)* prohibido estacionar *or Esp* aparcar, estacionamiento prohibido; *US* **p. lot** *Esp* aparcamiento *m*, *RP* playa *f* de estacionamiento, *Col* parqueadero *m*; **p. meter** parquímetro *m*; **p. space** estacionamiento *m*, sitio *m or* hueco *m* para estacionar

parliament ['pɑ:ləmənt] *n* parlamento *m*

parliamentary [pɑ:lə'mentərɪ] *adj* parlamentario(a)

parlour, *US* **parlor** ['pɑ:lə(r)] *n* salón *m*

parochial [pə'rəʊkɪəl] *adj* parroquial; *Pej (narrow-minded)* de miras estrechas

parody ['pærədɪ] *n* parodia *f*

parole [pə'rəʊl] *n* *Jur* libertad *f* condicional; **on p.** en libertad bajo palabra

parquet ['pɑ:keɪ] *n* **p. floor** suelo *m* de parqué

parrot ['pærət] *n* loro *m*, papagayo *m*

parry ['pærɪ] *vt* parar

parsimonious [pɑ:sɪ'məʊnɪəs] *adj* tacaño(a)

parsley ['pɑ:slɪ] *n* perejil *m*

parsnip ['pɑ:snɪp] *n* chirivía *f*

parson ['pɑ:sən] *n* cura *m*

part [pɑ:t] **1** *n* **(a)** *(portion, element)* parte *f*; *(episode)* capítulo *m*; *Tech* pieza *f*; **for the most p.** en la mayor parte **(b)** *Cin & Th* papel *m*; **to take p. in sth** participar en algo **(c)** *(place)* lugar *m*; **in these parts** por estos lugares **(d)** **for my p.** por mi parte; **to take sb's p.** tomar partido por algn **(e)** *US (in hair)* raya *f*, *Col, Méx, Ven* carrera *f*
   2 *adj (partial)* parcial
   3 *adv (partly)* en parte
   4 *vt (separate)* separar; **to p. one's hair** hacerse raya *or Col, Méx, Ven* carrera (en el pelo)
   5 *vi* separarse; *(say goodbye)* despedirse
   ▸ **part with** *vt insep* separarse de

partial ['pɑ:ʃəl] *adj* parcial; **to be p. to sth** ser aficionado(a) a algo

participant [pɑ:'tɪsɪpənt] *n* participante *mf*; *(in competition)* concursante *mf*

participate [pɑ:'tɪsɪpeɪt] *vi* participar **(in en)**

participation [pɑ:tɪsɪ'peɪʃən] *n* participación *f*

participle ['pɑ:tɪsɪpəl] *n* participio *m*

particle ['pɑ:tɪkəl] *n* partícula *f*

particular [pə'tɪkjʊlə(r)] **1** *adj* **(a)** *(special)* particular, especial; **in this p. case** en este caso concreto; **that p. person** esa persona en particular **(b)** *(fussy)* exigente
   2 *npl* **particulars** pormenores *mpl*; **to take down sb's particulars** anotar los datos personales de algn

particularly [pə'tɪkjʊləlɪ] *adv* particularmente, especialmente

parting ['pɑ:tɪŋ] **1** *n (separation)* separación *f*; *(farewell)* despedida *f*; *Br (in hair)* raya *f*, *Col, Méx, Ven* carrera *f*
   2 *adj* de despedida

partisan [pɑ:tɪ'zæn, 'pɑ:tɪzæn] **1** *n* *Mil* guerrillero(a) *m,f*; *(supporter)* partidario(a) *m,f*
   2 *adj (supporter)* a ultranza; *(of party)* partidista

partition [pɑ:'tɪʃən] **1** *n (wall)* tabique *m*; *(of country)* partición *f*
   2 *vt* dividir

partly ['pɑ:tlɪ] *adv* en parte

partner ['pɑ:tnə(r)] **1** *n* compañero(a) *m,f*; *(in dancing, tennis)* pareja *f*; *(hus-*

band) marido *m; (wife)* mujer *f; Com* socio(a) *m,f*
  2 *vt* acompañar

partnership ['pɑ:tnəʃɪp] *n (relationship)* vida *f* en común; *Com* sociedad *f*

partridge ['pɑ:trɪdʒ] *n* perdiz pardilla

part-time ['pɑ:t'taɪm] **1** *adj (work etc)* de tiempo parcial
  2 *adv* a tiempo parcial

party ['pɑ:tɪ] **1** *n* (a) *(celebration)* fiesta *f* (b) *(group)* grupo *m* (c) *Pol* partido *m;* **p. political broadcast** espacio *m* electoral
  2 *adj* de fiesta

pass [pɑ:s] **1** *n* (a) *(of mountain)* desfiladero *m* (b) *(permit)* permiso *m;* **bus p.** abono *m* de autobús (c) *Sport* pase *m*
  2 *vt* (a) *(go past) (person, place)* pasar junto a; *(frontier)* pasar; *(overtake)* adelantar; (b) *(exam, law)* aprobar; *Jur* **to p. sentence** dictar sentencia
  3 *vi* (a) *(go past)* pasar; *(procession)* desfilar; *(car)* adelantar; *Sport* hacer un pase; **we passed on the stairs** nos cruzamos en la escalera (b) *(in exam)* aprobar

▸ **pass away** *vi Euph* pasar a mejor vida
▸ **pass by** *vt sep* pasar de largo
  2 *vi* pasar
▸ **pass for** *vt insep* pasar por
▸ **pass off 1** *vt sep* hacer pasar; **to p. oneself off as sth** hacerse pasar por algo
  2 *vi (happen)* transcurrir
▸ **pass on 1** *vt sep (hand on)* transmitir
  2 *vi Euph* pasar a mejor vida
▸ **pass out** *vi (faint)* desmayarse; *Mil* graduarse
▸ **pass over** *vt insep* (a) *(aircraft)* volar por (b) *(disregard)* pasar por alto
▸ **pass up** *vt sep Fam (opportunity)* dejar pasar; *(offer)* rechazar

passable ['pɑ:səbəl] *adj (road)* transitable; *(acceptable)* pasable

passage ['pæsɪdʒ] *n* (a) *(alleyway)* callejón *m; (hallway)* pasillo *m* (b) *(movement)* tránsito *m; Naut* travesía *f* (c) *Mus & Lit* pasaje *m*

passageway ['pæsɪdʒweɪ] *n (interior)* pasillo *m; (exterior)* pasaje *m*

passbook ['pɑ:sbʊk] *n* libreta *f* de banco

passenger ['pæsɪndʒə(r)] *n* pasajero(a) *m,f*

passer-by [pɑ:sə'baɪ] *n (pl* **passers-by** [pɑ:səz'baɪ] *)* transeúnte *mf*

passing ['pɑ:sɪŋ] **1** *n* (a) *(of time)* transcurso *m;* **in p.** de pasada (b) *(of law)* aprobación *f*
  2 *adj* que pasa; *(glance)* rápido(a); *(thought)* pasajero(a)

passion ['pæʃən] *n* pasión *f;* **p. fruit** granadilla *f*

passionate ['pæʃənɪt] *adj* apasionado(a)

passive ['pæsɪv] *adj* pasivo(a); **p. smoker** fumador(a) pasivo(a)

Passover ['pɑ:səʊvə(r)] *n* Pascua *f* de los judíos

passport ['pɑ:spɔ:t] *n* pasaporte *m*

password ['pɑ:swɜ:d] *n* contraseña *f*

past [pɑ:st] **1** *n* pasado *m;* **in the p.** en el pasado; **to have a p.** tener antecedentes
  2 *adj* pasado(a); *(former)* anterior; **in the p. weeks** en las últimas semanas
  3 *adv* por delante; **to run p.** pasar corriendo
  4 *prep (beyond)* más allá de; *(more than)* más de; **he's p. forty** pasa de los cuarenta (años); *Br* **it's five p. ten** son las diez y cinco; *Fam* **to be p. it** estar muy carroza

pasta ['pæstə] *n* pasta *f,* pastas *fpl*

paste [peɪst] **1** *n* pasta *f,* *(glue)* engrudo *m*
  2 *vt (stick)* pegar; *(put paste on)* engomar

pastel ['pæstəl] *adj & n* pastel *(m)*

pasteurized ['pæstjəraɪzd] *adj* pasteurizado(a)

pastille ['pæstɪl] *n* pastilla *f*

pastime ['pɑ:staɪm] *n* pasatiempo *m*

pastor ['pɑ:stə(r)] *n* pastor *m*

pastoral ['pɑ:stərəl] *adj* pastoral

pastry ['peɪstrɪ] *n (dough)* pasta *f; (cake)* pastel *m,* Col, CSur torta *f*

pasture ['pɑ:stʃə(r)] *n* pasto *m*

pasty¹ ['pæstɪ] *n Culin* empanada *f,* pastel *m* de carne

pasty² ['peɪstɪ] *adj* (**pastier, pastiest**) *(complexion)* pálido(a)

pat [pæt] **1** *n (caress)* caricia *f; (tap)* palmadita *f; Fig* **to give sb a p. on the back** felicitar a algn
  2 *vt* acariciar; **to p. sb on the back** dar a algn una palmadita en la espalda

patch [pætʃ] *n (of material)* parche *m; Br (of land)* terreno *m; (of colour, light)* mancha *f; Br Fam* **to be going through a bad p.** estar pasando por una mala racha
▸ **patch up** *vt sep (wounded person)* hacer una cura *or Méx, RP* curación de urgencia a; **to p. things up** *(after argument)* limar asperezas

patchwork ['pætʃwɜ:k] **1** *n* labor *f* de retales
  2 *adj (quilt etc)* hecho(a) con retales distintos

patchy ['pætʃɪ] *adj* (**patchier, patchiest**) *(colour, performance)* desigual; *(knowledge)* incompleto(a)

pâté ['pæteɪ] *n* paté *m*

patent ['pætənt, *Br* 'peɪtənt] **1** *n Com* patente *f*
 2 *adj (obvious)* patente, evidente
 3 *vt Com* patentar

patently [*Br* 'peɪtəntlɪ *US* 'pætəntlɪ] *adv* **it is p. obvious** está clarísimo

paternal [pə'tɜːnəl] *adj* paternal; *(grandmother etc)* paterno(a)

paternity [pə'tɜːnɪtɪ] *n* paternidad *f*

path [pɑːθ] *n* camino *m*, sendero *m*; *(route)* ruta *f*; *(of missile)* trayectoria *f*

pathetic [pə'θetɪk] *adj (pitiful)* patético(a); *Fam (hopeless)* malísimo(a); **she was a p. sight** daba lástima verla

pathological [pæθə'lɒdʒɪkəl] *adj* patológico(a)

pathologist [pə'θɒlədʒɪst] *n* patólogo(a) *m,f*

pathology [pə'θɒlədʒɪ] *n* patología *f*

pathos ['peɪθɒs] *n* patetismo *m*

pathway ['pɑːθweɪ] *n* camino *m*, sendero *m*

patience ['peɪʃəns] *n* **(a)** *(quality)* paciencia *f*; **to lose one's p. with sb** perder la paciencia con algn **(b)** *Br Cards* solitario *m*

patient ['peɪʃənt] **1** *adj* paciente; **to be p. with sb** tener paciencia con algn
 2 *n Med* paciente *mf*

patio ['pætɪəʊ] *n* patio *m*

patriot ['pætrɪət, 'peɪtrɪət] *n* patriota *mf*

patriotic [pætrɪ'ɒtɪk] *adj (person)* patriota; *(speech, act)* patriótico(a)

patrol [pə'trəʊl] **1** *n* patrulla *f*; **p. car** coche *m* or*Am* carro *m* or*CSur* auto *m* patrulla
 2 *vt* patrullar por

patrolman [pə'trəʊlmən] *n US* policía *m*

patron ['peɪtrən] *n* **(a)** *(of charity)* patrocinador(a) *m,f*; *(of arts)* mecenas *m inv*; **p. saint** (santo(a)) patrón(ona) **(b)** *(customer)* cliente(a) *m,f* habitual

patronize ['pætrənaɪz] *vt* **(a)** *(arts)* fomentar; *(shop)* ser cliente(a) *m,f* habitual de; *(club etc)* frecuentar **(b)** *Pej (person)* tratar con condescendencia

patronizing ['pætrənaɪzɪŋ] *adj Pej* condescendiente

patter¹ ['pætə(r)] **1** *n (of rain)* repiqueteo *m*; *(of feet)* pasito *m*
 2 *vi (rain)* repiquetear; *(feet)* hacer ruido sordo

patter² ['pætə(r)] *n Fam* labia *f*; *(of salesman)* discursillo preparado

pattern ['pætən] *n Sewing* patrón *m*; *(design)* dibujo *m*; *(on material)* estampado *m*; *Fig (of behaviour)* modelo *m*

paunch [pɔːntʃ] *n* barriga *f*, panza *f*, *Chile* guata *f*

pauper ['pɔːpə(r)] *n* pobre *mf*

pause [pɔːz] **1** *n* pausa *f*; *(silence)* silencio *m*
 2 *vi* hacer una pausa; *(be silent)* callarse

pave [peɪv] *vt* pavimentar; *(with stones)* empedrar; *Fig* **to p. the way for sth/sb** preparar el terreno para algo/algn

pavement ['peɪvmənt] *n* **(a)** *Br (beside road)* acera *f*, *CSur* vereda *f*, *CAm, Méx* banqueta *f* **(b)** *US (roadway)* calzada *f*

pavilion [pə'vɪljən] *n* pabellón *m*; *Br Sport (changing rooms)* vestuarios *mpl*

paving ['peɪvɪŋ] *n (on road)* pavimento *m*; *(on floor)* enlosado *m*; *(with stones)* empedrado *m*; **p. stone** losa *f*

paw [pɔː] **1** *n (foot)* pata *f*; *(of cat)* garra *f*, *(of lion)* zarpa *f*
 2 *vt (of lion)* dar zarpazos a; *Pej (of person)* manosear, sobar

pawn¹ [pɔːn] *n (in chess)* peón *m*; *Fig* **to be sb's p.** ser el juguete de algn

pawn² [pɔːn] *vt* empeñar

pawnbroker ['pɔːnbrəʊkə(r)] *n* prestamista *mf*

pawnshop ['pɔːnʃɒp] *n* casa *f* de empeños

pay [peɪ] **1** *n (wages)* paga *f*, sueldo *m*; **p.** *Br* **packet** or*US* **envelope** sobre *m* de la paga; **p.** *Br* **rise** or*US* **raise** aumento *m* del sueldo; **p. slip** nómina *f*
 2 *vt (pt & pp* **paid)** **(a)** *(person, money, bill)* pagar; **to be** or **get paid** cobrar **(b)** *(attention)* prestar; *(homage)* rendir; *(visit)* hacer; **to p. sb a compliment** halagar a algn **(c)** *(be profitable for)* compensar
 3 *vi* **(a)** *(give payment)* pagar; **to p. for sth** pagar (por) algo **(b)** *(be profitable)* ser rentable
 ▸ **pay back** *vt sep* reembolsar; *Fig* **to p. sb back** vengarse de algn
 ▸ **pay in** *vt sep (money) Esp* ingresar, *Am* depositar
 ▸ **pay off** **1** *vt sep (debt)* liquidar; *(mortgage)* cancelar
 2 *vi (be successful)* dar resultado
 ▸ **pay out** *vt sep (spend)* gastar **(on** en)
 ▸ **pay up** *vi* pagar

payable ['peɪəbəl] *adj* pagadero(a)

pay-as-you-go ['peɪəzjʊ'gəʊ] *n (with mobile phone)* prepago *m*

payday ['peɪdeɪ] *n* día *m* de pago

PAYE [piːeɪwaɪ'iː] *n Br (abbr* **pay-as-you-earn)** retención *f* del impuesto sobre la renta

payee [peɪ'iː] *n* portador(a) *m,f*

payment ['peɪmənt] *n* pago *m*; *(of cheque)* cobro *m*; **advance p.** anticipo *m*; **down p.** entrada *f*; **monthly p.** mensualidad *f*

payoff ['peɪɒf] n Fam (reward) compensación f; (bribe) soborno m, Méx mordida f, RP coima f

pay-per-view ['peɪpə'vjuː] n pago m por visión

payroll ['peɪrəʊl] n nómina f

PC ['piː'siː] **1** n (**a**) Br (abbr Police Constable) agente mf de policía (**b**) (abbr personal computer) PC m
2 adj (abbr politically correct) políticamente correcto(a)

pc (abbr per cent) p.c.

PDA [piːdiː'eɪ] n (abbr personal digital assistant) PDA m, asistente m personal

PE ['piː'iː] n Sch (abbr physical education) educación física

pea [piː] n guisante m, Am arveja f, Carib, Méx chícharo m

peace [piːs] n paz f; (calm) tranquilidad f; at or in p. en paz; **p. and quiet** tranquilidad; **to make p.** hacer las paces; (of countries) firmar la paz

peaceable ['piːsəbəl] adj pacífico(a)

peaceful ['piːsfʊl] adj (demonstration) pacífico(a); (place) tranquilo(a)

peace-keeping ['piːskiːpɪŋ] adj pacificador(a); **p. forces** fuerzas fpl de pacificación

peach [piːtʃ] n melocotón m, Am durazno m

peacock ['piːkɒk] n pavo m real

peak [piːk] n (of cap) visera f; (of mountain) pico m; (summit) cima f; Fig cumbre f; **p. hours** horas fpl punta; **p. period** horas de mayor consumo; **p. season** temporada alta

peal [piːl] n (of bells) repique m; **p. of thunder** trueno m; **peals of laughter** carcajadas fpl

peanut ['piːnʌt] n cacahuete m, Andes, Carib, RP maní m, CAm, Méx cacahuate m; **p. butter** mantequilla f or crema f de cacahuete or Andes, Carib, RP maní or CAm, Méx cacahuate

pear [peə(r)] n pera f

pearl [pɜːl] n perla f

peasant ['pezənt] adj & n campesino(a) (m,f)

peat [piːt] n turba f; **p. bog** turbera f

pebble ['pebəl] n guijarro m; (small) china f

pecan [Br 'piːkən, US pɪ'kæn] n pacana f

peck [pek] **1** n (of bird) picotazo m; Fam (kiss) besito m
2 vt (of bird) picotear; Fam (kiss) dar un besito a
3 vi **to p. at one's food** picar la comida

pecking order ['pekɪŋɔːdə(r)] n Fig jerarquía f

peckish ['pekɪʃ] adj Br Fam **to be p.** tener un poco de hambre or Esp gusa

peculiar [pɪ'kjuːlɪə(r)] adj (odd) extraño(a); (particular) característico(a)

peculiarity [pɪkjuːlɪ'ærɪtɪ] n (oddity) rareza f; (characteristic) característica f, peculiaridad f

pedal ['pedəl] **1** n pedal m
2 vi pedalear

pedantic [pɪ'dæntɪk] adj pedante

peddle ['pedəl] vt & vi Com vender de puerta en puerta; **to p. drugs** traficar con drogas

peddler ['pedlə(r)] n (of drugs) traficante mf

pedestal ['pedɪstəl] n pedestal m; Fig **to put sb on a p.** poner a algn sobre un pedestal

pedestrian [pɪ'destrɪən] **1** n peatón(ona) m,f; **p. crossing** paso m de peatones
2 adj Pej prosaico(a)

pediatrician [piːdɪə'trɪʃən] n US = paediatrician

pedigree ['pedɪgriː] **1** n linaje m; (family tree) árbol genealógico; (of animal) pedigrí m
2 adj (animal) de raza

pedometer [pɪ'dɒmɪtə(r)] n podómetro m, cuentapasos m inv

pedophile ['piːdəʊfaɪl] n US = paedophile

pee [piː] Fam **1** n pis m
2 vi hacer pis

peek [piːk] **1** n ojeada f
2 vi **to p. at sth** mirar algo a hurtadillas

peel [piːl] **1** n (of fruit) piel f; (of orange, lemon) cáscara f
2 vt (fruit) pelar
3 vi (paint) desconcharse; (wallpaper) despegarse; (skin) pelarse

peeler ['piːlə(r)] n **potato p.** pelapatatas m inv

peelings ['piːlɪŋz] npl peladuras fpl, mondaduras fpl

peep¹ [piːp] n (sound) pío m

peep² [piːp] n (glance) ojeada f, (furtive look) mirada furtiva
2 vi **to p. at sth** echar una ojeada a algo; **to p. out from behind sth** dejarse ver detrás de algo

peephole ['piːphəʊl] n mirilla f

peer¹ [pɪə(r)] n (equal) igual mf; Br (noble) par m; **p. group** grupo parejo

peer² [pɪə(r)] vi mirar detenidamente; (shortsightedly) mirar con ojos de miope

peerage ['pɪərɪdʒ] n título m de nobleza

peeved [piːvd] *adj Fam* fastidiado(a), de mal humor

peevish ['piːvɪʃ] *adj* malhumorado(a)

peg [peg] **1** *n* clavija *f*; *(for coat, hat)* percha *f*
2 *vt (clothes)* tender; *(prices)* fijar

pejorative [pɪ'dʒɒrətɪv] *adj* peyorativo(a)

Pekinese [piːkə'niːz] *adj & n* pequinés(esa) *(m,f)*

Peking [piː'kɪŋ] *n* Pekín

pelican ['pelɪkən] *n* pelícano *m*; *Br* **p. crossing** paso *m* de peatones

pellet ['pelɪt] *n* bolita *f*; *(for gun)* perdigón *m*

pelt¹ [pelt] *n (skin)* pellejo *m*

pelt² [pelt] **1** *vt* **to p. sb with sth** tirar algo a algn
2 *vi Fam* **(a)** **it was pelting (down)** *(raining)* diluviaba, *Esp* caían chuzos de punta **(b)** **to p. along** *(rush)* correr a toda prisa

pelvis ['pelvɪs] *n* pelvis *f*

pen¹ [pen] **1** *n (for writing)* pluma *f* *(estilográfica)*; *(ballpoint)* bolígrafo *m*, *Chile* lápiz *m* (de pasta), *Col, Ecuad, Ven* esferográfica *f*, *Méx* pluma *f*, *RP* birome *f*
2 *vt* escribir

pen² [pen] **1** *n (enclosure)* corral *m*; *(for sheep)* redil *m*; *(for children)* corralito *m*
2 *vt* **to p. in** acorralar

penal ['piːnəl] *adj* penal

penalize ['piːnəlaɪz] *vt* castigar; *Sport* penalizar

penalty ['penltɪ] *n (punishment)* pena *f*; *Sport* castigo *m*; *Ftb* penalti *m*, *Am* penal; **to pay the p. for sth** cargar con las consecuencias de algo; **p. area** área *f* de castigo

penance ['penəns] *n* penitencia *f*

pence [pens] *pl of* **penny**

pencil ['pensɪl] *n* lápiz *m*; **p. case** estuche *m* de lápices; **p. sharpener** sacapuntas *m inv*

pendant ['pendənt] *n* colgante *m*

pending ['pendɪŋ] **1** *adj* pendiente
2 *prep* a la espera de; **p. a decision** *(until)* hasta que se tome una decisión

pendulum ['pendjʊləm] *n* péndulo *m*

penetrate ['penɪtreɪt] **1** *vt* penetrar; *Fig* adentrarse en
2 *vi* penetrar

penetrating ['penɪtreɪtɪŋ] *adj (look)* penetrante; *(mind)* perspicaz; *(sound)* agudo(a)

penfriend ['penfrend] *n* amigo(a) *m,f* por carta

penguin ['pengwɪn] *n* pingüino *m*

penicillin [penɪ'sɪlɪn] *n* penicilina *f*

peninsula [pɪ'nɪnsjʊlə] *n* península *f*

penis ['piːnɪs] *n* pene *m*

penitent ['penɪtənt] *adj Rel* penitente; *(repentant)* arrepentido(a)

penitentiary [penɪ'tenʃərɪ] *n US* cárcel *f*, penal *m*

penknife ['pennaɪf] *n* navaja *f*, cortaplumas *m inv*

penniless ['penɪlɪs] *adj* **to be p.** estar sin un centavo *or Esp* duro

penny ['penɪ] *n (pl* **pennies, pence)** *Br* penique *m*; *US* centavo *m*

penpal ['penpæl] *n US* = **penfriend**

pension ['penʃən] *n* pensión *f*; **retirement p.** jubilación *f*

pensioner ['penʃənə(r)] *n* jubilado(a) *m,f*

pensive ['pensɪv] *adj* pensativo(a)

pentagon ['pentəgɒn] *n US Pol* **the P.** el Pentágono

Pentecost ['pentɪkɒst] *n* Pentecostés *m*

penthouse ['penthaʊs] *n* ático *m*

pent-up ['pentʌp] *adj* reprimido(a)

penultimate [pɪ'nʌltɪmɪt] *adj* penúltimo(a)

people ['piːpəl] *npl* **(a)** *(as group)* gente *f*, *(individuals)* personas *fpl*; **many p.** mucha gente; **old p.'s home** asilo *m* de ancianos; **p. say that …** se dice que …; **some p.** algunas personas **(b)** *(citizens)* ciudadanos *mpl*; *(inhabitants)* habitantes *mpl*; **the p.** el pueblo **(c)** *(nation)* pueblo *m*, nación *f*

pep [pep] *n Fam* ánimo *m*, energía *f*; **p. talk** discurso *m* enardecedor
▸ **pep up** *vt sep Fam* animar

pepper ['pepə(r)] **1** *n (spice)* pimienta *f*; *(vegetable)* pimiento *m*, *Méx* chile *m*, *RP* ají *m*, *Col, Ven* pimentón *m*; **black p.** pimienta negra; *Br* **p. pot** pimentero *m*; **red/green p.** pimiento rojo/verde; **p. mill** molinillo *m* de pimienta
2 *vt Fig* **peppered with** salpicado(a) de

peppermint ['pepəmɪnt] *n* menta *f*; *(sweet)* pastilla *f* de menta

per [pɜː(r)] *prep* por; **five times p. week** cinco veces a la semana; **p. cent** por ciento; **p. day/annum** al *or* por día/año; **p. capita** per cápita

perceive [pə'siːv] *vt (see)* percibir

percentage [pə'sentɪdʒ] *n* porcentaje *m*

perceptible [pə'septəbəl] *adj (visible)* perceptible; *(sound)* audible; *(improvement)* sensible

perception [pə'sepʃən] *n* percepción *f*

perceptive [pə'septɪv] *adj* perspicaz

perch¹ [pɜːtʃ] *n (fish)* perca *f*

perch² [pɜːtʃ] **1** *n (for bird)* percha *f*
2 *vi (bird)* posarse (**on** en)

percolate ['pɜːkəleɪt] **1** *vt* filtrar; **percolated coffee** café *m* de cafetera
2 *vi* filtrarse

percolator ['pɜːkəleɪtə(r)] *n* cafetera *f*

percussion [pə'kʌʃən] *n* percusión *f*

perennial [pə'renɪəl] *adj Bot* perenne

perfect 1 *adj* ['pɜːfɪkt] perfecto(a); **he's a p. stranger to us** nos es totalmente desconocido; **p. tense** tiempo perfecto
2 *vt* [pə'fekt] perfeccionar

perfection [pə'fekʃən] *n* perfección *f*

perfectly ['pɜːfɪktlɪ] *adv* perfectamente; *(absolutely)* completamente

perforate ['pɜːfəreɪt] *vt* perforar

perforation [pɜːfə'reɪʃən] *n* perforación *f*; *(on stamps etc)* perforado *m*

perform [pə'fɔːm] **1** *vt (task)* ejecutar, realizar; *(piece of music)* interpretar; *Th* representar
2 *vi (machine)* funcionar; *Mus* tocar, interpretar; *Th* actuar

performance [pə'fɔːməns] *n (of task)* ejecución *f*, realización *f*; *Mus* interpretación *f*; *Th* representación *f*; *Sport* actuación *f*; *(of machine etc)* rendimiento *m*

performer [pə'fɔːmə(r)] *n Mus* intérprete *mf*; *Th* actor *m*, actriz *f*

perfume ['pɜːfjuːm] *n* perfume *m*

perfunctory [pə'fʌŋktərɪ] *adj* superficial

perhaps [pə'hæps, præps] *adv* tal vez, quizá(s), *Am* talvez

peril ['perɪl] *n (risk)* riesgo *m*; *(danger)* peligro *m*

perilous ['perɪləs] *adj (risky)* arriesgado(a); *(dangerous)* peligroso(a)

perilously ['perɪləslɪ] *adv* peligrosamente

perimeter [pə'rɪmɪtə(r)] *n* perímetro *m*

period ['pɪərɪəd] **1** *n* (**a**) *(stretch of time)* período *m*; *(stage)* etapa *f* (**b**) *Educ* clase *f* (**c**) *US (full stop)* punto *m* (**d**) *(menstruation)* regla *f*
2 *adj (dress, furniture)* de época

periodic [pɪərɪ'ɒdɪk] *adj* periódico(a)

periodical [pɪərɪ'ɒdɪkəl] **1** *adj* periódico(a)
2 *n* revista *f*

periodically [pɪərɪ'ɒdɪklɪ] *adv* de vez en cuando

peripheral [pə'rɪfərəl] **1** *adj* periférico(a)
2 *n Comput* unidad periférica

perish ['perɪʃ] *vi* perecer; *(material)* echarse a perder

perishable ['perɪʃəbəl] *adj* perecedero(a)

perjury ['pɜːdʒərɪ] *n* perjurio *m*

perk [pɜːk] *n Br Fam* extra *m*

▸ **perk up** *vi (person)* animarse; *(after illness)* reponerse

perky ['pɜːkɪ] *adj* (**perkier, perkiest**) animado(a), alegre

perm [pɜːm] **1** *n* permanente *f*
2 *vt* **to have one's hair permed** hacerse la permanente

permanent ['pɜːmənənt] *adj* permanente; *(address, job)* fijo(a)

permeate ['pɜːmɪeɪt] **1** *vt* impregnar
2 *vi* **to p. through sth** *(liquid)* filtrarse a través de algo; *(fear, suspicion)* extenderse por algo

permissible [pə'mɪsəbəl] *adj* admisible

permission [pə'mɪʃən] *n* permiso *m*

permissive [pə'mɪsɪv] *adj* permisivo(a)

permit 1 *n* ['pɜːmɪt] permiso *m*; *Com* licencia *f*
2 *vt* [pə'mɪt] **to p. sb to do sth** permitir a algn hacer algo

pernicious [pə'nɪʃəs] *adj* pernicioso(a)

perpendicular [pɜːpən'dɪkjələ(r)] **1** *adj* perpendicular; *(cliff)* vertical
2 *n* perpendicular *f*

perpetrate ['pɜːpɪtreɪt] *vt* cometer

perpetrator ['pɜːpɪtreɪtə(r)] *n* autor(a) *m,f*

perpetual [pə'petʃʊəl] *adj (noise)* continuo(a); *(arguing)* interminable; *(snow)* perpetuo(a)

perplex [pə'pleks] *vt* dejar perplejo(a)

perplexing [pə'pleksɪŋ] *adj* desconcertante

persecute ['pɜːsɪkjuːt] *vt* perseguir; *(harass)* acosar

persecution [pɜːsɪ'kjuːʃən] *n* persecución *f*; *(harassment)* acoso *m*

perseverance [pɜːsɪ'vɪərəns] *n* perseverancia *f*

persevere [pɜːsɪ'vɪə(r)] *vi* perseverar

Persian ['pɜːʒən] *adj* persa; **P. Gulf** golfo Pérsico

persist [pə'sɪst] *vi* empeñarse (**in** en)

persistence [pə'sɪstəns] *n* empeño *m*

persistent [pə'sɪstənt] *adj (person)* perseverante; *(smell etc)* persistente; *(continual)* constante

person ['pɜːsən] *n (pl people)* persona *f*; *(individual)* individuo *m*; **in p.** en persona

personable ['pɜːsənəbəl] *adj (handsome)* bien parecido(a); *(pleasant)* amable

personal ['pɜːsənəl] *adj* (**a**) *(private)* personal; *(friend)* íntimo(a); **p. computer** ordenador *m* *Am* computadora *f* personal; **p. column** anuncios *mpl* personales; **p. pronoun** pronombre *m* personal (**b**) *(in person)* en persona; **he will make a p. appearance** estará aquí en persona (**c**) *Pej (comment etc)* indiscreto(a)

personality [pɜːsəˈnælɪti] *n* personalidad *f*

personally [ˈpɜːsənəli] *adv (for my part)* personalmente; *(in person)* en persona

personify [pɜːˈsɒnɪfaɪ] *vt* personificar, encarnar

personnel [pɜːsəˈnel] *n* personal *m*

perspective [pəˈspektɪv] *n* perspectiva *f*

Perspex® [ˈpɜːspeks] *n* plexiglás® *m*

perspiration [pɜːspəˈreɪʃən] *n* transpiración *f*

perspire [pəˈspaɪə(r)] *vi* transpirar

persuade [pəˈsweɪd] *vt* persuadir; **to p. sb to do sth** persuadir a algn para que haga algo

persuasion [pəˈsweɪʒən] *n* persuasión *f*; *(opinion, belief)* credo *m*

persuasive [pəˈsweɪsɪv] *adj* persuasivo(a)

pert [pɜːt] *adj* pizpireta, coqueto(a)

pertain [pəˈteɪn] *vi* estar relacionado(a) (**to** con)

pertinent [ˈpɜːtɪnənt] *adj (relevant)* pertinente; **p. to** relacionado(a) con, a propósito de

perturbing [pəˈtɜːbɪŋ] *adj* inquietante

Peru [pəˈruː] *n* Perú

peruse [pəˈruːz] *vt Fml* leer

Peruvian [pəˈruːvɪən] *adj & n* peruano(a) *(m,f)* ·

pervade [pəˈveɪd] *vt (of smell)* penetrar; *(of light)* difundirse por; *Fig (of influence)* extenderse por

pervasive [pɜːˈveɪsɪv] *adj (smell)* penetrante; *(influence)* extendido(a)

perverse [pəˈvɜːs] *adj (wicked)* perverso(a); *(contrary)* contrario(a) a todo

perversion [*Br* pəˈvɜːʃən, *US* pəˈvɜːrʒən] *n Med & Psy* perversión *f*; *(of justice, truth)* desvirtuación *f* ⸱

pervert 1 *n* [ˈpɜːvɜːt] *Med* pervertido(a) *m,f* (sexual)
  2 *vt* [pəˈvɜːt] pervertir; *(justice, truth)* desvirtuar

pessimism [ˈpesɪmɪzəm] *n* pesimismo *m*

pessimist [ˈpesɪmɪst] *n* pesimista *mf*

pessimistic [pesɪˈmɪstɪk] *adj* pesimista

pest [pest] *n* (**a**) *Zool* animal nocivo; *Bot* planta nociva (**b**) *Fam (person)* pelma *mf*; *(thing)* lata *f*

pester [ˈpestə(r)] *vt* molestar, *Esp* incordiar

pesticide [ˈpestɪsaɪd] *n* pesticida *m*

pet [pet] **1** *n* (**a**) *(animal)* animal doméstico (**b**) *(favourite)* preferido(a)

m,f; Fam (addressing sb) cariño *m*
  2 *adj (favourite)* preferido(a)
  3 *vt* acariciar
  4 *vi Fam (sexually) Esp* darse *or* pegarse el lote, *Am* manosearse

petal [ˈpetəl] *n* pétalo *m*

peter [ˈpiːtə(r)] **1** *n US Fam (penis)* pilila *f*, pito *m*
  2 *vi* **to p. out** agotarse

petite [pəˈtiːt] *adj* menuda, chiquita

petition [pɪˈtɪʃən] *n* petición *f*

petrify [ˈpetrɪfaɪ] *vt Literary* petrificar; *Fig* **they were petrified** se quedaron de piedra

petrol [ˈpetrəl] *n Br* gasolina *f*, *RP* nafta *f*; **p. can** bidón *m* de gasolina *or RP* nafta; **p. pump** surtidor *m* de gasolina *or RP* nafta; **p. station** gasolinera *f*, estación *f* de servicio, *Andes* grifo *m*; **p. tank** depósito *m* de gasolina, *RP* tanque *m* de nafta

> ⚲ Note that the Spanish word **petróleo** is a false friend and is never a translation for the English word **petrol**. In Spanish **petróleo** means "oil, petroleum".

petroleum [pəˈtrəʊlɪəm] *n* petróleo *m*

petticoat [ˈpetɪkəʊt] *n* enaguas *fpl*

petty [ˈpeti] *adj* (**pettier, pettiest**) *(trivial)* insignificante; *(small-minded)* mezquino(a); **p. cash** dinero *m* para gastos pequeños; *Naut* **p. officer** sargento *m* de marina

petulant [ˈpetjʊlənt] *adj* malhumorado(a)

> ⚲ Note that the Spanish word **petulante** is a false friend and is never a translation for the English word **petulant**. In Spanish, **petulante** means "opinionated, arrogant".

pew [pjuː] *n* banco *m* de iglesia; *Br Fam* **take a p.!** ¡siéntate!

pewter [ˈpjuːtə(r)] *n* peltre *m*

phantom [ˈfæntəm] *adj & n* fantasma *(m)*

pharmaceutical [fɑːməˈsjuːtɪkəl] *adj* farmacéutico(a)

pharmacist [ˈfɑːməsɪst] *n* farmacéutico(a) *m,f*

pharmacy [ˈfɑːməsɪ] *n* farmacia *f*

phase [feɪz] **1** *n* fase *f*
  2 *vt* **to p. sth in/out** introducir/retirar algo progresivamente

PhD [piːeɪtʃˈdiː] *n* *(abbr* **Doctor of Philosophy)** *(person)* Doctor(a) *m,f* en Filosofía

pheasant [ˈfezənt] *n* faisán *m* (vulgar)

phenomena [fɪˈnɒmɪnə] *pl of* **phenomenon**

phenomenal [fɪ'nɒmɪnəl] *adj* fenomenal

phenomenon [fɪ'nɒmɪnən] *n (pl* **phenomena**) fenómeno *m*

phial [faɪəl] *n* frasco *m*

philanthropist [fɪ'lænθrəpɪst] *n* filántropo(a) *m,f*

philately [fɪ'lætəlɪ] *n* filatelia *f*

Philippines ['fɪlɪpi:nz] *npl* **the P.** las (Islas) Filipinas

philosopher [fɪ'lɒsəfə(r)] *n* filósofo(a) *m,f*

philosophical [fɪlə'sɒfɪkəl] *adj* filosófico(a)

philosophy [fɪ'lɒsəfɪ] *n* filosofía *f*

phlegm [flem] *n* flema *f*

phlegmatic [fleg'mætɪk] *adj* flemático(a)

phobia ['fəʊbɪə] *n* fobia *f*

phone [fəʊn] *n* = **telephone**

phonecard ['fəʊnka:d] *n* tarjeta telefónica

phone-in ['fəʊnɪn] *n Fam* = programa de radio o televisión con línea telefónica abierta

phonetic [fə'netɪk] **1** *adj* fonético(a)
  2 *n* **phonetics** fonética *f*

phoney ['fəʊnɪ] **1** *adj* (**phonier, phoniest**) *(thing)* falso(a); *(person)* farsante
  2 *n (person)* farsante *mf*

phosphate ['fɒsfeɪt] *n* fosfato *m*

photo ['fəʊtəʊ] *n* foto *f*

photocopier ['fəʊtəʊkɒpɪə(r)] *n* fotocopiadora *f*

photocopy ['fəʊtəʊkɒpɪ] **1** *n* fotocopia *f*
  2 *vt* fotocopiar

photogenic [fəʊtəʊ'dʒenɪk] *adj* fotogénico(a)

photograph ['fəʊtəgræf, 'fəʊtəgrɑ:f] **1** *n* fotografía *f;* **black and white/colour p.** fotografía en blanco y negro/en color
  2 *vt* fotografiar

photographer [fə'tɒgrəfə(r)] *n* fotógrafo(a) *m,f*

photography [fə'tɒgrəfɪ] *n* fotografía *f*

phrase [freɪz] **1** *n* frase *f;* **p. book** libro *m* de frases
  2 *vt* expresar

physical ['fɪzɪkəl] *adj* físico(a); **p. education** educación física

physically ['fɪzɪkəlɪ] *adv* físicamente; **p. handicapped** minusválido(a); **to be p. fit** estar en forma

physician [fɪ'zɪʃən] *n* médico(a) *m,f*

physicist ['fɪzɪsɪst] *n* físico(a) *m,f*

physics ['fɪzɪks] *n sing* física *f*

physiological [fɪzɪə'lɒdʒɪkəl] *adj* fisiológico(a)

physiology [fɪzɪ'ɒlədʒɪ] *n* fisiología *f*

physiotherapist [fɪzɪəʊ'θerəpɪst] *n* fisioterapeuta *mf*

physique [fɪ'zi:k] *n* físico *m*

pianist ['pɪənɪst] *n* pianista *mf*

piano [pɪ'ænəʊ] *n* piano *m*

piccolo ['pɪkələʊ] *n* flautín *m*

pick [pɪk] **1** *n* (a) *(tool)* pico *m*, piqueta *f* (b) **take your p.** *(choice)* elige el que quieras
  2 *vt* (a) *(choose)* escoger; *(team)* seleccionar (b) *(flowers, fruit)* recoger, *Esp* coger (c) *(scratch)* hurgar; **to p. one's nose** hurgarse la nariz (d) *(lock)* forzar
  3 *vi* **to p. at one's food** comer sin ganas

▸ **pick off** *vt sep (remove)* quitar (b) *(shoot)* matar uno a uno

▸ **pick on** *vt insep (persecute)* meterse con

▸ **pick out** *vt sep (choose)* elegir; *(distinguish)* distinguir; *(identify)* identificar

▸ **pick up 1** *vt sep* (a) *(object on floor)* recoger, *Esp* coger; *(telephone)* descolgar; **to p. oneself up** levantarse (b) *(collect)* recoger; *(shopping, person)* buscar; **to p. up speed** ganar velocidad (c) *(acquire)* conseguir; *(learn)* aprender
  2 *vi (improve)* mejorarse, ir mejorando; *(prices)* subir

pickaxe, *US* **pickax** ['pɪkæks] *n* piqueta *f*

picket ['pɪkɪt] **1** *n* piquete *m;* **p. line** piquete
  2 *vt* piquetear
  3 *vi* hacer piquete

pickle ['pɪkəl] **1** *n* (a) *Br (sauce)* = salsa agridulce a base de trocitos de fruta y verduras (b) *Fam (mess)* lío *m*, apuro *m*
  2 *vt Culin* conservar en adobo *or* escabeche; **pickled onions** cebollas *fpl* en vinagre

pick-me-up ['pɪkmɪʌp] *n Fam* reconstituyente *m*, tónico *m*

pickpocket ['pɪkpɒkɪt] *n* carterista *mf*

pick-up ['pɪkʌp] *n Br* **p. (arm)** *(on record player)* brazo *m;* **p. (truck)** furgoneta *f*

picnic ['pɪknɪk] **1** *n* comida *f* de campo, picnic *m*
  2 *vi* hacer una comida de campo

pictorial [pɪk'tɔ:rɪəl] *adj* ilustrado(a)

picture ['pɪktʃə(r)] **1** *n* (a) *(painting)* cuadro *m;* *(drawing)* dibujo *m;* *(portrait)* retrato *m;* *(photo)* foto *f;* *(illustration)* ilustración *f;* **p. book** libro ilustrado; **p. postcard** tarjeta *f* postal (b) *TV* imagen *f;* *Cin* película *f; Br* **to go to the pictures** ir al cine
  2 *vt (imagine)* imaginarse

picturesque [pɪktʃə'resk] *adj* pintoresco(a)

pie [paɪ] n (of fruit) tarta f, pastel m; (of meat, fish) empanada f, pastel, Col, CSur torta f; (pasty) empanadilla f

piece [piːs] n (**a**) (of food) pedazo m, trozo m; (of paper) trozo; (part) pieza f; **a p. of advice** un consejo; **a p. of news** una noticia; **to break sth into pieces** hacer algo pedazos; Fig **to go to pieces** perder el control (de sí mismo(a)) (**b**) Lit & Mus obra f, pieza f (**c**) (coin) moneda f (**d**) (in chess) pieza f; (in draughts) ficha f

▸ **piece together** vt sep (facts) reconstruir; (jigsaw) hacer

piecemeal ['piːsmiːl] adv (by degrees) poco a poco, a etapas; (unsystematically) desordenadamente

piecework ['piːswɜːk] n trabajo m a destajo; **to be on p.** trabajar a destajo

pier [pɪə(r)] n embarcadero m, muelle m; (promenade) = paseo de madera que entra en el mar

pierce [pɪəs] vt perforar; (penetrate) penetrar en

piercing ['pɪəsɪŋ] adj (sound etc) penetrante

piety ['paɪɪtɪ] n piedad f

pig [pɪg] n (**a**) (animal) cerdo m (**b**) Fam (greedy person) comilón(ona) m,f, glotón(ona) m,f, Am chancho m; (unpleasant person) cerdo(a) m,f, asqueroso(a) m,f, Am chancho m (**c**) Fam Pej (policeman) Esp madero m, Andes paco m, Méx tamarindo m, RP cana f

pigeon ['pɪdʒɪn] n paloma f; Culin & Sport pichón m

pigeonhole ['pɪdʒɪnhəʊl] n casilla f

piggy ['pɪgɪ] n **p. bank** hucha f, Am alcancía f (en forma de cerdito)

pigheaded [pɪg'hedɪd] adj terco(a), cabezota

piglet ['pɪglɪt] n cerdito m, lechón m

pigment ['pɪgmənt] n pigmento m

pigskin ['pɪgskɪn] n piel f de cerdo

pigsty ['pɪgstaɪ] n pocilga f

pigtail ['pɪgteɪl] n trenza f; (bullfighter's) coleta f

pike [paɪk] n (fish) lucio m

pilchard ['pɪltʃəd] n sardina f

pile¹ [paɪl] **1** n montón m

2 vt amontonar

3 vi Fam **to p. into** meterse atropella-damente en

▸ **pile up 1** vt sep (things) amontonar; (riches, debts) acumular

2 vi amontonarse

pile² [paɪl] n (on carpet) pelo m; **thick p.** pelo largo

piles [paɪlz] npl Med almorranas fpl, hemorroides fpl

pile-up ['paɪlʌp] n Aut choque m en cadena

pilfer ['pɪlfə(r)] vt & vi hurtar, Esp sisar

pilgrim ['pɪlgrɪm] n peregrino(a) m,f

pilgrimage ['pɪlgrɪmɪdʒ] n peregrinación f

pill [pɪl] n píldora f, pastilla f; **to be on the p.** estar tomando la píldora (anti-conceptiva)

pillage ['pɪlɪdʒ] vt & vi pillar, saquear

pillar ['pɪlə(r)] n pilar m, columna f; Br **p. box** buzón m

pillion ['pɪljən] n asiento trasero (de una moto)

pillow ['pɪləʊ] n almohada f

pillowcase ['pɪləʊkeɪs] n funda f de almohada

pilot ['paɪlət] **1** n piloto m

2 adj (trial) piloto inv; **p. light** piloto m; **p. scheme** proyecto piloto

3 vt pilotar

pimp [pɪmp] n proxeneta m, Esp chulo m, RP cafiolo m

pimple ['pɪmpəl] n grano m, espinilla f

PIN [pɪn] n (abbr **personal identification number**) **P. (number)** PIN m

pin [pɪn] **1** n (for sewing) alfiler m; (bolt) clavija f; Br (of electric plug) clavija f; (in bowling) bolo m; (brooch, badge) pin m; **pins and needles** hormigueo m

2 vt (on board) clavar con chinchetas; (garment etc) sujetar con alfileres; **to p. sb against a wall** tener a algn contra una pared; Fig **to p. one's hopes on sth** poner sus esperanzas en algo; Fam **to p. a crime on sb** endosar un delito a algn

▸ **pin down** vt sep Fig **to p. sb down** hacer que algn se comprometa

pinafore ['pɪnəfɔː(r)] n (apron) delantal m; **p. dress** Esp pichi m, CSur, Méx jumper m

pinball ['pɪnbɔːl] n flipper m, máquina f de petacos

pincers ['pɪnsəz] npl (on crab) pinzas fpl; (tool) tenazas fpl

pinch [pɪntʃ] **1** n (nip) pellizco m; Fig Br **at or US in a p.** en caso de apuro; **a p. of salt** una pizca de sal

2 vt pellizcar; Br Fam (steal) afanar, Esp levantar

3 vi (shoes) apretar

> 🖉 Note that the Spanish verb **pinchar** is a false friend and is never a translation for the English verb **to pinch**. In Spanish **pinchar** means "to prick, to puncture".

pincushion ['pɪnkʊʃən] n acerico m

pine¹ [paɪn] *n (tree)* pino *m*; **p. cone** piña *f*

pine² [paɪn] *vi* **to p. (away)** consumirse, morirse de pena; **to p. for sth/sb** echar de menos *or* añorar algo/a algn, *Am* extrañar algo/a algn

pineapple ['paɪnæpəl] *n* piña *f*, *RP* ananá *m*

ping [pɪŋ] *n* sonido metálico; *(of bullet)* silbido *m*

Ping-Pong® ['pɪŋpɒŋ] *n* ping-pong® *m*

pink [pɪŋk] **1** *n (colour)* rosa *m*; *Bot* clavel *m*
2 *adj (colour)* rosa *inv*; *Pol Fam* rojillo(a)

pinnacle ['pɪnəkəl] *n (of building)* pináculo *m*; *(of mountain)* cima *f*, pico *m*; *Fig (of success)* cumbre *f*

pinpoint ['pɪnpɔɪnt] *vt* señalar

pinstripe ['pɪnstraɪp] *adj* a rayas

pint [paɪnt] *n* pinta *f*; *Br Fam* **a p. (of beer)** una pinta (de cerveza)

pioneer [paɪə'nɪə(r)] **1** *n (settler)* pionero(a) *m,f*; *(forerunner)* precursor(a) *m,f*
2 *vt* ser pionero(a) en

pious ['paɪəs] *adj* piadoso(a), devoto(a); *Pej* beato(a)

pip¹ [pɪp] *n (seed)* pepita *f*

pip² [pɪp] *n (sound)* señal (corta); *(on dice)* punto *m*

pipe [paɪp] **1** *n* **(a)** *(tube)* conducto *m*, tubería *f*; *(of organ)* caramillo *m*; *Fam* **the pipes** *(bagpipes)* la gaita **(b)** *(for smoking)* pipa *f*; **p. cleaner** limpiapipas *m inv*; *Fig* **p. dream** sueño *m* imposible
2 *vt (water)* llevar por tubería; *(oil)* transportar por oleoducto; **piped music** hilo *m* musical

▸ **pipe down** *vi Fam* callarse

▸ **pipe up** *vi Fam* hacerse oír

pipeline ['paɪplaɪn] *n* tubería *f*, cañería *f*; *(for gas)* gasoducto *m*; *(for oil)* oleoducto *m*

piper ['paɪpə(r)] *n* gaitero(a) *m,f*

piping ['paɪpɪŋ] **1** *n (for water, gas etc)* tubería *f*, cañería *f*
2 *adj* **p. hot** bien caliente

piquant ['pi:kənt] *adj* picante; *(fig)* intrigante

pique [pi:k] **1** *n* enojo *m*
2 *vt* herir

pirate ['paɪrɪt] *n* pirata *m*; **p. edition** edición *f* pirata; **p. radio** emisora *f* pirata; **p. ship** barco *m* pirata

pirouette [pɪru'et] **1** *n* pirueta *f*
2 *vi* hacer piruetas

Pisces ['paɪsi:z] *n* Piscis *m inv*

piss [pɪs] *very Fam* **1** *vi* mear
2 *n* meada *f*

pissed [pɪst] *adj very Fam* **(a)** *Br (drunk)* *Esp, Méx* pedo *inv*, *Col* caído(a), *RP* en pedo **(b)** *US (angry)* cabreado(a)

pistachio [pɪs'tɑ:ʃɪəʊ] *n (nut)* pistacho *m*

pistol ['pɪstəl] *n* pistola *f*

piston ['pɪstən] *n* pistón *m*

pit¹ [pɪt] **1** *n* hoyo *m*; *(large)* hoya *f*; *(coal mine)* mina *f* de carbón; *Th* platea *f*; **the pits** *(in motor racing)* los boxes
2 *vt* **to p. one's wits against sb** medirse con algn

pit² [pɪt] *n (of cherry)* hueso *m*, pipo *m*, *RP* carozo *m*; *US (of peach, plum)* hueso, *RP* carozo *m*

pitch [pɪtʃ] **1** *vt* **(a)** *(throw)* lanzar, arrojar **(b)** *(tent)* armar
2 *n* **(a)** *Mus (of sound)* tono *m* **(b)** *esp Br Sport* campo *m*, cancha *f*

pitch-black [pɪtʃ'blæk], **pitch-dark** [pɪtʃ'dɑ:k] *adj* negro(a) como la boca del lobo

pitched [pɪtʃt] *adj* **p. battle** batalla *f* campal

pitcher ['pɪtʃə(r)] *n (container)* cántaro *m*, jarro *m*

pitchfork ['pɪtʃfɔ:k] *n* horca *f*

piteous ['pɪtɪəs] *adj* lastimoso(a)

pitfall ['pɪtfɔ:l] *n* dificultad *f*, obstáculo *m*

pith [pɪθ] *n (of orange)* piel blanca; *Fig* meollo *m*

pithy ['pɪθɪ] *adj* (**pithier, pithiest**) *Fig* contundente

pitiful ['pɪtɪfʊl] *adj (producing pity)* lastimoso(a); *(terrible)* lamentable

pitiless ['pɪtɪlɪs] *adj* despiadado(a), implacable

pittance ['pɪtəns] *n* miseria *f*

pity ['pɪtɪ] **1** *n* **(a)** *(compassion)* compasión *f*, piedad *f*; **to take p. on sb** compadecerse de algn **(b)** *(shame)* lástima *f*, pena *f*; **what a p.!** ¡qué pena!, ¡qué lástima!
2 *vt* compadecerse de; **I p. them** me dan pena

pivot ['pɪvət] **1** *n* pivote *m*
2 *vi* girar sobre su eje

pizza ['pi:tsə] *n* pizza *f*; **p. parlour** pizzería *f*

placard ['plækɑ:d] *n* pancarta *f*

placate [plə'keɪt] *vt* aplacar, apaciguar

place [pleɪs] **1** *n* **(a)** *(location)* sitio *m*, lugar *m*; **to be in/out of p.** estar en/fuera de su sitio; **to take p.** tener lugar **(b)** *(seat)* sitio *m*; *(on bus)* asiento *m*; *(at university)* plaza *m*; **to change places with sb** intercambiar el sitio con algn; **to take sb's p.** sustituir a algn **(c)** *(position on scale)* posición *f*; *(social position)* rango *m*; **in the first p.**

en primer lugar (**d**) *(house)* casa *f*; *(building)* lugar *m*; **we're going to his p.** vamos a su casa

2 *vt* (**a**) *(put)* poner, colocar; **to p. an order with sb** hacer un pedido a algn (**b**) *(face, person)* recordar; *(in job)* colocar en un empleo

placid ['plæsɪd] *adj* apacible

plagiarize ['pleɪdʒəraɪz] *vt* plagiar

plague [pleɪg] **1** *n (of insects)* plaga *f*; *Med* peste *f*

2 *vt* **to p. sb with requests** acosar a algn a peticiones

plaice [pleɪs] *n (pl* **plaice**) *(fish)* platija *f*

plaid [plæd, pleɪd] *n (cloth)* tejido *m* escocés

plain [pleɪn] **1** *adj* (**a**) *(clear)* claro(a), evidente; *Fig* **he likes p. speaking** le gusta hablar con franqueza (**b**) *(simple)* sencillo(a); *(chocolate)* amargo(a); *(flour)* sin levadura; **in p. clothes** vestido(a) de paisano; **the p. truth** la verdad lisa y llana (**c**) *(unattractive)* poco atractivo(a)

2 *n Geog* llanura *f*, llano *m*

plainly ['pleɪnlɪ] *adv* claramente; *(simply)* sencillamente; **to speak p.** hablar con franqueza

plaintiff ['pleɪntɪf] *n* demandante *mf*

plaintive ['pleɪntɪv] *adj* lastimero(a)

plait [plæt] **1** *n* trenza *f*

2 *vt* trenzar

plan [plæn] **1** *n (scheme)* plan *m*, proyecto *m*; *(drawing)* plano *m*

2 *vt* (**a**) *(for future)* planear, proyectar; *(economy)* planificar (**b**) *(intend)* pensar, tener la intención de; **it wasn't planned** no estaba previsto

3 *vi* hacer planes; **to p. on doing sth** tener la intención de hacer algo

plane¹ [pleɪn] **1** *n* (**a**) *Math* plano *m*; *Fig* nivel *m* (**b**) *Fam Av* avión *m*

2 *adj Geom* plano(a)

3 *vi (glide)* planear

plane² [pleɪn] *n (tool)* cepillo *m*

2 *vt* cepillar

plane³ [pleɪn] *n Bot* **p. (tree)** plátano *m*

planet ['plænɪt] *n* planeta *m*

plank [plæŋk] *n* tabla *f*, tablón *m*

planner ['plænə(r)] *n* planificador(a) *m,f*

planning ['plænɪŋ] *n* planificación *f*; **family p.** planificación familiar; *Br* **p. permission** licencia *f* de obras

plant¹ [plɑːnt] **1** *n* planta *f*

2 *vt (flowers)* plantar; *(seeds)* sembrar; *(bomb)* colocar

plant² [plɑːnt] *n (factory)* planta *f*, fábrica *f*; *(machinery)* maquinaria *f*

plantation [plæn'teɪʃən] *n* plantación *f*

plaque [plæk] *n* placa *f*; *(on teeth)* sarro *m*

plasma ['plæzmə] *n* plasma *m*; *Comput* **p. screen** pantalla *f* de plasma

plaster ['plɑːstə(r)] **1** *n Constr* yeso *m*; *Med* escayola *f*; *Br (sticking)* **p.** tirita® *f*, *Am* curita *f*; **p. of Paris** yeso mate

2 *vt Constr* enyesar; *Fig (cover)* cubrir (**with** de)

plastered ['plɑːstəd] *adj Fam* borracho(a), trompa

plasterer ['plɑːstərə(r)] *n* yesero(a) *m,f*

plastic ['plæstɪk] **1** *n* plástico *m*

2 *adj (cup, bag)* de plástico; **p. surgery** cirugía plástica

Plasticine® ['plæstɪsiːn] *n* plastilina® *f*

plate [pleɪt] **1** *n* (**a**) *(for food)* plato *m* (**b**) *(sheet)* placa *f*; **gold p.** chapa *f* de oro; **p. glass** vidrio cilindrado *m* (**c**) *(in book)* grabado *m*, lámina *f*

2 *vt* chapar

plateau ['plætəʊ] *n* meseta *f*

platform ['plætfɔːm] *n* (**a**) *(raised flat surface)* plataforma *f*; *(stage)* estrado *m*; *(at meeting)* tribuna *f* (**b**) *Rail* andén *m*; **p. ticket** billete *m* de andén (**c**) *Pol (programme)* programa *m*

platinum ['plætɪnəm] *n* platino *m*

platitude ['plætɪtjuːd] *n* lugar *m* común, tópico *m*

platoon [plə'tuːn] *n Mil* pelotón *m*

platter ['plætə(r)] *n* fuente *f*

plausible ['plɔːzəbəl] *adj* plausible

play [pleɪ] **1** *vt* (**a**) *(game)* jugar a; *(team)* jugar contra (**b**) *(instrument, tune)* tocar; **to p. a CD** poner un CD *(in play, film)* interpretar; *Fig* **to p. a part in sth** participar en algo

2 *vi* (**a**) *(children)* jugar (**with** con); *(animals)* juguetear (**b**) *Sport* jugar; *Fig* **to p. for time** tratar de ganar tiempo (**c**) *(joke)* bromear (**d**) *Mus* tocar; *(instrument)* sonar

3 *n* (**a**) *Th* obra *f* de teatro (**b**) *Sport* juego *m* (**c**) *Tech & Fig (movement)* juego *m*; **a p. on words** un juego de palabras

▸ **play around** *vi (waste time)* gandulear; *(be unfaithful)* tener líos

▸ **play down** *vt sep* minimizar, quitar importancia a

▸ **play on** *vt insep (take advantage of)* aprovecharse de; *(nerves etc)* exacerbar

▸ **play up 1** *vt sep (annoy)* dar la lata a, fastidiar

2 *vi Br (child, injury etc)* dar guerra

playboy ['pleɪbɔɪ] *n* playboy *m*

player ['pleɪə(r)] *n Sport* jugador(a) *m,f*; *Mus* músico(a) *m,f*; *Th (man)* actor *m*; *(woman)* actriz *f*

playful ['pleɪfʊl] *adj* juguetón(ona)

playground ['pleɪɡraʊnd] *n* patio *m* de recreo

playgroup ['pleɪɡruːp] *n* jardín *m* de infancia

playing ['pleɪɪŋ] *n* juego *m*; **p. card** carta *f*, naipe *m*; **p. field** campo *m* de deportes

playmate ['pleɪmeɪt] *n* compañero(a) *m,f* de juego

play-off ['pleɪɒf] *n Sport* partido *m* de desempate

playpen ['pleɪpen] *n* corralito *m or* parque *m* (de niños)

playschool ['pleɪskuːl] *n* escuela *f* infantil, guardería *f*

plaything ['pleɪθɪŋ] *n* juguete *m*

playtime ['pleɪtaɪm] *n* (*at school*) recreo *m*

playwright ['pleɪraɪt] *n* dramaturgo(a) *m,f*

PLC, plc [piːel'siː] *n Br* (*abbr* **public limited company**) ≃ S.A.

plea [pliː] *n* (**a**) (*request*) petición *f*, súplica *f*, *Am* pedido *m*; (*excuse*) pretexto *m*, disculpa *f* (**b**) *Jur* alegato *m*

plead [pliːd] **1** *vt* (**a**) *Jur & Fig* **to p. sb's cause** defender la causa de algn (**b**) *to p.* **ignorance** (*give as excuse*) alegar ignorancia

2 *vi* (**a**) (*beg*) rogar, suplicar; **to p. with sb to do sth** suplicar a algn que haga algo (**b**) *Jur* **to p. guilty/not guilty** declararse culpable/inocente

pleasant ['plezənt] *adj* agradable

pleasantry ['plezəntrɪ] *n* cumplido *m*

please [pliːz] **1** *vt* (*give pleasure to*) agradar, complacer; (*satisfy*) satisfacer; *Fam* **p. yourself** como quieras; **easy/hard to p.** poco/muy exigente

2 *vi* (*give pleasure*) complacer, agradar

3 *adv* por favor; **may I? – p. do** ¿me permite? – desde luego; **p. do not smoke** (*sign*) se ruega no fumar; **yes, p.** sí, por favor

pleased [pliːzd] *adj* (*happy*) contento(a); (*satisfied*) satisfecho(a); **p. to meet you!** ¡encantado(a)!, ¡mucho gusto!; **to be p. about sth** alegrarse de algo

pleasing ['pliːzɪŋ] *adj* (*pleasant*) agradable, grato(a); (*satisfactory*) satisfactorio(a)

pleasure ['pleʒə(r)] *n* placer *m*; **it's a p. to talk to him** da gusto hablar con él; **to take great p. in doing sth** disfrutar mucho haciendo algo; **with p.** con mucho gusto

pleat [pliːt] **1** *n* pliegue *m*

2 *vt* hacer pliegues en

pledge [pledʒ] **1** *n* promesa *f*, (*token of love etc*) señal *f*; (*guarantee*) prenda *f*

2 *vt* (*promise*) prometer; (*pawn*) empeñar

plentiful ['plentɪfʊl] *adj* abundante

plenty ['plentɪ] *n* abundancia *f*; **p. of books** muchos libros; **p. of time** tiempo de sobra; **we've got p.** tenemos de sobra

Plexiglas® ['pleksɪɡlɑːs] *n US* plexiglás® *m*

pliable ['plaɪəbəl] *adj* flexible

pliers ['plaɪəz] *npl* alicates *mpl*, tenazas *fpl*

plight [plaɪt] *n* situación *f* grave

plimsolls ['plɪmsəlz] *npl Br* zapatos *mpl* de tenis

plinth [plɪnθ] *n* plinto *m*

plod [plɒd] *vi* andar con paso pesado; *Fig* **to p. on** perseverar; *Fig* **to p. through a report** estudiar laboriosamente un informe

plodder ['plɒdə(r)] *n* trabajador(a) *m,f*/ estudiante *mf* tenaz

plonk¹ [plɒŋk] *vt esp Br Fam* dejar caer

plonk² [plɒŋk] *n Br Fam* (*cheap wine*) vino *m* peleón

plot¹ [plɒt] **1** *n* (**a**) (*conspiracy*) complot *m* (**b**) *Th & Lit* (*story*) argumento *m*, trama *f*

2 *vt* (**a**) (*course, route*) trazar (**b**) (*scheme*) fraguar

3 *vi* conspirar, tramar

plot² [plɒt] *n Agr* terreno *m*; (*for building*) solar *m*; **vegetable p.** campo *m* de hortalizas

plough [plaʊ] **1** *n* arado *m*

2 *vt* arar

3 *vi* **to p. into sth** chocar contra algo

▸ **plough back** *vt sep* (*profits*) reinvertir

plow [plaʊ] *n, vt & vi US =* **plough**

ploy [plɔɪ] *n* estratagema *f*

pluck [plʌk] **1** *vt* (**a**) (*hair, feathers*) arrancar (**out of** de) (**b**) (*flower*) arrancar (**c**) (*chicken*) desplumar (**d**) (*guitar*) puntear

2 *n* (*courage*) valor *m*, ánimo *m*

▸ **pluck up** *vt sep* **to p. up courage** armarse de valor

plucky ['plʌkɪ] *adj* (**pluckier, pluckiest**) valiente

plug [plʌɡ] **1** *n* (**a**) (*in bath etc*) tapón *m* (**b**) *Elec* enchufe *m*, clavija *f*; **two-/three-pin p.** clavija bipolar/tripolar

2 *vt* (**a**) (*hole*) tapar (**b**) *Fam* (*publicize*) dar publicidad a; (*idea etc*) hacer hincapié en

▸ **plug in** *vt sep* enchufar

plughole ['plʌɡhəʊl] *n* desagüe *m*

plum [plʌm] **1** *n* (*fruit*) ciruela *f*

2 *adj* **a p. job** *Esp* un chollo *or Méx* churro (de trabajo), *RP* un laburazo

plumage ['pluːmɪdʒ] *n* plumaje *m*

plumb [plʌm] **1** adv Fam **p. in the middle** justo en medio; US **he's p. crazy** está completamente loco

2 vt Fig **to p. the depths** tocar fondo

plumber ['plʌmə(r)] n fontanero(a) m,f, Méx, RP, Ven plomero(a) m,f

plumbing ['plʌmɪŋ] n (occupation) fontanería f, Méx, RP, Ven plomería f; (system) tuberías fpl, cañerías fpl

plume [pluːm] n penacho m

plummet ['plʌmɪt] vi (bird, plane) desplomarse, caer en picado or Am picada; Fig (prices) bajar vertiginosamente; (morale) caer a plomo

plump¹ [plʌmp] adj (person) relleno(a); (baby) rechoncho(a)

▸ **plump down** vt sep dejar caer

▸ **plump up** vt sep (cushions) ahuecar

plump² [plʌmp] vi **to p. for sth** optar por algo

plunder ['plʌndə(r)] **1** vt saquear

2 n (action) saqueo m, pillaje m; (loot) botín m

plunge [plʌndʒ] **1** vt (immerse) sumergir; (thrust) arrojar

2 vi (dive) lanzarse, zambullirse; Fig (fall) caer, hundirse; (prices) desplomarse

3 n (dive) zambullida f; Fig (fall) desplome m; **to take the p.** dar el paso decisivo

plunger ['plʌndʒə(r)] n Tech émbolo m; (for pipes) desatascador m

pluperfect [pluːˈpɜːfɪkt] n pluscuamperfecto m

plural ['plʊərəl] adj & n plural (m)

plus [plʌs] **1** prep **three p. four makes seven** tres más cuatro hacen siete

2 n Math signo m más; Fig (advantage) ventaja f

plush [plʌʃ] **1** n felpa f

2 adj Fam lujoso(a), Esp muy puesto(a)

plutonium [pluːˈtəʊnɪəm] n plutonio m

ply [plaɪ] **1** vt **to p. one's trade** ejercer su oficio; **to p. sb with drinks** no parar de ofrecer copas a algn

2 vi (ship) ir y venir; **to p. for hire** ir en busca de clientes

plywood ['plaɪwʊd] n madera contrachapada

PM [piːˈem] n Br (abbr **Prime Minister**) primer(a) ministro(a) m,f

p.m. [piːˈem] (abbr **post meridiem**) después del mediodía; **at 2 p.m.** a las dos de la tarde

PMT [piːemˈtiː] n (abbr **premenstrual tension**) tensión f premenstrual

pneumatic [njʊˈmætɪk] adj neumático(a)

pneumonia [njuːˈməʊnɪə] n pulmonía f

PO [piːˈəʊ] n (abbr **Post Office**) oficina f de correos; **PO Box** apartado m de correos, CAm, Carib, Méx casilla f postal, Andes, RP casilla de correos

poach¹ [pəʊtʃ] vt (a) **to p. fish/game** pescar/cazar furtivamente (b) Fam Fig (steal) birlar

poach² [pəʊtʃ] vt Culin (egg) escalfar; (fish) hervir

poacher ['pəʊtʃə(r)] n pescador/cazador furtivo

pocket ['pɒkɪt] **1** n (a) (in trousers, jacket) bolsillo m, CAm, Méx, Perú bolsa f; Fig **to be £10 in/out of p.** salir ganando/perdiendo 10 libras; **p. money** dinero m para gastos (b) (of air) bolsa f (c) (of resistance) foco m

2 vt (money) embolsarse

pocketbook ['pɒkɪtbʊk] n US (wallet) cartera f; (handbag) Esp bolso m, Col, CSur cartera f, Méx bolsa f

pocketknife ['pɒkɪtnaɪf] n navaja f

pod [pɒd] n vaina f

podcast ['pɒdkɑːst] n podcast m

podgy ['pɒdʒɪ] adj (podgier, podgiest) Br gordinflón(ona), regordete

podiatrist [pəˈdaɪətrɪst] n US pedicuro(a) m,f

podium ['pəʊdɪəm] n podio m

poem ['pəʊɪm] n poema m

poet ['pəʊɪt] n poeta mf

poetic [pəʊˈetɪk] adj poético(a)

poetry ['pəʊɪtrɪ] n poesía f

poignant ['pɔɪnjənt] adj conmovedor(a)

point [pɔɪnt] **1** n (a) (sharp end) punta f (b) (place) punto m; Fig **p. of no return** punto sin retorno (c) (quality) **good/bad p.** cualidad buena/mala (d) (moment) **at that p.** en aquel momento; **to be on the p. of doing sth** estar a punto de hacer algo (e) (score) punto m, tanto m (f) (in argument) punto m; **I take your p.** entiendo lo que quieres decir (g) (purpose) propósito m; **I don't see the p.** no veo el sentido; **there's no p. in going** no merece la pena ir; **to come to the p.** llegar al meollo de la cuestión (h) (on scale) punto m; (in share index) entero m; **six p. three** seis coma tres (i) Geog punta f (j) **points** Aut platinos mpl; Br Rail agujas fpl

2 vt (way etc) señalar, indicar; **to p. a gun at sb** apuntar a algn con una pistola

3 vi señalar, indicar; **to p. at sth/sb** señalar algo/a algn con el dedo

▸**point out** *vt sep* indicar, señalar; *(mention)* hacer resaltar

point-blank ['pɔɪnt'blæŋk] **1** *adj* a quemarropa; *(refusal)* rotundo(a)
  2 *adv (shoot)* a quemarropa; *(refuse)* rotundamente

pointed ['pɔɪntɪd] *adj (sharp)* puntiagudo(a); *Fig (comment)* intencionado(a); *(cutting)* mordaz

pointedly ['pɔɪntɪdlɪ] *adv Fig (significantly)* con intención; *(cuttingly)* con mordacidad

pointer ['pɔɪntə(r)] *n* (**a**) *(indicator)* indicador *m*, aguja *f*; *(for map)* puntero *m* (**b**) *(dog)* perro *m* de muestra

pointless ['pɔɪntlɪs] *adj* sin sentido

poise [pɔɪz] **1** *n (bearing)* porte *m*; *(self-assurance)* aplomo *m*
  2 *vt Fig* **to be poised to do sth** estar listo(a) para hacer algo

poison ['pɔɪzən] **1** *n* veneno *m*
  2 *vt* envenenar

poisoning ['pɔɪzənɪŋ] *n* envenenamiento *m*; *(by food etc)* intoxicación *f*

poisonous ['pɔɪzənəs] *adj (plant, snake)* venenoso(a); *(gas)* tóxico(a); *Fig (rumour)* pernicioso(a)

poke [pəʊk] *vt (with finger or stick)* dar con la punta del dedo/del bastón a; **to p. one's head out** asomar la cabeza; **to p. the fire** atizar el fuego

▸**poke about, poke around** *vi* fisgonear, hurgar

▸**poke out** *vt sep (eye)* sacar

poker¹ ['pəʊkə(r)] *n (for fire)* atizador *m*

poker² ['pəʊkə(r)] *n Cards* póquer *m*

poker-faced ['pəʊkəfeɪst] *adj Fam* de cara impasible

poky ['pəʊkɪ] *adj* (**pokier, pokiest**) *Fam Pej* minúsculo(a); **a p. little room** un cuartucho

Poland ['pəʊlənd] *n* Polonia

polar ['pəʊlə(r)] *adj* polar; **p. bear** oso *m* polar

Pole [pəʊl] *n* polaco(a) *m,f*

pole¹ [pəʊl] *n* palo *m*; **p. vault** salto *m* con pértiga

pole² [pəʊl] *n Geog* polo *m*; *Fig* **to be poles apart** ser polos opuestos

police [pə'liːs] **1** *npl* policía *f*; **p. car** coche *m or Am* carro *m or CSur* auto *m* de policía; *Br* **p. constable** policía *m or* Esp guardia *m* de policía; **p. force** cuerpo *m* de policía; **p. record** antecedentes *mpl* penales; **p. state** estado *m* policial; **p. station** comisaría *f*
  2 *vt* vigilar

policeman [pə'liːsmən] *n* policía *m*

policewoman [pə'liːswʊmən] *n* (mujer *f*) policía *f*

policy ['pɒlɪsɪ] *n Pol* política *f*; *(of company)* norma *f*, principio *m*; *Ins* póliza *f* (de seguros)

polio ['pəʊlɪəʊ] *n* poliomielitis *f*

Polish ['pəʊlɪʃ] **1** *adj* polaco(a)
  2 *n* (**a**) **the P.** los polacos (**b**) *(language)* polaco *m*

polish ['pɒlɪʃ] **1** *vt* pulir; *(furniture)* encerar; *(shoes)* limpiar; *(silver)* sacar brillo a
  2 *n* (**a**) *(for furniture)* cera *f*; *(for shoes)* betún *m*; *(for nails)* esmalte *m* (**b**) *(shine)* brillo *m*; *Fig (refinement)* refinamiento *m*

▸**polish off** *vt sep Fam (work)* despachar; *(food)* zamparse

▸**polish up** *vt sep Fig* perfeccionar

polished ['pɒlɪʃt] *adj Fig (manners)* refinado(a); *(style)* pulido(a); *(performance)* impecable

polite [pə'laɪt] *adj* educado(a)

politeness [pə'laɪtnɪs] *n* educación *f*

politic ['pɒlɪtɪk] *adj* prudente

political [pə'lɪtɪkəl] *adj* político(a)

politically [pə'lɪtɪklɪ] *adv* políticamente; **p. correct** políticamente correcto(a)

politician [pɒlɪ'tɪʃən] *n* político(a) *m,f*

politics ['pɒlɪtɪks] *n sing* política *f*

polka ['pɒlkə] *n (dance)* polca *f*; **p. dot** lunar *m*

poll [pəʊl] **1** *n* (**a**) *(voting)* votación *f*; **the polls** las elecciones; **to go to the polls** acudir a las urnas (**b**) *(survey)* encuesta *f*
  2 *vt (votes)* obtener

pollen ['pɒlən] *n* polen *m*

polling ['pəʊlɪŋ] *n* votación *f*; **p. booth** cabina *f* electoral; **p. station** colegio *m* electoral

pollute [pə'luːt] *vt* contaminar

pollution [pə'luːʃən] *n* contaminación *f*, polución *f*; **environmental p.** contaminación ambiental

polo ['pəʊləʊ] *n Sport* polo *m*; *Br* **p. neck (sweater)** suéter *m or Esp* jersey *m or Col* saco *m or RP* pulóver *m* de cuello alto *or* de cisne

polyester [pɒlɪ'estə(r)] *n* poliéster *m*

polyethylene [pɒlɪ'eθɪliːn] *n US* polietileno *m*

polymer ['pɒlɪmə(r)] *n Chem* polímero *m*

Polynesia [pɒlɪ'niːʒɪə] *n* Polinesia

polystyrene [pɒlɪ'staɪriːn] *n* poliestireno *m*

polythene ['pɒlɪθiːn] *n Br* polietileno *m*

polyunsaturated [pɒlɪʌn'sætjʊreɪtɪd] *adj* poliinsaturado(a)

pomegranate ['pɒmɪgrænɪt] *n* granada *f*

pomp [pɒmp] *n* pompa *f*
pompom ['pɒmpɒm], **pompon** ['pɒm-pɒn] *n* borla *f*, pompón *m*
pompous ['pɒmpəs] *adj* (*person*) presumido(a); (*speech*) rimbombante
pond [pɒnd] *n* estanque *m*
ponder ['pɒndə(r)] **1** *vt* considerar
 2 *vi* **to p. over sth** meditar sobre algo
ponderous ['pɒndərəs] *adj* pesado(a)
pong [pɒŋ] *n Br Fam* tufo *m*
pontoon¹ [pɒn'tu:n] *n Constr* pontón *m*
pontoon² [pɒn'tu:n] *n Br Cards* veintiuna *f*
pony ['pəʊnɪ] *n* poney *m*
ponytail ['pəʊnɪteɪl] *n* cola *f* de caballo
poo [pu:] *n Fam* caca *f*
poodle ['pu:dəl] *n* caniche *m*
poof [puf] *n Br Fam Pej* maricón *m*, marica *m*
pool¹ [pu:l] *n* (*of water, oil etc*) charco *m*; (*pond*) estanque *m*; (*in river*) pozo *m*; (**swimming**) **p.** piscina *f*, *Méx* alberca *f*, *RP* pileta *f*
pool² [pu:l] **1** *n* (**a**) (*common fund*) fondo *m* común (**b**) **typing p.** servicio *m* de mecanografía (**c**) *US* (*snooker*) billar americano (**d**) *Br* **the pools** las quinielas *fpl*, *Arg* el Prode, *Col, CRica* el totogol
 2 *vt* (*funds*) reunir; (*ideas, resources*) juntar
poor [pʊə(r)] **1** *adj* pobre; (*quality*) malo(a); *Fam* **you p. thing!** ¡pobrecito!
 2 *npl* **the p.** los pobres
poorly ['pʊəlɪ] **1** *adv* (*badly*) mal
 2 *adj* (**poorlier, poorliest**) (*ill*) mal, malo(a)
pop [pɒp] **1** *vt* (*burst*) hacer reventar; (*cork*) hacer saltar
 2 *vi* (**a**) (*burst*) reventar; (*cork*) saltar (**b**) *Fam* **I'm just popping over to Ian's** voy un momento a casa de Ian
 3 *n* (**a**) (*noise*) pequeña explosión (**b**) *Fam* (*drink*) gaseosa *f* (**c**) *US Fam* (*father*) papá *m* (**d**) *Fam Mus* música *f* pop; **p. singer** cantante *mf* pop
▸ **pop in** *vi Fam* entrar un momento, pasar
popcorn ['pɒpkɔːn] *n* palomitas *fpl* de maíz, *RP* pochoclo *m*
Pope [pəʊp] *n* **the P.** el Papa
poplar ['pɒplə(r)] *n* álamo *m*
poppy ['pɒpɪ] *n* amapola *f*
Popsicle® ['pɒpsɪkəl] *n US* polo *m*
populace ['pɒpjʊləs] *n* (*people*) pueblo *m*
popular ['pɒpjʊlə(r)] *adj* popular; (*fashionable*) de moda; (*common*) corriente
popularity [pɒpjʊ'lærɪtɪ] *n* popularidad *f*
popularize ['pɒpjʊləraɪz] *vt* popularizar

populate ['pɒpjʊleɪt] *vt* poblar
population [pɒpjʊ'leɪʃən] *n* población *f*; **the p. explosion** la explosión demográfica
pop-up menu ['pɒpʌp'menju:] *n Comput* menú *m* desplegable
porcelain ['pɔːsəlɪn] *n* porcelana *f*
porch [pɔːtʃ] *n Br* (*entrance*) zaguán *m*; *US* (*veranda*) terraza *f*
porcupine ['pɔːkjʊpaɪn] *n* puerco *m* espín
pore¹ [pɔː(r)] *vi* **to p. over sth** leer *or* estudiar algo detenidamente
pore² [pɔː(r)] *n Anat* poro *m*
pork [pɔːk] *n* (*carne f de*) cerdo *m or Am* chancho *m*
pornography [pɔː'nɒgrəfɪ] *n* pornografía *f*
porous ['pɔːrəs] *adj* poroso(a)
porpoise ['pɔːpəs] *n* marsopa *f*
porridge ['pɒrɪdʒ] *n* gachas *fpl* de avena
port¹ [pɔːt] *n* (*harbour*) puerto *m*; **p. of call** puerto de escala
port² [pɔːt] *n Naut & Av* babor *m*
port³ [pɔːt] *n* (*wine*) vino *m* de Oporto, oporto *m*
portable ['pɔːtəbəl] *adj* portátil
portal ['pɔːtəl] *n Comput* (*web page*) portal *m*
portent ['pɔːtent] *n Fml* augurio *m*
porter ['pɔːtə(r)] *n* (*at station*) mozo *m* de equipaje; *esp Br* (*at hotel*) portero(a) *m,f*, conserje *mf*; *US* (*on train*) mozo *m*
portfolio [pɔːt'fəʊlɪəʊ] *n* (*file*) carpeta *f*; (*of artist, politician*) cartera *f*
porthole ['pɔːthəʊl] *n* portilla *f*
portion ['pɔːʃən] *n* (*part, piece*) parte *f*, porción *f*; (*of food*) ración *f*
▸ **portion out** *vt sep* repartir
portly ['pɔːtlɪ] *adj* (**portlier, portliest**) corpulento(a)
portrait ['pɔːtreɪt] *n* retrato *m*
portray [pɔː'treɪ] *vt* (*paint portrait of*) retratar; (*describe*) describir; *Th* representar
Portugal ['pɔːtjʊgəl] *n* Portugal
Portuguese [pɔːtjʊ'giːz] **1** *adj* portugués(esa)
 2 *n* (*person*) portugués(esa) *m,f*; (*language*) portugués *m*
pose [pəʊz] **1** *vt* (*problem*) plantear; (*threat*) representar
 2 *vi* (*for painting*) posar; *Pej* (*behave affectedly*) hacer pose; **to p. as** hacerse pasar por
 3 *n* (*stance*) postura *f*; *Pej* (*affectation*) pose *f*

posh [pɒʃ] *adj Br Fam* elegante, de lujo; *(person, accent)* Esp pijo(a), Méx fresa, RP (con)cheto(a)

position [pə'zɪʃən] **1** *n* (**a**) *(physical posture)* posición *f*; *(location)* situación *f*; *(rank)* rango *m*; **to be in a p. to do sth** estar en condiciones de hacer algo (**b**) *(opinion)* postura *f* (**c**) *(job)* puesto *m*
  2 *vt* colocar

positive ['pɒzɪtɪv] *adj* positivo(a); *(sign)* favorable; *(proof)* incontrovertible; *(sure)* seguro(a); *Fam (absolute)* auténtico(a)

possess [pə'zes] *vt* poseer; *(of fear)* apoderarse de

possessed [pə'zest] *adj* poseído(a)

possession [pə'zeʃən] *n* posesión *f*; **possessions** bienes *mpl*

possessive [pə'zesɪv] *adj* posesivo(a)

possibility [pɒsɪ'bɪlɪtɪ] *n* posibilidad *f*; **possibilities** *(potential)* potencial *m*

possible ['pɒsɪbəl] *adj* posible; **as much as p.** todo lo posible; **as often as p.** cuanto más mejor; **as soon as p.** cuanto antes

possibly ['pɒsɪblɪ] *adv* posiblemente; *(perhaps)* tal vez, quizás; **I can't p. come** no puedo venir de ninguna manera

post¹ [pəʊst] **1** *n (of wood)* poste *m*
  2 *vt (affix)* poner, pegar

post² [pəʊst] **1** *n (job)* puesto *m*; US **trading p.** factoría *f*
  2 *vt Br (assign)* destinar

post³ [pəʊst] *esp Br***1** *n (mail)* correo *m*; **by p.** por correo; **p. office** oficina *f* de correos; **P. Office Box** apartado *m* de correos, *CAm, Carib, Méx* casilla *f* postal, *Andes, RP* casilla de correos
  2 *vt (letter)* echar al correo; **to p. sth to sb** mandar algo por correo a algn

postage ['pəʊstɪdʒ] *n* franqueo *m*

postal ['pəʊstəl] *adj* postal, de correos; *Br* **p. code** código *m* postal; *Br* **p. order** giro *m* postal; **p. vote** voto *m* por correo

postbox ['pəʊstbɒks] *n Br* buzón *m* (de correos)

postcard ['pəʊstkɑːd] *n* (tarjeta *f*) postal *f*

postcode ['pəʊstkəʊd] *n Br* código *m* postal

postdate [pəʊst'deɪt] *vt (cheque)* extender con fecha posterior

poster ['pəʊstə(r)] *n* póster *m*; *(advertising)* cartel *m*

posterior [pɒ'stɪərɪə(r)] **1** *n Hum* trasero *m*, pompis *m*
  2 *adj* posterior

posterity [pɒ'sterɪtɪ] *n* posteridad *f*

postgraduate [pəʊst'grædjʊɪt] **1** *n* posgraduado(a) *m,f*
  2 *adj* de posgraduado

posthumous ['pɒstjʊməs] *adj* póstumo(a)

postman ['pəʊstmən] *n Br* cartero *m*

postmark ['pəʊstmɑːk] *n* matasellos *m inv*

postmaster ['pəʊstmɑːstə(r)] *n* administrador *m* de correos; **p. general** director *m* general de correos

postmortem [pəʊst'mɔːtəm] *n* autopsia *f*

postpone [pəs'pəʊn] *vt* aplazar

postscript ['pəʊsskrɪpt] *n* posdata *f*

posture ['pɒstʃə(r)] **1** *n* postura *f*; *(affected)* pose *f*
  2 *vi* adoptar una pose

postwar ['pəʊstwɔː(r)] *adj* de la posguerra

posy ['pəʊzɪ] *n* ramillete *m*

pot [pɒt] **1** *n (container)* tarro *m*, pote *m*; *(for cooking)* olla *f*; *(for flowers)* maceta *f*; *Fam* **to go to p.** irse al garete *or Am* al diablo
  2 *vt (plant)* poner en una maceta

potassium [pə'tæsɪəm] *n* potasio *m*

potato [pə'teɪtəʊ] *n (pl* **potatoes)** patata *f*, *Am* papa *f*

potent ['pəʊtənt] *adj* potente

potential [pə'tenʃəl] **1** *adj* potencial, posible
  2 *n* potencial *m*

potentially [pə'tenʃəlɪ] *adv* en potencia

pothole ['pɒthəʊl] *n Geol* cueva *f*; *(in road)* bache *m*

potholing ['pɒthəʊlɪŋ] *n Br* espeleología *f*

potion ['pəʊʃən] *n* poción *f*, pócima *f*

potluck [pɒt'lʌk] *n Fam* **to take p.** conformarse con lo que haya

potted ['pɒtɪd] *adj (food)* en conserva; *(plant)* en maceta *or* tiesto

potter¹ ['pɒtə(r)] *n* alfarero(a) *m,f*

potter² ['pɒtə(r)] *vi Br* **to p. about** *or* **around** entretenerse

pottery ['pɒtərɪ] *n (craft, place)* alfarería *f*; *(objects)* cerámica *f*

potty¹ ['pɒtɪ] *adj* (**pottier, pottiest)** *Br Fam* pirado(a), *Col* corrido(a), *CSur* rayado(a), *Méx* zafado(a)

potty² ['pɒtɪ] *n Fam* orinal *m*

pouch [paʊtʃ] *n* (**a**) *(for money)* saquito *m*; *(for ammunition)* morral *m*; *(for tobacco)* petaca *f* (**b**) *Zool* bolsa *f* abdominal

poultry ['pəʊltrɪ] *n (live)* aves *fpl* de corral; *(food)* pollos *mpl*

pounce [paʊns] *vi* **to p. on** abalanzarse encima de

pound¹ [paʊnd] **1** *vt (strike)* aporrear
  2 *vi (heart)* palpitar; *(walk heavily)* andar con paso pesado

pound² [paʊnd] *n (money, weight)* libra *f*

pound³ [paʊnd] *n (for dogs)* perrera *f; (for cars)* depósito *m* de coches

pour [pɔː(r)] **1** *vt* echar, verter; **to p. sb a drink** servirle una copa a algn

2 *vi* correr, fluir; **it's pouring with rain** está lloviendo a cántaros

▸ **pour out** *vt sep* echar, verter; *Fig* **to p. one's heart out to sb** desahogarse con algn

pouring ['pɔːrɪŋ] *adj (rain)* torrencial

pout [paʊt] **1** *vi* hacer pucheros

2 *n* puchero *m*

poverty ['pɒvətɪ] *n* pobreza *f*

poverty-stricken ['pɒvətɪstrɪkən] *adj* necesitado(a); **to be p.** vivir en la miseria

powder ['paʊdə(r)] **1** *n* polvo *m;* **p. compact** polvera *f;* **p. keg** polvorín *m;* **p. puff** borla *f;* **p. room** baño *m or Esp* servicios *mpl or CSur* toilette *m* de señoras

2 *vt* **to p. one's nose** ponerse polvos en la cara; *Euph* ir a los servicios *or* al tocador

powdered ['paʊdəd] *adj (milk)* en polvo

power ['paʊə(r)] **1** *n* **(a)** *(physical strength)* fuerza *f, (energy)* energía *f* **(b)** *Elec* **to cut off the p.** cortar la corriente; *esp Br* **p. point** enchufe *m;* **p. station** central *or Andes, RP* usina eléctrica **(c)** *(capacity)* capacidad *f*, facultad *f* **(d)** *(authority)* poder *m; (nation)* potencia *f; (influence)* influencia *f;* **to be in p.** estar en el poder **(e)** *Tech* potencia *f; (output)* rendimiento *m*

2 *vt* propulsar, impulsar

powerboat ['paʊəbəʊt] *n* lancha (motora)

powerful ['paʊəfʊl] *adj (strong)* fuerte; *(influential)* poderoso(a); *(remedy)* eficaz; *(engine, machine)* potente; *(emotion)* fuerte; *(speech)* conmovedor(a)

powerless ['paʊəlɪs] *adj* impotente, ineficaz

pp *(abbr* **pages)** págs., pp

PR [piː'ɑː(r)] *(abbr* **public relations)** *n* relaciones públicas

practicable ['præktɪkəbəl] *adj* factible

practical ['præktɪkəl] *adj* práctico(a); *(useful)* útil; *(sensible)* adecuado(a)

practicality [præktɪ'kælɪtɪ] *n (of suggestion, plan)* factibilidad *f,* **practicalities** detalles prácticos

practically ['præktɪkəlɪ] *adv (almost)* casi

practice ['præktɪs] **1** *n* **(a)** *(habit)* costumbre *f* **(b)** *(exercise)* práctica *f; Sport* entrenamiento *m; Mus* ensayo *m;* **to be out of p.** no estar en forma **(c)** *(way of doing sth)* práctica *f;* **in p.** en la práctica; **to put sth into p.** poner algo en práctica **(d)** *(of profession)* ejercicio *m* **(e)** *(place)*

(of doctors) consultorio *m; (of lawyers)* bufete *m* **(f)** *(clients) (of doctors)* pacientes *mpl; (of lawyers)* clientela *f*

2 *vt & vi US* = **practise**

practicing ['præktɪsɪŋ] *adj US* = **practising**

practise ['præktɪs] **1** *vt* practicar; *(method)* seguir; *(principle)* poner en práctica; *Mus* ensayar; *(profession)* ejercer

2 *vi* practicar; *Sport* entrenar; *Mus* ensayar; *(doctor)* practicar; *(lawyer)* ejercer

practising ['præktɪsɪŋ] *adj (doctor etc)* en ejercicio; *(Christian etc)* practicante

practitioner [præk'tɪʃənə(r)] *n Br Med* **general p.** médico(a) *m,f* de cabecera

pragmatic [præg'mætɪk] *adj* pragmático(a)

prairie ['preərɪ] *n* pradera *f, US* llanura *f*

praise [preɪz] **1** *n* alabanza *f*

2 *vt* alabar, elogiar

praiseworthy ['preɪzwɜːðɪ] *adj* loable

pram [præm] *n Br* cochecito *m* de niño

prance [prɑːns] *vi (horse)* encabritarse; **to p. about** *(person)* pegar brincos

prank [præŋk] *n* broma *f; (of child)* travesura *f*

prat [præt] *n Br Fam* soplagaitas *mf inv, Am* pendejo(a) *m,f*

prawn [prɔːn] *n* gamba *f, Am* camarón *m*

pray [preɪ] *vi* rezar, orar

prayer [preə(r)] *n* rezo *m*, oración *f; (entreaty)* súplica *f;* **p. book** misal *m*

preach [priːtʃ] *vi* predicar

preacher ['priːtʃə(r)] *n* predicador(a) *m,f*

precarious [prɪ'keərɪəs] *adj* precario(a)

precaution [prɪ'kɔːʃən] *n* precaución *f*

precede [prɪ'siːd] *vt* preceder

precedence ['presɪdəns] *n* preferencia *f*, prioridad *f;* **to take p. over sth/sb** tener prioridad sobre algo/algn

precedent ['presɪdənt] *n* precedente *m*

preceding [prɪ'siːdɪŋ] *adj* precedente

precinct ['priːsɪŋkt] *n* **(a)** *Br (area)* **pedestrian/shopping p.** zona *f* peatonal/comercial **(b)** *US (administrative, police division)* distrito *m; (police station)* comisaría *f* (de policía)

> *Note that the Spanish word* **precinto** *is a false friend and is never a translation for the English word* **precinct.** *In Spanish* **precinto** *means "seal".*

precious ['preʃəs] **1** *adj* precioso(a); **p. stones** piedras preciosas

2 *adv Fam* **p. little/few** muy poco/pocos

precipice ['presɪpɪs] *n* precipicio *m*

precipitate 1 vt [prɪˈsɪpɪteɪt] precipitar; Fig arrojar
2 adj [prɪˈsɪpɪtət] precipitado(a)

precise [prɪˈsaɪs] adj preciso(a), exacto(a); (meticulous) meticuloso(a)

precisely [prɪˈsaɪslɪ] adv (exactly) precisamente, exactamente; **p.!** ¡eso es!, ¡exacto!

precision [prɪˈsɪʒən] n precisión f

preclude [prɪˈkluːd] vt excluir; (misunderstanding) evitar

precocious [prɪˈkəʊʃəs] adj precoz

preconceived [priːkənˈsiːvd] adj preconcebido(a)

precondition [priːkənˈdɪʃən] n condición previa

precursor [prɪˈkɜːsə(r)] n precursor(a) m,f

predator [ˈpredətə(r)] n depredador m

predecessor [ˈpriːdɪsesə(r)] n antecesor(a) m,f

predetermine [priːdɪˈtɜːmɪn] vt predeterminar

predicament [prɪˈdɪkəmənt] n apuro m, aprieto m

predict [prɪˈdɪkt] vt predecir, pronosticar

predictable [prɪˈdɪktəbəl] adj previsible

prediction [prɪˈdɪkʃən] n pronóstico m

predispose [priːdɪˈspəʊz] vt to be predisposed to do sth estar predispuesto(a) a hacer algo

predominant [prɪˈdɒmɪnənt] adj predominante

predominantly [prɪˈdɒmɪnəntlɪ] adv en su mayoría

predominate [prɪˈdɒmɪneɪt] vi predominar

pre-empt [prɪˈempt] vt adelantarse a

preen [priːn] vt to p. oneself (of bird) arreglarse las plumas; Fig (of person) pavonearse

prefab [ˈpriːfæb] n Br Fam (house) casa prefabricada

prefabricated [priːˈfæbrɪkeɪtɪd] adj prefabricado(a)

preface [ˈprefɪs] **1** n prefacio m
2 vt prologar

prefect [ˈpriːfekt] n Br Educ monitor(a) m,f

prefer [prɪˈfɜː(r)] vt preferir; I p. coffee to tea prefiero el café al té

preferable [ˈprefərəbəl] adj preferible (to a)

preferably [ˈprefərəblɪ] adv preferentemente

preference [ˈprefərəns] n preferencia f; (priority) prioridad f; to give p. to sth dar prioridad a algo

preferential [prefəˈrenʃəl] adj preferente

prefix [ˈpriːfɪks] n prefijo m

pregnancy [ˈpregnənsɪ] n embarazo m

pregnant [ˈpregnənt] adj (woman) embarazada; (animal) preñada; Fig **a p. pause** una pausa cargada de significado

prehistoric(al) [priːhɪˈstɒrɪk(əl)] adj prehistórico(a)

prejudge [priːˈdʒʌdʒ] vt prejuzgar

prejudice [ˈpredʒʊdɪs] **1** n (bias) prejuicio m; (harm) perjuicio m
2 vt (bias) predisponer; (harm) perjudicar

prejudiced [ˈpredʒʊdɪst] adj parcial; **to be p. against/in favour of** estar predispuesto(a) en contra/a favor de

preliminary [prɪˈlɪmɪnərɪ] **1** adj preliminar; Sport (round) eliminatorio(a)
2 n preliminares preliminares mpl

prelude [ˈpreljuːd] n preludio m

premarital [priːˈmærɪtəl] adj prematrimonial

premature [preməˈtjʊə(r), ˈpremətʊə(r)] adj prematuro(a)

prematurely [preməˈtjʊəlɪ, ˈpremətjʊəlɪ] adv antes de tiempo

premeditate [prɪˈmedɪteɪt] vt (crime) premeditar

premenstrual [priːˈmenstrʊəl] adj **p. tension** tensión f premenstrual

premier [ˈpremjə(r)] **1** n Pol primer(a) ministro(a) m,f
2 adj primer, primero(a)

premiere [ˈpremɪeə(r)] n Cin estreno m

premise [ˈpremɪs] n premisa f

premises [ˈpremɪsɪz] npl local m; **on the p.** en el local

premium [ˈpriːmɪəm] n Com, Fin & Ind prima f; **to be at a p.** tener sobreprecio; Fig estar muy solicitado(a); Br **p. bonds** = bonos numerados emitidos por el Gobierno británico, cuyo comprador entra en un sorteo mensual de premios en metálico

premonition [premənˈɪʃən] n presentimiento m

preoccupied [priːˈɒkjʊpaɪd] adj preocupado(a); **to be p. with sth** preocuparse por algo

prep [prep] n Br Fam deberes mpl; **p. school** = colegio privado para alumnos de entre 7 y 13 años

prepacked [priːˈpækt] adj empaquetado(a)

prepaid [priːˈpeɪd] adj con el porte pagado

preparation [prepəˈreɪʃən] n preparación f; (plan) preparativo m

preparatory [prɪ'pærətərɪ] *adj* preparatorio(a), preliminar; **p. school** *Br* = colegio privado para alumnos de entre 7 y 13 años; *US* = escuela secundaria privada

prepare [prɪ'peə(r)] **1** *vt* preparar; **to p. to do sth** prepararse *or Am* alistarse para hacer algo
2 *vi* prepararse, *Am* alistarse (**for** para)

prepared [prɪ'peəd] *adj (ready)* preparado(a); **to be p. to do sth** *(willing)* estar dispuesto(a) a hacer algo

preponderance [prɪ'pɒndərəns] *n* preponderancia *f*

preposition [prepə'zɪʃən] *n* preposición *f*

preposterous [prɪ'pɒstərəs] *adj* absurdo(a), ridículo(a)

prerequisite [pri:'rekwɪzɪt] *n* condición *f* previa

prerogative [prɪ'rɒgətɪv] *n* prerrogativa *f*

preschool [pri:'sku:l] *adj* preescolar

prescribe [prɪ'skraɪb] *vt (set down)* prescribir; *Med* recetar; *Fig (recommend)* recomendar

prescription [prɪ'skrɪpʃən] *n Med* receta *f*

presence ['prezəns] *n* presencia *f*; *(attendance)* asistencia *f*; *Fig* **p. of mind** presencia de ánimo

present¹ ['prezənt] **1** *adj* **(a)** *(in attendance)* presente; *Ling* **p. tense** (tiempo *m*) presente *m*; **to be p. at** estar presente en **(b)** *(current)* actual
2 *n (time)* presente *m*, actualidad *f*; **at p.** actualmente; **for the p.** de momento; **up to the p.** hasta ahora

present² **1** *vt* [prɪ'zent] **(a)** *(give as gift)* regalar; *(medal, prize etc)* entregar; **to p. sb with sth** obsequiar a algn con algo **(b)** *(report etc)* presentar; *(opportunity)* ofrecer; *(problem)* plantear **(c)** *(introduce)* *(person, programme)* presentar
2 *n* ['prezənt] *(gift)* regalo *m*; *(formal)* obsequio *m*

presentable [prɪ'zentəbəl] *adj* presentable; **to make oneself p.** arreglarse

presentation [prezən'teɪʃən] *n* **(a)** *(of person)* presentación *f*; **p. ceremony** ceremonia *f* de entrega **(b)** *(formal talk)* exposición *f*, charla *f* *(con la ayuda de gráficos, diapositivas, etc)*

present-day ['prezəntdeɪ] *adj* actual, de hoy en día

presenter [prɪ'zentə(r)] *n Br Rad* locutor(a) *m,f*; *TV* presentador(a) *m,f*

presently ['prezəntlɪ] *adv (soon)* dentro de poco; *US (now)* ahora

preservation [prezə'veɪʃən] *n* conservación *f*

preservative [prɪ'zɜ:vətɪv] *n* conservante *m*

preserve [prɪ'zɜ:v] **1** *vt* **(a)** *(keep)* mantener **(b)** *Culin* conservar
2 *n* **(a)** *(hunting)* coto *m* **(b)** *Culin* conserva *f*

preside [prɪ'zaɪd] *vi* presidir

presidency ['prezɪdənsɪ] *n* presidencia *f*

president ['prezɪdənt] *n Pol* presidente(a) *m,f*; *US Com* director(a) *m,f*, gerente *mf*

presidential [prezɪ'denʃəl] *adj* presidencial

press [pres] **1** *vt* **(a)** *(push, squeeze)* apretar; *(grapes)* prensar; *(trousers etc)* planchar **(b)** *(pressurize)* presionar; **to p. sb to do sth** acosar a algn para que haga algo
2 *vi* **(a)** *(push)* apretar; **to p. against sth/sb** apretarse contra algo/algn; **to p. (down) on sth** hacer presión sobre algo **(b)** *(be urgent)* **time is pressing** el tiempo apremia
3 *n* **(a)** *(machine)* prensa *f*; **to go to p.** *(of newspaper)* entrar en prensa **(b)** *Press* **the p.** la prensa; **p. agency** agencia *f* de prensa; **p. conference** rueda *f* de prensa
▶ **press on** *vi* seguir adelante

pressed [prest] *adj* **to be (hard) p. for** andar escaso(a) de; **I'd be hard p. to do it** me costaría mucho hacerlo

pressing ['presɪŋ] *adj* apremiante, urgente

press-up ['presʌp] *n Br* flexión *f* (de brazos)

pressure ['preʃə(r)] *n* presión *f*; *Med & Met* **high/low p.** altas/bajas presiones; **p. cooker** olla *f* a presión; **p. gauge** manómetro *m*; *Fig* **to bring p. (to bear) on sb** ejercer presión sobre algn

pressurize ['preʃəraɪz] *vt Fig* presionar; **pressurized cabin** cabina presurizada

prestige [pre'sti:ʒ] *n* prestigio *m*

prestigious [pres'tɪdʒəs] *adj* prestigioso(a)

presumably [prɪ'zju:məblɪ] *adv* es de suponer que

presume [prɪ'zju:m] **1** *vt* suponer, presumir; **we p. so/not** suponemos que sí/no
2 *vi (suppose)* suponer

presumption [prɪ'zʌmpʃən] *n* **(a)** *(supposition)* suposición *f* **(b)** *(boldness)* osadía *f*; *(conceit)* presunción *f*

presumptuous [prɪ'zʌmptjʊəs] *adj* impertinente

📖 Note that the Spanish word **presuntuoso** is a false friend and is never a translation for the English word **presumptuous**. In Spanish, **presuntuoso** means "vain" and "pretentious".

presuppose [priːsə'pəʊz] *vt* presuponer

pretence [prɪ'tens] *n* (**a**) *(deception)* fingimiento *m*; **false pretences** estafa *f*; **under the p. of** so pretexto de (**b**) *(claim)* pretensión *f*

pretend [prɪ'tend] **1** *vt (feign)* fingir, aparentar; *(claim)* pretender
2 *vi (feign)* fingir

pretense [prɪ'tens] *n US* = **pretence**

pretention [prɪ'tenʃən] *n* pretensión *f*

pretentious [prɪ'tenʃəs] *adj* presuntuoso(a), pretencioso(a)

pretext ['priːtekst] *n* pretexto *m*; **on the p. of** so pretexto de

pretty ['prɪtɪ] **1** *adj* (**prettier, prettiest**) bonito(a), *Am* lindo(a)
2 *adv Fam* bastante; **p. much the same** más o menos lo mismo

prevail [prɪ'veɪl] *vi* (**a**) *(predominate)* predominar (**b**) *(be successful)* prevalecer (**c**) **to p. upon** *or* **on sb to do sth** *(persuade)* persuadir *or* convencer a algn para que haga algo

prevailing [prɪ'veɪlɪŋ] *adj (wind)* predominante; *(opinion)* general; *(condition, fashion)* actual

prevalent ['prevələnt] *adj* predominante; *(illness)* extendido(a)

prevaricate [prɪ'værɪkeɪt] *vi* andar con ambages

prevent [prɪ'vent] *vt* impedir; *(accident)* evitar; *(illness)* prevenir; **to p. sb from doing sth** impedir a algn hacer algo; **to p. sth from happening** evitar que pase algo

prevention [prɪ'venʃən] *n* prevención *f*

preventive [prɪ'ventɪv] *adj* preventivo(a)

preview ['priːvjuː] *n (of film etc)* preestreno *m*

previous ['priːvɪəs] **1** *adj* anterior, previo(a); **p. conviction** antecedente *m* penal
2 *adv* **p. to going** antes de ir

previously ['priːvɪəslɪ] *adv* anteriormente, previamente

prewar ['priːwɔː(r)] *adj* de antes de la guerra

prey [preɪ] **1** *n* presa *f*; *Fig* víctima *f*
2 *vi* **to p. on** alimentarse de

price [praɪs] **1** *n* precio *m*; **what p. is that coat?** ¿cuánto cuesta el abrigo?; **p. list** lista *f* de precios; **p. tag** etiqueta *f*
2 *vt (put price on)* poner un precio a; *(value)* valorar

priceless ['praɪslɪs] *adj* que no tiene precio

pricey ['praɪsɪ] *adj* (**pricier, priciest**) *Fam* carillo(a)

prick [prɪk] **1** *vt* picar; **to p. one's finger** pincharse el dedo; *Fig* **to p. up one's ears** aguzar el oído
2 *n* (**a**) *(with pin)* pinchazo *m* (**b**) *Vulg (penis) Esp* polla *f*, *Am* verga *f*, *Méx* pito *m*, *RP* pija *f* (**c**) *Vulg (person) Esp* gilipollas *mf inv*, *Am* pendejo(a) *m,f*, *RP* forro *m*

prickle ['prɪkəl] **1** *n* espina *f*; *(spike)* pincho *m*; *(sensation)* picor *m*
2 *vt & vi* pinchar, picar

prickly ['prɪklɪ] *adj* (**pricklier, prickliest**) espinoso(a); *Fig (touchy)* enojadizo(a); **p. heat** = sarpullido por causa del calor; **p. pear** higo chumbo, *Am* tuna *f*

pride [praɪd] **1** *n* orgullo *m*; *(arrogance)* soberbia *f*; **to take p. in sth** enorgullecerse de algo
2 *vt* **to p. oneself on** enorgullecerse de

priest [priːst] *n* sacerdote *m*, cura *m*

priestess ['priːstɪs] *n* sacerdotisa *f*

priesthood ['priːsthʊd] *n (clergy)* clero *m*; *(office)* sacerdocio *m*

prig [prɪg] *n* gazmoño(a) *m,f*, mojigato(a) *m,f*

prim [prɪm] *adj* (**primmer, primmest**) **p. (and proper)** remilgado(a)

primaeval [praɪ'miːvəl] *adj* primitivo(a)

primarily ['praɪmərɪlɪ] *adv* ante todo

primary ['praɪmərɪ] **1** *adj* fundamental, principal; **of p. importance** primordial; **p. colour** color primario; **p. education/ school** enseñanza/escuela primaria
2 *n US Pol* (elección) primaria

primate¹ ['praɪmeɪt] *n Rel* primado *m*

primate² ['praɪmeɪt] *n Zool* primate *m*

prime [praɪm] **1** *adj* (**a**) *(principal)* principal, primordial; **P. Minister** primer(a) ministro(a) (**b**) *(first-rate)* de primera; **p. number** número primo
2 *n* **in the p. of life** en la flor de la vida
3 *vt (pump, engine)* cebar; *(surface)* imprimar; *Fig (prepare)* preparar

primer¹ ['praɪmə(r)] *n (textbook)* cartilla *f*

primer² ['praɪmə(r)] *n (paint)* imprimación *f*

primeval [praɪ'miːvəl] *adj* = **primaeval**

primitive ['prɪmɪtɪv] *adj* primitivo(a); *(method, tool)* rudimentario(a)

primrose ['prɪmrəʊz] *n* primavera *f*

Primus® ['praɪməs] *n* infiernillo *m*, camping-gas *m inv*, *Am* primus *m inv*

prince [prɪns] *n* príncipe *m*; **P. Charming** Príncipe Azul

princess [prɪn'ses] *n* princesa *f*

principal ['prɪnsɪpəl] **1** *adj* principal
2 *n Educ* director(a) *m,f*, *Th (in play)* protagonista *mf* principal

principle ['prɪnsɪpəl] n principio m; **in p.** en principio; **on p.** por principio

print [prɪnt] **1** vt (a) (book) imprimir; (newspaper) publicar; Fig grabar; **printed matter** impresos mpl (b) (write) escribir con letra de imprenta
2 n (a) (of hand, foot) huella f (b) (written text) letra f; **out of p.** agotado(a) (c) Tex estampado m (d) Art grabado m; Phot copia f
▸ **print out** vt sep Comput imprimir

printer ['prɪntə(r)] n (person) impresor(a) m,f; (machine) impresora f

printing ['prɪntɪŋ] n (industry) imprenta f; (process) impresión f; (print run) tirada f; **p. press** prensa f

print-out ['prɪntaʊt] n Comput impresión f; (copy) copia impresa

prior ['praɪə(r)] adj previo(a), anterior; **p. to leaving** antes de salir

priority [praɪ'ɒrɪtɪ] n prioridad f

prise [praɪz] vt **to p. sth open** abrir algo con palanca; **to p. sth off** arrancar algo

prism ['prɪzəm] n prisma f

prison ['prɪzən] n cárcel f, prisión f

prisoner ['prɪzənə(r)] n preso(a) m,f; **to hold sb p.** detener a algn; **p. of war** prisionero(a) m,f de guerra

privacy ['praɪvəsɪ, 'prɪvəsɪ] n intimidad f

private ['praɪvɪt] **1** adj (a) privado(a); (secretary) particular; (matter) personal; (letter) confidencial; **one's p. life** la vida privada de uno; **p.** (notice) (on road) carretera privada; (on gate) propiedad privada; (on envelope) confidencial; **p. detective,** Fam **p. eye** detective privado(a); **p. school** escuela privada
2 n Mil soldado raso

privately ['praɪvɪtlɪ] adv en privado; (personally) personalmente

privatize ['praɪvɪtaɪz] vt privatizar

privet ['prɪvɪt] n alheña f

privilege ['prɪvɪlɪdʒ] n privilegio m

privileged ['prɪvɪlɪdʒd] adj privilegiado(a)

privy ['prɪvɪ] **1** adj Br **P. Council** Consejo Privado; **to be p. to sth** estar enterado(a) de algo
2 n (lavatory) retrete m

prize [praɪz] **1** n premio m
2 adj (first-class) de primera (categoría or clase)
3 vt (value) apreciar, valorar

prize-giving ['praɪzgɪvɪŋ] n distribución f de premios

prizewinner ['praɪzwɪnə(r)] n premiado(a) m,f

pro¹ [prəʊ] n pro m; **the pros and cons of an issue** los pros y los contras de una cuestión

pro² [prəʊ] n Fam profesional mf, Méx profesionista mf

pro- [prəʊ] pref (in favour of) pro-

proactive [prəʊ'æktɪv] adj **to be p.** tomar la iniciativa

probability [prɒbə'bɪlɪtɪ] n probabilidad f

probable ['prɒbəbəl] adj probable

probably ['prɒbəblɪ] adv probablemente

probation [prə'beɪʃən] n Jur **to be on p.** estar en libertad condicional; **to be on two months' p.** (at work) trabajar dos meses de prueba

probe [prəʊb] **1** n Med & (in outer space) sonda f; (investigation) sondeo m
2 vt Med sondar; (investigate) investigar
▸ **probe into** vt insep investigar

problem ['prɒbləm] n problema m

problematic(al) [prɒblə'mætɪk(əl)] adj problemático(a); **it's p.** tiene sus problemas

procedure [prə'siːdʒə(r)] n procedimiento m; (legal, business) gestión f, trámite m

proceed [prə'siːd] vi seguir, proceder; **to p. to do sth** ponerse a hacer algo; **to p. to the next matter** pasar a la siguiente cuestión

proceedings [prə'siːdɪŋz] npl (of meeting) actas fpl; (measures) medidas fpl; Jur proceso m

proceeds ['prəʊsiːdz] npl ganancias fpl

process ['prəʊses] **1** n proceso m; (method) método m, sistema m; **in the p. of** en vías de
2 vt (information) tramitar; (food) tratar; Comput procesar

processing ['prəʊsesɪŋ] n (of information) evaluación f; Comput tratamiento m

procession [prə'seʃən] n desfile m; Rel procesión f

processor ['prəʊsesə(r)] n Comput procesador m

proclaim [prə'kleɪm] vt proclamar, declarar

proclamation [prɒklə'meɪʃən] n proclamación f

procrastinate [prəʊ'kræstɪneɪt] vi dejar las cosas para después

procure [prə'kjʊə(r)] vt conseguir, procurarse

prod [prɒd] vt (with stick etc) golpear; (push) empujar

prodigal ['prɒdɪgəl] adj pródigo(a)

prodigious [prə'dɪdʒəs] *adj* prodigioso(a)

prodigy ['prɒdɪdʒɪ] *n* prodigio *m*

produce 1 *vt* [prə'dju:s] (**a**) *(create) (food, goods)* producir (**b**) *Th* dirigir; *Rad & TV* realizar; *Cin* producir (**c**) *(give birth to)* dar a luz a (**d**) *(document)* enseñar; *(bring out)* sacar
2 *n* ['prɒdju:s] productos *mpl*; **p. of Spain** producto *m* de España

producer [prə'dju:sə(r)] *n* (**a**) *(of crops, goods)* productor(a) *m,f* (**b**) *(of film, play, radio or TV programme)* productor(a) *m,f*

product ['prɒdʌkt] *n* producto *m*

production [prə'dʌkʃən] *n* (**a**) *(manufacture)* producción *f*; **p. line** cadena *f* de producción (**b**) *(play)* montaje *m*; *(film, radio or TV programme)* producción *f*

productive [prə'dʌktɪv] *adj* productivo(a)

productivity [prɒdʌk'tɪvɪtɪ] *n* productividad *f*

profane [prə'feɪn] *adj (secular)* profano(a); *(language)* blasfemo(a)

profess [prə'fes] *vt (faith)* profesar; *(opinion)* expresar; *(claim)* pretender

profession [prə'feʃən] *n* profesión *f*

professional [prə'feʃənəl] **1** *adj* profesional; *(soldier)* de profesión; *(polished)* de gran calidad
2 *n* profesional *mf*

professor [prə'fesə(r)] *n* *Univ Br* catedrático(a) *m,f*; *US* profesor(a) *m,f*

proficiency [prə'fɪʃənsɪ] *n (in language)* capacidad *f*; *(in skill)* pericia *f*

proficient [prə'fɪʃənt] *adj (in language)* experto(a); *(in skill)* hábil

profile ['prəʊfaɪl] *n* perfil *m*; **in p.** de perfil

profit ['prɒfɪt] **1** *n* (**a**) *(of company, on deal)* beneficio *m*; **to make a p. on** sacar beneficios de (**b**) *(advantage)* provecho *m*
2 *vi* *Fig* sacar provecho; **to p. from** aprovecharse de

profitability [prɒfɪtə'bɪlɪtɪ] *n* rentabilidad *f*

profitable ['prɒfɪtəbəl] *adj Com* rentable; *Fig (worthwhile)* provechoso(a)

profiteer [prɒfɪ'tɪə(r)] **1** *n* especulador(a) *m,f*
2 *vi* obtener beneficios excesivos

profound [prə'faʊnd] *adj* profundo(a)

profuse [prə'fju:s] *adj* profuso(a), abundante

profusely [prə'fju:slɪ] *adv* con profusión; **to sweat p.** sudar mucho

profusion [prə'fju:ʒən] *n* profusión *f*, abundancia *f*

prognosis [prɒg'nəʊsɪs] *n Med* pronóstico *m*; *Fig (prediction)* augurio *m*

program ['prəʊgræm] *Comput* **1** *n* programa *m*
2 *vi & vt* programar
3 *US* = **programme**

programer ['prəʊgræmər] *n* *US* = **programmer**

programme ['prəʊgræm] **1** *n* programa *m*; *(plan)* plan *m*
2 *vt* (**a**) *(plan)* planear, planificar (**b**) *(computer)* programar

programmer ['prəʊgræmə(r)] *n* programador(a) *m,f*

progress 1 *n* ['prəʊgres] progreso *m*; *(development)* desarrollo *m*; *Med* mejora *f*; **to make p.** hacer progresos; **in p.** en curso
2 *vi* [prəʊ'gres] avanzar; *(develop)* desarrollar; *(improve)* hacer progresos; *Med* mejorar

progressive [prə'gresɪv] *adj (increasing)* progresivo(a); *Pol* progresista

progressively [prə'gresɪvlɪ] *adv* progresivamente

prohibit [prə'hɪbɪt] *vt* prohibir; **to p. sb from doing sth** prohibir a algn hacer algo

prohibitive [prə'hɪbɪtɪv] *adj* prohibitivo(a)

project 1 *n* ['prɒdʒekt] proyecto *m*; *(plan)* plan *m*; *Educ* trabajo *m*; *US* **(housing) p.** = urbanización con viviendas de protección oficial
2 *vt* [prə'dʒekt] proyectar, planear
3 *vi* *(stick out)* sobresalir

projectile [prə'dʒektaɪl] *n Fml* proyectil *m*

projection [prə'dʒekʃən] *n* (**a**) *(over-hang)* saliente *m* (**b**) *Cin* proyección *f* (**c**) *(forecast)* proyección *f*

projector [prə'dʒektə(r)] *n Cin* proyector *m*

proletariat [prəʊlɪ'teərɪət] *n* proletariado *m*

prolific [prə'lɪfɪk] *adj* prolífico(a)

prologue ['prəʊlɒg] *n* prólogo *m*

prolong [prə'lɒŋ] *vt* prolongar

prom [prɒm] *n Br Fam (seafront)* paseo marítimo; *Br (concert)* = concierto sinfónico en que parte del público está de pie; *US (school dance)* = baile de fin de curso

promenade [prɒmə'nɑ:d] **1** *n Br (at seaside)* paseo marítimo
2 *vi* pasearse

prominence ['prɒmɪnəns] *n* prominencia *f*; *Fig (importance)* importancia *f*

prominent ['prɒmɪnənt] *adj (standing out)* saliente; *Fig (important)* importante; *(famous)* eminente

promiscuous [prəˈmɪskjʊəs] *adj* promiscuo(a)

promise [ˈprɒmɪs] **1** *n* promesa *f*; **to show p.** ser prometedor(a)
2 *vt & vi* prometer

promising [ˈprɒmɪsɪŋ] *adj* prometedor(a)

promontory [ˈprɒməntərɪ] *n* promontorio *m*

promote [prəˈməʊt] *vt* ascender; *(product)* promocionar; *(ideas)* fomentar; *Ftb* **they've been promoted** han subido

promoter [prəˈməʊtə(r)] *n* promotor(a) *m,f*

promotion [prəˈməʊʃən] *n (in rank)* promoción *f*, ascenso *m*; *(of product)* promoción *f*; *(of arts etc)* fomento *m*

prompt [ˈprɒmpt] **1** *adj (quick)* rápido(a); *(punctual)* puntual
2 *adv* **at two o'clock p.** a las dos en punto
3 *vt* (a) *(motivate)* incitar; **to p. sb to do sth** instar a algn a hacer algo (b) *(actor)* apuntar

promptly [ˈprɒmptlɪ] *adv (quickly)* rápidamente; *(punctually)* puntualmente

prone [prəʊn] *adj* (a) **to be p. to do sth** ser propenso(a) a hacer algo (b) *Fml (face down)* boca abajo

prong [prɒŋ] *n* punta *f*, diente *m*

pronoun [ˈprəʊnaʊn] *n* pronombre *m*

pronounce [prəˈnaʊns] **1** *vt* pronunciar; *Fml (declare)* declarar
2 *vi Fml* **to p. on sth** opinar sobre algo

pronounced [prəˈnaʊnst] *adj* pronunciado(a)

pronouncement [prəˈnaʊnsmənt] *n Fml* declaración *f*

pronunciation [prənʌnsɪˈeɪʃən] *n* pronunciación *f*

proof [pruːf] **1** *n* prueba *f*
2 *adj* (a) *(secure)* a prueba de (b) **this rum is 70 per cent p.** este ron tiene 70 grados
3 *vt* impermeabilizar

prop¹ [prɒp] **1** *n (support)* puntal *m*; *Fig* sostén *m*
2 *vt (support)* apoyar; *Fig* sostener
▸ **prop up** *vt sep* apoyar

prop² [prɒp] *n Fam Th* accesorio *m*

propaganda [prɒpəˈgændə] *n* propaganda *f*

propel [prəˈpel] *vt* propulsar

propeller [prəˈpelə(r)] *n* hélice *f*

propelling pencil [prəˈpelɪŋˈpensəl] *n Br* portaminas *m inv*

propensity [prəˈpensɪtɪ] *n Fml* propensión *f*

proper [ˈprɒpə(r)] *adj* (a) *(correct)* correcto(a); *(real)* verdadero(a); **he isn't a**

p. doctor no es médico de verdad (b) *(appropriate) (time, place)* adecuado(a), apropiado(a) (c) *(characteristic)* propio(a); *Ling* **p. noun** nombre propio

properly [ˈprɒpəlɪ] *adv (suitably, correctly, decently)* correctamente; **it wasn't p. closed** no estaba bien cerrado; **she refused, quite p.** se negó, y con razón

property [ˈprɒpətɪ] *n* (a) *(quality)* propiedad *f* (b) *(possession)* propiedad *f*, posesión *f*; **personal p.** bienes *mpl*; **public p.** dominio público (c) *(estate)* finca *f*

prophecy [ˈprɒfɪsɪ] *n* profecía *f*

prophesy [ˈprɒfɪsaɪ] *vt (predict)* predecir; *Rel* profetizar

prophet [ˈprɒfɪt] *n* profeta *mf*

proportion [prəˈpɔːʃən] *n* proporción *f*; *(part, quantity)* parte *f*; **in p. to** or **with** en proporción a

proportional [prəˈpɔːʃənəl] *adj* proporcional (**to** a); *Pol* **p. representation** representación *f* proporcional

proportionate [prəˈpɔːʃənɪt] *adj* proporcional

proposal [prəˈpəʊzəl] *n* propuesta *f*; *(suggestion)* sugerencia *f*; **p. of marriage** propuesta de matrimonio

propose [prəˈpəʊz] **1** *vt* proponer; *(suggest)* sugerir; *Fml (intend)* tener la intención de
2 *vi* declararse

proposition [prɒpəˈzɪʃən] *n* propuesta *f*; *Math* proposición *f*

proprietor [prəˈpraɪətə(r)] *n* propietario(a) *m,f*

propriety [prəˈpraɪətɪ] *n (decency)* decoro *m*

propulsion [prəˈpʌlʃən] *n* propulsión *f*

prosaic [prəʊˈzeɪɪk] *adj* prosaico(a)

prose [prəʊz] *n Lit* prosa *f*; *Educ* texto *m* para traducir

prosecute [ˈprɒsɪkjuːt] *vt* procesar

prosecution [prɒsɪˈkjuːʃən] *n (action)* proceso *m*, juicio *m*; **the p.** la acusación

prosecutor [ˈprɒsɪkjuːtə(r)] *n* acusador(a) *m,f*

prospect 1 *n* [ˈprɒspekt] *(outlook)* perspectiva *f*; *(hope)* esperanza *f*; **the job has prospects** es un trabajo con porvenir
2 *vt* [prəˈspekt] explorar
3 *vi* **to p. for gold/oil** buscar oro/petróleo

prospective [prəˈspektɪv] *adj (future)* futuro(a); *(possible)* eventual, probable

prospector [prəˈspektə(r)] *n* **gold p.** buscador(a) *m,f* del oro

prospectus [prəˈspektəs] *n* prospecto *m*

prosper [ˈprɒspə(r)] *vi* prosperar

prosperity [prɒ'sperɪtɪ] n prosperidad f
prosperous ['prɒspərəs] adj próspero(a)
prostate ['prɒsteɪt] n Anat **p. (gland)** próstata f
prostitute ['prɒstɪtjuːt] n prostituta f
prostitution [prɒstɪ'tjuːʃən] n prostitución f
prostrate ['prɒstreɪt] adj (face down) boca abajo; **p. with grief** deshecho(a) de dolor
protagonist [prəʊ'tægənɪst] n protagonista mf
protect [prə'tekt] vt proteger; (interests etc) salvaguardar; **to p. sb from sth** proteger a algn de algo
protection [prə'tekʃən] n protección f
protective [prə'tektɪv] adj protector(a)
protégé ['prɒtəʒeɪ] n protegido m
protégée ['prɒtəʒeɪ] n protegida f
protein ['prəʊtiːn] n proteína f
protest 1 n ['prəʊtest] protesta f; (complaint) queja f
　　2 vt [prə'test] US protestar en contra de
　　3 vi Br protestar
Protestant ['prɒtɪstənt] adj & n protestante (mf)
protester [prə'testə(r)] n manifestante mf
protocol ['prəʊtəkɒl] n protocolo m
prototype ['prəʊtətaɪp] n prototipo m
protracted [prə'træktɪd] adj prolongado(a)
protrude [prə'truːd] vi Fml sobresalir
protuberance [prə'tjuːbərəns] n Fml protuberancia f
proud [praʊd] adj orgulloso(a); (arrogant) soberbio(a)
prove [pruːv] **1** vt (demonstrate) probar, demostrar; Math comprobar; **to p. oneself** dar pruebas de valor
　　2 vi (turn out) it proved to be disastrous resultó ser desastroso(a)
proverb ['prɒvɜːb] n refrán m, proverbio m
provide [prə'vaɪd] **1** vt proporcionar; (supplies) suministrar, proveer
　　2 vi proveer; **to p. for sb** mantener a algn
provided [prə'vaɪdɪd] conj **p. (that)** con tal de que
providing [prə'vaɪdɪŋ] conj = **provided**
province ['prɒvɪns] n provincia f; Fig (field of knowledge) campo m
provincial [prə'vɪnʃəl] **1** adj provincial; Pej provinciano(a)
　　2 n Pej (person) provinciano(a) m,f
provision [prə'vɪʒən] n provisión f; (supply) suministro m; **provisions** (food) provisiones fpl, víveres mpl

provisional [prə'vɪʒənəl] adj provisional
proviso [prə'vaɪzəʊ] n (pl **provisos,** US **provisoes**) **with the p. that** a condición de que
provocation [prɒvə'keɪʃən] n provocación f
provocative [prə'vɒkətɪv] adj provocador(a); (flirtatious) provocativo(a)
provoke [prə'vəʊk] vt provocar
prow [praʊ] n proa f
prowess ['praʊɪs] n destreza f
prowl [praʊl] **1** n merodeo m; **to be on the p.** merodear, rondar
　　2 vi merodear; Fam **to p. about** or **around** rondar
prowler ['praʊlə(r)] n Fam merodeador m
proximity [prɒk'sɪmɪtɪ] n proximidad f; **in p. to, in the p. of** cerca de
proxy ['prɒksɪ] n Jur (power) poderes mpl; (person) apoderado(a) m,f; **by p.** por poderes
prudence ['pruːdəns] n prudencia f
prudent ['pruːdənt] adj prudente
prudish ['pruːdɪʃ] adj remilgado(a)
prune¹ [pruːn] n ciruela pasa
prune² [pruːn] vt (roses etc) podar; Fig acortar
pry [praɪ] vi curiosear, husmear; **to p. into sth** entrometerse en algo
PS, ps [piː'es] (abbr **postscript**) P.S., P.D.
psalm [sɑːm] n salmo m
pseudo- ['sjuːdəʊ] pref pseudo-, seudo-
pseudonym ['sjuːdənɪm] n (p)seudónimo m
psyche ['saɪkɪ] n psique f
psychiatric [saɪkɪ'ætrɪk] adj psiquiátrico(a)
psychiatrist [saɪ'kaɪətrɪst] n psiquiatra mf
psychiatry [saɪ'kaɪətrɪ] n psiquiatría f
psychic ['saɪkɪk] **1** adj psíquico(a)
　　2 n médium mf
psychoanalysis [saɪkəʊə'nælɪsɪs] n psicoanálisis f
psychoanalyst [saɪkəʊ'ænəlɪst] n psicoanalista mf
psychological [saɪkə'lɒdʒɪkəl] adj psicológico(a)
psychologist [saɪ'kɒlədʒɪst] n psicólogo(a) m,f
psychology [saɪ'kɒlədʒɪ] n psicología f
psychopath ['saɪkəʊpæθ] n psicópata mf
psychosomatic [saɪkəʊsə'mætɪk] adj psicosomático(a)
psychotherapist ['saɪkəʊ'θerəpɪst] n psicoterapeuta mf

psychotherapy ['saɪkəʊ'θerəpɪ] *n* psicoterapia *f*

psychotic [saɪ'kɒtɪk] *adj & n* psicótico(a) *(m,f)*

PT [piː'tiː] *n (abbr* **physical training**) educación física

PTA [piːtiː'eɪ] *n (abbr* **Parent-Teacher Association**) = asociación de padres de alumnos y profesores, ≃ APA *f*

PTO, pto [piːtiː'əʊ] *(abbr* **please turn over**) sigue

pub [pʌb] *n Br Fam* bar *m*, pub *m*

puberty ['pjuːbətɪ] *n* pubertad *f*

pubic ['pjuːbɪk] *adj* púbico(a)

public ['pʌblɪk] **1** *adj* público(a); **to make sth p.** hacer público(a) algo; *Com* **to go p.** *(of company)* pasar a cotizar en Bolsa; **p. address system** (sistema *m* de) megafonía *f*; *Br* **p. company** empresa pública; *Br* **p. convenience** servicios *o Esp* aseos públicos; **p. holiday** día festivo *o Am* feriado; *Br* **p. house** pub *m*, taberna *f*; *Br* **p. limited company** sociedad anónima; **p. opinion** opinión pública; *Br* **p. prosecutor** fiscal *m*; **p. relations** relaciones públicas; **p. school** *Br* colegio privado; *US* colegio público; **p. transport** transporte público

2 *n* **the p.** el público; **in p.** en público

publican ['pʌblɪkən] *n Br* dueño(a) *m,f* de un "pub"

publication [pʌblɪ'keɪʃən] *n* publicación *f*

publicity [pʌ'blɪsɪtɪ] *n* publicidad *f*

publicize ['pʌblɪsaɪz] *vt (make public)* hacer público(a); *(advertise)* hacer publicidad a

public-spirited [pʌblɪk'spɪrɪtɪd] *adj* de espíritu cívico

publish ['pʌblɪʃ] *vt* publicar, editar

publisher ['pʌblɪʃə(r)] *n (person)* editor(a) *m,f*; *(firm)* (casa *f*) editorial *f*

publishing ['pʌblɪʃɪŋ] *n (business)* industria *f* editorial; **p. company** *or* **house** casa *f* editorial

pucker ['pʌkə(r)] *vt (lips, brow)* fruncir, arrugar

pudding ['pʊdɪŋ] *n Culin* pudín *m*; *Br (dessert)* postre *m*; **Christmas p.** = pudín a base de frutos secos típico de Navidad; **p. basin** cuenco *m*; **steamed p.** budín *m*

puddle ['pʌdəl] *n* charco *m*

Puerto Rican ['pweətəʊ'riːkən] *adj & n* portorriqueño(a) *(m,f)*, puertorriqueño(a) *(m,f)*

Puerto Rico ['pweətəʊ'riːkəʊ] *n* Puerto Rico

puff [pʌf] **1** *n (of wind)* racha *f*; *(of smoke)* nube *f*; **p. pastry** pasta *f* de hojaldre

2 *vi (person)* jadear, resoplar; *(train)*

echar humo; **to p. on a cigarette** dar chupadas *or Esp* caladas *or Am* pitadas a un cigarrillo

3 *vt (cigarette)* dar una calada a

▸ **puff up** *vi* hincharse

puffy ['pʌfɪ] *adj (* **puffier, puffiest**) hinchado(a)

pugnacious [pʌg'neɪʃəs] *adj* belicoso(a)

puke [pjuːk] *vi Fam* echar la papa, devolver

pull [pʊl] **1** *n* (a) *(act of pulling)* tirón *m*, *Am salvo RP* jalón *m*; **to give sth a p.** dar un tirón *or Am salvo RP* jalón a algo (b) *(attraction)* atracción *f*; *(influence)* enchufe *m*

2 *vt* (a) *(tug)* dar un tirón *or Am salvo RP* jalón a; **to p. the trigger** apretar el gatillo; **to p. to pieces** hacer pedazos; *Fig* poner por los suelos; *Fig* **to p. sb's leg** tomar el pelo a algn (b) *(draw)* tirar, arrastrar (c) *(draw out)* sacar (d) *Fam (people)* atraer

3 *vi (drag)* tirar, *Am salvo RP* jalar

▸ **pull apart** *vt sep* desmontar; *Fig (criticize)* poner por los suelos

▸ **pull down** *vt sep (building)* derribar

▸ **pull in 1** *vt sep (crowds)* atraer

2 *vi (train)* entrar en la estación; *(stop)* parar

▸ **pull off 1** *vt sep Fam (carry out)* llevar a cabo

2 *vi (vehicle)* arrancar

▸ **pull out 1** *vt sep (withdraw)* retirar

2 *vi Aut* **to p. out to overtake** salir para adelantar

▸ **pull over** *vi (driver)* parar en *Esp* el arcén *or Méx* el acotamiento

▸ **pull through** *vi* reponerse, restablecerse

▸ **pull together** *vt sep* **to p. oneself together** calmarse

▸ **pull up 1** *vt sep* (a) *(uproot)* desarraigar (b) *(chair)* acercar

2 *vi (stop)* pararse

pulley ['pʊlɪ] *n* polea *f*

pullover ['pʊləʊvə(r)] *n* suéter *m*, *Esp* jersey *m*, *RP* pulóver *m*

pulp [pʌlp] *n (of paper, wood)* pasta *f*; *(of fruit)* pulpa *f*

pulpit ['pʊlpɪt] *n* púlpito *m*

pulsate [pʌl'seɪt] *vi* vibrar, palpitar

pulse¹ [pʌls] *n Anat* pulso *m*

pulse² [pʌls] *n Bot & Culin* legumbre *f*

pumice ['pʌmɪs] *n* **p. (stone)** piedra *f* pómez

pummel ['pʌməl] *vt* aporrear

pump¹ [pʌmp] **1** *n* bomba *f*

2 *vt* bombear; **to p. sth in/out** meter/sacar algo con una bomba

▸ **pump out** *vt sep (empty)* vaciar

▸ **pump up** *vt sep (tyre)* inflar
pump² [pʌmp] *n Br (shoe)* zapatilla *f*
pumpkin ['pʌmpkɪn] *n* calabaza *f*, *Andes, RP* zapallo *m*, *Col, Carib* ahuyama *f*
pun [pʌn] *n* juego *m* de palabras
punch¹ [pʌntʃ] **1** *n (for making holes)* perforadora *f*; *(for tickets)* taladradora *f*; *(for leather etc)* punzón *m*
  2 *vt (make hole in)* perforar; *(ticket)* picar; *(leather)* punzar
punch² [pʌntʃ] **1** *n (blow)* puñetazo *m*; *(in boxing)* pegada *f*; *Fig* **it lacks p.** le falta fuerza; **p. line** remate *m (de un chiste)*
  2 *vt (with fist)* dar un puñetazo a
punch³ [pʌntʃ] *n (drink)* ponche *m*
punch-up ['pʌntʃʌp] *n Fam* pelea *f*
punctual ['pʌŋktjʊəl] *adj* puntual
punctuate ['pʌŋktjʊeɪt] *vt* puntuar; *Fig* salpicar
punctuation [pʌŋktjʊ'eɪʃən] *n* puntuación *f*
puncture ['pʌŋktʃə(r)] **1** *n* pinchazo *m*, *Guat, Méx* ponchadura *f*
  2 *vt (tyre)* pinchar, *Guat, Méx* ponchar
pundit ['pʌndɪt] *n Fam* experto(a) *m,f*
pungent ['pʌndʒənt] *adj (smell)* acre; *(taste)* fuerte
punish ['pʌnɪʃ] *vt* castigar
punishable ['pʌnɪʃəbəl] *adj* castigable, punible
punishment ['pʌnɪʃmənt] *n* castigo *m*
punk [pʌŋk] *n Fam* (**a**) *(person)* punk *mf*, **p. (music)** *(música f)* punk *m* (**b**) *US (contemptible person)* desgraciado(a) *m,f*
punt [pʌnt] **1** *n (boat)* batea *f*
  2 *vi* ir en batea
punter ['pʌntə(r)] *n (gambler)* jugador(a) *m,f*; *(customer)* cliente(a) *m,f*
puny ['pju:nɪ] *adj* (**punier, puniest**) enclenque, endeble
pup [pʌp] *n* cachorro(a) *m,f*
pupil¹ ['pju:pəl] *n Educ* alumno(a) *m,f*
pupil² ['pju:pəl] *n Anat* pupila *f*
puppet ['pʌpɪt] *n* títere *m*
puppy ['pʌpɪ] *n* cachorro(a) *m,f*, perrito *m*
purchase ['pɜ:tʃɪs] **1** *n* compra *f*
  2 *vt* comprar; **purchasing power** poder adquisitivo
purchaser ['pɜ:tʃɪsə(r)] *n* comprador(a) *m,f*
pure [pjʊə(r)] *adj* puro(a)
purée ['pjʊəreɪ] *n* puré *m*
purely [pjʊəlɪ] *adv* simplemente
purge [pɜ:dʒ] **1** *n* purga *f*
  2 *vt* purgar
purify ['pjʊərɪfaɪ] *vt* purificar

puritanical [pjʊərɪ'tænɪkəl] *adj* puritano(a)
purity ['pjʊərɪtɪ] *n* pureza *f*
purl [pɜ:l] *vi (in knitting)* hacer punto del revés
purple ['pɜ:pəl] *adj* morado(a), purpúreo(a); **to go p. (in the face)** ponerse morado(a)
purport [pɜ:'pɔ:t] *vi Fml* pretender; **to p. to be sth** pretender ser algo
purpose ['pɜ:pəs] *n* (**a**) *(object, aim)* propósito *m*, objeto *m*; **on p.** a propósito (**b**) *(use)* finalidad *f*
purposeful ['pɜ:pəsfʊl] *adj (resolute)* decidido(a), resoluto(a)
purr [pɜ:(r)] *vi (cat)* ronronear; *(engine)* zumbar
purse [pɜ:s] **1** *n Br (for coins)* monedero *m*; *US (bag)* *Esp* bolso *m*, *Col, CSur* cartera *f*, *Méx* bolsa *f*; *(prize money)* premio *m* en metálico
  2 *vt* **to p. one's lips** apretarse los labios
purser ['pɜ:sə(r)] *n* contador(a) *m,f*
pursue [pə'sju:] *vt (criminal)* perseguir; *(person)* seguir; *(pleasure)* buscar; *(career)* ejercer
pursuer [pə'sju:ə(r)] *n Fml* perseguidor(a) *m,f*
pursuit [pə'sju:t] *n (of criminal)* persecución *f*; *(of animal)* caza *f*; *(of pleasure)* búsqueda *f*; *(pastime)* pasatiempo *m*
purveyor [pə'veɪə(r)] *n Fml* proveedor(a) *m,f*
pus [pʌs] *n* pus *m*
push [pʊʃ] **1** *n* empujón *m*, *CAm, Méx* aventón *m*; *Fig (drive)* brío *m*, dinamismo *m*
  2 *vt* (**a**) *(in general)* empujar; *(button)* pulsar, apretar; **to p. one's finger into a hole** meter el dedo en un agujero (**b**) *Fig (pressurize)* instar; *(harass)* acosar; *Fam* **to be (hard) pushed for time** estar apurado(a) *or RP* corto(a) de tiempo (**c**) *Fam (product)* promover; **to p. drugs** pasar droga
  3 *vi* empujar
▸ **push aside** *vt sep (object)* apartar
▸ **push in** *vi* colarse
▸ **push off** *vi (in boat)* desatracar; *Fam* **p. off!** ¡lárgate!
▸ **push on** *vi (continue)* seguir adelante
▸ **push through** *vt sep* abrirse paso entre
pushchair ['pʊʃtʃeə(r)] *n Br* sillita *f* (de ruedas)
pusher ['pʊʃə(r)] *n Fam (of drugs)* camello *m*, *Am* dealer *m*
pushover ['pʊʃəʊvə(r)] *n Fam* **it's a p.** está chupado; **she's a p.** es un ligue fácil

push-up ['pʊʃʌp] *n* flexión *f* (de brazos)

pushy ['pʊʃɪ] *adj* (**pushier, pushiest**) *Fam* agresivo(a)

puss [pʊs], **pussy** ['pʊsɪ] *n Fam* minino *m*

put [pʊt] **1** *vt* (*pt & pp* put) (**a**) (*place*) poner; (*carefully*) colocar; (*insert*) meter; **to p. sb to bed** acostar a algn; **to p. a picture up on the wall** colgar un cuadro en la pared (**b**) (*present*) presentar, exponer; **to p. a question to sb** hacer una pregunta a algn (**c**) (*express*) expresar, decir; **to p. sth simply** explicar algo de manera sencilla (**d**) (*estimate*) calcular (**e**) (*money*) ingresar; (*invest*) invertir

2 *vi Naut* **to p. to sea** zarpar

3 *adv* **to stay p.** quedarse quieto(a)

▸ **put about** *vt sep* (*rumour*) hacer correr

▸ **put across** *vt sep* (*idea etc*) comunicar

▸ **put aside** *vt sep* (*money*) ahorrar; (*time*) reservar

▸ **put away** *vt sep* (*tidy away*) recoger; *Fam* (*eat*) zamparse; (*save*) (*money*) ahorrar

▸ **put back** *vt sep* (*postpone*) aplazar; **to p. the clock back** retrasar la hora

▸ **put by** *vt sep* (*money*) ahorrar

▸ **put down** *vt sep* (*set down*) dejar; (*suppress*) sofocar; (*humiliate*) humillar; (*criticize*) criticar; (*animal*) provocar la muerte de; (*write down*) apuntar

▸ **put down to** *vt sep* achacar a

▸ **put forward** *vt sep* (*theory*) exponer; (*proposal*) hacer; **to p. one's name forward for sth** presentarse como candidato(a) para algo

▸ **put in 1** *vt sep* (*install*) instalar; (*complaint, request*) presentar; (*time*) pasar

2 *vi Naut* hacer escala (**at** en)

▸ **put off** *vt sep* (*postpone*) aplazar; **to p. sb off doing sth** quitarle *or Am* sacarle a algn las ganas de hacer algo

▸ **put on** *vt sep* (*clothes*) poner, ponerse; (*show*) montar; (*concert*) dar; (*switch on*) (*radio*) poner; (*light*) encender; *Am* prender; (*water, gas*) abrir; **to p. on weight** aumentar de peso; **to p. on the brakes** frenar; *Fig* **to p. on a straight face** poner cara de serio(a)

▸ **put out** *vt sep* (**a**) (*light, fire*) apagar (**b**) (*place outside*) sacar (**c**) (*extend*) (*arm*) extender; (*tongue*) sacar; (*hand*) tender (**d**) (*spread*) (*rumour*) hacer correr (**e**) (*annoy*) molestar; (*inconvenience*) incordiar (**f**) (*anger*) **to be p. out by sth** *Esp* enfadarse *or Am* enojarse por algo

▸ **put through** *vt sep Tel* **p. me through to Pat, please** póngame con Pat, por favor

▸ **put together** *vt sep* (*join*) unir, reunir; (*assemble*) armar, montar

▸ **put up** *vt sep* (*raise*) levantar, subir; (*picture*) colocar; (*curtains*) colgar; (*building*) construir; (*tent*) armar; (*prices*) subir, aumentar; (*accommodate*) alojar, hospedar; **to p. up a fight** ofrecer resistencia

▸ **put up to** *vt sep* **to p. sb up to sth** incitar a algn a hacer algo

▸ **put up with** *vt insep* aguantar, soportar

putrid ['pjuːtrɪd] *adj Fml* putrefacto(a)

putt [pʌt] **1** *n* tiro *m* al hoyo

2 *vt & vi* tirar al hoyo

putting ['pʌtɪŋ] *n* **p. green** minigolf *m*

putty ['pʌtɪ] *n* masilla *f*

puzzle ['pʌzəl] **1** *n* rompecabezas *m inv*; (*crossword*) crucigrama *m*; *Fig* (*mystery*) misterio *m*

2 *vt* dejar perplejo(a); **to be puzzled about sth** no entender algo

▸ **puzzle over** *vt insep* **to p. over sth** dar vueltas a algo (en la cabeza)

puzzling ['pʌzlɪŋ] *adj* extraño(a), curioso(a)

PVC [piːviːˈsiː] *n* (*abbr* **polyvinyl chloride**) PVC *m*

pygmy ['pɪgmɪ] *n* pigmeo(a) *m,f*; *Fig* enano(a) *m,f*

pyjamas [pəˈdʒɑːməz] *npl* pijama *m*, *Am* piyama *m or f*

pylon ['paɪlən] *n* torre *f* (de conducción eléctrica)

pyramid ['pɪrəmɪd] *n* pirámide *f*

Pyrenees [pɪrəˈniːz] *npl* **the P.** los Pirineos

Pyrex® ['paɪreks] *n* pírex® *m*

python ['paɪθən] *n* pitón *m*

Q, q [kju:] *n (the letter)* Q, q *f*

quack [kwæk] **1** *n* (a) *(of duck)* graznido *m* (b) *Br Fam Pej or Hum (doctor)* matasanos *m inv*
2 *vi* graznar

quad [kwɒd] *n Fam* (a) *Br (of school, university)* patio *m* interior (b) *(quadruplet)* cuatrillizo(a) *m,f*

quadrangle ['kwɒdræŋgəl] *n* (a) *Geom* cuadrángulo *m* (b) *(courtyard)* patio *m* interior

quadruple ['kwɒdropəl, kwɒ'dru:pəl] **1** *n* cuádruplo *m*
2 *adj* cuádruple
3 *vt* cuadruplicar
4 *vi* cuadruplicarse

quadruplet ['kwɒdroplɪt, kwɒ'dru:plɪt] *n* cuatrillizo(a) *m,f*

quagmire ['kwægmaɪə(r), 'kwɒgmaɪə(r)] *n (land)* cenagal *m*

quail¹ [kweɪl] *n (bird)* codorniz *f*

quail² [kweɪl] *vi Fig* encogerse

quaint [kweɪnt] *adj (picturesque)* pintoresco(a); *(original)* singular

quake [kweɪk] **1** *vi* temblar
2 *n Fam* temblor *m* de tierra

Quaker ['kweɪkə(r)] *n* cuáquero(a) *m,f*

qualification [kwɒlɪfɪ'keɪʃən] *n* (a) *(ability)* aptitud *f* (b) *(requirement)* requisito *m* (c) *(diploma etc)* título *m* (d) *(reservation)* reserva *f*

qualified ['kwɒlɪfaɪd] *adj* (a) *(having diploma)* titulado(a); *(competent)* capacitado(a); **q. teacher** profesor(a) titulado(a) (b) **q. approval** *(modified)* aprobación *f* condicional

qualify ['kwɒlɪfaɪ] **1** *vt* (a) *(entitle)* capacitar (b) *(modify)* modificar; *(statement)* matizar; *Ling* calificar
2 *vi* (a) **to q. as** *(doctor etc)* sacar el título de; **when did you q.?** ¿cuándo terminaste la carrera? (b) *(in competition)* quedar clasificado(a)

qualifying ['kwɒlɪfaɪɪŋ] *adj (round, exam)* eliminatorio(a)

quality ['kwɒlɪtɪ] *n* (a) *(excellence)* calidad *f*; **q. control** control *m* de calidad; *Br* **q. newspapers** prensa *f* no sensacionalista (b) *(attribute)* cualidad *f*

qualm [kwɑ:m] *n* (a) *(scruple)* escrúpulo *m* (b) *(doubt)* duda *f*

quandary ['kwɒndərɪ, 'kwɒndrɪ] *n* **to be in a q.** estar en un dilema

quango ['kwæŋgəʊ] *(abbr* **quasi-autonomous non-governmental organization)** *n Br* = organismo público semiindependiente

quantity ['kwɒntɪtɪ] *n* cantidad *f*

quarantine ['kwɒrəntiːn] *n* cuarentena *f*

quarrel ['kwɒrəl] **1** *n (argument)* riña *f*, pelea *f*; *(disagreement)* desacuerdo *m*
2 *vi (argue)* pelearse, reñir; **to q. with sth** discrepar de algo

quarrelsome ['kwɒrəlsəm] *adj* camorrista

quarry¹ ['kwɒrɪ] *Min* **1** *n* cantera *f*
2 *vt* extraer

quarry² ['kwɒrɪ] *n* presa *f*

quart [kwɔ:t] *n (measurement)* = cuarto de galón *(Br = 1,13 l; US = 0,94 l)*

quarter ['kwɔ:tə(r)] **1** *n* (a) *(fraction, of orange, of moon)* cuarto *m*; **a q. of an hour** un cuarto de hora (b) *(in telling time) Br* **it's a q. to three,** *US* **it's a q. of three** son las tres menos cuarto; **it's a q.** *Br* **past** *or US* **after six** son las seis y cuarto (c) *US (coin)* cuarto *m* (de dólar) (d) *(district)* barrio *m* (e) **quarters** *(lodgings)* alojamiento *m* (f) *US Mus* **q. note** negra *f*
2 *vt* (a) *(cut into quarters)* dividir en cuartos (b) *(accommodate)* alojar

quarterback ['kwɔ:təbæk] *n US* quarterback *m Méx* mariscal *m* de campo

quarterfinal ['kwɔ:tə'faɪnəl] *n Sport* cuarto *m* de final

quarterly ['kwɔ:təlɪ] **1** *adj* trimestral
2 *n* publicación *f* trimestral
3 *adv* trimestralmente

quartermaster ['kwɔ:təmɑ:stə(r)] *n Mil* oficial *m* de intendencia

quartet(te) [kwɔ:'tet] *n* cuarteto *m*

quartz [kwɔ:ts] *n* cuarzo *m*; **q. watch** reloj *m* de cuarzo

quash [kwɒʃ] *vt Jur* anular; *(uprising)* aplastar

quasi ['kwɑ:zɪ, 'kweɪzaɪ] *pref* cuasi

quaver ['kweɪvə(r)] **1** n (**a**) Br Mus corchea f (**b**) (in voice) temblor m
2 vi (voice) temblar

quay(side) ['kiː(saɪd)] n muelle m

queasy ['kwiːzɪ] adj (**queasier, queasiest**) **to feel q.** (ill) tener náuseas

queen [kwiːn] n (**a**) (of country) reina f (**b**) Fam Pej loca f, marica m

queer [kwɪə(r)] **1** adj (strange) extraño(a), raro(a)
2 n Fam Pej marica m, maricón m

quell [kwel] vt reprimir

quench [kwentʃ] vt apagar

querulous ['kwerʊləs, 'kwerjʊləs] adj Fml quejumbroso(a)

query ['kwɪərɪ] **1** n (question) pregunta f
2 vt (ask questions about) preguntar acerca de; (have doubts about) poner en duda

quest [kwest] n Literary búsqueda f

question ['kwestʃən] **1** n pregunta f; **to ask sb a q.** hacer una pregunta a algn; **he did it without q.** lo hizo sin rechistar; **to call sth into q.** poner algo en duda; **that's out of the q.!** ¡ni hablar!; **q. mark** signo m de interrogación; Fig interrogante m
2 vt (ask questions of) hacer preguntas a; (interrogate) interrogar; (query) poner en duda

questionable ['kwestʃənəbəl] adj (doubtful) dudoso(a); (debatable) discutible

questionnaire [kwestʃə'neə(r)] n cuestionario m

queue [kjuː] Br **1** n cola f
2 vi **to q. (up)** hacer cola

quibble ['kwɪbəl] **1** n pega f
2 vi poner pegas (with a); Fam buscarle tres pies al gato

quiche [kiːʃ] n quiche m or f

quick [kwɪk] adj (**a**) (fast) rápido(a); **a q. look** un vistazo; **a q. snack** un bocado; **be q.!** ¡date prisa!, Am ¡apúrate! (**b**) (clever) espabilado(a); (wit) agudo(a) (**c**) **she has a q. temper** Esp se enfada or Am se enoja con nada

quicken ['kwɪkən] **1** vt acelerar; **to q. one's pace** acelerar el paso
2 vi (speed up) acelerarse

quickly ['kwɪklɪ] adv rápidamente, de prisa

quickness ['kwɪknɪs] n (**a**) (speed) rapidez f (**b**) (of wit) agudeza f, viveza f

quicksand ['kwɪksænd] n arenas movedizas

quicksilver ['kwɪksɪlvə(r)] n mercurio m

quick-witted [kwɪk'wɪtɪd] adj agudo(a)

quid [kwɪd] n (pl **quid**) Br Fam (pound) libra f

quiet ['kwaɪət] **1** n (**a**) (silence) silencio m (**b**) (calm) tranquilidad f
2 adj (**a**) (silent) silencioso(a); (street) tranquilo(a); **keep q.!** ¡silencio! (**b**) (calm) tranquilo(a) (**c**) (person) reservado(a) (**d**) (not showy) (clothes) sobrio(a); (colours) apagado(a)
3 vt US calmar
4 vi US calmarse

quieten ['kwaɪətən] **1** vt (silence) callar; (calm) calmar
2 vi (silence) callarse; (calm) calmarse
▸ **quieten down** Br **1** vt sep calmar
2 vi calmarse

quietly ['kwaɪətlɪ] adv (**a**) (silently) silenciosamente; **he spoke q.** habló en voz baja (**b**) (calmly) tranquilamente (**c**) (discreetly) discretamente

quietness ['kwaɪətnɪs] n (**a**) (silence) silencio m (**b**) (calm) tranquilidad f

quill [kwɪl] n (feather, pen) pluma f; (of porcupine) púa f

quilt [kwɪlt] **1** n edredón m
2 vt acolchar

quin [kwɪn] n Fam quintillizo(a) m,f

quinine ['kwɪniːn, US 'kwaɪnaɪn] n quinina f

quint [kwɪnt] n US Fam = **quin**

quintessential [kwɪntɪ'senʃəl] adj fundamental

quintet(te) [kwɪn'tet] n quinteto m

quintuple ['kwɪntjʊpəl, kwɪn'tjuːpəl] **1** n quíntuplo m
2 adj quíntuplo(a)
3 vt quintuplicar
4 vi quintuplicarse

quintuplet ['kwɪntjʊplɪt, kwɪn'tjuːplɪt] n quintillizo(a) m,f

quip [kwɪp] **1** n salida f; (joke) chiste m
2 vi bromear

quirk [kwɜːk] n (**a**) (peculiarity) manía f (**b**) (of fate) arbitrariedad f

quit [kwɪt] **1** vt (pt & pp **quitted** or **quit**) (**a**) (leave) dejar, abandonar (**b**) **q. making that noise!** ¡deja de hacer ese ruido!
2 vi (**a**) (go) irse; (give up) abandonar (**b**) (resign) dimitir
3 adj **let's call it quits** dejémoslo estar

> 🖉 Note that the Spanish verb **quitar** is a false friend and is never a translation for the English verb **to quit**. In Spanish **quitar** means both "to remove" and "to take away".

quite [kwaɪt] adv (**a**) (entirely) totalmente; **she's q. right** tiene toda la razón (**b**) (rather) bastante; **q. a while** un buen rato; **that's q. enough!** ¡ya está bien!; **it's**

q. something es increíble (**c**) *(exactly)*
exactamente; **q. (so)!** ¡efectivamente!
quiver¹ [ˈkwɪvə(r)] *vi* temblar
quiver² [ˈkwɪvə(r)] *n (for arrows)* aljaba *f*,
carcaj *m*
quiz [kwɪz] **1** *n Rad & TV* **q. show** concurso *m*
2 *vt* hacer preguntas a
quizzical [ˈkwɪzɪkəl] *adj* (**a**) *(bemused)*
burlón(ona) (**b**) *(enquiring)* curioso(a)
quorum [ˈkwɔːrəm] *n* quórum *m inv*

quota [ˈkwəʊtə] *n* (**a**) *(proportional share)*
cuota *f*, parte *f* (**b**) *(prescribed amount,
number)* cupo *m*
quotation [kwəʊˈteɪʃən] *n* (**a**) *Lit* cita *f*; **q.
marks** comillas *fpl* (**b**) *Fin* cotización *f*
quote [kwəʊt] **1** *vt* (**a**) *(cite)* citar (**b**) *Com*
to q. a price dar un presupuesto (**c**) *Fin*
cotizar
   2 *n* (**a**) *Lit* cita *f* (**b**) *Com* presupuesto *m*
quotient [ˈkwəʊʃənt] *n* cociente *m*

R

R, r [ɑː(r)] *n (the letter)* R, r *f*

rabbi ['ræbaɪ] *n* rabí *m*, rabino *m*

rabbit ['ræbɪt] **1** *n* conejo(a) *m,f*; **r. hutch** conejera *f*
2 *vi Fam* **to r. (on)** enrollarse

rabble ['ræbəl] *n Pej* **the r.** el populacho

rabies ['reɪbiːz] *n* rabia *f*

RAC [ɑːreɪ'siː] *n Br (abbr* **Royal Automobile Club)** = organización británica de ayuda al automovilista, *Esp* ≃ RACE *m, Arg* ≃ ACA *m*

raccoon [rə'kuːn] *n* mapache *m*

race¹ [reɪs] **1** *n* **(a)** *Sport* carrera *f* **(b)** *Br* **the races** las carreras (de caballos)
2 *vt* **(a)** **I'll r. you!** ¡te echo una carrera! **(b)** *(car, horse)* hacer correr **(c)** *(engine)* acelerar
3 *vi (go quickly)* correr; *(pulse)* acelerarse

race² [reɪs] *n (people)* raza *f*

racecourse ['reɪskɔːs] *n Br* hipódromo *m*

racehorse ['reɪshɔːs] *n* caballo *m* de carreras

racer ['reɪsə(r)] *n Sport* **(a)** *(person)* corredor(a) *m,f* **(b)** *(bicycle)* bicicleta *f* de carreras; *(car)* coche *m or Am* carro *m or CSur* auto *m* de carreras

racetrack ['reɪstræk] *n (for cars, people, bikes)* pista *f; US (for horses)* hipódromo *m*

racial ['reɪʃəl] *adj* racial

racing ['reɪsɪŋ] **1** *n* carreras *fpl*
2 *adj* de carreras; **r. bicycle** bicicleta *f* de carreras; **r. car** coche *m or Am* carro *m or CSur* auto *m* de carreras

racism ['reɪsɪzəm] *n* racismo *m*

racist ['reɪsɪst] *adj & n* racista *(mf)*

rack [ræk] **1** *n* **(a)** *(shelf)* estante *m; (for clothes)* percha *f;* **luggage r.** portaequipajes *m inv;* **roof r.** baca *f* **(b)** *(for torture)* potro *m*
2 *vt Literary (torment)* atormentar; *Fam Fig* **to r. one's brains** devanarse los sesos

racket¹ ['rækɪt] *n (a) (din)* estruendo *m, Esp* jaleo *m* **(b)** *(swindle)* timo *m; (shady business)* chanchullo *m*

racket² ['rækɪt] *n Sport* raqueta *f*

racquet ['rækɪt] *n* = **racket²**

racy ['reɪsɪ] *adj (**racier, raciest**) (lively)* vivo(a); *(risqué)* atrevido(a)

radar ['reɪdɑː(r)] *n* radar *m*

radiance ['reɪdɪəns] *n* resplandor *m*

radiant ['reɪdɪənt] *adj* radiante, resplandeciente

radiate ['reɪdɪeɪt] *vt* irradiar; *Fig* **she radiated happiness** rebosaba de alegría

radiation [reɪdɪ'eɪʃən] *n* radiación *f*

radiator ['reɪdɪeɪtə(r)] *n* radiador *m*

radical ['rædɪkəl] *adj* radical

radii ['reɪdɪaɪ] *pl of* **radius**

radio ['reɪdɪəʊ] *n* radio *f;* **on the r.** en *or* por la radio; **r. station** emisora *f* (de radio)

radioactive [reɪdɪəʊ'æktɪv] *adj* radiactivo(a)

radio-controlled [reɪdɪəʊkən'trəʊld] *adj* teledirigido(a)

radiography [reɪdɪ'ɒɡrəfɪ] *n* radiografía *f*

radiology [reɪdɪ'ɒlədʒɪ] *n* radiología *f*

radiotherapy [reɪdɪəʊ'θerəpɪ] *n* radioterapia *f*

radish ['rædɪʃ] *n* rábano *m*

radius ['reɪdɪəs] *n (pl* **radii)** radio *m;* **within a r. of** en un radio de

RAF [ɑːreɪ'ef] *n Br (abbr* **Royal Air Force)** = fuerzas aéreas británicas

raffle ['ræfəl] **1** *n* rifa *f*
2 *vt* rifar

raft [rɑːft] *n* balsa *f*

rafter ['rɑːftə(r)] *n* viga *f* de madera

rag [ræɡ] *n (a) (torn piece)* harapo *m* **(b)** *(for cleaning)* trapo *m* **(c)** *Fam* **rags** *(clothes)* trapos *mpl* **(d)** *Pej Press* periodicucho *m*

rag-and-bone ['ræɡən'bəʊn] *adj Br* **r. man** trapero *m*

rage [reɪdʒ] **1** *n (a) (fury)* cólera *f* **(b)** *Fam* **it's all the r.** hace furor
2 *vi* **(a)** *(person)* rabiar, estar furioso(a) **(b)** *Fig (storm, sea)* rugir; *(wind)* bramar

ragged ['ræɡɪd] *adj* **(a)** *(clothes)* hecho(a) jirones **(b)** *(person)* harapiento(a) **(c)** *(edge)* mellado(a) **(d)** *Fig (uneven)* desigual

raging ['reɪdʒɪŋ] *adj* **(a)** *(angry)* furioso(a) **(b)** *Fig (sea)* embravecido(a) **(c)** *(intense)* feroz; *(storm)* violento(a)

raid [reɪd] **1** *n Mil* incursión *f; (by police)* redada *f; (robbery etc)* atraco *m*

2 *vt Mil* hacer una incursión en; *(of police)* hacer una redada en; *(rob)* asaltar; *Fam* **to r. the larder** vaciar la despensa

raider ['reɪdə(r)] *n (invader)* invasor(a) *m,f*

rail [reɪl] *n* (**a**) *(railing)* baranda *f, Esp* barandilla *f* (**b**) *Rail* carril *f;* **by r.** *(send sth)* por ferrocarril; *(travel)* en tren

railcard ['reɪlkɑːd] *n Br* **family/young person's r.** = tarjeta familiar/juvenil para obtener billetes de tren con descuento

railing ['reɪlɪŋ] *n (metal post)* reja *f;* **railings** *(fence)* verja *f*

railroad ['reɪlrəʊd] *n US* ferrocarril *m*

railway ['reɪlweɪ] *n Br* ferrocarril *m;* **r. line, r. track** vía férrea; **r. station** estación *f* de ferrocarril

railwayman ['reɪlweɪmən] *n Br* ferroviario *m*

rain [reɪn] **1** *n* lluvia *f;* **in the r.** bajo la lluvia
2 *vi* llover; **it's raining** llueve

rainbow ['reɪnbəʊ] *n* arco *m* iris

raincoat ['reɪnkəʊt] *n* impermeable *m*

raindrop ['reɪndrɒp] *n* gota *f* de lluvia

rainfall ['reɪnfɔːl] *n (falling of rain)* precipitación *f;* *(amount)* pluviosidad *f*

rainforest ['reɪnfɒrɪst] *n* selva *f* tropical

rainy ['reɪnɪ] *adj* (**rainier, rainiest**) lluvioso(a)

raise [reɪz] **1** *n US* aumento *m* (de sueldo)
2 *vt* (**a**) *(lift)* levantar; *(voice)* levantar (**b**) *(prices)* aumentar (**c**) *(money)* reunir (**d**) *(issue)* plantear (**e**) *(crops, children)* criar (**f**) *(standards)* mejorar

raisin ['reɪzən] *n* pasa *f*

rake¹ [reɪk] **1** *n (garden-tool)* rastrillo *m;* *(for fire)* hurgón *m*
2 *vt (leaves)* rastrillar; *(fire)* hurgar; *(with machine gun)* barrer

rake² [reɪk] *n (dissolute man)* calavera *m,* libertino *m*

rally ['rælɪ] **1** *n* (**a**) *(gathering)* reunión *f; Pol* mitin *m* (**b**) *Aut* rallye *m* (**c**) *(in tennis)* jugada *f*
2 *vt (support)* reunir
3 *vi* recuperarse

▸ **rally round** *vi* **her family rallied round** su familia la arropó

RAM [ræm] *n Comput (abbr* **random access memory)** RAM *f*

ram [ræm] **1** *n* (**a**) *Zool* carnero *m* (**b**) *Tech* maza *f*
2 *vt* (**a**) *(drive into place)* hincar; *(cram)* embutir; *Fam* **to r. sth home** hacer algo patente (**b**) *(crash into)* chocar con

ramble ['ræmbəl] **1** *n (walk)* caminata *f*
2 *vi* (**a**) *(walk)* hacer una excursión a pie (**b**) *Fig (digress)* divagar

rambler ['ræmblə(r)] *n* (**a**) *(person)* excursionista *mf* (**b**) *Bot* rosal *m* trepador

rambling ['ræmblɪŋ] *adj* (**a**) *(incoherent)* incoherente (**b**) *(house)* laberíntico(a) (**c**) *Bot* trepador(a)

ramp [ræmp] *n* (**a**) *(to ease access)* rampa *f* (**b**) *(to plane)* escalerilla *f*

rampage 1 *n* ['ræmpeɪdʒ] **to be on the r.** desmandarse
2 *vi* [ræm'peɪdʒ] **to r. about** comportarse como un/una loco(a)

rampant ['ræmpənt] *adj* incontrolado(a); **corruption is r.** la corrupción está muy extendida

rampart ['ræmpɑːt] *n* muralla *f*

ramshackle ['ræmʃækəl] *adj* destartalado(a)

ran [ræn] *pt of* **run**

ranch [rɑːntʃ] *n US* rancho *m,* hacienda *f*

rancher ['rɑːntʃə(r)] *n US* ranchero(a) *m,f*

rancid ['rænsɪd] *adj* rancio(a)

rancour, *US* **rancor** ['ræŋkə(r)] *n Fml* rencor *m*

random ['rændəm] **1** *n* **at r.** al azar
2 *adj* fortuito(a); **r. selection** selección hecha al azar

randy ['rændɪ] *adj* (**randier, randiest**) *Br Fam* caliente, *Esp, Méx* cachondo(a)

rang [ræŋ] *pt of* **ring**

range [reɪndʒ] **1** *n* (**a**) *(of mountains)* cordillera *f,* sierra *f* (**b**) *US (open land)* pradera *f* (**c**) *(choice)* surtido *m;* *(of products)* gama *f* (**d**) *firing r.* campo *m* de tiro (**e**) *(of missile)* alcance *m;* **at close r.** de cerca (**f**) *(cooker)* fogón *m,* cocina *f* or *Col, Méx, Ven* estufa *f* de carbón
2 *vi (extend)* extenderse (**to** hasta); **prices r. from £5 to £20** los precios oscilan entre 5 y 20 libras

ranger ['reɪndʒə(r)] *n* (**a**) *(forest)* **r.** guardabosques *mf inv* (**b**) *US Mil* comando *m*

rank¹ [ræŋk] **1** *n* (**a**) *Mil (row)* fila *f;* **the ranks** los soldados rasos (**b**) *(position in army)* graduación *f;* *(in society)* rango *m* (**c**) *Br* **(taxi) r.** parada *f* de taxis
2 *vt (classify)* clasificar
3 *vi (figure)* figurar; **to r. above/below sb** figurar por encima/debajo de algn; **to r. with** estar al mismo nivel que

rank² [ræŋk] *adj Fml (foul-smelling)* fétido(a)

ransack ['rænsæk] *vt (plunder)* saquear; *(rummage in)* registrar

ransom ['rænsəm] *n* rescate *m;* **to hold sb to r.** pedir rescate por algn; *Fig* poner a algn entre la espada y la pared

rant [rænt] *vi* vociferar; *Fam* **to r. and rave** pegar gritos

rap [ræp] **1** n (a) (blow) golpe seco; (on door) golpecito m (b) Mus rap m
2 vt & vi (knock) golpear

rape¹ [reɪp] Jur **1** n violación f
2 vt violar

rape² [reɪp] n Bot colza f

rapeseed ['reɪpsiːd] n **r. oil** aceite m de colza

rapid ['ræpɪd] **1** adj rápido(a)
2 n **rapids** (in river) rápidos mpl

rapidity [rə'pɪdɪtɪ] n rapidez f

rapist ['reɪpɪst] n violador(a) m,f

rapper ['ræpə(r)] n rapero(a) m,f

rapport [ræ'pɔː(r)] n compenetración f

rapture ['ræptʃə(r)] n éxtasis m

rapturous ['ræptʃərəs] adj muy entusiasta

rare¹ [reə(r)] adj raro(a), poco común

rare² [reə(r)] adj (steak) poco hecho(a)

rarefied ['reərɪfaɪd] adj enrarecido(a)

rarely ['reəlɪ] adv raras veces

raring ['reərɪŋ] adj Fam **to be r. to do sth** morirse de ganas de hacer algo

rarity ['reərɪtɪ] n rareza f

rascal ['rɑːskəl] n granuja mf

rash¹ [ræʃ] n (a) Med erupción f, sarpullido m (b) Fig (of robberies etc) racha f

rash² [ræʃ] adj (reckless) impetuoso(a); (words, actions) precipitado(a), imprudente

rasher ['ræʃə(r)] n Br **r. (of bacon)** loncha f de tocino or Esp beicon

raspberry ['rɑːzbərɪ] n frambuesa f

rasping ['rɑːspɪŋ] adj áspero(a)

rat [ræt] n (a) (animal) rata f; **r. poison** raticida m (b) US Fam (informer) soplón(ona) m,f, chivato(a) m,f

rate [reɪt] **1** n (a) (ratio) índice m, tasa f; **at any r.** (at least) al menos; (anyway) en cualquier caso (b) (cost) precio m; Fin (of interest, exchange) tipo m, tasa f (c) **at the r. of** (speed) a la velocidad de; (quantity) a razón de (d) Br **(business) rates** impuestos mpl municipales (para empresas)
2 vt (a) (estimate) estimar (b) (evaluate) tasar (c) (consider) considerar

rateable ['reɪtəbəl] adj Br **r. value** valor m catastral

ratepayer ['reɪtpeɪə(r)] n Br contribuyente mf

rather ['rɑːðə(r)] adv (a) (quite) más bien, bastante; (very much so) muy (b) (more accurately) mejor dicho; **r. than** (instead of) en vez de; (more than) más que (c) **she would r. stay here** (prefer to) prefiere quedarse aquí

ratify ['rætɪfaɪ] vt ratificar

rating ['reɪtɪŋ] n (a) (valuation) tasación f; (score) valoración f (b) TV **(programme) ratings** índice m de audiencia (c) Naut marinero m sin graduación

ratio ['reɪʃɪəʊ] n razón f; **in the r. of** a razón de

ration ['ræʃən] **1** n (a) (allowance) ración f (b) **rations** víveres mpl
2 vt racionar

rational ['ræʃənəl] adj racional

rationale [ræʃə'nɑːl] n base f

rationalize ['ræʃənəlaɪz] vt racionalizar

rattle ['rætəl] **1** n (a) (of train, cart) traqueteo m; (of metal) repiqueteo m; (of glass) tintineo m (b) (toy) sonajero m; (instrument) carraca f
2 vt (a) (keys etc) hacer sonar (b) Fam (unsettle) poner nervioso(a)
3 vi sonar; (metal) repiquetear; (glass) tintinear

rattlesnake ['rætəlsneɪk] n serpiente f de cascabel

raucous ['rɔːkəs] adj estridente

ravage ['rævɪdʒ] Fml **1** npl **ravages** estragos mpl
2 vt asolar, devastar

rave [reɪv] **1** vi (a) (be delirious) delirar (b) (be angry) enfurecerse (at con) (c) Fam (show enthusiasm) entusiasmarse (about por)
2 adj Fam **r. review** crítica f muy favorable

raven ['reɪvən] n cuervo m

ravenous ['rævənəs] adj **I'm r.** tengo un hambre que no veo

ravine [rə'viːn] n barranco m

raving ['reɪvɪŋ] adj Fam **r. mad** loco(a) de atar

ravishing ['rævɪʃɪŋ] adj (person) encantador(a)

raw [rɔː] adj (a) (uncooked) crudo(a) (b) (not processed) bruto(a); **r. material** materia prima (c) (emotion) instintivo(a) (d) **r. deal** trato injusto (e) US (inexperienced) novato(a)

ray¹ [reɪ] n rayo m; Fig **r. of hope** rayo de esperanza

ray² [reɪ] n (fish) raya f

rayon ['reɪɒn] n rayón m

raze [reɪz] vt arrasar

razor ['reɪzə(r)] n (for shaving) maquinilla f de afeitar; **r. blade** hoja f de afeitar

R & D [ɑːrən'diː] n (abbr **Research and Development**) I+D

Rd (abbr **Road**) calle f, c/

re [riː] prep respecto a, con referencia a

reach [riːtʃ] **1** vt (a) (arrive at) llegar a (b) (contact) localizar

2 *vi* **to r. for sth** (tratar de) alcanzar algo; **to r. out** extender la mano

3 *n* alcance *m*; **out of r.** fuera del alcance; **within r.** al alcance

react [rɪˈækt] *vi* reaccionar

reaction [rɪˈækʃən] *n* reacción *f*

reactionary [rɪˈækʃənərɪ] *adj & n* reaccionario(a) *(m,f)*

reactor [rɪˈæktə(r)] *n* reactor *m*

read [riːd] **1** *vt (pt & pp* **read** [red]*)* (**a**) *(book, newspaper, letter)* leer (**b**) *Br Univ* estudiar (**c**) *(of dial)* marcar; *(of signpost, text)* decir

2 *vi* leer

▸ **read out** *vt sep* leer en voz alta

readable [ˈriːdəbəl] *adj* (**a**) *(interesting)* interesante (**b**) *(legible)* legible

reader [ˈriːdə(r)] *n* (**a**) *(person)* lector(a) *m,f* (**b**) *(book)* libro *m* de lectura (**c**) *Br Univ* profesor(a) *m,f* adjunto(a)

readership [ˈriːdəʃɪp] *n Press* lectores *mpl*

readily [ˈredɪlɪ] *adv* (**a**) *(easily)* fácilmente; **r. available** disponible en el acto (**b**) *(willingly)* de buena gana

readiness [ˈredɪnɪs] *n* (**a**) *(preparedness)* preparación *f* (**b**) *(willingness)* buena disposición

reading [ˈriːdɪŋ] *n* (**a**) *(action, pastime)* lectura *f* (**b**) *(interpretation)* interpretación *f* (**c**) *(of laws, bill)* presentación *f*

readjust [riːəˈdʒʌst] **1** *vt* reajustar

2 *vi (adapt oneself)* adaptarse

ready [ˈredɪ] *adj* (**readier, readiest**) (**a**) *(prepared)* listo(a), preparado(a); **r., steady, go!** ¡preparados, listos, ya! (**b**) **r. to** *(about to)* a punto de (**c**) *(to hand)* a mano; **r. cash** dinero *m* en efectivo (**d**) *(willing)* dispuesto(a)

ready-cooked [ˈredɪˈkʊkt] *adj* precocinado(a)

ready-made [ˈredɪˈmeɪd] *adj* confeccionado(a); *(food)* preparado(a)

real [rɪəl] *adj* (**a**) *(danger, fear, effort)* real; *Fam* **for r.** de veras (**b**) *(genuine)* auténtico(a); **r. leather** piel legítima (**c**) *US Com* **r. estate** bienes *mpl* inmuebles; **r. estate agent** agente inmobiliario

realism [ˈrɪəlɪzəm] *n* realismo *m*

realistic [rɪəˈlɪstɪk] *adj* realista

reality [rɪˈælɪtɪ] *n* realidad *f*; **in r.** en realidad

realization [rɪəlaɪˈzeɪʃən] *n* (**a**) *(understanding)* comprensión *f* (**b**) *(of plan, assets)* realización *f*

realize [ˈrɪəlaɪz] *vt* (**a**) *(become aware of)* darse cuenta de (**b**) *(assets, plan)* realizar

really [ˈrɪəlɪ] *adv* verdaderamente, realmente; **I r. don't know** no lo sé de verdad; **r.?** ¿de veras?

realm [relm] *n (kingdom)* reino *m*; *Fig (field)* terreno *m*

realtor [ˈrɪəltə(r)] *n US* agente inmobiliario(a)

ream [riːm] *n (of paper)* resma *f*

reap [riːp] *vt Agr* cosechar; *Fig* **to r. the benefits** llevarse los beneficios

reappear [riːəˈpɪə(r)] *vi* reaparecer

reappraisal [riːəˈpreɪzəl] *n* revaluación *f*

rear¹ [rɪə(r)] **1** *n* (**a**) *(back part)* parte *f* de atrás (**b**) *Fam (buttocks)* trasero *m*

2 *adj* trasero(a); **r. entrance** puerta *f* de atrás

rear² [rɪə(r)] **1** *vt* (**a**) *(breed, raise)* criar (**b**) *(lift up)* levantar

2 *vi* **to r. up** *(horse)* encabritarse

rearguard [ˈrɪəɡɑːd] *n* retaguardia *f*

rearmament [riːˈɑːməmənt] *n* rearme *m*

rearrange [riːəˈreɪndʒ] *vt* (**a**) *(furniture)* colocar de otra manera (**b**) *(appointment)* fijar otra fecha para

rear-view [ˈrɪəvjuː] *adj* **r. mirror** (espejo *m)* retrovisor *m*

reason [ˈriːzən] **1** *n* (**a**) *(cause, motive)* motivo *m*, razón *f*; **for no r.** sin razón; **for some r.** por algún motivo (**b**) *(good sense)* razón *f*; **it stands to r.** es lógico; **to listen to r.** atender a razones, *Am* atender a razones

2 *vi* (**a**) **to r. with sb** convencer a algn (**b**) *(argue, work out)* razonar

reasonable [ˈriːzənəbəl] *adj* (**a**) *(fair)* razonable (**b**) *(sensible)* sensato(a) (**c**) *(average)* regular

reasonably [ˈriːzənəblɪ] *adv* *(fairly)* bastante

reasoning [ˈriːzənɪŋ] *n* razonamiento *m*

reassurance [riːəˈʃʊərəns] *n* consuelo *m*

reassure [riːəˈʃʊə(r)] *vt* (**a**) *(comfort)* tranquilizar (**b**) *(restore confidence)* dar confianza a

reassuring [riːəˈʃʊərɪŋ] *adj* consolador(a)

rebate [ˈriːbeɪt] *n* devolución *f*; **tax r.** devolución fiscal

> $\wp$ Note that the Spanish verb **rebatir** is a false friend and is never a translation for the English word **rebate**. In Spanish **rebatir** means "to refute".

rebel 1 *adj & n* [ˈrebəl] rebelde *(mf)*

2 *vi* [rɪˈbel] rebelarse, sublevarse (**against** contra)

rebellion [rɪˈbeljən] *n* rebelión *f*

rebellious [rɪˈbeljəs] *adj* rebelde

rebound 1 *n* ['ri:baʊnd] *(of ball)* rebote *m*; *Fig* **on the r.** de rebote
2 *vi* [rɪ'baʊnd] *(ball)* rebotar

rebuff [rɪ'bʌf] **1** *n* desaire *m*
2 *vt* desairar

rebuild [ri:'bɪld] *vt* reconstruir

rebuke [rɪ'bju:k] **1** *n* reproche *m*
2 *vt* reprochar

rebut [rɪ'bʌt] *vt* refutar

recalcitrant [rɪ'kælsɪtrənt] *adj Fml* recalcitrante

recall [rɪ'kɔ:l] *vt* (a) *(soldiers, products)* hacer volver; *(ambassador)* retirar (b) *(remember)* recordar

recant [rɪ'kænt] *vi Fml* retractarse

recap 1 *vt & vi* [ri:'kæp] resumir; **to r.** en resumen
2 *n* ['ri:kæp] recapitulación *f*

recapitulate [ri:kə'pɪtjʊleɪt] *vt & vi Fml* recapitular

recapture [ri:'kæptʃə(r)] *vt Fig* recuperar

recd *Com (abbr* **received)** recibido(a)

recede [rɪ'si:d] *vi* retroceder; **to have a receding hairline** tener entradas

receipt [rɪ'si:t] *n* (a) *(act)* recepción *f*; **to acknowledge r. of sth** acusar recibo de algo (b) *Com (paper)* recibo *m* (c) **receipts** *(takings)* recaudación *f*

receive [rɪ'si:v] *vt* (a) *(be given, get)* recibir (b) *Jur (stolen goods)* ocultar (c) *(welcome)* acoger (d) *Rad & TV* captar

receiver [rɪ'si:və(r)] *n* (a) *(person)* receptor(a) *m,f* (b) *Jur (of stolen goods)* perista *mf* (c) *(of telephone)* auricular *m*, *RP, Ven* tubo *m*

recent ['ri:sənt] *adj* reciente; **in r. years** en los últimos años

recently ['ri:səntlɪ] *adv* hace poco, recientemente

receptacle [rɪ'septəkəl] *n* receptáculo *m*

reception [rɪ'sepʃən] *n* (a) *(welcome)* recibimiento *m* (b) *(party)* recepción *f*; **wedding r.** banquete *m* de boda *or Andes* matrimonio *or RP* casamiento (c) **r. (desk)** recepción *f* (d) *Rad & TV* recepción *f*

receptionist [rɪ'sepʃənɪst] *n* recepcionista *mf*

receptive [rɪ'septɪv] *adj* receptivo(a)

recess ['ri:ses, rɪ'ses] *n* (a) *(in a wall)* hueco *m* (b) *(secret place)* escondrijo *m* (c) *US Educ* recreo *m*; *Pol* período *m* de vacaciones

recession [rɪ'seʃən] *n* recesión *f*

recharge [ri:'tʃɑ:dʒ] *vt (battery)* recargar

rechargeable [ri:'tʃɑ:dʒəbəl] *adj* recargable

recipe ['resɪpɪ] *n Culin* receta *f*; *Fig* fórmula *f*

recipient [rɪ'sɪpɪənt] *n* receptor(a) *m,f*, *(of letter)* destinatario(a) *m,f*

> *Note that the Spanish word* **recipiente** is a false friend and is never a translation for the English word **recipient**. In Spanish **recipiente** means "receptacle, container".

reciprocate [rɪ'sɪprəkeɪt] **1** *vt (favour etc)* devolver
2 *vi* hacer lo mismo

recital [rɪ'saɪtəl] *n* recital *m*

recite [rɪ'saɪt] *vt & vi* recitar

reckless ['reklɪs] *adj (unwise)* imprudente; *(fearless)* temerario(a)

reckon ['rekən] **1** *vt* (a) *(calculate)* calcular; *(count)* contar (b) *Fam (think)* creer; *(consider)* considerar
2 *vi (calculate)* calcular; *(count)* contar
► **reckon on** *vt insep* contar con

reckoner ['rekənə(r)] *n* **ready r.** tabla *f* de cálculo

reckoning ['rekənɪŋ] *n* cálculo *m*; **by my r.** ... según mis cálculos ...; *Fig* **day of r.** día *m* del juicio final

reclaim [rɪ'kleɪm] *vt* (a) *(recover)* recuperar; *(demand back)* reclamar (b) *(marshland etc)* convertir

recline [rɪ'klaɪn] *vi* recostarse, reclinarse

reclining [rɪ'klaɪnɪŋ] *adj* recostado(a); **r. seat** asiento *m* abatible

recluse [rɪ'klu:s] *n* solitario(a) *m,f*

> *Note that the Spanish word* **recluso** is a false friend and is never a translation for the English word **recluse**. In Spanish **recluso** means "prisoner".

recognition [rekəg'nɪʃən] *n* reconocimiento *m*; *(appreciation)* apreciación *f*; **changed beyond all r.** irreconocible

recognizable [rekəg'naɪzəbəl] *adj* reconocible

recognize ['rekəgnaɪz] *vt* reconocer

recoil 1 *n* ['ri:kɔɪl] *(of gun)* culatazo *m*; *(of spring)* aflojamiento *m*
2 *vi* [rɪ'kɔɪl] (a) *(gun)* dar un culatazo; *(spring)* aflojarse (b) *(in fear)* espantarse

recollect [rekə'lekt] *vt* recordar

recollection [rekə'lekʃən] *n* recuerdo *m*

> *Note that the Spanish word* **recolección** is a false friend and is never a translation for the English word **recollection**. In Spanish **recolección** means "harvest, collection".

recommend [rekə'mend] *vt* recomendar

recommendation [rekəmen'deɪʃən] *n* recomendación *f*

recompense ['rekəmpens] **1** n recompensa f; Jur indemnización f
2 vt recompensar; Jur indemnizar

reconcile ['rekənsaɪl] vt (two people) reconciliar; (of ideas) conciliar; **to r. oneself to** resignarse a

recondition [ri:kən'dɪʃən] vt (engine) revisar

reconnaissance [rɪ'kɒnɪsəns] n Mil reconocimiento m

reconnoitre, US **reconnoiter** [rekə-'nɔɪtə(r)] vt Mil reconocer

reconsider [ri:kən'sɪdə(r)] vt reconsiderar

reconstruct [ri:kən'strʌkt] vt reconstruir

reconstruction [ri:kən'strʌkʃən] n reconstrucción f

record 1 n ['rekɔ:d] (a) (account) relación f; (of meeting) actas fpl(**b**) (document) documento m; **public records** archivos mpl (**c**) Mus disco m; **r. player** tocadiscos m inv (**d**) Sport récord m
2 vt [rɪ'kɔ:d] (a) (relate) hacer constar; (note down) apuntar (**b**) (record, voice) grabar

recorded [rɪ'kɔ:dɪd] adj Br **r. delivery** correo certificado; **r. message** mensaje grabado

recorder [rɪ'kɔ:də(r)] n (a) (person) registrador(a) m,f; Jur magistrado(a) m,f (**b**) Mus flauta f

recording [rɪ'kɔ:dɪŋ] n (registering) registro m; (recorded music, message etc) grabación f

recount [rɪ'kaʊnt] vt (tell) contar

re-count 1 vt ['ri:'kaʊnt] Pol volver a contar
2 n ['ri:kaʊnt] Pol recuento m

recoup [rɪ'ku:p] vt (losses etc) recuperar

recourse [rɪ'kɔ:s] n **to have r. to** recurrir a

recover [rɪ'kʌvə(r)] **1** vt (items, lost time) recuperar; (consciousness) recobrar
2 vi (from illness etc) reponerse

recovery [rɪ'kʌvərɪ] n (a) (retrieval) recuperación f (**b**) (from illness) restablecimiento m

re-create [ri:kri'eɪt] vt recrear

recreation [rekrɪ'eɪʃən] n (a) (leisure) ocio m, esparcimiento m (**b**) Educ (playtime) recreo m

recreational [rekrɪ'eɪʃənəl] adj recreativo(a); US **r. vehicle** autocaravana f, casa f caravana

recrimination [rɪkrɪmɪ'neɪʃən] n reproche m

recruit [rɪ'kru:t] **1** n recluta m
2 vt (soldiers) reclutar; (workers) contratar

recruitment [rɪ'kru:tmənt] n (of soldiers) reclutamiento m; (of employees) contratación f

rectangle ['rektæŋgəl] n rectángulo m

rectangular [rek'tæŋgjʊlə(r)] adj rectangular

rectify ['rektɪfaɪ] vt rectificar

rector ['rektə(r)] n (a) Rel párroco m (**b**) Scot Educ director(a) m,f

recuperate [rɪ'ku:pəreɪt] vi reponerse

recur [rɪ'kɜ:(r)] vi repetirse

⚠ Note that the Spanish verb **recurrir** is a false friend and is never a translation for the English verb **to recur**. In Spanish **recurrir** means "to appeal, to resort".

recurrence [rɪ'kʌrəns] n repetición f, reaparición f

recurrent [rɪ'kʌrənt] adj constante; Med recurrente

recycle [ri:'saɪkəl] vt reciclar

recycling [ri:'saɪklɪŋ] n reciclaje m; **r. bank** ecopunto m

red [red] **1** adj (redder, reddest) rojo(a); **r. light** semáforo m en rojo; **r. wine** vino tinto; **to go r.** ponerse colorado(a); **to have r. hair** ser pelirrojo(a); Fig **r. herring** truco m para despistar; Fam **to roll out the r. carpet for sb** recibir a algn con todos los honores; **R. Cross** Cruz Roja; **R. Indian** piel roja mf; **R. Riding Hood** Caperucita Roja; **R. Sea** Mar Rojo; **r. tape** papeleo m
2 n (a) (colour) rojo m (**b**) Fin **to be in the r.** estar en números rojos

redcurrant ['redkʌrənt] n grosella roja

redden ['redən] **1** vi (blush) enrojecerse, ponerse colorado(a)
2 vt (make red) teñir de rojo

reddish ['redɪʃ] adj rojizo(a)

redeem [rɪ'di:m] vt (a) (regain) recobrar; (voucher) canjear (**b**) (debt) amortizar (**c**) (film, novel etc) salvar (**d**) Rel redimir; Fig **to r. oneself** redimirse

redeeming [rɪ'di:mɪŋ] adj compensatorio(a); **his only r. feature** lo único que le salva

redemption [rɪ'dempʃən] n Fml (a) (of debt) amortización f (**b**) Rel redención f; **beyond r.** sin remedio

redeploy [ri:dɪ'plɔɪ] vt redistribuir

red-handed [red'hændɪd] adj **he was caught r.** en Esp cogieron or Am agarraron con las manos en la masa

redhead ['redhed] n pelirrojo(a) m,f

red-hot [red'hɒt] adj (a) (very hot) candente (**b**) Fam (passionate) ardiente (**c**) *Fam* **r. news** noticia(s) *f(pl)* de última hora

redial [riːˈdaɪəl] *n Tel* **r. (feature)** (botón *m* de) rellamada *f*

redirect [riːdɪˈrekt] *vt* (**a**) *(funds)* redistribuir (**b**) *(letter)* remitir a la nueva dirección

red-light [redˈlaɪt] *adj Fam* **r. district** *Esp* barrio chino, *Am* zona roja

redo [riːˈduː] [*pt* **redid** [riːˈdɪd], *pp* **redone** [riːˈdʌn]] *vt* rehacer

redouble [riːˈdʌbəl] *vt* redoblar

redress [riːˈdres] *Fml* **1** *n* reparación *f*
2 *vt* reparar

redskin [ˈredskɪn] *n* piel roja *mf*

reduce [rɪˈdjuːs] *vt* (**a**) *(make smaller, lower)* reducir; *(price, product)* rebajar (**b**) *(in rank)* degradar (**c**) *Culin (sauce)* espesar (**d**) *Med* recomponer

reduction [rɪˈdʌkʃən] *n* reducción *f*; *Com (in purchase price)* descuento *m*, rebaja *f*

redundancy [rɪˈdʌndənsɪ] *n Br (dismissal)* despido *m*

redundant [rɪˈdʌndənt] *adj* (**a**) *(superfluous)* redundante (**b**) *Br Ind* **to be made r.** perder el empleo; **to make sb r.** despedir a algn

reed [riːd] *n* (**a**) *Bot* caña *f* (**b**) *Mus* caramillo *m*

reef [riːf] *n* arrecife *m*

reek [riːk] **1** *n* tufo *m*
2 *vi* apestar

reel [riːl] **1** *n* (**a**) *(spool)* bobina *f*, carrete *m* (**b**) *Scot Mus* danza *f* tradicional
2 *vi (stagger)* tambalearse

re-elect [riːɪˈlekt] *vt* reelegir

ref [ref] *n* (**a**) *Fam Sport* árbitro(a) *m,f* (**b**) *Com (abbr* **reference***)* ref

refectory [rɪˈfektərɪ] *n* refectorio *m*

refer [rɪˈfɜː(r)] **1** *vt* mandar, enviar; **to r. a matter to a tribunal** remitir un asunto a un tribunal
2 *vi* (**a**) *(allude)* referirse, aludir (**to a**) (**b**) **to r. to** *(consult)* consultar

referee [refəˈriː] **1** *n* (**a**) *Sport* árbitro(a) *m,f* (**b**) *Br (for job application)* garante *mf*
2 *vt Sport* arbitrar

reference [ˈrefərəns] *n* (**a**) *(consultation)* consulta *f*; *(source)* referencia *f*; **with r. to** referente a, con referencia a; **r. book** libro *m* de consulta; **r. library** biblioteca *f* de consulta (**b**) *Br (from employer)* informe *m*, referencia *f*

referendum [refəˈrendəm] *n* referéndum *m*

refill **1** *n* [ˈriːfɪl] (**a**) *(replacement)* recambio *m*, carga *f* (**b**) *Fam (drink)* **a r.** otra copa
2 *vt* [riːˈfɪl] rellenar

refine [rɪˈfaɪn] *vt* refinar

refined [rɪˈfaɪnd] *adj* refinado(a)

refinement [rɪˈfaɪnmənt] *n* refinamiento *m*

refinery [rɪˈfaɪnərɪ] *n* refinería *f*

reflect [rɪˈflekt] **1** *vt (light, attitude)* reflejar
2 *vi (think)* reflexionar; **to r. on sth** meditar sobre algo

reflection [rɪˈflekʃən] *n* (**a**) *(indication, mirror image)* reflejo *m* (**b**) *(thought)* reflexión *f*; **on r.** pensándolo bien (**c**) *(criticism)* crítica *f*

reflector [rɪˈflektə(r)] *n (of vehicle)* catafaro *m*

reflex [ˈriːfleks] *n* reflejo *m*

reflexive [rɪˈfleksɪv] *adj* reflexivo(a)

reform [rɪˈfɔːm] **1** *n* reforma *f*; **r. school** reformatorio *m*
2 *vt* reformar

reformation [refəˈmeɪʃən] *n* reforma *f*

reformatory [rɪˈfɔːmətərɪ] *n* reformatorio *m*

reformer [rɪˈfɔːmə(r)] *n* reformador(a) *m,f*

refrain [rɪˈfreɪn] **1** *n Mus* estribillo *m*; *Fig* lema *m*
2 *vi* abstenerse (**from** de)

refresh [rɪˈfreʃ] *vt* refrescar

refresher [rɪˈfreʃə(r)] *n* **r. course** cursillo *m* de reciclaje

refreshing [rɪˈfreʃɪŋ] *adj* refrescante; **a r. change** un cambio muy agradable

refreshment [rɪˈfreʃmənt] *n* refresco *m*

refrigerator [rɪˈfrɪdʒəreɪtə(r)] *n* nevera *f*, frigorífico *m*, *Andes* frigider *m*, *RP* heladera *f*

refuel [riːˈfjuːəl] *vi* repostar combustible

refuge [ˈrefjuːdʒ] *n* refugio *m*, cobijo *m*; **to take r.** refugiarse

refugee [refjʊˈdʒiː] *n* refugiado(a) *m,f*

refund **1** *n* [ˈriːfʌnd] reembolso *m*
2 *vt* [rɪˈfʌnd] reembolsar, devolver

refurbish [riːˈfɜːbɪʃ] *vt* redecorar .

refusal [rɪˈfjuːzəl] *n* negativa *f*; **to have first r. on sth** tener la primera opción en algo

refuse¹ [rɪˈfjuːz] *vt* rechazar; **to r. sb sth** negar algo a algn
2 *vi* negarse

refuse² [ˈrefjuːs] *n* basura *f*; **r. collector** basurero(a) *m,f*

refute [rɪˈfjuːt] *vt* refutar, rebatir

regain [rɪˈgeɪn] *vt* recuperar; *(consciousness)* recobrar

regal [ˈriːgəl] *adj* regio(a)

regard [rɪˈgɑːd] **1** *n* (**a**) *(concern)* consideración *f*, respeto *m*; **with r. to** respecto a

(**b**) *(esteem)* estima *f* (**c**) **regards** *(good wishes)* saludos *mpl*, *CAm, Col, Ecuad* saludes *fpl*; **give him my regards** dale recuerdos de mi parte
2 *vt* (**a**) *(consider)* considerar (**b**) **as regards** *(regarding)* respecto a

regarding [rɪˈgɑːdɪŋ] *prep* respecto a

regardless [rɪˈgɑːdlɪs] **1** *prep* **r. of** sin tener en cuenta; **r. of the outcome** pase lo que pase
2 *adv* a toda costa

regime [reɪˈʒiːm] *n* régimen *m*

regiment [ˈredʒɪmənt] **1** *n* regimiento *m*
2 *vt* regimentar

regimental [redʒɪˈmentəl] *adj* del regimiento

region [ˈriːdʒən] *n* región *f*; **in the r. of** alrededor de, del orden de

regional [ˈriːdʒənəl] *adj* regional

regionalism [ˈriːdʒənəlɪzəm] *n* regionalismo *m*

register [ˈredʒɪstə(r)] **1** *n* registro *m*
2 *vt* (**a**) *(record)* registrar (**b**) *(letter)* certificar (**c**) *(show)* mostrar
3 *vi* *(for course)* inscribirse; *Univ* matricularse

registered [ˈredʒɪstəd] *adj* certificado(a); *Br* **r. letter** carta certificada; **r. trademark** marca registrada

registrar [redʒɪˈstrɑː(r), ˈredʒɪstrɑː(r)] *n* (**a**) *(record keeper)* registrador(a) *m,f* (**b**) *Br Med* = médico de grado superior en un hospital (**c**) *Univ* secretario(a) *m,f* general

registration [redʒɪˈstreɪʃən] *n* inscripción *f*; *Univ* matrícula *f*; *Br Aut* **r. number** matrícula *f*

registry [ˈredʒɪstrɪ] *n* registro *m*; *Br* **r. office** registro civil; **to get married in a r. office** casarse por lo civil

regret [rɪˈgret] **1** *n* *(remorse)* remordimiento *m*; *(sadness)* pesar *m*; **regrets** *(excuses)* excusas *fpl*; **to have no regrets** no arrepentirse de nada
2 *vt* arrepentirse de, lamentar

regretful [rɪˈgretfʊl] *adj* arrepentido(a)

regrettable [rɪˈgretəbəl] *adj* lamentable

regroup [riːˈgruːp] **1** *vt* reagrupar
2 *vi* reagruparse

regular [ˈregjʊlə(r)] **1** *adj* (**a**) *(features, pulse, verb)* regular (**b**) *(usual)* normal (**c**) *(staff)* permanente (**d**) *(frequent)* frecuente (**e**) **r. army** tropas *fpl* regulares (**f**) *US Fam* **a r. guy** un tío legal, *Am* un tipo derecho
2 *n* *(customer)* cliente *mf* habitual

regularity [regjʊˈlærɪtɪ] *n* regularidad *f*

regularly [ˈregjʊləlɪ] *adv* con regularidad

regulate [ˈregjʊleɪt] *vt* regular

regulation [regjʊˈleɪʃən] **1** *n* (**a**) *(control)* regulación *f* (**b**) *(rule)* regla *f*
2 *adj* reglamentario(a)

rehabilitation [riːəbɪlɪˈteɪʃən] *n* rehabilitación *f*; **r. centre** centro *m* de reinserción

rehearsal [rɪˈhɜːsəl] *n* ensayo *m*

rehearse [rɪˈhɜːs] *vt & vi* ensayar

reign [reɪn] **1** *n* reinado *m*
2 *vi* reinar

reigning [ˈreɪnɪŋ] *adj* **r. champion** campeón(ona) *m,f* actual

reimburse [riːɪmˈbɜːs] *vt* reembolsar

rein [reɪn] *n* *(for horse)* rienda *f*; *Fig* **he gave free r. to his emotions** dio rienda suelta a sus emociones

reindeer [ˈreɪndɪə(r)] *n* reno *m*

reinforce [riːɪnˈfɔːs] *vt* *(strengthen)* reforzar; *(support)* apoyar; **reinforced concrete** hormigón *or Am* concreto armado

reinforcement [riːɪnˈfɔːsmənt] *n* (**a**) *(of wall, structure)* refuerzo *m* (**b**) *Mil* **reinforcements** refuerzos *mpl*

reinstate [riːɪnˈsteɪt] *vt* *(to job)* reincorporar

reiterate [riːˈɪtəreɪt] *vt* reiterar

reject 1 *n* [ˈriːdʒekt] (**a**) *Com* **rejects** artículos defectuosos (**b**) *Fam Pej (person)* desecho *m*
2 *vt* [rɪˈdʒekt] rechazar

rejection [rɪˈdʒekʃən] *n* rechazo *m*

rejoice [rɪˈdʒɔɪs] *vi* regocijarse (**at** *or* **over de**)

rejuvenate [rɪˈdʒuːvɪneɪt] *vt* rejuvenecer; *Fig* revitalizar

relapse [rɪˈlæps] **1** *n* (**a**) *Med* recaída *f*; **to have a r.** sufrir una recaída (**b**) *(into crime, alcoholism)* reincidencia *f*
2 *vi* recaer

relate [rɪˈleɪt] **1** *vt* (**a**) *(connect)* relacionar (**b**) *(tell)* relatar
2 *vi* relacionarse

related [rɪˈleɪtɪd] *adj* (**a**) *(linked)* relacionado(a) (**to** con) (**b**) **to be r. to sb** ser pariente de algn

relation [rɪˈleɪʃən] *n* (**a**) *(link)* relación *f*; **in** *or* **with r. to** respecto a; **it bears no r. to what we said** no tiene nada que ver con lo que dijimos (**b**) *(member of family)* pariente *mf*

relationship [rɪˈleɪʃənʃɪp] *n* (**a**) *(link)* relación *f* (**b**) *(between people)* relaciones *fpl*; **to have a good/bad r. with sb** llevarse bien/mal con algn

relative [ˈrelətɪv] **1** *n* pariente *mf*
2 *adj* relativo(a)

relatively [ˈrelətɪvlɪ] *adv* relativamente

relax [rɪ'læks] **1** vt (muscles, rules) relajar **2** vi relajarse

relaxation [ri:læk'seɪʃən] n (a) (rest) descanso m, relajación f (b) (of rules) relajación f (c) (pastime) distracción f

relaxed [rɪ'lækst] adj relajado(a); (peaceful) tranquilo(a)

relaxing [rɪ'læksɪŋ] adj relajante

relay 1 n ['ri:leɪ] (a) (of workers) relevo m (b) Rad & TV **r. station** repetidor m (c) Sport **r. (race)** carrera f de relevos **2** vt [rɪ'leɪ] (a) (pass on) difundir (b) Rad & TV retransmitir

release [rɪ'li:s] **1** n (a) (of prisoner) liberación f, puesta f en libertad; (of gas) escape m (b) Com puesta f en venta (c) Cin estreno m (d) (record) disco m **2** vt (let go) soltar; (prisoner) poner en libertad; (gas) despedir (b) Com poner en venta (c) Cin estrenar (d) (record) publicar

relegate ['relɪgeɪt] vt (a) (consign) relegar (b) Br Ftb **to be relegated** bajar a una división inferior

relent [rɪ'lent] vi ceder; (storm) aplacarse

relentless [rɪ'lentlɪs] adj implacable

relevance ['reləvəns] n pertinencia f

relevant ['reləvənt] adj pertinente (to a); **it is not r.** no viene al caso

> *𝒧* Note that the Spanish word **relevante** is a false friend and is never a translation for the English word **relevant**. In Spanish **relevante** means "outstanding, important".

reliability [rɪlaɪə'bɪlɪtɪ] n (a) (of person) formalidad f (b) (of car, machine) fiabilidad f, Am confiabilidad f

reliable [rɪ'laɪəbəl] adj (person, machine) fiable, Am confiable; **a r. car** un coche seguro; **a r. source** una fuente fidedigna

reliably [rɪ'laɪəblɪ] adv **to be r. informed that** saber de buena tinta que

reliant [rɪ'laɪənt] adj **to be r. on** depender de

relic ['relɪk] n (a) Rel reliquia f (b) (reminder of past) vestigio m

relief [rɪ'li:f] n (a) (from pain, anxiety) alivio m (b) (help) auxilio m, ayuda f; US **to be on r.** cobrar un subsidio (c) Art & Geog relieve m

relieve [rɪ'li:v] vt (a) (alleviate) (pain, anxiety) aliviar; (monotony) romper (b) (take over from) relevar (c) Euph **to r. oneself** hacer sus necesidades (d) **to r. sb of sth** (burden, obligation) quitar algo a algn

relieved [rɪ'li:vd] adj aliviado(a), tranquilizado(a)

religion [rɪ'lɪdʒən] n religión f

religious [rɪ'lɪdʒəs] adj religioso(a)

relinquish [rɪ'lɪŋkwɪʃ] vt renunciar a; **to r. one's hold on sth** soltar algo

relish ['relɪʃ] **1** n (a) (enjoyment) deleite m (b) Culin condimento m **2** vt agradar

relocate [ri:ləʊ'keɪt] vt trasladar

reluctance [rɪ'lʌktəns] n desgana f

reluctant [rɪ'lʌktənt] adj reacio(a); **to be r. to do sth** estar poco dispuesto(a) a hacer algo

reluctantly [rɪ'lʌktntlɪ] adv de mala gana, a regañadientes

rely [rɪ'laɪ] vi contar (on con), confiar (on en)

remain [rɪ'meɪn] **1** vi (a) (stay) permanecer, quedarse (b) (be left) quedar; **it remains to be seen** está por ver **2** npl **remains** restos mpl

remainder [rɪ'meɪndə(r)] n resto m

remaining [rɪ'meɪnɪŋ] adj restante

remand [rɪ'mɑ:nd] Jur **1** vt remitir; **remanded in custody** en prevención **2** n detención f; **on r.** detenido(a)

remark [rɪ'mɑ:k] **1** n comentario m **2** vt comentar, observar

> *𝒧* Note that the Spanish verb **remarcar** is a false friend and is never a translation for the English word **remark**. In Spanish **remarcar** means "to stress, to underline".

remarkable [rɪ'mɑ:kəbəl] adj extraordinario(a); (strange) curioso(a)

remedial [rɪ'mi:dɪəl] adj reparador(a); **r. classes** clases fpl para niños atrasados en los estudios

remedy ['remɪdɪ] **1** n remedio m **2** vt remediar

remember [rɪ'membə(r)] **1** vt (a) (recall) acordarse de, recordar (b) **r. me to your mother** dale recuerdos a tu madre **2** vi acordarse, recordar; **I don't r.** no me acuerdo

remembrance [rɪ'membrəns] n **in r. of** en recuerdo de; Br **R. Day** or **Sunday** día m de homenaje a los caídos (en las guerras mundiales)

remind [rɪ'maɪnd] vt recordar; **r. me to do it** recuérdame que lo haga; **she reminds me of your sister** me recuerda a tu hermana; **that reminds me** ahora que me acuerdo

reminder [rɪ'maɪndə(r)] n recordatorio m, aviso m

reminisce [remɪ'nɪs] vi rememorar

reminiscent [remɪ'nɪsənt] adj Fml nostálgico(a); **to be r. of** recordar

remiss [rɪ'mɪs] *adj (negligent)* descuidado(a)

remission [rɪ'mɪʃən] *n* (a) *Med* remisión *f* (b) *Jur* perdón *m*

remit [rɪ'mɪt] *vt* (a) *(send)* remitir (b) *Jur* referir a otro tribunal

remittance [rɪ'mɪtəns] *n* (a) *(sending)* envío *m* (b) *(payment)* giro *m*, pago *m*

remnant ['remnənt] *n* resto *m*; **remnants** *(of cloth)* retales *mpl*

remold ['riːməʊld] *n US* = **remould**

remorse [rɪ'mɔːs] *n* remordimiento *m*

remorseful [rɪ'mɔːsfʌl] *adj* lleno(a) de remordimiento

remorseless [rɪ'mɔːslɪs] *adj* despiadado(a)

remote [rɪ'məʊt] *adj* (a) *(far away)* remoto(a); **r. control** mando *m* a distancia (b) *(isolated)* aislado(a) (c) *(possibility)* remoto(a); **I haven't the remotest idea** no tengo la más mínima idea

remote-controlled [rɪ'məʊtkən'trəʊld] *adj* teledirigido(a)

remotely [rɪ'məʊtlɪ] *adv* (a) *(vaguely)* vagamente (b) *(distantly)* en lugar aislado

remould ['riːməʊld] *n Br Aut* neumático recauchutado, *Col, Méx* llanta *or Arg* goma recauchutada

removable [rɪ'muːvəbəl] *adj (detachable)* que se puede quitar

removal [rɪ'muːvəl] *n* (a) *Br (moving house)* mudanza *f*; **r. van** camión *m* de mudanzas (b) *(of stain etc)* eliminación *f*

remove [rɪ'muːv] *vt* (a) *(move)* quitar, *Am* sacar; **to r. one's make-up** desmaquillarse; **to r. one's name from a list** tachar su nombre de una lista (b) *(from office)* despedir

> ⚠ Note that the Spanish verb **remover** is a false friend and is never a translation for the English verb **remove**. In Spanish **remover** means "to move over, to turn over, to stir".

removed [rɪ'muːvd] *adj* **far r. from** muy diferente de

remover [rɪ'muːvə(r)] *n* **make-up r.** desmaquillador *m*; **nail varnish r.** quitaesmalte *m*; **stain r.** quitamanchas *m inv*

remuneration [rɪmjuːnə'reɪʃən] *n Fml* remuneración *f*

renaissance [rə'neɪsəns] **1** *n* renacimiento *m*; **the R.** el Renacimiento **2** *adj* renacentista

rend [rend] *vt (pt & pp rent) Fml* rasgar

render ['rendə(r)] *vt Fml* (a) *(give)* dar (b) *(make)* hacer (c) *Com* presentar (d) *(translate)* traducir

rendering ['rendərɪŋ] *n* (a) *(of song, piece of music)* interpretación *f* (b) *(translation)* traducción *f*

rendezvous ['rɒndɪvuː] **1** *n* (a) *(meeting)* cita *f* (b) *(place)* lugar *m* de reunión **2** *vi* reunirse

renegade ['renɪgeɪd] *n* renegado(a) *m,f*

renew [rɪ'njuː] *vt (contract etc)* renovar; *(talks etc)* reanudar; **with renewed vigour** con renovadas fuerzas

renewal [rɪ'njuːəl] *n (of contract etc)* renovación *f*; *(of talks etc)* reanudación *f*

renounce [rɪ'naʊns] *vt Fml* renunciar

renovate ['renəveɪt] *vt* renovar, hacer reformas en

renown [rɪ'naʊn] *n* renombre *m*

renowned [rɪ'naʊnd] *adj* renombrado(a)

rent¹ [rent] **1** *n* (a) *(for building, car, TV)* alquiler *m* (b) *(for land)* arriendo *m* **2** *vt* (a) *(building, car, TV)* alquilar, *Méx* rentar (b) *(land)* arrendar

rent² [rent] *pt & pp of* **rend**

rental ['rentəl] *n (of house etc)* alquiler *m*

renunciation [rɪnʌnsɪ'eɪʃən] *n Fml* renuncia *f*

reorganize [riː'ɔːgənaɪz] *vt* reorganizar

rep [rep] *n Fam* (a) *Com* representante *mf* (b) *Th* teatro *m* de repertorio

repaid [riː'peɪd] *pt & pp of* **repay**

repair [rɪ'peə(r)] **1** *n* reparación *f*, arreglo *m*; **in good/bad r.** en buen/mal estado **2** *vt* (a) *(shoes, clothes, road)* arreglar; *(car, machine)* reparar (b) *(make amends for)* reparar

repartee [repɑː'tiː] *n* réplica aguda

repatriate [riː'pætrɪeɪt] *vt* repatriar

repay [riː'peɪ] *vt (pt & pp* **repaid***)* devolver; **to r. a debt** liquidar una deuda; **to r. a kindness** devolver un favor

repayment [riː'peɪmənt] *n* pago *m*

repeal [rɪ'piːl] *Jur* **1** *n* revocación *f* **2** *vt* revocar

repeat [rɪ'piːt] **1** *vt* repetir; **to r. oneself** repetirse **2** *n (repetition)* repetición *f*; *TV* reposición *f*

repeated [rɪ'piːtɪd] *adj* repetido(a)

repeatedly [rɪ'piːtɪdlɪ] *adv* repetidas veces

repel [rɪ'pel] *vt* (a) *(fight off)* repeler (b) *(disgust)* repugnar

repellent [rɪ'pelənt] **1** *adj* repelente; **water-r.** impermeable **2** *n (insect)* r. repelente *m* (antiinsectos)

repent [rɪ'pent] *vt & vi* arrepentirse (de)

repentance [rɪ'pentəns] *n* arrepentimiento *m*

repercussion [riːpəˈkʌʃən] n repercusión f; **to have repercussions for** or **on** tener repercusiones en or sobre

repertoire [ˈrepətwɑː(r)] n repertorio m

repertory [ˈrepətərɪ] n Th teatro m de repertorio

repetition [repɪˈtɪʃən] n repetición f

repetitive [rɪˈpetɪtɪv] adj repetitivo(a)

replace [rɪˈpleɪs] vt (a) (put back) volver a poner en su sitio (b) (substitute for) sustituir, reemplazar

replacement [rɪˈpleɪsmənt] n (a) (returning) reemplazo m (b) (person) sustituto(a) m,f (c) (part) pieza f de recambio

replay [ˈriːpleɪ] n repetición f

replenish [rɪˈplenɪʃ] vt (a) (fill up) rellenar (b) **to r. stocks** reponer las existencias

replete [rɪˈpliːt] adj Fml repleto(a)

replica [ˈreplɪkə] n réplica f

reply [rɪˈplaɪ] 1 n respuesta f, contestación f
2 vi responder, contestar

report [rɪˈpɔːt] 1 n (a) (account) informe m, Andes, CAm, Méx, Ven reporte m; Br **school r.** informe escolar (b) (piece of news) noticia f (c) Press, Rad & TV reportaje m
2 vt (a) **it is reported that ...** se dice que ... (b) (tell authorities about) denunciar (c) Press hacer un reportaje sobre
3 vi (a) (of committee member etc) hacer un informe (b) Press hacer un reportaje (c) (for duty etc) presentarse

reported [rɪˈpɔːtɪd] adj **r. speech** estilo indirecto

reportedly [rɪˈpɔːtɪdlɪ] adv Fml según se dice

reporter [rɪˈpɔːtə(r)] n periodista mf

repose [rɪˈpəʊz] Fml 1 n reposo m
2 vt & vi reposar

repossess [riːpəˈzes] vt **our house has been repossessed** el banco ha ejecutado la hipoteca de nuestra casa

reprehensible [reprɪˈhensəbəl] adj reprensible, censurable

represent [reprɪˈzent] vt representar

representation [reprɪzenˈteɪʃən] n (a) (of facts, in Parliament) representación f (b) Fml **representations** protesta f

representative [reprɪˈzentətɪv] 1 adj representativo(a)
2 n (a) (of company, on committee) representante mf (b) US Pol diputado(a) m,f

repress [rɪˈpres] vt reprimir, contener

repressed [rɪˈprest] adj **to be r.** estar reprimido(a)

repression [rɪˈpreʃən] n represión f

repressive [rɪˈpresɪv] adj represivo(a)

reprieve [rɪˈpriːv] 1 n (a) Jur indulto m (b) Fig alivio m
2 vt Jur indultar

reprimand [ˈreprɪmɑːnd] 1 n reprimenda f
2 vt reprender

reprint 1 n [ˈriːprɪnt] reimpresión f
2 vt [riːˈprɪnt] reimprimir

reprisal [rɪˈpraɪzəl] n represalia f

reproach [rɪˈprəʊtʃ] 1 n reproche m; **beyond r.** intachable
2 vt reprochar

reproachful [rɪˈprəʊtʃfʊl] adj reprobador(a)

reproduce [riːprəˈdjuːs] 1 vt reproducir
2 vi reproducirse

reproduction [riːprəˈdʌkʃən] n reproducción f

reproof [rɪˈpruːf] n Fml reprobación f, censura f

reprove [rɪˈpruːv] vt Fml reprobar, censurar

reptile [ˈreptaɪl] n reptil m

republic [rɪˈpʌblɪk] n república f

republican [rɪˈpʌblɪkən] adj & n republicano(a) (m,f); US Pol **R. Party** Partido Republicano

repudiate [rɪˈpjuːdɪeɪt] vt Fml (a) (reject) rechazar (b) (not acknowledge) negarse a reconocer

repugnant [rɪˈpʌgnənt] adj repugnante

repulse [rɪˈpʌls] vt rechazar

repulsive [rɪˈpʌlsɪv] adj repulsivo(a)

reputable [ˈrepjʊtəbəl] adj (company etc) acreditado(a); (person, products) de toda confianza

reputation [repjʊˈteɪʃən] n reputación f

repute [rɪˈpjuːt] n Fml reputación f

reputed [rɪˈpjuːtɪd] adj supuesto(a); **to be r. to be** ser considerado(a) como

reputedly [rɪˈpjuːtɪdlɪ] adv según se dice

request [rɪˈkwest] 1 n petición f, solicitud f, Am pedido m; **available on r.** disponible a petición de los interesados; Br **r. stop** (for bus) parada f discrecional
2 vt pedir, solicitar

require [rɪˈkwaɪə(r)] vt (a) (need) necesitar, requerir (b) (demand) exigir

requirement [rɪˈkwaɪəmənt] n (a) (need) necesidad f (b) (demand) requisito m

⚠️ Note that the Spanish word **requerimiento** is a false friend and is never a translation for the English word **requirement**. In Spanish **requerimiento** means both "entreaty" and "writ, injunction".

requisite ['rekwɪzɪt] *Fml* **1** *adj* requerido(a)
  2 *n* requisito *m*
requisition [rekwɪ'zɪʃən] **1** *n* requisición *f*
  2 *vt* requisar
rescind [rɪ'sɪnd] *vt Fml (contract)* rescindir; *(law)* abrogar
rescue ['reskjuː] **1** *n* rescate *m*; **r. team** equipo *m* de rescate
  2 *vt* rescatar
rescuer ['reskjʊə(r)] *n* rescatador(a) *m,f*
research [rɪ'sɜːtʃ] **1** *n* investigación *f*; **R. and Development** Investigación más Desarrollo
  2 *vt & vi* investigar
researcher [rɪ'sɜːtʃə(r)] *n* investigador(a) *m,f*
resemblance [rɪ'zembləns] *n* semejanza *f*
resemble [rɪ'zembəl] *vt* parecerse a
resent [rɪ'zent] *vt* ofenderse por
resentful [rɪ'zentfʊl] *adj* ofendido(a)
resentment [rɪ'zentmənt] *n* resentimiento *m*
reservation [rezə'veɪʃən] *n* reserva *f*, *Am* reservación *f*
reserve [rɪ'zɜːv] **1** *n* (**a**) *(supply)* reserva *f*; **to keep sth in r.** guardar algo de reserva (**b**) *Sport* suplente *mf* (**c**) *Mil* **reserves** reservas *fpl*
  2 *vt* reservar
reserved [rɪ'zɜːvd] *adj* reservado(a)
reservoir ['rezəvwɑː(r)] *n* embalse *m*, pantano *m*; *Fig* reserva *f*
reshape [riː'ʃeɪp] *vt* rehacer; *Fig* reorganizar
reshuffle [riː'ʃʌfəl] *n Pol* remodelación *f*
reside [rɪ'zaɪd] *vi Fml* residir
residence ['rezɪdəns] *n Fml (home)* residencia *f*; *(address)* domicilio *m*; *(period of time)* permanencia *f*
resident ['rezɪdənt] *adj & n* residente *(mf)*; *US Med* = médico que ha cumplido la residencia y prosigue con su especialización; **to be r. in** estar domiciliado(a) en
residential [rezɪ'denʃəl] *adj* residencial
residual [rɪ'zɪdjʊəl] *adj* residual
residue ['rezɪdjuː] *n* residuo *m*
resign [rɪ'zaɪn] **1** *vt* (**a**) *(give up)* dimitir (**b**) **to r. oneself to sth** resignarse a algo
  2 *vi (from job)* dimitir
resignation [rezɪg'neɪʃən] *n* (**a**) *(from a job)* dimisión *f* (**b**) *(acceptance)* resignación *f*
resigned [rɪ'zaɪnd] *adj* resignado(a)
resilience [rɪ'zɪlɪəns] *n* resistencia *f*
resilient [rɪ'zɪlɪənt] *adj (strong)* resistente
resin ['rezɪn] *n* resina *f*

resist [rɪ'zɪst] **1** *vt* (**a**) *(not yield to)* resistir (**b**) *(oppose)* oponerse a
  2 *vi* resistir
resistance [rɪ'zɪstəns] *n* resistencia *f*
resistant [rɪ'zɪstənt] *adj* **to be r. to sth** *(change, suggestion)* mostrarse remiso(a) a aceptar algo, mostrar resistencia a algo; *(disease)* ser resistente a algo
resit [riː'sɪt] *vt Br (exam)* volver a presentarse a
resolute ['rezəluːt] *adj* resuelto(a), decidido(a)
resolution [rezə'luːʃən] *n* resolución *f*
resolve [rɪ'zɒlv] **1** *n* resolución *f*
  2 *vt* resolver; **to r. to do** resolverse a hacer
  3 *vi* resolverse
resonant ['rezənənt] *adj* resonante
resort [rɪ'zɔːt] **1** *n* (**a**) *(place)* lugar *m* de vacaciones; **tourist r.** centro turístico (**b**) *(recourse)* recurso *m*; **as a last r.** como último recurso
  2 *vi* recurrir (**to** a)

  ℐ Note that the Spanish word **resorte** is a false friend and is never a translation for the English word **resort**. In Spanish **resorte** means both "spring" and "means".

resound [rɪ'zaʊnd] *vi* resonar; *Fig* tener resonancia ✦
resounding [rɪ'zaʊndɪŋ] *adj* **a r. failure** un fracaso total; **a r. success** un éxito rotundo
resource [rɪ'sɔːs] *n* recurso *m*
resourceful [rɪ'sɔːsfʊl] *adj* ingenioso(a)
respect [rɪ'spekt] **1** *n* (**a**) *(deference)* respeto *m*; **to pay one's respects to sb** presentar sus respetos a algn (**b**) *(relation, reference)* respecto *m*; **in that r.** a ese respecto; **with r. to** con referencia a
  2 *vt* respetar
respectable [rɪ'spektəbəl] *adj* respetable; *(clothes)* decente
respectful [rɪ'spektfʊl] *adj* respetuoso(a)
respective [rɪ'spektɪv] *adj* respectivo(a)
respectively [rɪ'spektɪvlɪ] *adv* respectivamente
respite ['respaɪt] *n Fml* respiro *m*
resplendent [rɪ'splendənt] *adj* resplandeciente
respond [rɪ'spɒnd] *vi* responder
response [rɪ'spɒns] *n* (**a**) *(reply)* respuesta *f* (**b**) *(reaction)* reacción *f*
responsibility [rɪspɒnsə'bɪlɪtɪ] *n* responsabilidad *f*

responsible [rɪ'spɒnsəbəl] *adj* responsable (**for** de); **to be r. to sb** tener que dar cuentas a algn

responsive [rɪ'spɒnsɪv] *adj* sensible

rest[1] [rest] **1** *n* (**a**) *(break)* descanso *m*; *US* **r. room** baño *m*, *Esp* servicios *mpl*, *CSur* toilette *m* (**b**) *(peace)* tranquilidad *f*; **at r.** *(object)* inmóvil (**c**) *(support)* apoyo *m*
2 *vt* (**a**) *(cause to repose)* descansar (**b**) *(lean)* apoyar; **to r. a ladder against a wall** apoyar una escalera contra una pared **3** *vi* (**a**) *(relax)* descansar (**b**) *(be calm)* quedarse tranquilo(a) (**c**) **it doesn't r. with me** no depende de mí

rest[2] [rest] *n* **the r.** *(remainder)* el resto, lo demás; **the r. of the girls** las demás chicas

restaurant ['restərɒnt] *n* restaurante *m*; *Br Rail* **r. car** coche *m* restaurante

restful ['restfʊl] *adj* relajante

restitution [restɪ'tjuːʃən] *n Fml* restitución *f*; **to make r.** restituir

restive ['restɪv] *adj* inquieto(a), nervioso(a)

restless ['restlɪs] *adj* agitado(a), inquieto(a)

restoration [restə'reɪʃən] *n* (**a**) *(giving back)* devolución *f* (**b**) *Br Hist* **the R.** la Restauración (**c**) *(of building, furniture)* restauración *f*

restore [rɪ'stɔː(r)] *vt* (**a**) *(give back)* devolver (**b**) *(re-establish)* restablecer (**c**) *(building etc)* restaurar

restrain [rɪ'streɪn] *vt* contener; **to r. one's anger** reprimir la cólera; **to r. oneself** contenerse

restrained [rɪ'streɪnd] *adj (person)* moderado(a); *(emotion)* contenido(a)

restraint [rɪ'streɪnt] *n* (**a**) *(restriction)* restricción *f*; *(hindrance)* traba *f* (**b**) *(moderation)* moderación *f*

restrict [rɪ'strɪkt] *vt* restringir, limitar

restriction [rɪ'strɪkʃən] *n* restricción *f*, limitación *f*

restrictive [rɪ'strɪktɪv] *adj* restrictivo(a)

result [rɪ'zʌlt] **1** *n* resultado *m*; **as a r. of** como consecuencia de
2 *vi* resultar; **to r. from** resultar de; **to r. in** causar

resume [rɪ'zjuːm] **1** *vt (journey, work, conversation)* reanudar; *(control)* reasumir
2 *vi* recomenzar

◢ *Note that the Spanish word **resumir** is a false friend and is never a translation for the English word **resume**. In Spanish **resumir** means "to sum up, to summarize".*

résumé ['rezjʊmeɪ] *n* (**a**) *(summary)* resumen *m* (**b**) *US (curriculum vitae)* currículum *(vitae) m*

resumption [rɪ'zʌmpʃən] *n (of journey, work, conversation)* reanudación *f*

resurface [riː'sɜːfɪs] **1** *vt (road)* rehacer el firme de
2 *vi Fig* resurgir

resurgence [rɪ'sɜːdʒəns] *n* resurgimiento *m*

resurrection [rezə'rekʃən] *n* resurrección *f*

resuscitate [rɪ'sʌsɪteɪt] *vt Med* reanimar

retail ['riːteɪl] **1** *n* venta *f* al por menor, *Am* menoreo *m*; **r. outlet** punto *m* de venta; **r. price** precio *m* de venta al público; *Br* **r. price index** Índice *m* de Precios al Consumo
2 *vt* vender al por menor
3 *vi* venderse al por menor
4 *adv* al por menor

retailer ['riːteɪlə(r)] *n* detallista *mf*

retain [rɪ'teɪn] *vt* (**a**) *(heat)* conservar; *(personal effects)* guardar (**b**) *(water)* retener (**c**) *(facts, information)* recordar

retainer [rɪ'teɪnə(r)] *n* (**a**) *(payment)* anticipo *m* sobre los honorarios (**b**) *(servant)* criado(a) *m,f*

retaliate [rɪ'tælɪeɪt] *vi* tomar represalias (**against** contra)

retaliation [rɪtælɪ'eɪʃən] *n* represalias *fpl*; **in r.** en represalia

retarded [rɪ'tɑːdɪd] *adj* retrasado(a)

retch [retʃ] *vi* tener náuseas

retentive [rɪ'tentɪv] *adj* retentivo(a)

rethink ['riːθɪŋk] *n Fam* **to have a r. about sth** volver a reflexionar sobre algo

reticent ['retɪsənt] *adj* reticente

retina ['retɪnə] *n* retina *f*

retinue ['retɪnjuː] *n* séquito *m*

retire [rɪ'taɪə(r)] **1** *vt* jubilar
2 *vi* (**a**) *(stop working)* jubilarse (**b**) *(from race)* retirarse; **to r. for the night** irse a la cama, acostarse

retired [rɪ'taɪəd] *adj* jubilado(a)

retiree [rɪtaɪə'riː] *n US* retirado(a) *m,f*

retirement [rɪ'taɪəmənt] *n* jubilación *f*

retiring [rɪ'taɪərɪŋ] *adj* (**a**) *(reserved)* reservado(a) (**b**) *(official)* saliente

retort [rɪ'tɔːt] **1** *n* réplica *f*
2 *vi* replicar

retrace [riː'treɪs] *vt (recall)* reconstruir; **to r. one's steps** volver sobre sus pasos

retract [rɪ'trækt] **1** *vt* (**a**) *(claws)* retraer; *(landing gear)* replegar (**b**) *(statement)* retirar
2 *vi* (**a**) *(claws)* retraerse; *(landing gear)* replegarse (**b**) *Fml* retractarse

retread ['riːtred] n Aut neumático m recauchutado, Col, Méx llanta f or Arg goma f recauchutada

retreat [rɪ'triːt] 1 n (a) Mil retirada f (b) (shelter) refugio m (c) Rel retiro m
2 vi retirarse (from de)

retrial ['riːtraɪəl] n Jur nuevo juicio

retribution [retrɪ'bjuːʃən] n represalias fpl

📖 Note that the Spanish word **retribución** is a false friend and is never a translation for the English word **retribution**. In Spanish **retribución** means "payment, reward".

retrieval [rɪ'triːvəl] n recuperación f; Comput **information r. system** sistema m de recuperación de datos

retrieve [rɪ'triːv] vt (a) (recover) recuperar; (of dog) cobrar; Comput recoger (b) (rescue) salvar

retriever [rɪ'triːvə(r)] n perro m cazador

retro ['retrəʊ] adj retro

retrograde ['retrəʊɡreɪd] adj retrógrado(a)

retrospect ['retrəʊspekt] n **in r.** retrospectivamente

retrospective [retrəʊ'spektɪv] 1 adj retrospectivo(a)
2 n Art (exposición f) retrospectiva f

return [rɪ'tɜːn] 1 n (a) (of person) regreso m, vuelta f; **by r. of post** a vuelta de correo; **in r. for** a cambio de; **many happy returns!** ¡felicidades!; **r. match** partido m de vuelta; Br **r. (ticket)** billete m de ida y vuelta (b) (of sth borrowed, stolen) devolución f (c) (profit) beneficio m, ganancia f (d) (interest) interés m
2 vt (give back) devolver; **r. to sender** (on envelope) devuélvase al remitente; **to r. sb's love** corresponder al amor de algn
3 vi (a) (come or go back) volver, regresar (b) (reappear) reaparecer

returnable [rɪ'tɜːnəbəl] adj (bottle) retornable

reunion [riː'juːnjən] n reunión f

reunite [riːjuː'naɪt] vt **to be reunited with** (after separation) reunirse con

reuse [riː'juːz] vt volver a utilizar, reutilizar

rev [rev] Fam Aut 1 n revolución f
2 vi **to r. (up)** acelerar el motor

revamp [riː'væmp] vt Fam modernizar, renovar

reveal [rɪ'viːl] vt (make known) revelar; (show) dejar ver

revealing [rɪ'viːlɪŋ] adj revelador(a)

reveille [rɪ'vælɪ] n diana f

revel ['revəl] vi disfrutar (**in** con); **to r. in doing sth** gozar muchísimo haciendo algo

revelation [revə'leɪʃən] n revelación f

revelry ['revəlrɪ] n jarana f, juerga f

revenge [rɪ'vendʒ] n venganza f; **to take r. on sb for sth** vengarse de algo en algn

revenue ['revɪnjuː] n renta f

reverberate [rɪ'vɜːbəreɪt] vi (a) (sound) reverberar (b) (ideas, news) resonar

reverberation [rɪvɜːbə'reɪʃən] n resonancia f

revere [rɪ'vɪə(r)] vt reverenciar

reverence ['revərəns] n reverencia f

reverend ['revərənd] Rel 1 adj reverendo(a); **R. Mother** reverenda madre
2 n (Protestant) pastor m; (Catholic) padre m

reverie ['revərɪ] n ensueño m

reversal [rɪ'vɜːsəl] n (a) (of order) inversión f (b) (of attitude, policy) cambio m total (c) Jur revocación f

reverse [rɪ'vɜːs] 1 adj inverso(a)
2 n (a) **quite the r.** todo lo contrario (b) (other side) (of cloth) revés m; (of coin) cruz f; (of page) dorso m (c) Aut **r. gear** marcha f atrás
3 vt (a) (order) invertir (b) (turn round) volver del revés (c) (change) cambiar totalmente (d) Br Tel **to r. the charges** poner una conferencia a cobro revertido
4 vi Aut dar marcha atrás

revert [rɪ'vɜːt] vi volver (**to** a)

review [rɪ'vjuː] 1 n (a) (examination) examen m (b) Press crítica f, reseña f (c) (magazine) revista f
2 vt (a) (examine) examinar (b) Mil **to r. the troops** pasar revista a las tropas (c) (book etc) hacer una crítica de

reviewer [rɪ'vjuːə(r)] n crítico(a) m,f

revile [rɪ'vaɪl] vt Fml injuriar

revise [rɪ'vaɪz] vt (a) (look over) revisar; Br (at school) repasar (b) (change) modificar

revision [rɪ'vɪʒən] n (a) (of text) revisión f; Br (at school) repaso m (b) (change) modificación f

revitalize [riː'vaɪtəlaɪz] vt revivificar

revival [rɪ'vaɪvəl] n (a) (of interest) renacimiento m; (of economy, industry) reactivación f; (of a country) resurgimiento m (b) Th reestreno m (c) Med reanimación f

revive [rɪ'vaɪv] 1 vt (a) (interest) renovar; (a law) restablecer; (economy, industry) reactivar; (hopes) despertar (b) Th reestrenar (c) Med reanimar
2 vi (a) (interest, hopes) renacer (b) Med volver en sí

revoke [rɪ'vəʊk] *vt* revocar; *(permission)* suspender

revolt [rɪ'vəʊlt] **1** *n* rebelión *f*, sublevación *f*
2 *vi* rebelarse, sublevarse
3 *vt* repugnar, dar asco a

revolting [rɪ'vəʊltɪŋ] *adj* repugnante

revolution [revə'lu:ʃən] *n* revolución *f*

revolutionary [revə'lu:ʃənərɪ] *adj & n* revolucionario(a) *(m,f)*

revolve [rɪ'vɒlv] **1** *vi* girar; *Fig* **to r. around** girar en torno a
2 *vt* hacer girar

> *Note that the Spanish verb **revolver** is a false friend and is never a translation for the English verb **to revolve**. In Spanish **revolver** means "to stir, to mix" and "to mess up".*

revolver [rɪ'vɒlvə(r)] *n* revólver *m*

revolving [rɪ'vɒlvɪŋ] *adj* giratorio(a)

revue [rɪ'vju:] *n* revista *f*

revulsion [rɪ'vʌlʃən] *n* repulsión *f*

reward [rɪ'wɔːd] **1** *n* recompensa *f*
2 *vt* recompensar

rewarding [rɪ'wɔːdɪŋ] *adj* provechoso(a)

rewind [riː'waɪnd] *(pt & pp rewound) vt (tape, film)* rebobinar

rewire [riː'waɪə(r)] *vt Elec* **to r. a house** poner nueva instalación eléctrica a una casa

reword [riː'wɜːd] *vt* expresar con otras palabras

rewound [riː'waʊnd] *pt & pp of rewind*

rewrite [riː'raɪt] *vt (pt rewrote* [riː'rəʊt]; *pp rewritten* [riː'rɪtən]) escribir de nuevo

rhapsody ['ræpsədɪ] *n Mus* rapsodia *f*

rhetoric ['retərɪk] *n* retórica *f*

rhetorical [rɪ'tɒrɪkəl] *adj* retórico(a)

rheumatism ['ru:mətɪzəm] *n* reuma *m*

rheumatoid ['ru:mətɔɪd] *adj* **r. arthritis** reuma *m* articular

Rhine [raɪn] *n* **the R.** el Rin

rhinoceros [raɪ'nɒsərəs] *n* rinoceronte *m*

rhododendron [rəʊdə'dendrən] *n* rododendro *m*

Rhone [rəʊn] *n* **the R.** el Ródano

rhubarb ['ru:bɑːb] *n* ruibarbo *m*

rhyme [raɪm] **1** *n* rima *f*; *(poem)* poema *m*
2 *vi* rimar

rhythm ['rɪðəm] *n* ritmo *m*

rib [rɪb] *n Anat* costilla *f*; **r. cage** caja torácica

ribald ['rɪbəld] *adj (humour)* verde

ribbon ['rɪbən] *n* cinta *f*; *(in hair etc)* lazo *m*; **torn to ribbons** hecho(a) jirones

rice [raɪs] *n* arroz *m*; **r. pudding** arroz con leche

rich [rɪtʃ] **1** *adj (person, food)* rico(a); *(soil)* fértil; *(voice)* sonoro(a); *(colour)* vivo(a)
2 *npl* **the r.** los ricos

riches ['rɪtʃɪz] *npl* riquezas *fpl*

richly ['rɪtʃlɪ] *adv* ricamente; **r. deserved** bien merecido(a)

richness ['rɪtʃnɪs] *n* riqueza *f*; *(of soil)* fertilidad *f*; *(of voice)* sonoridad *f*; *(of colour)* viveza *f*

rickets ['rɪkɪts] *n sing Med* raquitismo *m*

rickety ['rɪkətɪ] *adj (chair etc)* cojo(a); *(car)* desvencijado(a)

ricochet ['rɪkəʃeɪ, 'rɪkəʃet] **1** *n* rebote *m*
2 *vi* rebotar

rid [rɪd] *vt (pt & pp rid)* librar; **to get r. of sth** deshacerse de algo; **to r. oneself of** librarse de

riddance ['rɪdəns] *n Fam* **good r.!** ¡ya era hora!

ridden ['rɪdən] *pp of ride*

riddle¹ ['rɪdəl] *n* **(a)** *(puzzle)* acertijo *m*, adivinanza *f* **(b)** *(mystery)* enigma *m*

riddle² ['rɪdəl] *vt (with bullets)* acribillar

ride [raɪd] **1** *n* paseo *m*, vuelta *f*; **a short bus r.** un corto trayecto en autobús; *Fam* **to take sb for a r.** tomar el pelo a algn
2 *vt (pt rode; pp ridden) (bicycle, horse)* montar en; **can you r. a bicycle?** ¿sabes montar *or Am* andar en bicicleta?
3 *vi* **(a)** *(on horse)* montar *or Am* andar a caballo **(b)** *(travel) (in bus, train etc)* viajar
▸ **ride out** *vt sep* sobrevivir; **to r. out the storm** capear el temporal

rider ['raɪdə(r)] *n (of horse) (man)* jinete *m*; *(woman)* amazona *f*; *(of bicycle)* ciclista *mf*; *(of motorbike)* motociclista *mf*

ridge [rɪdʒ] *n (crest of a hill)* cresta *f*; *(hillock)* loma *f*; *(of roof)* caballete *m*; *Met* área *m*

ridicule ['rɪdɪkju:l] **1** *n* burla *f*
2 *vt* burlarse de

ridiculous [rɪ'dɪkjʊləs] *adj* ridículo(a)

riding ['raɪdɪŋ] *n* equitación *f*; **r. breeches** pantalones *mpl* de montar; **r. school** escuela hípica

rife [raɪf] *adj* abundante; **rumour is r. that …** corre la voz de que …; **to be r. with** abundar en

riffraff ['rɪfræf] *n Fam* chusma *f*, gentuza *f*

rifle¹ ['raɪfəl] *n* fusil *m*, rifle *m*; **r. range** campo *m* de tiro

rifle² ['raɪfəl] *vt* desvalijar

rift [rɪft] *n* **(a)** *Geol* falla *f* **(b)** *Fig (in friendship)* ruptura *f*; *Pol (in party)* escisión *f*; *(quarrel)* desavenencia *f*

rig [rɪg] **1** n (**a**) *Naut* aparejo m (**b**) **(oil) r.** *(onshore)* torre f de perforación; *(offshore)* plataforma petrolífera
2 vt *Pej* amañar
▸ **rig out** vt sep *Fam* ataviar
▸ **rig up** vt sep improvisar, *Esp* apañar
rigging [ˈrɪgɪŋ] n aparejo m, jarcia f
right [raɪt] **1** adj (**a**) *(not left)* derecho(a) (**b**) *(correct)* correcto(a); *(time)* exacto(a); **to be r.** tener razón; **r.?** ¿vale? (**c**) *(true)* cierto(a) (**d**) *(suitable)* adecuado(a); **the r. time** el momento oportuno (**e**) *(proper)* apropiado(a) (**f**) *Fam (healthy)* bien (**g**) *Br Fam (complete)* auténtico(a) (**h**) **r. angle** ángulo recto
2 n (**a**) *(right side)* derecha f (**b**) *(right hand)* mano derecha (**c**) *Pol* **the R.** la derecha (**d**) *(lawful claim)* derecho m; **in one's own r.** por derecho propio; **r. of way** *(across land)* derecho de paso; *(on roads)* prioridad f (**e**) **r. and wrong** el bien y el mal
3 adv (**a**) *(correctly)* bien; **it's just r.** es justo lo que hace falta (**b**) **r. away** *(immediately)* en seguida, inmediatamente, *CAm, Méx* ahorita (**c**) *(to the right)* a la derecha; **r. and left** a diestro y siniestro (**d**) *(directly)* directamente; **go r. on** sigue recto; **r. at the top** en todo lo alto; **r. to the end** hasta el final
4 vt (**a**) *(correct)* corregir (**b**) *(put straight)* enderezar
righteous [ˈraɪtʃəs] adj *(upright)* recto(a)
rightful [ˈraɪtful] adj legítimo(a)
right-hand [ˈraɪthænd] adj derecho(a); **r. drive** conducción f por la derecha; **r. side** lado derecho; *Fam* **r. man** brazo derecho
right-handed [raɪtˈhændɪd] adj *(person)* que usa la mano derecha; *(tool)* para la mano derecha
rightly [ˈraɪtlɪ] adv debidamente; **and r. so** y con razón
right-wing [ˈraɪtwɪŋ] adj de derechas, derechista
right-winger [raɪtˈwɪŋə(r)] n derechista mf
rigid [ˈrɪdʒɪd] adj rígido(a)
rigidity [rɪˈdʒɪdɪtɪ] n rigidez f, inflexibilidad f
rigmarole [ˈrɪgmərəʊl] n *Fam (process)* engorro m, *Esp* latazo m; *(speech)* rollo m, galimatías m inv
rigor [ˈrɪgər] n *US* = **rigour**
rigorous [ˈrɪgərəs] adj riguroso(a)
rigour [ˈrɪgə(r)] n rigor m, severidad f
rile [raɪl] vt *Fam (annoy)* fastidiar, irritar, *Am* enojar
rim [rɪm] n *(edge)* borde m; *(of wheel)* llanta f; *(of spectacles)* montura f

rind [raɪnd] n *(of fruit, cheese)* corteza f
ring¹ [rɪŋ] **1** n (**a**) *(sound of bell)* toque m; *(of doorbell, alarm clock)* timbre m (**b**) *Tel* llamada f
2 vt *(pt* **rang**, *pp* **rung)** (**a**) *(bell)* tocar; *Fig* **it rings a bell** me suena (**b**) *Br (on phone)* llamar (por teléfono) a, *RP* hablar a
3 vi (**a**) *(bell, phone etc)* sonar (**b**) **my ears are ringing** tengo un pitido en los oídos (**c**) *Tel* llamar
▸ **ring back** vt sep *Br Tel* volver a llamar
▸ **ring off** vi *Br Tel* colgar
▸ **ring out** vi resonar
▸ **ring up** vt sep *Br Tel* llamar (por teléfono) a, *RP* hablar a
ring² [rɪŋ] **1** n (**a**) *(metal hoop)* aro m; **curtain r.** anilla f; **r. binder** archivador m *or* carpeta f de anillas, *RP* bibliorato m (**b**) *(for finger)* anillo m, sortija f (**c**) *(circle)* círculo m; *Br* **r. road** carretera f de circunvalación (**d**) *(group of people)* corro m; *(of spies)* red f; *(of thieves)* banda f (**e**) *(arena)* pista f; *(for boxing)* cuadrilátero m; *(for bullfights)* ruedo m
2 vt *(surround)* rodear
ringing [ˈrɪŋɪŋ] n *(of bell)* toque m, repique m; *(in ears)* pitido m
ringleader [ˈrɪŋliːdə(r)] n cabecilla mf
ringlet [ˈrɪŋlɪt] n tirabuzón m
ringtone [ˈrɪŋtəʊn] n *(of mobile phone)* melodía f
rink [rɪŋk] n pista f; **ice r.** pista de hielo
rinse [rɪns] **1** n **to give sth a r.** enjuagar *or Esp* aclarar algo
2 vt *(clothes, dishes)* enjuagar, *Esp* aclarar; **to r. one's hands** enjuagarse las manos
riot [ˈraɪət] **1** n *(uprising)* disturbio m; **to run r.** desmandarse; **r. police** policía f antidisturbios (**b**) *Fig (of colour)* profusión f
2 vi amotinarse
rioter [ˈraɪətə(r)] n amotinado(a) m,f
riotous [ˈraɪətəs] adj (**a**) *(behaviour, mob)* descontrolado(a) (**b**) *Fam (party, living)* desenfrenado(a)
rip [rɪp] **1** n *(tear)* rasgón m
2 vt rasgar, rajar; **to r. one's trousers** rajarse los pantalones
3 vi rasgarse, rajarse
▸ **rip off** vt sep *Fam* **to r. sb off** clavar *or Esp* timar a algn
▸ **rip up** vt sep hacer pedacitos
ripcord [ˈrɪpkɔːd] n cuerda f de apertura
ripe [raɪp] adj (**a**) *(fruit)* maduro(a) (**b**) *(ready)* listo(a); **the time is r.** es el momento oportuno
ripen [ˈraɪpən] vt & vi madurar

rip-off ['rɪpɒf] n Fam timo m, Col, RP cagada f

ripple ['rɪpəl] 1 n (a) (on water, fabric) onda f (b) (sound) murmullo m
2 vt (water) ondular
3 vi (a) (water) ondularse (b) (applause) extenderse

rise [raɪz] 1 n (a) (of slope, hill) cuesta f (b) (of waters) crecida f (c) (in prices, temperature) subida f; Br (pay) r. aumento m (de sueldo) (d) to give r. to ocasionar
2 vi (pt rose; pp risen ['rɪzən]) (a) (land etc) elevarse (b) (waters) crecer; (river) nacer; (tide) subir; (wind) levantarse (c) (sun, moon) salir (d) (voice) alzarse (e) (in rank) ascender (f) (prices, temperature) subir; (wages) aumentar (g) (curtain) subir (h) (from bed) levantarse (i) (stand up) levantarse; Fig (city, building) erguirse
▸ **rise above** vt insep estar por encima de
▸ **rise up** vi (rebel) sublevarse

rising ['raɪzɪŋ] 1 adj (sun) naciente; (tide) creciente; (prices) en aumento; r. damp humedad f
2 n (a) (of sun) salida f (b) (rebellion) levantamiento m

risk [rɪsk] 1 n riesgo m; at r. en peligro; at your own r. por su cuenta y riesgo; to take risks arriesgarse
2 vt arriesgar; I'll r. it correré el riesgo

risky ['rɪskɪ] adj (riskier, riskiest) arriesgado(a)

risqué ['rɪskeɪ] adj atrevido(a); (joke) picante

rite [raɪt] n rito m; the last rites la extremaunción

ritual ['rɪtjʊəl] adj & n ritual (m)

rival ['raɪvəl] 1 adj & n rival (mf)
2 vt rivalizar con

rivalry ['raɪvəlrɪ] n rivalidad f

river ['rɪvə(r)] n río m; down/up r. río abajo/arriba

river-bank ['rɪvəbæŋk] n orilla f, ribera f

river-bed ['rɪvəbed] n lecho m

rivet ['rɪvɪt] 1 n Tech remache m, roblón m
2 vt Tech remachar; Fig cautivar

riveting ['rɪvɪtɪŋ] adj Fig fascinante

roach [rəʊtʃ] n US Fam (cockroach) cucaracha f, Chile barata f

road [rəʊd] n (a) (in general) carretera f; Br A/B r. carretera nacional/secundaria; main r. carretera principal; r. accident accidente m de tráfico; r. safety seguridad f vial; r. sign señal f de tráfico; r. Br works or US work obras fpl (b) (in town) calle f (c) (path, track) camino m

roadblock ['rəʊdblɒk] n control m policial

roadhog ['rəʊdhɒg] n Fam loco(a) m,f del volante, dominguero(a) m,f

roadside ['rəʊdsaɪd] n borde m de la carretera; r. restaurant/café restaurante m/cafetería f de carretera

roadway ['rəʊdweɪ] n calzada f

roadworthy ['rəʊdwɜːðɪ] adj (vehicle) en buen estado

roam [rəʊm] 1 vt vagar por, rondar
2 vi vagar

roar [rɔː(r)] 1 n (of lion) rugido m; (of bull, sea, wind) bramido m; (of crowd) clamor m
2 vi (lion, crowd) rugir; (bull, sea, wind) bramar; (crowd) clamar; Fig to r. with laughter reírse a carcajadas

roaring ['rɔːrɪŋ] adj a r. success un éxito clamoroso; to do a r. trade hacer un negocio redondo

roast [rəʊst] 1 adj (meat) asado(a); r. beef rosbif m
2 n Culin asado m
3 vt (meat) asar; (coffee, nuts) tostar
4 vi asarse

rob [rɒb] vt robar; (bank) atracar

robber ['rɒbə(r)] n ladrón(ona) m,f; bank r. atracador(a) m,f

robbery ['rɒbərɪ] n robo m

robe [rəʊb] n (ceremonial) toga f; (dressing gown) bata f

robin ['rɒbɪn] n petirrojo m

robot ['rəʊbɒt] n robot m

robust [rəʊ'bʌst] adj (sturdy) robusto(a)

rock [rɒk] 1 n (a) (substance, large stone) roca f; Fig on the rocks (marriage) a punto de fracasar; (whisky) con hielo (b) US (stone) piedra f (c) Br (sweet) stick of r. = barra de caramelo de menta que se vende sobre todo en localidades costeras y lleva el nombre del lugar impreso (d) Mus música f rock; r. and roll rock and roll m
2 vt (a) (chair) mecer; (baby) acunar (b) (shake) hacer temblar; Fig (shock) conmover
3 vi (a) (move to and fro) mecerse (b) (shake) vibrar

rock-bottom ['rɒk'bɒtəm] adj bajísimo(a); r. prices precios regalados

rockery ['rɒkərɪ] n jardín m de rocas

rocket ['rɒkɪt] 1 n cohete m; r. launcher lanzacohetes m inv
2 vi Fam (prices) dispararse

rocking-chair ['rɒkɪntʃeə(r)] n mecedora f

rocking-horse ['rɒkɪŋhɔːs] n caballito m de balancín

rocky ['rɒkɪ] adj (rockier, rockiest) rocoso(a); Fam Fig (unsteady) inseguro(a); the R. Mountains las Montañas Rocosas

rod [rɒd] *n (of metal)* barra *f*; *(stick)* vara *f*; **fishing r.** caña *f* de pescar

rode [rəʊd] *pt of* **ride**

rodent ['rəʊdənt] *n* roedor *m*

roe[1] [rəʊ] *n Zool* **r. (deer)** corzo(a) *m,f*

roe[2] [rəʊ] *n (fish eggs)* hueva *f*

rogue [rəʊg] *n* granuja *m*

role, rôle [rəʊl] *n* papel *m*; **to play a r.** desempeñar un papel

roll [rəʊl] **1** *n* (**a**) *(of paper, film)* rollo *m* (**b**) *(bread)* panecillo *m*, *Méx* bolillo *m* (**c**) *(list of names)* lista *f*, nómina *f* (**d**) *(of drum)* redoble *m*; *(of thunder)* fragor *m*
  2 *vt* (**a**) *(ball)* hacer rodar (**b**) *(cigarette)* liar (**c**) *(push)* empujar
  3 *vi* (**a**) *(ball)* rodar (**b**) *(animal)* revolcarse (**c**) *(ship)* balancearse (**d**) *(drum)* redoblar; *(thunder)* retumbar

▸ **roll about, roll around** *vi* rodar (de acá para allá)

▸ **roll by** *vi (years)* pasar

▸ **roll in** *vi Fam* (**a**) *(arrive)* llegar (**b**) *(money)* llegar a raudales

▸ **roll over** *vi* dar una vuelta

▸ **roll up 1** *vt sep* enrollar; *(blinds)* subir; **to r. up one's sleeves** (ar)remangarse
  2 *vi Fam (arrive)* llegar

roll-call ['rəʊlkɔːl] *n* **to have a r.** pasar lista

roller ['rəʊlə(r)] *n* (**a**) *Tech* rodillo *m*; **r. blades** patines *mpl* en línea; **r. coaster** montaña rusa; **r. skates** patines *mpl* (de ruedas) (**b**) *(large wave)* ola *f* grande (**c**) *(for hair)* rulo *m*, *Chile* tubo *m*, *RP* rulero *m*

rolling ['rəʊlɪŋ] **1** *adj* (**a**) *Rail* **r. stock** material *m* rodante (**b**) *(countryside)* ondulado(a)
  2 *n* rodamiento *m*; *(of ground)* apisonamiento *m*; **r. pin** rodillo *m* (de cocina)

ROM [rɒm] *n Comput (abbr* **read-only memory)** ROM *f*

Roman ['rəʊmən] *adj & n* romano(a) *(m,f)*; **R. Catholic** católico(a) (romano(a)); **R. law** derecho romano; **R. numerals** números romanos

Romance [rəʊ'mæns] *adj Ling* románico(a), romance; **R. languages** lenguas románicas

romance [rəʊ'mæns] **1** *n* (**a**) *(tale)* novela romántica (**b**) *(love affair)* aventura amorosa (**c**) *(romantic quality)* lo romántico
  2 *vi* fantasear

Romania [rəʊ'meɪnɪə] *n* Rumanía

Romanian [rə'meɪnɪən] **1** *adj* rumano(a)
  2 *n (person)* rumano(a) *m,f*; *(language)* rumano *m*

romantic [rəʊ'mæntɪk] *adj & n* romántico(a) *(m,f)*

Rome [rəʊm] *n* Roma

romp [rɒmp] **1** *n* jugueteo *m*
  2 *vi* juguetear

rompers ['rɒmpəz] *npl* pelele *m*

roof [ruːf] **1** *n (pl* **roofs** [ruːfs, ruːvz]) (**a**) *(of building)* tejado *m*; *Fam Fig* **to go through the r.** *(of prices)* estar por las nubes; *(with anger)* subirse por las paredes (**b**) *Aut* techo *m*; **r. rack** baca *f* (**c**) *(of mouth)* cielo *m*
  2 *vt* techar

roofing ['ruːfɪŋ] *n* materiales *mpl* usados para techar

rooftop ['ruːftɒp] *n* tejado *m*; *Fig* **to shout sth from the rooftops** proclamar algo a los cuatro vientos

rook [rʊk] *n* (**a**) *(bird)* grajo *m* (**b**) *(in chess)* torre *f*

rookie ['rʊkɪ] *n US Fam* novato(a) *m,f*

room [ruːm] *n* (**a**) *(in house)* habitación *f*, cuarto *m*; *(in hotel)* habitación *f*; *(bedroom)* dormitorio *m*, *Am* cuarto *m*, *CAm, Col, Méx* recámara *f*; **single r.** habitación individual; **r. service** servicio *m* de habitaciones (**b**) *(space)* sitio *m*, espacio *m*, *Am* lugar *m*, *Andes* campo *m*; **to make r. (for sb)** hacer sitio *or Am* lugar *or Andes* campo (para *or* a algn)

rooming-house ['ruːmɪnhaʊs] *n US* casa *f* de huéspedes, pensión *f*

roommate ['ruːmmeɪt] *n* compañero(a) *m,f* de habitación

roomy ['ruːmɪ] *adj* (**roomier, roomiest**) amplio(a)

roost [ruːst] **1** *n* palo *m*, percha *f*; **(hen) r.** gallinero *m*; *Fig* **to rule the r.** llevar la batuta
  2 *vi* posarse

rooster ['ruːstə(r)] *n esp US* gallo *m*

root[1] [ruːt] **1** *n* raíz *f*; **to take r.** echar raíces
  2 *vt* arraigar
  3 *vi* arraigar

▸ **root out, root up** *vt sep* arrancar de raíz

root[2] [ruːt] *vi (search)* buscar; **to r. about** *or* **around for sth** hurgar en busca de algo

root[3] [ruːt] *vi Fam* **to r. for a team** animar a un equipo

rope [rəʊp] **1** *n* (**a**) *(thin)* cuerda *f*; *(thick)* soga *f*; *Naut* cabo *m* (**b**) *Fam Fig* **to know the ropes** estar al tanto
  2 *vt (package)* atar; *(climbers)* encordar

> *Note that the Spanish word* **ropa** *is a false friend and is never a translation for the English word* **rope**. *In Spanish* **ropa** *means "clothes".*

▸ **rope in** *vt sep Fam* enganchar

▸ **rope off** *vt sep* acordonar

rop(e)y ['rəʊpɪ] adj (**ropier, ropiest**) Br Fam (unreliable) flojo(a); (ill) pachucho(a), Am flojo(a)

rosary ['rəʊzərɪ] n rosario m

rose¹ [rəʊz] pt of **rise**

rose² [rəʊz] n (a) Bot rosa f; **r. bed** rosaleda f; **r. bush** rosal m (b) (colour) rosa m (c) (of watering can) alcachofa f

rosé ['rəʊzeɪ] n (vino m) rosado m

rosebud ['rəʊzbʌd] n capullo m de rosa

rosemary ['rəʊzmərɪ] n romero m

rosette [rəʊ'zet] n (of ribbons) escarapela f

roster ['rɒstə(r)] n lista f

rostrum ['rɒstrəm] n estrado m

> ✍ Note that the Spanish word **rostro** is a false friend and is never a translation for the English word **rostrum**. In Spanish, **rostro** means "face".

rosy ['rəʊzɪ] adj (**rosier, rosiest**) (a) (complexion) sonrosado(a) (b) Fig (future) prometedor(a)

rot [rɒt] 1 n (a) (decay) putrefacción f; **dry r.** putrefacción de la madera (b) Br Fam (nonsense) sandeces fpl, Am pendejadas fpl
2 vt pudrir
▸ **rot away** vt sep acabar, concluir

rota ['rəʊtə] n Br lista f

rotary ['rəʊtərɪ] 1 n US (for traffic) rotonda f
2 adj rotatorio(a), giratorio(a)

rotate [rəʊ'teɪt] 1 vt (a) (revolve) hacer girar (b) (jobs, crops) alternar
2 vi (revolve) girar

rotating [rəʊ'teɪtɪŋ] adj rotativo(a)

rotation [rəʊ'teɪʃən] n rotación f

rote [rəʊt] n **by r.** de memoria

rotten ['rɒtən] adj (a) (decayed) podrido(a); (tooth) picado(a) (b) Fam (very bad) malísimo(a); Fam **I feel r.** me siento Esp fatal or Am pésimo

rouble ['ru:bəl] n rublo m

rouge [ru:ʒ] 1 n colorete m
2 vt poner colorete a

rough [rʌf] 1 adj (a) (surface, skin) áspero(a); (terrain) accidentado(a); (sea) agitado(a); (weather) tempestuoso(a) (b) (violent) violento(a) (c) (wine) áspero(a) (d) Fam **to feel r.** encontrarse fatal (e) (approximate) aproximado(a); **r. draft** borrador m (f) (harsh) severo(a)
2 adv duramente; Fam Fig **to sleep r.** dormir a la intemperie or Am al raso
3 vt Fam **we had to r. it** nos las arreglamos or Esp apañamos como pudimos

roughage ['rʌfɪdʒ] n (substance) fibra f

rough-and-ready ['rʌfən'redɪ] adj improvisado(a)

roughen ['rʌfən] vt poner áspero(a)

roughly ['rʌflɪ] adv (a) (crudely) toscamente (b) (clumsily) torpemente (c) (not gently) bruscamente (d) (approximately) aproximadamente

roulette [ru:'let] n ruleta f

round [raʊnd] 1 adj redondo(a); **r. trip** viaje m de ida y vuelta
2 n (a) (series) serie f; **r. of talks** ronda f de negociaciones (b) (of ammunition) cartucho m; (salvo) salva f (c) (of drinks) ronda f, Am vuelta f (d) (in golf) partido m (e) (in boxing) round m (f) (in a competition) eliminatoria f
3 adv **all year r.** durante todo el año; **to invite sb r.** invitar a algn a casa
4 prep alrededor de; **r. here** por aquí; **it's just r. the corner** está a la vuelta de la esquina, RP queda a la vuelta
5 vt (turn) dar la vuelta a
▸ **round off** vt sep acabar, concluir
▸ **round on** vt insep (attack) atacar
▸ **round up** vt sep (cattle) acorralar, rodear; (people) reunir

roundabout ['raʊndəbaʊt] 1 n Br (a) (merry-go-round) tiovivo m, carrusel m, RP calesita f (b) (for cars) rotonda f, Esp glorieta f
2 adj indirecto(a)

rounders ['raʊndəz] n Br = juego parecido al béisbol

roundly ['raʊndlɪ] adv completamente, totalmente

round-shouldered ['raʊnd'ʃəʊldəd] adj cargado(a) de espaldas

round-trip ['raʊnd'trɪp] US adj (ticket) de ida y vuelta

round-up ['raʊndʌp] n (a) (of cattle) rodeo m; (of suspects) redada f (b) (summary) resumen m

rouse [raʊz] vt despertar; (stir up) suscitar

rousing ['raʊzɪŋ] adj (cheer) entusiasta; (applause) caluroso(a); (speech, song) conmovedor(a)

rout [raʊt] 1 n aniquilación f
2 vt aniquilar

route [ru:t] 1 n (a) (of traveller, plane, ship) ruta f; (of bus) línea f; Fig camino m; **r. map** mapa m de carreteras (b) US **R.** ≃ carretera f nacional
2 vt encaminar

routine [ru:'ti:n] 1 n (a) (habit) rutina f (b) Th número m
2 adj rutinario(a)

roving ['rəʊvɪŋ] adj errante; **r. reporter** enviado(a) m,f especial

row¹ [rəʊ] n fila f, hilera f; US **r. house** casa f adosada; Fig **three times in a r.** tres veces seguidas

row² [rəʊ] vt & vi (in a boat) remar

row³ [raʊ] **1** n (**a**) (quarrel) pelea f, bronca f (**b**) (noise) jaleo m; (protest) escándalo m
2 vi pelearse

rowboat ['rəʊbəʊt] n US bote m or barca f de remos

rowdy ['raʊdɪ] **1** adj (**rowdier, rowdiest**) (**a**) (noisy) ruidoso(a); (disorderly) alborotador(a) (**b**) (quarrelsome) camorrista
2 n camorrista mf

rowing ['rəʊɪŋ] n remo m; esp Br **r. boat** bote m de remos

royal ['rɔɪəl] **1** adj real; **r. blue** azul marino; **the R. Family** la Familia Real
2 n Fam miembro m de la Familia Real

royally ['rɔɪəlɪ] adv Fig magníficamente

royalty ['rɔɪəltɪ] n (**a**) (royal persons) miembro(s) m(pl) de la Familia Real (**b**) **royalties** derechos mpl de autor

RPI [ɑːpiːˈaɪ] n (abbr **Retail Price Index**) IPC m, Índice m de Precios al Consumo

rpm [ɑːpiːˈem] n (abbr **revolutions per minute**) r.p.m.

RSPCA [ɑːrespiːsiːˈeɪ] n Br (abbr **Royal Society for the Prevention of Cruelty to Animals**) ≃ Sociedad f Protectora de Animales

RSVP [ɑːresviːˈpiː] (abbr **répondez s'il vous plaît**) se ruega contestación, S.R.C.

Rt Hon Br Pol (abbr (**the**) **Right Honourable**) = tratamiento que se da a los diputados en el Parlamento británico, ≃ Su Señoría

rub [rʌb] **1** n **to give sth a r.** frotar algo
2 vt frotar; (hard) restregar; (massage) friccionar
3 vi rozar (**against** contra)
▸ **rub down** vt sep rotar; (horse) almohazar; (surface) raspar
▸ **rub in** vt sep (**a**) (cream etc) frotar con (**b**) Fam **don't r. it in** no me lo refriegues
▸ **rub off 1** vt sep (erase) borrar
2 vi Fig **to r. off on sb** influir en algn
▸ **rub out** vt sep borrar
▸ **rub up** vt sep Fam Fig **to r. sb up the wrong way** fastidiar a algn

rubber¹ ['rʌbə(r)] n (**a**) (substance) goma f, Am hule m; **r. band** goma; **r. stamp** tampón m (**b**) Br (eraser) goma f (de borrar) (**c**) Fam (condom) goma f, Méx impermeable m, RP forro m

rubber² ['rʌbə(r)] n (in bridge) rubber m

rubbery ['rʌbərɪ] adj (elastic) elástico(a)

rubbish ['rʌbɪʃ] n (**a**) Br (refuse) basura f; Br **r. bin** cubo m or Am bote m de la basura; **r. dump** or **tip** vertedero m (**b**) Fam (worthless thing) birria f (**c**) Fam (nonsense) tonterías fpl

rubble ['rʌbəl] n escombros mpl

rubric ['ruːbrɪk] n rúbrica f

ruby ['ruːbɪ] n rubí m

rucksack ['rʌksæk] n mochila f

ructions ['rʌkʃənz] npl Fam jaleo m

rudder ['rʌdə(r)] n timón m

ruddy ['rʌdɪ] adj (**ruddier, ruddiest**) (**a**) (complexion) rojizo(a), colorado(a) (**b**) Br Fam (damned) maldito(a)

rude [ruːd] adj (**a**) (impolite) maleducado(a); (foul-mouthed) grosero(a); **don't be r. to your mother** no le faltes al respeto a tu madre (**b**) (abrupt) **a r. awakening** un despertar repentino

rudimentary [ruːdɪˈmentərɪ] adj rudimentario(a)

rudiments ['ruːdɪmənts] npl rudimentos mpl

rue [ruː] vt arrepentirse de

rueful ['ruːfʊl] adj (regretful) arrepentido(a); (sad) triste

ruff [rʌf] n (collar) gorguera f

ruffian ['rʌfɪən] n canalla m

ruffle ['rʌfəl] vt (water) agitar; (hair) despeinar; Fig **to r. sb's feathers** hacer esp Esp enfadar or esp Am enojar a algn

ruffled ['rʌfəld] adj (**a**) (hair) alborotado(a); (clothes) en desorden (**b**) (perturbed) perturbado(a)

rug [rʌg] n alfombra f, alfombrilla f

rugby ['rʌgbɪ] n rugby m; **r. league** rugby a trece; **r. union** rugby a quince

rugged ['rʌgɪd] adj (**a**) (terrain) accidentado(a) (**b**) (features) marcado(a) (**c**) (character) vigoroso(a)

rugger ['rʌgə(r)] n Br Fam rugby m

ruin ['ruːɪn] **1** n ruina f; **ruins** ruinas fpl, restos mpl; **in ruins** en ruinas
2 vt arruinar; (spoil) estropear

ruined ['ruːɪnd] adj (building) en ruinas

rule [ruːl] **1** n (**a**) (principle, regulation) regla f, norma f; **to work to r.** hacer una huelga de celo; **as a r.** por regla general (**b**) (government) dominio m; (of monarch) reinado m; **r. of law** imperio m de la ley
2 vt & vi (**a**) (govern) gobernar; (of monarch) reinar (**b**) (decide) decidir; (decree) decretar (**c**) (draw) tirar
▸ **rule out** vt sep descartar

ruled [ruːld] adj rayado(a)

ruler ['ruːlə(r)] n (**a**) (of country) gobernante mf (**b**) (for measuring) regla f

ruling ['ruːlɪŋ] **1** adj (in charge) dirigente; Fig (predominant) predominante; **the r. party** el partido en el poder
2 n Jur fallo m

rum [rʌm] n ron m

Rumania [ruːˈmeɪnɪə] n = Romania

Rumanian [ruːˈmeɪnɪən] adj & n = Romanian

rumble ['rʌmbəl] **1** n (a) (of thunder, gunfire) rugido m, retumbo m (b) (of stomach) gruñido m
2 vi (a) (thunder) retumbar (b) (stomach) gruñir

ruminate ['ruːmɪneɪt] vi (chew, ponder) rumiar

rummage ['rʌmɪdʒ] vi revolver (**through** en); US **r. sale** (in store) liquidacion f de saldos; (for charity) rastrillo benéfico

rumour, US **rumor** ['ruːmə(r)] **1** n rumor m; **r. has it that ...** se dice que ...
2 vt **it is rumoured that** se rumorea que

rump [rʌmp] n (of animal) ancas fpl; Fam Hum (of person) trasero m; **r. steak** filete m de lomo

rumpus ['rʌmpəs] n Fam jaleo m, bronca f, Esp follón m

run [rʌn] **1** n (a) (act of running) carrera f; **on the r.** fugado(a); **to go for a r.** hacer footing; Fig **in the long r.** a largo plazo (b) (trip) (in car) vuelta f (c) (sequence) serie f (d) (in stocking) carrera f
2 vt (pt ran; pp run) (a) (distance) correr; **to r. a race** correr en una carrera (b) (drive) llevar (c) (house, business) llevar; (company) dirigir; (organize) organizar (d) (fingers) pasar (e) Comput **to r. a program** ejecutar un programa
3 vi (a) (person) correr (b) (colour) desteñirse (c) (water, river) correr; **to leave the tap running** dejar el grifo abierto; Fam **your nose is running** se te caen los mocos (d) (operate) (machine) funcionar (**on** con) (e) Pol **to r. for president** presentarse como candidato a la presidencia (f) (range) oscilar (**between** entre) (g) **shyness runs in the family** la timidez le viene de familia (h) Cin & Th estar en cartel

▸ **run about** vi corretear

▸ **run across** vt insep (meet) tropezar con

▸ **run away** vi fugarse; (horse) desbocarse

▸ **run down 1** vt insep (stairs) bajar corriendo
2 vt sep (a) (in car) atropellar (b) (criticize) criticar
3 vi (battery) agotarse; (clock) pararse

▸ **run in** vt sep Aut rodar

▸ **run into** vt insep (a) (room) entrar corriendo en (b) (people, problems) tropezar con (c) (crash into) chocar contra

▸ **run off 1** vt sep (print) tirar
2 vi escaparse

▸ **run on 1** vt sep Typ enlazar
2 vi (meeting) continuar

▸ **run out** vi (a) (exit) salir corriendo (b) (come to an end) agotarse; (of contract) vencer; **to r. out of** quedarse sin

▸ **run over 1** vt sep (in car) atropellar
2 vt insep (rehearse) ensayar
3 vi (overflow) rebosar

▸ **run through** vt insep (a) (of river) pasar por (b) (read quickly) echar un vistazo a (c) (rehearse) ensayar

▸ **run up** vt sep (a) (flag) izar (b) (debts) acumular

▸ **run up against** vt insep tropezar con

runaway ['rʌnəweɪ] **1** n fugitivo(a) m,f
2 adj (person) huido(a); (horse) desbocado(a); (vehicle) incontrolado(a); (inflation) galopante; (success) clamoroso(a)

rundown ['rʌndaʊn] n Fam **to give sb a r.** poner a algn al tanto

run-down [rʌnˈdaʊn] adj (a) (exhausted) agotado(a) (b) (dilapidated) ruinoso(a)

rung¹ [rʌŋ] pp of ring¹

rung² [rʌŋ] n (of ladder) escalón m, peldaño m

runner ['rʌnə(r)] n (a) (person) corredor(a) m,f (b) Br **r. bean** Esp judía f verde, Bol, RP chaucha f, Méx ejote m

runner-up [rʌnərˈʌp] n subcampeón(ona) m,f

running ['rʌnɪŋ] **1** n (a) **he likes r.** le gusta correr; Fig **to be in the r. for sth** tener posibilidades de conseguir algo (b) (of company) dirección f (c) (of machine) funcionamiento m
2 adj (a) **r. commentary** comentario m en directo; **r. costs** costos mpl de mantenimiento; Pol **r. mate** candidato m a la vicepresidencia; **r. water** agua f corriente (b) **three weeks r.** tres semanas seguidas

runny ['rʌnɪ] adj (runnier, runniest) blando(a); (egg) crudo(a); (butter) derretido(a); (nose) que moquea

run-of-the-mill ['rʌnəvðəˈmɪl] adj corriente y moliente

runt [rʌnt] n Fam enano(a) m,f

run-up ['rʌnʌp] n (to elections) preliminares mpl

runway ['rʌnweɪ] n Av pista f (de aterrizaje y despegue or Am decolaje)

rupee [ruːˈpiː] n rupia f

rupture ['rʌptʃə(r)] **1** n (a) Med hernia f (b) Fig ruptura f

2 *vt* (**a**) **to r. oneself** herniarse (**b**) *(break)* romper

rural ['ruərəl] *adj* rural

ruse [ruːz] *n* ardid *m*, astucia *f*

rush¹ [rʌʃ] *n Bot* junco *m*

rush² [rʌʃ] **1** *n* (**a**) *(hurry)* prisa *f*, *Am* apuro *m*; **the r. hour** *Esp* la hora *f* punta, *Am* la hora *f* pico (**b**) *(demand)* demanda *f*
2 *vt* (**a**) *(task)* hacer de prisa; *(person)* meter prisa a; **to r. sb to hospital** llevar a algn urgentemente al hospital (**b**) *(attack)* abalanzarse sobre; *Mil* tomar por asalto
3 *vi* *(go quickly)* precipitarse
▸ **rush about** *vi* correr de un lado a otro
▸ **rush into** *vt insep Fig* **to r. into sth** hacer algo sin pensarlo bien
▸ **rush off** *vi* irse corriendo

rusk [rʌsk] *n* = galleta dura para niños

Russia ['rʌʃə] *n* Rusia

Russian ['rʌʃən] **1** *adj* ruso(a)
2 *n* (**a**) *(person)* ruso(a) *m,f* (**b**) *(language)* ruso *m*

rust [rʌst] **1** *n* (**a**) *(substance)* herrumbre *f* (**b**) *(colour)* pardo rojizo
2 *vt* oxidar
3 *vi* oxidarse

rustic ['rʌstɪk] *adj* rústico(a)

rustle ['rʌsəl] **1** *n* crujido *m*
2 *vt* *(papers etc)* hacer crujir
3 *vi* *(steal cattle)* robar ganado

rustproof ['rʌstpruːf] *adj* inoxidable

rusty ['rʌstɪ] *adj* (**rustier, rustiest**) oxida-do(a); *Fam Fig* **my French is a bit r.** tengo el francés un poco oxidado

rut [rʌt] *n* (**a**) *(furrow)* surco *m*; *(groove)* ranura *f* (**b**) *Fig* **to be in a r.** ser esclavo de la rutina (**c**) *Zool* celo *m*

ruthless ['ruːθlɪs] *adj* despiadado(a)

RV [ɑː'viː] *n US* (*abbr* **recreational vehicle**) autocaravana *f*, casa *f* or coche *m* caravana

rye [raɪ] *n* centeno *m*; **r. bread** pan *m* de centeno; **r. grass** ballica *f*; *US* **r. (whiskey)** whisky *m* de centeno

S, s [es] *n (the letter)* S, s *f*

Sabbath ['sæbəθ] *n (Jewish)* sábado *m*; *(Christian)* domingo *m*

sabbatical [sə'bætɪkəl] *adj* sabático(a)

sabotage ['sæbətɑːʒ] **1** *n* sabotaje *m*
  2 *vt* sabotear

saccharin ['sækərɪn] *n* sacarina *f*

sachet ['sæʃeɪ] *n* bolsita *f*, sobrecito *m*

sack [sæk] **1** *n* (**a**) *(bag)* saco *m* (**b**) *Fam* **to get the s.** ser despedido(a); *Fam* **to give sb the s.** despedir a algn
  2 *vt* (**a**) *Fam* despedir (**b**) *Mil* saquear

sacking ['sækɪŋ] *n Tex* arpillera *f*

sacrament ['sækrəmənt] *n* sacramento *m*

sacred ['seɪkrɪd] *adj* sagrado(a)

sacrifice ['sækrɪfaɪs] **1** *n* sacrificio *m*
  2 *vt* sacrificar

sacrificial [sækrɪ'fɪʃəl] *adj* **s. lamb** chivo expiatorio

sacrilege ['sækrɪlɪdʒ] *n* sacrilegio *m*

sacrosanct ['sækrəʊsæŋkt] *adj* sacrosanto(a)

sad [sæd] *adj* (**sadder, saddest**) triste; **how s.!** ¡qué pena!

sadden ['sædən] *vt* entristecer

saddle ['sædəl] **1** *n (for horse)* silla *f* (de montar); *(of bicycle etc)* sillín *m*
  2 *vt (horse)* ensillar; *Fam* **to s. sb with sth** encajar *or Esp, Méx* encasquetar algo a algn

saddlebag ['sædəlbæg] *n* alforja *f*

sadist ['seɪdɪst] *n* sádico(a) *m,f*

sadistic [sə'dɪstɪk] *adj* sádico(a)

sadly ['sædlɪ] *adv (reply, smile)* tristemente; **s., this is so** así es, por desgracia

sadness ['sædnɪs] *n* tristeza *f*

sadomasochism [seɪdəʊ'mæsəkɪzəm] *n* sadomasoquismo *m*

SAE [eseɪ'iː] *n Br (abbr stamped addressed envelope)* sobre franqueado con la dirección del remitente

safari [sə'fɑːrɪ] *n* safari *m*; **s. park** reserva *f*

safe [seɪf] **1** *adj* (**a**) *(unharmed)* ileso(a); *(out of danger)* a salvo; **s. and sound** sano(a) y salvo(a) (**b**) *(not dangerous)* inocuo(a) (**c**) *(secure, sure)* seguro(a) (**d**) *(driver)* prudente
  2 *n (for money etc)* caja *f* fuerte

safe-conduct [seɪf'kɒndʌkt] *n* salvoconducto *m*

safe-deposit [seɪfdɪ'pɒzɪt] *n* **s. (box)** cámara blindada

safeguard ['seɪfgɑːd] **1** *n (protection)* salvaguarda *f*; *(guarantee)* garantía *f*
  2 *vt* proteger, salvaguardar

safekeeping [seɪf'kiːpɪŋ] *n* custodia *f*

safely ['seɪflɪ] *adv* (**a**) *(without danger)* sin riesgos (**b**) **to arrive s.** llegar sin incidentes

safety ['seɪftɪ] *n* seguridad *f*; **s. first!** ¡la seguridad ante todo!; **s. belt** cinturón *m* de seguridad; **s. net** red *f* de protección; **s. pin** imperdible *m, Am* alfiler *m* de gancho, *CAm, Méx* seguro *m*

saffron ['sæfrən] *n* azafrán *m*

sag [sæg] *vi* (**a**) *(roof)* hundirse; *(wall)* pandear; *(wood, iron)* combarse; *(flesh)* colgar (**b**) *Fig (spirits)* flaquear

saga ['sɑːgə] *n (story)* saga *f*; *Fig* **a s. of corruption** una historia interminable de corrupción

sage¹ [seɪdʒ] **1** *adj (wise)* sabio(a)
  2 *n (person)* sabio(a) *m,f*

sage² [seɪdʒ] *n* salvia *f*

Sagittarius [sædʒɪ'teərɪəs] *n* Sagitario *m*

Sahara [sə'hɑːrə] *n* **the S.** el Sahara

Saharan [sə'hɑːrən] *adj* saharaui, sahariano(a)

said [sed] **1** *adj* dicho(a)
  2 *pt & pp of* **say**

sail [seɪl] **1** *n* (**a**) *(canvas)* vela *f*; **to set s.** zarpar (**b**) *(trip)* paseo *m* en barco
  2 *vt (ship)* gobernar; *Literary* navegar
  3 *vi* (**a**) *(ship, person)* navegar (**b**) *(set sail)* zarpar

▸ **sail through** *vt insep Fam* **he sailed through university** en la universidad todo le fue sobre ruedas

sailboat ['seɪlbəʊt] *n US* velero *m*

sailing ['seɪlɪŋ] *n* navegación *f*; *(yachting)* vela *f*; *Fam* **it's all plain s.** es todo coser y cantar; *Br* **s. boat** (barco *m*) velero *m*; **s. ship** barco *m* de vela

sailor ['seɪlə(r)] *n* marinero *m*

saint [seɪnt] *n* santo(a) *m,f*, *(before all masculine names except those beginning* **Do** *or* **To)** San; *(before feminine names)*

Santa; **S. Dominic** Santo Domingo; **S. Helen** Santa Elena; **S. John** San Juan; **All Saints' Day** Día *m* deTodos los Santos

saintly ['seɪntlɪ] *adj* (**saintlier, saintliest**) santo(a)

sake [seɪk] *n* **for the s. of** por (el bien de); **for your own s.** por tu propio bien

salad ['sæləd] *n* ensalada *f*; **potato s.** ensalada de patatas *or Am* papas; **s. bowl** ensaladera *f*; *Br* **s. cream** salsa *f* tipo mahonesa; **s. dressing** aderezo *m or Esp* aliño *m* para la ensalada

salami [sə'lɑːmɪ] *n* salami *m*, *Am* salame *m*

salary ['sælərɪ] *n* salario *m*, sueldo *m*

sale [seɪl] *n* (**a**) *(action)* venta *f*; **for** *or* **on s.** en venta; **sales department** departamento *m* comercial; **sales figures** cifra *f* de ventas; **sales manager** jefe(a) *m,f* de ventas; **sales tax** impuesto *m* de venta (**b**) *(at low prices)* rebajas *fpl*

salesclerk ['seɪlzklɑːk] *n US* dependiente(a) *m,f*

salesman ['seɪlzmən] *n* (**a**) *(in shop)* dependiente *m* (**b**) *(for company)* comercial *m*, vendedor *m*

salesroom ['seɪlzruːm] *n* sala *f* de subastas

saleswoman ['seɪlzwʊmən] *n* (**a**) *(in shop)* dependienta *f* (**b**) *(for company)* comercial *f*, vendedora *f*

salient ['seɪlɪənt] *adj Fig* sobresaliente

saliva [sə'laɪvə] *n* saliva *f*

sallow ['sæləʊ] *adj* cetrino(a)

salmon ['sæmən] **1** *n* salmón *m* **2** *adj* (de color) salmón

salmonella [sælmə'nelə] *n Biol & Med (bacteria)* salmonela *f*; *(food poisoning)* salmonelosis *f*

salon ['sælɒn] *n* salón *m*

saloon [sə'luːn] *n* (**a**) *(on ship)* cámara *f* (**b**) *US (bar)* taberna *f*, bar *m*; *Br* **s. (bar)** bar de lujo (**c**) *Br (car)* turismo *m*

salt [sɔːlt] **1** *n* sal *f*; *Fig* **to take sth with a pinch of s.** creer algo con reservas; **bath salts** sales de baño; **smelling salts** sales aromáticas
2 *adj* salado(a)
3 *vt* (**a**) *(cure)* salar (**b**) *(add salt to)* echar sal a

saltcellar ['sɔːltselə(r)], *US* **saltshaker** ['sɔːltʃeɪkə(r)] *n* salero *m*

saltwater ['sɔːltwɔːtə(r)] *adj* de agua salada

salty ['sɔːltɪ] *adj* (**saltier, saltiest**) salado(a)

salubrious [sə'luːbrɪəs] *adj* salubre, sano(a)

salutary ['sæljʊtərɪ] *adj (experience)* beneficioso(a); *(warning)* útil

salute [sə'luːt] **1** *n (greeting)* saludo *m*
2 *vt* (**a**) *Mil* saludar (**b**) *Fig (achievement etc)* aplaudir
3 *vi Mil* saludar

salvage ['sælvɪdʒ] **1** *n* (**a**) *(of ship etc)* salvamento *m*, rescate *m* (**b**) *(objects recovered)* objetos recuperados (**c**) *Jur* derecho *m* de salvamento
2 *vt (from ship etc)* rescatar

salvation [sæl'veɪʃən] *n* salvación *f*; **S. Army** Ejército *m* de Salvación

Samaritan [sə'mærɪtən] *n* samaritano(a) *m,f*; **the Samaritans** los Samaritanos, *Esp* ≈ el teléfono de la Esperanza

same [seɪm] **1** *adj* mismo(a); **at that very s. moment** en ese mismísimo momento; **at the s. time** *(simultaneously)* al mismo tiempo; *(however)* sin embargo; **in the s. way** del mismo modo; **the two cars are the s.** los dos coches son iguales
2 *pron* **the s.** el mismo/la misma/lo mismo; *Fam* **the s. here** lo mismo digo yo; *Fam* **the s. to you!** ¡igualmente!
3 *adv* del mismo modo, igual; **all the s., just the s.** sin embargo, aun así; **it's all the s. to me** (a mí) me da igual *or* lo mismo

sample ['sɑːmpəl] **1** *n* muestra *f*
2 *vt (wines)* catar; *(dish)* probar

sanatorium [sænə'tɔːrɪəm] *n* sanatorio *m*

sanctimonious [sæŋktɪ'məʊnɪəs] *adj* beato(a)

sanction ['sæŋkʃən] **1** *n* (**a**) *(authorization)* permiso *m* (**b**) *(penalty)* sanción *f* (**c**) *Pol* **sanctions** sanciones *fpl*
2 *vt* sancionar

sanctity ['sæŋktɪtɪ] *n (sacredness)* santidad *f*; *(of marriage)* indisolubilidad *f*

sanctuary ['sæŋktjʊərɪ] *n* (**a**) *Rel* santuario *m* (**b**) *Pol* asilo *m* (**c**) *(for birds, animals)* reserva *f*

sand [sænd] **1** *n* arena *f*; **s. castle** castillo *m* de arena; **s. dune** duna *f*
2 *vt* **to s. (down)** lijar

sandal ['sændəl] *n* sandalia *f*, *Andes, CAm* ojota *f*, *Méx* guarache *m*

sandalwood ['sændəlwʊd] *n* sándalo *m*

sandbag ['sændbæg] *n* saco *m* terrero *or m* de arena, *RP* bolsa *f* de arena

sandbox ['sændbɒks] *n US* arenal *m*

sandpaper ['sændpeɪpə(r)] *n* papel *m* de lija

sandpit ['sændpɪt] *n Br (in playground etc)* recinto *m* de arena

sandshoe ['sændʃuː] *n Br* playera *f*

sandstone ['sændstəʊn] *n* arenisca *f*

sandwich ['sænwɪdʒ, 'sænwɪtʃ] **1** *n (with sliced bread)* sándwich *m*; *(with French*

bread) Esp bocadillo *m, Am* sándwich *m, CSur* sándwiche *m, Méx* torta; *Educ* **s. course** curso teórico-práctico
  2 *vt* intercalar; **it was sandwiched between two lorries** quedó encajonado entre dos camiones

sandy ['sændɪ] *adj* (**sandier, sandiest**) (a) *(earth, beach)* arenoso(a) (b) *(hair)* rubio rojizo

sane [seɪn] *adj (not mad)* cuerdo(a); *(sensible)* sensato(a)

> 🖉 Note that the Spanish word **sano** is a false friend and is never a translation for the English word **sane**. In Spanish **sano** means "healthy".

sang [sæŋ] *pt of* **sing**

sanitarium [sænɪ'teərɪəm] *n US* sanatorio *m*

sanitary ['sænɪtərɪ] *adj* sanitario(a); *(hygienic)* higiénico(a); **s.** *Br* **towel** *or US* **napkin** compresa *f, Am* toalla *f* higiénica

sanitation [sænɪ'teɪʃən] *n* sanidad (pública); *(plumbing)* sistema *m* de saneamiento

sanity ['sænɪtɪ] *n* cordura *f*, juicio *m*; *(good sense)* sensatez *f*

> 🖉 Note that the Spanish word **sanidad** is a false friend and is never a translation for the English word **sanity**. In Spanish **sanidad** means "health".

sank [sæŋk] *pt of* **sink²**

Santa Claus ['sæntə'klɔːz] *n* Papá Noel *m*, San Nicolás *m*

sap¹ [sæp] *n Bot* savia *f*

sap² [sæp] *vt (undermine)* minar; *Fig* agotar

sap³ [sæp] *n Fam (gullible person)* papanatas *mf inv, Esp* pardillo(a) *m,f*

sapling ['sæplɪŋ] *n Bot* árbol *m* joven

sapphire ['sæfaɪə(r)] *n* zafiro *m*

sarcasm ['sɑːkæzəm] *n* sarcasmo *m*

sarcastic [sɑː'kæstɪk] *adj* sarcástico(a)

sardine [sɑː'diːn] *n* sardina *f*

Sardinia [sɑː'dɪnɪə] *n* Cerdeña *f*

sardonic [sɑː'dɒnɪk] *adj* sardónico(a)

sari ['sɑːrɪ] *n* sari *m*

SASE [eseɪes'iː] *n US (abbr* **self-addressed stamped envelope**) sobre franqueado con la dirección del remitente

sash¹ [sæʃ] *n* faja *f*

sash² [sæʃ] *n* **s. window** ventana *f* de guillotina

sat [sæt] *pt & pp of* **sit**

Satan ['seɪtən] *n* Satán *m*, Satanás *m*

satanic [sə'tænɪk] *adj* satánico(a)

satchel ['sætʃəl] *n* cartera *f* de colegial

satellite ['sætəlaɪt] *n* satélite *m*; **s. dish** antena parabólica

satin ['sætɪn] *n* satén *m*; **s. finish** *(acabado m)* satinado *m*

satire ['sætaɪə(r)] *n* sátira *f*

satirical [sə'tɪrɪkəl] *adj* satírico(a)

satisfaction [sætɪs'fækʃən] *n* satisfacción *f*

satisfactory [sætɪs'fæktərɪ] *adj* satisfactorio(a)

satisfied ['sætɪsfaɪd] *adj* satisfecho(a)

satisfy ['sætɪsfaɪ] *vt* (a) *(person, curiosity)* satisfacer (b) *(condition, demand)* cumplir (c) *(convince)* convencer

satisfying ['sætɪsfaɪɪŋ] *adj* satisfactorio(a); *(pleasing)* agradable; *(meal)* que llena

saturate ['sætʃəreɪt] *vt* saturar (**with** de); **saturated fats** grasas *fpl* saturadas

Saturday ['sætədɪ] *n* sábado *m*

sauce [sɔːs] *n* (a) *(for food)* salsa *f* (b) *Br Fam (impudence)* descaro *m*

saucepan ['sɔːspən] *n* cacerola *f*; *(large)* olla *f*

saucer ['sɔːsə(r)] *n* platillo *m*

saucy ['sɔːsɪ] *adj* (**saucier, sauciest**) *Fam* fresco(a)

Saudi Arabia ['saʊdɪə'reɪbɪə] *n* Arabia Saudí

Saudi Arabian ['saʊdɪə'reɪbɪən] *adj & n* saudita *(mf)*, saudí *(mf)*

sauna ['sɔːnə] *n* sauna *f, Am* sauna *m or f*

saunter ['sɔːntə(r)] **1** *n* paseo *m*
  2 *vi* pasearse

sausage ['sɒsɪdʒ] *n (raw)* salchicha *f*; *(cured)* salchichón *m*; *(spicy)* chorizo *m*; *Fam* **s. dog** perro *m* salchicha; *Br* **s. roll** empanada *f* de carne

sauté ['səʊteɪ] **1** *adj* salteado(a)
  2 *vt* saltear

savage ['sævɪdʒ] **1** *adj* (a) *(ferocious)* feroz; *(cruel)* cruel; *(violent)* salvaje (b) *(primitive)* salvaje
  2 *n* salvaje *mf*
  3 *vt (attack)* embestir; *Fig (criticize)* criticar despiadadamente

save [seɪv] **1** *vt* (a) *(rescue)* salvar, rescatar; *Fig* **to s. face** salvar las apariencias (b) *(put by)* guardar; *(money, energy, time)* ahorrar; *(food)* almacenar; **it saved him a lot of trouble** le evitó muchos problemas
  2 *vi* (a) **to s. (up)** ahorrar (b) **to s. on paper** *(economize)* ahorrar papel
  3 *n Ftb* parada *f*
  4 *prep Literary* salvo, excepto

saving ['seɪvɪŋ] *n* (**a**) *(of time, money)* ahorro *m* (**b**) **savings** ahorros *mpl*; **savings account** cuenta *f* de ahorros

saviour, *US* **savior** ['seɪvjə(r)] *n* salvador(a) *m,f*

savour, *US* **savor** ['seɪvə(r)] **1** *n* sabor *m*, gusto *m*
   2 *vi* saborear

savoury, *US* **savory** ['seɪvərɪ] *adj (tasty)* sabroso(a); *(salted)* salado(a); *(spicy)* picante

saw¹ [sɔː] **1** *n (tool)* sierra *f*
   2 *vt & vi (pt* sawed; *pp* sawed *or* sawn*)* serrar
   ▸ **saw up** *vt sep* serrar (**into** en)

saw² [sɔː] *pt of* **see¹**

sawdust ['sɔːdʌst] *n* (a) serrín *m*

sawed-off [sɔːd'ɒf] *adj US =* **sawn-off**

sawmill ['sɔːmɪl] *n* aserradero *m*, serrería *f*

sawn [sɔːn] *pp of* **saw¹**

sawn-off ['sɔːnɒf] *adj* recortado(a); **s. shotgun** escopeta *f* de cañones recortados

saxophone ['sæksəfəʊn] *n* saxofón *m*

say [seɪ] **1** *vt (pt & pp* said*)* decir; **it goes without saying that ...** huelga decir que ...; **it is said that ...** se dice que ...; **not to s. ...** por no decir ...; **that is to s.** es decir; **to s. yes/no** decir que sí/no; *Fam* **I s.!** ¡oiga!; **what does the sign s.?** ¿qué pone en el letrero?; **shall we s. Friday then?** ¿quedamos el viernes, pues?
   2 I have no s. in the matter no tengo ni voz ni voto en el asunto; **to have one's s.** dar su opinión

saying ['seɪɪŋ] *n* refrán *m*, dicho *m*

scab [skæb] *n* (**a**) *Med* costra *f* (**b**) *Fam* esquirol *mf*, *Am* rompehuelgas *mf inv*

scaffold ['skæfəld] *n (for execution)* patíbulo *m*

scaffolding ['skæfəldɪŋ] *n Constr* andamio *m*

scald [skɔːld] **1** *n* escaldadura *f*
   2 *vt* escaldar

scale¹ [skeɪl] *n (of fish, on skin)* escama *f*; *(in boiler)* incrustaciones *fpl*

scale² [skeɪl] **1** *n* (**a**) *(for measuring, of pay rates)* escala *f*; **on a large s.** a gran escala; **to s.** a escala; **s. model** maqueta *f* (**b**) *(of problem, changes)* escala *f*, magnitud *f* (**c**) *Mus* escala *f*
   2 *vt (climb)* escalar
   ▸ **scale down** *vt sep (drawing)* reducir a escala; *(production)* reducir

scales [skeɪlz] *npl* **(pair of) s.** *(shop, kitchen)* balanza *f*; *(bathroom)* báscula *f*

scallop ['skɒləp] *n* (**a**) *(mollusc)* vieira *f* (**b**) *(shell)* venera *f*

scalp [skælp] **1** *n* cuero cabelludo
   2 *vt* arrancar el cuero cabelludo a

scalpel ['skælpəl] *n* bisturí *m*

scamper ['skæmpə(r)] *vi* corretear

scampi ['skæmpɪ] *n* gambas empanadas

scan [skæn] **1** *vt* (**a**) *(scrutinize)* escrutar; *(horizon)* otear (**b**) *(glance at)* ojear (**c**) *(of radar)* explorar
   2 *n Med* exploración ultrasónica; *(in gynaecology etc)* ecografía *f*

scandal ['skændəl] *n* (**a**) *(outrage)* escándalo *m*; **what a s.!** ¡qué vergüenza! (**b**) *(gossip)* chismorreo *m*, *Esp* cotilleo *m*

scandalous ['skændələs] *adj* escandaloso(a)

Scandinavia [skændɪ'neɪvɪə] *n* Escandinavia

Scandinavian [skændɪ'neɪvɪən] *adj & n* escandinavo(a) *(m,f)*

scanner ['skænə(r)] *n Med & Comput* escáner *m*

scant [skænt] *adj* escaso(a)

scanty ['skæntɪ] *adj (scantier, scantiest)* escaso(a); *(meal)* insuficiente; *(clothes)* ligero(a)

scapegoat ['skeɪpgəʊt] *n* chivo expiatorio

scar [skaː(r)] *n* cicatriz *f*

scarce [skeəs] *adj* escaso(a); *Fig* **to make oneself s.** largarse

scarcely ['skeəslɪ] *adv* apenas

scarcity ['skeəsɪtɪ] *n* escasez *f*; *(rarity)* rareza *f*

scare [skeə(r)] **1** *n (fright)* susto *m*; *(widespread alarm)* pánico *m*; **bomb s.** amenaza *f* de bomba
   2 *vt* asustar, espantar; *Fam* **to be scared stiff** estar muerto(a) de miedo
   ▸ **scare away, scare off** *vt sep* ahuyentar

scarecrow ['skeəkrəʊ] *n* espantapájaros *m inv*

scarf [skaːf] *n (pl* scarfs *or* scarves*) (long, woollen)* bufanda *f*; *(square)* pañuelo *m*; *(silk)* fular *m*

scarlet ['skaːlɪt] **1** *adj* escarlata
   2 *n* escarlata *f*; **s. fever** escarlatina *f*

scarves [skaːvz] *pl of* **scarf**

scary ['skeərɪ] *adj (scarier, scariest) Fam (noise, situation)* aterrador(a), espantoso(a); *(film, book)* de miedo

scathing ['skeɪðɪŋ] *adj* mordaz, cáustico(a)

scatter ['skætə(r)] **1** *vt* (**a**) *(papers etc)* esparcir, desparramar (**b**) *(crowd)* dispersar
   2 *vi* dispersarse

scatterbrained ['skætəbreɪnd] *adj Fam* ligero(a) de cascos; *(forgetful)* despistado(a)

scattered ['skætəd] *adj* **s. showers** chubascos aislados

scavenger ['skævɪndʒə(r)] *n* (**a**) *(person)* rebuscador(a) *m,f*, trapero *m* (**b**) *(animal)* (animal *m*) carroñero(a) *mf*

scenario [sɪ'nɑːrɪəʊ] *n* (**a**) *Cin* guión *m* (**b**) *(situation)* situación *f* hipotética

scene [siːn] *n* (**a**) *Th, Cin & TV* escena *f* (**b**) *(place)* lugar *m*, escenario *m* (**c**) **to make a s.** *(fuss)* hacer una escena, *Esp* montar un número

scenery ['siːnərɪ] *n* (**a**) *(landscape)* paisaje *m* (**b**) *Th* decorado *m*

scenic ['siːnɪk] *adj (picturesque)* pintoresco(a)

scent [sent] **1** *n* (**a**) *(smell)* olor *m*; *(of food)* aroma *m* (**b**) *(perfume)* perfume *m* (**c**) *(in hunting)* pista *f*
2 *vt (add perfume to)* perfumar; *(smell)* olfatear; *Fig* presentir

sceptic ['skeptɪk] *adj* escéptico(a)

sceptical ['skeptɪkəl] *adj* escéptico(a)

scepticism ['skeptɪsɪzəm] *n* escepticismo *m*

sceptre ['septə(r)] *n* cetro *m*

schedule ['ʃedjuːl, *US* 'skedʒʊəl] **1** *n* (**a**) *(plan, agenda)* programa *m*; *(timetable)* horario *m*; **on s.** a la hora (prevista); **to be behind s.** llevar retraso (**b**) *(list)* lista *f*, *(inventory)* inventario *m*
2 *vt (plan)* programar, fijar

scheduled ['ʃedjuːld, *US* 'skedʒʊəld] *adj* previsto(a), fijo(a); **s. flight** vuelo *m* regular

scheme [skiːm] **1** *n* (**a**) *(plan)* plan *m*; *(project)* proyecto *m*; *(idea)* idea *f*; **colour s.** combinación *f* de colores (**b**) *(plot)* intriga *f*; *(trick)* ardid *m*
2 *vi (plot)* tramar, intrigar

scheming ['skiːmɪŋ] *adj* intrigante, maquinador(a)

schism ['sɪzəm] *n* cisma *m*

schizophrenic [skɪtsəʊ'frenɪk] *adj & n* esquizofrénico(a) *(m,f)*

schmuck [ʃmʌk] *n US Fam* lelo(a) *m,f*

scholar ['skɒlə(r)] *n (learned person)* erudito(a) *m,f*, *(pupil)* alumno(a) *m,f*

scholarly ['skɒləlɪ] *adj* erudito(a)

scholarship ['skɒləʃɪp] *n* (**a**) *(learning)* erudición *f* (**b**) *(grant)* beca *f*; **s. holder** becario(a) *m,f*

school [skuːl] **1** *n* (**a**) *(for children)* (up to 14) colegio *m*, escuela *f*; (from 14 to 18) instituto *m*; **s. friend** amigo(a) *m,f* del colegio; **s. year** año *m* escolar (**b**) *US (university)* universidad *f* (**c**) *(university* department) facultad *f* (**d**) *(group of artists)* escuela *f*
2 *vt (teach)* enseñar; *(train)* formar

schoolbook ['skuːlbʊk] *n* libro *m* de texto

schoolboy ['skuːlbɔɪ] *n* alumno *m*

schoolchild ['skuːltʃaɪld] *n* alumno(a) *m,f*

schooldays ['skuːldeɪz] *npl* años *mpl* de colegio

schoolgirl ['skuːlgɜːl] *n* alumna *f*

schooling ['skuːlɪŋ] *n* educación *f*, estudios *mpl*

schoolmaster ['skuːlmɑːstə(r)] *n* profesor *m*; *(primary school)* maestro *m*

schoolmistress ['skuːlmɪstrɪs] *n* profesora *f*; *(primary school)* maestra *f*

schoolteacher ['skuːltiːtʃə(r)] *n* profesor(a) *m,f*; *(primary school)* maestro(a) *m,f*

schooner ['skuːnə(r)] *n Naut* goleta *f*

sciatica [saɪ'ætɪkə] *n* ciática *f*

science ['saɪəns] *n* ciencia *f*; *(school subject)* ciencias; **s. fiction** ciencia-ficción *f*

scientific [saɪən'tɪfɪk] *adj* científico(a)

scientist ['saɪəntɪst] *n* científico(a) *m,f*

scintillating ['sɪntɪleɪtɪŋ] *adj* brillante

scissors ['sɪzəz] *npl* tijeras *fpl*; **a pair of s.** unas tijeras

scoff¹ [skɒf] *vi (mock)* mofarse (**at** de)

scoff² [skɒf] *vt Br Fam (eat)* zamparse

scold [skəʊld] *vt* regañar, reñir

scone [skəʊn, skɒn] *n* bollo *m*, pastelito *m*

scoop [skuːp] *n* (**a**) *(for flour)* pala *f*; *(for ice cream)* cucharón *m*; *(amount)* palada *f*, cucharada *f* (**b**) *Press* exclusiva *f*
▸ **scoop out** *vt sep (flour etc)* sacar con pala; *(water) (from boat)* achicar
▸ **scoop up** *vt sep* recoger

scooter ['skuːtə(r)] *n (child's)* patinete *m*; *(adult's)* Vespa® *f*

scope [skəʊp] *n* (**a**) *(range)* alcance *m*; *(of undertaking)* ámbito *m* (**b**) *(freedom)* libertad *f*

scorch [skɔːtʃ] *vt (singe)* chamuscar

scorching ['skɔːtʃɪŋ] *adj Fam* abrasador(a)

score [skɔː(r)] **1** *n* (**a**) *Sport* tanteo *m*; *Cards & (in golf)* puntuación *f*; *(result)* resultado *m*; **on that s.** a ese respecto (**c**) *(twenty)* veintena *f* (**d**) *Mus (of opera)* partitura *f*; *(of film)* música *f*
2 *vt* (**a**) *(goal)* marcar; *(points)* conseguir (**b**) *(wood)* hacer una muesca en; *(paper)* rayar
3 *vi* (**a**) *Sport* marcar un tanto; *Ftb* marcar un gol (**b**) *Fam* ligar (**with** con)
▸ **score out** *vt sep (word etc)* tachar

scoreboard ['skɔːbɔːd] n marcador m

scorer ['skɔːrə(r)] n (a) (goal striker) goleador m (b) (scorekeeper) encargado(a) m,f del marcador

scorn [skɔːn] **1** n desprecio m
2 vt despreciar

scornful ['skɔːnfʊl] adj desdeñoso(a)

Scorpio ['skɔːpɪəʊ] n Escorpio m, Escorpión m

scorpion ['skɔːpɪən] n alacrán m, escorpión m

Scot [skɒt] n escocés(esa) m,f

Scotch [skɒtʃ] **1** adj escocés(esa); US **S. tape**® cinta adhesiva, Esp celo® m, CAm, Méx Durex® m
2 n (whisky) whisky m escocés

scot-free ['skɒt'friː] adj impune

Scotland ['skɒtlənd] n Escocia

Scots [skɒts] **1** adj escocés(esa)
2 n (dialecto m) escocés m

Scotsman ['skɒtsmən] n escocés m

Scotswoman ['skɒtswʊmən] n escocesa f

Scottish ['skɒtɪʃ] adj escocés(esa)

scoundrel ['skaʊndrəl] n sinvergüenza mf, canalla m

scour¹ [skaʊə(r)] vt (clean) fregar, restregar

scour² [skaʊə(r)] vt (search) (countryside) rastrear; (building) registrar

scourge [skɜːdʒ] n Fig azote m

scout [skaʊt] **1** n Mil explorador(a) m,f; Sport & Cin cazatalentos m inv; **boy s.** boy m scout
2 vi Mil reconocer el terreno; **to s. around for sth** andar en busca de algo

scowl [skaʊl] **1** vi fruncir el ceño; **to s. at sb** mirar a algn con ceño
2 n ceño m

scrabble ['skræbəl] vi escarbar; Fig **to s. around for sth** revolver todo para encontrar algo

scraggy ['skrægɪ] adj (scraggier, scraggiest) delgado(a), flacucho(a)

scram [skræm] vi Fam largarse, Esp, RP pirarse; **s.!** ¡largo!

scramble ['skræmbəl] **1** vi trepar; **to s. for** pelearse por; **to s. up a tree** trepar a un árbol
2 vt (a) Culin **scrambled eggs** huevos revueltos (b) Rad & Tel (message) codificar; (broadcast) interferir
3 n (climb) subida f; Fig **it's going to be a s.** (rush) va a ser muy apresurado

scrap¹ [skræp] **1** n (a) (small piece) pedazo m; **there isn't a s. of truth in it** no tiene ni un ápice de verdad; **s. (metal)** chatarra f; **s. dealer** or **merchant** chatarrero(a) m,f; **s.**

paper papel m de borrador; **s. yard** (for cars) cementerio m de coches (b) **scraps** restos mpl; (of food) sobras fpl
2 vt (discard) desechar; Fig (idea) descartar

scrap² [skræp] Fam **1** n (fight) pelea f
2 vi pelearse (**with** con)

scrapbook ['skræpbʊk] n álbum m de recortes

scrape [skreɪp] **1** vt (paint, wood) raspar; (knee) arañarse, hacerse un rasguño en
2 vi (make noise) chirriar; (rub) rozar
3 n Fam (trouble) lío m
▸**scrape through** vi Fam (exam) aprobar por los pelos
▸**scrape together** vt sep reunir a duras penas

scraper ['skreɪpə(r)] n rasqueta f

scrapheap ['skræphiːp] n (dump) vertedero m

scratch [skrætʃ] **1** n (a) (on skin, paintwork) arañazo m; (on record) raya f (b) (noise) chirrido m (c) Fig **to be up to s.** dar la talla; Fig **to start from s.** partir de cero
2 adj **s. team** equipo improvisado
3 vt (a) (with nail, claw) arañar, rasguñar; (paintwork) rayar (b) (to relieve itching) rascarse

scratchcard ['skrætʃkɑːd] n tarjeta f de rasca y gana, Arg ≃ raspadita f

scrawl [skrɔːl] **1** n garabatos mpl
2 vt (message etc) garabatear
3 vi hacer garabatos

scrawny ['skrɔːnɪ] adj (scrawnier, scrawniest) flaco(a)

scream [skriːm] **1** n chillido m; **screams of laughter** carcajadas fpl
2 vt (insults etc) gritar
3 vi chillar; **to s. at sb** chillar a algn

scree [skriː] n pedregal m

screech [skriːtʃ] **1** n (of person) chillido m; (of tyres, brakes) chirrido m
2 vi (person) chillar; (tyres) chirriar

screen [skriːn] **1** n (a) (movable partition) biombo m (b) Fig cortina f (c) Cin, TV & Comput pantalla f
2 vt (a) (protect) proteger; (conceal) tapar (b) (candidates) seleccionar (c) (show) (film) proyectar; (for first time) estrenar (d) Med examinar

screening ['skriːnɪŋ] n (a) (of film) proyección f; (for first time) estreno m (b) Med exploración f

screenplay ['skriːnpleɪ] n guión m

screw [skruː] **1** n (a) (for fixing) tornillo m (b) (propeller) hélice f
2 vt (a) (fix) atornillar; **to s. sth down** or

in or on fijar algo con tornillos (**b**) *Vulg Esp* follar, *Am* coger

▸ **screw up** *vt sep* (**a**) *(piece of paper)* arrugar; *(one's face)* torcer (**b**) *very Fam (ruin)* joder

screwdriver ['skru:draɪvə(r)] *n* destornillador *m*, *Am* desatornillador *m*

scribble ['skrɪbəl] **1** *n* garabatos *mpl*
2 *vt (message etc)* garabatear
3 *vi* hacer garabatos

script [skrɪpt] *n* (**a**) *(writing)* escritura *f*; *(handwriting)* letra *f*; *Typ* letra cursiva (**b**) *(in exam)* escrito *m* (**c**) *Cin* guión *m*

Scripture ['skrɪptʃə(r)] *n* Holy S. Sagrada Escritura

scroll [skrəʊl] *n* rollo *m* de pergamino

scrounge [skraʊndʒ] *Fam* **1** *vi* gorrear, *Esp* gorronear; **to s. (around) for** buscar; **to s. off sb** vivir a costa de algn
2 *vt* gorrear, *Esp* gorronear

scrounger ['skraʊndʒə(r)] *n Fam Esp, Méx* gorrón(ona) *m,f*, *RP* garronero(a) *m,f*

scrub¹ [skrʌb] *n (undergrowth)* maleza *f*

scrub² [skrʌb] **1** *vt* (**a**) *(floor, pots)* fregar (**b**) *Fam (cancel)* borrar
2 *n (cleaning)* fregado *m*

scruff [skrʌf] *n* pescuezo *m*, cogote *m*

scruffy ['skrʌfɪ] *adj* (**scruffier, scruffiest**) *Fam* desaliñado(a)

scrum [skrʌm] *n Esp* melé *f*, *Am* scrum *f*; **s. half** *Esp* medio (de) melé *mf*, *Am* medio scrum *mf*

scruple ['skru:pəl] *n* escrúpulo *m*

scrupulous ['skru:pjʊləs] *adj* escrupuloso(a)

scrupulously ['skru:pjʊləslɪ] *adv* **s. honest** sumamente honrado(a)

scrutinize ['skru:tɪnaɪz] *vt* escudriñar

scrutiny ['skru:tɪnɪ] *n* escrutinio *m*

scuba diving ['sku:bədaɪvɪŋ] *n* buceo *m*, submarinismo *m (con botellas de oxígeno)*

scuff [skʌf] *vt (floor)* rayar; *(one's feet)* arrastrar

scuffle ['skʌfəl] **1** *n* pelea *f*
2 *vi* pelearse (**with** con)

scullery ['skʌlərɪ] *n Br* fregadero *m*, trascocina *f*

sculptor ['skʌlptə(r)] *n* escultor(a) *m,f*

sculpture ['skʌlptʃə(r)] *n* escultura *f*

scum [skʌm] *n* (**a**) *(on liquid)* espuma *f* (**b**) *Fig* escoria *f*

scupper ['skʌpə(r)] *vt Br Fam (plan etc)* desbaratar

scurrilous ['skʌrɪləs] *adj (abusive)* difamatorio(a)

scurry ['skʌrɪ] *vi (run)* corretear; *(hurry)* apresurarse; **to s. away** or **off** escabullirse

scuttle¹ ['skʌtəl] *n* cubo *m*; **coal s.** cubo del carbón

scuttle² ['skʌtəl] *vt (ship)* barrenar

scuttle³ ['skʌtəl] *vi* **to s. away** or **off** escabullirse

scythe [saɪð] **1** *n* guadaña *f*
2 *vt* guadañar

sea [si:] *n* mar *m* or *f*; **by the s.** a orillas del mar; **out at s.** en alta mar; **to go by s.** ir en barco; **to put to s.** zarpar; *Fig* **to be all at s.** estar desorientado(a); **s. breeze** brisa marina; *Fig* **s. change** metamorfosis *f*; **s. level** nivel *m* del mar; **s. lion** león marino; **s. water** agua *f* de mar

seabed ['si:bed] *n* fondo *m* del mar

seaboard ['si:bɔ:d] *n US* costa *f*, litoral *m*

seafood ['si:fu:d] *n* marisco *m*, *Am* mariscos *mpl*

seafront ['si:frʌnt] *n* paseo marítimo

seagull ['si:gʌl] *n* gaviota *f*

seal¹ [si:l] *n Zool* foca *f*

seal² [si:l] **1** *n* (**a**) *(official stamp)* sello *m* (**b**) *(airtight closure)* cierre hermético; *(on bottle)* precinto *m*
2 *vt* (**a**) *(with official stamp)* sellar; *(with wax)* lacrar (**b**) *(close)* cerrar; *(make airtight)* cerrar herméticamente (**c**) *(determine)* **this sealed his fate** esto decidió su destino

▸ **seal off** *vt sep (pipe etc)* cerrar; *(area)* acordonar

seam [si:m] *n* (**a**) *Sewing* costura *f*; *Tech* juntura *f*; *Fam* **to be bursting at the seams** *(room)* rebosar de gente (**b**) *Geol & Min* veta *f*, filón *m*

seaman ['si:mən] *n* marinero *m*

seamy ['si:mɪ] *adj* (**seamier, seamiest**) *Fig* sórdido(a)

séance ['seɪɑ:ns] *n* sesión *f* de espiritismo

seaplane ['si:pleɪn] *n* hidroavión *m*

seaport ['si:pɔ:t] *n* puerto marítimo

search [sɜ:tʃ] **1** *vt (files etc)* buscar en; *(building, suitcase)* registrar; *(person)* cachear; *(one's conscience)* examinar
2 *vi* buscar; **to s. through** registrar
3 *n* búsqueda *f*, *(of building etc)* registro *m*; *(of person)* cacheo *m*; **in s. of** en busca de; *Comput* **s. engine** motor *m* de búsqueda; **s. party** equipo *m* de salvamento; **s. warrant** orden *f* de registro

searching ['sɜ:tʃɪŋ] *adj (look)* penetrante; *(question)* indagatorio(a)

searchlight ['sɜ:tʃlaɪt] *n* reflector *m*

seashell ['si:ʃel] *n* concha marina

seashore ['si:ʃɔ:(r)] *n (beach)* playa *f*

seasick ['si:sɪk] *adj* mareado(a); **to get s.** marearse

seaside ['si:said] n playa f, costa f; **s. resort** lugar turístico de veraneo; **s. town** pueblo costero

season¹ ['si:zən] n época f; (of year) estación f; (for sport etc) temporada f; **the busy s.** la temporada alta; **the rainy s.** la estación de lluvias; **in s.** (fruit) en sazón; (animal) en celo; Br **s. ticket** abono m

season² ['si:zən] vt Culin sazonar

seasonal ['si:zənəl] adj estacional

seasoned ['si:zənd] adj (a) Culin sazonado(a) (b) Fig (campaigner) curtido(a), avezado(a)

seasoning ['si:zənɪŋ] n condimento m, aderezo m

seat [si:t] **1** n (a) (chair, in vehicle) asiento m; (in theatre, cinema) butaca f; **to take a s.** sentarse; Aut **s. belt** cinturón m de seguridad (b) (in parliament) escaño m
  2 vt (a) (guests etc) sentar (b) (accommodate) tener cabida para

seating ['si:tɪŋ] n asientos mpl

seaweed ['si:wi:d] n alga (marina)

seaworthy ['si:wɜ:ðɪ] adj en condiciones de navegar

sec [sek] n Fam (abbr **second**) segundo m

secede [sɪ'si:d] vi separarse (**from** de)

secluded [sɪ'klu:dɪd] adj retirado(a), apartado(a)

second¹ ['sekənd] **1** adj segundo(a); **every s. day** cada dos días; **it's the s. highest mountain** es la segunda montaña más alta; **on s. thought(s) ...** pensándolo bien ...; **to have s. thoughts about sth** dudar de algo; **to settle for s. best** conformarse con lo que hay
  2 n (a) (in series) segundo(a) m,f; **Charles the S.** Carlos Segundo; **the s. of October** el dos de octubre (b) Aut (gear) segunda f (c) Com **seconds** artículos defectuosos
  3 vt (motion) apoyar
  4 adv **to come s.** terminar en segundo lugar

second² ['sekənd] n (time) segundo m; Fam **in a s.** enseguida; Fam **just a s.!** ¡un momentito!; **s. hand** (of watch, clock) segundero m

secondary ['sekəndərɪ] adj secundario(a); Br **s. school** escuela secundaria

second-class ['sekənd'klɑ:s] **1** adj Br (ticket, carriage) de segunda (clase)
  2 adv **to travel s.** viajar en segunda

second-hand ['sekənd'hænd] adj & adv de segunda mano

secondly ['sekəndlɪ] adv en segundo lugar

secondment [sɪ'kɒndmənt] n Br traslado m temporal

second-rate ['sekənd'reɪt] adj de segunda categoría

secrecy ['si:krəsɪ] n secreto m; **in s.** en secreto

secret ['si:krɪt] **1** adj secreto(a); **to keep sth s.** mantener algo en secreto; **s. ballot** votación secreta
  2 n secreto m; Fig clave f; **in s.** en secreto; **to keep a s.** guardar un secreto

secretarial [sekrɪ'teərɪəl] adj de secretario(a)

secretary ['sekrətrɪ] n secretario(a) m,f; **S. of State** Br ministro(a) m,f con cartera; US ministro(a) m,f de Asuntos Exteriores

secretion [sɪ'kri:ʃən] n secreción f

secretive ['si:krɪtɪv] adj reservado(a)

secretly ['si:krɪtlɪ] adv en secreto

sect [sekt] n secta f

sectarian [sek'teərɪən] adj & n sectario(a) (m,f)

section ['sekʃən] n (a) (part) sección f, parte f; (of law) artículo m; (of community) sector m; (of orchestra, department) sección (b) (cut) corte m

sector ['sektə(r)] n sector m

secular ['sekjʊlə(r)] adj (school, teaching) laico(a); (music, art) profano(a); (priest) seglar, secular

secure [sɪ'kjʊə(r)] **1** adj seguro(a); (window, door) bien cerrado(a); (ladder etc) firme
  2 vt (a) (make safe) asegurar (b) (fix) (rope, knot) sujetar, fijar; (object to floor) afianzar; (window, door) cerrar bien (c) (obtain) conseguir, obtener

security [sɪ'kjʊərɪtɪ] n (a) (stability, safety) seguridad f (b) Fin (for loan) fianza f (c) Fin **securities** valores mpl

sedan [sɪ'dæn] n (a) Hist **s. chair** silla f de manos (b) US Aut turismo m

sedate [sɪ'deɪt] **1** adj sosegado(a)
  2 vt sedar

sedation [sɪ'deɪʃən] n sedación f

sedative ['sedətɪv] adj & n sedante (m)

sediment ['sedɪmənt] n sedimento m; (of wine) poso m

seduce [sɪ'dju:s] vt seducir

seduction [sɪ'dʌkʃən] n seducción f

seductive [sɪ'dʌktɪv] adj seductor(a)

see¹ [si:] vt & vi (pt **saw**; pp **seen**) (a) (with eyes, perceive) ver; **let's s.** a ver; **s. page 10** véase la página 10; **to s. the world** recorrer el mundo; **s. you (later)/soon!** ¡hasta luego/pronto! (b) (meet with) ver, tener cita con; **they are seeing each other** (of couple) salen juntos (c) (understand) entender; **as far as I can s.** por lo visto; **I s.**

ya veo (d) **to s. sb home** acompañar a algn a casa

▸ **see about** *vt insep (deal with)* ocuparse de

▸ **see off** *vt sep (say goodbye to)* despedirse de

▸ **see out** *vt sep* (a) *(show out)* acompañar hasta la puerta (b) *(survive)* sobrevivir

▸ **see through 1** *vt insep* **Fam to s. through sb** verle el plumero a algn

2 *vt sep* (a) **I'll s. you through** puedes contar con mi ayuda; **£20 should s. me through** con 20 libras me las apaño (b) **to s. sth through** *(carry out)* llevar algo a cabo

▸ **see to** *vt insep (deal with)* ocuparse de

see² [si:] *n* Rel sede *f*; **the Holy S.** la Santa Sede

seed [si:d] **1** *n* (a) *Bot* semilla *f*; *(of fruit)* pepita *f*; **to go to s.** *(of plant)* granar; *Fig (of person)* descuidarse (b) *(in tennis) (player)* cabeza *mf* de serie

2 *vt* (a) *(sow with seed)* sembrar (b) *(grapes)* despepitar (c) *(in tennis)* preseleccionar

seedling ['si:dlɪŋ] *n* plantón *m*

seedy ['si:dɪ] *adj* (**seedier, seediest**) *Fam (bar etc)* sórdido(a); *(clothes)* raído(a); *(appearance)* desaseado(a)

seeing ['si:ɪŋ] *conj* **s. that** visto que, dado que

seeing-eye dog ['si:ɪŋaɪ'dɒɡ] *n US* perro *m* lazarillo

seek [si:k] **1** *vt (pt & pp* **sought**) (a) *(look for)* buscar (b) *(advice, help)* solicitar

2 *vt* buscar; **to s. to do sth** procurar hacer algo

▸ **seek after** *vt insep* buscar; **much sought after** *(person)* muy solicitado(a); *(thing)* muy cotizado(a)

seem [si:m] *vi* parecer; **I s. to remember his name was Colin** creo recordar que su nombre era Colin; **it seems to me that he** parece que; **so it seems** eso parece

seeming ['si:mɪŋ] *adj* aparente

seemingly ['si:mɪŋlɪ] *adv* aparentemente, según parece

seen [si:n] *pp of* **see**

seep [si:p] *vi* **to s. through/into/out** filtrarse por/en/de

seesaw ['si:sɔ:] **1** *n* balancín *m*, subibaja *m*

2 *vi (prices, mood)* fluctuar

seethe [si:ð] *vi* bullir, hervir; *Fig* **to s. with anger** rabiar; **to s. with people** rebosar de gente

see-through ['si:θru:] *adj* transparente

segment ['seɡmənt] *n* segmento *m*; *(of orange)* gajo *m*

segregate ['seɡrɪɡeɪt] *vt* segregar (**from** de)

segregation [seɡrɪ'ɡeɪʃən] *n* segregación *f*

seize [si:z] *vt (grab)* agarrar, *Esp* coger; *Jur (property, drugs)* incautar; *(assets)* secuestrar; *(territory)* tomar; *(arrest)* detener; **to s. an opportunity** aprovechar una ocasión; **to s. power** hacerse con el poder

▸ **seize on** *vt insep (chance)* agarrar; *(idea)* aferrarse a

▸ **seize up** *vi* agarrotarse

seizure ['si:ʒə(r)] *n* (a) *Jur (of property, drugs)* incautación *f*; *(of newspaper)* secuestro *m*; *(arrest)* detención *f* (b) *Med* ataque *m* (de apoplejía)

seldom ['seldəm] *adv* rara vez, raramente

select [sɪ'lekt] **1** *vt (thing)* escoger, elegir; *(team)* seleccionar

2 *adj* selecto(a)

selected [sɪ'lektɪd] *adj* selecto(a), escogido(a); *(team, player)* seleccionado(a); *Lit* **s. works** obras escogidas

selection [sɪ'lekʃən] *n (choosing)* elección *f*; *(people or things chosen)* selección *f*; *(range)* surtido *m*

selective [sɪ'lektɪv] *adj* selectivo(a)

self [self] *n (pl* **selves**) uno(a) mismo(a), sí mismo(a); *Psy* **the s.** el yo

self- [self] *pref* auto-

self-addressed envelope ['selfədrest-'envələʊp] *n* sobre dirigido a uno mismo

self-adhesive [selfəd'hi:sɪv] *adj* autoadhesivo(a)

self-assured [selfə'ʃʊəd] *adj* seguro(a) de sí mismo(a)

self-catering [self'keɪtərɪŋ] *adj* sin servicio de comida

self-centred, *US* **self-centered** [self-'sentəd] *adj* egocéntrico(a)

self-confessed [selfkən'fest] *adj* confeso(a)

self-confidence [self'kɒnfɪdəns] *n* confianza *f* en sí mismo(a)

self-confident [self'kɒnfɪdənt] *adj* seguro(a) de sí mismo(a)

self-conscious [self'kɒnʃəs] *adj* cohibido(a)

self-contained [selfkən'teɪnd] *adj (flat)* con entrada propia; *(person)* independiente

self-control [selfkən'trəʊl] *n* autocontrol *m*

self-defence, *US* **self-defense** [self-dɪ'fens] *n* autodefensa *f*

self-discipline [self'dɪsɪplɪn] *n* autodisciplina *f*

self-employed [selfɪm'plɔɪd] *adj (worker)* autónomo(a)

self-esteem [selfɪ'stiːm] *n* amor propio, autoestima *f*

self-evident [self'evɪdənt] *adj* evidente, patente

self-governing [self'gʌvənɪŋ] *adj* autónomo(a)

self-help [self'help] *n* autoayuda *f*

self-important [selfɪm'pɔːtənt] *adj* engreído(a), presumido(a)

self-indulgent [selfɪn'dʌldʒənt] *adj* inmoderado(a)

self-interest [self'ɪntrɪst] *n* egoísmo *m*

selfish ['selfɪʃ] *adj* egoísta

selfishness ['selfɪʃnɪs] *n* egoísmo *m*

selfless ['selflɪs] *adj* desinteresado(a)

self-made ['selfmeɪd] *adj* **s. man** hombre *m* que se ha hecho a sí mismo

self-pity [self'pɪtɪ] *n* autocompasión *f*

self-portrait [self'pɔːtreɪt] *n* autorretrato *m*

self-possessed [selfpə'zest] *adj* sereno(a), dueño(a) de sí mismo(a)

self-preservation [selfprezə'veɪʃən] *n (instinct of)* **s.** instinto *m* de conservación

self-raising ['selfreɪzɪŋ] *adj* **s. flour** *Esp* harina *f* con levadura, *Am* harina *f* con polvos de hornear, *RP* harina *f* leudante

self-reliant [selfrɪ'laɪənt] *adj* autosuficiente

self-respect [selfrɪ'spekt] *n* amor propio, dignidad *f*

self-righteous [self'raɪtʃəs] *adj* santurrón(ona)

self-rising ['selfraɪzɪŋ] *adj US* = **self-raising**

self-sacrifice ['selfsækrɪfaɪs] *n* abnegación *f*

self-satisfied [self'sætɪsfaɪd] *adj* satisfecho(a) de sí mismo(a)

self-service [self'sɜːvɪs] **1** *n (in shop etc)* autoservicio *m*
2 *adj* de autoservicio

self-sufficient [selfsə'fɪʃənt] *adj* autosuficiente

self-taught [self'tɔːt] *adj* autodidacta

sell [sel] **1** *vt (pt & pp* **sold)** vender
2 *vi* venderse; **this record is selling well** este disco se vende bien
3 *n* **hard/soft s.** *(in advertising)* publicidad agresiva/discreta

▸ **sell off** *vt sep* vender; *(goods)* liquidar

▸ **sell out 1** *vi* **to s. out to the enemy** claudicar ante el enemigo
2 *vt sep Com* **we're sold out of sugar** se nos ha agotado el azúcar; *Th* **sold out** *(sign)* agotadas las localidades

sell-by date ['selbaɪdeɪt] *n Com* fecha *f* límite de venta

seller ['selə(r)] *n* vendedor(a) *m,f*

selling ['selɪŋ] *n* venta *f*; **s. point** atractivo *m* comercial; **s. price** precio *m* de venta

Sellotape® ['seləteɪp] **1** *n Br* cinta adhesiva, *Esp* celo *m*, *CAm*, *Méx* Durex® *m*
2 *vt* pegar *or* fijar con celo

sell-out ['selaʊt] *n* **(a)** *Th* éxito *m* de taquilla **(b)** *(act of disloyalty)* claudicación *f*

selves [selvz] *pl of* **self**

semaphore ['seməfɔː(r)] *n* semáforo *m*

semblance ['sembləns] *n* apariencia *f*; **there was some s. of truth in it** había algo de verdad en ello

semen ['siːmen] *n* semen *m*

semester [sɪ'mestə(r)] *n* semestre *m*

semi- ['semɪ] *pref* semi-

semicircle ['semɪsɜːkəl] *n* semicírculo *m*

semicolon [semɪ'kəʊlən] *n* punto y coma *m*

semiconductor ['semɪkən'dʌktə(r)] *n* semiconductor *m*

semidetached [semɪdɪ'tætʃt] *Br* **1** *adj* adosado(a)
2 *n* chalé adosado, casa adosada

semifinal [semɪ'faɪnəl] *n* semifinal *f*

seminar ['semɪnɑː(r)] *n* seminario *m*

seminary ['semɪnərɪ] *n* seminario *m*

semitrailer ['semɪtreɪlə(r)] *n US* semirremolque *m*

semolina [semə'liːnə] *n* sémola *f*

senate ['senɪt] *n* **(a)** *Pol* senado *m* **(b)** *Univ* claustro *m*

senator ['senətə(r)] *n* senador(a) *m,f*

send [send] **1** *vt (pt & pp* **sent) (a)** *(letter)* enviar, mandar; *(radio signal)* transmitir; *(rocket, ball)* lanzar; **he was sent to prison** lo mandaron a la cárcel; **to s. sth flying** tirar algo **(b)** **to s. sb mad** *(cause to become)* volver loco(a) a algn
2 *vi* **to s. for sb** mandar llamar a algn; **to s. for sth** encargar algo

▸ **send away 1** *vt sep (dismiss)* despedir
2 *vi* **to s. away for sth** escribir pidiendo algo

▸ **send back** *vt sep (goods etc)* devolver; *(person)* hacer volver

▸ **send in** *vt sep (application etc)* mandar; *(troops)* enviar

▸ **send off** *vt sep* **(a)** *(letter etc)* enviar; *(goods)* despachar **(b)** *Ftb (player)* expulsar

▸ **send on** *vt sep (luggage) (ahead)* facturar; *(later)* mandar (más tarde)

▸ **send out** *vt sep* **(a)** *(person)* echar **(b)** *(invitations)* enviar **(c)** *(emit)* emitir

►**send up** *vt sep* (**a**) *(rocket)* lanzar; *(smoke)* echar (**b**) *Br Fam (parody)* parodiar, remedar

sender ['sendə(r)] *n* remitente *mf*

sendoff ['sendɒf] *n Fam* despedida *f*

senile ['si:naɪl] *adj* senil

senior ['si:nɪə(r)] **1** *adj* (**a**) *(in age)* mayor; **William Armstrong S.** William Armstrong padre; **s. citizen** jubilado(a) *m,f* (**b**) *(in rank)* superior; *(with longer service)* más antiguo(a); *Mil* **s. officer** oficial *mf* de alta graduación

2 *n* (**a**) **she's three years my s.** *(in age)* me lleva tres años (**b**) *US Educ* estudiante *mf* del último curso

seniority [si:nɪ'ɒrɪtɪ] *n* antigüedad *f*

sensation [sen'seɪʃən] *n* sensación *f*; **to be a s.** ser un éxito; **to cause a s.** causar sensación

sensational [sen'seɪʃənəl] *adj (marvellous)* sensacional; *(exaggerated)* sensacionalista

sense [sens] **1** *n* (**a**) *(faculty)* sentido *m*; *(feeling)* sensación *f*; **s. of direction/ humour** sentido *m* de la orientación/del humor (**b**) *(wisdom)* sentido *m* común, juicio *m*; **common s.** sentido común (**c**) *(meaning)* sentido *m*; *(of word)* significado *m*; **in a s.** en cierto sentido; **it doesn't make s.** no tiene sentido (**d**) **to come to one's senses** recobrar el juicio

2 *vt* sentir, percatarse de

senseless ['senslɪs] *adj* (**a**) *(absurd)* insensato(a), absurdo(a) (**b**) *(unconscious)* sin conocimiento

sensibility [sensɪ'bɪlɪtɪ] *n* (**a**) *(sensitivity)* sensibilidad *f* (**b**) **sensibilities** susceptibilidad *f*

sensible ['sensɪbəl] *adj* (**a**) *(wise)* sensato(a) (**b**) *(choice)* acertado(a) (**c**) *(clothes, shoes)* práctico(a), cómodo(a)

> ✍ Note that the Spanish word **sensible** is a false friend and is never a translation for the English word **sensible**. In Spanish **sensible** means both "sensitive" and "perceptible, significant".

sensitive ['sensɪtɪv] *adj* (**a**) *(person)* sensible; *(touchy)* susceptible (**b**) *(skin)* delicado(a); *(document)* confidencial

sensitivity [sensɪ'tɪvɪtɪ] *n* sensibilidad *f*

sensor ['sensə(r)] *n* sensor *m*

sensual ['sensjʊəl] *adj* sensual

sensuous ['sensjʊəs] *adj* sensual

sent [sent] *pt & pp of* **send**

sentence ['sentəns] **1** *n* (**a**) *Ling* oración *f*, frase *f* (**b**) *Jur* sentencia *f*; **to pass s. on sb**

imponer una pena a algn; **life s.** cadena perpetua

2 *vt Jur* condenar

sentiment ['sentɪmənt] *n* (**a**) *(sentimentality)* sensiblería *f* (**b**) *(feeling)* sentimiento *m* (**c**) *(opinion)* opinión *f*

sentimental [sentɪ'mentəl] *adj* sentimental

sentry ['sentrɪ] *n* centinela *m*

separate 1 *vt* ['sepəreɪt] separar (**from** de); *(divide)* dividir (**into** en); *(distinguish)* distinguir

2 *vi* separarse

3 *adj* ['sepərɪt] separado(a); *(different)* distinto(a); *(entrance)* particular

4 *npl* **separates** ['sepərɪts] *(clothes)* piezas *fpl*

separately ['sepərɪtlɪ] *adv* por separado

separation [sepə'reɪʃən] *n* separación *f*

separatist ['sepərɪtɪst] *n* separatista *mf*

September [sep'tembə(r)] *n* se(p)tiembre *m*

septic ['septɪk] *adj* séptico(a); **to become s.** *(of wound)* infectarse; **s. tank** fosa séptica

sequel ['si:kwəl] *n* secuela *f*; *(of film etc)* continuación *f*

sequence ['si:kwəns] *n* (**a**) *(order)* secuencia *f*, orden *m* (**b**) *(series)* serie *f*, sucesión *f*; *Cin* **film s.** secuencia *f*

Serbia ['sɜ:bɪə] *n* Serbia

Serbian ['sɜ:bɪən] *adj & n* Serbio (*m,f*)

serenade [serɪ'neɪd] *n* serenata *f*

serene [sɪ'ri:n] *adj* sereno(a), tranquilo(a)

sergeant ['sɑ:dʒənt] *n Mil* sargento *mf*; *(of police)* ≃ oficial *mf* de policía; **s. major** sargento *mf* mayor

serial ['sɪərɪəl] *n* (**a**) *Rad & TV* serial *m*; *(soap opera)* radionovela *f*, telenovela *f* (**b**) **s. number** número *m* de serie

serialize ['sɪərɪəlaɪz] *vt* *(in newspaper, magazine)* publicar por entregas; *(on TV)* emitir en forma de serial

series ['sɪəri:z] *n* (*pl* **series**) serie *f*; *(of books)* colección *f*; *(of concerts, lectures)* ciclo *m*

serious ['sɪərɪəs] *adj* (**a**) *(solemn, earnest)* serio(a); **I am s.** hablo en serio (**b**) *(causing concern)* grave

seriously ['sɪərɪəslɪ] *adv* (**a**) *(in earnest)* en serio (**b**) *(dangerously, severely)* gravemente

seriousness ['sɪərɪəsnɪs] *n* gravedad *f*, seriedad *f*; **in all s.** hablando en serio

sermon ['sɜ:mən] *n* sermón *m*

serpent ['sɜ:pənt] *n* serpiente *f*

serrated [sɪ'reɪtɪd] *adj* dentado(a)

serum ['sɪərəm] *n* suero *m*

servant ['sɜːvənt] *n (domestic)* criado(a) *m,f*, *Fig* servidor(a) *m,f*

serve [sɜːv] **1** *vt* (**a**) *(master, cause)* servir (**b**) *(customer)* atender a (**c**) *(in tennis)* servir (**d**) **it serves him right** bien merecido lo tiene
  2 *vi* (**a**) *(carry out duty)* servir; **to s. on a committee** ser miembro de una comisión (**b**) *(in tennis)* servir
  3 *n (in tennis)* servicio *m*

▸ **serve out, serve up** *vt sep* servir

server ['sɜːvə(r)] *n Comput* servidor *m*

service ['sɜːvɪs] **1** *n* (**a**) *(with army, firm)* servicio *m*; **at your s.!** ¡a sus órdenes!; **s. (charge) included** servicio incluido; **s. area** área *m* de servicio; **s. industry** sector *m* de servicios; **s. station** estación *f* de servicio (**b**) *Mil* **the Services** las Fuerzas Armadas (**c**) *(maintenance)* revisión *f* (**d**) *Rel* oficio *m*; *(mass)* misa *f* (**e**) *(in tennis)* servicio *m*
  2 *vt (car, machine)* revisar

serviceable ['sɜːvɪsəbəl] *adj* (**a**) *(fit for use)* útil, servible (**b**) *(practical)* práctico(a)

serviceman ['sɜːvɪsmən] *n* militar *m*

serviette [sɜːvɪ'et] *n Br* servilleta *f*

servile ['sɜːvaɪl] *adj* servil

serving ['sɜːvɪŋ] *n (portion)* ración *f*; **s. spoon** cuchara *f* de servir

sesame ['sesəmɪ] *n* sésamo *m*

session ['seʃən] *n* (**a**) *(period of activity)* sesión *f*; **to be in s.** estar reunido(a); *(of Parliament, court)* celebrar una sesión (**b**) *Educ (academic year)* año académico

set¹ [set] **1** *vt (pt & pp set)* (**a**) *(put, place)* poner, colocar; *(trap)* poner (**for** para); **the novel is s. in Moscow** la novela se desarrolla en Moscú; **to s. fire to sth** prender fuego a algo; **to s. sb free** poner en libertad a algo (**b**) *(time, price)* fijar; *(record)* establecer; **to s. one's watch** poner el reloj en hora (**c**) *(bone)* encajar (**d**) *(arrange)* arreglar; **he s. the words to music** puso música a la letra; **to s. the table** poner la mesa (**e**) *(exam, homework)* poner; *(example)* dar; *(precedent)* sentar
  2 *vi* (**a**) *(sun, moon)* ponerse (**b**) *(jelly, jam)* cuajar; *(cement)* fraguar; *(bone)* encajarse (**c**) **to s. to** *(begin)* ponerse a
  3 *n* (**a**) *(stage)* Cin plató *m*; *Th* escenario *m*; *(scenery)* decorado *m*
  4 *adj* (**a**) *(task, idea)* fijo(a); *(date, time)* señalado(a); *(opinion)* inflexible; **s. phrase** frase hecha; **to be s. on doing sth** estar empeñado(a) en hacer algo (**b**) *(ready)* listo(a)

▸ **set about** *vt insep* (**a**) *(begin)* empezar (**b**) *(attack)* agredir

▸ **set aside** *vt sep (time, money)* reservar; *(differences)* dejar de lado

▸ **set back** *vt sep* (**a**) *(delay)* retrasar; *(hinder)* entorpecer (**b**) *Fam (cost)* costar

▸ **set down** *vt sep (luggage etc)* dejar (en el suelo); *Br (passengers)* dejar

▸ **set in** *vi (winter, rain)* comenzar; **panic s. in** cundió el pánico

▸ **set off 1** *vi (depart)* salir
  2 *vt sep* (**a**) *(bomb)* hacer estallar; *(burglar alarm)* hacer sonar; *(reaction)* desencadenar (**b**) *(enhance)* hacer resaltar

▸ **set out 1** *vi* (**a**) *(depart)* salir; **to s. out for ...** partir hacia ... (**b**) **to s. out to do sth** proponerse hacer algo
  2 *vt sep (arrange)* disponer; *(present)* presentar

▸ **set up 1** *vt sep* (**a**) *(position)* colocar; *(statue, camp)* levantar; *(tent, stall)* montar (**b**) *(business etc)* establecer; *Fam* montar; *(committee)* constituir; *Fam* **you've been s. up!** ¡te han timado!
  2 *vi* establecerse

set² [set] *n* (**a**) *(series)* serie *f*; *(of golf clubs etc)* juego *m*; *(of tools)* estuche *m*; *(of books)* colección *f*; *(of teeth)* dentadura *f*; **chess s.** juego de ajedrez; **s. of cutlery** cubertería *f* (**b**) *(of people)* grupo *m*; *Pej (clique)* camarilla *f* (**c**) *Math* conjunto *m* (**d**) *(in tennis)* set *m* (**e**) **TV s.** televisor *m*

setback ['setbæk] *n* revés *m*, contratiempo *m*

settee [se'tiː] *n* sofá *m*

setting ['setɪŋ] *n* (**a**) *(background)* marco *m*; *(of novel, film)* escenario *m* (**b**) *(of jewel)* engaste *m*

settle ['setəl] **1** *vt* (**a**) *(put in position)* colocar (**b**) *(decide on)* acordar; *(date, price)* fijar; *(problem)* resolver; *(differences)* arreglar (**c**) *(debt)* pagar (**d**) *(nerves)* calmar; *(stomach)* asentar (**e**) *(establish) (person)* instalar
  2 *vi* (**a**) *(bird, insect)* posarse; *(dust)* depositarse; *(liquid)* asentarse; **to s. into an armchair** acomodarse en un sillón (**b**) *(put down roots)* afincarse; *(in a colony)* asentarse (**c**) *(child, nerves)* calmarse (**d**) *(pay)* pagar; **to s. out of court** llegar a un acuerdo amistoso

▸ **settle down** *vi* (**a**) *(put down roots)* instalarse; *(marry)* casarse (**b**) **to s. down to work** ponerse a trabajar (**c**) *(child)* calmarse; *(situation)* normalizarse

▸ **settle for** *vt insep* conformarse con

▸ **settle in** *vi (move in)* instalarse; *(become adapted)* adaptarse

▸ **settle with** *vt sep (pay debt to)* ajustar cuentas con

settlement ['setəlmənt] n (a) (agreement) acuerdo m (b) (of debt) pago m (c) (colony) asentamiento m; (village) poblado m

settler ['setlə(r)] n colono m

setup ['setʌp] n (system) sistema m; (situation) situación f; Fam montaje m

seven ['sevən] adj & n siete (m inv)

seventeen [sevən'ti:n] adj & n diecisiete (m inv), diez y siete (m inv)

seventeenth [sevən'ti:nθ] 1 adj & n decimoséptimo(a) (m,f)
2 n (fraction) decimoséptima parte

seventh ['sevənθ] 1 adj & n séptimo(a) (m,f)
2 n séptimo m

seventy ['sevəntɪ] adj & n setenta (m inv)

sever ['sevə(r)] vt (cut) cortar; Fig (relations) romper

several ['sevərəl] 1 adj (a) (more than a few) varios(as) (b) (different) distintos(as)
2 pron algunos(as)

severance ['sevərəns] n (of relations etc) ruptura f; **s. pay** indemnización f por despido

severe [sɪ'vɪə(r)] adj severo(a); (climate, blow) duro(a); (illness, loss) grave; (pain) intenso(a)

severity [sɪ'verɪtɪ] n (of person, criticism, punishment) severidad f; (of climate) rigor m; (of illness) gravedad f; (of pain) intensidad f; (of style) austeridad f

Seville [sə'vɪl] n Sevilla

sew [səʊ] vt & vi (pt sewed; pp sewed or sewn) coser

▸ **sew up** vt sep (stitch together) coser; (mend) remendar

sewage ['su:ɪdʒ] n aguas fpl residuales

sewer ['su:ə(r)] n alcantarilla f, cloaca f

sewerage ['su:ərɪdʒ] n alcantarillado m

sewing ['səʊɪŋ] n costura f; **s. machine** máquina f de coser

sewn [səʊn] pp of sew

sex [seks] n sexo m; **s. education** educación f sexual; **to have s. with sb** tener relaciones sexuales con algn; **s. appeal** sex-appeal m

sexist ['seksɪst] adj & n sexista (mf)

sexual ['seksjʊəl] adj sexual

sexuality [seksjʊ'ælɪtɪ] n sexualidad f

sexy ['seksɪ] adj (sexier, sexiest) Fam sexi, erótico(a)

shabby ['ʃæbɪ] adj (shabbier, shabbiest) (a) (garment) raído(a); (house) desvencijado(a); (person) (in rags) harapiento(a); (unkempt) desaseado(a) (b) (treatment) mezquino(a)

shack [ʃæk] n casucha f, Esp chabola f, CSur,Ven rancho m

shackles ['ʃækəlz] npl grilletes mpl, grillos mpl; Fig trabas fpl

shade [ʃeɪd] 1 n (a) (shadow) sombra f; **in the s.** a la sombra (b) (eyeshade) visera f; (lampshade) pantalla f; US (blind) persiana f (c) (of colour) tono m, matiz m; Fig (of meaning) matiz m (d) Fam **shades** gafas fpl orAm anteojos mpl de sol
2 vt (from sun) proteger contra el sol

shadow ['ʃædəʊ] 1 n (a) (shade) sombra f (b) Br **the S. Cabinet** el gabinete de la oposición
2 vt Fig seguir la pista a

shadowy ['ʃædəʊɪ] adj (dark) oscuro(a); (hazy) vago(a)

shady ['ʃeɪdɪ] adj (shadier, shadiest) (place) a la sombra; (suspicious) (person) sospechoso(a); (deal) turbio(a)

shaft [ʃɑ:ft] n (a) (of tool, golf club) mango m (b) Tech eje m (c) (of mine) pozo m; (of lift, elevator) hueco m (d) (beam of light) rayo m

shaggy ['ʃægɪ] adj (shaggier, shaggiest) (hairy) peludo(a); (long-haired) melenudo(a); (beard) desgreñado(a)

shake [ʃeɪk] 1 n sacudida f
2 vt (pt shook; pp shaken ['ʃeɪkən]) (carpet etc) sacudir; (bottle) agitar; (dice) mover; (building) hacer temblar; **the news shook him** la noticia le conmocionó; **to s. hands with sb** estrechar la mano a algn; **to s. one's head** negar con la cabeza
3 vi (person, building) temblar; **to s. with cold** tiritar de frío

▸ **shake off** vt sep (a) (dust etc) sacudirse (b) Fig (bad habit) librarse de; (cough, cold) quitarse orAm de encima; (pursuer) dar esquinazo a

▸ **shake up** vt sep Fig (shock) trastornar; (reorganize) reorganizar

shake-up ['ʃeɪkʌp] n Fig reorganización f

shaky ['ʃeɪkɪ] adj (shakier, shakiest) (hand, voice) tembloroso(a); (step) inseguro(a); (handwriting) tembón(ona)

shall [ʃæl, unstressed ʃəl] v aux

En el inglés hablado, y en el escrito en estilo coloquial, el verbo **shall** se contrae de manera que **I/you/he** etc **shall** se transforman en **I'll/you'll/he'll** etc. La forma negativa **shall not** se transforma en **shan't**.

(a) (used to form future tense) (first person only) **I s.** or **I'll buy it** lo compraré; **I s.** not or **I shan't say anything** no diré nada (b) (in suggestions, offers) **s. I close the door?** ¿cierro la puerta?; **s. I mend it for you?**

¿quieres que te lo repare?; **s. we go?** ¿nos vamos? (**c**) *(emphatic, command, threat) (all persons)* **we s. overcome** venceremos; **you s. leave immediately** te irás enseguida

shallow ['ʃæləʊ] *adj* poco profundo(a); *Fig* superficial

sham [ʃæm] **1** *adj* falso(a); *(illness etc)* fingido(a)
　2 *n* (**a**) *(pretence)* engaño *m*, farsa *f* (**b**) *(person)* fantoche *m*
　3 *vt* fingir, simular
　4 *vi* fingir

shambles ['ʃæmbəlz] *n sing* confusión *f*; **the performance was a s.** la función fue un desastre

shame [ʃeɪm] **1** *n* (**a**) *(disgrace, guilt)* vergüenza *f*, *Am salvo RP* pena *f*; **to put to s.** *(far outdo)* eclipsar, sobrepasar (**b**) *(pity)* pena *f*, lástima *f*; **what a s.!** ¡qué pena!, ¡qué lástima!
　2 *vt* avergonzar, *Am salvo RP* apenar; *(disgrace)* deshonrar

shamefaced ['ʃeɪmfeɪst] *adj* avergonzado(a), *Am salvo RP* apenado(a)

shameful ['ʃeɪmfʊl] *adj* vergonzoso(a)

shameless ['ʃeɪmlɪs] *adj* desvergonzado(a)

shampoo [ʃæm'puː] **1** *n* champú *m*
　2 *vt* lavar con champú; **to s. one's hair** lavarse el pelo

shamrock ['ʃæmrɒk] *n* trébol *m*

shandy ['ʃændɪ] *n Br* cerveza *f* con gaseosa, *Esp* clara *f*

shan't [ʃɑːnt] = **shall not**

shantytown ['ʃæntɪtaʊn] *n Esp* barrio *m* de chabolas, *Am* barriada *f*, *Perú* pueblo *m* joven, *Arg, Bol* villa *f* miseria, *Chile* callampa *f*, *Méx* ciudad *f* perdida, *Urug* cantegril *m*

shape [ʃeɪp] **1** *n* (**a**) *(form)* forma *f*; *(shadow)* silueta *m*; **to take s.** tomar forma (**b**) **in good/bad s.** *(condition)* en buen/mal estado; **to be in good s.** *(health)* estar en forma
　2 *vt* dar forma a; *(clay)* modelar; *(stone)* tallar; *(character)* formar; *(destiny)* determinar; **star-shaped** con forma de estrella
　3 *vi* *(also s. up)* tomar forma; **to s. up well** *(events)* tomar buen cariz; *(person)* hacer progresos

shapeless ['ʃeɪplɪs] *adj* amorfo(a), informe

shapely ['ʃeɪplɪ] *adj* (**shapelier, shapeliest**) escultural

share [ʃeə(r)] **1** *n* (**a**) *(portion)* parte *f* (**b**) *Fin* acción *f*; **s. index** índice *m* de la Bolsa; **s. prices** cotizaciones *fpl*

　2 *vt* (**a**) *(divide)* dividir (**b**) *(have in common)* compartir
　3 *vi* compartir

▸ **share out** *vt sep* repartir

shareholder ['ʃeəhəʊldə(r)] *n* accionista *mf*

shark [ʃɑːk] *n* (**a**) *(fish)* tiburón *m* (**b**) *Fam (swindler)* estafador(a) *m,f*; **loan s.** usurero(a) *m,f*

sharp [ʃɑːp] **1** *adj* (**a**) *(razor, knife)* afilado(a), *Am* filoso(a); *(needle, pencil)* puntiagudo(a) (**b**) *(bend)* cerrado(a) (**c**) *(contrast)* marcado(a) (**d**) *(clever)* listo(a); *(quick-witted)* avispado(a) (**e**) *(cunning)* astuto(a) (**e**) *(pain, cry)* agudo(a) (**f**) *(sour)* acre (**g**) *(temper)* arisco(a); *(tone)* seco(a) (**h**) *Mus* sostenido(a)
　2 *adv* **at two o'clock s.** *(exactly)* a las dos en punto
　3 *n Mus* sostenido *m*

sharpen ['ʃɑːpən] *vt* (**a**) *(knife)* afilar; *(pencil)* sacar punta a (**b**) *Fig (desire, intelligence)* agudizar

sharpener ['ʃɑːpənə(r)] *n* *(for knife)* afilador *m*; *(for pencil)* sacapuntas *m inv*

sharp-eyed ['ʃɑːpaɪd] *adj* con ojos de lince

sharply ['ʃɑːplɪ] *adv* (**a**) *(abruptly)* bruscamente (**b**) *(clearly)* marcadamente

shat [ʃæt] *pt & pp of* **shit**

shatter ['ʃætə(r)] **1** *vt* hacer añicos; *(nerves)* destrozar; *(hopes)* frustrar
　2 *vi* hacerse añicos

shattered ['ʃætəd] *adj Fam* **to be s.** *(stunned)* quedarse destrozado(a); *Br (exhausted)* estar rendido(a), *Méx* estar camotes

shave [ʃeɪv] **1** *n* afeitado *m*; **to have a s.** afeitarse; *Fig* **to have a close s.** escaparse por los pelos
　2 *vt* (*pt* **shaved**; *pp* **shaved** *or* **shaven** ['ʃeɪvən]) *(person)* afeitar; *(wood)* cepillar
　3 *vi* afeitarse

shaver ['ʃeɪvə(r)] *n* (**electric**) **s.** máquina *f* de afeitar

shaving ['ʃeɪvɪŋ] *n* (**a**) *(of wood)* viruta *f* (**b**) **s. brush** brocha *f* de afeitar; **s. cream** crema *f* de afeitar; **s. foam** espuma *f* de afeitar

shawl [ʃɔːl] *n* chal *m*, *Am* rebozo *m*

she [ʃiː] *pers pron* ella *(usually omitted in Spanish, except for contrast)*

she- [ʃiː] *pref (of animal)* hembra; **s.-cat** gata *f*

sheaf [ʃiːf] *n* (*pl* **sheaves**) *Agr* gavilla *f*; *(of arrows)* haz *m*; *(of papers, banknotes)* fajo *m*

shear [ʃɪə(r)] **1** *vt* (*pt* **sheared**; *pp* **shorn** or **sheared**) (*sheep*) esquilar; **to s. off** cortar
2 *vi* esquilar ovejas

shears [ʃɪəz] *npl* tijeras *fpl* (grandes)

sheath [ʃiːθ] *n* (a) (*for sword*) vaina *f*; (*for knife, scissors*) funda *f* (b) (*contraceptive*) preservativo *m*

sheaves [ʃiːvz] *pl of* **sheaf**

shed¹ [ʃed] *n* (*in garden*) cobertizo *m*; (*for cattle*) establo *m*; (*in factory*) nave *f*, *Andes, Carib, RP* galpón *m*

shed² [ʃed] *vt* (*pt & pp* **shed**) (a) (*clothes*) despojarse de; (*unwanted thing*) deshacerse de; **the snake s. its skin** la serpiente mudó de piel (b) (*blood, tears*) derramar

sheen [ʃiːn] *n* brillo *m*

sheep [ʃiːp] *n* (*pl* **sheep**) oveja *f*

sheepdog [ʃiːpdɒg] *n* perro *m* pastor

sheepish [ʃiːpɪʃ] *adj* avergonzado(a)

sheepskin [ʃiːpskɪn] *n* piel *f* de carnero

sheer [ʃɪə(r)] *adj* (a) (*utter*) total, puro(a) (b) (*cliff*) escarpado(a); (*drop*) vertical (c) (*stockings, cloth*) fino(a)

sheet [ʃiːt] *n* (a) (*on bed*) sábana *f* (b) (*of paper*) hoja *f*; (*of tin, glass, plastic*) lámina *f*; (*of ice*) capa *f*

sheik(h) [ʃeɪk] *n* jeque *m*

shelf [ʃelf] *n* (*pl* **shelves**) (*on bookcase*) estante *m*; (*in cupboard*) tabla *f*; **shelves** estantería *f*

shell [ʃel] **1** *n* (a) (*of egg, nut*) cáscara *f*; (*of pea*) vaina *f*; (*of tortoise etc*) caparazón *m*; (*of snail etc*) concha *f* (b) (*of building*) armazón *m* (c) (*mortar etc*) obús *m*, proyectil *m*; (*cartridge*) cartucho *m*; **s. shock** neurosis *f* de guerra
2 *vt* (a) (*peas*) desvainar; (*nuts*) pelar (b) *Mil* bombardear

shellfish [ʃelfɪʃ] *n* (*pl* **shellfish**) marisco *m*, mariscos *mpl*

shelter [ʃeltə(r)] **1** *n* (a) (*protection*) abrigo *m*, amparo *m*; **to take s. (from)** refugiarse (de) (b) (*place*) refugio *m*; (*for homeless*) asilo *m*; **bus s.** marquesina *f*
2 *vt* (a) (*protect*) abrigar, proteger (b) (*take into one's home*) ocultar
3 *vi* refugiarse

sheltered [ʃeltəd] *adj* (*place*) abrigado(a); **to lead a s. life** vivir apartado(a) del mundo

shelve [ʃelv] *vt* *Fig* (*postpone*) dar carpetazo a

shelves [ʃelvz] *pl of* **shelf**

shelving [ʃelvɪŋ] *n* estanterías *fpl*

shepherd [ʃepəd] **1** *n* pastor *m*; **s.'s pie** = pastel de carne picada con puré de patatas or *Am* papas
2 *vt* *Fig* **to s. sb in** hacer entrar a algn

sheriff [ʃerɪf] *n* *Br* = representante de la Corona; *Scot* ≃ juez *mf* de primera instancia; *US* sheriff *m*

sherry [ʃerɪ] *n* jerez *m*

Shetland [ʃetlənd] *n* the **S. Isles**, **S.** las Islas Shetland; **S. wool** lana *f* Shetland

shield [ʃiːld] **1** *n* (a) (*of knight*) escudo *m*; (*of policeman*) placa *f* (b) (*on machinery*) blindaje *m*
2 *vt* proteger (**from** de)

shift [ʃɪft] **1** *n* (a) (*change*) cambio *m*; *US Aut* (**gear**) **s.** cambio de velocidades (b) (*period of work, group of workers*) turno *m*; **to be on the day s.** hacer el turno de día
2 *vt* (*change*) cambiar; (*move*) cambiar de sitio, trasladar
3 *vi* (*move*) moverse; (*change place*) cambiar de sitio; (*opinion*) cambiar; (*wind*) cambiar de dirección

shiftless [ʃɪftlɪs] *n* perezoso(a), vago(a)

shiftwork [ʃɪftwɜːk] *n* trabajo *m* por turnos

shifty [ʃɪftɪ] *adj* (**shiftier**, **shiftiest**) (*look*) furtivo(a); (*person*) sospechoso(a)

shilling [ʃɪlɪŋ] *n* *Formerly* chelín *m*

shimmer [ʃɪmə(r)] **1** *vi* relucir; (*shine*) brillar
2 *n* luz trémula, reflejo trémulo; (*shining*) brillo *m*

shin [ʃɪn] *n* espinilla *f*, *RP* canilla *f*; **s. pad** espinillera *f*, *RP* canillera *f*

shine [ʃaɪn] **1** *vi* (*pt & pp* **shone**) (a) (*light*) brillar; (*metal*) relucir (b) *Fig* (*excel*) sobresalir (**at** en)
2 *vt* (a) (*lamp*) dirigir (b) (*pt & pp* **shined**) (*polish*) sacar brillo a; (*shoes*) limpiar
3 *n* brillo *m*, lustre *m*

shingle [ʃɪŋgəl] *n* (a) (*pebbles*) guijarros *mpl* (b) (*roof tile*) tablilla *f*

shingles [ʃɪŋgəlz] *n sing* *Med* herpes *m*

shining [ʃaɪnɪŋ] *adj* *Fig* (*outstanding*) ilustre

shiny [ʃaɪnɪ] *adj* (**shinier**, **shiniest**) brillante

ship [ʃɪp] **1** *n* barco *m*, buque *m*
2 *vt* (a) (*take on board*) embarcar (b) (*transport*) transportar (en barco); (*send*) enviar, mandar

shipbuilding [ʃɪpbɪldɪŋ] *n* construcción *f* naval

shipment [ʃɪpmənt] *n* (a) (*act*) transporte *m* (b) (*load*) consignación *f*, envío *m*

shipper [ʃɪpə(r)] *n* (*person*) cargador(a) *m,f*

shipping [ʃɪpɪŋ] *n* (a) (*ships*) barcos *mpl*; **s. lane** vía *f* de navegación (b) (*loading*) embarque *m*; *(transporting)* transporte *m* (en barco); **s. company** compañía naviera

shipshape ['ʃɪpʃeɪp] *adj & adv* en perfecto orden

shipwreck ['ʃɪprek] **1** *n* naufragio *m*
  2 *vt* **to be shipwrecked** naufragar

shipyard ['ʃɪpjɑːd] *n* astillero *m*

shire [ʃaɪə(r)] *n Br* condado *m*

shirk [ʃɜːk] **1** *vt (duty)* faltar a; *(problem)* eludir
  2 *vi* gandular

shirt [ʃɜːt] *n* camisa *f*; **in s. sleeves** en mangas de camisa; *Fam* **keep your s. on!** ¡no te sulfures!

shit [ʃɪt] *Vulg* **1** *n (excrement)* mierda *f*; *(mess)* porquería *f*, mierda *f*; **to** *Br* **have or** *US* **take a s.** cagar
  2 *vt (pt & pp* **shitted** *or* **shat** [ʃæt]) **to s. oneself** *(defecate)* cagarse (encima); *(be scared)* cagarse *or Esp* jiñarse de miedo

shiver ['ʃɪvə(r)] **1** *vi (with cold)* tiritar; *(with fear)* temblar, estremecerse
  2 *n (with cold, fear)* escalofrío *m*

shoal [ʃəʊl] *n (of fish)* banco *m*

shock [ʃɒk] **1** *n* **(a)** *(jolt)* choque *m*; **s. absorber** amortiguador *m*; **s. wave** onda expansiva **(b)** *(upset)* conmoción *f*; *(scare)* susto *m* **(c)** *Med* shock *m*
  2 *vt (upset)* conmover; *(startle)* sobresaltar; *(scandalize)* escandalizar

shocking ['ʃɒkɪŋ] *adj* **(a)** *(causing horror)* espantoso(a), *Fam (very bad)* horroroso(a) **(b)** *(disgraceful)* escandaloso(a) **(c)** **s. pink** rosa chillón

shod [ʃɒd] *pt & pp of* **shoe**

shoddy ['ʃɒdɪ] *adj* (**shoddier, shoddiest**) *(goods)* de mala calidad; *(work)* chapucero(a)

shoe [ʃuː] **1** *n* **(a)** *(for person)* zapato *m*; **shoes** calzado *m*; **s. polish** betún *m*; **s. repair (shop)** remiendo *m* de zapatos; **s. shop,** *US* **s. store** zapatería *f* **(b)** *(for horse)* herradura *f* **(c)** **(brake) s.** zapata *f*
  2 *vt (pt & pp* **shod**) *(horse)* herrar

shoebrush ['ʃuːbrʌʃ] *n* cepillo *m* para los zapatos

shoehorn ['ʃuːhɔːn] *n* calzador *m*

shoelace ['ʃuːleɪs] *n* cordón *m* (de zapatos)

shoestring ['ʃuːstrɪŋ] *n Fig* **to do sth on a s.** hacer algo con poquísimo dinero

shone [ʃɒn, *US* ʃəʊn] *pt & pp of* **shine**

shoo [ʃuː] **1** *interj* ¡fuera!
  2 *vt* **to s. (away)** espantar

shook [ʃʊk] *pt of* **shake**

shoot [ʃuːt] **1** *n Bot* retoño *m*; *(of vine)* sarmiento *m*
  2 *vt (pt & pp* **shot**) **(a)** *(fire at)* pegar un tiro a; *(kill)* matar; *(execute)* fusilar; *(hunt)*

cazar; **to s. dead** matar a tiros **(b)** *(missile, glance)* lanzar; *(bullet, ball)* disparar **(c)** *(film)* rodar, filmar; *Phot* fotografiar
  3 *vi* **(a)** *(with gun)* disparar (**at sb** a algn); **to s. at a target** tirar al blanco; *Ftb* **to s. at the goal** chutar a puerta **(b)** **to s. past** *or* **by** pasar flechado(a)

▸ **shoot down** *vt sep (aircraft)* derribar

▸ **shoot out** *vi (person)* salir disparado(a); *(water)* brotar; *(flames)* salir

▸ **shoot up** *vi* **(a)** *(flames)* salir; *(water)* brotar; *(prices)* dispararse **(b)** *Fam (inject drugs)* pincharse, *Esp* chutarse

shooting ['ʃuːtɪŋ] **1** *n* **(a)** *(shots)* tiros *mpl*; *(murder)* asesinato *m*; *(hunting)* caza *f*; **s. star** estrella *f* fugaz **(b)** *(of film)* rodaje *m*
  2 *adj (pain)* punzante

shoot-out ['ʃuːtaʊt] *n* tiroteo *m*

shop [ʃɒp] **1** *n* **(a)** *(for goods)* tienda *f*; *(large store)* almacén *m*; **s. assistant** dependiente(a) *m,f*; **s. window** escaparate *m*, *Am* vidriera *f*, *Am* vitrina *f* **(b)** *(workshop)* taller *m*; **s. floor** *(place)* planta *f*; *(workers)* obreros *mpl*; **s. steward** enlace *mf* sindical
  2 *vi* hacer compras; **to go shopping** ir de compras

shopkeeper ['ʃɒpkiːpə(r)] *n* tendero(a) *m,f*

shoplifter ['ʃɒplɪftə(r)] *n* ladrón(ona) *m,f* (de tiendas)

shopper ['ʃɒpə(r)] *n* comprador(a) *m,f*

shopping ['ʃɒpɪŋ] *n (purchases)* compra *fpl*, *Am* compras *fpl*; **s. bag/basket** bolsa *f*/ cesta *f* de la compra; **s. centre** *or* **precinct** centro *m* comercial

shopsoiled ['ʃɒpsɔɪld], *US* **shopworn** ['ʃɒpwɔːn] *adj* deteriorado(a)

shore [ʃɔː(r)] *n (of sea, lake)* orilla *f*; *US (beach)* playa *f*; *(coast)* costa *f*; **to go on s.** desembarcar

▸ **shore up** *vt sep* apuntalar

shorn [ʃɔːn] *pp of* **shear**

short [ʃɔːt] **1** *adj* **(a)** *(physically)* corto(a); *(person)* bajo(a), *Méx* chaparro(a), *RP* petiso(a); **in the s. term** a corto plazo; **s. circuit** cortocircuito *m*; **s. cut** atajo *m*; **s. story** relato corto, cuento *m*; **s. wave** onda corta **(b)** *(brief)* corto(a), breve; **"Bob" is s. for "Robert"** "Bob" es el diminutivo de "Robert"; **in s.** en pocas palabras **(c)** **to be s. of breath** faltarle a uno la respiración; **to be s. of food** andar escaso(a) de comida
  2 *adv* **(a)** **to pull up s.** pararse en seco **(b)** **to cut s.** *(holiday)* interrumpir; *(meeting)* suspender; **we're running s. of coffee** se nos está acabando el café **(c)** **s. of** *(except)* excepto, menos

shortage [ˈʃɔːtɪdʒ] *n* escasez *f*

shortbread [ˈʃɔːtbred] *n* mantecado *m*

short-change [ʃɔːtˈtʃeɪndʒ] *vt* **to s. sb** no devolver el cambio completo a algn; *Fig* timar a algn

short-circuit [ʃɔːtˈsɜːkɪt] **1** *vt* provocar un cortocircuito en
2 *vi* tener un cortocircuito

shortcomings [ˈʃɔːtkʌmɪŋz] *npl* defectos *mpl*

shortcrust [ˈʃɔːtkrʌst] *n* **s. pastry** pasta brisa

shorten [ˈʃɔːtən] *vt (skirt, visit)* acortar; *(word)* abreviar; *(text)* resumir

shortfall [ˈʃɔːtfɔːl] *n* déficit *m*

shorthand [ˈʃɔːthænd] *n* taquigrafía *f*; *Br* **s. typist** taquimecanógrafo(a) *m,f*

short-list [ˈʃɔːtlɪst] *vt* poner en la lista de seleccionados

short-lived [ʃɔːtˈlɪvd] *adj* efímero(a)

shortly [ˈʃɔːtlɪ] *adv (soon)* dentro de poco; **s. after** poco después

short-range [ˈʃɔːtreɪndʒ] *adj* de corto alcance

shorts [ʃɔːts] *npl* (a) *(short trousers)* pantalones *mpl* cortos; **a pair of s.** un pantalón corto (b) *US (underpants)* calzoncillos *mpl*

short-sighted [ʃɔːtˈsaɪtɪd] *adj (person)* miope; *Fig (plan etc)* sin visión de futuro

short-staffed [ʃɔːtˈstɑːft] *adj* escaso(a) de personal

short-tempered [ʃɔːtˈtempəd] *adj* de mal genio

short-term [ˈʃɔːttɜːm] *adj* a corto plazo

shot¹ [ʃɒt] *n* (a) *(act, sound)* tiro *m*, disparo *m* (b) *(pellets)* perdigones *mpl* (c) *(person)* tirador(a) *m,f* (d) *Ftb (kick)* tiro *m* (a puerta); *(in billiards, cricket, golf)* golpe *m* (e) *(attempt)* tentativa *f*; **to have a s. at** **sth** intentar hacer algo (f) *(injection)* inyección *f*; *Fam* pinchazo *m* (g) *(drink)* trago *m* (h) *Phot* foto *f*; *Cin* toma *f*

shot² [ʃɒt] *pt & pp of* **shoot**

shotgun [ˈʃɒtgʌn] *n* escopeta *f*

should [ʃʊd, *unstressed* ʃəd] *v aux*

En el inglés hablado, y en el escrito en estilo coloquial, la forma negativa **should not** se transforma en **shouldn't**.

(a) *(duty)* deber; **all employees s. wear helmets** todos los empleados s. wear llevar casco; **he s. have been an architect** debería haber sido arquitecto (b) *(probability)* deber de; **he s. have finished by now** ya debe de haber acabado; **this s. be interesting** esto promete ser interesante (c) *(conditional*

use) **if anything strange s. happen** si pasara algo raro (d) **I s. like to ask a question** quisiera hacer una pregunta

shoulder [ˈʃəʊldə(r)] **1** *n* (a) *(of person)* hombro *m*; **s. blade** omóplato *m*; **s. strap** *(of garment)* tirante *m*, *CSur* bretel *m*; *(of bag)* correa *f*; *Br Aut* **hard s.** arcén *m*, *Andes* berma *f*, *Méx* acotamiento *m*, *RP* banquina *f*, *Ven* hombrillo *m* (b) *(of meat)* paletilla *f* (c) *US Aut* arcén *m*, *Andes* berma *f*, *Méx* acotamiento *m*, *RP* banquina *f*, *Ven* hombrillo *m*
2 *vt Fig (responsibilities)* cargar con

shout [ʃaʊt] **1** *n* grito *m*
2 *vt* gritar
3 *vi* gritar; **to s. at sb** gritar a algn
▸ **shout down** *vt sep* abuchear

shouting [ˈʃaʊtɪŋ] *n* gritos *mpl*, vocerío *m*

shove [ʃʌv] **1** *n Fam* empujón *m*
2 *vt* empujar; **to s. sth into one's pocket** meterse algo en el bolsillo a empellones
3 *vi* empujar; *(jostle)* dar empellones
▸ **shove off** *vi Fam* largarse
▸ **shove up** *vi Fam (move along)* correrse

shovel [ˈʃʌvəl] **1** *n* pala *f*; **mechanical s.** excavadora *f*
2 *vt* mover con pala *or* a paladas

show [ʃəʊ] **1** *vt* (*pt* **showed**; *pp* **shown** *or* **showed**) (a) *(ticket etc)* mostrar; *(painting etc)* exponer; *(film)* poner (b) *(display)* demostrar (c) *(explain)* explicar (d) *(temperature, way etc)* indicar (e) *(prove)* demostrar (f) *(conduct)* llevar; **to s. sb in** hacer pasar a algn; **to s. sb to the door** acompañar a algn hasta la puerta
2 *vi (be visible)* notarse
3 *n* (a) *(display)* demostración *f* (b) *(outward appearance)* apariencia *f* (c) *(exhibition)* exposición *f*; **on s.** expuesto(a) (d) *Th (entertainment)* espectáculo *m*; *(performance)* función *f*; *Rad & TV* programa *m*; **s. business** *or Fam* **biz** *m* el mundo del espectáculo
▸ **show off 1** *vt sep* (a) *(highlight)* hacer resaltar (b) *Fam (flaunt)* hacer alarde de
2 *vi Fam* farolear
▸ **show up 1** *vt sep* (a) *(reveal)* sacar a luz; *(highlight)* hacer resaltar (b) *Fam (embarrass)* dejar en evidencia
2 *vi* (a) *(stand out)* destacarse (b) *Fam (arrive)* aparecer

showdown [ˈʃəʊdaʊn] *n* enfrentamiento *m*

shower [ˈʃaʊə(r)] **1** *n* (a) *(rain)* chubasco *m*, chaparrón *m* (b) *Fig (of stones, insults)* lluvia *f* (c) *(bath)* ducha *f*, *Col, Méx, Ven* regadera *f*; **to have a s.** ducharse
2 *vt* (a) *(spray)* rociar (b) *Fig* **to s. gifts/**

praise on sb colmar a algn de regalos/ elogios
  3 *vi* ducharse

showerproof ['ʃaʊəpruːf] *adj* impermeable

showery ['ʃaʊərɪ] *adj* lluvioso(a)

showing ['ʃəʊɪŋ] *n (of film)* proyección *f*

showjumping ['ʃəʊdʒʌmpɪŋ] *n* hípica *f*

shown [ʃəʊn] *pp of* **show**

show-off ['ʃəʊf] *n Fam* fanfarrón(ona) *m,f, Esp* fantasma *mf*

showpiece ['ʃəʊpiːs] *n (in exhibition etc)* obra maestra; *Fig (at school etc)* modelo *m*

showroom ['ʃəʊruːm] *n Com* exposición *f; Art* galería *f*

showy ['ʃəʊɪ] *adj* (**showier, showiest**) llamativo(a)

shrank [ʃræŋk] *pt of* **shrink**

shrapnel ['ʃræpnəl] *n* metralla *f*

shred [ʃred] **1** *n* triza *f; (of cloth)* jirón *m; (of paper)* tira *f*
  2 *vt (paper)* hacer trizas; *(vegetables)* rallar

shredder ['ʃredə(r)] *n (for waste paper)* trituradora *f; (for vegetables)* rallador *m*

shrew [ʃruː] *n* (a) *Zool* musaraña *f* (b) *Fig (woman)* arpía *f*

shrewd [ʃruːd] *adj* astuto(a); *(clearsighted)* perspicaz; *(wise)* sabio(a); *(decision)* acertado(a)

shriek [ʃriːk] **1** *n* chillido *m;* **shrieks of laughter** carcajadas *fpl*
  2 *vi* chillar

shrill [ʃrɪl] *adj* agudo(a), estridente

shrimp [ʃrɪmp] *n Br* camarón *m,* quisquilla *f; US (prawn)* gamba *f*

shrine [ʃraɪn] *n (tomb)* sepulcro *m; (chapel)* capilla *f; (holy place)* lugar sagrado

shrink [ʃrɪŋk] **1** *vt (pt* **shrank;** *pp* **shrunk)** encoger
  2 *vi* (a) *(clothes)* encoger(se) (b) *(savings)* disminuir (c) **to s. (back)** echarse atrás; **to s. from doing sth** no tener valor para hacer algo
  3 *n Fam (psychiatrist)* psiquiatra *mf*

shrinkage ['ʃrɪŋkɪdʒ] *n* (a) *(of cloth)* encogimiento *m; (of metal)* contracción *f* (b) *(of savings etc)* disminución *f*

shrink-wrapped ['ʃrɪŋkræpt] *adj* envuelto(a) en plástico

shrivel ['ʃrɪvəl] **1** *vt* **to s. (up)** encoger; *(plant)* secar; *(skin)* arrugar
  2 *vi* encogerse; *(plant)* secarse; *(skin)* arrugarse

shroud [ʃraʊd] **1** *n Rel* sudario *m*
  2 *vt Fig* envolver

Shrove Tuesday ['ʃrəʊv'tjuːzdɪ] *n* martes *m* de carnaval

shrub [ʃrʌb] *n* arbusto *m*

shrubbery ['ʃrʌbərɪ] *n* arbustos *mpl*

shrug [ʃrʌg] **1** *vt* **to s. one's shoulders** encogerse de hombros
  2 *vi* encogerse de hombros
  3 *n* encogimiento *m* de hombros
▸ **shrug off** *vt sep* no dejarse desanimar por

shrunk [ʃrʌŋk] *pp of* **shrink**

shrunken ['ʃrʌŋkən] *adj* encogido(a)

shudder ['ʃʌdə(r)] **1** *n* (a) *(of person)* estremecimiento *m* (b) *(of machinery)* sacudida *f*
  2 *vi* (a) *(person)* estremecerse (b) *(machinery)* dar sacudidas

shuffle ['ʃʌfəl] **1** *vt* (a) *(feet)* arrastrar (b) *(papers etc)* revolver; *(cards)* barajar
  2 *vi* (a) *(walk)* andar arrastrando los pies (b) *Cards* barajar

shun [ʃʌn] *vt (person)* esquivar; *(responsibility)* rehuir

shunt [ʃʌnt] *vt Rail* cambiar de vía; *Elec* derivar

shut [ʃʌt] **1** *vt (pt & pp* **shut)** cerrar
  2 *vi* cerrarse
  3 *adj* cerrado(a)
▸ **shut down 1** *vt sep (factory)* cerrar
  2 *vi (factory)* cerrar
▸ **shut off** *vt sep (gas, water etc)* cortar
▸ **shut out** *vt sep* (a) *(lock out)* dejar fuera a (b) *(exclude)* excluir
▸ **shut up 1** *vt sep* (a) *(close)* cerrar (b) *(imprison)* encerrar (c) *Fam (silence)* callar
  2 *vi Fam (keep quiet)* callarse

shutdown ['ʃʌtdaʊn] *n* cierre *m*

shutter ['ʃʌtə(r)] *n* (a) *(on window)* contraventana *f,* postigo *m* (b) *Phot* obturador *m*

shuttle ['ʃʌtəl] **1** *n* (a) *(in weaving)* lanzadera *f* (b) *Av* puente aéreo; **(space) s.** transbordador *m* espacial
  2 *vi* ir y venir

shuttlecock ['ʃʌtəlkɒk] *n* volante *m*

shy [ʃaɪ] **1** *adj* (**shyer, shyest** *or* **shier, shiest**) *(timid)* tímido(a), *Am salvo RP* penoso(a); *(reserved)* reservado(a)
  2 *vi (horse)* espantarse **(at** de); *Fig* **to s. away from doing sth** negarse a hacer algo

shyness ['ʃaɪnɪs] *n* timidez *f*

Siberia [saɪ'bɪərɪə] *n* Siberia

sibling ['sɪblɪŋ] *n Fml (brother)* hermano *m; (sister)* hermana *f;* **siblings** hermanos

Sicily ['sɪsɪlɪ] *n* Sicilia

sick [sɪk] *adj* (**a**) *(ill)* enfermo(a); **s. leave** baja *f* por enfermedad; **s. pay** subsidio *m* de enfermedad (**b**) **to feel s.** *(about to vomit)* tener ganas de devolver; **to be s.** devolver (**c**) *Fam (fed up)* harto(a) (**d**) *Fam (mind, joke)* morboso(a); **s. humour** humor negro

sickbay ['sɪkbeɪ] *n* enfermería *f*

sicken ['sɪkən] **1** *vt (make ill)* poner enfermo; *(revolt)* dar asco a
2 *vi (fall ill)* enfermar

sickening ['sɪkənɪŋ] *adj* nauseabundo(a); *(revolting)* repugnante; *(horrifying)* escalofriante

sickle ['sɪkəl] *n* hoz *f*

sickly ['sɪklɪ] *adj* (**sicklier, sickliest**) (**a**) *(person)* enfermizo(a) (**b**) *(taste)* empalagoso(a) *(smile)* forzado(a)

sickness ['sɪknɪs] *n* (**a**) *(illness)* enfermedad *f* (**b**) *(nausea)* náuseas *fpl*

side [saɪd] **1** *n* (**a**) *(side)* (of house, box, square) lado *m*; *(of coin, sheet of paper)* cara *f*, *(of hill)* ladera *f* (**b**) *(of body)* costado *m*; *(of animal)* ijar *m*; **by my s.** a mi lado; **s. by s.** juntos (**c**) *(edge)* borde *m*; *(of lake, river)* orilla *f* (**d**) *Fig (aspect)* aspecto *m* (**e**) *(team)* equipo *m*; *Pol* partido *m*; **she's on our s.** está de nuestro lado; **to take sides with sb** ponerse de parte de algn; **s. effect** efecto secundario; **s. entrance** entrada *f* lateral; **s. street** calle *f* lateral
2 *vi* **to s. with sb** ponerse de parte de algn

sideboard ['saɪdbɔːd] *n* aparador *m*

sideburns ['saɪdbɜːnz], *Br* **sideboards** ['saɪdbɔːdz] *npl* patillas *fpl*

sidelight ['saɪdlaɪt] *n Aut* luz *f* lateral, piloto *m*

sideline ['saɪdlaɪn] *n* (**a**) *Sport* línea *f* de banda (**b**) *Com (product)* línea suplementaria; *(job)* empleo suplementario

sidelong ['saɪdlɒŋ] *adj* de reojo

side-saddle ['saɪdsædəl] **1** *n* silla *f* de amazona
2 *adv* **to ride s.** montar a la inglesa

sideshow ['saɪdʃəʊ] *n* atracción secundaria

sidestep ['saɪdstep] *vt (issue)* esquivar

sidetrack ['saɪdtræk] *vt Fig (person)* despistar

sidewalk ['saɪdwɔːk] *n US* acera *f*, *CSur* vereda *f*, *CAm, Méx* banqueta *f*

sideways ['saɪdweɪz] **1** *adj (movement)* lateral; *(look)* de reojo
2 *adv* de lado

siding ['saɪdɪŋ] *n (on railway)* apartadero *m*; *(connected at only one end to main track)* vía *f* muerta

sidle ['saɪdəl] *vi* **to s. up to sb** acercarse furtivamente a algn

siege [siːdʒ] *n* sitio *m*, cerco *m*; **to lay s. to** sitiar

sieve [sɪv] **1** *n (fine)* tamiz *m*; *(coarse)* criba *f*
2 *vt (fine)* tamizar; *(coarse)* cribar

sift [sɪft] *vt (sieve)* tamizar; *Fig* **to s. through** examinar cuidadosamente

sigh [saɪ] **1** *vi* suspirar
2 *n* suspiro *m*

sight [saɪt] **1** *n* (**a**) *(faculty)* vista *f*; **at first s.** a primera vista; **to catch s. of** divisar; **to know by s.** conocer de vista; **to lose s. of sth/sb** perder algo/a algn de vista (**b**) *(range of vision)* vista *f*; **within s.** a la vista; **to come into s.** aparecer (**c**) *(spectacle)* espectáculo *m* (**d**) *(on gun)* mira *f*; *Fig* **to set one's sights on** tener la mira puesta en (**e**) **the sights** *(of city)* los lugares de interés
2 *vt* ver; *(land)* divisar

sightseeing ['saɪtsiːɪŋ] *n* turismo *m*; **to go s.** hacer turismo

sign [saɪn] **1** *n* (**a**) *(symbol)* signo *m* (**b**) *(gesture)* gesto *m*, seña *f*; *(signal)* señal *f* (**c**) *(indication)* señal *f*; *(trace)* rastro *m*, huella *f* (**d**) *(notice)* anuncio *m*; *(board)* letrero *m*
2 *vt* (**a**) *(letter etc)* firmar (**b**) *Ftb* fichar
3 *vi* firmar
▸ **sign on** *vi Br (worker)* firmar un contrato; *Br Fam* = registrarse para recibir el seguro de desempleo, *Esp* apuntarse al paro; *(regularly)* ir a firmar *or Esp* sellar
▸ **sign up** **1** *vt sep (soldier)* reclutar; *(worker)* contratar
2 *vi (soldier)* alistarse; *(worker)* firmar un contrato

signal ['sɪgnəl] **1** *n* señal *f*; *Rad & TV* sintonía *f*; *Rail* **s. box** garita *f* de señales
2 *vt* (**a**) *(message)* transmitir por señales (**b**) *(direction etc)* indicar
3 *vi (with hands)* hacer señales; *(in car)* señalar

signalman ['sɪgnəlmən] *n* guardavía *m*

signature ['sɪgnɪtʃə(r)] *n (name)* firma *f*; *Rad & TV* **s. tune** sintonía *f*

signet ['sɪgnɪt] *n* **s. ring** (anillo *m* de) sello *m*

significance [sɪgˈnɪfɪkəns] *n (meaning)* significado *m*; *(importance)* importancia *f*

significant [sɪgˈnɪfɪkənt] *adj (meaningful)* significativo(a); *(important)* importante

significantly [sɪgˈnɪfɪkəntlɪ] *adv (markedly)* sensiblemente

signify ['sɪgnɪfaɪ] *vt* (**a**) *(mean)* significar (**b**) *(show, make known)* indicar

signpost ['saɪnpəʊst] *n* poste *m* indicador

Sikh [siːk] *adj & n* sij *(mf)*

silence ['saɪləns] **1** *n* silencio *m*
2 *vt* acallar; *(engine)* silenciar

silencer ['saɪlənsə(r)] *n* (**a**) *(on gun)* silenciador *m* (**b**) *Br (on car)* silenciador *m*

silent ['saɪlənt] *adj* silencioso(a); *(not talkative)* callado(a); *(film)* mudo(a); **be s.!** ¡cállate!; **to remain s.** guardar silencio

silently ['saɪləntlɪ] *adv* silenciosamente

silhouette [sɪluːˈet] *n* silueta *f*

silicon ['sɪlɪkən] *n* silicio *m*; **s. chip** chip *m* (de silicio)

silk [sɪlk] **1** *n* seda *f*
2 *adj* de seda

silky ['sɪlkɪ] *adj* (**silkier, silkiest**) *(cloth)* sedoso(a); *(voice etc)* aterciopelado(a)

sill [sɪl] *n (of window)* alféizar *m*

silly ['sɪlɪ] *adj* (**sillier, silliest**) tonto(a)

silo ['saɪləʊ] *n* silo *m*

silt [sɪlt] *n* cieno *m*
▸ **silt up** *vi* obstruirse con cieno

silver ['sɪlvə(r)] **1** *n* (**a**) *(metal)* plata *f* (**b**) *Br (coins)* monedas *fpl* plateadas *(de entre 5 y 50 peniques)* (**c**) *(tableware)* vajilla *f* de plata
2 *adj* de plata; **s. foil** *(tinfoil)* papel *m* de aluminio; **s. paper** papel de plata; **s. wedding** bodas *fpl* de plata

silver-plated [sɪlvəˈpleɪtɪd] *adj* plateado(a)

silversmith ['sɪlvəsmɪθ] *n* platero(a) *m,f*

silverware ['sɪlvəweə(r)] *n* vajilla *f* de plata

silvery ['sɪlvərɪ] *adj* plateado(a)

similar ['sɪmɪlə(r)] *adj* parecido(a), semejante (**to** a); **to be s.** parecerse

similarity [sɪmɪˈlærɪtɪ] *n* semejanza *f*

similarly ['sɪmɪləlɪ] *adv* (**a**) *(as well)* igualmente (**b**) *(likewise)* del mismo modo, asimismo

simile ['sɪmɪlɪ] *n* símil *m*

simmer ['sɪmə(r)] **1** *vt* cocer a fuego lento
2 *vi* cocerse a fuego lento
▸ **simmer down** *vi Fam* calmarse

simpering ['sɪmpərɪŋ] *adj* melindroso(a)

simple ['sɪmpəl] *adj* (**a**) *(uncomplicated)* sencillo(a); **s. interest** interés *m* simple (**b**) *(natural)* natural (**c**) *(foolish)* simple; *(naïve)* ingenuo(a); *(dim)* de pocas luces

simplicity [sɪmˈplɪsɪtɪ] *n* (**a**) *(easiness)* sencillez *f* (**b**) *(naïveté)* ingenuidad *f*

simplify ['sɪmplɪfaɪ] *vt* simplificar

simply ['sɪmplɪ] *adv* (**a**) *(plainly)* sencillamente (**b**) *(only)* simplemente, sólo

simulate ['sɪmjʊleɪt] *vt* simular

simulator ['sɪmjʊleɪtə(r)] *n* **flight s.** simulador *m* de vuelo

simultaneous [sɪməlˈteɪnɪəs] *adj* simultáneo(a)

simultaneously [sɪməlˈteɪnɪəslɪ] *adv* simultáneamente

sin [sɪn] **1** *n* pecado *m*
2 *vi* pecar

since [sɪns] **1** *adv* (**ever**) **s.** desde entonces; **long s.** hace mucho tiempo; **it has s. come out that ...** desde entonces se ha sabido que ...
2 *prep* desde; **she has been living here s. 1975** vive aquí desde 1975
3 *conj* (**a**) *(time)* desde que; **how long is it s. you last saw him?** ¿cuánto tiempo hace que lo viste por última vez? (**b**) *(because, as)* ya que, puesto que

sincere [sɪnˈsɪə(r)] *adj* sincero(a)

sincerely [sɪnˈsɪəlɪ] *adv* sinceramente; **Yours s.** *(in letter)* Atentamente

sincerity [sɪnˈserɪtɪ] *n* sinceridad *f*

sinew ['sɪnjuː] *n (tendon)* tendón *m*; *(in meat)* nervio *m*

sinful ['sɪnfʊl] *adj (person)* pecador(a); *(act, thought)* pecaminoso(a); *Fig (waste etc)* escandaloso(a)

sing [sɪŋ] **1** *vt (pt* **sang**; *pp* **sung**) cantar
2 *vi (person, bird)* cantar; *(kettle, bullets)* silbar

singe [sɪndʒ] *vt* chamuscar

singer ['sɪŋə(r)] *n* cantante *mf*

singing ['sɪŋɪŋ] *n (art)* canto *m*; *(songs)* canciones *fpl*; *(of kettle)* silbido *m*

single ['sɪŋgəl] **1** *adj* (**a**) *(solitary)* solo(a) (**b**) *(only one)* único(a) (**c**) *(not double)* sencillo(a); **s. bed/room** cama *f*/habitación *f* individual (**d**) *(unmarried)* soltero(a)
2 *n* (**a**) *Br Rail* billete *m or Am* boleto *m or Am* pasaje *m* sencillo *or* de ida (**b**) *(record)* single *m* (**c**) *Sport* **singles** individuales *mpl*
▸ **single out** *vt sep (choose)* escoger; *(distinguish)* distinguir

single-breasted ['sɪŋgəl'brestɪd] *adj (suit, jacket)* recto(a)

single-handed ['sɪŋgəl'hændɪd] *adj & adv* sin ayuda

single-minded ['sɪŋgəl'maɪndɪd] *adj* resuelto(a)

singlet ['sɪŋglɪt] *n Br* camiseta *f* (de tirantes *or Am* breteles)

singly ['sɪŋglɪ] *adv (individually)* por separado; *(one by one)* uno por uno

singular ['sɪŋgjʊlə(r)] **1** *adj* (**a**) *Ling* singular (**b**) *Fml (outstanding)* excepcional (**c**) *Fml (unique)* único(a)
2 *n Ling* singular *m*

singularly ['sɪŋɡjʊləlɪ] *adv* excepcionalmente

sinister ['sɪnɪstə(r)] *adj* siniestro(a)

sink¹ [sɪŋk] *n (in kitchen)* fregadero *m; (in bathroom)* lavabo *m, Am* lavamanos *m inv*

sink² [sɪŋk] **1** *vt (pt* sank; *pp* sunk) **(a)** *(ship)* hundir, echar a pique; *Fig (hopes)* acabar con **(b)** *(hole, well)* cavar; *(post, knife, teeth)* hincar
 2 *vi* **(a)** *(ship)* hundirse **(b)** *Fig* **my heart sank** se me cayó el alma a los pies **(c)** *(sun)* ponerse **(d)** **to s. to one's knees** hincarse de rodillas
 ▸ **sink in** *vi (penetrate)* penetrar; *Fig* **it hasn't sunk in yet** todavía no me he/se ha/*etc* hecho a la idea

sinner ['sɪnə(r)] *n* pecador(a) *m,f*

sinus ['saɪnəs] *n* seno *m* (nasal)

sip [sɪp] **1** *n* sorbo *m*
 2 *vt* sorber, beber a sorbos

siphon ['saɪfən] *n* sifón *m*
 ▸ **siphon off** *vt sep (liquid)* sacar con sifón; *Fig (funds, traffic)* desviar

sir [sɜː(r)] *n Fml* **(a)** *(form of address)* señor *m;* **yes, s.** sí, señor **(b)** *(title)* **S. Walter Raleigh** Sir Walter Raleigh

siren ['saɪrən] *n* sirena *f*

sirloin ['sɜːlɔɪn] *n* solomillo *m*

sissy ['sɪsɪ] *n Fam (coward)* miedica *mf*

sister ['sɪstə(r)] *n* **(a)** *(relation)* hermana *f* **(b)** *Br Med* enfermera *f* jefe **(c)** *Rel* hermana *f;* **s. Teresa** sor Teresa

sister-in-law ['sɪstərɪnlɔː] *n* cuñada *f*

sit [sɪt] **1** *vt (pt & pp* sat) **(a)** *(child etc)* sentar **(in/on** en) **(b)** *Br (exam)* presentarse a
 2 *vi* **(a)** *(action)* sentarse **(b)** *(be seated)* estar sentado(a) **(c)** *(object)* estar; *(be situated)* hallarse; *(person)* quedarse **(d)** *(assembly)* reunirse
 ▸ **sit back** *vi* recostarse
 ▸ **sit down** *vi* sentarse
 ▸ **sit in** *vt insep* asistir sin participar en
 ▸ **sit out** *vt sep* aguantar hasta el final
 ▸ **sit through** *vt insep* aguantar
 ▸ **sit up** *vi* **(a)** *(from lying position)* incorporarse **(b)** *(stay up late)* quedarse levantado(a)

sitcom ['sɪtkɒm] *n TV* telecomedia *f* (de situación)

site [saɪt] **1** *n* **(a)** *(area)* lugar *m;* **building s.** solar *m; (under construction)* obra *f* **(b)** *(location)* situación *f;* **nuclear testing s.** zona *f* de pruebas nucleares
 2 *vt* situar

sit-in ['sɪtɪn] *n Fam (demonstration)* sentada *f; (strike)* huelga *f* de brazos caídos

sitting ['sɪtɪŋ] **1** *n (of committee)* sesión *f; (in canteen)* turno *m*
 2 *adj Br* **s. room** sala *f* de estar

situated ['sɪtjʊeɪtɪd] *adj* situado(a), ubicado(a)

situation [sɪtjʊ'eɪʃən] *n* **(a)** *(circumstances)* situación *f* **(b)** *(job)* puesto *m; Br* **situations vacant** *(in newspaper)* ofertas de trabajo

six [sɪks] *adj & n* seis *(m inv)*

sixteen [sɪks'tiːn] *adj & n* dieciséis *(m inv),* diez y seis *(m inv)*

sixteenth [sɪks'tiːnθ] **1** *adj & n* decimosexto(a) *(m,f)*
 2 *n (fraction)* dieciseisavo *m*

sixth [sɪksθ] **1** *adj* sexto(a); *Br Educ* **the s. form** = últimos dos cursos del bachillerato británico previos a los estudios superiores; *Br Educ* **s. former** = estudiante de los dos últimos cursos del bachillerato británico
 2 *n* **(a)** *(in series)* sexto(a) *m,f* **(b)** *(fraction)* sexto *m,* sexta parte

sixty ['sɪkstɪ] *adj & n* sesenta *(m inv)*

sizable ['saɪzəbəl] *adj* = **sizeable**

size [saɪz] *n* tamaño *m; (of garment)* talla *f; (of shoes)* número *m; (of person)* estatura *f; (scope)* alcance *m;* **what s. do you take?** *(garment)* ¿qué talla tienes?; *(shoes)* ¿qué número calzas?
 ▸ **size up** *vt sep (person)* juzgar; *(situation, problem)* evaluar

sizeable ['saɪzəbəl] *adj (building etc)* (bastante) grande; *(sum)* considerable; *(problem)* importante

sizzle ['sɪzəl] *vi* chisporrotear

skate¹ [skeɪt] **1** *n* patín *m*
 2 *vi* patinar

skate² [skeɪt] *n (fish)* raya *f*

skateboard ['skeɪtbɔːd] *n* monopatín *m, RP* skate *m*

skater ['skeɪtə(r)] *n* patinador(a) *m,f*

skating ['skeɪtɪŋ] *n* patinaje *m;* **s. rink** pista *f* de patinaje

skeleton ['skelɪtən] **1** *n* **(a)** *(of person)* esqueleto *m* **(b)** *(of building)* armazón *m* **(c)** *(outline)* esquema *m*
 2 *adj (staff, service)* reducido(a); **s. key** llave maestra

skeptic ['skeptɪk] *n US* = **sceptic**

skeptical ['skeptɪkəl] *adj US* = **sceptical**

skepticism ['skeptɪsɪzəm] *n US* = **scepticism**

sketch [sketʃ] **1** *n* **(a)** *(preliminary drawing)* bosquejo *m,* esbozo *m; (drawing)* dibujo *m; (outline)* esquema *m; (rough draft)* boceto *m* **(b)** *Th & TV* sketch *m*
 2 *vt (draw)* dibujar; *(preliminary drawing)* bosquejar, esbozar

sketch-book ['sketʃbʊk], **sketch-pad** ['sketʃpæd] *n* bloc *m* de dibujo

sketchy ['sketʃɪ] *adj* (**sketchier, sketchiest**) *(incomplete)* incompleto(a); *(not detailed)* vago(a)

skewer ['skjʊə(r)] *n* pincho *m*, broqueta *f*

ski [skiː] **1** *n* esquí *m*
2 *adj* de esquí; **s. boots** botas *fpl* de esquiar; **s. jump** *(action)* salto *m* con esquís; **s. lift** telesquí *m*; *(with seats)* telesilla *f*; **s. pants** pantalón *m* de esquiar; **s. resort** estación *f* de esquí; **s. stick** *or* **pole** bastón *m* de esquiar
3 *vi* esquiar; **to go skiing** ir a esquiar

skid [skɪd] **1** *n* patinazo *m*
2 *vi* patinar

skier ['skiːə(r)] *n* esquiador(a) *m,f*

skiing ['skiːɪŋ] *n* esquí *m*

skilful ['skɪlfʊl] *adj* hábil, diestro(a)

skill [skɪl] *n* (**a**) *(ability)* habilidad *f*, destreza *f*; *(talent)* don *m* (**b**) *(technique)* técnica *f*

skilled [skɪld] *adj* (**a**) *(dextrous)* hábil, diestro(a); *(expert)* experto(a) (**b**) *(worker)* cualificado(a)

skillet ['skɪlɪt] *n US* sartén *f*

skillful ['skɪlfʊl] *adj US* = **skilful**

skim [skɪm] **1** *vt* (**a**) *(milk)* *Esp* quitar la nata a, *Am* sacar la crema a; **skimmed milk** leche desnatada (**b**) *(brush against)* rozar; **to s. the ground** *(bird, plane)* volar a ras de suelo
2 *vi Fig* **to s. through a book** hojear un libro

skimp [skɪmp] *vt & vi (food, material)* escatimar; *(work)* chapucear

skimpy ['skɪmpɪ] *adj* (**skimpier, skimpiest**) *(shorts)* muy corto(a); *(meal)* escaso(a)

skin [skɪn] **1** *n* (**a**) *(of person, animal)* piel *f*; *(of face)* cutis *m*; *(complexion)* tez *f* (**b**) *(of fruit, sausage)* piel *f*; *(of lemon)* cáscara *f*; *(peeling)* mondadura *f*
2 *vt* (**a**) *(animal)* despellejar (**b**) *(graze)* arañar

skin-deep [skɪn'diːp] *adj* superficial

skin-diving ['skɪndaɪvɪŋ] *n* buceo *m*, submarinismo *m*

skinhead ['skɪnhed] *n Fam* cabeza *mf* rapada

skinny ['skɪnɪ] *adj* (**skinnier, skinniest**) *Fam* flaco(a)

skin-tight ['skɪntaɪt] *adj (clothing)* muy ajustado(a)

skip¹ [skɪp] **1** *n (jump)* salto *m*, brinco *m*
2 *vi (jump)* saltar, brincar; *(with rope)* saltar a la cuerda *or Esp* comba; *Fig* **to s. over sth** saltarse algo
3 *vt Fig* saltarse

skip² [skɪp] *n Br (for rubbish)* contenedor *m*

skipper ['skɪpə(r)] *n Naut & Sport Fam* capitán(ana) *m,f*

skipping ['skɪpɪŋ] *n* (saltos *mpl* a la) cuerda *f or Esp* comba *f*; *Br* **s. rope** *Esp* comba *f, Am* cuerda *f* de saltar

skirmish ['skɜːmɪʃ] *n* escaramuza *f*

skirt [skɜːt] **1** *n* falda *f, CSur* pollera *f*
2 *vt (town etc)* rodear; *(coast)* bordear; *Fig (problem)* esquivar

skirting ['skɜːtɪŋ] *n Br* **s. (board)** zócalo *m*, rodapié *m*

skit [skɪt] *n* sátira *f*, parodia *f*

skittle ['skɪtəl] *n* (**a**) *(pin)* bolo *m* (**b**) **skittles** *(game)* (juego *m* de los) bolos *mpl*, boliche *m*

skive [skaɪv] *vi Br Fam (avoid work)* zafarse, *Esp* escaquearse

skulk [skʌlk] *vi (hide)* esconderse; *(prowl)* merodear; *(lie in wait)* estar al acecho

skull [skʌl] *n Anat* cráneo *m; Fam* calavera *f*

skunk [skʌŋk] *n* mofeta *f*

sky [skaɪ] *n* cielo *m*; **s. blue** azul *m* celeste

skydiving ['skaɪdaɪvɪŋ] *n* caída *f* libre (en paracaídas)

skylight ['skaɪlaɪt] *n* tragaluz *m*, claraboya *f*

skyline ['skaɪlaɪn] *n (of city)* perfil *m*

skyscraper ['skaɪskreɪpə(r)] *n* rascacielos *m inv*

slab [slæb] *n (of stone)* losa *f*, *(of chocolate)* tableta *f*; *(of cake)* trozo *m*

slack [slæk] **1** *adj* (**a**) *(not taut)* flojo(a) (**b**) *(lax)* descuidado(a); *(lazy)* vago(a) (**c**) *(market)* flojo(a); **business is s.** hay poco negocio
2 *n (in rope)* parte floja

slacken ['slækən] **1** *vt* (**a**) *(rope)* aflojar (**b**) *(speed)* reducir
2 *vi* (**a**) *(rope)* aflojarse; *(wind)* amainar (**b**) *(trade)* aflojar
► slacken off *vi* disminuirse

slacker ['slækə(r)] *n Fam* vago(a) *m,f*, tirado(a) *m,f, Méx* flojo(a) *m,f*

slacks [slæks] *npl* pantalones *mpl* ajustados

slag [slæg] *n* (**a**) *Min* escoria *f*; **s. heap** escorial *m* (**b**) *Br very Fam (woman)* fulana *f, Esp* cualquiera *f, Col, Méx* piruja *f*
► slag off *vt sep Br Fam (criticize)* criticar, *Esp* poner a parir a, *Méx* viborear

slain [sleɪn] **1** *npl* **the s.** los caídos
2 *pp of* **slay**

slam [slæm] **1** *n (of door)* portazo *m*
2 *vt (bang)* cerrar de golpe; **to s. sth down on the table** soltar algo sobre la

mesa de un palmetazo; **to s. the door** dar un portazo; **to s. on the brakes** dar un frenazo

3 *vi (door)* cerrarse de golpe

slander ['slɑːndə(r)] **1** *n* difamación *f*, calumnia *f*

2 *vt* difamar, calumniar

slang [slæŋ] *n* argot *m*

slant [slɑːnt] **1** *n* (**a**) *(of ground)* cuesta *f*, pendiente *f*; *(of roof)* inclinación *f* (**b**) *Fig (point of view)* punto *m* de vista

2 *vt Fig (problem etc)* enfocar subjetivamente

3 *vi* inclinarse

slanting ['slɑːntɪŋ] *adj* inclinado(a)

slap [slæp] **1** *n* palmada *f*; *(in face)* bofetada *f*

2 *adv Fam* **he ran s. into the fence** se dio de lleno contra la valla; **s. in the middle of ...** justo en medio de ...

3 *vt* pegar con la mano; *(hit in face)* dar una bofetada a; **to s. sb on the back** dar a algn una palmada en la espalda

slapdash [slæp'dæʃ] *adj Fam* descuidado(a); *(work)* chapucero(a)

slapstick ['slæpstɪk] *n* bufonadas *fpl*, payasadas *fpl*

slap-up ['slæpʌp] *adj Br Fam* **s. meal** comilona *f*

slash [slæʃ] **1** *n Fam Typ* barra oblicua

2 *vt* (**a**) *(with knife)* acuchillar; *(with sword)* dar un tajo a (**b**) *Fig (prices)* rebajar

slat [slæt] *n* tablilla *f*, listón *m*

slate [sleɪt] **1** *n* pizarra *f*; *Fig* **to wipe the s. clean** hacer borrón y cuenta nueva

2 *vt Fam* vapulear, *Esp* poner por los suelos, *Méx* viborear

slaughter ['slɔːtə(r)] **1** *n (of animals)* matanza *f*; *(of people)* carnicería *f*

2 *vt (animals)* matar; *(people)* matar brutalmente; *(in large numbers)* masacrar

slaughterhouse ['slɔːtəhaʊs] *n* matadero *m*

Slav [slɑːv] *adj & n* eslavo(a) *(m,f)*

slave [sleɪv] **1** *n* esclavo(a) *m,f*; **s. trade** trata *f* de esclavos

2 *vi* **to s. (away)** dar el callo

slavery ['sleɪvərɪ] *n* esclavitud *f*

Slavonic [slə'vɒnɪk] *adj* eslavo(a)

slay [sleɪ] *vt (pt* slew; *pp* slain*)* matar

sleazy ['sliːzɪ] *adj* (**sleazier, sleaziest**) sórdido(a)

sledge [sledʒ], *US* **sled** [sled] **1** *n* trineo *m*

2 *vi* montar en trineo

sledgehammer ['sledʒhæmə(r)] *n* almádena *f*

sleek [sliːk] *adj (hair)* lustroso(a); *(appearance)* impecable

sleep [sliːp] **1** *n* sueño *m*; **to go to s.** dormirse; **my foot has gone to s.** se me ha dormido el pie; *Fig* **to send to s.** (hacer) dormir

2 *vi (pt & pp* slept*)* dormir; *Fam* **to s. like a log** dormir como un lirón

▸ **sleep in** *vi Br (oversleep)* quedarse dormido(a); *(have a lie-in)* quedarse en la cama

▸ **sleep with** *vt insep Fam* **to s. with sb** acostarse con algn

sleeper ['sliːpə(r)] *n* (**a**) *(person)* durmiente *mf*; **to be a heavy s.** tener el sueño pesado (**b**) *Br Rail (on track)* traviesa *f* (**c**) *Rail (coach)* coche-cama *m*; *(berth)* litera *f*

sleeping ['sliːpɪŋ] *adj* **s. bag** saco *m* de dormir, *Col, Méx* sleeping *m* (bag), *RP* bolsa *f* de dormir; **S. Beauty** la Bella durmiente; **s. car** coche-cama *m*; *Br Com* **s. partner** socio(a) comanditario(a); **s. pill** somnífero *m*

sleepless ['sliːplɪs] *adj* **to have a s. night** pasar la noche en blanco

sleepwalker ['sliːpwɔːkə(r)] *n* sonámbulo(a) *m,f*

sleepy ['sliːpɪ] *adj* (**sleepier, sleepiest**) soñoliento(a); **to be** *or* **feel s.** tener sueño

sleet [sliːt] **1** *n* aguanieve *f*

2 *vi* **it's sleeting** cae aguanieve

sleeve [sliːv] *n (of garment)* manga *f*; *(of record)* funda *f*

sleigh [sleɪ] *n* trineo *m*; **s. bell** cascabel *m*

sleight [slaɪt] *n* **s. of hand** juego *m* de manos

slender ['slendə(r)] *adj* (**a**) *(thin)* delgado(a) (**b**) *Fig (hope, chance)* remoto(a)

slept [slept] *pt & pp of* **sleep**

slew [sluː] *pt of* **slay**

slice [slaɪs] **1** *n* (**a**) *(of bread)* rebanada *f*; *(of ham)* loncha *f*; *(of beef etc)* tajada *f*; *(of lemon etc)* rodaja *f*; *(of cake)* trozo *m* (**b**) *(utensil)* pala *f*

2 *vt (food)* cortar a rebanadas/lonchas/rodajas; *(divide)* partir

slick [slɪk] **1** *adj* (**a**) *(programme, show)* logrado(a) (**b**) *(skilful)* hábil, mañoso(a)

2 *n* (**oil**) **s.** marea negra

slide [slaɪd] **1** *n* (**a**) *(act)* resbalón *m* (**b**) *(in prices etc)* baja *f* (**c**) *(in playground)* tobogán *m* (**d**) *Phot* diapositiva *f*; **s. projector** proyector *m* de diapositivas (**e**) *Br (for hair)* pasador *m*

2 *vt (pt & pp* slid [slɪd]*)* deslizar; *(furniture)* correr

3 *vi (on purpose)* deslizarse; *(slip)* resbalar

sliding ['slaɪdɪŋ] adj (door, window) corredizo(a); Fin **s. scale** escala f móvil

slight [slaɪt] 1 adj (a) (small) pequeño(a); **not in the slightest** en absoluto (b) (build) menudo(a); (slim) delgado(a); (frail) delicado(a) (c) (trivial) leve
2 n (affront) desaire m
3 vt (a) (scorn) despreciar (b) (snub) desairar

slightly ['slaɪtlɪ] adv (a little) ligeramente, algo

slim [slɪm] 1 adj (slimmer, slimmest) (a) (person) delgado(a) (b) Fig (resources) escaso(a); (hope, chance) remoto(a)
2 vi adelgazar

slime [slaɪm] n (mud) lodo m, cieno m; (of snail) baba f

slimming ['slɪmɪŋ] 1 adj (diet, pills) para adelgazar; (food) que no engorda
2 n (process) adelgazamiento m

slimy ['slaɪmɪ] adj (slimier, slimiest) (a) (muddy) lodoso(a); (snail) baboso(a) (b) Fig (person) zalamero(a)

sling [slɪŋ] 1 n (a) (catapult) honda f; (child's) tirador m (b) Med cabestrillo m
2 vt (pt & pp slung) (throw) tirar

slingshot ['slɪŋʃɒt] n US tirachinas m inv

slink [slɪŋk] vi (pt & pp slunk) **to s. off** escabullirse

slip [slɪp] 1 n (a) (slide) resbalón m (b) (mistake) error m; (moral) desliz m; **a s. of the tongue** un lapsus linguae (c) (of paper) trocito m
2 vi (a) (slide) resbalar (b) Med dislocarse; **slipped disc** vértebra dislocada (c) (move quickly) ir de prisa (d) (standards etc) deteriorarse
3 vt (a) (slide) dar a escondidas (b) **it slipped my memory** se me fue de la cabeza
▸ **slip away** vi (person) escabullirse
▸ **slip off** vt sep (clothes) quitarse rápidamente
▸ **slip on** vt sep (clothes) ponerse rápidamente
▸ **slip out** vi (a) (leave) salir (b) Fig **the secret slipped out** se le escapó el secreto
▸ **slip up** vi Fam (blunder) cometer un desliz

slipper ['slɪpə(r)] n zapatilla f

slippery ['slɪpərɪ] adj resbaladizo(a)

slip-road ['slɪprəʊd] n Br (onto motorway) carril m de incorporación or aceleración; (out of motorway) carril m de salida or deceleración

slipshod ['slɪpʃɒd] adj descuidado(a); (work) chapucero(a)

slip-up ['slɪpʌp] n Fam (blunder) desliz m

slipway ['slɪpweɪ] n grada f

slit [slɪt] 1 n (opening) hendidura f; (cut) corte m, raja f
2 vt (pt & pp slit) cortar, rajar

slither ['slɪðə(r)] vi deslizarse

sliver ['slɪvə(r)] n (of wood, glass) astilla f; (of ham) loncha f

slob [slɒb] n Fam (untidy person) cerdo(a) m,f, Esp guarro(a) m,f; (lazy person) dejado(a) m,f, tirado(a) m,f

slog [slɒg] Fam 1 n **it was a bit of a s.** fue un aburrimiento or Esp tostonazo (de trabajo); **it's a long s.** (walk) hay un buen trecho or Esp una buena tirada
2 vi (pt & pp slogged) (work hard) trabajar como un(a) negro(a), Esp dar el callo

slogan ['sləʊgən] n (e)slogan m, lema m

slop [slɒp] 1 vi **to s. (over)** derramarse; **to s. about** chapotear
2 vt derramar

slope [sləʊp] 1 n (incline) cuesta f, pendiente f; (up) subida f; (down) bajada f; (of mountain) ladera f; (of roof) vertiente f
2 vi inclinarse; **to s. up/down** subir/bajar en pendiente
▸ **slope off** vi Br Fam escabullirse

sloping ['sləʊpɪŋ] adj inclinado(a)

sloppy ['slɒpɪ] adj (sloppier, sloppiest) Fam descuidado(a); (work) chapucero(a); (appearance) desaliñado(a)

slot [slɒt] 1 n (a) (for coin) ranura f; (opening) rendija f; **s. machine** (for gambling) (máquina f) tragaperras f inv; (vending machine) distribuidor automático (b) Rad & TV espacio m
2 vt (place) meter; (put in) introducir
3 vi **to s. in** or **together** encajar

sloth [sləʊθ] n Fml (laziness) pereza f

slouch [slaʊtʃ] vi andar or sentarse con los hombros caídos

Slovakia [sləʊ'vækɪə] n Eslovaquia

Slovakian [sləʊ'vækɪən] adj & n eslovaco(a) (m,f)

Slovene ['sləʊviːn] 1 adj esloveno(a)
2 n (a) (person) esloveno(a) m,f (b) (language) esloveno m

Slovenia [sləʊ'viːnɪə] n Eslovenia

Slovenian [sləʊ'viːnɪən] adj & n = Slovene

slovenly ['slʌvənlɪ] adj descuidado(a); (appearance) desaliñado(a); (work) chapucero(a)

slow [sləʊ] 1 adj (a) (not fast) lento(a); **in s. motion** a cámara lenta; **to be s. to do sth** tardar or Am demorar en hacer algo (b) *(clock)* atrasado(a) (**c**) *(stupid)* lento(a), torpe

2 *adv* despacio, lentamente

3 *vt (car)* reducir la marcha de; *(progress)* retrasar

4 *vi* **to s. down** *or* **up** ir más despacio; *(in car)* reducir la velocidad

slowly ['sləʊlɪ] *adv* despacio, lentamente

sludge [slʌdʒ] *n (mud)* fango *m*, lodo *m*

slug [slʌg] **1** *n* (**a**) *Zool* babosa *f* (**b**) *US Fam (bullet)* posta *f* (**c**) *Fam (blow)* porrazo *m*

2 *vt Fam (hit)* aporrear

sluggish ['slʌgɪʃ] *adj* (**a**) *(river, engine)* lento(a); *Com* flojo(a) (**b**) *(lazy)* perezoso(a)

sluice [slu:s] *n (waterway)* canal *m*

sluicegate ['slu:sgeɪt] *n* esclusa *f*

slum [slʌm] *n (district)* barrio *m* bajo; *(on outskirts)* arrabal *m*, suburbio *m*; *(house)* tugurio *m*

slumber ['slʌmbə(r)] *Fml* **1** *n (sleep)* sueño *m*

2 *vi* dormir

slump [slʌmp] **1** *n* (**a**) *(drop in sales etc)* bajón *m* (**b**) *(economic depression)* crisis económica

2 *vi* (**a**) *(sales etc)* caer de repente; *(prices)* desplomarse; *(the economy)* hundirse; *Fig (morale)* hundirse (**b**) *(fall)* caer

slung [slʌŋ] *pt & pp of* **sling**

slunk [slʌŋk] *pt & pp of* **slink**

slur [slɜ:(r)] **1** *n* (**a**) *(stigma)* mancha *f*; *(slanderous remark)* calumnia *f*

2 *vt (word)* tragarse

slush [slʌʃ] *n* (**a**) *(melting snow)* nieve medio fundida (**b**) *Fam* sentimentalismo *m* (**c**) *US Fam* **s. fund** fondos *mpl* para corrupción *or Esp* corruptelas

slut [slʌt] *n very Fam Pej* (**a**) *(untidy woman)* marrana *f*, *Esp* guarra *f* (**b**) *(whore)* fulana *f*

sly [slaɪ] *adj* **(slyer, slyest** *or* **slier, sliest)** (**a**) *(cunning)* astuto(a) (**b**) *(secretive)* furtivo(a) (**c**) *(mischievous)* travieso(a) (**d**) *(underhand)* malicioso(a)

smack¹ [smæk] **1** *n* (**a**) *(slap)* bofetada *f* (**b**) *(sharp sound)* ruido sonoro

2 *vt* (**a**) *(slap)* dar una bofetada a (**b**) *(hit)* golpear; *Fig* **to s. one's lips** relamerse

smack² [smæk] *vi Fig* **to s. of** oler a

small [smɔ:l] **1** *adj* (**a**) *(not large)* pequeño(a), *Am* chico(a) (**b**) *(in height)* bajo(a) (**c**) *(scant)* escaso(a); **s. change** cambio *m*, suelto *m*, *Am* vuelto *m* (**d**) *(minor)* insignificante; **s. businessmen** pequeños comerciantes; **s. talk** charloteo *m* (**e**) *(increase)* ligero(a)

2 *n* **s. of the back** región *f* lumbar

smallholder ['smɔ:lhəʊldə(r)] *n Br* minifundista *mf*

small-minded [smɔ:l'maɪndɪd] *adj* mezquino(a)

smallpox ['smɔ:lpɒks] *n* viruela *f*

smarmy ['smɑ:mɪ] *adj* **(smarmier, smarmiest)** *Fam* cobista, zalamero(a)

smart [smɑ:t] **1** *adj* (**a**) *(elegant)* elegante (**b**) *(clever)* listo(a), inteligente; *Fam* **s. alec(k)** sabelotodo *mf*, listillo(a) *m,f*, *Méx*, *RP* vivo(a) *m,f* (**c**) *(quick)* rápido(a); *(pace)* ligero(a)

2 *vi* (**a**) *(sting)* picar, escocer (**b**) *Fig* sufrir

smarten ['smɑ:tən] **1** *vt* **to s. (up)** arreglar

2 *vi* **to s. (oneself) up** arreglarse

smartly ['smɑ:tlɪ] *adv* (**a**) *(elegantly)* elegantemente (**b**) *(quickly)* rápidamente, con rapidez

smash [smæʃ] **1** *n* (**a**) *(loud noise)* estrépito *m*; *(collision)* choque violento (**b**) *(in tennis)* smash *m*

2 *vt* (**a**) *(break)* romper; *(shatter)* hacer pedazos; *(crush)* aplastar (**b**) *(destroy)* destrozar; *(defeat)* aplastar (**c**) *(record)* fulminar

3 *vi (break)* romperse; *(shatter)* hacerse pedazos; *(crash)* estrellarse; *(in tennis)* hacer un mate

▸ **smash up** *vt sep Fam (car)* hacer pedazos; *(place)* destrozar

smashing ['smæʃɪŋ] *adj Br Fam* genial, *Méx* padre, *RP* bárbaro(a)*

smattering ['smætərɪŋ] *n* **he had a s. of French** hablaba un poquito de francés

smear [smɪə(r)] **1** *n* (**a**) *(smudge)* mancha *f*; **s. (test)** citología *f* (**b**) *Fig (defamation)* calumnia *f*

2 *vt* (**a**) *(butter etc)* untar; *(grease)* embadurnar (**b**) *(make dirty)* manchar (**c**) *Fig (defame)* calumniar, difamar

smell [smel] **1** *n* (**a**) *(sense)* olfato *m* (**b**) *(odour)* olor *m*

2 *vt (pt & pp* **smelled** *or* **smelt)** oler; *Fig* olfatear

3 *vi* oler (**of** a); **it smells good/like lavender** huele bien/a lavanda; **he smelt of whisky** olía a whisky

smelly ['smelɪ] *adj* **(smellier, smelliest)** *Fam* maloliente, apestoso(a)

smelt¹ [smelt] *vt (ore)* fundir

smelt² [smelt] *pt & pp of* **smell**

smidgen ['smɪdʒən] *n Fam* pizca *f*

smile [smaɪl] **1** *n* sonrisa *f*

2 *vi* sonreír; **to s. at sb** sonreír a algn; **to s. at sth** reírse de algo

smiling ['smaɪlɪŋ] *adj* sonriente, risueño(a)

smirk [smɜːk] **1** *n (conceited)* sonrisa satisfecha; *(foolish)* sonrisa boba
  2 *vi (conceitedly)* sonreír con satisfacción; *(foolishly)* sonreír bobamente
smith [smɪθ] *n* herrero *m*
smithereens [smɪðəˈriːnz] *npl* **to smash/blow sth to s.** hacer algo añicos
smithy [ˈsmɪðɪ] *n* herrería *f*
smitten [ˈsmɪtən] *adj Fam* **to be s. with sb** estar enamorado(a) de algn
smock [smɒk] *n (blouse)* blusón *m*; *(worn in pregnancy)* blusón de premamá; *(overall)* bata *f*
smog [smɒg] *n* niebla tóxica, smog *m*
smoke [sməʊk] **1** *n* humo *m*; **s. bomb** bomba *f* de humo; **s. screen** cortina *f* de humo
  2 *vi* fumar; *(chimney etc)* echar humo
  3 *vt* **(a)** *(tobacco)* fumar; **to s. a pipe** fumar en pipa **(b)** *(fish, meat)* ahumar
smoked [sməʊkt] *adj* ahumado(a)
smokeless [ˈsməʊklɪs] *adj* **s. fuel** combustible *m* sin humo; **s. zone** zona *f* libre de humos
smoker [ˈsməʊkə(r)] *n* **(a)** *(person)* fumador(a) *m,f* **(b)** *Rail* vagón *m* de fumadores
smoking [ˈsməʊkɪŋ] *n* **no s.** *(sign)* prohibido fumar
smoky [ˈsməʊkɪ] *adj* (**smokier, smokiest**) **(a)** *(chimney)* humeante; *(room)* lleno(a) de humo; *(atmosphere)* cargado(a) (de humo); *(taste)* ahumado(a) **(b)** *(colour)* ahumado(a)
smolder [ˈsməʊldə(r)] *vi US* = smoulder
smooth [smuːð] **1** *adj* **(a)** *(surface)* liso(a); *(skin)* suave; *(road)* llano(a) **(b)** *(beer, wine)* suave **(c)** *(flowing)* fluido(a) **(d)** *(flight)* tranquilo(a); *(transition)* sin problemas **(e)** *Pej (slick)* zalamero(a)
  2 *vt* **(a)** *(hair etc)* alisar **(b)** *(plane down)* limar
▸ **smooth out** *vt sep (creases)* alisar; *Fig (difficulties)* allanar; *(problems)* resolver
▸ **smooth over** *vt sep Fig* **to s. things over** limar asperezas
smoothie [ˈsmuːðɪ] *n* **(a)** *Fam Pej (person)* zalamero(a) *m,f* **(b)** *(drink)* = zumo de fruta con yogur o leche
smoothly [ˈsmuːðlɪ] *adv* sobre ruedas
smoothy [ˈsmuːðɪ] *n* = smoothie
smother [ˈsmʌðə(r)] *vt* **(a)** *(asphyxiate)* asfixiar; *(suffocate)* sofocar **(b)** *Fig (cover)* cubrir (**with** de)
smoulder [ˈsməʊldə(r)] *vi (fire)* arder sin llama; *Fig (passions)* arder; **smouldering hatred** odio *m* latente
smudge [smʌdʒ] **1** *n (stain)* mancha *f*; *(of ink)* borrón *m*

  2 *vt* manchar; *(piece of writing)* emborronar
smug [smʌg] *adj* (**smugger, smuggest**) engreído(a)
smuggle [ˈsmʌgəl] *vt* pasar de contrabando
smuggler [ˈsmʌglə(r)] *n* contrabandista *mf*
smuggling [ˈsmʌglɪŋ] *n* contrabando *m*
smutty [ˈsmʌtɪ] *adj* (**smuttier, smuttiest**) *Fam* obsceno(a); *(joke)* verde; *(book, film etc)* pornográfico(a)
snack [snæk] *n* tentempié *m*, *Esp* piscolabis *m inv*, *Méx* botana *f*; **s. bar** cafetería *f*
snag [snæg] **1** *n* **(difficulty)** pega *f*, problemilla *m*
  2 *vt (clothing)* enganchar
snail [sneɪl] *n* caracol *m*
snake [sneɪk] *n (big)* serpiente *f*; *(small)* culebra *f*
snap [snæp] **1** *n* **(a)** *(noise)* ruido seco; *(of branch, fingers)* chasquido *m* **(b)** *(bite)* mordisco *m* **(c)** *Phot* (foto *f*) instantánea *f*
  2 *adj (sudden)* repentino(a)
  3 *vt* **(a)** *(branch etc)* partir (en dos) **(b)** *(make noise)* **to s. one's fingers** chasquear los dedos; **to s. sth shut** cerrar algo de golpe **(c)** *Phot* sacar una foto de
  4 *vi* **(a)** *(break)* romperse **(b)** *(make noise)* hacer un ruido seco **(c)** *(whip)* chasquear; **to s. shut** cerrarse de golpe **(d)** **to s. at sb** *(dog)* intentar morder a algn; *Fam (person)* hablar en mal tono a algn
▸ **snap off 1** *vt sep (branch etc)* arrancar
  2 *vi (branch etc)* separarse
▸ **snap up** *vt sep Fam* **to s. up a bargain** llevarse una ganga
snappy [ˈsnæpɪ] *adj* (**snappier, snappiest**) *Fam* **(a)** *(quick)* rápido(a); **look s.!, make it s.!** ¡date prisa! **(b)** *(stylish)* elegante **(c)** *(short-tempered)* irritable
snapshot [ˈsnæpʃɒt] *n* (foto *f*) instantánea *f*
snare [sneə(r)] **1** *n* trampa *f*
  2 *vt (animal)* cazar con trampa; *Fig (person)* hacer caer en la trampa
snarl¹ [snɑːl] **1** *n* gruñido *m*
  2 *vi* gruñir
snarl² [snɑːl] **1** *n (in wool)* maraña *f*
  2 *vt* **to s. (up)** *(wool)* enmarañar; *(traffic)* atascar; *(plans)* enredar
snatch [snætʃ] **1** *n* **(a)** *Fam (theft)* robo *m*; **bag s.** tirón *m* **(b)** *(fragment)* fragmentos *mpl*
  2 *vt* **(a)** *(grab)* arrebatar **(b)** *Fam (steal)* robar; *(kidnap)* secuestrar

3 *vi* **to s. at sth** intentar agarrar *or Esp* coger algo

sneak [sni:k] **1** *n Br Fam Esp* chivato(a) *m,f*, *Méx* hocicón(ona) *m,f*, *RP* buchón(ona) *m,f*

2 (*pt & pp* **sneaked** *or US* **snuck**) *vt* **to s. sth out of a place** sacar algo de un lugar a escondidas

3 *vi* (**a**) **to s. off** escabullirse; **to s. in/out** entrar/salir a hurtadillas (**b**) *Fam* **to s. on sb** (*tell tales*) ir con cuentos, *Esp* chivarse

sneaker ['sni:kə(r)] *n US* playera *f*

sneaky ['sni:kɪ] *adj* (**sneakier, sneakiest**) solapado(a)

sneer [snɪə(r)] *vi* **to s. at** hacer un gesto de desprecio a

sneeze [sni:z] **1** *n* estornudo *m*
2 *vi* estornudar

sniff [snɪf] **1** *n* (*by person*) aspiración *f*; (*by dog*) husmeo *m*
2 *vt* (*flower etc*) oler; (*suspiciously*) husmear; (*snuff etc*) aspirar; (*glue*) esnifar
3 *vi* aspirar por la nariz

snigger ['snɪgə(r)] **1** *n* risa disimulada
2 *vi* reír disimuladamente; **to s. at sth** burlarse de algo

snip [snɪp] **1** *n* (**a**) (*cut*) tijeretada *f*, (*small piece*) recorte *m* (**b**) *Br Fam* (*bargain*) *Esp* chollo *m*, *Am* regalo *m*
2 *vt* cortar a tijeretazos

sniper ['snaɪpə(r)] *n* francotirador(a) *m,f*

snippet ['snɪpɪt] *n* (*of cloth, paper*) recorte *m*; (*of conversation*) fragmento *m*

snivel ['snɪvəl] *vi* lloriquear

snivelling ['snɪvəlɪŋ] *adj* llorica

snob [snɒb] *n* (e)snob *mf*

snobbery ['snɒbərɪ] *n* (e)snobismo *m*

snobbish ['snɒbɪʃ] *adj* (e)snob

snooker ['snu:kə(r)] *n* snooker *m*, billar ruso

snoop [snu:p] *vi* fisgonear, *Esp* fisgar

snooty ['snu:tɪ] *adj* (**snootier, snootiest**) *Fam* (e)snob

snooze [snu:z] *Fam* **1** *n Esp* siestecilla *f*, *Am* siestita *f*
2 *vi* echarse una *Esp* siestecilla *or Am* siestita

snore [snɔ:(r)] **1** *n* ronquido *m*
2 *vi* roncar

snoring ['snɔ:rɪŋ] *n* ronquidos *mpl*

snorkel ['snɔ:kəl] *n* (*of swimmer*) tubo *m* de respiración; (*of submarine*) esnórquel *m*

snort [snɔ:t] **1** *n* resoplido *m*
2 *vi* resoplar

snot [snɒt] *n Fam* mocos *mpl*

snout [snaʊt] *n* (*of animal, gun etc*) morro *m*

snow [snəʊ] **1** *n* nieve *f*; **s. shower** nevada *f*
2 *vi* nevar; **it's snowing** está nevando
3 *vt Fig* **to be snowed under with work** estar agobiado(a) de trabajo

snowball ['snəʊbɔ:l] **1** *n* bola *f* de nieve
2 *vi Fig* aumentar rápidamente

snowbound ['snəʊbaʊnd] *adj* aislado(a) por la nieve

snowdrift ['snəʊdrɪft] *n* ventisquero *m*

snowdrop ['snəʊdrɒp] *n* campanilla *f* de invierno

snowfall ['snəʊfɔ:l] *n* nevada *f*

snowflake ['snəʊfleɪk] *n* copo *m* de nieve

snowman ['snəʊmæn] *n* hombre *m* de nieve

snowplough, US snowplow ['snəʊplaʊ] *n* quitanieves *m inv*

snowshoe ['snəʊʃu:] *n* raqueta *f* (de nieve)

snowstorm ['snəʊstɔ:m] *n* nevasca *f*

snowy ['snəʊɪ] *adj* (**snowier, snowiest**) (*mountain*) nevado(a); (*climate*) nevoso(a); (*day*) de nieve

Snr (*abbr* **Senior**) **Neil Smith S.** Neil Smith padre

snub [snʌb] **1** *n* (*of person*) desaire *m*; (*of offer*) rechazo *m*
2 *vt* (*person*) desairar; (*offer*) rechazar

snub-nosed ['snʌbnəʊzd] *adj* de nariz respingona

snuck [snʌk] *US pt & pp of* **sneak**

snuff [snʌf] *n* rapé *m*

snug [snʌg] *adj* (**snugger, snuggest**) (**a**) (*cosy*) cómodo(a) (**b**) (*tightfitting*) ajustado(a)

snuggle ['snʌgəl] *vi* **to s. down in bed** acurrucarse en la cama; **to s. up to sb** arrimarse a algn

snugly ['snʌglɪ] *adv* **to fit s.** (*clothes*) quedar ajustado(a); (*object in box etc*) encajar

so [səʊ] **1** *adv* (**a**) (*to such an extent*) tanto; **he was so tired that ...** estaba tan cansado que ...; **it's so long since ...** hace tanto tiempo que ...; *Fam* **so long!** ¡hasta luego! (**b**) (*degree*) tanto; **a week or so** una semana más o menos; **we loved her so (much)** la queríamos tanto; *Fam* **he's ever so handsome!** ¡es tan guapo! (**c**) (*thus, in this way*) así, de esta manera; **and so on, and so forth** y así sucesivamente; **if so** en este caso; **I think/hope so** creo/ espero que sí; **I told you so** ya te lo dije; **so far** hasta ahora *or* allí; **so they say** eso dicen (**d**) (*also*) **I'm going to Spain – so am I** voy a España – yo también

2 *conj* (**a**) (*expresses result*) así que; **so you like England, do you?** ¿así que te gusta Inglaterra, pues?; *Fam* **so what?** ¿y qué? (**b**) *(expresses purpose)* para que; **I'll put the key here so (that) everyone can see it** pongo la llave aquí para que todos la vean

soak [səʊk] **1** *vt (washing, food)* remojar; *(cotton, wool)* empapar (**in** en)
2 *vi (washing, food)* estar en remojo
▸ **soak in** *vi* penetrar
▸ **soak up** *vt sep* absorber

soaking ['səʊkɪŋ] *adj (object)* empapado(a); *(person)* calado(a) hasta los huesos

so-and-so ['səʊənsəʊ] *n Fam* **Mr S.** Don Fulano (de tal); *Pej* **an old s.** un viejo imbécil

soap [səʊp] **1** *n* (**a**) *(for washing)* jabón *m*; **s. flakes** jabón en escamas; **s. powder** jabón en polvo (**b**) *TV* **s. (opera)** culebrón *m*
2 *vt* enjabonar

soapsuds ['səʊpsʌdz] *npl* espuma *f* (de jabón)

soapy ['səʊpɪ] *adj* (**soapier, soapiest**) jabonoso(a); *(hands)* cubierto(a) de jabón

soar [sɔː(r)] *vi (bird, plane)* remontar el vuelo; *Fig (skyscraper)* elevarse; *(hopes, prices)* aumentar

sob [sɒb] **1** *n* sollozo *m*
2 *vi* sollozar

sober ['səʊbə(r)] *adj (not drunk, moderate)* sobrio(a); *(sensible)* sensato(a); *(serious)* serio(a); *(colour)* discreto(a)
▸ **sober up** *vi* **he sobered up** se le pasó la borrachera

so-called ['səʊkɔːld] *adj* supuesto(a), llamado(a)

soccer ['sɒkə(r)] *n* fútbol *m*

sociable ['səʊʃəbəl] *adj (gregarious)* sociable; *(friendly)* amistoso(a)

social ['səʊʃəl] *adj* social; **s. class** clase *f* social; **s. climber** arribista *mf*; **S. Democratic** socialdemócrata; *US* **s. insurance** seguro *m* social; **s. security** seguridad *f* social; **the s. services** los servicios sociales; **s. work** asistencia *f* social; **s. worker** asistente(a) *m,f* social

socialist ['səʊʃəlɪst] *adj & n* socialista *(mf)*

socialite ['səʊʃəlaɪt] *n* vividor(a) *m,f*

socialize ['səʊʃəlaɪz] **1** *vi* alternar, mezclarse con la gente
2 *vt* socializar

socially ['səʊʃəlɪ] *adv* socialmente

society [sə'saɪətɪ] *n* (**a**) *(in general)* sociedad *f*; **the consumer s.** la sociedad de consumo; **(high) s.** la alta sociedad; **s. column** ecos *mpl* de sociedad (**b**) *(club)* asociación *f* (**c**) *Literary (company)* compañía *f*

sociologist [səʊsɪ'ɒlədʒɪst] *n* sociólogo(a) *m,f*

sociology [səʊsɪ'ɒlədʒɪ] *n* sociología *f*

sock [sɒk] *n* calcetín *m*, *CSur* zoquete *m*

socket ['sɒkɪt] *n* (**a**) *(of eye)* cuenca *f* (**b**) *Elec* enchufe *m*

sod[1] [sɒd] *n Fml (piece of turf)* terrón *m*

sod[2] [sɒd] *Br very Fam* **1** *n* (**a**) *(person)* mamón(ona) *m,f*, *Méx* mamila *mf*, *RP* choto(a) *m,f*; **the lazy s.!** ¡qué tío más vago!; **poor s.!** ¡pobre diablo! (**b**) **I've done s. all today** *(nothing)* hoy no he pegado ni golpe
2 *vt* **s. it!** *Esp* ¡joder!, *Méx* ¡chin!, *RP* ¡la puta!

soda ['səʊdə] *n* (**a**) *Chem* sosa *f*; **baking s.** bicarbonato sódico (**b**) **s. water** soda *f* (**c**) *US (fizzy drink)* gaseosa *f*

sodden ['sɒdən] *adj* empapado(a)

sodium ['səʊdɪəm] *n* sodio *m*

sofa ['səʊfə] *n* sofá *m*; **s. bed** sofá cama *m*

soft [sɒft] *adj* (**a**) *(not hard)* blando(a); **s. drinks** refrescos *mpl*; **s. drugs** drogas blandas; **s. toy** muñeco *m* de peluche (**b**) *(skin, colour, hair, light, music)* suave; *(breeze, steps)* ligero(a) (**c**) *(lenient)* permisivo(a) (**d**) *(voice)* bajo(a)

softball ['sɒftbɔːl] *n* = juego parecido al béisbol jugado en un campo más pequeño y con una pelota más blanda

soften ['sɒfən] **1** *vt (leather, heart)* ablandar; *(skin)* suavizar; *Fig (blow)* amortiguar
2 *vi (leather, heart)* ablandarse; *(skin)* suavizarse

softly ['sɒftlɪ] *adv (gently)* suavemente; *(quietly)* silenciosamente

softness ['sɒftnɪs] *n* (**a**) *(of ground)* blandura *f* (**b**) *(of hair, skin)* suavidad *f* (**c**) *(foolishness)* estupidez *f*

software ['sɒftweə(r)] *n Comput* software *m*; **s. package** paquete *m*

soggy ['sɒgɪ] *adj* (**soggier, soggiest**) empapado(a); *(bread)* pastoso(a)

soil [sɔɪl] **1** *n (earth)* tierra *f*
2 *vt (dirty)* ensuciar; *Fig (reputation)* manchar

soiled [sɔɪld] *adj* sucio(a)

solace ['sɒlɪs] *n Fml* consuelo *m*

solar ['səʊlə(r)] *adj* solar

sold [səʊld] *pt & pp of* **sell**

solder ['sɒldə(r)] **1** *n* soldadura *f*
2 *vt* soldar

soldier ['səʊldʒə(r)] *n* soldado *m*; *(officer)* militar *m*; **toy s.** soldadito *m* de plomo
▸ **soldier on** *vi Fig* continuar contra viento y marea

sole¹ [səʊl] *n (of foot)* planta *f*; *(of shoe, sock)* suela *f*

sole² [səʊl] *n (fish)* lenguado *m*

sole³ [səʊl] *adj (only)* único(a)

solely ['səʊllɪ] *adv* únicamente

solemn ['sɒləm] *adj* solemne

solicit [sə'lɪsɪt] **1** *vt (request)* solicitar **2** *vi (prostitute)* abordar a los clientes

solicitor [sə'lɪsɪtə(r)] *n Br* abogado(a) *m,f*

solid ['sɒlɪd] **1** *adj* (a) *(not liquid)* sólido(a); *(firm)* firme (b) *(not hollow, pure) (metal)* macizo(a) (c) *(of strong material)* resistente **2** *n* sólido *m*

solidarity [sɒlɪ'dærɪtɪ] *n* solidaridad *f*

solidify [sə'lɪdɪfaɪ] *vi* solidificarse

solidly ['sɒlɪdlɪ] *adv* sólidamente; **s. built** *(house etc)* de construcción sólida; **to work s.** trabajar sin descanso

soliloquy [sə'lɪləkwɪ] *n* soliloquio *m*

solitaire [sɒlɪteə(r)] *n* solitario *m*

solitary ['sɒlɪtərɪ] *adj* (a) *(alone)* solitario(a); *(secluded)* apartado(a) (b) *(only)* solo(a)

solitude ['sɒlɪtjuːd] *n* soledad *f*

solo ['səʊləʊ] *n* solo *m*

soloist ['səʊləʊɪst] *n* solista *mf*

solstice ['sɒlstɪs] *n* solsticio *m*

soluble ['sɒljʊbəl] *adj* soluble

solution [sə'luːʃən] *n* solución *f*

solve [sɒlv] *vt* resolver, solucionar

solvent ['sɒlvənt] *adj & n* solvente *(m)*

sombre, *US* **somber** ['sɒmbə(r)] *adj (dark)* sombrío(a); *(gloomy)* lúgubre; *(pessimistic)* pesimista

some [sʌm] **1** *adj* (a) *(with plural nouns)* unos(as), algunos(as); *(several)* varios(as); *(a few)* unos(as) cuantos(as); **there were s. roses** había unas rosas; **s. more peas** más guisantes (b) *(with singular nouns)* algún/alguna; *(a little)* un poco de; **there's s. wine left** queda un poco de vino; **would you like s. coffee?** ¿quiere café? (c) *(certain)* cierto(a), alguno(a); **to s. extent** hasta cierto punto; **s. people say that ...** algunas personas dicen que ... (d) *(unspecified)* algún/alguna; **for s. reason or other** por una razón o por otra; **s. day** algún día (e) *(quite a lot of)* bastante; **s. years ago** hace algunos años **2** *pron* (a) *(people)* algunos(as), unos(as); **s. go by bus and s. by train** unos van en autobús y otros en tren (b) *(objects)* algunos(as); *(a few)* unos(as) cuantos(as); *(a little)* algo, un poco; *(certain ones)* algunos(as) **3** *adv* **s. thirty cars** unos treinta coches

somebody ['sʌmbədɪ] *pron* alguien; **s. else** otro(a)

somehow ['sʌmhaʊ] *adv* (a) *(in some way)* de alguna forma (b) *(for some reason)* por alguna razón

someone ['sʌmwʌn] *pron* = **somebody**

someplace ['sʌmpleɪs] *adv US* = **somewhere**

somersault ['sʌməsɔːlt] **1** *n* voltereta *f*; *(by acrobat etc)* salto *m* mortal; *(by car)* vuelta *f* de campana **2** *vi* dar volteretas; *(acrobat etc)* dar un salto mortal; *(car)* dar una vuelta de campana

something ['sʌmθɪŋ] *pron & n* algo; **s. to eat/drink** algo de comer/beber; **are you drunk or s.?** ¿estás borracho o qué?; **s. must be done** hay que hacer algo; **she has a certain s.** tiene un no sé qué; **is s. the matter?** ¿le pasa algo?; **s. else** otra cosa; **s. of the kind** algo por el estilo

sometime ['sʌmtaɪm] *adv* algún día; **s. last week** un día de la semana pasada; **s. next year** durante el año que viene

sometimes ['sʌmtaɪmz] *adv* a veces, de vez en cuando

somewhat ['sʌmwɒt] *adv Fml* algo, un tanto

somewhere ['sʌmweə(r)] *adv* (a) *(in some place)* en alguna parte; *(to some place)* a alguna parte; **s. else** *(in some other place)* en otra parte; *(to some other place)* a otra parte; **s. or other** no sé dónde (b) **s. in the region of** *(approximately)* más o menos

son [sʌn] *n* hijo *m*; **eldest/youngest s.** hijo mayor/menor

song [sɒŋ] *n* canción *f*; *(of bird)* canto *m*

songwriter ['sɒŋraɪtə(r)] *n* compositor(a) *m,f* (de canciones)

sonic ['sɒnɪk] *adj* sónico(a)

son-in-law ['sʌnɪnlɔː] *n* yerno *m*

sonnet ['sɒnɪt] *n* soneto *m*

sonny ['sʌnɪ] *n Fam* hijo *m*, hijito *m*

soon [suːn] *adv* (a) *(within a short time)* pronto, dentro de poco; *(quickly)* rápidamente; **s. after midnight** poco después de medianoche; **s. afterwards** poco después (b) **as s. as I arrived** en cuanto llegué; **as s. as possible** cuanto antes (c) *(preference)* **I would just as s. stay at home** prefiero quedarme en casa

sooner ['suːnə(r)] *adv* (a) *(earlier)* más temprano; **s. or later** tarde o temprano; **the s. the better** cuanto antes mejor (b) **no s. had he finished than he fainted** *(immediately after)* nada más acabar se desmayó (c) **I would s. do it alone** *(rather)* prefiero hacerlo yo solo

soot [sʊt] n hollín m

soothe [suːð] vt (calm) tranquilizar; (pain) aliviar

sop [sɒp] n (concession) favor m; (bribe) soborno m

▸ **sop up** vt sep empapar

sophisticated [səˈfɪstɪkeɪtɪd] adj sofisticado(a)

sophomore [ˈsɒfəmɔː(r)] n US Univ = estudiante de segundo curso

soporific [sɒpəˈrɪfɪk] adj soporífero(a)

sopping [ˈsɒpɪŋ] adj Fam s. (wet) como una sopa

soppy [ˈsɒpɪ] adj (soppier, soppiest) Fam sensiblero(a), Esp ñoño(a)

soprano [səˈprɑːnəʊ] n soprano mf

sorcerer [ˈsɔːsərə(r)] n brujo m

sorceress [ˈsɔːsərɪs] n bruja f

sordid [ˈsɔːdɪd] adj sórdido(a)

sore [sɔː(r)] **1** adj (a) (painful) dolorido(a); **to have a s. throat** tener dolor de garganta (b) Fam (annoyed) esp Esp enfadado(a), enojado(a) (**about** por); **to feel s. about sth** estar resentido(a) por algo
2 n llaga f

sorely [ˈsɔːlɪ] adv (greatly) enormemente; **she will be s. missed** se la echará muchísimo de menos, Am se la extrañará muchísimo

sorrow [ˈsɒrəʊ] n pena f, dolor m

sorrowful [ˈsɒrəʊfʊl] adj afligido(a)

sorry [ˈsɒrɪ] **1** adj (sorrier, sorriest) (a) **I feel very s. for her** me da mucha pena (b) (pitiful) triste (c) **to be s. (about sth)** sentir (algo); **I'm s. I'm late** siento llegar tarde
2 interj (a) (apology) ¡perdón! (b) Br (for repetition) ¿cómo?

sort [sɔːt] **1** n (a) (kind) clase f, tipo m; (brand) marca f; **it's a s. of teapot** es una especie de tetera (b) **he is a musician of sorts** tiene algo de músico; **there's an office of sorts** hay una especie de despacho (c) **s. of** en cierto modo
2 vt (classify) clasificar

▸ **sort out** vt sep (a) (classify) clasificar; (put in order) ordenar (b) (problem) arreglar, solucionar

sorting [ˈsɔːtɪŋ] n s. office sala f de batalla

SOS [esəʊˈes] n S.O.S. m

so-so [ˈsəʊsəʊ] adv Fam así así, regular

soufflé [ˈsuːfleɪ] n soufflé m, suflé m

sought [sɔːt] pt & pp of seek

soul [səʊl] n (a) (spirit) alma f (b) **he's a good s.** (person) es muy buena persona (c) Mus soul m

soul-destroying [ˈsəʊldɪstrɔɪɪŋ] adj (boring) monótono(a); (demoralizing) desmoralizador(a)

soulful [ˈsəʊlfʊl] adj conmovedor(a)

sound¹ [saʊnd] **1** n (a) (in general) sonido m; (noise) ruido m; **s. effects** efectos sonoros (b) Geog estrecho m
2 vt (bell, trumpet) tocar; **to s. the alarm** dar la señal de alarma
3 vi (a) (trumpet, bell, alarm) sonar (b) (give an impression) parecer; **it sounds interesting** parece interesante (c) Naut & Med sondar

▸ **sound out** vt sep sondear

sound² [saʊnd] **1** adj (a) (healthy) sano(a); (in good condition) en buen estado (b) (safe, dependable) seguro(a); (correct) acertado(a); (logical) lógico(a) (c) (basis etc) sólido(a) (d) (sleep) profundo(a)
2 adv **to be s. asleep** estar profundamente dormido(a)

sounding [ˈsaʊndɪŋ] n Naut sondeo m

soundly [ˈsaʊndlɪ] adv (a) (logically) razonablemente (b) (solidly) sólidamente (c) **to sleep s.** dormir profundamente

soundproof [ˈsaʊndpruːf] adj insonorizado(a)

soundtrack [ˈsaʊndtræk] n banda sonora

soup [suːp] n sopa f; (thin, clear) caldo m; Fam **in the s.** en un apuro; **s. dish** plato hondo; **s. spoon** cuchara sopera

sour [saʊə(r)] adj (a) (fruit, wine) agrio(a); (milk) cortado(a); **to go s.** (milk) cortarse; (wine) agriarse; Fig (situation) empeorar (b) Fig (person) amargado(a)

source [sɔːs] n fuente f; (of infection) foco m

south [saʊθ] **1** n sur m; **in the s. of England** en el sur de Inglaterra; **to the s. of York** al sur de York
2 adj del sur; **S. Africa** Sudáfrica; **S. African** sudafricano(a) (m,f); **S. Korea** Corea del Sur; **S. Pole** Polo m Sur
3 adv (location) al sur; (direction) hacia el sur

southeast [saʊθˈiːst] **1** n sudeste m
2 adj sudeste
3 adv (location) al sudeste; (direction) hacia el sudeste

southeasterly [saʊθˈiːstəlɪ] adj del sudeste

southerly [ˈsʌðəlɪ] adj (direction) hacia el sur; (point) al sur; (wind) del sur

southern [ˈsʌðən] adj del sur, meridional; **S. Europe** Europa del Sur; **the s. hemisphere** el hemisferio sur

southerner [ˈsʌðənə(r)] n sureño(a) m,f

southward [ˈsaʊθwəd] adj & adv hacia el sur

southwest [saυθ'west] **1** *n* suroeste *m*
2 *adj* suroeste
3 *adv (location)* al suroeste; *(direction)* hacia el suroeste

southwesterly [saυθ'westəlı] *adj* del suroeste

souvenir [su:və'nıə(r)] *n* recuerdo *m*, souvenir *m*

sovereign ['sɒvrın] **1** *n* (a) *(monarch)* soberano(a) *m,f* (b) *Hist (coin)* soberano *m*
2 *adj* soberano(a)

sovereignty ['sɒvrəntı] *n* soberanía *f*

soviet ['səυvıət] **1** *n* (a) *(council)* soviet *m* (b) **the Soviets** los soviéticos
2 *adj* soviético(a); *Hist* **S. Union** Unión Soviética

sow[1] [səυ] *vt (pt* **sowed***; pp* **sowed** *or* **sown**) sembrar

sow[2] [saυ] *n Zool* cerda *f*, puerca *f*, *Am* chancha *f*

sown [səυn] *pp of* **sow**

soy [sɔı] *n* soja *f*; **s. sauce** salsa *f* de soja

soya ['sɔıə] *n* soja *f*; **s. bean** semilla *f* de soja

spa [spɑː] *n* balneario *m*

space [speıs] **1** *n* (a) *(room)* espacio *m*, sitio *m*; **in a confined s.** en un espacio reducido (b) *(outer space)* espacio *m*; **s. age** era *f* espacial; **s. shuttle** transbordador *m* espacial; **s. station** estación *f* espacial
2 *vt (also* **s. out)** espaciar, separar

spacecraft ['speıskrɑːft] *n (pl* **spacecraft)** nave *f* espacial

spaced out [speıst'aυt] *adj Fam (dazed)* atontado(a)

spaceman ['speısmən] *n* astronauta *m*, cosmonauta *m*

spaceship ['speısʃıp] *n* nave *f* espacial

spacing ['speısıŋ] *n* **double s.** doble espacio *m*

spacious ['speıʃəs] *adj* espacioso(a), amplio(a)

spade[1] [speıd] *n (for digging)* pala *f*

◦ *Note that the Spanish word* **espada** *is a false friend and is never a translation for the English word* **spade***. In Spanish* **espada** *means "sword".*

spade[2] [speıd] *n Cards* pica *f*

spaghetti [spə'getı] *n* espaguetis *mpl*

Spain [speın] *n* España

spam [spæm] *Comput* **1** *n* correo *m* basura
2 *vi* enviar correo basura

span [spæn] **1** *n (of wing)* envergadura *f*; *(of hand)* palmo *m*; *(of arch)* luz *f*; *(of road)* tramo *m*; *(of time)* lapso *m*; **life s.** vida *f*

2 *vt (river etc)* extenderse sobre, atravesar; *(period of time etc)* abarcar
3 *pt of* **spin**

Spaniard ['spænjəd] *n* español(a) *m,f*

spaniel ['spænjəl] *n* perro *m* de aguas

Spanish ['spænıʃ] **1** *adj* español(a)
2 *n* (a) *(language)* español *m*, castellano *m* (b) *pl* **the S.** los españoles

Spanish-speaking ['spænıʃspiːkıŋ] *adj* de habla española, hispanohablante

spank [spæŋk] *vt* zurrar

spanner ['spænə(r)] *n Br* llave *f* plana *(herramienta)*; *Fam* **to throw a s. in the works** estropear los planes

spar[1] [spɑː(r)] *n Naut* palo *m*, verga *f*

spar[2] [spɑː(r)] *vi* (a) *(boxers)* entrenarse (b) *(argue)* discutir

spare [speə(r)] **1** *vt* (a) *(do without)* prescindir de; **I can't s. the time** no tengo tiempo (b) *(begrudge)* escatimar (c) *(show mercy to)* perdonar (d) **s. me the details** ahórrate los detalles
2 *adj (left over)* sobrante; *(surplus)* de sobra, de más; **s. part** (pieza *f* de) recambio *m*; **s. room** cuarto *m* de los invitados; **s. wheel** rueda *f* de recambio *or RP* auxilio, *Méx* llanta *f* de refacción
3 *n Aut* (pieza *f* de) recambio *m*

sparing ['speərıŋ] *adj* **to be s. with praise** escatimar elogios; **to be s. with words** ser parco(a) en palabras

sparingly ['speərıŋlı] *adv* en poca cantidad

spark [spɑːk] **1** *n* chispa *f*; *Aut* **s. plug** bujía *f*
2 *vi* echar chispas

▶ **spark off** *vt sep* desatar

sparking ['spɑːkıŋ] *adj* **s. plug** bujía *f*

sparkle ['spɑːkəl] **1** *vi (diamond, glass)* centellear, destellar; *(eyes)* brillar
2 *n (of diamond, glass)* centelleo *m*, destello *m*; *(of eyes)* brillo *m*

sparkling ['spɑːklıŋ] *adj* (a) *(diamond, glass)* centelleante; *(eyes)* brillante; **s. wine** vino espumoso (b) *Fig (person, conversation)* vivaz

sparrow ['spærəυ] *n* gorrión *m*

sparse [spɑːs] *adj (thin)* escaso(a); *(scattered)* esparcido(a); *(hair)* ralo(a)

Spartan ['spɑːtən] *adj & n* espartano(a) *(m,f)*

spasm ['spæzəm] *n* (a) *Med* espasmo *m*; *(of coughing)* acceso *m* (b) *(of anger, activity)* arrebato *m*

spasmodic [spæz'mɒdık] *adj* (a) *Med* espasmódico(a) (b) *(irregular)* irregular

spastic ['spæstık] *adj & n Med* espástico(a) *(m,f)*

spat [spæt] *pt & pp of* spit¹
spate [speɪt] *n* (**a**) *(of letters)* avalancha *f*; *(of words)* torrente *m*; *(of accidents)* racha *f* (**b**) *Br (river)* desbordamiento *m*; **to be in full s.** estar crecido(a)
spatter ['spætə(r)] *vt* salpicar (**with** de)
spatula ['spætjʊlə] *n* espátula *f*
spawn [spɔːn] **1** *n* (*of fish, frogs*) huevas *fpl*
  2 *vi* (*fish, frogs*) frezar
  3 *vt Fig Pej* generar
speak [spiːk] **1** *vt* (*pt* spoke; *pp* spoken) (**a**) *(utter)* decir; **to s. the truth** decir la verdad (**b**) *(language)* hablar
  2 *vi* (**a**) *(gen)* hablar, *esp Am* conversar, *Méx* platicar; **roughly speaking** a grandes rasgos; **so to s.** por así decirlo; **speaking of …** a propósito de …; **to s. to sb** hablar *or esp Am* conversar *or Méx* platicar con algn (**b**) *(make a speech)* pronunciar un discurso; *(take the floor)* tomar la palabra (**c**) *Tel* hablar; **speaking!** ¡al habla!; **who's speaking, please?** ¿de parte de quién?
▸ **speak for** *vt insep (person, group)* hablar en nombre de; **it speaks for itself** es evidente
▸ **speak out** *vi* **to s. out against sth** denunciar algo
▸ **speak up** *vi* hablar más fuerte; *Fig* **to s. up for sb** intervenir a favor de algn
speaker ['spiːkə(r)] *n* (**a**) *(in dialogue)* interlocutor(a) *m,f*; *(at conference)* conferenciante *mf*, *Am* conferencista *mf*; *(public)* s. orador(a) *m,f* (**b**) *(of language)* hablante *mf* (**c**) *(loudspeaker)* altavoz *m*, *Am* altoparlante *m*, *Méx* bocina *f*
spear [spɪə(r)] *n* lanza *f*; *(javelin)* jabalina *f*; *(harpoon)* arpón *m*
spearhead ['spɪəhed] *vt* encabezar
spec [spek] *n Fam* **on s.** sin garantías
special ['speʃəl] **1** *adj* especial; *(specific)* específico(a); *(exceptional)* extraordinario(a); **s. delivery** envío *m* urgente; **s. effects** efectos *mpl* especiales
  2 *n Rad & TV* programa *m* especial
specialist ['speʃəlɪst] *n* especialista *mf*
speciality [speʃɪ'ælɪtɪ] *n esp Br* especialidad *f*
specialize ['speʃəlaɪz] *vi* especializarse (**in** en)
specially ['speʃəlɪ] *adv (specifically)* especialmente; *(on purpose)* a propósito
specialty ['speʃəltɪ] *n US* = **speciality**
species ['spiːʃiːz] *n (pl* species*)* especie *f*
specific [spɪ'sɪfɪk] *adj* específico(a); *(definite)* concreto(a); *(precise)* preciso(a); **to be s.** concretar
specifically [spɪ'sɪfɪklɪ] *adv (exactly)* específicamente; *(expressly)* expresamente; *(namely)* en concreto

specifications [spesɪfɪ'keɪʃənz] *npl (of machine)* especificaciones *fpl or* características *fpl* técnicas
specify ['spesɪfaɪ] *vt* especificar, precisar
specimen ['spesɪmɪn] *n (sample)* muestra *f*; *(example)* ejemplar *m*; **urine/tissue s.** espécimen de orina/tejido
speck [spek] *n (of dust)* mota *f*; *(stain)* manchita *f*; *(small trace)* pizca *f*
speckled ['spekəld] *adj* moteado(a)
specs [speks] *npl Fam (spectacles)* gafas *fpl*
spectacle ['spektəkəl] *n* (**a**) *(display)* espectáculo *m* (**b**) **spectacles** *(glasses)* gafas *fpl*, *Am* lentes *mpl*, *Am* anteojos *mpl*
spectacular [spek'tækjʊlə(r)] **1** *adj* espectacular, impresionante
  2 *n Cin & TV* (gran) espectáculo *m*
spectator [spek'teɪtə(r)] *n* espectador(a) *m,f*
spectre, *US* **specter** ['spektə(r)] *n* espectro *m*, fantasma *m*
spectrum ['spektrəm] *n* espectro *m*
speculate ['spekjʊleɪt] *vi* especular
speculation [spekjʊ'leɪʃən] *n* especulación *f*
sped [sped] *pt & pp of* speed
speech [spiːtʃ] *n* (**a**) *(faculty)* habla *f*; *(pronunciation)* pronunciación *f*; **freedom of s.** libertad *f* de expresión (**b**) *(address)* discurso *m*; **to give a s.** pronunciar un discurso (**c**) *Ling* **part of s.** parte *f* de la oración
speechless ['spiːtʃlɪs] *adj* mudo(a), boquiabierto(a)
speed [spiːd] **1** *n* velocidad *f*; *(rapidity)* rapidez *f*; **at top s.** a toda velocidad; **s. limit** límite *m* de velocidad
  2 *vi* (**a**) *(pt & pp* sped*) (go fast)* ir corriendo; *(hurry)* apresurarse; **to s. along** *(car etc)* ir a toda velocidad; **to s. past** pasar volando (**b**) *(pt & pp* speeded*) (exceed speed limit)* conducir con exceso de velocidad
▸ **speed up 1** *vt sep* acelerar; *(person)* meter prisa a
  2 *vi (person)* darse prisa, *Am* apurarse
speedboat ['spiːdbəʊt] *n* lancha rápida
speeding ['spiːdɪŋ] *n* exceso *m* de velocidad
speedometer [spɪ'dɒmɪtə(r)] *n* velocímetro *m*
speedway ['spiːdweɪ] *n* (**a**) *(racing)* carreras *fpl* de motos (**b**) *(track)* pista *f* de carreras
speedy ['spiːdɪ] *adj* (speedier, speediest) veloz, rápido(a)
spell¹ [spel] **1** *vt (pt & pp* spelt *or* spelled*) (letter by letter)* deletrear; *Fig (denote)*

significar; **how do you s. your name?**
¿cómo se escribe su nombre?
2 *vi* **she can't s.** comete faltas de
ortografía
▸ **spell out** *vt sep Fig* explicar con detalle

spell² [spel] *n (magical)* hechizo *m*,
encanto *m*

spell³ [spel] *n* (**a**) *(period)* período *m*;
(short period) rato *m*; *Met* **cold s.** ola *f* de
frío (**b**) *(shift)* turno *m*

spellbound ['spelbaʊnd] *adj* hechizado(a), embelesado(a)

spell-checker ['speltʃekə(r)] *n Comput*
corrector *m* ortográfico

spelling ['spelɪŋ] *n* ortografía *f*

spelt [spelt] *pt & pp of* **spell¹**

spend [spend] *vt (pt & pp spent)* (**a**)
(money) gastar (**on** en) (**b**) *(time)* pasar;
to s. time on sth dedicar tiempo a algo

spending ['spendɪŋ] *n* gastos *mpl*; **s.
money** dinero *m* de bolsillo; **s. power**
poder adquisitivo

spendthrift ['spendθrɪft] *adj & n* derrochador(a) *(m,f)*

spent [spent] **1** *adj* gastado(a)
2 *pt & pp of* **spend**

sperm [spɜːm] *n* esperma *m*; **s. bank** banco
m de esperma; **s. whale** cachalote *m*

spew [spjuː] *vt* **to s. (up)** vomitar

sphere [sfɪə(r)] *n* esfera *f*

spice [spaɪs] **1** *n* (**a**) *(seasoning)* especia *f*
(**b**) *(interest, excitement)* chispa *f*
2 *vt* (**a**) *(food)* sazonar (**b**) **to s. (up)**
(story etc) salpimentar

spick-and-span [spɪkən'spæn] *adj (very
clean)* limpísimo(a); *(well-groomed)* acicalado(a)

spicy ['spaɪsɪ] *adj* (**spicier, spiciest**) (**a**)
Culin sazonado(a); *(hot)* picante (**b**) *Fig
(story etc)* picante

spider ['spaɪdə(r)] *n* araña *f*; *Br* **s.'s** *or US* **s.
web** telaraña *f*

spike¹ [spaɪk] *n (sharp point)* punta *f*;
(metal rod) pincho *m*; *(on railing)* barrote
m; *Sport (on shoes)* clavo *m*

spike² [spaɪk] *n Bot* espiga *f*

spiky ['spaɪkɪ] *adj* (**spikier, spikiest**)
puntiagudo(a); *(hairstyle)* de punta

spill [spɪl] **1** *vt (pt & pp spilled or spilt*
[spɪlt]) derramar
2 *vi (liquid)* derramarse
▸ **spill over** *vi* desbordarse

spin [spɪn] **1** *vt (pt span or spun; pp spun)*
(**a**) *(wheel etc)* hacer girar; *(washing)*
centrifugar (**b**) *(cotton, wool)* hilar;
(spider's web) tejer
2 *vi (wheel etc)* girar; *Av* caer en barrena;
Aut patinar

3 *n* (**a**) *(turn)* vuelta *f*, giro *m* (**b**) *Sport*
efecto *m* (**c**) *Br* **to go for a s.** *(ride)* dar una
vuelta (**d**) *Pol (on news story)* sesgo *m*; **s.
doctor** asesor(a) político(a) *(para dar
buena prensa a un partido o político)*

spinach ['spɪnɪtʃ] *n* espinacas *fpl*

spinal ['spaɪnəl] *adj* espinal, vertebral; **s.
column** columna *f* vertebral; **s. cord**
médula *f* espinal

spindly ['spɪndlɪ] *adj* (**spindlier, spindliest**) *Fam (long-bodied)* larguirucho(a);
(long-legged) zanquilargo(a)

spin-dryer [spɪn'draɪə(r)] *n* secador *m*
centrífugo

spine [spaɪn] *n* (**a**) *Anat* columna *f*
vertebral, espinazo *m*; *(of book)* lomo *m*
(**b**) *Zool* púa *f*; *Bot* espina *f*

spineless ['spaɪnlɪs] *adj Fig (weak)* sin
carácter

spinning ['spɪnɪŋ] *n* (**a**) *(of cotton etc)*
(act) hilado *m*; *(art)* hilandería *f*; **s. wheel**
rueca *f* (**b**) **s. top** peonza *f*

spin-off ['spɪnɒf] *n (by-product)* derivado
m; *Fig* efecto secundario

spinster ['spɪnstə(r)] *n* soltera *f*

spiral ['spaɪərəl] **1** *n* espiral *f*
2 *adj* en espiral; **s. staircase** escalera *f* de
caracol

spire ['spaɪə(r)] *n (of church)* aguja *f*

spirit¹ ['spɪrɪt] *n* (**a**) *(soul)* espíritu *m*,
alma *f*; *(ghost)* fantasma *m* (**b**) *(attitude)*
espíritu *m*; *(mood)* humor *m* (**c**) *(courage)*
valor *m*; *(liveliness)* ánimo *m*; *(vitality)*
vigor *m* (**d**) **spirits** *(mood)* humor *m*; **to
be in good spirits** estar de buen humor

spirit² ['spɪrɪt] *n* (**a**) *Chem* alcohol *m*; **s.
level** nivel *m* de aire (**b**) **spirits** *(alcoholic
drinks)* licores *mpl*

spirited ['spɪrɪtɪd] *adj (person, attempt)*
valiente; *(horse)* fogoso(a); *(attack)*
enérgico(a)

spiritual ['spɪrɪtjʊəl] *adj* espiritual

spit¹ [spɪt] **1** *vt (pt & pp spat)* escupir
2 *vi* escupir; *Fam* **he's the spitting image
of his father** es el vivo retrato de su
padre
3 *n (saliva)* saliva *f*

spit² [spɪt] *n Culin* asador *m*

spite [spaɪt] **1** *n* (**a**) *(ill will)* rencor *m*,
ojeriza *f* (**b**) **in s. of** a pesar de, pese a; **in
s. of the fact that** a pesar de que, pese a
que
2 *vt (annoy)* fastidiar

spiteful ['spaɪtfʊl] *adj (person)* rencoroso(a); *(remark)* malévolo(a); *(tongue)*
viperino(a)

spittle ['spɪtəl] *n* saliva *f*

spittoon [spɪ'tuːn] *n* escupidera *f*

splash [splæʃ] **1** *vt* salpicar
2 *vi* (**a**) **to s. (about)** *(in water)* chapotear (**b**) *(water etc)* salpicar
3 *n* (**a**) *(noise)* chapoteo *m* (**b**) *(spray)* salpicadura *f*; *Fig (of colour)* mancha *f*
▸ **splash out** *vi Fam* tirar la casa por la ventana

spleen [spliːn] *n Anat* bazo *m*

splendid ['splendɪd] *adj* espléndido(a)

splendour, *US* **splendor** ['splendə(r)] *n* esplendor *m*

splint [splɪnt] *n* tablilla *f*

splinter ['splɪntə(r)] **1** *n* *(wood)* astilla *f*; *(bone, stone)* esquirla *f*; *(glass)* fragmento *m*; **s. group** grupo *m* disidente
2 *vi* (**a**) *(wood etc)* astillarse (**b**) *Pol* escindirse

split [splɪt] **1** *n* *(crack)* grieta *f*, hendidura *f*; *(tear)* desgarrón *m*; *Fig (division)* cisma *m*; *Pol* escisión *f*
2 *adj* partido(a); **in a s. second** en una fracción de segundo
3 *vt (pt & pp* **split)** (**a**) *(crack)* agrietar; *(cut)* partir; *(tear)* rajar; *(atom)* desintegrar (**b**) *(divide)* dividir (**c**) *(share out)* repartir (**d**) *Pol* escindir
4 *vi* (**a**) *(crack)* agrietarse; *(into two parts)* partirse; *(garment)* rajarse (**b**) *(divide)* dividirse (**c**) *Pol* escindirse
▸ **split up 1** *vt sep (break up)* partir; *(divide up)* dividir; *(share out)* repartir
2 *vi (couple)* separarse

splutter ['splʌtə(r)] *vi (person)* balbucear; *(candle, fat)* chisporrotear; *(engine)* petardear

spoil [spɔɪl] **1** *vt (pt & pp* **spoiled** *or* **spoilt)** (**a**) *(ruin)* estropear, echar a perder (**b**) *(child)* mimar a; **to be spoilt for choice** tener demasiadas cosas para elegir
2 *vi (food)* estropearse

spoilsport ['spɔɪlspɔːt] *n Fam* aguafiestas *mf inv*

spoilt [spɔɪlt] **1** *adj* (**a**) *(food, merchandise)* estropeado(a) (**b**) *(child)* mimado(a)
2 *pt & pp of* **spoil**

spoke¹ [spəʊk] *pt of* **speak**

spoke² [spəʊk] *n (of wheel)* radio *m*, rayo *m*

spoken ['spəʊkən] *pp of* **speak**

spokesman ['spəʊksmən] *n* portavoz *m*

spokeswoman ['spəʊkswʊmən] *n* portavoz *f*

sponge [spʌndʒ] **1** *n* esponja *f*; *Fig* **to throw in the s.** arrojar la toalla; *Br* **s. cake** bizcocho *m*
2 *vt (wash)* lavar con esponja
3 *vi Fam* vivir de gorra

▸ **sponge off, sponge on** *vt insep* vivir a costa de

sponger ['spʌndʒə(r)] *n Fam* gorrero(a) *m,f, Esp, Méx* gorrón(ona) *m,f, RP* garronero(a) *m,f*

spongy ['spʌndʒɪ] *adj* (**spongier, spongiest**) esponjoso(a)

sponsor ['spɒnsə(r)] **1** *vt* patrocinar; *Fin* avalar; *(support)* respaldar
2 *n* patrocinador(a) *m,f, Fin* avalador(a) *m,f*

sponsorship ['spɒnsəʃɪp] *n* patrocinio *m*; *Fin* aval *m*; *(support)* respaldo *m*

spontaneous [spɒn'teɪnɪəs] *adj* espontáneo(a)

spoof [spuːf] *n Fam* (**a**) *(parody)* burla *f* (**b**) *(hoax)* engaño *m*

spooky ['spuːkɪ] *adj* (**spookier, spookiest**) *Fam* espeluznante

spool [spuːl] *n* bobina *f*, carrete *m*

spoon [spuːn] **1** *n* cuchara *f*; *(small)* cucharita *f*
2 *vt* sacar con cuchara; *(serve)* servir con cuchara

spoon-feed ['spuːnfiːd] *vt (baby)* dar de comer con cuchara a; *Fig (spoil)* mimar

spoonful ['spuːnfʊl] *n* cucharada *f*

sporadic [spə'rædɪk] *adj* esporádico(a)

sport [spɔːt] **1** *n* (**a**) *(activity)* deporte *m* (**b**) *Fam* **he's a good s.** es buena persona; **be a s.!** ¡sé amable!
2 *vt (display)* lucir

sporting ['spɔːtɪŋ] *adj* deportivo(a)

sports [spɔːts] *adj* **s. car** coche *m* or *Am* carro *m* or *CSur* auto *m* deportivo; **s. centre** polideportivo *m*; *Br* **s. jacket** chaqueta *f* or *Am* saco *m* de sport

sportsman ['spɔːtsmən] *n* deportista *m*

sportsmanlike ['spɔːtsmənlaɪk] *adj* deportivo(a)

sportsmanship ['spɔːtsmənʃɪp] *n* deportividad *f*

sportswear ['spɔːtsweə(r)] *n (for sport)* ropa *f* de deporte; *(casual clothes)* ropa (de) sport

sportswoman ['spɔːtswʊmən] *n* deportista *f*

sporty ['spɔːtɪ] *adj* (**sportier, sportiest**) *Fam* deportivo(a)

spot [spɒt] **1** *n* (**a**) *(dot)* punto *m*; *(on fabric)* lunar *m* (**b**) *(stain)* mancha *f* (**c**) *(pimple)* grano *m* (**d**) *(place)* sitio *m*, lugar *m*; **on the s.** allí, presente; **to be in a tight s.** estar en un apuro; **to put sb on the s.** poner a algn en un aprieto (**e**) *Br Fam (small amount) (of rain, wine)* gota *f*; **a s. of bother** una problemilla
2 *vt (notice)* darse cuenta de, notar; *(see)* ver

spotless ['spɒtlɪs] *adj (very clean)* impecable; *Fig (reputation etc)* intachable

spotlight ['spɒtlaɪt] *n* foco *m*; *Aut* faro *m* auxiliar; *Fig* **to be in the s.** ser objeto de la atención pública

spot-on [spɒt'ɒn] *adj Br Fam* exacto(a)

spotted ['spɒtɪd] *adj (with dots)* con puntos; *(fabric)* con lunares; *(speckled)* moteado(a)

spotty ['spɒtɪ] *adj* (**spottier, spottiest**) *Pej* con granos

spouse [spaʊs] *n* cónyuge *mf*

spout [spaʊt] **1** *n (of jug)* pico *m*; *(of teapot)* pitorro *m*
2 *vt Fam (nonsense)* soltar
3 *vi* **to s. out/up** *(liquid)* brotar

sprain [spreɪn] **1** *n* esguince *m*
2 *vt* torcer; **to s. one's ankle** torcerse el tobillo

sprang [spræŋ] *pt of* **spring**²

sprawl [sprɔːl] **1** *vi* (**a**) *(sit, lie)* tumbarse (**b**) *(city, plant)* extenderse
2 *n (of city)* extensión *f*

spray¹ [spreɪ] **1** *n* (**a**) *(of water)* rociada *f*; *(from sea)* espuma *f*; *(from aerosol)* pulverización *f* (**b**) *(aerosol)* spray *m*; *(for plants)* pulverizador *m*; **s. can** aerosol *m*
2 *vt (water)* rociar; *(insecticide, perfume)* pulverizar

spray² [spreɪ] *n (of flowers)* ramita *f*

spread [spred] **1** *n* (**a**) *(of ideas)* difusión *f*; *(of disease, fire)* propagación *f*; *(of terrorism)* generalización *f* (**b**) *(for bread)* **cheese s.** queso *m* para untar (**c**) *Fam (large meal)* banquetazo *m*
2 *vt (pt & pp* **spread***)* (**a**) *(unfold)* desplegar; *(lay out)* extender (**b**) *(butter etc)* untar (**c**) *(news)* difundir; *(rumour)* hacer correr; *(disease, fire)* propagar; *(panic)* sembrar
3 *vi* (**a**) *(stretch out)* extenderse; *(unfold)* desplegarse (**b**) *(news)* difundirse; *(rumour)* correr; *(disease)* propagarse

spread-eagled [spred'iːgəld] *adj* despatarrado(a)

spreadsheet ['spredʃiːt] *n Comput* hoja *f* de cálculo

spree [spriː] *n* juerga *f*; **to go on a s.** ir de juerga

sprig [sprɪg] *n* ramita *f*

sprightly ['spraɪtlɪ] *adj* (**sprightlier, sprightliest**) *(nimble)* ágil; *(energetic)* enérgico(a); *(lively)* animado(a)

spring¹ [sprɪŋ] **1** *n* (**a**) *(season)* primavera *f*
2 *adj* primaveral; **s. onion** cebolleta *f*, *RP* cebolla *f* de verdeo; **s. roll** rollo *m* de primavera, *RP* arrollado *m* de primavera

spring² [sprɪŋ] **1** *n* (**a**) *(of water)* manantial *m*, fuente *f* (**b**) *(of watch etc)* resorte *m*; *(of mattress)* muelle *m*; *Aut* ballesta *f*
2 *vi* (*pt* **sprang**, *pp* **sprung**) (**a**) *(jump)* saltar; **the lid sprang open** la tapa se abrió de golpe (**b**) *(appear)* aparecer (de repente)
3 *vt* (**a**) **to s. a leak** hacer agua (**b**) *Fig (news, surprise)* dar de golpe
▶ **spring up** *vi* aparecer; *(plants)* brotar; *(buildings)* elevarse; *(problems)* surgir

springboard ['sprɪŋbɔːd] *n* trampolín *m*

spring-clean [sprɪŋ'kliːn] *vt* limpiar a fondo

springtime ['sprɪŋtaɪm] *n* primavera *f*

springy ['sprɪŋɪ] *adj* (**springier, springiest**) *(bouncy)* elástico(a); *Fig (step)* saltarín

sprinkle ['sprɪŋkəl] *vt (with water)* rociar (**with** de); *(with sugar)* espolvorear (**with** de)

sprint [sprɪnt] **1** *n* esprint *m*
2 *vi* esprintar

sprinter ['sprɪntə(r)] *n* esprínter *mf*, velocista *mf*

sprout [spraʊt] **1** *vi (bud)* brotar; *Fig* crecer rápidamente
2 *n* (**Brussels**) **sprouts** coles *fpl* or *CSur* repollitos *mpl* de Bruselas

spruce¹ [spruːs] *n Bot* picea *f*

spruce² [spruːs] *adj (neat)* pulcro(a); *(smart)* apuesto(a)
▶ **spruce up** *vt sep* acicalar

sprung [sprʌŋ] *pp of* **spring**

spry [spraɪ] *adj* (**sprier, spriest**) *(nimble)* ágil; *(active)* activo(a); *(lively)* vivaz

spun [spʌn] *pt & pp of* **spin**

spur [spɜː(r)] **1** *n* (**a**) *(for riding)* espuela *f* (**b**) *Fig (stimulus)* acicate *m*; **on the s. of the moment** sin pensarlo
2 *vt* (**a**) *(horse)* espolear (**b**) *Fig* incitar

spurious ['spjʊərɪəs] *adj* falso(a), espurio(a)

spurn [spɜːn] *vt Fml* desdeñar, rechazar

spurt [spɜːt] **1** *n* (**a**) *(of liquid)* chorro *m* (**b**) *Fig (of activity etc)* racha *f*; *(effort)* esfuerzo *m*
2 *vi* (**a**) *(liquid)* chorrear (**b**) *(make an effort)* hacer un último esfuerzo; *(accelerate)* acelerar

spy [spaɪ] **1** *n* espía *mf*
2 *vt Fml (see)* divisar
3 *vi* espiar (**on** a)

spyhole ['spaɪhəʊl] *n* mirilla *f*

spying ['spaɪɪŋ] *n* espionaje *m*

squabble ['skwɒbəl] **1** *n* riña *f*, pelea *f*
2 *vi* reñir, pelearse (**over** or **about** por)

squad [skwɒd] *n Mil* pelotón *m*; *(of police)* brigada *f*; *Sport* equipo *m*; **drugs s.** brigada antidroga

squadron ['skwɒdrən] *n Mil* escuadrón *m*; *Av* escuadrilla *f*; *Naut* escuadra *f*

squalid ['skwɒlɪd] *adj (very dirty)* asqueroso(a); *(poor)* miserable; *(motive)* vil

squall[1] [skwɔːl] *n (wind)* ráfaga *f*

squall[2] [skwɔːl] *vi* chillar, berrear

squalor ['skwɒlə(r)] *n (dirtiness)* mugre *f*, *(poverty)* miseria *f*

squander ['skwɒndə(r)] *vt (money)* derrochar, despilfarrar; *(time)* desperdiciar

square [skweə(r)] **1** *n* (a) *(shape)* cuadro *m*; *(on chessboard, crossword)* casilla *f* (b) *(in town)* plaza *f* (c) *Math* cuadrado *m*
2 *adj* (a) *(in shape)* cuadrado(a) (b) *Math (metre, root)* cuadrado(a) (c) **a s. meal** una buena comida (d) *(old-fashioned)* carroza; *(conservative)* carca
3 *vt* (a) *Math* elevar al cuadrado (b) *(settle)* arreglar
4 *vi (agree)* cuadrar (**with** con)

squarely ['skweəlɪ] *adv (directly)* directamente, de lleno

squash[1] [skwɒʃ] **1** *n Br (drink)* **orange/lemon s.** (bebida *f* a base de) concentrado *m* de naranja/limón
2 *vt (crush)* aplastar
3 *vi* aplastarse

squash[2] [skwɒʃ] *n Sport* squash *m*

squash[3] [skwɒʃ] *n US (vegetable)* calabacín *m*

squat [skwɒt] **1** *adj (person)* rechoncho(a)
2 *vi* (a) *(crouch)* agacharse, sentarse en cuclillas (b) *(in building)* ocupar ilegalmente
3 *n Br (illegally occupied dwelling)* casa *f* ocupada *(ilegalmente)*

squatter ['skwɒtə(r)] *n* ocupante *mf* ilegal, okupa *mf*

squawk [skwɔːk] **1** *n* graznido *m*
2 *vi* graznar

squeak [skwiːk] **1** *n (of mouse)* chillido *m*; *(of hinge, wheel)* chirrido *m*; *(of shoes)* crujido *m*
2 *vi (mouse)* chillar; *(hinge, wheel)* chirriar, rechinar; *(shoes)* crujir

squeaky ['skwiːkɪ] *adj* (**squeakier, squeakiest**) chirriante; *(voice)* chillón(ona); *(shoes)* que crujen

squeal [skwiːl] **1** *n (of animal, person)* chillido *m*
2 *vi* (a) *(animal, person)* chillar (b) *Fam (inform)* chivarse

squeamish ['skwiːmɪʃ] *adj* muy sensible

squeeze [skwiːz] **1** *vt* apretar; *(lemon etc)* exprimir; *(sponge)* estrujar; **to s. paste**

out of a tube sacar pasta de un tubo apretando
2 *vi* **to s. in** apretujarse
3 *n* (a) *(pressure)* estrujón *m*; **a s. of lemon** unas gotas de limón (b) *(of hand)* apretón *m*; *(hug)* abrazo *m*; *(crush)* apiñamiento *m*; **credit s.** reducción *f* de créditos

squelch [skweltʃ] *vi* chapotear

squid [skwɪd] *n* calamar *m*; *(small)* chipirón *m*

squiggle ['skwɪɡəl] *n* garabato *m*

squint [skwɪnt] **1** *n* (a) *(eye defect)* **to have a s.** tener estrabismo (b) *Br (quick look)* ojeada *f*, vistazo *m*
2 *vi* (a) *(have an eye defect)* tener estrabismo (b) **to s. at sth** *(glance)* echar un vistazo a algo; *(with eyes half-closed)* mirar algo con los ojos entrecerrados

squirm [skwɜːm] *vi* retorcerse; *(with embarrassment)* ruborizarse, avergonzarse, *Am* apenarse

squirrel ['skwɪrəl] *n* ardilla *f*

squirt [skwɜːt] **1** *n (of liquid)* chorro *m*
2 *vt* lanzar a chorro
3 *vi* **to s. out** salir a chorros

Sr (abbr **Senior**) **Thomas Smith, Sr** Thomas Smith, padre

Sri Lanka [sriːˈlæŋkə] *n* Sri Lanka

St (a) (abbr **Saint**) S./Sto./Sta. (b) (abbr **Street**) c/

st *Br* (abbr **stone**) = peso que equivale a 6,348 kg

stab [stæb] **1** *n (with knife)* puñalada *f*; *(of pain)* punzada *f*
2 *vt* apuñalar

stabbing ['stæbɪŋ] *adj (pain)* punzante

stability [stəˈbɪlɪtɪ] *n* estabilidad *f*

stabilize ['steɪbɪlaɪz] **1** *vt* estabilizar
2 *vi* estabilizarse

stable[1] ['steɪbəl] *adj* estable

stable[2] ['steɪbəl] *n* cuadra *f*, caballeriza *f*

stack [stæk] **1** *n (pile)* montón *m*; *Fam* **he's got stacks of money** está forrado
2 *vt (pile up)* amontonar, apilar; *Fig* **the odds are stacked against us** todo está en contra nuestra

stadium ['steɪdɪəm] *n* estadio *m*

staff [stɑːf] **1** *n* (a) *(personnel)* personal *m*; *Mil* estado *m* mayor; **s. meeting** claustro *m*; *Br* **s. nurse** enfermera cualificada (b) *(stick)* bastón *m*; *(of shepherd)* cayado *m*
2 *vt* proveer de personal

staffroom ['stɑːfruːm] *n* sala *f* de profesores

stag [stæɡ] *n* ciervo *m*, venado *m*; *Fam* **s. party** despedida *f* de soltero

stage [steɪdʒ] **1** n (**a**) (*platform*) plataforma f (**b**) (*in theatre*) escenario m; **s. door** entrada f de artistas; **s. fright** miedo escénico; **s. manager** director(a) m,f de escena (**c**) (*phase*) (*of development, journey, rocket*) etapa f; (*of road, pipeline*) tramo m; **at this s. of the negotiations** a estas alturas de las negociaciones; **in stages** por etapas
2 vt (**a**) (*play*) poner en escena, montar (**b**) (*arrange*) organizar; (*carry out*) llevar a cabo

stagecoach ['steɪdʒkəʊtʃ] n diligencia f

stagger ['stæɡə(r)] **1** vi tambalearse
2 vt (**a**) (*amaze*) asombrar (**b**) (*hours, work*) escalonar

staggering ['stæɡərɪŋ] adj asombroso(a)

stagnant ['stæɡnənt] adj estancado(a)

stagnate [stæɡ'neɪt] vi estancarse

staid [steɪd] adj (*person*) conservador(a); (*manner, clothes*) serio(a), formal

stain [steɪn] **1** n (**a**) (*mark*) mancha f; **s. remover** quitamanchas m inv (**b**) (*dye*) tinte m
2 vt (**a**) (*mark*) manchar (**b**) (*dye*) teñir
3 vi mancharse

stained [steɪnd] adj **s. glass window** vidriera f de colores

stainless ['steɪnlɪs] adj (*steel*) inoxidable

stair [steə(r)] n escalón m, peldaño m; **stairs** (*flight*) escalera f

staircase ['steəkeɪs] n escalera f

stake¹ [steɪk] **1** n (*stick*) estaca f; (*for plant*) rodrigón m; (*post*) poste m
2 vt **to s. (out)** cercar con estacas

stake² [steɪk] **1** n (**a**) (*bet*) apuesta f; **the issue at s.** el tema en cuestión; **to be at s.** (*at risk*) estar en juego (**b**) (*investment*) interés m
2 vt (*bet*) apostar; (*invest*) invertir; **to s. a claim to sth** reivindicar algo

stale [steɪl] adj (*food*) pasado(a); (*bread*) duro(a)

stalemate ['steɪlmeɪt] n (*in chess*) tablas fpl; Fig **to reach s.** llegar a un punto muerto

stalk¹ [stɔːk] n (*of plant*) tallo m; (*of fruit*) rabo m

stalk² [stɔːk] **1** vt (*of hunter*) cazar al acecho; (*of animal*) acechar
2 vi **he stalked out of the room** salió esp Esp enfadado or esp Am enojado de la habitación

stalker ['stɔːkə(r)] n = persona que sigue o vigila obsesivamente a otra

stall [stɔːl] **1** n (**a**) (*in market*) puesto m; (*at fair*) caseta f (**b**) (*stable*) establo m; (*stable compartment*) casilla f de establo (**c**) Br Cin & Th **the stalls** el patio de butacas

2 vt (*hold off*) retener
3 vi (**a**) Aut pararse, Esp calarse; Av perder velocidad (**b**) (*delay*) **to s. (for time)** intentar ganar tiempo

stallion ['stæljən] n semental m

stalwart ['stɔːlwət] n incondicional mf

stamina ['stæmɪnə] n resistencia f

stammer ['stæmə(r)] **1** n tartamudeo m
2 vi tartamudear

stamp [stæmp] **1** n (**a**) (*postage stamp*) sello m, Am estampilla f, CAm, Méx timbre m; **s. album** álbum m de sellos; **s. collector** filatelista mf; **s.** Br **duty** or US **tax** póliza f, = impuesto de transmisiones patrimoniales (**b**) (*rubber stamp*) tampón m; (*for metals*) cuño m (**c**) (*with foot*) patada f
2 vt (**a**) (*with postage stamp*) poner el sello a; Br **stamped addressed envelope**, US **self-addressed stamped envelope** sobre franqueado con la dirección del remitente (**b**) (*with rubber stamp*) sellar (**c**) **to s. one's feet** patear; (*in dancing*) zapatear
3 vi patear

⎰ Note that the Spanish word **estampa** is a false friend and is never a translation for the English word **stamp**. In Spanish **estampa** means "print, image".

▸ **stamp out** vt sep Fig (*racism etc*) acabar con; (*rebellion*) sofocar

stampede [stæm'piːd] **1** n estampida f; Fig (*rush*) desbandada f
2 vi desbandarse; Fig (*rush*) precipitarse

stance [stæns] n postura f

stand [stænd] **1** n (**a**) (*position*) posición f, postura f; **to make a s.** resistir (**b**) (*of lamp, sculpture*) pie m (**c**) (*market stall*) puesto m; (*at fair*) caseta f; (*at exhibition*) stand m (**d**) (*platform*) plataforma f; (*in stadium*) gradas fpl, Esp graderío m; US (*witness box*) estrado m
2 vt (pt & pp **stood**) (**a**) (*place*) poner, colocar (**b**) (*tolerate*) aguantar, soportar
3 vi (**a**) (*be upright*) estar de pie or parado(a); (*get up*) levantarse; (*remain upright*) quedarse de pie or Am parado(a); **s. still!** ¡estáte quieto(a)! (**b**) (*be situated*) estar, encontrarse (**c**) (*remain valid*) seguir vigente (**d**) **as things s.** tal como están las cosas (**e**) Pol presentarse

▸ **stand back** vi (*allow sb to pass*) abrir paso

▸ **stand by 1** vi (**a**) (*do nothing*) quedarse sin hacer nada (**b**) (*be ready*) estar listo(a)
2 vt insep (*person*) apoyar a; (*promise*) cumplir con; (*decision*) atenerse a

▸ **stand down** vi Fig retirarse

▸ **stand for** vt insep (**a**) (*mean*) significar (**b**) (*represent*) representar (**c**) (*tolerate*) aguantar

▸ **stand in** *vi* sustituir

▸ **stand in for** *vt insep* sustituir

▸ **stand out** *vi (mountain etc)* destacarse (**against** contra); *Fig (person)* destacar

▸ **stand up** *vi (get up)* ponerse de pie, *Am* pararse; *(be standing)* estar de pie; *Fig* **it will s. up to wear and tear** es muy resistente; *Fig* **to s. up for sb** defender a algn; *Fig* **to s. up to sb** hacer frente a algn

standard ['stændəd] **1** *n* (a) *(level)* nivel *m*; **s. of living** nivel de vida (b) *(criterion)* criterio *m* (c) *(norm)* norma *f*, estándar *m*
2 *adj* normal, estándar; **s. lamp** lámpara *f* de pie

standardize ['stændədaɪz] *vt* normalizar

standby ['stændbaɪ] *n* (a) *(thing)* recurso *m* (b) *(person)* suplente *mf*; **to be on s.** *Mil* estar de retén; *Av* estar en la lista de espera; **s. ticket** billete *m* sin reserva

stand-in ['stændɪn] *n* suplente *mf*; *Cin* doble *mf*

standing ['stændɪŋ] **1** *adj* (a) *(not sitting)* de pie; *(upright)* recto(a); **to give sb a s. ovation** ovacionar a algn de pie; **there was s. room only** no quedaban asientos (b) *(committee, invitation)* permanente; *Br* **s. order** pago fijo
2 *n* (a) *(social position)* rango *m* (b) *(duration)* duración *f*; *(in job)* antigüedad *f*

stand-offish [stænd'ɒfɪʃ] *adj Fam* distante

standpoint ['stændpɔɪnt] *n* punto *m* de vista

standstill ['stændstɪl] *n* **at a s.** *(car, traffic)* parado(a); *(industry)* paralizado(a); **to come to a s.** *(car, traffic)* pararse; *(industry)* paralizarse

stand-up ['stændʌp] *adj* **s. comic** o **comedian** = humorista que basa su actuación en contar chistes al público solo desde el escenario

stank [stæŋk] *pt of* **stink**

staple[1] ['steɪpəl] **1** *n (fastener)* grapa *f*, *Chile* corchete *m*, *RP* ganchito *m*
2 *vt* grapar

staple[2] ['steɪpəl] **1** *adj (food)* básico(a); *(product)* de primera necesidad
2 *n (food)* alimento básico

stapler ['steɪplə(r)] *n* grapadora *f*, *Am* engrapadora *f*, *Chile* corchetera *f*, *RP* abrochadora *f*

star [stɑː(r)] **1** *n* estrella *f*
2 *adj* estelar
3 *vt Cin* tener como protagonista a
4 *vi Cin* **to s. in a movie** protagonizar una película

starboard ['stɑːbəd] *n* estribor *m*

starch [stɑːtʃ] **1** *n* almidón *m*
2 *vt* almidonar

stardom ['stɑːdəm] *n* estrellato *m*

stare [steə(r)] **1** *n* mirada fija
2 *vi* mirar fijamente

starfish ['stɑːfɪʃ] *n* estrella *f* de mar

stark [stɑːk] *adj (landscape)* desolado(a); *(décor)* austero(a); **the s. truth** la dura realidad; **s. poverty** la miseria

stark-naked ['stɑːkneɪkɪd] *adj Fam* en cueros

starling ['stɑːlɪŋ] *n* estornino *m*

starry ['stɑːrɪ] *adj* (**starrier, starriest**) estrellado(a)

starry-eyed [stɑːrɪ'aɪd] *adj (idealistic)* idealista; *(in love)* enamorado(a)

start [stɑːt] **1** *n* (a) *(beginning)* principio *m*, comienzo *m*; *(of race)* salida *f*; **for a s.** para empezar; **from the s.** desde el principio; **to make a fresh s.** volver a empezar (b) *(advantage)* ventaja *f* (c) *(jump)* sobresalto *m*
2 *vt* (a) *(begin)* empezar, comenzar; **to s. doing sth** empezar a hacer algo (b) *(cause)* causar, provocar (c) *(found)* fundar; **to s. a business** montar un negocio (d) *(set in motion)* arrancar
3 *vi* (a) *(begin)* empezar, comenzar; *(engine)* arrancar; **starting from Monday** a partir del lunes (b) *(take fright)* asustarse, sobresaltarse

▸ **start off** *vi* (a) *(begin)* empezar, comenzar; **to s. off by/with** empezar por/con (b) *(leave)* salir, ponerse en camino

▸ **start up 1** *vt sep (engine)* arrancar
2 *vi* empezar; *(car)* arrancar

starter ['stɑːtə(r)] *n* (a) *Sport (official)* juez *mf* de salida; *(competitor)* competidor(a) *m,f* (b) *Aut* motor *m* de arranque (c) *Culin* entrada *f*

starting ['stɑːtɪŋ] *n* **s. block** taco *m* de salida; **s. point** punto *m* de partida; **s. post** línea *f* de salida

startle ['stɑːtəl] *vt* asustar

startling ['stɑːtlɪŋ] *adj* (a) *(frightening)* alarmante (b) *(news etc)* asombroso(a); *(coincidence)* extraordinario(a)

starvation [stɑː'veɪʃən] *n* hambre *f*

starve [stɑːv] **1** *vt* privar de comida; *Fig* **he was starved of affection** fue privado de cariño
2 *vi* pasar hambre; **to s. to death** morirse de hambre

starving ['stɑːvɪŋ] *adj* hambriento(a); *Fam* **I'm s.!** ¡estoy muerto(a) de hambre!

state [steɪt] **1** *n* (a) *(condition, situation)* estado *m*; **s. of emergency** estado de emergencia; **s. of mind** estado de ánimo;

to be in no fit s. to do sth no estar en condiciones de hacer algo (**b**) *(country, administrative region)* estado *m*; *Fam* **the States** los Estados Unidos; *US* **s. highway** ≃ carretera *f* nacional; *US* **S. Department** Departamento *m* de Estado, = Ministerio de Asuntos *or Am* Relaciones Exteriores estadounidense

2 *adj* (**a**) *Pol* estatal; **s. education** enseñanza pública; **s. ownership** propiedad *f* del Estado (**b**) *(ceremonial)* de gala; **s. visit** visita *f* oficial

3 *vt* declarar, afirmar; *(case)* exponer; *(problem)* plantear

stated ['steɪtɪd] *adj* indicado(a)

stately ['steɪtlɪ] *adj* (**statelier, stateliest**) majestuoso(a); **s. home** casa solariega

statement ['steɪtmənt] *n* (**a**) *(of opinion)* declaración *f*; **official s.** comunicado *m* oficial; *Jur* **to make a s.** prestar declaración (**b**) *Fin* estado *m* de cuenta; **monthly s.** balance *m* mensual

statesman ['steɪtsmən] *n* estadista *m*

static ['stætɪk] **1** *adj* estático(a)

2 *n Rad* ruido *m*

station ['steɪʃən] **1** *n* (**a**) *(for trains, buses)* estación *f*; *US* **s. wagon** *(car)* ranchera *f*, *Esp* coche *m* modelo familiar (**b**) *(position)* puesto *m* (**c**) *(social standing)* rango *m*

2 *vt (place)* colocar; *Mil* apostar

stationary ['steɪʃənərɪ] *adj (not moving)* inmóvil; *(unchanging)* estacionario(a)

stationer ['steɪʃənə(r)] *n* papelero(a) *m,f*; **s.'s (shop)** papelería *f*

stationery ['steɪʃənərɪ] *n (paper)* papel *m* de escribir; *(pens, ink etc)* artículos *mpl* de escritorio

stationmaster ['steɪʃənmɑːstə(r)] *n* jefe *m* de estación

statistic [stə'tɪstɪk] *n* estadística *f*

statistical [stə'tɪstɪkəl] *adj* estadístico(a)

statistics [stə'tɪstɪks] **1** *n sing (science)* estadística *f*

2 *npl (data)* estadísticas *fpl*

statue ['stætjuː] *n* estatua *f*

stature ['stætʃə(r)] *n (physical build)* estatura *f*; *(reputation)* talla *f*, estatura *f*

status ['steɪtəs] *n* estado *m*; **social s.** estatus *m*; **s. symbol** signo *m* de prestigio; **s. quo** status quo *m*

statute ['stætjuːt] *n* estatuto *m*

statutory ['stætjʊtərɪ] *adj* reglamentario(a); *(offence)* contemplado(a) por la ley; *(right)* legal; *(holiday)* oficial

staunch [stɔːntʃ] *adj* incondicional, acérrimo

stave [steɪv] *n Mus* pentagrama *m*

▸ **stave off** *vt sep (repel)* rechazar; *(avoid)* evitar; *(delay)* aplazar

stay[1] [steɪ] **1** *n Esp, Méx* estancia *f*, *Am* estadía *f*

2 *vi* (**a**) *(remain)* quedarse, permanecer (**b**) *(reside temporarily)* alojarse; **she's staying with us for a few days** ha venido a pasar unos días con nosotros

3 *vt Fig* **to s. the course** aguantar hasta el final; **staying power** resistencia *f*

▸ **stay in** *vi* quedarse en casa

▸ **stay on** *vi* quedarse

▸ **stay out** *vi* **to s. out all night** no volver a casa en toda la noche

▸ **stay up** *vi* no acostarse

stay[2] [steɪ] *n (rope)* estay *m*, viento *m*

stead [sted] *n* in sb's s. en lugar de algn; **to stand sb in good s.** resultar muy útil a algn

steadfast ['stedfɑst, 'stedfɑːst] *adj* firme

steadily ['stedɪlɪ] *adv (improve)* constantemente; *(walk)* con paso seguro; *(gaze)* fijamente; *(rain, work)* sin parar

steady ['stedɪ] **1** *adj* (**steadier, steadiest**) firme, seguro(a); *(gaze)* fijo(a); *(prices)* estable; *(demand, speed)* constante; *(pace)* regular; *(worker)* aplicado(a); **s. job** empleo fijo

2 *vt (table etc)* estabilizar; *(nerves)* calmar

3 *vi (market)* estabilizarse

steak [steɪk] *n* filete *m*, bistec *m*, *RP* bife *m*

steal [stiːl] (*pt* **stole**; *pp* **stolen**) **1** *vt* robar; **to s. a glance at sth** echar una mirada furtiva a algo; **to s. the show** llevarse todos los aplausos

2 *vi* (**a**) *(rob)* robar (**b**) *(move quietly)* moverse con sigilo; **to s. away** escabullirse

stealth [stelθ] *n* sigilo *m*

stealthily ['stelθɪlɪ] *adv* a hurtadillas

stealthy ['stelθɪ] *adj* (**stealthier, stealthiest**) sigiloso(a), furtivo(a)

steam [stiːm] **1** *n* vapor *m*; *Fam* **to let off s.** desahogarse; **s. engine** máquina *f* de vapor

2 *vt Culin* cocer al vapor

3 *vi (give off steam)* echar vapor; *(bowl of soup etc)* humear

▸ **steam up** *vi (window etc)* empañarse

steamer ['stiːmə(r)] *n Naut* vapor *m*

steamroller ['stiːmrəʊlə(r)] *n* apisonadora *f*

steamship ['stiːmʃɪp] *n* vapor *m*

steamy ['stiːmɪ] *adj* (**steamier, steamiest**) lleno(a) de vapor

steel [stiːl] **1** *n* acero *m*; **s. industry** industria *f* siderúrgica

2 *vt Fig* **to s. oneself to do sth** armarse de valor para hacer algo

steelworks ['sti:lwɜ:ks] *npl* acería *f*

steep¹ [sti:p] *adj (hill etc)* empinado(a); *Fig (price, increase)* excesivo(a)

steep² [sti:p] *vt (washing)* remojar; *(food)* poner en remojo

steeple ['sti:pəl] *n* aguja *f*

steeplechase ['sti:pəltʃeɪs] *n* carrera *f* de obstáculos

steer [stɪə(r)] **1** *vt* dirigir; *(car)* conducir, *Am* manejar; *(ship)* gobernar
2 *vi (car)* conducir, *Am* manejar; *Fig* **to s. clear of sth** evitar algo

steering ['stɪərɪŋ] *n* dirección *f*; **assisted s.** dirección asistida; **s. wheel** volante *m*, *Andes* timón *m*

stem [stem] **1** *n* **(a)** *(of plant)* tallo *m*; *(of glass)* pie *m*; *(of pipe)* tubo *m* **(b)** *(of word)* raíz *f*
2 *vi* **to s. from** derivarse de
3 *vt (blood)* restañar; *(flood, attack)* contener

stench [stentʃ] *n* hedor *m*

stencil ['stensəl] *n* **(a)** *(for artwork etc)* plantilla *f* **(b)** *(for typing)* cliché *m*

step [step] **1** *n* **(a)** *(movement, sound)* paso *m*; **s. by s.** poco a poco **(b)** *(measure)* medida *f*; **a s. in the right direction** un paso acertado **(c)** *(stair)* peldaño *m*, escalón *m* **(d)** **steps** *(flight)* escalera *f*
2 *vi* dar un paso; **s. this way, please** haga el favor de pasar por aquí; **to s. aside** apartarse

▸ **step down** *vi* dimitir

▸ **step forward** *vi (volunteer)* ofrecerse

▸ **step in** *vi* intervenir

▸ **step up** *vt sep* aumentar

stepbrother ['stepbrʌðə(r)] *n* hermanastro *m*

stepchild ['steptʃaɪld] *n* hijastro(a) *m,f*

stepdaughter ['stepdɔ:tə(r)] *n* hijastra *f*

stepfather ['stepfɑ:ðə(r)] *n* padrastro *m*

stepladder ['steplædə(r)] *n* escalera *f* de tijera

stepmother ['stepmʌðə(r)] *n* madrastra *f*

stepping-stone ['stepɪŋstəʊn] *n* pasadera *f*; *Fig* trampolín *m*

stepsister ['stepsɪstə(r)] *n* hermanastra *f*

stepson ['stepsʌn] *n* hijastro *m*

stereo ['sterɪəʊ] **1** *n* estéreo *m*
2 *adj* estéreo, estereofónico(a)

stereotype ['sterɪətaɪp] *n* estereotipo *m*

sterile ['steraɪl] *adj (barren)* estéril

sterilize ['sterɪlaɪz] *vt* esterilizar

sterling ['stɜ:lɪŋ] **1** *n* libras *fpl* esterlinas; **s. silver** plata *f* de ley; **the pound s.** la libra esterlina
2 *adj (person, quality)* excelente

stern¹ [stɜ:n] *adj (severe)* severo(a)

stern² [stɜ:n] *n Naut* popa *f*

steroid ['sterɔɪd] *n* esteroide *m*

stethoscope ['steθəskəʊp] *n* estetoscopio *m*

stew [stju:] **1** *n* estofado *m*, cocido *m*
2 *vt (meat)* guisar, estofar; *(fruit)* cocer

steward ['stjuəd] *n (on estate)* administrador *m*; *(on ship)* camarero *m*; *(on plane)* auxiliar *m* de vuelo

stewardess ['stjuədɪs] *n (on ship)* camarera *f*; *(on plane)* auxiliar *f* de vuelo, azafata *f*, *Am* aeromoza *f*

stick¹ [stɪk] *n* **(a)** *(of wood)* palo *m*; *(walking stick)* bastón *m*; *(of dynamite)* cartucho *m*; *Br Fam* **to live in the sticks** vivir en el quinto infierno *or Esp* pino **(b)** *Fam* **to give sb s.** dar caña a algn

stick² [stɪk] **1** *vt (pt & pp* **stuck)** **(a)** *(push)* meter; *(knife)* clavar; **he stuck his head out of the window** asomó la cabeza por la ventana **(b)** *Fam (put)* meter **(c)** *(with glue etc)* pegar **(d)** *Fam (tolerate)* soportar, aguantar
2 *vi* **(a)** *(become attached)* pegarse **(b)** *(window, drawer)* atrancarse; *(machine part)* encasquillarse

▸ **stick at** *vt insep* perseverar en

▸ **stick by** *vt insep (friend)* ser fiel a; *(promise)* cumplir con

▸ **stick out 1** *vi (project)* sobresalir; *(be noticeable)* resaltar
2 *vt sep (tongue)* sacar; *Fig* **to s. one's neck out** jugarse el tipo

▸ **stick to** *vt insep (principles)* atenerse a

▸ **stick up 1** *vi (project)* sobresalir; *(hair)* ponerse de punta
2 *vt sep* **(a)** *(poster)* fijar **(b)** *(hand etc)* levantar

▸ **stick up for** *vt insep* defender

sticker ['stɪkə(r)] *n (label)* etiqueta adhesiva; *(with slogan)* pegatina *f*

sticking-plaster ['stɪkɪŋ'plɑ:stə(r)] *n Br (to cover wound)* tirita® *f*, *Am* curita *m or f*; *(to keep bandage in place)* esparadrapo *m*

stickler ['stɪklə(r)] *n* meticuloso(a) *m,f*; **to be a s. for detail** ser muy detallista

stick-up ['stɪkʌp] *n US Fam* atraco *m*, asalto *m*

sticky ['stɪkɪ] *adj* **(stickier, stickiest)** pegajoso(a); *(label)* engomado(a); *(weather)* bochornoso(a); *Fam (situation)* difícil

stiff [stɪf] **1** *adj* **(a)** *(rigid)* rígido(a), tieso(a); *(collar, lock)* duro(a); *(joint)* entumecido(a); *(machine part)* atascado(a); **to have a s. neck** tener tortícolis

(**b**) *Fig (test)* difícil; *(punishment)* severo(a); *(price)* excesivo(a); *(drink)* fuerte; *(person) (unnatural)* estirado(a)
  2 *n Fam (corpse)* fiambre *m*

stiffen ['stɪfən] **1** *vt (fabric)* reforzar; *(collar)* almidonar; *Fig (resistance)* fortalecer
  2 *vi (person)* ponerse tieso(a); *(joints)* entumecerse; *Fig (resistance)* fortalecerse

stiffness ['stɪfnɪs] *n* rigidez *f*

stifle ['staɪfəl] **1** *vt* sofocar; *(yawn)* reprimir
  2 *vi* ahogarse, sofocarse

stifling ['staɪflɪŋ] *adj* sofocante, agobiante

stigma ['stɪgmə] *n* estigma *m*

stile [staɪl] *n* = escalones para pasar por encima de una valla

stiletto [stɪ'letəʊ] *n* zapato *m* de tacón *or Am* taco de aguja

still [stɪl] **1** *adv* (**a**) *(up to this time)* todavía, aún, *Am* siempre (**b**) *(with comp adj & adv) (even)* aún; **s. colder** aún más frío (**c**) *(nonetheless)* no obstante, con todo (**d**) *(however)* sin embargo (**e**) *(motionless)* quieto; **to stand s.** no moverse
  2 *adj (calm)* tranquilo(a); *(peaceful)* sosegado(a); *(silent)* silencioso(a); *(motionless)* inmóvil; *Art* **s. life** naturaleza muerta

stillborn ['stɪlbɔːn] *adj* nacido(a) muerto(a)

stillness ['stɪlnɪs] *n* calma *f*; *(silence)* silencio *m*

stilt [stɪlt] *n* zanco *m*

stilted ['stɪltɪd] *adj* afectado(a)

stimulant ['stɪmjʊlənt] *n* estimulante *m*

stimulate ['stɪmjʊleɪt] *vt* estimular

stimulating ['stɪmjʊleɪtɪŋ] *adj* estimulante

stimulus ['stɪmjʊləs] *n* (*pl* **stimuli** ['stɪmjʊlaɪ]) estímulo *m*; *Fig* incentivo *m*

sting [stɪŋ] **1** *n (part of bee, wasp)* aguijón *m*; *(wound)* picadura *f*; *(burning)* escozor *m*; *Fig (of remorse)* punzada *f*; *Fig (of remark)* sarcasmo *m*
  2 *vt (pt & pp* **stung**) picar; *Fig (of conscience)* remorder; *Fig (of remark)* herir en lo vivo
  3 *vi* picar

stingy ['stɪndʒɪ] *adj* (**stingier, stingiest**) *Fam (person)* tacaño(a); *(amount)* escaso(a); **to be s. with** escatimar

stink [stɪŋk] **1** *n* peste *m*, hedor *m*
  2 *vi (pt* **stank** *or* **stunk;** *pp* **stunk**) apestar, heder (**of** a)

stinking ['stɪŋkɪŋ] **1** *adj (smelly)* apestoso(a); *Fam* **to have a s. cold** tener un catarro bestial
  2 *adv Fam* **he's s. rich** está podrido de dinero, *Méx* tiene un chorro de lana

stint [stɪnt] **1** *n (period)* período *m*, temporada *f*; *(shift)* turno *m*; **he did a two-year s. in the navy** sirvió durante dos años en la Marina
  2 *vt* escatimar

stipulate ['stɪpjʊleɪt] *vt* estipular

stipulation [stɪpjʊ'leɪʃən] *n* estipulación *f*

stir [stɜː(r)] **1** *n Fig* revuelo *m*
  2 *vt* (**a**) *(liquid)* remover (**b**) *(move)* agitar (**c**) *Fig (curiosity, interest)* despertar; *(anger)* provocar
  3 *vi (move)* rebullirse

▸ **stir up** *vt sep Fig (memories, curiosity)* despertar; *(passions)* excitar; *(anger)* provocar; *(revolt)* fomentar

stirring ['stɜːrɪŋ] *adj* conmovedor(a)

stirrup ['stɪrəp] *n* estribo *m*

stitch [stɪtʃ] **1** *n* (**a**) *Sewing* puntada *f*; *(in knitting)* punto *m*; *Med* punto (de sutura); *Fam* **we were in stitches** nos tronchábamos de risa (**b**) *(pain)* punzada *f*
  2 *vt Sewing* coser; *Med* suturar, dar puntos a

stoat [stəʊt] *n* armiño *m*

stock [stɒk] **1** *n* (**a**) *(supply)* reserva *f*; *Com (goods)* existencias *fpl*, stock *m*; *(selection)* surtido *m*; **out of s.** agotado(a); **to have sth in s.** tener existencias de algo; *Fig* **to take s. of** evaluar (**b**) *Fin* capital *m* social; **stocks and shares** acciones *fpl*, valores *mpl*; **S. Exchange** Bolsa *f* (de valores); **s. market** bolsa *f* (**c**) *Culin* caldo *m*; **s. cube** cubito *m* de caldo (**d**) *(descent)* estirpe *f*
  2 *adj (excuse, response)* de siempre; *(phrase)* gastado(a)
  3 *vt* (**a**) *(have in stock)* tener existencias de (**b**) *(provide)* abastecer, surtir (**with** de); *(cupboard)* llenar (**with** de)

▸ **stock up** *vi* abastecerse (**on** *or* **with** de)

stockbroker ['stɒkbrəʊkə(r)] *n* corredor(a) *m,f* de Bolsa

stockholder ['stɒkhəʊldə(r)] *n US* accionista *mf*

stocking ['stɒkɪŋ] *n* media *f*; **a pair of stockings** unas medias

stockist ['stɒkɪst] *n* distribuidor(a) *m,f*

stockpile ['stɒkpaɪl] **1** *n* reservas *fpl*
  2 *vt* almacenar; *(accumulate)* acumular

stocks [stɒks] *npl Hist* cepo *m*

stocktaking ['stɒkteɪkɪŋ] *n Com* inventario *m*

stocky ['stɒkɪ] *adj* (**stockier, stockiest**) *(squat)* rechoncho(a); *(heavily built)* fornido(a)

stodgy ['stɒdʒɪ] *adj* (**stodgier, stodgiest**) *(food)* indigesto(a); *Fig (book, person)* pesado(a)

stoical ['stəʊɪkəl] *adj* estoico(a)

stoke [stəʊk] *vt (poke)* atizar; **to s. (up)** *(feed)* alimentar

stole¹ [stəʊl] *pt of* **steal**

stole² [stəʊl] *n* estola *f*

stolen ['stəʊlən] *pp of* **steal**

stolid ['stɒlɪd] *adj* impasible

stomach ['stʌmək] **1** *n* estómago *m*; **s. ache** dolor *m* de estómago; **s. upset** trastorno gástrico
2 *vt Fig* aguantar

stone [stəʊn] **1** *n* (**a**) *(material, piece of rock)* piedra *f*; *(on grave)* lápida *f* (**b**) *(of fruit)* hueso *m*, *RP* carozo *m* (**c**) *Br (weight)* = peso que equivale a 6,348 kg
2 *adj* de piedra

stone-cold [stəʊn'kəʊld] *adj* helado(a)

stoned [stəʊnd] *adj Fam (drugged)* colocado(a); *(drunk)* como una cuba

stone-deaf [stəʊn'def] *adj* sordo(a) como una tapia

stonework ['stəʊnwɜːk] *n* mampostería *f*

stony ['stəʊnɪ] *adj* (**stonier, stoniest**) *(ground)* pedregoso(a); *Fig (look, silence)* glacial

stood [stʊd] *pt & pp of* **stand**

stool [stuːl] *n* (**a**) *(seat)* taburete *m* (**b**) *Med* heces *fpl*

stoop [stuːp] *vi* (**a**) *(have a stoop)* andar encorvado(a) (**b**) *(bend)* **to s. down** inclinarse, agacharse (**c**) *Fig* **to s. to** rebajarse a; **he wouldn't s. so low** no se rebajaría tanto

stop [stɒp] **1** *n* (**a**) *(halt)* parada *f*, alto *m*; **to come to a s.** pararse; **to put a s. to sth** poner fin a algo (**b**) *(break)* pausa *f*; *(for refuelling etc)* escala *f* (**c**) *(for bus, tram)* parada *f* (**d**) *(punctuation mark)* punto *m*
2 *vt* (**a**) *(person, vehicle)* parar; *(conversation)* interrumpir; *(pain, abuse etc)* poner fin a (**b**) *(payments)* suspender; *(cheque)* anular (**c**) **to s. doing sth** dejar de hacer algo; **s. it!** ¡basta ya! (**d**) *(prevent)* evitar; **to s. sb from doing sth** impedir a algn hacer algo
3 *vi* (**a**) *(person, moving vehicle)* pararse, detenerse (**b**) *(cease)* acabarse, terminar

▸ **stop by** *vi Fam* visitar

▸ **stop off** *vi* pararse un rato

▸ **stop over** *vi (spend the night)* pasar la noche; *(for refuelling etc)* hacer escala

▸ **stop up** *vt sep (hole)* tapar

stopgap ['stɒpgæp] *n (thing)* medida *f* provisional; *(person)* sustituto(a) *m,f*

stopover ['stɒpəʊvə(r)] *n* parada *f*; *Av* escala *f*

stoppage ['stɒpɪdʒ] *n* (**a**) *(of game, payments)* suspensión *f*; *(of work)* paro *m*; *(strike)* huelga *f*; *(deduction)* deducción *f* (**b**) *(blockage)* obstrucción *f*

stopper ['stɒpə(r)] *n* tapón *m*

stop-press [stɒp'pres] *n* noticias *fpl* de última hora

stopwatch ['stɒpwɒtʃ] *n* cronómetro *m*

storage ['stɔːrɪdʒ] *n* almacenaje *m*, almacenamiento *m*; **s. battery** acumulador *m*; **s. heater** placa acumuladora

store [stɔː(r)] **1** *n* (**a**) *(stock)* provisión *f* (**b**) **stores** víveres *mpl* (**c**) *(warehouse)* almacén *m* (**d**) *esp US (shop)* tienda *f*; **department s.** gran almacén *m*
2 *vt* (**a**) *(furniture, computer data)* almacenar; *(keep)* guardar (**b**) **to s. (up)** acumular

storekeeper ['stɔːkiːpə(r)] *n US* tendero(a) *m,f*

storeroom ['stɔːruːm] *n* despensa *f*

storey ['stɔːrɪ] *n* piso *m*

stork [stɔːk] *n* cigüeña *f*

storm [stɔːm] **1** *n* tormenta *f*; *(with wind)* vendaval *m*; *Fig (uproar)* revuelo *m*; *Fig* **she has taken New York by s.** ha cautivado a todo Nueva York
2 *vt* tomar por asalto
3 *vi (with rage)* echar pestes

stormy ['stɔːmɪ] *adj* (**stormier, stormiest**) *(weather)* tormentoso(a); *Fig (discussion)* acalorado(a); *(relationship)* tempestuoso(a)

story¹ ['stɔːrɪ] *n* historia *f*; *(tale, account)* relato *m*; *(article)* artículo *m*; *(plot)* trama *f*; *(joke)* chiste *m*; *(rumour)* rumor *m*; **it's a long s.** sería largo de contar; **tall s.** cuento chino

story² ['stɔːrɪ] *n US* = **storey**

storybook ['stɔːrɪbʊk] *n* libro *m* de cuentos

storyteller ['stɔːrɪtelə(r)] *n* cuentista *mf*

stout [staʊt] **1** *adj* (**a**) *(fat)* gordo(a), corpulento(a) (**b**) *(strong)* fuerte (**c**) *(brave)* valiente; *(determined)* firme
2 *n (beer)* cerveza negra

stoutly ['staʊtlɪ] *adv* resueltamente

stove [stəʊv] *n* (**a**) *(for heating)* estufa *f* (**b**) *(cooker)* cocina *f*, *Col, Méx, Ven* estufa *f*

stow [stəʊ] *vt* (**a**) *(cargo)* estibar (**b**) *(put away)* guardar

▸ **stow away** *vi (on ship, plane)* viajar de polizón

stowaway ['stəʊəweɪ] *n* polizón *mf*

straddle ['strædəl] *vt* (**a**) *(horse etc)* sentarse a horcajadas sobre (**b**) *Fig (embrace)* abarcar

straggle ['strægəl] *vi* (**a**) *(lag behind)* rezagarse (**b**) *(spread untidily)* desparramarse

straggler ['stræglə(r)] *n* rezagado(a) *m,f*

straight [streɪt] **1** *adj* (**a**) *(not bent)* recto(a), derecho(a); *(hair)* liso(a) (**b**) *(honest)* honrado(a); *(answer)* sincero(a); *(refusal)* rotundo(a)
2 *adv* (**a**) *(in a straight line)* en línea recta (**b**) *(directly)* directamente, derecho; **keep s. ahead** sigue todo recto (**c**) **s. away** en seguida

straighten ['streɪtən] *vt (sth bent)* enderezar, poner derecho(a); *(tie, picture)* poner bien; *(hair)* alisar
▸ **straighten out** *vt sep (problem)* resolver

straight-faced ['streɪt'feɪst] *adj* con la cara seria

straightforward [streɪt'fɔ:wəd] *adj* (**a**) *(honest)* honrado(a); *(sincere)* franco(a) (**b**) *Br (simple)* sencillo(a)

strain¹ [streɪn] **1** *vt* (**a**) *(rope etc)* estirar; *Fig* crear tensiones en (**b**) *Med* torcer(se); *(eyes, voice)* forzar; *(heart)* cansar (**c**) *(liquid)* filtrar; *(vegetables, tea)* colar
2 *vi (pull)* tirar (**at** de)
3 *n* (**a**) *(from pulling)* tensión *f*; *(from pushing)* presión *f* (**b**) *(mental stress)* agobio *m* (**c**) *(of ankle)* torcedura *f* (**d**) *Mus* **strains** son *m*

strain² [streɪn] *n* (**a**) *(breed)* raza *f* (**b**) *(streak)* vena *f*

strained ['streɪnd] *adj* (**a**) *(muscle)* torcido(a); *(eyes)* cansado(a); *(voice)* forzado(a) (**b**) *(atmosphere)* tenso(a)

strainer ['streɪnə(r)] *n* colador *m*

strait [streɪt] *n* (**a**) *Geog* estrecho *m* (**b**) *(difficulty)* **in dire straits** en un gran aprieto

straitjacket ['streɪtdʒækɪt] *n* camisa *f* de fuerza

strait-laced [streɪt'leɪst] *adj* remilgado(a)

strand¹ [strænd] *vt* *Fig (person)* abandonar; **to leave stranded** dejar plantado(a)

strand² [strænd] *n (of thread)* hebra *f*; *(of hair)* pelo *m*

strange [streɪndʒ] *adj* (**a**) *(unknown)* desconocido(a); *(unfamiliar)* nuevo(a) (**b**) *(odd)* raro(a), extraño(a)

stranger ['streɪndʒə(r)] *n (unknown person)* desconocido(a) *m,f*; *(outsider)* forastero(a) *m,f*

strangle ['strængəl] *vt* estrangular

stranglehold ['strængəlhəʊld] *n* **to have a s. on sb** tener a algn agarrado(a) por el cuello

strangulation [strængjʊ'leɪʃən] *n* estrangulación *f*

strap [stræp] **1** *n (of leather)* correa *f*; *(on bag)* bandolera *f*; *(on dress, bra)* tirante *m*, *Am* bretel *m*
2 *vt* atar con correa

strapping ['stræpɪŋ] *adj Fam* fornido(a), robusto(a)

strata ['strɑːtə] *pl of* stratum

strategic [strə'tiːdʒɪk] *adj* estratégico(a)

strategy ['strætɪdʒɪ] *n* estrategia *f*

stratosphere ['strætəsfɪə(r)] *n* estratosfera *f*

stratum ['strɑːtəm] *n (pl* **strata**) estrato *m*

straw [strɔ:] *n* (**a**) *(dry stalks)* paja *f*; *Fig* **to clutch at straws** agarrarse a un clavo ardiente; *Fam* **that's the last s.!** ¡eso ya es el colmo! (**b**) *(for drinking)* pajita *f*, *Méx* popote *m*

strawberry ['strɔːbərɪ] *n* fresa *f*, *CSur* frutilla *f*

stray [streɪ] **1** *vi (from path)* desviarse; *(get lost)* extraviarse
2 *n* animal extraviado
3 *adj (bullet)* perdido(a); *(animal)* callejero(a)

streak [striːk] **1** *n* (**a**) *(line)* raya *f*; **s. of lightning** rayo *m* (**b**) *(in hair)* reflejo *m* (**c**) *Fig (of genius etc)* vena *f*; *Fig (of luck)* racha *f*
2 *vt* rayar (**with** de)
3 *vi* **to s. past** pasar como un rayo

stream [striːm] **1** *n* (**a**) *(brook)* arroyo *m*, riachuelo *m* (**b**) *(of water, air)* flujo *m*; *(of blood)* chorro *m*; *(of light)* raudal *m* (**c**) *(of people)* oleada *f*
2 *vi* (**a**) *(liquid)* correr (**b**) **to s. in/out/ past** *(people etc)* entrar/salir/pasar en tropel

streamer ['striːmə(r)] *n (paper ribbon)* serpentina *f*

streamlined ['striːmlaɪnd] *adj* (**a**) *(car)* aerodinámico(a) (**b**) *(system, method)* racionalizado(a)

street [striːt] *n* calle *f*; **the man in the s.** el hombre de la calle; **s. map, s. plan** (plano *m*) callejero *m*

streetcar ['striːtkɑ:(r)] *n US* tranvía *m*

streetlamp ['striːtlæmp] *n* farola *f*

streetwise ['striːtwaɪz] *adj* espabilado(a)

strength [streŋθ] *n* (**a**) *(of person)* fuerza *f*; *(of rope, nail)* resistencia *f*; *(of emotion, colour)* intensidad *f*; *(of alcohol)* graduación *f* (**b**) *(ability)* punto *m* fuerte

strengthen ['streŋθən] **1** *vt* (**a**) *(wall, building)* reforzar; *(character)* fortalecer (**b**) *(intensify)* intensificar

2 *vi* (**a**) *(gen)* reforzarse (**b**) *(intensify)* intensificarse

strenuous ['strenjʊəs] *adj* (**a**) *(denial)* enérgico(a); *(effort, life)* intenso(a) (**b**) *(exhausting)* fatigoso(a), cansado(a)

stress [stres] **1** *n* (**a**) *Tech* tensión *f* (**b**) *Med* estrés *m* (**c**) *(emphasis)* hincapié *m*; *(on word)* acento *m*
2 *vt (emphasize)* subrayar; *(word)* acentuar

stressed [strest] *adj (person)* estresado(a)

stressful ['stresfʊl] *adj* estresante

stretch [stretʃ] **1** *vt (elastic)* estirar; *(wings)* desplegar
2 *vi (elastic)* estirarse; *Fig* **my money won't s. to it** mi dinero no me llegará para eso
3 *n* (**a**) *(length)* trecho *m*, tramo *m* (**b**) *(of land)* extensión *f*; *(of time)* intervalo *m*

> ⏃ Note that the Spanish verb **estrechar** is a false friend and is never a translation for the English verb **stretch**. In Spanish **estrechar** means "to make narrow", "to tighten".

▸ **stretch out 1** *vt sep (arm, hand)* alargar; *(legs)* estirar
2 *vi* (**a**) *(person)* estirarse (**b**) *(countryside, years etc)* extenderse

stretcher ['stretʃə(r)] *n* camilla *f*

strew [struː] *vt (pt strewed; pp strewed or strewn* [struːn]*)* esparcir

stricken ['strɪkən] *adj (with grief)* afligido(a); *(with illness)* aquejado(a); *(by disaster etc)* afectado(a); *(damaged)* dañado(a)

strict [strɪkt] *adj* (**a**) *(person, discipline)* estricto(a) (**b**) *(absolute)* absoluto(a)

strictly ['strɪktlɪ] *adv* (**a**) *(categorically)* terminantemente (**b**) *(precisely)* estrictamente; **s. speaking** en sentido estricto

stride [straɪd] **1** *n* zancada *f*, tranco *m*; *Fig (progress)* progresos *mpl*
2 *vi (pt strode; pp stridden* ['strɪdən]*)* **to s. (along)** andar a zancadas

strident ['straɪdənt] *adj (voice, sound)* estridente; *(protest etc)* enérgico(a)

strife [straɪf] *n* conflictos *mpl*

strike [straɪk] **1** *vt (pt & pp struck)* (**a**) *(hit)* pegar, golpear (**b**) *(collide with)* chocar contra; *(of bullet, lightning)* alcanzar (**c**) *(match)* encender, *Am* prender (**d**) **the clock struck three** el reloj dio las tres (**e**) *(oil, gold)* descubrir (**f**) *(impress)* impresionar; **it strikes me …** me parece …
2 *vi* (**a**) *(attack)* atacar; *(disaster)* sobrevenir (**b**) *(clock)* dar la hora (**c**) *(workers)* declararse en huelga

3 *n* (**a**) *(by workers)* huelga *f*; **to call a s.** convocar una huelga (**b**) *Mil* ataque *m*
▸ **strike back** *vi* devolver el golpe
▸ **strike down** *vt sep* fulminar, abatir
▸ **strike out 1** *vt sep (cross out)* tachar
2 *vi* **to s. out at sb** arremeter contra algn
▸ **strike up** *vt insep* (**a**) *(friendship)* trabar; *(conversation)* entablar (**b**) *(tune)* empezar a tocar

striker ['straɪkə(r)] *n* (**a**) *(worker)* huelguista *mf* (**b**) *Fam Ftb* marcador(a) *m,f*

striking ['straɪkɪŋ] *adj (eye-catching)* llamativo(a); *(noticeable)* notable; *(impressive)* impresionante

string [strɪŋ] **1** *n* (**a**) *(cord)* cuerda *f*; *Fig* **to pull strings for sb** enchufar a algn; **s. bean** judía *f* verde, *Bol, RP* chaucha *f*, *CAm* ejote *m*, *Col, Cuba* habichuela *f*, *Chile* poroto *m* verde, *Ven* vainita *f* (**b**) *(of events)* cadena *f*; *(of lies)* sarta *f* (**c**) *(of racket, guitar)* cuerda *f*; *Mus* **the strings** los instrumentos de cuerda
2 *vt (pt & pp strung)* (**a**) *(beads)* ensartar (**b**) *(racket etc)* encordar (**c**) *(beans)* quitar la hebra a

stringed [strɪŋd] *adj (instrument)* de cuerda

stringent ['strɪndʒənt] *adj* severo(a), estricto(a)

strip¹ [strɪp] **1** *vt* (**a**) *(person)* desnudar; *(bed)* quitar la ropa de; *(paint)* rascar, quitar, *Am* sacar (**b**) *Tech* **to s. (down)** desmontar
2 *vi (undress)* desnudarse; *(perform striptease)* hacer un striptease
▸ **strip off 1** *vt sep* quitar, *Am* sacar
2 *vi (undress)* desnudarse

strip² [strɪp] *n* tira *f*; *(of land)* franja *f*; *(of metal)* fleje *m*; *Br* **football s.** indumentaria *f*; **s. cartoon** historieta *f*; **s. lighting** alumbrado *m* fluorescente; **to tear sb off a s.** echar una bronca a algn

stripe [straɪp] *n* raya *f*; *Mil* galón *m*

striped [straɪpt] *adj* rayado(a), a rayas

stripper ['strɪpə(r)] *n* artista *mf* de striptease

strive [straɪv] *vi (pt strove; pp striven* ['strɪvən]*)* **to s. to do sth** esforzarse por hacer algo

strobe [strəʊb] *n* **s. lighting** luces estroboscópicas

strode [strəʊd] *pt of* **stride**

stroke [strəʊk] **1** *n* (**a**) **a s. of luck** un golpe de suerte (**b**) *(of pen)* trazo *m*; *(of brush)* pincelada *f* (**c**) *(caress)* caricia *f* (**d**) *Med* apoplejía *f*
2 *vt* acariciar

stroll [strəʊl] **1** *vi* dar un paseo
2 *n* paseo *m*

stroller ['strəʊlə(r)] *n US (for baby)* cochecito *m*

strong [strɒŋ] **1** *adj* (**a**) *(powerful)* fuerte (**b**) *(durable)* sólido(a) (**c**) *(firm, resolute)* firme (**d**) *(colour)* intenso(a); *(light)* brillante

2 *adv* fuerte; **to be going s.** *(business)* ir fuerte; *(elderly person)* conservarse bien

strongbox ['strɒŋbɒks] *n* caja *f* fuerte

stronghold ['strɒŋhəʊld] *n Mil* fortaleza *f*; *Fig* baluarte *m*

strongly ['strɒŋlɪ] *adv* fuertemente

strongroom ['strɒŋruːm] *n* cámara acorazada

stroppy ['strɒpɪ] *adj* (**stroppier, stroppiest**) *Br Fam* **to be s.** *(by nature)* tener mal genio *or Esp* mal café; *(in a mood)* estar de mal humor *or Esp* de mal café

strove [strəʊv] *pt of* **strive**

struck [strʌk] *pt & pp of* **strike**

structural ['strʌktʃərəl] *adj* estructural

structure ['strʌktʃə(r)] *n* estructura *f*; *(building, monument)* construcción *f*

struggle ['strʌgəl] **1** *vi* luchar

2 *n* lucha *f*; *(physical fight)* pelea *f*

strum [strʌm] *vt (guitar)* rasguear

strung [strʌŋ] *pt & pp of* **string**

strut [strʌt] *vi* pavonearse

stub [stʌb] **1** *n (of cigarette)* colilla *f*; *(of pencil)* cabo *m*; *(of cheque)* matriz *f*

2 *vt* (**a**) *(strike)* golpear (**b**) **to s. (out)** apagar

stubble ['stʌbəl] *n (in field)* rastrojo *m*; *(on chin)* barba *f* de tres días

stubborn ['stʌbən] *adj* (**a**) *(person)* terco(a), testarudo(a) (**b**) *(stain)* difícil (**c**) *(refusal)* rotundo(a)

stucco ['stʌkəʊ] *n* estuco *m*

stuck [stʌk] *pt & pp of* **stick²**

stuck-up [stʌk'ʌp] *adj Fam* creído(a)

stud¹ [stʌd] **1** *n (on clothing)* tachón *m*; *(on football boots) Esp* taco *m*, *RP* tapón *m*; *(on shirt)* botonadura *f*

2 *vt (decorate)* tachonar (**with** de); *Fig (dot, cover)* salpicar (**with** de)

stud² [stʌd] *n (horse)* semental *m*

student ['stjuːdənt] *n* estudiante *mf*; **s. teacher** profesor(a) *m,f* en prácticas

studio ['stjuːdɪəʊ] *n TV & Cin* estudio *m*; *(artist's)* taller *m*; **s. (apartment** *or Br* **flat)** estudio

studious ['stjuːdɪəs] *adj* estudioso(a)

studiously ['stjuːdɪəslɪ] *adv* cuidadosamente

study ['stʌdɪ] **1** *vt.* estudiar; *(facts etc)* examinar, investigar; *(behaviour)* observar

2 *vi* estudiar; **to s. to be a doctor** estudiar para médico

3 *n* (**a**) *(investigation, report)* estudio *m*; **s. group** grupo *m* de trabajo (**b**) *(room)* despacho *m*, estudio *m*

stuff [stʌf] **1** *vt* (**a**) *(container)* llenar (**with** de); *Culin* rellenar (**with** con *or* de); *(animal)* disecar (**b**) *(cram)* atiborrar (**with** de)

2 *n Fam* (**a**) *(substance)* cosa *f* (**b**) *(things)* cosas *fpl*

stuffing ['stʌfɪŋ] *n Culin* relleno *m*

stuffy ['stʌfɪ] *adj* (**stuffier, stuffiest**) (**a**) *(room)* mal ventilado(a); *(atmosphere)* cargado(a) (**b**) *(pompous)* estirado(a); *(narrow-minded)* de miras estrechas

stumble ['stʌmbəl] *vi* tropezar, dar un traspié; *Fig* **to s. across** *or* **on** *or* **upon** tropezar *or* dar con

stumbling ['stʌmblɪŋ] *n* **s. block** escollo *m*

stump [stʌmp] **1** *n* (**a**) *(of pencil)* cabo *m*; *(of tree)* tocón *m*; *(of arm, leg)* muñón *m* (**b**) *(in cricket)* estaca *f*

2 *vt (puzzle)* confundir; **to be stumped** estar perplejo(a)

stun [stʌn] *vt (of blow)* aturdir; *Fig (of news etc)* sorprender

stung [stʌŋ] *pt & pp of* **sting**

stunk [stʌŋk] *pt & pp of* **stink**

stunning ['stʌnɪŋ] *adj (blow)* duro(a); *(news)* sorprendente; *Fam (woman, outfit)* fenomenal

stunt¹ [stʌnt] *vt (growth)* atrofiar

stunt² [stʌnt] *n* (**a**) *Av* acrobacia *f* (**b**) *publicity* **s.** truco publicitario (**c**) *Cin* escena peligrosa; **s. man** doble *m*

stunted ['stʌntɪd] *adj* enano(a), mal desarrollado(a)

stupefy ['stjuːpɪfaɪ] *vt (of alcohol, drugs)* aturdir; *Fig (of news etc)* dejar pasmado(a)

stupendous [stjuː'pendəs] *adj (wonderful)* estupendo(a)

stupid ['stjuːpɪd] *adj* estúpido(a), imbécil

stupidity [stjuː'pɪdɪtɪ] *n* estupidez *f*

stupor ['stjuːpə(r)] *n* estupor *m*

sturdy ['stɜːdɪ] *adj* (**sturdier, sturdiest**) robusto(a), fuerte; *(resistance)* enérgico(a)

stutter ['stʌtə(r)] **1** *vi* tartamudear

2 *n* tartamudeo *m*

sty [staɪ] *n (pen)* pocilga *f*

sty(e) [staɪ] *n Med* orzuelo *m*

style [staɪl] **1** *n* (**a**) *(manner, sophistication)* estilo *m*; *(of dress)* modelo *m* (**b**) *(fashion)* moda *f* (**c**) **to live in s.** *(elegance)* vivir a lo grande

2 *vt (hair)* marcar

stylish ['staɪlɪʃ] *adj* con estilo

stylist ['staɪlɪst] *n (hairdresser)* peluquero(a) *mf*

stylus ['staɪləs] *n (of record player)* aguja *f*

suave [swɑːv] *adj* amable, afable; *Pej* zalamero(a)

> 📖 Note that the Spanish word **suave** is a false friend and is never a translation for the English word **suave**. In Spanish, **suave** means both "smooth" and "soft".

sub [sʌb] *n Fam* (**a**) *(to magazine)* suscripción *f*; *(to club)* cuota *f* (**b**) *(substitute)* suplente *mf*

sub- [sʌb] *pref* sub-

subconscious [sʌb'kɒnʃəs] **1** *adj* subconsciente
2 *n* **the s.** el subconsciente

subcontract [sʌbkən'trækt] *vt* subcontratar

subcontractor [sʌbkən'træktə(r)] *n* subcontratista *mf*

subdivide [sʌbdɪ'vaɪd] *vt* subdividir (**into** en)

subdue [səb'djuː] *vt* (**a**) *(nation, people)* sojuzgar (**b**) *(feelings)* dominar (**c**) *(colour, light)* atenuar

subdued [səb'djuːd] *adj* (**a**) *(person, emotion)* callado(a) (**b**) *(voice, tone)* bajo(a) (**c**) *(light)* tenue; *(colour)* apagado(a)

subject ['sʌbdʒɪkt] **1** *n* (**a**) *(citizen)* súbdito *m* (**b**) *(topic)* tema *m*; **s. matter** materia *f*; *(contents)* contenido *m* (**c**) *Educ* asignatura *f* (**d**) *Ling* sujeto *m*
2 *adj* **s. to** *(law, tax)* sujeto(a) a; *(conditional upon)* previo(a)
3 *vt* [səb'dʒekt] someter

subjective [səb'dʒektɪv] *adj* subjetivo(a)

subjunctive [səb'dʒʌŋktɪv] **1** *adj* subjuntivo(a)
2 *n* subjuntivo *m*

sublet [sʌb'let] *vt & vi* subarrendar

sublime [sə'blaɪm] *adj* sublime

submachine-gun [sʌbmə'ʃiːngʌn] *n* metralleta *f*

submarine ['sʌbməriːn] *n* submarino *m*

submerge [səb'mɜːdʒ] *vt* sumergir; *(flood)* inundar; *Fig* **submerged in ...** sumido(a) en ...

submission [səb'mɪʃən] *n* (**a**) *(yielding)* sumisión *f* (**b**) *(of documents)* presentación *f* (**c**) *(report)* informe *m*

submissive [səb'mɪsɪv] *adj* sumiso(a)

submit [səb'mɪt] **1** *vt* (**a**) *(present)* presentar (**b**) *(subject)* someter (**to** a)
2 *vi (surrender)* rendirse

subnormal [sʌb'nɔːməl] *adj* subnormal

subordinate [sə'bɔːdɪnɪt] *adj & n* subordinado(a) *(m,f)*

subpoena [səb'piːnə] *Jur* **1** *n* citación *f*
2 *vt* citar

subscribe [səb'skraɪb] *vi (to magazine)* suscribirse (**to** a); *(to opinion, theory)* adherirse (**to** a)

subscriber [səb'skraɪbə(r)] *n* abonado(a) *m,f*

subscription [səb'skrɪpʃən] *n (to magazine)* suscripción *f*; *(to club)* cuota *f*

subsequent ['sʌbsɪkwənt] *adj* subsiguiente

subsequently ['sʌbsɪkwəntlɪ] *adv* posteriormente

subside [səb'saɪd] *vi (land)* hundirse; *(floodwater)* bajar; *(wind, anger)* amainar

subsidence [səb'saɪdəns] *n (of land)* hundimiento *m*; *(of floodwater)* bajada *f*; *(of wind)* amaine *m*

subsidiary [səb'sɪdɪərɪ] **1** *adj (role)* secundario(a)
2 *n Com* sucursal *f*, filial *f*

subsidize ['sʌbsɪdaɪz] *vt* subvencionar

subsidy ['sʌbsɪdɪ] *n* subvención *f*

subsistence [səb'sɪstəns] *n* subsistencia *f*

substance ['sʌbstəns] *n* (**a**) *(matter)* sustancia *f* (**b**) *(essential element)* esencia *f* (**c**) **a woman of s.** *(wealth)* una mujer acaudalada

substantial [səb'stænʃəl] *adj* (**a**) *(solid)* sólido(a) (**b**) *(sum, loss)* importante; *(difference, improvement)* notable; *(meal)* abundante

substantiate [səb'stænʃɪeɪt] *vt* respaldar

substitute ['sʌbstɪtjuːt] **1** *vt* sustituir; **to s. X for Y** sustituir X por Y
2 *n (person)* suplente *mf*; *(thing)* sucedáneo *m*

substitution [sʌbstɪ'tjuːʃən] *n* sustitución *f*; *Sport* sustitución *f*, cambio *m*

subtitle ['sʌbtaɪtəl] *n* subtítulo *m*

subtle ['sʌtəl] *adj* sutil; *(taste)* delicado(a); *(remark)* ingenioso(a); *(irony)* fino(a)

subtlety ['sʌtəltɪ] *n* sutileza *f*; *(of remark)* ingeniosidad *f*; *(of irony, joke)* finura *f*

subtotal ['sʌbtəʊtəl] *n* subtotal *m*

subtract [səb'trækt] *vt* restar

subtraction [səb'trækʃən] *n* resta *f*

suburb ['sʌbɜːb] *n* barrio periférico; **the suburbs** las afueras

suburban [sə'bɜːbən] *adj* suburbano(a)

suburbia [sə'bɜːbɪə] *n* barrios residenciales periféricos

subversive [səb'vɜːsɪv] *adj & n* subversivo(a) *(m,f)*

subway ['sʌbweɪ] *n* (a) *Br* (*underpass*) paso subterráneo (b) *US* (*underground railway*) metro *m*, *RP* subte *m*

succeed [sək'siːd] 1 *vi* (a) (*person*) tener éxito; (*plan*) salir bien; **to s. in doing sth** conseguir hacer algo (b) (*follow after*) suceder; **to s. to** (*throne*) suceder a
2 *vt* (*monarch*) suceder a

succeeding [sək'siːdɪŋ] *adj* sucesivo(a)

success [sək'ses] *n* éxito *m*

> 🖉 Note that the Spanish word **suceso** is a false friend and is never a translation for the English word **success**. In Spanish **suceso** means both "event, occurrence" and "incident".

successful [sək'sesfʊl] *adj* de éxito, exitoso(a); (*business*) próspero(a); (*marriage*) feliz; **to be s. in doing sth** lograr hacer algo

successfully [sək'sesfʊlɪ] *adv* con éxito

succession [sək'seʃən] *n* sucesión *f*, serie *f*; **in s.** sucesivamente

successive [sək'sesɪv] *adj* sucesivo(a), consecutivo(a)

successor [sək'sesə(r)] *n* sucesor(a) *m,f*

succinct [sək'sɪŋkt] *adj* sucinto(a)

succumb [sə'kʌm] *vi* sucumbir (**to** a)

such [sʌtʃ] 1 *adj* (a) (*of that sort*) tal, semejante; **artists s. as Monet** artistas como Monet; **at s. and s. a time** a tal hora; **in s. a way that** de tal manera que (b) (*so much, so great*) tanto(a); **he's always in s. a hurry** siempre anda con tanta prisa; **she was in s. pain** sufría tanto
2 *adv* (*so very*) tan; **it's s. a long time ago** hace tanto tiempo; **she's s. a clever woman** es una mujer tan inteligente; **s. a lot of books** tantos libros; **we had s. good weather** hizo un tiempo tan bueno

suchlike ['sʌtʃlaɪk] 1 *adj* tal
2 *pron* (*things*) cosas *fpl* por el estilo; (*people*) gente *f* por el estilo

suck [sʌk] 1 *vt* (*by pump*) aspirar; (*liquid*) sorber; (*lollipop, blood*) chupar
2 *vi* (*person*) chupar; (*baby*) mamar
▸ **suck in** *vt sep* (*of whirlpool*) tragar

sucker ['sʌkə(r)] *n* (a) *Fam* primo(a) *m,f*, bobo(a) *m,f* (b) *Zool* ventosa *f*; *Bot* chupón *m*

suckle ['sʌkəl] *vt* (*of mother*) amamantar

suction ['sʌkʃən] *n* succión *f*

sudden ['sʌdən] *adj* (a) (*hurried*) súbito(a), repentino(a) (b) (*unexpected*) imprevisto(a) (c) (*abrupt*) brusco(a); **all of a s.** de repente

suddenly ['sʌdənlɪ] *adv* de repente

suds [sʌdz] *npl* espuma *f* de jabón, jabonaduras *fpl*

sue [suː, sjuː] *Jur* 1 *vt* demandar
2 *vi* presentar una demanda; **to s. for divorce** solicitar el divorcio

suede [sweɪd] *n* ante *m*, gamuza *f*; (*for gloves*) cabritilla *f*

suet ['suːɪt] *n* sebo *m*

suffer ['sʌfə(r)] 1 *vt* (a) (*endure*) (*loss, defeat, pain*) sufrir (b) (*tolerate*) aguantar, soportar
2 *vi* sufrir; **to s. from** sufrir de

sufferer ['sʌfərə(r)] *n* *Med* enfermo(a) *m,f*

suffering ['sʌfərɪŋ] *n* (*affliction*) sufrimiento *m*; (*pain, torment*) dolor *m*

suffice [sə'faɪs] *vi* *Fml* bastar, ser suficiente

sufficient [sə'fɪʃənt] *adj* suficiente, bastante

sufficiently [sə'fɪʃəntlɪ] *adv* suficientemente, bastante

suffix ['sʌfɪks] *n* sufijo *m*

suffocate ['sʌfəkeɪt] 1 *vt* asfixiar
2 *vi* asfixiarse

suffocating ['sʌfəkeɪtɪŋ] *adj* (*heat*) agobiante, sofocante

suffrage ['sʌfrɪdʒ] *n* sufragio *m*

suffuse [sə'fjuːz] *vt* *Literary* bañar, cubrir (**with** de)

sugar ['ʃʊgə(r)] 1 *n* azúcar *m or f*; **s. beet** remolacha (azucarera), *Méx* betabel (azucarero); **s. bowl** azucarero *m*; **s. cane** caña *f* de azúcar
2 *vt* azucarar, echar azúcar a

sugary ['ʃʊgərɪ] *adj* (a) (*like sugar*) azucarado(a) (b) *Fig* (*insincere*) zalamero(a); (*over-sentimental*) sentimentaloide

suggest [sə'dʒest] *vt* (a) (*propose*) sugerir (b) (*advise*) aconsejar (c) (*indicate, imply*) indicar

suggestion [sə'dʒestʃən] *n* (a) (*proposal*) sugerencia *f* (b) (*trace*) sombra *f*; (*small amount*) toque *m*

suggestive [sə'dʒestɪv] *adj* (a) (*reminiscent, thought-provoking*) sugerente (b) (*remark*) insinuante

suicidal [sjuː'saɪdəl] *adj* suicida

suicide ['sjuːɪsaɪd] *n* suicidio *m*; **s. bombing** atentado *m* suicida con bomba

suit [suːt, sjuːt] 1 *n* (a) (*clothes*) traje *m*, *Andes*, *RP* terno *m* (b) *Jur* pleito *m* (c) *Cards* palo *m*
2 *vt* (a) (*be convenient to*) convenir a, venir bien a (b) (*be right, appropriate for*) ir bien a; **red really suits you** el rojo te favorece mucho; **they are well suited** están hechos el uno para el otro (c) (*please*) **s. yourself!** ¡como quieras!

suitable ['sjuːtəbəl] *adj* (*convenient*) conveniente; (*appropriate*) adecuado(a);

the most s. woman for the job la mujer más indicada para el puesto

suitably ['sju:təblɪ] *adv (correctly)* correctamente; *(properly)* adecuadamente

suitcase ['su:tkeɪs] *n* maleta *f*, *Méx* petaca *f*, *RP* valija *f*

suite [swi:t] *n* (a) *(of furniture)* juego *m* (b) *(of hotel rooms, music)* suite *f*

suitor ['sju:tə(r)] *n Literary (wooer)* pretendiente *m*

sulfur ['sʌlfə(r)] *n US* = **sulphur**

sulfuric [sʌl'fjʊərɪk] *n US* = **sulphuric**

sulk [sʌlk] *vi* enfurruñarse

sulky ['sʌlkɪ] *adj* (**sulkier, sulkiest**) malhumorado(a), enfurruñado(a)

sullen ['sʌlən] *adj* hosco(a); *(sky)* plomizo(a)

sulphur ['sʌlfər] *n* azufre *m*

sulphuric [sʌl'fjʊərɪk] *adj* sulfúrico(a)

sultan ['sʌltən] *n* sultán *m*

sultana [sʌl'tɑ:nə] *n esp Br (raisin)* pasa *f* de Esmirna

sultry ['sʌltrɪ] *adj* (**sultrier, sultriest**) (a) *(muggy)* bochornoso(a) (b) *(seductive)* sensual

sum [sʌm] *n* (a) *(arithmetic problem, amount)* suma *f* (b) *(total amount)* total *m*; *(of money)* importe *m*
▸ **sum up 1** *vt sep* resumir
2 *vi* resumir; **to s. up ...** en resumidas cuentas ...

summarize ['sʌmərɪz] *vt & vi* resumir

summary ['sʌmərɪ] **1** *n* resumen *m*
2 *adj* sumario(a)

summer ['sʌmə(r)] **1** *n* verano *m*
2 *adj (holiday etc)* de verano; *(weather)* veraniego(a); *(resort)* de veraneo

summerhouse ['sʌməhaʊs] *n* cenador *m*, glorieta *f*

summertime ['sʌmətaɪm] *n* verano *m*

summit ['sʌmɪt] *n* (a) *(of mountain)* cima *f*, cumbre *f* (b) *Pol* **s. (meeting)** cumbre *f*

summon ['sʌmən] *vt* (a) *(meeting, person)* convocar (b) *(aid)* pedir (c) *Jur* citar
▸ **summon up** *vt sep (resources)* reunir; **to s. up one's courage** armarse de valor

summons ['sʌmənz] **1** *n sing* (a) *(call)* llamada *f*, llamamiento *m* (b) *Jur* citación *f* judicial
2 *vt Jur* citar

sumptuous ['sʌmptjʊəs] *adj* suntuoso(a)

sun [sʌn] **1** *n* sol *m*
2 *vt* **to s. oneself** tomar el sol

sunbathe ['sʌnbeɪð] *vi* tomar el sol

sunbed ['sʌnbed] *n (in garden)* tumbona *f*; *(with sunlamp)* solario *m*

sunburn ['sʌnbɜ:n] *n (burn)* quemadura *f* de sol

sunburnt ['sʌnbɜ:nt] *adj (burnt)* quemado(a) por el sol; *(tanned)* bronceado(a)

Sunday ['sʌndɪ] *n* domingo *m inv*; **S. newspaper** periódico *m* del domingo; **S. school** catequesis *f*

sundial ['sʌndaɪəl] *n* reloj *m* de sol

sundown ['sʌndaʊn] *n US* anochecer *m*

sundry ['sʌndrɪ] **1** *adj* diversos(as), varios(as)
2 *n* (a) *Fam* **all and s.** todos sin excepción (b) *Com* **sundries** artículos diversos; *(expenses)* gastos diversos

sunflower ['sʌnflaʊə(r)] *n* girasol *m*

sung [sʌŋ] *pp of* **sing**

sunglasses ['sʌnglɑ:sɪz] *npl* gafas *fpl* or *Am* anteojos *mpl* de sol

sunk [sʌŋk] *pp of* **sink**

sunlamp ['sʌnlæmp] *n* lámpara *f* solar

sunlight ['sʌnlaɪt] *n* sol *m*, luz *f* del sol

sunlit ['sʌnlɪt] *adj* iluminado(a) por el sol

sunny ['sʌnɪ] *adj* (**sunnier, sunniest**) (a) *(day)* de sol; *(place)* soleado(a); **it is s.** hace sol (b) *Fig (smile, disposition)* alegre; *(future)* prometedor(a)

sunrise ['sʌnraɪz] *n* salida *f* del sol

sunroof ['sʌnru:f] *n Aut* techo corredizo

sunset ['sʌnset] *n* puesta *f* del sol

sunshade ['sʌnʃeɪd] *n* sombrilla *f*

sunshine ['sʌnʃaɪn] *n* sol *m*, luz *f* del sol

sunstroke ['sʌnstrəʊk] *n* insolación *f*

suntan ['sʌntæn] *n* bronceado *m*; **s. oil** crema protectora; **s. lotion** (aceite *m*) bronceador *m*

super ['su:pə(r)] *adj Fam* genial, *Am* salvo *RP* chévere, *Méx* padre, *RP* bárbaro(a)

super- ['su:pə(r)] *pref* super-, sobre-

superannuation [su:pərænjʊ'eɪʃən] *n Br* jubilación *f*, pensión *f*

superb [sʊ'pɜ:b] *adj* espléndido(a)

supercilious [su:pə'sɪlɪəs] *adj (condescending)* altanero(a); *(disdainful)* desdeñoso(a)

superficial [su:pə'fɪʃəl] *adj* superficial

superfluous [su:'pɜ:flʊəs] *adj* sobrante, superfluo(a); **to be s.** sobrar

superglue ['su:pəglu:] *n* pegamento rápido

superhuman [su:pə'hju:mən] *adj* sobrehumano(a)

superimpose [su:pərɪm'pəʊz] *vt* sobreponer

superintendent [su:pərɪn'tendənt] *n* (a) *(police officer) (in UK)* comisario(a) *m,f*, *(in US)* comisario(a) *m,f* jefe (b) *US (of apartment building)* portero(a) *m,f*

superior [suːˈpɪərɪə(r)] **1** *adj* (**a**) *(better, more senior)* superior (**b**) *(haughty)* altivo(a)
2 *n* superior(a) *m,f*

superiority [suːpɪərɪˈɒrɪtɪ] *n* superioridad *f*

superlative [suːˈpɜːlətɪv] **1** *adj* superlativo(a)
2 *n Ling* superlativo *m*

superman [ˈsuːpəmæn] *n* superhombre *m*, supermán *m*

supermarket [ˈsuːpəmɑːkɪt] *n* supermercado *m*

supermodel [ˈsuːpəmɒdəl] *n* supermodelo *f*, top model *f*

supernatural [suːpəˈnætʃərəl] **1** *adj* sobrenatural
2 *n* **the s.** lo sobrenatural

superpower [ˈsuːpəpaʊə(r)] *n Pol* superpotencia *f*

supersede [suːpəˈsiːd] *vt Fml* suplantar

supersonic [suːpəˈsɒnɪk] *adj* supersónico(a)

superstar [ˈsuːpəstɑː(r)] *n* superestrella *f*

superstition [suːpəˈstɪʃən] *n* superstición *f*

superstitious [suːpəˈstɪʃəs] *adj* supersticioso(a)

superstore [ˈsuːpəstɔː(r)] *n Com* hipermercado *m*, gran superficie *f*

supertanker [ˈsuːpətæŋkə(r)] *n* superpetrolero *m*

supervise [ˈsuːpəvaɪz] *vt* supervisar; *(watch over)* vigilar

supervision [suːpəˈvɪʒən] *n* supervisión *f*

supervisor [ˈsuːpəvaɪzə(r)] *n* supervisor(a) *m,f*; *US (of apartment building)* portero(a) *m,f*

supper [ˈsʌpə(r)] *n* cena *f*; **to have s.** cenar

supplant [səˈplɑːnt] *vt* suplantar

supple [ˈsʌpəl] *adj* flexible

supplement 1 *n* [ˈsʌplɪmənt] suplemento *m*
2 *vt* [ˈsʌplɪment] complementar

supplementary [sʌplɪˈmentərɪ] *adj* adicional

supplier [səˈplaɪə(r)] *n* suministrador(a) *m,f*; *Com* proveedor(a) *m,f*

supply [səˈplaɪ] **1** *n* (**a**) *(provision)* abastecimiento *m*, suministro *m*; **s. and demand** oferta *f* y demanda (**b**) **supplies** *(food)* víveres *mpl*; *Mil* pertrechos *mpl*
2 *vt* (**a**) *(provide)* suministrar (**b**) *(with provisions)* aprovisionar (**c**) *(information)* facilitar (**d**) *Com* surtir

support [səˈpɔːt] **1** *n* (**a**) *(moral)* apoyo *m* (**b**) *(funding)* ayuda económica
2 *vt* (**a**) *(weight etc)* sostener (**b**) *Fig*

(back) apoyar; *(substantiate)* respaldar (**c**) *Sport* ser (hincha) de (**d**) *(sustain)* mantener; *(feed)* alimentar

supporter [səˈpɔːtə(r)] *n Pol* partidario(a) *m,f*; *Sport* hincha *mf*

supportive [səˈpɔːtɪv] *adj* **he was s.** apoyó mucho, fue muy comprensivo

suppose [səˈpəʊz] *vt* suponer; *(presume)* creer; **I s. not/so** supongo que no/sí; **you're not supposed to smoke in here** no está permitido fumar aquí dentro; **you're supposed to be in bed** deberías estar acostado(a) ya

supposed [səˈpəʊzd] *adj* supuesto(a)

supposedly [səˈpəʊzdlɪ] *adv* teóricamente

suppress [səˈpres] *vt* suprimir; *(feelings, laugh etc)* contener; *(news, truth)* callar; *(revolt)* sofocar

supremacy [sʊˈpreməsɪ] *n* supremacía *f*

supreme [sʊˈpriːm] *adj* supremo(a); **with s. indifference** con total indiferencia; *US Jur* **S. Court** Tribunal *m* Supremo, *Am* Corte *f* Suprema

supremely [sʊˈpriːmlɪ] *adv* sumamente

surcharge [ˈsɜːtʃɑːdʒ] *n* recargo *m*

sure [ʃʊə(r)] **1** *adj* seguro(a); **I'm s. (that) ...** estoy seguro(a) de que ...; **make s. that it's ready** asegúrate de que esté listo; **s. of oneself** seguro(a) de sí mismo(a); *Fam* **s. thing!** ¡claro!
2 *adv* (**a**) *(of course)* claro (**b**) *(certainly)* seguro; *US* **it s. is cold** qué frío que hace (**c**) **s. enough** efectivamente

surely [ˈʃʊəlɪ] *adv (without a doubt)* sin duda; **s. not!** ¡no puede ser!

surety [ˈʃʊərɪtɪ] *n* (**a**) *(sum)* fianza *f* (**b**) *(person)* fiador(a) *m,f*; **to stand s. for sb** ser fiador de algn

surf [sɜːf] **1** *n (waves)* oleaje *m*; *(foam)* espuma *f*
2 *vt Comput* **to s. the Net** navegar por Internet
3 *vi Sport* hacer surf

surface [ˈsɜːfɪs] **1** *n* superficie *f*; *(of road)* firme *m*
2 *adj* superficial; **s. area** área *f* de la superficie; **by s. mail** por vía terrestre *or* marítima
3 *vt (road)* revestir
4 *vi (submarine etc)* salir a la superficie; *Fam (wake up)* levantarse

surface-to-air [ˈsɜːfɪstʊˈeə(r)] *adj* **s. missile** misil *m* tierra-aire

surfboard [ˈsɜːfbɔːd] *n* tabla *f* de surf

surfeit [ˈsɜːfɪt] *n Fml* exceso *m*

surfer [ˈsɜːfə(r)] *n* surfista *mf*

surfing [ˈsɜːfɪŋ] *n* surf *m*, surfing *m*

surge [sɜːdʒ] **1** n (**a**) (growth) alza f (**b**) (of sea, sympathy) oleada f; Fig (of anger, energy) arranque m
2 vi **to s. forward** (people) avanzar en tropel

surgeon ['sɜːdʒən] n cirujano(a) m,f

surgery ['sɜːdʒərɪ] n (**a**) (operation) cirugía f (**b**) Br (consulting room) consultorio m; **s. hours** horas fpl de consulta

surgical ['sɜːdʒɪkəl] adj quirúrgico(a); **s. spirit** alcohol m de 90°

surly ['sɜːlɪ] adj (**surlier, surliest**) (bad-tempered) hosco(a), malhumorado(a); (rude) maleducado(a)

surmount [sɜːˈmaʊnt] vt superar, vencer

surname ['sɜːneɪm] n apellido m

surpass [sɜːˈpɑːs] vt superar

surplus ['sɜːpləs] **1** n (of goods) excedente m; (of budget) superávit m
2 adj excedente

surprise [səˈpraɪz] **1** n sorpresa f; **to take sb by s.** Esp coger or Am agarrar desprevenido(a) a algn
2 adj (visit) inesperado(a); **s. attack** ataque m sorpresa
3 vt (astonish) sorprender; **I'm not surprised that …** no me extraña que …

surprising [səˈpraɪzɪŋ] adj sorprendente

surprisingly [səˈpraɪzɪŋlɪ] adv sorprendentemente, de modo sorprendente

surrealist [səˈrɪəlɪst] adj & n surrealista (mf)

surrender [səˈrendə(r)] **1** n Mil rendición f; (of weapons) entrega f; Ins rescate m
2 vt Mil rendir; (right) renunciar a
3 vi (give in) rendirse

surreptitious [sʌrəpˈtɪʃəs] adj subrepticio(a)

surrogate ['sʌrəgɪt] n Fml sustituto(a) m,f; **s. mother** madre f de alquiler

surround [səˈraʊnd] **1** n marco m, borde m
2 vt rodear

surrounding [səˈraʊndɪŋ] **1** adj circundante
2 npl **surroundings** (of place) alrededores mpl, cercanías fpl

surveillance [sɜːˈveɪləns] n vigilancia f

survey 1 n ['sɜːveɪ] (**a**) (of building) inspección f; (of land) reconocimiento m (**b**) (of trends etc) encuesta f (**c**) (overall view) panorama m
2 vt [səˈveɪ] (**a**) (building) inspeccionar; (land) medir (**b**) (trends etc) hacer una encuesta sobre (**c**) (look at) contemplar

surveyor [səˈveɪə(r)] n agrimensor(a) m,f; **quantity s.** aparejador(a) m,f

survival [səˈvaɪvəl] n supervivencia f

survive [səˈvaɪv] **1** vi sobrevivir; (remain) perdurar
2 vt sobrevivir a

survivor [səˈvaɪvə(r)] n superviviente mf

susceptible [səˈseptəbəl] adj (to attack) susceptible (**to** a); (to illness) propenso(a) (**to** a)

suspect 1 adj ['sʌspekt] (dubious) sospechoso(a)
2 n sospechoso(a) m,f
3 vt [səˈspekt] (**a**) (person) sospechar (**of** de); (plot, motives) recelar de (**b**) (think likely) imaginar, creer

suspend [səˈspend] vt suspender; (pupil) expulsar por un tiempo

suspended [səˈspendɪd] adj suspendido(a); Jur **s. sentence** condena f condicional

suspender [səˈspendə(r)] n (**a**) Br (for stocking, sock) liga f; **s. belt** liguero m (**b**) US **suspenders** (for trousers) tirantes mpl

suspense [səˈspens] n (uncertainty) incertidumbre f; (in movie) Esp suspense m, Am suspenso m; **to keep sb in s.** mantener a algn en la incertidumbre

suspension [səˈspenʃən] n (**a**) (of car) suspensión f (**b**) (of pupil, employee) expulsión f temporal (**c**) **s. bridge** puente m colgante

suspicion [səˈspɪʃən] n (**a**) (belief of guilt) sospecha f (**b**) (notion, feeling) presentimiento m (**c**) (small amount) asomo m

suspicious [səˈspɪʃəs] adj (**a**) (arousing suspicion) sospechoso(a) (**b**) (distrustful) receloso(a); **to be s. of sb** desconfiar de algn

suss out [sʌs] vt sep Br Fam (person) calar; (system) Esp coger or Am agarrar el truco a; **I haven't sussed out how it works yet** todavía no me he enterado de cómo funciona

sustain [səˈsteɪn] vt (**a**) (weight, growth, life) sostener (**b**) (nourish) mantener (**c**) Jur (objection) admitir (**d**) (injury etc) sufrir

sustainable [səˈsteɪnəbəl] adj (development) sostenible

sustained [səˈsteɪnd] adj sostenido(a)

sustenance ['sʌstənəns] n sustento m

SUV [esjuːˈviː] n (abbr **sport-utility vehicle**) todoterreno m

swab [swɒb] **1** n (cotton wool) algodón m; (for specimen) frotis m
2 vt (wound) limpiar

swagger ['swægə(r)] **1** n pavoneo m
2 vi pavonearse

swallow¹ ['swɒləʊ] **1** n (of drink, food) trago m

2 vt (**a**) (drink, food) tragar (**b**) Fig (believe) tragarse
3 vi tragar

▸ **swallow up** vt sep Fig (**a**) (engulf) tragar (**b**) (eat up) consumir

swallow² ['swɒləʊ] n (bird) golondrina f

swam [swæm] pt of **swim**

swamp [swɒmp] **1** n ciénaga f
2 vt (**a**) (boat) hundir (**b**) Fig inundar (**with** or **by** de)

swan [swɒn] **1** n cisne m
2 vi Fam **to s. around** pavonearse; **to s. around doing nothing** hacer el vago

swap [swɒp] **1** n Fam intercambio m
2 vt cambiar

▸ **swap round**, **swap over** vt sep (switch) cambiar

swarm [swɔːm] **1** n enjambre m
2 vi (bees) enjambrar; Fig **Rye was swarming with tourists** Rye estaba lleno de turistas

swarthy ['swɔːðɪ] adj (**swarthier**, **swarthiest**) moreno(a)

swastika ['swɒstɪkə] n esvástica f, cruz gamada

swat [swɒt] vt aplastar

swathe [sweɪð] vt (bind up) envolver

sway [sweɪ] **1** n (**a**) (movement) balanceo m (**b**) **to hold s. over sb** dominar a algn
2 vi (**a**) (swing) balancearse, mecerse (**b**) (totter) tambalearse
3 vt Fig (persuade) convencer

swear [sweə(r)] **1** vt (pt **swore**; pp **sworn**) (vow) jurar; **to s. an oath** prestar juramento
2 vi (**a**) (formally) jurar, prestar juramento (**b**) (curse) soltar tacos, decir palabrotas; (blaspheme) jurar; **to s. at sb** echar pestes contra algn

swear-word ['sweəwɜːd] n palabrota f

sweat [swet] **1** n (perspiration) sudor m; Fam (hard work) trabajo duro
2 vi (perspire) sudar; Fig (work hard) sudar la gota gorda
3 vt Fam **to s. it out** aguantar

sweater ['swetə(r)] n suéter m, Esp jersey m, RP pulóver m

sweatshirt ['swetʃɜːt] n sudadera f, Col, RP buzo m

sweaty ['swetɪ] adj (**sweatier**, **sweatiest**) sudoroso(a)

Swede [swiːd] n (person) sueco(a) m,f

swede [swiːd] n esp Br (vegetable) nabo sueco

Sweden ['swiːdən] n Suecia

Swedish ['swiːdɪʃ] **1** adj sueco(a)
2 n (**a**) (language) sueco m (**b**) **the S.** los suecos

sweep [swiːp] **1** n (**a**) (with broom) barrido m, Am barrida f (**b**) (**chimney**) **s.** deshollinador(a) m,f
2 vt (pt & pp **swept**) (floor etc) barrer
3 vi (**a**) (with broom) barrer (**b**) **to s. in/out/past** entrar/salir/pasar rápidamente

▸ **sweep aside** vt sep apartar bruscamente; Fig (objections) rechazar

▸ **sweep away** vt sep (**a**) (dust) barrer (**b**) (of storm) arrastrar

▸ **sweep up** vi barrer

sweeper ['swiːpə(r)] n (**a**) (machine) barredora f (**b**) Ftb líbero m

sweeping ['swiːpɪŋ] adj (**a**) (broad) amplio(a); **a s. statement** una declaración demasiado general (**b**) (victory) aplastante (**c**) (reforms, changes etc) radical

sweet [swiːt] **1** adj (**a**) (taste, wine) dulce; (sugary) azucarado(a); **to have a s. tooth** ser goloso(a); **s. pea** guisante m de olor; **s. shop** confitería f (**b**) (pleasant) agradable; (smell) fragante; (sound) melodioso(a) (**c**) (person, animal) encantador(a)
2 n (**a**) Br (confectionery) dulce m; (**boiled**) **s.** caramelo m (**b**) (dessert) postre m

sweet-and-sour ['swiːtən'saʊə(r)] adj agridulce

sweetcorn ['swiːtkɔːn] n maíz tierno, Andes, RP choclo m, Méx elote m

sweeten ['swiːtən] vt (**a**) (tea etc) azucarar (**b**) Fig (temper) aplacar; **to s. the pill** suavizar el golpe

sweetener ['swiːtənə(r)] n (for tea, coffee) edulcorante m

sweetheart ['swiːthɑːt] n (**a**) (boyfriend) novio m; (girlfriend) novia f (**b**) (dear, love) cariño m, amor m

sweetness ['swiːtnɪs] n dulzura f; (of smell) fragancia f; (of sound) suavidad f

swell [swel] **1** n (of sea) marejada f, oleaje m
2 adj US Fam genial, Méx padre, RP bárbaro(a)
3 vi (pt **swelled**; pp **swollen**) (part of body) hincharse; (river) subir

▸ **swell up** vi hincharse

swelling ['swelɪŋ] n hinchazón f; Med tumefacción f

sweltering ['sweltərɪŋ] adj agobiante

swept [swept] pt & pp of **sweep**

swerve [swɜːv] **1** n (**a**) (by car) viraje m (**b**) Sport (by player) regate m
2 vi (**a**) (car) dar un viraje brusco (**b**) Sport (player) dar un regate

swift [swɪft] **1** adj rápido(a), veloz
2 n (bird) vencejo m (común)

swiftly ['swɪftlɪ] *adv* rápidamente

swig [swɪg] *Fam* **1** *n* trago *m*
2 *vt Esp* pimplar, *Am* tomar

swill [swɪl] **1** *n* (**a**) *(food) (for pigs)* sobras *fpl* para los cerdos; *Pej (for people)* bazofia *f* (**b**) *(rinse)* enjuague *m*
2 *vt* (**a**) *(rinse)* enjuagar (**b**) *Fam (drink)* beber a grandes tragos
▸**swill out** *vt sep (rinse)* enjuagar, *Esp* aclarar

swim [swɪm] **1** *vi* (*pt* **swam**; *pp* **swum**) nadar; **to go swimming** ir a nadar; *Fam* **my head is swimming** la cabeza me da vueltas
2 *vt (the Channel)* pasar a nado
3 *n* baño *m*; **to go for a s.** ir a nadar *or* bañarse

swimmer ['swɪmə(r)] *n* nadador(a) *m,f*

swimming ['swɪmɪŋ] *n* natación *f*; **s. cap** gorro *m* de baño; **s. costume** traje *m* de baño, *Esp* bañador *m*, *Ecuad, Perú, RP* malla *f*; **s. pool** piscina *f*, *Méx* alberca *f*, *RP* pileta *f*; **s. trunks** *Esp* bañador *m (de hombre)*, *Ecuad, Perú, RP* malla *f (de hombre)*

swimsuit ['swɪmsuːt] *n* traje *m* de baño, *Esp* bañador *m*, *Ecuad, Perú, RP* malla *f*

swindle ['swɪndəl] **1** *n* estafa *f*
2 *vt* estafar

swindler ['swɪndlə(r)] *n* estafador(a) *m,f*

swine [swaɪn] *n* (**a**) *(pl* **swine**) *(pig)* cerdo *m*, puerco *m*, *Am* chancho *m* (**b**) *(pl* **swines**) *Fam (person)* canalla *mf*, cochino(a) *m,f*

swing [swɪŋ] **1** *n* (**a**) *(movement) (of rope, chain)* balanceo *m*, vaivén *m*; *Fig (in votes etc)* viraje *m* (**b**) *(in golf)* swing *m* (**c**) *(plaything)* columpio *m* (**d**) *(rhythm)* ritmo *m*; **in full s.** en plena marcha
2 *vi* (*pt & pp* **swung**) (**a**) *(move to and fro)* balancearse; *(arms, legs)* menearse; *(on swing)* columpiarse (**b**) *(turn)* girar; **he swung round** dio media vuelta
3 *vt (cause to move to and fro)* balancear; *(arms, legs)* menear

swingeing ['swɪndʒɪŋ] *adj Br* drástico(a)

swipe [swaɪp] **1** *n* golpe *m*
2 *vt* (**a**) *(hit)* dar un tortazo a (**b**) *Fam (steal)* afanar, birlar

swirl [swɜːl] **1** *n* remolino *m*; *(of cream, smoke)* voluta *f*
2 *vi* arremolinarse

swish [swɪʃ] **1** *adj Fam (smart)* elegante
2 *vt (tail)* menear
3 *vi (whip)* dar un chasquido; *(skirt)* crujir

Swiss [swɪs] **1** *adj* suizo(a)
2 *n (pl* **Swiss**) *(person)* suizo(a) *m,f*

switch [swɪtʃ] **1** *n* (**a**) *Elec* interruptor *m* (**b**) *(changeover)* cambio repentino; *(exchange)* intercambio *m* (**c**) *US Rail* agujas *fpl*
2 *vt* (**a**) *(jobs, direction)* cambiar de (**b**) *(allegiance)* cambiar (**to** por); *(attention)* desviar (**to** hacia)
▸**switch off** *vt sep* apagar
▸**switch on** *vt sep* encender, *Am* prender
▸**switch over** *vi* cambiar (**to** a)

switchboard ['swɪtʃbɔːd] *n* centralita *f*, *Am* conmutador *m*

Switzerland ['swɪtsələnd] *n* Suiza

swivel ['swɪvəl] **1** *n* **s. chair** silla giratoria
2 *vt & vi* girar

swollen ['swəʊlən] **1** *adj (ankle, face)* hinchado(a); *(river, lake)* crecido(a)
2 *pp of* **swell**

swoon [swuːn] **1** *n* desmayo *m*
2 *vi* desmayarse

swoop [swuːp] **1** *n* (**a**) *(of bird)* calada *f*; *(of plane)* (vuelo *m* en) picado *m or Am* picada *f* (**b**) *(by police)* redada *f*
2 *vi* (**a**) *(plane, bird)* volar en picado *or Am* picada (**b**) *(police)* hacer una redada

swop [swɒp] *n & vt* = **swap**

sword [sɔːd] *n* espada *f*

swordfish ['sɔːdfɪʃ] *n* pez *m* espada

swore [swɔː(r)] *pt of* **swear**

sworn [swɔːn] **1** *adj* jurado(a)
2 *pp of* **swear**

swot [swɒt] *vi Br Fam* matarse estudiando, *Esp* empollar, *RP* tragar (**for** para)

swum [swʌm] *pp of* **swim**

swung [swʌŋ] *pt & pp of* **swing**

sycamore ['sɪkəmɔː(r)] *n* (**a**) *Br* sicomoro *m* (**b**) *US (plane tree)* plátano *m*

syllable ['sɪləbəl] *n* sílaba *f*

syllabus ['sɪləbəs] *n* programa *m* de estudios

symbol ['sɪmbəl] *n* símbolo *m*

symbolic [sɪm'bɒlɪk] *adj* simbólico(a)

symbolize ['sɪmbəlaɪz] *vt* simbolizar

symmetry ['sɪmɪtrɪ] *n* simetría *f*

sympathetic [sɪmpə'θetɪk] *adj* (**a**) *(showing pity)* compasivo(a) (**b**) *(understanding)* comprensivo(a); *(kind)* amable

> ♪ Note that the Spanish word **simpático** is a false friend and is never a translation for the English word **sympathetic**. In Spanish **simpático** means "nice, likeable".

sympathize ['sɪmpəθaɪz] *vi* (**a**) *(show pity)* compadecerse (**with** de) (**b**) *(understand)* comprender

sympathizer ['sɪmpəθaɪzə(r)] *n* simpatizante *mf*

sympathy ['sɪmpəθɪ] *n* (**a**) *(pity)* compasión *f* (**b**) *(condolences)* pésame *m*; **letter of s.** pésame; **to express one's s.** dar el pésame (**c**) *(understanding)* comprensión *f*

> ♪ Note that the Spanish word **simpatía** is a false friend and is never a translation for the English word **sympathy**. In Spanish **simpatía** means "liking, affection".

symphony ['sɪmfənɪ] *n* sinfonía *f*

symposium [sɪm'pəʊzɪəm] *n* simposio *m*

symptom ['sɪmptəm] *n* síntoma *m*

symptomatic [sɪmptə'mætɪk] *adj* sintomático(a)

synagogue ['sɪnəɡɒɡ] *n* sinagoga *f*

synchronize ['sɪŋkrənaɪz] *vt* sincronizar

syndicate ['sɪndɪkɪt] *n* corporación *f*; **newspaper s.** sindicato periodístico

syndrome ['sɪndrəʊm] *n* síndrome *m*

synonym ['sɪnənɪm] *n* sinónimo *m*

synonymous [sɪ'nɒnɪməs] *adj* sinónimo(a) (**with** de)

synopsis [sɪ'nɒpsɪs] *n* sinopsis *f inv*

syntax ['sɪntæks] *n* sintaxis *f inv*

synthesis ['sɪnθɪsɪs] *n* (*pl* **syntheses** ['sɪnθɪsiːz]) síntesis *f inv*

synthesizer ['sɪnθɪsaɪzə(r)] *n* sintetizador *m*

synthetic [sɪn'θetɪk] *adj* sintético(a)

syphilis ['sɪfɪlɪs] *n* sífilis *f*

syphon ['saɪfən] *n* = **siphon**

Syria ['sɪrɪə] *n* Siria

Syrian ['sɪrɪən] *adj & n* sirio(a) *(m,f)*

syringe [sɪ'rɪndʒ] *n* jeringa *f*, jeringuilla *f*

syrup ['sɪrəp] *n* jarabe *m*, almíbar *m*

system ['sɪstəm] *n* sistema *m*; *Fam* **the s.** el orden establecido; *Comput* **systems analyst** analista *mf* de sistemas

systematic [sɪstɪ'mætɪk] *adj* sistemático(a)

T, t [tiː] *n (the letter)* T, t *f*

t *(abbr* **ton(s))* tonelada(s) *f(pl) (Br = 1.016 kilos; US = 907 kilos)*

ta [tɑː] *interj Br Fam* gracias

tab [tæb] *n* (**a**) *(flap)* lengüeta *f; (label)* etiqueta *f; Fam* **to keep tabs on sb** vigilar a algn (**b**) *US Fam (bill)* cuenta *f*

tabby ['tæbɪ] *n* **t. (cat)** gato(a) romano(a)

table ['teɪbəl] **1** *n* (**a**) *(furniture)* mesa *f;* **to lay** *or* **set the t.** poner la mesa; **t. lamp** lámpara *f* de mesa; **t. mat** salvamanteles *m inv;* **t. tennis** ping-pong® *m*, tenis *m* de mesa; **t. wine** vino *m* de mesa (**b**) *(of figures)* tabla *f*, cuadro *m;* **t. of contents** índice *m* de materias

2 *vt (motion, proposal) Br* presentar; *US* posponer

tablecloth ['teɪbəlklɒθ] *n* mantel *m*

tablespoon ['teɪbəlspuːn] *n* cucharón *m*

tablespoonful ['teɪbəlspuːnfʊl] *n* cucharada *f* grande

tablet ['tæblɪt] *n* (**a**) *Med* pastilla *f* (**b**) *(of stone)* lápida *f*

tableware ['teɪbəlweə(r)] *n* vajilla *f*

tabloid ['tæblɔɪd] *n* periódico *m* de pequeño formato; **t. press** prensa sensacionalista

taboo [tə'buː] *adj & n* tabú *(m)*

tabulate ['tæbjʊleɪt] *vt* disponer en listas

tacit ['tæsɪt] *adj* tácito(a)

taciturn ['tæsɪtɜːn] *adj* taciturno(a)

tack [tæk] **1** *n* (**a**) *(small nail)* tachuela *f* (**b**) *Sewing* hilván *m* (**c**) *Naut* amura *f; (distance)* bordada *f; Fig* **to change t.** cambiar de rumbo

2 *vt* (**a**) **to t. sth down** clavar algo con tachuelas (**b**) *Sewing* hilvanar

3 *vi Naut* virar de bordo

▸ **tack on** *vt sep (add)* añadir

tackle ['tækəl] **1** *n* (**a**) *(equipment)* aparejos *mpl;* **fishing t.** aparejos de pescar (**b**) *(challenge) (in football)* entrada *f; (in rugby, American football)* placaje *m, Am* tackle *m*

2 *vt* agarrar; *(task)* emprender; *(problem)* abordar; *(in football)* entrar a; *(in rugby, American football)* hacer un placaje a, *Am* tacklear

tacky¹ ['tækɪ] *adj* (**tackier, tackiest**) pegajoso(a)

tacky² ['tækɪ] *adj* (**tackier, tackiest**) *Fam (tasteless)* chabacano(a), ordinario(a)

tact [tækt] *n* tacto *m*, diplomacia *f*

tactful ['tæktfʊl] *adj* diplomático(a)

tactic ['tæktɪk] *n* táctica *f;* **tactics** táctica *f*

tactical ['tæktɪkəl] *adj* táctico(a)

tactless ['tæktlɪs] *adj* *(person)* poco diplomático(a); *(question)* indiscreto(a)

tadpole ['tædpəʊl] *n* renacuajo *m*

taffy ['tæfɪ] *n US* caramelo *m* de melaza

tag [tæg] *n* (**a**) *(label)* etiqueta *f* (**b**) *(saying)* coletilla *f*

▸ **tag along** *vi Fam* pegarse

▸ **tag on** *vt sep (add to end)* añadir

tai chi [taɪ'tʃiː] *n* tai-chi *m*

tail [teɪl] **1** *n* (**a**) *(of animal, plane)* cola *f;* **t. end** cola (**b**) *(of shirt)* faldón *m;* **to wear tails** ir de frac; **t. coat** frac *m* (**c**) **tails** *(of coin)* cruz *f*, *Andes, Ven* sello *m, Méx* sol *m, RP* ceca *f*

2 *vt Fam (follow)* seguir de cerca

▸ **tail away, tail off** *vi* desvanecerse

tailback ['teɪlbæk] *n Br* caravana *f*

tail-gate ['teɪlgeɪt] **1** *n Aut* puerta trasera

2 *vt US* conducir *or Am* manejar pegado a, pisar los talones a

taillight ['teɪllaɪt] *n Aut* faro *m* trasero

tailor ['teɪlə(r)] **1** *n* sastre *m;* **t.'s (shop)** sastrería *f*

2 *vt (suit)* confeccionar; *Fig* adaptar

tailor-made [teɪlə'meɪd] *adj* hecho(a) a la medida

tailwind ['teɪlwɪnd] *n* viento *m* de cola

taint [teɪnt] *vt* contaminar; *Fig* corromper

tainted ['teɪntɪd] *adj* contaminado(a); *(reputation)* manchado(a)

take [teɪk] **1** *vt (pt* **took**; *pp* **taken)** (**a**) *(grasp)* tomar, *Esp* coger, *Am* agarrar; **to t. an opportunity** aprovechar una oportunidad; **to t. hold of sth** agarrar algo; **to t. sth from one's pocket** sacarse algo del bolsillo; **t. your time!** ¡tómate el tiempo que quieras!; **to t. a bath** bañarse; **to t. care (of oneself)** cuidarse; **his car takes six people** caben seis personas en su coche; **is this seat taken?** ¿está ocupado

este asiento?; **to t. a decision** tomar una decisión; **to t. a liking/dislike to sb** tomar cariño/antipatía a algn; **to t. a photograph** sacar una fotografía; **t. the first road on the left** *esp Esp* coja la *or Am* agarre por la primera a la izquierda; **to t. the train** tomar *or esp Esp* coger el tren (**b**) *(accept)* aceptar; *(earn)* **to t. so much per week** recaudar tanto por semana (**c**) *(win)* ganar; *(prize)* llevarse (**d**) *(eat, drink)* tomar; **to t. drugs** drogarse (**e**) **she's taking (a degree in) law** estudia derecho; **to t. an exam (in …)** examinarse (de …) (**f**) *(person to a place)* llevar (**g**) *(endure)* aguantar (**h**) *(consider)* considerar (**i**) **I t. it that …** supongo que …; **what do you t. me for?** ¿por quién me tomas? (**j**) *(require)* requerir; **it takes an hour to get there** se tarda una hora en llegar hasta allí (**k**) **to be taken ill** enfermar
2 *n Cin* toma *f*

▸ **take after** *vt insep* parecerse a

▸ **take apart** *vt sep (machine)* desmontar

▸ **take away** *vt sep* (**a**) *(carry off)* llevarse (**b**) **to t. sth away from sb** quitar *or Am* sacar algo a algn (**c**) *Math* restar

▸ **take back** *vt sep* (**a**) *(give back)* devolver; *(receive back)* recuperar (**b**) *(withdraw)* retractarse

▸ **take down** *vt sep* (**a**) *(lower)* bajar (**b**) *(demolish)* derribar (**c**) *(write)* apuntar

▸ **take in** *vt sep* (**a**) *(shelter, lodge)* alojar, acoger (**b**) *Sewing* meter (**c**) *(include)* abarcar (**d**) *(understand)* entender (**e**) *(deceive)* engañar

▸ **take off 1** *vt sep* (**a**) *(remove)* quitar, *Am* sacar; **he took off his jacket** se quitó *or Am* se sacó la chaqueta (**b**) *(lead or carry away)* llevarse (**c**) *(deduct)* descontar (**d**) *(imitate)* imitar burlonamente
2 *vi (plane)* despegar, *Am* decolar

▸ **take on** *vt sep* (**a**) *(undertake)* encargarse de (**b**) *(acquire)* tomar (**c**) *(employ)* contratar (**d**) *(compete with)* competir con

▸ **take out** *vt sep* sacar, quitar; **he's taking me out to dinner** me ha invitado a cenar fuera

▸ **take over 1** *vt sep Com & Pol* tomar posesión de; **the rebels took over the country** los rebeldes se apoderaron del país
2 *vi* **to t. over from sb** relevar a algn

▸ **take to** *vt insep (become fond of)* tomar *or Esp* coger cariño a; **to t. to drink** darse a la bebida

▸ **take up** *vt sep* (**a**) *Sewing* acortar (**b**) *(accept)* aceptar; *(adopt)* adoptar (**c**) **I've taken up the piano/French** he empezado a tocar el piano/a aprender francés (**d**) *(occupy)* ocupar

takeaway ['teɪkəweɪ] *Br* **1** *n (food)* comida *f* para llevar; *(restaurant)* restaurante *m* que vende comida para llevar
2 *adj (food)* para llevar

take-home pay ['teɪkhəʊm'peɪ] *n* sueldo neto

taken ['teɪkən] *pp of* **take**

takeoff ['teɪkɒf] *n* (**a**) *(plane, economy)* despegue *m*, *Am* decolaje *m* (**b**) *(imitation)* imitación burlona

takeout ['teɪkaʊt] *US* **1** *n (food)* comida *f* para llevar
2 *adj (food)* para llevar

takeover ['teɪkəʊvə(r)] *n Com* absorción *f*; **military t.** golpe *m* de estado; **t. bid** oferta pública de adquisición, OPA *f*

takings ['teɪkɪŋz] *npl Br Com* recaudación *f*

talc [tælk] *n* talco *m*

talcum powder ['tælkəmpaʊdə(r)] *n (polvos mpl de)* talco *m*

tale [teɪl] *n* cuento *m*; **to tell tales** contar chismes

talent ['tælənt] *n* talento *m*

talented ['tæləntɪd] *adj* dotado(a)

talk [tɔːk] **1** *vi (talk)* hablar, *CAm, Méx* platicar; *(chat)* charlar; *(gossip)* chismorrear; *Fam* **now you're talking!** ¡eso sí que me interesa!
2 *vt* **to t. nonsense** decir tonterías; **to t. sense** hablar con sentido común; **to t. shop** hablar del trabajo
3 *n* (**a**) *(conversation)* conversación *f*, *CAm, Méx* plática *f* (**b**) *(words)* palabras *fpl*; **he's all t.** no hace más que hablar (**c**) *(rumour)* rumor *m*; *(gossip)* chismes *mpl* (**d**) *(lecture)* charla *f*

▸ **talk into** *vt sep* **to t. sb into sth** convencer a algn para que haga algo

▸ **talk out of** *vt sep* **to t. sb out of sth** disuadir a algn de que haga algo

▸ **talk over** *vt sep* discutir

talkative ['tɔːkətɪv] *adj* hablador(a)

talking ['tɔːkɪŋ] *n* **no t. please!** ¡silencio, por favor!; **t. book** audiolibro *m*; **t. point** tema *m* de conversación

talking-to ['tɔːkɪŋtuː] *n Fam* sermón *m*, *Esp* rapapolvo *m*

tall [tɔːl] *adj* alto(a); **a tree 10 m t.** un árbol de 10 m (de alto); **how t. are you?** ¿cuánto mides?; *Fig* **that's a t. order** eso es mucho pedir

tally ['tælɪ] **1** *vi* **to t. with sth** corresponderse con algo

2 n Com apunte m; **to keep a t. of** llevar la cuenta de

talon ['tælən] n garra f

> 📖 Note that the Spanish word **talón** is a false friend and is never a translation for the English word **talon**. In Spanish, **talón** means both "heel" and "cheque".

tambourine [tæmbə'riːn] n pandereta f

tame [teɪm] **1** adj (a) (animal) domado(a); (by nature) manso(a); (person) dócil (b) (style) soso(a)
2 vt domar

tamper ['tæmpə(r)] vi **to t. with** (text) adulterar; (records, an entry) falsificar; (lock) intentar forzar

tampon ['tæmpɒn] n tampón m

tan [tæn] **1** n (a) (colour) marrón rojizo (b) (of skin) bronceado m, Esp moreno m
2 adj (colour) marrón rojizo
3 vt (a) (leather) curtir (b) (skin) broncear
4 vi ponerse moreno(a)

tang [tæŋ] n sabor m fuerte

tangent ['tændʒənt] n tangente f; Fig **to go off at a t.** salirse por la tangente

tangerine [tændʒə'riːn] n clementina f

tangible ['tændʒəbəl] adj tangible

tangle ['tæŋgəl] n (of thread) maraña f; Fig lío m; Fig **to get into a t.** hacerse un lío

tangled ['tæŋgəld] adj enredado(a), enmarañado(a)

tank [tæŋk] n (a) (container) depósito m (b) Mil tanque m

tanker ['tæŋkə(r)] n Naut tanque m; (for oil) petrolero m; Aut camión m cisterna

Tannoy® ['tænɔɪ] n (sistema m) de megafonía f

tantalize ['tæntəlaɪz] vt atormentar

tantalizing ['tæntəlaɪzɪŋ] adj atormentador(a)

tantamount ['tæntəmaʊnt] adj **t. to** equivalente a

tantrum ['tæntrəm] n rabieta f

tap¹ [tæp] **1** vt golpear suavemente; (with hand) dar una palmadita a
2 vi **to t. at the door** llamar suavemente a la puerta
3 n golpecito m; **t. dancing** claqué m

tap² [tæp] **1** n Br (for water) grifo m, Chile, Col, Méx llave f, RP canilla f; Fig **funds on t.** fondos mpl disponibles
2 vt (a) (stick with tape) pegar con cinta adhesiva; Fig **I've got him/it taped** lo tengo controlado (b) (record) grabar

tape [teɪp] **1** n (a) (ribbon) cinta f; **sticky t.** cinta adhesiva; **t. measure** cinta métrica (b) (for recording) cinta (magnetofónica)

t. recorder magnetófono m, cassette m; **t. recording** grabación f
2 vt (a) (stick with tape) pegar (con cinta adhesiva) (b) (record) grabar (en cinta)

taper ['teɪpə(r)] **1** vi estrecharse; (to a point) afilarse
2 n (candle) vela f

▸ **taper off** vi ir disminuyendo

tapestry ['tæpɪstrɪ] n tapiz m

tapping ['tæpɪŋ] n (a) (of tree) sangría f; (of resources) explotación f (b) Tel intervención f ilegal de un teléfono

tar [tɑː(r)] n alquitrán m

target ['tɑːgɪt] n (a) (object aimed at) blanco m; **t. practice** tiro m al blanco (b) (purpose) meta f

tariff ['tærɪf] n tarifa f, arancel m

tarmac® ['tɑːmæk] **1** n (a) (substance) alquitrán m (b) Av pista f de aterrizaje
2 vt alquitranar

tarnish ['tɑːnɪʃ] vt deslustrar

tarpaulin [tɑː'pɔːlɪn] n lona f

tart¹ [tɑːt] n Br Culin tarta f

tart² [tɑːt] adj (taste) ácido(a), agrio(a)

tart³ [tɑːt] Fam **1** n fulana f, Méx piruja f
2 vt Br **to t. oneself up** emperifollarse

tartan ['tɑːtən] n tartán m

tartar ['tɑːtə(r)] n (a) Chem tártaro m (b) Culin **sauce** salsa tártara

task [tɑːsk] n tarea f; **to take sb to t.** reprender a algn; Mil **t. force** destacamento m (de fuerzas)

tassel ['tæsəl] n borla f

taste [teɪst] **1** n (a) (sense) gusto m; (flavour) sabor m; **it has a burnt t.** sabe a quemado (b) (sample) (of food) bocado m; (of drink) trago m; **to give sb a t. of his own medicine** pagar a algn con la misma moneda (c) (liking) afición f; **to have a t. for sth** gustarle a uno algo (d) **in bad t.** de mal gusto; **to have (good) t.** tener (buen) gusto
2 vt (sample) probar
3 vi **to t. of sth** saber a algo

tasteful ['teɪstful] adj de buen gusto

tasteless ['teɪstlɪs] adj (a) (food) soso(a) (b) (in bad taste) de mal gusto

tasty ['teɪstɪ] adj (**tastier, tastiest**) sabroso(a)

tattered ['tætəd] adj hecho(a) jirones

tatters ['tætəz] npl **in t.** hecho(a) jirones

tattoo¹ [tæ'tuː] n Mil retreta f

tattoo² [tæ'tuː] **1** vt tatuar
2 n (mark) tatuaje m

tatty ['tætɪ] adj (**tattier, tattiest**) Fam ajado(a), Esp sobado(a)

taught [tɔːt] pt & pp of **teach**

taunt [tɔːnt] **1** *vt* **to t. sb with sth** echar algo en cara a algn
2 *n* pulla *f*

Taurus ['tɔːrəs] *n* Tauro *m*

taut [tɔːt] *adj* tenso(a), tirante

tavern ['tævən] *n* taberna *f*

tawdry ['tɔːdrɪ] *adj* (**tawdrier, tawdriest**) hortera

tawn(e)y ['tɔːnɪ] *adj* leonado(a), rojizo(a)

tax [tæks] **1** *n* impuesto *m*; **t. free** exento(a) de impuestos; **t. collector** recaudador(a) *m,f* (de impuestos); **t. evasion** evasión *f* fiscal; **t. return** declaración *f* de renta
2 *vt* (**a**) (*goods, income*) gravar; (*people*) cobrar impuestos a (**b**) (*patience etc*) poner a prueba

taxable ['tæksəbəl] *adj* imponible

taxation [tæk'seɪʃən] *n* impuestos *mpl*

taxi ['tæksɪ] **1** *n* taxi *m*; **t. driver** taxista *mf*; **t.** *Br* **rank** *or US* **stand** parada *f* de taxis
2 *vi* (*aircraft*) rodar por la pista

taxidermy ['tæksɪdɜːmɪ] *n* taxidermia *f*

taxing ['tæksɪŋ] *adj* exigente

taxpayer ['tækspeɪə(r)] *n* contribuyente *mf*

TB [tiː'biː] *n* (*abbr* **tuberculosis**) tuberculosis *f inv*

tea [tiː] *n* (**a**) (*plant, drink*) té *m*; **t. bag** bolsita *f* de té; **t. break** descanso *m*; *Br* **t. cosy** cubretetera *f*; **t. leaf** hoja *f* de té; **t. service** *or* **set** juego *m* de té; **t. towel** trapo *m* *or* paño *m* (de cocina); *RP* repasador *m* (**b**) (*snack*) merienda *f*; (**high**) **t.** merienda-cena *f*

teach [tiːtʃ] **1** *vt* (*pt & pp* **taught**) enseñar; (*subject*) dar clases de; **to t. sb** (**how**) **to do sth** enseñar a algn a hacer algo; *US* **to t. school** ser profesor(a)
2 *vi* dar clases, ser profesor(a)

teacher ['tiːtʃə(r)] *n* profesor(a) *m,f*; (*in primary school*) maestro(a) *m,f*

teaching ['tiːtʃɪŋ] *n* enseñanza *f*

teacup ['tiːkʌp] *n* taza *f* de té

teak [tiːk] *n* teca *f*

team [tiːm] *n* equipo *m*; (*of oxen*) yunta *f*

team-mate ['tiːmmeɪt] *n* compañero(a) *m,f* de equipo

teamwork ['tiːmwɜːk] *n* trabajo *m* en equipo

teapot ['tiːpɒt] *n* tetera *f*

tear¹ [tɪə(r)] *n* lágrima *f*; **to be in tears** estar llorando; **t. gas** gas lacrimógeno

tear² [teə(r)] **1** *vt* (*pt* **tore**; *pp* **torn**) (**a**) (*rip*) rasgar (**b**) (*snatch*) **to t. sth out of sb's hands** arrancarle algo de las manos a algn

2 *vi* (**a**) (*cloth*) rajarse (**b**) **to t. along** ir a toda velocidad
3 *n* desgarrón *m*; (*in clothes*) rasgón *m*
▸ **tear down** *vt sep* derribar
▸ **tear off** *vt sep* arrancar
▸ **tear out** *vt sep* arrancar
▸ **tear up** *vt sep* (**a**) (*document, photo*) romper, hacer pedazos (**b**) (*uproot*) arrancar de raíz

tearful ['tɪəfʊl] *adj* lloroso(a)

tearoom ['tiːruːm] *n* *Br* = **teashop**

tease [tiːz] **1** *vt* tomar el pelo a
2 *n* bromista *mf*

teashop ['tiːʃɒp] *n* *Br* salón *m* de té

teaspoon ['tiːspuːn] *n* cucharilla *f*

teaspoonful ['tiːspuːnfʊl] *n* cucharadita *f*

teat [tiːt] *n* (*of animal*) teta *f*; (*of bottle*) tetina *f*

teatime ['tiːtaɪm] *n* *esp Br* hora *f* del té

technical ['teknɪkəl] *adj* técnico(a); *Br* **t. college** escuela *f* de formación profesional

technicality [teknɪ'kælɪtɪ] *n* detalle técnico

technically ['teknɪkəlɪ] *adv* (*theoretically*) en teoría

technician [tek'nɪʃən] *n* técnico(a) *m,f*

technique [tek'niːk] *n* técnica *f*

techno ['teknəʊ] *n* tecno *m*

technological [teknə'lɒdʒɪkəl] *adj* tecnológico(a)

technology [tek'nɒlədʒɪ] *n* tecnología *f*

teddy bear ['tedɪbeə(r)] *n* oso *m* de felpa

tedious ['tiːdɪəs] *adj* tedioso(a), aburrido(a)

tee [tiː] *n* (*in golf*) tee *m*

teem [tiːm] *vi* **to t. with** rebosar de; *Fam* **it was teeming down** llovía a cántaros

teenage ['tiːneɪdʒ] *adj* adolescente

teenager ['tiːneɪdʒə(r)] *n* adolescente *mf*

teens [tiːnz] *npl* adolescencia *f*

teeshirt ['tiːʃɜːt] *n* camiseta *f*, *Méx* playera, *RP* remera *f*

teeter ['tiːtə(r)] *vi* balancearse

teeth [tiːθ] *pl of* **tooth**

teethe [tiːð] *vi* echar los dientes

teething ['tiːðɪŋ] *n* **t. ring** chupador *m*; *Fig* **t. troubles** dificultades *fpl* iniciales

teetotaller [tiː'təʊtələ(r)] *n* abstemio(a) *m,f*

TEFL ['tefəl] *n* (*abbr* **Teaching of English as a Foreign Language**) enseñanza *f* del inglés como idioma extranjero

telecommunications ['telɪkəmjuːnɪ'keɪʃənz] *n sing* telecomunicaciones *fpl*

telegram ['telɪgræm] *n* telegrama *m*

telegraph ['telɪgrɑːf] **1** n telégrafo m; **t. pole** poste telegráfico
2 vt & vi telegrafiar

telemarketing [telɪmɑːkɪtɪŋ] n Com telemarketing m

telepathy [tɪˈlepəθɪ] n telepatía f

telephone ['telɪfəʊn] **1** n teléfono m; **t. banking** telebanca f; Br **t. booth** or **box** cabina (telefónica); **t. call** llamada telefónica, Am llamado telefónico; **t. directory** guía telefónica, Am directorio m de teléfonos; **t. number** número m de teléfono
2 vt telefonear, llamar por teléfono a, Am hablar por teléfono a

telephonist [tɪˈlefənɪst] n Br telefonista mf

telephoto ['telɪfəʊtəʊ] adj **t. lens** teleobjetivo m

teleprinter ['telɪprɪntə(r)] n teletipo m

telesales [telɪˈseɪlz] npl Com televenta f, ventas fpl por teléfono

telescope ['telɪskəʊp] **1** n telescopio m
2 vi plegarse (como un catalejo)
3 vt plegar

telescopic [telɪˈskɒpɪk] adj (umbrella) plegable

teleshopping ['telɪʃɒpɪŋ] n Com telecompra f

televise ['telɪvaɪz] vt televisar

television ['telɪvɪʒən] n televisión f; **t. programme** programa m de televisión; **t. (set)** televisor m

teleworker ['telɪwɜːkə(r)] n teletrabajador(a) m,f

teleworking ['telɪwɜːkɪŋ] n teletrabajo m

telex ['teleks] **1** n télex m
2 vt enviar por télex

tell [tel] **1** vt (pt & pp **told**) (a) (say) decir; (relate) contar; (inform) comunicar; **to t. lies** mentir; **to t. sb about sth** contarle algo a algn; **you're telling me!** ¡a mí me lo vas a contar! (b) (order) mandar; **to t. sb to do sth** decir a algn que haga algo (c) (distinguish) distinguir; **to know how to t. the time** saber decir la hora (d) **all told** en total
2 vi (a) (reveal) reflejar (b) **who can t.?** (know) ¿quién sabe? (c) (have effect) notarse; **the pressure is telling on her** está acusando la presión
▸ **tell off** vt sep Fam (scold) **to t. sb off (for)** echar una reprimenda or Esp bronca a algn (por)

teller ['telə(r)] n (in bank etc) cajero(a) m,f

telling ['telɪŋ] adj (action) eficaz; (blow, argument) contundente

telltale ['telteɪl] n acusica mf, Esp chivato(a) m,f; **t. signs** señales reveladoras

telly ['telɪ] n Br Fam **the t.** la tele

temp [temp] n Fam trabajador(a) m,f temporal

temper ['tempə(r)] **1** n (a) (mood) humor m; **to keep one's t.** no perder la calma; **to lose one's t.** perder los estribos (b) (temperament) **to have a bad t.** tener (mal) genio
2 vt (in metallurgy) templar; Fig suavizar

temperament ['tempərəmənt] n temperamento m

temperamental [tempərəmentəl] adj temperamental

temperate ['tempərɪt] adj (a) (language, criticism) moderado(a) (b) (climate) templado(a)

temperature ['temprɪtʃə(r)] n temperatura f; **to have a t.** tener fiebre

tempest ['tempɪst] n Literary tempestad f

temple¹ ['tempəl] n Archit templo m

temple² ['tempəl] n Anat sien f

tempo ['tempəʊ] n tempo m

temporary ['tempərərɪ] adj temporal, Am temporario(a); (office, arrangement, repairs) provisional, Am temporario(a)

tempt [tempt] vt tentar; **to t. providence** tentar la suerte; **to t. sb to do sth** incitar a algn a hacer algo

temptation [tempˈteɪʃən] n tentación f

tempting ['temptɪŋ] adj tentador(a)

ten [ten] adj & n diez (m inv)

tenable ['tenəbəl] adj (opinion) sostenible

tenacious [tɪˈneɪʃəs] adj tenaz

tenancy ['tenənsɪ] n (of house) alquiler m; (of land) arrendamiento m

tenant ['tenənt] n (of house) inquilino(a) m,f; (of farm) arrendatario(a) m,f

tend¹ [tend] vi (be inclined) tender, tener tendencia (**to** a)

tend² [tend] vt (care for) cuidar

tendency ['tendənsɪ] n tendencia f

tender¹ ['tendə(r)] adj (affectionate) cariñoso(a); (compassionate) compasivo(a); (meat) tierno(a)

tender² ['tendə(r)] **1** vt ofrecer; **to t. one's resignation** presentar la dimisión
2 vi Com **to t. for** sacar a concurso
3 n (a) Com oferta f (b) **legal t.** moneda f de curso legal

tenderness ['tendənɪs] n ternura f

tendon ['tendən] n tendón m

tenement ['tenɪmənt] n **t. (building)** bloque m de apartamentos or Esp pisos or Arg departamentos

tenet ['tenɪt] n principio m

tennis ['tenɪs] *n* tenis *m*; **t. ball** pelota *f* de tenis; **t. court** pista *f* de tenis; **t. player** tenista *mf*; **t. racket** raqueta *f* de tenis; **t. shoe** zapatilla *f* de tenis

tenor ['tenə(r)] *n Mus* tenor *m*

tense¹ [tens] *adj* tenso(a)

tense² [tens] *n Ling* tiempo *m*

tension ['tenʃən] *n* tensión *f*

tent [tent] *n* tienda *f* de campaña, *Am* carpa *f*; **t. peg** estaca *f*

tentacle ['tentəkəl] *n* tentáculo *m*

tentative ['tentətɪv] *adj* (a) *(not definite)* de prueba (b) *(hesitant)* indeciso(a)

tenterhooks ['tentəhʊks] *npl Fig* **on t.** sobre ascuas

tenth [tenθ] **1** *adj & n* décimo(a) *(m,f)*
2 *n (fraction)* décimo *m*

tenuous ['tenjʊəs] *adj* (a) *(connection)* tenue (b) *(argument)* flojo(a)

tenure ['tenjʊə(r)] *n* (a) *(of office)* ocupación *f* (b) *(of property)* arrendamiento *m*

tepid ['tepɪd] *adj* tibio(a)

term [tɜːm] **1** *n* (a) *(period)* período *m*; *Educ* trimestre *m*; **t. of office** mandato *m*, legislatura *f*; **in the long/short t.** a largo/corto plazo (b) *(word)* término *m*; *Fig* **in terms of money** en cuanto al dinero (c) **terms** *(conditions)* condiciones *fpl*; **to come to terms with** hacerse a la idea de (d) **to be on good/bad terms with sb** tener buenas/malas relaciones con algn
2 *vt* calificar de

terminal ['tɜːmɪnəl] **1** *adj* terminal; **t. cancer** cáncer incurable
2 *n* terminal *f*

terminate ['tɜːmɪneɪt] **1** *vt* terminar; **to t. a pregnancy** abortar
2 *vi* terminarse

termini ['tɜːmɪnaɪ] *pl of* **terminus**

terminology [tɜːmɪ'nɒlədʒɪ] *n* terminología *f*

terminus ['tɜːmɪnəs] *n (pl* **termini)** terminal *m*

terrace ['terəs] *n* (a) *(on hillside)* terraza *f* (b) *(outside cafe, hotel)* terraza *f* (c) *Br (of houses)* hilera *f* de casas adosadas (d) *Br Ftb* **the terraces** las gradas

terraced ['terəst] *adj Br (hillside)* en terrazas; *Br (house, row)* adosado(a)

terrain [tə'reɪn] *n* terreno *m*

terrestrial [tɪ'restrɪəl] *adj* terrestre

terrible ['terəbəl] *adj* horrible, terrible

terribly ['terəblɪ] *adv* tremendamente mal, *Esp* fatal

terrier ['terɪə(r)] *n* terrier *m*

terrific [tə'rɪfɪk] *adj* (a) *Fam (excellent)* estupendo, genial (b) *(extreme)* tremendo(a)

terrify ['terɪfaɪ] *vt* aterrorizar

terrifying ['terɪfaɪɪŋ] *adj* aterrador(a)

territory ['terɪtərɪ] *n* territorio *m*

terror ['terə(r)] *n* terror *m*

terrorism ['terərɪzəm] *n* terrorismo *m*

terrorist ['terərɪst] *adj & n* terrorista *(mf)*

terrorize ['terəraɪz] *vt* aterrorizar

terry ['terɪ] *n* **t. towel** toalla *f* de rizo

terse [tɜːs] *adj (curt)* lacónico(a)

tertiary ['tɜːʃɪərɪ] *adj Br Educ* superior

test [test] **1** *vt* probar, someter a una prueba; *(analyse)* analizar; *Med* hacer un análisis de
2 *n* prueba *f*, examen *m*; **to put to the t.** poner a prueba; **to stand the t.** pasar la prueba; **t. match** partido *m* internacional; **t. pilot** piloto *m* de pruebas; **t. tube** probeta *f*; **t.-tube baby** niño *m* probeta

testament ['testəmənt] *n* testamento *m*; **Old/New T.** Antiguo/Nuevo Testamento

testicle ['testɪkəl] *n* testículo *m*

testify ['testɪfaɪ] **1** *vt* declarar
2 *vi Fig* **to t. to sth** atestiguar algo

testimonial [testɪ'məʊnɪəl] *n* recomendación *f*

testimony ['testɪmənɪ] *n* testimonio *m*, declaración *f*

tetanus ['tetənəs] *n* tétano(s) *m inv*

tether ['teðə(r)] **1** *n* ronzal *m*; *Fig* **to be at the end of one's t.** estar hasta la coronilla
2 *vt (animal)* atar

Texas ['teksəs] *n* Tejas

text [tekst] **1** *n* texto *m*; **t. (message)** mensaje *m* de texto
2 *vt (send text message to)* enviar un mensaje de texto a

textbook ['tekstbʊk] *n* libro *m* de texto

textile ['tekstaɪl] **1** *n* tejido *m*
2 *adj* textil

texture ['tekstʃə(r)] *n* textura *f*

Thai [taɪ] *adj & n* tailandés(esa) *(m,f)*

Thailand ['taɪlænd] *n* Tailandia

Thames [temz] *n* **the T.** el Támesis

than [ðæn, *unstressed* ðən] *conj* que; *(with numbers)* de; **he's older t. me** es mayor que yo; **I have more/less t. you** tengo más/menos que tú; **more interesting t. we thought** más interesante de lo que creíamos; **more t. once** más de una vez; **more t. ten people** más de diez personas

thank [θæŋk] *vt* agradecer; **t. you** gracias

thankful ['θæŋkfʊl] *adj* agradecido(a)

thankless ['θæŋklɪs] *adj (task)* ingrato(a)

thanks [θæŋks] *npl* gracias *fpl*; **no t.** no gracias; **many t.** muchas gracias; **t. for phoning** gracias por llamar; **t. to** gracias a

Thanksgiving [θæŋks'gɪvɪŋ] *n US* **T. (Day)** Día *m* de Acción de Gracias

that [ðæt, *unstressed* ðət] **1** *dem pron* (*pl* **those**) (**a**) (*in near to middle distance*) ése *m*, ésa *f*; (*further away*) aquél *m*, aquélla *f*; **this one is new but t. is old** éste es nuevo pero ése es viejo (**b**) (*indefinite*) eso; (*remote*) aquello; **after t.** después de eso; **like t.** así; **t.'s right** eso es; **t.'s where I live** allí vivo yo; **what's t.?** ¿qué es eso?; **who's t.?** ¿quién es? (**c**) (*with relative*) el/la; **all those I saw** todos los que vi

2 *dem adj* (*pl* **those**) (*masculine*) ese; (*feminine*) esa; (*further away*) (*masculine*) aquel; (*feminine*) aquella; **at t. time** en aquella época; **t. book** ese/aquel libro; **t. one** ése/aquél

3 *rel pron* (**a**) (*subject, direct object*) que; **all (t.) you said** todo lo que dijiste; **the letter (t.) I sent you** la carta que te envié (**b**) (*governed by preposition*) que, el/la que, los/las que, el/la cual, los/las cuales; **the car (t.) they came in** el coche en el que vinieron (**c**) (*when*) que, en que; **the moment (t.) you arrived** el momento en que llegaste

> El pronombre relativo **that** puede omitirse salvo cuando es sujeto de la oración subordinada.

4 *conj* que; **come here so (t.) I can see you** ven aquí (para) que te vea; **he said (t.) he would come** dijo que vendría

> La conjunción **that** se puede omitir cuando introduce una oración subordinada.

5 *adv* así de, tanto, tan; **cut off t. much** córteme un trozo así de grande; **I don't think it can be t. old** no creo que sea tan viejo; **we haven't got t. much money** no tenemos tanto dinero

thatched [θætʃt] *adj* cubierto(a) con paja; **t. cottage** casita *f* con techo de paja; **t. roof** techo *m* de paja

thaw [θɔː] **1** *vt* (*snow*) derretir; (*food, freezer*) descongelar

2 *vi* descongelarse; (*snow*) derretirse

3 *n* deshielo *m*

the [ðə, *before vowel sound* ðɪ, *emphatic* ðiː] **1** *def art* (**a**) (*singular*) el/la; (*plural*) los/las; **at/to t.** al/a la; *pl* a los/a las; **of** or **from t.** del/de la; *pl* de los/de las; **t. Alps** los Alpes; **t. right time** la hora exacta; **t. voice of t. people** la voz del pueblo; (*omitted*) **George t. Sixth** Jorge Sexto (**c**) **by t. day** al día; **by t. dozen** a docenas (**d**)

(with adjectives used as nouns) **t. elderly** los ancianos (**e**) *(indicating kind)* **he's not t. person to do that** no es de los que hacen tales cosas (**f**) *(enough)* **he hasn't t. patience to wait** no tiene suficiente paciencia para esperar

2 *adv* **t. more t. merrier** cuantos más mejor; **t. sooner t. better** cuanto antes mejor

theatre, *US* **theater** ['θɪətə(r)] *n* teatro *m*

theatre-goer, *US* **theater-goer** ['θɪətə-gəʊə(r)] *n* aficionado(a) *m,f* al teatro

theatrical [θɪ'ætrɪkəl] *adj* teatral

theft [θeft] *n* robo *m*; **petty t.** hurto *m*

their [ðeə(r)] *poss adj* su; *pl* sus

theirs [ðeəz] *poss pron* (el) suyo/(la) suya; *pl* (los) suyos/(las) suyas

them [ðem, *unstressed* ðəm] *pers pron pl* (**a**) (*direct object*) los/las; (*indirect object*) les; **I know t.** los/las conozco; **I shall tell t. so** se lo diré (a ellos/ellas); **it's t.!** ¡son ellos!; **speak to t.** hábleles (**b**) (*with preposition*) ellos/ellas; **walk in front of t.** camine delante de ellos; **they took the keys away with t.** se llevaron las llaves; **both of t., the two of t.** los dos; **neither of t.** ninguno de los dos; **none of t.** ninguno de ellos

theme [θiːm] *n* tema *m*; **t. tune** sintonía *f*

themselves [ðəm'selvz] *pers pron pl* (*as subject*) ellos mismos/ellas mismas; (*as direct or indirect object*) se; (*after a preposition*) sí mismos/sí mismas; **they did it by t.** lo hicieron ellos solos

then [ðen] **1** *adv* (**a**) (*at that time*) entonces; **since t.** desde entonces; **there and t.** en el acto; **till t.** hasta entonces (**b**) (*next, afterwards*) luego (**c**) (*anyway*) de todas formas (**d**) (*in that case*) entonces; **go t.** pues vete

2 *conj* entonces

3 *adj* **the t. president** el entonces presidente

theology [θɪ'ɒlədʒɪ] *n* teología *f*

theoretic(al) [θɪə'retɪk(əl)] *adj* teórico(a)

theoretically [θɪə'retɪklɪ] *adv* teóricamente

theory ['θɪərɪ] *n* teoría *f*

therapeutic [θerə'pjuːtɪk] *adj also Fig* terapéutico(a)

therapist ['θerəpɪst] *n* terapeuta *mf*

therapy ['θerəpɪ] *n* terapia *f*

there [ðeə(r), *unstressed* ðə(r)] **1** *adv* (**a**) (*indicating place*) allí, allá; (*nearer speaker*) ahí; **here and t.** acá y allá; **in t.** ahí dentro; **is Peter t.?** ¿está Peter? (**b**) (*emphatic*) **that man t.** aquel hombre (**c**) (*unstressed*) **t. is .../t. are ...** hay ...; **t. were many cars** había muchos coches; **t.**

were six of us éramos seis (**d**) (*in respect*) **t.'s the difficulty** ahí está la dificultad

2 *interj* **so t.!** ¡ea!; **t., t.** bien, bien

thereabouts [ˈðeərəbaʊts], *US* **thereabout** [ˈðeərəbaʊt] *adv* **in Cambridge or t.** en Cambridge o por allí cerca; **at four o'clock or t.** a las cuatro o así

thereafter [ðeərˈɑːftə(r)] *adv* a partir de entonces

thereby [ˈðeəbaɪ] *adv* por eso *or* ello

therefore [ˈðeəfɔː(r)] *adv* por lo tanto, por eso

thermal [ˈθɜːməl] **1** *adj* (*spring*) termal; *Phys* térmico(a)

2 *n Met* corriente térmica

thermometer [θəˈmɒmɪtə(r)] *n* termómetro *m*

Thermos® [ˈθɜːməs] *n* **T. (flask)** termo *m*

thermostat [ˈθɜːməstæt] *n* termostato *m*

thesaurus [θɪˈsɔːrəs] *n* diccionario *m* de sinónimos

these [ðiːz] **1** *dem adj pl* estos(as)

2 *dem pron pl* éstos(as); *see* **this**

thesis [ˈθiːsɪs] *n* (*pl* **theses** [ˈθiːsiːz]) tesis *f inv*

they [ðeɪ] *pron pl* (**a**) (*personal use*) ellos/ ellas (*usually omitted in Spanish, except for contrast*); **t. are dancing** están bailando; **t. are rich** son ricos (**b**) (*stressed*) **t. alone** ellos solos; **t. themselves told me** me lo dijeron ellos mismos (**c**) (*with relative*) los/las (**d**) (*indefinite*) **that's what t. say** eso es lo que se dice; **t. say that …** se dice que …

thick [θɪk] **1** *adj* (**a**) (*book etc*) grueso(a); **a wall 2 m t.** un muro de 2 m de espesor (**b**) (*dense*) espeso(a) (**c**) *Fam* (*stupid*) tonto(a)

2 *adv* densamente

3 *n* **to be in the t. of it** estar metido(a) de lleno

thicken [ˈθɪkən] **1** *vt* espesar

2 *vi* espesarse; *Fig* (*plot*) complicarse

thickness [ˈθɪknɪs] *n* (*of wall etc*) espesor *m*; (*of wire, lips*) grueso *m*; (*of liquid, woodland*) espesura *f*

thickset [θɪkˈset] *adj* (*person*) rechoncho(a)

thick-skinned [θɪkˈskɪnd] *adj Fig* poco sensible

thief [θiːf] *n* (*pl* **thieves** [θiːvz]) ladrón(ona) *m,f*

thigh [θaɪ] *n* muslo *m*

thimble [ˈθɪmbəl] *n* dedal *m*

thin [θɪn] *adj* (**thinner, thinnest**) (**a**) (*not thick*) delgado(a); **a t. slice** una loncha fina (**b**) (*hair, vegetation*) ralo(a); (*liquid*) claro(a); (*population*) escaso(a) (**c**) *Fig*

(*voice*) débil; **a t. excuse** un pobre pretexto

2 *vt* **to t. (down)** (*paint*) diluir

thing [θɪŋ] *n* (**a**) (*object*) cosa *f*; **my things** (*clothing*) mi ropa *f*; (*possessions*) mis cosas *fpl*; **for one t.** en primer lugar; **the t. is …** resulta que …; **what with one t. and another** entre unas cosas y otras; **as things are** tal como están las cosas (**b**) **poor little t.!** ¡pobrecito(a)!

think [θɪŋk] **1** *vt* (*pt & pp* **thought**) (**a**) (*believe*) pensar, creer; **I t. so/not** creo que sí/no (**b**) **I thought as much** yo me lo imaginaba

2 *vi* (**a**) (*reflect*) pensar (**of** *or* **about** en); **give me time to t.** dame tiempo para reflexionar; **to t. ahead** prevenir (**b**) (*have as opinion*) opinar, pensar; **to t. highly of sb** apreciar a algn; **what do you t.?** ¿a ti qué te parece? (**c**) **just t.!** ¡imagínate!

▸ **think out** *vt sep* meditar; **a carefully thought-out answer** una respuesta razonada

▸ **think over** *vt sep* reflexionar; **we'll have to t. it over** lo tendremos que pensar

▸ **think up** *vt sep* imaginar, idear

thinking [ˈθɪŋkɪŋ] *adj* racional

think-tank [ˈθɪŋktæŋk] *n Fam* grupo *m* de expertos

thinly [ˈθɪnlɪ] *adv* poco, ligeramente

third [θɜːd] **1** *adj* tercero(a); (*before masculine singular noun*) tercer; (**on**) **the t. of March** el tres de marzo; **the T. World** el Tercer Mundo; **t. party insurance** seguro *m* a terceros

2 *n* (**a**) (*in series*) tercero(a) *m,f* (**b**) (*fraction*) tercio *m*, tercera parte

thirdly [ˈθɜːdlɪ] *adv* en tercer lugar

third-rate [ˈθɜːdreɪt] *adj* de calidad inferior

thirst [θɜːst] *n* sed *f*

thirsty [ˈθɜːstɪ] *adj* (**thirstier, thirstiest**) sediento(a); **to be t.** tener sed

thirteen [θɜːˈtiːn] *adj & n* trece (*m inv*)

thirteenth [θɜːˈtiːnθ] **1** *adj & n* decimotercero(a) *m,f*

2 *n* (*fraction*) decimotercera parte

thirtieth [ˈθɜːtɪɪθ] **1** *adj & n* trigésimo(a) *m,f*

2 *n* (*fraction*) trigésima parte

thirty [ˈθɜːtɪ] *adj & n* treinta (*m inv*)

this [ðɪs] **1** *dem adj* (*pl* **these**) (*masculine*) este; (*feminine*) esta; **t. book/these books** este libro/estos libros; **t. one** éste/ésta

2 *dem pron* (*pl* **these**) (**a**) (*indefinite*) esto; **it was like t.** fue así (**b**) (*place*) **t. is where we met** fue aquí donde nos conocimos (**c**) (*time*) **it should have come before t.**

debería haber llegado ya (**d**) *(specific person or thing)* éste *m*, ésta *f*; **I prefer these to those** me gustan más éstos que aquéllos; *(introduction)* **t. is Mr Álvarez** le presento al Sr. Álvarez; *Tel* **t. is Julia (speaking)** soy Julia
3 *adv* **he got t. far** llegó hasta aquí; **t. small/big** así de pequeño/grande

thistle ['θɪsəl] *n* cardo *m*

thong [θɒŋ] *n* (**a**) *(for fastening)* correa *f* (**b**) *(underwear)* tanga *f* (**c**) *US, Austr (sandal)* chancleta *f*, chancla *f*

thorax ['θɔːræks] *n* tórax *m*

thorn [θɔːn] *n* espina *f*

thorough ['θʌrə] *adj (careful)* minucioso(a); *(work)* concienzudo(a); *(knowledge)* profundo(a); **to carry out a t. enquiry into a matter** investigar a fondo un asunto

thoroughbred ['θʌrəbred] **1** *adj (horse)* de pura sangre
2 *n (horse)* pura sangre *mf*

thoroughfare ['θʌrəfeə(r)] *n (road)* carretera *f*; *(street)* calle *f*

thoroughly ['θʌrəlɪ] *adv (carefully)* a fondo; *(wholly)* completamente

those [ðəʊz] **1** *dem pron pl* ésos(as); *(remote)* aquéllos(as); **t. who** los que/las que
2 *dem adj pl* esos(as); *(remote)* aquellos(as); *see* **that**

though [ðəʊ] **1** *conj* aunque; **strange t. it may seem** por (muy) extraño que parezca; **as t.** como si; **it looks as t. he's gone** parece que se ha ido
2 *adv* sin embargo

thought [θɔːt] **1** *n* (**a**) *(act of thinking)* pensamiento *m*; **what a tempting t.!** ¡qué idea más tentadora! (**b**) *(reflection)* reflexión *f* (**c**) **it's the t. that counts** *(intention)* lo que cuenta es la intención
2 *pt & pp of* **think**

thoughtful ['θɔːtfʊl] *adj (pensive)* pensativo(a); *(considerate)* atento(a)

thoughtless ['θɔːtlɪs] *adj (person)* desconsiderado(a); *(action)* irreflexivo(a)

thousand ['θaʊzənd] *adj & n* mil *(m inv)*; **thousands of people** miles de personas

thousandth ['θaʊzənθ] **1** *adj* milésimo(a)
2 *n* (**a**) *(in series)* milésimo(a) *m,f* (**b**) *(fraction)* milésima parte

thrash [θræʃ] **1** *vt* dar una paliza a
2 *vi* **to t. about** *or* **around** agitarse
▸ **thrash out** *vt sep* discutir a fondo

thrashing ['θræʃɪŋ] *n (beating, defeat)* paliza *f*

thread [θred] **1** *n* (**a**) *(of cotton, nylon)* hilo *m*; **length of t.** hebra *f* (**b**) *(of screw)* rosca *f*

2 *vt* (**a**) *(needle)* enhebrar (**b**) **to t. one's way (through)** colarse (por)

threadbare ['θredbeə(r)] *adj* raído(a)

threat [θret] *n* amenaza *f*

threaten ['θretən] *vt* amenazar; **to t. to do sth** amenazar con hacer algo

threatening ['θretənɪŋ] *adj* amenazador(a)

threateningly ['θretənɪŋlɪ] *adv* de modo amenazador

three [θriː] *adj & n* tres *(m inv)*

three-dimensional ['θriːdɪ'menʃənəl] *adj* tridimensional

threefold ['θriːfəʊld] **1** *adj* triple
2 *adv* tres veces; **to increase t.** triplicarse

three-piece ['θriːpiːs] *adj* **t. suit** traje *m* de tres piezas; **t. suite** tresillo *m*

three-ply ['θriːplaɪ] *adj* de tres hebras

three-wheeler [θriː'wiːlə(r)] *n Aut* coche *m* de tres ruedas; *(tricycle)* triciclo *m*

thresh [θreʃ] *vt* trillar

threshold ['θreʃəʊld] *n* umbral *m*; *Fig* **to be on the t. of** estar a las puertas *or* en los umbrales de

threw [θruː] *pt of* **throw**

thrifty ['θrɪftɪ] *adj* (**thriftier, thriftiest**) económico(a), ahorrador(a)

thrill [θrɪl] **1** *n* (**a**) *(excitement)* emoción *f* (**b**) *(quiver)* estremecimiento *m*
2 *vt (excite)* emocionar; *(audience)* entusiasmar

thriller ['θrɪlə(r)] *n* thriller *m*

thrilling ['θrɪlɪŋ] *adj* emocionante

thrive [θraɪv] *vi* (*pt* **thrived** *or* **throve**; *pp* **thrived** *or* **thriven** ['θrɪvən]) (**a**) *(person)* rebosar de salud (**b**) *Fig (business)* prosperar; **he thrives on it** le viene de maravilla

thriving ['θraɪvɪŋ] *adj Fig* próspero(a)

throat [θrəʊt] *n* garganta *f*

throb [θrɒb] **1** *n* *(of heart)* latido *m*; *(of machine)* zumbido *m*
2 *vi (heart)* latir; *(machine)* zumbar; **my head is throbbing** me va a estallar la cabeza

throes [θrəʊz] *npl* **to be in one's death t.** estar agonizando; *Fig* **in the t. of ...** en pleno(a) ...

thrombosis [θrɒm'bəʊsɪs] *n Med* trombosis *f inv*

throne [θrəʊn] *n* trono *m*

throng [θrɒŋ] **1** *n* multitud *f*, gentío *m*
2 *vi* apiñarse
3 *vt* atestar

throttle ['θrɒtəl] **1** *n* **t. (valve)** *(of engine)* válvula reguladora
2 *vt (person)* estrangular
▸ **throttle back** *vt sep (engine)* desacelerar

through [θruː] **1** prep (**a**) (place) a través de, por; **to look t. the window** mirar por la ventana (**b**) (time) a lo largo de; **all t. his life** durante toda su vida; US **Tuesday t. Thursday** desde el martes hasta el jueves inclusive (**c**) (by means of) por, mediante; **I learnt of it t. Jack** me enteré por Jack (**d**) (because of) a or por causa de; **t. ignorance** por ignorancia
2 adj **a t. train** un tren directo; **t. traffic** tránsito m
3 adv (**a**) (from one side to the other) de un lado a otro; **to let sb t.** dejar pasar a algn; Fig **socialist/French t. and t.** socialista/francés por los cuatro costados (**b**) **I'm t. with him** he terminado con él (**c**) Tel **to get t. to sb** comunicar con algn; **you're t.** ¡hablen!

throughout [θruː'aʊt] **1** prep por todo(a); **t. the year** durante todo el año
2 adv (place) en todas partes; (time) todo el tiempo

throve [θrəʊv] pt of **thrive**

throw [θrəʊ] **1** vt (pt **threw**; pp **thrown**) (**a**) (with hands) (in general) tirar, Am aventar; (ball, javelin) lanzar; (rider) desmontar; Fig **he threw a fit** le dio un ataque; Fig **to t. a party** dar una fiesta (**b**) (disconcert) desconcertar
2 n tiro m, lanzamiento m; (in wrestling) derribo m
▸ **throw away** vt sep (rubbish) tirar, Am botar; (money) malgastar; (opportunity) perder
▸ **throw in** vt sep (**a**) (ball, javelin) lanzar; Sport sacar de banda; Fig **to t. in the towel** arrojar la toalla (**b**) (add) añadir; (in deal) incluir (gratis)
▸ **throw off** vt sep (person, thing) deshacerse de; (clothes) quitarse
▸ **throw out** vt sep (rubbish) tirar; (person) echar
▸ **throw up 1** vt sep (**a**) (dust, dirt) levantar (**b**) (facts, information) poner de manifiesto
2 vi Fam vomitar, devolver

throwaway ['θrəʊəweɪ] adj desechable

throw-in ['θrəʊɪn] n Sport saque m de banda

thrown [θrəʊn] pp of **throw**

thru [θruː] prep, adj & adv US Fam = **through**

thrush [θrʌʃ] n (bird) tordo m, zorzal m

thrust [θrʌst] **1** vt (pt & pp **thrust**) empujar con fuerza; **he t. a letter into my hand** me puso una carta violentamente en la mano
2 n (push) empujón m; Av & Phys empuje m

thud [θʌd] n ruido sordo

thug [θʌg] n (lout) gamberro m; (criminal) criminal m

thumb [θʌm] **1** n pulgar m
2 vt (**a**) (book) hojear (**b**) Fam (hitch) **to t. a lift** hacer autostop or dedo, CAm, Méx, Perú pedir aventón
▸ **thumb through** vt insep (book) hojear

thumbtack ['θʌmtæk] n US Esp chincheta f, Am chinche m

thump [θʌmp] **1** n (**a**) (sound) ruido sordo (**b**) (blow) porrazo m
2 vt golpear
3 vi (**a**) **to t. on the table** golpear la mesa (**b**) (heart) latir ruidosamente

thunder ['θʌndə(r)] **1** n trueno m; **t. of applause** estruendo m de aplausos
2 vi tronar

thunderbolt ['θʌndəbəʊlt] n (lighting) rayo m; Fig (news) bomba f

thunderclap ['θʌndəklæp] n trueno m

thunderous ['θʌndərəs] adj Fig ensordecedor(a)

thunderstorm ['θʌndəstɔːm] n tormenta f

thundery ['θʌndərɪ] adj (weather) tormentoso(a)

Thursday ['θɜːzdɪ] n jueves m

thus [ðʌs] adv así, de esta manera; **and t. … así que …**

thwart [θwɔːt] vt frustrar, desbaratar

thyme [taɪm] n tomillo m

thyroid ['θaɪrɔɪd] n tiroides f inv

tiara [tɪ'ɑːrə] n diadema f; Rel tiara f

tic [tɪk] n tic m

tick¹ [tɪk] **1** n (**a**) (sound) tic-tac m (**b**) Br Fam **I'll do it in a t.** ahora mismo lo hago (**c**) (mark) marca f de visto bueno
2 vi hacer tic-tac
3 vt marcar
▸ **tick off** vt sep (**a**) (mark) marcar con una señal de visto bueno (**b**) Br Fam (reprimand) echar una bronca a
▸ **tick over** vi Aut funcionar al ralentí

tick² [tɪk] n (insect) garrapata f

ticket ['tɪkɪt] n (**a**) (for train, plane, lottery) billete m, Am boleto m, esp Am pasaje m; (for theatre, cinema) entrada f, Col, Méx boleto; **t. collector** revisor(a) m,f; **t. office** taquilla f, Am boletería f; **t. tout** or US **scalper** reventa mf (**b**) (receipt) recibo m (**c**) (label) etiqueta f (**d**) Aut multa f

tickle ['tɪkəl] **1** vt hacer cosquillas a
2 vi hacer cosquillas
3 n cosquillas fpl

ticklish ['tɪklɪʃ] adj **to be t.** tener cosquillas

tick-tack-toe [tɪktæk'təʊ] n US tres en raya m

tidal ['taɪdəl] *adj* de la marea; **t. wave** ola *f* gigante

tidbit ['tɪdbɪt] *n US* = titbit

tiddlywinks ['tɪdlɪwɪŋks] *n sing (game)* pulga *f*

tide [taɪd] *n* (**a**) *(of sea)* marea *f*; **high/low t.** marea alta/baja (**b**) *(of events)* curso *m*; **the t. has turned** han cambiado las cosas; **to go against the t.** ir contra corriente

tidings ['taɪdɪŋz] *npl Fml* noticias *fpl*

tidy ['taɪdɪ] **1** *adj* (**tidier, tidiest**) (**a**) *(room, habits)* ordenado(a) (**b**) *(appearance)* arreglado(a)
 2 *vt* arreglar; **to t. away** poner en su sitio
 3 *vi* **to t. (up)** ordenar las cosas

tie [taɪ] **1** *vt (shoelaces etc)* atar; **to t. a knot** hacer un nudo
 2 *vi Sport* empatar (**with** con)
 3 *n* (**a**) *(link)* lazo *m*, vínculo *m* (**b**) *Fig (hindrance)* atadura *f* (**c**) *(item of clothing)* corbata *f* (**d**) *Sport (draw)* empate *m*; *(match)* eliminatoria *f*, partido *m* de clasificación

▸ **tie down** *vt sep* sujetar; *Fig* **to be tied down** estar atado(a); *Fig* **to t. sb down to a promise** obligar a algn a cumplir una promesa

▸ **tie up** *vt sep* (**a**) *(parcel, dog)* atar (**b**) *(deal)* concluir (**c**) *(capital)* inmovilizar; *Fig* **I'm tied up just now** de momento estoy muy ocupado(a)

tiebreaker ['taɪbreɪkə(r)] *n* tie-break *m*

tiepin ['taɪpɪn] *n* alfiler *m* de corbata

tier [tɪə(r)] *n (of seats)* fila *f*; *(in stadium)* grada *f*; **four-t. cake** pastel *m* de cuatro pisos

tiger ['taɪgə(r)] *n* tigre *m*

tight [taɪt] **1** *adj* (**a**) *(knot, screw)* apretado(a); *(clothing)* ajustado(a); *(seal)* hermético(a); **my shoes are too t.** me aprietan los zapatos; *Fig* **to be in a t. corner** estar en un apuro (**b**) *(scarce)* escaso(a); **money's a bit t.** estamos escasos de dinero (**c**) *(mean)* agarrado(a) (**d**) *Fam (drunk)* alegre, *Esp* piripi
 2 *adv* estrechamente; *(seal)* herméticamente; **hold t.** agárrate fuerte; **shut t.** bien cerrado(a); **to sit t.** no moverse de su sitio

tighten ['taɪtən] **1** *vt (screw)* apretar; *(rope)* tensar; *Fig* **to t. (up) restrictions** intensificar las restricciones
 2 *vi* apretarse; *(cable)* tensarse

tightfisted [taɪt'fɪstɪd] *adj* tacaño(a)

tightrope ['taɪtrəʊp] *n* cuerda floja; **t. walker** funámbulo(a) *m,f*

tights [taɪts] *npl (woollen)* leotardos *mpl*, *Col* medias *fpl* veladas, *RP* cancanes *mpl*; *Br (nylon, silk)* medias *fpl*, pantis *mpl*

tile [taɪl] **1** *n (of roof)* teja *f*; *(glazed)* azulejo *m*; *(for floor)* baldosa *f*
 2 *vt (roof)* tejar; *(wall)* poner azulejos en, *Esp* alicatar; *(floor)* embaldosar

tiled [taɪld] *adj (roof)* de tejas; *(wall)* con azulejos, *Esp* alicatado(a); *(floor)* embaldosado(a)

till¹ [tɪl] *n (for cash)* caja *f*

till² [tɪl] *vt (field)* labrar, cultivar

till³ [tɪl] **1** *prep* hasta; **from morning t. night** de la mañana a la noche; **t. then** hasta entonces
 2 *conj* hasta que

tiller ['tɪlə(r)] *n Naut* caña *f* del timón

tilt [tɪlt] **1** *n* (**a**) *(angle)* inclinación *f* (**b**) **(at) full t.** *(speed)* a toda velocidad
 2 *vi* **to t. over** volcarse; **to t. (up)** inclinarse
 3 *vt* inclinar

timber ['tɪmbə(r)] *n (wood)* madera *f* (de construcción); *(trees)* árboles *mpl*; **(piece of) t.** viga *f*

time [taɪm] **1** *n* (**a**) *(in general)* tiempo *m*; **all the t.** todo el tiempo; **for some t. (past)** desde hace algún tiempo; **I haven't seen him for a long t.** hace mucho (tiempo) que no lo veo; **in a short t.** en poco tiempo; **in no t.** en un abrir y cerrar de ojos; **in t.** a tiempo; **in three weeks' t.** dentro de tres semanas; **to take one's t. over sth** hacer algo con calma; *Fam* **to do t.** cumplir una condena; **t. bomb** bomba *f* de relojería; **t. limit** límite *m* de tiempo; *(for payment etc)* plazo *m*; **t. switch** interruptor *m* electrónico automático; **t. zone** huso horario
 (**b**) *(era)* época *f*, tiempos *mpl*; **a sign of the times** un signo de los tiempos; **to be behind the times** tener ideas anticuadas
 (**c**) *(point in time)* momento *m*; **(at) any t. (you like)** cuando quiera; **at no t.** en ningún momento; **at that t.** (en aquel) entonces; **at the same t.** al mismo tiempo; **at times** a veces; **from t. to t.** de vez en cuando; **he may turn up at any t.** puede llegar en cualquier momento; **in good t.** con anticipación; **on t.** puntualmente; **what's the t.?** ¿qué hora es?
 (**d**) *(time of day)* hora *f*; **and about t. too!** ¡ya era hora!; **in good t.** con anticipación; **on t.** puntualmente; **what's the t.?** ¿qué hora es?
 (**e**) **t. of year** época *f* del año
 (**f**) **to have a good/bad t.** pasarlo bien/mal
 (**g**) *(occasion)* vez *f*; **four at a t.** cuatro a la vez; **next t.** la próxima vez; **several times over** varias veces; **three times running** tres veces seguidas; **t. after t.** una y otra vez

(**h**) *(in multiplication)* **three times four** tres (multiplicado) por cuatro; **four times as big** cuatro veces más grande (**i**) *Mus* compás *m*; **in t.** al compás
2 *vt* (**a**) *(speech)* calcular la duración de; *Sport (race)* cronometrar (**b**) *(choose the time of)* escoger el momento oportuno para

time-consuming ['taɪmkənsjuːmɪŋ] *adj* que ocupa mucho tiempo

time-lag ['taɪmlæg] *n* intervalo *m*

timeless ['taɪmlɪs] *adj* eterno(a)

timely ['taɪmlɪ] *adj* (**timelier, timeliest**) oportuno(a)

timer ['taɪmə(r)] *n (device)* temporizador *m*

timetable ['taɪmteɪbəl] *n* horario *m*

timid ['tɪmɪd] *adj* tímido(a)

timing ['taɪmɪŋ] *n* (**a**) *(timeliness)* oportunidad *f*; *(coordination)* coordinación *f*; **your t. was wrong** no calculaste bien (**b**) *Sport* cronometraje *m*

tin [tɪn] 1 *n* (**a**) *(metal)* estaño *m*; **t. plate** hojalata *f* (**b**) *esp Br (container)* lata *f*, *Am* tarro *m*
2 *vt (food)* enlatar; **tinned food** conservas *fpl*

tinfoil ['tɪnfɔɪl] *n* papel *m* de estaño

tinge [tɪndʒ] 1 *n* tinte *m*, matiz *m*
2 *vt* teñir

tingle ['tɪŋgəl] *vi* **my feet are tingling** siento un hormigueo en los pies

tinker ['tɪŋkə(r)] 1 *n Pej* calderero(a) *m,f*
2 *vi* **stop tinkering with the radio** deja de toquetear la radio

tinkle ['tɪŋkəl] *vi* tintinear

tin-opener ['tɪnəʊpənə(r)] *n* abrelatas *m inv*

tinsel ['tɪnsəl] *n* oropel *m*

tint [tɪnt] 1 *n* tinte *m*, matiz *m*
2 *vt* teñir; **to t. one's hair** teñirse el pelo

tiny ['taɪnɪ] *adj* (**tinier, tiniest**) pequeñito(a); **a t. bit** un poquitín

tip¹ [tɪp] 1 *n (end)* punta *f*, *(of cigarette)* colilla *f*; **it's on the t. of my tongue** lo tengo en la punta de la lengua
2 *vt* poner cantera a; **tipped with steel** con punta de acero

tip² [tɪp] 1 *n* (**a**) *(gratuity)* propina *f* (**b**) *(advice)* consejo *m* (**c**) *Sport (racing)* pronóstico *m*
2 *vt* (**a**) *(give money to)* dar una propina a (**b**) *Sport* pronosticar
▸ **tip off** *vt sep (police)* dar el chivatazo a

tip³ [tɪp] 1 *n Br* **rubbish t.** vertedero *m*
2 *vt* inclinar; *Br (rubbish)* verter
3 *vi* **to t. (up)** ladearse; *(cart)* bascular
▸ **tip over** 1 *vt sep* volcar
2 *vi* volcarse

tipple ['tɪpəl] *Fam* 1 *vi* empinar el codo, *Am* tomar
2 *n* bebida alcohólica; **what's your t.?** ¿qué te gusta beber?

tipsy ['tɪpsɪ] *adj* (**tipsier, tipsiest**) contentillo(a)

tiptoe ['tɪptəʊ] 1 *vi* caminar *or Esp* andar de puntillas; **to t. in/out** entrar/salir de puntillas
2 *n* **on t.** de puntillas

tiptop ['tɪptɒp] *adj Fam* de primera

tire¹ [taɪə(r)] *n US =* **tyre**

tire² [taɪə(r)] 1 *vt* cansar; **to t. sb out** agotar a algn
2 *vi* cansarse; **to t. of doing sth** cansarse de hacer algo

tired ['taɪəd] *adj* cansado(a); **t. out** rendido(a); **to be t.** estar cansado(a); **to be t. of sth** estar harto(a) de algo

tiredness ['taɪədnɪs] *n (fatigue)* cansancio *m*, fatiga *f*

tireless ['taɪəlɪs] *adj* incansable

tiresome ['taɪəsəm] *adj* pesado(a)

tiring ['taɪərɪŋ] *adj* agotador(a)

tissue ['tɪʃuː, 'tɪsjuː] *n* (**a**) *Biol* tejido *m* (**b**) *Tex* tisú *m*; **t. paper** papel *m* de seda (**c**) *(handkerchief)* pañuelo *m* de papel, kleenex® *m*

tit¹ [tɪt] *n* **to give t. for tat** devolver la pelota

tit² [tɪt] *n very Fam (breast)* teta *f*, *Méx* chichi *f*, *RP* lola *f*

titbit ['tɪtbɪt] *n* tentempié *m*, refrigerio *m*

titillate ['tɪtɪleɪt] *vt* excitar

title ['taɪtəl] *n* (**a**) *(of book, chapter)* título *m*; *Cin* **credit titles** ficha técnica; **t. page** portada *f*; **t. role** papel *m* principal (**b**) *Jur* título *m* de propiedad

titter ['tɪtə(r)] 1 *vi* reírse nerviosamente; *(foolishly)* reírse tontamente
2 *n* risa ahogada; *(foolish)* risilla tonta

titular ['tɪtjʊlə(r)] *adj* titular

TM *n (abbr* **trademark)** marca registrada

to [tuː, *unstressed before vowels* tʊ, *before consonants* tə] 1 *prep* (**a**) *(with place)* a; *(expressing direction)* hacia; **from town to town** de ciudad en ciudad; **he went to France/Japan** fue a Francia/Japón; **I'm going to Mary's** voy a casa de Mary; **it is 30 miles to London** Londres está a 30 millas; **the train to Madrid** el tren de Madrid; **to the east** hacia el este; **to the right** a la derecha; **what school do you go to?** ¿a qué escuela vas?
(**b**) *(time)* a; **from day to day** de día en día; **from two to four** de dos a cuatro; *Br* **it's ten to (six)** son (las seis) menos diez, *Am salvo RP* faltan diez (para las seis)
(**c**) *(as far as)* hasta; **accurate to a**

millimetre exacto(a) hasta el milímetro

(**d**) *(with indirect object)* **he gave it to his cousin** se lo dio a su primo; **what's that to you?** ¿qué te importa a ti?

(**e**) *(towards a person)* **he was very kind to me** se portó muy bien conmigo

(**f**) *(of)* de; **heir to an estate** heredero *m* de una propiedad; **adviser to the president** consejero *m* del presidente

(**g**) **to come to sb's assistance** acudir en ayuda de algn; **to everyone's surprise** para sorpresa de todos; **to this end** con este fin

(**h**) **to the best of my knowledge** que yo sepa

(**i**) *(compared to)* **that's nothing to what I've seen** eso no es nada en comparación con lo que he visto yo

(**j**) *(in proportion)* **one house to the square kilometre** una casa por kilómetro cuadrado; **six votes to four** seis votos contra cuatro

(**k**) *(about)* **what did he say to my suggestion?** ¿qué contestó a mi sugerencia?

2 with infin (**a**) *with simple infinitives* **to** *is not translated but is shown by the verb endings;* **to buy** comprar; **to come** venir

(**b**) *(in order to)* para; *(with verbs of motion or purpose)* a, por; **he did it to help me** lo hizo para ayudarme; **he stopped to talk** se detuvo a hablar; **he fought to convince them** luchó por convencerlos

(**c**) *various verbs followed by dependent infinitives take particular prepositions* (a, de, en, por, con, para *etc*) *and others take no preposition;* see *the entry of the verb in question*

(**d**) *(with adj and infin)*a, de; **difficult to do** difícil de hacer; **ready to listen** dispuesto(a) a escuchar; **too hot to drink** demasiado caliente para bebérselo

(**e**) *(with noun and infin)* **the first to complain** el primero en quejarse; **this is the time to do it** éste es el momento de hacerlo; **to have a great deal to do** tener mucho que hacer

(**f**) *(expressing following action)* **he awoke to find the light still on** al despertarse encontró la lámpara todavía encendida

(**g**) *(with verbs of ordering, wishing etc)* **he asked me to do it** me pidió que lo hiciera

(**h**) *(expressing obligation)* **fifty employees are to go** cincuenta empleados deben ser despedidos; **to have to do sth** tener que hacer algo

(**i**) *(replacing infin)* **go if you want to** váyase si quiere

3 *adv* **to go to and fro** ir y venir; **to push the door to** encajar la puerta

toad [təʊd] *n* sapo *m*

toadstool ['təʊdstuːl] *n* Esp seta venenosa, *Am* hongo (venenoso)

toast¹ [təʊst] *Culin* **1** *n* pan tostado; **a slice of t.** una tostada
2 *vt* tostar

toast² [təʊst] **1** *n (drink)* brindis *m inv*; **to drink a t. to** brindar por
2 *vt* brindar por

toaster ['təʊstə(r)] *n* tostador *m* (de pan)

tobacco [tə'bækəʊ] *n* tabaco *m*

tobacconist [tə'bækənɪst] *n* Br estanquero(a) *m,f*; Br **t.'s (shop)** estanco *m*, CSur quiosco *m*, Méx estanquillo *m*

toboggan [tə'bɒgən] *n* tobogán *m*

today [tə'deɪ] **1** *n* hoy *m*
2 *adv* hoy; *(nowadays)* hoy en día; **a week t.** justo dentro de una semana

toddler ['tɒdlə(r)] *n* niño(a) *m,f* que empieza a andar; **the toddlers** los pequeñitos

toddy ['tɒdɪ] *n (drink)* ponche *m*

to-do [tə'duː] *n* lío *m*, jaleo *m*

toe [təʊ] **1** *n* dedo *m* del pie; **big t.** dedo gordo
2 *vt* **to t. the line** conformarse

toenail ['təʊneɪl] *n* uña *f* del dedo del pie

toffee ['tɒfɪ] *n* caramelo *m*

together [tə'geðə(r)] *adv* junto, juntos(as); **all t.** todos juntos; **t. with** junto con; **to bring t.** reunir

toil [tɔɪl] **1** *n* trabajo duro
2 *vi* afanarse, trabajar (duro); **to t. up a hill** subir penosamente una cuesta

toilet ['tɔɪlɪt] *n* (**a**) Br *(in house)* cuarto *m* de baño, retrete *m*; *(in public place)* baño(s) *m(pl)*, Esp servicio(s) *m(pl)*, CSur toilette *f*; **t. paper** or **tissue** papel higiénico; **t. roll** rollo *m* de papel higiénico (**b**) *(washing etc)* aseo *m (personal)*; **t. bag** neceser *m*; **t. soap** jabón *m* de tocador

toiletries ['tɔɪlɪtrɪz] *npl* artículos *mpl* de aseo

token ['təʊkən] **1** *n* (**a**) *(sign)* señal *f*; **as a t. of respect** en señal de respeto (**b**) *Com* vale *m*; **book t.** vale para comprar libros
2 *adj* simbólico(a)

told [təʊld] *pt & pp of* tell

tolerable ['tɒlərəbəl] *adj* tolerable

tolerance ['tɒlərəns] *n* tolerancia *f*

tolerant ['tɒlərənt] *adj* tolerante

tolerate ['tɒləreɪt] *vt* tolerar

toll¹ [təʊl] **1** *vt* tocar
2 *vi* doblar

toll² [təʊl] *n* (**a**) *(charge)* peaje *m*, Méx cuota *f* (**b**) *(loss)* pérdidas *fpl*; **the death t.** el número de víctimas mortales

toll-free [təʊl'friː] US **1** adj **t. number** (número m de) teléfono m gratuito
2 adv (call) gratuitamente

tomato [tə'mɑːtəʊ, US tə'meɪtəʊ] n (pl **tomatoes**) tomate m, Méx jitomate m

tomb [tuːm] n tumba f, sepulcro m

tomboy ['tɒmbɔɪ] n marimacho f

tombstone ['tuːmstəʊn] n lápida f sepulcral

tomcat ['tɒmkæt] n gato (macho)

tomorrow [tə'mɒrəʊ] **1** n mañana m; **the day after t.** pasado mañana
2 adv mañana; **see you t.!** ¡hasta mañana!; **t. night** mañana por la noche; **t. week** dentro de ocho días a partir de mañana

ton [tʌn] n tonelada f; Fam **tons of** montones de

tone [təʊn] **1** n tono m
2 vi **to t. (in) with sth** armonizar con algo
► tone down vt sep atenuar

tone-deaf [təʊn'def] adj **to be t.** no tener oído musical

tongs [tɒŋz] npl (for sugar, hair) tenacillas fpl; (fire) t. tenazas fpl

tongue [tʌŋ] n (a) (in mouth) lengua f; Fig **to say sth t. in cheek** decir algo con la boca pequeña; **t. twister** trabalenguas m inv (b) (of shoe) lengüeta f; (of bell) badajo m

tongue-tied ['tʌŋtaɪd] adj mudo(a) (por la timidez)

tonic ['tɒnɪk] **1** n (a) Med tónico m (b) (drink) tónica f
2 adj tónico(a)

tonight [tə'naɪt] adv & n esta noche

tonnage ['tʌnɪdʒ] n (of ship) tonelaje m

tonne [tʌn] n = **ton**

tonsil ['tɒnsəl] n amígdala f; **to have one's tonsils out** ser operado(a) de las amígdalas

tonsillitis [tɒnsɪ'laɪtɪs] n amigdalitis f

too [tuː] adv (a) (besides) además (b) (also) también (c) (excessively) demasiado; **t. much money** demasiado dinero; **£10 t. much** 10 libras de más; **t. frequently** con demasiada frecuencia; **t. old** demasiado viejo

took [tʊk] pt of **take**

tool [tuːl] n (utensil) herramienta f

toolbox ['tuːlbɒks] n caja f de herramientas

toot [tuːt] Aut **1** vt tocar
2 vi tocar la bocina

tooth [tuːθ] n (pl **teeth**) (a) (of person) diente m; (molar) muela f; Fig **to fight t. and nail** luchar a brazo partido (b) (of saw) diente m; (of comb) púa f

toothache ['tuːθeɪk] n dolor m de muelas

toothbrush ['tuːθbrʌʃ] n cepillo m de dientes

toothpaste ['tuːθpeɪst] n pasta dentífrica

toothpick ['tuːθpɪk] n mondadientes m inv

top¹ [tɒp] **1** n (a) (upper part) parte f de arriba; (of hill) cumbre f, cima f; (of tree) copa f; **from t. to bottom** de arriba (a) abajo; **on t. of** encima de; Fig **on t. of it all** ... para colmo ...; **t. hat** sombrero m de copa (b) (surface) superficie f (c) (of list etc) cabeza f (d) (of bottle etc) tapa f, tapón m (e) (garment) camiseta f (f) (best) lo mejor (g) Fig **at the t. of one's voice** a voz en grito
2 adj (a) (part) superior, de arriba; **the t. floor** el último piso; **t. coat** (of paint) última mano (b) (highest) más alto(a); Br Aut **t. gear** directa f (c) (best) mejor
3 vt (a) (place on top of) coronar (b) Th **to t. the bill** encabezar el reparto
► top up vt sep llenar hasta el tope; **to t. up the petrol tank** llenar el depósito; Fig **and to t. it all** y para colmo

top² [tɒp] n (toy) peonza f

topic ['tɒpɪk] n tema m

> 🖉 Note that the Spanish word **tópico** is a false friend and is never a translation for the English word **topic**. In Spanish **tópico** means "cliché".

topical ['tɒpɪkəl] adj de actualidad

top-level ['tɒplevəl] adj de alto nivel

topmost ['tɒpməʊst] adj (el) más alto/ (la) más alta

topple ['tɒpəl] **1** vi (building) venirse abajo; **to t. (over)** volcarse
2 vt volcar; Fig (government) derrocar

top-secret ['tɒp'siːkrɪt] adj de alto secreto

topsy-turvy ['tɒpsɪ'tɜːvɪ] adj & adv al revés; (in confusion) en desorden, patas arriba

top-up ['tɒpʌp] n Br **top-up card** (for mobile phone) tarjeta f de recarga; **t. fees** (charged by university) = derechos de matrícula suplementarios

torch [tɔːtʃ] n Br (electric) linterna f

tore [tɔː(r)] pt of **tear**

torment 1 vt [tɔː'ment] atormentar
2 n ['tɔːment] tormento m, suplicio m

torn [tɔːn] pp of **tear**

tornado [tɔː'neɪdəʊ] n tornado m

torpedo [tɔː'piːdəʊ] n torpedo m

torrent ['tɒrənt] n torrente m

torrential [tɒ'renʃəl] adj torrencial

torrid ['tɒrɪd] adj tórrido(a)

torso ['tɔːsəʊ] n torso m

tortoise ['tɔːtəs] n tortuga f (de tierra)

tortoiseshell ['tɔːtəsʃel] adj de carey

tortuous ['tɔːtjʊəs] adj (path) tortuoso(a); (explanation) enrevesado(a)

torture ['tɔːtʃə(r)] 1 vt torturar; Fig atormentar
  2 n tortura f; Fig tormento m

Tory ['tɔːrɪ] adj & n Br Pol conservador(a) (m,f)

toss [tɒs] 1 vt (a) (ball) tirar; **to t. a coin** echar a cara o cruz, Méx echar a águila o sol, RP echar a cara o seca (b) (throw about) sacudir
  2 vi (a) (move about) agitarse; **to t. and turn** dar vueltas en la cama (b) Sport **to t. (up)** sortear
  3 n (a) (of ball) lanzamiento m; (of coin) sorteo m (a cara o cruz) (b) (of head) sacudida f

tot¹ [tɒt] n (a) **(tiny) t.** (child) nene(a) m,f (b) (of whisky etc) trago m

tot² [tɒt] vt Br **to t. up** sumar

total ['təʊtəl] 1 n total m; (in bill) importe m; **grand t.** suma f total
  2 adj total
  3 vt sumar
  4 vi **to t. up to** ascender a

totalitarian [təʊtælɪˈteərɪən] adj totalitario(a)

totally ['təʊtəlɪ] adv totalmente

tote [təʊt] n Fam Sport totalizador m

tote bag ['təʊtbæg] n US petate m

totem ['təʊtəm] n tótem m

totter ['tɒtə(r)] vi tambalearse

touch [tʌtʃ] 1 vt (a) (physically) tocar; Fig **to t. on a subject** tocar un tema (b) (equal) igualar (c) (move) conmover
  2 vi tocarse; Fig **it was t. and go whether we caught the train** estuvimos a punto de perder el tren
  3 n (a) (act of touching) toque m (b) (sense of touch) tacto m (c) **it was a nice t. of his** fue un detalle de su parte; **to put the finishing touches to sth** dar los últimos toques a algo (d) (ability) habilidad f (e) (contact) contacto m; **to be/get/keep in t. with sb** estar/ponerse/mantenerse en contacto con algn; **to be out of t. with sth** no estar al tanto de algo (f) (small amount) pizca f (g) Sport **in t.** fuera de banda
  ▸ **touch down** vi (plane) aterrizar
  ▸ **touch off** vt sep desencadenar
  ▸ **touch up** vt sep (picture) retocar

touchdown ['tʌtʃdaʊn] n (a) (of plane) aterrizaje m; (of space capsule) amerizaje m (b) (in American football) ensayo m

touched [tʌtʃt] adj (a) (moved) emocionado(a) (b) Fam (crazy) Esp tocado(a) del ala, Am zafado(a)

touching ['tʌtʃɪŋ] adj conmovedor(a)

touchline ['tʌtʃlaɪn] n línea f de banda

touchy ['tʌtʃɪ] adj (**touchier, touchiest**) Fam (person) susceptible; (subject) delicado(a)

tough [tʌf] 1 adj (material, competitor etc) fuerte, resistente; (test, criminal, meat) duro(a); (punishment) severo(a); (problem) difícil
  2 n (person) matón m

toughen ['tʌfən] vt endurecer

toupee ['tuːpeɪ] n tupé m

tour [tʊə(r)] 1 n (a) (journey) viaje m; **package t.** viaje organizado (b) (of monument etc) visita f; (of city) recorrido turístico (c) Sport & Th gira f; **on t.** de gira
  2 vt (a) (country) viajar por (b) (building) visitar (c) Th estar de gira en
  3 vi estar de viaje

tourism ['tʊərɪzəm] n turismo m

tourist ['tʊərɪst] n turista mf; **t. centre** centro m de información turística; Av **t. class** clase f turista

tournament ['tʊənəmənt] n torneo m

tousled ['taʊzəld] adj (hair) despeinado(a)

tout [taʊt] 1 vt Com tratar de vender; Br (tickets) revender
  2 vi = salir a la caza y captura de compradores
  3 n Com gancho m

tow [təʊ] 1 n **to take a car in t.** remolcar un coche; US **t. truck** grúa f
  2 vt remolcar

towards [təˈwɔːdz, tɔːdz] prep (a) (direction, time) hacia (b) (with regard to) hacia, (para) con; **our duty t. others** nuestro deber para con los demás; **what is your attitude t. religion?** ¿cuál es su actitud respecto a la religión?

towel ['taʊəl] 1 n toalla f; **hand t.** toallita f; **t.** Br **rail** or US **bar** toallero m
  2 vt **to t. dry** secar con una toalla

towelling ['taʊəlɪŋ] n felpa f

tower ['taʊə(r)] 1 n torre f
  2 vi **to t. over** or **above sth** dominar algo

towering ['taʊərɪŋ] adj impresionante, enorme

town [taʊn] n ciudad f; (small) pueblo m; **to go into t.** ir al centro; Fam **to go to t.** tirar la casa por la ventana; Br **t. council** ayuntamiento m; Br **t. councillor** concejal(a) m,f; **t. hall** ayuntamiento m; **t. planning** urbanismo m

townspeople ['taʊnzpiːpəl] npl ciudadanos mpl

towpath ['təʊpɑːθ] n sendero m a lo largo de un canal

towrope ['təʊrəʊp] n cable m de remolque

toxic ['tɒksɪk] adj tóxico(a)

toy [tɔɪ] **1** n juguete m
2 vi to t. with an idea acariciar una idea; to t. with one's food comer sin gana

toyshop ['tɔɪʃɒp] n juguetería f

trace [treɪs] **1** n (**a**) (sign) indicio m, vestigio m (**b**) (tracks) rastro m
2 vt (**a**) (drawing) calcar (**b**) (plan) bosquejar (**c**) (locate) seguir la pista de

tracing ['treɪsɪŋ] n t. paper papel m de calco

track [træk] **1** n (**a**) (trail) rastro m; to keep/lose t. of sb no perder/perder de vista a algn (**b**) (pathway) camino m; to be on the right/wrong t. ir por el buen/mal camino (**c**) Sport pista f; (for motor racing) circuito m; Fig t. record historial m (**d**) Rail vía f; Fig he has a one-t. mind tiene una única obsesión (**e**) (on record, CD) canción f (**f**) US Educ = cada una de las divisiones del alumnado en grupos por niveles de aptitud
2 vt seguir la pista de; (with radar) seguir la trayectoria de
▸ **track down** vt sep (locate) localizar

tracksuit ['træksuːt] n Esp chándal m, Méx pants m, RP jogging m

tract¹ [trækt] n (expanse) extensión f

tract² [trækt] n (treatise) tratado m; (pamphlet) folleto m

traction ['trækʃən] n tracción f

tractor ['træktə(r)] n tractor m

trade [treɪd] **1** n (**a**) (profession) oficio m; by t. de oficio (**b**) Com comercio m; it's good for t. es bueno para los negocios; the building t. (la industria de) la construcción; t. name nombre m comercial; t. union sindicato m; t. unionist sindicalista mf
2 vi comerciar (in en)
3 vt to t. sth for sth trocar algo por algo
▸ **trade in** vt sep dar como entrada

trademark ['treɪdmɑːk] n marca f (de fábrica); registered t. marca registrada

trader ['treɪdə(r)] n comerciante mf

tradesman ['treɪdzmən] n (shopkeeper) tendero m

trading ['treɪdɪŋ] n comercio m; Br t. estate polígono m industrial

tradition [trə'dɪʃən] n tradición f

traditional [trə'dɪʃənəl] adj tradicional

traffic ['træfɪk] **1** n (**a**) (vehicles) tráfico m; US t. circle rotonda f; t. island isleta f; t. jam atasco m; t. lights semáforo m; Br t. warden ≃ guardia mf urbano(a) (**b**) (trade) tráfico m
2 vi (pt & pp trafficked) to t. in drugs traficar con droga

trafficker ['træfɪkə(r)] n traficante mf

tragedy ['trædʒɪdɪ] n tragedia f

tragic ['trædʒɪk] adj trágico(a)

trail [treɪl] **1** vt (**a**) (drag) arrastrar (**b**) (follow) rastrear
2 vi (**a**) (drag) arrastrarse (**b**) to t. behind rezagarse
3 n (**a**) (track) pista f, rastro m (**b**) (path) senda f, camino m (**c**) (of smoke) estela f

trailer ['treɪlə(r)] n (**a**) Aut remolque m (**b**) US Aut (caravan) caravana f (**c**) Cin trailer m, avance m

train [treɪn] **1** n (**a**) Rail tren m (**b**) (of vehicles) convoy m; (of followers) séquito m; (of events) serie f (**c**) (of dress) cola f
2 vt (**a**) (teach) formar; Sport entrenar; (animal) amaestrar; (voice etc) educar (**b**) (gun) apuntar (on a); (camera) enfocar (on a)
3 vi prepararse; Sport entrenarse

trainee [treɪ'niː] n aprendiz(a) m,f

trainer ['treɪnə(r)] n (**a**) Sport entrenador(a) m,f; (of dogs) amaestrador(a) m,f; (of lions) domador(a) m,f (**b**) Br trainers (shoes) zapatillas fpl de deporte

training ['treɪnɪŋ] n (instruction) formación f; Sport entrenamiento m; (of animals) amaestramiento m; (of lions) doma f; to go into t. empezar el entrenamiento; vocational t. formación profesional

traipse [treɪps] vi Fam dar vueltas y vueltas, Esp estar en danza

trait [treɪt] n rasgo m

traitor ['treɪtə(r)] n traidor(a) m,f

trajectory [trə'dʒektərɪ] n trayectoria f

tram [træm], **tramcar** ['træmkɑː(r)] n Br tranvía m

tramp [træmp] **1** vi caminar con pasos pesados, marchar
2 n (person) vagabundo(a) m,f; Pej she's a t. es una fulana or Col, Méx piruja or RP reventada

> ◈ Note that the Spanish word **trampa** is a false friend and is never a translation for the English word **tramp**. In Spanish **trampa** means both "trap" and "trick".

trample ['træmpəl] vt to t. down the grass pisotear la hierba; to t. sth underfoot pisotear algo

trampoline ['træmpəliːn] n cama elástica

> ♪ Note that the Spanish word **trampolín** is a false friend and is never a translation for the English word **trampoline**. In Spanish **trampolín** means both "diving board" and "ski jump".

trance [trɑːns] n trance m

tranquil ['træŋkwɪl] adj tranquilo(a)

tranquillity, US **tranquility** [træŋ'kwɪlɪtɪ] n tranquilidad f

tranquillizer, US **tranquilizer** ['træŋkwɪlaɪzə(r)] n tranquilizante m

transact [træn'zækt] vt negociar

transaction [træn'zækʃən] n (procedure) tramitación f; (deal) transacción f

transatlantic [trænzət'læntɪk] adj transatlántico(a)

transcend [træn'send] vt trascender

transcribe [træn'skraɪb] vt transcribir

transcript ['trænskrɪpt] n transcripción f

transcription [træn'skrɪpʃən] n transcripción f

transfer 1 vt [træns'fɜː(r)] trasladar; (funds) transferir; Jur ceder; Ftb traspasar; US Rail hacer transbordo
2 n ['trænsfɜː(r)] **(a)** (of employee, prisoner) traslado m; (of funds) transferencia f; Jur cesión f; Ftb traspaso m **(b)** (picture, design) calcomanía f **(c)** US Rail transbordo m

transform [træns'fɔːm] vt transformar

transformation [trænsfə'meɪʃən] n transformación f

transformer [træns'fɔːmə(r)] n Elec transformador m

transfusion [træns'fjuːʒən] n Med transfusión f (de sangre)

transgenic [trænz'dʒiːnɪk] adj transgénico(a)

transgress [trænz'gres] vi Fml transgredir

transient ['trænzɪənt] adj transitorio(a)

transistor [træn'zɪstə(r)] n transistor m

transit ['trænzɪt] n tránsito m; **in t.** de tránsito

transition [træn'zɪʃən] n transición f

transitive ['trænzɪtɪv] adj transitivo(a)

transitory ['trænzɪtərɪ] adj transitorio(a)

translate [træns'leɪt] vt traducir

translation [træns'leɪʃən] n traducción f

translator [træns'leɪtə(r)] n traductor(a) m,f

translucent [trænz'luːsənt] adj translúcido(a)

transmission [trænz'mɪʃən] n transmisión f

transmit [trænz'mɪt] vt transmitir

transmitter [trænz'mɪtə(r)] n Rad (set) transmisor m; Rad & TV (station) emisora f

transparency [træns'pærənsɪ] n Phot diapositiva f

transparent [træns'pærənt] adj transparente

transpire [træn'spaɪə(r)] vi (happen) ocurrir; **it transpired that ...** ocurrió que ...

transplant 1 vt [træns'plɑːnt] trasplantar
2 n ['trænsplɑːnt] trasplante m

transport 1 vt [træns'pɔːt] transportar
2 n ['trænspɔːt] transporte m; **t. aircraft/ ship** avión m/buque m de transporte; Br **t. café** bar m de carretera

transportation [trænspɔː'teɪʃən] n transporte m

transsexual [træn(z)'seksjʊəl] n transexual mf

transvestite [trænz'vestaɪt] n Fam travestido(a) m,f, Esp travestí mf

trap [træp] **1** n trampa f; **t. door** trampilla f; Th escotillón m
2 vt atrapar

trapeze [trə'piːz] n trapecio m

trappings ['træpɪŋz] npl parafernalia f

trash [træʃ] n (inferior goods) bazofia f; US (rubbish) basura f; Fig **to talk a lot of t.** decir tonterías; US **t. can** cubo m de la basura

trashy ['træʃɪ] adj (trashier, trashiest) Fam de pacotilla, Esp cutre, Méx gacho(a)

trauma ['trɔːmə] n trauma m

traumatic [trɔː'mætɪk] adj traumático(a)

travel ['trævəl] **1** vi **(a)** (person) viajar; **to t. through** recorrer **(b)** (vehicle) circular; (news, sound, electricity) propagarse
2 vt recorrer
3 n viajar m; **t. agency** agencia f de viajes

traveller, US **traveler** ['trævələ(r)] n viajero(a) m,f; **t.'s** Br **cheque** or US **check** cheque m de viaje

travelling, US **traveling** ['trævəlɪŋ] **1** adj (salesman) ambulante
2 n viajes mpl, (el) viajar m; **I'm fond of t.** me gusta viajar; **t. expenses** gastos mpl de viaje

travel-sick ['trævəlsɪk] adj Br **to be** or **feel t.** estar mareado(a)

travesty ['trævɪstɪ] n parodia f burda

> ♪ Note that the Spanish word **travestí** is a false friend and is never a translation for the English word **travesty**. In Spanish **travestí** means "transvestite".

trawler ['trɔːlə(r)] n barco m de arrastre

tray [treɪ] n (for food) bandeja f; (for letters) cesta f (para la correspondencia)

treacherous ['tretʃərəs] *adj* (a) *(person)* traidor(a); *(action)* traicionero(a) (b) *(dangerous)* peligroso(a)

treachery ['tretʃərɪ] *n* traición *f*

treacle ['tri:kəl] *n Br* melaza *f*

tread [tred] 1 *vi (pt* **trod;** *pp* **trod** or **trodden)** pisar; **to t. on** pisar

2 *vt* (a) *(step on)* pisar (b) **to t. water** mantenerse a flote verticalmente

3 *n* (a) *(step)* paso *m; (sound)* ruido *m* de pasos (b) *(of tyre)* banda *f* de rodadura

treadmill ['tredmɪl] *n (in gym)* tapiz *m* rodante, cinta *f* de footing or de correr

treason ['tri:zən] *n* traición *f*

treasure ['treʒə(r)] 1 *n* tesoro *m*

2 *vt (keep)* guardar como oro en paño; *(value)* apreciar muchísimo

treasurer ['treʒərə(r)] *n* tesorero(a) *m,f*

treasury ['treʒərɪ] *n* tesorería *f*; **the T.** *(in UK)* el tesoro (público), ≃ (el Ministerio de) Economía; **the Department of the T.** *(in US)* el tesoro (público), ≃ (el Ministerio de) Hacienda; **T. bill** bono *m* del Tesoro

treat [tri:t] 1 *n* (a) *(present)* regalo *m* (b) *(pleasure)* placer *m*

2 *vt* (a) *(person, illness)* tratar; **to t. badly** maltratar (b) *(regard)* considerar (c) **he treated them to dinner** les invitó a cenar

treatise ['tri:tɪz] *n* tratado *m*

treatment ['tri:tmənt] *n* (a) *(of person)* trato *m* (b) *(of subject, patient)* tratamiento *m*

treaty ['tri:tɪ] *n* tratado *m*

treble ['trebəl] 1 *adj* (a) *(triple)* triple (b) *Mus* **t. clef** clave *f* de sol; **t. voice** voz *f* de tiple

2 *vt* triplicar

3 *vi* triplicarse

tree [tri:] *n* árbol *m*; **apple/cherry t.** manzano *m*/cerezo *m*

treetop ['tri:tɒp] *n* copa *f*

trek [trek] 1 *n (journey)* camino largo; *Fam (walk)* caminata *f*

2 *vi (pt & pp* **trekked)** hacer un viaje largo y difícil; *Fam (walk)* ir caminando

trellis ['trelɪs] *n* enrejado *m*

tremble ['trembəl] *vi* temblar, estremecerse

trembling ['tremblɪŋ] *adj* tembloroso(a)

tremendous [trɪ'mendəs] *adj (huge)* enorme; *(success)* arrollador(a); *(shock etc)* tremendo(a); *Fam (marvellous)* estupendo(a)

tremor ['tremə(r)] *n* temblor *m*

trench [trentʃ] *n* (a) *(ditch)* zanja *f*; *Mil* trinchera *f* (b) **t. coat** trinchera *f*

trend [trend] 1 *n (tendency)* tendencia *f*; *(fashion)* moda *f*

2 *vi* tender **(to** or **towards** hacia)

trendy ['trendɪ] *adj* **(trendier, trendiest)** *Fam (person)* modernillo(a) *m,f*, *RP* modernoso(a) *m,f, (clothes)* a la última

trepidation [trepɪ'deɪʃən] *n* turbación *f*

trespass ['trespəs] *vi* entrar sin autorización

> *Note that the Spanish verb **traspasar** is a false friend and is never a translation for the English verb **trespass**. In Spanish **traspasar** means "to go through, to cross", "to transfer" and "to exceed".*

trespasser ['trespəsə(r)] *n* intruso(a) *m,f*

trestle ['tresəl] *n* caballete *m*

trial ['traɪəl] *n* (a) *Jur* proceso *m*, juicio *m* (b) *(test)* prueba *f*; **on t.** a prueba; **by t. and error** a fuerza de equivocarse (c) **trials** *(competition)* concurso *m* (d) **trials** *(suffering)* sufrimiento *m*; **trials and tribulations** tribulaciones *fpl*

triangle ['traɪæŋgəl] *n* triángulo *m*

triangular [traɪ'æŋgjʊlə(r)] *adj* triangular

tribe [traɪb] *n* tribu *f*

tribunal [traɪ'bju:nəl] *n* tribunal *m*

tributary ['trɪbjʊtərɪ] *n (river)* afluente *m*

tribute ['trɪbju:t] *n* (a) *(payment)* tributo *m* (b) *(mark of respect)* homenaje *m*; **to pay t. to** rendir homenaje a

trice [traɪs] *n Fam* **in a t.** en un abrir y cerrar de ojos

trick [trɪk] 1 *n* (a) *(ruse)* ardid *m*; *(dishonest)* engaño *m; (in question)* trampa *f* (b) *(practical joke)* broma *f*; **to play a t. on sb** gastarle una broma a algn; *(malicious)* jugar una mala pasada a algn (c) *(of magic, knack)* truco *m*; **that'll do the t.!** ¡eso es exactamente lo que hace falta! (d) *Cards* baza *f*

2 *vt* engañar; **to t. sb out of sth** quitar or *Am* sacarle algo a algn a base de engaños

trickery ['trɪkərɪ] *n* engaños *mpl*, trampas *fpl*

trickle ['trɪkəl] 1 *vi* discurrir; *(water)* gotear

2 *n* hilo *m*

tricky ['trɪkɪ] *adj* **(trickier, trickiest)** *(person)* astuto(a); *(situation, mechanism)* delicado(a)

tricycle ['traɪsɪkəl] *n* triciclo *m*

tried [traɪd] *pt & pp of* **try**

trifle ['traɪfəl] 1 *n* (a) *(insignificant thing)* bagatela *f*; **he's a t. optimistic** es ligeramente optimista (b) *Br Culin* = postre de bizcocho, gelatina, frutas y *Esp* nata or *Am* crema de leche

2 *vi* **to t. with** tomar a la ligera

trifling ['traɪflɪŋ] adj insignificante, trivial

trigger ['trɪgə(r)] **1** n (of gun) gatillo m; (of mechanism) disparador m
2 vt **to t. (off)** desencadenar

trill [trɪl] n (of music, bird) trino m; Ling vibración f

trilogy ['trɪlədʒɪ] n trilogía f

trim [trɪm] **1** adj (**trimmer, trimmest**) (neat) aseado(a); **to have a t. figure** tener buen tipo
2 vt (a) (cut) recortar; Fig (expenses) disminuir (b) (decorate) adornar
3 n (a) (condition) estado m; Naut asiento m (b) (cut) recorte m

trimming ['trɪmɪŋ] n (a) (cut) recorte m (b) (on clothes) adorno m (c) Culin **trimmings** guarnición f

trinket ['trɪŋkɪt] n baratija f

trio ['triːəʊ] n trío m

trip [trɪp] **1** n (a) (journey) viaje m; (excursion) excursión f; **to go on a t.** ir de excursión (b) Fam **to be on a t.** (on drugs) estar colocado(a)
2 vi (a) **to t. (up)** (stumble) tropezar (**over** con); Fig (err) equivocarse (b) **to t. along** ir con paso ligero
3 vt **to t. sb (up)** poner la zancadilla a algn; Fig hacer caer a algn

tripe [traɪp] n (a) Culin mondongo m, Esp callos mpl, Chile chunchules mpl (b) Fam (nonsense) tonterías fpl, bobadas fpl

triple ['trɪpəl] **1** adj triple
2 vt triplicar
3 vi triplicarse

triplet ['trɪplɪt] n trillizo(a) m,f

triplicate ['trɪplɪkɪt] adj **in t.** por triplicado

tripod ['traɪpɒd] n trípode m

trite [traɪt] adj (sentiment) banal; (subject) trillado(a)

triumph ['traɪəmf] **1** n triunfo m
2 vi triunfar

triumphant [traɪˈʌmfənt] adj triunfante

trivia ['trɪvɪə] npl trivialidades fpl

trivial ['trɪvɪəl] adj trivial, banal

trod [trɒd] pt & pp of **tread**

trodden ['trɒdən] pp of **tread**

trolley ['trɒlɪ] n Br carro m

trombone [trɒmˈbəʊn] n trombón m

troop [truːp] **1** n (a) (of people) grupo m (b) Mil **troops** tropas fpl
2 vi **to t. in/out/off** entrar/salir/marcharse en tropel

trooper ['truːpə(r)] n (a) (soldier) soldado m (de caballería o división acorazada) (b) US (policeman) policía mf

trooping ['truːpɪŋ] n Br **t. the colour** = ceremonia de homenaje a la bandera de un regimiento

trophy ['trəʊfɪ] n trofeo m

tropic ['trɒpɪk] n trópico m

tropical ['trɒpɪkəl] adj tropical

trot [trɒt] **1** vi trotar
2 n trote m; **to go at a t.** ir al trote; Br Fam **on the t.** (in succession) seguidos(as)

trouble ['trʌbəl] **1** n (a) (misfortune) desgracia f (b) (problems) problemas mpl; **to be in t.** estar en un lío; **to cause sb t.** ocasionar problemas a algn; **to get sb out of t.** sacar a algn de un apuro; **the t. is that …** lo que pasa es que … (c) (effort) esfuerzo m; **it's no t.** no es ninguna molestia; **it's not worth the t.** no merece la pena; **to take the t. to do sth** molestarse en hacer algo (d) (conflict) conflicto m (e) Med enfermedad f; **to have liver t.** tener problemas de hígado
2 vt (a) (affect) afligir; (worry) preocupar; **that doesn't t. him at all** eso le tiene sin cuidado (b) (bother) molestar
3 vi molestarse

troubled ['trʌbəld] adj agitado(a)

troublemaker ['trʌbəlmeɪkə(r)] n alborotador(a) m,f

troubleshooter ['trʌbəlʃuːtə(r)] n Ind = persona encargada de solucionar problemas

troublesome ['trʌbəlsəm] adj molesto(a)

trough [trɒf] n (a) (drinking) **t.** abrevadero m; (feeding) **t.** pesebre m (b) (of wave) seno m (c) Geog & Met depresión f

trounce [traʊns] vt dar una paliza a

troupe [truːp] n Th compañía f

trousers ['traʊzəz] npl pantalones mpl; **a pair of t.** unos pantalones

trousseau ['truːsəʊ] n ajuar m

trout [traʊt] n trucha f

trowel ['traʊəl] n (a) (builder's) palustre m (b) (for gardening) desplantador m

truant ['truːənt] n Br **to play t.** faltar a clase, Esp hacer novillos, Méx irse de pinta

truce [truːs] n tregua f

truck¹ [trʌk] n (a) Br Rail vagón m (b) Aut camión m; **t. driver** camionero(a) m,f, CAm, Méx trailero(a) m,f, US **t. farm** huerta f; US **t. farmer** hortelano(a) m,f

truck² [trʌk] n (a) **to have no t. with** no estar dispuesto a tolerar (b) US verduras fpl; **t. farm** huerta f; **t. farming** cultivo m de hortalizas

trucker ['trʌkə(r)] n US (lorry driver) camionero(a) m,f, CAm, Méx trailero(a) m,f

truculent ['trʌkjʊlənt] adj agresivo(a), airado(a)

ℓ Note that the Spanish word **truculento** is a false friend and is never a translation for the English word **truculent**. In Spanish, **truculento** means "horrifying, terrifying".

trudge [trʌdʒ] *vi* caminar con dificultad

true [truː] *adj* (**truer, truest**) (**a**) *(factually correct)* cierto(a), verdadero(a); **it's t. that …** es verdad que …; **to come t.** cumplirse, hacerse realidad (**b**) *(faithful)* fiel (**c**) *(aim)* acertado(a)

truffle ['trʌfəl] *n* trufa *f*

truly ['truːlɪ] *adv* verdaderamente; **really and t.?** ¿de veras?; **yours t.** *(at end of letter)* atentamente

trump [trʌmp] *Cards* **1** *n* triunfo *m*
2 *vt* fallar

trumped-up ['trʌmptʌp] *adj* inventado(a)

trumpet ['trʌmpɪt] *n* trompeta *f*

trumpeting ['trʌmpɪtɪŋ] *n* (of elephant) berrido *m*

truncheon ['trʌntʃən] *n* *Br* porra *f* (de policía)

trundle ['trʌndəl] *vi* rodar

trunk [trʌŋk] *n* (**a**) *(of tree, body)* tronco *m* (**b**) *(of elephant)* trompa *f* (**c**) *(luggage)* baúl *m* (**d**) *Br Tel* **t. call** llamada *f* or *Am* llamado *m* de larga distancia, *Esp* conferencia *f*; **t. road** carretera *f* principal (**e**) *US (of car)* maletero *m*, *CAm, Méx* cajuela *f*, *RP* baúl *m*

trunks [trʌŋks] *npl* (**bathing**) **t.** bañador *m* (de hombre)

truss [trʌs] **1** *vt* *(tie)* atar
2 *n* (**a**) *Constr* cuchillo *m* de armadura (**b**) *Med* braguero *m*

trust [trʌst] **1** *n* (**a**) *(belief)* confianza *f*; **breach of t.** abuso *m* de confianza (**b**) *Jur* fideicomiso *m* (**c**) *Fin* trust *m*
2 *vt* (**a**) *(hope)* esperar (**b**) *(rely upon)* fiarse de; **to t. sb with sth** confiar algo a algn
3 *vi* confiar (**in** en)

trusted ['trʌstɪd] *adj* de fiar

trustee [trʌs'tiː] *n* *Jur* fideicomisario(a) *m,f*; *(in bankruptcy)* síndico *m*

trustful ['trʌstful], **trusting** ['trʌstɪŋ] *adj* confiado(a)

trustworthy ['trʌstwɜːðɪ] *adj* (person) fiable, de confianza, *Am* confiable; (information) fidedigno(a), fiable, *Am* confiable

trusty ['trʌstɪ] *adj* (**trustier, trustiest**) fiel, leal

truth [truːθ] *n* verdad *f*; **to tell the t.** decir la verdad

truthful ['truːθful] *adj* (person) veraz, sincero(a); (testimony) verídico(a)

truthfully ['truːθfulɪ] *adv* sinceramente

try [traɪ] **1** *vt* *(pt & pp* **tried**) (**a**) *(attempt)* intentar; **to t. to do sth** tratar de *or* intentar hacer algo (**b**) *(test)* probar, ensayar; **to t. sb's patience** poner a prueba la paciencia de algn (**c**) *Jur* juzgar
2 *vi* intentar
3 *n* (**a**) *(attempt)* tentativa *f*, intento *m* (**b**) *Sport* ensayo *m*
▸ **try on** *vt sep* *(dress)* probarse
▸ **try out** *vt sep* probar

trying ['traɪɪŋ] *adj* (person) molesto(a), pesado(a); **to have a t. time** pasar un mal rato

tsar [zɑː(r)] *n* zar *m*

T-shirt ['tiːʃɜːt] *n* camiseta *f*, *Méx* playera, *RP* remera *f*

tub [tʌb] *n* (**a**) *(container)* tina *f*, cuba *f* (**b**) *(bath)* bañera *f*, *Am* tina *f*, *Am* bañadera *f*

tuba ['tjuːbə] *n* tuba *f*

tubby ['tʌbɪ] *adj* (**tubbier, tubbiest**) rechoncho(a)

tube [tjuːb] *n* (**a**) *(pipe, container)* tubo *m*; *(in tyre)* cámara *f* (de aire) (**b**) *Br Fam* **the t.** *(underground)* el metro, *RP* el subte

tuberculosis [tjʊbɜːkjʊ'ləʊsɪs] *n* tuberculosis *f*

tubing ['tjuːbɪŋ] *n* tubería *f*; **(piece of) t.** *(trozo m de)* tubo *m*

tubular ['tjuːbjʊlə(r)] *adj* tubular

tuck [tʌk] **1** *vt* **to t. in the bedclothes** remeter la ropa de la cama; **to t. sb in** arropar a algn; **to t. one's shirt into one's trousers** meterse la camisa por dentro (de los pantalones)
2 *n* *Sewing* pliegue *m*
▸ **tuck in** *vi Fam* devorar

Tuesday ['tjuːzdɪ] *n* martes *m*

tuft [tʌft] *n* (of hair) mechón *m*

tug [tʌg] **1** *vt* *(pull at)* tirar de; *(haul along)* arrastrar; *Naut* remolcar
2 *n* (**a**) *(pull)* tirón *m*; **t. of war** *(game)* lucha *f* de la cuerda; *Fig* lucha encarnizada (**b**) *Naut* remolcador *m*

tugboat ['tʌgbəʊt] *n* remolcador *m*

tuition [tjuː'ɪʃən] *n* instrucción *f*; **private t.** clases *fpl* particulares; **t. fees** honorarios *mpl*

tulip ['tjuːlɪp] *n* tulipán *m*

tumble ['tʌmbəl] **1** *vi* (person) caerse; *(acrobat)* dar volteretas; *(building)* venirse abajo
2 *vt* volcar
3 *n* (**a**) *(fall)* caída *f* (**b**) **t. dryer** secadora *f*

tumbledown ['tʌmbəldaʊn] *adj* en ruinas

tumbler ['tʌmblə(r)] *n* vaso *m*

tummy ['tʌmɪ] *n Fam* barriga *f, Chile* guata *f*

tumour, *US* **tumor** ['tjuːmə(r)] *n* tumor *m*

tumult ['tjuːmʌlt] *n* tumulto *m*

tuna ['tjuːnə] *n* atún *m*, bonito *m*

> Note that the Spanish word **tuna** is a false friend and is never a translation for the English word **tuna**. In Spanish **tuna** means "group of student minstrels".

tune [tjuːn] **1** *n* (a) *(melody)* melodía *f; Fig* **to change one's t.** cambiar de tono (b) *Mus* tono *m*; **in/out of t.** afinado/desafinado; **to sing out of t.** desafinar
   2 *vt Mus* afinar
   3 *vi Rad & TV* **to t. in to a station** sintonizar una emisora
▸ **tune up** *vi* afinar los instrumentos

tuneful ['tjuːnfʊl] *adj* melodioso(a)

tuner ['tjuːnə(r)] *n* (a) *(of pianos)* afinador(a) *m,f* (b) *Rad & TV (knob)* sintonizador *m*

tunic ['tjuːnɪk] *n* túnica *f*

tuning ['tjuːnɪŋ] *n* (a) *Mus* afinación *f*; **t. fork** diapasón *m* (b) *Rad & TV* **t. in** sintonización *f*

Tunisia [tjuːˈnɪzɪə] *n* Túnez

Tunisian [tjuːˈnɪzɪən] *adj & n* tunecino(a) *(m,f)*

tunnel ['tʌnəl] **1** *n* túnel *m; Min* galería *f*
   2 *vt* **to t. through** abrir un túnel a través de

turban ['tɜːbən] *n* turbante *m*

turbine ['tɜːbaɪn] *n* turbina *f*

turbulent ['tɜːbjʊlənt] *adj* turbulento(a)

tureen [təˈriːn] *n* sopera *f*

turf [tɜːf] *n* (a) *(grass)* césped *m*; *(peat)* turba *f* (b) *Br* **t. accountant** *(in horse racing)* corredor(a) *m,f* de apuestas
▸ **turf out** *vt sep Br Fam* **to t. sb out** poner a algn de patitas en la calle

Turk [tɜːk] *n* turco(a) *m,f*

Turkey ['tɜːkɪ] *n* Turquía

turkey ['tɜːkɪ] *n* pavo *m; Méx* guajolote *m*

Turkish ['tɜːkɪʃ] **1** *adj* turco(a)
   2 *n (language)* turco *m*

turmoil ['tɜːmɔɪl] *n* confusión *f*

turn [tɜːn] **1** *vt* (a) *(wheel, handle)* girar; *(key, omelette)* dar la vuelta a; **to t. sth inside out** volver algo del revés; **to t. a page** volver una hoja; **to t. one's head/gaze** volver la cabeza/mirada *(towards* hacia); **to t. the corner** doblar *or Am* voltear la esquina; *Fig* **he's turned forty** ha cumplido los cuarenta (b) *(change)*

transformar *(into* en) (c) *(on lathe)* tornear
   2 *vi* (a) *(rotate)* girar (b) *(turn round)* volverse, dar la vuelta; **to t. to sb** volverse hacia algn; *Fig (for help)* acudir a algn; **to t. upside down** volcarse; *Fig* **to t. on sb** volverse contra algn (c) *(become)* volverse; **the milk has turned sour** la leche se ha cortado
   3 *n* (a) *(of wheel)* vuelta *f*; **done to a t.** *(meat)* en su punto (b) *(change of direction)* cambio *m* de dirección; *(in road)* curva *f*; **to take a t. for the better** empezar a mejorar; **left/right t.** giro *m* a la izquierda/a la derecha; *US Aut* **t. signal** intermitente *m, Col, Ecuad, Méx* direccional *m or f* (c) **to do sb a good t.** hacer un favor a algn (d) *Med* ataque *m* (e) *(in game, queue)* turno *m*, vez *f*; **it's your t.** te toca a ti; **to take turns (at doing sth),** *Br* **to take it in turns (to do sth)** turnarse (para hacer algo) (f) *Th* número *m* (g) **t. of phrase** giro *m*
▸ **turn aside 1** *vt sep* desviar
   2 *vi* desviarse
▸ **turn away 1** *vt sep (person)* rechazar
   2 *vi* volver la cabeza
▸ **turn back 1** *vt sep (person)* hacer retroceder; *(clock)* retrasar
   2 *vi* volverse
▸ **turn down** *vt sep* (a) *(gas, radio etc)* bajar (b) *(reject)* rechazar (c) *(fold)* doblar
▸ **turn in** *Fam* **1** *vt sep (person)* entregar a la policía
   2 *vi* acostarse
▸ **turn off 1** *vt sep (electricity)* desconectar; *(gas, light)* apagar; *(water)* cerrar
   2 *vi* desviarse
▸ **turn on** *vt sep (electricity)* encender, *Am* prender; *(tap, gas)* abrir; *(machine)* poner en marcha; *Fam* **it turns me on** me encanta
▸ **turn out 1** *vt sep* (a) *(extinguish)* apagar (b) *(eject)* echar; *(empty)* vaciar (c) *(produce)* producir
   2 *vi* (a) *(attend)* asistir (b) **it turns out that ...** resulta que ...; **things have turned out well** las cosas han salido bien
▸ **turn over 1** *vt sep (turn upside down)* poner al revés; *(page)* dar la vuelta a
   2 *vi* volverse
▸ **turn round 1** *vt sep* volver
   2 *vi (rotate)* girar, dar vueltas
▸ **turn up 1** *vt sep* (a) *(collar)* levantar; **to t. up one's shirt sleeves** arremangarse; **turned-up nose** nariz respingona (b) *Rad & TV* subir
   2 *vi* (a) *Fig* **something is sure to t. up** algo saldrá (b) *(arrive)* llegar, presen-

tarse; **no one turned up** nadie se presentó (**c**) *(attend)* asistir

turning ['tɜːnɪŋ] *n* (**a**) *Fig* **t. point** punto decisivo (**b**) *(in road)* salida *f*

turnip ['tɜːnɪp] *n* nabo *m*

turnout ['tɜːnaʊt] *n* asistencia *f*

turnover ['tɜːnəʊvə(r)] *n Com (sales)* facturación *f*; *(of goods)* movimiento *m*

turnpike ['tɜːnpaɪk] *n US* autopista *f* de peaje

turnstile ['tɜːnstaɪl] *n* torniquete *m*

turntable ['tɜːnteɪbəl] *n (for record)* plato *m* (giratorio)

turn-up ['tɜːnʌp] *n Br (of trousers)* vuelta *f*

turpentine ['tɜːpəntaɪn] *n* (esencia *f* de) trementina *f*

turquoise ['tɜːkwɔɪz] **1** *n (colour, stone)* turquesa *f*
2 *adj* **t. (blue)** azul turquesa

turret ['tʌrɪt] *n* torrecilla *f*

turtle ['tɜːtəl] *n Br* tortuga (marina); *US (tortoise)* tortuga *f*

turtledove ['tɜːtəldʌv] *n* tórtola *f*

turtleneck ['tɜːtəlnek] *n* a **t. (sweater)** un suéter *or Esp* jersey de cuello alto

tusk [tʌsk] *n* colmillo *m*

tussle ['tʌsəl] *n* pelea *f*, lucha *f*

tutor ['tjuːtə(r)] *n Br Univ* tutor(a) *m,f*; **private t.** profesor(a) *m,f* particular

tutorial [tjuːˈtɔːrɪəl] *n Br Univ* tutoría *f*, seminario *m*

tuxedo [tʌkˈsiːdəʊ] *n US* smoking *m*

TV [tiːˈviː] *n (abbr* **television)** televisión *f*

twang [twæŋ] **1** *n* (**a**) *(of instrument)* sonido *m* vibrante (**b**) **nasal t.** gangueo *m*
2 *vt* puntear
3 *vi (string)* vibrar

tweak [twiːk] *vt* pellizcar

tweed [twiːd] *n* cheviot *m*

tweezers ['twiːzəz] *npl* pinzas *fpl*

twelfth [twelfθ] **1** *adj & n* duodécimo(a) *(m,f)*
2 *n (fraction)* duodécimo *m*

twelve [twelv] *adj & n* doce *(m inv)*

twentieth ['twentɪəθ] **1** *adj & n* vigésimo(a) *(m,f)*
2 *n (fraction)* vigésimo *m*

twenty ['twentɪ] *adj & n* veinte *(m inv)*

twice [twaɪs] *adv* dos veces; **he's t. as old as I am** tiene el doble de años que yo

twiddle ['twɪdəl] **1** *vt* dar vueltas a; **to t. one's moustache** mesarse el bigote; **to t. one's thumbs** estar mano sobre mano
2 *vi* **to t. with sth** juguetear con algo

twig¹ [twɪg] *n* ramilla *f*

twig² [twɪg] *vi Br Fam* darse cuenta

twilight ['twaɪlaɪt] *n* crepúsculo *m*

twin [twɪn] **1** *n* mellizo(a) *m,f*; **identical twins** gemelos (idénticos); **t. brother/sister** hermano gemelo/hermana gemela; **t. beds** camas *fpl* gemelas
2 *vt* hermanar

twine [twaɪn] **1** *n* bramante *m*
2 *vt* entretejer
3 *vi* **to t. round sth** enroscarse alrededor de algo

twinge [twɪndʒ] *n (of pain)* punzada *f*; *Fig* **t. of conscience** remordimiento *m*

twinkle ['twɪŋkəl] *vi (stars)* centellear; *(eyes)* brillar

twinkling ['twɪŋklɪŋ] *n (of stars)* centelleo *m*; *Fig* **in the t. of an eye** en un abrir y cerrar de ojos

twirl [twɜːl] **1** *vt* girar rápidamente
2 *vi (spin)* girar rápidamente; *(dancer)* piruetear
3 *n (movement)* giro rápido; *(of dancer)* pirueta *f*

twist [twɪst] **1** *vt* torcer; *(sense)* tergiversar; **to t. one's ankle** torcerse el tobillo
2 *vi (smoke)* formar volutas; *(path)* serpentear
3 *n* (**a**) *(of yarn)* torzal *m* (**b**) *(movement)* torsión *f*; *Med* torcedura *f*; *Fig* **to give a new t. to sth** dar un nuevo enfoque a algo (**c**) *(in road)* vuelta *f* (**d**) *(dance)* twist *m*

twit [twɪt] *n Br Fam* lerdo(a) *m,f*, *Esp* memo(a) *m,f*

twitch [twɪtʃ] **1** *vt* dar un tirón a
2 *vi* crisparse; **his face twitches** tiene un tic en la cara

twitter ['twɪtə(r)] **1** *vi* gorjear
2 *n* gorjeo *m*

two [tuː] **1** *adj* dos *inv*; *Fig* **to be in** *or* **of t. minds about sth** estar indeciso(a) respecto a algo
2 *n* dos *m inv*; *Fig* **to put t. and t. together** atar cabos

two-faced ['tuːˈfeɪst] *adj* hipócrita

twofold ['tuːfəʊld] *adj* doble

two-party ['tuːpɑːtɪ] *adj* **t. system** bipartidismo *m*

two-piece ['tuːpiːs] **1** *adj* de dos piezas
2 *n (suit)* traje *m* de dos piezas

two-seater ['tuːsiːtə(r)] *adj & n* biplaza *(m)*

twosome ['tuːsəm] *n* pareja *f*

two-time ['tuːtaɪm] *vt Fam* **to t. sb** engañar *or Esp* pegársela a algn

two-way ['tuːweɪ] *adj* (**a**) *(street)* de dos direcciones (**b**) **t. radio** aparato *m* emisor y receptor

tycoon [taɪˈkuːn] *n* magnate *m*

type [taɪp] **1** *n* (**a**) *(kind)* tipo *m*, clase *f*; *(brand)* marca *f*; *(of car)* modelo *m* (**b**) *Typ* carácter *m*; *(print)* caracteres *mpl*

2 *vt & vi (with typewriter)* escribir a máquina; *(with word processor)* escribir en *Esp* el ordenador *or Am* la computadora

typecast ['taɪpkɑːst] *vt* encasillar

typescript ['taɪpskrɪpt] *n* texto *m* escrito a máquina

typeset ['taɪpset] *vt* componer

typesetter ['taɪpsetə(r)] *n* (**a**) *(person)* cajista *mf* (**b**) *(machine)* máquina *f* para componer tipos

typewriter ['taɪpraɪtə(r)] *n* máquina *f* de escribir

typewritten ['taɪprɪtən] *adj* escrito(a) a máquina

typhoid ['taɪfɔɪd] *n* **t. (fever)** fiebre tifoidea

typhoon [taɪ'fuːn] *n* tifón *m*

typical ['tɪpɪkəl] *adj* típico(a)

typify ['tɪpɪfaɪ] *vt* tipificar

typing ['taɪpɪŋ] *n* mecanografía *f*

typist ['taɪpɪst] *n* mecanógrafo(a) *m,f*

tyrannical [tɪ'rænɪkəl] *adj* tiránico(a)

tyrannize ['tɪrənaɪz] *vt* tiranizar

tyranny ['tɪrənɪ] *n* tiranía *f*

tyrant ['taɪrənt] *n* tirano(a) *m,f*

tyre [taɪə(r)] *n* neumático *m, Am* llanta *f*; **t. pressure** presión *f* de los neumáticos

U, u [ju:] *n (the letter)* U, u *f*

U [ju:] *adj (film)* ≃ (apta) para todos los públicos

ubiquity [ju:'bɪkwɪtɪ] *n* ubicuidad *f*

udder ['ʌdə(r)] *n* ubre *f*

UFO, ufo ['ju:ef əʊ, 'ju:fəʊ] *n (abbr unidentified flying object)* OVNI *m*

ugh [ʌχ] *interj* ¡uf!, ¡puf!

ugly ['ʌglɪ] *adj* (**uglier, ugliest**) feo(a); *(situation)* desagradable; *Fig* **u. duckling** patito feo

UK [ju:'keɪ] *n (abbr United Kingdom)* R.U. *m*

Ukraine [ju:'kreɪn] *n* **the U.** Ucrania

ulcer ['ʌlsə(r)] *n (sore)* llaga *f*, *(internal)* úlcera *f*

ulterior [ʌl'tɪərɪə(r)] *adj (motive)* oculto(a)

ultimate ['ʌltɪmɪt] *adj* (**a**) *(final)* último(a); *(aim)* final (**b**) *(basic)* esencial

ultimately ['ʌltɪmɪtlɪ] *adv* (**a**) *(finally)* finalmente (**b**) *(basically)* en el fondo

ultimatum [ʌltɪ'meɪtəm] *n* ultimátum *m*

ultrasound ['ʌltrəsaʊnd] *n* ultrasonido *m*

ultraviolet [ʌltrə'vaɪəlɪt] *adj* ultravioleta

umbilical [ʌm'bɪlɪkəl] *adj* **u. cord** cordón *m* umbilical

umbrella [ʌm'brelə] *n* paraguas *m inv*, *Col* sombrilla *f*

umpire ['ʌmpaɪə(r)] **1** *n* árbitro *m* **2** *vt* arbitrar

umpteen [ʌmp'ti:n] *adj Fam* muchísimos(as), la tira de

umpteenth [ʌmp'ti:nθ] *adj* enésimo(a)

UN [ju:'en] *n (abbr United Nations (Organization))* ONU *f*

unabashed [ʌnə'bæʃt] *adj* descarado(a); **to be u. (by or at)** no sentir vergüenza *or Am* pena (de or por)

unable [ʌn'eɪbəl] *adj* incapaz; **to be u. to do sth/anything** no poder hacer algo/ nada

unacceptable [ʌnək'septəbəl] *adj* inaceptable

unaccompanied [ʌnə'kʌmpənɪd] *adj* solo(a)

unaccountable [ʌnə'kaʊntəbəl] *adj* inexplicable

unaccounted-for [ʌnə'kaʊntɪdfɔ:(r)] *adj* **to be u.** faltar

unaccustomed [ʌnə'kʌstəmd] *adj* he's **u. to this climate** no está muy acostumbrado a este clima

unaffected [ʌnə'fektɪd] *adj* (**a**) *(undamaged, untouched)* no afectado(a) (**by** por) (**b**) *(indifferent)* indiferente (**by a**) (**c**) *(natural) (person)* natural; *(style)* llano(a)

unaided [ʌn'eɪdɪd] *adj* sin ayuda, solo(a)

unanimous [ju:'nænɪməs] *adj* unánime

unannounced [ʌnə'naʊnst] *adj* sin avisar

unanswered [ʌn'ɑ:nsəd] *adj* sin contestar

unapproachable [ʌnə'prəʊtʃəbəl] *adj* inabordable, inaccesible

unarmed [ʌn'ɑ:md] *adj* desarmado(a)

unashamed [ʌnə'ʃeɪmd] *adj* descarado(a)

unasked [ʌn'ɑ:skt] *adv* **u. (for)** *(unrequested)* no solicitado(a); *(spontaneous)* espontáneo(a)

unassuming [ʌnə'sju:mɪŋ] *adj* sin pretensiones

unattached [ʌnə'tætʃt] *adj* (**a**) *(independent)* libre; *(loose)* suelto(a) (**b**) *(person)* soltero(a) y sin compromiso

unattainable [ʌnə'teɪnəbəl] *adj* inalcanzable

unattended [ʌnə'tendɪd] *adj (counter etc)* desatendido(a); **to leave a child u.** dejar a un niño solo

unattractive [ʌnə'træktɪv] *adj* poco atractivo(a)

unauthorized [ʌn'ɔ:θəraɪzd] *adj* (**a**) *(person)* no autorizado(a) (**b**) *(trade etc)* ilícito(a), ilegal

unavailable [ʌnə'veɪləbəl] *adj* **to be u.** no estar disponible

unavoidable [ʌnə'vɔɪdəbəl] *adj* inevitable; *(accident)* imprevisible

unaware [ʌnə'weə(r)] *adj* **to be u. of sth** ignorar algo

unawares [ʌnə'weəz] *adv* (**a**) *(unexpectedly)* desprevenido(a) (**b**) *(without knowing)* inconscientemente

unbalanced [ʌn'bælənst] *adj* desequilibrado(a)

unbearable [ʌn'beərəbəl] *adj* insoportable

unbeatable [ʌn'biːtəbəl] *adj (team)* invencible; *(price, quality)* inmejorable

unbelievable [ʌnbɪ'liːvəbəl] *adj* increíble

unbend [ʌn'bend] *vi Fam Fig* relajarse

unbia(s)sed [ʌn'baɪəst] *adj* imparcial

unblock [ʌn'blɒk] *vt (sink, pipe)* desatascar

unborn [ʌn'bɔːn] *adj* sin nacer, nonato(a)

unbreakable [ʌn'breɪkəbəl] *adj* irrompible; *Fig* inquebrantable

unbroken [ʌn'brəʊkən] *adj* **(a)** *(whole)* intacto(a) **(b)** *(uninterrupted)* continuo(a) **(c)** *(record)* imbatido(a)

unbutton [ʌn'bʌtən] *vt* desabrochar

uncalled-for [ʌn'kɔːldfɔː(r)] *adj (inappropriate)* insensato(a); *(unjustified)* inmerecido(a)

uncanny [ʌn'kænɪ] *adj* misterioso(a), extraño(a)

unceasing [ʌn'siːsɪŋ] *adj* incesante

uncertain [ʌn'sɜːtən] *adj* **(a)** *(not certain)* incierto(a); *(doubtful)* dudoso(a); **in no u. terms** claramente **(b)** *(hesitant)* indeciso(a)

uncertainty [ʌn'sɜːtəntɪ] *n* incertidumbre *f*

unchanged [ʌn'tʃeɪndʒd] *adj* igual

unchecked [ʌn'tʃekt] *adj* **(a)** *(unrestrained)* desenfrenado(a) **(b)** *(not examined)* no comprobado(a)

uncivilized [ʌn'sɪvɪlaɪzd] *adj (tribe)* incivilizado(a), salvaje; *(not cultured)* inculto(a)

uncle ['ʌŋkəl] *n* tío *m*

unclear [ʌn'klɪə(r)] *adj* poco claro(a)

uncomfortable [ʌn'kʌmftəbəl] *adj* incómodo(a); **to make things u. for** complicarle la vida a

uncommon [ʌn'kɒmən] *adj* **(a)** *(rare)* poco común; *(unusual)* extraordinario(a) **(b)** *(excessive)* excesivo(a)

uncommonly [ʌn'kɒmənlɪ] *adv* **not u.** con cierta frecuencia

uncompromising [ʌn'kɒmprəmaɪzɪŋ] *adj* intransigente; **u. honesty** sinceridad absoluta

unconcerned [ʌnkən'sɜːnd] *adj* indiferente (**about** a)

unconditional [ʌnkən'dɪʃənəl] *adj* incondicional; **u. refusal** negativa rotunda

unconnected [ʌnkə'nektɪd] *adj* no relacionado(a)

unconscious [ʌn'kɒnʃəs] **1** *adj* **(a)** *(not awake)* inconsciente **(b)** *(unintentional)* involuntario(a)
2 *n* **the u.** el inconsciente

unconsciousness [ʌn'kɒnʃəsnɪs] *n Med* pérdida *f* del conocimiento

unconstitutional [ʌnkɒnstɪ'tjuːʃənəl] *adj* inconstitucional, anticonstitucional

uncontested [ʌnkən'testɪd] *adj Pol* **u. seat** escaño *m* ganado sin oposición

uncontrollable [ʌnkən'trəʊləbəl] *adj* incontrolable; *(desire)* irresistible

unconventional [ʌnkən'venʃənəl] *adj* poco convencional, original

unconvincing [ʌnkən'vɪnsɪŋ] *adj* poco convincente

uncooperative [ʌnkəʊ'ɒpərətɪv] *adj* poco cooperativo(a)

uncouth [ʌn'kuːθ] *adj (rude)* grosero(a)

uncover [ʌn'kʌvə(r)] *vt* destapar; *Fig* descubrir

undamaged [ʌn'dæmɪdʒd] *adj (article etc)* sin desperfectos; *(person)* indemne; *(reputation)* intacto(a)

undaunted [ʌn'dɔːntɪd] *adj* firme, impávido(a)

undecided [ʌndɪ'saɪdɪd] *adj* **(a)** *(person)* indeciso(a) **(b)** *(issue)* pendiente; **it's still u.** está aún por decidir

undefeated [ʌndɪ'fiːtɪd] *adj* invicto(a)

undefined [ʌndɪ'faɪnd] *adj* indeterminado(a)

undeniable [ʌndɪ'naɪəbəl] *adj* innegable

under ['ʌndə(r)] **1** *prep* **(a)** *(beneath)* debajo de, bajo, *Am* abajo de; **u. the sun** bajo el sol **(b)** *(less than)* menos de; **incomes u. £1,000** ingresos inferiores a 1.000 libras; **u. age** menor de edad **(c)** *(of rank)* de rango inferior a **(d)** *(ruled by)* **u. Caesar** bajo César **(e)** *(subject to)* bajo; **u. arrest** detenido(a); **u. cover** a cubierto; **u. obligation** en la obligación de; **u. the circumstances** dadas las circunstancias; *Fig* **I was u. the impression that …** tenía la impresión de que … **(f)** *(according to)* según, conforme a
2 *adv* abajo, debajo

under- ['ʌndə(r)] *pref (below)* sub-, infra-; *(insufficiently)* insuficientemente

underarm ['ʌndərɑːm] **1** *adj* **u. deodorant** desodorante *m* para las axilas
2 *adv Sport* por debajo del hombro

undercarriage ['ʌndəkærɪdʒ] *n* tren *m* de aterrizaje

undercharge [ʌndə'tʃɑːdʒ] *vt* cobrar menos de lo debido

underclothes ['ʌndəkləʊðz] *npl* ropa *f* interior

undercoat ['ʌndəkəʊt] *n (of paint)* primera mano

undercover [ʌndə'kʌvə(r)] *adj* secreto(a)

undercurrent ['ʌndəkʌrənt] *n* (a) *(in sea)* corriente submarina (b) *Fig* sentimiento *m* latente

undercut [ʌndə'kʌt] *vt (pt & pp* **undercut)** *Com* vender más barato que

underdeveloped [ʌndədɪ'veləpt] *adj* subdesarrollado(a)

underdog ['ʌndədɒg] *n* desvalido(a) *m,f*

underestimate [ʌndər'estɪmeɪt] *vt* infravalorar

underexposure [ʌndərɪk'spəʊʒə(r)] *n Phot* subexposición *f*

underfed [ʌndə'fed] *adj* subalimentado(a)

underfoot [ʌndə'fʊt] *adv* en el suelo

undergo [ʌndə'gəʊ] *vt (pt* **underwent**; *pp* **undergone** [ʌndə'gɒn]) *(experience);* *(change)* sufrir; *(test etc)* pasar por

undergraduate [ʌndə'grædjʊɪt] *n* estudiante *mf* universitario(a)

underground 1 *adj* ['ʌndəgraʊnd] subterráneo(a); *Fig* clandestino(a)
2 *n* (a) *Pol* movimiento clandestino (b) *Br* **the u.** *(train)* el metro, *RP* el subte
3 *adv* [ʌndə'graʊnd] *Fig* **to go u.** pasar a la clandestinidad

undergrowth ['ʌndəgrəʊθ] *n* maleza *f*

underhand 1 *adj* ['ʌndəhænd] *(method)* ilícito(a); *(person)* solapado(a)
2 *adv* [ʌndə'hænd] bajo cuerda

underline [ʌndə'laɪn] *vt* subrayar

underling ['ʌndəlɪŋ] *n Pej* mandado(a) *m,f*

underlying [ʌndə'laɪɪŋ] *adj (basic)* fundamental

undermine [ʌndə'maɪn] *vt* socavar, minar

underneath [ʌndə'ni:θ] **1** *prep* debajo de, bajo
2 *adv* abajo, debajo
3 *adj* de abajo
4 *n* parte *f* inferior

undernourished [ʌndə'nʌrɪʃt] *adj* desnutrido(a)

underpaid [ʌndə'peɪd] *adj* mal pagado(a)

underpants ['ʌndəpænts] *npl* calzoncillos *mpl*, *Chile* fundillos *mpl*, *Méx* calzones *mpl*

underpass ['ʌndəpɑːs] *n* paso subterráneo

underprivileged [ʌndə'prɪvɪlɪdʒd] **1** *adj* desfavorecido(a)
2 *npl* **the u.** los menos favorecidos

underrate [ʌndə'reɪt] *vt* subestimar, infravalorar

under-secretary [ʌndə'sekrətərɪ] *n* subsecretario(a) *m,f*

undershirt ['ʌndəʃɜːt] *n US* camiseta *f*

underside ['ʌndəsaɪd] *n* parte *f* inferior

underskirt ['ʌndəskɜːt] *n* combinación *f*

understand [ʌndə'stænd] *vt & vi (pt & pp* **understood)** (a) *(comprehend)* entender, comprender; **do I make myself understood?** ¿me explico? (b) *(assume, believe)* entender; **she gave me to u. that ...** me dio a entender que ... (c) *(hear)* tener entendido (d) **to u. one another** entenderse

understandable [ʌndə'stændəbəl] *adj* comprensible

understanding [ʌndə'stændɪŋ] **1** *n* (a) *(intellectual grasp)* entendimiento *m*, comprensión *f* (b) *(interpretation)* interpretación *f* (c) *(agreement)* acuerdo *m* (d) **on the u. that ...** a condición de que ...
2 *adj* comprensivo(a)

understatement [ʌndə'steɪtmənt] *n* **to make an u.** minimizar, subestimar; **to say that the boy is rather clever is an u.** decir que el chico es bastante listo es quedarse corto

understood [ʌndə'stʊd] **1** *adj* (a) **I wish it to be u. that ...** que conste que ... (b) *(agreed on)* convenido(a) (c) *(implied)* sobreentendido(a)
2 *pt & pp of* **understand**

understudy ['ʌndəstʌdɪ] *n* suplente *mf*

undertake [ʌndə'teɪk] *vt (pt* **undertook**; *pp* **undertaken** [ʌndə'teɪkən]) (a) *(responsibility)* asumir; *(task, job)* encargarse de (b) *(promise)* comprometerse a

undertaker ['ʌndəteɪkə(r)] *n* empresario(a) *m,f* de pompas fúnebres; **u.'s** funeraria *f*

undertaking [ʌndə'teɪkɪŋ] *n* (a) *(task)* empresa *f* (b) *(promise)* compromiso *m*

undertone ['ʌndətəʊn] *n* **in an u.** en voz baja

undertook [ʌndə'tʊk] *pt of* **undertake**

underwater [ʌndə'wɔːtə(r)] **1** *adj* submarino(a)
2 *adv* bajo el agua

underwear ['ʌndəweə(r)] *n* ropa *f* interior

underwent [ʌndə'went] *pt of* **undergo**

underworld ['ʌndəwɜːld] *n (criminals)* hampa *f*, bajos fondos

underwrite [ʌndə'raɪt] *vt (pt* **underwrote**; *pp* **underwritten)** (a) *(guarantee)* garantizar, avalar (b) *(insure)* asegurar

underwriter ['ʌndəraɪtə(r)] n (a) *Fin* suscriptor(a) m,f (b) *(insurer)* asegurador(a) m,f

underwritten [ʌndə'rɪtən] pp of **underwrite**

underwrote [ʌndə'rəʊt] pt of **underwrite**

undesirable [ʌndɪ'zaɪrəbəl] adj & n indeseable (mf)

undeterred [ʌndɪ'tɜːd] adj sin inmutarse; **u. by** sin arredrarse ante

undid [ʌn'dɪd] pt of **undo**

undies ['ʌndɪz] npl Fam bragas fpl

undignified [ʌn'dɪgnɪfaɪd] adj *(attitude etc)* indecoroso(a)

undisciplined [ʌn'dɪsɪplɪnd] adj indisciplinado(a)

undisclosed [ʌndɪs'kləʊzd] adj sin revelar

undiscovered [ʌndɪs'kʌvəd] adj sin descubrir

undisguised [ʌndɪs'gaɪzd] adj Fig no disimulado(a)

undisputed [ʌndɪ'spjuːtɪd] adj *(unchallenged)* incontestable; *(unquestionable)* indiscutible

undivided [ʌndɪ'vaɪdɪd] adj **to give one's u. attention** prestar toda la atención

undo [ʌn'duː] vt (pt undid; pp undone) (a) *(knot)* deshacer; *(button)* desabrochar (b) *(put right)* enmendar

undoing [ʌn'duːɪŋ] n perdición f

undone¹ [ʌn'dʌn] adj *(unfinished)* inacabado(a)

undone² [ʌn'dʌn] **1** adj *(knot etc)* deshecho(a); **to come u.** *(shoelace)* desatarse; *(button, blouse)* desabrocharse; *(necklace etc)* soltarse
2 pp of **undo**

undoubted [ʌn'daʊtɪd] adj indudable

undress [ʌn'dres] **1** vt desnudar
2 vi desnudarse

undressed [ʌn'drest] adj *(naked)* desnudo(a)

undue [ʌn'djuː] adj (a) *(excessive)* excesivo(a) (b) *(improper)* indebido(a)

undulate ['ʌndjʊleɪt] vi ondular, ondear

unduly [ʌn'djuːlɪ] adv excesivamente

unearth [ʌn'ɜːθ] vt desenterrar

unearthly [ʌn'ɜːθlɪ] adj (a) *(being)* sobrenatural (b) Fam *(din)* espantoso(a); **at an u. hour** a una hora intempestiva

uneasy [ʌn'iːzɪ] adj (a) *(worried)* preocupado(a); *(disturbing)* inquietante (b) *(uncomfortable)* incómodo(a)

uneconomic(al) [ʌniːkə'nɒmɪk(əl)] adj poco económico(a)

uneducated [ʌn'edjʊkeɪtɪd] adj inculto(a)

unemployed [ʌnɪm'plɔɪd] **1** adj desempleado(a), Esp parado(a), Am desocupado(a); **to be u.** estar desempleado(a) or Esp en (el) paro or Am desocupado(a)
2 npl **the u.** los desempleados, Esp los parados, Am los desocupados

unemployment [ʌnɪm'plɔɪmənt] n desempleo m, Esp paro m, Am desocupación f; **u. benefit, US u. compensation** subsidio m de desempleo or Am de desocupación

unending [ʌn'endɪŋ] adj interminable

unenviable [ʌn'envɪəbəl] adj poco envidiable

unequal [ʌn'iːkwəl] adj desigual

unequivocal [ʌnɪ'kwɪvəkəl] adj inequívoco(a)

uneven [ʌn'iːvən] adj (a) *(not level)* desigual; *(bumpy)* accidentado(a) (b) *(variable)* irregular

uneventful [ʌnɪ'ventfʊl] adj sin acontecimientos

unexceptional [ʌnɪk'sepʃənəl] adj ordinario(a)

unexpected [ʌnɪk'spektɪd] adj *(unhoped for)* inesperado(a); *(event)* imprevisto(a)

unexplained [ʌnɪks'pleɪnd] adj inexplicado(a)

unfailing [ʌn'feɪlɪŋ] adj indefectible; *(incessant)* constante; *(patience)* inagotable

unfair [ʌn'feə(r)] adj injusto(a); *Sport* sucio(a)

unfaithful [ʌn'feɪθfʊl] adj *(friend)* desleal; *(husband, wife)* infiel

unfamiliar [ʌnfə'mɪljə(r)] adj *(unknown)* desconocido(a); *(not conversant)* no familiarizado(a) *(with con)*

unfashionable [ʌn'fæʃənəbəl] adj pasado(a) de moda; *(ideas etc)* poco popular

unfasten [ʌn'fɑːsən] vt *(knot)* desatar; *(belt, clothing)* desabrochar

unfavourable, US **unfavorable** [ʌn'feɪvərəbəl] adj desfavorable; *(criticism)* adverso(a); *(winds)* contrario(a)

unfeeling [ʌn'fiːlɪŋ] adj insensible

unfinished [ʌn'fɪnɪʃt] adj inacabado(a); **u. business** un asunto pendiente

unfit [ʌn'fɪt] adj (a) *(thing)* inadecuado(a); *(person)* no apto(a) *(for para)* (b) *(incompetent)* incompetente (c) *(physically)* incapacitado(a); **to be u.** no estar en forma

unflinching [ʌn'flɪntʃɪŋ] adj (a) *(determined)* resuelto(a) (b) *(fearless)* impávido(a)

unfold [ʌn'fəʊld] **1** vt (**a**) (sheet) desdoblar; (newspaper) abrir (**b**) (plan, secret) revelar
2 vi (**a**) (open up) abrirse; (landscape) extenderse (**b**) (plot) desarrollarse (**c**) (secret) descubrirse

unforeseeable [ʌnfə'siːəbəl] adj imprevisible

unforeseen [ʌnfɔː'siːn] adj imprevisto(a)

unforgettable [ʌnfə'getəbəl] adj inolvidable

unforgivable [ʌnfə'gɪvəbəl] adj imperdonable

unfortunate [ʌn'fɔːtʃənɪt] adj (person, event) desgraciado(a); (remark) desafortunado(a); **how u.!** ¡qué mala suerte!

unfortunately [ʌn'fɔːtʃənɪtlɪ] adv desgraciadamente, por desgracia

unfounded [ʌn'faʊndɪd] adj infundado(a)

unfriendly [ʌn'frendlɪ] adj (**unfriendlier, unfriendliest**) antipático(a), poco amistoso(a)

unfulfilled [ʌnfʊl'fɪld] adj **to feel u.** sentirse insatisfecho(a)

unfurl [ʌn'fɜːl] vi desplegarse

unfurnished [ʌn'fɜːnɪʃt] adj sin amueblar

ungainly [ʌn'geɪnlɪ] adj (gait) desgarbado(a)

ungodly [ʌn'gɒdlɪ] adj (**ungodlier, ungodliest**) (behaviour) impío(a); Fam Fig **at an u. hour** a una hora intempestiva

ungrateful [ʌn'greɪtfʊl] adj (person) desagradecido(a); (task) ingrato(a)

unguarded [ʌn'gɑːd] adj (**a**) (unprotected) desatendido(a); (imprudent) desprevenido(a) (**b**) (frank) franco(a)

unhappiness [ʌn'hæpɪnɪs] n (**a**) (sadness) tristeza f (**b**) (wretchedness) desdicha f

unhappy [ʌn'hæpɪ] adj (**unhappier, unhappiest**) (**a**) (sad) triste (**b**) (wretched) desgraciado(a), infeliz; (unfortunate) desafortunado(a)

unharmed [ʌn'hɑːmd] adj ileso(a), indemne

unhealthy [ʌn'helθɪ] adj (**unhealthier, unhealthiest**) (**a**) (ill) enfermizo(a) (**b**) (unwholesome) malsano(a)

unheard [ʌn'hɜːd] adj (**a**) **her request went u.** su petición no fue atendida (**b**) **u. of** (outrageous) inaudito(a); (without precedent) sin precedente

unhelpful [ʌn'helpfʊl] adj (person) poco servicial; (criticism, advice) poco constructivo(a)

unhesitating [ʌn'hezɪteɪtɪŋ] adj resuelto(a)

unhook [ʌn'hʊk] vt (from hook) descolgar; (clothing) desabrochar

unhurt [ʌn'hɜːt] adj ileso(a), indemne

unhygienic [ʌnhaɪ'dʒiːnɪk] adj antihigiénico(a)

unidentified [ʌnaɪ'dentɪfaɪd] adj **u. flying object** objeto volador no identificado, ovni m

unification [juːnɪfɪ'keɪʃən] n unificación f

uniform ['juːnɪfɔːm] adj & n uniforme (m)

uniformity [juːnɪ'fɔːmɪtɪ] n uniformidad f

unify ['juːnɪfaɪ] vt unificar

unilateral [juːnɪ'lætərəl] adj unilateral

unimaginative [ʌnɪ'mædʒɪnətɪv] adj **to be u.** (of person) tener poca imaginación; (of book, choice) ser muy poco original, no tener originalidad

unimportant [ʌnɪm'pɔːtənt] adj poco importante

uninformed [ʌnɪn'fɔːmd] adj (opinion) sin fundamento

uninhabited [ʌnɪn'hæbɪtɪd] adj despoblado(a)

uninhibited [ʌnɪn'hɪbɪtɪd] adj sin inhibición

uninspired [ʌnɪn'spaɪəd] adj (person) falto(a) de inspiración; (performance) insulso(a)

uninspiring [ʌnɪn'spaɪərɪŋ] adj que no inspira

unintelligible [ʌnɪn'telɪdʒəbəl] adj ininteligible, incomprensible

unintentional [ʌnɪn'tenʃənəl] adj involuntario(a)

unintentionally [ʌnɪn'tenʃənəlɪ] adv sin querer

uninterested [ʌn'ɪntərestɪd] adj poco interesado(a)

uninteresting [ʌn'ɪntrɪstɪŋ] adj poco interesante

uninterrupted [ʌnɪntə'rʌptɪd] adj ininterrumpido(a)

union ['juːnjən] **1** n (**a**) (of countries) unión f (**b**) (organization) sindicato m (**c**) US **the U.** los Estados Unidos; Br **U. Jack** bandera f del Reino Unido
2 adj sindical

unique [juː'niːk] adj único(a)

unison ['juːnɪsən] n Mus unisonancia f; Fig (harmony) armonía f; **in u.** al unísono

unit ['juːnɪt] n (**a**) (subdivision) unidad f; **monetary u.** unidad monetaria; Br Fin **u. trust** sociedad f de inversiones (**b**) (piece of furniture) módulo m; **kitchen u.** mueble m de cocina (**c**) Tech grupo m; Comput **central processing u.** procesador m central; **visual display u.** monitor m (**d**) *(department)* servicio *m* (e) *(team)* equipo *m*

unite [juːˈnaɪt] **1** *vt* unir
  2 *vi* unirse

united [juːˈnaɪtɪd] *adj* unido(a); **U. Kingdom** Reino Unido; **U. States (of America)** Estados Unidos (de América); **U. Nations** Naciones Unidas

unity [ˈjuːnɪtɪ] *n* unidad *f*; *(harmony)* armonía *f*

universal [juːnɪˈvɜːsəl] *adj* universal

universe [ˈjuːnɪvɜːs] *n* universo *m*

university [juːnɪˈvɜːsɪtɪ] **1** *n* universidad *f*
  2 *adj* universitario(a)

unjust [ʌnˈdʒʌst] *adj* injusto(a)

unkempt [ʌnˈkempt] *adj* descuidado(a); *(hair)* despeinado(a); *(appearance)* desaliñado(a)

unkind [ʌnˈkaɪnd] *adj (not nice)* poco amable; *(cruel)* despiadado(a)

unknowingly [ʌnˈnəʊɪŋlɪ] *adv* inconscientemente, inadvertidamente

unknown [ʌnˈnəʊn] **1** *adj* desconocido(a); **u. quantity** incógnita *f*
  2 *n* **the u.** lo desconocido

unlawful [ʌnˈlɔːfʊl] *adj (not legal)* ilegal

unleaded [ʌnˈledɪd] *adj* **u.** *Br* **petrol** *or US* **gasoline** gasolina *f or RP* nafta *f* sin plomo

unleash [ʌnˈliːʃ] *vt* (a) *(dog)* soltar (b) *Fig (release)* liberar; *(provoke)* desencadenar

unless [ʌnˈles] *conj* a menos que, a no ser que

unlike [ʌnˈlaɪk] **1** *adj* diferente, distinto(a)
  2 *prep* a diferencia de

unlikely [ʌnˈlaɪklɪ] *adj* (a) *(improbable)* poco probable (b) *(unusual)* raro(a)

unlimited [ʌnˈlɪmɪtɪd] *adj* ilimitado(a)

unlisted [ʌnˈlɪstɪd] *adj US Tel* que no figura en la guía (telefónica)

unload [ʌnˈləʊd] *vt & vi* descargar

unlock [ʌnˈlɒk] *vt* abrir (con llave)

unluckily [ʌnˈlʌkɪlɪ] *adv* desafortunadamente, por desgracia

unlucky [ʌnˈlʌkɪ] *adj* (**unluckier, unluckiest**) *(unfortunate)* desgraciado(a); **to be u.** *(person)* tener mala suerte; *(thing)* traer mala suerte

unmade [ˈʌnmeɪd] *adj (bed)* deshecho(a), sin hacer

unmanageable [ʌnˈmænɪdʒəbəl] *adj (people)* ingobernable; *(child, hair)* incontrolable

unmanned [ʌnˈmænd] *adj (spacecraft etc)* no tripulado(a)

unmarried [ʌnˈmærɪd] *adj* soltero(a)

unmask [ʌnˈmɑːsk] *vt Fig (plot)* descubrir

unmistak(e)able [ʌnmɪsˈteɪkəbəl] *adj* inconfundible

unmistak(e)ably [ʌnmɪsˈteɪkəblɪ] *adv* sin lugar a dudas

unmitigated [ʌnˈmɪtɪɡeɪtɪd] *adj* (a) *(absolute)* absoluto(a); *(liar)* rematado(a) (b) *(grief)* profundo(a)

unmoved [ʌnˈmuːvd] *adv* **to watch/ listen u.** observar/escuchar impertérrito(a)

unnamed [ʌnˈneɪmd] *adj (anonymous)* anónimo(a)

unnatural [ʌnˈnætʃərəl] *adj* (a) *(against nature)* antinatural; *(abnormal)* anormal (b) *(affected)* afectado(a)

unnecessary [ʌnˈnesɪsərɪ] *adj* innecesario(a), inútil; **it's u. to add that ...** sobra añadir que ...

unnoticed [ʌnˈnəʊtɪst] *adj* desapercibido(a); **to let sth pass u.** pasar algo por alto

unobserved [ʌnɒbˈzɜːvd] *adj* inadvertido(a)

unobtainable [ʌnəbˈteɪnəbəl] *adj* inasequible, inalcanzable

unobtrusive [ʌnəbˈtruːsɪv] *adj* discreto(a)

unoccupied [ʌnˈɒkjʊpaɪd] *adj (house)* desocupado(a); *(seat)* libre

unofficial [ʌnəˈfɪʃəl] *adj* no oficial; *Ind* **u. strike** huelga *f* no apoyada por los sindicatos

unorthodox [ʌnˈɔːθədɒks] *adj* (a) *(behaviour etc)* poco ortodoxo(a) (b) *Rel* heterodoxo(a)

unpack [ʌnˈpæk] **1** *vt (boxes)* desembalar; *(suitcase)* deshacer, *Am* desempacar
  2 *vi* deshacer la(s) maleta(s)

unpaid [ʌnˈpeɪd] *adj* (a) *(work, volunteer)* no retribuido(a) (b) *(bill, debt)* impagado(a)

unpalatable [ʌnˈpælətəbəl] *adj* desagradable

unparalleled [ʌnˈpærəleld] *adj* (a) *(in quality)* incomparable (b) *(without precedent)* sin precedente

unpardonable [ʌnˈpɑːdənəbəl] *adj* imperdonable

unperturbed [ʌnpəˈtɜːbd] *adj* impasible

unpleasant [ʌnˈplezənt] *adj* desagradable (**to** con)

unpleasantness [ʌnˈplezəntnɪs] *n* disgusto *m*

unplug [ʌnˈplʌɡ] *vt* desenchufar

unpopular [ʌnˈpɒpjʊlə(r)] *adj* impopular; **to make oneself u.** ganarse la antipatía de todos

unprecedented [ʌnˈpresɪdentɪd] *adj* sin precedente

unpredictable [ʌnprɪ'dɪktəbəl] adj imprevisible

unprepared [ʌnprɪ'peəd] adj (speech etc) improvisado(a); (person) desprevenido(a)

unprincipled [ʌn'prɪnsɪpəld] adj sin escrúpulos

unprintable [ʌn'prɪntəbəl] adj (word, comment) malsonante

unproductive [ʌnprə'dʌktɪv] adj (inefficient) improductivo(a); (fruitless) infructuoso(a)

unprofessional [ʌnprə'feʃənəl] adj (unethical) poco profesional; (substandard) de aficionado(a)

unprotected [ʌnprə'tektɪd] adj indefenso(a)

unprovoked [ʌnprə'vəʊkt] adj gratuito(a)

unpublished [ʌn'pʌblɪʃt] adj inédito(a)

unpunished [ʌn'pʌnɪʃt] adj impune

unqualified [ʌn'kwɒlɪfaɪd] adj (a) (without qualification) sin título; (incompetent) incompetente (b) (unconditional) incondicional; (denial) rotundo(a); (endorsement) sin reserva; (success) total

unquestionable [ʌn'kwestʃənəbəl] adj indiscutible

unquestioning [ʌn'kwestʃənɪŋ] adj incondicional; (obedience) ciego(a)

unravel [ʌn'rævəl] **1** vt desenmarañar **2** vi desenmarañarse

unreadable [ʌn'riːdəbəl] adj (a) (handwriting) ilegible (b) (book) imposible de leer

unreal [ʌn'rɪəl] adj irreal

unrealistic [ʌnrɪə'lɪstɪk] adj poco realista

unreasonable [ʌn'riːzənəbəl] adj poco razonable; (demands) desmedido(a); (prices) exorbitante; (hour) inoportuno(a)

unrecognizable [ʌnrekəg'naɪzəbl] adj irreconocible

unrefined [ʌnrɪ'faɪnd] adj (a) (sugar, oil etc) sin refinar (b) (person) tosco(a), basto(a)

unrelated [ʌnrɪ'leɪtɪd] adj (not connected) no relacionado(a)

unrelenting [ʌnrɪ'lentɪŋ] adj (behaviour) implacable; (struggle) encarnizado(a)

unreliable [ʌnrɪ'laɪəbəl] adj (a) (person) de poca confianza (b) (information) que no es de fiar; (machine) poco fiable

unrelieved [ʌnrɪ'liːvd] adj (boredom) total

unremitting [ʌnrɪ'mɪtɪŋ] adj (a) (efforts etc) incesante (b) (person) incansable

unrepentant [ʌnrɪ'pentənt] adj impenitente

unreserved [ʌnrɪ'zɜːvd] adj (praise, support) sin reserva

unreservedly [ʌnrɪ'zɜːvɪdlɪ] adv sin reserva

unrest [ʌn'rest] n (social etc) malestar m; **political u.** agitación política

unrivalled, US **unrivaled** [ʌn'raɪvəld] adj sin par, sin rival

unroll [ʌn'rəʊl] vt desenrollar

unruffled [ʌn'rʌfəld] adj Fig tranquilo(a)

unruly [ʌn'ruːlɪ] adj (unrulier, unruliest) (a) (child) revoltoso(a) (b) (hair) rebelde

unsafe [ʌn'seɪf] adj (dangerous) peligroso(a); (risky) inseguro(a); **to feel u.** sentirse expuesto(a)

unsaid [ʌn'sed] adj it's better left u. más vale no decir nada; **much was left u.** quedó mucho por decir

unsatisfactory [ʌnsætɪs'fæktərɪ] adj insatisfactorio(a); **it's most u.** deja mucho que desear

unsavoury, US **unsavory** [ʌn'seɪvərɪ] adj desagradable

unscathed [ʌn'skeɪðd] adj ileso(a), indemne

unscrew [ʌn'skruː] vt destornillar

unscrupulous [ʌn'skruːpjʊləs] adj sin escrúpulos

unseemly [ʌn'siːmlɪ] adj impropio(a)

unseen [ʌn'siːn] **1** adj invisible; (unnoticed) inadvertido(a) **2** n Br Educ = texto no trabajado en clase

unselfish [ʌn'selfɪʃ] adj desinteresado(a)

unsettle [ʌn'setəl] vt perturbar

unsettled [ʌn'setəld] adj (a) (person) nervioso(a); (situation) inestable (b) (weather) inestable (c) (matter, debt) pendiente (d) (land) sin colonizar

unshaven [ʌn'ʃeɪvən] adj sin afeitar

unsightly [ʌn'saɪtlɪ] adj feo(a), desagradable

unskilled [ʌn'skɪld] adj (worker) no cualificado(a); (work) no especializado(a)

unsociable [ʌn'səʊʃəbəl] adj insociable, huraño(a)

unsophisticated [ʌnsə'fɪstɪkeɪtɪd] adj (a) (naïve) ingenuo(a) (b) (simple) poco sofisticado(a)

unsound [ʌn'saʊnd] adj (a) (unstable) inestable; **of u.. mind** demente (b) (fallacious) falso(a)

unspeakable [ʌn'spiːkəbəl] adj (a) (pain) indecible (b) (conditions, squalor) inefable

unspoken [ʌnˈspəʊkən] *adj* (**a**) *(tacit)* tácito(a) (**b**) *(feeling)* interior, secreto(a)

unstable [ʌnˈsteɪbəl] *adj* inestable

unsteady [ʌnˈstedɪ] *adj* *(not firm)* inestable; *(table, chair)* cojo(a); *(hand, voice)* tembloroso(a)

unstinting [ʌnˈstɪntɪŋ] *adj* pródigo(a) (**in** en)

unstuck [ʌnˈstʌk] *adj* **to come u.** despegarse; *Fig* venirse abajo

unsuccessful [ʌnsəkˈsesfʊl] *adj* (**a**) *(fruitless)* fracasado(a); *(useless)* vano(a) (**b**) *(businessman etc)* fracasado(a); *(candidate)* derrotado(a); **to be u. at sth** no tener éxito con algo

unsuccessfully [ʌnsəkˈsesfʊlɪ] *adv* sin éxito, en vano

unsuitable [ʌnˈsuːtəbəl] *adj* (**a**) *(person)* no apto(a) (**b**) *(thing)* inadecuado(a); *(remark)* inoportuno(a); *(time)* inconveniente

unsuited [ʌnˈsuːtɪd] *adj* (**a**) *(person)* no apto(a); *(thing)* impropio(a) (**to** para) (**b**) *(incompatible)* incompatible

unsure [ʌnˈʃʊə(r)] *adj* poco seguro(a)

unsuspecting [ʌnsəˈspektɪŋ] *adj* confiado(a); **he went in u.** entró sin sospechar nada

unswerving [ʌnˈswɜːvɪŋ] *adj* firme

unsympathetic [ʌnsɪmpəˈθetɪk] *adj* *(unfeeling)* impasible; *(not understanding)* poco comprensivo(a)

untangle [ʌnˈtæŋgəl] *vt* desenredar, desenmarañar

untapped [ʌnˈtæpt] *adj* *(resource)* sin explotar

untarnished [ʌnˈtɑːnɪʃt] *adj Fig* sin mancha

untenable [ʌnˈtenəbəl] *adj* insostenible

unthinkable [ʌnˈθɪŋkəbəl] *adj* impensable, inconcebible

untidy [ʌnˈtaɪdɪ] *adj* (**untidier, untidiest**) *(room, person)* desordenado(a); *(hair)* despeinado(a); *(appearance)* desaseado(a)

untie [ʌnˈtaɪ] *vt* desatar; *(free)* soltar

until [ʌnˈtɪl] **1** *conj* hasta que; **she worked u. she collapsed** trabajó hasta desfallecer; **u. she gets back** hasta que vuelva
2 *prep* hasta; **u. now** hasta ahora; **u. ten o'clock** hasta las diez; **not u. Monday** hasta el lunes no

untimely [ʌnˈtaɪmlɪ] *adj* (**a**) *(premature)* prematuro(a) (**b**) *(inopportune)* inoportuno(a); *(hour)* intempestivo(a)

untold [ʌnˈtəʊld] *adj* (**a**) *(indescribable)* indecible (**b**) *Fig (loss, wealth)* incalculable (**c**) *(not told)* sin contar

untouchable [ʌnˈtʌtʃəbəl] *adj & n* intocable *(mf)*

untoward [ʌntəˈwɔːd] *adj* (**a**) *(unfortunate)* desafortunado(a) (**b**) *(adverse)* adverso(a)

untrained [ʌnˈtreɪnd] *adj* (**a**) *(unskilled)* sin preparación profesional (**b**) *(inexpert)* inexperto(a)

untrue [ʌnˈtruː] *adj* (**a**) *(false)* falso(a) (**b**) *(unfaithful)* infiel (**c**) *(inexact)* inexacto(a)

untrustworthy [ʌnˈtrʌstwɜːðɪ] *adj* (**a**) *(person)* de poca confianza (**b**) *(source)* no fidedigno(a)

untruthful [ʌnˈtruːθfʊl] *adj* *(person)* embustero(a), mentiroso(a); *(story, reply)* falso(a)

unused [ʌnˈjuːzd] *adj* (**a**) *(car)* sin usar; *(flat etc)* sin estrenar; *(stamp)* sin matar (**b**) *(not in use)* que ya no se utiliza (**c**) [ʌnˈjuːst] *(unaccustomed)* desacostumbrado(a) (**to** a)

unusual [ʌnˈjuːʒʊəl] *adj* *(rare)* insólito(a), poco común; *(original)* original; *(exceptional)* excepcional

unusually [ʌnˈjuːʒʊəlɪ] *adv* excepcionalmente

unveil [ʌnˈveɪl] *vt* descubrir

unwanted [ʌnˈwɒntɪd] *adj* *(attentions, baby)* no deseado(a); *(clothes, trinkets)* desechado(a)

unwarranted [ʌnˈwɒrəntɪd] *adj* injustificado(a); *(remark)* gratuito(a)

unwavering [ʌnˈweɪvərɪŋ] *adj* *(loyalty)* constante, firme; *(courage)* inquebrantable

unwelcome [ʌnˈwelkəm] *adj* *(visitor)* molesto(a); *(visit)* inoportuno(a); *Fig (news etc)* desagradable

unwell [ʌnˈwel] *adj* malo(a), indispuesto(a)

unwieldy [ʌnˈwiːldɪ] *adj* *(difficult to handle)* poco manejable; *(clumsy)* torpe

unwilling [ʌnˈwɪlɪŋ] *adj* **to be u. to do sth** no estar dispuesto a hacer algo

unwillingly [ʌnˈwɪlɪŋlɪ] *adv* de mala gana

unwind [ʌnˈwaɪnd] **1** *vt* *(pt & pp un-*wound**)** desenrollar
2 *vi* (**a**) *(string, wool)* desenrollarse (**b**) *(relax)* relajarse

unwise [ʌnˈwaɪz] *adj* imprudente, desaconsejable

unwitting [ʌnˈwɪtɪŋ] *adj* involuntario(a)

unworkable [ʌnˈwɜːkəbəl] *adj* *(not feasible)* impracticable; *(suggestion)* irrealizable

unworthy [ʌnˈwɜːðɪ] *adj* indigno(a)

unwound [ʌnˈwaʊnd] *pt & pp of* **unwind**

unwrap [ʌn'ræp] *vt* (*gift*) desenvolver; (*package*) deshacer

unwritten [ʌn'rɪtən] *adj* no escrito(a); (*agreement*) verbal

unyielding [ʌn'jiːldɪŋ] *adj* inflexible

unzip [ʌnzɪp] (*pt & pp* **unzipped**) *vt* abrir la cremallera *or Am* el cierre de

up [ʌp] **1** *prep* (**a**) (*movement*) **to climb up the mountain** escalar la montaña; **to walk up the street** caminar *or Esp* andar por la calle (**b**) (*position*) en lo alto de; **further up the street** más adelante (en la misma calle); **halfway up the ladder** a mitad de la escalera
2 *adv* (**a**) (*upwards*) arriba, hacia arriba; (*position*) arriba; **from £10 up** de 10 libras para arriba; **halfway up** a medio camino; **right up (to the top)** hasta arriba (del todo); **to go/come up** subir; **this side up** (*sign*) este lado hacia arriba
(**b**) **the moon is up** ha salido la luna
(**c**) (*towards*) hacia; **to come** *or* **go up to sb** acercarse a algn; **to walk up and down** ir de un lado a otro
(**d**) (*in, to*) **he's up in Yorkshire** está en Yorkshire
(**e**) (*increased*) **bread is up** el pan ha subido
(**f**) **it's up for discussion** se está discutiendo; **up for sale** en venta
(**g**) *Fam* **something's up** pasa algo; **what's up (with you)?** ¿qué pasa (contigo)?
(**h**) **to be up against sth** enfrentarse con algo
(**i**) **up to** (*as far as, until*) hasta; **I can spend up to £5** puedo gastar un máximo de 5 libras; **up to here** hasta aquí; **up to now** hasta ahora
(**j**) **to be up to** (*depend on*) depender de; (*be capable of*) estar a la altura de; **I don't feel up to doing it today** hoy no me encuentro con fuerzas para hacerlo; **it's not up to much** no vale gran cosa
(**k**) **he's up to sth** está tramando algo
3 *adj* (**a**) (*out of bed*) levantado(a) (**b**) (*finished*) terminado(a); **time's up** (ya) es la hora
4 *vt Fam* aumentar
5 *n Fig* **ups and downs** altibajos *mpl*

up-and-coming ['ʌpən'kʌmɪŋ] *adj* prometedor(a)

upbringing ['ʌpbrɪŋɪŋ] *n* educación *f*

update [ʌp'deɪt] *vt* actualizar, poner al día

upgrade 1 *vt* [ʌp'greɪd] (**a**) (*promote*) ascender (**b**) (*improve*) mejorar la calidad de (**c**) *Comput* (*software, hardware*) actualizar
2 *n* ['ʌpgreɪd] *Comput* actualización *f*

upheaval [ʌp'hiːvəl] *n* trastorno *m*

upheld [ʌp'held] *pt & pp of* **uphold**

uphill 1 *adj* ['ʌphɪl] ascendente; *Fig* arduo(a)
2 *adv* [ʌp'hɪl] cuesta arriba

uphold [ʌp'həʊld] *vt* (*pt & pp* **upheld**) sostener

upholstery [ʌp'həʊlstəri] *n* tapizado *m*, tapicería *f*

upkeep ['ʌpkiːp] *n* mantenimiento *m*

up-market ['ʌpmɑːkɪt] *adj* de categoría

upon [ə'pɒn] *prep Fml* en, sobre; **once u. a time …** érase una vez …; **u. my word** (mi) palabra de honor

upper ['ʌpə(r)] **1** *adj* (**a**) (*position*) superior; **u. storey** piso de arriba; *Fig* **to have the u. hand** llevar la delantera (**b**) (*in rank*) alto(a); **the u. class** la clase alta; **the U. House** la Cámara Alta
2 *n* (*of shoe*) pala *f*

upper-class ['ʌpə'klæs] *adj* de la clase alta

uppermost ['ʌpəməʊst] *adj* más alto(a); *Fig* **it was u. in my mind** era lo que me preocupaba más

upright ['ʌpraɪt] **1** *adj* (**a**) (*vertical*) vertical (**b**) (*honest*) honrado(a)
2 *adv* derecho
3 *n Ftb* (*post*) poste *m*

uprising ['ʌpraɪzɪŋ] *n* sublevación *f*

uproar ['ʌprɔː(r)] *n* tumulto *m*, alboroto *m*

uproot [ʌp'ruːt] *vt* (*plant*) arrancar de raíz

upset [ʌp'set] **1** *vt* (*pt & pp* **upset**) (**a**) (*overturn*) volcar; (*spill*) derramar (**b**) (*shock*) trastornar; (*worry*) preocupar; (*displease*) disgustar (**c**) (*spoil*) desbaratar (**d**) (*make ill*) sentar mal a
2 *adj* (*shocked*) alterado(a); (*displeased*) disgustado(a); **to have an u. stomach** sentirse mal del estómago
3 *n* ['ʌpset] (**a**) (*reversal*) revés *m* (**b**) *Sport* resultado inesperado

upshot ['ʌpʃɒt] *n* resultado *m*

upside down ['ʌpsaɪd'daʊn] *adj & adv* al revés

upstage [ʌp'steɪdʒ] *vt Fam* eclipsar

upstairs [ʌp'steəz] **1** *adv* al piso de arriba; **she lives u.** vive en el piso de arriba
2 *n* piso *m* de arriba

upstart ['ʌpstɑːt] *n* advenedizo(a) *m,f*

upstream [ʌp'striːm] *adv* río arriba

uptake ['ʌpteɪk] *n Fam* **to be quick on the u.** cogerlas al vuelo

uptight [ʌp'taɪt] *adj Fam* nervioso(a)

up-to-date [ʌptə'deɪt] *adj* (**a**) (*current*) al día (**b**) (*modern*) moderno(a)

uptown ['ʌptaʊn] *n US* zona *f* residencial

upturn ['ʌptɜːn] n mejora f

upward ['ʌpwəd] adj ascendente

upward(s) ['ʌpwəd(z)] adv hacia arriba; **from ten (years) u.** a partir de los diez años; *Fam* **u. of** algo más de

uranium [jʊ'reɪnɪəm] n uranio m

urban ['ɜːbən] adj urbano(a)

urbane [ɜː'beɪn] adj urbano(a), cortés

urchin ['ɜːtʃɪn] n (a) (child) pilluelo(a) m,f (b) **sea u.** erizo m de mar

urge [ɜːdʒ] 1 vt (a) (encourage) instar; (plead) exhortar (b) (advocate) preconizar; **to u. that sth should be done** insistir en que se haga algo
2 n impulso m

▸ **urge on** vt sep animar a

urgency ['ɜːdʒənsɪ] n urgencia f

urgent ['ɜːdʒənt] adj urgente; (need, tone) apremiante

urinal [jʊ'raɪnəl] n (toilet) urinario m; (bowl) orinal m

urinate ['jʊərɪneɪt] vi orinar

urine ['jʊərɪn] n orina f

URL [juːɑː'rel] n Comput (abbr **uniform resource locator**) URL m

urn [ɜːn] n (a) (decorative, funerary) urna f (b) **tea u.** tetera f grande

Uruguay ['jʊərəgwaɪ] n Uruguay

Uruguayan [jʊərə'gwaɪən] adj & n uruguayo(a) (m,f)

US [juː'es] n (abbr **United States**) EE.UU. mpl

us [ʌs, unstressed əs] pers pron (a) (as object) nos; **let's forget it** olvidémoslo (b) (after prep) nosotros(as); **he's one of us** es de los nuestros (c) (after v **to be**) nosotros(as); **she wouldn't believe it was us** no creía que fuéramos nosotros (d) Fam me; **give us a kiss!** ¡dame un beso!

USA [juːes'eɪ] n (abbr **United States of America**) EE.UU. mpl

usage ['juːsɪdʒ] n (a) (habit, custom) costumbre f (b) Ling uso m

use 1 vt [juːz] (a) (utilize) usar, utilizar; **what is it used for?** ¿para qué sirve?; **to u. force** hacer uso de la fuerza (b) (consume) consumir, gastar (c) (take unfair advantage of) aprovecharse de (d) Fam **I could u. a drink** no me vendría mal un trago
2 n [juːs] (a) (utilization) uso m; **directions for u.** modo de empleo; **in u.** en uso; **not in u.** (on lift) no funciona; **ready for u.** listo para usar; **to make (good) u. of sth** aprovechar algo; **to put to good u.** sacar partido de (b) (application) aplicación f (c) (usefulness) utilidad f; **it's no u.** es inútil; **what's the u.?** ¿para

qué?; Fam **it's no u. crying** no sirve de nada llorar; **of u.** útil; **to be of u.** servir

3 v aux used to ['juːstə] soler, acostumbrar; **where did you u. to live?** ¿dónde vivías (antes)?

> Como verbo auxiliar, aparece siempre en la forma **used to**. Se traduce al español por el verbo principal en pretérito imperfecto, o por el pretérito imperfecto de **soler** más infinitivo.

▸ **use up** vt sep acabar

use-by date ['juːzbaɪdeɪt] n Com fecha f de caducidad

used adj (a) [juːzd] (second-hand) usado(a) (b) [juːst] **to be u. to** estar acostumbrado(a) a

useful ['juːsfʊl] adj útil; (practical) práctico(a); Br **to come in u.** venir bien

usefulness ['juːsfʊlnɪs] n utilidad f

useless ['juːslɪs] adj inútil

user ['juːzə(r)] n (a) (of road, dictionary, computer) usuario(a) m,f (b) Fam (of drugs) drogadicto(a) m,f

user-friendly [juːzə'frendlɪ] adj also Comput de fácil manejo

usher ['ʌʃə(r)] 1 n (a) Cin & Th acomodador(a) m,f (b) (in court etc) ujier m
2 vt **to u. in** Cin & Th acomodar; (at home) hacer pasar; **to u. out** acompañar hasta la puerta

USSR [juːeses'ɑː(r)] n Hist (abbr **Union of Soviet Socialist Republics**) URSS f

usual ['juːʒʊəl] 1 adj corriente, normal; **as u.** como siempre; **at the u. hour** a la hora habitual; **earlier than u.** más pronto que de costumbre; **the u. problems** los problemas de siempre
2 n lo habitual; **out of the u.** fuera de lo común

usually ['juːʒʊəlɪ] adv normalmente

usurp [juː'zɜːp] vt usurpar

utensil [juː'tensəl] n utensilio m; **kitchen utensils** batería f de cocina

uterus ['juːtərəs] n útero m

utilitarian [juːtɪlɪ'teərɪən] adj (a) (in philosophy) utilitarista (b) (useful) utilitario(a)

utility [juː'tɪlɪtɪ] n (a) (usefulness) utilidad f; **u. room** cuarto m de planchar; (for storage) trascocina f (b) **(public) u.** empresa f de servicio público

utilize ['juːtɪlaɪz] vt utilizar

utmost ['ʌtməʊst] 1 adj sumo(a); **of the u. importance** de suma importancia
2 n máximo m; **to do** or **try one's u.** hacer todo lo posible; **to the u.** al máximo, a más no poder

utopian [juː'təʊpɪən] adj utópico(a)

utter¹ [ˈʌtə(r)] *vt (words)* pronunciar; *(sigh)* dar; *(cry, threat)* lanzar

utter² [ˈʌtə(r)] *adj* total, completo(a)

utterance [ˈʌtərəns] *n* declaración *f*

utterly [ˈʌtəlɪ] *adv* completamente, totalmente

U-turn [ˈjuːtɜːn] *n* cambio *m* de sentido; *Pol* giro *m* de 180 grados

V, v [viː] *n (the letter)* V, v *f*

V *(abbr* **volt(s))** V

v (**a**) *(abbr* **verse**) v (**b**) *(abbr* **versus**) contra

vacancy ['veɪkənsɪ] *n* (**a**) *(job)* vacante *f* (**b**) *(room)* habitación *f* libre; **no vacancies** *(sign)* completo

vacant ['veɪkənt] *adj* (**a**) *(empty)* vacío(a) (**b**) *(job)* vacante; *Br* **situations v.** *(in newspaper)* ofertas de trabajo (**c**) *(free, not in use)* libre

vacate [və'keɪt] *vt (flat)* desalojar

vacation [və'keɪʃən] **1** *n Br Univ & US* vacaciones *fpl;* **on v.** de vacaciones
2 *vi US* pasar las vacaciones (**in/at** en)

vacationer [və'keɪʃənə(r)] *n US* turista *mf; (in summer)* veraneante *mf*

vaccinate ['væksɪneɪt] *vt* vacunar

vaccination [væksɪ'neɪʃən] *n Med* vacunación *f*

vaccine ['væksiːn] *n* vacuna *f*

vacuum ['vækjʊəm] **1** *n* vacío *m;* **v. cleaner** aspiradora *f; Br* **v. flask** termo *m*
2 *vt (carpet, room)* pasar la aspiradora por

vacuum-packed ['vækjʊəm'pækt] *adj* envasado(a) al vacío

vagina [və'dʒaɪnə] *n* vagina *f*

vagrant ['veɪgrənt] *adj & n* vagabundo(a) *(m,f)*

vague [veɪg] *adj (imprecise)* vago(a), impreciso(a); *(indistinct)* borroso(a)

vain [veɪn] *adj* (**a**) *(proud)* vanidoso(a), presumido(a) (**b**) *(hopeless)* vano(a); **in v.** en vano

valentine ['væləntaɪn] *n* (**a**) *(card)* = tarjeta que se manda el Día de los Enamorados (**b**) *(sweetheart)* novio(a) *m,f*

valet ['vælɪt, 'væleɪ] *n* ayuda *m* de cámara

valiant ['væljənt] *adj* valiente

valid ['vælɪd] *adj* válido(a); **no longer v.** caducado(a)

validate ['vælɪdeɪt] *vt* validar

valley ['vælɪ] *n* valle *m*

valour, *US* **valor** ['vælə(r)] *n* valor *m*

valuable ['væljʊəbəl] **1** *adj* valioso(a), de valor
2 *npl* **valuables** objetos *mpl* de valor

valuation [væljʊ'eɪʃən] *n* (**a**) *(act)* valoración *f* (**b**) *(price)* valor *m*

value ['væljuː] **1** *n* valor *m;* **50 pence is good v.** 50 peniques es un buen precio; **to get good v. for money** sacarle jugo al dinero; *Br* **v.-added tax** impuesto *m* sobre el valor añadido *or Am* agregado
2 *vt* valorar

valve [vælv] *n* (**a**) *Anat & Tech* válvula *f* (**b**) *Rad* lámpara *f*

vampire ['væmpaɪə(r)] *n* vampiro *m*

van [væn] *n* (**a**) *Aut* furgoneta *f* (**b**) *Br Rail* furgón *m*

vandal ['vændəl] *n* vándalo(a) *m,f, Esp* gamberro(a) *m,f*

vandalism ['vændəlɪzəm] *n* vandalismo *m, Esp* gamberrismo *m*

vandalize ['vændəlaɪz] *vt* destruir, destrozar

vanguard ['vængɑːd] *n* vanguardia *f*

vanilla [və'nɪlə] *n* vainilla *f*

vanish ['vænɪʃ] *vi* desaparecer

vanity ['vænɪtɪ] *n* vanidad *f;* **v. bag** *or* **case** neceser *m*

vantage ['vɑːntɪdʒ] *n* ventaja *f;* **v. point** posición estratégica

vapor ['veɪpər] *n US =* **vapour**

vaporizer ['veɪpəraɪzə(r)] *n (device)* vaporizador *m; (spray)* pulverizador *m*

vapour ['veɪpə(r)] *n* vapor *m; (on windowpane)* vaho *m;* **v. trail** estela *f* de humo

variable ['veərɪəbəl] *adj & n* variable *(f)*

variance ['veərɪəns] *n Fml* **to be at v.** no concordar; **to be at v. with sb** estar en desacuerdo con algn

variant ['veərɪənt] *n* variante *f*

variation [veərɪ'eɪʃən] *n* variación *f*

varicose ['værɪkəʊs] *adj* **v. veins** varices *fpl*

varied ['veərɪd] *adj* variado(a), diverso(a)

variety [və'raɪtɪ] *n* (**a**) *(diversity)* variedad *f; (assortment)* surtido *m;* **for a v. of reasons** por razones diversas (**b**) **v. show** espectáculo *m* de variedades

various ['veərɪəs] *adj* diversos(as), varios(as)

varnish ['vɑːnɪʃ] **1** n barniz m; Br nail v. esmalte m de uñas
2 vt barnizar; Br (nails) esmaltar

vary ['veərɪ] vi variar; **prices v. from £2 to £4** los precios oscilan entre 2 y 4 libras; **to v. in size** variar de tamaño

varying ['veərɪŋ] adj **with v. degrees of success** con más o menos éxito

vase [Br vɑːz, US veɪs] n jarrón m

⚠ Note that the Spanish word **vaso** is a false friend and is never a translation for the English word **vase**. In Spanish **vaso** means both "glass" and "vessel".

---

vasectomy [və'sektəmɪ] n Med vasectomía f

Vaseline® ['væsɪliːn] n vaselina f

vast [vɑːst] adj vasto(a); (majority) inmenso(a)

VAT [viːeɪ'tiː, væt] n Br (abbr **value-added tax**) IVA m

vat [væt] n cuba f, tina f

Vatican ['vætɪkən] n **the V.** el Vaticano

vault¹ [vɔːlt] n bóveda f; (for wine) bodega f; (tomb) cripta f; (of bank) cámara acorazada, Am bóveda f de seguridad

vault² [vɔːlt] **1** vt & vi saltar
2 n salto m

vaunt [vɔːnt] vt Fml jactarse de, hacer alarde de

VCR [viːsiː'ɑː(r)] n (abbr **video cassette recorder**) (aparato m de) vídeo m or Am video m

VD [viː'diː] n (abbr **venereal disease**) enfermedad venérea

VDU [viːdiː'juː] n (abbr **visual display unit**) monitor m

veal [viːl] n ternera f

veer [vɪə(r)] vi (ship) virar; (car) girar

vegan ['viːgən] n vegetariano(a) m,f, vegetariano(a) m,f estricto(a)

vegeburger ['vedʒɪbɜːgə(r)] n hamburguesa vegetariana

vegetable ['vedʒtəbəl] n (food) verdura f, hortaliza f; **v. garden** huerta f, huerto m

vegetarian [vedʒɪ'teərɪən] adj & n vegetariano(a) m,f

vegetation [vedʒɪ'teɪʃən] n vegetación f

vehement ['viːɪmənt] adj vehemente

vehicle ['viːɪkəl] n vehículo m

veil [veɪl] **1** n velo m
2 vt velar

vein [veɪn] n vena f

velocity [vɪ'lɒsɪtɪ] n velocidad f

velvet ['velvɪt] n terciopelo m

velvety ['velvɪtɪ] adj aterciopelado(a)

vendetta [ven'detə] n vendetta f

vending ['vendɪŋ] n **v. machine** máquina expendedora

vendor ['vendɔː(r)] n vendedor(a) m,f

veneer [vɪ'nɪə(r)] n (a) (covering) chapa f (b) Fig apariencia f

venerable ['venərəbəl] adj venerable

venereal [vɪ'nɪərɪəl] adj venéreo(a)

Venetian [vɪ'niːʃən] adj & n veneciano(a) (m,f); **v. blind** persiana f graduable

Venezuela [venɪ'zweɪlə] n Venezuela

Venezuelan [venɪ'zweɪlən] adj & n venezolano(a) (m,f)

vengeance ['vendʒəns] n venganza f; Fam **it was raining with a v.** llovía con ganas

Venice ['venɪs] n Venecia

venison ['venɪsən] n carne f de venado

venom ['venəm] n veneno m

venomous ['venəməs] adj venenoso(a); Fig **v. tongue** lengua viperina

vent [vent] **1** n (a) (opening) abertura f, orificio m; (grille) rejilla f de ventilación; **air v.** respiradero m (b) (of volcano) chimenea f
2 vt Fig (feelings) descargar

ventilate ['ventɪleɪt] vt ventilar

ventilation [ventɪ'leɪʃən] n ventilación f

ventilator ['ventɪleɪtə(r)] n ventilador m

ventriloquist [ven'trɪləkwɪst] n ventrílocuo(a) m,f

venture ['ventʃə(r)] **1** vt arriesgar, aventurar; **he didn't v. to ask** no se atrevió a preguntarlo
2 vi arriesgarse; **to v. out of doors** atreverse a salir
3 n empresa arriesgada, aventura f; Com **business/joint v.** empresa comercial/colectiva

venue ['venjuː] n (a) (meeting place) lugar m de reunión (b) (for concert etc) local m

Venus ['viːnəs] n (goddess) Venus f; (planet) Venus m

veranda(h) [və'rændə] n porche m, terraza f

verb [vɜːb] n verbo m

verbal ['vɜːbəl] adj verbal

verbatim [və'beɪtɪm] **1** adj textual
2 adv textualmente

verbose [vɜː'bəʊs] adj pródigo(a) en palabras

verdict ['vɜːdɪkt] n (a) Jur veredicto m, fallo m (b) (opinion) opinión f, juicio m

verge [vɜːdʒ] **1** n (a) (margin) borde m; Fig **on the v. of** al borde de; Fig **to be on the v. of doing sth** estar a punto de hacer algo (b) Br (of road) arcén m, Andes berma f, Méx acotamiento m, RP banquina f, Ven hombrillo m
2 vi rayar (**on** en)

verification [verɪfɪ'keɪʃən] *n* verificación *f*, comprobación *f*

verify ['verɪfaɪ] *vt* verificar, comprobar

veritable ['verɪtəbəl] *adj* auténtico(a)

vermicelli [vɜːmɪ'tʃelɪ] *n* fideos *mpl*

vermin ['vɜːmɪn] *npl* (**a**) *(animals)* bichos *mpl*, sabandijas *fpl* (**b**) *Fig* gentuza *f*

vermouth ['vɜːməθ] *n* vermú *m*, vermut *m*

verruca [və'ruːkə] *n* verruga *f*

versatile ['vɜːsətaɪl] *adj (person)* polifacético(a); *(object)* versátil

verse [vɜːs] *n* (**a**) *(stanza)* estrofa *f* (**b**) *(poetry)* versos *mpl*, poesía *f* (**c**) *(of song)* copla *f* (**d**) *(of Bible)* versículo *m*

versed [vɜːst] *adj* to be (well) v. in ser (muy) versado en

version ['vɜːʃən, 'vɜːʒən] *n* (**a**) *(account)* versión *f*; **stage v.** adaptación *f* teatral (**b**) *Aut* modelo *m*

versus ['vɜːsəs] *prep* contra

vertebra ['vɜːtɪbrə] *n* (*pl* **vertebras** *or* **vertebrae** ['vɜːtɪbriː]) vértebra *f*

vertical ['vɜːtɪkəl] *adj & n* vertical (*f*)

vertigo ['vɜːtɪgəʊ] *n* vértigo *m*

verve [vɜːv] *n* vigor *m*, brío *m*

very ['verɪ] **1** *adv* (**a**) *(extremely)* muy; **to be v. hungry** tener mucha hambre; **v. much** muchísimo; **v. well** muy bien (**b**) *(emphatic)* **at the v. latest** como muy tarde; **at the v. least** como mínimo; **the v. best** el mejor de todos; **the v. first/last** el primero/último de todos; **the v. same day** el mismo día

2 *adj* (**a**) **at the v. end/beginning** al final/principio de todo (**b**) *(precise)* **at this v. moment** en este mismo momento; **her v. words** sus palabras exactas; **in the v. middle** justo en medio (**c**) *(mere)* **the v. thought of it!** ¡sólo con pensarlo!

vespers ['vespəz] *npl* vísperas *fpl*

vessel ['vesəl] *n* (**a**) *(container)* vasija *f* (**b**) *Naut* buque *m*, nave *f* (**c**) *Anat & Bot* vaso *m*

vest [vest] **1** *n* (**a**) *Br (undershirt)* camiseta *f* de tirantes *or Am* breteles (**b**) *US* chaleco *m*

2 *vt Jur* **by the power vested in me …** por los poderes que se me han conferido …

vested ['vestɪd] *adj Fin & Jur* **v. interests** derechos adquiridos; *Fig* intereses *mpl* creados

vestibule ['vestɪbjuːl] *n* vestíbulo *m*

vestige ['vestɪdʒ] *n* vestigio *m*

vestry ['vestrɪ] *n* sacristía *f*

vet [vet] **1** *n* veterinario(a) *m,f*

2 *vt Br* someter a investigación, examinar

veteran ['vetərən] *n Mil* ex combatiente *mf*; *Fig* veterano(a) *m,f*

veterinarian [vetərɪ'neərɪən] *n US* veterinario(a) *m,f*

veterinary ['vetərɪnərɪ] *adj* veterinario(a); **v. medicine** veterinaria *f*; *Br* **v. surgeon** veterinario(a) *m,f*

veto ['viːtəʊ] **1** *n* (*pl* **vetoes**) veto *m*

2 *vt Pol* vetar; *(suggestion etc)* descartar

vexed [vekst] *adj* (**a**) *(annoyed)* molesto(a), disgustado(a); *(angry) esp Esp* enfadado(a), *esp Am* enojado(a) (**b**) *(much debated)* controvertido(a)

VHF [viːeɪtʃ'ef] *(abbr* **very high frequency**) VHF

via ['vaɪə] *prep* por, vía

viable ['vaɪəbəl] *adj* viable, factible

viaduct ['vaɪədʌkt] *n* viaducto *m*

vibrant ['vaɪbrənt] *adj* (**a**) *(sound)* vibrante (**b**) *Fig (personality)* vital; *(city)* animado(a)

vibrate [vaɪ'breɪt] *vi* vibrar (**with** de)

vibration [vaɪ'breɪʃən] *n* vibración *f*

vicar ['vɪkə(r)] *n* párroco *m*

vicarage ['vɪkərɪdʒ] *n* casa *f* del párroco

vicarious [vɪ'keərɪəs] *adj* experimentado(a) por otro; *(punishment)* sufrido(a) por otro

vice¹ [vaɪs] *n* vicio *m*

vice² [vaɪs] *n Br (tool)* torno *m* de banco

vice- [vaɪs] *pref* vice-; **v.-chairman** vicepresidente *m*; **v.-chancellor** rector(a) *m,f*; **v.-president** vicepresidente(a) *m,f*

vice versa [vaɪs'vɜːsə] *adv* viceversa

vicinity [vɪ'sɪnɪtɪ] *n* (*area)* vecindad *f*; **in the v. of** *(geographic location)* cerca de, en las inmediaciones de; *(amount)* alrededor de

vicious ['vɪʃəs] *adj (violent)* violento(a); *(malicious)* malintencionado(a); *(cruel)* cruel; **v. circle** círculo vicioso

victim ['vɪktɪm] *n* víctima *f*

victimize ['vɪktɪmaɪz] *vt* perseguir, tratar injustamente

victor ['vɪktə(r)] *n* vencedor(a) *m,f*

victorious [vɪk'tɔːrɪəs] *adj* victorioso(a)

victory ['vɪktərɪ] *n* victoria *f*

video ['vɪdɪəʊ] *n* vídeo *m*, *Am* video *m*; **v. camera** cámara *f* de vídeo *or Am* video; **v. cassette** cinta *f* de vídeo *or Am* video; **v. game** videojuego *m*; **v. (cassette) recorder** (aparato *m* de) vídeo *or Am* video; **v. tape** cinta de vídeo *or Am* video

video-tape ['vɪdɪəʊteɪp] *vt* grabar (en vídeo)

vie [vaɪ] *vi* competir (**against** *or* **with** con)

Vienna [vɪ'enə] *n* Viena

Viennese [vɪə'niːz] *adj & n* vienés(esa) *(m,f)*

Vietnam [vjet'næm] *n* Vietnam

view [vjuː] **1** *n* (a) *(sight)* vista *f*, panorama *m*; **in full v.** completamente visible; **on v.** a la vista; **to come into v.** aparecer; *Fig* **in v. of the fact that …** dado que … (b) *(opinion)* opinión *f*; **point of v.** punto *m* de vista; **to take a dim v. of** ver con malos ojos (c) *(aim)* fin *m*; **with a v. to** con la intención de
2 *vt* (a) *(look at)* mirar; *(house etc)* visitar (b) *(consider)* contemplar; *(topic, problem)* enfocar

viewer ['vjuːə(r)] *n* (a) *TV* televidente *mf* (b) *Phot* visionador *m*

viewfinder ['vjuːfaɪndə(r)] *n* visor *m*

viewpoint ['vjuːpɔɪnt] *n* punto *m* de vista

vigil ['vɪdʒɪl] *n* vigilia *f*

vigilant ['vɪdʒɪlənt] *adj* alerta

vigilante [vɪdʒɪ'læntɪ] *n* **v. group** patrulla ciudadana

vigorous ['vɪgərəs] *adj* vigoroso(a), enérgico(a)

vigour, *US* **vigor** ['vɪgə(r)] *n* vigor *m*

vile [vaɪl] *adj* (a) *(evil)* vil, infame (b) *(disgusting)* repugnante (c) *Fam (awful)* horrible

vilify ['vɪlɪfaɪ] *vt* denigrar

villa ['vɪlə] *n* (a) *(in country)* casa *f* de campo (b) *Br* chalet *m*

village ['vɪlɪdʒ] *n* *(small)* aldea *f*; *(larger)* pueblo *m*

villager ['vɪlɪdʒə(r)] *n* aldeano(a) *m,f*

villain ['vɪlən] *n* villano(a) *m,f*; *Cin & Th* malo(a) *m,f*

vinaigrette [vɪneɪ'gret] *n* vinagreta *f*

vindicate ['vɪndɪkeɪt] *vt* justificar, vindicar

vindictive [vɪn'dɪktɪv] *adj* vengativo(a)

vine [vaɪn] *n* vid *f*; *(climbing)* parra *f*

vinegar ['vɪnɪgə(r)] *n* vinagre *m*

vineyard ['vɪnjəd] *n* viña *f*, viñedo *m*

vintage ['vɪntɪdʒ] **1** *n* (a) *(crop, year)* cosecha *f* (b) *(season)* vendimia *f* (c) *(era)* era *f*
2 *adj* (a) *(wine)* añejo(a) (b) *(classic)* clásico(a); **v. car** coche *m* de época

vinyl ['vaɪnɪl] *n* vinilo *m*

viola [vɪ'əʊlə] *n* viola *f*

violate ['vaɪəleɪt] *vt* violar

violence ['vaɪələns] *n* violencia *f*

violent ['vaɪələnt] *adj* violento(a)

violet ['vaɪəlɪt] **1** *n* (a) *Bot* violeta *f* (b) *(colour)* violeta *m*
2 *adj* violeta

violin [vaɪə'lɪn] *n* violín *m*

violinist [vaɪə'lɪnɪst] *n* violinista *mf*

VIP [viːaɪ'piː] *n* *Fam (abbr* **very important person)** VIP *mf*

viper ['vaɪpə(r)] *n* víbora *f*

virgin ['vɜːdʒɪn] **1** *n* virgen *f*; **the V. Mary** la Virgen María; **to be a v.** ser virgen
2 *adj* virgen

virginity [və'dʒɪnɪtɪ] *n* virginidad *f*

Virgo ['vɜːgəʊ] *n* Virgo *m*

virile ['vɪraɪl] *adj* viril

virtual ['vɜːtjʊəl] *adj* virtual; *Comput* **v. reality** realidad *f* virtual

virtually ['vɜːtjʊəlɪ] *adv (almost)* prácticamente

virtue ['vɜːtjuː] *n* virtud *f*; **by v. of** en virtud de

virtuous ['vɜːtjʊəs] *adj* virtuoso(a)

virulent ['vɪrʊlənt] *adj* virulento(a)

virus ['vaɪrəs] *n* virus *m inv*; *Comput* **v. check** detección *f* de virus

visa ['viːzə] *n* visado *m*, *Am* visa *f*

vis-à-vis [viːzɑː'viː] *prep* (a) *(regarding)* respecto a (b) *(opposite)* frente a

viscose ['vɪskəʊs] *n* viscosa *f*

viscount ['vaɪkaʊnt] *n* vizconde *m*

vise [vaɪs] *n US* = **vice**²

visibility [vɪzɪ'bɪlɪtɪ] *n* visibilidad *f*

visible ['vɪzɪbəl] *adj* visible

vision ['vɪʒən] *n* (a) *(apparition)* visión *f* (b) *(eyesight)* vista *f*

visit ['vɪzɪt] **1** *vt* (a) *(person)* visitar, hacer una visita a (b) *(place)* visitar, ir a
2 *n* visita *f*; **to pay sb a v.** hacerle una visita a algn

visiting ['vɪzɪtɪŋ] *adj* **v. card** tarjeta *f* de visita; *Med* **v. hours** horas *fpl* de visita; *Sport* **v. team** equipo *m* visitante

visitor ['vɪzɪtə(r)] *n* (a) *(guest)* invitado(a) *m,f*; **we've got visitors** tenemos visita (b) *(in hotel)* cliente(a) *m,f* (c) *(tourist)* turista *mf*

visor ['vaɪzə(r)] *n* visera *f*

> ⎙ Note that the Spanish word **visor** is a false friend and is never a translation for the English word **visor**. In Spanish **visor** means "viewfinder".

vista ['vɪstə] *n* vista *f*, panorama *m*

visual ['vɪʒʊəl] *adj* visual; **v. aids** medios *mpl* visuales

visualize ['vɪʒʊəlaɪz] *vt* (a) *(imagine)* imaginar(se) (b) *(foresee)* prever

vital ['vaɪtəl] *adj* (a) *(lively)* enérgico(a) (b) *(essential)* fundamental (c) *(decisive)* decisivo(a); *Fam* **v. statistics** medidas *fpl* del cuerpo de la mujer (d) *Med (function, sign)* vital

vitality [vaɪ'tælɪtɪ] n vitalidad f
vitally ['vaɪtəlɪ] adv it's v. important es de vital importancia
vitamin ['vɪtəmɪn, US 'vaɪtəmɪn] n vitamina f
viva ['vaɪvə] n Br examen m oral
vivacious [vɪ'veɪʃəs] adj vivaz
vivacity [vɪ'væsɪtɪ] n viveza f, vivacidad f
vivid ['vɪvɪd] adj (a) (bright, lively) vivo(a), intenso(a) (b) (graphic) gráfico(a)
vivisection [vɪvɪ'sekʃən] n vivisección f
vixen ['vɪksən] n zorra f
V-neck(ed) ['viːnek(t)] adj de (cuello de) pico
vocabulary [və'kæbjʊlərɪ] n vocabulario m
vocal ['vəʊkəl] adj vocal; v. cords cuerdas fpl vocales
vocalist ['vəʊkəlɪst] n cantante mf
vocation [vəʊ'keɪʃən] n vocación f
vocational [vəʊ'keɪʃənəl] adj profesional; v. training formación f profesional
vociferous [vəʊ'sɪfərəs] adj (a) (protest) enérgico(a) (b) (noisy) clamoroso(a)
vodka ['vɒdkə] n vodka m
vogue [vəʊg] n boga f, moda f; in v. de moda
voice [vɔɪs] 1 n voz f; to lose one's v. quedarse afónico(a); Fig at the top of one's v. a voz en grito; Comput v. mail buzón m de voz
2 vt (a) (express) manifestar (b) Ling sonorizar
void [vɔɪd] 1 adj (a) v. of sin (b) Jur nulo(a), inválido(a)
2 n vacío m
volatile ['vɒlətaɪl] adj volátil
volcanic [vɒl'kænɪk] adj volcánico(a)
volcano [vɒl'keɪnəʊ] n (pl volcanoes) volcán m
volition [və'lɪʃən] n Fml of one's own v. por voluntad propia
volley ['vɒlɪ] 1 n (a) (of shots) descarga f (b) Fig (of stones, insults) lluvia f (c) (in tennis, football) volea f
2 vt (in tennis, football) volear
volleyball ['vɒlɪbɔːl] n voleibol m
volt [vəʊlt] n voltio m
voltage ['vəʊltɪdʒ] n voltaje m
voluble ['vɒljʊbəl] adj locuaz

🖉 Note that the Spanish word **voluble** is a false friend and is never a translation for the English word **voluble**. In Spanish, **voluble** means "fickle, changeable".

volume ['vɒljuːm] n (a) (of sound) volumen m (b) (capacity) capacidad f (c) (book) volumen m, tomo m; Fig to speak volumes decirlo todo
voluntary ['vɒləntərɪ] adj voluntario(a); v. organization organización benéfica
volunteer [vɒlən'tɪə(r)] 1 n voluntario(a) m,f
2 vt (help etc) ofrecer
3 vi (a) (put self forward) ofrecerse (for para) (b) Mil alistarse como voluntario
voluptuous [və'lʌptjʊəs] adj voluptuoso(a)
vomit ['vɒmɪt] 1 vt & vi vomitar
2 n vómito m
voracious [vɒ'reɪʃəs] adj voraz
vortex ['vɔːteks] n (pl vortices ['vɔːtɪsiːz]) vórtice m; Fig vorágine f
vote [vəʊt] 1 n voto m; (voting) votación f; v. of confidence voto de confianza; to take a v. on sth someter algo a votación; to have the v. tener derecho al voto
2 vt (a) (in ballot) votar (b) (elect) elegir (c) Fam (propose) proponer
3 vi votar; to v. for sb votar a algn
voter ['vəʊtə(r)] n votante mf
voting ['vəʊtɪŋ] n votación f
vouch [vaʊtʃ] vi to v. for sth/sb responder de algo/por algn
voucher ['vaʊtʃə(r)] n Br vale m
vow [vaʊ] 1 n voto m
2 vt jurar
vowel ['vaʊəl] n vocal f
voyage ['vɔɪdʒ] n viaje m; (crossing) travesía f; to go on a v. hacer un viaje (en barco)
vulgar ['vʌlgə(r)] adj (coarse) vulgar, ordinario(a); (in poor taste) de mal gusto
vulgarity [vʌl'gærɪtɪ] n (coarseness) vulgaridad f, ordinariez f; (poor taste) mal gusto m
vulnerable ['vʌlnərəbəl] adj vulnerable
vulture ['vʌltʃə(r)] n buitre m
vulva ['vʌlvə] n vulva f

W, w ['dʌbəljuː] n (the letter) W, w f

W (a) (abbr West) O (b) (abbr Watt(s)) W

wad [wɒd] n (of paper) taco m; (of cotton wool) bolita f; (of banknotes) fajo m

waddle ['wɒdəl] vi caminar or andar como un pato

wade [weɪd] vi caminar por el agua; **to w. across a river** vadear un río

▸**wade through** vt insep hacer con dificultad; **I'm wading through the book** me cuesta mucho terminar el libro

wading pool ['weɪdɪŋpuːl] n US piscina f para niños

wafer ['weɪfə(r)] n barquillo m; Rel hostia f

waffle¹ ['wɒfəl] n (food) Esp gofre m, Am wafle m

waffle² ['wɒfəl] Br Fam 1 vi meter mucha paja; **to w. on** parlotear
2 n paja f

waft [wɑːft, wɒft] 1 vt llevar por el aire
2 vi flotar (por or en el aire)

wag [wæg] 1 vt menear
2 vi (tail) menearse

wage [weɪdʒ] 1 n wage(s) salario m, sueldo m; **w. earner** asalariado(a) m,f; **w. freeze** congelación f salarial; **w. packet** (envelope) sobre m de la paga; (money) salario m
2 vt (campaign) realizar (**against** contra); **to w. war (on)** hacer la guerra (a)

wager ['weɪdʒə(r)] 1 n apuesta f
2 vt apostar

waggle ['wægəl] 1 vt menear
2 vi menearse

wa(g)gon ['wægən] n (horse-drawn) carro m; Br Rail vagón m

wail [weɪl] 1 n lamento m, gemido m
2 vi (person) lamentar, gemir

waist [weɪst] n Anat cintura f; Sewing talle m

waistcoat ['weɪstkəʊt] n Br chaleco m

waistline ['weɪstlaɪn] n Anat cintura; Sewing talle m

wait [weɪt] 1 n espera f; (delay) demora f; **to lie in w.** estar al acecho
2 vi (a) (in general) esperar; **I can't w. to see her** me muero de ganas de verla; **while you w.** en el acto; **to keep sb**
waiting hacer esperar a algn (b) Br **to w. at table** servir mesas

▸**wait about, wait around** vi esperar

▸**wait on** vt insep servir

waiter ['weɪtə(r)] n camarero m, Andes, RP mozo m, Chile, Ven mesonero m, Col, Guat, Méx, Salv mesero m

waiting ['weɪtɪŋ] n **no w.** (sign) prohibido detenerse; **w. list** lista f de espera; **w. room** sala f de espera

waitress ['weɪtrɪs] n camarera f, Andes, RP moza f, Chile, Ven mesonera f, Col, Guat, Méx, Salv mesera f

waive [weɪv] vt Fml (rule) no aplicar

wake¹ [weɪk] 1 vt (pt woke; pp woken) **to w. sb (up)** despertar a algn
2 vi **to w. (up)** despertar(se)
3 n (for dead) velatorio m, Am velorio m

wake² [weɪk] n (in water) estela f; Fig **in the w. of** tras

waken ['weɪkən] vt Literary despertar

Wales [weɪlz] n (el país de) Gales

walk [wɔːk] 1 n (a) (long) caminata f; (short) paseo m; **it's an hour's w.** está a una hora de camino; **to go for a w.** dar un paseo; **to take the dog for a w.** sacar a pasear al perro (b) (gait) andares mpl, modo m de caminar or Esp andar (c) **people from all walks of life** gente f de toda condición
2 vt (a) **we walked her home** la acompañamos a casa (b) (dog) pasear
3 vi (a) (move on foot) caminar, Esp andar (b) (as opposed to riding, driving) ir caminando or Esp andando

▸**walk away** vi irse (caminando or Esp andando); Fig **to w. away with a prize** llevarse un premio

▸**walk into** vt insep (a) (place) entrar en; Fig (trap) caer en (b) (bump into) chocarse contra

▸**walk out** vi salir; Ind declararse en huelga; **to w. out on sb** abandonar a algn

▸**walk up** vi **to w. up to sb** abordar a algn

walkabout ['wɔːkəbaʊt] n Br (of politician) paseo m entre la multitud

walker ['wɔːkə(r)] n paseante mf; Sport marchador(a) m,f

walkie-talkie [wɔːkɪ'tɔːkɪ] *n* walkie-talkie *m*

walking ['wɔːkɪŋ] **1** *n* caminar *m*, *Esp* andar *m*; *(hiking)* excursionismo *m*
　　2 *adj* **at w. pace** a paso de marcha; **w. shoes** zapatos *mpl* de andar; **w. stick** bastón *m*

Walkman® ['wɔːkmən] *n* (*pl* **Walkmans**) walkman® *m*

walkout ['wɔːkaʊt] *n Ind* huelga *f*

walkover ['wɔːkəʊvə(r)] *n* **it was a w.** fue pan comido

walkway ['wɔːkweɪ] *n* paso *m* de peatones

wall [wɔːl] *n* (**a**) *(freestanding, exterior)* muro *m*; *Fig* **to have one's back to the w.** estar entre la espada y la pared; **city w.** muralla *f*; **garden w.** tapia *f* (**b**) *(interior)* pared *f*; **w. map** mapa *m* mural (**c**) *Ftb* barrera *f*
　▸ **wall up** *vt sep (door, fireplace)* tabicar

walled [wɔːld] *adj (city)* amurallado(a); *(garden)* cercado(a) con tapia

wallet ['wɒlɪt] *n* cartera *f*

wallflower ['wɔːlflaʊə(r)] *n* (**a**) *Bot* alhelí *m* (**b**) *Fam* **to be a w.** ser un convidado de piedra

wallop ['wɒləp] *Fam* **1** *n* tortazo *m*, golpetazo *m*, *Méx* madrazo *m*
　　2 *vt* (**a**) *(hit)* dar un tortazo *or* golpetazo a (**b**) *(defeat)* dar una buena paliza a

wallow ['wɒləʊ] *vi* revolcarse (**in** en); *Fig* **to w. in self-pity** sumirse en la auto-compasión

wallpaper ['wɔːlpeɪpə(r)] **1** *n* papel pintado
　　2 *vt* empapelar

wally ['wɒlɪ] *n Br Fam* idiota *mf*, *Esp* chorra *mf*

walnut ['wɔːlnʌt] *n* nuez *f*; *(tree, wood)* nogal *m*

walrus ['wɔːlrəs] *n* morsa *f*

waltz [wɔːls] **1** *n* vals *m*
　　2 *vi* bailar un vals

wan [wɒn] *adj* (**wanner, wannest**) pálido(a); *(look, smile)* apagado(a)

wand [wɒnd] *n* (**magic**) **w.** varita (mágica)

wander ['wɒndə(r)] **1** *vt* **to w. the streets** vagar por las calles
　　2 *vi* (**a**) *(aimlessly)* vagar, errar; **to w. about** deambular; **to w. in/out** entrar/ salir sin prisas (**b**) *(stray)* desviarse; *(mind)* divagar; **his glance wandered round the room** recorrió el cuarto con la mirada

wandering ['wɒndərɪŋ] *adj* errante; *(tribe)* nómada; *(speech)* divagador(a)

wane [weɪn] *vi* menguar; *(interest)* decaer

wangle ['wæŋgəl] *vt Fam* agenciarse

wank [wæŋk] *Br Vulg* **1** *n* paja *f*
　　2 *vi* hacerse una *or Am* la paja

wanker ['wæŋkə(r)] *n Br Vulg Esp* gilipollas *mf inv*, *Am* pendejo(a) *m,f*

want [wɒnt] **1** *n* (**a**) *(lack)* falta *f*; **for w. of** por falta de (**b**) *(poverty)* miseria *f*
　　2 *vt* (**a**) *(desire)* querer, desear; **to w. to do sth** querer hacer algo (**b**) *Fam (need)* necesitar; **the grass wants cutting** hace falta cortar el césped (**c**) *(seek)* buscar; **you're wanted on the phone** te llaman al teléfono
　▸ **want for** *vt insep* carecer de; **to w. for nothing** tenerlo todo

wanted [wɒntɪd] *adj (on police poster)* se busca; **w., a good cook** *(advertisement)* se necesita buen cocinero

wanting ['wɒntɪŋ] *adj* (**a**) **she is w. in tact** le falta tacto (**b**) **he was found w.** no daba la talla

wanton ['wɒntən] *adj* (**a**) *(motiveless)* sin motivo; **w. cruelty** crueldad gratuita (**b**) *(unrestrained)* desenfrenado(a); *(licentious)* lascivo(a)

WAP [wæp] *n Comput* (*abbr* **Wireless Application Protocol**) WAP *m*; **W. phone** teléfono *m* WAP

war [wɔː(r)] *n* guerra *f*; **to be at w.** (**with**) estar en guerra (con); *Fig* **to declare/ wage w. on** declarar/hacer la guerra a; **w. crime** crimen *m* de guerra

warble ['wɔːbəl] *vi* gorjear

ward [wɔːd] *n* (**a**) *(of hospital)* sala *f* (**b**) *Jur* pupilo(a) *m,f*; **w. of court** pupilo(a) bajo tutela judicial (**c**) *Br Pol* distrito *m* electoral
　▸ **ward off** *vt sep (blow)* parar, desviar; *(attack)* rechazar; *(danger)* evitar; *(illness)* prevenir

warden ['wɔːdən] *n* (**a**) *(of institution, hostel)* guardián(ana) *m,f*; **game w.** guardia *m* de coto (**b**) *US (of prison)* director(a) *m,f*, alcaide(esa) *m,f*

warder ['wɔːdə(r)] *n Br (in prison)* vigilante *mf*

wardrobe ['wɔːdrəʊb] *n* (**a**) *(cupboard)* armario *m*, ropero *m* (**b**) *(clothes)* guardarropa *m* (**c**) *Th* vestuario *m*

warehouse ['weəhaʊs] *n* almacén *m*

wares [weəz] *npl* mercancías *fpl*

warfare ['wɔːfeə(r)] *n* guerra *f*

warhead ['wɔːhed] *n* (**nuclear**) **w.** ojiva *f* nuclear

warm [wɔːm] **1** *adj* (**a**) *(water)* tibio(a); *(hands)* caliente; *(climate)* cálido(a); **a w. day** un día de calor; **I am w.** tengo calor; **it is (very) w. today** hoy hace (mucho) calor; **w. clothing** ropa *f* de abrigo (**b**)

(welcome, applause) cálido(a)
 2 *vt* calentar; *Fig* alegrar
 3 *vi* calentarse; **to w. to sb** cogerle simpatía a algn

▸**warm up 1** *vt sep* **(a)** *(food, room)* calentar **(b)** *(audience)* animar
 2 *vi* **(a)** *(engine)* calentarse **(b)** *(dancer, athlete)* calentar, hacer calentamiento **(c)** *Fig (audience, party)* animarse

warm-blooded [wɔːm'blʌdɪd] *adj* de sangre caliente

warm-hearted [wɔːm'hɑːtɪd] *adj* afectuoso(a)

warmly ['wɔːmlɪ] *adv Fig* calurosamente; *(thank)* con efusión

warmth [wɔːmθ] *n (heat)* calor *m*; *Fig* cordialidad *f*

warn [wɔːn] *vt* avisar **(of** de), advertir **(about/against** sobre/contra); **they warned me not to go** me advirtieron que no fuera; **to w. sb that** advertir a algn que

warning ['wɔːnɪŋ] **1** *adj* **w. light** piloto *m*; **w. sign** señal *f* de aviso
 2 *n* **(a)** *(of danger)* advertencia *f*, aviso *m* **(b)** *(replacing punishment)* amonestación *f* **(c)** *(notice)* aviso *m*; **without w.** sin previo aviso

warp [wɔːp] **1** *vt* **(a)** *(wood)* alabear, combar **(b)** *Fig (mind)* pervertir
 2 *vi* alabearse, combarse

warrant ['wɒrənt] **1** *n* **(a)** *Jur* orden *f* judicial; **death w.** sentencia *f* de muerte **(b)** *(authorization note)* cédula *f*; *Com* bono *m*
 2 *vt* **(a)** *(justify)* justificar **(b)** *(guarantee)* garantizar

warranty ['wɒrəntɪ] *n Com* garantía *f*

warren ['wɒrən] *n* conejera *f*; *Fig* laberinto *m*

warrior ['wɒrɪə(r)] *n* guerrero(a) *m,f*

Warsaw ['wɔːsɔː] *n* Varsovia

warship ['wɔːʃɪp] *n* buque *m* or barco *m* de guerra

wart [wɔːt] *n* verruga *f*

wartime ['wɔːtaɪm] *n* tiempos *mpl* de guerra

wary ['weərɪ] *adj* **(warier, wariest)** cauteloso(a); **to be w. of doing sth** dudar en hacer algo; **to be w. of sth/sb** recelar de algo/algn

was [wɒz] *pt of* **be**

·**wash** [wɒʃ] **1** *n* **(a)** *(action)* lavado *m*; **to have a w.** lavarse **(b)** *(of ship)* estela *f*; *(sound)* chapoteo *m*
 2 *vt* **(a)** *(clean)* lavar; *(dishes)* fregar; **to w. one's hair** lavarse el pelo **(b)** *(of sea, river)* arrastrar
 3 *vi* **(a)** *(person)* lavarse; *(do the laundry)* hacer la colada **(b)** *(lap)* batir

▸**wash away** *vt sep (of sea)* llevarse; *(traces)* borrar

▸**wash off** *vi* lavar, quitar *or Am* sacar lavando

▸**wash out 1** *vt sep* **(a)** *(stain)* quitar lavando **(b)** *(bottle)* enjuagar
 2 *vi* quitarse lavando

▸**wash up** *vt sep Br (dishes)* fregar
 2 *vi* **(a)** *Br* fregar los platos **(b)** *US* lavarse rápidamente

washable ['wɒʃəbəl] *adj* lavable

washbasin ['wɒʃbeɪsən], *US* **washbowl** ['wɒʃbəʊl] *n* lavabo *m*, *Am* lavamanos *m inv*

washcloth ['wɒʃklɒθ] *n US* manopla *f*

washer ['wɒʃə(r)] *n (on tap)* zapata *f*, junta *f*

washing ['wɒʃɪŋ] *n (action)* lavado *m*; *(of clothes)* colada *f*; *(dirty)* **w.** ropa sucia; **to do the w.** hacer la colada; **w. line** tendedero *m*; **w. machine** lavadora *f*, *RP* lavarropas *m inv*; **w. powder** detergente *m*

washing-up [wɒʃɪŋ'ʌp] *n Br* **(a)** *(action)* fregado *m*; **w. bowl** palangana *f* or *Esp* barreño *m* para lavar los platos; **w. liquid** (detergente *m*) lavavajillas *m inv* **(b)** *(dishes)* platos *mpl* (para fregar)

washout ['wɒʃaʊt] *n Fam* fracaso *m*

washroom ['wɒʃruːm] *n US* lavabo *m*, baño *m*, *Esp* servicios *mpl*, *CSur* toilette *f*

wasp [wɒsp] *n* avispa *f*

wastage ['weɪstɪdʒ] *n* pérdidas *fpl*

waste [weɪst] **1** *adj* **(a)** *(unwanted)* desechado(a); **w. food** restos *mpl* de comida; **w. products** productos *mpl* de desecho **(b)** *(ground)* baldío(a)
 2 *n* **(a)** *(unnecessary use)* desperdicio *m*; *(of resources, effort, money)* derroche *m*; *(of time)* pérdida *f*; **to go to w.** echarse a perder **(b)** *(leftovers)* desperdicios *mpl*; *(rubbish)* basura *f*; **radioactive w.** desechos radioactivos; *Br* **w. disposal unit** trituradora *f* (de desperdicios); **w. pipe** tubo *m* de desagüe
 3 *vt (squander)* desperdiciar, malgastar; *(resources)* derrochar; *(money)* despilfarrar; *(time)* perder

▸**waste away** *vi* consumirse

wasteful ['weɪstfʊl] *adj* derrochador(a)

wasteland ['weɪstlænd] *n* baldío *m*

wastepaper [weɪst'peɪpə(r)] *n* **w. basket** *or* **bin** papelera *f*, *Méx* bote *m*

watch [wɒtʃ] **1** *n* **(a)** *(look-out)* vigilancia *f*; **to keep a close w. on sth/sb** vigilar algo/a algn muy atentamente **(b)** *Mil (body)* guardia *f*, *(individual)* centinela *m*; **to be on w.** estar de guardia **(c)** *(timepiece)* reloj *m*

2 *vt* (**a**) *(observe)* mirar, observar (**b**) *(keep an eye on)* vigilar; *(with suspicion)* acechar (**c**) *(be careful of)* tener cuidado con; *Fig* **to w. one's step** ir con pies de plomo

3 *vi* *(look)* mirar, observar; **w. out!** ¡cuidado!

► **watch out for** *vt insep (be careful of)* tener cuidado con

watchband ['wɒtʃbænd] *n US* = **watch-strap**

watchdog ['wɒtʃdɒg] *n* perro *m* guardián; *Fig* guardián(ana) *m,f*

watchful ['wɒtʃfʊl] *adj* vigilante

watchmaker ['wɒtʃmeɪkə(r)] *n* relojero(a) *m,f*

watchman ['wɒtʃmən] *n* vigilante *m*; **night w.** *(of site)* vigilante nocturno

watchstrap ['wɒtʃstræp] *n Br* correa *f* (de reloj)

watchtower ['wɒtʃtaʊə(r)] *n* atalaya *f*

water ['wɔːtə(r)] **1** *n* (**a**) *(liquid, element)* agua *f*; **w. bottle** cantimplora *f*; **w. lily** nenúfar *m*; **w. main** conducción *f* de aguas; **w. polo** waterpolo *m*; **w. sports** deportes acuáticos; **w. tank** depósito *m* de agua; **territorial waters** aguas jurisdiccionales; *Fig* **it's all w. under the bridge** ha llovido mucho desde entonces (**b**) **to pass w.** orinar

2 *vt (plants)* regar

3 *vi* **my eyes are watering** me lloran los ojos; **my mouth watered** se me hizo la boca agua

► **water down** *vt sep (drink)* aguar

watercolour, *US* **watercolor** ['wɔːtə-kʌlə(r)] *n* acuarela *f*

watercress ['wɔːtəkres] *n* berro *m*

waterfall ['wɔːtəfɔːl] *n* cascada *f*; *(very big)* catarata *f*

waterfront ['wɔːtəfrʌnt] *n (shore)* orilla *f* del agua; *(harbour)* puerto *m*

watering ['wɔːtərɪŋ] *n (of plants)* riego *m*; **w. can** regadera *f*; **w. place** abrevadero *m*

waterline ['wɔːtəlaɪn] *n* línea *f* de flotación

waterlogged ['wɔːtəlɒgd] *adj* anegado(a)

watermark ['wɔːtəmaːk] *n* filigrana *f*

watermelon ['wɔːtəmelən] *n* sandía *f*

waterproof ['wɔːtəpruːf] **1** *adj (material)* impermeable; *(watch)* sumergible

2 *n (coat)* impermeable *m*

watershed ['wɔːtəʃed] *n Geog* línea divisoria de aguas; *Fig* punto decisivo

water-skiing ['wɔːtəskiːɪŋ] *n* esquí acuático

watertight ['wɔːtətaɪt] *adj* hermético(a)

waterway ['wɔːtəweɪ] *n* vía *f* fluvial

waterworks ['wɔːtəwɜːks] *npl (for treating water)* central *f* de abastecimiento de agua; *Fig* **to turn on the w.** ponerse a llorar (a voluntad)

watery ['wɔːtərɪ] *adj* (**a**) *(soup)* aguado(a); *(coffee)* flojo(a) (**b**) *(eyes)* lacrimoso(a) (**c**) *(pale)* pálido(a)

watt [wɒt] *n* vatio *m*

wave [weɪv] **1** *n* (**a**) *(at sea)* ola *f* (**b**) *(in hair)* & *Rad* onda *f* (**c**) *Fig (of anger, strikes etc)* oleada *f* (**d**) *(gesture)* saludo *m* con la mano

2 *vt* (**a**) *(flag, stick)* agitar; *(brandish)* blandir (**b**) *(hair)* ondular

3 *vi* (**a**) *(person)* **she waved (to me)** *(greeting)* me saludó con la mano; *(goodbye)* se despidió (de mí) con la mano; *(signal)* me hizo señas con la mano (**b**) *(flag)* ondear; *(corn)* ondular

wavelength ['weɪvleŋθ] *n* longitud *f* de onda

waver ['weɪvə(r)] *vi (hesitate)* vacilar (**between** entre); *(voice)* temblar; *(courage)* flaquear

wavy ['weɪvɪ] *adj* (**wavier, waviest**) ondulado(a)

wax¹ [wæks] **1** *n* cera *f*

2 *vt* encerar

wax² [wæks] *vi* (**a**) *(moon)* crecer (**b**) **to w. lyrical** exaltarse

waxworks ['wækswɜːks] *n sing* museo *m* de cera

way [weɪ] **1** *n* (**a**) *(route)* camino *m*; *(road)* vía *f*, camino; **a letter is on the w.** una carta está en camino; **on the w.** en el camino; **on the w. here** de camino para aquí; **out of the w.** apartado(a); **to ask the w.** preguntar el camino; **to go the wrong w.** ir por el camino equivocado; **to lose one's w.** perderse; **to make one's w. through the crowd** abrirse camino entre la multitud; **which is the w. to the station?** ¿por dónde se va a la estación?; *Fig* **she went out of her w. to help** se desvivió por ayudar; **w. in** entrada *f*; **w. out** salida *f*; *Fig* **the easy w. out** la solución fácil; **I can't find my w. out** no me encuentro la salida; **on the w. back** en el viaje de regreso; **on the w. up/down** en la subida/bajada; **there's no w. through** el paso está cerrado; **you're in the w.** estás estorbando; **(get) out of the w.!** ¡quítate de en medio!; *Fig* **to get sth/sb out of the w.** desembarazarse de algo/algn; **I kept out of the w.** me mantuve a distancia; *Aut* **right of w.** prioridad *f*; **there's a wall in the w.** hay un muro en medio; **to give w.** ceder; *Aut* ceder el paso

(**b**) *(direction)* dirección *f*; **come this w.**

venga por aquí; **which w. did he go?** ¿por dónde se fue?; **that w.** por allá; **the other w. round** al revés
(**c**) *(distance)* distancia *f*; **a long w. off** lejos; *Fig* **he'll go a long w.** llegará lejos; *Fig* **we've come a long w.** hemos hecho grandes progresos
(**d**) **to get under w.** *(travellers, work)* ponerse en marcha; *(meeting, match)* empezar
(**e**) *(means, method)* método *m*, manera *f*; **do it any w. you like** hazlo como quieras; **I'll do it my w.** lo haré a mi manera
(**f**) *(manner)* modo *m*, manera *f*; **in a friendly w.** de modo amistoso; **one w. or another** de un modo o de otro; **the French w. of life** el estilo de vida francés; **the w. things are going** tal como van las cosas; **to my w. of thinking** a mi modo de ver; *Fam* **no w.!** ¡ni hablar!; **she has a w. with children** tiene un don para los niños; **by w. of** a modo de; **either w.** en cualquier caso; **in a w.** en cierto sentido; **in many ways** desde muchos puntos de vista; **in some ways** en algunos aspectos; **in no w.** de ninguna manera
(**g**) *(custom)* hábito *m*, costumbre *f*; **to be set in one's ways** tener costumbres arraigadas
(**h**) *(state)* estado *m*; **leave it the w. it is** déjalo tal como está; **he is in a bad w.** está bastante mal
(**i**) **by the w.** a propósito; **in the w. of business** en el curso de los negocios
2 *adv Fam* mucho, muy; **it was w. off target** cayó muy desviado del blanco; **w. back in 1940** allá en 1940

waylay ['weɪ'leɪ] *vt* *(pt & pp* **waylaid** ['weɪ'leɪd]*)* (**a**) *(attack)* atacar por sorpresa (**b**) *Fig (intercept)* abordar, detener

wayside ['weɪsaɪd] *n Fig* **to fall by the w.** quedarse en el camino

wayward ['weɪwəd] *adj* rebelde; *(capricious)* caprichoso(a)

WC [dʌblju:'si:] *n (abbr* **water closet)** wáter *m*, váter *m*

we [wi:] *pers pron* nosotros(as) *(usually omitted in Spanish, except for contrast)*

weak [wi:k] *adj* débil; *(argument, excuse)* pobre; *(team, piece of work, tea)* flojo(a)

weaken ['wi:kən] **1** *vt* debilitar; *(argument)* quitar fuerza a
2 *vi* debilitarse

weakling ['wi:klɪŋ] *n* enclenque *mf*

weakness ['wi:knɪs] *n* debilidad *f*; *(character flaw)* punto flaco

wealth [welθ] *n* riqueza *f*; *Fig* abundancia *f*

wealthy ['welθɪ] *adj* **(wealthier, wealthiest)** rico(a)

wean [wi:n] *vt (child)* destetar; *Fig* **to w. sb from** *or* **off a habit** quitar *or Am* sacarle una mala costumbre a algn

weapon ['wepən] *n* arma *f*

wear [weə(r)] **1** *vt (pt* **wore**; *pp* **worn)** (**a**) *(clothes)* llevar puesto, vestir; *(shoes)* llevar puestos, calzar; **he wears glasses** lleva gafas; **to w. black** vestirse de negro (**b**) *(erode)* desgastar
2 *vi* **to w. (thin/smooth)** desgastarse (con el roce); *Fig* **my patience is wearing thin** se me está acabando la paciencia
3 *n* (**a**) *(clothing)* ropa *f*; **leisure w.** ropa de sport (**b**) *(use) (of clothes)* uso *m* (**c**) *(deterioration)* desgaste *m*; **normal w. and tear** desgaste natural
▸ **wear away 1** *vt sep* erosionar
2 *vi (stone etc)* erosionarse; *(inscription)* borrarse
▸ **wear down 1** *vt sep (heels)* desgastar; *Fig* **to w. sb down** vencer la resistencia de algn
2 *vi* desgastarse
▸ **wear off** *vi (effect, pain)* pasar, desaparecer
▸ **wear out 1** *vt sep* gastar; *Fig* agotar
2 *vi* gastarse

wearily ['wɪərɪlɪ] *adv* con cansancio

wearisome ['wɪərɪsəm] *adj* fatigoso(a)

weary ['wɪərɪ] **1** *adj* **(wearier, weariest)** (**a**) *(tired)* cansado(a) (**b**) *(fed up)* harto(a)
2 *vt* cansar
3 *vi* cansarse (**of** de)

weasel ['wi:zəl] *n* comadreja *f*

weather ['weðə(r)] **1** *n* tiempo *m*; **the w. is fine** hace buen tiempo; *Fig* **to feel under the w.** no encontrarse bien; **w. chart** mapa meteorológico; **w. forecast** parte meteorológico; **w. vane** veleta *f*
2 *vt Fig (crisis)* aguantar; *Fig* **to w. the storm** capear el temporal

weather-beaten ['weðəbi:tən] *adj* curtido(a)

weathercock ['weðəkɒk] *n* veleta *f*

weatherman ['weðəmæn] *n* hombre *m* del tiempo

weave [wi:v] **1** *n* tejido *m*
2 *vt (pt* **wove**; *pp* **woven)** (**a**) *Tex* tejer (**b**) *(intertwine)* entretejer (**c**) *(intrigues)* tramar
3 *vi (person, road)* zigzaguear

weaver ['wi:və(r)] *n* tejedor(a) *m,f*

web [web] *n* (**a**) *(of spider)* telaraña *f* (**b**) *(of lies)* sarta *f* (**c**) *Comput* **the W.** la Web; **w. page** página *f* web; **w. site** sitio *m* web

webbed [webd] *adj (foot)* palmeado(a)

webcam ['webkæm] *n* cámara *f* web

wed [wed] *vt Literary (pt & pp* **wed** *or* **wedded**) casarse con

wedding ['wedɪŋ] *n* boda *f, Andes* matrimonio *m, RP* casamiento *m;* **w. cake** tarta *f or* pastel *m* de boda; **w. day** día *m* de la boda; **w. dress** traje *m* de novia; **w. present** regalo *m* de boda; **w. ring** alianza *f*

wedge [wedʒ] **1** *n* (**a**) *(for door, wheel)* cuña *f,* calzo *m* (**b**) *(of cake, cheese)* trozo *m* grande
   2 *vt* calzar; **to be wedged tight** *(object)* estar completamente atrancado(a)

Wednesday ['wenzdɪ] *n* miércoles *m*

wee¹ [wiː] *adj esp Scot* pequeñito(a)

wee² [wiː] *Br Fam* **1** *n* pipí *m*
   2 *vi* hacer pipí

weed [wiːd] **1** *n Bot* mala hierba
   2 *vt* (**a**) *(garden)* escardar (**b**) *Fig* **to w. out** eliminar
   3 *vi* escardar

weedkiller ['wiːdkɪlə(r)] *n* herbicida *m*

weedy ['wiːdɪ] *adj* (**weedier, weediest**) *Pej* debilucho(a)

week [wiːk] *n* semana *f;* **a w. (ago)** today/yesterday hoy hace/ayer hizo una semana; **a w.** today justo dentro de una semana; **last/next w.** la semana pasada/que viene; **once a w.** una vez por semana; **w. in, w. out** semana tras semana

weekday ['wiːkdeɪ] *n* día *m* laborable

weekend [wiːk'end] *n* fin *m* de semana

weekly ['wiːklɪ] **1** *adj* semanal
   2 *adv* semanalmente; **twice w.** dos veces por semana
   3 *n Press* semanario *m*

weep [wiːp] **1** *vi (pt & pp* **wept**) llorar; **to w. with joy** llorar de alegría
   2 *vt (tears)* derramar

weeping ['wiːpɪŋ] *adj* **w. willow** sauce *m* llorón

weigh [weɪ] **1** *vt* (**a**) *(measure)* pesar (**b**) *(consider)* ponderar (**c**) **to w. anchor** levar anclas
   2 *vi* pesar

▸ **weigh down** *vt sep* sobrecargar

▸ **weigh in** *vi* (**a**) *Sport* pesarse (**b**) *Fam (join in)* intervenir

▸ **weigh up** *vt sep (matter)* evaluar; *(person)* formar una opinión sobre; **to w. up the pros and cons** sopesar los pros y los contras

weight [weɪt] *n* (**a**) *(of person, object)* peso *m;* **to lose w.** adelgazar; **to put on w.** subir de peso (**b**) *(of clock, scales)* pesa *f* (**c**) *Fig* **that's a w. off my mind** eso me quita *or Am* saca un peso de encima

weighting ['weɪtɪŋ] *n Br (on salary)* suplemento *m* de salario

weightlifter ['weɪtlɪftə(r)] *n* halterófilo(a) *m,f*

weightlifting ['weɪtlɪftɪŋ] *n* halterofilia *f,* levantamiento *m* de pesos

weighty ['weɪtɪ] *adj* (**weightier, weightiest**) pesado(a); *Fig (problem, matter)* importante, grave; *(argument)* de peso

weir [wɪə(r)] *n* presa *f*

weird [wɪəd] *adj* raro(a), extraño(a)

welcome ['welkəm] **1** *adj (person)* bienvenido(a); *(news)* grato(a); *(change)* oportuno(a); **to make sb w.** acoger a algn calurosamente; **you're w.!** ¡no hay de qué!
   2 *n (greeting)* bienvenida *f*
   3 *vt* acoger; *(more formally)* darle la bienvenida a; *(news)* acoger con agrado; *(decision)* aplaudir

welcoming ['welkəmɪŋ] *adj (person)* acogedor(a); *(smile)* de bienvenida

weld [weld] *vt* soldar

welfare ['welfeə(r)] *n* (**a**) *(well-being)* bienestar *m;* **animal/child w.** protección *f* de animales/de menores; **w. work** asistencia *f* social; **w. worker** asistente *mf* social (**b**) *US (social security)* seguridad *f* social

well¹ [wel] *n* (**a**) *(for water, oil)* pozo *m* (**b**) *(of staircase, lift)* hueco *m* (**c**) *(of court, hall)* hemiciclo *m*

▸ **well up** *vi* brotar

well² [wel] **1** *adj* (**a**) *(healthy)* bien; **are you keeping w.?** ¿estás bien de salud?; **to get w.** reponerse (**b**) *(satisfactory)* **all is w.** todo va bien; **it's just as w.** menos mal (**c**) **it is as w. to remember that** conviene recordar que
   2 *adv* (**better, best**) (**a**) *(properly)* bien; **he has done w. (for himself)** ha prosperado; **the business is doing w.** el negocio marcha bien; **she did w. in the exam** el examen le fue bien; **w. done!** ¡muy bien!; **he took it w.** lo tomó a bien (**b**) *(thoroughly)* bien; **I know it only too w.** lo sé de sobra; *Culin* **w. done** muy hecho(a) (**c**) **he's w. over thirty** tiene treinta años bien cumplidos; **w. after six o'clock** mucho después de las seis (**d**) *(easily, with good reason)* **he couldn't very w. say no** difícilmente podía hacer que no; **I may w. do that** puede que haga eso (**e**) **as w.** también; **as w. as** así como; **children as w. as adults** tanto niños como adultos
   3 *interj* (**a**) *(surprise)* ¡bueno!, ¡vaya!; **w. I never!** ¡no me digas! (**b**) *(agreement, question, resignation)* bueno; **very w.** bueno; **w.?** ¿y bien? (**c**) *(doubt)* pues; **w.,**

I don't know pues, no sé (**d**) *(resumption)* w., as I was saying pues (bien), como iba diciendo

well-behaved ['welbɪheɪvd] *adj (child)* formal, educado(a)

well-being ['welbiːɪŋ] *n* bienestar *m*

well-built ['welbɪlt] *adj (building etc)* de construcción sólida; *(person)* fornido(a)

well-earned ['welɜːnd] *adj* merecido(a)

well-educated [wel'edʊkeɪtd] *adj* culto(a)

well-heeled ['welhiːld] *adj Fam* ricachón(ona), forrado(a), *Esp* con pelas, *Am* con plata

well-informed ['welɪnfɔːmd] *adj* bien informado(a)

wellington ['welɪŋtən] *n Br* wellingtons, w. boots botas *fpl* de agua *or* goma *or Méx*, *Ven* caucho

well-known ['welnəʊn] *adj* (bien) conocido(a)

well-mannered ['welmænəd] *adj* educado(a)

well-meaning [wel'miːnɪŋ] *adj* bien intencionado(a)

well-off [wel'ɒf] *adj (rich)* acomodado(a)

well-read [wel'red] *adj* culto(a)

well-spoken [wel'spəʊkən] *adj* con acento culto

well-to-do [weltə'duː] *adj* acomodado(a)

well-wisher ['welwɪʃə(r)] *n* admirador(a) *m,f*

Welsh [welʃ] **1** *adj* galés(esa); **W. rarebit** = tostada con queso fundido
2 *n* (**a**) *(language)* galés *m* (**b**) **the W.** los galeses

Welshman ['welʃmən] *n* galés *m*

Welshwoman ['welʃwʊmən] *n* galesa *f*

welterweight ['weltəweɪt] *n* (peso *m*) wélter *m*

wench [wentʃ] *n Old-fashioned* moza *f*

went [went] *pt of* go

wept [wept] *pt & pp of* weep

were [wɜː(r), *unstressed* wə(r)] *pt of* be

west [west] **1** *n* oeste *m*, occidente *m*; in/to the w. al oeste; *Pol* the W. los países occidentales
2 *adj* del oeste, occidental; the W. Indies las Antillas; W. Indian antillano(a)
3 *adv* al oeste, hacia el oeste

westerly ['westəlɪ] *adj (wind)* del oeste

western ['westən] **1** *adj* del oeste, occidental; W. Europe Europa Occidental
2 *n Cin* western *m*, película *f* del oeste

westward ['westwəd] *adj* in a w. direction hacia el oeste

westwards ['westwədz] *adv* hacia el oeste

wet [wet] **1** *adj* (wetter, wettest) (**a**) *(soaked)* mojado(a); *(damp)* húmedo(a); *Fig* w. blanket aguafiestas *mf inv*; w. paint *(sign)* recién pintado; w. through *(person)* calado(a) hasta los huesos; *(thing)* empapado(a); w. suit traje isotérmico (**b**) *(rainy)* lluvioso(a) (**c**) *Br Fam (person)* soso(a)
2 *vt (pt & pp* wet) mojar; to w. oneself orinarse

whack [wæk] **1** *vt (hit hard)* dar un porrazo *or Méx* madrazo a
2 *n* (**a**) *(blow)* porrazo *m*, *Méx* madrazo *m* (**b**) *Fam (share)* parte *f*, porción *f*

whale [weɪl] *n* ballena *f*

wharf [wɔːf] *n (pl* wharves [wɔːvz]) muelle *m*

what [wɒt, *unstressed* wət] **1** *adj* (**a**) *(direct question)* qué; w. (sort of) bird is that? ¿qué tipo de ave es ésa?; w. good is that? ¿para qué sirve eso? (**b**) *(indirect question)* qué; ask her w. colour she likes pregúntale qué color le gusta
2 *pron* (**a**) *(direct question)* qué; w. are you talking about? ¿de qué estás hablando?; w. about your father? ¿y tu padre (qué)?; w. about going tomorrow? ¿qué te parece si vamos mañana?; w. can I do for you? ¿en qué puedo servirle?; w. did it cost? ¿cuánto costó?; w. did you do that for? ¿por qué hiciste eso?; w. (did you) say? ¿cómo?; w. does it sound like? ¿cómo suena?; w. is happening? ¿qué pasa?; w. is it? *(definition)* ¿qué es?; *(what's the matter)* ¿qué pasa?; w.'s it called? ¿cómo se llama?; w.'s this for? ¿para qué sirve esto?
(**b**) *(indirect question)* qué, lo que; he asked me w. I thought me preguntó lo que pensaba; I didn't know w. to say no sabía qué decir
(**c**) **(and) w.'s more** y además; come w. may pase lo que pase; guess w.! ¿sabes qué?; it's just w. I need es exactamente lo que necesito
(**d**) *(in exclamations)* w. a goal! ¡qué *or* vaya golazo!; w. a lovely picture! ¡qué cuadro más bonito!
3 *interj (surprise, indignation)* ¡cómo!; w., no dessert? ¿cómo, no hay postre?

whatever [wɒt'evə(r), *unstressed* wət-'evə(r)] **1** *adj* (**a**) *(any)* cualquiera que; at w. time you like a la hora que quieras; of w. colour no importa de qué color (**b**) *(with negative)* nothing w. nada en absoluto; with no interest w. sin interés alguno
2 *pron* (**a**) *(what)* w. happened? ¿qué pasó? (**b**) *(anything, all that)* (todo) lo que; do w. you like haz lo que quieras (**c**) *(no matter what)* don't tell him, w. you

do no se te ocurra decírselo; **w. (else) you find** cualquier (otra) cosa que encuentres; **he goes out w. the weather** sale haga el tiempo que haga

whatsoever [wɒtsəʊ'evə(r)] *adj* **any-thing w.** cualquier cosa; **nothing w.** nada en absoluto

wheat [wiːt] *n* trigo *m*; **w. germ** germen *m* de trigo

wheedle ['wiːdəl] *vt* **to w. sb into doing sth** engatusar a algn para que haga algo; **to w. sth out of sb** sonsacar algo a algn halagándole

wheel [wiːl] **1** *n* rueda *f*
2 *vt (bicycle)* empujar
3 *vi* (a) *(bird)* revolotear (b) **to w. round** girar sobre los talones

wheelbarrow ['wiːlbærəʊ] *n* carretilla *f*

wheelchair ['wiːltʃeə(r)] *n* silla *f* de ruedas

wheeze [wiːz] *vi* respirar con dificultad, resollar

when [wen] **1** *adv* (a) *(direct question)* cuándo; **since w.?** ¿desde cuándo?; **w. did he arrive?** ¿cuándo llegó? (b) *(indirect question)* cuándo; **tell me w. to go** dime cuándo debo irme (c) *(on which)* cuando, en que; **the days w. I work** los días en que trabajo
2 *conj* (a) *(with time)* cuando; **I'll tell you w. she comes** se lo diré cuando llegue; **w. he was a boy ...** de niño ... (b) *(whenever)* cuando (c) *(given that, if)* si (d) *(although)* aunque

whence [wens] *adv Fml Literary (from where)* de dónde

whenever [wen'evə(r)] **1** *conj (when)* cuando; *(every time)* siempre que
2 *adv* **w. that might be** sea cuando sea

where [weə(r)] *adv* (a) *(direct question)* dónde; *(direction)* adónde; **w. are you going?** ¿adónde vas?; **w. did we go wrong?** ¿en qué nos equivocamos?; **w. do you come from?** ¿de dónde es usted? (b) *(indirect question)* dónde; *(direction)* adónde; **tell me w. you went** dime adónde fuiste (c) *(at, in which)* donde; *(direction)* adonde, a donde (d) *(when)* cuando

whereabouts 1 *adv* [weərə'baʊts] **w. do you live?** ¿por dónde vives?
2 *n* ['weərəbaʊts] paradero *m*

whereas [weər'æz] *conj* (a) *(but, while)* mientras que (b) *Jur* considerando que

whereby [weə'baɪ] *adv* por el/la/lo cual

whereupon [weərə'pɒn] *conj Fml* después de lo cual

wherever [weər'evə(r)] **1** *conj* donde-quiera que; **I'll find him w. he is** le

encontraré dondequiera que esté; **sit w. you like** siéntate donde quieras
2 *adv (direct question)* adónde

wherewithal ['weəwɪðɔːl] *n Fam* pelas *fpl*

whet [wet] *vt* **to w. sb's appetite** abrir el apetito a algn

whether ['weðə(r)] *conj* (a) *(if)* si; **I don't know w. it is true** no sé si es verdad; **I doubt w. he'll win** dudo que gane (b) **w. he comes or not** venga o no

which [wɪtʃ] **1** *adj* (a) *(direct question)* qué; **w. colour do you prefer?** ¿qué color prefieres?; **w. one?** ¿cuál?; **w. way?** ¿por dónde? (b) *(indirect question)* qué; **tell me w. dress you like** dime qué vestido te gusta (c) **by w. time** y para entonces; **in w. case** en cuyo caso
2 *pron* (a) *(direct question)* cuál/cuáles; **w. of you did it?** ¿quién de vosotros lo hizo?
(b) *(indirect question)* cuál/cuáles; **I don't know w. I'd rather have** no sé cuál prefiero
(c) *(defining relative)* que; *(after preposition)* que, el/la cual, los/las cuales, el/la que, los/las que; **here are the books (w.) I have read** aquí están los libros que he leído; **the accident (w.) I told you about** el accidente del que te hablé; **the car in w. he was travelling** el coche en (el) que viajaba; **this is the one (w.) I like** éste es el que me gusta
(d) *(non-defining relative)* el/la cual, los/las cuales; **I played three sets, all of w. I lost** jugué tres sets, todos los cuales perdí
(e) *(referring to a clause)* lo cual, lo que; **he won, w. made me very happy** ganó, lo cual or lo que me alegró mucho

whichever [wɪtʃ'evə(r)] **1** *adj* el/la que, cualquiera que; **I'll take w. books you don't want** tomaré los libros que no quieras; **w. system you choose** cualquiera que sea el sistema que elijas
2 *pron* el/la que

whiff [wɪf] *n* (a) *(quick smell)* ráfaga *f*; *(of air, smoke)* bocanada *f* (b) *Fam (bad smell)* tufo *m*

while [waɪl] **1** *n* (a) *(length of time)* rato *m*, tiempo *m*; **in a little w.** dentro de poco; **once in a w.** de vez en cuando (b) **it's not worth your w. staying** no merece la pena que te quedes
2 *conj* (a) *(time)* mientras; **he fell asleep w. driving** se durmió mientras conducía (b) *(although)* aunque (c) *(whereas)* mientras que

▸**while away** *vt sep* **to w. away the time** pasar el rato

whilst [waɪlst] *conj Br* = **while**

whim [wɪm] *n* capricho *m*, antojo *m*

whimper ['wɪmpə(r)] **1** n quejido m
2 vi lloriquear

whine [waɪn] vi (a) *(child)* lloriquear;
(with pain) dar quejidos (b) *(complain)*
quejarse (c) *(engine)* chirriar

whip [wɪp] **1** n (a) *(for punishment)* látigo
m; *(for riding)* fusta f (b) Br Pol = oficial
encargado(a) de la disciplina de un
partido
2 vt (a) *(as punishment)* azotar; *(horse)*
fustigar (b) Culin batir; **whipped cream**
Esp nata montada, Am crema batida (c)
Fam *(steal)* mangar
▸ **whip away** vt sep arrebatar
▸ **whip up** vt sep *(passions, enthusiasm)*
avivar; *(support)* incrementar

whipping ['wɪpɪŋ] n Fig **w. boy** cabeza f
de turco

whip-round ['wɪpraʊnd] n Br Fam colecta f

whir [wɜː(r)] vi = **whirr**

whirl [wɜːl] **1** n giro m; Fig torbellino m
2 vt **to w. sth round** dar vueltas a or hacer
girar algo
3 vi **to w. round** girar con rapidez; *(leaves
etc)* arremolinarse; **my head's whirling**
me está dando vueltas la cabeza

whirlpool ['wɜːlpuːl] n remolino m

whirlwind ['wɜːlwɪnd] n torbellino m

whirr [wɜː(r)] vi zumbar, runrunear

whisk [wɪsk] **1** n Culin batidor m; *(electric)*
batidora f
2 vt Culin batir
▸ **whisk away, whisk off** vt sep quitar
bruscamente, llevarse de repente

whisker ['wɪskə(r)] n **whiskers** *(of person)*
patillas fpl; *(of cat)* bigotes mpl

whisky, US **whiskey** ['wɪskɪ] n whisky m

whisper ['wɪspə(r)] **1** n (a) *(sound)*
susurro m (b) *(rumour)* rumor m
2 vt decir en voz baja
3 vi susurrar

whistle ['wɪsəl] **1** n (a) *(instrument)* pito m
(b) *(sound)* silbido m, pitido m
2 vt *(tune)* silbar
3 vi *(person, kettle, wind)* silbar; *(train)*
pitar

white [waɪt] **1** adj blanco(a); **to go w.**
(face) palidecer; *(hair)* encanecer; **w.
coffee** café m con leche; **w. hair** pelo
cano; **a w. Christmas** una Navidad con
nieve; Fig **a w. lie** una mentira piadosa; US
the W. House la Casa Blanca; Pol **w. paper**
libro blanco; **w. sauce** bechamel f, Col,
CSur salsa f blanca
2 n (a) *(colour, person, of eye)* blanco m
(b) *(of egg)* clara f (c) **whites** ropa f
blanca

white-collar ['waɪtkɒlə(r)] adj **w. worker**
empleado m de oficina

whiteness ['waɪtnɪs] n blancura f

whitewash ['waɪtwɒʃ] **1** n (a) *(paint)* cal f
(b) Fam *(cover-up)* encubrimiento m
2 vt (a) *(wall)* enjalbegar, blanquear (b)
Fam *(cover up)* encubrir

whiting ['waɪtɪŋ] n *(pl* whiting) *(fish)*
pescadilla f

Whitsun ['wɪtsən] n Pentecostés m

whittle ['wɪtəl] vt cortar en pedazos; **to w.
away at** roer; Fig **to w. down** reducir poco
a poco

whiz(z) [wɪz] vi (a) *(sound)* silbar (b) **to
w. past** pasar volando; Fam **w. kid** joven
mf dinámico(a) y emprendedor(a)

who [huː] pron (a) *(direct question)* quién/
quiénes; **w. are they?** ¿quiénes son?; **w. is
it?** ¿quién es? (b) *(indirect question)*
quién; **I don't know w. did it** no sé quién
lo hizo (c) rel *(defining)* que; **those w.
don't know** los que no saben (d) rel
(non-defining) quien/quienes, el/la cual,
los/las cuales; **Elena's mother, w. is very
rich …** la madre de Elena, la cual es muy
rica …

whodun(n)it [huː'dʌnɪt] n Fam novela f/
película f de suspense

whoever [huː'evə(r)] pron (a) *(anyone
that, no matter who)* quienquiera que; **w.
you are** quienquiera que seas; **give it to
w. you like** dáselo a quien quieras; **w. said
that is a fool** el que dijo eso es un tonto
(b) *(direct question)* **w. told you that?**
¿quién te dijo eso?

whole [həʊl] **1** adj (a) *(entire)* entero(a),
íntegro(a); **a w. week** una semana entera;
he took the w. lot se los llevó todos (b) *(in
one piece)* intacto(a)
2 n (a) *(single unit)* todo m, conjunto m;
as a w. en su totalidad (b) *(all)* totalidad f;
the w. of London todo Londres (c) **on the
w.** en general

wholefood ['həʊlfuːd] n alimentos mpl
integrales

wholehearted ['həʊl'hɑːtɪd] adj *(enthusiastic)* entusiasta; *(sincere)* sincero(a);
(unreserved) incondicional

wholemeal ['həʊlmiːl] adj Br integral

wholesale ['həʊlseɪl] Com **1** n compraventa f al por mayor, Am mayoreo m
2 adj al por mayor; Fig total
3 adv al por mayor; Fig en su totalidad

wholesaler ['həʊlseɪlə(r)] n mayorista mf

wholesome ['həʊlsəm] adj sano(a)

wholly ['həʊllɪ] adv enteramente, completamente

whom [huːm] pron Fml (a) *(direct
question) (accusative)* a quién; **w. did you**

talk to? ¿con quién hablaste?; *(after preposition)* **of/from w.?** ¿de quién?; **to w. are you referring?** ¿a quién te refieres? (**b**) *rel (accusative)* que, a quien/a quienes; **those w. I have seen** aquéllos a quien(es) he visto (**c**) *rel (after preposition)* quien/quienes, el/la cual, los/las cuales; **my brothers, both of w. are miners** mis hermanos, que son mineros los dos

En la actualidad, sólo aparece en contextos formales. **Whom** se puede sustituir por **who** en todos los casos salvo cuando va después de preposición.

whooping cough ['hu:pɪŋkɒf] *n* tos ferina

whopping ['wɒpɪŋ] *adj Fam* enorme

whore [hɔː(r)] *n very Fam Pej* puta *f*

whose [hu:z] **1** *pron* (**a**) *(direct question)* de quién/de quiénes; **w. are these gloves?** ¿de quién son estos guantes?; **w. is this?** ¿de quién es esto? (**b**) *(indirect question)* de quién/de quiénes; **I don't know w. these coats are** no sé de quién son estos abrigos (**c**) *rel* cuyo(s)/cuya(s); **the man w. children we saw** el hombre a cuyos hijos vimos
2 *adj* **w. car/house is this?** ¿de quién es este coche/esta casa?

why [waɪ] **1** *adv* por qué; *(for what purpose)* para qué; **w. did you do that?** ¿por qué hiciste eso?; **w. not go to bed?** ¿por qué no te acuestas?; **I don't know w. he did it** no sé por qué lo hizo; **that is w. I didn't come** por eso no vine; **there's no reason w. you shouldn't go** no hay motivo para que no vayas
2 *interj* (**a**) *(fancy that!)* ¡toma!, ¡vaya!; **w., it's David!** ¡sí es David! (**b**) *(protest, assertion)* sí, vamos

wick [wɪk] *n* mecha *f*

wicked ['wɪkɪd] *adj* (**a**) *(evil)* perverso(a), malo(a) (**b**) *Fam (appalling)* asqueroso(a); *(temper)* de perros

wicker ['wɪkə(r)] **1** *n* mimbre *m*
2 *adj* de mimbre

wickerwork ['wɪkəwɜːk] *n (material)* mimbre *m*; *(articles)* artículos *mpl* de mimbre

wicket ['wɪkɪt] *n (in cricket) (stumps)* palos *mpl*

wide [waɪd] **1** *adj* (**a**) *(road, trousers)* ancho(a); *(gap, interval)* grande; **it is 10 m w.** tiene 10 m de ancho (**b**) *(area, knowledge, support, range)* amplio(a); **w. interests** intereses muy diversos (**c**) *(off target)* desviado(a)
2 *adv* **from far and w.** de todas partes; **to open one's eyes w.** abrir los ojos de par

en par; **w. apart** muy separados(as); **w. awake** completamente despierto(a); **w. open** abierto(a) de par en par; **with mouth w. open** boquiabierto(a)

wide-angle ['waɪdæŋgəl] *adj Phot* **w. lens** gran angular *m*

widely ['waɪdlɪ] *adv (travel etc)* extensamente; *(believed)* generalmente; **he is w. known** es muy conocido

widen ['waɪdən] **1** *vt* ensanchar; *(interests)* ampliar
2 *vi* ensancharse

wide-ranging ['waɪd'reɪndʒɪŋ] *adj (interests)* muy diversos(as); *(discussion)* amplio(a); *(study)* de gran alcance

widespread ['waɪdspred] *adj (unrest, belief)* general; *(damage)* extenso(a); **to become w.** generalizarse

widow ['wɪdəʊ] *n* viuda *f*

widowed ['wɪdəʊd] *adj* enviudado(a)

widower ['wɪdəʊə(r)] *n* viudo *m*

width [wɪdθ] *n* (**a**) *(dimension)* anchura *f* (**b**) *(of material, swimming pool)* ancho *m*

wield [wiːld] *vt (weapon)* blandir; *Fig (power)* ejercer

wife [waɪf] *n (pl wives)* mujer *f*, esposa *f*

wig [wɪg] *n* peluca *f*

wiggle ['wɪgəl] **1** *vt (finger etc)* menear; **to w. one's hips** contonearse
2 *vi* menearse

Wight [waɪt] *n* Isle of W. Isla *f* de Wight

wild [waɪld] **1** *adj* (**a**) *(animal, tribe)* salvaje; **w. beast** fiera *f* (**b**) *(plant)* silvestre (**c**) *(landscape)* agreste; **the W. West** el Salvaje Oeste (**d**) *(temperament, behaviour)* alocado(a); *(appearance)* desordenado(a); *(passions etc)* desenfrenado(a); *(laughter, thoughts)* loco(a); *(applause)* fervoroso(a); *Fam Fig* **she is w. about him/about tennis** está loca por él/por el tenis
2 *adv Fig* **to run w.** *(children)* desmandarse
3 *n* **in the w.** en el estado salvaje

wildcat ['waɪldkæt] *n* (**a**) *(animal)* gato *m* montés (**b**) *Ind* **w. strike** huelga *f* salvaje

wilderness ['wɪldənɪs] *n* desierto *m*

wildfire ['waɪldfaɪə(r)] *n* **to spread like w.** correr como la pólvora

wildlife ['waɪldlaɪf] *n* fauna *f*; **w. park** parque *m* natural

wildly ['waɪldlɪ] *adv* (**a**) *(rush round etc)* como un(a) loco(a); *(shoot)* sin apuntar; *(hit out)* a tontas y a locas (**b**) **w. enthusiastic** loco(a) de entusiasmo; **w. inaccurate** totalmente erróneo(a)

wilful, *US* **willful** ['wɪlfʊl] *adj* (**a**) *(stubborn)* terco(a) (**b**) *Jur* premeditado(a)

will¹ [wɪl] **1** *n* (**a**) *(resolve)* voluntad *f*; **good/ill w.** buena/mala voluntad; **of my own free w.** por mi propia voluntad (**b**) *Jur (testament)* testamento *m*; **to make one's w.** hacer testamento

2 *vt* fate willed that ... el destino quiso que ...

will² [wɪl] *v aux* (*pt* **would**)

En el inglés hablado, y en el escrito en estilo coloquial, el verbo **will** se contrae de manera que **I/you/he** *etc* **will** se transforman en **I'll, you'll, he'll** *etc* y el verbo **would** se contrae de manera que **I/you/he** *etc* **would** se transforman en **I'd, you'd, he'd** *etc*. Las formas negativas **will not** y **would not** se transforman en **won't** y **wouldn't**.

(**a**) *(future) (esp second & third person)* **they'll come** vendrán; **w. he be there? – yes, he w.** ¿estará allí? – sí, estará); **you'll tell him, won't you?** se lo dirás, ¿verdad?; **don't forget, w. you!** ¡que no se te olvide, vale!; **she won't do it** no lo hará

(**b**) *(command)* **you w. be here at eleven!** ¡debes estar aquí a las once!

(**c**) *(future perfect)* **they'll have finished by tomorrow** habrán terminado para mañana

(**d**) *(willingness)* **be quiet, w. you! – no, I won't!** ¿quiere callarse? – no quiero; **I won't have it!** ¡no lo permito!; **you have a drink? – yes, I w.** ¿quiere tomar algo? – sí, por favor; **won't you sit down?** ¿quiere sentarse?

(**e**) *(custom)* **accidents w. happen** siempre habrá accidentes

(**f**) *(persistence)* **if you w. go out without a coat** ... si te empeñas en salir sin abrigo ...

(**g**) *(probability)* **he'll be on holiday now** ahora estará de vacaciones

(**h**) *(ability)* **the lift w. hold ten people** en el ascensor caben diez personas

willing ['wɪlɪŋ] *adj (obliging)* complaciente; **I'm quite w. to do it** lo haré con mucho gusto; **to be w. to do sth** estar dispuesto(a) a hacer algo

willingly ['wɪlɪŋlɪ] *adv* de buena gana

willingness ['wɪlɪŋnɪs] *n* buena voluntad

willow ['wɪləʊ] *n* **w. (tree)** sauce *m*

willpower ['wɪlpaʊə(r)] *n* (fuerza *f* de) voluntad *f*

willy ['wɪlɪ] *n Br Fam* pito *m*, pilila *f*

willy-nilly ['wɪlɪ'nɪlɪ] *adv* por gusto o por fuerza

wilt [wɪlt] *vi* marchitarse

wily ['waɪlɪ] *adj* (**wilier, wiliest**) astuto(a)

wimp [wɪmp] *n Fam (physically)* debilucho(a) *m,f*; *(lacking character)* blandengue *mf*

win [wɪn] **1** *n* victoria *f*

2 *vt* (*pt & pp* **won**) (**a**) *(battle, race, election)* ganar; *(prize)* llevarse; *(victory)* conseguir (**b**) *Fig (sympathy, friendship)* ganarse; *(praise)* cosechar; **to w. sb's love** conquistar a algn

3 *vi* ganar

▸ **win back** *vt sep* recuperar

▸ **win over** *vt sep (to cause, idea)* atraer (**to** a); *(voters, support)* ganarse

▸ **win through** *vi* conseguir triunfar

wince [wɪns] *vi* tener un rictus de dolor

winch [wɪntʃ] *n* cigüeña *f*, torno *m*

wind¹ [wɪnd] **1** *n* (**a**) *(air current)* viento *m*; *Fig* **to get w. of sth** olerse algo; **w. farm** parque eólico; **w. tunnel** túnel aerodinámico (**b**) *(breath)* aliento *m*; **to get one's second w.** recobrar el aliento (**c**) *Med* flato *m*, gases *mpl* (**d**) **w. instrument** instrumento *m* de viento

2 *vt* **to be winded** quedarse sin aliento

wind² [waɪnd] **1** *vt* (*pt & pp* **wound**) (**a**) *(on to a reel)* enrollar; **to w. a bandage round one's finger** vendarse el dedo (**b**) **to w. on/back** *(film, tape)* avanzar/rebobinar (**c**) *(clock)* dar cuerda a

2 *vi (road, river)* serpentear

▸ **wind down 1** *vt sep (window)* bajar

2 *vi Fam (person)* relajarse

▸ **wind up 1** *vt sep* (**a**) *(roll up)* enrollar (**b**) *(business etc)* cerrar; *(debate)* clausurar (**c**) *(clock)* dar cuerda a

2 *vi (meeting)* terminar

windfall ['wɪndfɔːl] *n Fig* ganancia inesperada

winding ['waɪndɪŋ] *adj (road, river)* sinuoso(a); *(staircase)* de caracol

windmill ['wɪndmɪl] *n* molino *m* (de viento)

window ['wɪndəʊ] *n* ventana *f*; *(of vehicle, ticket office etc)* ventanilla *f*; **(shop) w.** escaparate *m*, *Am* vidriera *f*, *Chile, Col, Méx* vitrina *f*; **to clean the windows** limpiar los cristales; **w. box** jardinera *f*; **w. cleaner** limpiacristales *mf inv*

windowpane ['wɪndəʊpeɪn] *n* vidrio *m* or cristal *m*

window-shopping ['wɪndəʊʃɒpɪŋ] *n* **to go w.** ir a mirar escaparates

windowsill ['wɪndəʊsɪl] *n* alféizar *m*

windpipe ['wɪndpaɪp] *n* tráquea *f*

windscreen ['wɪndskriːn], *US* **windshield** ['wɪndʃiːld] *n* parabrisas *m inv*; **w. washer** lavaparabrisas *m inv*; **w. wiper** limpiaparabrisas *m inv*

windsurfing ['wɪndsɜ:fɪŋ] *n* **to go w.** ir a hacer windsurf *or* tabla a vela

windswept ['wɪndswept] *adj* (*landscape*) expuesto(a) a los vientos; (*person, hair*) despeinado(a) (por el viento)

windy ['wɪndɪ] *adj* (**windier, windiest**) (*weather*) ventoso(a); (*place*) desprotegido(a) del viento; **it is very w. today** hoy hace mucho viento

wine [waɪn] *n* vino *m*; **w. cellar** bodega *f*; **w. list** lista *f* de vinos; **w. merchant** vinatero(a) *m,f*; **w. tasting** cata *f* de vinos; **w. vinegar** vinagre *m* de vino

wineglass ['waɪnɡlɑ:s] *n* copa *f* (para vino)

wing [wɪŋ] *n* (**a**) (*of bird, plane*) ala *f* (**b**) (*of building*) ala *f* (**c**) *Br Aut* aleta *f*; **w. mirror** retrovisor externo (**d**) *Th* (**in the**) **wings** (entre) bastidores *mpl* (**e**) *Ftb* banda *f* (**f**) *Pol* ala *f*; **the left w.** la izquierda

winger ['wɪŋə(r)] *n Ftb* extremo *m*

wink [wɪŋk] **1** *n* guiño *m*
2 *vi* (**a**) (*person*) guiñar (el ojo) (**b**) (*light*) parpadear

winner ['wɪnə(r)] *n* ganador(a) *m,f*

winning ['wɪnɪŋ] *adj* (*person, team*) ganador(a); (*number*) premiado(a); (*goal*) decisivo(a); **w. post** meta *f*

winnings ['wɪnɪŋz] *npl* ganancias *fpl*

winter ['wɪntə(r)] **1** *n* invierno *m*
2 *adj* de invierno; **w. sports** deportes *mpl* de invierno
3 *vi* invernar

wintry ['wɪntrɪ] *adj* (**wintrier, wintriest**) invernal

wipe [waɪp] *vt* limpiar; **to w. one's brow** enjugarse la frente; **to w. one's feet/nose** limpiarse los pies/las narices
▸ **wipe away** *vt sep* (*tear*) enjugar
▸ **wipe off** *vt sep* quitar frotando; **to w. sth off the blackboard/the tape** borrar algo de la pizarra/de la cinta
▸ **wipe out** *vt sep* (**a**) (*erase*) borrar (**b**) (*army*) aniquilar; (*species etc*) exterminar
▸ **wipe up** *vt sep* limpiar

wiper ['waɪpə(r)] *n Aut* limpiaparabrisas *m inv*

wire [waɪə(r)] **1** *n* (**a**) (*in general*) alambre *m*; *Elec* cable *m*; *Tel* hilo *m*; **w. cutters** cizalla *f* (**b**) (*telegram*) telegrama *m*
2 *vt* (**a**) **to w. (up) a house** poner la instalación eléctrica de una casa; **to w. (up) an appliance to the mains** conectar un aparato a la red eléctrica (**b**) (*information*) enviar por telegrama

wireless ['waɪəlɪs] **1** *n Old-fashioned* radio *f*
2 *adj Comput* wireless, inalámbrico(a)

wiring ['waɪərɪŋ] *n* (*network*) cableado *m*; (*action*) instalación *f* del cableado

wiry ['waɪərɪ] *adj* (**wirier, wiriest**) (*hair*) basto(a) y rizado(a) *or Méx* quebrado(a); (*person*) fibroso(a)

wisdom ['wɪzdəm] *n* (**a**) (*learning*) sabiduría *f*, saber *m* (**b**) (*good sense*) (*of person*) cordura *f*; (*of action*) sensatez *f* (**c**) **w. tooth** muela *f* del juicio

wise [waɪz] *adj* (**a**) (*knowledgeable*) sabio(a); **a w. man** un sabio; **the Three W. Men** los Reyes Magos (**b**) (*remark*) juicioso(a); (*decision*) acertado(a); **it would be w. to keep quiet** sería prudente callarse

wisecrack ['waɪzkræk] *n Fam* chiste *m*, salida *f* ingeniosa

wisely ['waɪzlɪ] *adv* (*with prudence*) sensatamente

wish [wɪʃ] **1** *n* (**a**) (*desire*) deseo *m* (**for** de); **to make a w.** pedir un deseo (**b**) **best wishes** felicitaciones *fpl*; **give your mother my best wishes** salude a su madre de mi parte; **with best wishes, Peter** (*at end of letter*) saludos cordiales, Peter
2 *vt* (**a**) (*want*) querer, desear; **I w. I could stay longer** me gustaría poder quedarme más tiempo; **I w. you had told me!** ¡ojalá me lo hubieras dicho!; **to w. to do sth** querer hacer algo (**b**) **to w. sb goodnight** darle las buenas noches a algn; **to w. sb well** desearle a algn mucha suerte
3 *vi* (*want*) desear; **as you w.** como quieras; **do as you w.** haga lo que quiera; **to w. for sth** desear algo

wishful ['wɪʃfʊl] *adj* **it's w. thinking** es hacerse ilusiones

wishy-washy ['wɪʃɪ'wɒʃɪ] *adj Fam* vacilante

wisp [wɪsp] *n* (*of wool, hair*) mechón *m*; (*of smoke*) voluta *f*

wistful ['wɪstfʊl] *adj* melancólico(a)

wit [wɪt] *n* (**a**) (*intelligence*) (*often pl*) inteligencia *f*; *Fig* **to be at one's wits' end** estar para volverse loco(a); *Fam Fig* **to have one's wits about one** ser despabilado(a) (**b**) (*humour*) ingenio *m*

witch [wɪtʃ] *n* bruja *f*; *Fig* **w. hunt** caza *f* de brujas

witchcraft ['wɪtʃkrɑ:ft] *n* brujería *f*

with [wɪð, wɪθ] *prep* con; **a room w. a bath** un cuarto con baño; **do you have any money w. you?** ¿traes dinero?; **the man w. the glasses** el hombre de las gafas; **he went w. me/you** fue conmigo/contigo; *Fam* **w. (sugar) or without (sugar)?** ¿con o sin azúcar?; **I have six w. this one** con éste tengo seis; **w. all his faults, I admire him** le admiro con todos sus defectos; **w.**

your permission con su permiso; **we're all w. you** (support) todos estamos contigo; **you're not w. me, are you?** (understand) no me entiendes, ¿verdad?; **he's w. Lloyds** trabaja para Lloyds; **she is popular w. her colleagues** todos sus colegas la estiman mucho; **to fill a vase w. water** llenar un jarrón de agua; **it is made w. butter** está hecho con mantequilla; **she put on weight w. so much eating** engordó de tanto comer; **to be paralysed w. fear** estar paralizado(a) de miedo; **w. experience** con la experiencia

withdraw [wɪð'drɔ:] **1** vt (pt **withdrew**; pp **withdrawn**) (**a**) (troops, offer, support) retirar; (from pocket) sacar; **to w. money from the bank** sacar dinero del banco (**b**) (statement, accusation) retirar; retractarse de; (plan, claim) renunciar a
2 vi retirarse

withdrawal [wɪð'drɔ:əl] n retirada f; (of statement) retractación f; (of complaint, plan) renuncia f; **w. symptoms** síndrome m de abstinencia

withdrawn [wɪð'drɔ:n] **1** adj (person) introvertido(a)
2 pp of **withdraw**

withdrew [wɪð'dru:] pt of **withdraw**

wither ['wɪðə(r)] vi (plant) marchitarse; (limb) atrofiarse

withering ['wɪðərɪŋ] adj (look) fulminante; (criticism) mordaz

withhold [wɪð'həʊld] vt (pt & pp **withheld** [wɪð'held]) (money) retener; (decision) aplazar; (consent) negar; (information) ocultar

within [wɪ'ðɪn] **1** prep (**a**) (inside) dentro de (**b**) (range) **the house is w. walking distance** se puede ir andando a la casa; **situated w. 5 km of the town** situado(a) a menos de 5 km de la ciudad; **w. sight of the sea** con vistas al mar; **Fig w. an inch of death** a dos dedos de la muerte (**c**) (time) **they arrived w. a few days of each other** llegaron con pocos días de diferencia; **w. the hour** dentro de una hora; **w. the next five years** durante los cinco próximos años
2 adv dentro; **from w.** desde dentro

with-it ['wɪðɪt] adj Fam **she is very w.** tiene ideas muy modernas; **to get w.** ponerse de moda

without [wɪ'ðaʊt] prep sin; **he did it w. my knowing** lo hizo sin que lo supiera yo; Fig **to do** or **go w. sth** (voluntarily) prescindir de algo; (forcibly) pasar(se) sin algo

withstand [wɪð'stænd] vt (pt & pp **withstood** [wɪð'stʊd]) resistir a; (pain) aguantar

witness ['wɪtnɪs] **1** n (**a**) (person) testigo mf; **w. box**, US **w. stand** barra f de los testigos (**b**) (evidence) **to bear w. to sth** dar fe de algo
2 vt (**a**) (see) presenciar, ser testigo de (**b**) Fig (notice) notar (**c**) Jur **to w. a document** firmar un documento como testigo

witticism ['wɪtɪsɪzəm] n ocurrencia f, agudeza f

witty ['wɪtɪ] adj (**wittier**, **wittiest**) ingenioso(a), agudo(a)

wives [waɪvz] pl of **wife**

wizard ['wɪzəd] n hechicero m, mago m

wizened ['wɪzənd] adj marchito(a), arrugado(a)

WMD ['dʌbəlju:em'di:] npl (abbr **weapons of mass destruction**) armas fpl de destrucción masiva

wobble ['wɒbəl] vi (table, ladder etc) tambalearse; (jelly) temblar

wobbly ['wɒblɪ] adj (**wobblier**, **wobbliest**) (chair, table) cojo(a); (shelf, ladder) tambaleante

woe [wəʊ] n Literary infortunio m; **w. betide you if I catch you!** ¡ay de ti si te cojo!

woeful ['wəʊfʊl] adj (**a**) (person) apesadumbrado(a), afligido(a) (**b**) (sight) penoso(a), deplorable; **w. ignorance** una ignorancia supina

wok [wɒk] n wok m, = sartén china con forma de cuenco

woke [wəʊk] pt of **wake**

woken ['wəʊkən] pp of **wake**

wolf [wʊlf] n (pl **wolves** [wʊlvz]) lobo m; Fig **a w. in sheep's clothing** un lobo con piel de cordero

woman ['wʊmən] n (pl **women**) mujer f; **old w.** vieja f; Fam **women's libber** feminista mf; Fam **women's lib** movimiento m feminista; **women's rights** derechos mpl de la mujer

womanhood ['wʊmənhʊd] n (adult) edad adulta de la mujer

womanizer ['wʊmənaɪzə(r)] n mujeriego m

womanly ['wʊmənlɪ] adj femenino(a)

womb [wu:m] n matriz f, útero m

women ['wɪmɪn] pl of **woman**

won [wʌn] pt & pp of **win**

wonder ['wʌndə(r)] **1** n (**a**) (miracle) milagro m; **no w. he hasn't come** no es de extrañar que no haya venido (**b**) (amazement) admiración f, asombro m
2 vt (**a**) (be surprised) sorprenderse (**b**) (ask oneself) preguntarse; **I w. why** ¿por qué será?
3 vi (**a**) (marvel) maravillarse; **to w. at**

sth admirarse de algo (**b**) **it makes you w.** (*reflect*) te hace pensar

wonderful ['wʌndəful] *adj* maravillo-so(a)

wonderfully ['wʌndəfulɪ] *adv* maravillo-samente

wont [wəunt] *Fml* **1** *adj* **to be w. to do sth** ser dado(a) a hacer algo
2 *n* costumbre *f*; **as is his w.** como acostumbra

won't [wəunt] = **will not**

woo [wuː] *vt Literary* (*court*) cortejar; *Fig* intentar congraciarse con

wood [wud] *n* (**a**) (*forest*) bosque *m* (**b**) (*material*) madera *f*; (*for fire*) leña *f*

woodcarving ['wudkɑːvɪŋ] *n* (**a**) (*craft*) tallado *m* en madera (**b**) (*object*) talla *f* en madera

woodcutter ['wudkʌtə(r)] *n* leñador(a) *m,f*

wooded ['wudɪd] *adj* arbolado(a)

wooden ['wudən] *adj* (**a**) (*made of wood*) de madera; **w. spoon/leg** cuchara *f*/pata *f* de palo (**b**) *Fig* rígido(a); (*acting*) sin expresión

woodlouse ['wudlaus] *n* cochinilla *f*

woodpecker ['wudpekə(r)] *n* pájaro carpintero

woodwind ['wudwɪnd] *n* **w. (instruments)** instrumentos *mpl* de viento de madera

woodwork ['wudwɜːk] *n* (**a**) (*craft*) carpintería *f* (**b**) (*of building*) maderaje *m*

woodworm ['wudwɜːm] *n* carcoma *f*

wool [wul] **1** *n* lana *f*; *Fig* **to pull the w. over sb's eyes** embaucar *or* dar el pego a algn
2 *adj* de lana

woollen, *US* **woolen** ['wulən] **1** *adj* (**a**) (*dress*) de lana (**b**) (*industry*) lanero(a)
2 *npl* **woollens** géneros *mpl* de lana *or* de punto

woolly, *US* **wooly** ['wulɪ] *adj* (**woollier**, **woolliest**, *US* **woolier**, **wooliest**) (**a**) (*made of wool*) de lana (**b**) *Fig* (*unclear*) confuso(a)

word [wɜːd] **1** *n* (**a**) (*spoken, written*) palabra *f*; **in other words ...** es decir ..., o sea ...; **words failed me** me quedé sin habla; *Fig* **a w. of advice** un consejo; *Fig* **I'd like a w. with you** quiero hablar contigo un momento; *Fig* **she didn't say it in so many words** no lo dijo de modo tan explícito; **in the words of the poet ...**, como dice el poeta ...; *Fig* **w. for w.** palabra por palabra; **w. processing** tratamiento *m* de textos; **w. processor** procesador *m* de textos
(**b**) *Fig* (*message*) mensaje *m*; **by w. of**

mouth de palabra; **is there any w. from him?** ¿hay noticias de él?; **to send w.** mandar recado
(**c**) *Fig* (*rumour*) voz *f*, rumor *m*
(**d**) *Fig* (*promise*) palabra *f*; **he's a man of his w.** es hombre de palabra
2 *vt* (*express*) formular; **a badly worded letter** una carta mal redactada

wording ['wɜːdɪŋ] *n* expresión *f*; **I changed the w. slightly** cambié algunas palabras

word-perfect [wɜːd'pɜːfekt] *adj* **to be w.** saberse el papel perfectamente

wordy ['wɜːdɪ] *adj* (**wordier**, **wordiest**) verboso(a)

wore [wɔː(r)] *pt of* **wear**

work [wɜːk] **1** *n* (**a**) (*labour*) trabajo *m*; **his w. in the field of physics** su labor en el campo de la física; **it's hard w.** cuesta trabajo (**b**) (*employment*) trabajo *m*, empleo *m*; **to be out of w.** no tener trabajo, *Esp* estar parado(a) (**c**) (*action*) obra *f*, acción *f*; **keep up the good w.!** ¡que siga así! (**d**) **a piece of w.** un trabajo; **a w. of art** una obra de arte (**e**) **works** obras *fpl*; **public works** obras (públicas) (**f**) **works** (*machinery*) mecanismo *m* (**g**) *Br* **works** (*factory*) fábrica *f*
2 *vt* (**a**) (*drive*) hacer trabajar; **to w. one's way up/down** subir/bajar a duras penas; *Fig* **to w. one's way up in a firm** trabajarse el ascenso en una empresa (**b**) (*machine*) manejar; (*mechanism*) accionar (**c**) (*miracles, changes*) operar, hacer (**d**) (*land*) cultivar; (*mine*) explotar (**e**) (*wood, metal etc*) trabajar
3 *vi* (**a**) (*person*) trabajar (**on** *or* **at** en); **to w. as a gardener** trabajar de jardinero (**b**) (*machine*) funcionar; **it works on gas** funciona con gas (**c**) (*drug*) surtir efecto; (*system*) funcionar bien; (*plan, trick*) salir bien (**d**) (*operate*) obrar; **to w. loose** soltarse; **we have no data to w. on** no tenemos datos en que basarnos

▸ **work off** *vt sep* (*fat*) eliminar trabajando; (*anger*) desahogar

▸ **work out 1** *vt sep* (**a**) (*plan*) idear; (*itinerary*) planear; (*details*) desarrollar (**b**) (*problem*) solucionar; (*solution*) encontrar; (*amount*) calcular; **I can't w. out how he did it** no me explico cómo lo hizo
2 *vi* (**a**) **things didn't w. out for her** las cosas no le salieron bien (**b**) **it works out at five each** sale a cinco cada uno (**c**) *Sport* hacer ejercicio

▸ **work through** *vi* penetrar (**to** hasta)

▸ **work up** *vt sep* (*excite*) acalorar; **to get worked up** excitarse; **to w. up enthusiasm (for)** entusiasmarse (con)

workable ['wɜːkəbəl] *adj* factible

workaholic [wɜːkə'hɒlɪk] *n Fam* trabajo-adicto(a) *m,f*

workbench ['wɜːkbentʃ] *n* obrador *m*

worker ['wɜːkə(r)] *n* trabajador(a) *m,f*; *(manual)* obrero(a) *m,f*

workforce ['wɜːkfɔːs] *n* mano *f* de obra

working ['wɜːkɪŋ] **1** *adj* (a) *(population, capital)* activo(a); **w. class** clase obrera; **w. man** obrero *m* (b) *(clothes, conditions, hours)* de trabajo; **w. day** día *m* laborable; *(number of hours)* jornada *f* laboral (c) **it is in w. order** funciona (d) *(majority)* suficiente; **w. knowledge** conocimientos básicos
2 *n* **workings** *(mechanics)* funcionamiento *m*; *Min* explotación *f*

workload ['wɜːkləʊd] *n* cantidad *f* de trabajo

workman ['wɜːkmən] *n (manual)* obrero *m*

workmanship ['wɜːkmənʃɪp] *n (appearance)* acabado *m*; *(skill)* habilidad *f*, arte *m*; **a fine piece of w.** un trabajo excelente

workmate ['wɜːkmeɪt] *n* compañero(a) *m,f* de trabajo

work-out ['wɜːkaʊt] *n* entrenamiento *m*

worksheet ['wɜːkʃiːt] *n* plan *m* de trabajo

workshop ['wɜːkʃɒp] *n* taller *m*

worktop ['wɜːktɒp] *n* encimera *f*

work-to-rule ['wɜːktəˈruːl] *n* huelga *f* de celo

world [wɜːld] *n* mundo *m*; **all over the w.** en todo el mundo; **the best in the w.** el mejor del mundo; *Ftb* **the W. Cup** los Mundiales; **w. record** récord *m* mundial; **w. war** guerra *f* mundial

world-class ['wɜːld'klɑːs] *adj* de categoría mundial

world-famous ['wɜːld'feɪməs] *adj* de fama mundial

worldly ['wɜːldlɪ] *adj* (**worldlier, worldliest**) mundano(a)

worldwide ['wɜːldwaɪd] *adj* mundial

worm [wɜːm] **1** *n* (a) *(in general)* gusano *m*; **(earth) w.** lombriz *f* (b) *Med* **worms** lombrices *fpl*
2 *vt* **to w. a secret out of sb** sonsacarle un secreto a algn

worn [wɔːn] **1** *adj* gastado(a), usado(a)
2 *pp of* **wear**

worn-out ['wɔːnaʊt] *adj (thing)* gastado(a); *(person)* rendido(a), agotado(a)

worried ['wʌrɪd] *adj* inquieto(a), preocupado(a)

worry ['wʌrɪ] **1** *vt* (a) *(cause anxiety to)* preocupar; **it doesn't w. me** me trae sin cuidado (b) *(pester)* molestar
2 *vi* preocuparse (**about** por); **don't w.** no te preocupes
3 *n (state)* inquietud *f*; *(cause)* preocupación *f*

worrying ['wʌrɪɪŋ] *adj* inquietante, preocupante

worse [wɜːs] **1** *adj (comp of* **bad**) peor; **he gets w. and w.** va de mal en peor; **to get w.** empeorar; *Fam* **w. luck!** ¡mala suerte!
2 *n* **a change for the w.** un empeoramiento; *Fig* **to take a turn for the w.** empeorar
3 *adv (comp of* **badly**) peor; **w. than ever** peor que nunca

worsen ['wɜːsən] *vt & vi* empeorar

worship ['wɜːʃɪp] **1** *vt* adorar
2 *n* (a) *(of deity)* adoración *f* (b) *(ceremony)* culto *m* (c) *Br* **His W. the Mayor** el señor alcalde; *Jur* **Your W.** Su Señoría

worshipper ['wɜːʃɪpə(r)] *n* devoto(a) *m,f*

worst [wɜːst] **1** *adj (superl of* **bad**) peor; **the w. part about it is that …** lo peor es que …
2 *n* (a) *(person)* el/la peor, los/las peores (b) **the w. of the storm is over** ya ha pasado lo peor de la tormenta
3 *adv (superl of* **badly**) peor; *Fig* **to come off w.** salir perdiendo

worth [wɜːθ] **1** *adj* (a) **to be w. £3** valer 3 libras; **a house w. £50,000** una casa que vale 50.000 libras (b) *(deserving of)* merecedor(a) de; **a book w. reading** un libro que merece la pena leer; **for what it's w.** por si sirve de algo; **it's w. your while, it's w. it** vale *or* merece la pena; **it's w. mentioning** es digno de mención
2 *n* (a) *(in money)* valor *m*; **£5 w. of petrol** gasolina por valor de 5 libras (b) *(of person)* valía *f*

worthless ['wɜːθlɪs] *adj* sin valor; *(person)* despreciable

worthwhile [wɜːθ'waɪl] *adj* valioso(a), que vale la pena

worthy ['wɜːðɪ] *adj* (**worthier, worthiest**) (a) *(deserving)* digno(a) (**of** de); *(winner, cause)* justo(a) (b) *(citizen)* respetable; *(effort, motives, action)* loable

would [wʊd, *unstressed* wəd] *v aux* (a) *(conditional)* **I w. go if I had time** iría si tuviera tiempo; **he w. have won but for that** habría ganado sí no hubiera sido por eso; **we w. if we could** lo haríamos si pudiéramos; **you w. have to choose me!** ¡tenías que elegirme precisamente a mí! (b) *(reported speech)* **he said that he w. come** dijo que vendría (c) *(willingness)* **the car wouldn't start** el coche no arrancaba; **they asked him to**

come but he **wouldn't** le invitaron a venir pero no quiso; **w. you do me a favour?** ¿quiere hacerme un favor? (**d**) *(wishing)* **he w. like to know why** quisiera saber por qué; **I'd rather go home** preferiría ir a casa; **w. you like a cigarette?** ¿quiere un cigarrillo? (**e**) *(custom)* **we w. go for walks** solíamos dar un paseo (**f**) **try as I w.** por mucho que lo intentara (**g**) *(conjecture)* **it w. have been about three weeks ago** debe haber sido hace unas tres semanas; **w. this be your cousin?** ¿será éste tu primo? (**h**) *(expectation)* **so it w. appear** según parece

would-be ['wʊdbiː] *adj* en potencia; **a w. politician** un aspirante a político; *Pej* **a w. poet** un supuesto poeta

wound¹ [waʊnd] *pt & pp of* **wind²**

wound² [wuːnd] **1** *n* herida *f*
  2 *vt* herir

wove [wəʊv] *pt of* **weave**

woven ['wəʊvən] *pp of* **weave**

wow [waʊ] *interj Fam* ¡hala!, *RP* ¡uau!

WP ['dʌbəljuː'piː] *n* (**a**) *(abbr* **word processor)** procesador *m* de textos (**b**) *(abbr* **word processing)** tratamiento *m* de textos

wrangle ['ræŋgəl] **1** *n* disputa *f*
  2 *vi* disputar (**over** por)

wrap [ræp] **1** *vt* **to w. (up)** envolver; **he wrapped his arms around her** la estrechó entre sus brazos; *Fam* **we wrapped up the deal** concluimos el negocio
  2 *vi Fam* **w. up well** abrígate (bien)
  3 *n (shawl)* chal *m; (cape)* capa *f*

wrapper ['ræpə(r)] *n (of sweet)* envoltorio *m; (of book)* sobrecubierta *f*

wrapping ['ræpɪŋ] *n* **w. paper** papel *m* de envolver

wreath [riːθ] *n (pl* **wreaths** [riːðz, riːθs]) *(of flowers)* corona *f;* **laurel w.** corona de laurel

wreck [rek] **1** *n* (**a**) *Naut* naufragio *m; (ship)* barco naufragado (**b**) *(of car, plane)* restos *mpl; (of building)* ruinas *fpl* (**c**) *Fig (person)* ruina *f*
  2 *vt* (**a**) *(ship)* hacer naufragar (**b**) *(car, machine)* destrozar (**c**) *Fig (health, life)* arruinar; *(plans, hopes)* desbaratar; *(chances)* echar a perder

wreckage ['rekɪdʒ] *n (of ship, car, plane)* restos *mpl; (of building)* ruinas *fpl*

wren [ren] *n* chochín *m*

wrench [rentʃ] **1** *n* (**a**) *(pull)* tirón *m* (**b**) *Med* torcedura *f* (**c**) *(tool) Br* llave inglesa; *US* llave
  2 *vt* **to w. oneself free** soltarse de un

tirón; **to w. sth off sb** arrebatarle algo a algn; **w. sth off/open** quitar/abrir algo de un tirón

wrestle ['resəl] *vi* luchar

wrestler ['reslə(r)] *n* luchador(a) *m,f*

wrestling ['reslɪŋ] *n* lucha *f*

wretch [retʃ] *n (poor)* **w.** desgraciado(a) *m,f*

wretched ['retʃɪd] *adj* (**a**) *(very bad) (weather, state, conditions)* deplorable; *(life, childhood)* desdichado(a) (**b**) **I feel w.** *(ill)* me siento fatal (**c**) *(contemptible)* despreciable (**d**) *Fam (for emphasis)* maldito(a), condenado(a)

wriggle ['rɪgəl] **1** *vt* menear
  2 *vi* **to w. (about)** *(worm)* serpentear; *(restless child)* moverse nerviosamente; **to w. free** escapar deslizándose

wring [rɪŋ] *vt (pt & pp* **wrung)** (**a**) *(clothes)* escurrir; *(hands)* retorcer (**b**) *Fig (extract)* arrancar, sacar

wringing ['rɪŋɪŋ] *adj* **to be w. wet** estar empapado(a)

wrinkle ['rɪŋkəl] **1** *n* arruga *f*
  2 *vt* arrugar
  3 *vi* arrugarse

wrist [rɪst] *n* muñeca *f*

wristwatch ['rɪstwɒtʃ] *n* reloj *m* de pulsera

writ [rɪt] *n* orden *f* judicial

write [raɪt] **1** *vt (pt* **wrote;** *pp* **written)** escribir; *(article)* redactar; *(cheque)* extender; *US* **to w. sb** escribir a algn
  2 *vi* escribir (**about** sobre); *Br* **to w. to sb** escribir a algn; **to w. for a paper** colaborar en un periódico
▸ **write back** *vi* contestar
▸ **write down** *vt sep* poner por escrito; *(note)* apuntar
▸ **write in** *vi* escribir
▸ **write off 1** *vt sep (debt)* condonar; *Fam (car)* cargarse, *Méx* dar en la madre, *RP* hacer bolsa
  2 *vi* **to w. off for sth** pedir algo por escrito
▸ **write out** *vt sep (cheque, recipe)* extender
▸ **write up** *vt sep (notes)* redactar; *(diary, journal)* poner al día

write-off ['raɪtɒf] *n* **the car's a w.** el coche está hecho una ruina

writer ['raɪtə(r)] *n (by profession)* escritor(a) *m,f; (of book, letter)* autor(a) *m,f*

writhe [raɪð] *vi* retorcerse

writing ['raɪtɪŋ] *n* (**a**) *(script)* escritura *f; (handwriting)* letra *f;* **in w.** por escrito (**b**) **writings** escritos *mpl* (**c**) *(action)* escritura *f;* **w. desk** escritorio *m*

written ['rɪtən] *pp of* **write**

wrong [rɒŋ] **1** *adj* (**a**) *(person)* equivo-
cado(a); **I was w. about that boy** me
equivoqué con ese chico; **to be w.** no
tener razón; **you're w. in thinking that ...**
te equivocas si piensas que ...
(**b**) *(answer, way)* incorrecto(a), equivo-
cado(a); **my watch is w.** mi reloj anda
mal; **to drive on the w. side of the road**
conducir *or Am* manejar por el lado
contrario de la carretera; **to go the w.
way** equivocarse de camino; *Tel* **I've got
the w. number** me he confundido de
número
(**c**) *(unsuitable)* impropio(a), inadecua-
do(a); *(time)* inoportuno(a); **to say the w.
thing** decir algo inoportuno
(**d**) *(immoral etc)* malo(a); **there's nothing
w. in that** no hay nada malo en ello;
what's w. with smoking? ¿qué tiene de
malo fumar?
(**e**) **is anything w.?** ¿pasa algo?; **something's w.** hay algo que no está bien;
what's w.? ¿qué pasa?; **what's w. with
you?** ¿qué te pasa?
2 *adv* mal, incorrectamente; **to get it w.**
equivocarse; *Fam* **to go w.** *(plan)* fallar,
salir mal

3 *n* (**a**) *(evil, bad action)* mal *m*; **you did
w. to hit him** hiciste mal en pegarle (**b**)
(injustice) injusticia *f*; *(offence)* agravio *m*;
the rights and wrongs of a matter lo justo
y lo injusto de un asunto (**c**) **to be in the
w.** *(be to blame)* tener la culpa
4 *vt (treat unfairly)* ser injusto(a) con;
(offend) agraviar

wrongdoing ['rɒŋduːɪŋ] *n* maldad *f*
wrongful ['rɒŋfʊl] *adj* injusto(a)
wrongly ['rɒŋlɪ] *adv* (**a**) *(incorrectly)*
incorrectamente (**b**) *(mistakenly)* equivocadamente (**c**) *(unjustly)* injustamente

wrote [rəʊt] *pt of* **write**
wrung [rʌŋ] *pt & pp of* **wring**
wry [raɪ] *adj* (**wrier, wriest** *or* **wryer,
wryest**) sardónico(a)

WTO ['dʌbəljuːtiːˈəʊ] *n (abbr* **World Trade
Organization)** OMC *f*
WWW *n Comput (abbr* **World Wide Web)**
WWW *f*

WYSIWYG ['wɪzɪwɪg] *n Comput (abbr
what you see is what you get)
WYSIWYG, = se imprime lo que ves

X, x [eks] *n (the letter)* X, x *f*

xenophobia [zenə'fəʊbɪə] *n* xenofobia *f*

Xerox® ['zɪərɒks] **1** *n* fotocopia *f*, xerocopia *f* **2** *vt* fotocopiar

Xmas ['krɪsməs, 'eksməs] *n (abbr* **Christmas**) Navidad *f*

X-ray ['eksreɪ] **1** *n (radiation)* rayo *m* X; *(picture)* radiografía *f*; **to have an X.** hacerse una radiografía **2** *vt* radiografiar

xylophone ['zaɪləfəʊn] *n* xilófono *m*, xilofón *m*

Y, y [waɪ] *n (the letter)* Y, y *f*

yacht [jɒt] *n* yate *m*; **y. club** club náutico

yachting ['jɒtɪŋ] *n Sport* navegación *f* a vela; *(competition)* regatas *fpl*

yachtsman ['jɒtsmən] *n* balandrista *m*

yachtswoman ['jɒtswʊmən] *n* balandrista *f*

yam [jæm] *n (a) (vegetable)* ñame *m* **(b)** *US (sweet potato)* Esp, Arg, Col, Ven batata *f*, Esp, Cuba, Urug boniato *m*, Andes, CAm, Méx camote *m*

Yank [jæŋk] *n Fam Br (person from the USA)* yanqui *mf*; *US (person from north-eastern USA)* = estadounidense procedente del nordeste del país

yank [jæŋk] *vt Fam* tirar; *(tooth)* arrancar

Yankee ['jæŋkɪ] *adj & n Pej* yanqui *(mf)*

yap [jæp] *vi (dog)* aullar; *Fam (person)* darle al pico

yard¹ [jɑːd] *n (measure)* yarda *f (aprox 0,914 m)*

yard² [jɑːd] *n* patio *m*; *US* jardín *m*

yardstick ['jɑːdstɪk] *n Fig* criterio *m*, norma *f*

yarn [jɑːn] *n (a) Sewing* hilo *m* **(b)** *(story)* historia *f*, cuento *m*; **to spin a y.** *(lie)* inventarse una historia

yawn [jɔːn] **1** *vi* bostezar
2 *n* bostezo *m*

yawning ['jɔːnɪŋ] *adj (gap)* profundo(a)

yd *(pl* yds*) (abbr* yard*)* yarda *f*

yeah [jeə] *adv Fam* sí

year [jɪə(r)] *n (a) (of calendar)* año *m*; **all y. round** durante todo el año; **last y.** el año pasado; **next y.** el año que viene; **y. in, y. out** año tras año; **I'm ten years old** tengo diez años **(b)** *Educ* curso *m*; **first-y. student** estudiante *mf* de primero

yearly ['jɪəlɪ] **1** *adj* anual
2 *adv* anualmente, cada año

yearn [jɜːn] *vi* **to y. for sth** anhelar algo

yearning ['jɜːnɪŋ] *n* anhelo *m* **(for** de)

yeast [jiːst] *n* levadura *f*

yell [jel] **1** *vi* gritar
2 *n* grito *m*, alarido *m*

yellow ['jeləʊ] **1** *adj* amarillo(a); *Tel* **Y. Pages®** páginas amarillas
2 *n* amarillo *m*

yelp [jelp] **1** *vi* aullar
2 *n* aullido *m*

yen [jen] *n (a) (currency)* yen *m* **(b)** **to have a y. for sth** tener ganas de algo

yeoman ['jəʊmən] *n Br* **Y. of the Guard** = alabardero de la Casa Real británica

yes [jes] **1** *adv* sí; **you said y.** dijiste que sí
2 *n* sí *m*

yesterday ['jestədeɪ] *adv & n* ayer *m*; **the day before y.** anteayer; **y. morning** ayer por la mañana

yet [jet] **1** *adv* **(a) not y.** aún no, todavía no; **as y.** hasta ahora; **I haven't eaten y.** no he comido todavía **(b)** *(in questions)* ya; **has he arrived y.?** ¿ha venido ya? **(c)** *(even)* más; **y. again** otra vez; **y. more** todavía más **(d)** *(eventually)* todavía, aún; **he'll win y.** todavía puede ganar
2 *conj* sin embargo

yew [juː] *n* tejo *m*

yield [jiːld] **1** *n* **(a)** *(of mine, interest)* rendimiento *m* **(b)** *Agr* cosecha *f* **(c)** *Fin* beneficio *m*
2 *vt* producir; *Agr* dar; *(money)* producir
3 *vi* **(a)** *(surrender, break)* ceder **(b)** *US Aut* ceder el paso

YMCA [waɪemsiː'eɪ] *n (abbr* **Young Men's Christian Association)** ACJ *f*, Asociación *f* Cristiana de Jóvenes *(que regenta hostales económicos)*

yob(bo) ['jɒb(əʊ)] *n Br Fam* vándalo(a) *m*, Esp gamberro(a) *m,f*, Perú, RP patotero *m*

yoga ['jəʊgə] *n* yoga *m*

yog(h)urt ['jɒgət] *n* yogur *m*

yoke [jəʊk] **1** *n* yugo *m*
2 *vt (oxen)* uncir; *Fig* unir

yokel ['jəʊkəl] *n Pej or Hum* palurdo(a) *m,f*, Esp paleto(a) *m,f*

yolk [jəʊk] *n* yema *f*

yonder ['jɒndə(r)] *adv* más allá

you [juː, *unstressed* jʊ] *pers pron*

In Spanish, the formal form **usted** takes a third person singular verb and **ustedes** takes a third person plural verb. In many Latin American countries, **ustedes** is the standard form of the second person plural and is not considered formal.

(**a**) *(subject) (usually omitted in Spanish, except for contrast) (singular)* tú, *esp RP* vos, *Fml* usted; *(plural) Esp* vosotros(as), *Am or Fml* ustedes; **have you got it?** *(singular)* ¿lo tienes tú?, *Fml* ¿lo tiene usted?; *(plural) Esp* ¿lo tenéis vosotros?, *Am or Fml* ¿lo tienen ustedes?

(**b**) *(direct object) (singular)* te, *Fml* lo(la); *(plural) Esp* os, *Am or Fml* los(las); **I can understand your son but not you** *(singular)* a tu hijo lo entiendo, pero a ti no, *Fml* a su hijo lo entiendo, pero a usted no; *(plural) Esp* a vuestro hijo lo entiendo, pero a vosotros no, *Am or Fml* a su hijo lo entiendo, pero a ustedes no

(**c**) *(indirect object) (singular)* te, *Fml* le; *(plural) Esp* os, *Am or Fml* les; **I gave y. the book** *(singular)* te di el libro, *Fml* le di el libro; *(plural) Esp* os di el libro, *Am or Fml* les di el libro!; **I told y.** *(singular)* te lo dije, *Fml* se lo dije; *(plural) Esp* os lo dije, *Am or Fml* se lo dije

(**d**) *(after preposition) (singular)* ti, *Fml* usted; *(plural) Esp* vosotros(as), *Am or Fml* ustedes; **I'm thinking of y.** *(singular)* pienso en ti, *Fml* pienso en usted; *(plural) Esp* pienso en vosotros, *Am or Fml* pienso en ustedes

(**e**) *(impersonal)* **y. don't do that kind of thing** esas cosas no se hacen

young [jʌŋ] **1** *adj (age)* joven; *(brother etc)* pequeño(a); **y. lady** señorita *f*; **y. man** joven *m*

2 *npl* (**a**) *(people)* **the y.** los jóvenes, la juventud (**b**) *(animals)* crías *fpl*

youngster [ˈjʌŋstə(r)] *n* muchacho(a) *m,f*

your [jɔː(r), *unstressed* jə(r)] *poss adj* (**a**) *(of one person)* tu, *Fml* su; **y. house** tu/su casa; **y. books** tus/sus libros; **it wasn't YOUR idea!** ¡no fue idea tuya! (**b**) *(of more than one person) Esp* vuestro(a), *Am or Fml* su; **y. house** *Esp* vuestra casa, *Am or Fml* su casa; **y. books** *Esp* vuestros libros, *Am or Fml* sus libros; **it wasn't YOUR idea!** *Esp* ¡no fue idea vuestra!, *Am or Fml* ¡no fue idea suya or de ustedes! (**c**) *(for parts of body, clothes) (translated by definite article)* **did you hit y. head?** ¿te has dado un golpe en la cabeza? (**d**) *(impersonal)* **smoking is bad for y. health** el tabaco perjudica la salud

yours [jɔːz] *poss pron*

> In Spanish, the forms **tuyo(a)**, **suyo(a)** and **vuestro(a)** require a definite article in the singular and in the plural when they are the subject of the phrase.

(**a**) *(of one person) (singular)* tuyo(a) *m,f*; *(plural)* tuyos(as) *m,fpl*; *(formal: singular)* suyo(a) *m,f*; *(formal: plural)* suyos(as)

m,fpl; **my house is big but y. is bigger** mi casa es grande, pero la tuya/suya es mayor; **this book is y.** este libro es tuyo/ ~suyo; **these books are y.** estos libros son tuyos/suyos; **a friend of y.** un amigo tuyo/suyo; **y. (sincerely/faithfully)** atentamente (**b**) *(of more than one person) (singular) Esp* vuestro(a), *Am or Fml* suyo(a); *(plural) Esp* vuestros(as), *Am or Fml* suyos(as); **this book is y.** este libro es vuestro/suyo; **these books are y.** estos libros son vuestros/suyos

yourself [jɔːˈself] *pron* (**a**) *(reflexive)* te; *(formal)* se; **have you hurt y.?** ¿te has hecho daño?; *(formal)* ¿se ha hecho daño?

(**b**) *(emphatic)* tú mismo *m*, tú misma *f*; *(formal)* usted mismo *m*, usted misma *f*; **did you do all the work y.?** ¿has hecho todo el trabajo tú solo?; *(formal)* ¿ha hecho todo el trabajo usted solo?; **you told me y.** me lo dijiste tú mismo; *(formal)* me lo dijo usted mismo; **you're not y. today** hoy no se te nota nada bien (**c**) *(after preposition)* ti; *(formal)* usted; **did you do this by y.?** ¿lo has hecho tú solo?; *(formal)* ¿lo ha hecho usted solo?; **do you live by y.?** ¿vives solo?; **did you buy it for y.?** ¿te lo has comprado para ti?; *(formal)* ¿se lo ha comprado para usted?

yourselves [jɔːˈselvz] *pron* (**a**) *(reflexive) Esp* os, *Am or Fml* se; **have you hurt y.?** *Esp* ¿os habéis hecho daño?, *Am or Fml* ¿se han hecho daño? (**b**) *(emphatic) Esp* vosotros(as) mismos(as), *Am or Fml* ustedes mismos(as); **did you do all the work y.?** *Esp* ¿habéis hecho todo el trabajo vosotros solos?, *Am or Fml* ¿han hecho todo el trabajo ustedes solos? (**c**) *(after preposition) Esp* vosotros(as), *Am or Fml* ustedes; **did you do this by y.?** *Esp* ¿lo habéis hecho vosotros solos?, *Am or Fml* ¿lo han hecho ustedes solos?; **did you buy it for y.?** *Esp* ¿os lo habéis comprado para vosotros?, *Am or Fml* ¿se lo han comprado para ustedes?

youth [juːθ] *n* (**a**) *(period)* juventud *f* (**b**) *(young man)* joven *m*; **y. club** club *m* juvenil; **y. hostel** albergue *m* juvenil

youthful [ˈjuːθfʊl] *adj* juvenil, joven

Yugoslavia [juːɡəʊˈslɑːvɪə] *n Formerly* Yugoslavia

Yugoslavian [juːɡəʊˈslɑːvɪən] *adj & n Formerly* yugoslavo(a) *(m,f)*

yuppie [ˈjʌpɪ] *n* yupi *mf*; **a y. restaurant** un restaurante de yupis

YWCA [ˈwaɪdʌbəljuːsiːˈeɪ] *n (abbr* **Young Women's Christian Association)** ACJ *f*, Asociación *f* Cristiana de Jóvenes *(que regenta hostales económicos)*

Z

Z, z [zed, US zi:] *n (the letter)* Z, z *f*

zany ['zeɪnɪ] *adj* (**zanier, zaniest**) *Fam* (**a**) *(mad)* *Esp* chiflado(a), *Am* zafado(a), *RP* rayado(a) (**b**) *(eccentric)* estrafalario(a)

zap [zæp] **1** *interj* ¡zas!
2 *vt Fam* (**a**) *(hit)* pegar (**b**) *(kill)* cargarse a
3 *vi TV* hacer zapping

zeal [zi:l] *n (enthusiasm)* entusiasmo *m*

zealous ['zeləs] *adj (enthusiastic)* entusiasta

zebra ['zi:brə, 'zebrə] *n* cebra *f*; *Br* **z. crossing** paso *m* de cebra

zenith ['zenɪθ] *n Astron* cenit *m*; *Fig* apogeo *m*

zero ['zɪərəʊ] *n* cero *m*; **z. hour** hora *f* cero

zest [zest] *n (eagerness)* entusiasmo *m*

zigzag ['zɪgzæg] **1** *n* zigzag *m*
2 *vi* zigzaguear

Zimbabwe [zɪm'bɑːbweɪ] *n* Zimbabue

zinc [zɪŋk] *n* cinc *m*, zinc *m*

zip [zɪp] **1** *n* (**a**) *Br* **z. (fastener)** cremallera *f*, *Am* cierre *m* (**b**) *Fam* brío *m*; *US* **z. code** código *m* postal
2 *vi* cerrarse con cremallera

▸ **zip by** *vi* pasar como un rayo

▸ **zip up** *vt sep* cerrar la cremallera *or Am* el cierre de; **to z. sb up** cerrar la cremallera *or Am* el cierre a algn

zipper ['zɪpə(r)] *n US* cremallera *f*, *Am* cierre *m*

zit [zɪt] *n Fam* grano *m*

zodiac ['zəʊdɪæk] *n* zodiaco *m*, zodíaco *m*

zombie ['zɒmbɪ] *n* zombie *mf*

zone [zəʊn] **1** *n* zona *f*
2 *vt* dividir en zonas

zoo [zu:] *n* zoo *m*

zoological [zu:ə'lɒdʒɪkəl] *adj* zoológico(a)

zoologist [zu:'ɒlədʒɪst] *n* zoólogo(a) *m,f*

zoology [zu:'ɒlədʒɪ] *n* zoología *f*

zoom [zu:m] **1** *n* (**a**) *(buzz)* zumbido *m* (**b**) **z. lens** zoom *m*, teleobjetivo *m*
2 *vi* (**a**) *(buzz)* zumbar (**b**) **to z. past** pasar volando

▸ **zoom in** *vi (camera)* acercarse rápidamente

zucchini [zu:'ki:nɪ] *n US* calabacín *m*, *CSur* zapallito *m*

Zulu ['zu:lu:] *adj & n* zulú *(mf)*